Gun Digest®

1994/48th Annual Edition

EDITED BY KEN WARNER

DBI BOOKS, INC.

ABOUT OUR COVERS

Innovation is nothing new to Heckler & Koch. For more than 40 years, HK engineering has been designing and manufacturing firearms that are on the cutting edge of high technology. Their latest effort, the USP (Universal Self-loading Pistol), can be seen in two versions on our front and back covers.

This is the first HK pistol designed especially for the demanding needs of the American shooter. Features favored by U.S. civilian, law enforcement and military users provided the design criteria for the USP, and its controls were, in fact, greatly influenced by the Government Model 1911 pistol. The USP can be safely carried "cocked and locked." The control lever, a combination safety and decocking lever, is frame mounted and quickly accessible, unlike slide-mounted safeties common on many pistols.

Using a modified Browning-type action with a special HK recoil reduction system, the USP is built to take the punishment of the most powerful 40-caliber loads. Unlike most 40s, this gun was *designed* as a 40, not scaled up from an existing 9mm model.

The USP's polymer frame is the result of technological experience gained by HK engineers in the development of the world's first composite-material pistols. It's light in weight, corrosion-free and high strength. The "grip panels" are stippled to provide a comfortable, non-slip surface. Even the magazine is made of a strong polymer with stainless steel reinforcements.

HK's modular approach to the internal components allows the USP control lever to be switched from the left to the right side for left-handed shooters, and permits changing the pistol from one type of firing mode to another—including combination double action and single action and double-action-only. Like a popular hamburger, you can have your new HK USP *your way*.

In addition to a wide selection of trigger/firing modes, the USP has an ambidextrous magazine release lever shielded by the trigger guard. The stepped grip at the rear, combined with the tapered magazine well, makes magazine changes speedy and precise. The position of the extended slide release lever allows easy operation without changing the grip of the shooting hand.

One of the most important and unique features of the new HK USP pistol is the mechanical recoil reduction system incorporated into the recoil/buffer spring assembly below the barrel. Designed primarily to buffer the slide and barrel and reduce recoil effects on the pistol's components, it also lowers the felt recoil for the shooter. The system is insensitive to ammunition types and requires no maintenance or adjustment.

This latest high-tech offering from HK is available in either 40 S&W with thirteen-shot magazine (front cover) or 9mm Parabellum with sixteen-shot magazine (back cover). Barrel length for both is 4.13 inches; weight 1.74 lbs. (40), 1.66 lbs. (9mm). Overall length is 6.90 inches. Standard sights are the three-dot system with tritium sights optionally available; both systems are adjustable for windage.

At Heckler & Koch, form follows function, and we think this form has a lot of attractive features.

GUN DIGEST STAFF

EDITOR-IN-CHIEF
Ken Warner

SENIOR STAFF EDITOR
Harold A. Murtz

ASSOCIATE EDITOR
Robert S.L. Anderson

PRODUCTION MANAGER
John L. Duoba

EDITORIAL/PRODUCTION ASSOCIATE
Jamie L. Puffpaff

ASSISTANT TO THE EDITOR
Lilo Anderson

CONTRIBUTING EDITORS
Bob Bell
Doc Carlson
Dean A. Grennell
Edward A. Matunas
Layne Simpson
Larry S. Sterett
Hal Swiggett
D.A. Warner
J.B. Wood
Don Zutz

EUROPEAN CORRESPONDENT
Raymond Caranta

ELECTRONIC PUBLISHING MANAGER
Nancy J. Mellem

GRAPHIC DESIGN
Jim Billy

MANAGING EDITOR
Pamela J. Johnson

PUBLISHER
Sheldon L. Factor

DBI BOOKS, INC.

PRESIDENT
Charles T. Hartigan

VICE PRESIDENT & PUBLISHER
Sheldon L. Factor

VICE PRESIDENT—SALES
John G. Strauss

TREASURER
Frank R. Serpone

Women's Shooting Sports Foundation

NSSF helped launch the Women's Shooting Sports Foundation to serve the increasing numbers of female hunters and shooters. Sue King is National Director, and Sporting Clays and summer biathlon will get the new group's early attention.

U.S. Tops CISM Shoot

The Conseil International Du Sport Militaire has been running competitions in twenty-four sports since 1946 or so. The latest shoot was a good one for the U.S. Among 351 participants from 27 countries, U.S. shooters managed eleven medals—and so the U.S. won its own Challenge trophy.

Eight New Hall-Of Famers

The two pre-1948 nominees to the International Hall of Fame were Walter Stokes, who won eight world rifle titles between 1921-1924, and Carl Osburn, who was a multiple rifle medalist at both the 1912 and 1920 games. The six post-1948 shooters nominated are rifle shooters Lanny Bassham, Jack Foster, Art Jackson and Jack Writer, and pistol shooters Joe Benner and Bill McMillan.

Two Really Big Names

Dr. Mikhail T. Kalashnikov, designer of Russia's best battle rifle,

visited William B. Ruger as his guest. The two exchanged gifts and cordially—and the Ruger company could not resist hinting at future cooperation between these two great names of the firearms world.

NSSF Out There Working

Apart from SHOT Shows and making Summer Biathlon shoots attract thousands and generating materials for school use and getting positive national and regional TV exposure for all kinds of shooting sports, NSSF is also down in the trenches—making, for instance, public service ad programs that work. This is one such ad.

NRA Tours Great Hunters

With eighteen well-known hunters as key speakers, NRA presented a positive hunting message in thirty-seven states and nearly sixty cities.

The NRA Great American Hunter Tour is NRA's new bid to remain a leader in the pro-hunting struggle.

Harry Reeves
1993

A legend in handgun shooting has been elected 1993's Outstanding American Handgunner. Harry Reeves was six times national NRA pistol champion.

J. Thompson Ruger
1944-1993

After a six-month fight against leukemia, Tom Ruger passed away January 31, 1993 at age 48. Prominence in the firearms industry came to him not only because, since 1971, he had worked for Sturm, Ruger & Co., Inc. He was a hard worker in NRA, Safari Club International, NSSF, ATA—and a contributor throughout the world of sporting guns. He left a lot too soon.

CONTENTS

FEATURES

DEPARTMENTS

CATALOG

WHEN YOU SPEND 1500 hours hunting grouse in central and western New York, between the years 1964 and 1985, you learn something about ruffed grouse hunting, as I did, although it may only be applicable to New York state grouse hunting. I have to say my limited ruffed grouse hunting experience in Pennsylvania was exactly like that in New York.

Real grouse hunters may scoff at my comments, but I had to learn all by myself. The only local man who was known as a grouse hunter was very uncommunicative. Reading about ruffed grouse hunting didn't

only certain places where you can consistently flush grouse. That area must contain four things:

First, it seems to have to be near water. I don't think I ever flushed grouse more than 200 yards from a source of water.

Second, the area has to have a source of food. New York state is littered with abandoned apple orchards and single apple trees abound in the woods. Some counties had 90 percent of their surface area under cultivation in the old days, so you are almost always hunting on an abandoned farm. Thorn apple trees also abound in the New York woods,

New York, the grouse season lasted then from early October through the end of January, and in some years through the end of February. I have shot grouse near the end of February and found their crops full of spruce needles. Apparently, the grouse eat them when the other food supplies are gone.

Fourth, there have to be small evergreen trees, preferably white pines where the lower branches are down at ground level. On really rough days, and you can get them in New York in February, when the temperature is below zero and there is a 40-mile-per-hour wind blowing,

Hunting RUFFED GROUSE

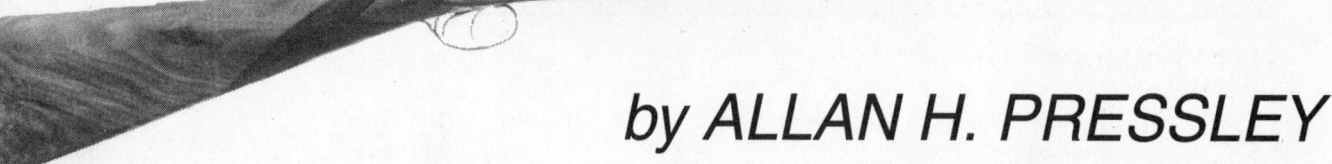

by ALLAN H. PRESSLEY

help me much. General hunters didn't seem to know much about hunting them and only said they were very hard to hit.

I learned four basic things about grouse: First, they are really hard to find; second, they are really hard to get to flush; third, they are *really* hard to hit; and fourth, they are sometimes hard to find if you do hit them. One thing I will warn you about—hunting grouse is an excuse to walk in the woods carrying a gun. If you want to walk in the woods and shoot a lot, I recommend that you take up Sporting Clays rather than grouse hunting.

I finally learned, after roaming the woods for many years, that there are

but I have never seen them in my native Pennsylvania. They are very small trees with miniature crab apples and really large thorns. I have only consistently flushed grouse where these two food trees exist. When I opened the crops of grouse shot early in the season, they were full of thorn apple pieces and whole thorn apples if they were small enough. I never could identify normal apple pieces, but the birds were always close to apple trees.

Third, there have to be large evergreen trees in the areas where they are found. Grouse normally roost in large evergreen trees. I have occasionally flushed them from these trees when I walked under them. In

the grouse will be sitting on the ground under the base of a small pine tree where the branches are down to the ground. Also, on this type of day, they will usually be in a narrow valley or a ravine, apparently to be out of the wind as much as possible.

When I found an area with these features, I would consistently flush grouse. If you can find a place where these things all exist within 400 yards of each other, you should find grouse in New York. Since both areas I lived and hunted in were hilly—our kind of hills, up to 800-foot-high ridges really—I don't know if they preferred narrow valleys and ravines or simply stayed there because that's what most of the terrain was like. When the sun came out after some rough weather, you could almost be sure to find the grouse on a sunny hillside. Pennsylvania hunters have told me that they find grouse on the tops of ridges, but I never found that to be

side. I never flushed grouse in a completely open field, but they will flush into an open field from a hedge row. With one exception, I have never flushed grouse within about 200 yards of a house or working barn or a used road. They don't like the presence of people or cars, so you can't be a road hunter and find grouse. The presence of grazing animals doesn't seem to bother them. I used to hunt a field which was mixed pasture and trees, with cattle in the field, and would occasionally flush a grouse out of a tree or from the ground there.

Grouse seem to be most consistently on the edges of things. When

woods, I did not flush grouse. I think they need room to fly and will not stay in thick brush where they can't fly. One guy I hunted with believed you should beat through the really thick stuff to push them into more open woods, but that never seemed to work. We never flushed grouse in the thinner woods after we had beat the thick stuff.

It seems that you have to kick a grouse in the butt, or your dog has to bite them, to get them to flush. They sit tight. After I had been hunting a few years, and the first year with my dog, I shot a rabbit one day. I cleaned it immediately right where it was shot, and while cleaning it, my dog wandered off. I stood in the same spot for 10 minutes calling the dog at the top of my voice. Finally she came back, and when she was within 20 yards of me she stopped, sniffed, turned to the right and pounced. A grouse flew up from that spot. That grouse had stayed there, while I shot the rabbit, while I cleaned the rabbit, and while I called the dog for 10 minutes!

I hunted grouse several years with other people with very poor success. Then my wife came home with a six-

Either mileage or hours—it takes plenty to bag grouse regularly.

so, either in New York or in the limited hunting I did in Pennsylvania.

Grouse are also found in hedge rows on working farms. They are ground birds and really don't like to fly much. They seem to use the hedge rows to move from woods to woods. If you have a dog to work down the hedge row, you can walk on one side. The grouse will flush to one side or the other and you have a 50-50 chance they will flush to your

hunting a woods bounded by fields on all sides, I always found the grouse on the edge of the woods, never in the center. When hunting an old second growth woods which abutted a more mature woods, the grouse were always on the boundary just inside the second growth. People claim that grouse are always in extremely thick brush, but I didn't find that to be so. If I had a very hard time walking through the

week-old mutt one day and named her "Honey." Because of the demands of work and some health problems, I was never sure when I could go hunting again, so I could not commit to other people. I started going by myself when possible, as a last-minute decision.

Honey could earn her keep by going with me. She was a mixed collie and beagle, certainly didn't have any bird hunting instincts, and I didn't know how to train a bird dog anyway. I trained her to stay close to me, so she made circles around me in the woods, going out about 20-30 yards and then coming back. Therefore, she was making a pattern around me that looked like one of those flower drawings that you make with a compass. Suddenly, it was obvious that there were a lot more grouse in the woods than I thought.

A dog—any dog—makes a big difference on grouse.

My average changed from three hours per flush to one hour per flush.

Basically, Honey and I were hunting a 60- to 70-yard-wide swath in the woods, versus the 10-yard-wide swath I was covering by hunting alone. I concluded that you needed a dog to hunt grouse. If she was going away from me and flushed a grouse 20 or 30 yards out, I could not get a shot off. However, she flushed more grouse in range toward me, or across in front of me, or the same behind me, than she flushed out of range, so I was much better off with her help. If the grouse flushed, then it was obvious that they were there. A friend of mine had a pure-bred collie that a neighbor of his borrowed frequently to hunt grouse. The neighbor said the collie was a good grouse dog because he flushed them.

When hunting a woods, I was usually hunting parallel to the edge and about 10 yards inside. If flushed, the grouse would tend to fly away, staying parallel to the edge and just inside the woods. They would set back down within 100-150 yards and could be flushed again. Sometimes I would flush what I thought was the same bird four times. However, each time they would flush further away so a shot didn't always present itself. One curious fact is that they don't seem to fly uphill; I never saw one fly uphill. They usually fly along the contour lines. Sometimes they will go downhill, depending on the cover. They will go out of cover rather than fly uphill. When deciding where to go to reflush them, this was the most important issue and it overrode the edge consideration. Occasionally, I noticed that the grouse would fly up above the tree tops and then away, but they wouldn't be visible until they were 40 yards or more away.

An old hunter told me that it is better to move and pause—that makes them nervous and they will be more likely to flush. I started doing this, moving 20 yards at a time and stopping for 10 seconds or so, where it was easier to swing my gun. That way, if a grouse flushed, it was easier to shoot at it. I noticed that grouse frequently flushed after taking a step or two from pausing, so the old hunter was right. Of course, a pointing dog would have been the answer, but I was told by a number of people that it was very difficult to get a dog to point on grouse. Besides, Honey would have been insanely jealous.

Honey and I hunted grouse together for the next thirteen years until she got too old to hunt. She died in her seventeenth year. With all this, we only flushed grouse once an hour on the average. I know because I kept track of it. I don't remember how often I got a shot, but I would say in less than half the flushes, mostly because I could not see the bird or because I could not get a shot off in time. You have to be dedicated to be a grouse hunter in New York! After Honey stopped hunting, I went alone for several more years, but my flushing average went way down because I was only covering a 10-yard-wide swath once again.

One other interesting fact I noticed was that grouse never flushed before 9 a.m. The local grouse hunter told me he also had found this to be true. He believed that the dew had to be dried before they would move. I used this as an excuse to get up at a normal time, have a leisurely breakfast, and then go hunting.

Remember, I said it is really, really difficult to hit grouse, especially for a non-clay bird shooter like I was then. There was no success for two years, but my stubborn nature kept me going. My J.P. Sauer double averaged 45 percent patterns in the right barrel (a normal Improved Cylinder) and 70 percent patterns in the left (a Full choke). At 10-15 yards, which was the normal shooting range, the IC barrel gave a fairly small pattern, but the right pattern was really tiny. I could have had the chokes opened, but this was my only shotgun until 1969, and it was used for all other small game.

Upon reading Francis Sell's "Put and Take Choke" in the 1966 GUN DIGEST, which told how to make spreader loads to open up the pattern, I immediately loaded some. With them, my right barrel would shoot about 30 percent which is basically a Cylinder bore, equivalent to a Skeet #1 or Skeet-in pattern. It gave a nice big pattern at 10 yards. All my first shots were between 10 and 20 yards; I don't remember a shot farther then that. The left would pattern 45 percent. I started hitting grouse with these big patterns.

This brings us to "Pressley's First Law of New York State Ruffed Grouse Hunting." You have to have a Cylinder bore pattern. If you don't, and you're not a person who can consistently break twenty-four or twenty-five at trap and Skeet, you are just wasting your time. In fact, anybody who uses a shotgun and doesn't pattern it is wasting his or her time, in my not-humble opinion. You will be absolutely amazed at how small the patterns are at 10 and 20 yards. My Full choke pattern was only $7^1/_2$ inches in diameter at 10 yards, and my 45 percent pattern went only 14 inches at the same distance. Using spreaders in my right barrel opened the pattern up to almost 20 inches at 10 yards.

The classic grouse gun is a light double, and I believe that is the best gun to use. You almost never need more than one shot anyway. Three are certainly useless. I have never seen anybody hunting upland game, waterfowl, or deer, hit anything with their third shot. My Sauer weighed $6^1/_2$ pounds, which is pretty light for an American 12-gauge double, but fairly standard for a European game gun. It had perfect balance, with the balance point $4^1/_2$ inches in front of the front trigger; that put the balance point exactly midway between my hands as I held the gun, and it came up as nicely and as quickly as any shotgun ever seen.

Whatever type of gun you choose, it must be light and properly balanced. If you have never had such a gun in your hands, it behooves you to try one. This brings up another important point about shooting at grouse: to get a grouse, the shots must be taken very fast, so whatever gun is used, you have to be able to bring it up quickly. Train yourself not to be startled by the sound of the grouse flushing; after all, that's what you're out there to hear. I could only get a shot off fast enough if I mounted the gun at the start of the hunt, and then, without moving my hands, carry the gun around at high port. I have fairly slow reactions, so this extreme measure was necessary on my part. One of the other things I trained myself to do was to start the gun up at the first sound of the flush, even if it wasn't obvious where it was. I could always swing around toward the bird, when I figured out where it was, as the gun was coming up. Maybe that's why, when I took the gun to a really good gunsmith a few years ago, he found a lot of small dents in the barrels, probably from hitting trees! My habit of pausing where I could swing the gun, however, usually allowed me to swing it without too much interference.

You will almost never get a clear shot at a grouse. They put a tree between you and them as soon as possible. Many times, I have seen them curving around as they went up to put the tree between me and them. So you have to shoot at them through trees and bushes. This tends to cut down the number of successful shots, but you must shoot or you will never get a grouse. It may be that old grouse hunters are reincarnated as grouse and know all the tricks.

For a while, I carried a normal load in my left barrel, to shoot them at long range when they went up over the trees. This tactic was never successful, so I reverted to a spreader load for the occasional close-in second shot. I used the classic trap load of $1^1/_8$ ounces of $7^1/_2$s in a 3-dram equivalent. You should not use a heavier load in a light European double; they are not made for them. The $7^1/_2$s put grouse down, and there is no sense using heavier shot if you don't have to, so you can have the greatest number of shot in your charge. Trying 9s, the grouse I was sure were hit (I saw their feathers ruffle from the impact), did not go down.

I would advise a beginning grouse hunter who needed a gun to seriously think of finding a light American double such as an L.C. Smith featherweight 12 or a light Ansley Fox 12. Either of them will get down to $6^1/_2$ pounds and would probably stand a diet of $1^1/_4$-ounce loads. If they didn't have open bores, they could be opened up by a competent gunsmith. You can always use spreader loads if you want to keep the original chokes intact. Do not use $1^1/_4$-ounce loads in light 12-gauge European shotguns; use lighter loads.

Science should study the brain tissue of grouse; they are much smarter than the size of their brains suggest. I have already mentioned that they will curve around as they take off to put a tree between you and them when a straight flight would keep them in the clear. They have flushed when I could not possibly shoot, as when going over a fence. One time, I decided I would outsmart a grouse. A grouse would frequently flush from under a small pine tree by a certain creek. I decided I would get the bugger. The creek was in a small depression about 6 feet wide and 4 feet deep. Coming up to the creek bed by the small pine on the other side, I stopped, mounted the gun, slipped off the safety, and waited for a minute. No flush. I scrambled down the side of the creek bed, stood on the near side of the water and did the same thing. No flush. I crossed the creek and did the same thing. Again, no flush. Giving up, I couldn't see anything under the tree and started up the other side of the depression. Out went a grouse from under the tree about 8 feet from my face and it scared the hell out of me. Naturally, I was not in a position to shoot, hanging on the side of the bank.

If you shoot at a grouse, you hope you will see it crumple and fall dead, but this isn't usually the case. You are generally shooting through a tree or bush. Also, they seem to be very tough—their breast muscles are enormous for the size of the bird, and getting shot in that area will not crumple them up. I have only seen them fold if a wing bone is broken or if they are hit in the head. Because of this, you have to look for a dead grouse some distance from where you shot.

This is where a dog is needed. Honey was able to find dead birds for me that I wouldn't have found by myself. They are incredibly hard to see lying on the leaf bed of the woods. I remember one time I shot a grouse on the edge of an old overgrown apple orchard through a dense bush. The grouse had trouble getting up, it was only about 5 yards away, and I was sure I hit it solidly. It flew up and over into a woods on the side of a hill. I went over to the woods where the grouse had entered, and since they never fly uphill, I turned left and went downhill. Since they always stay on the edge of the woods, I walked about 10 yards inside the woods. I went about 50 yards and found a dead warm grouse which had to be the one I had just shot. Its breast had the most pellets in it of any grouse I had ever taken. I was quite pleased with myself for finding this bird because I had applied all my theories and they had worked; also I was glad that the grouse was not wasted.

Some people cut the breast out of the bird and just eat that. Since it is so damned much work to get one, I always carefully pluck each bird and eat every morsel! My wife has tried all the standard cooking recipes and they have always been delicious. The breast meat is surprisingly good;, the rest is a little tough. One thing I like about grouse hunting over deer hunting—it is a hell of a lot easier to carry a grouse out of the woods than a deer! Good luck. ●

IHAVE ENJOYED 22 rimfire rifles for years, but never gave the 22 WMR more than a casual thought until C. Rodney James' excellent article, "The Quiet Ones" (GUN DIGEST 47th edition), sparked my interest. After having written in detail on the Long Rifle and the 22 Short, readers brought to my attention that the 22 WMR had somehow escaped my scrutiny. This came as no surprise, but realizing why says a lot about riflemen in general.

You see, there are two types of riflemen: The practical "hunter" is usually a farmer, rancher, police officer or soldier for whom the rifle is a tool for a specific job; the precision experimenter is often a scientist, engineer or active target competitor, but always a dedicated tinkerer and paper puncher. Those who know me and my writings know I am of the latter group. While I hunt occasionally, it is not a consuming passion for me. Ken Warner is, without question, a "hunter" who sometimes gets frustrated with my propensity for number crunching. In giving me this assignment he could have said, "Don't give us the meaning of life in 4000 words at .95 level of confidence, just tell us what works, and why!"

Twenty years ago, Ken told me about the joy of his favorite "Florida gun," a Winchester Model 61 22 WMR pumpgun, and how effective his Mossberg bolt-action 22 WMR "Chuckster" had been. All I could think about while he waxed nostalgically was, "Why should I buy factory loads that cost four times as much as 22 Long Rifles, when 9 grains of #2400 and a 40-grain Hornet softpoint, or 7 grains of Unique and with a #225415 cast bullet in my 222 or 223 Remington, will do the same thing?" My carefully prepared small game handloads were more accurate than the best 22 WMR I had ever seen. I also could rationalize they were cheaper than 22 WMR ammo, as long as I didn't consider my time in working up the loads and carefully assembling them.

You see, for the experimenter, the intellectual stimulation associated with working up a new load substitutes for planning the hunt, and seeing it work on paper is the thrill of the chase. For most hunters, load development is simply a chore which subtracts from time afield. Of course, I know a few serious hunters are dedicated, seeking that perfect handload that will increase their chances of success, but they are really closet experimenters.

The suburban hunter reads more about hunting than doing it, but many farmers and ranchers would rather spend their leisure time hunting than reloading. For these users, the 22 WMR has considerable merit. They don't use more than a box of ammo a month, so $7 per box of fifty 22 WMRs is a bargain compared to $10 or more for a box of twenty 223 Remingtons. Realistically, ammo cost isn't that big an issue for them, anyway.

C. Rodney James stated that the 22 WMR is ballistically "half a Hornet, and twice a Long Rifle." This sums up the 22 WMR as a rifle cartridge. It is the best rimfire for the occasional shooter and hunter who doesn't reload. It is ideal for quiet varminting in settled areas where the report of a centerfire rifle alarms the livestock and neighbors, or where there are legal restrictions on use of centerfire rifles. For these folks, 50 yards of additional effective range compared to the 22 Long Rifle is significant.

Handgun hunters find the 22 WMR much more effective than the 22 LR. I have always thought it made more sense as a handgun round than as a rifle cartridge. That is because it is highly accurate in single shot pistols such as the T/C Contender, and gives 22 LR "rifle-like" ballistics in handgun barrels of

LOOKING AGAIN

Ruger's M77 in 22 WMR shoots with the 22 LR version and gives 50 yards more effective killing range.

by C.E. HARRIS

6 inches or more. It also provides added flexibility and power in convertible revolvers like the Ruger Single-Six, when you want more energy without having to buy a second gun. While not my first choice as a defense gun, the 22 WMR is probably a better choice than most small revolvers and autos. I can tell you that, when fired in a small room, its report and muzzle flash are far out of proportion to its caliber and energy.

In my limited experience, the 22 WMR is overly destructive on small game for the pot unless used with the 40-grain FMJ bullet. If I wanted a more effective small game cartridge than the 22 LR, which would do for the usual rabbits, squirrels, plus woodchucks and the occasional turkey, I would much prefer a 25-20, 32 H&R Magnum or 32-20 in a Rook rifle. The 40-grain JHP 22 WMR loads are very effective on animals the size of woodchucks and foxes, but make fur burgers of rabbits and squirrels unless you stick to head shots. Even those make a mess of the game bag. FMJs are ideal for trappers and meat hunters, but are more prone to ricochet than 22 LR hollowpoints.

When the 22 WMR was introduced by Winchester in 1959, it was envisioned as a 125-yard cartridge, with flatter trajectory and comparable accuracy to the 22 Long Rifle. It does that. The original published ballistics were 2000 fps with a 40-grain jacketed bullet. Current test barrel figures are 1910 fps for the common 40-grain loads, 1650 for the heavier 50-grain Federal, and 2200 fps for the new 30.5-grain CCI +V. When chronographing typical sporters, you can expect as much as 150-200 fps less than that.

In my experience, the 40-grain JHP is the best all-around load, because at least you can switch to FMJs of the same brand as needed without a significant change in zero. If you are zeroed for 40s and switch to 50s or +Vs, all bets are off. The JHP loads are a bit more destructive than 22 LR hollowpoints, but less so than Yellow Jackets or Stingers, because they do not expand as explosively. The FMJs do little more damage than a 22 LR solid. I haven't tried the new CCI 30.5-grain +V, but am told it anchors chucks more positively than 40-grain JHPs because of better expansion, but ruins meat animals.

C. Rodney James wondered why none of the factories offer a heavy barrel varmint rifle for the 22 WMR. I think he answered his own question when he mentioned the distinction between "hunting" rifles and "precision" rifles. The typical factory sporter weighs 7 pounds with scope, whereas a "precision" rimfire rifle is analogous to a varmint or silhouette rifle. These weigh 9+ pounds and are usually custom-made by experimenters like myself. Experts in the industry, like Bill Ruger, know hunters who buy their rifles at Wal-Mart don't buy heavy barreled varmint rifles, but want light, trim, slick-looking sporters. A few serious and monied "hunter-experimenters" buy the heavy, accurate and expensive 22 WMR rifles like Anschutz 1416s and HK 300s, but the market for these is very limited. The average experimenter will probably build his own.

Single shot BSA Martini target rifles are viable candidates for 22 WMR conversion, but other rifles designed for 22 LR ammunition are dangerous to convert to 22 WMR. This is only partly because of the difference in bore and groove dimensions (22 LR barrels are .217-inch bore and .222-inch groove diameter, whereas 22 WMR runs .219-inch bore and .224-inch groove). It is more significant that typical 22 sporters do not provide adequate support for the cartridge case, will not feed the

AT THE 22 WMR

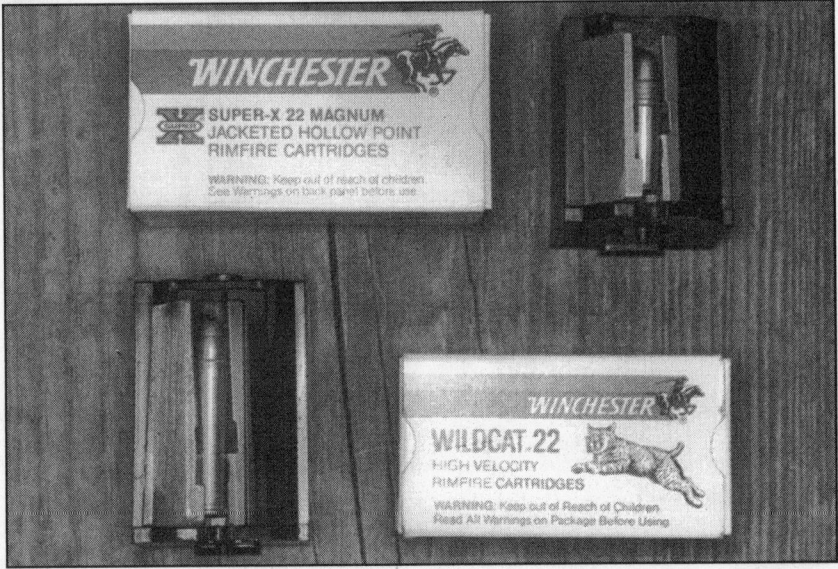

Changes in the M77 are mostly associated with the magazine—which include receiver and inletting modification.

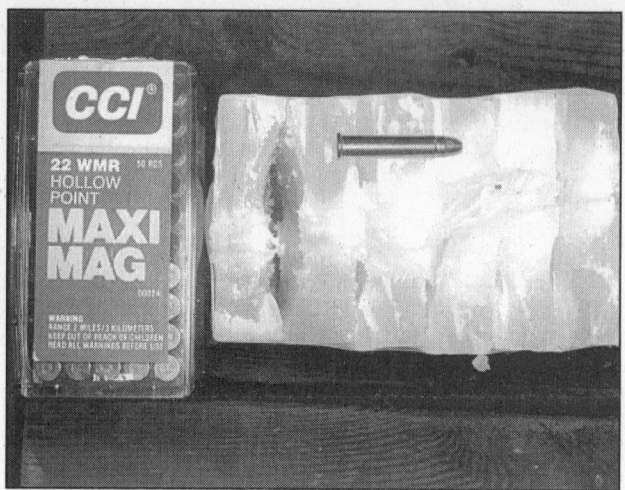

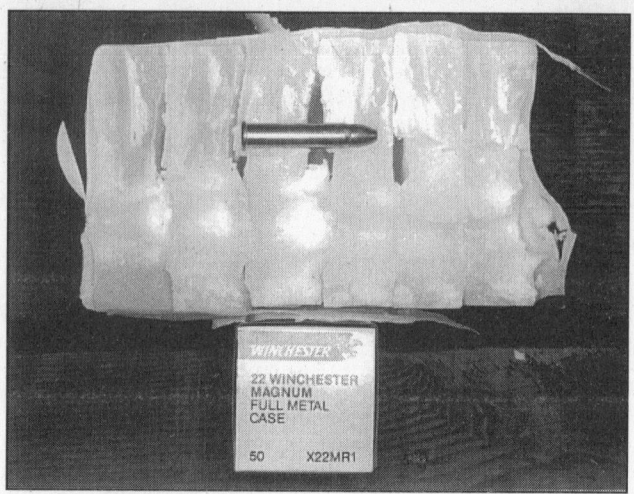

The 22 WMR hollowpoint, this one by CCI, does what hollowpoints do, only more violently than the 22 LR.

In full metal case, as in this Winchester ammo, the 22 WMR is ideal for trappers and meat hunters, the writer believes.

22 WMR ACCURACY RESULTS
Average of Five Consecutive Five-Shot Groups at 100 Yards From Benchrest with Target Telescope

Ten five-shot groups were fired with each ammo in the custom heavy barrel to establish a baseline. The two samples of five groups with each sporter rifle were pooled to provide comparable sample sizes for statistical comparisons.

Ammunition	Standard M77/22 WMR Avg. spread (ins.) #47469	Avg. spread (ins.) #47833	T-Test #47469 v. #47833	Pooled Avg. (ins.)	Heavy Barrel Avg. spread (ins.)	T-Test Std. v. Hvy.	Test Result	Row Mean By Ammo
CCI 40-grain FMJ	2.65	1.53	T=3.002[1]	2.09	1.05	T=3.002	Heavy Better	1.57[4]
CCI 40-grain JHP	1.72	1.47	T=0.916[2]	1.59	1.49	T=0.571	No Improvement	1.54[4]
Fed. 40-grain FMJ	4.77	3.75	T=1.372[2]	4.27	1.82	T=6.129	Heavy Better	3.04[5]
Fed. 50-grain JHP	1.50	1.76	T=0.704[2]	1.60	1.63	T=0.203	No Improvement	1.62[4]
Win. 40-grain FMJ	2.45	2.87	T=0.922[2]	2.63	1.45	T=4.632	Heavy Better	2.04[4]
Win. 40-grain JHP	2.14	1.58	T=1.745[3]	1.86	1.22	T=2.916	Heavy Better	1.54[4]
Column Mean	2.54	2.16		2.34	1.44			

[1]Rifle #47833 is significantly more accurate that #49469 with this ammunition.
[2]Rifles #47833 and #49469 did not prove significantly different with the majority of ammunitions tested.
[3]Rifle #47833 showed a marginally significant preference for this ammunition over #47469, but showed less than .95 confidence based on this limited sample.
[4]The overall differences in accuracy between these ammunitions are not statistically significant.
[5]Federal 40-grain was the least accurate ammunition tested, and the difference is statistically significant from the other brands. It is not known whether this performance is attributed to this type as a whole, or of this was simply a below-average production lot.

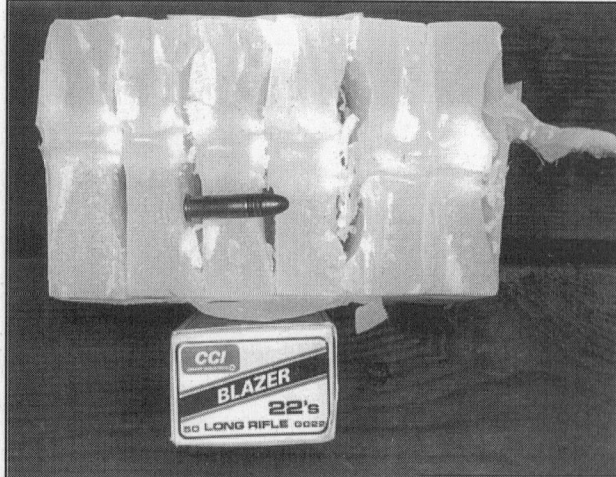

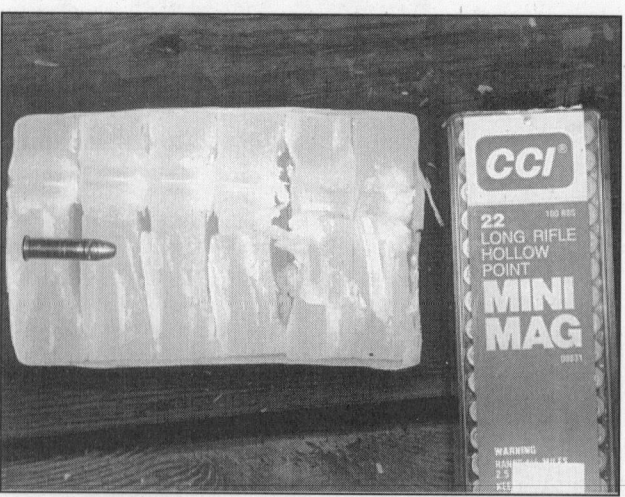

This is what the standard 40-grain lead 22 LR bullet does, this example being a CCI Blazer, which is great as far as it goes.

The hollowpoint 22 LR, this a CCI Mini Mag, provides—within its range—sufficient immediate disruption of tissue to be effective on small game.

longer round, and generally aren't strong enough to handle the WMR's higher pressure levels.

Factory 22 WMR bolt-action sporters like the Marlin 882 and Ruger M77/22 WMR are well within the reach of the average worker and generally shoot 2-inch five-shot groups at 100 yards with ordinary ammo, or perhaps 1½-inch with selected lots they like. The pumps and lever guns such as the Rossi 625A and Winchester 9422M group about double that, which is OK, since they are 50-yard woods rifles rather than open-country varmint guns. I've seen the Anschutz and HK sporters average less than 1-inch five-shot 100-yard groups with imported RWS ammunition, but an inch to 1½ inches is realistic with the U.S. stuff.

My favorite-ever 22 rimfire rifle is a customized Ruger M77/22 with heavy barrel by Arlington, VA, gunsmith James C. Coleman. I wanted to see if C. Rodney James' idea of making a "precision" 22 WMR rifle was feasible. Jim wanted to know also, as he had been asked by potential customers and didn't know the answer. We decided that I could test 22 WMR using my glass-bedded, "switch-barrel" M77/22 rifle by simply adding a heavy 22 WMR barrel to my existing assortment and using the rifle as a single shot. George Wilson of Wilson Arms Co. (63 Leetes Island Road, Branford, CT 06405) provided a 22 WMR barrel blank of the same type he supplies for the Ruger. This was chambered with a SAAMI-dimensioned 22 WMR pressure-velocity barrel reamer. Ten consecutive five-shot groups were fired using a 36x Leupold target scope on the rifle to establish baseline performance for each ammunition.

Later, two production Ruger M77/22 WMR sporters with factory plain barrels and sporting chambers were tested for comparison, firing five consecutive five-shot groups with each ammunition. Results from the two sporters were pooled to provide a comparable sample size to the baseline series fired in the heavy barrel. A total of 300 rounds were fired with six ammunitions in the two sporters, plus the same total number of rounds in the heavy barrel.

The Ruger M77/22 WMR has much in common with the 22 Long Rifle version. The receiver appears the same, but some differences are necessary in the trigger guard

assembly to accommodate the longer magazine of the 22 WMR cartridge. Magazine capacity is reduced by one round to nine cartridges, compared to ten rounds in the 22 LR version. There are corresponding changes in stock inletting to accommodate the altered trigger guard and magazine assembly, but otherwise the rifles are remarkably alike.

Both Ruger M77/22 WMRs were nicely made and finished, but suffered from the same complaint. The trigger pulls were *very* heavy. You could actually lift the bare rifle (without scope) on the cocked trigger. I appreciate that in today's product liability climate manufacturers must be cautious, but a trigger pull which exceeds the weight of the rifle is excessive. An excessively heavy trigger pull will frustrate some users into uneducated tinkering, which may cause more safety problems than had the rifle left the plant with a safe, but usable 3½- to 5-pound trigger pull in the first place. Fortunately, the trigger mechanism on the M77/22 is a simple propped-sear design, and a skilled gunsmith *(Not an amateur—please: KW)* can greatly improve it by careful stoning and replacement of the trigger return spring with a slightly less beefy one. I must note here that the user's manual cautions against any alterations.

The two Ruger M77/22 WMRs shot quite well, averaging slightly over 2 minutes for a total of thirty five-shot groups at 100 yards with each rifle, using six different kinds of ammunition. This equals the grouping expected of average 22 Long Rifle high-velocity ammunition fired from a comparable rifle at the same range.

To compare the accuracy of our 22 WMR results, it is useful to know that the best lots of high-velocity 22 LR ammunition average under 1.5 inches for ten-shot groups at 100 yards from a heavy target rifle. Good standard-velocity and match 22 LR ammunition is expected to group under 1.2 inches. In my experience, accurate 22 sporters produce five-shot extreme spreads which approximate ten-shot groups from a heavy target rifle using the same ammo.

The most accurate 22 WMR ammunition in the sporters was CCI 40-grain JHP, although it ranked fourth out of six in the Wilson heavy barrel. It averaged 1.59 inches for the pooled sample of five targets from the two sporters and 1.49 inches in the heavy barrel. The Federal

50-grain JHP ranked second in the sporters, averaging 1.60 inches, although it ranked fifth out of six in the heavy barrel at 1.63 inches. The best ammunition in the heavy Wilson-barreled Ruger was CCI 40-grain FMJ at 1.05 inches for ten consecutive five-shot groups at 100 yards, though it ranked fourth out of six brands in the sporters at 2.09 inches.

The 22 WMR ammunition ranking dead last was Federal 40-grain FMJ, which averaged 4.27 inches in the two sporters and 1.82 inches in the heavy barrel with target telescope. Of the six U.S. ammunitions tested, four showed significant accuracy improvement in the heavy, Wilson-barreled custom Ruger with minimum, pressure-barrel chamber. CCI

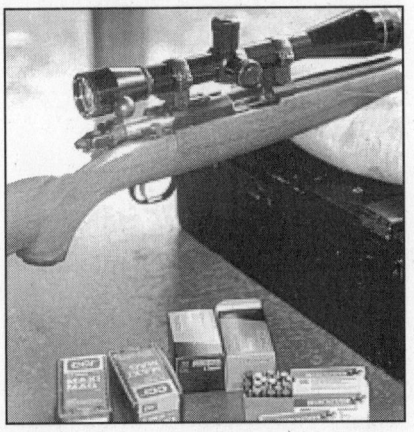

The 22 WMR ammo offers enough variety to suit needs and to permit accuracy matching.

40-grain JHP and Federal 50-grain JHP did not show significant improvement in the heavy barrel, but gave average performance in all the rifles tested. Complete test results are summarized in the accompanying table.

So the moral is the 22 WMR remains a fine choice for the hunter who doesn't reload and wants 50 yards more effective range than a 22 LR. It is about as accurate as 22 LR, not any better, but it reaches a good bit farther. The accuracy enthusiast who expects selected lots of 22 WMR to group like Eley Tenex from his target or silhouette rifle will surely be disappointed. He's better off working up a reduced load for his favorite centerfire varmint rifle if he wants something quieter and less destructive. That's what this experimenter will continue to do. In the meantime, Ken Warner will end up with this Ruger M77/22 WMR, and I know he's going to be delighted with it. ●

Late-issue German WWII K98k.

The third locking lug in the 98's receiver bridge is not its sole distinguishing feature, but is usually held to be the most important single distinction between the M98 and its predecessors.

THE MOST IMPORTANT RIFLE

by JIM THOMPSON

GREATNESS IN firearms is a pretty subjective judgement. But when a gun is nearing its hundredth birthday, hasn't been out of production for much longer than somebody's coffeebreak, and is still a favorite of hunters and precision shooters everywhere, calling it great may be an understatement. About the closest estimate one can acquire of the quantities of the Mauser Model 98 produced thus far is somewhere between 91 million and 125 million. It's hard to come up with a firmer figure, for the rifle was produced in twenty or more countries, most of which used it as a military rifle, and another large group of nations produced clones, copies and ripoffs of the original, often in quan-

tities so vast they couldn't give a production figure if they wanted, and they don't want.

Only the Russian AK-47 design comes anywhere close to the production figures of the Model 98. It's probably not that close, but no one knows for sure. The Chinese and Japanese produced Model 98 rifles and copies in vast quantities, both for themselves and for client states. The Belgians, Poles, Austrians, Czechs, Iranians, Yugoslavs, Turks, Spaniards, Argentines, Brazilians, Mexicans and others produced military M98s in quantity; others produced near-copies and "improvements" for military use like the U.S. M1903 and '03A3. (Yes, the Mauser firm was paid at least $400,000 in

royalties until at least 1914.) There were also the U.S/British P17/P14 "Enfields" and the late French MAS derivatives in this category.

And that's just the military rifles. Handmade Model 98s in calibers up to 50 Browning are still being turned out by builders like Fred Wells of Prescott, Arizona. French, Dutch, British and Italian sporting rifles and actions have been made in standard, miniature and magnum lengths. The Finnish Sakos and the Swedish Carl Gustaf and Husqvarna are all 98-type actions. Many of the countries which used the 98 as a military rifle produced and most *still* produce the action as a hunting piece. The famous Swiss annual *Waffen Digest* recently (1992 edition)

Marking on standard German K98k of WWII vintage, circa 1944.

carried a couple of unusual announcements: One was descriptive of a "new" product called *Mauser Jagdrepetierer Modell 98*, a rather familiar model introduced by the mother firm, Mauser-Werke, Oberndorf-am-Neckar, absent from the thriving market for their most famous product for 46 years. Waffen Frankonia also introduced their new K98k military rifle, actually a reworked and specification updated military rifle with new parts and stocks, as and where necessary.

So why introduce—at fairly high prices, incidentally—technology almost a century old as a new product

process is that such rifles can be built up slowly, on a sort of self-regulating installment plan, adding a new trigger in January, scope or mount in March, stock in June or July, total refinish some other year. That you cannot do with a new rifle which comes in a fancy box.

But there's more to the Mauser 98 saga. From 1898 to about 1962, military Mausers were built in considerable variety. All specifications called for minimum vise-secured accuracy level *under* two minutes of angle. Most performed better. Of course, given the limitations of a broad V rear sight and skinny front blade, or

repeat to shooters and collectors that hardness very decidedly *is not strength*; most materials in use today develop their strengths at hardness levels way below the vogue of forty years ago, and are, in fact, dangerous at high hardness levels. Hardness is relevant in any respect only to a given material in a given application and lately, more often than not, optimum strengths are obtained at levels far below what was popular thirty to forty years ago. When someone in a gun store begins to talk hardness level as some kind of quality determinant, your best response is to turn

EVER MADE

uct at a time of worldwide economic recession? Simply put: demand. The Mauser 98 is closer to a true basic product than nearly any other firearm, and though the analogy seems strained, it occupies a market position similar to eggs, flour or rice. If one needs an accurate rifle for hunting, sniping, experimenting or target shooting, the ancient three-lug "safety" action is a fine place to start. Indeed, structurally, there's little to choose between any M98 and the latest bolt guns from, say, Weatherby or Remington; there have been refinements, but the nuts and bolts have been very similar for a long time, and almost anything in the way of doo-dads one can imagine or concoct for a Model 70 Winchester can be acquired, built or purchased for the Mauser.

Of course, for civilians, even purchasing an old military action for very little money and doing the full custom job on it doesn't save a penny over a top-of-the-line commercial product. The main difference is, when the consumer reworks his own Model 98, he gets *exactly* what he wants—no more, no less—and if he can do some or all of the work, he really can save a few bucks. What is unique about this time-honored

pyramidal "barleycorn" post, shooter-limited factors meant such a level of accuracy was seldom maintained in the field. There were no mystery alloys used in Model 98 Mausers, and if the odd stamped or roughly soldered or welded part found its way onto a wartime K98k, it was always someplace where it bore little stress. The 98s were made for so long that whole metallurgical techniques changed, but, surprisingly, this had almost no impact on the rifle's quality or durability. Even the military finishes of the rifles generally exceeded the workaday qualities of most of today's civilian firearms.

Most original specification rifles from about 1898 through World War II used what are today considered rather primitive ordnance steels, but carefully heat-treated so that while the core remained very soft, the surface was often as high as 62 on the Rockwell C scale. FN rifles and many from Eastern Europe used tighter dimensional tolerances overall, used far more sophisticated metallurgy, and show lower hardness figures. However, this latter group comprises generally superior actions, far more durable. I am often compelled to

on your heel and leave. The very strongest bolt actions in the world, the Japanese Arisakas, are quite soft. Dimensions, design, venting and strength determine the overall safety and quality of a rifle action; hardness alone as a factor is bunk. Read *Hatcher's Notes* to get a more specific idea of how these matters translate to reality.

The engineering factors which made the M98 a landmark were simple progressions from the M1892-1896 designs, but they were significant enough that few countries could avoid discarding whatever they had been using to adopt the new system. Rifles just three to ten years old in military service became second-line *materiel* in most of the world. The third or "emergency" locking lug, the inside receiver ring collar, and the vastly improved, safer, more reliable firing mechanism with its lockout to prevent premature ignition with a broken firing pin, combined with a conglomerate of earlier Mauser evolutionary features and improved metallurgy to produce a rifle which looked and worked very much like its predecessors. In terms of safety under rough conditions and rapid-fire, though, the Model 98 stood alone.

This assortment is only a part of the new cornucopia of Mauser 98 delight brought to us by the changing world picture. The author's point is that any one of them in barely decent condition is a fine rifle for real rifle work.

It surprises many collectors and shooters that relatively few Mausers were actually built by the designing firm. "Few" is, of course, a relative term: The Oberndorf factory produced millions. But almost from the beginning, demand was so vast and deep that firms in Europe and elsewhere were licensed to produce the guns. Loewe, DWM, Steyr, Sauer and Son, Fabrique Nationale, the Czech works at BRNO, Radom in Poland, all the German government arsenals and all their subcontractors, and as many as a hundred small factories in Central Europe were producing actions and/or complete rifles by the mid-1920s.

If one wishes to analyze the impact Paul Mauser had on the world, he should dig through the cartridge specifications in one of the better reloading manuals and refer back to Paul Mauser's 1880s and 1890s cartridges. He'll find almost every currently popular medium-power rifle cartridge owes much to the compatible cartridges Mauser designed from their inception to be quickly and cheaply adapted to standard rifle actions. The Mauser originals—7.92x57, 7x57, 7.65x53 (sometimes called 7.65x54)—and the Brenneke cartridges developed in direct consultation with the Mauser firm do not resemble the 308, 30/06, 270 and others by accident; from case heads to bottlenecks, modern cartridge configurations are virtually all derived from original Mauser ideas.

Before World War I, the Turks, Argentines, Chileans, Mexicans, Brazilians and many others had adopted the military 98. By the mid-1930s, there were already so many Model 98 Mauser versions and variants that a complete listing would've been almost impossible. And by the late 1940s, another World War later, such a catalog was literally impossible. Many countries had ordered rifles in that period from several manufacturers and in several configurations and lengths. Rifles were also refurbished, of course, and calibers were sometimes changed.

Brazil, at one time or another, for example, ordered quantities of rifles from virtually all the major European manufacturers and in 1954 began to manufacture receivers at Itajuba Arsenal. So when one says "Brazilian Mauser," he may be describing a Model 1908 29-inch long rifle, similar to the German Gew.98 or K98a revision built by DWM; a Czech 08/34, almost identical to the Nazi K98k but with a 22-inch barrel and in 7mm; the Oberndorf-built M1935 long rifle, essentially a later clone of the original Model 1908, the "2nd Variation" 08/34; various rifles shortened to 24 inches and barrels rebored to 30-06 and appropriately modified; the M1954, a 30-06 rifle receiver built as such, but completed with parts left over from all kinds of surplus rifles, including German 98ks; or as many as a dozen other fairly obscure variants ordered in small quantities for special purposes or from firms unwilling to advance

FN—are very handy to gunsmiths who wish to stock actions that can be delivered in a variety of configurations.

However, the differences in size are minimal; a person chooses one or the other usually based upon aesthetics or, more commonly, what's available at a given time. The truly short or miniature actions and the magnum length units are either carefully modified and sectioned militaries or civilian actions. Virtually any Model 98 action that has been checked for cracks and has been rebarreled with correct headspace is quite safe for any standard cartridge which can be stuffed into it. Smiths have become adept at opening up magazines and adapting receivers even to the longer magnum rounds.

But I have always been fond of shooting military rifles, in general, and Mausers, in particular, in their

bought used specimens of other country's service rifles after both World Wars, and may have gotten some from the Soviets. So the variety was startling. I saw several hundred rifles, which ranged from truly odd-ball 16½- to 17-inch barreled 8mm carbines to standard German-issue Gewehr 98s from World War I, German Standard Modell rifles, K98ks in German-issue style and complete with World War II fits and codes, and just about everything else one can imagine finding its way to that part of the world. Since these rifles saw as much as sixty years of hard duty, most were pretty beat up, though some were far better than average.

Springfield Sporters (Penn Run, PA) brought in most of the Model 98 Mauser supply from Yugoslavia. These were mostly rebuilt in Yugoslavia, and to very high standards. There were several variants, including the enormous quantity of VZ.24/G.24t rifles captured from the Waffen SS; K98ks and refurbished G.98s from the same source; Yugoslavian-built pre- and post-World War II rifles; Czech contract rifles from the late '20s and the '30s; and oddments of other Central European Mausers captured by the Yugoslavians.

These rifles, in addition to being well-maintained and beautifully rebuilt, contain more of the "if this rifle could talk" history collectors appreciate than most other hardware on the market and genuinely deserve a place in any European Mauser collection, despite—maybe because of—the applied Yugoslavian markings. They're also good actions for conversion, although most bear mint-like 8mm barrels, and throwing them out would be foolish. Century International Arms supplied virtually all the Latin American Mausers pictured within this article. If the close-ups reveal anything, it's that the "export" guns were often made to higher standards than those for German domestic consumption. And why not? Foreign contracts were open to competitive commercial bid and nothing was locked in automatically. Most were made to very high standards, like the best sporting rifles of the period. And since I had an opportunity to compare directly with German rifles of the same years, it was pretty obvious that finish quality was higher on the DWM, Steyr, and even Mauser/Oberndorf guns for Latin America. What was interesting was

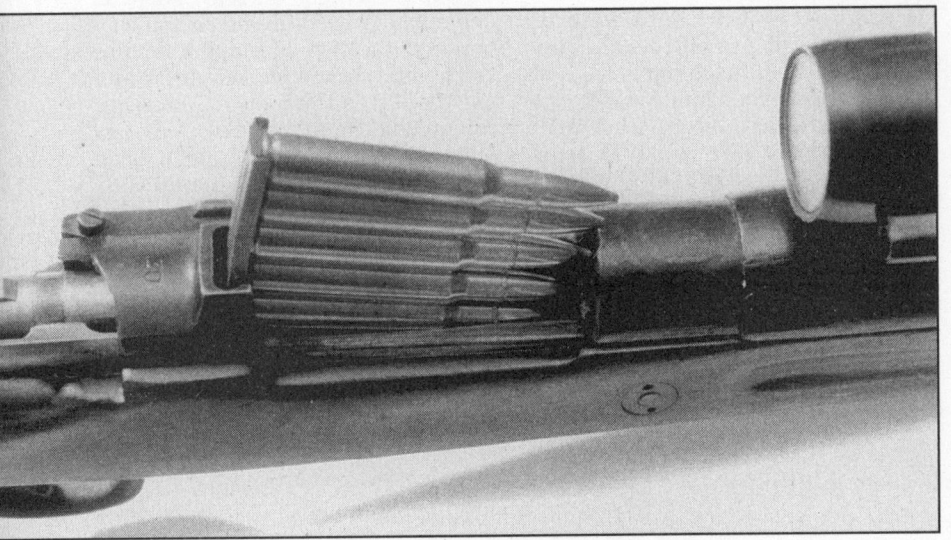

FN-built Peruvian M1946 short rifle accepting five rounds in a stripper clip of the 30-06 for which these post-WWII rifles were chambered.

normal credit to the Brazilian government and therefore delivered only on a cash in advance basis.

The most common general action configuration of the M98 Mauser is the so-called "large ring, standard length." The receiver ring measures 1.410 inches. The "small ring" rifles measure 1.3 inches. There are also differences in overall configuration, but the ring size is readily discernible and is, therefore, the main identifier. The standard action is 8.75 inches long; the "short" action measures 8.5 inches in length and, at 43 ounces, is 2 ounces lighter than the standard length. There are also large ring, small thread actions which accept M93/95-style barrels, and these—especially those built by

original configurations. The performance is surprising, the variety amazing, and the original cartridges are at least as good as the 30-06 and 7.62x51mm rounds to which many were later converted.

In the six years or so since GCA '68 was modified to allow curio and relic firearms to enter the country again, quite a variety of Mausers have entered. The pictures accompanying and the information with them will supply some specifics, but I'll relate some general data here.

The first big batch of Mausers to enter the U.S. recently arrived from China, and encompassed virtually all eras and nearly all manufacturers. The Chinese ordered millions, made more millions, apparently the shooting quality delivered down-range.

Before developing that data, however, let me note that every Mauser I shot that's pictured here was in the very best available condition. This cost me extra; it'll cost you extra, but it's dollars well spent. It always pays off. Of course, this caution does not apply so much if you're doing a full-house sporter conversion; Century sells actions in various conditions, already stripped of their barrels and wood; often, complete rifles in fair to good condition cost less than the actions. But if you mean to do any shooting as-is, get the best condition available. If you're a collector, this is especially true. Pay the extra money, and it'll always be reflected in the gun's long-term value. It also always costs much more to restore a clunker than to purchase a better rifle in the first place.

It's also wise to shoot the best ammo you can. Surprisingly, the quality of surplus ammo is now very high. The FN Belgian 7.65mm Argentine and the San Francisco (Argentina) 7.65 shot as well as any military ammo I've ever shot. Yugoslavian PrviPartizan and Yugoslavian surplus 8mm, also from Century, performed beautifully and very accurately, as did the Yugoslavian 7x57.

Several of the rifles shot very close to MOA, and the Peruvian M1935 7.65—which looked quite rough but sported a superb bore—actually delivered a $7/8$-inch group at just over 100 yards. The 7mm long rifles also performed exceptionally, especially the two M1935 Brazilian Mausers, one of which was the proverbial gnat's eyelash below the Peruvian gun in on-target performance. The Chilean Steyr M1912 was not far behind. Even the ugly M1954 Brazilian—as rough a rifle as I've ever seen and dared to fire, but sporting a pristine bore and perfect headspace even by commercial standards—performed right up to the standards of my National Match M1 in 30-06. The Yugoslavian PrviPartizan 7mm 175-grain loading shot to point of aim in the Brazilian M1935 at 300 yards, but with the sights set for 100 meters. The trajectory suggested high velocity and excellent power, but I determined—since there were no signs of high pressure—chronographing was unnecessary.

The little Argentine M1909 carbines—one an Argentine-built DGFM, the other a DWM from Germany—delivered $1^1/_2$-inch groups at 100 yards. Those are five-shot groups. I fired three rounds of Norma's excellent softpoints per gun and did a little better.

Again, as noted early on, these were best groups. No Model 98 sight is quite discriminatory enough to deliver this sort of accuracy anyway, except from a rest, and even then, eyesight limitations and the hard realities of real shooting don't allow the shooter to do that consistently. But the potential is there. I've lately been recommending B-Square's long eye relief scope setups because they don't demand anything be drilled or ground up, and the military Mausers thus retain their collector's value. Also, the stripper loading capability is maintained, and the bolt handles need not be modified.

I'd be remiss if I didn't mention the tradeoff equation with high-powered rifles. That is, the little $6^1/_2$- to $7^1/_2$-pound carbines are light and handy, but the Mauser buttplate is downright abusive, and short barrels generate serious muzzleblast. The 29-inch barreled long rifles are cumbersome, but sweet to shoot and easy to balance, even over long sessions. The 22- to 24-inch barreled guns, as one might expect, are about midway between the two. Military ammo in 7mm and 8mm is loaded stiffer and shoots better than most American commercial ammo; in fact, I recommend RWS or Norma factory loads in 7.92x57JS (8mm) or handloads. American 8mm is so underloaded that European publications list it as a whole different caliber.

Paul Mauser died in 1914. But you can bet on it: Come 2014, his last major rifle design will be alive, well, and living almost everywhere. ●

A composite "Kar.98b," made in 8mm to approximate the interwar German specification, bearing parts from at least six countries, but primarily comprising a Greek-issue FN 24/30 action, German M1936 "Olympic" target barrel and Argentine stock, with fittings from Turkey, Austria and elsewhere. Shoots well.

by W.E. SPRAGUE

TRICKS and TREATS

I CAN THINK OF no other handgun that pistolsmiths have tuned, rebuilt, and modified to suit more goals and purposes than the M1911 45 ACP. The 45 automatic, as it's commonly called, reigns supreme in the realm of conventional bullseye shooting, dominates freestyle combat matches, is a potent contender in the sport of metallic silhouette shooting, and has only the 44 Magnum double-action revolver as a practical rival in bowling-pin competitions. And, of course, it has long since been accepted as the one to beat in the area of self-defense.

As a result of its widespread use, more modifications, adaptations and accessories have probably been devised for the M1911 than for any other handgun in history. Judging from the number of ads in the vari-

This otherwise stock 45 has no less than ten drop-ins and add-ons from as many different suppliers.

for your 45

Drop-ins that might make a difference

ous shooting magazines, it's probably safe to say that more such modifications, adaptations and accessories exist for the 45 than for all other handguns combined. And though many of these require the services of a gunsmith, what are commonly called "add-on" or "drop-in" parts comprise the bulk of the trade and hold the greatest interest for the largest number of shooters. These are accessories of a type that can be installed at home with very little trouble, and range from simple, redesigned replacement parts on up through such major components as frames, slides and barrels.

Where barrels are concerned, the 45 owner can choose from a generous menu of replacements, including extended barrels that can be ported, or fitted with compensators, to help reduce recoil and promote faster follow-up shots. But whether extended or standard length, perhaps the most popular are corrosion-resistant stainless steel barrels.

While offered by many suppliers, these were pioneered back in the early 1970s by Bar-Sto Precision Machine, and today Bar-Sto offers them for virtually every pistol on the

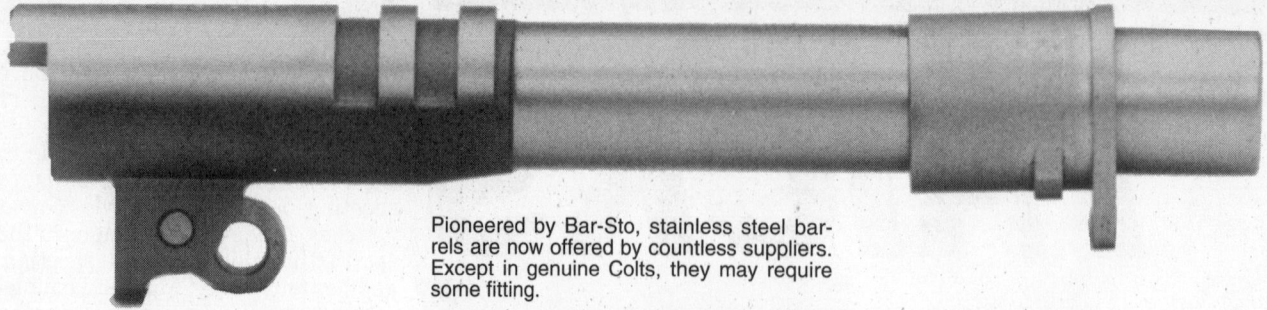

Pioneered by Bar-Sto, stainless steel barrels are now offered by countless suppliers. Except in genuine Colts, they may require some fitting.

market, including, of course, the 45. With prices starting at about $135, Bar-Sto barrels are superbly finished, held to close dimensional tolerances, and include refinements such as radiused chamber mouths to help eliminate feeding problems. And, while their match-grade barrels must be professionally fitted, their standard barrels, for either the Government Model or Commander, can be had as drop-in units, providing the pistol is a genuine Colt. Barrels for clones and copies, Bar-Sto warns, may or may not require fitting; it depends on how faithful the copy is to the Colt.

A number of suppliers now offer stainless steel barrels that come with their own compensator units. Brownells, for example, widely known as a primary source for gunsmith tools and supplies, also offers a wide assortment of brand-name gun parts and accessories, including a dozen or so different "comp kits," as these barrel/compensator units are commonly called. The installation of most of them requires the services of a gunsmith, but several can be had as true drop-in units for either competition or self-defense guns.

One such is the Quadra-Comp II, developed by Centaur Systems. Priced at about $269.95, and available either directly from Centaur or through Brownells, it consists of a 5.5-inch bushingless tapered stainless barrel with a radiused chamber mouth; a dual-ported, dual-chambered compensator; a buffered, captive recoil spring with full-length recoil guide rod; and Centaur's exclusive adjustable slide stop system.

This latter piece is perhaps the most unusual feature of the Quadra-Comp II. The slide stop—which comes with a small roller, a specially dimensioned barrel link, and several shims of varying thickness—has a groove milled into the top of its link pin contact area. By "stacking" the proper selection of shims in the groove (initially, a matter of trial and error), then topping them with the

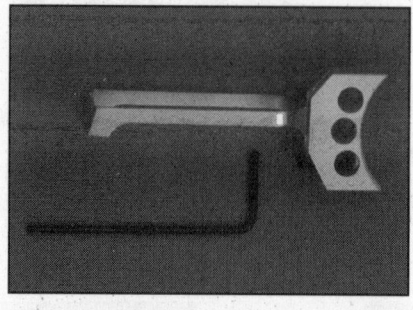

Lightweight replacement triggers, such as this ultra-light from Wilson, are available from many different suppliers.

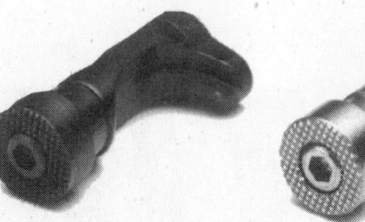

Extended magazine catches—these from Ed Brown Products—provide a more positive magazine "drop."

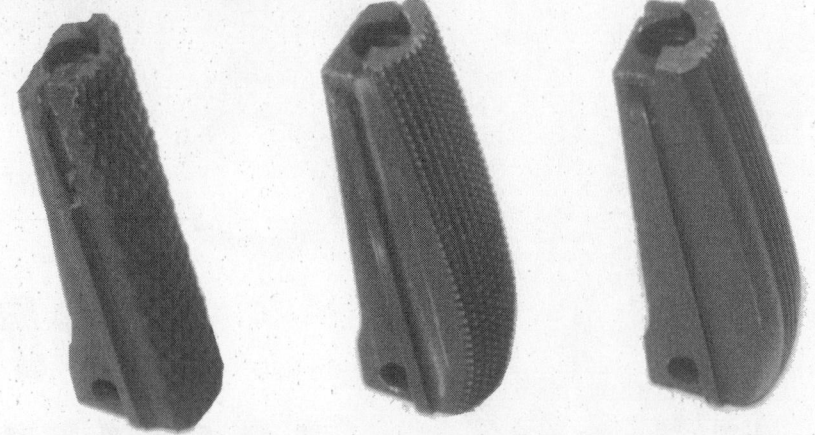

Whichever—straight, standard, checkered, not—mainspring housing, it's there today.

roller, consistent lock-up, and so greater accuracy, is achieved by a camming action that forces the chamber end of the barrel up against the rear of the slide, while forcing the muzzle end down against the front in sort of a V-block fashion. Extra shims, supplied with the system, can be used to compensate for wear.

This same slide stop system is part of another drop-in offering from Centaur. Called the Quadra-Lok "T" and priced at $179.95, it includes a stainless barrel (without a compensator) and a so-called universal bushing—which the latter, according to Centaur, fits any 45 slide, providing solid muzzle support and making the entire unit transferable to any M1911. Meant to enhance the accu-

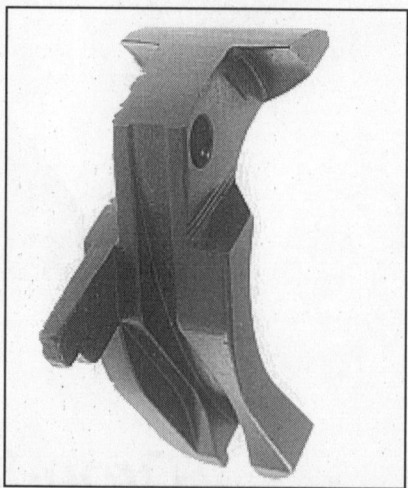

Replacement grip safeties are made with a broad extension to keep the web of the hand from being pinched by the hammer.

racy of Tactical Class IPSC competition pistols, it will, of course, do the same for plain-vanilla 45s.

A far less costly means of improving the accuracy of a stock-barreled 45 is the Wilson-Dwyer Combat Group Gripper, a modified recoil spring guide from Wilson's Gun Shop. Retailing at around $26.95 for either the Government Model or the Commander, it has a special barrel link with a cam on its leading edge

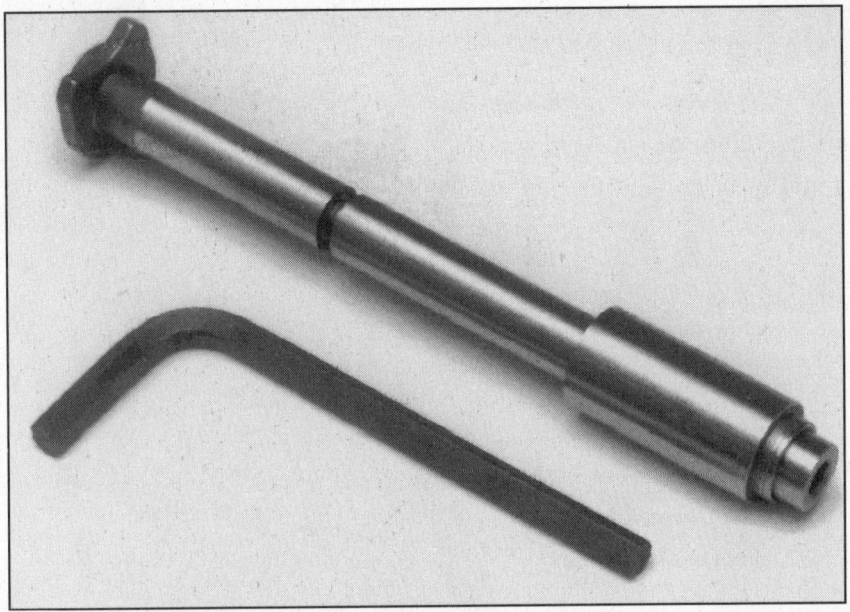

Full-length recoil guide rods—this from Ed Brown Products—keep the recoil spring from kinking or binding.

that engages a leaf spring in the rear of the guide; thus, as the slide moves forward into battery, the link is forced up and forward by the spring, which in turn forces the barrel up into the locking lugs in the slide. The result is a more consistent lock-up and greater accuracy than might be obtained in a standard production gun. In fact, according to many experts, the Gripper can provide a greater increase in accuracy than can be achieved with any other drop-in or accessory.

With the 45 that's fired a *lot*, it's a very good idea to protect it from the recurrent rearward impact of its slide, which, over time, can result in a cracked frame. So, for years now, several different suppliers have

offered recoil buffers designed to do just that. Typical of these is the type made by Bar-Sto. Priced at $30 for either the Government Model or Commander, and made from the same quality stainless that Bar-Sto uses in its barrels, it consists of a standard recoil spring guide fitted with a strong spring-loaded plunger that extends beyond the forward end of the guide to contact the slide during recoil. When compressed by the

Designed to promote consistent lock-up, the Wilson-Dwyer Group Gripper seems to do more to improve the accuracy of a stock 45 than any other drop-in or accessory.

Precision made magazines, such as these from Wilson, have special followers, extra-power springs and pads or bumpers to aid rapid magazine change.

moving slide, the plunger slows the final part of its rearward travel, thus easing the blow when it strikes the usual arresting surface. In addition, as the slide moves forward into battery, the plunger spring accelerates its closing, often improving feeding by supplying more energy to carry the cartridge forward.

Yet another way to offset the effects of the recoiling slide is Wilson's Combat Shok-Buff kit. With a price tag of only $6.75, the basic kit consists of a heavy-duty recoil spring and two injection-moulded poly fiber buffers, one of which is meant to be sandwiched between the spring and the pistol's recoil spring guide. Of the same shape and approximate thickness of the metal stop at the rear of the guide itself, the poly fiber buffer, good for 1000 rounds of hardball, absorbs the final impact of the rearward-moving slide. The poly fiber buffers, in packs of six, can be had without the heavy-duty spring for the same modest price, while at the top end of the price scale ($36.95) is what might be called the deluxe version of the kit. This consists of six poly fiber buffers, an extra-power firing pin spring, a heavy-duty recoil spring, a "softball" target spring, and a full-length recoil guide rod and plug.

Full-length recoil guide rods, meant to take the place of the standard recoil spring guide, are in themselves popular drop-in items. These help to promote smoother functioning and longer recoil spring life by keeping the recoil spring from kink-

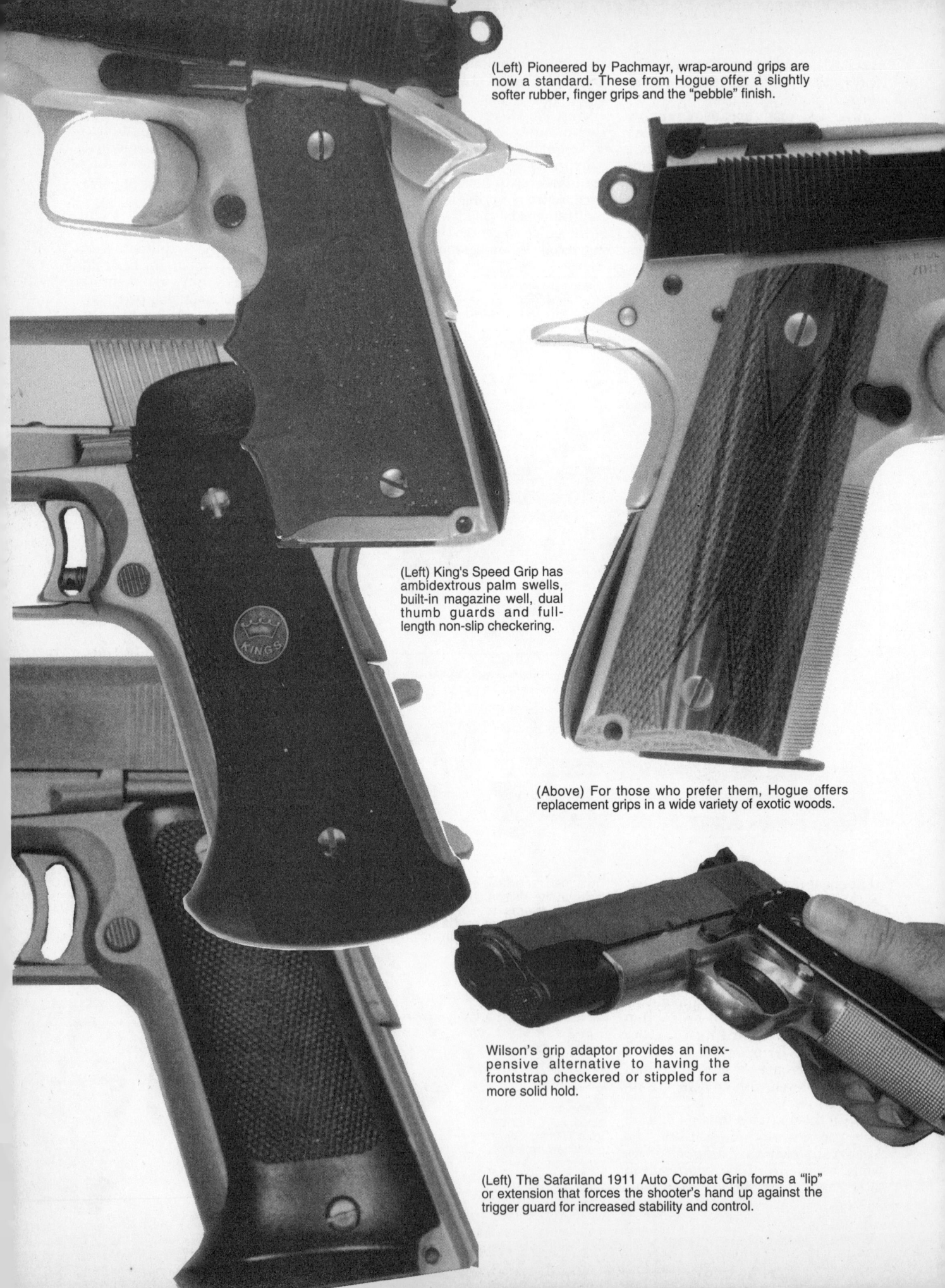

(Left) Pioneered by Pachmayr, wrap-around grips are now a standard. These from Hogue offer a slightly softer rubber, finger grips and the "pebble" finish.

(Left) King's Speed Grip has ambidextrous palm swells, built-in magazine well, dual thumb guards and full-length non-slip checkering.

(Above) For those who prefer them, Hogue offers replacement grips in a wide variety of exotic woods.

Wilson's grip adaptor provides an inexpensive alternative to having the frontstrap checkered or stippled for a more solid hold.

(Left) The Safariland 1911 Auto Combat Grip forms a "lip" or extension that forces the shooter's hand up against the trigger guard for increased stability and control.

ing or binding against the slide, which can slow the movement of the slide, and thus the cycling rate, whenever the gun is fired. They come with their own specially designed spring plugs and, often as not, are two-piece affairs joined by fine precision threads for ease of assembly. Typical of these is the two-piece unit designed by Ed Brown, renowned gunsmith and head of Ed Brown Products. At a cost of about $27.50, it's available for either the Government Model or Commander.

Some suppliers offer full-length recoil guide rods that incorporate additional features. Wilson's, for example, has a two-piece rod, priced at $39.95, that includes their afore-mentioned Group Gripper as part of its design, thus affording the standard 45 with a factory barrel the advantages of a full-length rod plus the consistent lock-up and improved accuracy of the Group Gripper.

Consistent lock-up and improved accuracy are also added features of a full-length guide designed by Accu-Systems and available either directly or from J.P. Enterprises. Called the Dual Action Buffer Spring System, this $69.95 drop-in is really a two-piece rod with the pieces permanently joined in overlapping sections by a stout roll pin, and with a secondary spring contained within the breech-end section. This, in combination with its heavy-duty recoil spring and a head designed to match the curves and angles of the barrel link and lug, applies upward tension on the barrel and keeps the slide from slamming against its stop.

Yet another "added-feature" full-length guide rod is one designed by master gunsmith Richard Heinie and available from

Because of its adjustable slide stop system, the Quadra-Comp II from Centaur Systems is one of the few drop-in comp kits that requires no gunsmith fitting whatsoever. (Bilal photo)

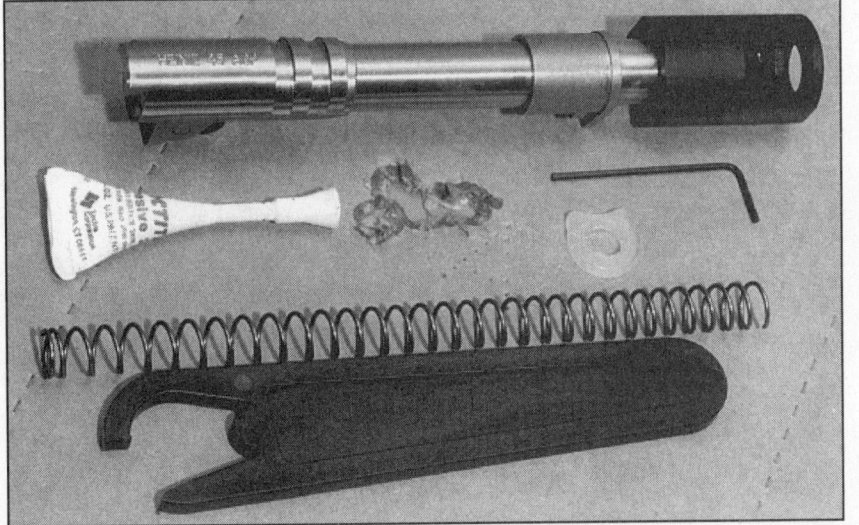

his company, Heinie Specialty Products. Priced at $65, it's made from heavy tungsten steel and, replacing the .5-ounce factory spring guide, adds 3.5 ounces of weight to the front of the pistol, thus reducing felt recoil and muzzle flip.

Richard Heinie's comp kit is a true drop-in for 99 percent of all Colts. Clones and copies, though, may require some fitting.

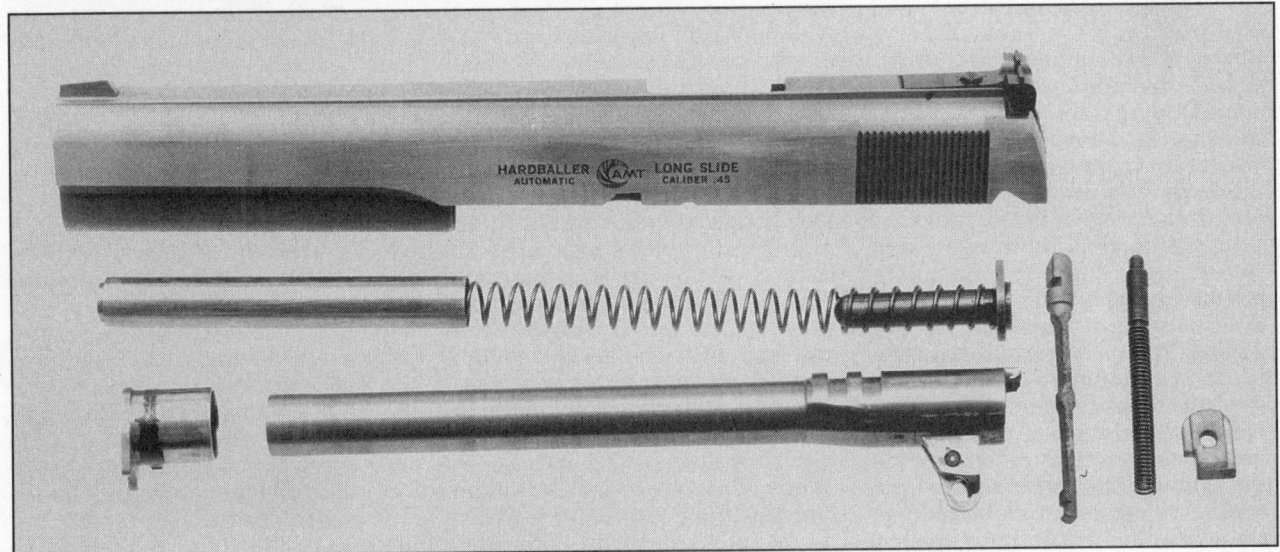

The Long Slide Kit from AMT, which includes a 7-inch stainless barrel and slide, replaces the entire upper assembly of a stock 45, providing a greater sight radius and thus improved accuracy.

Characterized by a familiar white "Y" rear-sight outline, Millet sights offer a wide variety of popular replacements for the M1911.

Low light sights, like Millet's Tritium Night Sight, utilize a minuscule amount of a radioactive isotope, allowing them to be seen even in total darkness.

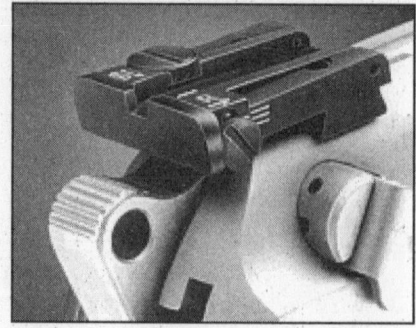

For the pistol owner who uses different bullet weights and loads, an adjustable rear sight, like this one from Pachmayr, is a highly desirable replacement.

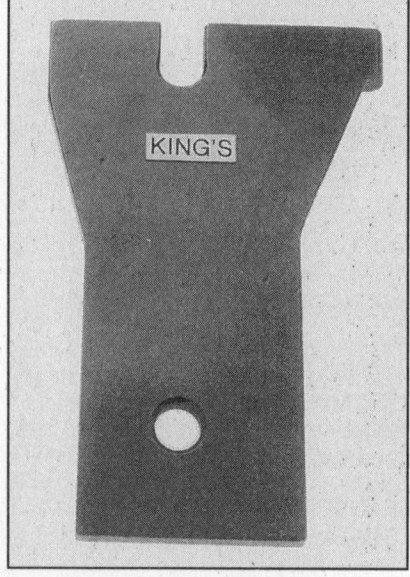

King's "arsenal-type" front-sight staking tool can be used by almost anyone with the ability to handle a file and mallet, and with it, a profusion of both fixed and adjustable sights becomes available to the 45 owner.

Lighter and less expensive than other red dot sights, the "epc" is chemically bonded to the gun, thus doing away with the need for a separate mount.

Two other popular items are redesigned replacements for the standard grip safety and mainspring housing. The former, another drop-in offered by virtually everyone in the trade, is made with a broad—or sometimes upswept—extension at its upper rear that sets back over the web of the hand to keep it from being pinched between the hammer and the tang of the standard safety. Often called a "beavertail" grip safety, it also helps position the gun more firmly in the hand.

Although many of the upswept versions require fitting and frame contouring by a competent gunsmith, the other type can usually be owner-installed quite easily, especially those made by King's Gunworks. Over the years, I've installed no less than a dozen of

King's #203 grip safeties ($33 for the Colt Series 70, $35.50 for the Series 80) without any fitting whatsoever. At comparable prices, King's also offers a model to fit the Springfield frame, and one that's notched to allow the use of a Commander hammer with the Colt Government Model pistol.

Two reasons for replacing the factory mainspring housing would be that the 45 owner either wants one that's checkered or one that's flat (and checkered), rather than arched, because it affords a more comfortable hold. If the pistol is a genuine Colt—clones and copies might need a bit of fitting—several suppliers can oblige. Wilson, for one, has deeply checkered steel housings, either flat or arched, at a cost of $36.95 in blue and $39.95 in stainless. Pachmayr, for another, offers drop-in housings covered in checkered rubber at either $18.95 or $19.95, depending on the style.

Lightweight replacement triggers, with either plastic or aluminum finger pieces—and most with adjustable screw-type trigger stops—are available from several different sources. Pachmayr has one with a self-lubricating nylon finger piece at a cost of $14.95, while Wilson offers one at $17.95 with an aluminum finger piece that's further lightened by a trio of holes drilled through it.

Replacement magazines of plain steel in both standard and increased capacity are available from several vendors. Generally, though, anything over a ten-round length tends to make the gun cumbersome. Far more popular are standard length and eight-round magazines in stainless steel. Precision-made, they usually incorporate such features as specially designed followers meant to eliminate feeding failures, extra-power springs to resist "spring set," and so-called combat pads or bumpers designed to facilitate a rapid change of magazines, while guarding against damage should the unit be dropped.

Worthy of special mention is the magazine made by Eagle International. Priced at $31.50, and available in either natural or blackened stainless steel, it holds *nine* rounds, instead of seven, without increasing its overall length beyond that of a seven- or even eight-round magazine equipped with a combat pad. Its secret seems to be a unique constant force spring that takes up very little space inside the body, thus allowing it to hold two more rounds than a standard type with its conventional spring compressed at the bottom. In any case, with one round in the chamber, the 45 equipped with an Eagle mag has more than a 42 percent increase in immediate firepower.

Aimpoint, pioneer of the electro-optical red dot, offers a wide variety of laser sights.

By projecting a red dot on the target, laser sights, like Alpec Team's Beam Shot, allow the shooter to concentrate on what he intends to shoot instead of his sight alignment.

Another popular item offered by several suppliers is the extended magazine catch. Designed to be more accessible to the shooter's thumb, it generally consists of a standard catch to which extra length is added by way of a "button" attached to its protruding end with a screw that sets flush to the surface of the button after installation. Typical examples are those available from Ed Brown Products at a cost of $29.95 for either a blued or stainless steel version, or $31.95 for a hard chromed stainless model.

The item most often replaced by the 45 owner would seem to be the pistol's factory grips. Accordingly, there seems to be an almost unlimited assortment of available replacements in exotic woods, rubber and various plastics, making a proper choice a matter of knowing exactly what the owner wants from his replacements.

For the shooter who wants a well-balanced blend of beauty and function, a fine line of quasi-custom grips is offered by David Wayland, long-time master craftsman and grip designer, whose business name is Wayland Precision Wood Products. Called Classic+ Grips, they follow the factory shape, but are made a bit fuller, incorporating subtle changes

that improve the hand-to-gun fit. A basic set in tropical wood with smooth finish and a German silver oval inlay (suitable for engraving) set in the right-hand panel costs $34.95, with hand-cut checkering, if desired, adding another $24 to $70, depending on the grade of checkering desired (deluxe, presentation, extra fine, etc.) and the number of lines per inch.

Similar replacements are available from Hogue Grips, a firm best known for its unique revolver Monogrip. The Hogue grips, though, more closely replicate the 45's original style, with the exception of one type that comes with finger grooves designed to enclose the pistol's front strap. Available in Pau Ferro, Goncalo Alves and comparable woods, they range in price from $34.95 to $42.95, depending on the style and kind of wood.

For those more interested in function than appearance, the choice is often a set of so-called wrap-arounds. Made of a tough synthetic rubber, or in some cases, a proprietary elastomer, they consist of a single piece, the center section or web of which completely encloses the smooth front strap of the grip frame, providing a positive, nonskid hold. The only problem confronting a would-be buyer would seem to be a confusing array of choices.

Pachmayr, for example, who introduced the concept back in 1974, now offers three different styles for the Government Model or Commander, each with slightly different features, and each at a cost of $30.50. Like all Pachmayr grips, they're made of tough neoprene rubber that affords positive contact with the shooter's hand and fingers. Further augmenting this contact, they are checkered to about 20 lines per inch.

Comparable wrap-around grips are offered by other suppliers, including Hogue. The Hogue grips, though, priced at $19.95, seem to be slightly larger in girth and are made from a slightly softer rubber. They're also made with finger grooves that force the hand up against the trigger guard for better recoil control. Instead of checkering, they have Hogue's customary "pebbled" finish.

A unique offering from Michaels of Oregon is a three-piece grip for the Colt Government Model and its various clones and siblings. It uses a separate center section or web, incorporating finger grooves, that locks into the cutouts of the grip frame by way of thin, integral "slabs" that approxi-

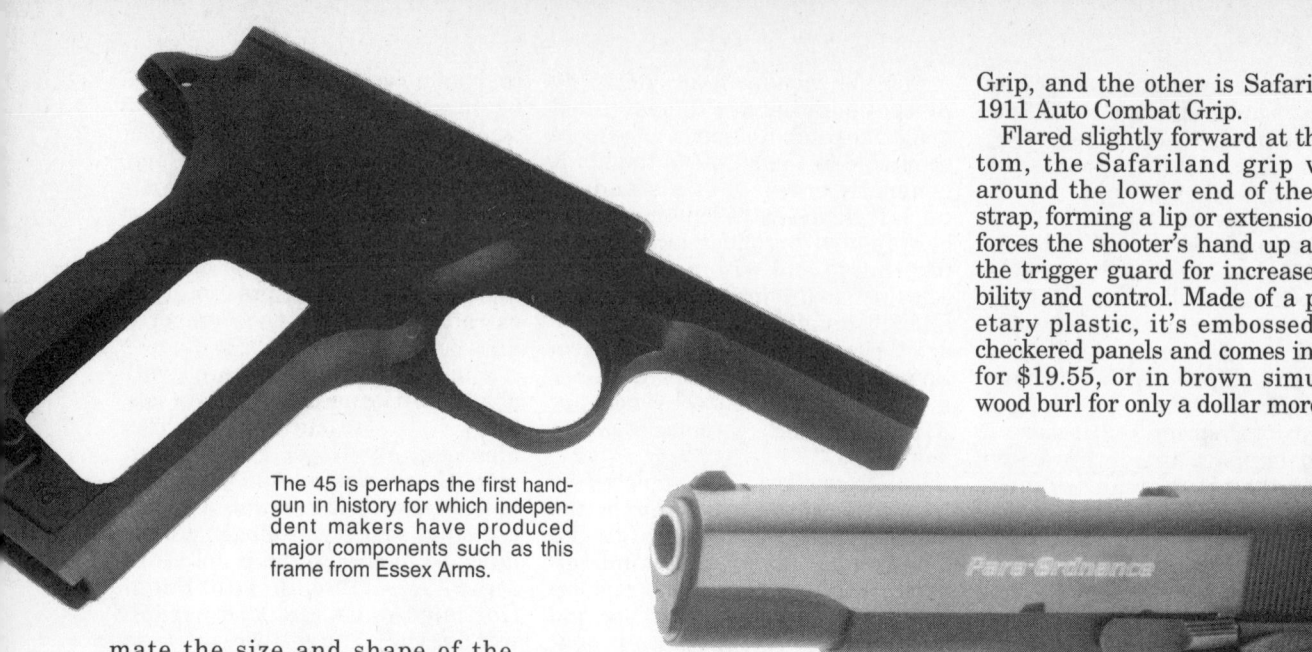

The 45 is perhaps the first handgun in history for which independent makers have produced major components such as this frame from Essex Arms.

Grip, and the other is Safariland's 1911 Auto Combat Grip.

Flared slightly forward at the bottom, the Safariland grip wraps around the lower end of the front strap, forming a lip or extension that forces the shooter's hand up against the trigger guard for increased stability and control. Made of a proprietary plastic, it's embossed with checkered panels and comes in black for $19.55, or in brown simulated wood burl for only a dollar more.

Para-Ordnance still offers its original frame assembly kit, which allows the 45 owner to convert his own pistol to high-capacity.

Replacement slides are also among the major components produced by independent makers such as Essex Arms.

mate the size and shape of the cutouts, after which it's secured by the grip panels. At a cost of $17.95 a set, they're precision-moulded reproductions of hand-carved hardwood masters and are made of a specially formulated elastomer that's both lighter in weight and firmer than rubber.

If wrap-around grips have any particular failing, it's that many 45 owners find their ubiquitous black to be aesthetically lacking. In an effort to offset this, Radical Concepts (formerly R. J. Renner Co.) offers one-piece wrap-around grips in color. Aptly named "Radical Grips," and priced at $19.95 each, they're made of a proprietary elastomer that's virtually immune to chemical attack from oils and solvents. They also offer their wrap-arounds with the choice of a center section featuring a "grid" of fourteen evenly spaced 5mm holes, into which the shooter's fingers are firmly compressed each time the gun is gripped, virtually locking the hand in place.

But, "grid grip" or plain, the most obvious feature is, of course, color. Besides the usual black, they come in a smoky gray that complements stainless steel, as well as in a veritable rainbow of other colors: royal blue, coral, lime and yellow. One might wonder about the virtue of colors, aside from aesthetics, that is, but there are some practical aspects. For example, some owners maintain a "wardrobe" of grips, changing them whenever they grow a bit bored with those on their guns. And some few others literally color-code their otherwise identical pistols according to caliber, permitting a quick selection.

There is yet another practical aspect that, hopefully, none of us will

ever have to discover the hard way. According to at least one legal expert, if ever the day should come that you find yourself in court, defending yourself for having used deadly force to stop a malicious intruder in your home, a set of colored grips could work to your advantage. It's not uncommon these days for a prosecutor (or a plaintiff's attorney in a civil case) to try to convince a jury that defendants in such cases are monsters of some kind who keep

a gun on hand, just waiting for a chance to do somebody in. Jurors, though, might find it hard to believe a "monster" would decorate his gun with a set of coral pink grips.

While that may sound a bit far-fetched to some of us, it certainly reflects one of the major purposes behind Radical's introduction of colored grips. As a company spokesman put it, "we want to make handguns look more like the sport equipment they are, and not the tools of crime that the media like to paint them."

Though not exactly wrap-arounds as such, there are two replacement grips for the 45 that accomplish much the same thing, and in one case, even more. One is King's Speed

Costing $49.95, the King's Speed Grip, made of a hard, black polymer, follows the same basic design, but incorporates several additional features, such as ambidextrous palm swells, a built-in magazine well, dual thumb guards, and full-length non-slip checkering. The swells provide a more hand-filling hold for either a right- or left-handed shooter, while for the shooter who prefers a high thumb hold, the twin guards prevent ejection failures caused by friction between the thumb and the rear-ward-moving slide.

For shooters who favor factory stocks, or those of similar design, the smooth front strap of the 45 is often a source of irritation, promoting, as it does, a slippery hold, especially in hot and humid climates or if the hand is wet or oily. And while having the frontstrap checkered seems an obvious cure, it's also quite expensive. A much less costly cure, priced at $14.95, is offered by Wilson's Gun Shop in the form of a special adapter. Available for either blued or stainless steel guns, it consists of a thin steel overlay, stamped with a checkered design, that completely encloses the frontstrap, and is held in place by the factory-design stocks.

Replacing the 45's original sights is a virtual "must" where many owners are concerned, but owing to the way in which the front sight is attached, installation generally calls for a gunsmith's services. King's, however, offers an "arsenal-type" front sight staking tool priced at $19.95. Of simple design, it can be used by almost anyone with a modicum of mechanical aptitude and the ability to handle a file and mallet; with its use, a profusion of both fixed and adjustable sights becomes available to the 45 owner.

King's offers several front/rear combinations, including a "target" version of the popular three-dot system priced at $39, and a "combat" version costing $32. Other outstanding sights can be had from other suppliers too numerous to individualize here; suffice it to say that the Brownells catalog devotes a good five pages to 45 replacement sights, all at comparable prices.

Popularized by competition shooters, the electro-optical "red dot" sight is yet another item finding favor with more and more non-competition shooters. It's fairly expensive, though, with Aimpoint, who pio-

neered the concept, charging $229.95 for its least expensive sight, the Model 3000, plus the cost of a suitable mount which adds another $59.95. A far less pricey red dot is the epc (all lower case letters, please) from Electro Prismatic Collimators at a cost of $149.50, with further savings affected by the fact that it doesn't require a mount. Considerably smaller and lighter than competitive red dot sights, it uses a unique chemical bonding system that attaches the sight directly to the slide—which means it can also be used with virtually any firearm.

For those who decide it's worth the price, the complex mating of optics and electronics that goes into this type of sight all but guarantees a hit by generating the illusion of a bright red dot on the target, obviating the need for the usual sight alignment, proper focusing of the eye on the front sight, and so forth. The same is true of laser sights, which have the added advantage of allowing the shooter to fix on the target instead of the gun or its sight, since that's where it actually puts its dot. Laser sights, though, are also fairly expensive. The Beam Shot from Alpec Team, for example, retails for $159, but the price includes a mount.

The M1911 is one of the few guns in history for which independent makers have produced major components. Essex Arms, for instance, offers both frames and slides, with a matte blue frame costing $125.80 and a matching slide $130.66. Still other suppliers offer major components, among them AMT (Arcadia Machine & Tool) which offers its Long Slide Kit (an entire upper assembly that includes a 7-inch stainless barrel and slide) for $259.99, or its Hardballer Kit (a comparable upper assembly, but in standard length) for $245.95.

Yet other suppliers offer the 45

owner a way to upgrade his seven-rounder to a high-capacity pistol holding thirteen rounds or more. Para-Ordnance, for example, sells a selection of three so-called frame assembly kits, two in steel and one in alloy. Each consists of a high-capacity "wide body" frame and compatible magazine, along with a recoil spring and guide, and a redesigned trigger and magazine release. Priced at $269, the alloy kit accommodates thirteen rounds, as does one of the steel kits, priced at $375. The remaining steel kit, priced at $385, holds fifteen rounds.

Another fifteen-rounder, considered by some to be the Rolls Royce of frame kits, is one designed and manufactured by Tripp Research and available from Chip McCormick. Priced at $665 (which price, at least in part, might account for the Rolls Royce comparison), it's called the Modular 1911 Frame Kit—so named because it is, in effect, a two-piece affair. It has a fully checkered grip and squared-off trigger guard made from a space-age polymer, and a slide-rail upper portion machined from a solid steel billet. The two materials, though, are bonded in such a way as to produce, in effect, a one-piece frame that's 42 percent lighter than even a standard 45 frame.

With such components available, it's possible for a 45 buff to assemble his own custom pistol, mixing and matching a choice of frames and slides along with the other parts mentioned here, producing a wide array of special features never made by Colt, nor imagined by John Browning.

Still other modified parts and accessories are available for the 45, including a good many more from the suppliers and manufacturers mentioned here, but space prohibits listing them all. A good idea is to send for their catalogs, or even better, the Brownells catalog ($3.75 to non-dealers), since it seems to give the best overview of what's available from almost everyone in the trade. Where any accessory is concerned, a closing word of caution is in order: Over the years, I've learned the wisdom of avoiding any accessory that requires a major alteration of the gun; should the accessory ever break, replacing it with a Colt or a GI part could be your only recourse, but one that's unavailable if the gun is substantially altered. With that said, there are endless tricks and treats awaiting your 45. ●

Thought by some to be the Rolls Royce of frame kits, the Modular 1911 from Chip McCormick combines space-age polymer parts with steel parts.

by C. Rodney James

The Stinger

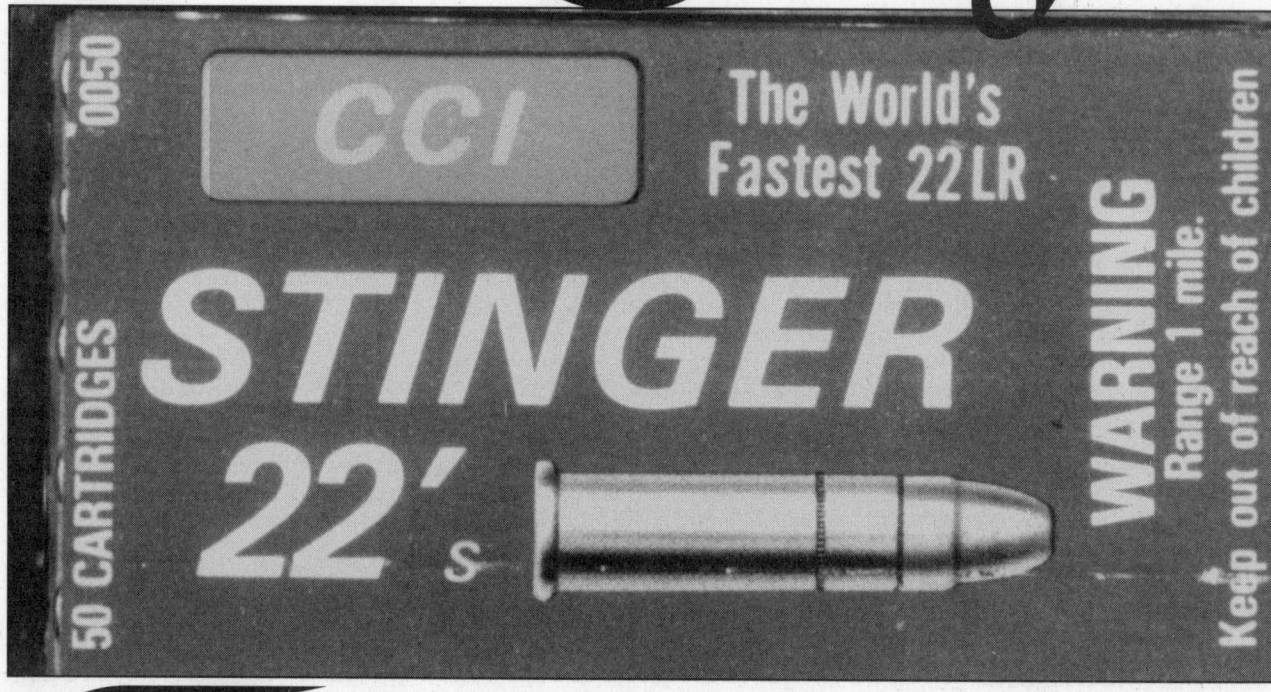

Legacy

CASCADE CARTRIDGE, Inc., entered the ammunition field in 1965 as a maker of rimfires to compete with the well-established Olin (Winchester/Western), Remington and Federal. As the new kids on the block, the CCI staff knew that if they were going to make it against the competition, they would not only have to win new customers, but woo those with ingrained brand loyalties—a formidable task indeed.

From the start, CCI realized that success in carving out a share of the market lay in innovation—offering something others did not. Critics and shooters alike were favorably impressed by the new CCI Mini-Mag and Mini-Group Long Rifles which gained a reputation for power and accuracy.

In 1972, CCI offered a new version of the 22 WMR. The CCI product differed from the rest in two important

respects. The case design featured an internal reinforcing belt of thick brass just forward of the head—a useful adjunct to prevent swelling, much appreciated by revolver and autoloader shooters. The bullet in the CCI magnum, dubbed the "Maxi-Mag," was also unique in that it was jacketed by electroplating a thin copper skin over the entire surface. The resulting bullet was less prone to damage in the feeding process than the Winchester magnum with its exposed lead point, and easier on the bore than the hard bronze of the Winchester jacket. It had the third advantage of holding the bullet together far better than an applied jacket which had a tendency to strip

times economically for the rimfire cartridge—the 1968 Gun Control Act had limited sales to those twenty-one and over, and paperwork and licensing requirements made many small grocery, hardware and bait stores quit the ammunition busi-

the 22 WMR, yet one that could be used in a conventional Long Rifle gun—making a premium quality hunting cartridge. CCI had originally produced power loads for construction fasteners which delivered high energy for driving spikes into metal and concrete. If the same could be applied to a bullet...

The initial work was commenced by Y.S. Hsu of the Development Engineering Department. The original concept was a duplex load of a solid propellent cylinder over a conventional powder charge. The plan was to flatten and extend the time/pressure curve with a long burn to accelerate a standard 40-grain bullet without excessive pressures. Impressive velocities were produced without excessive pressures, but *uniform* velocities were never achieved.

This limited success, however, was enough to bring about resurrection of the idea for a magnumized Long Rifle in July of 1975, when Kenneth Alexander was assigned to the R&D department as a development engineer. Pressure limits for both the Long Rifle and WMR cartridges are essentially the same. The greater case capacity of the magnum allows the use of a larger charge of slower burning powder for an extended burn yielding a velocity about double that of the standard-velocity Long Rifle with the same 40-grain bullet.

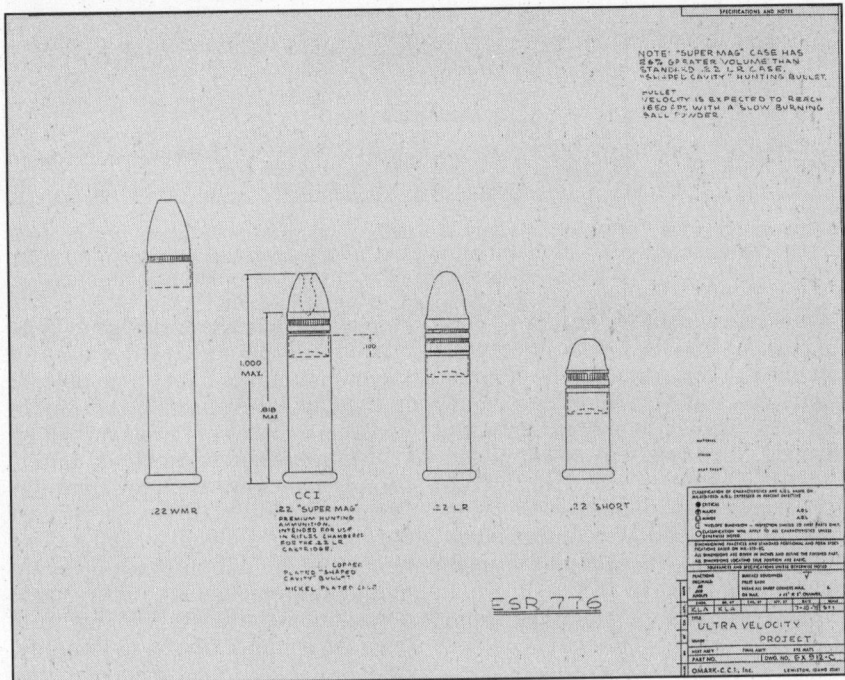

off. These advances, however, were mere grace notes compared to the innovation that brought about the second rimfire revolution in the late 1970s. (What could be called the first rimfire revolution took place between 1927-1931 with the introduction of noncorrosive priming and high-velocity loadings.)

Though the early '70s were bad

ness—CCI brought out the Stinger. It was a good idea.

Details of the origins of the 22 Stinger cartridge are obscure, but the idea evolved from staff discussions involving the possibility of pushing a Long Rifle bullet to 1600 fps—a round with ballistic efficiency above the high-velocity Long Rifle hollowpoint and approaching that of

With the limiting factor of the 1-inch overall length of the Long Rifle, the most practical strategy was to increase the case length while decreasing the bullet weight. The actual design work fell to Ken Alexander, who prepared the initial drawing for a cartridge with a .1-inch longer case, gaining an additional 26 percent internal capacity

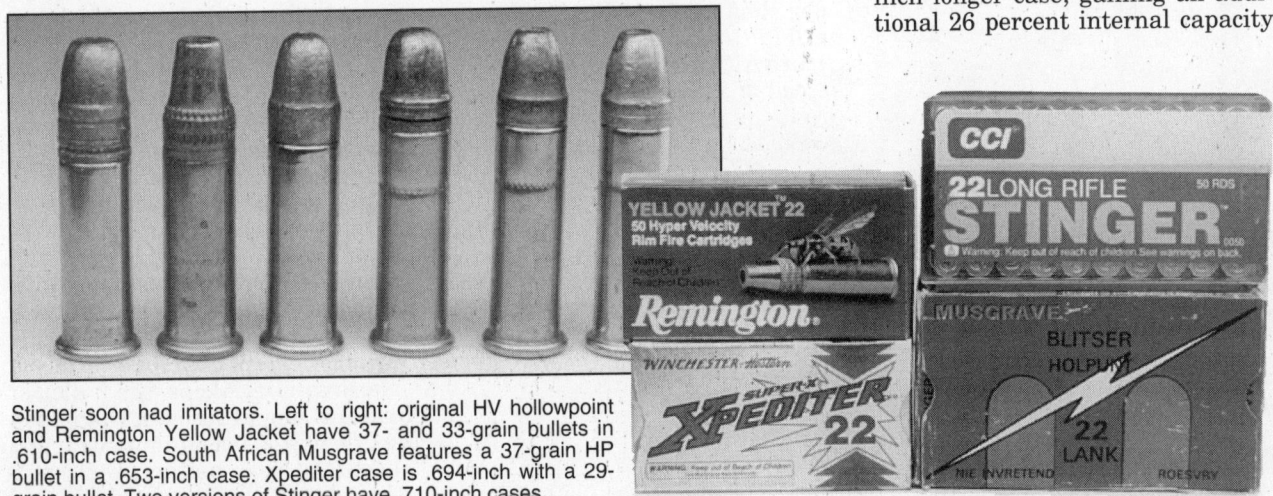

Stinger soon had imitators. Left to right: original HV hollowpoint and Remington Yellow Jacket have 37- and 33-grain bullets in .610-inch case. South African Musgrave features a 37-grain HP bullet in a .653-inch case. Xpediter case is .694-inch with a 29-grain bullet. Two versions of Stinger have .710-inch cases.

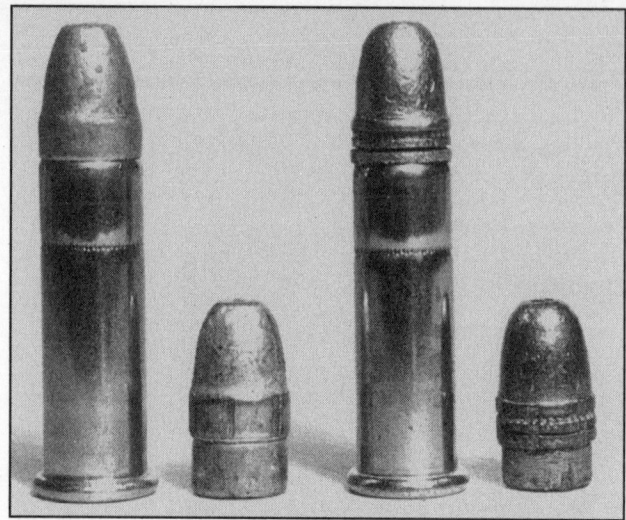

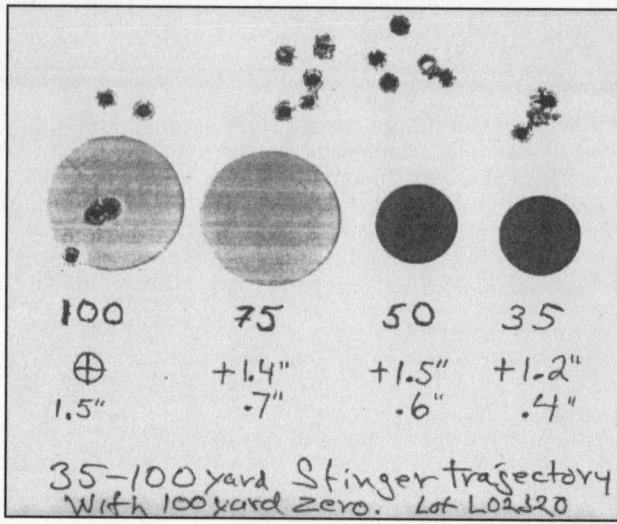

Stinger and Xpediter look much alike, but the Winchester cartridge was abandoned before it was ever perfected. Distortions in case crimp and bullet knurling probably affected accuracy.

The flat trajectory of Stinger zeros at about 20 yards and again at 100, with a vertical rise and fall of an inch and a half through the 52. With a lot of ammunition, groups don't open until past 75 yards.

when loaded with a 32-grain hollow-point bullet.

Initial ballistics tests were run using these bullets in standard cases with a variety of powders, one of which produced velocities of 1500 fps within normal pressures. CCI thereby anticipated the Remington, Federal and Winchester Yellow Jacket, Spitfire and Super-Max cartridges.

In February of 1976, a test lot of longer cases was prepared, loaded with 32-grain bullets. Velocities averaged 1643 fps. Throughout the spring and summer, fine tuning was done on the case length, bullet design and weight, eliminating the original cannelured design in favor of a smooth, wide driving band to make it look as much like the 22 WMR as possible. This would

enhance the image of "magnum" performance. The bullet weight was trimmed to 30.5 grains. The "Penta-point" nose cavity used in Speer bullets was adopted to enhance product identity. The case was nickel-plated to give the round a distinctive appearance—an idea taken from the time Western and Winchester introduced the first Super-X and Super-Speed Long Rifles in 1931.

Later production lots of powders from Hercules produced 1684 fps with a charge of 3.7 grains of powder, as compared to the normal 2 grains for a standard Long Rifle. Loading problems, however, plagued development and required building a new crimping machine for the special round. The final touch was packaging the cartridges in an all-plastic slide-top box—a declaration that *here* was a premium-quality cartridge.

It was decided that in order to compete in the marketplace with the Long Rifle, the new Long Rifle-compatible cartridge had to equal its accuracy. This meant an extreme spread of 3 inches for five ten-shot groups at 100 yards. Test groups averaged 1.5 to 2.5 inches. The next

step was to test the cartridge in guns other than the match rifles used in the ballistics lab. Every available 22 in the Quality Assurance test lab, in addition to dozens of arms owned by CCI employees, were tried. Later, sample lots were sent to "friendly" firearms manufacturers for trial in both new and obsolete arms. The new cartridge did not work perfectly in all guns, but this is a natural phenomenon of the Long Rifle, which is not *really* standardized to this day. In most arms, performance was excellent; even handguns recorded notably higher velocities, although the slower burning powder was primarily devised to make use of rifle-length barrels.

The last step was to give the new creation a name. Contenders included "Super Mini-Mag," "22 CCI Magnum," and "5.51mm CCI Magnum." The two former were discarded for fear of compromising the Mini Mag should something go wrong in the marketplace, the latter because of the absence of specified Long Rifle compatibility. "Long Rifle" still appeared on the box, but a trade name was needed to designate the cartridge as something *new!* "Stinger" finally beat out "White Lightning," the second choice.

One fact not generally known about the Stinger is that it is still constantly evolving. Most Long Rifle ammunition, once on the market, remains that way with little if any variation, except perhaps a variety of coloring materials on the bullet or case and similar cosmetic changes in box design. Throughout Stinger's seventeen-year history, CCI engineers have continued to test and

Bullet on the left is from a woodchuck killed with the Stinger. The other was fired into wet snow and expanded to .35-inch.

develop the cartridge. During this process, the discovery was made that case nickel-plating had more than cosmetic benefits when an experimental lot of unplated brass cases were found to give much harder extraction than nickeled ones. Brass, of course, tarnishes and corrodes over time, which would enhance this problem. Nickel cases are almost impervious to such corrosion, thus handling and long-term storage problems are minimized.

The first serious problem in the marketplace occurred when cases burst in Model XV Llama auto pistols. Inspection revealed undersized bore and chamber dimensions in the Llama, raising the question that there might be other problem guns out there as well. A new warning label was issued satisfying corporate lawyers and saving Stinger from oblivion. While a product can be made foolproof, it can't be made damn-fool proof, and an ammunition maker faces the uneasy prospect of seeing his ammunition fired in substandard, ancient and faulty guns with unhappy results, which in today's litigious society can spell disaster for the maker.

Public reaction to the Stinger was overwhelmingly favorable, as writer after writer heaped such praise upon the new cartridge that plant employees began swearing to one another they had it on the best of authority that Stingers killed stuff 30 percent deader. The bullet did have an exceptionally explosive effect.

Although sample ammunition came into the possession of competitors early on, other ammunition companies decided to wait before jumping in with Stinger knockoffs, allowing CCI to grab a good market-share in the first year-plus of sales. Convinced CCI was onto a good thing, Winchester rushed a hastily conceived Stinger clone on the market called "Xpediter." In this author's experience, *no* gun ever performed well with this cartridge. While velocity of the 29-grain bullet was equal or slightly ahead of Stinger, accuracy was terrible. Tests with several lots of Xpediter through a Model 52 Winchester failed to keep groups inside 3 inches at 75 yards, while good lots of Stingers would group well under an inch at that range.

Explanations for Xpediter's failure vary; some factors appeared to be the heavy, at times uneven, knurl on the bullet and an inability to get even base expansion and a good crimp on the case without damaging the bul-

Stinger variations may interest collectors. Left to right: Type 1, Type 2, brass case, zinc-plated case, grooved bullet, .015-inch shorter case, .030-inch-shorter case and shot loading.

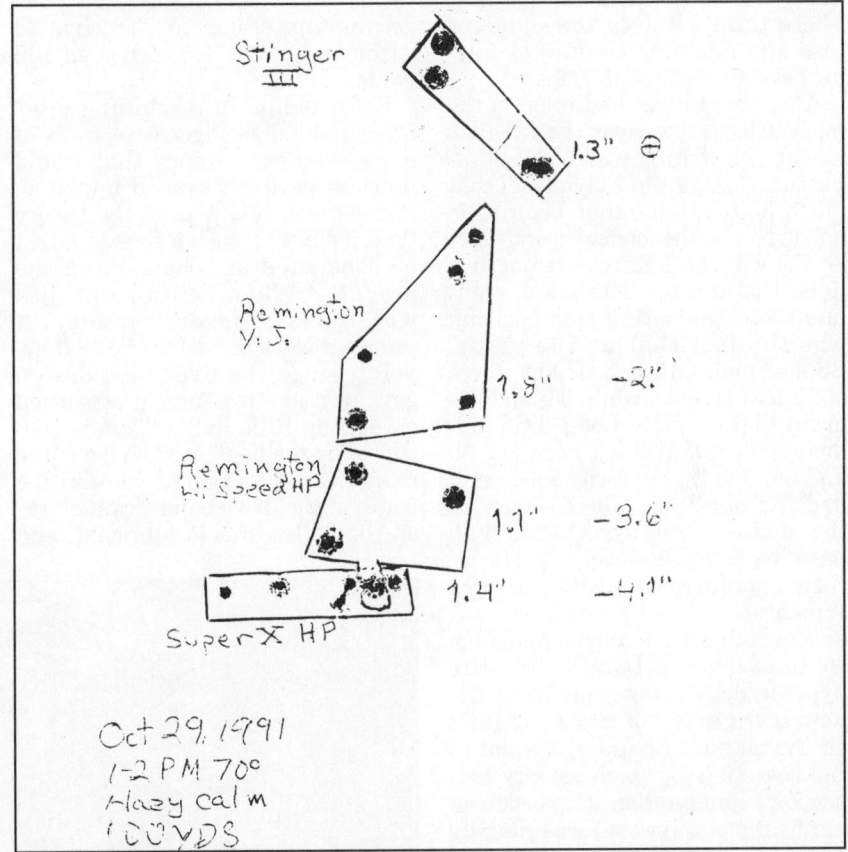

With a 100-yard zero for the Stinger, others drop by the way. Top to bottom: Stinger, Yellow Jacket, Remington Hi-Speed HP and Super-X HP. Fired into sheets of solid plywood at 100 yards, the following accuracy and penetration/expansion results were obtained from a M52 Winchester rifle, 28-inch barrel, sandbag rest:

STINGER VS. OTHER 22 LONG RIFLE LOADS

Load	MV (fps)	Penetration (ins.)	Expansion (ins.)	Five-Shot 100-Yard Group (ins.)
22 CCI Stinger	1643	1.3	.335	1.1-1.8*
22 W-W Super-X HP	1317	1.2	.327	1.4
22 Remington Hi-Speed HP	1335	1.2	.340	1.1
22 Remington YJ HP	1421	1.3	.340	1.8

*1.4 Four-Group Avg. HP:Hollowpoint; YJ:Yellow Jacket.

New small headstamp assures less distortion of the head in manufacture.

let—a process CCI had spent considerable time perfecting. After a couple of years, Xpediter was dropped in favor of a truncated-cone hollowpoint with a 33-grain bullet which was essentially the equivalent of Remington's Yellow Jacket and Federal's Spitfire, which came out about the same time as Xpediter. These three all used the standard case and produce velocities averaging between 1400 to 1500 fps.

After the Stinger had been on the market for a few years, revisionists among the writing clan began hinting that Stinger wasn't *really* all that much better than other Long Rifle hollowpoints, the louder report, higher velocity and flatter trajectory notwithstanding. The main argument substantiating this position was the fact that at 100 yards, Stinger maintained a striking force of 78 foot pounds, while 36- and 37-grain high-velocity Long Rifle hollowpoints maintained between 85 and 86, and high-velocity solids still had 93 foot pounds. There is more to the successful hunting equation than paper ballistics, however.

In comparative tests using a Winchester Model 52 rifle—a suitable arm to get the maximum ballistic bang from a Long Rifle—the hyper-velocity Stinger produced the *flattest trajectory* of any Long Rifle on the market. Accuracy is equal to the best 22 hyper/high-velocity hollowpoint ammunition. Expansion in hard targets (plywood) was roughly equivalent at short ranges, and greater at 100 yards with deeper penetration than the high-velocity hollowpoint bullet. In tests in wet snow, Stingers always expanded to .35-inch or more while high-velocity hollowpoint expansion was erratic—sometimes nil. Thus, claims of Stinger's increased lethality would seem well justified.

As has been mentioned earlier, Stinger is in a constant state of evolution. In 1978, Stingers saw a reduction in velocity to today's standard of 1640 fps with a marked increase in accuracy as the original 3.7-grain loading was dropped in favor of 2.7 grains of a new powder. My own tests made with 1977 ammunition achieved five-shot groups averaging 1.7 inches at 75 yards and 2.3 inches at a 100 yards. Groups from lots with the new powder run from .7-inch to .75-inch at 75 yards and 1.1 to 1.8 inches at 100 yards.

Refinements in machining processes yielded stronger case walls of more even consistency that would function perfectly even if unplated. Plating was retained on the theory that, if omitted, such a change might be construed as "cheapening the product." When Penta-point dies wore out, however, roundpoint punches were used for the hollowpoint, since the five-sided design gave no real advantage in expansion on a Long Rifle bullet. This is controlled by the depth and shape of the cavity. Other variations were in the width of the drive bands, cannelures on the bullet to hold lubricant, and

various styles of crimping. The latest change is the small, shallow "C" headstamp on all of CCI's rimfires. This is not simply a new cosmetic wrinkle, but results in less head distortion and thus a rounder head of more even rim thickness and, subsequently, a more even spread of priming material inside, all of which yields improved accuracy.

The success of Stinger led to a logical outgrowth with the introduction of a 22 WMR version of the Stinger called "+V." Like the Stinger, the +V, introduced in 1988, featured a lighter bullet (30 grains) with a deep five-sided cavity in the nose, seated in a nickeled case. The +V delivered a flat trajectory and velocity in excess of 2000 fps—very close to the vaunted Remington 5mm Magnum, but usable in a 22 WMR gun and without the problems that plagued the Remington. The excellent shooting qualities of the +V have been reflected in its sales.

The Stinger served to establish CCI as a major innovator in the field, giving the company a strong foothold as a producer of specialty or "niche" products as they are known in the trade. Such niches are often spurned and ignored by Remington and Winchester.

What is in the future at CCI? Within a year, lead-free primers for safer indoor shooting, possibly a run of 22 Winchester Automatic and/or 22 WRF for those of us who balk at the $20 per box collectors charge for these (sadly) obsolete 22s. Whatever it may be, it will appeal to shooters who want some extra something. ●

Big brother of the Stinger is the +V Magnum. The 30-grain jacketed bullet features a single crimping cannelure and large Penta-point cavity.

Anatomy of a Legend...

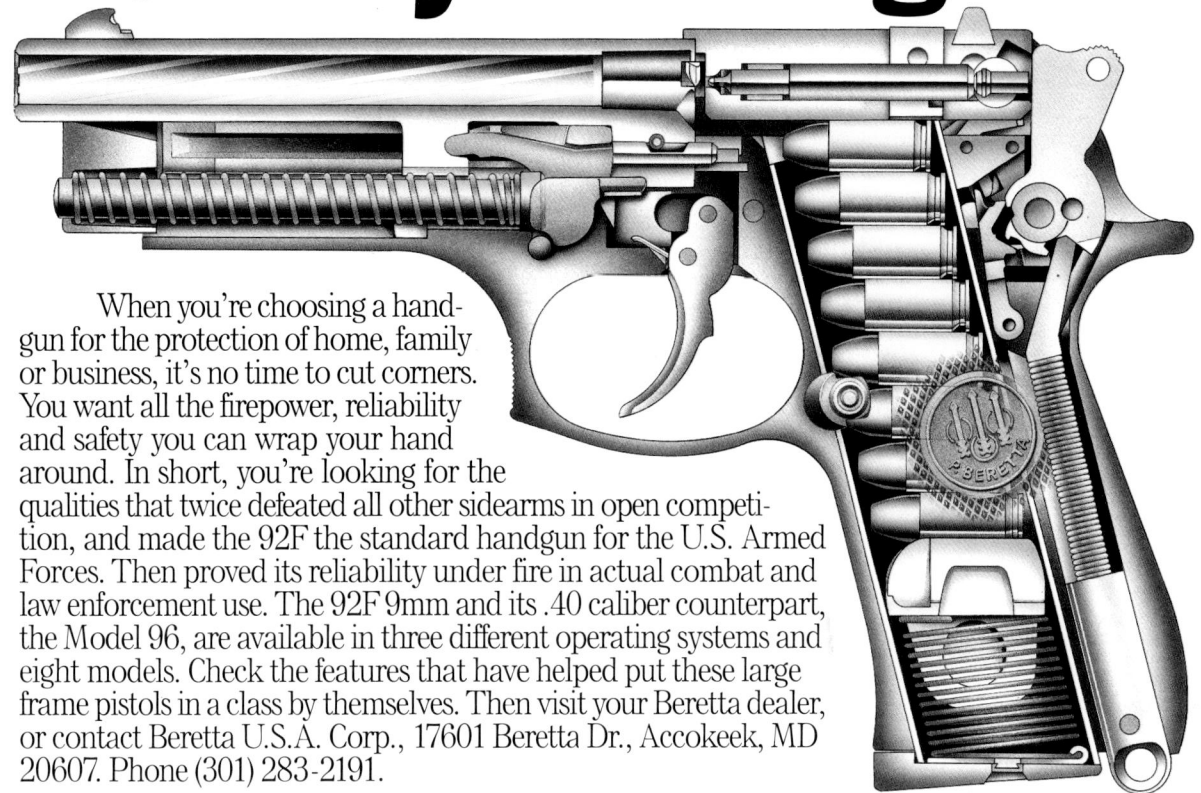

When you're choosing a handgun for the protection of home, family or business, it's no time to cut corners. You want all the firepower, reliability and safety you can wrap your hand around. In short, you're looking for the qualities that twice defeated all other sidearms in open competition, and made the 92F the standard handgun for the U.S. Armed Forces. Then proved its reliability under fire in actual combat and law enforcement use. The 92F 9mm and its .40 caliber counterpart, the Model 96, are available in three different operating systems and eight models. Check the features that have helped put these large frame pistols in a class by themselves. Then visit your Beretta dealer, or contact Beretta U.S.A. Corp., 17601 Beretta Dr., Accokeek, MD 20607. Phone (301) 283-2191.

any way you want it.

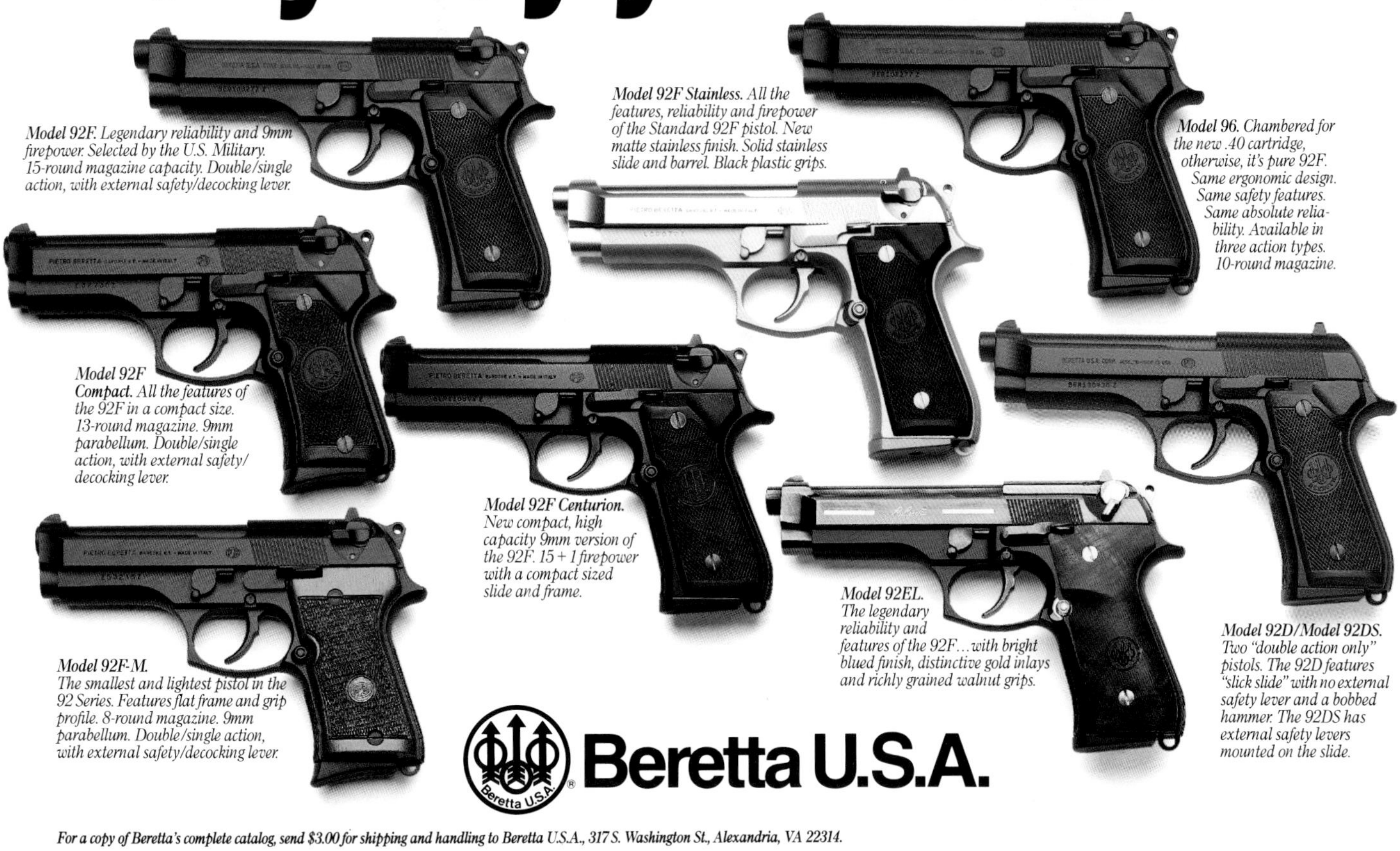

Model 92F. Legendary reliability and 9mm firepower. Selected by the U.S. Military. 15-round magazine capacity. Double/single action, with external safety/decocking lever.

Model 92F Stainless. All the features, reliability and firepower of the Standard 92F pistol. New matte stainless finish. Solid stainless slide and barrel. Black plastic grips.

Model 96. Chambered for the new .40 cartridge, otherwise, it's pure 92F. Same ergonomic design. Same safety features. Same absolute reliability. Available in three action types. 10-round magazine.

Model 92F Compact. All the features of the 92F in a compact size. 13-round magazine. 9mm parabellum. Double/single action, with external safety/decocking lever.

Model 92F Centurion. New compact, high capacity 9mm version of the 92F. 15 + 1 firepower with a compact sized slide and frame.

Model 92EL. The legendary reliability and features of the 92F...with bright blued finish, distinctive gold inlays and richly grained walnut grips.

Model 92D/Model 92DS. Two "double action only" pistols. The 92D features "slick slide" with no external safety lever and a bobbed hammer. The 92DS has external safety levers mounted on the slide.

Model 92F-M. The smallest and lightest pistol in the 92 Series. Features flat frame and grip profile. 8-round magazine. 9mm parabellum. Double/single action, with external safety/decocking lever.

Beretta U.S.A.®

For a copy of Beretta's complete catalog, send $3.00 for shipping and handling to Beretta U.S.A., 317 S. Washington St., Alexandria, VA 22314.

Desert Eagle .357/.41/.44/.50 Magnum For serious shooters, this semi-auto is big, powerful, accurate and shootable. Excellent for handgun hunting, silhouette and recreational shooting.

Mountain Eagle .22 LR ▶ This lightweight, affordable pistol is perfect for recreational shooting, including varmint hunting and plinking. The ammo's inexpensive, too.

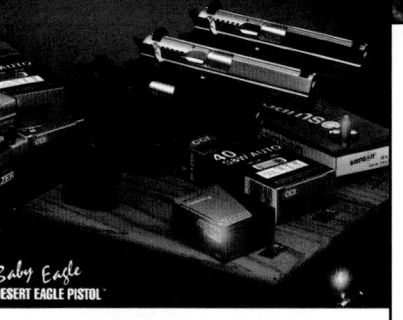

.50 MAGNUM
.22 LR
Gold-plated
BASIC BLACK
Massive Firepower
Lightweight
BOOM!
HUNTING
Plinking
SELF-DEFENSE
.30-06
9mm/.40 S&W
Single-shot
SEMI-AUTO SEMI-AUTO SEMI-AUTO

A Multi-Purpose Pistol That's Highly Reliable And Accurate.

This little bundle of power gets its pedigree as a precise, dependable weapon from the Desert Eagle Pistol. The Baby Eagle's elegant lines and comfortable hold make it a natural extension of the hand that fires it. With an extra long slide rail, polygonal rifling and short barrel recoil, it's a lightning fast, on-target pistol you can count on. Ideal for target, plinking, self-defense and law enforcement use.

Weighing in at only 38 ounces, the Baby Eagle is lightweight to carry and comfortable to shoot. But as a

chip off the Desert Eagle block, it's got the high capacity and heavy-duty, all-steel construction that give you the confidence you'd expect from a larger pistol. 9mm, .40 S&W, and .41 AE. Conversion kits are available. At your favorite dealer now.

MAGNUM RESEARCH, INC.
7110 University Avenue NE
Minneapolis, MN 55432
(612) 574-1868

Baby Eagle 9mm/.40 S&W/.41 AE This semi-auto is reliable, accurate and comfortable. For recreation, self-defense or law enforcement, it's the best.

Lone Eagle (.30-06, .444 Marlin ▶ & more) This new single-shot HuntingPistol combines unique design and a smart price with exceptional accuracy in more than a dozen large calibers.

Sell the hottest pistols for today's shooter: the Desert Eagle, Mountain Eagle, Baby Eagle and Lone Eagle. Call Magnum Research for a free dealer kit and a complete list of distributors, or call your favorite distributor.

MAGNUM RESEARCH, INC.
7110 University Avenue N.E.
Minneapolis, Minnesota 55432
612-574-1868 • 1-800-772-6168

IF YOU CAN FIND A SCOPE THIS BRIGHT FOR LESS MONEY, JUMP ON IT.

The Whitetail Classic. It shames the "big buck" scopes.

Whitetail is getting the reputation for being brighter and working harder than a lot of the more expensive scopes. Feature for feature, these scopes perform as good as or better than a lot of scopes that cost twice as much.

This year we're introducing a new 50 MM model. It gives sharper visibility in low light because of its extra-large, camera-quality objective lenses.

In fact, all of our Whitetail models come with 100% multi-coated objective, and ocular lenses.

They are all waterproof, shockproof, and designed for guys that hunt hard.

BEAUTIFULLY STYLED
Each model features a handsome Whitetail medallion on the saddle. 7 versions come in our rugged BlackGranite® non-glare, finish.

TEN WHITETAIL CHOICES
We make ten models so you can get the scope that best matches your rifle and your type of hunting.

BINOCULARS TO MATCH
Look into our compact Whitetail binoculars that match our BlackGranite scopes. They are rubber-covered, have camera-quality multi-coated optics and our Whitetail medallion on the bridge. In 8x25 Wide Angle or 10x25 WA.

Send $3 for a full line catalogue to: Simmons Outdoor Corporation. 201 Plantation Oak Drive, Thomasville, GA 31792

SIMMONS®

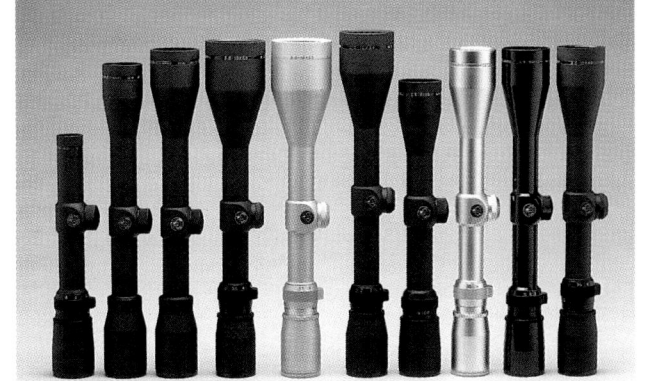

7 Wide Angle Combinations: 1.5-5x20MM, 4x32MM, 4x40MM, 3.5-10x50MM, 2-10x44MM, 2.5-8x36MM, and 3.5-10x40MM.

THE SIG SAUER P 226...
Full-Time Safety, Impressive Firepower

Firepower? When your situation demands maximum firepower, the Sig Sauer P 226 will always deliver. Developed specifically for today's law enforcement officer, the Sig Sauer P 226 can deliver 16, 9mm rounds (21 optional) rapid-fire at outstanding accuracy. Adjustable high-contrast sights provide easy target acquisition even when visibility is diminished.

Safe...Always! The unique multiple internal safety and decocking feature make the P 226 the safest gun you can carry under *any* conditions. The loaded and decocked weapon puts the hammer in register with the safety intercept notch, so firing is possible only when the trigger is pulled.

It is the perfect transitional weapon from revolver to semi-automatic. Now being carried by many elite law enforcement agencies in the U.S. and Europe, it has proven itself to be the most efficient, safe and reliable handgun in the world.

Contact us today for the name of your nearest Sigarms dealer. He's anxious to show you the safest ...and most effective gun you can carry.

SIGARMS

SIGARMS, Inc.,
Industrial Drive,
Exeter, NH 03833

THE SIG SAUER P 226...YOUR TACTICAL EDGE!

Leather goods courtesy of Don Hume, Inc.

by ROB LUCAS

M'ZEE *and the* MARMOTA

Typical groundhog setup in alfalfa, with the 2.5x Alaskan scope and the sticks.

THE LAST BLAZING sliver of afternoon sun burned out above my green hillside. With both of us in shadow now, I felt the chill of evening watching the big boy feed in shoulder-high grass halfway up. I looked at him through the scope for the first time: He was big all right, and ugly, facing left and showing me just the top of his black-and-brown backline. I crawled the last five yards to a coffin-sized berm and peeked over the top. No way to get closer, just above 45 yards. I squirmed into a sitting position and raised the 404 Jeffery Nitro Express, propping the forearm solidly on the berm. I saw his head was up again and he was looking straight at me. I pushed the safety forward, shoving the crosshairs onto his shoulder. The Jeffery boomed, sending 370 grains of lead on its way. At the shot, I jumped up and reloaded quickly and watched for movement. Nothing.

With my heart pounding in my ears, I walked up the hill and found my prey stone dead with his nose in the dirt.

As Mr. Selby might have said to Mr. Ruark, *piga* (Swahili for "hit"). And most definitely *kufa* (Swahili for "dead"). Down and jolly well dead.

In this sixteenth 404 Jeffery kill of the summer, I was concerned about bullet performance and so flopped him over for a look-see. Yellowed buck teeth, long and efficient-looking digging claws, blackish belly pelt so thin I could count the fleas—maybe an 18-pounder. I saw where the lead .423-inch bullet had smashed through fur and shoulder joint and left a .75-inch exit hole. Best performance yet.

And he was a she, a she *groundhog* (Appalachian for "marmota monax"). Woodchuck and whistlepig, too. And she was taken with the big-bore *bundouki* (Swahili for "rifle").

Before you decide I'm crazy for killing groundhogs with a Cape buffalo caliber, be advised that I proposed a whitetail/404 scenario for this piece. But *M'zee* (Swahili for "Old Geezer"), the Editor, wanted *marmota monax*. I naturally assumed it was because he was hitting the *pombe* (Swahili for "booze") jar. (I tell you, this Africa stuff gets in your blood.) I had shot one or two groundhogs in my life, but wasn't hooked on them. Well, the first varmint safari was a little weird, with some apparent contradictions, but after three months and three dozen groundhogs, and some 250 rounds of jacketed and cast bullets fired in the field and at the range, I think we're onto something. And I think I know why he wanted groundhogs and not deer.

That first groundhog shot with my

404 Jeffery was an event. Armed with this 45-70 equivalent rifle, a 2.5x scope, and a dozen 400-grain Barnes softpoints loaded at magnum pistol velocity with a drop factor of over 3 feet at 200 yards and BIG TIME ricochet potential, I leaned over the hood of the car and glassed 300 acres of rolling green alfalfa pasture bordering a ripening Illinois cornfield. Groundhog holes, looking like little brown weed-choked volcanoes, lots of them, were far out there. Within 30 seconds, I spotted one busy critter at around 450 yards. I looked down at the Leupold Alaskan on my 404 and felt pretty ridiculous. My partner made a crack about turning the elevation screw. Undaunted, we jumped into the *lorry* (English for "truck") and bumped along at 2 miles an hour, trying to look like a farm implement. We drove to within 200 yards of the target before it dashed 6 feet and disappeared. The next groundhog let us get within 150 yards.

I needed a confidence builder. I decided to check the 404's zero at 50 yards and so brought out our portable bullet trap, a cardboard box filled with telephone books and a target pasted in front. Those first 404 varmint loads consisted of 28 grains of IMR-4198 and Federal 215 primers behind Barnes 400-grain softpoints, the ones with the .049-inch pure copper jackets, for a chronographed velocity of 1175 fps. It was a fun load, quiet, almost no recoil. Three of these had shot in one hole for me at the range, but I hadn't tried them on anything but paper. I loaded one of my cigar-sized cartridges into the rifle and fired at the telephone book trap: The Barnes slug blew a hole out the back of the trap and scattered pieces of Yellow Pages for 10 feet. Embarrassing for a varmint load.

"Might be a touch too hot," my partner observed.

"This was not my idea," I responded.

But they were the only 404 loads I had, so we tried sneaking up on a third feeding groundhog in the truck. He saw us coming two football fields away and ducked down.

"Kwenda" (Swahili for "I quit"), I said to my partner, who had just returned from his first African safari, booked his second, and had thoroughly infected both of us with the Ruark bug. "Scratch this plan, I gotta get closer."

Long-range shooting with big-glass scopes, small calibers and

A 404 Jeffery works on varmints.

exploding bullets was a sport I called prairie dog hunting. Taking those first three hogs with my 222 and Hornady SXs would have been no contest. Nor were the eighty or so dairy cows observing us from their side of the barbed-wire fence a problem; I was used to single-loading and carefully picking my shots around Wyoming and South Dakota livestock out to 300 yards. Here the whole idea was to get close and shoot close, African style. Here, I didn't want to risk a miss with a hard-shelled 400-grain bullet. I had sworn a sacred oath not to fire my groundhog cannon from farther out than 50 yards.

"Never fear, *Bwana*" (Swahili for "dude"), my partner replied. "Disorientation is the key. We will pull the Zimbabwe Sneak on him. They use it for *punda*—that's zebra to you, son." He showed me a hog feeding in a freshly mown strip of alfalfa grass a quarter-mile in front of us. Its escape route, weeds and a tall mound of sun-baked dirt where our host couldn't cut any closer with his John Deere, was but 6 feet from him.

We hopped in the truck, cruised up to within 75 yards of the groundhog hole, and I dived out the passenger side carrying 404 Jeffery, binoculars and shooting sticks. As my partner drove past the hole with the

radio blasting, I duck-walked and then low-crawled through the alfalfa, 404 Jeffery N.E. cradled in my elbows like an M-16, to a small rise where I could look down at the groundhog hole 35 yards below.

I had serious doubts about this stunt, but was in a safe position to try a shot. I took my time getting into a sitting position with the 404, forearm pinched in the cross-sticks and 2.5x Alaskan aimed at the entrance to the hole. A minute or so went by. Off to my right, I heard the sound of the transmission shifting, the engine idling at high revs, as my partner stopped the truck on high ground in plain view of the hole. It was a beautiful, clear morning.

Another minute went by. Then the most unlikely thing happened; Mr. Groundhog popped his head out of the hole to look for Mr. Fox, found him 400 yards away, and so jumped all the way out of the hole to continue breakfast. Like clockwork thereafter, every 8 to 10 seconds he sat up on his hind legs and stared at the idling car, assuring himself it was still there. All I had to do was time his movement, wait for a perfect chest shot, and let drive with 400 grains of lead.

I missed that first groundhog, watching in amazement as he spun and scurried into his hole. But damn!...hunting him up close was a sporting proposition for any African heavyweight. Later, I came to think maybe I did hit him right, but the Barnes slug simply drilled right through him without leaving even a drop of blood. I don't know.

The Zimbabwe Sneak technique could possibly endanger *marmota monax monax* as a species. We knocked off five of them using the Sneak the first day out, all shot within our self-imposed maximum range of 50 yards. At times, I found myself crawling through the alfalfa listening to the receding sound of the engine and having to stifle a diabolical laugh, *knowing* I'd sit up and see my next victim on his hind legs straining his neck to look in the wrong direction. Half an hour after the first one, we used the Sneak to get inside 40 yards, where I spied a tan-colored male hog—*kufa*—he did *not* make it back to his hole. Then I crawled inside 50 yards and put the crosshairs at bellybutton height on another upright groundhog, and shot him dead center through the body with a 400-grain bullet. We watched that 15-pound hog jump in the air, roll backwards, and then haul full-speed a dozen yards to the hole. *Piga*, but not *kufa sana*, dead.

Inspecting the scene of that bullet failure, we found where the big Barnes softpoint had dug an 18-inch-long trough in the dirt before burying in the green hillside.

From a couple days shooting at the range and one day of actual groundhog hunting with a 404 Jeffery, there were two things I had learned for sure: One, reduced heavy-bullet loads had the accuracy for varmint hunting, but a *bwana* needs much better bullet performance from his *bundouki* than I got. True, the .049-inch jacketed softpoints were all I had, but no excuses from here on. I ordered a mould for a 370-grain wheelweight bullet from Colorado Shooters Supply, but had to wait four weeks for it. Second, using the Zimbabwe Sneak technique, or something similar to get close, and hunting *marmota monax monax* with an elephant rifle is not only possible, but in fact it's a blast. I had so much confidence in the Sneak that I tried it next with iron sights.

Looking for any kind of bullet expansion, I drilled the noses of two dozen Barnes 400-grainers, creating what looked like 375-grain truncated hollow-cavity handgun bullet. At the 50-yard range, they shot about as well as unaltered Barnes bullets. I

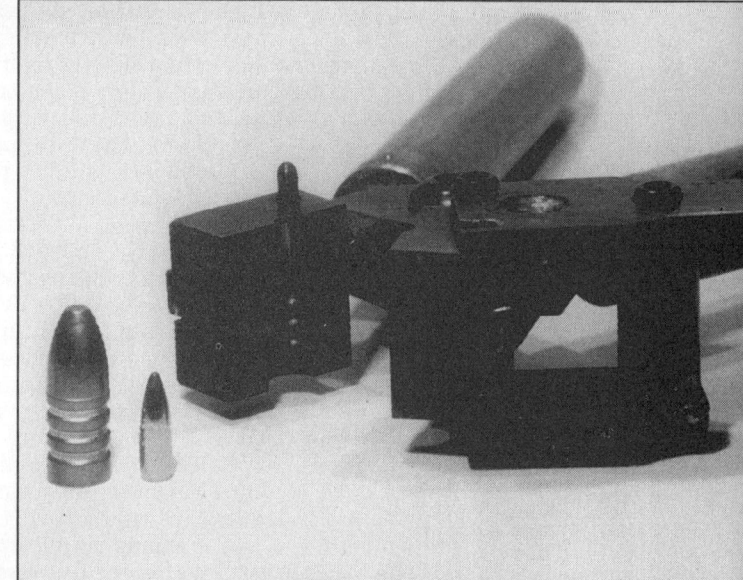

This is the Hoch mould and its bullet. That wee little thing is a 22-caliber Nosler bullet.

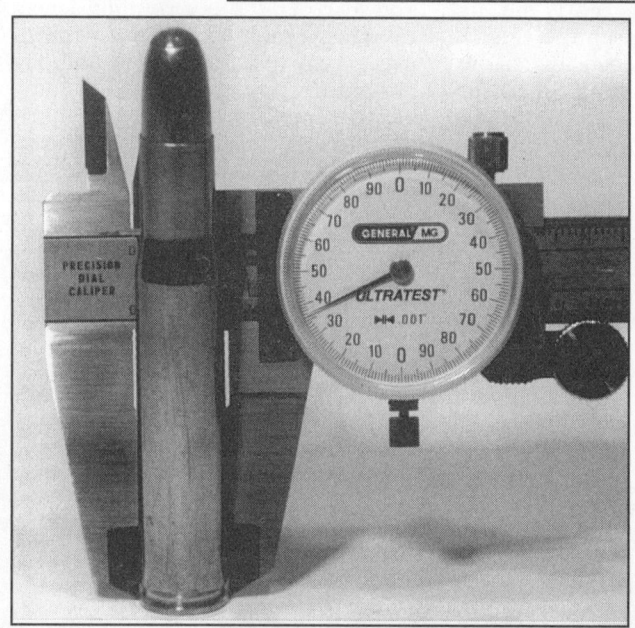

Turned out the rim of the standard 404 Jeffery case was too snug for the rifle's extractor hook, a good thing to find out in Illinois, not Africa.

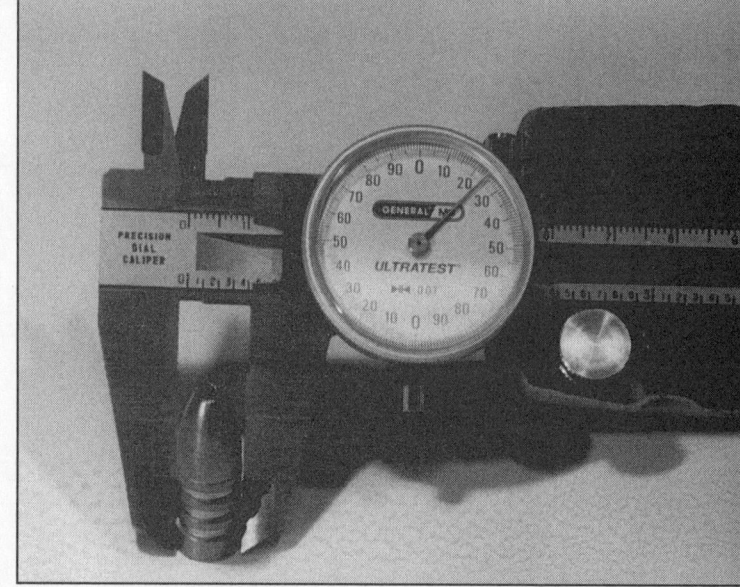

This hollowpoint .424-inch lead bullet made from wheel-weights is simply lightning on ground-hogs.

had one of these mangled slugs in the chamber and a backup in my shirt pocket on the memorable August afternoon when I doubled on groundhogs using the 404's Jaeger iron sights.

My partner dropped me off below one particular Sneaky Pete's weed-patched abode, and while watching for him to show himself, two other groundhogs sat up in the alfalfa on my right, both about 25 yards away. I held a shade low and fired. Both hogs ran like hell for their holes, but only one of them stopped for a last peek at me. I rolled him with my backup round. The Jaeger front bead showed up small but razor sharp against a backdrop of dark brown *marmota* fur. The truncated hollowpoints ripped clean through, one in the neck and the other the upper chest, but both apparently did just enough internal damage to stop them after a short dash. Better, but still far short of 222/55 SX performance.

I fired the Barnes 375-grain cavity-point into telephone books and saw why it couldn't anchor a groundhog either. At 1200 fps, three of them penetrated an average 9 inches while slightly riveting the nose cavities before being stopped, same lack of expansion as unaltered Barnes JSPs. The .049-inch Barnes jacket was just too thick to allow expansion at low velocity.

Waiting for Dave Farmer's mould to arrive, I loaded up the last of my original Barnes softpoints over 28 grains of IMR-4198, traded the 2.5x Alaskan for a Leupold 1.5-5x Vari-X III, and went to the range to practice from the sitting position. I had shot a dozen groundhogs and learned a little about hunting and hunting bullets, a little about large varmints. But most important, I knew for certain that my 404 Jeffery African stopping rifle *worked*. The gun had performed flawlessly, feeding, firing and ejecting the big rounds. I was thinking of raiding the bank account, me and my *manamouki* (Swahili for "woman"), and heading for Zimbabwe. Luckily, there were more groundhogs to shoot. My African stopping rifle, built for reliability, had a major bug in it, and it's not too far-fetched to say that Illinois groundhogs may have saved my African bacon.

Like other serious hunters, I had put together an African safari rifle using all the right parts: A 375 H&H-length Interarms action with "Whitworth" stamped on the side, one of Sam Mays' last Apex barrels in .423-inch bore, Jaeger banded front sight and wide English rear, Grizel drop magazine and barrel band, Blackburn trigger, Jantz safety, Ottmar rust bluing job and all Tertin gunsmithing. In 1986, I had the great fortune to meet Dale Goens in Las Vegas after he'd had some health problems, and he shot me a price for his best-grade wood and finest checkering that I could not turn down. In the six years that followed, I fired my wonderful 404 Jeffery safari rifle a total of thirty times with hot expensive 401-grain RWS "vollmantel rundkopf" Cape buffalo loads. It wasn't until my *marmota* safaris that I learned I owned a single-shot stopping rifle, one that wouldn't eject an empty case with a full magazine underneath.

(Right) The setting is agricultural, but the sitting and the crossed sticks are tactical—sound lessons in game shooting.

(Above) Yep, it's big stuff all right. Here are the Barnes 400-grain JSP and a 370-grain cast bullet from a Farmer mould.

At the rifle range where I did the target work for this project, a large sign in front of every bench reads "Single Load Only." Single loading a bolt-action rifle, either at the public shooting facility or in wide-open prairie dog towns, is a good safety habit. But not many single shots go to Africa. With permission from the range officer, I sat down with my cross-sticks and loaded three in the magazine and one in the chamber. I pulled the trigger, drew back the bolt, and learned I needed either a claw extractor or the hook on this one trimmed back.

The rim diameter of the standard 404 Jeffery runs .537-inch and the rim of the standard belted 375 case goes .530-inch. The claw extractor hook on the 375 bolt face was an extra tight fit on the fatter rim of the 404, plus it was slightly humped in the middle. I thought this tight extractor hook was good because I sure as hell didn't want to leave a fired case in the chamber with a buffalo bearing down on me.

Trouble was, the hook bite was *too*

good. While the action would extract and eject fired cases with an empty magazine, and it would feed and eject magazine loads of my 400 Barnes dummy rounds all day and all night, the combination of a fired case, with its lack of inertia, and full magazine was no-go. With spring pressure from the full magazine below and the extractor hanging onto the fired case too tightly, the smart rap of the ejector simply left the extracted case lying sideways on the rail. A jam, in other words, every time.

But the repair to my 404's extractor had to wait. Groundhog populations were busy padding their fat layers for the long winter's hibernation, and I had a sleek new wheel-weight cast bullet to try on them.

In doing the research on short-range reduced loads for a big-bore rifle, I rediscovered that 350- to 500-grain slugs at 1300-1500 fps were turn-of-century state of the art for target shooting, even out to 1000 yards. The old bottlenecked 40-70 Sharps with a 330-grain bullet at

1450 was known as a splendid long-range match cartridge, as was the 44-90 Sharps with a 470-grain bullet at only 1300 fps. I decided not to handicap myself with a blunt, short-range-only slug. Taking the correct trim-to and overall cartridge length for the 404 Jeffery and my rifle's slugged chamber and bore measurements, Dave Farmer at Colorado Shooters Supply copied a modern 40-caliber bullet already in his catalog and modified it to 423-caliber and 370 grains of weight. He added a little weight in the ogive area and moved the front driving band forward. The groove diameter in my rifle is .423-inch and Dave's mould drops bullets that cool off to mike .424-inch and weigh 370-372 grains starting from wheelweights. Perfect.

I lubed the first fifty of them with beeswax and loaded them up. I shot them over an Oehler 33 chronograph at the 100-yard range using the super-accurate 28-grain load of IMR-4198 and the Federal 215 primer, no special wadding. At 1270 fps average, the best group was five big holes in 1¼ inches. I tried the 30-grain load and recorded an average velocity of 1331 fps, but less accuracy; and 34 grains gave 1375 fps and fair accuracy. With that load zeroed 3 inches high at 100 yards, I fired two groups at 200-yard targets just for drill. The better group was 4 inches wide and 5 inches tall, with its center only 20 inches below the point of aim.

The improved trajectory over the 400-grain Barnes was due to 200 more foot-seconds and the streamlined shape of Dave Farmer's cast bullet. I guessed that if I were *dead certain* of the exact range, and just *had* to shoot a groundhog two football fields away with a large-diameter bullet, these cast bullets could hit them one out of every two tries. But with the Zimbabwe Sneak, I could get as close as I wanted to most any groundhog. I stayed with a 50-yard zero, but adjusted my self-imposed maximum range to 75 yards using the tried-and-deadly 28-grain load.

Summer days were growing shorter; fall was in the air. The first morning out, we hunted almost to noon before seeing a groundhog. They finally showed themselves when the chill lifted and the sun burned the glistening dew off the alfalfa leaves. The Zimbabwe Sneak continued to produce close-range groundhog encounters, and I shot three in quick succession at between 30 and 60 yards with the variable Leupold set

Iron sights, regulated for 401-grain RWS factory loads, put reduced load for varmints high and right.

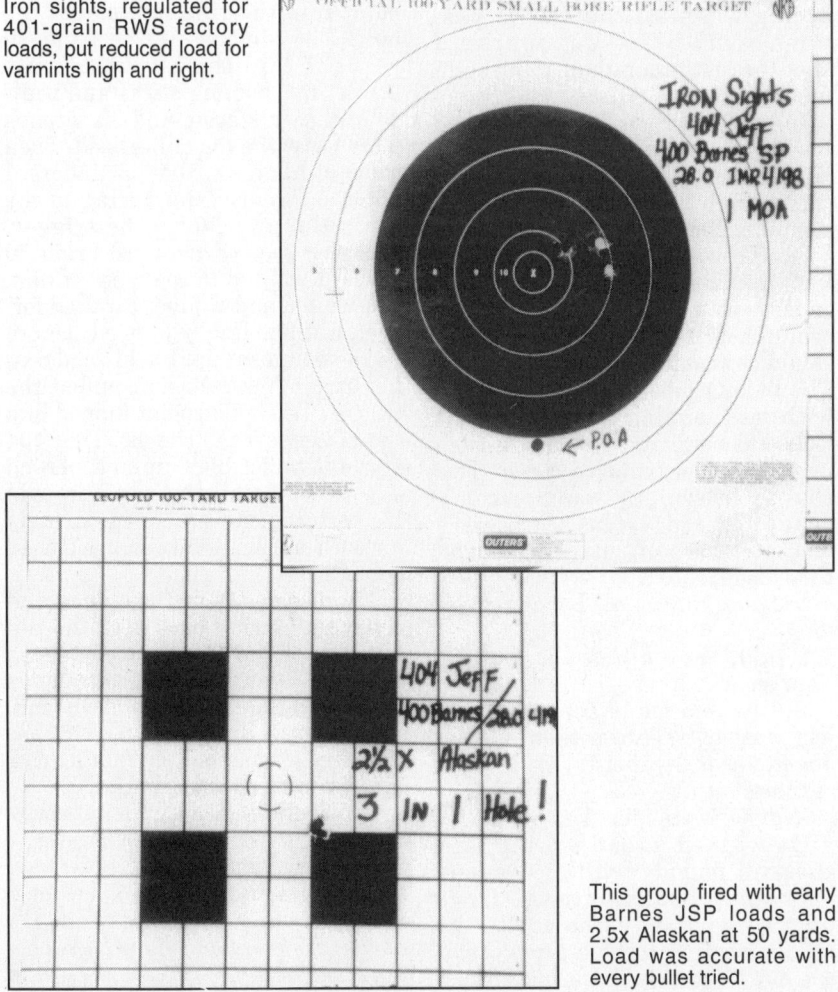

This group fired with early Barnes JSP loads and 2.5x Alaskan at 50 yards. Load was accurate with every bullet tried.

on 5. The performance of the cast bullet was much better than the Barnes JSP, but still not as conclusive as any small-caliber, high-velocity bullet. Three hogs shot, three cast slugs passed all the way through, but partially broke up if they struck bone. No hog crawled more than a few feet after being steamrolled by one these monsters. One final adjustment was needed.

The secret to the cast lead hollowpoint bullet fired from a rifle, I was advised, was not so much the diameter of the hole, but the depth, For small game, the experts said, drill it right down to the first driving band. Using a 3/8-inch variable-speed drill clamped into a portable stand and some very sharp bits, and a little patience, I drilled a 1/2-inch pilot hole halfway down to the first driving band and then opened it up with an 1/8-inch bit. A full 35 grains of lead came out, leaving me with a wicked looking 335-grain hollowpoint.

By the time the 404 Jeffery FLHPV (frangible lead hollowpoint varmint) bullet was ready for field testing, it was October and there were damn few surviving groundhogs left in the main alfalfa patch. We knew of at least a dozen hogs living in holes in the hill fence line between the alfalfa and the feed lot pasture, but the fence line was strictly off limits, not because of the cows, but because we could only drive the safari truck where the alfalfa crop was recently cut. Along the barbed wire, it was still a foot tall. It appeared that the summer *marmota* safari was over and the 404 FLHPV, like the Chicago Cubs, had to wait until next year.

"You boys quittin' already?" the landowner asked, as we stopped by his house to thank him for the three months of great groundhog shooting. "There's no limit you know. And I know you ain't got 'em all!"

I shook my head and explained the situation. He said it was a little wet on that side of the property. Then he put on his cap, climbed up on his John Deere, and cut us a fenceline swath 10-feet wide where we could hunt his pastures from front to back. We couldn't drive it, but we could walk it. The generous gesture gave us another two weeks of afternoon and weekend hunting, added to our license, and showed us a walking variation of the Zimbabwe Sneak to use in the spring when all the alfalfa pastures would be too wet to drive. I shot the last groundhog of the summer on October 12th.

In mid-afternoon, my partner and I walked the fence line with our rifles on our shoulders, sipping hot coffee from a Thermos bottle and scanning the rolling grass ahead of us for brown parts sticking up. Our freshly mowed walking lane was cut as close as a Lake Forest lawn; any groundhog trying to dash across it would be visible for a half mile away. The blue October sky was streaked with low-hanging flat clouds that looked like winter. I spotted the feeding hog and we ambled closer. This chunky brown guy waddled confidently to the edge of his hole beside a crooked fencepost, glared at us and then disappeared.

"*Bwana Marmota*," he said, grinning.

I said, "*Tao bundouki*, buddy. Your shot."

But he told me to get *my* gun. "I just want to walk over that hill yonder and hear the shot."

"Sure?"

"*Ndio*" (Swahili for "You bet").

He walked ahead whistling a cheerful melody while I dropped back and blended into the fence line. I jogged 50 yards across the muddy pasture to high ground and sat down, quickly fed a fat African cartridge tipped with a cast hollowpoint into the rifle and closed the bolt. The shot would be from 70 yards. I laid the 10-pound rifle across my shooting sticks and waited still as a statue, and 30 seconds later I saw the top of his head. Then some of his neck, then shoulders. I felt the forearm checkering in my left palm and found the trigger. This hog seemed nervous. From 70 yards, I wanted to see more of him, so I waited and waited. I waited forever, until he finally jumped clear of the hole and sat up. I held dead center under his neck and pulled the trigger. The hollowpoint flipped him completely over in the air. That 404 varmint bullet blew up and plowed a 1-inch hole all the way through. He disintegrated as devastatingly as with a 222 Remington with an SX or a Blitz.

My partner heard the shot and came sauntering back over the hill with the Thermos bottle. "There must be twenty more groundhogs feeding on the downslope of this hill. Next year...I bring out the 375. We could try a boom box.... What a great idea for hunting woodchucks."

Groundhogs, woodchucks, whistlepigs, *marmota monax*, whatever.

And now, as to why *M'zee* wanted them and not the deer? I know for a fact...(*Actually, he doesn't, but it's obvious: This would have been boring about deer. KW*) ●

SHOTGUNS

Browning's Sweet Sixteen was a gun from the 1930s—1937 to be exact—and it's still with us, matter of fact.

OF THE THIRTIES

The Great Depression didn't depress gun designers.

WHENEVER WE SEE books or magazine articles written about the Great Depression of the 1930s, we also see photos of bread lines, destitute people living in the packing crates of Hoovervilles, downtrodden individuals selling pencils on Wall Street, and stock market speculators diving out of windows. It was a terrible time, so we're told, and economists and historians have filled library shelves with tomes detailing the causes and social consequences. To make things worse, I suppose, I was born just as the whole blasted thing got started.

But as a kid growing up in the countryside, I can't say I really noticed the economic plight we were supposed to have been suffering. Moreover, as I became a sort of teenage gun nut in the following 1940s, I found a pretty good bevy of guns to capture my interest. And since World War II basically halted the production of sporting guns from 1941 through 1945-46, it became obvious that many of the guns used from the aftermath of WWII into the 1960s were developments of the supposedly depressed 1930s. Indeed, a detailed look into gunmaking of the 1930s will make any shotgun fancier ask if that depression was really depressing. From where I sit, the 1930s were actually a mighty lively period when it comes to bird guns, mighty lively.

This was essentially the time when side-by-sides had lost favor and repeaters were coming on strong. The reverberations from the 1929 stock market crash had hardly subsided when Remington introduced a pumpgun design which, in my humble opinion, was the slickest high-quality trombone gun ever made, namely the Model 31. It was eventually made from 1931 until 1949 in 12-, 16-, and 20-gauge, and a variety of grades were produced: riot, Skeet, trap, field, and an upgraded field version known as the

by DON ZUTZ

The writer's father and the neat little Winchester Model 42 410 that popped out of the Depression years and popped a few cottontails, too.

Remington's Model 32 was America's first step to a quality over/under, introduced during the depressed 1930s and a no-foolin' shooter.

struck, Winchester already had a successful pumpgun, the "Perfect Repeater"—the Model 12. But they didn't stand pat. In 1933, Winchester announced the introduction of a cute little slide action chambered for the then-new 3-inch 410 shotshell. Known as the Model 42, it was a scaled-down version of the larger Model 12, and it immediately won hearts. The Model 42 was to last in field, Skeet and pigeon grades until 1963. My father liked to run beagles, and he carried a Full-choked M42 behind the hounds to pick off cottontails or to drop an occasional ringneck or ruffed grouse that bolted ahead of the floppy-ear hounds named Duke, Sport, Tarzan (he was a tough one), Sam, or Rusty. The

Model 31H or "Hunter's Special."

But if one believes Remington was a bit gutsy for introducing a new model just as a depression got underway, he'll have to revamp his thinking. For just a year later, in 1932, Remington took the wraps off a spanking new over/under—the Model 32. Talk about flying into the teeth of adversity! Not only was the Great Depression rolling, but the over/under concept hadn't yet been popularly accepted by American wingshots. However, the Model 32 lasted a decade, being squelched mainly by WWII. It also was made in a variety of grades. Perhaps the most successful M32 variant was the Skeet grade, but I once had a field-grade M32 and felt that it, with plain barrel, was a good-pointing birdgun, especially on passing game.

Remington's main stateside competitor at the time was Winchester, and Winchester wasn't sitting on its heels, either. Almost unheralded, the company brought out a new side-by-

side that was to undergo an evolutionary process which would make it a premier American smoothbore. This was the to-be-famous Model 21. At the time, the powers-that-be at Winchester wanted a quality double to compete with the Parkers, the Foxes, Smiths, and Lefevers, and apparently no depression was going to stop them. Just because the stock market crashed in 1929 didn't mean everyone was going to stop hunting and shooting, so the company went through with its plans to enter the double-barrel market. Earlier in its history, Winchester had sold some European-made side-by-sides, but the Model 21 was its own in-house fowling piece. At first the Model 21 was just a better gun, a semi-production item given more great care in assembly and finish than basic run-of-the-mill doubles, and it would be years before it took on a custom gun status. But the Model 21 was indeed a Depression baby.

By the time the Great Depression

M42 was also the ranking 410 Skeet gun for more than a few tournament seasons, and I must have owned a half dozen of them when they could be had for $100-$150. Like a genius, I sold or traded them all early on for less than I paid for them. Today, any one of the M42 Skeet guns I owned would be worth $500-$1,000 to a collector. In general, my stock market dealings are somewhat sharper than my gun trades, but I digress. The point is that one of the neatest 410 slide actions ever to come down the pike did so at the depths of the Great Depression.

Winchester also took a hard look at the Model 12 during the 1930s, and various new models of it were introduced. By that time, the game of Skeet shooting had become popular; Skeet fields had popped up all over the country. And the game was employing the smaller gauges as well as the big 12-bore. So Winchester wound up and made the M12 in 28-gauge, beginning in 1935 and continuing until 1958. At the same time, Winchester announced the availability of the Model 12 Heavy Duck Gun, which was a beefed-up version of the M12 made for the oncoming 3-inch magnum load. It was about this same period when federal legislation mandated the use of a magazine plug to reduce repeater capacity to three shells. Also in 1935, Winchester introduced the Improved Modified and Improved Cylinder chokes; hitherto, the main M12 chokes had been Cylinder, Modified and Full.

The years 1932-1934 seem to have been especially hard for gunmakers, and it isn't surprising to find that, in 1937 and 1939, Winchester brought out some lower-priced shotguns. The

Remington bought the grand old Parker works in the depths of the 1930s and brought out Skeet grade doubles with the gracefully long beavertail forend.

One of the great all-time pumpguns, the Remington Model 31, debuted in 1931. This Skeet grade has a steel Cutts up front. If they made 'em any smoother, nobody'd believe it!

1937 entry was the "Steelbilt" Model 37 single shot, a so-called "semi-hammerless" affair that collectors are now fighting over. A good M37 Winchester should bring well over $100 on today's gun trading market, which is totally amazing. However, the Model 37 was one of the first, if not the first, single shots to have a relatively modern comb height and beavertail-like (semi-beavertail, actually) forend for easy gripping and effective pointing. I happen to have a 16-gauge Model 37, and it's fun to take it afield upon occasion for auld lang syne.

The 1939 Winchester entry was the Model 24 side-by-side, which has been described as two Model 37 single shots slapped together. Designed as a cheaply constructed double of the knockabout type, the Model 24 actually had excellent pointing qualities, too, with a full, raised comb and a semi-beavertail forend *a la* the Model 37. Although I like the way an M24 points, its trigger positions (it is

a twin-triggered gun) are such that the recoil inflicts pain both against the trigger finger when it pulls the rear dingus and against the second finger as the trigger guard is driven backward. The M24 was made to fit a price range induced by the Depression; it was cheaply made and sold, and I for one am astonished by the prices some collectors will pay for this former knockabout of no important value when it was in its heyday.

One of the least known of Winchester's Depression-era efforts was the Model 40 autoloader. This gun was developed during the late 1930s when John M. Browning's patents for an autoloading gun ran out, and it was an attempt to build a more streamlined selfloader by using a rounded receiver rear. The Model 40 was made in 12-gauge only and was introduced in 1940. Because of a weakness at the juncture of receiver and action spring housing, it barely lasted a year and sold somewhat less than 19,000 copies. A Model 40 in

excellent condition is a scarce item these days, as so many were returned to the factory because of the defect and were replaced by Model 12s. Aside from the weakness, however, the Model 40 wasn't a bad pointing autoloader.

Remington and Winchester weren't the only gun companies that had to scramble for a living during the Depression, of course. In 1937, Marlin introduced the Model 90 over/under, which was popular enough so that Marlin brought it back after WWII and improved it with a single trigger. Although a healthy 7½-pounder in 12-gauge, the Model 90 was a different gun in 16- and 20-gauge, scaling about 6½ pounds and moving spiritedly. Anyone interested in an old-time 16 could do a lot worse than hunt up a Marlin Model 90 on the gun traders' market.

With the sporting world starting to see over/unders, Savage Arms also took a crack at the market. In 1938,

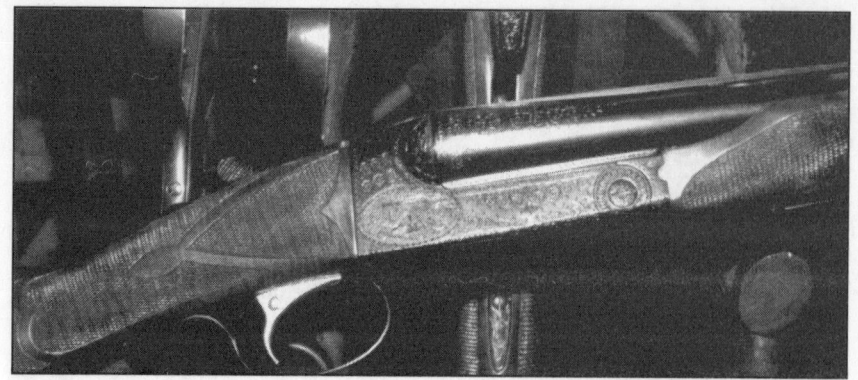

The Winchester Model 21, introduced directly into the teeth of the Great Depression, went on to outlive the likes of Smiths, Foxes, Parkers and Ithacas. This is a Pigeon Grade.

The Model 37 Ithaca, being shot here in Deerslayer styling, was introduced in 1937 and overcame the Depression to become an outstanding hunter's gun. It folded before the inflation of the 1980s. Now there's a Model 87.

nicely. At one time, several of my acquaintances used the 16-gauge Model 37 Ithaca as a split-the-difference gun, one that carried easier than the 12, but nevertheless packed enough pellets for upland purposes. After a certain amount of shooting, the Model 37s slicked up and were good field companions. The bottom feeding and ejecting feature of the M37 never endeared them to clay target shooters, and that may have been one of their downfalls. Even today, veteran Skeet and trap shoot-

they came out with a pair of break actions that were conceptually excellent. One was the Model 420 over/under; the other was the Model 220 single shot. A slightly heavier gun than the Model 90 Marlin, the Model 420 was also made in a deluxe grade known as the Model 430. The Models 420/430 have side ribs joining the barrels as opposed to the split-barrels of the Model 90 (which may have accounted for some of the weight differential), but overall the Savage stackbarrel had a favorable profile with a nicely swept forend and comfortable pistol grip. Despite its genuinely handsome appearance, the Model 430 didn't return from WWII.

The Savage Model 220 single shot was one of the few break-action singles ever to sport a sliding top tang safety rather than a visible hammer spur. As such guns went, the M220 also had fair stock dimensions and an acceptable forearm. A couple of my friends had 220s back in the 1940s, and they served well. Hunters wedded to the top tang safety slide should have grand sport trying for a brace of partridge with the ol' Model 220. Again, the interesting thing to note is that these Savages were on the drawing board during the depths of the Great Depression; thus, some-

body was thinking ahead and wasn't afraid that this was the end of the world.

Over in Ithaca, New York, a new repeating-gun venture was getting underway as the economic debacle ran its course. Once a foremost maker of side-by-sides, the Ithaca Gun Co., under the direction of Lou Smith, who was a brother of the famous L.C. Smith, was in trouble. Doubles appeared to be on the way out, and the Depression was definitely eating into the sale of high-quality pieces. Hit by this double whammy, Lou Smith turned to repeaters that could be made cheaper and sold less expensively. But which design should Ithaca pursue?

As history tells it, Remington was having some patent problems with the Model 17 pumpgun, which had been designed by John M. Browning, and Lou Smith knew of this and waited in the wings. When the Model 17's patent expired, Smith began making a very similar gun known as the Model 37 pumpgun.

A featherweight slide action, the Model 37 was for decades Ithaca's staff of life. The gun was trim, easy carrying, reasonably streamlined, and possessed of a light frontal segment that enhanced eye-hand coordination. In other words, it pointed

ers hate to be on a squad with somebody (especially a beginner) who hacks around with a bottom-ejecting pump that must be chambered from the magazine tube. But for hunting, the M17/M37 concept works out very well, and the Model 37, which was made in 12, 16, and 20 gauges by Ithaca with each gun scaled to the gauge, made a strong comeback after WWII.

Makers of other side-by-sides also fell on hard times. Stevens once made some excellent doubles, but with the on-rush of repeaters and the economic collapse, it had to resort to cheaper guns for sales. Perhaps the most depressing thing about the entire Great Depression was the Stevens-made Springfield Model 311, which came out in 1931. The Springfield designation was eventually dropped and it became a pure Stevens. In 1936, Stevens tried to upgrade the Model 311 by giving it some checkering, a single trigger, and a rubber recoil pad plus a different catalog number—the Model 530. In general, however, the Model 311 concept sold only because it was inexpensive compared to other guns, and both it and its stablemate-to-be, the 1940-introduced Fox Model B, have continued to falter in quality.

The 1930s' demand for cheap shotguns apparently prompted Stevens to bring out bolt-action smoothbores, such as the Model 58 410-bore and the Model 258, a 20-gauge item. Both had box magazines that kept the ammo centered between the shooter's hands, and the guns (despite being bolt actions) weren't all that bad on a handling basis. But Stevens also made a tubular-magazined 410 in the 1930s, and advertised at just 6 pounds, it promised to be a hunter's delight. When placed on a scale, though, the M59 came to 7 pounds, and with a tubular magazine stuffed with loads, the gun was excessively muzzle heavy. Aside from the fact that these Stevens guns kept some folks shooting, they hardly added to the glory of American gunmaking.

Over at Lefever, a hammerless double known as the Grade A Hammerless was developed for 1934. This was an attempt to split the gap between the knockabout Nitro Special and the upper grades of Lefevers, which weren't selling worth shucks. To a certain extent, this Anson & Deeley-type boxlock wasn't a bad gun, and it was also turned out in Skeet grade with substantial checkering panels on the grip and classy beavertail forend.

Also in 1934, the red ink flowed in torrents over the ledgers of the now-vaunted Parker establishment, and Remington bought the Meriden, CT works, eventually moving Parker production to the Remington plant at Ilion, NY. One interesting outcome of this transition was that Remington encouraged production of the Skeet-grade Parkers. There's a Skeet-grade Trojan in the Remington museum. Hunters who now want a tie with yesteryear in the form of a neat upland double can't do much better than a Skeet-grade Parker, Lefever, or Winchester Model 21, especially in the smaller gauges like 16 and 20.

Why did gunmakers introduce all these new designs and concepts in the Depression-racked 1930s? Some of them might have been on the drawing board well before the Depression hit. But for many companies, I'm certain that it made good business sense to offer the public new ideas for whatever sales could be generated. For not everyone is hurt by a Depression; some people will always have money. And not everyone will be out of work entirely. So the companies scrambled for sales, and out of it all came some models that are now desirable collectors' items or shooters.

The fact that Skeet shooting grew during the 1930s, and that trap shooting still held the big Grand American Handicap, should tell us that the shotgun sports didn't collapse entirely with the stock market in 1929. In fact, as one considers the great ol' bird guns that came out of the supposedly depressed '30s—the Winchester M12 in 28-gauge; the Winchester Models 42 and 21; the slick-stroking Remington Model 31; Ithaca's family of featherweight Model 37s; the Skeet-grade Parkers, Foxes, and Lefevers; and the first Yankee strides toward over/unders, to name a few—we find that there was some sunlight in an otherwise bleak economic period, anyway. In fact, it sorta makes one look forward with interest to the next Great Depression, doesn't it? ●

The first honest-to-gosh 12-gauge Magnum repeater was Winchester's Model 12, with 3-inch chamber and a slug of factory-installed lead in its butt.

by GENE GANGAROSA, JR.

STEYR'S GB:

TOO GOOD TOO SOON?

This GB pistol was produced about midway through the Steyr production run.

WHY DO SOME guns persist for years or decades and make firearms history, while others appear only briefly and then fade into obscurity? That answer might be that the guns that last are good and the ones that don't are no good, but while this may sometimes be true, in many cases it is not. The factors influencing acceptance or rejection are often more complex than any one simple explanation, and a very good gun may fail for any number of reasons.

Consider the story of the Steyr GB. Steyr-Daimler-Puch, a world-renowned Austrian manufacturer of military and sporting firearms—as well as trucks and heavy machinery—officially introduced this pistol in 1981. However, the GB's ancestry

really dates back to the latter days of World War II, to the gas-delayed operating mechanism of a prototype German assault rifle and to experimental pistols Walther was building that were less expensive to manufacture than the P-38. By 1969, the Austrian government was thinking of replacing its aging collection of P-38 and FN Hi-Power pistols, and they requested that Steyr, Austria's chief manufacturer of military equipment, develop a new pistol. Steyr studied the late-war German firearms and then painstakingly began developing and testing their own design. The Austrian handgun took the form of a large double-action pistol with an eighteen-shot, double-column magazine. It became

known as the "Gas Bremse," German for "Gas Brake," or by the initials GB.

Before Steyr built and marketed the GB design under its own auspices, Les Rogak, a Steyr importer, received in the 1970s a set of manufacturing drawings for the new pistol. Whether he got the plans for publicity purposes to announce Steyr's upcoming handgun or actually had permission to build the pistol under his own name (the advantage of that arrangement for Steyr being deniability if the gun should fail) is not clear. In any event, he set up a manufacturing firm called L.E.S. or Rogak, Incorporated in Morton Grove, Illinois, and began building the pistol in stainless steel as the Rogak P-18, a reference to the enormous magazine capacity. What resulted was a gun whose troubled history ominously foreshadowed that of the later GB, which it strongly resembled.

Seemingly, the Rogak had a lot going for it. Its advanced design and stainless steel construction, combined with the highest-capacity production magazine available on any automatic pistol seemed to give it great potential for success.

Unfortunately, several factors conspired against the Rogak. First of all, the 9mm Parabellum chambering simply wasn't that popular in the United States in the late 1970s. This was almost seven years before the U.S. armed forces adopted a 9mm automatic pistol. What limited demand existed for 9mm pistols was adequately served by the Smith & Wesson Model 39 and the various surplus war-era Lugers, P-38s, Radoms, etc. Even those desiring a high-capacity pistol were more likely to buy a Smith & Wesson Model 59 or a Browning Hi-Power than the futuristic-looking Rogak. Those whose tastes ran to the exotic had the new Beretta Model 92 or even, for a lot more money the SIG P-210 or CZ-76 to choose from.

But what really killed the Rogak was poor workmanship. So bad was its manufacturing quality that the leaky gas delay mechanism did not work. Instead, it was made to work as a simple blowback pistol by the addition of fiber buffers around the barrel. Despite good accuracy, the gun gained a reputation for choking on ammunition and earned the derogatory nickname of "Jammatic."

Steyr took legal action to halt its manufacture, but even without a lawsuit the gun's reliability problems would very likely have been all the nails its coffin ever needed. P-18 production ceased in the late 1970s or early 1980s after Rogak, Incorporated had made about 2,300 guns. Not surprisingly Steyr has little good to say about Les Rogak.

Steyr resumed the project, and all further development work on the GB occurred in Austria. Testing continued, with modifications undertaken to correct the Rogak's deficiencies. The magazine lips were strengthened and thickened to make loading less painful and to improve feeding reliability. A decocking lever replaced the Rogak's manual safety. The contours of the front sight, muzzle, hammer, and slide stop were all rounded off for easier carry. Steyr also put the magazine release at the rear of the trigger guard instead of at the bottom rear of the grip as in the Rogak. Most importantly the workmanship of the male bushing was improved to enable it to seal the breech during firing, thus achieving the full potential of the braking mechanism. In the only two retrograde steps, the Rogak's well-contoured rounded trigger guard gave way to a square trigger guard to promote a two-handed hold with the first finger of the support hand on the front edge of the trigger guard, and regular carbon steel replaced the Rogak's stainless construction.

By 1980 Steyr had finalized the design, so their pistol is sometimes referred to as the "GB-80." Although it externally resembled the Rogak and was the same size, the redesigned GB had the absolutely superb fit and finish for which Steyr has long been famous.

With a length of 8.5 inches and a 5.3-inch barrel, and weighing about 35 ounces unloaded, the GB was the same size as the Beretta Model 92. Grips were usually checkered black plastic, though some specimens with steel grips have been reported. The gas delay mechanism was interesting and quite ingenious, as it allowed a strong pistol without the need for a breech-locking mechanism or massive recoil spring. Basically, the GB used some of the expanding powder gases from a fired round to form a counterpressure that delayed the opening of the slide until the bullet exited the barrel, allowing the gases to escape. The gases used to lock the slide came from two holes drilled at the midpoint of the barrel, and vented into a chamber sealed by the barrel bushing. Once chamber pressures decreased to the point where the shooter was not in danger, the slide cycled to the rear, ejecting the spent cartridge, and then forward, chambering the next round from the magazine.

The system used by Steyr was simpler and stronger than comparable mechanisms used in the competing Heckler & Koch P7 series of pistols, as it required no pistons or other moving parts. It also did not appreciably reduce the muzzle velocity and hence the energy, of the 9mm cartridge it fired; in fact, the GB's muzzle velocities were competitive with those of other modern 9mm pistols. The fixed barrel was attached solidly to the frame and used polygonal rifling in the bore, both innovations promoting above-average accuracy. The frame was composed of two steel halves welded together, a technique borrowed from wartime German experimentation. Another interesting production shortcut was that the trigger guard, a part integral with the frame in most handguns, was made as a separate piece and then pinned in place. In the earlier design that had led to the Rogak, the frame, including the trigger guard, had been machined as a single piece in the traditional manner. Steyr's redesign greatly improved and simplified the pistol's manufacture. The refined gun was simple, functional, and rugged: it used fewer than fifty parts, compared to over seventy for the Beretta Model 92.

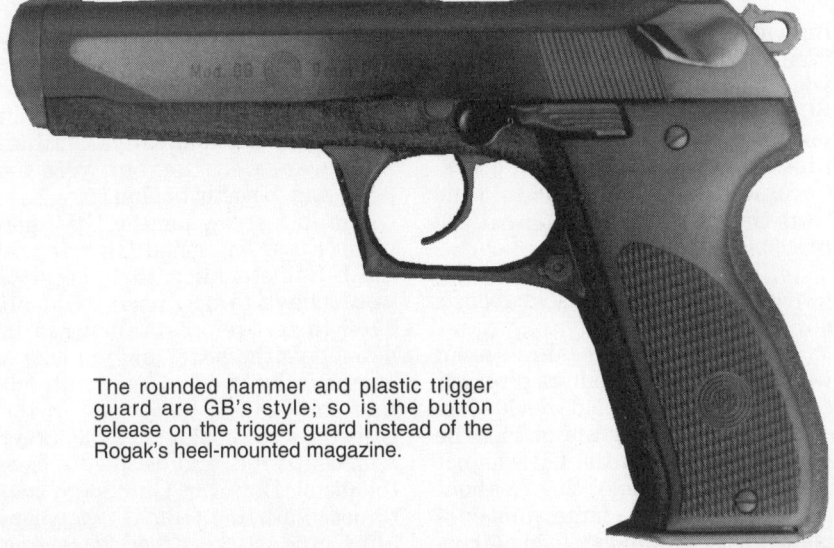

The rounded hammer and plastic trigger guard are GB's style; so is the button release on the trigger guard instead of the Rogak's heel-mounted magazine.

The modified GB had a lot going for it when it finally appeared in 1981, after an extended and agonizing research and development phase that had lasted for more than a decade. Steyr had eliminated the reliability problems that killed the Rogak, and they lavished excellent workmanship on the new gun. The company felt that the GB was at least as good as anything else in the slowly-growing 9mm market and should sell well.

But fortune decreed otherwise. The first setback occurred in the 25,000-pistol Austrian government contract, a number established as sufficient to replace the PP, P-38 and Hi-Power pistols in that country's military and police inventories. The GB was a shoo-in to win this contest until a then-unknown designer named Gaston Glock unveiled his new pistol, the Glock 17, with which Glock won the order in 1983.

Disappointed, and humiliated at being beaten in its native country, Steyr turned next to the United States XM9 military handgun trials. In November, 1983, the U.S. Army published a formal Request for Test Samples, for which Steyr submitted 30 Model GB pistols. The Army conducted the XM9 trials from February through August, 1984, during which time the GB competed against entries from Beretta, Colt, FN, Heckler & Koch, SIG Sauer, Smith & Wesson, and Walther. The M9 contract called for over 315,000 pistols (later increased to almost 500,000), and would have put Steyr solidly on the map with its first military centerfire pistol since the legendary Steyr-Hahn of 1912.

But this happy outcome was not to be. Although the GB won high marks from its American examiners for its good handling and its accuracy, and had already seen some use by members of Special Forces, its reliability in this testing series was less than that of the control weapon, the M1911A1. This shortcoming caused the Army to eliminate it from the competition on May 4, 1984, and Beretta's Model 92SB-F went on to win.

With the GB's loss of two important military trials, Steyr realized that the GB, despite police sales to Pakistan and Lebanon, and some unofficial use as an individual weapon by police officers in other places, was not generating sufficient sales in the extremely competitive military and police service gun market. Consequently, Steyr made

The GB quickly disassembles into the five assemblies shown here. On this later gun, Gun South's legend is stamped on the top surface of the slide.

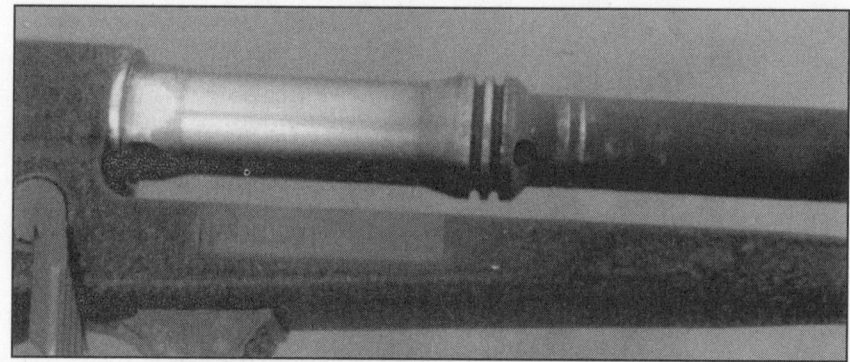

The GB's barrel is screwed into the receiver and remains fixed at all times. Holes in its thickened midsection vent gases into the chamber formed by the slide and barrel bushing. The disassembly latch is turned down.

increased efforts to sell the GB to civilians, and from 1983 on they widely advertised it in the United States and Europe. Over the next few years, the GB became a popular pistol among civilian shooters. Several gun dealers have told me that they had no trouble selling these big guns. One dealer in particular liked the GB a great deal, owned one himself, and sold about a dozen of them.

Then Steyr, which had stayed with the GB throughout its protracted development period, decided in 1986 to discontinue the pistol. The main problem with the GB was not mechanical, but marketing. Without a firm contract for a large number of pistols from a well-established cus-

tomer, preferably a major police department or military force, the company did not feel that it could commit enough resources to the gun to build it economically. Civilian sales were welcome, but were too fickle and variable to plan on.

The last straw for the GB came when Steyr informed Gun South, the U.S. distributor, that the price would have to be raised by about $150 to recover costs incurred in developing the pistol and to make it economically viable. Gun South felt that the GB would not sell in the United States at close to $700. Steyr soon concurred, and decided to drop the pistol. However, Gun South continued importing GBs for two years after production ceased, receiving

A late-production Rogak P-18, serial number 2229, owned by the author, was the immediate production forerunner of the GB. The tight 25-yard five-shot group is typical of this specimen.

The author's GB shoots extremely well with Silvertip 115-grain hollowpoints. This five-shot group, fired offhand at 25 feet, measures one inch across.

their final shipment of 633 pistols on November 25, 1988.

A late advertisement for the GB appeared in the fall of 1988 in the 1989 edition of the *Sportman's Gun Annual*. This listed the GB at $595 suggested retail, a price identical to that of the Beretta Model 92F, while the SIG P226 retailed at the time for $780. Neither Beretta nor SIG was having any trouble selling pistols to the American public, and neither, perhaps, would Steyr, had they been more patient. On the other hand, both Beretta and SIG had received U.S. armed forces approval and the SIG P226, while not being ordered by the military, was enjoying a tremendous quantity of police business, in addition to strong civilian sales. In contrast, the GBs inability to secure a passing score in government testing seriously hurt it in the fierce competition for official orders. The GB was also hurt by its association with the failed Rogak and, perhaps, by its unconventional appearance.

Despite the GB's woes, the pistol received almost unanimous praise from some very discriminating users—the gun writers who reviewed it. From 1981 on, Wiley Clapp, Joe Poyer, Pete Dickey, J.B. Wood, Massad Ayoob and others all spoke highly of the GB's features, performance, and quality of workmanship. Their comments included such statements as: "one of the best shooting, most versatile handguns made in 9mmP chambering...a delight to shoot... a likable gun" (Clapp); "everyone who shot the pistol remarked on the mild recoil...the grip is contoured in such a manner that it cuddles nicely into your hand...the GB functioned flawlessly" (Poyer); "superb quality...more than 300 rounds of assorted 9mm ammu-

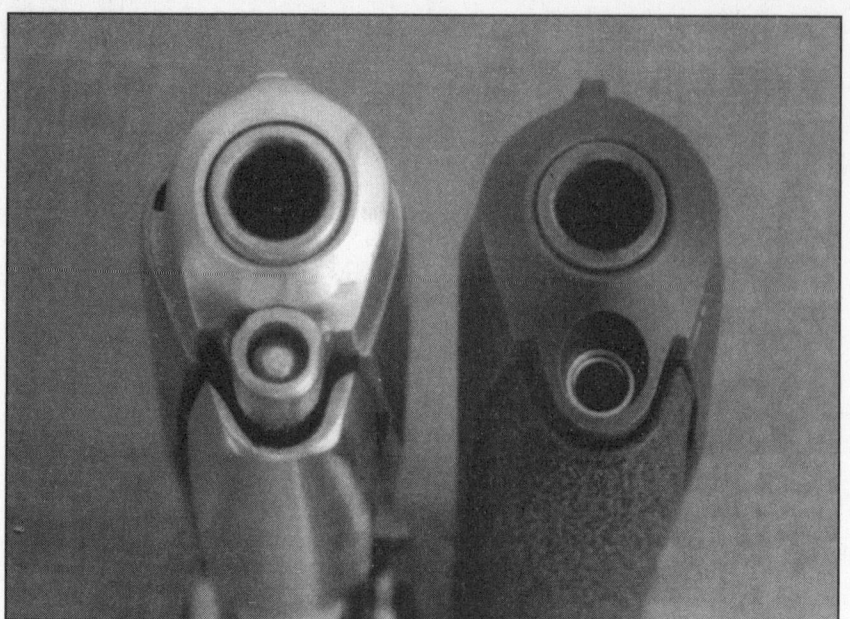

The Rogak's muzzle cap (left) shows typical workmanship. The large gap at upper left incapacitated the gas-locking system, and the pistol was made to function as a blowback. Fit and finish on Steyr's GB is shown at right.

nition was run through the Steyr with accuracy and comfort to the shooter. There were no malfunctions of any kind" (Dickey); "excellent" (Ayoob); "superb" (Wood). These are the words of men who make their living using guns, and their praise indicates that the GB is indeed a fine pistol.

A rare negative view of the GB was expressed by Rene Smeets, a Belgian gun writer highly regarded in Europe. Co-writing *Great Combat Handguns* with Leroy Thompson in 1987, Smeets acknowledged the GB as "very accurate indeed," but described it as "enormous" and "bulky," and added, "range tests suggest that the GB-80 is not a success...the handling of the GB-80 came as an unpleasant surprise...the handling qualities of the big Steyr pistol not only negate its accuracy but also reduce its value as a combat weapon." But Smeets was definitely of a minority opinion here, and in the same book he spoke favorably of the handling of Beretta's Model 92SB, a gun of almost identical dimensions to the GB.

Modern features abounded on the GB, which was ahead of its time. It is a gun that could still sell today in terms of what it has to offer, and is by no means outdated. A partial list of its desirable features follows: a spring-loaded decocking lever which safely lowers the hammer onto a loaded chamber and then returns to the fire position, leaving the pistol ready for an instantaneous first shot; double-action trigger mecha-

nism; firing pin lock that remains in place until the trigger reaches its rearward travel; three-dot luminous sighting system; a fixed barrel promoting above-average accuracy; double-column, eighteen-round magazine (more than any other production Wondernine, although the Ram-Line company makes aftermarket eighteen-round magazines for several popular fifteen-shot 9mm pistols); chrome-lined, polygonally-rifled barrel; steel frame; virtually indestructible finish; and smooth, rounded contours throughout, even on the sights and operating controls. It gives many the impression that it is a bigger gun than it actually is; the reality is that the GB, while large, is extraordinarily well-engineered for easy handling. No heavier or bulkier than the Beretta Model 92, it offers competitive features and handling with three extra shots and a steel, not alloy, frame.

Estimates of total GB production vary. Steyr gives "about 15,000" as the number, while Gun South estimates from serial numbers of pistols received in the United States that the final production approached 20,000. Gun South revealed to me that the company received thousands of letters of protest upon Steyr's decision to drop the pistol, indicating that the GB was building a large following among civilians at the time it was discontinued.

It is difficult to fault Steyr for discontinuing an unprofitable gun. In

1986, they could not have foreseen that the 9mm market in the United States was on the verge of an enormous expansion after the Beretta's military acceptance. But while Steyr's underestimation of the American 9mm market following the Beretta's marketing coup is understandable, less understandable is the way that Steyr missed some valuable earlier opportunities to market the GB.

For example, in the early '80s the company built several prototype models of a single-action target version that did very well in European and American IPSC matches. Due to the GB's gas-delayed recoil design, the pistol was especially well suited to the fitting of a compensator. Yet Steyr chose to ignore this

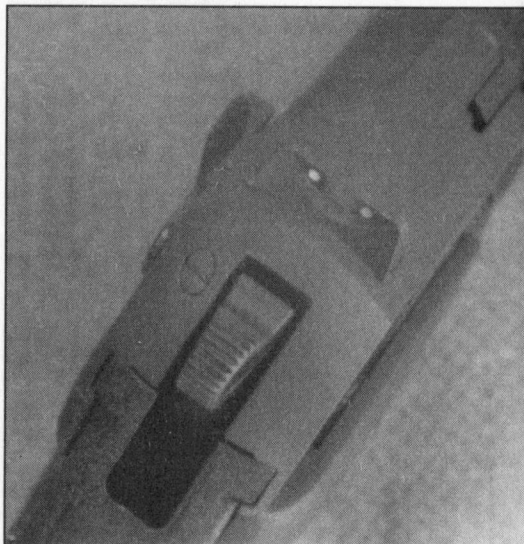

Steyr rounded everything off on the GB to make a smooth-carrying handgun.

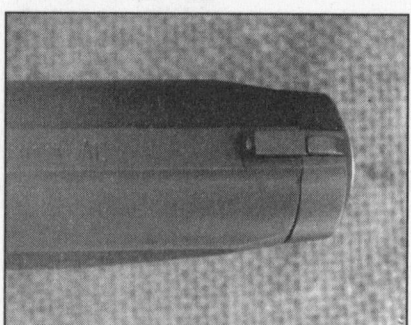

GB's front sight is also well-rounded for a snagproof draw. Note the white luminous dot to match the two-dot rear.

rich advertising field, contenting themselves with making small numbers of a lengthened barrel/compensator assembly that could be added to a standard GB pistol by substituting it for the standard muzzle bushing. Steyr also made experimental machine-pistol versions with extended magazines and a three-shot burst capability; Beretta successfully markets a similar weapon, the Model 93R, modeled after their Model 92 pistol, to police and paramilitary forces, but Steyr took their design no further. Alternate calibers might have been a possibility also, adapting the GB's excellent gas-braking mechanism to other cartridges.

Discriminating shooters today recognize that the GB, despite its unhappy history and untimely end, was and remains a fine combat handgun. While many owners are holding onto theirs in hopes of the

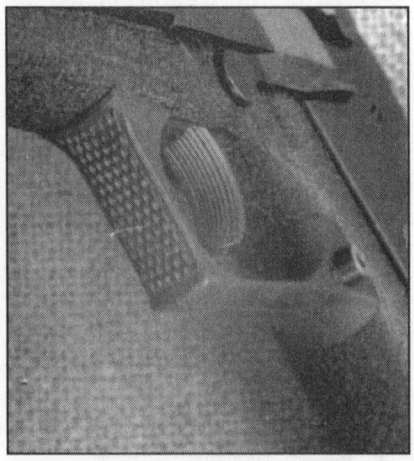

Trigger guard offered coarse checkering; the trigger had deep grooves in it. Some late GBs had smooth triggers. Guard is a separate piece, usually plastic, but sometimes metal.

gun becoming a collector's piece, the GB shoots too well to let it sit unused in its box. It is incredibly accurate for a combat pistol. Recoil is low, thanks to the gas delay mechanism and the ample weight of the pistol. And reliability is not generally a problem with a variety of hollowpoint and jacketed ammunition, though cast lead bullets cause gas port fouling after several hundred rounds.

From a collector's standpoint, the GB is an interesting pistol, as it is rather rare, there are several distinct variations, and prices are quite low. The Rogak P-18 was made in two variations, with the standard finish model selling in 1991 for about $350 and the high-polish variation for about $400. Getting to the true GB, the military variation, the last model available in the United States in 1987-1988, sold in 1991 for about $450 in mint condition. Only 937 of these military GBs were imported into the United States. They had dull, smooth epoxy-finished frames and a Parkerized slide, and some may have had metal trigger guards. Their appearance was unattractive, a gray-green reminiscent of late Nazi-era Mauser-Werke "Gray Ghost" P-38s. I once owned one of these late GBs and found it to be plagued with unreliable feeding, though that may not be true of this variation in general.

The commercial model GB is by far the most common, with several thousand still extant. There were two variations of markings on the

commercial guns imported into the United States. Early guns (examples noted in the P 3000 serial number range) had the importer given as "Secaucus N.J." stamped on the left slide flat. Mid-production versions, including my own, serial number P 08501, had the new importer's mark "Gun South, Inc., Trussv. Al." stamped on the upper portion of the slide. On the latest guns, the Gun South address was given as "B'ham." The last models made had a spur hammer instead of a rounded one and a smooth trigger instead of the earlier grooved type. With an improved hammer spring, this version had the best trigger pull of the entire GB line.

The commercial guns had a black epoxy crinkled finish, giving the frame a rough texture that makes the gun easy to hold, while the slide had a high-polish blued finish on the flats and a matte blued surface on the balance of the slide. For a commercial model in mint condition, $525 is Fjestad's top price listed in the 1991 *Blue Book of Gun Values*.

The Steyr GB proves that even a well-designed, superbly-built gun with the backing of a world-renowned and experienced firearms manufacturer can fail. Mechanical characteristics aside, political and economic factors also play a major role. The GB was a fine handgun that deserved better fortune than it got. Happily, it is still available used at reasonable prices and is well worth getting, either as a collector's item or as a good shooter. ●

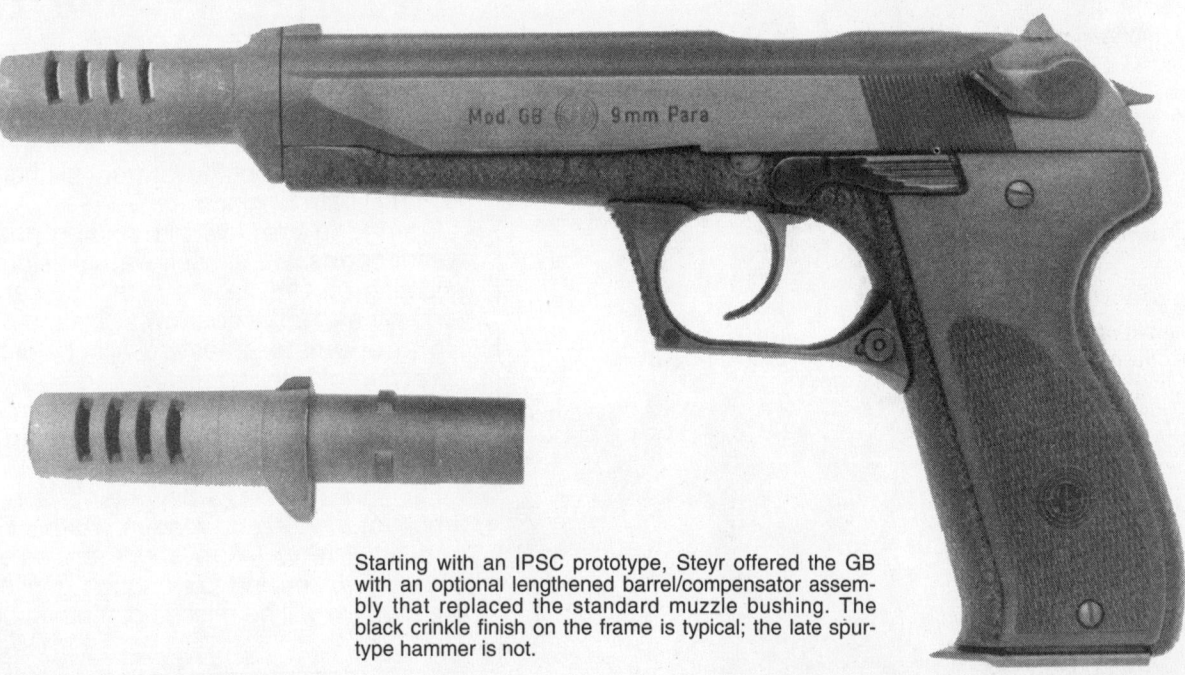

Starting with an IPSC prototype, Steyr offered the GB with an optional lengthened barrel/compensator assembly that replaced the standard muzzle bushing. The black crinkle finish on the frame is typical; the late spur-type hammer is not.

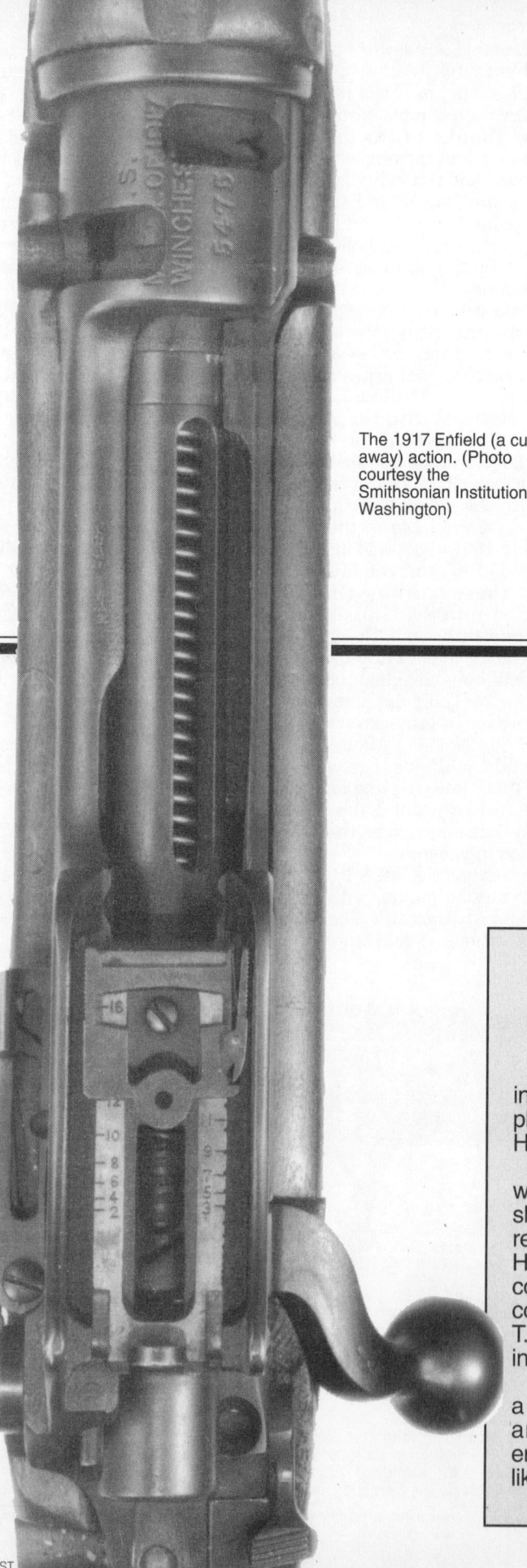

The 1917 Enfield (a cut-away) action. (Photo courtesy the Smithsonian Institution, Washington)

BRITAIN OFTEN HAS been inadequately prepared for her wars, but not always. This article tells how her preparations to build a new super rifle prior to World War I served not only her own purposes, but later those of her ally, the United States. Ironically, the preparations flowed from British troubles during the Boer War, where the Boers, using Mausers, had usually outshot the British. The press called for a Mauser-actioned service rifle. More realistically, Lord Roberts advocated better rifle training.

Plans for a new rifle began in 1910. On August 26th, the Small Arms Committee was requested by the Director of Artillery to "consider a new mechanism for a new magazine rifle, also any other points, *exclusive of ballistics*, which you may think necessary." This Committee was a typical British institution, which had been founded some years earlier to advise in such matters. It

THE

was not universally admired; indeed, the February, 1905, issue of *Arms and Explosives* was acid in its criticism of the Committee to which it referred as "nothing more than a chance assembly of officeholders." This was overly harsh, and Skennerton is probably right in saying that the Committee's advice was a "good cross section of professional opinion and experience."[1]

The Committee met on September 2nd and advised a rifle which was to be used by cavalry and infantry, of approximately the same size as the existing 303 rifle, but with a one-piece stock. It should retain the butt trap, as well as the principles for attaching the bayonet and supporting the barrel, but the nosecap would be lightened in as far as this was compatible with the proper support of the bayonet. The handguard would run the full length of the barrel, and a barrel of 2 pounds 14 ounces was advised.

Furthermore, the recoil was to be about the same as that of the existing rifle. The magazine, which was not to have a cut-off, would carry ten rounds and be charger-loaded with a rimless cartridge. The action, which was one of the fundamental alterations to be incorporated, was to be a Mauser type, giving strength, reliability and symmetry. Forward locking lugs would be used together with a secondary safety shoulder to the bolt. The bolt head should be either detachable or solid with the bolt. A rotary bolt movement would produce primary extraction, and the extractor would not rotate with the bolt. The trigger was to be connected to the body of the action and not the trigger guard. The safety catch could be locked in both cocked and fired positions. Finally, the striker would be controlled by the cocking piece.

The sights—which eventually turned out to be one of the most advanced and praised aspects of the whole development—were, if possible, to incorporate an aperture backsight calibrated up to 1600 yards and a battle sight (also aperture) for use up to 700 yards. The long-range sight from the Lee-Enfield was to be retained for greater distances.

Further reflection on September 12th led to the recommendations being confirmed, save that the bolt head was to be revolving and detachable. The action would cock on opening by the rotation of the bolt, the handle of which was to be as near the trigger as possible. By November 3rd the Royal Small Arms Factory at Enfield Lock was instructed to produce a design for such a rifle, and also a rifle for experimental purposes. The design for the rifle and the aperture sight (from Hythe) was ready by December 13th, when the assistant superintendant attended upon the Small Arms

ACTION

That Served

TWO ARMIES

by WILFRID WARD

committee, and by April 3rd he again came bringing an experimental 276-caliber rifle. It was suggested that a different nosecap be fitted and that a bead fore-sight be provided for use with the aperture sight. In addition, a battle sight (not so far included) would be added. The stock in front of the body was also considered too thick. The rifle then underwent rapid-fire trials leading to various minor alterations. Troubles were encountered with the ejection and the sight.

At this stage, the caliber of the new weapon had not yet been decided. The choice was between .276-inch and .256-inch. A series of trials were held in which the 276 caliber was very much more successful, resulting in a report, Minute 1197A, that considered the 276 caliber to have achieved a result which was "very fair for an experimental rifle with experimental ammunition."

The smaller caliber was abandoned quite soon thereafter.

We need not pursue the detailed history of the new rifle through its experimental stages, save to say that the chief source of its difficulties was enabling it to cope with the 276-caliber cartridge. This extremely powerful round generated high pressures, which in turn caused excess heat, extraction difficulties and bulged barrels, even in the two specially designed experimental rifles produced at Enfield for the purpose of the trials. Designated the Experimental Pattern Rifles 1911 Models A and B, they were followed in 1912 by two further models: the Experimental Pattern Rifle

1912, Models 1 and 2. More tests took place in June, 1912, and December 1912, at Hythe—the latter sighting trials. It was also at this stage that the difficulties encountered with the ten-shot magazine led the next experimental rifles to be fitted with five-round magazines; a modification of design which was not only incorporated into the Pattern 1913, but its successor the Pattern 1914. The use was licensed by Mauser and, almost incredibly, full royalty payments were made after the end of hostilities on the whole production. By this stage, the experiments on the design were finished, and a trial order for a nominal 1,000 weapons

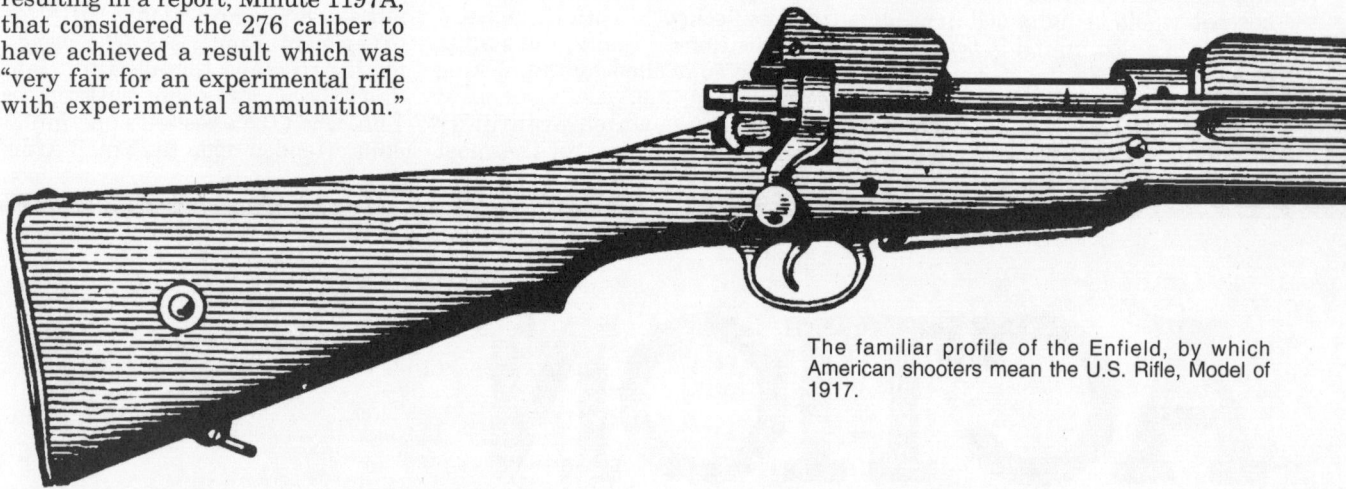

The familiar profile of the Enfield, by which American shooters mean the U.S. Rifle, Model of 1917.

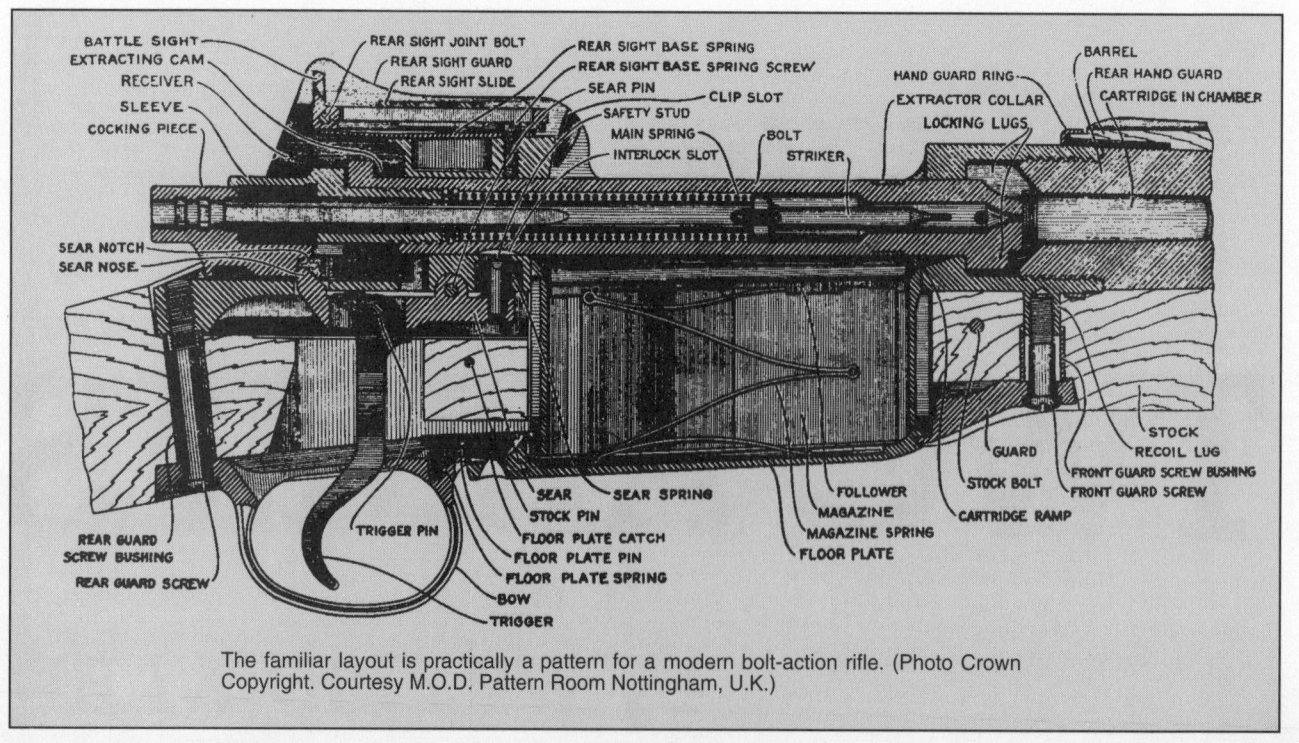

The familiar layout is practically a pattern for a modern bolt-action rifle. (Photo Crown Copyright. Courtesy M.O.D. Pattern Room Nottingham, U.K.)

was put in hand at the Enfield manufactory. The new weapon was designated the "Rifle, Magazine, Enfield, .276-inch" and was officially so described by the War Office on March 15, 1913. These arms were distributed to troops in the British Isles, Egypt and South Africa, in order that they might undergo the most thorough tests.

A variety of advantages were claimed over the 303. Greater power in the cartridge gave flatter trajectory and higher muzzle velocity, while greater strength (which was needed for this cartridge) was provided. Yet this was achieved with simplification and reduction of components. In particular, the

returned to store, were converted to 470 caliber for use against snipers' plates—armored firing port covers—and at least one was tried in France. Similar use had been made of heavy-caliber big game rifles, and the latter turned out to be more efficient. These were superseded by the introduction of armor-piercing 303 rifle ammunition. The P13 again was retired, and re-emerged only briefly as an idea in similar context in the 1930s (see below). Its positively final appearance was during the 1939-45 war, when a number were rebuilt and reissued as sniper rifles. (I am indebted to Mr. David Penn for calling my attention to these.)

The specifications for the substitute rifle, designated "Rifle, Magazine, .303-inch, Pattern 1914," were approved in October, 1914, and six examples made from the improved version of the 1913 trials rifle were ready in April, 1915. The new pattern was simpler to make than the Lee-Enfield, nonetheless production did not go smoothly, or indeed at all, in Britain. B.S.A., one of Britain's principal arms manufacturers, declined the contract. An order was placed with Vickers for 200,000 rifles to be delivered at a rate of 2000 per week from July 31, 1915, and rise to 3000 a week from November 27. For a variety of reasons, the Vickers rifles were at first

front-locking bolt gave the hoped-for advantage of greater rigidity to both body and bolt. The action and bolt could be stripped without tools. The one-piece stocking allowed a lighter nosecap to be used. This improved the balance, and was not only cheaper to produce, but less likely to break. The aperture backsight was particularly successful, giving the rifle an increased sightbase. In addition, there was a fixed aperture battle sight. Other advantages were the heavier barrel, made possible by other weight savings. The magazine, being entirely within the stock, was less susceptible to accidental damage; moreover it remained open when empty. Overall, it was claimed the rifle showed a general improvement in ease of handling.

While these qualities were justifiably claimed for the rifle itself, the combination with the new cartridge was far less successful. Had it not been for the outbreak of war, the problems (largely occasioned by the power of the 276 round) would probably have been overcome. The problem was being considered during the summer of 1914. Eventually, the authorities decided to use the new rifle, but with the well-tried, though less powerful, 303 cartridge.

This was not quite the end of the P13, because in late 1915 some of the original thousand P13s, by then

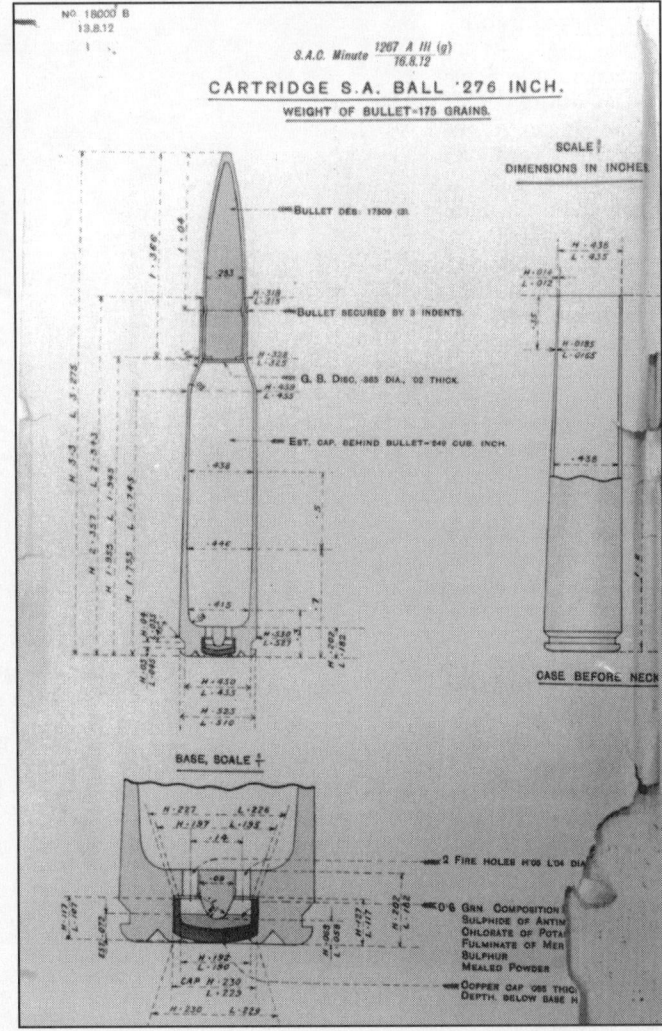

Small Arms Committee Minute setting out detail of 276 cartridge for P13 rifle. (Photo Crown Copyright. Courtesy of M.O.D. Pattern Room Nottingham, U.K.)

Camouflaged sniper using P14. Though the picture is clearly posed, it was almost only in this way that the rifle saw active service. It was very successful. (Photo courtesy Imperial War Museum)

delayed, and later the project was abandoned with only a few prototypes to show for it.

In the United States, the arms industry was more accommodating, and contracts were entered into by Winchester Repeating Arms Company of New Haven, Connecticut; Remington Arms Company of Delaware; and Remington Arms Company of Ilion, New York, to make 2000, 6000, and 3000, rifles a day to a total of 3,400,000 in all, for a staggering total of $102,500,000. Tools and gauges were dispatched from Britain, and a British military inspectorate was established in the United States. Again, progress was not smooth, and a renegotiation of the contracts was deemed necessary. This was completed on December 31, 1916. The new grand total for rifles was 1,811,764. Difficulties had also arisen over the actual cost of the work done. These were sorted out by the British representatives. Britain had agreed to pay all expenses and to buy the plant on completion of the orders.

Before this could happen, however, the United States entered the war as Britain's ally. By the spring of 1917, it was apparent the Enfield S.M.L.E. 303 rifle had served satisfactorily in the trenches, and the 303 Pattern 14 was needed only in a specialized role for snipers and reserve troops. (This policy continued after the 1939-1945 war, and can be vouched for by the author, aged 13, who met his first P14, aged about 30, in 1945 in his school cadet force.) Accordingly, production was

Home Guard Corporal Batcherlor's expression of happy anticipation seemed too good to miss. He was a veteran and probably had experience bayonet fighting during the 1914 war. (Photo courtesy Imperial War Museum)

brought to an end, with an approximate total of 1,233,000, Pattern 14s being produced. The 604,901 rifles made at Eddystone by Remington Arms Company were the most expensive, and together with bayonet and scabbard cost $43.75 each; those from Winchester (225,008) $36.82; while those from Remington Arms UMC (403,126) came out at $28.38 each. Soon after this, the whole enterprise was sold by Britain to the American government at a price of $9,000,000. This was a big loss, but by this stage it was clear that Britain's needs would be covered by 303 Lee-Enfields. The expanding U.S. Army,

behaved irresponsibly. Perhaps this was occasioned by the fact that the companies concerned were being offered contracts of almost undreamed of size, and as good businessmen they felt compelled to accept first and work out later. Also, in fairness to those involved, one must remember that in the end American industry did find a way. The combination of unpreparedness, tight inspection procedures, lack of enough expert labor (particularly toolmakers) and pressure for fast production was just too much for success. Had the British government insisted on its contractual rights, the likely outcome would have been the

1914-1918 war), her small military arms industry preserved, and an acceptable compromise reached.

This was not quite the end of the P13/P14 concept in the British service. Apart from the use of the existing 303 rifles for sniping and in lesser theatres, and the later use by the Home Guard of Model 1917s (see below), there was one final flirtation with the action in 1936. That year, the Small Arms Committee decided that a rifle with armor-piercing capability was desirable. The result was the "Rifle, Magazine, Experimental, .276 High Velocity." It fired a rimless magnum 276 round and was shaped in the style of a sporting rifle. There were also mounts for a telescopic sight. In 1939, B.S.A. made two prototypes with Mauser-type bolt systems and a built-in five-round magazine. History, however, repeated itself and the same problems of overheating and bullet stripping were encountered, as with the P13. Eventually the war led to a final repetition—the scheme was scrapped. The rifle was called after Captain J.R. Ainley who led the design team.[2]

After the sale by Britain, the first necessity was a complete evaluation of the rifle from an American viewpoint. This led to the abandonment of the 303 caliber in favor of the 30-06 rimless round. Next, and in some ways even more important, interchangeability of parts was introduced. These decisions, like the British one to replace the experimental 276 with the well-tried 303, turned out well for America both militarily and commercially. Interchangeability of parts cut production times greatly, and whilst the P14 had only been turned out at about fifty a day, in one day a record 250 Model 1917s were produced. Setting the caliber at 30-06 was clearly a wise decision. As well as the obvious convenience of keeping to one caliber, the performance of the rimmed cartridge had left a lot to be desired, particularly in terms of feeding from the magazine. When the new model arrived in American military hands, *Arms and Explosives* (Sept. 1,1917) tells us that the new rifle received a sympathetic welcome, a reaction not always accorded to new weapons by soldiers. Though doubts had been expressed in advance, the action showed itself quite strong enough to cope with the Springfield round, which had a chamber pressure of some 10,000 pounds more than the 303.

By the time the United States

Strengthened M17 with grenade throwing device used by British Home Guard. (Photo courtesy Imperial War Museum)

on the other hand, was shorter of weapons than it had been at any time since the earlier part of the Civil War. The solution was a statesmanlike one, and a success.

Pausing to ask oneself how great a success the new rifle had been up to this point, the answer is only a limited one. Blame must go in many different directions, and a high proportion be laid to bad luck. Nonetheless, there were those who

ruin of two if not all of the contracting manufacturers. As it was, a substantial sum was saved from the ruins ($9,000,000) by the sale of the whole plant and apparatus to the United States. The balance of the British contract arms were to be completed whilst at the same time work began on the new U.S. rifles. This way Britain's new ally was armed with a first-class rifle (now accepted as the best used in the

This is the 276 experimental rifle made in 1912. (Photo Crown Copyright. Courtesy M.O.D. Pattern Room Nottingham, U.K.)

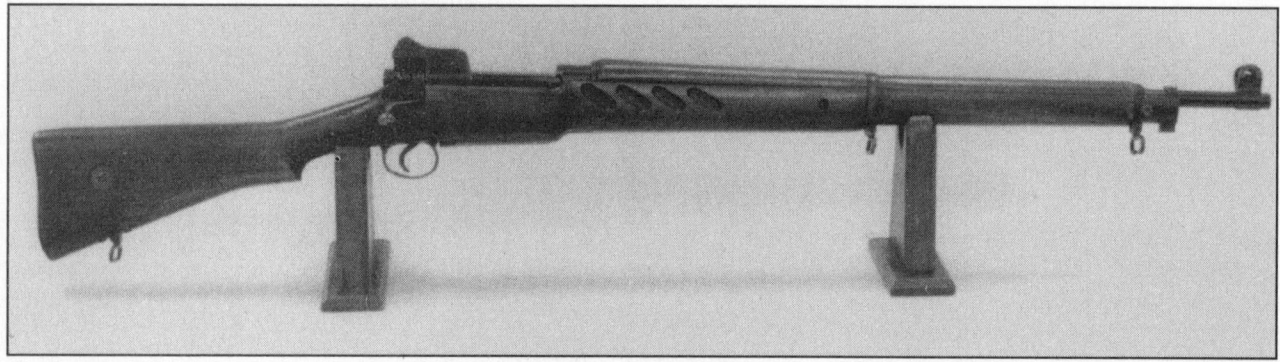

Finally, the 276 Pattern 1913 Rifle looked like this. (Photo Crown Copyright. Courtesy M.O.D. Pattern Room Nottingham, U.K.)

This is the sealed Pattern 1914 Sniper rifle with offset telescopic sight. Mounting the sight directly over the line of the bore obstructed charger loading. (Photo Crown Copyright. Courtesy M.O.D. Pattern Room Nottingham, U.K.)

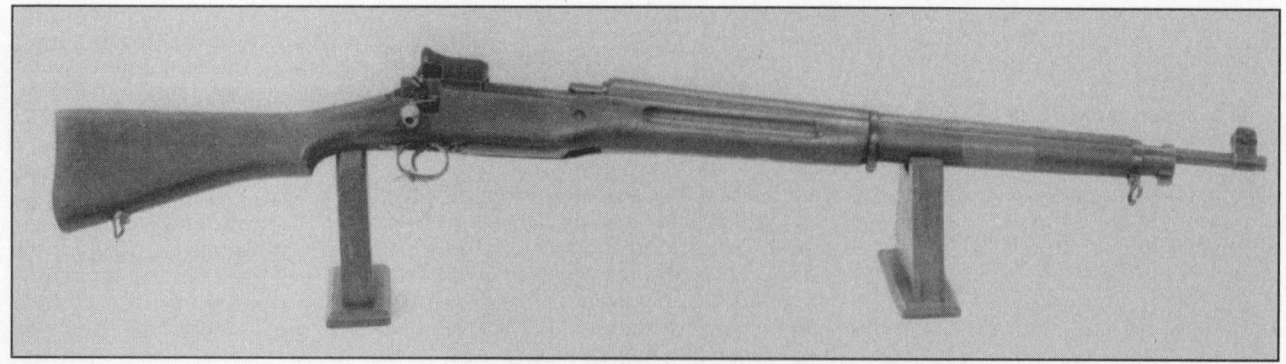

Here is a Winchester-made Model 1917 exported to Britain and used by Home Guard. Note painted band distinguishing from 303 P14.

troops got to France, the pattern of trench warfare was well established. That most war-like of Americans, Captain Herbert W. McBride (author of *A Rifleman Went to War* and one of the most famous snipers of the era) had missed the South African War because he was not British. Not to be caught a second time by such a technicality, in 1914 he enlisted in the Canadian forces and was in France from 1915 to 1917. He did his sniping with the Canadian Ross rifle, but formed a favorable impression of the Model 1917 when he had returned to the U.S. as an instructor. (The rifle is also said by the Editor and Wiley Clapp to have been used by Sergeant York in his famous exploit. Doubts are cast on this by Dr. Ezell and an anonymous 1969 *American Rifleman* writer, who both attribute a Springfield to him. The latter article includes York holding a Springfield pictured with his son. In light of such a conflict of authorities, one can only say that if he had had one, it would probably have done him very well! Silencing 35 machine guns, killing 25 and capturing 132 Germans, all with a rifle and a Government 45, doesn't just depend on the make of the rifle.)

There is no doubt that the American version of the Enfield rifle was a great improvement upon its 303 relation. It was simplified, incorporating most of the good points of the P14 and the Springfield. At the same time, there is no reason to doubt that, had the original development at Enfield not been interrupted by war, a first-class rifle would have emerged. The post-sale development was on strictly American lines. Thus, when one examines the ultra-rare trench-firing device (which I illustrate by courtesy of the Springfield Armory Museum and the Museums and Parks Service), one finds the designer has departed from the British system of raising the whole rifle in a frame containing a separate trigger mechanism, and has hinged the butt, thus permitting the rifle's own trigger and optical sight to be used. The development of the equally rare Pedersen Device, which converted the 1917—only a few made—into a semi-automatic rifle, was brought to an end with the arrival of peace. In 1934, though not acting for the U.S. government, Remington produced a "Model 1934" as an export to Honduras. Argentina, too, is reputed to have received rifles.

Rumors of the new version of the Enfield had crossed the Atlantic to

Model 1917 closeup of backsight. The aperture battle sight, horizontal when the main sight is raised, can be seen at the base of the backsight. (Photo Crown Copyright. Courtesy M.O.D. Pattern Room Nottingham, U.K.)

Arms and Explosives by April, 1917, together with justifiable comment on the superiority of the British aperture sight. Final details of the various changes were not published until August, 1917. In the September 1st issue, despite the very strict British censorship, the same paper reported more. The U.S. press, forgetting that the action had been originally designed for the powerful 276 round, expressed fears that the 52,000 pounds of pressure generated by the 30-06 cartridge would prove too much for an action which had only handled the 42,000 pounds of the 303 round. In fact, the 30-06 and the original 276 produced roughly the same pressures. The reaction of the American users was almost universally favorable, although this must have been hard in some instances, bearing in mind that a great deal of the design was still foreign, and that it largely displaced a popular American rifle. The American decision had been to embody chosen changes, but only if they would not occasion delay in production of the new weapon.

Arms and the Man welcomed the new arrival, praising the heavy barrel and the rimless cartridge. (In fairness we must not lose sight of the fact that the P13 was designed for such a cartridge.) The writer, however, hit on the greatest merit, namely the aperture backsight. This, he considered, would make the rifle "stand apart from all others." It was a true prophecy. His other comment that the new naming of the rifle the "U.S. Rifle Model 1917" was "an extraordinary fate for a weapon designed by the British Small Arms Committee" had a ring of jingoism about it, which might have seemed more appropriate from Enfield rather than Washington D.C. Even the proudest Briton could not but agree with one comment that its most striking feature was its "entire lack of beauty."[3]

It would have been too much to hope for that everyone would get it right, though they probably tried harder then in matters of weapons than they do today. The *New York Sun* attacked the change with the headline "Why Our Forces in France Must Use Inferior Rifle," and continued to say that the U.S. Expeditionary Force was to use British Lee-Enfield rifles, recham-

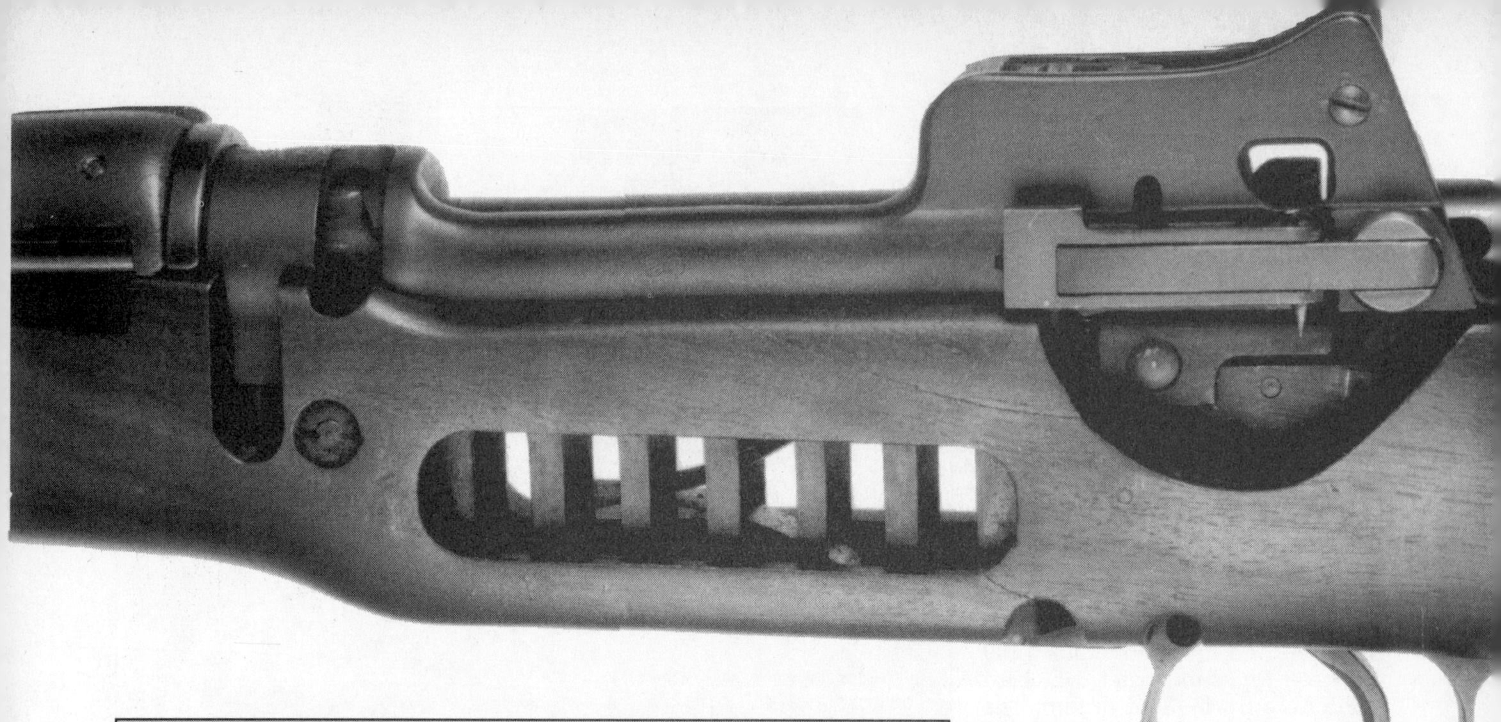

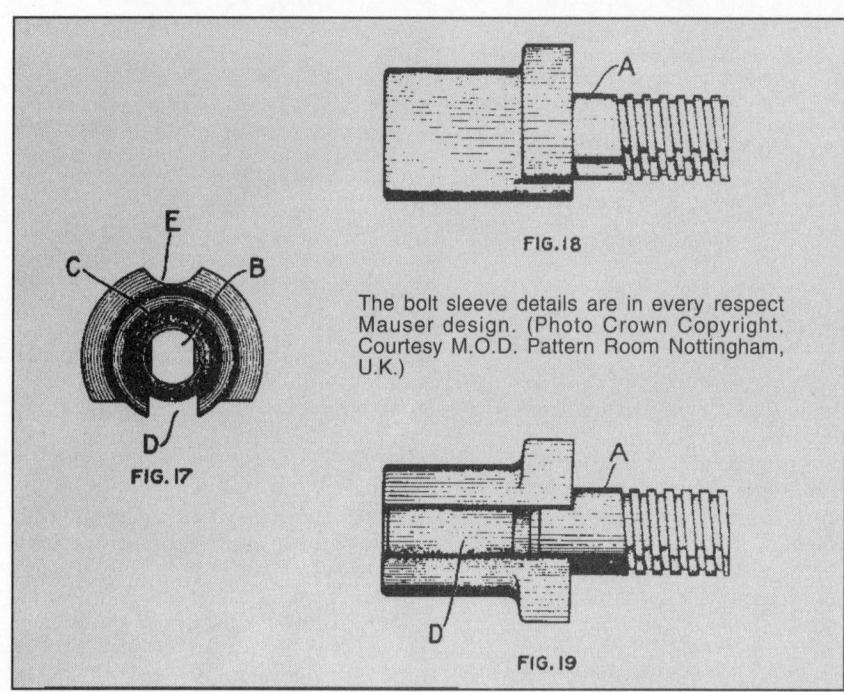

FIG.18

FIG.17

The bolt sleeve details are in every respect Mauser design. (Photo Crown Copyright. Courtesy M.O.D. Pattern Room Nottingham, U.K.)

FIG.19

Cutaway Model 1917, close-up of action, right side. (Photo courtesy the Smithsonian Institution Washington)

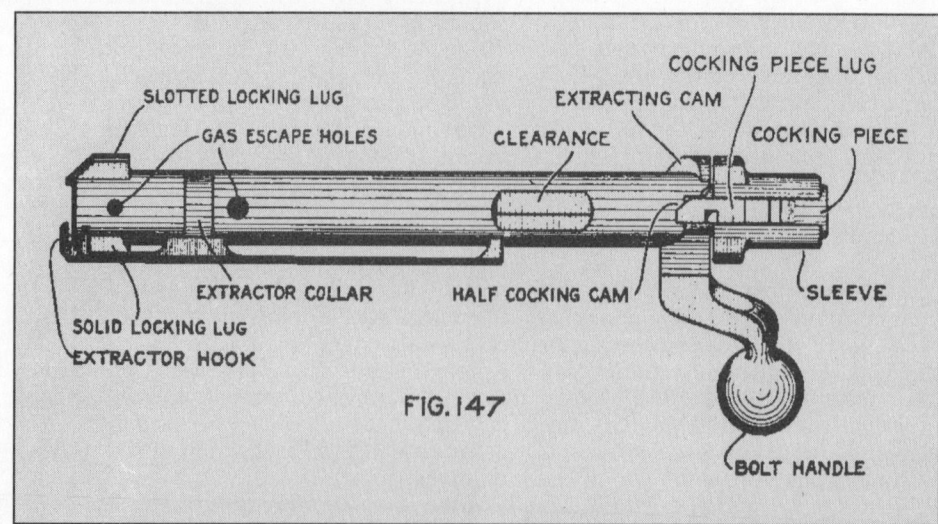

SLOTTED LOCKING LUG
GAS ESCAPE HOLES
COCKING PIECE LUG
EXTRACTING CAM
CLEARANCE
COCKING PIECE
EXTRACTOR COLLAR
HALF COCKING CAM
SLEEVE
SOLID LOCKING LUG
EXTRACTOR HOOK

FIG.147

BOLT HANDLE

Seen from below, the 1917 bolt is clearly a Mauser layout. (Photo Crown Copyright. Courtesy M.O.D. Pattern Room Nottingham, U.K.)

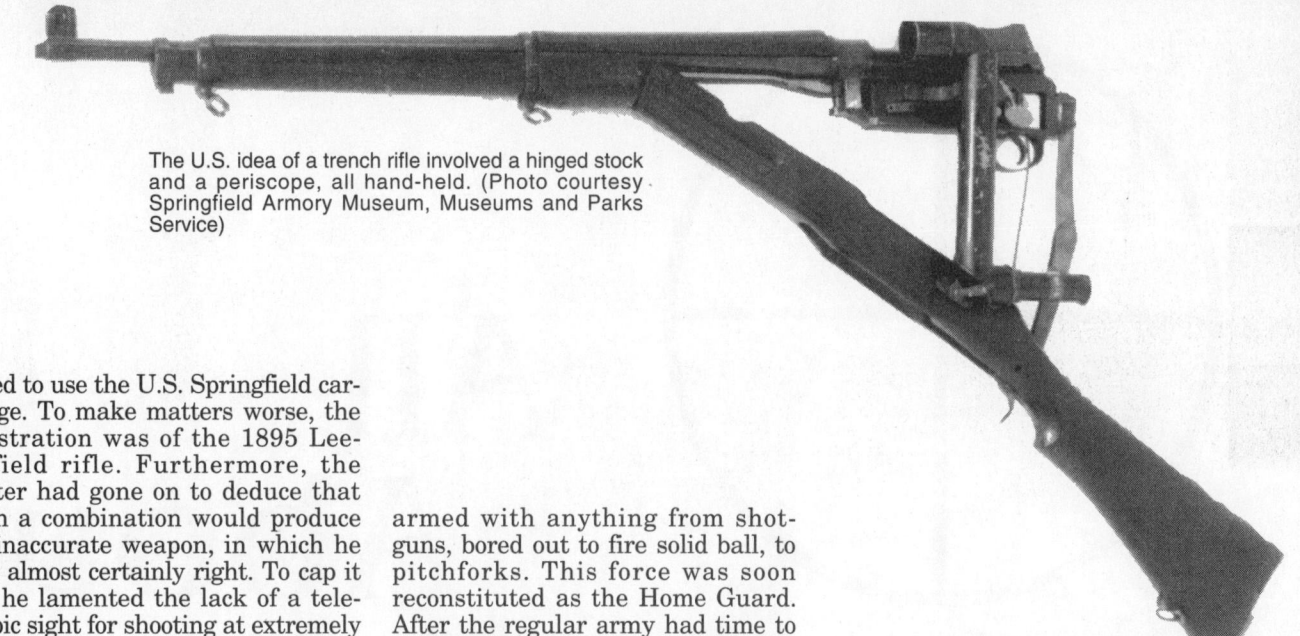

The U.S. idea of a trench rifle involved a hinged stock and a periscope, all hand-held. (Photo courtesy Springfield Armory Museum, Museums and Parks Service)

bered to use the U.S. Springfield cartridge. To make matters worse, the illustration was of the 1895 Lee-Enfield rifle. Furthermore, the writer had gone on to deduce that such a combination would produce an inaccurate weapon, in which he was almost certainly right. To cap it all, he lamented the lack of a telescopic sight for shooting at extremely long ranges.

Such errors at such a time could not go uncorrected, and the NRA's former president, General George W. Wingate, joined Captain Mattice, the officer in charge of the U.S. Enfield project, to correct the record in *Arms and the Man*. Mr. Skerrett (the author) was said to have shown that he had done considerable research, but "that he was not a practical rifleman." The General's conclusion was that "to enable the soldier to shoot with greatest accuracy and rapidity, the modified Enfield is to my mind superior to the Springfield as the latter is now sighted."

One could continue to quote contemporary sources, but suffice it to say that the near-unanimous view on both sides of the Atlantic was that the "Modified Enfield" was the finest rifle yet developed. Like every other manufacturing process, it had its problems. The Model 1917's were the difficulties encountered in heat-treating the rifle, both at Eddystone and Springfield. It was not absolutely without fault, but it was infinitely ahead of its competitors on both sides of the conflict.

By 1939, the U.S. was re-equipping itself with the semi-automatic Garand, thus the Model 1917 no longer occupied as high a place as it had at the end of hostilities in 1918. Though downgraded to "limited standard" in 1943, it was by no means finished, and appropriately many thousands were exported to Britain under the Lend-Lease agreement. At the beginning of the 1939 war in Britain, home defense was in the hands of the Local Defense Volunteers, who were armed with anything from shotguns, bored out to fire solid ball, to pitchforks. This force was soon reconstituted as the Home Guard. After the regular army had time to reorganize itself and replenish its supplies after the vast losses suffered in the retreat from France in 1940, official attention was turned to the Home Guard. From the status of peasant skirmishers, it became a well-armed, if elderly, force, officered and manned largely by seasoned soldiers who had been service in the 1914 war. In such hands, the Model 1917 was a potent and valued weapon. To distinguish them from the 303 caliber P14, the 30-06 Model 1917 rifles were marked with a red band. Though the cartridges of the two rifles were not interchangeable, considerable logistic problems must have arisen from the presence of both rifles in the same units. The P14, too, had not been battle-tested apart from sniping and was restricted to reserve units and a variety of non-standard formations.

Thus, this great and under-used action returned to the country of its origin. By the accidents of timing, it was too late for effective and prolonged service with European users other than for snipers in its 303 form in World War I, and too early for much war service in its 30-06 form in World War II. Speculation can be dangerous, but had the beginning of the 1914 conflict come later, or its end been further prolonged, it seems highly likely that either the Pattern 1913 or the Model 1917 would have earned itself a much more notable place in the history of infantry weapons than circumstances allowed. Moreover, it is no accident that the P14 actions are still greatly sought after as the basis for custom target rifles in Britain today.●

Acknowledgements

I am particularly indebted to Mr. Herbert Woodend of the M O D Pattern Room, Nottingham; to Mr. David Penn, keeper of firearms at the Imperial War Museum; and its trustees for their help and guidance in the preparation of this article and for the opportunity to photograph their exhibits. In addition, I owe thanks to Dr. Ed Ezell and the Smithsonian Institution for photographs of the cutaway Model 1917, and to The Springfield Armory Museum and the National Parks Service for the opportunity to photograph the trench-firing Model 1917 device. Mr. Pete Dickey of the NRA of America provided me with relevant extracts from *Arms and The Man*, and Dr. DeWitt Bailey and Mr. W.S. Curtis those from *Arms and Explosives*. Finally, I refer those readers who seek further information on this very interesting subject to Mr. Skennerton's invaluable work *The U.S. Enfield*, where once again he has almost certainly produced the metaphorical, if not the actual, last word on the subject.

Wilfrid Ward

Footnotes
[1]Ian Skennerton, *The U.S. Enfield* (Margate, Australia: Ian Skennerton, 1983) p.2.

[2]Herbert Woodend, *British Rifles: A Catalogue of the Enfield Pattern Room* (No HMSO, 1981).

[3]"A Causerie About Rifles," *Arms and the Man* (Washington DC: NRA, June, 1918).

This design is an industry classic. Heavy posts stand out against thick cover and the thin lines obscure nothing.

All About Modern SCOPE

On A LIST OF THE most significant advances in telescopic sight design of the past generation, better reticle design would be at or near the top. Reticle styles or configurations have been a source of interest and fascination to shooters for many years. About three decades back, the Bausch & Lomb Co. of Rochester, New York, introduced a variable 2.5-8x scope employing a tapered crosshair. Like most scopes of that period, the reticle was located in the first focal plane. This was OK, except the crosshairs would move off center when even a modest amount of windage or elevation adjustment was applied. During that period, both Bausch & Lomb and Leupold were able to get around this negative feature by having windage and elevation adjustments in their respective mounts.

In the case of variable power scopes, the reticles were in the first focal plane, but the variable power system was to the rear of the reticle. This meant that when the image was "zoomed" larger, enlargement of the reticle had to go along with it. When viewed at low power, the reticle was proportionate to the image, but then when the scope was zoomed to, say, 9x power, the reticle appeared to "grow" disproportionately. This was obviously a problem for the user. Bausch & Lomb conceived the idea that if the crosshairs were tapered, this feature would be less objectionable, and they were probably correct.

The Germans had long ago used the combination of posts and crosshairs in a manner that placed the tapered posts in front of the normal crosshair which produced a pretty good pattern. It had to be a very time-consuming manufacturing process, however, and consequently relatively expensive. My thought was there must be a simpler method by which the tapered reticle pattern could be accomplished. At my desk I had an ordinary 12-inch rule. The thin brass edging strip had come loose so I carefully removed it. Holding each end between my thumb and forefinger, I gave the strip a 180-degree twist. Presto! I had half of my tapered crosshair. The concept was sound and it provided a starting point, so I turned to some key people at Leupold for assistance. By running some of our regular reticle wire of that period through a small set of rollers, manageable wire ribbons were produced that could be soldered to the brass reticle frames with the all-important 180-degree twist, and we were in business with a new, all-metal reticle pattern at a fairly economical production cost.

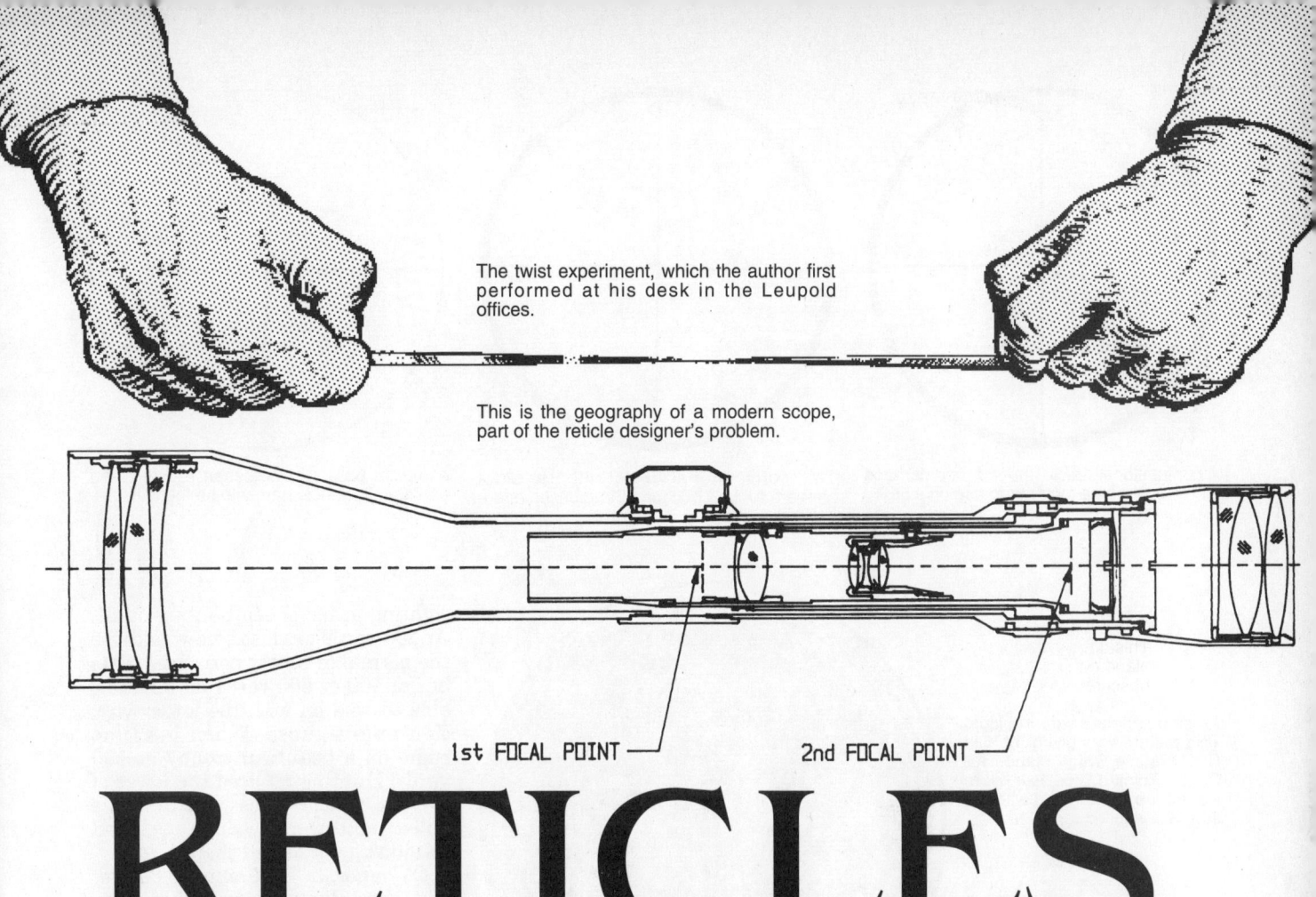

The twist experiment, which the author first performed at his desk in the Leupold offices.

This is the geography of a modern scope, part of the reticle designer's problem.

1st FOCAL POINT   2nd FOCAL POINT

RETICLES

by JACK V. SLACK

There was one major drawback to this fabrication system, however. At the intersection of the flattened wires, where they met "on edge," recoil tended to cause a peening action that over time would cause sort of a "dot" to develop. Hardly a positive feature! Leupold's tool and die people developed the idea that instead of rolling the reticle wire into a flat ribbon, we should simply press it flat in a die in such a manner that only the heavier or wider area would be pressed. Therefore, the unpressed section was left untouched. Of course, this is easier said than done; considerable development time and cost was to follow. In the end, the reticles fashioned in this manner were stronger and better, and the peening problem ended.

This process provided an avenue to develop the now well-known Duplex pattern, developed by Leupold, employing a step-down instead of a taper. Of course, other reticle patterns and combinations followed, but, far and away, the now well-established Duplex style was to be the front runner. It would be difficult to come up with the total number made, but we are talking in the hundreds of thousands in the years since its introduction in 1962. This would number into the millions, taking in the whole industry.

Most everyone, I am sure, is aware that the first reticles were of the simple crosshair style, probably beginning with early transits or optical levels. Nothing could be simpler, and even today it still holds true. The first rifle scopes, dating way back over 100 years and beyond, had crosshair reticles. In North America (including Canada), a reticle style that was quite popular for a time was the post and crosshair. I have

particular reference to the tapered flat top post that extended somewhat above the horizontal wire. It is supposed that its one-time popularity was due to the fact that this style of post better accommodated the transition from "iron sights" to the rifle scope. The tapered post seemed more nearly like the rifle's front sight.

It is probably just as well, too, that we stay with the simpler patterns, otherwise the gadgetry and clutter become a distraction. The late Jack O'Connor once told me of an incident that happened when he was sheep hunting with Fred Huntington (then head of RCBS). I believe the story beyond doubt since Huntington had asked Leupold to make up a couple of 4xs with a dual horizontal crosshair having a predetermined distance between the wires. Huntington, according to O'Connor, had spent a fair amount of time

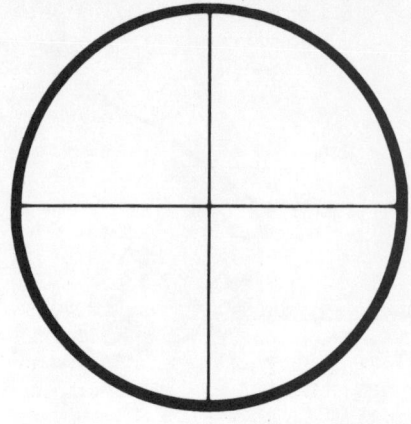

A conventional reticle, indeed, and perhaps the very first type ever put to use on a rifle.

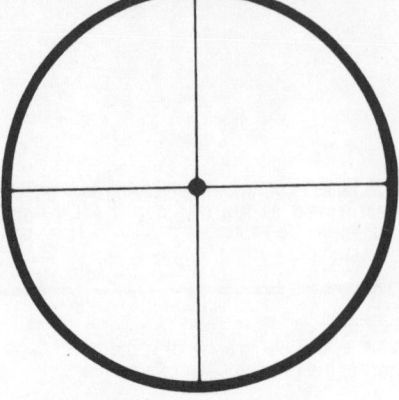

This conventional target-shooter's dot appears to float because the crosshairs are extremely fine.

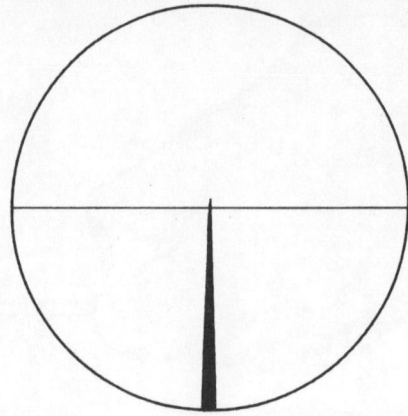

A typical post and crosshair reticle of an earlier period, now hardly to be found.

Twisted flattened wire in place. This pattern was given the title CPC Reticle which stands for Center Pointed Crosshair. Here we are looking forward with the eyepiece section removed.

Rifle great Townsend Whelen, an early scope sight advocate, generated this book on the subject for Samworth Publications. Note the reticles.

sighting-in his sheep hunting outfit. At 300 yards or closer, he would use the normal or center horizontal wire, but at 500 or 600 yards he would be able to hold on with the lower wire. You might guess: When his time came on a beautiful trophy at 150 yards, Huntington used the lower of the two reticle wires which put his bullet right over the ram's back and he didn't get a second chance.

O'Connor, in his *Complete Book of Rifles and Shotguns,* had this to say:

> Many types of reticles have been designed since the telescope sight came into being. For the most part, American scope makers go in for simple reticles, whereas the Germans, and other Europeans, have always liked them complicated. Fancy reticles fascinate the uninstructed beginner; the old-timer or practical hunter wants them simple.

A large segment of European hunters have adopted American cartridges and, yes, even U.S.-made rifles. However, by and large, they tend to stick by their European-style reticles. To us these appear rather gross. I have even heard the reference, "It looks like a fence post!" There is probably a good reason, though, for this preference. For the most part, hunting in Europe is done at closer ranges and quite frequently from shooting stands. A very long shot would be in the neighborhood of 200 yards. The really big difference, however, is the fact that the hunter has probably climbed up to his stand in total darkness. He would expect his big moment would come at the very break of dawn. The light obviously would be very poor and the typical North American scope reticle is virtually invisible. So, under certain conditions, the European

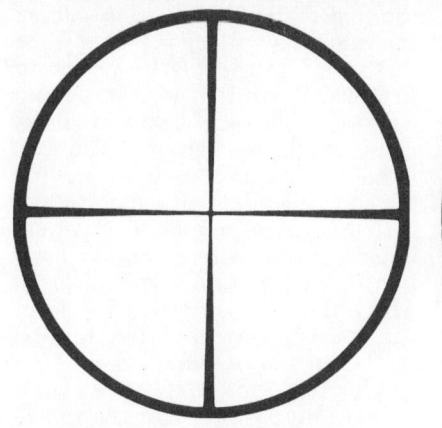
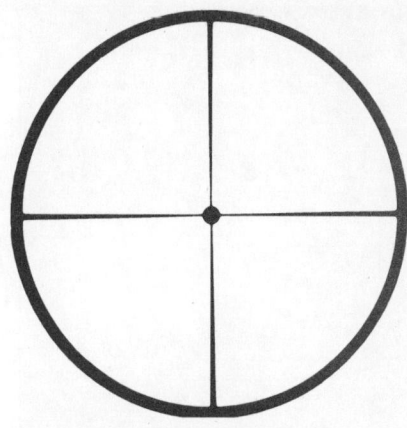

The CPC reticle is a steady taper down to its intersection, leading your eye to the center.

This reticle has a prominent dot coupled with a thin version of the CPC crosshairs.

hunter's "fence post" reticles have their place.

Someone once said that the one sure thing you can count on is *change*. It is noteworthy that the European large objective scope is catching on in the U.S. Most domestic scope manufacturers and some of the imports from the Orient are now offering the larger objective scopes in at least one model. Going along with the larger objective is a more prominent reticle. The same pattern may be retained, but usually a heavier material is used.

All this seems to point to the fact that North American hunters, too, are finding that as game becomes harder to come by, early morning or late evening hunting can have its rewards and a good chance should not be passed up even in dimmer light conditions, where such is legal.

What material are scope reticles fabricated from? Are spider webs used? I'm often asked that. I am told that at Leupold for a long time only platinum wire has been used in metallic reticle fabrication. Their target dots, on the other hand, are suspended or attached to fine glass-fiber filaments, which take the place of the black widow spider webs once used. This obviously is more convenient in several ways. The glass fibers must be attached to the reticle frame or holder by cementing them in place. The platinum wire, flattened, or otherwise, is held in place with soft solder; nothing else is as strong or durable.

Another reticle material that has more recently been put into use for dot fabrication is tungsten. This wire can be drawn to .00015-inch and holds promise of being even better than glass fiber. The crosshair filament that supports the dot must be separated or spaced apart by a distance equal to the diameter of the dot itself, which has been formed from an epoxy material. A special department at Leupold handles this specialized work.

A sort of freakish occurrence, fortunately infrequent, is the burn-out of the dot reticle! The dot and its supporting filament can be melted or burned out given certain conditions. This can happen without the individual being aware until he takes aim to find no usable aiming point! If the sun should enter the objective parallel to the optical axis, the damage will take place in a few seconds. This only seems to happen with the so-called "floating dot" which would be supported by a nonmetallic filament. Where this supporting member is of a metallic wire, there seems to be no problem. It therefore is assumed that the wire takes the heat away from the center or the dot's location. All this sounds as if the dot is pretty delicate, and it is, but apart from the above, once installed and surrounded by the body of the scope, the reticle is amazingly rugged and able to stand up to very severe recoil or rough handling.

Virtually all scope makers prefer to stick with what I call mechanical-type reticles, rather than a reticle "printed" on a glass surface. A mechanically formed reticle is one stretched across the reticle frame and soldered or glued in place and, therefore, suspended within the reticle frame. This is, by far, the most desirable method of fabricating a reticle from the standpoint of simplicity as well as economics. This does, however, tend to limit the availability of styles or patterns. But with over 90 percent of demand being for the Duplex style, it can hardly be said that there is any great demand for something totally different.

At Leupold, nearly all popular reticles are made using a pressed wire

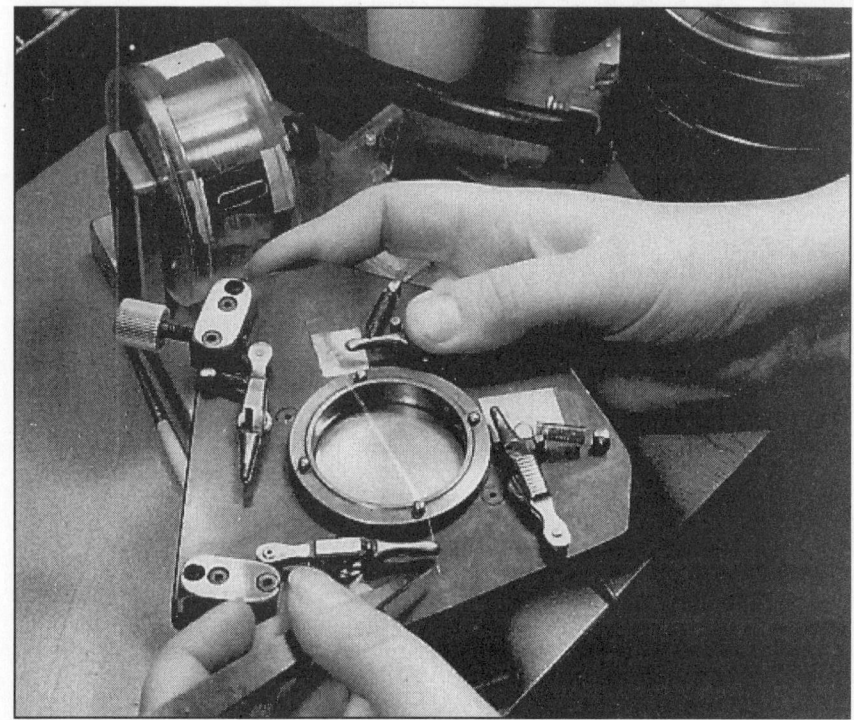

Applying the metallic wire to the holding fixture in a production situation, fully tooled. Job takes three minutes.

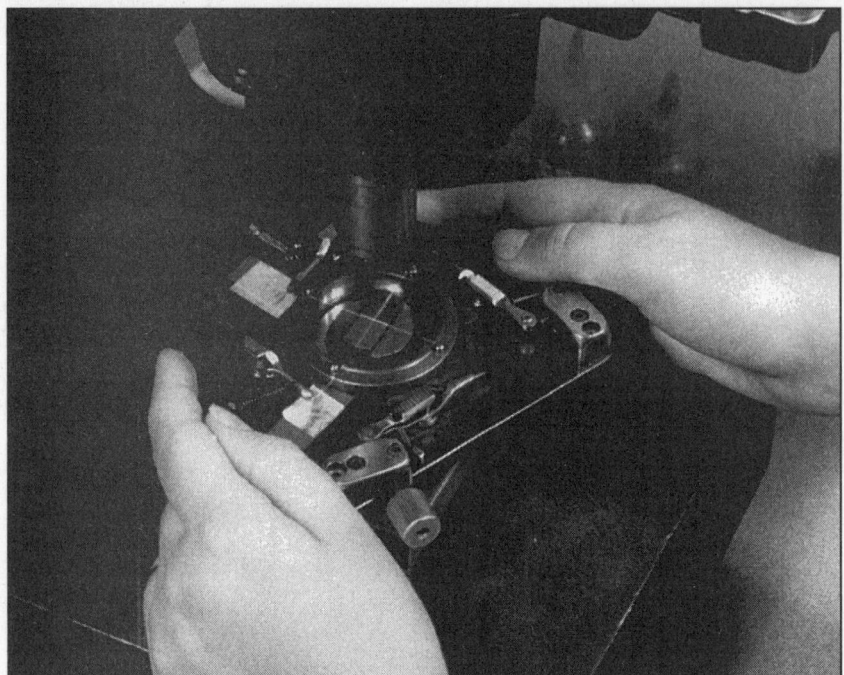

The pressing operation showing fixture and two-part die that just squeezes the desired reticle in place.

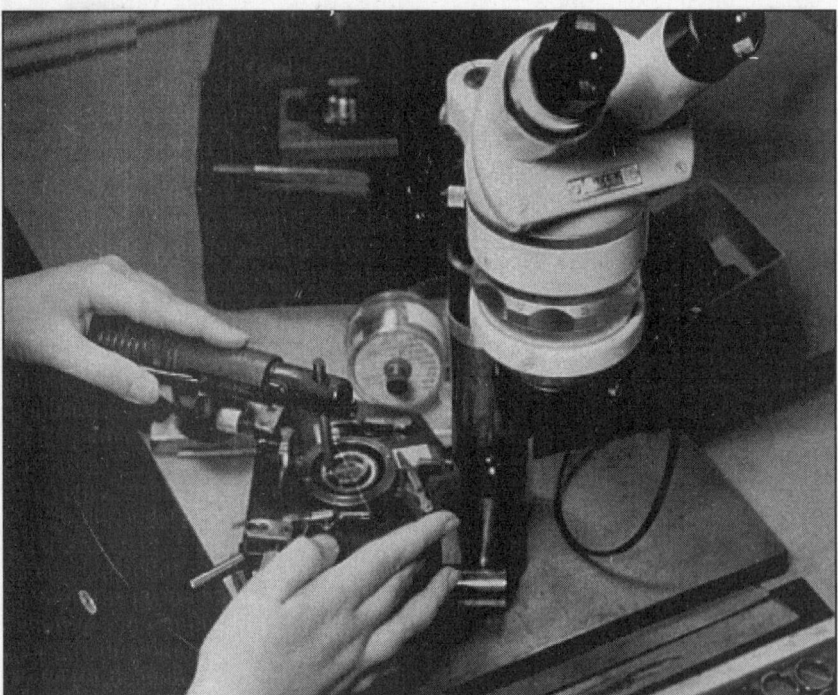

After proper alignment is attained, soldering is the final step. The dot reticles are a little more trouble, take more time.

the edge of the four opposing sides of the ring. The housing is placed (slots up) in a fixture for the pressing process. Platinum wire is strung across the slots and held in position using an alligator-type clip. The wire is held in position under a specific tension depending on what style of reticle is being made. The reticle housing, with wire strung in position, is then put on a special press where the wire is flattened to form the specific reticle style (Duplex, CPC, Post and Duplex).

A special microscope is then swung into position over the reticle to aid in aligning the platinum wire so it forms a perfect perpendicular cross. Tiny flecks of solder are then placed in the four slots of the housing where the wire is being held. An electrode is touched near the slots which melts the solder and fuses the wire to the reticle housing. The pressed wire reticle subassembly takes about three minutes to produce.

Manufacturing a Dot reticle is a more delicate and time-consuming process largely because the wire is much finer and there is no wire pressing in this process. The reticle housing for the Dot looks similar to that used for pressed wire-style reticles, except two opposing slots in the housing are cut slightly deeper. The housing is placed in a special holder (slots up). Extremely fine tungsten wire is strung over the slots and held in position. Because two slots in the reticle housing are cut slightly deeper, there is a slight gap between the two wires at the intersection. Wires are aligned using a microscope and glued into position using epoxy.

To form the Dot in the middle of the crosshair, a tiny amount of black epoxy is placed between the non-touching intersection of the crosshairs. The size of the Dot can be controlled by the depth of the two deeper slots machined on the reticle housing. The deeper the slots, the more space between the two wires, the bigger the Dot. The Dot reticle takes about seven minutes to produce.

In his book titled *Telescopic Rifle Sights* published in 1944, Colonel Townsend Whelen advocates the rather heavy flat-top post reticle. It is shown on the cover of his book (see page 62). This, of course, was one man's view of almost fifty years ago. This style of reticle would go over like a proverbial lead balloon with today's shooter/hunter. The Duplex reigns supreme. ●

production method. Three components are used in the manufacture of this subassembly: platinum wire, silver solder and a brass reticle housing. The reticle housing is machined from brass and resembles a wedding ring with four shallow slots cut on

Expect Scattered Clouds All Weekend.

THE MODEL 11-87™ PREMIER® SPORTING CLAYS: IT'S ALSO AN IDEAL UPLAND GAME GUN.

If there ever was a sport which combined the mind game of golf with the quick reflexes of tennis, it has to be Sporting Clays. Introducing the Model 11-87™ Premier® Sporting Clays—it can give you the edge you need to break more targets. And, after all, isn't that what it's all about? Point it and you'll swear this 12's a 20; it's a good 3/4 lb. lighter than any Model 11-87 you've ever tried. Its new, light contour barrel, shorter magazine and fore-end put the center of balance right where you want it— between your hands. Note how its rounded butt pad makes gun mounting easy. A matte-finished receiver top, barrel, and rib eliminate reflections. A lengthened forcing cone in its 26" or 28" barrel means better pattern uniformity and reduced recoil. The competition trigger pulls cleanly, breaks crisply. All five Rem™ Choke tubes are knurled for quick changes, with or without tools. And, when you buy this shotgun, you even get a custom-fitted hard case. Best of all, this Model 11-87 is so light and quick in the field, it's our bet you'll use it as much on feathered birds as clay ones. **Remington** DUPONT

IT'S WHAT YOU'RE SHOOTING FOR.

WE'RE LEADING THE WAY INTO THE FUTURE!

WITNESS

Multi-caliber versatility for the twenty-first century. Even more than today, the citizens of the future will look for economy and value. The versatile WITNESS will still fill the bill. With models for competition, duty, home defense and casual plinking...sizes from standard to subcompact...ported and unported slides...both standard length and extra-long compensated barrels...six calibers from .22 to .45 ACP...there's a WITNESS for everybody and every purpose. Best of all, all current and future WITNESS top ends are interchangeable on almost any WITNESS standard size frame! So starting with just a single frame, a value-minded citizen with an eye to the future can create a complete multi-purpose collection. A very futuristic approach, if you ask us.

ASTRA

The dawn of a new era of high performance super pistols. No pistols in the world are as ahead of their time as the A-75 and A-100. The mighty little A-75 (9mm, .40 S&W) is ASTRA's brand new selective double/single action super-compact. With all-steel construction, adjustable three-dot sights, and a triple safety system including a de-cocking lever, the sleek little A-75 promises to be ASTRA's hottest model yet and one of the most popular compact pistols in the United States. The double-action A-100 (9mm, .40 S&W, .45 ACP) is an equal in both quality and function to some other popular pistols costing twice as much. It comes with a law enforcement-approved de-cocking lever and a new higher capacity magazine.

Want to be prepared for the future? It's here today.

See the complete line of EAA products at your local firearms dealer, or send $2 for our current color catalog. Dealers, send your current FFL, retail tax certificate and your phone number for a FREE catalog.

EUROPEAN AMERICAN ARMORY CORP.

P.O. Box 3498, Bright Station ▪ Hialeah, FL 33013 ▪ 305/688-4442

© EAA 1993

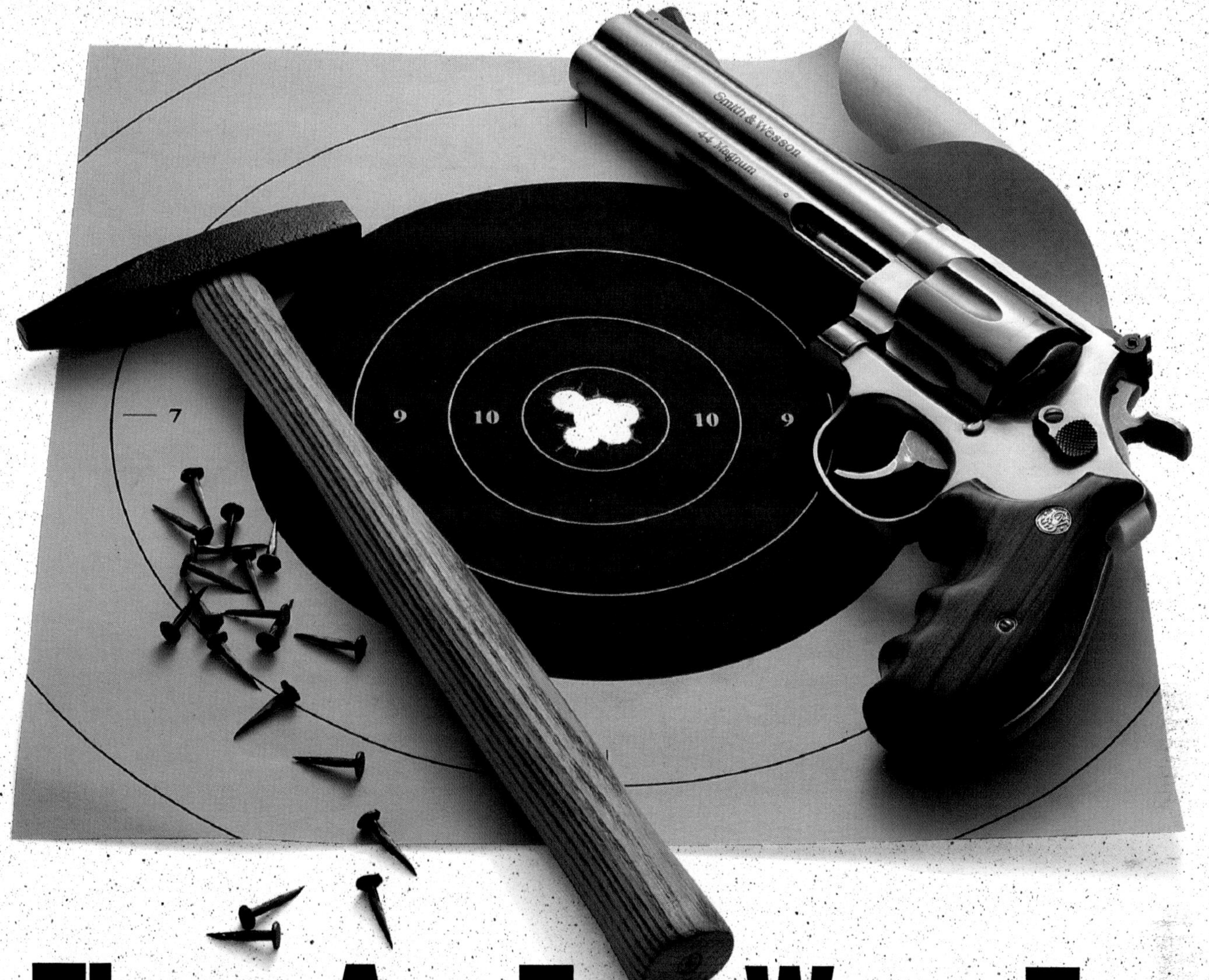

There Are Two Ways To Drive Tacks.

Driving tacks with a hammer is work. Driving tacks with a Smith & Wesson Model 29 or 629 classsic is pure shooting fun.

Featuring a full-lug barrel, chamfered cylinder, interchangeable front sights, target hammer and trigger, and optional silhouette sight package, the Smith & Wesson's family of Classics has taken .44 Magnum accuracy to a new level.

Whatever your game is—steel rams at 200 meters or whitetails at 50 yards—the Smith & Wesson Model 29 and 629 Classics deliver the accuracy and endurance you demand.

Another American Classic By Smith & Wesson.

RUGER

Sporting Firearms

Sporting firearms built by Ruger are known worldwide for perfect performance, exclusive design, and classic style. Ruger manufacturing methods and proud Ruger people produce these perfect firearms efficiently, and Ruger quality reaches the buyer reasonably priced. From top to bottom: 77/22RS $424.00; Ruger Express $1550.00; No. 1 International $656.00; Sporting Clays $1285.00.*

*Suggested Retail Prices

by LAYNE SIMPSON

RIFLE REVIEW

IT IS BECOMING extremely difficult for rifle manufacturers to come up with anything new—most of the slots are filled. So, for 1993, we're getting new variations of existing models. An example is a new autoloading rifle in 22 WMR that's actually a rimfire version of an existing centerfire rifle. Then we have other old rifles with new stocks, new barrels, new calibers and new materials. Some even look like what American manufacturers think European hunters want in a big game rifle. An old single shot bolt-action varmint rifle with solid-bottom receiver is back, as is a rifle that floats. Nestled inside the synthetic stock of a new version of an old varmint rifle is an aluminum bedding block. A quick-handling little bolt-action carbine, the one that caused thousands of woods hunters to hang up their lever actions, is now available with a Mannlicher-style full stock. On a sadder note, the most versatile single shot centerfire ever designed is gasping for breath like a carp out of water.

As chamberings go, a speedy 7mm-caliber belted wildcat is now available in three factory rifles, and one of those companies is factory-loading the cartridge. If you think that's something, a big, fast 30-caliber wildcat that burns over 100 grains of powder per trigger squeeze and makes lots of noise may be on the verge of achieving the same fate. Two of my favorite close-to-medium range varmint cartridges are the 22 Hornet and 218 Bee, simply

northwestern America.

Manufacturers of autoloading target rifles have caught the accuracy bug, and this report includes three that will consistently shoot five bullets into minute-of-angle groups and smaller. Let's now see what's new and exciting for '93, item by item.

A-Square

A-Square is now offering the 7mm STW chambering in its custom bolt-action rifles, the Hannibal built around a 1917 Enfield, and the Caesar on the Remington Model 700, either with walnut or fiberglass stocks. Unprimed cases and loaded ammunition with the 7mm STW headstamp are available. Two A-Square fac-

because their voices are so soft and you can get lots of shots from a pound of powder. Both are now available in the most handsome single shot rifle introduced during the 20th century. Other cartridges finding new homes during '93 are the 35 Whelen, 22 PPC, 6mm PC and 404 Jeffery. The 250-3000 Savage almost did, but we'll have to wait another year for it. Then there's the new rimmed 416-caliber cartridge which is just the ticket for a double rifle.

This is a big year for the 22 rimfire. A new autoloader is black all over and has a plastic heart, a new reproduction of an old bolt action is here, and we may see what many consider the world's most handsome bolt action ever built rise up from its ashes in

Simpson's suggestion produced USRAC's Model 70 Sporting Sharpshooter. This one is the first chambered for his 7mm STW cartridge.

tory loads feature the Nosler 140-grain Ballistic Tip at 3500 fps for deer-size game and a moose/elk/bear load with the Nosler 160-grain Partition at 3250 fps. According to the catalog, the latter loading packs almost 2600 foot pounds of energy at 300 yards compared to 2100 foot pounds for the firm's 7mm Remington Magnum load. There's also the possibility of a third 7mm STW load with the Sierra 160-grain spitzer boattail at 3250 fps.

Sometime back, I opined that the hunting world is ready for a domesticated version of Roy Weatherby's old 30-378 Magnum, formed by necking down the 378 Weatherby Magnum case and a favorite of 1000-yard benchrest competitors. There are worse

cartridges to choose for reaching across wide canyons and dropping elk-size game. I have 9½-pound big game rifles chambered for two versions of this cartridge. One is the original 30-378 Weatherby Magnum, and the other is called the 300 Kong. In 26-inch barrels, these cartridges push the 180- and 200-grain Nosler Partition along at 3500 and 3300 fps, and deliver as much punch at 300 yards as does the 30-06 at the muzzle. At any rate, Art Alphin of A-Square read my "wish list" and later informed me that he will introduce just such a cartridge in factory-loaded form and offer rifles chambered for it. Basically, his is the full-length 416

Rigby case necked down. Art hasn't come up with a name for it, but for now it can accurately be described as a 30-378 Weatherby Magnum without a belt on its case. It probably will be very much like the 30 wildcat Melvin Forbes of Ultra Light Arms has been playing with.

Brown Precision

Back in 1979, when fleaweight big game rifles were quite scarce, I had Chet Brown build me what he called the Model 600 Super Light in 7mm SGLC. Built around a lightened Remington Model 600 action, the little 600 SL had a Kevlar stock and a soda straw-thin 20-inch barrel that measured .494-inch at its muzzle. According to my postal scale, it weighed 4 pounds, 9 ounces. With a 1-inch carrying sling, four cartridges, and a Leupold 4x Compact held in place with a Weaver mount, it weighed 5 pounds, 14 ounces. I still have the 600 SL and it has dropped many whitetails since Brown built it.

Today, Chet Brown offers several models of custom rifles and handguns, most built around Remington's Models 700, Seven and XP-100 actions. As might be expected, all wear Brown Precision synthetic stocks. His latest creation, the Pro Hunter Elite, is available with a list of options about as long as my arm. To name but a few: 18- to 26-inch barrel lengths, barrel band-type front sight with brass bead and optional white flip-up night sight, electroless nickel or black Teflon finish, trapdoor grip cap for storing a detachable peep sight, Talley quick-detach scope mount, dropped extra-capacity magazine box, and muzzle-brake. The Pro Hunter Elite wears a Shilen stainless steel barrel and is available in virtually any factory or wildcat chambering you can think of.

Browning

Browning's BAR is the only autoloading sporting rifle available in the 338 Winchester, 7mm Remington and 270 Weatherby Magnum chamberings. Other options are 243, 270, 308 and 30-06. Celebrating its 25th anniversary during 1993, the 8 1/2-pound autoloader has been upgraded and redesignated the BAR Mark II Safari. The changes include a new bolt release that speeds up loading a round in the chamber. Lock back the bolt, insert a charged magazine, trip the bolt latch, and the chamber is loaded. The enlarged trigger guard has more room for a glove-clad finger, and the trigger assembly is now easily removed for cleaning by pushing out its two retaining pins. In the newly modified gas handling system, the port is designed for cleaner operation and improved reliability. The redesigned buffering system reduces wear and stress on the action during cycling. The BAR Mark II is available with or without open sights.

With its huge bolt shroud, butterknife bolt handle, Schnabel-style forearm, matte metal finish, and dull wood fin-

ish, the new Euro-Bolt is best described as the old A-Bolt with a new Germanic look. In fact, that's exactly what it is. Its chamberings are 270 and 30-06 (22-inch barrel) and 7mm Remington Magnum (26-inch barrel). Nominal weight is 7 pounds for the

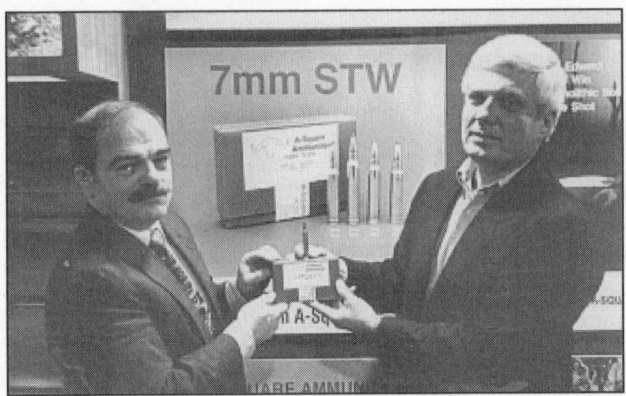

Art Alphin (left) presents the author with the first box of 7mm STW ammunition manufactured by A-Square, all long since shot up by Simpson, no doubt.

standard caliber and 7 1/2 pounds for the magnum.

Chapuis USA

Like most double-barrel rifles, the Chapuis AGEX Express side-by-side ain't exactly cheap. Prices range from $8500 for the standard grade gun to over $35,000 for the high grade. Its chamberings are 30-06, 300 Winchester Magnum, 7x65R, 8x57R, 9.3x74R, 375 H&H Magnum, 470 Nitro Express, 416 Rigby, and 416R Chapuis. A rimmed cartridge, this particular 416 was designed by Art Alphin of A-Square who just happens to make the ammunition. Loaded with a 400-grain bullet at 2400 fps, it duplicates 416 Rigby performance at relatively low chamber pressures that are compatible with a double rifle.

Clifton Arms

Brent Clifton makes some of the world's best synthetic stocks. I know this to be true because two of my big game rifles and one of my varmint rifles wear his stocks. Brent's operation now includes building fine custom rifles. He will put together a rifle around any suitable action, but considers the new Winchester Model 70 with claw extractor and Ruger's Model 77 Mark II awfully tough to beat for the money. One I recently lusted after was built for Jeff Cooper on a Kimber Model 89 action.

Called the Kimber Crusher, it was in 460 G&A caliber and had a six-round drop magazine. The rifle also had a Clifton-Wickert ghost ring aperture on its receiver bridge. Out front, a .04-inch-wide strip of gold was hammered vertically into a

.1-inch-wide ramped square blade. Nice work. Naturally, the rifle had a Clifton fiberglass stock. Don't be surprised if I someday take just such an outfit to Africa, or possibly a 375 H&H or 358 STA version to Alaska.

Cooper Arms

Cooper Arms of Stevensville, Montana, now offers two versions of its bolt-action rifle. The 22 rimfire has three locking lugs at about the mid-point of its bolt and a 45-degree bolt rotation. Its fully

adjustable trigger leaves the factory at 40 ounces, and the match-grade, Shilen barrel (chrome moly or stainless) is free-floating and has a heavy sporter contour. The standard AA grade Claro walnut stock has an oil finish, and 22-line checkering is standard. For a few dollars more, you can have AAA Claro of French walnut with a four-panel checkering layout. Overall length of the 8-pound rifle is 42 1/2 inches.

Called the Model 38, the centerfire Cooper is available in two wildcat chamberings called the 22 CCM and 17 CCM. Its action has three locking lugs at the front of the bolt, and its stock options are the same as for the rimfire rifle.

Eagle Arms, Inc.

I'm still having great fun with Eagle Arms' H-BAR target rifle that I mentioned in last year's report. It has a

Chet Brown of Brown Precision with his new Pro Hunter Elite in 416 Remington Magnum—enough gun.

heavy Hart barrel in 223 and wears a Leupold 6.5-20x Vari-X-III. Several new handloads consistantly average less than minute-of-angle for five, five-shot groups. They include the Speer 52-grain hollowpoint, Sierra 55-grain flat-base, or Nosler 55-grain Ballistic Tip seated atop 28.0 grains Reloder 15 for 3250 to 3300 feet per second.

Gibbs

In addition to the Midland and Parker-Hale lines of sporting rifles, Gibbs is offering various tired old soldiers who starred in military conflicts of yesteryear. They include the No. 1 Mk. III, No. 4 Mk. I, No. 5 Mk. I and the P-14 Enfield rifles; Turkish '93 Mauser; German '98 Mauser; M-1 Garand; and the M-1 Carbine, the latter in standard and paratrooper versions. Then there's the single shot BSA Martini Cadet Australian training rifle in 22 Long Rifle. Several decades ago, when you could buy the Martini Cadet action for 12 bucks, I had a custom rifle in 222 Rimmed built around one. Dave Talley stocked it and did all the metal work, including a barrel rib for attaching a Unertl scope and a transverse safety button in the trigger guard—nice little varmint rig. The 222 Rimmed was developed in Australia and, as its name implies, is a rimmed version of Remington's 222. If I were building such a rifle today, I would come up with about the same performance from a rimmed cartridge by necking down the 357 Maximum case.

Jarrett Rifles, Inc.

One of my favorite deer rifles was built several years ago around a Remington Model Seven action by Kenny Jarrett. A switch-barrel gun, it wears a McMillan fiberglass stock, the one that more or less copies the shape of the factory wood stock. The rifle has three barrels, a 20-inch Broughton in 243 Winchester Improved, a 21-inch Lilja in 6.5 SGLC, and a 20-inch Hart in 7mm SGLC. Average muzzle diameter of the barrels is .800-inch. As Model Sevens go, it's relatively heavy at 8³/₄ pounds with 1.5-6x Schmidt

& Bender scope, but that doesn't matter as I have other rifles made for walking more and sitting less. The little rifle is quite accurate. Its groups average less than half an inch at the 100-yard benchrest with some in the quarter-minute-of-angle category.

More recently, Jarrett introduced a lighter version of the same rifle. Called the "Walkabout," it weighs less than 8 pounds. I have not shot one of these, but I am told that the average weight with a Leupold 3-9x compact scope is between 7 and 7¹/₂ pounds. In addition to the three chamberings I've already mentioned, it's available in a number of short-cartridge chamberings, including 223, 223 Improved, 6x45mm, 6x47mm, 7mmTCU, 22-250 Improved, 243, 6mm Remington, 6mm Improved, 6.5-08, 7mm-08, 308, 308 Improved and 358 Winchester.

Jarrett is now making his own benchrest-grade stainless steel barrels. Button-rifled, they are used exclusively on his custom rifles and are available for installation by other gunsmiths. Most calibers are available and standard contours range from lightweight for big game rifles to medium weight for varmint rifles to heavyweight for target rifles. I have one in 30-378 on a Weatherby Mark V action, and its quality is top-notch.

Kimber

In March of '93, Greg Warne, who along with his father, Jack, founded Kimber, informed me he has now bought the Kimber name back. Warne has also pur-

chased various and sundry equipment used to manufacture those handsome little rifles. God willing and the creek don't rise, Greg intends to bring back the Model 82. If he does, I'll tell you all about it next time we meet.

Knight's Manufacturing

The SR-25 in 7.62x51mm caliber is basically an updated version of Eugene E. Stoner's fine AR-15. Available in two models, both wearing match-grade barrels with Remington's 5R rifling, its development was a joint effort between Stoner and KMC officials. The receiver is made of lightweight, high tensile strength, aircraft-grade aluminum alloy. Basically the standard rifle looks like a 30-caliber M-16 and weighs 8³/₄ pounds. It comes with a two minute-of-angle (MOA) accuracy guarantee. Five- and ten-round detachable magazines are available. The SR-25 Match weighs 10³/₄ pounds, has a heavier free-floated barrel, a cylindrical forearm, and a rail machined into the top of its receiver for mounting a scope with Weaver-type rings. Its accuracy is guaranteed at less than one MOA.

Lakefield

The line of economy-grade 22 rimfire rifles offered by this Canadian company keeps growing like weeds in the turnip patch. I count thirteen. Most unique is the Mark II bolt action with a left-hand action. With its bolt handle, safety-lever, and ejection port over where southpaws prefer them to be, it's a true mirror-image of the right-hand Mark II. Then we have the Mark I,

a single shot boltgun with rifled or smoothbore barrel. The Model 64B is a sleek autoloader that reminds me a bit of the old Winchester Model 490 which, I believe, was manufactured in Canada. It has a ten-round detachable magazine, 20¹/₄-inch barrel, hardwood stock, and 5¹/₂ pounds of weight. Lakefield also offers single shot and repeating heavy barrel target and metallic silhouette rifles with left- and right-hand actions. Each comes in a hard plastic carrying case.

Dan Lilja

In addition to making benchrest-grade barrels in calibers from 22 to 416, Dan Lilja also builds super accurate rifles for big game hunting, varmint shooting and benchrest competition. I'm using two of his barrels on custom Jarrett rifles and am quite happy with them. A Remington 700 switch-barrel gun wears one. It is chambered for the 358 Shooting Times Alaskan, the 8mm Remington Magnum case necked up and fireformed to less body taper and a 30-degree shoulder angle. I used that rifle to take brown bear in southeastern Alaska during '91. The other barrel was installed on a Model Seven switch-barrel rifle by Lilja. It is chambered for the 6.5 SGLC. That's the 7mm-08 Remington case necked down and improved, or simply the old 7mm SGLC necked down. I did it in response to the many letters I've received from readers who want 6.5x55mm Swedish Mauser performance from a cartridge short enough to work in a short action. I've yet to bag

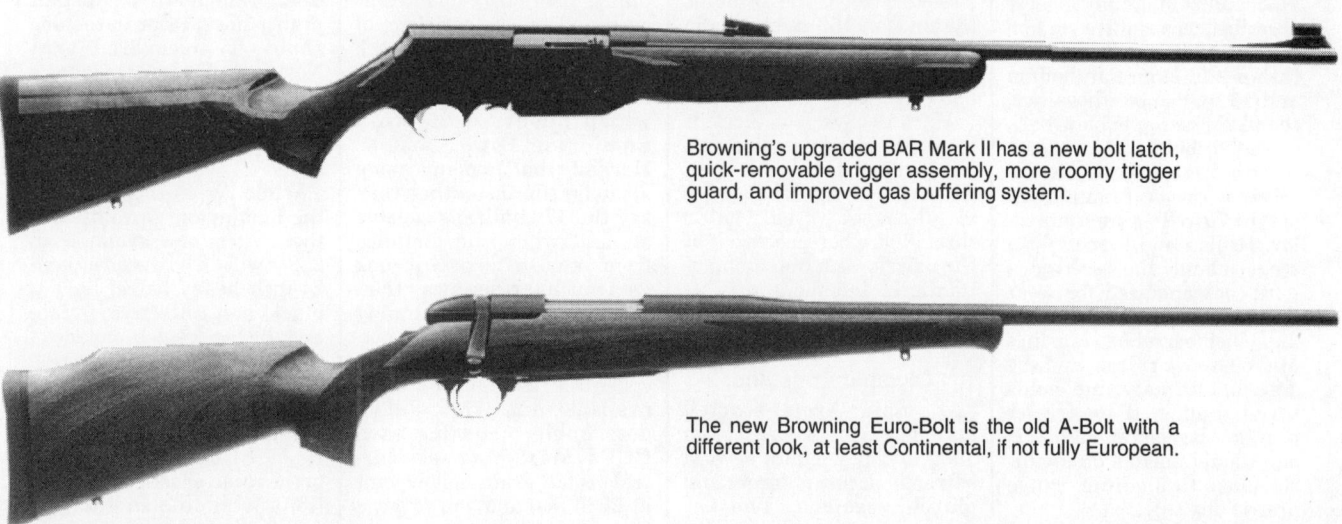

Browning's upgraded BAR Mark II has a new bolt latch, quick-removable trigger assembly, more roomy trigger guard, and improved gas buffering system.

The new Browning Euro-Bolt is the old A-Bolt with a different look, at least Continental, if not fully European.

Art Alphin of A-Square holds a Chapuis double in 416 Chapuis while Rene Chapuis of Chapuis Armes holds the new cartridge. The thing behind them is a sort of symbol.

tramatch, International Match and Multimatch are flat-top versions with receivers that utilize Weaver rings to mount the scope low and close to the axis of the barrel. They also have a free-floating aluminum handguard. Now for the really interesting part, these rifles are available in many calibers including 9mm Luger, 40 S&W, 10mm Auto, 45 ACP, 41 AE, 7.62x39mmR, 6x45mm, 22 PPC, 6mm PPC, 257 PPC, 7mm PPC and, of course, 223 Remington.

Precision Imports

Back in GUN DIGEST No. 46, I you told about shooting prototype 17 Rimfire Magnum ammunition loaded by Federal in a Mauser Model 201 while on a hunt with Dick Cantu of Precision Imports. Dick recently informed me that the 17 rimfire was dead even before it stumbled from the starting gate. As I understand it, none of the major ammunition manufacturers who have experimented with the Teeny Seventeen have been able to reach muzzle velocities much faster than 2500 fps without experiencing chamber pressure problems. And since the lightweight 17-caliber projectile is greatly

lightweight, easy-on-the-shoulder prairie dog rifle that will consistently drop them at 200 paces. This is assuming, of course, that you do your thing and the wind doesn't.

Remington

During October of 1992, I was one of the first five hunters to harvest a big game animal with a prototype 338-caliber, 250-grain big game bullet that Winchester planned to introduce in 1993 as the Black Talon Failsafe. In 338 Winchester Magnum, the rifle I used to bag a Colorado elk is one I'd like to see Remington offer. I removed the stainless steel barreled action of a Model 700 SS from its synthetic stock and dropped it into the laminated wood stock of a Model 700 ADL LS. It looks good, feels good, has maintained its zero perfectly and weighs exactly 9 pounds with its Bausch & Lomb 1.5-6x scope and Leupold Dual-Dovetail mount. Shall we call it the Model 700 ADL LSS?

Another Remington I've been quite pleased with is a Model 700 Varmint Synthetic in 223 with a Burris 12x scope. During summer of '92, I spent several days in Mon-

anything but paper targets with the little cartridge, but find it to be extremely accurate with the Speer 120-grain spitzer and Nosler 120-grain Ballistic Tip pushed along at 2800 to 2900 feet per second by Hodgdon's H-380 or Hercules' Reloder 19.

Marlin

Chambered for the 22 WMR cartridge, Marlin's new Model 922 Magnum is best described as a rimfire version of its centerfire autoloading carbines in 9mm Parabellum and 45 ACP. Like those two, the 922M action is blow-back operated, but unlike its centerfire littermates, its receiver is carved from a block of type 7075-T6 aluminum alloy. Drilled and tapped for a scope mount, the receiver is hard-coat anodized for wear and corrosion resistance. The 20 1/2-inch barrel has Marlin's Micro-Groove rifling, and the detachable magazine holds seven rounds. If its trigger proves to be good enough, this one should make a dandy little close-to-medium range prairie dog rifle.

The Model 60SS in 22 Long Rifle and Model 883SS in 22 WMR are Marlin's first stainless steel rifles. The former is the old Model 60 autoloader in new clothing, and the latter is a new version of the old Model 883 bolt action.

Marlin's new Gun Lock is available in two models, one for handguns, the other for rifles and shotguns. Pass its vinyl-coated steel cable through the bore, secure it at the muzzle with the combination lock, and the gun is secured from young hands and inquiring minds.

Olympic Arms, Inc.

Olympic Arms started manufacturing the AR-15 in 1982 and now offers several extremely accurate target and match versions. The Ul-

Marlin's 922M is a rimfire version of the 9mm and 45-caliber Camp Carbines, brought out first in 22 WMR with aluminum receiver.

dependent on extremely high impact velocity for humane kills on even the smaller varmints, I seriously doubt that such a slowpoke cartridge of that caliber would ever set the world afire in popularity. I've used the 17 Hornet Improved which pushes a 25-grain Remington Power-Lokt or Hornady hollowpoint along about 500 fps faster than they say the 17 rimfire is capable of, and when the distance from muzzle to prairie dog gets much farther away than 100 yards, it starts running out of steam fast.

On the brighter side, the excellent little Mauser 201 is available in 22 WMR. Fill its detachable magazine with CCI's Maxi-Mag +V cartridges (30-grain hollowpoint at 2200 fps) and you've got a

tana with one while trying to see how many Nosler 50-grain Ballistic Tip bullets I could rain down on distant prairie dogs. Prior to the dog shoot, I discovered that Nosler's bullet and Hodgdon's H335 averaged just under half an inch for five shots at 100 yards in Remington's rifle.

While I'm on the subject of the Remington Varmint Synthetic, it is now available in 220 Swift. The receiver and 24-inch heavy barrel have a black non-reflective finish, and the black stock is made of fiberglass reinforced with Kevlar and graphite. Its action rests in a precision-machined bedding block that extends from the locking lug to the receiver tang. Other options available in this ex-

This Model Seven with its Mannlicher-style fullstock of laminated wood and 20-inch barrel is from Remington's Custom Shop—not yet a catalog item.

tremely accurate rifle are 223, 22-250 and 308.

The classic chambering in the Model 700 Classic for 1993 is the outstandingly accurate, but now sadly neglected, 222 Remington, a cartridge that once dominated benchrest competition and owned a big chunk of varmint-shooting territory. The rifle has a short action and 24-inch sporter-weight barrel with 1:14-inch rifling pitch. The limited production series of 700 Classics started with the 7x57mm Mauser back in 1981.

Seems like everybody is introducing what is commonly described as a "European"-style bolt-action rifle. The truth of the matter is, the new Model 700 European is nothing more exotic than the Model 700 BDL with a non-reflective satin-finished stock. Both have a Monte Carlo-style buttstock, black plastic grip cap and forearm tip, and whiteline spacers.

Last year, Remington dropped its stainless steel Model 700 ADL barreled action with blind magazine into a synthetic stock shaped similarly to the stock of the Mountain Rifle and introduced it as the Model 700 Stainless Synthetic. This year, that rifle has a hinged floorplate and is now called the Model 700 BDL Stainless Synthetic. It's available in fourteen calibers

ranging from 223 to 338. Nominal weight is 7 pounds, and barrel lengths are 22 inches for standard calibers and 24 inches for the belted magnums. Also new for '93 is the 6¼-pound Model 700 Mountain Rifle Stainless Synthetic with a 22-inch barrel in 25-06, 270, 280 or 30-06. It has the Mountain Rifle barreled action, but with a blind magazine.

Moreover, 1993 brings us a new look for the Model 7400 autoloader and 7600 pump gun. Called "Special Purpose," both have American walnut with cut checkering and a non-reflective finish, and quick-detach sling swivels with nylon carrying sling. The metal wears a black matte skin. As a bonus, Special Purpose 7400 and 7600 rifles come from the factory with a hard plastic case made from, believe it or not, recycled plastic pop bottles. Since the case is green, one can only assume its parents contained a popular uncola.

Remington now offers three rifles in 35 Whelen. Joining the 35-caliber Model 600 slide action and Model 700 bolt is the Model 7400 autoloader. It's the first autoloading rifle ever offered in James Howe's fine old cartridge.

One of the new items from Tim McCormack and his talented Custom Shop crew is

the Model Seven MS. Made of laminated wood and featuring cut checkering at its wrist and forearm, the Mannlicher-style fullstock terminates at the muzzle of a 20-inch barrel with a blued steel nose cap. Weighing 6¾ pounds, the Seven MS is available in 222, 223, 22-250, 243, 6mm Remington, 250-3000 Savage, 257 Roberts, 7mm-08, 308, 35 Remington, 6.5 Remington Magnum and 350 Remington Magnum. I've held one of these neat little carbines in my hands, and it handles and feels as good as it looks. Also new from the Custom Shop is the Model 700 Safari KS Stainless with a stainless steel barreled action. Its Kevlar-reinforced fiberglass stock has moulded-in 18-line checkering and a battleship gray finish. Available with a 22- or 24-inch barrel, the 7¼-pound 700 SKSS is available in 375 H&H, 416 Remington Magmun and 458 Winchester Magnum.

The 17 Remington is a new chambering for the standard-production Model Seven. In this caliber, the little-rifle-that-could comes from the factory with no open sights on its 18½-inch barrel. A new economy-grade variation of the Model Seven has a hardwood stock (with no checkering) and a 12³/₁₆-inch length

of pull for those among us with short arms. It weighs 6 pounds, is available in 243, 6mm or 7mm-08, and will set you back about $100 less than the Model Seven with shiny walnut and cut checkering.

It's as black as a crow's heart, tough as dirt, and except for its Model 700-style sights, 20-inch barrel, ten-round detachable magazine, and a few other small component parts, the new 4½-pound Model 22 Viper is made of injection-moulded resin. Even its receiver, which is grooved for scope mounting, is made of the tough synthetic stuff. Other Viper features include a two-stage trigger, last-shot hold-open device on the bolt, and twin sears designed to prevent firing should the gun be accidentally dropped. It is 40 inches long and sells for less than the Ruger 10/22. I shot a Viper back in January. It's the kind of rifle you don't mind throwing behind the seat of your pickup and forgetting until a skunk raids the hen house.

As American-made, 22-caliber rimfire bolt actions go, the Remington Model 541-T is one of most accurate available. It now has a heavy-barrel mate called the Model 541-THB. This 6½-pound tackdriver comes with a five-

(Text continues on page 72)

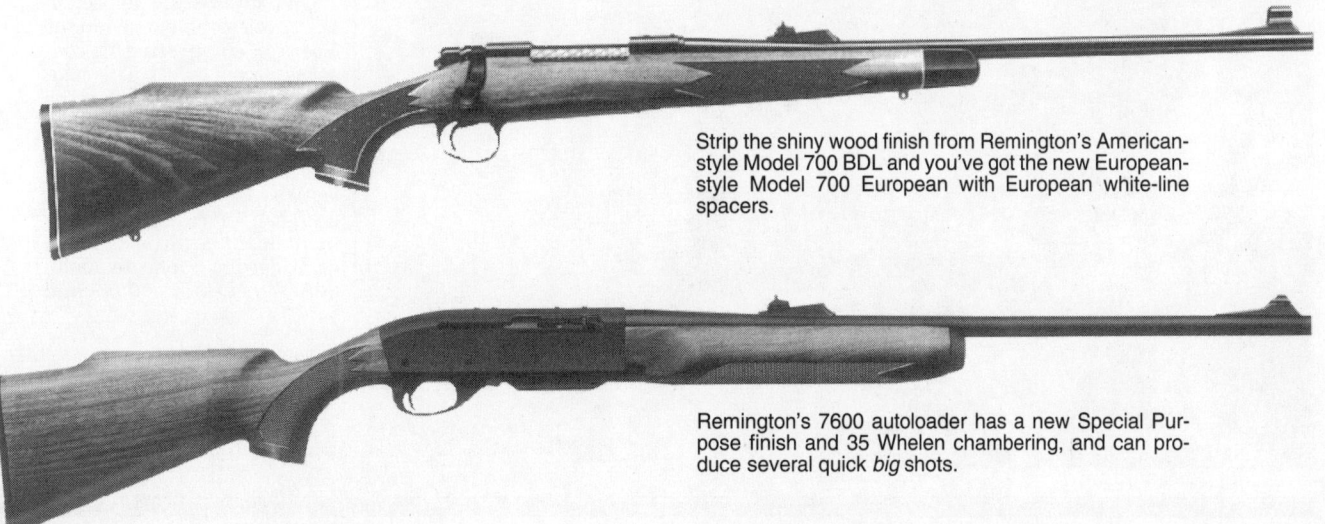

Strip the shiny wood finish from Remington's American-style Model 700 BDL and you've got the new European-style Model 700 European with European white-line spacers.

Remington's 7600 autoloader has a new Special Purpose finish and 35 Whelen chambering, and can produce several quick *big* shots.

CASELESS CARTRIDGES ARRIVE

Here are the UCC-91 5.7mm cartridges together with standard 223 rounds.

THE TIME IS not coming when you can have a high-powered rifle firing caseless rounds—that time is here. At the annual SHOT Show in Houston in January, 1993, Voere of Austria showed their VEC 91 rifle and its cartridges. Some gun writers have already taken game with the rifle.

It's been a while getting here. Years ago, Daisy had a try with a low-powered caseless combination here in the U.S. on the commercial market. More recently, H&K was very close with the G-11 military rifle, but got into, they said, corporate and government problems, and their development is adrift on a sea of peace and unification.

Voere believes the time is now. Their first is a 22—caliber 5.7x26 UCC, it's labelled. The cartridge is a cute little thing—a short yellow cylinder of plastic with a bullet poking out one end and a rudimentary rim shaped into the other, in case you ever want to unload the chambered round without firing. It delivers ballistics about like the 223 Remington or, you could also say, right up to NATO standard.

Fire control is no more complex than the cartridge. Primer material, of a sort percussion doesn't affect, is plugged into the rear of the cartridge and is fired by electricity. The trigger mechanism is, in essence, a switch;

there are, of course, batteries, but no moving parts.

The major benefits claimed for the whole system are manifold: Ammunition is lighter and smaller, therefore the rifle is likewise. There is no empty case to handle after the shot. Ignition of the round is virtually instantaneous. The resulting simplicity, Voere says, contributes to a high degree of accuracy and reliability. Reports thus far bear out the claims.

The ammo has undergone all manner of examination concerning its suitability for field use—durability, reaction to water and dampness,

and so forth—and is, they say, right up there with conventional ammunition.

It all burns—primer and charge—when fired. There is no residue; it all goes up the flue. Will it burn if ignited by an open fire? The company states it "burns slowly like nitrocellulose" if thus ignited. It burns, then, like unconfined smokeless powder.

And what of obturation? The rifle's action handles that. In sum, the chamber pressure pushes the steel of the shaped bolt face firmly into its seat. This requires precision in manufacture, of course, but the rifle is, after all, to be made in Austria.

The igniting force is not an ordinary electrical spark. It is semi-conductor controlled; the primer responds only to the correct voltages and impulses. Random electricity is unlikely to fire this cartridge.

One interesting aspect of the caseless phenomenon, as Voere is engineering it, concerns power levels. The company has announced that the same chamber could be managed to handle several powder charges. Indeed, they were so specific as to say that a 30-caliber rifle in development might be furnished with cartridges to duplicate 30-30, 308 Winchester, 30-06 and

Nothing in the gun system at this point is going to be mysterious for the shooter.

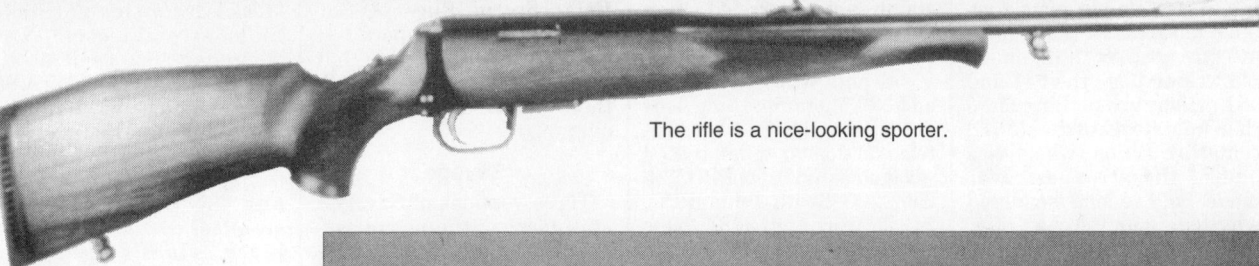

The rifle is a nice-looking sporter.

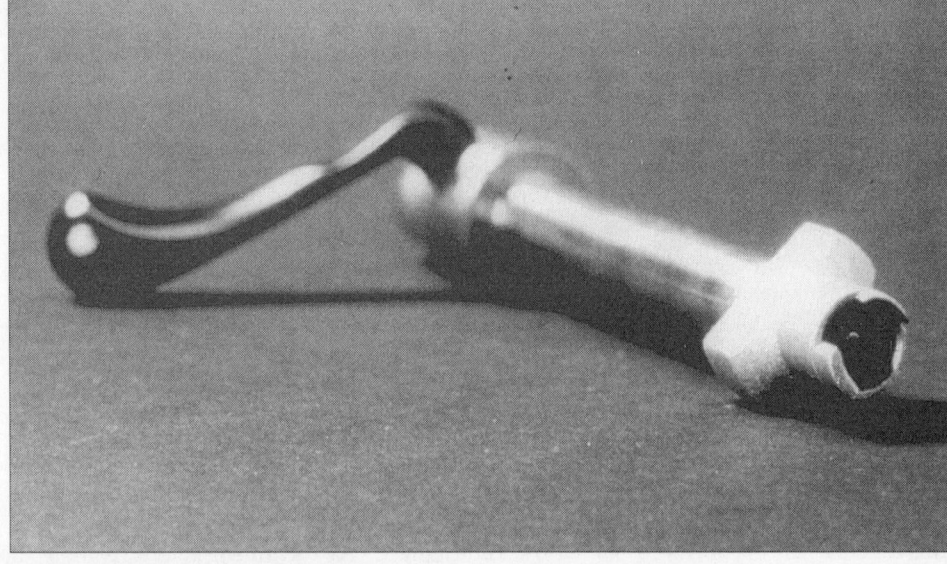

The bolt face seals the combustion chamber by its shape and by being prestressed when in firing position.

This cutaway round shows how simple things can be if you have enough factory.

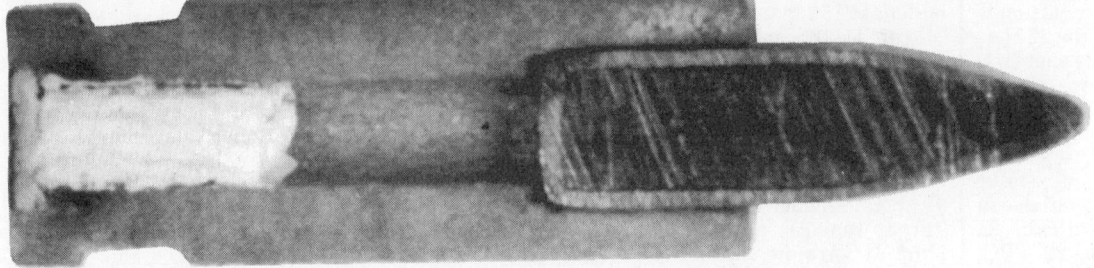

300 Magnum power in turn and at the user's option.

That's fascinating stuff. One wouldn't want to get mixed up, of course, and—absent a genuine recoil-handling feature—the very lightweight 30-caliber rifle would have its drawbacks. In a precision setup, adjusting the sighting from load to load might not be too difficult.

And the benefits would be genuine. Whether one considers adapting the single arm to a wide range of conditions and targets or simply likes the idea of practicing with a "30-30" and shooting a "30-06" in the field, it's an appealing possibility. And such versatility is doubtless not without military application.

It is customary for those who develop new things to believe in them strongly. Certainly, Voere believes in its rifle (VEC 91 means Voere Electronic Caseless 91) and the cartridges developed for it (UCC means Usel Caseless Cartridge for the ammunition developer). Correspondence from Voere says, flatly, their system is as important for the 21st century as the Mauser '98 was for the 20th century. Certainly, there is much to say of it we have not the space to discuss.

Here are a few of the subjects that Voere thinks important:

●Safety: The electrical system, specially proofed against the environment,

should be far easier to render safe.
●Reliability: Properly engineered electrical systems are found, all over industry, to be more reliable than mechanical systems.
●Accuracy: This system removes the cartridge case, a major source of variables, from consideration, while at the same time the metered ignition impulse is less variable than the standard system.

Voere isn't talking much about any but theoretical cost savings at this point. Obviously, the cartridge case is the most expensive part of conventional ammo; not so obviously there may be expenses—considerable

ones—in concocting caseless rounds not present in the standard technology. For right now, it's less bang for the buck.

The rifle itself is a nice, light European bolt-action sporter. Except for the off-on switch and the funny little rounds, it functions like a bolt-action sporter should, even if it is a milestone.

There are changes to come. Already Swarosports, the U.S. representative, a subsidiary of Swarovski Optik North America, has changed its name to JägerSports, Ltd. And they have chosen a name for the rifle as well: It's the Lightning Bolt, and the ammo is Lightning Fire. Stay tuned.

Ken Warner

(Text continued from page 69) round detachable magazine, but a ten-rounder is available at extra cost. With its multiple locking lugs, the 541 and 581 actions are nothing more than miniatures of the old 788 centerfire action, which was one of the strongest ever made. So, I've long wondered why Remington doesn't offer the 541-T and its economy-grade mate, the 581-S, in 22 WMR. The new 541-THB in

30-06), All Weather with stainless steel barreled action and synthetic stock (243, 270, 7mm Remington Magnum, 30-06 and Winchester's 300 and 338 Magnums), and Target with stainless steel barreled action in a laminated wood stock (223, 22 PPC, 22-250, 220 Swift, 6mm PPC, 243, 25-06 and 308). New chamberings are 6.5x55mm Swedish in the Mark II Standard and 404 Jeffery in

postpaid to Customer Service Dept., Sturm, Ruger & Co., Inc., Guild Rd., Newport, NH 03773. This is assuming that your 1-inch rings are still in their unopened factory packaging.

Savage

Three versions of Savage's stainless/synthetic bolt-action big game rifle are now available. All feature stainless steel barreled actions and

bags, its laminated wood stock is brown in color, has a high, straight comb, and Wundhammer swell at its wrist. The Model 112FVSS should also be at your Savage dealer by the time this report is published. Also in 223 or 22-250, its action and 26-inch barrel are stainless steel. It wears a black, classic-style synthetic stock replete with moulded-in checkering and

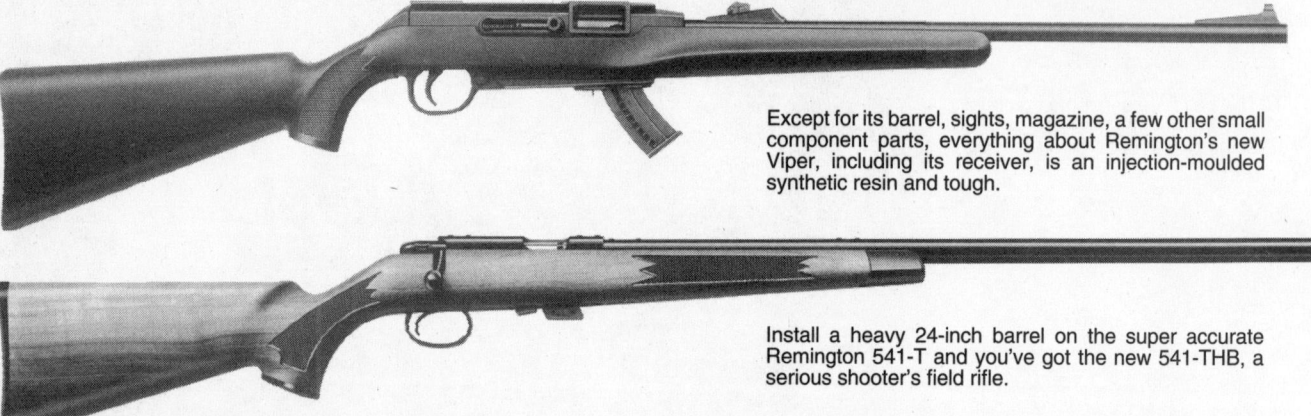

Except for its barrel, sights, magazine, a few other small component parts, everything about Remington's new Viper, including its receiver, is an injection-moulded synthetic resin and tough.

Install a heavy 24-inch barrel on the super accurate Remington 541-T and you've got the new 541-THB, a serious shooter's field rifle.

that caliber would make a fine close-to-medium range prairie dog and groundhog rifle. In fact, I believe the action is strong enough for the 22 Hornet. Would a single shot 541-THB in that caliber be fun or what?

Ruger

Ruger's handsome No. 1 single shot is now available in 26 chamberings with the 22 Hornet, 218 Bee, 22 PPC, 6mm PPC, 270 Weatherby Magnum, 404 Jeffery and 416 Rigby being some of the more recent additions. I used to hunt big game a lot with No. 1 rifles and still hunt with them some. My all-time favorite models are the 1-A Light Sporter (22-inch barrel and Alexander Henry-style forearm) for standard cartridges and the 1-S Medium Sporter (same as the 1-A except for its 26-inch barrel) for the belted magnums up to 338-caliber.

Production of the original Model 77 rifle, which was sometimes described as "the rifle with the fake '98 Mauser extractor," ceased in November 1991. During 1993, its replacement, the Model 77 Mark II with an extractor of true controlled-feed design, will be offered in three new versions: International with 18-inch barrel and Mannlicher-style fullstock (243, 270, 308 and

the Mark II Magnum. A-Square offers 404 ammunition loaded with a 400-grain bullet at 2150 fps.

I can see thousands of varmint shooters lusting after a pair of Ruger's new centerfire and rimfire heavy-barrel rifles. Both have a stainless steel barreled action and laminated wood stock. The 9¾-pound Model 77 Mark II Target replaces last year's Mark II Varmint and has a heavy 26-inch barrel in 223, 22 PPC, 22-250, 220 Swift, 6mm PPC, 243, 25-06 and 308. Its two-stage trigger is said to be adjustable down to a feathery 24-ounce letoff.

According to a Ruger official, the Model 77/22 Varmint is just the ticket for picking off distant targets while making a minimum amount of noise. Chambered for Winchester's 22 WMR, it has a heavy 24-inch free-floating barrel with 1:16-inch rifling pitch. Its laminated wood stock is outfitted with a hard rubber butt-pad and quick-detach sling swivel posts.

Standard-height, 30mm scope mounting rings for Model 77 Mark II rifles are now available from Ruger. Rifles that come from the factory with rings will have the 1-inchers (25.4mm) which can be traded for the new 30mm rings by sending them

synthetic stocks. Available in 270, 7mm Remington Magnum, 30-06 and 300 Winchester Magnum, the Model 116FCS has a detachable magazine that holds five standard cartridges or four belted magnums. Change the magazine to Paul Mauser's staggered-column design, add the 223, 243 and 338 Winchester Magnum options, and you've got the Model 116FSS. Then we have the Model 116FSK Kodiak, which is sure to become a favorite with Alaskan brown bear hunters and guides who'll use it for backup work. It's available in 338 Winchester Magnum only and has Savage's "Shock-Suppressor" multiple-port muzzlebrake at the far end of its 22-inch barrel. Like all Savage rifles, these three models come from the factory with a gun lock that locks the trigger from use by tiny hands. The new Savage big game rifles weigh from 7 to 7¼ pounds, depending on barrel length and caliber.

In the varmint rifle department, Savage has three on the runway and one possibly waiting in the hanger. Ready for the 1993 season is the 9½-pound Model 112BV with a heavy 26-inch barrel in 223 or 22-250. Designed specifically for field shooting over sand-

a recoil pad. Then we have the Model 112FVS which has a 26-inch heavy barrel 223 or 22-250 and a single shot action with solid-bottom receiver. It wears the same synthetic stock as the Model 112FVSS. Not quite ready for the '93 season is a rifle I've asked Savage officials to introduce during 1994. I'm shooting a prototype in 223, and it's a genuine tackdriver. Drop the single shot barreled action into the laminated wood stock of the Model 112BV and you've got it. Who knows, it might even be called the Model 112BVS.

Sako/Tikka

The new Model 995 Hunter is Sako's answer to the economy-grade bolt-action big game rifle question. In a nutshell, it has three locking lugs at the front of its bolt, an extremely light (and surprisingly flexible) polyurethane stock, and a trigger guard/floorplate assembly of aluminum alloy. The stock has hard rubber shims beneath its recoil pad which can be removed to shorten its length of pull. Sako's new scope mounting rings fit the familiar dovetailed receiver and have split plastic shims which allow them to be used with scopes having 1-inch or 30mm tubes.

Survival Arms

Remember the Charter Arms 22-caliber AR-7 Explorer Carbine? It had an eight-round detachable magazine, a 16½-inch aluminum alloy barrel with steel liner, and a weight of 2½ pounds. Its barrel and receiver could be taken down and stowed in the hollow Cycolac buttstock. It's back, but is now available from Survival Arms, Inc., of Cocoa, Florida. Like Ivory soap, it floats.

Thompson/Center

Try explaining this one: Like the T/C Contender single shot pistol, the TCR '87 single shot rifle is extremely versatile due to its interchangable barrel design. With one receiver and buttstock and several barrels, you can do big game, small game and varmints with it. Attach a smoothbore shotgun barrel and the TCR big game rifle becomes a bird gun. Attach a rifled shotgun barrel and you've transformed it into an extremely accurate deer gun. That spells major versatility with minor capital invest-

be mixed and matched with those of blued steel. The SP (Small People) Model Contender Carbine with its short 12-inch pull and 16¼-inch barrel is now available in 22 Long Rifle, 410 bore, 30-30, 35 Remington and 375 Winchester. If its owner grows longer arms, the short buttstock is easily replaced by another with a standard length of pull.

Perhaps more important than any of this is the fact that the U.S. Supreme Court has ruled the use of a T/C carbine conversion kit with the Contender pistol receiver is now legal. Even so, T/C's carbine conversion kits are not available for sale in California.

Ultra Light Arms

Back in January of '92, Ultra Light Arms president Melvin Forbes showed me a small game rig that owners of his big game rifles will simply be unable to resist. At first glance, the lightweight little rig appeared to be just another Model 20 centerfire. Closer examination confirmed that it was similar in appearance to the Model 20, but chambered for the 22

USRAC

I'm convinced nobody at U.S. Repeating Arms Company ever sleeps. If they did, they wouldn't have time to introduce so many new goodies each year. And 1993 is certainly no exception. For starters, there are now 16 standard-production Model 70 variations available. According to my quick count, if you bought every variation in every available caliber, you'd be the proud owner of 110 Model 70s. Add one each of the four Custom Shop Model 70s in their various calibers and your battery grows to just over 125 rifles.

From the USRAC Custom Shop, we have the Model 70 Custom Sharpshooter which is guaranteed to shoot five bullets into half an inch at 100 yards. This rifle was actually introduced in 1992, but too late to be included in last year's "Rifle Review." With its Leupold 6.5-20x Vari-X-III, the 300 Winchester Magnum Sharpshooter, with which I've been punching holes in paper, weighs 12½ pounds. It averaged .55-inch for twenty-five five-shot groups fired

Custom Shop hand-laps the locking lugs and trues up the face of the receiver ring. The action is then sent to a barrelmaker who specializes in building super accurate rifled tubes. The barreled action then goes to a maker of fiberglass stocks. After stock and barreled action are joined together, the outfit ends up back at the Custom Shop for final proof testing and accuracy check. The rifle I worked with had a McMillan stock and Schneider barrel.

In April of 1992, while having lunch with a couple of USRAC officials, I was informed that, during 1993, the Custom Shop would add the 7mm Shooting Times Westerner to its list of options for the Model 70. For the benefit of those who are not familiar with the 7mm STW, it is the 8mm Remington Magnum case necked down. At any rate, when asked in which Model 70 variation the new chambering should become available, I suggested that a new and lighter version of the Sharpshooter target rifle be created for big game hunting. Three months after that discussion took place, I received the

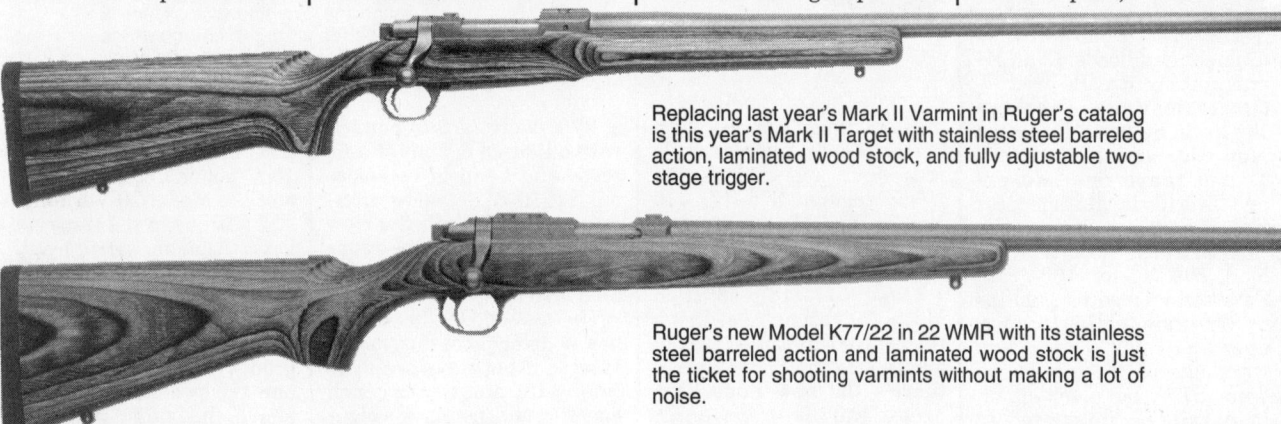

Replacing last year's Mark II Varmint in Ruger's catalog is this year's Mark II Target with stainless steel barreled action, laminated wood stock, and fully adjustable two-stage trigger.

Ruger's new Model K77/22 in 22 WMR with its stainless steel barreled action and laminated wood stock is just the ticket for shooting varmints without making a lot of noise.

ment. Unlike the Contender pistol, though, the rifle has been anything but successful. In other words, it has never sold very well. Now you know why Thompson/Center has dropped the TCR rifle from its catalog. It is still available, but only by special order to the T/C Custom Shop.

Back to things positive, the Contender Carbine is now available in a stainless steel version with walnut or DuPont Rynite stock. Its 21-inch barrel is available in 22 Long Rifle, 22 Long Rifle Match, 22 Hornet, 223, 30-30, 45 Colt/410, and 410 smoothbore. Incidentally, stainless steel components can

Long Rifle cartridge. The Ultra Light Model 20RF is available in a single shot or repeater version, the latter with a five-round detachable magazine. It has a 22-inch barrel, weighs a nominal 5½ pounds, and its trim synthetic stock has a tough DuPont Imron finish. Color options are the same as for Ultra Light centerfire rifles. Buy one during 1993 and you'll also receive the recipe for Patty Forbes' sinfully delicious chocolate chip cookies. A rimfire version of Melvin's Model 20 REB bolt-action pistol may be just a wish or two away.

during the first range session. Three loads averaged less than half an inch—Sierra 190-grain MatchKing and 82.0 grains of H1000, Nosler 150-grain Ballistic Tip and 74.0 grains of H4350, and the 180-grain Ballistic Tip seated atop 71.0 grains of H4350. Not bad considering a 54-ounce trigger which is far too heavy for precision work. The Sharpshooter has a fiberglass stock, an extremely heavy 26-inch barrel, and is also available in 308, 223 and 22-250.

Interestingly enough, the Sharpshooter is built by outside subcontractors. First, a craftsman in the USRAC

very first "Sporting Sharpshooter" built by USRAC. It was also the first Winchester in 7mm STW to leave the factory. Introduced in that caliber, as well as 270 and 300 Winchester Magnum, the new rifle was officially unveiled to the public at the SHOT Show in January, 1993.

Just as I had specified to USRAC officials, the Model 70 Sporting Sharpshooter has a 26-inch stainless steel barrel and a battleship gray-finished fiberglass stock of classic style. The stock has a lightly textured finish, a solid recoil pad, quick-detach sling

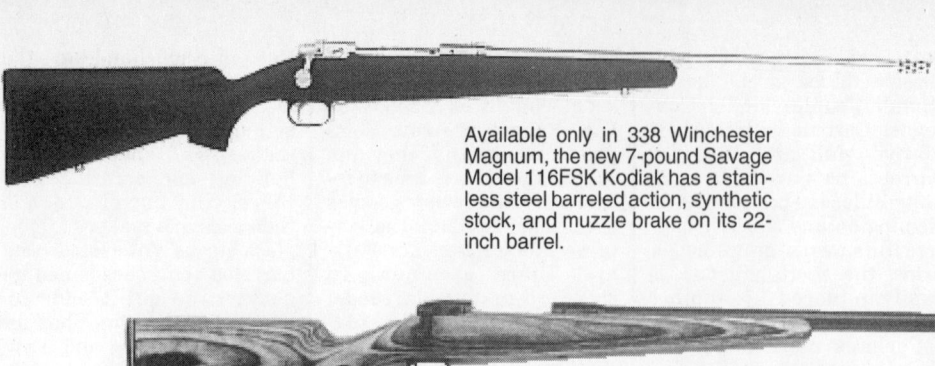

Available only in 338 Winchester Magnum, the new 7-pound Savage Model 116FSK Kodiak has a stainless steel barreled action, synthetic stock, and muzzle brake on its 22-inch barrel.

The 9½-pound Savage Model 112BV varmint rifle has a laminated wood stock and 26-inch barrel in 223 and 22-250.

USRAC's version of the Winchester Model 52 Sporter is basically the same as Browning's version.

swivel posts, and moulded checkering at its wrist and forearm. Fresh from its box, the rifle weighed 8½ pounds. A Leupold 3.5-10x Vari-X-III with Dual-Dovetail mount increased that by a pound. During its first range session, the new Sporting Sharpshooter averaged .71-inch for twenty-five, five-shot groups with five different handloads. At an average of .53-inch, the most accurate load was Nosler's 140-grain Ballistic Tip seated atop 81.0 grains of H1000. That just happens to be one of my favorite long-range deer and pronghorn recipes for this cartridge. A favorite elk load, the Nosler 160-grain Partition pushed to 3300 fps by 87.0 grains of H5010, averaged .81-inch. Those who want one of these rifles in 7mm STW, but don't handload, will be interested to know A-Square is making the ammunition.

Several Model 70 variations now share the controlled-feed action with claw extractor which was introduced by USRAC in 1989 on its then-new Super Grade rifle. From the Custom Shop, there are the Model 70 Custom Grade and Model 70 Custom Express. The former is basically a more expensive version of the standard-production Super Grade with fancier wood. This one is available in a number of chamberings, including 7mm STW. The Custom Express is basically a more expensive version of the standard-pro-

The new 7¼-pound Model 70 DBM-S has a detachable box magazine, a synthetic stock, and is available in eight chamberings from 223 to 300 Winchester Magnum.

duction Super Express with better wood, Express-style rear sight, and calibers 375 H&H Magnum, 375 JRS, 416 Remington Magnum, 458 Winchester Magnum and 470 Capstick.

Three standard-production Model 70 variants now have the controlled-feed action. In addition to the Super Grade, there's the new Super Express and Featherweight Classic. The new Super Express with its pre-'64 style action replaces the old Super Express with its post-'64 action, but that's only part of the good news—the retail price is the same. At least it is during 1993. Except for its controlled-feed action and higher price tag, the new Model 70 Featherweight Classic is the same as a regular Model 70 Featherweight. If I had to pick the four most handsome American-made big game rifles of current production that cost less than $1000, two would be Model 70s, one being the Featherweight Classic. For now, its only chamberings are 270, 280 and 30-06. Mine,

a 270, weighs 8¾ pounds with a Bausch & Lomb 1.5-6x scope and Leupold two-piece mount. In case you're interested, the bolt with the claw extractor weighs an ounce more than the standard Model 70 bolt.

The new Model 70 DBM-S has a detachable box magazine, a fiberglass/graphite composite stock, a 24-inch barrel and a nominal weight of 7¼ pounds. Its calibers are 223, 22-250, 243, 270, 7mm Remington Magnum, 308, 30-06 and 300 Winchester Magnum.

Last year's wood-stocked Model 70 DBM is now available in the same eight calibers as this year's synthetic-stocked version. The Model 70 Stainless Synthetic has two new chamberings for '93, 270 and 30-06.

The receiver of the new Model 70 Heavy Varmint rests on an aluminum bedding block nestled in a synthetic stock. The stock has a flat-bottomed forearm for shooting over a sandbag, and a heavy 26-inch stainless

steel barrel in 223, 22-250, 243 or 308. Nominal weight is 10¾ pounds. The old wood-stocked Model 70 Varmint is still with us in the same calibers, the same barrel length, and for less money.

U.S. Repeating Arms Company is now owned by the same foreign investment group that owns Browning, and the two companies even share the same president. This is why USRAC is now offering the same Japanese-built reproduction of the old Winchester Model 52 Sporter that was offered a few years back by Browning. The new "Winchester Model 52B Sporter" weighs 7 pounds, has a 24-inch barrel, fully adjustable Micro-Motion trigger, fancy walnut stock with cut checkering, Model 70 Super Grade-style quick-detach sling swivels, a detachable magazine that holds five 22 Long Rifle cartridges. They say production will stop at 6000 units.

The Winchester Model 9422 is the only lever-action 22 rimfire that was designed from the ground up to handle the chamber pressures of the 22 WMR cartridge. It's now available in three versions: Standard with cut-checkered American walnut, Wintuff with laminated wood, and WinCam with multi-colored laminated wood. Average weight is 6¼ pounds and overall length is a handy 37⅛ inches, including 20 inches of barrel. The receiver is grooved for scope mounting and the rifle is easily taken down with a few twists of a coin. The tubular magazine of the magnum version holds eleven cartridges. The other one works with 21 Short, 17 Long or 15 Long Rifle cartridges. I consider the 9422 one of the finest, best-handling and most handsome small game rifles available and never cease to be puzzled to see so few sold each year.

Volquartsen Custom, Ltd.

Last year I reported on Tom Volquartsen's precision transformation of Ruger's 10/22 autoloader into a super accurate little small game rifle. It's also just the ticket for competitive matches such as the Chevy Truck Team Challenge. If you missed my report, the handy little tackdriver averaged an incredible .511-inch for five ten-shot groups at 50 yards with

Eley Tenex, .640-inch with Winchester Super Silhouette, and .644-inch with CCI Green Tag. Its titanium trigger broke at a marvelous 38 ounces, had zero creep, and was fitted with an adjustable over-travel stop. This year, Federal's new Gold Medal Ultramatch ammo averaged .629-inch in the little quickshooter.

Volquartsen has two new projects in the works. One is a tack-driving squirrel, bunny, and close-to-medium range prairie dog rifle built around a Ruger Model 77/22 action in 22 Long Rifle or 22 WMR. The other is a new super accurate 22 WMR autoloader to be built from scratch in Volquartsen's shop. I won't be surprised to see it average well under minute of angle with CCI, RWS and Winchester ammo. If he does and it does, I'll fill you in on the details in next year's report.

Weatherby

During the early 1960s, before Remington introduced its 7mm-08, and before every company who is anybody was offering extremely lightweight rifles, I decided to build one by converting a dainty little Weatherby Varmintmaster in 22-250 to a wildcat called the 7mm SGLC. Back then, I described

the 7mm SGLC as the 308 Winchester case necked down and blown out to the improved shape. I now describe it as an improved version of Remington's 7mm-08. I liked the 7mm caliber Varmintmaster so much I used it to bag a few elk, moose, pronghorn, and a lot of deer with it in North America. I also took the little rifle to Africa where it accounted for various antelope ranging in size from impala to greater kudu. My "Big Gamemaster" eventually became a switch-barrel rig with two other barrels in 22-250 and 250 Savage Improved.

I'm saying all of this because despite my several suggestions to Roy Weatherby, I could never convince him that his Varmintmaster in 250-3000 Savage would sell like fresh donuts to a family of starving ants. In fact, I was never able to convince him that the big game rifle of the future would be relatively light in weight.

I have news, both good and bad. On pages 18 and 19 of the 1993 Weatherby catalog is the rifle I've long wanted to see the South Gate firm introduce. Called the Whitetail Deluxe, it is nothing more or less than the Varmintmaster in 250-3000 Savage. Measuring 41¼ inches overall with its 22-inch lightweight barrel, the handsome little deer rifle weighs a mere 6 pounds. Now for the bad news. Ed Weatherby tells me it is doubtful that any 25-caliber Varmintmasters will reach American soil before 1994.

It was the U.S. military who, back in the 1950s, asked Roy Wetherby to conduct experiments to see how fast bullets of conventional design could be driven from a shoulder-fired rifle. So, Roy necked down his 378 Magnum case to 30-caliber and seated a lightweight bullet atop lots of powder. He managed to squeeze 5000 fps from his prototype rifle, and while working with the same cartridge, other wildcatters later exceeded 6000 fps with lightweight bullets custom-made by Ray Speer.

More recently, I mentioned to Ed Weatherby that a Mark V rifle chambered for Roy's old 30-378 might sell to today's hunters. Such a cartridge would also put the Weatherby firm a step or two ahead of its competition in ve-

locity, like it was during days of yesteryear. So, Ed sent me a Mark V action, asked me to have a prototype rifle built around it, and to let him know how fast the 30-378 would run in a rifle light enough to tote up a mountain. Built by Kenny Jarrett, the rifle has one of his 26-inch barrels with a 1:12-inch twist and a Clifton fiberglass stock. With a Leupold 3.5-10x Vari-X-III and Dual-Dovetail mount, it pushes my postal scale to 10¼ pounds. That's no flyweight, but I've carried heavier rifles for weeks in Africa and lived to tell about it. Depending on the brand of 180-grain bullet, the 30-378 averages 3450 to 3525 fps, and its rifle will consistently keep three inside an inch. Zeroed 3 inches high at 100 yards, a good 180-grain spitzer is down about 5 inches at 400 yards, where it is still packing over 2900 foot pounds of energy. In comparison, the 300 Weatherby delivers 2400 foot pounds at 400 yards.

If Weatherby decides to introduce such a rig, it will be built by an outside subcontractor who specializes in building super accurate rifles. Since it will be capable of shooting minute of angle, it will be called Accumark. Norma, the maker of Weatherby ammunition, is already making 378 Magnum cases, so squeezing their necks on down and loading 150-, 180- and 200-grain 30-caliber bullets to respective velocities of 3700, 3500 and 3300 fps should represent no big deal. We'll see. ●

Melvin Forbes, president of Ultra Light Arms, Inc., shows off the first Model 20 rifle built in 22 Long Rifle.

(Editor's note: Layne's new book, The Custom Government Model Pistol, *has 650 pages and over 400 photographs from pistolsmiths across the country who specialize in Colt's 1911 pistol as well as the new breed of high-capacity versions of same from Caspian, Para-Ordnance and McCormick. It is published by Wolfe Publishing, and autographed copies are available from the author for $30 at Highcountry Press, 104 Holly Tree Lane, Simpsonville, SC 29681. Please add $5 per book for foreign orders.)*

GETTING DOWN

"YOU GUYS are lagging too far back. Stick to me like a shadow. Be ready. Things can happen purty fast."

The two pilgrims I was guiding weren't staying close enough to suit me. I hate to have to continue telling folks to stay within arm's reach, but with the technique I was working that day, it was a must that they be at my elbow, guns ready.

Turkey season was nearly over; the birds were just plain "skeery." They'd learned the best places to feed were in the deep dry creek bottoms, any cove which had big old burr oaks hugging its sides. Acorns from a burr oak are as big as an English walnut, but a turkey gobbler will eat them. Whole. You'd think they'd choke.

I'd no sooner learned where the birds were hanging out during the winter afternoons when I began hunting them there. What this entailed was to ease slowly along the top of the ridges and, when possible, to sneak quietly to the edge, and peer down into the darkness of the bottom in hopes of spying birds there feeding on the nuts. Or to hear them scratching in the leaves.

It's a relentless job, takes no end of walking and, when changing from one ridge to the next, some dogged climbing down and then up canyon walls. It's not for sissy hunters.

When a guide has hunters booked, it's his job to find game, along with methods to bring clients and game together inside easy gunshot. I'd had good luck on such hunts through the years, so knew what to expect. The fact was I had put two other hunters into turkeys only a couple days earlier using the same method. It requires no end of patience, some shoe-leather, and a big gob of "stick-with-it."

My two hunters had stuck with me for upward of an hour, when once again, like a hundred other times, I gingerly eased out to where the ridge broke over, scrutinizing the bottom as it came in sight, doing this ever so slowly as I realized I was also silhouetted against the sky.

Wouldn't've mattered how sneaky I'd looked into that hollow because I'd come out dead above the turkeys. Not missing a thing, they saw me in the same second. Our eyes met. Turkey gobblers just come a'hellin' up out of there, wings flapping, beards bouncing off their chests, those old he-turkeys suddenly decided they didn't like the company.

"Shoot! Gobblers! Shoot!"

Falling aside so I'd be clear, glancing around as I did, I could see that my two pilgrims were lagging behind, but they were near enough that the turkeys all but blew their hats off as the birds exploded from the tree-filled bottom.

The hunter farthest from me got his act together in jig time, cutting down on a bird booming from the hollow on his side, whereon it slewed back toward earth, cartwheeling among the branches of a small oak. It'd no more'n crashed when the other man's gun cut loose. Then it was over. Turkey hunting, any kind of hunting, can be that way. Nothing, then moments later, back-slapping, laughing, a great day to be hunting.

To the beginner, all of this might have appeared as nothing but blind luck. Like the luck of a blind hog looking for acorns. But it so happens that over the years I'd noticed the turkeys would abandon their usual habitat at higher elevations, then they'd haunt the bottoms, gulping down those huge acorns which had fallen from the big burr oaks. Though there was plenty of food higher up, foods the birds ordinarily preferred, they would go to the oak trees down low. My technique was to wait 'til mid-morn, when the droves, singles, pairs, and what-have-you, had finished morning toiletries, whereon they'd head for the coves, hollows, and bottoms to feed on acorns. Another reason for waiting until mid-morning to begin hunting was to give the sun time to climb up to where it would illuminate the dark areas under the oak trees, making the birds easier to see. About an hour before sundown, it's getting too dark for the same reason, so I usually cease hunting in this manner at that time.

So it is simply a matter of walking the ridges, easing over to peer down into the bottoms from time to time, backing away, walking quietly 50 yards or so, then while slipping over to the edge very slowly, scan the cover as it comes into view, walk another 40 or 50 yards, and do this over and over. I don't walk the edge continuously because turkeys farther along the bottom could see me before I get into range, and run off. Invariably, I'll put a hunter into turkeys before the day is up. The bulk of the time I'll either see or hear the birds before they know I'm around, but the average hunter will have trouble making them out before the birds get spooked, which results in running or flying shots. This use of terrain in hunting wild turkeys has served me all across the United States and into Mexico.

I've read numerous times that it's all but impossible to walk up on turkeys, or to stalk them, which is a tub of hogwash written by someone who thinks they are a turkey hunter and, truthfully, haven't learned the meaning of the words. Turkeys are often credited with having the keenest eyesight of American wildlife, which is probably so, and they also have extremely good hearing, which, amazingly, can pinpoint sound sources to the inch. But if the wild turkey were a super-bird, it would be a waste of time to hunt them. No one would ever shoot one.

Not only can the birds be hunted by stillhunting, bushwacking, belly-crawling, sneaking, stalking, ambush, or whatever else you want to call your hunting methods, but they can also be called to the hunter. All of these tactics are further enhanced by a person's use of terrain, either the ground cover, the terrain itself, or in knowing how the game uses it.

Whitetail bucks have a sense for remaining in heavy cover when a doe would walk across open ground. The older the buck, the more he'll do this. So, to hunt Old Many-Points, you'd stick to heavy woods. I've seen deer drives where the hunters made the drive so that the animals would be driven toward open country. Then the old boys would have a fit 'cause the animals kept circling back through them. A deer wants to get to cover. It'll run right past you to get there.

A wild goose is just the opposite. It wants to feed and rest smack out in the open, where the nearest bush which

TO EARTH by DWAIN BLAND

would hide a coyote or bobcat is some distance from there. You can use this trait of wild geese in hunting them. Set up your decoy spread far from brush, fencelines, anything which will screen predators, including man.

Many times I've hunted honkers on the open plains on which the only cover was the green wheat I was lying in, it being perhaps 5 or 6 inches in height. No, it won't hide any hunter, but by arranging a spread of several dozen decoys, then laying down among them, with a few stuck in the ground around my head and along my body, I'm easily hidden to the point that incoming geese have all but landed on me. What's more, a call being used in among the decoys is much more of an enticement than one 40 yards from the spread. Geese can be stalked when conditions are right, as can ducks, on flat prairie country, though there will be times when the birds will have landed in an area where this is impossible. Back during the '30s, my brother and I, and a few of our farming buddies, killed the bulk of our waterfowl through stalking. We had a few wooden blocks, over which we took lots of ducks, but much of the time our kill was when we snuck up on them.

Have you ever laid down on your stomach, then looked across your front yard while you rested your chin on the ground? No, I'm sure you haven't. Try it. Most lawns have some roll to them, what's known to some of us as the lay of the land. Rolling plains country has humps and dips all but imperceptible to a person standing erect. Stretched out on it, on your belly, you'll see that there are mounds, hillocks, tiny hollows, which will help to hide a crawling hunter. You can belly-crawl on such cover behind very little of it to screen your straight-in approach. Add a few clumps of weeds, grass, small fallen trees, sticks, rocks, leaf piles, any kind of ground cover, then you have the makings of a successful sneak. I've belly-crawled everything from prairie chickens to wild hogs, with deer, ducks, geese, grouse, quail, and other stuff thrown in for good measure. And heck knows how many turkeys, from Florida to high in Mexico's Sierra Madres. Belly-crawling is the only way to

get into easy gunshot of many kinds of game, under certain conditions. The average hunter has never tried it. I know that, because I've guided many, many folks who have told me after a stalk, "That's the first time I ever did that."

Bellying takes lots and lots of patience. Sometimes the odds will seem insurmountable, particularly when it appears you'll have to belly for 200 or 300 yards, perhaps over rocks and gravel, or through sandburs, or even water. A couple times when hunting Florida, I've had to belly-crawl across patches of water, and other times among burned-off palmettoes, so I came out of them wet, or smudged up from the burned-off prairie. One day north of Lake Okeechobee, a client bellied along back of me through burned-off stuff, but the big old trophy hog didn't know we were around before we were inside 30 yards, and though he then became suspicious to the point of walking toward us, the old critter couldn't make us out as hunters. If we'd stood erect, he'd have lit out while we were just beginning the stalk.

Hogs have poor sight, but our stalk was aligned to prevent the hog from

getting wind of us. As with all hunting methods, nothing helps in using terrain more than knowledge of the game you're hunting, its lifestyle, daily habits, and particularly what habitat it will be using during the hunting season. The Osceola wild turkey, which is found in south Florida, is ordinarily easy to stalk, as is all game in that state. Florida has so much thick cover it is also an obstacle. But I can recall an old patriarch I spied one morning, feeding out on open pasture, 100 yards from thick cover. The prairie had a few clumps of grass on it, scattered about, and by keeping my eyes glued to him, then freezing absolutely stone-still when he was head-up, looking around, I managed to slip inside 25 yards where I killed him with a muzzle-loader. This took time, but I only had a 100-yard crawl, and I was there to hunt turkeys. Florida seems to me one of the easiest places on Earth to hunt, simply because of all the ground clutter, brush, palmettoes, water, and other terrain features which will hide a hunter or cause game to walk toward him. If that isn't enough, the weather is mild.

Years ago, I began making it a prac-

In open parklands and mountain meadows, a hunter can remain quiet, lean back against a tree, and have a clear shot at game to the edge of range. By using ridges, hollows, depressions and other physical features of the terrain, he can shorten the range or extend it.

tice to order topographical maps of areas I intended to hunt, particularly if I had never hunted on like terrain. I still follow this line, studying these maps intensively before traveling to the area, acquainting myself with landmarks, roads, any and all large geophysical objects which I can relate to once I am afoot. Topo maps will give a person an inkling of how the ground lays, ridges, creek bottoms, and the steepness of hills and mountains; but as to how much actual roll there is in the ground, and the tiny bumps and gullies, you'll have to wait until arriv-

ing on the site to ascertain this for yourself. Size of trees, density of woods, and how much ground clutter and brush there is can't be told from topo maps either.

Binoculars are a must for a stalking hunter. They enable him to study terrain to pick an approach on sighted game. Many times I have been able to use terrain to approach inside easy shotgun range of all sorts of game simply because my field glasses were hanging around my neck and not back in the truck where so many hunters leave them. The first whitetail I killed

was because I could study the cover between us, then easily belly-crawl into shooting distance, in the end poking my long rifle over a brushpile to kill him.

The hunter who doesn't tote binoculars when hunting plains country Rio Grande turkeys is simply penalizing himself. Probably I've used field glasses in hunting Rio Grandes several hundred times, so many ending successfully because of the instruments' enormous help in studying the lay of the ground.

Will the quarry be at that location by the time the stalk is made? Are its habits such that it may have wandered off? If so, would you know where to? What about trophy heads? Will the planned route bring you to within easy range? These are but a few of the questions you'll need to answer before beginning the sneak.

If the quarry is waterfowl, you may need to consider wind direction and speed. Ducks and geese flush into the wind, but in a strong wind can flare back away from the gun on lift-off, *unless* they are diver ducks, which must run a few steps to flush. If you're stalking big game animals, you can never forget these animals' sense of smell. If they get a scent of you—could be after a long stalk, you ease up—they're gone. You are positive they didn't see you. No, but did they get a whiff instead?

Big game also has a terrific sense of hearing—if you must crawl through dry leaves, or across rocks and shale, you need to consider the noise you'll make. I came to a large area of dead leaves one morning while bellying toward a buck. Hoping I could fool the deer, I bawled like a small calf a couple times as I sneaked across the leaves. I sounded like a Sherman tank thrashing around in those things, but the buck, and the does he was with, paid me no mind whatever. I didn't try to hide the sound, because this would have been a tip-off to the deer something was amiss. It was a gamble, but I got the eight-pointer.

Of course, game like wild hogs, javelinas, along with other large game, will show no signs of alarm at noises made by a stalking hunter in select areas, so long as it sounds much like other animals, cattle, or livestock native to the area. Try to cover it, to make as few sounds as possible, anything which may sound like a predator stealthily stalking game, and all of them become acutely alert. Water, once it is above shoe top depth, has no equal for enabling the hunter to make a successful sneak, *if* a person can

The hunter pictured here shows the use of shadows so as to be less easily seen by game. The parts of him which are in the shade are completely hidden, while those areas in the sunshine could be detected by any alert game bird or animal—if he moved them.

Today's abundant variety of camouflage clothing gives the hunter a wide range of choices, each suitable to various types of cover and terrain found around the United States. Makes both the ambush and the stalk easier.

(Right) Deer seldom look up, so the hunter locates in a tree; don't try it on turkeys, as they are tree-oriented.

(Below) Goose hunters can use the lay of the land when putting out a decoy on open ground, which is where all geese prefer to land. Geese will be easily attracted and a hunter can be hidden easily.

The hunter should study the terrain he intends to hunt in any manner possible, prior to leaving the vehicle, if this can be done. Using this knowledge, along with a topography map, the hunter can then begin planning what country he wants to hunt.

remain on his feet. I've belly-crawled in water, some of which was next to having ice on it, but this requires not only a tremendous amount of dedication, but also a large dose of being nuts.

Belly-crawling, by its very nature, can be hazardous, to you and the gun you're carrying. Sometimes it's muddy; quite often there are rocks, gravel, goathead stickers, sandburs; and I've had clients who were afraid we'd crawl onto snakes. I've wiggled through brushpiles, but only one thing has stopped me dead in my tracks a couple of times—wild blackberry tangles. You just don't go through them, you go around; and it's the same with any tangle covered with thorn-laden vines.

Safety must be considered. Carrying a gun in such close proximity to the ground can cause the barrel to become clogged with snow, mud, water, or get loose sand in the action. I have no problem with these when carrying a modern double, as I can gently open the action and look down each barrel, even when close to game. Most can be blown free by blowing down the barrels, then inserting the loads back in the chambers. I can recall times when I have had to rummage around for a long stick, or weed stalk, to dislodge objects in the barrels. Nowadays, while toting old blackpowder side-by-side doubles, I can no longer look down the barrels, or blow objects free, so I must take greater precautions.

There are two techniques utilized in toting a firearm while bellying over

terrain. One is the Army method, wherein the gun is cradled over the arms, more or less in the crook of the elbows. This is fine for short guns, such as the newer automatics and carbines. It is exceedingly hard on elbows, which take much of the brunt of crawling.

I never use it, but carry the gun in one hand, using the other and both legs to crawl. Of course, many stalks can be made on hands and knees into easy gunshot range, but others require the final stages lower to the ground. The hands-and-knees approach requires that the gun be carried in one hand, ordinarily the right hand for right-handed shooters, the left for southpaws. I'm rarely afield without leather gloves, simply because any type of crawling can be extremely hard on the hands. The main thing is to be careful not to get anything in the gun barrel, and as little as possible in the action. Many times I've seen guns unloaded, then swished back and forth in a pond, or creek, to wash out mud, debris, and sand after a seige of old-fashioned belly-crawling.

An important aspect of low, close-to-the-ground stalking is range estimation. Many times I've been in open

country, particularly open prairie, and have crawled to game, but as there were absolutely no reference marks, nothing to relate to, I couldn't shoot until positive I was within easy killing distance.

One warm, dew-laden morning in south Florida, I spied a turkey gobbler strutting far out on a burned area of palmettoes. I crawled on hands and knees as far as possible, but when I came to the end of cover I began calling to the bird, and to the hen with the gobbler. Though the old he-turkey paid me no mind, the hen commenced a conversation, then walked my way. I cut off the calling when she came by, but when the gobbler came along back of her a ways, blossomed out in full strut, the bird seemed awfully short. I didn't know if he was just a small adult gobbler, or if he was farther away than I thought. At last, he marched behind a big clump of unburned palmetto, and in that instant I stood erect, thus getting a good look at the distance between us. No problem. The old bird was inside 20 yards and I nailed him when he came back into view.

So, knowing your game, its size, and age, may help you in making a correct decision on distance. Many times on prairies, I have had to wait until game was behind cover, or had its head turned, enabling me to raise up for a quick look-see, to get a solid picture of the distance to other objects or to game. Knowing the size of the game helps. A 200-pound buck can look the same as a 125-pound deer at varying ranges, but you may kill one, and not the other, if you shoot at too long a range.

Knowing game habits is of tremendous help in stalking, particularly concerning the time of day, food habits, and how game moves throughout the

Patience is a virtue
Possess it if you can
Seldom found in woman
Never in a man.

course of a day's time. Weather also enters into this. If you are attempting to sneak within range of a flock of feeding honkers, but a hard wind is blowing, the birds may stay beyond gunshot if you've crawled toward them with the wind, in your face. Geese feed into the wind and they can move along at a brisk pace, so if you have a long crawl, your shot might be a 60-yarder. On the other hand, if no wind is blowing, the geese could be inside 40 yards, as the birds feed any which direction when there is no breeze.

"Stay in the shadows."

I've told that to so many clients I probably do it in my sleep. Shadows, or shade, are the best hunter helpers found anywhere if the sun is shining. Even on gray days, a hunter should remain near cover, any kind of terrain objects which will help hide his approach. The best still-hunter invariably chooses routes near trees, brush, rocks—always in the shadows—to break his outline and screen his approach. Countless times—hundreds—I have walked into easy killing distance of wild turkeys simply because I was utilizing all of the terrain features available while easing through cover, remaining in the shade with each possible chance it was available, and combining this with a very thorough knowledge of the wild turkey, and where I could expect to find the birds at various times of day. I keep

using wild turkeys as examples, not only because this is what I've guided for so many years, but also because of the acute wariness of the birds.

Hundreds of those turkeys which I walked into were unexpected. I knew I was in areas where turkeys were to be found, but I had to find them. I did, but whereas so many hunters would scare the birds before coming into killing range, I often come onto them inside easy killing distance. Of course, many are flushing shots, but anyone who hunts any type of bird should be a good wing shot. I grew to shooting age during an era where it was unethical to shoot birds on the ground. You just didn't shoot birds which weren't flying.

Anyone can walk up on wild turkeys if they'll stick to a few self-imposed rules. And this goes for any wild game; it can all be stalked successfully, time after time. First, study its habits, what it eats, where it's found, all of these in relation to various times of day, the days as these relate to your season dates. You must study your quarry thoroughly—all ages of it from the young to the trophy.

Next, you must know your gun. And make an attempt to become as good with it as possible. You owe this to any living game animal or bird you intend to hunt. The best hunters are invariably good shots. Then, use top quality loads and, above all, use self-restraint. Know the gun's limitations, and make up your mind you'll stick with them.

Last week, while reading a story in an outdoor magazine, I came across something in an article on hunting which stuck in my gizzard. The hunter says, ". .. I had to settle for a shot at 50 yards...," and this man was, at the time, shooting a shotgun. Now, among myself and all the old boys I've been hunting around all my life, from one end of these states to the other, I have yet to see a shotgun which would kill consistently at 50 yards. Few shotguns will kill half of the time at 50 yards. Worse, few hunters can estimate ranges at that distance, and the average hunter who would consider shooting at such a distance would also shoot at 60 to 70 yards, and farther. Don't listen to all these tales about long-distance

killing. Don't settle for a long shot; make up your mind you're a hunter and you'll shoot from considerably closer.

Camouflage clothing is new to some of us old hunters who put in many years hunting before it came on the market. We had no such thing before World War II, but did afterward.

Camo has taken some of the hunt out of hunting, making it so much easier to remain hidden that many hunters have lost touch with the old arts of stalking, still-hunting, bushwacking, and other related forms of bagging wild game. I suppose if all camouflage clothing were suddenly lost to mankind, many hunters would give up the thought of taking a wild bird or animal, simply because they would no longer have the advantage of remaining motionless, whereon so much of wildlife seemingly is unaware of their presence.

Some of my hunting is with camos, some is without. When decked out in no-see-um clothing, I can remain out in front of cover, but when I don't, I have to get behind cover. It's that simple.

Camouflage is older than man himself. Look at all the upland game birds. Each one's instincts tell it when to remain like a rock, whereon these birds blend in with their habitat to be unseeable. An elk stands quietly in the pole pines; a whitetail buck lies frozen as a hunter walks by a few feet from him; a big turkey gobbler hunkers, belly down on the leaves—all are examples of how wild creatures counter the advance of predators. We can all take lessons from such critters as rattlesnakes, coyotes, the majestic Bengal tiger, the slinking bobcat, or a copperhead stretched out on a leafy ridge in Alabama. Which came first, the oak tree or the snake's skin? Both blend like whiskey and branch water. A copperhead lying among a bunch of dead leaves is like looking for an Indian-head penny in a penny arcade. Beyond its perfect camouflage, Old Copperhead lies silent, watching and waiting, then stalking, gliding so easy along the forest floor, always studying its victim, watching, waiting, making sure it's inside easy killing distance. Time means nothing to this hunter.

Patience. Old Copperhead is patience animated. Yes, we need to take some lessons from these best of all hunters: Slow down. Watch. Wait. Stick to the shadows. Make dead sure of the range. You may need to get down to earth, on your belly.

The best of hunters do. ●

BOLT-ACTION SHOT-GUNS

by John Malloy

In the years following WWII, a Sears J.C. Higgins bolt-action shotgun, often with a surplus Army pack as a gamebag, became a common sight in the woods of America.

"A BOLT-ACTION SHOTGUN!" exclaimed the young duck hunter on the shore.

As I nosed my canoe into the landing, he could not help commenting on the gun strapped on top of my decoy bags. As we discussed the results of our hunts, I realized that hunters of his generation had probably not seen the bolt-action shotgun in common use as members of mine had.

To him, the bolt-action shotgun was a novelty, something strange and unusual, something not quite right.

Even during its period of extensive use, the bolt-action shotgun was the ugly duckling of the shotgun world. Its existence would have been hard to prove by reading books on shotgun handling. Most shotgun books and articles completely ignored it. When it was mentioned, it was often with an apology that such things even existed.

Such treatment is a bit unfair. True, bolt-action shotguns have little collector value, and hardly anyone

In a year long past, the writer attempts to wait out a southeast Texas bushytail, his gun a 16-gauge Mossberg Model 190K.

Some European muzzleloaders were converted into single shot bolt-action shotguns. This 12-gauge specimen has had the old lock recess filled and covered with a veneer.

brings one out to impress his shooting friends.

Yet, the bolt-action shotgun, although born in Europe, is as American as apple pie. Only in America did the widespread use of the bolt-action smoothbore for sporting use develop. Almost unnoticed, it played important roles in American shooting history.

No one seems to have felt that the birth of the bolt-action shotgun was important enough to record. It probably occurred during the latter part of the 1800s. Most governments were converting their obsolete muzzleloaders to a breech-loading system of some sort, or selling them to others who sometimes did so.

In Europe—familiar with the early bolt systems of the Prussian needle gun and the French Chassepot—some of the conversions became bolt actions. With the introduction of self-contained shotshells, some of the conversions became bolt-action shotguns.

After World War I, numbers of German Mauser rifles were converted in Germany into bolt-action shotguns. These guns use the rifle's box magazine to hold an extra shell, making a two-shot repeater.

Because the receiver had been bored to accept the large shotgun barrel, the bolt's locking lugs no longer contacted metal. Locking was accomplished only by the small safety lug at the rear of the bolt. Although some of these Mauser shotguns were used for years, they are considered of marginal safety.

During the 1920s, Japanese Muratas were made into bolt-action shotguns. A small number were

reportedly made for sale to South American settlers.

At a later time, British rifles were also made into bolt-action shotguns. SMLE 303-caliber rifles were converted into 410-bore single shot shotguns. The guns were apparently used as colonial military arms, for guard or foraging purposes.

Although bolt-action shotguns have seen some use throughout the world, the widespread use of the bolt-action smoothbore for sporting purposes is limited to America, where it began as an outgrowth of World War I. Many American soldiers were introduced to bolt-action rifles during that conflict and sought similar firearms after returning home.

At the close of the war, Winchester Repeating Arms Company, one of the largest suppliers of firearms and ammunition, was aware that its manufacturing capacity was no longer needed for military production. To keep its facilities operating, the firm branched into other lines of merchandise, including tools and hardware. With its other new products, Winchester introduced postwar firearms that were departures from its previous offerings.

Along with the immediately popular Model 52 target rifle, Winchester offered several light, small-bore shotguns in 1920. To appeal to the bolt-action-conscious returning servicemen, two of the new shotguns were bolt actions. Interestingly, their model numbers were based on their bore diameters.

The Model 36 was a simple, manually cocked single shot chambered for the 9mm rimfire shotshell. Although export sales were better, its low power made it a poor seller in America. It was discontinued in 1927.

The Model 41 had better acceptance. Chambered for the $2^{1}/_{2}$-inch 410 shell, this new bolt-action shotgun was at least adequate for hunting small game. The 410 had been introduced to America shortly before World War I. A gun by Winchester in that chambering went a long way to assure the widespread popularity of the new load. In 1932, Winchester brought out the 3-inch 410, and the Model 41 was chambered for the then-new shell. The well-made single shot was light enough for a boy to use, but its larger size also suited it for adult use.

After WWI, large numbers of German Mauser rifles were made into two-shot bolt-action shotguns. Because the locking is accomplished only by the small safety lug, their safety is considered marginal.

British SMLE rifles have been converted to single shot 410 bolt-action shotguns. They were reportedly used by colonial troops for guard duty and foraging.

Within a year, however, Winchester introduced its second 410—the Model 42 slide-action shotgun, chambered for the new 3-inch shell. The bolt-action model was dropped from the line soon after.

In the early 1930s, America was in the depths of the Great Depression. In those hard times, many people with little previous interest in hunting recognized the benefits of supplementing the family food supply with game. A demand for inexpensive guns, especially those that could be used by family youngsters, began to grow.

In 1933, about the time Winchester decided to discontinue the Model 41, two other American companies—Mossberg and Stevens—entered the bolt-action shotgun market. Their new 410 guns were repeaters. They were made by simple production methods and sold at low prices.

Priced just above single shot guns, they provided repeating shotguns at a fraction of the cost of the double barrel, pump, or semi-automatic offerings then available.

The young Mossberg firm, founded fourteen years earlier in 1919, had made only its four-barrel "Brownie" pistol and 22-caliber rifles previously. The first Mossberg bolt-operated shotgun was the Model 80, a four-shot repeater with a fixed (non-detachable) box magazine. It was replaced in 1936 by the Model 83, which could handle 3-inch shells. A three-shot 20-gauge version, the Model 85, was introduced in 1934.

In 1939, both 410 and 20-gauge guns were redesigned. The new models—83B and 85B, respectively—both had three-shot capacity. The 20-gauge also sported a detachable magazine for the first time. Produc-

tion of these guns was suspended during World War II.

The Stevens firm had been a division of Savage Arms Corporation since 1926. Savage had not previously marketed shotguns prior to acquiring Stevens. The new bolt actions expanded the company's line of products. The Stevens offerings for 1933 were the Model 38 with a detachable box ("clip") magazine, and the Model 39 with a tubular magazine. Both guns could handle the 3-inch 410 shell.

In 1937, modifications were made to the guns and the model numbers were changed to 58 and 59. A 20-gauge box magazine version was also added during that year. The new gun was the Model 258.

Like their Mossberg counterparts, production of Stevens bolt-action shotguns was suspended for the war effort after the United States entered World War II.

By the end of that conflict, vast numbers of young American men had been exposed to firearms and shooting. Glad to be done with the war, many of them wanted to continue shooting afterwards and became interested in hunting. A joke of the time was that returning GIs were primarily interested in two things—and the second one was hunting.

Because of the demand for hunting guns, production of postwar bolt-action shotguns rose to great numbers. Quick and inexpensive to manufacture, rugged and effective in the field, the postwar crop of bolt-action shotguns became available shortly after the war's end. Not elegant by traditional shotgun standards, they fulfilled a need and performed well.

The Mossberg guns went back into

production in 1946. Offered with three interchangeable choke tubes, they were now the Models 83D (410) and 85D (20-gauge).

In 1950, a 16-gauge version was offered, and adjustable chokes were introduced for the first time as factory-installed equipment on low-priced guns. Mossberg guns with this "C-lect-Choke" bear the "K" model suffix. By 1956, a 12-gauge model was available. Model designations had become 183 for the 410, 185 for the 20-gauge, 190 for the 16 and 195 for the new 12-gauge. Recoil pads for all except the 410 were added.

By the mid-1960s, Mossberg offered a redesigned bolt action that could use the 3-inch magnum shells becoming popular. Model numbers became 395 (12-gauge), 390 (16-gauge) and 385 (20-gauge). With their double locking lugs, center-mounted slide safety and rear-positioned bolt handle for quicker operation, these guns perhaps represented the high point of bolt-action shotgun development.

Several variants of the new series guns were offered. In 1968, a rifle-sighted "Slugster" was made with a 24-inch barrel. In 1982, responding to the popularity of the Marlin 36-inch-barrel "Goose Gun," Mossberg added a 12-gauge Full-choke model with a 38-inch barrel.

One of the most interesting variants of this series was the Model 595 A5, designed as a low-price police and guard gun. The fierce-looking shotgun had an 18½-inch barrel, a sling and a long five-shot box magazine that gave it a paramilitary look.

Introduced in 1983, it had a short production run. By 1986, after producing perhaps more bolt-action shotguns than all other manufacturers combined, Mossberg phased those guns out of their product line.

Except for some single shot 410s made in the '60s, all Mossberg bolt-action shotguns have been box-magazine repeaters. They have been marketed under the New Haven brand, and also as "house brands" for several different retail companies.

After World War II, Stevens resumed production of their Models 58, 59 and 258 in late 1945. With only minor changes, the two 410s and the 20 formed the bolt-action shotgun line until 1954, when a heavier action for 12- and 16-gauges was introduced. "Model 58" was also used for the new guns.

During the 1960s, the box-magazine 410s were redesigned. The new guns were simpler and had bolt han-

dles positioned to the rear for quicker operation.

The big-gauge Stevens boltactions were dropped from the line after 1973. The tubular-magazine 410, which had been made without a major change for forty years, was also discontinued in that year. The last Stevens bolt-action shotgun, the Model 58 410 box-magazine repeater, lasted until 1980. The Stevens bolt-action line had begun with that type almost half a century earlier.

In the early 1940s, Harrington & Richardson was already established in the low-price shotgun field with their single shot line. The firm designed a bolt-action shotgun, the H&R "Game Gun." That gun, offered in 16- and 20-gauge, featured a long

six-shot tubular magazine that extended under the barrel beyond the forearm.

Its limited production was discontinued during World War II. When the company resumed bolt-action shotgun production in 1949, a redesigned model was introduced. Perhaps because of the necessity of plugging the long magazine for waterfowl hunting, the new "Gamester" Model 348 was a three-shot gun. The short tubular magazine was concealed entirely within the forearm. It was offered only in 12- and 16-gauge.

The year 1953 saw the introduction of the Model 349, the Gamester Deluxe. It was the same basic gun with an adjustable choke and recoil pad. In 1957, a lighter version, the Model 351 Huntsman was introduced.

Shortly afterward, however, during 1958, Harrington & Richardson discontinued their bolt-action shotgun line. All the H&R bolt-action models were tubular magazine repeaters that loaded through a port in the underside of the stock forearm.

Between 1950 and 1953, the firm of Kessler Arms Corporation, of Silver Creek, New York, produced bolt-action shotguns. All Kessler bolt guns were box-magazine repeaters, with both detachable and non-detachable versions made. Plain barrels and models with a compensator/adjustable choke were offered. Gauges were 12, 16 and 20.

An interesting note on the Kesslers: Although the guns were not serial numbered, they had the month and year of assembly stamped on the underside of the barrel. The marks remain hidden inside the stock barrel channel.

The Kessler safety control is also worth noting. Most other brands of bolt-action smoothbores used some form of forward-rearward safety control with no uniformity as to the "safe" and "fire" positions. The Kessler safety was placed in an "up" position when the trigger was blocked. An easily remembered downward movement of the thumb as the gun was raised would then make it ready to fire.

Kessler guns were made as "house brand" firearms also. Those made for Montgomery Ward were marked "Western Field." I have seen one specimen marked "Spiegel Huntmaster." It apparently had been made for that large mail-order firm.

After Kessler went out of business,

Mike Malloy, the writer's older son, twelve years old in this 1988 photo, is armed with a 20-gauge Mossberg 185K as he heads to his position for a Texas dove hunt.

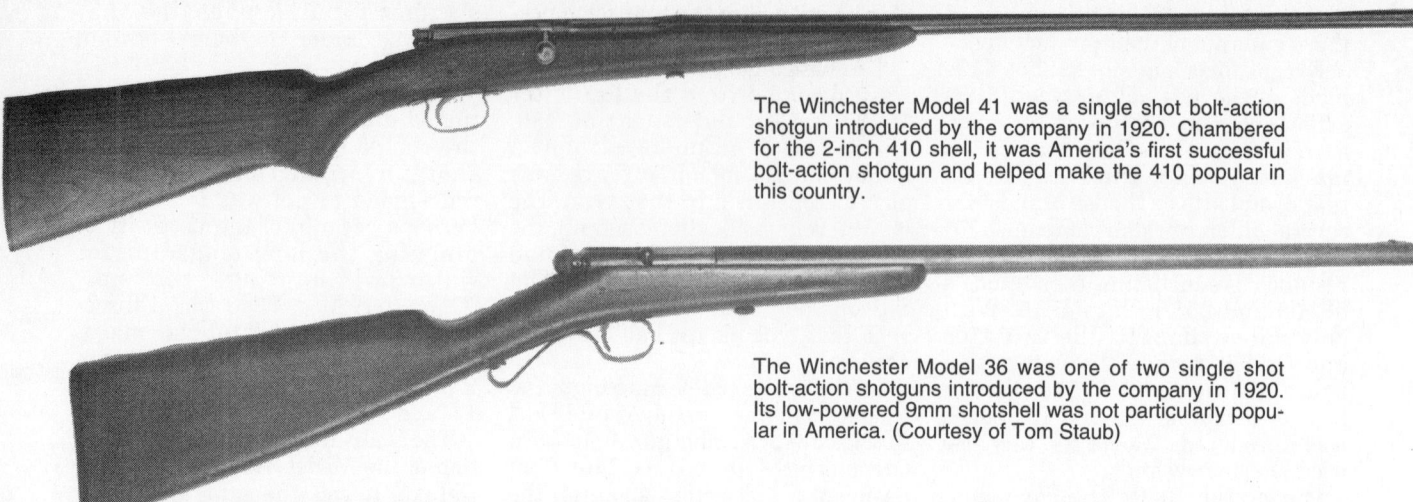

The Winchester Model 41 was a single shot bolt-action shotgun introduced by the company in 1920. Chambered for the 2-inch 410 shell, it was America's first successful bolt-action shotgun and helped make the 410 popular in this country.

The Winchester Model 36 was one of two single shot bolt-action shotguns introduced by the company in 1920. Its low-powered 9mm shotshell was not particularly popular in America. (Courtesy of Tom Staub)

the unsold guns and parts inventory were acquired by Numrich Arms Corporation. The large New York parts company sold the remaining Kessler guns by mail order. The supply apparently was gone by the middle '50s.

Your writer has a soft spot for the ungainly, clumsy-looking Kesslers.

My first shotgun was a 16-gauge Kessler. Not knowing that I was supposed to be at a disadvantage, I learned the basics of shotgun shooting with it, and it gave years of reliable service.

Marlin had been a strong competitor in the U.S. shotgun market during the late 1890s and the early

decades of the 1900s. However, the firm entered the postwar period with only one shotgun—the limited-production Model 90 over/under—in its line.

In 1955, Marlin offered its first bolt-action repeating shotgun. In 12-gauge only, with an adjustable choke as an option, the gun was marketed

The year is 1975 and the scene is a camp gun rack amid the Florida palmetto growth. The writer and his young companions felt well-armed with a 22 revolver, three 22 rifles and three bolt-action shotguns.

as the Marlin Model 55 Hunter. By the early 1960s, 20-gauge and 16-gauge versions were also offered.

Marlin saw a market for specialty guns. The company brought out a long-barrel "Goose Gun" in 1962, a short-barrel "Swamp Gun" in 1964, a "Slug Gun" in 1973, and, in 1976, their Model 5510 "Supergoose" 10-gauge. The latter is the largest bolt-action shotgun ever produced. It stayed in the line until 1986.

Marlin bolt-action shotguns were

Model 55 "Goose Gun," three decades after its introduction, is the only one still remaining in the Marlin line. It is also the only bolt-action shotgun now being made in America.

A number of hunters still swear by the old Goose Gun with its 3-inch chamber and its long 36-inch barrel. Velocity increase is probably minor, but once the gun starts swinging, it follows through. It also shoots "quieter," because more powder burns inside the barrel; when the muzzle

buck and Company. In 1947, Sears offered a bolt-action shotgun with a long tubular magazine. It was unlike any manufacturer's current model.

Produced for Sears by High Standard Manufacturing Company, the guns were offered as the J.C. Higgins Model 10. The "J.C. Higgins" trademark had been used previously for sporting goods marketed by Sears. It was named after John Higgins, a former director of the company. The "C" had been added to make

After WWII, Mossberg, having made bolt-action shotguns since the Depression, introduced its bolt-action line with several interchangeable choke tubes. This is a Model 185D in 20-gauge.

During the decades after WWII, Mossberg continually improved its bolt-action shotgun line, adding adjustable chokes, recoil pads, rear sighting bars and a redesigned bolt. This late 20-gauge 185K was made in the early 1960s.

During the 1960s, Mossberg introduced a new series of big-gauge bolt-action shotguns. The guns, like this 12-gauge Model 395K, had 3-inch chambers, a rear-positioned bolt handle and dual locking lugs.

also marketed under the Glenfield name. As the Glenfield Model 50, the basic gun was the same, but had fewer embellishments and a stock of a hardwood other than walnut. It drifted in and out of the Marlin line according to demand. Marlin also made some house brand guns. I have seen one marked "American Eagle."

With the exception of a 410 single shot made during the 1960s, all Marlin bolt-action shotguns have been repeaters with detachable box magazines. At the time of this writing, the

blast does occur, it is farther from the shooter's face.

Most nationwide retailers such as Montgomery Ward, Western Auto and others offered bolt-action shotguns which were current models of one of those manufacturers previously mentioned. These were essentially identical to the manufacturers' guns, but were stamped with the retailer's house brand.

An exception was the J.C. Higgins bolt-action shotgun marketed during the postwar period by Sears, Roe-

the sound of the name flow better.

The six-shot guns were made in 12-, 16- and 20-gauge. They were similar in appearance and function to the short-lived H&R Game Gun, which had been discontinued during World War II. The connection between the H&R design and the High Standard-produced Sears guns is not known, but apparently there was one. Not only do the guns look alike and function in the same manner, but it has been reported that the bolts will interchange.

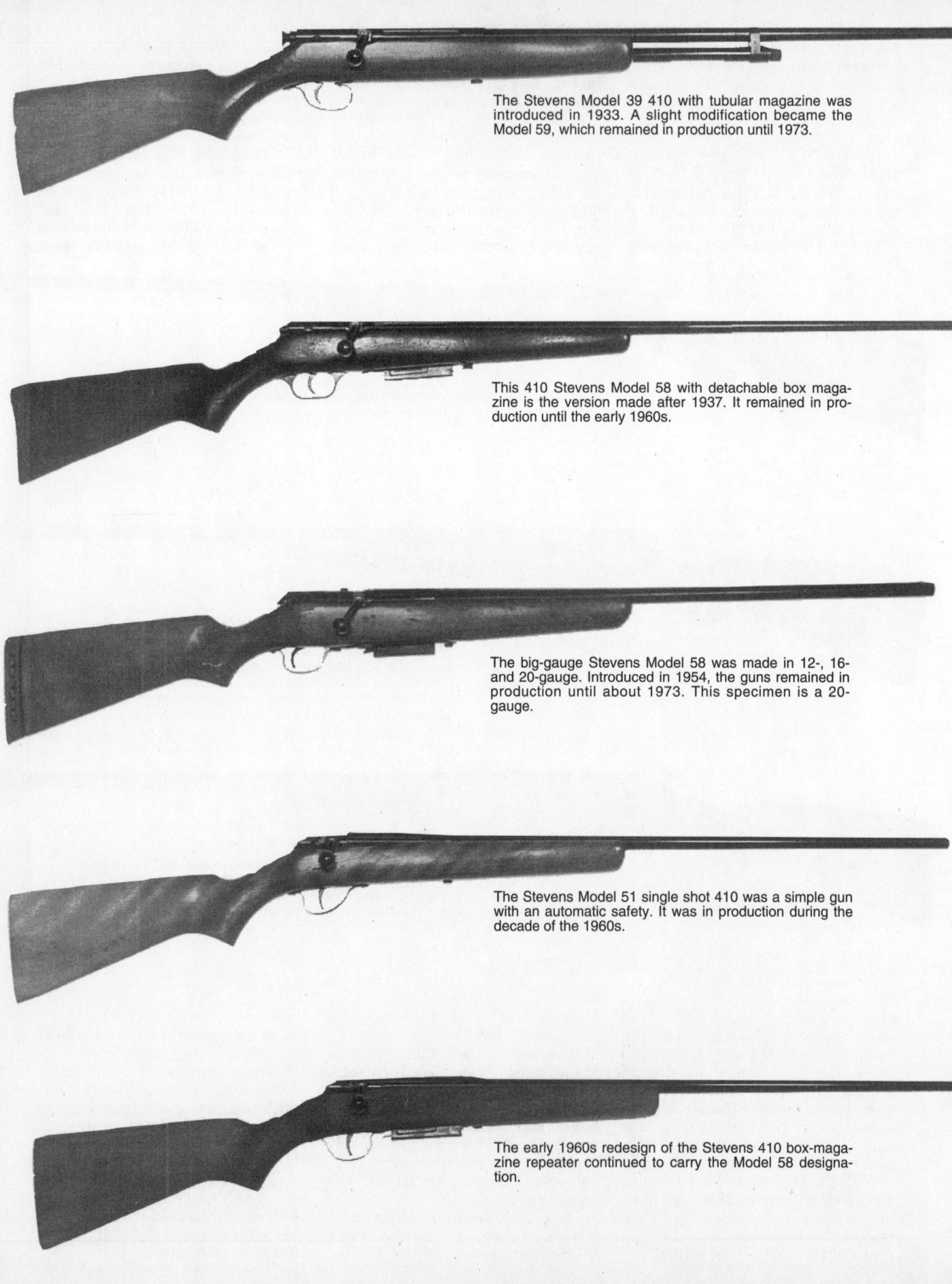

The Stevens Model 39 410 with tubular magazine was introduced in 1933. A slight modification became the Model 59, which remained in production until 1973.

This 410 Stevens Model 58 with detachable box magazine is the version made after 1937. It remained in production until the early 1960s.

The big-gauge Stevens Model 58 was made in 12-, 16- and 20-gauge. Introduced in 1954, the guns remained in production until about 1973. This specimen is a 20-gauge.

The Stevens Model 51 single shot 410 was a simple gun with an automatic safety. It was in production during the decade of the 1960s.

The early 1960s redesign of the Stevens 410 box-magazine repeater continued to carry the Model 58 designation.

mechanically the same as the Model 11 but with a different stock, was offered in 1963.

The Sears contract was a mixed blessing for High Standard. It did allow the maker to move to a larger and better factory location in 1950. Still, having so much of their production going to one customer made High Standard vulnerable to any change in Sears policies. The manufacturer found itself making more and more guns, but receiving less and less per gun. The almost two-decade-old relationship ended in 1964.

In 1965, Sears followed the practice of other retailers and offered the current models of Stevens bolt-actions as house-brand shotguns. And High Standard brought out a small number of bolt-action shotguns under their own name, changing the model number from 14 to 514.

We will probably never know exactly how many bolt-action shotguns have been made. Most were made when few companies serial numbered shotguns, especially low-priced ones. Even if records were kept by the manufacturers, several have since gone out of business.

The figures certainly run into many hundreds of thousands, perhaps well into the millions. All these guns seem to have been made with hardly any notice. Firearms professionals and the shooting press paid little attention to them. As a saying goes, no one seems to have liked them except people. And, of course,

The original J.C. Higgins Model 10 does not have that model designation on the gun. Instead, the guns will bear "Model 583." The number "583." is Sears' manufacturer code for that particular gun. Numbers following the decimal represent the variations and modifications, for parts-supply purposes.

The Sears distribution network made it possible for a tremendous number of these guns to be sold.

Although few people knew their background, they became common hunting guns.

In 1958, the Model 11 was introduced. The long magazine was dropped, and the shorter two-shot magazine tube was contained within the forearm. With its rearward-sloping trigger guard and metal forend cap, its appearance was still unlike any other shotgun being made. The final variation, the Model 14,

Made from 1949 until 1953, the Model 348 Gamester was Harrington & Richardson's first postwar bolt-action shotgun. The two-shot tubular magazine was contained entirely inside the forearm, and the gun loaded through a port on the underside.

the companies that made them.

No matter what company made them, most American bolt-action shotguns have certain common characteristics.

They are strong for the ammunition used, and the simple mechanism is rugged and reliable. They have greater opening and closing leverage than other types of shotguns; they may chamber and extract swollen or deformed shells that might jam other actions. Relatively inexpensive as new guns, they are now generally a great bargain in the used gun market. These characteristics make the bolt-action a good utility or "extra" shotgun. Its simplicity also makes it particularly suitable for bad weather use.

Richard Arnold, a British author, wrote in the postwar years in that country where the double shotgun was then considered the only suitable type for a sportsman. Arnold held the opinion that, for hunting in very bad conditions, "the bolt-action repeating shotgun...is about the best bet."

Arnold's 1958 shotgun book probably raised the eyebrows of some Britons. It contains this interesting statement:

Indeed, for the person who can only afford one shotgun for general-purpose shooting at pests, game and wildfowl, and who at the same time may have the opportunity of shooting deer, the bolt-action repeating shotgun as produced by Mossberg, Stevens, H&R or J.C. Higgins is the best possible buy for him.

Americans in the postwar years had already figured that out!

Besides their versatility, bolt-action shotguns are generally the easiest type on which to mount sling swivels, a factor when a hunter needs both hands free. For hunting with slugs, some models were easily fitted with iron sights. Marlin bolt actions were regularly drilled and tapped for a Lyman peep sight. Removal of the bolt allows adjustment of sights by bore sighting. A friend of mine, a Methodist minister and an ardent hunter, used a 12-gauge Mossberg fitted with a scope

for use with slugs in "shotgun only" areas.

Although shotguns are generally acknowledged to be unsurpassed as home defense weapons, bolt actions are seldom, if ever, mentioned. Yet, bolt actions are the only common shotguns to offer a detachable magazine. If safety considerations dictate an unloaded gun in the house, it is easier to slip in a loaded clip in the dark than it is to load another type with loose shells.

In a home with small children, removal of both the magazine and the bolt make the gun safe, safer than almost any other type of shotgun. In an emergency, the bolt and a loaded magazine can be quickly replaced.

The only real fault with the bolt-action shotgun is its slow operation.

As a user of bolt-action shotguns since my youth, I must admit that I have experienced the frustration of not being able to get off a follow-up shot after missing a zig-zagging dove. I have also faced the embarrassment of having a hunting com-

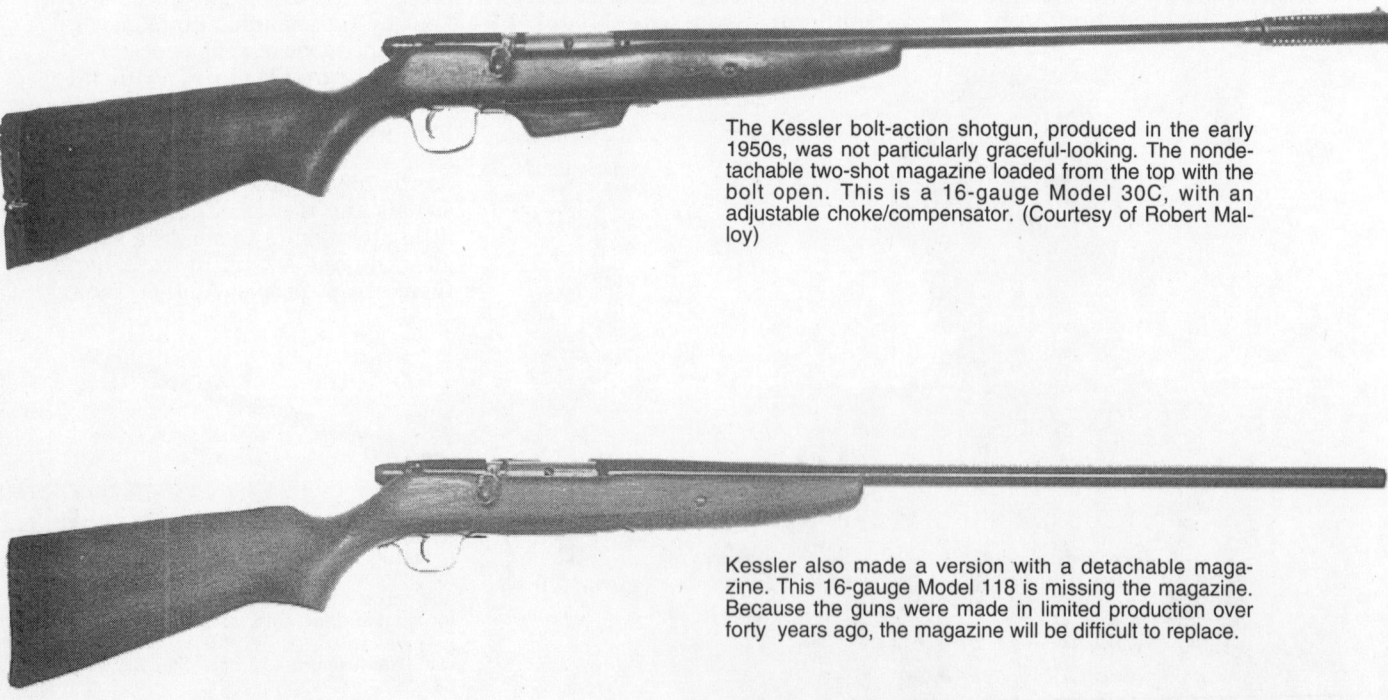

The Kessler bolt-action shotgun, produced in the early 1950s, was not particularly graceful-looking. The nondetachable two-shot magazine loaded from the top with the bolt open. This is a 16-gauge Model 30C, with an adjustable choke/compensator. (Courtesy of Robert Malloy)

Kessler also made a version with a detachable magazine. This 16-gauge Model 118 is missing the magazine. Because the guns were made in limited production over forty years ago, the magazine will be difficult to replace.

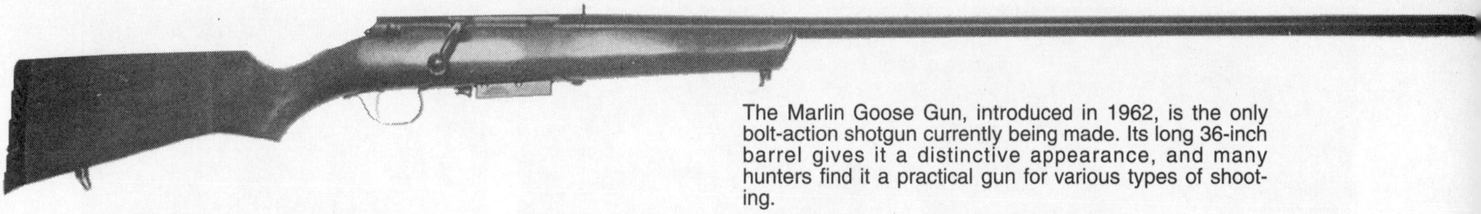

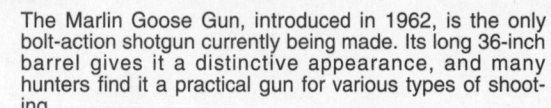

The Marlin Goose Gun, introduced in 1962, is the only bolt-action shotgun currently being made. Its long 36-inch barrel gives it a distinctive appearance, and many hunters find it a practical gun for various types of shooting.

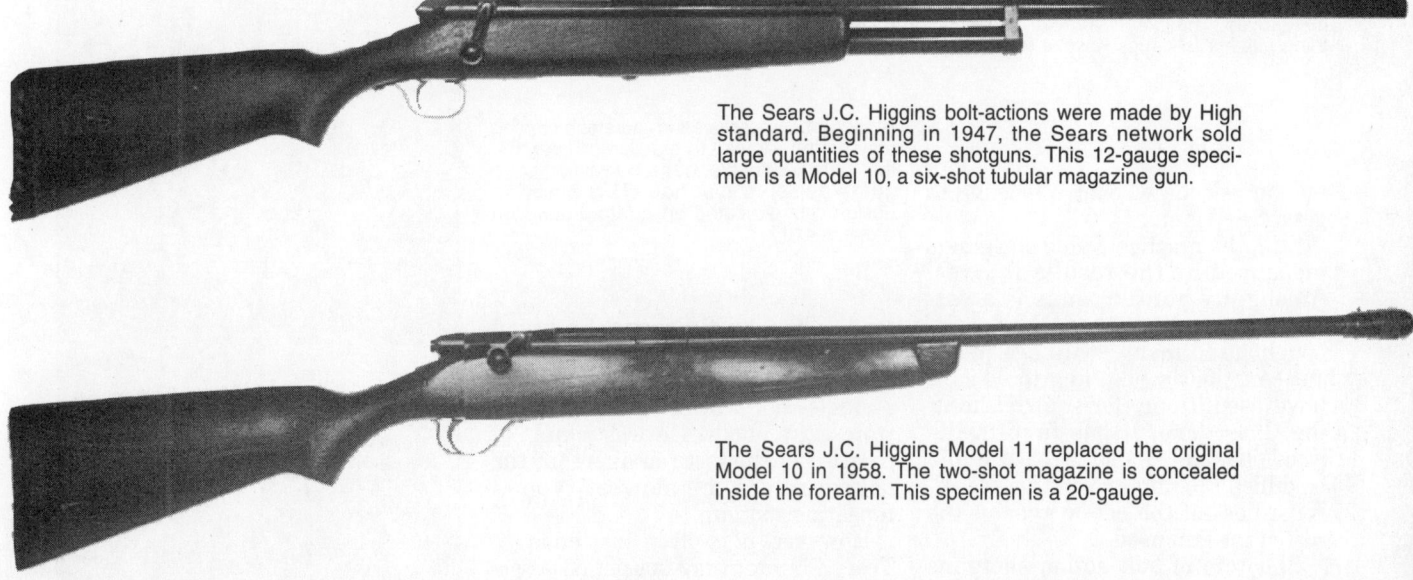

Florida duck hunter Bill Benda reflects on the wood duck he has just retrieved. He bagged the handsome drake with the long-barrel Marlin Goose Gun strapped to his kayak.

The Sears J.C. Higgins bolt-actions were made by High standard. Beginning in 1947, the Sears network sold large quantities of these shotguns. This 12-gauge specimen is a Model 10, a six-shot tubular magazine gun.

The Sears J.C. Higgins Model 11 replaced the original Model 10 in 1958. The two-shot magazine is concealed inside the forearm. This specimen is a 20-gauge.

The year is 1958, and the scene is an excursion into the Florida mangroves. The writer, younger and skinnier, feels ready for anything with his 16-gauge Kessler Model 30C in his hands.

A young boy interested in gunstock carving may not be allowed to practice on grandfather's Parker double, but a bolt-action shotgun may serve just fine. This pleasing design was executed on a late-production Stevens 410.

panion ask me when I was going to get a "real" gun.

Still, the practical value of a gun is measured by the results it gives. Among my hunting guns is a battered 20-gauge Stevens Model 58, bought used many years ago. Without consciously planning to do so, I have used it only for squirrel hunting. *Every* shot it has fired in the woods has killed a squirrel. It would be difficult to improve on that record, regardless of the action type or the cost of the gun used.

Shooters of bolt-action shotguns tend to be realistic, though. A friend once remarked with a smile that his bolt-action repeater was actually just a single-shot with a handy place to store extra shells. He was joking, of course, but the fact remains that the bolt action is the slowest type of repeating shotgun.

However, it is often fast enough. True, a hunter may not get off a second shot at an exploding covey of quail. However, a double on ducks cupping their wings over the decoys would not be out of the question.

Lack of speed aside, the versatile bolt-action shotgun had (and still has) much going for it. In today's world, one of its outstanding features is its low price on the resale market. This is of some importance even for those with no desire to own one.

Those of us interested in shooting, hunting and other gun-related activities realize that new people must constantly become a part of the firearms fraternity if these interests are to survive. The price of many desirable guns can be prohibitively high for a new shooter. The low cost of bolt-action shotguns, on the other hand, allows newcomers to acquire serviceable firearms. That second-hand bolt model from the used gun rack can give a new shooter a versatile shotgun that can handle many shooting situations.

Gun collecting is an activity that draws people—shooters and non-shooters alike—into the firearms fraternity. A newcomer will soon find that it is difficult start a good Colt, Winchester or Kentucky collection. However, the seemingly endless varieties of bolt-action shotguns form a field that is virtually unexplored. Such guns provide a low-cost opportunity for a beginning collector to get into the activity.

In either case, more people become fellow gun owners, with a stake in the future of firearms ownership.

We know now that bolt-action shotguns have played a quiet, but real, part in the history of our country. After World War I, they helped make the small-bore shotgun popular; they put meat on many tables during the Depression; and they gave a great boost to promoting American interest in hunting and shooting after World War II.

Bolt-action shotguns are more than just useful guns. They are a true part of America's history. ●

Selected Bibliography

Arnold, Richard. *Automatic and Repeating Shotguns.* New York: A.S. Barnes, 1958.

Brown, Pete. "The Mossberg Story," *Gun Digest,* 17th Ed. p. 120-124. Chicago: Gun Digest Co., 1963.

Dickey, Pete. "Savage Private Brands," *American Rifleman,* v. 130, no. 3 (March 1982) p. 69-70.

Goodman, Geoff. "Bolt-Action Shotguns In My Experience," *American Rifleman,* v. 133, no. 12 (December 1985) p. 56.

deHaas, Frank. *Bolt Action Rifles.* Northfield,IL: DBI Books, 1971.

Keith, Elmer. *Shotguns By Keith.* New York: Bonanza, 1967.

Malloy, John. "Bolt-Action Shotguns," *American Rifleman,* vol. 128, no. 6 (June 1980) p. 40-41, 86.

Petty, Charles E. "High Standard— The Final Days," *Shooting Industry,* v. 31, no. 12 (December 1986) p. 100-103.

Rakusan, J. "The Bolt-Action Shotgun," *Guns Illustrated,* 22nd ed. (1990) p.65-67.

Swearengen, Thomas F. *The World's Fighting Shotgun.* Alexandria, VA: Ironside, 1978.

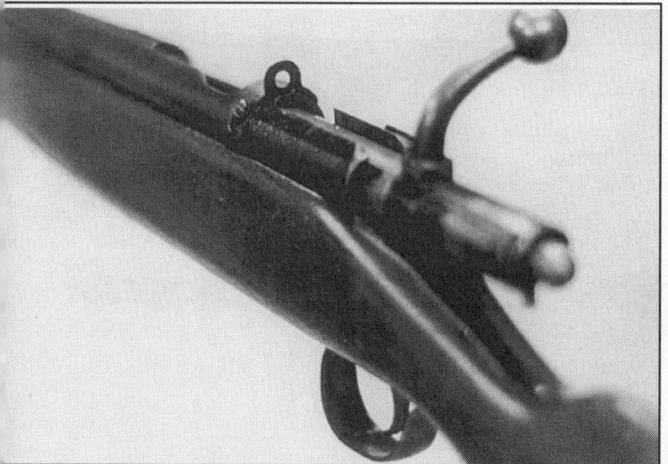

Although only Marlin bolt-action shotguns were regularly drilled and tapped for peep sights, simple sights for close-range slug use can be made at a home workbench. Removal of the bolt allowed bore sighting of this gun, a J.C. Higgins Model 10.

EDITOR'S NOTE

The late Gough Thomas Garwood wrote on the shotgun (as Gough Thomas) for decades in England. In one of his little books, he brought his engineer's training to bear on the game gun, examining and discussing moments of inertia and such. To hardly anyone's surprise, his principal conclusion in that discussion was that the British best quality game gun provided great inertial moments. To, no doubt, nearly everyone's surprise, he appended the further thought that American small-bore bolt-action guns felt great, too.

Ken Warner

Introduced in 1983 as a low-cost police and guard gun, Mossberg's Model 595 AP5 has a paramilitary appearance. This display at the 1985 NRA Meetings was perhaps its last public appearance. All Mossberg bolt-action shotguns were dropped from the company's line the following year.

by DOC CARLSON

BLACKPOWDER REVIEW

that is formulated to work with the new Super Lube 2000, a specially designed lube that they say holds down powder fouling when using slugs. Their Super Slug will come prelubed in plastic tubes holding ten of the prelubed bullets. The tube is flexible and can be easily carried in the pocket, making the carrying of prelubed bullets easier and less of a mess. There are also "Quick Chargers" which are the same flexible tubing in short sections that will hold one bullet and the powder charge.

Connecticut Valley Arms has increased their accessory line also. They have a pre-loader called the Second

hold six caps ready to put on the nipple. It will work equally well on inline or conventional guns. This is a very nicely designed, very inexpensive accessory that percussion shooters will be pleased with. At $3.95, a hunter can afford to have several in his gear.

CVA also has a new parts book that lists all their guns, past and present, with parts pictures and lists. If you own any of the CVA line of guns, it's a good investment at $8.95.

Speaking of parts, **Taylor & Co.** has a 225-page *Spare Parts Book for Italian Muzzleloading Firearms*. This book lists most all of the Italian

MUZZLE-LOADING is in for another great year. The frontloading family of firearms is alive and very well. At the Shooting, Hunting and Outdoor Show in Houston, I looked over all the goodies that will be showing up on your dealers shelves by the time this sees print.

There were fewer radically new guns to be seen this year. I think this shows that manufacturers are pretty comfortable with their lines in the firearms category. What was very much in evidence was an upgrading of existing guns and the addition of a great many gadgets and accessories.

One of the companies that has shown enormous growth in their product line is **White Muzzleloading Systems**. Started by veteran hunter Gary White, this outfit brought its first gun, an inline, to the marketplace in 1991. The White System concept is based on the use of their rifles combined with specially designed bullets to get maximum performance on game. These are hunting guns. Their design is based upon tried and true inline developments with a large dose of Gary White's experience-based innovation.

The White gun line was expanded this year to include a stainless steel version of their inline using a composite stock. This one will find favor with the hunter as it has to be almost impervious to weather. Of great interest to me and other more traditional shooters, they are also bringing out a sidelock rifle that resembles

Yep. Looks like a centerfire breechloader, scope and all, but it's T/C's 50-caliber inline Thunder Hawk.

Dixie Gun Works joins the inline parade with this offering.

Why not a thumbholer? This is Modern Muzzle Loading's version.

the English sporting rifles that were very popular a century or so ago. The sidelock gun is in the prototype stage and might be on dealers' shelves by mid-year. The gun uses the same barrel configuration as the inline guns and is intended to fire the White Super Slug that is the backbone of the shooting system. I will enjoy getting my hands on one of these when they are available.

White has brought out a full line of accessories made with the hunter in mind: A sling to fit the swivels on their rifles and a new cleaning solution

Shot which is calibrated on the side of the tube to act as a powder measure. The charger will hold a ball or bullet and the measured charge of powder for a quick second shot. The charger also has a socket on the side that slips over the ramrod to use as a "T" handle when seating your bullet. This is a real help in the hunting field when a fouled barrel resists your efforts to ram down a charge.

Another CVA accessory that caught my eye was their Rapid Capper. This tool combines a plastic cap box with fingers around the edge that

guns, showing exploded views and parts name listings, along with the maker and maker's part numbers. It should help considerably when hunting parts for some of the imported muzzleloaders. If you own any of the Italian-built muzzleloaders, this would be a darn good investment at $13.95, it would seem.

Taylor is well known for quality U.S. musket reproductions of Civil War vintage—the 1861 Springfield, C.S. Richmond Musket and the 1853 three-band Enfield. They have added a well-done

Brown Bess 1762. They also have a full line of cap and ball revolvers, plus Kentucky- and Hawken-style rifles. I was very interested to note that they are going to import a decent-looking copy of the Sharps Business Rifle. This gun will be available in 45-70 only with double-set triggers and a 28-inch barrel. If this gun shoots as good as it looks, it should find a ready acceptance among the blackpowder cartridge shooters.

Traditions, Inc. is importing three new high-quality match rifles. All are Italian guns and include an Alex Henry Target Rifle, a Creedmoor Style Long Range Rifle and a Hawken Match Rifle. These guns are in the prototype stage of development, but may be part of the line by mid-year. These are top-quality guns and priced accordingly, but I'm sure they will find a ready market among those looking for quality, good looks and top accuracy.

Traditions has added a small change to many of their conventional side-hammer hunting guns and are now bending the hammer slightly to the right so that it will be more available to thumb-cock with gloves on in the hunting field, especially when a scope is mounted. Just a small thing, but something that will be appreciated by hunters, among others.

There is one new gun that really deserves mention. **Sile Distributors** was showing a new muzzleloader that will really attract attention, and probably the ire, of the traditional shooter. The gun is basically an inline type of action, but it is based on the '98 Mauser action. The gun looks like any other '98 Mauser sporter until you open the bolt. The bolt is modified so that it fires a shotgun primer that is seated in the rear end of the barrel. The breech end of the barrel is recessed for this primer and, after firing when the bolt is opened, the primer is pulled out by the extractor and ejected the same as a fired shell. Other than that, the gun functions like any other inline. Certainly something different.

October Country, the leather shooting bag folks, are making up standard and deluxe shooter's kits. These are available in either flint or percussion and contain one of their fine pouches and all the gear necessary to run either a flint or percussion muzzleloader in the field. The Basic Hunter's Kit has a small belt pouch and the basics to deal with your rifle. The Deluxe Hunter's Kit uses their Freetrapper shoulder bag with needed gear of a more deluxe nature. They are also going to put out a couple of their more popular bags in kit form for those who like to build things and save a few bucks at the same time.

Thompson/Center Arms Co. was one of the first to bring the mass-produced muzzleloader to the American consumer. They are still a leader in the industry and continue to expand their line. Their newest addition is the Thunder Hawk, an inline-action muzzleloader. This follows the trend to these guns by various other manufacturers. The T/C gun is stocked with American black walnut and has a rubber recoil pad and sling swivels. It is drilled and tapped to take the T/C Quick Release scope mounting system. The 21-inch barrel is rifled with a 1:38-inch twist and is intended for use with slug bullets, sabots or conventional patched round ball. At a retail of $275, this one brings T/C quality to this style rifle at a very reasonable price.

The folks at T/C also are now making their conventional sidelock rifle in stainless steel and Rynite stock for those who like the more traditional-style rifle, but also like the weather resistance, durability and ease of maintenance of modern materials. Called the Grey Hawk, this rifle is available in 50-caliber with a 24-inch barrel. The little Scout rifle will also be offered with the rugged Rynite stock.

An addition to the T/C line, accessory-wise, is a ball discharger that uses CO_2 cartridges to silently blow the load out of percussion, flintlock or inline guns. I have used one of these outfits for some time, and it is very much preferable to the use of the screw-type ball pullers. It gives the shooter a safe way to unload a gun that was misloaded for whatever reason and allows the hunter to unload at the end of a hunt without dirtying the rifle or scaring game with the noise of firing it. Every shooter should have one of these in his

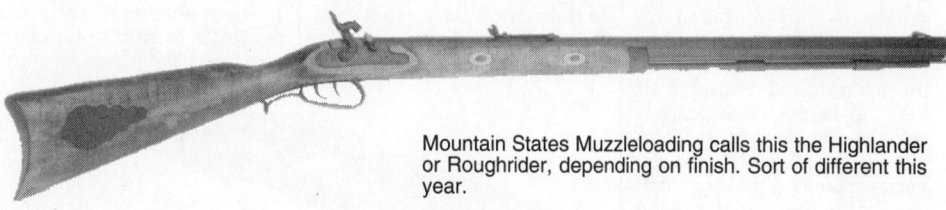

Mountain States Muzzleloading calls this the Highlander or Roughrider, depending on finish. Sort of different this year.

or her kit. At $35, it is not a small investment, but the convenience and safety certainly make up for the price. At least, every shooting range, club or hunting camp should have one.

Modern Muzzle Loading Inc., the folks that started the revolution in the inline style of rifle, have further refined their line of these rifles, adding a thumbhole-stocked version in either blued steel or stainless called the Knight Hawk. The composite thumbhole stock is available in either standard black or simulated burl walnut. I can attest that the burl walnut version looks more like wood than wood does, if that's possible. A standard stock, again composite, is available with the Mossy Oak Treestand camouflage pattern, intended for use in, where else, treestands. These guns are priced in the $500 to $700 range.

The Modern Muzzle Loading folks also are still offering their lower priced version of their inline gun. Called the Knight Legend and priced at $289, this is a popular hunting rifle with many.

A new accessory by these folks is their ballistics guide. This is a slide rule-style calculator that allows the shooter to figure out the ballistics of a particular load in advance. The two-sided heavy cardboard slide rule is set up for 50-caliber on one

This is MMLI's Mossy Oak inline rifle, ready for the treestand.

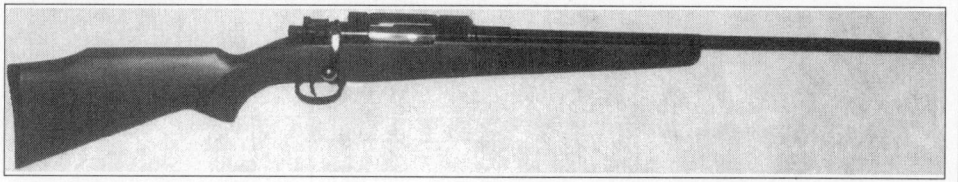

Sile Distributors builds an inline muzzleloader with a Model '98 Mauser action.

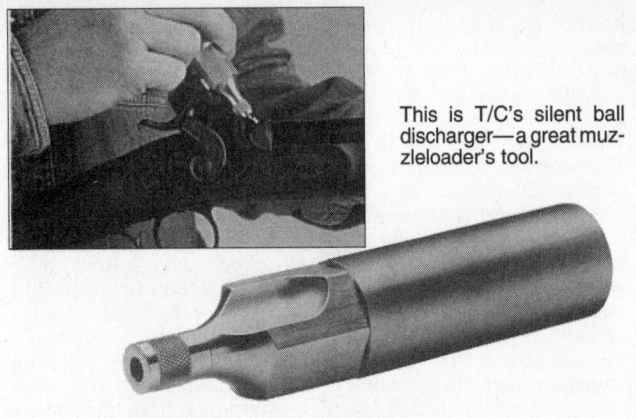

This is T/C's silent ball discharger—a great muzzleloader's tool.

side and 54 on the other. Loads of 80, 90, 100 or 110 grains can be matched up with sabot/jacketed bullet, sabot/lead bullet, pure lead bullet or patched round ball loadings to give velocities, energy in foot pounds and trajectories at 25, 50, 100 or 150 yards. This is a tool that will especially find favor among hunters. The guide will show what changing the powder charge, for example, will do to the ballistics of various projectiles. It will also show, unequivocally, that with any loading, trajectories are such that shots beyond 100 yards are very "iffy" unless one really knows both the range and the ballistics of the load. It also shows that the foot pounds of striking energy drop rather dramatically beyond 100 yards. This is a great pocket reference for the shooter, and especially the hunter, to carry.

Mountain States Muzzleloading is showing a new rifle called the Highlander or Roughrider, depending upon whether the metal is blued or browned. This rifle is available in either 45, 50 or 54 calibers with a deep (.010- to .012-inch) rifling, twisted 1:66 inches for patched round ball. The gun looks very much like the old CVA Mountain Rifle that was very popular a few years ago and was aban-

doned for whatever reason. I'm glad to see this rifle back in the marketplace. It's a good traditional rifle and priced within the range of most—

$249.95. The whole Mountain States line includes some traditional-looking guns of very good quality with a custom-made look. Most all their guns are available as kits.

Gonic Arms continues to add refinements to their inline guns. They are adding special bullet designs and custom touches such as full-length Mannlicher-style stocks and such. If inlines are your cup of tea, you should write for their catalog and price list. Your local dealer may well have them in stock also.

Dixie Gun Works needs no introduction to most blackpowder shooters. They also continue to carry one of the most complete lines of reproduction guns around. A couple of their newest additions are on both ends of the traditional scale. On the one hand, they are bringing in one of the best reproductions of a U.S. musket that I have seen in some time, the 1816, and at the opposite end is an inline gun that is strictly modern in design and look. If you don't have Dixie's catalog, you should send them four bucks and get it. It's got a lot of good

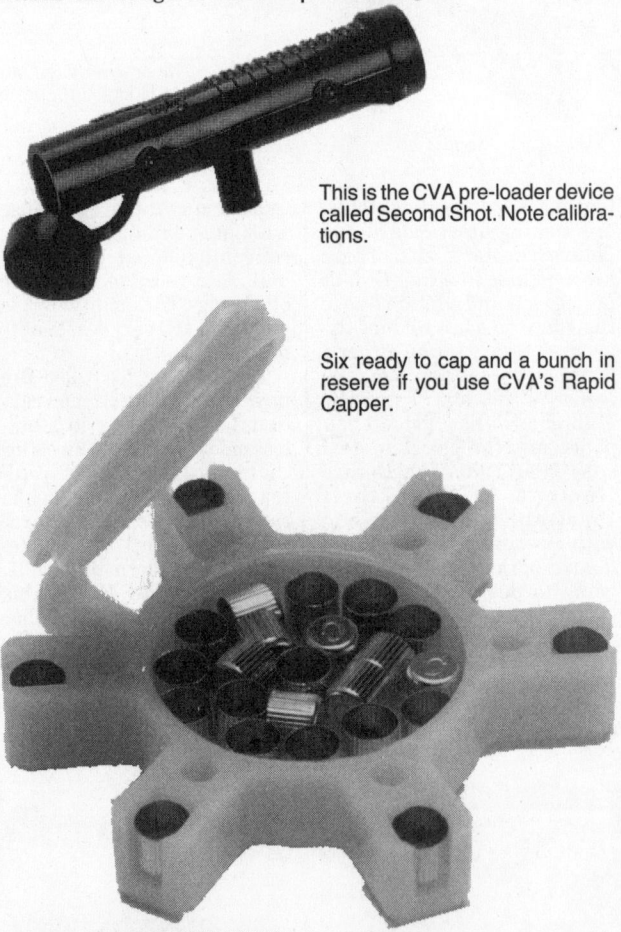

This is the CVA pre-loader device called Second Shot. Note calibrations.

Six ready to cap and a bunch in reserve if you use CVA's Rapid Capper.

reading and reference material in it, besides showing their complete line of guns and gear.

A few things showed up in the ammunition department that are worth a look. **Hodgdon Powder Co.** has a new lube called Pyro Patch that is especially formulated to work with Pyrodex and keep fouling to a minimum while protecting the barrel. It will work equally well with blackpowder also. Hodgdon is also out with a new plastic pouring spout that will fit their Pyrodex cans to make pouring charges or filling horns and flasks easier and safer with less spillage.

Goex Powder Company, the only U.S. maker of blackpowder, is celebrating their 80th anniversary. To commemorate this event, they are putting out their powder in a special can. These cans will be used all this year and are sure to become a collector's item down the road. I would sure rat-hole some of these.

While on the subject of blackpowder, I talked to a representative of a new powder company called **Petro-Explo Inc.** They are importing a blackpowder called Elephant Brand. The powder is made in Brazil and appears to be the same as we are used to, at least as far as looks go. It will remain to be seen how this new import powder will function in sporting arms.

Hornady Manufacturing, the bullet people, are putting out a new shooter's kit that contains 4 ounces of Pyrodex, a box of percussion caps and a box of twenty of their Great Plains bullets. This should be well received by those who want to try the Hornady bullets or who have just bought a rifle and want to pick up the basics to shoot it. Very convenient.

Another bullet company, **Buffalo Bullet Company**, is putting out a Variety Pack. This has ten round balls with lubed patches, ten saboted boattail bullets and ten prelubricated Buffalo Bullet conicals packaged in a reusable plastic box with basic loading data. This is available in both 50 and 54 calibers and allows the shooter to try the different bullets that Buffalo puts out. They can be tested for accuracy and ease of loading without buying larger packages of each bullet. ●

Pyro patch lube—specially for Pyrodex but OK with the black stuff.

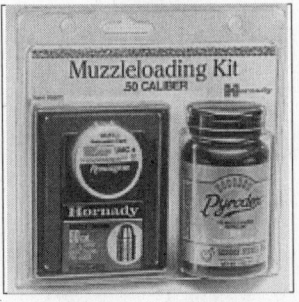

Caps, powder and balls in one package from Hornady.

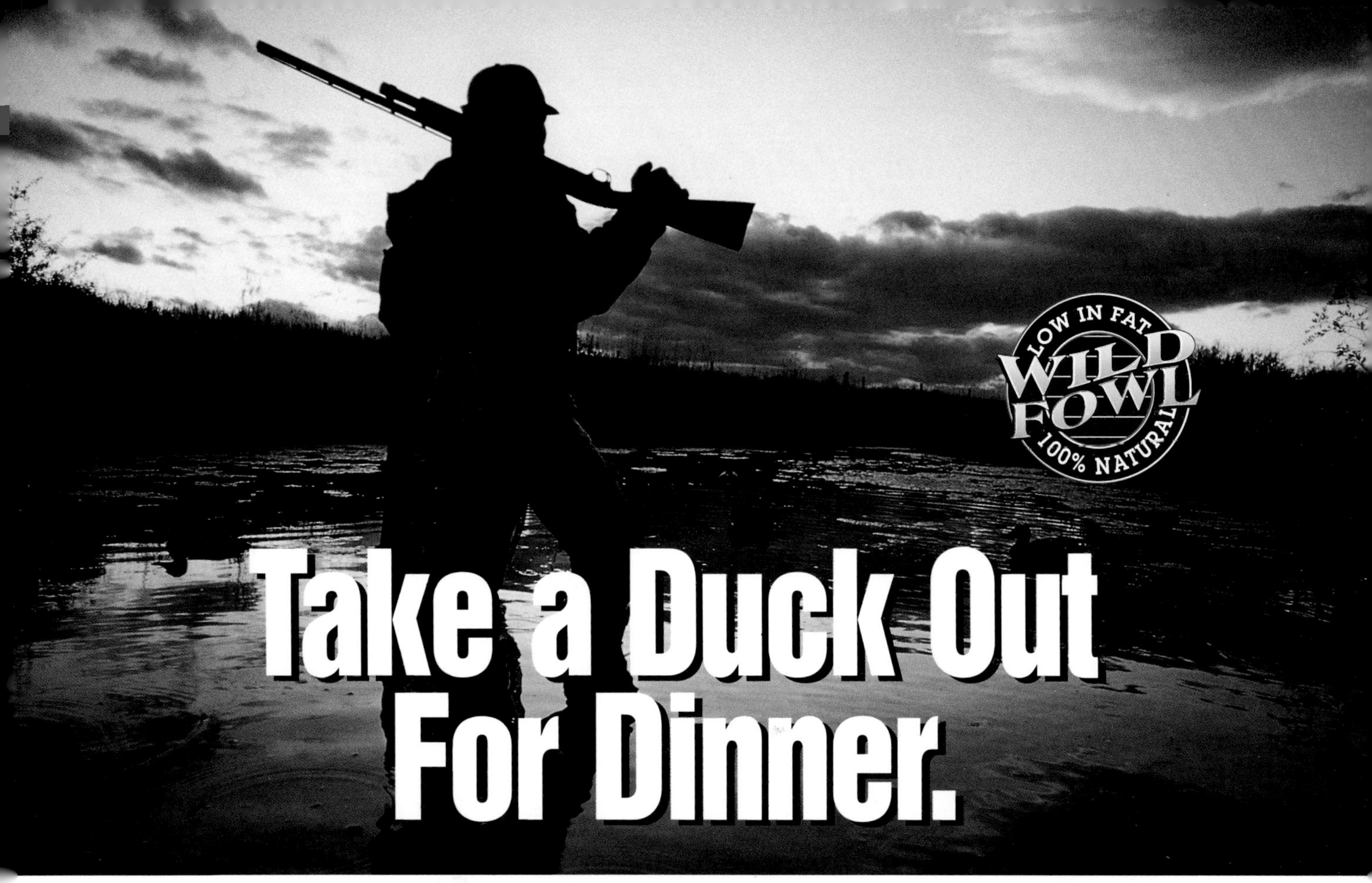

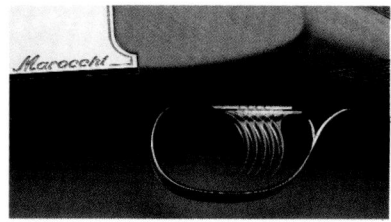

Many competitors claim their safes are fire resistant by just adding fire insulating materials. In reality, they leave your guns and valuables at serious risk.

Browning's Sierra Fire Safe is the first affordable burglary/fire resistant safe that is *independently laboratory tested and certified* to be fire resistant. Certified tests were conducted in a furnace where temperatures exceeded 1,200° F; the temperature of an average house fire. After exposure to this fire for 32 minutes, Browning's Sierra Fire Safe interior temperatures were substantially below the 350° F temperature at which paper burns. In fact, the average temperature inside the safe was well below 300° F.

Unlike many so-called fire-resistant safes, the *complete* Sierra safe itself has been tested and certified fire resistant — not just the insulating material.

For more facts, write Browning, One Browning Place, Dept. G05, Morgan, Utah 84050-9326. For the Browning dealers near you, call 1-800-333-3288.

America's Number One Crime Fighter.

What would happen to your guns in a 1200° fire?

Nothing, if you buy the right fire safe.

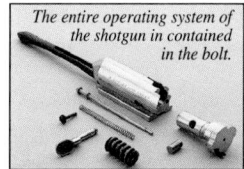
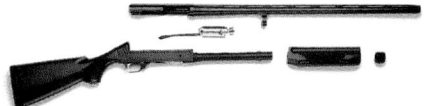

by RAYMOND CARANTA

THE GUNS OF EUROPE

THE EXPRESS RIFLE RETURNS

IN EARLY TIMES, Europe felt a strong attraction for double shotguns because they offered the obvious and simplest solution for providing two fast shots. Early rifles, however, were mostly single shot for the sake of accuracy and economy. Double flintlock rifles were custom-made, mostly for boar hunting in the woods, but, in spite of their compactness, their use was never widespread because they were heavy and expensive.

It is during the percussion period of the 19th century that double rifles became more popular, when hunters were confronted, in the colonies, with ferocious wild animals of huge size, often at close range.

When powerful centerfire metallic cartridges and efficient repeating mechanisms were developed during the last quarter of that century, the use of double rifles was strictly limited to hunting the most dangerous species in jungles. They were much more expensive than competitive bolt-action designs and less accurate beyond 100 yards.

Then, the famous British gunmaker William W. Greener defined the Express rifle in the 1881 edition of his book, *The Shotgun*: "...The Express rifle bears on the principle of a strong load of powder, combined with a light expansive bullet, a long pitch rifled bore and a high muzzle velocity..."

There was no double barrel mentioned and any modern rifle would fit this definition. The turn of the century was the moment of the greatest British Empire glory and that of the Express rifle's triumph in Africa and the Far East.

Soon, however, with the railway, motor cars and trucks, standardization was the master word, ferocious wild animals were reduced to book or movie fictions in most areas, and expensive Express rifles gave way to hundreds of cheaper Mauser bolt-action variations.

Some doubles were still made in Great Britain and Central Europe, but they were on the verge of entering history. Things were still changing and, about twenty years ago, in most European countries, the hunting rifle and shotgun capacity was limited to three shots, while the use of buckshot was prohibited. This led hunters formerly using shotguns for big game to turn toward rifles or, at least, slug shooting and to reconsider the available gun designs.

It was soon demonstrated that bolt-action rifles did not permit *fast* second shots, while three-shot self-loading models were more complicated and harder to maintain than doubles, for the illusive benefit of a rarely used third round. In Central Europe, double rifles slowly returned to fashion, while French, Spanish and Italian companies were not long to design double slug guns in 12-gauge (smooth or rifled) for boar

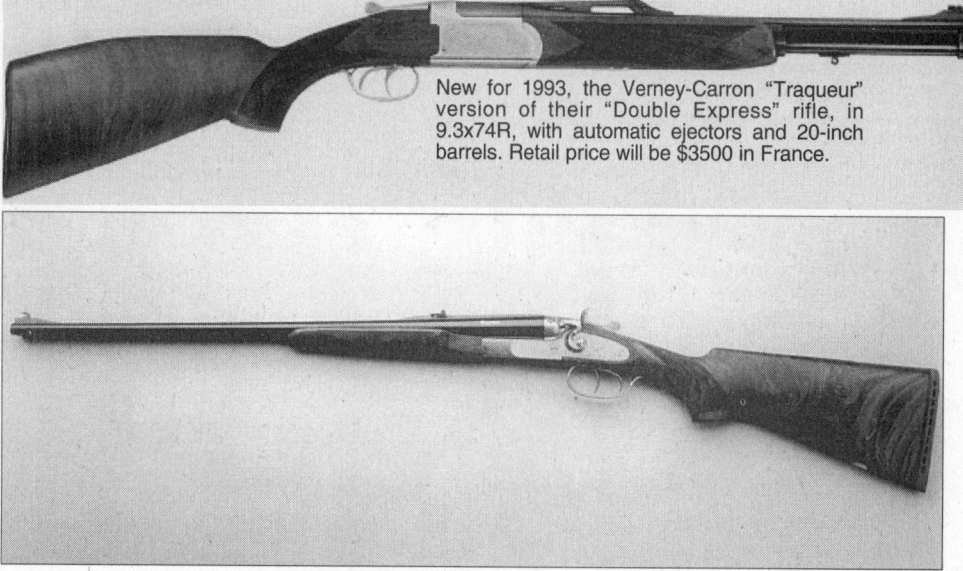

New for 1993, the Verney-Carron "Traqueur" version of their "Double Express" rifle, in 9.3x74R, with automatic ejectors and 20-inch barrels. Retail price will be $3500 in France.

The Bernardelli Minerva Express is a modern external hammer side-by-side available in most modern calibers.

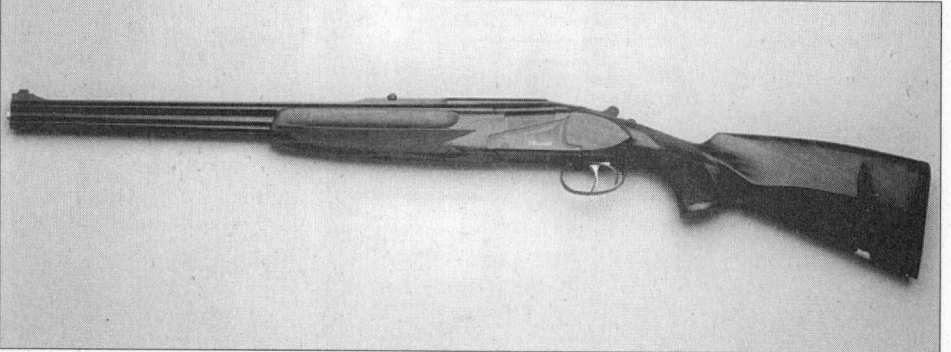

A nice Bernardelli VB 2000 over/under rifle available in 7x65R, 30-06 and 9.3x74R.

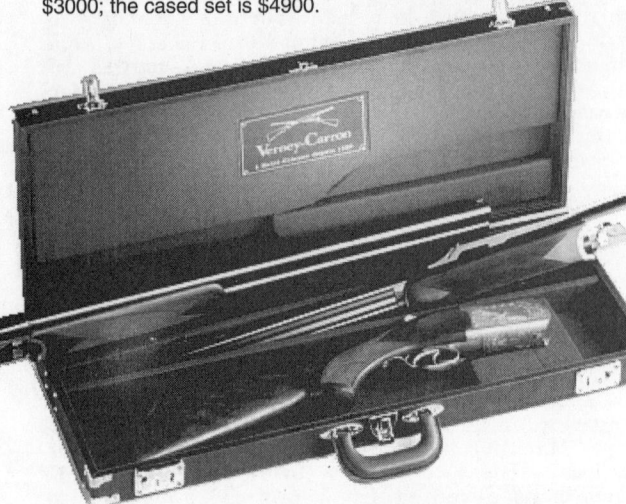

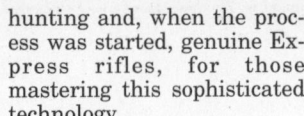

A French Verney-Carron cased Sagittaire Double Express, available in 7x65R, 8x57JRS or 9.3x74R, with spare 20- or 12-gauge barrels. French retail price, rifle alone, is about $3000; the cased set is $4900.

hunting and, when the process was started, genuine Express rifles, for those mastering this sophisticated technology.

Now, 12-gauge slug guns are mostly made as over/under propositions by Beretta, Bernardelli, Chapuis, Nikko, Marocchi, SGS, Verney-Carron, Zanoletti and Antonio Zoli. Most popular side-by-sides of this configuration are those made by Bernardelli,

Renato Gamba, Gaucher, Verney-Carron, Zanoletti and Antonio Zoli, to this writer's knowledge. However, it must be kept in mind that custom-made double "slug guns" can be obtained from most European gunmakers on request at a reasonable increase of price.

With the exception of sidelock models or some special brands, this kind of gun can be purchased in France for

(Right) A cased Chapuis classical side-by-side rifle in 9.3x74R with spare smoothbore barrels.

A custom Italian Zoli over/under with sidelocks and scope—in the grand Teutonic style.

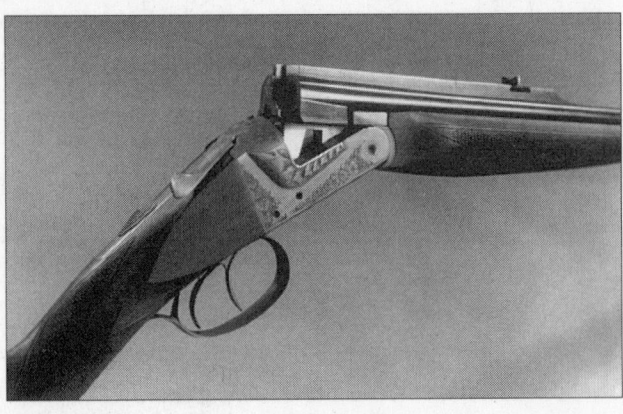

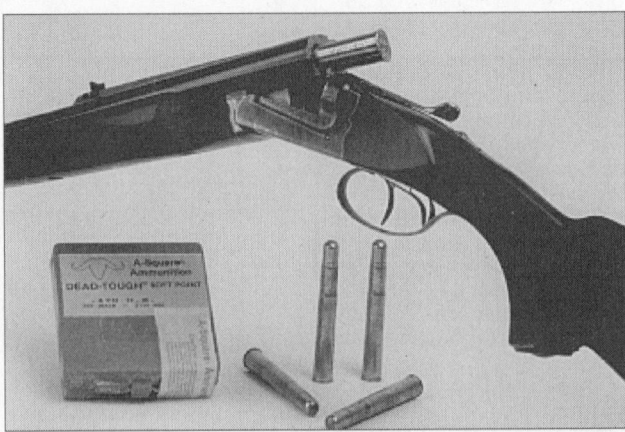

German Heym over/under Model 55B boxlock rifle available in many small to medium calibers from 22 Hornet up to 300 Winchester Magnum. About $8000 in France.

French Gaucher side-by-side Double Express rifle. Retail price in France is slightly above $2500.

Chapuis Brousse boxlock rifle chambered in 470 Nitro Express. Price may vary from $1500 to $4000.

Chapuis Safari Express rifle chambered in 375 Holland & Holland. The French retail price varies from $4000 to $8000.

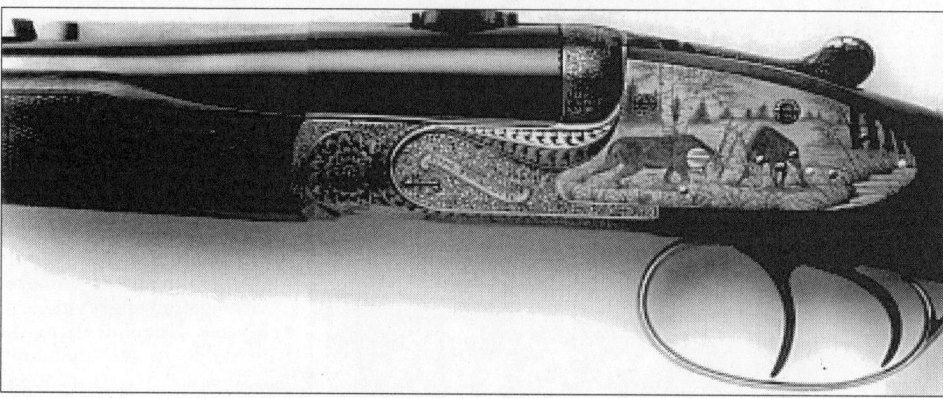

A very classical Belgian Francotte side-by-side rifle of the best quality. In the sidelock configuration, the export price exceeds $27,000. Boxlocks cost about half this price.

A superb Beretta Model 455 EELL Express available in 375 H&H, 458 Winchester Magnum, 470 Nitro Express and 416 Rigby. This removable sidelock side-by-side rifle is a beauty, but it costs more than $50,000 in Europe.

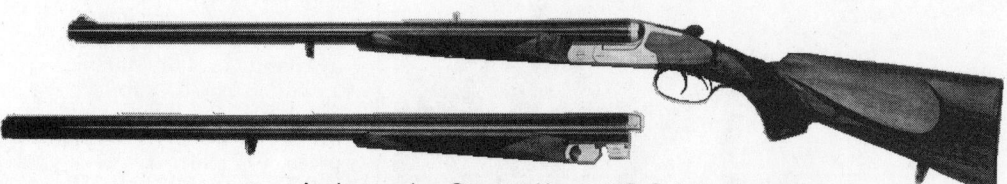

An impressive German Heym 88B Safari side-by-side chambered in big bore calibers, from 375 H&H to 500 Nitro Express, with spare 20-gauge smoothbore barrels. Cost of the rifle, alone: $12,000 in France.

less than $3000. In this connection, it must be stated these are not "Express" rifles according to William W. Greener's definition, as they are designed for conventional 12-gauge slugs and not for high-velocity light bullet loads. Such guns are normally used for hunting boar within about 60 yards, with a maximum practical range of 90 yards, shooting from a given barrel with a tested or targeted load. By the way, when ordering such guns, it is recommended to specify the load and range, and request a test target, factory fired from both barrels.

Besides the outstanding custom British (Holland & Holland, Westley-Richards, etc.) and Belgian (such as Francotte and Lebeau-Courally, for instance) guns, which cost fortunes and command lead times expressed in years, genuine Express rifles are available from reputable gunmakers such as Beretta, Bernardelli, BRNO, Browning, Chapuis, Dumoulin, Ferlach, Fias, Renato Gamba, Gaucher, Heym, Krieghoff, Juch, Kufsteiner, Waffenstube, Merkel, Perazzi, Perrin, Perugini-Visini, Victor Sarasqueta, Sauer, Sidna, Sodia, Tikka, Verney-Carron, Wolf, Zanardini, Angelo Zoli and Antonio Zoli. Of course, most gunmakers producing Express rifles also list "Drillings" and combination rifles along the same designs, within the same price brackets.

Prices are extremely variable, starting, for instance, from about $2000 for a simple Sidna over/under chambered in 7x65R or 9.3x74R (retail price in France) and going up to $12,000 for a Heym Model 88B Safari; lead times must be negotiated in accordance with caliber and finish requirements.

About calibers: Besides the usual American standards, the 7x65R (140- to 173-grain bullet at 2900/2500 fps) and 9.3x74R (270- to 293-grain bullet at 2460/2280 fps) are the most popular, as the first covers most forest and mountain game, and the second the heaviest European animals in battue. Besides these conventional models, special rifles are made on request in the so-called British "African" calibers for special people, but they do not fall in the common hunter's outfit. Among this

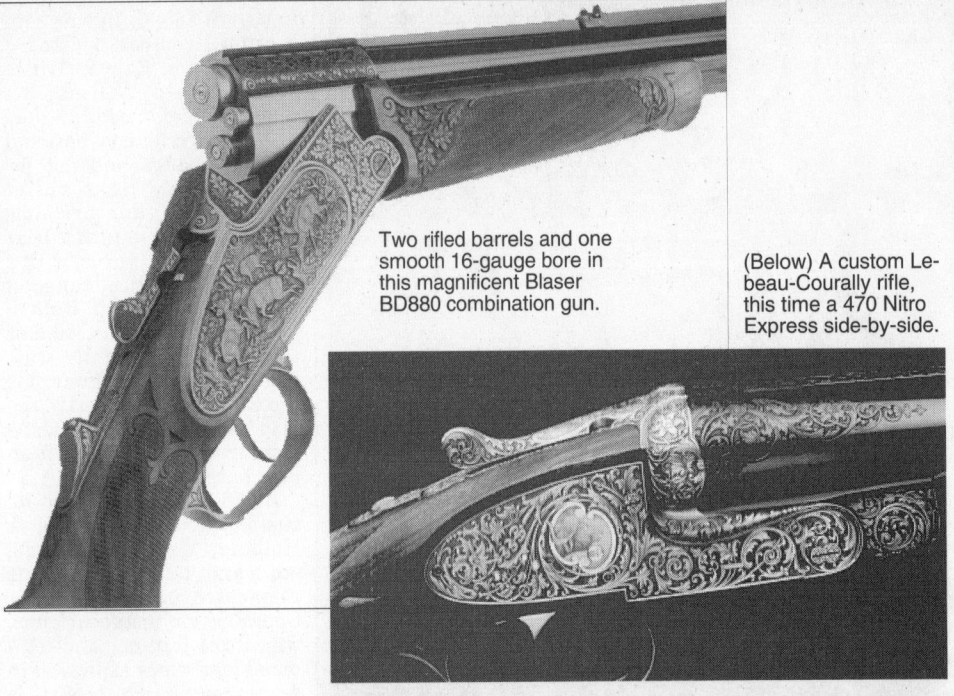

Two rifled barrels and one smooth 16-gauge bore in this magnificent Blaser BD880 combination gun.

(Below) A custom Lebeau-Courally rifle, this time a 470 Nitro Express side-by-side.

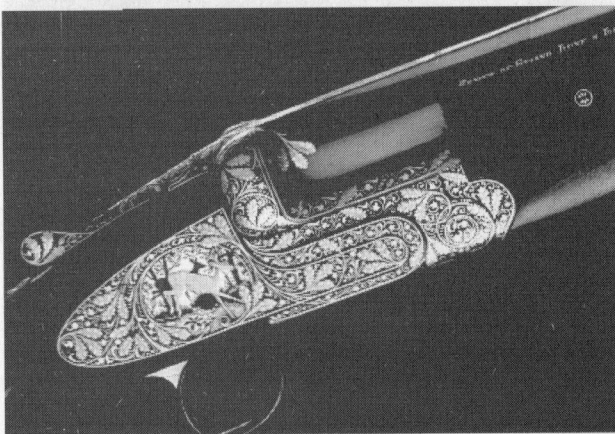

A rich Belgian Lebeau-Courally "three-gold" sidelock over/under in 9.3x74R caliber.

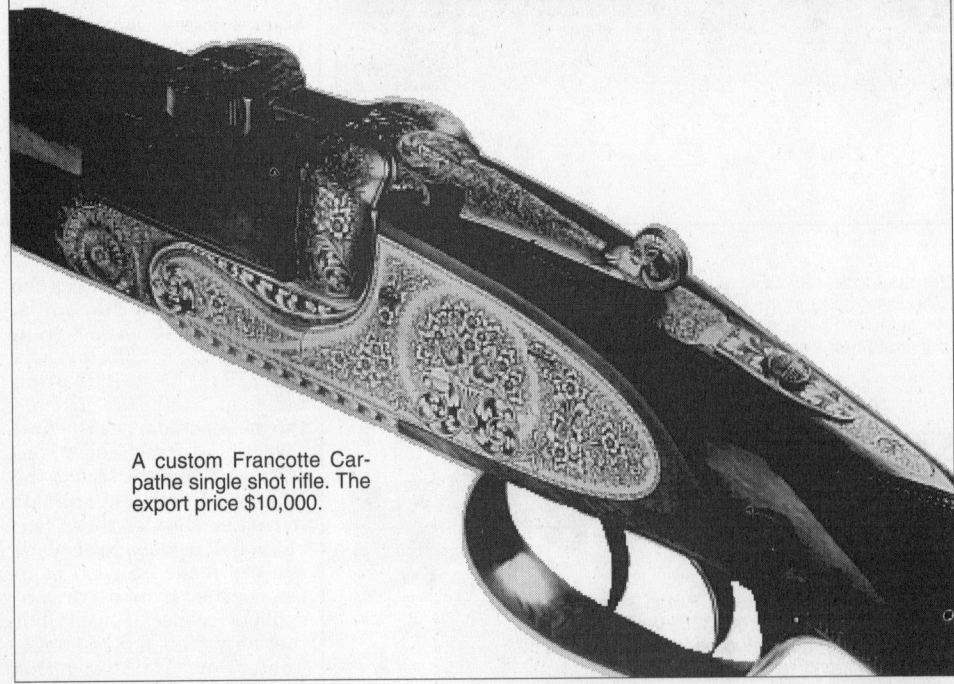

A custom Francotte Carpathe single shot rifle. The export price $10,000.

year's news relating to the Express rifle world in Europe, let us mention the following items:

- **Bernardelli** offers two fine Express rifles: the outside hammer Minerva Express side-by-side available in all classical calibers and the VB 2000 over/under chambered in 9.3x74R, 30-06 and 7x65R.
- **Blaser** has developed a Wolfram tubular device fitted in the stock, reducing, they say, the felt recoil by 20 percent.
- **Chapuis** has released this year, in co-operation with A-Square, a beautiful side-by-side AGEX Express rifle, marketed in the United States and chambered in 375 H&H, 470 Nitro Express, 416 Rigby and, in a new caliber, 416 Chapuis, which duplicates the 416 Rigby ballistics at a lower pressure.
- **Francotte** has the Carpathe single shot mountain rifle with sidelock, available in all popular calibers, with custom engraving.
- **Heym**'s Euro drilling is available in most popular calibers, with reinforced light alloy receiver. There's an Express bolt-action rifle chambered in 375 H&H, 378 Weatherby Magnum, 404 Jeffery, 416 Rigby, 500 Nitro Express, 450 Ackley, 460 Weatherby Magnum and 500 A-Square; and Express 88B, 88BBS and 88F Safari side-by-sides are made, the latter chambered in 375 H&H, 458 Winchester Magnum, 470 Nitro Express and 500 Nitro Express.
- **Lebeau-Courally** makes a custom over/under "three-gold" Express rifle chambered in 9.3x74R. It comes with 22-inch barrels and is decorated with rich gold inlays in three colors. Also a Safari side-by-side Express, with Bohler steel barrels, 26 inches long.
- **Zanardini**'s custom side-by-side 403 Oxford Express rifle chambered in 9.3x74R, with gold and ivory inlays. Standard deluxe model available in 444 Marlin, 7x65R, 6.5x57R, 9.3x74R, 375 H&H, 458 Winchester Magnum, 465 Nitro Express, 577 Nitro Express, 600 Nitro Express and 375 Flanged Nitro Express Magnum. ●

by CLARENCE E. ELLIS

The Rubber Band Gun is hardly a show gun, but it really works.

THE RUBBER BAND GUN

The nickname is meaningless; the performance is outstanding.

Sectioned fired and unfired bullets and loaded rounds flank a loaded 300-grain Hornady FMJ. On the left, the 300-grain Swift recovered from a Cape buffalo and an unfired Swift; on the right, a 270-grain Hornady from a gemsbok and an unfired Hornady.

THE MORNING AIR in the Chobe district of Botswana was still a couple hours away from losing its chill. Wisps of smoke from cigarettes hand-rolled from newspapers issued from the blankets that hid the three Bushman trackers huddled behind the cab of the Land Cruiser. Closer inspection would have revealed three pairs of beady little eyeballs scanning the sandy track we were traversing. The fresh tracks on our tire marks of yesterday, they had just asserted, were a lioness following a buffalo cow. At the first announcement of this detailed analysis of dimples in the sand, given from the back of a pickup traveling at about 20 mph, Professional Hunter Mike Watson called a halt, and we dismounted for a white man's look. It certainly was a lion track and a large hoof print, as anybody standing over

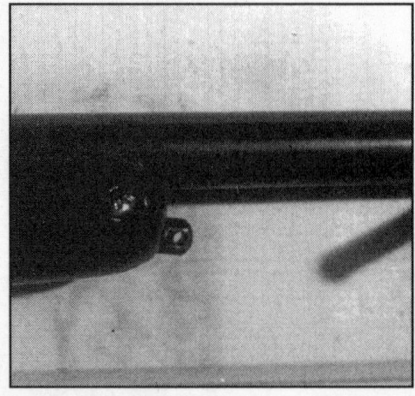

The Rubber Band 375 once sported a gorgeous Claro walnut stock, but common sense came to prevail.

the clearer prints could tell after a few minutes' scrutiny.

I guess everyone else was looking at the tracks because, minutes later, I was the first to spot the three gray forms, barely visible over the brush, as they cruised along on a parallel course about 100 yards to our left. "Eland!" I hissed, and slapped the truck roof.

My mind registered the mats of forehead hair that told me they were bulls, and the gray hides that told they were old bulls, while my hands cranked a round into the chamber of my 375 H&H. All eyes were on the eland in the few seconds it took to stop the truck. Oddly enough, the eland stopped just as fast and stared back. My feet had the temerity to propel me up onto a fuel drum, thus giving me a somewhat clear view of two of the bulls, one of which was under the crosshairs of my 4x Leupold.

"Right one!" Mike hissed.

Naturally, I was on the left one. Under normal circumstances, the eland and our driver would have simultaneously popped their clutches, leaving me draped over the tailgate with multiple broken parts. An ethical purist (or a pure ethicist)

would have dismounted and spent the rest of the day tracking the eland on foot, possibly (but not probably) catching them, but getting no shot due to the dense brush resulting from an ample rainy season.

None of the aforementioned occurred. On the contrary, I shifted the scope and directed a 300-grain Swift to the base of the right bull's throat with nary a thought about morality, ethics or the latest Paris fashions. My brain prefers one thought at a time, and at the moment that idea was to kill eland. Following the short and prompt disappearance of all three bulls amidst much crashing of brush, my brain switched to: "Get down off this drum, you blithering idiot, before you get dumped on your fool head!"

A resounding thud from the bush coincided with the driver popping the clutch and killing the engine. Then, with the dignity befitting my fifty years, I dismounted and strolled over to examine my marksmanship.

The bullet had cut the main arteries over the heart, and the initial headlong rush deposited voluminous quantities of blood over considerable landscape. Mike, observing the bullet hole about an inch from the cen-

This front swivel is located where it never bashes the hand.

ter of the throat, inquired if that's where I intended to shoot him. "No," I responded calmly, "I intended to hit dead center."

Modesty may be becoming, but lacking that, I try for honesty.

That afternoon, after I placed another Swift into the limited amount of visible chest of a zebra nearly hidden by brush 150 yards from us, Mike concluded I actually could shoot. My first shot, the previous day, was not an auspicious start. On that occasion, I placed my Swift

Ellis finds a Wundhammer swell essential for fast, accurate offhand shooting.

into the southeast end of a northeast-bound sable. Given that a 300-grain Swift at a remaining velocity of about 1950 fps has a good chance of resulting in damaged parts, we collected said sable in short order. It was shortly post-zebra that Mike proclaimed the 375 shot like a rubber band. I didn't quite follow the logic, but he seemed happy, so I assumed it was in some way complimentary.

The Rubber Band Gun began life, humbly, as a P-17 Enfield, but in its later years retired from the military, shed its uniform, and became a handsome, highly polished 375 H&H by the addition of a Douglas premium barrel and a stock carved from a gorgeous blank of Claro walnut. In that form, it had accompanied me up the mountains and through the devil's club on Kodiak Island, and on a grand tour of all known varieties of thorn tree in South Africa. It rode a battered scabbard on a horse named Bear Bait through the slide alders above the Toad River in British Columbia. In most ways, it was an entirely satisfactory companion, but one of us was pretty slow about pointing at a lung-shot Kodiak bear when he emerged from the willows.

As a consequence, the Claro walnut stock was in a gun cabinet in Colorado while the rest of us chased lions in Botswana. There are legions of people offended by fiberglass stocks. They will grudgingly give glass stocks their due as being practical, but they won't admit to *liking* them. The 375 wears my first attempt at fitting and finishing a glass stock, and although my artistic sensibilities died some time ago, I won't say it looks good.

On the other hand, after a couple days of tracking lions as they twisted and turned through the brush and led us on a slalom through significant quantities of displeased elephants, I came to appreciate how beautiful that stock really was. Weight, balance and fit were so perfect that even after hours on the trail it jumped to my shoulder in an instant, pointing unerringly at the threatening bush or clump of grass. Ah, the memories that come rushing back every time I fondle the sweaty

A rifle for the dangerous stuff should come rapidly to the shoulder, pointing at your target even when you aren't really prepared. The Rubber Band Gun does.

The 375 at bottom is essentially a weight and balance match of the 30-06 factory job above it. The top rifle shows better fiberglass stock work, Ellis claims.

fingerprints pressed deeply into the fiberglass shell.

After a time, we gave up chasing lions in the Chobe and moved to the Okavango Delta to chase lions. We'd run out of herbivores to work out our lionless frustrations on in the Chobe, but a whole new assortment awaited us in the Delta. Cape buffalo, wildebeeste, tsessebe, warthog, lechwe, impala, reedbuck, kudu and sitatunga were in abundance as were the pussycats. I'd planned to use my 280 a lot here, but only carried it briefly to snuff a gold medal lechwe and a sitatunga better than I and most other hunters deserve to even see. We looked for, or followed, lion tracks most of every day, and toward evening would head back to the island we were camped on and pick out an outstanding specimen of something to stalk. Sometimes I shot, sometimes we walked away. Critters were abundant and we got real picky. We finally caught a pride of lions, and none being worth shooting, we walked away from them, too.

One morning a Cape buffalo briefly considered ramming our dugout canoe, but a 300-grain Swift tucked under his chin diminished his apparent hostility. He gave us a fright shortly after sinking when, after we poled over to him, a shifting of internal gases caused him to bob to the surface with a loud moan. I switched to 270-grain Hornady

spirepoints in the 375 for plains game, taking tsessebe and wildebeeste. John Coleman, who had over twenty years of professional hunting in Africa under his belt when I first hunted that continent with him a few years ago, once commented he'd never seen a wildebeeste dropped in its tracks by a body shot. I took mine at about 100 yards while resting against a tree. High brush prevented a heart shot, so I held on his shoulders just at brush line, which was halfway up (or down, if you prefer). Hornady intersected wildebeeste at about 2400 fps, and departed soon thereafter to prune a few palm fronds. An ample exit hole would have contributed to a good blood trail, but the only movement was 3 feet vertically downward. Tactical nuclear warheads may cause more rapid death, but I doubt it.

Having devastated the Okavangon wildlife, we emplaned for the Kalahari Desert in search of more excitement. It was a short wait. The engine on the old Beaver quit abruptly midway between noplace and noplace else. Following an awkward silence, the embarrassed pilot switched gas tanks, and we proceeded with hardly a loss of speed or altitude, although one of us passengers did spill a little beer.

The Kalahari had more vegetation than I'd expect from a desert,

and the trees couldn't be blamed on the recent rainy season. It did have the expected complement of sand. It behooves the hunter to keep his spiffy Safari-Grade Thunderstick in a soft case while motorized in this environment. Even a grain or two of sand in the right spot can cause some annoying stoppages to hunters equipped with non-military rifle actions. My P-17, conversely, had cellophane tape over the muzzle and a large rubber band (cut from an inner tube) over the scope lenses as its sole protection during days of searching for leopard tracks. When called upon to go bang, it did. But then, who ever saw a little sand on a rubber band ruin its snap?

A solid sitting position with a tight sling can bring out the excellent long-range accuracy of the 375 H&H cartridge in a good rifle.

Having a chance to observe a small variety of shiny new 375s from both sides of the Atlantic, I see they have agreed on the general form—heavy varminter. Makes sense to me. Elephant is about as heavy as a varmint can get. Either they have deduced (correctly, no doubt) that the average bloke bound for Africa needs all the weight he can carry to tolerate the recoil, should he actually shoot the gun himself to sight-in, or, agreeing with the current dictum that the absolute minimum needed to kill a Cape buffalo is a 400-grain 40-caliber bullet, have balanced their 375s like silhouette rifles—perfect for deliberate offhand shots at standing non-dangerous game because they obviously wouldn't be used on any of the nasties. Given my preference for that configuration when I built the 375, I can't figure out why I didn't put on a heavier barrel. The Red Gods must watch over some fools sometimes. Maybe they somehow sensed that I was going to be one of the few who actually used the 375.

The balance point on my P-17 is at the front guard screw, and that massive action coupled with a fiberglass stock and relatively light barrel truly puts the weight between the hands, just like the grouse hunters want. We didn't flush any grouse, but after an exciting chase lasting about six hours, we did flush a tom leopard. Although I am at best half-fast, I snapped a shot at him before he had a chance to start jinking from side to side. The bullet cut the skin on the top of his skull and his shoulders. Slowed him down a bunch, but didn't trouble him for long. Old Doc Ellis' magic cure-all painkiller took care of that.

In theory, if you believe all you read, a fast-handling rifle doesn't hold steady for a deliberate, precise, long shot. That, in my view, is why you learn to use a sling. At a good 250 yards, I gave a hartebeeste the Hornady-in-the-middle-of-the-shoulder treatment. He expired just as fast as the wildebeeste at half the distance. My shooting position bore a resemblance to prone and kneeling both; I've learned to use available objects for rests every time possible, and the sling for further stability. Although 250 yards is not a particularly long shot, I did have to fit the bullet through the brush and among the other seven hartebeeste who were dancing around, ready to bolt.

The current fashion rage is to place the front sling swivel on a barrel band on the hard kickers. Having loosely held the forearm of my 375 when it wore its heavy wood stock, I can understand why. The swivel goes about halfway through the hand and smarts a bit. I don't see anything wrong with barrel-band swivels on short-range stopping rifles that will usually be used with the sling removed, 458s, for instance. On a long-range rifle like the 375 (or the current crop of 416s), the barrel-band swivel prevents you from using the sling to enhance your chances of connecting on those 200-plus-yard shots because the point of impact will shift on most such rifles when you go from a tight sling to no sling. This shift can easily exceed a foot at 100 yards. The simple solution, which I copied from the Steyr-Mannlicher Professional model with the nylon stock, is to place the swivel in the end of the forend. It works.

The pistol grip on my 375 has a Wundhammer swell which I personally find essential, for good offhand shooting. It positions my hand the same all the time, and because I point the rifle with my right hand (the left is only support), it ensures a consistent hold. On the hard kickers, it also allows the right hand to take a share of the recoil.

Other hunters passing through camp were attracted to the Rubber Band Gun by its unloveliness. It would look right in place in Alaska, but Africa is where a fancy custom rifle *can* tenderly be withdrawn from a padded gun case, gently carried on a variety of stalks, and see much use but few dings. The Rubber Band Gun was never cased for three weeks. The black paint became chipped and gouged, the recoil pad was crumbling and held intact by duct tape, the stock had stains of mud and blood. Polite folks, those other hunters. Nobody sneered. Looked askance at, yes. Mike would invariably note the looks and proclaim how he loved that gun...shot like a rubber band.

Immediate understanding never dawned. Nobody asked what he meant by that—just slightly shook their heads like the poor chap had been out in the sun too long. Other PHs generally looked awhile, finally picked it up and handled it awhile, pointed it a few times, studied it longer, put it down and looked some more. Draw your own conclusions.

Three weeks ended too soon, and I departed, never having asked Mike just exactly what "shoots like a rubber band" really means. Didn't really matter by then. The 375 did everything I asked it to, so a derogatory comment would have not been accepted as valid, and a compliment would have been gilding the lily. It did everything I demanded, and did it well. I can't ask for more. That's not true, I can *ask* for a lot more, but I doubt the rifle will buy me another such hunt in Africa. ●

This is not a recommended shooting position with a hard-kicking rifle, but the Rubber Band Gun barely broke the skin once, under similar conditions.

The author has never been known to pass a good rest in the field, regardless of the

With a 25-inch barrel and nearly 9 pounds of heft, the Rubber Band Gun is not a typical mountain rifle, which is small comfort to, thus far, a Kodiak bear and some mule deer.

by DON ZUTZ

SHOTGUN REVIEW

THERE MAY BE some revamped or upgraded rifles around with a few new cartridge chamberings. Some oddball magnification combos have been worked out for variable-powered scope sights. The Lord knows we have more 9mm semi-automatic pistol designs than a nervous gink can shake the proverbial stick at after a pot of hot coffee.

But for all that, 1993 seems to be an even better year for shotgunners. Without too much hoopla, the industry has been busy filling gaps, developing new models, and improving on established pieces. None of this is superfluous. Most serves a definite purpose. The guns can be all-rounders or niche items, economy models or big-ticket stuff; there are old names and new, big bores and small, target types and game guns. Whatever. But unless one studies all the magazines and catalogs, and unless he's had a chance to mosey down the aisles of the SHOT Show in Houston's Astrodomain, he's probably well behind the news curve on this full range of the scattergun spectrum.

American Arms, Inc.

Take this well-established importer, for example. Bowing to customer demand for some short-barreled turkey guns in the heavy gauges at entry-level prices, American

Winchester's name can again appear on the neat little Model 42 410 pumpgun, but the company would prefer it to be USRAC/Winchester. Still a neat smallbore.

Arms has introduced a pair of new break actions for this specialty. The TS/OU 12 is a 24-inch-barreled over/under chambered for the 3½-inch 12-gauge magnum, while the WT/OU is a 26-inch-barreled 10-gauge magnum. Both have non-reflective finishes, sling swivels, checkered grips, single selective triggers and choke tubes. There is also a 28-inch-barreled version of the 12-gauge known as the WS/OU 12 which is suggested for waterfowling with the 3½-inch 12-gauge shotshell.

Benelli

Everyone was wondering when it would happen, and now it has—Benelli's Montefeltro autoloader is coming out in 20-gauge. Based on the rotary bolt system, which means it's recoil-operated rather than gas-urged, this smallbore variant of the in-

creasingly popular Super 90 scales but 5¾ pounds with a 26-inch, ventilated rib barrel. The stock drop is adjustable, and it carries like a wand.

Also new from Benelli is a Sporting Special version of the 12-gauge M1 Super 90 with just an 18½-inch barrel for turkey hunting. This gun bears the black synthetic stock/forend assembly, a dull metal finish, and what Benelli calls the "ghost ring" sights to accurately center the tight, Full-choked patterns used on gobblers. Moreover, the Super Black Eagle—still the only semi-auto to handle the 3½-inch 12-gauge round—is now available with the black synthetic stock and forend plus matte metal finish and 24-inch, choke-tubed barrel. A shim kit lets the hunter adjust comb drop to his individual needs. I have

The Benelli Super Black Eagle remains the only semi-auto chambered for the 3½-inch 12-gauge magnum, only now the gun can be had with a black synthetic stock/forearm treatment.

always enjoyed the way these Benelli autoloaders point with the ease of a responsive over/under.

Beretta

Beretta has quietly let the Model A303 slip out of sight while bringing on line the spe-

cialized Skeet, trap and Deluxe grades of the newer Model A390ST. The A390ST Super Trap features adjustable, interchangeable comb heights with length-of-pull adjustments as well. The ventilated rib is elevated for target acquisition and visibility.

In the lower price ranges, Beretta has introduced a new autoloader known as the Vittoria. This has a Benelli Montefeltro action, and it is quite legal, etc., because Beretta owns a huge chunk of Benelli. The Vittoria will handle all 12-gauge ammo in the 2¾- and 3-inch lengths and potencies, just as will the Benelli Super 90. However, the Vittoria has a plain-Jane finish without checkering, but with sling swivels, giving it a European flair and workhorse appearance.

In over/unders, Beretta has introduced a so-called Continental Course Sporting Clays gun, emphasizing a semi-rise rib and adjustable length-of-pull. Also new are the Model 686 Onyx Hunter Sport and Model 686 Hunter Sport O/Us, which are offered at entry-level pricing. Both have generous 12.5mm ribs and the stereotyped, rounded recoil pad heel for quick mounting. The guns can be used for both Sporting Clays and hunting via the Mobilchoke features.

Browning

Browning's line of shotguns for 1993 is a kind of blow-out of all sorts of ideas, some solid and some racy. Leading the pack is the BAS-10, a 10-gauge autoloader. If it feels and functions like an overgrown copy of the now-obsolete Winchester Super-X Model 1, it's because that is what it happens to be. Strip both, and you'll see the similarity.

The 10-bore is getting more than its share of attention these days, thanks to goose hunters who use buckets of bulky steel pellets and turkey hunters who ram 2¼-ounce charges of lead shot. To meet a demand for an upgraded gun in this gauge, Browning is introducing a Pigeon Grade BPS-10 with selected walnut, a high-gloss finish and some gold work on the receiver.

In a more dubious vein, however, some target-grade Brownings like the BT-99 will be splashed with bright red on an otherwise black stock and forend. Also new on the Browning rack is the B325 Sporting Clays gun. A similar gun, although not necessarily the same, has been winning heavily in British and European Sporting Clays. It has the favored European combo of a full pistol grip with a schnabel forend and a broad, flat rib. The exact overseas version of the B325, which is made for Browning by Miroku of Japan, is being handled by British Sporting Arms (914/677-8303) of Millbrook, NY, and Bell's Legendary Country Wear (516/679-1158) of Bellmore, NY. These overseas samples have responsive, lightweight barrels as opposed to the heavy-walled, over-bored barrels used on Browning Sporting Clays guns sold stateside.

Harrington & Richardson 1871, Inc.

This great old name in Yankee gunmaking seems to have re-established itself with an expanding line of break-action singles under both the H&R 1871 and New England Firearms brand names. New for 1993 is a junior-sized, 20-gauge turkey model with full-coverage camouflage. Also at hand is a synthetic-stocked survival gun with a thumbhole stock and carrying strap. Both 10-gauge magnum and 3½-inch 12-gauge magnum singles are available.

Ithaca

Ithaca Gun continues to struggle on a long comeback trail. The Model 87 Deerslayer II has some rifle-like qualities built into it for improved slug accuracy. The barrel is fully rifled and is integrated with the receiver for stability. The barrel is free-floated to reduce vibrations. The 20-gauge, field-grade smoothbore can still be had with the English-style straight grip.

only the Kemen models are thousands of dollars cheaper. The Kemen O/Us can be had in many different configurations with various rib widths and styles. Likewise, Kemen will make barrels that fit the Perazzi (except MX-3) for less than a Perazzi set. Kemen is distributed stateside by Derek Partridge, Box 22, Alpha Terrace, Glendale, CA 91208-2137.

Magtech

A relatively new name in stateside shotgunning, the Magtech slide-action shotgun is made in Brazil by Companhia Brasileira de Cartuchos (CBC). This is a utilitarian pump sans frills, except for a ventilated rib and a beavertail forend on the field model. Closely resembling the Remington Model 870, the Magtech pump's main claim to fame is a low price, the retail figure barely topping

Marocchi

Within their price range, the Marocchi over/unders are underrated bird and target guns. The Avanza has been around for a few seasons, and it is a fine lightweight stack-barrel for birds at just 6½ to 6¾ pounds in 12-gauge! That's 20-gauge weight in a 12-bore field piece, and in my experience the recoil is entirely manageable afield.

A 1993 addition to the Marocchi line is the Conquista, an over/under Sporting Clays gun that'll work out beautifully on upland game as well. It has the European schnabel forend, full pistol grip for control, and an adjustable trigger pull weight. The monoblock is jeweled, bores are honed, and the body has a soft patina appearance for elegance. Barrels of 28, 30, and 32 inches are available, and five choke tubes come along for the ride.

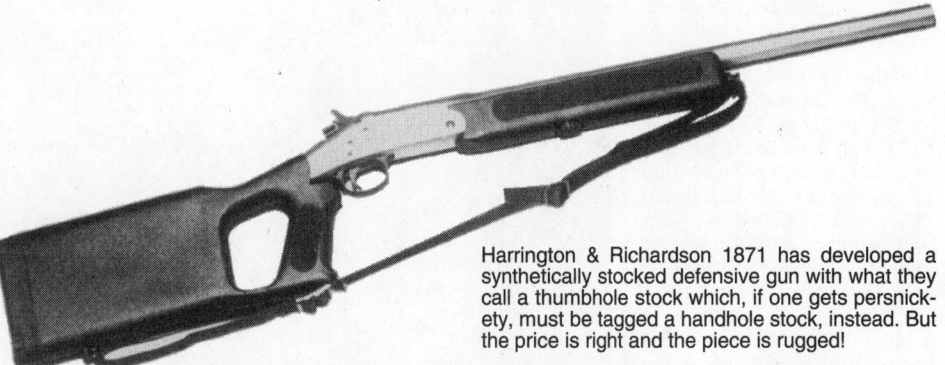

Harrington & Richardson 1871 has developed a synthetically stocked defensive gun with what they call a thumbhole stock which, if one gets persnickety, must be tagged a handhole stock, instead. But the price is right and the piece is rugged!

Kemen

Kemen over/unders are Iberian versions of the famed Italian over/under target guns, such as the Perazzi—

two hundred clams. The stock/forearm assemblies of all grades are Brazilian hardwood, and a slug model is made with a 24-inch cylinder bore.

Merkel

The well-known GSI, Inc., formerly known as Guns South, has really gotten into this outstanding German

One of the outstanding sporting clays guns is the Browning B325 which, with lightweight barrel, has been finding its way to these shores via Canada.

Beretta's Model A390ST has now replaced the former Model A303 in all grades. The writer took this one from the dove fields of Colombia, S.A., to the goose marshes of Wisconsin, then south again to the mallard holes of Stuttgart, Arkansas—with perfect performances all the way.

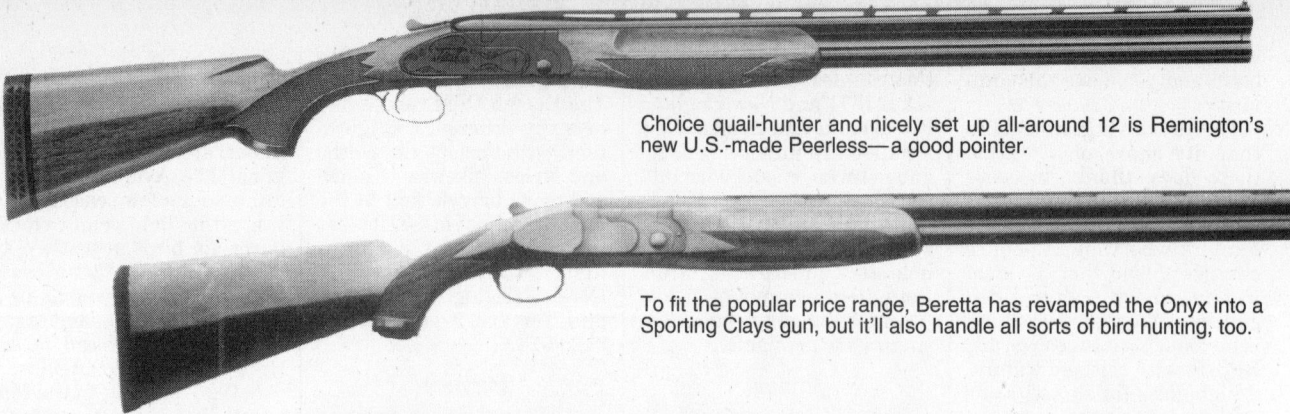

Choice quail-hunter and nicely set up all-around 12 is Remington's new U.S.-made Peerless—a good pointer.

To fit the popular price range, Beretta has revamped the Onyx into a Sporting Clays gun, but it'll also handle all sorts of bird hunting, too.

line. Both the O/Us and SxSs are being imported with a wide selection always on hand. Some changes have been made. GSI has convinced Merkel to open the bore diameters for Western shotshells, and a Sporting Clays side-by-side is scheduled for later in 1993. Merkel fanciers might wish to shop quickly, however, as the Westernization of former East German workers will cause prices to climb steadily during the next several years.

Mossberg

Although announced last year, the Mossberg Model 9200 autoloader is only now coming off production lines. It is a versatile, gas-operated 12-gauge that can handle all $2^3/_4$- and 3-inch loads without any need for adjustments or barrel changing. Different models are available, with or without camouflage. There is a slug version with a rifled barrel and cantilever scope mount called the Trophy Slugster. Two different camouflage patterns—Mossy Oak and OFM Marsh—bedeck the turkey and waterfowl guns, respectively. Meanwhile, the Mossberg pumpgun line remains pretty much the same except for the inclusion of an upgraded model of the 835 Ulti-Mag which now sports walnut instead of stained hardwood and has a high-gloss finish. Looks good and is a step up for Mossberg.

Parker Reproductions

Although out of production for several seasons, there is still a good inventory of Parker Reproductions, which may say something about the velocity with which finely finished doubles sell in these United States nowadays. However, something fresh has been added. The promised sets of 16-gauge barrels

The Merkel guns are back—in both over/under and side-by-side styles—and in solid hands at GSI, Inc. The author likes 'em in his hands, too! They are among the very best-pointing over/unders for field work, if not *the* best!

are being fitted to 500 20-gauge frames by Krieghoff to form a trim 16/20 combo. These will be made in D and A-1 Special models.

What some buffs perhaps don't know is that custom engraving is available at the company's shop for the A-1 Special. This is one of the big-ticket items mentioned at the top of this review, but all these Parker Reproductions are among the most beautifully finished doubles around today.

Powell Doubles

One of the great names in British gunmaking is that of William Powell. Finely made and known as "the Purdeys of Birmingham," Powell game guns are once again available through an American distributor: Bell's Legendary Country Wear (22 Circle Dr., Bellmore, NY 11710). Along with the great Powell sidelocks, there is the Powell Heritage boxlock which, like the Westley Richards droplock, has detachable locks that can be removed via the floorplate. Bell's handles some overseas Sporting Clays guns, such as the Browning B325 with lightweight barrels.

Remington

Perhaps I'm prejudiced because I swatted so many quail with it on the Kansas prairie with but a couple misses, but Remington's new Peerless over/under is an extraordinarily pointable stackbarrel for a production-grade piece that'll probably sell below $1000. With a 28-inch barrel assembly, it is responsive yet disciplined. And the fit is akin to that of the great ol' Model 1100 autoloader, which lined up for just about everybody. In fact, the 12-gauge Peerless feels to me like the 20-gauge M1100. At about $7^1/_2$ pounds with 28-inch tubes, it carries easily and has an attractive appearance, what with its sideplates bearing light scroll and the same dog images as the former Model 3200. They're all American-made, and the chaps at Ilion, New York, ought to sell a million of 'em.

last year are slow in showing up. In the target grades, however, SKB offers the most economical entrance into the trap combo market, and the guns feature lengthened forcing cones, slight over-bores, and long, competition-type choke tubes.

boldy capped, and a forend with a diagonally cut tip. No more is that the only profile. Today's Weatherby O/Us—the Orion and Athena—can also be had in the Classic Field grade, which finds the stock with more shotgunny lines. The grips are semi-pis-

only for 2¾-inch loads, is compact. The barrel is 26 inches with three Winchokes provided.

Now that the paper shuffling is over and both Browning and Winchester/USRAC are owned by the same French outfit, GIAT, the roof which

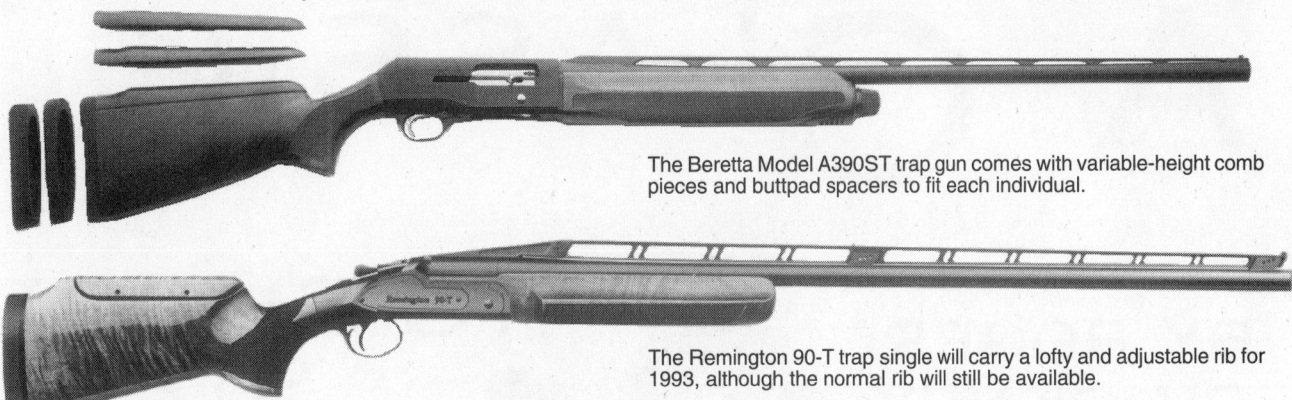

The Beretta Model A390ST trap gun comes with variable-height comb pieces and buttpad spacers to fit each individual.

The Remington 90-T trap single will carry a lofty and adjustable rib for 1993, although the normal rib will still be available.

Otherwise, the Remington shotgun line has been bolstered by a turkey variation of the SP-10 autoloader, it being decked out in camo and a stumpy 23-inch, choke-tubed barrel. Some models of the 11-87 and 870 are also being given the full-length camouflage treatment in the Special Purpose (SP) mode, and there will be fully rifled barrels for the 11-87 and 870 before the snow flies. The Special Purpose deer and waterfowl guns will be outfitted with black synthetic stock/forend assemblies.

For trap shooters, the

Tar-Hunt

It is a moot question as to whether the Tar-Hunt 12-gauge slug gun fits a shotgun column. We may, in fact, have to start a whole new category for slug stuff: Rifled barrels which lob gobs of lead and solid copper are hardly smoothbore scatterguns! But the Tar-Hunt custom-made, bolt-actioned, 12-gauge slug outfit has a tremendous reputation for accuracy. Made with the same features as a benchrest rifle, it minimizes vibrations and plunks shotgun slugs and sabots into

tols with a round knob, the finish is an oil treatment instead of gloss, and the forearm is slender. In short, it's a European flavoring rather than the former Weatherby/California treatment. The guns look good and point nicely. And Weatherby's custom shop will now build a custom stackbarrel to your specs, including an English straight grip, if that's your pleasure.

Winchester/USRAC

Each year, Winchester/USRAC changes the etched or rolled engraving on a Model 1300 pump or 1400 auto-

fits over both businesses allows Winchester/USRAC to participate in the Winchester reproduction parade that Browning began years ago. Thus, the Winchester/USRAC catalog now contains promise of a revived Model 12 20-gauge pump gun. The run will be 5000 guns, Grade I (4000) and Grade IV (1000). A special issue gun will be made for Ducks Unlimited chapters with waterfowl engraving on a silvery receiver.

Finally, back in the Winchester line is an over/under which is being brought from Italy under the style of Model 1001 (pronounced Ten-0-One), to keep from confusing it with the original Model 101. The M1001 is in field and Sporting Clays persuasions, and the sporter feels pretty good with a 30-inch set of tubes. Both grades have back-

This is Remington's 870 SPS-Deer—synthetic stock, rifled barrel, the right sights.

CVC's Classic Sporter looks like, but is not, a 101 and is made in Connecticut in this style and as a waterfowler.

Remington 90-T will be made with a high ventilated rib that is adjustable for point-of-impact patterning.

SKB

SKB keeps turning out some extremely attractive over/unders. A 28-gauge Sporting Clays O/U is at hand, as are some custom engraved guns by Angelo Bee. Folks will have to inquire about the Bee pieces directly. The side-by-sides that were introduced so promisingly

neat little clusters at 100 yards. It's actually a 12-gauge rifle.

Weatherby

When the late Roy Weatherby first introduced over/unders to complement his line of sporting arms, the shotguns invariably bore the lines and features of his Mark V Magnum rifle, namely, whiteline spacers, a full pistol grip

loader and comes up with a gun-of-the-year. This time it's two of 'em: The Model 1300 became the National Wild Turkey Federation GOTY when the company put a gray/black laminated stock/-forearm assembly on a 22-inch-barreled version; the Model 1400 popped forth as the Quail Unlimited piece, emphasis on the compact receiver which, dimensioned

bored barrels, long forcing cones, and the new WinPlus choke tubes to match the wider bores. Can you get them mixed up with the original WinChoke tubes? Hardly, as the WinPlus units are considerably longer for a lengthier choke taper. The Sporting Clays model has a broad 10mm rib and silver nitrated receiver, while the field grade is nicely blued. ●

BRINGING BACK A CLASSIC...

TO SHOOT STEEL SHOT

BY ROGER PINCKNEY

DUCK HUNTING IS a sport heavy-laden with tradition. There is the pre-dawn ritual of black coffee, sweet rolls, old friends, anxious dogs, boats and decoys. There are father and son reunions on opening day, ponds and sloughs shot over by the same family for 50 years, retriever bloodlines fine-tuned through a dozen canine generations. These traditions have been pursued by many with an almost religious intensity. How else can one explain the devotion of a million-plus waterfowlers who take to the marshes, enduring discomfort and the dangers of drowning and hypothermia for a smidgen of meat that ultimately costs upward of $40 per pound?

These traditions were sprung somewhat severely in the 1980s when the U.S. Fish and Wildlife Service mandated the use of steel shot for hunting waterfowl. Studies made as early as 1916, it was claimed, had shown spent lead shot were winding up in the gizzards of feeding ducks and geese and were causing heavy metal poisoning. Critics pointed out that steel made great guns, automobiles and baby carriages, but damned poor projectiles and predicted that many birds would be lost to crippling instead. Thousands of hunters continued to shoot lead and many were fined by state and federal wardens.

The controversy over lead versus steel continues and will likely do so for the foreseeable future as manufacturers experiment with other nontoxic alternatives. The bottom line is that while Grandpa's decoys and call may be cherished artifacts and used yearly, his shotgun most likely is not. The old guns, no matter how slick and sound, will not stand up to the pounding of steel shot. Most have been reverently laid to rest and replaced by machine-finished wonders with barrels as hard as ball bearings.

Like many other Americans who came of age in the middle years of the century, I grew up shooting a Winchester Model 12. The Model 12 is the only pump shotgun thus far elevated to classic status by American hunters. It was developed by Thomas C. Johnson and first offered to the public in 20-gauge in 1912. Other gauges followed, from 12 to 28. It soon got a reputation for

being fast-pointing and utterly reliable. Winchester dubbed it "the perfect repeater" and sold around two million of them.

Then, in the early 1960s, their marketing experts warned the American public would not tolerate a pump shotgun that cost over $100. By 1964, the Model 12 cost a whole $9 more than that. It was discontinued, except for a few custom trap and Skeet guns and replaced by a model that was "more compatible to modern machining techniques," meaning that it contained aluminum and stamped steel parts. Three years later, what few Model 12s dealers still had in stock were selling for twice the intended price. I found mine on the used gun rack in a little country store and was happy to give $150 for it.

The Winchester and I soon became fast friends. I shot greenheads in the Carolina ricefields, canvasbacks over

It's a real one all right—marked for the 3-inch chamber and all.

Iowa corn, geese on the Dakota prairie. But when I was faced with the cruel reality of putting steel shot though it, I sadly hung it on the wall and bought one of those new, rough-hewn, dull-finished 12-gauge pumps, with a 3-inch chamber and interchangeable chokes.

In fairness, I should say that I liked the new gun well enough. Once I unlearned all the basic scattergun principles I had grown up with, I did tolerably well. But one afternoon during a furious late-season bluebill shoot, I heard a metallic tinkle in the bottom of the boat and was instantly reduced to having a single shot repeater. I banged away one shot at a time, and finally managed to get my limit.

Picking up the decoys, I tried to remember how long I had been using them. Most were purchased, well-used, from a neighbor whose age and declining health forced him to give up the sport. A few were survivors of

the half-dozen my father gave me for my 16th birthday. Then I pondered my boat, old enough to perhaps have been a lifeboat on the Ark, but watertight nevertheless. My little motor's serial number dated it from 1968, but it always started on the third pull. My only new piece of equipment was my gun. My broken gun.

I thought it over on the way back to shore. I considered bringing my Model 12 back from retirement and modifying it to handle steel. I had put maybe ten boxes of shells through it for each of the last 20 years, but it was still clean and tight. But then it had only a 2³/₄-inch chamber, a definite handicap when shooting steel. And then there was the collector's value. The last really nice original Model 12 I had seen for sale bore a price tag of nearly $500. Once I started whittling on it, its value would be cut in half.

Before I could further consider this dubious enterprise, I got a late afternoon visit from an old hunting buddy. He had spent the day at a farm auction and had come back with an old pump shotgun. When he got home and tried to fire it, he found it would not extract the fired shells from the chamber. I have a reputation as a gun tinkerer, so he asked me if I thought I could fix it. If it was worth the trouble, that is. He flipped the seat of his pickup forward and hauled out a tattered gun case. He unzipped it and handed me a Winchester Model 12 Heavy Duck Gun.

Now I consider myself a quiet man, a comtemplative man, a man not easily given up to high emotion. But when I held that shotgun, released the belt and worked the butter smooth slide, I could hear my pulse pounding in my ears. I asked how much he gave for it. He said maybe too much if it wouldn't work. I pressed him further and found he had bid it up to $220. I offered to give him what he paid for it and to stand the costs of repairs myself. We shook on it before either had the chance to change his mind.

It wasn't much to look at. The bluing was just about gone, the buttstock cracked, the recoil pad turned to mush. And long ago some miscreant had cut the barrel and installed an adjustable choke, known derisively in these parts as a "wonder winder." The failure to extract proved no great problem. Years before, after purchasing my first Model 12, I had garnered a selection of spare parts. I had a spare firing pin, a bolt release, an ejector, extractor and various springs and screws. I had packed them into a little plastic box in anticipation of repairs I was sure would come. After 20 years, the box remained unopened. After a couple of hours and much head scratching, I was able to get the gun to function as new. The other repairs and modifications promised to involve considerable expense, so before I proceeded further, I decided to consult more knowledgeable authorities.

It seemed logical to first contact Winchester and ask about long-term effects of running steel through a Model 12. But the Winchester of yore, the producer of the gun that won the West, the coveted pre-war Model 70, and the perfect repeater is no more. Firearms facilities had been purchased by a consortium known as "The U.S. Repeating Arms Corp." Ammunition is being made by Olin in East Alton, Illinois, and somebody, somewhere, owned the rights to the expensive stackbarrels made in Japan. But who wound up with liability, repair and customer relations? I tried an 800 number for Olin and lucked out. After being on hold for a relatively short time, I was able to talk to somebody who cared.

A week later, I got a reply from Olin on genuine red and orange Winchester stationery. They told me my Heavy Duck Gun was one of a mere 19,000 that were made between 1936 and 1964. My gun's serial number told them it left the factory just after World War II, though component parts probably dated from before 1941. They cautioned against using steel shot larger than BBs or BBBs and predicted I'd get the best results from an "Improved-Modified" choke.

Next, I investigated my options for re-choking. A nationally known gunsmithing firm offered "steel compatible" replacement barrels for about a week's wages. A firm in a nearby city offered to custom-fit a barrel off the newer Model 1200 for a little less. Other options included sweating in a stainless choke tube or, in the odd chance that the old Winchester's barrel walls were thick enough, machining in threads for a screw-in choke system.

I finally decided to take the gun to Mike Partain of Fergus Falls, Minnesota. Fergus Falls is in a county that boasts 1000 lakes and is the unrivaled goose capital of the region. It is a town where folks take their shotguns seriously and Partain is as serious as his clientele. He is one of

Here's how the duck gun looked—good to great on the inside, clean to worn outside.

Many old Model 12s just can't handle steel shot as-is. This nickel-steel barrel dusted the shooter's toes with F-shot.

(Below) Reaming gently by hand for the new screw-in chokes—with a thousandth to spare.

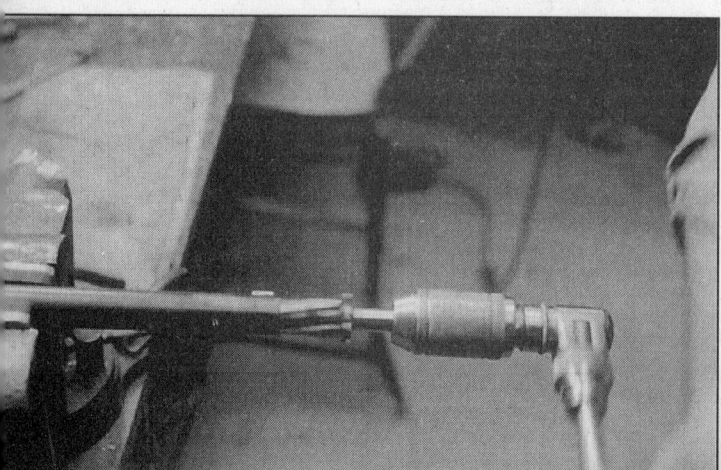

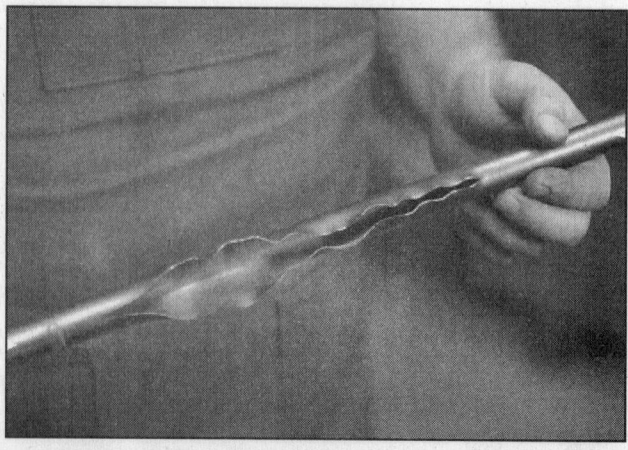

the few gunsmiths who lavish the same attention to detail on scatterguns as rifles. He speaks knowledgeably of choke restrictions, forcing cone angles and barrel wall thickness. One evening I had the privilege of looking over his shoulder as he worked on my Heavy Duck Gun.

He began by stripping the barrel off and holding it securely in a padded vise. He gently heated the adjustable choke to loosen threads bonded by forty years of rust and powder residue, unscrewed it and cut off the threaded portion of the barrel. I put a tape to it and discovered we had a generous 28 inches left to play with. Partain ran a snap gauge around the inside diameter, passed a micrometer over the outside and announced we could install screw-in chokes because we had one single thousandth of an inch to spare.

Next came reaming and tapping, a time-consuming job since with every few revolutions of reamer and tap, the tool had to be removed, washed clean of chips and reinserted in the hole. When he was done, we were able to install an Improved Cylinder choke tube with just finger pressure.

Partain also suggested lengthening the forcing cone by cutting it down to about a 3-degree angle. This would make an easier passage for the unforgiving steel as it was funneled down from chamber to bore size. He cut and then carefully honed the new cone, polishing out all marks left by the reamer. I left him with instructions to repair the stock, to replace the old oil-soaked recoil pad and to blue the gun, taking special care to leave all barrel stampings, numbers and proofmarks crisp and clear.

It seemed ages until he called me. Empires rose and fell. Glaciers came and went, as did the goose opener and the duck opener a week later. The second week into our 30-day short duck season, I got a call from Mike Partain. He apologized and told me he had been working to the wee hours trying to get all his waterfowling cutomers into their blinds on time. He had 10-gauge autos that wouldn't feed, pumps that wouldn't extract, a ventilated rib that flapped in the breeze and a Belgian Browning A-5 that somebody had run over with a four-wheel-drive. But the Model 12 was finally ready, choked, blued and padded. The bill was just over $300.

He had it laid out in a display case when I arrived. If my pulse pounded

Now it's a pair—the old faithful below, the new faithful above—of 12s.

the first time I beheld it, this time it nearly took my breath away. Partain picked it up and went over the finer points of the job for me. He showed me how he had avoided blurring even the finest number or letter in the patent information stamped upon the barrel. He pointed with pride to the hand-crafted front ramp and the 1950s vintage white bead affixed to it. The choke tube projected about an inch and a half beyond the end of the barrel. This was the only visable concession to modernity. He cautioned that the extended choke should always be used with steel, since it put most of the stress outside the relatively thin-walled barrel. He included another tube that screwed up flush with the muzzle that could be used if the situation permitted the use of lead shot. I took it from him and worked the action. It was as slick and tight as any Model 12 I have ever seen.

I was in the blind with it at daybreak the following morning. I had chosen a sheltered bay on a local lake. A hard freeze that night had put the first skim of ice upon the prairie potholes and woodland ponds. I reasoned this would drive puddle ducks to deeper water and there would also be a chance of picking up some early arriving divers. Being a true believer in Murphy's Law, I had lashed the Model 12 to

the boat seat during the deep water crossing. My hunting partner and I put out two small sets of decoys, one of mallards, the other of divers. We pulled up into the cattails, spread out our camo netting and waited.

We did not have to wait long. The ducks came sailing in at first light. Woodies and teal headed right for the blocks; mallards were a little more standoffish, but came close enough to get shot at, too. A flock of ring-necked ducks buzzed the decoys and two of them were added to our limit. We had our three birds each in less than half an hour.

The Heavy Duck Gun performed flawlessly, as I knew it would. There was something very familiar in the way it came to my shoulder, and my success out where the feathers were reflected it. I shot better than I had in years.

We picked up our ducks and headed home. On the way back across the lake, I assessed my situation. I had just shot what I hoped would be the first of many limits with a classic shotgun. Not just any classic, mind you, but the "perfect repeater." It was a gun that would last me the rest of my days, providing nobody stole it and I didn't drop it overboard. And it had cost me just a tad more than most currently produced pump shotguns. I was one happy man.

Reviving Old Reliable...

...shooting steel shot through an original Parker

by JOHN ROSS

The Steel Shot Special from Parker Reproductions is a side-by-side gunner's dream on geese.

BEYOND THE TREES at the end of the close-cropped cornfield, we heard geese, crooning in the late January afternoon wind.

"Get down," guide Tom Cornicelli said. "They're comin'." He called and flagged, and the birds answered. "Take the ones on the right," he told me. "Now!"

Up through the bundled cornstalks, I pushed the old Parker, swinging left to right to pick up the bird, and then back with it as it hit the gas and began to climb up away from the stuffed decoys on the ground. I don't remember shooting, but the bird somersaulted and crashed to the ground, stone cold dead. A dose of Winchester's #1 shot, steel of course, had dropped that Canada like it had been hit with a pole axe. The Parker'd worked its magic once more, and I became convinced that it has a new life.

Shooting steel shot in a classic American scattergun is taboo. Steel shot will bulge the barrels, perhaps causing tubes to separate from ribs. It'll score the bores, causing barrels to burst. The pressure is more than the soft steel in those old guns can withstand. So runs conventional wisdom.

Yet, every day, a gunsmith somewhere opens up the chokes on an American double so a hunter can carry his old friend out to the blind, once in a while, for a couple of ducks and a memory.

Nostalgia is part of hunting tradition, and there's no more important name in American shotgunning tradition than Parker. It took me nearly twenty years of trading shotguns before a weathered VH grade settled into my battery.

Barrels patinaed grey, receiver silver with no trace of original case colors, stock sans finish in some spots—this Parker looks as homely as Jake, Jim Peterson's venerable, old setter whose coat has weathered poorly from a dozen unkind seasons.

But like Jake, the Parker is solid and staunch. The pigeon shooter from Reading, who'd bought it new in 1906, shot it hard but kept it clean. Its bores are still pristine. It locks up crisply with the lever a little right of center. And, Lord, how that gun fits. When I take the Parker afield, I feel a kinship with the old man who owned it first.

When steel shot became mandatory, I thought the Parker would be relegated to the gun rack. Steel shot and old side-by-sides don't mix, everyone told me. And so the Parker sat while I considered my options.

For a season, I hunted with a loaned Steel Special made by Parker

(Above) Ross ran 500 rounds of steel shot through his Parker's tubes to see if bore dimensions would enlarge. There was no change.

(Left) Chapman's practiced eye finds no flaw in the nearly ninety-year-old bores.

Reproductions. What a beautiful gun. It sprang to my shoulder and swung on birds just like we'd grown up together. Its 28-inch tubes were choked Improved Cylinder and Modified, and it delivered good patterns in the 50 to 60 percent range with various fodder at 50 yards. The shotgun was pure Parker; all the parts will interchange with originals. But the stock, of highly figured walnut, had a little less drop, catering to the tastes of today's shooters, according to Jack Skeuse, president of Reagent Chemical and Research, which in partnership with Winchester, reincarnated the Parker gun.

Had the sweepstakes called my number, I'd have bought that gun in an instant, but the $3500 or so price tag was a little salty for my wallet. It's hard to let a work of art like the Parker Reproduction get muddy and scratched, as a shotgun must, in a goose pit.

The easiest option would have been to buy a set of barrels from Parker Reproductions and fit them to the old Parker's frame. At $1000 or so, this would have been a viable solution. But my VH frame is a #2, and Parker Reproduction's 12-gauge barrels are designed only for the #1½ frame. According to LeFever & Sons in Lee Center, New York, barrels designed for a #1½ frame cannot be used on a #2 action.

Briley, in Houston, could create a monobloc from my existing barrels and then add heavier tubes specially designed for steel shot. The price of this varies, of course, but one can expect to spend something in the neighborhood of $1200 or more. That, too, seems a bit rich for my blood.

Then I talked to Paul Chapman,

Cautions About Converting Old Doubles To Use Steel Shot

1. I don't recommend it.
2. Barrels need to be of first quality steel, Fox's Chromeox or Krupp Fluid Steel, for example.
3. The action should be solid and tight.
4. Bores should not be too tight. Some 12-gauge doubles have bore diameters of .725-inch. The Parker's tubes mike .730-inch.
5. Chokes should not be too tight either. About .020-inch constriction is the most that's required for steel shot.
6. Barrel wall thickness at the muzzle should be no thinner than .020-inch, .030-inch is better.
7. Follow the recommendations of the manufacturer of the gun, if the company is still in business. Browning, for example, would not recommend shooting steel through a Superposed.

Paul Chapman

This nice Canada went head over heels for a load of #1s, the biggest shot Ross will fire through his original Parker.

head gunsmith at Griffin & Howe in Bernardsville, New Jersey.

"Anybody ever convert an old Parker to shoot steel shot?"

"We don't recommend it," he said.

"What if a customer were really insistent?"

It could be done, he told me, less than eager to undertake the project.

There is more than a little risk in shooting steel shot through old American doubles. Steel shot lacks the malleability and lubricity of lead. A charge of steel shot racing down the bore will cause a shotgun barrel to expand and contract, slightly. The thicker the barrel, the less the expansion. Where the barrels thin at the choke, expansion can become permanent, a bulge.

Also, a steel pellet trapped outside the wad can score the bore, creating a zone of weakness that may eventually lead to a split barrel.

In short, as experts have written for the past two decades, shooting steel in old double guns isn't highly recommended. Experts agree that shooting steel in an old double is likely to ruin it.

But I was curious. What if the Parker's waterfowling were limited to birds over decoys where shots are seldom more than 25 to 30 yards?

For geese, there would be no need for pellets larger than #1s, an ample number of which can be held in a 2³/₄-inch, 1¹/₄-ounce load.

If I restricted the Parker's steel diet to loads no heavier than that, could I extend the life of the shotgun another generation?

Maybe.

What would happen if the forcing cones were lengthened, reducing pressure in the initial constriction of the shot column to bore diameter?

What if, rather than opening up the chokes from Full and Modified to Modified and Improved Cylinder, only the Full barrel was reamed to Modified and the Modified tube left as is? That way there'd still be plenty of steel in the critical choke area, and the tendency for a permanent bulge would be reduced.

In discussing the project with Chapman, he said that several G&H clients have reworked Parkers and Winchester 21s to handle steel. But he didn't recommend it. All clients who have such work done sign waivers absolving G&H from liability should the gun fail as a result of shooting steel shot.

I pressed him about lengthening the chambers on the Parker from 2³/₄ inches to 3 inches, but there he drew

the line. No way, he said. The pressure might be more than the action could take.

"Are you sure you want to shoot steel through this gun," he asked.

My logic (or illogic, you be the judge) ran this way. A couple of years ago, I'd broken the Parker's stock at its wrist and repaired it. While the seam is hidden in the checkering, it can be seen under careful inspection. Thus, the collector's value of the Parker is reduced.

I wanted to know how much steel shot one could shoot through the Parker before the tubes showed signs of bulging or incipient failure. Whether the gun survived or failed ought to provide an informative article.

And finally, I really wanted to keep hunting waterfowl with the shotgun that fits me best.

My Parker is ideally suited for conversion to handle steel shot. It is built on the #2 frame, which was the standard for all of Parker's 12-gauge guns prior to 1917. After that, the #1¹/₂ frame was used for most 12-bores. The older frame is stronger.

The barrels on my VH grade are 30 inches long. Bore diameter is .730- or .732-inch, depending on

Patterns were dense enough to portend success on New Jersey's big Canadas.

The author finds no joy in, but no way to avoid, patterning the Parker off the bench.

encourages me to limit my shots with this ammo in the Parker to 25 to 35 yards.

Both bores produced similar patterns as far as density was concerned. However, the tube opened up by Griffin & Howe tended to center the point of aim better than the original Modified tube that shoots a little high and to the right.

Once the gun was patterned, my plan was to run 1000 rounds through it to see if and when it would fail. At Paradise Valley range, close to my home at the Delaware Water Gap, I showed up to shoot Skeet with #1 steel loads for geese. Range officer Howard Franco and gunsmith George Geiger thought I was nuts.

Hell, I'm lousy at hitting clay birds with loads of #8s or #9s. Trying to bust those spinning platters with #1s was a real exercise in frustration; there are only about 125 pellets in a 1$1/4$-ounce charge. But off and on over three weeks, I shot twenty rounds of Skeet with the Parker and steel shot.

After each 100 shells, we measured the diameter of the chokes to see if any expansion had occurred. We stopped the formal tests at 500 rounds. There was no bulge or enlargement in either barrel. Nor were there signs of scoring by errant pellets trapped between wad and bore.

Later that winter, I put another hundred rounds of various steel shot through the Parker with no deterioration in bore dimensions. Rather than continue the tests out to the original goal of 1000 rounds, I called a halt to testing and began hunting.

Six hundred rounds of steel shot is a lot of shells. Even in my neck of the woods, where limits are more generous than in other places in the East, the average gunner hunting geese over decoys shoots eight or ten shells before limiting out.

If I take the Parker out a couple of times a year, which is my intent, I'll shoot less than a box of shells through it each season. Thus, the 600 rounds of steel I've shot through the Parker equals twenty-four years of hunting.

At that rate, according to the folks at Griffin & Howe, the gun will last through my lifetime and that of my kids.

From now on out, the Parker will be hunted with steel a couple of times each season, just enough to refresh my memories of the time when Americans made great doubles and the side-by-side was *sine qua non* in a blind.

whose mike you read. The barrel thickness at the muzzle is about .025-inch, stout enough to withstand flexing under a charge of steel shot.

And the shotgun is tight. There's no lateral or horizontal play.

We did the deed. Paul opened up the Full barrel to .710-inch, matching precisely the constriction of the Modified tube. He tightened up the action by fitting a new bolt plate. That was it. The price for the work was less than $200.

I hied myself to the range,

benched the gun and patterned each barrel with 1$1/4$-ounce loads of #1 steel shot for geese, and #4s for ducks. An average of five rounds per bore showed 42 percent of the #1 shot, and 46 percent of the #4 shot, in a 30-inch circle at 50 yards.

My usual procedure is to pattern shotguns at the maximum effective range. That way I know I have a gauge of performance in a worst-case scenario, such as that mistaken shot at a fleeing bird. Knowing that patterns get pretty thin at 50 yards

Parker Repro's Steel Shot Special can digest a variety of shot sizes with no risk to the bore.

CUSTOM GUNS

▲▼ DENNIS ERHARDT

Single square bridge Mauser in 7x57 offers metal-work by Rayburn and Billingsley, engraving by Koevenig and English walnut stock from Angelo & Little.

▲▼ BRIAN R. SKEOCH

Turkish Mauser 7x57 stocked in French walnut in pure classic profile and checkered 24 l.p.i.

▲▼ CHARLES ENLOW

Sako in 25-06 with Douglas barrel, London Guns add-ons, special metalwork and stocked in California English with big-gun style.

▼ JERRY FISHER

Mauser in 270 has lots of Burgess metalwork, but all final finish in wood and metal by the maker.

▼ JAMES C. TUCKER

Voere in 30-06 has English walnut stock, skeleton cap and buttplate; other metalwork by Heilman. (Waller photo)

▼ R.H. DEVEREAUX

Lapped and trued Sako magnum is maker's penultimate piece in 338, with California English checkered 22 l.p.i.

▼ MAURICE OTTMAR

Hagn action has Donnely barrel in 38-55. Sights by Axtell; engraving by Kehr; stock is Turkish walnut. (Hughes photo)

▼ FRED WELLS

This is a 510 Wells big gun with integral milled rib—all done in house.

▼ STEVEN DODD HUGHES

Winchester High-Wall in 30-40 offers a Melani octagonal barrel with integral fittings, and 19th-century style. (Hughes photo)

▲▼ CHARLES ENLOW

Ruger is a 270, weighing 9 pounds; stock is black walnut. London Guns and Biesen fittings.

▼ JOHN M. BOLTIN

Sako in 7mm-08 with tang safety, accessories from Talley and McFarlin. Elaborate checkering is 26 l.p.i.

▲ COREY O. HUEBNER

Winchester High-Wall is now a 30-40, stocked in seedling English walnut. Engraved by Jerome Glimm.

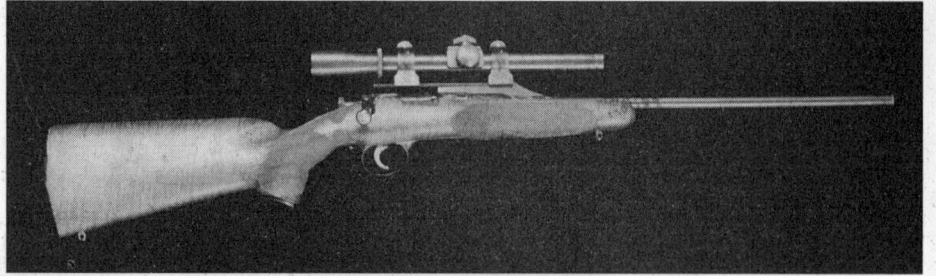

◀▲ JOHN M. BOLTIN

Elaborate Chipmunk 22 has Snapp and McFarlin metal-work and gold inlays, and engraving by Lisa Tomalin. Checkering is 26 l.p.i.

ART OF THE ENGRAVER

▼ HEIDEMARIE HIPTMAYER

▼ BILLY BURGESS

▼ GEOFFROY GOURNET

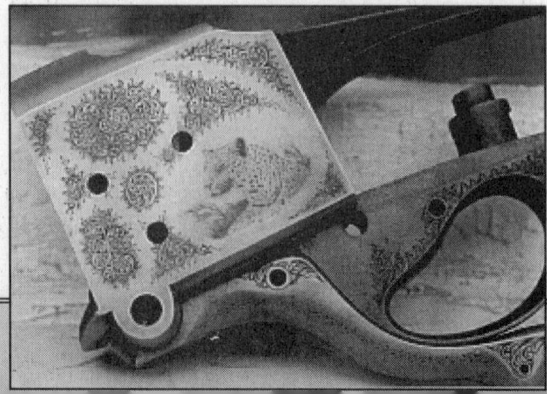

▲ DAVE VORHES

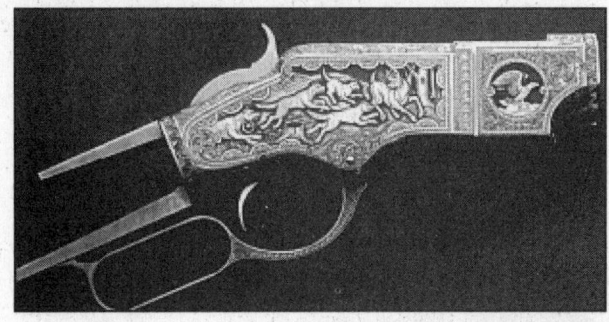
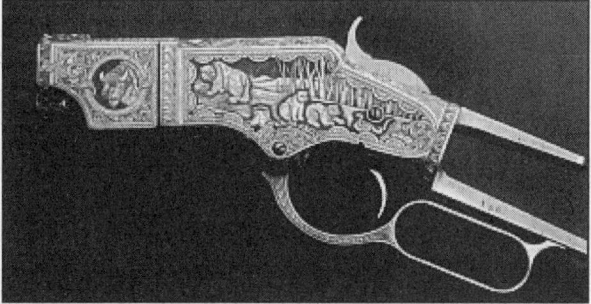

▲ TONY TUSCANO

▲ RACHEL WELLS

◄ GEOFFROY
GOURNET

▲ LISA TOMALIN

▲ CLAUS WILLIG

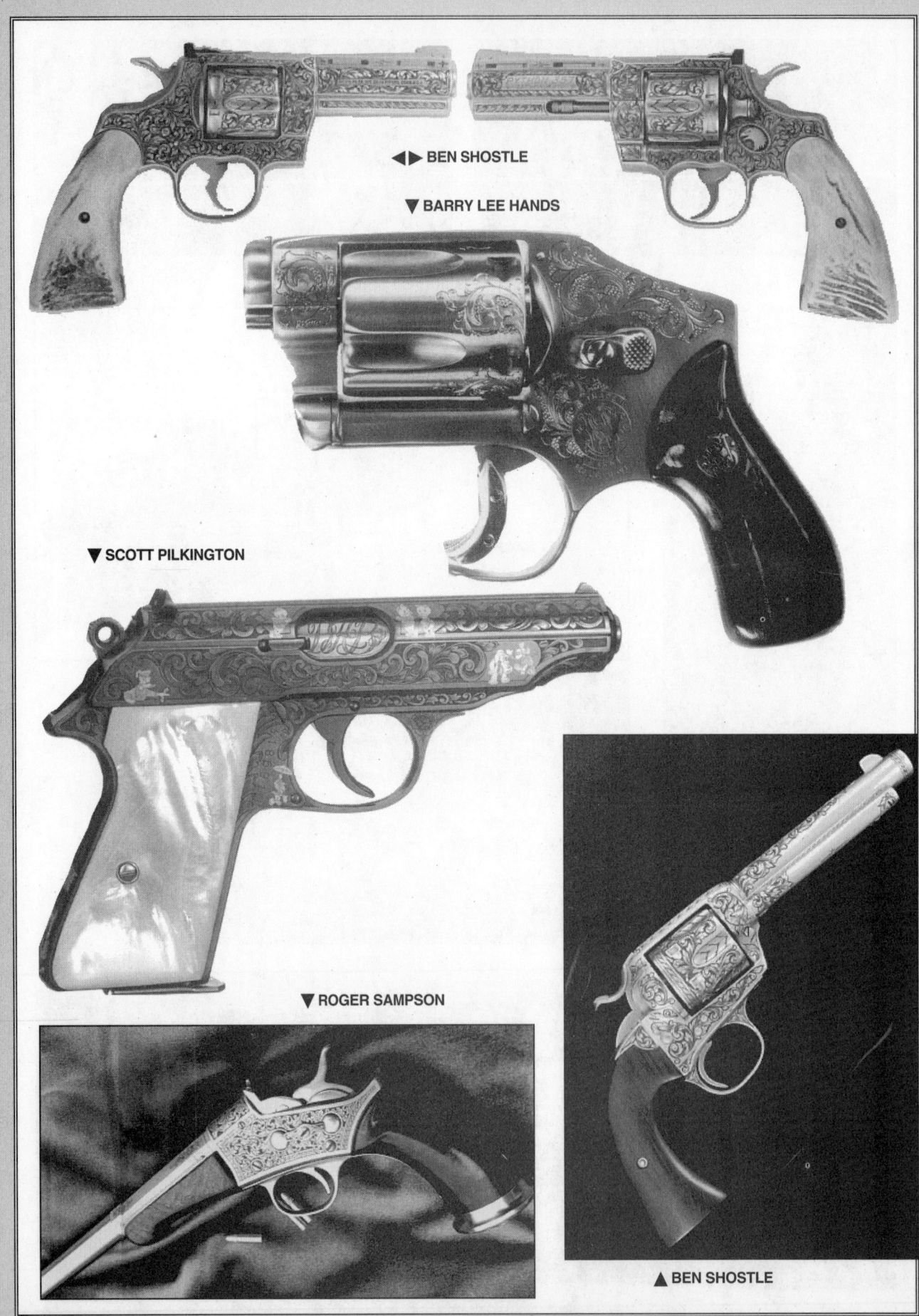

◀▶ BEN SHOSTLE

▼ BARRY LEE HANDS

▼ SCOTT PILKINGTON

▼ ROGER SAMPSON

▲ BEN SHOSTLE

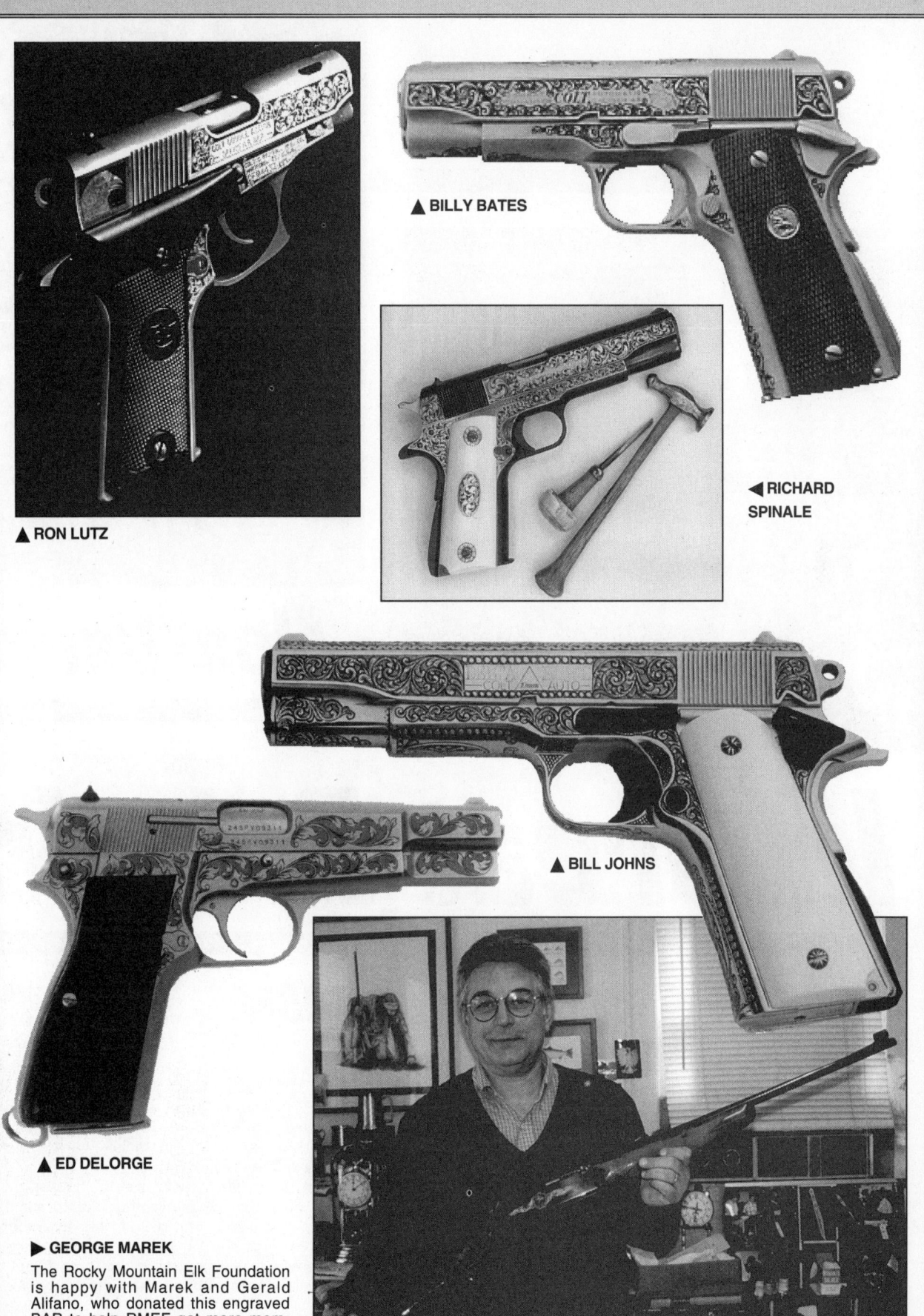

▲ RON LUTZ

▲ BILLY BATES

◀ RICHARD SPINALE

▲ BILL JOHNS

▲ ED DELORGE

▶ GEORGE MAREK

The Rocky Mountain Elk Foundation is happy with Marek and Gerald Alifano, who donated this engraved BAR to help RMEF get more members.

Gun Users

& Non-Users

In Great Britain

by SIDNEY DU BROFF

(Above left) British policemen guarding the Israeli Embassy now are armed.

(Above right) Author Du Broff on a good day despite the efforts of the anti-hunters.

THE SCHOOLMISTRESS dashed from her school and out into the street when she saw the Bobby approach. "Officer, officer," she cried in a panic. "We've just had the most terrible thing happen."

"Calm yourself, Miss," the man in blue said, immediately taking charge of the situation. "Tell me what it's about."

"We're having our Christmas party, and Father Christmas (Santa Claus) hasn't turned up."

"That is a problem, Miss," the policeman said, obvious concern in his voice.

"The children will be so disappointed. I don't know what to do."

"Never mind, Miss. Not to worry"

On his two-way radio, standard equipment for every cop in Britain, the Bobby contacted his station and explained the situation. "Is it all right if I fill in for an hour or so?" the cop asked.

"Sure, go right ahead," came the reply. "We can't let those kids down, now can we? Good luck, and remember to say "Ho, ho, ho..."

And he did, too. Santa's white cotton beard and mustache kept falling off to

reveal the policeman's own black mustache. But apparently the kids didn't mind, or at least were prepared to tolerate an otherwise jolly St. Nick with two mustaches, each of a different color.

This is a true story. This is the way British policemen like to see themselves, and this is the way the British public likes to see their police. The vast majority of the force do not carry guns, nor do they wish to do so. They view themselves as social workers, pleased and proud to stand in when Santa is unavoidably detained.

Britain is a highly decentralized nation. Consequently, things like guns will come under the regulations as interpreted in the local fiefdom by whomever holds power and whomever feels most strongly one way or the other. The police in one area will regard sporting arms as a quite normal part of life, with possession posing threat to neither life, limb nor the local gas station. Whereas in the county next door, anybody with a gun, or who wants to own a gun, is considered a potential stick-up man, if not actually a blood-thirsty murderer.

Britain is also a small country, with a lot of people in it. England, with an area of 6000 square miles—less than the state of Illinois—has about fifty million people in it, stepping on each other's toes. You can be sure that whatever one group wants, there's going to be another group opposed to them having it. The reality of today's Britain has many sides to it, many segments, something like an orange, but, unlike the orange and its segments, they have little in common and, for the most part, do not even like each other.

The police themselves are divided, with the ones who want to play social worker in opposition to those who understand the need to be adequately armed and trained in the use of those arms. It is the sportsman who is getting squeezed in between.

Let's look at the gun users, the gun owners, and the gun haters—here, at least, making the distinction between those who use them for sport, for anti-social purposes, and for the protection of our society. And let's look at the police, who don't always know when guns should and shouldn't be used.

Not long ago, a policeman, one of three in a patrol car (none of whom was armed), strode over to a vehicle whose occupants appeared suspicious and was shot. The second officer rushing over to investigate, also was shot; while the third was run over first with the front wheels, then with the back, and afterward shot—to be sure he was dead.

Britons were shocked, but there was a lot more to come. A policeman, tackling a man in the process of robbing a liquor store, was shot and paralyzed from the chest down, and lingered in that condition for about seven years before he died.

A young female police officer, Yvonne Fletcher, was shot by a Libyan, from inside the Libyan Embassy in London, and laid in a heap on the ground. She had been engaged to a fellow officer. That engagement had been abruptly canceled, and the whole nation mourned for the young woman. They laid flowers on the ground where she had fallen, and the hearts of the nation went out to the young man who was her fiance.

The list goes on and on and on.

Arms were provided, still in very limited numbers, to supplement the relatively few to which the police had previous access.

As a result, a man by the name of Stephen Waldorf, a film editor, was shot in his car by police. They thought he was somebody else. He was expected to die from his wounds, but miraculously survived.

On another occasion, armed police entered a home in search of a suspect. John Stonehouse, age 5, whose father was being sought, laid in bed with the covers pulled over his head, obscuring him from view. A policeman set his loaded, and cocked, revolver down; the gun went off and killed the boy.

Not long after, police broke into the home of a West Indian woman in south London, in search of her son, who wasn't there, and managed to shoot her by mistake. The son had been before the courts on fourteen separate occasions, charged with forty-two offenses, and was now being sought, suspected of firing at police with a sawed-off shotgun.

The woman's death resulted in another Brixton riot, which had been waiting to happen. The jewelry stores in the area were looted, as well as other stores with contents considered worthwhile. Houses were burned; cars set alight. Two women were raped, one of them by a gang, and there were fifty-eight burglaries. The police were, by and large, impotent, ever cognizant of the charge of racial bias and the use of undue force.

Clearly there was something wrong; this semi-armed police force was an obvious menace.

Of the 120,000 police in Britain, 12,000 volunteers have been trained in the use of firearms (another report claims the number is 14,000), with 4000 of those in London. The question is, "Have they had enough training?" The answer is, "No."

Before the police shot Stephen Waldorf, officers were given four days of arms instruction. After they shot him, this was increased to two weeks, with refresher courses required every three months. They use 38 Smith & Wesson revolvers and 9mm Browning autos. They do a fairly vigorous simulator course, and if they pass with a 70 percent grade, they are issued the Pink Card, which entitles them to carry a gun. This does not mean they are going to; it only means they are *allowed* to—if, and when, such a need should arise.

It was too bad that Police Constable Roger Brereton hadn't tried for a Pink Card, and that he wasn't armed, the day he confronted Michael Ryan, whom he might have shot before Ryan shot him. Adequately armed, Officer Brereton might have ended the slaughter which Ryan had begun earlier, and which later continued.

That day, in and around the village of Hungerford, where he lived (about sixty miles west of London), Michael Ryan, using mainly an AK-47—as a semi-automatic—killed fourteen people, including his own mother. He wounded sixteen others, missed some more at whom he had shot, and ultimately holed up in the school he had once attended. Obviously not a very well-adjusted person, Ryan continued his spree for about seven hours, during which time it was reported a police marksman had Ryan in his sights for a full minute, but did not shoot, unwilling, he said, to have the killer's death on his conscience. Ultimately, Michael Ryan, age 27, and a devoted son (according to those who knew him), took his own life.

This incident has brought down the most devastating avalanche of demands for even tighter gun controls, currently the most stringent in Western Europe, directed at those who shoot for sport. How Ryan got hold of, and was allowed to keep, an AK-47 and most of the other arms reported to be in his arsenal, requires answers to a number of questions, directed mainly at his local police constabulary. Ryan had a history of emotional instability, which should have precluded him from permission to possess these arms. Yet the police in *his area* gave that permission. While at the same time, many police, represented by the Association of Chief Police Officers, are making the most articulate demands that guns—any kind of gun—in the hands of a sporting gun user should be drastically curtailed.

On one occasion, the police did get it right: At a stakeout, they confronted three armed men attempting to rob a payroll truck. (These are not manned by armed personnel.) The robbers, holding a hostage, refused to surrender. A single policeman killed two of them and wounded the third, which led to outcries in the press and parliament for stricter controls on the use of firearms by the police—lest Britain become, they said, like the United States.

For those in Britain who would like to fire a handgun for sport, it is necessary to find and join a local gun club, and attend regularly. The prospective shooter may well meet a couple of guys who live just down the block, whom he didn't know shot. Of course he didn't know; those guys didn't casually talk about it. People don't readily talk about such things. Gun people are under siege in Britain; no point in making it worse by idle chatter. In Britain today, however, it is easier to buy an illegal handgun than a legal one—and cheaper, too, by all accounts.

The aspiring sport shooter is not allowed to buy a gun—not right away. It will take about a year before he can be judged competent and reliable. Police thinking, you can be pretty sure, also has it that in an argument with family or friend, the gun owner might resort to the gun.

Burglars in Britain are given what is virtually a free hand; to impede their functioning within your home by the employment of your gun—or even a club—will land you before the court where you will be prosecuted.

Want a 22 rifle? Look for a club where they fire rifles. If you have any idea that you're going to take it out in the country and plink away at a tin can, forget it. If you have a place to use it—a farm or a friendly farmer who says you can come there to shoot vermin (rabbits, squirrels)—they will issue you a certificate that says so. But go somewhere else to fire that rifle and that will put a quick finish to your shooting days.

For some time in Britain, police policy has been to discourage rifle and pistol ownership, to *actively discourage* it. Their success can be judged by the fact that there are twenty-five percent fewer firearms certificate holders today than there were fifteen years ago. The police would consider this a great victory, though it is obviously a hollow one, when one considers there has been an increase of illegally held firearms in the hands of criminals which greatly exceeds twenty-five percent.

"Today," one pleased-with-himself copper put it to a friend of mine whom he had successfully talked out of renewing his firearms certificate, "you have to fight for your certificate."

And fight I did. I decided I wanted a drilling. The police sat on the application for a long time. When I made inquiries, they pounced. They didn't think I ought to have a drilling—they didn't think I ought to have the rifles I had. They were after my certificate! But I wasn't going to be among the twenty-five-percent statistic. When I made my position unmistakably clear

(Above) Du Broff, clinging to his rifle, filled with fear that it will be snatched from him.

(Left) Clay pigeon shooters come in all sizes and ages, but all must have shotgun certificates at hand.

(Right) Policeman with German shepherd, considered by some more formidable than a gun.

(Left) A policeman stands guard over a bank delivery as bags of coins are thrown from hand to hand.

and took a very firm stand, they decided it would be more expedient to pick on somebody with a little less determination.

Buying a shotgun also requires permission from the police; a law dating from 1967 had it that this would eliminate crime, but it didn't, since no criminals applied for a shotgun certificate. Then along came Michael Ryan with his AK-47, which he had apparently kept in the garden sheds along with his other licensed arms. It was something of a surprise that he was allowed to keep this, and other arms, so casually, in view of the stringent regulations governing firearms in this country, to which we all conform.

Though an obvious police failure, it was the more than one million licensed and carefully regulated gun owners who were considered culpable by the police, newspapers, television, radio and large segments of the population. The Association of Chief Police Officers had indeed some strange bedfellows as their allies, in the shape, for example, of the radical Left.

As gun owners, we have been getting the message loud and clear in the U.K. for many years. We are all under threat and we had better organize for the pending battle if we are going to save our guns. Until now, we haven't done this to the extent we should. Perhaps it stems from the fact that gun owners in Britain tend to be extremely solid citizens and fail to comprehend that anything they do should be considered anti-social.

The Labour Party, with its profoundly socialist orientation, would like sporting guns removed from the hands of sportsmen. To use them for hunting is not considered, by them, sufficient justification for owning one; many among them object to the killing of animals for sport.

The British Broadcasting Corporation, a state-owned body, in theory public-controlled, is riddled by the Left and far Left and takes every opportunity it can to make a case against gun ownership, and generally stir up the populace into permanent hostility, ignoring the facts it doesn't like.

The Animal Rights protesters burned down the clubhouse of the London Gun Company Gun Club, where only clay pigeons are shot.

My own shoot borders on grounds controlled by the local water authority, who has designated its patch as a conservation area. The water authority has allowed in those who would like to observe the wildlife. But it wasn't long before the "observers" turned into "wardens" who were trying to get our shooting banned. They harassed us every year, during the whole of the season, going so far as to erect plywood figures with guns and streamers attached, which they hoped would deter the geese and cause them to take another route. Hearing our gunfire, they would phone the police, who soon became aware they were being used, as instruments of the Looney Left, to harass us. They—the "Looney Left"—are an element normally eager to destroy the power of the police and, while they

A plywood figure erected by anti-hunters to divert geese from flight over a shooting lease.

Police controlling a peaceful political demonstration in peaceful London use horses.

A part of the role of the police is to ensure that demonstrations of whatever shade be allowed to take place.

themselves use the democratic processes, would like to see democracy suspended in preference to their own system.

A swan was found dead on the shore of our lake. You can probably guess who found it. Swans in Britain are generally the Queen's property and fall under the protection of her long arms; the demise of one, however it might occur, is an occasion for profound concern.

Swans, like other creatures, die, sometimes of old age, as well as numerous other causes, but this one, the "wardens" claimed, had been shot. The implication was someone in our shooting club had done it, which, when reason prevails, seems most unlikely. They did, however, reap maximum benefit from that swan corpse, displaying it as "Exhibit A" for the benefit of the local press, who were only too pleased to project us as heartless killers and direct further hostility toward hunters and hunting.

We reached a compromise that permitted us two days of duck and goose shooting from a blind along our shore. But no longer would any of us be permitted to walk around the lakes, putting up the odd duck, or walk about on the farm where it was possible to encounter some snipe as well as a reasonable amount of doves. Basically, we have lost and lost a lot. We were never in violation of the law, but yet a group of people could come along and compel us to refrain from doing what we had every right to do, contrary to our own interests. What are they likely to be demanding next time, considered in the light of their victory this time?

As Britain has changed, so too has the role of the police. The trouble is, they aren't sure what their role is, or at least there is serious disagreement among them as to what it should be. This has led to extremely low morale and the departure of many competent police officers. The police, very rarely on the take, heavily depend upon the support and approval of the public. They like to be Jolly Old St. Nick come Christmas time, but that facet of their functioning has all but disappeared, and the reality of Britain today is one of violence and fear.

We all fear for our safety and for our property. There's a break-in every ninety seconds and a car is stolen every thirty. Maybe we won't get mugged or raped, but the possibility remains distinctly real, which has to engender considerable anxiety. The elderly man who successfully fought off a group of young attackers on the London underground train was prosecuted because he had employed a sword stick, considered a concealed weapon, and missed going to prison only by the virtue of his advanced years.

Young boys—and girls—attack the elderly, often in their homes, sometimes pretending they are there to offer assistance; the elderly, and even the crippled, are targeted by virtue of being less able to offer any kind of defense. And Britain, despite its lax ways with criminals, has the highest prison population in Western Europe. Unable to protect our homes, the police have borrowed the American concept of Neighborhood Watch. It has been effective and reduced our break-ins considerably in some areas, sending the burglars off to other less watchful districts, but not really serving as a deterrent to crime.

London in particular is highly vulnerable. The Irish Republican Army has brought its war to the English capital, detonating bombs in department stores and attacking the innocent. They even managed to get into the House of Parliament to commit murder. In Brighton, on the south coast, during the Conservative Party convention, they planted a bomb that almost killed the Prime Minister, paralyzed the wife of a Cabinet Minister, and killed a number of others.

An Arab shot the Israeli Ambassador. Arabs wage war in London against Israel and against each other. The British Foreign Office, with its deep affinity for the Arabs, has turned a blind eye to their importation of arms and explosives in diplomatic bags, which had always been immune from surveillance. One Arab walked up to another one on a busy London street and shot him at point-blank range. The victim's crime, as a cartoonist on an Arab newspaper, had been to depict some Arab group or another in an unfavorable light.

All diplomats are vulnerable.

There are occasional gang wars.

There are drug-related problems.

The police have taken heed, though not nearly enough. If they are going to play Santa, they had better have appropriate arms stashed away in that bag. At Heathrow Airport, for example, the police now carry Heckler & Koch submachine guns. Their arsenal also includes Enfield sniper rifles, Remington pump-action shotguns and other assorted weaponry. As previous events have shown, it is too little and too late, serving now as only a partial deterrent. This ambivalence over arms must be overcome once and for all if today's police are to live in today's world and be anywhere near effective in it.

They must also learn to make the distinction between arms meant for sporting purposes and other kinds. It would seem obvious to most of the rest of us, but too many of the British police have never learned to make that distinction. Like so much in Britain that is decentralized, attitudes between constabularies differ enormously, with one being quite reasonable, while another remains completely intransigent.

Departing not long ago from Gatwick, London's second airport, I presented my ticket and my shotgun at the check-in desk. They took my ticket and other baggage, but weren't allowed to take the gun. They were, however, obligated to press the button that summoned the police, two of whom duly arrived to confront me. I presented them with my guns—cased—which they held in obvious discomfort, and the one charged with talking asked, "Do you have your shotgun certificate?"

I always have my shotgun certificate, except when I'm in the shower—and even then, it's close at hand. (Get caught with your shotgun and without your shotgun certificate on your person, you could easily wind up at the police station.)

Later, we conferred with the Home Office, who rule the police, and not the other way around (though there are those making every effort to reverse the process). They made it apparent the police were to end their harassment and to stop exceeding their authority. Consequently, when next a group of people appeared with guns at Gatwick, bound for St. Petersburg, Florida, USA, to compete in a clay shoot, there wasn't a single cop around to ask for the certificates of those eighteen armed men and women.

Maybe somebody somewhere was learning. Maybe there was still hope that the people who are supposed to be protecting us, and not persecuting us, will, in the end, be able to make the distinction between sporting arms and other kinds, as well as the differences between the people who use them.

●

Some people have waited years to see these beautiful little numbers again. 12, 42, 52.

Model 12 in 20 Gauge

Model 42

Model 52B

Wait No Longer to Own a Classic Tradition.

If you missed your chance the first time, don't miss it again. Make your claim on three of the greatest Winchester guns of all time: the Model 42, the Model 12 in 20 gauge, and the Model 52B.

Model 12 in 20 gauge. Effortless slide action function and delightful balance. Few 20 gauge guns come close to the handling grace of the 20 gauge Model 12. Choose the beautiful Grade I version or the engraving and gold highlights of the Grade IV.

Model 42. This is the .410 bore pump shotgun that evolved from the famous Model 12. Upon its introduction, sixty years ago, it instantly became famous for its superb handling characteristics.

Model 52B Sporting. Many regard the 52 as the premier rimfire bolt action of all time. With its superb trigger system, sculpted cheekpiece and proven accuracy, the 52 should be at the top of your list of lifetime must-haves.

Don't wait a minute too long. All three guns are in limited edition quantities.

WINCHESTER®

For a Free Catalog write:
U.S. Repeating Arms Company, Dept. U036,
275 Winchester Ave., New Haven, Connecticut 06511.
Winchester is a registered trademark licensed
from Olin Corporation.

YOU COULD SPEND YEARS PUTTING TOGETHER A RELOADING BENCH LIKE THIS. OR, YOU COULD SPEND MINUTES.

A BENCH IN A BOX. ROCK CHUCKER PRESS, 5•0•5 RELOADING SCALE, SPEER RELOADING MANUAL, UNIFLOW POWDER MEASURE, ROTARY CASE TRIMMER-II KIT, HEX KEY SET, CASE LUBE KIT, CASE LOADING BLOCK, AUTOMATIC PRIMER FEED, POWDER FUNNEL, PRIMER TRAY II AND DEBURRING TOOL. DIES AND SHELLHOLDERS SOLD SEPARATELY.

At RCBS, we believe you should spend a lifetime using your reloading equipment, not accumulating it. That's why we created the Rock Chucker Master® Reloading Kit. It contains the world's most popular press, the Rock Chucker, plus all the accessories you need to reload like an expert. It costs considerably less than you'd pay for these items separately. It expands easily to progressive operation, with a Piggyback™ II conversion unit, which means you'll never outgrow it. Plus, it's guaranteed for life or forever, whichever happens to come first. So if you're ready to start reloading, spend your time wisely: visit your local RCBS dealer today.

RCBS®

TO DO IT RIGHT.

SCOPES AND MOUNTS

by BOB BELL

IT'S NOT UNUSUAL for questions about shooting to be chewed over in hunting camp, but I was a bit surprised by one from a pal last fall. I'd just shivered into my old Kara Koram mummy bag, wondering if our hard-pressed tent was gonna hang tough against the fierce snow-grainy winds sweeping across the high Wyoming plains, when he said, "Hey, Shooter, you're always messing with scopes, so tell me something. How can the image seen through a scope be brighter than what you see with only the eye when all manufacturers admit that no scope transmits all the light it receives? I mean, how can 80 or 90 percent of something be more than 100 percent?"

I threw a glance to see if he was kidding, but he didn't seem to be. So I said, "Easy. Scopes gather light."

"I don't understand that. Neither do others, apparently, because I read somewhere that such a thing is impossible, that there's no such thing as light gathering."

"Well, maybe 'gathering' isn't the perfect description of what happens when light passes through a scope, but I can't think of a better one. Just visualize the situation—what happens when you look at something with the eye alone and then with a scope..."

In the first case, the light available to the eye's retina is that which passes through its pupil, a circle with a diameter that varies from about 2 to 7 millimeters, depending upon ambient light intensity. Under the worst light conditions you might be hunting in—almost full dark—its diameter is about 7mm. That means the retina receives 100 percent of whatever light is available that can pass through a 7mm circle.

Suppose we interpose a scope between the eye and the light source. Now, instead of light directly striking the eye's pupil, it first strikes the objective lens of the scope. This lens—the entrance pupil of the scope—is much larger than the eye's pupil. Perhaps it's 42mm, as with a 6x42mm scope. That means the exit pupil *of the scope* is 7mm (objective diameter in millimeters divided by scope magnification), which in this case exactly equals the entrance pupil of the eye. Thus all of the light which strikes the scope's 42mm objective, except that which is reflected from its outer surface plus whatever is lost in transmission through the scope, is compressed or "gathered" into a beam which will enter the shooter's eye. You have more light in a smaller area, therefore its intensity is greater. How much more? Since areas of circles are proportionate to the square of their diameters, 36 times more light strikes a 42mm objective lens than a 7mm eye pupil (42 squared = 1764; 7 squared = 49; 1764 divided by 49 = 36).

Even if only 80 percent of the light that strikes the objective lens actually reaches the user's eye, it is still about 30 times as much as the 100 percent delivered by the eye's pupil alone. It's a matter of the different areas of the two circles.

Naturally, scope exit pupil diameters rarely exactly equal eye entrance pupil diameters. If the former is larger, some of the light transmitted by the scope never reaches the retina. But what does arrive is still much greater than would be admitted by just the eye pupil.

When it's truly dark, the biggest objective lens and best optical system you can get won't transmit much light. That is, 30 or 40 times 0 is still 0. On the other hand, in bright sunlight, when the eye's pupil contracts to almost nothing, the target image is still bright even though only a tiny fraction of the transmitted light is utilized.

"At least that's the way I see it," I said. "Okay?"

A snore was the only response.

Oh, well. Here's this year's rundown:

Bausch & Lomb has introduced a complete new line of riflescopes this year. It's called the Elite—the same name they gave to their top line of binoculars announced last year. Actually, there are two series of Elite scopes, the 4000 and the 3000. The former is the more expensive, with retail prices ranging from $479.95 for the 1.5-6x36mm to $587.95 for the 6-24x40mm. There's also a 2.5-10x40mm at $533.95 and rumors are circulating about a straight 10x40mm for special super-precise work with a list price of more than double the 6-24x.

The 3000 series includes 3-9x50mm, 2-7x32mm, 3-9x40mm and 4-12x40mm models at prices from $281.95 to $369.95.

All Elites have fully multi-coated lenses; black anodized internal tubes, with crinkle finish to minimize reflection; reticle attached with screws, a metal ring and sealant instead of just a sealant; erector assembly made of aluminum and brass instead of just aluminum; and a spring behind

Bob Wise did the work, shooter Bell the fun; ballistics by a 338-08 and sighting by Leupold—even the buck looks pleased.

B&L's goal with their new Elites was to combine the optics of a top target scope with the durability of a great hunting scope. A few years of hard use should tell us how successful they were.

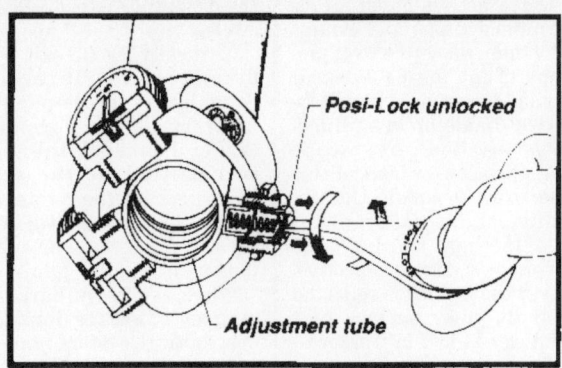

Posi-Lock unlocked

Adjustment tube

Posi-Lock in unlocked position

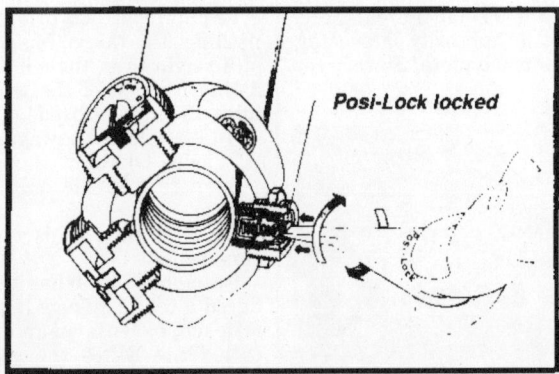

Posi-Lock locked

Posi-Lock in locked position

(Above) The Burris Posi-Lock system snugs up tight the erector lens tube after windage and elevation adjustments are made, preventing any internal movement due to recoil, falls or whatever.

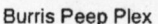

If you look closely at the bottom of the adjustment turret on this 2.5-10x Signature Series Burris, you can see where the Posi-Lock is installed.

aged to get the critters in the scope. The little Balvar had been set at 6x ever since I mounted it, and through it I could see those horns shining like a black V against the dun background. For an instant, the horizontal crosswire lay just above their tips and my finger pressed the trigger. When the rifle settled after the recoil, the does were scattering and the buck was on the ground, motionless. A few minutes later we were bent over it, studying the impact. The bullet had entered the back of the neck, about 16 inches down from my 200-yard zero, so it was out there a ways.

"Luck of the Irish," TR said.

"Nah," I lied. "I always do it that way." Well, sometimes. And it helps to have a crystal-clear scope on the top deck when it's time to try. Like maybe this 1.5-6x B&L. It provides an awful lot of optics for its size.

Bushnell continues to offer a wide assortment of models in their Trophy, Banner and Sportview lines, including the 3-9x Armor-Sight which features a graphite composition tube that's lighter than alu-

at dawn and dusk. High mounting rings will be required, especially on heavy-barreled rifles, but that's a small price to pay for such optical efficiency.

Burris has a number of new items this year, including one—the Posi-Lock—which they claim is the most significant advance in scope design in the last fifty years. So we'll start with that.

In summary, the Posi-Lock makes it possible to lock the internal optics of a scope in position after the rifle is sighted in. This prevents recoil, rough hunting use or temperature changes from affecting the scope's zero. Some of a scope's internal optics are housed in a tube which is held in place by springs. The springs are necessary so the shooter can make windage and elevation adjustments by moving the spring-supported tube. However, some compression of these springs can occur during recoil, permitting the internal components to move slightly. If the normal spring expansion does not return the tube to precisely the same position after every shot, point of aim will change and accuracy will suffer.

Posi-Lock replaces the springs of a conventional adjusting system with a key-retractable steel post. In use, the shooter loosens the Posi-Lock screw, makes any required sighting adjustments, then tightens the P-L screw, locking the internal tube and

all adjustable objective lenses to cushion impact and force the lens to remain in alignment. The power change ring is designed to maximize torque, and adjustable objectives have a 270-degree range for extremely precise movement. The 4000 series has two extra lenses (the 3000, one) to improve resolution and color correction and minimize aberration. Internal quarter-minute clicks (eighth-minute in 6-24x) are audible and finger adjustable.

The Elites are Bausch & Lomb's response to their own question: Why can't the optical and mechanical performance of the best target scopes be built into a scope that's as practical and durable as the best hunting scopes? It's too soon to say whether that question has been answered in full—it takes an awful lot of shooting to determine the

durability of a scope—but there's no doubt the Elites have taken a giant stride in that direction.

Might mention that last October I put a 1.5-6x B&L Balvar on a favorite long-range rifle, my M700 Remington 7mm Remington Magnum, and took it to Wyoming for pronghorns. It put three shots in less than 1½ inches at 200 yards when I zeroed it with 165-grain Extended Range Remington ammo. So the first kill, a doe walking broadside at about 235, was nothing to get excited about. Just bang, plop. The buck took a bit more doing. It was running straight away from me, leading a small bunch of does, and my buddy TR was shouting, "Hold for 400, hold for 400!" I wasn't sure about my range estimate, but I had to hold somewhere, so from a sprawled rest position I man-

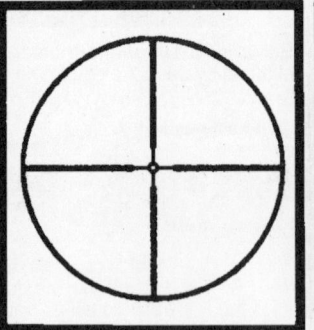

Burris Peep Plex

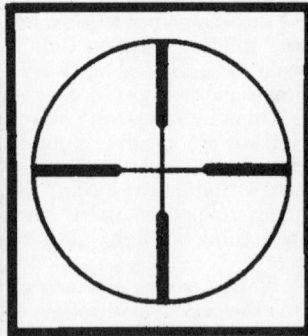

Burris Heavy Plex

Two new Burris reticles—one for teensy targets, one for big ones.

minum and nearly impervious to field hazards. An interesting new Banner is the 3-9x56mm. The huge objective gives an exit pupil of 6+mm even at top power, which means it will provide a very bright target image for long-range deer snipers even

its contained optics into position. Posi-Lock is available as an option on Burris Signature Series variable-power scopes.

New Burris scopes are a 2-8x Signature, 3.5-10x50mm Fullfield and 2-7x LER handgun model. The first is intended for hunters who use the lighter mountain rifles, but don't want to sacrifice the image quality of a full-size scope. The enlarged internal lenses of the Signature models, discussed in earlier reviews, enhance the performance of this medium-size 2-8x. The new 3.5-10x is Burris' first scope with a 50mm objective. Like all Fullfields, it is 100 percent American-made, and, of course, is intended for use when ambient light is poor to bad. The 2-7x LER is the latest in a long line of handgun scopes from this Colorado company. At top power, it provides precise aiming ability for load testing or small varmint shooting, while the lower powers make it suitable for deer, boar and whatever in close up situations. Eye relief at 2x is 7-27 inches, and 8-15 inches at 7x. Burris president John McCarty says this 2-7x LER is built to take the recoil of the biggest handguns (which I suppose includes the cannons my ol' buddy J.D. Jones creates), so everyone oughta be happy.

Burris also is offering a pair of new scope reticles this year as options in a number of their models. The Peep Plex

ner crosswire section of the new reticle is no heavier than that of the regular Plex, so precise aiming can be done with it. Seems to me the receiver-mounted 1.5x Shotgun model with Heavy Plex reticle and its 62-foot field ought to be just the ticket on a dangerous game rifle.

Europtik Ltd's "From Jena" scope line (translated from the earlier "aus Jena" name) now consists of four straight powers and three variables: 4x36mm, 6x36mm, 6x42mm, 8x56mm, 1.5-6x42mm, 2-8x42mm and 2.5-10x56mm. As with the earlier models, the single-mag models are built on thick-walled 26mm aluminum alloy tubes (steel available), the variables on 30mm tubes. All reticles are etched on glass, with seven styles offered, from plain crosshairs through German-style posts, dots and combinations thereof. Adjustments for windage and eleva-

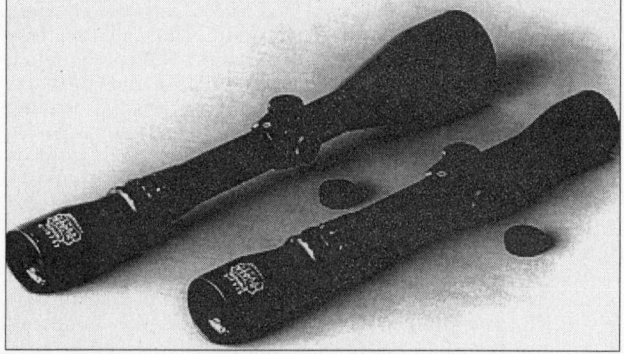

Leupold's new Vari-X III varies sorta uniquely—from 4.5x—but that oughta be just the ticket for the hunter whose close shots tend to be at medium range.

has an open circle at what would otherwise be the intersection of the fine crosshairs. At top magnification of the various variables in which it's offered, the opening or subtension of the circle is approximately 1 MOA. The new Heavy Plex has a different purpose. It's intended for use at short range where rapid target acquisition is necessary, so is offered in the smaller variables and low-power Shotgun Fullfields. The four outer bars of the Plex reticle are almost twice as thick as those in a standard Plex reticle; however, the in-

tion are internal clicks. Values differ in each model, from 0.20 in the 8x56 to 0.31 in the 1.5-6x.

Jerry Holden's **Iron-sighter** See-Thru mount is now made for the new Remington M522 22 Viper, Mossberg's M500 Slugster and M835 Slug Gun, Thompson/-Center's Greyhawk and Thunderhawk, Traditions' T-93 Custom Rifle/Carbine, and S&W's M29 Classic, all in High Profile models. A Low Profile version, featuring a somewhat flattened see-thru tunnel, is also available for a whole batch of guns.

Leupold's latest Vari-X III is interesting for its unusual magnification range, 4.5-14x. The 3-1 ratio is common enough, but I can't remember another variable with those exact powers. This scope could be especially useful on a semi-open-country big game rifle—that is, one to be used in areas of scattered woods, grassy hillsides and plains. Pronghorns and deer, both mulies and whitetails, can be found in such places, and this 4.5-14x with its field of 21-7.5 feet seems adaptable to such hunting. Despite its high power, this scope is only 12.4 inches long and weighs but 14.5 ounces—almost identical to Leupold's earlier 3.5-10x50mm. It has a 40mm objective lens which is adjustable for range, and either Duplex or Heavy Duplex reticle.

Leupold also has a new tactical scope intended primarily for law enforcement work. Called the Mark 4 M3-6x, it

If you're a cop on an anti-terrorist squad, you oughta take a look at Leupold's latest, their Mark 4 M3-6x.

features a one-piece 30mm main tube made from a solid bar of aircraft-grade aluminum. Finished wall thickness is 0.1-inch, and it has the same bullet-drop compensation dials already available on the Mark 4 M3-10x model. All lenses have Multicoat 4 treatment, and the scope's finish is matte black, for obvious reasons.

There hasn't been time to

use either of these scopes yet, but I'd like to mention another Leupold which came through for me in December. It's a Vari-X II 1-4x and it's aboard a wildcat 338-08 gunsmith Jim Peightal put together for me. On the tenth day of Pennsylvania's buck season last December, in a blinding snowstorm, Bob Wise kicked up a nice buck through a wide brushy fence row about 120 yards below me. Visibility was so bad, I knew my only chance would be when it crossed a farm lane separating the fence row from another big brush corner. Now, it doesn't take a scared buck long to go 15 feet, but I somehow managed to find him in the Leupold and get off a shot just as he disappeared. I heard the bullet whack and found him, a nice eight-point, in the snowy brush along the far edge of the lane. The 175-grain Barnes X-Bullet had angled completely through. It was the kind of shot a low-power scope with a big field is made for...which is why I like little variables for big game.

Optolyth-USA recently informed me they will be distributing the Pecar line of riflescopes, but I have no other details. Pecars, quite a few years ago, were imported by Charles Leavell of South Carolina. They were high-grade scopes which at that time were known for an unusual feature—interchangeable reticles.

Pentax has added two scopes to their LightSeeker line, the SG Plus 2.5x and a 3.5-10x50mm. The smaller model is intended for deep woods use, apparently by shotgunners (thus, SG) pursuing turkeys and whitetails with either shot or slugs, though there's no good reason not to mount it on a rifle. Its reticle, however, is designed

Here are two of the Pecar line of scopes now being distributed in the U.S. by Optolyth-USA.

for smoothbore use, as at its center it features a circle which encloses 30 inches at 40 yards and contains fine crosshairs. The circle, when properly zeroed, will show precisely where the bulk of a pattern will strike, or when using slugs, the shooter can sight-in with the crosshair intersection. (Whether a given gun will be in zero with both shot and slug at the same time can't be predicted, but can be easily determined by testfiring. It would be great if it worked out that way.) The tube of this 2.5x is slightly enlarged at the front to enclose a 22mm objective lens. Field is 55 feet, which is good for thick cover shooting.

The 3.5-10x50mm, of course, is intended for precise shot placement at any hunting range, especially when the light is bad. Which is to

Model 788 Remington 7mm-08 that's been lathe-turned and whittled down to 7 pounds woods ready. That's the rig I was carrying in a multiple-deer area early last winter when the drivers bounced a pair of whitetails out of the woods and into a broad snowcovered field. They were flat-out running, nose to tail and broadside to me at maybe 140 yards, when I swung through the first one. It rolled up in a pile, forcing the second one

This new little LightSeeker from Pentax is designed for deep woods hunting and has a special reticle to do the job.

Schmidt & Bender's latest is this 3-12x50, a wide enough power spread for any big game and a big enough objective for lots of light at the top end.

The newest Zeiss: 2.5-10x48mm—a pound and a half of top optics.

say, the kind of opportunities that often come up in the South, when watching the fields around the swamps where the little SG 2.5x would be used.

Redfield currently markets over three dozen scope models, from the large Ultimate Illuminators to a couple for the 22 rimfire, including handgun models and a 1-4x shotgun scope with 6-inch eye relief which permits mounting ahead of an unaltered Mauser or Springfield bolt (see last year's "Scopes and Mounts" review). All of which means there is little or no need for additional models at this time, and none have been introduced. Many of the current scopes are now offered with a choice of finishes—black matte or nickel matte to match the finish of a gun or satisfy the hunter's ideas. Conventional black and unconventional Realtree Camo are also offered on some models—both scopes and mounts.

An old—very old—Redfield 1-4x is Weaver-mounted on my dirty-weather deer gun, a

into a wild legs-flying leap to clear it—a sight the little scope's large field let me see clearly—and my next 140-grain Nosler dropped the second only yards farther on. It was a wild few seconds—the kind this rig was made for, and not the first time it's come through for me. As I said, this Redfield is kinda old, but I'm not replacing it. We've been through too much together.

Schmidt & Bender scopes are now distributed in this country through Dietrich Apel, Brook Road, Meriden, NH 03770, according to Hans Bender, who told me that S&B does not have the capacity to produce enough scopes to satisfy the marketing plans of Leica Camera, Inc., the former distributor. Regardless, this top-quality line will still be available to American hunters.

Currently, ten Schmidt & Bender models are offered, with a choice of steel or light metal (with rail mounting) construction: 1½x15, 4x36, 6x42, 8x56 and 10x42 straight powers, and 1¼-

4x20, 1½-6x42, 2½-10x56, 3-12x50 and 4-12x42 variables. Obviously, one or another of these will handle any big game requirement on earth, as well as most varmint shooting situations.

New this year is the 3-12x50, which like all S&B variables has a center tube diameter of 30mm. (Fixed powers are built on 26mm tubes, which is so close to 1 inch that the difference doesn't matter, except in scope rings.) The 3-12x50 was designed as a compromise between the twilight scopes with 56mm objectives and the smaller models intended for normal light conditions. Despite its slightly smaller objective, at 12x this new scope has a twilight factor of 24.5, which is higher than the 21 TF rating of an 8x56.

(The twilight factor, incidentally, is simply a mathematical rating calculated by multiplying the unobstructed diameter of the objective lens in millimeters by the magnification, and taking the square root of the product. Thus, 12 x 50 = 600, and the square root of this is 24.5. Theoretically, the higher this number, the more efficient a given scope is when ambient light is bad. But this assumes that lens quality, optical and mechanical design, etc., are equal in the scopes being compared. As pointed out in the Schmidt & Bender catalog, this is not always the case. Such a formula simply does not consider quality. S&B *does* consider quality. I've thoroughly tested a number of their models over the years, and they've always been top-level stuff.)

Shepherd scopes, as we wrote some years ago, have a unique Dual Reticle System which makes all sorts of useful things possible—one-shot zeroing, adaption for wind without losing basic zero, etc. The most conspicuous part of the DRS is a series of decreasing-size circles strung on a vertical line beneath the basic crosshair intersection. Separation is such that each circle matches bullet drop at 100-yard intervals from 300 to 1000. Circles are sized to subtend 18 inches at those ranges, so in use the shooter finds the circle which best encloses an 18-inch (withers-to-brisket) area on a deer, holds dead on and shoots. Reticles with different circle separations—one or another of which will match most of today's high-velocity loads—are available. Recently, reticles matching the trajectories of Layne Simpson's 7mm Shooting Times Westerner, the Weatherby magnums, the 338-378 and other screamers have been added.

Steiner has added an 8x56 to their Penetrator-Infrared riflescope line, which also includes a 6x42, 1.5-6x42 and 3-12x56. These PI scopes have a special infrared lens coating so they will transmit more light in the red and infrared end of the spectrum, which includes the brown and tan hues typical of many game animals, and less at the opposite end, where blue and green are typical of haze and foliage. Thus, the PI scopes are said to provide more color contrast between animals and their surroundings than other scopes.

All Penetrators come with transparent covers which permit fast shooting in emergencies and an accordion eyecup to block out sidelights. New this year is the 7B reticle, a heavy plex style intended for low light contitions in North America. Opposing post ends have a separation of 56 inches at 100 yards, the approximate length of a whitetailed deer, which can be useful in determining range.

Swarovski has two lines of big game scopes, the Habicht Nova, which can be thought of as their European line, and the Habicht Nova A, which

alloy tubes. The Nova A-AL models (4x32, 6x36, 1.5-4.5x20 and 3-9x36) all have 1-inch center tubes and are of alloy construction.

Seven German-style reticles are offered in the Nova models; they are located in the first (objective) focal plane, thus always subtend the same amount and can be used as a range-finding assist if target size is known. Four reticle styles are available in the Nova A scopes, including the popular Plex and the favorite of yesteryear, the post and crosswire, in the 1.5-4.5x only. Nova A reticles are in the second focal plane, so sub-

side mount for installing one of their scopes or the ProPoint on the BRNO CZ75-85 auto, Colt M1911 or Springfield/TA 90 STD. The base is machined of aircraft aluminum alloy and attaches rigidly to the pistol frame with hex screws. Rings are 30mm steel. Tasco is also supplying their World Class no-drill, no-tap shotgun bases for easy installation on the ventilated rib of many smoothbores.

Thompson/Center currently has four Recoil Proof Compact scopes intended primarily for their own Contender carbines and assorted muzzleloaders, but also us-

at the front of each base prevent ring slippage. Rings, which are split vertically and sculptured nicely, are available in three heights in 0.125-inch increments and three diameters, 1-inch, 26mm and 30mm. Each has a thumb-operated lever for quick detachment. Slotted thumb knobs or machine screws are available for more permanent installation, if preferred. Testing has indicated that scopes replace to within 1/2-MOA after removal.

Weaver's seven riflescopes cover all shooting situations except benchrest (the KT15x is their highest power, about half the magnification the super-serious paper-punchers prefer). At the bottom end, they start at unit power with the V1-3x, a neat little scope that has an 88-foot field at bottom power and almost 4 inches of eye relief, qualities that highly recommend it for thick cover or dangerous game use. In between, they offer the K2.5, K4, K6, V3-9x and V2-10x. And there's another scope for archery hunters, the BOWeaver. It's made with either one- or three-dot green-glowing reticle (intensity automatically decreases in dim light, eliminating blind-out). Needs no batteries, so is legal in all states and accepted by Pope & Young.

This is the way Tasco's new Competition mount gets their Propoint on an autoloader.

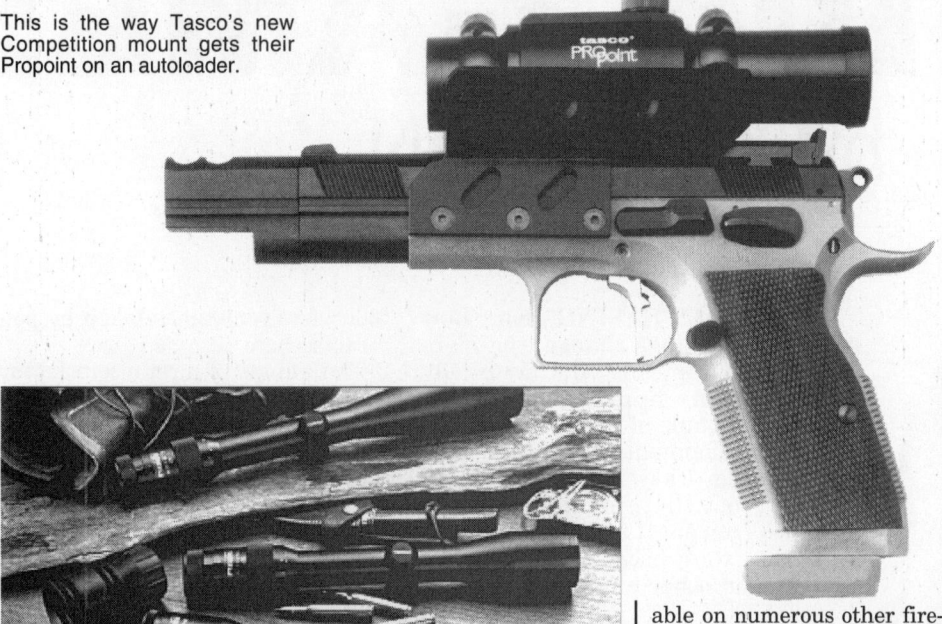

Steiner applies an infrared coating to the Penetrator lenses to make more contrast between animal and background colors.

Williams is perhaps best known for their extensive lines of scope mounts—it's hard to think of a gun they can't latch a glass sight onto—but they also offer two lines of big game scopes, the Twilight and Guideline II series. These medium- to low-priced scopes are tough, durable and dependable, and made in all the usual powers topping out with the 3-9x.

Zeiss has a new variable in their Z-series, the Diavari 2.5-10x48mm T*. At 14+ inches and 24 ounces, and being built on a 30mm tube, this scope obviously is not intended for a featherweight rifle, but where those factors are unimportant, this model has a great deal to recommend it—primarily, optics. We've come to expect that quality from Zeiss, and in our experience they've always delivered. Not on the cheap, of course. List price on this 2.5-10x48 is about $1400. But as somebody once said, you pays your money and you takes your choice. ●

tends toward American ideas. In fact, the latter are often designated Nova A-AL, the terminology indicating American Lightweight.

There are seven scopes in the Nova line, three straight powers built on 26mm tubes with enlarged ocular and objective units (4x32, 6x42 and 8x56), and four variables built on 30mm tubes (1.5-6x42, 2.2-9x42, 3-12x56 and 3-12x50P). The last has an adjustable objective for parallax correction and is made with steel tube only, as is the 4x32. Other Novas are available with either steel or light

tend less of the target as the power is increased.

We've used several Swarovski scopes over the years, and all have been absolutely top quality.

Tasco's latest addition to their World Class scope line is a 3-9x40mm which features the Opti-Centered 30-30 range-finding reticle, Super-Con multilayer coating and, most importantly, stainless steel construction. This Miami-based company is also now supplying, in addition to numerous other scopes, binoculars and optical-related items, a Competition Pistol

able on numerous other firearms. The RPC line includes a 4x32, 1.5-5x and two 3-9xs. Interestingly, a new quick release mounting system makes for easy scope removal when iron sight use is wanted. A spring-loaded plunger attached to the bottom of the rings holds the scope to a screw-installed base. For quick removal, the scope is pulled rearward, the front end tilted up, and the scope and rings lifted off. Remounting is done in reverse order and is just as quick, and is said to replace to zero.

Warne Mfg. Co. has for several years now been supplying an extensive range of excellent quick-detachable scope mounts, all machined from solid steel. Two- and one-piece bases are made, their top surfaces being rail-type dovetails with large areas of engagement with the rings. Raised recoil shoulders

AIR GUNS
ON BIG GAME!
by J.I. GALAN

THAT OLD SAYING about how the more things change, the more they stay the same, flutters briefly through my mind when I think about a couple of high-powered airgun developments of recent years. And when I say "high-powered," I mean just that, for the two guns which I am about to discuss are modern-day throwbacks to a time when deer and other animals of similar bulk were sometimes taken by powerful big-bore airguns.

The annals of airgun lore feature such notables as King Ludwig VIII of Hessen, Germany, an avid hunter who in the early 1700s used airguns routinely during his hunting forays. Good ole King Ludwig was credited with bagging a respectable number of wild boar and stag with his trusty large-bore pneumatic gun. On one particular occasion, it was reported that the king shot and killed a large stag at a distance of 154 paces with his favorite airgun.

Nearly one century later and in the New World, a powerful airgun accompanied explorers Lewis and Clark in their famous 1804-1806 expedition through then-uncharted wilderness. The chronicles of the expedition show seventeen different instances in which that airgun is specifically mentioned. The airgun in question was apparently a pneumatic utilizing the butt reservoir system popular at the time. It was used at

There is no doubt that the Farco is a man-sized gun in every respect. Author found it to be simple to operate and maintain.

least once to kill deer during the journey. Many Indians, already familiar with the muzzleloaders of the period, seemed to have been fearful of this powerful airgun, due to its lack of flash and smoke, plus its relative quietness.

Game animals haven't been the only live targets to fill the sights of high-power airguns in centuries gone by. During the 1790s, when Napoleon Bonaparte's armies marched across much of Europe, the airgun was used for awhile to snipe at French soldiers. Austrian sharpshooters armed with the Girandoni pattern 1780 repeating pneumatic rifle caused so much dread among Bonaparte's troops that the French high command issued an order that any Austrian soldier caught with one of the deadly air rifles was to be summarily executed as an assassin. The Girandoni military air rifle could fire twenty 51-caliber balls without reloading and had an effective killing range of about 150 yards. Even by today's high-tech standards, those 18th-century military air rifles would be awesome, indeed.

The foregoing clearly illustrates that if the technology to produce such tremendously powerful airguns existed more than 200 years ago, it was only a matter of time before someone in this day and age decided to resurrect the concept. Given the huge impetus that airguns, in general, have enjoyed during the last quarter century, the appearance of airguns intended primarily for hunting game much larger than rabbits,

squirrels and such—typical airgun quarry for a long time—does not come as a surprise. It really didn't come as a surprise, either, when our Editor asked me to look into the matter and prepare a report on the two most powerful airguns in production today, the ARS Farco and the Airrow A-8S Stealth.

The Farco has been available in the U.S for a few years, imported by Air Rifle Specialists. Manufactured in the Philippines, this gun has always been intended as a serious hunting arm in a country whose government practically bans the possession of firearms by the general public. Faced with such firearms laws, many Filipino hunters and shooters turned to airguns long ago as the only practical alternative.

The Farco was really designed as a single-shot shotgun with a 28-gauge (51-caliber) cylinder bore barrel. In that capacity, this interesting airgun is routinely used in the Philippines to hunt pheasant, dove, quail and even duck. It is powered by CO_2 which is charged into the gun via a standard 10-ounce CO_2 bottle. The gun's gas reservoir holds about $4\frac{1}{2}$ ounces of CO_2, which yields thirty to thirty-five shots before recharging is needed. The CO_2 bottle is simply screwed into the intake valve at the front of the reservoir tube—running below the barrel—and the bottle's spigot valve is opened for a short while until the gun is fully pressurized.

The shotshells for the Farco consist of 1-inch-long brass tubes open

at both ends. Each of these can hold approximately 240 #8 shot, or 12 #4 Buck pellets, to give you an idea of the load size. The shells are closed at each end with cardboard or cork wads made with a special "cookie-cutter" tool supplied with the gun. A load of #8 shot throws a rather dense pattern about 14 inches across at 10 yards, at an MV of approximately 405 fps. This load exceeds 100 foot pounds of muzzle energy and is potent enough to kill small game at up to 25 yards or so.

The Farco may not be the handsomest airgun around, but it is certainly practical and lots of fun to shoot. Overall, this gun measures $48\frac{1}{2}$ inches and weighs a comfortable 7 pounds. Its barrel, receiver and CO_2 reservoir tube are made of brass with a non-reflective, silvery finish. This contrasts nicely with the light-colored oil-finished hardwood stock. Currently, the Farco retails for just under $400.

Of course, in order to go after prey larger than pheasant, duck and the like, the Farco must be loaded with something other than birdshot or even buckshot. Davis Schweisinger, owner of Air Rifle Specialists, turned the Farco into an eminently viable hunting arm for medium game by utilizing a single projectile of suitable caliber. He chose a .433-inch lead ball, held in a plastic sabot of the kind used in modern muzzleloading rifles. The ball and sabot combination are simply pressed into the open-ended shotshell, thereby turning the Farco into a superb slug gun. The saboted 120-grain lead ball develops a muzzle velocity of approximately 625 fps in the Farco, which results in a muzzle energy of just over 104 foot pounds. That's quite a respectable figure by current airgun standards.

In order to field-test the combination of the Farco with saboted ball, Schweisinger journeyed south last summer, going after wild boar in the vast expanse of the Dixie Wildlife Safaris ranch in Lake Wales, Florida. The result was the clean taking of a 79-pound boar, dropped instantly with one single head shot from the scoped Farco, at a distance of approximately 30 yards. According to Schweisinger, the ball punched through the thickest part of the skull at the front, going through the brain and finally ending up about 6 inches into the neck area—impressive, indeed.

Those inch-long brass shotshells can hold a wide variety of shot loads, making the Farco a highly versatile hunting arm.

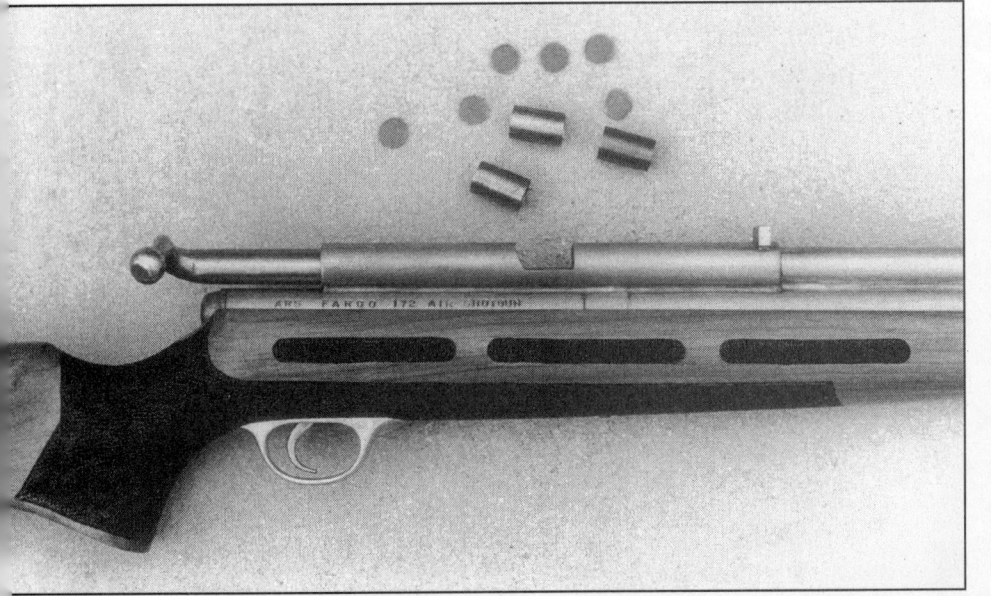

Davis Schweisinger, president of ARS, proudly poses with a wild boar taken in a Florida hunt. (Photo courtesy ARS)

Single projectile load for the Farco consists of a .433-inch, 120-grain ball with plastic sabot. Arrow indicates deformed ball taken out of boar killed with the Farco. (ARS photo)

Author puts the incredible Airrow A-8S 1P through its paces.

The Airrow A-8S Stealth can only be described as awesome, in the full sense of the word. I had the privilege of testing one of the first Stealth production guns way back in 1989, and even then it was a most extraordinary airgun. The intervening years have seen this device refined to a much higher level of sophistication.

In its basic form, the Airrow A-8S Stealth is really a unique concept, capable of shooting crossbow-length arrows at twice the speed of conventional archery equipment. The A-8S works with CO_2 as well as compressed air, and with the latter is capable of launching a broadhead-tipped hunting bolt at more than 500 fps. This remarkable gun is constructed mostly of aircraft-grade aluminum and stainless steel, in modular form that allows quick and easy takedown for transport in a compact attache-style carrying case. The whole setup would look quite natural on the set of a James Bond film or, for that matter, in a bunch of real-world places where state-of-the-art shooting technology is required. Besides shooting hunting arrows with tremendous velocity and accuracy, the Airrow gun, in its several versions, can be used as a line-throwing gun, underwater spear gun, tranquilizer gun for wildlife management work and (last but not least) as a rather esoteric anti-personnel weapon in paramilitary operations.

The basic Airrow A-8S with standard 16-inch archery barrel measures 33½ inches overall with its CAR-15 collapsible stock fully extended. Light weight is paramount here, and the A-8S tips the scales at just under 4½ pounds with a 1.5-5x20mm factory-supplied telescope mounted. A cursory look might mistake the Airrow for an M-16 or AR-15, given its all-black matte finish, carrying handle and overall military styling.

In the performance department, the Airrow A-8S Stealth with its recently developed pneumatic trigger is quite outstanding. Using CO_2 as propellant—at around 850 psi of pressure—from a 7-ounce tank that screws into the front of the receiver, the Airrow can launch a 320-grain, 16-inch aluminum bolt with field-point at a muzzle velocity of approximately 367 fps, for a muzzle energy of over 95 foot pounds. A 260-grain carbon arrow of the same length will develop a muzzle velocity of 396 fps

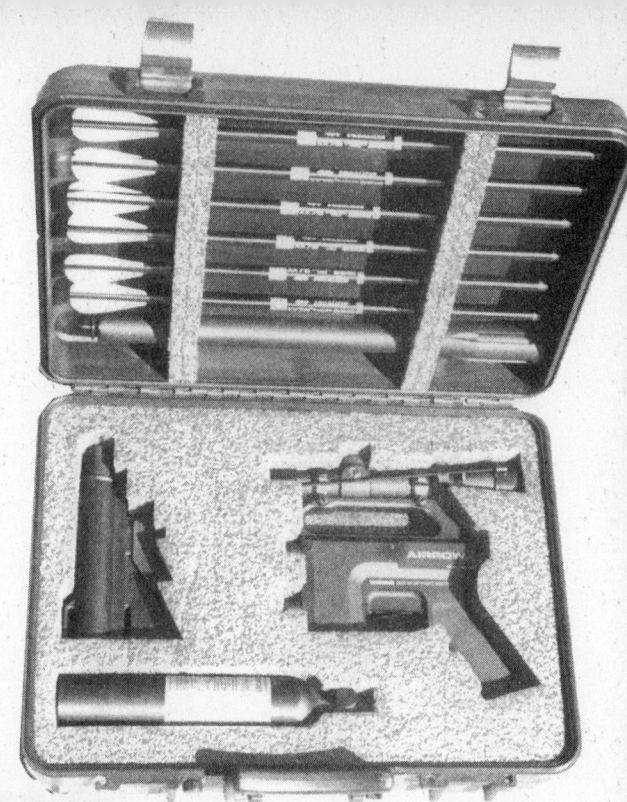

The Airrow A-8S 1P (pneumatic trigger model) is the latest bolt-shooting version of this amazing airgun. It comes in a special compartmentalized attache, case with arrows.

The new Airrow A-8S RB Stealth comes with a rifled barrel in .25-inch caliber, but other calibers, including .38-inch, are optional. This will be a limited production gun. (Photo courtesy SMW, Inc.)

or so. The aforementioned CO_2 tank will yield somewhere between twenty-eight and thirty-five shots when used in an ambient temperature of 70 degrees F.

Switching over to compressed air, at an average pressure of 3000 psi, the Airrow will launch the same 320-grain bolt at approximately 608 fps, while the 260-grain carbon bolt will reach an incredible 660 fps of MV. The resulting muzzle energies are 267 and 251 foot pounds respectively. The down side of the equation is that compressed air will allow only around twelve full-power shots, compared to more than twice that number—at more sedate velocities—when CO_2 is used.

Not content to leave things there, the designers of the Airrow are ready

The Airrow A-8S Stealth has taken its share of deer, like these two Virginia whitetails. (Photo courtesy SMW, Inc.)

Wild turkeys, too, have fallen to the amazing Airrow. (Photo courtesy SMW, Inc.)

The Airrow is a modern hunting arm that clearly surpasses the crossbow in terms of power, accuracy and practical range.

to launch yet another version of this amazing airgun. The new gun features a rifled barrel in 25-caliber and will be available on a very limited basis only, through licensed FFL dealers. Optional barrels in .177-, .20-, .22- and .38-inch caliber (with polygonal rifling) will be offered also.

As you might expect, all this state-of-the-art magnum airgun technology does not come cheap. The bolt-shooting A-8S 1P (pneumatic trigger) Airrow carries a retail price tag of $1599, while the A-8S RB (rifled barrel) model with pneumatic trigger goes for a cool $2167. Obviously, these airguns live in the province of truly dedicated enthusiasts with fat pocketbooks. I can sure keep Mama and the kids in beans and jeans for a long time with that kind of coin. By the way, the Airrow is manufactured by Swivel Machine Works, Inc.

Just to give you an idea of the performance figures involved, with the rifled-barrel Airrow, using compressed air at 3000 psi and a $23^3/_4$-inch barrel, this gun can shoot a 25-caliber Beeman Ram Point pellet (27.1 grains) at an average MV of 1275 fps. That gives a muzzle energy of 97.8 foot pounds. From a 17-inch barrel, the MV drops to 1166 fps, for an energy of 81.8 foot pounds. The accuracy obtained with the rifled-barrel Airrow in 25-caliber is reported to be quite respectable also, with quarter-size groups at 50 yards as the rule. Although I did not have the opportunity to test a rifled-barrel version for this article, I did test one of the latest bolt-shooting versions with pneumatic trigger. The discharge report is slightly more pronounced than that heard from a high-power pneumatic rifle, but it is still below that of a typical 22 LR firearm.

The Airrow has already taken a sizable number of deer and turkey, cleanly and efficiently. Thus, there is no doubt whatsoever that this airgun can perform satisfactorily as a full-fledged hunting arm, easily surpassing the modern crossbow in many instances in terms of power, range and accuracy.

Both the Airrow and the Farco represent a new breed of hunting airgun that hasn't been seen for the better part of two centuries. Which sort of proves that the more things change, the more they tend to come full circle. ●

by DEAN A. GRENNELL

HANDLOADING UPDATE

THE FIRST STEP in preparing a report such as this is to consult the previous year's edition to see what was covered in it, so as not to chew my cabbage twice. All too often, it's a little disconsolating to discover several of the things I'd planned to discuss were covered a year ago.

This, however, is the year **Hornady** got their Apex shotshell loaders into production. There are two versions, a standard and an automatic. You can start with the standard and later retrofit it to various levels of automation. Currently, the Apex loaders are available in 12-, 20- and 28-gauge, as well as 410-bore. They've also added handy new items for the shotshell reloader, such as the Stack N' Pack, a metal box that holds twenty-five loads for convenient packaging, and they can also furnish new shotshell boxes in the popular gauges.

RCBS rounded out its first half-century in 1993, having seen its inception in a tool shed behind the dry-cleaning shop operated by Fred Huntington's father in 1943, when Fred produced his first sets of bullet swaging dies. The initials, if you didn't know, stand for Rock Chuck Bullet Swage.

Huntington went on to design and produce the RCBS A-2 press. The design was sixteen years old in 1959 when I acquired my A-2, which remains the press that gets the most use around my own loading bench. It featured compound leverage and the ability to drop spent primers

neatly into a tin can positioned on a shelf beneath it.

A corporate entity called **Omark** bought up **Speer**, **CCI**, **Outers**, **Weaver** and **RCBS**, then sold them to **Blount** in 1985. The RCBS A-2 press was dropped some while back, but they still offer five other press designs, ranging from the cute and handy little Partner through the

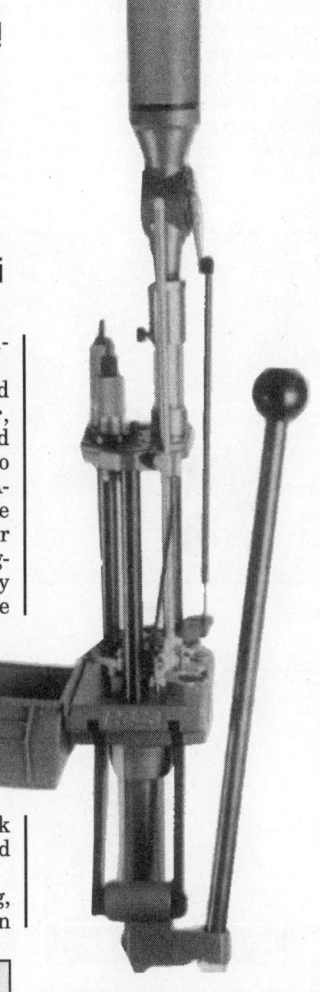

RCBS AmmoMaster

Reloader Special-5, the Rock Chucker, the Auto 4x4 and the AmmoMaster.

The AmmoMaster is a big, highly versatile press that can

be configured to serve nearly any reloading application. Set up as a single-stage unit, it can handle cartridges up to the 50 BMG, possibly larger ones, or on down to the 25 ACP, if you don't mind a touch of overkill. Add the

Single-to-Auto Kit and it becomes a progressive that indexes either manually or automatically.

The RCBS Piggyback II unit can be installed on the RCBS Rock Chucker, Reloader Special-3 or Reloader Special-5 presses, to provide a comparable degree of automation. The RCBS Auto 4x4 press is said to be capable of producing about 500 reloads per hour, and it will load handgun ammunition or rifle ammo up through the 30-06 Springfield.

The RCBS Uniflow powder measure now can be converted to a micrometer-type unit by means of two different diameters of UPM micrometer adjustment screws, permitting recording of the setting that delivered a given charge weight, for easy, simple return to that adjustment.

Operation of progressive loading presses inevitably poses the specter of verifying that one and only one charge of powder gets dropped into every single case, and RCBS offers a powder checker die and a lock-out die to provide peace of mind about that.

Until quite recent times, the 9mm Makarov pistols have been rarely encountered in this country, but quantities of surplus guns in that exotic caliber are being imported from former Soviet Bloc members, and RCBS now has 9mm Makarov die sets with tungsten carbide sizing dies. Newly added to the RCBS line of bullet moulds is the No. 9mm-100-RN which turns out a round-nosed bullet weighing 100 grains at a diameter of .365-inch. That's right, the bullet diameter is .010-inch larger than the

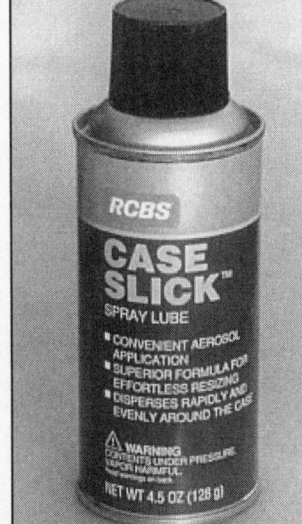

RCBS Case Slick spray lube

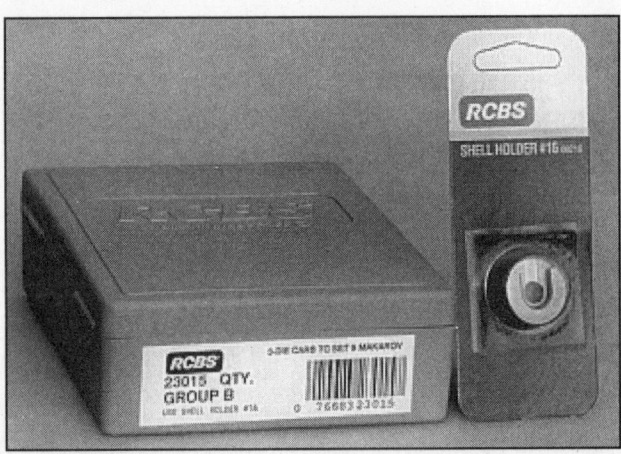

RCBS 9mm Makarov 3-die set and Shellholder #16

.355- (or .356) inch we've been accustomed to using for cartridges such as the 9mm Parabellum. RCBS also has added a .365-inch sizing die for their lube/sizer.

Other new RCBS bullet moulds include the No. 30-180-FN, a gas-checked flat-nose sized to .309-inch and weighing 180 grains for reloading 30-caliber cartridges. Also new this year is the No. 416-350-FN, likewise gas-checked and intended for such cartridges as the 416 Remington Magnum, 416 Weatherby Magnum or 416 Rigby.

RCBS now has a spray can lube they call Case Slick to ease the effort required for full-length case resizing. Not only does it work exceedingly well in that application, but I've been using it as a swaging lube with highly satisfactory results. The spray propellant is carbon dioxide, so it poses no problem to the upper ozone.

If there is a cartridge that has gotten solidly established as a legend in its own time, it would have to be the 6mm PPC or 6mm PPC USA, as its co-designer Dr. Lou Palmisano prefers to call it. A problem has been the availability of the cases, so I note the 1993 catalog from **Redding/SAECO** lists case-forming dies for making the 6mm PPC from 7.62x39mm parent cases. The set consists of a 6mm Form #1 die ($37.50), a 6mm PPC trim die ($28.50) and a #12E extended shellholder ($10). The 7.62x39mm brass is reasonably plentiful, so this may well be the solution many fans of the 6mm PPC have been seeking.

Several new designs have

been added to Redding's line of SAECO bullet moulds. They now have a .311-inch, 180-grain flatpoint gas-check (FPGC) for the 303 British, No. 305; a 100-grain semi-wadcutter bevel-base (SWCBB) and a 118-grain flatpoint to size to .313-inch for 32-caliber, Nos. 326 and 322A; a 124-grain SWCGC and a 140-grain SWC for 9mmP or 38 Super, Nos. 924 and 383; as well as a 100-grain round-nose in what they call a 9.2mm size at .365-inch for the 9mm Makarov, No. 940. They also have a trim die for making 9mm Makarov cases from 9mmP brass.

For the 38/357 size, there is a new 148-grain wadcutter with a single grease groove, the No. 053; a 155-grain SWCBB for the 40/10mm, (040); a 365-grain RNGC for the 416 calibers (916); a 200-grain wadcutter for the 44, (944); a 160-grain SWC for the 45 ACP/AR, (062-B); and a 255-grain SWCGC for the 45 Long Colt, (No. 945).

Also new is the Redding straight-line benchrest competition bullet seating die with a micrometer knob that can be zeroed to any desired setting for precise control of

Forster Ultra bullet seater die

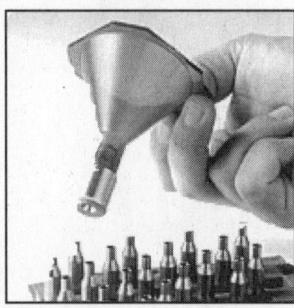
The adapter from Hornady seals around the mouths of 17-caliber cases. They have a 17-caliber drop sleeve for the Pro-Jector loader as well.

Dillon D-Terminator electronic scale

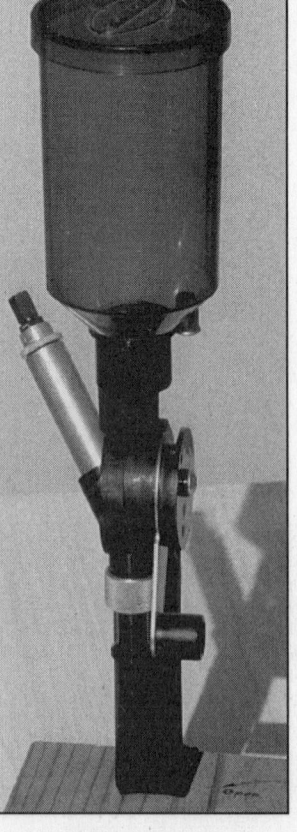
Lee Perfect Powder Measure

the bullet ogive position in relation to the commencement of the rifling. These retail at $79.50 and are offered for all the calibers popular for benchrest competition.

Forster Products has introduced their Ultra bullet seater die, with a micrometer adjustment, available in no fewer than fifty-one different calibers. It offers full and precise support of both the case and bullet throughout the entire seating operation. For those of you who already own a Forster benchrest seater die, a four-piece kit is available to upgrade to the new design.

For those who use Forster's excellent case trimmer, there is now a power adapter that can be operated with power screwdrivers turning at 140 rpm or higher, or with a small electric drill. For reloaders with access to a drill press, Forster has a power case trimmer base that can be C-clamped to the bed of the drill press for fast and effortless trimming, using the same collets and pilots as the regular trimmer. They note it works exceptionally well with their outside neck turner accessory.

Forster continues to market the Bonanza Model B-2 Co-Ax loading press with an innovative shellholder and a system that enables the operator to change dies in a matter of just a few seconds.

Lee Precision continues to make and market bullet moulds in what they term their Micro Band design. The bullet shank has many shallow grooves and, in most instances, they can be loaded and used as-cast, with no need for further sizing. Lee also supplies their Liquid Alox Lubricant and the Micro Band bullets are designed to be tumble-lubed. That affords a quick and highly convenient approach for making up a large quantity of cast bullets, all ready to use.

Lee's six-cavity commercial moulds are capable of turning out 100 bullets in about six minutes, and all you need is something such as an empty oatmeal carton in which to apply the Liquid Alox and a sheet of wax paper upon which to decant the bullets for the lube to set up. Newly added to the Lee line is their Perfect Powder Measure, with its adjustment stem graduated in cubic centimeters. It's

Midway heater base for lube/sizer

supplied with a chart giving the density of the various powders in grains per cubic centimeter and that makes fairly quick work of adjusting the measure to throw the desired charge weight.

In the area of new sources of loading data, **Hodgdon Powder Company** has brought out their *No. 26 Data Manual* and **Lyman** has published the 47th edition of the *Lyman Reloading Handbook*. The Hodgdon book is still so new I've yet to see a copy. The LRH-47 is at hand, however, all 480 8½x11-inch pages of it.

I don't know what manner of yardstick was used to decide which cartridges to include in the LRH-47 and which to leave out. The 357 Remington Maximum is covered in the section of loads for the Remington Model XP-100 and Thompson/Center Contender. The 445 Super Mag, a.k.a. 445 Gates, is not listed, nor is the 41 Action Express and 50 Action Express. The 40 S&W is covered and, according to a note in the data booklet from Accurate Arms, data for the 40 S&W can be used for the 41 Action Express, so long as you don't get too intrepidly carried away.

As in earlier editions, the LRH-47 carries quite a bit of load data for use with cast bullets, particularly cast bullets from Lyman moulds, and many of the listed loads give the pressure in CUP.

Fans of the 220 Swift cartridge will find some interesting data listed in the LRH-47. On pages 212 and 213 are loads that take a 40-grain Speer Spire Point bullet to a maximum of 4385 fps. The 45-grain Sierra Spitzer peaks out at 4219 fps, and the 50-grain Sierra SP Blitz gets to 4081 fps. All of those are maximum loads, to be approached from the underside with appropriate caution. The pressure listings for the quoted loads are left blank.

A recently added item is the *Lyman Reloading Data Log*, designed with direct input from shooters and reloaders to offer the most complete and easy-to-use format available anywhere. The 8½x11-inch sheets are bound in pad form and three-hole-punched for easy insertion in a loose-leaf binder.

Dillon Precision has added an electronic scale they're listing as the D-Terminator. It has a maximum capacity of 1500 grains (or 95 grams) and a sensitivity of 0.1-grain or 0.01-gram. It's powered by a 9-volt battery or an AC adapter and both are included in the introductory price of $199.95.

Dillon's Model RL 1050 progressive press will reload cartridge cases from 380 ACP through 30-06 Springfield, and its production capability is said to be on the order of 1300 rounds per hour; roughly one round every 2.77 seconds. It retails for $1049.95, complete with dies for one caliber, plus shipping and handling.

Somewhat more painlessly priced is Dillon's Model XL 650 press at $374.95 for the basic machine, with an automatic case feeder available at $119.95, and a powder-check system for another $49.95, with shipping and handling

costs in addition to the quoted prices.

Thompson Bullet Lube Company offers four different formulas to meet the needs and requirements of casters and shooters in today's market. They are designated as Bear Lube Cold, Bear Lube Heat, Blue Angel and Red Angel. The Bear Lube Cold requires a temperature of about 90F/32C to flow and fill the bullet grooves properly. The Bear Lube Heat is a medium-hard lube that requires a temperature of 110F/43C. Lazy Lube is the same as Bear Lube Heat, but made to flow through an automated Star lube/sizer.

Blue Angel requires a temperature of 125-140F/52-60C and it melts at 165F/74C. It is dry and non-sticky. Red Angel needs a temperature of 180F/82C and melts at 240F/116C. Midway markets a lube/sizer heater that works well with any of the Thompson lubes, and it is drilled and tapped to accept all of the popular lube/sizer units.

Dave Corbin, head honcho of **Corbin Manufacturing & Supply**, has been putting some wear on his thinking cap again. The firm specializes in equipment and supplies for swaging bullets, and Corbin has come up with something he calls Bullet Balls. These are lightweight spheres of linear polyethylene plastic, and you can pack one or more into the base of your jacket when swaging bullets, going on to put some amount of lead core up in the front of it. That produces a bullet with a full-length airframe, rela-

tively light in overall weight for the sake of reduced recoil, but with its center of gravity well to the front. The possibilities of the approach are distinctly intriguing.

Corbin can supply swaging dies for the .416-inch bullet diameter for those intent upon working with that burly caliber. I have one of the Ruger Model 77 Magnum rifles in 416 Rigby and have been having so much fun with it as to border upon the downright indecent.

Now it's true you can buy 416 bullets in weights up around 400 to 420 grains or even heavier, but if you loft those forth at any respectable velocities, the recoil will just about rip your shoulder off by the bloody, writhing roots.

What I did was to run some 210-grain Hornady No. 4103 FMJ-FP bullets up into the nose-forming die of the Corbin 416 set, bumping them up from .410- to .416-inch diameter and making neat-looking round-nose FMJs out of them in the process. With half the weight of a 420-grain, recoil isn't all that much worse than a really severe cold.

The powder that really made the 210-grain bullets perform in the 416 Rigby Ruger turned out to be

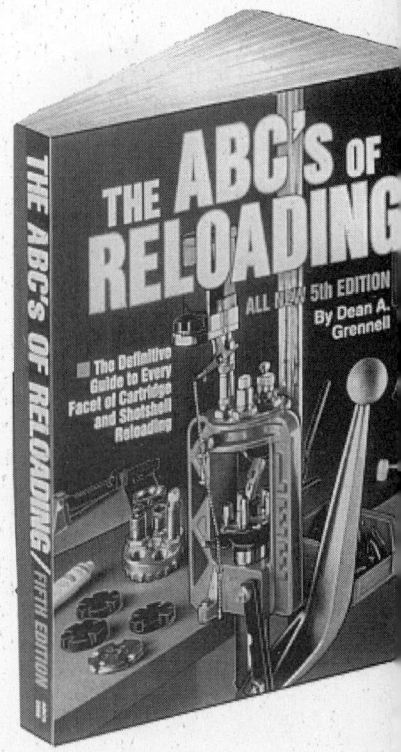
The ABC's of Reloading from DBI Books, Inc.

Accurate Arms No. 2015 BR. With cautiously increased charge weights and the ballistics listed in fps/fpe format, the quoted number of grains of 2015 BR delivered as follows, with the 210-grain HCG (Hornady/Corbin/Grennell) bullets:

AA 2015 BR Powder

86.5 grains	3094/4465
91.0 grains	3173/4696
94.4 grains	3298/5073
97.0 grain	3407/5414
100.2 grains	3509/5743

All five of the above rounds were fired at a single aiming paster from a distance of 100 yards, with velocities varying by 415 fps and a standard deviation of approximately 168.5428729 fps. The entire group showed a center-spread of 1.739 inches, with the best four into 1.106—that's pretty close to one minute-of-angle.

The fifth charge increase got us pretty close to three foot-tons of muzzle energy, at a velocity that wouldn't seem unduly shabby in a 22-250 Remington, but with a bullet weighing about four times as much. We decided to tie it off at that point.

As you may know, swaging enables one to "bump-up" bullets to a larger diameter quite readily, although it's by no means as easy and simple to bring the diameter down to a smaller figure. Since that particular test session, I have bumped up some 135-grain Nosler 10mm bullets to .416-inch girth and they show a lot of interesting promise. I look forward to trying those in the big Ruger to see if I can obtain velocities in the range of the 220 Swift, but that has

H&G TCFH designs that include the 62-grain No. 333 in 38 and the 87-grain No. 350 in 44 size. All have a single grease groove, are flat on either end and measure just .250-inch from front to back. The designation was dreamed up by Wayne Gibbs and it stands for Tuna Can From Hell. All that notwithstanding, the TCFH concept has its practical aspects. Loaded one at a time, they deliver fine accuracy and modest recoil for short-range plinking and target practice. You don't really need a massive gob of lead to

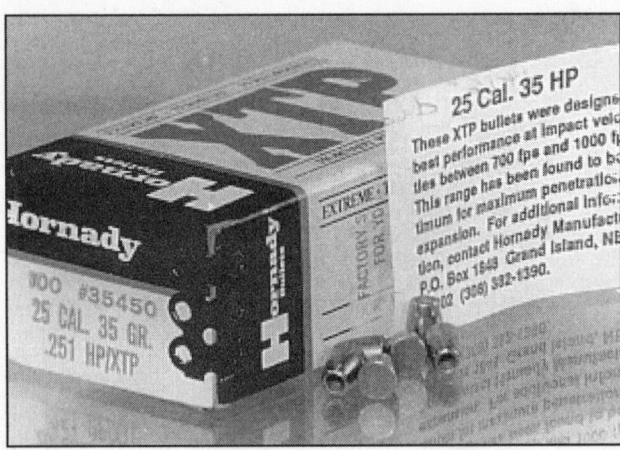

XTP bullets in 25-caliber from Hornady.

Left bullet was "bumped up" to .416-inch diameter.

Lyman's 47th Reloading Handbook

416 Rigby

to wait until I get the current batch of copy deadlines off the nape of my neck.

Loyd D. "Butch" Catron operates **Uvalde Machine & Tool** in the Texas town of that name. He makes and markets the UM&T Berdan Depriming Tool, designed to deprime Berdan primed cases, 30-caliber or larger, made to NATO standards since 1965. The flash holes in pre-1965 cases will be too small for the locating/extracting (L/E) pins to enter. The two pins are guided into the two flash holes and the exposed end of the tool is tapped with a hammer or mallet, with the case head resting in a shellholder or a similar support large enough to provide clearance for the ejected primer. The tools are available in manual or press-type patterns, at $38 plus $5 S&H, plus sales tax to Texas addresses.

Hensley & Gibbs recently added a TCFH design in 41 Magnum. It's their mould number 368 and it weighs 79 grains when cast in linotype alloy. It joins the other two

penetrate target paper. What's more, they make your casting alloy deliver a great many additional bullets.

Depending upon the case being reloaded, it may be possible to load two, three, perhaps even four of the TCFH bullets into a single round, although more than two may introduce more complexity than many of us feel we really need.

A copy of the current H&G charts of mould designs may be obtained by sending a business-length, self-addressed, stamped envelope to Mrs. Sharon Gibbs, Box 10, Murphy, OR 97533. Be patient, as your request may arrive when they are waiting for a fresh version to get back from the printer.

Along the way, I managed to eke forth a fifth edition of *ABC'S of Reloading*, which is published by those wonderful folks who bring you GUN DIGEST. It calls to mind an observation once made by the late Walt Kelly, creator of the comic strip, Pogo: "Them fifths are great for celebrating." ●

Building an...

ALMOST-SERIOUS RIFLE

The older some shooters get, the bigger their rifles.

by Wilf MacGlais

SEVERAL YEARS AGO, one of the better outdoor writers introduced a new magnum cartridge via an article praising its performance on caribou. Our hero's choice of quarry seemed a bit odd at the time, considering that a goodly percentage of Eskimos were still bagging their caribou with cartridges as small as the 22 Hornet.

One of the all-time greats once said he would be willing to take on any and all North American game, including the larger species of bears, with a 257 Roberts. There was a day when I would have been willing to take them on with my 22 High Power, but I had an excuse: I was a none-too-bright fifteen-year-old who had dropped a couple of Pacific Coast blacktail bucks in their tracks, one short standing shot each.

As hunting conditions have evolved over the years, so have men's notions on the adequacy of certain older cartridges when used on our larger big game species. One cannot deliver a mortal wound to a big game animal and have him take off as though stung by a bee without suffering a change of opinion. This is not to say that we need the 338 Winchester (or any other magnum) for caribou, but experience has led me to distance myself from the High Power a great deal farther than our letter writer ever distanced himself from the 257.

George Jacobsen, a man with a *lot* of technical and field experience, made the point in the April, 1974, *American Rifleman*. In the process of taking 200-plus head of African antelope over a period of three years, Jacobsen had found that the 30-06 could be less than adequate when used under less than ideal conditions. Conversely, Jacobsen found that the 350 Rigby Magnum, which is ballistically an identical twin of the 35 Whelen, performed very well indeed when called upon to handle the more difficult shots. We could further belabor the point, but we digress.

The seeds from which this article sprouted came not from Jacobsen's article, which dealt primarily with bullet performances, but from an article by C.E. Harris. Said seeds have been a long time coming to fruition. Relying upon information found in my NRA *Gunsmithing Manual* (early edition) rather than any innate mechanical ability, I have put together a few fairly respectable looking rifles over the years. I recently got around to attempting a copy of the handsome 35 Whelen whose creation Harris had covered in detail in the September, 1975, *American Rifleman*. There are, however, a few departures.

Harris had based his rifle on the highly acclaimed pre-1964 Model 70 Winchester. At various times, I have owned three Model 70s—all like Harris' of pre-war manufacture. It has long seemed to me that they suffered the common shortcoming (admittedly to a lesser degree than most) of all of the so called "improved" Mauser types in that they failed to measure up to the original '98. To put it in stronger terms: For some years now, my views have coincided with those of the opinionated few who consider the pre-'64 Model 70 the world's most overrated rifle action.

My project was based upon an FN deluxe Mauser action that was purchased by mail some thirty years back from N.F. Strebe, who was a regular advertiser in the *Rifleman* in those dear-departed pre-1968 gun law days. It now sports a new, Flaig-installed Douglas barrel. Its third stock was carved from an exceptionally dense Claro walnut blank from Calico Hardwoods (also a former *Rifleman* advertiser). My cheekpiece design would probably bring pained expressions to the faces of some stockmakers, but all who have seen it have been polite enough to comment on its good looks.

The barreled action was glass-bedded from its tang to a point just short of the tip of the forearm. A deep channel was cut in the forearm and the action and magazine areas of the stock were undercut. Laminated in with resin, glass cloth, and flock during the bedding process, this created what is, in effect, a strongback.

Much ado is made by some experts about allowing contact only at the receiver ring flat, rear of the recoil lug, and bottom of the tang, when bedding the action. This oft-repeated dogma harks back to the pre-glass-bedding era—to those early days when even the experts sometimes resorted to shims to achieve their three-point bedding. It is pertinent only in those cases where the wood (which has the potential to move) is in contact with the action. Our experience has been that when the glass bedding is sufficiently thick (upwards of ⅛-inch), total contact is a positive thing. This is seen in the benchrester's glued-in actions.

We relieve actions only at the *bottom* of the recoil lug and the last half-inch of the bottom of the tang. *Release agent-coated* actions bedded

in this manner are best tapped out with the aid of a mallet and a pair of stockmaker's guide screws.

Two short sections of threaded steel rod act as blind crossbolts at the front and rear of the magazine well. With a clamped-on straight edge acting as a guide, a ⅜-inch hole was drilled at a 30-degree angle from the tang area down through the center of the stock's wrist, to allow the glassing in of a section of ⁵⁄₁₆-inch threaded rod.

One end of the rod was heated with an acetylene torch and bumped up, then forged into a rectangle. It was ground where needed, reheated, and bent to a 30-degree open level. It was then bored, first with a ¹⁷⁄₆₄-inch bit to receive the rear guard screw, then counter-bored ⅜-inch to fit the boss on the tang, and finally cut to its proper length.

The guard screw bushing was shortened to suit, and with the rod in place, the action and guard were tried for fit. The rod (together with the bushing) was glassed in as a separate operation with the stock positioned butt down. This procedure eliminates the need for any unsightly relieving of the wood at the rear of the tang, as well as preventing fractures in the wrist (including the type seen in Harris' stock).

The weak link in the bolt-action chain (exacerbated in those with hinged floorplates) is in the front tang area of the guard. It is not all that unusual for a bedded-in-wood guard to move enough in a frequently fired, heavily recoiling rifle to have produced a darkened compression mark here. We increased the metal-to-wood bearing surface by using the Moto Tool to carefully undercut the wood in the tang area, enough to slide in a dural "washer" that had been drilled ½-inch then lightly filed to fit the guard screw boss. The washer (which will need slotting) plus a mock-up of the hinge extension when used in conjunction with a hinged floorplate—illustrated—is, of course, glass-bedded simultaneously with the guard.

Early on we had tried slightly oversized aluminum mock-ups of the floorplate hinge extension and the trigger when bedding in guards. Unfortunately, even though they were tapered and waxed to facilitate their release, they had an annoying tendency to lock in. This led to our return to wood mock-ups (used here) which are easily chipped out.

Another dogma-fraught subject is that concerning the use of a few pounds of upward pressure on the

barrel at the forearm tip to reduce vibration and thus improve accuracy. This rifle's fairly heavy #3 1:12-inch-twist barrel shoots very well free-floated back to the parallel section of the barrel reinforce. Clearance in the free-floated area (holding to date) was created by applying a strip of 2-inch-wide cellophane tape to the underside of the barrel prior to glass bedding. To avoid wrinkles, two short lengths of tape were applied at right angles to the bore in the tapered area of the swell.

Some recommend the use of electrician's tape to provide clearance in those areas needing same, such as the magazine. Our experience here has been that a layer of masking tape, over which a layer of cellophane tape has been applied, does a much better job. Being that they are difficult to tape, the *bottoms* of the recoil lug and tang are brushed with a coat of thick latex paint and allowed to dry before bedding. Any holes or depressions that could contribute to the locking in of the action or guard are filled in with candle drippings. Ordinary paste wax is our release agent.

Upon completion of the glass-bedding, the stock was sanded with #500 wet or dry and warmed in the sun before applying each of its five coats of Birchwood Casey Tru Oil.

A new Timney Sportsman trigger replaced the stiff FN single-stage job. The FN bolt head safety, which had occasionally self-disengaged when hunting with the rifle slung from one's shoulder, was put to less serious use. It was replaced with a Precision Metalsmithing side swing shroud/safety. This one is a bit tricky and fellow amateurs taking on this job will find it a challenge.

Having had ring trouble with the one Herkner (the make used by Harris) scope mount that I have owned, I wasn't troubled by its discontinuance. The Bausch and Lomb 1½-6x scope rides in the fourth set of Kimber mounts. These mounts work every bit as well as did the top mounts on a Griffin & Howe Express rifle I formerly owned. They also (with a second set of rings) allow instant replacement with a sighted-in back-up scope should the occasion arise.

Emboldened by the progress to this point, I decided to attempt the metal work on the barrel, which I had originally planned to farm out. This, too, is tricky. Since I don't intend to shoot lion at night by the light of a carbide lamp (or any other source of illumination) as did John

Taylor, the auxiliary iron sights are a departure from the Holland & Holland night sights used by Harris. This change eliminated the need for an expensive, wrist-weakening, trapped grip cap as well.

The front sight is a Precision Metalsmithing Custom Band Ramp with sourdough blade. The rear is a Dakota Express Rear Island and blade. With the aid of the indispensable Dremel Moto Tool and a bit of Prussian blue, the base of the rear island was contoured to fit the barrel taper.

Another departure was a barrel band sling swivel base by London Guns. Although there seems to be an abundance of information on the silver soldering process, there is little pertaining to the proper aligning of the parts themselves on the barrel.

Left to my own devices, I first cen-

Above-bore heights of the front and rear sight blades were copied from those on my Whitworth 375 H&H. In addition to assuring a line of sight above the scope mount bases, this created a practical high comb/open-sight combination.

At this juncture, the barreled action and guard were polished first with Brownell's 555 black polishing compound on a hard-felt wheel, followed by gray and white on their individual muslin wheels. The metal work was hot-water blued using Brownell's Dicropan IM—following all instructions to the letter. To prevent possible rusting, the dowel sections used to plug the chamber and muzzle were removed forthwith to allow drying and oiling of the bore.

Before moving on to the shooting bench, I should note that handload-

The new rifle's performance at the benchrest could be called predictable. Temporarily glass-bedded in a lopped off VZ 24 stock with a 12x Redfield scope, the 12-inch-twist barreled action had, with 200-grain round-nose bullets, produced three-shot test groups that averaged just over a minute of angle. These stubby slugs had produced groups that were almost twice as large when shot in the discarded 14-inch-twist Whelen barrel.

With most experts recommending use of a 14- or 16-inch twist, this disparity would seem to fly in the face of conventional wisdom.

As anticipated, the long-throated 12-inch-twist Douglas barrel does an excellent job of digesting the longer 250- and 300-grain bullets as well. I did, however, run into trouble with the iron sights. This was the direct

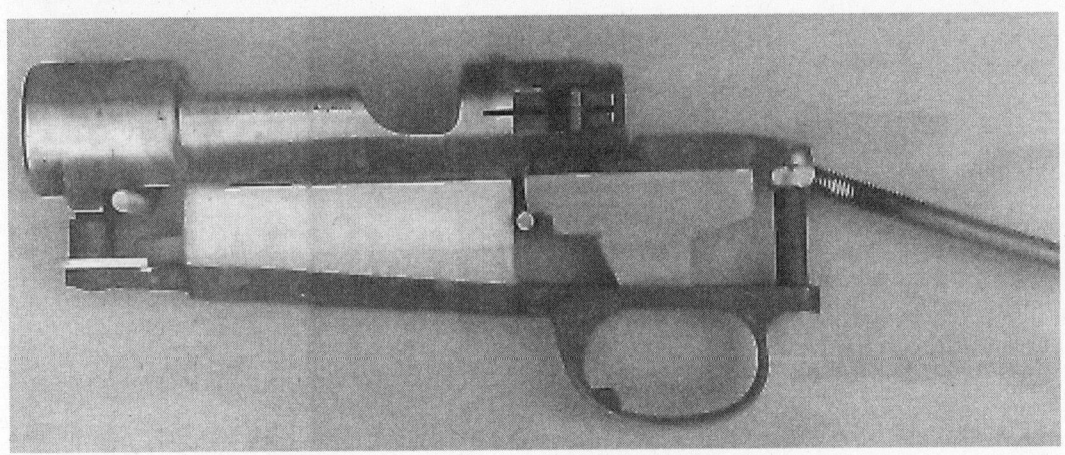

Illustrated here on a BRNO action and Mark X guard are the author's wrist reinforcement rod, shortened rear guard screw bushing, blind through bolts, trigger and floorplate hinge extension mock-ups and tang washer.

tered the swivel base by aligning it with the action flat with the aid of a sling swivel and an accurate level. The front and rear sights were similarly aligned with the aid of the level and a machinist's parallel clamp, then witness-marked for soldering. Held to the scribe marks by their bands, the swivel base and front sight were silver soldered.

There were two points of concern regarding the rear sight base: 1) With the use of the 8-40 screws that came with the sight, there was a chance of ruining the barrel by accidentally drilling through into the bore; 2) That the heat required for silver soldering might weaken the critical swell area.

In a drill press, drilling the holes without accidentally going through into the bore proved less of a chore than we had feared. The overheating question was handled by the use of Brownell's Force 44 low-heat solder.

ers may find, as had I some time back, that *used* 30-06 brass does not take well to being stretched out to receive .358-inch bullets. Even though case throats were first scrubbed out with a bore brush, run over a graphite-lubricated 8 expander button, and allowed to "rest," necking up to .358-inch resulted in a high percentage of cracked necks. The solution here has been to make up all loads with unfired Frankford Arsenal match cases.

I should also mention that handloaders whose previous experience has been limited to the flatter shooting cartridges, which can produce a near-common downrange point of impact with a wide spectrum of bullet weights, will find themselves in a new ball game when taking on the Whelen. With its sights set to zero a 200-grain Hornady spirepoint at 200 yards, my Whelen will put the 300-grain Barnes bullet 19 inches low.

result of my short-sighted use of the lighter (less expensive) bullets when sighting in. Fortunately, before too much of the rear sight had been filed off, I caught this mistake. They now zero the 300-grain Barnes round-nose bullet at 160 yards.

This being my second 35 Whelen, the new rifle's performance in the field was equally predictable. To date, this rifle has accounted for one good-sized male black bear that was hit in the seat of the pants at a full 200 yards—a far longer shot than some of the purveyors of corral-dust-inflated shooting distances would have us believe. Drilled end to end by a 300-grain Barnes round-nose bullet, he dropped like the proverbial armload of wet sacks.

Although it will never qualify as a work of art, the satisfaction derived from the creation of this rifle justified the effort twice over. Its utility is a bonus. ●

by HAL SWIGGETT

HANDGUNS TODAY:

SIXGUNS AND OTHERS

NEW FOR this year?

Enough to make it interesting.

BF Pistol is in new hands and with some updating.

Charco, Inc. (formerly Charter Arms) is delivering revolvers.

Colt's stainless steel Anaconda now is made in 45 Colt.

A pair of new derringers (make that three).

Wesson Firearms with a lot of new machinery, two new guns, compensated barrel assemblies...

...and a lot more a few lines down. Let's go alphabetical and see what happens.

American Derringer

Bob Saunders' original Model 1, listed at 15 ounces, is offered in more than sixty chamberings. Ultra Lightweight, 7½ ounces; Lightweight, 10 ounces; Texas Commemorative, 16 ounces; Alaskan Survival, 16½ ounces; Model 6 410 or 45 Colt, 21 ounces. There's a DA 38 in four chamberings, 14½ ounces; a High Standard-type 22 in Long Rifle or Magnum,

11 ounces; and the legendary Semmerling. This one looks like an autoloader, holds five 45 ACP rounds, measures 5.2x3.1x1 inches and features a lightning-fast manual slide action. I've shot this gun. You'll have to see it to believe it. Then there is the stainless steel Pen pistol. It transforms from a pen to a legal pistol in two seconds. Chambered for 22 Long Rifle, 25 Auto or 32 Auto.

Anschutz

Anschutz Exemplar pistols have an improved rear sight so finely tuned it can change the point of impact $^{3}/_{10}$-inch at 100 feet with each click. There's a two-stage trigger factory set at 9.85 ounces. I no longer have to ask for this fine pistol in 22 WMR. There is one. Only one. See the "Testfire" article, page 174.

Test-firing Mitchell Arms adjustable sight single-action 45 Colt. Mitchell was right—Hal did like it.

Proof there is one 22 Magnum Anschutz Exemplar pistol.

Armscorp

This company offers three versions of their Model 200: 4-inch 38 Special (Police); 2½-inch 38 Special (Detective Chief); and 4-inch Thunder Chief in 38 Special, 22 Magnum Rimfire and 22 Long Rifle. All are six-shot. Grips are rubber or wood.

BF Pistol

This single shot of fallingblock design is offered in a multitude of calibers and is primarily aimed at silhouette shooters. My test pistol is chambered for 7-30 Waters, has 12 inches of barrel and is topped with Jim Herringshaw's Maxi-Mount holding a 7x Burris. Factory Federal 120-grain loads, through Ken Oehler's Model 35P, run 2328 fps. My first homemades, both with Nosler 120-grain Ballistic Tips, move out at 2160 (36 grains of W-748) and 2067 (37.5 grains of H-414). Winchester primers are all I use. My only problem—I have lost my trigger finger—is that my middle finger is not so educated. It's a smart finger; it will learn. Accuracy? Superb! From the E. Arthur Brown Company.

Charco

These fine little revolvers are again being offered. Three versions: Bulldog Pug (44 Special), Off Duty (38 Special/22 Long Rifle) and Undercover (38 Special/32

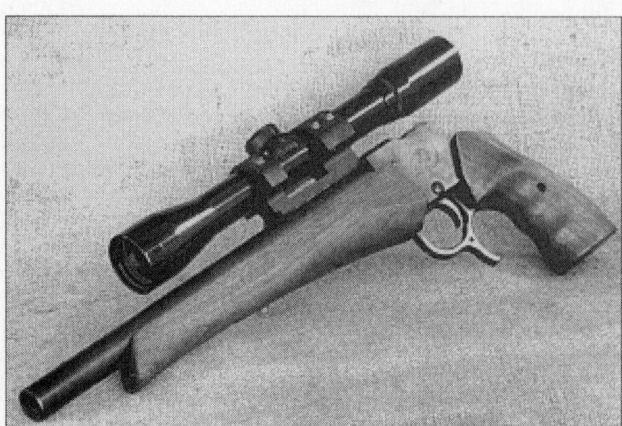

European American Armory's Big Bore Bounty Hunter with fixed or adjustable sights and 5½- or 7½-inch barrel.

BF Pistol chambered for 7-30 Waters and topped with Burris' 7x scope and Herringshaw's Maxi-Mount.

Magnum). Barrel length on 44s is 2½ inches—the others 2 inches. Charco, the company, has new machinery and updated equipment, and Nick Ecker, head man, is real excited about getting back to work. He also wants you to remember all Charter Arms revolvers wear a Lifetime Maintenance Policy.

Colt

Anaconda is *it* so far as Colt double actions are concerned. I have shot their 44 Magnum extensively. It truly is a beauty. Looks like an overgrown Python. It's a shame they didn't carry that theme all the way through. Inside, it is a Cobra. Not bad, but inside the Python is a whole bunch better.

Colt's catalog lists only the Anaconda and their introduced-in-1927 Colt Detective Special in revolvers. Read into that what you will. If interested in this Anaconda, could be you'd best buy one in a hurry. It has 6 inches of barrel, good sights and black neoprene "pebbled" combat-style grips.

European American Armory

The Big Bore Bounty Hunter single action comes with fixed or adjustable sights and 5½- or 7½-inch barrels. Cartridges include 357 Magnum, 44 Magnum or 45 Colt. Guns are manufactured by the H. Weihrauch Company in Germany.

Harrington & Richardson

H&R's Sportsman 999 has been around a long time and withstood those tests. One of these was my second to be personally owned "way back

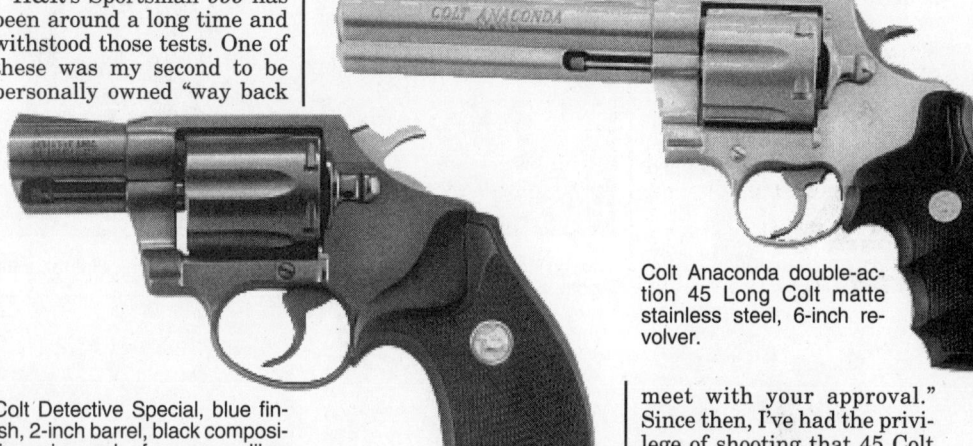

Colt Anaconda double-action 45 Long Colt matte stainless steel, 6-inch revolver.

there." Barrel lengths are 4 or 6 inches, 22 Short, Long or Long Rifle, and they are nine-shot. With adjustable sights, I'd best add. A lot of gun for their cost, and now it's in production again.

HJS Arms

Herman Seminiano's HJS Arms company is located as far south as can be in Texas—Brownsville to be specific. His American-made derringers are two: Frontier is four-barreled with positive rotating firing pin, stainless steel, 5½ ounces of weight and 22 Long Rifle only. Lone Star weighs 6 ounces and is single shot—38 S&W or 380 Auto.

Magnum Research

Magnum Research has renamed their SSP-91 single shot pistol to conform, I assume, with their other Eagles. The single shot is now called Lone Eagle. It's the same pistol offering fourteen chamberings from 22 Hornet through 444 Marlin. This one offers quick-change, but the switch includes a complete receiver/barrel—not just barrels. This means each is FFL registered.

Mitchell Arms

Last year, I mentioned Don Mitchell saying, "This time I have a single action that will meet with your approval." Since then, I've had the privilege of shooting that 45 Colt single action with its 5½-inch barrel. Not only does it look like the original, it s-o-u-n-d-s like the original. Cock it slowly and it spells C-O-L-T. I like that. Not only that, but it shoots the way it looks and sounds. Made in Italy, not Hartford, but it speaks C-O-L-T and not Italian.

Remington

The XP-100 bolt-action Remington pistol was introduced in 1963, chambered to accept their 221 Remington Fire Ball cartridge featuring a 50-grain bullet at 2650 fps. Three decades later, all sorts of things have happened to XPs. My collection includes

Nick Ecker, Charco executive, holds his company's Charter Arms Bulldog Pug.

Colt Detective Special, blue finish, 2-inch barrel, black composition grips and, of course, caliber 38 Special.

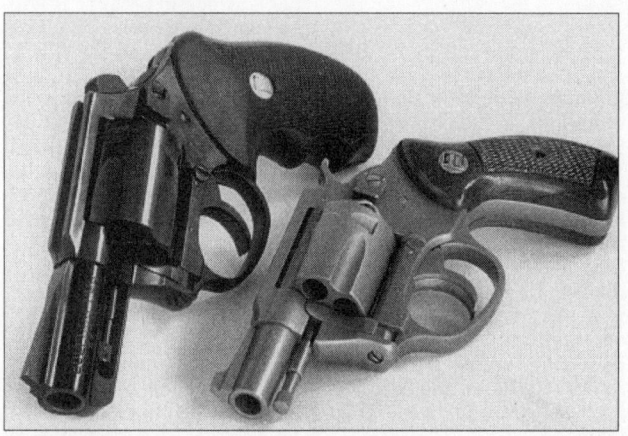

Charter Arms 2½-inch Bulldog Pug 44 Special and stainless 2-inch Undercover 38 Special.

four: 223 rechambered to 22-250, 7mm BR rechambered to 284 (by SSK Industries), 35 Remington and an "R" 250 Savage. New this time around are two wood-stocked production models. The Silhouette wears a newly contoured 10½-inch barrel and is chambered for their 7mm BR cartridge. The stock is American walnut and mid-handle. The Hunter is 14⅜ inches of barrel contoured same as the Silhouette. Its stock, same style as above, is laminated light and dark wood. Chamberings are 223 Remington, 7mm BR, 35 Remington and 7mm-08 Remington. The Silhouette wears adjustable sights; Hunter is drilled and tapped for scope mounting.

Rossi

Interarms has added a 3¼-

Though Freedom Arms has no new offerings this year, Hal feels there is no finer single action than the Model 353 357 Magnum.

Texas Arms Defender is offered in 9mm Luger, 38 Special, 357 Magnum, 40 S&W, 44 Magnum, 45 Auto and 45 Colt/410.

HJS Arms' 4-barreled Frontier derringer is offered in 22 Long Rifle only.

New for this year from North American Arms is a belt buckle to hold their Long Rifle-frame minis.

inch stainless steel 357 Magnum Comp Gun to the Model 971 series. These M971s feature square-notch rear sights with white outline, front sight blued with red insert, ejector rod shroud integral with their barrels and combat styled, contoured rubber grips.

Ruger

The fertile mind of Bill Ruger never rests. This time his company offers three innovations, and destined to be number one popular is their Vaquero single action. Based on the New Model Blackhawk, but in the form of Colt's SAA, Vaquero's barrel lengths are 4⅝, 5½, and 7½ inches. Chamberings are 45 Colt, 44-40 Winchester and 44 Magnum. Vaquero's "color case-hardened" frame enhances the blued and polished barrel, cylinder and grip frame.

The cute little Ruger Bearcat is back. Its demise in 1973

caused it to be immediately extra valuable to collectors. Those first were two: standard with aluminum frame and Super built of steel. There are two this time also—blue and stainless steel. Plus a minor difference in that the cylinder is a bit lengthier (frame too, obviously) because it will be issued with two cylinders: 22 Long Rifle and 22 WMR. All this plus all of Ruger's safety innovations.

And now the SP101 is offered as hammerless and double-action-only in 38 Special +P+ or 357 Magnum. The 357 will handle all bullet weights and the 38 all +P and +P+ ammo.

Smith & Wesson

"Outdoorsmen interested in carrying a serious handgun will want to check out the 629 Mountain Gun from S&W." Those are the first two lines of S&W's press release, and they're right. This one is

Harrington & Richardson's Model 999 Sportsman double action has been around since 1950, and it is still doing well.

stainless steel, 4-inch barrel, 44 Magnum and, believe it or not, it's drilled and tapped for scope mounting. It is delivered with Hogue's round-butt rubber Monogrip, a pinned black ramp front sight and adjustable rear black blade. This one is a limited edition,

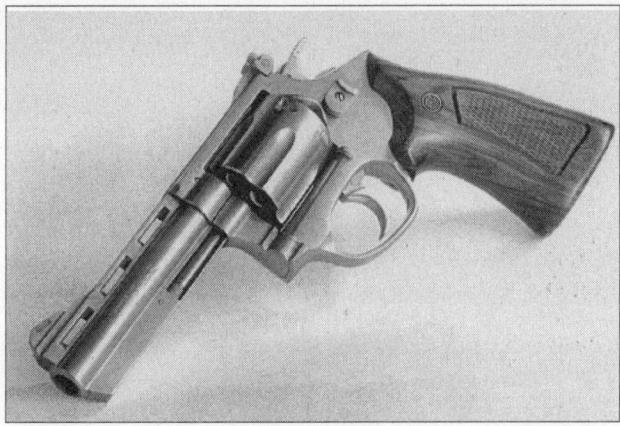
Rossi's 4-inch 38 Special stainless steel double action is vent-ribbed and has good sights. Hal had to buy this one for Wilma.

making it available only for a short time.

There's now a Model 442 Centennial five-shot, 38 Special, aluminum alloy frame, cylinder of carbon steel and 2-inch barrel. Finish on this hammerless revolver is low-luster matte blue or satin nickel.

Taurus

You are going to need their catalog. There are twenty listings as "new." From 32 H&R Magnum six-shot with adjustable sights in barrel lengths of 3 or 4 inches through 357 Magnum/38 Special six-shot with adjustable sights. My favorite Taurus revolvers are two—both stainless steel and both 4-inch barreled. The first is an adjustable sight nine-shot 22 Long Rifle (pistolsmithed to perfection by Teddy Jacobson's Actions by "T"). The other is a fixed-sight 44 Special.

Texas Arms

A new kid on the block, Greg Bond manufactures the Texas Arms Defender—an "Old West"-style 1880s der-

Bill Grover took this sika buck during the "Handgun Meat Hunt For The Needy" on the Y.O. Ranch using one of this Improved #5 right-hand 45 Colt revolvers.

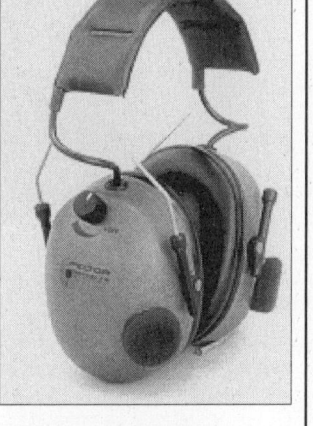
Swiggett finds Peltor's Tactical 7 ideally suited to range shooting because it allows conversation to be heard yet shuts out *all* noise from shooting. He often wears it while hunting, especially from blinds or stands.

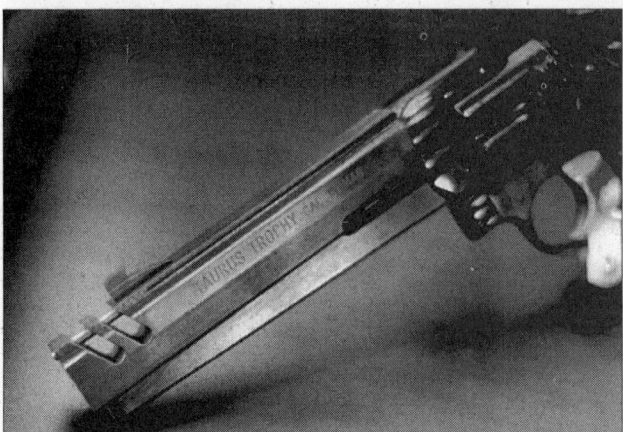
Taurus Trophy 357 Magnum comp-barreled double action—so new it isn't in their catalog.

Smith & Wesson's new Model 629 Mountain Gun in 44 Magnum has 4-inch barrel, is of stainless steel, has adjustable sights and is issued with the Hogue monogrips you see.

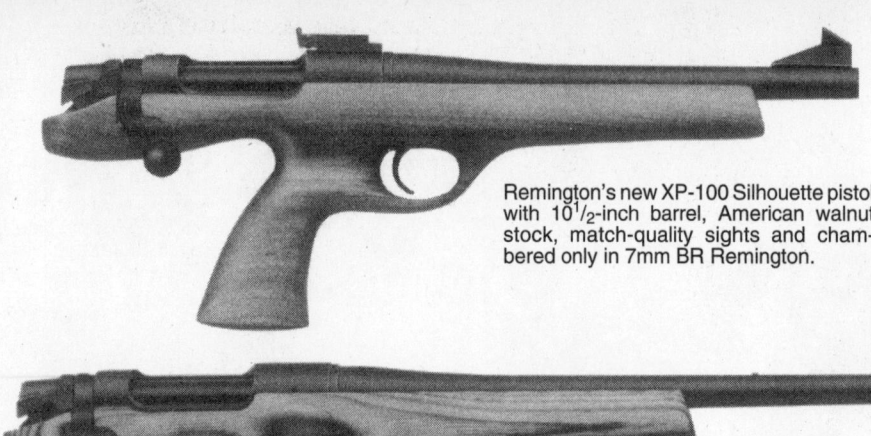

Remington's new XP-100 Silhouette pistol with 10^1/$_2$-inch barrel, American walnut stock, match-quality sights and chambered only in 7mm BR Remington.

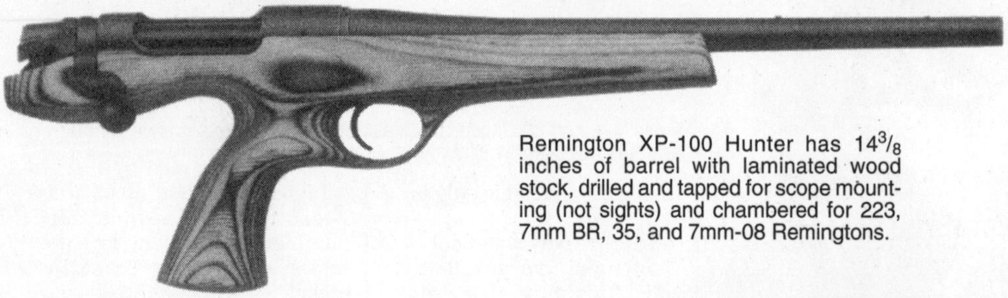

Remington XP-100 Hunter has 14^3/$_8$ inches of barrel with laminated wood stock, drilled and tapped for scope mounting (not sights) and chambered for 223, 7mm BR, 35, and 7mm-08 Remingtons.

ter, 30-30, 22 WMR and 22 Long Rifle. The test? To check out point of impact when changing barrels. A three-shot group was fired, that barrel removed, another installed, another three-shot group, etc. Twice around—meaning those same four barrels were reinstalled, in the same order, and three more shots fired into the original group. To say I was amazed puts it mildly. All six bullets printed so close together as to make it the shooter's fault should even a jackrabbit be missed—at 100 yards. The real kicker came with the 375 Winchester. The initial three shots were in 1^7/$_{16}$ inches. The next three printed *inside* the first group. This with Winchester factory 200-grain loads.

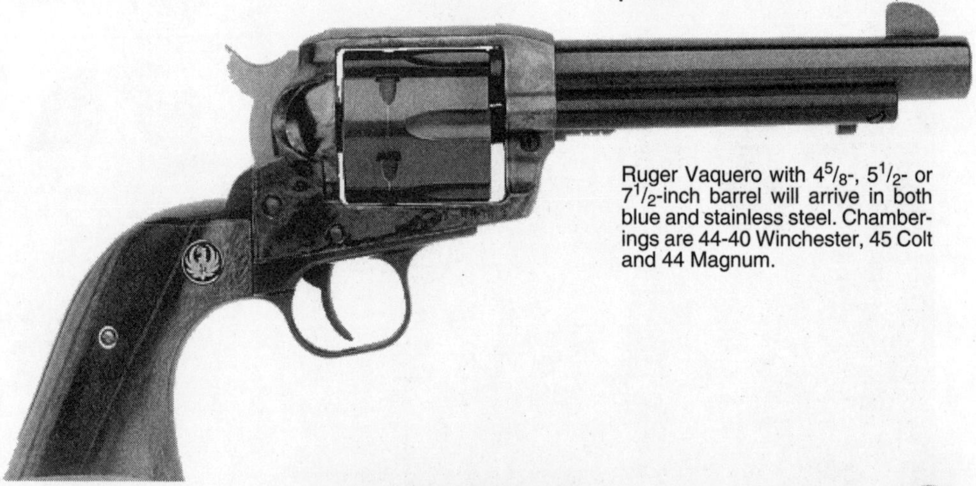

ringer. It has a rebounding hammer, retracting firing pins and a cross-bolt safety. Greg goes on to describe it as the safest derringer ever manufactured. Chamberings offered are 9mm Luger, 38 Special, 357 Magnum, 40 S&W, 44 Magnum, 45 Auto and 45 Colt/410. Sights are three-dot combat. Other features include a removeable trigger guard, automatic shell extractor and octagon barrels.

Texas Longhorn Arms

Bill Grover, with his Improved Number Five single action (the one built for right-hand shooters), has an all-new manufacturing facility. It's a lot bigger, plus it contains a lot of new equipment. In other words, he is in full production with guns being delivered. And now there is more. Several years back, I introduced two mighty cute little single shot pistols with the message that his plans included getting them on the market. They will be, as you read this, in full production. Called "Jezebel," they are 22s, Long Rifle and WMR.

Thompson/Center

Contender pistols are now offered in stainless steel. And, the rest of the story, all blue barrels will fit these stainless frames and/or all stainless barrels will mate with blue frames. I have just completed a test using one T/C "Hunter" 12-inch barrel with a Muzzle Tamer, one 14-inch barrel and two 16^1/$_4$-inch barrels. Calibers were 375 Winches-

Ruger Vaquero with 4^5/$_8$-, 5^1/$_2$- or 7^1/$_2$-inch barrel will arrive in both blue and stainless steel. Chamberings are 44-40 Winchester, 45 Colt and 44 Magnum.

The Bearcat is back in blue or stainless steel and with two cylinders: 22 Long Rifle and 22 WMR. It now has Ruger's transfer bar safety system. Barrel length is 4 inches.

A new double-action-only model of the compact Ruger SP101 features a spurless hammer and no single-action notch. Both 38 Special +P and 357 Magnum revolvers have 2^1/$_4$-inch barrels.

Wesson Firearms

Several new items: A stainless steel five-shot 2-inch barrel 38 Special +P, Model 738P by nomenclature, weighs 23 ounces on my postal scale and drops the hammer at an even 4 pounds. Another is a fixed-barrel, 6-inch, stainless steel revolver with lockup tight as a drum and trigger pull, are you ready for this, of 32 ounces—an even 2 pounds. This one weighs 46 ounces. There are compensated barrel assemblies for 44 Magnum, 445 SuperMag and 357 SuperMag, winding up Wes-

Wesson *fixed-barrel* 6-inch stainless 357 Magnum. This one, sent for testing, locked up tight as a drum and featured a 2-pound trigger pull.

Wesson 2-inch stainless steel 38 Special +P. Sounds heard from this Palmer, Massachusetts, plant indicate there might be a 357 Magnum in this format before long. Interchangeable barrels, of course.

Taurus' Tom Conrad shows us their new stainless steel, adjustable sighted 44 Special.

Smith & Wesson Model 442 Centennial Lightweight 38 Special is five-shot with 2-inch barrel, has a concealed hammer, and is offered in matte blue or satin nickel with rubber combat grips by Michaels of Oregon.

son's new-for-this-year items. Overall length of compensated barrel assemblies are $1\frac{1}{2}$ inches longer than the noted barrel length.

Competitor Corporation

Remember Remington's great little 5mm Rimfire? It's back, but not in rimfire! Al Straitiff has, in stock, ready for delivery, 5mm centerfire brass, bullets and reloading dies. A kit, reloading dies, shellholder, 100 bullets and 50 cases (headstamp 5mm RMCF) will set you back $79.95. This for those of us fortunate to own a 5mm Thompson/Center barrel. Should your 5mm Remington be a rifle, Al is prepared to ship, with the aforementioned items, a conversion kit for $119.95. This is a 38-grain bullet at 2100 fps, same as the original.

One more: Straitiff now has everything he needs to start production of 14-caliber barrels. You truly smallbore fans might want to get in on this.

Peltor

I shoot a lot and can still hear soft sounds, sing in a choir, tune my trumpet, a lot of things folks much younger gave up on years ago. How come? I've done my best to protect my ears. Even back fifty and more years when we were often laughed at and sometimes called "sissies" among the nicer refererences. The past two or more years, all my protection has been placed in Peltor's Tactical 7 Stereo-Long-Ear. It blocks out any and all loud noise, yet allows normal conversation to be clearly understood. I've even used mine on deer and turkey stands. Animals approaching can be heard long before they can be sighted. So far as I'm concerned, it is the best.

FSPI

Firearm Safety Products, Inc., offers the TriggerShield that warns children, or other unauthorized persons, not to handle a firearm. It covers the entire trigger area of most guns, yet leaves that firearm accessible to the owner. Constructed of Celanese Celcon, internal ratchets self-tighten to hold the specially blended rubber/neoprene-padded sides snugly against the trigger. Removal of this Trigger-Shield takes only a few seconds, even in the dark. This company also offers Trigger Alarm, a device offering the same protection as TriggerShield plus an alarm that sounds if the device is tampered with or removed from the firearm. This could come in mighty handy if you have children in the home. ●

by J. B. WOOD

HANDGUNS TODAY:

AUTOLOADERS

Designed in 40 S&W, the new USP from Heckler & Koch is also offered in 9mm.

Especially for left-handers—with all controls on the right and ejection to the left—from Rocky Mountain Arms.

Colt's M1991A1 Commander—the 45 shorter with a burr hammer.

The Baby Eagle from Magnum Research comes in 9mm, 40 S&W and 41AE. Earlier, it was the Jericho.

It HAS BEEN called the P.08, the Parabellum, and has had other military designations. Most people here just give it the name of its designer—Luger. Only one company can use that name, though: Stoeger. They registered it as a trademark many years ago.

Mitchell Arms calls it the American Eagle P-08, and it is a beautiful recreation of the classic pistol in stainless steel. It is appropriately chambered for the 9mm Luger cartridge. The gun is made in Houston, Texas, and the fit and finish are excel-lent. So far, I have fired around 400 rounds through mine, and it functions perfectly. The big surprise is the price—not cheap, but less than you'd expect. In other news from Mitchell, their re-makes of the Hi-Standard pistols are well under way.

Another 9mm that I recently tried and liked was the **Colt** Model 2000 All American, the polymer-frame version. It was reliable and accurate, and the DA-only trigger was smooth. Its handling qualities were particularly nice. The grip reminds me of the old Remington Model 51 pistol, a perfect shape. Colt now offers a conversion kit with a shorter (3^3/$_4$-inch) barrel for the Model 2000. More recent news from Colt is the introduction of two reduced-size versions of their 1991A1 pistol. Both are in 45 Auto. One is the M1991A1 Commander, differing from the full-sized gun only in length and hammer spur shape. The other is

One of the smallest of the double-action nines, Astra's A-75 from EAA can also be had in 40.

New from Bersa, via Eagle Imports, the 9mm Thunder 9 has elegant lines.

the M1991A1 Compact, which is $1\frac{1}{2}$ inches shorter and $\frac{3}{8}$-inch less in height.

With a look toward the competitive shooter, **Smith & Wesson** is offering a Limited Series pistol called the 356 TSW. Its special cartridge meets the IPSC "major power factor," and it has all of the features that are usually added to competition guns, right out of the box. Also new from S&W was the Special Edition Model 5906, with a special finish and a Novak Lo-Mount Carry rear sight. Early in 1993, this special edition was already sold out.

New from **Sturm, Ruger & Company** is the 40 S&W KP91DAO with a spurless hammer and no external levers other than the slide latch. As the designation indicates, it is double-action-only. The Eastern Region U.S. Forest Service has adopted the new pistol as their standard sidearm. Also new from Ruger is the P-93, a compact 9mm in DA-only or decock-only. It

weighs only 24 ounces and has a full fifteen-round magazine capacity.

Speaking of compact 9mm pistols, **Taurus** has a beauty—the new PT-908. It's only 1.1 inches wide, with a 3.8-inch barrel, and just 7.05 inches in overall length. Its single-column magazine holds eight rounds. It has a double-action trigger and a frame-mounted three-position safety. The sights are three-dot style. Versions in 40 S&W and 45 Auto are planned.

Eagle Imports has the new **Bersa** Thunder 9, a full-sized but slim fifteen-shot 9mm with selective double action. It has all of the mechanical features that have become standard on pistols in this category, and several special ones. These include an ambidextrous slide release and safety-levers, an adjustable trigger stop, and superb ergonomics. All of the Bersa pistols are of high quality, and the price will be competitive.

European American Armory now has the **Astra** line, and a new "super compact" pistol in 9mm and 40 S&W, the Astra A-75. It is just $6\frac{1}{2}$ inches overall, with a $3\frac{1}{2}$-inch barrel. The trigger is selective double action, and there is a frame-mounted decocking lever. Magazine capacity is eight rounds in 9mm and seven rounds in 40 S&W. Of course, EAA also still has the Witness and the other fine Tanfoglio pistols from Italy.

In the full-sized pistols chambered for 40 S&W, I have tried two versions of the **AMT** On Duty, a DA-only and a regular double action with a decocking lever. Both guns performed flawlessly, and they were pleasant to shoot. The nicely shaped grip spread out the slightly higher felt recoil of the 40 S&W cartridge. Both versions are also offered in 9mm. I have also fired the new DAO version of the Back Up, and it is a little jewel.

Among the other new pistols I have tried recently were

two versions of the Centurion from **Beretta**. The Centurion has the frame of the full-sized Model 92FS and Model 96, with the slide and barrel of the Compact version, about a half-inch shorter. This gives a smaller carrying size with a full magazine capacity in both chamberings, 9mm and 40 S&W. As always with Beretta pistols, the Centurions performed perfectly with all loads.

The 9mm **Sigarms** P228 now has an additional military designation. As the "M11 Compact Pistol," it is the new substitute-standard sidearm for military police, flight crews, armor crews, CID agents, general officers and other special applications. The P228 was already in use by some departments of the FBI, DEA, FAA and other federal law encorcement groups. One important difference in the M11 is the sights—it has three-dot tritium night sights. These, of course, are offered as optional accesso-

J.B. Wood with the American Eagle P-08 from Mitchell Arms.

ries on the civilian P228 and the other Sigarms pistols.

As an outgrowth of their work on a prototype SOCOM pistol for the U.S. Special Operations Command, **Heckler & Koch** now has a new commercial pistol, the USP (Universal Self-loading Pistol). Available in 9x19mm and 40 S&W, it was designed as a 40, not upscaled to that cartridge. The gun is more conventional in appearance and features than the other H&K pistols and is offered in DAO and regular selective double ac-

tion. Notable is a set of grooves in the front extension of the frame for laser mounting.

Added to the Eagle line at **Magnum Research** is the Baby Eagle, which is diminutive only in comparison with their massive Desert Eagle. Made by IMI in Israel, it is offered in 9mm, 40 S&W and 41AE. It is essentially the same as the Jericho pistol, imported earlier by KBI, and it has the same outstanding ergonomics. There are similarities to the CZ-75, but with

This is the new compact version of the 357 Magnum pistol from Coonan Arms.

some fine IMI design touches, such as full-length inside slide rails.

KBI, Incorporated once again has the well-made pistols from Hungary that were based on the FN Hi-Power, in single-action and double-action versions. They also have the excellent PMK-380 and SMC-380, resembling, respectively, the Walther PP and PPK. I have fired a PMK-380 extensively, and its per-

formance has been perfect. In the medium-frame DA 380 Auto category, it is a good choice.

Rocky Mountain Arms is making mirror-image pistols of Model 1911 design for left-handed shooters. These are custom-grade guns made of stainless steel and finished in DuPont Teflon-S. The price is not low, but quality costs. At the other end of the price scale, **MKS Supply** has the

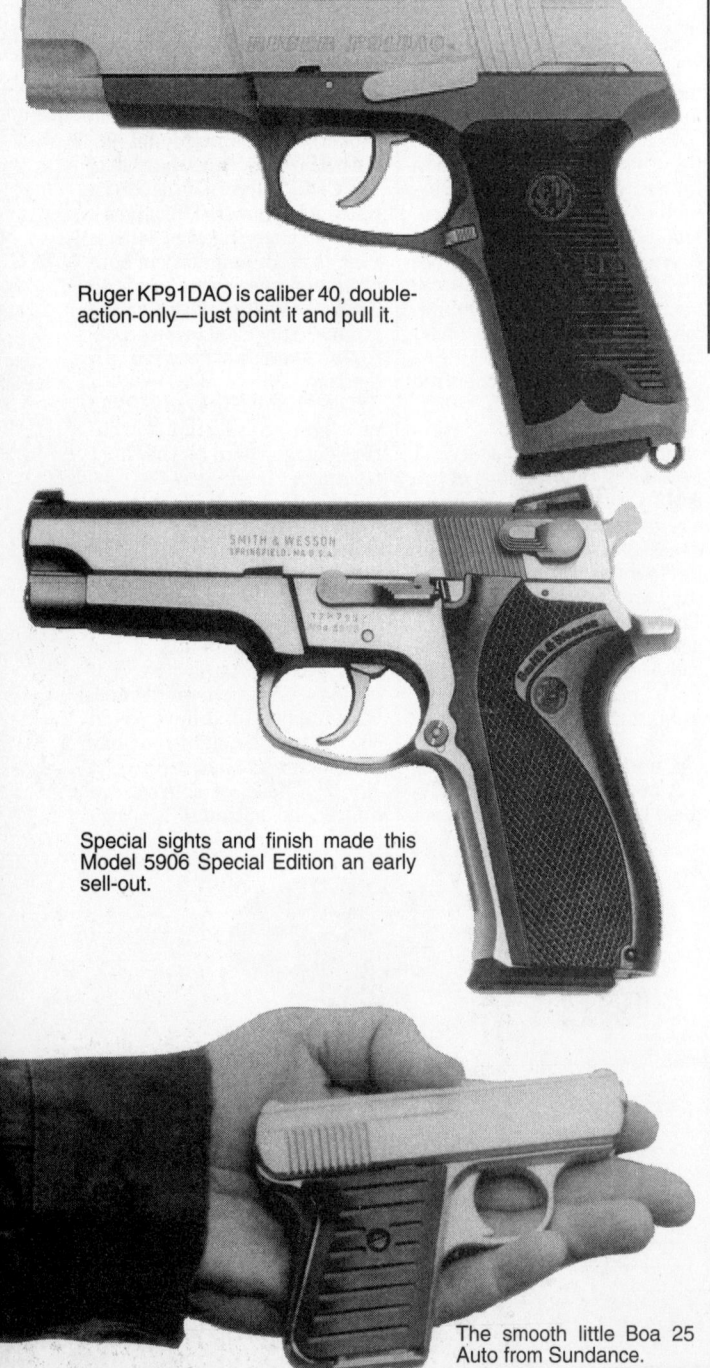

Ruger KP91DAO is caliber 40, double-action-only—just point it and pull it.

Special sights and finish made this Model 5906 Special Edition an early sell-out.

The smooth little Boa 25 Auto from Sundance.

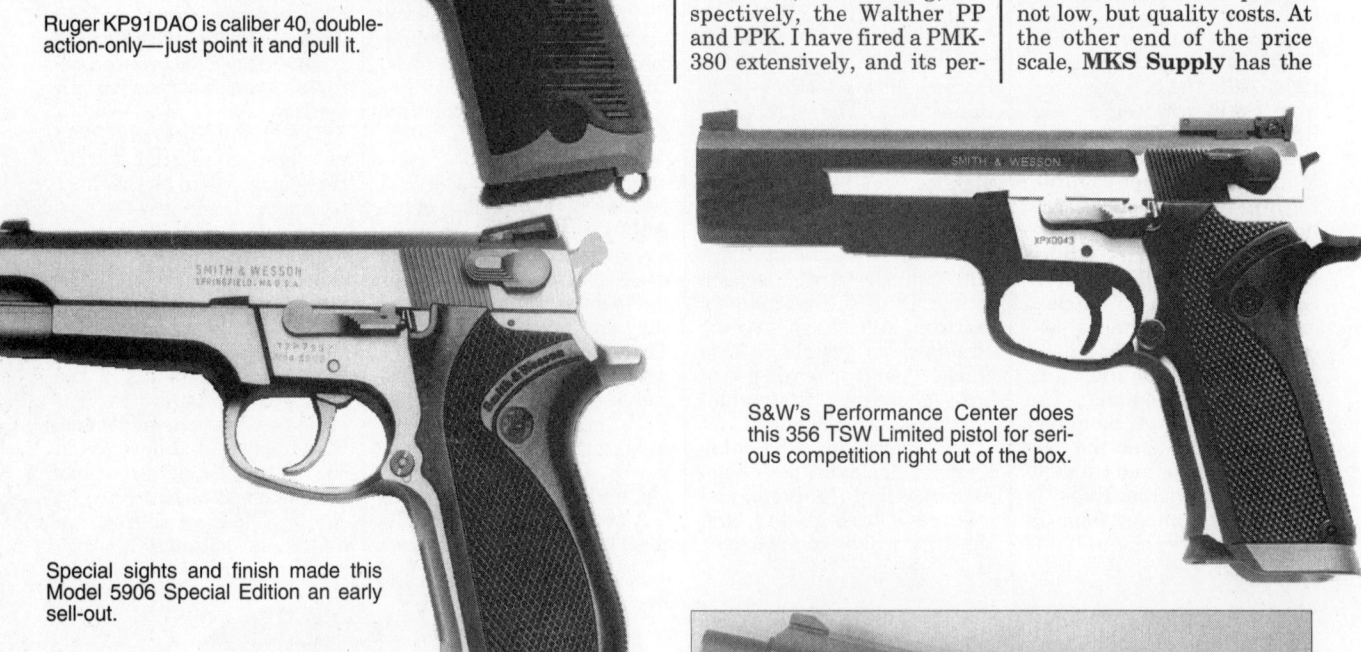

S&W's Performance Center does this 356 TSW Limited pistol for serious competition right out of the box.

L.A.R.'s Grizzly now comes in 50 Action Express, a big bore for sure.

9mm JS-Compact, a smaller version of the single-action blowback nine. Elitists may sneer, but I have tried the JS pistols in 9mm and 45 Auto, and they are quite reliable.

L.A.R., maker of the Grizzly, has now chambered it for the formidable 50 Action Express cartridge, so now there are two pistols with a half-inch bore. The other, in case you just joined us, is the 50 Desert Eagle from Magnum Research. Blount-CCI loads the round commercially.

While we're in the magnum-caliber category, I must mention that **Coonan Arms** is introducing a compact version of their sleek and beautifully made 357 Magnum pistol. I recently handled a prototype, and it was impressive. Just 7.8 inches overall, it has a 3.9-inch barrel, about an inch shorter than the full-sized gun. The height is 5.3 inches, and the magazine holds six rounds, one less than the big one.

The slim and small 9mm and 40 S&W DAO Sabre from **American Arms** is still in the works, but it will take a little longer, as Sites in Italy is experimenting with different materials. Meanwhile, look for a larger special-purpose 9mm pistol from American Arms in the near future.

I have handled the prototype, and the engineering is outstanding in its simplicity. That's all I can say about it, right now.

While working to get their DAO AT-9 and AT-40 into production, **Accu-Tek** has announced a version of their 380 pistol with a double-column twelve-round magazine. It is designated the Model HC-380SS. In stainless steel, it has a single-action trigger, an external hammer, and a slide-mounted firing pin block safety. The Accu-Tek guns are well-made and moderately priced.

It hasn't been announced, but I have seen it—a **Ram-Line** Exactor pistol with an all-steel slab-sided barrel. It gives the Exactor some extra weight that many shooters will appreciate. **Intratec** has a new 9mm DAO pistol, very small, a superb redesign of the Sirkis (or Sardius) SD9. I recently fired a neat little 25 Auto from **Sundance**, the Boa. Compact and inexpensve, it has both manual and grip safeties.

Olympic Arms, well-known for their excellent recreation of the Safari Arms pistols, has a new project: Watch for the return of the 22 LR Whitney Wolverine, with a few subtle improvements. The Wolverine may have looked a little too "space age" for its time, but now it will fit right in. And, mechanically, it is a fine design.

Yes, the old reliable Raven 25 Auto is still being made, by a new company called **Phoenix Arms**, in Ontario, California. Also, Phoenix has new external-hammer pistols in 22 LR and 25 Auto, the HP22 and HP25. These will have a suggested retail price of just under a hundred dollars, but they look like they cost much more. A very neat little pistol.

My writing colleague Jerry Ahern has designed several holsters in black nylon, suede-lined, including a shoulder rig called the "Tri-Speed." Among several notable features is an extra strap that can be used as a second thumbbreak, a pull-through, or a double-snap lock-down. The rig is totally ambidextrous, and two basic sizes fit a long list of revolvers and pistols. For more information, the address is Ahern Enterprises, Box 186, Commerce, GA 30529. ●

The Ahern Tri-Speed shoulder rig comes with a multi-purpose extra strap.

Accu-Tek's HC-380SS holds twelve rounds of 380 ACP and has single-action lockwork.

The new 9mm compact pistol from Taurus, the PT-908, is both slim and short, and holds eight rounds.

Beretta Centurion offers a compact barrel-slide unit on a full-size frame.

In 40 S&W, this is the AMT On Duty, decocker version—a full-sized pistol for serious work.

ROSS RUDD'S

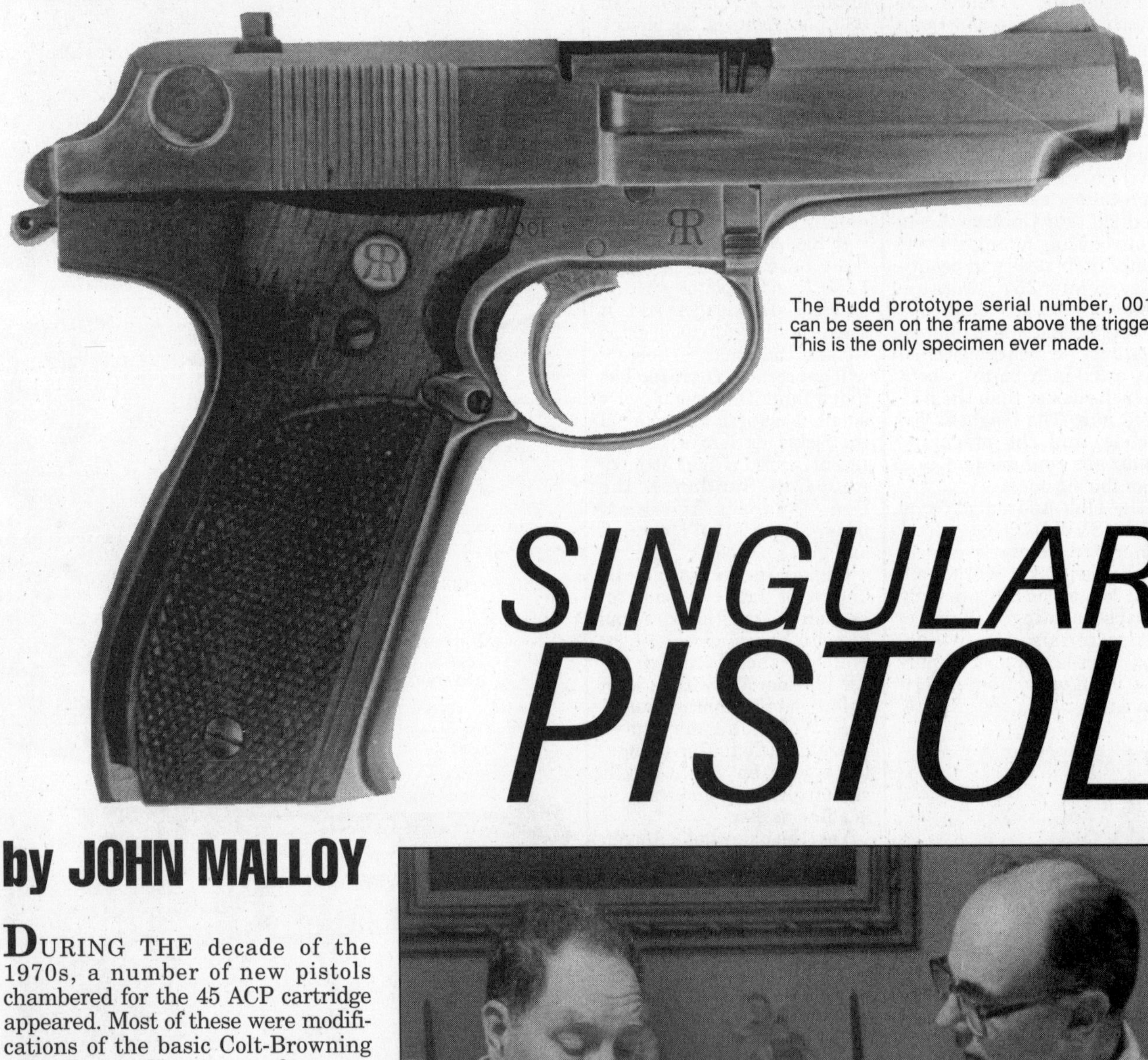

The Rudd prototype serial number, 001, can be seen on the frame above the trigger. This is the only specimen ever made.

SINGULAR
PISTOL

by JOHN MALLOY

DURING THE decade of the 1970s, a number of new pistols chambered for the 45 ACP cartridge appeared. Most of these were modifications of the basic Colt-Browning 1911 design. However, a few were based on new and original concepts. One of the most interesting was the 45-caliber Rudd pistol.

The designer, Ross Rudd, was born in Toronto, Canada, in 1915. His family moved to Springfield, Massachusetts, during World War I when he was only two years old. He grew up in Springfield and was interested in firearms throughout his early years.

As he grew, he thought more and more about the design of firearms and ammunition. At about age 16, he came up with an idea for what he thought would be an improved mili-

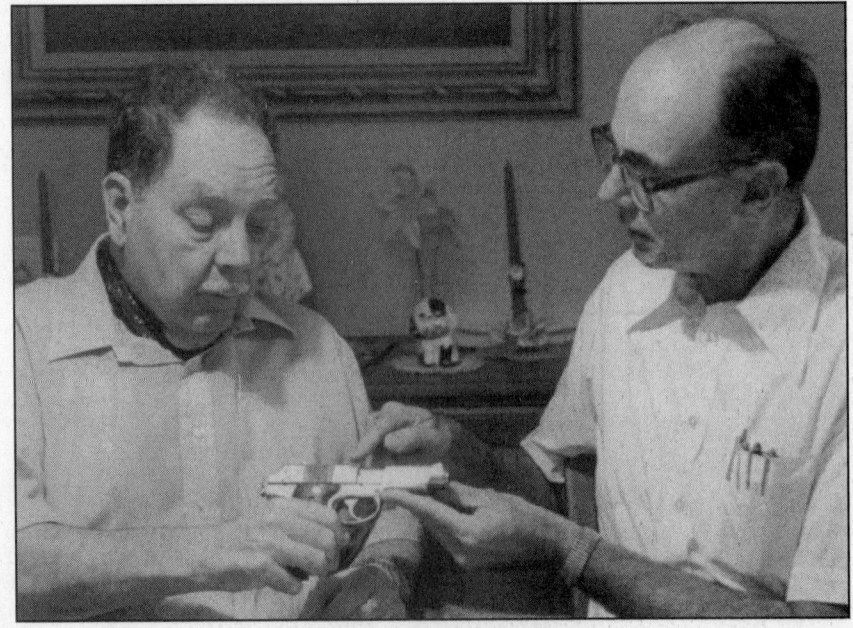

Ross Rudd, left, the inventor of the Rudd pistol, discusses the locking mechanism of his pistol with Malloy.

tary bullet and submitted the design to the War Department. The concept involved triangular skirts of jacket material that extended rearward from the base of the bullet. Rudd reasoned that the skirts would close during flight, streamlining the bullet without the additional weight of a traditional boattail design.

The idea was evaluated by none other than Townsend Whelen, the noted firearms authority, who was then Commandant of Springfield

arms while at Savage and may have been one of the first to try converting a Thompson to operate without the Blish lock.

Although he takes no credit for the modifications, while at Savage he suggested simplifying the Thompson design by eliminating the Blish lock, compensator, barrel fins, hammer, adjustable sight and detachable stock. All these modifications were later incorporated into the M1 and M1A1 Thompsons.

His duties included qualifying troops for marksmanship at the National Guard range at Golden, Colorado. Most of the firing was done with the then-new M-1 Carbine. Rudd recalled an incident in which one recruit was having trouble qualifying, although the young man had hunted extensively and had a reputation as an excellent shot.

It turned out that the new soldier, recently from the hills, had seldom worn shoes before entering the Army. He somehow could not seem to shoot well with his feet covered. Rudd was skeptical, but shrugged and allowed the man to shoot barefoot. He qualified easily!

Late in 1942, Rudd went to England. His unit was transported over on the Queen Mary. Because it was so much faster than most warships, the Queen Mary sailed alone, without an escort, depending on its speed for protection against the Germans.

In England, Rudd worked primarily on bomb selection, bomb disposal and chemical warfare assignments. He never abandoned his interest in firearms or his inventive streak. He designed a booster to increase the rate of fire of the 50-caliber Browning machinegun. This allowed more shots to be fired at fast-moving enemy fighters during brief encounters. The device worked, but was not adopted.

At the end of the war, he saw the German V2 rocket and began to develop an interest in rockets and missiles.

After discharge from the service, he moved to California, where he combined his interests and experience with aircraft, firearms and missiles. He worked as an aerospace engineer for Pratt & Whitney, Douglas Aircraft and Lockheed. The projects on which he worked included various missiles, the Aegena space vehicle and the redesigned armament for the Army's Cheyenne attack helicopter.

By the early 1970s, Rudd had come up with the idea for a new pistol locking system which allowed a fixed barrel to be used.

He formed Rudd Arms Company and developed the concept into reality while living in Northridge, California. The resulting pistol had a separate bolt that moved inside the slide. This bolt had a lug at the lower rear portion that would lock down

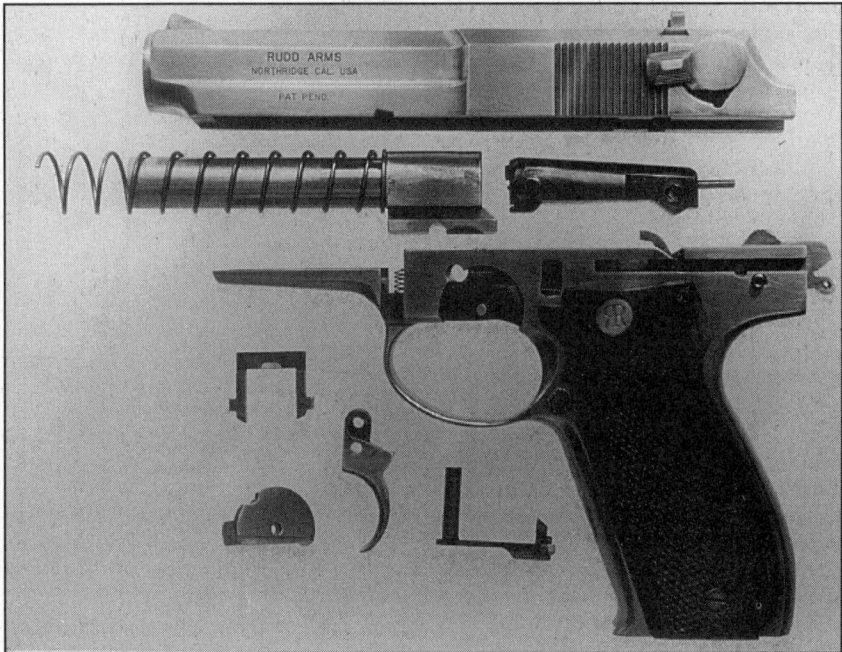

The Rudd pistol field-stripped. The fixed barrel is installed rearward into the frame, where it is locked into place by the slide stop. The relatively simple design contains only 29 parts, compared to the traditional Colt's 49 parts.

Armory. Whelen pointed out that the muzzle blast caused by the expanding propellant gases would distort the triangular skirts as the bullet left the muzzle. Nevertheless, he was impressed by the teenager's initiative. He invited young Rudd to the Armory and personally gave him a tour of the facilities.

In September, 1939, Great Britain went to war against Germany barely twenty-five years after entering World War I against the same enemy. The British were poorly prepared for war. Fortunately America— "The Great Arsenal of Democracy"—was able to begin manufacturing arms for British forces.

In 1940, Rudd moved to Chicopee Falls, Massachusetts, to take a position with Savage Arms. The company had received military contracts for the British Enfield No. 4 rifle and for the Thompson submachine gun. Rudd worked with both

Rudd Pistol Specifications	
Caliber	45 ACP
Length	8.13 inches
Height	5 inches
Barrel Length	4.7 inches
Slide Width	1.05 inches
Weight	36 ounces
Magazine Capacity	7 cartridges

Rudd entered the U.S. Army in 1942, serving as an ordnance officer attached to the 8th Air Force at Lowry Field, near Denver. He demonstrated the use of the Thompson submachine gun, with which he was, of course, very familiar. It was a rare case of having the right man for the job.

into a recess in the pistol's frame. The system was designed, of course, to delay the opening of the slide until chamber pressures dropped.

It is obvious that if the locking recess in the frame and the corresponding bolt lug were at right angles to the thrust applied through the bolt, the action would never unlock, regardless of the force applied. However, if the angle is changed, then—at some point—the force will begin to cam the bolt lug up out of engagement with the frame recess.

The bolt, however, cannot move up until it, in turn, begins to cam back the slide. The slide resists this, because it is held forward by inertia and the pressure of the recoil spring.

Most of the force of firing the shot is absorbed by the mass of the pistol's parts; only a part of this force is used to cam the bolt open. This arrangement provides a substantial delay during which the bullet can leave the barrel and the chamber pressure drops.

The prototype pistol was made in California and proved that the system was a sound one. The pistol can remain locked about three times longer than one based on the Colt-Browning system.

The Rudd is a handsome pistol and feels good in the hand. In appearance, the grip might be that of an enlarged Smith & Wesson Model 39. The angle of the grip is within a few degrees of that of the Colt 1911, which is comfortable to most shooters. The center of gravity is farther rearward than is usual. This makes the pistol fairly compact for its caliber and would allow a substantially longer barrel before the feel became muzzle heavy.

Operation is simple and without complications. The magazine release is thumb-operated on the left side of the frame. The magazine itself is similar to that of a 45-caliber Colt 1911, but the baseplate angle has been changed so that it is parallel to the top of the pistol. A Colt magazine will, however, function in the Rudd.

When the slide is retracted, initial movement cams the rear of the bolt

up out of its recess and allows the slide to be opened. A thumb-latch on the left will lock it open. This latch and the magazine release are in conventional positions for those familiar with the Colt 1911.

The reach to the trigger is comfortable. The trigger mechanism is what has now come to be considered conventional: double action for the first shot, then single action for succeeding shots. The mainspring is contained within the hammer, aiding the compactness of the design.

The slide-mounted safety is designed to be operated by the right thumb. It is not ambidextrous, but the location is now more-or-less traditional for double-action, semi-automatic pistols. There is nothing new or unusual that must be learned to operate the Rudd pistol.

Takedown for field-stripping is simple. The magazine is first removed. A stirrup latch at the front of the trigger guard is then pulled down. The slide can now go back far enough to disengage from the frame slots. The rear of the slide can be lifted and the slide moved forward off the barrel. The recoil spring surrounds the barrel and can now be removed. The bolt can be removed from its guideway slots in the slide. Then, with the removal of the slide latch, the barrel can be pulled forward out of its frame slot.

Rudd saw multiple advantages to his system. The fixed barrel does not move during the firing cycle and has the potential for great accuracy. Because the barrel is easily removable, one of longer or shorter length could be quickly installed. Interchange of calibers could be accomplished by change of the barrel, breechblock and magazine. Also, for some military applications, a fixed barrel allows easy mounting of a silencer.

Longer lock time generally means less felt recoil. The design allows the pistol to be fired in any attitude—straight up, sideways or upsidedown.

After his development work on the pistol, Rudd adapted the concept to a rifle. He designed a receiver that would work on the Armalite AR-18 frame. The open area above the trigger mechanism required that the bolt lug lock into the top, rather than the bottom, of the receiver. However, the Rudd lock works equally well in any direction.

Because the receiver, unlike the pistol slide, was fixed, an extra part—the bolt carrier—was designed. The bolt operates within this

Ross Rudd, with his 45-caliber pistol on the table before him, shows the function of the Rudd locking system, using a large demonstration model made of wood and aluminum.

carrier. The carrier is necessary to allow opening the bolt by hand.

The rifle was made in 223-caliber. A number of different locking angles were considered. An angle was chosen that kept the bolt locked as long as possible, yet gave perfect functioning. There was no measurable case expansion, with fired cases dropping easily back into the chamber. The resulting rifle was simpler than the original gas-operated design.

The inventor pointed out that the Rudd lock could also be adapted for machinegun use. The absence of a gas system or recoiling barrel would simplify using various types of belt and magazine feeding.

In 1979, Rudd left California. He moved back to Massachusetts, with the idea of having the pistol produced for commercial and military markets.

With the slide off the frame, we see the relationship of the barrel, breechblock and frame in firing position. The locking lug at the lower rear of the breechblock is in the locking recess in the frame above the rear portion of the grip panel. The cam slots in the slide will mate with the cam lugs on the side of the breechblock.

flat sides to provide more sure contact area. Other modifications, which included changes to the trigger, trigger bar and the shape of the hammer, were planned.

To provide a dramatic introduction, the first 2000 pistols would have frames and slides made of titanium. Use of this metal would combine strength and corrosion resistance while reducing the weight by a full 10 ounces. The standard model would be of stainless steel. Aluminum alloy frames and other calibers were scheduled for later introduction.

In 1983, a pre-production public announcement offered the Rudd pistol for sale. However, with established companies having troubles, newly formed RACOM found the financial climate very difficult. The expected financing did not materialize, and production never began. No commercial Rudd pistols were ever made.

Rudd never abandoned his faith in his design. He continued to promote it while waiting for better times. Then, toward the latter part of the decade, he experienced a series of

The prototype pistol attracted considerable attention, and a number of favorable writeups appeared in the shooting press. Rudd discussed manufacturing arrangements with a number of people in the firearms industry. The Inventors Club of America honored him for his pistol design.

However, the late 1970s and early 1980s were a period of inflation and economic uncertainty. Even the giant automobile manufacturers were experiencing financial difficulties and laying off workers. Rudd could not interest an established firearms company in producing his design.

A new company, RACOM, was formed. The name was an acronym for Rudd Arms Company of Massachusetts. Manufacturing arrangements were made with Cogswell Manufacturing Company of Agawam, Massachusetts, for production of the pistol. That company had been in

The Rudd pistol looks good and feels good to most people who have handled it. The grip is a comfortable one, and the trigger reach is satisfactory in either the double-action or single-action positions.

business since 1912 and had experience making firearms parts.

Based on experience with the prototype, the redesign of some features was planned. The side lugs on the bolt would be made larger and with

The Rudd's bolt carrier with the enclosed bolt can be seen through the ejection port. The protrusion on the top of the receiver contains the recess into which the bolt locks.

With the forearm removed, it is plain that no gas tubes or gas-operated rods were designed into the Rudd rifle.

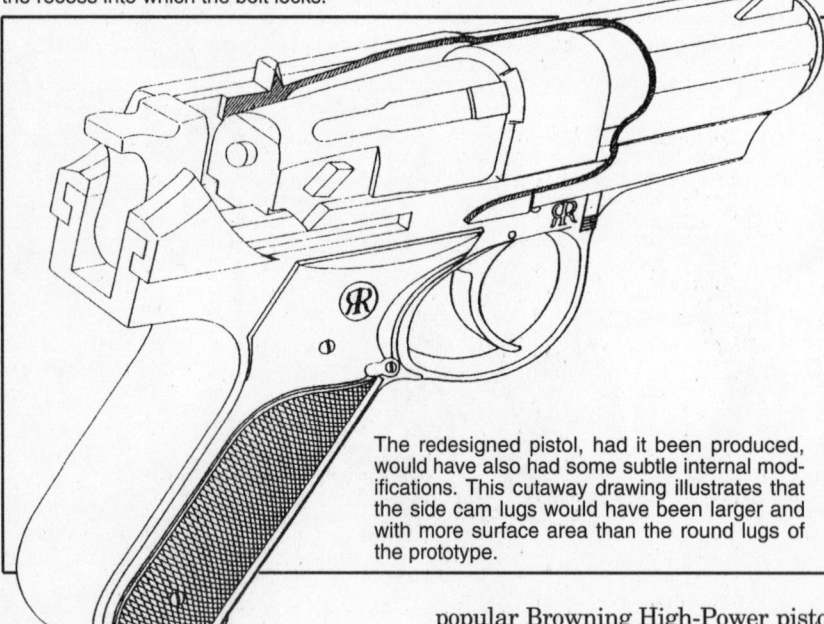

The redesigned pistol, had it been produced, would have also had some subtle internal modifications. This cutaway drawing illustrates that the side cam lugs would have been larger and with more surface area than the round lugs of the prototype.

life-threatening medical problems. A move from the North, to a milder climate, was indicated. He and his wife now live quietly in Florida, not far from the coast of the Gulf of Mexico.

The inventor still is in communication with people in the firearms world. His active mind has designed a simple mechanism to convert the popular Browning High-Power pistol to double-action firing and an anti-aircraft sight which provides a built-in lead.

Expanding his interests to automobiles, he has recently designed a suspension system which would give today's short-wheelbase cars a "long-wheelbase" ride.

His biggest interest remains the Rudd locking mechanism. Because of the current crowded pistol market, he favors his lock for rifle use now. He maintains contact with represen-tatives of the firearms industry and has hopes that an established manufacturer will produce his design.

The Rudd pistol was ahead of its time in many respects. Although the prototype was made as a 45 ACP, the design lends itself to caliber changes as well as barrel-length changes. The double-action mechanism, stainless steel construction and other features now considered standard were innovative when the Rudd came on the scene. The fixed barrel mounting and rigid breech locking system are still in a class by themselves.

The Colt-Browning locking system, with its dropping barrel, still dominates the centerfire pistol world. Most largebore pistols use this system.

Only a few other recoil lock systems (predominantly the underblock on the P38/Beretta and, to a lesser extent, methods such as the PA-15 rotating barrel) are used on regularly produced pistols. All require the barrel to move during operation.

The only fixed-barrel centerfire pistols of recent production fall into two categories: simple blowbacks at one end of the scale and complex gas-operated pistols at the other.

The Rudd pistol stands alone—a full-power, yet rather compact pistol—with some special characteristics related to its fixed barrel and unique recoil locking system. The capabilities of the design can hardly be considered as known from the limited testing of the single prototype specimen.

America, with its large shooting population and varied uses for firearms, is still the proving ground of most new firearms. We can only speculate as to what effect the production of this American design in the decade past might have had. Few others have looked as good, felt as good or had more potential than the Rudd pistol. ●

GUN GUARD
THE·EVOLUTION·OF·DESIGN

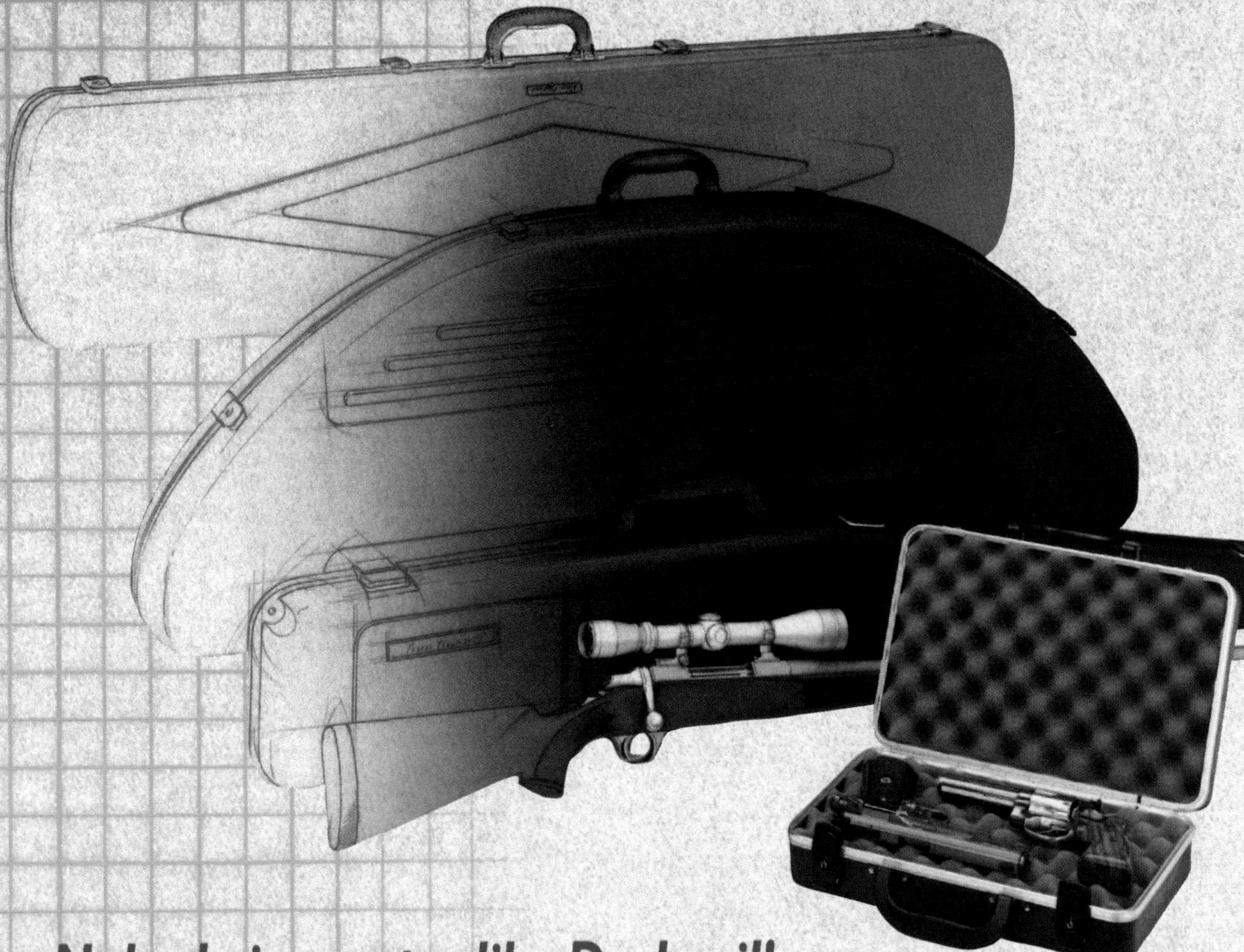

Nobody innovates like Doskocil!

You've always counted on Gun Guard to offer a full line of cases, and this year we are expanding and introducing the hottest cases on the market.

Our **XLT Bow Case** is the premier bow case with unique features such as key lockable metal latches and a two-piece fold down handle. The popular styling and affordable pricing of the new **Scoped Rifle/Shotgun Case** has received rave reviews. And with the introduction of the new **All-Weather Series**, there are finally affordable water-tight cases available.

Other new cases added to our line-up include the **XLT-12 Pistol Case**, the **Double Bow**

Case, and back by popular demand are the **Black Wildlife Series Cases**.

If you haven't seen these exciting new products, ask your distributor to see the 1993 Gun Guard catalog.

Take another look at Doskocil. Don't let the evolution of design pass you by.

Doskocil Mfg. Co. Inc.
P.O. Box 1246
Arlington, Tx. 76004-1246

Endless Versatility

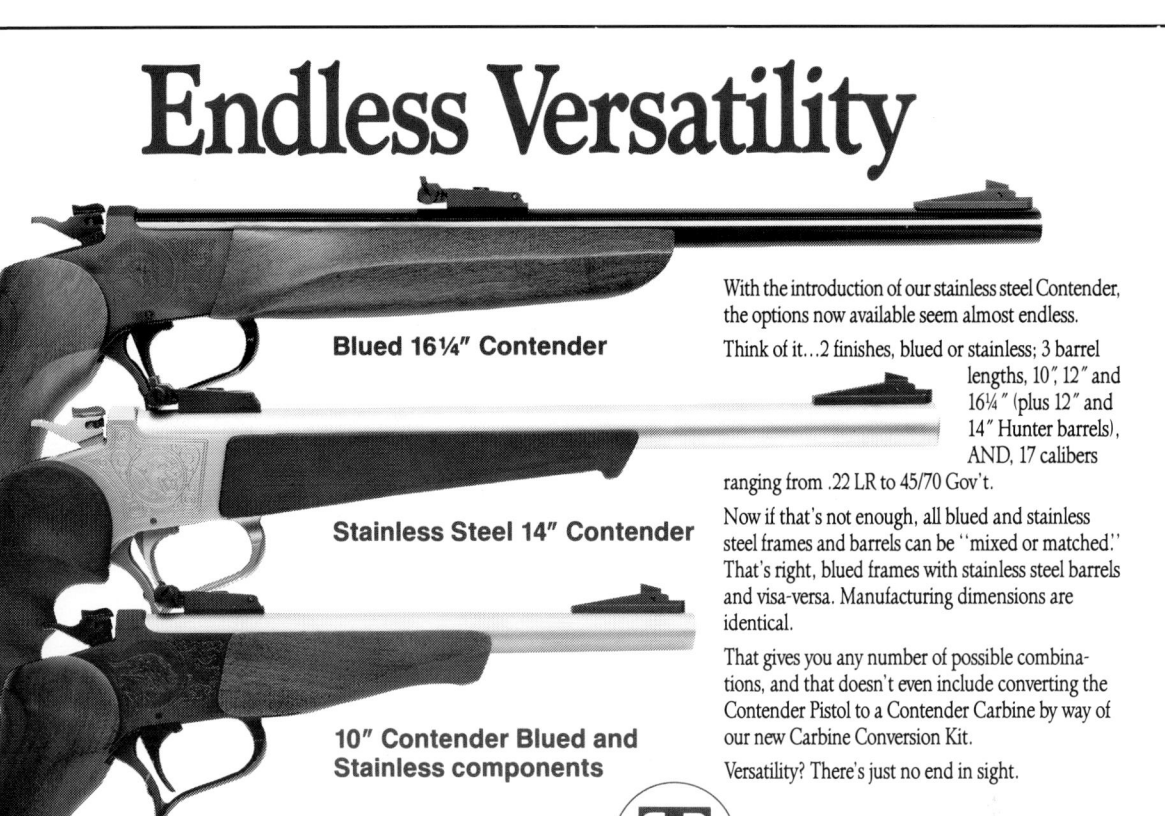

Blued 16¼" Contender

Stainless Steel 14" Contender

10" Contender Blued and Stainless components

With the introduction of our stainless steel Contender, the options now available seem almost endless.

Think of it...2 finishes, blued or stainless; 3 barrel lengths, 10", 12" and 16¼" (plus 12" and 14" Hunter barrels), AND, 17 calibers ranging from .22 LR to 45/70 Gov't.

Now if that's not enough, all blued and stainless steel frames and barrels can be "mixed or matched." That's right, blued frames with stainless steel barrels and visa-versa. Manufacturing dimensions are identical.

That gives you any number of possible combinations, and that doesn't even include converting the Contender Pistol to a Contender Carbine by way of our new Carbine Conversion Kit.

Versatility? There's just no end in sight.

The Ultimate Hunting Handgun

Write for our free catalog

THOMPSON/CENTER
ARMS COMPANY, INC.
P.O. BOX 5002, DEPT. GD4
FARMINGTON ROAD
ROCHESTER, NEW HAMPSHIRE 03867

A Versatile, Lightweight Carbine weighing in at 5 lbs. 3 oz. that will "Fill the hands" of most men.

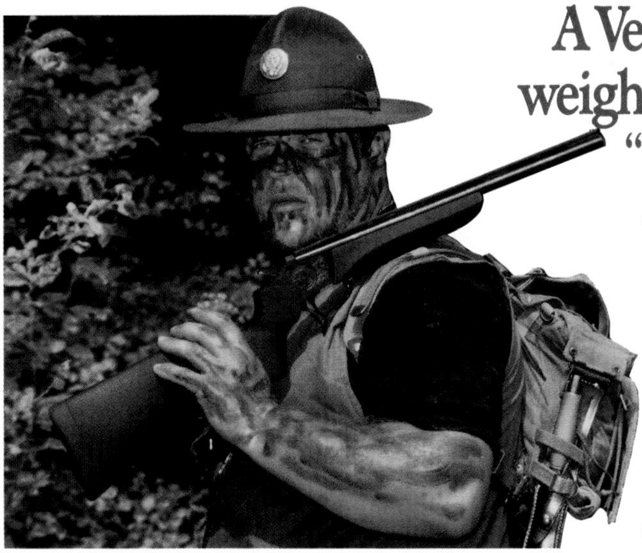

They don't come anymore versatile. The T/C Contender Carbine is chambered for 12 cartridges; potent varmint rounds like the .22 Hornet, .17 Rem. and .223 Rem., and proven deer cartridges like the 30-30 Win., 7-30 Waters, 35 Rem., and the .375 Winchester. Barrels interchange in seconds, which literally means you can be hunting squirrels one day and going after monster swamp bucks the next.

Our special youth model is equipped with a shorter buttstock (12" pull) and a 16¼" barrel. Instant barrel interchangeability means the Contender Carbine can become his or her "first" .22, "first" shotgun (.410 gauge) or "first" centerfire rifle. No other gun on the market offers this versatility. It breaks down easily and can be stowed away as a survival gun with 1, 2 or even 3 barrels. Or it can simply be the gun you take with you "just in case."

It's a serious rifleman's rifle, a great introductory rifle, and just a whole lot of fun.

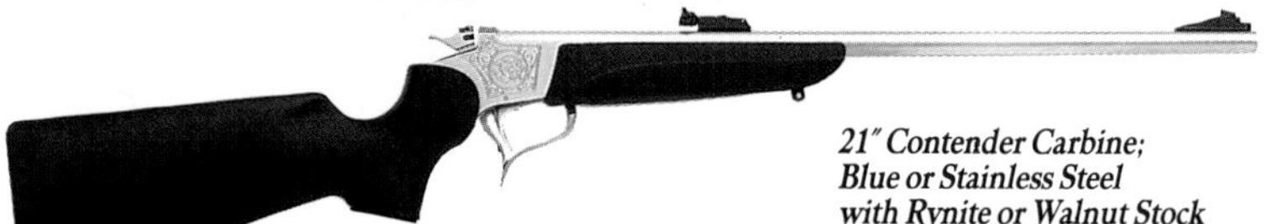

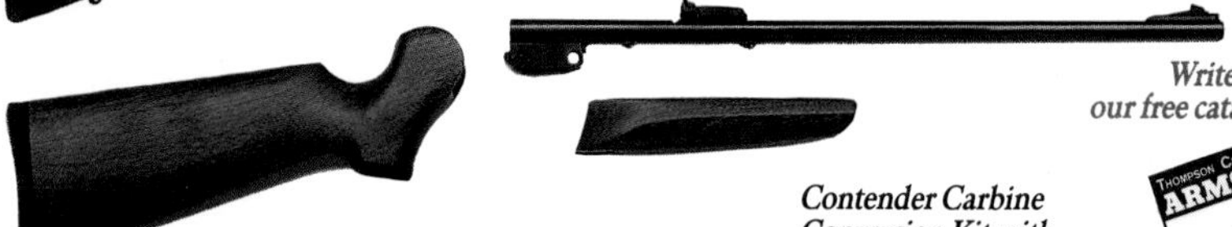

21" Contender Carbine; Blue or Stainless Steel with Rynite or Walnut Stock

Own a Contender Pistol?

We now have kits which will convert your pistol to a legal carbine in less time than it takes to put your hunting gear on. It's that simple.

Contender Carbine Conversion Kit with Rynite or Walnut Stock

Write for our free catalog

THOMPSON/CENTER
ARMS COMPANY, INC.
P.O. BOX 5002, DEPT. GD4
FARMINGTON ROAD
ROCHESTER, NEW HAMPSHIRE 03867

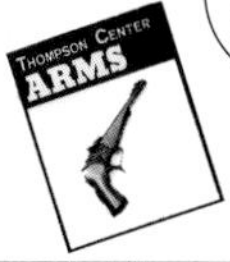

The Shape of Things to Come from —

RidgeBack HUNTER™

NEW FOR 1993!

Inner Frame LOCKBACK™

Blackie Collins Designs

W. R. Case & Sons Cutlery Company
Owens Way
Bradford, PA 16701

Made in U.S.A.

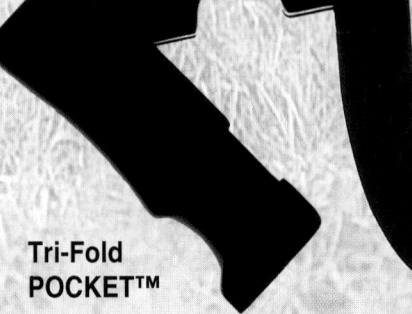
Tri-Fold POCKET™

Uncle Jack's
KRAG

Finally, it gets out on the prairie.

by JOHN HAVILAND

I FIGURED MY late uncle, Jack Potts, left me his 30-40 Krag as a message for me to take the rifle pronghorn antelope hunting.

The last time I saw Jack, he was in a veteran's home. He was failing, having had both legs amputated because of bad circulation. I knew hunting was the only subject that could cheer him up, so when we got around to talking about rifles, I mentioned a couple of magnum rifles I had recently bought. Jack wondered at the extravagance of owning more than one hunting rifle. He owned a 30-40 Krag and had used it for decades for all his big game hunting.

As I was leaving, I told Jack I was headed antelope hunting for a week. His eyes brightened up. Although he had lived his whole life in western Montana, except for World War II, he had never traveled to the prairies of eastern Montana to hunt antelope. He said that was one of his few regrets and wished me luck.

It was no surprise when Jack died that winter. It did surprise me that he left me his 30-40. Then I thought about it. If he couldn't hunt the prairie, at least his rifle could.

Jack's gun had started as a U.S.

military rifle from the Springfield Armory, a Model 1898. Nearly 263,000 were produced, making it the most common Krag.

The Krag's action is both the rifle's appeal and its weakness. A slight bit of upward pressure with the palm of the hand against the bolt handle pops the action open and the bolt glides back like water out of a glass. If nothing else, owning a Krag is worth it just to slide the bolt back and forth in the action. The bolt only has one forward lug and it locks in the bottom front of the receiver. A guide rib on the body of the bolt acts as a safety locking lug. When the bolt is closed, the guide rib turns in the right front edge of the bridge of the action. This rib slides through a slot in the receiver bridge when the bolt is moved back and forth, keeping the bolt from binding and giving the bolt its smooth slide.

The lunch box-like magazine protruding on the right side of the action identifies the Krag. I like the magazine because shells can be added without opening the bolt. But it adds weight and bulk to the rifle. About the only precaution to keep cartridges from jamming in the mag-

azine when loading is to make sure the bullets are pointed forward when the cartridges are dropped in. When the gate is shut, a follower lines up the cartridges into the magazine well and feeds them up and around to the opening in the receiver. A magazine cutoff lever in the down position on the left rear of the receiver holds down the top cartridge so the bolt cannot pick it up and converts the rifle to a single shot. Such a complicated magazine of machined parts would surely add $100 to the price of a rifle today.

Jack's rifle, like a good percentage of all Krags, had been sporterized. The military stock was replaced with sporting-style wood with a pistol grip and black forearm tip. The comb is full and high, so the bolt just clears it. My eye lines up with the rear sight without having to lift my cheek from the comb. Someone checkered a simple point pattern on the grip and forearm. The checkering lacks points on the diamonds and has plenty of run-overs around the borders. I wouldn't doubt some ranch hand did the job during Montana's cold winter nights when the snow drifts were so deep he couldn't get to town.

The barrel had been cut to 25 inches from 30, and crowned. An inside barrel band was fitted about three-fourths of the way up the forearm to hold the stock against the barrel. A Lyman blade front sight was added on a barrel band at the muzzle. An aperture sight of unknown make was mounted on the bolt just ahead of the leaf safety. I can never remember whether the leaf is positioned to the left or the right for the safety, so I put a spot of red paint on the leaf when it's on the left to show the rifle is ready to fire.

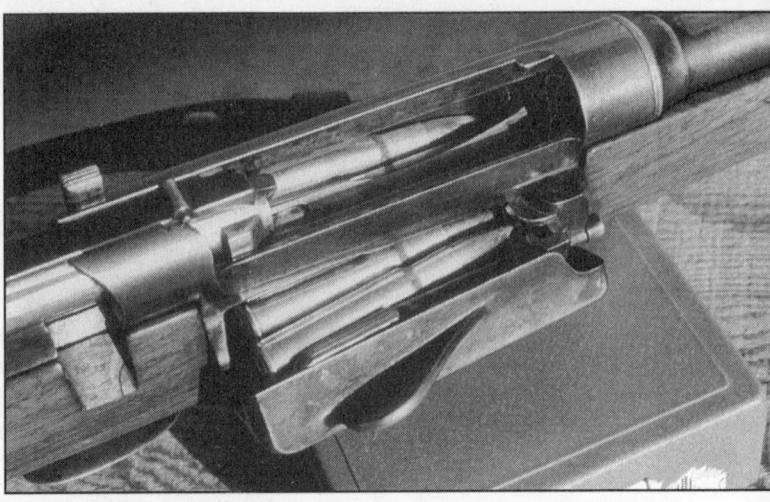
The distinctive magazine sets the Krag apart from other bolt-action rifles. Just make sure the bullets are pointed forward.

A few loaded Winchester Silvertip cartridges came along with the rifle. On my first trip to the range with the gun, I stopped by the local gun, hiking boot and camping gear store and bought a box of Remington 180-grain shells. The rifle had not been fired for fifteen years, yet the old cartridges and new Remingtons hit right on at 100 yards. I shot four three-shot strings, each grouping into 2³/₈ inches.

I went to a gun show that weekend with the intent of buying a couple hundred empty 30-40 cases. The lady at the table selling brass said she was all out of 30-40s. People don't realize it, she said, but the 30-40 is very popular with reloaders. Next, I called two reloading suppliers advertised in *Shotgun News*. Both were backordered on 30-40s. A third phone call located a supply and I ordered 250 new, empty Remingtons.

Several reloading books showed velocities of up to 2400 fps with 180-grain bullets in the 30-40. But these were all shot from 30-inch barrels.

I settled on a middle load of Hodgdon's 322 and a 180-grain Sierra Spitzer boattail bullet. The cartridges assembled easily through RCBS loading dies. The Sierra bullets had a velocity of 2277 fps from the 25-inch barrel, pretty slow but still fast enough for a 150-yard or, at the outside, a 200-yard shot. The bullets landed right on at 100 yards. They also grouped exactly at 2³/₈ inches.

In early August, I took the rifle to the range one last time before antelope season. I shot a box of shells from various positions, mainly for the pleasurable feel of working the bolt back and forth. I never noticed it before, but the Krag was a heavy rifle. It weighs an honest 9 pounds. Maybe I was just used to modern rifles with plastic stocks, skinny barrels, and aluminum floorplates and trigger guards.

As I was leaving, a fellow showed up at the benches with a 303 British Lee-Enfield. He had a scope on the rifle and shot some 2- and 3-inch groups. I decided I would try one

Old-timers must know this sight, but there's no name on it. Works great.

more group with the Krag. My three 180 Sierras clustered into one inch. He looked at my group, but didn't say a word. Neither did I.

In mid-October, my son and I loaded the pickup with camping gear and our rifles and headed east for the antelope prairie. A rancher along the eastern edge of the Musselshell River gave us permission to hunt. When I mentioned we were going to camp out, he showed me on a map the location of the abandoned homestead where he had grown up in the 1930s and said it was a good place to pitch a tent.

We drove out and inspected what was left of the homestead. The log walls of the one-room house still stood strong, but the roof had fallen in. The outbuildings had crumbled. Cottontail rabbits infested the place. Other than being on the prairie instead of in a mountain valley, the homestead looked exactly like the place where Uncle Jack, my mother and their six other brothers and sisters had grown up.

Paul missed a shot at a buck across a wide basin that afternoon. Because of the slope of the ground, I had only a vague idea of the range. I told him to hold a good 2 feet over the buck's back. The obedient thirteen-year-old he is, Paul did. The bullet launched from his 7mm-08

landed in the dirt, sailing over the top of the buck.

The next day we walked the prairie. According to the map, we walked 14 miles. Paul stalked a couple of herds containing bucks, but they ran wild when he tried crawling within range.

We were trudging back to the pickup when I spotted three antelope lying in the sage. Paul crawled up to the crest of the ridge. The antelope stood and Paul shot. A big doe ran, then fell dead. Paul paced off the distance of the shot at 60 yards. That's the kind of shot I needed for the 30-40.

We broke camp and headed west of the Musselshell where my antelope tag was valid on the Mike Murphy ranch. Murphy was in the corral doctoring calves when we arrived. In addition to ranching, Murphy runs Bull Mountain Outfitters (POB 286, Musselshell, MT 59059, 406/947-3337). Murphy directed us to another abandoned homestead to camp.

The Bull Mountains are a plateau rising above the prairie of Ponderosa pines interspersed with pastures of grass. The antelope bed and hide in the trees. But because of the trees, they cannot rely on their eyesight as much for safety and are very skittish.

My buck taken with Uncle Jack's 30-40 Krag and 180-grain bullet, and an iron-sighted fusillade.

Handloads or factory, Jack's Krag, iron-sighted, holds 'em well under three inches.

Paul and I drove the back roads and climbed each knob to glass the country. From one overlook, I spotted twenty antelope at the head of a valley. The spotting scope showed two average bucks in the bunch, but we left them alone. At sundown, I spotted a lone buck several miles away, grazing under a sparse covering of pines. His horns looked extremely tall through the spotting scope.

Paul built a campfire that night, and sat next to the fire on an old chair left in the log cabin. Coyotes howled at the stars. During the night, Canada geese flew over the tent between two reservoirs. I went to sleep listening to their calling.

We looked for the lone buck all the next morning, and headed back toward camp at noon for lunch. When I stopped to open a gate, Paul spotted the white of a dozen antelope grazing in a long pasture. A buck with good prongs and hook to the horn tips stood in the middle of the herd. A ravine paralleled one side of the pasture.

We slipped into an eroded cut in the ground that led to the ravine, and I peeked over the edge to where I had marked the antelope. They still grazed in the same place. The range was a long 300 yards, much too far for the 30-40.

I noticed a shallow cut in the ground between us and the antelope that emptied into the ravine we had used to hide our approach. We retraced our steps and crawled up the cut. The wind blew from us toward the antelope, but I hoped it would pass to their side. The last few yards, I heard an antelope snort and I looked up over the rise. The herd was all bunched together, trying to confirm with their eyes what their noses had warned them.

They stood within easy range, with the buck in the front. I dared not shoot, though, lest my bullet plow through the whole bunch. They finally turned and ran single file over the hill and out of sight. I ran to the top of the hill and watched them run a mile into a basin. They never came out.

"Ready for another hike?" I asked Paul.

"Lunch first," he replied.

We finished our apples below the rim of the basin. I used a patch of trees as cover to look for the antelope. They lay in the middle of the open. As we started crawling around the yucca and cactus to close the distance, I glanced back at Paul a couple times. The cactus was getting the best of him. I went on by myself the last 50 yards. Over and over, I lay the Krag in front of me then crawled

up to it. Finally, the antelope came into view between the bayonets of the yucca. The animal saw my rear end wiggling along above the cover and stood up.

I brought the Krag up and twisted off the safety, my elbows planted in the soft prairie dirt. The buck stood alone, quartering toward me. The blade of the front sight rested on its shoulder. The slack went out of the trigger and the rifle fired. The buck still stood there. I had missed! I sat up. The antelope ran to the right, the buck in the rear.

I ran another shell into the chamber. The front sight swung ahead of the buck, far enough that the buck's breast rode at the left edge of the aperture. He staggered at the second shot. He stopped and I hit him again. He wobbled over the crest of the hill before I could shoot again.

I expected to find the buck dead over the hill, but he wasn't. Instead, he stood head down out on a flat. Paul joined me and we sneaked down a draw toward the buck. I rested my back against a pine and estimated the range. The first shot fell low. The buck fell as a crack came back from the second shot.

What a rotten fusillade that had been. I never did see where my very first shot hit, even though the range was only a bit over 100 yards. The second shot hit the buck high in front of the hips. The third shot hit high on his right front leg. Because the range was unknown, the fourth shot hit low in the dirt. On the last shot, the buck was almost blotted out by the front sight at a range Paul paced off at 250 yards.

The 30-40 has a flat enough trajectory, perfect for me when antelope hunting because I like to stalk antelope and shoot at a moderate range. If the 30-40 was my only antelope rifle, I would mount a scope on it. I never realized before how much I relied on the look of game through a scope to estimate range. But I have other rifles with scopes. The aperture sight will remain on Uncle Jack's rifle.

Back at camp, Paul helped me hang the buck in the shade of the log cabin. I smelled strong cigarette smoke as I worked on the buck with my knife. It smelled just like the Prince Albert from the red can Jack used to roll.

The smoke must have come from last night's campfire. I looked at the ashes, but the fire was dead. The empty chair from the cabin stared back at me. ●

The High-Tech Steyr SPP

The new Steyr SPP is a rugged, state-of-the-art semi-auto sporting and defense pistol.

The SPP looks extremely menacing, particularly from its business end!

ONE NEW 9mm pistol which has become available just recently is worthy of close scrutiny, both by virtue of its novel design as well as its manufacturer. Steyr-Mannlicher has been synonymous with top-quality, innovative firearms for a very long time and really needs little in the way of introduction. Steyr's AUG assault rifle has already earned a well-deserved reputation.

Now enters the 9mm Steyr SPP—Special Purpose Pistol—where design relies heavily on synthetics. The entire outer frame/receiver is made of a synthetic material called IXEF 1313. IXEF 1313 is described as being extremely tough, possessing an expansion modulus similar to that of steel. The outer envelope or frame is divided into two parts. The upper section houses the bolt and barrel subassemblies, while the lower half with the pistol grip contains the trigger and safety mechanisms.

The SPP has been ergonomically designed from beginning to end, and this becomes particularly evident in the area of the pistol grip. It has to be one of the most comfortable grips that I have ever encountered, with just the right size and slant. It also incorporates horizontal grooves along its front and rear surfaces, for a positive hold even with wet or sweaty hands. The sides of the frame, just ahead of the trigger, also have longitudinal grooves on both sides.

The trigger guard is large enough and schnabel-shaped at the front to permit a firm, steady hold by the supporting hand during firing. At the extreme lower front end of the frame, there is a fairly large integral spur intended to prevent the supporting hand from sliding forward and ahead of the muzzle. The top of the receiver has a rail moulded right into it that allows the use of a variety of optronic sights.

All in all, the synthetic outer frame/receiver of the SPP is quite rugged, with an eminently practical nonreflective matte black finish. The barrel/bolt assembly has a phosphated finish that's also extremely hard-wearing.

The SPP is over a foot long and over 6 inches high—not exactly highly concealable. The SPP is, in fact, the civilian semi-auto version of the Steyr TMP machine pistol. The SPP and TMP are very close in appearance and overall dimension. The only major visual difference is the TMP's rather ample "coke bottle" forward grip, while the SPP has no such appendage.

The SPP weighs just 3.2 pounds with a fully loaded fifteen-round double-column synthetic magazine in place. There are also thirty-round magazines. My test pistol functioned flawlessly with both, using a variety of 9mm fodder.

The SPP's barrel assembly includes the barrel guide subassembly and a plastic muzzle sleeve. The actual barrel measures $5\frac{1}{8}$ inches. The system is a truly unique delayed blowback with a rotating barrel, so the entire action is rigidly locked during firing. Perceived recoil is greatly reduced in comparison to other 9mm pistols of similar size employing the straight blowback system and heavy, massive bolts. All of this translates into greater potential accuracy, along with an improvement in

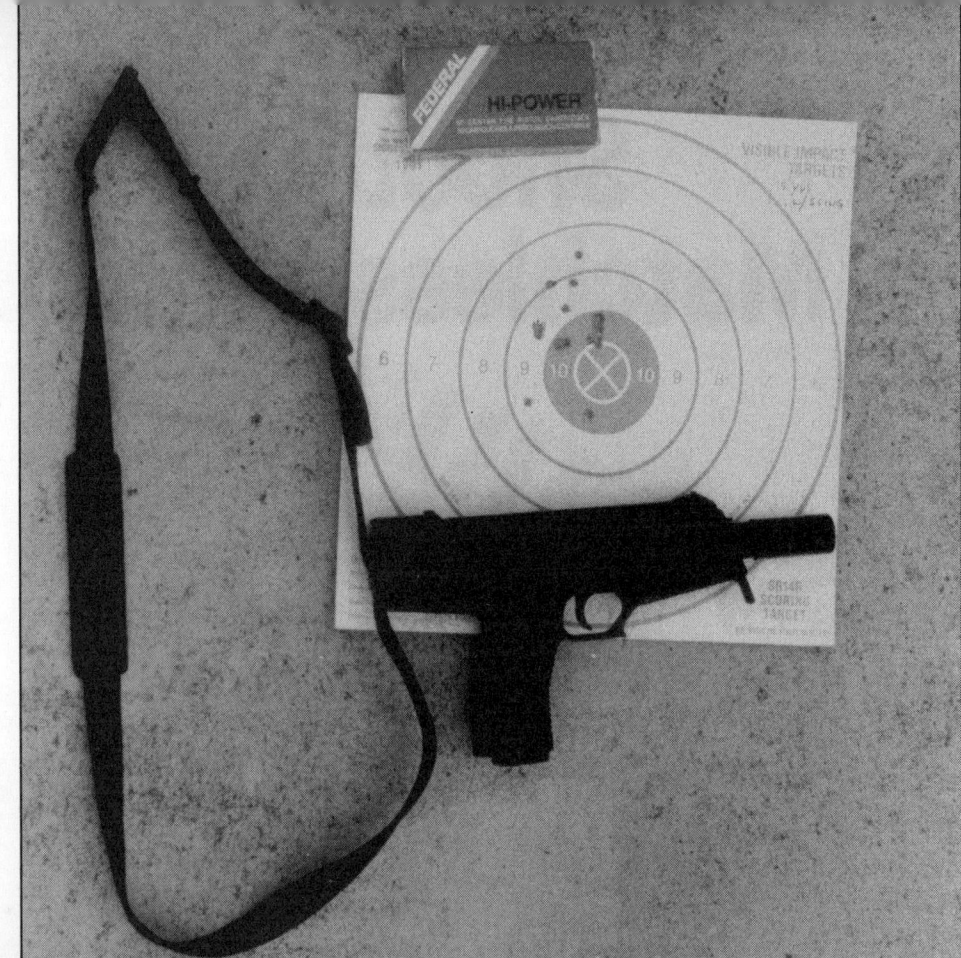

Typical fifteen-shot group at 15 yards, rapid fire, shows pretty darned good grouping, Particularly in a defensive situation.

The Steyr TMP (Tactical Machine Pistol) is the selective-fire cousin of the SPP.

recovery time between shots.

The SPP can be fitted with a telesight or an electronic sight, but its own sights are entirely adequate for most situations. This is not, after all, a target gun, nor is it intended for long-range shooting. The rear sight has a square notch that is wide enough to allow light on both sides of the front post. Windage adjustments are carried out via a simple slotted head screw. The front sight is a stout, round post, adjustable for elevation through a screw located on the inside of the upper receiver. Thus, the pistol must be partially field-stripped in order to make occasional elevation adjustments.

The moulded cocking handle is right behind the rear sight, flush with the rear of the upper receiver. It is easy and quick to operate with either hand.

The SPP also gets high marks for clever simplicity and safety in the trigger system. The trigger itself is synthetic, nicely curved with a wide and smooth finger contact surface. The trigger has a mostly straight sliding movement of nearly $1/4$-inch. The let-off pressure was extremely consistent at around $9^{1}/_{2}$ pounds. The manually operated cross-bolt trigger safety is simple; there is also an automatic safety mechanism that locks the internal hammer.

How does the SPP shoot? Well, I can only tell you that the sample on test did not hiccup even once in firing nearly four hundred rounds of assorted 9mm ammo. The SPP digested all kinds of factory ammo—FMJ as well as a variety of hollowpoints—with alacrity.

As far as handling characteristics go, the SPP felt really nice and maneuverable, even in rapid fire. The optional carrying strap can actually double as a highly viable support in aimed fire. As long as the strap is kept taut, highly accurate fire can be delivered with this pistol out to 75 yards or so. The strap is also quite useful in other ways. It allows the SPP—as well as its selective-fire cousin, the TMP—to be comfortably carried slung from the shoulder underneath a loose-fitting jacket or trenchcoat. Bodyguards and other protection professionals can readily appreciate this. Even without the strap, in a typical two-handed combat hold, the SPP is a fearsome defensive handgun. Based on looks alone, there is a very good chance that any potential attacker would be quickly persuaded to desist when confronted by an SPP.

The importer, GSI, indicates that the SSP is " . . . ideal for boaters and other outdoorsmen who require a durable, low-maintenance firearm." I couldn't agree more. Obviously, the size of this pistol just about rules out personal carry except, as noted earlier, in highly specialized scenarios. As a sporting and home defense handgun, however, the SPP would be quite useful. Its suggested retail price is $895.
J.I. Galan

Shooting The Matchless Matchlock

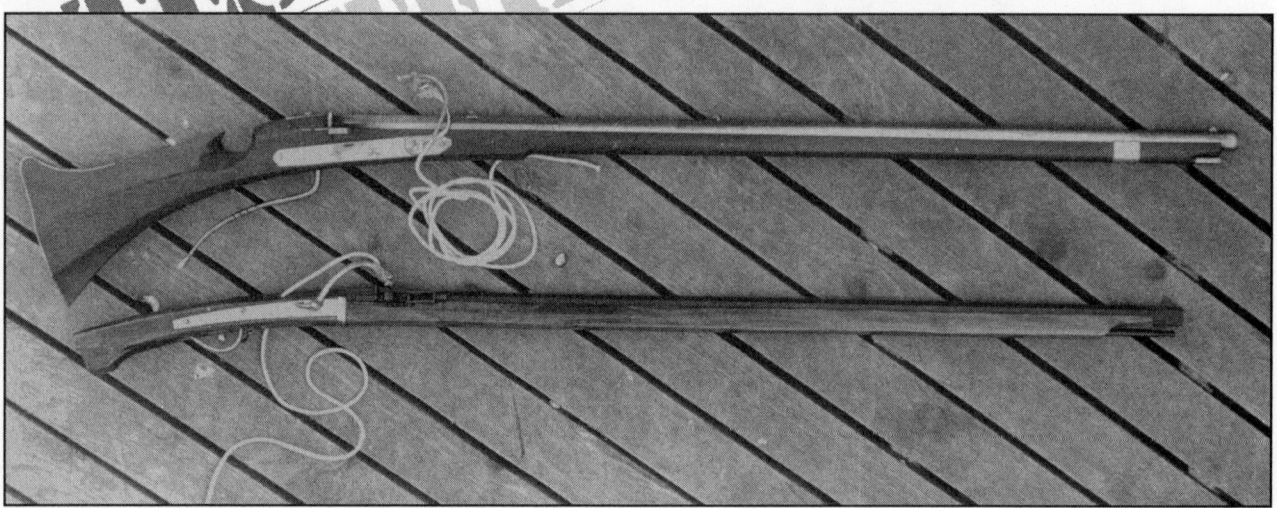

The English/Continental style of matchlock musket is at top, the Japanese below.

THE FIRST very primitive firearms came into use in the 13th century. The first recorded reference to the use of firearms occurred between 1230 and 1248 in Spain. The dates are merely approximate—we didn't have Dan Rather around then to report on the new invention.

The first guns were large cannons or something similar, but it wasn't long before smaller versions were adopted, one that allowed the new "doomsday weapon" to be carried and used by one man. The first hand cannons were fired by the use of a hot wire or smoldering bit of rope that was hand-inserted into a touchhole in the barrel. The gun usually consisted of a barrel fixed to a long shaft, similar to a pike.

In use, one man held the gun and another touched the igniter to the touchhole. Not the most efficient method of waging war, but, we're told, the banging of the handheld cannons scared the hell out of horses and spread disorder among mounted troops. It probably scared the first foot troops to face the new invention as well. The hand cannon was described in the accounts of Edward III dated 1374 and 1375.

As soon as the hand cannon came into common use, it was a short step for someone to figure out how to fix a mechanism to the barrel or stock of the gun to hold and control use of the igniting system. Somewhere around 1440 this happened and the individually fired gun, similar to what we know today, was born. By 1470 or so, they had figured out that if the piece of rope used for the igniter was

soaked in saltpeter, it would burn evenly and not be as likely to go out at an inopportune time. Called a match or slow match, this rope-like ignition system was in use until the end of the 17th century by most of the armies of the world.

The forms of guns that used the self-firing matchlock system ranged from barrels with rudimentary stocks that were merely held in both hands to more elaborate stocks that had provision for the butt to be held against the chest, cheek or, finally, the shoulder. The crossbow of the time used the same type of stocks and sighting, so it isn't too hard to understand why the gun developed so rapidly to resemble the form we use today. The "Arquebus," as it was called by the French, or "Hakenbuchse" as it was

called by the Germans, was usually fired off a rest, a forked stick carried by the soldier. The rest was needed because of the rather long firing sequence of the matchlock. These forked sticks, or possibly the shape of the holder for the match, which was curved in shape, were probably responsible for the name which meant "hook gun" in both languages.

By the mid-16th century, the matchlock Arquebus was rather sophisicated in design and very similar in shape and form to the gun of today. The general form of the hand-held firearm has not changed very much over the centuries. Combined with the invention of rifling around 1500, the individually handled firearm had been birthed and warfare would never be the same again.

A member of the Japanese team prepares to fire his Tanegashima-style matchlock during the International Muzzleloading competition in 1980 at Quantico, Virginia.

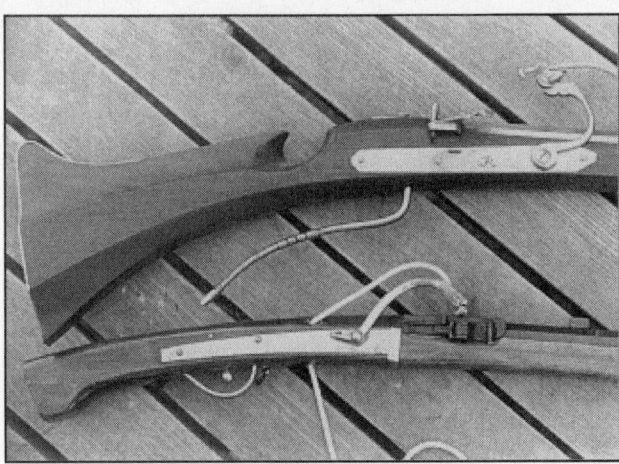

Manipulating the two matchlock systems is different, the "feel" is different, but the follow-through has to be the same.

Incidentally, well into the 1700s, it still wasn't understood why a spinning projectile flew straighter. It was known that spinning arrows and bullets were more accurate, but the simple physics of the phenomenon eluded folks of the time. One explanation that was advanced by a Bavarian named Moretius in 1522 was that it was impossible for a demon to ride astride a spinning object and move it out of its trajectory. His rationale for this was that the heavenly bodies spun and were demon and devil free, but the earth, which as everyone knew, didn't spin, was infected by devils and demons. This made perfect sense at the time.

Just to prove that the more things change, the less they do, matchlocks are back! There are a couple of matchlock guns on the market. The International Muzzleloading Competitions, which are shot every other year around the world, have shooting programs for these guns. It would appear that the matchlock has been effectively saved from being relegated to the same historical niche that holds dinosaurs and the hula hoop.

When GUN DIGEST suggested I do a shooting test of the reproduction matchlocks on the market, I accepted

with a great deal of interest. I enjoy shooting primitive firearms and the matchlock is about as primitive as it gets! My first exposure to this type gun was during my attendance at a couple of the World Muzzleloading matches that were held in the United States, one in Quantico, Virginia, in 1980, and the other this last summer in Camp Perry, Ohio. The accuracy impressed me both times.

I had also seen something akin to the matchlock years before at a primitive muzzleloading match. Two brothers fired a flintlock match using a rifle with a broken frizzen. The frizzen broke during the match at some time or another and the two fired the rest of the match with one brother doing the aiming and the other firing the gun on command with a cigarette touched to the pan. As I recall, while they didn't win the match, they didn't do all that badly, if you don't count the singed fingers of the firing brother.

At any rate, I contacted Dixie Gun Works and Navy Arms Company for the loan of a couple of these old-timey, steeped-in-tradition muzzleloaders which, in due time, arrived.

The first I got involved with was the Tanegashima. It's

pronounced just like its spelled Tan-e-ga-shima. This gun, as the name would suggest, is a replica of a Japanese gun made in the village of Kunitomo, near the town of Kyoto, and used in the 17th century. The gun is pretty typical of the Japanese guns of the 17th and 18th centuries. The original pattern was copied, according to legend, from guns that were recovered from the wreck of a Portuguese trading vessel in the mid-1500s. The style does resemble Portuguese guns of the time.

What makes this gun unique is that there is no buttstock, as we normally recognize it. The stock ends in an elongated pistol grip, and the gun is intended to be shot while this grip is held against the cheek. The stock is made of cherry wood, as were the originals, with brass trim and furniture. The lock is brass and consists of a spring-loaded "serpentine" or hammer. This is cocked by moving it upward. The serpentine is then released by pulling a knob-shaped trigger fixed in the normal place for such things. The steel pan is topped by a pivoting cover that the shooter moves out of the way before firing.

The barrel is steel, 15/16-inch octagon, of 50-caliber and browned. The bore is smooth as were the originals. Sights are a double aperture arrangement that work reasonably well, reminding one of a tube-type sight that was in vogue much later in firearms development. The stock extends to the muzzle and a wooden ramrod completes the picture.

An interesting sidelight is

that the Japanese never did use the flintlock system of ignition. They relied upon the matchlock up until well into the 19th century and then went to the percussion form of ignition, skipping the flintlock intermediate step altogether. They were certainly aware of the system, as the Samurai warrior class carried a small version of the flintlock that was used to light their pipes, but it was never used on a firearm. I suspect that the reason was that the use of the matchlock took some training and if flintlocks had ever gotten into the hands of the general population, the day of the warlord, with his cadre of well-trained warriors ruling the local folks, would have come to a rather early and violent end. Obviously, modern gun control schemes are nothing new.

In use, the Tanegashima matchlock is loaded like any other muzzle-loading arm. I used the recommended charge of 50 grains of FFFg black-powder with a .490-inch round ball patched with .015-inch Wonder-lubed patching. The match or fuse is then clamped in the serpentine or hammer, using a small wedge of wood to hold it in place. The excess wicking (it comes in long ropes) is threaded through a brass-lined hole in the stock, there for that purpose. The excess is then wrapped around the stock. As the match burns and shortens, it is advanced in the serpentine and fed up from the coil around the stock. When the match, wick or fuse, however you wish to call it, is lit, it burns with a glowing coal on the end. It doesn't flame but smolders, being made of

The cheek-stocked Japanese matchlock is surprisingly mild, recoil-wise. Accuracy is acceptable for a smooth-bored gun.

For hunting purposes, a blind that will hide hand movement when adjusting the "match" in the cock jaws is an advantage.

The overly large priming powder pan gives much more flash and smoke than one is used to from the standard flintlock gun.

cotton rope. With the serpentine (so-called because of its snaky look) cocked, the glowing end of the match is about 1/4- to 1/2-inch above the pan.

When one is ready to fire, the cover is swiveled off the top of the pan and the stock is placed against the cheek, the sights aligned, and the trigger is pulled. This drops the match into the pan causing ignition that is very similar to a flintlock. Firing is instantaneous upon pan ignition.

The thing that makes one somewhat jumpy shooting the Tangeshima is that, with the match so close over the pan, there is a very real chance of ignition before one is ready. This happens because, as you can imagine, sparks occasionally drop off the burning match. If this happens and the pan is open, the gun can fire. During the time from opening the pan and taking the sight to pulling the trigger, a very real chance of pre-

ignition exists. Therefore, it takes real concentration to put this chance of accidental firing out of your mind and work on sight alignment, and such. The prefiring doesn't happen very often but, then, it doesn't have to for it to get in your mind. The experience is somewhat like pulling the trigger on a modern rifle, only to have the sear release and then hang up for an undetermined length of time. Trying to quickly pick up a sight picture and get ready for the firing is—well, you get the picture. In spite of all this, matchlocks are fun to shoot and certainly a challenge.

One safety rule that must never be ignored in using the matchlock is that the match is never lit until you are ready to fire and have the barrel pointing downrange in a safe direction. You should never, never reload a matchlock without removing the match from the gun. It should either

be put out or, as the International Competition shooters do, put into a box with a lid so that there is no chance of the match igniting the powder charge during loading. Should this occur, I greatly doubt anyone could hold the bullet in the barrel with the ramrod until the pressure goes down.

The other gun I worked with was a replica of the English matchlock that figured prominently in the early settlement of America. This "Longgun" was in use during the 1600s in England and was probably the gun that was most often seen in the hands of the Pilgrims and the Jamestown folks.

The gun is very plainly styled, as were the originals. It features a Getz barrel of 72-caliber. The 44-inch barrel is octagon for the first 11 inches from the breech then converts to round and ends with a cannon-shaped muzzle. Definitely

not the bell-shaped blunderbus that the Pilgrims are often erroneously pictured as carrying. The barrel is finished in the white. This gun, too, is smoothbored. The stock is walnut and nicely done. The buttstock is similar to guns that we are all familiar with but much wider. It has a polygonal cross-section and flares distinctly at the butt. The buttplate is a piece of sheet iron that fits the end of the wood very well, but has tool marks in evidence, as was correct for the guns of this period.

The quality of this gun is nice, but it retains a crude look, for lack of a better term. This is intentional. The gun is made as a perfect replica of guns of this era and, as such, does not show some of the niceties of fit and finish that came along later.

The mechanism of this gun is different from the Japanese gun. The serpentine is back action, that is, it lowers backward toward the shooter instead of moving forward as with a more conventional, for today, front or forward action. The serpentine has a jaw that is clamped by a thumb screw to hold the match. The loose coils of the match are then held in the hand or wrapped around the stock in the grip area.

The trigger is a long lever that is squeezed with the firing hand. The pulling of this lever toward the stock lowers the serpentine with its glowing match into the pan. The total movement of the match during this process is an arc of about 4 inches. The serpentine is not snapped down by spring pressure—it is lowered by the movement of the lever-type trigger and can be lowered slowly or fast, depending on how fast the lever is squeezed. The pan also has a cover on it that swivels sideways off the pan to open the powder to the match. This must be done before shooting, as with the Tangeshima. The match is far enough from the pan with this gun that premature firings are unlikely.

I used 80 grains FFFg blackpowder with a .690-inch round ball patched with a .020-inch Wonder patch for shooting this gun. I settled on the 80-grain charge because that was the standard charge for military muskets of similar bore size. This is roughly a

3-dram equivalent load in a 12-gauge smoothbore.

How did the shooting go? Very well, as a matter of fact. I was impressed with the accuracy of the guns. I was aware that a well patched round ball in a smooth-bored gun will shoot pretty much with a rifle out to 50 yards or so, but I wondered how much the rather slow lock time of the matchlock would effect accuracy. Surprisingly, it shot about the same as a flintlock or wheellock firearm, once the sequence of firing was mastered. Two-inch groups at 25 yards were the norm and 2- to 3-inch groups at 50 yards were very attainable with both guns.

One other thing that I worried about was shooting the Tangeshima with the stock held against my cheek. I have been well abused by muzzle-loading guns that were too short or had a comb too high and had no illusions about how recoil ramming into one's cheekbone felt. I was not looking foward to it. To say that I had a slight flinch when I first fired the Japanese gun would be an understatement similar to saying the Titanic was scratched by an iceberg. I ducked, cringed and cried piteously. Amazingly, there was no discomfort! The cheek stock works very well and can be shot very accurately. Recoil with the 50-caliber gun was not the least disconcerting. Now, I'm not going to cut the buttstock off all my hunting guns or anything like that, but the cheekstock does work.

Both guns performed very well through the testing that I gave them. The only problem that I encountered was that the muzzle on the English gun was very sharp and tended to shave the side of the ramrod when loading and cleaning. This would have been easily fixed by merely breaking the edge with a crown.

After wringing out both guns, and since the deer season was on, I tried the English matchlock in the hunting field. No, sorry to say, I did not kill the record buck for 1992. Matter of fact, I didn't get a chance to do in a deer. The day I used the gun, I had a group of them coming to my stand, but they chose a fork in the trail that took them about 75 yards from me, as opposed to the 35 yards or so had they picked the correct trail. Luck of the draw, as they say. I guess that's why they call it hunting.

At any rate, I proved to myself that the matchlock would be a viable hunting gun, if range restrictions inherent to a smoothbore are observed. Shots beyond 50 yards are best passed up. The ignition form is usable in the hunting field, especially when hunting from a blind. If a blind is used, it is easier to light the slow match and position it (also reposition it as it burns down) in the jaws of the serpentine without the movement spooking game. I cheated slightly, using a butane lighter to light the match. A true traditionalist would have used flint and steel, but I felt I was tempting fate enough as it was. At least I didn't use an in-line matchlock.

After testing the two guns, I know our forefathers were not quite as handicapped by their arms as I had imagined. True, high wind or rain will ruin the day of the *Arque-busier*, but, by and large, they are fairly efficient. Until the advent of the flintlock and wheellock, the American Indian was likely better armed with his bow and arrow, at least for use in the forests of America. But, from behind walls and fixed positions, the matchlock was a pretty good firearm.

To my knowledge, these two guns are the only reproduction matchlocks on the market. There may be a few folks that will custom-build, but these are the only ones that I am aware of being more or less mass produced. The English style is made in a one-man shop and can be ordered with some custom features. The cost for this gun runs slightly over $800, with the Japanese-made Tanegashima coming in at just under $500. Dixie Gun Works carries both guns in their catalog and Navy Arms also carries the Tanegashima. Both are museum-quality reproductions and will qualify for International Competition, which means a gun must be a faithful, screw for screw, copy of an existing antique firearm, so both guns are obviously "right." If you are interested in understanding how our early forefathers hunted and protected themselves, here's your chance. I'll guarantee you'll draw a crowd at the range. *J.W. Carlson*

Calico's 100-Shooter

Muzzle-end view. Scary and very 21st century.

NOW, I'M A handgunner first, last, and always, but decided I needed a 22 rifle. My gun safe was only big enough for my handgun cases, but when I measured the Calico with its stock folded, I found it would fit. So I bought it. At the time, I didn't know the barrel was easily removable by unscrewing the fluted nut that held it fast. After reading the instruction manual (always do this when you purchase any firearm) and discovering this, I found the rifle, with barrel detached, would fit into a Gun Guard four-pistol case, of which I happened to have a spare. Neat.

Finally, to the range. I was initially disappointed with the gun's accuracy, but, boy, was it fun to blast 100 rounds so fast without a reload! I burned a lot of ammo that day. And after more shooting, I decided I'd keep the Calico, so I bought a scope mount and scope, and spent time with it.

Finding a rest was always a problem, and I bought a bipod that clamped to the barrel—no good, not enough adjustments and not too steady. A Harris Bipod barrel clamp would not work on the Calico because not enough barrel was exposed. Then, I bought a quick detachable sling stud and some J.B. Weld epoxy. After I removed the handguard, I placed tape on the outside, covering some of the vent holes on the bottom of the handguard. I then positioned the stud, and filled the inside of the guard with epoxy, firmly anchoring the stud. When I installed the bipod on the stud, I added two

(Left) Author having gun, empty in the air, and empty magazine about to happen.

CHRONOGRAPH & ACCURACY

Load	Group Avg. (ins.)	MV (fps)
PMC Sidewinder	1.525	1199
Win. Wildcat	1.70	1174
Fed. Hi-Power	1.36	1205
Fed. American Eagle	1.00	1227
Rem. Thunderbolt	1.72	1194
CCI Blazer	1.22	1159
Win. T-22	.98	
CCI Mini Mag	1.70	
Eley Club	1.18	
PMC Target	1.32	

Chronograph and accuracy are the result of the best 10-shot groups fired at 50 yards.

(Below) Calico breaks down into these major components and fits in convenient luggage.

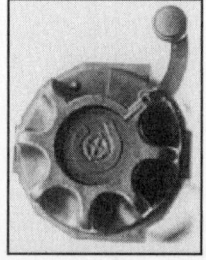

New crank-equipped magazine is lots easier to use and quicker into action as well.

CALICO M-100 SPECIFICATIONS

WEIGHT: Carbine, no magazine, 4.2 pounds; magazine, empty, 14 ounces; carbine loaded, 5.7 pounds; magazine with 100 rounds, 24 ounces
LENGTH: Stock folded, 29.8 inches; stock extended, 35.8 inches
HEIGHT: 7.3 inches
WIDTH: 2.2 inches
AMMUNITION: 22 LR only
MAGAZINE CAPACITY: 102 rounds
BARREL LENGTH: 16.1 inches
BARREL RIFLING: RH 6 grooves
SIGHT RADIUS: 12.2 inches
OPERATION: Blowback, semi-auto

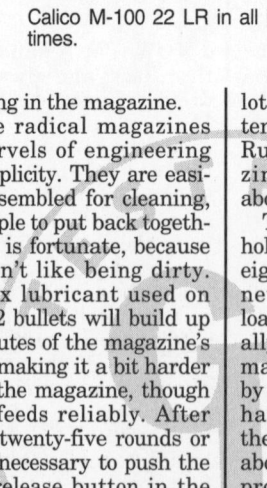

Calico M-100 22 LR in all its glory—scoped, bipodded, stock extended and ready to go 100 times.

screws. I now have a very handy, high-capacity plinker that is a 24-karat ball to shoot.

Now to some of the warts and wrinkles:

The first problem that arose was with the spring that works with the bolt hold-open lever. It fell out repeatedly, and I've finally just left it out. The lever is easily used without it.

Then the pin for that same lever backed out repeatedly. A touch of LocTite fixed that.

During the extensive accuracy and reliability testing, I found it decidedly does *not* like the truncated cone bullet shape. Sometimes they will feed, sometimes they jam. All other ammo works flawlessly, if you remember to wind up the spring in the magazine.

Those radical magazines are marvels of engineering and simplicity. They are easily disassembled for cleaning, and simple to put back together. This is fortunate, because they don't like being dirty. The wax lubricant used on many 22 bullets will build up in the flutes of the magazine's carrier, making it a bit harder to load the magazine, though it still feeds reliably. After loading twenty-five rounds or so, it is necessary to push the spring-release button in the center of the winding knob to take the tension off the magazine spring. It also helps to occasionally lightly rap the magazine to make loading a bit easier. All in all, loading 100 rounds in the magazine is

lots easier than loading ten, ten-round magazines for my Ruger Mark II. The magazines do need cleaning at about 700-800 rounds.

The magazine's witness holes tell you when you have eight, forty-nine and (on the newer ones) ninety rounds loaded. Total capacity is actually 102 rounds. The earlier magazines can be identified by the lack of a fold-out crank handle. When fully loaded, the magazine spring is given about seventeen full turns to produce tension for feeding. The newer magazines have a clutch that prevents over-winding. The slick thing about these magazines is they can be left fully loaded, and the tension spring then wound only when needed.

The sights are a U-notch and post. The iron sights are usable with the scope mounted. The rear sight is adjustable for windage only, and the front sight is adjustable for elevation.

Usually, 700 or 800 rounds between cleanings would not be a problem, but this little critter goes through ammunition so fast, you might find yourself having to clean it in the middle of the day, if you have friends shooting with you. You are unlikely to shoot that many rounds yourself in one session, due to the shape of the trigger and the heavy trigger pull. I'd gauge it to be on the order of 17-18 pounds, with *lots* of creep and over-travel. I'd normally have something done about a trig-

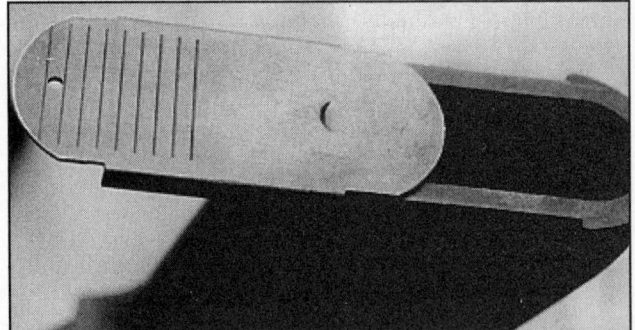

Quick-release sling swivel stud epoxied into bottom of handguard for bipod—the writer's add-on.

Pistol grip storage area—not nearly big enough for ammo.

Oldies, But Goodies: Sealed Eights

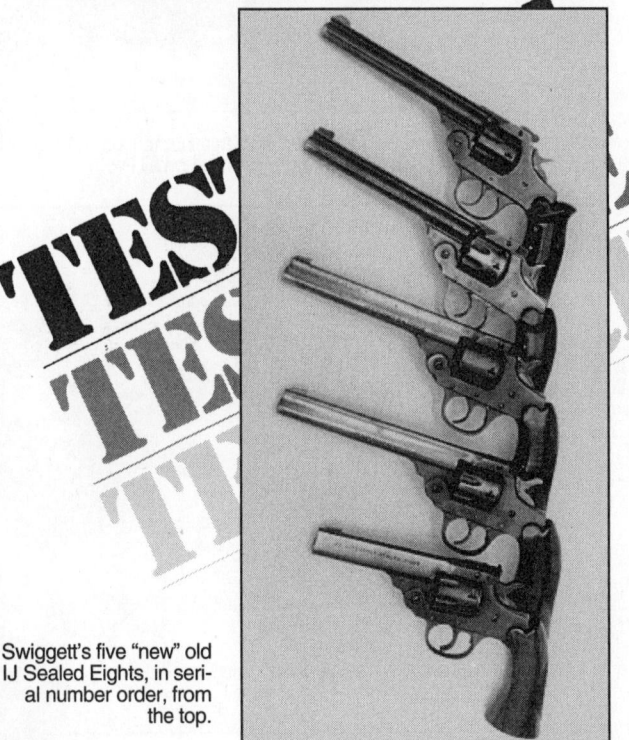

Swiggett's five "new" old IJ Sealed Eights, in serial number order, from the top.

ger like this, but this time I decided it might save me some money to leave it like it is. Otherwise, I'd keep shooting, and ammunition costs could become a major part of my budget.

The accuracy is pretty average, in my estimation. Groups at 50 yards have run from a best of .98-inch using Winchester T-22 target ammo to about 2.75 inches with Remington Viper 22s. Not outstanding, but the bunnies will never know the difference. I have been able to get only one sub-1-inch group.

Cleaning without a teardown is a hit-and-miss deal, but I've found that dental picks, Q-Tips and Break-Free will get you going again when you don't feel like doing the job right. I know we'd all rather shoot than clean, any day.

The Calico is easily hand-fed single rounds with the magazine removed. Ejection is to the right rear and downward. The rifle comes with sling swivels and has a hollow pistol grip with a sliding cover, so some goodies can be stored there if need be. I don't think it would be ammunition! The safety is ambidextrous with markings on only the left side. The collapsible buttstock works flawlessly and can be shortened for smaller shooters. You do want to keep your left hand clear of the operating handle, or it will receive a smart slap.

I've thought about selling the little Calico a few times. That trigger is an abomination, and it just isn't a handgun, but the darn thing just grows on you. Besides, I just have to own one of those "evil, deadly, vicious, mean-looking assault rifles."

Upon ejecting an unfired round from the Calico, I noticed the nose of the bullet was smeared badly. Aha! There's the reason for the mediocre accuracy. A letter was sent to Calico, but no response. Knowing firearms companies tend to hurry to help folks, I mailed another letter. The reply came back, "Send us the gun." I did. A week and a day later, I had the M-100 back in my sweaty hands, eager to take it to the range. The repair order stated they'd chamfered the chamber and modified the ramp. I didn't see any marks on the magazine feed ramp, but the rear of the barrel had been lightly chamfered. Finally, I got to the range. Running a few rounds through the action, there was no sign of the smearing. Eagerly, I fired a series of groups, again at 50 yards. Well, my Calico will now feed truncated cone bullets, but accuracy was as before. I've owned my Calico for several years, and there was no charge for the service. Heck, they even cleaned it for me! Now that's service.

Thanks, Calico. *R.B. Albach*

SEALED EIGHTS were built from 1931 through 1957, and I have no idea as to how many were sold. Mine was purchased in 1933, by my grandfather, and given to me on my twelfth birthday. We left southeastern Kansas in September of 1936. Our guns stayed there.

Now I own five—thanks to GUN DIGEST readers—plus a Trigger Cocking Single Action, which I never knew existed, and a Target Sealed Eight. Could be we'll talk about that trigger cocker later.

My acquisitions run from a four-digit serial number through five digits, then five digits with an L in front, and another with a T in that same spot. The first to move in came from El Paso, Texas. It is like-new and in its original factory box with labels and instructions intact. Plus, it

has just 4 inches of barrel. This length I've not seen in any ad or used-gun value lists.

I have no idea how much my grandfather paid for mine, but a reader from Wisconsin sent a listing dated 1940 with "my" revolver listed at $18.50 with special sights. Minus those "special sights," it was priced at $16.

My library goes back to the 1944 First Annual Edition of the GUN DIGEST ($5.95 by the way). On page 127, "my" revolver is listed at $30 and described as "The best target revolver made by Iver Johnson."

I have shot four of my five new guns somewhat extensively. One, the four-digit (lowest) serial number, is obviously without those special sights; in fact, the front sight is knife-blade thin. The rear looks like a pair of knife

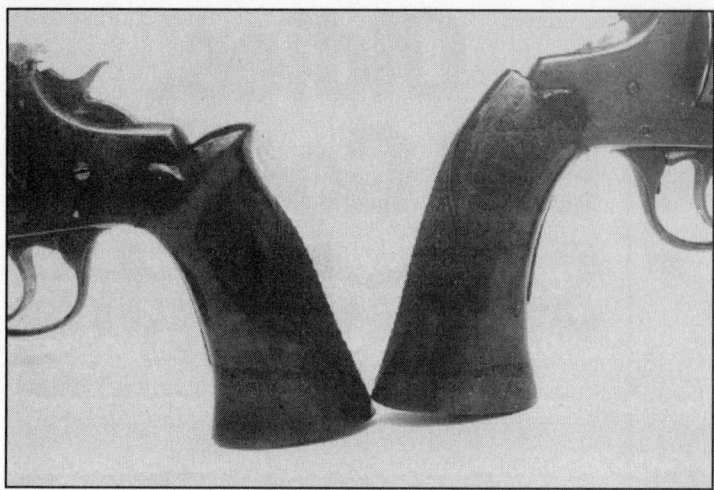

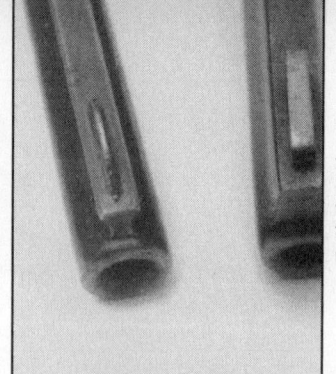

The four-digit numbered revolver wears this knife-blade up front; other blade is easier to shoot.

Hal's four-digit numbered IJ is fitted with this hump-backed grip, the others are like the one on the right. Checkering is identical on all five.

Rear sight on his four-digit revolver is shown on the right. The other four have the same as on the left.

One of his collection, the lowest L-number with no cylinder flutes, has cuts on the outside of each of the eight chambers. It is the only one so made.

.22 SUPERSHOT SEALED EIGHT

That they are, in fact, 22 Supershot Sealed Eights is identified on the four-incher's barrel. All are stamped this identical way.

blades side-by-side with slightly rounded tops. This gun's grip is different than the others—the same checkering pattern and wood, but with a "hump" at the top. Rather comfortable, I must say.

The other four easily keep a cylinder full, all eight shots, in 1½ to 2 inches at fifteen or so steps—cottontail/squirrel shooting distances. That's with me shooting.

Shooting for this review was done with Federal Hi-Power Hollow Point, CCI Mini Mag Hollow Point, Remington High Velocity Hollow Point and Winchester Silhouette, the same ammo I would use for those cottontails and squirrels.

Each gun was fired twenty rounds with each of the four cartridges. The figures that follow are averages from those twenty-round readings. This was done with Ken Oehler's Model 35P chronograph—the first of those three screens at 8 feet.

Federal Hi-Power HPs clocked, please keep this order in mind, 934, 904, 956, 905 and 933 feet per second (fps).

CCI Mini Mag HPs ran 988, 914, 1014, 995 and 979.

Remington High Velocity HPs turned in 945, 884, 970, 995 and 958.

Winchester's Silhouette zipped through those three screens at 874, 844, 925, 937 and 888 fps.

The punchline?

That last reading for each cartridge was the 4-incher's effort. It turned in higher velocities than the 6-inch guns seven times out of those twenty listings. Sort of dispells that short-barrel theory, doesn't it?

Trigger pulls on these old guns checked out at 4, 5½, 4, 5¼ and 5¼ pounds. Very nice, actually.

The two older guns have slender barrels with an integral and distinctive rib, and weigh 20 ounces each, even though their sights are different. Then, one has the same barrel configuration of those following, but no cylinder flutes, and weighs 28½ ounces. Number four, same features as above except the cylinder is fluted, tips my scale at 28½ ounces, same as the gun lacking flutes. The last, my 4-incher, wears the same barrel style as those two in front, with the same sights, and weighs 25½ ounces.

All, from that very early gun to one of the last, have the same checkering pattern on their grip.

Yes, I have several more modern guns in my collection of 22s. But, just to make a stab at my early teen years of 1933, '34 and '35, number two in this collection will be my table (cottontail) revolver for 1993. In spite of being fifty-eight years older and with cataract implants in both eyes, I'm a bit like that little train chugging its way up a mountain, I think I can, I think I can, I think I can.

Hal Swiggett

Interarms' 7.62x39 Mini-Mark X As A Scout Rifle

The little gun measures up to any field use commensurate with its power.

Lots of room around the extended-eye-relief scope lets the shooter see what's happening.

Good on paper and easy on the shoulder, the Little Scout taught Harris a thing or two.

Atop its aluminum adapter plate, the recycled 1903A3 sight doesn't even get in the way of scope use.

MY TESTFIRE OF the 7.62x39 Interarms Mini-Mark X in GUN DIGEST, 47th edition, speculated on its potential as a handy "walking-around rifle" following the general concept of Jeff Cooper's Scout Rifle. I thought a handy 7.62x39 bolt-gun with quick-detachable, forward-mounted scope and auxiliary iron sights would make a fine utility rifle for use on small game, varmints and the occasional deer. The Interarms Mini-Mark X so-modified is handy, attractive and useful.

The usual Scout Rifle is a bolt action chambered for a full-power military cartridge, such as the 308 Winchester. It is a meter long and is intended to weigh under 7 pounds with scope. The forward-mounted Burris "Scout Scope" is available in either 1.5x or 2.5x, has 7-11 inches eye relief, and is mounted ahead of the receiver ring so that no bolt handle modification is required to military actions. The ability to reload using stripper clips is retained if the action accommodates them. Ex-military bolt actions such as the '98 Mauser or '03 Springfield are usual candidates for a full-power Scout

Rifle. The Interarms Mini-Mark X 7.62x39 is well inside these parameters, meeting all but the provision for a clip slot. However, intended as a "walking-around" rifle, it needs no clip slot for its three-shot magazine.

The low-powered Scout Scope has a small field of view, but this is not the problem it would be with a conventional mounting arrangement, as you can readily see around it. This enables the user to pick up and follow moving targets in snap-shooting. It is also far better suited for longer range precision work than the usual military iron battle sights.

When using a 308 Winchester Scout for sporting use, firing a round such as the 308 Winchester, a 150-grain factory load provides an optimum point-blank range of about 260 yards. This assumes a 1.5-inch scope height above bore, and a maximum 3-inch bullet rise above line of sight, which is appropriate for deer-sized game. Sighted dead-on at 25 yards, it will reach its

maximum trajectory height at about 125 yards, cross the line of sight again at about 225 yards, and drops 3 inches low at 260.

Some users think such a rig in a caliber like the 308 Winchester, 30-06 or 7x57 Mauser makes an ideal deer rifle. Then if that is so, where does a "Little Scout" in 7.62x39 fit?

I see the 7.62x39 "Little Scout" as the modern-day replacement for the lever-action 30-30 carbine—a handy, but *close* range deer and varmint gun. With 125-grain spitzers, as used in factory loads, the 7.62x39 has about the same striking energy at 50 yards that the 308 Winchester does at 300. With only about 1500 foot pounds of energy at the muzzle, 1300 at 50 yards and 1100 at 100, it is a marginal deer load, and definitely isn't a long-range number, so let's not kid ourselves. It works OK on small Eastern deer, seldom over 150 pounds within 100 yards or so.

For varmints and fun shooting, however, there is less difference in trajectory

between the 7.62x39 and the 308 than you might think. With typical 125-grain factory loads, the 7.62x39 should be zeroed about from $1\frac{1}{2}$ to $1\frac{3}{4}$ inches high at 50 yards. This provides a maximum bullet rise of 3 inches at 100 yards. The trajectory crosses the line of sight again at 186 yards, and is 3 inches low at 217 yards. In terms of practical hitting ability you have a 50-yard difference from the 308 Winchester. This makes the Little Scout great for off-season practice, banging the iron critters with inexpensive surplus ammo, or as a starter rifle for the beginner who is shy of recoil.

Before trying this little rifle, I had not fooled with the Scout Rifle concept. I was skeptical of the forward-mounted scope, as I was uncertain it would work at all. But everyone who has shot it liked it, and it works.

An interesting wrinkle Larry Wright did on this job was to install auxiliary iron sights, and provide for quick and easy scope removal and replacement without loss of zero. He used a Ruger Mini-14 band and ramp front sight, and a surplus military 03A3 Springfield rear peep. The latter is mounted on an aluminum base made to fit the existing drilled and tapped holes in the receiver bridge. Remarkably, the irons don't get in the way of the scope, and you don't even notice them.

Wright epoxied the left windage screw on the Burris Scout Scope base so the scope can be removed and replaced without loss of zero, when the right screw is snugged until the slot lines up. The zero then repeats close enough for field work. The dovetail base on the front scope ring should have a light film of grease so the dovetail doesn't wear if you swap between irons and scope frequently.

We zeroed the iron sights so that when "bottomed," a squirrel load with 110-grain bullet and 5 grains of Bullseye strikes at the top of the front sight at 50 yards. Handloaded 150-grain Remington 30-30 softpoints with 24.5 grains of Hercules RL-7 hit 3-inches above the front sight at 50 yards, which gives a useful point-blank range to 200 yards on deer-sized targets. The Chinese Ball or factory softpoints with this sight setting are 7 inches high at 50 yards, which gives a maximum 8-inch bullet rise and a 300-meter battle-sight range, the same as an SKS, which is fine for ringing the gong back to 300 meters.

We found that 150-grain handloaded 30-30 bullets struck 5.5-inches higher at 100 yards than the scope zero than the 125-grain loads did. The squirrel load strikes about 5 inches low at 25 yards with the same sight setting, rather than being "close enough" as we usually expect it to be with a 308 or 30-06. If we were doing this again, we'd make the peep sight base of steel and $1/16$-inch lower than we did, or as low as you can get it, so as to get a useful zero with factory loads, while leaving some room for adjustment with the pipsqueak stuff, without having to go with a higher front sight.

Overall we're pleased with the experiment, which could probably be improved upon by others after reading this. Ken Warner now has the rifle. It was fun.   *C.E. Harris*

One-of-a-Kind 22 Magnum Anschutz

One-of-a-kind Anschutz Exemplar 22 Magnum rimfire fully rigged and ready for small varmint shooting.

Hal's expression says, "I like it!"

FOUR 25-YARD groups—each five shots with six different loadings from three companies—averaged .3728-inch. A total of 120 rounds were fired to construct that average group, made at an average velocity of 1685 feet per second (fps) from a 10-inch barrel. I thought this not all that bad for a gun Mr. Dieter Anschutz proclaimed "See, no good!" in March of 1992.

I'd best qualify that: Anschutz builds the most accurate rimfire rifles in the world, proven Olympic championship rifles. The group he proclaimed "See, no good!" was fired on his test range in the Anschutz plant, Ulm, Germany. From their vise at 50 meters, it measured .512-inch with four touching in .327-inch. Average velocity of the Dynamit Nobel rounds was 1700-1750 fps.

My tests with American ammunition didn't come up to that done in the Anschutz plant. My average came from half a dozen loads from three companies and a bit more than doubled his when moved on out to 50 yards. However—and there is always that—my best five-shot group, doubled because it was shot at only 25 yards, is only .053-inch larger than the one rated "See, no good!"

Maybe we'd best go back to the beginning.

My first mention of an Anschutz 22 *Magnum* pistol was in 1988 (GUN DIGEST 42nd ed.) and found to be in error. Not mine—I simply quoted their incorrect release. But it did start the ball bouncing. The 1989 43rd Annual Edition of GD pointed out I was still trying to get an Exemplar in 22 WMR and Anschutz was still refusing.

This continued on through 1990, when Anschutz introduced the 22 *Hornet* in the Exemplar pistol. Finally in 1992, by the time GUN DIGEST got out, there was, in fact, one 22 Magnum rimfire Exemplar pistol. Between the time my section was written and the book was published, I visited the Anschutz plant and "See, no good!" took place.

With its 10-inch barrel and topped with Leupold's new and very excellent 2.5-8x LER scope, my one-and-only "Exemplar Cal. 22 Magnum" (that's what is stamped on the barrel) pistol weighs in at 4 pounds, 6 ounces. Magazine capacity is four rounds, making it five-shot with a cartridge chambered. The trigger pull is a traditional Anschutz Exemplar two-stage and is as crisp as breaking glass at 27 ounces.

About the way it shoots: My best group came from Federal's new Classic Hollow

All test shots were fired over solid rests through Ken Oheler's Model 35P chronograph.

Barrel marking is unequivocal—this is the one.

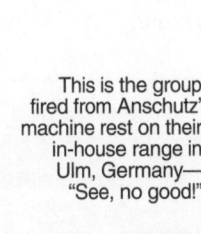

Cal .22 Magnum

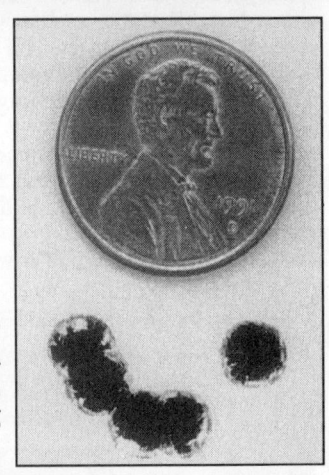

This is the group fired from Anschutz' machine rest on their in-house range in Ulm, Germany—"See, no good!"

Point, .190-inch (remember, 25 yards), and those five shots averaged 1360 fps. This cartridge, by the way, was the slowest of all tested. Move this on out to 100 yards and, should it hold true, we are talking about .76-inch, but give it an expansion ratio of 25 percent, and it still will be in 1-inch at 100 yards.

My second-best group came from CCI's speedster Maxi Mag +V. It clocked 2013 fps and measured .198-inch.

Carry such figures out to 125 yards, maximum in my opinion for small varmints, and they are still in the ball-park for jackrabbit-sized game with 2¼-inch groups or a bit more for Winchester solids. Both Federal Classic Hollow Point and CCI Maxi

Mag +V should hold to 1¼ to 1½ inches at 125 yards. This kind of accuracy is plenty good for prairie dogs, Columbia ground squirrels and the like. Even if an additional 25 yards were to be added, putting those targets at 150 yards, more would be hit than missed, if, obviously, shooters do their parts.

Put another way, how far is this from the majority of 22 Hornet rifles? At this last-mentioned 150 yards?

I would like to have included German-made cartridges, but could not get my hands on any. They might have done a bit better, but frankly I doubt it. Anyway, my point with Dieter Anschutz was a simple one. I felt his Exemplar pistol so chambered would be great

for small varmints. Mr. Anschutz thinks in terms of gold medals. My thinking is field shooter-style—Columbia ground squirrels, prairie dogs and jackrabbits.

Could be we are both right.

This Exemplar was built to

prove Anschutz's point. In so doing, he proved mine, and then presented it to me as, "The Only Anschutz Exemplar Pistol Ever To Be So Chambered."

Time will tell, or so be it. We'll see.   *Hal Swiggett*

The Numbers

Cartridge	Group avg. (in.)	MV (fps)
Federal Classic Hollow Point	.255	1348*
CCI Maxi Mag +V	.267	2025
CCI Maxi Mag	.399	1746
Federal Classic Solid	.414	1655
Winchester Hollow Point	.439	1659
Winchester Solid	.463	1677

All shots taken from solid rest at 25 yards. Velocities at 10 feet through Oehler's Model 35P.
*These are the numbers as recorded when they are fired. No explanation.

When the chips are down, elite units...
PICK A 45 FOR STOPPING POWER

(Below) Colt's offensive handgun system offers a stainless heavy-duty *big* pistol in 45 ACP. It has muzzlebrake, suppressor mount and laser aiming device mount built in. Long grip holds ten-round single-stack magazine.

THE SERVICES went for the 9mm pistol, but plenty of military units never stopped using the 45. That's likely to continue as developments like Colt's offensive handgun weapon system see service.

The New Colt is a short-recoil-operated semi-automatic with a rotating barrel. Receiver, slide, barrel and muzzlebrake are stainless steel; the design goal is a weapon that fires 60,000 rounds before the frame and slide wear out.

The U.S. Special Operations Command (USSOCOM), which directs such units as Navy SEALs, Army Rangers, and the Air Force Special Operations Wing, was pretty specific as to cartridge and other details. Colt chose a single-stack magazine to get maximum reliability, for instance.

Modestly enough, Colt says the gun was designed to "outperform and outlast any other handgun in the world." Given the size and layout of the result, it very likely might.

Ken Warner

Unique design consists of six major components: (1) stainless steel slide, (2) one piece muzzlebrake/barrel bushing, (3) barrel with integral locking lugs, (4) recoil spring assembly, (5) stainless steel receiver, and (6) ten-round magazine.

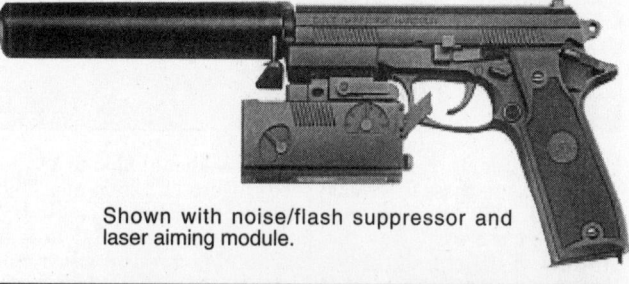

Shown with noise/flash suppressor and laser aiming module.

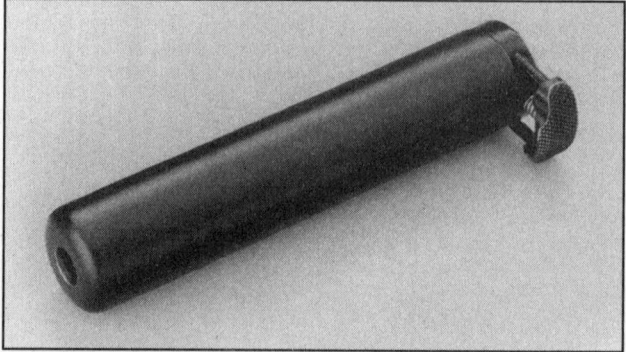

Noise/flash suppressor may be used with the slide unlocked or locked for noise attenuation. Unit is easily mounted by spring-loaded thumb latch.

by LARRY S. STERETT

UTILITY GUNS

UTILITY (yoo-til'i-te) 1. The condition or quality of being useful;...5. In utilitarianism, the principle of the greatest good for the greatest number. -adj. Of the lowest U.S. Government grade of meat.

Only the word useful above actually fits the category of the guns under discussion here, but the definition for serviceable shotguns and handguns for under $200-$250 is next to impossible. Good, previously owned arms of this type are available, but new arms are not exactly plentiful.

Centerfire Rifles

Dealers handling Century International Arms products have access to several utility-handles have been turned down, low-swing safeties have been installed, along with a two-piece Weaver-type scope mount base, and the whole unit fitted in a black Rynite stock with recoil pad and swivel studs. Both the P-14 and 98 Sporters have been refinished to excellent condition.

For those shooters wanting a real utility gun with less frill, there's a Mexican M1910 Mauser Sporter in 30-06. Rebored, rechambered, and refinished, this sporter features a 23-inch barrel, a weight of approximately 8 pounds, a cut-down military stock and issue sights. The Enfield No. IV Sporter in 303 British features a new American walnut pistol grip stock and refinished metal surfaces. Featuring a barrel length of just over 25 inches, a ten-round magazine capacity, and a weight of approximately $7^{3}/_{4}$ pounds, the Enfield is capable of taking most game huntable in North America. The 303 British cartridge has also been used to take even elephants, but that use is not exactly recommended.

Century also has inexpensive Lee-Enfield Sporters—the No. 1 MK III and No. 4 MK I feature cut-down military stocks and issue sights. These range in condition from good to very good, and the metal surfaces retain the military finish. Caliber is 303 British. All for under $150.

Samco Global Arms has two sporter rifles: one called the Spanish Sporter is based on the M1916 Spanish Mauser, while the second, called the German Sporter, is based on the M95 Mauser action. Both rifles have been reblued and fitted with Williams front and rear sights. The barrel length on the Spanish model is 20 inches, chambered for the 308 Winchester cartridge; this rifle features a European hardwood stock with walnut finish, Monte Carlo, and checkering. The German Sporter has a 24-inch barrel, chambered for the 7mm Mauser cartridge, a Monte Carlo walnut stock with checkering, and bolt handle altered to accommodate a scope. Both rifles are available without sights, if desired, and they still cost less than $250. Samco also has the M1916 Spanish Mauser in unsporterized form, but rebored and chambered for the 308 Winchester cartridge; this rifle has issue sights, stock and hardware, and is truly a utility rifle suitable for deer-sized game and at a price of about half that of the sporterized rifles.

Gibbs Rifle Co. has several utility-grade hunting rifles,

New England Firearms Ultra Varmint rifle is available in 223 or 22-250 Remington chamberings. It has 1:12-inch twist, a heavyweight barrel, and a trigger which has been tuned for a better than usual let-off. (Scope not included.)

"utility man" could be adapted, as in..."capable of playing several positions," or "to serve in several capacities." In a manner of speaking, a utility gun is a type of shotgun, handgun or rifle that is low-priced, but serviceable under a variety of conditions.

Following World War II, the Johnson Automatics Company changed a number of M1917 Enfield rifles into what he of Johnson Light Machine Gun fame called a **knockabout** rifle. It was not exactly a beauty, but it was definitely useful, and a rifle which could be carried in a scabbard, in a Country Cadillac, or even left in the barn for utility duty when needed. Today, such rifles can still be produced, but finding good, type rifles capable of bagging big game from deer to elephant, although that might be pushing it a bit. And the price should be around $250, or less. These include the Centurion P-14 Sporter in 7mm Remington Magnum or 300 Winchester Magnum. Built on reconditioned P-14 actions, with new 24-inch commercial barrels, and Bell & Carlson black fiberglass stock, including recoil pad, the P-14 Sporters weigh approximately 8 pounds, without sights. They come mounted with a one-piece Weaver-type scope mount base. The Centurion 98 Sporter is based on the Mauser 98 action, with new 22-inch commercial barrels in 308 Winchester, 270 Winchester or 30-06. The bolt all priced under $250. These include the Mauser 98 Sporter with new barrel in 243, 270, 308 Winchester or 30-06, topped with new ramp front sight and flip-up open rear. The stock is a Monte Carlo design of hardwood with walnut finish, and the receiver is drilled and tapped for scope mounts. An even

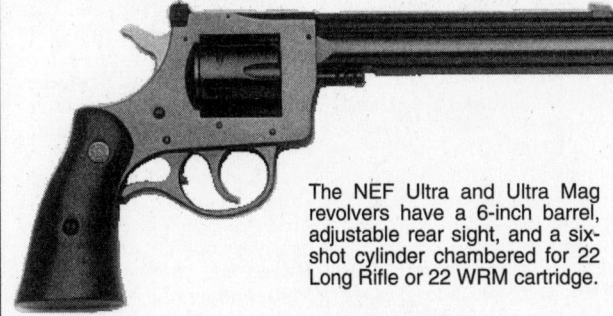

The NEF Ultra and Ultra Mag revolvers have a 6-inch barrel, adjustable rear sight, and a six-shot cylinder chambered for 22 Long Rifle or 22 WRM cartridge.

more economical model is the Economy 98 Sporter, which is available chambered only for the 8mm Mauser cartridge; it does have sporting sights, and the stock is of walnut-finished hardwood, with checkering.

Two other Gibbs Sporters—the M53 and the MK III Enfield—use the issue sights and the original calibers: 7.62x54R and 303 British.

Carlo. It comes with a scope mount base, but no sights. The break-action single shot with a center-mounted outside hammer is no beauty, but it is definitely functional and useful. NEF has the Handi-Rifle, which is basically the same gun, but with a walnut-stained hardwood stock, without checkering, and in some versions without the Monte Carlo. Chamberings

small game classic, easy to operate. In 22 WRM, it covers a lot of country.

Century International has imported a couple of Russian rimfire rifles, both bolt actions. Retailing for under $150, these rifles—the T0Z-17-1 and the T03-17—have 21-inch barrels, five-round magazines, and weigh under $5\frac{1}{2}$ pounds. Both rifles have checkered hardwood stocks,

Feather Industries has a rimfire rifle that comes just under the $250 price tag. The AT-22 weighs under $3\frac{1}{2}$ pounds (empty), has a 17-inch barrel, a twenty-round magazine capacity, and a telescoping stock that permits an overall length of 26 inches. It is also available with a fixed polymer stock at a higher price for those shooters wanting such a stock; a retro-fit

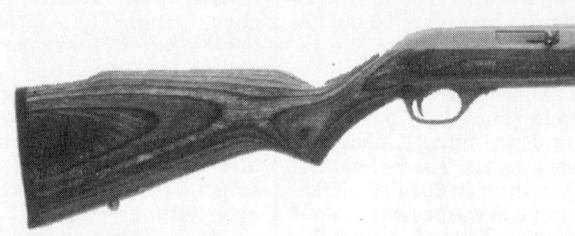

Marlin's Model 60 Stainless Steel rimfire rifle is one of the most graceful of the utility guns, sort of the top of the line utility.

The M53 has had the barrel cut down, the bayonet lug removed, the metal parts reblued and the stock sporterized and refinished. The MK III Enfield has a new lightweight synthetic stock complete with pistol grip, recoil pad and sling swivels. Both the 7.62x54R and 303 British cartridges are capable of taking any game on which the 30-06 is normally used.

There are many SKS and other KS-90 (MAK-90), NHM-90 and NHM-91 models, all chambered for the 7.62x39mm cartridge, as well as some versions in 223 (5.56mm). Dealers have several versions available, including some fitted with synthetic sporter stocks re-

include the 22 Hornet, 223 Remington, 243 Winchester, 270 Winchester, 30-30 and 45-70 Gov't. The barrel length is 22 inches, and the weight is approximately 7 pounds.

Rimfire Rifles

Utility-type rimfire rifles that are not U.S.-manufactured, and still priced under $250, are limited mainly to imports from China or Brazil. Interarms dealers will have both the Norinco ATD and JW-15 models available, and these are both excellent. The ATD is a copy of the Browning Model 24 autoloader. It features an all-steel receiver (drilled and tapped for scope mount) and barrel, checkered stock and forearm of hard-

open sights and receivers grooved to accept tip-off scope mounts. Century also imports the Norinco JW-27 rifle, another bolt-action design chambered for the 22 Long Rifle cartridge.

Ruko Products distributes the rimfire rifles and shotguns manufactured by Armscor (Arms Corporation of the Philippines). The Model 14P is a bolt-action, detachable box magazine design with 23-inch barrel and mahogany stock. (A five-round magazine is standard, but a ten-round magazine is available.) The sights are open, but the receiver is dovetailed for tip-off scope mounts. The M20P is an autoloader with straight blowback action and

stock is also available.

Single shot rimfire rifles are becoming rather rare, but Lakefield Arms in Ontario, Canada, has the Mark I, available in four versions, include two smoothbores for use with shot cartridges. Featuring a self-cocking bolt action with thumb-operated rotary safety, the Mark I has a one-piece walnut-finished hardwood stock with impressed checkering on two of the versions; two of the versions are adult-size and two are youth-size. The barrel lengths are 19 and $20\frac{3}{4}$ inches, and the rifles weigh from 5 to $5\frac{1}{2}$ pounds. There are also four repeating rifles, two for right-handed shooters and two for lefties, one each adult and

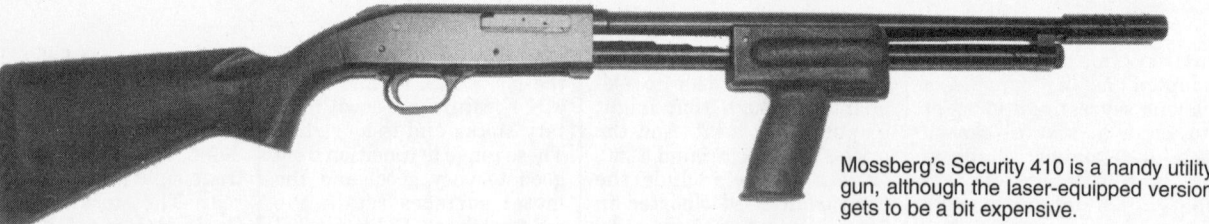

Mossberg's Security 410 is a handy utility gun, although the laser-equipped version gets to be a bit expensive.

placing the issue stocks.

So far as U.S.-manufactured utility guns go, about the only firm actually making complete rifles that cost under $250, and are not rimfires, is New England Firearms/H&R 1871. There's a new Ultra Varmint rifle in a choice of 223 Remington or 22-250 Remington. With a barrel length of 22 inches, and a weight in the 7- to 8-pound range, the Ultra Varmint features a hand-checkered curly maple stock, with Monte

wood, and the same rapid takedown for which the Model 24 was famous. The JW-15 is a bolt-action rifle with Model 70-type safety that locks both the firing pin and bolt. The receiver is dovetailed to accept scope mounts, but the rifle comes with open rear and hooded front sights. Interarms also has the Rossi M62 pump-action rifle in several versions for under $250. Based on the Winchester M90, and available in rifle or carbine versions, the M62 is a

fifteen-round detachable box magazine. It's a good, durable rifle and an excellent value. Two other versions—the M20C carbine, which has a barrel length of $16\frac{1}{2}$ inches and is stocked to resemble the Ruger 10/22, and the M50, which is stocked slightly different and has a perforated barrel shroud to resemble the PPS-50—use the same receiver. There are deluxe versions, at a higher price, of both the M20P and the M14P rifles.

youth. The Mark II rifles are basically the same as the Mark I, except for a ten-round detachable box magazine. Stocks, barrel lengths, weights, etc., are identical for practical purposes. All of these rifles can be purchased for well under $150.

Lakefield has one semi-automatic rimfire rifle—the 64B. It has a weight of $5\frac{1}{2}$ pounds, barrel length of $20\frac{1}{4}$ inches, and a stock similar to that on the bolt-action rifles. (All the Lakefield stocks are of the Monte Carlo style, and all the receivers are grooved or dovetailed for use with tip-off scope mounts.) The 64B is made in right-hand version only, and it uses the same ten-round detachable box magazine as the Mark II bolt actions. These rifles are excellent values in what is becoming a shrinking field. Lakefield also manufactures rimfire target rifles—the 91R, 91T, 92S, 90B (Biath-

and a weight of approximately 36 ounces.

Grendel produces the P-30 and P-30M autoloading pistols that retail for under $250. The pistols are chambered for the 22 WMR cartridge, have a thirty-round magazine, and differ mainly in barrel length. They have fixed sights and an empty weight of under 22 ounces, which is something to consider if backpacking or weight is a prime consideration.

combo unit which includes barrels for both cartridges, and the retail is right at the $250 mark. The Tokarev has features of some of the best Swiss designs of the pre-WWII period, and reportedly OSS agents liked the pistol because of its slimness and reliability.

Shotguns

Most of the Maverick line of pump-action shotguns, which

gauge models can be obtained with fixed or choke tube barrels. All for under $135.

Summary

There is a market for good, reliable utility sporting arms—rifles (rimfire and centerfire), shotguns and handguns—but there just are not many such arms available. Synthetic stocks, such as those used on the Maverick shotguns, seem to be more

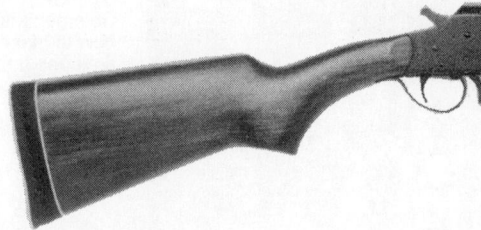

The IGA Reuna Youth shotgun from Stoeger is definitely one of the types farmers used to leave in the barn for utility use.

lon), which are available in right- or left-hand versions—but these are more expensive and are not what we're defining as utility rifles.

Marlin manufactures a line of promotional rifles—no frills—which are suitable for utility guns. These include the models 25N, 15YN, 25MN, 60, 60SS (which is a beauty with a price tag of under $175), 70HC and 70P. Some are in 22 WMR, but most are chambered for the 22 Long Rifle cartridge. Barrel lengths range from $16^{1}/_{4}$ inches to 22 inches. These are probably covered elsewhere in this edition.

One of the best values in rimfire autoloading rifles, in this shooter's opinion, is still the Ruger 10/22 in either blued or stainless, just as one of the best handgun values is the standard Ruger Mark II rimfire pistol. The designs are time-tested, and the guns are reasonably priced.

Handguns

There are not many utility handguns available for under $200. NEF has had their standard revolver with swing-out cylinders in nine-shot 22 rimfire with 4-inch barrel, blued or nickel finish, plus a five-shot blued version in 32 H&R. The top of the line is the Ultra with a 6-inch barrel and blued finish. The Ultra is available chambered for regular 22 Long Rifle or the 22 WMR cartridge, and it is priced under $200. Featuring an adjustable rear sight, as opposed to a fixed rear sight on the standard model, the Ultra has a rib on the barrel,

Magnum Research's Mountain Eagle is an excellent utility pistol. Tipping the scales at less than $1^{1}/_{2}$ pounds, it has a 6-inch barrel and a magazine capacity of fifteen rounds of standard or high-speed 22 Long Rifle cartridges. At 25 yards, it is capable of producing five-shot groups measuring less than 2 inches, center-to-center, and it costs under $250.

Intratec Firearms has the TEC-22T pistol with a 4-inch barrel and thirty-round magazine capacity for utility users who like the machine pistol look. It weighs under $2^{1}/_{2}$ pounds, loaded, and retails for under $160 with blued finish, or with a Tec-Kote finish for a double sawbuck and some change more.

In the big bore category, about the only good, reasonably priced pistol is the Helwan Brigadier. In 9mm Parabellum, with a barrel length of $4^{1}/_{2}$ inches, the Helwan is none other than the time-tested Beretta design based on the Walther P-38. It has an eight-round magazine, all-steel construction, ribbed synthetic stocks, and a sensible price for a 9mm autoloader.

K-Sports Imports distributes the Chinese-manufactured Model 54-1 and 213B pistols, which are versions of the famed Tokarev pistol in original 7.62x25mm and 9mm Parabellum. These pistols have an eight-round magazine capacity, barrel length of $4^{1}/_{2}$ inches, and a weight of under 2 pounds. Navy Arms has the same pistol as the TU-90, including a

are probably covered elsewhere, are priced under $250. Even the Mossberg Home Security 410, which is suitable for some utility chores such as rat control around the barn, fits in the price range. The Maverick shotguns feature synthetic stocks, are available in 12-gauge only, and are chambered for 3-inch shells. Barrel lengths range from $18^{1}/_{2}$ to 30 inches. One—the Model 91—is chambered for $3^{1}/_{2}$-inch shells.

KBI, Inc., imports the Baikal shotguns from the former USSR. The single shot model, the IJ-18M, has a barrel length of 26 or 28 inches, depending on the gauge—12 or 20, or 410-bore—chambered for $2^{3}/_{4}$- or 3-inch shells. This shotgun is a hammerless design, with under-lever opening, a cross-bolt safety, and chrome-lined fixed-choke barrel. This shotgun is commonly found throughout the former USSR, and it retails here for under $125.

Stoeger Industries' Reuna single barrel shotgun from Brazil has to be one of the crudest-appearing shotguns on the market. Yet, it will do the job of a utility gun. The stock and forearm are of Brazilian hardwood with a lacquered or oil finish. The chrome-lined barrel, and the receiver with under-lever opening, are steel. A center-mounted outside hammer is standard, as is an extractor, and lengths of the 3-inch chambered barrels range from 22 inches (Youth model) to 28 inches. The 410 versions are available with fixed chokes, but the 20- and 12-

common, and such stocks, being non-warping or swelling, are an asset to a utility gun. Even rifle and handgun manufacturers are starting to add them to their lines, as seen by some of the Remington, Weatherby and Winchester rifles, and the Magnum Research Mountain Eagle and Ruger's 22/45 pistols to mention a few. There are many more after-market stocks for rifles available at present than there are such stocks being provided on factory rifles. Stainless steel is also becoming more common on all arms, as are matte black finishes on non-stainless metal parts. Screw-in choke tubes are available on almost all currently manufactured shotguns, including some of the lower-priced models, and even rifle barrels and/or rifled choke tubes for shooting slugs.

A combination of such materials in an autoloading or pump-action rifle (centerfire and rimfire), shotgun or autoloading pistol (centerfire and rimfire), would make ideal utility guns. Remington had the correct idea several years ago with their Sportsman rifle and shotgun—plain, no frills, based on tested designs, but with hardwood stocks at the time, since synthetics were not well accepted then. Synthetic stocks on rifles and shotguns have been around for over fifty years, but the early versions did have a few problems. Still the price has to be right, which is less than what is generally available today. Maybe tomorrow! ●

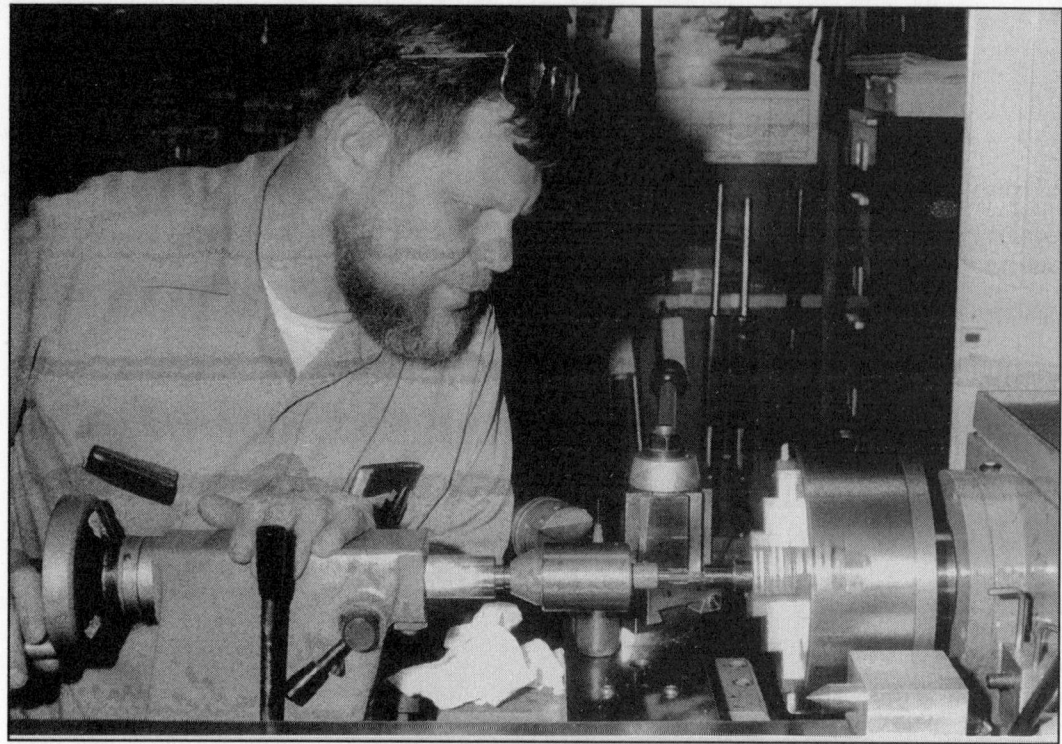

It's almost all in the chamber, and Jim Coleman knows how to make the right one happen in a semi-auto.

MAKE AN ACCURATE

Ruger 10/22 with bull barrel works well in the field and shoots 3/4-inch 50-yard groups with CCI standard ammo.

THE CONCEPT OF an autoloading 22 rifle which is both handy *and* highly accurate is very attractive. How often have you lost the opportunity for a second shot at a squirrel or other small game because the action noise and movement of your hand spooked the animal? Semi-autos mask the action noise with the report of the rifle.

If you can, as well, use subsonic ammunition—it doesn't provide the supersonic "crack" which accompanies the "whiz-bang" stuff—game targets are often unaware of that first shot. The shooter who remains motionless after a near-miss often gets a follow-up shot.

The tough part of shooting the semi-auto on squirrels is that many autoloaders simply aren't accurate enough for clean kills, except at short range. Part of that is because light rifles are hard to hold steadily, but there is also an inherent limitation in the design compromises made to obtain safe and reliable functioning. The few

If your rifle functions reliably with standard-velocity or match ammunition (an iffy thing with some autoloaders), you might reduce your benchrest ten-shot group sizes to 1½ inches at 50 yards. A few autoloaders do better with a particular ammunition they like, if you can discover what that is and then hoard some. Most 22 bolt actions, when scoped, will easily beat an inch for ten-shot groups at 50 yards. A very few will approach half that with good match ammunition. The obvious way to make an accurate 22 autoloader is to do what Navy gunsmiths did for CISM competition.

The January, 1990, issue of *American Rifleman* shows a heavy target barrel from a Winchester 52 and custom McMillan target stock installed on a Ruger 10/22. The rig certainly looks interesting, but is hardly the type of thing I would want to carry up the ridges. It's also a little strange to put $500 worth of gunsmithing into a $150 rifle!

shows several series of five-shot, 50-yard groups with high-velocity ammunition averaging from 1.3-1.8 inches. That implies that ten-shot groups, which are the usual industry standard for 22 rimfire ammunition testing, would be in the "ordinary" 2-inch range. Shucks, a third of normal-production Ruger 10/22s will shoot 1½-inch ten-shot groups from a rest with CCI Green Tag, straight from the box!

From 1984-86, I observed thousands of rounds fired through 10/22s every day at the Newport, New Hampshire, Ruger factory. Occasionally, range staff would conduct audit shoots of normal production. When I was with the company, it was not unusual to get a dozen rifles from a rack of thirty which would shoot 1½-inch ten-shot groups at 50 yards with CCI Green Tag, and function reliably, too, with seldom a bobble.

The various test results I've seen on the Clark-Custom don't seem like much of an accuracy improve-

by C.E. HARRIS

22 SEMI-AUTO

semi-auto 22 rifles you see that are consistently accurate are greatly prized by their owners, most of whom know their rifles are aberrations.

Squirrels have tiny vital areas. The maximum effective range for a small game rifle is determined by the longest distance you can confidently fire a 1-inch, five-shot group from a field position. I have found that ten-shot benchrest groups under controlled conditions on the range approximate what I can expect for five-shot groups under field conditions shooting from an improvised rest. This realistically limits the *average* 22 autoloader to 30-40 yards.

Because there was no accuracy data, I could not determine from the *Rifleman* article how well the Navy-CISM rifle really shot.

Shortly afterward, several magazine articles described the Clark-Custom Ruger 10/22 autoloader built for the Chevy Truck Sportsman's Team Challenge. It has a 21½-inch heavy Douglas barrel and supposed match-type chamber, but retained the Ruger's trim sporter stock. This makes a handsome 7-pound package which appears to have obvious field utility, but the developed accuracy reported in several write-ups I've seen was uninspiring. The March, 1991, issue of *American Rifleman*

ment from my memories of factory testing the 10/22, considering that the custom gunsmithing added about $300 to the cost of the basic rifle! The NRA tech staff tried Eley Tenex ammunition in the Clark rifle, but it malfunctioned and no accuracy data were reported. We don't know what the Clark-Custom would do with good ammo when tuned to function reliably with it.

If you watched the 1991 Chevy Truck Sportsman's Team Challenge last year on ESPN, you probably noticed the shooters lost time clearing jams. I have watched this tape several times, and it made the lasting impression that the gun modification wasn't completely worked out.

Scoped—it's a 6x Unertl—Norinco proved to be so good as-is it was left alone—the exception that proves the rule.

The Ruger 10/22 is, generally, one of the most reliable 22 autoloaders ever made. Feeding malfunctions will occur in some autoloaders with standard-velocity ammunition, because it doesn't provide as sharp an impulse to work the mechanism. If the action spring is balanced for high-velocity rounds, the usual case with U.S.-made autoloaders, standard-velocity rounds don't provide full compression of the action spring, and the shorter bolt stroke reduces the bolt closing force imparted by the action spring. This condition gets worse when the gun gets dirty.

The traditional 22 Long Rifle SAAMI-dimentioned "match" chamber isn't suited for use in autoloaders. This is because additional force is required to seat a 22 Long Rifle round that last $1/10$-inch or so into the origin of rifling in the match chamber. This increased resistance causes failures of the bolt to close fully, because semi-autos depend upon the inertia of the closing bolt to seat the round. It is necessary to adjust forcing cone depth to the particular ammunition when the tighter body diameter, match-type chamber is used.

It is no secret that the accuracy potential of a 22 rifle is determined by its chamber. The SAAMI-dimensioned 22 Long Rifle sporting chamber is seldom capable of much better than $1^{1}/_{2}$-inch groups at 50 yards, no matter how heavy the barrel is or what kind of ammunition you try. However, many 22 semi-auto target pistols group well under 2 inches at 50 yards with match ammunition when scoped or fired from a machine rest. If you cast the chamber of a 22 rimfire match pistol, you will find it doesn't have the usual sporting chamber. It doesn't have the same chamber that match rifles do either. It is something in between, which is exactly what we are looking for.

The Ruger Mark II Government Model pistol uses a shallower 2-degree leade angle in the forcing cone of the chamber, rather than the standard 5 degrees. This permits the chamber body length (measured from the rim seat to the start of the forcing cone) to be shortened to .670-.700-inch length, which is a compromise compared to the .600-inch of the SAAMI-dimensioned 22 LR match chamber or .775-inch in the SAAMI sporting chamber.

While this chamber greatly reduces free bullet travel compared to the sporting chamber, engraving force on the round being chambered is far less than the SAAMI-dimensioned match chamber. A safe, reliable autoloader which functions with anything and isn't fussy about cleaning requires about $1/16$-inch longer body length than the SAAMI match or Winchester 52D chamber. I recommend the gunsmith making rifles for the average user adopt a chamber as shown in the accompanying drawing. It includes a .228-inch base diameter, .670-inch minimum body length with up to +.030-inch if needed for reliable function, .225-inch mouth diameter, and 2-degree forcing cone. In my humble opinion, the chamber illustrated is the best way to go for all but the most serious accuracy requirements. It will also work well in manually operated repeaters and semi-auto pistols.

Serious shooters after pure accuracy, who are willing to select specific ammunition and clean carefully, can use the Winchester 52D or Freeland-type chamber in autoload-

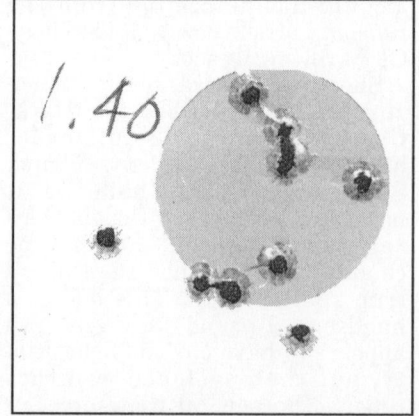
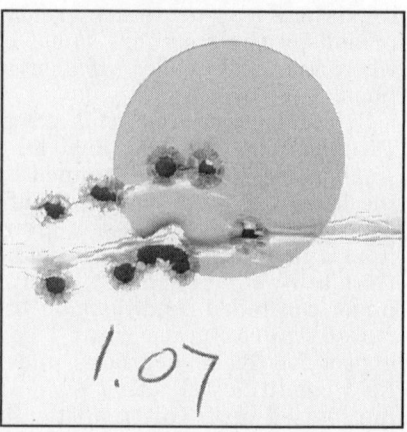

The second-best and second-worst of ten-shot at 50 yards with a factory ATD demonstrate that some rifles should be left as-is.

ers like the Browning or Ruger and can expect accuracy which rivals a boltgun. The Winchester 52D chamber has a .580-inch body length, whereas the similar Freeland type is .600-inch. Both have a 2-degree forcing cone which engraves a round of Eley Tenex to about the second cannelure upon chambering.

This chamber generally works well as long as the guns are well tuned to function smoothly and are kept clean. The shorter Winchester 52D and Freeland-type chambers may sometimes experience malfunctions with foreign ammunition exceeding SAAMI maximum bullet diameter, or if the chamber is used in rifles with light breech bolts or weaker action springs. These rifles and manually operated slam-feeders with little chambering leverage, such as the old discontinued Winchester Models 1890, 1906, 61 and 62, require the chamber body be lengthened about 1/16-inch to obtain reliable functioning. Gunsmiths wanting to ensure reliable functioning in autoloaders which will work with any ammunition and go 1000 rounds or more between cleanings should try this lengthened chamber.

A viable expedient for gunsmiths not wanting to buy special tooling is to use a 22-caliber centerfire rifle throating reamer (usually .2245- to .2250-inch diameter with a 1 1/2- or 3-degree angle) to carefully lengthen the SAAMI-dimensioned match chamber approximately, but not appreciably more than, 1/16-inch. The exact body *length* is not critical as long as chamber *diameter* is maintained as close as possible to the SAAMI maximum cartridge diameter of .225-inch. A round of the chosen ammunition dropped by its own wieght into the chamber should stop about 1/16-inch short of the rim seat, versus 1/8-inch or so for the usual match chamber. Lengthening the match chamber slightly reduces resistance to chambering while preserving a close fit of cartridge to chamber, which is essential to best accuracy.

Simply shortening the sporting chamber by stopping the reamer before it cuts to the full .775-inch depth from the rim seat does *not* work, because chamber *diameter* is more important than length. Running a 2-degree, .225-inch diameter rifle throater 1/16-inch into a SAAMI match chamber only enlarges the average of a series of ten-shot groups about 10 percent.

This is insignificant. Further deepening the chamber *another* 1/16-inch increases group size by 15-18 percent over the original match chamber, which is only marginally significant. But enlarging the body diameter of the same chamber only .005-inch by cleaning it up with a sporting reamer, just enough to get reliable semiautomatic functioning, *doubles* group size compared to the Winchester 52D-type chamber. You don't need to be a statistician to see that doesn't work.

We fired several factory 22 autoloaders to get a baseline for comparison. These included a Ruger 10/22, a Browning Grade I autoloader, a Norinco ATD copy of the Browning from Interarms, and a circa-1970 Remington Model 77 Apache. All of them shot remarkably alike. The Remington did not function reliably with all standard-velocity ammunition, but the Ruger 10/22, the Browning and the ATD did. The ATD shot fully as well as the Browning, a pleasant

Norinco ATD with Eley Subsonic HP.

If you are unwilling to test a parade of 22 autoloaders until you find an accurate one, the least expensive way to get a tackdriver is to install a Brownells liner in a factory barrel, with a proper chamber. I recommend use of the SAAMI-dimensioned match or Winchester 52D-style reamer, adjusting the forcing cone not more than .060-inch deeper with a 22 centerfire rifle throater until rounds chamber and extract easily, but are engraved for about 1/16-inch when extracted without firing. Arlington, VA, gunsmith Jim Coleman has found that relined barrels with good chambers average under an inch, with the best ammunition being 3/4-inch or so. However, because the light factory barrel contours are whippy, they are very difficult to hold steadily. Getting consistent grouping remains a problem, so a heavier replacement barrel is the preferred option if you want the "all-out-accurate" autoloader.

At Coleman's suggestion, we

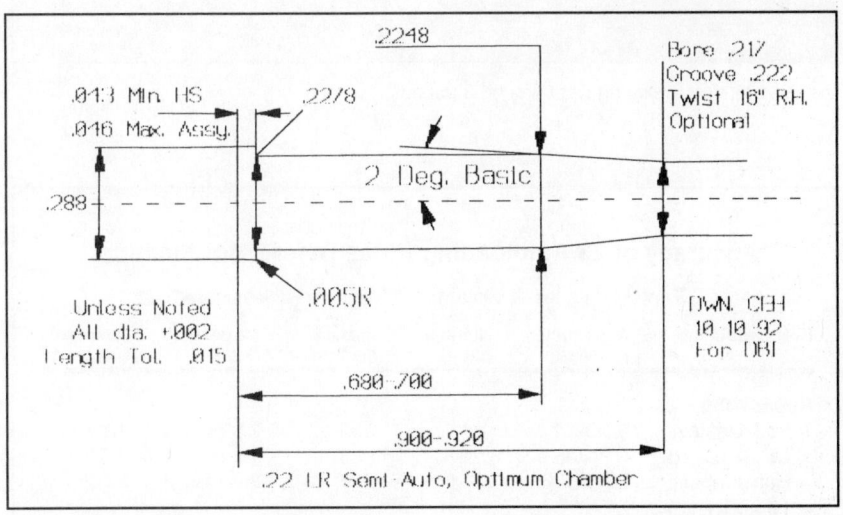

.22 LR Semi-Auto, Optimum Chamber

surprise. I had intended to reline the ATD as an experiment, and then shoot it again for comparison. But when I saw the targets with CCI Standard Velocity and Eley Subsonic Hollowpoints, my chosen squirrel ammunition, I took Jim Coleman's advice that "if it ain't broke, Mister, don't fix it!"

Our results suggest that over the long run most 22 autoloaders will average 2 inches or so for five ten-shot groups with high-velocity ammunition. Standard-velocity ammunition was more accurate, averaging about 1 1/4 inches. The Browning approached 1-inch with Eley Tenex ammo, as did the

decided to see how well we could get an all-out-autoloader to shoot—heavy barrel, target scope, the works. George Wilson of the Wilson Arms Co. provided several blanks of the same type he supplied to Ruger for producing the 10/22. These are 1137 steel and 15/16-inch diameter, providing a finished barrel 20 inches long. Fitting these cylindrical blanks on a Ruger 10/22 and a Browning autoloader, we reached our goal—an autoloader which would average under an inch for a long series of ten-shot groups at 50 yards. We also proved to our satisfaction that the Winchester 52D chamber or something similar with a gradual forcing

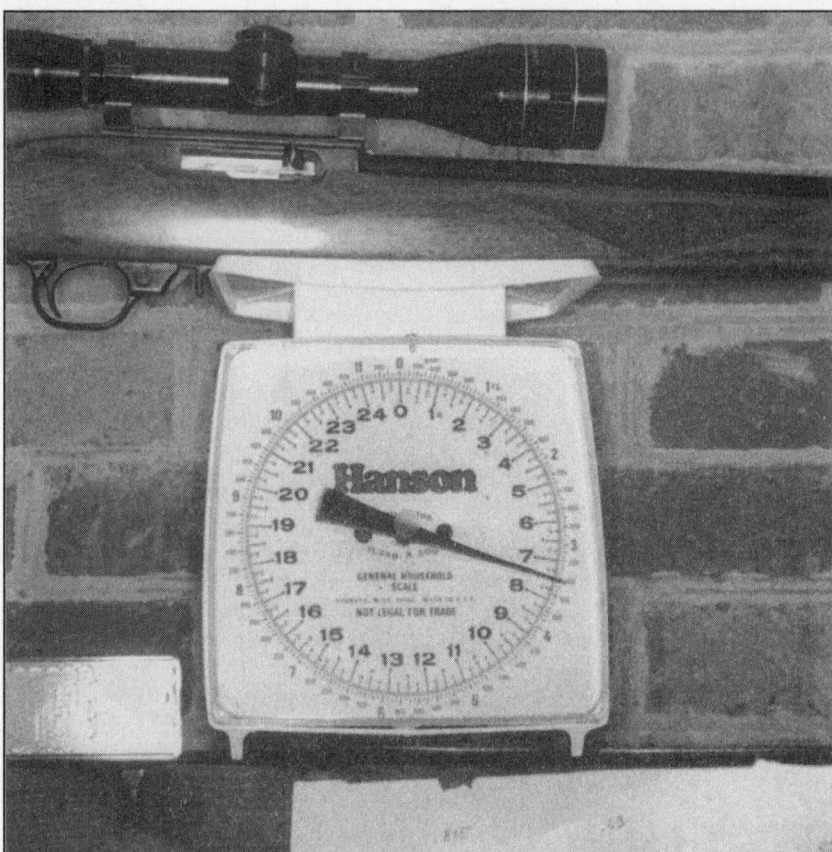

The bull-barreled Browning went around 8 pounds.

cone, optionally up to 1/16-inch longer (depending on the intended ammunition and your cleaning habits), was necessary.

Our early trials with the SAAMI-dimensioned match chamber in the Browning produced malfunctions. Once the gun was dirty, we blew off a few case heads from slamfires. One of these is illustrated. I would caution people never to use the SAAMI-dimensioned match chamber in an autoloader.

Actually, two heavy Wilson Arms

Burst cases can happen to the regular SAAMI-spec match chamber in a 22 semi-auto.

Accuracy of 22 Autoloading Rifles Before Modification

Ten-shot groups at 50 yards with 6x scope unless noted

Rifle and Ammo	Ammunition Lot No.	Number of tgts.	Smallest (ins.)	Largest (ins.)	Average (ins.)
Ruger 10/22					
Fed. Lightning	3A-9721	5	1.55	2.09	1.80
CCI Grn. Tag	C19V05	5	1.36	1.99	1.64
Hansen Std.	8609-123	5	1.36	2.43	2.03
Browning Grade I					
CCI Std.	K08V14	5	0.99	1.99	1.49
CCI Blazer	K10P16	5	1.75	2.63	2.21
Fed. Lightning	3A-9721	5	1.29	2.29	1.65
Eley Tenex	WL300	5	1.08	2.15	1.17
Eley Subsonic	RG26	5	1.36	1.64	1.52
Eley P100	LM165	5	0.92	1.99	1.19
Norinco ATD (open sights at 50 yards)					
CCI Std.	K08V14	10	1.25	2.02	1.66
CCI Blazer	K10P16	10	1.69	2.68	2.02
repeat Norinco ATD (with 6x Unertl Small Game Scope)					
CCI Std.	K08V14	10	0.81	1.51	1.23
CCI Blazer	K10P16	10	1.12	2.05	1.55
Eley Subsonic	RG26	10	0.76	1.64	1.12
Remington Nylon 77 Apache (circa 1970s) with Weaver B4 scope					
CCI Std.	K08V14	5	0.72	1.69	1.29
CCI Blazer	K10P16	5	1.24	2.02	1.55

Co. barrels were fitted to the Browning 22 autoloader, chambered to Winchester 52D dimensions. One barrel had the normal 16-inch twist and the other was 14-inch twist, as used by Clark in his custom target pistols, which we tried just to see if it made any difference. It didn't. The average of *fifty* ten-shot groups in the Browning autoloader using an assortment of high-velocity, standard and match ammunitions at 50 yards was .99-inch with the 16-inch twist barrel and .95-inch with the 14-inch twist. Eley Tenex averaged under 3/4-inch in both barrels, CCI Green Tag, CCI Standard Velocity and Eley Subsonic HP averaged under an inch. None of the high-velocity ammo averaged over 1.2 inches.

Looking at the Clark-Custom Squirrel Rifle advertised recently in several shooting publications, we decided to shorten the barrel on the 14-inch twist Browning heavy barrel. The results were gratifying. Ten consecutive ten-shot groups with Eley Tenex averaged 0.67-inch, a significant improvement from the 0.74-inch average produced by the same

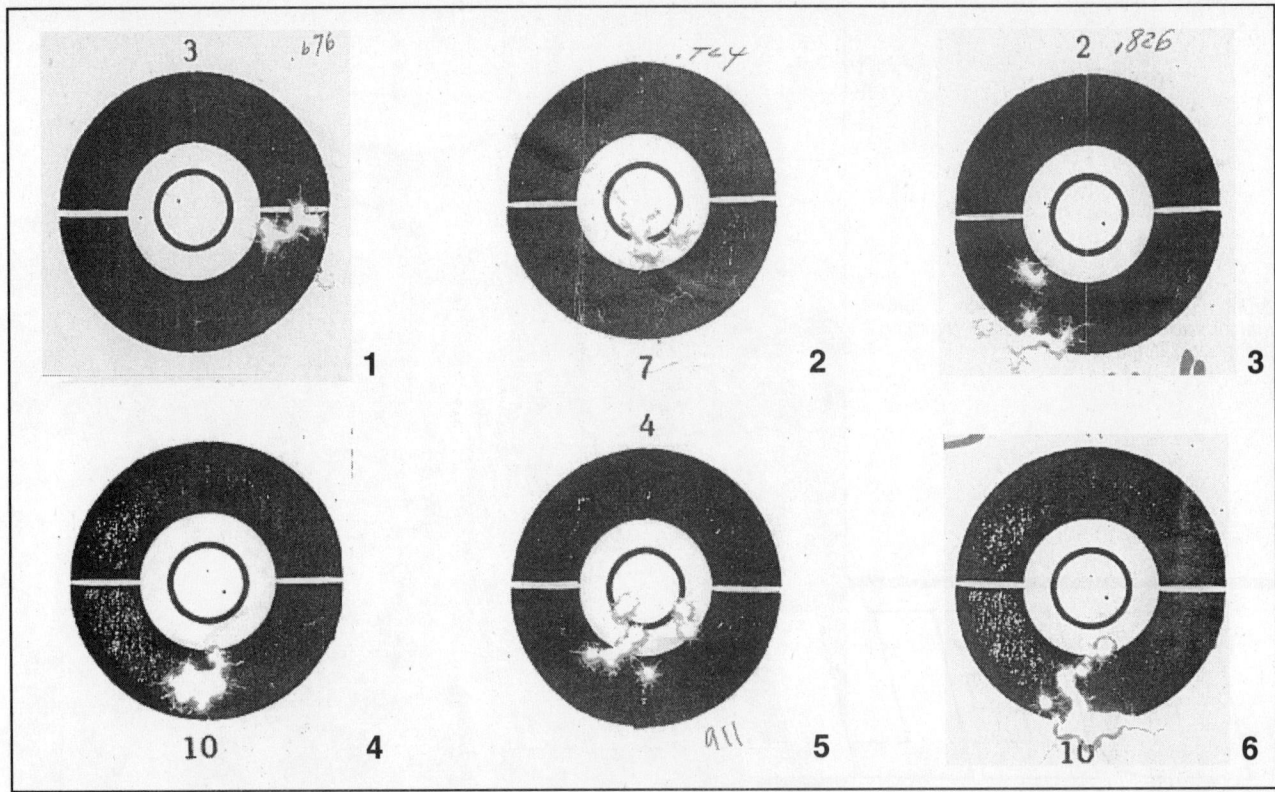

All these were shot through a Winchester 52D-chambered heavy barrel of 16$\frac{1}{2}$-inch length fitted to a Browning 22 semi-auto rifle. Targets 1 and 2 show a best group of .424-inch—ten shots at 50 yards—and a more typical group at .67-inch made with excellent Eley Tenex target ammo. Targets 3 and 4 show a best of .483-inch and a typical .826-inch group, this time with CCI Standard Velocity cartridges. Targets 5 and 6 were made with Eley Subsonic hollowpoints—a typical .911-inch group and a best at .778-inch. This was an accurate 22 semi-auto, indeed.

barrel when shot at 20-inch length. Results obtained with CCI Standard Velocity and Eley Subsonic HP were essentially unchanged from the same barrel at 20 inches, being 0.71- and 0.89-inch, respectively.

The accuracy obtained with heavy 20-inch barrel and Winchester 52D chamber on the Ruger 10/22 was similar. Nineteen ten-shot groups with CCI Standard Velocity averaged 0.75-inch, with the largest just over an inch and the smallest under a half-inch. With Eley Practice 100, eleven ten-shot groups at 50 yards averaged 0.71-inch, with nothing over an inch. Federal Lightning high velocity averaged just under an inch for a smaller fifty-shot sample. We were very pleased with this, because the rifle is accurate, reliable and works with anything we have tried in it. So, the moral is, you *can* have an accurate 22 autoloader. If you don't want a heavy rifle or don't want to spend a tub of money on a heavy custom barrel, reline it (and don't tell anybody). Let them think you have one of those "rare" factory autoloaders that happens to shoot well! •

Accuracy of Autoloading Rifles After Rebarreling

Rifle and Ammo	Ammunition Lot. No.	Number of tgts.	Smallest (ins.)	Largest (ins.)	Average (ins.)
Ruger 10/22 with Wilson Arms					
16-inch-twist bull barrel and Winchester 52D chamber					
CCI Std.	K08V14	19	0.55	0.92	0.75
Eley P100	LM165	11	0.63	0.80	0.71
Fed. Lightning	3A-9721	5	0.79	0.99	0.89
Browning autoloader after rebarreling					
with 16-inch-twist Wilson Arms barrel and Winchester 52D chamber					
CCI Std.	K08V14	10	0.60	1.29	0.91
CCI Blazer	K10P16	10	0.70	1.69	1.10
Eley Tenex	WL300	5	0.42	0.97	0.71
Eley P100	LM165	10	0.88	1.52	1.13
Eley Subsonic	RG26	5	0.86	1.25	0.98
FC Lightning	3A-9721	10	0.91	1.13	1.00
Browning 22 autoloader after rebarreling					
with 14-inch-twist Wilson Arms barrel and Winchester 52D chamber					
CCI Std.	K08V14	10	0.48	0.90	0.74
CCI Blazer	K10P16	10	0.88	1.40	1.19
Eley Tenex	WL300	5	0.56	0.88	0.75
Eley P100	LM165	10	0.87	1.09	0.99
Eley Subsonic	RG26	5	0.71	1.01	0.85
Fed. Lightning	3A-9721	10	0.73	1.45	1.09
Reshoot of Browning 22 autoloader					
with 14-inch-twist Wilson Arms Barrel after shortening barrel to 16$\frac{1}{4}$ inches					
CCI Std.	K08V14	10	0.48	0.85	0.71
Eley Tenex	WL300	10	0.42	0.92	0.67
Eley Subsonic	RG26	10	0.78	1.0	0.89

Brunton 10x50 served Bell well for a summer of varmint shooting and on Wyoming pronghorns in the fall.

BELL ON BINOCULARS

What's new, what's good in a basic hunter's tool

by BOB BELL

Nᴇxᴛ ᴛᴏ ᴀ good gun and boots, maybe a knife, a hunter's most useful piece of equipment is a good binocular. Actually, in the field, he will use the binocular far more than the gun—probably an hour or more on average for every shot fired at varmints, and sometimes far more than that for each shot at big game. Just imagine how handicapped a sheep or goat or pronghorn hunter would be without a top-quality binocular. Good optics can be a great

help, even for whitetails and elk, when you go into the thick stuff after them. Binoculars make it possible to examine small details at long range and in poor light, and ultimately that can mean the difference between success and failure on a hunt. Things have changed the last few years, so here's a rundown on what's current in the binocular field:

Bausch & Lomb has a 7x36 in their top-line Elite series, and the new unit is a runaway best seller. Only 5½ inches high and 26 ounces, this 7x36 features phase-correction coating (PC-3) to significantly increase resolving power by overcoming the phase-shift inherent in roof prisms. The result is a razor sharp image. (PC-3 is available at extra cost on the older 8x42 and 10x42 Elites.) An example of the precision to which the new 7x36 is assembled is shown in its 90-degree roof prism, which is held to an accuracy of less than 5 millionths of an inch. Maximum light transmission is achieved by multicoating all air/glass surfaces, and the 7x36 can be focused as close as 12 feet, for use by birders. The unit has a soft rubber covering for protection, and the diopter setting has thirteen precise click stops, to compensate for eyes of unequal strength.

We might mention that the 7x36 PC-3 Elite has a list price of $1704 at this writing, which might be a bit steep for most of us, though it's doubtless worth its cost. Top quality never comes cheap, and the best last a lifetime. Nevertheless, Bausch & Lomb markets three other binocular lines: the Discoverer, which tops out at about $650; the Custom, which goes to $535 or so; and the Legacy, with its most expensive model an 8-24x50mm zoom at about $325. So the buyer who favors B&L has a choice, although the Medalist series has been discontinued. Numerous models are available in straight or zoom powers, standards or compacts; some are armored, wide angle, fogproof/waterproof; all are center focus.

Brunton/Lakota, long known for their compasses, knives and other outdoor equipment, recently introduced several lines of binoculars. The Eterna porro prism series includes a 7x42, a 10x50 and, brand new, a 6x30 monocular. These feature advanced coatings (ruby in color) to block some 96 percent of the harmful ultraviolet and infrared light rays. The Eternas have long eye relief for easy use with glasses.

We used a 10x50 Eterna for a summer of chuck hunting, plus a Wyoming pronghorn hunt, and found it excellent. It takes only a tiny movement of the adjusting ring to cover the entire focusing range. The monocular just came in for testing—too late for a report here, but we hope to use it in deer season.

Brunton also offers several Compact and mid-size Tracker binoculars in 7x, 8x and 10x models. All are roof prism designs, and several models have long eye relief and ruby coating. One 10x design has a wide angle field. Brunton binoculars have gray rubber armoring with finger-contoured depressions for sure gripping.

Burris now has four entries in their Fullfield series of binoculars— 7x35, 8x40, 10x50 and a compact 8x25. The three conventional size models have porro prisms and a Focus Lock, which allows adjustment at an optimum distance and locking in that setting. The 8x25 has a roof prism and center focus. All are armor-coated and have multi-coated optics.

Bushnell is adding eight new models to the PowerView line introduced last year, but the only ones on which information is available at this writing are three compacts—a center-focus, porro prism 8x25, and two folding roof prisms, an 8x21 and a 10x21. New models will be of contemporary styling, with matte black rubber covering. The earlier PowerViews—a conventional 8x30 and wide angles in 7x35 and 10x50—are still available. Of traditional silhouette, they, too, have fully coated optics, rubber covering and Bushnell's Insta-Focus system. The Spectator series also has a new compact entry, a 10x24 porro prism design. It, too, has contemporary body styling with neoprene covering, is only 4 inches high and weighs but $8\frac{1}{2}$ ounces.

Also new is the Bushnell Autofocus, a 10x25 with built-in compartment for the AA batteries which provide its power. The main power switch has an automatic

Bob Wise says the 8x56 Swarovski is unsurpassed for chucks in the Back 40 or prairie/mountain use on big game.

This 7x36 is newest addition to Bausch & Lomb's Elite line. It has phase correction coating to get the ultimate optics out of its room prism system.

Bushnell's new 10x24 Spectator is a porro prism compact with gray neoprene covering that is only four inches high, weighs only 8.5 ounces.

Bushnell 7x35 PowerView is a wide angle, Insta-Focus design. Shown here with black armoring, it's also available with camo covering.

Jason 10x25 GlassesOn compact has extended eye relief for those who wear eye/shooting glasses. A similar 8x21 is also available now.

shut-off, one fingertip button provides automatic focusing, and there are two fingertip buttons for special focusing situations. Individual eyepieces can be adjusted to accommodate different users. Focusing is as close as $6\frac{1}{2}$ feet.

The low-priced PowerView series is replacing the earlier Ensign line, while the somewhat higher priced Spectators give hunters a wide choice of items. Rubber armored, Insta-Focus wide-angle models are offered in 7x35, 8x40 and 10x50; there are 7-15x35mm and 7-21x40mm zooms; a roof prism 8x42; compacts in 5x25, 8x23 and 10x24; and wide-angle folding roof prisms in 8x21 and 10x25. And for those who need the highest light transmission, Bushnell has a pair of 7x50 Marine models with individual focus in either black or yellow armor.

Jason Empire, now part of B&L/Bushnell, struck an optical chord a few years back with their Perma Focus binoculars, a fixed-focus design that essentially let the viewer's eyes make any necessary adjustments. They followed this with their GlassesOn model, a wide angle which gave a full field of view while wearing glasses—without fooling with eyecups or rubber extensions. Now they have five binoculars called the GlassesOn Perma Focus series, the name deriving from Jason's combination of these features in the same models. Currently available are standard-size 7x35, 7x50 and 10x50 binoculars, and 8x21 and 10x25 compacts. On all of these, cushioned eyeglass guards gently position the binocular's eyepieces against the user's glasses, and the 18mm eye relief delivers the full image to the entrance pupil of the eye. Jason supplies many other models, in sizes and styles suited for most purposes. Prices are low-medium.

Leica's 42 BA series of German-made binoculars (7x42, 8x42 and 10x42) are judged by many hunters to be unsurpassed. Now there is a Leica 8x32 BA which features the same level of design and technology: An intricate optical system based on glass with high refractive indices, multiple coating of all glass/air surfaces and additional phase-correction coating, and extremely accurate alignment and parallelism of both optical systems. Eyepieces have sliding eyecups to provide eyeglass wearers a full field, and the entire focusing range from closeup to "forever" is covered with less than one rotation of the central drive. Focusing is internal—no outer lens or eyepiece part is moved, so no air, dust or moisture can enter—and there is a multi-function drive for easy focusing, diopter adjustment and storing the diopter setting all in one place. The diecast aluminum body is protected by black shock-absorbent polyurethane armoring. This 8x32 BA weighs 22 ounces, has a 4mm exit pupil, a twilight factor of 16, minimum focusing distance of $10\frac{1}{2}$ feet, and a field of 443 feet at 1000 yards. List price is $1425.

For those interested in even higher-tech units, Leica is also offering their Geovid 7x42 BDA. This binocular's optical and mechanical qualities are enhanced by state of the art opto-electronics that provide near-perfect orientation. In the Geovid, an eye-safe infra-red distance meter measures the range to any target between 25 and 1500 meters with an acuracy of one meter. Range is shown via an LED display in the center of the field. Direction to the target is determined by a solid sensor electronic compass which shows the azimuth on another LED display. Practical applications of the Geovid will be obvious to wilderness hunters, rescue teams and others...assuming the $6000 list price is no deterrent.

Leupold has just added (early '93) two new roof prism center-focus binoculars to their line, 8x32 and 10x42 models. They offer the user a continuous simultaneous focus capability, and are similar to last year's 8x30 and 10x40 individual focus

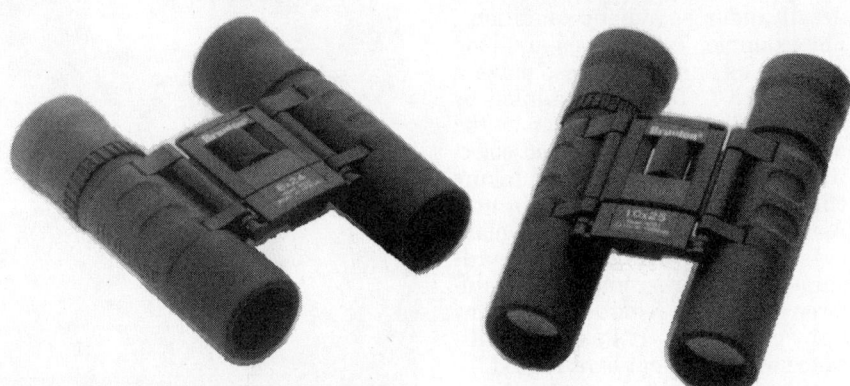

Brunton 8x24 and 10x25 Eterna compacts have 18mm eye relief, to give full fields of view to eyeglass wearers, and have Ruby coated lenses to reduce harmful infrared and ultra violet rays.

models. They have the same straightline optics system, multi-coated glass surfaces and fold-down eyecups. These two new models bring the Leupold line to nine, the earlier ones being 7x30, 9x35 and 10x40 glasses built with porro prisms, the two roof prisms mentioned above, and 9x25 and 10x28 Gold Ring pocket models, also utilizing roof prisms.

These Leupolds are the first U.S.-made binoculars in two decades, and their quality matches the company's outstanding riflescopes. The seven larger models are designed to give exit pupils of 4mm, which results in twilight factor ratings of about 15 to 20. Even the Leupold pocket models have TFRs of 15 and 17, so work well under tough hunting conditions. (TFR is a measure of an opti-

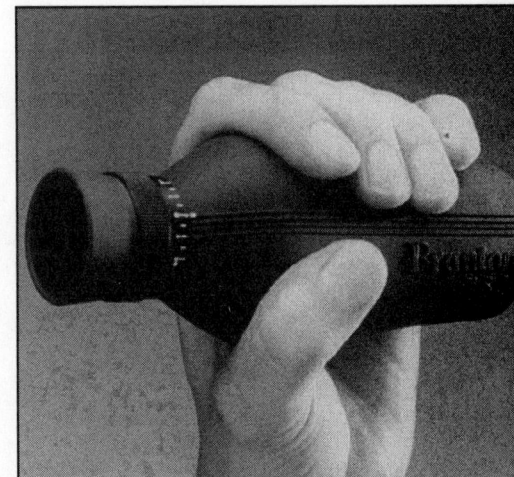

6x30 Brunton monocular is only six inches high, weighs 11.5 ounces, has finger-grooved barrel for easy gripping.

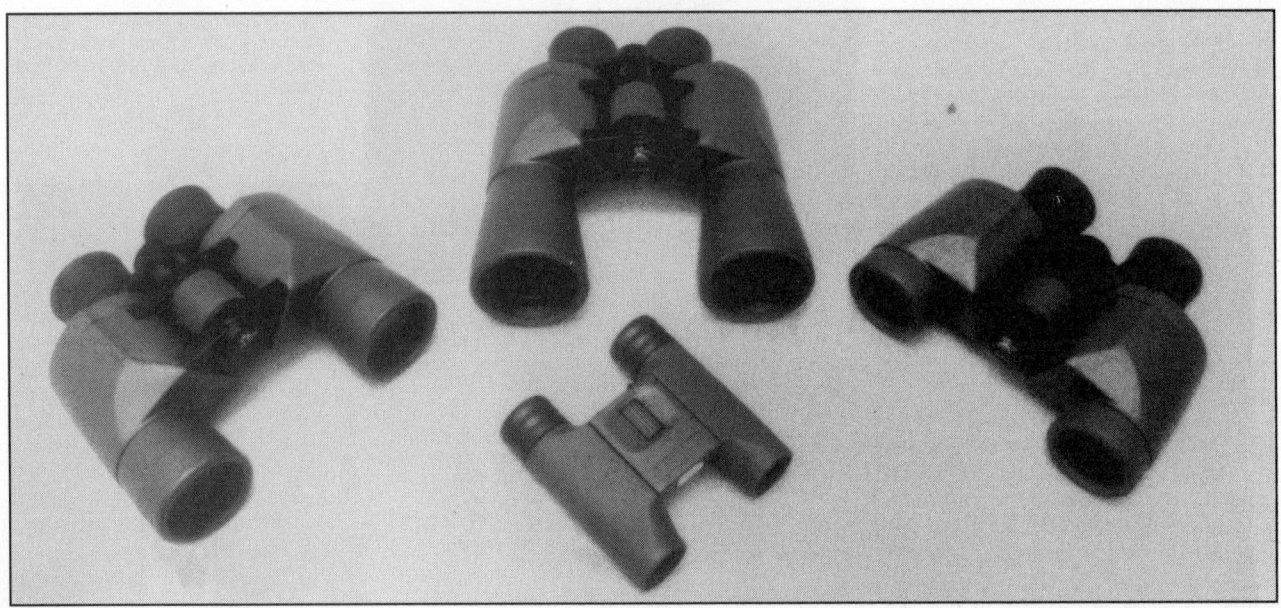

Burris binocular line includes these Fullfield models: 8x40, 10x50 and 7x35 featuring porro prisms, and the roof prism Mini 8x25.

cal system's capability of revealing detail under poor light conditions. For example, 7x50 binoculars, long popular as "night glasses," have a TFR of 18.7. TFR is calculated by multiplying the unit's power by the diameter of the unobstructed objective lens in millimeters, and taking the square root of the product. Assuming binoculars of equal quality—material, design, workmanship—TFR allows comparison of different models in regard to use in low light conditions. It has no significance when ambient light is good.)

Nikon has added two models to their top-of-the-line Criterion series. Called the Execulite IIs, they are 8x32 and 10x40 additions to the 9x30 and 12x36 Execulite models. Both are central-focus roof prism designs with rubber-covered all-metal bodies, and both feature precision-ground BAK4 high index prisms. These give an ideal optical axis between the objective lens and eyepiece, creating a sharp full field without color fringing. Prices are in the $700 range.

Nikon also has added an 8x40 unit to their StayFocus Plus II series of binoculars. With this series of 7x, 8x and 10x models, the viewer can line up an infinity mark and lock the focus into place. The binocular will then be in focus at from 40-80 feet, depending upon magnification, to infinity. Other new Nikons available include a pair of shirt-pocket size Sportstars in 8x20 and 10x25 and an ergonomically designed 10x25 Travelite III. Most of these are in the $200 range.

Pentax is another optical company, perhaps best known for their fine riflescopes, which also makes binoculars. Fact is, they have several lines totaling ten models at this writing. These range in size from pocket models of 7x and 9x with 20mm objectives and inverted porro prisms to a 9x63 roof prism center-focusing model and 16x50 center-focusing porro prism unit. Other models in the last category include 8x, 10x and 12x units with 24mm objectives, and 8x42, 10x42 and 8x56 glasses with central-focusing roof prism designs.

All of these Pentax models have objective units created of two lenses in one group; eyepieces are more complex—with three or four elements in one, two or three groups—depending upon a particular binocular's design. Weights run from 8 ounces for the Jupiter mini models to 44 ounces for the 9x63 DCF. The

This 8x32 BA joins Leica's 42-series of binoculars, giving hunters still another choice among these world-famous glasses.

For 1993, Leupold is introducing two roof prism models. In 8x32 and 10x42, they feature central focusing and straightline optics.

New StayFocus 8x40 Plus II from Nikon permits locking the focus at a convenient distance for fast usage.

Nikon's 10x40 Execulite II fits neatly between their 9x30 and 12x36 models in the Criterion series

This 9x63 DCF is neither the largest nor the smallest binocular in the Pentax line, but it does represent the high quality of all. Its 7mm exit pupil means it will perform to an extremely high level when ambient light conditions are bad.

Redfield binoculars, as some of their riflescopes, can be had with a camouflage finish, if desired, or black if your taste is more traditional.

These are Swarovski's latest models in their SLC (Slender—Long-lasting—Compact) line, the 10x42 and 7x42. They have Swaratop multi-layer coating, phase corrected roof prisms, and interior focusing.

16x50 PCF weighs only 32½ ounces. Diopter adjustments run from two to four in different models. Some are continuously variable, others have click adjustments, and some have a locking central fingertip adjustment. Most eyepieces have collapsible-type eyecup rings.

Redfield currently offers conventional-size waterfproof binoculars, 7x35 and 10x50, with either camo or black armor finish. These roof prism models feature a built-in compass on the adjusting knob and soft rubber eyecups that fold back for eyeglass wearers. Weights are 21 and 29 ounces.

Redfield also has two compact binoculars, both with roof prisms. The smaller one is an 8x24 which weighs under 10 ounces; perhaps more interesting is a 6-15x24 zoom model, as it provides a wide range of magnification in a small package. At 16 ounces, it's heavier than many compacts, but it's only 5 inches long, so can be conveniently tucked inside the shirt.

Swarovski Optik, Austria's largest manufacturer in the field of teleoptics (binoculars, riflescopes, telescopes), at present is supplying sixteen binocular models in conventional sizes from 6x30 to 10x50. That's about the only aspect in which Swarovskis might be considered conventional. These are top-grade items, many of them featuring a design in which the optical core is immovably cast in a shockproof shell of polyurethane, with prisms and lenses cemented into place. This makes them waterproof to a pressure depth of 4.35 psi. Objective lenses of some models are equipped with fixed optical-quality glass covers for further protection; focusing is therefore totally within the optical system.

Swarovski binoculars also receive their Swarotop treatment, a multi-layer, broadband lens coating which reduces light reflections over the entire spectrum, and especially in the region of maximal retinal sensitivity. Here, it is said, the degree of reflection is reduced to less than 0.2 percent, which supplies brilliant images to the viewer.

At various times, we've had the opportunity to use several Swarovskis for some months. The 8x20B Habicht compact went everywhere with us one deer season, its weight and bulk of no consequence at all, its optics outstanding whenever called upon. Even more impressive optically, due to the size difference, were the 8x56B-SL and 10x50-SL. As Ol' Elmer would have put it, these almost permitted a view of the Promised Land. They're bulky, fairly heavy (especially the 8x56), and expensive (like $1000+), but you sure can see with them. As an example, I happened to have the 10x50 along when I was checking the impact of my 40XB-BR 222 at 300 yards. After shooting, I snugged the 10x50 Swarovski into the sandbag and took a look at the target...and could make out the 22-caliber holes in the white some seven inches under my aiming point. If that doesn't impress you at the moment, I'd suggest you try it with your pet binocular.

Tasco, too, has an extensive line of binoculars—a number of lines, in fact. These include, but aren't limited to, the Titan, World Class, World Class Plus and InFocus. They come in all configurations from compacts to standard sizes and zooms to wide angles, in magnifications from 3x to

ed for military situations, but they are impractical for hunters. Therefore, Zeiss developed the 20x60S. This binocular has its prisms mechanically mounted on a cardanic suspension system which allows all relevant optical components to "sway" in line with any hand movement. As a result, the light rays always fall on the same image plane, even those which are not parallel due to shaking or quivering of the user's hands. This is said to permit clear recognition of a 15mm (⁶/₁₀-inch) object at 1000 meters—without a tripod.

The central-focusing 20x60S has the Zeiss T* multicoating, five-element eyepieces which give a full field (50 and 1000 meters) while wearing glasses, internal focusing (as close as 14 meters), and rubber armoring. Its twilight factor is 34.6—almost twice that of a 7x50 night glass. It's large, of course, 10.8x6.3 inches, and heavy, 58.6 ounces. But in the field it actually

replaces two optical units, a binocular and a spotting scope, so it's considerably lighter than their combined weights.

The 20x60S obviously is not for everyone, but for the specialist whose demands are the toughest and who has $4725 to spare...

At the other end of the size category, Zeiss now produces four DesignSelection pocket binoculars, including a 4x12BT* and a 6x18BT*, which barely top 6 ounces in weight. These focus as close as 1 and 2 meters respectively, which makes them ideal for studying small animals or exotic blossoms, and have fields of 552 and 366 feet at 1000 yards. These lower power compacts are recent additions to the 8x20BT* and 10x25BT* pocket models introduced earlier. They weigh only 6.5 and 7.1 ounces. All four Design-Selection models are central focusing, with multicoated phase-corrected roof prisms, and all fold neatly into snug-fitting carrying cases. ●

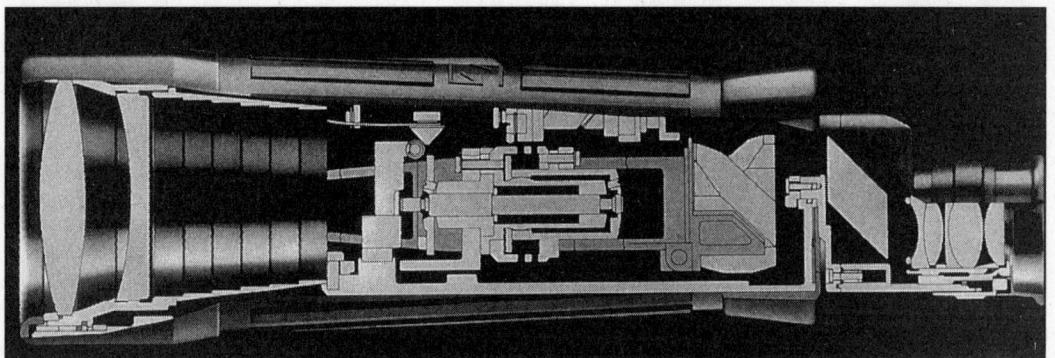

Schematic of the Zeiss 20x60S's innards.

20x. Several monoculars are also available.

There are simply too many Tascos to discuss individually in a review such as this, but we should mention that one of the 7x50s, Model 322BCW, is designed as a navigational tool. In addition to being waterproof, it is fitted with a red illuminated compass and a rangefinder; the latter, coupled with a built-in calculator, measures either your distance from, or the size of, far away objects.

Zeiss continues to cover the optics field with German-made gear. Perhaps their most interesting binocular is the incredible 20x60S ("S" for stabilized). It has been long recognized that conventional high-magnification binoculars are impractical in hand-held situations, their inevitable wiggle making small detail resolution impossible. Gyro-stabilized systems have been creat-

Nobody ever said the Zeiss 20x60S was small.... but, oh, what it can do.

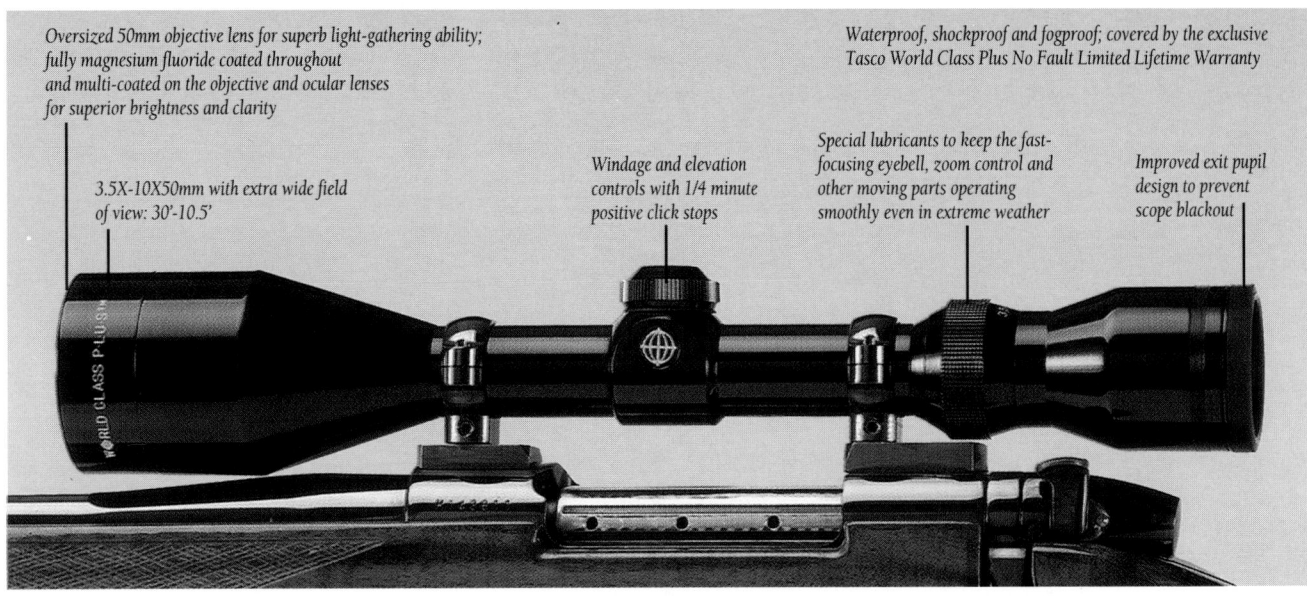

Oversized 50mm objective lens for superb light-gathering ability; fully magnesium fluoride coated throughout and multi-coated on the objective and ocular lenses for superior brightness and clarity

Waterproof, shockproof and fogproof; covered by the exclusive Tasco World Class Plus No Fault Limited Lifetime Warranty

3.5X-10X50mm with extra wide field of view: 30'-10.5'

Windage and elevation controls with 1/4 minute positive click stops

Special lubricants to keep the fast-focusing eyebell, zoom control and other moving parts operating smoothly even in extreme weather

Improved exit pupil design to prevent scope blackout

"SATISFACTION GUARANTEED"

"If our Tasco World Class Plus™ riflescopes don't meet your expectations for quality, performance and value, we'll give you your money back."

I founded Tasco in 1951 and we've been designing, refining and improving binoculars and scopes year after year ever since. Now I'd like you to share my pride and a little of the excitement that I've experienced in the creation of our Tasco World Class Plus™ line.

Building on the proven record of performance and customer satisfaction enjoyed by our World Class™ line, our research and development department set out to take that quality to a new level of excellence and they succeeded. The result is Tasco World Class *PLUS*, a line with a *Performance Level Uniquely Superior*. But don't take my word for it. Experience Tasco World Class Plus™ first hand. And I'll help you do just that with the following personal offer from me to you.

Buy any Tasco World Class Plus™ riflescope. If you don't like it, return it with your receipt from your local authorized Tasco World Class Plus™ dealer for a full refund. Yes, you read it right. I'll give you your money back if you buy a Tasco World Class Plus™ riflescope and don't agree with my enthusiasm for this exceptional line of optics. It's that simple.

See your authorized Tasco World Class Plus™ dealer today and look into Tasco World Class Plus.™ Discover a line that demonstrates edge-to-edge sharpness, complete clarity and unusual brightness. Add to this the Tasco World Class Plus™ No Fault Warranty which guarantees that should the product be damaged and fail to operate, it will be repaired or replaced free of charge (except for a nominal handling charge)...and you'll be sold. On Tasco World Class Plus.™ A uniquely superior product. You've got my word on that...and the guarantee of complete satisfaction or your money back.

George G. Rosenfield
Founder and President

tasco®

P.S. For more information on purchasing Tasco World Class Plus™ products and how to get in on this offer, contact your sporting goods dealer or write/call Tasco, Dept. 000, P.O. Box 520080, Miami, FL 33152/(305) 591-3670, ext. 315.

©1993 Tasco Sales, Inc.

We put the choice in your hands.

Innovation is nothing new to Heckler & Koch. For more than forty years, HK engineering has been unsurpassed in the design and manufacture of quality firearms. The new Heckler & Koch USP (Universal Self-loading Pistol) is the first HK pistol designed especially for you, the American shooter. And each USP variant gives you a distinct choice. Choice of fire modes. Choice of controls. Choice of conditions of carry.

Special features favored by U.S. law enforcement, military, and civilian users provided the design criteria for the USP. Its controls are uniquely American — influenced by such famous pistols as the Government Model 1911. And like the Model 1911, the USP can be safely carried "cocked and locked".

The control lever, a combination safety and decocking lever, is frame mounted and quickly accessible, unlike the slide mounted safeties common on many other pistols.

The modular design of the internal parts allows the control lever on the USP to be switched from the left to the right side of the pistol to accommodate left handed shooters. The USP can also be converted from one type of fire mode to another.* This includes combination double-action and single-action modes and a double action only mode. All fire modes are available with, or without, a manual safety.

USP FIRE MODES & CONTROL FUNCTIONS
*conversion by HK armorer only

	Double Action	Single Action	Double Action Only	Control Lever (Left Side)	Control Lever (Right Side)	Control Lever (Manual Safety)	Control Lever (Decocking)	Control Lever (No Decocking)	Caliber Availability
Variant 1	●	●		●		●	●		.40 S&W / 9mm
Variant 2	●	●			●	●	●		.40 S&W / 9mm
Variant 3	●	●		●		●			.40 S&W / 9mm
Variant 4	●	●			●	●			.40 S&W / 9mm
Variant 5			●	●		●		●	.40 S&W / 9mm
Variant 6			●		●	●		●	.40 S&W / 9mm
Variant 7			●					●	.40 S&W / 9mm
Variant 9	●	●		●			●	●	.40 S&W / 9mm
Variant 10	●	●			●	●		●	.40 S&W / 9mm

Another unique feature of the HK USP is the patented mechanical recoil reduction system. This system is incorporated into the recoil and buffer spring assembly located below the barrel. Designed primarily to cushion the slide and barrel during firing, it reduces recoil effects on internal pistol components and also lowers the recoil forces felt by the shooter.

This recoil reduction system was tested and proven in the HK .45 ACP Handgun recently designed for the U.S. Special Operations Command (SOCOM). Using the same system as the USP, the "SOCOM pistol" fired more than 30,000 +P cartridges without damage to any components. The buffering effect of the recoil reduction system plays a major role in ensuring the durability of the HK USP, especially when you consider the punishment inflicted on any pistol that fires a steady diet of powerful .40 S&W cartridges.

A special "HE" (Hostile Environment) finish protects all metal parts of the USP from the worst types of corrosion and wear, including prolonged exposure to salt water.

At Heckler & Koch, form follows function. All HK pistols are designed and manufactured to meet the operational requirements of the most demanding users. Users like you. The new HK USP is no exception. In a world of compromise, some don't.

USP
Handgun innovation for the next century.

For more information and the location of your nearest Authorized Dealer, contact:
**Heckler & Koch, Inc.
21480 Pacific Blvd.
Sterling, Virginia 20166 USA
TEL. (703) 450-1900**

Heckler & Koch supports the rights of Americans to own and use firearms for sport, hunting, recreation, and self-defense. For every HK firearm sold, Heckler & Koch, Inc. will donate $1.00 to the American Shooting Sports Council (ASSC), a national organization dedicated to preserving the Second Amendment rights of all Americans.

AUTOLOADER
Classics

A nostalgic sale of classic 22 rifles. Never before and never again will you find prices like these. We have over 2000 miscellaneous 22-caliber rifles produced during the 1940s, '50s, '60s, NRA very good to excellent.   —*Shotgun News*

AND THERE THEY were—murky, black and white photographs of that rogue's gallery of rifles that had robbed me of my money, my youth, a part of my sanity, but above all my tender, fervid belief in the American way of gunmaking. Shoving *Shotgun News* in the furnace, I watched flames consume the reminder of the past. Classics! Everything that isn't an assault rifle or a magnum seems to be a classic. Old frustrations began boiling over onto fresh memories of recent articles purporting to be critical evaluations.

"Prices like in the good old days." Those *bad* old days began for me in 1966 when, at sixteen, I decided I'd come of age—which meant I'd had it with thumbing single cartridges into the chamber of my little 614 Remington 22 single shot. It was time for a *real* rifle and some *real* hunting. Didn't my friend Billy have a repeater? Didn't my cousin stalk deer and bear in Canada? Hadn't my grandfather once outshot Annie Oakley? Yes, but my immediate fam-

ily was not exactly keen on guns. My father's consent eventually came in the statement: "Don't shoot yourself in the foot, huh?"

The event which started me on the road to autoloader land, however, was no Kansas tornado. Through the largess of a neighbor recently returned from the national trap shoot at Vandalia, a stack of those multicolored advertising brochures volplaned into my life. There were ammunition handbooks, price lists and even full-color comic books wherein a sage old party named "Doc Peters" handed a boy, who had just fired a "pop gun" shot missing a distant coyote, one of his "Peters 22s" which in the next panel went screaming hell-for-leather like a 30-06 right to the heart. I wasn't that impressed because I knew the real 30-06 of 22s came in that old yellow and blue box marked "Super X."

The pamphlets I studied into the night were those three-color, fully illustrated items with titles on the order of "Sporting Firearms By

Remington." Inside, ducks rose, moose lurched and grizzly bears stood menacingly on hind legs, all held in check by rifles and shotguns poised scepter-like above them. A boy grinning in clear-eyed determination posed—rifle at the ready—as a rabbit bounded in front of him, while beside the boy his trusty hound rushed in for the retrieval—all in a rural landscape stretching emptily to the horizon. I knew what I needed all right: a rifle for those fast-running shots. And on the following page there it was...a Remington 550 autoloader in the hands of a sturdy outdoorsman, aimed at a snarling wolverine in the act of raiding the man's larder.

There weren't many wolverines around Columbus, Ohio, at that time, and our trusty hound was a Pekinese; the Peke had recently made a valiant, though unsuccessful, attempt to capture several mallards who had come by our Indiana lake cottage in search of handouts. Puffing like a walrus, tail drooping

by C. RODNEY JAMES

like a wet flag above the water, he barely made it to shore. His heart was there, but like me, he simply lacked the right equipment.

The 550 Remington was described as "man-sized," "streamlined," "dependable," "the perfect gun for a person who likes fast shooting." It would also fire 22 Short, Long and Long Rifle cartridges interchangeably and automatically without

one or more cuts on the sides. While many firearms writers advise shooters to pre-check rimfire ammunition and avoid using imperfect bullets for serious shooting, none of them, at least at that time, had anything to say about damage to bullets in the feeding and loading process—a problem which is at its worst in 22 rimfire autoloaders using soft lead bullets.

rawhide, would have been ideal to hold the breech plug against the pressure of the recoil springs while at the same time turning it to engage the threaded portion of the plug with the threaded portion of the receiver.

The Model 550 action was a cornucopia of parts, as cunningly engineered as a Swiss music box, and included a floating chamber which made possible the interchangeable use of three lengths of rimfires. That floating chamber, in spite of, or perhaps because of, my efforts to keep it clean, soon began to float in importune ways. The net effect was to produce bulges on the cases which then jammed the action as they swelled to fill the gap created by the improper fit of the chamber. One day, I noticed a crescent-shaped piece of metal had been broken from the thin edge of the breech. The rifle went back to Remington. I don't think I was charged for a new barrel, at least I can't call up any hostile feelings over the incident. I managed several rabbit hunts where I saw a few rabbits in brief tail flashes as they disappeared into the underbrush. My major impression of those events was of that 43½-inch rifle pulled sideways by every passing shrub as I threaded my way through Ohio woodlands.

"Don't shoot yourself in the foot, huh?"

adjustment. Wow! In retrospect, I can't think why anyone in his right mind would mix up a handful of cartridges in this manner except to see if it were possible. I tried it once, and it was. Before purchasing the 550, I gave long consideration to a Model 63 Winchester autoloader, resting sleek and tempting in a gray carton which bore an illustration of a hunter moving stealthily through autumn woods. Money has a way of deciding such matters, and, in 1966, $70 for the Winchester 63 was a lot of scratch for a sixteen-year-old of limited means. The Remington was under fifty bucks.

While it would indeed shoot all three lengths of rimfires, the Long Rifle cartridges seemed the most accurate. Try as I might, using a variety of brands, I could not get that 550 to group under 5 inches at 75 yards. I soon discovered the journey to the chamber, via the tubular magazine under the barrel, left the bullets with their noses flattened, sometimes bent in the case and bearing

As I continued shooting, I became aware of the second of this rifle's idiosyncrasies—it didn't like fouling. In the first 50 rounds, the firing and ejection process took place with a simultaneous *crack!* It had separated to a *crack-chalack* at 100 rounds. At 150, the operation was a *crack! chick-chack* with a noticeable lag in the movement of the bolt after firing. At 200 rounds, the bolt had to be closed manually with a bump on the operating handle. That meant it was cleaning time.

The tolerances in my 550 must have been very close for it to gum up that quickly. Western ball-powder ammunition—my beloved Super-X—was the worst culprit in this respect. Liberal applications of Hoppe's Number 9 extended shooting time, but still the days that the gun had to be dismounted came all too frequently.

My younger brother was often drafted to assist in this job, which he referred to as a "steel-thumb" operation. Such a thumb, fleshed with

There was, though, one moment the 550 lived up to its promise. It was early spring when we arrived at the lake cottage to find towels and bedding chewed to a pulp, tea kettles stuffed with acorns, and droppings in the sugar bowl among other places—the results of a winter-long occupation by unknown rodents.

I stood on the ground, rifle ready, watching as my daddy bend to peer into a suspicious-looking hole near the top of the chimney that probably led to the attic. The next instant he recoiled with a little shriek of surprise causing the ladder on which he stood to tip back in a balancing act I had not before witnessed, outside a circus.

Before the ladder returned to the support of the house, a scurry of small animals erupted from the hole,

leaping and gliding into the trees. The leashed Peke roared in outrage as one of the flying squirrels landed in front of us to dash up a nearby oak, pursued by the better part of a magazine-worth of bullets, one of which met him at a point about 30 feet above the ground. That was the only fast-running shot I can claim to this day. The remaining squirrels wisely abandoned our cottage for the splendor of a hotel owner's place down the road, where I heard they did extensive damage to some upholstery and devoured part of a Celotex ceiling. Later that year, the Remington began bulging cases again, and I traded it in.

My second autoloader was a Stevens Model 87, which I have since heard referred to as the "bird cage" autoloader. For some inexplicable reason, the left side of the receiver was vented with grill-like slots. It was as long as the Remington and was also a bullet chewer, grouping its shots in a 12-inch pattern at a hundred yards. It had an unusual feature wherein the operating handle could be pushed through the bolt and the rifle used as a bolt-action repeater. By pushing it at a particular point, the action could be locked open for cleaning. Sometimes the handle moved all by itself, allowing more than one squirrel and barn rat to live a while longer. The action, other than the bolt group, was made of stampings, pinned together and attached to the barrel by screws which worked loose on firing, eventually jamming the action on a live round as it emerged from the tube magazine. Removal was accomplished by working the cartridge out *very* gingerly with a screwdriver. The Stevens went the way of the Remington before my luck ran out.

My thoughts returned to that neat little Winchester 63, but by this time it was gone from the catalog and the sporting goods counter at $70, appearing on gun-show tables at $125. Outrageous! Winchester, however, had brought out a nifty-looking number called the Model 77. The one on display looked as good as the catalog photo, although I was somewhat

put off by the plastic trigger guard and magazine housing. By this time, I was convinced the heavy spring of the tube-loaders was the main cause of battered inaccurate bullets, thus the solution was a box magazine. Unfortunately, this meant sacrificing half the tube-loader's capacity for those running shots.

It seemed to me a sacrilege to put plastic on a Winchester, but Remington had just brought out a rifle entirely stocked in plastic. I thought the Model 77 looked like a BB gun. The salesman assured me the new plastics were solid stuff, and he was right. Neither guard nor housing ever caused any problems. Perhaps distracted by the plastic and concentrating on the feeding of the cartridges, I failed to notice a tool gouge about an inch inside the muzzle and a crack in the forend of the stock. The smiling salesman had run out of smiles when I returned the rifle, refusing me another. I would have to negotiate with Winchester.

The letter from New Haven informed me that the stock had been cracked by my mishandling and the bore flaw was a rust pit, probably resulting from my leaving the rifle out in the rain. I wrote a blistering reply pointing out that the *single* gouge had chipped edges in the manner of a tool mark, and if I had left it out in the rain why was there no evidence of corrosion on the exterior?

I suggested a second examination

including a close look at the stock to observe how varnish, applied at the factory, had run into the crack and dried there long before the rifle came to me, and they apologized, promising no charges for repairs. I waited. The company was experiencing labor problems at that time, which might explain why six months elapsed before the rifle was returned with a new stock, a new barrel, a letter saying they hoped I hadn't experienced "too much inconvenience" and a smashed rear sight. Back it went.

When I finally had the opportunity to try the 77, I found that sun glare from the highly polished receiver virtually obliterated the low-lying rear sight. A strip of friction tape cured this, but did nothing for the problem that soon developed with the sear. One squeeze of the trigger yielded two very fast shots and a jammed action. That was it for the 77, which was in possesion of the Winchester company for more than six of the twelve months I owned it.

I borrowed a Browning autoloader from a friend—not the 22 BAR, but the original patent, a version of which was made for many years by Remington as their Model 241. The new one ejected hot empties down my shirt sleeve, in addition to putting twin notches on the sides of each bullet it chambered. With a price in excess of $70, it was the most costly autoloader then on the market.

There weren't many wolverines around Columbus, Ohio...

I was now thoroughly convinced undamaged bullets and a heavy barrel held the key to autoloader accuracy, a notion I now believe to be half true—the half about undamaged bullets. The Mossberg 350K autoloader was solidly built, used a box magazine, but was subject to a fair number of jams and still shaved and scarred the bullets it loaded. It passed briefly through my life, receiving little scorn, for by this time I had little left to give. I traded it on a secondhand Winchester 52B bolt-action target rifle which I'm happy to say has blessed me with twenty-five years of accurate, problem-free shooting.

It would be nice if I could say the story ends here, that I shot happily ever after, but that wasn't the case. About a week later, Sturm, Ruger & Co. presented their addition to the autoloader family—the 10/22—and about a week after that, my brother bought one. Had he lost all powers of reason? Had he learned nothing from my experience? I counseled

nylon, rotary-cored magazine. The bullets, on examination, bore not a nick or scrape from this process. He favored me with a grin I clearly remember and still find intensely annoying.

We went shooting in a gravel pit where I proceeded to pick off bottle caps at 50 yards, advising him not to bother trying as he would waste ammunition in the attempt.

"Well, of course," he said, "with a big clunky gun like that with a scope on it, I'm surprised you can't hit them at a hundred." He then tossed a beer can up a nearby bank and blazed away, hitting it several times as it bounced and skittered to the bottom.

"Can you do that? You've gotta have a *little* gun to get those quickies." Suppressing anger, I waited for something to go wrong with the Ruger. A dozen years passed. Nothing did.

As time passed, there were assassinations, a war in Vietnam. I finished a doctorate and took a teaching

knows I should have known better, but I bought it. Once home I was unable to fully load any of the three magazines I had acquired or to feed a single cartridge into the chamber. Receipt in hand, I returned with the unfired rifle.

The salesman regarded me with a look of contempt as he began loading the magazine I handed him. The bullets stuck. He tried another, three, four, five, jabbing angrily at the cartridges with a screwdriver. They refused to budge. Stepping back, waiting for the sound of an exploding 22, I asked for my money back.

There seem to be two types of French Canadians—those who are cultured and charming, and the sort I was dealing with. Perhaps he'd had a fight with his wife or boss, possibly he was feeling the keen edge of some political outrage committed by Separatists, Federalists or some outside exploiter of Quebecers— Britishers, English Canadians, Americans. Whatever the reason, his refusals to do anything beyond telling me to send the rifle to the factory and complain to the Marcos government were adamant and vehement. His language became infused with "chalices," "sacraments," "tabernacles" and other swear words peculiar to the French language and Quebec culture. Oh deja vu, it was like the Winchester 77 only worse. For an instant I may have considered hitting him, then realized he was probably armed. The memory of a news story flashed to mind—a gun store robbery by F.L.Q. terrorists, an employee murdered, gun store owners armed to the teeth ready to shoot. My God, it was this very store! I became reasonable, accommodating—"I'm sure we can work something out. Look, forget I said I was calling a lawyer. How about applying the cost to something else?" He stopped shouting long enough to ask what I wanted.

There wasn't much, and what there was wasn't very good— Canadian-made Cooey bolt-action 22s, grungy-looking Lee-Enfields, an assortment of nondescript shotguns. If I'd had my wits about me, I would

> *In 1955, $70 was a lot of scratch for a 16-year-old...*

him, finally asking point-blank if he wanted to wind up sobbing like a child or simply staring into space muttering to himself—a broken man. His replies were cryptic: "moulded nylon, stainless steel throat, rotary core, positive functioning."

He then proceeded to snap the bolt quickly, chambering and ejecting the contents of the Ruger's moulded

post in Montreal, Quebec. One day, I wandered into a gun store and found myself staring at a 22 autoloader with a mahogany stock, a muzzle-brake and a box magazine that held fifteen shots. Like the good old tube guns, here was one you could load on Sunday and shoot all week. The rifle was a Squibman, made in the Philippines. What more can I say? I was an experienced adult. God

have asked for ammunition, taken whatever I could use at whatever inflated price he quoted and fled the place, but my eye was caught by a flier advertising a French 22 autoloader—a Gevarm. As drowning men are said to grasp at straws, I snatched up the paper, thrusting it at him. "Let's see one of these."

"I've got one," he replied, in a voice indicating I had better like it. The Gevarm cost $20 more than the Squibman, but was of better quality and had available a twenty-shot magazine. Whee! The takedown was incredibly simple. There were few moving parts, no extractor, ejector, hammer or firing pin. It fired from an open bolt position in the manner of a Sten gun, discharging the round by striking the rimfire case the full width of its head with a raised ridge on the bolt face. At home, I went to the basement to run cartridges through the action, catching the bolt to avoid firing them. To my amazement, they fed flawlessly. I tested it at a friend's farm. The bolt slammed the cartridges home, firing them all right, but bursting the heads. The reason was obvious: The ridge had not been milled properly. I was not about to return to the shop on Bleury St. to be told: "Back to Saint Etienne (calice!). Complain to Giscard (tabernac!)."

With a diamond file—the bolt was too hard for an ordinary steel one—I slimmed the bolt-face ridge. The operation was a success. The rifle never jammed, fouled or even slowed down after well over 2000 rounds without cleaning. It would even digest 22 Longs! Accuracy was fair—1½-inch groups at 35 yards. Spoiled by the 52, I wished the Gevarm would group a bit closer. I brought it back to Ohio where it has continued to function without a hitch.

I've thought about selling it, but no one at gun shows seems interested. "It functions well," a little voice in my brain tells me, "quit while you're ahead." The little voice was ignored at a recent show where I again saw that familiar gray box with the hunter on it. Inside was a new or

like-new Winchester 63, but the price was up from $125 to an incredible $560, "...and worth every penny of it," said the man behind the table. "It's a classic."

I no longer look in those boxes at gun shows for the same reason I do not glance in open coffins, on the off chance I might recognize the occupant.

Before squirrel season, I stopped at a gun store in search of some 22 Winchester Automatic ammunition—the necessary fodder for my original 1903 Winchester, the forerunner of the Model 63. The '03, too, is a classic, but not so much in demand because of its special cartridge, discontinued in 1982, and now double or triple Long Rifle price if you can find them. I bought the last the owner had. We discussed squirrel hunting, and I commented on the unusual accuracy of the '03 autoloader I had bought for $212, with a trade for a so-so 1810 musket, and how I was subsequently able to spin an article about the rifle which covered the cash outlay (*Guns Illustrated* 1985).

He raised his eyebrows ever so slightly, letting me know I was accepted as someone more than the average nerd who bangs away at a few squirrels, missing most of those he sees. He spoke of keeping his family in squirrel and rabbit meat during the Depression, of serving as a range instructor during World War

II. There were trophy plaques and targets with tight groups of holes on the walls, adding a solid credibility to his modest telling of these events.

"Want to see something?" he asked.

"Of course," I replied in anticipation of being witness to some special treasure. He ambled to the back room to return with a rifle whose walnut stock glowed with the shine

I waited for something to go wrong with the Ruger.

that only comes from years of careful, but regular, use.

"Ever see one of these?"

The breath chilled in my lungs. "I *had* one once. It was..."

He cut me off saying, "Ah ha," his face glowing with an inner light at having found a kindred soul. "This 550 Remington is a straight shooter, particularly with the 22 Short. The floating chamber never causes any problems with Shorts. I really had to work to find it. The Shorts don't disturb the other squirrels. I like to slip up on them. I'll tell you, there's nothing like it for those quick shots when they run. I rarely miss one."

I nodded, trying to mould my features to mirror the worldly-wise look he gave me. Speaking with the conviction I hoped would mask the envy and regretful feelings of an "also-ran," I answered in a voice resonate with experience drawn from two decades and two countries. "Yeah, I know *exactly* what you mean—the perfect rifle for those quick running shots." ●

by BILL WOODWARD

A Well-Traveled Friend By Sako

It WAS 1969 in Germany. A young lieutenant stood in the Base Rod and Gun Club, admiring the rows of Merkels, Berettas and Mannlichers. My eyes, however, kept coming back to a Sako. The hang-tag read, "243 Winchester-Biathlon Model." The price was $112—ridiculously low, even then.

I was fresh from two years at the Air Force Marksmanship School in San Antonio. That assignment had been perfect for a young man enthusiastic about guns and hunting. Olympic shooters, master gunsmiths and gifted coaches made the school a rich resource of shooting knowledge. That knowledge was reflected in the personal firearms of the staff. Several NCOs owned startling arrays of hunting weapons. There were Schultz & Larsens, Francottes and British double rifles. Sakos were very popular, especially in 243 Winchester. I had filed that fact away.

Now, I hefted the rifle the clerk handed me and made the decision quickly. My travel pay covered the rifle's cost; I had $37 left. With it I bought the least expensive scope in the case—a Redfield 2¾x.

During the next three years, I used the rifle and 100-grain Normas on the small German roe deer. Shots just behind the shoulder anchored the 50-pound deer cleanly and decisively. The Sako's 9-pound weight and broad forearm perfectly suited it to hunting from a highseat. However, German hunting law prohibited using the 243 on wild boar or red deer. I remember thinking the Germans had a lot to learn about ballistics.

Eventually, the Sako became too much gun to lug easily through the woods. A German gunsmith cut the 24-inch barrel to 20 inches. Now the Sako weighed just 8 pounds. It was considerably handier, but I had created a rifle with a real identity crisis—a heavy barrel without

much barrel topped by a low-power scope best suited to a light sporter.

What it *was* suited to was smooth offhand shooting. There was a running boar range on the base, and the Sako's solid weight and light recoil made it ideal for tracking the cardboard image of a

boar as it streaked across the opening.

Eventually, I drew a tour in Colorado and used the rifle on mule deer and antelope. The short barrel carried well in

Tasco World Class 3x9 scope and the rifle's short, 20-inch barrel make it an easy-handling medium-game rifle. (Nolt photo)

Woodward with a good antelope and his Sako 243.

the Rockies. The rifle's compact weight sat solidly in the hands, making it a perfect hunting rifle. The Redfield's post reticle and broad field of view put me on game quickly. The Sako was growing on me.

In the mid-'70s, I was assigned to Belgium, and back to Germany again. I acquired several rifles, but seldom used them. The Sako continued to play a central role in my hunting. It also played an important role in my life.

One evening, I sat with a *forstmeister* in a *hochsitz* in the Black Forest. My host used a beech leaf to imitate the bleating sound of a roe doe in heat. He called several times, resting as much as three minutes between calls. Finally, a buck burst into the field before us. The forstmeister saw through his glasses that the animal had a broken front leg. "This buck you must shoot," he said. I raised the Sako and dropped the animal with a shoulder shot.

That evening the local hunters gathered at the Gasthaus to honor the buck and celebrate the cleansing of the forest. There were plates of wienerschnitzel, red cabbage and the inevitable white wine. I returned to my quarters late that night, filled with the warmth of the jaegers' hospitality. The gracious lady to whom I was married had long since gone to bed. I skinned the buck out on the kitchen table and considered where to hang him. As I washed my hands in the bathroom, my eyes fixed on the massive, industrial-strength shower head. I snubbed the buck up to the fixture. Then, for good measure, I wrapped one of my wife's embroidered sheets around the carcass and went to bed. At 6 am, my wife arose to take a shower. There was a scream. Several weeks later, I was a bachelor again.

In 1980, I took the Sako to southwest Africa as a backup rifle. My 30-06 developed scope problems, so I used the 243 on the smaller plains game. It worked well on springbok, steinbok, duiker—even warthog.

A month before, a Dutch hunter had lost a boar shot too far back with a 375 H&H. With the 243, only a head shot would be acceptable, counselled my professional hunter. The hunter and I sat with our backs against a

Warthog and jackal were taken in southwest Africa in 1980, shooting 100-grain Core-Lokt bullets.

(Below) When his 30-06 developed scope problems, Woodward's Sako 243 worked well on all the smaller African plains game.

(Below) The Sako took springbok in the Kalahari Desert, again with 100-grain Core-Lokts.

Paula Woodward and rancher Terry Jenkins. She took this Wyoming mule deer with the Sako.

Paula also bagged this antelope buck with the 243.

camel thorn tree, watching the waterhole and not moving. The African sun became a huge red ball hanging on the horizon. Finally, the sun disappeared and the cold hand of evening gripped the veldt. The francolin partridge fled the water. As they flew, there was a fierce snort and a huge warthog emerged from the bush. His tusks gleamed in the half light, as he walked to the water's edge. The post reticle settled between the tusks, then moved higher. The Sako bucked gently as the 100-grain Core-Lokt took the boar squarely between the eyes. He fell on his side, twitched once and was still. His tusks measured a respectable nine inches.

In 1982, I remarried. Paula was also in the Air Force and developed a real interest in hunting. We retired in 1984 and eventually settled in Wyoming's Bighorn Mountains. I began to reload seriously and poured hundreds of rounds through the Sako, shooting prairie dogs. A 3x9 Tasco World Class scope replaced the well-used Redfield. My favorite varmint bullet became the Hornady 70-grain SXSP in front of 37 grains of H-380 and a magnum primer. This load is well below max, but it gives me consistent 3/4-inch, 100-yard groups from a clean barrel.

I've collected quite a battery of rifles over the years. Even so, the stocky, light-recoiling Sako gets the nod whenever the deer and antelope seasons roll around. Paula used the rifle to take her first antelope and her first mule deer, a huge buck with antlers 26 inches high. The antelope eluded us for three days and was finally taken at 280 paces; the mulie at about 80 yards. Each fell to a single bullet.

I've tried every type of 243 bullet suitable for medium game—from the 100-grain premium bonded variety to more frangible 85-grainers. I've settled on two. For whitetail under 150 yards, I use Hornady's 87-grain boattail hollowpoint with 47 grains of H-450. For longer range shooting, I rely on 36 grains of IMR-4064 behind Sierra 100-grain boattail spirepoints. This load chronographs right at 2800 fps in the Sako's stubby barrel. Both bullets shoot well under an inch at 100 yards. The Sako has had an estimated 5000 rounds through it. So, to compensate for throat erosion, I seat bullets out, just short of the lands.

Am I sold on the 243? The answer is yes. And no. I've taken more than fifty head of game on three continents with my beloved Sako. It's a perfect game rifle for shooting at long ranges.

But hitting and killing cleanly are two different things. That's why, as I get older, the distance at which I'm willing to take game with the Sako shortens. I believe that the 243 is over-extended when it comes to making *quick*, clean kills on animals in the 200-pound class. In my experience, it is also over-extended on medium game at distances over 200 yards—even with precise bullet placement. Mark Twain said it about parents—as the years have passed, it's amazing how smart the Germans have become.

The Sako remains my favorite rifle. Anything else in my hands on opening day seems clumsy, "whippy" and out-of-place. Over the years this one good gun has become the standard by which I judge all other rifles. ●

One Good Gun

by RODERICK S. CARMAN

A Classic Gets To Africa

As I CROUCHED as silently and unobtrusively as possible on the banks of the Chiredze River in southern Zimbabwe, I watched the double-spiral horns of the first greater kudu I had ever seen in the wild move slowly through the brush about seventy-five yards away. My young professional hunter whispered that this was a large bull with good but rather narrow horns. The kudu was moving slowly and very cautiously to our left, stopping for long periods to gaze suspiciously in our direction. As I gripped the 270 and prepared to take a shot if offered, I recalled the long journey this rifle and I had made together from its conception, completion and use over a period of more than thirty years.

Struggling as a newly married college student at the University of Colorado in the early 1960s, I still had the dream of years—of someday having and using a fine custom rifle in the classic tradition. Influenced by many outdoor authors, but notably Jack O'Connor, I had by that time definite ideas about what my dream rifle should be. I believe my views of form and proportion were shaped early on by pictures of English rifles, Rigbys and Jefferys. This led me to appreciate the American classic rifle as done by Griffin & Howe, Al Biesen and others I first saw in articles by authors such as O'Connor.

Thus it was that I was psychologically (if not financially) primed to respond to a modest advertisement on page 87 of the December, 1959, issue of *American Rifleman*. This ad announced the availability of custom rifle and shotgun stocks, "Handmade, exactly to your specifications. From $100 up. All work guaran-

teed." What caught my eye, however, was the rifle pictured. It was an elegantly stocked Mauser of beautiful proportions. It appeared to be of dark walnut with a solid recoil pad and a sling swivel band on the barrel. Although obviously of large bore, there was nothing heavy or ponderous about this rifle. It had the graceful look of a thoroughbred. The address given in the ad was in Denver, only 25 miles away! The name of the craftsman who had placed the ad was unknown to me, but I knew that I would have to get to Denver and look up this fellow, this Jerry Fisher.

My first efforts were not

quickly rewarded. The address given turned out to be an abandoned structure with no tenants. A passerby said he thought the "gunsmith" who had been there briefly had closed up and gone

Here's the photo that started the public career of Woodward's Jerry Fisher-stocked 270.

"somewhere up in the mountains." In Colorado, that could cover a lot of territory. In fact it was several months later, after all sorts of detective work, that I located not Jerry, but his wife Marge, at their home (and Jerry's workshop) on Lookout Mountain, just west of Denver. Marge's comment was, "You found us from that ad in the *Rifleman*? Wow, you must be serious."

Jerry had only recently finished his training at the Colorado School of Trades in Denver and I don't think customers were exactly beating down the doors at this point. I tried to *appear* serious as I talked with Marge about my

The 270, its owner and impala taken in southern Zimbabwe.

48th EDITION **201**

Sighting in the 270 in preparation for African hunt, summer of '92.

reaction to the rifle in the ad, and what I would like to discuss as a project with Jerry. I didn't mention that I didn't even own a big game rifle at that time (having hocked my old Model 70 to pay tuition) and that the idea of $100 for a *stock* was about as sensible for me as a down payment on a new Ferrari.

On my next visit, Jerry was at home, and while Grace and his Marge got acquainted, he and I began to discover that we were kindred souls in our love of classic rifles. Many then-current custom rifles were afflicted with hideous lines and grotesque adornments, so those of us who savored the classic lines of older artists like A.G. Minar, Al Linden, Bob Owen and Tom Shelhamer shared our enthusiasms with almost conspiratorial glee. Jerry showed me photos not only of stocks he had made, but old, faded pictures of the works of others he admired. Jerry was candid about things he had done on request, but didn't really like. We seemed to be together every step of the way. I didn't know how, but I knew that I was going to have a Jerry Fisher rifle.

Without ever placing a formal order or even calculating a final cost, the plans were made. I am reminded of something I read by an automotive journalist about his having raced sports cars as a college student that he now couldn't even afford to drive on the street. He said, "Money was no object—we didn't have any."

The same was true for me. Somehow, through a complicated series of barters and creative financing, I acquired a new Winchester Model 70 Featherweight 270—what else? This I delivered to Jerry,

and he, in the meantime, showed me a nice blank of "French" which he thought would take the fine checkering for which he would later become famous. We agreed that the stock should reflect the English tradition of trim lines, including a thin, short forend. This was especially radical at the time, since almost everyone seemed to agree that big game rifles needed a lot of wood out front.

The pistol grip was to be small in circumference and the stock straight in order to provide support for scope use and to minimize recoil. We threw away the aluminum trigger guard and floorplate and replaced them with a steel assembly offered at that time by Griffin & Howe. The front sight was replaced with a Redfield hooded ramp. A checkered steel buttplate and grip cap were used, and Jerry himself checkered and thinned the bolt handle. Grace and I made trips to Lookout Mountain almost every weekend to visit and to check on the progress of our "classic." We even talked of its potential suitability for the exotic plains game of such faraway hunting fields as Africa.

When it was finished, the rifle was a thing of startling beauty and absolutely ruinous cost. My recollection is that the total came to just about $400, not counting the Model 70 or the Redfield Bear Cub 4x scope and Buehler mount. Grace agreed that certain members of her family should never learn of this secret, lest it irrevocably confirm their earlier conclusion that marrying me was an act of madness. As they say, "For better or for worse."

Given the stupendous cost and exquisite beauty of my new rifle, I experienced the

first symptoms of what I like to call *Collector's Disease*. Since I think this syndrome is fairly widespread and, like malaria, tends to recur, I will briefly describe it so others can recognize and treat themselves and friends. Basically, this disease consists of the delusional belief that fine firearms should never actually be used, that, paradoxically, the better they are designed and crafted, the more they become candidates for collection rather than use.

"You actually use that rifle for hunting?" is a question I am often asked by carriers of this disease trying to reinfect me.

Even though I felt the onset of collectionist symptoms early in my possession of this 270, a certain immunity was provided by the knowledge that, given our critical financial condition, I had to start using it immediately to put venison on the table or Grace and I (and new arrival Sean) would undoubtedly starve. *Collector's Disease* does not thrive among the poor. Also, in moments of lucidity, I was able to recall that having a fine, classic rifle to *use* was the original inspiration for all this effort.

So it was that in the fall of 1962, the first head of big game fell to the new rifle. I bagged two nice fat does on a ranch near Maybell, Colorado. We were managing an apartment building in Boulder and one of the tenants, a student, got us permission to hunt on the property in return for a share of the meat. They were the first of many deer and antelope over the years to provide challenge for the 270 and sustenance for the Carmans.

I was enormously happy with this first custom rifle, and I was surprised and pleased when it began to be admired by others. Jerry sent a picture of it to John Amber, then-Editor of the GUN DIGEST, and it was included in the Custom Guns section of the 18th edition (1964). In April of that year, I received a letter from Jack O'Connor which began:

"I remember that picture of your Model 70 in the GUN DIGEST. I thought it an extremely handsome rifle. I am going to have Fisher stock a rifle for me. I met the chap in Portland and I believe he is a most excellent workman."

Jack ran the same picture

of the 270 in an article entitled, "Stocks for Hunting Rifles" which appeared in the December, 1964, issue of *Outdoor Life*. The rifle appeared again in the 20th Edition of the GUN DIGEST, this time in an article on extreme "California-style" custom stocks. Finally, Buehler used it in ads to display his scope mounts. It has picked up a few minor dings over the years, and it now wears a Leupold scope in a two-piece Buehler mount, but to my eye, at least, its beauty has increased as it has aged and its wood has slightly darkened.

The Fisher rifle shoots as well as ever, with favored handloads going under an inch at 100 yards. I currently use 150-grain Nosler Partition bullets with H-4831 for all my hunting with it, and it produces a chronographed 2930 fps out of its 22-inch barrel. As I write this, I still have some antelope burger in the freezer from last year's hunt with this load. Accuracy runs around 1^1/$_2$ MOA with this bullet and powder, and it was with this combination that I confronted that Gray Ghost of a kudu in southern Africa.

As I continued to watch, I felt the reassuring familiarity of the 270 in my hands and experienced the deep satisfaction of dreams realized. Despite the almost nagging insistence of my professional hunter that I use the larger Kimber 375 I had brought along for buffalo, I was confident that the essential correctness of the 270s design and the balanced combination of its precision and power would render my classic more than adequate for our elk-like quarry. After it disappeared momentarily, melting away as kudu do, we shortly saw the bull going up the river bank opposite, about 150 yards away. At the critical moment, it paused and looked back. The shot was made and the kudu went down. Once again the classic had done its job, and I was glad that my confidence in it had not wavered.

In addition to the kudu, I was able to use my old 270 to take bush pig, bushbuck, impala and duiker. I even used it as my only defense and to assist in finishing off a rogue buffalo which had been injured by a poacher's snares, but those are other stories. ●

by ROBERT SHERWOOD

A Sweeter Sixteen: Finally

THE PARKER-HALE Model 640-E side-by-side 16-gauge represented a 180-degree turn in my approach to shotgunning. It was a gun I really wanted. For the better part of an erratic lifetime, I had forced a fitting of self to shotgun, learning to do with what I had for the times being—and those were often long times. Those scatterguns mostly lacked any hint of balance, and offered the handling qualities of post-augers. They were what I could buy on my occasional, meager salaries after I had met all my enforceable obligations. They threw as good as they were held, and that last was small privilege. I did, over the sere years, kill a lot of birds with clunky guns.

Tides and fortunes are hard to call; I found myself employed permanently at a better-than-living wage, and debtless, too, as I entered my declining years. I also found my fowling piece of many years, a Fox-Savage Model B, was shedding its buttstock in splintered installments. The new job was in the chukar capital of Nevada, so I sent a check and specs to Reinhart Fajen for a utility-type stock to suit my garden-grade shotgun.

My tax refund check beat the replacement stock to the mailbox, and I wondered why I was restocking a shotgun I had to warp myself to fit, anyway? I could no longer plead poverty—that left insanity. I got out the GUN DIGEST and found the portion listing side-by-side doubles. There were many I couldn't afford; my limit was $1000, and I didn't quite want to reach it.

But there was a Parker-Hale, of English name and clean English lines, with 26-inch barrels bored Improved and Modified, double-trig-

Parker-Hale 16 in its new habitat.

gered, for a price pleasant to behold. It looked something like a Cogswell & Harrison I once borrowed to hunt ruffed grouse. It appeared also to have features in common with a Webley & Scott 16-gauge I was privileged to shoot doves with on one of the better afternoons of a haphazard life. I had tasted many a vat of beer, but I could recognize champagne, and I and Precision Sports of Cortland, New York, came to a swift understanding.

The gun still looked like champagne when I took it out of the box. It had been through several stages—it was made in Spain by the ancient Basque firm of Ugartechea, on order by and to specifications of the British firm, which shipped it to the American outlet. It had all three names on it. It was a nice gun and more so, weighing about 6 pounds and wearing nice-grained and fine-checkered stocks of European walnut. The buttstock was a marvel of slim-wristed grace, with a perfect angle of drop for my neck and reach. It passed a heft test; balance lived there. It had tasteful English-style engraving.

I carried it a lot that summer, just to get used to it, and I shot clays with it when I could get someone to throw them for me. I noted that I got the discs lined up quickly and powdered an astonishing number of them.

September found son and self with shotguns and dogs ranging across grassy ridges in Idaho's Bonneville County, looking for sharptails. Half the sun was looking over the rim when dogs did something smart, and the cackling grouse came up before us. I spotted one out a ways and quartering that no one else was going to shoot at. The

Author and Dog, gun and an Idaho sharptail limit. It's a good gun for big country.

Parker-Hale came up and poised, almost on its own; I pulled the back trigger and feathers flew. I couldn't have made that shot with a lot of guns I've carried.

The next and limiting sharptail came out from under the dog's nose and whizzed around a dense chokecherry thicket, trying to put brush between me and her. I had almost a millisecond to get off a shot before she vanished behind the limbs. She vanished tumbling in the high grass instead, as I yanked the front trigger, and then it was up to Dog. As he brought the bird to me, I pondered the fact that this shotgun handled so well I wasn't even conscious of the line-up-swing-aim-squeeze sequence I had practiced so tediously with my earlier scatterguns. I was probably going through all the motions, but so swiftly I wasn't aware of them. The gun fit.

We left the sharptail country, after son Tom filled, and went after forest grouse in the aspen of the higher benches. The first blue grouse Salty Dog found was another tight test. He flushed and streaked low, cross-ridge, through the brushtops, trying to put the ridge between him and shot, and I had one clear glimpse to shoot at before he got out of range. It was enough. Later I doubled on ruffed grouse whisking through the green leaves and white trunks of the aspen forest. Sure, I missed a bird now and then. But I was

making more tough shots than I could remember making before with any other shotgun.

Shooting improved through the Idaho hunting, and then I returned to Nevada for the chukar opening. There are more tough shots than any other kind in chukar hunting, the birds are about as predictable as hogs on roller skates, and they sometimes run a long ways carrying a lot of shot.

Morning one: Dog threw a classic point, I walked up, and four chukars got up a good 30 yards out. It was a one-shot go; I lined one at a good 40 yards and pulled the Modified trigger. He folded, feathers danced in the air, and six more birds flushed 10 yards in front of Dog. The Improved barrel had an unfired shell in it, and it worked. The bird glided down about 70 yards away, but Salty had him after a search and a chase. The final test was later in the day, when a single flushed quar-

tering to my right and down-hill. This has always been a tough shot for me, but I made it.

I made a lot of good shots that season. It was a tough season; birds were few and wild-flushing. It was a year furnishing few opportunities, comparatively; gun-handling qualities and dog ability made it successful anyway. It was either Havilah Babcock or Buck Rutledge who wrote: "If you finish a day unashamed of your shooting and proud of your dog, you have had good hunting, kill numbers not-withstanding."

I get a lot of questions and some criticisms on my shotgun choice; there are answers for some of them. One friend uses an autoloader, and he sometimes takes four chukars on a covey rise. Maybe I can't think that big. Also, chukars are tough, and they often run like pheasants or more so. If I double on them and both birds run, it is about all Dog and I can do to find the pair of

them. I have never handled an auto or pump gun that felt as good to me as does a good double, and I doubt if I would get as many hits with any other action type as I do with a double I like. Also, I want the instant choice of chokes that only a double affords.

Other friends openly question my choice of double triggers over the selective single type. I have shot some fine shotguns with selective single triggers, but I often find myself on the fumble while the bird is on the fly. I can select my barrel easier with two triggers to pick from.

Why the gauge? The 16 is on the fade. I can't argue that. Shotgun gauge choice is a subjective matter, at least to me. I have owned mostly 16-gauge guns. I haven't felt overgunned in the quail coverts or undergunned while hunting turkeys. I stock lots of wads and cases. And hope.

Knowing scribes have praised heavier guns for holding qualities, especially in late season. They are welcome to them. Late or early, I can align a light and balanced double on a bird with greater surety and swiftness than I can heavier doubles and much more so than I can any pump or semi-auto.

Other knowing scribes have praised sidelocks over boxlocks for the handling qualities I prize. I have shot quality sidelocks and more expensive boxlocks than mine; there is a difference. Perhaps I am a coarse country boy; the difference is not that big to me.

Good days are made of good components, such as is this gun. I'll always remember one, a late Sunday in the 1991 season. We came off the Sterrett Rim, with four chukars bulging the game pocket of my shell vest; Dog quartered and circled in his never-tiring search pattern through the lava jumbles. Then he locked up, and a single towered in the classic rise, silhouetted over the setting sun when I caught him with the Modified barrel. Salty Dog searched him out of a hole in the slide rocks for me, and we went to the truck which wasn't far. I didn't have a limit, but I had all the birds I wanted to pick that evening. I had a gun and a dog I wouldn't trade for any others. I wondered how the poor people were doing. ●

Salty Dog was born to follow a 16, except when he leads it.

Sako's 375 Carbine

WHEN I WAS young and dinosaurs ruled the earth, I became a devout believer in the cartridge that was and is one of the greatest hunting cartridges extant—the 375 Holland & Holland Magnum.

Many thousands, possibly hundreds of thousands, of words of praise have been heaped on this cartridge that has been around since 1912.

There might have been magic floating around then because the 375 has proven to be almost "magical."

All the different makes and models of rifles chambered for this old timer have exhibited a level of accuracy for me that is truly scary. Even in out-of-the-box condition, I have *never* found a solidly bedded 375 that would not shoot into

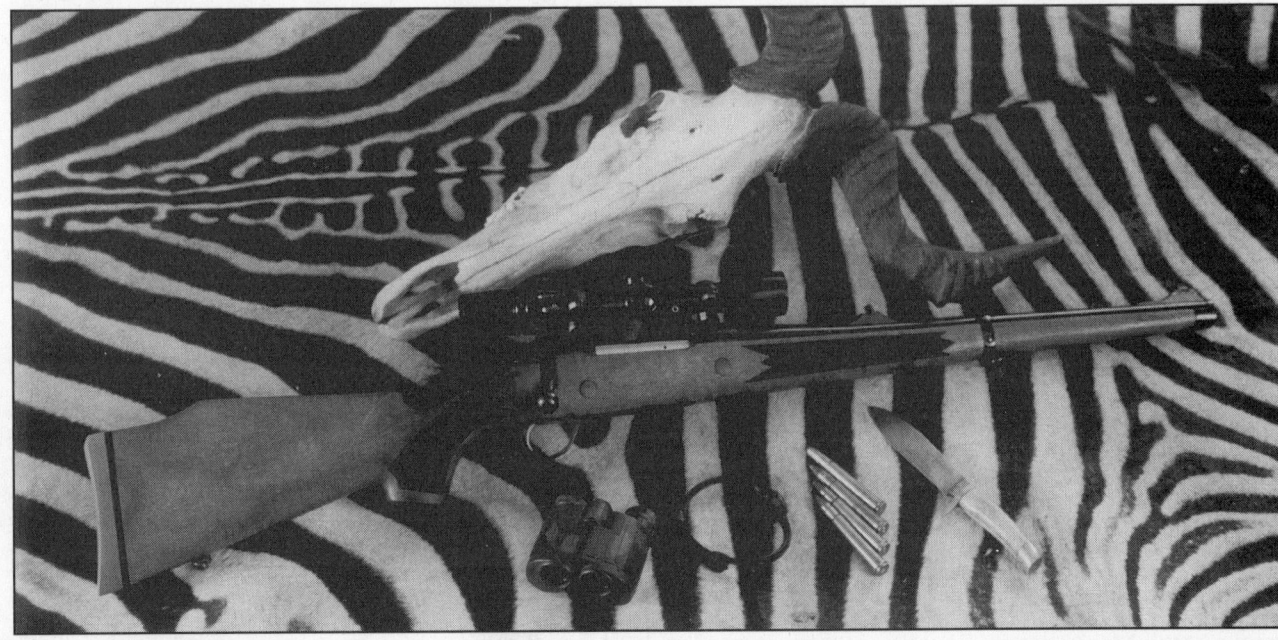

(Above) The short-barreled 375 H&H carbine from Sako is the apogee of the author's rifle experience.

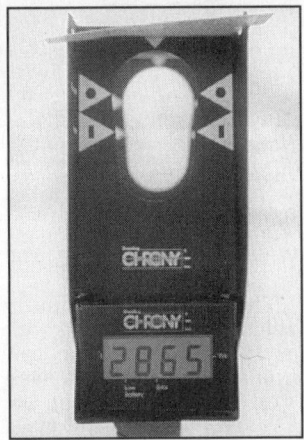

Favorite deer load clocked an honest 2865 fps out of the Sako carbine's 18½-inch barrel.

The author actually shoots up to 200 rounds at a session of 375 Holland and Holland Magnum from the bench.

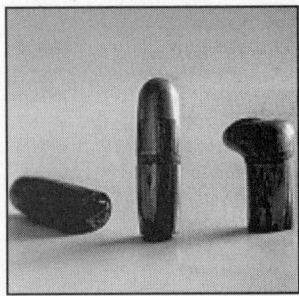

Three 300-grain RWS solids recovered from Cape buffalo after penetrating over three feet. The bullet on the right broke *both* shoulders and mushroomed nicely, but never broke up.

One of the reasons the 375 H&H is a perfect choice for hunting big game from deer to Cape buffalo around the world. You are never undergunned.

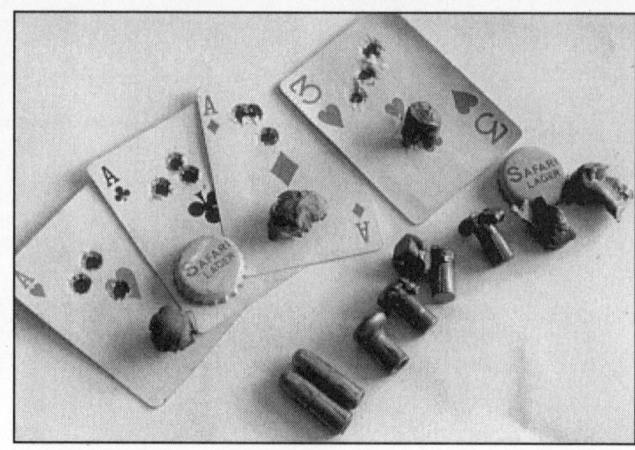
Writer has never found a rifle chambered for the 375 H&H Magnum cartridge that would not shoot very well.

less than two inches at a hundred meters. That *is* amazing. For some other cartridges, I have spent years looking for just the right handload to turn a mediocre shooter into a tackdriver, but I have never found a 375 load that refuses to shoot like it was developed just for the rifle in question.

After ten years of shooting a whole bunch of handloads and taking my two pet 375 H&H rifles to Africa, where I was born again a true 375 believer—both my professional hunters had 375 bolt actions and double rifles—I decided there was no reason to hunt big game with any other rifle or any other caliber.

I did take a lot of more or less good natured ribbing the first time I showed up at deer camp with what was dubbed "the elephant rifle." The laughing stopped when a nice whitetail buck paused for a few seconds in some fairly heavy scrub brush. Before witnesses, I held just a little high, set the set trigger and, resting the forend on my gloved hand which was resting on a handy stump, touched the front trigger. The six-point buck dropped as if struck by lightning at well over two hundred paces. The 235-grain Speer bullet penetrated the chest cavity and lodged in a tree directly behind the buck, and the buck literally never moved from his tracks. We recovered the bullet after taking pictures of it resting exactly halfway through the eight-inch locust.

For the following three years, I hunted deer with the 375 and never fired more than one round per deer: It was almost a joke in camp. One bitter cold afternoon, I ran into another hunter from our camp while I was driving the thickets. He just looked at me quizzically and said, "I heard you shoot your cannon early this morning. How big was he?"

That kind of performance really builds confidence. I was convinced that the 375 H&H was not only the best cartridge for deer and all other big game, it was the only cartridge for me. The only little thing that bothered me was weight of the rifles. They were heavy, as in *real* heavy when compared to my wife's little 243 Remington Model 600.

My Ruger No. 1 goes over 10 pounds with scope, mounts and sling; my customized Whitworth Mauser is even heavier. The Whitworth is also sort of long in the barrel department for hunting in thick brush. The Ruger is shorter by several inches, but still awfully heavy for a slogging through the snow and heavy brush rifle. I dreamed about a 375 H&H that would be as handy to use as my old commercial Mauser carbine chambered for the 8x60 cartridge.

I decided that I was going to allow myself to get extravagant and have a 375 H&H carbine built just for me. It would have a short barrel and a Mannlicher-style stock made of good, strong, straight-grained walnut, nothing too fancy, just a solid 375 H&H hunting carbine.

I then spent several months doing one of the things that I enjoy most,

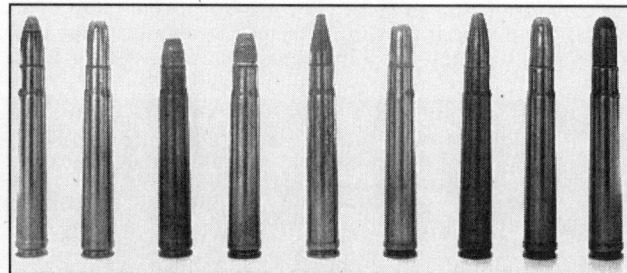
Here are nine different loads tested through the handy, little Sako carbine: Left to right—WW Silvertip, WW Solid, 230-grain cast bullet, 296-grain cast bullet, 300-grain RWS conepoint, 300-grain RWS solid, 235-grain Speer spitzer, 300-grain Hornady softpoint, 300-grain Hornady solid. No load shot over 2½ inches at 100 meters.

dreaming about my new rifle and looking through catalogs at actions, barrels, stocks, scope mounts, triggers, scopes and other neat little modifications that I wanted in this custom 375 H&H carbine. As most of my dream projects tend to be, the dream carbine was far beyond the capability of my new rifle fund.

I wasn't about to give up. Somehow, I would find a 375 H&H carbine, somewhere. If even a dummy like me realized how superb a hunting rifle this little carbine would make, there had to be someone, somewhere, making one as a production rifle. Well, there was and it's a Sako.

Sako offers, in off-the-shelf fullstock carbines alone, no less than 14 different chamberings in two different action lengths. There are 22-250 Remington, 243 Winchester, 7mm-08 and 308 Winchester chamberings in a short action. In the long action are 25-06 Winchester, 6.5x55, 270 Winchester, 7x64, 30-06, 7mm Remington Magnum, 300 Winchester Magnum, 338

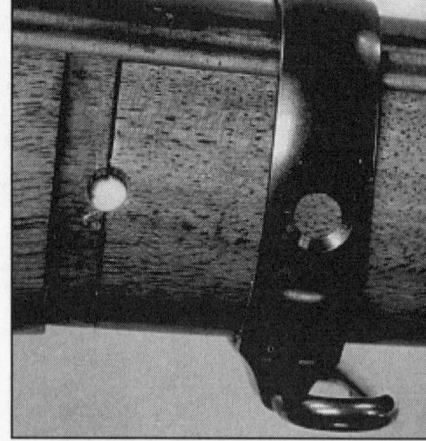
One of the secrets of the Sako: The long forearm is actually two separate pieces of wood. The joint is hidden under the barrel band.

Winchester Magnum, 9.3x62 and 375 H&H Magnum.

The 375 H&H Magnum weighs in at 7¾ pounds with an 18½-inch barrel, excellent iron sights in place, a solid steel barrel band far up the forearm, Continental-style sling swivels and a solid steel box magazine that holds three rounds. Mine arrived on

by BRUCE D. WOODS

Friday. I had already pulled my old Bushnell 3-9x and I proceeded to slap it onto the carbine. I took several boxes from my stash of reloaded ammunition and loaded up my range box with all of my various and sundry "possibles," including my sissy bag.

If you think that I'm going to fire two or three hundred rounds of 300-grain, 375 H&H from the bench without a sissy bag, you have another think coming. I have had my fill of double vision and low-grade concussions—I don't need to be *that* macho.

I bore-sighted the Sako over the bags at 25 meters and proceeded to fire eight rounds to allow the mounts and scope to seat themselves. I then retightened all of the screws and added a drop of red Loctite and returned the rifle to my nice warm car while I took a break. I had planned to shoot eight different loads that had performed superbly in my other rifles. Then I was planning some rapid-fire exercises offhand and without the sissy bag to check feeding, ejection, trigger pull, practical accuracy and overall performance.

At the bench, the Sako carbine was a joyous thing to behold. It would shoot just over an inch with every load I had ever used. It just seemed to like to shoot little tiny, groups, even in rapid fire.

From the shoulder, I could place my rounds inside of a five-inch circle at 100 meters. The recoil, which I had expected to be fairly stiff, didn't feel any different than the recoil from my other and much heavier 375 H&H rifles. And the carbine was almost as slick as my ancient 8x60 commercial Mauser carbine.

I now believe this little carbine, chambered for 375 H&H Magnum, will provide a lifetime of big game hunting anywhere in the world. It will make a dandy African rifle, a super deer rifle and will provide an Alaskan and thick timber hunter with an extra bonus of knockdown power.

If you happen to see me out in the Pennsylvania woods next deer season, in Tanzania some September or in northern Canada in the thick timber, chances are that I'll be toting a 375. It will be a Sako carbine. ●

Just One Ithaca 37

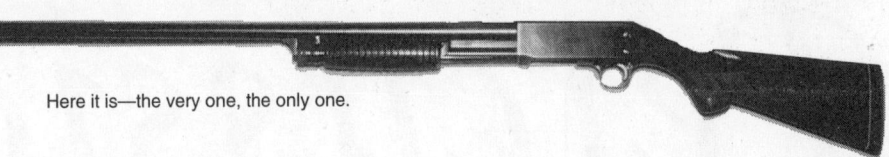

Here it is—the very one, the only one.

IT WAS A MAGIC moment in my life. I was fourteen years old. I had saved up money from my *Des Moines Register* paper route and was about to make my second big purchase in 1957. The first was a starter set of Spiegel catalog golf clubs. I had owned a genuine Red Ryder BB gun and had shot dad's 22 rifle regularly and his Winchester Model 12 occasionally. I was hooked. I wanted a shotgun so that I could also shoot trap and hunt pheasants and rabbits with my dad.

Back in the '50s, it seemed you were either a Winchester man or a Remington man. A few well-off fellows had Brownings. A few less fortunate others had other brands that weren't quite up to the image of the big names. Since my finances were slim, dad was scouting the want ads for any serviceable gun that would fill the bill. His shotgun biases (then) favored 12-gauges and pump guns.

The magic moment came at last. We went to see a 12-gauge Ithaca Model 37 Featherweight advertised for $50. It was the standard model and with a 30-inch Full-choke barrel. The bluing was a bit worn and it had been used, but not abused. After my father examined it, I put it up to my shoulder and it was a good fit. It was at least a pound lighter and felt a lot more comfortable than dad's Model 12. Despite my obvious drooling over this wonderful machine, my dad bargained with him and offered him $35; the sale price was $42 which included four boxes of miscellaneous reloads.

My dad was once again the hero of my life. I was so happy I offered to let him use it the next time we went trap shooting. To my surprise, he said, "No." He didn't particularly like the Model 37 especially since they were light (more recoil) and because their actions are a bit noisier than the 870 or Model 12. He shot it a couple of times right after we got it, just to make sure it worked properly and was safe.

The Ithaca was my wonder gun. I used it for trap and all manner of hunting. It brought many rabbits, pheasants, etc., to the Sunday dinner table. It brought down a fat doe at the edge of an Iowa cornfield 15 minutes after deer season opened. It has never malfunctioned and still is 100 percent original.

A couple years after I got my Model 37, dad started a part-time gun/shooting supplies business. His shotgun interests got wider: He started using over/under doubles for trap and Skeet; he shot 20-gauge as well as 12; he owned and used Remingtons and other brands as well as Winchesters.

Then one fall, he and his hunting buddies got the bug for deer hunting. Dad, being the perfectionist, took several shotguns, with several chokes, with two different brands of shotgun slugs out to sight-in. It was an all-day affair. He came home with an armload of shot-up targets and was disheartened (and sore). None of the many combinations he had tried were accurate

enough at 50 yards to suit him. It was Saturday night, next Saturday the season started.

There was, however, one combination he hadn't tried—my old Ithaca with its 30-inch Full-choke barrel. So Sunday afternoon, he took my gun out to the range and tried it. It was the most accurate combination he had tried. That next Friday night, he asked me if he could borrow my gun. Of course, I didn't mind. My mom had a wonderful time chiding my dad about his thousands of dollars worth of fancy shotguns staying in the closet while he took my $42 gun out to hunt. She enjoyed it immensely.

So the Model 37 is the only shotgun I've ever owned. That Full choke is humbling on quail and pigeon shoots, but it works on everything else.

Every once in a while, my dad and I will talk about the old days in Iowa together (he's retired in Arizona), and he'll ask me about my "corn-shucker" as he calls it (and he'll still remind me that it kicks too much compared to a Model 12). I'm always happy to relate that it is still going strong. In fact, I recently won a trophy at a club shoot for "slug shooting at 50 yards." The old Model 37 using standard 1-ounce Remington slugs beat out newer shotguns, most of which had special slug barrels using more exotic types of slugs. Ye old Ithaca is still my deer gun where rifles aren't allowed.

In my eyes, that makes my Ithaca Model 37 "One Good Gun." ●

The Best British Percussion Wheelgun

by JACK BARTLETT

This was the first double-trigger Tranter revolver.

DURING THE 19th century, there were nigh on 2000 gunmakers practicing their trade in the midland city of Birmingham, England. Though many of these craftsmen produced "best" shotguns and rifles, many earned their crust by producing cheap "trade" guns, weapons crude and nasty, destined to be swapped in Africa for whatever was going. Other members of the trade concentrated on securing contracts to supply rifles and pistols to the participants in the numerous wars being fought around the globe.

Previous to the year 1817, firearms were crafted entirely by skilled hands using forge, hammer and anvil. But after that magic year, the gunmakers very, very slowly commenced to employ crude machinery, first powered by water wheel and subsequently by steam engines. In the year 1851, Colonel Colt was to upset the new apple carts of the British gunmakers. On that date, a huge exhibition of the products of worldwide industry was staged at the Crystal Palace in London, and the gallant Colonel displayed to the British public the pocket, dragoon and the more popular Navy percussion revolvers. All were built of interchangeable components, enabling arms damaged in action to be cannibalized in the field.

In that same year, the astute Colonel was also to set the British gun trade in uproar. The blighter opened a revolver factory at Pimlico, in London, powered by a 30-horsepower steam engine, where the unskilled hands of some 200 British boys, girls and adults, supervised by skilled American foremen, were to manufacture by the system of "mass production" the individual components for the three models of Colt revolver. The implications of this system brought forth the wrath of both the British gunmaker and his skilled handcraftsmen, who roared "that all chambered revolvers are bad, but Colt's is not the best even of the bad ones."

Despite this highly inaccurate criticism, British military purchasing boards ensured that the British army and navy were equipped with considerable numbers of Colt Navy 36-caliber handguns. In addition, many of these most popular of the Colt models were privately purchased by the officer corps and were employed in the Kaffir Wars in South Africa, the Indian Mutiny, and the Crimean War.

Unhappily, after these conflicts, two criticisms about the Navy Colt were voiced in the British press. In the first place, the small bullet, traveling at extremely high velocity, gave the pistoleer a long range, but the British officers were usually indulging in a hand-to-hand melee where long range was not required, and the small bullet proved to be sadly deficient in stopping power when employed 'gainst a savage and fanatical dusky opponent. Secondly, in a hand-to-hand fight, the single-action Colt proved slower in discharging successive shots than a trigger-cocking revolver.

To meet the demand for a rapidly cocked handgun which carried a

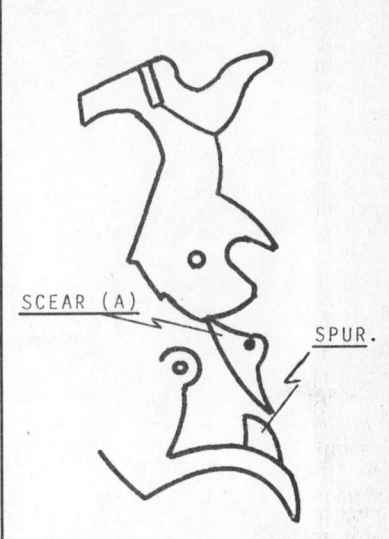

When using the single-trigger Tranter, the hammer is cocked and held by the engagement of the sear with the bent. Pressure on the trigger causes the spur behind the trigger to enter a slot in the action body until it forces the sear out of engagement with the bent, causing the hammer to fall under the pressure of the mainspring.

knockdown bullet, one Robert Adams, who traded as a gunmaker in the city of London, designed, manufactured and offered the British pistol-owning fraternity a massive five-chambered wheelgun, having no hammer spur, whose cylinder was revolved and the arm fired by a straight-through pull on the trigger.

The Rhodda/Tranter, with its breech-loading cylinder fitted, having the fired cases ejected into the hand.

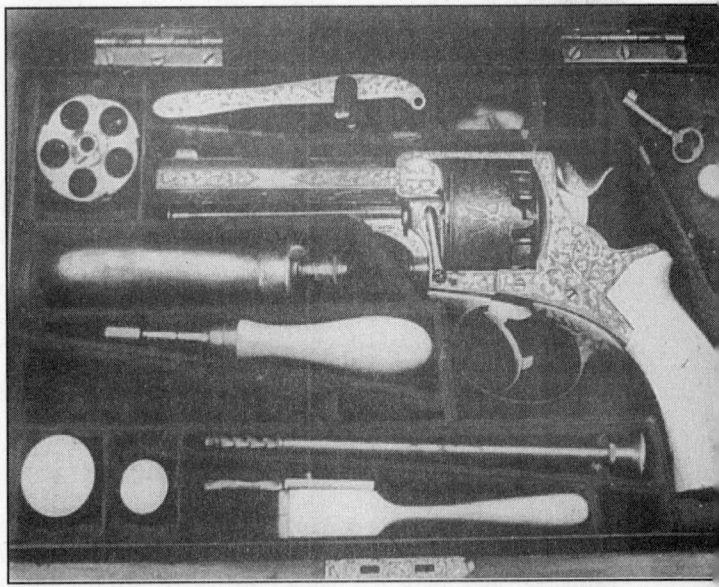

The superb Rhodda (Calcutta)/Tranter wheelgun, cased with its two interchangeable cylinders, which belongs now to John Slough.

A British subaltern officer of the 67th Regiment, having led his platoon into an obvious trap in the 1840 war 'gainst the Afghans, tries to supplement his men's rifle fire with his percussion Adams despite the impossible range.

Adams' revolver could be obtained in 38-bore (or .497-inch) and threw a slug capable of instantly downing even the most virile opponent.

The mould for the first model Adams revolver cast a bullet with a spigot on its rear. In the pistol case lay a wad punch which produced felt wads of a slightly larger diameter than the bullet. These wads were then threaded onto the spike protruding from the tail of the bullet.

To load the Adams, a charge of blackpowder was dropped into each chamber and the combined missile with its attached wad pushed home with the pistolero's little finger. Though this idea was excellent for quick loading and discharge in the clinical atmosphere of a pistol range, it was not so good in active service. A mounted officer found that the motion of his horse shook the combination bullet out of its chambers and jammed his weapon. Besides, if the greased wads were not an extremely tight fit, the danger of a sympathetic discharge when the flash from the fired charge ignited the powder in t'other chambers was ever present, a circumstance which did the shooter's hand no good at all.

Eventually, the first model Adams was supplanted by the Beaumont/Adams, a double-action piece possessing a robust rammer which forced down a tightly fitting naked slug. Despite the considerable improvement to the original design, the house of Adams was to be challenged by another British revolver manufacturer, one William Tranter, who was to produce wheelguns whose craftsmanship, finish, engraving and mechanism were to outshine all other handguns then on the market.

William Tranter was born in the year 1816, the scion of an affluent family whose cash came from their blacksmithing business. He was eventually to be apprenticed to the trade of the gunmaker. On completion of his trade training, his family purchased a partnership in a Birmingham firm of gunmakers—Hollis, Sheath & Tranter—but our Bill was obsessed with the idea of things modern; like Colt, he was sold on the idea of mass production.

He left the partnership and installed steam machinery in a rented factory, and the venture was a great success, enabling him to accept many subcontracts from other gunmakers, including Adams. If an internal examination of the frames of many of the Adams percussion revolvers still existing today is carried out, one may find the letters "WT" stamped thereon. These components emanated from Tranter's steam-driven plant.

Our Bill's active brain led him full-time into the revolver manufacturing game. His first difficulty was the fact that Adams had beaten him to the post with the early patents, particularly Adams' first which protected the idea of forging a revolver frame and barrel in one unit. Fortunately, Tranter was able to secure a license from Adams to use this patent, paying a fee for each revolver produced.

Tranter endeavoured to satisfy the requirements of the officer corps who had to plunge into a melee 'gainst dusky, bearded, fanatical faces, sword in right hand, revolver in left, leading their companies and platoons. As we can see from the advertisement for the first Tranter five-chambered model, there was no spur for cocking on the rear of the hammer. A peculiar second trigger extends below the trigger guard, and the pistoleer's second finger was placed on this trigger. Pressure on this secondary trigger draws the hammer to full cock, thus enabling the weapon to be fired by a normal "single action" type of pressure on the normal trigger with the first finger.

pistolero had first to fumble unfolding the secondary trigger.

Bill Tranter therefore listened to the critics, particularly one guy who wrote in the military press: "Nobody wants to have to play 'cornet a'piston' on his pistol in a hot action". Therefore, William re-designed his handgun, producing it as as a single trigger, double-action weapon. These superb revolvers were built in 38-bore (.497-inch); 54-bore (440-inch); 80-bore (.392-inch); and finally the little guy, 120-bore (.310-inch). Your ancient scribe, despite his four-score years, is lucky enough to possess an 80-bore late model Tranter in immaculate condition, and nothing delights the old devil more than casting a slew of bullets, dipping their bases in Tranter's patent mixture of wax and tallow, and firing them in his club range in a disused quarry.

The bane of all early revolvers (both cap and ball and breech-loading) using the mucky blackpowder as its fodder was that the fouling tended to gum up the works so that the cylinder finally refused to revolve. It was, however, recorded in a test carried out in the year 1858 that a Tranter revolver employing bullets anointed with his "Patent Compound" was fired 500 times without malfunction.

Remarkably enough, although this superb arm was far ahead of its time, workmanship and design being far superior to the product of any other British manufacturer,

Tranter's weapons left his huge factory bearing only a tiny stamp indicating that they were "Tranter's Patent," while on the topstrap was engraved, in quite large lettering, the retailer's name and address. In the case of old Jack's revolver, the retailer's name is "E. Whistler, The Strand, London" and indeed the trade label pasted inside the lid of the walnut case is Whistler's and not Tranter's. Whistler was no gunmaker, but a type of pawnbroker who specialised in helping "toffs" and army officers who were temporarily strapped for cash by purchasing and reselling at a considerable profit their firearms, and surplus uniforms and saddlery as well.

Despite the fact that none of Tranter's revolvers bore the manufacturer's name in large script, one can pick any old book about experiences in the Indian Mutiny, the Maori wars or the Crimean conflict, and find that the writer invariably refers to his personal arm as a "Tranter."

The diameter of the bullets cast in the Tranter mould in old Jack's possession is .392-inch, and as the mouth of the chambers measured .400-inch, they were easily inserted. Since the chambers were bored on a taper measuring .388-inch at its base, the rammer ensured that the lubricated slugs were an extremely tight fit, thus virtually eliminating sympathetic discharge.

Cap and ball Tranters were manu-

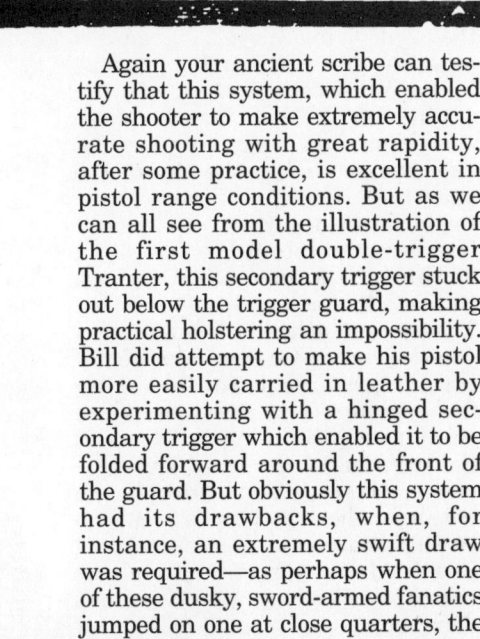

Again your ancient scribe can testify that this system, which enabled the shooter to make extremely accurate shooting with great rapidity, after some practice, is excellent in pistol range conditions. But as we can all see from the illustration of the first model double-trigger Tranter, this secondary trigger stuck out below the trigger guard, making practical holstering an impossibility. Bill did attempt to make his pistol more easily carried in leather by experimenting with a hinged secondary trigger which enabled it to be folded forward around the front of the guard. But obviously this system had its drawbacks, when, for instance, an extremely swift draw was required—as perhaps when one of these dusky, sword-armed fanatics jumped on one at close quarters, the

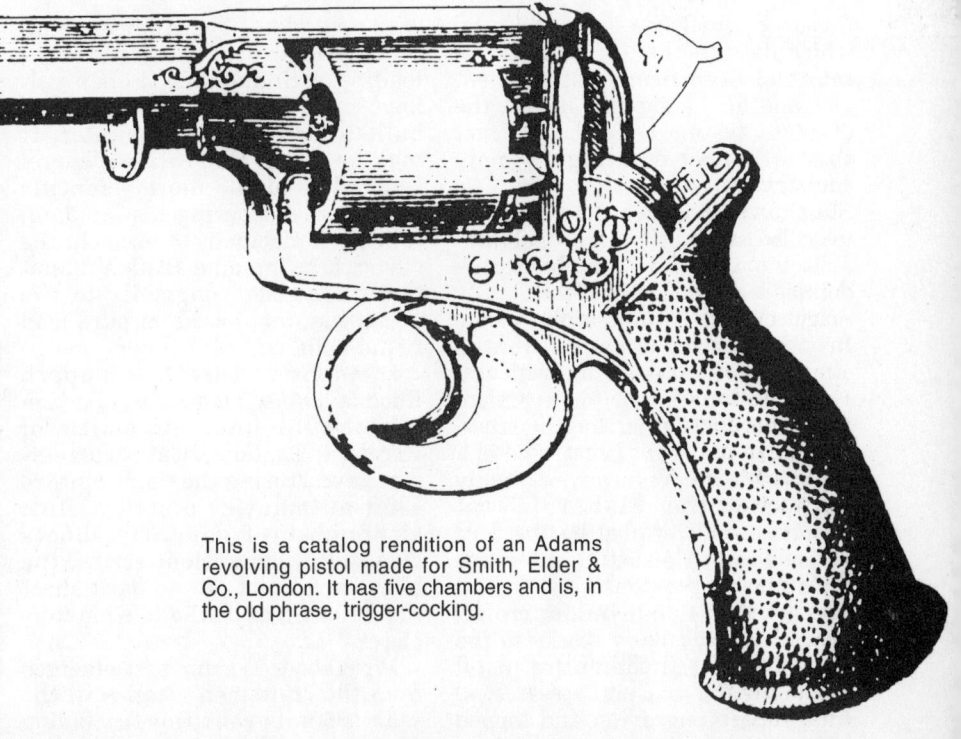

This is a catalog rendition of an Adams revolving pistol made for Smith, Elder & Co., London. It has five chambers and is, in the old phrase, trigger-cocking.

A heavy caliber, quick-shooting revolver was necessary when fighting the tough Zulus in South Africa.

factured until the year 1870, by which date the breech-loading system had been firmly established. Demand for handguns built on the obsolete system reflected the fact that a traveler entering a remote country store in either Africa or South America would find that metallic cartridges were unobtainable, tho' the trader had blackpowder, pig lead and caps a'plenty.

It therefore became a ploy of the British revolver manufacturers to offer their cased revolvers with two cylinders, one bored for a rimfire cartridge and t'other for the traditional cap and ball. Illustrated is a superb Tranter revolver, originally built for the Maharajah of Jodphore and retailed by the firm of Rhodda of Calcutta, and under their direction extensively worked over by traditional Indian craftsmen who fitted ivory stocks to the butt, smothered the entire pistol (including the case and accessories) with superb engraving and topped

with gold plate. The rimfire metallic cartridge used in the breech-loading cylinder is .442-inch caliber, while the mould cast 54-bore bullets for the other cylinder. It may be noted that while Colonel Colt adopted the more scientific method of measuring his handgun calibers in decimals of an inch, the old stick-in-the-mud British manufacturers stuck doggedly to the ancient system based on pure lead round balls.

Incidently, this last superb Rhodda Tranter is in the collection of John Slough, gunsmith of Hereford, England, who is currently manufacturing the 9mm Spitfire semi-automatic pistols. But, although he frequently shoots alongside your ancient scribe, the blighter will not let old Jack shoot the Tranter and Rhodda masterpiece!

My 80-bore Tranter first emerged from the craftsmen's hands in the year 1859; its condition, including

the bore, is pristine. Carefully loaded with a quarter-dram of blackpowder together with a patent lubricated bullet, shooting from a rest enables the old devil to achieve a standard of accuracy quite equal to that given by his S&W 38 Special.

William Tranter was to leave this planet and depart for the great shooting ground in the sky in the year 1885. He left behind a thriving business, together with an original directorship in the formation of the well-known Birmingham Small Arms Company. After Tranter's death, his large factory was leased to George Kynoch (of later explosive manufacturing fame) where the premises were employed in building the Kynoch Schlund revolver and Gras-type rifles. Despite substantial contracts for the sale of these weapons to the Transvaal government of South Africa, the enterprise was not to survive long after Tranter's departure. ●

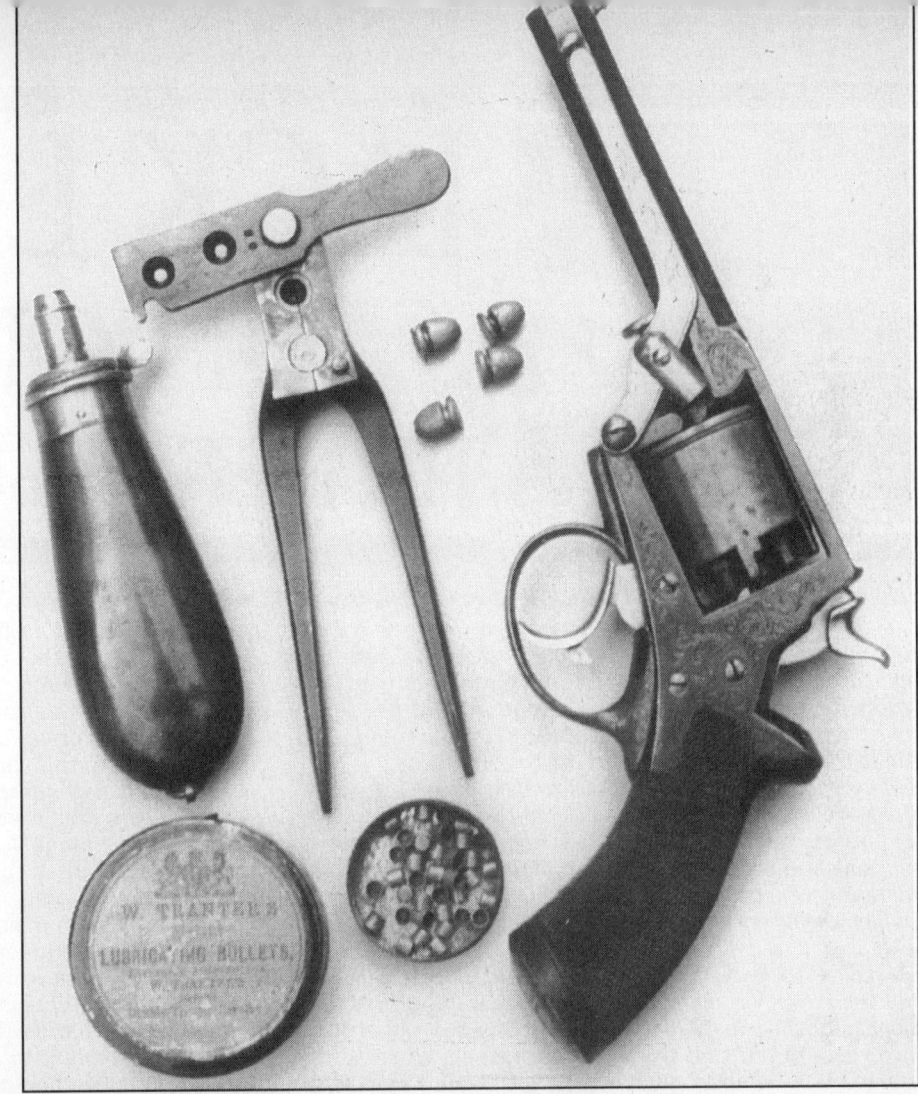

Old Jack's 80-bore Tranter, together with the "makings" to get her a'thundering. It is, of course, what Yankees call a pocket pistol.

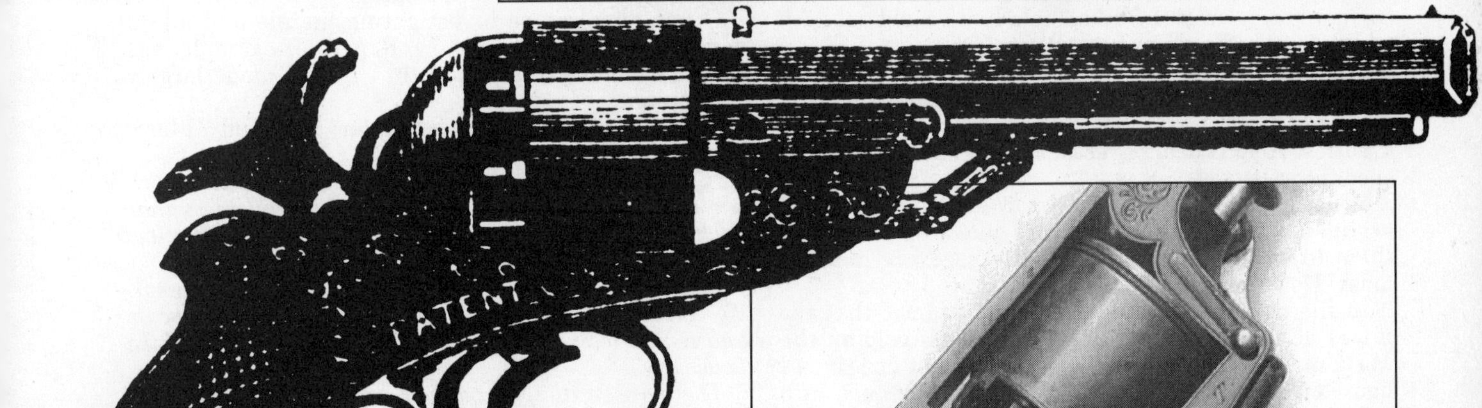

G.H. Daw's patent revolvers were cocked with thumb or self-acting with trigger—the fire control pattern that survived longest.

The safety catch, which locks the cylinder by engaging behind a nipple, made this Tranter pretty safe.

JACK LEWIS
ON GUNS
PRICES (and) HYPE

Getting something straight right away, he advised of two things: First, this is that same Jack Lewis who has owned and operated Gun World *magazine more or less safely for some time now; and, second, he did not write what we print here for* GUN DIGEST. *He wrote it for another DBI book, but it's good reading, anyway.*

The paragraphs by Lewis were written as introductions—to an entire book and then to three sections therein—but we print them here as the nearly private contemplations of a man, a professional, who doesn't have a lot more to learn about his subject. This is Jack Lewis himself, on the prices of guns and other things:

THE NINTH EDITION of *The Gun Digest Book of Modern Gun Values* contains 560 pages. The first edition, published in 1976, had only 288 pages, but it took two years to put that first edition together. When I first started talking about such a book with Chuck Hartigan, current honcho of DBI Books, I told him I could put such a book together in six months. Wrong.

I have found the succeeding volumes difficult for what appears a simple reason. With each edition, I tend to develop a theory as to what influences the prices of used firearms. A good deal of research goes into these developed theories.

When it is time to prepare a new edition of MGV, as we call it, I dust off the old theories and attempt to apply them to what is happening in the used gun market today. However, the theories no longer fit.

In the past, I have theorized, for instance, that the prices of guns tend to follow the price of gold on the world market. That proved to be the case at one time. I figured that used arms prices had much in common with inflation and that individuals bought guns as a hedge against such financial fluctuations. That seemed to be the case for a year or two, but many of those guns no longer are worth what they once brought in an era of double-digit inflation and 20 percent interest.

Avoiding further philosophy, let us simply say that gun prices do change—downward as well as upward.

If we compare prices of used handguns listed in this edition to those of the eighth edition, which was published in 1991, the first thing we are likely to note is that, for the most part, prices have not changed all that much for the vast majority of the pistols and revolvers listed.

There are numerous reasons for this stagnation. First, of course, has been the state of the economy. With interest rates remaining low, the rate of inflation has risen little and there has been little investment in handguns as a hedge against that periodic problem. Another reason for the lack of action is the fact that the floodgates have been opened and thousands of used firearms are coming out of Europe at prices usually lower than we have been used to paying in this country.

In the matter of citizens who simply want a handgun for home protection, there are plenty of them available it seems. In some areas, local legislation is making it comparatively difficult to buy a gun legally so these used guns are lying in cases waiting for the would-be buyers to come up with the paperwork.

But possibly the greatest effect on the used handgun market has been new materials either being introduced or now in varying stages of development. Introduction of the Glock series with their plastic frames has caused other manufacturers to start incorporating tough, high-impact plastics in their own models.

Other makers are investigating metals and alloys new to the firearms industry. Ruger, for example, has been developing a handgun that will be made largely of titanium.

When is all this going to get better? Truthfully, I have no answers. Do you?

It is not often in a long career spent tap-dancing with one toe almost always in the journalism business that Jack Lewis has asked a question when he doesn't know the answer. But that one sounds heartfelt.

And he's right. His own long series of MGVs proves it. We can all—all us experts—believe we know, but events and reality often confound the theory and the belief. Like Lewis says.

There are verities, of course. Some are not always positive verities mind you. As Lewis also knows.

Just as in selling new automobile models or the latest mousetrap, there is a good deal of hype involved in the firearms business. It isn't like it used to be. The modern-day Sam Colts and John M. Brownings don't just go to the workbench, design a rifle, then take it to a firearms company whose bosses are standing in line, looking for a chance to put the new gun into production.

The rifle business is particularly demanding and planners constantly are looking for the unusual gimmick that customers will just demand to have, and which no other manufacturer will be able to offer—for one season, at least.

There are two schools of thought regarding firearms, in general, of course. Some want highly decorated guns that they can hang on a wall for others to admire, but the greater number of gun buyers are after a firearm that is built for practical use. This latter type of thinking has led to virtually all of the U.S. rifle manufacturers turning to stainless steel and various breeds of plastic for recent models.

Rumor has it that combining stainless steel barrels and ugly but functional plastic stocks on the classic Model 110 rifle virtually saved Savage Arms from oblivion and put this old-line company back in the marketplace.

It is said there are no secrets in the firearms business, and in the United States, at least, that would appear to be true. Every company seems to know what its competitors are doing and what they will be attempting to sell. Thus, they tend to watch each other's marketing strategy to learn what is selling. It doesn't take long to climb on the bandwagon.

Today, all of the major arms companies that used to push beautiful wood, hand-checkering and exquisite bluing have included the stainless and plastic models in their lines.

So there you have it. The Almighty is not always on the side of the better mousetrap. Something, however, is always on the side of the better (more effective) hype.

Is it all just advertising? Actually not. There's good stuff there, in amongst the dross. That's the way Jack Lewis sees the recent history of shotguns and shotgunning.

There was a period in this country when a certain type of shotgunner seemed to be more interested in what was termed "pride of ownership" than he was in shooting.

This individual made a great thing of collecting highly decorated side-by-side doubles of both U.S. and European manufacture. He would drag one of these art pieces out of a locked gun cabinet, caress it lovingly, then throw it to his shoulder and swing on the chandelier. This move was meant to illustrate the

shotgun's exquisite balance and pointability which seemed to equate with the dollars spent in collecting the gem.

No doubt there still are some of these gunowners about; there must be. However, the manufacturers in this country seem to be concentrating less on the high-ticket guns than in getting good, solid shooting machines into the hands of hunters and clay target shooters.

From my own observations, there are two—no, three—types of scattergunners who have been responsible for this business-like approach to gun furnishing: Sporting Clays shooters, turkey-takers and deer hunters.

One of the charms of the Sporting Clays challenge is that it can be fired with just about any type of shotgun, except possibly a single-shot, and I suspect some of those have seen competition, too. This sport was developed to get away from the equipment race that seemed to have become a big part of competitive trap and Skeet.

No matter what the purpose, arms manufacturers quickly began incorporating subtle changes in existing designs and labeling them as Sporting Clays guns. The range of prices is broad and one cannot help but wonder whether the equipment race is in full swing once again.

The other facet which threatens to bring the shotgun market out of the doldrums is hunting; specifically, two types of hunting.

The wild turkey is found in big numbers in nearly all of our states these days, and having both fall and spring turkey seasons has caused hunter interest—and participation—to increase dramatically.

It stands to reason that one has to have a special shotgun for turkey-taking, right? Manufacturers have pushed this "specialty gun" concept, and gun shops and sporting goods stores now are loaded with shotguns that are totally camouflaged. Hiding metal, wood and synthetics is so well done, one wonders how many shotguns are lost in the woods each year. Whether this helps fool turkeys is something else to wonder about, of course.

A third shooting sport that has brought the shotgun to the fore is deer hunting. An increasing number of states are limiting deer hunting to rifle-sighted, slug or buckshot-hurling smoothbores. Much of this has to do with the supposed threat created by long-range rifles to encroaching housing tracts and other evidences of civilization. A shotgun is supposed to be safer for everyone and everything involved, except the deer.

What this all comes down to is the fact that there are some excellent bargains among used shotguns that have been traded so the former owner could upgrade and compete in the equipment race.

And here we see the old pro slipping up and letting the guy who knows sneak through. It's the old pro who identifies the three biggest current influences on smoothbore designs—very conventional stuff. The guy who knows, however, cynically—a little—and whimsically—a lot—wonders how important gun camouflage is, whether or not the Sporting Clays game is another equipment race, which it is, and if the shotguns-only laws provide safe deer hunting.

And in the end, you note, this guy who knows gets back to business, the business of explaining, of telling how it is. In this case, his reader gets bargains from the guys who are playing the new games.

So that's him—Jack Lewis, a guy who knows. Kind of shows on him, doesn't it?
Ken Warner

Modern Gun Values, 9th edition, published by DBI Books, Inc., Northbrook, IL, 560 pages, $20.95.

by EDWARD A. MATUNAS

AMMUNITION, BALLISTICS AND COMPONENTS

HERE WE ARE again. It is hard to believe that there is a full year between each of these efforts. Perhaps my continued good luck (another successful safari completed, a new home built in the boonies, and by the time this is being read I will be packing for another safari) is keeping me just busy enough to keep time moving quickly. However, I will admit that a few less than kind shooters have suggested that time moves fastest for those of us who are members of the "older" folks group. But, what do they know anyway?

As stated last year, ballistics for new loads are no longer incorporated into the body of our text (so that we can devote our space to more of the new items). Instead, all new ballistics appear in the tables following this section. This method seems to work well and will be continued in the future.

The Remington Safari Grade ammo in 375 H&H with the Swift A-Frame bullets that was discussed in these pages last edition has since been used extensively on safari. Ditto for the 338 load of like type. They both proved better than perfect, bashing and anchoring all sorts of critters from tiny 100-pound antelope to giant eland weighing close to a ton. And, as we will discuss in a moment, there is more of this great ammo.

The more I hunt, the more enamored I become with high-performance hunting

troduced new big game bullets which will retain almost all of their mass, supply that deep penetration, and still expand to a very large frontal area diameter. Today's hunters have bullet performance choices that folks not too long ago wouldn't have dreamed possible. Let's hope the manufacturers keep up the great development work.

Readers who find a particular round or component extremely satisfactory, or an extreme disappointment, are invited to write me with the details of their experiences. No, there isn't time for individual responses, but your input can help with a foundation for good pass-it-along material. No matter how many critters I collect each year,

A premium bullet went from stem to stern, a measured 55 inches, in this very handsome kudu. Performance like this is no longer the domain of reloads only. Indeed the photo was a direct result of Remington Safari Grade factory ammo use.

bullets—those that retain most of their original mass and nonetheless expand fully. Such bullets deliver all the shock of lesser types which sometimes expand so violently that they shed most of their mass very quickly. But, unlike the lesser types, these premium bullets will penetrate very, very deeply. I recovered one A-Frame bullet that expanded to more than double diameter, retained 95 percent of its original weight, and penetrated one African critter for a measured 55 inches. Performance like that is what impresses hunters with their cartridge, bullet choice and prowess.

Not to be left behind, Winchester and Federal have in-

Write me at: E. Matunas, P.O. Box 511, Moosup, CT 06354. If you want to gamble on the far-out chance of a response, enclose a stamped self-addressed envelope.

A timely tip to serious big game hunters: There are still opportunities to hunt Africa in the old traditional way—on foot and away from most of humanity. But Africa, like the rest of the world, is changing fast. If you dream of going, do it as soon as possible. It is still affordable. Wait too long and you just may miss it.

But, before I get off onto too many tangents, let's get right to those items that I feel are the best of this year's new ammunition and component introductions:

Federal

Gee, I can still remember being forced to reload because the quality in hunting bullets that I wanted was simply not available in factory rifle ammunition. Now there are plenty to choose from. Federal has opted now to use the Trophy Bonded Bearclaw bullets in a number of premium hunting loads. This is in addition to the existing loads with Nosler Partition bullets. Federal omits reference to the "Bearclaw" nomenclature of these Trophy Bonded bullets, but they are the same. Superb penetration, positive mushrooming and very high weight retention are all here. (I enjoy sounding like a broken record when it comes to game bullet performance.) The Trophy Bonded bullet is made from solid copper bars. The rear two-thirds of the bullet is

Getting close is all part of the testing. How else would I find out if the bullets hold together at max velocity?

your experiences will help with evaluations. I am especially interested in your success, or lack of it, with the various new premium bullets.

solid copper. The front end has a lead core which is bonded to the jacket. Weight retention after double diameter expansion is typically

Remington's new 200-grain A-Frame bullet in their Safari Grade ammo will help get the job done on applications previously thought beyond the capability of the 300 Winchester Magnum cartridge.

about 95 percent. Great accuracy, too. Beautiful!

The calibers and bullet weights offered with the Trophy Bonded bullets are 270 Winchester 140-grain; 30-06 Springfield 165-grain; 300 Winchester Magnum 200-grain; 338 Winchester Magnum 225-grain; and 375 H&H Magnum 300-grain. Between these and the other Federal Premium cartridges loaded with Nosler Partition bullets, the hunter can find a perfect load for many applications.

The 7mm-08 is no longer a proprietary cartridge. Federal is loading it with a 140-grain Nosler Partition. This should add a lot of game performance to an accurate cartridge.

A Hydra-Shok 155-grain bullet is now available in Federal's Premium ammo for the 40 S&W. Other new handgun ammo loads are a 9mm 147-grain and a 357 Magnum 140-grain. Gold Medal target loads for the 9mm, 38 Special, 44 Magnum and 45 ACP are also new. The Gold Medal target load line of rifle ammo will include loads for 223 Remington, 308 Winchester and 30-06 Springfield.

Federal is now loading some of the finest 22 Long Rifle ammo available. This ammo was originally developed for the U.S. Shooting Team and was used successfully in the 1992 Olympics to win gold and silver medals. Three grades of this ammo are offered—Ultramatch, Match and Target. If accuracy is important to you, give this ammo a try.

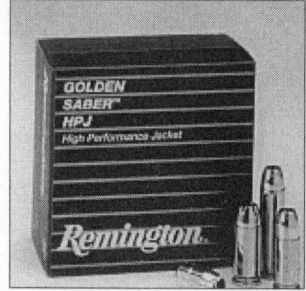

Golden Saber bullets give Remington a challenger in the new high-performance handgun-round arena—the best weights in the most popular calibers.

There are a lot of new steel shot pellet sizes in Federal's various shotshell loadings this year. New heavy game and dove loads also have been added, as well as some new paper-cased 12-gauge target loads. Also, Federal's 12-gauge 2³/₄-inch saboted slug load continues to prove to be the most accurate slug load I have ever used!

Remington

There has been a lot happening at Remington over the past several years which has again led to the introduction of a lot of new ammo for the year. I heaped a lot of praise on the past intro-

duction of Remington's SafariGrade ammunition which, in my opinion, uses the very best hunting bullets available—Swift A-Frame softpoints and Barnes Super Solids. The line has now been expanded to include the 300 Winchester Magnum loaded with a 200-grain Swift A-Frame. This specific weight is a very wise choice, as when a hunter is knowledgeable enough to understand the need for a premium-grade bullet, there is likely to also be an understanding of the need for a heavyweight one. The introduction of this load is the reason for my renewed interest in the 300 Winchester Magnum.

Remington Extended Range brand ammo has two new loads—a 135-grain 270 Winchester and 160-grain 30-30 Winchester. Both of these are flat-base bullets with a lot of computer-aided design to maximize ballistic coefficient and enhance downrange ballistics. Both deliver great accuracy. Interestingly enough, after all these years of 150- and 170-grain 30-30 bullets,

we are back to the original century-ago weight of 160 grains.

As a direct challenge to Winchester's successful Black Talon handgun bullets, Remington now has the Golden Saber bullet in loads for one-hand guns. The new bullet is another of the recent breed that is designed to optimize penetration while still affording the shock associated with a properly expanded bullet. High weight retention is always the answer to such requirements, and it appears that the Remington effort is very successful. The bullet jacket is

heavy walled of solid cartridge brass with cut-through nose expansion grooves. Nose jacket expansion stops at about 1.65 calibers and does not fold back against the bullet shank. The hollowpoint is designed to aid expansion yet avoid core loss during penetration. This is a good idea that really works and is extremely accurate to boot. Availability includes 125-grain 38 Special and 357 Magnum; 147-grain 9mm Luger; 180-grain 40 S&W; and 230-grain 45 ACP. Obviously, Remington has selected bullet weights which have proven the very best choices when push and shove goes to deadly force.

New, too, is a 147-grain flat-nosed full-metal-case Match Grade load for the 9mm Luger. Bullet design was geared to positive feeding in as many models as can be had from a single style projectile. Nice!

The new 12-gauge 2³/₄-inch Copper Solid Sabot slug load is *not* ideal for use in smoothbore shotguns. It was designed specifically for rifled barrels. Unlike other similar offerings, Remington uses a one-piece sabot designed not unlike their Accelerator cartridge sabots. Remington claims consistent 2¹/₂-inch 100-yard groups.

The new slug is unique. It is solid copper and non-expanding in the traditional sense of forming a permanent nose mushroom. But the front four petals forming a "crossed slot" in the nose will open to at least double diameter before breaking off after limited penetration, and then become separate projectiles that weigh about 20 grains each. These will penetrate in random directions. Missed the vitals? Maybe not with this new load.

Remington has also redesigned their traditional Foster-type 12-gauge shotgun slugs. The result is noticeably improved accuracy. A needed change!

Other new shotshell loads include Premier grade field types in 12-, 16- and 20-gauge. These give the advantages of extra-hard plated shot (best possible patterns). In effect, these are target-load quality with field-size shot. There is a new Heavy Dove load in 12- and 20-gauge. Simply ¹/₈-ounce more

Remington's new all-copper saboted 12-gauge slug promises rifle-like accuracy in rifled slug barrels.

shot—1¹/₈-ounce for the larger bore and 1 ounce for the smaller gauge. A 20-gauge target load with an extra ¹/₈-ounce (1 full ounce) is also being offered for those who want the little gauge to be more competitive in 12-gauge situations. I like the idea.

Steel shot loads receive another upgrade. All steel shotshells have gotten the "Wet-Proof" treatment. No more rusting and subsequent fusing of pellets. Pellets are now plated, and crimps and primers are sealed against

Even on light game, the Trophy Bonded Bullets used in Federal's newest rifle ammunition can prove very effective. This impala was taken with a Trophy Bonded bullet at an extreme range, where lesser bullets sometimes fail. Expansion was complete, as was penetration.

water penetration. Shot sizes run from TT through 6.

Swift

Swift makes what surely is one of the best, if not the very best in the world, premium softpoint hunting bullets. I suspect that Swift A-Frame bullets first gained a reputation among a select few, but extensively experienced, hunters. Their fame in Africa is getting to be, at the very least, most impressive. The A-Frame's basic construction is not unlike the more familiar Nosler Partition. There are, however, several differences,

the most important being the front core is bonded to the jacket. So when the bullet is fully expanded, it retains its mushroom and about 90 percent (often even more) of its original weight.

My field experience with these bullets began when Remington started the exclusive use of them for the soft-point loads in their Safari Grade ammo. Results on game were far better than I would have thought possible.

Swift makes a lot of bullet weights and diameters for turning reloads into the finest

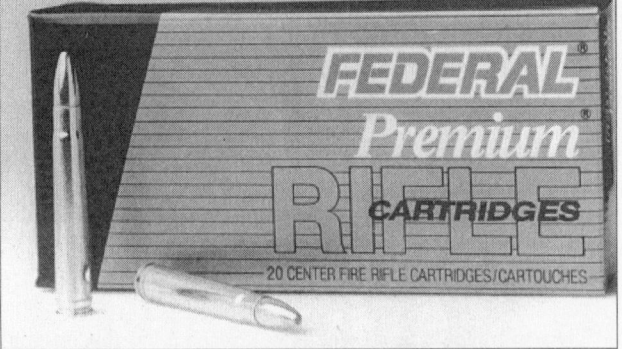

The monster basher of the new Trophy Bonded bullet loadings by Federal is a 300-grain 375 H&H Magnum loading; there's a 140-grain 270, too, and others.

hunting ammo possible. Thirty-caliber weights include 165-, 180- and the mentioned 200-grain. Bullets of 33-caliber are made in weights of 225, 250 and 275. The latter is a dandy for making a real monster masher out of a 338 Winchester Magnum. There are 35-caliber bullets in 225- and 250-grain weight and 9mm weights of 250 and 300 grains. Besides the 300-grain bullet mentioned for

.375-inch diameter, there is a 250-grain bullet. And how about .411-inch in weights of 350 and 400? In addition to the already mentioned .416-inch bullets, there are 400- and 500-grain weights in 45-caliber. If you want the finest big game bullets I have ever used, and this selection includes your favorite diameters, I promise you won't be disappointed.

These are not cheap, but considering all the costs of a good hunt, it is not unreasonable to pay from about $65 to $95 for fifty bullets. And, my good reader, minute-of-angle groups are possible with all of these that I have used.

Nosler

'Tis no secret, if you read any of the stuff that follows my bylines, that I have a very warm spot in my heart for Nosler Partition bullets. Seems some folks, based on my mail, do not fully understand how these work. The front 40 percent or so of the bullet expands early and rapidly. This allows a Partition to deliver maximum shock value, even when the critters are small. The front end continues to expand until there is nothing left to expand (velocity of the bullet and thickness

of the quarry permitting). The mushroom may even be eventually wiped completely away if you are using a large enough cartridge (read: high terminal velocity). At this point, penetration about equals the depth at which many mushrooming bullets stop forward movement. Complete penetration, with expansion continuing all the way, is accomplished on most broadside shots when game is

of the appropriate size for the bullet being used.

After that, a Partition continues to penetrate much as a solid would. All of this extra penetration is possible as the bullet will retain about 60 percent of its weight, even if the mushroom front portion is completely wiped away. Dependent upon circumstances, the rear section may continue front end first or it may tumble, traveling rear end first through the remainder of its wound channel. It is this extra penetration (combined with all that good early expansion) that makes the Partition a better killer than lesser bullets. If you have enough momentum (terminal velocity) for the bullet to penetrate past the mush point, then that is what happens, and it's all plus performance. Partition choices range from 85 grains in 6mm to 300 grains in .375-inch diameter.

Nosler handgun bullets seem to be heading toward the money-saving bulk packs. There are now eight bullets available only in the 250-bullet pack size.

While the number of Nosler Solid Base bullets was whittled down considerably last year, there is a new one this year. It is a bullet they make for Federal to load in 7-30 Waters cartridges—a 120-grain cannelured flatpoint. I guess it helps to have several outlets for each item. Or have factory fodder sales come to a standstill?

Winchester

The big news from the Illinois Winchester folks is the new big game rifle bullet which they have named after their successful deep-penetrating Black Talon handgun bullets. They start with 30-

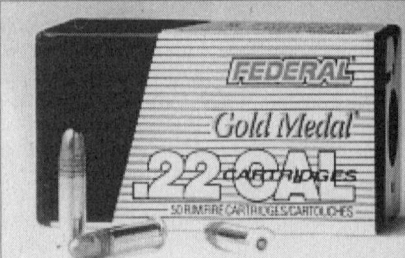

Match-grade 22 Long Rifle ammo is being loaded by Federal in three grades, Ultramatch, Match and Target. The worth of this ammo has already been proven by Olympic champions.

Do Swift bullets work well? This 700-pound zebra squared off with a single one, and it proved terminal. Penetration on a quartering shot was complete. The grins of Eric Matunas and professional hunter "Willie" Finaughty tell how the story went for ten critters with ten shots—A-Frames all.

all other modern high-performance handgun bullets are judged. It was the first of what is destined to be a long list of the get-any-job-done bullets. After a very successful introduction in semi-automatic cartridges, Winchester is now loading revolver rounds with this bullet. And they are using heavyweight bullets—a 180-grain for the 357 Magnum and a 250-grain for the 44 Magnum. Maybe Hal Swiggett will now agree there is finally a good 44 Magnum factory hunting load? Weight retention of 100 percent and good expansion should get the job done, even

$1\frac{1}{8}$-ounce load of No. 8 lead pellets. Velocity is 1235 fps., which should about balance out to lead target load velocity at the downrange distances at which clays are broken.

Other new shotshell loads include a 12-gauge Foster-type slug load in the 3-inch shell. It will add a lot of punch to guns which will shoot it accurately, as it has 3000 foot pounds of energy at the muzzle. Another new load is a 20-gauge 1-ounce target shell for competing with 12-gauge guns, or for informal shooting when you really want to grind up those clays. It would also make a great small bird load.

caliber 180-grain bullets in the 308, 30-06 and 300 Winchester Magnum cartridges. There also will be a 250-grain 338 Winchester Magnum load. All will be sold with a Black Talon Fail Safe Supreme logo.

Do not be confused by the nomenclature. This bullet is different from those used in its namesake handgun rounds. The front end of this new bullet in many ways resembles a Barnes all-copper X-Bullet. The four nose petals which form the "hollow" tip are designed to expand to 1.5x calibers and to retain 100 percent weight. A Winchester photo showed a unique secondary area of expansion immediately behind the four nose petals. The rear section is filled with lead, and thus the bullet is denser than the Barnes type. The whole affair is coated with a black-colored compound which adds lubricity to the bullet. Anything that cuts down on the barrel fouling of the new generation copper bullets is a great idea! No ammo was available at this writing for tests. If we

Nosler Partitions, which work so well on the heaviest of game, also perform their special magic on the smallest of critters. This 30 pounds or so of duiker is a trophy in its own right, as its four-inch horns attest. It was dropped with a single 180-grain Partition bullet fired from a T/C 30-30 Contender. The same load took 120-pound impala and an assortment of 600-pound critters with the shooting done by Eric Matunas.

can get a supply of 338 Winchester Magnum ammo before safari time, we can give it a good working out.

The Black Talon handgun bullet by Winchester may well become the one by which

through bone.

A steel shot target shotgun load is available for those who shoot in places where lead shot use has been banned. It uses 1 ounce of No. 7 shot and has a pellet count similar to a

Because the velocity of this load is a bit less than the $\frac{7}{8}$-ounce target loads, recoil is only a tad more. The Olin folks are using an orange hull on their standard-velocity field loads—called Super-X

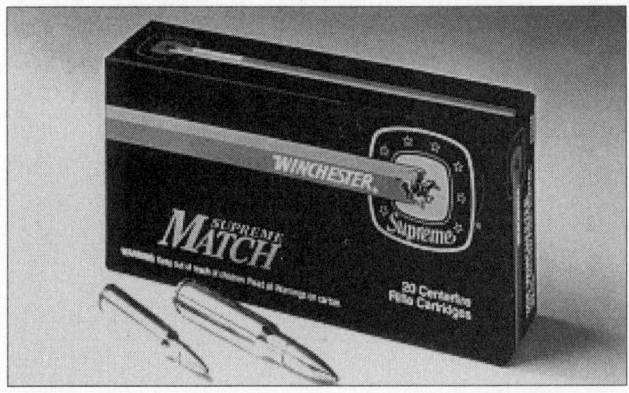

Match-grade ammo from Winchester for the 223 and 308 will be welcomed by accuracy-minded target shooters.

Heavy Black Talon-bulleted loads in the 357 and 44 Magnum should prove ideal for handgun hunting applications.

Small Game Hunter. This should make it easier not to leave any litter behind. We all pick up our empties, don't we?

When attempting to duplicate Winchester shotshell target loads, the reloader, for a long time, has been able to purchase the same powder, wads, and even the same shot used to assemble factory ammo. But the primer used in current factory ammo has been unavailable to the reloader. Now, for the first time, this is no longer true. Enter the new AATP primer. Now you can precisely match every component in a factory AA target load. Nice!

Blount

Blount, as most will recall, is the parent company of CCI, Speer, RCBS, Outers, and Weaver. Their CCI Blazer line of ammo (non-reloadable, Berdan-primed, aluminum case) has a lot of appeal to factory ammo shooters who want to save money by not having to purchase a reusable brass case. The popularity of this ammo is such that every year sees a few new loads. This year it is a 44 Special with a 200-grain "Gold Dot Bullet" and a 44 Magnum mid-velocity range (1200 fps) 240-grain softpoint.

As most readers are aware, there have been a great deal of new and improved jacketed handgun bullets. Various police agency testing is causing a demand for handgun bullets which will expand, not lose any mass, and penetrate

deeply. Speer's answer to this need is their "Gold Dot Bullets," so named for the bit of Uni-Cor jacket that shows in the center of the bullet's mushroom. These new handgun bullets have shown 97 percent weight retention in some tests, while still displaying dramatic expansion. These are all of the plated-to-the-core jacket construction and feature an eight-sided hollowpoint cavity. There are seven bullets of this type: 115-, 124-, and 147-grain 9mm; 155- and 180-grain 40-caliber; 185- and 230-grain 45-caliber. Prices range from about $11 to $16 per hundred.

There are two new TNT hollowpoint rifle bullets this year. These are a 70-grain

.243-inch and a 125-grain .308-inch. TNT bullets feature internal fluting for 90 percent of the jacket length. This means explosive performance on varmints at normal ranges and less likelihood of ricochets, too. These will expand at ranges where other bullets fail. Real nice for the serious varmint shooter!

If you are fairly new to premium big game bullets, we suggest you take a look at Speer's Grand Slam and African Grand Slam bullets. These give greatly enhanced performance for a not-too-great price premium. If you pursue anything bigger than deer or antelope, premium bullets are a real asset to the hunt.

Lyman's 47th Reloading Handbook has more information and data than any other similar publication. It is a must for every reloader's bench/library—Matunas, who edited it, says so.

Barnes

Barnes has been in the bullet business for a long time. However, they are enjoying an increased profile during recent years. No doubt that the enviable reputation of their true solid bullets has increased as more and more U.S. sportsmen hunt Africa. This has helped get the Barnes name in front of more reloaders. Also, their X-Bullet, a solid that expands—or if you prefer, an expanding bul-

Barnes all-copper X-Bullets retain high mass with reliable four-petal expansion and are available in a very wide range of calibers and weights.

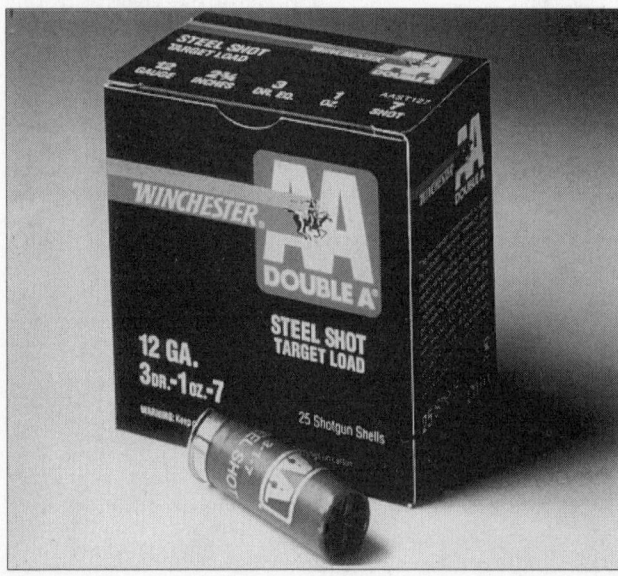

Is steel shot becoming the new standard? Here is a target load using steel pellets as assembled by Winchester.

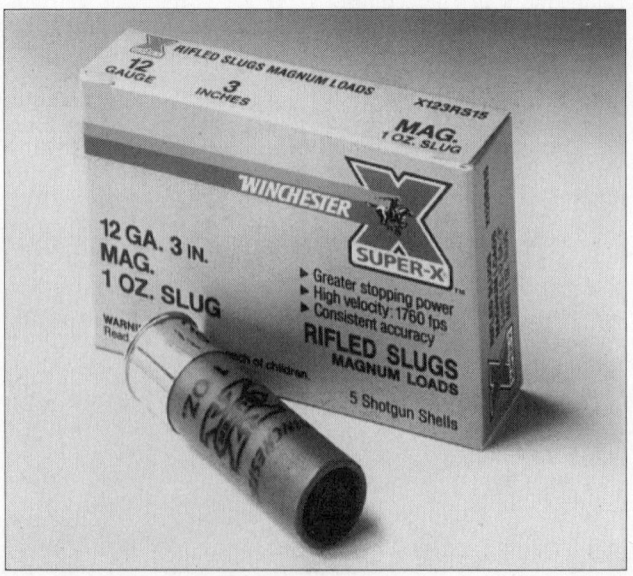

Winchester is now offering a 12-gauge 3-inch magnum Foster-type—3000 foot pounds of muzzle energy.

CCI Blazer's new 44 Special load has a 200-grain jacketed hollow-point bullet. Terminal ballistics are printed on the box, a thoughtful idea.

Another new Blazer load is a 240-grain softpoint for the 44 Magnum. It, too, has ballistics printed on the box.

let that has no separate core—is also responsible for the increased and deserved interest. Some shooters have noted that X-Bullets tend to foul bores more than the run-of-the-mill types. So, Barnes has introduced a new bore cleaner—CR-10. And to help the popularity of their bullets there is the *Barnes Number One Reloading Manual*. Both items will help the shooter/re-loader and Barnes.

There are a lot of new X-bullets for those who insist on deep penetration with reliable expansion. New are 100-grain weights in .264-, .277-, and .308-inch diameters. A 110-grain .308-inch, a 200-grain .323-inch, a 180-grain .358-inch, and finally a 210-grain .375-inch are the other latest offerings. New solids are monstrous 750- and 850-grain .510-inch bullets.

The X-Bullet approach will be used on new 9mm, 44- and 45-caliber handgun bullets, which may be about ready as this is read.

Hornady

At one time, if you wanted Weatherby ammo, you bought it from Weatherby. Then came PMC and Remington. Now, Hornady has Weatherby ammunition in two calibers—7mm and 300. The 28-caliber load comes with a 175-grain bullet and the 30-caliber load with a

180-grain bullet.

Muzzleloading fans can now buy their needs as packaged ammo. A box of twenty Hornady Great Plains hollow-base, hollowpoint conical bullets in 45- or 50-caliber, or fifteen in 54-caliber, with 100 percussion caps (Remington #11) and a 4-ounce jar of powder (Hodgdon Pyrodex) are all in one neat little pack. Should make getting what you need a bit easier as dealers will be more apt to stock these convenient packs. Price will be about $17.

For metallic silhouette handgun shooting, full-metal-cased bullets which stay together have the best chance of imparting sufficient momentum to dump the target. And jacketed bullets with no lead exposed at the base can be very accurate. Hornady's new Crimp Lock Silhouette handgun bullets provide both of these features. The bullet is fully jacketed at the base and the jacket is crimped over the nose end of the bullet like a shotshell case. Nifty idea that works in 44-caliber 240-grain. Other calibers and weights to follow? You betcha!

Midway

If you reload and do not have a Midway catalog (1-800-243-3220), you are missing a good thing. Many dealers do not stock the items that the more sophisticated

reloader wants. Inexpensive (very) bulk brass, Swift A-Frame bullets, Norma-brand components, Barnes X-Bullets and solid bullets, almost every reloading handbook printed, bulk bullets from the major ammunition makers, muzzleloading balls and conicals, and about any other reloading component (and more) that you can think of, they have it all. It is the low-cost brass and hard-to-find items that get most of my attention. There is no place locally that I can get 400-grain Swift A-Frame bullets and 416 Rigby cases.

Also, if you are one of those who load for the 50 BMG round, you know just how expensive and hard to find suitable components can be.

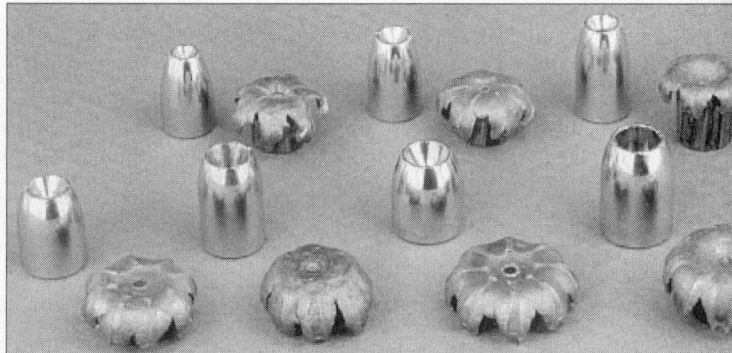

The new Gold Dot Speer bullets offer deep penetration as a result of expansion without loss of bullet mass and include 115-, 124- and 147-grain weight in 9mm diameter (rear row). Foreground left are 155- and 180-grain 40-caliber, and foreground right are 185- and 230-grain 45-caliber.

Midway has primers, bullets and cases for this cartridge.

Hodgdon

Hodgdon's latest handbook, *Data Manual #26*, is essential if you load with any of Hodgdon's powders, especially so if you use one of their latest propellants which are so new as not to be covered elsewhere. Also, this manual lists data for powders of the other major brands of propellants. The shotshell loading information section has also been notably revised.

Hodgdon has been introducing a new series of Australian-manufactured powders. The first of these was called Clays, and its performance as a 12-gauge target load powder is noteworthy. It also performs nicely in many popular handgun cartridges including 38 Special, 40 S&W and 45 ACP.

The other powders in this

series are Universal Clays and International Clays. Had anyone asked me, I would not have included the word Clays in the nomenclature, so as to avoid any potential confusion. Universal has loading applications similar to Hercules Unique. That makes it a very useful shotgun/handgun propellant. International is primarily a target load shotshell powder somewhat slower burning than Clays, and hence it will be very useful for 20-gauge fans.

Other New Data

Throwing away the old and getting the new information from powder manufacturers is not only good advice, but essential to safety. The Hercules 1992 data manual con-

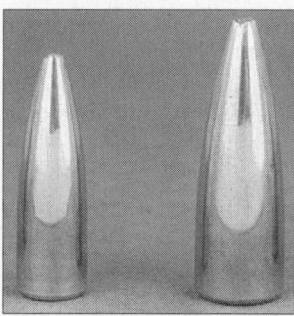

The two new super-explosive TNT bullets from Speer are a 70-grain in .243-inch diameter and one of 125 grains for .308-inch diameter.

tains a heap of new info, and if you don't have it, you should. For this year, there is a supplement containing data for Sporting Clays loads. It is also free and available at your favorite Hercules outlet. If you have not looked at a Hercules manual for a number of years, you will really be impressed with how the data listings have been expanded in all areas—rifle, handgun and shotgun.

Lyman has published the long awaited 47th edition of their reloading handbook. It is *greatly* expanded and nearly all of the editorial is completely new. You can find almost any technical question answered in one of its many parts. I know this to be true because I edited this effort. Scads of new data, lots of new cartridges, and more tips and techniques than you might ever hope for. Buy it and read it—you will be a more accomplished and knowledgeable reloader.

DBI Books' latest in smoothbore info is about to be published. *Reloading For Shotgunners*, 3rd edition, is *all new* and greatly expanded. Not much is published on shotshell reloading, and this one is really quite complete. Plenty of new data, over 2000 loads, hard-to-find shotshell ballistics, how-to, and an all-new format make this effort essential. Step-by-step reloading for the beginner and advanced pro are also included. No shotshell loading bench can be complete without this book. It was written by a most pleasant sort of fellow—yours truly.

Accurate's newest loading data book is quite enormous compared to earlier editions. You owe it to yourself to get a copy from an Accurate powder dealer if you use any of their propellants.

Garrett Cartridges

Garrett Cartridges has reduced, and wisely so, the number of 45-70 loads that they offer. The 45-70 Magnum load is gone—too great a chance of someone attempting to use it in one of the weak-actioned 45-70 rifles. Older inventories of this ammo should be used only exactly in accordance to label instructions. The 405- and 500-grain 45-70 loads are also gone. The 415-grain super-hard alloy bullet survives and is the sole future offering for this cartridge.

No changes to report in the 44 Magnum Garrett ammo line. The 280-, 310- and 330-grain extra-hard alloy bullets in this caliber have proven to provide near unbelievable penetration for this caliber.

They make fine hunting loads. These make the Washington state legal requirements for elk hunting *if* you have your sales receipt for the rounds in your pocket.

Gramp's Antique Cartridges

The number of inquiries I get annually for odd-ball ammo components is somewhat staggering. Gramp's Antique Cartridges can fill a very large percentage of the requests for these items. For example, proprietor Ellwood Epps offers everlasting cartridge cases in 577 Snider, 577/450, 43 Mauser, 42 Spanish, 11mm Gras, 450/400, 43 Egyptian, #2 Musket, 50-110 Winchester, 50-70 Government, 11x55R Turkish, and 461 No. 1 Gibbs.

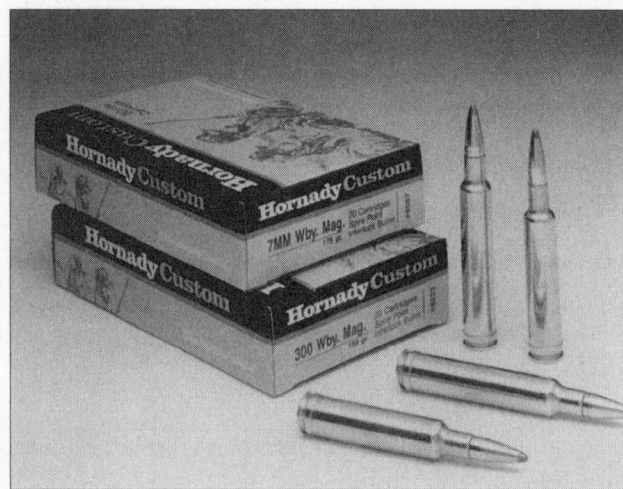

A new source of Weatherby cartridges in 7mm and 30-caliber is Hornady—175-grain in 7mm and 180-grain in 300 Weatherby Magnum.

Bertram drawn brass cases are available from GAC in the following calibers: 45 Basic 2.6-inch, 45 Basic 3.25-inch, 44 Sharps, 45-90, 40-90 Sharps, 40-82, 40-72, 40-65, 405 Winchester, 405 Basic 3.25-inch Bell, 38-72, 38-56, 35 Winchester, 33 Winchester, 30-30 Basic, 28-30 Stevens and 25-20 Single Shot. If you are looking for English calibers, you can select drawn brass for all of the following: 240 Flanged, 240 Belted, 6.5x58mmR, 7mm Rigby, 7mm H&H, 7x72mmR, 310 Cadet, 300 Sherwood, 300 Rook, 318 Rimless, 375 Flanged, 400/375 Belted, 400/360 Purdey, 400/360 Westley Richards, 400 Nitro 3-inch, and 450 Nitro.

And there are a lot more calibers available, too numerous to list here, including many metric rifle and some handgun cartridges. Also, Epps has reloading dies for many of these. Perhaps a phone call to Canada can resurrect one of your favorite possessions from wall hanger to a useful shooter.

Buffalo Bullet Company

Buffalo continues to offer a very wide range of muzzle-loading projectiles. They have balls, conicals and sabots to fit a wide range of applications and barrel twists. I used a number of their saboted units in 50-caliber this year. Accuracy was so good that I am afraid to give specifics, for fear someone who can't shoot and load well will fail to dupli-

cate my performances.

These saboted bullets are available in 45-, 50- and 54-caliber, and in several weights for each. The heaviest weights are for use in slow-twist barrels. Check local law before hunting with saboted bullets as these are

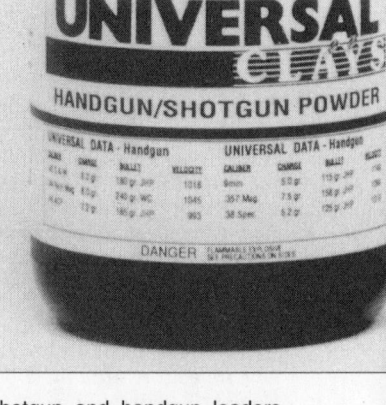

Shotgun and handgun loaders have a new source of fun—Hodgdon's new Clays series of powders which include Clays, Universal (shown) and International.

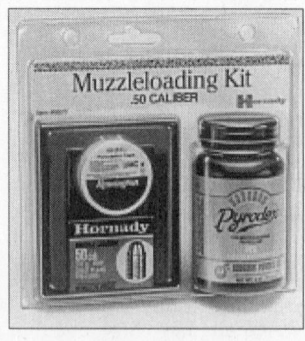

A convenient way to purchase muzzle-loading "ammo" is Hornady's new kit which gives you a choice of several bullet weights in each of 45-, 50- and 54-caliber and comes complete with enough caps and powder to use up all the bullets.

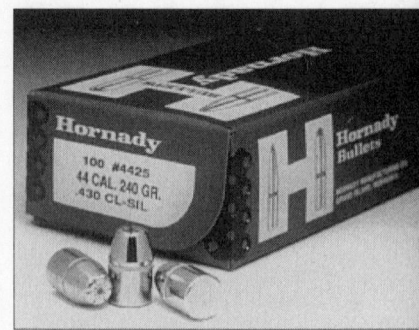

For more metallic silhouette handgun target bash, there is the new Hornady Crimp Lock Silhouette 240-grain 44-caliber bullet. Other weights and diameters soon.

not legal in all muzzleloading jurisdictions.

Buffalo also has more than a dozen conical bullets for 45-, 50-, 54- and 58-caliber front-stuffers. These are hollow-points, semipoints, round-noses, hollow-bases, and flat-bases available in almost all combinations of these. Yes, lots of round balls, too. I have shot more than a dozen big game animals with Buffalo bullets and a 50-caliber Thompson/Center Renegade. Each was a one-shot kill!

Cartridges Unlimited

If you do not reload, but nonetheless want to shoot an old-timer of U.S. or European ancestry, try calling Bill Smith at Cartridges Unlimited. While the list of calibers available is far too long for these pages, a sampling includes: 219 Zipper, 25-36 Marlin, 32-25 Stevens, 351 Winchester, 401 Winchester,

Even if it is hard to pronounce, V.O. is determined to become a factor in the U.S. propellant market.

Impact offers a wide range of handgun target and service loads at modest prices.

44 Evans, 5.6x61mm VH, 8x52 Siamese, 7mm Nambu, 10.4 Italian, 455 Webley and on and on and on. Bill says callers are welcomed on Saturdays and Sundays. Looking over their price list, it seems quite fair. Most items are actually affordable for frequent shooting, being priced more like currently available standard ammo—$10 to $28 per twenty rounds.

Cascade Custom Bullets

A great many custom bullet makers have come into existence during the past ten years. Each maker usually chooses to specialize in one or two diameters to keep the manufacturing cost manageable at their entry level. Some of these bullets, despite their hand-assembly methods, offer no real advantage in accuracy or controlled expansion for hunting as compared to standard-grade commercial bullets. Still, this outfit's Double-Lock bullets look like they would do a grand job in the hunting field. The design seems to be well thought out with no expense being spared for the sake of production

ease or ultimate market positioning.

The Double-Lock bullets, available at this writing only in .338-inch diameter, use a polycarbonate tip (a la Nosler's Ballistic Tip) which ensures early expansion even on smaller game or at extended ranges. This tip also eliminates battered bullet noses caused by recoil when the round is in the magazine. The front half of the bullet will continue to expand as long as the bullet has sufficient energy remaining to cause continued penetration. Expansion is stopped at a specific point by a heavy shoulder between the front and rear core sections. These bullets are not true partition types as there is joining of the front and rear cores at the center of the bullet via a small orifice. However, the partial partition appears to be more than heavy enough to guarantee that expansion will be halted. The solid lead core is bonded to the jacket, ensuring that weight retention will be maximized.

The base of the Double-Lock (Safari Grade) bullet is a rebated boattail to ensure minimum velocity loss at greater ranges. Some will like this feature enormously, but I would just as soon have a flat-base for a hunting bullet, though there are no major drawbacks to either type. There is a Premium Grade bullet also offered. This is described as sans polycarbonate tip and bonded core. I fail to see what this lesser grade offers as compared to a Nosler Partition at less than half the price. Contact Gene Lewis for more information.

VihtaVuori Oy

That's a real mouthful unless you happen to be Finnish or a student of languages. V.O. is trying to become the new kid on the reloading propellant block. But they are not new to powder manufacture, having been doing so for more than seventy years. They sell powder to a lot of countries for both military and sporting applications, even to U.S. ammo makers. And they do have data to support their 100-series rifle powders and 300-series handgun and shotshell powders.

Everything currently has a decidedly European flavor. Based on my near-decade of propellant marketing for Winchester, V.O. has a tough row to hoe. Still, the product is top quality and supported by good data. Indeed, the data booklet I reviewed contains a bunch of info that many reloaders would find enlightening. Good luck to the importers. For more info contact Robert Trownsell at Kaltron-Pettibone, 1241 Ellis Street, Bensenville, IL 60106 708-350-1606.

Miscellaneous

In the way of new cartridges, we now have a 416 Chapuis, a round that reportedly produces 416 Rigby/Remington ballistics at chamber pressures even lower than the Rigby. This so the round, as made by A-Square, can be used in double rifles, especially those made and chambered by Chapuis Arms.

A short while ago, I wrote a piece for *Guns Magazine* which could have been considered a modest appeal for beltless magnum cartridges. The article had no sooner been printed when Imperial Magnum Corporation ran an ad for their new series of cartridge cases. There were 7mm, 300, 311, 338 and 360 IM listed. These use a beltless case of 3.450-inch length with a rim diameter of .532-inch. They require the same bolt face and action length as the 375 H&H. IMC is claiming higher velocity due to increased case body diameter as compared to similar cartridges. Nonetheless, I would like these loaded to normal velocities at reduced chamber pressure—I am real tired of cartridges that produce more than 60,000 psi. Imperial Magnum says loaded ammo should appear next year. Perhaps.

Fiocchi of America imports shotshells from Italy. These tend to get to the consumer at bargain prices as compared to domestic ammunition. Like Remington and Winchester, Fiocchi now offers a 12-gauge target load using steel shot; though at 7/8-ounce of shot, it is somewhat lighter than the other brands. Nice load, if controlling recoil is important. Unlike most steel shot loads, this round uses a wad set-up that incorporates a cushioned leg section.

Recently, I have had the opportunity to burn up several

Steel shot loads that won't rust are sure to please waterfowl hunters. Plated shot, sealed crimps and primers are what get the job done.

cases of Activ Sporting Clays shotshell loads. One of these uses a spreader wad for those close-in shots, and another was a handicap load for the long shots. Both loads performed as expected and burned very, very clean. This is an especially nice feature if you use a semi-automatic shotgun.

Safari Classic Bullets offers you a chance to get bullets the way you want them. Variations in nose ogive, tip type, thin jackets, thick jackets, all lead, bullet weights and cannelure are all possible, just so long as what you need is .375-inch in diameter. Requirements from 38-55 to 378 Weatherby can be handled. Call Joe Arrington and tell him what you have in mind.

Ballard Built Custom Bullets is a fine source for hard-to-find .475- and .510-inch diameter bullets. Either diameter can be had in weights from 300 to 600 grains.

Conclusion

The main thrust in ammo and component development still seems to be the development of sophisticated hunting bullets. In that I consider myself a serious hunter, it is with delight that I test some of the new crop of such bullets each year in Africa. Most have proven quite effective. Those which have failed simply are forgotten, and very quickly. The accuracy levels of many of the premium bullets now used in factory big game ammunition is superb. For example, Remington's Swift A-Frame-bulleted Safari Grade ammo in 375 H&H has consistently provided minute-of-angle groups in two of my Ruger Mk. IIs. This wipes away the old and once true adage that factory ammo has better hunting bullets, but gives up a bit of accuracy. Some factory loads now have the best available hunting bullets and a superb level of accuracy—a level that many reloaders would be hard pressed to duplicate. Ammunition and components seem to be getting better each year. And that's splendid because I really enjoy proving this on critters around the world. ●

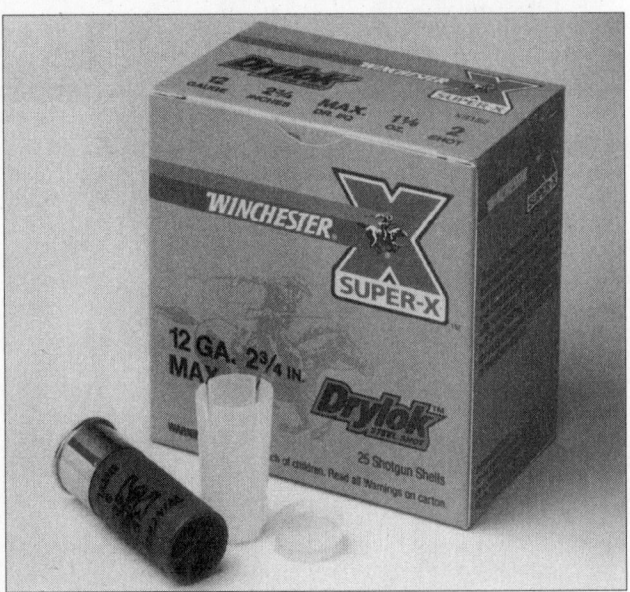

Water resistant steel shot loads are also available from Winchester.

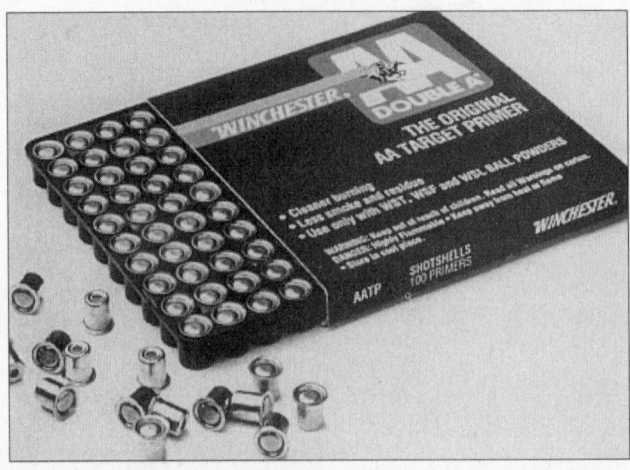

With the new availability of Winchester's AATP shotshell primer, the reloader can now duplicate every component in factory AA target loads. Perfect reloads.

UNSURPASSED STOPPING POWER.

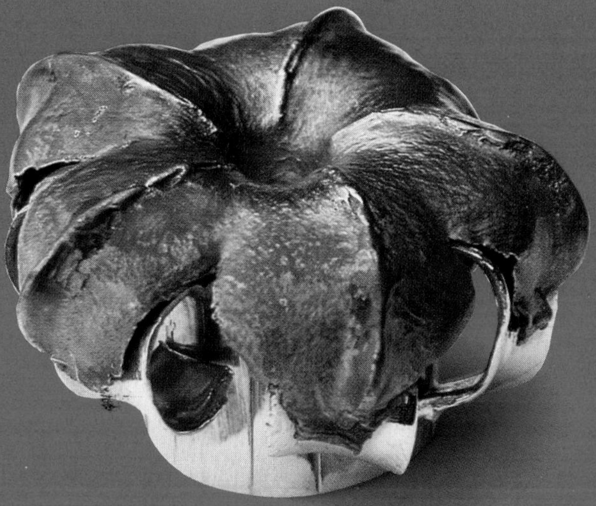

THAT'S A CLAIM WE CAN EXPAND ON.

Starfire™

No other handgun bullet delivers greater expansion or stopping power for home and personal protection or hunting. Starfire truly represents the cutting edge of bullet technology. The key to its broad, reliable expansion is in its patented rib and flute design. Five sharp-edged ribs stretch apart on impact, hyperexpanding the bullet to approximately twice its original diameter. Starfire penetrates deep, with virtually no fragmentation or weight loss.

The unique ribs also provide stabilizing central mass and weight for straighter, truer flight and superb accuracy.

Starfire. From PMC ammunition. Now available in all popular calibers. Ask your ammunition dealer.

If you're seriously looking for the ultimate in stopping power, please try Starfire. It will expand your views on handgun ammunition.

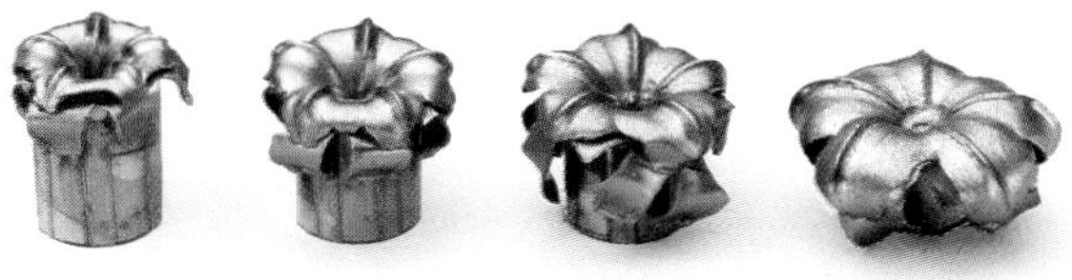

NOTHING HITS HARDER

PMC™
AMMUNITION
ELDORADO™
CARTRIDGE CORPORATION
Boulder City, Nevada 89005

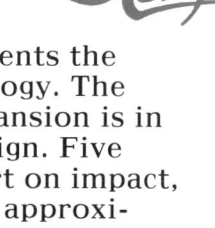

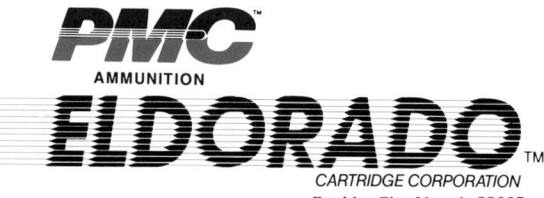

Realtree All-Purpose Camouflage

Now in its second year, Realtree All-Purpose camouflage has proven itself the most effective, most versatile camouflage available. Hunters have used All-Purpose successfully in all regions of the United States, Canada, Mexico, and elsewhere. No matter what game you pursue — whitetail deer, turkey, dove, ducks, geese, elk, pronghorn, or other — Realtree All-Purpose is quite simply the best camouflage you can choose.

Effective camouflage does two things: 1) It conceals the hunter by blending in with the natural surroundings. 2) It "breaks up" the human outline. *Realtree All-Purpose* does these two things better than any other camouflage on the market. How? By using not only trees, leaves, and limbs, but also open spaces — just like the patches of ground or sky found in all natural settings. These "holes" in the pattern keep All-Purpose from "closing up" at a distance, and effectively break up a hunter's outline by "separating" an arm or leg form the rest of the hunter.

BILL JORDAN'S
REALTREE®
America's Most Versatile Camo Pattern.™

THE CLASS OF 45

Three Classic Semiautomatics from the first name in 45 ACPs.

Colt's trusty service 45 is now back, in three distinctive models:

The Colt M1991A1™ takes off where the original G.I. 45 left off. Serial numbers run consecutively from our last batch in 1945.

The Colt M1991A1™ Commander features a barrel 3/4" shorter than standard, with a full-size grip for better control and 7-round magazine capacity.

The Colt M1991A1™ Compact is 1-1/4" shorter and 3/4" less in height. It has the legendary stopping power of its big brother, in a more concealable package.

Remember, the 45 ACP semiautomatics you can rely on are the ones that proudly display the Colt trademark. See them at your Colt dealer today.

1991A1

1991A1 Commander

1991A1 Compact

COLT®

Colt's Manufacturing Company, Inc. P.O. Box 1868, Hartford, CT 06144-1868

Warning: Be a safe shooter – never chamber a round until you are ready to shoot. Always read and follow the instruction manual which accompanies each firearm. Free instruction manuals are available upon request.

	Caliber	Bullet weight grains	Muzzle	-VELOCITY (fps)-				Muzzle	-ENERGY (ft. lbs.)-				-TRAJ. (in.)-				Approx. Price per box
				100 yds.	200 yds.	300 yds.	400 yds.		100 yds.	200 yds.	300 yds.	400 yds.	100 yds.	200 yds.	300 yds.	400 yds.	
17	17 Remington	25	4040	3284	2644	2086	1606	906	599	388	242	143	+2.0	+1.7	-4.0	-17.0	$15
	221 Fireball	50	2800	2137	1580	1180	988	870	507	277	155	109	0.0	-7.0	-28.0	NA	$14
22	22 Hornet	45	2690	2042	1502	1128	948	723	417	225	127	90	0.0	-7.7	-31.0	NA	$27**
	218 Bee	46	2760	2102	1550	1155	961	788	451	245	136	94	0.0	-7.2	-29.0	NA	$46**
	222 Remington	50	3140	2602	2123	1700	1350	1094	752	500	321	202	+2.0	-0.4	-11.0	-33.0	$11.
	222 Remington	55	3020	2562	2147	1773	1451	1114	801	563	384	257	+2.0	-0.4	-11.0	-33.0	$11.
	22 PPC	52	3400	2930	2510	2130	NA	1335	990	730	525	NA	+2.0	=1.4	-5.0	NA	NA
	223 Remington	40	3650	3010	2450	1950	1530	1185	805	535	340	265	+2.0	+1.0	-6.0	-22.0	$12
	223 Remington	52/53	3330	2882	2477	2106	1770	1305	978	722	522	369	+2.0	+0.6	-6.5	-21.5	$14.
	223 Remington	55	3240	2748	2305	1906	1556	1282	922	649	444	296	+2.0	-0.2	-9.0	-27.0	$12.
	223 Remington	60	3100	2712	2355	2026	1726	1280	979	739	547	397	+2.0	+0.2	-8.0	-24.7	$15
	223 Remington	64	3020	2621	2256	1920	1619	1296	977	723	524	373	+2.0	-0.2	-9.3	-23.0	$14.
	223 Remington	69	3000	2720	2460	2210	1980	1380	1135	925	750	600	+2.0	+0.8	-5.8	-17.5	$15.
	222 Rem. Mag.	55	3240	2748	2305	1906	1556	1282	922	649	444	296	+2.0	-0.2	-9.0	-27.0	$13
	225 Winchester	55	3570	3066	2616	2208	1838	1556	1148	836	595	412	+2.0	+1.0	-5.0	-20.0	$19.
	224 Wea. Mag.	55	3650	3192	2780	2403	2057	1627	1244	943	705	516	+2.0	+1.2	-4.0	-17.0	$32
	22-250 Rem.	40	4000	3320	2720	2200	1740	1420	980	660	430	265	+2.0	+1.8	-3.0	-16.0	$13
	22-250 Rem.	52/55c	3680	3137	2656	2222	1832	1654	1201	861	603	410	+2.0	+1.3	-4.0	-17.0	$13.
	22-250 Rem.	60	3600	3195	2826	2485	2169	1727	1360	1064	823	627	+2.0	+2.0	-2.4	-12.3	$19
	220 Swift	50	3780	3158	2617	2135	1710	1586	1107	760	506	325	+2.0	+1.4	-4.4	-17.9	NA
	220 Swift	55	3650	3194	2772	2384	2035	1627	1246	939	694	506	+2.0	+2.0	-2.6	-13.4	$19
	220 Swift	60	3600	3199	2824	2475	2156	1727	1364	1063	816	619	+2.0	+1.6	-4.1	-13.1	$19
	22 Savage H.P	71	2790	2340	1930	1570	1280	1225	860	585	390	190	+2.0	-1.0	-10.4	-35.7	NA
6mm (24)	6mm BR Rem.	100	2550	2310	2083	1870	1671	1444	1185	963	776	620	+2.5	-0.6	-11.8	NA	$20
	6mm PPC	70	3140	2750	2400	2070	NA	1535	1175	895	665	NA	+2.0	+1.4	-5.0	NA	NA
	243 Winchester	60	3600	3110	2660	2260	1890	1725	1285	945	680	475	+2.0	+1.8	-3.3	-15.5	$15
	243 Winchester	75/80	3350	2955	2593	2259	1951	1993	1551	1194	906	676	+2.0	+0.9	-5.0	-19.0	$15.
	243 Winchester	85	3320	3070	2830	2600	2380	2080	1770	1510	1280	1070	+2.0	+1.2	-4.0	-14.0	$15
	243 Winchester*	100	2960	2697	2449	2215	1993	1945	1615	1332	1089	882	+2.5	+1.2	-6.0	-20.0	$15.
	243 Winchester	105	2920	2689	2470	2261	2062	1988	1686	1422	1192	992	+2.5	+1.6	-5.0	-18.4	NA
	6mm Remington	80	3470	3064	2694	2352	2036	2139	1667	1289	982	736	+2.0	+1.1	-5.0	-17.0	$16.
	6mm Remington*	100	3100	2829	2573	2332	2104	2133	1777	1470	1207	983	+2.5	+1.6	-5.0	-17.0	$16.
	6mm Remington	105	3060	2822	2596	2381	2177	2105	1788	1512	1270	1059	+2.5	+1.1	-3.3	-15.0	NA
	240 Wea. Mag.	87	3500	3202	2924	2663	2416	2366	1980	1651	1370	1127	+2.0	+2.0	-2.0	-12.0	$32
	240 Wea. Mag *	100	3395	3106	2835	2581	2339	2559	2142	1785	1478	1215	+2.5	+2.8	-2.0	-11.0	$43
25	25-20 Win.	86	1460	1194	1030	931	858	407	272	203	165	141	0.0	-23.5	NA	NA	$35**
	25-35 Win.	117	2230	1866	1545	1282	1097	1292	904	620	427	313	+2.5	-4.2	-26.0	NA	$23.
	250 Savage	100	2820	2504	2210	1936	1684	1765	1392	1084	832	630	+2.5	+0.4	-9.0	-28.0	$18.
	257 Roberts	100	2980	2661	2363	2085	1827	1972	1572	1240	965	741	+2.5	-0.8	-5.2	-21.6	$20.
	257 Roberts	117	2780	2411	2071	1761	1488	2009	1511	1115	806	576	+2.5	-0.2	-10.2	-32.6	$17.
	257 Roberts +P*	120	2780	2560	2360	2160	1970	2060	1750	1480	1240	1030	+2.5	+1.2	-6.4	-23.6	$17
	257 Roberts	122	2600	2331	2078	1842	1625	1831	1472	1169	919	715	+2.5	0.0	-10.6	-31.4	NA
	25-06 Rem.	87	3440	2995	2591	2222	1884	2286	1733	1297	954	686	+2.0	+1.1	-2.5	-14.4	$17
	25-06 Rem.	90	3440	3043	2680	2344	2034	2364	1850	1435	1098	827	+2.0	+1.8	-3.3	-15.6	$17.
	25-06 Rem.	100	3230	2893	2580	2287	2014	2316	1858	1478	1161	901	+2.0	+0.8	-5.7	-18.9	$17
	25-06 Rem.	117	2990	2770	2570	2370	2190	2320	2000	1715	1465	1246	+2.5	+1.0	-7.9	-26.6	$17
	25-06 Rem.	120	2990	2730	2484	2252	2032	2382	1985	1644	1351	1100	+2.5	+1.2	-5.3	-19.6	$17.
	25-06 Rem.	122	2930	2706	2492	2289	2095	2325	1983	1683	1419	1189	+2.5	+1.8	-4.5	-17.5	NA
	257 Wea. Mag.	87	3825	3456	3118	2805	2513	2826	2308	1870	1520	1220	+2.0	+2.7	-0.3	-7.6	$32
	257 Wea. Mag.	100	3555	3237	2941	2665	2404	2806	2326	1920	1576	1283	+2.5	+3.2	0.0	-8.0	$32
	257 Wea. Mag.*	120	3300	3056	2823	2599	2388	2902	2489	2124	1800	1520	+2.5	+3.2	-4.1	-18.4	$47
6.5	6.5x50mm Jap.	139	2360	2160	1970	1790	1620	1720	1440	1195	985	810	+2.5	-1.0	-13.5	NA	NA
	6.5x50mm Jap.	156	2070	1830	1610	1430	1260	1475	1155	900	695	550	+2.5	-4.0	-23.8	NA	NA
	6.5x52mm Car.	139	2580	2360	2160	1970	1790	2045	1725	1440	1195	985	+2.5	0.0	-9.9	-29.0	NA
	6.5x52mm Car.	156	2430	2170	1930	1700	1500	2045	1630	1285	1005	780	+2.5	-1.0	-13.9	NA	NA
	6.5x55mm Swe.*	139/140	2850	2640	2440	2250	2070	2525	2170	1855	1575	1330	+2.5	+1.6	-5.4	-18.9	NA
	6.5x55mm Swe.	156	2650	2370	2110	1870	1650	2425	1950	1550	1215	945	+2.5	0.0	-10.3	-30.6	NA
	6.5 Rem. Mag.	120	3210	2905	2621	2353	2102	2745	2248	1830	1475	1177	+2.5	+1.7	-4.1	-16.3	Disc.
	264 Win. Mag.	140	3030	2782	2548	2326	2114	2854	2406	2018	1682	1389	+2.5	+1.4	-5.1	-18.0	$23.

CAUTION: PRICES CHANGE, CHECK AT GUNSHOP.

Caliber	Bullet weight grains	Muzzle	100 yds.	200 yds.	300 yds.	400. yds.	Muzzle	100 yds.	200 yds.	300 yds.	400 yds.	100 yds.	200 yds.	300 yds.	400 yds.	Approx. Price per box
				-VELOCITY (fps)-					-ENERGY (ft. lbs.)-					-TRAJ. (in.)-		
270 Winchester	100	3430	3021	2649	2305	1988	2612	2027	1557	1179	877	+2.0	+1.0	-4.9	-17.5	$17.
270 Winchester	130	3060	2776	2510	2259	2022	2702	2225	1818	1472	1180	+2.5	+1.4	-5.3	-18.2	$17.
270 Winchester	135†	3000	2780	2570	2369	2178	2697	2315	1979	1682	1421	+2.5	+1.4	-6.0	-17.6	$21
270 Winchester*	140†	2940	2700	2480	2260	2060	2685	2270	1905	1590	1315	+2.5	+1.8	-4.6	-17.9	$21
270 Winchester* 150	2850	2585	2336	2100	1879	2705	2226	1817	1468	1175	+2.5	+1.2	-6.5	-22.0	$17.
270 Wea. Mag.	100	3760	3380	3033	2712	2412	3139	2537	2042	1633	1292	+2.0	+2.4	-1.2	-10.1	$32
270 Wea. Mag.	130	3375	3119	2878	2649	2432	3287	2808	2390	2026	1707	+2.5	+2.9	-0.9	-9.9	$32
270 Wea. Mag.*	150	3245	3036	2837	2647	2465	3507	3070	2681	2334	2023	+2.5	+2.6	-1.8	-11.4	$47
7mm BR	140	2215	2012	1821	1643	1481	1525	1259	1031	839	681	+2.0	-3.7	-20.0	NA	$20
7mm Mauser*	139/140	2660	2435	2221	2018	1827	2199	1843	1533	1266	1037	+2.5	0.0	-9.6	-27.7	$17
7mm Mauser	145	2690	2442	2206	1985	1777	2334	1920	1568	1268	1017	+2.5	+0.1	-9.6	-28.3	$17.
7mm Mauser	154	2690	2490	2300	2120	1940	2475	2120	1810	1530	1285	+2.5	+0.8	-7.5	-23.5	$17
7mm Mauser	175	2440	2137	1857	1603	1382	2313	1774	1340	998	742	+2.5	-1.7	-16.1	NA	$17
7 x 30 Waters	120	2700	2300	1930	1600	1330	1940	1405	990	685	470	+2.5	-0.2	-12.3	NA	$17.
7mm-08 Rem.	120	3000	2725	2467	2223	1992	2398	1979	1621	1316	1058	+2.0	0.0	-7.6	-22.3	$17
7mm-08 Rem.*	140	2860	2625	2402	2189	1988	2542	2142	1793	1490	1228	+2.5	+0.8	-6.9	-21.9	$17
7mm-08 Rem.	154	2715	2510	2315	2128	1950	2520	2155	1832	1548	1300	+2.5	+1.0	-7.0	-22.7	NA
7x64mm Bren.	154	2820	2610	2420	2230	2050	2720	2335	1995	1695	1430	+2.5	+1.4	-5.7	-19.9	NA
7x64mm Bren.*	160	2850	2669	2495	2327	2166	2885	2530	2211	1924	1667	+2.5	+1.6	-4.8	-17.8	NA
284 Winchester	150	2860	2595	2344	2108	1886	2724	2243	1830	1480	1185	+2.5	+0.8	-7.3	-23.2	$23.
280 Remington	120	3150	2866	2599	2348	2110	2643	2188	1800	1468	1186	+2.0	+0.6	-6.0	-17.9	$17
280 Remington	140	3000	2758	2528	2309	2102	2797	2363	1986	1657	1373	+2.5	+1.4	-5.2	-18.3	$17.
280 Remington*	150	2890	2624	2373	2135	1912	2781	2293	1875	1518	1217	+2.5	+0.8	-7.1	-22.6	$17
280 Remington	160†	2840	2637	2442	2556	2078	2866	2471	2120	1809	1535	+2.5	+0.8	-6.7	-21.0	$19.
280 Remington	165	2820	2510	2220	1950	1701	2913	2308	1805	1393	1060	+2.5	+0.4	-8.8	-26.5	$17
7x61mm S&H Sup.	154	3060	2720	2400	2100	1820	3200	2520	1965	1505	1135	+2.5	+1.8	-5.0	-19.8	NA
7mm Rem. Mag.*†	139/140c	3150	2930	2710	2510	2320	3085	2660	2290	1960	1670	+2.5	+2.4	-2.4	-12.7	$21
7mm Rem. Mag.	150/154	3110	2830	2585	2320	2085	3221	2667	2196	1792	1448	+2.5	+1.6	-4.6	-16.5	$21.
7mm Rem. Mag.*	160/162	2950	2730	2520	2320	2120	3090	2650	2250	1910	1600	+2.5	+1.8	-4.4	-17.8	$26
7mm Rem. Mag.	165	2900	2699	2507	2324	2147	3081	2669	2303	1978	1689	+2.5	+1.2	-5.9	-19.0	NA
7mm Rem. Mag.	175	2860	2645	2440	2244	2057	3178	2718	2313	1956	1644	+2.5	+1.0	-6.5	-20.7	$21.
7mm Wea. Mag.	140	3225	2970	2729	2501	2283	3233	2741	2315	1943	1621	+2.5	+2.0	-3.2	-14.0	$21
7mm Wea. Mag.	154	3260	3023	2799	2586	2382	3539	3044	2609	2227	1890	+2.5	+2.8	-1.5	-10.8	$32
7mm Wea. Mag.*	160	3200	3004	2816	2637	2464	3637	3205	2817	2469	2156	+2.5	+2.7	-1.5	-10.6	$47
7mm Wea. Mag.	165	2950	2747	2553	2367	2189	3188	2765	2388	2053	1756	+2.5	+1.8	-4.2	-16.4	NA
7mm Wea. Mag.	175c	2910	2693	2486	2288	2098	3293	2818	2401	2033	1711	+2.5	+1.2	-5.9	-19.4	$32
30 Carbine	110	1990	1567	1236	1035	923	977	600	373	262	208	0.0	-13.5	NA	NA	$27**
303 Savage	190	1890	1612	1372	1183	1055	1507	1096	794	591	469	+2.5	-7.6	NA	NA	$23
30 Remington	170	2120	1822	1555	1328	1153	1696	1253	913	666	502	+2.5	-4.7	-26.3	NA	$18
30-30 Win.	55	3400	2693	2085	1570	1187	1412	886	521	301	172	+2.0	0.0	-10.2	-35.0	$16
30-30 Win.	125	2570	2090	1660	1320	1080	1830	1210	770	480	320	+2.0	-2.6	-19.9	NA	NA
30-30 Win.	150	2390	1973	1605	1303	1095	1902	1296	858	565	399	+2.5	-3.2	-22.5	NA	$13.
30-30 Win.	160†	2300	1997	1719	1473	1268	1879	1416	1050	771	571	+2.5	-2.9	-20.2	NA	$14
30-30 Win.*	170	2200	1895	1619	1381	1191	1827	1355	989	720	535	+2.5	-5.8	-23.6	NA	$13.
300 Savage	150	2630	2354	2094	1853	1631	2303	1845	1462	1143	886	+2.5	-0.4	-10.1	-30.7	$17.
300 Savage	180	2350	2137	1935	1754	1570	2207	1825	1496	1217	985	+2.5	-1.6	-15.2	NA	$17.
30-40 Krag	180	2430	2213	2007	1813	1632	2360	1957	1610	1314	1064	+2.5	-1.4	-13.8	NA	$19.
7.65x53mm Arg.	180	2590	2390	2200	2010	1830	2685	2280	1925	1615	1345	+2.5	0.0	-27.6	NA	NA
307 Winchester	150	2760	2321	1924	1575	1289	2530	1795	1233	826	554	+2.5	-1.5	-13.6	NA	Disc.
307 Winchester	180	2510	2179	1874	1599	1362	2519	1898	1404	1022	742	+2.5	-1.6	-15.6	NA	$20.
7.5x55 Swiss	180	2650	2450	2250	2060	1880	2805	2390	2020	1700	1415	+2.5	+0.6	-8.1	-24.9	NA
308 Winchester	55	3770	3215	2726	2286	1888	1735	1262	907	638	435	+2.0	+1.4	-3.8	-15.8	$19
308 Winchester	150	2820	2533	2263	2009	1774	2648	2137	1705	1344	1048	+2.5	+0.4	-8.5	-26.1	$17.
308 Winchester	165	2700	2440	2194	1963	1748	2670	2180	1763	1411	1199	+2.5	0.0	-9.7	-28.5	$18
308 Winchester	168	2680	2493	2314	2143	1979	2678	2318	1998	1713	1460	+2.5	0.0	-8.9	-25.3	$18.
308 Winchester	178	2620	2415	2220	2034	1857	2713	2306	1948	1635	1363	+2.5	0.0	-9.6	-27.6	$21
308 Winchester*	180	2620	2393	2178	1974	1782	2743	2288	1896	1557	1269	+2.5	-0.2	-10.2	-28.5	$17.
30-06 Spfd.	55	4080	3485	2965	2502	2083	2033	1483	1074	764	530	+2.0	+1.9	-2.1	-11.7	$19
30-06 Spfd.	125	3140	2780	2447	2138	1853	2736	2145	1662	1279	953	+2.0	+1.0	-6.2	-21.0	$17.
30-06 Spfd.	150	2910	2617	2342	2083	1853	2820	2281	1827	1445	1135	+2.5	+0.8	-7.2	-23.4	$17.
30-06 Spfd.	152	2910	2654	2413	2184	1968	2858	2378	1965	1610	1307	+2.5	+1.0	-6.6	-21.3	$21
30-06 Spfd.*	165	2800	2534	2283	2047	1825	2872	2352	1909	1534	1220	+2.5	+0.4	-8.4	-25.5	$19.
30-06 Spfd.	168	2710	2522	2346	2169	2003	2739	2372	2045	1754	1497	+2.5	+0.4	-8.0	-23.5	$20

27

7mm

30

CAUTION: PRICES CHANGE, CHECK AT GUNSHOP.

	Caliber	Bullet weight grains	Muzzle	100 yds.	200 yds.	300 yds.	400. yds.	Muzzle	100 yds.	200 yds.	300 yds.	400 yds.	100 yds.	200 yds.	300 yds.	400 yds.	Approx. Price per box
				-VELOCITY (fps)-					-ENERGY (ft. lbs.)-					-TRAJ. (in.)-				
30 (cont.)	30-06 Spfd.	178	2720	2511	2311	2121	1939	2924	2491	2111	1777	1486	+2.5	+0.4	-8.2	-24.6	$21
	30-06 Spfd.*	180	2700	2469	2250	2042	1846	2913	2436	2023	1666	1362	+2.5	0.0	-9.3	-27.0	$17.
	30-06 Spfd.	220	2410	2130	1870	1632	1422	2837	2216	1708	1301	988	+2.5	-1.7	-16.0	NA	$17.
30 Mag	308 Norma Mag.	180	3020	2820	2630	2440	2270	3645	3175	2755	2385	2050	+2.5	+2.0	-3.5	-14.8	NA
	300 H&H Magnum*	180	2880	2640	2412	2196	1990	3315	2785	2325	1927	1583	+2.5	+0.8	-6.8	-21.7	$25.
	300 H&H Magnum	220	2550	2267	2002	1757	NA	3167	2510	1958	1508	NA	+2.5	-0.4	-12.0	NA	NA
	300 Win. Mag.	150	3290	2951	2636	2342	2068	3605	2900	2314	1827	1424	+2.5	+1.9	-3.8	-15.8	$22.
	300 Win. Mag.	165	3100	2877	2665	2462	2269	3522	3033	2603	2221	1897	+2.5	+2.4	-3.0	-16.9	$24
	300 Win. Mag.	178	2980	2769	2568	2375	2191	3509	3030	2606	2230	1897	+2.5	+1.4	-5.0	-17.6	$27
	300 Win. Mag.*	180	2960	2745	2540	2344	2157	3501	3011	2578	2196	1859	+2.5	+1.2	-5.5	-18.5	$22.
	300 Win. Mag.	190	2885	2691	2506	2327	2156	3511	3055	2648	2285	1961	+2.5	+1.2	-5.7	-19.0	$25.
	300 Win. Mag.*	200c	2825	2595	2376	2167	1970	3545	2991	2508	2086	1742	+2.5	+1.6	-4.7	-17.2	NA
	300 Win. Mag.	220	2680	2448	2228	2020	1823	3508	2927	2424	1993	1623	+2.5	0.0	-9.5	-27.5	$22.
	300 Wea. Mag.	110	3900	3441	3038	2652	2305	3714	2891	2239	1717	1297	+2.0	+2.6	-0.6	-8.7	$32
	300 Wea. Mag.	150	3600	3307	3033	2776	2533	4316	3642	3064	2566	2137	+2.5	+3.2	0.0	-8.1	$32
	300 Wea. Mag.	165	3450	3210	3000	2792	2593	4360	3796	3297	2855	2464	+2.5	+3.2	0.0	-7.8	N.A
	300 Wea. Mag.	178	3120	2902	2695	2497	2308	3847	3329	2870	2464	2104	+2.5	-1.7	-3.6	-14.7	$39
	300 Wea. Mag.*	180	3120	2866	2667	2400	2184	3890	3284	2758	2301	1905	+2.5	+1.7	-3.8	-15.0	$56
	300 Wea. Mag.	190	3030	2830	2638	2455	2279	3873	3378	2936	2542	2190	+2.5	+1.6	-4.3	-16.0	$35
	300 Wea. Mag.	220	2850	2541	2283	1984	1736	3967	3155	2480	1922	1471	+2.5	+0.4	-8.5	-26.4	$35
31	32-20 Win.	100	1210	1021	913	834	769	325	231	185	154	131	0.0	-32.3	NA	NA	$22**.
	303 British	150	2685	2441	2210	1992	1787	2401	1984	1627	1321	1064	+2.5	+0.6	-8.4	-26.2	$19
	303 British	180	2460	2124	1817	1542	1311	2418	1803	1319	950	687	+2.5	-1.8	-16.8	NA	$17
	7.62x39mm Rus.	123/125	2300	2030	1780	1550	1350	1445	1125	860	655	500	+2.5	-2.0	-17.5	NA	$15.
	7.62x54mm Rus.	146	2950	2730	2520	2320	NA	2820	2415	2055	1740	NA	+2.5	+2.0	-4.4	-17.7	NA
	7.62x54mm Rus.	180	2580	2370	2180	2000	1820	2650	2250	1900	1590	1100	+2.5	0.0	-9.8	-28.5	NA
	7.7x58mm Jap.	180	2500	2300	2100	1920	1750	2490	2105	1770	1475	1225	+2.5	0.0	-10.4	-30.2	NA
8mm	8x57mm JS Mau.	165	2850	2520	2210	1930	1670	2965	2330	1795	1360	1015	+2.5	+1.0	-7.7	NA	NA
	32 Win.Special	170	2250	1921	1626	1372	1175	1911	1393	998	710	521	+2.5	-3.5	-22.9	NA	$14.
	8mm Mauser	170	2360	1969	1622	1333	1123	2102	1464	993	671	476	+2.5	-3.1	-22.2	NA	$17.
	8mm Rem. Mag.	185	3080	2761	2464	2186	1927	3896	3131	2494	1963	1525	+2.5	+1.4	-5.5	-19.7	$27
	8mm Rem. Mag.	220	2830	2581	2346	2123	1913	3912	3254	2688	2201	1787	+2.5	+0.6	-7.6	-23.5	Disc.
33	338 Win. Mag.	200	2960	2658	2375	2110	1862	3890	3137	2505	1977	1539	+2.5	+1.0	-6.7	-22.3	$26.
	338 Win. Mag.*	210	2830	2590	2370	2150	1940	3735	3130	2610	2155	1760	+2.5	+1.4	-6.0	-20.9	NA
	338 Win. Mag.*	225	2785	2517	2266	2029	1808	3871	3165	2565	2057	1633	+2.5	+0.4	-8.5	-25.9	$26.
	338 Win. Mag.*	250	2660	2456	2261	2075	1898	3927	3348	2837	2389	1999	+2.5	+0.2	-9.0	-26.2	$26
	340 Wea. Mag.*	210	3250	2991	2746	2515	2295	4924	4170	3516	2948	2455	+2.5	1.9	-1.8	-11.8	$56
	340 Wea. Mag.*	250	3000	2806	2621	2443	2272	4995	4371	3812	3311	2864	+2.5	+2.0	-3.5	-14.8	$56
	338 A-Square	250	3120	2799	2500	2220	1958	5403	4348	3469	2736	2128	+2.5	+2.7	-1.5	-10.5	NA
34	348 Winchester	200	2520	2215	1931	1672	1443	2820	2178	1656	1241	925	+2.5	-1.4	-14.7	NA	$40.
35	357 Magnum	158	1830	1427	1138	980	883	1175	715	454	337	274	0.0	-16.2	-33.1	NA	$25**.
	35 Remington	150	2300	1874	1506	1218	1039	1762	1169	755	494	359	+2.5	-4.1	-26.3	NA	$16
	35 Remington	200	2080	1698	1376	1140	1001	1921	1280	841	577	445	+2.5	-6.3	-17.1	-33.6	$15.
	356 Winchester	200	2460	2114	1797	1517	1284	2688	1985	1434	1022	732	+2.5	-1.8	-17.1	NA	$31.
	356 Winchester	250	2160	1911	1682	1476	1299	2591	2028	1571	1210	937	+2.5	-3.7	-22.2	NA	$31.
	358 Winchester	200	2490	2171	1876	1619	1379	2753	2093	1563	1151	844	+2.5	-1.6	-15.6	NA	$31.
	350 Rem. Mag.	200	2710	2410	2130	1870	1631	3261	2579	2014	1553	1181	+2.5	-0.2	-10.0	-30.1	$29
	35 Whelen	200	2675	2378	2100	1842	1606	3177	2510	1958	1506	1145	+2.5	-0.2	-10.3	-31.1	$18
	35 Whelen	250	2400	2197	2005	1823	1652	3197	2680	2230	1844	1515	+2.5	-1.2	-13.7	NA	$18
	358 Norma Mag.	250	2800	2510	2230	1970	1730	4350	3480	2750	2145	1655	+2.5	+1.0	-7.6	-25.2	NA
9.3	9.3x57mm Mau.	286	2070	1810	1590	1390	1110	2710	2090	1600	1220	955	+2.5	-2.6	-22.5	NA	NA
	9.3 x 62mm Mau.	286	2360	2089	1844	1623	NA	3538	2771	2157	1670	1260	+2.5	-1.6	-21.0	NA	NA
	9.3 x 64mm	286	2700	2505	2318	2139	1968	4629	3984	3411	2906	2460	+2.5	+2.7	-4.5	-19.2	NA
	9.3 x 74Rmm	286	2360	2089	1844	1623	NA	3538	2771	2157	1670	NA	+2.5	-2.0	-11.0	NA	NA
375	38-55 Win.	255	1320	1190	1091	1018	963	987	802	674	587	525	0.0	-23.4	NA	NA	$25.
	375 Winchester	200	2200	1841	1526	1268	1089	2150	1506	1034	714	527	+2.5	-4.0	-26.2	NA	$26.
	375 Winchester	250	1900	1647	1424	1239	1103	2005	1506	1126	852	676	+2.5	-6.9	-33.3	NA	$26.
	375 N.E. 2½"	270	2000	1740	1507	1310	NA	2398	1815	1362	1026	NA	+2.5	-6.0	-30.0	NA	NA
	375 Flanged	300	2450	2150	1886	1640	NA	3998	3102	2369	1790	NA	+2.5	-2.4	-17.0	NA	NA
	375 H&H Magnum	250	2670	2450	2240	2040	1850	3955	3335	2790	2315	1905	+2.5	-0.4	-10.2	-28.4	NA
	375 H&H Magnum	270	2690	2420	2166	1928	1707	4337	3510	2812	2228	1747	+2.5	0.0	-10.0	-29.4	$29.
	375 H&H Magnum*	300c	2530	2245	1979	1733	1512	4263	3357	2608	2001	1523	+2.5	-1.0	-10.5	-33.6	$35
	375 Wea. Mag.	300	2700	2420	2157	1911	1685	4856	3901	3100	2432	1891	+2.5	-0.4	-10.7	-	NA

CAUTION: PRICES CHANGE, CHECK AT GUNSHOP.

Caliber	Bullet weight grains	VELOCITY (fps) Muzzle	100 yds.	200 yds.	300 yds.	400. yds.	ENERGY (ft. lbs.) Muzzle	100 yds.	200 yds.	300 yds.	400 yds.	TRAJ. (in.) 100 yds.	200 yds.	300 yds.	400 yds.	Approx. Price per box
375 (cont.)																
378 Wea. Mag.	270	3180	2976	2781	2594	2415	6062	5308	4635	4034	3495	+2.5	+2.6	-1.8	-11.3	$71
378 Wea. Mag.	300	2929	2576	2252	1952	1680	5698	4419	3379	2538	1881	+2.5	+1.2	-7.0	-24.5	$77
375 A-Square	300	2920	2626	2351	2093	1850	5679	4594	3681	2917	2281	+2.5	+1.4	-6.0	-21.0	NA
40 38-40 Win.	180	1160	999	901	827	764	538	399	324	273	233	0.0	-33.9	NA	NA	$42**
450/400-3"	400	2150	1932	1730	1545	1379	4105	3316	2659	2119	1689	+2.5	-4.0	-9.5	-30.3	NA
41 416 Taylor	400	2350	2117	1896	1693	NA	4905	3980	3194	2547	NA	+2.5	-1.2	-15.0	NA	NA
416 Hoffman	400	2380	2145	1923	1718	1529	5031	4087	3285	2620	2077	+2.5	-1.0	-14.1	NA	NA
416 Rigby	350	2600	2449	2303	2162	2026	5253	4661	4122	3632	3189	+2.5	-1.8	-10.2	-26.0	NA
416 Rigby	400	2370	2063	1780	1527	1312	4988	3778	2815	2171	1529	+2.5	-1.7	-17.0	NA	NA
416 Rigby	410	2370	2110	1870	1640	1440	5115	4050	3165	2455	1895	+2.5	-2.4	-17.3	-39.0	NA
416 Rem. Mag.*	350	2520	2270	2034	1814	1611	4935	4004	3216	2557	2017	+2.5	-0.8	-12.6	-35.0	$74
416 Rem. Mag.*	400	2400	2175	1962	1763	1579	5115	4201	3419	2760	2214	+2.5	-1.5	-14.6	NA	$74
416 Wea. Mag.*	400	2700	2397	2115	1852	1613	6474	5104	3971	3047	2310	+2.5	0.0	-10.1	-30.4	$96
425 404 Jeffrey	400	2150	1924	1716	1525	NA	4105	3289	2614	2064	NA	+2.5	-4.0	-22.1	NA	NA
425 Express	400	2400	2160	1934	1725	NA	5115	4145	3322	2641	NA	+2.5	-1.0	-14.0	NA	NA
44 44-40 Win.	200	1190	1006	900	822	756	629	449	360	300	254	0.0	-33.3	NA	NA	$35**
44 Rem. Mag.	210†	1920	1477	1155	982	880	1719	1017	622	450	361	0.0	-17.6	NA	NA	$14.
44 Rem. Mag.	240	1760	1380	1114	970	878	1650	1015	661	501	411	0.0	-17.6	NA	NA	$13.
444 Marlin	240	2350	1815	1377	1087	941	2942	1753	1001	630	472	+2.5	-15.1	-31.0	NA	$20
444 Marlin	265	2120	1733	1405	1160	1012	2644	1768	1162	791	603	+2.5	-6.0	-32.2	NA	Disc.
45 45-70 Govt.	300	1810	1497	1244	1073	969	2182	1492	1031	767	625	0.0	-14.8	NA	NA	$21.
45-70 Govt.	405	1330	1168	1055	977	918	1590	1227	1001	858	758	0.0	-24.6	NA	NA	$21
458 Win. Mag.	350	2470	1990	1570	1250	1060	4740	3065	1915	1205	870	+2.5	-2.5	-21.6	NA	NA
458 Win. Mag.	400	2450	2295	2146	2002	1865	5330	4678	4089	3560	3080	+2.5	-0.1	-10.3	-29.2	NA
458 Win. Mag.	465	2220	1999	1791	1601	NA	5088	4127	3312	2646	NA	+2.5	-2.0	-17.7	NA	NA
458 Win. Mag.	500	2040	1823	1623	1442	1237	4620	3689	2924	2308	1839	+2.5	-3.5	-22.0	NA	$63.
458 Win. Mag.	510	2040	1770	1527	1319	1157	4712	3547	2640	1970	1516	+2.5	-4.1	-25.0	NA	$40.
450 N.E.-3¼"	465	2190	1970	1765	1577	NA	4952	4009	3216	2567	NA	+2.5	-3.0	-20.0	NA	NA
450 N.E.-3¼"	500	2150	1920	1708	1514	NA	5132	4093	3238	2544	NA	+2.5	-4.0	-22.9	NA	NA
450 No. 2	465	2190	1970	1765	1577	NA	4952	4009	3216	2567	NA	+2.5	-3.0	-20.0	NA	NA
450 No. 2	500	2150	1920	1708	1514	NA	5132	4093	3238	2544	NA	+2.5	-4.0	-22.9	NA	NA
458 Lott	465	2380	2150	1932	1730	NA	5848	4773	3855	3091	NA	+2.5	-1.0	-14.0	NA	NA
458 Lott	500	2300	2062	1838	1633	NA	5873	4719	3748	2960	NA	+2.5	-1.6	-16.4	NA	NA
450 Ackley Mag	465	2400	2169	1950	1747	NA	5947	4857	3927	3150	NA	+2.5	-1.0	-13.7	NA	NA
450 Ackley Mag.	500	2320	2081	1855	1649	NA	5975	4085	3820	3018	NA	+2.5	-1.2	-15.0	NA	NA
460 Short A-Sq.	500	2420	2175	1943	1729	NA	6501	5250	4193	3319	NA	+2.5	-0.8	-12.8	NA	NA
460 Wea. Mag.	500	2700	2404	2128	1869	1635	8092	6416	5026	3878	2969	+2.5	+0.6	-8.9	-28.0	$72
475 500/465 N.E.	480	2150	1917	1703	1507	NA	4926	3917	3089	2419	NA	+2.5	-4.0	-22.2	-	NA
470 Rigby	500	2150	1912	1693	1494	NA	5132	4058	3182	2478	NA	+2.5	-4.0	-23.0	NA	NA
470 Nitro Ex.	480	2190	1954	1735	1536	NA	5111	4070	3210	2515	NA	+2.5	-3.5	-20.8	NA	NA
470 Nitro Ex.	500	2150	1890	1650	1440	1270	5130	3965	3040	2310	1790	+2.5	-4.3	-24.0	NA	NA
475 No. 2	500	2200	1955	1728	1522	NA	5375	4243	3316	2573	NA	+2.5	-3.2	-20.9	NA	NA
50 505 Gibbs	525	2300	2063	1840	1637	NA	6166	4922	3948	3122	NA	+2.5	-3.0	-18.0	NA	NA
58 500 N.E.-3"	570	2150	1928	1722	1533	NA	5850	4703	3752	2975	NA	+2.5	-3.7	-22.0	NA	NA
500 N.E.-3"	600	2150	1927	1721	1531	NA	6158	4947	3944	3124	NA	+2.5	-4.0	-22.0	NA	NA
495 A-Square	570	2350	2117	1896	1693	NA	5850	4703	3752	2975	NA	+2.5	-1.0	-14.5	NA	NA
495 A-Square	600	2280	2050	1833	1635	NA	6925	5598	4478	3562	NA	+2.5	-2.0	-17.0	NA	NA
500 A-Square	600	2380	2144	1922	1766	NA	7546	6126	4920	3922	NA	+2.5	-3.0	-17.0	NA	NA
500 A-Square	707	2250	2040	1841	1567	NA	7947	6530	5318	4311	NA	+2.5	-2.0	-17.0	NA	NA
577 Nitro Ex.	750	2050	1793	1562	1360	NA	6990	5356	4065	3079	NA	+2.5	-5.0	-26.0	NA	NA

Notes: N.A. in vel. or eng. column = This data not available from manufacturer. N.A.in trajectory column = Bullet has fallen more than 3 feet below line of sight and further hold-over is not practical. A - in any column means the data was not available at press time. Wea. Mag. = Weatherby Magnum. Spfd. = Springfield. A-Sq. = A-Square. N.E.= Nitro Express. Some manufacturers do not supply suggested retail prices. Others did not get their pricing to us before press time. All pricing can vary dependent on the exact brand and style of ammo selected and/or the retail outlet from which you make your purchase. Pricing has been rounded to the nearest dollar and represent our best estimate of average pricing. An * after the cartridge name means these loads are available with Nosler Partition bullets or Swift A-Frame bullets. Listed pricing may or may not reflect this bullet type. ** = These are packed 50 to box, all others are 20 to box. A + = special limited production. A † = new bullet weight this year.

CAUTION: PRICES CHANGE, CHECK AT GUNSHOP.

Caliber	Bullet Wt. Grs.	Velocity (fps)			Energy (ft. lbs.)			Mid-Range Traj. (in.)		Bbl. Lgth. (in.)	Est. Price /box
		MV	50 yds.	100 yds.	ME	50 yds.	100 yds.	50 yds.	100 yds.		
221 Rem. Fireball	50	2650	2380	2130	780	630	505	0.2	0.8	10½"	$14
25 Automatic	35	900	813	742	63	51	43	NA	NA	2"	$18
25 Automatic	45	815	730	655	65	55	40	1.8	7.7	2"	$21.
25 Automatic	50	760	705	660	65	55	50	2.0	8.7	2"	$17.
7.62 Tokarev	87	1390	NA	NA	365	NA	NA	0.6	NA	4½"	NA
30 Luger	93†	1220	1110	1040	305	255	225	0.9	3.5	4½"	$34.
30 Carbine	110	1790	1600	1430	785	625	500	0.4	1.7	10"	$27.
32 S&W	88	680	645	610	90	80	75	2.5	10.5	3"	$18.
32 S&W Long	98	705	670	635	115	100	90	2.3	10.5	4"	$17.
32 Short Colt	80	745	665	590	100	80	60	2.2	9.9	4"	$19.
32 Long Colt	82	755	715	675	100	95	85	2.0	8.7	4"	Disc.
32 H&R Magnum	85	1100	1020	930	230	195	165	1.0	4.3	4½"	NA
32 H&R Magnum	95	1030	940	900	225	190	170	1.1	4.7	4½"	NA
32 Automatic	60	970	895	835	125	105	95	1.3	5.4	4"	$22.
32 Automatic	71	905	855	810	130	115	95	1.4	5.8	4"	$19.
380 Automatic	85/88	990	920	870	190	165	145	1.2	5.1	4"	$20.
380 Automatic	90	1000	890	800	200	160	130	1.2	5.5	3¾"	$19.
380 Automatic	95/100	955	865	785	190	160	140	1.4	5.9	4"	$19.
38 Automatic	130	1040	980	925	310	275	245	1.0	4.7	4½"	Disc.
38 Super Auto +P	115	1300	1145	1040	430	335	275	0.7	3.3	5"	$24
38 Super Auto +P	125/130	1215	1100	1015	425	350	300	0.8	3.6	5"	$20.
9mm Luger	88	1500	1190	1010	440	275	200	0.6	3.1	4"	$23
9mm Luger	90	1360	1112	978	370	247	191	NA	NA	4"	$26
9mm Luger	95	1300	1140	1010	350	275	215	0.8	3.4	4"	NA
9mm Luger	115	1155	1045	970	340	280	240	0.9	3.9	4"	$21.
9mm Luger	123/125	1110	1030	970	340	290	260	1.0	4.0	4"	$23
9mm Luger	140	935	890	850	270	245	225	1.3	5.5	4"	$23
9mm Luger	147	990	940	900	320	290	265	1.1	4.9	4"	$28.
9mm Luger +P	115	1250	1113	1019	399	316	265	0.8	3.5	4"	$25
9mm Federal	115	1280	1130	1040	420	330	280	0.7	3.3	4"V	NA
38 S&W	145	685	650	620	150	135	125	2.4	10.0	4"	$18.
38 Short Colt	125	730	685	645	150	130	115	2.2	9.4	6"	$18
38 Special	110	945	895	850	220	195	175	1.3	5.4	4"V	$24.
38 (Multi-Ball)	140	830	730	505	215	130	80	2.0	10.6	4"V	$9*
38 Special	148	710	635	565	165	130	105	2.4	10.6	4"V	$16.
38 Special	158	755	725	690	200	185	170	2.0	8.3	4"V	$18.
38 Special	200	635	615	595	180	170	155	2.8	11.5	4"V	Disc.
38 Special +P	95	1175	1045	960	290	230	195	0.9	3.9	4"V	$24.
38 Special +P	110	995	925	870	240	210	185	1.2	5.1	4"V	$23.
38 Special +P	125	945	900	860	250	225	205	1.3	5.4	4"V	$24.
38 Special +P	129	945	910	870	255	235	215	1.3	5.3	4"V	NA
38 Special +P	147/150c	884	NA	NA	264	NA	NA	NA	NA	4"V	$27.
38 Special +P	158	890	855	825	280	255	240	1.4	6.0	4"V	$20.
357 Magnum	110	1295	1095	975	410	290	230	0.8	3.5	4"V	$25.
357 (med. Vel.)	125	1220	1075	985	415	315	270	0.8	3.7	4"V	$24
357 Magnum	125	1450	1240	1090	585	425	330	0.6	2.8	4"V	$25.
357 (Multi-Ball)	140	1155	830	665	420	215	135	1.2	6.4	4"V	$10*
357 Magnum	140	1360	1195	1075	575	445	360	0.7	3.0	4"V	$24
357 Magnum	145	1290	1155	1060	535	430	360	0.8	3.5	4"V	$26.
357 Magnum	150†/158	1235	1105	1015	535	430	360	0.8	3.5	4"V	$25.
357 Magnum	180	1145	1055	985	525	445	390	0.9	3.9	4"V	$24
357 Rem. Maximum	158	1825	1590	1380	1170	885	670	0.4	1.7	10½"	$12*
40 S&W	155	1140	1026	958	447	362	309	0.9	4.1	4"	$28.
40 S&W	180	985	936	893	388	350	319	1.4	5.0	4"	$32.
10mm Automatic	155	1125	1046	986	436	377	335	0.9	3.9	5"	$26.
10mm Automatic	170	1340	1165	1145	680	510	415	0.7	3.2	5"	$31
10mm Automatic	175	1290	1140	1035	650	505	420	0.7	3.3	5½"	$11*.
10mm Auto.(FBI)	180	950	905	865	361	327	299	1.5	5.4	4"	$16*.
10mm Automatic	180	1030	970	920	425	375	340	1.1	4.7	5"	$16*.
10mm Auto H.V.	180†	1240	1124	1037	618	504	430	0.8	3.4	5"	$15*
10mm Automatic	200	1160	1070	1010	495	510	430	0.9	3.8	5"	$17*.
41 Action Exp.	180	1000	947	903	400	359	326	0.5	4.2	5"	$14*
41 Rem. Magnum	170	1420	1165	1015	760	515	390	0.7	3.2	4"V	$31
41 Rem. Magnum	175	1250	1120	1030	605	490	410	0.8	3.4	4"V	$14*.
41 (Med. Vel.)	210	965	900	840	435	375	330	1.3	5.4	4"V	$28
41 Rem. Magnum	210	1300	1160	1060	790	630	525	0.7	3.2	4"V	$13*.
44 S&W Special	180	980	NA	NA	383	NA	NA	NA	NA	6½"	NA
44 S&W Special	200†	875	825	780	340	302	270	1.2	6.0	6"	$19
44 S&W Special	200	1035	940	865	475	390	335	1.1	4.9	6½"	$13*.
44 S&W Special	240/246	755	725	695	310	285	265	2.0	8.3	6½"	$26.
44 Rem. Magnum	180	1610	1365	1175	1035	745	550	0.5	2.3	4"V	$14*
44 Rem. Magnum	200	1400	1192	1053	870	630	492	0.6	NA	6½"	NA
44 Rem. Magnum	210	1495	1310	1165	1040	805	635	0.6	2.5	6½"	$14*
44 (Med. Vel.)	240	1000	945	900	535	475	435	1.1	4.8	6½"	$28
44 R.M.(Jacketed)	240	1180	1080	1010	740	625	545	0.9	3.7	4"V	$13*.
44 R.M. (Lead)	240	1350	1185	1070	970	750	610	0.7	3.1	4"V	$28
44 Rem. Magnum	250	1180	1100	1040	775	670	600	0.8	3.6	6½"V	$17*
44 Rem. Magnum	300	1200	1100	1026	959	806	702	NA	NA	7½"	$17
45 Automatic	185	1000	940	890	410	360	325	1.1	4.9	5"	$11*.
45 Auto. (Match)	185	770	705	650	245	204	175	2.0	8.7	5"	$27.
45 Auto (Match)	200	940	890	840	392	352	312	2.0	8.6	5"	NA
45 Automatic	200	975	917	860	421	372	328	1.4	5.0	5"	NA
45 Automatic	230	830	800	675	355	325	300	1.6	6.8	5"	$11*.
45 Automatic	Shot	This data not available									
45 Automatic +P	185	1140	1040	970	535	445	385	0.9	4.0	5"	$28
45 Win. Magnum	230	1400	1230	1105	1000	775	635	0.6	2.8	5"	$14*.
45 Auto. Rim	230	810	775	730	335	305	270	1.8	7.4	5½"	Disc.
45 Colt	200	1000	938	889	444	391	351	1.3	4.8	5½"	NA
45 Colt	225	960	890	830	460	395	345	1.3	5.5	5½"	$13*.
45 Colt	250/255	860	820	780	410	375	340	1.6	6.6	5½"	$11*.
50 Action Exp.	325	1400	1209	1075	1414	1055	835	0.2	2.3	6"	$24*

Notes: Blanks are available in 32 S&W, 38 S&W, and 38 Special. V after barrel length indicates test barrel was vented to produce ballistics similar to a revolver with a normal barrel-to-cylinder gap. Ammo prices are per 50 rounds except when marked with an * which signifies a 20 round box. Not all loads are available from all ammo manufacturers. Listed loads are those made by Remington, Winchester, Federal, and others. DISC. is a discontinued load. Prices are rounded to nearest whole dollar and will vary with brand and retail outlet. † = new bullet, or bullet weight this year. A "c" indicates a change in data.

RIMFIRE AMMUNITION—BALLISTICS AND PRICES

Cartridge type	Bullet Wt. Grs.	Type	Velocity (fps) 22½" Barrel			Energy (ft. lbs.) 22½" Barrel			Velocity (fps) 6" Barrel		Energy (ft lbs) 6" Barrel		Approx. Price Per Box	
			Muzzle	50 Yds.	100 Yds.	Muzzle	50 Yds.	100 Yds.	Muzzle	50 Yds.	Muzzle	50 Yds.	50 Rds.	100 Rds.
22 Short Blank			Not applicable										3.52	N.A.*
22 CB Short	29		725	667	610	34	29	24	706	—	32	—	1.92	N.A.*
22 Short Match	29		830	752	695	44	36	31	786	—	39	—	—	N.A.
22 Short Std. Vel.	29		1045	—	810	70	—	42	865	—	48	—	Discontinued	
22 Short High Vel.	29		1095	—	903	77	—	53	—	—	—	—	1.76	N.A.*
22 Short H.V. H.P.	27		1120	—	904	75	—	49	—	—	—	—	—	N.A.
22 CB Long	29		725	667	610	34	29	24	706	—	32	—	2.33	N.A.
22 Long Std. Vel.	29		1180	1038	946	90	69	58	1031	—	68	—	—	N.A.
22 Long High Vel.	29		1240	—	962	99	—	60	—	—	—	—	2.33	N.A.
22 L.R. Match type	40		1070	970	890	100	80	70	940	—	78	—	—	N.A.
22 L.R. Std. Vel.	40		1138	1047	975	116	97	84	1027	925	93	76	1.68	N.A.*
22 L.R. High Vel.	40		1255	1110	1017	140	109	92	1060	—	100	—	1.60	3.20*
22 L.R. H.V. Sil.	42		1220	—	1003	139	—	94	1025	—	98	—	1.68	N.A.*
22 L.R. H.V. H.P.	36/38		1280	1126	1010	131	101	82	1089	—	95	—	1.60	3.20*
22 L.R. Shot	—	#11 or #12	1047	—	—	—	—	—	950	—	—	—	4.56	N.A.
22 L.R. Hyper Vel	36		1410	1187	1056	159	113	89	—	—	—	—	2.80	N.A.
22 L.R. Hyper H.P	32/33/34		1500	1240	1075	165	110	85	—	—	—	—	2.80	N.A.
22 Win. Mag.	30		2200	1750	1373	322	203	127	1610	—	—	—	—	N.A.
22 Win. Mag.	40		1910	1490	1326	324	197	156	1428	—	181	—	6.16	N.A.*
22 Win. Mag.	50		1650	—	1280	300	—	180	—	—	—	—	N.A.	N.A.
22 Win. Mag. Shot	—	#11	1126	—	—	—	—	—	—	—	—	—	N.A.	N.A.

Note: The actual ballistics obtained with your firearm can vary considerably from the advertised ballistics. Also ballistics can vary from lot to lot with the same brand and type load. Prices can vary with manufacturer and retail outlet. A — in the price column indicates this size packaging currently unavailable.

SHOTSHELL LOADS AND PRICES

Dram Equivalent	Shot Ozs.	Load Style	Shot Sizes	Avg. Brands	Nominal Price /box	Velocity (fps)
10 Gauge 3½" Magnum						
4½	2¼	premium	BB, 2, 4, 6	Win., Fed., Rem.	$33	1205
4½	2¼	premium	4, 6	Win., Fed.	$13*	1205
4¼	2	high velocity	BB, 2, 4	Rem.	$22	1210
4½	2¼	duplex	4x6	Rem.	$14*	1205
Max	18 pellets	premium	00 buck	Fed., Win.	$7**	1100
Max	54 pellets	premium	4 buck	Win.	Disc.	1100
4¼	1¾	steel	T, BBB, BB, 1, 2, 3	Win., Rem.	$27	1260
4¼	1¾	steel duplex	TxBB, BBBx1	Rem.	$12**	1260
Mag	1⅝	steel	T, BBB	Win.	$27	1285
4⅝	1⅝	steel	F, T, BBB	Fed.	$26	1350
Max	1¾	slug, rifled	slug	Fed.	NA	1280
12 Gauge 3½" Magnum						
Max	2¼	premium	4, 6	Fed., Rem., Win.	$13*	1150
Max	18 pellets	premium	00 buck	Fed., Win.	$7**	1100
4⅛	1 9/16	steel	F, T, BB, 1, 2	Win., Fed.	$22	1335
12 Gauge 3" Magnum						
4	2	premium	BB, 2, 4, 5, 6	Win., Fed., Rem.	$9*	1175
4	2	duplex	4x6	Rem.	$10	1175
4	1⅞	premium	BB, 2, 4, 6	Win., Fed., Rem.	$19	1210
4	1⅞	duplex	BBx4, 2x4, 2x6, 4x6	Rem.	$9*	1210
4	1⅝	premium	2, 4, 5, 6	Win., Fed., Rem.	$18	1290
4	24 pellets	buffered	1 buck	Win., Fed., Rem.	$5**	1040
4	15 pellets	buffered	00 buck	Win., Fed., Rem.	$6**	1210
4	10 pellets	buffered	000 buck	Win., Fed., Rem.	$6**	1225
4	41 pellets	buffered	4 buck	Win., Fed., Rem.	$6**	1210
Max	1¼	slug, rifled	slug	Fed.	NA	1600
Max	1	slug, rifled	slug, magnum	Win., Rem.	$5**	1760
Max	1	saboted slug	slug	Win.	$10**	1550
3⅝	1⅜	steel	F, T, BBB, BB, 1, 2, 3, 4	Win., Fed., Rem.	$19	1275
3⅝	1⅜	steel duplex	BBBx1, BBx2, 1x3	Rem.	$8*	1275
4	1¼	steel	F, T, BBB, BB, 1, 2, 3, 4, 6	Win., Fed., Rem.	$18	1375
4	1¼	steel duplex	BBx1, BBx2, BBx4, 1x3, 2x6	Rem.	$8*	1375
12 gauge 2¾"						
Max	1⅝	magnum	4, 5, 6	Win.	$8*	1250
3¾	1½	magnum	BB, 2, 4, 5, 6	Win., Fed., Rem.	$16	1260
3¾	1½	duplex	BBx4, 2x4, 2x6, 4x6	Rem.	$9*	1260
3¾	1¼	high velocity	BB, 2, 4, 5, 6, 7½, 8, 9	Win., Fed., Rem.	$13	1330
3½	1¼	mid velocity	7, 8, 9	Win.	Disc.	1275
3¼	1¼	standard velocity	6, 7½, 8, 9	Win., Fed., Rem.	$11	1220
3¼	1⅛	standard velocity	4, 6, 7½, 8, 9	Win., Fed., Rem.	$9	1255
3¼	1	standard velocity	6, 7½, 8	Rem., Fed.	$6	1290
3¼	1¼	target	7½, 8, 9	Win., Fed., Rem.	$10	1220
3	1⅛	target	7½, 8, 9, 7½x8	Win., Fed., Rem.	$7	1200
2¾	1⅛	target	7½, 8, 8½, 9, 7½x8	Win., Fed., Rem.	$7	1145
2¼	1⅛	target	7½, 8, 8½, 9	Rem., Fed.	$7	1080
3½	1	target	10	Fed.	NA	1350
3¼	28grams(1oz)	target	7½, 8, 9	Win., Fed., Rem.	$8	1290
2¾	1	target	8½	Fed.	NA	1180
3¾	8 pellets	buffered	000 buck	Win., Fed., Rem.	$4**	1325
4	12 pellets	premium	00 buck	Win., Fed., Rem.	$5**	1290
3¾	9 pellets	buffered	00 buck	Win., Fed., Rem.	$19	1325
3¾	12 pellets	buffered	0 buck	Win., Fed., Rem.	$4**	1275
4	20 pellets	buffered	1 buck	Win., Fed., Rem.	$4**	1075
3¾	16 pellets	buffered	1 buck	Win., Fed., Rem.	$4**	1250
4	34 pellets	premium	4 buck	Fed., Rem.	$5**	1250
3¾	27 pellets	buffered	4 buck	Win., Fed., Rem.	$4**	1325
Max	1	saboted slug	slug	Win., Fed.	$10**	1450
Max	1¼	slug, rifled	slug	Fed.	NA	1520
Max	1	slug, rifled	slug, magnum	Rem.	$5**	1680
Max	1	slug, rifled	slug	Win., Fed., Rem.	$4**	1610
3	1#	steel	7	Win.	$11	1235
3½	1¼	steel	T, BBB, BB, 1, 2, 3, 4, 5, 6	Win., Fed., Rem.	$18	1275
3½	1¼	steel duplex	BBx2, 1x3	Rem.	$8*	1275
3¾	1⅛	steel	BB, 1, 2, 3, 4, 5, 6	Win., Fed., Rem.	$16	1365
3¾	1⅛	steel duplex	BBx1, BBx2, BBx4, 1x3, 2x6	Rem.	$7*	1365
3¾	1	steel	2, 4, 6	Win., Fed.	$13	1390
16 Gauge 2¾"						
3¼	1¼	magnum	2, 4, 6	Win., Fed., Rem.	$16	1260
3¼	1⅛	high velocity	4, 6, 7½	Win., Fed., Rem.	$12	1295
2¾	1⅛	standard velocity	6, 7½, 8	Fed., Rem.	$9	1185
2½	1	promotional	6, 7½, 8	Win., Fed., Rem.	$6	1165
Max	15/16	steel	2, 4	Fed.	NA	1300
Max	⅞	steel	2, 4	Win.	$16	1300
3	12 pellets	buffered	1 buck	Win., Fed., Rem.	$4**	1225
Max	4/5	slug, rifled	slug	Win., Fed., Rem.	$4**	1570
20 Gauge 3" Magnum						
3	1¼	premium	2, 4, 6, 7½	Win., Fed., Rem.	$15	1185
Max	18 pellets	buck shot	2 buck	Fed.	NA	1200
Max	24 pellets	buffered	3 buck	Win.	$5**	1150
2¾	20 pellets	buck	3 buck	Rem.	$4**	1200
3¼	1	steel	1, 2, 3, 4, 5, 6	Win., Fed., Rem.	$15	1330
20 Gauge 2¾"						
2¾	1⅛	magnum	4, 6, 7½	Win., Fed., Rem.	$14	1175
2¾	1	high velocity	4, 5, 6, 7½, 8, 9	Win., Fed., Rem.	$12	1220
2½	1	standard velocity	6, 7½, 8	Win., Rem., Fed.	$6	1165
2½	⅞	promotional	6, 7½, 8	Win., Rem.	$6	1210
2½	1#	target	8, 9	Win., Rem.	$8	1165
2½	⅞	target	8, 9	Win., Fed., Rem.	$8	1200
Max	20 pellets	buffered	3 buck	Win., Fed.	$4	1200
Max	⅝	slug, saboted	slug	Win.	$9**	1400
2¾	⅝	slug, rifled	slug	Rem.	$4**	1580
Max	¾	slug, rifled	slug	Win., Fed.	$4**	1570
Max	¾	steel	4, 6	Win., Fed.	$14	1425
28 Gauge 2¾"						
2	1	high velocity	6, 7½, 8	Win.	$12	1125
2¼	¾	high velocity	6, 7½, 8	Win., Fed., Rem.	$11	1295
2	¾	target	9	Win., Fed., Rem.	$9	1200
410 Bore 3"						
Max	1 1/16	high velocity	4, 5, 6, 7½, 8, 9	Win., Fed., Rem.	$10	1135
410 Bore 2½"						
Max	½	high velocity	4, 6, 7½	Win., Fed., Rem.	$9	1245
Max	⅕	slug, rifled	slug	Win., Fed., Rem.	$4**	1815
1½	½	target	9	Win., Fed., Rem.	$8	1200

NOTES: * = 10 rounds per box. ** = 5 rounds per box. Pricing variations and number of rounds per box can occur with type and brand of ammunition. Listed pricing is for load style and box quantity shown. Not every brand is available in all shot size variations. Some manufacturers do not provide suggested list prices. All prices rounded to nearest whole dollar. The price you pay will vary dependent upon outlet of purchase. # = new load spec this year. A "c" indicates a change in data.

SHOOTER'S MARKETPLACE

REPLACEMENT RIFLE STOCKS

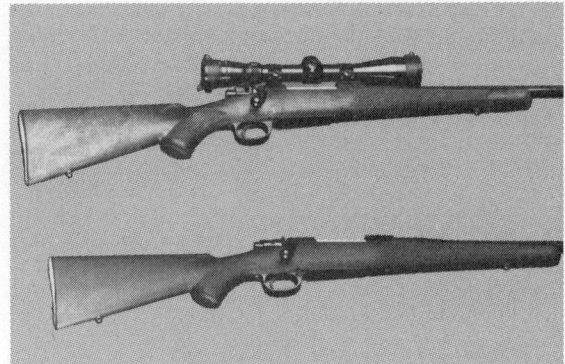

Butler Creek is expanding their Classic Series of replacement rifle stocks.

The Military Mauser 98K and Howa 1500 stocks are available with cheekpiece and classic straight stock. The Classic Series is manufactured using space-age polymers made to withstand hunting and weather abuse.

Butler Creek's trademark of raised checkering and slim pistol grip area with classic straight stock has been expanded to include recoil pads. Their stocks are designed to be quiet and comfortable and improve accuracy.

Classic Series stocks are available in Field ($115) and Deluxe Texturized ($145) finishes. For further information, contact Butler Creek Corp.

BUTLER CREEK CORP.

22LR/1911 CONVERSION UNIT

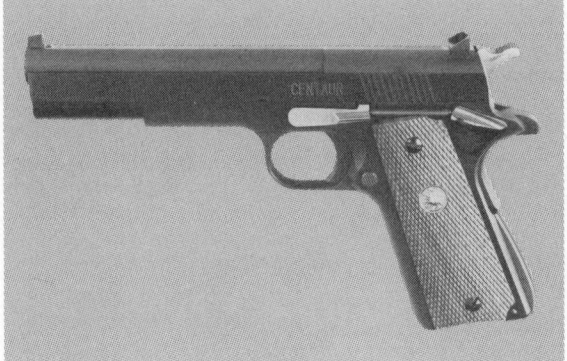

Ray Herriott, designer of the popular Quadra-Comp Drop-in Barrel System, has employed the newest CAD technology to create Centaur's new 22LR Caliber Top-End Conversion for the Colt M1911, Commander, Officer's Model and their clones.

The conversion unit comes complete with slide, hammer spring, recoil guide and spring, plus magazine—everything you need but the ammo to convert your own 1911 (or variant) into a semi-auto rimfire.

The kit retails for $299.99 and requires no fitting or gunsmithing skills to install. Call or write for more information or send $2.00 for Centaur's newest catalog.

CENTAUR SYSTEMS, INC.

FULL-LENGTH SYNTHETIC STOCKS

Butler Creek recently introduced new sporterized full-length synthetic stocks for Ruger's 10/22 and Mini 14/30 rifles.

These stocks were developed for shooters wanting to upgrade their Ruger rifle with a strong, full-length, lightweight synthetic stock.

They are available in standard and deluxe texturized finishes and come with rifle pad and swivel studs.

Butler Creek stocks are manufactured with the most advanced polymers. Weighing less than 2 pounds, these "all weather" stocks are very quiet and are impervious to changes in weather conditions.

Butler Creek offers a lifetime warranty. For further information, contact Butler Creek Corp.

BUTLER CREEK CORP.

See manufacturers' addresses on page 269.

RUGGED LASER BEAM ACCURACY

Advanced semiconductor laser technology brings high-tech precision and affordable quality to the experienced shooter. Alpec's Beam Shot™ laser sight projects a red hot point of laser light right on target, providing the greatest accuracy possible.

With Alpec's rugged mounts, the Beam Shot is tough enough for combat shooting, and compatible with most popular semi-automatic, rifles, shotguns and revolvers.

The Beam Shot adjusts for windage and elevation by a precise X-Y lead screw mechanism. Their optical-grade lens focuses the <5 mW laser light for the greatest intensity, distance and visibility. The laser is activated by a removable pressure switch mounted on the grip of the firearm.

For a catalog, call or write Alpec.

ALPEC TEAM, INC.

ADJUSTABLE BORE SAVER ROD GUIDES

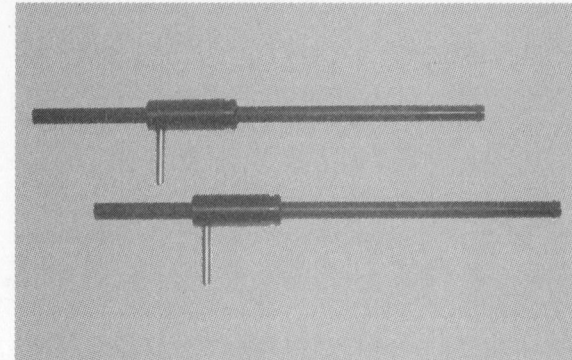

The Dewey Bore Saver cleaning rod guide replaces the bolt in your action while cleaning. The cleaning rod enters the bore straight, without harming the chamber or throat. Made from anodized aluminum in six bore sizes, the Delrin rod guide collar with threaded brass adjustment pin allows for quick adjustment to any bolt length. Chamber-sealing O-rings prohibit solvents from entering the action, trigger and magazine areas. On some rifles, the bolt stop will retain the rod guide by using the groove on the guide collar.

The guide can be used with all cleaning rods; all models fit .695- to .700-inch bolt diameter rifles. All guides allow brush clearance through tube I.D. and come with spare O-rings and O-ring assembly tool. Weatherby models available. Write for information.

J. DEWEY MANUFACTURING CO., INC.

CUSTOM GUNSTOCKS

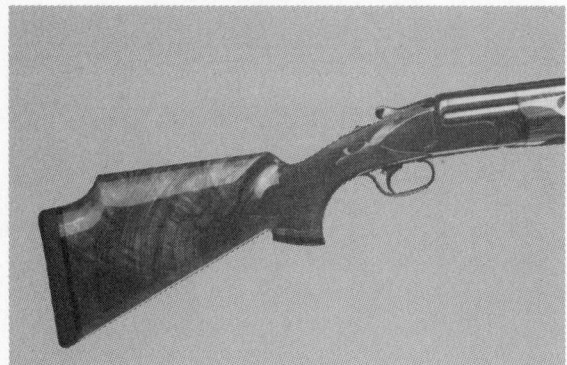

Wenig Custom Gunstocks is a newly established company that prides itself on fine woods and skilled craftsmanship.

President Fred Wenig and Vice President Elbert Smith have over 100 years of combined experience and specialize in custom-built gunstocks for trap, Skeet, Sporting Clay and classic guns. Custom checkering is performed by Darrell Smith.

Wood selections are Claro walnut, American walnut, English walnut and laminated birch. The Try-Stock is used to properly fit a shooter's gun. Pictured above is the "New American Style" gunstock.

Blanks will be sent on approval and customer's wood machined upon request. Call or write for an appointment and price lists.

WENIG CUSTOM GUNSTOCKS, INC.

TRITIUM NIGHT SIGHTS

Trijicon® self-luminous iron sight blades are exceptionally strong and bright night sights for handguns. The sharply defined 3-Dot aiming system improves accuracy potential for both day and night shooting. With inlaid white rings and glowing tritium sapphire dots, Trijicon Night Sights are impervious to cleaning solutions and carry a 10-year warranty against loss of illumination.

Trijicon is a leading supplier to handgun manufacturers, with customers who include: State Police agencies, major city police departments, federal agencies, military special forces.

Over 80 models to choose from for popular handguns and rifles. New adjustable models. Custom models by special order. Made in U.S.A.

TRIJICON, INC.

See manufacturers' addresses on page 269.

DOUBLE-ACTION AUTOLOADER

The Hungarian FEG PMK-380 autoloader is currently being imported by K.B.I. The PMK-380 is a 380 ACP double-action patterned after the Walther PP.

Each PMK-380 features a blue anodized aluminum alloy frame, thumb safety, high luster blued steel slide, serrated hammer, black composite grips (with thumbrest), ramp front sight and dovetailed rear sight that is windage adjustable.

The PMK-380 is a slightly "up-sized" cousin of the K.B.I. SMC-380.

Each autoloader comes complete with a pair of seven-round magazines and cleaning rod. Suggested retail: $279.00. For more information, see your local dealer or contact K.B.I. directly.

K.B.I., INC.

NEW 9MM SEMI-AUTO

The single-action FEG 9mm PJK-9HP is currently being imported by K.B.I. This 13-round pistol is patterned after the Browning Hi-Power currently in use by most NATO members.

Each PJK-9HP features high luster, blued-steel construction, a thumb safety, combat serrated hammer, ramp front sight and rear dovetail sight adjustable for windage.

Additionally, the PJK-9HP comes complete with a pair of 13-round magazines and a cleaning rod. An industrial hard chrome finish version is also available.

Suggested retail for the blued version is $314.00. For more information, see your local dealer or contact K.B.I. directly.

K.B.I., INC.

HUNGARIAN 380 AUTOLOADER

K.B.I. recently started importing the Hungarian FEG SMC-380, a 380 ACP semi-auto patterned after the Walther PPK.

Each SMC-380 double-action auto features a blue anodized aluminum alloy frame and a high luster blued steel slide.

Additional features include a serrated hammer, composite target grips (with thumbrest), ramp front sight and rear dovetail sight that is adjustable for windage.

A pair of six-round magazines and cleaning rod is included with each semi-auto.

Suggested retail price: $299.00. See your local dealer for more information, or contact K.B.I. directly via mail, phone or fax.

K.B.I., INC.

NEW RUSSIAN MAKAROV

Makarov's have been showing up in surplus for some time now. K.B.I., Inc., is currently importing the Makarov in "new, commercial production" form.

Chambered for the 9mm Makarov (9x18mm), the K.B.I. double-action model IJ-70 features high luster blued steel frame and slide, decocking lever, slide-mounted safety, fully adjustable sights and checkered plastic grips.

Each Makarov comes with a pair of eight-round magazines, cleaning rod and leather holster (with cleaning rod holder and spare magazine pouch).

Suggested retail for the entire rig is $229.00. Write K.B.I. for more information.

K.B.I., INC.

See manufacturers' addresses on page 269.

NEW FIXED-BARREL REVOLVERS

Wesson Firearms Co. offers a nice line of revolvers in blue carbon steel or stainless steel, chambered for 22LR on up to 445 Supermag.

Wesson's new line of accurate and reliable fixed-barrel revolvers is offered in 357 or 44 Magnum. Their Compensated Barrel Assemblies for big-bore revolvers are said to reduce muzzle flip 50 percent over standard barrel assemblies.

Wesson's addition to the personal defense and home protection market is the Model 738 P, a five-shot revolver rated for +P 38 Special ammunition.

All Wesson revolvers (except the Supermag Series) carry a 10-year warranty. For a brochure of Wesson's full product line, send $2.00 along with a catalog request.

WESSON FIREARMS CO., INC.

STEEL SHOT COMPONENTS

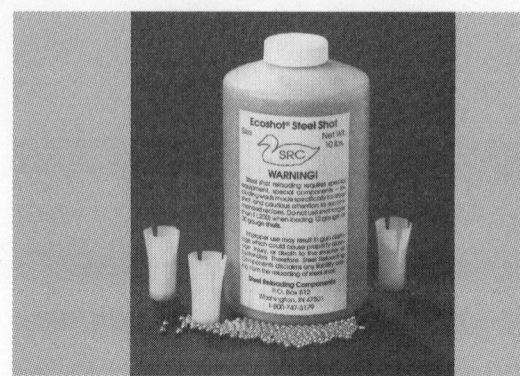

Steel Reloading offers SAAMI-approved steel shot in sizes No. 8 through F in zinc and copper-plated versions for improved resistance against rust and better patterning performance.

Their new wad line includes 12-gauge 2³⁄₄", 3", 3¹⁄₂" and 10-gauge 3¹⁄₂", "beefed-up" to prevent pinholing.

Steel Reloading has spent the last year developing new, safe loads for their steel shot components. All loads were checked by piezoelectric transducer. Each bag of wads comes with a data book which currently lists over 50 proven loads.

Their new reloading manual includes expert advice from writers such as L.P. Brezny, Don Zutz, Tom Armbrust and Brook Elliott. See your nearest stocking dealer or call Steel Reloading directly.

STEEL RELOADING COMPONENTS, INC.

CLAY TARGET TRAPS

The easy cocking, lay-on loading of Trius Traps make them easy to operate. With singles, doubles and piggy-back doubles, Trius offers seven trap models. The Birdshooter offers quality at an affordable price; the Model 92 is a best seller with high-angle clip and can thrower; the Trapmaster offers sit-down comfort plus pivoting action.

The Model SC92 is a heavy-duty trap designed for permanent installation that will throw all Sporting Clay targets except battue and rabbit; the Model BAT2 throws single and double battue targets. The Rabbitmaster throws "rabbit disc" clay targets along the ground; the Squirrelmaster holds five "rabbit disc" targets that roll down a ramp and across the ground when released. Free catalog available.

TRIUS TRAPS

NEW SHOOTING GLASSES

New Randolph Ranger shooting glasses serve to combine a number of desirable shooter-oriented features—safety, comfort, visual acuity and flexibility.

Interchangeable polycarbonate lenses, available in clear, yellow, orange, purple, vermillion, grey and brown, are shatterproof and distortion-free. Frame welds were designed for rugged outdoor use and are guaranteed for life.

The Ranger comes packaged in a bigger-than-life shotgun shell complete with choice of three lenses, PVC cable covers, cleaning cloth and durable carrying case.

For more information, write, call or fax Ranger Shooting Glasses, or ask for Randolph Ranger at your local gun dealer or sporting goods store.

RANGER SHOOTING GLASSES.

See manufacturers' addresses on page 269.

CUSTOM 22 RIMFIRE RIFLE

The Custom Team Challenger™ combines the speed and reliability of Ruger's 10/22 semi-automatic 22 rimfire action with the accuracy and features available only in a custom rifle.

The Challenger has a classic-style Brown Precision lightweight fiberglass or Kevlar stock with wide, flat-bottom forearm for off-hand or rest shooting. The re-worked action has an extended magazine release, simplified bolt release and finely tuned trigger.

All chrome-moly or stainless barrels installed by Brown are custom-length Shilen match-grade .920" diameter straight barrels or, upon request, lightweight tapered barrels. Features a match-grade chamber and custom crown. Available in blue, stainless, or a combination. Catalog $3.00.

BROWN PRECISION, INC.

PRECISION RIFLE REST

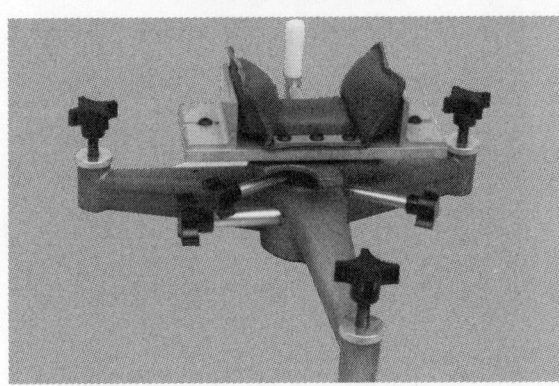

Bald Eagle Precision Machine Co. makes a beautiful rifle rest perfect for the serious benchrester or dedicated varminter. The rest is constructed of aircraft-quality aluminum and weighs in at 7 pounds, 12 ounces.

It's nicely finished with three coats of Imron Clear. Height adjustments are made with a rack and pinion and a mariner wheel. A fourth leg allows lateral movement on the bench.

Bald Eagle offers approximately 56 models to choose from, including windage adjustments, right or left hand, cast aluminum or cast iron. "Standard Rest" with rifle stop and bag pictured above.

Prices: $99.95 to $260.00. For more information or a free brochure, contact Bald Eagle.

BALD EAGLE PRECISION MACHINE CO.

GUN PARTS CATALOG

The Gun Parts Corporation, one of the world's largest suppliers of gun parts (formerly Numrich Arms Parts Div.), offers a newly updated 18th Edition Catalog—a standard reference for gunsmiths, shooters, collectors and military organizations worldwide.

Its 650-plus pages contain complete listings and prices for more than 400 million gun parts currently in stock.

Machinegun, military, U.S., foreign, commercial and antique gun parts are included, as well as hundreds of schematic drawings.

To order, U.S. customers send $5.95; foreign surface mail orders $10.95. Write The Gun Parts Corp. for airmail quote.

THE GUN PARTS CORP.

RIMFIRE CARTRIDGE GAUGE

The Rimfire Cartridge Gage, from Bald Eagle Precision Machine Co., can improve overall group size by up to 25% by sorting rimfire ammo into uniform rim-thickness lots.

The more consistent the rim thickness, the more consistent the ignition of the primer and powder charge, and the firing pin travel remains uniform from shot-to-shot.

The Cartridge Gage is a snap to use—grab a box or two of your favorite flavor of rimfire ammo and start sorting. It is ideal for BR-50 benchrest competitors and serious small game hunters.

Normally $80.00, mention *Shooter's Marketplace* and it's only $74.95. Write Bald Eagle for a free brochure.

BALD EAGLE PRECISION MACHINE CO.

See manufacturers' addresses on page 269.

QUICK-DETACHABLE SWIVEL

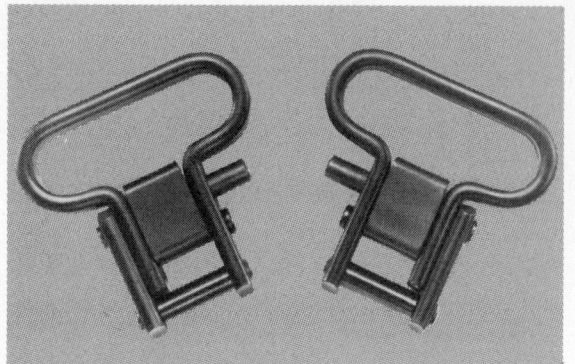

Boonie Packer is offering a new, quick-detachable sling swivel—the Safari.

Its strong, patented automatic locking system is engineered to stay locked; however, the design allows for easy-on, easy-off use. The loop of the new Safari sling swivel is guaranteed never to pull out and it doesn't squeak.

Simply designed and American-made, the Safari can be used with slings with 1" swivels and fits standard quick-detachable studs. Price per pair: $7.49 (blued); $8.99 nickeled.

Boonie Packer offers a free 8-page brochure to *Shooter's Marketplace* readers. For more information, write Boonie Packer directly or call toll-free.

BOONIE PACKER PRODUCTS

QUALITY GUNSTOCK BLANKS

Cali'co Hardwoods has been cutting superior-quality shotgun and rifle blanks for more than 31 years. Cali'co supplies blanks to many of the major manufacturers—Browning, Weatherby, Ruger, Holland & Holland, to name a few—as well as custom gunsmiths the world over.

Profiled rifle blanks are available, ready for inletting and sanding. Cali'co sells superior California hardwoods in Claro walnut, French walnut, Bastogne, maple and myrtle.

Cali'co offers good, serviceable blanks and some of the finest exhibition blanks available. Satisfaction guaranteed.

Color catalog, retail and dealer price list (FFL required) free upon request.

CALI'CO HARDWOODS, INC.

MAGNUM DERRINGER

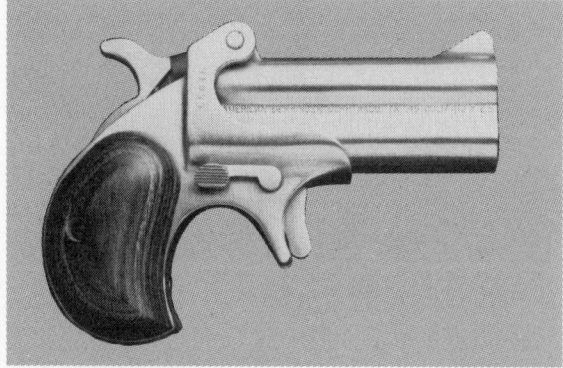

The Model 1, 45 Colt/410, from American Derringer Corp. was designed as the ultimate short-range back-up pistol.

More than ten years were spent developing and refining this pistol; it is one of the smallest and most powerful pocket pistols ever made.

Built from the finest high-tensile-strength stainless steel, it has the strength to handle even the 44 Magnum cartridge. More than 60 different rifle and pistol calibers are available.

Classic styling and smooth lines give this derringer a classic look. The gun is finished with a high polish (looks like nickel plate) or satin finish. All guns equipped with rosewood, bacote or walnut; other grips available at extra cost.

AMERICAN DERRINGER CORP.

NEW FIREARM SAFETY LOCK

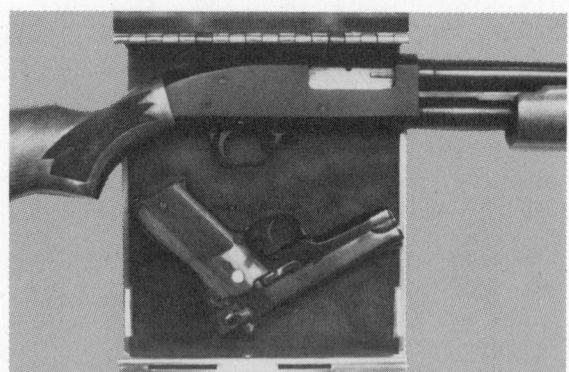

Insta Guard from Necessary Concepts, Inc., is a newly patented firearm safety lock which locks firearms away from children and intruders, yet allows access in seconds—even in the dark.

Available in two rubber-lined models in heavy-gauge stainless steel with the proven Simplex push-button combination lock. Both models can be bolted securely at any height—to a closet wall or bed frame, or in a vehicle, trailer or boat.

The Model 1100 locks any single handgun or shotgun; the Model 1200 locks a handgun and shotgun, up to three handguns or a modern military weapon.

For complete information, contact Necessary Concepts, Inc., directly. Dealer inquiries welcome (FFL required).

NECESSARY CONCEPTS, INC.

See manufacturers' addresses on page 269.

ADJUSTABLE DISC APERTURE

Hunters are constantly faced with continually changing light conditions. A receiver sight with a fixed aperture is adequate for only one light condition.

The Merit Hunting Disc aperture is instantly adjustable from .025- to .155-inch in diameter, allowing a clear sight picture to be maintained under changing conditions.

The aperture leaves are supported to withstand recoil from heavy calibers, and the shank is tapered to provide solid lock-up of the disc to your receiver sight.

Contact Merit Corp. for a free copy of their brochure describing this and other sighting aids for shooters.

MERIT CORP.

SHOOTING GLASSES APERTURE

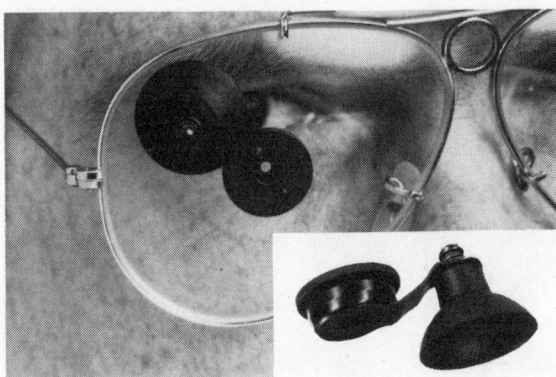

Pistol shooters can see their sights and target clearly with the Merit Optical Attachment and its instantly adjustable diameter aperture.

An aperture (pinhole) increases the eyes' depth of field (range of focus) dramatically.

The optical attachment is instantly adjustable from .022- to .156-inch in diameter to accommodate different light conditions. The sights and target will be in clear focus.

Additionally, using an aperture improves a shooter's concentration by helping him maintain a consistent head position. This device works equally well with bifocals, trifocals or plain-lensed shooting glasses.

Contact Merit Corp. for a free brochure.

MERIT CORP.

COMPACT 357 AUTOLOADER

The Cadet from Coonan Arms, Inc., is one of the only "compact" 357 semi-auto magnum pistols on the market today.

Handcrafted from high-quality stainless steel, the Cadet offers a 6+1 capacity, weighs 39 ounces and has a 3.9-inch barrel length. The Cadet is American-made and features a linkless bull barrel, full-length guide rod, and extended slide catch and thumblock for one-hand operation.

Like all Coonan pistols, the reliable and accurate Cadet uses standard 357 Magnum ammunition. Other options available include porting for less felt recoil.

Available through most major distributors and gun dealers; contact Coonan for more information or a free catalog. Be sure to mention *Shooter's Marketplace*.

COONAN ARMS, INC.

357 MAGNUM AUTOLOADER

Coonan Arms, Inc., manufacturer of one of the finest 357 semi-auto pistols currently on the market, is offering variations on their standard Model "B" 5-inch 357 (top)—a 6-inch model ideal for handgun hunters (middle); and the Factory Comp., a favorite with competitive shooters (bottom).

All models are handcrafted from high-quality stainless steel and are American-made. Features include a linkless barrel system plus extended slide catch and thumblock for one-hand operation. Capacity is 8+1; all use standard 357 Magnum ammunition. A 38+P conversion kit is also offered.

Available through most major distributors and gun dealers; contact Coonan for more information or a free catalog. Be sure to mention *Shooter's Marketplace*.

COONAN ARMS, INC.

NEW AMMUNITION SERVICE

New England Ammunition Co. offers a comprehensive selection of Hansen Cartridge Co. products.

All ammunition has been designed to fit the needs of avid American target shooters, plinkers, hunters and reloaders. It's all newly manufactured, non-corrosive, boxer-primed and fully reloadable. There are over 70 items available.

New England Ammunition Co. offers many unique and specialty calibers at reasonable prices, such as the 9mm Makarov full metal jacket and hollowpoint, as well as such standbys as the 30-06 softpoint.

Write New England Ammunition Co. for pricing information and ordering instructions.

NEW ENGLAND AMMUNITION CO.

ALL-TERRAIN TARGET HOLDER

The Targ-A-Tote™ provides the ultimate in convenience and precision whenever it is impractical to go to a formal range. It can be set up safely virtually anywhere in about a minute.

The Targ-A-Tote comes assembled and folds flat to save or reuse. Extendable tripod legs give stability on slopes to 35°. A built-in level allows the unit to be set plumb every time for best groups—no wasted shots.

The target board and all parts are replaceable. It is designed for professionals, handloaders, varmint hunters and other serious shooters for calibers 22 rimfire and larger.

Targ-A-Tote sells for $69.95 plus $9.50 shipping and handling.

Call or write R-Tech for more information.

R-TECH CORP.

MUZZLE-LOADING HUNTING RIFLE

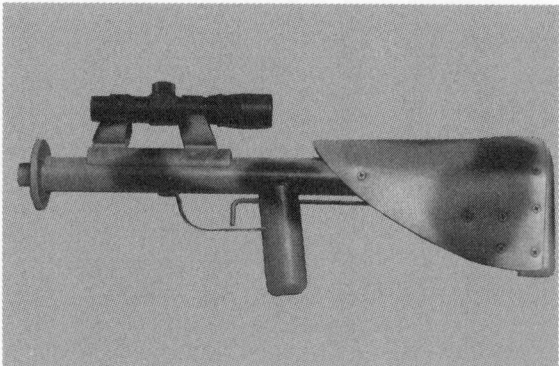

This high-tech blackpowder Bullpup hunting rifle packs power and accuracy into an extremely compact, lightweight package.

Custom overall lengths run from 18" to 26". Available in 50- and 54-caliber with large, soft buttpad, the barrel is massive at the breech with a fast, aggressive taper.

A heavy, metal rollover cheekpiece protects the face from flash; a large flange at the muzzle keeps the left hand out of harm's way; and the bullet starter protects the crown and promotes accuracy.

The Bullpup fits easily into an open backpack. The sling allows "hands free" carry in the "ready" position. The scope base is secured to the barrel sleeve, allowing use of a wide variety of mechanical, optical and laser sighting systems. Send $2 for brochure.

SOUND TECHNOLOGY

COMPLETE GUNSMITHING SERVICES

Walker Arms Co., Inc., one of the nation's oldest firearm repair services, provides factory-authorized warranty service for many of the world's best firearm manufacturers.

Walker Arms also provides warranty firearm repairs for major U.S. retailers, and is one of the southeast's largest parts distributors.

The combined 108 years of experience of their five professional gunsmiths is available to assist customers with all of their gunsmithing needs. Services include installation of screw-in chokes, barrel, sight and action work, metal and wood finishing, custom-made guns, antique gun restoration and firearm appraisals.

Write for a free brochure and shipping information.

WALKER ARMS CO., INC.

See manufacturers' addresses on page 269.

SHOOTER'S MARKETPLACE

GUN BOOKS & MAGAZINES

Wolfe Publishing Co. offers a large selection of hunting and firearms books, art prints and magazines for serious outdoor and gun enthusiasts.

They offer three of America's foremost sporting magazines–*Hunting Horizons,* a journal dedicated to the hunt; *Rifle,* an excellent firearms journal; and *Handloader,* the only magazine devoted exclusively to reloading.

If you want to expand your firearms knowledge and want more than mass media gun magazines, Wolfe publications are for you.

The Wolfe catalog lists more than 100 books for the sportsman's library and sells for $1.00—mention *Shooter's Marketplace* and it's free. Contact Wolfe Publishing Co. for more information.

WOLFE PUBLISHING CO.

COMPLETE NEW LINE OF TARGETS

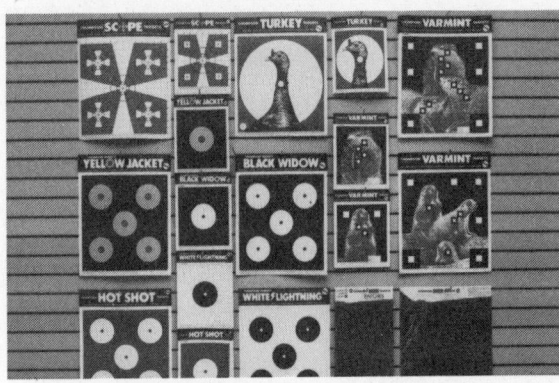

Thompson Target Technology offers a complete target line for the competitor and non-professional, as well as range shooter and hunter/sportsman.

Using a scientific approach to how the eye adjusts to color and light, their targets give shooters the optimum in sight-to-target alignment.

Their line includes scope alignment, conventional bullseye, turkey patterning, varmint, benchrest, deer and animal targets for gun and bow.

The new human silhouette series for police, security and self-defense are used in ranges throughout the country.

See your local dealer or send $5.95 for complete 14-target sample pack and catalog ($2.00 for catalog only).

THOMPSON TARGET TECHNOLOGY

22 RIMFIRE ACCURACY GAUGE

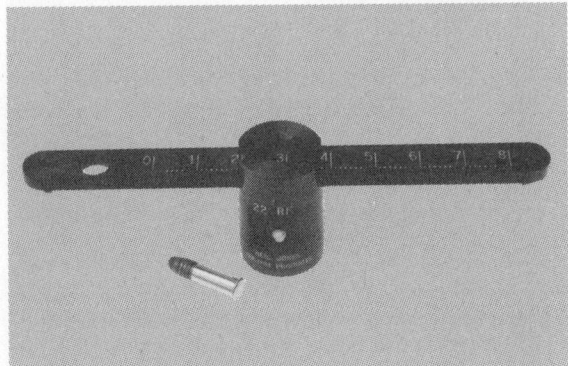

The 22 Rimfire Accuracy Gauge from Neil Jones Custom Products measures the thickness of the cartridge rim and enables ammunition to be sorted for consistent headspacing. The use of this gauge helps eliminate flyers, which results in smaller groups.

The rimfire gauge has been used for 15 years by thousands of satisfied customers. It is 100% safe, with nothing to wear out or break. It is easily modified for use with 22 Rimfire Magnum ammunition.

Shooter's Marketplace readers can send for a free catalog of prices and information on this and other Neil Jones accuracy products for shooters and handloaders.

NEIL JONES CUSTOM PRODUCTS

PORTABLE GUN REST/CLEANING BOX

Whether shooting "red-clay," "whitetail" or "black-powder," the Gun-Box from Timber Heirloom Products will last for generations.

This solid oak shooting/cleaning box with protective oil finish has a felt-lined tray and two large storage compartments. A center compartment keeps containers upright, while a hideaway area organizes cleaning equipment.

The fold-out gun rest features full-length piano hinges and heavy-duty tool box catches. This, coupled with the non-marring bumpers, provides the ultimate gun rest for cleaning or shooting.

Send check or money order for $119.95 plus $5.00 shipping/handling to Timber Heirloom Products, or send $1.00 for brochure.

TIMBER HEIRLOOM PRODUCTS

See manufacturers' addresses on page 269.

SHOOTER'S MARKETPLACE

NEW SMOKELESS PROPELLANTS

Powders with a purpose are what V-Propellants from Vihtavuori Oy are all about. Ammunition manufacturers such as Sako, Eley, Remington and Federal frequently choose V-Propellants when assembling rimfire ammunition and optimizing specific cartridges. Now, reloaders can obtain these powders to get the best from specific cartridges and bullet weights.

For eye-opening information on pressure, optimized powder charges, case volume, seating depth, ambient temperature effect, accuracy, loading data for the thirteen different V-Powders, and more, the V-Propellant Guide is a must. Reloaders, dealers and master distributors should write or call for a free copy of the guide.

VIHTAVUORI OY

CARTRIDGES FOR COLLECTORS

James Tillinghast's *Cartridges for Collectors List* contains over 1000 cartridges for sale: patent ignition, rimfire, pistol, rifle, shotgun. It also lists American and foreign books and catalogs available. Send $2.00 for a single cartridge list; $8.00 for the next five, a real "bargin."

Also offered is the *Antique Ammunition Price Guide #1*—8½x11, 64 pages, well illustrated. Regular price: $6.00; special price: $3.50 prepaid. The cartridge list is free with the purchase of the price guide.

Tillinghast is looking to buy cartridge collections, accumulations, box lots and rare singles of all types. He also purchases gun catalogs, gun powder tins, and gun and ammunition related advertising material.

JAMES C. TILLINGHAST

MILITARY/POLICE RANGING SYSTEM

The SN-4 Omni-Purpose Tactical Format Military and Police Sighting and Ranging System is available from U.S. Optics. It features custom-made 1-4x variable power front focal plane (no shift center of impact) and circle dot reticle (etched glass).

A fixed eyepiece with European-style rapid focus diopters, 30mm tube, and fully multi-coated, waterproof, ruggedized construction are standard.

This is a 10-lens element system with extra wide field of view. Bullet Drop Compensator calculated for 223- or 308-caliber.

Choice of reticles, knobs and finishes is offered. The GP-4, the hunting version of the SN-4, is also available. Contact U.S. Optics for more information.

U.S. OPTICS TECHNOLOGIES, INC.

RE-ENERGIZING SERRATED KNIVES

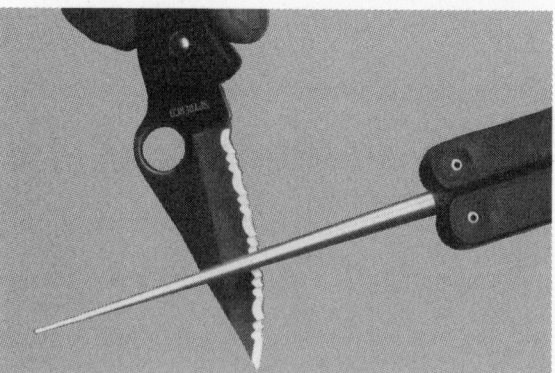

Diamond Machining Technology, Inc., offers a pocket Serrated Knife Sharpener that quickly restores the edges of serrated knives and other cutting tools. The sharpener is a 4-inch cone that tapers in diameter from ⅟₁₆- to ¼-inch, the most common serration sizes found on cutting tools.

The knife sharpener is coated with micronized diamond crystals in coarse or fine grit. The diamond abrasive quickly sharpens one serration at a time, restoring knives and tools to peak efficiency.

The sharpener is part of DMT's Diafold™ line of sharpening tools. Diafold sharpeners are housed in a plastic case that unfolds into a convenient handle.

More information and a full-line catalog of precision products are available.

DIAMOND MACHINING TECHNOLOGY, INC.

See manufacturers' addresses on page 269.

SHOOTER'S MARKETPLACE

2.4X NIGHT VISION SCOPE

Formerly unavailable in America, the HiTEK II Military Night Vision Scope is now offered here by HiTEK.

It uses starlight technology, requiring only the stars and/or moon to make subjects clearly visible. And with the optional Laser Illuminator (mounted in the handgrip), the unit will perform in total darkness.

The HiTEK II has 2.4x magnification with a field of vision not less than 15°. Features include a daylight filter, delayed-action shutoff, camera adapter, handgrip or tripod mount, standard 9V battery, and leatherette carrying bag.

With a variety of uses, the units are sold brand-new (not surplus) for $495 and carry a 30-day money-back guarantee along with a 1-year warranty.

Contact HiTEK for a catalog and dealer pricing.

HITEK INTERNATIONAL

4.7X NIGHT VISION SCOPE

Featuring 60,000x light amplification, the HiTEK 10 Military Night Vision Scope was originally designed for assaults in urban areas. It has an Image Tube Protection System to guard against sudden flashes of light, plus a daylight filter and 4.7x magnification.

Rugged and versatile, the water-resistant HiTEK 10 is adaptable to most Single Lens Reflex cameras and Pro-Video recorders. An optional Laser Illuminator allows use in total darkness.

The HiTEK 10 is available for $1495, including standard 9V batteries, leatherette carrying bag and shoulder strap. The unit is tripod-mountable, features an adjustable sight, and accepts a variety of standard lenses.

HiTEK 10 comes with a 30-day guarantee and 1-year warranty. Contact HiTEK for a free catalog and pricing.

HITEK INTERNATIONAL

NIGHT VISION RIFLE SCOPE

The HiTEK NS2 Military Night Vision Rifle Scope offers top-of-the-line starlight technology and rugged dependability for only $1895.

Features include 90,000x light amplification, interchangeable lens and ocular, and an Image Tube Protection System. The NS2 is recoil-proof, uses a standard mount and is adaptable to most Single Lens Reflex cameras and Pro-Video recorders.

Powered by a standard 9V battery, the patented NS2 has a daylight filter and adjustable sight. Designed for the KGB, Russian commandos and the military, they are sold new (not surplus), with a 30-day money-back guarantee and 1-year warranty. Overnight delivery is available.

Contact HiTEK for a free catalog and dealer pricing.

HITEK INTERNATIONAL

NIGHT VISION BINOCULAR

The HiTEK 3B Military Night Vision Binocular delivers superior 90,000x light amplification for only $1895.

This rugged, versatile binocular was designed for the KGB, Russian commandos and the military, and comes with a top-of-the-line Image Tube Protection System. Powered by four standard AA batteries, the 3B is convertible for day and night use, and features interchangeable lens and ocular. It is adaptable to most Single Lens Reflex cameras and can be tripod-mounted.

Magnification is 4.7x with a 12° field of vision; the sight is adjustable. All units are sold new, not surplus, and come with a 30-day money-back guarantee and a 1-year warranty.

Contact HiTEK for a free catalog and dealer pricing.

HITEK INTERNATIONAL

See manufacturers' addresses on page 269.

INDUSTRIAL SEWING MACHINE

The Bull, an industrial-grade sewing machine from Ferdinand, has the unique ability to sew forward and backward on Kevlar, ballistic nylon, canvas and plastic.

Its extra foot lift allows up to 7/8" of the toughest leather to be sewn. Because of its delicate touch, the machine can sew from 2 to 12 stitches per inch on material as light as a dollar bill.

Ferdinand offers a money-back guarantee on all their products. A complete machine shop and skilled staff can rebuild leather stitchers from as early as 1890. Ferdinand's line of sewing machines is intended for professional and advanced hobbyist usage.

Call toll-free from the U.S. or Canada for complete information.

FERDINAND, INC.

RIFLE/PISTOL RELOADING CATALOG

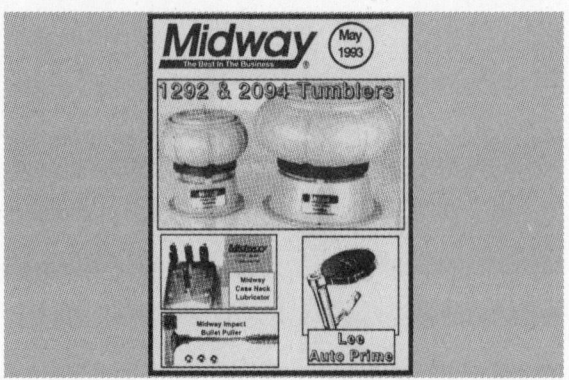

Midway Arms' 52-page catalog contains one of the world's largest selections of reloading and shooting products for rifles and pistols.

The catalog features products from nearly every manufacturer of reloading equipment and accessories. There are over 8,000 products offered to help beginning and serious shooters perfect their reloading skills.

For example, handloaders who are looking for bulk-pack bullets or brass will find Midway's selection quite extensive, with attractive prices.

Midway's staff has been providing reloaders with fast, friendly service since 1977, with free shipping and handling on every order. Call or write for their free catalog.

MIDWAY ARMS, INC.

LINSEED RUBBING OIL

Old World Oil Products has been offering best-quality linseed oil for over a decade. Long recognized as *the* professional gun stock finish, linseed oil brings out the full character and quality of a walnut gun stock.

This linseed oil is available in red or amber shades and is perfect for the expert refinishing of old gun lumber or the complete and total enhancement of a brand new gun stock.

This product is also ideal for maintaining original, oil-finished stocks.

Each bottle of linseed oil comes complete with instructions. Simply send $7.50 for a 4-oz. bottle of red or amber Old World Linseed Oil. Catalogs are not available.

OLD WORLD OIL PRODUCTS

CONVERSION KITS

Jonathan Arthur Ciener offers conversion kits to change your firearm from its standard caliber to 22 LR in just a few seconds for target practice, plinking or small game hunting.

Installation does not require permanent alteration of the firearm, which can be changed back to its original caliber quickly.

Ciener manufactures 22 LR Conversion Kits for the AR15 or M16, Mini-14 and AC556, AK47/S or AK84/S rifles, the 1911A1, Beretta 92 and Taurus PT92 pistols, plus others.

Prices start at $99 and you can order direct since no FFL is required. For more information on these and other Ciener products, send $5 for a catalog or $15 for a catalog and distinctive logo T-shirt.

JONATHAN ARTHUR CIENER, INC.

See manufacturers' addresses on page 269.

NEW ADJUSTABLE BORE GUIDE

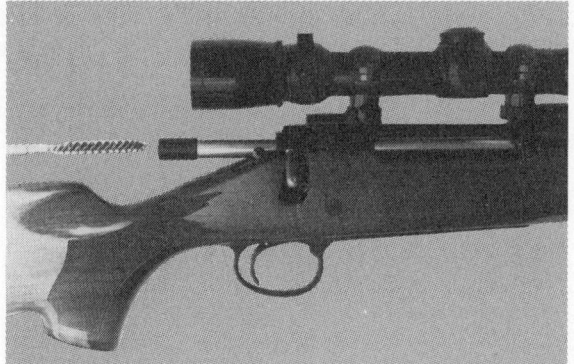

The new precision-machined XL Model Chamber-All™ Bore Guides feature an anodized aluminum tube and special Delrin® fittings. The Bore Guide simply replaces the bolt for cleaning. A slide-adjustable bolt collar with threaded pin locks solidly into any length action. A bore brush or jag will feed easily through the funneled entry guide.

Model XL-101 (.270" I.D.) is suitable for cleaning 17- to 25- caliber barrels, Model XL-202 (.338" I.D.) for 25- to 30-caliber/8mm barrels. Both fit centerfire firearms with .695" to .700" bolt diameters. Optional bolt collars are available to fit Weatherby Vanguard, Tika, and Sako A1 and A2 actions.

Retail: $23.95 each (plus S&H). Ask your dealer, or send for free information.

STONEY POINT PRODUCTS, INC.

NEW SEE-THROUGH SCOPE MOUNT

J.B. Holden Co. introduced the patented Iron-sighter® "See-Thru" scope mount line in 1967. Today, the Ironsighter two-way sighting option is accepted as standard. The Holden Wide Ironsighters are one of their most recent developments; the 700 series Ironsighters are now available for most centerfire, rimfire and muzzleloading rifles as well as many handguns and shotguns.

Holden offers a superior aluminum alloy which is as much as 60% stronger than the materials found in similar products. When combined with solid engineering designs, added metal thickness in high-stress areas, and precision-machined contact surfaces, Holden mounts will withstand the heaviest types of use.

J.B. HOLDEN CO.

NEW BULLET SEATING GAUGE

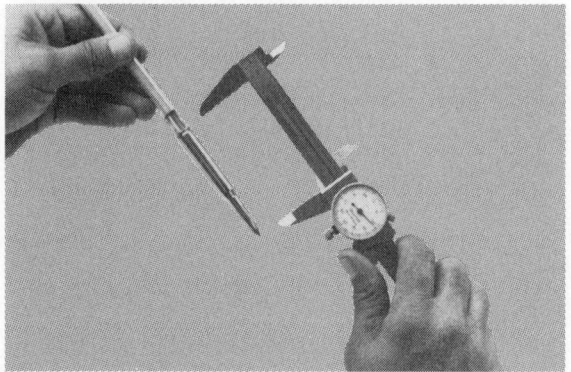

The new Chamber-All™ OAL Gauge can significantly improve shooting accuracy by establishing proper bullet seating depth. After it is removed from the firearm, a special port in the tool allows a caliper to measure from the case's base to bullet tip. This dimension determines proper bullet seating depth.

The precision-machined gauge works with all bolt-actions and single shots and retails for $34.95, complete with choice of Modified Case. Modified Cases are factory altered (neck I.D. .002" oversize and case head threaded) so they may be used interchangeably. Modified Cases are $3.95 each, available in many sizes (SAAMI specifications). Wildcat and improved cartridge brass can be factory-modified for $6.50 each (plus S&H). Ask your dealer, or send for free information.

STONEY POINT PRODUCTS, INC.

NEW BLACKPOWDER SCOPE MOUNT

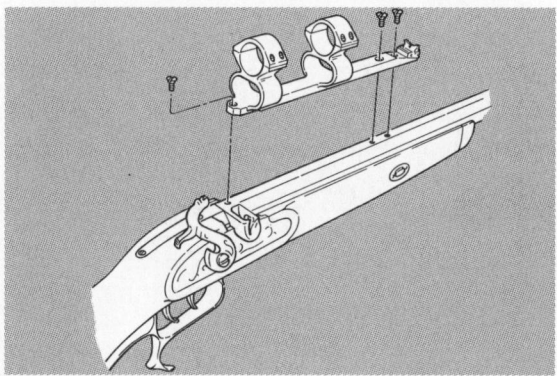

Recent innovations from the J.B. Holden Co. include the new Ironsighter® 365, 375 and 385 Black Powder Scope Mounts for popular 1991 and later Thompson/Center rifles.

This unique product, which attaches to factory-drilled holes on the barrel, offers an adjustable rear sight, see-through scope rings and mounting base which are precision-machined from a single piece of high-strength alloy. The result is a product designed for stability and durability. As the lead product in the constantly expanding line of Holden no-gunsmithing blackpowder scope mounts, each of these new Ironsighters provides superior strength and mounting stability.

Write for a catalog and serial number list of drilled and tapped T/C barrels.

J.B. HOLDEN CO.

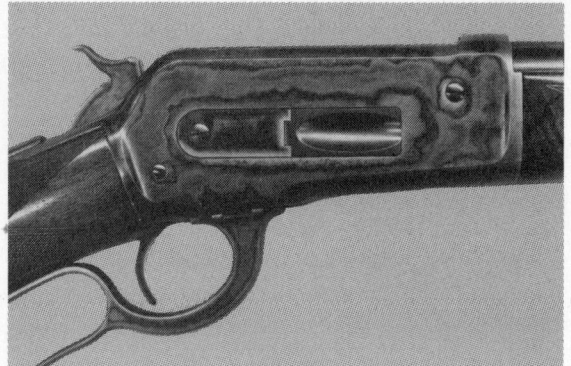

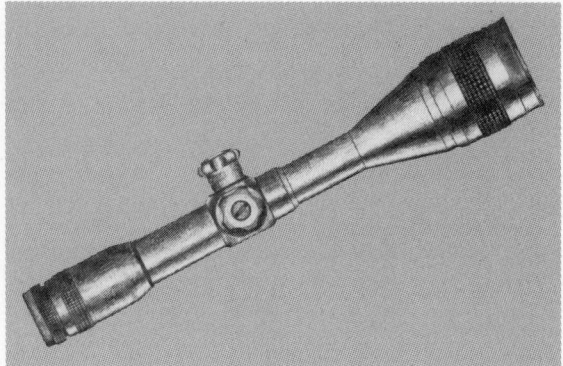

See manufacturers' addresses on page 269.

SHOOTER'S MARKETPLACE

RIFLED SHOTGUN BARRELS

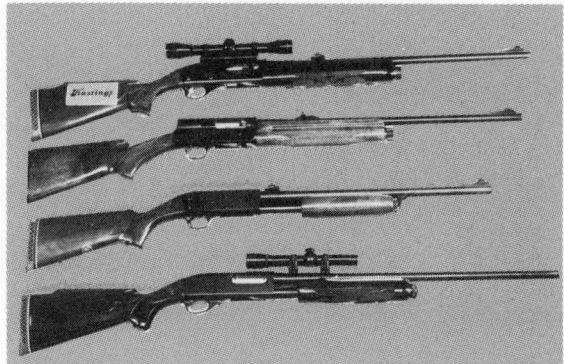

The Hastings Paradox Rifled Slug Barrel puts rifle-like accuracy within the reach and budget of every shotgun hunter. The rifled bore has a 1:34 twist for increased slug stability and superb accuracy. These are the only rifled slug barrels sold as exact replacement barrels for most popular single-barrel 12-gauge guns (no fitting required).

Barrels are offered in 20" and 24" lengths and are equipped with rifle sights or scope mount blocks. The popular Cantilever Scope Mount barrel has an extended mount to allow the use of a standard eye relief scope. All barrels have a high-polish blued finish and are proof-tested and serial numbered.

Paradox barrels are available from select gunshops or directly from Hastings. Call for more information.

HASTINGS BARRELS

SELF-ADHESIVE RECOIL PAD

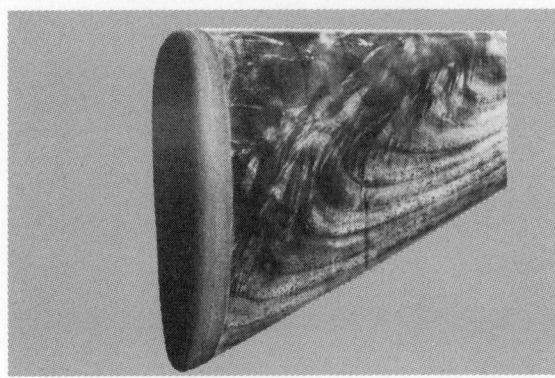

Add-A-Pad, for rifles or shotguns, can be installed in minutes by simply pressing a pad on the end of the butt, trimming it with a sharp knife and then sanding it to the exact shape of the stock.

Add-A-Pad is made from a shock-absorbent blended neoprene with a specially formulated adhesive backing.

The package includes two 1/4-inch and one 1/2-inch pads allowing the use of any one pad or a combination of pads to build a recoil pad up to 1-inch thick. The result is an economical pad which looks professionally installed.

Add-A-Pad costs $10.95 and comes with complete installation instructions. Call or write Palsa Outdoor Products for more information.

PALSA OUTDOOR PRODUCTS

QUICK-CHANGE MUZZLE BRAKE

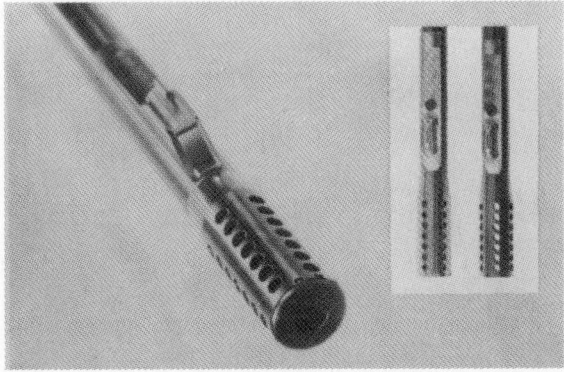

The Hastings Quick-Change Muzzle Brake is right at home on the range or in the woods.

The HQC tames recoil and muzzle jump by deflecting expanding gases perpendicular to the bore. This reduces the pounding taken during extended shooting sessions and helps eliminate flinching.

All effective muzzle brakes do increase noise for the shooter (this is not a problem on the range when ear protection is worn, but can be a problem when hunting). The HQC is unique in that a quick rotation of the outer sleeve seals the gas ports deactivating the brake and returns noise levels to normal.

Hastings installs the HQC on most centerfire rifles. It's available in stainless steel or blued finish. Contact Hastings for complete details.

HASTINGS BARRELS

CHOKE TUBE INSTALLATION

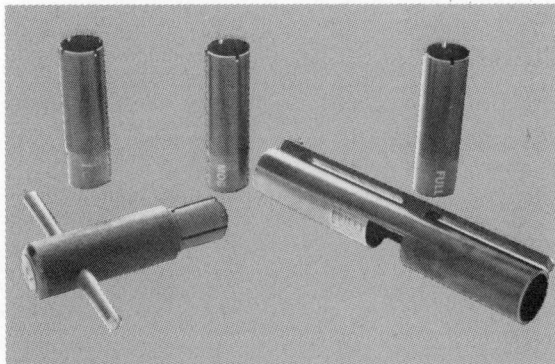

Now you can hunt everything from close-flushing woodcock to high-flying geese with a single gun. That's the versatility you'll enjoy with a Briley Screw-in Choke System.

If outstanding patterns with target loads, turkey loads, steel or buckshot are your goal, there is a Briley System right for the job. Briley tubes can currently be installed in nearly any shotgun of any gauge, including most single-barrel guns, plus thin-walled over/unders and side-by-sides.

Hastings is the master distributor and installer of Briley Chokes. They have perfected installation to ensure correct point of impact (tubes are concentric with the bore and fit to exacting tolerances). Call for complete information.

HASTINGS BARRELS

See manufacturers' addresses on page 269.

SHOTGUN SADDLE MOUNTS

B-Square shotgun saddle mounts are now available for most popular 12-gauge guns. These newly designed mounts straddle the receiver and fit the top of the gun tightly. All mounts have a standard dovetail base and "see-thru" design. Standard dovetail rings can be used.

B-Square shotgun mounts do not require gunsmithing, have a blued finish and attach to the gun's side with included hardware. Saddle mounts are available for Remington 870/1100 and 11/87; Mossberg 500, 5500 and 835; Winchester 1400/1300/1200; Ithaca 37/87; and Browning A-5 shotguns.

The mounts retail for $49.95 at your local dealer, or call B-Square toll-free. A catalog featuring the complete line of B-Square products is available for $2.00.

B-SQUARE CO.

CHOKE TUBE SPEED WRENCH

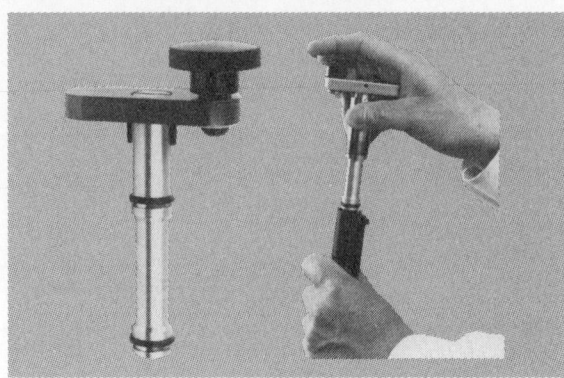

The Texas Twister choke tube speed wrench from B-Square is currently available for most 12-gauge shotguns.

The wrench inserts into the choke tube so it can be cranked in or out of the bore, and has a bore guide to prevent crooked starts and damaged threads. The T-handle is designed to break stubborn tubes loose so they can be cranked out easily and quickly.

Texas Twister wrenches are available for Briley, Beretta, Browning, Mossberg, Weatherby, Remington, Ruger, SKB and Winchester 12-gauge shotguns.

Retail price is $29.95 at your local dealer, or call B-Square toll-free. A catalog featuring the complete line of B-Square products is available for $2.00.

B-SQUARE CO.

LASER SIGHT MOUNTING SYSTEM

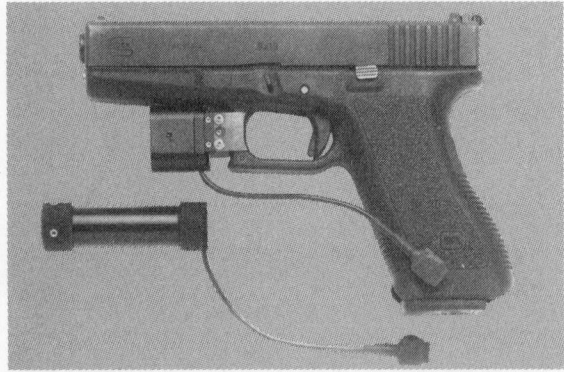

The BSL-1 Laser Sight, B-Square's newest laser sight mounting system, can now be interchanged with the Over/Under Laser Sight.

This unique mounting system uses a dovetail trigger guard mount in which either laser sight can be installed. This versatility allows shooters to move their BSL-1 or O/U laser sight to any number of guns with these special dovetail mounts.

B-Square lasers come in blued or stainless finish and feature a pulsating beam, sealed circuitry, common batteries, 5 mW of power and a lifetime warranty.

Laser mounts are available for most popular firearms. For more information, see your local dealer or call B-Square toll-free. A catalog featuring the complete line of B-Square products is available for $2.00.

B-SQUARE CO.

SCREW KITS

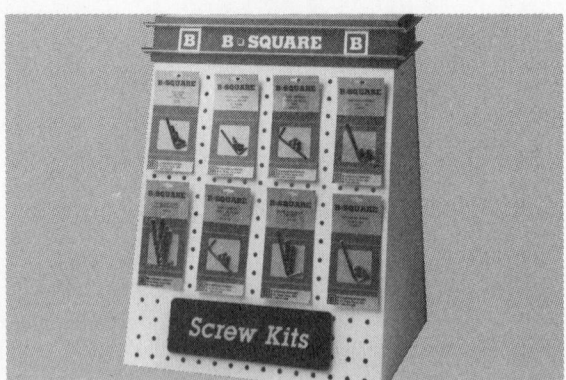

B-Square has become known within the industry as the source for screws—especially those hard-to-find, "must have" firearm screws we all need at some time.

B-Square screws are available in a variety of sizes and uses. All screw kits include a wrench and the appropriate number of socket head screws plus one extra. Available screw kit categories include base screws, trigger guard/action screws, grip screws, ring screws, plug screws and Smith & Wesson sideplate screws.

B-Square screw kit display units for retailers are now available. For additional information about display units and/or screw kits, call B-Square Co. toll-free.

B-SQUARE CO.

See manufacturers' addresses on page 269.

GUNSMITH TOOLS

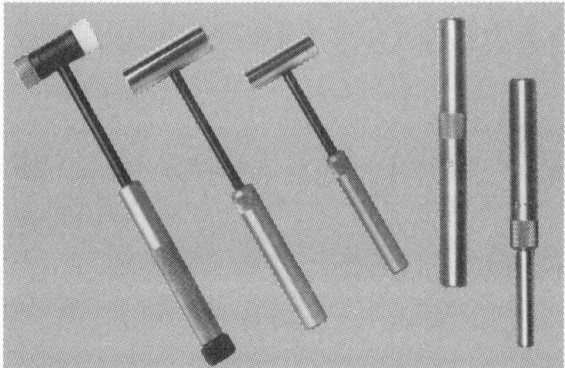

B-Square brass hammers and punches are famous for their design and quality. For the professional and hobby gunsmith, solid brass-headed hammers are perfect for dent removal and setting work in machine vises.

They provide the right sensitivity and feel for gunsmithing and other delicate jobs. Hammers are available in three weights: 2.5 ounces, 5 ounces and 10 ounces.

B-Square solid brass drifts are for driving out gunsights and large pins without damage. The set of two knurled 1/4" diameter and 3/8" diameter punches retails for $9.95 at your local dealer.

Call B-Square toll-free for a catalog featuring their complete line of tools and accessories.

B-SQUARE CO.

NO-GUNSMITHING SCOPE MOUNTS

B-Square Co. offers a complete line of scope mounts for pistols, revolvers, shotguns, sporting rifles and military rifles. Installation of any B-Square scope mount is simple and requires no gunsmithing.

Most mounts feature a "see-thru" standard dovetail base which accepts all standard dovetail (Weaver) rings. Scope mounts are available in blued and stainless finish and come with socket head screws.

New mounts are always being developed at B-Square. For additional information, ask your dealer or call B-Square toll-free. A 32-page catalog featuring the complete line of B-Square products is available for $2.00.

B-SQUARE CO.

COMPETITION GEAR

B-Square has a new shooting accessory line for competitive shooters.

Mounting systems are now available for CZ 75/Tanfoglio and Colt/Para Ordnance 1911 handguns. The mounts attach to tapped holes on the side of the gun. All standard optical sight and dovetail rings can be used. Drill jigs for each model can be purchased to ensure perfect installation of the sight mount.

Slide pulls and magazine bumpers for race guns are also available from B-Square.

Competition mounts retail for $99.50 at your local dealer, or call B-Square toll-free. A catalog featuring the complete line of B-Square products is available for $2.00.

B-SQUARE CO.

NEW BIPOD MODELS

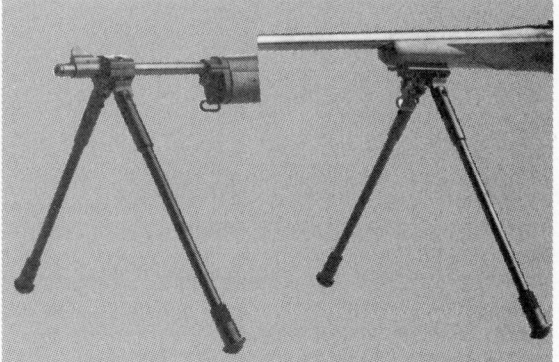

The new bipod from B-Square is currently available in two attachment models—barrel clamp and swivel stud. Featuring extendable legs in two lengths—7" to 11" and 11" to 17"—they're easy to install and require no gunsmithing or stock alteration. They are designed to swivel 15° for instant leveling on uneven ground.

B-Square bipods can be set up quickly, are fully machined and have no stampings, protrusions, springs or levers. When not in use, the legs fold up against the stock for a clean profile.

These bipods are available for $59.95 at your local dealer, or call B-Square toll-free. A catalog featuring the complete line of B-Square products is available for $2.00.

B-SQUARE CO.

See manufacturers' addresses on page 269.

SHOOTER'S MARKETPLACE

LASER/ELECTRONIC SIGHT MOUNTS

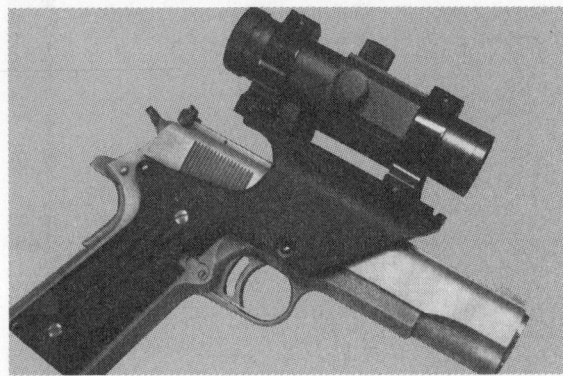

Aimtech offers a full line of unique scope, electronic sight and laser mounting systems. Right-side auto-pistol mounts, saddle shotgun mounts, double decker bow mounts, see-through solid rifle and muzzleloader mounts, as well as their patented revolver and Glock mount, were all designed with the convenience of the shooter in mind.

Highest-quality computer-aided design/manufacture and modern heat-treated alloy combine to make them among the best looking, best feeling mounts in the industry.

Aimtech products are available through all major distributors and quality gun dealers.

Write or call the manufacturer for more information or a free catalog.

AIMTECH MOUNT SYSTEMS

FREE BULLETS FROM 22 CASES

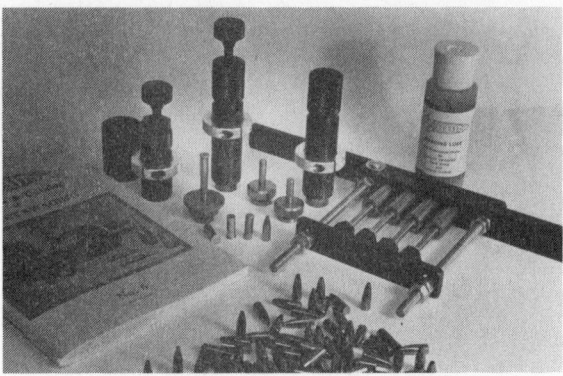

For over two decades, shooters have been making their own free 224 and 6mm bullets from fired 22 LR cases with the help of Corbin Bullet Swage Kits.

The BSD-224 and BSD-243 sets work with a regular reloading press, turning empty 22 cases and scrap lead into precision bullets at no cost. Weight is fully adjustable; accuracy is outstanding, with less bore wear than conventional jacketed bullets. Kit price, each caliber: $349.50.

Corbin produces swaging systems for a variety of other calibers as well, and recently introduced jacket-maker kits, available in any caliber. The Corbin Cannelure Tool will put factory-perfect cannelures on any bullet from 224 to 458 for $39.50. Illustrated 200-page book, $6. Contact Corbin for more information.

CORBIN , INC.

SHOTGUN SHELL RELOADING WADS

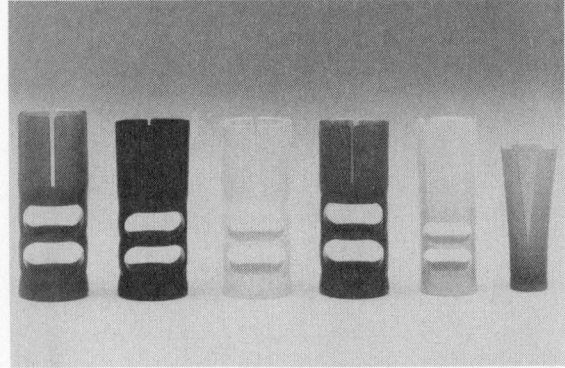

Jerry Haselbauer Products offers shotgun shell reloading wads currently available in 12- and 20-gauge and 410-bore; 28-gauge and other sizes soon to follow.

These Competitive Edge wads have a unique design which develops slightly higher speed with lower chamber pressure. This allows loading 1/2- to 1-grain less powder, which is an added savings in reloading.

Competitive Edge wads are available direct from Haselbauer for $11.25 per 1,000 (includes shipping to the lower 48 states). Jerry Haselbauer Products is in the process of implementing a mail-order program for shooters nationwide.

Send SASE for more information.

JERRY HASELBAUER PRODUCTS

COMPETITION 'HAWK AND KNIFE COMBO

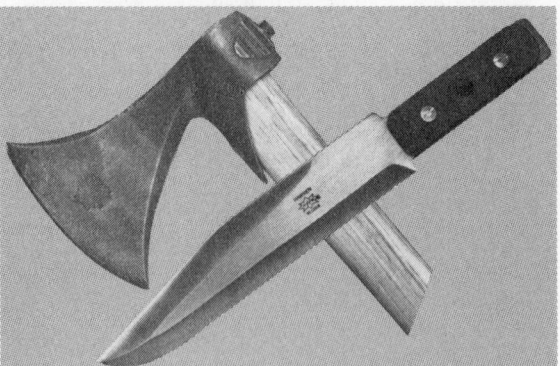

The tomahawk and knife pictured above were specially designed for competition throwing according to NMLRA rules. Knifemaker Harry McEvoy says this tomahawk is the ultimate in throwing design.

Its elongated throat lowers throwing stress leverage and impact stress on the handle, reducing breakage. Patented Head-Lok® design secures head to handle better than any other method. Comes with a 'hawk blade cover.

The Hawken "Bowie" has ideal weight and balance for competition throwing. Its semi-sharp clip edge can be handle *or* blade thrown. Comes with leather belt scabbard.

Their illustrated instruction book *Stick with the Winners* is included with each 'hawk or knife.

THE HAWKEN SHOP

See manufacturers' addresses on page 269.

AMBIDEXTROUS HANDGUN LASER

The Duty Grade laser by Laser Devices was designed with the law enforcement customer in mind. Upgraded, sophisticated and easy to install, it has been computer-designed to fit each handgun. The handgun remains field-strippable and does not require modification.

The ambidextrous switch allows the user to turn the unit on and off from the same side, or turn it on from the right side and off from the left, or vice versa.

The laser is a true 5 mW and is also available in the infra-red spectrum. In addition, LDI offers leather duty holsters at a special price when laser and holster are purchased together.

For an instructional video and/or catalog, contact Laser Devices, Inc.

LASER DEVICES, INC.

HANDGUN LASER SIGHTS

Laser Devices offers a large selection of below-the-barrel laser sights such as the BA-2. Once the BA-2 is mounted onto a handgun, laser and firearm become one. The patented trigger guard makes installation easy; the handgun does not require any modification. Since the unit is mounted under the barrel, it does not interfere with the open sight. It is available in blue or stainless finish.

Along with 14 years of experience, Laser Devices offers their customers a lifetime warranty on all diode laser sights and a true 5 mW output. All diode lasers are also available in the infra-red spectrum. A variety of accessories are also offered.

For an instructional video and/or catalog, contact Laser Devices, Inc.

LASER DEVICES, INC.

REVOLVER LASER SIGHTS

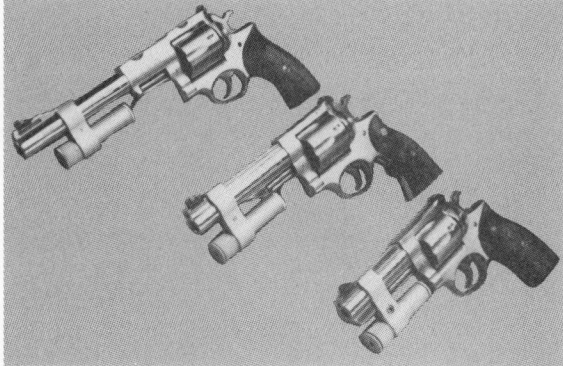

Laser Devices is currently offering a wide variety of laser sights that have been specifically designed for revolvers.

The BA-3 laser sight, mounted under the revolver's barrel, is computer designed to fit a specific revolver. The unit has a true 5 mW power output and a range of approximately 500 yards.

Working on a standard 3- or 6-Volt lithium battery, the BA-3 laser sight will provide many hours of shooting.

The BA-3 is also available in the infra-red spectrum. It is offered in blue or stainless finish and has a lifetime warranty.

For a free catalog call Laser Devices, Inc. and mention *Shooter's Marketplace*.

LASER DEVICES, INC.

M16/AR-15 LASER SIGHT

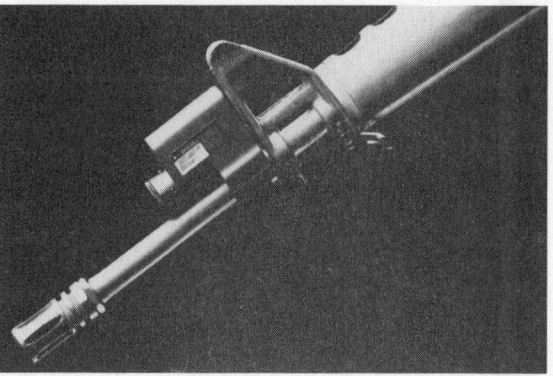

Laser Devices recently introduced the latest addition to an already extensive line of laser sights—the Model AR-2.

This small and compact laser unit fits above the barrel and in front of the open sight of the M16 or AR-15 rifle.

Due to its low parallax, only minor adjustments are necessary to align the laser beam to its preferred shooting distance.

A true 5 mW output and 15 hours of continuous battery life will give the user complete confidence in any situation.

This laser is available in the infra-red spectrum and comes with a lifetime warranty.

For a free catalog, call Laser Devices, Inc.

LASER DEVICES, INC.

VARIABLE CHOKE FOR SPORTING CLAYS

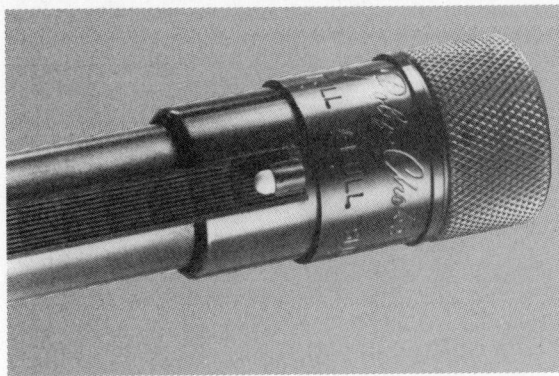

Poly-Choke from Marble Arms will convert any single-barrel shotgun into a fast-shooting, super-versatile Sporting Clays gun with a full array of chokes. Used for years by hunters, Poly-Choke now offers unlimited possibilities for the Sporting Clays shooter.

With a twist of an external sleeve, you can choose from nine different choke settings for the patterns wanted from station to station. And no fussing with loose choke tubes or wrenches.

Marble Arms will shorten your barrel, if necessary, and professionally install the standard model for $77.25; ventilated model for $85.50 (both plus shipping).

Send your original or spare barrel to Marble Arms for installation. Write for a free catalog.

MARBLE ARMS CORP.

HOME HANDGUN SECURITY

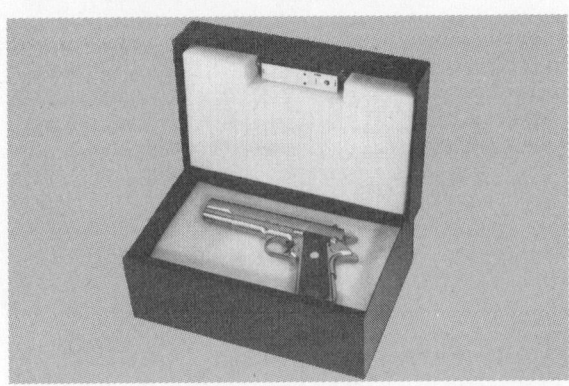

Sportsman's Communicators offers a Ready Response Safe Box for home/office handgun storage. Childproof and secure, it can also be opened in 5 seconds—in the dark.

It features a telescoping lid, 20-gauge steel-welded joints and a concealed piano hinge. It is portable, though can be pre-drilled for bolting in place. Set your choice of 2,000 combinations in minutes.

Internal foam pads hold gun in place (holds two 6" barrel guns). It is offered in brown or grey—a hand-tooled Deco box in antique brown or ebony is also available. Prices: 12"x8"x4" $85.95; 16"x8"x4" $95.95; 12"x8"x4" Deco $92.95. Add $6.00 postage and handling.

For more information or to order direct, call Sportsman's Communicators toll-free.

SPORTSMAN'S COMMUNICATORS

SOMETHING FOR THE LADIES

TomBoy, Inc., was established for women interested in hunting and fishing sports.

Founded by women, TomBoy, Inc., publishes *Tomboy*, the first magazine for women hunters and anglers.

The TomBoy Club is the first women's hunting and fishing club to go national. It provides a much-needed resource for women who want to learn and experience these sports.

Learning resources, outdoor clothing and equipment for women have not been readily available (until now) because women have not let their interest in these sports be known. Hence, Tomboy's logo: "We're Breaking the Silence."

They need your support. Write or call TomBoy, Inc.

TOMBOY, INC.

NEW OPTICS WITH UV AND IR COATING

New optical coatings technology is applied to the Brunton line of Eterna binoculars. The Eterna line offers the shooter one of the most advanced optical systems in the world. Special optical path design allows the user to wear shooting glasses, eyeglasses or sunglasses without having tunnel vision.

Camera-grade optics are fully multi-coated to reduce reflection. Brunton also adds a revolutionary "ruby" coating which eliminates all of the harmful ultraviolet (UV) and infrared (IR) light and reduces glare over water or snow.

This hunters/shooters optical system provides incredibly clear viewing, crisp detail and improved light transmission.

BRUNTON U.S.A.

See manufacturers' addresses on page 269.

ACCESSORY/SERVICE BROCHURE

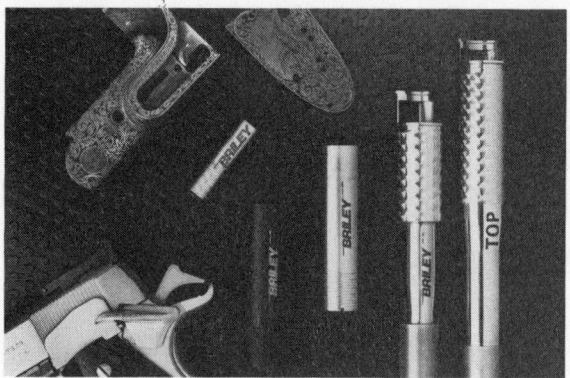

This Houston-based firm is well-known for providing precision products to the avid shotgunner. The Briley tradition of attention to detail and complete customer satisfaction keeps the hunter and competition shooter happy.

Their brochure describes Briley's line of shotgun and now pistol and revolver services. Briley has added a new division for the discerning handgun enthusiast.

Everything from screw-in chokes to competition Skeet tubes to pistol and revolver customizing and accessories is available. Briley offers an extensive line of products and services for the shotgunner and handgunner.

Write or call toll-free for a free brochure.

BRILEY MANUFACTURING, INC.

SCREW-IN CHOKES

Briley screw-in chokes produce reliable, uniform patterns. This system allows the shooter the complete choke control necessary to utilize the full spectrum of ammunition available to today's shotgunner.

There are new innovations in chokes, as well. The unique "Comp-Choke" gives the shooter not only reliable patterns, but aids in second-shot recovery time by porting gases upward at the muzzle.

Total steel shot compatibility is also available with the screw-in choke system. Even the largest shot sizes are usable through their steel shot chokes. Briley also offers exclusive choke designs and constrictions for turkey hunters.

Write or call toll-free for a free brochure.

BRILEY MANUFACTURING, INC.

PISTOL CUSTOMIZING/ACCESSORIES

Briley Manufacturing has a new fully specialized Pistol Division. For the dedicated handgun enthusiast, Briley offers some of the finest modifications, customizing, repair parts and accessories currently available.

Compensators, extended slide releases, thumb guards, squared trigger guards and more are just some of the services currently available from the new division.

The Pistol Division is currently manufacturing custom slides, barrels, custom titanium compensators and other unique accessories for the discerning handgun shooter and competitor.

Briley also offers complete, conventional repair services for all makes of handguns.

BRILEY MANUFACTURING, INC.

CUSTOM SHOTGUN REBARRELING

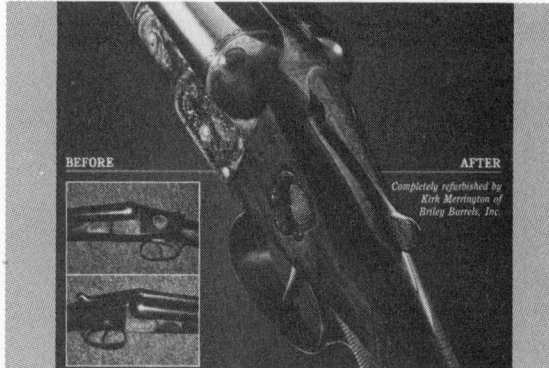

Briley has added a new custom department that is dedicated to the refurbishing of over/under and side-by-side shotgun barrels.

Briley can now fully restore a set of unshootable shotgun barrels. Barrels that have been severely dented, have rusted or have even burst during firing (due to a bore obstruction) can virtually all be saved.

Additionally, Briley can manufacture a set of new barrels (any make) for any gun, can provide new or custom ribs, and can completely strip, clean and/or repair the action.

This new Briley department also offers custom engraving services and complete stock repair and refinishing.

Write or call for more details.

BRILEY MANUFACTURING, INC.

See manufacturers' addresses on page 269.

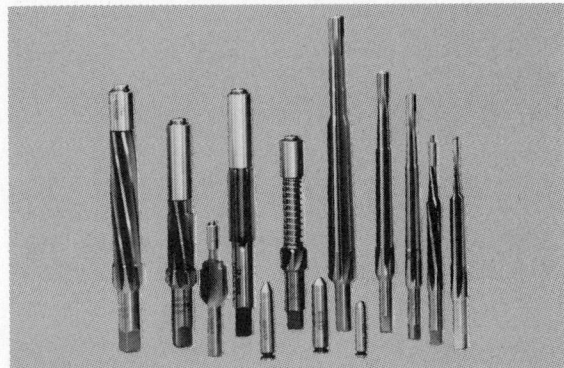
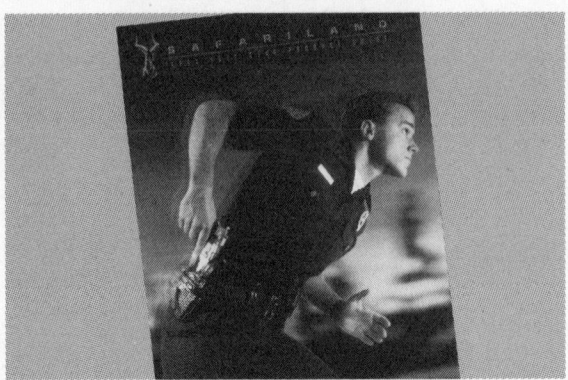

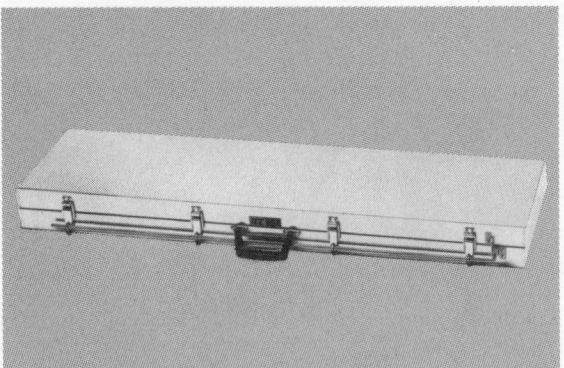

SHOOTER'S MARKETPLACE

NEW SPINNING TARGETS

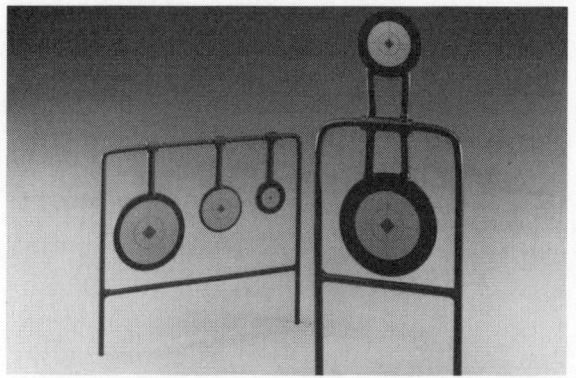

Birchwood Casey is offering a new line of circle spinners, silhouette swingers and action targets.

Purchased recently from the Steidle Corporation, the World of Targets® name will now be marketed by Birchwood Casey. Pictured above are the Qualifier Triple Action and Double Mag Circle Spinners, which are among the 25 metallic action targets they feature.

Offered in models designed for 22 rimfire as well as centerfire handguns up to 44 Magnum, the spinner targets provide challenging shooting practice. Each portable, easy-to-use target is solid steel hung from a durable, welded steel frame to provide years of service. The exclusive shatterproof finish will not chip or flake off like painted finishes. See your dealer or write Birchwood Casey direct for a free catalog.

BIRCHWOOD LABORATORIES, INC.

ELECTRONIC HEARING PROTECTOR

Silencio's RSX-87 Rangesafe electronic hearing protector has a 20 millisecond shutdown on sounds exceeding 85 dB; yet amplifies harmless noise, normal conversation, range commands and low level sounds in the field. The direction of sound is enhanced by the state-of-the-art stereo circuitry.

Stereophonic reception is created by the dual speakers and microphones. Separate volume controls allow adjustments for hearing variances.

The RSX-87 is powered by two 9V batteries, and is available with camouflage earcups in addition to the standard earcups.

For information on all Silencio products available, check with your local gun dealer or contact Silencio directly.

SILENCIO

COMPOSITE GUN STOCKS

Bell & Carlson recently announced its new Premier line of gunstocks. The Premier handcrafted composite stocks feature leading-edge design and innovative engineering.

The Varmint Special pictured above is an example of the new line; the stock provides outstanding accuracy along with shooting comfort.

The Premier line is available in six finishes, including the award-winning wood-grain and camouflage finishes.

Bell & Carlson has a fully staffed custom fitting department to help satisfy each customer's unique requirements.

Call or write Bell & Carlson for more information about their new gunstocks.

BELL & CARLSON, INC.

WRAPAROUND SHOOTING GLASSES

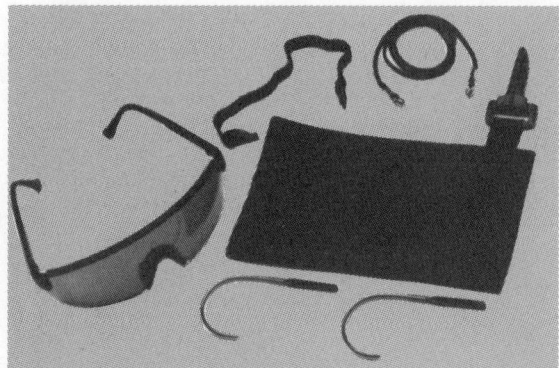

The comfortable line of Wrapps shooting glasses has deluxe, almost total U.V. blocking, polycarbonate, wraparound lenses weighing just 1-ounce. In a recent test, these high-impact lenses withstood a full-frontal shotgun blast.

Wrapps were designed with comfort, style, protection and affordability in mind.

Each pair of Wrapps includes a nylon case with belt clip, cleaning cloth, interchangeable and adjustable cable and paddle type temples, and safety cord plus elastic retainer strap. Available in yellow, gray, green, vermilion and clear lens colors. Wrapps are also available without the accessories.

For more information on all Silencio products, check with your local gun dealer or contact Silencio.

SILENCIO

See manufacturers' addresses on page 269.

FOLDING BIPODS

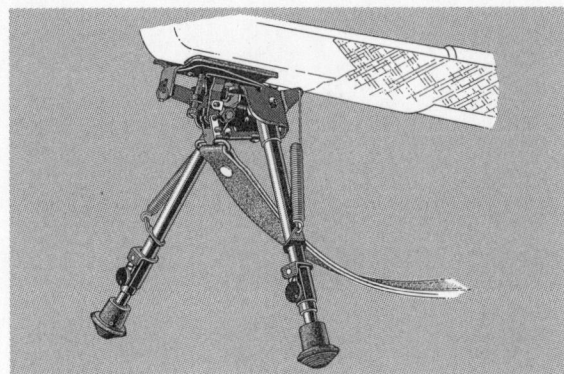

Harris Bipods clamp securely to most stud-equipped bolt-action rifles and are quick-detachable. With adapters, they will fit some other guns. On all models except the Model LM, folding legs have completely adjustable spring-return extensions. The sling swivel attaches to the clamp. This time-proven design is manufactured with heat-treated steel and hard alloys and has a black anodized finish.

Series S Bipods rotate 45° for instant leveling on uneven ground. Hinged base has tension adjustment and buffer springs to eliminate tremor or looseness in crotch area of bipod. They are otherwise similar to non-rotating Series 1A2.

Eleven models are available from Harris Engineering; literature is free.

HARRIS ENGINEERING, INC.

SCOPE GUARDS

Scopeguard™, available from Anderson Manufacturing Co., Inc., protects scopes from weather, shock and scratches. It is made of $1/8$" neoprene rubber bonded to nylon, and there's even an extra layer of protection over the windage and elevation adjustments.

Because it stretches, Scopeguard will fit virtually all scopes. It is available in two sizes—small for pistol or compact scopes, and regular for most other scopes. It comes with Huntbands™ so the ends can be pulled up quickly to take a shot.

Available in black or tree camo, manufacturer list price is $14.99.

For a free brochure call or write Anderson Manufacturing Co., Inc.

ANDERSON MANUFACTURING CO., INC.

FULL-AUTO PUBLICATION

Full-auto enthusiasts can turn to *Machine Gun News* each month for an arsenal of information about Title 2 firearms and other types of exotic weaponry.

This magazine features interesting articles, product reports, ammunition tests, industry interviews, legislative updates and events.

Advertising, both classified and display, offers hard-to-find firearms, hard-to-find parts, accessories and more.

The one-year subscription price is $29.95; single copy price $4. *Machine Gun News* is mailed with a protective cover to ensure privacy.

Mention *Shooter's Marketplace* when ordering from Lane Publishing and receive a free sample issue of *Machine Gun News*.

LANE PUBLISHING

NEW SIGHTING DEVICES

Lohman Manufacturing, makers of one of the most complete lines of game call products, has added two new items to their Sight-Vise line.

The Sight-Vise Model SSV-2 and SSV-3 are improved rifle/shotgun and pistol sighting devices. The SSV-2 clamps to the gun to reduce recoil and provide a solid rest for accurate, precise shotgun patterning or rifle sighting. It also holds guns securely for scope mounting, cleaning or repair work.

The SSV-3 securely clamps pistol barrels for sighting-in scopes or iron-sighted handguns. A V-Block attachment can be inserted to accommodate any handgun action.

These products were designed for both serious and pleasure shooters. Contact Lohman for more information.

LOHMAN MANUFACTURING CO., INC.

See manufacturers' addresses on page 269.

WOOD-GRAIN SYNTHETIC STOCK

Ram-Line introduces a synthetic wood stock that offers beauty and strength. The Wood-Tech is guaranteed against breakage as long as you own it.

Underneath the simulated wood stock finish is the classic Syn-Tech stock. The Wood-Tech offers the same strength, weather-proof accuracy, field-proven reliability and drop-in simplicity as all Syn-Tech stocks. It comes field-equipped with a Hunter Re-Actor pad and Uncle Mike's quick detachable/quick adjustable sling.

Twenty-eight models are available for actions like Interarms, Mauser, Remington, Ruger and Winchester; new stocks are available for Weatherby Mark V, Savage, Sako and more. Retail price $159.97 plus $5.00 shipping/handling! Call or write for a catalog.

RAM-LINE, INC.

GLOCK 17 REPLACEMENT MAG

Ram-Line announces a reliable steel magazine for the Glock 17 pistol. Made of heat-treated alloy, it holds a full factory load of 17 rounds, but drops free from the gun.

Ram-Line's unique insert protects the magazine release from metal latch tabs. Without this insert, the release can fail to hold the magazine in the well.

Further, a spacer provides a smooth surface for the rounds to glide upon, assuring reliable feeding. A polymer baseplate matches the Glock finish.

Available with a lifetime guarantee in blued (item MGK 9617 $24.97) or stainless steel (item MGK 9617S $28.97). Other 9mm magazines are also available including Browning, Beretta, Ruger, S&W, Taurus, Sig Sauer and more.

For more information contact Ram-Line.

RAM-LINE, INC.

NEW CARBINE STOCKS

You can preserve the military look of your SKS, M-1 Carbine, Ruger 10/22, Mini 14 or Marlin with Ram-Line's military-type folding stock made from high-impact modified polymers that won't chip, crack or warp. The stock adjusts for length of pull, and comes with pistol grip storage and Uncle Mike's sling swivel studs.

Or, you can sporterize the SKS, M-1 Carbine or 10/22 with a nearly-unbreakable Syn-Tech classic carbine stock with "krinkle" texturing, checkering, moulded-in color, studs and shoulder pad.

Both SKS stocks come with an injection-moulded upper-ventilated handguard—an extra-cost accessory on the others. Prices range from $64.97 to $69.97. No gunsmithing is required.

RAM-LINE, INC.

REPLACEMENT RUGER 10/22 MAGAZINES

Ram-Line is introducing a new 25-round magazine for the Ruger 10/22. While the 22 Maverick was designed for Yellow Jacket, Viper, and other hard-to-feed ammunition, it will also handle any other Long Rifle offering. The unique red follower and semi-transparent color allow easy round count, plus special markings (engraved bullet heads) show when there are 10 and 20 rounds remaining.

This single-column magazine retails for $9.97 and features a trapdoor for quick cleaning and an easy loading spring.

All Ram-Line products carry a lifetime warranty for repair or replacement. The Ruger 10/22 is a registered trademark of Sturm, Ruger & Co.

For more information contact Ram-Line, Inc.

RAM-LINE, INC.

See manufacturers' addresses on page 269.

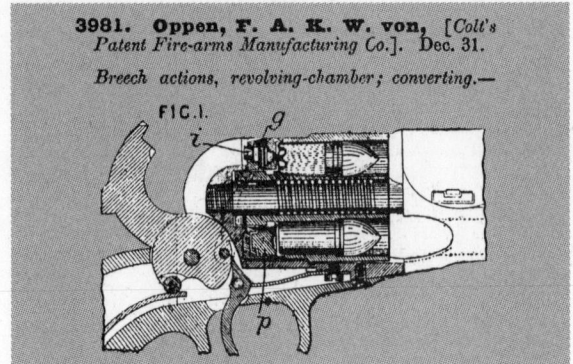

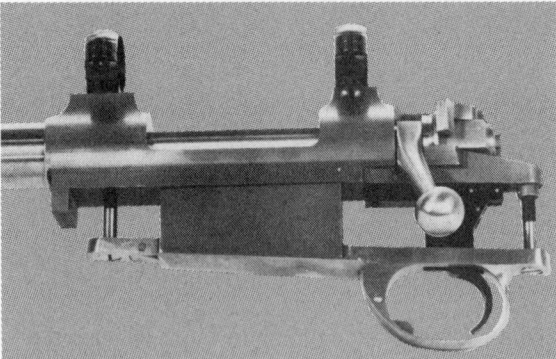
See manufacturers' addresses on page 269.

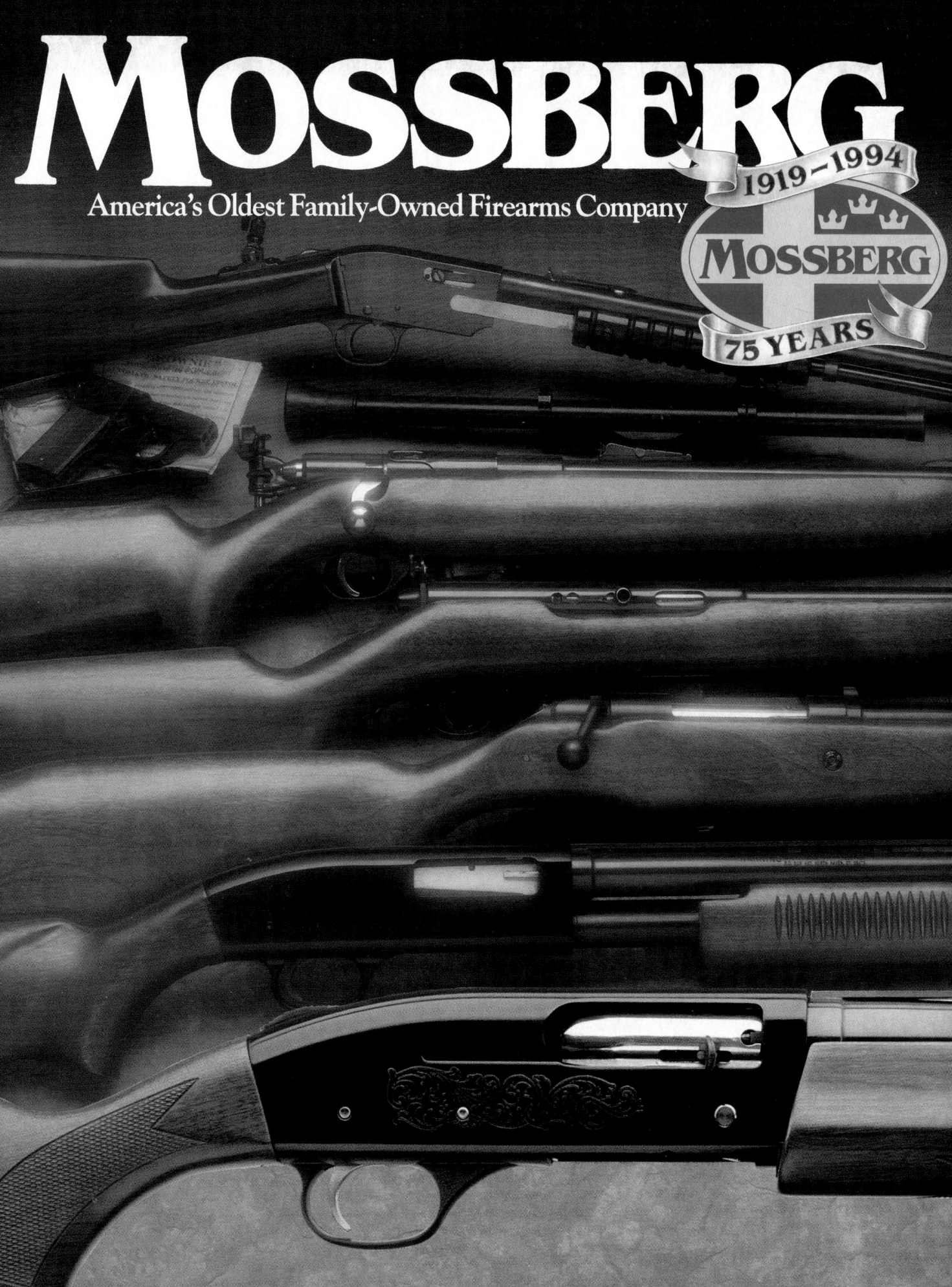

The Founder, Oscar F. Mossberg, flanked by
sons, Harold (left) and Iver (right).

Current President &
CEO, Oscar's
grandson, Alan
Mossberg, flanked by
sons, Jonathan (left)
and A. Iver (right).

FOUR GENERATIONS OF AMERICAN GUNMAKING

*Snapshots. They not only reflect the generations of a
family, they reflect the generations of gunmaking tradition
at O.F. Mossberg & Sons, Inc.*

As America's oldest family-owned firearms company,
O.F. Mossberg & Sons has provided generations of
hunters, sportsmen and law enforcement officers with
well designed, solidly crafted and reasonably priced
firearms. Starting in 1919 with the innovative "Brownie"
.22 caliber pistol, Oscar Mossberg set a standard of
technical inventiveness and manufacturing excellence
that continues today.

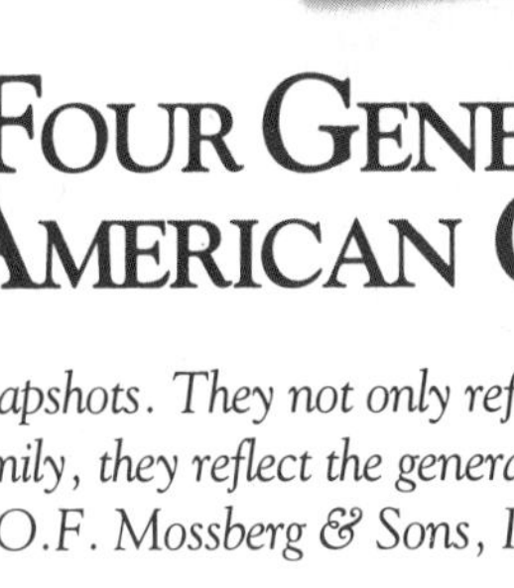

In 1922, the Model K pump rifle introduced the world to
"the Mossberg .22". Through the ensuing years,
generations of Americans, young and old, sharpened
their marksmanship with Mossberg .22's. Many
embarked on their competitive target shooting careers
looking through the sights of a Mossberg target rifle like
the Model 146B. Others spent untold hours plinking at
tin cans and other informal targets with one of
Mossberg's .22 autoloading rifles.

Shotgunners looking for a reasonably priced repeater to
replace their tip-up single barrel guns were quick to
recognize the value of the Mossberg bolt action shotgun.
In the 1940's and 50's, these guns established a
reputation for robust, hard working value that all
Mossberg shotguns continue to live up to.

Over three decades ago, Mossberg crafted the pump
shotgun that heralded a period of extraordinary growth.
The Model 500 grew to become the most successful
firearm in the company's history. It introduced several
new generations of shooters to Mossberg value.

Today, on the eve of Mossberg's 75th year, dedicated
company employees and the Mossberg family remain
committed to the concepts of innovation and value on
which Oscar Mossberg founded the company. The
innovative 3 1/2 inch Model 835 Pump Shotgun and the
remarkably priced 9200 Autoloader are just two
examples of this continuing commitment.

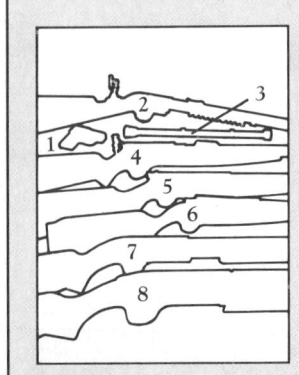

1. Brownie .22 Pistol, 1919 – 1932
2. Model K .22 Rifle, 1922 – 1931
3. Model 6 Telescopic Sight & Mount, 1934
4. Model 42M(C) .22 Rifle, 1940 – 1950
5. Model 152 Autoloading .22 Carbine, 1948 – 1958
6. Model 385 Bolt Action 20 gauge, 1947 – 1985
7. Model 500 Pump Action 20 gauge, 1962 – present
8. New Model 9200 Autoloader 12 gauge, 1993 – present

MOSSY OAK® 9200 Semiautomatic (#49434 shown) Includes: • Full MOSSY OAK Tree Stand camo finish • 24" vent rib magnum barrel • 4 AccuChoke tubes including one Extra-Full turkey choke tube for lead shot • MOSSY OAK sling with QD swivels and posts • Cablelock® for safe storage when not in use.

The Perfect Blend

Nobody offers you more shotgun camouflage options than Mossberg. You can choose our all-purpose camo pattern which we call Mossberg **OFM CAMO**, or our all new spray-applied **OFM MARSH** fall season pattern. You can also match your hunting outfit exactly with our **MOSSY OAK®**, and **REALTREE®** patterns. All four are tough, durable finishes built to last in the field.

The 835 Ulti-Mag™, 9200 Semi-Auto and Model 500 are all available, with a full, muzzle-to-butt Mossberg **OFM CAMO** or **OFM MARSH** pattern right out of the box. This finish gives turkey, deer and waterfowl hunters an advantage by blending with a wide variety of camo patterns and backgrounds.

Our Model 9200 is the only semi-auto available in the **MOSSY OAK** Tree Stand pattern This is a unique two-dimensional camo pattern that combines the blending capabilities of original **MOSSY OAK** Bottomland with a bold overlay of limbs and branches.

Introduced last year, the 835 Ulti-Mag is again available in its super successful Brown Leaf **REALTREE®** camo. The colors are olive brown, brown, tan, green and black. It blends naturally with earth tones as well as greener backgrounds.

Model 835 ULTI-MAG (#60034 shown)
Includes: • Full **REALTREE®** pattern camo finish • 24" vent rib barrel • 4 ACCU-MAG™ choke tubes including one Extra Full turkey choke tube for lead shot (#95251) Drilled and tapped receiver • **REALTREE** sling with QD swivels and posts • Cablelock for safe storage when not in use

Experienced hunters know they must remain hidden from their quarry. Nobody helps you like Mossberg.

Our camo shotguns also come with some not-so-standard features. A matching camo sling with QD swivels and posts is included with each gun.

Receivers are drilled and tapped for scope mounting on 835 and 500 models.

The **MOSSY OAK** 9200 and the **REALTREE** 835 Ulti-Mag were designated the 1992 NWTF Turkey Hunters' Guns of the Year. Their popularity will continue with turkey hunters throughout the States.

New REALTREE Accessory Barrels

A fully rifled 24" barrel with integral scope mount (#91820 shown) 24" fully rifled barrel with iron sights (#91803), a 24" smooth bore barrel with rifle sights (#91800), and a 28" vent rib Accu-Mag barrel (#91815) are all available in matching REALTREE finish as accessories. See page 13 for details.

NOTE: REALTREE CAMO Scope is for demonstration purposes only and is not available from Mossberg. (Redfield Optics Scope).

New Ghost Ring™ Turkey Gun

This new Mossberg **OFM CAMO** Model 500 turkey gun was just introduced last year. It features a **Ghost Ring** sighting system and an **AccuChoke** barrel with an Extra-Full turkey choke tube for lead shot. This unique sight provides a quicker target picture and improved accuracy. The Mossberg turkey tube is designed for maximum effectiveness at 30 yards. See page 11 for turkey tube details.

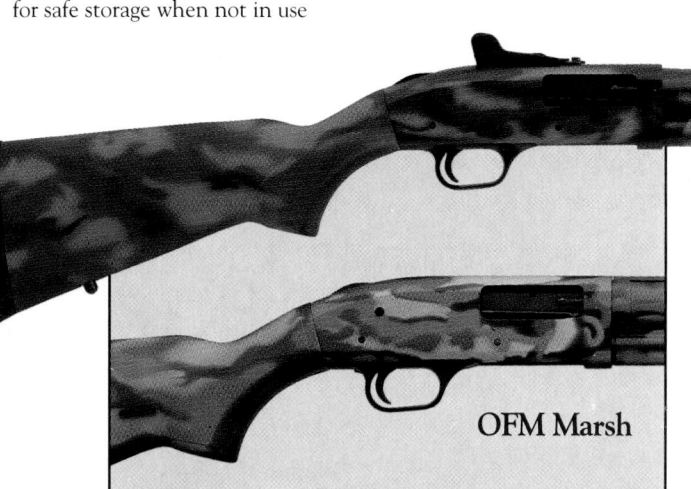

OFM Woodland

OFM Marsh

NEW OFM CAMO

Nobody knows camo guns like Mossberg. That's why the new OFM Marsh and OFM Woodland Camo Patterns are so effective. Using exclusive patterns and specially designed equipment, Mossberg created this new camo to work with virtually any clothing pattern and yet be far less costly. Available on Model 500 & 835 Ulti-Mag Pumps and 9200 Autoloaders, OFM Camo delivers remarkable effectiveness at a savings.

Model 9200 (#49420 shown) Includes: •Engraved aluminum receiver • Fires 3" Magnum and 2 3/4" 12 ga. field loads • 28" vent rib barrel • American Walnut cut-checkered stock and forearm • 3 ACCU-CHOKE tubes • 5 round capacity • Dual shell stops • Ambidextrous top tang safety • Steel-to-steel lockup • Wide vent rib with white front bead and brass midpoint sight • Field plug for magazine tube • Interchangeable rifle barrels and stocks within this model • Cablelock® for safe storage when not in use

The New 9200 Regal Autoloader
Shoots Both Magnum and Light Load Ammo!

The Model 9200 fires any sequence of 12 gauge loads, from 2 3/4" trap to 3" Magnums. No barrels to change, no buttons to push, no adjustments to make.

Fire mixed loads or identical loads. The 9200's unique gas regulating system instantly compensates for varied pressures developed by a wide range of shot shell loads. For example, when firing low brass loads, the system remains essentially closed, with all available gases used to cycle the action. That means controlled rapid cycling and strong reliable ejection.

With heavier loads, the system opens to release any gas not needed to work the action, assuring controlled bolt velocity, minimized stress on internal parts and diminished recoil.

Available now, the 9200, like all Mossberg shotguns, gives you "more gun for the money" - packing in extra features like a full 5-shot capacity with 2 3/4" shells, super-strong lightweight alloy receiver, an ambidextrous safety, self-adjusting action bars and a solid steel-to-steel lockup of bolt and barrel extension.

The 9200 combines its flawless gas system with modern styling usually found only on autoloaders costing much more. Cut checkering on both buttstock and forearm provide a sure grip for hunter and target shooter alike. The chromed bolt sets off the rich black finished receiver. A thoroughbred in form and function, all at a Mossberg affordable price.

Lifetime Limited Warranty

The popular priced Model 9200 is backed by a lifetime limited warranty, for the original purchaser. This warranty covers defects in materials and manufacture, so be sure to read the complete warranty statement included with every Model 9200 autoloader. Great gun, great service.

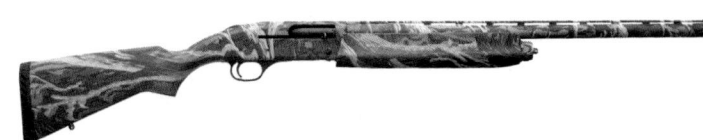

Model 9200 (#49434 shown) Includes: • Full MOSSY OAK® Tree Stand pattern camo finish • 12 ga. 24" magnum vent rib barrel • 4 ACCU-CHOKE tubes including one Extra-Full turkey choke tube for lead shot (#95240) • MOSSY OAK® sling with QD swivels and posts • Cablelock for safe storage when not in use

Model 6000 (#46401 shown) Includes: • Aluminum receiver • 28" vent rib barrel • Fires 2 3/4" non-magnum loads • Walnut finish stock • 5 round capacity • Modified ACCU-CHOKE tube • Two year limited warranty (Read complete warranty statement for details).

The Low-Priced 6000 Semi-Auto Is Loaded With Value

The Mossberg 6000 is an economical, high performance 12 gauge semiautomatic shotgun with designated magnum and non-magnum barrels to compensate for the power differences of magnum and non-magnum ammunition.

Magnum barrels shoot both 2 3/4" and 3" magnum loads. Their smaller gas ports regulate the bolt's speed and help reduce the felt recoil of magnum loads. Non-magnum barrels are designed to shoot standard 2 3/4" loads and light 2 3/4" target loads.

Our Model 6000s are the most economical autoloading shotguns you can buy.

Model 9200 USST (#49403 shown) Includes • 12 ga 26" barrel • 4 ACCU-CHOKE tubes including a skeet tube (#95235) • United States Shooting Team custom engraved receiver • Walnut finish stock and forearm • Cablelock for safe storage when not in use

An Autoloader For Those Who Said They'd Never Own One

If you've been holding out on the decision to buy an autoloader, take a good look at the Model 9200. You'll find a high performance shotgun that handles beautifully, functions reliably and costs significantly less than other autoloaders.

Mossberg design engineers built convenient features into the 9200, such as fast convenient take-down, traditional top tang safety and a full 5 round capacity with 2 3/4" shells. From buttstock to muzzle, the Model 9200 was created to appeal to the novice autoloader shooter and long time target busters.

A. Gas pressure enters the gas cylinder.
B. The gas exerts a force against all surfaces including the front face of the inertia weight assembly which functions the action.
C. Excess pressure forces the valves off their seats which vents the excess pressure.

U.S. Shooting Team

After extensive testing at the U.S. Olympic Shooting Center in Colorado Springs, CO, the Model 9200 USST is endorsed by the U. S. Shooting Team.

"This is an excellent performing firearm "

Lloyd Woodhouse— Shotgun Coach, U.S. Shooting Team

US U.S. SHOOTING TEAM

Used with the express consent of the United States Shooting Team.

SAFETY TIP *Keep your finger off the trigger until you are ready to shoot.*

Combo Models – An Automatic Start To Your Shooting System

If you need more versatility than a single barrel can provide, combination slug and shot shell barrels give you an economical solution to a wide variety of shooting needs.

Model 9200 Combo (#49443 shown) Includes: • 12 ga. 28" vent rib barrel • 3 ACCUCHOKE tubes • High-gloss American walnut DUAL-COMB™ stock • 24" fully rifled barrel with integral scope mount • Cablelock for safe storage when not in use.

NOTE: Scope is for demonstration purposes only and is not available from Mossberg . (Bushnell Optics).

The new 9200 Trophy Slugster model combines the patented Mossberg Dual-Comb™ stock, with the fully rifled accuracy of the Trophy barrel. Cantilevered scope base provides quick, easy scope mounting.

The New 835 Regal
Unbeatable Power and Versatility

The Mossberg 835 Ulti-Mag™ is the most powerful and versatile 12 gauge shotgun ever made. Some thirty years ago, Mossberg was the first manufacturer to offer 3" chambers instead of just 2 3/4" chambers on all shotguns. Now we offer the 3 1/2" Ulti-Mag with **new high-gloss American walnut** DualComb™ stocks for added beauty and performance. The Dual-Comb provides for two sighting positions: one higher for slug shooting with a scope; the other lower for field shooting with a shot shell barrel. It's a shooting system without compromise.

The Ulti-Mag is the first shotgun designed to handle 3 1/2" 12 gauge shot shells that equate to 96% of 10 gauge power! More versatile than the 10 gauge, the Ulti-Mag has the unique advantage of also chambering 12 gauge 3" and even 2 3/4" shells.

This capability, coupled with interchangeable barrels, truly makes the Ulti-Mag a shooting system for all seasons.

The Mossberg 835 Ulti-Mag is also the first production hunting gun with a fully back-bored barrel. Back-boring has been used for years by custom gunsmiths as a method to improve patterns and reduce recoil on competition target guns.

There's also a new high-energy-absorbing recoil pad on the Regal series to tame the kick of 3 1/2" ammo.

Versatile power, and interchangeable choke tubes and barrels mean more than just convenience. As your target changes—trap, to upland, to waterfowl or big game— the 835 Ulti-Mag adapts. It shoulders, swings and sights the same every time, adding to your shooting comfort and proficiency.

Model 835 (#60110 shown) Includes: • DUAL-COMB high-gloss American walnut stock • 12 ga. 28" vent rib barrel • 6-round capacity with 2 3/4" shot shells • 3 1/2" chamber • Back-bored barrel • Double slide bars • Twin extractors • Dual shell stops • Ambidextrous top tang safety • Anti-jam elevator • Steel-to-steel lockup • Wide vent rib with white front bead and brass midpoint sight • Aluminum engraved receiver • Field plug for magazine • 4 choke tubes • Interchangeable barrels and stocks within this model • Cablelock for safe storage when not in use

The Special Value 835 Field Grade

835 Field Grade models are available with walnut finish stock and forearm, blued finish and one modified choke tube. See the specifications on Pages 14 and 15 for complete details on these economical models.

835 Combo Models– The Ultimate Shooting System

The 835 Ulti-Mag is available in combo versions with Trophy or rifle sight barrel, and Dual-Comb stock. All combos include an Accu-Mag™ shot shell barrel with ventilated rib.

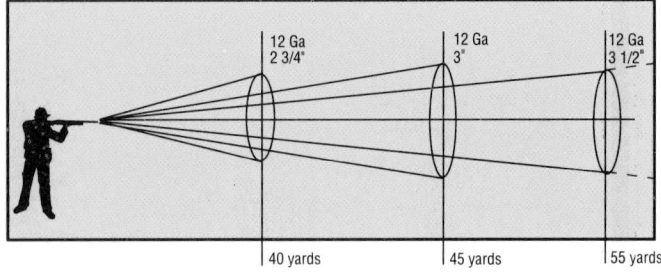

Model 835 ULTI-MAG with REALTREE Camo (#60034 shown) Includes: • Complete REALTREE camo finish • Drilled and tapped receiver for mounting a scope base • 12 ga. 24" vent rib barrel • Three ACCU-MAG choke tubes plus one Extra-Full turkey choke tube for lead shot • REALTREE sling with QD swivels and posts • Cablelock for safe storage when not in use

EXTRA FULL
TURKEY CHOKE
LEAD SHOT ONLY

(#95251)

The 835 Ulti-Mag was designated the 1992 NWTF Turkey Hunters' Gun of the Year by the National Wild Turkey Federation and is the only pump shotgun available in brown leaf REALTREE camo.

A fully rifled 24" slug barrel with integral scope mount (#91820), a 24" fully rifled barrel with iron sights (#91803), a 24" smooth bore barrel with rifle sights (#91800), and a 28" vent rib Accu-Mag barrel (#91815) are all available in matching REALTREE finish as accessories. See page 13 for details.

Accu-Mag tubes are the first internal, flush-fitting choke tubes that give you both durability and optimum pattern for either lead or steel shot.

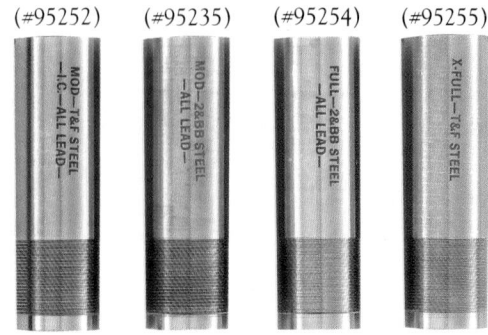

(#95252) (#95235) (#95254) (#95255)

| MOD–T&F STEEL –I.C.–ALL LEAD– | MOD–2&BB STEEL –ALL LEAD– | FULL–2&BB STEEL –ALL LEAD– | X-FULL–T&F STEEL |

Each ACCU-MAG tube is clearly marked to tell you the choke patterns it will produce with lead and steel shot.

THE 12 GAUGE 3 1/2" MAGNUM

12 Ga 2 3/4"	12 Ga 3"	12 Ga 3 1/2"
40 yards	45 yards	55 yards

The relatively new 12 gauge 3 1/2" magnum shot shell was designed for the Mossberg 835 Ulti Mag shotgun. Although it has found great favor as a lead shot turkey round, it is also widely used as a steel shot waterfowl load. The magnum power and larger shot capacity produce denser patterns at extended ranges. Waterfowlers are able to fill their pattern with larger size steel shot virtually equal in number and performance to their once familiar lead shot loads.

Sharpening The Focus

The Trophy Slugster™ is best described as a serious slug shooting machine! With its 12 gauge fully rifled barrel, intregal scope mount and Dual-Comb™ stock, it further redefines modern slug shooting, averaging 3" groups at 100 yards. It is available in pump Models 835 and 500 as well as in our new Model 9200 Semi-Auto.

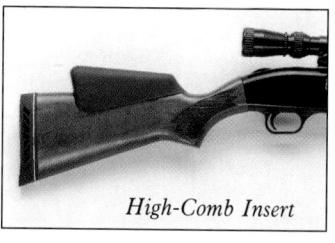

High-Comb Insert

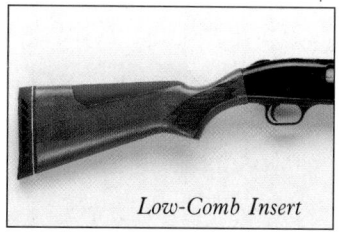

Low-Comb Insert

The New Dual-Comb stock is just what the name implies; two comb inserts provide the shooter with optimum sighting positions. One height for slug shooting with a scope, the other for field shooting with one of the many Mossberg shot shell barrel options.

This unique stock design lets you quickly and easily change from one comb height to another by unscrewing a single bolt. We even supply the Allen wrench.

The Trophy Slugster scope mount is permanently affixed to the barrel and has a cantilever design that places the scope over the receiver. This gives you normal eye relief, 3 1/2" to 4" and a solid foundation that keeps the scope properly aligned with the barrel, even after the barrel has been removed and reinstalled. The "Weaver Style" base has four mounting grooves – or ring slots – that will accept a wide variety of scopes.

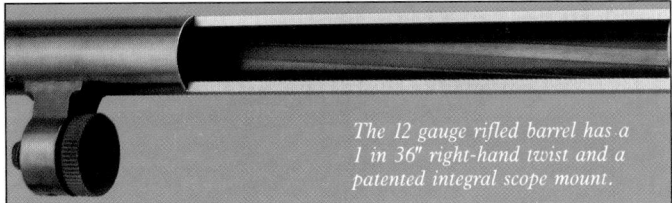

The 12 gauge rifled barrel has a 1 in 36" right-hand twist and a patented integral scope mount.

The Trophy Slugster gives you the consistent accuracy and proper eye relief that only a fully rifled gun with a permanent scope base and a high-comb stock could offer. The Trophy Slugster is a true shooting system.

Model 835

(#60132 shown) Includes:
• 6-round capacity with 2 3/4" shells • 3 1/2" chamber • Fully rifled 12 ga. 24" barrel • Hi -gloss American walnut DUAL-COMB stock • Integral scope mount • Double slide bars • Twin extractors • Dual shell stops • Ambidextrous top tang safety • Anti-jam elevator • Steel-to-steel lockup • Aluminum receiver • Field plug for magazine • Interchangable barrels within models • Cablelock® for safe storage when not in use

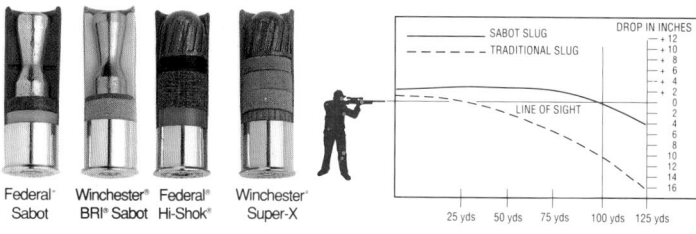

Federal Sabot · Winchester® BRI® Sabot · Federal® Hi-Shok® · Winchester® Super-X

Trophy Slugster Combos– A Shooting System For The Serious Shooter

Trophy Slugster combos are available for Models 835, 500 and 9200.

All Trophy Slugster combos come with a 28" barrel for shot shells, in addition to the fully rifled slug barrel. You can easily and economically change the Trophy Slugster back and forth between slug gun and field shotgun.

Model 500 TROPHY SLUGSTER Combo (#50043 shown)
Includes: • Fully rifled 12 ga. 24" barrel • Integral scope mount • Walnut finish DUAL-COMB stock •28" vent rib barrel • 3 ACCU-CHOKE™ tubes • QD swivel posts • Cablelock for safe storage when not in use

Model 9200 Semi-Auto TROPHY SLUGSTER (#49432 shown)
Includes: •Fully rifled 12 ga. 24" barrel • Integral scope mount • High gloss American walnut DUAL-COMB stock • QD swivel posts •Cablelock for safe storage when not in use

NOTE: The Dual-Comb stock is available as an accessory (#95059). See page 12.

Mossberg Wrote the Book on Slug Shooting

Extensive research went into the development of the Trophy Slugster. Mossberg compiled and published its findings in an elaborate and detailed book filled with charts, ballistics, and penetration information concerning a wide range of shotgun slug ammunition. It's called *Mossberg's Guide to Modern Slug Shooting. . .and More!*, by R.W. "Bob" Zwirz. To get your copy send a check for $9.95 payable to O. F. Mossberg and Sons, Inc.

#95506

Model 500 (#50136 shown) Includes: • 20 ga. 26" vent rib barrel • 3 ACCU-CHOKE tubes • Walnut finish stock and forearm • 6 round capacity. with 2 3/4" shells • 3" chamber • Double shell stops • Ambidextrous top tang safety • Anti-jam elevator • Steel-to-steel lockup • Aluminum receiver • 3-round field plug • Wide vent rib with white front bead and brass mid point sight • Interchangeable barrels and stocks within model and gauge • Cablelock for safe storage when not in use

Building On Precedents

This is the best selling pump action shotgun in the world. And, it provided the foundation for the guns that met the 3000-round MILSPEC endurance test, setting new records for durability and reliability in military shotguns.

The Model 500 has introduced important innovations to American shotgunners, such as 2 3/4" and 3" capabilities in the same gun, lightweight alloy receiver and top receiver safety. The original design has been constantly improved and modified into the basis for the extensive Mossberg shooting system available today.

The endurance and unique anti-jam features- like a solid steel-to-steel lockup between the bolt and the barrel extension, double slide bars, twin extractors, dual shell latches and anti-jam elevator system were pioneered on the 500. The elevator remains up when the action is closed to aid in loading, unloading, and cleaning. Also,

the cartridge stop and interrupter are designed for easy removal to further facilitate maintenance and cleaning. It is the pump shotgun by which all others are measured.

Versatile

The Mossberg 500 has a 3" chamber that will fire everything from light 2 3/4" target loads to the heaviest 3" magnum loads.

You can get a multitude of different gauges, finishes, barrel lengths, and choke variations on the model 500. The proportionally scaled .410 and 20 gauge guns come in a blued finish with synthetic or hardwood stocks, and the 12 gauge guns come with a blued finish and synthetic or hardwood stocks or traditional Mossberg camo finish. Variations are available in 20", 22", 24", 26" and 28" barrel lengths with a variety of inter-changeable choke tube systems as well as fixed choke models. See pages 12, 13, 14 and 15 for specifications and availability of accessory choke tubes.

Some of the many design innovations pioneered in the Mossberg Model 500 since its inception include:

- 6 shot capacity with 2 3/4" shells
- Factory combo shooting systems
- Anti-jam pump feed system
- Dual comb buttstock
- Factory applied camo finish
- Factory synthetic stocks
- Factory fully rifled barrels
- Integral shotgun scope mount
- Cablelock with every gun
- Lowest priced accessory barrels

Model 500 Combos –The Proud Beginning Of The Shooting System Tradition

There are economically priced combo packages available with Accu-Choke shot shell barrels, and 18 1/2" cylinder bore or 24" slug barrels. The slug barrels are available with Trophy or rifle sights and rifled and smooth

For more detailed information about the combos available, see the Specifications section on pages 14 and 15.

NEW Turkey Model 500 12 Gauge (#50126 shown) Includes: • **24" Accu barrel** with **rifle sights** • Extra-Full turkey tube for lead shot (#95240) • Walnut finish stock and forearm • QD swivel posts and receiver drilled and tapped for scope mount • Blued matte finish steel parts • Cablelock for safe storage when not in use.

New Muzzleloader Combo – Extend Your Hunting Season

Now Mossberg Model 500 owners can experience the excitement of bringing down a big buck on black powder without spending big bucks to do it.

The new Mossberg Muzzleloader Conversion Barrel turns the Mossberg 12 gauge, Model 500 6-shot, pump action shotgun into a Muzzleloader in seconds.

Model 500 Muzzleloader Combo 12 Gauge (#50153 shown) Includes: • 24" rifled bore, rifle sight slug barrel • .50 caliber 24" rifled muzzleloading barrel with ramrod • Hardwood stock and forearm • Cablelock for safe storage when not in use.

NOTE: Muzzleloader barrel (#95302) is also available as an accessory. See accessory listing.

Important Note: Due to the extremely hard nature of steel shot, Mossberg recommends that choke tubes be removed and reinserted periodically to ensure tubes are not peened tight by the force of steel shot impact.

Model 500 in .410 bore (#50104 shown). Also available in Bantam size with synthetic stock (#50149). Fixed full choke.

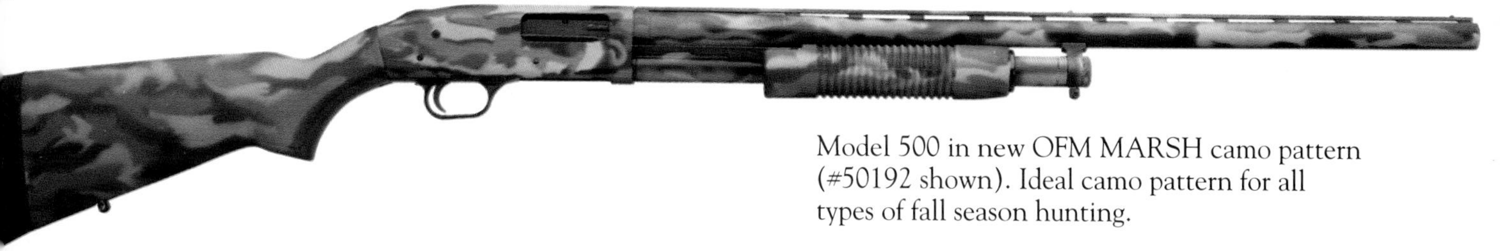

Model 500 in new OFM MARSH camo pattern (#50192 shown). Ideal camo pattern for all types of fall season hunting.

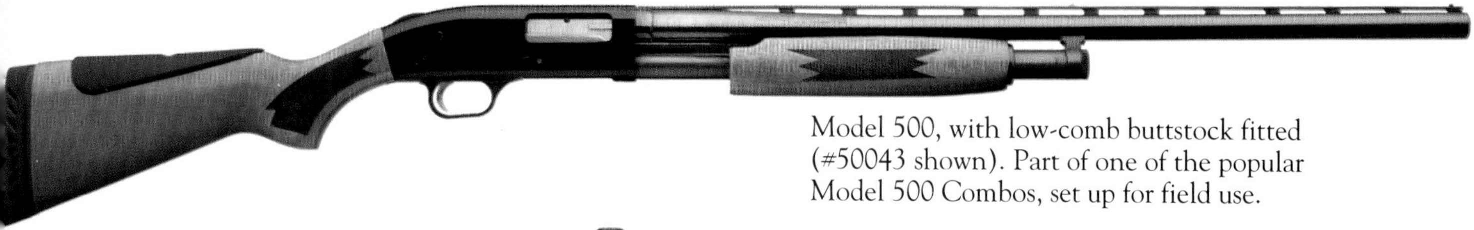

Model 500, with low-comb buttstock fitted (#50043 shown). Part of one of the popular Model 500 Combos, set up for field use.

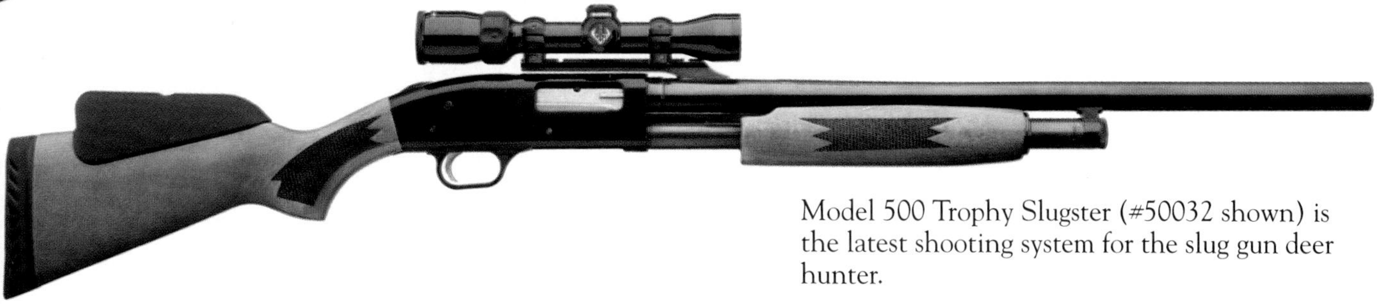

Model 500 Trophy Slugster (#50032 shown) is the latest shooting system for the slug gun deer hunter.

New Hard Cased Combo

The ultimate in a shooting system for 1993. Model 500 (#50160 shown) includes both 28" vent rib and 24" smooth bore slug barrel, all in its own molded hard case. Case also available as accessory (#95350).

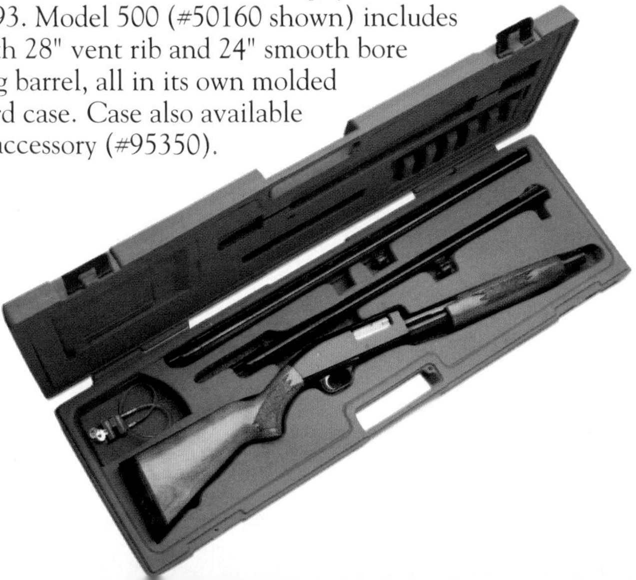

20 Gauge Bantam

The Bantam stock is one inch shorter than a standard stock. Plus, reduced dimensions in the hand grip area make it easier for smaller hands to hold the hand grip and reach the trigger. A special 22" barrel was chosen to reduce the overall weight and make the 500 Bantam easier to swing. This is a true fully featured downsized shotgun. The Bantam stock is available as an accessory(#95020).

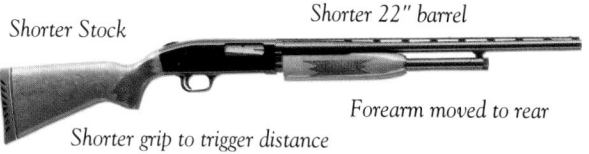

Shorter Stock

Shorter 22" barrel

Forearm moved to rear

Shorter grip to trigger distance

Model 500 BANTAM 20 Gauge (#50132 shown) Includes: • True compact scale • 22" vent rib barrel • Cablelock for safe storage when not in use.

Persuaders And Cruisers

The Special Purpose Model 500 and 590 series shotguns have the same design as the guns that outperformed all competitors in the tough MILSPEC endurance standard set by the U.S. Military. Used by all branches of the Armed Forces and police departments worldwide, they have also found great favor among competition shooters.

Model 500

The Model 500 is available in 12 or 20 gauge. The 12 gauge is offered with 6- or 8-shot capacity. It comes with blued or parkerized finish, wood or synthetic field stock, and bead or rifle sight. Many variations of the 500 come with a pistol grip kit at no extra cost.

Model 590

This is the commercially available version of the 9-shot military shotgun that met the MILSPEC 3443E standard including the 3000-round endurance test. All 590s have drilled and tapped receivers to accept the Ghost Ring™ sight.

Mariner™ 500 & 590

All components of the Mariner 500 and 590 guns are specially treated inside and out with Marinecote™ to resist corrosion when used around water.

In salt-spray tests conducted by an independent laboratory, parts protected with Marinecote actually provided better resistance to corrosion than gun parts made of stainless steel.

Marinecote is an innovative Teflon® and nickel formula that penetrates into the pores of the metal to provide deep corrosion protection. The extra hardness of the nickel with the lubricating characteristics of Teflon result in reduced wear on all moving parts.

Intimidator™ 500 & 590

The Intimidator possesses all the reliability and features of the Model 500 or 590, plus it has a powerful, rugged, .35-ounce laser sight built into the forearm.

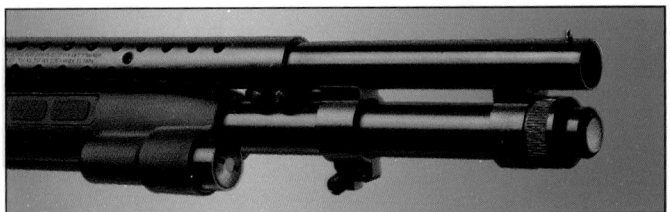

When activated by applying pressure to a touchpad, the laser sight emits a bright red laser dot that can be centered on the target assuring accuracy.

Model 500 MARINER
(#50273 shown) Includes: •
Marinecote® finish • 12ga. 18 1/2" cyl. bore barrel • Pistol grip kit • 6-shot capacity with 2 3/4" shells • 3" chambers • Double slide bars • Twin extractors • Dual shell latches • Ambidextrous top receiver safety • Anti-jam elevator • Steel-to-steel lockup • Aluminum receiver • Synthetic stock and forearm • QD swivel posts • Cablelock® for safe storage when not in use

Ghost Ring™ Sight Models 500 & 590

Models 500 and 590 shotguns are also available with a Ghost Ring sighting system. This sight has proven to be a superior metallic sight by providing a quicker target picture and improved accuracy.

With practice, the eye is trained to "ghost out" the rear sight, so you're only concerned with two points of reference –the front sight and the target.

The Ghost Ring sighting system has a drift adjustable front sight blade and a rear sight that adjusts for both windage and elevation. Strong side plates protect the sight so your setting remains intact under the most rugged conditions.

A Ghost Ring sight kit is also available as an accessory (#95300) and as a barrel and sight kit (#95303).

  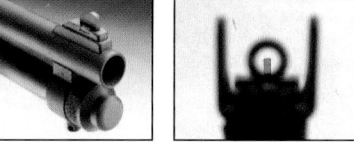

Rear sight   *Front sight blade*   *Ghost Ring sighting system*

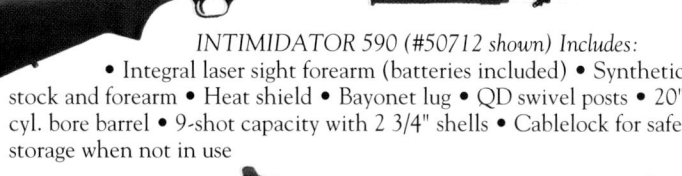

INTIMIDATOR 590 (#50712 shown) Includes:
• Integral laser sight forearm (batteries included) • Synthetic stock and forearm • Heat shield • Bayonet lug • QD swivel posts • 20" cyl. bore barrel • 9-shot capacity with 2 3/4" shells • Cablelock for safe storage when not in use

GHOST RING 500 (#50402 shown) Includes:
• GHOST RING Sight • 18 1/2" cyl. bore barrel • QD swivel posts • Synthetic stock and forearm • 6-shot capacity with 2 3/4" shells • Cablelock for safe storage when not in use

MODEL 500(#50521 shown) Includes: • Pistol grip kit • Parkerized finish • 18 1/2" cyl. bore barrel • 6-shot capacity with 2 3/4" shells • Synthetic stock and forearm • QD swivel posts • Cablelock for safe storage when not in use

Pistol grip kits are available in 12, 20 and .410. see page 12.

DANGER
LASER RADIATION
DO NOT STARE INTO BEAM
OR VIEW DIRECTLY WITH
OPTICAL INSTRUMENTS
5 MW. MAX OUTPUT
CLASS IIIa LASER PRODUCT

See page 12 for laser information.

AMMUNITION GUIDE

Hunting With Steel Shot

Hunting with steel shot is rapidly becoming the rule, rather than the exception. Today, steel shot laws affect nearly every flyway in North America. That means changing loads. And, more importantly, changing hunting habits.

Steel shot is 30% lighter than lead shot, but is loaded to shoot with increased <u>initial</u> velocity. This lighter pellet weight, however, means velocity will drop more quickly. To compensate, change your forward lead.

At 20 yards, you won't need to make any noticeable change. At 40 yards, lead your bird about 5 or 6 inches more that you would with lead shot.

Another way to make the adjustment to steel is to make it act more like lead. Since steel is lighter than lead, go about two shot sizes larger. That way a pellet of #2 steel will have about the same velocity, deliver similar energy, and require the same forward lead as #4 lead through the ranges. Patterns stay dense because there are more pellets per ounce of steel than lead, and steel pellets deform less, which means fewer stray out of the pattern. A shotgun shell has a fixed amount of room for shot, and the larger steel shot takes up more of that room. So if you really want pattern density of #2 steel to match more closely to that of #4 lead, you must increase shot weight. The model 835 12 gauge 3 1/2" Magnum was designed to solve this problem. It delivers a bigger load of larger steel shot at extended ranges.

The Mossberg Turkey Tube

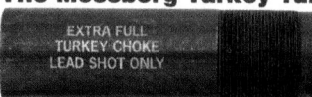

The Mossberg Turkey Hunting Extra-Full Choke Tube for lead shot was designed to deliver a tight and effective pattern for a head shot at 30 yards. 30 yards is the average distance for birds taken with a shotgun based on a 3-year average compiled by the NWTF.

We strongly recommend that hunters call turkeys within 30 yards where the pattern is most effective and avoid the risk of a crippling shot at longer range.

LEAD SHOT WITH MOSSBERG ACCU-II CHOKE TUBES

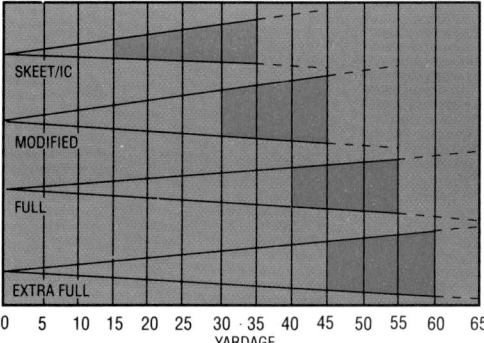

STEEL SHOT WITH MOSSBERG ACCU-STEEL AND ACCU-MAG CHOKE TUBES

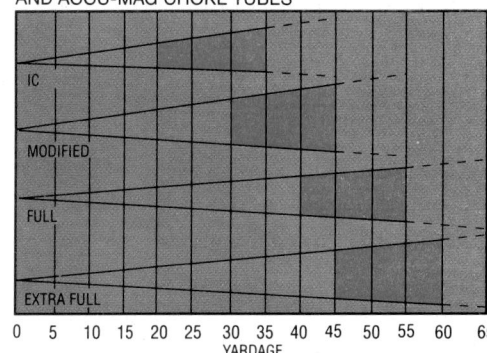

SHADED AREA REPRESENTS MOST EFFECTIVE USE OF SHOT

PATTERN/PELLET DENSITY GUIDE

The pattern densities shown here are for moderate shot sizes #5 and #6. Larger, heavier shot will increase your range and smaller, lighter shot will decrease your range to some degree.

LEAD

LEAD & STEEL SHOT SIZE AND AVERAGE PELLET COUNT

Lead shot sizes:	9	8 1/2	8	7 1/2	6	5	4	2	BB
Pellet diameter (inches) (mm)	.080 2.30	.085 2.16	.090 2.29	.095 2.41	.110 2.79	.120 3.05	.130 3.30	.150 3.81	.180 4.57
1/2 oz.	292	249	205	175	112	85	67	43	25
11/16 oz.	402	342	282	241	155	117	93	60	34
3/4 oz.	439	373	307	262	169	127	101	65	37
7/8 oz.	512	435	359	306	197	149	118	76	44
1 oz.	585	497	410	350	225	170	135	87	50
1 1/8 oz.	658	559	461	394	253	191	152	98	56
1 1/4 oz.	731	621	512	437	281	212	169	109	62
1 3/8 oz.	804	683	564	481	309	234	186	120	69
1 1/2 oz.	877	745	615	525	337	255	202	130	75
1 5/8 oz.	951	808	666	569	366	276	219	141	81
1 7/8 oz.	1097	932	769	656	422	319	253	163	94
2 oz.	1170	994	820	700	450	340	270	174	100
2 1/4 oz.	1316	1118	922	787	506	382	304	196	112

STEEL

Steel shot sizes:	6	5	4	3	2	1	BB	BBB	T	F
Pellet diameter (inches) (mm)	.11 2.79	.12 3.05	.13 3.30	.14 3.56	.15 3.81	.16 4.06	.18 4.57	.19 4.83	.20 5.08	.22 5.59
3/4 oz.	236	182	144	118	94	77	54	46	39	30
15/16 oz.	295	228	180	143	117	97	67	58	49	37
1 oz.	315	243	192	158	125	103	72	62	52	40
1 1/8 oz.	354	273	216	178	141	116	81	70	58	45
1 1/4 oz.	394	304	240	197	156	129	90	77	65	50
1 3/8 oz.	433	334	264	217	172	142	99	85	71	55
1 1/2 oz.	472	364	288	237	187	154	108	93	78	60
1 9/16 oz.	492	380	300	247	195	161	112	97	81	62
1 5/8 oz.	512	395	312	257	203	167	117	101	84	65

LEAD

LEAD & STEEL GAME SELECTION GUIDE

	WOODCOCK	RUFFED GROUSE	PHEASANTS	QUAIL	HUNGARIAN PARTRIDGE	OTHER GROUSE CHUKAR PARTRIDGE	DOVES & PIGEONS	RABBITS	WOODCOCK SNIPE, RAIL	SQUIRRELS	WILD TURKEY	CROWS	FOX
SIZE	7-1/2	6	5	7-1/2	6	5	6	4	7-1/2	4	2	5	BB
	8	7-1/2	6	8	7-1/2	6	7-1/2	5	8	5	4	6	2
	9	8	7-1/2	9	8	7-1/2	8	6	9	6	5	7-1/2	4
							9				6		

STEEL

BIRDS/RANGE	RECOMMENDED STEEL SHOT SIZES	RECOMMENDED MINIMUM SHOT WT.
Ducks under 35 yds.	2,3,4,5,6	3/4 oz. +
Ducks 35-45 yds.	BB,1,2,3	1 oz. +
Ducks 45 yds. or more	BB,1,2	1-1/8 oz. +
Small Geese under 45 yds.	BBB,BB,1	1-1/4 oz. +
Large Geese, any range/ Small Geese over 45 yds.	F,T,BBB,BB	1-1/4 oz. +

LEAD

LEAD VS. STEEL PELLET ENERGY COMPARISON

SHOT TYPE/SIZE	MUZZLE VELOCITY (F.P.S.)	PELLET ENERGY IN FOOT/POUNDS AT RANGE (YARDS)			
		30	40	50	60
lead 7-1/2	1330	1.6			
lead 6	1330	3.0	2.3		
lead 4	1330	5.6	4.4	3.4	
lead 2	1330	9.5	7.5	6.1	4.9
lead BB	1330	15.0	12.0	10.0	

The minimum energy required depends on the type of game being hunted.

STEEL

SHOT TYPE/SIZE	MUZZLE VELOCITY (F.P.S.)	PELLET ENERGY IN FOOT/POUNDS AT RANGE (YARDS)			
		30	40	50	60
steel 6	1365	1.8			
steel 4	1365	3.5	2.5		
steel 3	1365	4.0	3.0		
steel 2	1365	6.0	4.4	3.4	
steel BB	1365	11.6	9.0	7.1	5.5
steel T	1365		13.0	10.0	8.5
steel F	1400		18.0	15.0	13.0

The minimum energy required depends on the type of waterfowl being hunted.

Ammunition information was compiled with the much appreciated help of Federal Cartridge Company and Winchester/Olin Corporation in conjunction with the Mossberg Research Department.

ACCESSORIES

When you buy a Mossberg shotgun, you start a personal shooting system that matches your needs exactly. Accessories are the key to the Mossberg Shooting System and we provide the widest selection of accessories in the industry.

Interchangeable barrels and choke tubes allow you to adapt your shotgun to an infinite variety of hunting and shooting situations from skeet and sporting clays to small game, upland birds, turkey, waterfowl and big game hunting. You can even convert a 12 gauge Model 500 to a muzzleloader. Some receivers and barrels can mount scopes, and specialized stocks can adapt your gun to a variety of shooting situations.

There are laser sighting systems, Ghost Ring™ sights, iron sights, heat shields, pistol grips, stocks, forearms and the most specialized choke tube collection ever offered.

Take a few minutes to look at the selection of accessories that fit your Mossberg, and have your local dealer order the options that customize your shooting system exactly to you and your shooting.

Look for a complete selection of Mossberg Shotgun Accessories on display at your local shooting sports retailer.

CHOKE TUBES

Accu-Choke Tubes (Models 500, 6000, 9200)

Gauge	Catalog#	Choke
12	95190	Full
12	95195	Modified
12	95200	Imp. Cylinder
20	95215	Full
20	95220	Modified
20	95225	Imp. Cylinder
12	95235	Skeet
12	95240	Extra-Full Turkey tube
12	95245	Improved Modified
12-20	95205	Choke Tube Wrench

Accu-Steel Choke Tubes (for best steel shot patterns)

Gauge	Catalog#	Choke	Shot Sizes
12	95110	Full	T,F,BB,1,2
12	95115	Full	4,6
12	95117	Extra-Full	T,F,BB,1,2
12	95120	Modified	All
20	95125	Full	4,6
20	95130	Modified	All
12-20	95205	Choke Tube Wrench	

Accu-Mag Choke Tubes (For Model 835 Only)

Gauge	Catalog#	Lead Shot	Steel Shot
12	95251	X- Full Turkey Tube	. . . . .
12	95252	Imp. Cyl.	Mod, T & F
12	95253	Modified	Mod, 2 & BB
12	95254	Full	Full, 2 & BB
12	95255	. , . . .	Extra-Full, T & F
12	95256	Skeet	. . . . .
12-20	95205	Choke Tube Wrench	

Note: Accu-Steel tubes and Accu-Choke may be used in the following choke tube guns: Mossberg®, Smith & Wesson®, Savage®, U.S. Repeating Arms® and Maverick®.

National Mossberg Collectors Association

N.M.C.A. is a club of sport shooters who have a mutual appreciation for the reliable firearms Mossberg has been producing since 1919.

It is officially recognized by O.F. Mossberg and Sons, Inc. and has steadily gained recognition since being formed.

For more information call (314)353-6401 or write:

N.M.C.A.
P.O. Box 22156
St. Louis, MO 63116

ACCESSORIES

Mossberg Models 500, 590 and 835 Accessories

Gauge	Catalog#	Fits	Description
12	95000	500 / 590	Pistol Grip Kit w/Q.D. Swivel Posts
20	95005	500	Pistol Grip Kit w/Q.D. Swivel Posts
410	95010	500	Pistol Grip Kit w/Q.D. Swivel Posts
410	95025	500	Bantam Stock (Synthetic)
20	95020	500	Bantam Stock (Walnut finish)
12	95059	500 / 590 / 835	Dual-Comb Birch Stock
12	95058	500 / 590 / 835	Dual-Comb - OFM Camo
12	95030	500 / 590 / 835	Synthetic Field Stock - Black
12	95056	500 / 590 / 835	Synthetic Field Stock - REALTREE®
12	95045	500 / 590 / 835	Synthetic Field Stock - OFM Camo
12	95035	500 / 590 / 835	Speedfeed™ Stock - Black
12	95050	500 / 590 / 835	Speedfeed Stock - OFM Camo
12	95051	500 / 590 / 835	Synthetic Forearm - Black
12	95054	500 / 590 / 835	Synthetic Forearm - REALTREE
12	95055	500 / 590 / 835	Synthetic Forearm - OFM Camo
12	95065	500 / 590	Barrel Heat Shield Kit - Blued
12	95066	500 / 590	Barrel Heat Shield Kit - Parkerized
12	95068	500 / 590	Barrel Heat Shield Kit - Marinecote
12-20	95300	500 / 590 / 835	Ghost Ring Sight Kit
12	95311	500 / 590 / 835	Intimidator Laser Forearm Assembly
ALL	95507		Cablelock
ALL	95530		Five-Pack Cablelock (Keyed Alike)
ALL	95350	500 / 835	Gun Case

Remington 870® Pump Accessories

Gauge	Catalog#	Description
12	95090	Speedfeed Stock - Black
12	95095	Speedfeed Stock - OFM Camo
12	95100	Synthetic Forearm - Black
12	95105	Synthetic Forearm - OFM Camo

Intimidator Laser Product Specifications

DANGER
LASER RADIATION
DO NOT STARE INTO BEAM OR VIEW DIRECTLY WITH OPTICAL INSTRUMENTS
5 MW. MAX OUTPUT
CLASS IIIa LASER PRODUCT

Size: Outside diameter 0.584 ± .002"
Length: 1.125 ± 0.015"
Weight: 0.35 oz. (10 grams)
Power output: 5 milliwatt max.
Wavelength: 670 Nanometer
Pulse rate: 10 Hz (50% duty cycle)
Range: 20 ft. outdoors (daylight)
50 yds. indoors
300 yds. outdoor (night)

Laser type: Diode
Power requirements: 9V.D.C.
Battery: Lithium $\frac{1}{3}$ N (3 Req'd) included
(12 gauge Intimidator models)
9V Rectangular (HS410)
Battery life: $1\frac{1}{4}$ hr. (min.) continuous use
4 hr. (min.) 3 sec. on/10 sec. off
Beam: Red. 2.5" - 3.5" dia. spot @ 100 yds.
Operating temperature range: 14° F to 122° F

ACCESSORY BARRELS

Model	Gauge	Catalog#	BBL	Chokes	Finish	Sight	Notes
500 PUMP ACTION EXTRA BARRELS 6-SHOT	12	90130	28 VR	Accu	Blued	Bead	
	12	90180	28 VR	Accu	OFM CAMO	Bead	
	12	90135	24 VR	Accu	Blued	Bead	
	12	90185	24 VR	Accu	OFM CAMO	Bead	
	12	90140	20 VR	Accu	Blued	Bead	
	12	90085	30 VR	Full	Blued	Bead	
	12	90005	30 PL	Full	Blued	Bead	
	12	90090	28 VR	Mod	Blued	Bead	
	12	90010	28 PL	Mod	Blued	Bead	
	12	90015	18.5 PL	Cyl. Bore	Blued	Bead	
	20	90136	26 VR	Accu	Blued	Bead	NEW
	20	90144	22 VR	Accu	Blued	Bead	NEW
	20	90035	18.5 PL	Cyl. Bore	Blued	Bead	NEW
	.410	90116	24 VR	Full	Blued	Bead	NEW
	.410	90045	18.5 PL	Cyl. Bore	Blued	Bead	NEW
500 PUMP ACTION 6-SHOT EXTRA BARRELS SLUGSTERS AND SPECIALTIES	12	90056	24 Trophy	Rifled Bore	Blued	Scope Base	
	12	95303	18.5 PL	Cyl. Bore	Blued	Ghost Ring	NEW Includes Rec. Sight Kit
	12	95302	24 Muzzleloader	Rifled Bore	Blued	Rifle	NEW 1:26 Right Hand Twist
	12	90049	24 PL	Rifled Bore	Blued	Rifle	
	12	90149	24 PL	Rifled Bore	OFM CAMO	Rifle	NEW
	12	90055	24 PL	Cyl. Bore	Blued	Rifle	
	12	90160	24 PL	Cyl. Bore	OFM CAMO	Rifle	
	12	90065	18.5 PL	Cyl. Bore	Blued	Rifle	NEW
	20	90062	24 PL	Rifled Bore	Blued	Rifle	
	20	90060	24 PL	Cyl. Bore	Blued	Rifle	
500 PUMP ACTION 8-SHOT EXTRA BARRELS	12	90241	28 VR	Accu.	Blued	Bead	
	12	90240	20 PL	Cyl. Bore	Blued	Rifle	
9200 SEMI-AUTO EXTRA BARRELS	12	90949	24 PL	Rifled Bore	Blued	Rifle	
	12	90955	24 PL	Cyl. Bore	Blued	Rifle	
	12	90950	24 PL	Rifled Bore	OFM CAMO	Rifle	
	12	90960	24 PL	Cyl. Bore	OFM CAMO	Rifle	
MODEL 6000 & 5500 MK II SEMI-AUTO EXTRA BARRELS	12	90685	24 PL	Rifled Bore	Blued	Rifle	Magnum & Non-Magnum
	12	90681	24 PL	Cyl. Bore	Blued	Rifle	Magnum & Non-Magnum
	12	90676	28 VR	Accu	Blued	Bead	Non-Magnum
	12	90691	28 VR	Accu	MOSSY OAK®	Bead	Magnum
	12	90684	28 VR	Accu-Steel	Blued	Bead	Magnum Full Tube only (#95110)
	12	90686	24 VR	Accu	Blued	Bead	Magnum
	12	90688	24 VR	Accu	OFM CAMO	Bead	Magnum
	12	90678	24 VR	Accu	Blued	Bead	Non-Magnum
835 PUMP ACTION EXTRA BARRELS 3-1/2″ CHAMBER	12	90820	24 Trophy	Rifled Bore	Blued	Scope Base	
	12-	91820	24 Trophy	Rifled Bore	REALTREE®	Scope Base	
	12	90802	24 PL	Rifled Bore	Blued	Rifle	
	12	90803	24 PL	Rifled Bore	OFM CAMO	Rifle	
	12	91803	24 PL	Rifled Bore	REALTREE®	Rifle	
	12	90800	24 PL	Cyl. Bore	Blued	Rifle	
	12	90801	24 PL	Cyl. Bore	OFM CAMO	Rifle	
	12	91800	24 PL	Cyl. Bore	REALTREE®	Rifle	
	12	90815	28 VR	Accu-Mag	Blued	Bead	
	12	90816	28 VR	Accu-Mag	OFM CAMO	Bead	
	12	91815	28 VR	Accu-Mag	REALTREE®	Bead	
	12	90810	24 VR	Accu-Mag	Blued	Bead	
	12	90811	24 VR	Accu-Mag	OFM CAMO	Bead	
	12	90823	18.5 PL	Cyl. Bore	Blued	Bead	
REMINGTON 870® PUMP ACTION REPLACEMENT BARRELS	12	90320	28 VR	Accu	Blued	Bead	
	12	90330	24 PL	Cyl. Bore	Blued	Rifle	
	12	90335	18.5 PL	Cyl. Bore	Blued	Bead	
	12	90302	24 Muzzleloader	Rifled	Blued	Rifle	
REMINGTON 1100® SEMI-AUTO REPLACEMENT BARRELS	12	90341	28 VR	Accu	Blued	Bead	
	12	90343	24 PL	Rifled Bore	Blued	Rifle	

PL — Plain   VR — Ventilated Rib Barrel
VR Barrels include white front and brass mid-point bead sights.

Accu-Barrels include IC, Mod and Full choke tubes.
Accu-Mag Barrels include (1) Extra-Full lead shot choke tube (#95251).

SPECIFICATIONS

Model	Gauge	Catalog#	Barrel	Chokes	Finish	Stock	2 3/4" Capacity	Overall Length (in.)	Approx. Weight (lbs.)	Notes
9200 SEMI-AUTOS	12	49420	28 VR	Accu	Blued	Walnut	5	48	7.7	NEW
	12	49425	24 VR	Accu	Blued	Walnut	5	44	7.3	NEW
	12	49432	24 Trophy Scope Base	Rifled Bore	Blued	Walnut	5	44	7.3	NEW Dual-comb Stock
	12	49444	24 Rifle Sights	Rifled Bore	Blued	Walnut	5	44	7.3	NEW
USST	12	49403	26 VR	Accu	Blued	Walnut	5	46	7.5	Includes Skeet Tube
9200 COMBOS	12	49443	28 VR / 24 Trophy Scope Base	Accu Rifled Bore	Blued	Walnut	5	48	7.7	NEW Dual-Comb Stock
	12	49464	28 VR / 24 Rifle Sights	Accu Rifled Bore	Blued	Walnut	5	48	7.7	NEW
6000 SEMI-AUTO	12	46401	28 VR Non-Magnum	Accu	Blued	Syn	5	48	7.7	NEW One "Modified" Tube only
	12	46402	28 VR Magnum	Accu	Blued	Syn	5	48	7.7	NEW One "Modified" Tube only
9200 CAMO	12	49434	24 VR	Accu (1)	MOSSY OAK ®(2)	Syn	5	44	7.3	NEW
	12	49490	28 VR	Accu	OFM MARSH (2)	Syn	5	48	7.7	NEW
9200 CAMO COMBO	12	49465	28 VR / 24 Rifle Sights	Accu Rifled Bore	OFM MARSH (2)	Syn	5	48	7.7	NEW
835 ULTI-MAG	12	60110	28 VR	Accu-Mag	Blued	Walnut	6	48.5	7.7	NEW Dual-Comb Stock
	12	60132	24 Trophy Scope Base	Rifled Bore	Blued	Walnut	6	44.5	7.3	NEW Dual-Comb Stock
	12	60120	28 VR	Accu-Mag	Blued	Walnut	6	48.5	7.7	NEW
835 REGAL COMBOS	12	60144	28 VR / 24 Trophy Scope Base	Accu-Mag Rifled Bore	Blued	Walnut	6	48.5	7.7	NEW Dual-Comb Stock
	12	60145	28 VR / 24 Rifle Sights	Accu-Mag Rifled Bore	Blued	Walnut	6	48.5	7.7	NEW Dual-Comb Stock
835 CAMO	12	60034	24 VR	Accu-Mag (1)	REALTREE® (6)	Syn	6	44.5	7.3	X-Full Tube — Replaces Imp. Cyl.
	12	60035	28 VR	Accu-Mag	REALTREE® (6)	Syn	6	48.5	7.7	NEW
	12	60015	28 VR	Accu-Mag	OFM CAMO (6)	Dual-Comb	6	48.5	7.7	
COMBO	12	60146	28 VR / 24 Rifle Sights	Accu-Mag Rifled Bore	OFM CAMO (6)	Dual-Comb	6	48.5	7.7	NEW
	12	60147	24 VR / 24 Rifle Sights	Accu-Mag Rifled Bore	REALTREE® (6)	Syn	6	48.5	7.7	NEW Includes Hard Case
835 FIELD GRADE ULTI-MAG	12	61120	28 VR	Accu-Mag	Blued	Wal-Fin	6	48.5	7.7	NEW ONE "Modified" Tube only
	12	61125	24 VR	Accu-Mag	Blued	Wal-Fin	6	44.5	7.3	NEW Turkey; One Extra-Full Tube only
835 FIELD GRADE COMBOS	12	61160	28 VR / 24 Rifled Sights	Accu-Mag Cyl. Bore	Blued	Wal-Fin	6	48.5	7.7	NEW One "Modified" Tube only
500 SPORTING	12	50120	28 VR	Accu	Blued	Wal-Fin	6	48	7.2	
	12	50130	20 VR	Accu	Blued (3)	Wal-Fin	6	40	7.0	
	12	50126	24 Rifle Sights	Accu (1)	Blued (3)	Wal-Fin	6	44	7.0	NEW Turkey One Extra-Full Tube only
	12	50065	28 VR	Modified	Blued	Wal-Fin	6	48	7.2	Fixed Choke
	12	50116	26 VR	Accu	Blued	Wal-Fin	6	46	7.1	NEW One "I.C." Tube Only
	12	50117	28 VR	Accu	Blued	Wal-Fin	6	48	7.2	NEW One "Modified" Tube Only
	20	50136	26 VR	Accu	Blued	Wal-Fin	6	46	7.1	
	20	50144	22 VR	Accu	Blue	Wal-Fin	6	42	6.9	Bantam
	20	50137	26 VR	Accu	Blued	Wal-Fin	6	46	7.0	NEW One "Modified" Tube only
	20	50132	22 VR	Accu	Blued	Wal-Fin	6	42	6.9	NEW One "Modified" Tube Only
	20	50139	26 VR	Accu	Blued	Wal-Fin	6	46	7.1	Bantam NEW One "I.C." Tube Only
	.410	50149	24 PL	Full	Blued	Syn	6	44	6.8	Bantam Fixed Choke
	.410	50104	24 VR	Full	Blued	Wal-Fin	6	44	6.8	Fixed Choke
500 SLUGSTERS	12	50032	24 Trophy Scope Base	Rifled Bore	Blued (4)	Wal-Fin	6	44	7.25	Dual-Comb Stock
	12	50044	24 Rifle Sights	Rifled Bore	Blued (3)	Wal-Fin	6	44	7.0	
	12	50045	24 Rifle Sights	Cyl. Bore	Blued (3)	Wal-Fin	6	44	7.0	NEW
	20	50050	24 Rifle Sights	Cyl. Bore	Blued (3)	Wal-Fin	6	44	6.9	
	20	50051	24 Rifle Sights	Rifled Bore	Blued (3)	Wal-Fin	6	44	6.9	
500 COMBOS	12	50043	28 VR / 24 Trophy Scope Base	Accu Rifled Bore	Blued (4)	Wal-Fin	6	48	7.2	Dual-Comb Stock
	12	50164	28 VR / 24 Rifle Sights	Accu Rifled Bore	Blued	Wal-Fin	6	48	7.2	
	12	50494	28 VR / 18.5 Bead Sight	Accu Cyl. Bore	Blued	Wal-Fin (5)	6	48	7.2	
	12	50150	28 PL / 24 Rifle Sights	Modified Cyl. Bore	Blued	Wal-Fin	6	48	7.2	Fixed Choke
	12	50483	28 PL / 18.5 PL	Modified Cyl. Bore	Blued	Wal-Fin (5)	6	48	7.2	Fixed Choke
	12	50160	28 VR / 24 Rifled Sights	Accu Cyl. Bore	Blued	Wal-Fin	6	48	7.2	NEW Includes Hard Case
	20	50182	26 VR / 24 Rifle Sights	Accu Rifled Bore	Blued	Wal-Fin	6	46	7.0	
	.410	50456	24 VR / 18.5 Bead Sight	Full Cyl. Bore	Blued	Wal-Fin	6	44	6.8	NEW Fixed Choke

Model	Gauge	Catalog#	Barrel	Chokes	Finish	Stock	2 3/4" Capacity	Overall Length (in.)	Approx. Weight (lbs.)	Notes
500 MUZZLELOADER COMBO	12 Muzzleloader	50152	28 VR / 24 Rifle Sights	Accu / Rifled Bore	Blued	Wal-Fin	6	48	7.2	.50 Caliber Muzzleloader Combo 1:26 Right Hand Twist
	12 Muzzleloader	50153	24 Rifle Sights / 24 Rifle Sights	Rifled Bore / Rifled Bore	Blued	Wal-Fin	6	44	7.0	NEW Includes .50 Cal. Muzzleloader Barrel
500 CAMO	12	50190	28 VR	Accu	OFM CAMO (6)	Syn	6	48	7.2	
	12	50192	28 VR	Accu	OFM MARSH (6)	Syn	6	48	7.2	
	12	50195	24 VR	Accu (1)	OFM CAMO (6)	Syn	6	44	7.1	Turkey
	12	50196	24 GRS	Accu (1)	OFM CAMO (2)	Syn	6	44	7.1	Turkey w/Ghost Ring Sights
CAMO COMBO	12	50217	28 VR / 24 Rifle Sights	Accu-Steel / Rifled Bore	OFM MARSH (6)	Syn	6 / 6	48	7.2	Combo - Full Tube only
500/590 MARINER	12	50273	18.5 Bead	Cyl. Bore (7)	Marinecote	Syn	6	38.5	6.75	
	12	50299	20 Bead	Cyl. Bore (7)	Marinecote	Syn	9	40	7.0	
500 SPECIAL PURPOSE	12	50404	18.5 Bead	Cyl. Bore (7)	Blued	Wal-Fin	6	38.5	6.75	
	12	50411	18.5 Bead	Cyl. Bore (7)	Blued	Syn	6	38.5	6.75	
	12	50521	18.5 Bead	Cyl. Bore (7)	Parkerized	Syn	6	38.5	6.75	
	12	50440	18.5 Bead	Cyl. Bore	Blued	Pistol Grip	6	28	5.6	Cruiser w/Heat Shield
	20	50451	18.5 Bead	Cyl. Bore (7)	Blued	Wal-Fin	6	38.5	6.7	
	20	50450	18.5 Bead	Cyl. Bore	Blued	Pistol Grip	6	28	5.5	NEW Cruiser
	20	50330	18.5 Bead	Cyl. Bore	Blued	Pistol Grip	6	28	5.5	NEW Cruiser w/Camper Case
	12	50570	20 Rifle Sights	Cyl. Bore (7)	Blued	Wal-Fin	8	40	7.0	
	12	50564	20 Bead	Cyl. Bore (7)	Blued	Wal-Fin	8	40	7.0	
	12	50579	20 Bead	Cyl. Bore (7)	Blued	Syn	8	40	7.0	
	12	50580	20 Bead	Cyl. Bore	Blued	Pistol Grip	8	28	5.2	Cruiser w/Heat Shield
	.410	50455	18.5 Bead	Cyl. Bore	Blued	Pistol Grip	6	28	5.3	NEW Cruiser
	.410	50335	18.5 Bead	Cyl. Bore	Blued	Pistol Grip	6	28	5.3	NEW Cruiser w/Camper Case
590 SPECIAL PURPOSE	12	50645	20 Bead	Cyl. Bore (8)	Blued	Syn	9	40	7.2	
	12	50650	20 Bead	Cyl. Bore (8)	Blued	Speedfeed	9	40	7.2	
	12	50660	20 Bead	Cyl. Bore (8)	Parkerized	Syn	9	40	7.2	
	12	50665	20 Bead	Cyl. Bore (8)	Parkerized	Speedfeed	9	40	7.2	
500/590 INTIMIDATOR LASER SIGHT	12	50704	18.5 Bead	Cyl. Bore (7)	Blued	Syn Laser	6	38.5	6.75	Batteries included
	12	50706	18.5 Bead	Cyl. Bore (7)	Parkerized	Syn Laser	6	38.5	6.75	Batteries included
	12	50712	20 Bead	Cyl. Bore (8)	Blued	Syn Laser	9	40	7.25	Batteries included
	12	50714	20 Bead	Cyl. Bore (8)	Parkerized	Syn Laser	9	40	7.25	Batteries included
500/590 GHOST RING SIGHT	12	50402	18.5 GRS	Cyl. Bore (4)	Blued	Syn	6	38.5	6.75	
	12	50517	18.5 GRS	Cyl. Bore (4)	Parkerized	Syn	6	38.5	6.75	
	12	50652	20 GRS	Cyl. Bore (9)	Blued	Syn	9	40	7.3	
	12	50663	20 GRS	Cyl. Bore (9)	Parkerized	Syn	9	40	7.3	

All models include a Mossberg Cablelock. All laser sight models include batteries. Accu models include I.C., Mod and Full choke tubes except SPECIAL VALUE models. Accu-Mag Regal models include 4 choke tubes marked for best I.C., Mod and Full lead shot patterns and best Mod. Full and Extra-Full patterns with steel shot.

(1) Includes additional lead shot Extra-Full Turkey tube.
(2) Includes camo sling with Q.D. swivels and posts.
(3) Includes Q.D. swivel posts, receivers drilled and tapped for scope mount.
(4) Includes Q.D. swivel posts.
(5) Includes pistol grip kit.
(6) Includes camo sling with Q.D. swivels and posts, receivers drilled and tapped for scope mount.

(7) Includes Q.D. swivel posts and pistol grip kit.
(8) Includes Q.D. swivel posts, bayonet lug and heat shield.
(9) Includes Q.D. swivel posts and bayonet lug.
VR — Ventilated Rib Barrel
GRS — Ghost Ring Sight
WAL-FIN — Walnut Finish

PL — Plain Barrel
SYN — Synthetic
BBL — Barrel

REALTREE® is a registered trademark of Spartan-Realtree Products, Inc.
MOSSY OAK® is a registered trademark of Haas Outdoors Inc.

Over the years, Mossberg shotgun innovations and "factory firsts" have included the following:

- Standard 3" chambers on all guns
- 6 shot capacity magazine, with 2 3/4" shells
- Factory combo shooting systems
- First 3 1/2" 12 gauge magnum

- Factory applied camo finishes
- Anti-jam pump feed system
- Choke tubes designed specifically for steel patterns
- Factory fully rifled slug barrels
- Factory synthetic stocks
- Cantilevered shotgun scope mount
- Muzzleloading accessory barrel
- Cablelock supplied with every gun
- Dual Comb stock
- Integrated factory laser sight
- Only current MILSpec pump gun
- Industry's lowest priced accessory barrels

CABLELOCK

Cablelock®

Improperly stored firearms in the home lead to accidental shootings every year.

At Mossberg, we believe this is unacceptable. As the world's largest manufacturer of pump action shotguns, we're trying to do something about it.

In addition to promoting safety by including an owner's manual with every shotgun we sell, we offer a variety of safety videos for both novice and experienced shooters.

We took the initiative to employ another effective safety step. Since October 1, 1989, every Mossberg shotgun delivered comes with its own safety Cablelock. It is our intent that no Mossberg shotgun ever be sold without this locking device.

It allows the firearm to be locked up when not in use, with complete confidence that it cannot be accidentally fired by someone without a key.

Owners of almost all types of shotguns, handguns and rifles can employ this easily adaptable locking system for their guns. The Cablelock can be purchased separately as an accessory and is made available to gun retailers nationwide.

As a community service, Cablelocks are also available to qualifying nonprofit organizations at a special price.

It is every gun owner's personal responsibility to make sure his or her guns do not accidentally injure others.

We recommend you lock up your firearm when not in use before someone you love gets hurt.

Collectibles & Video Tapes

As part of an ongoing effort to stress safety and safe firearms handling, Mossberg offers three gun safety videos. Two are hosted by noted actor and sportsman Steve Kanally.

To order any of these videos or collectibles, please indicate the catalog number of the merchandise and quantity desired. Include $1.50 for shipping and handling and mail a check or money order (no cash please) to: O.F. Mossberg and Sons, Inc.
Product Service Department
P.O. Box 497
North Haven, CT 06473-9844
Note: Connecticut residents please add Connecticut sales tax.

#95520 — *A Family Guide to Handgun Safety (60 min)*

#95519 — *A Family Guide to Rifle and Shotgun Safety (45 min)*

#95551
#95552
#95521
#95513
Front
#95506
#95550
#95527
#95510
#95526
#95714

Item		Catalog#	Sug. Retail
VHS Home Security Video	(11 min)	95504	$9.95
VHS Shotgun Safety Video	(45 min)	95519	29.95
VHS Handgun Safety Video	(60 min)	95520	29.95
Slug Shooting Guide	(96 pages)	95506	9.95
Lock-Back Knife		95510	10.00
Mossberg Patch		95526	2.00
Mossberg Mesh Hat — Blue		95513	5.00
Law Enforcement Patch		95527	2.00
Law Enforcement Mesh Hat — Black		95521	5.00
Coffee Mug		95550	10.00
Sporting Clays Cap — Neon Pink		95551	5.00
Sporting Clays Cap — Neon Lime		95552	5.00
Clay Target T-Shirt (S, M, L, XL)		95714	11.00

O.F. MOSSBERG & SONS, INC.
7 Grasso Avenue
P.O. Box 497
North Haven, CT 06473-9844

RIFLE STOCKS

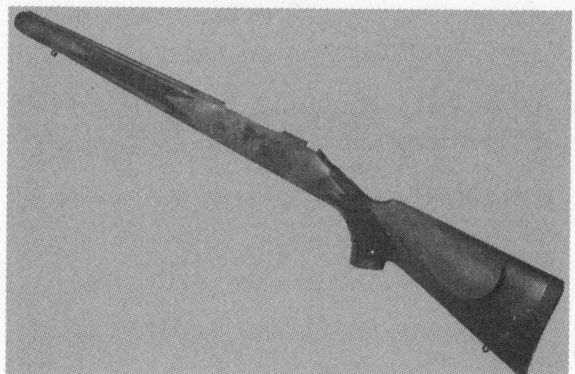

Six Enterprises' injection-moulded rifle and shotgun stocks are manufactured using the latest in thermoplastic technology.

By using a glass-reinforced plastic, they are able to ensure the durability, light weight and accuracy of synthetic stocks. Additionally, very close manufacturing tolerances allow for the production of one of the finest "drop-in" stocks available today.

All stocks feature classic styling and come with moulded rubber recoil pad and Uncle Mike's sling swivel studs. Checkering available on most models. Their unique moulded finish is designed so that further exterior finishing is not needed.

Call, write or fax for a free catalog showing their complete product line.

SIX ENTERPRISES

COMPACT DOUBLE-ACTION PISTOL

The new Hungarian FEG P9RK pistol with Browning Hi-Power styling is available from Century International Arms. This double-action uses the popular 9mm Parabellum round. Though compact, it is similar in many ways to its full-size brother, the P9R.

Features include a recurved trigger guard bow for target shooting; standard walnut wood panels with checkering ribs on frame back and frontstrap finger grooves; front and rear fixed sights; a double-column 15-round magazine; and hammer block safety. The barrel is 4 1/8" — 7 1/2" overall—and weighs 33.6 ounces (empty). Brand new with blued finish, the P9RK comes in a box complete with cleaning rod and spare magazine.

More information is available in their free 1993 catalog. Dealers and distributors welcome.

CENTURY INTERNATIONAL ARMS, INC.

SCOPE RINGS AND BASES

Six Enterprises offers a set of fully adjustable scope rings and bases for the ultimate in scope mounting. With this mounting system, scopes can be optically centered for maximum efficiency.

The adjustable height of the scope above the bore effectively lengthens point-blank range, and allows the shooter with glasses to get behind the scope easier. It also minimizes interference between ear muffs and stock.

Bases are available in flat, radius and dovetail configurations. Windage and elevation adjustments are made with Allen wrenches; everything locks into place.

Scope rings and bases $150.00 a set. Call, write or fax for a free catalog showing their complete product line.

SIX ENTERPRISES

RECHAMBERED SEMIAUTO

Century International Arms now offers the Czech 52 pistol rechambered for 9mm Parabellum and the powerful M48 7.62 Tokarev round.

Incorporating a system patented in 1910 by Paul Mauser, the Czech 52 features both active and passive safety systems. A single action with eight-round magazine and fixed sights, the barrel is 4.9"—8 1/4" overall—and weighs 2 1/4 pounds (empty).

The Czech pistol comes boxed in "excellent" condition, complete with an extra magazine, cleaning rod, lanyard and issue holster.

More information on this and other products available from Century International is available in their free 1993 catalog. Dealers and distributors welcome.

CENTURY INTERNATIONAL ARMS, INC.

See manufacturers' addresses on page 269.

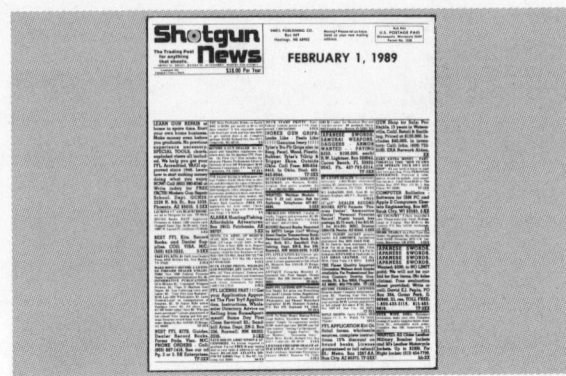
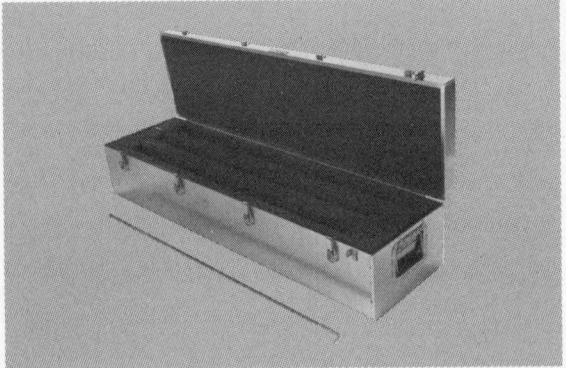

10/22 TARGET HAMMER

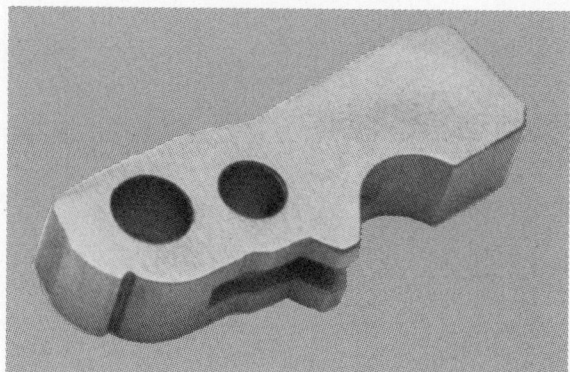

This new target hammer from Volquartsen Custom is designed to give the stock Ruger 10/22 a superb "trigger job" by simply installing it in place of the factory hammer. No stoning or fitting is required to the sear or springs.

This hammer may appear similar to the production hammer, but is geometrically advanced in the sear engagement area. It is hard plated for superior hardness and lubricity. Trigger pull is reduced to $1^1/_3$ pounds to $1^3/_4$ pounds depending on the gun.

The target hammer sells for $33.00 plus $4.00 shipping and handling, satisfaction guaranteed.

To receive a 38-page catalog, send $4.00; mention *Shooter's Marketplace* and that catalog is yours for just $3.00.

VOLQUARTSEN CUSTOM LTD.

NEW LASER SIGHTS

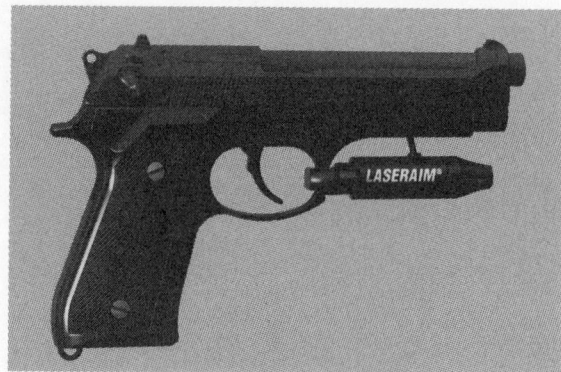

Laseraim, one of the world's leaders in laser sights, features a full line for 1994. Laseraim laser sights project an intense bright red dot directly on the target—up to $1^1/_2$ miles away. Utilizing the latest in solid-state laser technology, the sights are powered by rechargeable NiCad batteries (included) and equipped with a free 9V in-field charger.

Ideal for hunting and target shooting, they can easily be mounted to handguns, rifles, shotguns, paintball guns, muzzleloaders, bows and crossbows with Laseraim's universal fit SmartMounts. SmartMounts require no gunsmithing and are available in a variety of models. Sighting-in the Laseraim sight is simple with the four windage/elevation adjustment screws.

Write, call or fax for a free catalog.

LASERAIM

RUGER 10/22 THUMBHOLE STOCK

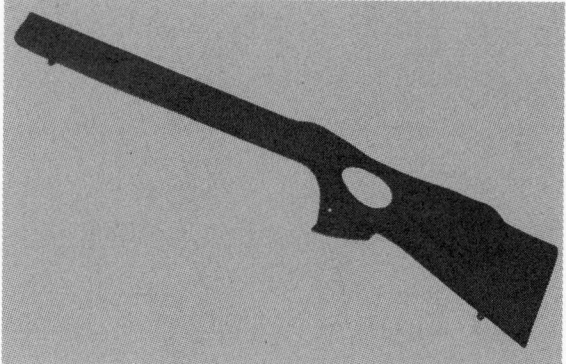

Volquartsen offers a drop-in, ready-to-shoot target stock for the heavy-barreled Ruger 10/22.

This multi-purpose stock is made from reinforced, high-density fiberglass to increase accuracy. The multiple pressure point pillar bedding design locks the action into the stock to eliminate shift and wobble. The thumbhole grip and Monte-Carlo cheekpiece allow a comfortable heads-up shooting position.

Included are front and rear swivels, an oversize front bedding screw and recoil pad. This $2^1/_2$-pound stock is available in black, red, blue and hunter green for $225; crotch walnut $250. Include $4 shipping and handling (add $4.50 for c.o.d.).

Send $4 for a Volquartsen catalog (mention *Shooter's Marketplace* and catalog is $3).

VOLQUARTSEN CUSTOM LTD.

NEW STAINLESS STEEL AUTOS

The new Laseraim Series II pistol lineup contains many standard features normally found only on expensive competition models. All Series II pistols have stainless steel construction, ramped barrels, accurized barrel bushings, built-in accessory mounts and more.

The Series II base model has fixed sights; however, several optional sights are available, including adjustable and adjustable tritium. Series II pistols are offered in value packages which include an Illusion electronic red dot sight or a Laseraim laser sight, mounts, mounting hardware and accessories.

The Series II pistol line is available in standard barrel (5") and Compact ($3^3/_8$"), in calibers 45 ACP, 40 S&W and 10mm (5" barrel only).

Call, write or fax for a free catalog.

LASERAIM ARMS

See manufacturers' addresses on page 269.

Shooter's Marketplace

MACHINE/TOOL CATALOG

The Blue Ridge Machinery & Tools #15 Catalog offers a complete selection of lathes, milling machines, shop supplies, tools, accessories, books, metals—aluminum, stainless steel, sheet metal, brass, bronze, copper tubing—and more for the gunsmithing and pistolsmithing trades.

Their catalog includes well-known names such as Emco Maier, Jet, Myford, South Bend, Sherline, Rusnok, Omatech, Wells Index and Toolmex. Products are also offered from Atlas Parts & Accessories, Baldor, Kalamazoo, Foredom, Palmgren, Royal, Trinco Niagara and Norton.

Catalog price is $1.00. Blue Ridge Machinery and Tools offers competitive prices and great service; contact the company for your machine shop needs.

BLUE RIDGE MACHINERY & TOOLS, INC.

MULTI-CALIBER ADAPTERS

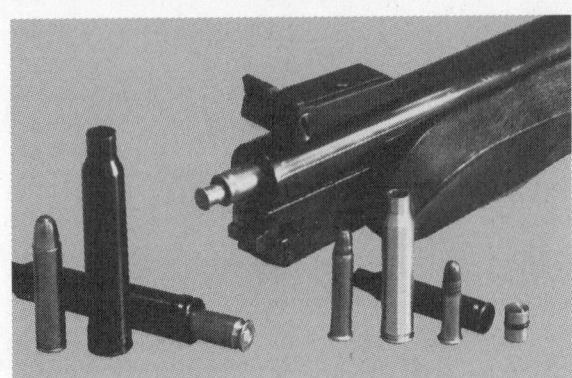

MCA Sports offers adapters and conversion devices for all types of firearms, including inserts for break-open shotguns and chamber adapters for rifles and pistols.

These inserts/adapters add versatility to any firearm. Big-bore shooters can practice on urban indoor ranges or take small game using the same rifle they used for big game hunting. For survival purposes, these adapters are unequaled, allowing a single rifle or pistol to fire a variety of ammunition. Wildcat and odd calibers are their specialty.

Write for prices; hundreds of combinations available. Offered in blue or stainless steel. Send self-addressed, stamped envelope (52¢ postage) to MCA Sports for information.

MCA SPORTS

CHECKERING TOOLS

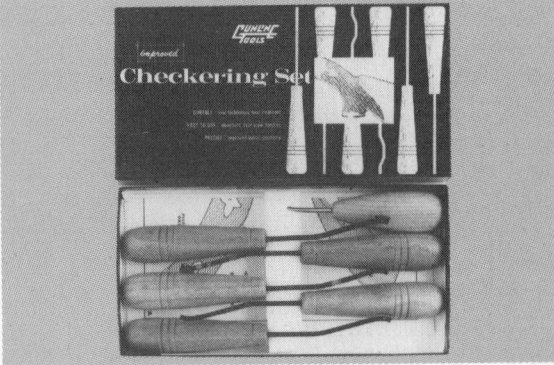

Gunline Checkering Tools are precisely made and come with illustrated instructions and easy-to-follow sample checkering patterns.

Easy to use, the cutting qualities and simple design of the checkering tools are useful for hobbyists and professional gunstockers.

Gunline offers a full line of medium and fine replaceable cutters from 16 to 28 lines per inch. They are available in 60° to 90°, in short and long size. Three types of handles are available, one with an offset rear-view feature.

Tool set prices start at $25.30 plus $3.00 shipping. The Camp Perry Set of six tools pictured above retails for $51.50. Call or write for a free brochure, prices and an order blank.

GUNLINE TOOLS

NEW RIFLE/CARTRIDGE FAMILY

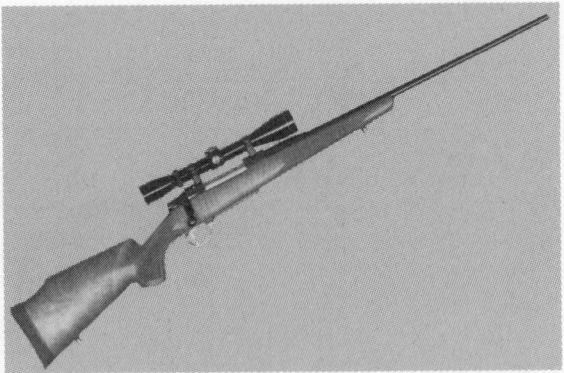

Imperial Magnum Corp. is offering a new family of rifles and cartridges designed to provide the highest velocities possible in each caliber.

The large-capacity and extra strong cartridge cases are designed for handloaders only. The beltless cases provide for more accurate headspacing, smoother feeding and simpler reloading.

Imperial production rifles have barreled actions by Sako and fiberglass stocks by McMillan and Pacific Research.

Custom rifles, chambering reamers/gauges, loading dies and unprimed cartridge cases are also available.

Write, phone or fax Imperial for free product information.

IMPERIAL MAGNUM CORP.

See manufacturers' addresses on page 269.

SHOOTER'S MARKETPLACE

YOUTH TURKEY GUN

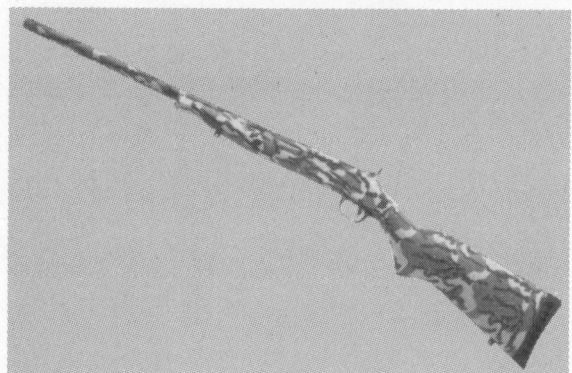

New England Firearms offers the first ever National Wild Turkey Federation sponsored Youth Turkey Gun. This 20-gauge, 3" chamber single shot with 22" barrel delivers excellent patterns and uses the same full-coverage Mossy Oak® Bottomland camo finish as last year's 10-gauge Turkey Special. Designed for young hunters, it offers a properly-sized full pistol grip stock, semi-beavertail forend and recoil pad. Perfect for turkey—as well as upland game and waterfowl—it has lower recoil than the adult-sized 12-gauge turkey guns currently available. Each gun features the NEF single shot action with patented transfer bar safety and automatic ejection. With every purchase, NEF will contribute to the N.W.T.F. habitat restoration program.

See your dealer for more information.

NEW ENGLAND FIREARMS

NEW SURVIVOR GUNS

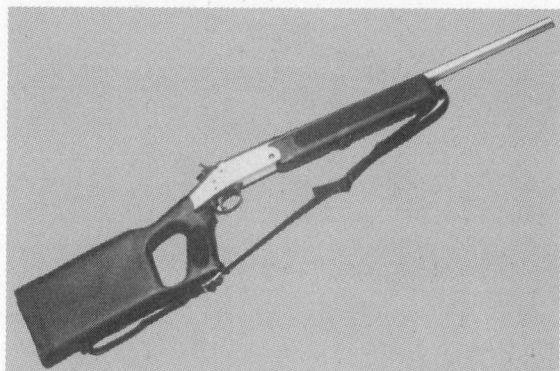

New England Firearms recently announced a new series of "Survivor" shotguns. With myriad uses besides survival, they are available in 12- and 20-gauge with blue or electroless nickel finish.

All Survivor guns feature the reliable and safe NEF action with patented transfer bar safety, plus a specially designed, high-impact, synthetic stock and forend. The stock is a modified thumbhole design with full pistol grip. The buttplate and forend are each attached with a large thumbscrew that allows access to storage compartments.

All barrels are 22", Modified Choke, and are chambered for 3" shotshells. Sling swivels and black nylon sling are standard.

See your local dealer for more information.

NEW ENGLAND FIREARMS

HANDY SINGLE SHOT RIFLE

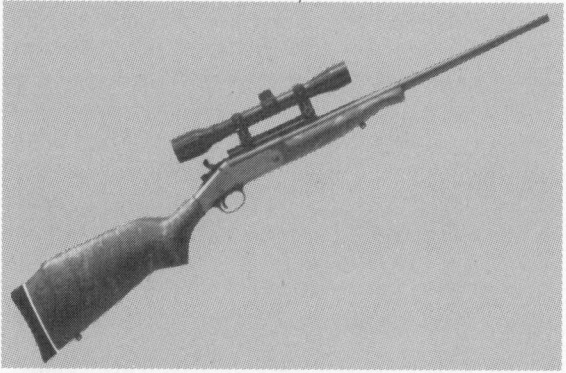

New England Firearms has added a new single shot to their Handi-Rifle family to fill the gap between their 243 Winchester and 30-06 Springfield. The American-made NEF SB2-270 is an excellent newcomer to this year's deer rifle scene. Each action is hand-tuned for the smooth let-off and crisp trigger pull required for the long-range capability of the cartridge.

The rifle features the NEF Handi-Rifle action with patented transfer bar safety and automatic ejection, plus a rebated muzzle to protect the rifling from accidental damage. It comes standard with scope mount, hammer extension and Monte Carlo stock with recoil pad; the stock and forend have sling swivel studs. Features walnut-finished, selected American hardwood stocks. See your local dealer for more information.

NEW ENGLAND FIREARMS

NEW SINGLE SHOT VARMINT RIFLES

H&R 1871, Inc., offers two new heavy barrel rifles which fill the need for highly accurate varmint rifles at affordable prices. Available in 223 Rem.—for budget-minded shooters—and 22-250 Rem.—for long-range hunters. Each action is hand-tuned for the smooth let-off and crisp trigger pull necessary for precise long-range work. Each varminter features the reliable and safe H&R single shot action with patented transfer bar safety and automatic ejection. The barrel features a heavy varmint-style profile and has a rebated muzzle to protect the rifling. Scope mount, hammer extension and Monte Carlo stock with Uncle Mike's® recoil pad are standard. Hand-checkered American Curly Maple stock and forend feature sling swivel studs. See your local dealer for more information.

H&R 1871, INC.

See manufacturers' addresses on page 269.

SHOOTER'S MARKETPLACE

CASELESS AMMO/RIFLE COMBO

JägerSport and Voere recently announced the distribution of the Voere/UCC caseless cartridge and electronic rifle system in the U.S. and Mexico. Delivery of the new Lightning Bolt Rifle and Lightning Fire Ammunition will begin September, 1993.

The new rifle and caseless ammunition will initially be offered in 223-caliber. The performance specifications of the new combination are said to be the same or better than standard 223-caliber ammo.

This rifle/ammunition combination offers extreme accuracy since the action has virtually "zero" lock-time and the propellant is consistent in pressure and velocity.

JägerSport is also distributing the full line of Voere centerfire and rimfire rifles.

JÄGERSPORT, LTD.

ECONOMICAL CLEANING KITS

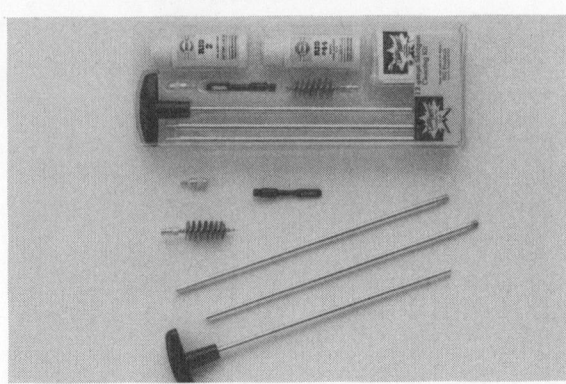

RIG Products, a leading manufacturer of gun cleaning gear since 1936, pays attention to detail and takes pride in their American-made products.

Their stainless steel RIG Rod™ is precision-machined, as are the products in their new Clean-Power™ line.

RIG's new lineup includes economical cleaning kits and aluminum rods. CleanPower patches, among the finest available, are made of densely woven 100 percent cotton twill fabric. Absorbing up to 10 times more than most patches, they come in six sizes to fit just about any gun.

The RIG Products line is available at sporting goods dealers and gun stores. Call, write or fax for a free brochure.

RIG PRODUCTS

DANGEROUS GAME ACTION

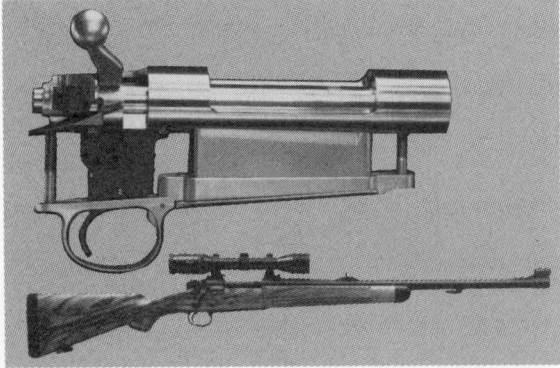

McMillan Gunworks, maker of the "Signature" rifle, now offers the "Talon," a fail-proof action developed for hunters facing the most dangerous game animals.

Handcrafted one-at-a-time, the Talon is an improved version of the pre-64 model 70 Winchester—in left- and right-hand models.

McMillan rifles are available with an array of options, calibers and accessories in sporting, heavy-caliber hunting, benchrest and prone/competition configuration—all developed from years of experience and technology.

Write, call, or fax McMillan Gunworks for more information.

Color catalog $2.00.

McMILLAN GUNWORKS, INC.

MATTE-SILVER SCOPES

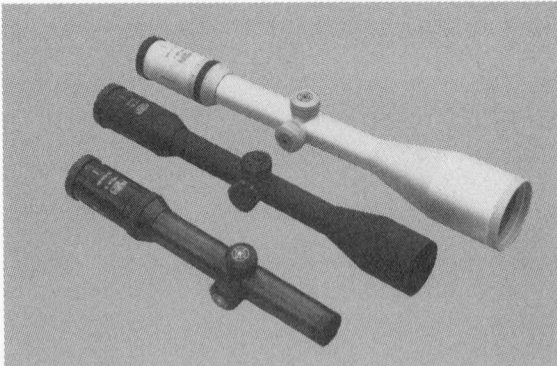

Kahles USA is offering silver-colored, anodized aluminum matte finish scopes to complement stainless steel barrels and rifles. This new finish is available in all of their variable power rifle scopes.

Kahles of Vienna, Austria is one of the world's oldest commercial manufacturers of premium rifle scopes. Their 1-inch and 30mm scopes are known for their rugged dependability, brilliance and light gathering ability. The KZF-84 is used by military and law enforcement specialists.

Kahles has over 90 years of optical engineering experience. Their scopes are offered direct to American hunters and shooters. Write or call for a color brochure and consumer price list. Dealers send signed copy of FFL for substantial discount.

KAHLES USA

See manufacturers' addresses on page 269.

SHOOTER'S MARKETPLACE

PERSONAL DEFENSE AMMUNITION

Glaser Safety Slug's state-of-the-art, professional-grade personal defense ammunition is offered in two bullet styles: Blue uses a #12 compressed shot core for maximum ricochet protection; and Silver uses a #6 compressed shot core for maximum penetration.

The Glaser Safety Slug manufacturing process results in outstanding accuracy with documented groups of less than 1" at 100 yards. This is one reason Glaser has been a top choice of professional and private law enforcement agencies worldwide for more than sixteen years.

Currently available in every caliber from 25 ACP through 30-06, plus 40 S&W, 10mm, 223 and 7.62x39.

Write Glaser Safety Slug for a free brochure.

GLASER SAFETY SLUG, INC.

NEW 30MM RED-DOT SIGHT

Aimpoint introduces a new 30mm electronic red dot optical sight with wide field of view—the AP 5000.

The main unit, designed for all types of pistols and revolvers, measures 5.5". On rifles and shotguns, where the rings need to be spaced farther apart, a 2" extender tube can be used.

The AP 5000 projects a small red dot into the 30mm parallax-free optical tube. Focusing and centering the dot is unnecessary; the shooter simply puts the dot on the target and shoots.

Available in blued or stainless finish, the AP 5000 comes complete with 30mm rings, polarizing filter and lens covers.

Suggested retail price is $319.95. For more information contact Aimpoint.

AIMPOINT, INC.

FEATHERWEIGHT BIPOD

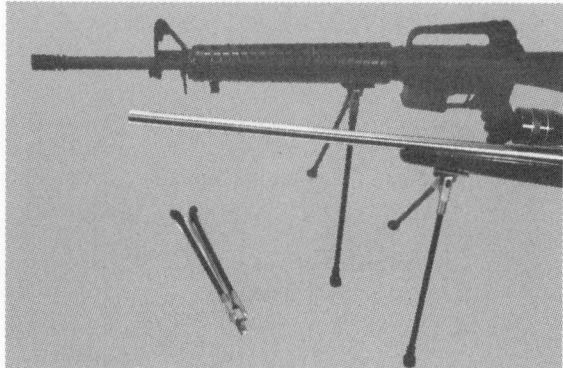

Weighing less than 6 ounces, half the usual weight, the Glaser/Cherokee bipod offers shooters the ultimate in strength (lifetime guarantee) and beauty. A frontal area less than a quarter of the size of other bipods greatly reduces snag hazards. Uneven terrain is automatically compensated for up to 33°. Deployment and retraction are single, silent, one-hand movements taking less than a second.

The bipod easily fits all sporter and varmint firearms, and most para-military firearms. The basic mount permits front or rear mounting to the forearm rather than the barrel for target accuracy. Glaser also offers hidden or quick-detachable custom mounting accessories.

Write Glaser Safety Slug for a free brochure.

GLASER SAFETY SLUG, INC.

NEW 2X RED-DOT SIGHT

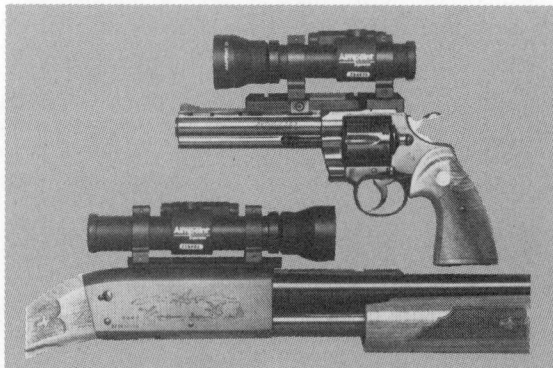

Aimpoint has developed a fixed, low-power electronic sight with floating red dot. The 30mm Aimpoint 5000 2-Power is one of the only sighting units with built-in magnification.

Shooters can now have the speed and accuracy of a red dot sight, combined with the advantages of a low-power scope.

Because the magnification is in the objective lens instead of the ocular lens (as with previous screw-in attachments), the dot covers only 1.5" at 200 yards.

The 5000 2-Power can be used on all types of firearms and is complete with 30mm rings and all accessories.

Suggested retail price for the Aimpoint 5000 2-Power is $399.95. Write Aimpoint for more information.

AIMPOINT, INC.

See manufacturers' addresses on page 269.

Shooter's Marketplace

TOP-QUALITY BULLET LUBE

Rooster Laboratories offers consistently high performance, professional high-melt cannelure bullet lubricants in a choice of two hardnesses. Both are available in 2"x 6" sticks for the commercial reloader, and 1"x 4" hollow and solid sticks.

With a 230°F melting point, both are ideal for indoor and outdoor shooting. Both bond securely to the bullet, thus remaining intact during shipping.

Zambini is a hard, tough version designed primarily for pistols. HVR is softer, but still firm. Designed primarily for high-velocity rifles, it is easier to apply; also excellent for pistols. Application requires the lubesizer be heated.

Prices: 2"x 6" sticks $4.00; 1"x 4" sticks $135.00 per 100. Contact Rooster for more information.

ROOSTER LABORATORIES

FIREARMS MARKETPLACE

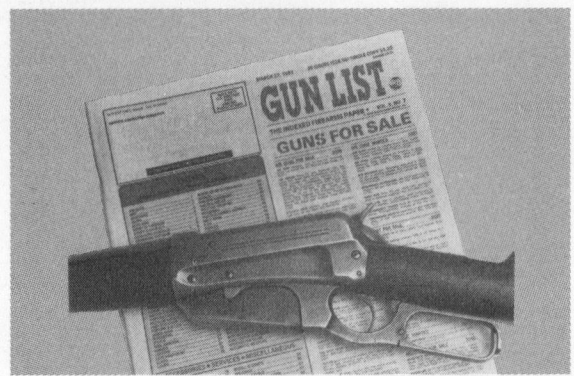

Gun List is a firearms publication for collectors and active shooters. Over 260,000 opportunities for buying, selling and trading nationwide are offered yearly. Each issue features numerous categories of quality firearms and related gun products from dealers, shops and individuals which provide opportunities to compare prices and quality.

Gun List indexes its products alphabetically in an easy-to-read format which allows readers to find their favorite collecting, hunting, reloading or shooting need quickly. Most firearms specialties are covered; nationwide gun show information is included.

A discount sample issue is $1.00. One-year subscription (26 issues) $24.95. Write or call for information.

GUN LIST

NEW RANGE FINDING SCOPE

Shepherd Scope offers a German-design Speed Focus eyepiece that provides razor sharp images with a twist of the rear ring.

The eyepiece remains rock solid throughout focusing and zooming.

Also available is an adjustable objective lens housing which will accept their sunshade. The scopes have a 340 hard matte finish that is extremely scratch resistant.

All scopes have Shepherd's patented dual reticle system that provides one-shot zeroing, instant range finding, bullet drop and constant visual verification of the original zero.

Call, write or fax Shepherd Scope direct for a free brochure.

SHEPHERD SCOPE LTD.

GLOCK MAGAZINE EXTENSIONS

La Prade offers extensions for Glock pistols that add two rounds to every standard Glock magazine. Instead of purchasing a complete magazine, the base plate is replaced with an extension.

The "2 plus 2" extension adds two rounds to 9mm and 40 S&W magazines; the "Super 2" extension adds two rounds to the 10mm and 45 magazines. The "Super 2" extension on a standard 45 Glock magazine provides a 15-round 45 or 10mm pistol for about half the cost of buying a new magazine.

The extensions come in a set of two for $9.00 prepaid ($10.00 prepaid insured); with a lifetime replacement guarantee.

A brochure detailing the rest of La Prade's magazine line is available for $1.00.

LA PRADE

See manufacturers' addresses on page 269.

SHOOTER'S MARKETPLACE

LIGHTWEIGHT, COMPACT BINOCULAR

The Swift Instrument 825 Compact Audubon, weighing only 26 ounces and standing just 5" tall, is the ideal glass for field or wood.

This armored, waterproof 7x compact binocular offers a broad field of vision with close focusing to 13 feet.

Its four-lens ocular system and magenta-coated optics with multi-coating on the ocular objective lens give a high resolving power that results in an extremely bright image under the most demanding conditions.

The 825 Compact Audubon is one of the latest in Swift Instruments' lineup of internationally known binoculars.

Write Swift Instruments for more information.

SWIFT INSTRUMENTS, INC.

UNIVERSAL RIFLESCOPE

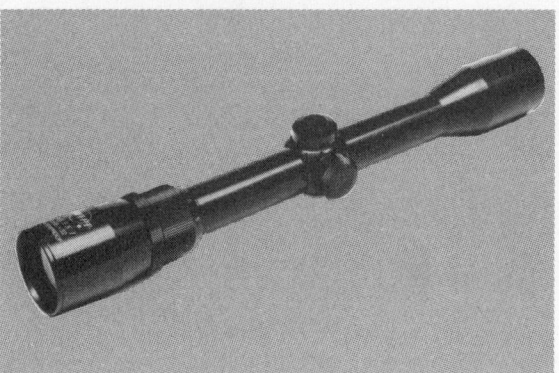

One of the most popular of the Swift Instruments line of riflescopes, the wide-angle, waterproof Model 656 features a maximum field of 40 feet at 100 yards at 3x and up to 14 feet at 9x. A maximum R.L.E. of 266 to 30 is provided by the 40mm objective lens. The Model 656 allows the shooter to easily pick up a moving target at the widest field and then zoom in for close up accuracy.

The multi-coated optical system features 11 lens elements; the Quadraplex reticle offers heavy posts to quickly line up the target and fine crosshairs for pinpoint results.

The Swift Model 656 Riflescope is available in regular, matte or silver finish and comes attractively gift-boxed. Write Swift Instruments for more information.

SWIFT INSTRUMENTS, INC.

VARIABLE POWER SPOTTING SCOPE

The 839 Searcher spotting scope from Swift Instruments offers maximum resolution in a compact body with its three-lens achromatic objective and orthoscopic eyepieces.

The variable power rotating head allows a choice of straight or 45° viewing with both 20x and 40x orthoscopic eyepieces. Additional accessories include 30x and 50x eyepieces.

The high resolving power of the Searcher makes this spotting scope perfect for telephotography with a camera adapter.

The Searcher weighs in at only 3 pounds and comes attractively gift-boxed.

Write Swift Instruments for more information about this and other products available.

SWIFT INSTRUMENTS, INC.

VARIABLE POWER RIFLESCOPE

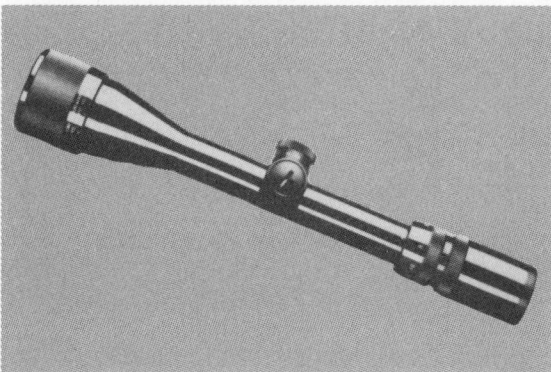

The Swift 664 from Swift Instruments meets the needs of just about everyone looking for a telescopic sight that can do double or even triple duty. The Swift 664 is a 4-12x (40mm objective lens) variable telescopic sight that features parallax adjustment from 5 meters all the way to infinity.

Big game hunters to varmint hunters to air rifle enthusiasts can find a use for the highly versatile Swift 664.

The 664 is fogproof and features superb multi-coated lenses, easy external adjustment for windage and elevation and self-centering quadraplex reticle, and comes in regular, matte or silver finish.

Write Swift Instruments for more information about this and other products available.

SWIFT INSTRUMENTS, INC.

See manufacturers' addresses on page 269.

NEW POTENT GUN PROTECTOR & LUBE

Chem-Pak's new Gun-Sav'r Protector and Lubricant is an ozone-friendly product formulated for the maximum care of fine firearms.

Gun Sav'r protects against corrosion from the elements including accidental immersion in salt water, handling, and long-term case, bag or rack storage. It also protects blackpowder bores for several days after a shoot, permitting a delay in flush cleaning.

Gun Sav'r provides smooth lubrication of moving parts. A heavy-duty additive, Tungsten disulfide, eliminates wear and provides continued improvement in slickness.

Available at your favorite gun supply shop. Write for free literature, fax or call their toll-free number. Dealer and distributor inquiries invited.

CHEM-PAK, INC.

GUN/HUNTING BOOKS & VIDEOS

Safari Press has a broad selection of books and videos on hunting and firearms. They publish titles on buffalo in Africa; woodcock hunting in the North; ducks along the Mississippi; Marco Polo sheep in Asia; elk in the Rockies; jaguar in South America; large-caliber double- and bolt-action rifles and shotguns; manufacturers such as Holland & Holland, Purdey's, Winchester and Fox; and British gunmakers.

Authors include Walter Bell, Craig Boddington, Geoffrey Boothroyd, Nash Buckingham, Peter Capstick, Gene Hill, Jack O'Connor, Jim Corbett, Elmer Keith, Frederick Selous and John Taylor.

All books have quality hard covers and are shipped worldwide. U.S. and Canadian customers send $1.00 for catalog; foreign, the equivalent of $2.00 in local stamps.

SAFARI PRESS

NEW GUNSTOCK FINISHES

Custom Oil and Pro-Custom Oil from Chem-Pak are newly developed, ozone-friendly, oil-modified urethane stock finishes.

A high-gloss finish, satin-sprayed finish and hand-rubbing liquid are available with instructions. Sprayed coatings are tack free in 30 to 45 minutes, which reduces dust collection; all finishes are run resistant. If recoat directions are followed, between coat or finish sanding or polishing is not required for sprayed finishes.

These hard finishes are tough enough to withstand hunting abuse and are water-resistant. All finishes were tested by professional finishers.

Available at your favorite gun supply shop. Write for free literature, fax or call their toll-free number. Dealer and distributor inquiries invited.

CHEM-PAK, INC.

PREMIUM SPOTTING SCOPES

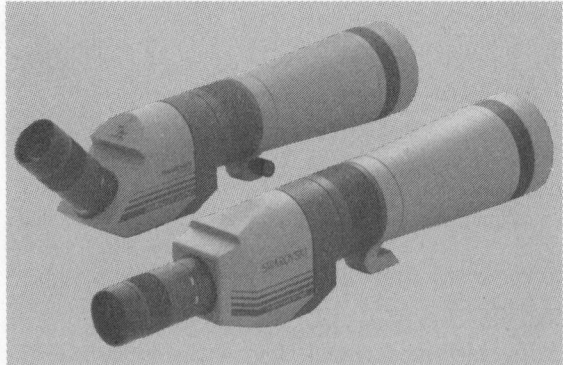

A new spotting scope has been added to Swarovski's non-extendable, premium scope line. The ST80 has optical performance characteristics similar to the AT80, which incorporates an angled eyepiece.

The ST80 comes with a straight-through eyepiece which allows faster and easier scope orientation for difficult-to-locate objects.

Since the scope bodies differ only in where the eyepiece is attached, Swarovski uses the same eyepiece and camera adapter system, allowing these accessories to be interchanged.

Other new spotting scope models from Swarovski are presently being introduced. Most of the components and accessories will be interchangeable within the system.

SWAROVSKI OPTIK NORTH AMERICA LTD.

See manufacturers' addresses on page 269.

GATLING GUN PLANS

Now you can own one. These quality blueprints allow scaling to other sizes or calibers (plans are for a 22 rimfire Gatling). Complete 40-page instruction book explains each part and how to make it. Finished Gatling has 10 rifled barrels (12" long) and is 20" in overall length. No castings required; all functioning internal parts.

The full-scale drawings are dimensioned and come complete with materials lists and notes describing how the parts were made and assembled. Includes drawings and instructions for making rifled barrels.

Original Gatling concepts have been fully adapted to obtainable materials and producible parts. Plans: $44.98. Send 3x5 self-addressed card to ensure correct shipment. Check or money order accepted.

R.G.-G., INC.

SPECIALTY RELOADING DIES

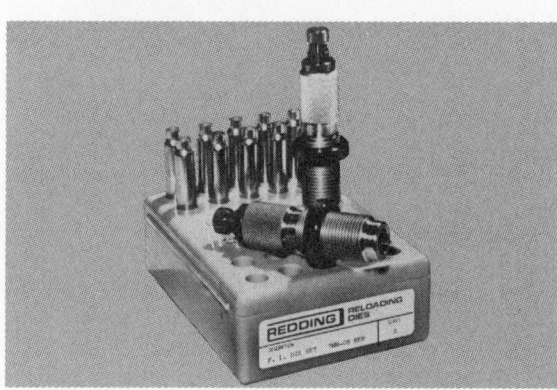

Redding Reloading has built a reputation equal to the quality of the reloading gear they produce, and they continue to expand their line of reloading dies that are available from stock.

The latest catalog from Redding lists dies for over 400 different calibers and a whole host of special-purpose dies. There are neck-sizing dies, benchrest competition dies, special-purpose crimping dies, trim dies, custom-made dies and a section on case forming that lists what is needed to form one caliber from another.

If you have something you've always wanted to shoot, or if you're contemplating building up a wildcat, contact Redding Reloading and they'll be happy to supply the dies.

REDDING RELOADING, INC.

SMOKELESS POWDERS

Accurate Arms offers the handloader a complete line of smokeless powders for handgun, rifle and shotshell reloading.

Depending upon the bulk/density of the propellant, Accurate Arms typically offers their powders in 1-, 4- or 8-pound containers.

Their current lineup includes Nitro 100 for 12-gauge shotshell applications; No. 2, No. 5, No. 7 and No. 9 for handgun applications; and 1680, 2015BR, 2230, 2460, 2495BR, 2520, 2700, 4350, 3100 and 8700 for rifle applications.

Accurate Arms currently offers a complete 32-page loading manual for their propellants free of charge, either through your local gun shop or by contacting Accurate Arms direct.

ACCURATE ARMS CO., INC.

PREMIUM BULLET MOULDS

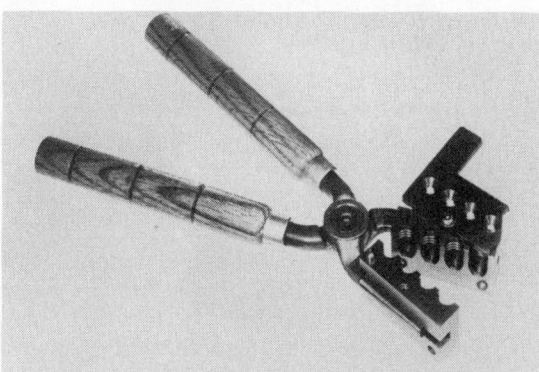

SAECO has long been regarded as one of the premier names in production bullet moulds by knowledgeable casters.

Several years ago, Redding Reloading purchased the remains of the old SAECO Reloading Company and is now producing the SAECO bullet mould line.

Redding has been constantly refining and adding to the lineup of sizes and styles to choose from and offers two-cavity and four-cavity blocks as standard items. Single-, three-, six- and eight-cavity moulds are also available on special order.

When you write or call Redding Reloading for a free catalog of SAECO products, be sure to mention you read about the SAECO lineup in *Shooter's Marketplace.*

REDDING RELOADING, INC.

See manufacturers' addresses on page 269.

HIGH-CAPACITY PISTOL

Cylinder & Slide offers the CST-1, a professionally tuned, high-capacity pistol.

The pistol is the Para Ordnance all-steel P-14 high-capacity semi-auto 45 with the new Slim Line frame. Custom combat features include: trigger pull of 4.5 pounds crisp; Gun Craft long aluminum match trigger with over travel stop; Brown high-grip beavertail grip safety; Brown narrow tactical ambidextrous thumb-safety; one-piece stainless steel guide rod; Bar-Sto match barrel bushing; Novak high-visibility low-mount fixed sights, and more.

The CST-1 is test-fired for reliability and zeroed for point of aim at 25 meters. Accuracy is 3" or better; target furnished. Comprehensive owner's manual supplied; contact Cylinder & Slide for information.

CYLINDER & SLIDE, INC.

PROFESSIONAL CUSTOM BULLETS

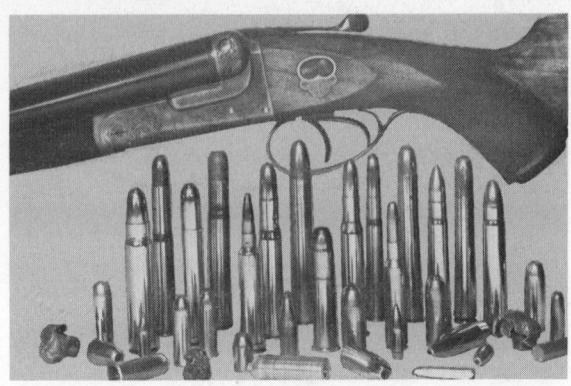

Star Custom Bullets has been making, testing and supplying custom bullets to hunters for ten years. Made particularly for heavy, dangerous game in Africa and Alaska, these superior bullets have been used successfully on elephant, Cape buffalo, lion and bear by hunters—especially professional hunters guiding and "backing up" clients.

Star incorporates ideas through continuing research of actual testing on dangerous game. They offer various solids and softnose bullets from .22 through .600 N.E. Individual customer specifications may be special-ordered.

To receive their current brochure free of charge, write Star Custom Bullets and mention *Shooter's Marketplace*.

STAR CUSTOM BULLETS

UNIQUE GUN CLEANING SYSTEM

Dunk-Kit is a very fast way to completely clean your pistol, rifle or shotgun. Dunk-Kit is a submersion-type gun cleaner. Soaking your firearm's action for an hour loosens the carbon and dirt, allowing it to be brushed out easily.

Revolver actions can be cleaned without disassembling; semi-auto pistols require only a field strip. Long gun actions and parts can be cleaned in half the normal time.

Dunk-Kit does not strip your gun dry; it leaves a light oil coating which protects and lubricates. Dunk-Kit is offered in two sizes—1³/₄ gallon, $40.95; and 4 gallon, $72.95 (prices include UPS delivery in the continental U.S.). Send $3.00 for a complete parts and custom pistolsmithing catalog (refundable).

CYLINDER & SLIDE, INC.

FLUORITE LENS SPOTTING SCOPE

Kowa Optimed's Prominar spotting scope features the only Fluorite 77mm lens on the market today. The Fluorite lens is unusual because it offers a sharper image, wider field of view and increased light-gathering capabilities of no less than 60% over conventional 60mm spotting scopes.

The Prominar is an ideal scope for the serious varmint hunter, big game hunter or dedicated benchrester.

The Kowa Optimed Prominar comes complete with bayonet mounting for easy eyepiece exchange. Seven fully interchangeable eyepieces are available from the manufacturer. An optional high-quality photo lens coupler is also offered.

Write or call for more information.

KOWA OPTIMED, INC.

See manufacturers' addresses on page 269.

SHOOTER'S MARKETPLACE

LEARN GUN REPAIR

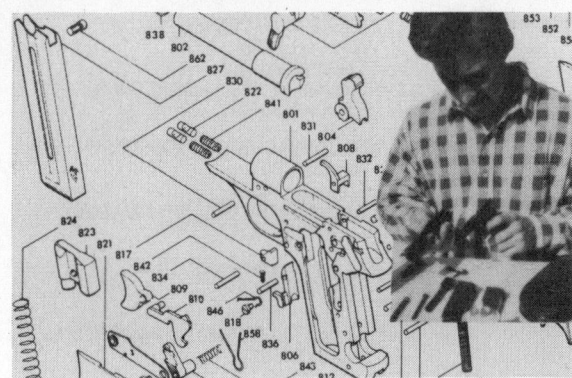

Modern Gun Repair School has taught gun repair the home-study way to more than 45,000 students since 1946. All courses are nationally accredited and approved for VA/GI benefits.

Courses include all lessons (including how to get your FFL), a tool kit, Powley Calculator and Powley Computer, GUN DIGEST, Gun Parts Catalog, mainspring vise, school binders, Brownell's Catalog, pull and drop gauge, trigger pull gauge, two parchment diplomas ready for framing and free consultation service, plus much more.

Enjoy your career; start your own business and make money in your spare time, too. No experience is needed. Write or call for free information; there's no obligation and no salesman will call.

MODERN GUN REPAIR SCHOOL

GUNSMITH SUPPLIES CATALOG

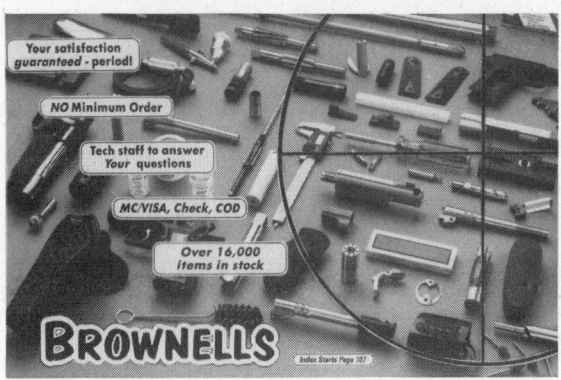

Since 1939, Brownells has been furnishing tools, supplies, fixtures and chemicals to professional gunsmiths and serious hobbyists worldwide. Their catalog features some of the finest equipment available for rebuilding, repairing, accurizing, engraving, checkering, bluing and building a complete gun.

All shipments are made from in-stock inventories and professional gunsmiths are available for technical support. As Frank Brownell says, "Our products, service, quality and reliability are guaranteed to satisfy you, our customer, 100%—period!"

Free catalog for full- and part-time gunsmiths and dealers; $3.75 for others—refunded on first $35 order. Information on FFL licensing procedures also available. MC/Visa, check and COD orders accepted.

BROWNELLS, INC.

SHOOTER'S MARKETPLACE
MANUFACTURERS' ADDRESSES

ACCURATE ARMS CO., INC. *(Pg. 267)*
Box SM'94
McEwen, TN 37101 (615-729-4207;
Fax 615-729-4217)

AIMPOINT, INC. *(Pg. 263)*
Attn: Dept. SM'94
580 Herndon Parkway, Suite 500
Herndon, VA 22070 (703-471-6828;
Fax 703-689-0575)

AIMTECH MOUNT SYSTEMS *(Pg. 248)*
(L&S Technologies, Inc.)
Attn: Dept. SM'94
P.O. Box 223
Thomasville, GA 31799 (912-226-4313;
Fax 912-227-0222)

ALPEC TEAM, INC. *(Pg. 232)*
Attn: Dept. SM'94
55 Oak Court
Danville, CA 94526 (510-820-1763;
Fax 510-820-8738)

AMERICAN DERRINGER CORP. *(Pg. 236)*
Attn: Dept. SM'94
127 N. Lacy Drive
Waco, TX 76705 (800-642-7817)

ANDERSON MANUFACTURING CO., INC.
(Pg. 254)
Attn: Dept. SM'94
P.O. Box 2640
Oak Harbor, WA 98277 (206-675-7300;
Fax 206-675-3939)

ARMORY PUBLICATIONS *(Pg. 256)*
Attn: Dept. SM'94
P.O. Box 4206
Oceanside, CA 92052 (619-757-3930;
Fax 619-722-4108)

BALD EAGLE PRECISION MACHINE CO.
(Pg. 235)
Attn: Dept. SM'94
101-K Allison Street
Lock Haven, PA 17745 (717-748-6772;
Fax 717-748-4443)

BELL & CARLSON, INC. *(Pg. 253)*
Attn: Dept. GD
509 N. 5th Street
Atwood, KS 67730 (800-634-8586;
Fax 913-626-9602)

BIRCHWOOD LABORATORIES, INC. *(Pg. 253)*
Attn: Dept. SM'94
7900 Fuller Road
Eden Prairie, MN 55344 (612-937-7933)

BLUE RIDGE MACHINERY & TOOLS, INC.
(Pg. 260)
Attn: Dept. SM'94
P.O. Box 536-GD
Hurricane, WV 25526 (800-872-6500;
Fax 304-562-5311)

BOONIE PACKER PRODUCTS *(Pg. 236)*
Attn: Dept. SM'94
P.O. Box 12204
Salem, OR 97309 (800-477-3244;
Fax 503-581-3191)

BRILEY MANUFACTURING, INC. *(Pg. 251)*
Attn: Dept. SM'94
1230 Lumpkin
Houston, TX 77043 (800-331-5718
or 713-932-6995; Fax 713-932-1043)

BROWNELLS, INC. *(Pg. 269)*
Attn: Dept. 231
200 S. Front Street
Montezuma, IA 50171 (515-623-5401;
Fax 515-623-3896)

BROWN PRECISION, INC. *(Pg. 235)*
Attn: Dept. SM'94
P.O. Box 270GD
Los Molinos, CA 96055 (916-384-2506;
Fax 916-384-1638)

BRUNTON U.S.A. *(Pg. 250)*
Attn: Dept. SM'94
620 E. Monroe Avenue
Riverton, WY 82501-4997 (307-856-6559;
Fax 307-856-1840)

B-SQUARE CO. *(Pg. 246, 247)*
Attn: Dept. SM'94
P.O. Box 11281
Ft. Worth, TX 76110-0281 (800-433-2909
or 817-923-0964; Fax 817-926-7012)

BUTLER CREEK CORP. *(Pg. 231)*
Attn: Dept. SM'94
290 Arden Drive
Belgrade, MT 59714 (406-388-1356;
Fax 406-388-7204)

CALI'CO HARDWOODS, INC. *(Pg. 236)*
Attn: Dept. SM'94
1648 Airport Blvd.
Windsor, CAL 95492 (707-546-4045;
Fax 707-546-4027)

CENTAUR SYSTEMS, INC. *(Pg. 231)*
New Products Division
Attn: Dept. SM'94
1602 Foothill Road
Kalispell, MT 59901 (Phone/Fax 406-755-8609)

CENTURY INTERNATIONAL ARMS, INC. *(Pg. 257)*
Attn: Dept. SM'94
P.O. Box 714
St. Albans, VT 05478 (802-527-1252;
Fax 802-527-0470)

CHEM-PAK, INC. *(Pg. 266)*
Attn: Dept. SM'94
11 Oates Avenue
Winchester, VA 22601 (800-336-9828;
Fax 703-722-3993)

JONATHAN ARTHUR CIENER, INC. *(Pg. 242)*
Attn: Dept. SM'94
8700 Commerce Street
Cape Canaveral, FL 32920 (407-868-2200;
Fax 407-868-2201)

CLYMER MANUFACTURING CO., INC. *(Pg. 252)*
Attn: Dept. SM'94
1645 W. Hamlin Road
Rochester Hills, MI 48309-3312 (313-853-5555;
Fax 313-853-1530)

COMPETITOR CORP., INC. *(Pg. 252)*
Gun Services
Attn: Dept. SM'94
P.O. Box 244
West Groton, MA 01472-0244 (508-448-3521;
Fax 603-673-4540)

COONAN ARMS, INC. *(Pg. 237)*
Attn: Dept. SM'94
840 Hampden Avenue
St. Paul, MN 55114 (Phone/Fax 612-646-0902)

CORBIN, INC. *(Pg. 248)*
Attn: Dept. SM'94
P.O. Box 2659
White City, OR 97503 (503-826-5211;
Fax 503-826-8669)

CRANDALL TOOL & MACHINERY CO. *(Pg. 256)*
Attn: Dept. SM'94
P.O. Box 569
Cadillac, MI 49601

CYLINDER & SLIDE, INC. *(Pg. 268)*
Attn: Dept. SM'94
245 E. 4th Street
Fremont, NE 68025 (402-721-4277;
Fax 402-721-0263)

J. DEWEY MANUFACTURING CO., INC. *(Pg. 232)*
Attn: Dept. SM'94
P.O. Box 2014
Southbury, CT 06488 (203-598-7912;
Fax 203-598-3119)

DIAMOND MACHINING TECHNOLOGY, INC.
(Pg. 240)
Attn: Dept. SM'94
85 Hayes Memorial Drive
Marlborough, MA 01752-1892 (508-481-5944;
Fax 508-485-3924)

D&J BULLET CO. & CUSTOM GUN SHOP, INC.
(Pg. 244, 258)
Attn: Dept. SM'94
Rt. 1, Box 223 A-1
Flatwoods, KY 41139 (Phone/Fax 606-836-2663)

FERDINAND, INC. *(Pg. 242)*
Attn: Dept. SM'94
P.O. Box 5, 201 Main Street
Harrison, ID 83833 (208-689-3012 or
800-522-6010; Canada 800-258-5266;
Fax 208-689-3142)

GLASER SAFETY SLUG, INC. *(Pg. 263)*
Attn: Dept. SM'94
P.O. Box 8223
Foster City, CA 94404 (800-221-3489;
Fax 415-345-8217)

GUNLINE TOOLS *(Pg. 260)*
Attn: Dept. SM'94
P.O. Box 478
Placentia, CA 92670 (714-528-5252;
Fax 714-572-4128)

GUN LIST *(Pg. 264)*
(Krause Publications)
Attn: Dept. ABAF8D
700 E. State Street
Iola, WI 54990-0001 (715-445-2214;
Fax 715-445-4087)

THE GUN PARTS CORP. *(Pg. 235)*
Attn: Dept. SM'94
Williams Lane
West Hurley, NY 12491 (914-679-2417;
Fax 914-679-5849)

H&R 1871, INC. *(Pg. 261)*
Attn: Dept. SM'94
60 Industrial Rowe
Gardner, MA 01440 (508-632-9393;
Fax 508-632-2300)

HARRIS ENGINEERING, INC. *(Pg. 254)*
Attn: Dept. SM'94
Route 1
Barlow, KY 42024 (502-334-3633;
Fax 502-334-3000)

JERRY HASELBAUER PRODUCTS *(Pg. 248)*
Attn: Dept. SM'94
P.O. Box 27629
Tucson, AZ 85726 (602-883-3391)

HASTINGS BARRELS *(Pg. 245)*
Attn: Dept. SM'94
P.O. Box 224
Clay Center, KS 67432 (913-632-3169;
Fax 913-632-6554)

THE HAWKEN SHOP *(Pg. 248)*
Attn: Dept. SM'94
P.O. Box 593
Oak Harbor, WA 98277 (206-679-4657;
Fax 206-675-1114)

HITEK INTERNATIONAL *(Pg. 241)*
Attn: Dept. SM'94
490 El Camino Real
Redwood City, CA 94063 (800-54-NIGHT;
Fax 415-363-1408)

J.B. HOLDEN CO. *(Pg. 243)*
Attn: Dept. SM'94
P.O. Box 700320
Plymouth, MI 48170 (313-455-4850;
Fax 313-455-4212)

IMPACT CASE CO. *(Pg. 252)*
Attn: Dept. SM'94
P.O. Box 9912
Spokane, WA 99209 (509-467-3303;
Fax 509-326-5436)

IMPERIAL MAGNUM CORP. *(Pg. 260)*
Attn: Dept. SM'94
1417 Main Street
Oroville, WA 98844 (604-495-3131;
Fax 604-495-2816)

JÄGERSPORT, LTD. *(Pg. 262)*
Attn: Dept. SM'94
One Wholesale Way
Cranston, RI 02920 (800-962-GUNS;
Fax 401-946-2587)

NEIL JONES CUSTOM PRODUCTS *(Pg. 239)*
Attn: Dept. SM'94
RD #1, Box 483A
Saegertown, PA 16433 (814-763-2769;
Fax 814-763-4228)

KAHLES USA *(Pg. 262)*
Attn: Dept. SM'94
P.O. Box 81071
Warwick, RI 02888 (800-752-4537;
Fax 401-946-2587)

K.B.I., INC. *(Pg. 233)*
Attn: Dept. SM'94
P.O. Box 6346
Harrisburg, PA 17112 (717-540-8518;
Fax 717-540-8567)

KK AIR INTERNATIONAL *(Pg. 258)*
Attn: Dept. SM'94
P.O. Box 9912
Spokane, WA 99209 (800-262-3322;
Fax 509-326-5436)

KOWA OPTIMED, INC. *(Pg. 268)*
Attn: Dept. SM'94
20001 S. Vermont Ave.
Torrance, CA 90502 (310-327-1913)

LANE PUBLISHING *(Pg. 254)*
Attn: Dept. SM'94
P.O. Box 759
Hot Springs, AR 71902 (501-623-4951;
Fax 501-23-9832)

LA PRADE *(Pg. 264)*
Attn: Dept. SM'94
Rt. 5, Box 240AD
Tazewell, TN 37879

LASER DEVICES, INC. *(Pg. 249)*
Attn: Dept. SM'94
2 Harris Court, A-4
Monterey, CA 93940 (408-373-0701;
Fax 408-373-0903)

LASERAIM *(Pg. 259)*
(Emerging Technologies, Inc.)
Attn: Dept. SM'94
P.O. Box 3548
Little Rock, AR 72203 (501-375-2227;
Fax 501-372-1445)

LASERAIM ARMS *(Pg. 259)*
(Sub. of Emerging Technologies, Inc.)
Attn: Dept. SM'94
P.O. Box 3548
Little Rock, AR 72203 (501-375-2227;
Fax 501-372-1445)

LOHMAN MANUFACTURING CO., INC. *(Pg. 254)*
Attn: Dept. SM'94
4500 Doniphan Drive
Neosho, MO 64850 (417-451-4438;
Fax 417-451-2576)

MARBLE ARMS CORP. *(Pg. 250)*
Attn: Dept. SM'94
P.O. Box 111
Gladstone, MI 49837 (906-428-3710)

MCA SPORTS *(Pg. 260)*
Attn: Dept. SM'94
P.O. Box 8868
Palm Springs, CA 92263 (619-770-2005)

MCMILLAN FIBERGLASS STOCKS, INC. *(Pg. 244)*
Attn: Dept. SM'94
21421 N. 14th Avenue
Phoenix, AZ 85027 (602-582-9635;
Fax 602-581-3825)

MCMILLAN GUNWORKS, INC. *(Pg. 262)*
Attn: Dept. SM'94
302 W. Melinda Lane
Phoenix, AZ 85027 (602-582-9627;
Fax 602-582-5178)

MERIT CORP. *(Pg. 237)*
Attn: Dept. SM'94
P.O. Box 9044
Schenectady, NY 12309 (518-346-1420)

MIDWAY ARMS, INC. *(Pg. 242)*
Attn: Dept. SM'94
5875-E W. Van Horn Tavern Rd.
Columbia, MO 65203 (314-445-6363;
Fax 314-446-1018)

MITCHELL ARMS, INC. *(Pg. 258)*
Attn: Dept. SM'94
3400 W. MacArthur Blvd., #1
Santa Ana, CA 92704 (714-957-5711;
Fax 714-957-5732)

MODERN GUN REPAIR SCHOOL *(Pg. 269)*
Attn: Dept. GJY'94
2538 North 8th Street, P.O. Box 5338
Phoenix, AZ 85010 (602-990-8346)

NECESSARY CONCEPTS, INC. *(Pg. 236)*
Attn: Dept. SM'94
P.O. Box 571
Deer Park, NY 11729 (516-321-8509)

NEW ENGLAND AMMUNITION CO. *(Pg. 238)*
Attn: Dept. SM'94
1771 Post Road East, Suite 223
Westport, CT 06880 (203-254-8048)

NEW ENGLAND FIREARMS *(Pg. 261)*
Attn: Dept. SM'94
60 Industrial Rowe
Gardner, MA 01440 (508-632-9393;
Fax 508-632-2300)

OLD WORLD OIL PRODUCTS *(Pg. 242)*
Attn: Dept. SM'94
3827 Queen Avenue, N.
Minneapolis, MN 55412 (612-522-5037)

PALSA OUTDOOR PRODUCTS *(Pg. 245)*
Attn: Dept. SM'94
P.O. Box 81336
Lincoln, NE 68501-1336 (800-456-9281;
Fax 402-488-2321)

RAM-LINE, INC. *(Pg. 255)*
Attn: Dept. SM'94
10601 W. 48th Ave., Suite #45
Wheat Ridge, CO 80033 (800-648-9624;
Fax 303-467-9833)

RANGER SHOOTING GLASSES *(Pg. 234)*
Randolph Advertising
Attn: Dept. SM'94
275 Centre St., Unit 17
Holbrook, MA 02343 (800-541-1405 or
617-961-6070; Fax 617-767-5239)

REDDING RELOADING, INC. *(Pg. 267)*
Attn: Dept. SM'94
1094 Starr Road
Cortland, NY 13045 (607-753-3331;
Fax 607-756-8445)

R.G.-G., INC. *(Pg. 267)*
Plans Coordinator
Attn: Dept. SM'94
P.O. Box 1261
Conifer, CO 80433-1261

RIG PRODUCTS *(Pg. 262)*
Attn: Dept. SM'94
87 Coney Island Drive
Sparks, NV 89431 (702-331-5666;
Fax 702-331-5669)

ROOSTER LABORATORIES *(Pg. 264)*
Attn: Dept. SM'94
P.O. Box 412514
Kansas City, MO 64141 (816-474-1622;
Fax 816-474-1307)

R-TECH CORP. *(Pg. 238)*
Attn: Dept. GD'94
P.O. Box 1281
Cottage Grove, OR 97424 (503-942-5126;
Fax 503-942-8624)

SAFARI PRESS *(Pg. 266)*
Attn: Dept. DG'94
P.O. Box 3095-GD94
Long Beach, CA 90803 (800-451-4788 or 714-894-9080)

SAFARILAND LTD., INC. *(Pg. 252)*
Attn: Dept. SM'94
3120 E. Mission Blvd.
Ontario, CAL 91761 (800-347-1200;
Fax 800-366-1669)

SHEPHERD SCOPE LTD. *(Pg. 264)*
Attn: Dept. GDA-1
Box 189
Waterloo, NE 68069 (402-779-2424;
Fax 402-779-4010)

THE SHOTGUN NEWS *(Pg. 258)*
Attn: Dept. SM'94, D. Clark
P.O. Box 669
Hastings, NE 68901

SILENCIO *(Pg. 253)*
Attn: Dept. SM'94
56 Coney Island Dr., Bldg. 22
Sparks, NV 88431 (800-648-1812;
Fax 702-359-1074)

SIX ENTERPRISES *(Pg. 257)*
Attn: Dept. SM'94
320-D Turtle Creek Court
San Jose, CA 95125 (408-999-0201;
Fax 408-999-0216)

SOUND TECHNOLOGY *(Pg. 238)*
Attn: Dept. SM'94
Box 391
Pelham, AL 35124 (205-664-5860)

SPORTSMAN'S COMMUNICATORS *(Pg. 250)*
Attn: Dept. SM'94
588 Radcliffe Avenue
Pacific Palisades, CA 90272 (800-538-3752)

STAR CUSTOM BULLETS *(Pg. 268)*
(Professional Hunter Supplies)
Attn: Dept. SM'94
P.O. Box 608, 468 Main St.
Ferndale, CA 95536 (707-786-4040;
Fax 707-786-9117)

STEEL RELOADING COMPONENTS, INC.
(Pg. 234)
Attn: Dept. SM'94
P.O. Box 812
Washington, IN 47501 (800-643-8188;
Fax 812-254-7269)

STONEY POINT PRODUCTS, INC. *(Pg. 243)*
Attn: Dept. SM'94
P.O. Box 5
Courtland, MN 56021-0005 (507-354-3360;
Fax 507-354-7236)

SWAROVSKI OPTIK NORTH AMERICA, LTD.
(Pg. 256, 266)
Attn: Dept. SM'94
One Wholesale Way
Cranston, RI 02920 (800-426-3089;
Fax 401-946-2587)

SWIFT INSTRUMENTS, INC. *(Pg. 265)*
Attn: Dept. SM'94
952 Dorchester Avenue
Boston, MA 02125 (617-436-2960; Fax 617-436-3232)

THOMPSON TARGET TECHNOLOGY *(Pg. 239)*
Attn: Dept. SM'94
618 Roslyn Avenue, S.W.
Canton, OH 44710 (216-453-7707;
Fax 216-478-4723)

JAMES C. TILLINGHAST *(Pg. 240)*
Attn: Dept. SM'94
P.O. Box 405DG
Hancock, NH 03449-27DG (603-525-4049)

TIMBER HEIRLOOM PRODUCTS *(Pg. 239)*
Attn: Dept. SM'94
618 Roslyn Avenue, S.W.
Canton, OH 44710 (216-453-7707;
Fax 216-478-4723)

TOMBOY, INC. *(Pg. 250)*
Attn: Dept. SM'94, Brandy Church
P.O. Box 846
Dallas, OR 97338 (503-623-8405)

TRIJICON, INC. *(Pg. 232)*
Attn: Dept. SM'94
P.O. Box 2130, Suite 37716
Farmington Hills, MI 48333 (313-553-4960;
Fax 313-553-6129)

TRIUS TRAPS *(Pg. 234)*
Attn: Dept. SM'94
221 S. Miami Avenue
Cleves, OH 45002 (513-941-5682;
Fax 513-941-7970)

DOUG TURNBULL RESTORATION *(Pg. 244)*
Attn: Dept. SM'94
P.O. Box 471
Holcomb, NY 14469 (716-657-6338)

U.S. OPTICS TECHNOLOGIES, INC. *(Pg. 240, 244)*
(Div. of Zeitz Optics, U.S.A.)
Attn: Dept. SM'94
1501 E. Chapman Ave., Ste. 306
Fullerton, CA 92631 (714-879-8922;
Fax 714-449-0941)

VIHTAVUORI OY *(Pg. 240)*
(Kaltron-Pettibone)
Attn: Dept. SM'94
1241 Ellis Street
Bensenville, IL 60106 (708-350-1116;
Fax 708-350-1606)

VOLQUARTSEN CUSTOM LTD. *(Pg. 259)*
Attn: Dept. SM'94
P.O. Box 271
Carroll, IA 51401 (712-792-4238;
Fax 712-792-2542)

WALKER ARMS CO., INC. *(Pg. 238)*
Attn: Dept. SM'94
499 County Road 820
Selma, AL 36701 (Service: 205-872-6231
or Parts: 205-875-8056)

WENIG CUSTOM GUNSTOCKS, INC. *(Pg. 232)*
Attn: Dept. SM'94
P.O. Box 249
Lincoln, MO 65338 (816- 547-3334;
Fax 816-547-2881)

WESSON FIREARMS CO., INC. *(Pg. 234)*
Attn: Dept. SM'94
Maple Tree Industrial Ctr.
Rt. 20, Wilbraham Rd.
Palmer, MA 01069 (413-267-4081;
Fax 413-267-3601)

WOLFE PUBLISHING CO. *(Pg. 239)*
Attn: Dept. SM'94
6471 Airpark Drive
Prescott, AZ 86301 (800-899-7810
or 602-445-7810; Fax 602-778-5124)

1994 GUN DIGEST

Complete Compact

CATALOG

GUNDEX®

G U N D E X

A listing of all the guns in the catalog, by name and model, alphabetically and numerically.

A

A-Square Caesar Bolt-Action Rifle, 347
A-Square Hannibal Bolt-Action Rifle, 347
A. Zoli Rifle-Shotgun O/U Combination Gun, 370
Accu-Tek Model AT-9 Auto Pistol, 282
Accu-Tek Model AT-25SS Auto Pistol, 282
Accu-Tek Model AT-25SSB Auto Pistol, 282
Accu-Tek Model AT-32SS Auto Pistol, 282
Accu-Tek Model AT-32SSB Auto Pistol, 282
Accu-Tek Model AT-40 Auto Pistol, 282
Accu-Tek Model AT-40B Auto Pistol, 282
Accu-Tek Model AT-380SS Auto Pistol, 282
Accu-Tek Model HC-380SS Auto Pistol, 282
Air Arms NJR 100 Air Rifle, 448
Air Arms SM 100 Air Rifle, 448
Air Arms TM 100 Air Rifle, 448
Air Arms XM 100 Air Rifle, 448
Airrow Model 6A Air Pistol, 442
Airrow Model 8S1P Stealth Air Rifle, 448
Airrow Model 8SRB Stealth Air Rifle, 448
Alpine Custom Grade Bolt-Action Rifle, 346
Alpine Supreme Grade Bolt-Action Rifle, 346
American Arms Brittany Double Shotgun, 409
American Arms Buckhorn Single Action Revolver, 327
American Arms Derby Double Shotgun, 410
American Arms Gentry Double Shotgun, 410
American Arms Grulla #2 Double Shotgun, 410
American Arms Model CX-22 DA Pistol, 282
American Arms Model P-98 Auto Pistol, 283
American Arms Model PK22 DA Pistol, 283
American Arms Model PX-22 Auto Pistol, 283
American Arms Regulator Single Actions, 327
American Arms Silver I O/U Shotgun, 399
American Arms Silver II O/U Shotgun, 399
American Arms Silver Skeet O/U Shotgun, 400
American Arms Silver Sporting O/U Shotgun, 400
American Arms Silver Trap O/U Shotgun, 400
American Arms Spectre DA Auto, 283
American Arms TS/SS 10 Double Shotgun, 410
American Arms TS/SS 12 Double Shotgun, 410
American Arms WS/OU 12, TS/OU 12 Shotguns, 400
American Arms WS/SS 10 Double Shotgun, 410
American Arms WT/OU 10 O/U Shotgun, 400
American Arms/Franchi Black Magic 48/AL, 389
American Arms/Franchi Falconet 2000 Shotgun, 399
American Arms/Franchi LAW-12 Shotgun, 417
American Arms/Franchi SPAS-12 Shotgun, 417
American Arms/Franchi Sporting 2000 Shotgun, 400
American Derringer 125th Anniv. Derringer, 333
American Derringer Alaskan Survivor Derringer, 333
American Derringer COP 357 Derringer, 334
American Derringer DA 38 Model, 334
American Derringer Lady Derringer, 333
American Derringer Mini COP Derringer, 334
American Derringer Model 1 Derringer, 333
American Derringer Model 3 Derringer, 333
American Derringer Model 4 Derringer, 333
American Derringer Model 6 Derringer, 333
American Derringer Model 7 Derringer, 333
American Derringer Model 10 Derringer, 333
American Derringer Semmerling LM-4, 333
American Derringer Texas Comm. Derringer, 333
AMT 45 ACP Hardballer Long Slide Pistol, 284
AMT 45 ACP Hardballer Pistol, 284
AMT Automag II Auto Pistol, 283
AMT Automag III Auto Pistol, 283
AMT Automag IV Auto Pistol, 283
AMT Backup Auto Pistol, 284
AMT Backup Double Action Only Auto, 284
AMT Government Model Auto Pistol, 284
AMT Lightning 25/22 Rifle, 371
AMT Lightning Small Game Hunting Rifle II, 371
AMT Magnum Hunter Auto rifle, 371
AMT On Duty DA Auto Pistol, 284
Anschutz 54.18 Standard Rifle, 382
Anschutz 54.18MS REP Deluxe Silhouette Rifle, 382
Anschutz 54.18MS Silhouette Rifle, 383
Anschutz 54.18MSL Silhouette Rifle, 383
Anschutz 64-MS, 64-MS Left Silhouette Rifle, 382
Anschutz 525 Deluxe Auto Rifle, 371
Anschutz 1416D/1516D Classic Bolt-Action Rifles, 377
Anschutz 1418D/1518D Mannlicher Rifles, 377

Anschutz 1700 FWT Bolt-Action Rifle, 377
Anschutz 1700D Bavarian Bolt-Action Rifle, 347
Anschutz 1700D Bavarian Bolt-Action Rifle, 377
Anschutz 1700D Bavarian Custom Meistergrade, 377
Anschutz 1700D Bavarian Meistergrade Rifle, 347
Anschutz 1700D Classic Bolt-Action Rifle, 347
Anschutz 1700D Classic Bolt-Action Rifle, 377
Anschutz 1700D Classic Meistergrade Rifle, 347
Anschutz 1700D Custom Bolt-Action Rifle, 347
Anschutz 1700D Custom Bolt-Action Rifle, 377
Anschutz 1700D Custom Meistergrade Rifle, 347
Anschutz 1700D Custom Meistergrade RF Rifle, 377
Anschutz 1700D Graphite Custom Rifle, 377
Anschutz 1700D Meistergrade Bolt-Action Rifle, 377
Anschutz 1733D Mannlicher Bolt-Action Rifle, 347
Anschutz 1803D Intermediate Match Rifle, 382
Anschutz 1808D RT Super Match 54 Target Rifle, 382
Anschutz 1827B Biathlon Rifle, 382
Anschutz 1903D Match Rifle, 382
Anschutz 1907 Match Rifle, 382
Anschutz 1907-L Match Rifle, 382
Anschutz 1910 Super Match II Rifle, 382
Anschutz 1911 Match Rifle, 382
Anschutz 1911-L Match Rifle, 382
Anschutz 1913 Super Match Left-Hand Rifle, 382
Anschutz 1913 Super Match Rifle, 382
Anschutz 2002 Match Air Rifle, 449
Anschutz 2002D RT Air Rifle, 449
Anschutz Achiever Bolt-Action Rifle, 376
Anschutz Exemplar Bolt-Action Pistol, 334
Anschutz Super Match 54 Target Model 2007 L.H., 383
Anschutz Super Match 54 Target Model 2007 Rifle, 383
Anschutz Super Match 54 Target Model 2013 L.H., 383
Anschutz Super Match 54 Target Model 2013 Rifle, 383
Arizaga Model 31 Double Shotgun, 410
Armoury R140 Hawken Rifle, 427
Armscor Model 14D Bolt-Action Rifle, 377
Armscor Model 14P Bolt-Action Rifle, 377
Armscor Model 20C Auto Rifle, 371
Armscor Model 20P Auto Rifle, 371
Armscor Model 50S Auto Rifle, 371
Armscor Model 1500 Bolt-Action Rifle, 377
Armscor Model 1600 Auto Rifle, 371
Armscor Model 1600R Auto Rifle, 371
Armscor Model 2000SC Auto Rifle, 371
Armscor Model AK22 Auto Rifle, 371
Armsport 1050 Series Double Shotgun, 410
Armsport 1863 Sharps Rifle, Carbine, 428
Armsport 1866 Sharps Carbine, 364
Armsport 1866 Sharps Rifle, 364
Armsport 2700 O/U Shotgun, 400
Armsport 2700 Series O/U Shotguns, 400
Armsport 2705 O/U Shotgun, 400
Armsport 2730/2731 O/U Shotguns, 400
Armsport 2733/2735 O/U Shotguns, 400
Armsport 2741 O/U Shotgun, 400
Armsport 2742 Sporting Clays O/U Shotgun, 400
Armsport 2744 Sporting Clays O/U Shotgun, 400
Armsport 2750 Sporting Clays O/U Shotgun, 400
Armsport 2751 Sporting Clays O/U Shotgun, 400
Armsport 2900 Tri-Barrel Shotgun, 400
Armsport Single Barrel Shotgun, 414
Army 1851 Percussion Revolver, 424
Army 1860 Percussion Revolver, 424
Arrieta Model 557 Double Shotgun, 410
Arrieta Model 570 Double Shotgun, 410
Arrieta Model 578 Double Shotgun, 410
Arrieta Model 600 Imperial Double Shotgun, 410
Arrieta Model 601 Imperial Tiro Double Shotgun, 410
Arrieta Model 801 Double Shotgun, 410
Arrieta Model 802 Double Shotgun, 410
Arrieta Model 803 Double Shotgun, 410
Arrieta Model 871 Double Shotgun, 410
Arrieta Model 872 Double Shotgun, 410
Arrieta Model 873 Double Shotgun, 410
Arrieta Model 874 Double Shotgun, 410
Arrieta Model 875 Double Shotgun, 410
Arrieta Sidelock Double Shotguns, 410
ARS AR6 Repeating Air Rifle, 448
ARS/Farco CO₂ Air Shotgun, 448
Astra A-70 Auto Pistol, 284
Astra A-75 Decocker Auto Pistol, 284

Astra A-100 Auto Pistol, 285
Auguste Francotte Bolt-Action Rifles, 350
Auguste Francotte Boxlock Double Rifle, 369
Auguste Francotte Boxlock Double Shotgun, 411
Auguste Francotte Sidelock Double Rifle, 369
Auguste Francotte Sidelock Double Shotgun, 412
Auto-Ordnance 40 S&W 1911A1 Auto Pistol, 285
Auto-Ordnance 1911A1 Auto Pistol, 285
Auto-Ordnance 1927A-3 Auto Rifle, 371
Auto-Ordnance Thompson 27 A-1, 337
Auto-Ordnance Thompson M-1, 337
Auto-Ordnance ZG-51 Pit Bull Auto, 285
AyA Boxlock Double Shotguns, 411
AyA Matador Double Shotgun, 411
AyA Model 1 Double Shotgun, 411
AyA Model 2 Double Shotgun, 411
AyA Model 4 Deluxe Double Shotgun, 411
AyA Model 4 Double Shotgun, 411
AyA Model 53 Double Shotgun, 411
AyA Model 56 Double Shotgun, 411
AyA Model XXV Boxlock Double Shotgun, 411
AyA Model XXV Sidelock Double Shotgun, 411
AyA Sidelock Double Shotguns, 411

B

Baby Bretton O/U Shotgun, 400
Baby Dragoon 1848 Percussion Revolver, 424
Baby Dragoon 1849 Pocket Percussion Revovler, 424
Baby Dragoon Wells Fargo Percussion Revolver, 424
Baby Eagle Auto Pistol, 285
Barrett Light-Fifty Model 82 A-1 Rifle, 338
Barrett Model 90 Bolt-Action Rifle, 347
Beeman Adder Air Pistol, 442
Beeman Air Wolf Air Rifle, 449
Beeman Carbine Model C1, 449
Beeman Classic Magnum Air Rifle, 449
Beeman Crow Magnum Air Rifle, 449
Beeman FX-1 Air Rifle, 449
Beeman Kodiak Air Rifle, 450
Beeman P-1 Magnum Air Pistol, 442
Beeman P-2 Match Air Pistol, 442
Beeman R1 Air Rifle, 450
Beeman R1 Carbine, 450
Beeman R1 Field Target Air Rifle, 450
Beeman R1 Laser Air Rifle, 450
Beeman R7 Air Rifle, 450
Beeman R8 Air Rifle, 450
Beeman R10 Air Rifles, 450
Beeman RX-1 Gas-Spring Magnum Air Rifle, 450
Beeman Super 7 Air Rifle, 450
Beeman Wolf Pup Air Rifle, 449
Beeman Wolf Pup Deluxe Air Rifle, 449
Beeman Wolverine Air Pistol, 443
Beeman/Feinwerkbau 65 MKI Air Pistol, 443
Beeman/Feinwerkbau 65 MKII Air Pistol, 443
Beeman/Feinwerkbau 102 Air Pistol, 443
Beeman/Feinwerkbau 300-S Mini-Match Air Rifle, 451
Beeman/Feinwerkbau 300-S Match Air Rifle, 451
Beeman/Feinwerkbau 601 Running Tgt. Rifle, 451
Beeman/Feinwerkbau 2600 Target Rifle, 383
Beeman/Feinwerkbau C5 CO₂ Rapid Fire Pistol, 443
Beeman/Feinwerkbau C20 CO₂ Pistol, 443
Beeman/Feinwerkbau C25 CO₂ Pistol, 443
Beeman/Feinwerkbau C25 Mini CO₂ Pistol, 443
Beeman/Feinwerkbau C60 CO₂ Air Rifle, 451
Beeman/Feinwerkbau C60 Running Target, 451
Beeman/Feinwerkbau Mini C60 Air Rifle, 451
Beeman/Feinwerkbau Model 601 Air Rifle, 451
Beeman/HW30 Air Rifle, 451
Beeman/HW50 Light/Sporter Target Air Rifle, 452
Beeman/HW55MM, HW55T Target Rifles, 451
Beeman/HW60J Bolt-Action Rifle, 347
Beeman/HW60J-ST Bolt-Action Rifle, 378
Beeman/HW70 Air Pistol, 443
Beeman/HW70A Air Pistol, 443
Beeman/HW77 Deluxe Air Rifle, Carbine, 452
Benelli Black Eagle Competition Auto Shotgun, 390
Benelli M1 Sporting Special Auto Shotgun, 390
Benelli M1 Super 90 Field Auto Shotgun, 390
Benelli M1 Super 90 Shotgun, 418
Benelli M1 Super 90 Tactical Shotgun, 418
Benelli M3 Super 90 Pump/Auto Shotgun, 418

Benelli Montefeltro Super 90 20-Gauge Shotgun, 390
Benelli Montefeltro Super 90 Auto Shotgun, 390
Benelli MP90S Match Pistol, 311
Benelli Super Black Eagle Auto Shotgun, 390
Benelli Super Black Eagle Slug Auto Shotgun, 390
Benjamin Sheridan 397, 392 Air Rifles, 452
Benjamin Sheridan CO2 Air Rifles, 452
Benjamin Sheridan CO2 Pellet Pistols, 444
Benjamin Sheridan E17 Pellet Pistol, 444
Benjamin Sheridan E20 Pellet Pistol, 444
Benjamin Sheridan E22 Pellet Pistol, 444
Benjamin Sheridan EB17 Pellet Pistol, 444
Benjamin Sheridan EB20 Pellet Pistol, 444
Benjam Sheridan EB22 Pellet Pistol, 444
Benjamin Sheridan F9 Air Rifle, 452
Benjamin Sheridan FB 9 Air Rifle, 452
Benjamin Sheridan 397, 392 Air Rifles, 452
Benjamin Sheridan G397, G392 Air Rifles, 452
Benjamin Sheridan GS397, GS392 Air Rifles, 451
Benjamin Sheridan H17, H20, H22 Pellet Pistols, 443
Benjamin Sheridan HB17, HB20, HB22 Pistols, 443
Benjamin Sheridan Pneumatic Air Rifles, 452
Benjamin Sheridan Pneumatic Pellet Pistols, 443
Benjamin Sheridan S397, S392 Air Rifles, 452
Beretta 390 Deluxe Auto Shotgun, 391
Beretta 390 Field Auto Shotgun, 391
Beretta 390 Field Matte Auto Shotgun, 391
Beretta 390 Super Trap, Super Skeet Shotguns, 391
Beretta 626 Onyx Double Shotgun, 411
Beretta 627EELL Double Shotgun, 411
Beretta 627EL Double Shotgun, 411
Beretta 682 Pigeon Silver O/U Shotgun, 402
Beretta 682 Skeet O/U Shotgun, 402
Beretta 682 Sporting Combo O/U Shotgun, 401
Beretta 682 Sporting O/U Shotgun, 401
Beretta 682 Super Skeet O/U Shotgun, 402
Beretta 682 Super Sport O/U Shotgun, 401
Beretta 682 Super Sporting O/U Shotgun, 401
Beretta 682 Super Trap O/U Shotgun, 402
Beretta 682 Trap Combo Sets, 402
Beretta 682 Trap Mono Shotgun, 402
Beretta 682 Trap O/U Shotgun, 402
Beretta 682 Trap Top Single Shotgun, 402
Beretta 686 English Course Sporting O/U Shotgun, 401
Beretta 686 Field O/U Shotgun, 401
Beretta 686 Hunter Sport O/U Shotgun, 401
Beretta 686 Onyx O/U Shotgun, 401
Beretta 686 Sporting Combo O/U Shotgun, 401
Beretta 686 Sporting O/U Shotgun, 401
Beretta 686 Ultralight O/U Shotgun, 401
Beretta 686EL O/U Shotgun, 401
Beretta 686L Silver O/U Shotgun, 401
Beretta 687 Sporting Combo O/U Shotgun, 401
Beretta 687 Sporting O/U Shotgun, 401
Beretta 687EELL O/U Shotgun, 401
Beretta 687EELL Skeet O/U Shotgun, 402
Beretta 687EELL Sporter O/U Shotgun, 401
Beretta 687EELL Trap O/U Shotgun, 402
Beretta 687EL O/U Shotgun, 401
Beretta 687EL Sporting O/U Shotgun, 401
Beretta 687L Field O/U Shotgun, 401
Beretta A-303 Auto Shotgun, 390
Beretta A-303 Sporting Clays Auto Shotgun, 390
Beretta A-303 Upland Model Auto Shotgun, 390
Beretta A-303 Youth Auto Shotgun, 390
Beretta ASE 90 Competition O/U Shotgun, 401
Beretta ASE 90 Sporting O/U Shotgun, 401
Beretta Express SSO6 Gold O/U Double Rifle, 368
Beretta Express SSO6 O/U Double Rifle, 368
Beretta Express SSO O/U Double Rifle, 368
Beretta Model 21 Auto Pistol, 286
Beretta Model 21 EL Auto Pistol, 286
Beretta Model 80 Series Auto Pistols, 285
Beretta Model 84F Auto Pistol, 285
Beretta Model 85F Auto Pistol, 285
Beretta Model 86 Auto Pistol, 285
Beretta Model 87 Auto Pistol, 285
Beretta Model 87 Long Barrel Pistol, 285
Beretta Model 89 Sport Auto Pistol, 285
Beretta Model 89 Target Pistol, 311
Beretta Model 92D Auto Pistol, 286
Beretta Model 92F Stainless Pistol, 286
Beretta Model 92F-EL Stainless Pistol, 286
Beretta Model 92F/92FS/96 Centurion Pistols, 286
Beretta Model 92FC Auto Pistol, 286
Beretta Model 92FS Auto Pistol, 285
Beretta Model 452 Sidelock Double Shotgun, 411
Beretta Model 452EELL Double Shotgun, 411

Beretta Model 455 SxS Express Rifle, 368
Beretta Model 455EELL SxS Express Rifle, 368
Beretta Model 950 BS Auto Pistol, 286
Beretta Model 1201F Auto Shotgun, 391
Beretta Model 1201FP3 Auto Shotgun, 418
Beretta Onyx Hunter Sport O/U Shotgun, 401
Beretta Onyx Sporting O/U Shotgun, 401
Beretta Over/Under Field Shotgun, 401
Beretta Series 682 Competition O/U Shotguns, 402
Beretta Side-by-Side Field Shotguns, 411
Beretta SO5 Combo O/U Shotgun, 401
Beretta SO5 O/U Shotgun, 401
Beretta SO6 O/U Shotgun, 401
Beretta SO9 O/U Shotgun, 401
Beretta SO5 Trap O/U Shotgun, 401
Beretta SO5 Skeet O/U Shotgun, 401
Beretta SO5 Sporting O/U Shotgun, 401
Beretta SO6 Trap O/U Shotgun, 401
Beretta SO6 Skeet O/U Shotgun, 401
Beretta SO6 Sporting O/U Shotgun, 401
Beretta SO6EELL Field O/U Shotgun, 401
Beretta Sporting Clays O/U Shotguns, 401
Beretta Vittoria Auto Shotgun, 391
Bersa Model 23 Auto Pistol, 286
Bersa Model 83 Auto Pistol, 286
Bersa Model 85 Auto Pistol, 286
Bersa Model 86 Auto Pistol, 286
Bersa Thunder 9 Auto Pistol, 287
BF Single Shot Pistol, 311
BF Unlimited Silhouette Pistol, 311
Bill Hanus Birdgun Double Shotguns, 412
Black Watch Scotch Pistol, 420
Blaser R84 Bolt-Action Rifle, 348
Bostonian Percussion Rifle, 428
BRNO 537 Sporter Bolt-Action Rifle, 348
BRNO 630 Standard Air Rifle, 452
BRNO 631 Deluxe Air Rifle, 452
BRNO Aeron-Tau CO2 Pistol, 444
BRNO Aeron-Tau-2000 Air Rifles, 452
BRNO ZKB 527 Fox Bolt-Action Rifle, 348
BRNO ZKK 600, 601, 602 Bolt-Action Rifles, 348
BRNO ZKM 452 Deluxe Bolt-Action Rifle, 377
BRNO ZKM 452 Standard Bolt-Action Rifle, 377
Brown Model One Single Shot Rifle, 364
Browning 325 Sporting Clays O/U Shotgun, 403
Browning A-500G Auto Shotgun, 391
Browning A-500G Sporting Clays Auto Shotgun, 391
Browning A-500R Auto Shotgun, 391
Browning A-500R Buck Special Auto Shotgun, 391
Browning A-Bolt 22 Bolt-Action Rifle, 378
Browning A-Bolt 22 Gold Medallion Rifle, 378
Browning A-Bolt Bolt-Action Rifle, 348
Browning A-Bolt Composite Stalker Rifle, 348
Browning A-Bolt Euro-Bolt Rifle, 349
Browning A-Bolt Gold Medallion Rifle, 349
Browning A-Bolt Hunter Bolt-Action Rifle, 348
Browning A-Bolt Left-Hand Bolt-Action Rifle, 348
Browning A-Bolt Medallion Bolt-Action Rifle, 348
Browning A-Bolt Micro Medallion, 349
Browning A-Bolt Short Action Composite Rifle, 349
Browning A-Bolt Short Action Hunter Rifle, 349
Browning A-Bolt Short Action Medallion Rifle, 349
Browning A-Bolt Stainless Stalker Rifle, 348
Browning Auto-5 Light 12 Auto Shotgun, 391
Browning Auto-5 Light 20 Auto Shotgun, 391
Browning Auto-5 Light 12 Buck Special Shotgun, 392
Browning Auto-5 Magnum 12 Auto Shotgun, 392
Browning Auto-5 Magnum 20 Auto Shotgun, 392
Browning Auto-5 Magnum Stalker Auto Shotgun, 392
Browning Auto-5 Stalker Auto Shotgun, 392
Browning Auto-22 Auto Rifle, 372
Browning Auto-22 Grade VI Auto Rifle, 372
Browning BAR Mark II Safari Magnum rifle, 338
Browning BAR Mark II Safari Rifle, 338
Browning BDA-380 DA Auto Pistol, 287
Browning BDM DA Auto Pistol, 287
Browning BL-22 Grade I Lever-Action Rifle, 375
Browning BL-22 Grade II Lever-Action Rifle, 375
Browning BPS Buck Special Pump Shotgun, 395
Browning BPS Game Gun Deer Special Shotgun, 395
Browning BPS Game Gun Turkey Special, 395
Browning BPS Ladies Model Pump Shotgun, 395
Browning BPS Pigeon Grade Pump Shotgun, 395
Browning BPS Pump Shotgun, 395
Browning BPS Stalker Pump Shotgun, 395
Browning BPS Youth Model Pump Shotgun, 395
Browning BSA 10 Auto Shotgun, 391
Browning BSA 10 Stalker Auto Shotgun, 391

Browning BT-99 Competition Trap Special, 414
Browning BT-99 Micro Pigeon Grade Shotgun, 414
Browning BT-99 Micro Shotgun, 414
Browning BT-99 Micro Signature Painted Shotgun, 414
Browning BT-99 Pigeon Grade Shotgun, 414
Browning BT-99 Plus Pigeon Grade Shotgun, 414
Browning BT-99 Plus Signature Painted Shotgun, 414
Browning BT-99 Plus Trap Shotgun, 414
Browning BT-99 Signature Painted Shotgun, 414
Browning Buck Mark 22 Pistol, 288
Browning Buck Mark Field 5.5 Pistol, 312
Browning Buck Mark Plus Pistol, 288
Browning Buck Mark Silhouette Pistol, 312
Browning Buck Mark Target 5.5 Gold Pistol, 312
Browning Buck Mark Target 5.5 Pistol, 312
Browning Buck Mark Unlimited Match Pistol, 312
Browning Buck Mark Varmint Pistol, 288
Browning Citori Gran Lightning O/U Shotgun, 402
Browning Citori GTI Sporting Clays O/U Shotgun, 403
Browning Citori Hunting Grade I O/U Shotgun, 402
Browning Citori Hunting Grade III O/U Shotgun, 402
Browning Citori Hunting Grade VI O/U Shotgun, 402
Browning Citori Lightning Grade I O/U Shotgun, 402
Browning Citori Lightning Grade III O/U Shotgun, 402
Browning Citori Lightning Grade VI O/U Shotgun, 402
Browning Citori O/U Shotgun, 402
Browning Citori O/U Skeet Shotgun, 402
Browning Citori Plus Trap Combo O/U Shotgun, 402
Browning Citori Plus Trap Grade I O/U Shotgun, 402
Browning Citori Plus Trap Pigeon Grade O/U, 402
Browning Hi-Power 40 S&W Pistol, 287
Browning Hi-Power Auto Pistol, 287
Browning Hi-Power Capitan Pistol, 287
Browning Hi-Power HP-Practical Pistol, 287
Browning Hi-Power Mark III Pistol, 287
Browning Lightning Sporting Clays O/U Shotgun, 402
Browning Lightning Sporting Clays Pigeon Grade, 402
Browning Micro Buck Mark Pistol, 288
Browning Micro Buck Mark Plus Pistol, 288
Browning Micro Citori Grade I O/U Shotgun, 402
Browning Micro Citori Grade III O/U Shotgun, 402
Browning Micro Citori Grade VI O/U Shotgun, 402
Browning Micro Citori O/U Shotgun, 402
Browning Micro Recoilless Trap Shotgun, 414
Browning Model 42 Pump Shotgun, 394
Browning Model 81 BLR Lever-Action Rifle, 342
Browning Model 81 Long Action BLR Rifle, 342
Browning Model 1885 Single Shot Rifle, 364
Browning Model 1886 High Grade Carbine, 342
Browning Model 1886 Lever-Action Carbine, 342
Browning O/U Grade I Skeet Set, 402
Browning O/U Skeet Grade I Shotgun, 402
Browning O/U Skeet Grade III Shotgun, 402
Browning O/U Skeet Grade VI Shotgun, 402
Browning O/U Trap Grade I Shotgun, 402
Browning O/U Trap Grade III Shotgun, 402
Browning O/U Trap Grade VI Shotgun, 402
Browning O/U Trap Shotgun, 402
Browning Recoilless Trap Shotgun, 414
Browning Special Sporting Clays O/U Shotgun, 403
Browning Superlight Citori Grade I O/U Shotgun, 402
Browning Superlight Citori Grade III O/U Shotgun, 402
Browning Superlight Citori Grade VI O/U Shotgun, 402
Browning Superlight Citori O/U Shotgun, 402
Bryco Model 38 Pistols, 288
Bryco Model 48 Pistols, 288
BSA Scorpion Air Pistol, 444
BSA Supersport Air Rifle, 453
BSA Superstar Air Rifle, 452

C

C. Sharps Arms 1875 Classic Sharps rifle, 367
C. Sharps Arms New Model 1874 Old Reliable, 367
C. Sharps Arms New Model 1875 Business Rifle, 367
C. Sharps Arms New Model 1875 Saddle Rifle, 367
C. Sharps Arms New Model 1875 Carbine, 367
C. Sharps Arms New Model 1875 Single Shot Rifle, 367
C. Sharps Arms New Model 1875 Sporting Rifle, 367
C. Sharps Arms New Model 1875 Tgt. & L.R. Rifle, 367
C.S. Richmond 1863 Musket, 436
Cabanas Esproncenda IV Bolt-Action Rifle, 378
Cabanas Leyre Bolt-Action Rifle, 378
Cabanas Master Bolt-Action Rifle, 378
Cabanas Mini 82 Youth Bolt-Action Rifle, 378
Cabanas Model R83 Bolt-Action Rifle, 378
Cabanas Phaser Bolt-Action Rifle, 378
Cabanas Pony Youth Bolt-Action Rifle, 378
Cabanas Varmint Model Bolt-Action Rifle, 378

GUNDEX

GUNDEX

Includes models suitable for several forms of competition and other sporting purposes.

ACCU-TEK MODEL AT-9 AUTO PISTOL
Caliber: 9mm Para., 7-shot magazine.
Barrel: 3.2".
Weight: 28 oz. **Length:** 6.25" overall.
Stocks: Black checkered nylon.
Sights: Blade front, rear adjustable for windage; three-dot system.
Features: Stainless steel construction. Double action only. Firing pin block with no external safeties. Lifetime warranty. Introduced 1992. Made in U.S. by Accu-Tek.
Price: Satin stainless **$270.00**
Price: Black finish over stainless **$275.00**

Accu-Tek AT-40 Auto Pistol
Same as the Model AT-9 except chambered for 40 S&W. Introduced 1992.
Price: Stainless **$270.00**
Price: Black finish over stainless (AT-40B) **$275.00**

ACCU-TEK MODEL HC-380SS AUTO PISTOL
Caliber: 380 ACP, 13-shot magazine.
Barrel: 2.75".
Weight: 28 oz. **Length:** 6" overall.
Stocks: Checkered black composition.
Sights: Blade front, rear adjustable for windage.
Features: External hammer; manual thumb safety with firing pin and trigger disconnect; bottom magazine release. Stainless finish. Introduced 1993. Made in U.S. by Accu-Tek.
Price: **$230.00**

ACCU-TEK MODEL AT-380SS AUTO PISTOL
Caliber: 380 ACP, 5-shot magazine.
Barrel: 2.75".
Weight: 20 oz. **Length:** 5.6" overall.
Stocks: Grooved black composition.
Sights: Blade front, rear adjustable for windage.
Features: Stainless steel frame and slide. External hammer; manual thumb safety; firing pin block, trigger disconnect. Lifetime warranty. Introduced 1992. Made in U.S. by Accu-Tek.
Price: Satin stainless **$182.00**
Price: Black finish over stainless (AT-380SSB) **$187.00**

Accu-Tek Model AT-32SS Auto Pistol
Same as the AT-380SS except chambered for 32 ACP. Introduced 1990.
Price: Satin stainless **$176.00**
Price: Black finish over stainless (AT-32SSB) **$181.00**

Accu-Tek Model AT-25SS Auto Pistol
Similar to the AT-380SS except chambered for 25 ACP with 7-shot magazine. Also available with aluminum frame and slide with 11-oz. weight. Introduced 1991.
Price: Satin stainless **$158.00**
Price: Black finish over stainless (AT-25SSB) **$163.00**

AMERICAN ARMS MODEL CX-22 DA AUTO PISTOL
Caliber: 22 LR, 8-shot magazine.
Barrel: 3⅓".
Weight: 22 oz. **Length:** 6⅓" overall.
Stocks: Checkered black polymer.
Sights: Blade front, rear adjustable for windage.
Features: Double action with manual hammer-block safety, firing pin safety. Alloy frame. Has external appearance of Walther PPK. Blue/black finish. Introduced 1990. Made in U.S. by American Arms, Inc.
Price: **$198.00**

AMERICAN ARMS MODEL PK22 DA AUTO PISTOL
Caliber: 22 LR, 8-shot magazine.
Barrel: 3.3".
Weight: 22 oz. **Length:** 6.3" overall.
Stocks: Checkered plastic.
Sights: Fixed.
Features: Double action. Polished blue finish. Slide-mounted safety. Made in the U.S. by American Arms, Inc.
Price: **$198.00**

Accu-Tek AT-9

Accu-Tek HC-380SS

Accu-Tek AT-380SS

American Arms PK22

AMERICAN ARMS MODEL P-98 AUTO PISTOL
Caliber: 22 LR, 8-shot magazine.
Barrel: 5".
Weight: 25 oz. **Length:** 8⅛" overall.
Stocks: Grooved black polymer.
Sights: Blade front, rear adjustable for windage.
Features: Double action with hammer-block safety, magazine disconnect safety. Alloy frame. Has external appearance of the Walther P-38 pistol. Introduced 1989. Made in U.S. by American Arms, Inc.
Price: $213.00

American Arms P-98

AMERICAN ARMS MODEL PX-22 AUTO PISTOL
Caliber: 22 LR, 7-shot magazine.
Barrel: 2.85".
Weight: 15 oz. **Length:** 5.39" overall.
Stocks: Black checkered plastic.
Sights: Fixed.
Features: Double action; 7-shot magazine. Polished blue finish. Introduced 1989. Made in U.S. From American Arms, Inc.
Price: $193.00

American Arms PX-22

American Arms Spectre

AMERICAN ARMS SPECTRE DA PISTOL
Caliber: 9mm Para., 30-shot; 45 ACP, 30-shot magazine.
Barrel: 6".
Weight: 4 lbs., 8 oz. **Length:** 13.75".
Stocks: Black nylon.
Sights: Post front adjustable for windage and elevation, fixed U-notch rear.
Features: Triple action blowback fires from closed bolt; ambidextrous safety and decocking levers; matte black finish; magazine loading tool. For standard velocity ammunition only. From American Arms, Inc.
Price: 9mm $429.00
Price: 45 ACP $457.00

AMT AUTOMAG II AUTO PISTOL
Caliber: 22 WMR, 9-shot magazine (7-shot with 3⅜" barrel).
Barrel: 3⅜", 4½", 6".
Weight: About 23 oz. **Length:** 9⅜" overall.
Stocks: Grooved carbon fiber.
Sights: Bl
Features: osed hammer. Slide flats hav er guard. Introduced 1986. F
Price: $375.95

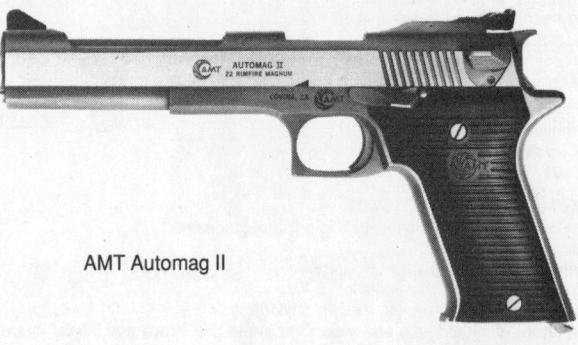

AMT Automag II

AMT AU
Caliber: 3
Barrel: 6
Weight: 4
Stocks: G
Sights: Blade front, adjustable rear.
Features: Stainless steel construction. Hammer-drop safety. Slide flats have brushed finish, rest is sandblasted. Introduced 1989. From AMT.
Price: $465.95

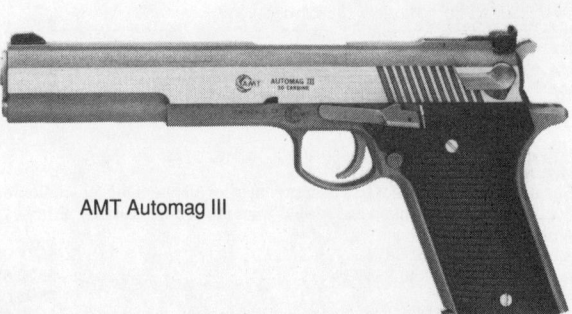

AMT Automag III

AMT AUTOMAG IV PISTOL
Caliber: 10mm Magnum, 45 Winchester Magnum, 6-shot magazine.
Barrel: 6.5" (45), 8⅝" (10mm only).
Weight: 46 oz. **Length:** 10.5" overall with 6.5" barrel.
Stocks: Carbon fiber.
Sights: Blade front, adjustable rear.
Features: Made of stainless steel with brushed finish. Introduced 1990. Made in U.S. by AMT.
Price: $679.99

AMT BACKUP AUTO PISTOL

Caliber: 380 ACP, 5-shot magazine.
Barrel: 2⅛".
Weight: 18 oz. **Length:** 5" overall.
Stocks: Carbon fiber.
Sights: Fixed, open, recessed.
Features: Concealed hammer, blowback operation; manual and grip safeties. All stainless steel construction. Smallest domestically-produced pistol in 380. From AMT.
Price: **$295.99**

AMT Backup DAO

AMT Backup Double Action Only Pistol

Similar to the standard Backup except has double-action-only mechanism, enlarged trigger guard, slide is rounded ar rear. Has 6-shot magazine. Introduced 1992. From AMT.
Price: **$295.99**

AMT ON DUTY DA PISTOL

Caliber: 9mm Para., 15-shot; 40 S&W, 11-shot; 45 ACP, 9-shot magazine.
Barrel: 4½".
Weight: 32 oz. **Length:** 7¾" overall.
Stocks: Smooth carbon fiber.
Sights: Blade front, rear adjustable for windage; three-dot system.
Features: Choice of DA with decocker or double action only. Inertia firing pin, trigger disconnector safety. Aluminum frame with steel recoil shoulder, stainless steel slide and barrel. Introduced 1991. Made in the U.S. by AMT.
Price: 9mm, 40 S&W **$469.99**
Price: 45 ACP **$529.99**

AMT On Duty

AMT 45 ACP HARDBALLER

Caliber: 45 ACP.
Barrel: 5".
Weight: 39 oz. **Length:** 8½" overall.
Stocks: Wrap-around rubber.
Sights: Adjustable.
Features: Extended combat safety, serrated matte slide rib, loaded chamber indicator, long grip safety, beveled magazine well, adjustable target trigger. All stainless steel. From AMT.
Price: **$529.99**
Price: Government model (as above except no rib, fixed sights) . . **$475.95**

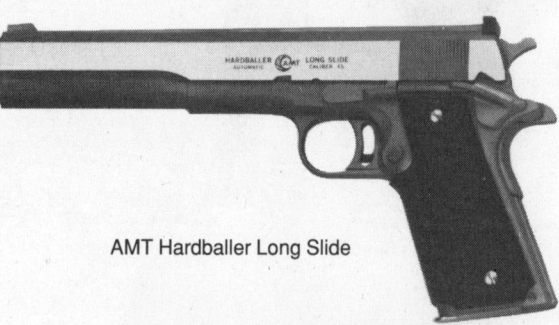

AMT Hardballer Long Slide

AMT 45 ACP HARDBALLER LONG SLIDE

Caliber: 45 ACP.
Barrel: 7". **Length:** 10½" overall.
Stocks: Wrap-around rubber.
Sights: Fully adjustable rear sight.
Features: Slide and barrel are 2" longer than the standard 45, giving less recoil, added velocity, longer sight radius. Has extended combat safety, serrated matte rib, loaded chamber indicator, wide adjustable trigger. From AMT.
Price: **$575.95**

CONSULT **Shooter's Marketplace** *Page 231, This Issue*

ASTRA A-70 AUTO PISTOL

Caliber: 9mm Para., 8-shot; 40 S&W, 7-shot magazine.
Barrel: 3.5".
Weight: 29.3 oz. **Length:** 6.5" overall.
Stocks: Checkered black plastic.
Sights: Blade front, rear adjustable for windage.
Features: All steel frame and slide. Checkered grip straps and trigger guard. Nickel or blue finish. Introduced 1992. Imported from Spain by European American Armory.
Price: Blue, 9mm Para. **$495.00**
Price: Blue, 40 S&W **$495.00**
Price: Nickel, 9mm Para. **$540.00**
Price: Nickel, 40 S&W **$540.00**

Astra A-75

Astra A-75 Decocker Auto Pistol

Same as the A-70 except has decocker system, different trigger, contoured pebble-grain grips. Introduced 1993. Imported from Spain by European American Armory.
Price: Blue, 9mm or 40 S&W **$575.00**
Price: Nickel, 9mm or 40 S&W **$620.00**
Price: Blue, 45 ACP **$595.00**
Price: Nickel, 45 ACP **$640.00**

CAUTION: PRICES CHANGE, CHECK AT GUNSHOP.

ASTRA A-100 AUTO PISTOL

Caliber: 9mm Para., 17-shot; 40 S&W, 13-shot; 45 ACP, 9-shot magazine.
Barrel: 3.9".
Weight: 29 oz. **Length:** 7.1" overall.
Stocks: Checkered black plastic.
Sights: Blade front, interchangeable rear blades for elevation, screw adjustable for windage.
Features: Selective double action. Decocking lever permits lowering hammer onto locked firing pin. Automatic firing pin block. Side button magazine release. Introduced 1993. Imported from Spain by European American Armory.
Price: Blue, 9mm, 40 S&W, 45 ACP **$625.00**
Price: As above, nickel **$660.00**
Price: Blue with night sights **$750.00**
Price: Nickel with night sights **$785.00**

AUTO-ORDNANCE 1911A1 AUTOMATIC PISTOL

Caliber: 9mm Para., 38 Super, 9-shot; 10mm, 45 ACP, 7-shot magazine.
Barrel: 5".
Weight: 39 oz. **Length:** 8½" overall.
Stocks: Checkered plastic with medallion.
Sights: Blade front, rear adjustable for windage.
Features: Same specs as 1911A1 military guns—parts interchangeable. Frame and slide blued; each radius has non-glare finish. Made in U.S. by Auto-Ordnance Corp.
Price: 45 cal. **$388.95**
Price: 9mm, 38 Super **$415.00**
Price: 10mm (has three-dot combat sights, rubber wrap-around grips) **$420.95**
Price: 45 ACP General Model (Commander style) **$427.95**
Price: Duo Tone (nickel frame, blue slide, three-dot sight system, textured black wrap-around grips) **$575.00**

Baby Eagle Auto

BERETTA MODEL 80 SERIES DA PISTOLS

Caliber: 380 ACP, 13-shot magazine (8-shot for M85F); 22 LR, 7-shot (M87), 22 LR, 8-shot (M89).
Barrel: 3.82".
Weight: About 23 oz. (M84/85); 20.8 oz. (M87). **Length:** 6.8" overall.
Stocks: Glossy black plastic (wood optional at extra cost).
Sights: Fixed front, drift-adjustable rear.
Features: Double action, quick takedown, convenient magazine release. Introduced 1977. Imported from Italy by Beretta U.S.A.
Price: Model 84F (380 ACP) **$525.00**
Price: Model 84F wood grips **$555.00**
Price: Model 84F nickel finish **$600.00**
Price: Model 85F nickel finish, 8-shot **$550.00**
Price: Model 85F plastic grips, 8-shot **$485.00**
Price: Model 85F wood grips, 8-shot **$510.00**
Price: Model 87, 22 LR, 7-shot magazine, wood grips **$490.00**
Price: Model 87 Long Barrel, 22 LR, single action **$510.00**
Price: Model 89 Sport Wood, single action, 22 LR **$735.00**

BERETTA MODEL 92FS PISTOL

Caliber: 9mm Para., 15-shot magazine.
Barrel: 4.9".
Weight: 34 oz. **Length:** 8.5" overall.
Stocks: Checkered black plastic; wood optional at extra cost.
Sights: Blade front, rear adjustable for windage.
Features: Double action. Extractor acts as chamber loaded indicator, squared trigger guard, grooved front- and backstraps, inertia firing pin. Matte finish. Introduced 1977. Made in U.S. and imported from Italy by Beretta U.S.A.
Price: With plastic grips **$625.00**
Price: With wood grips **$645.00**

Auto-Ordnance 1911A1

Auto-Ordnance ZG-51 Pit Bull Auto

Same as the 1911A1 except has 3½" barrel, weighs 36 oz. and has an over-all length of 7¼". Available in 45 ACP only; 7-shot magazine. Introduced 1989.
Price: **$420.95**

Auto-Ordnance 40 S&W 1911A1

Similar to the standard 1911A1 except has 4½" barrel giving overall length of 7¾", and weighs 37 oz. Has three-dot combat sight system, black rubber wrap-around grips, 8-shot magazine. Introduced 1991.
Price: **$427.95**

BABY EAGLE AUTO PISTOL

Caliber: 9mm Para., 40 S&W, 41 A.E.
Barrel: 4.37".
Weight: 35 oz. **Length:** 8.14" overall.
Stocks: High-impact black polymer.
Sights: Combat.
Features: Double-action mechanism; polygonal rifling; ambidextrous safety. Introduced 1992. Imported by Magnum Research.
Price: 9mm Para., 40 S&W, 41 A.E. **$569.00**
Price: Conversion kit, 9mm Para. to 41 A.E. **$239.00**

Beretta Model 84F

Beretta Model 86

Similar to the 380-caliber Model 85 except has tip-up barrel for first-round loading. Barrel length is 4.33", overall length of 7.33". Has 8-shot magazine, walnut or plastic grips. Introduced 1989.
Price: **$510.00**

Beretta Model 92FS

Beretta Model 92FC Pistol
Similar to the Beretta Model 92FS except has cut down frame, 4.3" barrel, 7.8" overall length, 13-shot magazine, weighs 31.5 oz. Introduced 1989.
Price: With plastic grips $625.00
Price: With wood grips $645.00
Price: For Trijicon sights, add $65.00

Beretta Models 92FS/96 Centurion Pistols
Same as the Model 92FS and 96 except uses slide and barrel (4.3") of the Compact version. Trijicon or three-dot sight systems. Plastic or wood grips. Available in 9mm or 40 S&W. Introduced 1992.
Price: Model 92FS Centurion, three-dot sights, plastic grips $625.00
Price: Model 92FS Centurion, wood grips $645.00
Price: Model 96 Centurion, three-dot sights, plastic grips $640.00
Price: For Trijicon sights, add $65.00

Beretta Model 92F Stainless Pistol
Same as the Model 92FS except has stainless steel barrel and slide, and frame of aluminum-zirconium alloy. Has three-dot sight system. Introduced 1992.
Price: $755.00
Price: Model 92F-EL Stainless (gold trim, engraved barrel, slide, frame, gold-finished safety-levers, trigger, magazine release, grip screws) . $1,240.00
Price: For Trijicon sights, add $65.00

Beretta Model 92D Pistol
Same as the Model 92FS except double action only and has bobbed hammer, no external safety. Introduced 1992.
Price: With plastic grips, three-dot sights $585.00
Price: As above with Trijicon sights $650.00

BERETTA MODEL 950 BS AUTO PISTOL
Caliber: 25 ACP, 8-shot.
Barrel: 2.5".
Weight: 9.9 oz. **Length:** 4.5" overall.
Stocks: Checkered black plastic or walnut.
Sights: Fixed.
Features: Single action, thumb safety; tip-up barrel for direct loading/unloading, cleaning. From Beretta U.S.A.
Price: Blue, 25 . . . . $180.00
Price: Nickel, 25 . . . . $210.00
Price: Engraved $260.00
Price: Matte blue $150.00

Beretta Model 21 Pistol
Similar to the Model 950 BS. Chambered for 22 LR and 25 ACP. Both double action. 2.5" barrel, 4.9" overall length. 7-round magazine on 22 cal.; 8-round magazine; available in nickel or blue finish. Both have walnut grips. Introduced in 1985.
Price: 22-cal. $235.00
Price: 22-cal., nickel finish $260.00
Price: 25-cal. $235.00
Price: 25-cal., nickel finish $260.00
Price: EL model, 22 or 25 . . . . $285.00
Price: Matte blue, plastic grips, 22 or 25 . . . . $185.00

BERSA MODEL 23 AUTO PISTOL
Caliber: 22 LR, 10-shot magazine.
Barrel: 3.5".
Weight: 24.5 oz. **Length:** 6.6" overall.
Stocks: Walnut with stippled panels.
Sights: Blade front, notch rear adjustable for windage; three-dot system.
Features: Double action; firing pin and magazine safeties. Available in blue or nickel. Introduced 1989. Distributed by Eagle Imports, Inc.
Price: Blue $281.95
Price: Nickel $314.95

BERSA MODEL 83, 85 AUTO PISTOLS
Caliber: 380 ACP, 7-shot (M83), 13-shot magazine (M85).
Barrel: 3.5".
Weight: 25.75 oz. **Length:** 6.6" overall.
Stocks: Walnut with stippled panels.
Sights: Blade front, notch rear adjustable for windage; three-dot system.
Features: Double action; firing pin and magazine safeties. Available in blue or nickel. Introduced 1989. Distributed by Eagle Imports, Inc.
Price: Model 85, blue $331.95
Price: Model 85, nickel $391.95
Price: Model 83 (as above, except 7-shot magazine), blue $281.95
Price: Model 83, nickel $314.95

Beretta Centurion

Beretta Model 96 Auto Pistol
Same as the Model 92F except chambered for 40 S&W. Ambidextrous triple safety mechanism with passive firing pin catch, slide safety/decocking lever, trigger bar disconnect. Has 10-shot magazine. Available with Trijicon or three-dot sights. Introduced 1992.
Price: Model 96F, plastic grips $640.00
Price: Model 96D, double action only, three-dot sights $605.00
Price: For Trijicon sights, add $65.00

Beretta 950BS

> Consult our Directory pages for the location of firms mentioned.

Bersa Model 85

BERSA MODEL 86 AUTO PISTOL
Caliber: 380 ACP, 13-shot magazine.
Barrel: 3.5".
Weight: 22 oz. **Length:** 6.6" overall.
Stocks: Wraparound textured rubber.
Sights: Blade front, rear adjustable for windage; three-dot system.
Features: Double action; firing pin and magazine safeties; combat-style trigger guard. Matte blue or satin nickel. Introduced 1992. Distributed by Eagle Imports, Inc.
Price: Matte blue $366.95
Price: Satin nickel $399.95

CAUTION: PRICES CHANGE, CHECK AT GUNSHOP.

BERSA THUNDER 9 AUTO PISTOL

Caliber: 9mm Para., 15-shot magazine.
Barrel: 4".
Weight: 30 oz. **Length:** 7⅜" overall.
Stocks: Checkered black polymer.
Sights: Blade front, rear adjustable for windage and elevation; three-dot system.
Features: Double action. Ambidextrous safety, decocking levers and slide release; internal automatic firing pin safety; reversible extended magazine release; adjustable trigger stop; alloy frame. Link-free locked breech design. Matte blue finish. Introduced 1993. Imported from Argentina by Eagle Imports, Inc.
Price: Blue only $414.95

Bersa Thunder 9

Browning BDA-380

BROWNING BDM DA AUTO PISTOL

Caliber: 9mm Para., 15-shot magazine.
Barrel: 4.73"
Weight: 31 oz. **Length:** 7.85" overall.
Stocks: Moulded black composition; checkered, with thumbrest on both sides.
Sights: Low profile removable blade front, rear screw adjustable for windage.
Features: Mode selector allows switching from DA pistol to "revolver" mode via a switch on the slide. Decocking lever/safety on the frame. Two redundant, passive, internal safety systems. All steel frame; matte black finish. Introduced 1991. Made in the U.S. From Browning.
Price: $559.95

BROWNING HI-POWER 9mm AUTOMATIC PISTOL

Caliber: 9mm Para., 13-shot magazine.
Barrel: 4²¹⁄₃₂".
Weight: 32 oz. **Length:** 7¾" overall.
Stocks: Walnut, hand checkered, or black Polyamide.
Sights: ⅛" blade front; rear screw-adjustable for windage and elevation. Also available with fixed rear (drift-adjustable for windage).
Features: External hammer with half-cock and thumb safeties. A blow on the hammer cannot discharge a cartridge; cannot be fired with magazine removed. Fixed rear sight model available. Ambidextrous safety available only with matte finish, moulded grips. Imported from Belgium by Browning.
Price: Fixed sight model, walnut grips $524.95
Price: 9mm with rear sight adj. for w. and e., walnut grips $571.95
Price: Mark III, standard matte black finish, fixed sight, moulded grips, ambidextrous safety $493.95
Price: Silver chrome, adjustable sight, Pachmayr grips $581.95

BROWNING BDA-380 DA AUTO PISTOL

Caliber: 380 ACP, 13-shot magazine.
Barrel: 3¹³⁄₁₆".
Weight: 23 oz. **Length:** 6¾" overall.
Stocks: Smooth walnut with inset Browning medallion.
Sights: Blade front, rear drift-adjustable for windage.
Features: Combination safety and de-cocking lever will automatically lower a cocked hammer to half-cock and can be operated by right- or left-hand shooters. Inertia firing pin. Introduced 1978. Imported from Italy by Browning.
Price: Blue $592.95
Price: Nickel $624.95

Browning BDM

Browning Capitan Hi-Power Pistol

Similar to the standard Hi-Power except has adjustable tangent rear sight authentic to the early-production model. Also has Commander-style hammer. Checkered walnut grips, polished blue finish. Reintroduced 1993. Imported from Belgium by Browning.
Price: $619.95

Browning Hi-Power HP-Practical Pistol

Similar to the standard Hi-Power except has silver-chromed frame with blued slide, wrap-around Pachmayr rubber grips, round-style serrated hammer and removable front sight, fixed rear (drift-adjustable for windage). Introduced 1991.
Price: $565.95
Price: With fully adjustable rear sight $612.95

Browning Hi-Power HP

Browning 40 S&W Hi-Power Pistol

Similar to the standard Hi-Power except chambered for 40 S&W, 10-shot magazine, weighs 35 oz., and has 4¾" barrel. Comes with matte blue finish, low profile front sight blade, drift-adjustable rear sight, ambidextrous safety, moulded polyamide grips with thumb rest. Introduced 1993. Imported from Belgium by Browning.
Price: $612.95

Browning Micro Buck Mark

Browning Buck Mark Varmint

BROWNING BUCK MARK 22 PISTOL

Caliber: 22 LR, 10-shot magazine.
Barrel: 5½".
Weight: 32 oz. **Length:** 9½" overall.
Stocks: Black moulded composite with skip-line checkering.
Sights: Ramp front, Browning Pro Target rear adjustable for windage and elevation.
Features: All steel, matte blue finish or nickel, gold-colored trigger. Buck Mark Plus has laminated wood grips. Made in U.S. Introduced 1985. From Browning.
Price: Buck Mark, blue **$234.95**
Price: Buck Mark, nickel finish with contoured rubber stocks **$274.95**
Price: Buck Mark Plus **$284.95**

Browning Micro Buck Mark

Same as the standard Buck Mark and Buck Mark Plus except has 4" barrel. Available in blue or nickel. Has 16-click Pro Target rear sight. Introduced 1992.
Price: Blue **$234.95**
Price: Nickel **$274.95**
Price: Micro Buck Mark Plus **$284.95**

Browning Buck Mark Varmint

Same as the Buck Mark except has 9⅞" heavy barrel with .900" diameter and full-length scope base (no open sights); walnut grips with optional forend, or finger-groove walnut. Overall length is 14", weight is 48 oz. Introduced 1987.
Price: **$354.95**

BRYCO MODEL 38 AUTO PISTOLS

Caliber: 22 LR, 32 ACP, 380 ACP, 6-shot magazine.
Barrel: 2.8".
Weight: 15 oz. **Length:** 5.3" overall.
Stocks: Polished resin-impregnated wood.
Sights: Fixed.
Features: Safety locks sear and slide. Choice of satin nickel, bright chrome or black Teflon finishes. Introduced 1988. From Jennings Firearms.
Price: 22 LR, 32 ACP, about **$109.95**
Price: 380 ACP, about **$129.95**

BRYCO MODEL 48 AUTO PISTOLS

Caliber: 22 LR, 32 ACP, 380 ACP, 6-shot magazine.
Barrel: 4".
Weight: 19 oz. **Length:** 6.7" overall.
Stocks: Polished resin-impregnated wood.
Sights: Fixed.
Features: Safety locks sear and slide. Choice of satin nickel, bright chrome or black Teflon finishes. Announced 1988. From Jennings Firearms.
Price: 22 LR, 32 ACP, about **$139.00**
Price: 380 ACP, about **$139.00**

Bryco Model 48

CALICO MODEL 110 AUTO PISTOL

Caliber: 22 LR, 100-shot magazine.
Barrel: 6".
Weight: 3.7 lbs. (loaded). **Length:** 17.9" overall.
Stocks: Moulded composition.
Sights: Adjustable post front, notch rear.
Features: Aluminum alloy frame; flash suppressor; pistol grip compartment; ambidextrous safety. Uses same helical-feed magazine as M-100 Carbine. Introduced 1986. Made in U.S. From Calico.
Price: **$301.90**

Calico M-110

Calico M-950

CALICO MODEL M-950 AUTO PISTOL

Caliber: 9mm Para., 50- or 100-shot magazine.
Barrel: 7.5".
Weight: 2.25 lbs. (empty). **Length:** 14" overall (50-shot magazine).
Stocks: Glass-filled polymer.
Sights: Post front adjustable for windage and elevation, fixed notch rear.
Features: Helical feed 50- or 100-shot magazine. Ambidextrous safety, static cocking handle. Retarded blowback action. Glass-filled polymer grip. Introduced 1989. From Calico.
Price: **$572.90**

CENTURY MODEL P9R PISTOL

Caliber: 9mm Para., 15-shot magazine.
Barrel: 4.6".
Weight: 35 oz. **Length:** 8" overall.
Stocks: Checkered walnut.
Sights: Blade front, rear drift adjustable for windage.
Features: Double action with hammer-drop safety. Polished blue finish. Comes with spare magazine. Imported from Hungary by Century International Arms.
Price: About **$263.00**
Price: Chrome finish, about **$375.00**

CAUTION: PRICES CHANGE, CHECK AT GUNSHOP.

CLARIDGE HI-TEC MODEL S, L, T PISTOLS

Caliber: 9mm Para., 18-shot magazine.
Barrel: 5" (S model); 7.5" (L model); 9.5" (T model).
Weight: 3 lbs., 2 oz. (L model). **Length:** 15.1" overall (L model).
Stocks: Moulded composition.
Sights: Adjustable post front in ring, open rear adjustable for windage.
Features: Aluminum or stainless frame. Telescoping bolt; floating firing pin. Safety locks the firing pin. Also available in 40 S&W and 45 ACP. Made in U.S. by Claridge Hi-Tec, Inc.
Price: Model S (5") **$419.50**
Price: Model L (7.5") **$466.50**
Price: Model T (target, 9.5") **$466.50**
Price: Model ZL-9 (7.5" with laser sight) **$776.50**
Price: Model ZT-9 (9.5" with laser sight) **$776.50**

Claridge Hi-Tec ZL-9

COLT ALL AMERICAN MODEL 2000 DA AUTO

Caliber: 9mm Para., 15-shot magazine.
Barrel: 4.5".
Weight: 29 oz. (polymer frame); 33 oz. (aluminum frame). **Length:** 7.5" overall.
Stocks: Checkered polymer.
Sights: Ramped blade front, rear drift-adjustable for windage. Three dot system.
Features: Double-action only. Moulded polymer or aluminum frame, blued steel slide. Internal striker block safety. Introduced 1991. Made in U.S. by Colt's Mfg. Co., Inc.
Price: Polymer frame **$575.00**
Price: Aluminum frame . . . . **NA**
Price: 3¾" barrel and bushing kit . . . . **NA**

COLT COMBAT COMMANDER AUTO PISTOL

Caliber: 38 Super, 9-shot; 45 ACP, 8-shot.
Barrel: 4¼".
Weight: 36 oz. **Length:** 7¾" overall.
Stocks: Rubber combat.
Sights: Fixed, glare-proofed blade front, square notch rear; three-dot system.
Features: Long trigger; arched housing; grip and thumb safeties.
Price: 45, blue **$694.95**
Price: 45, stainless **$749.95**
Price: 38 Super, stainless **$749.95**

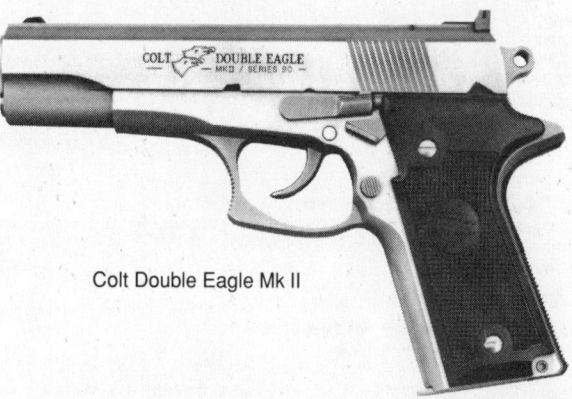

Colt All American 2000

Colt Lightweight Commander MK IV/Series 80

Same as Commander except high strength aluminum alloy frame, rubber combat grips, weight 27½ oz. 45 ACP only.
Price: Blue **$694.95**

COLT DOUBLE EAGLE MKII/SERIES 90 DA PISTOL

Caliber: 45 ACP, 8-shot magazine.
Barrel: 4½", 5".
Weight: 39 ozs. **Length:** 8½" overall.
Stocks: Black checkered Xenoy thermoplastic.
Sights: Blade front, rear adjustable for windage. High profile three-dot system. Colt Accro adjustable sight optional.
Features: Made of stainless steel with matte finish. Checkered and curved extended trigger guard, wide steel trigger; decocking lever on left side; traditional magazine release; grooved frontstrap; bevelled magazine well; extended grip guard; rounded, serrated combat-style hammer. Announced 1989.
Price: **$695.95**
Price: Combat Comm., 45, 4½" bbl. **$695.95**

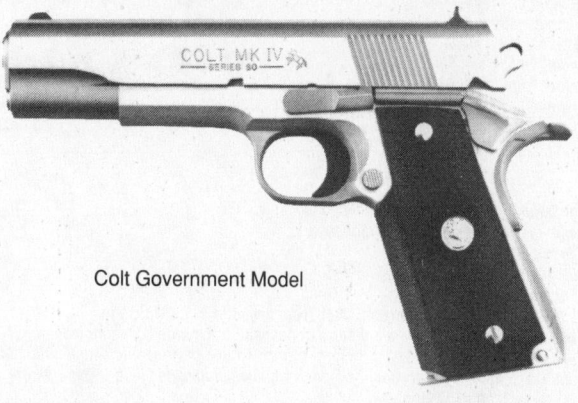

Colt Double Eagle Mk II

Colt Double Eagle Officer's ACP

Similar to the regular Double Eagle except 45 ACP only, 3½" barrel, 34 oz., 7¼" overall length. Has 5¼" sight radius. Also offered in Lightweight version weighing 25 oz. Introduced 1991.
Price: Standard or Lightweight **$695.95**

COLT GOVERNMENT MODEL MK IV/SERIES 80

Caliber: 38 Super, 9-shot; 45 ACP, 8-shot magazine.
Barrel: 5".
Weight: 38 oz. **Length:** 8½" overall.
Stocks: Rubber combat.
Sights: Ramp front, fixed square notch rear; three-dot system.
Features: Grip and thumb safeties and internal firing pin safety, long trigger.
Price: 45 ACP, blue **$693.95**
Price: 45 ACP, stainless **$738.95**
Price: 45 ACP, bright stainless **$813.95**
Price: 38 Super, blue **$704.95**
Price: 38 Super, stainless **$727.95**
Price: 38 Super, bright stainless **$819.95**

Colt Government Model

Colt 10mm Delta Elite

Similar to the Government Model except chambered for 10mm auto cartridge. Has three-dot high profile front and rear combat sights, rubber combat stocks with Delta medallion, internal firing pin safety, and new recoil spring/buffer system. Introduced 1987.
Price: Blue $765.95

Colt Combat Elite MK IV/Series 80

Similar to the Government Model except has stainless frame with ordnance steel slide and internal parts. High profile front, rear sights with three-dot system, extended grip safety, beveled magazine well, rubber combat stocks. Introduced 1986.
Price: 45 ACP, STS/B $841.95
Price: 38 Super, STS/B $852.95

COLT GOVERNMENT MODEL 380

Caliber: 380 ACP, 7-shot magazine.
Barrel: 3¼".
Weight: 21¾ oz. **Length:** 6" overall.
Stocks: Checkered composition.
Sights: Ramp front, square notch rear, fixed.
Features: Scaled-down version of the 1911A1 Colt G.M. Has thumb and internal firing pin safeties. Introduced 1983.
Price: Blue $432.95
Price: Nickel $483.95
Price: Stainless $463.95
Price: Pocketlite 380, blue $432.95

Colt Mustang Plus II

Similar to the 380 Government Model except has the shorter barrel and slide of the Mustang. Introduced 1988.
Price: Blue $432.95
Price: Stainless $463.95

COLT MODEL 1991 A1 AUTO PISTOL

Caliber: 45 ACP, 7-shot magazine.
Barrel: 5".
Weight: 38 oz. **Length:** 8.5" overall.
Stocks: Checkered black composition.
Sights: Ramped blade front, fixed square notch rear, high profile.
Features: Parkerized finish. Continuation of serial number range used on original G.I. 1911-A1 guns. Comes with one magazine and moulded carrying case. Introduced 1991.
Price: $499.95

Colt Model 1991 A1 Commander Auto Pistol

Similar to the Model 1991 A1 except has 4¼" barrel. Parkerized finish. 7-shot magazine. Comes in moulded case. Introduced 1993.
Price: $499.95

COLT OFFICER'S ACP MK IV/SERIES 80

Caliber: 45 ACP, 6-shot magazine.
Barrel: 3½".
Weight: 34 oz. (steel frame); 24 oz. (alloy frame). **Length:** 7¼" overall.
Stocks: Rubber combat.
Sights: Ramp blade front with white dot, square notch rear with two white dots.
Features: Trigger safety lock (thumb safety), grip safety, firing pin safety; long trigger; flat mainspring housing. Also available with lightweight alloy frame and in stainless steel. Introduced 1985.
Price: Blue $694.95
Price: L.W., blue finish $694.95
Price: Stainless $739.95
Price: Bright stainless $814.95

COONAN 357 MAGNUM PISTOL

Caliber: 357 Mag., 7-shot magazine.
Barrel: 5".
Weight: 42 oz. **Length:** 8.3" overall.
Stocks: Smooth walnut.
Sights: Interchangeable ramp front, rear adjustable for windage.
Features: Stainless and alloy steel construction. Unique barrel hood improves accuracy and reliability. Linkless barrel. Many parts interchange with Colt autos. Has grip, hammer, half-cock safeties, extended slide latch. Made in U.S. by Coonan Arms, Inc.
Price: 5" barrel $720.00
Price: 6" barrel $755.00
Price: With 6" compensated barrel $999.00

Colt Government Pocketlite

Colt Mustang 380, Mustang Pocketlite

Similar to the standard 380 Government Model. Mustang has steel frame (18.5 oz.), Pocketlite has aluminum alloy (12.5 oz.). Both are ½" shorter than 380 G.M., have 2¾" barrel. Introduced 1987.
Price: Mustang 380, blue $432.95
Price: As above, nickel $483.95
Price: As above, stainless $463.95
Price: Mustang Pocketlite, blue $432.95
Price: Mustang Pocketlite STS/N $463.95

Colt 1991A1 Compact

Colt Model 1991 A1 Compact Auto Pistol

Similar to the Model 1991 A1 except has 3½" barrel. Overall length is 7", and gun is ⅜" shorter in height. Comes with one 6-shot magazine, moulded case. Introduced 1993.
Price: $499.95

Coonan Compact 357

Coonan Compact 357 Magnum Cadet Pistol

Similar to the 357 Magnum full-size gun except has 3.9" barrel, shorter frame, 6-shot magazine. Weight is 39 oz., overall length 7.8". Linkless bull barrel, full-length recoil spring guide rod, extended slide latch. Introduced 1993. Made in U.S. by Coonan Arms, Inc.
Price: $841.00

CZ 75 AUTO PISTOL

Caliber: 9mm Para., 15-shot magazine.
Barrel: 4.7".
Weight: 34.3 oz. **Length:** 8.1" overall.
Stocks: High impact checkered plastic.
Sights: Square post front, rear adjustable for windage; three-dot system.
Features: Single action/double action design; choice of black polymer, matte or high-polish blue finishes. All-steel frame. Imported from the Czech Republic by Action Arms, Ltd.
Price: Black polymer finish **$485.00**
Price: Matte blue **$505.00**
Price: High-polish blue **$519.00**

CZ 75 Compact

CZ 75 Compact Auto Pistol

Similar to the CZ 75 except has 13-shot magazine, 3.9" barrel and weighs 32 oz. Has removable front sight, non-glare ribbed slide top. Trigger guard is squared and serrated; combat hammer. Introduced 1993. Imported from the Czech Republic by Action Arms, Ltd.
Price: Black polymer finish **$519.00**
Price: Matte blue **$545.00**
Price: High-polish blue **$565.00**

CZ 85 Combat Auto Pistol

Same as the CZ 85 except has walnut grips, round combat hammer, fully adjustable rear sight, extended magazine release. Trigger parts coated with friction-free beryllium copper. Introduced 1992. Imported from the Czech Republic by Action Arms, Ltd.
Price: Black polymer finish **$625.00**

CZ 85 Auto Pistol

Same gun as the CZ 75 except has ambidextrous slide release and safety-levers; non-glare, ribbed slide top; squared, serrated trigger guard; trigger stop to prevent overtravel. Introduced 1986. Imported from the Czech Republic by Action Arms, Ltd.
Price: Black polymer finish **$515.00**
Price: Matte blue **$529.00**
Price: High-polish blue **$559.00**

CZ 83 DOUBLE-ACTION PISTOL

Caliber: 380 ACP, 12-shot magazine.
Barrel: 3.8".
Weight: 26.2 oz. **Length:** 6.8" overall.
Stocks: High impact checkered plastic.
Sights: Removable square post front, rear adjustable for windage; three-dot system.
Features: Single action/double action; ambidextrous magazine release and safety. Blue finish; non-glare ribbed slide top. Imported from the Czech Republic by Action Arms Ltd.
Price: **$389.00**

CZ 83 DA

DAEWOO DP51 AUTO PISTOL

Caliber: 9mm Para., 13-shot magazine.
Barrel: 4.1".
Weight: 28.2 oz. **Length:** 7.48" overall.
Stocks: Checkered composition.
Sights: Blade front, square notch rear drift adjustable for windage.
Features: Patented tri-action mechanism. Ambidextrous manual safety and magazine catch, half-cock and firing pin block. Alloy frame, squared trigger guard. Matte black finish. Introduced 1991. Imported from Korea by Firstshot.
Price: **$369.50**

Daewoo DP51

Davis P-32

DAVIS P-32 AUTO PISTOL

Caliber: 32 ACP, 6-shot magazine.
Barrel: 2.8".
Weight: 22 oz. **Length:** 5.4" overall.
Stocks: Laminated wood.
Sights: Fixed.
Features: Choice of black Teflon or chrome finish. Announced 1986. Made in U.S. by Davis Industries.
Price: **$87.50**

DAVIS P-380 AUTO PISTOL

Caliber: 380 ACP, 5-shot magazine.
Barrel: 2.8".
Weight: 22 oz. **Length:** 5.4" overall.
Stocks: Black composition.
Sights: Fixed.
Features: Choice of chrome or black Teflon finish. Introduced 1991. Made in U.S. by Davis Industries.
Price: **$98.00**

Desert Eagle Magnum

Desert Industries Double Deuce

E.A.A. Witness

E.A.A. WITNESS DA AUTO PISTOL

Caliber: 9mm Para., 16-shot magazine; 10mm Auto, 10-shot magazine; 38 Super, 40 S&W, 12-shot magazine; 45 ACP, 10-shot magazine.
Barrel: 4.72".
Weight: 35.33 oz. **Length:** 8.10" overall.
Stocks: Checkered rubber.
Sights: Undercut blade front, open rear adjustable for windage.
Features: Double-action trigger system; squared-off trigger guard; frame-mounted safety. Introduced 1991. Imported from Italy by European American Armory.
Price: 9mm, blue $550.00
Price: 9mm, satin chrome $595.00

E.A.A. EUROPEAN MODEL AUTO PISTOLS

Caliber: 32 ACP or 380 ACP, 7-shot magazine.
Barrel: 3.88".
Weight: 26 oz. **Length:** 7⅜" overall.
Stocks: European hardwood.
Sights: Fixed blade front, rear drift-adjustable for windage.
Features: Chrome or blue finish; magazine, thumb and firing pin safeties; external hammer; safety-lever takedown. Imported from Italy by European American Armory.
Price: Blue $225.00
Price: Blue/chrome $249.00
Price: Chrome $249.00
Price: Blue/gold $260.00
Price: Ladies Model $299.00

DESERT EAGLE MAGNUM PISTOL

Caliber: 357 Mag., 9-shot; 41 Mag., 44 Mag., 8-shot; 50 Magnum, 7-shot.
Barrel: 6", 10", 14" interchangeable.
Weight: 357 Mag.—62 oz.; 41 Mag., 44 Mag.—69 oz.; 50 Mag.—72 oz.
Length: 10¼" overall (6" bbl.).
Stocks: Wraparound plastic.
Sights: Blade on ramp front, combat-style rear. Adjustable available.
Features: Rotating three-lug bolt; ambidextrous safety; combat-style trigger guard; adjustable trigger optional. Military epoxy finish. Satin, bright nickel, hard chrome, polished and blued finishes available. Imported from Israel by Magnum Research, Inc.
Price: 357, 6" bbl., standard pistol $789.00
Price: As above, stainless steel frame $839.00
Price: 41 Mag., 6", standard pistol $799.00
Price: 41 Mag., stainless steel frame $849.00
Price: 44 Mag., 6", standard pistol $899.00
Price: As above, stainless steel frame $949.00
Price: 50 Magnum, 6" bbl., standard pistol $1,249.00

DESERT INDUSTRIES WAR EAGLE PISTOL

Caliber: 9mm Para., 14-shot magazine; 10mm, 13-shot; 40 S&W, 14-shot; 45 ACP, 12-shot.
Barrel: 4".
Weight: 35.5 oz. **Length:** 7.5" overall.
Stocks: Rosewood.
Sights: Fixed.
Features: Double action; matte-finished stainless steel; slide mounted ambidextrous safety. Announced 1986. From Desert Industries, Inc.
Price: $795.00

DESERT INDUSTRIES DOUBLE DEUCE, TWO BIT SPECIAL PISTOLS

Caliber: 22 LR, 6-shot; 25 ACP, 5-shot.
Barrel: 2½".
Weight: 15 oz. **Length:** 5½" overall.
Stocks: Rosewood.
Sights: Special order.
Features: Double action; stainless steel construction with matte finish; ambidextrous slide-mounted safety. From Desert Industries, Inc.
Price: 22 . . . . $399.95
Price: 25 (Two-Bit Special) $399.95

Price: 9mm, blue slide, chrome frame $595.00
Price: 9mm Compact, blue, 13-shot $550.00
Price: As above, blue slide, chrome frame, or all-chrome $595.00
Price: 40 S&W or 41 A.E., blue $595.00
Price: As above, blue slide, chrome frame, or all-chrome $650.00
Price: 40 S&W or 41 A.E. Compact, 8-shot, blue $595.00
Price: As above, blue slide, chrome frame, or all-chrome $650.00
Price: 45 ACP, blue $695.00
Price: As above, blue slide, chrome frame, or all-chrome $750.00
Price: 45 ACP Compact, 8-shot, blue $695.00
Price: As above, blue slide, chrome frame or all-chrome $750.00
Price: 9mm/40 S&W Combo, blue, compact or full size $825.00
Price: As above, blue/chrome, compact or full size $875.00
Price: 9mm/40 S&W/41 A.E. Tri Caliber, blue, compact or full size . . $995.00
Price: As above, blue/chrome $1,050.00
Price: 9mm or 40 S&W Carry Comp, blue $775.00
Price: As above, blue/chrome $825.00
Price: As above, 45 ACP $1,010.00

> Consult our Directory pages for
> the location of firms mentioned.

E.A.A. European 380/DA Pistol

Similar to the standard European except in 380 ACP only, with double-action trigger mechanism. Available in blue, chrome or blue/chrome finish. Introduced 1992. From European American Armory.
Price: Blue $275.00
Price: Chrome $299.00
Price: Blue/chrome $299.00
Price: Blue/gold $310.00
Price: Ladies Model $365.00

CAUTION: PRICES CHANGE, CHECK AT GUNSHOP.

ERMA KGP68 AUTO PISTOL
Caliber: 32 ACP, 6-shot, 380 ACP, 5-shot.
Barrel: 4".
Weight: 22½ oz. **Length:** 7⅜" overall.
Stocks: Checkered plastic.
Sights: Fixed.
Features: Toggle action similar to original "Luger" pistol. Action stays open after last shot. Has magazine and sear disconnect safety systems. Imported from Germany by Mandall Shooting Supplies.
Price: $499.95

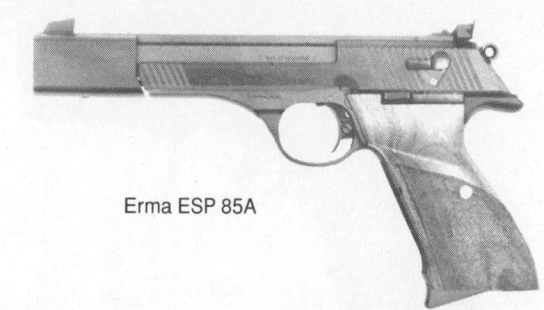

Erma ESP 85A

ERMA SPORTING PISTOL MODEL ESP 85A
Caliber: 22 LR, 8-shot; 32 S&W Long, 5-shot.
Barrel: 6".
Weight: 39.9 oz. **Length:** 10" overall.
Stocks: Checkered walnut with thumbrest. Adjustable target stocks optional.
Sights: Interchangeable blade front, micro. rear adjustable for windage and elevation.
Features: Interchangeable caliber conversion kit available; adjustable trigger, trigger stop. Imported from Germany by Precision Sales Int'l. Introduced 1988.
Price: 22 LR $1,228.00
Price: 32 S&W Long $1,284.00
Price: 22 LR, chrome $1,449.00
Price: 22 LR conversion unit $689.00
Price: 32 S&W conversion unit $746.00

FALCON AUTO PISTOL
Caliber: 10mm, 40 S&W, 10-shot magazine, 45 ACP, 8-shot magazine.
Barrel: 5".
Weight: 37.5 oz. **Length:** 8.5" overall.
Stocks: Black Du Pont Zytel with stipple finish.
Sights: Post front, rear adjustable for windage and elevation; Tri-Square system.
Features: Double-action with passive firing pin lock, decocking lever, ambidextrous thumb safety levers; reversible magazine release; beveled magazine well; stainless steel magazine. Black slide, stainless frame. Announced 1990. Made in U.S. by Falcon Industries.
Price: 10mm, 40 S&W, 45 ACP $795.00

FEG B9R

FEG B9R AUTO PISTOL
Caliber: 380 ACP, 15-shot magazine.
Barrel: 4".
Weight: 25 oz. **Length:** 7" overall.
Stocks: Hand-checkered walnut.
Sights: Blade front, drift-adjustable rear.
Features: Hammer-drop safety; grooved backstrap; squared trigger guard. Comes with spare magazine. Introduced 1993. Imported from Hungary by Century International Arms.
Price: About $312.00

FEG FP9 AUTO PISTOL
Caliber: 9mm Para., 14-shot magazine.
Barrel: 5".
Weight: 35 oz. **Length:** 7.8" overall.
Stocks: Checkered walnut.
Sights: Blade front, windage-adjustable rear.
Features: Full-length ventilated rib. Polished blue finish. Comes with extra magazine. Introduced 1993. Imported from Hungary by Century International Arms.
Price: About $269.00

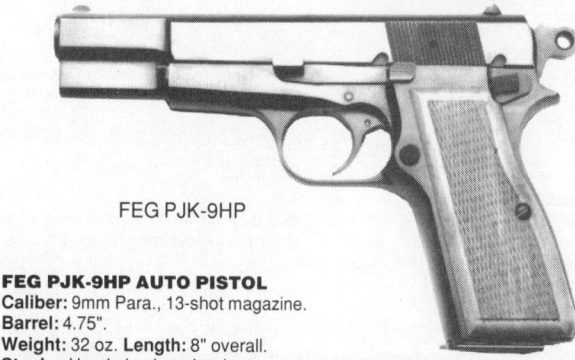

FEG PJK-9HP

FEG PJK-9HP AUTO PISTOL
Caliber: 9mm Para., 13-shot magazine.
Barrel: 4.75".
Weight: 32 oz. **Length:** 8" overall.
Stocks: Hand-checkered walnut.
Sights: Blade front, rear adjustable for windage.
Features: Single action; polished blue or hard chrome finish; rounded combat-style serrated hammer. Comes with two magazines and cleaning rod. Imported from Hungary by K.B.I., Inc.
Price: Blue $329.00
Price: Hard chrome $435.00

FEG PMK-380 AUTO PISTOL
Caliber: 380 ACP, 7-shot magazine.
Barrel: 4".
Weight: 21 oz. **Length:** 7" overall.
Stocks: Checkered black nylon with thumbrest.
Sights: Blade front, rear adjustable for windage.
Features: Double action; anodized aluminum frame, polished blue slide. Comes with two magazines, cleaning rod. Introduced 1992. Imported from Hungary by K.B.I., Inc.
Price: $249.00

FEG PMK-380

FEG SMC-380 AUTO PISTOL
Caliber: 380 ACP, 6-shot magazine.
Barrel: 3.5".
Weight: 18.5 oz. **Length:** 6.1" overall.
Stocks: Checkered composition with thumbrest.
Sights: Blade front, rear adjustable for windage.
Features: Patterned after the PPK pistol. Alloy frame, steel slide; double action. Blue finish. Comes with two magazines, cleaning rod. Imported from Hungary by K.B.I.
Price: $299.00

Glock 19

Glock 21

Glock 21 Auto Pistol
Similar to the Glock 17 except chambered for 45 ACP, 13-shot magazine. Overall length is 7.59", weight is 25.2 oz. (without magazine). Fixed or adjustable rear sight. Introduced 1991.
Price: **$638.49**

Glock 23 Auto Pistol
Similar to the Glock 19 except chambered for 40 S&W, 13-shot magazine. Overall length is 6.85", weight is 20.6 oz. (without magazine). Fixed or adjustable rear sight. Introduced 1990.
Price: **$579.95**

Grendel P-12

FEG P9R AUTO PISTOL
Caliber: 9mm Para., 15-shot magazine.
Barrel: 4.6".
Weight: 35 oz. **Length:** 7.9" overall.
Stocks: Checkered walnut.
Sights: Blade front, rear adjustable for windage.
Features: Double-action mechanism; slide-mounted safety. All-Steel construction with polished blue finish. Comes with extra magazine. Introduced 1993. Imported from Hungary by Century International Arms.
Price: About **$262.00**

GLOCK 17 AUTO PISTOL
Caliber: 9mm Para., 17-shot magazine.
Barrel: 4.49".
Weight: 21.9 oz. (without magazine). **Length:** 7.28" overall.
Stocks: Black polymer.
Sights: Dot on front blade, white outline rear adjustable for windage.
Features: Polymer frame, steel slide; double-action trigger with "Safe Action" system; mechanical firing pin safety, drop safety; simple takedown without tools; locked breech, recoil operated action. Adopted by Austrian armed forces 1983. NATO approved 1984. Imported from Austria by Glock, Inc.
Price: With extra magazine, magazine loader, cleaning kit **$579.95**
Price: Model 17L (6" barrel) **$768.25**

Glock 19 Auto Pistol
Similar to the Glock 17 except has a 4" barrel, giving an overall length of 6.85" and weight of 20.99 oz. Magazine capacity is 15 rounds. Fixed or adjustable rear sight. Introduced 1988.
Price: **$579.95**

Glock 20 10mm Auto Pistol
Similar to the Glock Model 17 except chambered for 10mm Automatic cartridge. Barrel length is 4.60", overall length is 7.59", and weight is 26.3 oz. (without magazine). Magazine capacity is 15 rounds. Fixed or adjustable rear sight. Comes with an extra magazine, magazine loader, cleaning rod and brush. Introduced 1990. Imported from Austria by Glock, Inc.
Price: **$638.49**

Glock 22 Auto Pistol
Similar to the Glock 17 except chambered for 40 S&W, 15-shot magazine. Overall length is 7.28", weight is 22.3 oz. (without magazine). Fixed or adjustable rear sight. Introduced 1990.
Price: **$579.95**

GRENDEL P-12 AUTO PISTOL
Caliber: 380 ACP, 11-shot magazine.
Barrel: 3".
Weight: 13 oz. **Length:** 5.3" overall.
Stocks: Checkered DuPont ST-800 polymer.
Sights: Fixed.
Features: Double action only with inertia safety hammer system. All steel frame; grip forms magazine well and trigger guard. Introduced 1992. Made in U.S. by Grendel, Inc.
Price: Blue **$175.00**
Price: Electroless nickel **$195.00**

GRENDEL P-30 AUTO PISTOL
Caliber: 22 WMR, 30-shot magazine.
Barrel: 5", 8".
Weight: 21 oz. (5" barrel). **Length:** 8.5" overall (5" barrel).
Stocks: Checkered Zytel.
Sights: Blade front, fixed rear.
Features: Blowback action with fluted chamber; ambidextrous safety, reversible magazine catch. Scope mount available. Introduced 1990.
Price: With 5" barrel **$225.00**
Price: With removable muzzlebrake (Model P-30M) **$235.00**
Price: With 8" barrel (Model P-30L) **$280.00**

GRENDEL P-31 AUTO PISTOL
Caliber: 22 WMR, 30-shot magazine.
Barrel: 11".
Weight: 48 oz. **Length:** 17.5" overall.
Stocks: Checkered black Zytel grip and forend.
Sights: Blade front adjustable for windage and elevation, fixed rear.
Features: Blowback action with fluted chamber. Ambidextrous safety. Matte black finish. Muzzlebrake. Scope mount optional. Introduced 1991. Made in the U.S. by Grendel, Inc.
Price: **$345.00**

HAMMERLI MODEL 212 AUTO PISTOL
Caliber: 22 LR, 8-shot magazine.
Barrel: 4.9".
Weight: 31 oz.
Stocks: Checkered walnut.
Sights: Blade front, rear adjustable for windage only.
Features: Polished blue finish. Imported from Switzerland by Mandall Shooting Supplies and Hammerli Pistols USA.
Price: About **$1,395.00**

HASKELL JS-45 CALIBER PISTOL
Caliber: 45 ACP, 7-shot magazine.
Barrel: 4.5".
Weight: 44 oz. **Length:** 7.95" overall.
Stocks: Checkered acetal resin.
Sights: Fixed; low profile.
Features: Internal drop-safe mechanism; all aluminum frame. Introduced 1991. From MKS Supply, Inc.
Price: Matte black **$149.95**
Price: Brushed nickel **$159.95**

Hammerli Model 212

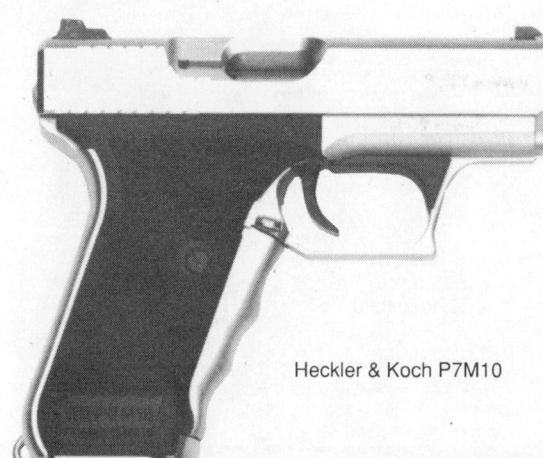

Heckler & Koch P7M10

Heckler & Koch SP89

Heckler & Koch USP

HECKLER & KOCH P7M8 AUTO PISTOL
Caliber: 9mm Para., 8-shot magazine.
Barrel: 4.13".
Weight: 29 oz. **Length:** 6.73" overall.
Stocks: Stippled black plastic.
Sights: Blade front, adjustable rear; three dot system.
Features: Unique "squeeze cocker" in frontstrap cocks the action. Gas-retarded action. Squared combat-type trigger guard. Blue finish. Compact size. Imported from Germany by Heckler & Koch, Inc.
Price: P7M8, blued **$1,059.00**
Price: P7M8, nickel **$1,059.00**
Price: P7M13 (13-shot capacity, ambidextrous magazine release, forged steel frame), blued **$1,284.00**
Price: P7M13, nickel **$1,284.00**

Heckler & Koch P7M10 Auto Pistol
Similar to the P7M8 except chambered for 40 S&W with 10-shot magazine. Weighs 43 oz., overall length is 6.9". Introduced 1992. Imported from Germany by Heckler & Koch, Inc.
Price: Blue **$1,314.00**
Price: Nickel **$1,314.00**

Heckler & Koch P7K3 Auto Pistol
Similar to the P7M8 and P7M13 except chambered for 22 LR or 380 ACP, 8-shot magazine. Uses an oil-filled buffer to decrease recoil. Introduced 1988.
Price: **$1,059.00**
Price: 22 LR conversion unit **$524.00**
Price: 32 ACP conversion unit **$228.00**

HECKLER & KOCH SP89 AUTO PISTOL
Caliber: 9mm Para., 15- or 30-shot magazine.
Barrel: 4.5".
Weight: 4.4 lbs. **Length:** 12.8" overall.
Stocks: Black high-impact plastic.
Sights: Post front, diopter rear adjustable for windage and elevation.
Features: Semi-auto pistol inspired by the HK94. Has special flash-hider forend. Introduced 1989. Imported from Germany by Heckler & Koch, Inc.
Price: **$1,324.00**

HECKLER & KOCH USP AUTO PISTOL
Caliber: 9mm Para., 16-shot magazine, 40 S&W, 13-shot magazine.
Barrel: 4.13".
Weight: 28 oz. (USP40). **Length:** 6.9" overall.
Stocks: Non-slip stippled black polymer.
Sights: Blade front, rear adjustable for windage.
Features: New HK design with polymer frame, modified Browning action with recoil reduction system, single control lever. Special "hostile environment" finish on all metal parts. Available in SA/DA, DAO, left- and right-hand versions. Introduced 1993. Imported from Germany by Heckler & Koch, Inc.
Price: Right-hand **$624.00**
Price: Left-hand **$644.00**

HELWAN "BRIGADIER" AUTO PISTOL
Caliber: 9mm Para., 8-shot magazine.
Barrel: 4.5".
Weight: 32 oz. **Length:** 8" overall.
Stocks: Grooved plastic.
Sights: Blade front, rear adjustable for windage.
Features: Polished blue finish. Single-action design. Cross-bolt safety. Imported by Interarms.
Price: **$262.00**

HERITAGE MODEL HA25 AUTO PISTOL
Caliber: 25 ACP, 6-shot magazine.
Barrel: 2½".
Weight: 12 oz. **Length:** 4⅝" overall.
Stocks: Smooth walnut.
Sights: Fixed.
Features: Exposed hammer, manual safety; open-top slide. Polished blue or chrome finish. Introduced 1993. Made in U.S. by Heritage Mfg., Inc.
Price: . . . . $69.95 to $89.95

Hi-Point C-9MM

HI-POINT FIREARMS MODEL C-9MM PISTOL
Caliber: 9mm Para., 8-shot magazine.
Barrel: 3.5".
Weight: 35 oz. **Length:** 6.7" overall.
Stocks: Textured acetal plastic.
Sights: Combat-style fixed three-dot system; low profile.
Features: Single-action design; frame-mounted magazine release. Scratch-resistant matte finish. Introduced 1993. From MKS Supply, Inc.
Price: $129.95

HUNGARIAN T-58 AUTO PISTOL
Caliber: 7.62mm and 9mm Para., 8-shot magazine.
Barrel: 4.5".
Weight: 31 oz. **Length:** 7.68" overall.
Stocks: Grooved composition.
Sights: Blade front, rear adjustable for windage.
Features: Comes with both barrels and magazines. Thumb safety locks hammer. Blue finish. Imported by Century International Arms.
Price: About $187.00

Hungarian T-58

IBERIA FIREARMS JS-40 S&W AUTO
Caliber: 40 S&W, 8-shot magazine.
Barrel: 4.5".
Weight: 44 oz. **Length:** 7.95" overall.
Stocks: Checkered acetal resin.
Sights: Fixed; low profile.
Features: Internal drop-safe mechansim; all aluminum frame. Introduced 1991. From MKS Supply, Inc.
Price: Matte black $149.95
Price: Brushed nickel $159.95

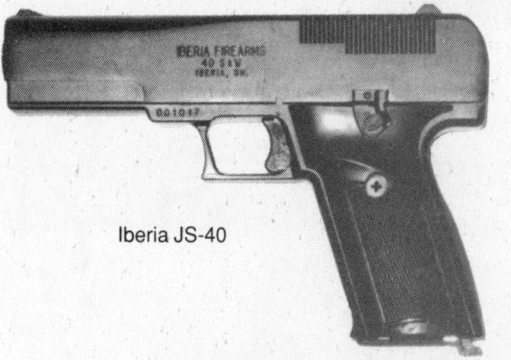

Iberia JS-40

INTRATEC CATEGORY 9 AUTO PISTOL
Caliber: 9mm Para., 8-shot magazine.
Barrel: 3".
Weight: 21 oz. **Length:** 5.5" overall.
Stocks: Textured black polymer.
Sights: Fixed channel.
Features: Black polymer frame. Announced 1993. Made in U.S. by Intratec.
Price: About $200.00

INTRATEC PROTEC-22, 25 AUTO PISTOLS
Caliber: 22 LR, 10-shot; 25 ACP, 8-shot magazine.
Barrel: 2½".
Weight: 14 oz. **Length:** 5" overall.
Stocks: Wraparound composition in gray, black or driftwood color.
Sights: Fixed.
Features: Double-action only trigger mechanism. Choice of black, satin or TEC-KOTE finish. Announced 1991. Made in U.S. by Intratec.
Price: 22 or 25, black finish $99.95
Price: 22 or 25, satin or TEC-KOTE finish $104.95

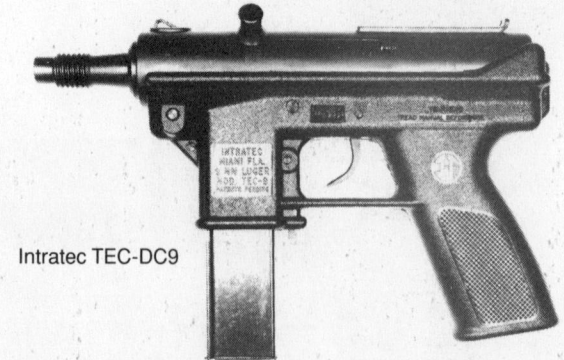

Intratec TEC-DC9

INTRATEC TEC-DC9 AUTO PISTOL
Caliber: 9mm Para., 32-shot magazine.
Barrel: 5".
Weight: 50 oz. **Length:** 12½" overall.
Stock: Moulded composition.
Sights: Fixed.
Features: Semi-auto, fires from closed bolt; firing pin block safety; matte blue finish. Made in U.S. by Intratec.
Price: $260.00
Price: TEC-DC9S (as above, except stainless) $353.00
Price: TEC-DC9K (finished with TEC-KOTE) $290.00

Intratec TEC-DC9M Auto Pistol
Similar to the TEC-DC9 except smaller. Has 3" barrel, weighs 44 oz.; 20-shot magazine. Made in U.S. by Intratec.
Price: $239.00
Price: TEC-DC9MS (as above, stainless) $330.00
Price: TEC-DC9MK (finished with TEC-KOTE) $270.00

CAUTION: PRICES CHANGE, CHECK AT GUNSHOP.

Jennings J-25

JENNINGS J-22, J-25 AUTO PISTOLS
Caliber: 22 LR, 25 ACP, 6-shot magazine.
Barrel: 2½".
Weight: 13 oz. (J-22). **Length:** 4¹⁵⁄₁₆" overall (J-22).
Stocks: Walnut on chrome or nickel models; grooved black Cycolac or resin-impregnated wood on Teflon model.
Sights: Fixed.
Features: Choice of bright chrome, satin nickel or black Teflon finish. Introduced 1981. From Jennings Firearms.
Price: J-22, about **$75.00**
Price: J-25, about **$89.95**

IVER JOHNSON COMPACT 25 ACP
Caliber: 25 ACP.
Barrel: 2".
Weight: 9.3 oz.
Stocks: Checkered composition.
Sights: Fixed.
Features: Ordnance steel construction with bright blue slide, matte blue frame, color case-hardened trigger. Comes in jewelry-type presentation box. Introduced 1991. From Iver Johnson.
Price: **$199.95**

IVER JOHNSON ENFORCER AUTO
Caliber: 30 M-1 Carbine, 15- or 30-shot magazine, or 9mm Para.
Barrel: 10½".
Weight: 4 lbs. **Length:** 18½" overall.
Stocks: American walnut with metal handguard.
Sights: Gold bead ramp front. Peep rear.
Features: Accepts 15- or 30-shot magazines. From Iver Johnson.
Price: 30 M-1 . . . . **$416.50**
Price: 9mm Para. **$448.95**

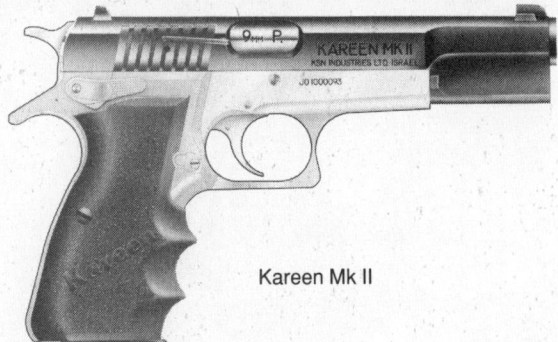

Kareen Mk II

L.A.R. GRIZZLY WIN MAG MK I PISTOL
Caliber: 357 Mag., 357/45, 10mm, 44 Mag., 45 Win. Mag., 45 ACP, 7-shot magazine.
Barrel: 5.4", 6.5".
Weight: 51 oz. **Length:** 10½" overall.
Stocks: Checkered rubber, non-slip combat-type.
Sights: Ramped blade front, fully adjustable rear.
Features: Uses basic Browning/Colt 1911A1 design; interchangeable calibers; beveled magazine well; combat-type flat, checkered rubber mainspring housing; lowered and back-chamfered ejection port; polished feed ramp; throated barrel; solid barrel bushings. Available in satin hard chrome, matte blue, Parkerized finishes. Introduced 1983. From L.A.R. Mfg., Inc.
Price: 45 Win. Mag. **$920.00**
Price: 357 Mag. **$933.00**
Price: Conversion units (357 Mag.) **$228.00**
Price: As above, 45 ACP, 10mm, 45 Win. Mag., 357/45 Win. Mag. . . **$214.00**

INTRATEC TEC-22T AUTO PISTOL
Caliber: 22 LR, 30-shot magazine.
Barrel: 4".
Weight: 30 oz. **Length:** 11³⁄₁₆" overall.
Stocks: Moulded composition.
Sights: Protected post front, front and rear adjustable for windage and elevation.
Features: Ambidextrous cocking knobs and safety. Matte black finish. Accepts any 10/22-type magazine. Introduced 1988. Made in U.S. by Intratec.
Price: **$157.00**
Price: TEC-22TK (as above, TEC-KOTE finish) **$178.95**

Iver Johnson Compact

KAREEN MK II AUTO PISTOL
Caliber: 9mm Para., 13-shot magazine.
Barrel: 4.75".
Weight: 32 oz. **Length:** 8" overall.
Stocks: Textured composition.
Sights: Blade front, rear adjustable for windage.
Features: Single-action mechanism; external hammer safety; magazine safety; combat trigger guard. Blue finish standard, optional two-tone or matte black. Optional Meprolight sights, improved rubberized grips. Comes with two magazines. Imported from Israel by J.O. Arms & Ammunition. Introduced 1969.
Price: . . . . **$389.00 to $525.00**

KIMEL AP9 AUTO PISTOL
Caliber: 9mm Para., 20-shot magazine.
Barrel: 5".
Weight: 3.5 lbs. **Length:** 11.8" overall.
Stocks: Checkered plastic.
Sights: Adjustable post front in ring, fixed open rear.
Features: Matte blue/black or nickel finish. Lever safety blocks trigger and sear. Fires from closed bolt. Introduced 1988. Made in U.S. Available from Kimel Industries.
Price: Matte blue/black **$264.00**
Price: Nickel finish **$274.00**
Price: Mini AP9 (3" barrel) **$258.00**
Price: Nickel finish **$268.00**
Price: Target AP9 (12" bbl., grooved forend, blue **$279.00**

L.A.R. Grizzly Win Mag

L.A.R. Grizzly Win Mag 8" & 10"
Similar to the standard Grizzly Win Mag except has lengthened slide and either 8" or 10" barrel. Available in 45 Win. Mag., 45 ACP, 357/45 Grizzly Win. Mag., 10mm or 357 Magnum. Introduced 1987.
Price: 8", 45 ACP, 45 Win. Mag., 357/45 Grizzly Win. Mag. **$1,313.00**
Price: As above, 10" **$1,375.00**
Price: 8", 357 Magnum **$1,337.50**
Price: As above, 10" **$1,400.00**

Laseraim Arms Series I

Laseraim Arms Series II Auto Pistol
Similar to the Series I except without compensator, has matte stainless finish. Standard Series II has 5" barrel, weighs 46 oz., Compact has 3⅜" barrel, weighs 43 oz. Blade front sight, rear adjustable for windage. Introduced 1993. Made in U.S. by Emerging Technologies, Inc.
Price: Standard or Compact **$529.00**

LLAMA COMPACT FRAME AUTO PISTOL
Caliber: 9mm Para., 9-shot, 40 S&W, 8-shot, 45 ACP, 7-shot.
Barrel: 4¼" (40 S&W), 4⁵⁄₁₆" (9mm, 45).
Weight: 37 oz.
Stocks: Smooth walnut.
Sights: Blade front, rear adjustable for windage.
Features: Scaled-down version of the Large Frame gun. Locked breech mechanism; manual and grip safeties. Introduced 1985. Imported from Spain by SGS Importers Int'l., Inc.
Price: Model XI-B (9mm Para.), blue **$314.95**
Price: As above, nickel **$363.95**
Price: Model XII-B (40 S&W), blue **$324.95**
Price: As above, nickel **$363.95**
Price: Model IX-B (45 ACP), blue **$324.95**
Price: As above, nickel **$363.95**

LLAMA LARGE FRAME AUTO PISTOL
Caliber: 38 Super, 40 S&W, 45 ACP.
Barrel: 5" (38 Super, 45 ACP), 5⅛" (40 S&W).
Weight: 40 oz. **Length:** 8½" overall.
Stocks: Checkered walnut.
Sights: Fixed.
Features: Grip and manual safeties, ventilated rib. Imported from Spain by SGS Importers Int'l., Inc.
Price: Model VIII (38 Super), blue **$324.95**
Price: As above, nickel **$363.95**
Price: Model XII-A (40 S&W), blue **$324.95**
Price: As above, nickel **$363.95**
Price: Model IX-A (45 ACP), blue **$324.95**
Price: As above, nickel **$363.95**

LLAMA XV, III-A SMALL FRAME AUTO PISTOLS
Caliber: 22 LR, 380.
Barrel: 3¹¹⁄₁₆".
Weight: 23 oz. **Length:** 6½" overall.
Stocks: Checkered plastic, thumbrest.
Sights: Fixed front, adjustable notch rear.
Features: Ventilated rib, manual and grip safeties. Imported from Spain by SGS Importers Int'l., Inc.
Price: Blue **$281.95**
Price: Satin Chrome **$314.95**

LLAMA M-82 DA AUTO PISTOL
Caliber: 9mm Para., 40 S&W, 15-shot magazine.
Barrel: 4¼".
Weight: 39 oz. **Length:** 8" overall.
Stocks: Matte black polymer.
Sights: Blade front, rear drift adjustable for windage. High visibility three-dot system.
Features: Double-action mechanism; ambidextrous safety. Introduced 1987. Imported from Spain by SGS Importers Int'l., Inc.
Price: **$584.95**

L.A.R. Grizzly 44 Mag MK IV
Similar to the Win. Mag. Mk I except chambered for 44 Magnum, has beavertail grip safety. Matte blue finish only. Has 5.4" or 6.5" barrel. Introduced 1991. From L.A.R. Mfg., Inc.
Price: **$933.00**

L.A.R. Grizzly 50 Mark V Pistol
Similar to the Grizzly Win Mag Mark I except chambered for 50 Action Express with 6-shot magazine. Weight, empty, is 56 oz., overall length 10⅝". Choice of 5.4" or 6.5" barrel. Has same features as Mark I, IV pistols. Introduced 1993. From L.A.R. Mfg., Inc.
Price: **$1,060.00**

LASERAIM ARMS SERIES I AUTO PISTOL
Caliber: 10mm Auto, 40 S&W, 8-shot, 45 ACP, 7-shot magazine.
Barrel: 5.5", with compensator.
Weight: 52 oz. **Length:** 10.5" overall.
Stocks: Pebble-grained black composite.
Sights: Blade front, fully adjustable rear.
Features: Single action; barrel compensator; stainless steel construction; ambidextrous safety-levers; extended slide release; matte black Teflon finish; integral mount for laser sight. Introduced 1993. Made in U.S. by Emerging Technologies, Inc.
Price: Standard **$599.00**
Price: Compact (3⅞" barrel, 40 S&W, 45 ACP only) **$599.00**

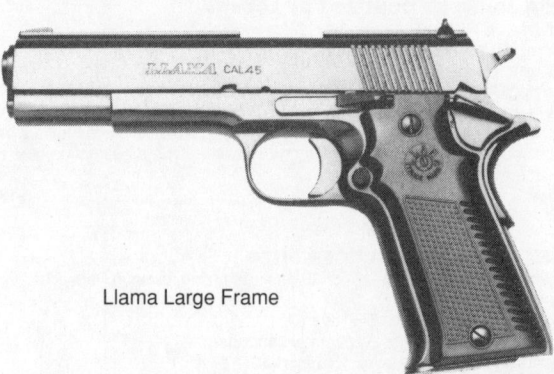

Llama Large Frame

Llama Small Frame

Llama M-82

CAUTION: PRICES CHANGE, CHECK AT GUNSHOP.

LORCIN L-22 AUTO PISTOL
Caliber: 22 LR, 9-shot magazine.
Barrel: 2.5".
Weight: 16 oz. **Length:** 5.25" overall.
Stocks: Black combat, or pink or pearl.
Sights: Fixed three-dot system.
Features: Available in chrome or black Teflon finish. Introduced 1989. From Lorcin Engineering.
Price: About **$79.95**

LORCIN L-25, LT-25 AUTO PISTOLS
Caliber: 25 ACP, 7-shot magazine.
Barrel: 2.4".
Weight: 14.5 oz. **Length:** 4.8" overall.
Stocks: Smooth composition.
Sights: Fixed.
Features: Available in choice of finishes: chrome, black Teflon or camouflage. Introduced 1989. From Lorcin Engineering.
Price: **$79.95**

Lorcin L-25

LORCIN L-32, L-380 AUTO PISTOLS
Caliber: 32 ACP, 380 ACP, 7-shot magazine.
Barrel: 3.5".
Weight: 27 oz. **Length:** 6.6" overall.
Stocks: Grooved composition.
Sights: Fixed.
Features: Black Teflon or chrome finish with black grips. Introduced 1992. From Lorcin Engineering.
Price: 32 ACP **$85.00**
Price: 380 ACP **$95.00**

Lorcin L-32

MAUSER MODEL 80 SA AUTO PISTOL
Caliber: 9mm Para., 13-shot magazine.
Barrel: 4.67".
Weight: 31.7 oz. **Length:** 8" overall.
Stocks: Checkered beechwood.
Sights: Blade front, rear adjustable for windage.
Features: Uses basic Hi-Power design. Polished blue finish. Introduced 1992. Imported from Germany by Precision Imports, Inc.
Price: **$372.00**

Mauser Model 90 DA Auto Pistols
Similar to the Mauser Model 80 except has double-action trigger system. Has 14-shot magazine, weighs 35.2 oz. Introduced 1992. Imported from Germany by Precision Imports, Inc.
Price: Model 90 DA **$399.00**
Price: Model 90 DA Compact (4.13" bbl., 7.4" overall, 33.5 oz.) . . . **$425.00**

MITCHELL ARMS AMERICAN EAGLE AUTO
Caliber: 9mm Para., 7-shot magazine.
Barrel: 4".
Weight: 29.6 oz. **Length:** 9.6" overall.
Stocks: Checkered walnut.
Sights: Blade front, fixed rear.
Features: Recreation of the American Eagle Parabellum pistol in stainless steel. Chamber loaded indicator. Made in U.S. From Mitchell Arms, Inc.
Price: **$695.00**

Mitchell American Eagle

MITCHELL ARMS SHARPSHOOTER AUTO PISTOL
Caliber: 22 LR, 10-shot magazine.
Barrel: 5.5" bull.
Weight: 42 oz. **Length:** 10.25" overall.
Stocks: Checkered walnut with thumbrest.
Sights: Ramp front, slide-mounted square notch rear adjustable for windage and elevation.
Features: Military grip. Slide lock; smooth gripstraps; push-button takedown. Announced 1992. From Mitchell Arms, Inc.
Price: Stainless steel **$364.00**

MITCHELL ARMS TROPHY II AUTO PISTOL
Caliber: 22 LR, 10-shot magazine.
Barrel: 5.5" bull, 7.25" fluted.
Weight: 44.5 oz. (5.5" barrel). **Length:** 9.75" overall (5.5" barrel).
Stocks: Checkered walnut with thumbrest.
Sights: Undercut ramp front, click-adjustable frame-mounted rear.
Features: Grip duplicates feel of military 45; positive action magazine latch; front- and backstraps stippled. Trigger adjustable for pull, over-travel; gold-filled roll marks, gold-plated trigger, safety, magazine release; push-button barrel takedown. Available in stainless steel. Announced 1992. From Mitchell Arms, Inc.
Price: Stainless steel **$479.00**

Mitchell Trophy II

Mitchell Arms Citation II Auto Pistol
Same as the Trophy II except has nickel-plated trigger, safety and magazine release, and has silver-filled roll marks. Available in stainless steel. Announced 1992. From Mitchell Arms, Inc.
Price: Stainless steel **$454.00**

Mountain Eagle

NAVY ARMS TT-OLYMPIA PISTOL
Caliber: 22 LR.
Barrel: 4.6".
Weight: 28 oz. **Length:** 8" overall.
Stocks: Checkered hardwood.
Sights: Blade front, rear adjsutable for windage.
Features: Reproduction of the Walther Olympia pistol. Polished blue finish. Introduced 1992. Imported by Navy Arms.
Price: $300.00

NORINCO NP-15 TOKAREV AUTO PISTOL
Caliber: 7.62x25mm, 8-shot magazine.
Barrel: 4.5".
Weight: 29 oz. **Length:** 7.7" overall.
Stocks: Grooved black plastic.
Sights: Fixed.
Features: Matte blue finish. Imported from China by China Sports, Inc.
Price: . . . . NA

NORINCO MODEL 59 MAKAROV DA PISTOL
Caliber: 9x18mm, 380 ACP, 8-shot magazine.
Barrel: 3.5".
Weight: 21 oz. **Length:** 6.3" overall.
Stocks: Checkered plastic.
Sights: Blade front, adjustable rear.
Features: Blue finish. Double action. Introduced 1990. Imported from China by China Sports, Inc.
Price: . . . . NA

Norinco 77B

OLYMPIC ARMS OA-93 AR PISTOL
Caliber: 223, 20- or 30-shot, 7.62x39mm, 5- or 30-shot magazine.
Barrel: 6", 9", 14"; 4140 steel or 416 stainless.
Weight: 4 lbs., 15 0z. **Length:** 15.75" overall (6" barrel).
Stocks: A2 stowaway pistol grip.
Sights: Cut-off carrying handle with scope rail attached.
Features: AR-15 receiver with special bolt carrier; short slotted aluminum handguard; button-cut 4140 chrome moly or broach-cut stainless barrel, Vortex flash suppressor. Introduced 1993. Made in U.S. by Olympic Arms, Inc.
Price: $952.00

MITCHELL ARMS SPORT-KING AUTO PISTOL
Caliber: 22 LR, 10-shot magazine.
Barrel: 4.5", 6.75".
Weight: 39 oz. (4.5" barrel).**Length:** 9" overall (4.5" barrel).
Stocks: Checkered black plastic.
Sights: Blade front, rear adjustable for windage.
Features: Military grip; standard trigger; push-button barrel takedown. All stainless steel. Announced 1992. From Mitchell Arms, Inc.
Price: $299.00

MOUNTAIN EAGLE AUTO PISTOL
Caliber: 22 LR, 15-shot magazine.
Barrel: 6.5".
Weight: 21 oz. **Length:** 10.6" overall.
Stocks: One-piece impact-resistant polymer in "conventional contour"; checkered panels.
Sights: Serrated ramp front with interchangeable blades, rear adjustable for windage and elevation; interchangeable blades.
Features: Injection moulded grip frame, alloy receiver; hybrid composite barrel replicates shape of the Desert Eagle pistol. Flat, smooth trigger. Introduced 1992. From Magnum Research.
Price: $239.00

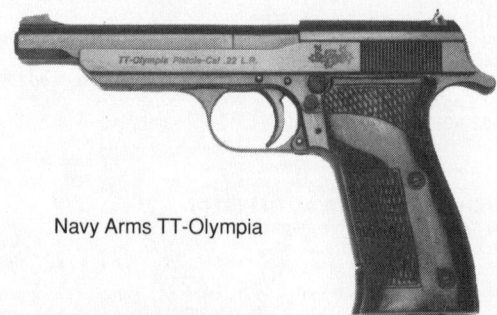

Navy Arms TT-Olympia

NORINCO MODEL 77B AUTO PISTOL
Caliber: 9mm Para., 8-shot magazine.
Barrel: 5".
Weight: 34 oz. **Length:** 7.5" overall.
Stocks: Checkered wood.
Sights: Blade front, adjustable rear.
Features: Uses trigger guard cocking, gas-retarded recoil action. Front of trigger guard can be used to cock the action with the trigger finger. Introduced 1989. Imported from China by China Sports, Inc.
Price: . . . . NA

CONSULT
SHOOTER'S MARKETPLACE
Page 231, This Issue

NORINCO M93 SPORTSMAN AUTO PISTOL
Caliber: 22 LR, 10-shot magazine.
Barrel: 4.6".
Weight: 26 oz. **Length:** 8.6" overall.
Stocks: Checkered composition.
Sights: Blade front, rear adjustable for windage.
Features: All steel construction with blue finish, Introduced 1992. Imported from China by Interarms.
Price: $238.00

NORINCO M1911A1 AUTO PISTOL
Caliber: 45 ACP, 7-shot magazine.
Barrel: 5".
Weight: 39 oz. **Length:** 8.5" overall.
Stocks: Checkered wood.
Sights: Blade front, rear adjustable for windage.
Features: Matte blue finish. Comes with two magazines. Imported from China by China Sports, Inc.
Price: . . . . NA

Para-Ordnance P12.45

PHOENIX ARMS MODEL RAVEN AUTO PISTOL
Caliber: 25 ACP, 6-shot magazine.
Barrel: 2⁷⁄₁₆".
Weight: 15 oz. **Length:** 4¾" overall.
Stocks: Smooth walnut, ivory-colored or black slotted plastic.
Sights: Ramped front, fixed rear.
Features: Available in blue, nickel or chrome finish. Made in U.S. Available from Phoenix Arms.
Price: **$69.95**

PSP-25 AUTO PISTOL
Caliber: 25 ACP, 6-shot magazine.
Barrel: 2⅛".
Weight: 9.5 oz. **Length:** 4⅛" overall.
Stocks: Checkered black plastic.
Sights: Fixed.
Features: All steel construction with polished finish. Introduced 1990. Made in the U.S. under F.N. license; distributed by K.B.I., Inc.
Price: Blue **$249.00**
Price: Hard chrome **$329.99**

ROCKY MOUNTAIN ARMS PATRIOT PISTOL
Caliber: 223, 5-, 20-, 30-shot magazine.
Barrel: 7", with Max Dynamic muzzle brake.
Weight: 6.5 lbs. **Length:** 21" overall.
Stocks: Black composition.
Sights: None furnished.
Features: Uses AR-type receiver with flat top for optical sight mount with Weaver-style bases. Finished in DuPont Teflon-S matte black or NATO green. Comes with black nylon case, one magazine. Introduced 1993. From Rocky Mountain Arms, Inc.
Price: **$1,095.00**

RUGER P89 AUTOMATIC PISTOL
Caliber: 9mm Para., 15-shot magazine.
Barrel: Weight: 32 oz. **Length:** 7.84" overall.
Stocks: Grooved black Xenoy composition.
Sights: Square post front, square notch rear adjustable for windage, both with white dot inserts.
Features: Double action with ambidextrous slide-mounted safety-levers. Slide is 4140 chrome moly steel or 400-series stainless steel, frame is a lightweight aluminum alloy. Ambidextrous magazine release. Blue or stainless steel. Introduced 1986; stainless introduced 1990.
Price: P89, blue, with extra magazine and magazine loading tool, plastic case **$410.00**
Price: KP89, stainless, with extra magazine and magazine loading tool, plastic case **$452.00**
Price: KP89X Convertible 30 Luger/9mm Para. **$497.00**

Ruger P89D Decocker Automatic Pistol
Similar to the standard P89 except has ambidextrous decocking levers in place of the regular slide-mounted safety. The decocking levers move the firing pin inside the slide where the hammer can not reach it, while simultaneously blocking the firing pin from forward movement—allows shooter to decock a cocked pistol without manipulating the trigger. Conventional thumb decocking procedures are therefore unnecessary. Blue or stainless steel. Introduced 1990.
Price: P89D, blue with extra magazine and loader, plastic case . . . **$410.00**
Price: KP89D, stainless, with extra magazine, plastic case **$452.00**

PARA-ORDNANCE P14.45 AUTO PISTOL
Caliber: 45 ACP, 13-shot magazine.
Barrel: 5".
Weight: 28 oz. (alloy frame). **Length:** 8.5" overall.
Stocks: Textured composition.
Sights: Blade front, rear adjustable for windage. High visibility three-dot system.
Features: Available with alloy, steel or stainless steel frame with black finish (silver or stainless gun). Steel and stainless steel frame guns weigh 38 oz. (P14.45), 35 oz. (P13.45), 33 oz. (P12.45). Grooved match trigger, rounded combat-style hammer. Double column, high-capacity magazine gives 14-shot total capacity (P14.45). Beveled magazine well. Manual thumb, grip and firing pin lock safeties. Solid barrel bushing. Introduced 1990. Made in Canada by Para-Ordnance.
Price: P14.45 . . . . **$716.25**
Price: P12.45 (11-shot magazine, 3½" bbl., 24 oz., alloy) **$650.00**
Price: P14.45E steel frame **$716.25**
Price: P12.45E steel frame **$708.75**

Phoenix Arms Model Raven

PHOENIX ARMS HP22, HP25 AUTO PISTOLS
Caliber: 22 LR, 11-shot (HP22), 25 ACP, 10-shot (HP25).
Barrel: 2⁷⁄₁₆".
Weight: 20 oz. **Length:** 5½" overall.
Stocks: Checkered composition.
Sights: Blade front, adjustable rear.
Features: Single action, exposed hammer; manual hold-open; button magazine release. Available in bright chrome, satin nickel, polished blue finish. Introduced 1993. Made in U.S. by Phoenix Arms.
Price: **$99.95**

> Consult our Directory pages for the location of firms mentioned.

ROCKY MOUNTAIN ARMS 1911A1-LH PISTOL
Caliber: 40 S&W, 45 ACP, 7-shot magazine.
Barrel: 5¼".
Weight: 37 0z. **Length:** 8¹³⁄₁₆" overall.
Stocks: Checkered walnut.
Sights: Red insert Patridge front, white outline rear click adjustable for windage and elevation.
Features: Fully left-handed pistol. Slide, frame, barrel made from stainless steel; working parts coated with Teflon-S. Single-stage trigger with 3½ lb. pull. Introduced 1993. Made in U.S. by Rocky Mountain Arms, Inc.
Price: **$1,395.00**

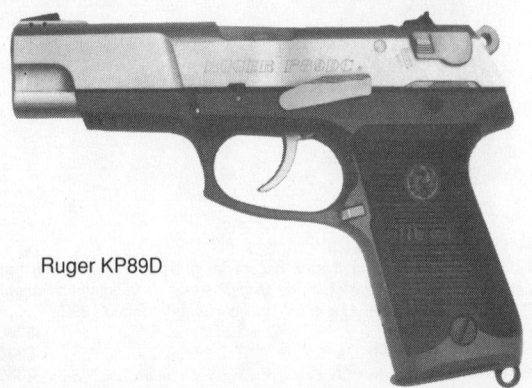

Ruger KP89D

Ruger P89 Double-Action Only Automatic Pistol

Same as the KP89 except operates only in the double-action mode. Has a bobbed, spurless hammer, gripping grooves on each side of the rear of the slide; no external safety or decocking lever. An internal safety prevents forward movement of the firing pin unless the trigger is pulled. Available in 9mm Para., stainless steel only. Introduced 1991.
Price: With lockable case, extra magazine, magazine loading tool . **$452.00**

Ruger P93 Compact Automatic Pistol

Similar to the P89 except has 3.9" barrel, 7.3" overall length, and weighs 31 oz. The forward third of the slide is tapered and polished to the muzzle. Front of the slide is crowned with a convex curve. Slide has seven finger grooves. Trigger guard bow is higher for better grip. Square post front sight, square notch rear drift adjustable for windage, both with white dot inserts. Slide is 400-series stainless steel, black-finished alloy frame. Available as decocker-only or double action-only. Introduced 1993.
Price: KP93DAO (double action only), KP93 (decocker) **$452.00**

Ruger KP90C

RUGER P90 AUTOMATIC PISTOL

Caliber: 45 ACP, 7-shot magazine.
Barrel: 4.50".
Weight: 33.5 oz. **Length:** 7.87" overall.
Stocks: Grooved black Xenoy composition.
Sights: Square post front, square notch rear adjustable for windage, both with white dot inserts.
Features: Double action with ambidextrous slide-mounted safety-levers which move the firing pin inside the slide where the hammer can not reach it, while simultaneously blocking the firing pin from forward movement. Stainless steel only. Introduced 1991.
Price: KP90 with lockable case, extra magazine **$488.65**

Ruger P90 Decocker Automatic Pistol

Similar to the P90 except has a manual decocking system. The ambidextrous decocking levers move the firing pin inside the slide where the hammer can not reach it, while simultaneously blocking the firing pin from forward movement—allows shooter to decock a cocked pistol without manipulating the trigger. Available only in stainless steel. Overall length 7.87", weight 34 oz. Introduced 1991.
Price: P90D with lockable case, extra magazine, and magazine loading tool **$488.65**

Ruger KP93DC

RUGER P91 DECOCKER AUTOMATIC PISTOL

Caliber: 40 S&W, 11-shot magazine.
Barrel: 4.50".
Weight: 33 oz. **Length:** 7.87" overall.
Stocks: Grooved black Xenoy composition.
Sights: Square post front, square notch rear adjustable for windage, both with white dot inserts.
Features: Ambidextrous slide-mounted decocking levers move the firing pin inside the slide where the hammer can not reach it while simultaneously blocking the firing pin from forward movement. Allows shooter to decock a cocked pistol without manipulating the trigger. Conventional thumb decocking procedures are therefore unnecessary. Stainless steel only. Introduced 1991.
Price: KP91D with lockable case, extra magazine, and magazine loading tool **$488.65**

Ruger 22/45 Mark II

Ruger 22/45 Mark II Pistol

Similar to the other 22 Mark II autos except has grip frame of Zytel that matchs the angle and magazine latch of the Model 1911 45 ACP pistol. Available in 4¾" standard, 5¼" tapered and 5½" bull barrel. Introduced 1992.
Price: KP4 (4¾" barrel) **$280.00**
Price: KP514 (5¼" barrel) **$330.00**
Price: KP512 (5½" bull barrel) **$330.00**

Ruger P91 Double-Action-Only Automatic Pistol

Same as the KP91D except operates only in the double-action mode. Has a bobbed, spurless hammer, gripping grooves on each side at the rear of the slide, no external safety or decocking levers. An internal safety prevents forward movement of the firing pin unless the trigger is pulled. Available in 40 S&W, stainless steel only. Introduced 1992.
Price: KP91DAO with lockable case, extra magazine, and magazine loading tool **$488.65**

RUGER MARK II STANDARD AUTO PISTOL

Caliber: 22 LR, 10-shot magazine.
Barrel: 4¾" or 6".
Weight: 36 oz. (4¾" bbl.). **Length:** 8⅝₁₆" (4¾" bbl.).
Stocks: Checkered plastic.
Sights: Fixed, wide blade front, square notch rear adjustable for windage.
Features: Updated design of the original Standard Auto. Has new bolt hold-open latch. 10-shot magazine, magazine catch, safety, trigger and new receiver contours. Introduced 1982.
Price: Blued (MK 4, MK 6) **$252.00**
Price: In stainless steel (KMK 4, KMK 6) **$330.25**

SAFARI ARMS CREST SERIES PISTOLS

Caliber: 9mm Para., 38 Super, 45 ACP, 7-shot magazine (standard), 6-shot (4-Star).
Barrel: 5" (standard), 4.5" (4-Star); 416 stainless steel.
Weight: 39 oz. (standard), 35.7 oz. (4-Star). **Length:** 8.5" overall (standard).
Stocks: Checkered walnut.
Sights: Ramped blade front, fully adjustable rear.
Features: Right- or left-hand models available. Long aluminum trigger, long recoil spring guide, extended safety and slide stop. Stainless steel. Introduced 1993. Made in U.S. by Safari Arms, Inc.
Price: Right-hand, standard **$740.00**
Price: Left-hand, standard **$880.00**
Price: Right-hand, 4-Star **$770.00**
Price: Left-hand, 4-Star **$910.00**

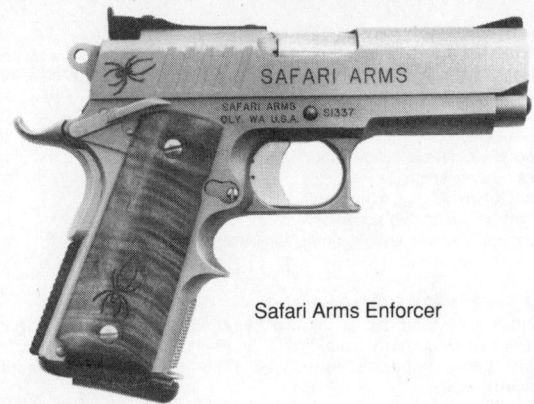

Safari Arms Enforcer

SAFARI ARMS ENFORCER PISTOL
Caliber: 45 ACP, 6-shot magazine.
Barrel: 3.8".
Weight: 36 oz. **Length:** 7.5" overall.
Stocks: Smooth walnut with etched black widow spider logo.
Sights: Ramped blade front, rear adjustable for windage and elevation.
Features: Extended safety, extended slide release; Commander-style hammer; beavertail grip safety; throated, ported, tuned, with cone-shaped barrel, no bushing. Parkerized matte black or satin stainless steel. From Safari Arms, Inc.
Price: $690.00

Safari Arms Enforcer Carrycomp II Pistol
Similar to the Enforcer except has Wil Schueman-designed hybrid compensator system. Introduced 1993. Made in U.S. by Safari Arms, Inc.
Price: $1,010.00

SAFARI ARMS G.I. SAFARI PISTOL
Caliber: 45 ACP, 7-shot magazine.
Barrel: 5".
Weight: 39.9 oz. **Length:** 8.5" overall.
Stocks: Checkered walnut.
Sights: Blade front, fixed rear.
Features: Beavertail grip safety, extended safety and slide release, Commander-style hammer. Barrel is chrome-lined 4140 steel; National Match 416 stainless optional. Parkerized matte black finish. Introduced 1991. Made in U.S. by Safari Arms, Inc.
Price: $430.00

SEECAMP LWS 32 STAINLESS DA AUTO
Caliber: 32 ACP Win. Silvertip, 6-shot magazine.
Barrel: 2", integral with frame.
Weight: 10.5 oz. **Length:** 4⅛" overall.
Stocks: Glass-filled nylon.
Sights: Smooth, no-snag, contoured slide and barrel top.
Features: Aircraft quality 17-4 PH stainless steel. Inertia-operated firing pin. Hammer fired double-action only. Hammer automatically follows slide down to safety rest position after each shot—no manual safety needed. Magazine safety disconnector. Polished stainless. Introduced 1985. From L.W. Seecamp.
Price: $375.00

SIG P-210-2 AUTO PISTOL
Caliber: 7.65mm or 9mm Para., 8-shot magazine.
Barrel: 4¾".
Weight: 31¾ oz. (9mm). **Length:** 8½" overall.
Stocks: Checkered black composition.
Sights: Blade front, rear adjustable for windage.
Features: Lanyard loop; matte finish. Conversion unit for 22 LR available. Imported from Switzerland by Mandall Shooting Supplies.
Price: P-210-2 Service Pistol $3,000.00

SIG SAUER P220 "AMERICAN" AUTO PISTOL
Caliber: 9mm, 38 Super, 45 ACP, (9-shot in 9mm and 38 Super, 7 in 45).
Barrel: 4⅜".
Weight: 28¼ oz. (9mm). **Length:** 7¾" overall.
Stocks: Checkered black plastic.
Sights: Blade front, drift adjustable rear for windage.
Features: Double action. De-cocking lever permits lowering hammer onto locked firing pin. Squared combat-type trigger guard. Slide stays open after last shot. Imported from Germany by SIGARMS, Inc.
Price: "American," blue (side-button magazine release, 45 ACP only) $780.00
Price: 45 ACP, blue, Siglite night sights $880.00
Price: K-Kote finish $850.00
Price: K-Kote, Siglite night sights $950.00

SIG SAUER P225 DA AUTO PISTOL
Caliber: 9mm Para., 8-shot magazine.
Barrel: 3.8".
Weight: 26 oz. **Length:** 7³⁄₃₂" overall.
Stocks: Checkered black plastic.
Sights: Blade front, rear adjustable for windage. Optional Siglite night sights.
Features: Double action. De-cocking lever permits lowering hammer onto locked firing pin. Square combat-type trigger guard. Shortened, lightened version of P220. Imported from Germany by SIGARMS, Inc.
Price: $775.00
Price: With Siglite night sights $875.00
Price: K-Kote finish $845.00
Price: K-Kote with Siglite night sights $945.00

SIG SAUER P230 DA AUTO PISTOL
Caliber: 32 ACP, 8-shot; 380 ACP, 7-shot.
Barrel: 3¾".
Weight: 16 oz. **Length:** 6½" overall.
Stocks: Checkered black plastic.
Sights: Blade front, rear adjustable for windage.
Features: Double action. Same basic action design as P220. Blowback operation, stationary barrel. Introduced 1977. Imported from Germany by SIGARMS, Inc.
Price: Blue $510.00
Price: In stainless steel (P230 SL) $595.00

SIG P-210-6 AUTO PISTOL
Caliber: 9mm Para., 8-shot magazine.
Barrel: 4¾".
Weight: 36.2 oz. **Length:** 8½" overall.
Stocks: Checkered black plastic; walnut optional.
Sights: Blade front, micro. adjustable rear for windage and elevation.
Features: Adjustable trigger stop; target trigger; ribbed frontstrap; sandblasted finish. Conversion unit for 22 LR consists of barrel, recoil spring, slide and magazine. Imported from Switzerland by Mandall Shooting Supplies.
Price: P-210-6 .... $3,200.00
Price: P-210-5 Target $3,500.00

SIG Sauer P220 "American"

SIG Sauer P230

SIG Sauer P228

SIG Sauer P226 DA Auto Pistol
Similar to the P220 pistol except has 15-shot magazine, 4.4" barrel, and weighs 26½ oz. 9mm only. Imported from Germany by SIGARMS, Inc.
Price: Blue $805.00
Price: With Siglite night sights $905.00
Price: Blue, double-action only $805.00
Price: Blue, double-action only, Siglite night sights $905.00
Price: K-Kote finish $875.00
Price: K-Kote, Siglite night sights $975.00
Price: K-Kote, double-action only $875.00
Price: K-Kote, double-action only, Siglite night sights $975.00

SIG Sauer P228 DA Auto Pistol
Similar to the P226 except has 3.86" barrel, with 7.08" overall length and 3.35" height. Chambered for 9mm Para. only, 13-shot magazine. Weight is 29.1 oz. with empty magazine. Introduced 1989. Imported from Germany by SIGARMS, Inc.
Price: Blue $805.00
Price: Blue, with Siglite night sights $905.00
Price: Blue, double-action only $805.00
Price: Blue, double-action only, Siglite night sights $905.00
Price: K-Kote finish $875.00
Price: K-Kote, Siglite night sights $975.00
Price: K-Kote, double-action only $875.00
Price: K-Kote, double-action only, Siglite night sights $975.00

SIG Sauer P229 DA Auto Pistol
Similar to the P228 except chambered for 40 S&W with 12-shot magazine. Has 3.86" barrel, 7.08" overall length and 3.35" height. Weight is 30.5 oz. Introduced 1991. Imported from Germany by SIGARMS, Inc.
Price: Blue $875.00
Price: Blue, double-action only $875.00

SMITH & WESSON MODEL .356 TSW LIMITED PISTOL
Caliber: 356 TSW, 15-shot magazine.
Barrel: 5".
Weight: 44 oz. **Length:** 8.5" overall.
Stocks: Checkered black composition.
Sights: Blade front drift adjustable for windage, fully adjustable Bo-Mar rear.
Features: Single action trigger. Stainless steel frame and slide, hand-fitted titanium-coated stainless steel bushing, match grade barrel. Extended magazine well and oversize release; magazine pads; extended safety. Checkered front strap. Introduced 1993. Available from Lew Horton Dist.
Price: About $1,300.00

Smith & Wesson .356 TSW

Smith & Wesson Model .356 TSW Compact Pistol
Similar to the .356 TSW Limited except has 3½" barrel, 12-shot magazine, Novak LoMount combat sights. Overall length 7", weight 37 oz. Introduced 1993. Available from Lew Horton Dist.
Price: .... NA

SMITH & WESSON MODEL 915 DA AUTO PISTOL
Caliber: 9mm Para., 15-shot magazine.
Barrel: 4".
Weight: 28.5 oz. **Length:** 7.5" overall.
Stocks: One-piece Xenoy, wraparound with straight backstrap.
Sights: Post front with white dot, fixed rear.
Features: Alloy frame, blue carbon steel slide. Slide-mounted decocking lever. Introduced 1992.
Price: $467.00

Smith & Wesson Model 915

SMITH & WESSON MODEL 422, 622 AUTO
Caliber: 22 LR, 10-shot magazine.
Barrel: 4½", 6".
Weight: 22 oz. (4½" bbl.). **Length:** 7½" overall (4½" bbl.).
Stocks: Checkered plastic (Field), checkered walnut (Target).
Sights: Field—serrated ramp front, fixed rear; Target—Patridge front, adjustable rear.
Features: Aluminum frame, steel slide, brushed blue finish; internal hammer. Introduced 1987. Model 2206 introduced 1990.
Price: Blue, 4½", 6", fixed sight $225.00
Price: As above, adjustable sight $278.00
Price: Stainless (Model 622), 4½", 6", fixed sight $272.00
Price: As above, adjustable sight $324.00

Smith & Wesson Model 2214

Smith & Wesson Model 2214 Sportsman Auto
Similar to the Model 422 except has 3" barrel, 8-shot magazine; dovetail Patridge front sight with white dot, fixed rear with two white dots; matte blue finish, black composition grips with checkered panels. Overall length 6⅛", weight 18 oz. Introduced 1990.
Price: $258.00

Smith & Wesson Model 2206 Auto
Similar to the Model 422/622 except made entirely of stainless steel with non-reflective finish. Weight is 35 oz. with 4½" barrel, 39 oz. with 6" barrel. Other specs are the same. Introduced 1990.
Price: With fixed sight $314.00
Price: With adjustable sight $370.00

SMITH & WESSON MODEL 3913/3914 DOUBLE ACTIONS
Caliber: 9mm Para., 8-shot magazine.
Barrel: 3½".
Weight: 26 oz. Length: 6¹³⁄₁₆" overall.
Stocks: One-piece Delrin wraparound, textured surface.
Sights: Post front with white dot, Novak LoMount Carry with two dots, adjustable for windage.
Features: Aluminum alloy frame, stainless slide (M3913) or blue steel slide (M3914). Bobbed hammer with no half-cock notch; smooth .304" trigger with rounded edges. Straight backstrap. Extra magazine included. Introduced 1989.
Price: Model 3913 . . . . $597.00
Price: Model 3914 . . . . $539.00

Smith & Wesson Model 3953DA Pistol
Same as the Models 3913/3914 except double-action only. Model 3953 has stainless slide with alloy frame. Overall length 7"; weight 25.5 oz. Extra magazine included. Introduced 1990.
Price: $597.00

Smith & Wesson Model 3913-NL Pistol
Same as the 3913/3914 LadySmith autos except without the LadySmith logo and it has a slightly modified frame design. Right-hand safety only. Has stainless slide on alloy frame; extra magazine included. Introduced 1990.
Price: $597.00

SMITH & WESSON MODEL 4006 DA AUTO
Caliber: 40 S&W, 11-shot magazine.
Barrel: 4".
Weight: 36 oz. Length: 7½" overall.
Stocks: Xenoy wraparound with checkered panels.
Sights: Replaceable post front with white dot, Novak LoMount Carry fixed rear with two white dots, or micro. click adjustable rear with two white dots.
Features: Stainless steel construction with non-reflective finish. Straight backstrap. Extra magazine included. Introduced 1990.
Price: With adjustable sights $743.00
Price: With fixed sight $715.00
Price: With fixed night sights $820.00

Smith & Wesson Model 4046 DA Pistol
Similar to the Model 4006 except is double-action only. Has a semi-bobbed hammer, smooth trigger, 4" barrel; Novak LoMount Carry rear sight, post front with white dot. Overall length is 7½", weight 39 oz. Extra magazine included. Introduced 1991.
Price: $715.00
Price: With fixed night sights $820.00

SMITH & WESSON MODEL 4013/4014, 4053 AUTOS
Caliber: 40 S&W, 7-shot magazine.
Barrel: 3½".
Weight: 26 oz. Length: 7" overall.
Stocks: One-piece Xenoy wraparound with straight backstrap.
Sights: Post front with white dot, fixed Novak LoMount Carry rear with two white dots.
Features: Models 4013/4014 are traditional double action; Model 4053 is double-action only; Models 4013, 4053 have stainless slide on alloy frame; 4014 has blued steel slide. Introduced 1991.
Price: Models 4013, 4053 . . . . $693.00
Price: Model 4014 . . . . $635.00

SMITH & WESSON MODEL 4026 DA AUTO
Caliber: 40 S&W, 11-shot magazine.
Barrel: 4".
Weight: 39 oz. Length: 7.5" overall.
Stocks: Xenoy one-piece wraparound.
Sights: Post front with white dot, Novak LoMount Carry rear with two white dots.
Features: Stainless steel. Has spring-loaded, frame-mounted decocking lever, magazine disconnector safety and firing pin safety. Matte finish. Bobbed hammer, smooth trigger. Introduced 1992.
Price: $731.00

Smith & Wesson 3913 LadySmith

Smith & Wesson Model 3913 LadySmith Auto
Similar to the standard Model 3913/3914 except has frame that is upswept at the front, rounded trigger guard. Comes in frosted stainless steel with matching gray grips. Grips are ergonomically correct for a woman's hand. Novak LoMount Carry rear sight adjustable for windage, smooth edges for snag resistance. Extra magazine included. Introduced 1990.
Price: $615.00

Smith & Wesson Model 4006

Smith & Wesson Model 4506

SMITH & WESSON MODEL 4500 SERIES AUTOS
Caliber: 45 ACP, 8-shot magazine (M4506, 4566/4586).
Barrel: 5" (M4506).
Weight: 41 oz. (4506). Length: 7⅛" overall (4516).
Stocks: Delrin one-piece wraparound, arched or straight backstrap on M4506, straight only on M4516.
Sights: Post front with white dot, adjustable or fixed Novak LoMount Carry on M4506.
Features: M4506 has serrated hammer spur. Extra magazine included. Contact Smith & Wesson for complete data. Introduced 1989.
Price: Model 4506, fixed sight $742.00
Price: Model 4506, adjustable sight $773.00
Price: Model 4566 (stainless, 4¼", traditional DA, ambidextrous safety) $742.00
Price: Model 4586 (stainless, 4¼", DA only) $742.00

Smith & Wesson Model 1006 Double-Action Auto

Similar to the Model 4506 except chambered for 10mm auto with 9-shot magazine. Available with either Novak LoMount Carry fixed rear sight with two white dots or adjustable micrometer-click rear with two white dots. All stainless steel construction; one-piece Delrin stocks with straight backstrap; curved backstrap available as option. Has 5" barrel, 8½" overall length, weighs 38 oz. with fixed sight. Rounded trigger guard with knurling. Extra magazine included. Introduced 1990.

Price: With fixed sight $769.00
Price: With adjustable sight $796.00

Smith & Wesson Model 1076 Auto

Same as the Model 1006 except has frame-mounted decocking lever, fixed sight only; traditional double-action mechanism. Extra magazine included. Introduced 1990.

Price: $778.00

SMITH & WESSON MODEL 5900 SERIES AUTO PISTOLS

Caliber: 9mm Para., 15-shot magazine.
Barrel: 4".
Weight: 28½ to 37½ oz. (fixed sight); 29 to 38 oz. (adj. sight). **Length:** 7½" overall.
Stocks: Xenoy wraparound with curved backstrap.
Sights: Post front with white dot, fixed or fully adjustable with two white dots.
Features: All stainless, stainless and alloy or carbon steel and alloy construction. Smooth .304" trigger, .260" serrated hammer. Extra magazine included. Introduced 1989.
Price: Model 5903 (stainless, alloy frame, traditional DA, adjustable sight, ambidextrous safety) **$693.00**
Price: As above, fixed sight **$662.00**
Price: Model 5904 (blue, alloy frame, traditional DA, adjustable sight, ambidextrous safety) **$645.00**
Price: As above, fixed sight **$616.00**
Price: Model 5906 (stainless, traditional DA, adjustable sight, ambidextrous safety) **$711.00**
Price: As above, fixed sight **$679.00**
Price: With fixed night sights **$784.00**
Price: Model 5946 (as above, stainless frame and slide) **$679.00**

Smith & Wesson Model 6904/6906 Double-Action Autos

Similar to the Models 5904/5906 except with 3½" barrel, 12-shot magazine (20-shot available), fixed rear sight, .260" bobbed hammer. Extra magazine included. Introduced 1989.

Price: Model 6904, blue **$590.00**
Price: Model 6906, stainless **$650.00**
Price: Model 6946 (stainless, DA only, fixed sights) **$650.00**
Price: With fixed night sights **$756.00**

> Consult our Directory pages for the location of firms mentioned.

SPHINX AT-380M AUTO PISTOL

Caliber: 380 ACP, 10-shot magazine.
Barrel: 3.27".
Weight: 25 oz. **Length:** 6.03" overall.
Stocks: Checkered plastic.
Sights: Fixed.
Features: Double-action-only mechanism, Chamber loaded indicator; ambidextrous magazine release and slide latch. Blued slide, bright Palladium frame, or bright Palladium overall. Introduced 1993. Imported from Switzerland by Sile Distributors, Inc.
Price: Two-tone **$571.95**
Price: Palladium finish **$629.95**

SPHINX AT-2000S DOUBLE-ACTION PISTOL

Caliber: 9mm Para., 9x21mm, 15-shot, 40 S&W, 11-shot magazine.
Barrel: 4.53".
Weight: 36.3 oz. **Length:** 8.03" overall.
Stocks: Checkered neoprene.
Sights: Fixed, three-dot system.
Features: Double-action mechanism changeable to double-action-only. Stainless frame, blued slide. Ambidextrous safety, magazine release, slide latch. Introduced 1993. Imported from Switzerland by Sile Distributors, Inc.
Price: 9mm, two-tone **$902.95**
Price: 9mm, Palladium finish **$989.95**
Price: 40 S&W, two-tone **$911.95**
Price: 40 S&W, Palladium finish **$998.95**

Smith & Wesson Model 1006

Smith & Wesson Model 6904

Sphinx AT-380M

Sphinx AT-2000S

Sphinx AT-2000H Auto Pistol
Similar to the AT-2000P except has shorter slide with 3.54" barrel, shorter frame, 10-shot magazine, with 7" overall length. Weight is 32.2 oz. Stainless frame with blued slide, or overall bright Palladium finish. Introduced 1993. Imported from Switzerland by Sile Distributors, Inc.
Price: 9mm, two-tone **$858.95**
Price: 9mm, Palladium finish **$945.95**
Price: 40 S&W, two-tone **$867.95**
Price: 40 S&W, Palladium **$954.95**

Sphinx AT-2000P, AT-2000PS Auto Pistols
Same as the AT-2000S except AT-2000P has shortened frame (13-shot magazine), 3.74" barrel, 7.25" overall length, and weighs 34 oz. Model AT-2000PS has full-size frame. Both have stainless frame with blued slide or bright Palladium finish. Introduced 1993. Imported from Switzerland by Sile Distributors, Inc.
Price: 9mm, two-tone **$858.95**
Price: 9mm, Palladium finish **$945.95**
Price: 40 S&W, two-tone **$867.95**
Price: 40 S&W, Palladium finish **$954.95**

SPORTARMS TOKAREV MODEL 213
Caliber: 9mm Para., 8-shot magazine.
Barrel: 4.5".
Weight: 31 oz. **Length:** 7.6" overall.
Stocks: Grooved plastic.
Sights: Fixed.
Features: Blue finish, hard chrome optional. 9mm version of the famous Russian Tokarev pistol. Made in China by Norinco. Imported by Sportarms of Florida. Introduced 1988.
Price: Blue, about **$150.00**
Price: Hard chrome, about **$179.00**

SPRINGFIELD INC. 1911A1 AUTO PISTOL
Caliber: 9mm Para., 9-shot; 38 Super, 10-shot; 45 ACP, 8-shot.
Barrel: 5".
Weight: 35.06 oz. **Length:** 8.59" overall.
Stocks: Checkered walnut.
Sights: Fixed low-profile combat-style.
Features: Beveled magazine well. All forged parts, including frame, barrel, slide. All new production. Introduced 1990. From Springfield Inc.
Price: Basic, 45 ACP, Parkerized **$449.00**
Price: Standard, 45 ACP, blued **$489.00**
Price: Basic, 45 ACP, stainless **$532.00**

Springfield Inc. 1911A1 Custom Carry Gun
Similar to the standard 1911A1 except has fixed three-dot low profile sights, Videki speed trigger, match barrel and bushing; extended thumb safety, beavertail grip safety; beveled, polished magazine well, polished feed ramp and throated barrel; match Commander hammer and sear, tuned extractor; lowered and flared ejection port; Shok Buff, full-length spring guide rod; walnut grips. Comes with two magazines with slam pads, plastic carrying case. Available in 45 ACP only. Introduced 1992. From Springfield Inc.
Price: . . . . **P.O.R.**

Springfield Inc. 1911A1 Factory Comp

STALLARD JS-9MM AUTO PISTOL
Caliber: 9mm Para., 8-shot magazine.
Barrel: 4.5".
Weight: 41 oz. **Length:** 7.72" overall.
Stocks: Textured acetal plastic.
Sights: Fixed, low profile.
Features: Single-action design. Scratch-resistant, non-glare blue finish. Introduced 1990. From MKS Supply, Inc.
Price: Matte black **$139.95**
Price: Brushed nickel **$149.95**

Sphinx AT-2000H

Springfield Inc. 1911A1

Springfield Inc. 1911A1 High Capacity Pistol
Similar to the Standard 1911A1 except available in 45 ACP and 9x21mm with 10-shot magazine (45 ACP), 16-shot magazine (9x21mm). Has Commander-style hammer, walnut grips, ambidextrous thumb safety, beveled magazine well, plastic carrying case. Blue finish only. Introduced 1993. From Springfield, Inc.
Price: 45 ACP **$799.00**
Price: 9x21mm **$879.00**
Price: 45 ACP Factory Comp$999.00

Springfield Inc. 1911A1 Factory Comp
Similar to the standard 1911A1 except comes with bushing-type dual-port compensator, adjustable rear sight, extended thumb safety, Videki speed trigger, and beveled magazine well. Checkered walnut grips standard. Available in 38 Super or 45 ACP, blue only. Introduced 1992.
Price: 38 Super **$899.00**
Price: 45 ACP **$869.00**

Springfield Inc. 1911A1 Champion Pistol
Similar to the standard 1911A1 except slide and barrel are ½" shorter. Has low-profile three-dot sight system. Comes with Commander hammer and walnut stocks. Available in 45 ACP only; blue or stainless. Introduced 1989.
Price: Blue **$513.00**
Price: Stainless **$558.00**
Price: Blue, comp **$829.00**

Springfield Inc. Product Improved 1911A1 Defender Pistol
Similar to the 1911A1 Champion except has tapered cone dual-port compensator system, rubberized grips. Has reverse recoil plug, full-length recoil spring guide, serrated frontstrap, extended thumb safety, Commander-style hammer with modified grip safety to match and a Videki speed trigger. Bi-Tone finish. Introduced 1991.
Price: 45 ACP **$959.00**

Springfield Inc. 1911A1 Compact Pistol
Similar to the Champion model except has a shortened slide with 4.025" barrel, 7.75" overall length. Magazine capacity is 7 shots. Has Commander hammer, checkered walnut grips. Available in 45 ACP only. Introduced 1989.
Price: Blued **$509.00**
Price: Bi-Tone (blue slide, stainless frame) **$829.00**
Price: Stainless **$558.00**

STAR FIRESTAR AUTO PISTOL
Caliber: 9mm Para., 7-shot; 40 S&W, 6-shot.
Barrel: 3.39".
Weight: 30.35 oz. **Length:** 6.5" overall.
Stocks: Checkered rubber.
Sights: Blade front, fully adjustable rear; three-dot system.
Features: Low-profile, combat-style sights; ambidextrous safety. Available in blue or weather-resistant Starvel finish. Introduced 1990. Imported from Spain by Interarms.
Price: Blue, 9mm **$460.00**
Price: Starvel finish 9mm **$492.00**
Price: Blue, 40 S&W **$488.00**
Price: Starvel finish, 40 S&W **$517.00**

Star Firestar

Star Firestar M45 Auto Pistol
Similar to the standard Firestar except chambered for 45 ACP with 6-shot magazine. Has 3.6" barrel, weighs 35 oz., 6.85" overall length. Reverse-taper Acculine barrel. Introduced 1992. Imported from Spain by Interarms.
Price: Blue **$525.00**
Price: Starvel finish **$553.00**

STAR MEGASTAR 45 ACP AUTO PISTOL
Caliber: 10mm, 45 ACP, 12-shot magazine.
Barrel: 4.6".
Weight: 47.6 oz. **Length:** 8.44" overall.
Stocks: Checkered composition.
Sights: Blade front, adjustable rear.
Features: Double-action mechanism; steel frame and slide; reverse-taper Ac-culine barrel. Introduced 1992. Imported from Spain by Interarms.
Price: Blue, 10mm **$693.00**
Price: Starvel finish, 10mm **$725.00**
Price: Blue, 45 ACP **$693.00**
Price: Starvel finish, 45 ACP **$725.00**

Star Model 31P

STAR MODEL 31P & 31PK DOUBLE-ACTION PISTOLS
Caliber: 9mm Para., 15-shot magazine.
Barrel: 3.86".
Weight: 30 oz. **Length:** 7.6" overall.
Stocks: Checkered black plastic.
Sights: Square blade front, square notch rear click-adjustable for windage and elevation.
Features: Double or single action; grooved front- and backstraps and trigger guard face; ambidextrous safety cams firing pin forward; removable backstrap houses the firing mechanism. Model 31P has steel frame; Model PK is alloy. Introduced 1984. Imported from Spain by Interarms.
Price: Model 31P, 40 S&W, blue, steel frame **$643.00**
Price: Model 31P, 40 S&W, Starvel finish, steel frame **$675.00**
Price: Model 31P, 9mm, blue, steel frame, ... **$580.00**
Price: Model 31P, 9mm, Starvel finish, steel frame **$612.00**
Price: Model 31PK, 9mm only, blue, alloy frame **$580.00**

STEYR SSP SEMI-AUTOMATIC PISTOL
Caliber: 9mm Para., 15- or 30-shot magazine.
Barrel: 5.9".
Weight: 42 oz. **Length:** 12.75" overall.
Stocks: Grooved synthetic.
Sights: Post front adjustable for elevation, open rear adjustable for windage.
Features: Delayed blowback, rotating barrel operating system. Synthetic upper and lower receivers. Drop and cross-bolt safeties. Rail mount for optics. Introduced 1993. Imported from Austria by GSI, Inc.
Price: **$895.00**

Steyr SSP

SUNDANCE BOA AUTO PISTOL
Caliber: 25 ACP, 7-shot magazine.
Barrel: 2½".
Weight: 16 oz. **Length:** 4⅞".
Stocks: Grooved ABS or smooth simulated pearl; optional pink.
Sights: Fixed.
Features: Patented grip safety, manual rotary safety; button magazine release; lifetime warranty. Bright chrome or black Teflon finish. Introduced 1991. Made in the U.S. by Sundance Industries, Inc.
Price: **$95.00**

Sundance BOA

SUNDANCE MODEL A-25 AUTO PISTOL
Caliber: 25 ACP, 7-shot magazine.
Barrel: 2.5".
Weight: 16 oz. **Length:** 4⅞" overall.
Stocks: Grooved black ABS or simulated smooth pearl; optional pink.
Sights: Fixed.
Features: Manual rotary safety; button magazine release. Bright chrome or black Teflon finish. Introduced 1989. Made in U.S. by Sundance Industries, Inc.
Price: **$79.95**

TAURUS MODEL PT 22/PT 25 AUTO PISTOLS
Caliber: 22 LR, 9-shot (PT 22); 25 ACP, 8-shot (PT 25).
Barrel: 2.75".
Weight: 12.3 oz. **Length:** 5.25" overall.
Stocks: Smooth Brazilian hardwood.
Sights: Blade front, fixed rear.
Features: Double action. Tip-up barrel for loading, cleaning. Blue only. Introduced 1992. Made in U.S. by Taurus International.
Price: 22 LR or 25 ACP **$182.00**

> Consult our Directory pages for the location of firms mentioned.

TAURUS MODEL PT 92AF AUTO PISTOL
Caliber: 9mm Para., 15-shot magazine.
Barrel: 4.92".
Weight: 34 oz. **Length:** 8.54" overall.
Stocks: Brazilian hardwood.
Sights: Fixed notch rear. Three-dot sight system.
Features: Double action, exposed hammer, chamber loaded indicator. Inertia firing pin. Imported by Taurus International.
Price: Blue **$473.00**
Price: Blue, Deluxe Shooter's Pak (extra magazine, case) **$501.00**
Price: Nickel **$511.00**
Price: Nickel, Deluxe Shooter's Pak (extra magazine, case) **$539.00**
Price: Stainless steel **$538.00**
Price: Stainless, Deluxe Shooter's Pak (extra magazine, case) . . . **$564.00**

Taurus PT 92AFC Compact Pistol
Similar to the PT-92 except has 4.25" barrel, 13-shot magazine, weighs 31 oz. and is 7.5" overall. Available in stainless steel, blue or satin nickel. Introduced 1991. Imported by Taurus International.
Price: Blue **$473.00**
Price: Blue, Deluxe Shooter's Pak (extra magazine, case) **$501.00**
Price: Nickel **$511.00**
Price: Nickel, Deluxe Shooter's Pak (extra magazine, case) **$539.00**
Price: Stainless steel **$538.00**
Price: Stainless, Deluxe Shooter's Pak (extra magazine and case) **$564.00**

TAURUS PT 100 AUTO PISTOL
Caliber: 40 S&W, 11-shot magazine.
Barrel: 5".
Weight: 34 oz.
Stocks: Smooth Brazilian hardwood.
Sights: Fixed front, drift-adjustable rear. Three-dot combat.
Features: Double action, exposed hammer. Ambidextrous hammer-drop safety; inertia firing pin; chamber loaded indicator. Introduced 1991. Imported by Taurus International.
Price: Blue **$482.00**
Price: Blue, Deluxe Shooter's Pak (extra magazine, case) **$510.00**
Price: Nickel **$521.00**
Price: Nickel, Deluxe Shooter's Pak (extra magazine, case) **$548.00**
Price: Stainless **$547.00**
Price: Stainless, Deluxe Shooter's Pak (extra magazine, case) . . . **$575.00**

Taurus PT 101 Auto Pistol
Same as the PT 100 except has micro-click rear sight adjustable for windage and elevation, three-dot combat-style. Introduced 1991.
Price: Blue **$522.00**
Price: Blue, Deluxe Shooter's Pak (extra magazine, case) **$549.00**
Price: Nickel **$564.00**
Price: Nickel, Deluxe Shooter's Pak (extra magazine, case) **$592.00**
Price: Stainless **$592.00**
Price: Stainless, Deluxe Shooter's Pak (extra magazine, case) . . . **$623.00**

TAURUS MODEL PT-908 AUTO PISTOL
Caliber: 9mm Para., 8-shot magazine.
Barrel: 3.8".
Weight: 30 oz. **Length:** 7.05" overall.
Stocks: Checkered black composition.
Sights: Drift-adjustable front and rear; three-dot combat.
Features: Double action, exposed hammer; manual ambidextrous hammer-drop; inertia firing pin; chamber loaded indicator. Introduced 1993. Imported by Taurus International.
Price: Blue **$473.00**
Price: Nickel **$511.00**
Price: Stainless steel **$538.00**

TAURUS MODEL PT58 AUTO PISTOL
Caliber: 380 ACP, 12-shot magazine.
Barrel: 4.01".
Weight: 30 oz. **Length:** 7.2" overall.
Stocks: Brazilian hardwood.
Sights: Integral blade on slide front, notch rear adjustable for windage. Three-dot system.
Features: Double action with exposed hammer; inertia firing pin. Introduced 1988. Imported by Taurus International.
Price: Blue **$423.00**
Price: Satin nickel **$454.00**
Price: Stainless steel **$481.00**

Taurus PT 99AF Auto Pistol
Similar to the PT-92 except has fully adjustable rear sight, smooth Brazilian walnut stocks and is available in stainless steel, polished blue or satin nickel. Introduced 1983.
Price: Blue **$512.00**
Price: Blue, Deluxe Shooter's Pak (extra magazine, case) **$540.00**
Price: Nickel **$554.00**
Price: Nickel, Deluxe Shooter's Pak (extra magazine, case) **$583.00**
Price: Stainless steel **$582.00**
Price: Stainless, Deluxe Shooter's Pak (extra magazine, case) . . . **$609.00**

Taurus PT92C

Taurus PT101

Taurus PT-908

WALTHER PP AUTO PISTOL

Caliber: 22 LR, 15-shot; 32 ACP, 380 ACP, 7-shot magazine.
Barrel: 3.86".
Weight: 23½ oz. **Length:** 6.7" overall.
Stocks: Checkered plastic.
Sights: Fixed, white markings.
Features: Double action; manual safety blocks firing pin and drops hammer; chamber loaded indicator on 32 and 380; extra finger rest magazine provided. Imported from Germany by Interarms.
Price: 22 LR **$948.00**
Price: 32 . . . . **$1,448.00**
Price: 380 . . . . **$1,492.00**
Price: Engraved models . . . . **On Request**

Walther PPK/S American Auto Pistol

Similar to Walther PP except made entirely in the United States. Has 3.27" barrel with 6.1" length overall. Introduced 1980.
Price: 380 ACP only **$627.00**
Price: As above, stainless **$627.00**

WALTHER P-38 AUTO PISTOL

Caliber: 9mm Para., 8-shot.
Barrel: 4¹⁵⁄₁₆".
Weight: 28 oz. **Length:** 8½" overall.
Stocks: Checkered plastic.
Sights: Fixed.
Features: Double action; safety blocks firing pin and drops hammer. Matte finish standard, polished blue, engraving and/or plating available. Imported from Germany by Interarms.
Price: **$1,000.00**
Price: Engraved models . . . . **On Request**

Walther P-5 Auto Pistol

Latest Walther design that uses the basic P-38 double-action mechanism. Caliber 9mm Para., barrel length 3½"; weight 28 oz., overall length 7".
Price: **$1,257.00**
Price: P-5 Compact **$1,257.00**

WALTHER MODEL TPH AUTO PISTOL

Caliber: 22 LR, 25 ACP, 6-shot magazine.
Barrel: 2¼".
Weight: 14 oz. **Length:** 5⅜" overall.
Stocks: Checkered black composition.
Sights: Blade front, rear drift-adjustable for windage.
Features: Made of stainless steel. Scaled-down version of the Walther PP/PPK series. Made in U.S. Introduced 1987. From Interarms.
Price: Blue or stainless steel, 22 or 25 . . . . **$473.00**

Walther P88 Compact

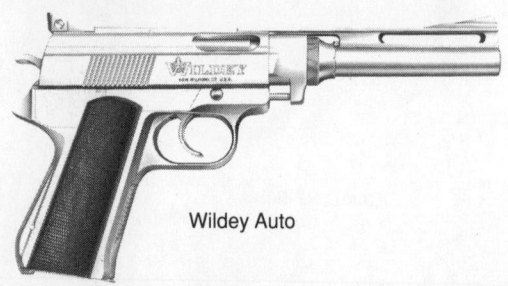

Wildey Auto

Walther PPK/S American

Walther PPK American Auto Pistol

Similar to Walther PPK/S except weighs 21 oz., has 6-shot capacity. Made in the U.S. Introduced 1986.
Price: Stainless, 380 ACP only **$627.00**
Price: Blue, 380 ACP only **$627.00**

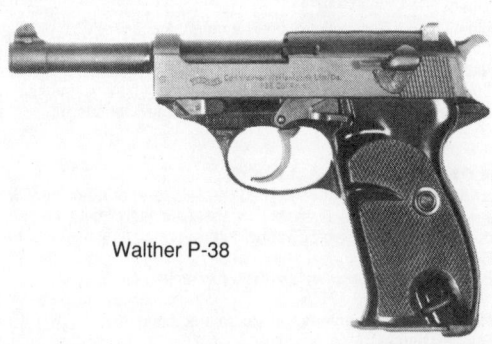

Walther P-38

Walther TPH

WALTHER P-88 AUTO PISTOL

Caliber: 9mm Para., 15-shot magazine.
Barrel: 4".
Weight: 31½ oz. **Length:** 7⅜" overall.
Stocks: Checkered black composition.
Sights: Blade front, rear adjustable for windage and elevation.
Features: Double action with ambidextrous decocking lever and magazine release; alloy frame; loaded chamber indicator; matte finish. Imported from Germany by Interarms.
Price: **$1,200.00**
Price: P-88 Compact (14-shot) **$1,200.00**

WILDEY AUTOMATIC PISTOL

Caliber: 10mm Wildey Mag., 11mm Wildey Mag., 30 Wildey Mag., 357 Peterbuilt, 45 Win. Mag., 475 Wildey Mag., 7-shot magazine.
Barrel: 5", 6", 7", 8", 10", 12", 14" (45 Win. Mag.); 8", 10", 12", 14" (all other cals.). Interchangeable.
Weight: 64 oz. (5" barrel). **Length:** 11" overall (7" barrel).
Stocks: Hardwood.
Sights: Ramp front (interchangeable blades optional), fully adjustable rear. Scope base available.
Features: Gas-operated action. Made of stainless steel. Has three-lug rotary bolt. Double or single action. Polished and matte finish. Made in U.S. by Wildey, Inc.
Price: . . . . **$1,175.00 to $1,495.00**

CAUTION: PRICES CHANGE, CHECK AT GUNSHOP.

Wilkinson "Sherry"

WILKINSON "SHERRY" AUTO PISTOL
Caliber: 22 LR, 8-shot magazine.
Barrel: 2⅛".
Weight: 9¼ oz. **Length:** 4⅜" overall.
Stocks: Checkered black plastic.
Sights: Fixed, groove.
Features: Cross-bolt safety locks the sear into the hammer. Available in all blue finish or blue slide and trigger with gold frame. Introduced 1985.
Price: $169.95

WILKINSON "LINDA" AUTO PISTOL
Caliber: 9mm Para., 31-shot magazine.
Barrel: 8⁵⁄₁₆".
Weight: 4 lbs., 13 oz. **Length:** 12¼" overall.
Stocks: Checkered black plastic pistol grip, maple forend.
Sights: Protected blade front, aperture rear.
Features: Fires from closed bolt. Semi-auto only. Straight blowback action. Cross-bolt safety. Removable barrel. From Wilkinson Arms.
Price: $412.00

HANDGUNS—COMPETITION HANDGUNS

Models specifically designed for classic competitive shooting sports.

Benelli MP90S

BENELLI MP90S MATCH PISTOL
Caliber: 22 Short, 22 LR, 32 S&W wadcutter, 5-shot magazine.
Barrel: 4.33".
Weight: 38.8 oz. **Length:** 11.81" overall.
Stocks: Stippled walnut match type with fully adjustable palm shelf; anatomically shaped.
Sights: Match type. Blade front, click-adjustable rear for windage and elevation.
Features: Fully adjustable trigger for pull and position, and is removable. Special internal weight box on sub-frame below barrel. Comes with loading tool, cleaning rods. Introduced 1993. Imported from Italy by European American Armory.
Price: $1,895.00

BF Single Shot

BF SINGLE SHOT PISTOL
Caliber: 22 LR, 357 Mag., 44 Mag., 7-30 Waters, 30-30 Win., 375 Win., 45-70; custom chamberings from 17 Rem. through 45-cal.
Barrel: 10", 10.75", 12", 15+".
Weight: 52 oz. **Length:** NA.
Stocks: Custom Herrett finger-groove grip and forend.
Sights: Undercut Patridge front, ½-MOA match-quality fully adjustable RPM Iron Sight rear; barrel or receiver mounting. Drilled and tapped for scope mounting.
Features: Rigid barrel/receiver; falling block action with short lock time; automatic ejection; air-gauged match barrels by Wilson or Douglas; matte black oxide finish standard, electroless nickel optional. Barrel has 11-degree recessed target crown. Introduced 1988. Made in U.S. by E.A. Brown Mfg.
Price: 10", no sights $499.95
Price: 10", RPM sights $564.95
Price: 10.75", no sights $529.95
Price: 10.75", RPM sights $594.95
Price: 12", no sights $562.95
Price: 12", RPM sights $627.95
Price: 15", no sights $592.95
Price: 15", RPM sights $658.95
Price: 10.75" Ultimate Silhouette (heavy barrel, special forend, RPM rear sight with hooded front, gold-plated trigger) $687.95

CONSULT **Shooter's Marketplace** Page 231, This Issue

BERETTA MODEL 89 TARGET PISTOL
Caliber: 22 LR, 8-shot magazine.
Barrel: 6"
Weight: 41 oz. **Length:** 9.5" overall.
Stocks: Target-type walnut with thumbrest.
Sights: Interchangeable blade front, fully adjustable rear.
Features: Single-action target pistol. Matte blue finish. Imported from Italy by Beretta U.S.A.
Price: $735.00

Beretta Model 89

BROWNING BUCK MARK SILHOUETTE

Caliber: 22 LR, 10-shot magazine.
Barrel: 9⅞".
Weight: 53 oz. **Length:** 14" overall.
Stocks: Smooth walnut stocks and forend, or finger-groove walnut.
Sights: Post-type hooded front adjustable for blade width and height; Pro Target rear fully adjustable for windage and elevation.
Features: Heavy barrel with .900" diameter; 12½" sight radius. Special sighting plane forms scope base. Introduced 1987. Made in U.S. From Browning.
Price: $394.95

Browning Buck Mark Target 5.5

Same as the Buck Mark Silhouette except has a 5½" barrel with .900" diameter. Has hooded sights mounted on a scope base that accepts an optical or reflex sight. Rear sight is a Browning fully adjustable Pro Target, front sight is an adjustable post that customizes to different widths, and can be adjusted for height. Contoured walnut grips with thumbrest, or finger-groove walnut. Matte blue finish. Overall length is 9⅝", weight is 35½ oz. Has 10-shot magazine. Introduced 1990. From Browning.
Price: $374.95
Price: Target 5.5 Gold (as above with gold anodized frame and top rib) $399.95

Browning Buck Mark Field 5.5

Same as the Target 5.5 except has hoodless ramp-style front sight and low profile rear sight. Matte blue finish, contoured or finger-groove walnut stocks. Introduced 1991.
Price: $374.95

Browning Buck Mark Target 5.5

Browning Buck Mark Unlimited Match

Same as the Buck Mark Silhouette except has 14" heavy barrel. Conforms to IHMSA 15" maximum sight radius rule. Introduced 1991.
Price: $469.95

COLT GOLD CUP NATIONAL MATCH MK IV/SERIES 80

Caliber: 45 ACP, 8-shot magazine.
Barrel: 5", with new design bushing.
Weight: 39 oz. **Length:** 8½".
Stocks: Rubber combat with silver-plated medallion.
Sights: Patridge-style front, Colt-Elliason rear adjustable for windage and elevation, sight radius 6¾".
Features: Arched or flat housing; wide, grooved trigger with adjustable stop; ribbed-top slide, hand fitted, with improved ejection port.
Price: Blue $885.95
Price: Stainless $948.95
Price: Bright stainless $1,018.95
Price: Delta Gold Cup (10mm, stainless) $975.95

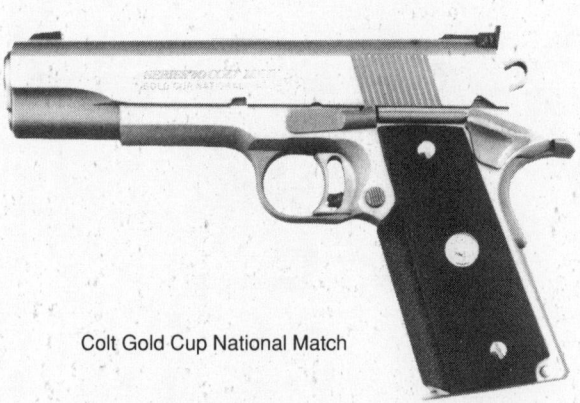
Colt Gold Cup National Match

COMPETITOR SINGLE SHOT PISTOL

Caliber: 22 LR through 50 Action Express, including belted magnums.
Barrel: 14" standard; 10.5" silhouette; 16" optional.
Weight: About 59 oz. (14" bbl.). **Length:** 15.12" overall.
Stocks: Ambidextrous; synthetic (standard) or laminated or natural wood.
Sights: Ramp front, adjustable rear.
Features: Rotary canon-type action cocks on opening; cammed ejector; interchangeable barrels, ejectors. Adjustable single stage trigger, sliding thumb safety and trigger safety. Matte blue finish. Introduced 1988. From Competitor Corp., Inc.
Price: 14", standard calibers, synthetic grip $364.90
Price: Extra barrels, from $132.95

E.A.A. EUROPEAN EA22T TARGET AUTO

Caliber: 22 LR, 12-shot.
Barrel: 6".
Weight: 40 oz. **Length:** 9.10" overall.
Stocks: Checkered walnut, with thumbrest.
Sights: Blade on ramp front, rear adjustable for windage and elevation.
Features: Blue finish. Finger-rest magazine. Imported by European American Armory Corp.
Price: $399.00

E.A.A. European EA22T

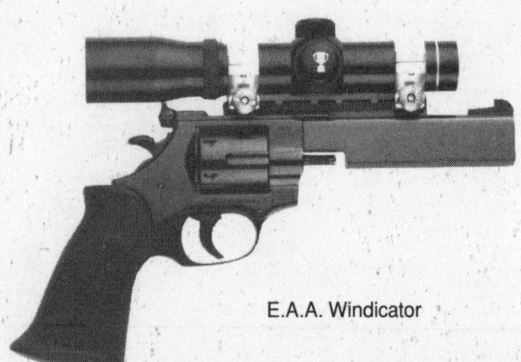
E.A.A. Windicator

E.A.A. WINDICATOR TARGET GRADE REVOLVERS

Caliber: 22 LR, 8-shot, 38 Special, 357 Mag., 6-shot.
Barrel: 6".
Weight: 50.2 oz. **Length:** 11.8" overall.
Stocks: Walnut, competition style.
Sights: Blade front with three interchangeable blades, fully adjustable rear.
Features: Adjustable trigger with trigger stop and trigger shoe; frame drilled and tapped for scope mount; target hammer. Comes with barrel weights, plastic carrying box. Introduced 1991. Imported from Germany by European American Armory.
Price: $499.00

CAUTION: PRICES CHANGE, CHECK AT GUNSHOP.

E.A.A. WITNESS GOLD TEAM AUTO

Caliber: 9mm Para., 9x21, 10mm Auto, 38 Super, 40 S&W, 45 ACP.
Barrel: 5.1".
Weight: 41.6 oz. **Length:** 9.6" overall.
Stocks: Checkered walnut, competition style.
Sights: Square post front, fully adjustable rear.
Features: Triple-chamber compensator; competition SA trigger; extended safety and magazine release; competition hammer; beveled magazine well; beavertail grip. Hand-fitted major components. Hard chrome finish. Match-grade barrel. From E.A.A. Custom Shop. Introduced 1992. From European American Armory.
Price: **$2,195.00**

E.A.A. Witness Gold Team

E.A.A. Witness Silver Team Auto

Similar to the Wittness Gold Team except has double-chamber compensator, paddle magazine release, checkered walnut grips, double-dip blue finish. Comes with Super Sight or drilled and tapped for scope mount. Built for the intermediate competition shooter. Introduced 1992. From European American Armory Custom Shop.
Price: 9mm Para., 9x21, 10mm Auto, 38 Super, 40 S&W, 45 ACP **$1,195.00**

ERMA ER MATCH REVOLVERS

Caliber: 22 LR, 32 S&W Long, 6-shot.
Barrel: 6".
Weight: 47.3 oz. **Length:** 11.2" overall.
Stocks: Stippled walnut, adjustable match-type.
Sights: Blade front, micrometer rear adjustable for windage and elevation.
Features: Polished blue finish. Introduced 1989. Imported from Germany by Precision Sales International.
Price: 22 LR or 32 S&W Long **$1,345.00**

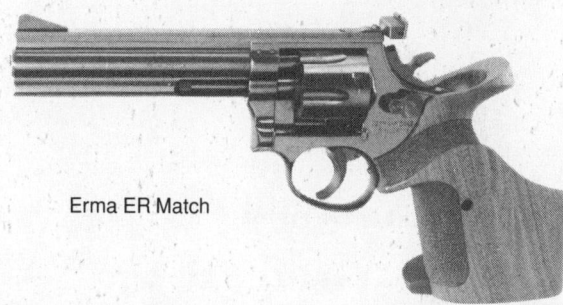

Erma ER Match

ERMA ESP 85A COMPETITION PISTOL

Caliber: 22 LR, 8-shot; 32 S&W, 5-shot magazine.
Barrel: 6".
Weight: 39 oz. **Length:** 10" overall.
Stocks: Match-type of stippled walnut; adjustable.
Sights: Interchangeable blade front, micrometer adjustable rear with interchangeable leaf.
Features: Five-way adjustable trigger; exposed hammer and separate firing pin block allow unlimited dry firing practice. Blue or matte chrome; right- or left-hand. Introduced 1988. Imported from Germany by Precision Sales International.
Price: 22 LR **$1,345.00**
Price: 22 LR, left-hand **$1,375.00**
Price: 22 LR, matte chrome **$1,568.00**
Price: 32 S&W **$1,400.00**

FREEDOM ARMS CASULL MODEL 252 SILHOUETTE

Caliber: 22 LR, 5-shot cylinder.
Barrel: 9.95".
Weight: 63 oz. **Length:** NA
Stocks: Black micarta, western style.
Sights: ⅛" Patridge front, Iron Sight Gun Works silhouette rear, click adjustable for windage and elevation.
Features: Stainless steel. Built on the 454 Casull frame. Two-point firing pin, lightened hammer for fast lock time. Trigger pull is 3 to 5 lbs. with pre-set overtravel screw. Introduced 1991. From Freedom Arms.
Price: Silhouette Class **$1,295.00**
Price: Extra fitted 22 WMR cylinder **$213.00**

Consult our Directory pages for the location of firms mentioned.

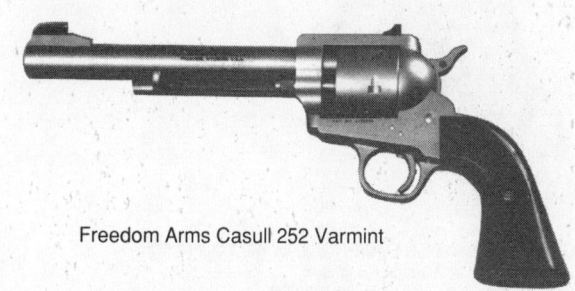

Freedom Arms Casull 252 Varmint

FAS 602 MATCH PISTOL

Caliber: 22 LR, 5-shot.
Barrel: 5.6".
Weight: 37 oz. **Length:** 11" overall.
Stocks: Walnut wraparound; sizes small, medium or large, or adjustable.
Sights: Match. Blade front, open notch rear fully adjustable for windage and elevation. Sight radius is 8.66".
Features: Line of sight is only 11/32" above centerline of bore; magazine is inserted from top; adjustable and removable trigger mechanism; single lever takedown. Full 5-year warranty. Imported from Italy by Nygord Precision Products.
Price: **$995.00**

FAS 601 Match Pistol

Similar to Model 602 except has different match stocks with adjustable palm shelf, 22 Short only for rapid fire shooting; weighs 40 oz., 5.6" bbl.; has gas ports through top of barrel and slide to reduce recoil; slightly different trigger and sear mechanisms. Imported from Italy by Nygord Precision Products.
Price: **$1,095.00**

FAS 603 Match Pistol

Similar to the FAS 602 except chambered for 32 S&W with 5-shot magazine; 5.3" barrel; 8.66" sight radius; overall length 11.0"; weighs 42.3 oz. Imported from Italy by Nygord Precision Products.
Price: **$1,050.00**

Freedom Arms Casull Model 252 Varmint

Similar to the Silhouette Class revolver except has 7.5" barrel, weighs 59 oz., has black and green laminated hardwood grips, and comes with brass bead front sight, express shallow V rear sight with windage and elevation adjustments. Introduced 1991. From Freedom Arms.
Price: Varmint Class **$1,248.00**
Price: Extra fitted 22 WMR cylinder **$213.00**

HAMMERLI MODEL 160/162 FREE PISTOLS

Caliber: 22 LR, single shot.
Barrel: 11.30".
Weight: 46.94 oz. **Length:** 17.52" overall.
Stocks: Walnut; full match style with adjustable palm shelf. Stippled surfaces.
Sights: Changeable blade front, open, fully adjustable match rear.
Features: Model 160 has mechanical set trigger; Model 162 has electronic trigger; both fully adjustable with provisions for dry firing. Introduced 1993. Imported from Switzerland by Hammerli Pistols USA.
Price: Model 160, about **$1,910.00**
Price: Model 162, about **$2,095.00**

HAMMERLI MODEL 208s PISTOL

Caliber: 22 LR, 8-shot magazine.
Barrel: 5.9".
Weight: 37.5 oz. **Length:** 10" overall.
Stocks: Walnut, target-type with thumbrest.
Sights: Blade front, open fully adjustable rear.
Features: Adjustable trigger, including length; interchangeable rear sight elements. Imported from Switzerland by Hammerli Pistols USA, Mandall Shooting Supplies.
Price: About **$1,695.00**

Hammerli 208s

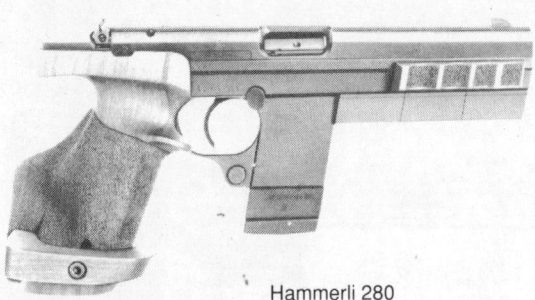

Hammerli 280

GAUCHER GP SILHOUETTE PISTOL

Caliber: 22 LR, single shot.
Barrel: 10".
Weight: 42.3 oz. **Length:** 15.5" overall.
Stocks: Stained hardwood.
Sights: Hooded post on ramp front, open rear adjustable for windage and elevation.
Features: Matte chrome barrel, blued bolt and sights. Other barrel lengths available on special order. Introduced 1991. Imported by Mandall Shooting Supplies.
Price: **$323.00**

Glock 17L

MITCHELL ARMS OLYMPIC I.S.U. AUTO PISTOL

Caliber: 22 Short, 10-shot magazine.
Barrel: 6.75" round tapered, with stabilizer.
Weight: 40 oz. **Length:** 11.25" overall.
Stocks: Checkered walnut with thumbrest.
Sights: Undercut ramp front, frame-mounted click adjustable square notch rear.
Features: Integral stabilizer with two removable weights. Trigger adjustable for pull and over-travel; blue finish; stippled front and backstraps; push-button barrel takedown. Announced 1992. From Mitchell Arms.
Price: **$599.00**

Ram-Line Exactor

HAMMERLI MODEL 280 TARGET PISTOL

Caliber: 22 LR, 6-shot; 32 S&W Long WC, 5-shot.
Barrel: 4.5".
Weight: 39.1 oz. (32). **Length:** 11.8" overall.
Stocks: Walnut match-type with stippling, adjustable palm shelf.
Sights: Match sights, micrometer adjustable; interchangeable elements.
Features: Has carbon-reinforced synthetic frame and bolt/barrel housing. Trigger is adjustable for pull weight, take-up weight, let-off, and length, and is interchangeable. Interchangeable metal or carbon fiber counterweights. Sight radius of 8.8". Comes with barrel weights, spare magazine, loading tool, cleaning rods. Introduced 1990. Imported from Switzerland by Hammerli Pistols USA and Mandall Shooting Supplies.
Price: 22-cal., about **$1,465.00**
Price: 32-cal., about **$1,650.00**

GLOCK 17L COMPETITION AUTO

Caliber: 9mm Para., 17-shot magazine.
Barrel: 6.02".
Weight: 23.3 oz. **Length:** 8.85" overall.
Stocks: Black polymer.
Sights: Blade front with white dot, fixed or adjustable rear.
Features: Polymer frame, steel slide; double-action trigger with "Safe Action" system; mechanical firing pin safety, drop safety; simple takedown without tools; locked breech, recoil operated action. Introduced 1989. Imported from Austria by Glock, Inc.
Price: **$768.25**

McMILLAN SIGNATURE JR. LONG RANGE PISTOL

Caliber: Any suitable caliber.
Barrel: To customer specs.
Weight: 5 lbs.
Stock: McMillan fiberglass.
Sights: None furnished; comes with scope rings.
Features: Right- or left-hand McMillan benchrest action of titanium or stainless steel; single shot or repeater. Comes with bipod. Introduced 1992. Made in U.S. by McMillan Gunworks, Inc.
Price: **$2,370.00**

McMILLAN WOLVERINE AUTO PISTOL

Caliber: 9mm Para., 10mm Auto, 38 Wadcutter, 38 Super, 45 Italian, 45 ACP.
Barrel: 6".
Weight: 45 oz. **Length:** 9.5" overall.
Stocks: Pachmayr rubber.
Sights: Blade front, fully adjustable rear; low profile.
Features: Integral compensator; round burr-style hammer; extended grip safety; checkered backstrap; skeletonized aluminum match trigger. Many finish options. Announced 1992. Made in U.S. by McMillan Gunworks, Inc.
Price: Combat or Competition Match **$1,500.00**

RAM-LINE EXACTOR TARGET PISTOL

Caliber: 22 LR, 15-shot magazine.
Barrel: 8.0".
Weight: 23 oz. **Length:** 12.3" overall.
Stocks: One-piece injection moulded in conventional contour; checkered side panels, ridged front and backstraps.
Sights: Ramp front with interchangeable .125" blade, rear adjustable for windage and elevation.
Features: Injection moulded grip frame, alloy receiver; hybrid composite barrel. Constant force sear spring gives 2.5-lb. trigger pull. Adapt-A-Barrel allows mounting weights, flashlight. Drilled and tapped receiver for scope mounting. Jewelled bolt. Comes with carrying case, test target. Introduced 1990. Made in U.S. by Ram-Line, Inc.
Price: **$279.97**

CAUTION: PRICES CHANGE, CHECK AT GUNSHOP.

Remington XP-100 Silhouette

Ruger Mark II Bull Barrel

Same gun as the Target Model except has 5½" or 10" heavy barrel (10" meets all IHMSA regulations). Weight with 5½" barrel is 42 oz., with 10" barrel, 52 oz.

Price: Blued (MK-512) **$310.50**
Price: Blued (MK-10) **$294.50**
Price: Stainless (KMK-10) **$373.00**
Price: Stainless (KMK-512) **$389.00**

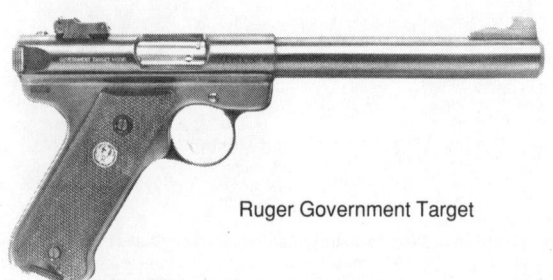

Ruger Government Target

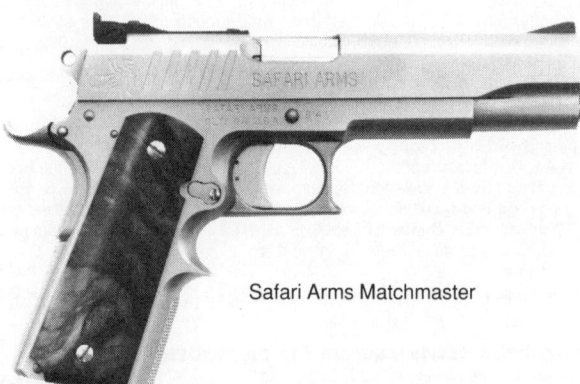

Safari Arms Matchmaster

SMITH & WESSON MODEL 41 TARGET

Caliber: 22 LR, 10-shot clip.
Barrel: 5½", 7".
Weight: 44 oz. **Length:** 9" overall.
Stocks: Checkered walnut with modified thumbrest, usable with either hand.
Sights: ⅛" Patridge on ramp base; S&W micro-click rear adjustable for windage and elevation.
Features: ⅜" wide, grooved trigger; adjustable trigger stop.
Price: S&W Bright Blue, satin matted top area **$753.00**

SMITH & WESSON MODEL 52 38 MASTER AUTO

Caliber: 38 Special (for mid-range W.C. with flush-seated bullet only), 5-shot magazine.
Barrel: 5".
Weight: 40 oz. with empty magazine. **Length:** 8⅝" overall.
Stocks: Checkered walnut.
Sights: ⅛" Patridge front, S&W micro-click rear adjustable for windage and elevation.
Features: Top sighting surfaces matte finished. Locked breech, moving barrel system; checked for 10-ring groups at 50 yards. Coin-adjustable sight screws. Dry-firing permissible if manual safety on.
Price: S&W Bright Blue **$908.00**

REMINGTON XP-100 SILHOUETTE PISTOL

Caliber: 7mm BR Rem., single shot.
Barrel: 10½".
Weight: 3⅞ lbs. **Length:** 17¼" overall.
Stock: American walnut.
Sights: Blade front, fully adjustable square notch rear.
Features: Mid-handle grip with scalloped contours for left- or right-handed shooters; match=type trigger; two-postion thumb safety. Matte blue finish.
Price: **$613.00**

RUGER MARK II TARGET MODEL AUTO PISTOL

Caliber: 22 LR, 10-shot magazine.
Barrel: 5¼", 6⅞".
Weight: 42 oz. **Length:** 11⅛" overall.
Stocks: Checkered hard plastic.
Sights: .125" blade front, micro-click rear, adjustable for windage and elevation. Sight radius 9⅜".
Features: Introduced 1982.
Price: Blued (MK-514, MK-678) **$310.50**
Price: Stainless (KMK-514, KMK-678) **$389.00**

Ruger Mark II Government Target Model

Same gun as the Mark II Target Model except has 6⅞" barrel, higher sights and is roll marked "Government Target Model" on the right side of the receiver below the rear sight. Identical in all aspects to the military model used for training U.S. armed forces except for markings. Comes with factory test target. Introduced 1987.
Price: Blued (MK-678G) **$356.50**
Price: Stainless (KMK-678G) **$427.29**

Ruger Stainless Government Competition Model 22 Pistol

Similar to the Mark II Government Target Model stainless pistol except has 6⅞" slab-sided barrel; the receiver top is drilled and tapped for a Ruger scope base adaptor of blued, chromemoly steel; comes with Ruger 1" stainless scope rings with integral bases for mounting a variety of optical sights; has checkered laminated grip panels with right-hand thumbrest. Has blued open sights with 9¼" radius. Overall length is 11⅛", weight 44 oz. Introduced 1991.
Price: KMK-678GC **$441.00**

SAFARI ARMS MATCHMASTER PISTOL

Caliber: 45 ACP, 7-shot magazine.
Barrel: 5"; National Match, stainless steel.
Weight: 38 oz. **Length:** 8.5" overall.
Stocks: Smooth walnut with etched scorpion logo.
Sights: Ramped blade front, rear adjustable for windage and elevation.
Features: Beavertail grip safety, extended safety, extended slide release, Commander-style hammer; throated, ported, tuned. Finishes: Parkerized matte black, or satin stainless steel. Available from Safari Arms, Inc.
Price: **$670.00**

Safari Arms Matchmaster Carrycomp I Pistol

Similar to the Matchmaster except has Wil Schueman-designed hybrid compensator system. Introduced 1993. Made in U.S. by Safari Arms, Inc.
Price: **$1,010.00**

Smith & Wesson Model 52

SPHINX AT-2000C COMPETITOR PISTOL

Caliber: 9mm Para., 9x21mm, 15-shot, 40 S&W, 11-shot.
Barrel: 5.31".
Weight: 40.56 oz. **Length:** 9.84" overall.
Stocks: Checkered neoprene.
Sights: Fully adjustable Bo-Mar or Tasco Pro-Point dot sight in Sphinx mount.
Features: Extended magazine release. Competition slide with dual-port compensated barrel. Two-tone finish only. Introduced 1993. Imported from Switzerland by Sile Distributors, Inc.
Price: With Bo-Mar sights (AT-2000CS) **$1,902.00**
Price: With Tasco Pro-Point and mount **$2,189.00**

Sphinx AT-2000GM Grand Master Pistol

Similar to the AT-2000C except has single-action-only trigger mechanism, squared trigger guard, extended beavertail grip, safety and magazine release; notched competition slide for easier cocking. Two-tone finish only. Has dual-port compensated barrel. Available with fully adjustable Bo-Mar sights or Tasco Pro-Point and Sphinx mount. Introduced 1993. Imported from Switzerland by Sile Distributors, Inc.
Price: With Bo-Mar sights (AT-2000GMS) **$2,893.00**
Price: With Tasco Pro-Point and mount (AT-2000GM) **$2,971.00**

SPRINGFIELD INC. 1911A1 BULLSEYE WADCUTTER PISTOL

Caliber: 45 ACP.
Barrel: 5".
Weight: 45 oz. **Length:** 8.59" overall (5" barrel).
Stocks: Checkered walnut.
Sights: Bo-Mar rib with undercut blade front, fully adjustable rear.
Features: Built for wadcutter loads only. Has full-length recoil spring guide rod, fitted Videki speed trigger with 3.5-lb. pull; match Commander hammer and sear; beavertail grip safety; lowered and flared ejection port; tuned extractor; fitted slide to frame; Shok Buff; beveled and polished magazine well; checkered front strap and steel mainspring housing (flat housing standard); polished and throated National Match barrel and bushing. Comes with two magazines with slam pads, plastic carrying case, test target. Introduced 1992. From Springfield Inc.
Price: . . . . **P.O.R.**

Springfield Inc. Entry Level Wadcutter Pistol

Similar to the 1911A1 Bullseye Wadcutter Pistol except has low-mounted Bo-Mar adjustable rear sight, undercut blade front; match throated barrel and bushing; polished feed ramp; lowered and flared ejection port; fitted Videki speed trigger with tuned 3.5-lb. pull; fitted slide to frame; Shok Buff; Pachmayr mainspring housing; Pachmayr grips. Comes with two magazines with slam pads, plastic carrying case, test target. Introduced 1992. From Springfield Inc.
Price: 45 ACP, blue, 5" only . . . . **P.O.R.**

Springfield Inc. 1911A1 N.M. Hardball Pistol

Similar to the 1911A1 Entry Level Wadcutter Pistol except has Bo-Mar adjustable rear sight with undercut front blade; fitted match Videki trigger with 4-lb. pull; fitted slide to frame; throated National Match barrel and bushing, polished feed ramp; Shok Buff; tuned extractor; Herrett walnut grips. Comes with one magazine, plastic carrying case, test target. Introduced 1992. From Springfield Inc.
Price: 45 ACP, blue . . . . **P.O.R.**

Springfield Inc. Trophy Master Expert Pistol

Similar to the 1911A1 Trophy Master Competition Pistol except has triple-chamber tapered cone compensator on match barrel with dovetailed front sight; lowered and flared ejection port; fully tuned for reliability. Comes with two magazines, plastic carrying case. Introduced 1992. From Springfield Inc.
Price: 45 ACP, Duotone finish . . . . **P.O.R.**

Sphinx AT-2000C Competitor

Sphinx AT-2000 GM Grand Master

Springfield Inc. Trophy Master Competition Pistol

Similar to the 1911A1 Entry Level Wadcutter Pistol except has brazed, serrated improved ramp front sight; extended ambidextrous thumb safety; match Commander hammer and sear; serrated rear slide; Pachmay flat mainspring housing; extended magazine release; beavertail grip safety; full-length recoil spring guide; Pachmayr wrap-around grips. Comes with two magazines with slam pads, plastic carrying case. Introduced 1992. From Springfield Inc.
Price: 45 ACP, blue . . . . **P.O.R.**

Springfield Inc. Trophy Master Distinguished Pistol

Has all the features of the 1911A1 Trophy Master Expert except is full-house pistol with Bo-Mar low-mounted adjustable rear sight; full-length recoil spring guide rod and recoil spring retainer; beveled and polished magazine well; Pachmayr grips. Duotone finish. Comes with five magazines with slam pads, plastic carrying case. From Springfield Inc.
Price: 45 ACP . . . . **P.O.R.**
Price: Trophy Master Distinguished Limited . . . . **P.O.R.**

THOMPSON/CENTER SUPER 14 CONTENDER

Caliber: 22 LR, 222 Rem., 223 Rem., 7mm TCU, 7-30 Waters, 30-30 Win., 35 Rem., 357 Rem. Maximum, 44 Mag., 10mm Auto, 445 Super Mag., single shot.
Barrel: 14".
Weight: 45 oz. **Length:** 17¼" overall.
Stocks: T/C "Competitor Grip" (walnut and rubber).
Sights: Fully adjustable target-type.
Features: Break-open action with auto safety. Interchangeable barrels for both rimfire and centerfire calibers. Introduced 1978.
Price: **$425.00**
Price: Extra barrels, blued **$200.00**

Thompson/Center Super 16 Contender

Same as the T/C Super 14 Contender except has 16¼" barrel. Rear sight can be mounted at mid-barrel position (10¾" radius) or moved to the rear (using scope mount position) for 14¾" radius. Overall length is 20¼". Comes with T/C Competitor Grip of walnut and rubber. Available in 22 LR, 22 WMR, 223 Rem., 7-30 Waters, 30-30 Win., 35 Rem., 44 Mag., 45-70 Gov't. Also available with 16" vent rib barrel with internal choke, caliber 45 Colt/410 shotshell.
Price: **$430.00**
Price: 45-70 Gov't **$435.00**
Price: Extra 16" barrels (blued) **$205.00**
Price: As above, 45-70 . . . . **$210.00**
Price: Super 16 Vent Rib (45-410) **$460.00**
Price: Extra vent rib barrel **$235.00**

Thompson/Center Super 14 Contender

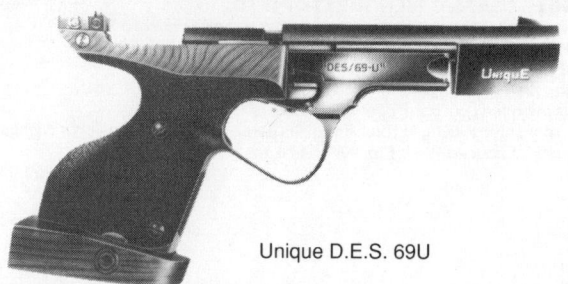

Unique D.E.S. 69U

Unique Model 2000-U

WALTHER GSP MATCH PISTOL
Caliber: 22 LR, 32 S&W wadcutter (GSP-C), 5-shot.
Barrel: 5¾".
Weight: 44.8 oz. (22 LR), 49.4 oz. (32). **Length:** 11.8" overall.
Stocks: Walnut, special hand-fitting design.
Sights: Fixed front, rear adjustable for windage and elevation.
Features: Available with either 2.2 lb. (1000 gm) or 3 lb. (1360 gm) trigger. Spare mag., bbl. weight, tools supplied in Match Pistol Kit. Imported from Germany by Interarms.
Price: GSP, with case **$1,843.00**
Price: GSP-C, with case **$2,545.00**
Price: 22 LR conversion unit for GSP-C (no trigger unit) . . . **$1,053.00**
Price: 22 Short conversion unit for GSP-C (with trigger unit) . . . **$1,495.00**
Price: 32 S&W conversion unit for GSP-C (no trigger unit) **$1,400.00**

Walther OSP Rapid-Fire Pistol
Similar to Model GSP except 22 Short only, stock has adjustable free-style hand rest.
Price: **$2,275.00**

WESSON FIREARMS MODEL 22 SILHOUETTE REVOLVER
Caliber: 22 LR, 6-shot.
Barrel: 10", regular vent or vent heavy.
Weight: 53 oz.
Stocks: Combat style.
Sights: Patridge-style front, .080" narrow notch rear.
Features: Single action only. Available in blue or stainless. Introduced 1989. From Wesson Firearms Co., Inc.
Price: Blue, regular vent **$459.72**
Price: Blue, vent heavy **$478.10**
Price: Stainless, regular vent **$488.84**
Price: Stainless, vent heavy **$516.40**

WESSON FIREARMS MODEL 40 SILHOUETTE
Caliber: 357 Maximum, 6-shot.
Barrel: 4", 6", 8", 10".
Weight: 64 oz. (8" bbl.). **Length:** 14.3" overall (8" bbl.).
Stocks: Smooth walnut, target-style.
Sights: ⅛" serrated front, fully adjustable rear.
Features: Meets criteria for IHMSA competition with 8" slotted barrel. Blue or stainless steel. Made in U.S. by Wesson Firearms Co., Inc.
Price: Blue, 4" **$488.00**
Price: Blue, 6" **$508.00**
Price: Blue, 8" **$550.94**
Price: Blue, 10" **$579.20**
Price: Stainless, 4" **$550.00**
Price: Stainless, 6" **$569.00**
Price: Stainless, 8" slotted **$571.57**
Price: Stainless, 10" **$651.16**

UNIQUE D.E.S. 32U RAPID FIRE MATCH
Caliber: 32 S&W Long wadcutter.
Barrel: 5.9".
Weight: 40.2 oz.
Stocks: Anatomically shaped, adjustable stippled French walnut.
Sights: Blade front, micrometer click rear.
Features: Trigger adjustable for weight and position; dry firing mechanism; slide stop catch. Optional sleeve weights. Introduced 1990. Imported from France by Nygord Precision Products.
Price: Right-hand, about **$1,295.00**
Price: Left-hand, about **$1,345.00**

UNIQUE D.E.S. 69U TARGET PISTOL
Caliber: 22 LR, 5-shot magazine.
Barrel: 5.91".
Weight: 35.3 oz. **Length:** 10.5" overall.
Stocks: French walnut target-style with thumbrest and adjustable shelf; hand-checkered panels.
Sights: Ramp front, micro. adj. rear mounted on frame; 8.66" sight radius.
Features: Meets U.I.T. standards. Comes with 260-gram barrel weight; 100, 150, 350-gram weights available. Fully adjustable match trigger; dry-firing safety device. Imported from France by Nygord Precision Products.
Price: Right-hand, about **$1,195.00**
Price: Left-hand, about **$1,245.00**

UNIQUE MODEL 2000-U MATCH PISTOL
Caliber: 22 Short, 5-shot magazine.
Barrel: 5.9".
Weight: 43 oz. **Length:** 11.3" overall.
Stocks: Anatomically shaped, adjustable, stippled French walnut.
Sights: Blade front, fully adjustable rear; 9.7" sight radius.
Features: Light alloy frame, steel slide and shock absorber; five barrel vents reduce recoil, three of which can be blocked; trigger adjustable for position and pull weight. Comes with 340-gram weight housing, 160-gram available. Introduced 1984. Imported from France by Nygord Precision Products.
Price: Right-hand, about **$1,350.00**
Price: Left-hand, about **$1,400.00**

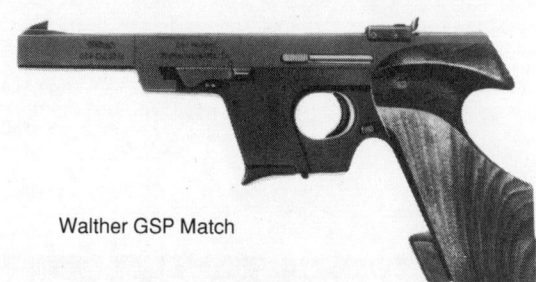

Walther GSP Match

Wesson Firearms Model 40

Wesson Firearms Model 445 Supermag Revolver
Similar size and weight as the Model 40 revolvers. Chambered for the 445 Supermag cartridge, a longer version of the 44 Magnum. Barrel lengths of 4", 6", 8", 10". Contact maker for complete price list. Introduced 1989. From Wesson Firearms Co., Inc.
Price: 4", vent heavy, blue **$539.00**
Price: As above, stainless **$615.00**
Price: 8", vent heavy, blue **$594.00**
Price: As above, stainless **$662.00**
Price: 10", vent heavy, blue **$615.00**
Price: As above, stainless **$683.00**
Price: 8", vent slotted, blue **$575.00**
Price: As above, stainless **$632.00**
Price: 10", vent slotted, blue **$597.00**
Price: As above, stainless **$657.00**

WESSON FIREARMS MODEL 322/7322 TARGET REVOLVER
Caliber: 32-20, 6-shot.
Barrel: 2.5", 4", 6", 8", standard, vent, vent heavy.
Weight: 43 oz. (6" VH). **Length:** 11.25" overall.
Stocks: Checkered walnut.
Sights: Red ramp interchangeable front, fully adjustable rear.
Features: Brigh blue or stainless. Introduced 1991. From Wesson Firearms Co., Inc.
Price: 6", blue $355.00
Price: 6", stainless $384.00
Price: 8", vent, blue $404.55
Price: 8", stainless $434.71
Price: 6", vent heavy, blue $412.20
Price: 6", vent heavy, stainless $441.32
Price: 8", vent heavy, blue $422.94
Price: 8", vent heavy, stainless $459.72

WICHITA INTERNATIONAL PISTOL
Caliber: 22 LR, 22 WMR, 32 H&R Mag., 357 Super Mag., 357 Mag., 7R, 7mm Super Mag., 7-30 Waters, 30-30 Win., single shot.
Barrel: 10", 10½", 14".
Weight: 3 lbs. 2 oz. (with 10", 10½" barrels).
Stocks: Walnut grip and forend.
Sights: Patridge front, adjustable rear. Wichita Multi-Range sight system optional.
Features: Made of stainless steel. Break-open action. Grip dimensions same as Colt 45 Auto. Drilled and tapped for furnished see-thru rings. Extra barrels are factory fitted. Introduced 1983. Available from Wichita Arms.
Price: International 10" $550.00
Price: International 14" $585.00
Price: Extra barrels, 10" $325.00
Price: Extra barrels, 14" $355.00

WICHITA SILHOUETTE PISTOL
Caliber: 308 Win. F.L., 7mm IHMSA, 7mm-308.
Barrel: 14 15/16".
Weight: 4½ lbs. **Length:** 21⅜" overall.
Stock: American walnut with oil finish. Glass bedded.
Sights: Wichita Multi-Range sight system.
Features: Comes with left-hand action with right-hand grip. Round receiver and barrel. Fluted bolt, flat bolt handle. Wichita adjustable trigger. Introduced 1979. From Wichita Arms.
Price: Center grip stock $1,150.00
Price: As above except with Rear Position Stock and target-type Lightpull trigger. $1,150.00

WICHITA CLASSIC SILHOUETTE PISTOL
Caliber: All standard calibers with maximum overall length of 2.800".
Barrel: 11¼".
Weight: 3 lbs., 15 oz.
Stocks: AAA American walnut with oil finish, checkered grip.
Sights: Hooded post front, open adjustable rear.
Features: Three locking lug bolt, three gas ports; completely adjustable Wichita trigger. Introduced 1981. From Wichita Arms.
Price: $2,950.00

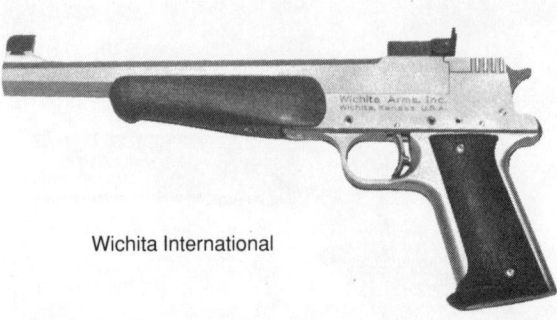

Wichita International

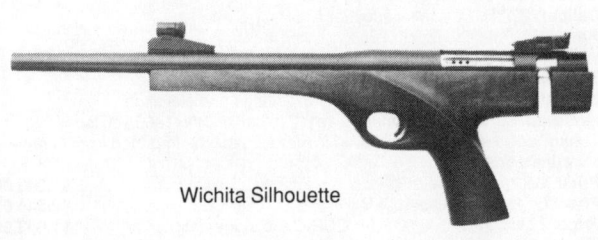

Wichita Silhouette

Includes models suitable for hunting and competitive courses for fire, both police and international.

CHARTER BULLDOG PUG REVOLVER
Caliber: 44 Spec., 5-shot.
Barrel: 2½".
Weight: 19½ oz. **Length:** 7" overall.
Stocks: Checkered walnut Bulldog.
Sights: Ramp-style front, fixed rear.
Features: Blue or stainless steel construction. Fully shrouded barrel. Reintroduced 1993. Made in U.S. by Charco, Inc.
Price: Blue $278.75
Price: Stainless steel $334.33

CHARTER OFF DUTY REVOLVER
Caliber: 22 LR, 6-shot, 38 Spec., 5-shot.
Barrel: 2".
Weight: 17 oz. (38 Spec.). **Length:** 6¼" overall.
Stocks: Checkered walnut.
Sights: Ramp-style front, fixed rear.
Features: Available in blue, stainless or electroless nickel. Fully shrouded barrel. Introduced 1993. Made in U.S. by Charco, Inc.
Price: Blue, 22 or 38 Spec. $208.83
Price: Stainless steel, 22 or 38 Spec. $267.83
Price: Electroless nickel, 22 or 38 Spec. $243.00

CHARTER POLICE UNDERCOVER REVOLVER
Caliber: 32 H&R Mag., 38 Spec., 6-shot.
Barrel: 2½".
Weight: 16 oz. (38 Spec.). **Length:** 6¼" overall.
Stocks: Checkered walnut.
Sights: Ramp-style front, fixed rear.
Features: Blue or stainless steel. Fully shrouded barrel. Reintroduced 1993. Made in U.S. by Charco, Inc.
Price: Blue $250.00
Price: Stainless $275.88

CAUTION: PRICES CHANGE, CHECK AT GUNSHOP.

COLT ANACONDA REVOLVER
Caliber: 44 Rem. Magnum, 45 Colt, 6-shot.
Barrel: 4", 6", 8".
Weight: 53 oz. (6" barrel). **Length:** 11⅝" overall.
Stocks: Combat-style black neoprene with finger grooves.
Sights: Red insert front, adjustable white outline rear.
Features: Stainless steel; full-length ejector rod housing; ventilated barrel rib; offset bolt notches in cylinder; wide spur hammer. Introduced 1990.
Price: **$584.95**
Price: 45 Colt, 6" barrel only **$584.95**

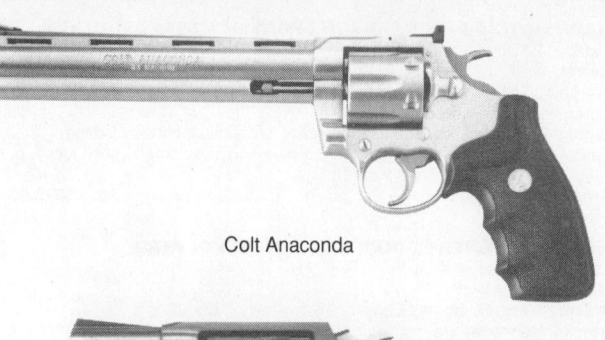

Colt Anaconda

COLT DETECTIVE SPECIAL REVOLVER
Caliber: 38 Special, 6-shot.
Barrel: 2".
Weight: 22 oz. **Length:** 6⅝" overall.
Stocks: Black composition.
Sights: Fixed. Ramp front, square notch rear.
Features: Glare-proof sights, grooved trigger, shrouded ejector rod. Colt blue finish. Reintroduced 1993.
Price: **$383.95**

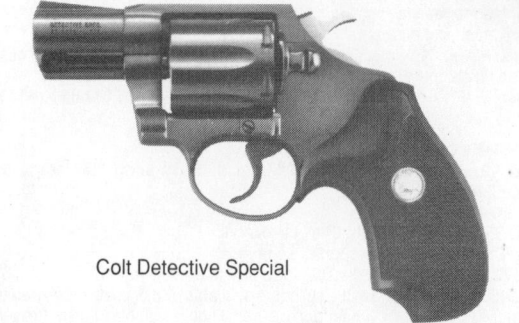

Colt Detective Special

COLT KING COBRA REVOLVER
Caliber: 357 Magnum, 6-shot.
Barrel: 4", 6".
Weight: 42 oz. (4" bbl.). **Length:** 9" overall (4" bbl.).
Stocks: Checkered rubber.
Sights: Red insert ramp front, adjustable white outline rear.
Features: Full-length contoured ejector rod housing, barrel rib. Introduced 1986.
Price: Stainless **$434.95**

COLT PYTHON REVOLVER
Caliber: 357 Magnum (handles all 38 Spec.), 6-shot.
Barrel: 4", 6" or 8", with ventilated rib.
Weight: 38 oz. (4" bbl.). **Length:** 9¼" (4" bbl.).
Stocks: Rubber wraparound.
Sights: ⅛" ramp front, adjustable notch rear.
Features: Ventilated rib; grooved, crisp trigger; swing-out cylinder; target hammer.
Price: Royal blue, 4", 6", 8" **$791.95**
Price: Stainless, 4", 6", 8" **$882.95**
Price: Bright stainless, 4", 6", 8" **$912.95**

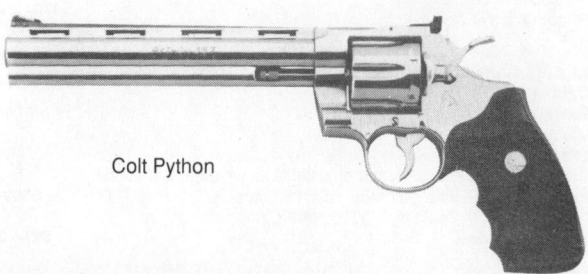

Colt Python

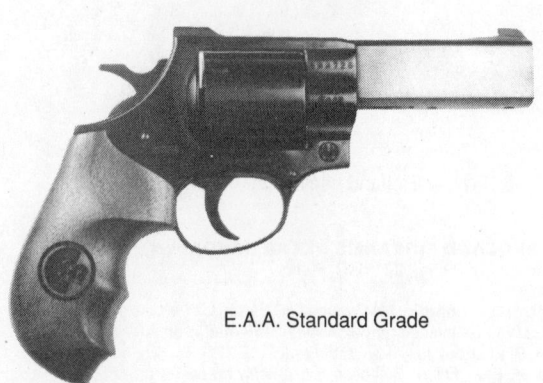

E.A.A. Standard Grade

E.A.A. STANDARD GRADE REVOLVERS
Caliber: 22 LR, 22 LR/22 WMR, 8-shot; 32 H&R Mag., 7-shot; 38 Special, 6-shot.
Barrel: 4", 6" (22 rimfire); 2" (32 H&R Mag.); 2", 4" (38 Special).
Weight: 38 oz. (22 rimfire, 4"). **Length:** 8.8" overall (4" bbl.).
Stocks: Hardwood with finger grooves.
Sights: Blade front, fixed or adjustable on rimfires; fixed only on 32, 38.
Features: Swing-out cylinder; hammer block safety; blue finish. Introduced 1991. Imported from Germany by European American Armory.
Price: 22 LR 4", 32 H&R 2", 38 Special 2" **$250.00**
Price: 38 Special, 4" **$275.00**
Price: 22 LR, 6" **$295.00**
Price: 22 LR/22 WMR combo, 4" **$350.00**
Price: As above, 6" **$375.00**

E.A.A. Tactical Grade Revolvers
Similar to the Standard Grade revolvers except in 38 Special only, 2" or 4" barrel, fixed sights. Compensator on 4", bobbed hammer (DA only) on 2" model. Introduced 1991. Imported from Germany by European American Armory.
Price: 2", bobbed hammer **$275.00**
Price: 4", compensator **$350.00**

ERMA ER-777 SPORTING REVOLVER
Caliber: 22 LR, 32 S&W, 357 Mag., 6-shot.
Barrel: 4", 5½".
Weight: 43.3 oz. **Length:** 9½" overall (4" barrel).
Stocks: Stippled walnut service-type.
Sights: Interchangeable blade front, micro-adjustable rear for windage and elevation.
Features: Polished blue finish. Adjustable trigger. Imported from Germany by Precision Sales Int'l. Introduced 1988.
Price: **$1,200.00**
Price: ER-772 (22 LR), ER-773 (32 S&W) **$1,265.00**

Erma ER-777

CAUTION: PRICES CHANGE, CHECK AT GUNSHOP.

HARRINGTON & RICHARDSON SPORTSMAN 999 REVOLVER
Caliber: 22 Short, Long, Long Rifle, 9-shot.
Barrel: 4", 6".
Weight: 30 oz. (4" barrel). **Length:** 8.5" overall.
Stocks: Walnut-finished hardwood.
Sights: Blade front adjustable for elevation, rear adjustable for windage.
Features: Top-break loading; polished blue finish; automatic shell ejection. Reintroduced 1992. From H&R 1871, Inc.
Price: $279.95

Harrington & Richardson Sportsman 999

HERITAGE SENTRY DOUBLE-ACTION REVOLVERS
Caliber: 38 Spec., 6-shot.
Barrel: 2", 4".
Weight: 23 oz. (2" barrel). **Length:** 6¼" overall (2" barrel).
Stocks: Magnum-style round butt; checkered plastic.
Sights: Ramp front, fixed rear.
Features: Pill-pin-type ejection; serrated hammer and trigger. Polished blue or chrome finish. Introduced 1993. Made in U.S. by Heritage Mfg., Inc.
Price: . . . . $104.95 to $129.95

Heritage Sentry

KORTH REVOLVER
Caliber: 22 LR, 22 Mag., 32 H&R Mag., 32 S&W Long, 357 Mag., 9mm Parabellum.
Barrel: 3", 4", 6".
Weight: 33 to 38 oz. **Length:** 8" to 11" overall.
Stocks: Checkered walnut, sport or combat.
Sights: Blade front, rear adjustable for windage and elevation.
Features: Four interchangeable cylinders available. Major parts machined from hammer-forged steel; cylinder gap of .002". High polish blue finish. Presentation models have gold trim. Imported from Germany by Mandall Shooting Supplies.
Price: With two cylinders $3,300.00

LLAMA COMANCHE REVOLVER
Caliber: 22 LR, 357 Mag.
Barrel: 4", 6".
Weight: 28 oz. **Length:** 9¼" (4" bbl.).
Stocks: Checkered walnut.
Sights: Fixed blade front, rear adjustable for windage and elevation.
Features: Ventilated rib, wide spur hammer. Satin chrome finish available. Imported from Spain by SGS Importers International., Inc.
Price: Blue finish $274.95

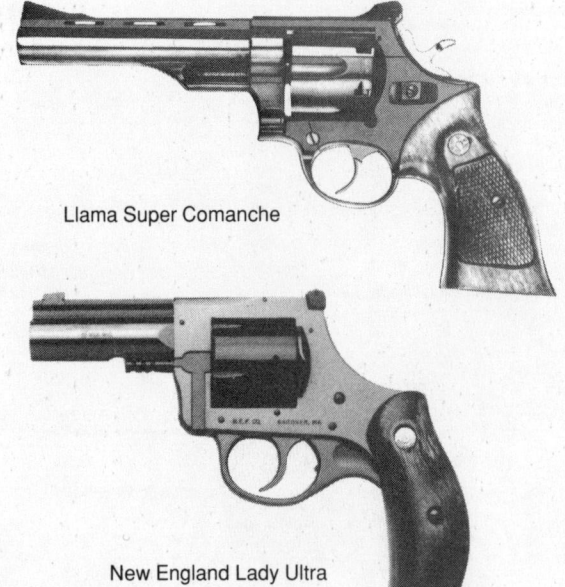

Llama Super Comanche

Llama Super Comanche Revolver
Similar to the Comanche except: large frame, 44 Mag. with 6", 8½" barrel, 6-shot cylinder; smooth, extra wide trigger; wide spur hammer; over-size walnut, target-style grips. Weight is 3 lbs., 2 oz. Blue finish only.
Price: 44 Mag. $366.95

NEW ENGLAND FIREARMS STANDARD REVOLVERS
Caliber: 22 LR, 9-shot; 32 H&R Mag., 5-shot.
Barrel: 2½", 4".
Weight: 26 oz. (22 LR, 2½"). **Length:** 8½" overall (4" bbl.).
Stocks: Walnut-finished American hardwood with NEF medallion.
Sights: Fixed.
Features: Choice of blue or nickel finish. Introduced 1988. From New England Firearms Co.
Price: 22 LR, 32 H&R Mag., blue $119.95
Price: 22 LR, 2½", 4", nickel, 32 H&R Mag. 2½" nickel $129.95

New England Lady Ultra

NEW ENGLAND FIREARMS LADY ULTRA REVOLVER
Caliber: 32 H&R Mag., 5-shot.
Barrel: 3".
Weight: 31 oz. **Length:** 7.25" overall.
Stocks: Walnut-finished hardwood with NEF medallion.
Sights: Blade front, fully adjustable rear.
Features: Swing-out cylinder; polished blue finish. Comes with lockable storage case. Introduced 1992. From New England Firearms Co.
Price: $149.95

NEW ENGLAND FIREARMS ULTRA REVOLVER
Caliber: 22 LR, 9-shot; 22 WMR, 6-shot.
Barrel: 4", 6".
Weight: 36 oz. **Length:** 10⅝" overall (6" barrel).
Stocks: Walnut-finished hardwood with NEF medallion.
Sights: Blade front, fully adjustable rear.
Features: Blue finish. Bull-style barrel with recessed muzzle, high "Lustre" blue/black finish. Introduced 1989. From New England Firearms.
Price: $149.95
Price: Ultra Mag 22 WMR $149.95

ROSSI MODEL 68 REVOLVER
Caliber: 38 Spec.
Barrel: 2", 3".
Weight: 22 oz.
Stocks: Checkered wood.
Sights: Ramp front, low profile adjustable rear.
Features: All-steel frame, thumb latch operated swing-out cylinder. Introduced 1978. Imported from Brazil by Interarms.
Price: 38, blue, 3" $227.00
Price: M68/2 (2" barrel), wood or rubber grips $238.00
Price: 3", nickel $232.00

ROSSI MODEL 88 STAINLESS REVOLVER
Caliber: 32 S&W, 38 Spec., 5-shot.
Barrel: 2", 3".
Weight: 22 oz. **Length:** 7.5" overall.
Stocks: Checkered wood, service-style.
Sights: Ramp front, square notch rear drift adjustable for windage.
Features: All metal parts except springs are of 440 stainless steel; matte finish; small frame for concealability. Introduced 1983. Imported from Brazil by Interarms.
Price: 3" barrel $262.00
Price: M88/2 (2" barrel), wood or rubber grips $275.00

CAUTION: PRICES CHANGE, CHECK AT GUNSHOP.

ROSSI MODEL 720 REVOLVER
Caliber: 44 Special, 5-shot.
Barrel: 3".
Weight: 27.5 oz. **Length:** 8" overall.
Stocks: Checkered rubber, combat style.
Sights: Red insert front on ramp, fully adjustable rear.
Features: All stainless steel construction; solid barrel rib; full ejector rod shroud. Introduced 1992. Imported from Brazil by Interarms.
Price: $332.00

Rossi 971 Comp

RUGER GP-100 REVOLVERS
Caliber: 38 Special, 357 Magnum, 6-shot.
Barrel: 3", 3" heavy, 4", 4" heavy, 6", 6" heavy.
Weight: 3" barrel—35 oz., 3" heavy barrel—36 oz., 4" barrel—37 oz., 4" heavy barrel—38 oz.
Sights: Fixed; adjustable on 4" heavy, 6", 6" heavy barrels.
Stocks: Ruger Santoprene Cushioned Grip with Goncalo Alves inserts.
Features: Uses action and frame incorporating improvements and features of both the Security-Six and Redhawk revolvers. Full length and short ejector shroud. Satin blue and stainless steel. Introduced 1988.
Price: GP-141 (357, 4" heavy, adj. sights, blue) $413.50
Price: GP-160 (357, 6", adj. sights, blue) $413.50
Price: GP-161 (357, 6" heavy, adj. sights, blue) $413.50
Price: GPF-330 (357, 3"), GPF-830 (38 Spec.) $397.00
Price: GPF-331 (357, 3" heavy), GPF-831 (38 Spec.) $397.00
Price: GPF-340 (357, 4"), GPF-840 (38 Spec.) $397.00
Price: GPF-341 (357, 4" heavy), GPF-841 (38 Spec.) $397.00
Price: KGP-141 (357, 4" heavy, adj. sights, stainless) $446.50
Price: KGP-160 (357, 6", adj. sights, stainless) $446.50
Price: KGP-161 (357, 6" heavy, adj. sights, stainless) $446.50
Price: KGPF-330 (357, 3", stainless), KGPF-830 (38 Spec.) $430.00
Price: KGPF-331 (357, 3" heavy, stainless), KGPF-831 (38 Spec.) . . $430.00
Price: KGPF-340 (357, 4", stainless), KGPF-840 (38 Spec.) $430.00
Price: KGPF-341 (357, 4" heavy, stainless), KGPF-841 (38 Spec.) . . $430.00

Consult our Directory pages for the location of firms mentioned.

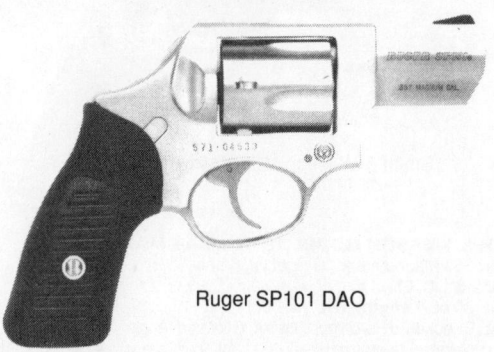

Ruger SP101 DAO

ROSSI MODEL 851 REVOLVER
Caliber: 38 Special, 6-shot.
Barrel: 3" or 4".
Weight: 27.5 oz. (3" bbl.). **Length:** 8" overall (3" bbl.).
Stocks: Checkered Brazilian hardwood.
Sights: Blade front with red insert, rear adjustable for windage.
Features: Medium-size frame; stainless steel construction; ventilated barrel rib. Introduced 1991. Imported from Brazil by Interarms.
Price: $280.00

ROSSI MODEL 971 REVOLVER
Caliber: 357 Mag., 6-shot.
Barrel: 2½", 4", 6", heavy.
Weight: 36 oz. **Length:** 9" overall.
Stocks: Checkered Brazilian hardwood. Stainless models have checkered, contoured rubber.
Sights: Blade front, fully adjustable rear.
Features: Full-length ejector rod shroud; matted sight rib; target-type trigger, wide checkered hammer spur. Introduced 1988. Imported from Brazil by Interarms.
Price: 4", stainless $315.00
Price: 6", stainless $315.00
Price: 4", blue $280.00
Price: 2½", stainless $320.00

Rossi Model 971 Comp Gun
Same as the Model 971 stainless except has 3¼" barrel with integral compensator. Overall length is 9", weight 32 oz. Has red insert front sight, fully adjustable rear. Checkered, contoured rubber grips. Introduced 1993. Imported from Brazil by Interarms.
Price: $320.00

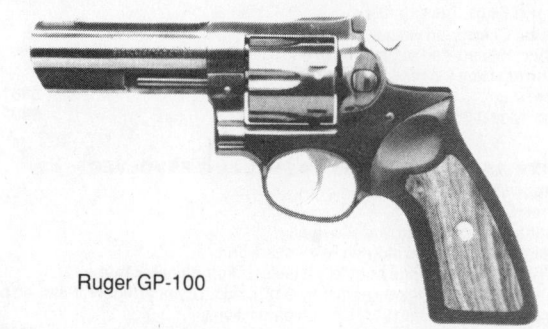

Ruger GP-100

RUGER SP101 REVOLVERS
Caliber: 22 LR, 32 H&R Mag., 6-shot, 9mm Para., 38 Special +P, 357 Mag., 5-shot.
Barrel: 2¼", 3¹⁄₁₆", 4".
Weight: 2¼"—25 oz.; 3¹⁄₁₆"—27 oz.
Sights: Adjustable on 22, 32, fixed on others.
Stocks: Ruger Santoprene Cushioned Grip with Xenoy inserts.
Features: Incorporates improvements and features found in the GP-100 revolvers into a compact, small frame, double-action revolver. Full-length ejector shroud. Stainless steel only. Introduced 1988.
Price: KSP-821 (2½", 38 Spec.) $408.00
Price: KSP-831 (3¹⁄₁₆", 38 Spec.) $408.00
Price: KSP-221 (2¼", 22 LR) $408.00
Price: KSP-240 (4", 22 LR) $408.00
Price: KSP-241 (4" heavy bbl., 22 LR) $408.00
Price: KSP-3231 (3¹⁄₁₆", 32 H&R) $408.00
Price: KSP-921 (2¼", 9mm Para.) $408.00
Price: KSP-931 (3¹⁄₁₆", 9mm Para.) $408.00
Price: KSP-321 (2¼", 357 Mag.) $408.00
Price: KSP-331 (3¹⁄₁₆", 357 Mag.) $408.00
Price: KSP-821L (2½", 38 Spec., double action only) $408.00
Price: KSP-32LXL (2½", 357 Mag., double action only) $408.00

Ruger SP101 Double-Action-Only Revolver
Similar to the standard SP101 except is double action only with no single-action sear notch. Has spurless hammer for snag-free handling, floating firing pin and Ruger's patented transfer bar safety system. Available with 2½" barrel in 38 Special +P and 357 Magnum only. Weight is 25½ oz., overall length 7.06". Natural brushed satin stainless steel. Introduced 1993.
Price: KSP821L (38 Spec.), KSP321XL (357 Mag.) $408.00

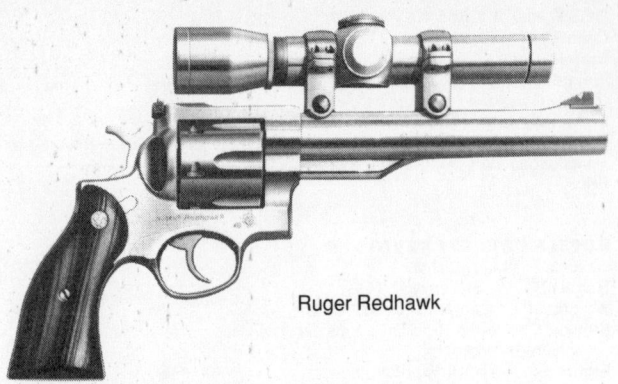

Ruger Redhawk

SMITH & WESSON MODEL 10 M&P REVOLVER
Caliber: 38 Special, 6-shot.
Barrel: 2", 4".
Weight: 30½ oz. **Length:** 9¼" overall.
Stocks: Checkered walnut, Service. Round or square butt.
Sights: Fixed, ramp front, square notch rear.
Price: Blue $361.00

Smith & Wesson Model 10 38 M&P Heavy Barrel
Same as regular M&P except: 4" heavy ribbed bbl. with ramp front sight, square rear, square butt, wgt. 33½ oz.
Price: Blue $361.00

SMITH & WESSON MODEL 13 H.B. M&P
Caliber: 357 and 38 Special, 6-shot.
Barrel: 3" or 4".
Weight: 34 oz. **Length:** 9⁵⁄₁₆" overall (4" bbl.).
Stocks: Checkered walnut, Service.
Sights: ⅛" serrated ramp front, fixed square notch rear.
Features: Heavy barrel, K-frame, square butt (4"), round butt (3").
Price: Blue $367.00
Price: Model 65, as above in stainless steel $402.00

SMITH & WESSON MODEL 14 FULL LUG REVOLVER
Caliber: 38 Special, 6-shot.
Barrel: 6", full lug.
Weight: 47 oz. **Length:** 11⅛" overall.
Stocks: Combat-style Morado with square butt.
Sights: Pinned Patridge front, adjustable micrometer click rear.
Features: Has .500" target hammer, .312" smooth combat trigger. Polished blue finish. Reintroduced 1991. Limited production.
Price: $442.00

SMITH & WESSON MODEL 15 COMBAT MASTERPIECE
Caliber: 38 Special, 6-shot.
Barrel: 4".
Weight: 32 oz. **Length:** 9⁵⁄₁₆" (4" bbl.).
Stocks: Checkered walnut. Grooved tangs.
Sights: Front, Baughman Quick Draw on ramp, micro-click rear, adjustable for windage and elevation.
Price: Blued $391.00

SMITH & WESSON MODEL 17 K-22 FULL LUG
Caliber: 22 LR, 6-shot.
Barrel: 4", 6".
Weight: 39 oz. (6" bbl.). **Length:** 11⅛" overall.
Stocks: Square butt Goncalo Alves, combat-style.
Sights: Patridge front with 6", serrated on 4", S&W micro-click rear adjustable for windage and elevation.
Features: Grooved tang, polished blue finish, full lug barrel. Introduced 1990.
Price: 4" $410.00
Price: 6" $449.00

Smith & Wesson Model 617 Full Lug Revolver
Similar to the Model 17 Full Lug except made of stainless steel. Has semi-target .375" hammer, .312" smooth combat trigger on 4"; 6"; 8⅜" available with either .312" smooth combat trigger or .400" serrated trigger and .500" target hammer. Introduced 1990.
Price: 4" $432.00
Price: 6", semi-target hammer, combat trigger $432.00
Price: 6", target hammer, target trigger $466.00
Price: 8⅜" $476.00

RUGER REDHAWK
Caliber: 44 Rem. Mag., 6-shot.
Barrel: 5½", 7½".
Weight: About 54 oz. (7½" bbl.). **Length:** 13" overall (7½" barrel).
Stocks: Square butt Goncalo Alves.
Sights: Interchangeable Patridge-type front, rear adjustable for windage and elevation.
Features: Stainless steel, brushed satin finish, or blued ordnance steel. Has a 9½" sight radius. Introduced 1979.
Price: Blued, 44 Mag., 5½", 7½" $458.50
Price: Blued, 44 Mag., 7½", with scope mount, rings $496.50
Price: Stainless, 44 Mag., 5½", 7½" $516.75
Price: Stainless, 44 Mag., 7½", with scope mount, rings $557.25

Ruger Super Redhawk Revolver
Similar to the standard Redhawk except has a heavy extended frame with the Ruger Integral Scope Mounting System on the wide topstrap. The wide hammer spur has been lowered for better scope clearance. Incorporates the mechanical design features and improvements of the GP-100. Choice of 7½" or 9½" barrel, both with ramp front sight base with Redhawk-style Interchangeable Insert sight blades, adjustable rear sight. Comes with Ruger "Cushioned Grip" panels of Santoprene with Goncalo Alves wood panels. Satin polished stainless steel, 44 Magnum only. Introduced 1987.
Price: KSRH-7 (7½"), KSRH-9 (9½") $589.00

Smith & Wesson Model 65

Smith & Wesson Model 15

Smith & Wesson Model 648 K-22 Masterpiece MRF
Similar to the Model 17 except made of stainless steel and chambered for 22 WMR cartridge. Available with 6" full-lug barrel only, combat-style square butt grips, combat trigger and semi-target hammer. Introduced 1991.
Price: $437.00

Smith & Wesson Model 19

SMITH & WESSON MODEL 19 COMBAT MAGNUM
Caliber: 357 Magnum and 38 Special, 6-shot.
Barrel: 2½", 4", 6".
Weight: 36 oz. **Length:** 9⁹⁄₁₆" (4" bbl.).
Stocks: Checkered hardwood, target. Grooved tangs.
Sights: Serrated ramp front 2½" or 4" bbl., red ramp on 4", 6" bbl., micro-click rear adjustable for windage and elevation.
Price: S&W Bright Blue, adj. sights . . . . $388.00 to $420.00

CAUTION: PRICES CHANGE, CHECK AT GUNSHOP.

SMITH & WESSON MODEL 27 357 MAGNUM REVOLVER
Caliber: 357 Magnum and 38 Special, 6-shot.
Barrel: 6".
Weight: 45½ oz. **Length:** 11⁵⁄₁₆" overall.
Stocks: Checkered walnut, Magna. Grooved tangs and trigger.
Sights: Serrated ramp front, micro-click rear, adjustable for windage and elevation.
Price: **$462.00**

Smith & Wesson Model 27

SMITH & WESSON MODEL 29 44 MAGNUM REVOLVER
Caliber: 44 Magnum, 6-shot.
Barrel: 6", 8³⁄₈".
Weight: 47 oz. (6" bbl.). **Length:** 11³⁄₈" overall (6" bbl.).
Stocks: Oversize target-type, checkered hardwood. Tangs and target trigger grooved, checkered target hammer.
Sights: ⅛" red ramp front, micro-click rear, adjustable for windage and elevation.
Price: S&W Bright Blue, 6", 8³⁄₈" **$526.00**
Price: Model 629 (stainless steel), 4", 6" **$557.00**
Price: Model 629, 8³⁄₈" barrel **$575.00**

Smith & Wesson Model 629

Smith & Wesson Model 29, 629 Classic Revolvers
Similar to the standard Model 29 and 629 except has full-lug 5", 6½" or 8³⁄₈" barrel; chamfered front of cylinder; interchangable red ramp front sight with adjustable white outline rear; Hogue square butt Santoprene grips with S&W monogram; the frame is drilled and tapped for scope mounting. Factory accurizing and endurance packages. Overall length with 5" barrel is 10½"; weight is 51 oz. Introduced 1990.
Price: Model 29 Classic, 5", 6½" **$567.00**
Price: As above, 8³⁄₈" **$578.00**
Price: Model 629 Classic (stainless), 5", 6½" **$598.00**
Price: As above, 8 ³⁄₈" **$617.00**

Smith & Wesson Model 629 Classic DX Revolver
Similar to the Classic Hunters except offered only with 6½" or 8³⁄₈" full-lug barrel; comes with five front sights: 50-yard red ramp; 50-yard black Patridge; 100-yard black Patridge with gold bead; 50-yard black ramp; and 50-yard black Patridge with white dot. Comes with combat-type grips with Carnuba wax finish and Hogue combat-style square butt conversion grip. Introduced 1991.
Price: Model 629 Classic DX, 6½" **$786.00**
Price: As above, 8³⁄₈" **$811.00**

Smith & Wesson Model 629 Classic DX

SMITH & WESSON MODEL 36, 37 CHIEFS SPECIAL & AIR-WEIGHT
Caliber: 38 Special, 5-shot.
Barrel: 2", 3".
Weight: 19½ oz. (2" bbl.); 13½ oz. (Airweight). **Length:** 6½" (2" bbl. and round butt).
Stocks: Checkered walnut, round or square butt.
Sights: Fixed, serrated ramp front, square notch rear.
Price: Blue, standard Model 36, 2" **$366.00**
Price: As above, 3" **$378.00**
Price: Blue, Airweight Model 37, 2" only **$394.00**
Price: As above, nickel, 2" only **$410.00**

Smith & Wesson Model 36LS LadySmith

Smith & Wesson Model 36LS, 60LS LadySmith
Similar to the standard Model 36. Available with 2" barrel. Comes with smooth, contoured rosewood grips with the S&W monogram. Has a speedloader cutout. Comes in a fitted carry/storage case. Introduced 1989.
Price: Model 36LS **$398.00**
Price: Model 60LS (as above except in stainless) **$450.00**

Smith & Wesson Model 60 Chiefs Special Stainless
Same as Model 36 except all stainless construction, 2" bbl. and round butt only.
Price: Stainless steel **$417.00**

Smith & Wesson Model 60 3" Full-Lug Revolver
Similar to the Model 60 Chief's Special except has 3" full-lug barrel, adjustable micrometer click black blade rear sight; rubber Uncle Mike's Custom Grade combat grips. Overall length 7½"; weight 24½ oz. Introduced 1991.
Price: **$443.00**

SMITH & WESSON MODEL 38 BODYGUARD
Caliber: 38 Special, 5-shot.
Barrel: 2".
Weight: 14½ oz. **Length:** 6⁵⁄₁₆" overall.
Stocks: Checkered walnut.
Sights: Fixed serrated ramp front, square notch rear.
Features: Alloy frame; internal hammer.
Price: Blue **$418.00**
Price: Nickel **$433.00**

Smith & Wesson Model 60 3"

CAUTION: PRICES CHANGE, CHECK AT GUNSHOP.

Smith & Wesson Model 49, 649 Bodyguard Revolvers
Same as Model 38 except steel construction, weight 20½ oz.
Price: Blued, Model 49 . . . . **$389.00**
Price: Stainless, Model 649 . . . . **$441.00**

SMITH & WESSON MODEL 57, 657 41 MAGNUM REVOLVERS
Caliber: 41 Magnum, 6-shot.
Barrel: 6".
Weight: 48 oz. **Length:** 11⅜" overall.
Stocks: Oversize target-type checkered Goncalo Alves.
Sights: ⅛" red ramp front, micro-click rear adjustable for windage and elevation.
Price: S&W Bright Blue, 6" **$466.00**
Price: Stainless, Model 657, 6" **$497.00**

SMITH & WESSON MODEL 63, 22/32 KIT GUN
Caliber: 22 LR, 6-shot.
Barrel: 2", 4".
Weight: 24 oz. (4" bbl.). **Length:** 8⅜" (4" bbl. and round butt).
Stocks: Checkered walnut, round or square butt.
Sights: Front, serrated ramp, micro-click rear, adjustable for windage and elevation.
Features: Stainless steel construction.
Price: 4" **$435.00**
Price: 2" round butt **$435.00**

SMITH & WESSON MODEL 65LS LADYSMITH
Caliber: 357 Magnum, 6-shot.
Barrel: 3".
Weight: 31 oz. **Length:** 7.94" overall.
Stocks: Rosewood, round butt.
Sights: Serrated ramp front, fixed notch rear.
Features: Stainless steel with frosted finish. Smooth combat trigger, service hammer, shrouded ejector rod. Comes with soft case. Introduced 1992.
Price: **$450.00**

SMITH & WESSON MODEL 66 STAINLESS COMBAT MAGNUM
Caliber: 357 Magnum and 38 Special, 6-shot.
Barrel: 2½", 4", 6".
Weight: 36 oz. **Length:** 9⁹⁄₁₆" overall.
Stocks: Checkered Goncalo Alves target.
Sights: Ramp front, micro-click rear adjustable for windage and elevation.
Features: Satin finish stainless steel.
Price: . . . . $437.00 to $447.00

SMITH & WESSON MODEL 586, 686 DISTINGUISHED COMBAT MAGNUMS
Caliber: 357 Magnum.
Barrel: 4", 6", full shroud.
Weight: 46 oz. (6"), 41 oz. (4").
Stocks: Goncalo Alves target-type with speed loader cutaway.
Sights: Baughman red ramp front, four-position click-adjustable front, S&W micrometer click rear (or fixed).
Features: Uses new L-frame, but takes all K-frame grips. Full-length ejector rod shroud. Smooth combat-type trigger, semi-target type hammer. Trigger stop on 6" models. Also available in stainless as Model 686. Introduced 1981.
Price: Model 586, blue, 4", from **$439.00**
Price: Model 686, stainless, from **$467.00**
Price: Model 686, 6", adjustable front sight **$499.00**
Price: Model 686, 8⅜" **$489.00**
Price: Model 686, 2½" **$457.00**

SMITH & WESSON MODEL 625-2 REVOLVER
Caliber: 45 ACP, 6-shot.
Barrel: 5".
Weight: 46 oz. **Length:** 11.375" overall.
Stocks: Pachmayr SK/GR Gripper rubber.
Sights: Patridge front on ramp, S&W micrometer click rear adjustable for windage and elevation.
Features: Stainless steel construction with .400" semi-target hammer, .312" smooth combat trigger; full lug barrel. Introduced 1989.
Price: **$562.00**

Smith & Wesson Model 442 Centennial Airweight
Similar to the Model 640 Centennial except has alloy frame giving weight of 15.8 oz. Chambered for 38 Special, 2" carbon steel barrel; carbon steel cylinder; concealed hammer; Uncle Mike's Custom Grade Santoprene grips. Fixed square notch rear sight, serrated ramp front. Introduced 1993.
Price: Blue **$418.00**
Price: Nickel **$433.00**

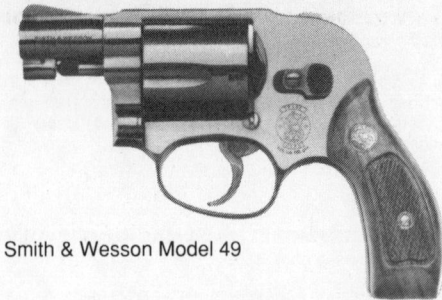

Smith & Wesson Model 49

SMITH & WESSON MODEL 64 STAINLESS M&P
Caliber: 38 Special, 6-shot.
Barrel: 2", 3", 4".
Weight: 34 oz. **Length:** 9⁵⁄₁₆" overall.
Stocks: Checkered walnut, Service style.
Sights: Fixed, ⅛" serrated ramp front, square notch rear.
Features: Satin finished stainless steel, square butt.
Price: **$402.00**

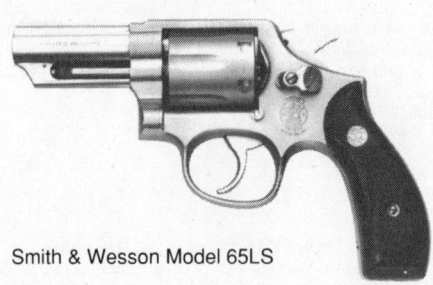

Smith & Wesson Model 65LS

Smith & Wesson Model 625-2

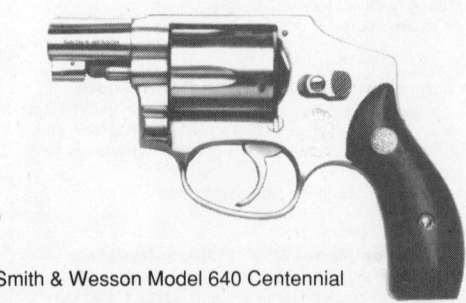

Smith & Wesson Model 640 Centennial

SMITH & WESSON MODEL 640, 940 CENTENNIAL
Caliber: 38 Special, 9mm Para., 5-shot.
Barrel: 2", 3".
Weight: 20 oz. **Length:** 6⁵⁄₁₆" overall.
Stocks: Round butt hardwood (M640), Santoprene (M940).
Sights: Serrated ramp front, fixed notch rear.
Features: Stainless steel version of the original Model 40 but without the grip safety. Fully concealed hammer, snag-proof smooth edges. Model 640 introduced 1990; Model 940 introduced 1991.
Price: Model 640 (38 Special) **$441.00**
Price: Model 940 (9mm Para., rubber grips) **$446.00**

Smith & Wesson Model 651

SMITH & WESSON MODEL 651 REVOLVER
Caliber: 22 WMR, 6-shot cylinder.
Barrel: 4".
Weight: 24½ oz. **Length:** 8¹¹/₁₆" overall.
Stocks: Checkered service Morado; square butt.
Sights: Red ramp front, adjustable micrometer click rear.
Features: Stainless steel construction with semi-target hammer, smooth combat trigger. Reintroduced 1991. Limited production.
Price: **$428.00**

> Consult our Directory pages for the location of firms mentioned.

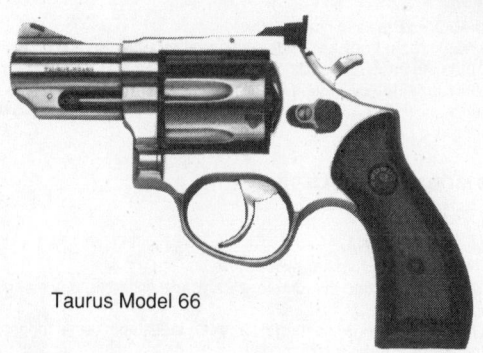

Taurus Model 66

SPORTARMS MODEL HS38S REVOLVER
Caliber: 38 Special, 6-shot.
Barrel: 3", 4".
Weight: 31.3 oz. **Length:** 8" overall (3" barrel).
Stocks: Checkered hardwood; round butt on 3" model, target-style on 4".
Sights: Blade front, adjustable rear.
Features: Polished blue finish; ventilated rib on 4" barrel. Made in Germany by Herbert Schmidt; Imported by Sportarms of Florida.
Price: About **$150.00**

TAURUS MODEL 66 REVOLVER
Caliber: 357 Magnum, 6-shot.
Barrel: 2.5", 4", 6".
Weight: 35 oz.(4" barrel).
Stocks: Checkered Brazilian hardwood.
Sights: Serrated ramp front, micro-click rear adjustable for windage and elevation. Red ramp front with white outline rear on stainlees models only.
Features: Wide target-type hammer spur, floating firing pin, heavy barrel with shrouded ejector rod. Introduced 1978. Imported by Taurus International.
Price: Blue, 2.5" **$292.00**
Price: Blue, 4", 6" **$290.00**
Price: Blue, 4", 6" compensated **$299.00**
Price: Stainless, 2.5" **$371.00**
Price: Stainless, 4", 6" **$368.00**
Price: Stainless, 4", 6" compensated **$375.00**

Taurus Model 65 Revolver
Same as the Model 66 except has fixed rear sight and ramp front. Available with 2.5" or 4" barrel only, round butt grip. Imported by Taurus International.
Price: Blue, 2.5" **$266.00**
Price: Blue, 4" **$264.00**
Price: Stainless, 2.5", 4" **$338.00**

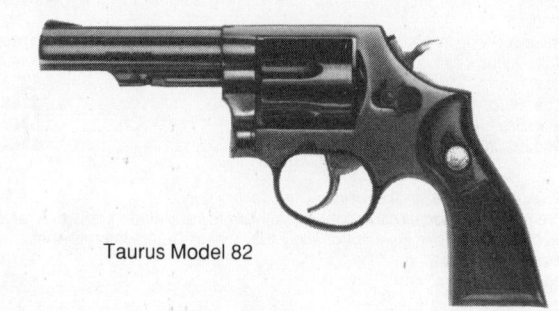

Taurus Model 82

TAURUS MODEL 80 STANDARD REVOLVER
Caliber: 38 Spec., 6-shot.
Barrel: 3" or 4".
Weight: 30 oz. (4" bbl.). **Length:** 9¼" overall (4" bbl.).
Stocks: Checkered Brazilian hardwood.
Sights: Serrated ramp front, square notch rear.
Features: Imported by Taurus International.
Price: Blue **$229.00**
Price: Stainless **$282.00**

TAURUS MODEL 82 HEAVY BARREL REVOLVER
Caliber: 38 Spec., 6-shot.
Barrel: 3" or 4", heavy.
Weight: 34 oz. (4" bbl.). **Length:** 9¼" overall (4" bbl.).
Stocks: Checkered Brazilian hardwood.
Sights: Serrated ramp front, square notch rear.
Features: Imported by Taurus International.
Price: Blue **$229.00**
Price: Stainless **$282.00**

TAURUS MODEL 85 REVOLVER
Caliber: 38 Spec., 5-shot.
Barrel: 2", 3".
Weight: 21 oz.
Stocks: Checkered Brazilian hardwood.
Sights: Ramp front, square notch rear.
Features: Blue, satin nickel finish or stainless steel. Introduced 1980. Imported by Taurus International.
Price: Blue, 2", 3" **$251.00**
Price: Stainless steel **$315.00**

TAURUS MODEL 83 REVOLVER
Caliber: 38 Spec., 6-shot.
Barrel: 4" only, heavy.
Weight: 34 oz.
Stocks: Oversize checkered Brazilian hardwood.
Sights: Ramp front, micro-click rear adjustable for windage and elevation.
Features: Blue or nickel finish. Introduced 1977. Imported by Taurus International.
Price: Blue **$241.00**
Price: Stainless **$292.00**

Taurus Model 85CH

Taurus Model 85CH Revolver
Same as the Model 85 except has 2" barrel only and concealed hammer. Smooth Brazilian hardwood stocks. Introduced 1991. Imported by Taurus International.
Price: Blue **$251.00**
Price: Stainless **$315.00**

TAURUS MODEL 86 REVOLVER

Caliber: 38 Spec., 6-shot.
Barrel: 6" only.
Weight: 34 oz. **Length:** 11¼" overall.
Stocks: Oversize target-type, checkered Brazilian hardwood.
Sights: Patridge front, micro-click rear adjustable for windage and elevation.
Features: Blue finish with non-reflective finish on barrel. Imported by Taurus International.
Price: $326.00

Taurus Model 86

TAURUS MODEL 94 REVOLVER

Caliber: 22 LR, 9-shot cylinder.
Barrel: 3", 4".
Weight: 25 oz.
Stocks: Checkered Brazilian hardwood.
Sights: Serrated ramp front, click-adjustable rear for windage and elevation.
Features: Floating firing pin, color case-hardened hammer and trigger. Introduced 1989. Imported by Taurus International.
Price: Blue $264.00
Price: Stainless $314.00

TAURUS MODEL 96 REVOLVER

Caliber: 22 LR, 6-shot.
Barrel: 6".
Weight: 34 oz. **Length:** NA.
Stocks: Checkered Brazilian hardwood.
Sights: Patridge-type front, micrometer click rear adjustable for windage and elevation.
Features: Heavy solid barrel rib; target hammer; adjustable target trigger. Blue only. Imported by Taurus International.
Price: $326.00

TAURUS MODEL 669 REVOLVER

Caliber: 357 Mag., 6-shot.
Barrel: 4", 6".
Weight: 37 oz., (4" bbl.).
Stocks: Checkered Brazilian hardwood.
Sights: Serrated ramp front, micro-click rear adjustable for windage and elevation.
Features: Wide target-type hammer, floating firing pin, full-length barrel shroud. Introduced 1988. Imported by Taurus International.
Price: Blue, 4", 6" $301.00
Price: Blue, 4", 6" compensated $308.00
Price: Stainless, 4", 6" $379.00
Price: Stainless, 4", 6" compensated $386.00

Taurus Model 689 Revolver

Same as the Model 669 except has full-length ventilated barrel rib. Available in blue or stainless steel. Introduced 1990. From Taurus International.
Price: Blue, 4" or 6" $313.00
Price: Stainless, 4" or 6" $392.00

TAURUS MODEL 761 REVOLVER

Caliber: 32 H&R Magnum, 6-shot.
Barrel: 6", heavy, solid rib.
Weight: 34 oz.
Stocks: Checkered Brazilian hardwood.
Sights: Patridge-type front, micro-click rear adjustable for windage and elevation.
Features: Target hammer, adjustable target trigger. Blue only. Introduced 1991. Imported by Taurus International.
Price: $326.00

Taurus Model 741 Revolver

Same as the Model 761 except with 3" or 4" heavy barrel only, serrated ramp front sight, micro click rear adjustable for windage and elevation. Introduced 1991. Imported by Taurus International.
Price: Blue, 3", 4" $254.00
Price: Stainless, 3", 4" $342.00

TAURUS MODEL 941 REVOLVER

Caliber: 22 WMR, 8-shot.
Barrel: 3", 4".
Weight: 27.5 oz. (4" barrel). **Length:** NA.
Stocks: Checkered Brazilian hardwood.
Sights: Serrated ramp front, rear adjustable for windage and elevation.
Features: Solid rib heavy barrel with full-length ejector rod shroud. Blue or stainless steel. Introduced 1992. Imported by Taurus International.
Price: Blue $290.00
Price: Stainless $346.00

TAURUS MODEL 441/431 REVOLVERS

Caliber: 44 Special, 5-shot.
Barrel: 3", 4", 6".
Weight: 40.4 oz. (6" barrel). **Length:** NA.
Stocks: Checkered Brazilian hardwood.
Sights: Serrated ramp front, micrometer click rear adjustable for windage and elevation.
Features: Heavy barrel with solid rib and full-length ejector shroud. Introduced 1992. Imported by Taurus International.
Price: Blue, 3", 4", 6" $307.00
Price: Stainless, 3", 4", 6" $386.00
Price: Model 431 (fixed sights), blue $281.00
Price: Model 431 (fixed sights), stainless $351.00

Taurus Model 761

Taurus Model 741

Taurus Model 941

THUNDER FIVE REVOLVER
Caliber: 45 Colt/410 shotshell, 2" and 3"; 5-shot cylinder.
Barrel: 2".
Weight: 48 oz. **Length:** 9" overall.
Stocks: Pachmayr checkered rubber.
Sights: Fixed.
Features: Double action with ambidextrous hammer-block safety; squared trigger guard; internal draw bar safety. Made of chrome moly steel, with matte blue finish. Announced 1991. From Tapco, Inc.
Price: $379.00

WESSON FIREARMS MODEL 8 & MODEL 14
Caliber: 38 Special (Model 8-2); 357 (14-2), both 6-shot.
Barrel: 2½", 4", 6", 8"; interchangeable.
Weight: 30 oz. (2½"). **Length:** 9¼" overall (4" bbl.).
Stocks: Checkered, interchangeable.
Sights: ⅛" serrated front, fixed rear.
Features: Interchangeable barrels and grips; smooth, wide trigger; wide hammer spur with short double-action travel. Available in stainless or Brite blue. Contact Wesson Firearms for complete price list.
Price: Model 8-2, 2½", blue $267.00
Price: As above except in stainless $311.00
Price: Model 714-2 Pistol Pac, stainless $522.00

Wesson Firearms Model 9-2, 15-2 & 32M Revolvers
Same as Models 8-2 and 14-2 except they have adjustable sight. Model 9-2 chambered for 38 Special, Model 15-2 for 357 Magnum. Model 32M is chambered for 32 H&R Mag. Same specs and prices as for 15-2 guns. Available in blue or stainless. Contact Wesson Firearms for complete price list.
Price: Model 9-2 or 15-2, 2½", blue $338.00
Price: As above except in stainless $366.00

Wesson Firearms Model 15 Gold Series
Similar to the Model 15 except has smoother action to reduce DA pull to 8-10 lbs.; comes with either 6" or 8" vent heavy slotted barrel shroud with bright blue barrel. Shroud is stamped "Gold Series" with the Wesson signature engraved and gold filled. Hammer and trigger are polished bright; rosewood grips. New sights with orange dot Patridge front, white triangle on rear blade. Introduced 1989.
Price: 6" . . . . NA
Price: 8" . . . . NA

WESSON FIREARMS MODEL 22 REVOLVER
Caliber: 22 LR, 22 WMR, 6-shot.
Barrel: 2½", 4", 6", 8"; interchangeable.
Weight: 36 oz. (2½"), 44 oz. (6"). **Length:** 9¼" overall (4" barrel).
Stocks: Checkered; undercover, service or over-size target.
Sights: ⅛" serrated, interchangeable front, white outline rear adjustable for windage and elevation.
Features: Built on the same frame as the Wesson 357; smooth, wide trigger with over-travel adjustment, wide spur hammer, with short double-action travel. Available in Brite blue or stainless steel. Contact Wesson Firearms for complete price list.
Price: 2½" bbl., blue $349.00
Price: As above, stainless $391.00
Price: With 4", vent. rib, blue $357.00
Price: As above, stainless $399.00
Price: Stainless Pistol Pac, 22 LR, blue $637.00

Wesson Model 32M

WESSON FIREARMS MODEL 41V, 44V, 45V REVOLVERS
Caliber: 41 Mag., 44 Mag., 45 Colt, 6-shot.
Barrel: 4", 6", 8", 10"; interchangeable.
Weight: 48 oz. (4"). **Length:** 12" overall (6" bbl.).
Stocks: Smooth.
Sights: ⅛" serrated front, white outline rear adjustable for windage and elevation.
Features: Available in blue or stainless steel. Smooth, wide trigger with adjustable over-travel; wide hammer spur. Available in Pistol Pac set also. Contact Wesson Firearms for complete price list.
Price: 41 Mag., 4", vent $433.55
Price: As above except in stainless $508.30
Price: 44 Mag., 4", blue $433.55
Price: As above except in stainless $508.30
Price: 45 Colt, 4", vent $433.55
Price: As above except in stainless $508.30

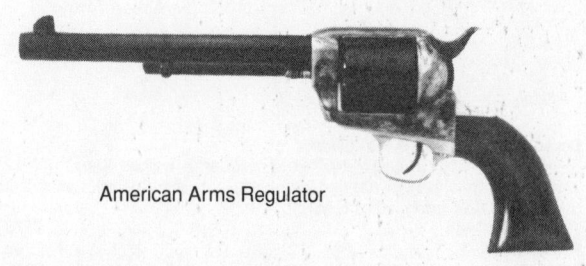

Wesson Model 738P

WESSON FIREARMS MODEL 738P REVOLVER
Caliber: 38 Special +P, 5-shot.
Barrel: 2".
Weight: 24.6 oz. **Length:** 6.5" overall.
Stocks: Pauferro wood or rubber.
Sights: Blade front, fixed notch rear.
Features: Designed for +P ammunition. Stainless steel construction. Introduced 1992. Made in U.S. by Wesson Firearms Co., Inc.
Price: $270.00

HANDGUNS—SINGLE-ACTION REVOLVERS

Both classic six-shooters and modern adaptations for hunting and sport.

AMERICAN ARMS REGULATOR SINGLE ACTIONS
Caliber: 357 Mag. 44-40, 45 Colt.
Barrel: 4¾", 5½", 7½".
Weight: 32 oz. (4¾" barrel) **Length:** 8⅛" overall (4¾" barrel).
Stocks: Smooth walnut.
Sights: Blade front, groove rear.
Features: Blued barrel and cylinder, brass trigger guard and backstrap. Introduced 1992. Imported from Italy by American Arms, Inc.
Price: Regulator, single cylinder $305.00
Price: Regulator, dual cylinder (44-40/44 Spec. or 45 Colt/45 ACP) . $349.00

American Arms Buckhorn Single Action
Similar to the Regulator single action except chambered for 44 Magnum. Available with 4¾", 6" or 7½" barrel. Overall length 11¾", weight is 44 oz. with 6" barrel. Introduced 1993. Imported from Italy by American Arms, Inc.
Price: $320.00

American Arms Regulator

CENTURY GUN DIST. MODEL 100 SINGLE ACTION
Caliber: 30-30, 375 Win., 444 Marlin, 45-70, 50-70.
Barrel: 6½" (standard), 8", 10", 12".
Weight: 6 lbs. (loaded). **Length:** 15" overall (8" bbl.).
Stocks: Smooth walnut.
Sights: Ramp front, Millett adjustable square notch rear.
Features: Highly polished high tensile strength manganese bronze frame, blue cylinder and barrel; coil spring trigger mechanism. Calibers other than 45-70 start at $1,500.00. Contact maker for full price information. Introduced 1975. Made in U.S. From Century Gun Dist., Inc.
Price: 6½" barrel, 45-70 . . . . $1,250.00

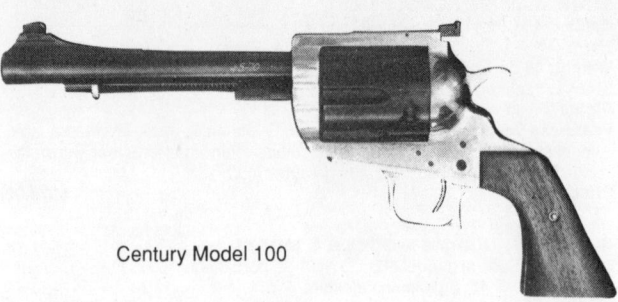

Century Model 100

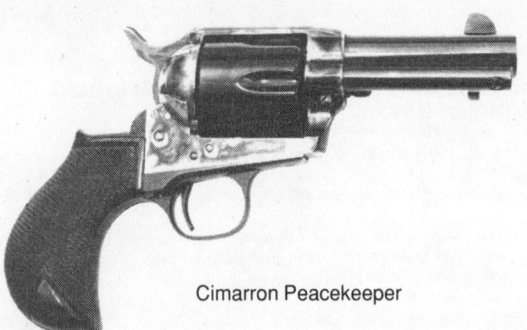

Cimarron Peacekeeper

CIMARRON PEACEKEEPER REVOLVER
Caliber: 357 Mag., 44 WCF, 44 Spec., 45 Colt, 6-shot.
Barrel: 3½", 4¾", with ejector.
Weight: 38 oz. (3$E1/2" barrel). **Length:** NA.
Stocks: Hand-checkered walnut.
Sights: Blade front, notch rear.
Features: Thunderer grip; color case-hardened frame with balance blued, or nickel finish. Introduced 1993. Imported by Cimarron Arms.
Price: Color case-hardened $459.00
Price: Nickeled $559.00

CIMARRON U.S. CAVALRY MODEL SINGLE ACTION
Caliber: 45 Colt.
Barrel: 7½".
Weight: 42 oz. **Length:** 13½" overall.
Stocks: Walnut.
Sights: Fixed.
Features: Has "A.P. Casey" markings; "U.S." plus patent dates on frame, serial number on backstrap, trigger guard, frame and cylinder, "APC" cartouche on left grip; color case-hardened frame and hammer, rest charcoal blue. Exact copy of the original. Imported by Cimarron Arms.
Price: $459.00

Cimarron Artillery Model Single Action
Similar to the U.S. Cavalry model except has 5½" barrel, weighs 39 oz., and is 11½" overall. U.S. markings and cartouche, case-hardened frame and hammer; 45 Colt only.
Price: $459.00

CIMARRON 1873 PEACEMAKER REPRO
Caliber: 22 LR, 22 WMR, 38 WCF, 357 Mag., 44 WCF, 44 Spec., 45 Colt.
Barrel: 4¾", 5½", 7½".
Weight: 39 oz. **Length:** 10" overall (4" barrel).
Stocks: Walnut.
Sights: Blade front, fixed or adjustable rear.
Features: Uses "old model" blackpowder frame with "Bullseye" ejector or New Model frame. Imported by Cimarron Arms.
Price: Peacemaker, 4¾" barrel $429.00
Price: Frontier Six Shooter, 5½" barrel $429.00
Price: Single Action Army, 7½" barrel $429.00

Cimarron 1873 Peacemaker

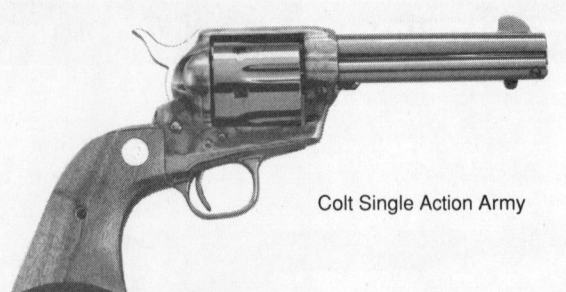

Colt Single Action Army

COLT SINGLE ACTION ARMY REVOLVER
Caliber: 44-40, 45 Colt, 6-shot.
Barrel: 4¾", 5½", 7½".
Weight: 40 oz. (4¾" barrel). **Length:** 10¼" overall (4¾" barrel).
Stocks: American walnut.
Sights: Blade front, notch rear.
Features: Available in full nickel finish with nickel grip medallions, or Royal Blue with color case-hardened frame, gold grip medallions. Reintroduced 1992.
Price: $1,273.95

DAKOTA 1875 OUTLAW REVOLVER
Caliber: 357, 44-40, 45 Colt.
Barrel: 7½".
Weight: 46 oz. **Length:** 13½" overall.
Stocks: Smooth walnut.
Sights: Blade front, fixed groove rear.
Features: Authentic copy of 1875 Remington with firing pin in hammer; color case-hardened frame, blue cylinder, barrel, steel backstrap and brass trigger guard. Also available in nickel, factory engraved. Imported by E.M.F.
Price: All calibers $465.00
Price: Nickel $550.00
Price: Engraved $600.00
Price: Engraved Nickel $710.00

Dakota 1890 Police Revolver
Similar to the 1875 Outlaw except has 5½" barrel, weighs 40 oz., with 12½" overall length. Has lanyard ring in butt. No web under barrel. Calibers 357, 44-40, 45 Colt. Imported by E.M.F.
Price: All calibers $470.00
Price: Nickel $560.00
Price: Engraved $620.00
Price: Engraved nickel $725.00

CAUTION: PRICES CHANGE, CHECK AT GUNSHOP.

E.A.A. BIG BORE BOUNTY HUNTER SA REVOLVERS
Caliber: 357 Mag., 41 Mag., 44-40, 44 Mag., 45 Colt, 6-shot.
Barrel: 4⅝", 5½", 7½".
Weight: 2.5 lbs. **Length:** 11" overall (5" barrel).
Stocks: Smooth walnut.
Sights: Blade front, grooved topstrap rear.
Features: Transfer bar safety; three position hammer; hammer forged barrel. Introduced 1992. Imported by European American Armory.
Price: Blue **$425.00**
Price: Color case-hardened frame **$440.00**
Price: Blue with gold-plated grip frame **$440.00**
Price: Chrome-plated **$475.00**

E.A.A. Big Bore Bounty Hunter

E.A.A. BOUNTY HUNTER REVOLVER
Caliber: 22 LR, 22 WMR, 6-shot cylinder.
Barrel: 4¾", 6", 9".
Weight: 32 oz. **Length:** 10" overall (4¾" barrel).
Stocks: European hardwood.
Sights: Blade front, rear adjustable for windage.
Features: Available in blue or blue/gold finish. Introduced 1991. From European American Armory Corp.
Price: 4¾", blue **$115.00**
Price: 4¾", blue, 22 LR/22 WMR combo **$135.00**
Price: 4¾", blue/gold, 22 LR/22 WMR combo **$145.00**
Price: 6", blue, 22 LR/22 WMR combo **$140.00**
Price: 6", blue/gold, 22 LR/22 WMR combo **$150.00**
Price: 9", blue, 22 LR/22 WMR combo **$155.00**
Price: 9", blue/gold, 22 LR/22 WMR combo **$165.00**

E.A.A. Bounty Hunter

FREEDOM ARMS PREMIER 454 CASULL
Caliber: 44 Mag., 45 Colt/45 ACP (optional cylinder), 454 Casull, 5-shot.
Barrel: 3", 4¾", 6", 7½", 10".
Weight: 50 oz. **Length:** 14" overall (7½" bbl.).
Stocks: Impregnated hardwood.
Sights: Blade front, notch or adjustable rear.
Features: All stainless steel construction; sliding bar safety system. Hunter Pak includes 7½" gun, sling and studs, aluminum carrying case with tool and cleaning kit. Lifetime warranty. Made in U.S.A.
Price: Field Grade (matte finish, Pachmayr grips), adjustable sights, 4¾", 6", 7½", 10" **$1,115.00**
Price: Field Grade, fixed sights, 4¾" only **$1,035.00**
Price: Field Grade, 44 Rem. Mag., adjustable sights, all lengths **$1,115.00**
Price: Premier Grade (brush finish, impregnated hardwood grips) adjustable sights, 4¾", 6", 7½", 10" **$1,385.00**
Price: Premier Grade, fixed sights, 7½" only **$1,298.00**
Price: Premier Grade, 44 Rem. Mag., adjustable sights, all lengths **$1,385.00**
Price: Premier Grade Hunter Pak, black micarta grips, no front sight base **$1,611.10**
Price: Premier Grade Hunter Pak, adjustable sight, black micarta grips **$1,711.35**
Price: Field Grade Hunter Pak, Pachmayr grips, 2x Leupold scope, Leupold rings and base, no front sight base **$1,332.85**
Price: Field Grade Hunter Pak, Pachmayr grips, low-profile adjustable sight **$1,408.85**
Price: Fitted 45 ACP or 45 Colt cylinder, add **$213.00**

Freedom 454 Field Grade

Dakota New Model Single-Action Revolvers
Similar to the standard Dakota except has color case-hardened forged steel frame, black nickel backstrap and trigger guard. Calibers 357 Mag., 44-40, 45 Colt only.
Price: **$490.00**
Price: Nickel **$636.00**

Freedom Arms Casull Model 353 Revolver
Similar to the Premier 454 Casull except chambered for 357 Magnum with 5-shot cylinder; 4¾", 6", 7½" or 9" barrel. Weighs 59 oz. with 7½" barrel. Standard model has adjustable sights, matte finish, Pachmayr grips, 7½" or 9" barrel; Silhouette has 9" barrel, Patridge front sight, Iron Sight Gun Works Silhouette adjustable rear, Pachmayr grips, trigger over-travel adjustment screw. All stainless steel. Introduced 1992.
Price: Field Grade **$1,115.00**
Price: Premier Grade (brushed finish, impregnated hardwood grips, Premier Grade sights) **$1,385.00**
Price: Silhouette **$1,213.80**

DAKOTA HARTFORD SINGLE-ACTION REVOLVERS
Caliber: 22 LR, 357 Mag., 32-20, 38-40, 44-40, 44 Spec., 45 Colt.
Barrel: 4¾", 5½", 7½".
Weight: 45 oz. **Length:** 13" overall (7½" barrel).
Stocks: Smooth walnut.
Sights: Blade front, fixed rear.
Features: Identical to the originanl Colts with inspector cartouche on left grip, original patent dates and U.S. markings. All major parts serial numbered using original Colt-style lettering, numbering. Bullseye ejector head and color case-hardening on frame and hammer. Introduced 1990. From E.M.F.
Price: **$600.00**
Price: Cavalry or Artillery **$655.00**
Price: Nickel plated **$760.00**
Price: Cattlebrand engraved nickel **$1,150.00**
Price: Scroll engraved **$840.00**
Price: Scroll engraved nickel **$1,000.00**

HERITAGE ROUGH RIDER REVOLVER
Caliber: 22 LR, 22 LR/22 WMR combo, 6-shot.
Barrel: 3", 4¾", 6½", 9".
Weight: 31 to 38 oz. **Length:** NA
Stocks: Smooth walnut.
Sights: Blade front, fixed rear.
Features: Hammer block safety. High polish blue finish, gold-tone screws, polished hammer. Introduced 1993. Made in U.S. by Heritage Mfg., Inc.
Price: . . . . **$104.95 to $139.95**

Heritage Rough Rider

MITCHELL SINGLE-ACTION ARMY REVOLVERS
Caliber: 357 Mag., 44 Mag., 45 ACP, 45 Colt, 6-shot.
Barrel: 4¾", 5½", 7½".
Weight: NA. **Length:** NA.
Stocks: One-piece walnut.
Sights: Serrated ramp front, fixed or adjustable rear.
Features: Color case-hardened frame, brass or steel backstrap/trigger guard; hammer-block safety. Bright nickel-plated model and dual cylinder models available. Contact importer for complete price list. Imported by Mitchell Arms, Inc.
Price: Cowboy, 4¾", Army 5½", Cavalry 7½", blue, 357,
45 Colt, 45 ACP **$399.00**
Price: As above, nickel **$439.00**
Price: 45 Colt/45 ACP dual cyl., blue **$549.00**
Price: As above, nickel **$588.00**
Price: Bat Masterson model, 45 Colt, 4¾", nickel **$439.00**

Mitchell Single Action

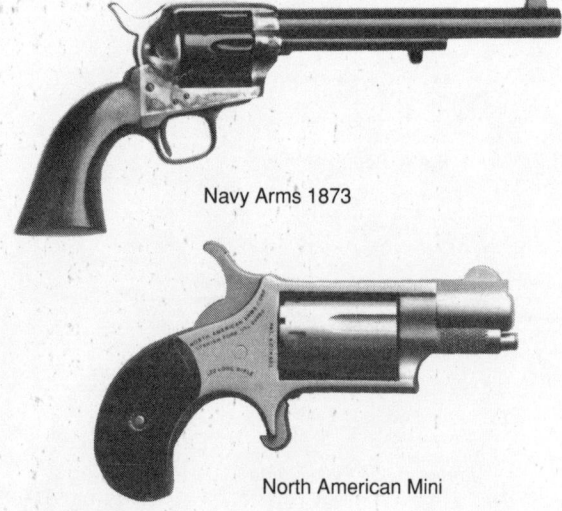

Navy Arms 1873

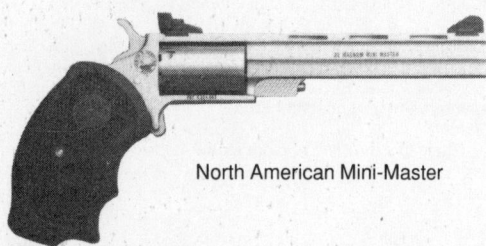

North American Mini

North American Mini-Master

PHELPS HERITAGE I, EAGLE I, GRIZZLY REVOLVERS
Caliber: 444 Marlin, 45-70, 50-70, 6-shot.
Barrel: 8", 12", 16" (45-70).
Weight: 5½ lbs. **Length:** 19½" overall (12" bbl.).
Stocks: Smooth walnut.
Sights: Ramp front, adjustable rear.
Features: Single action; polished blue finish; safety bar. From Phelps Mfg. Co.
Price: 8", 45-70 or 444 Marlin, about **$1,085.00**
Price: 12", 45-70 or 444 Marlin, about **$1,165.00**
Price: 8", 50-70, about **$1,550.00**

Ruger Blackhawk

NAVY ARMS 1873 SINGLE-ACTION REVOLVER
Caliber: 44-40, 45 Colt, 6-shot cylinder.
Barrel: 3", 4¾", 5½", 7½".
Weight: 36 oz. **Length:** 10¾" overall (5½" barrel).
Stocks: Smooth walnut.
Sights: Blade front, groove in topstrap rear.
Features: Blue with color case-hardened frame, or nickel. Introduced 1991. Imported by Navy Arms.
Price: Blue **$370.00**
Price: Nickel **$435.00**
Price: 1873 U.S. Cavalry Model (7½", 45 Colt, arsenal markings) . **$455.00**
Price: 1895 U.S. Artillery Model (as above, 5½" barrel) **$455.00**

NORTH AMERICAN MINI-REVOLVERS
Caliber: 22 LR, 22 WMR, 5-shot.
Barrel: 1⅛", 1⅝".
Weight: 4 to 6.6 oz. **Length:** 3⅝" to 6⅛" overall.
Stocks: Laminated wood.
Sights: Blade front, notch fixed rear.
Features: All stainless steel construction. Polished satin and matte finish. Engraved models available. From North American Arms.
Price: 22 LR, 1⅛" bbl. **$164.50**
Price: 22 LR, 1⅝" bbl. **$164.50**
Price: 22 WMR, 1⅝" bbl. **$184.50**
Price: 22 WMR, 1⅛" or 1⅝" bbl. with extra 22 LR cylinder . . . **$219.50**

> ### Consult our Directory pages for the location of firms mentioned.

NORTH AMERICAN MINI-MASTER
Caliber: 22 LR, 22 WMR, 5-shot cylinder.
Barrel: 4".
Weight: 10.7 oz. **Length:** 7.75" overall.
Stocks: Checkered hard black rubber.
Sights: Blade front, white outline rear adjustable for elevation, or fixed.
Features: Heavy vent barrel; full-size grips. Non-fluted cylinder. Introduced 1989.
Price: Adjustable sight, 22 WMR or 22 LR **$267.50**
Price: As above with extra WMR/LR cylinder **$302.50**
Price: Fixed sight, 22 WMR or 22 LR **$257.50**
Price: As above with extra WMR/LR cylinder **$292.50**

North American Black Widow Revolver
Similar to the Mini-Master except has 2" Heavy Vent barrel. Built on the 22 WMR frame. Non-fluted cylinder, black rubber grips. Available with either Millett Low Profile fixed sights or Millett sight adjustable for elevation only. Overall length 5⅞", weight 8.8 oz. From North American Arms.
Price: Adjustable sight, 22 LR or 22 WMR **$235.50**
Price: As above with extra WMR/LR cylinder **$270.50**
Price: Fixed sight, 22 LR or 22 WMR **$225.50**
Price: As above with extra WMR/LR cylinder **$260.50**

RUGER BLACKHAWK REVOLVER
Caliber: 30 Carbine, 357 Mag./38 Spec., 41 Mag., 45 Colt, 6-shot.
Barrel: 4⅝" or 6½", either caliber; 7½" (30 Carbine, 45 Colt only).
Weight: 42 oz. (6½" bbl.). **Length:** 12¼" overall (6½" bbl.).
Stocks: American walnut.
Sights: ⅛" ramp front, micro-click rear adjustable for windage and elevation.
Features: Ruger interlock mechanism, independent firing pin, hardened chrome moly steel frame, music wire springs throughout.
Price: Blue, 30 Carbine (7½" bbl.), BN31 . . . . **$328.00**
Price: Blue, 357 Mag. (4⅝", 6½"), BN34, BN36 . . . . **$328.00**
Price: Blue, 357/9mm Convertible (4⅝", 6½"), BN34X, BN36X . . **$343.50**
Price: Blue, 41 Mag., 45 Colt (4⅝", 6½"), BN41, BN42, BN45 . . **$328.00**
Price: Stainless, 357 Mag. (4⅝", 6½"), KBN34, KBN36 . . . . . . **$404.00**

Ruger Bisley

Ruger New Super Bearcat

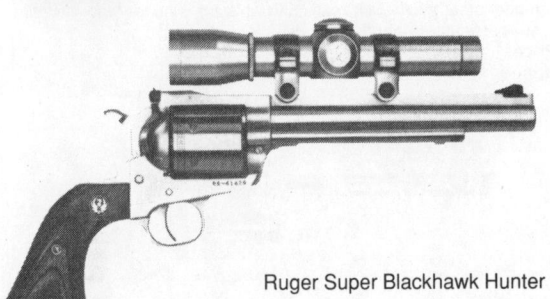

Ruger SSM Single-Six

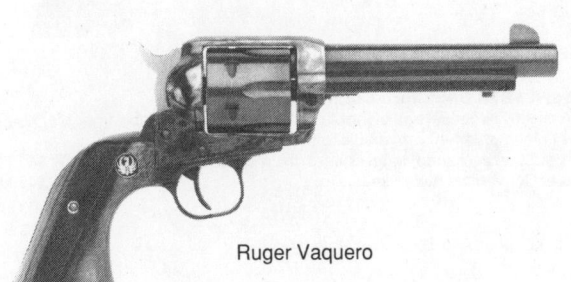

Ruger Super Blackhawk Hunter

Ruger Vaquero

SPORTARMS MODEL HS21S SINGLE ACTION
Caliber: 22 LR or 22 LR/22 WMR combo, 6-shot.
Barrel: 5½".
Weight: 33.5 oz. **Length:** 11" overall.
Stocks: Smooth hardwood.
Sights: Blade front, rear drift adjustable for windage.
Features: Available in blue with imitation stag or wood stocks. Made in Germany by Herbert Schmidt; Imported by Sportarms of Florida.
Price: 22 LR, blue, "stag" grips, about **$100.00**
Price: 22 LR/22 WMR combo, blue, wood stocks, about **$120.00**

Ruger Bisley Single-Action Revolver
Similar to standard Blackhawk except the hammer is lower with a smoothly curved, deeply checkered wide spur. The trigger is strongly curved with a wide smooth surface. Longer grip frame has a hand-filling shape. Adjustable rear sight, ramp-style front. Has an unfluted cylinder and roll engraving, adjustable sights. Chambered for 357, 41, 44 Mags. and 45 Colt; 7½" barrel; overall length of 13". Introduced 1985.
Price: **$391.00**

RUGER NEW SUPER BEARCAT SINGLE ACTION
Caliber: 22 LR/22 WMR, 6-shot.
Barrel: 4".
Weight: 23 oz. **Length:** 8⅞" overall.
Stocks: Smooth rosewood with Ruger medallion.
Sights: Blade front, fixed notch rear.
Features: Reintroduction of the Ruger Super Bearcat with slightly lengthened frame, Ruger patented transfer bar safety system. Comes with two cylinders. Available in blue or stainless steel. Introduced 1993. From Sturm, Ruger & Co.
Price: SBC4, blue **$298.00**
Price: KSBC4, stainless **$325.00**

RUGER SUPER SINGLE-SIX CONVERTIBLE
Caliber: 22 LR, 6-shot; 22 WMR in extra cylinder.
Barrel: 4⅝", 5½", 6½", or 9½" (6-groove).
Weight: 34½ oz. (6½" bbl.). **Length:** 11¹³⁄₁₆" overall (6½" bbl.).
Stocks: Smooth American walnut.
Sights: Improved Patridge front on ramp, fully adjustable rear protected by integral frame ribs.
Features: Ruger interlock mechanism, transfer bar ignition, gate-controlled loading, hardened chrome moly steel frame, wide trigger, music wire springs throughout, independent firing pin.
Price: 4⅝", 5½", 6½", 9½" barrel **$281.00**
Price: 5½", 6½" bbl. only, stainless steel **$354.00**

Ruger SSM Single-Six Revolver
Similar to the Super Single-Six revolver except chambered for 32 H&R Magnum (also handles 32 S&W and 32 S&W Long). Weight is about 34 oz. with 6½" barrel. Barrel lengths: 4⅝", 5½", 6½", 9½". Introduced 1985.
Price: **$281.00**

Ruger Bisley Small Frame Revolver
Similar to the Single-Six except frame is styled after the classic Bisley "flat-top." Most mechanical parts are unchanged. Hammer is lower and smoothly curved with a deeply checkered spur. Trigger is strongly curved with a wide smooth surface. Longer grip frame designed with a hand-filling shape, and the trigger guard is a large oval. Adjustable dovetail rear sight; front sight base accepts interchangeable square blades of various heights and styles. Has an unfluted cylinder and roll engraving. Weight about 41 oz. Chambered for 22 LR and 32 H&R Mag., 6½" barrel only. Introduced 1985.
Price: **$328.75**

RUGER SUPER BLACKHAWK
Caliber: 44 Magnum, 6-shot. Also fires 44 Spec.
Barrel: 5½", 7½", 10½".
Weight: 48 oz. (7½" bbl.), 51 oz. (10½" bbl.). **Length:** 13⅜" overall (7½" bbl.).
Stocks: American walnut.
Sights: ⅛" ramp front, micro-click rear adjustable for windage and elevation.
Features: Ruger interlock mechanism, non-fluted cylinder, steel grip and cylinder frame, square back trigger guard, wide serrated trigger and wide spur hammer.
Price: Blue (S45N, S47N, S411N) **$378.50**
Price: Stainless (KS45N, KS47N, KS411N) **$413.75**
Price: Stainless KS47NH Hunter with scope rings, 7½" **$479.50**

RUGER VAQUERO SINGLE-ACTION REVOLVER
Caliber: 44-40, 44 Magnum, 45 Colt, 6-shot.
Barrel: 4⅝", 5½", 7½".
Weight: 41 oz. **Length:** 13⅜" overall (7½" barrel).
Stocks: Smooth rosewood with Ruger medallion.
Sights: Blade front, fixed notch rear.
Features: Uses Ruger's patented transfer bar safety system and loading gate interlock with classic styling. Blued model has color case-hardened finish on the frame, the rest polished and blued. Stainless model is polished. Introduced 1993. From Sturm, Ruger & Co.
Price: BNV44 (4⅝"), BNV445 (5½"), BNV45 (7½"), blue **$394.00**
Price: KBNV44 (4⅝"), KBNV455 (5½"), KBNV45 (7½"), stainless . **$394.00**

TEXAS LONGHORN ARMS GROVER'S IMPROVED NO. FIVE
Caliber: 44 Magnum, 6-shot.
Barrel: 5½".
Weight: 44 oz. **Length:** NA.
Stocks: Fancy AAA walnut.
Sights: Square blade front on ramp, fully adjustable rear.
Features: Music wire coil spring action with double locking bolt; polished blue finish. Handmade in limited 1,200-gun production. Grip contour, straps, over-sized base pin, lever latch and lockwork identical copies of Elmer Keith design. Lifetime warranty to original owner. Introduced 1988.
Price: **$985.00**

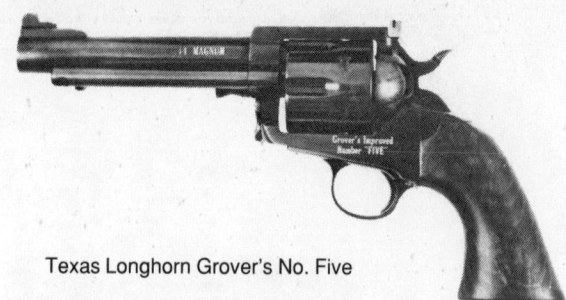

Texas Longhorn Grover's No. Five

TEXAS LONGHORN ARMS RIGHT-HAND SINGLE ACTION
Caliber: All centerfire pistol calibers.
Barrel: 4¾".
Weight: NA. **Length:** NA.
Stocks: One-piece fancy walnut, or any fancy AAA wood.
Sights: Blade front, grooved topstrap rear.
Features: Loading gate and ejector housing on left side of gun. Cylinder rotates to the left. All steel construction; color case-hardened frame; high polish blue; music wire coil springs. Lifetime guarantee to original owner. Introduced 1984. From Texas Longhorn Arms.
Price: South Texas Army Limited Edition—handmade, only 1,000 to be produced; "One of One Thousand" engraved on barrel **$1,500.00**

Texas Longhorn Arms Texas Border Special
Similar to the South Texas Army Limited Edition except has 3½" barrel, bird's-head style grip. Same special features. Introduced 1984.
Price: **$1,500.00**

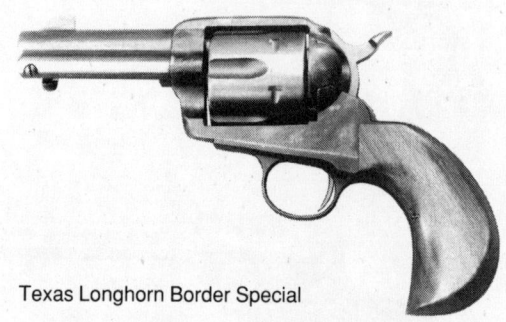

Texas Longhorn Border Special

Texas Longhorn Arms Sesquicentennial Model Revolver
Similar to the South Texas Army Model except has ¾-coverage Nimschke-style engraving, antique golden nickel plate finish, one-piece elephant ivory grips. Comes with handmade solid walnut presentation case, factory letter to owner. Limited edition of 150 units. Introduced 1986.
Price: **$2,500.00**

Texas Longhorn Arms Cased Set
Set contains one each of the Texas Longhorn Right-Hand Single Actions, all in the same caliber, same serial numbers (100, 200, 300, 400, 500, 600, 700, 800, 900). Ten sets to be made (#1000 donated to NRA museum). Comes in hand-tooled leather case. All other specs same as Limited Edition guns. Introduced 1984.
Price: **$5,750.00**
Price: With ¾-coverage "C-style" engraving **$7,650.00**

Texas Longhorn Arms West Texas Flat Top Target
Similar to the South Texas Army Limited Edition except choice of barrel length from 7½" through 15"; flat-top style frame; ⅛" contoured ramp front sight, old model steel micro-click rear adjustable for windage and elevation. Same special features. Introduced 1984.
Price: **$1,500.00**

UBERTI 1873 CATTLEMAN SINGLE ACTIONS
Caliber: 38 Spec., 357 Mag., 44 Spec., 44-40, 45 Colt/45 ACP, 6-shot.
Barrel: 4¾", 5½", 7½"; 44-40, 45 Colt also with 3".
Weight: 38 oz. (5½" bbl.). **Length:** 10¾" overall (5½" bbl.).
Stocks: One-piece smooth walnut.
Sights: Blade front, groove rear; fully adjustable rear available.
Features: Steel or brass backstrap, trigger guard; color case-hardened frame, blued barrel, cylinder. Imported from Italy by Uberti USA.
Price: Steel backstrap, trigger guard, fixed sights **$410.00**
Price: Brass backstrap, trigger guard, fixed sights **$365.00**

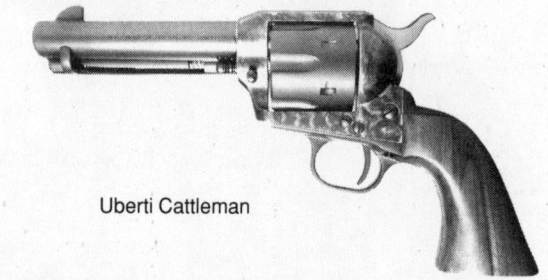

Uberti Cattleman

Uberti 1873 Buckhorn Single Action
A slightly larger version of the Cattleman revolver. Available in 44 Magnum or 44 Magnum/44-40 convertible, otherwise has same specs.
Price: Steel backstrap, trigger guard, fixed sights **$410.00**
Price: Convertible (two cylinders) **$460.00**

UBERTI 1875 SA ARMY OUTLAW REVOLVER
Caliber: 357 Mag., 44-40, 45 Colt, 6-shot.
Barrel: 7½".
Weight: 44 oz. **Length:** 13¾" overall.
Stocks: Smooth walnut.
Sights: Blade front, notch rear.
Features: Replica of the 1875 Remington S.A. Army revolver. Brass trigger guard, color case-hardened frame, rest blued. Imported by Uberti USA.
Price: **$405.00**
Price: 45 Colt/45 ACP convertible **$450.00**

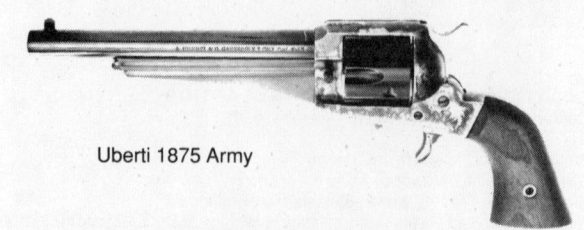

Uberti 1875 Army

UBERTI 1890 ARMY OUTLAW REVOLVER
Caliber: 357 Mag., 44-40, 45 Colt, 6-shot.
Barrel: 5½".
Weight: 37 oz. **Length:** 12½" overall.
Stocks: American walnut.
Sights: Blade front, groove rear.
Features: Replica of the 1890 Remington single action. Brass trigger guard, rest is blued. Imported by Uberti USA.
Price: **$410.00**
Price: 45 Colt/45 ACP convertible **$415.00**

CAUTION: PRICES CHANGE, CHECK AT GUNSHOP.

Specially adapted single-shot and multi-barrel arms.

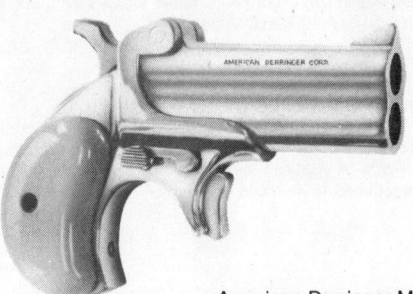

American Derringer Model 1

AMERICAN DERRINGER MODEL 3
Caliber: 38 Special.
Barrel: 2.5".
Weight: 8.5 oz. **Length:** 4.9" overall.
Stocks: Rosewood.
Sights: Blade front.
Features: Made of stainless steel. Single shot with manual hammer block safety. Introduced 1985. From American Derringer Corp.
Price: **$120.00**

American Derringer Model 7 Ultra Lightweight
Similar to Model 1 except made of high strength aircraft aluminum. Weighs 7½ oz., 4.82" o.a.l., rosewood stocks. Available in 22 LR, 32 H&R Mag., 380 ACP, 38 Spec., 44 Spec. Introduced 1986.
Price: 22 LR **$200.00**
Price: 38 Spec. **$202.50**
Price: 380 ACP **$199.95**
Price: 32 H&R Mag. **$202.50**
Price: 44 Spec. **$500.00**

American Derringer Texas Commemorative
A Model 1 Derringer with solid brass frame, stainless steel barrel and rosewood grips. Available in 38 Speical, 44-40 Win., or 45 Colt. Introduced 1987.
Price: 38 Spec. **$215.00**
Price: 44-40 or 45 Colt **$320.00**

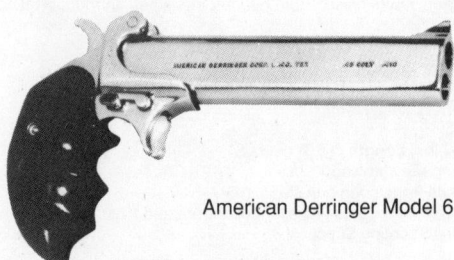

American Derringer Model 6

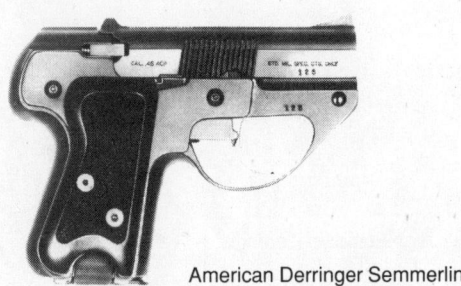

American Derringer Semmerling

AMERICAN DERRINGER MODEL 1
Caliber: 22 LR, 22 WMR, 30 Luger, 30-30 Win., 32 ACP, 380 ACP, 38 Spec., 9mm Para., 357 Mag., 357 Maximum, 10mm, 40 S&W, 41 Mag., 38-40, 44-40 Win., 44 Spec., 44 Mag., 45 Colt, 45 ACP, 410-bore (2½").
Barrel: 3".
Weight: 15½ oz. (38 Spec.). **Length:** 4.82" overall.
Stocks: Rosewood, Zebra wood.
Sights: Blade front.
Features: Made of stainless steel with high-polish or satin finish. Two-shot capacity. Manual hammer block safety. Introduced 1980. Available in almost any pistol caliber. Contact the factory for complete list of available calibers and prices. From American Derringer Corp.
Price: 22 LR or WMR . . . . **$212.50 to $225.00**
Price: 38 Spec. **$219.00**
Price: 357 Maximum **$265.00**
Price: 357 Mag. **$250.00**
Price: 9mm, 380, ... **$215.00**
Price: 10mm, 40 S&W **$250.00**
Price: 44 Spec., ... **$320.00**
Price: 44-40 Win., 45 Colt, 45 Auto Rim . . . **$320.00**
Price: 30-30, 41, 44 Mags., 45 Win. Mag. . . **$375.00**
Price: 45-70, single shot **$312.00**
Price: 45 Colt, 410, 2½" **$320.00**
Price: 45 ACP, 10mm Auto **$250.00**
Price: 125th Anniversary model (brass frame, stainless bbl., 44-40, 45 Colt, 38 Spec.) **$320.00**
Price: Alaskan Survival model (45-70 upper, 410-45 Colt lower) . . . **$387.50**

American Derringer Model 4
Similar to the Model 1 except has 4.1" barrel, overall length of 6", and weighs 16½ oz.; chambered for 3" 410-bore shotshells or 45 or 44 Magnum Colt. Can be had with 45-70 upper barrel and 3" 410-bore or 45 Colt bottom barrel. Made of stainless steel. Manual hammer block safety. Introduced 1985.
Price: 3" 410/45 Colt (either barrel) **$352.00**
Price: 3" 410/45 Colt or 45-70 (Alaskan Survival model) **$387.50**
Price: 44 Magnum with oversize grips **$422.00**

American Derringer Model 6
Similar to the Model 1 except has 6" barrels chambered for 3" 410 shotshells or 45 Colt, rosewood stocks, 8.2" o.a.l. and weighs 21 oz. Shoots either round for each barrel. Manual hammer block safety. Introduced 1986.
Price: High polish or satin finish **$387.50**
Price: Gray matte finish **$362.50**

American Derringer Model 10 Lightweight
Similar to the Model 1 except frame is of aluminum, giving weight of 10 oz. Available in 45 Colt or 45 ACP only. Matte gray finish. Introduced 1989.
Price: 45 Colt **$320.00**
Price: 45 ACP **$250.00**
Price: Model 11 (38 Spec., aluminum bbls., wgt. 11 oz.) **$205.00**

American Derringer Lady Derringer
Same as the Model 1 except has tuned action, is fitted with scrimshawed synthetic ivory grips; chambered for 32 H&R Mag. and 38 Spec.; 22 LR, 22 WMR, 380 ACP, 357 Mag., 9mm Para., 45 ACP, 45 Colt/410 shotshell available at extra cost. Deluxe Grade is highly polished; Deluxe Engraved is engraved in a pattern similar to that used on 1880s derringers. All come in a French fitted jewelry box. Introduced 1991.
Price: Deluxe Grade **$235.00**
Price: Deluxe Engraved Grade **$750.00**

AMERICAN DERRINGER SEMMERLING LM-4
Caliber: 9mm Para., 7-shot magazine; 45 ACP, 5-shot magazine.
Barrel: 3.625".
Weight: 24 oz. **Length:** 5.2" overall.
Stocks: Checkered plastic on blued guns, rosewood on stainless guns.
Sights: Open, fixed.
Features: Manually-operated repeater. Height is 3.7", width is 1". Comes with manual, leather carrying case, spare stock screws, wrench. From American Derringer Corp.
Price: Blued **$1,750.00**
Price: Stainless steel **$1,875.00**

AMERICAN DERRINGER DA 38 MODEL
Caliber: 9mm Para., 38 Spec., 357 Mag., 40 S&W.
Barrel: 3".
Weight: 14.5 oz. **Length:** 4.8" overall.
Stocks: Rosewood, walnut or other hardwoods.
Sights: Fixed.
Features: Double-action only; two-shots. Manual safety. Made of satin-finished stainless steel and aluminum. Introduced 1989. From American Derringer Corp.
Price: 38 Spec. **$250.00**
Price: 9mm Para. **$275.00**
Price: 357 Mag., 40 S&W **$300.00**

ANSCHUTZ EXEMPLAR BOLT-ACTION PISTOL
Caliber: 22 LR, 5-shot; 22 Hornet, 5-shot.
Barrel: 10", 14".
Weight: 3½ lbs. **Length:** 17" overall.
Stock: European walnut with stippled grip and forend.
Sights: Hooded front on ramp, open notch rear adjustable for windage and elevation.
Features: Uses Match 64 action with left-hand bolt; Anschutz #5091 two-stage trigger set at 9.85 oz. Receiver grooved for scope mounting; open sights easily removed. Introduced 1987. Imported from Germany by Precision Sales International.
Price: 22 LR **$499.50**
Price: 22 LR, left-hand **$499.50**
Price: 22 LR, 14" barrel **$522.00**
Price: 22 Hornet (no sights, 10" bbl.) **$822.00**

DAVIS DERRINGERS
Caliber: 22 LR, 22 WMR, 25 ACP, 32 ACP.
Barrel: 2.4".
Weight: 9.5 oz. **Length:** 4" overall.
Stocks: Laminated wood.
Sights: Blade front, fixed notch rear.
Features: Choice of black Teflon or chrome finish; spur trigger. Introduced 1986. Made in U.S. by Davis Industries.
Price: **$64.90**

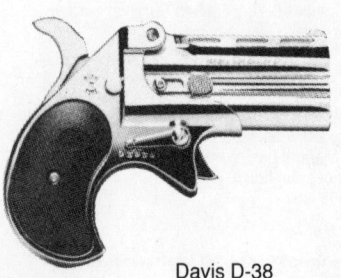

Davis D-38

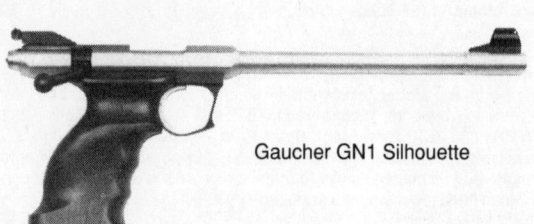

Gaucher GN1 Silhouette

HIGH STANDARD DERRINGER
Caliber: 22 LR, 22 WMR, 2-shot.
Barrel: 3.5".
Weight: 11 oz. **Length:** 5.12" overall.
Stocks: Black composition.
Sights: Fixed.
Features: Double action, dual extraction. Hammer-block safety. Blue finish. Introduced 1990. Made in U.S. by American Derringer Corp.
Price: **$169.50**

AMERICAN DERRINGER COP 357 DERRINGER
Caliber: 38 Spec. or 357 Mag., 4-shot.
Barrel: 3.14".
Weight: 16 oz. **Length:** 5.53" overall.
Stocks: Rosewood.
Sights: Fixed.
Features: Double-action only. Four shots. Made of stainless steel. Introduced 1990. Made in U.S. by American Derringer Corp.
Price: **$375.00**

American Derringer Mini COP Derringer
Similar to the COP 357 except chambered for 22 WMR. Barrel length of 2.85", overall length of 4.95", weight is 16 oz. Double action with automatic hammer-block safety. Made of stainless steel. Grips of rosewood, walnut or other hardwoods. Introduced 1990. Made in U.S. by American Derringer Corp.
Price: **$312.50**

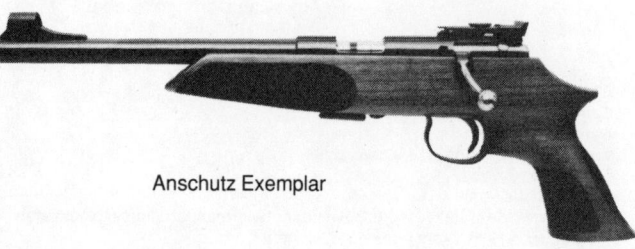

Anschutz Exemplar

DAVIS D-38 DERRINGER
Caliber: 38 Special.
Barrel: 2.75".
Weight: 11.5 oz. **Length:** 4.65" overall.
Stocks: Textured black synthetic.
Sights: Blade front, fixed notch rear.
Features: Alloy frame, stee-lined barrels, steel breech block. Plunger-type safety with integral hammer block. Chrome or black Teflon finish. Introduced 1992. Made in U.S. by Davis Industries.
Price: **$89.90**

FEATHER GUARDIAN ANGEL PISTOL
Caliber: 22 LR/22 WMR.
Barrel: 2".
Weight: 12 oz. **Length:** 5" overall.
Stocks: Black composition.
Sights: Fixed.
Features: Uses a pre-loaded two-shot drop-in "magazine." Stainless steel construction; matte finish. From Feather Industries. Introduced 1988.
Price: **$119.95**

GAUCHER GN1 SILHOUETTE PISTOL
Caliber: 22 LR, single shot.
Barrel: 10".
Weight: 2.4 lbs. **Length:** 15.5" overall.
Stock: European hardwood.
Sights: Blade front, open adjustable rear.
Features: Bolt action, adjustable trigger. Introduced 1990. Imported from France by Mandall Shooting Supplies.
Price: About **$319.95**
Price: Model GP Silhouette **$380.00**

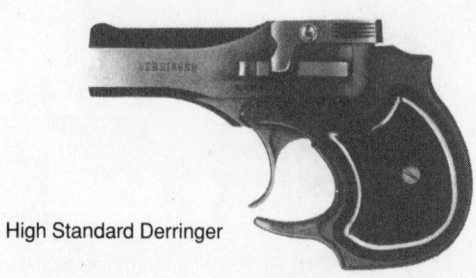

High Standard Derringer

HJS FRONTIER FOUR DERRINGER
Caliber: 22 LR.
Barrel: 2".
Weight: 5½ oz. **Length:** 3¹⁵⁄₁₆" overall.
Stocks: Black plastic.
Sights: None.
Features: Four barrels fire with rotating firing pin. Stainless steel construction. Introduced 1993. Made in U.S. by HJS Arms, Inc.
Price: **$160.00**

HJS LONE STAR DERRINGER
Caliber: 380 ACP, 38 S&W.
Barrel: 2".
Weight: 6 oz. **Length:** 3¹⁵⁄₁₆" overall.
Stocks: Black plastic.
Sights: Groove.
Features: Stainless steel Construction. Beryllium copper firing pin. Button-rifled barrel. Introduced 1993. Made in U.S. by HJS Arms, Inc.
Price: **$180.00**

ITHACA X-CALIBER SINGLE SHOT
Caliber: 22 LR, 44 Mag.
Barrel: 10", 15".
Weight: 3¼ lbs. **Length:** 15" overall (10" barrel).
Stocks: Goncalo Alves grip and forend on Model 20; American walnut on Model 30.
Sights: Blade on ramp front; Model 20 has adjustable, removable target-type rear. Drilled and tapped for scope mounting.
Features: Dual firing pin for RF/CF use. Polished blue finish.
Price: 22 LR, 10", 44 Mag., 10" or 15" **$270.00**
Price: 22 LR/44 Mag. combo, 10" and 15" **$365.00**
Price: As above, both 10" barrels **$365.00**

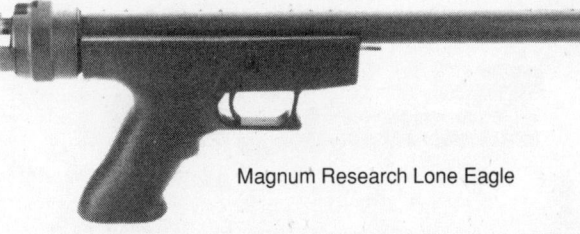

Magnum Research Lone Eagle

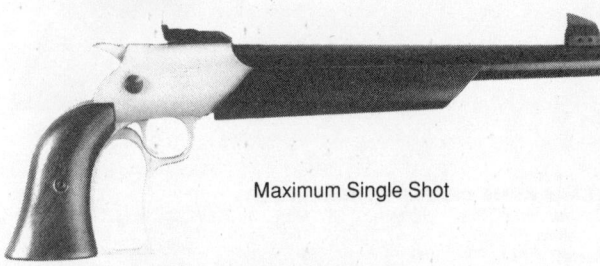

Maximum Single Shot

New Advantage Derringer

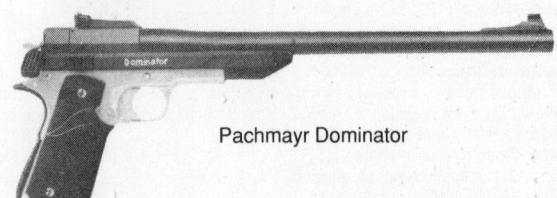

Pachmayr Dominator

HJS Frontier Four

MANDALL/CABANAS PISTOL
Caliber: 177, pellet or round ball; single shot.
Barrel: 9".
Weight: 51 oz. **Length:** 19" overall.
Stock: Smooth wood with thumbrest.
Sights: Blade front on ramp, open adjustable rear.
Features: Fires round ball or pellets with 22 blank cartridge. Automatic safety; muzzlebrake. Imported from Mexico by Mandall Shooting Supplies.
Price: **$139.95**

MAGNUM RESEARCH LONE EAGLE SINGLE SHOT PISTOL
Caliber: 22 Hornet, 223, 22-250, 243, 7mm BR, 7mm-08, 30-30, 308, 30-06, 357 Max., 35 Rem., 358 Win., 44 Mag., 444 Marlin.
Barrel: 14", interchangable.
Weight: 4lbs., 3 oz. to 4 lbs., 7 oz. **Length:** 15" overall.
Stocks: Composition, with thumbrest.
Sights: None furnished; drilled and tapped for scope mounting and open sights. Open sights optional.
Features: Cannon-type rotating breech with spring-activated ejector. Ordnance steel with matte blue finish. Cross-bolt safety. External cocking lever on left side of gun. Introduced 1991. Available from Magnum Research, Inc.
Price: Complete pistol **$344.00**
Price: Barreled action only **$254.00**
Price: Scope base **$14.00**
Price: Adjustable open sights **$35.00**

MAXIMUM SINGLE SHOT PISTOL
Caliber: 22 LR, 22 Hornet, 22 BR, 223 Rem., 22-250, 6mm BR, 6mm-223, 243, 250 Savage, 6.5mm-35, 7mm TCU, 7mm BR, 7mm-35, 7mm INT-R, 7mm-08, 7mm Rocket, 7mm Super Mag., 30 Herrett, 30 Carbine, 308 Win., 7.62 x 39, 32-20, 357 Mag., 357 Maximum, 358 Win., 44 Mag.
Barrel: 8¾", 10½", 14".
Weight: 61 oz. (10½" bbl.); 78 oz. (14" bbl.). **Length:** 15", 18½" overall (with 10½" and 14" bbl., respectively).
Stocks: Smooth walnut stocks and forend.
Sights: Ramp front, fully adjustable open rear.
Features: Falling block action; drilled and tapped for M.O.A. scope mounts; integral grip frame/receiver; adjustable trigger; Douglas barrel (interchangeable). Introduced 1983. Made in U.S. by M.O.A. Corp.
Price: Stainless receiver, blue barrel **$622.00**
Price: Stainless receiver, stainless barrel **$677.00**
Price: Extra blued barrel **$164.00**
Price: Extra stainless barrel **$222.00**
Price: Scope mount **$52.00**

NEW ADVANTAGE ARMS DERRINGER
Caliber: 22 LR, 22 WMR, 4-shot.
Barrel: 2½".
Weight: 15 oz. **Length:** 4½" overall.
Stocks: Smooth walnut.
Sights: Fixed.
Features: Double-action mechanism, four barrels, revolving firing pin. Rebounding hammer. Blue or stainless. Reintroduced 1989. From New Advantage Arms Corp.
Price: 22 LR, 22 WMR, blue, about **$199.00**
Price: As above, stainless, about **$229.00**

PACHMAYR DOMINATOR PISTOL
Caliber: 22 Hornet, 223, 7mm-06, 308, 35 Rem., 44 Mag., single shot.
Barrel: 10½" (44 Mag.), 14" all other calibers.
Weight: 4 lbs. (14" barrel). **Length:** 16" overall (14" barrel).
Stocks: Pachmayr Signature system.
Sights: Optional sights or drilled and tapped for scope mounting.
Features: Bolt-action pistol on 1911A1 frame. Comes as complete gun. Introduced 1988. From Pachmayr.
Price: Either barrel **$524.50**

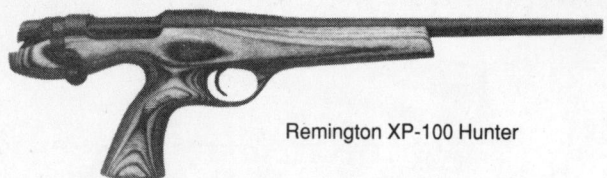

Remington XP-100 Hunter

Remington XP-100R KS

RPM XL SINGLE SHOT PISTOL

Caliber: 22 LR, 22 WMR, 225 Win., 25 Rocket, 6.5 Rocket, 32 H&R Mag., 357 Max., 357 Mag., 30-30 Win., 30 Herrett, 357 Herrett, 41 Mag., 44 Mag., 454 Casull, 375 Win., 7mm UR, 7mm Merrill, 30 Merrill, 7mm Rocket, 270 Ren, 270 Rocket, 270 Max., 45-70.
Barrel: 8" slab, 10¾", 12", 14" bull; .450" wide rib, matted to prevent glare.
Weight: About 60 oz. **Length:** 12¼" overall (10¾" bbl.).
Stocks: Smooth Goncalo with thumb and heel rest.
Sights: Front .100" blade, Millett rear adjustable for windage and elevation. Hooded front with interchangeable post optional.
Features: Blue finish, hard chrome optional. Barrel is drilled and tapped for scope mounting. Cocking indicator visible from rear of gun. Has spring-loaded barrel lock, positive hammer block thumb safety. Trigger adjustable for weight of pull and over-travel. For complete price list contact RPM.
Price: Regular ¾" frame, right-hand action $807.50
Price: As above, left-hand action $832.50
Price: Wide ⅞" frame, right-hand action $857.50
Price: Extra barrel, 8", 10¾" $287.50
Price: Extra barrel, 12", 14" $357.50

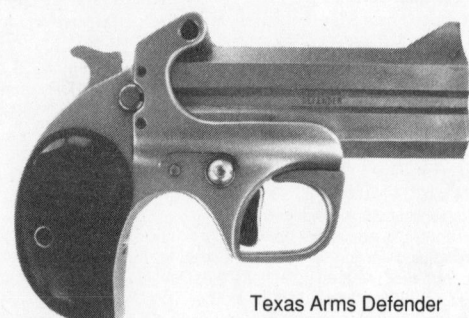

Texas Arms Defender

TEXAS LONGHORN "THE JEZEBEL" PISTOL

Caliber: 22 Short, Long, Long Rifle, single shot.
Barrel: 6".
Weight: 15 oz. **Length:** 8" overall.
Stocks: One-piece fancy walnut grip (right- or left-hand), walnut forend.
Sights: Bead front, fixed rear.
Features: Handmade gun. Top-break action; all stainless steel; automatic hammer block safety; music wire coil springs. Barrel is half-round, half-octagon. Announced 1986. From Texas Longhorn Arms.
Price: About $250.00

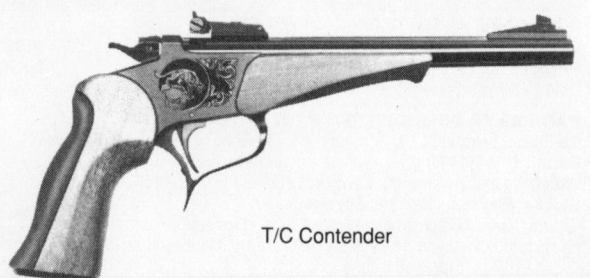

T/C Contender

REMINGTON XP-100 HUNTER PISTOL

Caliber: 223 Rem., 7mm BR Rem., 7mm-08 Rem., 35 Rem., single shot.
Barrel: 14½".
Weight: 4½ lbs. **Length:** 21¼" overall.
Stocks: Laminated wood with contoured grip.
Sights: None furnished. Drilled and tapped for scope mounting.
Features: Mid-handle grip design with scalloped contours for right- or left-handed shooters; two-position safety. Matte blue finish. Introduced 1993.
Price: $532.00

Remington XP-100 Custom HB Long Range Pistol

Similar to the XP-100 "Varmint Special" except chambered for 223 Rem., 22-250, 7mm-08 Rem., 35 Rem., 250 Savage, 6mm BR, 7mm BR, 308. Offered with standard 14½" barrel with adjustable rear leaf and front bead sights, or with heavy 15½" barrel without sights. Custom Shop 14½" barrel, Custom Shop English walnut stock in right- or left-hand configuration. Action tuned in Custom Shop. Weight is under 4½ lbs. (heavy barrel, 5½ lbs.). Introduced 1986.
Price: Right- or left-hand $945.00

Remington XP-100R KS Repeater Pistol

Similar to the Custom Long Range Pistol except chambered for 223 Rem., 22-250, 7mm-08 Rem., 250 Savage, 308, 350 Rem. Mag., and 35 Rem., and has a blind magazine holding 5 rounds (7mm-08 and 35), or 6 (223 Rem.). Comes with a rear-handle, synthetic stock of Du Pont Kevlar to eliminate the transfer bar between the forward trigger and rear trigger assembly. Fitted with front and rear sling swivel studs. Has standard-weight 14½" barrel with adjustable leaf rear sight, bead front. The receiver is drilled and tapped for scope mounts. Weight is about 4½ lbs. Introduced 1990. From Remington Custom Shop.
Price: $840.00

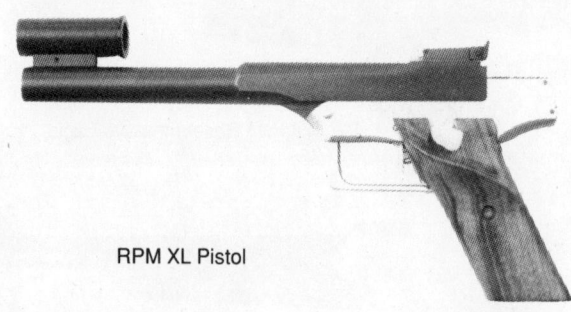

RPM XL Pistol

TEXAS ARMS DEFENDER DERRINGER

Caliber: 9mm Para., 38 Spec., 357 Mag., 40 S&W, 44 Mag., 45 ACP, 45 Colt/410.
Barrel: 3", 3.5".
Weight: 21 oz. **Length:** 5" overall.
Stocks: Smooth wood.
Sights: Blade front, fixed rear.
Features: Interchangeable barrels; retracting firing pins; rebounding hammer; cross-bolt safety; removable trigger guard; automatic extractor. Matte finish stainless steel. Introduced 1993. Made in U.S. by Texas Arms.
Price: $310.00
Price: Extra barrel sets $100.00

THOMPSON/CENTER CONTENDER

Caliber: 7mm TCU, 30-30 Win., 22 LR, 22 WMR, 22 Hornet, 223 Rem., 270 Ren, 7-30 Waters, 32-20 Win., 357 Mag., 357 Rem. Max., 44 Mag., 10mm Auto, 445 Super Mag., 45/410, single shot.
Barrel: 10", tapered octagon, bull barrel and vent. rib.
Weight: 43 oz. (10" bbl.). **Length:** 13¼" (10" bbl.).
Stocks: T/C "Competitor Grip." Right or left hand.
Sights: Under-cut blade ramp front, rear adjustable for windage and elevation.
Features: Break-open action with automatic safety. Single-action only. Interchangeable bbls., both caliber (rim & centerfire), and length. Drilled and tapped for scope. Engraved frame. See T/C catalog for exact barrel/caliber availability.
Price: Blued (rimfire cals.) $415.00
Price: Blued (centerfire cals.) $415.00
Price: Extra bbls. (standard octagon) $190.00
Price: 45/410, internal choke bbl. $210.00

CAUTION: PRICES CHANGE, CHECK AT GUNSHOP.

T/C Stainless Super 14

Thompson/Center Contender Hunter Package
Package contains the Contender pistol in 223, 7-30 Waters, 30-30, 375 Win., 357 Rem. Maximum, 35 Rem., 44 Mag. or 45-70 with 12" or 14" barrel with T/C's Muzzle Tamer, a 2.5x Recoil Proof Long Eye Relief scope with lighted reticle, q.d. sling swivels with a nylon carrying sling. Comes with a suede leather case with foam padding and fleece lining. Introduced 1990. From Thompson/Center Arms.
Price: 12" barrel **$695.00**
Price: 14" barrel **$705.00**

UBERTI ROLLING BLOCK TARGET PISTOL
Caliber: 22 LR, 22 WMR, 22 Hornet, 357 Mag., single shot.
Barrel: 9⅞", half-round, half-octagon.
Weight: 44 oz. **Length:** 14" overall.
Stocks: Walnut grip and forend.
Sights: Blade front, fully adjustable rear.
Features: Replica of the 1871 rolling block target pistol. Brass trigger guard, color case-hardened frame, blue barrel. Imported by Uberti USA.
Price: **$380.00**

ULTRA LIGHT ARMS MODEL 20 REB HUNTER'S PISTOL
Caliber: 22-250 thru 308 Win. standard. Most silhouette calibers and others on request. 5-shot magazine.
Barrel: 14", Douglas No. 3.
Weight: 4 lbs.
Stock: Composite Kevlar, graphite reinforced. Du Pont Imron paint in green, brown, black and camo.
Sights: None furnished. Scope mount included.
Features: Timney adjustable trigger; two-position, three-function safety; benchrest quality action; matte or bright stock and metal finish; right- or left-hand action. Shipped in hard case. Introduced 1987. From Ultra Light Arms.
Price: **$1,600.00**

WICHITA MASTER PISTOL
Caliber: 6mm BR, 7mm BR, 243, 7mm-08, 22-250, 308, 3 or 5-shot magazine.
Barrel: 13", 14.875".
Weight: 4.5 lbs. (13" barrel). **Length:** NA.
Stock: American walnut with oil finish; glass bedded.
Sights: Hooded post front, open adjustable rear.
Features: Comes with left-hand action with right-hand grip. round receiver and barrel. Wichita adjustable trigger. Introduced 1991. From Wichita Arms.
Price: **$1,500.00**

Thompson/Center Stainless Contender
Same as the standard Contender except made of stainless steel with blued sights, black Rynite forend and ambidextrous finger-groove grip with a built-in rubber recoil cushion that has a sealed-in air pocket. Receiver has a different cougar etching. Available with 10" bull barrel in 22 LR, 22 LR Match, 22 Hornet, 223 Rem., 30-30 Win., 357 Mag., 44 Mag., 45 Colt/410. Introduced 1993.
Price: **$445.00**
Price: 45 Colt/410 . . . . **$465.00**

Thompson/Center Stainless Super 14, Super 16 Contender
Same as the standard Super 14 and Super 16 except they are made of stainless steel with blued sights. Both models have black Rynite forend and finger-groove, ambidextrous grip with a built-in rubber recoil cushion that has a sealed-in air pocket. Receiver has a different cougar etching. Available in 22 LR, 22 LR Match, 22 Hornet, 223 Rem., 30-30 Win., 35 Rem. (Super 14), 45-70 (Super 16 only), 45 Colt/410. Introduced 1993.
Price: 14" bull barrel **$455.00**
Price: 16¼" bull barrel **$460.00**
Price: 45 Colt/410, 14" **$475.00**
Price: 45 Colt/410, 16" **$480.00**

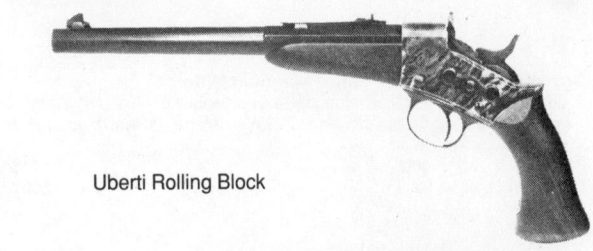

Uberti Rolling Block

Ultra Light Model 20

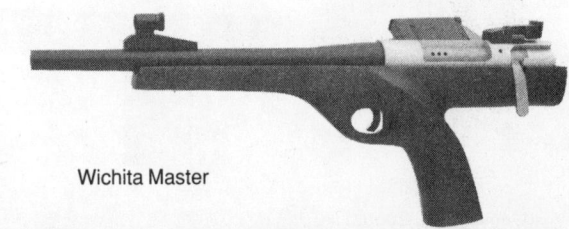

Wichita Master

CENTERFIRE RIFLES—AUTOLOADERS

Includes models for hunting, adaptable to and suitable for certain competition.

Thompson M1

Auto-Ordnance Thompson M1
Similar to the Model 27 A-1 except is in the M-1 configuration with side cocking knob, horizontal forend, smooth unfinned barrel, sling swivels on butt and forend. Matte black finish. Introduced 1985.
Price: **$712.50**

AUTO-ORDNANCE 27 A-1 THOMPSON
Caliber: 45 ACP, 30-shot magazine.
Barrel: 16".
Weight: 11½ lbs. **Length:** About 42" overall (Deluxe).
Stock: Walnut stock and vertical forend.
Sights: Blade front, open rear adjustable for windage.
Features: Recreation of Thompson Model 1927. Semi-auto only. Deluxe model has finned barrel, adjustable rear sight and compensator; Standard model has plain barrel and military sight. From Auto-Ordnance Corp.
Price: Deluxe **$735.00**
Price: 1927A5 Pistol (M27A1 without stock; wgt. 7 lbs.) **$704.00**
Price: 1927A1C Lightweight model **$707.00**

BARRETT LIGHT-FIFTY MODEL 82 A-1 AUTO
Caliber: 50 BMG, 10-shot detachable box magazine.
Barrel: 29".
Weight: 28.5 lbs. **Length:** 57" overall.
Stock: Composition with Sorbothane recoil pad.
Sights: Open, iron and 10x scope.
Features: Semi-automatic, recoil operated with recoiling barrel. Three-lug locking bolt; muzzlebrake. Self-leveling bipod. Fires same 50-cal. ammunition as the M2HB machinegun. Introduced 1985. From Barrett Firearms.
Price: From **$6,750.00**

CONSULT
Shooter's Marketplace
Page 231, This Issue

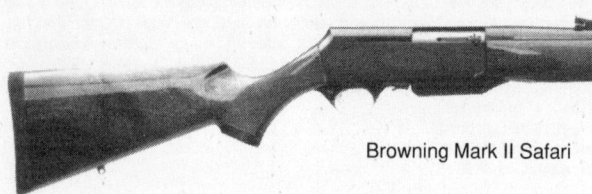

Browning Mark II Safari

BROWNING BAR MARK II SAFARI SEMI-AUTO RIFLE
Caliber: 243, 270, 30-06, 308.
Barrel: 22" round tapered.
Weight: 7⅜ lbs. **Length:** 43" overall.
Stock: French walnut p.g. stock and forend, hand checkered.
Sights: Gold bead on hooded ramp front, click adjustable rear, or no sights.
Features: Has new bolt release lever; removable trigger assembly with larger trigger guard; redesigned gas and buffer systems. Detachable 4-round box magazine. Scroll-engraved receiver is tapped for scope mounting. Mark II Safari introduced 1993. Imported from Belgium by Browning.
Price: Safari, with sights **$664.95**
Price: Safari, no sights **$647.95**

Browning BAR Mark II Safari Magnum Rifle
Same as the standard caliber model, except weighs 8⅜ lbs., 45" overall, 24" bbl., 3-round mag. Cals. 7mm Mag., 270 Wea. Mag., 300 Win. Mag., 338 Win. Mag. Introduced 1993.
Price: Safari, with sights **$713.95**
Price: Safari, no sights **$697.95**

Calico Model M-951

CALICO MODEL M-900 CARBINE
Caliber: 9mm Para., 50- or 100-shot magazine.
Barrel: 16.1".
Weight: 3.7 lbs. (empty). **Length:** 28½" overall (stock collapsed).
Stock: Sliding steel buttstock.
Sights: Post front adjustable for windage and elevation, fixed notch rear.
Feature: Helical feed 50- or 100-shot magazine. Ambidextrous safety, static cocking handle. Retarded blowback action. Glass-filled polymer grip. Introduced 1989. From Calico.
Price: **$617.90**

Calico Model M-951 Tactical Carbine
Similar to the M-900 Carbine except has an adjustable forward grip, long compensator, and 16.1" barrel. 9mm Para., 50- or 100-shot magazine. Introduced 1990. Made in U.S. by Calico.
Price: **$661.90**
Price: M-951-S (as above except fixed buttstock) **$674.90**

Century FAL Sporter

CENTURY INTERNATIONAL M-14 SEMI-AUTO RIFLE
Caliber: 308 Win., 20-shot magazine.
Barrel: 22".
Weight: 8.25 lbs. **Length:** 40.8" overall.
Stock: Walnut with rubber recoil pad.
Sights: Protected blade front, fully adjustable aperture rear.
Features: Gas-operated; forged receiver; Parkerized finish. Imported from China by Century International Arms.
Price: About **$468.95**

CENTURY INTERNATIONAL FAL SPORTER RIFLE
Caliber: 308 Win.
Barrel: 20.75".
Weight: 9 lbs., 13 oz. **Length:** 41.125" overall.
Stock: Bell & Carlson thumbhole sporter.
Sights: Protected post front, adjustable aperture rear.
Features: Matte blue finish; rubber butt pad. From Century International Arms.
Price: About **$625.00**

CLARIDGE HI-TEC C CARBINE
Caliber: 9mm Para., 18-shot magazine.
Barrel: 16.1".
Weight: 4 lbs., 9 oz. **Length:** 31.7" overall.
Stock: Walnut.
Sights: Adjustable post front in ring, open rear adjustable for windage.
Features: Aluminum or stainless frame. Telescoping bolt, floating firing pin. Safety locks the firing pin. Sight radius of 20.1". Accepts same magazines as Claridge Hi-Tec pistols. Can be equipped with scope or Aimpoint sight. Also available in 40 S&W and 45 ACP. Made in U.S. From Claridge Hi-Tec, Inc.
Price: **$525.50**
Price: Model LEC-9 (as above with graphite composite stock) . . . **$579.00**
Price: Model ZLEC-9 (as above with laser sight) **$898.50**

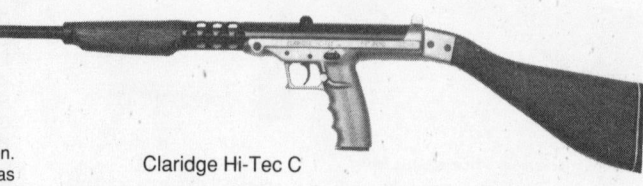

Claridge Hi-Tec C

CAUTION: PRICES CHANGE, CHECK AT GUNSHOP.

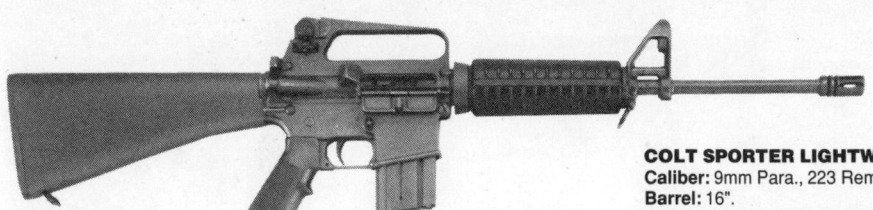

Colt Sporter Lightweight

COLT SPORTER LIGHTWEIGHT RIFLE
Caliber: 9mm Para., 223 Rem., 7.62x39mm, 5-shot magazine.
Barrel: 16".
Weight: 6.7 lbs. (223); 7.1 lbs. (9mm Para.). **Length:** 34.5" overall extended.
Stock: Composition stock, grip, forend.
Sights: Post front, rear adjustable for windage and elevation.
Features: 5-round detachable box magazine, flash suppressor, sling swivels. Forward bolt assist included. Introduced 1991.
Price: $877.95
Price: 7.62x39mm $859.95

Eagle Arms EA-15

EAGLE ARMS EA-15 AUTO RIFLE
Caliber: 223 Rem., 30-shot magazine.
Barrel: 20".
Weight: About 7 lbs. **Length:** 39" overall.
Stock: Black composition; trapdoor-style buttstock.
Sights: Post front, fully adjustable rear.
Features: Upper and lower receivers have push-type pivot pin for easy takedown. Receivers hard coat anodized. E2-style forward assist mechanism. Integral raised M-16A2-type fence around magazine release button. Introduced 1989. Made in U.S. by Eagle Arms, Inc.
Price: $800.00

Eagle Arms EA-15 Action Master Auto Rifle
Same as the EA-15 Standard Model except has a one-piece international-style upper receiver for scope mounting, no front sight; solid aluminum handguard tube; free-floating 20" Douglas Premium fluted barrel; muzzle compensator; NM trigger group and bolt carrier group. Weighs about 8 lbs., 5 oz. Introduced 1991. Made in U.S. by Eagle Arms, Inc.
Price: $1,075.00

Eagle Arms EA-15 Golden Eagle Auto Rifle
Same as the EA-15 Standard Model except has E2-style National Match rear sight with ½-MOA adjustments, elevation-adjustable NM front sight with set screw; 20" Douglas Premium extra-heavy match barrel with 1:9" twist; NM trigger group and bolt carrier group. Weight about 12 lbs., 12 oz. Introduced 1991. Made in U.S. by Eagle Arms, Inc.
Price: $1,075.00

Consult our Directory pages for the location of firms mentioned.

Eagle Arms EA-15 E1, E2 Carbines
Same as the EA-15 Standard Model except has collapsible carbine-type buttstock, 16" heavy carbine barrel. Weighs about 5 lbs., 14 oz. (E1), 6 lbs., 2 oz. (E2). Introduced 1989. Made in U.S. by Eagle Arms, Inc.
Price: E1 Carbine $845.00
Price: E2 Carbine (.73" dia. bbl., NM sights) $895.00

Eagle Arms EA-15 E2 H-BAR Auto Rifle
Same as the EA-15 Golden Eagle except has 20" standard heavy match barrel with 1:9" twist. Weighs about 8 lbs., 9 oz. Introduced 1989. Made in U.S. by Eagle Arms, Inc.
Price: $890.00
Price: With standard sights $895.00

Feather Model F9

FEATHER AT-9 SEMI-AUTO CARBINE
Caliber: 9mm Para., 25-shot magazine.
Barrel: 17".
Weight: 5 lbs. **Length:** 35" overall (stock extended); 26½" (closed).
Stock: Telescoping wire, composition pistol grip.
Sights: Hooded post front, adjustable aperture rear.
Features: Semi-auto only. Matte black finish. From Feather Industries. Announced 1988.
Price: $499.95
Price: Model F9 (fixed stock) $534.95

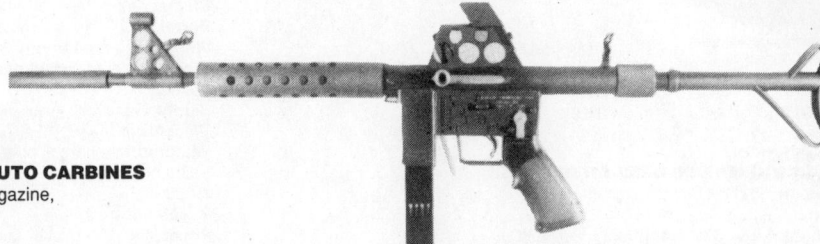

Federal XC900

FEDERAL ENGINEERING XC900/XC450 AUTO CARBINES
Caliber: 9mm Para., 32-shot; 45 ACP, 16-shot magazine,
Barrel: 16.5" (with flash hider).
Weight: 8 lbs. **Length:** 34.5" overall.
Stock: Quick-detachable tube steel.
Sights: Hooded post front, Williams adjustable rear; sight bridge grooved for scope mounting.
Features: Quick takedown; all-steel Heli-arc welded construction; internal parts industrial hard chromed. Made in U.S. by Federal Engineering Corp.
Price: Includes receiver cap, sling, swivels $639.00

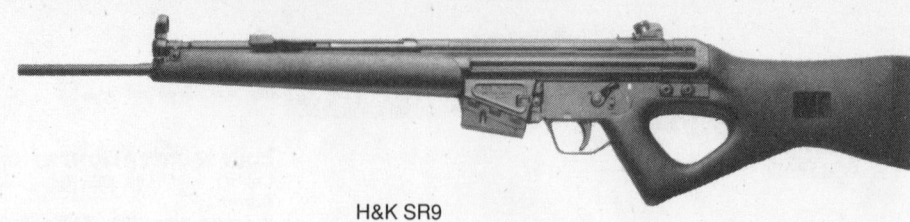

H&K SR9

HECKLER & KOCH SR9 RIFLE
Caliber: 308 Win., 5-shot magazine.
Barrel: 19.7", bull.
Weight: 11 lbs. **Length:** 42.4" overall.
Stock: Kevlar reinforced fiberglass with thumbhole; wood grain finish.
Sights: Post front, aperture rear adjustable for windage and elevation.
Features: A redesigned version of the HK91 rifle. Comes standard with bull barrel with polygonal rifling. Uses HK clawlock scope mounts. Introduced 1990. Imported from Germany by Heckler & Koch, Inc.
Price: **$1,369.00**

Heckler & Koch SR9(T) Target Rifle
Same as the SR9 rifle except has MSG90 adjustable buttstock, trigger group from the PSG1 Marksman's Rifle, and the PSG1 contoured pistol grip with palm shelf. Introduced 1992. Imported from Germany by Heckler & Koch, Inc.
Price: **$1,799.00**

FEG SA-85M AUTOLOADING RIFLE
Caliber: 7.62x39, 6-shot magazine.
Barrel: 16.3".
Weight: 7 lbs., 10 oz. **Length:** 34.7" overall.
Stock: Hardwood handguard and thumbhole buttstock.
Sights: Cylindrical post front, tangent rear adjustable for windage and elevation.
Features: Matte finish. Chrome-lined barrel. Imported from Hungary by K.B.I., Inc.
Price: **$499.00**

IBUS M17S 223 BULLPUP RIFLE
Caliber: 223, 20-shot magazine.
Barrel: 22".
Weight: 8.8 lbs. **Length:** 31½" overall.
Stock: Zytel glass-filled nylon.
Sights: None furnished. Comes with scope mount for Weaver-type rings.
Features: Gas-operated, short-stroke piston system. Ambidextrous magazine release. Introduced 1993. Made in U.S. by Quality Parts Co.
Price: **$975.00**

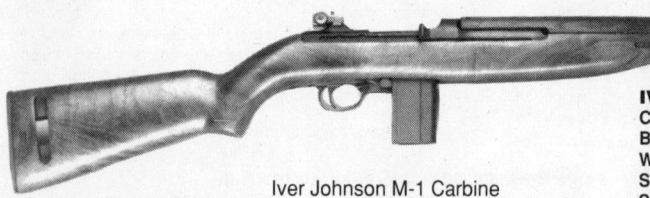

Iver Johnson M-1 Carbine

IVER JOHNSON M-1 CARBINE
Caliber: 30 U.S. Carbine, or 9mm Para.
Barrel: 18" four-groove.
Weight: 6½ lbs. **Length:** 35½" overall.
Stock: Glossy-finished hardwood or walnut; or collapsible wire.
Sights: Click-adjustable peep rear.
Features: Gas-operated semi-auto carbine. 15-shot detachable magazine. Made in U.S.A.
Price: 30 cal., Parkerized finish, hardwood stock, metal handguard . **$349.95**
Price: 30 cal., Parkerized finish, walnut stock and handguard **$384.95**
Price: 9mm, hardwood stock, metal handguard **$365.00**
Price: 9mm, walnut stock and handguard **$399.00**
Price: 30 cal., collapsible wire stock **$443.00**
Price: 9mm, collapsible wire stock **$448.95**

Iver Johnson 50th Anniversary M-1 Carbine
Same as the standard Iver Johnson 30-caliber M-1 Carbine except has deluxe walnut stock with red, white and blue circular enameled American flag embedded in the stock, and gold-filled roll-engraving with the words "50th Anniversary 1941-1991" on the slide. Parkerized finish. Introduced 1991. From Iver Johnson Arms.
Price: **$384.95**

KIMEL AR9 SEMI-AUTOMATIC RIFLE
Caliber: 9mm Para., 20-shot magazine.
Barrel: 16¼".
Weight: 6.5 lbs. **Length:** 33" overall.
Stock: Folding buttstock, checkered plastic grip.
Sights: Adjustable post front in ring, fixed open rear.
Features: Fires from closed bolt; lever safety blocks trigger and sear; vented barrel shroud. Matte blue/black or nickel finish. Introduced 1991. Made in U.S. From Kimel Industries.
Price: Blue/black finish **$369.00**

Kimel AR9

Marlin Model 9N

MARLIN MODEL 9 CAMP CARBINE
Caliber: 9mm Para., 12-shot magazine.
Barrel: 16½", Micro-Groove® rifling.
Weight: 6¾ lbs. **Length:** 35½" overall.
Stock: Walnut-finished hardwood; rubber buttpad; Mar-Shield® finish; swivel studs.
Sights: Ramp front with orange post, cutaway Wide-Scan™ hood, adjustable open rear.
Features: Manual bolt hold-open; Garand-type safety, magazine safety; loaded chamber indicator; receiver drilled, tapped for scope mounting. Introduced 1985.
Price: **$374.05**
Price: Model 9N (nickel-Teflon finish) **$421.90**

NORINCO MAK 90 SEMI-AUTO RIFLE
Caliber: 7.62x39, 5-shot magazine.
Barrel: 16.25".
Weight: 8 lbs., 3 oz. **Length:** 35.5" overall.
Stock: Walnut-finished thumbhole with recoil pad.
Sights: Adjustable post front, open adjustable rear.
Features: Chrome-lined barrel; forged receiver; black oxide finish. Comes with extra magazine, oil bottle, cleaning kit, sling. Imported from China by Century International Arms.
Price: About **$312.00**

Marlin Model 45 Carbine
Similar to the Model 9 except chambered for 45 ACP, 7-shot magazine. Introduced 1986.
Price: **$374.05**

Olympic CAR-310

QUALITY PARTS SHORTY E-2 CARBINE

Caliber: 223, 30-shot magazine.
Barrel: 16".
Weight: NA. **Length:** NA.
Stock: Telescoping buttstock.
Sights: Adjustable post front, adjustable aperture rear.
Features: Patterned after Colt M-16A2. Chrome-lined barrel with manganese phosphate finish. Has E-2 lower receiver with push-pin. From Quality Parts Co.
Price: **$850.00**
Price: E-2 Carbine Dissipator (M-16A2 handguard, E-2 sight, fixed or telescoping stock) **$895.00**
Price: As above with A-1 sight, fixed or telescoping stock **$875.00**

OLYMPIC ARMS CAR SERIES CARBINES

Caliber: 223, 20- or 30-shot; 9mm Para., 34-shot; 45 ACP, 16-shot; 10mm, 40 S&W, 41 A.E., 15-shot; 7.62x39mm, 5- or 30-shot.
Barrel: 16".
Weight: 7 lbs. **Length:** 34" overall (stock extended).
Stock: Telescoping butt.
Sights: Post front adjustable for elevation, rear adjustable for windage.
Features: Based on the AR-15 rifle. Has A2 Stowaway pistol grip and stock. Introduced 1982. Made in U.S. by Olympic Arms, Inc.
Price: CAR-15, 223 caliber **$650.00**
Price: CAR-9, 9mm Para. **$700.00**
Price: CAR-45, 45 ACP **$730.00**
Price: CAR-40, 40 S&W **$780.00**
Price: CAR-41, 41 A.E. **$780.00**
Price: CAR-310, 10mm **$850.00**
Price: 7.62x39mm **$700.00**

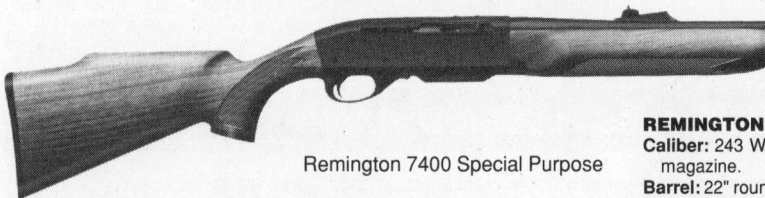

Remington 7400 Special Purpose

Remington Model 7400 Special Purpose Auto Rifle

Similar to the standard Model 7400 except chambered only for 270 and 30-06, non-glare finish on the American walnut stock. All exposed metal has non-reflective matte black finish. Comes with quick-detachable sling swivels and camo-pattern Cordura carrying sling. Introduced 1993.
Price: **$503.00**

REMINGTON MODEL 7400 AUTO RIFLE

Caliber: 243 Win., 270 Win., 280 Rem., 308 Win., 30-06, 35 Whelan, 4-shot magazine.
Barrel: 22" round tapered.
Weight: 7½ lbs. **Length:** 42" overall.
Stock: Walnut, deluxe cut checkered p.g. and forend. Satin or high-gloss finish.
Sights: Gold bead front sight on ramp; step rear sight with windage adjustable.
Features: Redesigned and improved version of the Model 742. Positive cross-bolt safety. Receiver tapped for scope mount. 4-shot clip mag. Introduced 1981.
Price: About **$503.00**
Price: Carbine (18½" bbl., 30-06 only) **$503.00**

Ruger Mini-14/5R

Ruger Mini Thirty Rifle

Similar to the Mini-14 Ranch Rifle except modified to chamber the 7.62x39 Russian service round. Weight is about 7 lbs., 3 oz. Has 6-groove barrel with 1-10" twist, Ruger Integral Scope Mount bases and folding peep rear sight. Detachable 5-shot staggered box magazine. Blued finish. Introduced 1987.
Price: Blue **$530.00**
Price: Stainless **$580.00**

RUGER MINI-14/5 AUTOLOADING RIFLE

Caliber: 223 Rem., 5-shot detachable box magazine.
Barrel: 18½". Rifling twist 1:7".
Weight: 6.4 lbs. **Length:** 37¼" overall.
Stock: American hardwood, steel reinforced.
Sights: Ramp front, fully adjustable rear.
Features: Fixed piston gas-operated, positive primary extraction. New buffer system, redesigned ejector system. Ruger S100RH scope rings included. 20-, 30-shot magazine available to police departments and government agencies only.
Price: Mini-14/5R, Ranch Rifle, blued, scope rings **$530.00**
Price: K-Mini-14/5R, Ranch Rifle, stainless, scope rings **$580.00**
Price: Mini-14/5, blued, no scope rings **$491.50**
Price: K-Mini-14/5, stainless, no scope rings **$542.00**

Springfield M-1A

SPRINGFIELD INC. M-1A RIFLE

Caliber: 7.62mm NATO (308), 5-, 10- or 20-shot box magazine.
Barrel: 25¹⁄₁₆" with flash suppressor, 22" without suppressor.
Weight: 8¾ lbs. **Length:** 44¼" overall.
Stock: American walnut with walnut colored heat-resistant fiberglass handguard. Matching walnut handguard available. Also available with fiberglass stock.
Sights: Military, square blade front, full click-adjustable aperture rear.
Features: Commercial equivalent of the U.S. M-14 service rifle with no provision for automatic firing. From Springfield Inc.
Price: Standard M-1A rifle, about **$1,239.00**
Price: National Match about **$1,539.00**
Price: Super Match (heavy premium barrel) about **$1,849.00**
Price: M1A-A1 Bush Rifle, walnut stock, about **$1,249.00**

Stoner SR-25

VOERE MODEL 2185 SEMI-AUTO RIFLE
Caliber: 7x64, 308, 30-06, 2-shot detachable magazine.
Barrel: 20".
Weight: 7¾ lbs. **Length:** 43½" overall.
Stock: European walnut with checkered grip and forend, ventilated rubber recoil pad. Oil finish.
Sights: Blade on ramp front, open adjustable rear. Receiver drilled and tapped for scope mounting.
Features: Gas-operated with three forward locking lugs; free-floating barrel; two-stage trigger; cocking indicator inside trigger guard. Imported from Austria by JagerSports, Ltd.
Price: About $1,950.00
Price: With Mannlicher-style full stock, about $2,015.00

STONER SR-25 STANDARD RIFLE
Caliber: 7.62 NATO, 20-shot magazine, 5-shot optional.
Barrel: 20".
Weight: 8.8 lbs. **Length:** 40.75" overall.
Stock: Black synthetic AR-15A2 design, synthetic round forend.
Sights: Fixed AR-15-style front sight tower, rear is adjustable for windage and elevation.
Features: Merges designs of the AR-10 and AR-15 rifles. Upper and lower receivers made of lightweight aircraft aluminum alloy. Quick-detachable carrying handle/rear sight assembly. Introduced 1993. Made in U.S. by Knight's Mfg. Co.
Price: $2,495.00

WILKINSON TERRY CARBINE
Caliber: 9mm Para., 31-shot magazine.
Barrel: 16³/₁₆".
Weight: 6 lbs., 3 oz. **Length:** 30" overall.
Stock: Maple stock and forend.
Sights: Protected post front, aperture rear.
Features: Semi-automatic blowback action fires from a closed breech. Bolt-type safety and magazine catch. Ejection port has automatic trap door. Receiver equipped with dovetail for scope mounting. Made in U.S. From Wilkinson Arms.
Price: $485.92

CENTERFIRE RIFLES—LEVER & SLIDE

Both classic arms and recent designs in American-style repeaters for sport and field shooting.

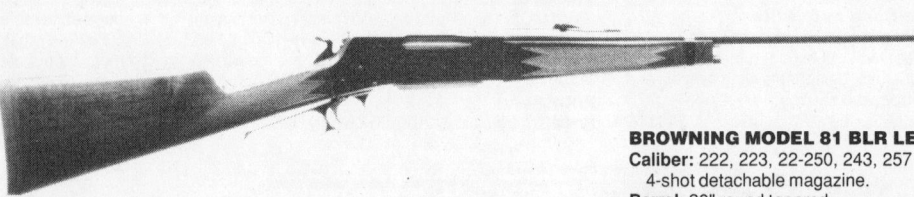

Browning Long Action BLR

Browning Model 81 Long Action BLR
Similar to the standard Model 81 BLR except has long acton to accept 30-06, 270 and 7mm Rem. Mag. Barrel lengths are 22" for 30-06 and 270, 24" for 7mm Rem. Mag. Has six-lug rotary bolt; bolt and receiver are full-length fluted. Fold-down hammer at half-cock. Weight about 8½ lbs., overall length 42½" (22" barrel). Introduced 1991.
Price: $539.95

BROWNING MODEL 81 BLR LEVER-ACTION RIFLE
Caliber: 222, 223, 22-250, 243, 257 Roberts, 7mm-08, 308 Win. or 358 Win., 4-shot detachable magazine.
Barrel: 20" round tapered.
Weight: 6 lbs., 15 oz. **Length:** 39¾" overall.
Stock: Walnut. Checkered straight grip and forend, high-gloss finish.
Sights: Gold bead on hooded ramp front; low profile square notch adj. rear.
Features: Wide, grooved trigger; half-cock hammer safety; fold-down hammer. Receiver tapped for scope mount. Recoil pad installed. Imported from Japan by Browning.
Price: With sights $509.95

Browning 1886 Carbine

CIMARRON 1860 HENRY REPLICA
Caliber: 44 WCF, 13-shot magazine.
Barrel: 24¼" (rifle), 22" (carbine).
Weight: 9½lbs. **Length:** 43" overall (rifle).
Stock: European walnut.
Sights: Bead front, open adjustable rear.
Features: Brass receiver amd buttplate. Uses original Henry loading system. Faithful to the original rifle. Introduced 1991. Imported by Cimarron Arms.
Price: $799.95

BROWNING MODEL 1886 LEVER-ACTION CARBINE
Caliber: 45-70, 8-shot magazine.
Barrel: 22".
Weight: 8 lbs., 3 oz. **Length:** 40.75" overall.
Stock: Satin-finished select walnut with metal crescent buttplate.
Sights: Blade front, open adjustable rear.
Features: Recreation of the original gun. Full-length magazine, classic-style forend with barrel band, saddle ring. Polished blue finish. Limited to 7000 guns. Introduced 1992. Imported from Japan by Browning.
Price: $749.95

Browning Model 1886 High Grade Carbine
Same as the standar Model 1886 Carbine except has high grade walnut with cut-checkered grip and forend and gloss finish. Receiver and lever are grayed steel. Receiver has scroll engraving and game scenes of mule deer and grizzly bear highlighted by a special gold plating and engraving process. Limited to 3000 guns. Introduced 1992.
Price: $1,175.00

CIMARRON 1866 WINCHESTER REPLICAS
Caliber: 22 LR, 22 WMR, 38 Spec., 44 WCF.
Barrel: 24¼" (rifle), 19" (carbine).
Weight: 9 lbs. **Length:** 43" overall (rifle).
Stock: European walnut.
Sights: Bead front, open adjustable rear.
Features: Solid brass receiver, buttplate, forend cap. Octagonal barrel. Faithful to the original Winchester '66 rifle. Introduced 1991. Imported by Cimarron Arms.
Price: Rifle $689.95
Price: Carbine $649.95

CIMARRON 1873 SHORT RIFLE
Caliber: 22 LR, 22 WMR, 357 Magnum, 44-40, 45 Colt.
Barrel: 20" tapered octagon.
Weight: 7.5 lbs. **Length:** 39" overall.
Stock: Walnut.
Sights: Bead front, adjustable semi-buckhorn rear.
Features: Has half "button" magazine. Original-type markings, including caliber, on barrel and elevator and "Kings" patent. From Cimarron Arms.
Price: $799.95

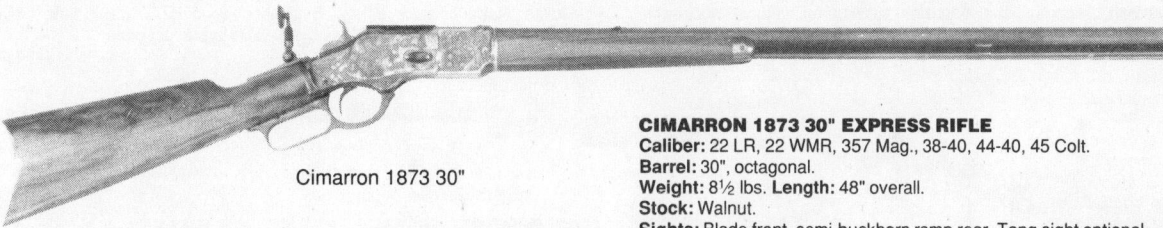

Cimarron 1873 30"

CIMARRON 1873 30" EXPRESS RIFLE
Caliber: 22 LR, 22 WMR, 357 Mag., 38-40, 44-40, 45 Colt.
Barrel: 30", octagonal.
Weight: 8½ lbs. **Length:** 48" overall.
Stock: Walnut.
Sights: Blade front, semi-buckhorn ramp rear. Tang sight optional.
Features: Color case-hardened frame; choice of modern blue-black or charcoal blue for other parts. Barrel marked "Kings improvement." From Cimarron Arms.
Price: $819.95

Cimarron 1873 Sporting Rifle
Similar to the 1873 Express except has 24" barrel with half-magazine.
Price: $799.95
Price: 1873 Saddle Ring Carbine, 19" barrel $729.95

Dixie 1873

E.M.F. 1866 YELLOWBOY LEVER ACTIONS
Caliber: 38 Spec., 44-40.
Barrel: 19" (carbine), 24" (rifle).
Weight: 9 lbs. **Length:** 43" overall (rifle).
Stock: European walnut.
Sights: Bead front, open adjustable rear.
Features: Solid brass frame, blued barrel, lever, hammer, buttplate. Imported from Italy by E.M.F.
Price: Rifle $848.00
Price: Carbine $825.00

DIXIE ENGRAVED 1873 RIFLE
Caliber: 44-40, 11-shot magazine.
Barrel: 20", round.
Weight: 7¾ lbs. **Length:** 39" overall.
Stock: Walnut.
Sights: Blade front, adjustable rear.
Features: Engraved and case-hardened frame. Duplicate of Winchester 1873. Made in Italy. From Dixie Gun Works.
Price: $995.00
Price: Plain, blued carbine $895.00

E.M.F. 1860 HENRY RIFLE
Caliber: 44-40 or 44 rimfire.
Barrel: 24.25".
Weight: About 9 lbs. **Length:** About 43.75" overall.
Stock: Oil-stained American walnut.
Sights: Blade front, rear adjustable for elevation.
Features: Reproduction of the original Henry rifle with brass frame and buttplate, rest blued. From E.M.F.
Price: Standard $1,100.10

E.M.F. MODEL 73 LEVER-ACTION RIFLE
Caliber: 357 Mag., 44-40, 45 Colt.
Barrel: 24".
Weight: 8 lbs. **Length:** 43¼" overall.
Stock: European walnut.
Sights: Bead front, rear adjustable for windage and elevation.
Features: Color case-hardened frame (blue on carbine). Imported by E.M.F.
Price: Rifle $1,050.00
Price: Carbine, 19" barrel $1,020.00

Marlin Model 336CS

MARLIN MODEL 336CS LEVER-ACTION CARBINE
Caliber: 30-30 or 35 Rem., 6-shot tubular magazine.
Barrel: 20" Micro-Groove®.
Weight: 7 lbs. **Length:** 38½" overall.
Stock: Select American black walnut, capped p.g. with white line spacers. Mar-Shield® finish; rubber buttpad; swivel studs.
Sights: Ramp front with Wide-Scan™ hood, semi-buckhorn folding rear adjustable for windage and elevation.
Features: Hammer-block safety. Receiver tapped for scope mount, offset hammer spur; top of receiver sand blasted to prevent glare.
Price: $404.30

MARLIN MODEL 444SS LEVER-ACTION SPORTER
Caliber: 444 Marlin, 5-shot tubular magazine.
Barrel: 22" Micro-Groove®.
Weight: 7½ lbs. **Length:** 40½" overall.
Stock: American black walnut, capped p.g. with white line spacers, rubber rifle buttpad. Mar-Shield® finish; swivel studs.
Sights: Hooded ramp front, folding semi-buckhorn rear adjustable for windage and elevation.
Features: Hammer-block safety. Receiver tapped for scope mount; offset hammer spur.
Price: $490.25

Marlin Model 30AS Lever-Action Carbine
Same as the Marlin 336CS except has walnut-finished hardwood p.g. stock, 30-30 only, 6-shot. Hammer-block safety. Adjustable rear sight, brass bead front.
Price: $344.25

Marlin Model 1894S

Marlin Model 1894CS Carbine
Similar to the standard Model 1894S except chambered for 38 Special/357 Magnum with full-length 9-shot magazine, 18½" barrel, hammer-block safety, brass bead front sight. Introduced 1983.
Price: $454.80

MARLIN MODEL 1894S LEVER-ACTION CARBINE
Caliber: 44 Special/44 Magnum, 10-shot tubular magazine.
Barrel: 20" Micro-Groove®.
Weight: 6 lbs. **Length:** 37½" overall.
Stock: American black walnut, straight grip and forend. Mar-Shield® finish. Rubber rifle buttpad; swivel studs.
Sights: Wide-Scan™ hooded ramp front, semi-buckhorn folding rear adjustable for windage and elevation.
Features: Hammer-block safety. Receiver tapped for scope mount, offset hammer spur, solid top receiver sand blasted to prevent glare.
Price: $454.80

Marlin Model 1894CL

Marlin Model 1894CL Classic
Similar to the 1894CS except chambered for 218 Bee, 25-20 and 32-20 Win. Has 6-shot tubular magazine. 22" barrel with 6-groove rifling, brass bead front sight, adjustable semi-buckhorn folding rear. Hammer-block safety. Weighs 6¼ lbs., overall length of 38¾". Bee has rubber rifle butt pad, swivel studs. Introduced 1988.
Price: $488.00

MARLIN MODEL 1895SS LEVER-ACTION RIFLE
Caliber: 45-70, 4-shot tubular magazine.
Barrel: 22" round.
Weight: 7½ lbs. **Length:** 40½" overall.
Stock: American black walnut, full pistol grip. Mar-Shield® finish; rubber buttpad; q.d. swivel studs.
Sights: Bead front with Wide-Scan™ hood, semi-buckhorn folding rear adjustable for windage and elevation.
Features: Hammer-block safety. Solid receiver tapped for scope mounts or receiver sights; offset hammer spur.
Price: $490.25

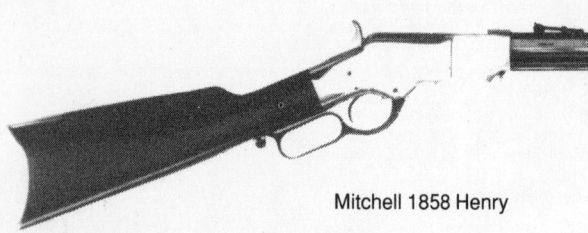

Mitchell 1858 Henry

MITCHELL 1866 WINCHESTER REPLICA
Caliber: 44-40, 13-shot.
Barrel: 24¼".
Weight: 9 lbs. **Length:** 43" overall.
Stock: European walnut.
Sights: Bead front, open adjustable rear.
Features: Solid brass receiver, buttplate, forend cap. Octagonal barrel. Faithful to the original Winchester '66 rifle. Introduced 1990. Imported by Mitchell Arms, Inc.
Price: $829.00

MITCHELL 1858 HENRY REPLICA
Caliber: 44-40, 13-shot magazine.
Barrel: 24¼".
Weight: 9.5 lbs. **Length:** 43" overall.
Stock: European walnut.
Sights: Bead front, open adjustable rear.
Features: Brass receiver and buttplate. Uses original Henry loading system. Faithful to the original rifle. Introduced 1990. Imported by Mitchell Arms, Inc.
Price: $999.00

MITCHELL 1873 WINCHESTER REPLICA
Caliber: 45 Colt, 13-shot.
Barrel: 24¼".
Weight: 9.5 lbs. **Length:** 43" overall.
Stock: European walnut.
Sights: Bead front, open adjustable rear.
Features: Color case-hardened steel receiver. Faithful to the original Model 1873 rifle. Introduced 1990. Imported by Mitchell Arms, Inc.
Price: $950.00

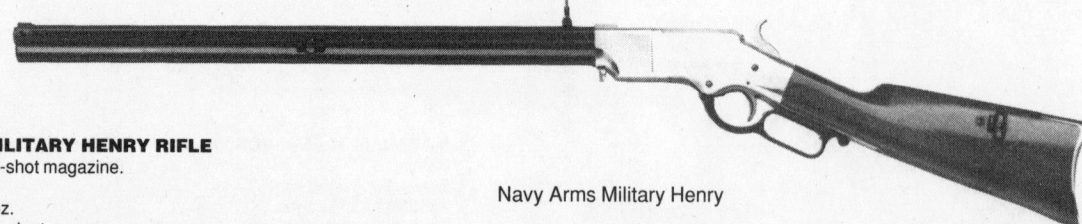

NAVY ARMS MILITARY HENRY RIFLE
Caliber: 44-40, 12-shot magazine.
Barrel: 24¼".
Weight: 9 lbs., 4 oz.
Stock: European walnut.
Sights: Blade front, adjustable ladder-type rear.
Features: Brass frame, buttplate, rest blued. Recreation of the model used by cavalry units in the Civil War. Has full-length magazine tube, sling swivels; no forend. Introduced 1991. Imported from Italy by Navy Arms.
Price: $875.00

Navy Arms Military Henry

Navy Arms Henry Trapper
Similar to the Military Henry Rifle except has 16½" barrel, weighs 7½ lbs. Brass frame and buttplate, rest blued. Introduced 1991. Imported from Italy by Navy Arms.
Price: $875.00

Navy Arms Iron Frame Henry
Similar to the Military Henry Rifle except receiver is blued or color case-hardened steel. Introduced 1991. Imported by Navy Arms.
Price: $895.00

Navy Arms Henry Carbine
Similar to the Military Henry rifle except has 22" barrel, weighs 8 lbs., 12 oz., is 41" overall; no sling swivels. Caliber 44-40. Introduced 1992. Imported from Italy by Navy Arms.
Price: $875.00

CONSULT
SHOOTER'S MARKETPLACE
Page 231, This Issue

NAVY ARMS 1866 YELLOWBOY RIFLE
Caliber: 44-40, 12-shot magazine.
Barrel: 24", full octagon.
Weight: 8½ lbs. **Length:** 42½" overall.
Stock: European walnut.
Sights: Blade front, adjustable ladder-type rear.
Features: Brass frame, forend tip, buttplate, blued barrel, lever, hammer.
Introduced 1991. Imported from Italy by Navy Arms.
Price: $710.00
Price: Carbine, 19" barrel $685.00

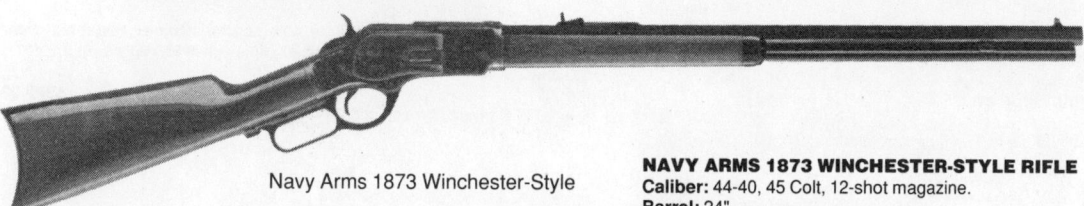

Navy Arms 1873 Winchester-Style

NAVY ARMS 1873 WINCHESTER-STYLE RIFLE
Caliber: 44-40, 45 Colt, 12-shot magazine.
Barrel: 24".
Weight: 8¼ lbs. **Length:** 43" overall.
Stock: European walnut.
Sights: Blade front, buckhorn rear.
Features: Color case-hardened frame, rest blued. Full-octagon barrel. Introduced 1991. Imported by Navy Arms.
Price: $840.00
Price: Carbine, 19" barrel $815.00

Navy Arms 1873 Sporting Rifle
Similar to the 1873 Winchester-Style rifle except has checkered pistol grip stock, 30" octagonal barrel (24" available). Introduced 1992. Imported by Navy Arms.
Price: $895.00

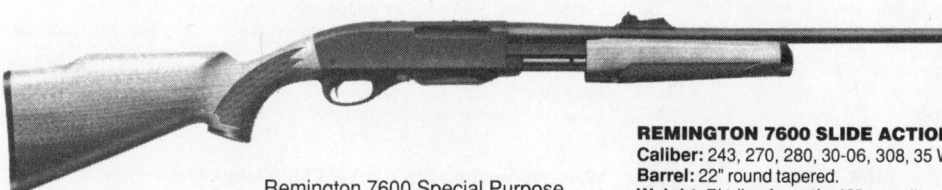

Remington 7600 Special Purpose

REMINGTON 7600 SLIDE ACTION
Caliber: 243, 270, 280, 30-06, 308, 35 Whelen.
Barrel: 22" round tapered.
Weight: 7½ lbs. **Length:** 42" overall.
Stock: Cut-checkered walnut p.g. and forend, Monte Carlo with full cheekpiece. Satin or high-gloss finish.
Sights: Gold bead front sight on matted ramp, open step adjustable sporting rear.
Feature: Redesigned and improved version of the Model 760. Detachable 4-shot clip. Cross-bolt safety. Receiver tapped for scope mount. Also available in high grade versions. Introduced 1981.
Price: About $480.00
Price: Carbine (18½" bbl., 30-06 only) $480.00

Remington Model 7600 Special Purpose Slide Action
Similar to the standard Model 7600 except chambered only for 270 and 30-06, non-glare finish on the American walnut stock. All exposed metal has non-reflective matte black finish. Comes with quick-detachable sling swivels and camo-pattern Cordura carrying sling. Introduced 1993.
Price: $480.00

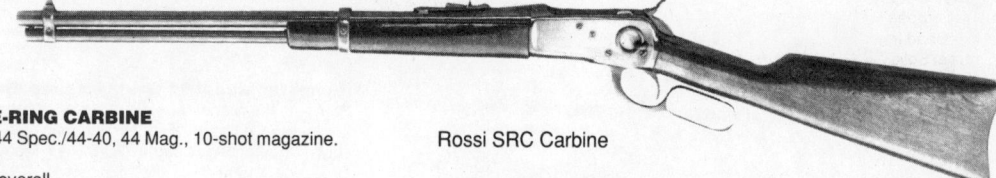

Rossi SRC Carbine

ROSSI M92 SRC SADDLE-RING CARBINE
Caliber: 38 Spec./357 Mag., 44 Spec./44-40, 44 Mag., 10-shot magazine.
Barrel: 20".
Weight: 5¾ lbs. **Length:** 37" overall.
Stock: Walnut.
Sights: Blade front, buckhorn rear.
Features: Recreation of the famous lever-action carbine. Handles 38 and 357 interchangeably. Has high-relief puma medallion inlaid in the receiver. Introduced 1978. Imported by Interarms.
Price: $350.00
Price: 44 Spec./44 Mag. (Model 65) $367.00

Rossi M92 SRS Short Carbine
Similar to the standard M92 except has 16" barrel, overall length of 33", in 38/357 only. Puma medallion on side of receiver. Introduced 1986.
Price: $350.00

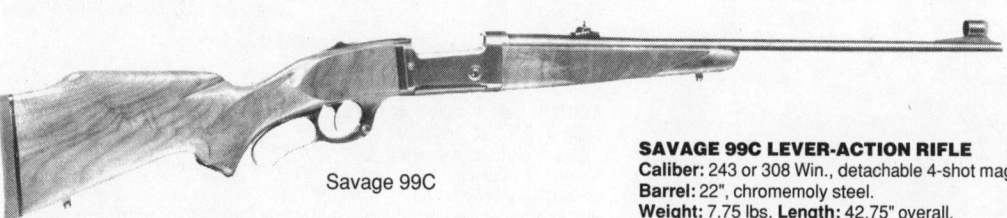

Savage 99C

SAVAGE 99C LEVER-ACTION RIFLE
Caliber: 243 or 308 Win., detachable 4-shot magazine.
Barrel: 22", chromemoly steel.
Weight: 7.75 lbs. **Length:** 42.75" overall.
Stock: Walnut with checkered p.g. and forend, Monte Carlo comb.
Sights: Hooded ramp front, adjustable ramp rear sight. Tapped for scope mounts.
Features: Grooved trigger, top tang slide safety locks trigger and lever. Brown rubber buttpad, q.d. swivel studs, push-button magazine release.
Price: $620.00

UBERTI HENRY RIFLE

Caliber: 44-40.
Barrel: 24¼", half-octagon.
Weight: 9.2 lbs. **Length:** 43¾" overall.
Stock: American walnut.
Sights: Blade front, rear adjustable for elevation.
Features: Frame, elevator, magazine follower, buttplate are brass, balance blue (also available in polished steel). Imported by Uberti USA.
Price: $895.00
Price: Henry Carbine (22¼" bbl.) $900.00
Price: Henry Trapper (16", 18" bbl.) $900.00

UBERTI 1873 SPORTING RIFLE

Caliber: 22 LR, 22 WMR, 38 Spec., 357 Mag., 44-40, 45 Colt.
Barrel: 24¼", 30", octagonal.
Weight: 8.1 lbs. **Length:** 43¼" overall.
Stock: Walnut.
Sights: Blade front adjustable for windage, open rear adjustable for elevation.

UBERTI 1866 SPORTING RIFLE

Caliber: 22 LR, 22 WMR, 38 Spec., 44-40, 45 Colt.
Barrel: 24¼", octagonal.
Weight: 8.1 lbs. **Length:** 43¼" overall.
Stock: Walnut.
Sights: Blade front adjustable for windage, rear adjustable for elevation.
Features: Frame, buttplate, forend cap of polished brass, balance charcoal blued. Imported by Uberti USA.
Price: $780.00
Price: Yellowboy Carbine (19" round bbl.) $720.00

Features: Color case-hardened frame, blued barrel, hammer, lever, buttplate, brass elevator. Also available with pistol grip stock ($100.00 extra). Imported by Uberti USA.
Price: $900.00
Price: 1873 Carbine (19" round bbl.) $890.00

Winchester 94 Side Eject

Winchester Model 94 Trapper Side Eject

Same as the Model 94 except has 16" barrel, 5-shot magazine in 30-30, 9-shot in 357 Magnum, 44 Magnum/44 Special, 45 Colt. Has stainless steel claw extractor, saddle ring, hammer spur extension, walnut wood.
Price: 30-30 . . . . $335.00
Price: 357 Mag., 44 Mag./44 Spec., 45 Colt $354.00

WINCHESTER MODEL 94 BIG BORE SIDE EJECT

Caliber: 307 Win., 356 Win., 6-shot magazine.
Barrel: 20".
Weight: 7 lbs. **Length:** 38⅝" overall.
Stock: American walnut. Satin finish.
Sights: Hooded ramp front, semi-buckhorn rear adjustable for windage and elevation.
Features: All external metal parts have Winchester's deep blue finish. Rifling twist 1:12". Rubber recoil pad fitted to buttstock. Introduced 1983. From U.S. Repeating Arms Co.
Price: $374.00

WINCHESTER MODEL 94 SIDE EJECT LEVER-ACTION RIFLE

Caliber: 30-30, 7x30 Waters, 32 Win. Spec., 6-shot tubular magazine.
Barrel: 20".
Weight: 6½ lbs. **Length:** 37¾" overall.
Stock: Straight grip walnut stock and forend.
Sights: Hooded blade front, semi-buckhorn rear. Drilled and tapped for scope mount. Post front sight on Trapper model.
Features: Solid frame, forged steel receiver; side ejection, exposed rebounding hammer with automatic trigger-activated transfer bar. Introduced 1984.
Price: Checkered walnut $362.00
Price: No checkering, walnut $335.00
Price: With WinTuff laminated hardwood stock, 30-30 only $335.00

Winchester Model 94 Ranger Side Eject Lever-Action Rifle

Same as Model 94 Side Eject except has 5-shot magazine, American hardwood stock and forend, post front sight. Introduced 1985.
Price: $296.00
Price: With 4x32 Bushnell scope, mounts $348.00

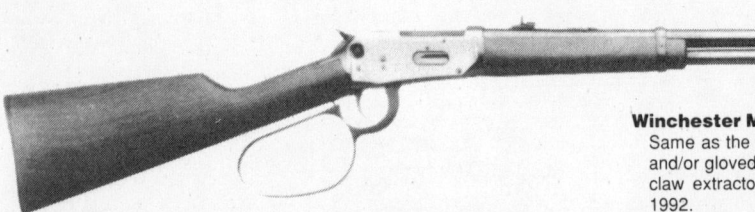

Winchester 94 Wrangler

Winchester Model 94 Wrangler Side Eject

Same as the Model 94 except has 16" barrel and large loop lever for large and/or gloved hands. Has 9-shot capacity (5-shot for 30-30), stainless steel claw extractor. Available in 30-30, 44 Magnum/44 Special. Reintroduced 1992.
Price: 30-30 . . . . $354.00
Price: 44 Magnum/44 Special $374.00

CENTERFIRE RIFLES—BOLT ACTION

Includes models for a wide variety of sporting and competitive purposes and uses.

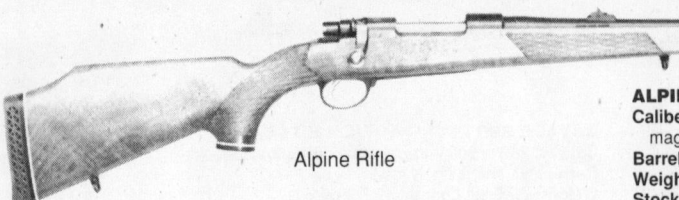

Alpine Rifle

ALPINE BOLT-ACTION RIFLE

Caliber: 22-250, 243 Win., 270, 30-06, 308, 7mm Rem. Mag., 8mm, 5-shot magazine (3 for magnum).
Barrel: 23" (std. cals.), 24" (mag.).
Weight: 7½ lbs.
Stock: European walnut. Full p.g. and Monte Carlo; checkered p.g. and forend; rubber recoil pad; white line spacers; sling swivels.
Sights: Ramp front, open rear adjustable for windage and elevation.
Features: Made by Firearms Co. Ltd. in England. Imported by Mandall Shooting Supplies.
Price: Custom Grade $395.00
Price: Supreme Grade $425.00

CAUTION: PRICES CHANGE, CHECK AT GUNSHOP.

A-Square Hannibal

A-SQUARE CAESAR BOLT-ACTION RIFLE
Caliber: 7mm Rem. Mag., 7mm STW, 30-06, 300 Win. Mag., 300 H&H, 300 Wea. Mag., 8mm Rem. Mag., 338 Win. Mag., 340 Wea. Mag., 338 A-Square, 9.3x62, 9.3x64, 375 Wea. Mag., 375 H&H, 375 JRS, 375 A-Square, 416 Hoffman, 416 Rem. Mag., 416 Taylor, 404 Jeffery, 425 Express, 458 Win. Mag., 458 Lott, 450 Ackley, 460 Short A-Square, 470 Capstick, 495 A-Square.
Barrel: 20" to 26" (no-cost customer option).
Weight: 8½ to 11 lbs.
Stock: Claro walnut with hand-rubbed oil finish; classic style with A-Square Coil-Chek® features for reduced recoil; flush detachable swivels. Customer choice of length of pull.
Sights: Choice of three-leaf express, forward or normal-mount scope, or combination (at extra cost).
Features: Matte non-reflective blue, double cross-bolts, steel and fiberglass reinforcement of wood from tang to forend tip; three-position positive safety; three-way adjustable trigger; expanded magazine capacity. Right- or left-hand. Introduced 1984. Made in U.S. by A-Square Co., Inc.
Price: Walnut stock **$2,550.00**
Price: Synthetic stock **$2,800.00**

A-SQUARE HANNIBAL BOLT-ACTION RIFLE
Caliber: 7mm Rem. Mag., 7mm STW, 30-06, 300 Win. Mag., 300 H&H, 300 Wea. Mag., 8mm Rem. Mag., 338 Win. Mag., 340 Wea. Mag., 338 A-Square Mag., 9.3x62, 9.3x64, 375 H&H, 375 Wea. Mag., 375 JRS, 375 A-Square Mag., 378 Wea. Mag., 416 Taylor, 416 Rem. Mag., 416 Hoffman, 416 Rigby, 416 Wea. Mag., 404 Jeffery, 425 Express, 458 Win. Mag., 458 Lott, 450 Ackley, 460 Short A-Square Mag., 460 Wea. Mag., 470 Capstick, 495 A-Square Mag., 500 A-Square Mag.
Barrel: 20" to 26" (no-cost customer option).
Weight: 9 to 11¾ lbs.
Stock: Claro walnut with hand-rubbed oil finish; classic style with A-Square Coil-Chek® features for reduced recoil; flush detachable swivels. Customer choice of length of pull. Available with synthetic stock.
Sights: Choice of three-leaf express, forward or normal-mount scope, or combination (at extra cost).
Features: Matte non-reflective blue, double cross-bolts, steel and fiberglass reinforcement of wood from tang to forend tip; Mauser-style claw extractor; expanded magazine capacity; two-position safety; three-way target trigger. Right-hand only. Introduced 1983. Made in U.S. by A-Square Co., Inc.
Price: Walnut stock **$2,495.00**
Price: Synthetic stock **$2,645.00**

Anschutz 1700D Classic

Anschutz 1700D Custom Rifles
Similar to the Classic models except have roll-over Monte Carlo cheekpiece, slim forend with Schnabel tip, Wundhammer palm swell on pistol grip, rosewood grip cap with white diamond insert. Skip-line checkering on grip and forend. Introduced 1988. Imported from Germany by PSI.
Price: **$1,416.00**
Price: Meistergrade (select stock, gold engraved trigger guard) . . **$1,615.00**

ANSCHUTZ 1700D CLASSIC RIFLES
Caliber: 22 Hornet, 5-shot clip; 222 Rem., 3-shot clip.
Barrel: 24", ¹³⁄₁₆ dia. heavy.
Weight: 7¾ lbs. **Length:** 43" overall.
Stock: Select European walnut with checkered pistol grip and forend.
Sights: Hooded ramp front, folding leaf rear; drilled and tapped for scope mounting.
Features: Adjustable single stage trigger. Receiver drilled and tapped for scope mounting. Introduced 1988. Imported from Germany by Precision Sales International.
Price: **$1,387.00**
Price: Meistergrade (select stock, gold engraved trigger guard) . . **$1,586.00**

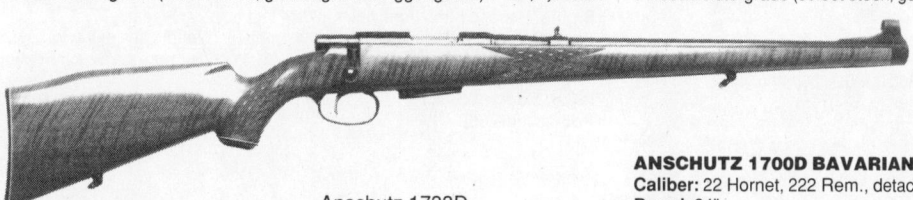

Anschutz 1733D

Anschutz 1733D Mannlicher Rifle
Similar to the 1700D Bavarian except chambered only for 22 Hornet and has Mannlicher stock. Uses improved Match 54 action with #5096 single-stage trigger with 2.6 lb. adjustable pull weight. Has 19.75" barrel, overall length of 39". Comes with sling swivels, Lyman folding rear sight and hooded ramp front, 4-shot magazine. Introduced 1993. Imported from Germany by Precision Sales International.
Price: **$1,537.00**

ANSCHUTZ 1700D BAVARIAN BOLT-ACTION RIFLE
Caliber: 22 Hornet, 222 Rem., detachable clip.
Barrel: 24".
Weight: 7¼ lbs. **Length:** 43" overall.
Stock: European walnut with Bavarian cheek rest. Checkered p.g. and forend.
Sights: Hooded ramp front, folding leaf rear.
Features: Uses the improved 1700 Match 54 action with adjustable trigger. Drilled and tapped for scope mounting. Introduced 1988. Imported from Germany by Precision Sales International.
Price: **$1,416.00**
Price: Meistergrade (select stock, gold engraved trigger guard) . . **$1,615.00**

Beeman/HW 60J

BARRETT MODEL 90 BOLT-ACTION RIFLE
Caliber: 50 BMG, 5-shot magazine.
Barrel: 29".
Weight: 22 lbs. **Length:** 45" overall.
Stock: Sorbothane recoil pad.
Sights: Scope optional.
Features: Bolt-action, bullpup design. Disassembles without tools; extendable bipod legs; match-grade barrel; high efficiency muzzlebrake. Introduced 1990. From Barrett Firearms Mfg., Inc.
Price: From **$3,650.00**

BEEMAN/HW 60J BOLT-ACTION RIFLE
Caliber: 222 Rem.
Barrel: 22.8".
Weight: 6.5 lbs. **Length:** 41.7" overall.
Stock: Walnut with cheekpiece; cut checkered p.g. and forend.
Sights: Hooded blade on ramp front, open rear.
Features: Polished blue finish; oil-finished wood. Imported from Germany by Beeman. Introduced 1988.
Price: **$945.00**

Blaser R84

BRNO 537 SPORTER BOLT-ACTION RIFLE
Caliber: 243, 270, 30-06 (internal 5-shot magazine), 308 (detachable 5-shot magazine).
Barrel: 23.6".
Weight: 7 lbs., 9 oz. **Length:** 44.7" overall.
Stock: Checkered walnut or synthetic.
Sights: Hooded ramp front, adjustable folding leaf rear.
Features: Improved standard size Mauser-style action with non-rotating claw extractor; externally adjustable trigger, American-style safety; streamlined bolt shroud with cocking indicator. Introduced 1992. Imported from the Czech Republic by Action Arms Ltd.
Price: Walnut stock **$669.00**
Price: Synthetic stock **$599.00**

BLASER R84 BOLT-ACTION RIFLE
Caliber: Std. cals.—22-250, 243, 6mm Rem., 25-06, 270, 280, 30-06; magnum cals.—257 Wea., 264 Win. Mag., 7mm Rem. Mag., 300 Win. Mag., 300 Wea., 338 Win. Mag., 375 H&H.
Barrel: 23" (24" in magnum cals.).
Weight: 7-7¼ lbs. **Length:** Std. cals.—41" overall (23" barrel).
Stock: Two-piece Turkish walnut. Solid black buttpad.
Sights: None furnished. Comes with low-profile Blaser scope mountings.
Features: Interchangeable barrels (scope mountings on barrel), and magnum/standard caliber bolt assemblies. Left-hand models available in all calibers. Imported from Germany by Autumn Sales, Inc.
Price: Right-hand, standard or magnum calibers **$2,300.00**
Price: Left-hand, standard or magnum calibers **$2,850.00**
Price: Interchangeable barrels, standard or magnum calibers **$600.00**

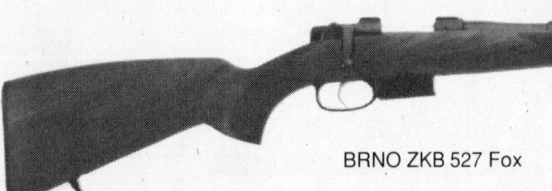

BRNO ZKB 527 Fox

BRNO ZKB 527 FOX BOLT-ACTION RIFLE
Caliber: 22 Hornet, 222 Rem., 223 Rem., detachable 5-shot magazine.
Barrel: 23½".

Weight: 6 lbs., 1 oz. **Length:** 42½" overall.
Stock: European walnut, with Monte Carlo, or synthetic.
Sights: Hooded front, open adjustable rear.
Features: Improved mini-Mauser action with non-rotating claw extractor; grooved receiver. Imported from the Czech Republic by Action Arms Ltd.
Price: Walnut stock **$655.00**
Price: Synthetic stock **$599.00**

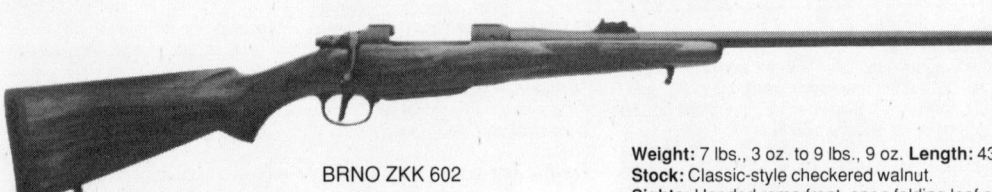

BRNO ZKK 602

BRNO ZKK 600, 601, 602 BOLT-ACTION RIFLES
Caliber: 7x57, 30-06, 270 (M600); 243, 308 (M601); 300 Win. Mag., 375 H&H, 458 Win. Mag. (M602), 5-shot magazine.
Barrel: 23½" (M600, 601); 25" (M602).

Weight: 7 lbs., 3 oz. to 9 lbs., 9 oz. **Length:** 43" overall (M601).
Stock: Classic-style checkered walnut.
Sights: Hooded ramp front, open folding leaf adjustable rear.
Features: Improved Mauser action with controlled feed, claw extractor; safety blocks triggers and locks bolt; sling swivels. Imported from the Czech Republic by Action Arms Ltd.
Price: Model 600, 601 . . . . **$609.00**
Price: Model 602 . . . . **$835.00**

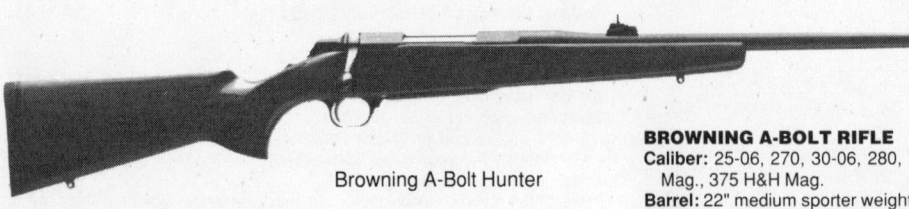

Browning A-Bolt Hunter

BROWNING A-BOLT RIFLE
Caliber: 25-06, 270, 30-06, 280, 7mm Rem. Mag., 300 Win. Mag., 338 Win. Mag., 375 H&H Mag.
Barrel: 22" medium sporter weight with recessed muzzle; 26" on mag. cals.
Weight: 6½ to 7½ lbs. **Length:** 44¾" overall (magnum and standard); 41¾" (short action).
Stock: Classic style American walnut; recoil pad standard on magnum calibers.
Features: Short-throw (60˚) fluted bolt, three locking lugs, plunger-type ejector; adjustable trigger is grooved and gold-plated. Hinged floorplate, detachable box magazine (4 rounds std. cals., 3 for magnums). Slide tang safety. Medallion has glossy stock finish, rosewood grip and forend caps, high polish blue. Introduced 1985. Imported from Japan by Browning.
Price: Medallion, no sights **$596.95**
Price: Hunter, no sights **$509.95**
Price: Hunter, with sights **$574.95**
Price: Medallion, 375 H&H Mag., with sights **$696.95**

> **Consult our Directory pages for the location of firms mentioned.**

Browning A-Bolt Stainless Stalker
Similar to the Hunter model A-Bolt except receiver is made of stainless steel; the rest of the exposed metal surfaces are finished with a durable matte silver-gray. Graphite-Fiberglass composite textured stock. No sights are furnished. Available in 270, 30-06, 7mm Rem. Mag., 375 H&H. Introduced 1987.
Price: **$664.95**
Price: Composite Stalker (as above, checkered stock) **$524.95**
Price: Left-hand, no sights **$684.95**
Price: 375 H&H, with sights **$764.95**
Price: 375 H&H, left-hand, with sights **$786.95**

Browning A-Bolt Left Hand
Same as the Medallion model A-Bolt except has left-hand action and is available only in 270, 30-06, 7mm Rem. Mag., 375 H&H. Introduced 1987.
Price: **$621.95**
Price: 375 H&H, with sights **$721.95**

CAUTION: PRICES CHANGE, CHECK AT GUNSHOP.

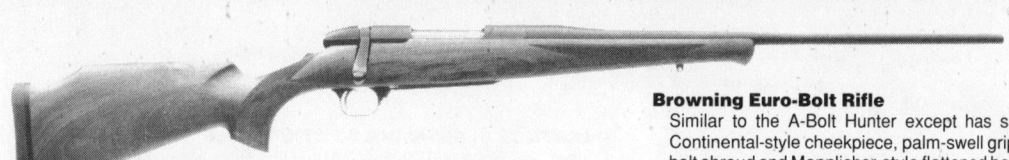

Browning Euro-Bolt

Browning A-Bolt Short Action

Similar to the standard A-Bolt except has short action for 22 Hornet, 223, 22-250, 243, 257 Roberts, 7mm-08, 284 Win., 308 chamberings. Available in Hunter or Medallion grades. Weighs 6½ lbs. Other specs essentially the same. Introduced 1985.

Price: Medallion, no sights $596.95
Price: Hunter, no sights $509.95
Price: Hunter, with sights $574.95
Price: Composite, no sights $524.95

Browning Euro-Bolt Rifle

Similar to the A-Bolt Hunter except has satin-finished walnut stock with Continental-style cheekpiece, palm-swell grip and schnabel forend, rounded bolt shroud and Mannlicher-style flattened bolt handle. Available in 30-06 and 270 with 22" barrel, 7mm Rem. Mag. with 26" barrel. Weighs about 6 lbs., 11 oz. Introduced 1993.

Price: $699.95

Browning A-Bolt Gold Medallion

Similar to the standard A-Bolt except has select walnut stock with brass spacers between rubber recoil pad and between the rosewood grip cap and forend tip; gold-filled barrel inscription; palm-swell pistol grip, Monte Carlo comb, 22 lpi checkering with double borders; engraved receiver flats. In 270, 30-06, 7mm Rem. Mag. only. Introduced 1988.

Price: $809.95

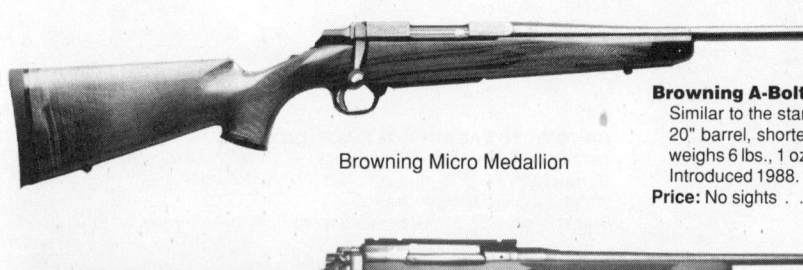

Browning Micro Medallion

Browning A-Bolt Micro Medallion

Similar to the standard A-Bolt except is a scaled-down version. Comes with 20" barrel, shortened length of pull (13⁵⁄₁₆"); three-shot magazine capacity; weighs 6 lbs., 1 oz. Available in 243, 308, 7mm-08, 257 Roberts, 223, 22-250. Introduced 1988.

Price: No sights $596.95

Century Centuion 14

CENTURY ENFIELD SPORTER #4

Caliber: 303 British, 10-shot magazine.
Barrel: 25.2".
Weight: 8 lbs., 5 oz. Length: 44.5" overall.
Stock: Beechwood with checkered p.g. and forend, Monte Carlo comb.
Sights: Blade front, adjustable aperture rear.
Features: Uses Lee-Enfield action; blue finish. Trigger pinned to receiver. Introduced 1987. From Century International Arms.
Price: About $156.00

CENTURY CENTURION 14 SPORTER

Caliber: 7mm Rem. Mag., 300 Win. Mag., 5-shot magazine.
Barrel: 24".
Weight: NA. Length: 43.3" overall.
Stock: Walnut-finished European hardwood. Checkered p.g. and forend. Monte Carlo comb.
Sights: None furnished.
Features: Uses modified Pattern 14 Enfield action. Drilled and tapped; scope base mounted. Blue finish. From Century International Arms.
Price: About $275.00

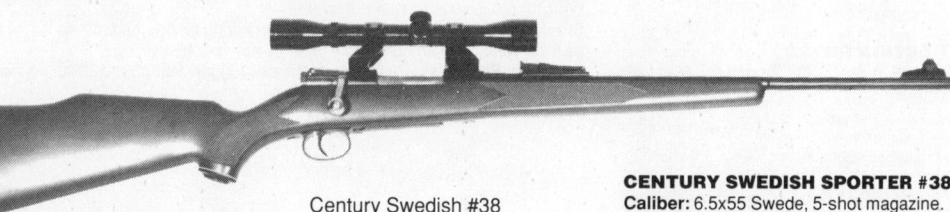

Century Swedish #38

CENTURY MAUSER 98 SPORTER

Caliber: 243, 270, 308, 30-06.
Barrel: 24".
Weight: NA. Length: 44" overall.
Stock: Black synthetic.
Sights: None furnished. Scope base installed.
Features: Mauser 98 action; bent bolt handle for scope use; low-swing safety; matte black finish; blind magazine. Introduced 1992. From Century International Arms.
Price: About $288.00

DAKOTA 22 SPORTER BOLT-ACTION RIFLE

Caliber: 22 LR, 22 Hornet, 5-shot magazine.
Barrel: 22".
Weight: About 6.5 lbs. Length: NA.
Stock: Claro or English walnut in classic design; 13.5" length of pull. Choice of grade. Point panel hand checkering. Swivel studs. Black butt pad.
Sights: None furnished; comes with mount bases.
Features: Combines features of Winchester 52 and Dakota 76 rifles. Full-sized receiver; rear locking lugs and bolt machined from bar stock. Trigger and striker-blocking safety; adjustable trigger. Introduced 1992. From Dakota Arms, Inc.
Price: $1,500.00

CENTURY SWEDISH SPORTER #38

Caliber: 6.5x55 Swede, 5-shot magazine.
Barrel: 24".
Weight: NA. Length: 44.1" overall.
Stock: Walnut-finished European hardwood with checkered p.g. and forend; Monte Carlo comb.
Sights: Blade front, adjustable rear.
Features: Uses M38 Swedish Mauser action; comes with Holden Ironsighter see-through scope mount. Introduced 1987. From Century International Arms.
Price: About $237.50

COOPER MODEL 38 CENTERFIRE SPORTER

Caliber: 17 CCM, 22 CCM, 3-shot magazine.
Barrel: 23¾" Shilen match.
Weight: 8 lbs. Length: 42½" overall.
Stock: Standard—AA Claro walnut with 22 lpi checkering, oil finish; Custom has AAA Claro or AA French walnut, beaded Monte Carlo cheekpiece.
Sights: None furnished.
Features: Action has three front locking lugs, 45-degree bolt rotation; fully adjustable single stage match trigger; swivel studs. Pachmayr butt pad. Introduced 1991. Made in U.S. by Cooper Arms.
Price: Standard $1,095.00
Price: Standard single shot $995.00
Price: Custom $1,295.00

Dakota 76 Classic

DAKOTA 76 CLASSIC BOLT-ACTION RIFLE
Caliber: 257 Roberts, 270, 280, 30-06, 7mm Rem. Mag., 338 Win. Mag., 300 Win. Mag., 375 H&H, 458 Win. Mag.
Barrel: 23".
Weight: 7½ lbs. **Length:** NA.
Stock: Medium fancy grade walnut in classic style. Checkered p.g. and forend; solid buttpad.
Sights: None furnished; drilled and tapped for scope mounts.
Features: Has many features of the original Model 70 Winchester. One-piece rail trigger guard assembly; steel grip cap. Adjustable trigger. Many options available. Left-hand rifle available at same price. Introduced 1988. From Dakota Arms, Inc.
Price: Short Classic **$2,300.00**

Dakota 76 Short Action Rifles
A scaled-down version of the standard Model 76. Standard chamberings are 22-250, 243, 6mm Rem., 250-3000, 7mm-08, 308, others on special order. Short Classic Grade has 21" barrel; Alpine Grade is lighter (6½ lbs.), has a blind magazine and slimmer stock. Introduced 1989.
Price: Short Classic **$2,300.00**

Dakota 76 Safari

DAKOTA 76 SAFARI BOLT-ACTION RIFLE
Caliber: 338 Win. Mag., 300 Win. Mag., 375 H&H, 458 Win. Mag.
Barrel: 23".
Weight: 8½ lbs. **Length:** NA.
Stock: Fancy walnut with ebony forend tip; point-pattern with wraparound forend checkering.
Sights: Ramp front, standing leaf rear.
Features: Has many features of the original Model 70 Winchester. Barrel band front swivel, inletted rear. Cheekpiece with shadow line. Steel grip cap. Introduced 1988. From Dakota Arms, Inc.
Price: Wood stock **$3,000.00**

Dakota 416 Rigby African
Similar to the 76 Safari except chambered for 404 Jeffery, 416 Rigby, 416 Dakota, 450 Dakota, 4-round magazine, select wood, two stock cross-bolts. Has 24" barrel, weight of 9-10 lbs. Ramp front sight, standing leaf rear. Introduced 1989.
Price: **$3,500.00**

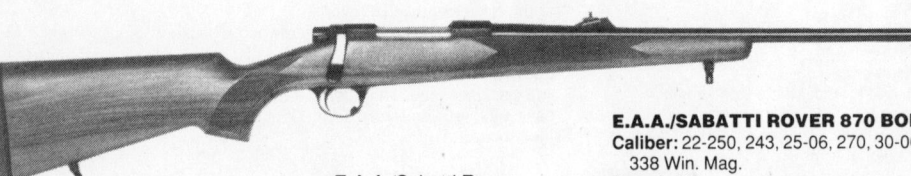

E.A.A./Sabatti Rover

E.A.A./SABATTI ROVER 870 BOLT-ACTION RIFLE
Caliber: 22-250, 243, 25-06, 270, 30-06, 308, 7mm Rem. Mag., 300 Win. Mag., 338 Win. Mag.
Barrel: 23".
Weight: 6.9 lbs. **Length:** 42.5" overall.
Stock: Walnut with straight comb, cut checkering on grip and forend.
Sights: Gold bead on ramp front, open adjustable rear.
Features: Blue finish. Positive safety locks trigger. Introduced 1986. Imported by European American Armory.
Price: **$550.00**

AUGUSTE FRANCOTTE BOLT-ACTION RIFLES
Caliber: 243, 270, 7x64, 30-06, 308, 300 Win. Mag., 338, 7mm Rem. Mag., 375 H&H, 458 Win. Mag.; others on request.
Barrel: 23½" to 26½".
Weight: 8 to 10 lbs.
Stock: Fancy European walnut. To customer specs.
Sights: To customer specs.
Features: Basically a custom gun, Francotte offers many options. Imported from Belgium by Armes de Chasse.
Price: . . . . **$9,000.00 to $15,000.00**

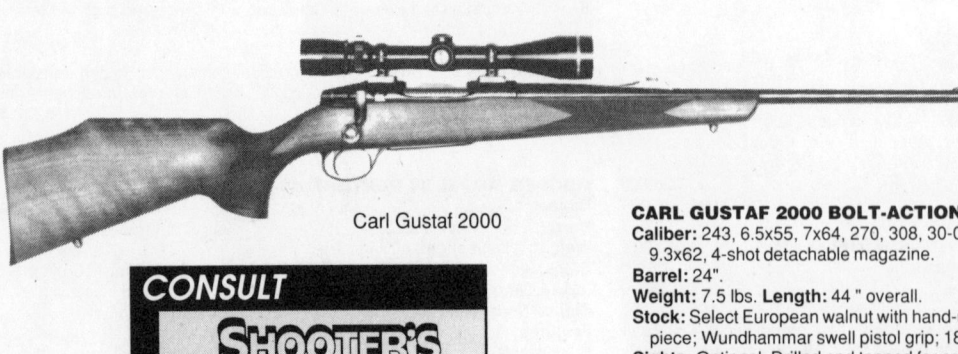

Carl Gustaf 2000

CARL GUSTAF 2000 BOLT-ACTION RIFLE
Caliber: 243, 6.5x55, 7x64, 270, 308, 30-06, 7mm Rem. Mag., 300 Win. Mag., 9.3x62, 4-shot detachable magazine.
Barrel: 24".
Weight: 7.5 lbs. **Length:** 44" overall.
Stock: Select European walnut with hand-rubbed oil finish; Monte Carlo cheekpiece; Wundhammar swell pistol grip; 18 l.p.i. checkering.
Sights: Optional. Drilled and tapped for scope mounting.
Features: Three-way adjustable single-stage, roller bearing trigger; three-position safety; triple front locking lugs; free-floating barrel; swivel studs. Comes with factory test target. Introduced 1991. Imported from Sweden by Precision Sales International.
Price: Without sights **$1,875.00**
Price: With sights **$1,985.00**

CAUTION: PRICES CHANGE, CHECK AT GUNSHOP.

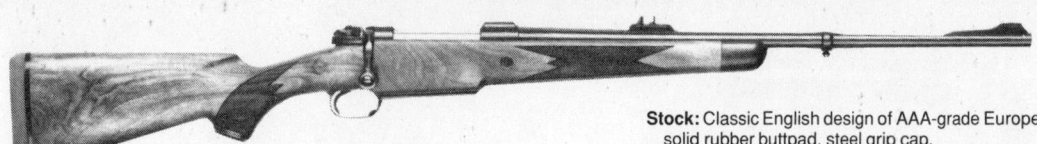

Heym Express

HEYM MAGNUM EXPRESS SERIES RIFLE
Caliber: 338 Lapua Mag., 375 H&H, 378 Wea. Mag., 416 Rigby, 500 Nitro Express 3", 460 Wea. Mag., 500 A-Square, 450 Ackley, 600 N.E.
Barrel: 24".
Weight: About 9.9 lbs. **Length:** 45¼" overall.

Stock: Classic English design of AAA-grade European walnut with cheekpiece, solid rubber buttpad, steel grip cap.
Sights: Adjustable post front on ramp, three-leaf express rear.
Features: Modified magnum Mauser action, Timney single trigger; special hinged floorplate; barrel-mouted q.d. swivel, q.d. rear; vertical double recoil lug in rear of stock. Introduced 1989. Imported from Germany by JagerSport, Ltd.
Price: **$6,500.00**
Price: For left-hand rifle, add **$595.00**
Price: 600 Nitro Express **$11,350.00**

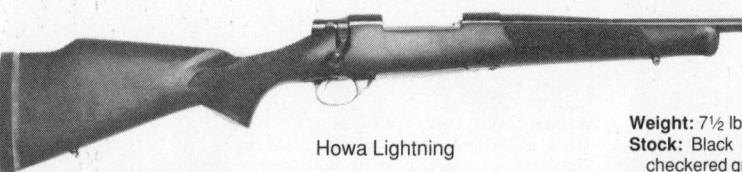

Howa Lightning

HOWA LIGHTNING BOLT-ACTION RIFLE
Caliber: 223, 22-250, 243, 270, 308, 30-06, 7mm Rem. Mag., 300 Win. Mag., 338 Win. Mag.
Barrel: 22", 24" magnum calibers.

Weight: 7½ lbs. **Length:** 42" overall (22" barrel).
Stock: Black Bell & Carlson Carbelite composite with Monte Carlo comb; checkered grip and forend.
Sights: None furnished. Drilled and tapped for scope mounting.
Features: Sliding thumb safety, hinged floorplate; polished blue/black finish. Introduced 1993. From Interarms.
Price: Standard calibers **$498.00**
Price: Magnum calibers **$517.00**

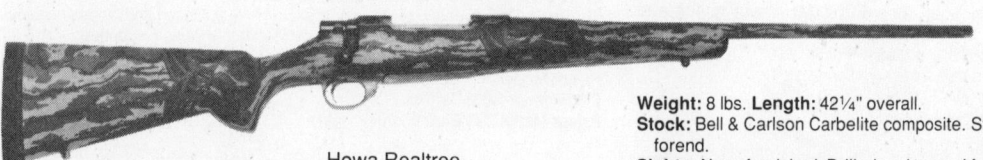

Howa Realtree

HOWA REALTREE CAMO RIFLE
Caliber: 270, 30-06, 5-shot magazine.
Barrel: 22".

Weight: 8 lbs. **Length:** 42¼" overall.
Stock: Bell & Carlson Carbelite composite. Straight comb; checkered grip and forend.
Sights: None furnished. Drilled and tapped for scope mouting.
Features: Completely covered with Realtree camo finish, except bolt. Sliding thumb safety, hinged floorplate; sling swivel studs, recoil pad. Introduced 1993. From Interarms.
Price: **$620.00**

Interarms Mark X Viscount

Interarms Mini-Mark X Rifle
Scaled-down version of the Mark X Viscount. Uses miniature M98 Mauser-system action, chambered for 223 Rem. and 7.62x39; 20" barrel. Overall length of 39¾", weight 6.35 lbs. Drilled and tapped for scope mounting. Checkered hardwood stock. Adjustable trigger. Introduced 1987. Imported from Yugoslavia by Interarms.
Price: Either caliber **$527.00**

INTERARMS MARK X VISCOUNT BOLT-ACTION RIFLE
Caliber: 22-250, 243, 25-06, 270, 7x57, 308, 30-06, 7mm Rem. Mag., 300 Win. Mag.
Barrel: 24".
Weight: 7 lbs. **Length:** 44" overall.
Stock: European hardwood with Monte Carlo comb, checkered grip and forend.
Sights: Blade on ramp front, open fully adjustable rear. Drilled and tapped for scope mounting.
Features: Polished blue finish. Uses Mauser system action with sliding thumb safety, hinged floorplate, adjustable trigger. Reintroduced 1987. Imported from Yugoslavia by Interarms.
Price: Standard calibers **$568.00**
Price: Magnum calibers **$590.00**

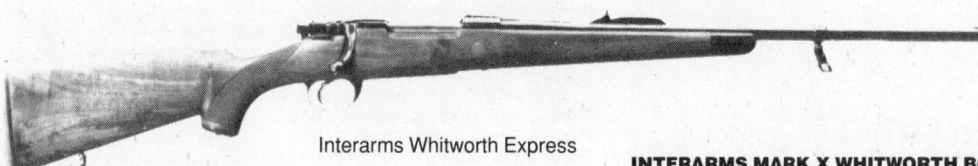

Interarms Whitworth Express

INTERARMS WHITWORTH EXPRESS RIFLE
Caliber: 375 H&H, 458 Win. Mag.
Barrel: 24".
Weight: 7½-8 lbs. **Length:** 44".
Stock: Classic English Express rifle design of hand checkered, select European walnut.
Sights: Ramp front with removable hood, three-leaf open sight calibrated for 100, 200, 300 yards on ¼-rib.
Features: Solid rubber recoil pad, barrel-mounted sling swivel, adjustable trigger, hinged floorplate, solid steel recoil cross bolt. From Interarms.
Price: 375, 458, with express sights **$870.00**

INTERARMS MARK X WHITWORTH BOLT-ACTION RIFLE
Caliber: 22-250, 243, 25-06, 270, 7x57, 308, 30-06, 7mm Rem. Mag., 300 Win. Mag., 5-shot magazine (3-shot for 300 Win. Mag.).
Barrel: 24".
Weight: 7 lbs. **Length:** 44" overall.
Stock: European walnut with checkered grip and forend, straight comb.
Sights: Hooded blade on ramp front, open fully adjustable rear.
Features: Uses Mauser system action with sliding thumb safety, hinged floorplate, adjustable trigger. Polished blue finish. Swivel studs. Imported from Yugoslavia by Interarms.
Price: Standard calibers **$700.00**
Price: Magnum calibers **$722.00**

Iver Johnson 5100A1

KDF K15 AMERICAN BOLT-ACTION RIFLE

Caliber: 25-06, 257 Wea. Mag., 270, 270 Wea. Mag., 7mm Rem. Mag., 30-06, 300 Win. Mag., 300 Wea. Mag., 338 Win. Mag., 340 Wea. Mag., 375 H&H, 411 KDF Mag., 416 Rem. Mag., 458 Win. Mag.; 4-shot magazine for standard calibers, 3-shot for magnums.
Barrel: 22" standard, 24" optional.
Weight: About 8 lbs. **Length:** 44" overall (24" barrel).
Stock: Laminated standard; Kevlar composite or AAA walnut in classic, schnabel or thumbhole styles optional.
Sights: None furnished; optional. Drilled and tapped for scope mounting.
Features: Three-lug locking design with 60˚ bolt lift; ultra-fast lock time; fully adjustable trigger. Options available. Introduced 1991. Made in U.S. by KDF, Inc.
Price: Standard calibers **$1,950.00**
Price: Magnum calibers **$2,000.00**

KRICO MODEL 700 BOLT-ACTION RIFLES

Caliber: 17 Rem., 222, 222 Rem. Mag., 223, 5.6x50 Mag., 243, 308, 5.6x57 RWS, 22-250, 6.5x55, 6.5x57, 7x57, 270, 7x64, 9.3x62, 6.5x68, 7mm Rem. Mag., 300 Win. Mag., 8x68S, 7.5 Swiss, 9.3x64, 6x62 Freres.
Barrel: 23.6" (std. cals.); 25.5" (mag. cals.).
Weight: 7 lbs. **Length:** 43.3" overall (23.6" bbl.).
Stock: European walnut, Bavarian cheekpiece.

Mauser Model 66

MAUSER MODEL 66 BOLT-ACTION RIFLE

Caliber: 243, 270, 308, 5.6x57, 6.5x57, 9.3x62, 7mm Rem. Mag., 300 Wea. Mag., 300 Win. Mag., 6.5x68, 8x68S, 9.3x64, 375 H&H, 458 Win. Mag. Three-shot magazine.
Barrel: 21" (Stutzen); 24" (standard cals.); 26" (magnum cals.).

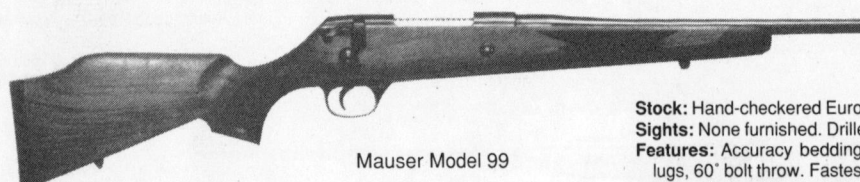

Mauser Model 99

MAUSER MODEL 99 BOLT-ACTION RIFLE

Caliber: 243, 25-06, 270, 308, 30-06, 5.6x57, 6.5x57, 7x57, 7x64 (standard cals.); 7mm Rem. Mag., 257 Wea. Mag., 270 Wea. Mag., 300 Wea. Mag., 300 Win. Mag., 338 Win. Mag., 375 H&H, 8x68S, 9.3x64 (magnum cals.); removable 4-shot magazine (std. cals.), 3-shot (magnum cals.).
Barrel: 24" (std.), 26" (mag.).
Weight: About 8 lbs. **Length:** 44" overall (std. cals.).

McMILLAN SIGNATURE CLASSIC SPORTER

Caliber: 22-250, 243, 6mm Rem., 7mm-08, 284, 308 (short action); 25-06, 270, 280 Rem., 30-06, 7mm Rem. Mag., 300 Win. Mag., 300 Wea. (long action); 338 Win. Mag., 340 Wea. (magnum action).
Barrel: 22", 24", 26".
Weight: 7 lbs. (short action).
Stock: McMillan fiberglass in green, beige, brown or black. Recoil pad and 1"

IVER JOHNSON MODEL 5100A1 LONG-RANGE RIFLE

Caliber: 50 BMG.
Barrel: 29", fully fluted, free-floating.
Weight: 36 lbs. **Length:** 51.5" overall.
Stocks: Composition. Adjustable drop and comb.
Sights: None furnished. Optional Leupold Ultra M1 16x scope.
Features: Bolt-action long-range rifle. Adjustable trigger. Rifle breaks down for transport, storage. From Iver Johnson.
Price: **$5,000.00**

KRICO MODEL 600 BOLT-ACTION RIFLE

Caliber: 222, 223, 22-250, 243, 308, 5.6x50 Mag., 4-shot magazine.
Barrel: 23.6".
Weight: 7.9 lbs. **Length:** 43.7" overall.
Stock: European walnut with Monte Carlo comb.
Sights: None furnished; drilled and tapped for scope mounting.
Features: Rubber recoil pad, sling swivels, checkered grip and forend. Polished blue finish. Imported from Germany by Mandall Shooting Supplies.
Price: **$1,295.00**

Sights: Blade on ramp front, open adjustable rear.
Features: Removable box magazine; sliding safety. Drilled and tapped for scope mounting. Imported from Germany by Mandall Shooting Supplies.
Price: Model 700 . . . . **$995.00**
Price: Model 700 Deluxe S **$1,495.00**
Price: Model 700 Deluxe **$1,025.00**
Price: Model 700 Stutzen (full stock) **$1,295.00**

Weight: 7.5 to 9.3 lbs. **Length:** 39" overall (std. cals.).
Stock: Hand-checkered European walnut, hand-rubbed oil finish. Rosewood forend and grip caps.
Sights: Blade front on ramp, open rear adjustable for windage and elevation.
Features: Telescopic short-stroke action; interchangeable, free-floated, medium-heavy barrels. Mini-claw extractor; adjustable single-stage trigger; internal magazine. Introduced 1989. Imported from Germany by Precision Imports, Inc.
Price: With Monte Carlo stock **$1,783.00**
Price: Stutzen (full-length stock) **$1,873.00**
Price: Safari model **$2,079.00**

Stock: Hand-checkered European walnut with rosewood grip cap.
Sights: None furnished. Drilled and tapped for scope mounting.
Features: Accuracy bedding with free-floated barrel, three front-locking bolt lugs, 60˚ bolt throw. Fastest lock time of any sporting rifle. Adjustable single-stage trigger. Silent safety locks bolt, sear, trigger. Introduced 1989. Imported from Germany by Precision Imports, Inc.
Price: Classic stock, oil finish, std. cals. **$1,130.00**
Price: As above, magnum cals. **$1,180.00**
Price: Classic stock, high luster finish, std. cals. . . . **$1,272.00**
Price: As above, magnum cals. **$1,322.00**
Price: Monte Carlo stock, oil finish, std. cals. **$1,130.00**
Price: As above, magnum cals. **$1,180.00**
Price: Monte Carlo stock, high luster finish, std. cals. . . **$1,272.00**
Price: As above, magnum cals. **$1,322.00**

swivels installed. Length of pull up to 14¼".
Sights: None furnished. Comes with 1" rings and bases.
Features: Uses McMillan right- or left-hand action with matte black finish. Trigger pull set at 3 lbs. Four-round magazine for standard calibers; three for magnums. Aluminum floorplate. Fibergrain and wood stocks optional. Introduced 1987. From McMillan Gunworks, Inc.
Price: **$2,299.00**

McMillan Alaskan

McMillan Signature Super Varminter

Similar to the Classic Sporter except has heavy contoured barrel, adjustable trigger, field bipod and special hand-bedded fiberglass stock (Fibergrain optional). Chambered for 223, 22-250, 220 Swift, 243, 6mm Rem., 25-06, 7mm-08 and 308. Comes with 1" rings and bases. Introduced 1989.
Price: **$2,370.00**

McMillan Signature Alaskan

Similar to the Classic Sporter except has match-grade barrel with single leaf rear sight, barrel band front, 1" detachable rings and mounts, steel floorplate, electroless nickel finish. Has wood Monte Carlo stock with cheekpiece, palm-swell grip, solid buttpad. Chambered for 270, 280 Rem., 30-06, 7mm Rem. Mag., 300 Win. Mag., 300 Wea., 358 Win., 340 Wea., 375 H&H. Introduced 1989.
Price: **$3,225.00**

McMillan Signature Titanium Mountain Rifle

Similar to the Classic Sporter except action made of titanium alloy, barrel of chromemoly steel. Stock is of graphite reinforced fiberglass. Weight is 5½ lbs. Chambered for 270, 280 Rem., 30-06, 7mm Rem. Mag., 300 Win. Mag. Fibergrain stock optional. Introduced 1989.
Price: **$2,995.00**

McMillan Classic Stainless

McMILLAN TALON SAFARI RIFLE

Caliber: 300 Win. Mag., 300 Wea. Mag., 338 Win. Mag., 300 H&H, 340 Wea. Mag., 375 H&H, 404 Jeffery, 416 Rem. Mag., 458 Win. Mag. (Safari Magnum); 378 Wea. Mag., 416 Rigby, 416 Wea. Mag., 460 Wea. Mag. (Safari Super Magnum).
Barrel: 24".
Weight: About 9-10 lbs. **Length:** 43" overall.
Stock: McMillan fiberglass Safari.
Sights: Barrel band front ramp, multi-leaf express rear.
Features: Uses McMillan Safari action. Has q.d. 1" scope mounts, positive locking steel floorplate, barrel band sling swivel. Match-grade barrel. Matte black finish standard. Introduced 1989. From McMillan Gunworks, Inc.
Price: Talon Safari Magnum **$3,570.00**
Price: Talon Safari Super Magnum **$4,120.00**

McMillan Classic Stainless Sporter

Similar to the Classic Sporter except barrel and action made of stainless steel. Same calibers, in addition to 416 Rem. Mag. Comes with fiberglass stock, right- or left-hand action in natural stainless, glass bead or black chrome sulfide finishes. Introduced 1990. From McMillan Gunworks, Inc.
Price: **$2,450.00**

McMILLAN TALON SPORTER RIFLE

Caliber: 25-06, 270, 280 Rem., 30-06 (Long Action); 7mm Rem. Mag., 300 Win. Mag., 300 Wea. Mag., 300 H&H, 338 Win. Mag., 340 Wea. Mag., 375 H&H, 416 Rem. Mag.
Barrel: 24" (standard).
Weight: About 7½ lbs. **Length:** NA.
Stock: Choice of walnut or McMillan fiberglass.
Sights: None furnished; comes with rings and bases. Open sights optional.
Features: Uses pre-'64 Model 70-type action with cone breech, controlled feed, claw extractor and three-position safety. Barrel and action are of stainless steel; chromemoly optional. Introduced 1991. From McMillan Gunworks, Inc.
Price: **$2,541.00**

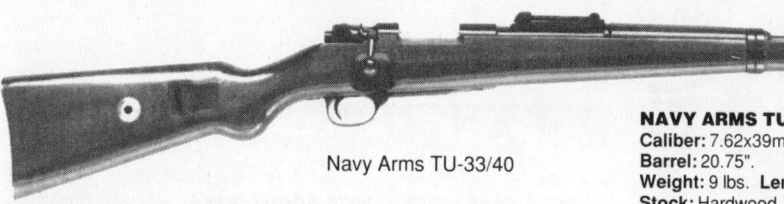

Navy Arms TU-33/40

MIDLAND 1500S SURVIVOR RIFLE

Caliber: 308, 5-shot magazine.
Barrel: 22".
Weight: 7 lbs. **Length:** 43" overall.
Stock: Black composite with recoil pad, Monte Carlo cheekpiece.
Sights: Hooded ramp front, open rear adjustable for windage.
Features: Stainless steel barreled action with satin chromed bolt. Introduced 1993. Made by Gibbs Rifle Co., distributed by Navy Arms.
Price: **$450.00**
Price: Model 1500C clip model **$480.00**

NAVY ARMS TU-33/40 CARBINE

Caliber: 7.62x39mm, 4-shot magazine.
Barrel: 20.75".
Weight: 9 lbs. **Length:** NA.
Stock: Hardwood.
Sights: Hooded barleycorn front, military V-notch adjustable rear.
Features: Miniature Mauser-style action. Comes with leather sling. Introduced 1992. Imported by Navy Arms.
Price: . . . . **NA**

> Consult our Directory pages for the location of firms mentioned.

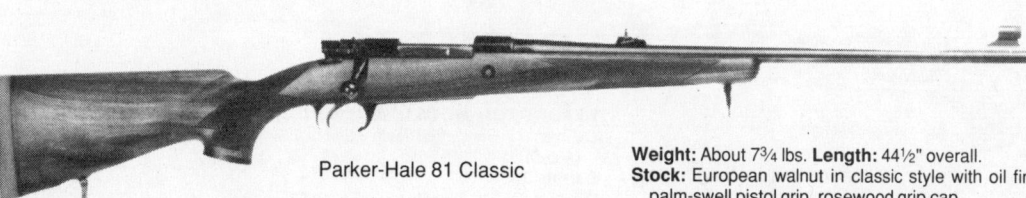

Parker-Hale 81 Classic

PARKER-HALE MODEL 81 CLASSIC RIFLE

Caliber: 22-250, 243, 6mm Rem., 270, 6.5x55, 7x57, 7x64, 308, 30-06, 300 Win. Mag., 7mm Rem. Mag., 4-shot magazine.
Barrel: 24".

Weight: About 7¾ lbs. **Length:** 44½" overall.
Stock: European walnut in classic style with oil finish, hand-cut checkering; palm-swell pistol grip, rosewood grip cap.
Sights: Drilled and tapped for open sights and scope mounting. Scope bases included.
Features: Uses Mauser-style action; one-piece steel, Oberndorf-style trigger guard with hinged floorplate; rubber buttpad; quick-detachable sling swivels. Introduced 1984. Made by Gibbs Rifle Co., distributed by Navy Arms.
Price: **$900.00**

Parker-Hale Model 81 Classic African Rifle

Similar to the Model 81 Classic except chambered only for 375 H&H and 9.3x62. Has adjustable trigger, barrel band front swivel, African express rear sight, engraved receiver. Classic-style stock has a solid buttpad, checkered pistol grip and forend. Introduced 1986. Made by Gibbs Rifle Co., distributed by Navy Arms.
Price: **$1,050.00**

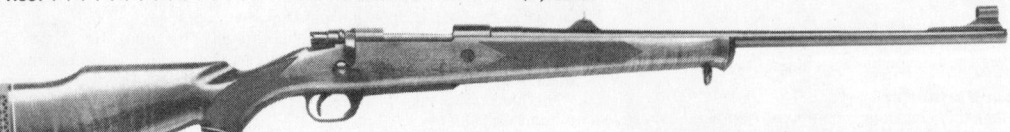

Parker-Hale 1100M

Parker-Hale Model 1100 Lightweight Rifle

Similar to the Model 81 Classic except has slim barrel profile, hollow bolt handle, alloy trigger guard/floorplate. The Monte Carlo stock has a schnabel forend, hand-cut checkering, swivel studs, palm-swell pistol grip. Comes with hooded ramp front sight, open Williams rear adjustable for windage and elevation. Same calibers as Model 81. Overall length is 43", weight 6½ lbs., with 22" barrel. Introduced 1984. Made by Gibbs Rifle Co., distributed by Navy Arms.
Price: **$510.00**

PARKER-HALE MODEL 2100 MIDLAND RIFLE

Caliber: 22-250, 243, 6mm, 270, 6.5x55, 7x57, 7x64, 308, 30-06, 300 Win. Mag., 7mm Rem. Mag.
Barrel: 22".
Weight: About 7 lbs. **Length:** 43" overall.
Stock: European walnut, cut-checkered pistol grip and forend; sling swivels.
Sights: Hooded post front, flip-up open rear.
Features: Mauser-type action has twin front locking lugs, rear safety lug, and claw extractor; hinged floorplate; adjustable single-stage trigger; silent side safety. Introduced 1984. Made by Gibbs Rifle Co., distributed by Navy Arms.
Price: **$390.00**
Price: Model 2600 (hardwood stock, no white spacers) **$375.00**

Parker-Hale Midland Model 2700 Lightweight Rifle

Similar to the Model 2100 Midland except has tapered lightweight barrel, aluminum trigger guard, lightened stock. Receiver drilled and tapped for scope mounting. Weighs 6.5 lbs. Not available in 300 Win. Mag. Introduced 1992. Made by Gibbs Rifle Co., distributed by Navy Arms.
Price: **$415.00**

Parker-Hale 1300C

Parker-Hale Model 2800 Midland Rifle

Similar to the Model 2100 Midland except has Monte Carlo stock of laminated birch. Not available in 300 Win. Mag. Made by Gibbs Rifle Co., distributed by Navy Arms.
Price: **$405.00**

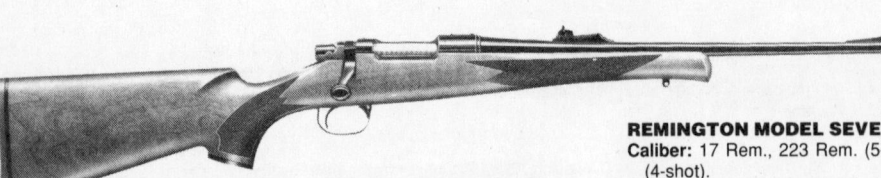

Remington Model Seven

Remington Model Seven Youth Rifle

Similar to the Model Seven except has hardwood stock with 12³⁄₁₆" length of pull and chambered for 6mm Rem., 243, 7mm-08. Introduced 1993.
Price: About **$425.00**

Parker-Hale Model 1000 Rifle

Similar to the Model 81 Classic except has walnut Monte Carlo stock, 22" barrel (24" in 22-250), weighs 7.25 lbs. Not available in 300 Win. Mag. Introduced 1992. Made by Gibbs Rifle Co., distributed by Navy Arms.
Price: **$495.00**
Price: Model 1000 Clip (detachable magazine) **$535.00**

PARKER-HALE MODEL 1100M AFRICAN MAGNUM

Caliber: 375 H&H, 458 Win. Mag.
Barrel: 24".
Weight: 9.5 lbs. **Length:** NA.
Stock: Checkered walnut with reinforcing lugs.
Sights: Hooded ramp front, shallow V open rear.
Features: Mauser-style 98 action with steel trigger guard, special lengthened steel magazine. Drilled and tapped for scope mounts. Made by Gibbs Rifle Co., distributed by Navy Arms.
Price: **$930.00**

PARKER-HALE MODEL 1200 SUPER RIFLE

Caliber: 22-250, 243, 6mm, 25-06, 270, 6.5x55, 7x57, 7x64, 308, 30-06, 8mm Mauser (standard action); 7mm Rem. Mag., 300 Win. Mag. (1200M Super Magnum).
Barrel: 24".
Weight: About 7½ lbs. **Length:** 44½" overall.
Stock: European walnut, rosewood grip and forend tips, hand-cut checkering; roll-over cheekpiece; palm-swell pistol grip; ventilated recoil pad; wraparound checkering.
Sights: Hooded post front, open rear.
Features: Uses Mauser-style action with claw extractor; gold-plated adjustable trigger; silent side safety locks trigger, sear and bolt; aluminum trigger guard. Introduced 1984. Made by Gibbs Rifle Co., distributed by Navy Arms.
Price: **$595.00**

Parker-Hale Model 1200 Super Clip Rifle

Same as the Model 1200 Super except has a detachable steel box magazine and steel trigger guard. Introduced 1984. Made by Gibbs Rifle Co., distributed by Navy Arms.
Price: **$640.00**

PARKER-HALE MODEL 1300C SCOUT RIFLE

Caliber: 243, 308, 10-shot magazine.
Barrel: 20".
Weight: 8.5 lbs. **Length:** 41" overall.
Stock: Checkered laminated birch.
Sights: None furnished. Drilled and tapped for scope mounting.
Features: Detachable magazine; muzzle brake; polished blue finish. Introduced 1992. Made by Gibbs Rifle Co., distributed by Navy Arms.
Price: **$525.00**
Price: With fixed 5-shot magazine **$495.00**

REMINGTON MODEL SEVEN BOLT-ACTION RIFLE

Caliber: 17 Rem., 223 Rem. (5-shot); 243, 6mm Rem., 7mm-08, 6mm, 308 (4-shot).
Barrel: 18½".
Weight: 6¼ lbs. **Length:** 37½" overall.
Stock: Walnut, with modified schnabel forend. Cut checkering.
Sights: Ramp front, adjustable open rear.
Features: Short-action design; silent side safety; free-floated barrel except for single pressure point at forend tip. Introduced 1983.
Price: About **$524.00**
Price: 17 Rem., about **$551.00**

CAUTION: PRICES CHANGE, CHECK AT GUNSHOP.

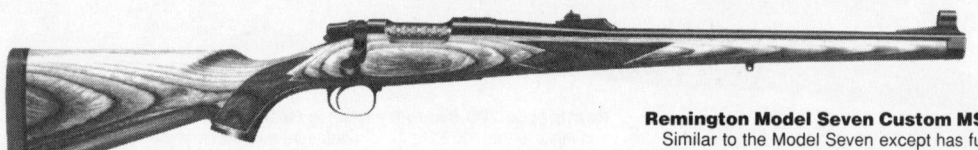

Remington Model Seven MS

Remington Model Seven Custom KS

Similar to the standard Model Seven except has custom finished stock of lightweight Kevlar aramid fiber and chambered for 223 Rem., 7mm-08, 308, 35 Rem. and 350 Rem. Mag. Barrel length is 20", weight 5¾ lbs. Comes with iron sights and is drilled and tapped for scope mounting. Special order through Remington Custom Shop. Introduced 1987.

Price: **$997.00**

Remington Model Seven Custom MS Rifle

Similar to the Model Seven except has full-length Mannlicher-style stock of laminated wood with straight comb, solid black recoil pad, black steel forend tip, cut checkering, gloss finish. Barrel length 20", weight 6¾ lbs. Availabloe in 222 Rem., 223, 22-250, 243, 6mm Rem., 7mm-08 Rem., 308, 350 Rem. Mag. Calibers 250 Savage, 257 Roberts, 35 Rem. available on special order. Polished blue finish. Introduced 1993. From Remington Custom Shop.

Price: About **$1,001.00**

Remington 700 BDL

Remington 700 BDL Bolt-Action Rifle

Same as the 700 ADL except chambered for 222, 223 (short action, 24" barrel), 22-250, 25-06, 6mm Rem. (short action, 22" barrel), 243, 270, 7mm-08, 280, 300 Savage, 30-06, 308; skip-line checkering; black forend tip and grip cap with white line spacers. Matted receiver top, quick-release floorplate. Hooded ramp front sight; q.d. swivels.

Price: About **$524.00**
Also available in 17 Rem., 7mm Rem. Mag., 300 Win. Mag. (long action, 24" barrel), 338 Win. Mag., 35 Whelen (long action, 22" barrel). Overall length 44½", weight about 7½ lbs.

Price: About **$551.00**
Price: Custom Grade, about **$2,296.00**

REMINGTON 700 ADL BOLT-ACTION RIFLE

Caliber: 243, 270, 308, 30-06 and 7mm Rem. Mag.
Barrel: 22" or 24" round tapered.
Weight: 7 lbs. **Length:** 41½" to 43½" overall.
Stock: Walnut. Satin-finished p.g. stock with fine-line cut checkering, Monte Carlo.
Sights: Gold bead ramp front; removable, step-adj. rear with windage screw.
Features: Side safety, receiver tapped for scope mounts.
Price: About **$439.00**
Price: 7mm Rem. Mag., about **$465.00**
Price: Model 700 ADL/LS (laminated stock, 243, 270, 30-06 only) . . **$485.00**
Price: As above, 7mm Rem. Mag. **$512.00**

Remington 700 BDL Varmint Special

Same as 700 BDL, except 24" heavy bbl., 43½" overall, weighs 9 lbs. Cals. 222, 223, 22-250, 243, 6mm Rem., 7mm-08 Rem. and 308. No sights.

Price: About **$557.00**

Remington 700 BDL European

Remington 700 BDL European Bolt-Action Rifle

Same as the 700 BDL except has oil-finished walnut stock and is chambered for 243, 270, 7mm-08, 280 Rem., 30-06 (22" barrel), 7mm Rem. Mag. (24" barrel). Introduced 1993.

Price: Standard calibers, about **$524.00**
Price: 7mm Rem. Mag., about **$551.00**

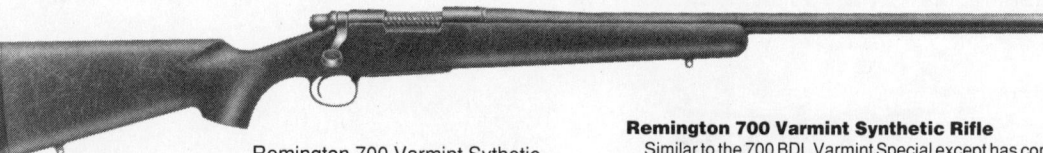

Remington 700 Varmint Sythetic

Remington 700 BDL SS Rifle

Similar to the 700 Stainless Synthetic rifle except has hinged floorplate, 24" standard weight barrel in all calibers; magnum calibers have magnum-contour barrel. No sights supplied, but comes drilled and tapped. Has corrosion-resistant follower and fire control, stainless BDL-style barreled action with fine matte finish. Synthetic stock has straight comb and cheekpiece, textured finish, positive checkering, plated swivel studs. Short action calibers—223, 243, 6mm Rem., 7mm-08 Rem., 308; standard long action—25-06, 270, 280 Rem., 30-06; magnums—7mm Rem. Mag., 7mm Wea. Mag., 300 Win. Mag., 300 Wea. Mag., 338 Win. Mag. Weighs 6¾-7 lbs. Introduced 1993.

Price: Standard calibers, about **$585.00**
Price: Magnum calibers, about **$612.00**

Remington 700 MTRSS Rifle

Similar to the 700 BDL SS except stainless steel barreled action with 22" barrel; textured black synthetic stock profiled like the Mountain Rifle with positive checkering, straight comb and cheekpiece. Available in 25-06, 270, 280 Rem., 30-06. Weighs 6¾ lbs. Introduced 1993.

Price: **$532.00**

Remington 700 Varmint Synthetic Rifle

Similar to the 700 BDL Varmint Special except has composite stock reinforced with DuPont Kevlar, fiberglass and graphite. Has aluminum bedding block that runs the full length of the receiver. Free-floating barrel. Metal has black matte finish; stock has textured black and gray finish and swivel studs. Available in 220 Swift, 223, 22-250, 308. Introduced 1992.

Price: **$632.00**

Remington 700 Stainless Synthetic Rifle

Similar to the 700 BDL except has stainless barrel, bolt and receiver with synthetic stock profiled like the Mountain Rifle, with blind magazine, corrosion-resistant follower, black textured finish, checkered pistol grip and forend, swivel studs. Matte-finished metal. Introduced 1992.

Price: 25-06, 270, 280, 30-06 . . . . **$532.00**
Price: 7mm Wea. Mag., 7mm Rem. Mag., 300 Win. Mag.,
338 Win. Mag. **$632.00**

Remington 700 BDL Left Hand

Same as 700 BDL except mirror-image left-hand action, stock. Available in 22-250, 243, 308, 270, 30-06 only.

Price: About **$548.00**
Price: 7mm Rem. Mag., 338 Win. Mag., about **$575.00**

Remington 700 Camo Synthetic

Remington 700 Safari

Similar to the 700 BDL except custom finished and tuned. In 8mm Rem. Mag., 375 H&H, 416 Rem. Mag. or 458 Win. Magnum calibers only with heavy barrel. Hand checkered, oil-finished stock in classic or Monte Carlo style with recoil pad installed. Delivery time is about 5 months.

Price: About **$999.00**
Price: Classic stock, left-hand **$1,063.00**
Price: Safari Custom KS (Kevlar stock), right-hand **$1,153.00**
Price: As above, left-hand **$1,215.00**
Price: Custom KS wood-grained stock, right-hand **$1,265.00**
Price: As above, left-hand **$1,327.00**

Remington 700 Custom KS Mountain Rifle

Similar to the 700 "Mountain Rifle" except custom finished with Kevlar reinforced resin synthetic stock. Available in both left- and right-hand versions. Chambered for 270 Win., 280 Rem., 30-06, 7mm Rem. Mag., 300 Win. Mag., 300 Wea. Mag., 35 Whelen, 338 Win. Mag., 8mm Rem. Mag., 375 H&H, all with 24" barrel only. Weight is 6 lbs., 6 oz. Introduced 1986.

Price: Right-hand **$997.00**
Price: Left-hand **$1,059.00**
Price: Stainless **$1,137.00**
Price: With wood-grained Kevlar stock, right-hand **$1,109.00**
Price: As above, left-hand **$1,172.00**

Remington 700 Camo Synthetic Rifle

Similar to the 700 BDL except has synthetic stock and the stock and metal (except bolt and sights) are fully camouflaged in Mossy Oak Bottomland camo. Comes with swivel studs, open adjustable sights. Available in 22-250, 243, 7mm-08, 270, 280, 30-06, 308, 7mm Rem. Mag., 300 Wea. Mag. Introduced 1992.

Price: Standard calibers **$568.00**
Price: Magnum calibers **$595.00**

Remington 700 Mountain Rifle

Similar to the 700 BDL weighs 6¾ lbs., has a 22" tapered barrel. Redesigned pistol grip, straight comb, contoured cheekpiece, satin stock finish, fine checkering, hinged floorplate and magazine follower, two-position thumb safety. Chambered for 243, 257 Roberts, 270 Win., 7x57, 7mm-08, 25-06, 280 Rem., 30-06, 308, 4-shot magazine. Overall length is 42½". Introduced 1986.

Price: About **$524.00**

REMINGTON 700 CLASSIC RIFLE

Caliber: 222 Remington only, 5-shot magazine.
Barrel: 24".
Weight: About 7¾ lbs. **Length:** 44½" overall.
Stock: American walnut, 20 lpi checkering on p.g. and forend. Classic styling. Satin finish.
Sights: None furnished. Receiver drilled and tapped for scope mounting.
Features: A "classic" version of the M700 ADL with straight comb stock. Fitted with rubber recoil pad. Sling swivel studs installed. Hinged floorplate. Limited production in 1993 only.

Price: About **$524.00**

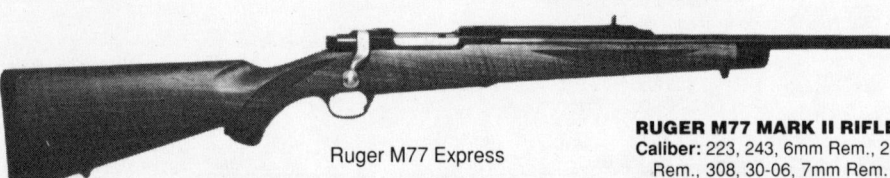

Ruger M77 Express

RUGER M77 MARK II MAGNUM RIFLE

Caliber: 375 H&H, 404 Jeffery, 4-shot magazine; 416 Rigby, 458 Win. Mag., 3-shot magazine.
Barrel: 26", with integral steel rib.
Weight: 9.25 lbs. (375, 404); 10.25 lbs. (416, 458). **Length:** 40.5" overall.
Stock: Circassian walnut with hand-cut checkering, swivel studs, steel grip cap, rubber butt pad.
Sights: Ramp front, three leaf express on serrated integral steel rib. Rib also serves as base for front scope ring.
Features: Uses an enlarged Mark II action with three-position safety, stainless bolt, steel trigger guard and hinged steel floorplate. Controlled feed. Introduced 1989.

Price: M77MKIIRSM **$1,550.00**

RUGER M77 MARK II RIFLE

Caliber: 223, 243, 6mm Rem., 257 Roberts, 25-06, 6.5x55 Swedish, 270, 280 Rem., 308, 30-06, 7mm Rem. Mag., 300 Win. Mag., 338 Win. Mag., 4-shot magazine.
Barrel: 20", 22"; 24" (magnums).
Weight: About 7 lbs. **Length:** 39¾" overall.
Stock: Hand-checkered American walnut; swivel studs, rubber butt pad.
Sights: None furnished. Receiver has Ruger integral scope mount base, comes with Ruger 1" rings. Some models have iron sights.
Features: Short action with new trigger and three-position safety. New trigger guard with redesigned floorplate latch. Left-hand model available. Introduced 1989.

Price: M77MKIIR (no sights **$558.00**
Price: M77MKIIRS (open sights) **$617.00**
Price: M77MKIILR (left-hand, 270, 30-06,
7mm Rem. Mag., 300 Win. Mag.) **$558.00**

Ruger M77RL

Ruger M77 All-Weather

Ruger M77RL Ultra Light

Similar to the standard M77 except weighs only 6 lbs., chambered for 223, 243, 308, 270, 30-06, 257; barrel tapped for target scope blocks; has 20" Ultra Light barrel. Overall length 40". Ruger's steel 1" scope rings supplied. Introduced 1983.

Price: M77MKIIRL **$592.46**

Ruger M77 Mark II All-Weather Stainless Rifle

Similar to the wood-stock M77 Mark II except all metal parts are of stainless steel, and has an injection-moulded, glass-fiber-reinforced Du Pont Zytel stock. Chambered for 223, 243, 270, 308, 30-06, 7mm Rem. Mag., 300 Win. Mag., 338 Win. Mag. Has the fixed-blade-type ejector, three-position safety, and new trigger guard with patented floorplate latch. Comes with integral Scope Base Receiver and 1" Ruger scope rings, built-in sling swivel loops. Introduced 1990.

Price: KM77MKIIRP **$558.00**

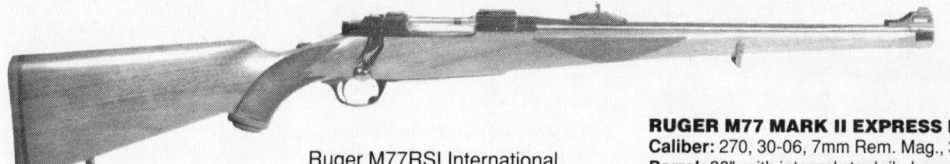

Ruger M77RSI International

Ruger M77RSI International Carbine

Same as the standard Model 77 except has 18½" barrel, full-length Mannlicher-style stock, with steel forend cap, loop-type steel sling swivels. Integral-base receiver, open sights, Ruger 1" steel rings. Improved front sight. Available in 243, 270, 308, 30-06. Weighs 7 lbs. Length overall is 38⅜".
Price: M77MKIIRSI **$623.44**

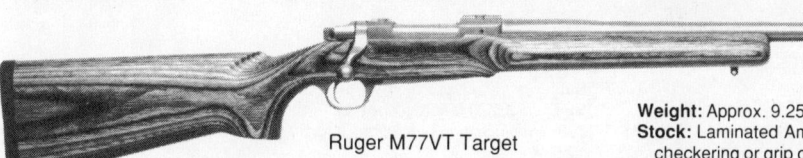

Ruger M77VT Target

RUGER M77VT TARGET RIFLE

Caliber: 22 PPC, 22-250, 220 Swift, 223, 243, 6mm PPC, 25-06, 308.
Barrel: 26" heavy stainless steel with matte finish.

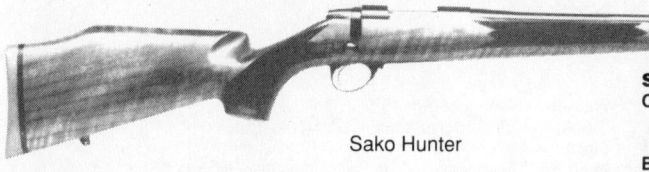

Sako Hunter

Sako Fiberclass Sporter

Similar to the Hunter except has a black fiberglass stock in the classic style, with wrinkle finish, rubber buttpad. Barrel length is 23", weight 7 lbs., 2 oz. Introduced 1985.
Price: 25-06, 270, 280 Rem., 30-06 . . . . **$1,310.00**
Price: 7mm Rem. Mag., 300 Win. Mag., 338 Win. Mag. **$1,325.00**
Price: 375 H&H, 416 Rem. Mag. **$1,340.00**

Sako Safari Grade Bolt Action

Similar to the Hunter except available in long action, calibers 338 Win. Mag. or 375 H&H Mag. or 416 Rem. Mag. only. Stocked in French walnut, checkered 20 lpi, solid rubber buttpad; grip cap and forend tip; quarter-rib "express" rear sight, hooded ramp front. Front sling swivel band-mounted on barrel.
Price: **$2,625.00**

Sako Classic

Sako Hunter LS Rifle

Same gun as the Sako Hunter except has laminated stock with dull finish. Chambered for same calibers. Also available in left-hand version. Introduced 1987.
Price: Medium action **$1,190.00**
Price: Long action, from **$1,155.00**
Price: Magnum cals., from **$1,175.00**
Price: 375 H&H, 416 Rem. Mag., from **$1,185.00**

RUGER M77 MARK II EXPRESS RIFLE

Caliber: 270, 30-06, 7mm Rem. Mag., 300 Win. Mag., 4-shot magazine.
Barrel: 22", with integral steel rib; barrel-mounted front swivel stud.
Weight: 7.5 lbs. **Length:** 42.125" overall.
Stock: Hand-checkered medium quality walnut with steel grip cap, black rubber butt pad, swivel studs.
Sights: Ramp front, open rear adjustable for windage and elevation mounted on rib.
Features: Mark II action with three-position safety, stainless steel bolt, steel trigger guard, hinged steel floorplate. Introduced 1991.
Price: M77EXPMKII **$1,550.00**

Weight: Approx. 9.25 lbs. **Length:** Approx. 44" overall.
Stock: Laminated American hardwood with flat forend, steel swivel studs; no checkering or grip cap.
Sights: Integral scope mount bases in receiver.
Features: Ruger diagonal bedding system. Ruger steel 1" scope rings supplied. Fully adjustable trigger. Steel floorplate and trigger guard. New version introduced 1992.
Price: KM77MKIIVT **$665.00**

SAKO HUNTER RIFLE

Caliber: 17 Rem., 222, 223 (short action); 22-250, 243, 7mm-08, 308 (medium action); 25-06, 270, 30-06, 7mm Rem. Mag., 300 Win. Mag., 338 Win. Mag., 375 H&H Mag., 300 Wea. Mag., 416 Rem. Mag. (long action).
Barrel: 22" to 24" depending on caliber.
Weight: 5¾ lbs. (short); 6¼ lbs. (med.); 7¼ lbs. (long).
Stock: Hand-checkered European walnut.
Sights: None furnished.
Features: Adj. trigger, hinged floorplate. Imported from Finland by Stoeger.
Price: 17 Rem., 222, 223 . . . . **$975.00**
Price: 22-250, 243, 308, 7mm-08 . . . . **$975.00**
Price: Long action cals. (except magnums) **$1,000.00**
Price: Magnum cals. **$1,020.00**
Price: 375 H&H, 416 Rem. Mag., from **$1,035.00**
Price: 300 Wea. **$1,035.00**

Sako Hunter Left-Hand Rifle

Same gun as the Sako Hunter except has left-hand action, stock with dull finish. Available in medium, long and magnum actions. Introduced 1987.
Price: Standard calibers, 22-250 to 7mm-08 . . . . **$1,055.00**
Price: Magnum calibers **$1,100.00**
Price: 375 H&H, 416 Rem. Mag. **$1,115.00**
Price: Deluxe, standard calibers, 25-06, 30-06 . . . . **$1,430.00**
Price: Deluxe, magnum calibers **$1,445.00**
Price: Deluxe, 375 H&H, 416 Rem. Mag. **$1,460.00**
Price: Long action, 25-06, 270, 280, 30-06 . . . . **$1,085.00**

Sako Classic Bolt Action

Similar to the Hunter except has classic-style stock with straight comb. Has 21¾" barrel, weighs 6 lbs. Matte finish wood. Introduced 1993. Imported from Finland by Stoeger.
Price: 243 . . . . **$975.00**
Price: 270, 30-06 . . . . **$1,000.00**
Price: 7mm Rem. Mag. **$1,020.00**
Price: Left-hand, 270 . . . . **$1,085.00**
Price: Left-hand, 7mm Rem. Mag. **$1,100.00**

Sako Deluxe Lightweight

Same action as Hunter except has select wood, rosewood p.g. cap and forend tip. Fine checkering on top surfaces of integral dovetail bases, bolt sleeve, bolt handle root and bolt knob. Vent. recoil pad, skip-line checkering, mirror finish bluing.
Price: 17 Rem., 222, 223, 22-250, 243, 308, 7mm-08 . . . . . **$1,325.00**
Price: 25-06, 270, 280 Rem., 30-06 . . . . **$1,365.00**
Price: 7mm Rem. Mag., 300 Win. Mag., 338 Win. Mag. **$1,380.00**
Price: 300 Wea., 375 H&H, 416 Rem. Mag. **$1,395.00**

Sako Mannlicher

Sako Super Deluxe Sporter

Similar to Deluxe Hunter except has select European walnut with high-gloss finish and deep-cut oak leaf carving. Metal has super high polish, deep blue finish. Special order only.
Price: **$2,790.00**

Sako Mannlicher-Style Carbine

Same as the Hunter except has full "Mannlicher" style stock, 18½" barrel, weighs 7½ lbs., chambered for 243, 25-06, 270, 308 and 30-06, 7mm Rem. Mag., 300 Win. Mag., 338 Win. Mag., 375 H&H. Introduced 1977. From Stoeger.
Price: 243, 308 . . . . **$1,130.00**
Price: 270, 30-06 . . . . **$1,165.00**
Price: 338 Win. Mag., 375 H&H **$1,180.00**
Price: 375 H&H **$1,200.00**

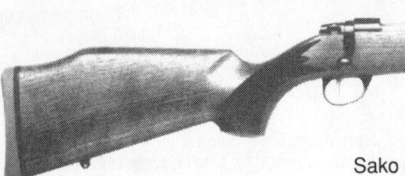

Sako Heavy Barrel

Sako Varmint Heavy Barrel

Same as std. Super Sporter except has beavertail forend; available in 17 Rem., 222, 223 (short action), 22 PPC, 6mm PPC (single shot), 22-250, 243, 308, 7mm-08 (medium action). Weight from 8¼ to 8½ lbs., 5-shot magazine capacity.
Price: 17 Rem., 222, 223 (short action) **$1,110.00**
Price: 22-250, 243, 308 (medium action) **$1,110.00**
Price: 22 PPC, 6mm PPC (single shot) **$1,330.00**

Sako TRG-S

SAKO TRG-S BOLT-ACTION RIFLE

Caliber: 243, 7mm-08, 270, 30-06, 7mm Rem. Mag., 300 Win. Mag., 338 Win. Mag., 375 H&H, 416 Rem. Mag., 5-shot magazine (4-shot for 375 H&H).
Barrel: 22", 24" (magnum calibers).

Weight: 7.75 lbs. **Length:** 45.5" overall.
Stock: Reinforced polyurethane with Monte Carlo comb.
Sights: None furnished.
Features: Resistance-free bolt with 60-degree lift. Recoil pad adjustable for length. Free-floating barrel, detachable magazine, fully adjustable trigger. Matte blue metal. Introduced 1993. Imported from Finland by Stoeger.
Price: 243, 7mm-08, 270, 30-06 . . . . **$730.00**
Price: Magnum calibers **$765.00**

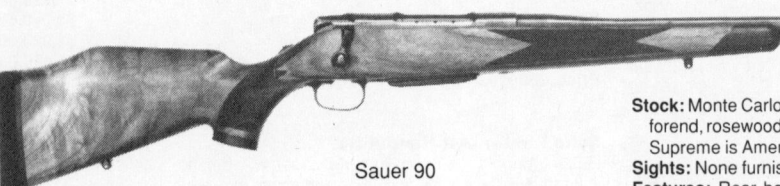

Sauer 90

SAUER 90 BOLT-ACTION RIFLE

Caliber: 270, 25-06, 30-06, 7mm Rem. Mag., 300 Win. Mag., 300 Wea. Mag., 338 Win., 375 H&H, 458 Win. Mag., 4-shot magazine for standard calibers, 3-shot for magnums.
Barrel: 24" (standard calibers), 26" (magnum calibers).
Weight: 7.25 to 8 lbs. **Length:** 44" overall (24" barrel).

Stock: Monte Carlo style with sculptured cheekpiece, hand-checkered grip and forend, rosewood grip cap and forend tip. Lux is European walnut with oil finish, Supreme is American walnut with high-gloss lacquer finish.
Sights: None furnished; drilled and tapped for scope mount.
Features: Rear bolt cam activated locking lug action with 65° bolt lift, fully adjustable gold-plated trigger, chamber-loaded signal pin, cocking indicator, tang-mounted slide safety. Detachable box magazine. Introduced 1986. Imported from Germany by G.U., Inc.
Price: Lux or Supreme **$1,495.00**
Price: With engraving LVL I **$2,495.00**
Price: With engraving LVL II **$3,095.00**
Price: With engraving LVL III **$3,395.00**
Price: With engraving LVL IV **$3,995.00**
Price: 458 Safari **$1,995.00**

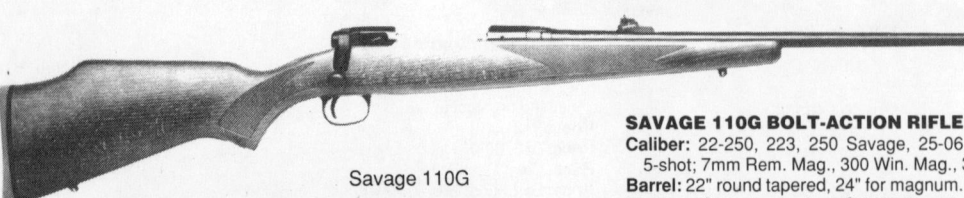

Savage 110G

SAVAGE 110G BOLT-ACTION RIFLE

Caliber: 22-250, 223, 250 Savage, 25-06, 7mm-08, 270, 308, 30-06, 243, 5-shot; 7mm Rem. Mag., 300 Win. Mag., 338 Win. Mag., 4-shot.
Barrel: 22" round tapered, 24" for magnum.
Weight: 6¾ lbs. **Length:** 42⅜" (22" barrel).
Stock: Walnut-finished checkered hardwood with Monte Carlo; hard rubber buttplate.
Sights: Ramp front, step adjustable rear.
Features: Top tang safety, receiver tapped for scope mount. Full-floating barrel; adjustable trigger. Introduced 1989.
Price: **$340.00**
Price: Left-hand, 30-06, 270, 7mm Rem. Mag. only, M110GLNS . . **$400.00**
Price: Model 110GNS (no sights) **$340.00**
Price: Model 110FNS (no sights, black composite stock) **$370.00**
Price: Model 110GC (removable box magazine, 30-06, 270, 7mm Rem. Mag., 300 Win. Mag.) **$375.00**

CAUTION: PRICES CHANGE. CHECK AT GUNSHOP.

CENTERFIRE RIFLES—BOLT ACTION

Savage 110CY Youth/Ladies Rifle
Similar to the Savage 110G except has walnut-finished hardwood stock with 12½" length of pull, and is chambered for 243 and 300 Savage. Comes with gun lock, ear plugs, sight-in target and shooting glasses. Introduced 1991.
Price: **$350.00**

Savage 110GXP3 Bolt-Action Rifle
Similar to the 110G except comes with 3-9x32 scope, rings and bases, Savage leather sling, swivels, gun lock, ear plugs, safety glasses and sight-in target. Available in 223, 22-250, 243, 270, 308, 30-06, 7mm Rem. Mag., 300 Win. Mag. Introduced 1991.
Price: **$397.00**

Savage 110FXP3 Bolt-Action Rifle
Same as the Savage 110F except has black composite stock and comes with a 3-9x32 scope, Kwik-Site rings and bases, Savage/Pathfinder leather sling, Uncle Mike's swivels, gun lock, ear plugs, shooting glasses and sight-in target. Chambered for 223, 22-250, 308, 243, 30-06, 270, 7mm Rem. Mag., 300 Win. Mag. Introduced 1991.
Price: **$390.00**

Savage 110WLE One of One Thousand Limited Edition Rifle
Similar to the Savage 110G except is chambered for 7x57mm Mauser, 250-3000 Savage and 300 Savage, and comes with high-luster #2 fancy-grade American walnut stock with cut checkering, swivel studs, and recoil pad. Highly polished barrel; the bolt has a laser-etched Savage logo. Included are gun lock, ear plugs, sight-in target and shooting glasses. Introduced 1992.
Price: About **$475.00**

Savage 110F Bolt-Action Rifle
Similar to the Model 110G except has a black Du Pont Rynite® stock with black buttpad, swivel studs, removable open sights. Same calibers as the 110G except 250 Savage, 25-06, 7mm-08. Introduced 1988.
Price: Right-hand only **$360.00**

Savage 110GV Varmint Rifle
Similar to the Model 110G except has medium-weight varmint barrel, no sights, receiver drilled and tapped for scope mounting. Calibers 22-250, 223 only. Introduced 1989.
Price: **$400.00**

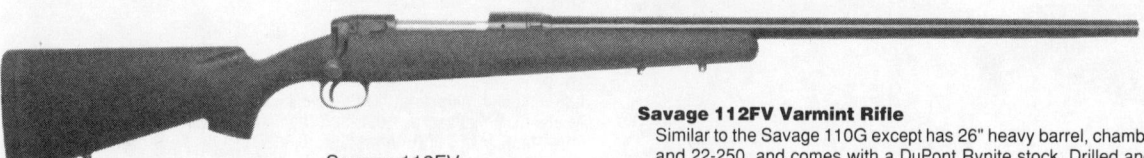

Savage 112FV

Savage 112FV Varmint Rifle
Similar to the Savage 110G except has 26" heavy barrel, chambered for 223 and 22-250, and comes with a DuPont Rynite stock. Drilled and tapped for scope mounts. Weight is 9 lbs. Included are gun lock, ear plugs, sight-in target and shooting glases. Reintroduced 1991.
Price: **$360.00**
Price: Model 112FVSS (as above except has stainless barrel, bolt handle, trigger guard, synthetic stock with positive checkering) **$460.00**

Savage 114CU Classic Ultra Rifle
Similar to the Savage 110G except comes with adjustable sights, a straight American walnut stock with high-gloss finish, cut checkering, grip cap and recoil pad. Removable box magazine hold five rounds (four for magnums). Chambered for 270, 30-06, 7mm Rem. Mag. and 300 Win. Mag. Introduced 1991.
Price: **$520.00**

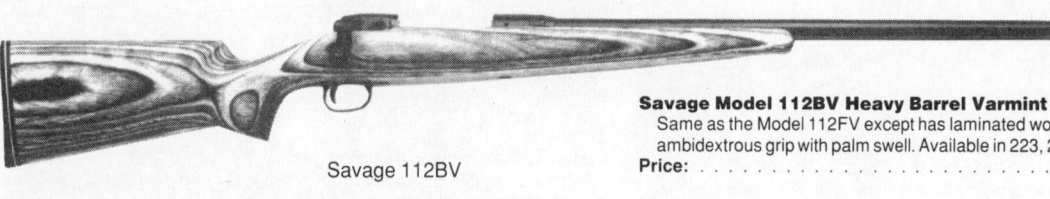

Savage 112BV

Savage Model 112BV Heavy Barrel Varmint Rifle
Same as the Model 112FV except has laminated wood stock with high comb, ambidextrous grip with palm swell. Available in 223, 22-250. Introduced 1993.
Price: **$460.00**

Savage Model 112FVS Varmint Rifle
Similar to the Model 112 FV except is a single shot with rigid, solid-bottom receiver. Available in 223, 22-250 and 220 Swift. Introduced 1993.
Price: **$360.00**

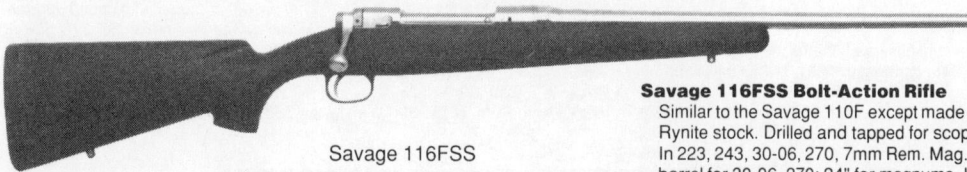

Savage 116FSS

Savage 116FSS Bolt-Action Rifle
Similar to the Savage 110F except made of stainless steel. Has black DuPont Rynite stock. Drilled and tapped for scope mounts; no open sights supplied. In 223, 243, 30-06, 270, 7mm Rem. Mag., 300 Win. Mag., 338 Win. Mag.; 22" barrel for 30-06, 270; 24" for magnums. Introduced 1991.
Price: **$500.00**
Price: Model 116FCS (as above with removable box magazine; cals. 30-06, 270, 7mm Rem. Mag., 300 Win. Mag. only) **$510.00**

Savage Model 116FSK Kodiak Rifle
Similar to the Model 116FSS except has "Shock Suppressor" recoil reducer. Available only in 338 Win. Mag., 22" barrel. Introduced 1993.
Price: **$510.00**

Savage 110FP

SAVAGE 110FP POLICE RIFLE
Caliber: 223, 308, 4-shot magazine.
Barrel: 24", heavy.
Weight: 9 lbs. **Length:** 45.5" overall.
Stock: Black Rynite composition.
Sights: None furnished. Receiver drilled and tapped for scope mounting.
Features: Matte finish on all metal parts. Double swivel studs on the forend for sling and/or bipod mount. Introduced 1990. From Savage Arms.
Price: **$400.00**

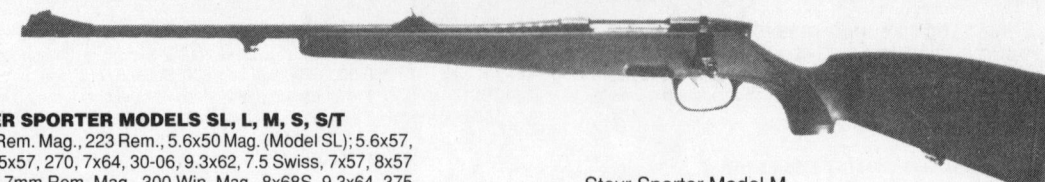

Steyr Sporter Model M

STEYR-MANNLICHER SPORTER MODELS SL, L, M, S, S/T
Caliber: 222 Rem., 222 Rem. Mag., 223 Rem., 5.6x50 Mag. (Model SL); 5.6x57, 243, 308 (Model L); 6.5x57, 270, 7x64, 30-06, 9.3x62, 7.5 Swiss, 7x57, 8x57 JS (Model M); 6.5x68, 7mm Rem. Mag., 300 Win. Mag., 8x68S, 9.3x64, 375 H&H, 458 Win. Mag. (Model S).
Barrel: 20" (full-stock), 23.6" (half-stock), 26" (magnums).
Weight: 6.8 to 7.5 lbs. **Length:** 39" (full-stock), 43" (half-stock).
Stock: Hand-checkered European walnut. Full Mannlicher or standard half-stock with Monte Carlo comb and rubber recoil pad.
Sights: Ramp front, open adjustable rear.
Features: Choice of single- or double-set triggers. Detachable 5-shot rotary magazine. Drilled and tapped for scope mounting. Model M actions available in left-hand models; S (magnum) actions available in half-stock only. Imported by GSI, Inc.

Price: Models SL, L, M, half-stock $2,023.00
Price: As above, full-stock $2,179.00
Price: Models SL, L Varmint, 26" heavy barrel $2,179.00
Price: Model M left-hand, half-stock (270, 30-06, 7x64) $2,179.00
Price: As above, full-stock (270, 7x57, 7x64, 30-06) $2,335.00
Price: Model S Magnum $2,179.00
Price: Model S/T, 26" heavy barrel (375 H&H, 9.3x64, 458 Win. Mag.) $2,335.00

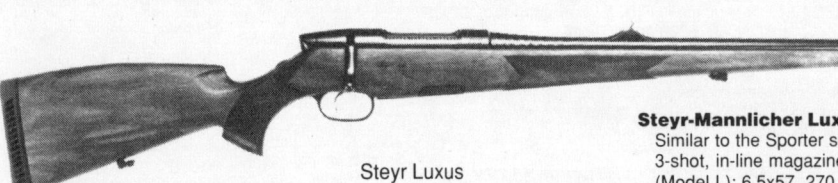

Steyr Luxus

Steyr-Mannlicher Model M Professional Rifle
Similar to the Sporter series except has black ABS Cycolac stock, Parkerized finish. Chambered for 6.5x57, 270, 7x64, 30-06, 9.3x62. Has 23.6" barrel, weighs 7.5 lbs. Imported by GSI, Inc.
Price: Without sights **$1,495.00**

Steyr-Mannlicher Luxus Model L, M, S
Similar to the Sporter series except has single set trigger, detachable steel 3-shot, in-line magazine, rear tang slide safety. Calibers: 5.6x57, 243, 308 (Model L); 6.5x57, 270, 7x64, 30-06, 9.3x62, 7.5 Swiss (Model M); 6.5x68, 7mm Rem. Mag., 300 Win. Mag., 8x68S (Model S). S (magnum) calibers available in half-stock only. Imported by GSI, Inc.
Price: Model L, M, half-stock $2,648.00
Price: As above, full-stock $2,804.00
Price: Model S (magnum) $2,804.00

Tikka Premium Grade

Tikka Premium Grade Rifles
Similar to the standard grade Tikka except has stock with roll-over cheekpiece, select walnut, rosewood grip and forend caps. Hand-checkered grip and forend. Highly polished and blued barrel. Introduced 1990. Imported from Finland by Stoeger.
Price: Standard calibers **$1,030.00**
Price: Magnum calibers **$1,070.00**

TIKKA BOLT-ACTION RIFLE
Caliber: 22-250, 223, 243, 270, 308, 30-06, 7mm Rem. Mag., 300 Win. Mag., 338 Win. Mag.
Barrel: 22½" (std. cals.), 24½" (magnum cals.).
Weight: 7⅛ lbs. **Length:** 43" overall (std. cals.).
Stock: European walnut with Monte Carlo comb, rubber buttpad, checkered grip and forend.
Sights: None furnished.
Features: Detachable four-shot magazine (standard calibers), three-shot in magnums. Receiver dovetailed for scope mounting. Introduced 1988. Imported from Finland by Stoeger Industries.
Price: Standard calibers $835.00
Price: Magnum calibers $860.00

Tikka Varmint/Continental Rifle
Similar to the standard Tikka rifle except has heavy barrel, extra-wide forend. Chambered for 22-250, 223, 243, 308. Introduced 1991. Made in Finland by Sako. Imported by Stoeger.
Price: **$1,090.00**

Tikka Whitetail/Battue Rifle
Similar to the standard Tikka rifle except has 20½" barrel with raised quarter-rib with wide V-shaped sight for rapid sighting. Chambered for 308, 270, 30-06, 7mm Rem. Mag., 300 Win. Mag., 338 Win. Mag. Made in Finland by Sako. Introduced 1991. Imported by Stoeger.
Price: 308, 270, 30-06 . . . . $860.00
Price: 7mm Rem. Mag., 300 Win. Mag., 338 Win. Mag. $895.00

Ultra Light Model 20

Ultra Light Arms Model 28, Model 40 Rifles
Similar to the Model 20 except in 264, 7mm Rem. Mag., 300 Win. Mag., 338 Win. Mag. (Model 28), 300 Wea. Mag., 416 Rigby (Model 40). Both use 24" Douglas Premium No. 2 contour barrel. Weight 5½ lbs., 45" overall length. KDF or ULA recoil arrestor built in. Any custom feature available on any ULA product can be incorporated.
Price: Right-hand, Model 28 or 40 . . . . **$2,900.00**
Price: Left-hand, Model 28 or 40 . . . . **$3,000.00**

ULTRA LIGHT ARMS MODEL 20 RIFLE
Caliber: 17 Rem., 22 Hornet, 222 Rem., 223 Rem. (Model 20S); 22-250, 6mm Rem., 243, 257 Roberts, 7x57, 7x57 Ackley, 7mm-08, 284 Win., 308 Savage. Improved and other calibers on request.
Barrel: 22" Douglas Premium No. 1 contour.
Weight: 4½ lbs. **Length:** 41½" overall.
Stock: Composite Kevlar, graphite reinforced. Du Pont imron paint colors— green, black, brown and camo options. Choice of length of pull.
Sights: None furnished. Scope mount included.
Features: Timney adjustable trigger; two-position three-function safety. Benchrest quality action. Matte or bright stock and metal finish. 3" magazine length. Shipped in a hard case. From Ultra Light Arms, Inc.
Price: Right-hand $2,400.00
Price: Model 20 Left Hand (left-hand action and stock) $2,500.00
Price: Model 24 (25-06, 270, 280 Rem., 30-06, 3⅜" magazine length) $2,500.00
Price: Model 24 Left Hand (left-hand action and stock) $2,600.00

VOERE VEC 91 LIGHTNING BOLT-ACTION RIFLE

Caliber: 5.7x26mm UCC (223-cal.) caseless, 5-shot magazine.
Barrel: 20".
Weight: 6 lbs. **Length:** 39'Overall.
Stock: European walnut with cheekpiece, checkered grip and schnabel forend.
Sights: Blade on ramp front, open adjustable rear.
Features: Fires caseless ammunition via electric ignition; two batteries housed in the pistol grip last for about 5000 shot. Trigger is adjustable from 5 oz. to 7 lbs. Bolt action has twin forward locking lugs. Top tang safety. Drilled and tapped for scope mounting. Ammunition available from importer. Introduced 1991. Imported from Austria by JagerSport, Ltd.
Price: About **$2,730.00**

Voere Model 2155, 2150 Bolt-Action Rifles

Similar to the Model 2165 except has conventional non-removable magazine, comes without sights (drilled and tapped); 22" barrel in standard calibers, 24" magnums. Imported from Austria by JagerSport, Ltd.
Price: Standard calibers—243, 270, 30-06, about **$910.00**
Price: Magnum calibers—7mm Rem. Mag.,
300 Win. Mag. (M2155M), about **$975.00**
Price: Model 2150 (as above with sights, deluxe walnut stock with hand-rubbed finish, barrel-mounted swivel), standard calibers, about . **$1,685.00**
Price: Model 2150M, 7mm Rem. Mag., 300 Win. Mag., about . . **$1,755.00**

VOERE MODEL 2165 BOLT-ACTION RIFLE

Caliber: 22-250, 243, 270, 7x57, 7x64, 308, 30-06 (standard), 7mm Rem. Mag., 300 Win. Mag., 9,3x64; 5-shot magazine for standard calibers, 3-shot for magnums.
Barrel: 22" (standard calibers), 24" (magnums).
Weight: 7-7½ lbs. **Length:** 44½" overall (22" barrel).
Stock: European walnut with Bavarian cheekpiece; schnabel forend tip; rosewood grip cap.
Sights: Ramp front, open adjustable rear.
Features: Built on Mauser 98-type action; tang safety; detachable box magazine. Comes with extra magazine. Imported from Austria by JagerSport, Ltd.
Price: Standard calibers, about **$1,425.00**
Price: Magnum calibers (Model 2165M), about **$1,495.00**

> Consult our Directory pages for the location of firms mentioned.

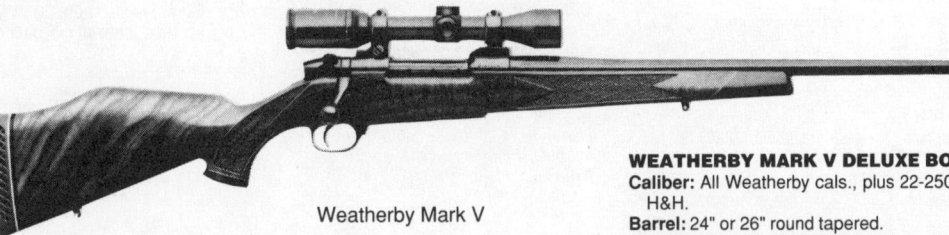

Weatherby Mark V

Weatherby Lazermark V Rifle

Same as standard Mark V except stock has extensive laser carving under cheekpiece on butt, p.g. and forend. Introduced 1981.
Price: 240, 257, 270, right-hand, 7mm, 300 Wea. Mag., right- or left-hand, 24" **$1,355.00**
Price: 240, 257, 270, 7mm Wea. Mag., 30-06, right-hand, 26" . **$1,368.00**
Price: 300 Wea. Mag., right- or left-hand, 340 Wea. Mag., right-hand, 26" **$1,403.00**
Price: 378 Wea. Mag., right-hand, 26" **$1,443.00**
Price: 416 Wea. Mag., right-hand, 26" **$1,489.00**
Price: 460 Wea. Mag., right-hand, 26" **$1,844.00**

WEATHERBY MARK V DELUXE BOLT-ACTION RIFLE

Caliber: All Weatherby cals., plus 22-250, 270, 30-06, 7mm Rem. Mag., 375 H&H.
Barrel: 24" or 26" round tapered.
Weight: 6½-10½ lbs. **Length:** 43¼"-46½" overall.
Stock: Walnut, Monte Carlo with cheekpiece, high luster finish, checkered p.g. and forend, recoil pad.
Sights: Optional (extra).
Features: Cocking indicator, adjustable trigger, hinged floorplate, thumb safety, quick detachable sling swivels.
Price: 224 Wea. Mag., 22-250, 26" **$1,196.00**
Price: 240, 257, 270, 7mm, 300 Wea. Mag., 30-06, right-hand, left-hand available, 24" **$1,225.00**
Price: 375 H&H, right-hand, 24" **$1,377.00**
Price: 240, 257, 270, 7mm Wea. Mag., 30-06, right-hand, 26" . . . **$1,239.00**
Price: 300 Wea. Mag., left-hand available, 340 Wea. Mag., right-hand, 26" **$1,270.00**
Price: 378 Wea. Mag., right-hand, 26" **$1,305.00**
Price: 416 Wea. Mag., right-hand, 26" **$1,346.00**

Weatherby Mark V Sporter

Weatherby Mark V Crown Custom Rifles

Uses hand-honed, engraved Mark V barreled action with fully-checkered bolt knob, damascened bolt and follower. Floorplate is engraved "Weatherby Custom." Super fancy walnut stock with inlays and stock carving. Gold monogram with name or initials. Right-hand only. Available in 240, 257, 270, 7mm, 300 Wea. Mag. or 30-06. Introduced 1989.
Price: From . . . . **$3,533.00** to **$4,933.00**
Price: For 340 Wea. Mag., add **$20.00**

Weatherby Weathermark Rifle

Similar to the Mark V rifle except has impregnated-color black composite stock with raised point checkering. Uses the Mark V action. Weighs 7.5 lbs. Right-hand only. Introduced 1992.
Price: 257, 270, 7mm, 300 Wea. Mag., 7mm Rem. Mag., 300 Win. Mag., 300 Win. Mag., right-hand, 24" **$599.00**
Price: 257, 270, 7mm Wea. Mag., right-hand, 26" **$625.00**
Price: 375 H&H, right-hand, 24" **$711.00**
Price: 270 Win., 30-06, right-hand, 22" **$599.00**
Price: 300, 340 Wea. Mag., right-hand, 26" **$625.00**

Weatherby Mark V Sporter Rifle

Same as the Mark V Deluxe without the embellishments. Metal has low-luster blue, Stock is Claro walnut with high-gloss epoxy finish, Monte Carlo comb, recoil pad. Introduced 1993.
Price: 257 270, 7mm, 300 Wea. Mag., 7mm Rem. Mag., 300, 338 Win. Mag., right-hand, 24" **$732.00**
Price: 375 H&H, right-hand, 24" **$833.00**
Price: 270 Win., 30-06, right-hand, 22" **$732.00**
Price: 300, 340 Wea. Mag., right-hand, 26" **$780.00**

Weatherby Mark V Safari Grade Custom Rifles

Uses the Mark V barreled action. Stock is of European walnut with satin oil finish, rounded ebony tip and cap, black presentation recoil pad, no white spacers, and pattern #16 fine-line checkering. Matte finish bluing, floorplate is engraved "Weatherby Safari Grade"; 24" barrel. Standard rear stock swivel, barrel band front swivel. Has quarter-rib rear sight with a stationary leaf and one folding shallow V leaf. Front sight is a hooded ramp with brass bead. Right- or left-hand. Allow 8-10 months delivery. Introduced 1985.
Price: 300 W.M. **$3,301.00**
Price: 340 W.M. **$3,321.00**
Price: 378 W.M. **$3,481.00**
Price: 416 W.M. **$3,534.00**
Price: 460 W.M. **$3,574.00**

CENTERFIRE RIFLES—BOLT ACTION

Weatherby Weathermark Alaskan Rifle
Same as the Weathermark except all metal plated with electroless nickel. Available in right-hand only. Introduced 1992.
Price: 257, 270, 7mm, 300 Wea. Mag., 7mm Rem. Mag., 300 Win. Mag., 338 Win. Mag.,right-hand, 24" **$799.00**
Price: 257, 270, 7mm Wea. Mag., right-hand, 26" **$833.00**
Price: 375 H&H, right-hand, 24" **$949.00**
Price: 270 Win., 30-06, right-hand, 22" **$799.00**
Price: 300, 340 Wea. Mag., right-hand, 26" **$833.00**

Weatherby Weatherguard Alaskan Rifle
Same as the Vanguard Weatherguard except all metal finished with electroless nickel. Available in 223, 243, 7mm-08, 270 Win., 7mm Rem. Mag., 308, 30-06, right-hand only, 24" barrel. Introduced 1992.
Price: **$699.00**

Weatherby Vanguard VGX

Weatherby Vanguard Classic Rifle
Similar to the Classicmark I except has rounded forend with black tip, black grip cap with walnut diamond inlay, 20 lpi checkering. Solid black recoil pad. Oil-finished stock. Available in 22-250, 243, 270, 7mm Rem. Mag., 30-06, 300 Win. Mag., 338 Win. Mag., 270 Wea. Mag., 300 Wea. Mag. Introduced 1989.
Price: **$549.00**

Weatherby Vanguard Classic No. 1 Rifle
Similar to the Vanguard VGX Deluxe except has a "classic" style stock without Monte Carlo comb, no forend tip. Has distinctive Weatherby grip cap. Satin finish on stock. Available in 223, 243, 270, 7mm-08, 7mm Rem. Mag., 30-06, 308; 24" barrel. Introduced 1989.
Price: **$549.00**

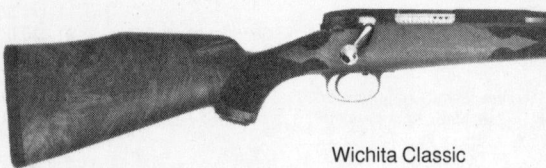
Wichita Classic

WICHITA VARMINT RIFLE
Caliber: 222 Rem., 222 Rem. Mag., 223 Rem., 22 PPC, 6mm PPC, 22-250, 243, 6mm Rem., 308 Win.; other calibers on special order.
Barrel: 20⅛".
Weight: 9 lbs. **Length:** 40⅛" overall.
Stock: AAA Fancy American walnut. Hand-rubbed finish, hand checkered, 20 lpi pattern. Hand-inletted, glass bedded, steel grip cap. Pachmayr rubber recoil pad.
Sights: None. Drilled and tapped for scope mounts.
Features: Right- or left-hand Wichita action with three locking lugs. Available as a single shot or repeater with 3-shot magazine. Checkered bolt handle. Bolt is hand fitted, lapped and jeweled. Side thumb safety. Firing pin fall is ³⁄₁₆". Non-glare blue finish. From Wichita Arms.
Price: Single shot **$2,250.00**

Weatherby Classicmark No. 1 Rifle
Similar to the Mark V except has straight comb stock of hand-selected American claro walnut with oil finish, 18 l.p.i. panel point checkering and a 1" Presentation recoil pad. All metal satin finished. Uses the Mark V action. Available in right- or left-hand versions. Introduced 1992.
Price: 240, 257, 270, 7mm, 300 Wea. Mag.,
7mm Rem. Mag., right-hand, 24" **$1,295.00**
Price: 375 H&H, right-hand, 26" **$1,425.00**
Price: 240, 257, 270, 7mm Wea. Mag., right-hand, 26" **$1,310.00**
Price: 270 Win., 30-06, right-hand, 22" **$1,295.00**
Price: 300, 340 Wea. Mag., right-hand, 26" **$1,323.00**
Price: 378 Wea. Mag., right-hand, 26" **$1,356.00**
Price: 416 Wea. Mag., right-hand, 26" **$1,411.00**
Price: 460 Wea. Mag., right-hand, 26" **$1,573.00**

WEATHERBY VANGUARD VGX DELUXE RIFLE
Caliber: 22-250, 243, 270, 270 Wea. Mag., 7mm Rem. Mag., 30-06, 300 Win. Mag., 300 Wea. Mag., 338 Win. Mag.; 5-shot magazine (3-shot for magnums).
Barrel: 24", No. 2 contour.
Weight: 7⅞-8½ lbs. **Length:** 44½" overall (22-250, 243 are 44").
Stock: Walnut with high luster finish; rosewood grip cap and forend tip.
Sights: Optional, available at extra cost.
Features: Fully adjustable trigger; side safety; rubber recoil pad. Introduced 1989. Imported from Japan by Weatherby.
Price: **$699.00**

Weatherby Vanguard Weatherguard Rifle
Has a forest green or black wrinkle-finished synthetic stock. All metal is matte blue. Has a 24" barrel, weighs 7½ lbs., measures 44½". In 223, 243, and 308; 40½" in 270, 7mm-08, 7mm Rem. Mag., 30-06. Accepts same scope mount bases as Mark V action. Introduced 1989.
Price: Right-hand only **$499.00**

WICHITA CLASSIC RIFLE
Caliber: 17-222, 17-222 Mag., 222 Rem., 222 Rem. Mag., 223 Rem., 6x47; other calibers on special order.
Barrel: 21⅛".
Weight: 8 lbs. **Length:** 41" overall.
Stock: AAA Fancy American walnut. Hand-rubbed and checkered (20 lpi). Hand-inletted, glass bedded, steel grip cap. Pachmayr rubber recoil pad.
Sights: None. Drilled and tapped for scope mounting.
Features: Available as single shot or repeater. Octagonal barrel and Wichita action, right- or left-hand. Checkered bolt handle. Bolt is hand-fitted, lapped and jeweled. Adjustable trigger is set at 2 lbs. Side thumb safety. Firing pin fall is ³⁄₁₆". Non-glare blue finish. From Wichita Arms.
Price: Single shot **$2,950.00**

Winchester Model 70 Sporter

WINCHESTER MODEL 70 SPORTER
Caliber: 22-250, 223, 243, 25-06, 270, 270 Wea., 30-06, 264 Win. Mag., 7mm Rem. Mag., 300 H&H, 300 Win. Mag., 300 Wea. Mag., 338 Win. Mag., 3-shot magazine.
Barrel: 24".
Weight: 7¾ lbs. **Length:** 44½" overall.
Stock: American walnut with Monte Carlo cheekpiece. Cut checkering and satin finish.
Sights: Optional hooded ramp front, adjustable folding leaf rear. Drilled and tapped for scope mounting.
Features: Three-position safety, stainless steel magazine follower; rubber buttpad; epoxy bedded receiver recoil lug. From U.S. Repeating Arms Co.
Price: With sights **$556.00**
Price: With bases and rings **$556.00**

CAUTION: PRICES CHANGE, CHECK AT GUNSHOP.

CENTERFIRE RIFLES—BOLT ACTION

Winchester Model 70 Win Tuff

Winchester Model 70 SM Sporter
Same as the Model 70 Sporter except has black composite, graphite-impregnated stock and matte-finished metal. Available in 223, 22-250, 243, 270, 308, 30-06, 7mm Rem. Mag., 300 Win. Mag., 338 Win. Mag., 375 H&H. Weighs about 7.8 lbs. Comes with scope bases and rings. Introduced 1992.
Price: **$576.00**
Price: 375 H&H **$604.00**

Winchester Model 70 Stainless

Winchester Model 70 Heavy Varmint

Winchester Model 70 Synthetic Heavy Varmint Rifle
Similar to the Model 70 Varmint except has fiberglass/graphite stock, 26" heavy stainless steel barrel, blued receiver. Weighs about 10¾ lbs. Available in 223, 22-250, 243, 308. Uses full-length Pillar Plus Accu Block bedding system. Introduced 1993.
Price: **$700.00**

Winchester Model 70 DBM Rifle
Same as the Model 70 Sporter except has detachable box magazine. Available in 223, 22-250, 243, 270, 308, 30-06, 7mm Rem. Mag., 300 Win. Mag. with 24" barrel. Introduced 1992.
Price: **$598.00**

Winchester Model 70 Featherweight

Winchester Model 70 Featherweight WinTuff
Same as the Model 70 Featherweight except has brown laminated stock. Available in 22-250, 223, 243, 270, 308, 30-06. Weighs 6.75-7 lbs. Comes with scope bases and rings. Introduced 1992.
Price: **$572.00**

Winchester Model 70 Featherweight Classic

Winchester Model 70 Sporter WinTuff
Same as the Model 70 Sporter except has classic-style brown laminated stock with sculpted cheekpiece, diamond point checkering, sling swivel studs, and contoured rubber recoil pad. Available in 270, 30-06, 7mm Rem. Mag., 300 Win. Mag., 300 Wea. Mag., 338 Win Mag. Weighs about 7.8 lbs. Comes with scope bases and rings. Introduced 1992.
Price: **$572.00**

Winchester Model 70 Stainless Rifle
Same as the Model 70 Sporter except has stainless steel barrel and action with matte gray finish, black composite stock impregnated with fiberglass and graphite, contoured rubber recoil pad. Available in 270, 30-06, 7mm Rem. Mag., 300 Win. Mag., 338 Win. Mag. (24" barrel), 3- or 5-shot magazine. Weighs 6.75 lbs. Introduced 1992.
Price: **$604.00**

Winchester Model 70 Varmint
Similar to the Model 70 Sporter except has heavy 26" barrel with counter-bored muzzle. Available in 22-250, 223, 243 and 308. Receiver bedded in sporter-style stock. Has rubber buttpad. Receiver drilled and tapped for scope mounting. Weight about 9 lbs., overall length 46". Introduced 1989.
Price: **$580.00**

Winchester Model 70 DBM-S Rifle
Same as the Model 70 DBM except has fiberglass/graphite composite stock. Available in 223, 22-250, 243, 270, 308, 30-06, 7mm Rem. Mag., 300 Win. Mag. Detachable box magazine, 24" barrel. Most calibers offered with choice of open sights or bases and rings. Introduced 1993.
Price: **$618.00**

Winchester Model 70 Featherweight
Available with standard action in 270 Win., 280 Rem., 30-06, 7mm Rem. Mag., 300 Win. Mag., short action in 22-250, 223, 243, 6.5x55, 7mm-08, 308; 22" tapered. Featherweight barrel; classic-style American walnut stock with Schnabel forend, wraparound checkering fashioned after early Model 70 custom rifle patterns. Red rubber buttpad, sling swivel studs. Weighs 6¾ lbs. (standard action), 6½ lbs. (short action). Introduced 1984.
Price: **$562.00**

Winchester Model 70 Featherweight Classic
Same as the Model 70 Featherweight except has claw controlled-round feeding system; action is bedded in a standard-grade walnut stock. Available in 270, 280 Rem., 30-06. Drilled and tapped for scope mounts; comes with rings and bases. Weighs 7.25 lbs. Introduced 1992.
Price: **$749.00**

WINCHESTER MODEL 70 LIGHTWEIGHT RIFLE

Caliber: 270, 280, 30-06 (standard action); 22-250, 223, 243, 308 (short action), both 5-shot magazine, except 6-shot in 223.
Barrel: 22".
Weight: 6¼ lbs. **Length:** 40½" overall (std.), 40" (short).
Stock: American walnut with satin finish, deep-cut checkering.
Sights: None furnished. Drilled and tapped for scope mounting.
Features: Three position safety; stainless steel magazine follower; hinged floorplate; sling swivel studs. Introduced 1984.
Price: Walnut $485.00

WINCHESTER MODEL 70 SUPER EXPRESS MAGNUM

Caliber: 375 H&H Mag., 458 Win. Mag., 3-shot magazine.
Barrel: 24" (375); 22" (458).
Weight: 8½ lbs.
Stock: American walnut with Monte Carlo cheekpiece. Wraparound checkering and finish.
Sights: Hooded ramp front, open rear.
Features: Controlled round feeding. Two steel cross bolts in stock for added strength. Front sling swivel stud mounted on barrel. Contoured rubber buttpad. From U.S. Repeating Arms Co.
Price: $816.00

Winchester Model 70 Custom Sporting Sharpshooter Rifle

Similar to the Custom Sharpshooter except has McMillan sporter-style, gray-finished composite stock, stainless steel Schneider barrel with natural matte finish, blued receiver. Available in 270, (24"), 7mm STW and 300 Win. Mag. (26"). Comes with rings and bases. Introduced 1993.
Price: $1,595.00

Winchester Ranger Rifle

Similar to Model 70 Lightweight except chambered only for 223, 243, 270, 30-06, with 22" barrel. American hardwood stock, no checkering, composition butt-plate. Metal has matte blue finish. Introduced 1985.
Price: $427.00
Price: Ranger Ladies/Youth, 243, 308 only, scaled-down stock . . . $443.00

WINCHESTER MODEL 70 SUPER GRADE

Caliber: 270, 30-06, 5-shot magazine; 7mm Rem. Mag., 300 Win. Mag., 338 Win. Mag., 3-shot magazine.
Barrel: 24".
Weight: About 7¾ lbs. **Length:** 44½" overall.
Stock: Walnut with straight comb, sculptured cheekpiece, wraparound cut checkering, tapered forend, solid rubber buttpad.
Sights: None furnished; comes with scope bases and rings.
Features: Controlled round feeding with stainless steel claw extractor, bolt guide rail, three-position safety; all steel bottom metal, hinged floorplate, stainless magazine follower. Introduced 1990. From U.S. Repeating Arms Co.
Price: $997.00

WINCHESTER MODEL 70 CUSTOM SHARPSHOOTER

Caliber: 223, 22-250, 308 Win., 300 Win. Mag.
Barrel: 24" (308), 26" (223, 22-250, 300 Win. Mag.).
Weight: 11 lbs. **Length:** 44.5" overall (24" barrel).
Stock: McMillan A-2 target style; glass bedded; recoil pad, swivel studs.
Sights: None furnished; comes with bases and rings.
Features: Hand-honed and fitted action, Schneider barrel. Matte blue finish. Introduced 1992. From U.S. Repeating Arms Co.
Price: $1,650.00

CENTERFIRE RIFLES—SINGLE SHOT

Classic and modern designs for sporting and competitive use.

Brown Model One

BROWN MODEL ONE SINGLE SHOT RIFLE

Caliber: 22 LR, 357 Mag., 44 Mag., 7-30 Waters, 30-30 Win., 375 Win., 45-70; custom chamberings from 17 Rem. through 45-caliber available.
Barrel: 22" or custom, bull or tapered.
Weight: 6 lbs. **Length:** NA.
Stock: Smooth walnut; custom takedown design by Woodsmith. Palm swell for right- or left-hand; rubber butt pad.
Sights: Optional. Drilled and tapped for scope mounting.
Features: Rigid barrel/receiver; falling block action with short lock time, automatic case ejection; air-gauged barrels by Wilson and Douglas. Muzzle has 11-degree target crown. Matte black oxide finish standard, polished and electroless nickel optional. Introduced 1988. Made in U.S. by E.A. Brown Mfg.
Price: $750.00

ARMSPORT 1866 SHARPS RIFLE, CARBINE

Caliber: 45-70.
Barrel: 28", round or octagonal.
Weight: 8.10 lbs. **Length:** 46" overall.
Stock: Walnut.
Sights: Blade front, folding adjustable rear. Tang sight set optionally available.
Features: Replica of the 1866 Sharps. Color case-hardened frame, rest blued. Imported by Armsport.
Price: $860.00
Price: With octagonal barrel $880.00
Price: Carbine, 22" round barrel $830.00

Browning Model 1885

BROWNING MODEL 1885 SINGLE SHOT RIFLE

Caliber: 223, 22-250, 30-06, 270, 7mm Rem. Mag., 45-70.
Barrel: 28".
Weight: About 8½ lbs. **Length:** 43½" overall.
Stock: Walnut with straight grip, schnabel forend.
Sights: None furnished; drilled and tapped for scope mounting.
Features: Replica of J.M. Browning's high-wall falling block rifle. Octagon barrel with recessed muzzle. Imported from Japan by Browning. Introduced 1985.
Price: $809.95

DAKOTA SINGLE SHOT RIFLE

Caliber: Most rimmed and rimless commercial calibers.
Barrel: 23".
Weight: 6 lbs. **Length:** 39½" overall.
Stock: Medium fancy grade walnut in classic style. Checkered grip and forend.
Sights: None furnished. Drilled and tapped for scope mounting.

Features: Falling block action with under-lever. Top tang safety. Removable trigger plate for conversion to single set trigger. Introduced 1990. Made in U.S. by Dakota Arms.
Price: $2,300.00
Price: Barreled action $1,650.00
Price: Action only $1,400.00

CAUTION: PRICES CHANGE, CHECK AT GUNSHOP.

DESERT INDUSTRIES G-90 SINGLE SHOT RIFLE
Caliber: 22-250, 220 Swift, 223, 6mm, 243, 25-06, 257 Roberts, 270 Win., 270 Wea. Mag., 280, 7x57, 7mm Rem. Mag., 30-06, 300 Win. Mag., 300 Wea. Mag., 338 Win. Mag., 375 H&H, 45-70, 458 Win. Mag.
Barrel: 20", 22", 24", 26"; light, medium, heavy.
Weight: About 7.5 lbs.
Stock: Walnut.
Sights: None furnished. Drilled and tapped for scope mounting.
Features: Cylindrical falling block action. All steel construction. Blue finish. Announced 1990. From Desert Industries, Inc.
Price: **$525.00**

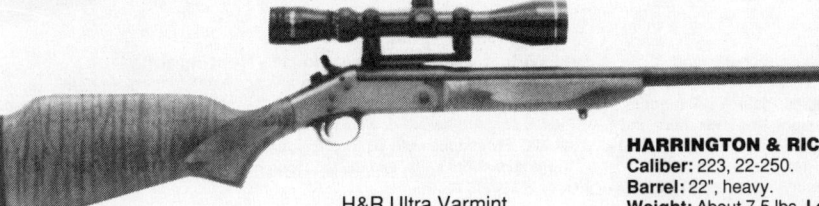

H&R Ultra Varmint

HARRINGTON & RICHARDSON ULTRA VARMINT RIFLE
Caliber: 223, 22-250.
Barrel: 22", heavy.
Weight: About 7.5 lbs. Length: NA.
Stock: Hand-checkered curly maple with Monte Carlo comb.
Sights: None furnished. Drilled and tapped for scope mounting.
Features: Break-open action with side-lever release, positive ejection. Comes with scope mount. Blued receiver and barrel. Swivel studs. Introduced 1993. From H&R 1971, Inc.
Price: **$249.95**

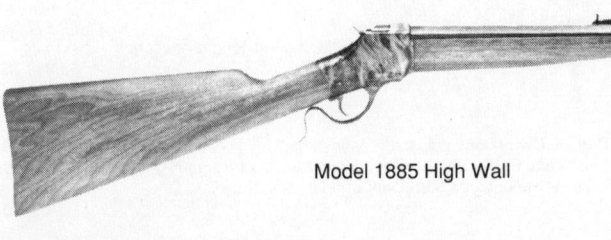

Model 1885 High Wall

MODEL 1885 HIGH WALL RIFLE
Caliber: 30-40 Krag, 32-40, 38-55, 40-65 WCF, 45-70.
Barrel: 26" (30-40), 28" all others. Douglas Premium #3 tapered octagon.
Weight: NA. Length: NA.
Stock: Premium American black walnut.
Sights: Marble's standard ivory bead front, #66 long blade top rear with reversible notch and elevator.
Features: Recreation of early octagon top, thick-wall High Wall with Coil spring action. Tand drilled, tapped for High Wall tand sight. Receiver, lever, hammer and breechblock color case-hardened. Introduced 1991. Avaiable from Montana Armory, Inc.
Price: **$1,095.00**

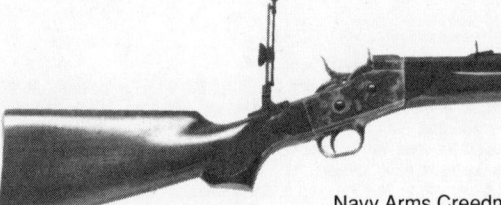

Navy Arms Creedmoor

Navy Arms #2 Creedmoor Rifle
Similar to the Navy Arms Buffalo Rifle except has 30" tapered octagon barrel, checkered full-pistol grip stock, blade front sight, open adjustable rear sight and Creedmoor tang sight. Introduced 1991. Imported by Navy Arms.
Price: **$695.00**

NAVY ARMS ROLLING BLOCK BUFFALO RIFLE
Caliber: 45-70.
Barrel: 26", 30".
Stocks: Walnut.
Sights: Blade front, adjustable rear.
Features: Reproduction of classic rolling block action. Available with full-octagon or half-octagon-half-round barrel. Color case-hardened action. From Navy Arms.
Price: **$510.00**

Navy Arms Sharps Cavalry Carbine
Similar to the Sharps Plains Rifle except has 22" barrel, overall length of 39", and weighs 7¾ lbs. Has blade front sight, military ladder-style rear, barrel band on forend. Color case-hardened action, rest blued. Introduced 1991. Imported by Navy Arms.
Price: **$650.00**

NAVY ARMS SHARPS PLAINS RIFLE
Caliber: 45-70.
Barrel: 28½".
Weight: 8 lbs., 10 oz. Length: 45¾" overall.
Stock: Checkered walnut butt and forend.
Sights: Blade front, open rear adjustable for windage.
Features: Color case-hardened action, rest blued. Introduced 1991. Imported by Navy Arms.
Price: **$715.00**

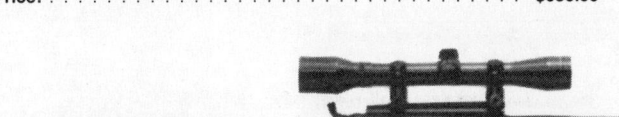
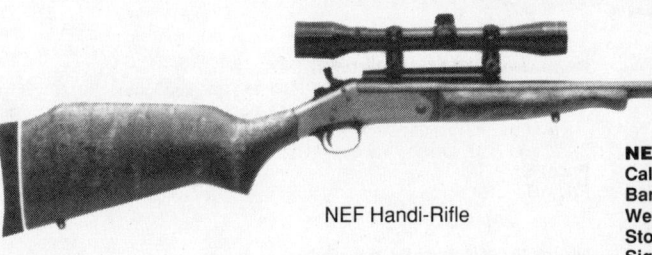

NEF Handi-Rifle

NEW ENGLAND FIREARMS HANDI-RIFLE
Caliber: 22 Hornet, 22-250, 223, 243, 30-30, 270, 30-06, 45-70.
Barrel: 22".
Weight: 7 lbs.
Stock: Walnut-finished hardwood.
Sights: Ramp front, folding rear. Drilled and tapped for scope mount; 22-250, 223, 243, 270, 30-06 have no open sights, come with scope mounts.
Features: Break-open action with side-lever release. The 243, 270 and 30-06 have recoil pad and Monte Carlo stock for shooting with scope. Swivel studs on all models. Blue finish. Introduced 1989. From New England Firearms.
Price: 22-250, 243, 270, 30-06 . . . . **$199.95**
Price: 22 Hornet, 223, 30-30, 45-70 . . . . **$189.95**

RED WILLOW ARMORY BALLARD NO. 5 PACIFIC
Caliber: 32-40 Win., 38-55, 40-65 Win., 40-70 Ballard, 40-85 Ballard, 45-70; other calibers on special order.
Barrel: 30", tapered octagon.
Weight: 10-11.5 lbs. **Length:** NA.
Stock: Oil-finished American walnut with crescent butt, schnabel forend.
Sights: Blade front, buckhorn rear.
Features: Exact recreation of the Ballard No. 5 Pacific; double-set triggers; under-barrel wiping rod; drilled and tapped for tang sight; ring lever. Mid- and long range sights, fancy wood, single trigger optionally available. Made in U.S. Introduced 1992. From Red Willow Tool & Armory, Inc.
Price: Standard model **$1,912.00**

Red Willow No. 5

Red Willow Armory Ballard No. 1½ Hunting Rifle
Similar to the Ballard No. 5 Pacific except has 30" medium-heavy tapered round barrel, no wiping rod, weighs 9 lbs. Has S-type lever, single trigger. Same calibers as No. 5 Pacific. Options include mid- and long range tang sights, Swiss tube with bead of Lyman globe front, fancy wood, double-set triggers, custom rifles. Introduced 1992. From Red Willow Tool & Armory, Inc.
Price: Standard model **$1,405.00**

Red Willow Armory Ballard No. 8 Union Hill Rifle
Similar to the Ballard No. 5 Pacific except has 30" part round-part octagon barrel; weighs 10 lbs. Oil-finished checkered American walnut stock with cheek rest, pistol grip, nickeled off-hand-style buttplate. Swiss tube sight with bead front, drilled and tapped for tang sight. Exact recreation of the original, with double-set triggers. Options include mid- and long range tang sights, Lyman globe front, fancy wood, single trigger, buckhorn rear sight, customs. Made in U.S. Introduced 1992. From Red Willow Tool & Armory, Inc.
Price: Standard model **$2,712.50**
Price: Deluxe model (has fancy wood and checkering, mid-range tang sight) **$3,212.50**

Red Willow Armory Ballard No. 4½ Target Rifle
Similar to the No. 5 Pacific except has single trigger, 30" part-round, part-octagon, medium-heavy barrel, full loop lever. Pistol grip stock has a checkered steel shotgun-style buttplate. Swiss bead front sight. Available in 32-40, 38-55, 40-63, 40-65, 40-85, 45-70. Introduced 1993. From Red Willow Tool & Armory, Inc.
Price: Standard model **$2,437.50**
Price: Deluxe model (fancy wood, checkering, long range tang sight) **$2,968.75**

REMINGTON-STYLE ROLLING BLOCK CARBINE
Caliber: 45-70.
Barrel: 30", octagonal.
Weight: 11¾ lbs. **Length:** 46½" overall.
Stock: Walnut.

Sights: Blade front, adjustable rear.
Features: Color case-hardened receiver, brass trigger guard, buttplate and barrel band, blued barrel. Imported from Italy by E.M.F.
Price: **$820.00**

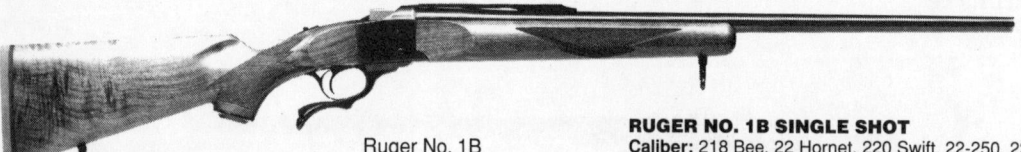

Ruger No. 1B

Ruger No. 1A Light Sporter
Similar to the No. 1B Standard Rifle except has lightweight 22" barrel, Alexander Henry-style forend, adjustable folding leaf rear sight on quarter-rib, dovetailed ramp front with gold bead. Calibers 243, 30-06, 270 and 7x57. Weight about 7¼ lbs.
Price: No. 1A **$634.00**
Price: Barreled action **$429.50**

Ruger No. 1H Tropical Rifle
Similar to the No. 1B Standard Rifle except has Alexander Henry forend, adjustable folding leaf rear sight on quarter-rib, ramp front with dovetail gold bead, 24" heavy barrel. Calibers 375 H&H, 404 Jeffery, 416 Rem. Mag. (weight about 8¼ lbs.), 416 Rigby, and 458 Win. Mag. (weight about 9 lbs.).
Price: No. 1H **$634.00**
Price: Barreled action **$429.50**

RUGER NO. 1B SINGLE SHOT
Caliber: 218 Bee, 22 Hornet, 220 Swift, 22-250, 223, 243, 6mm Rem., 25-06, 257 Roberts, 270, 280, 30-06, 7mm Rem. Mag., 300 Win. Mag., 338 Win. Mag., 270 Wea., 300 Wea.
Barrel: 26" round tapered with quarter-rib; with Ruger 1" rings.
Weight: 8 lbs. **Length:** 43⅜" overall.
Stock: Walnut, two-piece, checkered p.g. and semi-beavertail forend.
Sights: None, 1" scope rings supplied for integral mounts.
Features: Under-lever, hammerless falling block design has auto ejector, top tang safety.
Price: **$634.00**
Price: Barreled action **$429.50**

Ruger No. 1S Medium Sporter
Similar to the No. 1B Standard Rifle except has Alexander Henry-style forend, adjustable folding leaf rear sight on quarter-rib, ramp front sight base and dovetail-type gold bead front sight. Calibers 218 Bee, 7mm Rem. Mag., 338 Win. Mag., 300 Win. Mag. with 26" barrel, 45-70 with 22" barrel. Weight about 7½ lbs. In 45-70.
Price: No. 1S **$634.00**
Price: Barreled action **$429.50**

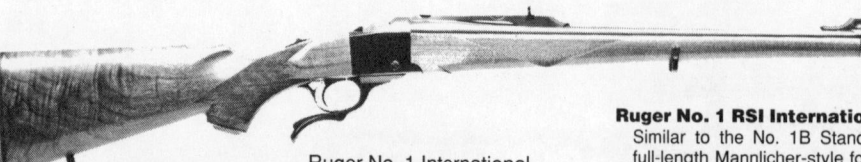

Ruger No. 1 International

Ruger No. 1 RSI International
Similar to the No. 1B Standard Rifle except has lightweight 20" barrel, full-length Mannlicher-style forend with loop sling swivel, adjustable folding leaf rear sight on quarter-rib, ramp front with gold bead. Calibers 243, 30-06, 270 and 7x57. Weight is about 7¼ lbs.
Price: No. 1 RSI **$656.00**
Price: Barreled action **$429.50**

Ruger No. 1V Special Varminter
Similar to the No. 1B Standard Rifle except has 24" heavy barrel. Semi-beavertail forend, barrel tapped for target scope block, with 1" Ruger scope rings. Calibers 22 PPC, 22-250, 220 Swift, 223, 6mm PPC, 25-06. Weight about 9 lbs.
Price: No. 1V **$634.00**
Price: Barreled action **$429.50**

CONSULT
SHOOTER'S MARKETPLACE
Page 231, This Issue

CAUTION: PRICES CHANGE, CHECK AT GUNSHOP.

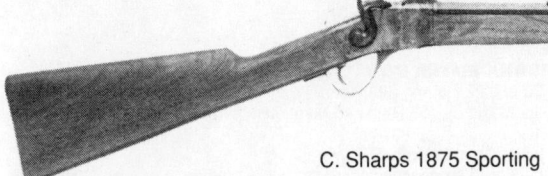

C. Sharps 1875 Sporting

C. SHARPS ARMS NEW MODEL 1874 OLD RELIABLE
Caliber: 40-50, 40-70, 40-90, 45-70, 45-90, 45-100, 45-110, 45-120, 50-70, 50-90, 50-140.
Barrel: 26", 28", 30" tapered octagon.
Weight: About 10 lbs. **Length:** NA.
Stock: American black walnut; shotgun butt with checkered steel buttplate; straight grip, heavy forend with schnabel tip.
Sights: Blade front, buckhorn rear. Drilled and tapped for tang sight.
Features: Recreation of the Model 1874 Old Reliable Sharps Sporting Rifle. Double set triggers. Reintroduced 1991. Made in U.S. by C. Sharps Arms. Available from Montana Armory, Inc.
Price: **$995.00**

C. Sharps Arms 1875 Classic Sharps
Similar to the New Model 1875 Sporting Rifle except has 26", 28" or 30" full octagon barrel, crescent buttplate with toe plate, Hartford-style forend with cast German silver nose cap. Blade front sight, Rocky Mountain buckhorn rear. Weight is 10 lbs. Introduced 1987. From C. Sharps Arms Co. and Montana Armory, Inc.
Price: **$1,075.00**

C. SHARPS ARMS NEW MODEL 1875 RIFLE
Caliber: 22LR, 32-40 & 38-55 Ballard, 38-56 WCF, 40-65 WCF, 40-90 3¼", 40-90 2⅝", 40-70 2¹⁄₁₀", 40-70 2¼", 40-70 2½", 40-50 1¹¹⁄₁₆", 40-50 1⅞", 45-90, 45-70, 45-100, 45-110, 45-120. Also available on special order only in 50-70, 50-90, 50-140.
Barrel: 24", 26", 30" (standard); 32", 34" optional.
Weight: 8-12 lbs.
Stocks: Walnut, straight grip, shotgun butt with checkered steel buttplate.
Sights: Silver blade front, Rocky Mountain buckhorn rear.
Features: Recreation of the 1875 Sharps rifle. Production guns will have case colored receiver. Available in Custom Sporting and Target versions upon request. Announced 1986. From C. Sharps Arms Co. and Montana Armory, Inc.
Price: 1875 Carbine (24" tapered round bbl.) **$725.00**
Price: 1875 Saddle Rifle (26" tapered oct. bbl.) **$825.00**
Price: 1875 Sporting Rifle (30" tapered oct. bbl.) **$850.00**
Price: 1875 Business Rifle (28" tapered round bbl.) **$775.00**

C. Sharps Arms New Model 1875 Target & Long Range
Similar to the New Model 1875 except available in all listed calibers except 22 LR; 34" tapered octagon barrel; globe with post front sight, Long Range Vernier tang sight with windage adjustments. Pistol grip stock with cheek rest; checkered steel buttplate. Introduced 1991. From C. Sharps Arms Co. and Montana Armory, Inc.
Price: **$1,165.00**

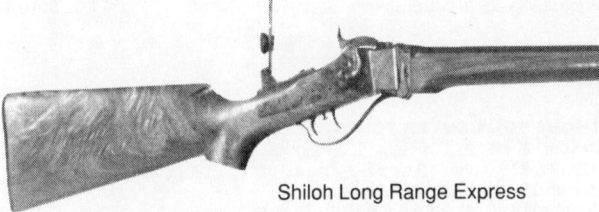

Shiloh Long Range Express

Shiloh Sharps 1874 Montana Roughrider
Similar to the No. 1 Sporting Rifle except available with half-octagon or full-octagon barrel in 24", 26", 28", 30", 34" lengths; standard supreme or semi-fancy wood, shotgun, pistol grip or military-style butt. Weight about 8½ lbs. Calibers 30-40, 30-30, 40-50x1¹¹⁄₁₆" BN, 40-70x2¹⁄₁₀" BN, 45-70x2¹⁄₁₀" ST. Globe front and tang sight optional.
Price: Standard supreme **$870.00**
Price: Semi-fancy **$950.00**

Shiloh Sharps 1874 Military Carbine
Has 22" round barrel with blade front sight and full buckhorn ladder-type rear. Military-style buttstock with barrel band on military-style forend. Steel buttplate, saddle bar and ring. Standard supreme grade only. Weight is about 8½ lbs. Calibers 40-70 BN, 45-70, 50-70. Introduced 1989.
Price: **$925.00**

SHILOH SHARPS 1874 LONG RANGE EXPRESS
Caliber: 40-50 BN, 40-70 BN, 40-90 BN, 45-70 ST, 45-90 ST, 45-110 ST, 50-70 ST, 50-90 ST, 50-110 ST, 32-40, 38-55, 40-70 ST, 40-90 ST.
Barrel: 34" tapered octagon.
Weight: 10½ lbs. **Length:** 51" overall.
Stock: Oil-finished semi-fancy walnut with pistol grip, shotgun-style butt, traditional cheek rest and accent line. Schnabel forend.
Sights: Globe front, sporting tang rear.
Features: Recreation of the Model 1874 Sharps rifle. Double set triggers. Made in U.S. by Shiloh Rifle Mfg. Co.
Price: **$995.00**
Price: Sporting Rifle No. 1 (similar to above except with 30" bbl., blade front, buckhorn rear sight) **$970.00**
Price: Sporting Rifle No. 3 (similar to No. 1 except straight-grip stock, standard wood) **$870.00**
Price: 1874 Hartford model **$1,033.00**

Shiloh Sharps 1874 Business Rifle
Similar to No. 3 Rifle except has 28" heavy round barrel, military-style buttstock and steel buttplate. Weight about 9½ lbs. Calibers 40-50 BN, 40-70 BN, 40-90 BN, 45-70 ST, 45-90 ST, 50-70 ST, 50-100 ST, 32-40, 38-55, 40-70 ST, 40-90 ST.
Price: **$875.00**
Price: 1874 Carbine (similar to above except 24" round bbl., single trigger—double set avail.) **$895.00**
Price: 1874 Saddle Rifle (similar to Carbine except has 26" octagon barrel, semi-fancy shotgun butt) **$925.00**

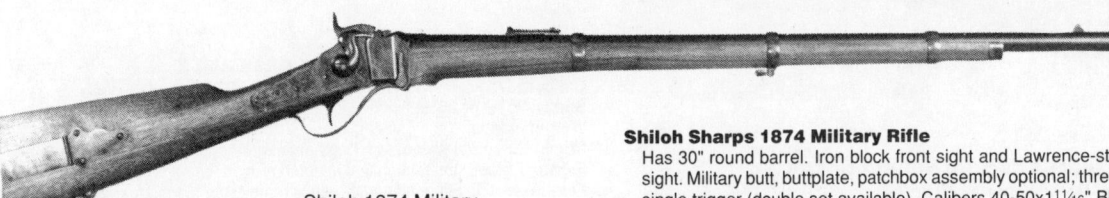

Shiloh 1874 Military

SHARPS 1874 OLD RELIABLE
Caliber: 45-70.
Barrel: 28", octagonal.
Weight: 9¼ lbs. **Length:** 46" overall.
Stock: Checkered walnut.
Sights: Blade front, adjustable rear.

Shiloh Sharps 1874 Military Rifle
Has 30" round barrel. Iron block front sight and Lawrence-style rear ladder sight. Military butt, buttplate, patchbox assembly optional; three barrel bands; single trigger (double set available). Calibers 40-50x1¹¹⁄₁₆" BN, 40-70x2¹⁄₁₀" BN, 40-90 BN, 45-70x2¹⁄₁₀" ST, 50-70 ST.
Price: **$995.00**

Features: Double set triggers on rifle. Color case-hardened receiver and buttplate, blued barrel. Imported from Italy by E.M.F.
Price: Rifle or carbine **$950.00**
Price: Military rifle, carbine **$860.00**
Price: Sporting rifle **$860.00**

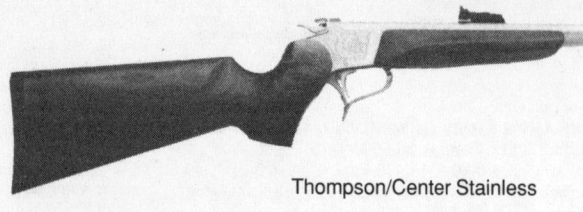

Thompson/Center Stainless

Thompson/Center Stainless Contender Carbine

Same as the blued Contender Carbine except made of stainless steel with blued sights. Available with walnut or Rynite stock and forend. Chambered for 22 LR, 22 Hornet, 223 Rem., 7-30 Waters, 30-30 Win., 410-bore. Youth model has walnut buttstock with 12" pull length. Introduced 1993.

Price: Walnut stock, forend **$490.00**
Price: Rynite stock, forend **$455.00**
Price: Youth model **$455.00**

Thompson/Center Contender Carbine Survival System

Combines the Rynite-stocked Contender Carbine with two 16¼" barrels—one chambered for 223 Rem., the other for 45 Colt/410 bore. The frame/buttstock assembly store in the camouflage Cordura case, measuring 25½"x6¾". Introduced 1991.

Price: **$635.00**

THOMPSON/CENTER CONTENDER CARBINE

Caliber: 22 LR, 22 Hornet, 223 Rem., 7mm T.C.U., 7x30 Waters, 30-30 Win., 357 Rem. Maximum, 35 Rem., 44 Mag., 410, single shot.
Barrel: 21".
Weight: 5 lbs., 2 oz. **Length:** 35" overall.
Stock: Checkered American walnut with rubber buttpad. Also with Rynite stock and forend.
Sights: Blade front, open adjustable rear.
Features: Uses the T/C Contender action. Eleven interchangeable barrels available, all with sights, drilled and tapped for scope mounting. Introduced 1985. Offered as a complete Carbine only.
Price: Rifle calibers **$460.00**
Price: Extra barrels, rifle calibers, each **$210.00**
Price: 410 shotgun **$480.00**
Price: Extra 410 barrel **$235.00**
Price: Rynite stock, forend **$425.00**
Price: As above, 21" vent. rib smoothbore 410 bbl. **$450.00**

Thompson/Center Contender Carbine Youth Model

Same as the standard Contender Carbine except has 16¼" barrel, shorter buttstock with 12" length of pull. Comes with fully adjustable open sights. Overall length is 29", weight about 4 lbs., 9 oz. Available in 22 LR, 22 WMR, 223 Rem., 7x30 Waters, 30-30, 35 Rem., 44 Mag. Also available with 16¼", rifled vent. rib barrel chambered for 45/410.

Price: **$425.00**
Price: With 45/410 barrel **$455.00**
Price: Extra barrels **$205.00**
Price: Extra 45/410 barrel **$235.00**
Price: Extra 45-70 barrel **$210.00**

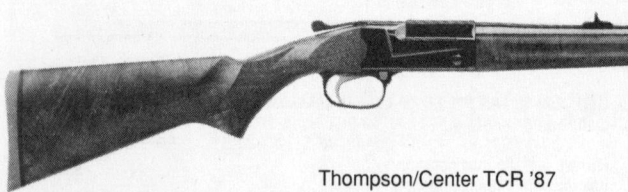

Thompson/Center TCR '87

UBERTI ROLLING BLOCK BABY CARBINE

Caliber: 22 LR, 22 WMR, 22 Hornet, 357 Mag., single shot.
Barrel: 22".
Weight: 4.8 lbs. **Length:** 35½" overall.
Stock: Walnut stock and forend.
Sights: Blade front, fully adjustable open rear.
Features: Resembles Remington New Model No. 4 carbine. Brass trigger guard and buttplate; color case-hardened frame, blued barrel. Imported by Uberti USA.
Price: **$460.00**

THOMPSON/CENTER TCR '87 SINGLE SHOT RIFLE

Caliber: 22 Hornet, 222 Rem., 223 Rem., 22-250, 243 Win., 270, 308, 7mm-08, 30-06, 32-40 Win., 12-ga. slug. Also 10-ga. and 12-ga. field barrels.
Barrel: 23" (standard), 25⅞" (heavy).
Weight: About 6¾ lbs. **Length:** 39½" overall.
Stock: American black walnut, checkered p.g. and forend.
Sights: None furnished.
Features: Break-open design with interchangeable barrels. Single-stage trigger. Cross-bolt safety. Introduced 1983. Made in U.S. by T/C. Available only through the T/C custom shop.
Price: With Medium Sporter barrel (223, 22-250, 7mm-08, 308, 32-40 Win.), about **$595.00**
Price: With Light Sporter barrel (22 Hornet, 222, 223, 22-250, 243, 270, 7mm-08, 308, 30-06), about **$595.00**
Price: 12-ga. slug barrel, about **$275.00**
Price: Extra Medium or Light Sporter barrel, about **$250.00**
Price: 10-, 12-ga. field barrels **$250.00**

DRILLINGS, COMBINATION GUNS, DOUBLE RIFLES

Designs for sporting and utility purposes worldwide.

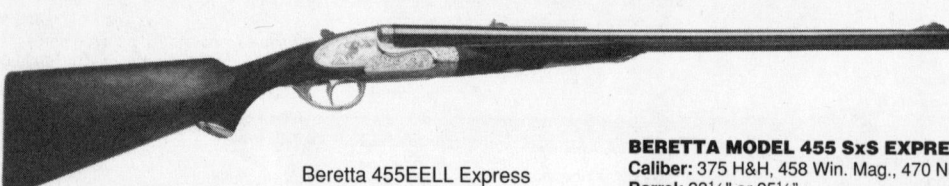

Beretta 455EELL Express

BERETTA EXPRESS SSO O/U DOUBLE RIFLES

Caliber: 375 H&H, 458 Win. Mag., 9.3x74R.
Barrel: 25.5".
Weight: 11 lbs.
Stock: European walnut with hand-checkered grip and forend.
Sights: Blade front on ramp, open V-notch rear.
Features: Sidelock action with color case-hardened receiver (gold inlays on SSO6 Gold). Ejectors, double triggers, recoil pad. Introduced 1990. Imported from Italy by Beretta U.S.A.
Price: SSO6 . . . . **$21,600.00**
Price: SSO6 Gold **$23,000.00**

BERETTA MODEL 455 SxS EXPRESS RIFLE

Caliber: 375 H&H, 458 Win. Mag., 470 NE, 500 NE 3", 416 Rigby.
Barrel: 23½" or 25½".
Weight: 11 lbs.
Stock: European walnut with hand-checkered grip and forend.
Sights: Blade front, folding leaf V-notch rear.
Features: Sidelock action with easily removable sideplates; color case-hardened finish (455), custom big game or floral motif engraving (455EELL). Double triggers, recoil pad. Introduced 1990. Imported from Italy by Beretta U.S.A.
Price: Model 455 . . . . **$36,000.00**
Price: Model 455EELL **$47,000.00**

CHAPUIS RGEXPRESS DOUBLE RIFLE
Caliber: 30-06, 7x65R, 8x57 JRS, 9.3x74R.
Barrel: 23.6".
Weight: 8-9 lbs. **Length:** NA.
Stock: Deluxe walnut with Monte Carlo comb, oil finish.
Sights: Bead on ramp front, adjustable express rear on quarter-rib.
Features: Boxlock action with long trigger guard, automatic ejectors, double hook Blitz system action with coil springs; coin metal finish; trap grip cap for extra front sight. Imported from France by Armes de Chasse.
Price: About . . . . **$7,000.00 to $8,500.00**

AUGUSTE FRANCOTTE BOXLOCK DOUBLE RIFLE
Caliber: 243, 270, 30-06, 7x64, 7x65R, 8x57JRS, 9.3x74R, 375 H&H, 470 N.E.; other calibers on request.
Barrel: 23.5" to 26".
Weight: NA. **Length:** NA.
Stock: Deluxe European walnut to customer specs; pistol grip or straight grip with Francotte cheekpiece; checkered butt; oil finish.
Sights: Bead front on long ramp, quarter-rib with fixed V rear.
Features: Side-by-side barrels; Anson & Deeley boxlock action with double triggers (front hinged), manual safety, floating firing pins and gas vent safety screws. Splinter or beavertail forend. English scroll engraving; coin finish or color case-hardening. Many options available. Imported from Belgium by Armes de Chasse.
Price: From about . . . . **$20,000.00 to $25,000.00**

Heym Model 55FW O/U Combo Gun
Similar to Model 55B O/U rifle except chambered for 12-, 16-, or 20-ga. (2¾" or 3") over 7x65R, 308, 30-06, 8x57JRS, 8x75 RS, 9.3x74R, 375 H&H, 458 Win. Mag., 470 N.E. Has solid rib barrel. Available with interchangeable shotgun and rifle barrels.
Price: Model 55FW boxlock **$3,900.00**
Price: Model 55BW (over/under rifle) **$5,715.00**

AUGUSTE FRANCOTTE SIDELOCK DOUBLE RIFLES
Caliber: 243, 7x64, 7x65R, 8x57JRS, 270, 30-06, 9.3x74R, 375 H&H, 470 N.E.; others on request.
Barrel: 23½" to 26".
Weight: 7.61 lbs. (medium calibers), 11.1 lbs. (mag. calibers).
Stock: Fancy European walnut; dimensions to customer specs. Straight or pistol grip style. Checkered butt, oil finish.
Sights: Bead on ramp front, leaf rear on quarter-rib; to customer specs.
Features: Custom made to customer's specs. Special extractor for rimless cartridges; back-action sidelocks; double trigger with hinged front trigger. Automatic or free safety. Wide range of options available. Imported from Belgium by Armes de Chasse.
Price: . . . . **$30,000.00** to **$36,000**

HEYM MODEL 55B O/U DOUBLE RIFLE
Caliber: 7x65R, 308, 30-06, 8x57JRS, 8x75 RS, 9.3x74R, 375 H&H, 458 Win. Mag., 470 N.E.
Barrel: 25".
Weight: About 8 lbs., depending upon caliber. **Length:** 42" overall.
Stock: Dark European walnut, hand-checkered p.g. and forend. Oil finish.
Sights: Silver bead front ramp, open V-type rear.
Features: Boxlock or full sidelock, Kersten double cross bolt, cocking indicators; hand-engraved hunting scenes. Options available include interchangeable barrels, Zeiss scopes in claw mounts, deluxe engravings and stock carving, etc. Imported from Germany by JagerSport, Ltd.
Price: Model 55B boxlock **$10,800.00**

HEYM MODEL 88B SIDE-BY-SIDE DOUBLE RIFLE
Caliber: 30-06, 8x57JRS, 9.3x74R, 375 H&H.
Barrel: 25".
Weight: 7½ lbs. (std. cals.), 8½ lbs. (mag.). **Length:** 42" overall.
Stock: Fancy French walnut, classic North American design.
Sights: Silver bead post on ramp front, fixed or three-leaf express rear.
Features: Action has complete coverage hunting scene engraving. Available as boxlock or with q.d. sidelocks. Imported from Germany by JagerSport, Ltd.
Price: Boxlock . . . . **$12,500.00 to $18,950.00**
Price: Sidelock, Model 88B-SS, from **$16,600.00**

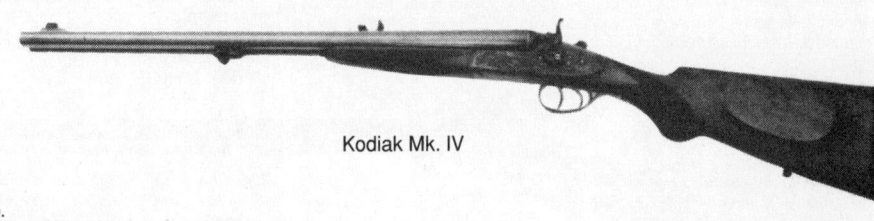

Kodiak Mk. IV

KODIAK MK. IV DOUBLE RIFLE
Caliber: 45-70.
Barrel: 24".
Weight: 10 lbs. **Length:** 42½" overall.
Stock: European walnut with semi-pistol grip.
Sights: Ramp front with bead, adjustable two-leaf rear.
Features: Exposed hammers, color case-hardened locks. Rubber recoil pad. Introduced 1988. Imported from Italy by Trail Guns Armory.
Price: About **$1,895.00**

KRIEGHOFF TECK O/U COMBINATION GUN
Caliber/Gauge: 12, 16, 20/22 Hornet, 222, 243, 270, 30-06, 308 and standard European calibers. O/U rifle also available in 458 Win. on special order.
Barrel: 25" on double rifle combo, 28" on O/U shotgun. Optional free-floating rifle barrel available.
Weight: 7-7½ lbs.
Stock: Hand-checkered European walnut with German-style grip and cheekpiece.
Sights: White bead front on shotgun, open or folding on rifle or combo.
Features: Boxlock action with non-selective single trigger or optional single/double trigger. Greener cross bolt. Ejectors standard on all but O/U rifle. Top tang safety. Light scroll engraving. Imported from Germany by Krieghoff International, Inc.
Price: From about . . . . **$7,995.00 to $9,500.00**
Price: Ulm (full sidelock model), from . . . . **$14,950.00 to 18,606.00**

MERKEL OVER/UNDER COMBINATION GUNS
Caliber/Gauge: 12, 16, 20 (2¾" chamber) over 22 Hornet, 5.6x50R, 5.6x52R, 222 Rem., 243 Win., 6.5x55, 6.5x57R, 7x57R, 7x65R, 308 Win., 30-06, 8x57JRS, 9.3x74R, 375 H&H.
Barrel: 25.6".
Weight: About 7.6 lbs. **Length:** NA.
Stock: Oil-finished walnut; pistol grip, cheekpiece.
Sights: Bead front, fixed rear.

KRIEGHOFF TRUMPF DRILLING
Caliber/Gauge: 12, 16, 20/22 Hornet, 222 Rem., 243, 270, 30-06, 308. Standard European calibers also available.
Barrel: 25". Shot barrels choked Imp. Mod. & Full. Optional free-floating rifle barrel available.
Weight: About 7½ lbs.
Stock: Hand-checkered European walnut with German-style grip and cheekpiece. Oil finish.
Sights: Bead front, automatic pop-up open rear.
Features: Boxlock action with double or optional single trigger, top tang shotgun safety. Fine, light scroll engraving. Imported from Germany by Krieghoff International, Inc.
Price: From about **$8,875.00**
Price: Neptun (full sidelock drilling), from about **$19,750.00**

Features: Kersten double cross-bolt lock; scroll-engraved, color case-hardened receiver; Blitz action; double triggers. Imported from Germany by GSI.
Price: Model 210E **$6,195.00**
Price: Model 211E (silver-grayed receivcer, fine hunting scene engraving) **$7,895.00**
Price: Model 213E (sidelock action, English-style, large scroll Arabesque engraving) **$14,695.00**
Price: Model 313E (as above, medium-scroll engraving) **$23,395.00**

DRILLINGS, COMBINATION GUNS, DOUBLE RIFLES

MERKEL DRILLINGS
Caliber/Gauge: 12, 20, 3" chambers, 16, 2¾" chambers; 22 Hornet, 5.6x50R Mag., 5.6x52R, 222 Rem., 243 Win., 6.5x55, 6.5x57R, 7x57R, 7x65R, 308, 30-06, 8x57JRS, 9.3x74R, 375 H&H.
Barrel: 25.6".
Weight: 7.9 to 8.4 lbs. depending upon caliber. **Length:** NA.
Stock: Oil-finished walnut with pistol grip; cheekpiece on 12-, 16-gauge.
Sights: Blade front, fixed rear.
Features: Double barrel locking lug with Greener cross-bolt; scroll-engraved, case-hardened receiver; automatic trigger safety; Blitz action; double triggers. Imported from Germany by GSI.
Price: Model 90 . . . . $6,895.00
Price: Model 90S (as above except has selective sear safety) . . $7,195.00
Price: Model 90K (manually cocked rifle system) $7,595.00
Price: Model 95 (silver-grayed receiver with fine hunting scene engraving) $7,895.00
Price: Model 95S (selective sear safety) $8,195.00
Price: Model 95K (manually cocked rifle system) $8,595.00

MERKEL OVER/UNDER DOUBLE RIFLES
Caliber: 22 Hornet, 5.6x50R Mag., 5.6x52R, 222 Rem., 243 Win., 6.5x55, 6.5x57R, 7x57R, 7x65R, 308, 30-06, 8x57JRS, 9.3x74R, 375 H&H.
Barrel: 25.6".
Weight: About 7.7 lbs., depending upon caliber. **Length:** NA.
Stock: Oil-finished walnut with pistol grip, cheekpiece.
Sights: Blade front, fixed rear.

Savage 24F-12T

Savage 24F-12T Turkey Gun
Similar to Model 24F except has camouflage Rynite stock and Full, Imp. Cyl., Mod. choke tubes. Available only in 22 Hornet or 223 over 12-gauge with 3" chamber. Introduced 1989.
Price: $420.00

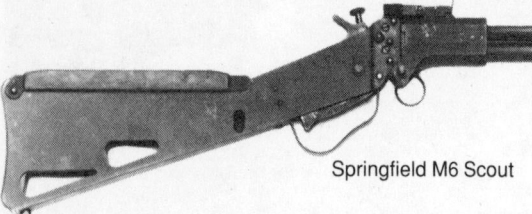

Springfield M6 Scout

TIKKA MODEL 412S COMBINATION GUN
Caliber/Gauge: 12 over 222, 308.
Barrel: 24" (Imp. Mod.).
Weight: 7⅝ lbs.
Stock: American walnut, with recoil pad. Monte Carlo style. Standard measurements 14"x1⅜"x2"x2⅜".
Sights: Blade front, flip-up-type open rear.
Features: Barrel selector on trigger. Hand-checkered stock and forend. Barrels are screw-adjustable to change bullet point of impact. Barrels are interchangeable. Introduced 1980. Imported from Italy by Stoeger.
Price: $1,255.00
Price: Extra barrels, from $720.00

TIKKA MODEL 412S DOUBLE RIFLE
Caliber: 9.3x74R.
Barrel: 24".
Weight: 8⅝ lbs.
Stock: American walnut with Monte Carlo style.
Sights: Ramp front, adjustable open rear.
Features: Barrel selector mounted in trigger. Cocking indicators in tang. Recoil pad. Valmet scope mounts available. Introduced 1980. Imported from Italy by Stoeger.
Price: With ejectors, 9.3x74R $1,470.00

MERKEL MODEL 160 SIDE-BY-SIDE DOUBLE RIFLE
Caliber: 22 Hornet, 5.6x50R Mag., 5.6x52R, 222 Rem., 243 Win., 6.5x55, 6.5x57R, 7x57R, 7x65R, 308, 30-06, 8x57JRS, 9.3x74R, 375 H&H.
Barrel: 25.6".
Weight: About 7.7 lbs., depending upon caliber. **Length:** NA.
Stock: Oil-finished walnut with pistol grip, cheekpiece.
Sights: Blade front on ramp, fixed rear.
Features: Sidelock action. Double barrel locking lug with Greener cross-bolt; fine engraved hunting scenes on sideplates; Holland & Holland ejectors; double triggers. Imported from Germany by GSI.
Price: $10,995.00

Features: Kersten double cross-bolt lock; scroll-engraved, case-hardened receiver; Blitz action with double triggers. Imported from Germany by GSI.
Price: Model 220E $10,795.00
Price: Model 221 E (silver-grayed receiver finish, hunting scene engraving) $12,295.00
Price: Model 223E (sidelock action, English-style large-scroll Arabesque engraving) $18,395.00
Price: Model 323E (as above with medium-scroll engraving) . . $27,595.00

SAVAGE 24F O/U COMBINATION GUN
Caliber/Gauge: 22 Hornet, 223, 30-30 over 12 (24F-12) or 22 LR, 22 Hornet, 223, 30-30 over 20-ga. (24F-20); 3" chambers.
Action: Takedown, low rebounding visible hammer. Single trigger, barrel selector spur on hammer.
Barrel: 24" separated barrels; 12-ga. has Full, Mod., Imp. Cyl. choke tubes, 20-ga. has fixed Mod. choke.
Weight: 7 lbs. **Length:** 40½" overall.
Stock: Black Rynite composition.
Sights: Ramp front, rear open adjustable for elevation. Grooved for tip-off scope mount.
Features: Removable butt cap for storage and accessories. Introduced 1989.
Price: 24F-12 . . . . $400.00
Price: 24F-20 . . . . $400.00

SPRINGFIELD INC. M6 SCOUT RIFLE/SHOTGUN
Caliber: 22 LR or 22 Hornet over 410-bore.
Barrel: 18.25".
Weight: 4.5 lbs. **Length:** 32" overall.
Stock: Steel, folding, with storage for 15 22 LR, four 410 shells.
Sights: Blade front, military aperture for 22; V-notch for 410.
Features: All-metal construction. Designed for quick disassembly and minimum maintenance. Folds for compact storage. Introduced 1982; reintroduced 1991. Made in U.S. by Springfield Inc.
Price: 22 LR/410 . . . . $199.00
Price: 22 Hornet/410 . . . . $219.00

> Consult our Directory pages for the location of firms mentioned.

A. ZOLI RIFLE-SHOTGUN O/U COMBO
Caliber/Gauge: 12-ga. over 222, 308 or 30-06.
Barrel: Combo—24"; shotgun—28" (Mod. & Full).
Weight: About 8 lbs. **Length:** 41" overall (24" bbl.).
Stock: European walnut.
Sights: Blade front, flip-up rear.
Features: Available with German claw scope mounts on rifle/shotgun barrels. Comes with set of 12/12 (Mod. & Full) barrels. Imported from Italy by Mandall Shooting Supplies.
Price: With two barrel sets $1,695.00
Price: As above with claw mounts, scope $2,495.00

Designs for hunting, utility and sporting purposes, including training for competition.

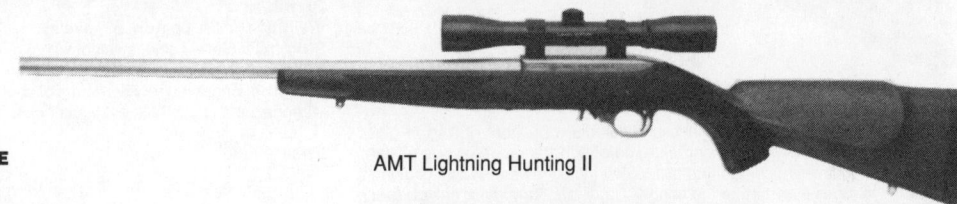

AMT Lightning Hunting II

AMT LIGHTNING 25/22 RIFLE
Caliber: 22 LR, 30-shot magazine.
Barrel: 18", tapered.
Weight: 6 lbs. **Length:** 26½" (folded), 37" (open).
Stock: Folding stainless steel.
Sights: Ramp front, fixed rear.
Features: Made of stainless steel with matte finish. Receiver dovetailed for scope mounting. Extended magazine release. Adjustable rear sight optionally available. Youth stock available. Introduced 1984. From AMT.
Price: **$295.99**

AMT MAGNUM HUNTER AUTO RIFLE
Caliber: 22 WMR, 10-shot rotary magazine.
Barrel: 22".
Weight: 6 lbs. **Length:** 40½" overall.
Stock: Black fiberglass-filled nylon; checkered grip and forend.

AMT Lightning Small-Game Hunting Rifle II
Same as the Lightning 25/22 except has conventional stock of black fiberglass-filled nylon, checkered at the grip and forend, and fitted with Uncle Mike's swivel studs. Removable recoil pad provides storage for ammo, cleaning rod and survival knife. No sights—receiver grooved for scope mounting. Has a 22" full-floating target weight barrel, weighs 6¾ lbs., overall length of 40½", 10-shot rotary magazine. Introduced 1992. From AMT.
Price: **$299.99**

Sights: None furnished; grooved for scope mounting.
Features: Stainless steel construction. Free-floating target-weight barrel. Removable recoil pad for storage of ammo, knife, etc. Introduced 1993. Made in U.S. by AMT.
Price: **$449.99**

Anschutz 525

ANSCHUTZ 525 DELUXE AUTO
Caliber: 22 LR, 10-shot clip.
Barrel: 24".

Weight: 6½ lbs. **Length:** 43" overall.
Stock: European hardwood; checkered pistol grip, Monte Carlo comb, beavertail forend.
Sights: Hooded ramp front, folding leaf rear.
Features: Rotary safety, empty shell deflector, single stage trigger. Receiver grooved for scope mounting. Introduced 1982. Imported from Germany by PSI.
Price: **$528.00**

ARMSCOR MODEL 1600 AUTO RIFLE
Caliber: 22 LR, 15-shot magazine.
Barrel: 19.5".
Weight: 6 lbs. **Length:** 38" overall.
Stock: Mahogany.
Sights: Post front, aperture rear.
Features: Resembles Colt AR-15. Matte black finish. Introduced 1987. Imported from the Philippines by Ruko Products.
Price: About **$189.00**
Price: M1600R (as above except has retractable buttstock, ventilated forend), about **$189.00**

ARMSCOR MODEL AK22 AUTO RIFLE
Caliber: 22 LR, 15- and 30-shot magazine.
Barrel: 18.5".
Weight: 7 lbs. **Length:** 36" overall.
Stock: Plain mahogany.
Sights: Post front, open rear adjustable for windage and elevation.
Features: Resembles the AK-47. Matte black finish. Introduced 1987. Imported from the Philippines by Ruko Products.
Price: About **$259.00**
Price: With folding steel stock, about **$289.00**

Armscor Model 2000SC

AUTO-ORDNANCE 1927A-3
Caliber: 22 LR, 10-, 30- or 50-shot magazine.
Barrel: 16", finned.
Weight: About 7 lbs.
Stock: Walnut stock and forend.
Sights: Blade front, open rear adjustable for windage and elevation.
Features: Recreation of the Thompson Model 1927, only in 22 Long Rifle. Alloy receiver, finned barrel.
Price: **$487.50**

ARMSCOR MODEL 20P AUTO RIFLE
Caliber: 22 LR, 15-shot magazine.
Barrel: 21".
Weight: 6.5 lbs. **Length:** 39.75" overall.
Stock: Walnut-finished mahogany.
Sights: Hooded front, rear adjustable for elevation.
Features: Receiver grooved for scope mounting. Blued finish. Introduced 1990. Imported from the Philippines by Ruko Products.
Price: About **$119.00**
Price: With checkered stock **$149.00**
Price: Model 20C (carbine-style stock, steel barrel band, buttplate) . **$139.00**
Price: Model 2000SC (as above except has checkered stock, fully adjustable sight, rubber buttpad, forend tip), about . . . . **NA**
Price: Model 50S (similar to Model 20P except has ventilated barrel shroud, and 30-shot magazine) **$199.00**

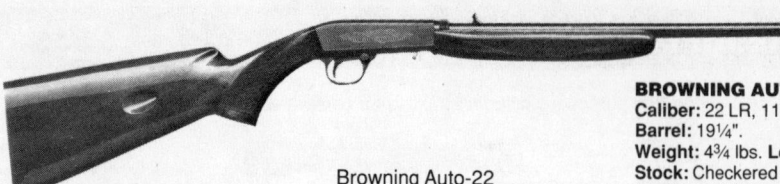

Browning Auto-22

Browning Auto-22 Grade VI

Same as the Grade I Auto-22 except available with either grayed or blued receiver with extensive engraving with gold-plated animals: right side pictures a fox and squirrel in a woodland scene; left side shows a beagle chasing a rabbit. On top is a portrait of the beagle. Stock and forend are of high-grade walnut with a double-bordered cut checkering design. Introduced 1987.

Price: Grade VI, blue or gray receiver **$708.95**

CALICO MODEL M-100 CARBINE

Caliber: 22 LR, 100-shot magazine.
Barrel: 16".
Weight: 5.7 lbs. (loaded). **Length:** 35.8" overall (stock extended).
Stock: Folding steel.
Sights: Post front adjustable for elevation, notch rear adjustable for windage.
Features: Uses alloy frame and helical-feed magazine; ambidextrous safety; removable barrel assembly; pistol grip compartment; flash suppressor; bolt stop. Made in U.S. From Calico.
Price: **$346.90**

E.A.A./SABATTI MODEL 1822 AUTO RIFLE

Caliber: 22 LR, 10-shot magazine.
Barrel: 18½" round tapered; bull barrel on Heavy and Thumbhole Heavy models.
Weight: 5¼ lbs. (Sporter). **Length:** 37" overall.
Stock: Stained hardwood; Thumbhole model has one-piece stock.
Sights: Bead front, folding leaf rear adjustable for elevation on Sporter model. Heavy and Thumbhole models only dovetailed for scope mount.
Features: Cross-bolt safety. Blue finish. Lifetime warranty. Introduced 1993. Imported from Italy by European American Armory.
Price: Sporter **$199.95**
Price: Heavy **$224.95**
Price: Thumbhole Heavy **$359.95**

Feather Model F2

BROWNING AUTO-22 RIFLE

Caliber: 22 LR, 11-shot.
Barrel: 19¼".
Weight: 4¾ lbs. **Length:** 37" overall.
Stock: Checkered select walnut with p.g. and semi-beavertail forend.
Sights: Gold bead front, folding leaf rear.
Features: Engraved receiver with polished blue finish; cross-bolt safety; tubular magazine in buttstock; easy takedown for carrying or storage. Imported from Japan by Browning.
Price: Grade I **$344.95**

Calico M-105

Calico Model M-105 Sporter

Similar to the M-100 except has hand-rubbed wood buttstock and forend. Weight is 4¾ lbs. Introduced 1987.
Price: **$376.90**

ERMA EM1 CARBINE

Caliber: 22 LR, 10-shot magazine.
Barrel: 18".
Weight: 5.6 lbs. **Length:** 35.5" overall.
Stock: Polished beech or oiled walnut.
Sights: Blade front, fully adjustable aperture rear.
Features: Blowback action. Receiver grooved for scope mounting. Imported from Germany by Mandall Shooting Supplies.
Price: **$499.95**

FEATHER AT-22 SEMI-AUTO CARBINE

Caliber: 22 LR, 20-shot magazine.
Barrel: 17".
Weight: 3.25 lbs. **Length:** 35" overall (stock extended).
Stock: Telescoping wire; composition pistol grip.
Sights: Protected post front, adjustable aperture rear.
Features: Removable barrel. Length when folded is 26". Matte black finish. From Feather Industries. Introduced 1986.
Price: **$249.95**
Price: Model F2 (fixed stock) **$279.95**

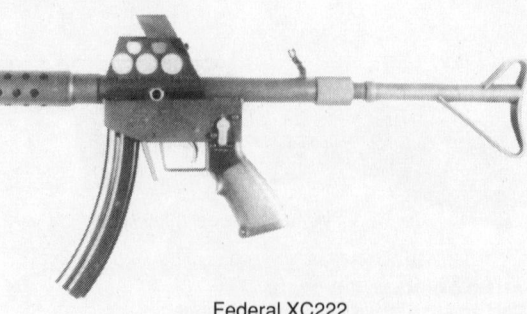

Federal XC222

> Consult our Directory pages for the location of firms mentioned.

FEDERAL ENGINEERING XC222 AUTO CARBINE

Caliber: 22 LR, 30-shot magazine.
Barrel: 16.5" (with flash hider).
Weight: 7.25 lbs. **Length:** 34.5" overall.
Stock: Quick-detachable tube steel.
Sights: Hooded post front, Williams adjustable rear; sight bridge grooved for scope mounting.
Features: Quick takedown; all-steel heli-arc welded construction; internal parts industrial hard chromed. Made in U.S. by Federal Engineering Corp.
Price: Includes receiver cap, sling, swivels **$459.00**

Grendel R-31

GRENDEL R-31 AUTO CARBINE
Caliber: 22 WMR, 30-shot magazine.
Barrel: 16".
Weight: 4 lbs. **Length:** 23.5" overall (stock collapsed).
Stock: Telescoping tube, Zytel forend.
Sights: Post front adustable for windage and elevation, aperture rear.
Features: Blowback action with fluted chamber; ambidextrous safety. Steel receiver. Matte black finish. Muzzle brake. Scope mount optional. Introduced 1991. Made in U.S. by Grendel, Inc.
Price: $385.00

KRICO MODEL 260 AUTO RIFLE
Caliber: 22 LR, 5-shot magazine.
Barrel: 19.6".
Weight: 6.6 lbs. **Length:** 38.9" overall.
Stock: Beech.
Sights: Blade on ramp front, open adjustable rear.
Features: Receiver grooved for scope mounting. Sliding safety. Imported from Germany by Mandall Shooting Supplies.
Price: $700.00

Lakefield Arms Model 64B

LAKEFIELD ARMS MODEL 64B AUTO RIFLE
Caliber: 22 LR, 10-shot magazine.
Barrel: 20".
Weight: 5½ lbs. **Length:** 40" overall.
Stock: Walnut-finished hardwood with Monte Carlo-type comb, checkered grip and forend.
Sights: Bead front, open adjustable rear. Receiver grooved for scope mounting.
Features: Thumb-operated rotating safety. Blue finish. Side ejection, bolt hold-open device. Introduced 1990. Made in Canada by Lakefield Arms Ltd.
Price: About $132.95

Marlin Model 60SS

Marlin Model 60SS Self-Loading Rifle
Same as the Model 60 except breech bolt, barrel and outer magazine tube are made of stainless steel; most other parts are either nickel-plated or coated to match the stainless finish. Monte Carlo stock is of black/gray Main birch laminate, and has nickel-plated swivel studs, rubber butt pad. Introduced 1993.
Price: $221.95

MARLIN MODEL 60 SELF-LOADING RIFLE
Caliber: 22 LR, 14-shot tubular magazine.
Barrel: 22" round tapered.
Weight: About 5½ lbs. **Length:** 40½" overall.
Stock: Walnut-finished Monte Carlo, full pistol grip; Mar-Shield® finish.
Sights: Ramp front, open adjustable rear.
Features: Matted receiver is grooved for scope mount. Manual bolt hold-open; automatic last-shot bolt hold-open.
Price: $148.75

Marlin Model 70HC

Marlin Model 990L Self-Loading Rifle
Similar to the Model 60 except has laminated hardwood stock with black rubber rifle butt pad and swivel studs, gold-plated steel trigger. Ramp front sight with brass bead and Wide-Scan hood, adjustable semi-buckhorn folding rear. Weighs 5.75 lbs. Introduced 1992. From Marlin.
Price: $215.50

MARLIN MODEL 70 HC AUTO
Caliber: 22 LR, 7- and 15-shot clip magazines.
Barrel: 18" (16-groove rifling).
Weight: 5 lbs. **Length:** 36¾" overall.
Stock: Walnut-finished hardwood with Monte Carlo, full p.g. Mar-Shield® finish.
Sights: Ramp front, adjustable open rear. Receiver grooved for scope mount.
Features: Receiver top has serrated, non-glare finish; cross-bolt safety; manual bolt hold-open.
Price: $168.90

Marlin Model 70P Papoose

Marlin Model 70P Papoose
Similar to the Model 70 HC except is a takedown model with easily removable barrel—no tools needed. Has 16¼" Micro-Groove® barrel, walnut-finished hardwood stock, ramp front, adjustable open rear sights, cross-bolt safety. Takedown feature allows removal of barrel without tools. Overall length is 35¼", weight is 3¼ lbs. Receiver grooved for scope mounting. Comes with zippered case. Introduced 1986.
Price: $195.50

Marlin Model 922

MARLIN MODEL 922 MAGNUM SELF-LOADING RIFLE
Caliber: 22 WMR, 7-shot magazine.
Barrel: 20.5".

MARLIN MODEL 995 SELF-LOADING RIFLE
Caliber: 22 LR, 7-shot clip magazine.
Barrel: 18" Micro-Groove®.
Weight: 5 lbs. **Length:** 36¾" overall.
Stock: American black walnut, Monte Carlo-style, with full pistol grip. Checkered p.g. and forend; white buttplate spacer; Mar-Shield® finish.

MITCHELL GALIL/22 AUTO RIFLE
Caliber: 22 LR, 20-shot magazine; 22 WMR, 10-shot magazine.
Barrel: 18".
Weight: 6.5 lbs. **Length:** 36" overall.
Stock: European walnut grip and forend with metal folding stock.
Sights: Post front adjustable for elevation, rear adjustable for windage.
Features: Replica of the Israeli Galil rifle. Introduced 1987. Imported by Mitchell Arms, Inc.
Price: 22 LR, fixed or folding stock $359.00
Price: 22 WMR, fixed or folding stock $359.00

MITCHELL PPS/50 RIFLE
Caliber: 22 LR, 20-shot magazine (50-shot drum optional).
Barrel: 16½".
Weight: 5½ lbs. **Length:** 33½" overall.
Stock: Walnut.
Sights: Blade front, adjustable rear.
Features: Full-length perforated barrel shroud. Matte finish. Introduced 1989. Imported by Mitchell Arms, Inc.
Price: With 20-shot "banana" magazine $359.00
Price: With 50-shot drum magazine $459.00

Weight: 6.5 lbs. **Length:** 39.75" overall.
Stock: American black walnut with Monte Carlo comb, swivel studs, rubber butt pad.
Sights: Ramp front with bead and removable Wide-Scan® hood, adjustable folding semi-buckhorn rear.
Features: Action based on the centerfire Model 9 Carbine. Receiver drilled and tapped for scope mounting. Automatic last-shot bolt holdopen; magazine safety. Introduced 1993.
Price: $362.95

Sights: Ramp bead front with Wide-Scan™ hood; adjustable folding semi-buckhorn rear.
Features: Receiver grooved for scope mount; bolt hold-open device; cross-bolt safety. Introduced 1979.
Price: $198.80

MITCHELL AK-22 SEMI-AUTO RIFLE
Caliber: 22 LR, 20-shot magazine; 22 WMR, 10-shot magazine.
Barrel: 18".
Weight: 6½ lbs. **Length:** 36" overall.
Stock: European walnut.
Sights: Post front, open adjustable rear.
Features: Replica of the AK-47 rifle. Wide magazine to maintain appearance. Imported from Italy by Mitchell Arms, Inc.
Price: 22 LR $359.00
Price: 22 WMR $359.00

MITCHELL MAS/22 AUTO RIFLE
Caliber: 22 LR, 20-shot magazine.
Barrel: 18".
Weight: 7½ lbs. **Length:** 28.5" overall.
Stock: Walnut butt, grip and forend.
Sights: Adjustable post front, flip-type aperture rear.
Features: Bullpup design resembles French armed forces rifle. Top cocking lever, flash hider. Introduced 1987. Imported by Mitchell Arms, Inc.
Price: 22 LR $359.00

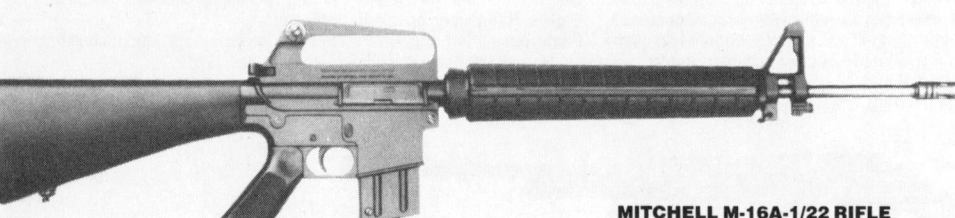

Mitchell M-16A1/22

Mitchell CAR-15/22 Semi-Auto Rifle
Similar to the M-16 A-1/22 rifle except has 16¾" barrel, telescoping butt, giving an overall length of 32" when collapsed. Adjustable post front sight, adjustable aperture rear. Scope mount available. Has 15-shot magazine. Replica of the CAR-15 rifle. Introduced 1990. Imported by Mitchell Arms, Inc.
Price: $359.00

MITCHELL M-16A-1/22 RIFLE
Caliber: 22 LR, 15-shot magazine.
Barrel: 20.5".
Weight: 7 lbs. **Length:** 38.5" overall.
Stock: Black composition.
Sights: Adjustable post front, adjustable aperture rear.
Features: Replica of the AR-15 rifle. Full width magazine. Comes with military-type sling. Introduced 1990. Imported by Mitchell Arms, Inc.
Price: 22 LR $359.00

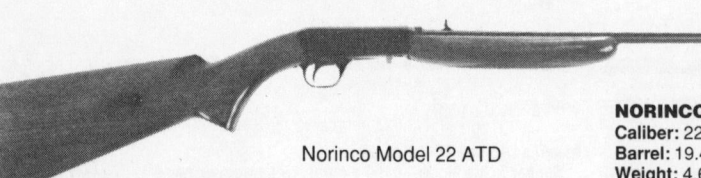

Norinco Model 22 ATD

NORINCO MODEL 22 ATD RIFLE
Caliber: 22 LR, 11-shot magazine.
Barrel: 19.4".
Weight: 4.6 lbs. **Length:** 36.6" overall.
Stock: Checkered hardwood.
Sights: Blade front, open adjustable rear.
Features: Browning-design takedown action for storage, transport. Cross-bolt safety. Tube magazine loads through buttplate. Blue finish with engraved receiver. Introduced 1987. Imported from China by Interarms.
Price: $168.00

RIMFIRE RIFLES—AUTOLOADERS

Remington 522 Viper

REMINGTON MODEL 522 VIPER AUTOLOADING RIFLE
Caliber: 22 LR, 10-shot magazine.
Barrel: 20".
Weight: 4⅝ lbs. **Length:** 40" overall.

Stock: Black synthetic with positive checkering, beavertail forend.
Sights: Bead on ramp front, fully adjustable open rear. Integral grooved rail for scope mounting.
Features: Synthetic stock and receiver with overall matte black finish. Has magazine safety, cocking indicator; manual and last-shot hold-open; trigger mechanism has primary and secondary sears; integral ejection port shield. Introduced 1993.
Price: **$159.00**

Remington 552BDL

REMINGTON 552BDL SPEEDMASTER RIFLE
Caliber: 22 S (20), L (17) or LR (15) tubular mag.
Barrel: 21" round tapered.

Weight: About 5¾ lbs. **Length:** 40" overall.
Stock: Walnut. Checkered grip and forend.
Sights: Bead front, step open rear adjustable for windage and elevation.
Features: Positive cross-bolt safety, receiver grooved for tip-off mount.
Price: About **$256.00**

Ruger K10/22RB

Ruger 10/22 Deluxe Sporter
Same as 10/22 Carbine except walnut stock with hand checkered p.g. and forend; straight buttplate, no barrel band, has sling swivels.
Price: Model 10/22 DSP **$254.50**

SURVIVAL ARMS AR-7 EXPLORER RIFLE
Caliber: 22 LR, 8-shot magazine.
Barrel: 16".
Weight: 2.5 lbs. **Length:** 34.5" overall; 16.5" stowed.
Stock: Moulded Cycolac; snap-on rubber butt cap.
Sights: Square blade front, aperture rear adjustable for elevation.
Features: Takedown design stores barrel and action in hollow stock. Light enough to float. Black, Silvertone or camouflage finish. Reintroduced 1992. From Survival Arms, Inc.
Price: Silver or camo **$150.00**
Price: Sporter (black finish with telescoping stock, 25-shot magazine) **$200.00**
Price: Wildcat (black finish with wood stock) **$150.00**

VOERE MODEL 2115 AUTO RIFLE
Caliber: 22 LR, 10-shot magazine.
Barrel: 18.1".
Weight: 5.75 lbs. **Length:** 37.7" overall.
Stock: Walnut-finished beechwood with cheekpiece; checkered pistol grip and forend.

RUGER 10/22 AUTOLOADING CARBINE
Caliber: 22 LR, 10-shot rotary magazine.
Barrel: 18½" round tapered.
Weight: 5 lbs. **Length:** 37¼" overall.
Stock: American hardwood with p.g. and bbl. band.
Sights: Brass bead front, folding leaf rear adjustable for elevation.
Features: Detachable rotary magazine fits flush into stock, cross-bolt safety, receiver tapped and grooved for scope blocks or tip-off mount. Scope base adaptor furnished with each rifle.
Price: Model 10/22 RB (blue) **$201.50**
Price: Model K10/22RB (bright finish stainless barrel) **$236.00**

TEXAS REMINGTON REVOLVING CARBINE
Caliber: 22 LR.
Barrel: 21".
Weight: 5¾ lbs. **Length:** 36" overall.
Stock: Smooth walnut.
Sights: Blade front, rear adjustable for windage and elevation.
Features: Brass frame, buttplate and trigger guard, blued cylinder and barrel. Introduced 1991. Imported from Italy by E.M.F.
Price: **$420.00**

Sights: Post front with hooded ramp, leaf rear.
Features: Clip-fed autoloader with single stage trigger, wing-type safety. Introduced 1984. Imported from Austria by JagerSport, Ltd.
Price: About **$585.00**

RIMFIRE RIFLES—LEVER & SLIDE ACTION

Classic and modern models for sport and utility, including training.

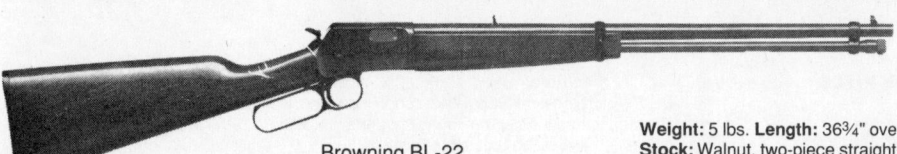

Browning BL-22

BROWNING BL-22 LEVER-ACTION RIFLE
Caliber: 22 S (22), L (17) or LR (15), tubular magazine.
Barrel: 20" round tapered.

Weight: 5 lbs. **Length:** 36¾" overall.
Stock: Walnut, two-piece straight grip Western style.
Sights: Bead post front, folding-leaf rear.
Features: Short throw lever, half-cock safety, receiver grooved for tip-off scope mounts. Imported from Japan by Browning.
Price: Grade I **$301.50**
Price: Grade II (engraved receiver, checkered grip and forend) . . . **$343.50**

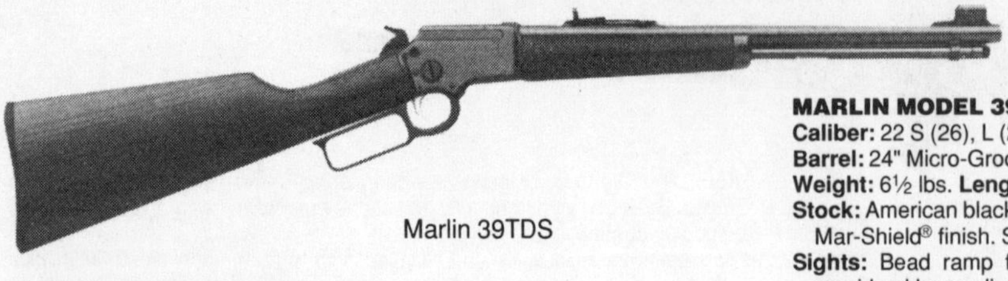

Marlin 39TDS

MARLIN 39TDS CARBINE
Caliber: 22 S (16), 22 L (12), 22 LR (11).
Barrel: 16½" Micro-Groove®.
Weight: 5¼ lbs. **Length:** 32⅝" overall.
Stock: American black walnut with straight grip; short forend with blued tip. Mar-Shield® finish.
Sights: Ramp front with Wide-Scan™ hood, adjustable semi-buckhorn folding rear.
Features: Takedown style, comes with carrying case. Hammer-block safety, rebounding hammer; blued metal, gold-plated steel trigger. Introduced 1988.
Price: With case **$418.85**

NORINCO EM-321 PUMP RIFLE
Caliber: 22 LR, 9-shot magazine.
Barrel: 19.5".
Weight: 6 lbs. **Length:** 37" overall.
Stock: Hardwood.
Sights: Blade front, open folding rear.
Features: Blue finish; grooved slide handle. Imported from China by China Sports, Inc.
Price: . . . . **NA**

Rossi Model 62 SAC

Rossi Model 62 SAC Carbine
Same as standard model except 22 LR only, has 16¼" barrel. Magazine holds slightly fewer cartridges.
Price: Blue **$227.00**
Price: Nickel **$245.00**

Winchester Model 9422

Winchester Model 9422 Magnum Lever-Action Rifle
Same as the 9422 except chambered for 22 WMR cartridge, has 11-round mag. capacity.
Price: Walnut **$393.00**
Price: With WinCam green stock **$393.00**
Price: With WinTuff brown laminated stock **$393.00**

MARLIN MODEL 39AS GOLDEN LEVER-ACTION RIFLE
Caliber: 22 S (26), L (21), LR (19), tubular magazine.
Barrel: 24" Micro-Groove®.
Weight: 6½ lbs. **Length:** 40" overall.
Stock: American black walnut with white line spacers at p.g. cap and buttplate; Mar-Shield® finish. Swivel studs; rubber buttpad.
Sights: Bead ramp front with detachable Wide-Scan™ hood, folding rear semi-buckhorn adjustable for windage and elevation.
Features: Hammer-block safety; rebounding hammer. Takedown action, receiver tapped for scope mount (supplied), offset hammer spur; gold-plated steel trigger.
Price: **$405.45**

REMINGTON 572BDL FIELDMASTER PUMP RIFLE
Caliber: 22 S (20), L (17) or LR (14), tubular magazine.
Barrel: 21" round tapered.
Weight: 5½ lbs. **Length:** 42" overall.
Stock: Walnut with checkered p.g. and slide handle.
Sights: Blade ramp front; sliding ramp rear adjustable for windage and elevation.
Features: Cross-bolt safety; removing inner magazine tube converts rifle to single shot; receiver grooved for tip-off scope mount.
Price: About **$269.00**

ROSSI MODEL 62 SA PUMP RIFLE
Caliber: 22 LR, 22 WMR.
Barrel: 23", round or octagonal.
Weight: 5¾ lbs. **Length:** 39¼" overall.
Stock: Walnut, straight grip, grooved forend.
Sights: Fixed front, adjustable rear.
Features: Capacity 20 Short, 16 Long or 14 Long Rifle. Quick takedown. Imported from Brazil by Interarms.
Price: Blue **$227.00**
Price: Nickel **$245.00**
Price: Blue, with octagonal barrel **$253.00**
Price: 22 WMR, as Model 59 . . . . **$280.00**

WINCHESTER MODEL 9422 LEVER-ACTION RIFLE
Caliber: 22 S (21), L (17), LR (15), tubular magazine.
Barrel: 20½".
Weight: 6¼ lbs. **Length:** 37⅛" overall.
Stock: American walnut, two-piece, straight grip (no p.g.).
Sights: Hooded ramp front, adjustable semi-buckhorn rear.
Features: Side ejection, receiver grooved for scope mounting, takedown action. From U.S. Repeating Arms Co.
Price: Walnut **$376.00**
Price: With WinTuff laminated stock **$376.00**

RIMFIRE RIFLES—BOLT ACTIONS & SINGLE SHOTS

Includes models for a variety of sports, utility and competitive shooting.

ANSCHUTZ ACHIEVER BOLT-ACTION RIFLE
Caliber: 22 LR, single shot adaptor.
Barrel: 19½".
Weight: 5 lbs. **Length:** 35½" to 36⅔" overall.
Stock: Walnut-finished hardwood with adjustable buttplate, vented forend, stippled pistol grip. Length of pull adjustable from 11⅞" to 13".
Sights: Hooded front, open rear adjustable for windage and elevation.
Features: Uses Mark 2000-type action with adjustable two-stage trigger. Receiver grooved for scope mounting. Designed for training in junior rifle clubs and for starting young shooters. Introduced 1987. Imported from Germany by Precision Sales International.
Price: **$395.00**
Price: Sight Set #1 . . . . **$67.00**

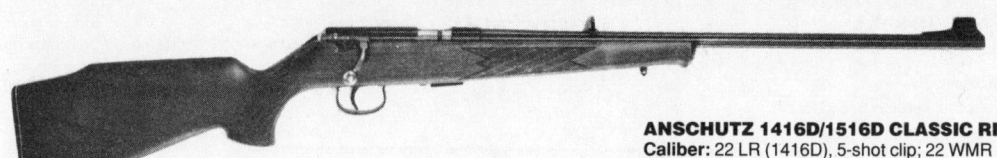

Anschutz 1416D/1516D

Anschutz 1418D/1518D Mannlicher Rifles
Similar to the 1416D/1516D rifles except has full-length Mannlicher-style stock, shorter 19¾" barrel. Weighs 5½ lbs. Stock has mahogany schnabel tip. Model 1418D chambered for 22 LR, 1518D for 22 WMR. Imported from Germany by Precision Sales International.
Price: 1418D **$1,053.00**
Price: 1518D **$1,073.00**

ANSCHUTZ 1700D CLASSIC RIFLES
Caliber: 22 LR, 5-shot clip.
Barrel: 23½", ¹³⁄₁₆ dia. heavy.
Weight: 7¾ lbs. Length: 42½" overall.
Stock: Select European walnut with checkered pistol grip and forend.
Sights: Hooded ramp front, folding leaf rear; drilled and tapped for scope mounting.
Features: Adjustable single stage trigger. Receiver drilled and tapped for scope mounting. Introduced 1988. Imported from Germany by Precision Sales International.
Price: 22 LR **$1,228.00**
Price: As above, Meistergrade (select walnut, gold engraved trigger guard), add **$199.00**

Anschutz 1700D Graphite Custom Rifle
Similar to the Model 1700D Custom except has McMillan graphite reinforced stock with roll-over cheekpiece. Has 22" barrel. No sights furnished, but drilled and tapped for scope mounting. Comes with embroidered sling, Michael's quick-detachable swivels. Introduced 1991.
Price: **$1,183.00**

> Consult our Directory pages for the location of firms mentioned.

ANSCHUTZ 1416D/1516D CLASSIC RIFLES
Caliber: 22 LR (1416D), 5-shot clip; 22 WMR (1516D), 4-shot clip.
Barrel: 22½".
Weight: 6 lbs. Length: 41" overall.
Stock: European walnut; Monte Carlo with cheekpiece, schnabel forend, checkered pistol grip and forend.
Sights: Hooded ramp front, folding leaf rear.
Features: Uses Model 1403 target rifle action. Adjustable single stage trigger. Receiver grooved for scope mounting. Imported from Germany by Precision Sales International.
Price: 1416D, 22 LR **$690.00**
Price: 1516D, 22 WMR **$716.00**
Price: 1416D Classic left-hand **$711.00**

Anschutz 1700D Custom Rifles
Similar to the Classic models except have roll-over Monte Carlo cheekpiece, slim forend with schnabel tip, Wundhammer palm swell on pistol grip, rosewood grip cap with white diamond insert. Skip-line checkering on grip and forend. Introduced 1988. Imported from Germany by Precision Sales International.
Price: 22 LR **$1,258.00**
Price: Custom 1700 Meistergrade (select walnut, gold engraved trigger guard), add **$199.00**

Anschutz 1700 FWT Bolt-Action Rifle
Similar to the Anschutz Custom except has McMillan fiberglass stock with Monte Carlo, roll-over cheekpiece, Wundhammer swell, and checkering. Comes without sights but the receiver is drilled and tapped for scope mounting. Has 22" barrel, single stage #5095 trigger. Weighs 6.25 lbs. Introduced 1989.
Price: With fiberglass stock **$1,118.00**
Price: As above, with Fibergrain stock **$1,327.00**

ANSCHUTZ 1700D BAVARIAN BOLT-ACTION RIFLE
Caliber: 22 LR, 5-shot clip.
Barrel: 24".
Weight: 7¼ lbs. Length: 43" overall.
Stock: European walnut with Bavarian cheek rest. Checkered p.g. and forend.
Sights: Hooded ramp front, folding leaf rear.
Features: Uses the Improved 1700 Match 54 action with adjustable 5096 trigger. Drilled and tapped for scope mounting. Introduced in 1988. Imported from Germany by Precision Sales International.
Price: 22 LR **$1,258.00**
Price: Custom 1700D Meistergrade (select walnut, gold engraved trigger guard), add **$199.00**

Armscor Model 14D

Armscor Model 1500 Rifle
Similar to the Model 14P except chambered for 22 WMR. Has 21.5" barrel, double lug bolt, checkered stock, weighs 6.5 lbs. Introduced 1987.
Price: About **$189.00**

ARMSCOR MODEL 14P BOLT-ACTION RIFLE
Caliber: 22 LR, 10-shot magazine.
Barrel: 23".
Weight: 7 lbs. Length: 41.5" overall.
Stock: Walnut-finished mahogany.
Sights: Bead front, rear adjustable for elevation.
Features: Receiver grooved for scope mounting. Blued finish. Introduced 1987. Imported from the Philippines by Ruko Products.
Price: About **$119.00**
Price: Model 14D Deluxe (checkered stock) **$139.00**

BRNO ZKM 452 Deluxe

BRNO ZKM 452 Deluxe
Same as the Standard except checked walnut stock with oil finish, sling swivels. Introduced 1992. Imported from the Czeck Republic by Action Arms, Ltd.
Price: **$349.00**
Price: With synthetic stock **$305.00**

BRNO ZKM-452 DELUXE BOLT-ACTION RIFLE
Caliber: 22 LR, detachable 5-shot magazine.
Barrel: 23.6".
Weight: 6.9 lbs. Length: 43.5" overall.
Stock: Checkered walnut.
Sights: Hooded bead front, open rear adjustable for windage and elevation.
Features: Dual claw extractors, safety locks firing pin. Blue finish; grooved receiver; oiled stock; sling swivels. Introduced 1992. Imported from the Czech Republic by Action Arms Ltd.
Price: **$349.00**
Price: With synthetic stock **$305.00**

BEEMAN/HW 60J-ST BOLT-ACTION RIFLE
Caliber: 22 LR.
Barrel: 22.8".
Weight: 6.5 lbs. **Length:** 41.7" overall.
Stock: Walnut with cheekpiece, cut checkered p.g. and forend.

Sights: Hooded blade on ramp front, open rear.
Features: Polished blue finish; oil-finished walnut. Imported from Germany by Beeman. Introduced 1988.
Price: $645.00

Browning A-Bolt 22

Browning A-Bolt Gold Medallion
Similar to the standard A-Bolt except stock is of high-grade walnut with brass spacers between stock and rubber recoil pad and between the rosewood grip cap and forend. Medallion-style engraving covers the receiver flats, and the words "Gold Medallion" are engraved and gold filled on the right side of the barrel. High gloss stock finish. Introduced 1988.
Price: No sights $496.95

CABANAS PHASER RIFLE
Caliber: 177.
Barrel: 19".
Weight: 6 lbs., 12 oz. **Length:** 42" overall.
Stock: Target-type thumbhole.
Sights: Blade front, open fully adjustable rear.
Features: Fires round ball or pellets with 22 blank cartridge. Imported from Mexico by Mandall Shooting Supplies.
Price: $159.95

Cabanas Espronceda IV Bolt-Action Rifle
Similar to the Leyre model except has full sporter stock, 18¾" barrel, 40" overall length, weighs 5½ lbs.
Price: $134.95

BROWNING A-BOLT 22 BOLT-ACTION RIFLE
Caliber: 22 LR, 22 WMR, 5-shot magazines standard.
Barrel: 22".
Weight: 5 lbs., 9 oz. **Length:** 40¼" overall.
Stock: Walnut with cut checkering, rosewood grip cap and forend tip.
Sights: Offered with or without open sights. Open sight model has ramp front and adjustable folding leaf rear.
Features: Short 60-degree bolt throw. Top tang safety. Grooved for 22 scope mount. Drilled and tapped for full-size scope mounts. Detachable magazines. Gold-colored trigger preset at about 4 lbs. Imported from Japan by Browning. Introduced 1986.
Price: A-Bolt 22, no sights $374.95
Price: A-Bolt 22, with open sights $384.95
Price: A-Bolt 22 WMR, no sights $429.95
Price: As above, with sights $439.95

CABANAS MASTER BOLT-ACTION RIFLE
Caliber: 177, round ball or pellet; single shot.
Barrel: 19½".
Weight: 8 lbs. **Length:** 45½" overall.
Stocks: Walnut target-type with Monte Carlo.
Sights: Blade front, fully adjustable rear.
Features: Fires round ball or pellet with 22-cal. blank cartridge. Bolt action. Imported from Mexico by Mandall Shooting Supplies. Introduced 1984.
Price: $159.95
Price: Varmint model (has 21½" barrel, 4½ lbs., 41" o.a.l., varmint-type stock) $119.95

Cabanas Leyre Bolt-Action Rifle
Similar to Master model except 44" overall, has sport/target stock.
Price: $149.95
Price: Model R83 (17" barrel, hardwood stock, 40" o.a.l.) $79.95
Price: Mini 82 Youth (16½" barrel, 33" o.a.l., 3½ lbs.) $69.95
Price: Pony Youth (16" barrel, 34" o.a.l., 3.2 lbs.) $69.95

Chipmunk Rifle

COOPER ARMS MODEL 36S SPORTER RIFLE
Caliber: 22 LR, 5-shot magazine.
Barrel: 23¾" Shilen match.
Weight: 8 lbs. **Length:** 42½" overall.
Stock: AA Claro walnut with 22 lpi checkering, oil finish; Custom has AAA Claro or AA French walnut.
Sights: None furnished.
Features: Action has three mid-bolt locking lugs, 45-degree bolt rotation; fully adjustable single stage match trigger; swivel studs. Pachmayr butt pad. Introduced 1991. Made in U.S. by Cooper Arms.
Price: Standard $995.00
Price: Custom $1,195.00

CHIPMUNK SINGLE SHOT RIFLE
Caliber: 22, S, L, LR, single shot.
Barrel: 16⅛".
Weight: About 2½ lbs. **Length:** 30" overall.
Stocks: American walnut, or camouflage.
Sights: Post on ramp front, peep rear adjustable for windage and elevation.
Features: Drilled and tapped for scope mounting using special Chipmunk base ($9.95). Made in U.S. Introduced 1982. From Oregon Arms.
Price: Standard $149.95
Price: Deluxe (better wood, checkering) $199.95

Dakota 22 Sporter

DAKOTA 22 SPORTER BOLT-ACTION RIFLE
Caliber: 22 LR, 22 Hornet, 5-shot magazine.
Barrel: 22".

Weight: About 6.5 lbs. **Length:** NA.
Stock: Claro or English walnut in classic design; 13.6" length of pull. Choice of grade. Point panel hand checkering. Swivel studs. Black butt pad.
Sights: None furnished; comes with mount bases.
Features: Combines features of Winchester 52 and Dakota 76 rifles. Full-sized receiver; rear locking lug and bolt machined from bar stock. Trigger and striker-blocking safety; adjustable trigger. Introduced 1992. From Dakota Arms, Inc.
Price: $995.00

CAUTION: PRICES CHANGE, CHECK AT GUNSHOP.

KRICO MODEL 300 BOLT-ACTION RIFLES
Caliber: 22 LR, 22 WMR, 22 Hornet.
Barrel: 19.6" (22 RF), 23.6" (Hornet).
Weight: 6.3 lbs. **Length:** 38.5" overall (22 RF).
Stock: Walnut-stained beech.
Sights: Blade on ramp front, open adjustable rear.

Features: Double triggers, sliding safety. Checkered grip and forend. Imported from Germany by Mandall Shooting Supplies.
Price: Model 300 Standard **$700.00**
Price: Model 300 Deluxe **$795.00**
Price: Model 300 Stutzen (walnut full-length stock) **$825.00**
Price: Model 300 SA (walnut Monte Carlo stock) **$750.00**

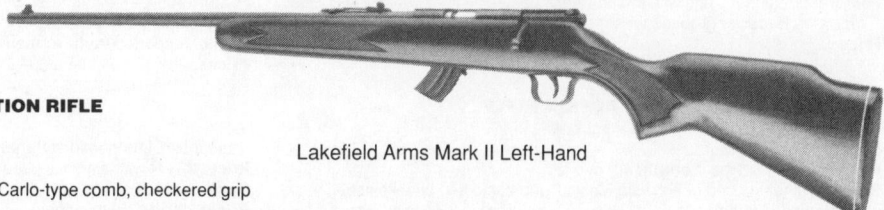

Lakefield Arms Mark II Left-Hand

LAKEFIELD ARMS MARK II BOLT-ACTION RIFLE
Caliber: 22 LR, 10-shot magazine.
Barrel: 20½".
Weight: 5½ lbs. **Length:** 39½" overall.
Stock: Walnut-finished hardwood with Monte Carlo-type comb, checkered grip and forend.
Sights: Bead front, open adjustable rear. Receiver grooved for scope mounting.
Features: Thumb-operated rotating safety. Blue finish. Introduced 1990. Made in Canada by Lakefield Arms Ltd.
Price: About **$124.95**
Price: Mark II-Y (youth), 19" barrel, 37" overall, 5 lbs. **$124.95**
Price: Mark II left-hand **$139.95**
Price: Mark II-Y (youth) left-hand **$139.95**

LAKEFIELD ARMS MARK I BOLT-ACTION RIFLE
Caliber: 22 LR, single shot.
Barrel: 20½".
Weight: 5½ lbs. **Length:** 39½" overall.
Stock: Walnut-finished hardwood with Monte Carlo-type comb, checkered grip and forend.
Sights: Bead front, open adjustable rear. Receiver grooved for scope mounting.
Features: Thumb-operated rotating safety. Blue finish. Rifled or smooth bore. Introduced 1990. Made in Canada by Lakefield Arms Ltd.
Price: About **$119.95**
Price: Mark I-Y (Youth), 19" barrel, 37" overall, 5 lbs. **$119.95**

Magtech Model MT-22C

MAGTECH MODEL MT-22C BOLT-ACTION RIFLE
Caliber: 22 S, L, LR, 6- and 10-shot magazines.
Barrel: 21" (six-groove).
Weight: 5¾ lbs. **Length:** 39" overall.
Stock: Brazilian hardwood.
Sights: Blade front, open rear adjustable for windage and elevation.
Features: Sliding wing-type safety; double extractors; red cocking indicator; receiver grooved for scope mount. Introduced 1991. Imported from Brazil by Magtech Recreational Products, Inc.
Price: About **$119.95**

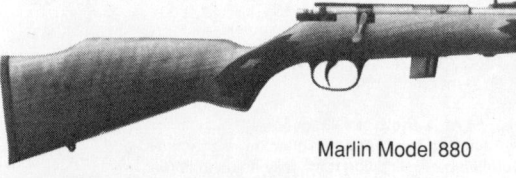

Marlin Model 880

Marlin Model 881 Bolt-Action Rifle
Same as the Marlin 880 except tubular magazine, holds 17 Long Rifle, 19 Long, 25 Short cartridges. Weighs 6 lbs.
Price: **$226.85**

MARLIN MODEL 880 BOLT-ACTION RIFLE
Caliber: 22 LR; 7-shot clip magazine.
Barrel: 22" Micro-Groove®.
Weight: 5½ lbs. **Length:** 41".
Stock: Monte Carlo American black walnut with checkered p.g. and forend. Rubber buttpad, swivel studs. Mar-Shield® finish.
Sights: Wide-Scan™ ramp front, folding semi-buckhorn rear adjustable for windage and elevation.
Features: Receiver grooved for scope mount. Introduced 1989.
Price: **$217.75**

Marlin Model 883 Bolt-Action Rifle
Same as Marlin 882 except tubular magazine holds 12 rounds of 22 WMR ammunition.
Price: **$248.90**
Price: Model 883N (nickel-Teflon finish) **$274.70**

Marlin Model 882 Bolt-Action Rifle
Same as the Marlin 880 except 22 WMR cal. only with 7-shot clip magazine; weight about 6 lbs. Comes with swivel studs.
Price: **$240.05**
Price: Model 882L (laminated hardwood stock) **$254.55**

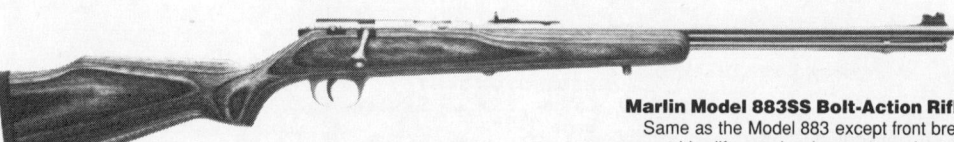

Marlin Model 883SS

Marlin Model 883SS Bolt-Action Rifle
Same as the Model 883 except front breech bolt, striker knob, trigger stud, cartridge lifter stud and outer magazine tube are of stainless steel; other parts are nickel-plated. Has two-tone brown laminated Monte Carlo stock with swivel studs, rubber butt pad. Introduced 1993.
Price: **$263.70**

Marlin Model 25MN Bolt-Action Rifle
Similar to the Model 25N except chambered for 22 WMR. Has 7-shot clip magazine, 22" Micro-Groove® barrel, walnut-finished hardwood stock. Introduced 1989.
Price: **$180.50**

Marlin Model 25N Bolt-Action Repeater
Similar to Marlin 880, except walnut-finished p.g. stock, adjustable open rear sight, ramp front.
Price: **$158.00**

MARLIN MODEL 15YN "LITTLE BUCKAROO"
Caliber: 22 S, L, LR, single shot.
Barrel: 16¼" Micro-Groove;rm.
Weight: 4¼ lbs. **Length:** 33¼" overall.
Stock: One-piece walnut-finished hardwood with Monte Carlo; Mar-Shield® finish.
Sights: Ramp front, adjustable open rear.
Features: Beginner's rifle with thumb safety, easy-load feed throat, red cocking indicator. Receiver grooved for scope mounting. Introduced 1989.
Price: **$152.15**

MAUSER MODEL 201 BOLT-ACTION RIFLE
Caliber: 22 LR, 22 WMR, 5-shot magazine.
Barrel: 21".
Weight: About 6.5 lbs. **Length:** 40" overall.
Stock: Walnut-stained beech with Monte Carlo comb and cheekpiece. Checkered grip and forend.
Sights: Available with or without sights.
Features: Hammer forged medium-heavy, free-floated barrel. Bolt has two front locking lugs, dual extractors. Adjustable trigger. Safety locks bolt, sear and trigger. Receiver accepts rail mounts and is drilled and tapped for scope

MAUSER MODEL 107 BOLT-ACTION RIFLE
Caliber: 22 LR, 5-shot magazine.
Barrel: 21.6".
Weight: 5.1 lbs. **Length:** 40" overall.
Stock: Walnut-stained beechwood with Monte Carlo, checkered grip and forend; sling swivels.
Sights: Hooded blade front, adjustable open rear.
Features: Dual extractors, 60-degree bolt throw; steel trigger guard and floorplate. Grooved receiver for scope mounting. Satin blue finish. Introduced 1992. Imported from Germany by Precision Imports, Inc.
Price: **$330.00**

mounting. Introduced 1989. Imported from Germany by Precision Imports, Inc.
Price: 22 LR with sights **$491.00**
Price: As above, no sights **$472.00**
Price: 22 WMR with sights **$534.00**
Price: As above, no sights **$515.00**
Price: Luxus, 22 LR with sights **$648.00**
Price: As above, no sights **$621.00**
Price: Luxus, 22 WMR with sights **$698.00**

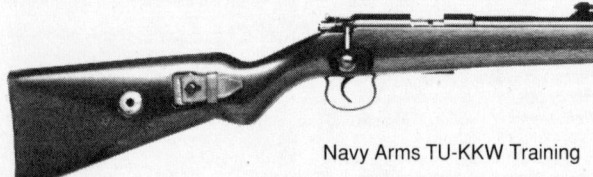

Navy Arms TU-KKW Training

NAVY ARMS TU-KKW TRAINING RIFLE
Caliber: 22 LR, 5-shot detachable magazine.
Barrel: 26".
Weight: 8 lbs. **Length:** 44" overall.
Stock: Walnut-stained hardwood.
Sights: Blade front, open rear adjustable for elevation; military style.
Features: Replica of the German WWII training rifle. Polished blue metal. Bayonet lug, cleaning rod, takedown disk in butt. Introduced 1991. Imported by Navy Arms.
Price: **$210.00**

Navy Arms TU-33/40 Carbine
Similar to the TU-KKW Training Rifle except has 20.75" barrel, weighs 7.5 lbs. Based on Mauser G.33/40 mountain carbine. Introduced 1992. Imported by Navy Arms.
Price: **$210.00**

Navy Arms TU-KKW Sniper Trainer
Same as the TU-KKW except comes with Type 89 2.75x scope with quick-detachable mount system. Introduced 1992. Imported by Navy Arms.
Price: **$285.00**

Consult our Directory pages for the location of firms mentioned.

Norinco JW-27

NORINCO JW-27 BOLT-ACTION RIFLE
Caliber: 22 LR, 5-shot magazine.
Barrel: 22.75".
Weight: 5 lbs., 14 oz. **Length:** 41.75" overall.
Stock: Walnut-finished hardwood with checkered grip and forend.
Sights: Dovetailed bead on blade front, fully adjustable rear.
Features: Receiver grooved for scope mounting. Blued finish. Introduced 1992. Imported from China by Century International Arms.
Price: About **$106.95**

NORINCO JW-15 BOLT-ACTION RIFLE
Caliber: 22 LR, 5-shot detachable magazine.
Barrel: 24".
Weight: 5 lbs., 12 oz. **Length:** 41¾" overall.
Stock: Walnut-stained hardwood.
Sights: Hooded blade front, open rear drift adjustable for windage.
Features: Polished blue finish; sling swivels; wing-type safety. Introduced 1991. Imported by Interarms, Navy Arms.
Price: About . . . . **$110.00 to $118.00**

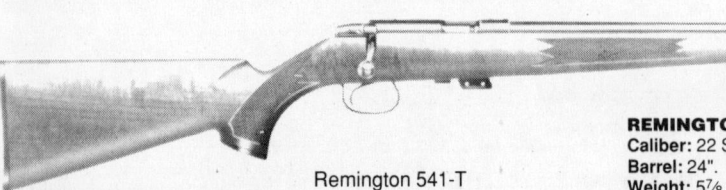

Remington 541-T

REMINGTON 541-T
Caliber: 22 S, L, LR, 5-shot clip.
Barrel: 24".
Weight: 5⅞ lbs. **Length:** 42½" overall.
Stock: Walnut, cut-checkered p.g. and forend. Satin finish.
Sights: None. Drilled and tapped for scope mounts.
Features: Clip repeater. Thumb safety. Reintroduced 1986.
Price: About **$371.00**

REMINGTON 40-XR RIMFIRE CUSTOM SPORTER
Caliber: 22 LR.
Barrel: 24".
Weight: 10 lbs. **Length:** 42½" overall.
Stock: Full-sized walnut, checkered p.g. and forend.
Sights: None furnished; drilled and tapped for scope mounting.
Features: Custom Shop gun. Duplicates Model 700 centerfire rifle.
Price: Grade I **$2,186.00**

CAUTION: PRICES CHANGE, CHECK AT GUNSHOP.

Remington 541-T Heavy Barrel

Remington 541-T HB Bolt-Action Rifle

Similar to the 541-T except has a heavy target-type barrel without sights. Receiver is drilled and tapped for scope mounting. American walnut stock with straight comb, satin finish, cut checkering, black checkered buttplate, black grip cap and forend tip. Weight is about 6½ lbs. Introduced 1993.
Price: **$397.00**

REMINGTON 581-S SPORTSMAN RIFLE

Caliber: 22 S, L or LR, 5-shot clip magazine.
Barrel: 24" round.
Weight: 4¾ lbs. **Length:** 42⅜" overall.
Stock: Walnut-finished hardwood, Monte Carlo with p.g.
Sights: Bead post front, screw adjustable open rear.
Features: Sliding side safety, wide trigger, receiver grooved for tip-off scope mounts. Comes with single shot adaptor. Reintroduced 1986.
Price: About **$204.00**

Ruger K77/22RSP

RUGER 77/22 RIMFIRE BOLT-ACTION RIFLE

Caliber: 22 LR, 10-shot rotary magazine; 22 WMR, 9-shot rotary magazine.
Barrel: 20".
Weight: About 5¾ lbs. **Length:** 39¾" overall.
Stock: Checkered American walnut or injection-moulded fiberglass-reinforced Du Pont Zytel with Xenoy inserts in forend and grip, stainless sling swivels.
Sights: Brass bead front, adjustable folding leaf rear or plain barrel with 1" Ruger rings.

Features: Mauser-type action uses Ruger's 10-shot rotary magazine. Three-position safety, simplified bolt stop, patented bolt locking system. Uses the dual screw barrel attachment system of the 10/22 rifle. Integral scope mounting system with 1" Ruger rings. Blued model introduced in 1983. Stainless steel model and blued model with the synthetic stock introduced in 1989.
Price: 77/22R (no sights, rings, walnut stock) **$402.00**
Price: 77/22RS (open sights, rings, walnut stock) **$424.00**
Price: 77/22RSP (open sights, rings, synthetic stock) **$353.00**
Price: K77/22RP (stainless, no sights, rings, synthetic stock) . . . **$397.00**
Price: K77/22RSP (stainless, open sights, rings, synthetic stock) . . **$419.00**
Price: 77/22RM (22 WMR, blue, walnut stock) **$402.00**
Price: K77/22RSMP (22 WMR, stainless, open sights, rings, synthetic stock) **$445.20**
Price: K77/22RMP (22 WMR, stainless, synthetic stock) **$419.00**
Price: 77/22RSM (22 WMR, blue, open sights, rings, walnut stock) . **$424.00**

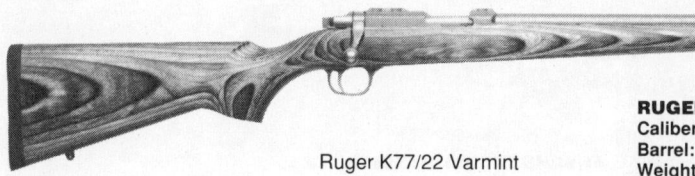

Ruger K77/22 Varmint

RUGER K77/22 VARMINT RIFLE

Caliber: 22 WMR, 9-shot detachable rotary magazine.
Barrel: 24", heavy.
Weight: 7.25 lbs. **Length:** 43.25" overall.
Stock: Laminated hardwood with rubber butt pad, quick-detachable swivel studs. No checkering or grip cap.
Sights: None furnished. Comes with Ruger 1" scope rings.
Features: Made of stainless steel with matte finish. Three-position safety, dual extractors. Stock has wide, flat forend. Introduced 1993.
Price: K77/22VBZ **$485.00**

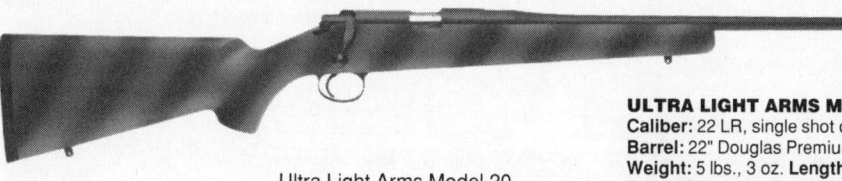

Ultra Light Arms Model 20

ULTRA LIGHT ARMS MODEL 20 RF BOLT-ACTION RIFLE

Caliber: 22 LR, single shot or 5-shot repeater.
Barrel: 22" Douglas Premium, #1 contour.
Weight: 5 lbs., 3 oz. **Length:** 41½" overall.
Stock: Composite Kevlar, graphite reinforced. Du Pont Imron paint; 13½" length of pull.
Sights: None furnished. Drilled and tapped for scope mounting.
Features: Available as either single shot or repeater with 5-shot removable magazine. Comes with scope mounts. Introduced 1993. Made in U.S. by Ultra Light Arms, Inc.
Price: **$800.00**

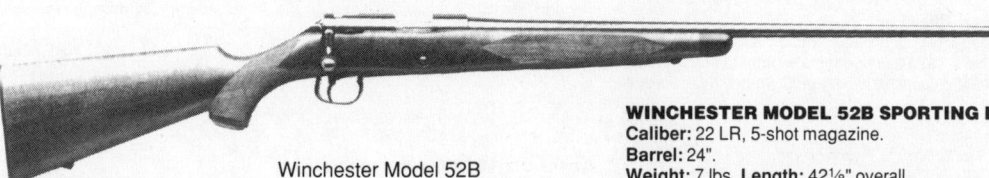

Winchester Model 52B

WINCHESTER MODEL 52B SPORTING RIFLE

Caliber: 22 LR, 5-shot magazine.
Barrel: 24".
Weight: 7 lbs. **Length:** 42⅛" overall.
Stock: Walnut, with sculpted cheekpiece.
Sights: None furnished. Drilled and tapped for scope mounting.
Features: Uses the Model 52C mechanism with stock configuration of the Model 52B. Has Micro-Motion trigger system of the original. Production limited to 6000 rifles. Reintroduced 1993. From U.S. Repeating Arms Co.
Price: **$576.00**

Includes models for classic American and ISU target competition and other sporting and competitive shooting.

ANSCHUTZ 64-MS, 64-MS LEFT SILHOUETTE
Caliber: 22 LR, single shot.
Barrel: 21½", medium heavy; ⅞" diameter.
Weight: 8 lbs. **Length:** 39½" overall.
Stock: Walnut-finished hardwood, silhouette-type.
Sights: None furnished. Receiver drilled and tapped for scope mounting.
Features: Uses Match 64 action. Designed for metallic silhouette competition. Stock has stippled checkering, contoured thumb groove with Wundhammer swell. Two-stage #5091 trigger. Slide safety locks sear and bolt. Introduced 1980. Imported from Germany by Precision Sales International.
Price: 64-MS **$912.00**
Price: 64-MS Left **$957.00**

ANSCHUTZ 1827B BIATHLON RIFLE
Caliber: 22 LR, 5-shot magazine.
Barrel: 21½".
Weight: 8½ lbs. with sights. **Length:** 42½" overall.
Stock: Walnut-finished hardwood; cheekpiece, stippled pistol grip and forend.
Sights: Globe front specially designed for Biathlon shooting, micrometer rear with hinged snow cap.
Features: Uses Match 54 action and nine-way adjustable trigger; adjustable wooden buttplate, Biathlon butthook, adjustable hand-stop rail. **Special Order Only.** Introduced 1982. Imported from Germany by Precision Sales International.
Price: Right-hand **$2,233.00**
Price: With Fortner straight-pull bolt **$3,449.00**
Price: As above, left-hand **$3,794.00**

ANSCHUTZ 1808D RT SUPER MATCH 54 TARGET
Caliber: 22 LR, single shot.
Barrel: 32½".
Weight: 9.4 lbs. **Length:** 50½" overall.
Stock: Walnut-finished European hardwood. Heavy beavertail forend; adjustable cheekpiece and buttplate. Stippled grip and forend.
Sights: None furnished. Grooved for scope mounting.
Features: Designed for Running Target competition. Nine-way adjustable single-stage trigger, slide safety. Introduced 1991. Imported from Germany by Precision Sales International.
Price: Right-hand **$1,759.00**

ANSCHUTZ 1903D MATCH RIFLE
Caliber: 22 LR, single shot.
Barrel: 25", ¾" diameter.
Weight: 8.6 lbs. **Length:** 43¾" overall.
Stock: Walnut-finished hardwood with adjustable cheekpiece; stippled grip and forend.
Sights: None furnished.
Features: Uses Anschutz Match 64 action and #5091 two-stage trigger. A medium weight rifle for intermediate and advanced Junior Match competition. Introduced 1987. Imported from Germany by Precision Sales International.
Price: Right-hand **$1,070.00**
Price: Left-hand **$1,143.00**
Price: #6823 sight set **$270.00**

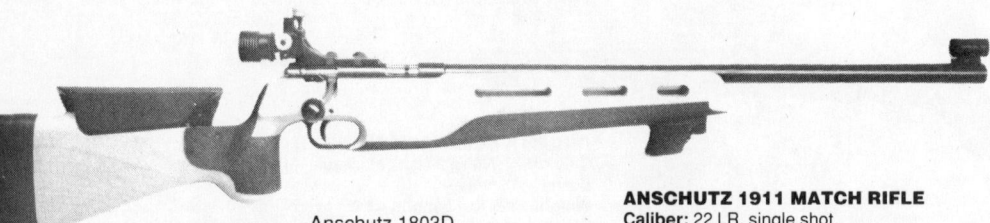

Anschutz 1803D

Anschutz 1803D Intermediate Match
Similar to the Model 1903D except has blonde-finished European hardwood stock, buttplate and cheekpiece have fewer adjustments. Takes Anschutz #6825 sight set (optional). Weight is 9.5 lbs. Introduced 1991.
Price: **$1,012.00**
Price: #6825 sight set **$250.00**

ANSCHUTZ 1911 MATCH RIFLE
Caliber: 22 LR, single shot.
Barrel: 27¼" round (1" dia.).
Weight: 11 lbs. **Length:** 46" overall.
Stock: Walnut-finished European hardwood; American prone style with Monte Carlo, cast-off cheekpiece, checkered p.g., beavertail forend with swivel rail and adjustable swivel, adjustable rubber buttplate.
Sights: None. Receiver grooved for Anschutz sights (extra). Scope blocks.
Features: Two-stage #5018 trigger adjustable from 2.1 to 8.6 oz. Extremely fast lock time. Imported from Germany by Precision Sales International.
Price: Right-hand, no sights **$2,086.00**
Price: M1911-L (true left-hand action and stock) **$2,209.00**

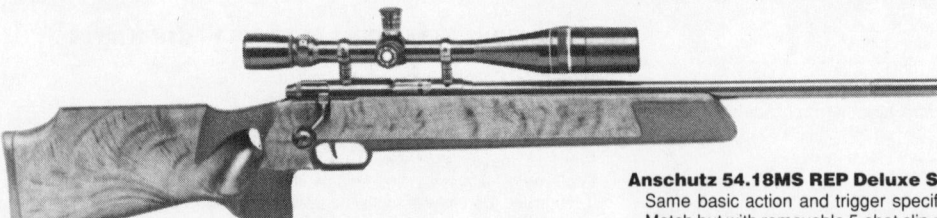

Anschutz 54.18MS REP

Anschutz 1913 Super Match Rifle
Same as the Model 1911 except European walnut International-type stock with adjustable cheekpiece, adjustable aluminum hook buttplate, adjustable hand stop, weight 15½ lbs., 46" overall. Imported from Germany by Precision Sales International.
Price: Right-hand, no sights **$2,980.00**
Price: M1913 left-hand **$3,148.00**

Anschutz 1907 Match Rifle
Same action as Model 1913 but with ⅞" diameter 26" barrel. Length is 44½" overall, weight 10 lbs. Blonde wood finish with vented forend. Designed for ISU requirements; suitable for NRA matches.
Price: Right-hand, no sights **$1,780.00**
Price: M1907-L (true left-hand action and stock) **$1,888.00**

Anschutz 54.18MS REP Deluxe Silhouette Rifle
Same basic action and trigger specifications as the Anschutz 1913 Super Match but with removable 5-shot clip magazine, 22" barrel extendable to 30" using optional extension and weight set. Receiver drilled and tapped for scope mounting. Silhouette stock with thumbhole grip is of fiberglass with walnut wood Fibergrain finish. Introduced 1990. Imported from Germany by Precision Sales International.
Price: 54.18MS REP Deluxe **$1,766.00**
Price: 54.18MS Standard with fiberglass stock **$2,055.00**

Anschutz 1910 Super Match II
Similar to the Super Match 1913 rifle except has a stock of European hardwood with tapered forend and deep receiver area. Hand and palm rests not included. Uses Match 54 action. Adjustable hook buttplate and cheekpiece. Sights not included. Introduced 1982. Imported from Germany by Precision Sales International.
Price: Right-hand **$2,660.00**
Price: Left-hand **$2,813.00**

COMPETITION RIFLES—CENTERFIRE & RIMFIRE

Anschutz 54.18MS Silhouette Rifle
Same basic features as Anschutz 1913 Super Match but with special metallic silhouette European hardwood stock and two-stage trigger. Has 22" barrel; receiver drilled and tapped.
Price: **$1,488.00**
Price: 54.18MSL (true left-hand version of above) **$1,594.00**

Consult our Directory pages for the location of firms mentioned.

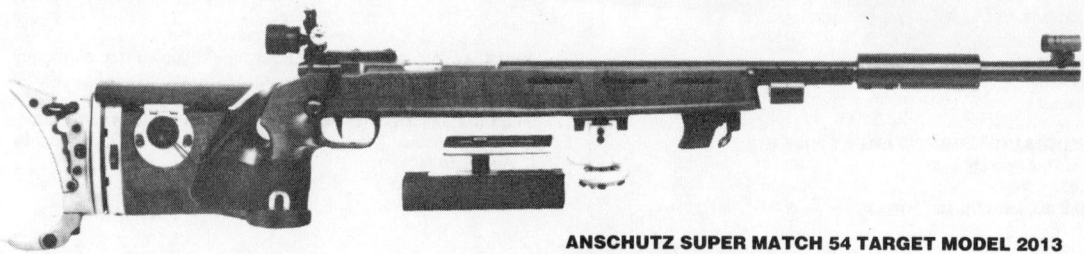

Anschutz 2013

Anschutz Super Match 54 Target Model 2007
Similar to the Model 2013 except has ISU Standard design European walnut stock. Sights optional. Introduced 1992. Imported from Germany by Precision Sales International.
Price: **$2,650.00**
Price: M2007 left-hand **$2,736.00**

ANSCHUTZ SUPER MATCH 54 TARGET MODEL 2013
Caliber: 22 LR.
Barrel: 19.75" (26" with tube installed).
Weight: 15.5 lbs. **Length:** NA.
Stock: European walnut; target adjustable.
Sights: Optional. Uses #6820 sight set.
Features: Improved Super Match 54 action, #5018 trigger give fastest consistent lock time for a production target rifle. Barrel is micro-honed; trigger has nine points of adjustment, two stages. Slide safety. Comes with test target. Introduced 1992. Imported from Germany by Precision Sales International.
Price: **$3,700.00**
Price: M2013 left-hand **$3,905.00**

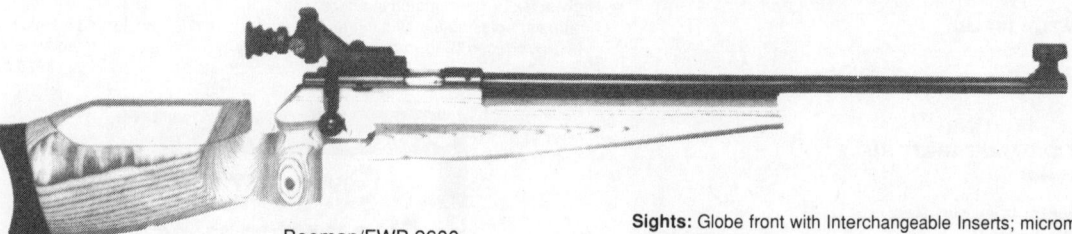

Beeman/FWB 2600

BEEMAN/FEINWERKBAU 2600 TARGET RIFLE
Caliber: 22 LR, single shot.
Barrel: 26.3".
Weight: 10.6 lbs. **Length:** 43.7" overall.
Stock: Laminated hardwood and hard rubber.

Sights: Globe front with Interchangeable Inserts; micrometer match aperture rear.
Features: Identical smallbore companion to the Beeman/FWB 600 air rifle. Free floating barrel. Match trigger has fingertip weight adjustment dial. Introduced 1986. Imported from Germany by Beeman.
Price: Right-hand **$1,695.00**
Price: Left-hand **$1,855.00**
Price: Free rifle, right-hand **$2,498.00**
Price: Free rifle, left-hand **$2,650.00**

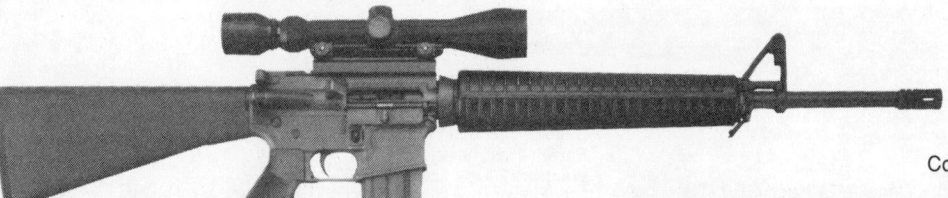

Colt Sporter Competition HBAR

Colt Sporter Competition HBAR Rifle
Similar to the Sporter Target except has flat-top receiver with integral Weaver-type base for scope mounting. Counter-bored muzzle, 1:9" rifling twist. Introduced 1991.
Price: Model R6700 . . . . **$989.95**

Colt Sporter Competition HBAR Range Selected Rifle
Same as the Sporter Competition HBAR #R6700 except is range selected for accuracy, and comes with 3-9x rubber armored scope, scope mount, carrying handle with iron sights, Cordura nylon carrying case. Introduced 1992.
Price: Model R6700CH **$1,489.95**

Colt Sporter Match HBAR Rifle
Similar to the Target Model except has heavy barrel, 800-meter rear sight adjustable for windage and elevation. Introduced 1991.
Price: **$938.95**

COLT SPORTER TARGET MODEL RIFLE
Caliber: 223 Rem., 5-shot magazine.
Barrel: 20".
Weight: 7.5 lbs. **Length:** 39" overall.
Stock: Composition stock, grip, forend.
Sights: Post front, aperture rear adjustable for windage and elevation.
Features: Five-round detachable box magazine, standard-weight barrel, flash suppressor, sling swivels. Has forward bolt assist. Military matte black finish. Model introduced 1991.
Price: **$897.95**

COOPER ARMS MODEL TRP-1 ISU STANDARD RIFLE
Caliber: 22 LR, single shot.
Barrel: 22".
Weight: 10 lbs. **Length:** 40.5" overall.
Stock: Walnut, competition style with adjustable cheekpiece and buttpad.
Sights: None furnished; accepts Anschutz sight packages.
Features: Action has three front locking lugs, 45-degree bolt rotation; fully adjustable single stage trigger; hand-lapped match grade Shilen stainless barrel. Introduced 1991. Made in U.S. by Cooper Arms.
Price: **$1,095.00**
Price: BR-50 (benchrest-style stock) **$995.00**
Price: MS-36 (oil-finished silhouette-style stock) **$995.00**

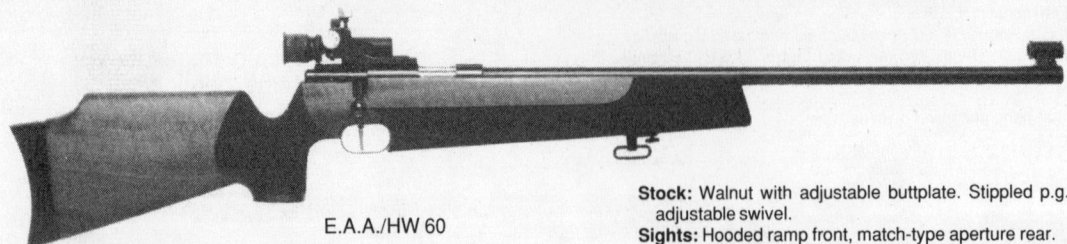

E.A.A./HW 60

E.A.A./WEIHRAUCH HW 60 TARGET RIFLE
Caliber: 22 LR, single shot.
Barrel: 26.8".
Weight: 10.8 lbs. **Length:** 45.7" overall.

Stock: Walnut with adjustable buttplate. Stippled p.g. and forend. Rail with adjustable swivel.
Sights: Hooded ramp front, match-type aperture rear.
Features: Adjustable match trigger with push-button safety. Left-hand version also available. Introduced 1981. Imported from Germany by European American Armory.
Price: Right-hand **$798.00**
Price: Left-hand **$878.95**

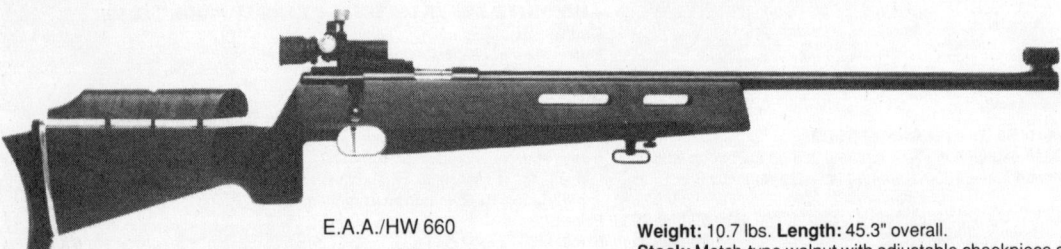

E.A.A./HW 660

E.A.A./HW 660 MATCH RIFLE
Caliber: 22 LR.
Barrel: 26".

Weight: 10.7 lbs. **Length:** 45.3" overall.
Stock: Match-type walnut with adjustable cheekpiece and buttplate.
Sights: Globe front, match aperture rear.
Features: Adjustable match trigger; stippled p.g. and forend; forend accessory rail. Introduced 1988. Imported from Germany by European American Armory.
Price: About **$875.00**

FINNISH LION STANDARD TARGET RIFLE
Caliber: 22 LR, single shot.
Barrel: 27⅝".
Weight: 10½ lbs. **Length:** 44⁹⁄₁₆" overall.
Stock: French walnut, target style.
Sights: Globe front, International micrometer rear.
Features: Optional accessories: palm rest, hook buttplate, forend stop and swivel assembly, buttplate extension, five front sight aperture inserts, three rear sight apertures, Allen wrench. Adjustable trigger. Imported from Finland by Mandall Shooting Supplies.
Price: Without sights **$695.00**
Price: Sight set **$195.00**

Heckler & Koch SR9 (TC)

HECKLER & KOCH SR9 (TC) TARGET RIFLE
Caliber: 308.
Barrel: 19.7" polygonal.
Weight: 10.9 lbs. **Length:** NA.
Stock: PSG1 adjustable buttstock.
Sights: Post front, aperture rear adjustable for windage and elevation.
Features: Target/competition version of the SR9 rifle. Has PSG1 butt, trigger group and contoured grip. Introduced 1993. Imported from Germany by Heckler & Koch, Inc.
Price: **$1,946.00**

HECKLER & KOCH PSG-1 MARKSMAN RIFLE
Caliber: 308, 5- and 20-shot magazines.
Barrel: 25.6", heavy.
Weight: 17.8 lbs. **Length:** 47.5" overall.
Stock: Matte black high impact plastic, adjustable for length, pivoting butt cap, vertically-adjustable cheekpiece; target-type pistol grip with adjustable palm shelf.
Sights: Hendsoldt 6x42 scope.
Features: Uses HK-91 action with low-noise bolt closing device; special forend with T-way rail for sling swivel or tripod. Gun comes in special foam-fitted metal transport case with tripod, two 20-shot and two 5-shot magazines, cleaning rod. Imported from Germany by Heckler & Koch, Inc. Introduced 1986.
Price: **$9,325.00**

KRICO MODEL 360 S2 BIATHLON RIFLE
Caliber: 22 LR, 5-shot magazine.
Barrel: 21.25".
Weight: 9 lbs., 15 oz. **Length:** 40.55" overall.
Stock: Biathlon design of black epoxy-finished walnut with pistol grip.
Sights: Globe front, fully adjustable Diana 82 match peep rear.
Features: Pistol-grip-activated action. Comes with five magazines (four stored in stock recess), muzzle/sight snow cap. Introduced 1991. Imported from Germany by Mandall Shooting Supplies.
Price: **$1,595.00**

KRICO MODEL 400 MATCH RIFLE
Caliber: 22 LR, 22 Hornet, 5-shot magazine.
Barrel: 23.2" (22 LR), 23.6" (22 Hornet).
Weight: 8.8 lbs. **Length:** 42.1" overall (22 RF).
Stock: European walnut, match type.
Sights: None furnished; receiver grooved for scope mounting.
Features: Heavy match barrel. Double-set or match trigger. Imported from Germany by Mandall Shooting Supplies.
Price: **$950.00**

Krico Model 360S Biathlon

KRICO MODEL 500 KRICOTRONIC MATCH RIFLE
Caliber: 22 LR, single shot.
Barrel: 23.6".
Weight: 9.4 lbs. **Length:** 42.1" overall.
Stock: European walnut, match type with adjustable butt.
Sights: Globe front, match micrometer aperture rear.
Features: Electronic ignition system for fastest possible lock time. Completely adjustable trigger. Barrel has tapered bore. Imported from Germany by Mandall Shooting Supplies.
Price: $3,950.00

KRICO MODEL 360S BIATHLON RIFLE
Caliber: 22 LR, 5-shot magazine.
Barrel: 21.25".
Weight: 9.26 lbs. **Length:** 40.55" overall.
Stock: Walnut with high comb, adjustable buttplate.
Sights: Globe front, fully adjustable Diana 82 match peep rear.
Features: Straight-pull action with 17.6-oz. match trigger. Comes with five magazines (four stored in stock recess), muzzle/sight snow cap. Introduced 1991. Imported from Germany by Mandall Shooting Supplies.
Price: $1,695.00

KRICO MODEL 600 SNIPER RIFLE
Caliber: 222, 223, 22-250, 243, 308, 4-shot magazine.
Barrel: 23.6".
Weight: 9.2 lbs. **Length:** 45.2" overall.
Stock: European walnut with adjustable rubber buttplate.
Sights: None supplied; drilled and tapped for scope mounting.
Features: Match barrel with flash hider; large bolt knob; wide trigger shoe. Parkerized finish. Imported from Germany by Mandall Shooting Supplies.
Price: $2,645.00

Krico Model 600 Match

Lakefield Model 92S

KRICO MODEL 600 MATCH RIFLE
Caliber: 222, 223, 22-250, 243, 308, 5.6x50 Mag., 4-shot magazine.
Barrel: 23.6".
Weight: 8.8 lbs. **Length:** 43.3" overall.
Stock: Match stock of European walnut with cheekpiece.
Sights: None furnished; drilled and tapped for scope mounting.
Features: Match stock with vents in forend for cooling, rubber recoil pad, sling swivels. Imported from Germany by Mandall Shooting Supplies.
Price: $1,250.00

LAKEFIELD ARMS MODEL 90B TARGET RIFLE
Caliber: 22 LR, 5-shot magazine.
Barrel: 21".
Weight: 8¼ lbs. **Length:** 39⅝" overall.
Stock: Natural finish hardwood with clip holder, carrying and shooting rails, butt hook, hand stop.
Sights: Target front with inserts, peep rear with ¼-minute click adjustments.
Features: Biathlon-style rifle with snow cap muzzle protector. Comes with five magazines. Introduced 1991. Made in Canada by Lakefield Arms.
Price: About $534.95
Price: left-hand, about $589.95

LAKEFIELD ARMS MODEL 91T TARGET RIFLE
Caliber: 22 LR, single shot.
Barrel: 25".
Weight: 8 lbs. **Length:** 43⅝" overall.
Stock: Target-type, walnut-finished hardwood.
Sights: Target front with inserts, peep rear with ¼-minute click adjustments.
Features: Comes with shooting rail and hand stop. Also available as 5-shot repeater as Model 91-TR. Introduced 1991. Made in Canada by Lakefield Arms.
Price: Model 91T $424.95
Price: Model 91-TR (repeater) $454.95
Price: Model 91-TR left-hand $499.95

Lakefield Arms Model 92S Silhouette Rifle
Similar to the Model 90B except has high-comb target-type stock of walnut-finished hardwood, one 5-shot magazine. Comes without sights, but receiver is drilled and tapped for scope base. Weight about 8 lbs. Introduced 1992. Made in Canada by Lakefield Arms.
Price: $364.95
Price: left-hand $399.95

Marlin Model 2000

MARLIN MODEL 2000 TARGET RIFLE
Caliber: 22 LR, single shot.
Barrel: 22" heavy, Micro-Groove® rifling, match chamber, recessed muzzle.
Weight: 8 lbs. **Length:** 41" overall.
Stock: High-comb fiberglass/Kevlar with stipple finish grip and forend.
Sights: Hooded front with seven aperture inserts, fully adjustable target rear peep.
Features: Stock finished with royal blue enamel. Buttplate adjustable for length of pull, height and angle. Aluminum forend rail with stop and quick-detachable swivel. Two-stage target trigger; red cocking indicator. Five-shot adaptor kit available. Introduced 1991. From Marlin.
Price: $559.50

COMPETITION RIFLES—CENTERFIRE & RIMFIRE

MAUSER MODEL 86-SR SPECIALTY RIFLE
Caliber: 308 Win., 9-shot detachable magazine.
Barrel: 25.6", fluted, 1:12 twist.
Weight: About 10.8 lbs. **Length:** 47.7" overall.
Stock: Laminated wood, fiberglass, or special match thumbhole wood. All have rail in forend and adjustable recoil pad.
Sights: None furnished. Competition metallic sights or scope mount optional.

Features: Match barrel with muzzlebrake. Action has two front bolt locking lugs. Action bedded in stock with free-floated barrel. Match trigger adjustable as single or two-stage; fully adjustable for weight, slack, and position. Silent safety locks bolt, firing pin. Introduced 1989. Imported from Germany by Precision Imports, Inc.
Price: With fiberglass stock **$3,921.00**
Price: With match thumbhole stock **$4,145.00**

McMillan M-86

McMillan COMBO M-87/M-88 50-CALIBER RIFLE
Caliber: 50 BMG, single shot.
Barrel: 29", with muzzlebrake.
Weight: About 21½ lbs. **Length:** 53" overall.
Stock: McMillan fiberglass.
Sights: None furnished.
Features: Right-handed McMillan stainless steel receiver, chromemoly barrel with 1:15 twist. Introduced 1987. From McMillan Gunworks, Inc.
Price: **$4,000.00**
Price: M-87R (5-shot repeater) "Combo" **$4,270.00**

McMillan 300 PHOENIX LONG RANGE RIFLE
Caliber: 300 Phoenix.
Barrel: 28".
Weight: 12.5 lbs. **Length:** NA.
Stock: Fiberglass with adjustable cheekpiece, adjustable butt plate.
Sights: None furnished; comes with rings and bases.
Features: Matte black finish; textured stock. Introduced 1992. Made in U.S. by McMillan Gunworks, Inc.
Price: **$2,995.00**

McMillan NATIONAL MATCH RIFLE
Caliber: 7mm-08, 308, 5-shot magazine.
Barrel: 24", stainless steel.
Weight: About 11 lbs. (std. bbl.). **Length:** 43" overall.
Stock: Modified ISU fiberglass with adjustable buttplate.
Sights: Barrel band and Tompkins front; no rear sight furnished.

McMillan Long Range

McMillan LONG RANGE RIFLE
Caliber: 300 Win. Mag., 7mm Rem. Mag., 300 Phoenix, 338 Lapua, single shot.
Barrel: 26", stainless steel, match-grade.

McMILLAN M-86 SNIPER RIFLE
Caliber: 308, 30-06, 4-shot magazine; 300 Win. Mag., 300 Phoenix, 3-shot magazine.
Barrel: 24", McMillan match-grade in heavy contour.
Weight: 11¼ lbs. (308), 11½ lbs. (30-06, 300). **Length:** 43½" overall.
Stock: Specially designed McHale fiberglass stock with textured grip and forend, recoil pad.
Sights: None furnished.
Features: Uses McMillan repeating action. Comes with bipod. Matte black finish. Sling swivels. Introduced 1989. From McMillan Gunworks, Inc.
Price: **$1,895.00**
Price: 300 Phoenix **$2,445.00**

McMILLAN M-89 SNIPER RIFLE
Caliber: 308 Win., 5-shot magazine.
Barrel: 28" (with suppressor).
Weight: 15 lbs., 4 oz.
Stock: McMillan fiberglass; adjustable for length; recoil pad.
Sights: None furnished. Drilled and tapped for scope mounting.
Features: Uses McMillan repeating action. Comes with bipod. Introduced 1990. From McMillan Gunworks, Inc.
Price: Standard (non-suppressed) **$2,200.00**

Features: McMillan repeating action with clip slot, Canjar trigger. Match-grade barrel. Available in right-hand only. Fibergrain stock, sight installation, special machining and triggers optional. Introduced 1989. From McMillan Gunworks, Inc.
Price: **$2,598.00**

Weight: 14 lbs. **Length:** 46½" overall.
Stock: Fiberglass with adjustable buttplate and cheekpiece. Adjustable for length of pull, drop, cant and cast-off.
Sights: Barrel band and Tompkins front; no rear sight furnished.
Features: Uses McMillan solid bottom single shot action and Canjar trigger. Barrel twist 1:12. Introduced 1989. From McMillan Gunworks, Inc.
Price: **$2,598.00**

Olymipc International

Olympic Arms Intercontinental Match Rifle
Similar to the Ultramatch/International Match except 20" barrel only, has woodgrain thumbhole buttstock, magazine well floorplate, 5-shot magazine. Introduced 1992. Made in U.S. by Olympic Arms, Inc.
Price: **$1,330.00**

OLYMPIC ARMS ULTRAMATCH/INTERNATIONAL MATCH RIFLES
Caliber: 223, 20- or 30-shot magazine.
Barrel: 20", 24", stainless steel.
Weight: 10 lbs., 3 oz. **Length:** 39½" overall (20" barrel).
Stock: A2 stowaway butt and grip.
Sights: Cut-off carrying handle with scope rail attached (Ultramatch); target peep on International Match.
Features: Based on the AR-15 rifle. Broach-cut, free-floating barrel with 1:10" or 1:8.5" twist; fluting optional. Introduced 1985. Made in U.S. by Olympic Arms, Inc.
Price: Ultramatch **$1,120.00**
Price: International Match **$1,200.00**

CAUTION: PRICES CHANGE, CHECK AT GUNSHOP.

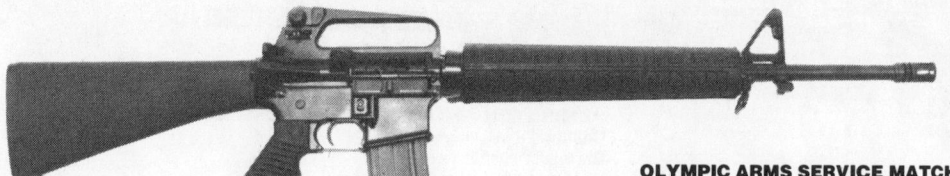

Olympic Service Match

OLYMPIC ARMS MULTIMATCH RIFLES
Caliber: 223, 20- or 30-shot magazine.
Barrel: 16" stainless steel.
Weight: 8 lbs., 2 oz. **Length:** 36" overall.
Stock: Telescoping or A2 stowaway butt and grip.
Sights: Post front, E2 rear (ML1); cut front, cut-off carrying handle with scope rail attached (ML2).
Features: Based on the AR-15 rifle. Barrel is broach-cut and free-floating with 1:10" or 1:8.5" twist. Introduced 1991. Made in U.S. by Olympic Arms, Inc.
Price: **$890.00**

OLYMPIC ARMS SERVICE MATCH RIFLE
Caliber: 223, 20- or 30-shot magazine.
Barrel: 20" stainless.
Weight: 8¾ lbs. **Length:** 39½" overall.
Stock: Black composition A2 standard stock.
Sights: Post front, fully adjustable aperture rear.
Features: Based on the AR-15 rifle. Conforms to all DCM standards. Barrel is broach-cut and free-floating with 1:10" or 1:8.5" twist; fluting optional. Introduced 1989. Made in U.S. by Olympic Arms, Inc.
Price: **$875.00**

Olympic Arms AR-15 Match Rifle
Similar to the Service Match except has cut-off carrying handle with scope rail attached, button-rifled 4140 ordnance steel or 416 stainless barrel with 1:9" twist standard, 1:7", 1:12", 1:14" twists optional. Weighs 8 lbs, 5 oz. Introduced 1993. Made in U.S. by Olympic Arms, Inc.
Price: **$690.00**

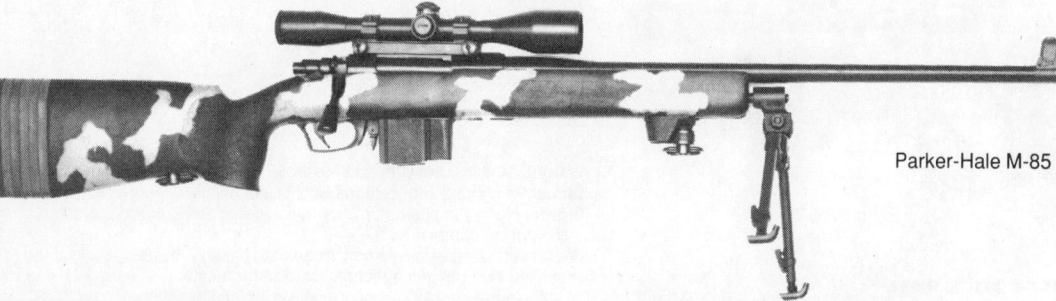

Parker-Hale M-85

PARKER-HALE M-87 TARGET RIFLE
Caliber: 308 Win., 243, 6.5x55, 308, 30-06, 300 Win. Mag. (other calibers on request), 5-shot detachable box magazine.
Barrel: 26" heavy.
Weight: About 10 lbs. **Length:** 45" overall.
Stock: Walnut target-style, adjustable for length of pull; solid buttpad; accessory rail with hand-stop. Deeply stippled grip and forend.
Sights: None furnished. Receiver dovetailed for Parker-Hale "Roll-Off" scope mounts.
Features: Mauser-style action with large bolt knob. Parkerized finish. Introduced 1987. Made by Gibbs Rifle Co., distributed by Navy Arms.
Price: **$1,500.00**

QUALITY PARTS V MATCH RIFLE
Caliber: 223, 30-shot magazine.
Barrel: 20", 24", 26"; 1:9" twist.
Weight: NA. **Length:** NA.
Stock: Composition.
Sights: None furnished; comes with scope mount base installed.
Features: Hand-built match gun. Barrel is .950" outside diameter with counter-bored crown: integral flash suppressor; upper receiver has brass deflector; free-floating steel handguard accepts laser sight, flashlight, bipod; 5-lb. trigger pull. From Quality Parts Co.
Price: From **$1,200.00**

PARKER-HALE M-85 SNIPER RIFLE
Caliber: 308 Win., 10-shot magazine.
Barrel: 24¼".
Weight: 12½ lbs (with scope). **Length:** 45" overall.
Stock: McMillan fiberglass (several color patterns available).
Sights: Post front adjustable for windage, fold-down rear adjustable for elevation.
Features: Comes with quick-detachable bipod, palm stop with rail; sling swivels; matte finish. Made by Gibbs Rifle Co., distributed by Navy Arms.
Price: Less scope **$1,950.00**

QUALITY PARTS XM-15-E2 TARGET MODEL RIFLE
Caliber: 223, 30-shot magazine.
Barrel: 20", 24", 26"; 1:7" or 1:9" twist; heavy.
Weight: NA. **Length:** NA.
Stock: Black composition.
Sights: Adjustable post front, adjustable aperture rear.
Features: Patterned after Colt M-16A2. Chrome-lined barrel with manganese phosphate exterior. Has E-2 lower receiver with push-pin. From Quality Parts Co.
Price: 20" match heavy barrel **$895.00**
Price: 24" match heavy barrel **$905.00**
Price: 26" match heavy barrel **$915.00**

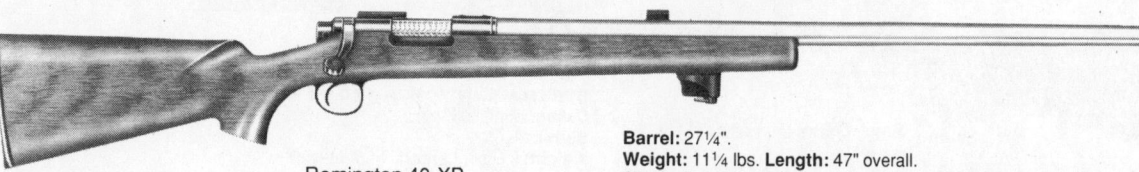

Remington 40-XB

Barrel: 27¼".
Weight: 11¼ lbs. **Length:** 47" overall.
Stock: American walnut or Kevlar with high comb and beavertail forend stop. Rubber non-slip buttplate.
Sights: None. Scope blocks installed.
Features: Adjustable trigger pull. Receiver drilled and tapped for sights.
Price: Standard s.s., stainless steel barrel, about **$1,109.00**
Price: Left-hand **$1,171.00**
Price: Model 40-XB KS **$1,265.00**
Price: Left-hand **$1,327.00**
Price: Extra for repeater model (KS) **$92.00**
Price: Extra for 2-oz. trigger **$155.00**

REMINGTON 40-XB RANGEMASTER TARGET CENTERFIRE
Caliber: 222 Rem., 222 Rem. Mag., 223, 220 Swift, 22-250, 6mm Rem., 243, 25-06, 7mm BR Rem., 7mm Rem. Mag., 30-338 (30-7mm Rem. Mag.), 300 Win. Mag., 7.62 NATO (308 Win.), 30-06, single shot.

Remington 40-XR KS

REMINGTON 40-XBBR KS

Caliber: 22 BR Rem., 222 Rem., 222 Rem. Mag., 223, 6mmx47, 6mm BR Rem.,
7.62 NATO (308 Win.).
Barrel: 20" (light varmint class), 24" (heavy varmint class).
Weight: 7¼ lbs. (light varmint class); 12 lbs. (heavy varmint class).
Length: 38" (20" bbl.), 42" (24" bbl.).
Stock: Kevlar.
Sights: None. Supplied with scope blocks.
Features: Unblued stainless steel barrel, trigger adjustable from 1½ lbs. to
3½ lbs. Special 2-oz. trigger at extra cost. Scope and mounts extra.
Price: With Kevlar stock **$1,345.00**
Price: Extra for 2-oz. trigger, about **$155.00**

REMINGTON 40-XR KS RIMFIRE POSITION RIFLE

Caliber: 22 LR, single shot.
Barrel: 24", heavy target.
Weight: 10 lbs. **Length:** 43" overall.
Stock: Kevlar. Position-style with front swivel block on forend guide rail.
Sights: Drilled and tapped. Furnished with scope blocks.
Features: Meets all ISU specifications. Deep forend, buttplate vertically adjustable, wide adjustable trigger.
Price: About **$1,265.00**

REMINGTON 40-XC KS NATIONAL MATCH COURSE RIFLE

Caliber: 7.62 NATO, 5-shot.
Barrel: 24", stainless steel.
Weight: 11 lbs. without sights. **Length:** 43½" overall.
Stock: Kevlar, position-style, with palm swell, handstop.
Sights: None furnished.
Features: Designed to meet the needs of competitive shooters firing the national match courses. Position-style stock, top loading clip slot magazine, anti-bind bolt and receiver, bright stainless steel barrel. Meets all ISU Army Rifle specifications. Adjustable buttplate, adjustable trigger.
Price: About **$1,345.00**

Sako TRG-21

SAKO TRG-21 BOLT-ACTION RIFLE

Caliber: 308 Win., 10-shot magazine.
Barrel: 25.75".
Weight: 10.5 lbs. **Length:** 46.5" overall.
Stock: Reinforced polyurethane with full adjustable cheekpiece and buttplate.
Sights: None furnished. Optional quick-detachable, one-piece scope mount base, 1" or 30mm rings.
Features: Resistance-free bolt, free-floating heavy stainless barrel, 60-degree bolt lift. Two-stage trigger is adjustable for length, pull, horizontal or vertical pitch. Introduced 1993. Imported from Finland by Stoeger.
Price: **$3,850.00**

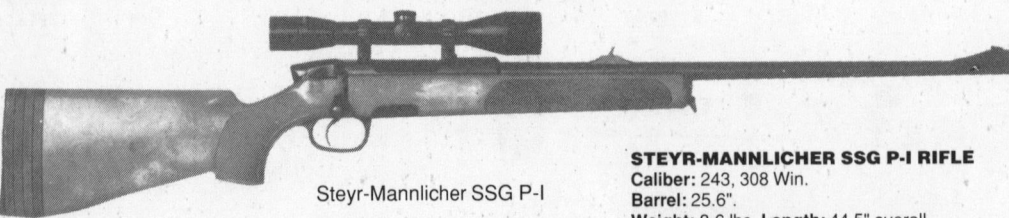

Springfield M-1A Match

STEYR-MANNLICHER MATCH SPG-UIT RIFLE

Caliber: 308 Win.
Barrel: 25.5".
Weight: 10 lbs. **Length:** 44" overall.
Stock: Laminated and ventilated. Special UIT Match design.
Sights: Steyr globe front, Steyr peep rear.
Features: Double-pull trigger adjustable for let-off point, slack, weight of first-stage pull, release force and length; buttplate adjustable for height and length. Meets UIT specifications. Introduced 1992. Imported from Austria by GSI, Inc.
Price: **$3,995.00**

SPRINGFIELD INC. M-1A SUPER MATCH

Caliber: 243, 7mm-08, 308 Win.
Barrel: 22", heavy Douglas Premium, or Hart stainless steel.
Weight: About 10 lbs. **Length:** 44.31" overall.
Stock: Heavy walnut competition stock with longer pistol grip, contoured area behind the rear sight, thicker butt and forend, glass bedded.
Sights: National Match front and rear.
Features: Has figure-eight-style operating rod guide. Introduced 1987. From Springfield Armory, Inc.
Price: About **$1,849.00**

Steyr-Mannlicher SSG P-I

STEYR-MANNLICHER SSG P-I RIFLE

Caliber: 243, 308 Win.
Barrel: 25.6".
Weight: 8.6 lbs. **Length:** 44.5" overall.
Stock: ABS Cycolac synthetic half-stock. Removable spacers in butt adjusts length of pull from 12¾" to 14".
Sights: Hooded blade front, folding leaf rear.
Features: Parkerized finish. Choice of interchangeable single- or double-set triggers. Detachable 5-shot rotary magazine (10-shot optional). Receiver grooved for Steyr and Bock Quick Detach mounts. Imported from Austria by GSI, Inc.
Price: Synthetic half-stock **$2,043.00**
Price: SSG-PII (as above except has large bolt knob, heavy bbl., no sights, forend rail) **$2,229.00**

Steyr-Mannlicher SSG P-III Rifle

Similar to the SSG P-I except has 26" heavy barrel, diopter match sight bases. Available in 308 only. Has H-S Precision Pro-Series stock (black only). Introduced 1992. Imported from Austria by GSI, Inc.
Price: **$3,162.00**

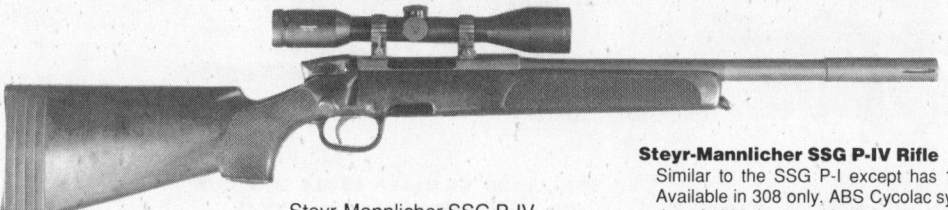

Steyr-Mannlicher SSG P-IV

Steyr-Mannlicher SSG P-IV Rifle
Similar to the SSG P-I except has 16.75" heavy barrel with flash hider. Available in 308 only. ABS Cycolac synthetic stock in green or black. Introduced 1992. Imported from Austria by GSI, Inc.
Price: **$2,603.00**

STONER SR-25 MATCH RIFLE
Caliber: 7.62 NATO, 20-shot magazine, 5-shot optional.
Barrel: 24" heavy match; 1:11.25" twist.
Weight: 10.75 lbs. **Length:** 44" overall.
Stock: Black synthetic AR-15A2 design. Full floating forend of glass-reinforced synthetic attaches to upper receiver at a single point.
Sights: None furnished. Has integral Weaver-style rail.
Features: Modified AR-15 trigger is adjustable for over-travel and sear engagement; AR-15-style seven-lug rotating bolt. Gas block rail takes detachable front sight. Introduced 1993. Made in U.S. by Knight's Mfg. Co.
Price: **$2,495.00**

Stoner SR-25 Match

TANNER 50 METER FREE RIFLE
Caliber: 22 LR, single shot.
Barrel: 27.7".
Weight: 13.9 lbs. **Length:** 44.4" overall.
Stock: Seasoned walnut with palm rest, accessory rail, adjustable hook buttplate.
Sights: Globe front with interchangeable inserts, Tanner micrometer-diopter rear with adjustable aperture.
Features: Bolt action with externally adjustable set trigger. Supplied with 50-meter test target. Imported from Switzerland by Mandall Shooting Supplies. Introduced 1984.
Price: About **$4,000.00**

TANNER STANDARD UIT RIFLE
Caliber: 308, 7.5mm Swiss, 10-shot.
Barrel: 25.9".
Weight: 10.5 lbs. **Length:** 40.6" overall.
Stock: Match style of seasoned nutwood with accessory rail; coarsely stippled pistol grip; high cheekpiece; vented forend.
Sights: Globe front with interchangeable inserts, Tanner micrometer-diopter rear with adjustable aperture.
Features: Two locking lug revolving bolt encloses case head. Trigger adjustable from ½ to 6½ lbs.; match trigger optional. Comes with 300-meter test target. Imported from Switzerland by Mandall Shooting Supplies. Introduced 1984.
Price: About **$4,700.00**

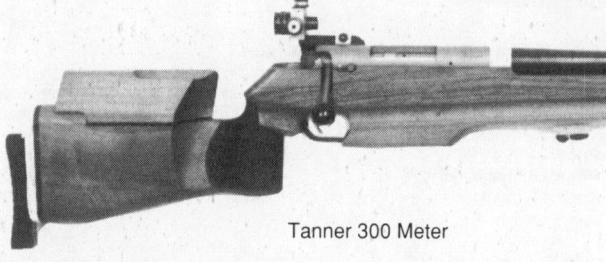

Tanner 300 Meter

WICHITA SILHOUETTE RIFLE
Caliber: All standard calibers with maximum overall cartridge length of 2.800".
Barrel: 24" free-floated Matchgrade.
Weight: About 9 lbs.
Stock: Metallic gray fiberthane with ventilated rubber recoil pad.
Sights: None furnished. Drilled and tapped for scope mounts.
Features: Legal for all NRA competitions. Single shot action. Fluted bolt, 2-oz. Canjar trigger; glass-bedded stock. Introduced 1983. From Wichita Arms.
Price: **$2,250.00**
Price: Left-hand **$2,400.00**

TANNER 300 METER FREE RIFLE
Caliber: 308 Win., 7.5 Swiss, single shot.
Barrel: 27.58".
Weight: 15 lbs. **Length:** 45.3" overall.
Stock: Seasoned walnut, thumbhole style, with accessory rail, palm rest, adjustable hook butt.
Sights: Globe front with interchangeable inserts, Tanner-design micrometer-diopter rear with adjustable aperture.
Features: Three-lug revolving-lock bolt design; adjustable set trigger; short firing pin travel; supplied with 300-meter test target. Imported from Switzerland by Mandall Shooting Supplies. Introduced 1984.
Price: About **$4,900.00**

SHOTGUNS—AUTOLOADERS

Includes a wide variety of sporting guns and guns suitable for various competitions.

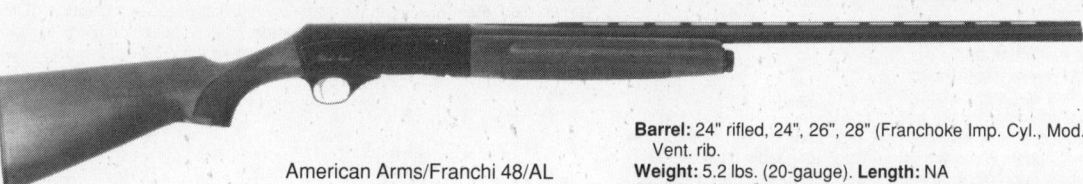

American Arms/Franchi 48/AL

AMERICAN ARMS/FRANCHI BLACK MAGIC 48/AL
Gauge: 12 or 20, 2¾" chamber.

Barrel: 24" rifled, 24", 26", 28" (Franchoke Imp. Cyl., Mod., Full choke tubes). Vent. rib.
Weight: 5.2 lbs. (20-gauge). **Length:** NA
Stock: 14¼"x1⅝"x2½". Walnut with checkered grip and forend.
Features: Recoil-operated action. Chrome-lined bore; cross-bolt safety. Imported from Italy by American Arms, Inc.
Price: **$609.00**
Price: 12-ga., 24" rifled slug, open sights **$640.00**

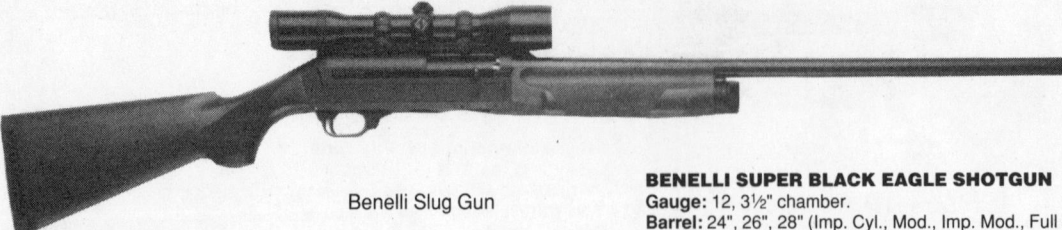

Benelli Slug Gun

BENELLI SUPER BLACK EAGLE SHOTGUN

Gauge: 12, 3½" chamber.
Barrel: 24", 26", 28" (Imp. Cyl., Mod., Imp. Mod., Full choke tubes).
Weight: 7 lbs., 5 oz. **Length:** 49⅝" overall (28" barrel).
Stock: European walnut with satin or gloss finish, or polumer. Adjustable for drop.
Sights: Bead front.
Features: Uses Montefeltro inertia recoil bolt system. Fires all 12-gauge shells from 2¾" to 3½" magnums. Introduced 1991. Imported from Italy by Heckler & Koch, Inc.
Price: **$1,079.00**

Benelli Super Black Eagle Slug Gun

Similar to the Benelli Super Black Eagle except has 24" E.R. Shaw Custom rifled barrel with 3" chamber, and comes with scope mount base. Uses the Montefeltro inertia recoil bolt system. Matte-finish receiver. Weight is 7.5 lbs., overall length 45.5". Introduced 1992. Imported from Italy by Heckler & Koch, Inc.
Price: **$1,079.00**

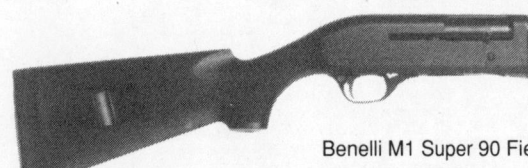

Benelli M1 Super 90 Field

BENELLI M1 SUPER 90 FIELD AUTO SHOTGUN

Gauge: 12, 3" chamber.
Barrel: 21", 24", 26", 28" (choke tubes).
Weight: 7 lbs., 4 oz.
Stock: High impact polymer.
Sights: Metal bead front.
Features: Sporting version of the military & police gun. Uses the rotating Montefeltro bolt system. Ventilated rib; blue finish. Comes with set of five choke tubes. Imported from Italy by Heckler & Koch, Inc.
Price: **$799.00**

Benelli Montefeltro Super 90 20-Gauge Shotgun

Similar to the 12-gauge Montefeltro Super 90 except chambered for 3" 20-gauge, 26" barrel (choke tubes), weighs 5 lbs., 12 oz. Has drop-adjustable walnut stock with gloss finish, blued receiver. Overall length 47.5". Introduced 1993. Imported from Italy by Heckler & Koch, Inc.
Price: **$824.00**

Benelli Montefeltro Super 90

Benelli Montefeltro Super 90 Shotgun

Similar to the M1 Super 90 except has checkered walnut stock with high-gloss finish. Uses the Montefeltro rotating bolt system with a simple inertia recoil design. Full, Imp. Mod., Mod., Imp. Cyl. choke tubes. Weight is 7-7½ lbs. Finish is matte black. Introduced 1987.
Price: 21", 24", 26", 28" **$824.00**
Price: Left-hand, 26", 28" **$844.00**
Price: 20-ga., Montefeltro Super 90, 26", 5¾ lbs. **$824.00**

BENELLI M1 SPORTING SPECIAL AUTO SHOTGUN

Gauge: 12, 3" chamber.
Barrel: 18.5" (Imp. Cyl. Mod., Full choke tubes).
Weight: 6 lbs., 8 oz. **Length:** 39.75" overall.
Stock: Sporting-style polymer with drop adjustment.
Sights: Ghost ring.
Features: Uses Montefeltro inertia recoil bolt system. Matte-finish receiver. Introduced 1993. Imported from Italy by Heckler & Koch, Inc.
Price: **$829.00**

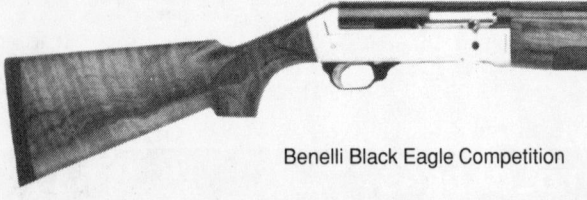

Benelli Black Eagle Competition

BENELLI BLACK EAGLE COMPETITION AUTO SHOTGUN

Gauge: 12, 3" chamber.
Barrel: 26", 28" (Full, Mod., Imp. Cyl., Imp. Mod., Skeet choke tubes). Mid-bead sight.
Weight: 7.1 to 7.6 lbs. **Length:** 49⅝" overall (26" barrel).
Stock: European walnut with high-gloss finish. Special competition stock comes with drop adjustment kit.
Features: Uses the Montefeltro rotating bolt inertia recoil operating system with a two-piece steel/aluminum etched receiver (bright on lower, blue upper). Drop adjustment kit allows the stock to be custom fitted without modifying the stock. Black lower receiver finish, blued upper. Introduced 1989. Imported from Italy by Heckler & Koch, Inc.
Price: **$1,099.00**

BERETTA A-303 AUTO SHOTGUN

Gauge: 12, 20, 2¾" or 3" chamber.
Barrel: 26", 28", Mobilchoke choke tubes.
Weight: About 6½ lbs., 20-gauge; about 7½ lbs., 12-gauge.
Stock: American walnut; hand-checkered grip and forend.
Features: Gas-operated action, alloy receiver, magazine cut-off, push-button safety. Mobilchoke models come with three interchangeable flush-mounted screw-in choke tubes. Imported from Italy by Beretta U.S.A. Introduced 1983.
Price: Mobilchoke, 20-ga. **$755.00**
Price: 12-ga. trap with standard trap stock **$735.00**
Price: 12- or 20-ga., Skeet **$735.00**
Price: A-303 Youth Gun, 20-ga., 2¾" or 3" chamber, 24" barrel . . . **$735.00**
Price: A-303 Sporting Clays with Mobilchoke, 12 or 20 . . . . **$835.00**

Beretta A-303 Upland Model

Similar to the field A-303 except 12- or 20-gauge, has 24" vent. rib barrel with Mobilchoke choke tubes, 2¾" chamber, straight English-style stock. Introduced 1989.
Price: **$735.00**

Beretta A390 Super Trap

Beretta 390 Super Trap, Super Skeet Shotguns

Similar to the 390 Field except have adjustable-comb stocks that allow height adjustments via interchangeable comb inserts. Rounded recoil pad system allows adjustments for length of pull. Wide ventilated rib with orange front sight. Factory ported barrels in 28" (fixed Skeet), 30", 32" (Mobilchoke tubes). Weight 7 lbs., 10 oz. In 12-gauge only, with 2¾" chamber. Introduced 1993. Imported from Italy by Beretta U.S.A.
Price: 390 Super Trap **$1,210.00**
Price: 390 Super Skeet **$1,160.00**

BERETTA 390 FIELD AUTO SHOTGUN
Gauge: 12, 3" chamber.
Barrel: 24", 26", 28", 30", Mobilchoke choke tubes.
Weight: About 7 lbs.
Stock: Select walnut. Adjustable drop and cast.
Features: Gas-operated action with self-compensating valve allows shooting all loads without adjustment. Alloy receiver, reversible safety; chrome-plated bore; floating vent. rib. Matte-finish models for turkey/waterfowl and Deluxe with gold, engraving also available. Introduced 1992. Imported from Italy by Beretta U.S.A.
Price: **$775.00**
Price: Model 390 Field (matte finish) **$775.00**
Price: Deluxe model **$935.00**

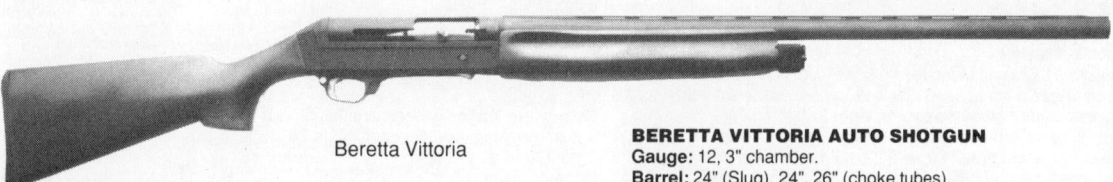

Beretta Vittoria

BERETTA MODEL 1201F AUTO SHOTGUN
Gauge: 12, 3" chamber.
Barrel: 24", 26", 28" vent. rib with Mobilchoke choke tubes.
Weight: 7 lbs., 4 oz.
Stock: Special strengthened technopolymer, matte black finish. Adjustable butt and recoil pad.
Features: Resists abrasion and adverse effects of water, salt and other damaging materials associated with tough field conditions. Imported from Italy by Beretta U.S.A. Introduced 1988.
Price: **$625.00**

BERETTA VITTORIA AUTO SHOTGUN
Gauge: 12, 3" chamber.
Barrel: 24" (Slug), 24", 26" (choke tubes).
Weight: 7 lbs.
Stock: Checkered walnut.
Features: Montefeltro-type short recoil action. Matte finish on wood and metal. Slug version has rifle sights and rifled choke tube. Comes with sling swivels. Introduced 1993. Imported from Italy by Beretta U.S.A.
Price: **$700.00**

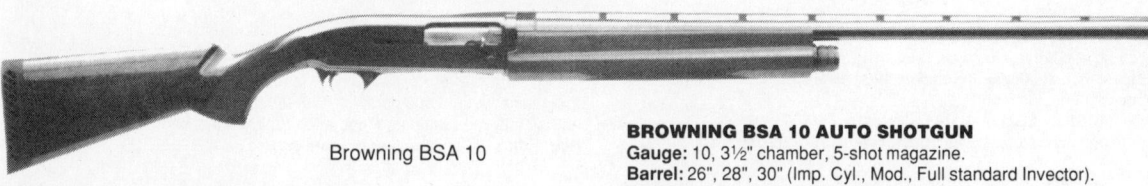

Browning BSA 10

Browning BSA 10 Stalker Auto Shotgun

Same as the standard BSA 10 except has non-glare metal finish and black graphite-fiberglass composite stock with dull finish and checkering. Introduced 1993. Imported by Browning.
Price: **$899.95**
Price: Extra barrel **$229.95**

BROWNING BSA 10 AUTO SHOTGUN
Gauge: 10, 3½" chamber, 5-shot magazine.
Barrel: 26", 28", 30" (Imp. Cyl., Mod., Full standard Invector).
Weight: 10 lbs, 7 oz. (28" barrel).
Stock: 14⅜"x1½"x2⅜". Select walnut with gloss finish, cut checkering, recoil pad.
Features: Short-stroke, gas-operated action, cross-bolt safety. Forged steel receiver with polished blue finish. Introduced 1993. Imported by Browning.
Price: **$899.95**
Price: Extra barrel **$229.95**

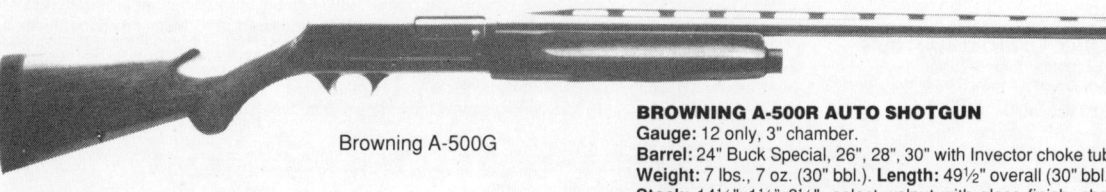

Browning A-500G

BROWNING A-500G AUTO SHOTGUN
Gauge: 12, 3" chamber.
Barrel: 26", 28", 30", Invector choke tubes. Ventilated rib.
Weight: 7 lbs., 14 oz. (26" bbl.). **Length:** 47½" overall.
Stock: 14⅜"x1½"x2". Select walnut with gloss finish, rounded pistol grip. Recoil pad standard.
Features: Gas-operated action with four-lug rotary bolt, cross-bolt safety. Interchangeable barrels. High-polish blue finish with light engraving on receiver and "A-500G" in gold color. Patented gas metering system to handle all loads. Built-in buffering system to absorb recoil, reduce stress on internal parts. Introduced 1990. Imported by Browning.
Price: **$652.95**
Price: Extra Invector barrels **$254.95**

BROWNING A-500R AUTO SHOTGUN
Gauge: 12 only, 3" chamber.
Barrel: 24" Buck Special, 26", 28", 30" with Invector choke tubes.
Weight: 7 lbs., 7 oz. (30" bbl.). **Length:** 49½" overall (30" bbl.).
Stock: 14¼"x1½"x2½"; select walnut with gloss finish; checkered p.g. and forend; black vent., recoil pad.
Sights: Metal bead front.
Features: Uses a short-recoil action with four-lug rotary bolt and composite and coil spring buffering system. Shoots all loads without adjustment. Has a magazine cut-off, Invector chokes. Introduced 1987. Imported from Belgium by Browning.
Price: **$559.95**
Price: A-500R Buck Special **$592.95**
Price: Extra Invector barrel **$199.95**
Price: 24" Buck Special barrel **$232.95**

Browning A-500G Sporting Clays
Same as the standard A-500G except has 28" or 30" Invector choke barrel, receiver has semi-gloss finish with "Sporting Clays" in gold lettering. Introduced 1992.
Price: **$652.95**

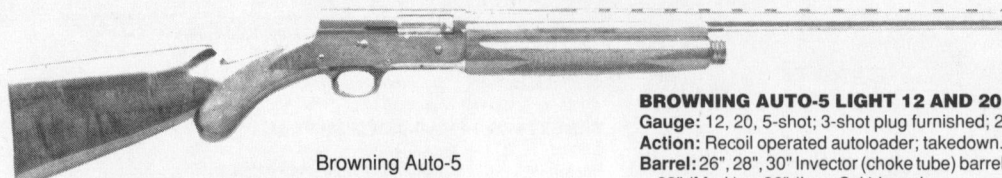

Browning Auto-5

CONSULT **Shooter's Marketplace** Page 231, This Issue

Browning Auto-5 Stalker

Similar to the Auto-5 Light and Magnum models except has matte blue metal finish and black graphite-fiberglass stock and forend. Stock is scratch and impact resistant and has checkered panels. Light Stalker has 2¾" chamber, 26" or 28" vent. rib barrel with Invector choke tubes, weighs 8 lbs., 1 oz. (26"). Magnum Stalker has 3" chamber, 28" or 30" back-bored vent. rib barrel with Invector choke tubes, weighs 8 lbs., 11 oz. (28"). Introduced 1992.
Price: Light Stalker **$734.95**
Price: Magnum Stalker **$756.95**

CHURCHILL TURKEY AUTOMATIC SHOTGUN

Gauge: 12, 3" chamber, 5-shot magazine.
Barrel: 25" (Mod., Full, Extra Full choke tubes).
Weight: 7 lbs. **Length:** NA.
Stock: Walnut with satin finish, hand checkering.
Features: Gas-operated action, magazine cut-off, non-glare metal finish. Gold-colored trigger. Introduced 1990. Imported by Ellett Bros.
Price: **$569.95**

COSMI AUTOMATIC SHOTGUN

Gauge: 12 or 20, 2¾" or 3" chamber.
Barrel: 22" to 34". Choke (including choke tubes) and length to customer specs. Boehler steel.
Weight: About 6¼ lbs. (20-ga.).
Stock: Length and style to customer specs. Hand-checkered exhibition grade

BROWNING AUTO-5 LIGHT 12 AND 20

Gauge: 12, 20, 5-shot; 3-shot plug furnished; 2¾" or 3" chamber.
Action: Recoil operated autoloader; takedown.
Barrel: 26", 28", 30" Invector (choke tube) barrel; also available with Light 20-ga. 28" (Mod.) or 26" (Imp. Cyl.) barrel.
Weight: 12-, 16-ga. 7¼ lbs.; 20-ga. 6⅜ lbs.
Stock: French walnut, hand checkered half-p.g. and forend. 14¼"x1⅝"x2½".
Features: Receiver hand engraved with scroll designs and border. Double extractors, extra bbls. Interchangeable without factory fitting; mag. cut-off; cross-bolt safety. All 12-gauge models except Buck Special and game guns have back-bored barrels with Invector Plus choke tubes. Imported from Japan by Browning.
Price: Light 12, 20, vent. rib., standard Invector **$719.95**
Price: Extra Invector barrel **$249.95**
Price: Light 12 Buck Special **$724.95**
Price: Extra fixed-choke barrel (Light 20 only) **$194.95**
Price: 12, 12 magnum, 20 Buck Special barrel **$259.95**
Price: Light 12, Hunting, Invector Plus **$734.95**

Browning Auto-5 Magnum 20

Same as Magnum 12 except 26" or 28" barrel with Invector choke tubes. With ventilated rib, 7½ lbs.
Price: Invector only **$742.95**
Price: Extra Invector barrel **$249.95**

Browning Auto-5 Magnum 12

Same as standard Auto-5 except chambered for 3" magnum shells (also handles 2¾" magnum and 2¾" HV loads). 28" Mod., Full; 30" and 32" (Full) bbls. Back-bored barrel comes with Invector choke tubes. 14"x1⅝"x2½" stock. Recoil pad. Wgt. 8¾ lbs.
Price: With standard Invector choke tubes **$742.95**
Price: Extra standard Invector barrel **$249.95**
Price: With back-bored barrel, Invector Plus **$756.95**
Price: Extra Invector Plus barrel **$269.95**

circassian walnut standard.
Features: Hand-made, essentially a custom gun. Recoil-operated auto with tip-up barrel. Made completely of stainless steel (lower receiver polished); magazine tube in buttstock holds 7 rounds. Double ejectors, double safety system. Comes with fitted leather case. Imported from Italy by Incor, Inc.
Price: From **$7,400.00**

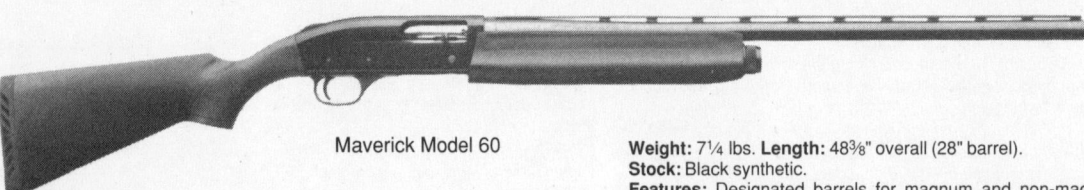

Maverick Model 60

MAVERICK MODEL 60 AUTO SHOTGUN

Gauge: 12, 2¾" or 3" chamber, 5-shot.
Barrel: 18½" (2¾" only, Cyl. bore), 24" (Full and Rifled choke tubes), 28" vent rib (Accu-Choke Mod. tube).

Weight: 7¼ lbs. **Length:** 48⅜" overall (28" barrel).
Stock: Black synthetic.
Features: Designated barrels for magnum and non-magnum loads. Blued receiver with action release button. Introduced 1993. Made in U.S. by Maverick Arms, Inc.
Price: 28" magnum or non-magnum **$279.00**
Price: Combo with 18½" and 28" barrels **$312.00**
Price: Turkey/Deer, Ghost Ring sights, tube combo **$324.00**

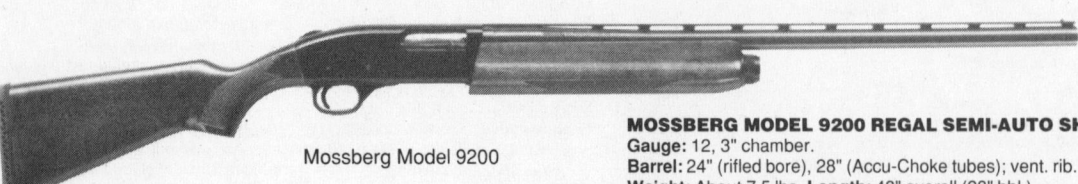

Mossberg Model 9200

MOSSBERG MODEL 9200 REGAL SEMI-AUTO SHOTGUN

Gauge: 12, 3" chamber.
Barrel: 24" (rifled bore), 28" (Accu-Choke tubes); vent. rib.
Weight: About 7.5 lbs. **Length:** 48" overall (28" bbl.).
Stock: Walnut with high-gloss finish.
Features: Shoots all 2¾" or 3" loads without adjustment. Alloy receiver, ambidextrous top safety. Introduced 1992.
Price: 28", vent rib **$374.00**
Price: Turkey, 24" vent rib **$374.00**
Price: Trophy, 24" with scope base, rifled bore, Dual-Comb stock . . **$393.00**
Price: 24", rifle sights, rifled bore **$374.00**
Price: Combo 24" Trophy with scope base, rifled bore, Dual-Comb, and 28" vent rib with Accu-Choke tubes **$441.00**
Price: Combo 24", rifle sights, rifled bore, and 28" vent rib, Accu-Choke tubes **$433.00**

Mossberg Model 9200 USST Auto Shotgun

Same as the Model 9200 Regal except has "United States Shooting Team" custom engraved receiver. Comes with 26" vent rib barrel with Accu-Choke tubes (including Skeet), walnut-finish stock and forend. Introduced 1993.
Price: **$374.00**

Mossberg Model 9200 Camo Shotgun

Same as the Model 9200 Regal except completely covered with Mossy Oak Tree Stand or OFM camouflage finish. Available with 24" or 28" barrel with Accu-Choke tubes, or 24" rifled bore with rifle sights, and 28" vent rib with Accu-Choke tubes as Combo model. All have synthetic stock and forend. Introduced 1993.
Price: Turkey, 24" vent rib, Mossy Oak finish **$436.00**
Price: 28" vent rib, Accu-Chokes, OFM camo finish **$393.00**
Price: Combo, 24", rifled bore, rifle sights, with 28" vent rib, Accu-Chokes, OFM camo finish **$456.000**

Mossberg Model 6000 Auto Shotgun

Similar to the Model 9200 Regal except comes only with 28" vent rib barrel— Magnum shoots 2¾" or 3" loads, Non-Magnum 2¾" only. Supplied with one Mod. Accu-Choke tube. Walnut-finish stock and forend. Introduced 1993.
Price: **$321.00**

Remington 11-87 Sporting Clays

REMINGTON 11-87 SPORTING CLAYS

Gauge: 12, 2¾" chamber
Barrel: 26", 28", vent. rib, Rem Choke (Skeet, Imp. Cyl., Mod., Full); Light Contour barrel. Medium height rib.
Weight: 7.5 lbs. **Length:** 46.5" overall (26" barrel).
Stock: 14³⁄₁₆"x1½"x2¼". Walnut, with cut checkering; sporting clays butt pad.
Features: Top of receiver, barrel and rib have matte finish; shortened magazine tube and forend; lengthened forcing cone; ivory bead front sight; competition trigger. Special no-wrench choke tubes marked on the outside. Comes in two-barrel fitted hard case. Introduced 1992.
Price: **$725.00**

Remington 11-87 Premier Skeet

Similar to 11-87 Premier except Skeet dimension stock with cut checkering, satin finish, two-piece buttplate; 26" barrel with Skeet or Rem Chokes (Skeet, Imp. Skeet). Gas system set for 2¾" shells only. Introduced 1987.
Price: **$669.00**
Price: Left-hand **$735.00**

REMINGTON 11-87 PREMIER SHOTGUN

Gauge: 12, 3" chamber.
Barrel: 26", 28", 30" Rem Choke tubes. Light Contour barrel.
Weight: About 8¼ lbs. **Length:** 46" overall (26" bbl.).
Stock: Walnut with satin or high-gloss finish; cut checkering; solid brown buttpad; no white spacers.
Sights: Bradley-type white-faced front, metal bead middle.
Features: Pressure compensating gas system allows shooting 2¾" or 3" loads interchangeably with no adjustments. Stainless magazine tube; redesigned feed latch, barrel support ring on operating bars; pinned forend. Introduced 1987.
Price: **$637.00**
Price: Left-hand **$699.00**
Price: Premier Cantilever Deer Barrel, scope rings, sling, swivels, Monte Carlo stock **$679.00**

Remington 11-87 Premier Trap

Similar to 11-87 Premier except trap dimension stock with straight or Monte Carlo combs; select walnut with satin finish and Tournament-grade cut checkering; 30" barrel with Rem Chokes (Trap Full, Trap Extra Full, Trap Super Full). Gas system set for 2¾" shells only. Introduced 1987.
Price: With straight stock, Rem Choke **$667.00**
Price: With Monte Carlo stock **$692.00**
Price: Left-hand, straight stock **$745.00**
Price: Left-hand, Monte Carlo stock **$761.00**

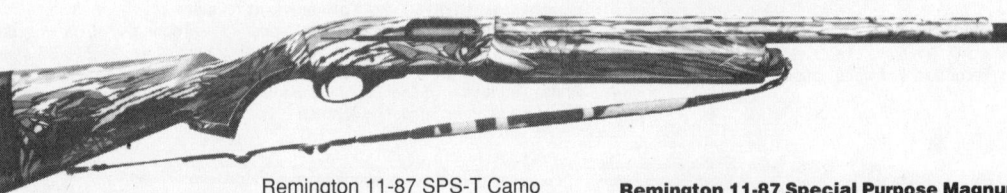

Remington 11-87 SPS-T Camo

Remington 11-87 SPS-T Camo Auto Shotgun

Similar to the 11-87 Special Purpose Magnum except with synthetic stock, 21" vent rib barrel with Super-Full Turkey (.665" diameter with knurled extension) and Imp. Cyl. Rem Choke tubes. Completely covered with Mossy Oak Green Leaf camouflage. Bolt body, trigger guard and recoil pad are non-reflective black. Introduced 1993.
Price: **$700.00**

Remington 11-87 Special Purpose Magnum

Similar to the 11-87 Premier except has dull stock finish, Parkerized exposed metal surfaces. Bolt and carrier have dull blackened coloring. Comes with 26" or 28" barrel with Rem Chokes, padded Cordura nylon sling and q.d. swivels. Introduced 1987.
Price: **$619.00**
Price: With synthetic stock and forend (SPS) **$619.00**
Price: Magnum-Turkey with synthetic stock (SPS-T) **$632.00**

Remington 11-87 Special Purpose Deer Gun

Similar to the 11-87 Special Purpose Magnum except has 21" barrel with rifle sights, rifled and Imp. Cyl. choke tubes. Gas system set to handle all 2¾" and 3" slug, buckshot, high velocity field and magnum loads. Not designed to function with light 2¾" field loads. Introduced 1987.
Price: **$599.00**
Price: With cantilever scope mount, rings **$653.00**

Remington 11-87 SPS-Deer Shotgun

Similar to the 11-87 Special Purpose Deer except has fully-rifled 21" barrel with rifle sights, black non-reflective, synthetic stock and forend, black carrying sling. Introduced 1993.
Price: **$625.00**

Remington 11-87 SPS-BG-Camo Deer/Turkey Shotgun

Similar to the 11-87 Special Purpose Deer Gun except completely covered with Mossy Oak Bottomland camouflage, comes with Super-Full Turkey Rem Choke tube of .665" diameter with knurled end-ring, Rifled choke tube insert, and an Imp. Cyl. tube. Synthetic stock and forend, quick-detachable swivels, camo Cordura carrying sling. Barrel is 21" with rifle sights, 3" chamber. Introduced 1993.
Price: **$683.00**

Remington 11-87 Special Purpose Synthetic Camo

Similar to the 11-87 Special Purpose Magnum except has synthetic stock and all metal (except bolt and trigger guard) and stock covered with Mossy Oak Bottomland camo finish. In 12-gauge only, 26", 28" vent. rib, Rem Choke. Comes with camo sling, swivels. Introduced 1992.
Price: **$687.00**

Remington 11-87 SPS-BG Camo

SHOTGUNS—AUTOLOADERS

Remington SP-10 Magnum Camo

Remington SP-10 Magnum-Camo Auto Shotgun

Similar to the SP-10 Magnum except buttstock, forend, receiver, barrel and magazine cap are covered with Mossy Oak Bottomland camo finish; bolt body and trigger guard have matte black finish. Comes with Extra-Full Turkey Rem Choke tube, 23" vent rib barrel with mid-rib bead and Bradley-style front sight, swivel studs and quick-detachable swivels, and a non-slip Cordura carrying sling in the same camo pattern. Introduced 1993.

Price: $1,105.00

REMINGTON SP-10 MAGNUM AUTO SHOTGUN

Gauge: 10, 3½" chamber, 3-shot magazine.
Barrel: 26", 30" (Full and Mod. Rem Chokes).
Weight: 11 to 11¼ lbs. **Length:** 47½" overall (26" barrel).
Stock: Walnut with satin finish. Checkered grip and forend.
Sights: Metal bead front.
Features: Stainless steel gas system with moving cylinder; ³⁄₈" ventilated rib. Receiver and barrel have matte finish. Brown recoil pad. Comes with padded Cordura nylon sling. Introduced 1989.

Price: $966.00

Remington SP-10 Magnum Turkey Combo

Combines the SP 10 with 26" or 30" vent. rib barrel, plus extra 22" rifle-sighted barrel with Mod., Full, Extra-Full Turkey Rem Choke tubes. Comes with camo sling, swivels. Introduced 1991.

Price: $1,104.00

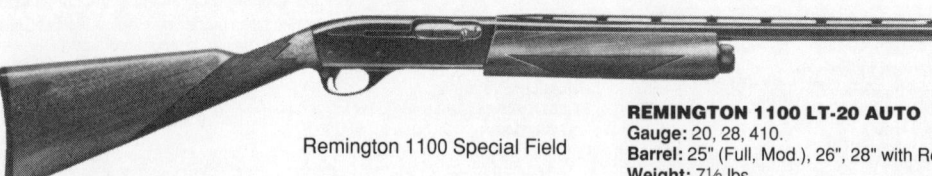

Remington 1100 Special Field

Remington 1100 Special Field

Similar to standard Model 1100 except 12- and 20-ga. only, comes with 21" Rem Choke barrel. LT-20 version 6½ lbs.; has straight-grip stock, shorter forend, both with cut checkering. Comes with vent. rib only; matte finish receiver without engraving. Introduced 1983.

Price: 12- and 20-ga., 21" Rem Choke, about $589.00

Remington 1100 20-Gauge Deer Gun

Same as 1100 except 20-ga. only, 21" barrel (Imp. Cyl.), rifle sights adjustable for windage and elevation; recoil pad with white spacer. Weight 7¼ lbs.

Price: About $532.00

REMINGTON 1100 LT-20 AUTO

Gauge: 20, 28, 410.
Barrel: 25" (Full, Mod.), 26", 28" with Rem Chokes.
Weight: 7½ lbs.
Stock: 14"x1½"x2½". American walnut, checkered p.g. and forend.
Features: Quickly interchangeable barrels. Matted receiver top with scroll work on both sides of receiver. Cross-bolt safety.

Price: With Rem Chokes, 20-ga. about $589.00
Price: 28 and 410 . . . . $633.00
Price: Youth Gun LT-20 (21" Rem Choke) $576.00
Price: 20-ga., 3" magnum $589.00

Remington 1100 LT-20 Tournament Skeet

Same as the 1100 except 26" barrel, special Skeet boring, vent. rib, ivory bead front and metal bead middle sights. 14"x1½"x2½" stock. 20-, 28-gauge, 410-bore. Weight 7½ lbs., cut checkering, walnut, new receiver scroll.

Price: Tournament Skeet (28, 410), about $670.00
Price: Tournament Skeet (20), about $670.00

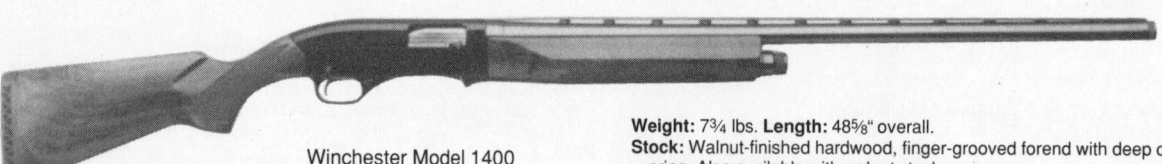

Winchester Model 1400

WINCHESTER MODEL 1400 SEMI-AUTO SHOTGUN

Gauge: 12 and 20, 2¾" chamber.
Barrel: 22", 26", 28" vent. rib with Winchoke tubes (Imp. Cyl., Mod., Full).

Weight: 7¾ lbs. **Length:** 48⅝" overall.
Stock: Walnut-finished hardwood, finger-grooved forend with deep cut checkering. Also available with walnut stock.
Sights: Metal bead front.
Features: Cross-bolt safety, front-locking rotary bolt, black serrated buttplate, gas-operated action. From U.S. Repeating Arms Co., Inc.

Price: Ranger, vent. rib with Winchoke $367.00
Price: As above with walnut stock (1400 Walnut) $407.00
Price: Ranger Deer barrel combo $423.00

SHOTGUNS—SLIDE ACTIONS

Includes a wide variety of sporting guns and guns suitable for competitive shooting.

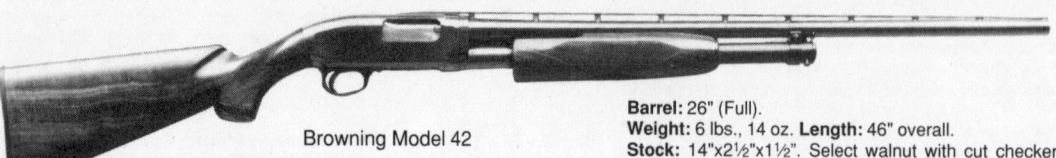

Browning Model 42

BROWNING MODEL 42 PUMP SHOTGUN

Gauge: 410-bore, 3" chamber.

Barrel: 26" (Full).
Weight: 6 lbs., 14 oz. **Length:** 46" overall.
Stock: 14"x2½"x1½". Select walnut with cut checkering, semi-gloss finish; Grade V has high-grade walnut.
Features: Reproduction of the Winchester Model 42. Has high post floating rib with grooved sighting plane; cross-bolt safety in trigger guard; polished blue finish. Limited to 6000 Grade I and 6000 Grade V guns. Introduced 1991. Imported from Japan by Browning.

Price: Model 42, Grade I $799.95
Price: Model 42, Grade V $1,360.00

CAUTION: PRICES CHANGE, CHECK AT GUNSHOP.

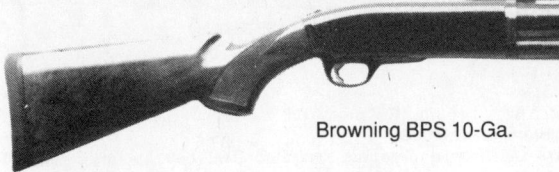

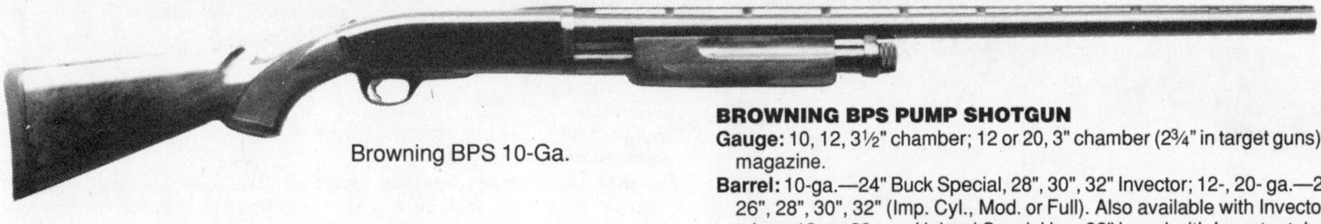

Browning BPS 10-Ga.

Browning BPS Stalker Pump Shotgun

Same gun as the standard BPS except all exposed metal parts have a matte blued finish and the stock has a durable black finish with a black recoil pad. Available in 10-ga. (3½") and 12-ga. with 3" or 3½" chamber, 22", 28", 30" barrel with Invector choke system. Introduced 1987.

Price: 12-ga., 3" chamber, Invector Plus $462.95
Price: 10-, 12-ga., 3½" chamber $584.95

Browning BPS Pigeon Grade Pump shotgun

Same as the standard BPS except has select high grade walnut stock and forend, and gold-trimmed receiver. Available in 12-gauge only with 26" or 28" vent. rib barrels. Introduced 1992.

Price: $599.95
Price: 10-gauge Waterfowl Model $749.95

Browning BPS Pump Shotgun (Ladies and Youth Model)

Same as BPS Upland Special except 20-ga. only, 22" Invector barrel, stock has pistol grip with recoil pad. Length of pull is 13¼". Introduced 1986.

Price: $442.95

BROWNING BPS PUMP SHOTGUN

Gauge: 10, 12, 3½" chamber; 12 or 20, 3" chamber (2¾" in target guns), 5-shot magazine.
Barrel: 10-ga.—24" Buck Special, 28", 30", 32" Invector; 12-, 20- ga.—22", 24", 26", 28", 30", 32" (Imp. Cyl., Mod. or Full). Also available with Invector choke tubes, 12- or 20-ga.; Upland Special has 22" barrel with Invector tubes. BPS 3" and 3½" have back-bored barrel.
Weight: 7 lbs., 8 oz. (28" barrel). **Length:** 48¾" overall (28" barrel).
Stock: 14¼"x1½"x2½". Select walnut, semi-beavertail forend, full p.g. stock.
Features: All 12-gauge 3" guns except Buck Special and game guns have back-bored barrels with Invector Plus choke tubes. Bottom feeding and ejection, receiver top safety, high post vent. rib. Double action bars eliminate binding. Vent. rib barrels only. All 12- and 20-gauge guns with 3" chamber available with fully engraved receiver flats at no extra cost. Each gsuge has its own unique game scene. Introduced 1977. Imported from Japan by Browning.

Price: 10-ga., Hunting, Invector $584.95
Price: 12-ga., 3½" Mag., Hunting, Invector Plus $584.95
Price: 12-ga., Hunting, Invector Plus $462.95
Price: 12-, 20-ga., Upland Special, Invector $442.95
Price: 10-ga. and 3½" 12-ga. Mag., Buck Special $589.95
Price: 12-ga. Buck Special $448.95

Browning BPS Game Gun Turkey Special

Similar to the Model 87 Supreme except has satin-finished walnut stock and dull-finished barrel and receiver. Receiver is drilled and tapped for scope mounting. Rifle-style stock dimensions and swivel studs. Has Extra-Full Turkey choke tube. Introduced 1992.

Price: $499.95

Browning BPS Game Deer

Browning BPS Game Gun Deer Special

Similar to the standard BPS except has newly designed receiver/magazine tube/barrel mounting system to eliminate play, heavy 20.5" barrel with rifle-type sights with adjustable rear, solid receiver scope mount, "rifle" stock dimensions for scope or open sights, sling swivel studs. Gloss-finish wood with checkering, polished blue metal. Introduced 1992.

Price: $527.95

Ithaca Model 87 Supreme

ITHACA MODEL 87 DEERSLAYER SHOTGUN

Gauge: 12, 20, 3" chamber.
Barrel: 20", 25" (Special Bore), or rifled bore.
Weight: 6 to 6¾ lbs.
Stock: 14"x1½"x2¼". American walnut. Checkered p.g. and slide handle.
Sights: Raybar blade front on ramp, rear adjustable for windage and elevation, and grooved for scope mounting.
Features: Bored for slug shooting. Bottom ejection, cross-bolt safety. Reintroduced 1988. From Ithaca Acquisition Corp.

Price: $391.00
Price: Deluxe $430.00
Price: Field Deerslayer, Basic $363.00

Ithaca Model 87 Turkey Gun

Similar to the Model 87 Supreme except comes with 22" or 24" (fixed Full or Full choke tube) barrel, either Camoseal camouflage or matte blue finish, oiled wood, blued trigger.

Price: With fixed choke, blue $380.00
Price: With choke tube, blue $394.00
Price: With fixed choke, Camoseal $422.00
Price: With choke tube, Camoseal $436.00

ITHACA MODEL 87 SUPREME PUMP SHOTGUN

Gauge: 12, 20, 3" chamber, 5-shot magazine.
Barrel: 26" (Imp. Cyl., Mod., Full tubes), 28" (Mod.), 30" (Full). Vent. rib.
Weight: 6¾ to 7 lbs.
Stock: 14"x1½"x2¼". Full fancy-grade walnut, checkered p.g. and slide handle.
Sights: Raybar front.
Features: Bottom ejection, cross-bolt safety. Polished and blued engraved receiver. Reintroduced 1988. From Ithaca Acquisition Corp.

Price: $668.00
Price: M87 Camo Vent. (28", Mod. choke tube, camouflage finish) . $457.00
Price: M87 English (20-ga., 24", 26", choke tubes) $462.50
Price: M87 Deluxe Vent, 12, 20, 26", 28", 30", choke tubes $462.50

Ithaca Deerslayer II Rifled Shotgun

Similar to the Deerslayer except has rifled 25" barrel and checkered American walnut stock and forend with high-gloss finish and Monte Carlo comb. Solid frame construction. Introduced 1988.

Price: 12 or 20 . . . . $525.00

Ithaca Model 87 Deluxe Pump Shotgun

Similar to the Model 87 Supreme Vent. Rib except comes with choke tubes in 25", 26", 28" (Mod.), 30" (Full). Standard-grade walnut.

Price: $463.00

Magtech Model 586-VR

MAGTECH MODEL 586-VR PUMP SHOTGUN
Gauge: 12, 3" chamber.
Barrel: 26", 28", choke tubes.

Weight: 8.5 lbs. **Length:** 46.5" overall (26" barrel).
Stock: Brazilian hardwood.
Features: Double action slide bars. Ventilated rib with bead front sight. Polished blue finish. Introduced 1993. Imported from Brazil by Magtech Recreational Products.
Price: Model 586-VR, about **$255.00**
Price: Model 586 (as above, plain barrel), about **$225.00**
Price: Model 586-S (24" barrel, rifle sights), about **$235.00**

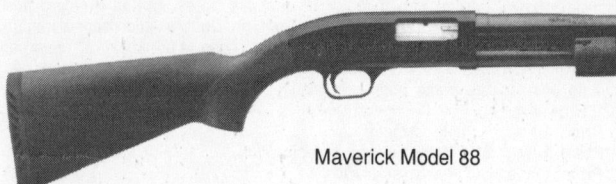

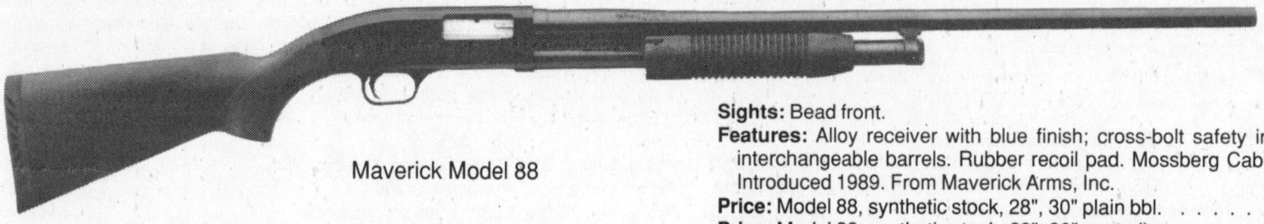

Maverick Model 88

MAVERICK MODELS 88, 91 PUMP SHOTGUNS
Gauge: 12, 3" chamber; 3½" chamber (Model 91).
Barrel: 18½" (Cyl.), 28" (Mod.), plain or vent. rib; 30" (Full), plain or vent. rib.
Weight: 7¼ lbs. **Length:** 48" overall with 28" bbl.
Stock: Black synthetic with ribbed synthetic forend.

Sights: Bead front.
Features: Alloy receiver with blue finish; cross-bolt safety in trigger guard; interchangeable barrels. Rubber recoil pad. Mossberg Cablelock included. Introduced 1989. From Maverick Arms, Inc.
Price: Model 88, synthetic stock, 28", 30" plain bbl. **$205.00**
Price: Model 88, synthetic stock, 28", 30" vent. rib **$212.00**
Price: Model 88, synthetic stock, 24" with rifle sights **$215.00**
Price: Model 88, synthetic stock, Combo 18½", 28" plain bbl. **$230.00**
Price: Model 88, synthetic stock, Combo 18½" (plain), 28" (vent. rib) **$238.00**
Price: Model 91, synthetic stock, 28" plain bbl. with one Full steel shot choke tube **$226.00**
Price: As above, vent. rib bbl. **$234.00**

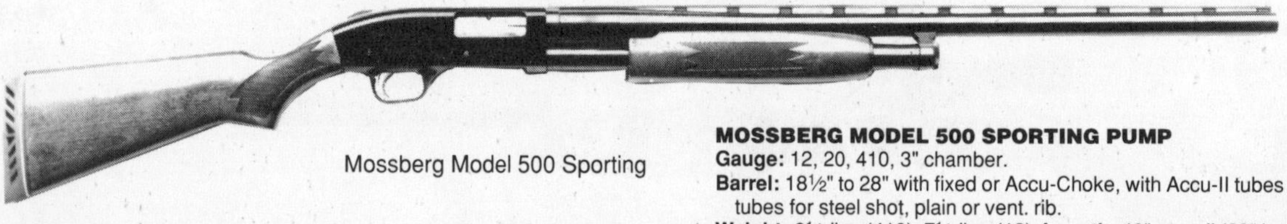

Mossberg Model 500 Sporting

Mossberg Model 500 Camo Pump
Same as the Model 500 Sporting Pump except 12-gauge only and entire gun is covered with special camouflage finish. Receiver drilled and tapped for scope mounting. Comes with q.d. swivel studs, swivels, camouflage sling, Mossberg Cablelock.
Price: From about **$299.00**
Price: Camo Combo (as above with extra Slugster barrel), from about **$353.00**

MOSSBERG MODEL 500 TROPHY SLUGSTER
Gauge: 12, 3" chamber.
Barrel: 24", rifled bore. Plain (no rib).
Weight: 7¼ lbs. **Length:** 44" overall.
Stock: 14" pull, 1⅜" drop at heel. Walnut; Dual Comb design for proper eye positioning with or without scoped barrels. Recoil pad and swivel studs.
Features: Ambidextrous thumb safety, twin extractors, dual slide bars. Comes with scope mount. Mossberg Cablelock included. Introduced 1988.
Price: Rifled bore, with scope mount **$327.00**
Price: Rifled bore, rifle sights **$300.00**
Price: Cyl. bore. rifle sights **$266.00**

MOSSBERG MODEL 500 SPORTING PUMP
Gauge: 12, 20, 410, 3" chamber.
Barrel: 18½" to 28" with fixed or Accu-Choke, with Accu-II tubes or Accu-Steel tubes for steel shot, plain or vent. rib.
Weight: 6¼ lbs. (410), 7¼ lbs. (12). **Length:** 48" overall (28" barrel).
Stock: 14"x1½"x2½". Walnut-stained hardwood. Checkered grip and forend.
Sights: White bead front, brass mid-bead.
Features: Ambidextrous thumb safety, twin extractors, disconnecting safety, dual action bars. Mossberg Cablelock included. From Mossberg.
Price: From about **$253.00**
Price: Sporting Combos (field barrel and Slugster barrel), from . . . **$281.00**

Mossberg Model 500 Muzzleloader Combo
Same as the Model 500 Sporting Pump except comes with 28" vent. rib Accu-Choke barrel with Imp. Cyl., Mod. and Full choke tubes and 24" fully rifled 50-caliber muzzle-loading barrel and ramrod. Uses #209 standard primer. Introduced 1992.
Price: **$399.00**

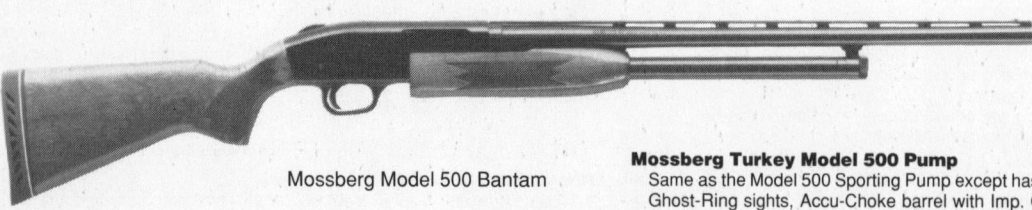

Mossberg Model 500 Bantam

Mossberg Model 500 Bantam Pump
Same as the Model 500 Sporting Pump except 20-gauge only, 22" vent. rib Accu-Choke barrel with three choke tubes; has 1" shorter stock, reduced length from pistol grip to trigger, reduced forend reach. Introduced 1992.
Price: **$253.00**
Price: Bantam Jake, Accu-Choke tubes, matte blue, Realtree camo on stock and forend **$318.00**

Mossberg Turkey Model 500 Pump
Same as the Model 500 Sporting Pump except has overall OFM camo finish, Ghost-Ring sights, Accu-Choke barrel with Imp. Cyl., Mod., Full, Extra-Full lead shot choke tubes, 24" barrel, swivel studs, camo sling. Introduced 1992.
Price: **$353.00**

Mossberg Field Grade Model 835 Pump Shotgun
Same as the Model 835 Regal except has walnut-stained hardwood stock and comes only with Modified choke tube, 28" barrel. Introduced 1992.
Price: **$284.00**
Price: Turkey, 24", Extra-Full choke tube **$284.00**
Price: Combo, 24" Cyl. bore, rifle sights, and 28" vent rib with Mod. tube **$321.00**

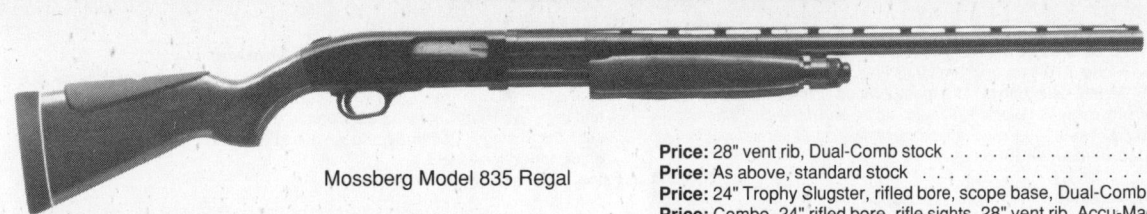

Mossberg Model 835 Regal

MOSSBERG MODEL 835 REGAL ULTI-MAG PUMP

Gauge: 12, 3½" chamber.
Barrel: 24" rifled bore, 24", 28", Accu-Mag with four choke tubes for steel or lead shot.
Weight: 7¾ lbs. **Length:** 48½" overall.
Stock: 14"x1½"x2½". Dual Comb. Walnut or camo synthetic; both have recoil pad.
Sights: White bead front, brass mid-bead.
Features: Shoots 2¾", 3" or 3½" shells. Backbored barrel to reduce recoil, improve patterns. Ambidextrous thumb safety, twin extractors, dual slide bars. Mossberg Cablelock included. Introduced 1988.

Price: 28" vent rib, Dual-Comb stock **$381.00**
Price: As above, standard stock **$374.00**
Price: 24" Trophy Slugster, rifled bore, scope base, Dual-Comb stock **$400.00**
Price: Combo, 24" rifled bore, rifle sights, 28" vent rib, Accu-Mag choke tubes, Dual-Comb stock **$429.00**
Price: Combo, 24" Trophy Slugster rifled bore, 28" vent rib, Accu-Mag choke tubes, Dual-Comb stock **$435.00**
Price: Realtree Camo Turkey, 24" vent rib, Accu-Mag Extra-Full tube, synthetic stock **$436.00**
Price: Realtree Camo, 28" vent rib, Accu-Mag tubes, synthetic stock **$436.00**
Price: Realtree Camo Combo, 24" rifled bore, rifle sights, 24" vent rib, Accu-Mag choke tubes, synthetic stock, hard case **$514.00**
Price: OFM Camo, 28" vent rib, Accu-Mag tubes, wood stock **$407.00**
Price: OFM Camo Combo, 24" rifled bore, rifle sights, 28" vent rib, Accu-Mag tubes, wood stock **$453.00**

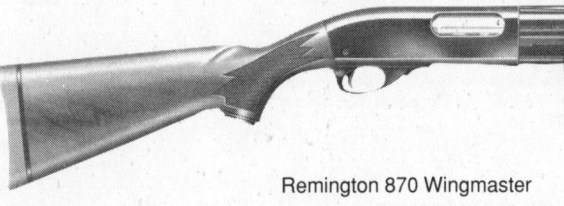

Remington 870 Wingmaster

Remington 870 Special Purpose Deer Gun

Similar to the 870 Wingmaster except available with 20" barrel with rifled and Imp. Cyl. choke tubes; rifle sights or cantilever scope mount with rings. Metal has black, non-glare finish, satin finish on wood. Recoil pad, detachable sling of camo Cordura nylon. Introduced 1989.
Price: With rifle sights, Monte Carlo stock **$412.00**
Price: With scope mount and rings, Monte Carlo stock **$497.00**

REMINGTON 870 WINGMASTER

Gauge: 12, 3" chamber.
Barrel: 26", 28", 30" (Rem Chokes). Light Contour barrel.
Weight: 7¼ lbs. **Length:** 46½" overall (26" bbl.).
Stock: 14"x2½"x1". American walnut with satin or high-gloss finish, cut-checkered p.g. and forend. Rubber buttpad.
Sights: Ivory bead front, metal mid-bead.
Features: Double action bars; cross-bolt safety; blue finish. Available in right- or left-hand style. Introduced 1986.
Price: **$469.00**
Price: Left-hand (28" only) **$529.00**
Price: Deer Gun (rifle sights, 20" bbl.) **$439.00**
Price: Deer Gun, left-hand, Monte Carlo stock **$495.00**
Price: LW-20 20-ga., vent. rib, 26", 28" (Rem Choke) **$460.00**

Remington 870 SPS-BG-Camo

Remington 870 SPS-Deer Shotgun

Similar to the 870 Special Purpose Deer excet has fully-rifled 20" barrel with rifle sights, black non-reflective, synthetic stock and forend, black carrying sling. Introduced 1993.
Price: **$385.00**

Remington 870 Marine Magnum

Similar to the 870 Wingmaster except all metal is plated with electroless nickel and has black synthetic stock and forend. Has 18" plain barrel (Cyl.), bead front sight, 7-shot magazine. Introduced 1992.
Price: **$448.00**

Remington 870 SPS-BG-Camo Deer/Turkey Shotgun

Similar to the 870 Special Purpose Deer Gun except completely covered with Mossy Oak Bottomland camouflage, comes with Super-Full Turkey Rem Choke tube of .665" diameter with knurled end-ring, Rifled choke tube insert, and an Imp. Cyl. tube. Synthetic stock and forend, quick-detachable swivels, camo Cordura carrying sling. Barrel is 20" with rifle sights, 3" chamber. Introduced 1993.
Price: **$443.00**

Remington 870 TC Trap

Same as the Model 870 except 12-ga. only, 30" Rem Choke, vent. rib barrel, Ivory front and white metal middle beads. Special sear, hammer and trigger assembly. 14⅜"x1½"x1⅞" stock with recoil pad. Hand fitted action and parts. Weight 8 lbs.
Price: Model 870TC Trap, Rem Choke, about **$613.00**
Price: TC Trap with Monte Carlo stock, about **$628.00**

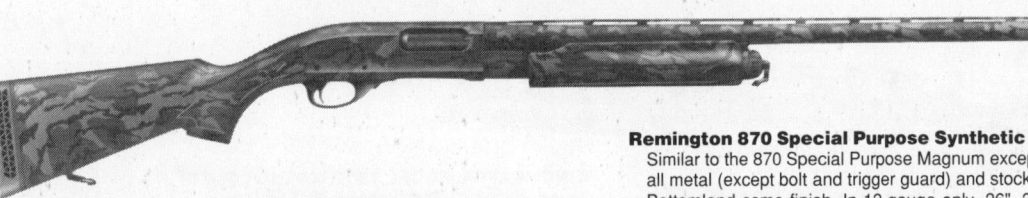

Remington 870 SPS Camo

Remington 870 Wingmaster Small Gauges

Same as the standard Model 870 Wingmaster except chambered for 20-ga. (2¾" and 3"), 28-ga., and 410-bore. The 20-ga. available with 26", 28" vent. rib barrel with Rem Choke tubes, high-gloss or satin wood finish; 28 and 410 available with 25" Full or Mod. fixed choke, satin finish only.
Price: 20-ga. **$460.00**
Price: 20-ga. Deer Gun, rifle sights **$412.00**
Price: 28 and 410 . . . . **$504.00**

Remington 870 Special Purpose Synthetic Camo

Similar to the 870 Special Purpose Magnum except has synthetic stock and all metal (except bolt and trigger guard) and stock covered with Mossy Oak Bottomland camo finish, In 12-gauge only, 26", 28" vent. rib, Rem Choke. Comes with camo sling, swivels. Introduced 1992.
Price: **$433.00**

Remington 870 Express Rifle-Sighted Deer Gun

Same as the Model 870 Express except comes with 20" barrel with fixed Imp. Cyl. choke, open iron sights, Monte Carlo stock. Introduced 1991.
Price: **$273.00**
Price: With fully rifled barrel **$304.00**

Remington 870 SPS Special Purpose Magnum

Similar to the Model 870 except chambered only for 12-ga., 3" shells, vent. rib. 26" or 28" Rem Choke barrel. All exposed metal surfaces are finished in dull, non-reflective black. Black synthetic stock and forend. Comes with padded Cordura 2" wide sling, quick-detachable swivels. Chrome-lined bores. Dark recoil pad. Introduced 1985.
Price: **$367.00**
Price: Magnum-Turkey (synthetic stock, forend) SPS-T **$393.00**

Remington 870 SPS-T Camo Pump Shotgun

Similar to the 870 Special Purpose Magnum except with synthetic stock, 21" vent rib barrel with Super-Full Turkey (.665" diameter with knurled extension) and Imp. Cyl. Rem Choke tubes. Completely covered with Mossy Oak Green Leaf camouflage. Bolt body, trigger guard and recoil pad are non-reflective black. Introduced 1993.
Price: **$447.00**

Remington 870 Special Field

Remington 870 Special Field

Similar to the standard Model 870 except comes with 21" barrel only, 3" chamber, choked Imp. Cyl., Mod., Full and Rem Choke; 12-ga. weighs 6¾ lbs., LW-20 weighs 6 lbs.; has straight-grip stock, shorter forend, both with cut checkering. Vent. rib barrel only. Introduced 1984.
Price: 12- or 20-ga., Rem Choke, about **$460.00**

Remington Model 870 Express Youth Gun

Same as the Model 870 Express except comes with 12½" length of pull, 21" barrel with Mod. Rem Choke tube. Hardwood stock with low-luster finish. Introduced 1991.
Price: **$277.00**

Remington 870 Express Turkey

Same as the Model 870 Express except comes with 3" chamber, 21" vent. rib turkey barrel and Extra-Full Rem Choke Turkey tube; 12-ga. only. Introduced 1991.
Price: **$292.00**

Remington 870 High Grades

Same as 870 except better walnut, hand checkering. Engraved receiver and barrel. Vent. rib. Stock dimensions to order.
Price: 870D, about **$2,509.00**
Price: 870F, about **$5,169.00**
Price: 870F with gold inlay, about **$7,752.00**

Remington 870 Express

Similar to the 870 Wingmaster except has a walnut-toned hardwood stock with solid, black recoil pad and pressed checkering on grip and forend. Outside metal surfaces have a black oxide finish. Comes with 26" or 28" vent. rib barrel with a Mod. Rem Choke tube. Introduced 1987.
Price: 12 or 20 .... **$277.00**
Price: Express Combo (with extra 20" Deer barrel), 12 or 20 .... **$376.00**
Price: Express 20-ga., 28" with Mod. Rem Choke tubes **$277.00**
Price: 410-bore **$292.00**

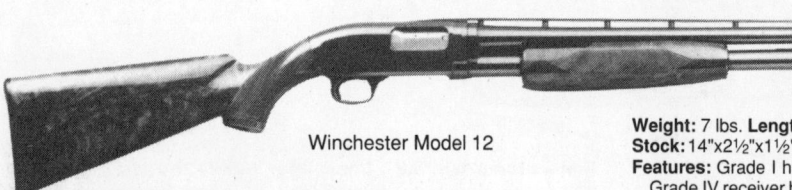

Winchester Model 12

WINCHESTER MODEL 12 PUMP SHOTGUN

Gauge: 20, 2¾" chamber, 5-shot magazine.
Barrel: 26" (Imp. Cyl.). Vent rib.

Weight: 7 lbs. **Length:** 45" overall.
Stock: 14"x2½"x1½". Select walnut with satin finish. Checkered grip and forend.
Features: Grade I has plain blued receiver; production limited to 4000 guns. Grade IV receiver has engraved game scenes and gold highlights identical to traditional Grade IV, and is limited to 1000 guns. Introduced 1993. From U.S. Repeating Arms Co.
Price: Grade I **$879.00**
Price: Grade IV **$1,431.00**

Winchester Model 42

WINCHESTER MODEL 42 HIGH GRADE SHOTGUN

Gauge: 410, 2¾" chamber.
Barrel: 26" (Full).
Weight: 7 lbs. **Length:** 45" overall.
Stock: 14"x2½"x1½". High grade walnut with checkered grip and forend.
Features: Engraved receiver with gold inlays. Production of only 850 guns. Introduced 1993. From U.S. Repeating Arms Co.
Price: **$1,617.00**

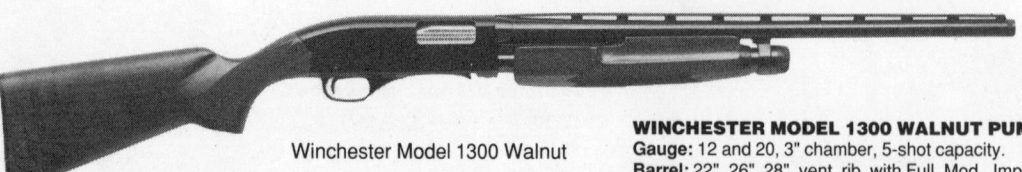

Winchester Model 1300 Walnut

WINCHESTER MODEL 1300 WALNUT PUMP

Gauge: 12 and 20, 3" chamber, 5-shot capacity.
Barrel: 22", 26", 28", vent. rib, with Full, Mod., Imp. Cyl. Winchoke tubes.
Weight: 6⅜ lbs. **Length:** 42⅝" overall.
Stock: American walnut, with deep cut checkering on pistol grip, traditional ribbed forend; high luster finish.
Sights: Metal bead front.
Features: Twin action slide bars; front-locking rotary bolt; roll-engraved receiver; blued, highly polished metal; cross-bolt safety with red indicator. Introduced 1984. From U.S. Repeating Arms Co., Inc.
Price: **$374.00**
Price: Model 1300 Ladies/Youth, 22" vent. rib **$312.00**

> Consult our Directory pages for the location of firms mentioned.

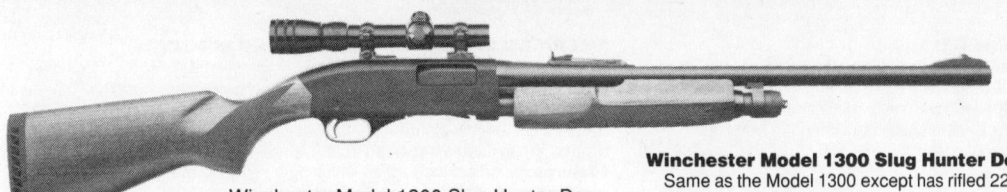

Winchester Model 1300 Slug Hunter Deer

Winchester Model 1300 Slug Hunter Deer Gun
Same as the Model 1300 except has rifled 22" barrel, walnut stock, rifle-type sights. Introduced 1990.
Price: Walnut stock **$445.00**
Price: Whitetails Unlimited model **$449.00**

Winchester Model 1300 Ranger Pump Gun Combo & Deer Gun
Similar to the standard Ranger except comes with two barrels: 22" (Cyl.) deer barrel with rifle-type sights and an interchangeable 28" vent. rib Winchoke barrel with Full, Mod. and Imp. Cyl. choke tubes. Drilled and tapped; comes with rings and bases. Available in 12- and 20-gauge 3" only, with recoil pad. Introduced 1983.
Price: Deer Combo with two barrels **$368.00**
Price: 12- or 20-ga., 22" (Cyl.) **$294.00**
Price: 12-ga., 22" rifled barrel **$333.00**
Price: 12-ga., 22" (Imp. Cyl., rifled sabot tubes) **$345.00**
Price: Combo 12-ga. with 18" (Cyl.) and 28" (Mod. tube) **$368.00**
Price: Rifled Deer Combo (22" rifled and 28" vent. rib barrels,
12 or 20-ga.) **$390.00**

CONSULT
SHOOTER'S MARKETPLACE
Page 231, This Issue

Winchester Model 1300 Turkey Gun
Similar to the standard Model 1300 Walnut except 12-ga. only, 22" barrel with Mod., Full and Extra Full Winchoke tubes, matte finish wood and metal. Comes with recoil pad, Cordura sling and swivels.
Price: With WinCam green camo laminated stock, about **$435.00**
Price: National Wild Turkey Federation Series III and IV **$458.00**

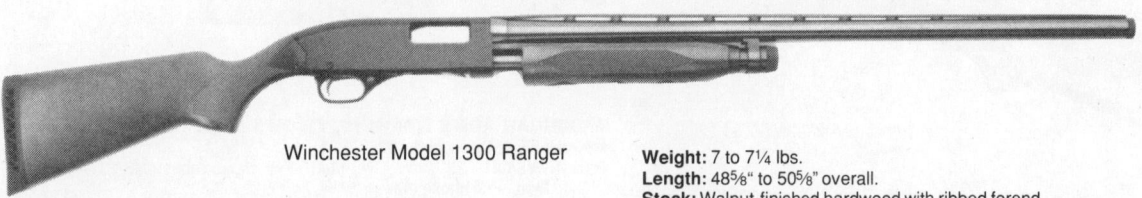

Winchester Model 1300 Ranger

WINCHESTER MODEL 1300 RANGER PUMP GUN
Gauge: 12 or 20, 3" chamber, 5-shot magazine.
Barrel: 26", 28" vent. rib with Full, Mod., Imp. Cyl. Winchoke tubes.

Weight: 7 to 7¼ lbs.
Length: 48⅝" to 50⅝" overall.
Stock: Walnut-finished hardwood with ribbed forend.
Sights: Metal bead front.
Features: Cross-bolt safety, black rubber recoil pad, twin action slide bars, front-locking rotating bolt. From U.S. Repeating Arms Co., Inc.
Price: Vent. rib barrel, Winchoke **$294.00**

SHOTGUNS—OVER/UNDERS

Includes a variety of game guns and guns for competitive shooting.

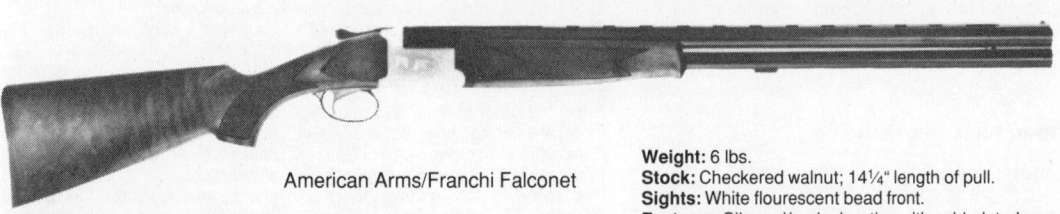

American Arms/Franchi Falconet

AMERICAN ARMS/FRANCHI FALCONET 2000 O/U
Gauge: 12, 2¾" chambers.
Barrel: 26" (Imp. Cyl., Mod., Full Franchoke tubes).

Weight: 6 lbs.
Stock: Checkered walnut; 14¼" length of pull.
Sights: White flourescent bead front.
Features: Silvered boxlock action with gold-plated game scene; single selective trigger; automatic selective ejectors. Reintroduced 1992. Imported from Italy by American Arms, Inc.
Price: **$1,419.00**

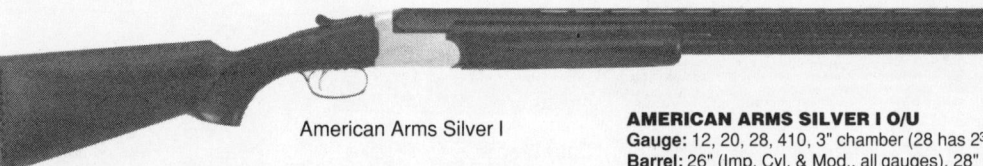

American Arms Silver I

American Arms Silver II Shotgun
Similar to the Silver I except 26" barrel (Imp. Cyl., Mod., Full choke tubes, 12- and 20-ga.), 28" (Imp. Cyl., Mod., Full choke tubes, 12-ga. only), 26" (Imp. Cyl. & Mod. fixed chokes, 28 and 410), 26" two-barrel set (Imp. Cyl. & Mod., fixed, 28 and 410); automatic selective ejectors. Weight is about 6 lbs., 15 oz. (12-ga., 26").
Price: **$699.00**
Price: 28, 410 . . . . **$719.00**
Price: Two-barrel set (28, 410) **$1,129.00**

AMERICAN ARMS SILVER I O/U
Gauge: 12, 20, 28, 410, 3" chamber (28 has 2¾").
Barrel: 26" (Imp. Cyl. & Mod., all gauges), 28" (Mod. & Full, 12, 20).
Weight: About 6¾ lbs.
Stock: 14⅛"x1⅜"x2⅜". Checkered walnut.
Sights: Metal bead front.
Features: Boxlock action with scroll engraving, silver finish. Single selective trigger, extractors. Chrome-lined barrels. Manual safety. Rubber recoil pad. Introduced 1987. Imported from Italy and Spain by American Arms, Inc.
Price: 12- or 20-gauge **$549.00**
Price: 28 or 410 . . . . **$609.00**

American Arms Silver Skeet O/U

Similar to the Silver II except has 28" ported barrels with elongated forcing cones, target-type vent. rib with two bead sights. Stock dimensions: 14⅜"x1⅜"x2⅜". Weighs 7 lbs., 6 oz. Comes with Skeet, Skeet, Imp. Cyl., Mod. choke tubes. Introduced 1992. Imported by American Arms, Inc.

Price: $899.00

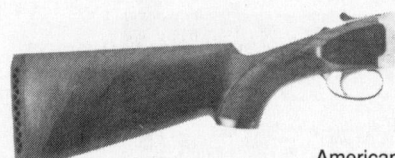

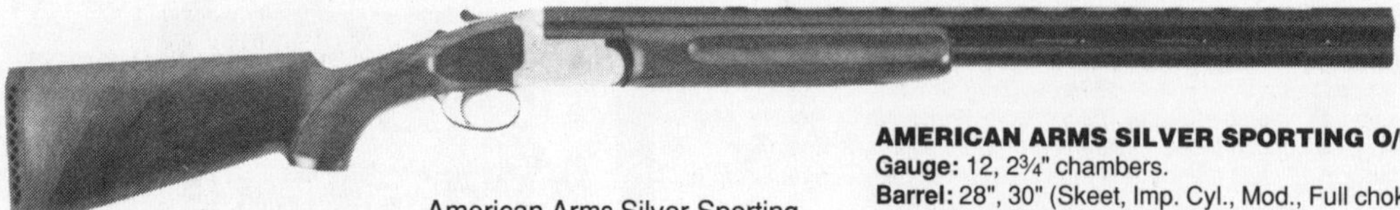

American Arms Silver Sporting

American Arms Silver Trap O/U

Similar to the Silver II except has 30" ported barrels with elongated forcing cones, target-type vent. rib with two sight beads. Stock dimensions: 14⅜"x1½"x1⅝". Weight is 7 lbs., 12 oz. Comes with Mod., Imp. Mod., Full, Full choke tubes. Introduced 1992. Imported by American Arms, Inc.

Price: $899.00

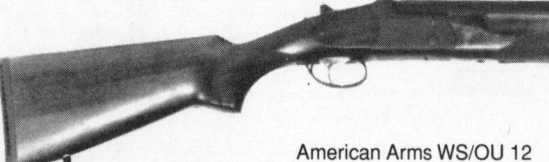

American Arms WS/OU 12

American Arms WT/OU 10 Shotgun

Similar to the WS/OU 12 except chambered for 10-gauge 3½" shell, 26" (Full & Full, choke tubes) barrel. Single selective trigger, extractors. Non-reflective finish on wood and metal. Imported by American Arms, Inc.

Price: $945.00

ARMSPORT 2700 O/U GOOSE GUN

Gauge: 10, 3½" chambers.
Barrel: 28" (Full & Imp. Mod.), 32" (Full & Full).
Weight: About 9.8 lbs.
Stock: European walnut.
Features: Boss-type action; double triggers; extractors. Introduced 1986. Imported from Italy by Armsport.
Price: Fixed chokes $1,190.00
Price: With choke tubes $1,299.00

ARMSPORT 2900 TRI-BARREL SHOTGUN

Gauge: 12, 3" chambers.
Barrel: 28" (Imp., Mod., Full).
Weight: 7¾ lbs.
Stock: European walnut.
Features: Has three barrels. Top-tang barrel selector; double triggers; silvered, engraved frame. Introduced 1986. Imported from Italy by Armsport.
Price: $3,400.00

AMERICAN ARMS/FRANCHI SPORTING 2000 O/U

Gauge: 12, 2¾" chambers.
Barrel: 28" (Skeet, Imp. Cyl., Mod., Full Franchoke tubes).
Weight: 7.75 lbs.
Stock: Checkered walnut.
Sights: White flourescent bead front.
Features: Blued boxlock action with single selective mechanical trigger, automatic selective ejectors; ported barrels. Introduced 1992. Imported from Italy by American Arms, Inc.
Price: $1,619.00

AMERICAN ARMS SILVER SPORTING O/U

Gauge: 12, 2¾" chambers.
Barrel: 28", 30" (Skeet, Imp. Cyl., Mod., Full choke tubes).
Weight: 7⅜ lbs. **Length:** 45½" overall.
Stock: 14⅜"x1½"x2⅜". Figured walnut, cut checkering; Sporting Clays quick-mount buttpad.
Sights: Target bead front.
Features: Boxlock action with single selective trigger, automatic selective ejectors; special broadway channeled rib; vented barrel rib; chrome bores. Chrome-nickel finish on frame, with engraving. Introduced 1990. Imported from Italy by American Arms, Inc.
Price: $899.00

AMERICAN ARMS WS/OU 12, TS/OU 12 SHOTGUNS

Gauge: 12, 3½" chambers.
Barrel: WS/OU—28" (Imp. Cyl., Mod., Full choke tubes); TS/OU—24" (Imp. Cyl., Mod., Full choke tubes).
Weight: 6 lbs., 15 oz. **Length:** 46" overall.
Stock: 14⅛"x1⅛"x2⅜". European walnut with cut checkering, black vented recoil pad, matte finish.
Features: Boxlock action with single selective trigger, automatic selective ejectors; chrome bores. Matte metal finish. Imported by American Arms, Inc.
Price: $719.00

ARMSPORT 2700 SERIES O/U

Gauge: 10, 12, 20, 28, 410.
Barrel: 26" (Imp. Cyl. & Mod.); 28" (Mod. & Full); vent. rib.
Weight: 8 lbs.
Stock: European walnut, hand-checkered p.g. and forend.
Features: Single selective trigger, automatic ejectors, engraved receiver. Imported by Armsport. Contact Armsport for complete list of models.
Price: M2733/2735 (Boss-type action, 12, 20, extractors) $790.00
Price: M2741 (as above with ejectors) $825.00
Price: M2730/2731 (as above with single trigger, screw-in chokes) . $975.00
Price: M2705 (410 bore, 26" Imp. & Mod., double triggers) $785.00
Price: M2742 Sporting Clays (12-ga., 28", choke tubes) $930.00
Price: M2744 Sporting Clays (20-ga., 26", choke tubes) $930.00
Price: M2750 Sporting Clays (12-ga., 28", choke tubes, sideplates) $1050.00
Price: M2751 Sporting Clays (20-ga., 26", choke tubes, sideplates) $1050.00

Baby Bretton

BABY BRETTON OVER/UNDER SHOTGUN

Gauge: 12 or 20, 2¾" chambers.
Barrel: 27½" (Cyl., Imp. Cyl., Mod., Full choke tubes).
Weight: About 5 lbs.
Stock: Walnut, checkered pistol grip and forend, oil finish.
Features: Receiver slides open on two guide rods, is locked by a large thumb lever on the right side. Extractors only. Light alloy barrels. Imported from France by Mandall Shooting Supplies.
Price: $895.00

Consult our Directory pages for the location of firms mentioned.

SHOTGUNS—OVER/UNDERS

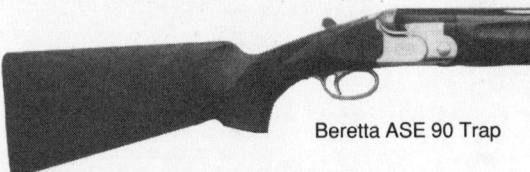

Beretta ASE 90 Trap

BERETTA MODEL 686 ULTRALIGHT O/U
Gauge: 12, 2¾" chambers.
Barrel: 26", 28", Mobilchoke choke tubes.
Weight: About 5 lbs., 13 oz.
Stock: Select American walnut with checkered grip and forend.
Features: Low-profile aluminum alloy receiver with titanium breech face insert. Matte black receiver finish with gold P. Beretta signature inlay. Single selective trigger; automatic safety. Introduced 1992. Imported from Italy by Beretta U.S.A.
Price: **$1,525.00**

BERETTA ASE 90 COMPETITION O/U SHOTGUN
Gauge: 12, 2¾" chambers.
Barrel: 28" (Pigeon, Sporting Clays, Skeet), 30" (Sporting Clays, Trap), Mobilchoke choke tubes on Sporting Clays, Trap; fixed chokes on Trap, Skeet, Pigeon. Trap model also available as Top Combo (30", 32" barrels or 30", 34").
Weight: About 8 lbs., 6 oz.
Stock: High grade walnut.
Features: Has drop-out trigger assembly, wide ventilated top and side ribs, hard-chrome bores. Competition-style receiver with coin-silver finish, gold inlay Pietro Beretta initials. Comes with hard case. Introduced 1992. Imported from Italy by Beretta U.S.A.
Price: Pigeon, Trap, Skeet **$8,070.00**
Price: Sporting Clays **$8,140.00**

Beretta 686EL

BERETTA ONYX HUNTER SPORT O/U SHOTGUN
Gauge: 12, 3" chambers.
Barrel: 28", 30" (Mobilchoke tubes).
Weight: 6 lbs., 13 oz.
Stock: Checkered American walnut.
Features: Intended for the beginning sporting clays shooter. Has wide, vented 12.5mm target rib, radiused recoil pad. Matte black finish on receiver and barrels. Introduced 1993. Imported from Italy by Beretta U.S.A.
Price: **$1,385.00**
Price: 686 Hunter Sport (as above except coin silver receiver with scroll engraving; 12- or 20-ga.) **$1,425.00**

BERETTA OVER/UNDER FIELD SHOTGUNS
Gauge: 12, 20, 28, and 410 bore, 2¾", 3" and 3½" chambers.
Barrel: 26" and 28" (Mobilchoke tubes).
Stock: Close-grained walnut.
Features: Highly-figured, American walnut stocks and forends, and a unique, weather-resistant finish on barrels. The 686 Onyx bears a gold P. Beretta signature on each side of the receiver. Imported from Italy by Beretta U.S.A.
Price: 686 Onyx **$1,355.00**
Price: 686 two bbl. set **$2,085.00**
Price: 686 Field **$1,355.00**
Price: 686L Silver (12, 20, polished silver receiver) **$1,385.00**
Price: 686EL (engraved sideplates, hard case) . . **$2,200.00**
Price: 687L Field **$1,870.00**
Price: 687 EL (gold inlays, sideplates) **$3,180.00**
Price: 687 EELL (engraved sideplates) . . . . . . **$4,625.00 to $5,130.00**

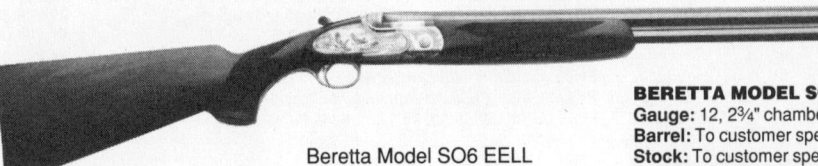

Beretta Model SO6 EELL

BERETTA SPORTING CLAYS SHOTGUNS
Gauge: 12 and 20, 2¾" chambers.
Barrel: 28", 30", Mobilchoke.
Stock: Close-grained walnut.
Sights: Luminous front sight and center bead.
Features: Equipped with Beretta Mobilchoke flush-mounted screw-in choke tube system. Models vary according to grade, from field-grade Beretta 686 Sporting with its floral engraving pattern, to competition-grade Beretta 682 Sporting with its brushed satin finish and adjustable length of pull to the 687 Sporting with intricately hand-engraved game scenes, fine line, deep-cut checkering. Imported from Italy by Beretta U.S.A.
Price: 682 Sporting, 30" (with case) **$2,605.00**
Price: 682 Super Sport, 28", 30", tapered rib . . **$2,715.00**
Price: 682 Sporting 20-gauge **$2,650.00**
Price: 682 Sporting Combo, 28" and 30" **$3,470.00**
Price: 686 Sporting **$1,940.00**
Price: 686 Onyx Sporting **$1,940.00**
Price: 686 English Course Sporting, 2¾" chambers, 28" . . **$2,015.00**
Price: 686 Sporting Combo, 28" and 30" **$2,600.00**
Price: 687 Sporting **$2,285.00**
Price: 687 Sporting (20-gauge) **$2,285.00**
Price: 687 EELL Sporter (hand engraved sideplates, deluxe wood) **$4,705.00**
Price: 687 Sporting Combo, 28" and 30" **$3,410.00**
Price: ASE 90 Sporting **$8,140.00**

BERETTA MODEL SO5, SO6, SO9 SHOTGUNS
Gauge: 12, 2¾" chambers.
Barrel: To customer specs.
Stock: To customer specs.
Features: SO5—Trap, Skeet and Sporting Clays models SO5 and SO5 EELL; SO6—SO6 and SO6 EELL are field models. SO6 has a case-hardened or silver receiver with contour hand engraving. SO6 EELL has hand-engraved receiver in a fine floral or "fine English" pattern or game scene, with bas-relief chisel work and gold inlays. SO6 and SO6 EELL are available with sidelocks removable by hand. Imported from Italy by Beretta U.S.A.
Price: SO5 Trap, Skeet, Sporting **$12,000.00**
Price: SO5 Combo, two-bbl. set **$15,500.00**
Price: SO6 Trap, Skeet, Sporting **$16,300.00**
Price: SO6 EELL Field, custom specs **$26,000.00**
Price: SO9 (12, 20, 28, 410, 26", 28", 30", any choke) **$28,500.00**

Beretta 687EL Sporting O/U
Similar to the 687 Sporting except has sideplates with gold inlay game scene, vent side and top ribs, bright orange front sight. Stock and forend are of high grade walnut with fine-line checkering. Available in 12-gauge only with 28" or 30" barrels and Mobilchoke tubes. Weight is 6 lbs., 13 oz. Introduced 1993. Imported from Italy by Beretta U.A.S.
Price: **$3,225.00**

Beretta 682 Super Sporting O/U
Similar to the 682 Sporting except has stock with adjustable comb that allows height adjustments via interchangeable inserts. Accessory recoil pad system and adjustable trigger allow length of pull changes. Factory ported barrels, raised tapered top rib with mid-rib bead, bright orange front sight. Available in 12-gauge only, 2¾" chambers, 28" 30", Mobilchoke tubes. Introduced 1993. Imported from Italy by Beretta U.S.A.
Price: **$2,925.00**

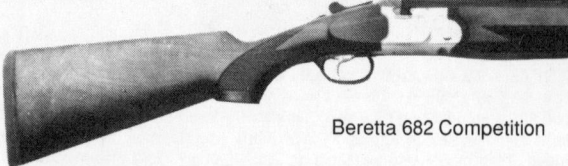

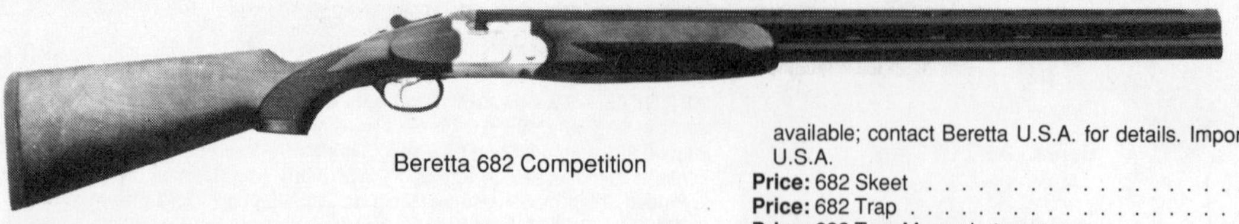

Beretta 682 Competition

BERETTA SERIES 682 COMPETITION OVER/UNDERS

Gauge: 12, 2¾" chambers.
Barrel: Skeet—26" and 28"; trap—30" and 32", Imp. Mod. & Full and Mobil-choke; trap mono shotguns—32" and 34" Mobilchoke; trap top single guns—32" and 34" Full and Mobilchoke; trap combo sets—from 30" O/U, 32" unsingle to 32" O/U, 34" top single.
Stock: Close-grained walnut, hand checkered.
Sights: Luminous front sight and center bead.
Features: Trap Monte Carlo stock has deluxe trap recoil pad. Various grades

available; contact Beretta U.S.A. for details. Imported from Italy by Beretta U.S.A.
Price: 682 Skeet $2,520.00
Price: 682 Trap $2,495.00
Price: 682 Trap Mono shotguns $3,400.00
Price: 682 Trap Top Single shotguns $2,650.00
Price: 682 Trap Combo sets . . . . . . $3,340.00 to $3,400.00
Price: 682 Pigeon Silver $2,760.00
Price: 687 EELL Trap . . . . $4,610.00 to $5,815.00
Price: 687 EELL Skeet (4-bbl. set) $8,040.00
Price: 682 Super Skeet (adjustable comb and butt pads, bbl. porting) $2,915.00
Price: 682 Super Trap (adjustable comb and butt pad, bbl. porting) . . . . $2,885.00 to $3,865.00

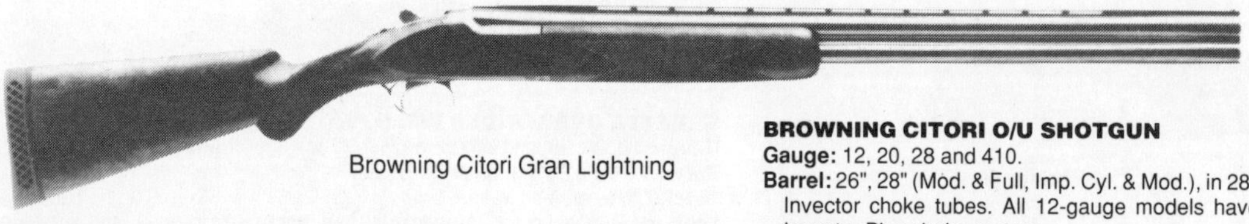

Browning Citori Gran Lightning

Browning Superlight Citori Over/Under

Similar to the standard Citori except available in 12, 20 with 24", 26" or 28" Invector barrels, 28 or 410 with 26" barrels choked Imp. Cyl. & Mod. or 28" choked Mod. & Full. Has straight grip stock, schnabel forend tip. Superlight 12 weighs 6 lbs., 9 oz. (26" barrels); Superlight 20, 5 lbs., 12 oz. (26" barrels). Introduced 1982.
Price: Grade I only, 28 or 410 . . . . $1,220.00
Price: Grade III, Invector, 12 or 20 . . . . $1,750.00
Price: Grade III, 28 or 410 . . . . $1,920.00
Price: Grade VI, Invector, 12 or 20 . . . . $2,540.00
Price: Grade VI, 28 or 410 . . . . $2,700.00
Price: Grade I Invector, 12 or 20 . . . . $1,215.00
Price: Grade I Invector, Upland Special (24" bbls.), 12 or 20 . . . $1,215.00

Browning Lightning Sporting Clays

Similar to the Citori Lightning with rounded pistol grip and classic forend. Has high post tapered rib or lower hunting-style rib with 30" back-bored Invector Plus barrels, ported or non-ported, 3" chambers. Gloss stock finish, radiused recoil pad. Has "Lightning Sporting Clays Edition" engraved and gold filled on receiver. Introduced 1989.
Price: Low-rib, ported $1,300.00
Price: High-rib, ported $1,360.00
Price: Pigeon Grade, low rib, ported $1,550.00
Price: Pigeon Grade, high rib, ported $1,488.00

Browning Citori Plus Trap Combo

Same as the Citori Plus Trap except comes with 34" single barrel with the 32" O/U model, or 32" or 34" single with the 30" O/U model. Introduced 1992.
Price: With fitted luggage case $3,300.00

Browning Citori O/U Skeet Models

Similar to standard Citori except 26", 28", 12-gauge, Invector Plus, (Skeet & Skeet) only; stock dimensions of 14⅜"x1½"x2", fitted with Skeet-style recoil pad; conventional target rib and high post target rib.
Price: Grade I Invector, 12-ga., Invector Plus (high post rib) $1,380.00
Price: Grade I, 20, 28 and 410 (high post rib) $1,315.00
Price: Grade III, 20, 28, 410 (high post rib) $1,860.00
Price: Grade VI, 20, 28, 410 (high post rib) $2,650.00
Price: Four barrel Skeet set—12, 20, 28, 410 barrels, with case, Grade I only $4,250.00
Price: Grade III, four-barrel set (high post rib) $4,860.00
Price: Grade VI, four-barrel set (high post rib) $5,500.00
Price: Grade I, three-barrel set $2,960.00
Price: Grade III, three-barrel set $3,560.00
Price: Grade VI, three-barrel set $4,200.00
Price: Grade III, 12-ga. Invector Plus $1,896.00
Price: Grade VI, 12-ga., Invector Plus $2,690.00

BROWNING CITORI O/U SHOTGUN

Gauge: 12, 20, 28 and 410.
Barrel: 26", 28" (Mod. & Full, Imp. Cyl. & Mod.), in 28 and 410. Also offered with Invector choke tubes. All 12-gauge models have back-bored barrels and Invector Plus choke system.
Weight: 6 lbs., 8 oz. (26" 410) to 7 lbs., 13 oz. (30" 12-ga.).
Length: 43" overall (26" bbl.).
Stock: Dense walnut, hand checkered, full p.g., beavertail forend. Field-type recoil pad on 12-ga. field guns and trap and Skeet models.
Sights: Medium raised beads, German nickel silver.
Features: Barrel selector integral with safety, automatic ejectors, three-piece takedown. Imported from Japan by Browning. Contact Browning for complete list of models and prices.
Price: Grade I, Hunting, Invector, 12 and 20 . . . . . $1,165.00
Price: Grade III, Hunting, Invector, 12 and 20 . . . . $1,715.00
Price: Grade VI, Hunting, Invector, 12 and 20 . . . . $2,485.00
Price: Grade I, Hunting, 28 and 410, fixed chokes . . . $1,155.00
Price: Grade III, Lightning, 28 and 410, fixed chokes . . . $1,900.00
Price: Grade VI, 28 and 410 Lightning, fixed chokes . . . $2,695.00
Price: Grade I, Lightning, Invector, 12, 20 . . . . . . $1,198.00
Price: Grade I, Hunting, 28", 30" only, 3½", Invector Plus $1,240.00
Price: Grade III, Lightning, Invector, 12, 20 . . . . . $1,745.00
Price: Grade VI, Lightning, Invector, 12, 20 . . . . . $2,530.00
Price: Gran Lightning, 26", 28", Invector $1,630.00

Browning Micro Citori Lightning

Similar to the standard Citori 20-ga. Lightning except scaled down for smaller shooter. Comes with 24" barrels with Invector choke system, 13¾" length of pull. Weighs about 6 lbs., 3 oz. Introduced 1991.
Price: Grade I $1,228.00
Price: Grade III $1,775.00
Price: Grade VI $2,515.00

Browning Citori Plus Trap Gun

Similar to the Grade I Citori Trap except comes only with 30" barrels with .745" over-bore, Invector Plus choke system with Full, Imp. Mod. and Mod. choke tubes; high post, ventilated, tapered, target rib for adjustable impact from 3" to 12" above point of aim. Available with or without ported barrels. Select walnut stock has high-gloss finish, Monte Carlo comb, modified beavertail forend and is fully adjustable for length of pull, drop at comb and drop at Monte Carlo. Has Browning Recoil Reduction System. Introduced 1989.
Price: Grade I, with ported barrel $1,950.00
Price: Grade I, non-ported barrel $1,925.00
Price: Pigeon Grade, ported barrels $2,140.00

Browning Citori O/U Trap Models

Similar to standard Citori except 12 gauge only; 30", 32" ported or non-ported (Full & Full, Imp. Mod. & Full, Mod. & Full) or Invector Plus, 34" single barrel in Combo Set (Full, Imp. Mod., Mod.), or Invector model; Monte Carlo cheek piece (14⅜"x1⅜"x1⅜"x2"); fitted with trap-style recoil pad; conventional target rib and high post target rib.
Price: Grade I, Invector Plus, ported bbls. $1,380.00
Price: Grade VI, Invector, high post target rib $2,520.00
Price: Grade III, Invector Plus Ported $1,896.00
Price: Grade IV, Invector Plus Ported $2,690.00

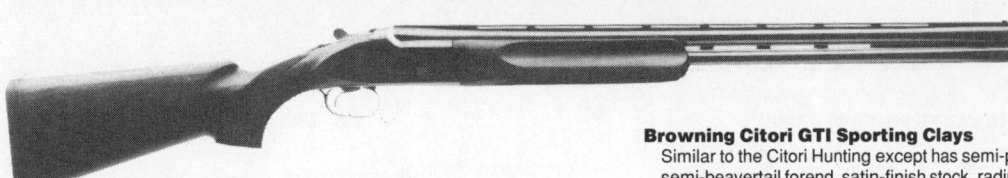

Browning Citori GTI

Browning Special Sporting Clays

Similar to the GTI except has full pistol grip stock with palm swell, gloss finish, 28", 30" or 32" barrels with back-bored Invector Plus chokes (ported or non-ported); high post tapered rib. Also available as 28" and 30" two-barrel set. Introduced 1989.
Price: With ported barrels **$1,360.00**

Browning Citori GTI Sporting Clays

Similar to the Citori Hunting except has semi-pistol grip with slightly grooved, semi-beavertail forend, satin-finish stock, radiused rubber buttpad. Has three interchangeable trigger shoes, trigger has three length of pull adjustments. Wide 13mm vent. rib, 28" or 30" barrels (ported or non-ported) with Invector Plus choke tubes. Ventilated side ribs. Introduced 1989.
Price: With ported barrels **$1,380.00**

Browning 325 Sporting Clays

BROWNING 325 SPORTING CLAYS

Gauge: 12, 20, 2¾" chambers.
Barrel: 12-ga.—28", 30", 32" (Invector Plus tubes), back-bored; 20-ga.—28", 30" (Imp. Mod. & Imp. Cyl.).

Weight: 7 lbs., 13 oz. (12-ga., 28").
Stock: 14¹³⁄₁₆" (+/-⅛")x1⁷⁄₁₆"x2³⁄₁₆" (12-ga.). Select walnut with gloss finish, cut checkering, schnabel forend.
Features: Grayed receiver with engraving, blued barrels. Barrels are ported on 12-gauge guns. Has 10mm wide vent rib. Comes with three interchangeable trigger shoes to adjust length of pull. Introduced in U.S. 1993. Imported by Browning.
Price: 12-ga. **$1,540.00**
Price: 20-ga. **$1,470.00**

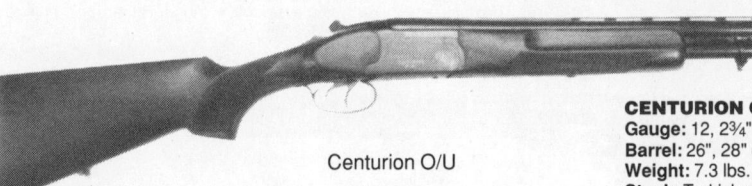

Centurion O/U

CHAPUIS OVER/UNDER SHOTGUN

Gauge: 12, 16, 20.
Barrel: 22", 23.6", 26.8", 27.6", 31.5", chokes to customer specs.
Weight: 5 to 8 lbs. **Length:** NA.
Stock: French walnut, straight English or pistol grip.
Features: Double hook blitz system boxlock action with automatic ejectors or extractors. Long trigger guard (most models), choice of raised solid rib, vent. rib or ultra light rib. Imported from France by Armes de Chasse.
Price: About . . . . **$4,000.00 to $5,000.00**

CENTURION OVER/UNDER SHOTGUN

Gauge: 12, 2¾" chambers.
Barrel: 26", 28" (Mod. & Full).
Weight: 7.3 lbs. **Length:** 42.5" overall (26" barrels).
Stock: Turkish walnut.
Features: Double triggers; sling swivels. Polished blue finish. Introduced 1993. Imported by Century International Arms.
Price: About **$350.00**

Connecticut Valley Classics Sporter

CONNECTICUT VALLEY CLASSICS CLASSIC SPORTER O/U

Gauge: 12, 3" chambers.
Barrel: 28", 30", 32" (Skeet, Imp. Cyl. Mod., Full CV choke tubes); elongated forcing cones.
Weight: 7¾ lbs. **Length:** 44⅞" overall (28" barrels).
Stock: 14½"x1½"x2⅛". American black walnut with hand-checkered grip and forend.
Features: Receiver duplicates Classic Doubles M101 specifications. Nitrided grayed or stainless receiver with fine engraving. Chrome-lined bores and chambers suitable for steel shot. Optionally available are CV Plus (2⅜" tubes) or Competition (2¾" Briley) choke tubes. Introduced 1993. Made in U.S. by Connecticut Valley Classics.
Price: Classic Sporter **$2,195.00**
Price: Classic Sporter Stainless **$2,395.00**

Connecticut Valley Classics Classic Field Waterfowler

Similar to the Classic Sporter except with 30" barrel only, blued, non-reflective overall finish. Interchangeable CV choke tube system includes Skeet, Imp. Cyl., Mod. Full tubes. Introduced 1993. Made in U.S. by Connecticut Valley Classics.
Price: **$1,895.00**

Charles Daly Lux Over/Under

Similar to the Field Grade except available in 12, 20, 28, 410-bore, has automatic selective ejectors, antique silver finish on frame, and has choke tubes for Imp. Cyl., Mod. and Full. Introduced 1989.
Price: **$699.00**

CHARLES DALY FIELD GRADE O/U

Gauge: 12 or 20, 3" chambers.
Barrel: 12- and 20- ga.—26" (Imp. Cyl. & Mod.), 12-ga.—28" (Mod. & Full).
Weight: 6 lbs., 15 oz. (12-ga.); 6 lbs., 10 oz. (20-ga.). **Length:** 43½" overall (26" bbl.).
Stock: 14⅛"x1⅜"x2⅜". Walnut with cut-checkered grip and forend. Black, vent. rubber recoil pad. Semi-gloss finish.
Features: Boxlock action with manual safety; extractors; single selective trigger. Color case-hardened receiver with engraving. Introduced 1989. Imported from Europe by Outdoor Sports Headquarters.
Price: **$475.00**

E.A.A./SABATTI SPORTING CLAYS PRO-GOLD O/U
Gauge: 12, 3" chambers.
Barrel: 28" or 30" with six choke tubes.
Weight: 7¼ lbs.
Stock: European walnut with gloss finish, checkered grip and forend. Special sporting clays recoil pad.
Features: Boxlock action with gold-plated single selective trigger, automatic ejectors. Engraved, blued receiver with gold inlays. Target-style flourescent bar front sight. Comes with lockable hard shell plastic case. Introduced 1993. Imported from Italy by European American Armory.
Price: **$999.00**

E.A.A./Sabatti Sporting Clays

E.A.A./SABATTI FALCON-MON OVER/UNDER
Gauge: 12, 20, 28, 410, 3" chambers.
Barrel: 26" or 28" (standard chokes).
Weight: 6.6 to 7.8 lbs.
Stock: Select walnut with cut checkering. Full pistol grip, beavertail forend. Gloss finish.
Features: Boxlock action with gold-plated single selective trigger, extractors; ventilated rib. Engraved, blued receiver. Lifetime warranty. Introduced 1993. Imported from Italy by European American Armory.
Price: 12 or 20 . . . . **$599.00**
Price: 28 or 410 . . . . **$675.00**

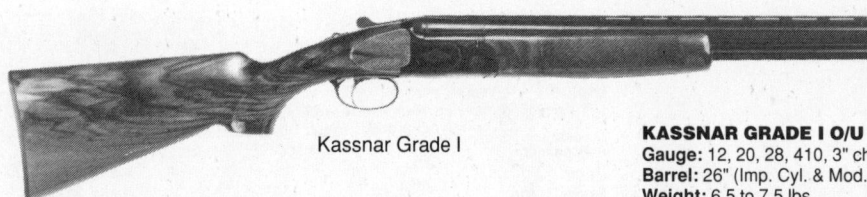

Kassnar Grade I

KASSNAR GRADE I O/U SHOTGUN
Gauge: 12, 20, 28, 410, 3" chambers.
Barrel: 26" (Imp. Cyl. & Mod.), 28" (Mod. & Full), 28" (choke tubes).
Weight: 6.5 to 7.5 lbs.
Stock: European walnut with checkered grip and forend.
Features: Boxlock action with single selective trigger; blued and engraved receiver; vent. rib. Imported by K.B.I., Inc.
Price: . . . . **$500.00** to **$750.00**

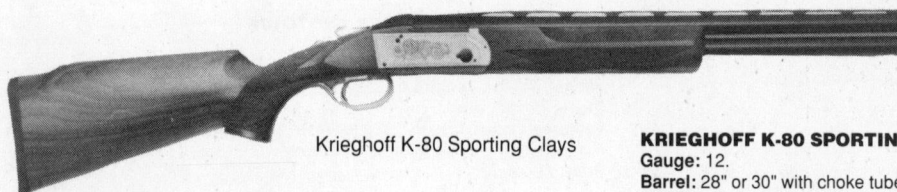

Krieghoff K-80 Sporting Clays

KRIEGHOFF K-80 SPORTING CLAYS O/U
Gauge: 12.
Barrel: 28" or 30" with choke tubes.
Weight: About 8 lbs.
Stock: #3 Sporting stock designed for gun-down shooting.
Features: Choice of standard or lightweight receiver with satin nickel finish and classic scroll engraving. Selective mechanical trigger adjustable for position. Choice of tapered flat or 8mm parallel flat barrel rib. Free-floating barrels. Aluminum case. Imported from Germany by Krieghoff International, Inc.
Price: Standard grade with five choke tubes **$7,350.00**

KRIEGHOFF K-80 SKEET SHOTGUN
Gauge: 12, 2¾" chambers.
Barrel: 28" (Skeet & Skeet, optional Tula or choke tubes).
Weight: About 7¾ lbs.
Stock: American Skeet or straight Skeet stocks, with palm-swell grips. Walnut.
Features: Satin gray receiver finish. Selective mechanical trigger adjustable for position. Choice of ventilated 8mm parallel flat rib or ventilated 8-12mm tapered flat rib. Introduced 1980. Imported from Germany by Krieghoff International, Inc.
Price: Standard, Skeet chokes **$6,290.00**
Price: As above, Tula chokes **$6,550.00**
Price: Lightweight model (weighs 7 lbs.), Standard **$6,290.00**
Price: Two-Barrel Set (tube concept), 12-ga., Standard **$10,935.00**
Price: Skeet Special (28", tapered flat rib, Skeet & Skeet choke tubes) **$6,895.00**

Krieghoff K-80 International Skeet
Similar to the Standard Skeet except has ½" ventilated Broadway-style rib, special Tula chokes with gas release holes at muzzle. International Skeet stock. Comes in fitted aluminum case.
Price: Standard grade **$6,995.00**

Krieghoff K-80 Four-Barrel Skeet Set
Similar to the Standard Skeet except comes with barrels for 12, 20, 28, 410. Comes with fitted aluminum case.
Price: Standard grade **$14,200.00**

Krieghoff K-80/RT Shotguns
Same as the standard K-80 shotguns except has a removable internally selective trigger mechanism. Can be considered an option on all K-80 guns of any configuration. Introduced 1990.
Price: RT (removable trigger) option on K-80 guns, add **$1,000.00**
Price: Extra pull trigger mechanisms **$1,275.00**

Krieghoff K-80 Trap

Weight: About 8½ lbs.
Stock: Four stock dimensions or adjustable stock available; all have palm-swell grips. Checkered European walnut.
Features: Satin nickel receiver. Selective mechanical trigger, adjustable for position. Ventilated step rib. Introduced 1980. Imported from Germany by Krieghoff International, Inc.
Price: K-80 O/U (30", 32", Imp. Mod. & Full), from **$6,695.00**
Price: K-80 Unsingle (32", 34", Full), Standard, from **$7,300.00**
Price: K-80 Combo (two-barrel set), Standard, from **$9,380.00**

KRIEGHOFF K-80 O/U TRAP SHOTGUN
Gauge: 12, 2¾" chambers.
Barrel: 30", 32" (Imp. Mod. & Full or choke tubes).

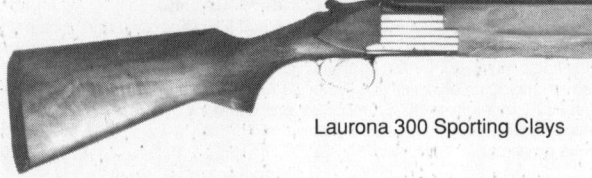

Laurona 300 Sporting Clays

LAURONA SILHOUETTE 300 SPORTING CLAYS
Gauge: 12, 2¾" or 3" chambers.
Barrel: 28", 29" (Multichoke tubes, flush-type or knurled).
Weight: 7 lbs., 12 oz.
Stock: 14⅜"x1⅜"x2½". European walnut with full pistol grip, beavertail forend. Rubber buttpad.
Features: Selective single trigger, automatic selective ejectors. Introduced 1988. Imported from Spain by Galaxy Imports.
Price: **$1,250.00**
Price: Silhouette Ultra-Magnum, 3½" chambers **$1,265.00**

LAURONA SILHOUETTE 300 TRAP
Same gun as the Silhouette 300 Sporting Clays except has 29" barrels, trap stock dimensions of 14⅜"x1⁷⁄₁₆"x1⅝", weighs 7 lbs., 15 oz. Available with flush or knurled Multichokes.
Price: **$1,310.00**

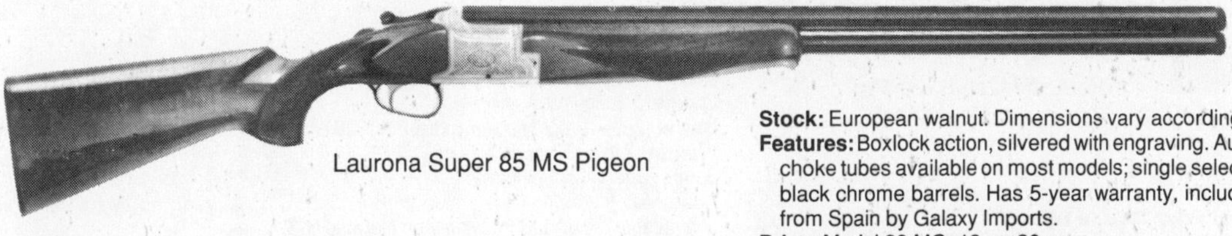

Laurona Super 85 MS Pigeon

Stock: European walnut. Dimensions vary according to model. Full pistol grip.
Features: Boxlock action, silvered with engraving. Automatic selective ejectors; choke tubes available on most models; single selective or twin single triggers; black chrome barrels. Has 5-year warranty, including metal finish. Imported from Spain by Galaxy Imports.
Price: Model 83 MG, 12- or 20-ga. **$1,215.00**
Price: Model 84S Super Trap (fixed chokes) **$1,340.00**
Price: Model 85 Super Game, 12- or 20-ga. **$1,215.00**
Price: Model 85 MS Super Trap (Full/Multichoke) **$1,390.00**
Price: Model 85 MS Super Pigeon **$1,370.00**
Price: Model 85 S Super Skeet, 12-ga. **$1,300.00**

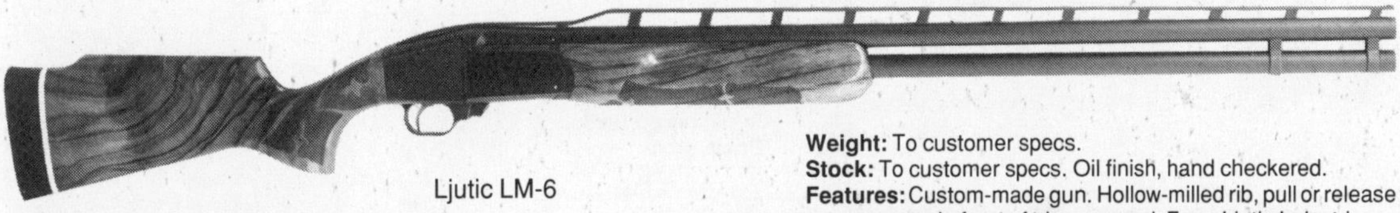

LAURONA SUPER MODEL OVER/UNDERS
Gauge: 12, 20, 2¾" or 3" chambers.
Barrel: 26", 28" (Multichoke), 29" (Multichokes and Full).
Weight: About 7 lbs.

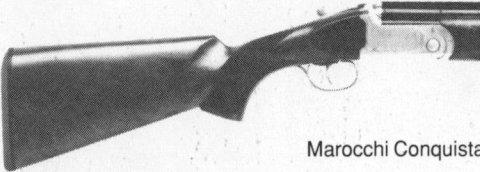

Ljutic LM-6

Weight: To customer specs.
Stock: To customer specs. Oil finish, hand checkered.
Features: Custom-made gun. Hollow-milled rib, pull or release trigger, pushbutton opener in front of trigger guard. From Ljutic Industries.
Price: Super Deluxe LM-6 O/U **$14,995.00**
Price: Over/under Combo (interchangeable single barrel, two trigger guards, one for single trigger, one for doubles) **$21,995.00**
Price: Extra over/under barrel sets, 29"-32" **$5,995.00**

LJUTIC LM-6 DELUXE O/U SHOTGUN
Gauge: 12.
Barrel: 28" to 34", choked to customer specs for live birds, trap, International Trap.

Marocchi Conquista

MAROCCHI CONQUISTA OVER/UNDER SHOTGUN
Gauge: 12, 2¾" chambers.
Barrel: 28", 30", 32" (Contre choke tubes).
Weight: 8 lbs.
Stock: 14½"-14⅞"x2¼"x1½"; American walnut with checkered grip and forend; sporting clays butt pad.
Sights: 16mm luminescent front.
Features: Has lower monoblock and frame profile. Fast lock time. Ergonomically-shaped trigger is adjustable for pull length and weight. Automatic selective ejectors. Coin-finished receiver, blued barrels. Comes with five choke tubes, hard case, stock wrinch. Introduced 1993. Imported from Italy by Precision Sales International.
Price: Grade I **$1,985.00**
Price: Grade II **$2,450.00**

MAROCCHI AVANZA O/U SHOTGUN
Gauge: 12 and 20, 3" chambers.
Barrel: 26" (Imp. Cyl. & Mod. or Imp. Cyl., Mod., Full Interchokes); 28" (Mod. & Full or Imp. Cyl. Mod., Full Interchokes).
Weight: 6 lbs., 6 oz. to 6 lbs., 13 oz.
Stock: 14"x2¼"x1½". Select walnut with cut checkering. Recoil pad.
Features: Single selective trigger, auto-mechanical barrel cycling, automatic selective ejectors, unbreakable firing pins. Ventilated top and middle ribs. Automatic safety. Introduced 1990. Imported from Italy by Precision Sales International.
Price: 12-ga., 26" or 28", fixed chokes **$769.00**
Price: As above, with Interchokes **$829.00**

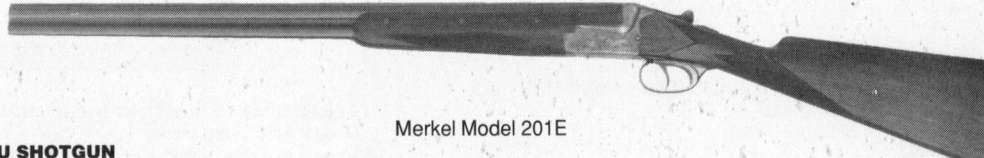

Merkel Model 201E

MERKEL MODEL 200E O/U SHOTGUN
Gauge: 12, 3" chambers, 16, 2¾" chambers, 20, 3" chambers.
Barrel: 12-, 16-ga.—28"; 20-ga.—26¾" (Imp. Cyl. & Mod., Mod. & Full). Solid rib.
Weight: About 7 lbs. (12-ga.).
Stock: Oil-finished walnut; straight English or pistol grip.
Features: Scroll engraved, color case-hardened receiver. Single selective or double triggers; ejectors. Imported from Germany by GSI.

Price: Model 200E **$3,395.00**
Price: Model 201E (as above except silver-grayed receiver with engraved hunting scenes) **$4,195.00**
Price: Model 202E (as above except has false sideplates, fine hunting scenes with Arabesque engraving) **$7,995.00**

Merkel Model 200E Skeet, Trap Over/Unders

Similar to the Model 200E except in 12-gauge only with 2¾" chambers, tapered ventilated rib, competition stock with full pistol grip, half-coverage Arabesque engraving on silver-grayed receiver. Single selective trigger only. Model 200ES has 26¾" (Skeet & Skeet) barrels; Model 200ET has 30" (Full & Full) barrles. Imported from Germany by GSI.

Price: Model 200ES **$4,995.00**
Price: Model 200ET **$4,795.00**
Price: Model 201ES (full-coverage engraving) **$5,595.00**
Price: Model 201ET (full-coverage engraving) **$5,395.00**
Price: Model 203ES (sidelock action, Skeet) **$9,795.00**
Price: Model 203ET (sidelock action, Trap) **$9,795.00**

Merkel Model 203E, 303E Over/Under Shotguns

Similar to the Model 200E except with Holland & Holland-style sidelocks, both quick-detachable: Model 203E with cranked screw, 303E with integral retracting hook. Model 203E has coil spring ejectors; 303E H&H ejectors. Both have silver-grayed receiver with English-style Arabesque engraving—large scrolls on 203E, medium on 303E. Imported from Germany by GSI.

Price: Model 203E **$9,695.00**
Price: Model 303E **$21,295.00**

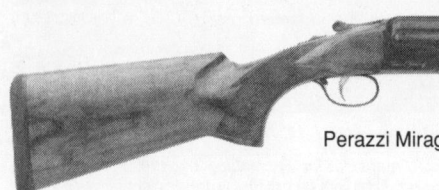

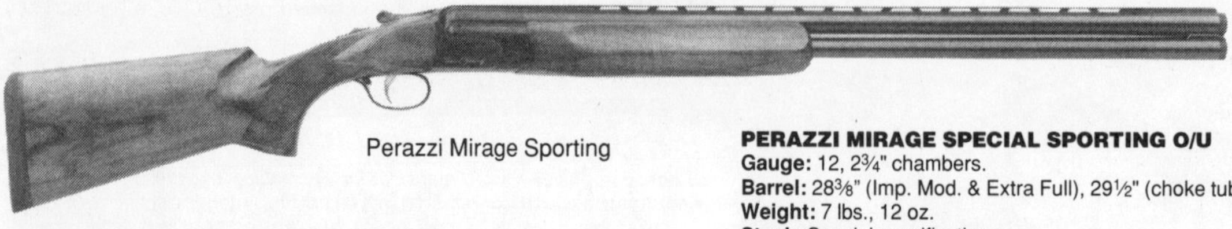

Perazzi Mirage Sporting

Perazzi Mirage Special Four-Gauge Skeet

Similar to the Mirage Sporting model except has Skeet dimensions, interchangeable, adjustable four-position trigger assembly. Comes with four barrel sets in 12, 20, 28, 410, flat ⁵⁄₁₆"x⁵⁄₁₆" rib.

Price: From **$17,500.00**

PERAZZI MIRAGE SPECIAL SPORTING O/U

Gauge: 12, 2¾" chambers.
Barrel: 28⅜" (Imp. Mod. & Extra Full), 29½" (choke tubes).
Weight: 7 lbs., 12 oz.
Stock: Special specifications.
Features: Has single selective trigger; flat ⁷⁄₁₆"x⁵⁄₁₆" vent. rib. Many options available. Imported from Italy by Perazzi U.S.A., Inc.
Price: **$8,100.00**

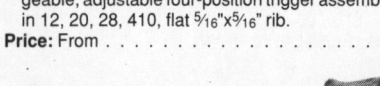

Perazzi Sporting Classic

Perazzi Sporting Classic O/U

Same as the Mirage Special Sporting except is deluxe version with select wood and engraving, Available with flush mount choke tubes, 29.5" barrels. Introduced 1993.

Price: From **$9,150.00**

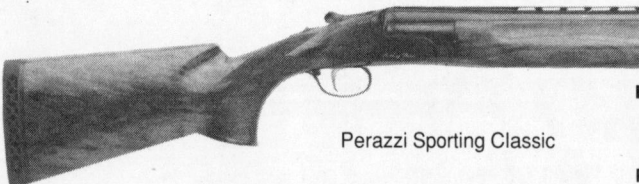

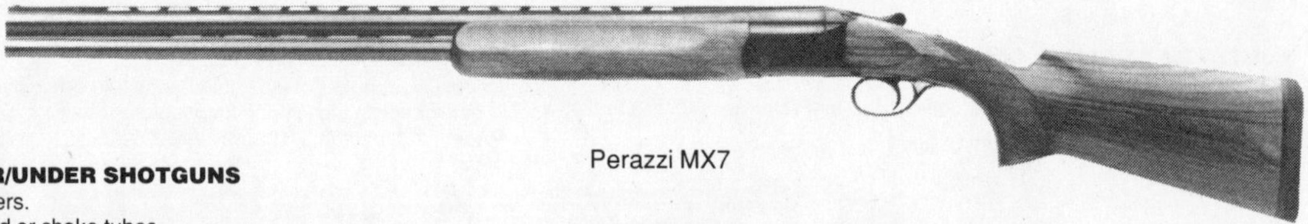

Perazzi MX7

PERAZZI MX7 OVER/UNDER SHOTGUNS

Gauge: 12, 2¾" chambers.
Barrel: 29.5", 31.5", fixed or choke tubes.
Weight: NA.
Stock: To customer specifications.
Features: Has fixed coil spring trigger mechanism; selective firing order. Available in combo or over/under configurations. Introduced 1992. Imported from Italy by Perazzi U.S.A.
Price: From **$6,100.00**

Perazzi Mirage Special Skeet Over/Under

Similar to the MX8 Skeet except has adjustable four-position trigger, Skeet stock dimensions.

Price: From **$7,700.00**

PERAZZI MX8/MX8 SPECIAL TRAP, SKEET

Gauge: 12, 2¾" chambers.
Barrel: Trap—29½" (Imp. Mod. & Extra Full), 31½" (Full & Extra Full). Choke tubes optional. Skeet—27⅝" (Skeet & Skeet).
Weight: About 8½ lbs. (Trap); 7 lbs., 15 oz. (Skeet).
Stock: Interchangeable and custom made to customer specs.
Features: Has detachable and interchangeable trigger group with flat V springs. Flat ⁷⁄₁₆" ventilated rib. Many options available. Imported from Italy by Perazzi U.S.A., Inc.
Price: From **$7,300.00**
Price: MX8 Special (adj. four-position trigger), from **$7,700.00**
Price: MX8 Special Single (32" or 34" single barrel, step rib), from **$7,300.00**
Price: MX8 Special Combo (o/u and single barrel sets), from . . . **$10,250.00**

Perazzi MX8/20 Over/Under Shotgun

Similar to the MX8 except has smaller frame and has a removable trigger mechanism. Available in trap, Skeet, sporting or game models with fixed chokes or choke tubes. Stock is made to customer specifications. Introduced 1993.

Price: From **$7,300.00**

PERAZZI MX9 SINGLE, OVER/UNDER SHOTGUNS

Gauge: 12, 2¾" chambers.
Barrel: 29.5", 31.5" (choke tubes).
Weight: NA.
Stock: Walnut; cheekpiece adjustable for elevation and cast.
Features: Comes with six pattern adjustment rib inserts. Vent side rib. Externally selective trigger. Available in single barrel, combo, over/under trap, Skeet, pigeon and sporting models. Introduced 1993. Imported from Italy by Perazzi U.S.A.
Price: From **$9,200.00**
Price: MX10 (fixed chokes, different rib), from **$9,450.00**

PERAZZI MX12 HUNTING OVER/UNDER

Gauge: 12, 2¾" chambers.
Barrel: 26", 27⅝", 28⅜", 29½" (Mod. & Full); choke tubes available in 27⅝", 29½" only (MX12C).
Weight: 7 lbs., 4 oz.
Stock: To customer specs; Interchangeable.
Features: Single selective trigger; coil springs used in action; schnabel forend tip. Imported from Italy by Perazzi U.S.A., Inc.
Price: From **$7,300.00**
Price: MX12C (with choke tubes), from **$7,700.00**

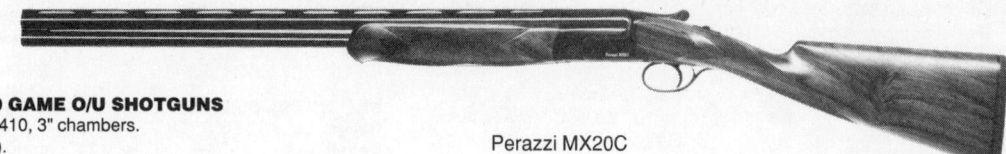

Perazzi MX20C

PERAZZI MX28, MX410 GAME O/U SHOTGUNS
Gauge: 28, 2¾" chambers, 410, 3" chambers.
Barrel: 26" (Imp. Cyl. & Full).
Weight: NA.
Stock: To customer specifications.
Features: Made on scaled-down frames proportioned to the gauge. Introduced 1993. Imported from Italy by Perazzi U.S.A.
Price: From **$14,600.00**

Perazzi MX20 Hunting Over/Under
Similar to the MX12 except 20-ga. frame size. Available in 20, 28, 410 with 2¾" or 3" chambers. 26" standard, and choked Mod. & Full. Weight is 6 lbs., 6 oz.
Price: From $7,650.00
Price: MX20C (as above, 20-ga. only, choke tubes), from $8,050.00

PIOTTI BOSS OVER/UNDER SHOTGUN
Gauge: 12, 20.
Barrel: 25" to 32", chokes as specified.
Weight: 6.5 to 8 lbs.
Stock: Dimensions to customer specs. Best quality figured walnut.
Features: Essentially a custom-made gun with many options. Introduced 1993. Imported from Italy by Wm. Larkin Moore.
Price: From **$34,0000.00**

> Consult our Directory pages for the location of firms mentioned.

Remington Peerless

Weight: 7¼ lbs. (26" barrels). **Length:** 43" overall (26" barrels).
Stock: 14³⁄₁₆"x1½"x2¼". American walnut with Imron gloss finish, cut-checkered grip and forend. Black, ventilated recoil pad.
Features: Boxlock action with removable sideplates. Gold-plated, single selective trigger, automatic safety, automatic ejectors. Fast lock time. Mid-rib bead, Bradley-type front. Polished blue finish with light scrollwork on sideplates, Remington logo on bottom of receiver. Introduced 1993.
Price: **$1,105.00**

REMINGTON PEERLESS OVER/UNDER SHOTGUN
Gauge: 12, 3" chambers.
Barrel: 26", 28", 30" (Imp. Cyl., Mod., Full Rem Chokes).

Ruger English Field

RUGER RED LABEL O/U SHOTGUN
Gauge: 12 and 20, 3" chambers.
Barrel: 26", 28" (Skeet, Imp. Cyl., Full, Extra-Full, Mod. screw-in choke tubes). Proved for steel shot.
Weight: About 7 lbs. (20-ga.); 7½ lbs. (12-ga.). **Length:** 43" overall (26" barrels).
Stock: 14"x1½"x2½". Straight grain American walnut. Checkered pistol grip and forend, rubber butt pad.
Features: Choice of blue or stainless receiver. Single selective mechanical trigger, selective automatic ejectors; serrated free-floating vent. rib. Comes with two Skeet, one Imp. Cyl., one Mod., one Full choke tube and wrench; Extra-Full tube available at extra cost. Made in U.S. by Sturm, Ruger & Co.
Price: Red Label with pistol grip stock **$1,157.50**
Price: English Field with straight-grip stock **$1,157.50**

Ruger Sporting Clays O/U Shotgun
Similar to the Red Label except 12-gauge only, 30" barrels back-bored to .744" diameter with stainless steel choke tubes. Weight is 7.75 lbs., overall length 47". Stock dimensions of 14⅛"x1½"x2½". Free-floating serrated vent. rib with brass front and mid-rib beads. No barrel side spacers. Comes with two Skeet, one Imp. Cyl., one Mod. choke tubes. Full and Extra-Full available at extra cost. Introduced 1992.
Price: **$1,285.00**

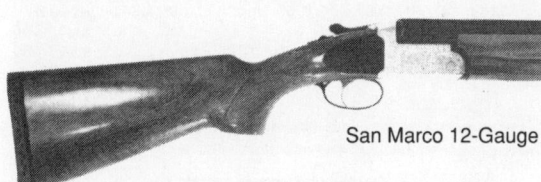

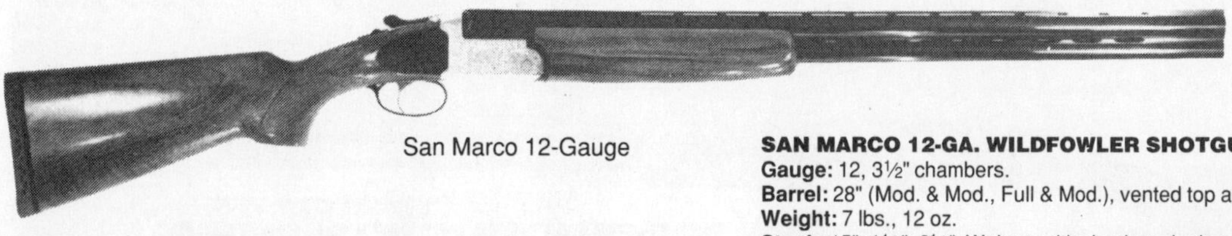

San Marco 12-Gauge

SAN MARCO 12-GA. WILDFOWLER SHOTGUN
Gauge: 12, 3½" chambers.
Barrel: 28" (Mod. & Mod., Full & Mod.), vented top and middle ribs.
Weight: 7 lbs., 12 oz.
Stock: 15"x1½"x2¼". Walnut, with checkered grip and forend.
Features: Chrome-lined bores with long forcing cones; single non-selective trigger; extractors on Standard, automatic ejectors on Deluxe; silvered, engraved action. Waterproof wood finish. Introduced 1990. Imported from Italy by Cape Outfitters.
Price: Standard **$595.00**
Price: Deluxe **$695.00**

San Marco Field Special O/U Shotgun
Similar to the 12-ga. Wildfowler except in 12-, 20- and 28-gauge with 3" chambers, 26" (Imp. Cyl. & Mod.) or 28" (Full & Mod.) barrels. Stock dimensions of 14¼"x1½"x1½". Weight of 5½ to 6 lbs. Engraved, silvered receiver, vented top and middle ribs, single trigger. Introduced 1990. Imported from Italy by Cape Outfitters.
Price: **$695.00**

SAN MARCO 10-GAUGE O/U SHOTGUN
Gauge: 10, 3½" chambers.
Barrel: 28" (Mod. & Mod.), 32" (Mod. & Full). Chrome lined.
Weight: 9 to 9½ lbs.
Stock: 15"x1⅜"x2⅛". Walnut.

Features: Solid ⅜" barrel rib. Long forcing cones. Double triggers, extractors; Deluxe grade has automatic ejectors. Engraved receiver with game scenes, matte finish. Waterproof finish on wood. Introduced 1990. Imported from Italy by Cape Outfitters.
Price: Standard grade **$795.00**
Price: Deluxe grade **$895.00**

SKB Model 685 Target

SKB Model 685 Over/Under Shotgun

Similar to the Model 505 Deluxe except has gold-plated trigger, semi-fancy American walnut stock, jeweled barrel block and fine engraving in silvered receiver, top lever, and trigger guard. Gold inlay on receiver, better walnut, ventilated side ribs. All 12-gauge barrels are back-bored, have lengthened forcing cones and longer choke tube system.

Price:		
Field	. . . .	$1,278.65
Two-barrel Field Set (12 & 20, 20 & 28 or 28 & 410)	. . . .	$1,813.65
Trap, Skeet	. . . .	$1,278.65
Two-barrel trap combo	. . . .	$1,706.65
Sporting Clays	. . . .	$1,332.15
Sporting Clays two-barrel set	. . . .	NA
Skeet Set (20, 28, 410)	. . . .	$2,562.65

SKB Model 885 Over/Under Trap, Skeet, Sporting Clays

Similar to the Model 685 except has engraved sideplates, top lever and trigger guard, select American walnut stock. All 12-gauge barrels are back-bored, have lengthened forcing cones and longer choke tube system.

Price: Field, Skeet/Trap $1,706.65

Stoeger/IGA ERA 2000 Over/Under Shotgun

Similar to the Condor I except available in 12-gauge only with 26" or 28" barrels, Full, Mod., and Imp. Cyl. choke tubes, single trigger. Introduced 1992. Imported from Brazil by Stoeger Industries.

Price: $665.00

SKB MODEL 505 DELUXE OVER/UNDER SHOTGUN

Gauge: 12, or 3"; 20, 3"; 28, 2¾"; 410, 3".
Barrel: 12-ga.—26", 28", 30", 32", 34" (Inter-Choke tube); 20-ga.—26", 28" (Inter-Choke tube); 28—26", 28" (Inter-Choke tube); 410—26", 28" (Imp. Cyl. & Mod., Mod. & Full). Ventilated side ribs.
Weight: 6.6 to 8.5 lbs. **Length:** 43" to 51⅜" overall.
Stock: 14⅛"x1½"x2³⁄₁₆". Hand checkered walnut with high-gloss finish. Target stocks available in standard and Monte Carlo.
Sights: Metal bead front (field), target style on Skeet, trap, Sporting Clays.
Features: Boxlock action; silver nitride finish with Field or Target pattern engraving, gold inlay; manual safety, automatic ejectors, single selective trigger. All 12-gauge barrels are back-bored, have lengthened forcing cones and longer choke tube system. Introduced 1987. Imported from Japan by G.U., Inc.

Price:		
Field	. . . .	$1,064.65
Two-barrel Field Set (12 & 20, 20 & 28 or 28 & 410)	. . . .	$1,599.65
Trap, Skeet	. . . .	$1,064.65
Two-barrel trap combo	. . . .	$1,492.65
Sporting Clays model	. . . .	$1,118.15
Skeet Set (20, 28, 410)	. . . .	$2,348.65

Price:		
Skeet Set (20, 28, 410)	. . . . . .	$3,204.65
Trap Combo	. . . .	$2,348.65
Field Set	. . . .	$2,348.65
Sporting Clays	. . . .	$1,760.15

STOEGER/IGA CONDOR I OVER/UNDER SHOTGUN

Gauge: 12, 20, 3" chambers.
Barrel: 26" (Full & Full, Imp. Cyl. & Mod.), 28" (Mod. & Full), or with choke tubes.
Weight: 6¾ to 7 lbs.
Stock: 14½"x1½"x2½". Oil-finished hardwood with checkered pistol grip and forend.
Features: Manual safety, single trigger, extractors only, ventilated top rib. Introduced 1983. Imported from Brazil by Stoeger Industries.

Price:		
	. . . .	$540.00
With choke tubes	. . . .	$582.00
Condor II (sames as Condor I except has double triggers, moulded buttplate)	. . . .	$432.00

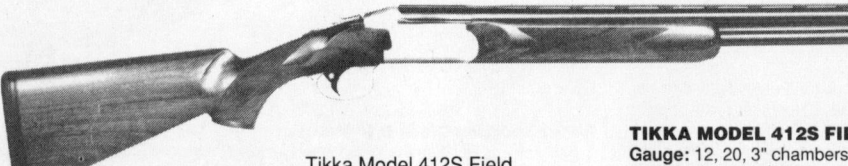

Tikka Model 412S Field

TECHNI-MEC MODEL 610 OVER/UNDER

Gauge: 10, 3½" chambers.
Barrel: 32" (Imp. Mod. & Full).
Stocks: Hand-checkered walnut.
Features: Single selective trigger; silvered engraved frame, blued barrels. Rubber recoil pad. Introduced 1991. Imported from Italy by Mandall Shooting Supplies.
Price: $1,200.00

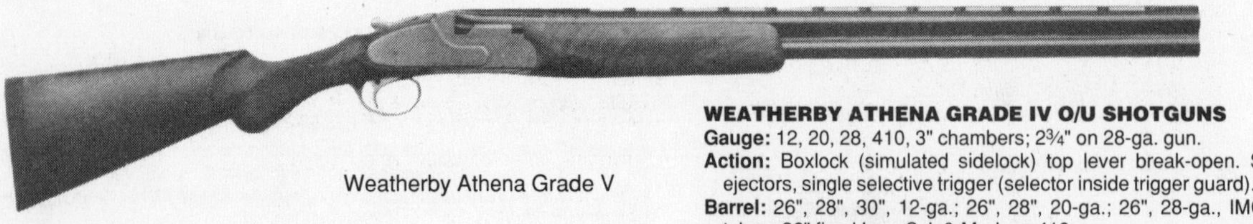

TIKKA MODEL 412S FIELD GRADE OVER/UNDER

Gauge: 12, 20, 3" chambers.
Barrel: 24", 26", 28", 30" with stainless steel screw-in chokes (Imp. Cyl, Mod., Imp. Mod., Full); 20-ga., 28" only.
Weight: About 7¼ lbs.
Stock: American walnut. Standard dimensions—13⁹⁄₁₀"x1½"x2²⁄₅". Checkered p.g. and forend.
Features: Free interchangeability of barrels, stocks and forends into double rifle model, combination gun, etc. Barrel selector in trigger; auto. top tang safety; barrel cocking indicators. Introduced 1980. Imported from Italy by Stoeger.
Price: Model 412S (ejectors) $1,155.00
Price: Model 412S Sporting Clays, 12-ga., 28", choke tubes $1,270.00

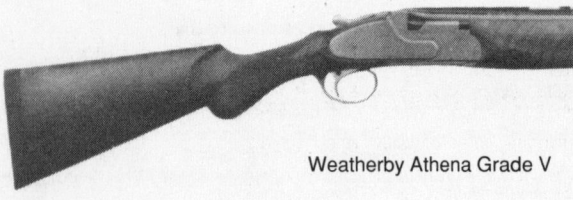

Weatherby Athena Grade V

Weatherby Athena Grade V Classic Field O/U

Similar to the Athena Grade IV except has rounded pistol grip, slender forend, oil-finished Claro walnut stock with fine-line checkering, Old English recoil pad. Sideplate receiver has rose and scroll engraving. Available in 12-gauge, 26", 28", 30", 20-gauge, 26", 28", all with 3" chambers. Introduced 1993.
Price: $2,450.00

WEATHERBY ATHENA GRADE IV O/U SHOTGUNS

Gauge: 12, 20, 28, 410, 3" chambers; 2¾" on 28-ga. gun.
Action: Boxlock (simulated sidelock) top lever break-open. Selective auto ejectors, single selective trigger (selector inside trigger guard).
Barrel: 26", 28", 30", 12-ga.; 26", 28", 20-ga.; 26", 28-ga., IMC Multi-Choke tubes; 26" fixed Imp. Cyl. & Mod. on 410.
Weight: 12-ga., 7⅜ lbs.; 20-ga. 6⅞ lbs.
Stock: American walnut, checkered p.g. and forend (14¼"x1½"x2½").
Features: Mechanically operated trigger. Top tang safety, Greener cross bolt, fully engraved receiver, recoil pad installed. IMC models furnished with three interchangeable flush-fitting choke tubes. Imported from Japan by Weatherby. Introduced 1982.
Price: 12-ga., IMC, 26", 28", 30" $1,950.00
Price: 20-ga., IMC, 26", 28" $1,950.00
Price: 28-ga., IMC, 26" $1,950.00
Price: 410-bore, fixed Imp. Cyl & Mod., 26" $1,950.00

Weatherby Orion II Classic Sporting

WEATHERBY ORION O/U SHOTGUNS
Gauge: 12, 20, 410, 3" chambers; 28, 2¾" chambers.
Barrel: Fixed choke, 12, 20, 28, 410—26", 28", 30" (Imp. Cyl. & Mod., Full & Mod., Skeet & Skeet); IMC Multi-Choke, 12, 20, Field models—26" (Imp. Cyl., Mod., Full, Skeet), 28" (Imp. Cyl., Mod., Full), 30" (Mod., Full); O/U Trap models—30", 32" (Imp. Mod., Mod., Full); Single bbl. Trap—32", 34" (Imp. Mod., Mod., Full).
Weight: 6½ to 9 lbs.
Stock: American walnut, checkered grip and forend. Rubber recoil pad. Dimensions for Field and Skeet models, 14¼"x1½"x2½".
Features: Selective automatic ejectors, single selective mechanical trigger. Top tang safety, Greener cross bolt. Orion I has plain blued receiver, no engraving; Orion II has engraved, blued receiver; Orion III has silver-gray receiver with engraving. Imported from Japan by Weatherby.

Weatherby Orion II, III Classic Field O/Us
Similar to the Orion II, Orion III except with rounded pistol grip, slender forend, oil-finished Claro walnut stock with fine-line checkering, Old English recoil pad. Sideplate receiver has rose and scroll engraving. Available in 12-gauge, 26", 28", 30" (IMC tubes), 20-gauge, 26", 28" (IMC tubes), 28-gauge, 26" (IMC tubes), 3" chambers. Introduced 1993.
Price: Orion II Classic Field **$1,150.00**
Price: Orion III Classic Field (12 and 20 only) **$1,350.00**

Price: Orion I, Field, 12, IMC, 26", 28", 30" **$1,050.00**
Price: Orion I, Field, 20, IMC, 26", 28" **$1,050.00**
Price: Orion II, Trap, 30", 32" **$1,207.00**
Price: Orion II, Single Barrel Trap, 32" **$1,207.00**
Price: Orion II, Skeet, 12 or 20, fixed chokes, 26" **$1,193.00**
Price: Orion III, Field, 12, IMC, 26", 28", 30" **$1,350.00**
Price: Orion III, Field, 20, IMC, 26", 28" **$1,350.00**

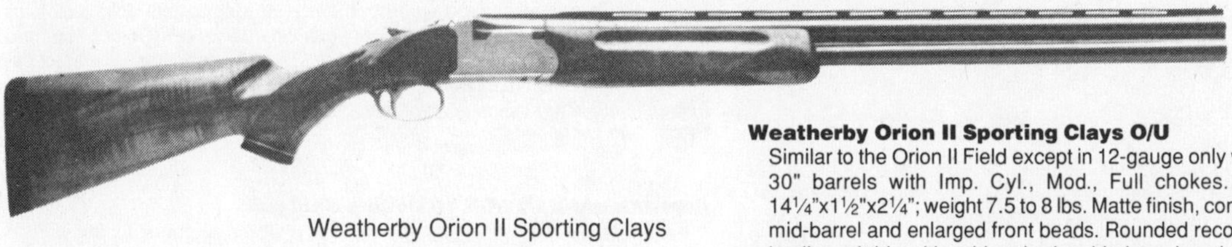

Weatherby Orion II Classic Sporting Clays O/U
Similar to the Orion II Sporting Clays except has rounded pistol grip, slender forend, oil-finished wood. Silver-gray nitride receiver has scroll engraving with clay pigeon monogram in gold-plate overlay. Stepped Broadway-style competition vent rib, vent side rib. Available in 12-gauge, 28" with choke tubes. Introduced 1993.
Price: **$1,249.00**

Weatherby Orion II Sporting Clays

Weatherby Orion II Sporting Clays O/U
Similar to the Orion II Field except in 12-gauge only with 2¾" chambers, 28", 30" barrels with Imp. Cyl., Mod., Full chokes. Stock dimensions are 14¼"x1½"x2¼"; weight 7.5 to 8 lbs. Matte finish, competition center vent. rib, mid-barrel and enlarged front beads. Rounded recoil pad. Receiver finished in silver nitride with acid-etched, gold-plate clay pigeon monogram. Barrels have lengthened forcing cones. Introduced 1992.
Price: **$1,249.00**

Winchester Model 1001 Field

WINCHESTER MODEL 1001 O/U SHOTGUN
Gauge: 12, 3" chambers.
Barrel: 28" (Imp. Cyl., Mod., Imp. Mod., Skeet WinPlus choke tubes).
Weight: 7 lbs. **Length:** 45" overall.
Stock: 14¼"x1½"x2". Select walnut with checkered grip and forend.
Features: Single selective inertia trigger, automatic ejectors; wide vent rib; back-bored barrels; matte-finished receiver top; receiver is blued and has scroll engraving. Introduced 1993. From U.S. Repeating Arms Co.
Price: **$1,099.00**

Winchester Model 1001 Sporting Clays O/U
Similar to the Field 1001 except has silver nitrate-finished receiver with special engraving incorporating a flying target, fuller pistol grip and radiused recoil pad. Ventilated rib is 10mm wide with mid-rib bead, white front bead. Available with 28" or 30" barrels with four WinPlus choke tubes. Stock dimensions are 14⅜"x1⅜"x2⅛"; weight 7¾ lbs. Introduced 1993.
Price: $1,253.00

PIETRO ZANOLETTI MODEL 2000 FIELD O/U
Gauge: 12 only.
Barrel: 28" (Mod. & Full).
Weight: 7 lbs.
Stock: European walnut, checkered grip and forend.

Sights: Gold bead front.
Features: Boxlock action with auto ejectors, double triggers; engraved receiver. Imported from Italy by Mandall Shooting Supplies. Introduced 1984.
Price: $895.00

SHOTGUNS—SIDE BY SIDES

Variety of models for utility and sporting use, including some competitive shooting.

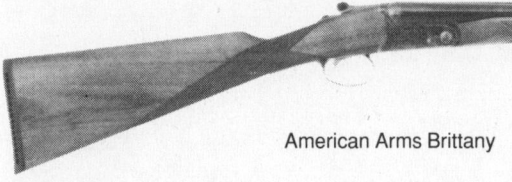

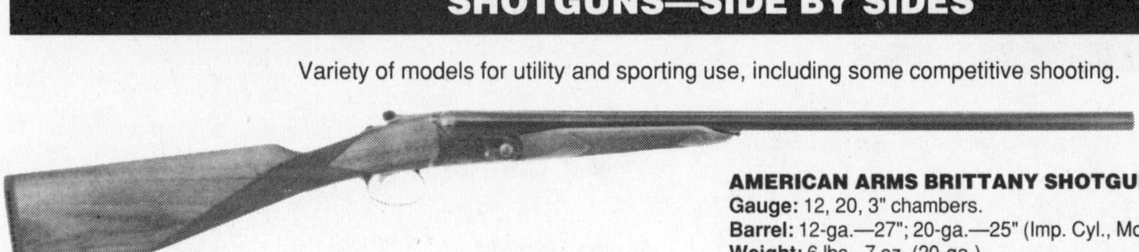

American Arms Brittany

AMERICAN ARMS BRITTANY SHOTGUN
Gauge: 12, 20, 3" chambers.
Barrel: 12-ga.—27"; 20-ga.—25" (Imp. Cyl., Mod., Full choke tubes).
Weight: 6 lbs., 7 oz. (20-ga.).
Stock: 14⅛"x1⅜"x2⅜". Hand-checkered walnut with oil finish, straight English-style with semi-beavertail forend.
Features: Boxlock action with case-color finish, engraving; single selective trigger, automatic selective ejectors; rubber recoil pad. Introduced 1989. Imported from Spain by American Arms, Inc.
Price: $763.00

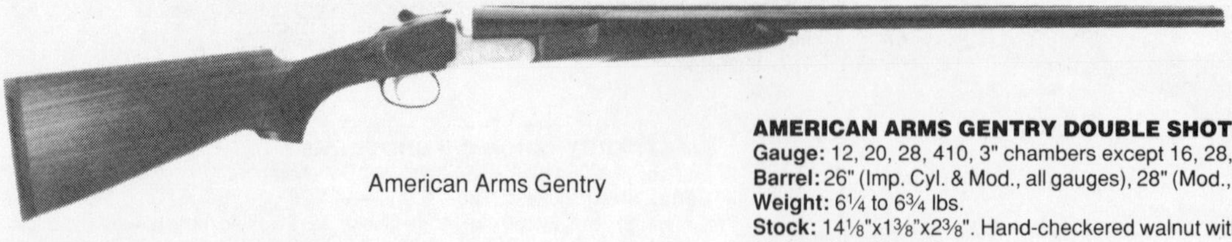

American Arms Gentry

American Arms Derby Side-by-Side
Has sidelock action with English-style engraving on the sideplates. Straight-grip, hand-checkered walnut stock with splinter forend, hand-rubbed oil finish. Single non-selective trigger, automatic selective ejectors. Same chokes, rib, barrel lengths as the Gentry. Has 5-year warranty. From American Arms, Inc.
Price: 12- or 20-ga. **$999.50**

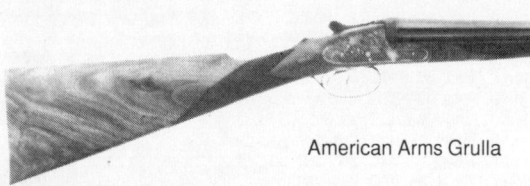

American Arms Grulla

AMERICAN ARMS WS/SS 10
Gauge: 10, 3½" chambers.
Barrel: 32" (Full & Full). Flat rib.
Weight: 10 lbs., 13 oz.
Stock: 14⁵⁄₁₆"x1⅜"x2⅜". Hand-checkered walnut with beavertail forend, full pistol grip, dull finish, rubber recoil pad.
Features: Boxlock action with double triggers and extractors. All metal has Parkerized finish. Comes with camouflaged sling, sling swivels, 5-year warranty. Introduced 1987. Imported from Spain by American Arms, Inc.
Price: **$639.00**

American Arms TS/SS 12 Side-by-Side
Similar to the WS/SS 10 except in 12-ga. with 3½" chambers, 26" barrels with Imp. Cyl., Mod., Full choke tubes, single selective trigger, extractors. Comes with camouflage sling, swivels, 5-year warranty. From American Arms, Inc.
Price: **$639.00**

ARMSPORT 1050 SERIES DOUBLE SHOTGUNS
Gauge: 12, 20, 410, 28, 3" chambers.
Barrel: 12-ga.—28" (Mod. & Full); 20-ga.—26" (Imp. & Mod.); 410—26" (Full & Full); 28-ga.—26" (Mod. & Full).
Weight: About 6¾ lbs.
Stock: European walnut.
Features: Chrome-lined barrels. Boxlock action with engraving. Imported from Italy by Armsport.
Price: 12, 20 . . . . **$785.00**
Price: 28, 410 . . . . **$860.00**

AMERICAN ARMS GENTRY DOUBLE SHOTGUN
Gauge: 12, 20, 28, 410, 3" chambers except 16, 28, 2¾".
Barrel: 26" (Imp. Cyl. & Mod., all gauges), 28" (Mod. & Full, 12 and 20 gauges).
Weight: 6¼ to 6¾ lbs.
Stock: 14⅛"x1⅜"x2⅜". Hand-checkered walnut with semi-gloss finish.
Sights: Metal bead front.
Features: Boxlock action with English-style scroll engraving, color case-hardened finish. Double triggers, extractors. Independent floating firing pins. Manual safety. Five-year warranty. Introduced 1987. Imported from Spain by American Arms, Inc.
Price: 12 or 20 . . . . **$625.00**
Price: 28 or 410 . . . . **$655.00**

AMERICAN ARMS GRULLA #2 DOUBLE SHOTGUN
Gauge: 12, 20, 28, 410.
Barrel: 12-ga.—28" (Mod. & Full); 26" (Imp. Cyl. & Mod.), all gauges.
Weight: 5 lbs., 13 oz. to 6 lbs., 4 oz.
Stock: Select walnut with straight English grip, splinter forend; hand-rubbed oil finish; checkered grip, forend, butt.
Features: True sidelock action with double triggers, detachable locks, automatic selective ejectors, cocking indicators, gas escape valves. Color case-hardened receiver with scroll engraving. English-style concave rib. Introduced 1989. Imported from Spain by American Arms, Inc.
Price: 12, 20, 28, 410 . . . . **$2,943.00**
Price: Two-barrel sets **$4,089.00**

American Arms TS/SS 10 Double Shotgun
Similar to the WS/SS 10 except has 26" (Full & Full choke tubes) barrels, raised solid rib. Double triggers, extractors. All metal and wood has matte finish. Imported by American Arms, Inc.
Price: **$639.00**

ARRIETA SIDELOCK DOUBLE SHOTGUNS
Gauge: 12, 16,,20, 28, 410.
Barrel: Length and chokes to customer specs.
Weight: To customer specs.
Stock: 14½"x1½"x2½" (standard dimensions), or to customer specs. Straight English with checkered butt (standard), or pistol grip. Select European walnut with oil finish.
Features: Essentially a custom gun with myriad options. Holland & Holland-pattern hand-detachable sidelocks, selective automatic ejectors, double triggers (hinged front) standard. Some have self-opening action. Finish and engraving to customer specs. Imported from Spain by Wingshooting Adventures.
Price: Model 557, auto ejectors, from **$2,750.00**
Price: Model 570, auto ejectors, from **$3,380.00**
Price: Model 578, auto ejectors, from **$3,740.00**
Price: Model 600 Imperial, self-opening, from **$4,990.00**
Price: Model 601 Imperial Tiro, self-opening, from **$5,750.00**
Price: Model 801, from **$7,950.00**
Price: Model 802, from **$7,950.00**
Price: Model 803, from **$5,850.00**
Price: Model 871, auto ejectors, from **$4,290.00**
Price: Model 872, self-opening, from **$9,790.00**
Price: Model 873, self-opening, from **$6,850.00**
Price: Model 874, self-opening, from **$7,950.00**
Price: Model 875, self-opening, from **$13,950.00**

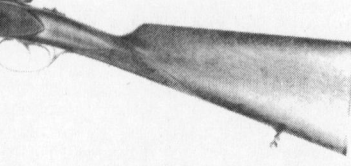

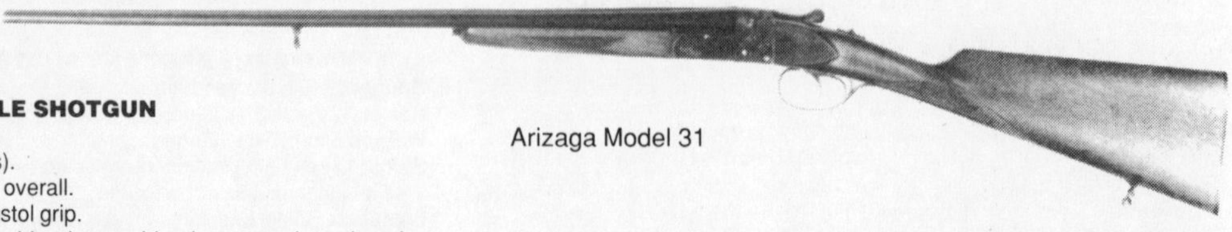

Arizaga Model 31

ARIZAGA MODEL 31 DOUBLE SHOTGUN
Gauge: 12, 16, 20, 28, 410.
Barrel: 26", 28" (standard chokes).
Weight: 6 lbs., 9 oz. **Length:** 45" overall.
Stock: Straight English style or pistol grip.
Features: Boxlock action with double triggers; blued, engraved receiver. Imported by Mandall Shooting Supplies.
Price: **$550.00**

AYA BOXLOCK SHOTGUNS

Gauge: 12, 16, 20, 28, 410.
Barrel: 26", 27", 28", depending upon gauge.
Weight: 5 to 7 lbs.
Stock: European walnut.
Features: Anson & Deeley system with double locking lugs; chopper lump barrels; bushed firing pins; automatic safety and ejectors; articulated front trigger. Imported by Armes de Chasse.
Price: Model XXV, 12 or 20 . . . . **$3,300.00**
Price: Model 4 Deluxe, 12, 16, 20, 28, 410 . . . . **$3,500.00**
Price: Model 4, 12, 16, 20, 28, 410 . . . . **$2,000.00**

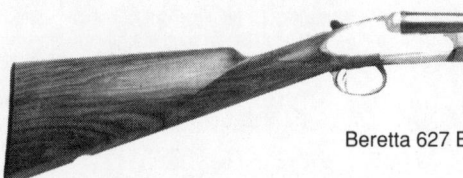

Beretta 627 EL

BERETTA SIDE-BY-SIDE FIELD SHOTGUNS

Gauge: 12 and 20, 3" chambers.
Barrel: 26" and 28" (Mobilchoke tubes).
Stock: Close-grained American walnut.
Features: Front and center beads on a raised ventilated rib. Onyx has P. Beretta signature on each side of the receiver, while a gold gauge marking is inscribed atop the rib. Imported from Italy by Beretta U.S.A.
Price: 626 Onyx **$1,870.00**
Price: 627 EL (gold inlays, sideplates) **$3,270.00**
Price: 627 EELL (engraved sideplates, pistol grip or straight English stock) **$5,405.00**

CHAPUIS SIDE-BY-SIDE SHOTGUN

Gauge: 12, 16, 20.
Barrel: 22", 23.6", 26.8", 27.6", 31.5", chokes to customer specs.
Weight: 5 to 10 lbs. **Length:** NA.
Stock: French walnut, straight English or pistol grip.
Features: Double hook Blitz system center sidelock action with notched action zone, automatic ejectors or extractors. Long trigger guard (most models), choice of raised solid rib, vent. rib or ultra light rib. Imported from France by Armes de Chasse.
Price: About . . . . **$4,000.00 to $5,000.00**

CHARLES DALY MODEL DSS DOUBLE

Gauge: 12, 20, 3" chambers.
Barrel: 26", choke tubes.
Weight: 6 lbs., 13 oz. (12-ga.). **Length:** 44.5" overall.
Stock: 14⅛"x1⅜"x2⅜". Figured walnut; pistol grip; cut checkering; black rubber recoil pad; semi-beavertail forend.
Features: Boxlock action with automatic selective ejectors, automatic safety, gold single trigger. Engraved, silvered frame. Introduced 1990. Imported by Outdoor Sports Headquarters.
Price: **$675.00**

AYA SIDELOCK DOUBLE SHOTGUNS

Gauge: 12, 16, 20, 28, 410.
Barrel: 26", 27", 28", 29", depending upon gauge.
Weight: NA.
Stock: Figured European walnut; cut checkering; oil finish.
Features: Sidelock actions with double triggers (articulated front), automatic safety, automatic ejectors, cocking indicators, bushed firing pins, replaceable hinge pins, chopper lump barrels. Many options available. Imported by Armes de Chasse.
Price: Model 1, 12 or 20, exhibition-quality wood **$7,000.00**
Price: Model 2, 12, 16, 20, 28, 410 . . . . **$3,700.00**
Price: Model 53, 12, 16, 20 . . . . **$5,300.00**
Price: Model 56, 12 only **$8,200.00**
Price: Model XXV, 12 or 20, Churchill-type rib **$4,300.00**
Price: Matador, 12 or 20, single selective trigger, pistol grip stock . **$2,000.00**

BERETTA MODEL 452 SIDELOCK SHOTGUN

Gauge: 12, 2¾" or 3" chambers.
Barrel: 26", 28", 30", choked to customer specs.
Weight: 6 lbs., 13 oz.
Stock: Dimensions to customer specs. Highly figured walnut; Model 452 EELL has walnut briar.
Features: Full sidelock action with English-type double bolting; automatic selective ejectors, manual safety; double triggers, single or single non-selective trigger on request. Essentially custom made to specifications. Model 452 is coin finished without engraving; 452 EELL is fully engraved. Imported from Italy by Beretta U.S.A.
Price: 452 . . . . **$22,000.00**
Price: 452 EELL **$30,500.00**

CRUCELEGUI HERMANOS MODEL 150 DOUBLE

Gauge: 12, 16 or 20, 2¾" chambers.
Action: Greener triple cross bolt.
Barrel: 20", 26", 28", 30", 32" (Cyl. & Cyl., Full & Full, Mod. & Full, Mod. & Imp. Cyl., Imp. Cyl. & Full, Mod. & Mod.).
Weight: 5 to 7¼ lbs.
Stock: Hand-checkered walnut, beavertail forend.
Features: Double triggers; color case-hardened receiver; sling swivels; chrome-lined bores. Imported from Spain by Mandall Shooting Supplies.
Price: **$450.00**

E.A.A./SABATTI SABA-MON DOUBLE SHOTGUN

Gauge: 12, 20, 28, 410, 3" chambers.
Barrel: 26" or 28" (standard chokes).
Weight: NA.
Stock: European walnut, straight English or pistol grip.
Features: Anson & Deeley-type boxlock action, single selective trigger, automatic selective ejectors. Blue finish. Introduced 1993. Imported from Italy by European American Armory.
Price: **$1,095.00**

FERLIB MODEL F VII DOUBLE SHOTGUN

Gauge: 12, 16, 20, 28, 410.
Barrel: 25" to 28".
Weight: 5½ lbs. (20-ga.).
Stock: Oil-finished walnut, checkered straight grip and forend.
Features: Boxlock action with fine scroll engraving, silvered receiver. Double triggers standard. Introduced 1983. Imported from Italy by Wm. Larkin Moore.
Price: F.VII **$7,500.00**
Price: F.VII SC **$9,000.00**
Price: F.VII SP Sideplate with gold **$13,000.00**

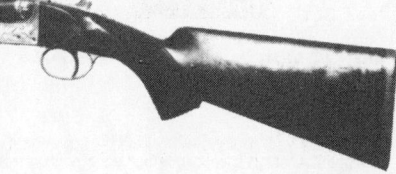

Francotte Boxlock

AUGUSTE FRANCOTTE BOXLOCK SHOTGUN

Gauge: 12, 16, 20, 28 and 410-bore, 2¾" or 3" chambers.
Barrel: 26" to 29", chokes to customer specs.
Weight: NA. **Length:** NA.
Stock: Deluxe European walnut to customer specs. Straight or pistol grip; checkered butt; oil finish; splinter or beavertail forend.
Sights: Bead front.
Features: Anson & Deeley boxlock action with double locks, double triggers (front hinged), manual or automatic safety, Holland & Holland ejectors. English scroll engraving, coin finish or color case-hardening. Many options available. Imported from Belgium by Armes de Chasse.
Price: From about . . . . **$16,000.00 to $20,000.00**

AUGUSTE FRANCOTTE SIDELOCK SHOTGUN
Gauge: 12, 16, 20, 28 and 410-bore, 2¾" or 3" chambers.
Barrel: 26" to 29", chokes to customer specs.
Weight: NA. **Length:** NA.
Stock: Deluxe European walnut to customer specs. Straight or pistol grip; checkered butt; oil finish; splinter or beavertail forend.

Garbi Model 100

Garbi Model 101 Side-by-Side
Similar to the Garbi Model 100 except is hand engraved with scroll engraving, select walnut stock. Better overall quality than the Model 100. Imported from Spain by Wm. Larkin Moore.
Price: From **$5,750.00**

Garbi Model 103A, B Side-by-Side
Similar to the Garbi Model 100 except has Purdey-type fine scroll and rosette engraving. Better overall quality than the Model 101. Model 103B has nickel-chrome steel barrels, H&H-type easy opening mechanism; other mechanical details remain the same. Imported from Spain by Wm. Larkin Moore.
Price: Model 103A, from **$7,100.00**
Price: Model 103B, from **$9,900.00**

BILL HANUS BIRDGUN DOUBLES
Gauge: 16, 20, 28.
Barrel: 26" (Skeet & Skeet).
Weight: About 6¼ lbs. (16-ga.).
Stock: Hand-checkered walnut; straight grip, semi-beavertail forend.

HATFIELD UPLANDER SHOTGUN
Gauge: 20, 3" chambers.
Barrel: 26" (Imp. Cyl. & Mod.).
Weight: 5¾ lbs.
Stock: Straight English style, special select XXX fancy maple. Hand-rubbed oil finish. Splinter forend.
Features: Double locking under-lug boxlock action; color case-hardened frame; single non-selective trigger. Grades differ in engraving, finish, gold work. Introduced 1988. From Hatfield.

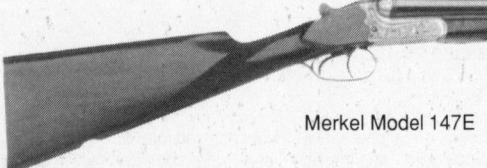

Merkel Model 147E

> Consult our Directory pages for the location of firms mentioned.

MERKEL MODEL 47LSC SPORTING CLAYS DOUBLE
Gauge: 12, 3" chambers.
Barrel: 28" with Briley choke tubes.
Weight: 7.2 lbs.
Stock: Fancy figured walnut with pistol grip, recoil pad. Beavertail forend.
Features: Anson & Deeley boxlock action with single selective trigger adjsutable for length of pull; H&H-type ejectors; white front sight with mid-rib bead; manual safety; cocking indicators; lengthened forcing cones; color case-hardened receiver with Arabesque engraving. Comes with fitted leather luggage case. Introduced 1993. Imported from Germany by GSI.
Price: **$2,995.00**

Sights: Bead front.
Features: True Holland & Holland sidelock action with double locks, double triggers (front hinged); manual or automatic safety; Holland & Holland ejectors. English scroll engraving, coin finish or color case-hardening. Many options available. Imported from Belgium by Armes de Chasse.
Price: From about . . . . **$20,000.00 to $25,000.00**

GARBI MODEL 100 DOUBLE
Gauge: 12, 16, 20, 28.
Barrel: 26", 28", choked to customer specs.
Weight: 5½ to 7½ lbs.
Stock: 14½"x2¼"x1½". European walnut. Straight grip, checkered butt, classic forend.
Features: Sidelock action, automatic ejectors, double triggers standard. Color case-hardened action, coin finish optional. Single trigger; beavertail forend, etc. optional. Five other models are available. Imported from Spain by Wm. Larkin Moore.
Price: From **$4,500.00**

Garbi Model 200 Side-by-Side
Similar to the Garbi Model 100 except has heavy-duty locks, magnum proofed. Very fine Continental-style floral and scroll engraving, well figured walnut stock. Other mechanical features remain the same. Imported from Spain by Wm. Larkin Moore.
Price: **$9,400.00**

Features: Color case-hardened boxlock action; raised Churchill rib; single non-selective trigger; auto ejectors, auto safety. Introduced 1991. Imported by Precision Sports.
Price: 16-, 20-ga. **$1,269.95**
Price: 28-ga. **$1,399.95**

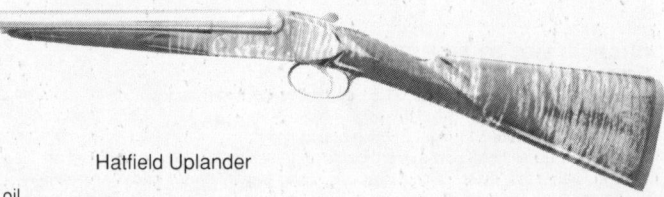

Hatfield Uplander

Price: Grade I **$1,995.00**
Price: Grade II **$2,595.00**
Price: Grades III through VIII, from **$3,500.00**

MERKEL MODEL 8, 47E SIDE-BY-SIDE SHOTGUNS
Gauge: 12, 3" chambers, 16, 2¾" chambers, 20, 3" chambers.
Barrel: 12-, 16-ga.—28"; 20-ga.—26¾" (Imp. Cyl. & Mod., Mod. & Full).
Weight: About 6¾ lbs. (12-ga.).
Stock: Oil-finished walnut; straight English or pistol grip.
Features: Anson & Deeley-type boxlock action with single selective or double triggers, automatic safety, cocking indicators. Color case-hardened receiver with standard Arabesque engraving. Imported from Germany by GSI.
Price: Model 8 (extractors only) **$1,295.00**
Price: Model 47E (H&H ejectors) **$1,595.00**
Price: Model 147 (extractors, silver-grayed receiver with hunting scenes) **$1,795.00**
Price: Model 147E (as above with ejectors) **$1,995.00**
Price: Model 122 (as above with false sideplates, fine engraving) . **$3,195.00**

Merkel Model 47S, 147S Side-by-Sides
Similar to the Model 122 except with Holland & Holland-style sidelock action with cocking indicators, ejectors. Silver-grayed receiver and sideplates have Arabesque engraving, engraved border and screws (Model 47S), or fine hunting scene engraving (Model 147S). Imported from Germany by GSI.
Price: Model 47S **$4,195.00**
Price: Model 147S **$5,195.00**
Price: Model 247S (English-style engraving, large scrolls) . . **$6,895.00**
Price: Model 347S (English-style engraving, medium scrolls) . **$7,895.00**
Price: Model 447S (English-style engraving, small scrolls) **$8,995.00**

PARKER REPRODUCTIONS SIDE-BY-SIDE SHOTGUN

Gauge: 12, 16/20 combo, 20, 28, 2¾" and 3" chambers.
Barrel: 26" (Skeet 1 & 2, Imp. Cyl. & Mod.), 28" (Mod. & Full, 2¾" and 3", 12, 20, 28; Skeet 1 & 2, Imp. Cyl. & Mod., Mod. & Full 16-ga. only).
Weight: 6¾ lbs. (12-ga.)
Stock: Checkered (26 lpi) AAA fancy California English or Claro walnut, skeleton steel and checkered butt. Straight or pistol grip, splinter or beavertail forend.
Features: Exact reproduction of the original Parker—parts interchange. Double or single selective trigger, selective ejectors, hard-chromed bores, designed

for steel shot. One, two or three (16-20, 20) barrel sets available. Hand-engraved snap caps included. Introduced 1984. Made by Winchester. Imported from Japan by Parker Division, Reagent Chemical.

Price:	
Price: D Grade, one-barrel set	$3,370.00
Price: Two-barrel set, same gauge	$4,200.00
Price: Two-barrel set, 16/20	$4,870.00
Price: Three-barrel set, 16/20/20	$5,630.00
Price: A-1 Special two-barrel set	$11,200.00
Price: A-1 Special three-barrel set	$13,200.00

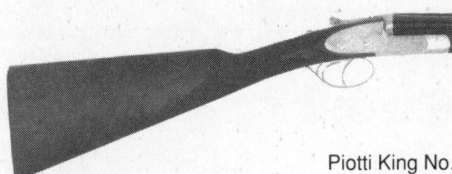

Piotti King No. 1

PIOTTI KING NO. 1 SIDE-BY-SIDE

Gauge: 12, 16, 20, 28, 410.
Barrel: 25" to 30" (12-ga.), 25" to 28" (16, 20, 28, 410). To customer specs. Chokes as specified.

Piotti Lunik Side-by-Side

Similar to the Piotti King No. 1 except better overall quality. Has Renaissance-style large scroll engraving in relief, gold crown in top lever, gold name and gold crest in forend. Best quality Holland & Holland-pattern sidelock ejector double with chopper lump (demi-bloc) barrels. Other mechanical specifications remain the same. Imported from Italy by Wm. Larkin Moore.
Price: From **$21,500.00**

Weight: 6½ lbs. to 8 lbs. (12-ga. to customer specs.).
Stock: Dimensions to customer specs. Finely figured walnut; straight grip with checkered butt with classic splinter forend and hand-rubbed oil finish standard. Pistol grip, beavertail forend, satin luster finish optional.
Features: Holland & Holland pattern sidelock action, automatic ejectors. Double trigger with front trigger hinged standard; non-selective single trigger optional. Coin finish standard; color case-hardened optional. Top rib; level, file-cut standard; concave, ventilated optional. Very fine, full coverage scroll engraving with small floral bouquets, gold crown in top lever, name in gold, and gold crest in forend. Imported from Italy by Wm. Larkin Moore.
Price: From **$19,900.00**

Piotti King Extra Side-by-Side

Similar to the Piotti King No. 1 except highest quality wood and metal work. Choice of either bulino game scene engraving or game scene engraving with gold inlays. Engraved and signed by a master engraver. Exhibition grade wood. Other mechanical specifications remain the same. Imported from Italy by Wm. Larkin Moore.
Price: From **$23,700.00**

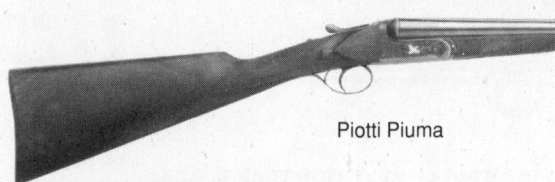

Piotti Piuma

PIOTTI PIUMA SIDE-BY-SIDE

Gauge: 12, 16, 20, 28, 410.
Barrel: 25" to 30" (12-ga.), 25" to 28" (16, 20, 28, 410).

Weight: 5½ to 6¼ lbs. (20-ga.).
Stock: Dimensions to customer specs. Straight grip stock with walnut checkered butt, classic splinter forend, hand-rubbed oil finish are standard; pistol grip, beavertail forend, satin luster finish optional.
Features: Anson & Deeley boxlock ejector double with chopper lump barrels. Level, file-cut rib, light scroll and rosette engraving, scalloped frame. Double triggers with hinged front standard, single non-selective optional. Coin finish standard, color case-hardened optional. Imported from Italy by Wm. Larkin Moore.
Price: From **$11,900.00**

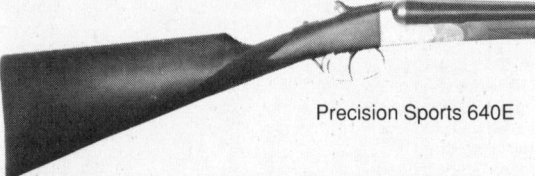

Precision Sports 640E

PRECISION SPORTS MODEL 600 SERIES DOUBLES

Gauge: 10, 3½" chambers; 12, 16, 20, 2¾" chambers; 28, 410, 3" chambers.
Barrel: 25", 26", 27", 28" (Imp. Cyl. & Mod., Mod. & Full).
Weight: 12-ga., 6¾-7 lbs.; 20-ga., 5¾-6 lbs.
Stock: 14½"x1½"x2½". Hand-checkered walnut with oil finish. "E" (English) models have straight grip, splinter forend, checkered butt. "A" (American) models have p.g. stock, beavertail forend, buttplate.
Features: Boxlock action; silvered, engraved action; automatic safety; ejectors or extractors. E-models have double triggers, concave rib (XXV models have Churchill-type rib); A-models have single, non-selective trigger, raised matte rib. Made in Spain by Ugartechea. Imported by Precision Sports. Introduced 1986.

Price: 640E (12, 16, 20; 26", 28"), extractors	$849.95
Price: 640E (28, 410 only), extractors	$939.95
Price: 640A (12, 16, 20; 26", 28"), extractors	$964.95
Price: 640A (28, 410 only), ejectors	$1,109.95
Price: 640M "Big Ten" (10-ga. 26", 30", 32", Full & Full)	$999.95
Price: 640 Slug Gun (12, 25", Imp. Cyl. & Imp. Cyl.)	$1,119.95
Price: 645E (12, 16, 20; 26", 28"), with ejectors	$1,089.95
Price: 645E (28, 410), with ejectors	$1,149.95
Price: 645A (12, 16, 20; 26", 28"), with ejectors	$1,199.95
Price: 645A (28, 410), ejectors	$1,309.95
Price: 645E-XXV (12, 16, 20; 25"), with ejectors	$1,099.95
Price: 645E-XXV (28, 410), with ejectors	$1,199.95
Price: 650E (12), extractors, choke tubes	$919.95
Price: 650A (12), extractors, choke tubes	$1,039.95
Price: 655E (12), ejectors, choke tubes	$1,149.95
Price: 655A (12), ejectors, choke tubes	$1,259.95

RIZZINI BOXLOCK SIDE-BY-SIDE

Gauge: 12, 16, 20, 28, 410.
Barrel: 25" to 30" (12-, 16-, 20-ga.), 25" to 28" (28, 410).
Weight: 5½ to 6¼ lbs. (20-ga.).
Stock: Dimensions to customer specs. Straight grip stock with checkered butt, classic splinter forend, hand-rubbed oil finish are standard; pistol grip, beavertail forend; satin luster finish optional.
Features: Anson & Deeley boxlock ejector double with chopper lump barrels. Level, file-cut rib, scalloped frame. Double triggers with hinged front optional, single non-selective standard. Coin finish standard. Imported from Italy by Wm. Larkin Moore.
Price: 12-, 20-ga., from **$23,000.00**
Price: 28, 410 bore, from **$25,500.00**

RIZZINI SIDELOCK SIDE-BY-SIDE

Gauge: 12, 16, 20, 28, 410.
Barrel: 25" to 30" (12-, 16-, 20-ga.), 25" to 28" (28, 410). To customer specs. Chokes as specified.
Weight: 6½ lbs. to 8 lbs. (12-ga. to customer specs).
Stock: Dimensions to customer specs. Finely figured walnut; straight grip with checkered butt with classic splinter forend and hand-rubbed oil finish standard. Pistol grip, beavertail forend, satin luster finish optional.
Features: Holland & Holland pattern sidelock action, auto ejectors. Double triggers with front trigger hinged optional; non-selective single trigger standard. Coin finish standard. Top rib level, file cut standard; concave optional. Imported from Italy by Wm. Larkin Moore.
Price: 12-, 20-ga., from **$40,000.00**
Price: 28, 410 bore, from **$46,000.00**

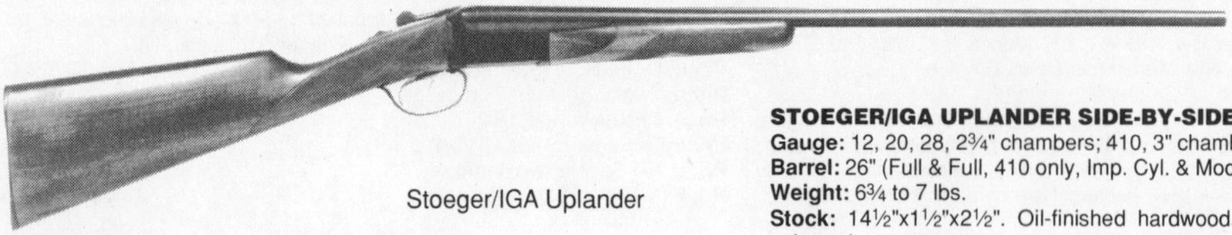

Stoeger/IGA Uplander

UGARTECHEA 10-GAUGE MAGNUM SHOTGUN
Gauge: 10, 3½" chambers.
Action: Boxlock.
Barrel: 32" (Full).
Weight: 11 lbs.
Stock: 14½"x1½"x2⅝". European walnut, checkered at pistol grip and forend.
Features: Double triggers; color case-hardened action, rest blued. Front and center metal beads on matted rib; ventilated rubber recoil pad. Forend release has positive Purdey-type mechanism. Imported from Spain by Mandall Shooting Supplies.
Price: **$699.50**

STOEGER/IGA UPLANDER SIDE-BY-SIDE SHOTGUN
Gauge: 12, 20, 28, 2¾" chambers; 410, 3" chambers.
Barrel: 26" (Full & Full, 410 only, Imp. Cyl. & Mod.), 28" (Mod. & Full).
Weight: 6¾ to 7 lbs.
Stock: 14½"x1½"x2½". Oil-finished hardwood. Checkered pistol grip and forend.
Features: Automatic safety, extractors only, solid matted barrel rib. Double triggers only. Introduced 1983. Imported from Brazil by Stoeger Industries.
Price: **$383.00**
Price: With choke tubes **$425.00**
Price: Coach Gun, 12, 20, 410, 20" bbls. **$367.00**

SHOTGUNS—BOLT ACTIONS & SINGLE SHOTS

Variety of designs for utility and sporting purposes, as well as for competitive shooting.

ARMSPORT SINGLE BARREL SHOTGUN
Gauge: 20, 3" chamber.
Barrel: 26" (Mod.).
Weight: About 6½ lbs.
Stock: Hardwood with oil finish.
Features: Chrome-lined barrel, manual safety, cocking indicator. Opening lever behind trigger guard. Imported by Armsport.
Price: **$100.00**

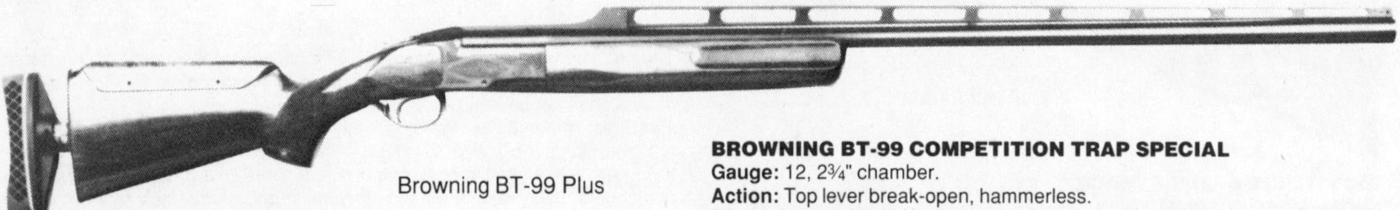

Browning BT-99 Plus

Browning BT-99 Plus Trap Gun
Similar to the Grade I BT-99 except comes with 32" or 34" barrel with .745" over bore, Invector Plus choke system with Full, Imp. Mod. and Mod. choke tubes; high post, ventilated, tapered, target rib adjustable from 3" to 12" above point of aim. Available with or without ported barrel. Select walnut stock has high-gloss finish, Monte Carlo comb, modified beavertail forend and is fully adjustable for length of pull, drop at comb and drop at Monte Carlo. Has Browning Recoil Reduction System. Introduced 1989.
Price: Grade I, with ported barrel **$1,780.00**
Price: Grade I, non-ported barrel **$1,765.00**
Price: Stainless, ported **$2,150.00**
Price: Pigeon Grade, ported **$1,985.00**
Price: Signature Painted, ported **$1,815.00**

BROWNING BT-99 COMPETITION TRAP SPECIAL
Gauge: 12, 2¾" chamber.
Action: Top lever break-open, hammerless.
Barrel: 32" or 34" with 1 1/32" wide high post floating vent. rib. Comes with Invector Plus choke tubes; .745" overbore.
Weight: 8 lbs. (32" bbl.).
Stock: French walnut; hand-checkered, full pistol grip, full beavertail forend; recoil pad. Trap dimensions with M.C. 14⅜"x1⅜"x1⅜"x2".
Sights: Ivory front and middle beads.
Features: Gold-plated trigger with 3½-lb. pull, deluxe trap-style recoil pad, automatic ejector, no safety. Available with either Monte Carlo or standard stock. Imported from Japan by Browning.
Price: Grade I Invector, Plus Ported barrels **$1,225.00**
Price: Stainless, ported **$1,650.00**
Price: Pigeon Grade, ported **$1,430.00**
Price: Signature Painted **$1,260.00**

Browning BT-99 Plus Micro
Similar to the standard BT-99 Plus except scaled down for smaller shooters. Comes with 28", 30", 32" or 34" barrel with adjustable rib system and buttstock with adjustable length of pull range of 13½" to 14". Also has Browning's recoil reducer system, ported barrels, Invector Plus choke system and back-bored barrel. Weight is about 8 lbs., 6 oz. Introduced 1991.
Price: With ported barrel **$1,780.00**
Price: With non-ported barrel **$1,765.00**
Price: Stainless, ported **$2,150.00**
Price: Pigeon Grade, ported **$1,985.00**
Price: Signature Painted**$1,815.00**

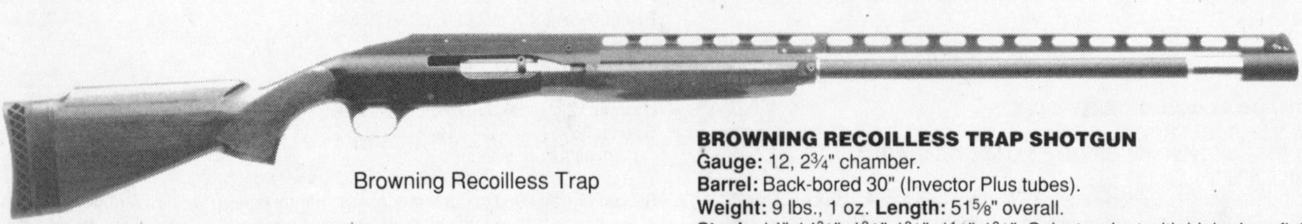

Browning Recoilless Trap

Browning Micro Recoilless Trap Shotgun
Same as the standard Recoilless Trap except has 27" barrel, weighs 8 lbs., 10 oz., and stock length of pull adjustable from 13" to 13¾", Overall length 47⅝". Introduced 1993. Imported by Browning.
Price: **$1,670.00**

BROWNING RECOILLESS TRAP SHOTGUN
Gauge: 12, 2¾" chamber.
Barrel: Back-bored 30" (Invector Plus tubes).
Weight: 9 lbs., 1 oz. **Length:** 51⅝" overall.
Stock: 14"-14¾"x1⅜"-1¾"x1⅛"-1¾". Select walnut with high gloss finish, cut checkering.
Features: Eliminates up to 72 percent of recoil. Mass of the inner mechansim (barrel, receiver and inner bolt) is driven forward when trigger is pulled, cancelling most recoil. Forend is used to cock action when the action is forward. Ventilated rib adjusts to move point of impact; drop at comb and length of pull adjustable. Introduced 1993. Imported by Browning.
Price: **$1,670.00**

DESERT INDUSTRIES BIG TWENTY SHOTGUN

Gauge: 20, 2¾" chamber.
Barrel: 19" (Cyl.).
Weight: 4¾ lbs. **Length:** 31¾" overall.
Stock: Fixed wire, with buttplate. Walnut forend and grip.

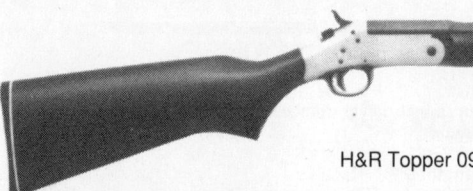

H&R Topper 098

Harrington & Richardson Topper Classic Youth Shotgun

Similar to the Topper Junior 098 except available in 20-gauge (3", Mod.), 410-bore (Full) with 3" chamber; 28-gauge, 2¾" chamber (Mod.); all have 22" barrel. Stock is American black walnut with cut-checkered pistol grip and forend. Ventilated rubber recoil pad with white line spacers. Blued barrel, blued frame. Introduced 1992. From H&R 1871, Inc.
Price: $139.95

H&R N.W.T.F. Turkey

Harrington & Richardson Topper Deluxe Model 098

Similar to the standard Topper 098 except 12-gauge only with 3½" chamber, 28" barrel with choke tube (comes with Mod. tube, others optional). Satin nickel frame, blued barrel, black-finished wood. Introduced 1992. From H&R 1871, Inc.
Price: $124.95

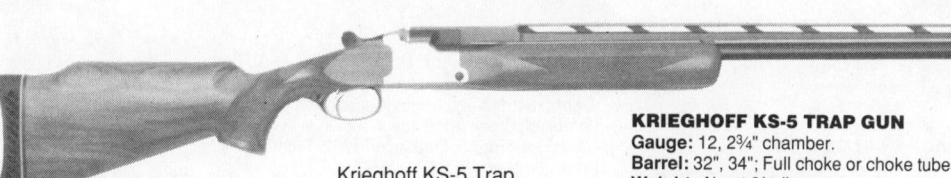

Krieghoff KS-5 Trap

Krieghoff KS-5 Special

Same as the KS-5 except the barrel has a fully adjustable rib and adjustable stock. Rib allows shooter to adjust point of impact from 50%/50% to nearly 90%/10%. Introduced 1990.
Price: $4,450.00

KRIEGHOFF K-80 SINGLE BARREL TRAP GUN

Gauge: 12, 2¾" chamber.
Barrel: 32" or 34" Unsingle; 34" Top Single. Fixed Full or choke tubes.
Weight: About 8¾ lbs.
Stock: Four stock dimensions or adjustable stock available. All hand-checkered European walnut.

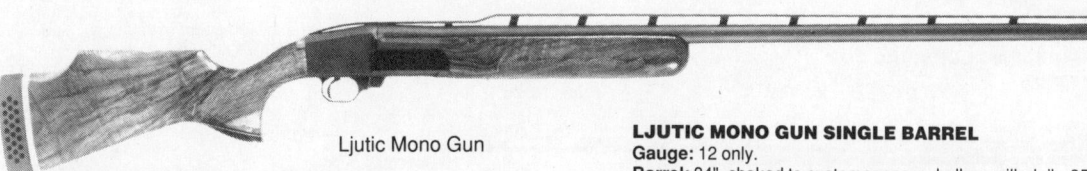

Ljutic Mono Gun

Ljutic LTX Super Deluxe Mono Gun

Super Deluxe version of the standard Mono Gun with high quality wood, extra-fancy checkering pattern in 24 lpi, double recessed choking. Available in two weights: 8¼ lbs. or 8¾ lbs. Extra light 33" barrel; medium-height rib. Introduced 1984. From Ljutic Industries.
Price: $5,595.00
Price: With three screw-in choke tubes $5,995.00

Stock: Bead front.
Features: Single shot action of all steel construction. Blue finish. Announced 1990. From Desert Industries, Inc.
Price: $189.95

HARRINGTON & RICHARDSON TOPPER MODEL 098

Gauge: 12, 20, 410, 3" chamber.
Barrel: 12 ga.—28" (Mod.); 20 ga.—26" (Mod.); 410 bore—26" (Full).
Weight: 5-6 lbs.
Stock: Black-finish hardwood with full pistol grip; semi-beavertail forend.
Sights: Gold bead front.
Features: Break-open action with side-lever release, automatic ejector. Satin nickel frame, blued barrel. Reintroduced 1992. From H&R 1871, Inc.
Price: $109.95
Price: Topper Junior 098 (as above except 22" barrel, 20-ga. (Mod.), 410-bore (Full), 12½" length of pull) $114.95

Harrington & Richardson N.W.T.F Turkey Mag

Similar to the Topper 098 except covered with Mossy Oak camouflage. Chambered for 12-gauge 3½" chamber, 24" barrel (comes with Turkey Full choke tube, others available); weighs 6 lbs., overall length 40". Comes with Mossy Oak sling, swivels, studs. Introduced 1992. From H&R 1871, Inc.
Price: $169.95

KRIEGHOFF KS-5 TRAP GUN

Gauge: 12, 2¾" chamber.
Barrel: 32", 34"; Full choke or choke tubes.
Weight: About 8½ lbs.
Stock: Choice of high Monte Carlo (1½"), low Monte Carlo (1⅜") or factory adjustable stock. European walnut.
Features: Ventilated tapered step rib. Adjustable trigger or optional release trigger. Satin gray electroless nickel receiver. Comes with fitted aluminum case. Introduced 1988. Imported from Germany by Krieghoff International, Inc.
Price: Fixed choke, cased $3,575.00
Price: With choke tubes $3,975.00

Features: Satin nickel finish with K-80 logo. Selective mechanical trigger adjustable for finger position. Tapered step vent. rib. Adjustable point of impact on Unsingle.
Price: Standard grade full Unsingle $7,300.00
Price: Standard grade full Top Single combo (special order), from $9,380.00
Price: RT (removable trigger) option, add $1,000.00

LJUTIC MONO GUN SINGLE BARREL

Gauge: 12 only.
Barrel: 34", choked to customer specs; hollow-milled rib, 35½" sight plane.
Weight: Approx. 9 lbs.
Stock: To customer specs. Oil finish, hand checkered.
Features: Totally custom made. Pull or release trigger; removable trigger guard contains trigger and hammer mechanism; Ljutic pushbutton opener on front of trigger guard. From Ljutic Industries.
Price: With standard, medium or Olympic rib, custom 32"-34" bbls. $4,495.00
Price: As above with screw-in choke barrel $4,695.00

LJUTIC RECOILLESS SPACE GUN SHOTGUN
Gauge: 12 only, 2¾" chamber.
Barrel: 30" (Full). Screw-in or fixed-choke barrel.
Weight: 8½ lbs.
Stock: 14½" to 15" pull length; universal comb; medium or large p.g.

Sights: Vent. rib.
Features: Pull trigger standard, release trigger available; anti-recoil mechanism. Revolutionary new design. Introduced 1981. From Ljutic Industries.
Price: From **$5,995.00**

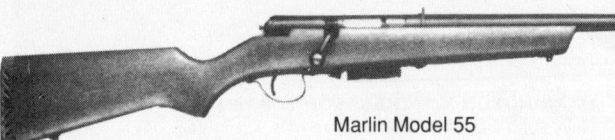

Marlin Model 55

MARLIN MODEL 55 GOOSE GUN BOLT ACTION
Gauge: 12 only, 2¾" or 3" chamber.

Action: Bolt action, thumb safety, detachable two-shot clip. Red cocking indicator.
Barrel: 36" (Full).
Weight: 8 lbs. **Length:** 56¾" overall.
Stock: Walnut-finished hardwood, p.g., ventilated recoil pad. Swivel studs, MarShield® finish.
Features: Brass bead front sight, U-groove rear sight.
Price: **$274.75**

NEW ENGLAND FIREARMS TURKEY AND GOOSE GUN
Gauge: 10, 3½" chamber.
Barrel: 28" (Full).
Weight: 9.5 lbs. **Length:** 44" overall.
Stock: American hardwood with walnut, or matte camo finish; ventilated rubber recoil pad.
Sights: Bead front.
Features: Break-open action with side-lever release; ejector. Matte finish on metal. Introduced 1992. From New England Firearms.
Price: Walnut-finish wood **$149.95**
Price: Camo finish, sling and swivels **$159.95**

New England Turkey

New England Firearms N.W.T.F. Shotgun
Similar to the Turkey/Goose Gun except completely covered with Mossy Oak camouflage finish; 24" barrel with interchangeable choke tubes (comes with Turkey Full, others optional); comes with Mossy Oak sling. Drilled and tapped for long eye relief scope mount. Introduced 1992. From New England Firearms.
Price: **$199.95**
Price: 20-ga., 24" (Mod.), Mossy Oak camo **$149.95**

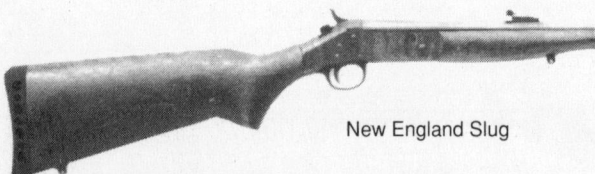

New England Slug

NEW ENGLAND FIREARMS TRACKER SLUG GUN
Gauge: 12, 20, 3" chamber.
Barrel: 24" (Cyl.).

Weight: 6 lbs. **Length:** 40" overall.
Stock: Walnut-finished hardwood with full pistol grip, recoil pad.
Sights: Blade front, fully adjustable rifle-type rear.
Features: Break-open action with side-lever release; blued barrel, color case-hardened frame. Introduced 1992. From New England Firearms.
Price: Tracker **$124.95**
Price: Tracker II (as above except fully rifled bore) **$129.95**

NEW ENGLAND FIREARMS STANDARD PARDNER
Gauge: 12, 20, 410, 3" chamber; 16, 28, 2¾" chamber.
Barrel: 12-ga.—28" (Full, Mod.); 16-ga.—28" (Full); 20-ga.—26" (Full, Mod.); 28-ga.—26" (Mod.); 410-bore—26" (Full).
Weight: 5-6 lbs. **Length:** 43" overall (28" barrel).
Stock: Walnut-finished hardwood with full pistol grip.

Sights: Bead front.
Features: Transfer bar ignition; break-open action with side-lever release. Introduced 1987. From New England Firearms.
Price: **$99.95**
Price: Youth model (20-ga., 410, 22" barrel, recoil pad) **$104.95**

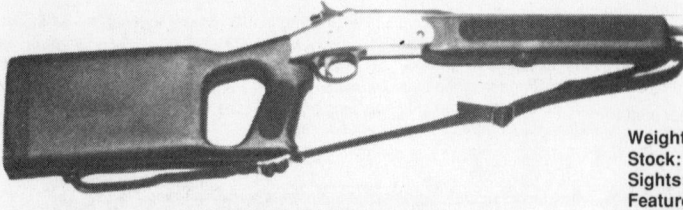

New England Survival

NEW ENGLAND FIREARMS SURVIVAL GUN
Gauge: 12, 20, 3" chamber.
Barrel: 22" (Mod.).

Weight: 6 lbs. **Length:** 36" overall.
Stock: Black polymer with thumbhole/pistol grip, sling swivels.
Sights: Bead front.
Features: Buttplate swings open to expose storage for extra ammunition. Blue or nickel finish. Introduced 1993. From New England Firearms.
Price: Blue **$129.95**
Price: Nickel **$149.95**

PERAZZI TM1 SPECIAL SINGLE TRAP
Gauge: 12, 2¾" chambers.
Barrel: 32" or 34" (Extra Full).
Weight: 8 lbs., 6 oz.
Stock: To customer specs; interchangeable.
Features: Tapered and stepped high rib; adjustable four-position trigger. Also available with choke tubes. Imported from Italy by Perazzi U.S.A., Inc.

Perazzi TM1

Price: From **$5,750.00**
Price: TMX Special Single (as above except special high rib), from **$5,950.00**

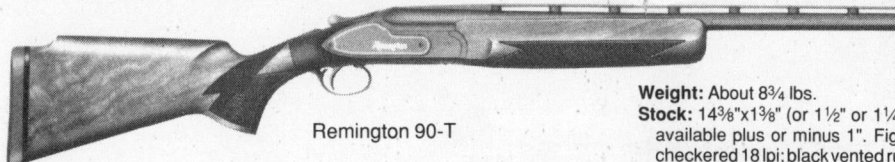

Remington 90-T

REMINGTON 90-T SUPER SINGLE SHOTGUN

Gauge: 12, 2¾" chamber.
Barrel: 30", 32", 34", fixed choke or Rem Choke tubes; ported or non-ported. Medium-high tapered, ventilated rib; white Bradley-type front bead, stainless center bead.

Weight: About 8¾ lbs.
Stock: 14⅜"x1⅜" (or 1½" or 1¼")x1½". Choice of drops at comb, pull length available plus or minus 1". Figured American walnut with low-luster finish, checkered 18 lpi; black vented rubber recoil pad. Cavity in forend and buttstock for added weight.
Features: Barrel is over-bored with elongated forcing cones. Removable sideplates can be ordered with engraving; drop-out trigger assembly. Metal has non-glare matte finish. Available with extra barrels in different lengths, chokes, extra trigger assemblies and sideplates, porting, stocks. Introduced 1990. From Remington.
Price: Depending on options **$2,995.00**
Price: With high post adjustable rib and adjustable comb . . . . **NA**

Snake Charmer II

SNAKE CHARMER II SHOTGUN

Gauge: 410, 3" chamber.
Barrel: 18¼".
Weight: About 3½ lbs. **Length:** 28⅝" overall.
Stock: ABS grade impact resistant plastic.
Features: Thumbhole-type stock holds four extra rounds. Stainless steel barrel and frame. Reintroduced 1989. From Sporting Arms Mfg., Inc.
Price: **$139.00**
Price: New Generation Snake Charmer (as above except with black carbon steel bbl.) **$129.00**

STOEGER/IGA REUNA SINGLE BARREL SHOTGUN

Gauge: 12, 2¾" chamber; 20, 410, 3" chamber.
Barrel: 12-ga.—26" (Imp. Cyl.), 28" (Full); 20-ga.—26" (Full); 410 bore—26" (Full).
Weight: 5¼ lbs.
Stock: 14"x1½"x2½". Brazilian hardwood.

Sights: Metal bead front.
Features: Exposed hammer with half-cock safety; extractor; blue finish. Introduced 1987. Imported from Brazil by Stoeger Industries.
Price: **$115.00**
Price: 12-, 20-ga., Full choke tube **$132.00**
Price: Youth model (20-ga., 410, 22" Full) **$127.00**

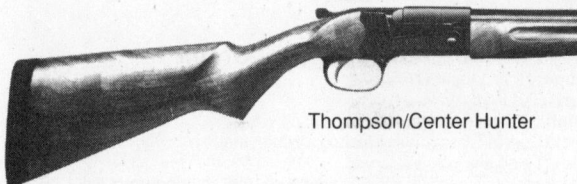

Thompson/Center Hunter

THOMPSON/CENTER TCR '87 HUNTER SHOTGUN

Gauge: 10, 12, 3½".
Barrel: 25" (Full).
Weight: 8 lbs.
Stock: Uncheckered walnut.
Sights: Bead front.
Features: Uses same receiver as TCR '87 rifle models, and stock has extra ⁷⁄₁₆" drop at heel. Choke designed for steel shot. Available only through the T/C custom shop. Introduced 1989. From Thompson/Center.
Price: About **$595.00**

SHOTGUNS—MILITARY & POLICE

Designs for utility, suitable for and adaptable to competitions and other sporting purposes.

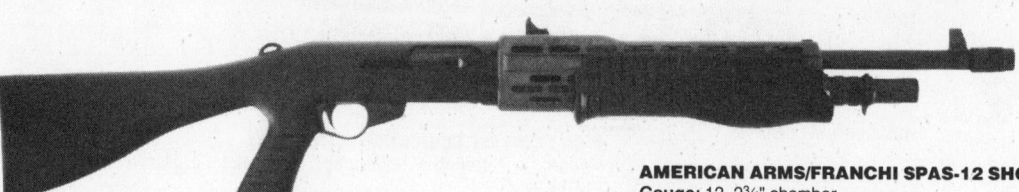

American Arms/Franchi SPAS-12

AMERICAN ARMS/FRANCHI SPAS-12 SHOTGUN

Gauge: 12, 2¾" chamber.
Barrel: 21½" (Cyl.), with muzzle protector.
Weight: 8¾ lbs. **Length:** 41" overall.
Stock: Black nylon with full pistol grip.
Sights: Blade front, aperture rear.
Features: Gas-operated semi-auto converts instantly to pump action; cross-bolt safety and secondary tactical lever safety; 7-shot tubular magazine; matte phosphate finish. Choke tubes available as accessories. Imported from Italy by American Arms, Inc.
Price: **$713.00**
Price: LAW-12 (as above except gas-operated action only) **$686.00**

Benelli M3 Super 90

Benelli M1 Super 90

Similar to the M3 Super 90 except is semi-automatic only, has overall length of 41" and weighs 7 lbs. Introduced 1986.

Price: Slug Gun with standard stock $724.00
Price: With pistol grip stock (Defense) $764.00
Price: With ghost ring sight system (standard stock) $764.00
Price: With ghost ring sight system, pistol grip stock (Defense) . . . $814.00

BENELLI M3 SUPER 90 PUMP/AUTO SHOTGUN

Gauge: 12, 3" chamber, 7-shot magazine.
Barrel: 19¾" (Cyl.).
Weight: 7 lbs., 8 oz. **Length:** 41" overall.
Stock: High-impact polymer with sling loop in side of butt; rubberized pistol grip on stock. Also folding stock model.
Sights: Post front, buckhorn rear adjustable for windage. Ghost ring system available.
Features: Combination pump/auto action. Alloy receiver with inertia recoil rotating locking lug bolt; matte finish; automatic shell release lever. Introduced 1989. Imported by Heckler & Koch, Inc.

Price: $919.00
Price: With Ghost Ring sight system $949.00
Price: With folding stock $1,029.00

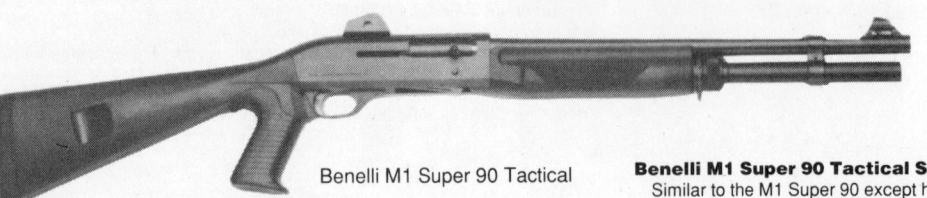

Benelli M1 Super 90 Tactical

Benelli M1 Super 90 Tactical Shotgun

Similar to the M1 Super 90 except has 18.5" barrel with Imp. Cyl., Mod., Full choke tubes, ghost ring sight system (tritium night sights optional), 7-shot magazine. In 12-gauge (3" chamber) only, matte-finish receiver. Overall length 39.75". Introduced 1993. Imported from Italy by Heckler & Koch, Inc.

Price: $829.00

Beretta Model 1201FP3

ITHACA MODEL 87 M&P DSPS SHOTGUNS

Gauge: 12, 3" chamber, 5- or 8-shot magazine.
Barrel: 20" (Cyl.).
Weight: 7 lbs.
Stock: Walnut.
Sights: Bead front on 5-shot, rifle sights on 8-shot.
Features: Parkerized finish; bottom ejection; cross-bolt safety. Reintroduced 1988. From Ithaca Acquisition Corp.

Price: M&P, 5-shot $322.00
Price: DSPS, 8-shot $322.00
Price: DSPS, 5-shot, nickel $422.00

BERETTA MODEL 1201FP3 AUTO SHOTGUN

Gauge: 12, 3" chamber.
Barrel: 20" (Cyl.).
Weight: 7.3 lbs. **Length:** NA
Stock: Special strengthened technopolymer, matte black finish.
Stock: Fixed rifle type.
Features: Has 6-shot magazine. Introduced 1988. Imported from Italy by Beretta U.S.A.

Price: $660.00
Price: Pistol grip model $705.00

Ithaca Model 87 Hand Grip Shotgun

Similar to the Model 87 M&P except has black polymer pistol grip and slide handle. In 12- or 20-gauge, 18½" barrel (Cyl.), 5-shot magazine. Reintroduced 1988.

Price: $323.00

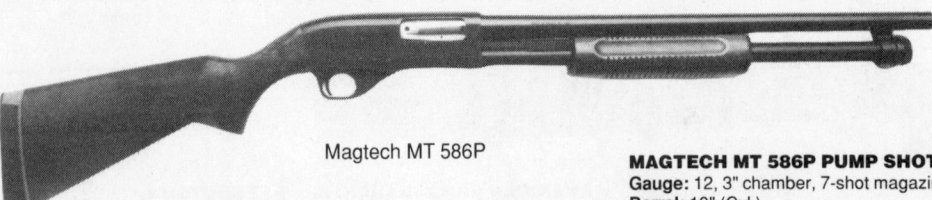

Magtech MT 586P

MAVERICK MODEL 60 AUTO SHOTGUN

Gauge: 12, 2¾" chamber, 6-shot.
Barrel: 18½" (Cyl.).
Weight: 7 lbs. **Length:** 38⅜" overall.
Stock: Black synthetic.
Sights: Bead front.
Features: Shoots 2¾" loads only. Blue finish. Introduced 1993. From Maverick Arms, Inc.

Price: $264.00

MAGTECH MT 586P PUMP SHOTGUN

Gauge: 12, 3" chamber, 7-shot magazine (8-shot with 2¾" shells).
Barrel: 19" (Cyl.).
Weight: 7.3 lbs. **Length:** 39.5" overall.
Stock: Brazilian hardwood.
Sights: Bead front.
Features: Dual action slide bars, cross-bolt safety. Blue finish. Introduced 1991. Imported from Brazil by Magtech Recreational Products.

Price: About $219.00

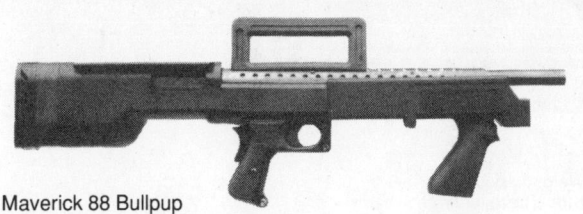

Maverick 88 Bullpup

MAVERICK MODEL 88 PUMP SECURITY SHOTGUN

Gauge: 12, 3" chamber, 6-shot.
Barrel: 18½" (Cyl.).
Weight: 6 lbs. **Length:** 38⅜" overall.
Stock: Black synthetic. Regular butt or pistol grip only.
Sights: Bead front.
Features: Blue finish. Ribbed pump handle. Introduced 1993. From Maverick Arms, Inc.
Price: **$199.00**

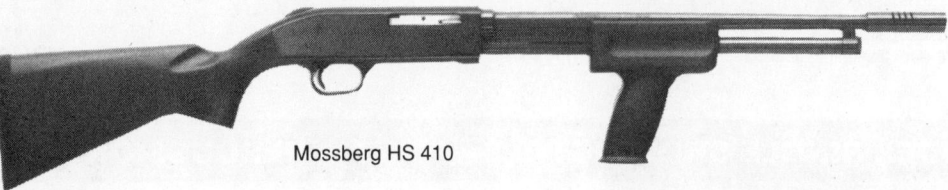

Mossberg 500 Security

Mossberg Model 500, 590 Ghost-Ring Shotguns

Similar to the Model 500 Security except has adjustable blade front, adjustable Ghost-Ring rear sight with protective "ears." Model 500 has 18.5" (Cyl.) barrel, 6-shot capacity; Model 590 has 20" (Cyl.) barrel, 9-shot capacity. Both have synthetic field stock. Mossberg Cablelock included. Introduced 1990. From Mossberg.
Price: Model 500, blue **$300.00**
Price: As above, Parkerized **$348.00**
Price: Model 590, blue **$359.00**
Price: As above, Parkerized **$406.00**

Mossberg Model 500, 590 Mariner Pump

Similar to the Model 500 or 590 Security except all metal parts finished with Marinecote, a Teflon and metal coating to resist rust and corrosion. Synthetic field stock; pistol grip kit included. Mossberg Cablelock included.
Price: 6-shot, 18½" barrel **$353.00**
Price: 9-shot, 20" barrel **$353.00**

Mossberg HS 410

MOSSBERG MODEL 590 SHOTGUN

Gauge: 12, 3" chamber.
Barrel: 20" (Cyl.).
Weight: 7¼ lbs.
Stock: Synthetic field or Speedfeed.

MAVERICK MODEL 88 BULLPUP SHOTGUN

Gauge: 12, 3" chamber; 6-shot magazine.
Barrel: 18½" (Cyl.).
Weight: 9½ lbs. **Length:** 26½" overall.
Stock: Bullpup design of high-impact plastics.
Sights: Fixed, mounted in carrying handle.
Features: Uses the Model 88 pump shotgun action. Cross-bolt and grip safeties. Mossberg Cablelock included. Introduced 1991. From Maverick Arms.
Price: **$291.00**

Maverick Model HS410 Shotgun

Similar to the Maverick Model 88 except chambered for 410, 3" shells; has pistol grip forend, thick recoil pad, muzzle brake and special spreader choke on the 18.5" barrel. Overall length is 37.5", weight is 6.25 lbs. Blue finish; synthetic field stock. Also available with integral Laser Sight forend. Cablelock included. Introduced 1993. From Maverick Arms, Inc.
Price: HS410 . . . . **$226.00**
Price: HS410 Laser **$366.00**

MOSSBERG MODEL 500 PERSUADER/CRUISER SECURITY SHOTGUNS

Gauge: 12, 20, 410, 3" chamber.
Barrel: 18½", 20" (Cyl.).
Weight: 7 lbs.
Stock: Walnut-finished hardwood or synthetic field.
Sights: Metal bead front.
Features: Available in 6- or 8-shot models. Top-mounted safety, double action slide bars, swivel studs, rubber recoil pad. Blue, Parkerized, Marinecote finishes. Pistol grip kit and Mossberg Cablelock included. **Price list not complete—contact Mossberg for full list.**
Price: 12- or 20-ga., 18½", blue, wood or synthetic stock, 6-shot . . **$251.00**
Price: As above, Parkerized finish, synthetic stock, 6-shot **$274.00**
Price: Cruiser, 12- or 20-ga., 18½", blue, pistol grip only **$242.00**
Price: As above, 410-bore **$280.00**
Price: 12-ga., 8-shot, blue, wood or synthetic stock **$251.00**
Price: As above with rifle sights **$272.00**

Mossberg Model 500, 590 Intimidator Shotguns

Similar to the Model 500 or 590 Security with synthetic stock except has integral Laser Sight built into the forend. Mossberg Cablelock included. Introduced 1990.
Price: Model 500, blue, 6-shot **$505.00**
Price: Model 500, Parkerized, 6-shot **$527.00**
Price: Model 590, blue, 9-shot **$556.00**
Price: Model 590, Parkerized, 9-shot **$601.00**

Mossberg HS 410

Mossberg Model HS410 Shotgun

Similar to the Model 500 Security pump except chambered for 410, 3" shells; has pistol grip forend, thick recoil pad, muzzle brake and has special spreader choke on the 18.5" barrel. Overall length is 37.5", weight is 6.25 lbs. Blue finish; synthetic field stock. Also available with integral Laser Sight forend. Mossberg Cablelock and video included. Introduced 1990.
Price: HS 410 . . . . **$253.00**
Price: HS 410 Laser **$451.00**

Mossberg Model 590

Sights: Metal bead front.
Features: Top-mounted safety, double slide action bars. Comes with heat shield, bayonet lug, swivel studs, rubber recoil pad. Blue, Parkerized or Marinecote finish. Mossberg Cablelock included. From Mossberg.
Price: Blue, synthetic stock **$305.00**
Price: Parkerized, synthetic stock **$351.00**
Price: Blue, Speedfeed stock **$319.00**
Price: Parkerized, Speedfeed stock **$366.00**

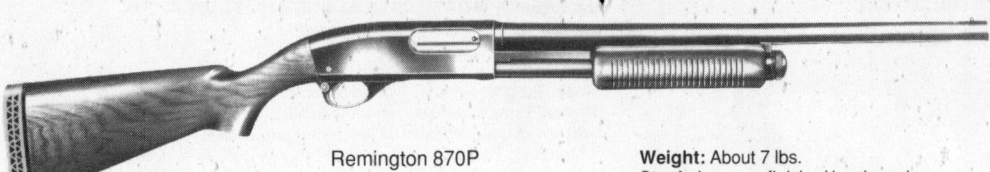

Remington 870P

REMINGTON 870P POLICE SHOTGUN
Gauge: 12, 3" chamber.
Barrel: 18", 20" (Police Cyl.), 20" (Imp. Cyl.).

Weight: About 7 lbs.
Stock: Lacquer-finished hardwood.
Sights: Metal bead front or rifle sights.
Features: Solid steel receiver, double action slide bars. Blued or Parkerized finish.
Price: 18" or 20", bead sight, about $356.00
Price: 20", rifle sights, about $383.00

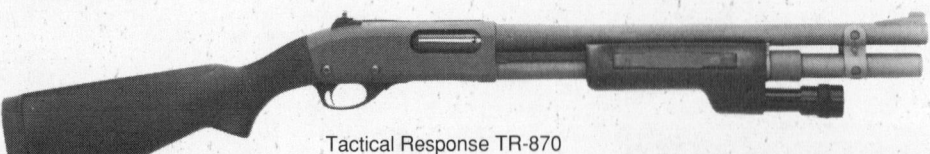

Tactical Response TR-870

TACTICAL RESPONSE TR-870 SHOTGUN
Gauge: 12, 3" chamber, 7-shot magazine.
Barrel: 18" (Cyl.).
Weight: 9 lbs. **Length:** 38" overall.
Stock: Fiberglass-filled polypropolene with non-snag recoil absorbing butt pad. Nylon tactical forend houses flashlight.
Sights: Trak-Lock ghost ring sight system. Front sight has tritium insert.

Features: Highly modified Remington 870P with Parkerized finish. Comes with nylon three-way adjustable sling, high visibility non-binding follower, high performance magazine spring, Jumbo Head safety, and Side Saddle extended 6-shot shell carrier on left side of receiver. Introduced 1991. From Scattergun Technologies, Inc.
Price: Standard model $695.00
Price: FBI model, 5-shot $665.00
Price: Patrol model, 5-shot, no Side Saddle $525.00
Price: Border Patrol model, 7-shot, standard forend $555.00
Price: Military model, 7-shot, bayonet lug $655.00
Price: K-9 model, 7-shot (Rem. 11-87 action) $755.00
Price: Urban Sniper, 7-shot, rifled bbl., Burris Scout scope, Rem. 11-87 action $1,095.00

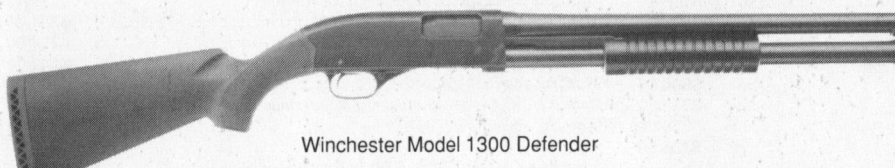

Winchester Model 1300 Defender

Winchester Model 1300 Stainless Marine Pump Gun
Same as the Defender except has bright chrome finish, stainless steel barrel, rifle-type sights only. Phosphate coated receiver for corrosion resistance.
Price: About $436.00

Winchester 8-Shot Pistol Grip Pump Security Shotguns
Same as regular Defender Pump but with pistol grip and forend of high-impact resistant ABS plastic with non-glare black finish. Introduced 1984.
Price: Pistol Grip Defender, about $270.00

WINCHESTER MODEL 1300 DEFENDER PUMP GUN
Gauge: 12, 20, 3" chamber, 5- or 8-shot capacity.
Barrel: 18" (Cyl.).
Weight: 6¾ lbs. **Length:** 38⅝" overall.
Stock: Walnut-finished hardwood stock and ribbed forend, or synthetic; or pistol grip.
Sights: Metal bead front.
Features: Cross-bolt safety, front-locking rotary bolt, twin action slide bars. Black rubber buttpad. From U.S. Repeating Arms Co.
Price: 8-shot, wood or synthetic stock $270.00
Price: 5-shot, wood stock $270.00

BLACKPOWDER SINGLE SHOT PISTOLS—FLINT & PERCUSSION

Dixie Charleville

BLACK WATCH SCOTCH PISTOL
Caliber: 577 (.500" round ball).
Barrel: 7", smoothbore.
Weight: 1½ lbs. **Length:** 12" overall.
Stock: Brass.
Sights: None.
Features: Faithful reproduction of this military flintlock. From Dixie Gun Works, E.M.F.
Price: . . . . $175.00 to $310.00

CHARLEVILLE FLINTLOCK PISTOL
Caliber: 69 (.680" round ball).
Barrel: 7½".
Weight: 48 oz. **Length:** 13½" overall.
Stock: Walnut.
Sights: None.
Features: Brass frame, polished steel barrel, iron belt hook, brass buttcap and backstrap. Replica of original 1777 pistol. Imported by Dixie Gun Works, E.M.F.
Price: . . . . $195.00 to $325.00

Consult our Directory pages for the location of firms mentioned.

CAUTION: PRICES CHANGE, CHECK AT GUNSHOP.

CVA Hawken

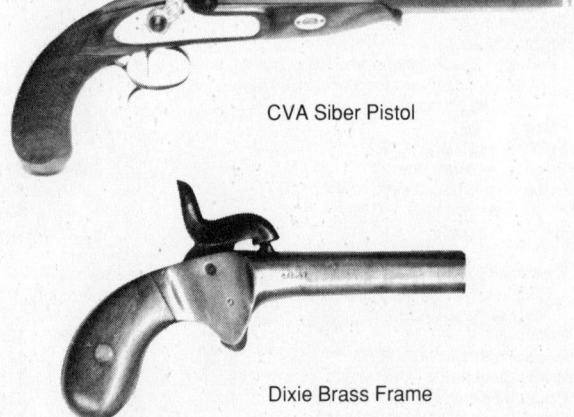

CVA Siber Pistol

Dixie Brass Frame

DIXIE LINCOLN DERRINGER
Caliber: 41.
Barrel: 2", 8 lands, 8 grooves.
Weight: 7 oz. **Length:** 5½" overall.
Stock: Walnut finish, checkered.
Sights: Fixed.
Features: Authentic copy of the "Lincoln Derringer." Shoots .400" patched ball. German silver furniture includes trigger guard with pineapple finial, wedge plates, nose, wrist, side and teardrop inlays. All furniture, lockplate, hammer, and breech plug engraved. Imported from Italy by Dixie Gun Works.
Price: With wooden case $285.95
Price: Kit (not engraved) $89.95

FRENCH-STYLE DUELING PISTOL
Caliber: 44.
Barrel: 10".
Weight: 35 oz. **Length:** 15¾" overall.
Stock: Carved walnut.
Sights: Fixed.
Features: Comes with velvet-lined case and accessories. Imported by Mandall Shooting Supplies.
Price: $295.00

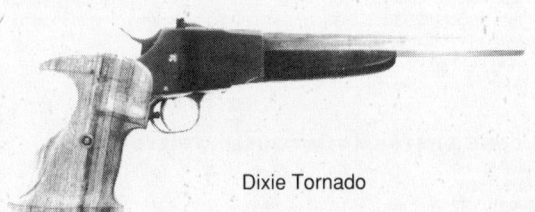

Dixie Tornado

CVA HAWKEN PISTOL
Caliber: 50.
Barrel: 9¾"; ¹⁵⁄₁₆" flats.
Weight: 50 oz. **Length:** 16½" overall.
Stock: Select hardwood.
Sights: Beaded blade front, fully adjustable open rear.
Features: Color case-hardened lock, polished brass wedge plate, nose cap, ramrod thimbles, trigger guard, grip cap. Hooked breech. Imported by CVA.
Price: $176.95
Price: Kit $109.95

CVA SIBER PISTOL
Caliber: 45.
Barrel: 10½".
Weight: 34 oz. **Length:** 15½" overall.
Stock: High-grade French walnut, checkered grip.
Sights: Barleycorn front, micro-adjustable rear.
Features: Reproduction of pistol made by Swiss watchmaker Jean Siber in the 1800s. Precision lock and set-trigger give fast lock time. Has engraved, polished steel barrel, trigger guard. Imported by CVA.
Price: $439.95

CVA VEST POCKET DERRINGER
Caliber: 44.
Barrel: 2½", brass.
Weight: 7 oz.
Stock: Two-piece walnut.
Features: All brass frame with brass ramrod. A muzzle-loading version of the Colt No. 3 derringer. Imported by CVA.
Price: Finished $69.95

DIXIE BRASS FRAME DERRINGER
Caliber: 41.
Barrel: 2½".
Weight: 7 oz. **Length:** 5½" overall.
Stock: Walnut.
Features: Brass frame, color case-hardened hammer and trigger. Shoots .395" round ball. Engraved model available. From Dixie Gun Works.
Price: Plain model $69.95
Price: Engraved model $95.50

DIXIE PENNSYLVANIA PISTOL
Caliber: 44 (.430" round ball).
Barrel: 10" (⅞" octagon).
Weight: 2½ lbs.
Stock: Walnut-stained hardwood.
Sights: Blade front, open rear drift-adjustable for windage; brass.
Features: Available in flint only. Brass trigger guard, thimbles, nosecap, wedgeplates; high-luster blue barrel. Imported from Italy by Dixie Gun Works.
Price: Finished $149.95
Price: Kit $119.95

DIXIE SCREW BARREL PISTOL
Caliber: .445".
Barrel: 2½".
Weight: 8 oz. **Length:** 6½" overall.
Stock: Walnut.
Features: Trigger folds down when hammer is cocked. Close copy of the originals once made in Belgium. Uses No. 11 percussion caps. From Dixie Gun Works.
Price: $89.00
Price: Kit $74.95

DIXIE TORNADO TARGET PISTOL
Caliber: 44 (.430" round ball).
Barrel: 10", octagonal, 1:22 twist.
Stocks: Walnut, target-style. Left unfinished for custom fitting. Walnut forend.
Sights: Blade on ramp front, micro-type open rear adjustable for windage and elevation.
Features: Grip frame style of 1860 Colt revolver. Improved model of the Tingle and B.W. Southgate pistol. Trigger adjustable for pull. Frame, barrel, hammer and sights in the white, brass trigger guard. Comes with solid brass, walnut-handled cleaning rod with jag and nylon muzzle protector. Introduced 1983. From Dixie Gun Works.
Price: $215.50

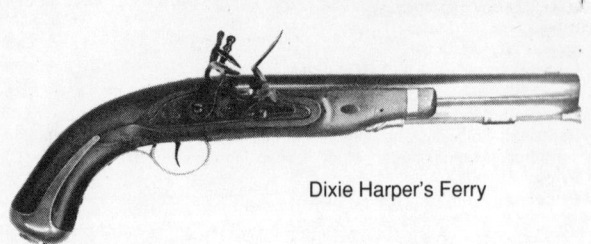

Dixie Harper's Ferry

HAWKEN PERCUSSION PISTOL
Caliber: 54.
Barrel: 9", octagonal.
Weight: 40 oz. **Length:** 14" overall.
Stock: Checkered walnut.
Sights: Blade front, fixed notch rear.
Features: German silver trigger guard, blued barrel. Imported from Italy by E.M.F.
Price: $370.00

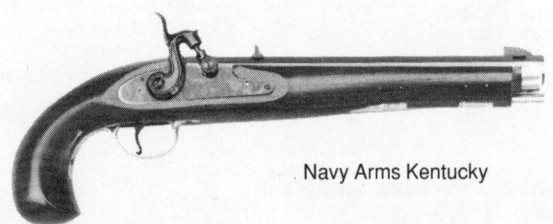

Navy Arms Kentucky

Lyman Plains Pistol

CHARLES MOORE FLINTLOCK PISTOL
Caliber: 45.
Barrel: 10", octagonal.
Weight: 36 oz. **Length:** 15" overall.
Stock: Checkered hardwood.
Sights: Blade front, fixed notch rear.
Features: German silver trigger guard, rest blued. Imported from Italy by E.M.F.
Price: $400.00

NAVY ARMS LE PAGE DUELING PISTOL
Caliber: 44.
Barrel: 9", octagon, rifled.
Weight: 34 oz. **Length:** 15" overall.
Stock: European walnut.
Sights: Adjustable rear.
Features: Single-set trigger. Polished metal finish. From Navy Arms.
Price: Percussion $475.00
Price: Single cased set, percussion $685.00
Price: Double cased set, percussion $1,290.00
Price: Flintlock, rifled $550.00
Price: Flintlock, smoothbore (45-cal.) $550.00
Price: Flintlock, single cased set $760.00
Price: Flintlock, double cased set $1,430.00

HARPER'S FERRY 1806 PISTOL
Caliber: 58 (.570" round ball).
Barrel: 10".
Weight: 40 oz. **Length:** 16" overall.
Stock: Walnut.
Sights: Fixed.
Features: Case-hardened lock, brass-mounted browned barrel. Replica of the first U.S. Gov't.-made flintlock pistol. Imported by Navy Arms, Dixie Gun Works, E.M.F.
Price: . . . . $249.95 to $405.00
Price: Kit (Dixie) $184.95

KENTUCKY FLINTLOCK PISTOL
Caliber: 44, 45.
Barrel: 10⅛".
Weight: 32 oz. **Length:** 15½" overall.
Stock: Walnut.
Sights: Fixed.
Features: Specifications, including caliber, weight and length may vary with importer. Case-hardened lock, blued barrel; available also as brass barrel flint Model 1821. Imported by Navy Arms (44 only), The Armoury, E.M.F.
Price: . . . . $145.00 to $207.00
Price: Brass barrel (E.M.F.) $265.00
Price: In kit form, from . . . . $90.00 to $112.00
Price: Single cased set (Navy Arms) $300.00
Price: Double cased set (Navy Arms) $515.00

Kentucky Percussion Pistol
Similar to flint version but percussion lock. Imported by The Armoury, E.M.F., Navy Arms, CVA (50-cal.).
Price: . . . . $141.95 to $250.00
Price: Brass barrel (E.M.F.) $275.00
Price: Steel barrel (Armoury) $179.00
Price: Single cased set (Navy Arms) $300.00
Price: Double cased set (Navy Arms) $515.00

LE PAGE PERCUSSION DUELING PISTOL
Caliber: 45.
Barrel: 10", rifled.
Weight: 40 oz. **Length:** 16" overall.
Stock: Walnut, fluted butt.
Sights: Blade front, notch rear.
Features: Double-set triggers. Blued barrel; trigger guard and buttcap are polished silver. Imported by Dixie Gun Works, E.M.F.
Price: . . . . $259.95 to $400.00

CONSULT **Shooter's Marketplace** Page 231, This Issue

LYMAN PLAINS PISTOL
Caliber: 50 or 54.
Barrel: 8", 1:30 twist, both calibers.
Weight: 50 oz. **Length:** 15" overall.
Stock: Walnut half-stock.
Sights: Blade front, square notch rear adjustable for windage.
Features: Polished brass trigger guard and ramrod tip, color case-hardened coil spring lock, spring-loaded trigger, stainless steel nipple, blackened iron furniture. Hooked patent breech, detachable belt hook. Introduced 1981. From Lyman Products.
Price: Finished $219.95
Price: Kit $179.95

MOORE & PATRICK FLINT DUELING PISTOL
Caliber: 45.
Barrel: 10", rifled.
Weight: 32 oz. **Length:** 14½" overall.
Stock: European walnut, checkered.
Sights: Fixed.
Features: Engraved, silvered lockplate, blue barrel. German silver furniture. Imported from Italy by Dixie Gun Works.
Price: $335.00

BLACKPOWDER SINGLE SHOT PISTOLS—FLINT & PERCUSSION

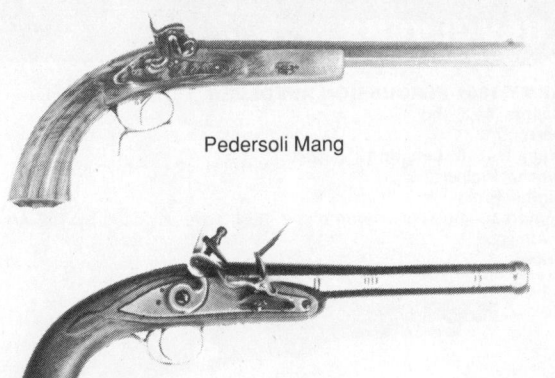

Pedersoli Mang

Dixie Queen Anne

THOMPSON/CENTER SCOUT PISTOL
Caliber: 45, 50 and 54.
Barrel: 12", interchangeable.
Weight: 4 lbs., 6 oz. **Length:** NA.
Stocks: American black walnut stocks and forend.
Sights: Blade on ramp front, fully adjustable Patridge rear.
Features: Patented in-line ignition system with special vented breech plug. Patented trigger mechanism consists of only two moving parts. Interchangeable barrels. Wide grooved hammer. Brass trigger guard assembly. Introduced 1990. From Thompson/Center.
Price: 45-, 50- or 54-cal. $315.00
Price: Extra barrel, 45-, 50- or 54-cal. $140.00

TRADITIONS BUCKSKINNER PISTOL
Caliber: 50.
Barrel: 10" octagonal, ¹⁵⁄₁₆" flats.
Weight: 40 oz. **Length:** 15" overall.
Stocks: Stained beech or laminated wood.
Sights: Blade front, rear adjustable for windage.
Features: Percussion ignition. Blackened furniture. Imported by Traditions, Inc.
Price: Beech stocks $157.00
Price: Laminated stocks $182.00

Traditions Pioneer

TRADITIONS TRAPPER PISTOL
Caliber: 50.
Barrel: 9¾", ⅞" flats.
Weight: 2¾ lbs. **Length:** 16" overall.
Stock: Beech.
Sights: Blade front, adjustable rear.
Features: Double-set triggers; brass buttcap, trigger guard, wedge plate, forend tip, thimble. From Traditions, Inc.
Price: $170.00
Price: Kit $130.00

TRADITIONS VEST POCKET DERRINGER
Caliber: 31.
Barrel: 2½", round.
Weight: 16 oz. **Length:** 5" overall.
Stocks: White composite.
Sights: Post front.
Features: Polished brass barrel and frame, blued trigger and screws. Imported by Traditions, Inc.
Price: $75.00

W. PARKER FLINTLOCK PISTOL
Caliber: 45.
Barrel: 11", rifled.
Weight: 40 oz. **Length:** 16½" overall.
Stock: Walnut.
Sights: Blade front, notch rear.
Features: Browned barrel, silver-plated trigger guard, finger rest, polished and engraved lock. Double-set triggers. Imported by Dixie Gun Works.
Price: $310.00

PEDERSOLI MANG TARGET PISTOL
Caliber: 38.
Barrel: 10.5", octagonal; 1:15" twist,
Weight: 2.5 lbs. **Length:** 17.25" overall.
Stock: Walnut with fluted grip.
Sights: Blade front, open rear adjustable for windage.
Features: Browned barrel, polished breech plug, rest color case-hardened. Imported from Italy by Dixie Gun Works.
Price: $595.00

QUEEN ANNE FLINTLOCK PISTOL
Caliber: 50 (.490" round ball).
Barrel: 7½", smoothbore.
Stock: Walnut.
Sights: None.
Features: Browned steel barrel, fluted brass trigger guard, brass mask on butt. Lockplate left in the white. Made by Pedersoli in Italy. Introduced 1983. Imported by Dixie Gun Works.
Price: $189.95
Price: Kit $138.50

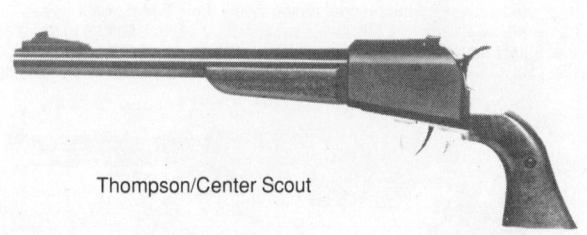

Thompson/Center Scout

TRADITIONS PHILADELPHIA DERRINGER
Caliber: 45.
Barrel: 3¼" octagonal, ⅞" flats.
Weight: 16 oz. **Length:** 7⅛" overall.
Stock: Stained beech.
Sights: Blade front.
Features: Color case-hardened percussion lock has coil mainspring. Brass furniture, engraved wedge plate. Imported by Traditions, Inc.
Price: $109.00
Price: Kit $82.00

TRADITIONS PIONEER PISTOL
Caliber: 45.
Barrel: 9⅝", ¹³⁄₁₆" flats.
Weight: 36 oz. **Length:** 15" overall.
Stock: Beech.
Sights: Blade front, fixed rear.
Features: V-type mainspring; 1:18" twist. Single trigger. German silver furniture, blackened hardware. From Traditions, Inc.
Price: $169.00
Price: Kit $119.00

TRADITIONS WILLIAM PARKER PISTOL
Caliber: 45 and 50.
Barrel: 10⅜", ¹⁵⁄₁₆" flats; polished steel.
Weight: 40 oz. **Length:** 17½" overall.
Stock: Walnut with checkered grip.
Sights: Brass blade front, fixed rear.
Features: Replica dueling pistol with 1:18" twist, hooked breech. Brass wedge plate, trigger guard, cap guard; separate ramrod. Double-set triggers. Polished steel barrel, lock. Imported by Traditions, Inc.
Price: $265.00

Army 1851

ARMY 1860 PERCUSSION REVOLVER
Caliber: 44, 6-shot.
Barrel: 8".
Weight: 40 oz. **Length:** 13⅝" overall.
Stocks: Walnut.
Sights: Fixed.
Features: Engraved Navy scene on cylinder; brass trigger guard; case-hardened frame, loading lever and hammer. Some importers supply pistol cut for detachable shoulder stock, have accessory stock available. Imported by American Arms, Cabela's, E.M.F., Navy Arms, The Armoury, Cimarron, Dixie Gun Works (half-fluted cylinder, not roll engraved), Euroarms of America (brass or steel model), Armsport, Mitchell, Traditions, Inc. (brass or steel), Uberti USA.
Price: About . . . . $92.95 to $300.00
Price: Single cased set (Navy Arms) $265.00
Price: Double cased set (Navy Arms) $430.00
Price: 1861 Navy: Same as Army except 36-cal., 7½" bbl., wgt. 41 oz., cut for shoulder stock; round cylinder (fluted avail.), from E.M.F., CVA (brass frame, 44-cal.), Cabela's, Mitchell . . . . . $99.95 to $249.00
Price: Steel frame kit (E.M.F., Mitchell, Navy, Euroarms) $125.00 to $187.00
Price: Colt Army Police, fluted cyl., 5½", 36-cal. (Cabela's) $96.95

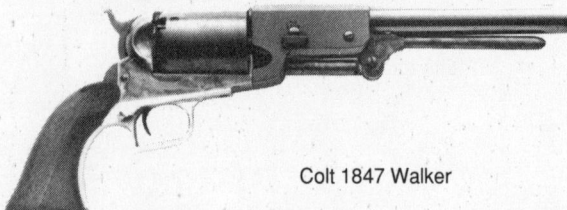

Colt 1847 Walker

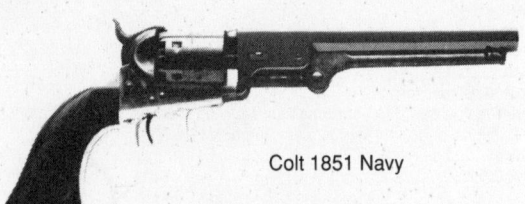

Colt 1851 Navy

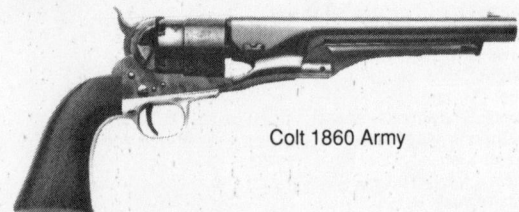

Colt 1860 Army

COLT 1860 ARMY PERCUSSION REVOLVER
Caliber: 44.
Barrel: 8", 7 groove, left-hand twist.
Weight: 42 oz.
Stocks: One-piece walnut.
Sights: German silver front sight, hammer notch rear.
Features: Steel backstrap cut for shoulder stock; brass trigger guard. Cylinder has Navy scene. Color case-hardened frame, hammer, loading lever. Reproduction of original gun with all original markings. From Colt Blackpowder Arms Co.
Price: $395.00

ARMY 1851 PERCUSSION REVOLVER
Caliber: 44, 6-shot.
Barrel: 7½".
Weight: 45 oz. **Length:** 13" overall.
Stocks: Walnut finish.
Sights: Fixed.
Features: 44-caliber version of the 1851 Navy. Imported by The Armoury, Armsport.
Price: $129.00

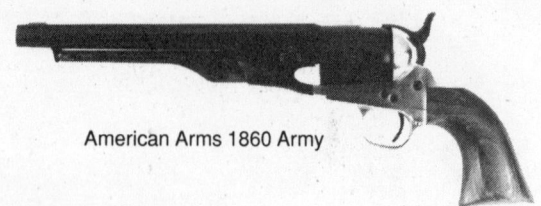

American Arms 1860 Army

BABY DRAGOON 1848, 1849 POCKET, WELLS FARGO
Caliber: 31.
Barrel: 3", 4", 5", 6"; seven-groove, RH twist.
Weight: About 21 oz.
Stock: Varnished walnut.
Sights: Brass pin front, hammer notch rear.
Features: No loading lever on Baby Dragoon or Wells Fargo models. Unfluted cylinder with stagecoach holdup scene; cupped cylinder pin; no grease grooves; one safety pin on cylinder and slot in hammer face; straight (flat) mainspring. From Armsport, Dixie Gun Works, Uberti USA, Cabela's.
Price: 6" barrel, with loading lever (Dixie Gun Works) $185.00
Price: 4" (Uberti USA) $295.00

CABELA'S PATERSON REVOLVER
Caliber: 36, 5-shot cylinder.
Barrel: 7½".
Weight: 24 oz. **Length:** 11½" overall.
Stocks: One-piece walnut.
Sights: Fixed.
Features: Recreation of the 1836 gun. Color case-hardened frame, steel backstrap; roll-engraved cylinder scene. Imported by Cabela's.
Price: $199.95

COLT 1847 WALKER PERCUSSION REVOLVER
Caliber: 44.
Barrel: 9", 7 groove, right-hand twist.
Weight: 73 oz.
Stocks: One-piece walnut.
Sights: German silver front sight, hammer notch rear.
Features: Made in U.S. Faithful reproduction of the original gun, including markings. Color case-hardened frame, hammer, loading lever and plunger. Blue steel backstrap, brass square-back trigger guard. Blue barrel, cylinder, trigger and wedge. From Colt Blackpowder Arms Co.
Price: $395.00

COLT 1849 POCKET DRAGOON REVOLVER
Caliber: 31.
Barrel: 4".
Weight: 24 oz. **Length:** 9½" overall.
Stocks: One-piece walnut.
Sights: Fixed. Brass pin front, hammer notch rear.
Features: Color case-hardened frame. No loading lever. Unfluted cylinder with engraved scene. Exact reproduction of original. From Colt Blackpowder Arms Co.
Price: $360.00

COLT 1851 NAVY PERCUSSION REVOLVER
Caliber: 36.
Barrel: 7½", octagonal, 7 groove left-hand twist.
Weight: 40½ oz.
Stocks: One-piece oiled American walnut.
Sights: Brass pin front, hammer notch rear.
Features: Faithful reproduction of the original gun. Color case-hardened frame, loading lever, plunger, hammer and latch. Blue cylinder, trigger, barrel, screws, wedge. Silver-plated brass backstrap and square-back trigger guard. From Colt Blackpowder Arms Co.
Price: $395.00

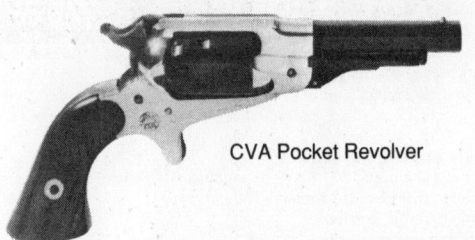

CVA Pocket Revolver

CVA Wells Fargo

Dixie Third Model Dragoon

GRISWOLD & GUNNISON PERCUSSION REVOLVER

Caliber: 36 or 44, 6-shot.
Barrel: 7½".
Weight: 44 oz. (36-cal.). **Length:** 13" overall.
Stocks: Walnut.
Sights: Fixed.
Features: Replica of famous Confederate pistol. Brass frame, backstrap and trigger guard; case-hardened loading lever; rebated cylinder (44-cal. only). Rounded Dragoon-type barrel. Imported by Navy Arms (as Reb Model 1860), E.M.F.
Price: About $229.00
Price: Single cased set (Navy Arms) $205.00
Price: Double cased set (Navy Arms) $335.00
Price: Reb 1860 (Navy Arms) $110.00
Price: As above, kit $90.00

LE MAT CAVALRY MODEL REVOLVER

Caliber: 44/65.
Barrel: 6¾" (revolver); 4⅞" (single shot).
Weight: 3 lbs., 7 oz.
Stocks: Hand-checkered walnut.
Sights: Post front, hammer notch rear.
Features: Exact reproduction with all-steel construction; 44-cal. 9-shot cylinder, 65-cal. single barrel; color case-hardened hammer with selector; spur trigger guard; ring at butt; lever-type barrel release. From Navy Arms.
Price: Cavalry model (lanyard ring, spur trigger guard) $595.00
Price: Army model (round trigger guard, pin-type barrel release) . . $595.00
Price: Naval-style (thumb selector on hammer) $595.00

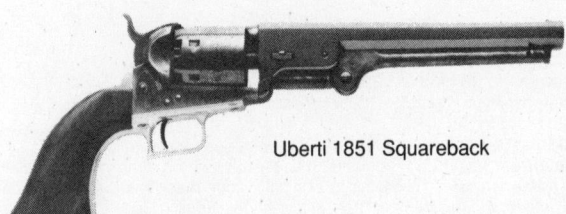

Uberti 1851 Squareback

CVA POCKET REVOLVER

Caliber: 31.
Barrel: 4", octagonal.
Weight: 15½ oz. **Length:** 7½" overall.
Stocks: Two-piece walnut.
Sights: Post front, grooved topstrap rear.
Features: Spur trigger, brass frame with blued barrel and cylinder. Introduced 1984. Imported by CVA.
Price: Finished $129.95

CVA WELLS FARGO MODEL

Caliber: 31.
Barrel: 4", octagonal.
Weight: 28 oz. (with extra cylinder). **Length:** 9" overall.
Stocks: Walnut.
Sights: Post front, hammer notch rear.
Features: Brass frame and backstrap; blue finish. Comes with extra cylinder. Imported by CVA.
Price: Brass frame, finished $129.95

DIXIE THIRD MODEL DRAGOON

Caliber: 44 (.454" round ball).
Barrel: 7⅜".
Weight: 4 lbs., 2½ oz.
Stocks: One-piece walnut.
Sights: Brass pin front, hammer notch rear, or adjustable folding leaf rear.
Features: Cylinder engraved with Indian fight scene. This is the only Dragoon replica with folding leaf sight. Brass backstrap and trigger guard; color case-hardened steel frame, blue-black barrel. Imported by Dixie Gun Works.
Price: $149.95

CVA Third Model Dragoon

Similar to the Dixie Third Dragoon except has 7½" barrel, weighs 4 lbs., 6 oz., blade front sight. Overall length of 14". 44-caliber, 6-shot.
Price: $279.95

DIXIE WYATT EARP REVOLVER

Caliber: 44.
Barrel: 12" octagon.
Weight: 46 oz. **Length:** 18" overall.
Stocks: Two-piece walnut.
Sights: Fixed.
Features: Highly polished brass frame, backstrap and trigger guard; blued barrel and cylinder; case-hardened hammer, trigger and loading lever. Navy-size shoulder stock ($45) will fit with minor fitting. From Dixie Gun Works.
Price: $130.00

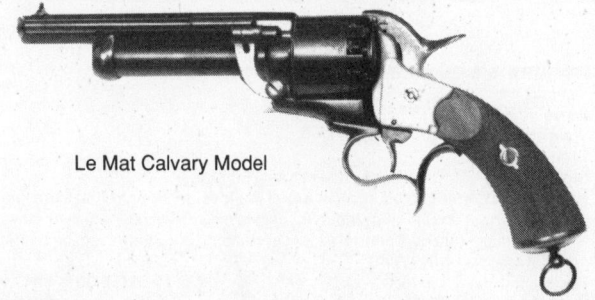

Le Mat Calvary Model

NAVY MODEL 1851 PERCUSSION REVOLVER

Caliber: 36, 44, 6-shot.
Barrel: 7½".
Weight: 44 oz. **Length:** 13" overall.
Stocks: Walnut finish.
Sights: Post front, hammer notch rear.
Features: Brass backstrap and trigger guard; some have 1st Model squareback trigger guard, engraved cylinder with navy battle scene; case-hardened frame, hammer, loading lever. Imported by American Arms, The Armoury, Cabela's, Mitchell, Navy Arms, E.M.F., Dixie Gun Works, Euroarms of America, Armsport, CVA (36-cal. only), Traditions, Inc., Uberti USA.
Price: Brass frame . . . . $125.00 to $280.00
Price: Steel frame . . . . $130.00 to $285.00
Price: Kit form . . . . $110.00 to $123.95
Price: Engraved model (Dixie Gun Works) $139.95
Price: Single cased set, steel frame (Navy Arms) $245.00
Price: Double cased set, steel frame (Navy Arms) $405.00
Price: Confederate Navy (Cabela's) $69.95

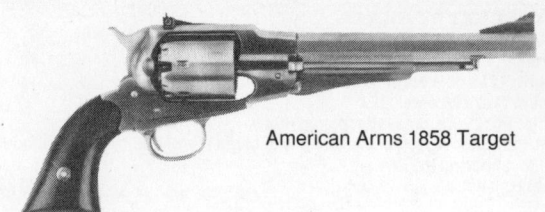

American Arms 1858 Target

CVA 1858 Target Revolver

Similar to the New Model 1858 Army revolver except has ramp-mounted blade front sight on 8" barrel, adjustable rear sight, overall blue finish. Imported by CVA.

Price: **$239.95**

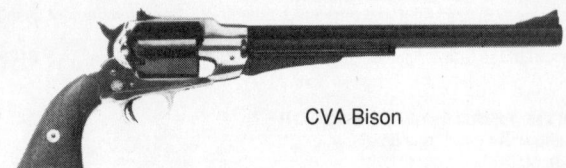

CVA Bison

CVA Bison Revolver

Similar to the CVA 1858 Target except has 10¼" octagonal barrel, 44-caliber, brass frame.

Price: Finished **$247.95**
Price: From Armsport **$222.00**

NAVY ARMS DELUXE 1858 REMINGTON-STYLE REVOLVER

Caliber: 44.
Barrel: 8".
Weight: 2 lbs., 13 oz.
Stocks: Smooth walnut.
Sights: Dovetailed blade front.
Features: First exact reproduction—correct in size and weight to the original, with progressive rifling; highly polished with blue finish; silver-plated trigger guard. From Navy Arms.
Price: Deluxe model **$365.00**

> Consult our Directory pages for the location of firms mentioned.

ROGERS & SPENCER PERCUSSION REVOLVER

Caliber: 44.
Barrel: 7½".
Weight: 47 oz. **Length:** 13¾" overall.
Stocks: Walnut.
Sights: Cone front, integral groove in frame for rear.
Features: Accurate reproduction of a Civil War design. Solid frame; extra large nipple cut-out on rear of cylinder; loading lever and cylinder easily removed for cleaning. From Euroarms of America (standard blue, engraved, burnished, target models), Navy Arms.
Price: . . . . $160.00 to **$240.00**
Price: Nickel-plated **$215.00**
Price: Engraved (Euroarms) **$286.00**
Price: Kit version **$95.00**
Price: Target version (Euroarms, Navy Arms) **$260.00**
Price: Burnished London Gray (Euroarms, Navy Arms) **$260.00**

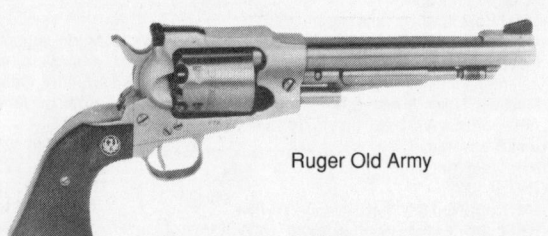

Ruger Old Army

Uberti 1861 Navy Percussion Revolver

Similar to 1851 Navy except has round 7½" barrel, rounded trigger guard, German silver blade front sight, "creeping" loading lever. Available with fluted or round cylinder. Imported by Uberti USA.

Price: Steel backstrap, trigger guard, cut for stock **$300.00**

CVA Colt Sheriff's Model

Similar to the Uberti 1861 Navy except has 5½" barrel, brass or steel frame, semi-fluted cylinder. In 36-caliber only.

Price: Brass frame, finished **$157.95**
Price: As above, brass frame, 44-cal. **$139.95**
Price: As above, kit **$129.95**
Price: Brass frame (Armsport) **$155.00**
Price: Steel frame (Armsport) **$193.00**

NEW MODEL 1858 ARMY PERCUSSION REVOLVER

Caliber: 36 or 44, 6-shot.
Barrel: 6½" or 8".
Weight: 40 oz. **Length:** 13½" overall.
Stocks: Walnut.
Sights: Blade front, groove-in-frame rear.
Features: Replica of Remington Model 1858. Also available from some importers as Army Model Belt Revolver in 36-cal., a shortened and lightened version of the 44. Target Model (Uberti USA, Navy Arms) has fully adjustable target rear sight, target front, 36 or 44. Imported by American Arms, Cabela's, CVA (as 1858 Army), Dixie Gun Works, Navy Arms, The Armoury, E.M.F., Euroarms of America (engraved, stainless and plain), Armsport, Mitchell, Traditions, Inc., Uberti USA.
Price: Steel frame, about . . . . $99.95 to **$280.00**
Price: Steel frame kit (Euroarms, Navy Arms) . . . . . $115.95 to **$150.00**
Price: Single cased set (Navy Arms) **$255.00**
Price: Double cased set (Navy Arms) **$420.00**
Price: Stainless steel Model 1858 (American Arms, Euroarms, Uberti USA, Cabela's, Navy Arms, Armsport, Traditions) . . . . . $169.95 to **$380.00**
Price: Target Model, adjustable rear sight (Cabela's, Euroarms, Uberti USA, Navy Arms, E.M.F.) . . . . $95.95 to **$399.00**
Price: Brass frame (CVA, Cabela's, Traditions, Navy Arms) $79.95 to **$212.95**
Price: As above, kit (CVA, Dixie Gun Works, Navy Arms) $145.00 to **$188.95**
Price: Remington "Texas" (Mitchell) **$199.00**
Price: Buffalo model, 44-cal. (Cabela's) **$109.95**
Price: Lawman model, 44-cal. (Cabela's) **$159.95**
Price: Police model, 36-cal. (Cabela's) **$99.95**
Price: Old Silver model, 44-cal. (Cabela's) **$199.95**

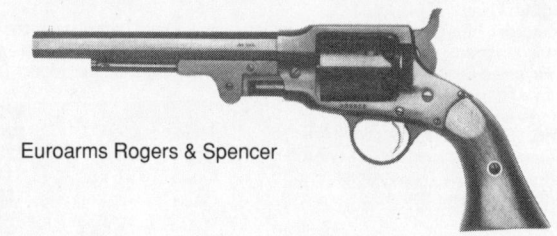

Euroarms Rogers & Spencer

POCKET POLICE 1862 PERCUSSION REVOLVER

Caliber: 36, 5-shot.
Barrel: 4½", 5½", 6½", 7½".
Weight: 26 oz. **Length:** 12" overall (6½" bbl.).
Stocks: Walnut.
Sights: Fixed.
Features: Round tapered barrel; half-fluted and rebated cylinder; case-hardened frame, loading lever and hammer; silver or brass trigger guard and backstrap. Imported by CVA (7½" only), Navy Arms (5½" only), Uberti USA (5½", 6½" only).
Price: About . . . . $143.95 to **$310.00**
Price: Single cased set with accessories (Navy Arms) **$360.00**

RUGER OLD ARMY PERCUSSION REVOLVER

Caliber: 45, 6-shot. Uses .457" dia. lead bullets.
Barrel: 7½" (6-groove, 16" twist).
Weight: 46 oz. **Length:** 13¾" overall.
Stocks: Smooth walnut.
Sights: Ramp front, rear adjustable for windage and elevation.
Features: Stainless steel; standard size nipples, chrome-moly steel cylinder and frame, same lockwork as in original Super Blackhawk. Also available in stainless steel. Made in USA. From Sturm, Ruger & Co.
Price: Stainless steel (Model KBP-7) **$428.00**
Price: Blued steel (Model BP-7) **$378.50**

BLACKPOWDER REVOLVERS

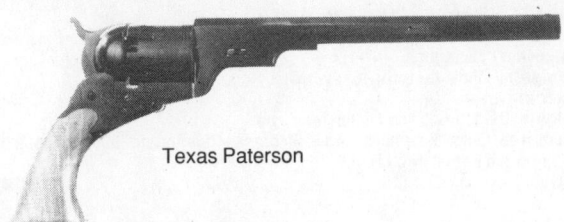

Texas Paterson

TEXAS PATERSON 1836 REVOLVER
Caliber: 36 (.376" round ball).
Barrel: 7½".
Weight: 42 oz.
Stocks: One-piece walnut.
Sights: Fixed.
Features: Copy of Sam Colt's first commercially-made revolving pistol. Has no loading lever but comes with loading tool. From Dixie Gun Works, Navy Arms, Uberti USA.
Price: About . . . . **$335.00 to $395.00**
Price: With loading lever (Uberti USA) **$450.00**
Price: Engraved (Navy Arms) **$465.00**

Uberti 2nd Model Dragoon Revolver
Similar to the 1st Model except distinguished by rectangular bolt cuts in the cylinder.
Price: **$325.00**

Uberti 3rd Model Dragoon Revolver
Similar to the 2nd Model except for oval trigger guard, long trigger, modifications to the loading lever and latch. Imported by Uberti USA.
Price: Military model (frame cut for shoulder stock, steel backstrap) **$330.00**
Price: Civilian (brass backstrap, trigger guard) **$325.00**

UBERTI 1862 POCKET NAVY PERCUSSION REVOLVER
Caliber: 36, 5-shot.
Barrel: 5½", 6½", octagonal, 7-groove, LH twist.
Weight: 27 oz. (5½" barrel). **Length:** 10½" overall (5½" bbl.).
Stocks: One-piece varnished walnut.
Sights: Brass pin front, hammer notch rear.
Features: Rebated cylinder, hinged loading lever, brass or silver-plated backstrap and trigger guard, color-cased frame, hammer, loading lever, plunger and latch, rest blued. Has original-type markings. From Uberti USA.
Price: With brass backstrap, trigger guard **$310.00**

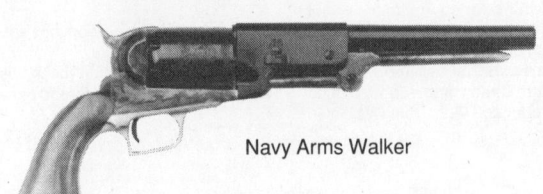

Navy Arms Walker

SHERIFF MODEL 1851 PERCUSSION REVOLVER
Caliber: 36, 44, 6-shot.
Barrel: 5".
Weight: 40 oz. **Length:** 10½" overall.
Stocks: Walnut.
Sights: Fixed.
Features: Brass backstrap and trigger guard; engraved navy scene; case-hardened frame, hammer, loading lever. Imported by E.M.F.
Price: Steel frame **$172.00**
Price: Brass frame **$140.00**

SPILLER & BURR REVOLVER
Caliber: 36 (.375" round ball).
Barrel: 7", octagon.
Weight: 2½ lbs. **Length:** 12½" overall.
Stocks: Two-piece walnut.
Sights: Fixed.
Features: Reproduction of the C.S.A. revolver. Brass frame and trigger guard. Also available as a kit. From Dixie Gun Works, Mitchell, Navy Arms.
Price: . . . . **$89.95 to $199.00**
Price: Kit form **$95.00**
Price: Single cased set (Navy Arms) **$230.00**
Price: Double cased set (Navy Arms) **$370.00**

UBERTI 1st MODEL DRAGOON
Caliber: 44.
Barrel: 7½", part round, part octagon.
Weight: 64 oz.
Stocks: One-piece walnut.
Sights: German silver blade front, hammer notch rear.
Features: First model has oval bolt cuts in cylinder, square-back flared trigger guard, V-type mainspring, short trigger. Ranger and Indian scene roll-engraved on cylinder. Color case-hardened frame, loading lever, plunger and hammer; blue barrel, cylinder, trigger and wedge. Available with old-time charcoal blue or standard blue-black finish. Polished brass backstrap and trigger guard. From Uberti USA.
Price: **$325.00**

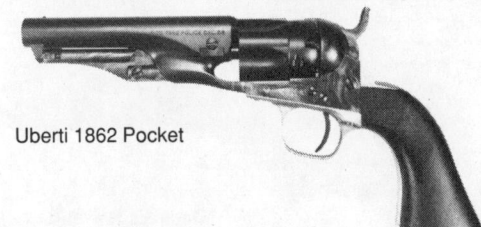

Uberti 1862 Pocket

WALKER 1847 PERCUSSION REVOLVER
Caliber: 44, 6-shot.
Barrel: 9".
Weight: 84 oz. **Length:** 15½" overall.
Stocks: Walnut.
Sights: Fixed.
Features: Case-hardened frame, loading lever and hammer; iron backstrap; brass trigger guard; engraved cylinder. Imported by American Arms, Cabela's, CVA, Navy Arms, Dixie Gun Works, Uberti USA, E.M.F., Cimarron, Traditions, Inc.
Price: About . . . . **$225.00 to $360.00**
Price: Single cased set (Navy Arms) **$385.00**

BLACKPOWDER MUSKETS & RIFLES

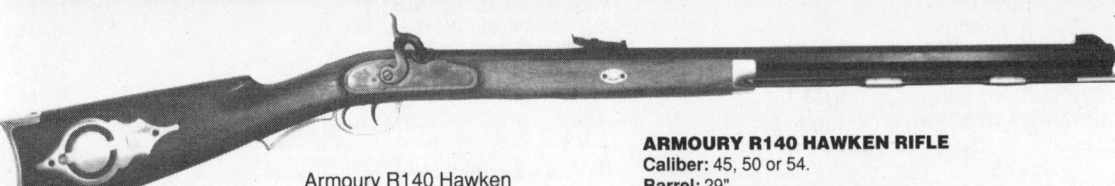

Armoury R140 Hawken

ARMOURY R140 HAWKEN RIFLE
Caliber: 45, 50 or 54.
Barrel: 29".
Weight: 8¾ to 9 lbs. **Length:** 45¾" overall.
Stock: Walnut, with cheekpiece.
Sights: Dovetail front, fully adjustable rear.
Features: Octagon barrel, removable breech plug; double set triggers; blued barrel, brass stock fittings, color case-hardened percussion lock. From Armsport, The Armoury.
Price: . . . . **$225.00 to $245.00**

ARMSPORT 1863 SHARPS RIFLE, CARBINE
Caliber: 45, 54.
Barrel: 28", round.
Weight: 8.4 lbs. **Length:** 46" overall.
Stock: Walnut.
Sights: Blade front, folding adjustable rear. Tang sight set optionally available.
Features: Replica of the 1863 Sharps. Color case-hardened frame, rest blued. Imported by Armsport.
Price: $780.00
Price: Carbine, 54 caliber, 22" barrel $755.00

BOSTONIAN PERCUSSION RIFLE
Caliber: 45.
Barrel: 30", octagonal
Weight: 7¼ lbs. **Length:** 46" overall.
Stock: Walnut.
Sights: Blade front, fixed notch rear.
Features: Color case-hardened lock, brass trigger guard, buttplate, patchbox. Imported from Italy by E.M.F.
Price: $285.00

Cabela's Accura 9000

Weight: About 7½ lbs. **Length:** 44" overall.
Stock: European walnut with Monte Carlo cheekpiece, checkered grip and forend.
Sights: Hooded front with interchangeable blades, open rear adjustable for windage and elevation.
Features: In-line ignition system with removable breech plug. Automatic safety and half-cock. Quick detachable sling swivels, schnabel forend tip, recoil pad. From Cabela's.
Price: Right or left-hand $399.95

CABELA'S ACCURA 9000 MUZZLELOADER
Caliber: 50, 54.
Barrel: 27"; 1:54 twist.

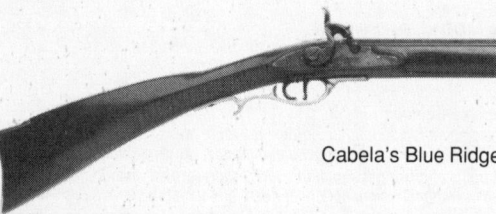

Cabela's Blue Ridge

CABELA'S BLUE RIDGE RIFLE
Caliber: 32, 36, 45, 50, 54.
Barrel: 39", octagonal.
Weight: About 7¾ lbs. **Length:** 55" overall.
Stock: American black walnut.
Sights: Blade front, rear drift adjustable for windage.
Features: Color case-hardened lockplate and cock/hammer, brass trigger guard and buttplate, double set, double-phased triggers. From Cabela's.
Price: Percussion $299.95
Price: Flintlock $319.95
Price: Squirrel Rifle, 32-cal., percussion $299.95
Price: As above, flintlock $319.95

Cabela's Blue Ridge Carbine
Similar to the Blue Ridge Rifle except has 28" barrel, weighs 6¼ lbs. Available in 50- or 54-caliber, From Cabela's.
Price: $259.95

Cabela's Swivel-Barrel

Weight: 10 lbs. **Length:** 40" overall.
Stock: Checkered American walnut.
Sights: Blade front, open rear adjustable for windage and elevation; one set for each barrel.
Features: Barrel assembly rotates for second shot. Back action mechanism. Monte Carlo comb, rubber butt pad; checkered pistol grip and forend panels. Introduced 1992. From Cabela's.
Price: $379.95

CABELA'S SWIVEL-BARREL RIFLE
Caliber: 50, 54.
Barrel: 23.75".

CABELA'S TAOS RIFLE
Caliber: 45, 50.
Barrel: 28¼".
Weight: 6 lbs., 11 oz. **Length:** 43¼" overall.
Stock: Oil-finished walnut.
Sights: Blade front, rear adjustable for windage.
Features: Carbine version of the Pennsylvania rifle. Adjustable double-set triggers. Imported by Cabela's.
Price: Percussion $229.95
Price: Flintlock $239.95

CABELA'S TRADITIONAL HAWKEN'S
Caliber: 45, 50, 54, 58.
Barrel: 29".
Weight: About 9 lbs.
Stock: Walnut.
Sights: Blade front, open adjustable rear.
Features: Flintlock or percussion. Adjustable double-set triggers. Polished brass furniture, color case-hardened lock. Imported by Cabela's.
Price: Percussion, right-hand $169.95
Price: Percussion, right-hand, kit $139.95
Price: Percussion, left-hand $174.95
Price: Flintlock, right-hand $189.95
Price: Flintlock kit $164.95

Cabela's Synthetic Hawken's Hunter
Similar to the Hawken's Hunter except has Bell & Carlson Carbelite black synthetic stock with rubber recoil pad. Available in percussion or flintlock, 50-, 54-, 58-caliber. From Cabela's.
Price: $179.95

> Consult our Directory pages for the location of firms mentioned.

Cabela's Hawken's Hunter Rifle
Similar to the Traditional Hawken's except has more modern stock style with rubber recoil pad, blued furniture, sling swivels. Percussion only, in 45-, 50-, 54- or 58-caliber.
Price: Right-hand $184.95
Price: Left-hand $189.95

BLACKPOWDER MUSKETS & RIFLES

CABELA'S ROLLING BLOCK MUZZLELOADER
Caliber: 50, 54.
Barrel: 26½" octagonal; 1:32" (50), 1:48" (54) twist.
Weight: About 9¼ lbs. **Length:** 43½" overall.
Stock: American walnut, rubber butt pad.
Sights: Blade front, adjustable buckhorn rear.
Features: Uses in-line ignition system, Brass trigger guard, color case-hardened hammer, block and buttplate; black-finished, engraved receiver; easily removable screw-in breech plug; black ramrod and thimble. From Cabela's.
Price: $269.95

Cabela's Rolling Block Muzzleloader Carbine
Similar to the rifle version except has 22¼" barrel, weighs 8¼ lbs. Has bead on ramp front sight, modern fully adjustable rear. From Cabela's.
Price: $249.95

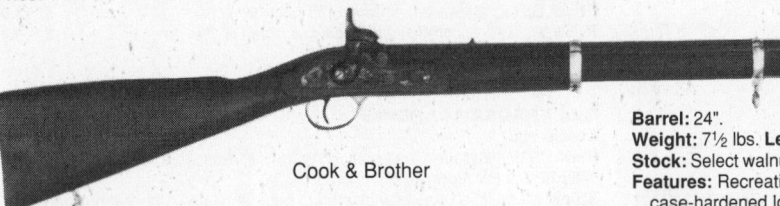

Cook & Brother

COOK & BROTHER CONFEDERATE CARBINE
Caliber: 58.

CABELA'S SHARPS SPORTING RIFLE
Caliber: 45, 54.
Barrel: 31", octagonal.
Weight: About 10 lbs. **Length:** 49" overall.
Stock: American walnut with checkered grip and forend.
Sights: Blade front, ladder-type adjustable rear.
Features: Color case-hardened lock and buttplate. Adjustable double set, double-phased triggers. From Cabela's.
Price: $595.00

Barrel: 24".
Weight: 7½ lbs. **Length:** 40½" overall.
Stock: Select walnut.
Features: Recreation of the 1861 New Orleans-made artillery carbine. Color case-hardened lock, browned barrel. Buttplate, trigger guard, barrel bands, sling swivels and nose cap of polished brass. From Euroarms of America.
Price: $366.00
Price: Cook & Brother rifle (33" barrel) $550.00

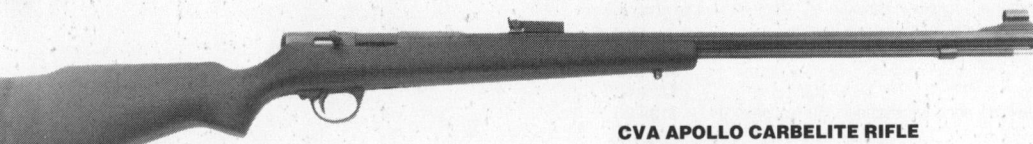

CVA Apollo Carbelite

CVA Apollo Shadow
Similar to the Apollo Carbelite except has black textured epoxicoat hardwood stock. Rifle length only with 27" barrel, 50- or 54- caliber.
Price: $314.95

CVA Apollo Sporter
Similar to the Apollo Carbelite except has walnut-stained hardwood stock, composition buttplate. Available only in 50-caliber, 25" barrel.
Price: $269.95

CVA APOLLO CARBELITE RIFLE
Caliber: 50, 54.
Barrel: 25", blued, round; 1:32" rifling.
Weight: 7½ lbs. **Length:** 43" overall.
Stock: Black Carbelite composite with fluted Monte Carlo comb, cheekpiece, full pistol grip. Sling swivel studs.
Sights: Bead on ramp front, fully adjustable click rear. Drilled and tapped for scope mounting or peep sight.
Features: In-line percussion system with push-pull bolt block safety system. One-piece blued barrel/receiver. Has loading window and foul weather cover. Vented for gas escape. From CVA.
Price: $349.95

CVA BUSHWACKER RIFLE
Caliber: 50.
Barrel: 26", octagonal; 15/16" flats; 1:48" twist.
Weight: 7.5 lbs. **Length:** 40" overall.
Stock: Walnut-stained hardwood.
Sights: Brass blade front, fixed semi-buckhorn open rear.
Features: Color case-hardened lockplate; single trigger with oversize blackened trigger guard; blued barrel, wedge plates. From CVA.
Price: Percussion only $159.95

CVA Express Rifle

CVA FRONTIER CARBINE
Caliber: 50.
Barrel: 24" octagon; 15/16" flats.
Weight: 6½ lbs. **Length:** 40" overall.
Stock: Selected hardwood.
Sights: Brass blade front, fixed open rear.
Features: Color case-hardened lockplate, V-type mainspring. Early style brass trigger with tension spring. Brass buttplate, trigger guard, wedge plate, nose cap, thimble. From CVA.
Price: Percussion $189.95
Price: Flintlock rifle $224.95
Price: Percussion Carbine kit $137.95

CVA EXPRESS RIFLE
Caliber: 50, 54.
Barrel: 28", round.
Weight: 9 lbs.
Stock: Walnut-stained hardwood.
Sights: Bead and post front, adjustable rear.
Features: Double rifle with twin percussion locks and triggers, adjustable barrels. Hooked breech. Introduced 1989. From CVA.
Price: Finished $525.95

CVA Frontier Hunter Carbine
Similar to the CVA Frontier Carbine except has conventional-style black rubber butt pad, black chrome furniture. Barrel is drilled and tapped for scope mounting. Fully adjustable rear sight. Overall length 40", weight 7.5 lbs., 50-caliber only. From CVA.
Price: $209.95

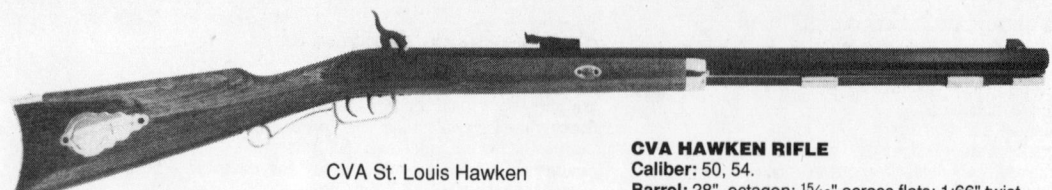

CVA St. Louis Hawken

CVA KENTUCKY RIFLE
Caliber: 50.
Barrel: 33½", rifled, octagon; ⅞" flats.
Weight: 7½ lbs. **Length:** 48" overall.
Stock: Select hardwood.
Sights: Brass Kentucky blade-type front, fixed open rear.
Features: Available in percussion only. Stainless steel nipple included. From CVA.
Price: Percussion $262.95
Price: Percussion kit $189.95

CVA STALKER RIFLE/CARBINE
Caliber: 50, 54.
Barrel: 24", 28"; octagonal; drilled and tapped for scope mounting; 1:32" twist.
Weight: 7.5 lbs. **Length:** 44" overall (rifle).
Stock: Walnut-stained hardwood with Monte Carlo comb, cheekpiece. Ventilated rubber recoil pad.
Sights: Beaded blade front, fully adjustable click rear.
Features: Color case-hardened lockplate; Hawken-style lock with bridle and fly, 45-degree offset hammer; single modern-style trigger. From CVA.
Price: 50, 54 rifle $217.95
Price: 50, 54 carbine $217.95
Price: Left-hand carbine $239.95
Price: Sierra Stalker Rifle (28", not drilled, tapped, 50-cal. only) . . . $189.95

CVA HAWKEN RIFLE
Caliber: 50, 54.
Barrel: 28", octagon; ¹⁵⁄₁₆" across flats; 1:66" twist.
Weight: 8 lbs. **Length:** 44" overall.
Stock: Select hardwood.
Sights: Beaded blade front, fully adjustable open rear.
Features: Fully adjustable double-set triggers; brass patch box, wedge plates, nosecap, thimbles, trigger guard and buttplate; blued barrel; color case-hardened, engraved lockplate. V-type mainspring. Percussion only. Hooked breech. Introduced 1981. From CVA.
Price: St. Louis Hawken, finished (50-, 54-cal.) $214.95
Price: As above, combo kit (50-, 54-cal. bbls.) $229.95

CVA TRACKER CARBINE
Caliber: 50.
Barrel: 21", half round, half octagon with ¹⁵⁄₁₆" flats; 1:32" twist.
Weight: 6.5 lbs. **Length:** 36" overall.
Stock: Matte finish walnut with straight grip; ventilated rubber recoil pad.
Sights: Beaded blade front, fully adjustable click rear.
Features: Color case-hardened lockplate, black-chromed furniture; drilled and tapped for scope mounting. From CVA.
Price: $254.95

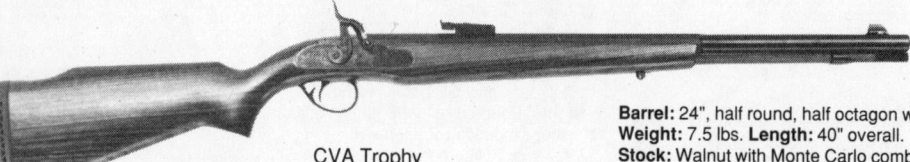

CVA Trophy

CVA TROPHY CARBINE
Caliber: 50, 54.

Barrel: 24", half round, half octagon with ¹⁵⁄₁₆" flats; 1:32" twist.
Weight: 7.5 lbs. **Length:** 40" overall.
Stock: Walnut with Monte Carlo comb, cheekpiece.
Sights: White bead on blade front, fully adjustable click rear.
Features: Color case-hardened lockplate, blued barrel, thimble. Modern-style stock; modern rifle trigger with over-sized guard; drilled and tapped for scope mounting. From CVA.
Price: $254.95

CVA VARMINT RIFLE
Caliber: 32.
Barrel: 24" octagonal; ⅞" flats; 1:48" rifling.
Weight: 6¾ lbs. **Length:** 40" overall.
Stock: Select hardwood.
Sights: Blade front, Patridge-style click adjustable rear.
Features: Brass trigger guard, nose cap, wedge plate, thinble and buttplate. Drilled and tapped for scope mounting. Color case-hardened lock. Single trigger. Imported by CVA.
Price: $234.95

DIXIE DELUX CUB RIFLE
Caliber: 40.
Barrel: 28".
Weight: 6½ lbs. .
Stock: Walnut.
Sights: Fixed.
Features: Short rifle for small game and beginning shooters. Brass patchbox and furniture. Flint or percussion. From Dixie Gun Works.
Price: Finished $335.00
Price: Kit $205.00

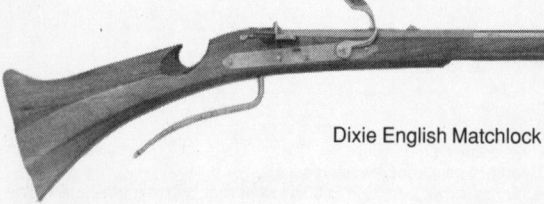

Dixie English Matchlock

DIXIE HAWKEN RIFLE
Caliber: 45, 50, 54.
Barrel: 30".
Weight: 8 lbs. **Length:** 46½" overall.
Stock: Walnut.
Sights: Blade front, adjustable rear.
Features: Blued barrel, double-set triggers, steel crescent buttplate. Imported by Dixie Gun Works.
Price: Finished $250.00
Price: Kit $220.00

DIXIE ENGLISH MATCHLOCK MUSKET
Caliber: 72.
Barrel: 44".
Weight: 8 lbs. **Length:** 57.75" overall.
Stock: Walnut with satin oil finish.
Sights: Blade front, open rear adjustable for windage.
Features: Replica of circa 1600-1680 English matchlock. Getz barrel with 11" octagonal area at rear, rest is round with cannon-type muzzle. All steel finished in the white. Imported by Dixie Gun Works.
Price: $825.00

BLACKPOWDER MUSKETS & RIFLES

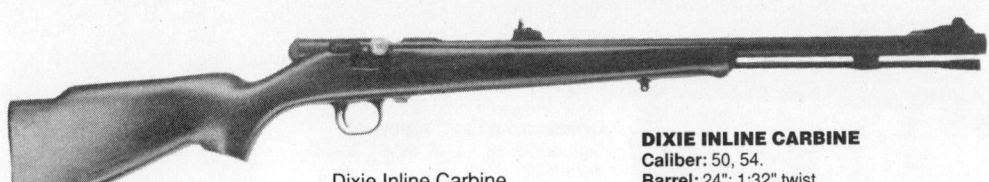

Dixie Inline Carbine

DIXIE TENNESSEE MOUNTAIN RIFLE

Caliber: 32 or 50.
Barrel: 41½", 6-groove rifling, brown finish. **Length:** 56" overall.
Stock: Walnut, oil finish; Kentucky-style.
Sights: Silver blade front, open buckhorn rear.
Features: Recreation of the original mountain rifles. Early Schultz lock, inter-changeable flint or percussion with vent plug or drum and nipple. Tumbler has fly. Double-set triggers. All metal parts browned. From Dixie Gun Works.
Price: Flint or percussion, finished rifle, 50-cal. $495.00
Price: Kit, 50-cal. $395.00
Price: Left-hand model, flint or percussion $450.00
Price: Left-hand kit, flint or perc., 50-cal. $360.00
Price: Squirrel Rifle (as above except in 32-cal. with ¹³⁄₁₆" barrel flats), flint or percussion $495.00
Price: Kit, 32-cal., flint or percussion $395.00

DIXIE INLINE CARBINE

Caliber: 50, 54.
Barrel: 24"; 1:32" twist.
Weight: 6.5 lbs. **Length:** 41" overall.
Stock: Walnut-finished hardwood with Monte Carlo comb.
Sights: Ramp front with red insert, open fully adjustable rear.
Features: Sliding "bolt" fully encloses cap and nipple. Fully adjustable trigger, automatic safety. Aluminum ramrod. Imported from Italy by Dixie Gun Works.
Price: $349.95

DIXIE 1863 SPRINGFIELD MUSKET

Caliber: 58 (.570" patched ball or .575" Minie).
Barrel: 50", rifled.
Stocks: Walnut stained.
Sights: Blade front, adjustable ladder-type rear.
Features: Bright-finish lock, barrel, furniture. Reproduction of the last of the regulation muzzleloaders. Imported from Japan by Dixie Gun Works.
Price: Finished $475.00
Price: Kit $330.00

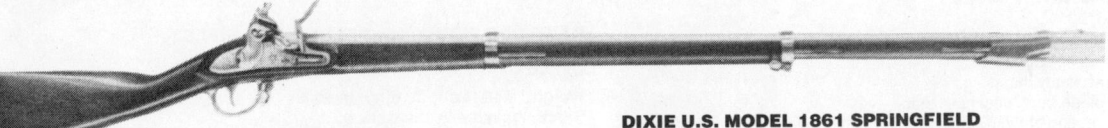

Dixie Model 1816

DIXIE U.S. MODEL 1816 FLINTLOCK MUSKET

Caliber: 69.
Barrel: 42", smoothbore.
Weight: 9.75 lbs. **Length:** 56.5" overall.
Stock: Walnut with oil finish.
Sights: Blade front.
Features: All metal finished "National Armory Bright"; three barrel bands with springs; steel ramrod with button-shaped head. Imported by Dixie Gun Works.
Price: $725.00

DIXIE U.S. MODEL 1861 SPRINGFIELD

Caliber: 58.
Barrel: 40".
Weight: About 8 lbs. **Length:** 55¹³⁄₁₆" overall.
Stock: Oil-finished walnut.
Sights: Blade front, step adjustable rear.
Features: Exact recreation of original rifle. Sling swivels attached to trigger guard bow and middle barrel band. Lockplate marked "1861" with eagle motif and "U.S. Springfield" in front of hammer; "U.S." stamped on top of buttplate. From Dixie Gun Works.
Price: $450.00
Price: Kit $420.00

Euroarms Volunteer

EUROARMS BUFFALO CARBINE

Caliber: 58.
Barrel: 26", round.
Weight: 7¾ lbs. **Length:** 42" overall.
Stock: Walnut.
Sights: Blade front, open adjustable rear.
Features: Shoots .575" round ball. Color case-hardened lock, blue hammer, barrel, trigger; brass furniture. Brass patchbox. Imported by Euroarms of America.
Price: $407.00

EUROARMS VOLUNTEER TARGET RIFLE

Caliber: .451.
Barrel: 33" (two-band), 36" (three-band).
Weight: 11 lbs. (two-band). **Length:** 48.75" overall (two-band).
Stock: European walnut with checkered wrist and forend.
Sights: Hooded bead front, adjustable rear with interchangeable leaves.
Features: Alexander Henry-type rifling with 1:20" twist. Color case-hardened hammer and lockplate, brass trigger guard and nose cap, rest blued. Imported by Euroarms of America.
Price: Two-band $670.00
Price: Three-band $700.00

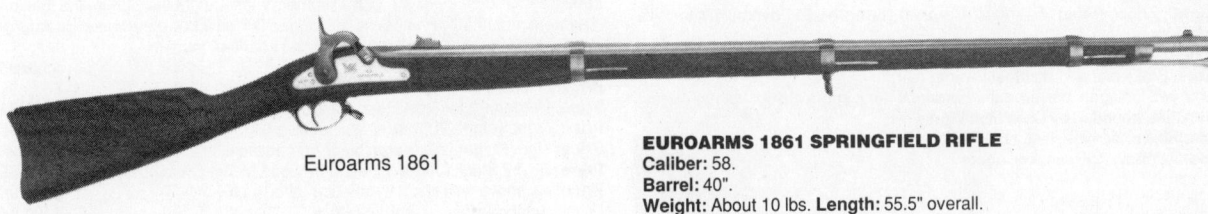

Euroarms 1861

EUROARMS 1861 SPRINGFIELD RIFLE

Caliber: 58.
Barrel: 40".
Weight: About 10 lbs. **Length:** 55.5" overall.
Stock: European walnut.
Sights: Blade front, three-leaf military rear.
Features: Reproduction of the original three-band rifle. Lockplate marked "1861" with eagle and "U.S. Springfield." Metal left in the white. Imported by Euroarms of America.
Price: $650.00

Gonic GA-87

GONIC GA-87 M/L RIFLE
Caliber: 30, 38, 44, 45, 50, 54, 20-ga.
Barrel: 26".
Weight: 6 to 6½ lbs. **Length:** 43" overall (Carbine).
Stock: American walnut with checkered grip and forend, or laminated stock.
Sights: Optional bead front, open or peep rear adjustable for windage and elevation; drilled and tapped for scope bases (included).
Features: Closed-breech action with straight-line ignition. Modern trigger mechanism with ambidextrous safety. Satin blue finish on metal, satin stock finish. Introduced 1989. From Gonic Arms, Inc.
Price: Standard rifle, no sights $493.38
Price: As above, with sights, from $535.95
Price: Deluxe Rifle, no sights, from $526.06
Price: As above, with sights, from $568.64
Price: Accessory 24" carbine barrel, from $190.49

Gonic Model 93 Magnum M/L Rifle
Similar to the GA-87 except has open bolt mechanism, single safety, 22" barrel and comes only in 50-caliber with open sights. Stock is either black wrinkle-finish wood or gray laminate. Introduced 1993. From Gonic Arms, Inc.
Price: $310.00

Hatfield Squirrel Rifle

HATFIELD SQUIRREL RIFLE
Caliber: 36, 45, 50.
Barrel: 39½", octagon, 32" on half-stock.
Weight: 7½ lbs. (32-cal.).
Stock: American fancy maple.
Sights: Silver blade front, buckhorn rear.
Features: Recreation of the traditional squirrel rifle. Available in flint or percussion with brass trigger guard and buttplate. From Hatfield Rifle Works. Introduced 1983.
Price: Full stock, percussion, Grade II $650.00
Price: As above, flintlock $650.00
Price: As above, Grade III, flint or percussion $750.00

HARPER'S FERRY 1803 FLINTLOCK RIFLE
Caliber: 54 or 58.
Barrel: 35".
Weight: 9 lbs. **Length:** 59½" overall.
Stock: Walnut with cheekpiece.
Sights: Brass blade front, fixed steel rear.
Features: Brass trigger guard, sideplate, buttplate; steel patch box. Imported by Euroarms of America, Navy Arms (54-cal. only).
Price: $512.00
Price: 54-cal. (Navy Arms) $555.00

HAWKEN RIFLE
Caliber: 45, 50, 54 or 58.
Barrel: 28", blued, 6-groove rifling.
Weight: 8¾ lbs. **Length:** 44" overall.
Stock: Walnut with cheekpiece.
Sights: Blade front, fully adjustable rear.
Features: Coil mainspring, double-set triggers, polished brass furniture. From Armsport, Ellett Bros., Navy Arms, E.M.F.
Price: . . . . $245.00 to $345.00
Price: 50-, 54-cal., right-hand, percussion (Ellett Bros.) $289.95
Price: 50-, 54-cal., left-hand, percussion (Ellett Bros.) $299.95
Price: 50-cal., right-hand, flintlock (Ellett Bros.) $309.95
Price: 50-cal., left-hand, flintlock (Ellett Bros.) $389.95

ITHACA-NAVY HAWKEN RIFLE
Caliber: 50.
Barrel: 32" octagonal, 1" dia.
Weight: About 9 lbs.
Stocks: Walnut.
Sights: Blade front, rear adjustable for windage.
Features: Hooked breech, 1⅞" throw percussion lock. Attached twin thimbles and under-rib. German silver barrel key inlays, Hawken-style toe and buttplates, lock bolt inlays, barrel wedges, entry thimble, trigger guard, ramrod and cleaning jag, nipple and nipple wrench. Introduced 1977. From Navy Arms.
Price: Complete, percussion $400.00
Price: Kit, percussion $360.00

Knight Mk-85 Hunter

KENTUCKIAN RIFLE & CARBINE
Caliber: 44.
Barrel: 35" (Rifle), 27½" (Carbine).
Weight: 7 lbs. (Rifle), 5½ lbs. (Carbine). **Length:** 51" overall (Rifle), 43" (Carbine).
Stock: Walnut stain.
Sights: Brass blade front, steel V-ramp rear.
Features: Octagon barrel, case-hardened and engraved lockplates. Brass furniture. Imported by Dixie Gun Works.
Price: Rifle or carbine, flint, about $259.95
Price: As above, percussion, about $249.95

Knight MK-85 Grand American Rifle
Similar to the MK-85 Hunter except comes with Shadow Black or Shadow Brown thumbhole stock. Hand-selected barrel and components. Comes with test target, hard gun case. Blue finish.
Price: $995.00
Price: As above except in stainless steel $1,095.00

KNIGHT MK-85 HUNTER RIFLE
Caliber: 50, 54.
Barrel: 24".
Weight: 7 lbs.
Stock: Classic walnut; recoil pad; swivel studs.
Sights: Hooded blade front on ramp, open adjustable rear.
Features: One-piece in-line bolt assembly with straight through in-line ignition system. Adjustable Featherweight trigger. Drilled and tapped for scope mounting. Made in U.S. From Modern Muzzle Loading, Inc.
Price: $529.95
Price: Stalker (laminated, colored stock), 50 or 54 . . . . $579.95
Price: Predator (stainless steel, composition stock), 50 or 54 . . . . $649.95
Price: Light Knight (20" barrel, walnut stock) $499.95
Price: Light Knight (20" barrel, black composite stock) $519.95
Price: BK-92 Black Knight (blued, hardwood Monte Carlo stock) . . $379.95
Price: As above with black synthetic-coated stock $349.95
Price: As above with composite stock $399.95
Price: LK-93 Knight Legend $289.95

KENTUCKY FLINTLOCK RIFLE

Caliber: 44, 45, or 50.
Barrel: 35".
Weight: 7 lbs. **Length:** 50" overall.
Stock: Walnut stained, brass fittings.
Sights: Fixed.
Features: Available in carbine model also, 28" bbl. Some variations in detail, finish. Kits also available from some importers. Imported by Navy Arms, The Armoury.
Price: About . . . . $217.95 to $345.00
Price: Percussion, 45 or 50-cal. (Navy Arms) $330.00

Kentucky Percussion Rifle

Similar to flintlock except percussion lock. Finish and features vary with importer. Imported by Navy Arms (45-cal.), The Armoury, CVA.
Price: About $259.95
Price: 50-cal. (Navy Arms) $330.00
Price: Kit, 50-cal. (CVA) $189.95

Navy Kodiak

LONDON ARMORY 2-BAND ENFIELD 1858

Caliber: .577" Minie, .575" round ball.
Barrel: 33".
Weight: 10 lbs. **Length:** 49" overall.
Stock: Walnut.
Sights: Folding leaf rear adjustable for elevation.
Features: Blued barrel, color case-hardened lock and hammer, polished brass buttplate, trigger guard, nosecap. From Navy Arms, Euroarms of America, Dixie Gun Works.
Price: . . . . $385.00 to $450.00
Price: Assembled kit (Euroarms of America) $364.00

LONDON ARMORY ENFIELD MUSKETOON

Caliber: 58, Minie ball.
Barrel: 24", round.
Weight: 7-7½ lbs. **Length:** 40½" overall.
Stock: Walnut, with sling swivels.
Sights: Blade front, graduated military-leaf rear.
Features: Brass trigger guard, nose cap, buttplate; blued barrel, bands, lockplate, swivels. Imported by Euroarms of America, Navy Arms.
Price: . . . . $300.00 to $370.00
Price: Kit $345.00

KODIAK MK. III DOUBLE RIFLE

Caliber: 54x54, 58x58, 50x50.
Barrel: 28", 5-groove, 1:48 twist.
Weight: 9½ lbs. **Length:** 43¼" overall.
Stock: Czechoslovakian walnut, hand-checkered.
Sights: Adjustable bead front, adjustable open rear.
Features: Hooked breech allows interchangeability of barrels. Comes with sling, swivels, bullet mould and bullet starter. Engraved lockplates, top tang and trigger guard. Locks and top tang polished, rest browned. Introduced 1976. Imported from Italy by Trail Guns Armory, Inc., Navy Arms.
Price: 50-, 54-, 58-cal. SxS $650.00
Price: Spare barrels, all calibers $395.50
Price: Spare barrels, 12-ga.x12-ga. $295.50

LONDON ARMORY 3-BAND 1853 ENFIELD

Caliber: 58 (.577" Minie, .575" round ball, .580" maxi ball).
Barrel: 39".
Weight: 9½ lbs. **Length:** 54" overall.
Stock: European walnut.
Sights: Inverted "V" front, traditional Enfield folding ladder rear.
Features: Recreation of the famed London Armory Company Pattern 1862 Enfield Musket. One-piece walnut stock, brass buttplate, trigger guard and nose cap. Lockplate marked "London Armoury Co." and with a British crown. Blued Baddeley barrel bands. From Dixie Gun Works, Euroarms of America, Navy Arms.
Price: About . . . . $350.00 to $485.00
Price: Assembled kit (Dixie, Euroarms of America) $425.00

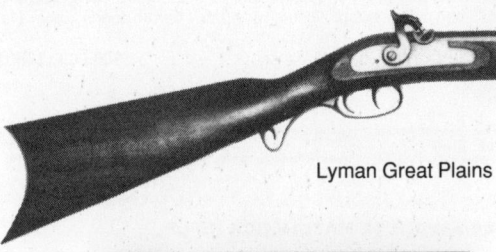

Lyman Great Plains

CONSULT **Shooter's Marketplace** Page 231, This Issue

LYMAN GREAT PLAINS RIFLE

Caliber: 50- or 54-cal.
Barrel: 32", 1:66 twist.
Weight: 9 lbs.
Stock: Walnut.
Sights: Steel blade front, buckhorn rear adjustable for windage and elevation and fixed notch primitive sight included.
Features: Blued steel furniture. Stainless steel nipple. Coil spring lock, Hawken-style trigger guard and double-set triggers. Round thimbles recessed and sweated into rib. Steel wedge plates and toe plate. Introduced 1979. From Lyman.
Price: Percussion $409.95
Price: Flintlock $439.95
Price: Percussion kit $329.95
Price: Flintlock kit $359.95
Price: Left-hand percussion $409.95
Price: Left-hand flintlock $439.95

LYMAN DEERSTALKER RIFLE

Caliber: 50, 54.
Barrel: 24", octagonal; 1:48 rifling.
Weight: 7½ lbs.
Stock: Walnut with black rubber buttpad.
Sights: Lyman #37MA beaded front, fully adjustable fold-down Lyman #16A rear.
Features: Stock has less drop for quick sighting. All metal parts are blackened, with color case-hardened lock; single trigger. Comes with sling and swivels. Available in flint or percussion. Introduced 1990. From Lyman.
Price: 50- or 54-cal., percussion $339.95
Price: 50- or 54-cal., flintlock $359.95
Price: 50- or 54-cal., percussion, left-hand $339.95
Price: 50-cal., flintlock, left-hand $359.95

Lyman Deerstalker Custom Carbine

Similar to the Deerstalker rifle except in 50-caliber only with 21" stepped octagon barrel; 1:24 twist for optimum performance with conical projectiles. Comes with Lyman 37MA front sight, Lyman 16A folding rear. Weighs 6¾ lbs., measures 38½" overall. Percussion or flintlock. Comes with Delrin ramrod, modern sling and swivels. Introduced 1991.
Price: Percussion $349.95
Price: Flintlock $374.95
Price: Percussion, left-hand $349.95

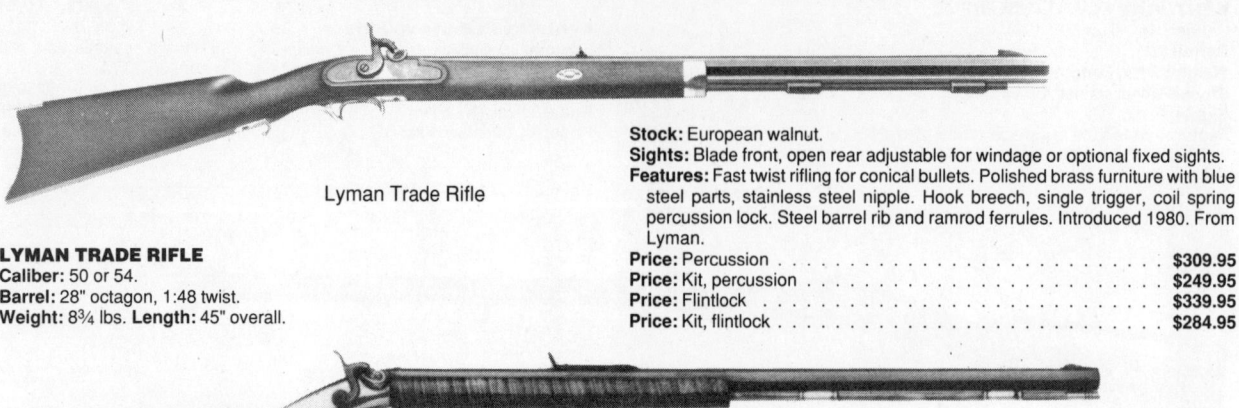

Lyman Trade Rifle

Stock: European walnut.
Sights: Blade front, open rear adjustable for windage or optional fixed sights.
Features: Fast twist rifling for conical bullets. Polished brass furniture with blue steel parts, stainless steel nipple. Hook breech, single trigger, coil spring percussion lock. Steel barrel rib and ramrod ferrules. Introduced 1980. From Lyman.

Price: Percussion **$309.95**
Price: Kit, percussion **$249.95**
Price: Flintlock **$339.95**
Price: Kit, flintlock **$284.95**

LYMAN TRADE RIFLE
Caliber: 50 or 54.
Barrel: 28" octagon, 1:48 twist.
Weight: 8¾ lbs. **Length:** 45" overall.

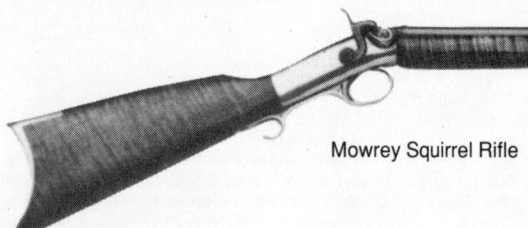

Mowrey Squirrel Rifle

MOWREY SQUIRREL RIFLE
Caliber: 32, 36 or 45.
Barrel: 28"; ¹³⁄₁₆" flats; 1:66" twist.
Weight: About 7.5 lbs. **Length:** 43" overall.
Stock: Curly maple; crescent buttplate.
Sights: German silver blade front, semi-buckhorn rear.
Features: Brass or steel boxlock action; cut-rifled barrel. Steel rifles have browned finish, brass have browned barrel. Adjustable sear and trigger pull. Made in U.S. by Mowrey Gun Works.
Price: Brass or steel **$350.00**
Price: Kit **$300.00**

Mowrey Silhouette Rifle
Similar to the Squirrel Rifle except in 40-caliber with 32" barrel. Available in brass or steel frame.
Price: Brass frame **$350.00**
Price: Steel frame **$350.00**
Price: Kit, brass or steel **$300.00**

Mowrey Plains Rifle
Similar to the Squirrel Rifle except in 50- or 54-caliber with 32" barrel. Available in brass or steel frame.
Price: Brass frame **$350.00**
Price: Steel frame **$350.00**
Price: Rocky Mountain Hunter (as above except 28" bbl.), brass . . **$350.00**
Price: As above, steel frame **$350.00**
Price: All above in kit form, ea. **$300.00**

Mowrey 1 N 30 Conical Rifle
Similar to the Squirrel Rifle except in steel frame only, 45-, 50- or 54-caliber. Has special 1:24" twist barrel for conical- and sabot-style bullets. The 50- and 54-caliber barrels have 1" flats.
Price: **$350.00**
Price: Kit **$300.00**

J.P. MURRAY 1862-1864 CAVALRY CARBINE
Caliber: 58 (.577" Minie).
Barrel: 23".
Weight: 7 lbs., 9 oz. **Length:** 39" overall.
Stock: Walnut.

Sights: Blade front, rear drift adjustable for windage.
Features: Browned barrel, color case-hardened lock, blued swivel and band springs, polished brass buttplate, trigger guard, barrel bands. From Navy Arms, Euroarms of America.
Price: . . . . **$300.00 to $380.00**

Navy Arms Japanese Matchlock

NAVY ARMS JAPANESE MATCHLOCK RIFLE
Caliber: 50.
Barrel: 41".
Weight: 8½ lbs. **Length:** 54¼" overall.
Stock: Stained hardwood.
Sights: Blade front, rear adjustable for windage.
Features: Replica of the matchlocks used by the Samurai. Brass lock, serpentine and trigger guard. Introduced 1991. Imported by Navy Arms.
Price: **$495.00**

NAVY ARMS MORTIMER FLINTLOCK RIFLE
Caliber: 54.
Barrel: 36".
Weight: 9 lbs. **Length:** 52¼" overall.
Stock: Checkered walnut.
Sights: Bead front, rear adjustable for windage.
Features: Waterproof pan, roller frizzen; sling swivels; browned barrel; external safety. Introduced 1991. Imported by Navy Arms.
Price: **$690.00**

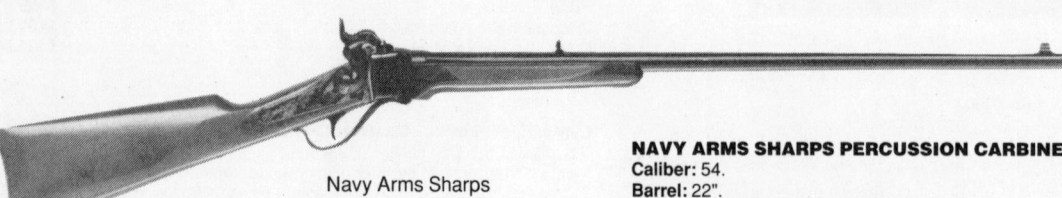

Navy Arms Sharps

NAVY ARMS SHARPS PERCUSSION CARBINE
Caliber: 54.
Barrel: 22".
Weight: 7¾ lbs. **Length:** 39" overall.
Stock: Walnut.
Sights: Blade front, military ladder-type rear.
Features: Color case-hardened action, blued barrel. Has saddle ring. Introduced 1991. Imported from Navy Arms.
Price: **$715.00**
Price: Sharps Plains rifle (28.5" barrel) **$715.00**

BLACKPOWDER MUSKETS & RIFLES

NAVY ARMS 1777 CHARLEVILLE MUSKET
Caliber: 69.
Barrel: 44⅝".
Weight: 10 lbs., 4 oz. **Length:** 59¾" overall.
Stock: Walnut.
Sights: Brass blade front.
Features: Exact copy of the musket used in the French Revolution. All steel is polished, in the white. Brass flashpan. Introduced 1991. Imported by Navy Arms.
Price: $690.00
Price: 1763 Standard Charleville Musket, finished $575.00
Price: As above, kit $450.00
Price: 1816 M.T. Wickham Musket $690.00

NAVY ARMS 1862 C.S. RICHMOND RIFLE
Caliber: 58.
Barrel: 40".
Weight: 10 lbs. **Length:** NA.
Stock: Walnut.
Sights: Blade front, adjustable rear.
Features: Copy of the three-band rifle musket made at Richmond Armory for the Confederacy. All steel polished bright. Imported by Navy Arms, Euroarms.
Price: $550.00
Price: From Euroarms $647.15

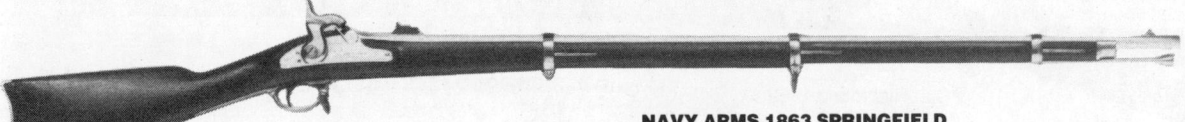

Navy Arms 1863

NAVY ARMS 1863 SPRINGFIELD
Caliber: 58, uses .575" Minie.
Barrel: 40", rifled.
Weight: 9½ lbs. **Length:** 56" overall.
Stock: Walnut.
Sights: Open rear adjustable for elevation.
Features: Full-size three-band musket. Polished bright metal, including lock. From Navy Arms.
Price: Finished rifle $550.00
Price: Kit $450.00

NAVY ARMS PENNSYLVANIA LONG RIFLE
Caliber: 32, 45.
Barrel: 40½".
Weight: 7½ lbs. **Length:** 56½" overall.
Stock: Walnut.
Sights: Blade front, fully adjustable rear.
Features: Browned barrel, brass furniture, polished lock with double-set triggers. Introduced 1991. Imported by Navy Arms.
Price: Percussion $395.00
Price: Flintlock $410.00

NAVY ARMS SMITH CARBINE
Caliber: 50.
Barrel: 21½".
Weight: 7¾ lbs. **Length:** 39" overall.
Stock: American walnut.
Sights: Brass blade front, folding ladder-type rear.
Features: Replica of the breech-loading Civil War carbine. Color case-hardened receiver, rest blued. Cavalry model has saddle ring and bar, Artillery model has sling swivels. Introduced 1991. Imported by Navy Arms.
Price: Cavalry model $600.00
Price: Artillery model $600.00

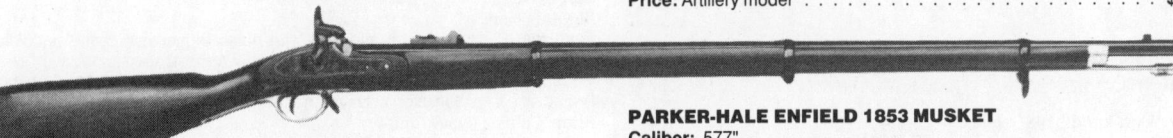

Parker-Hale 1853

PARKER-HALE ENFIELD 1853 MUSKET
Caliber: .577".
Barrel: 39", 3-groove cold-forged rifling.
Weight: About 9 lbs. **Length:** 55" overall.
Stock: Seasoned walnut.
Sights: Fixed front, rear step adjustable for elevation.
Features: Three-band musket made to original specs from original gauges. Solid brass stock furniture, color hardened lockplate, hammer; blued barrel, trigger. Made by Gibbs Rifle Co., distributed by Navy Arms.
Price: $585.00

PARKER-HALE ENFIELD PATTERN 1858 NAVAL RIFLE
Caliber: .577".
Barrel: 33".
Weight: 8½ lbs. **Length:** 48½" overall.
Stock: European walnut.
Sights: Blade front, step adjustable rear.
Features: Two-band Enfield percussion rifle with heavy barrel. Five-groove progressive depth rifling, solid brass furniture. All parts made exactly to original patterns. Made by Gibbs Rifle Co., distributed by Navy Arms.
Price: $550.00

PARKER-HALE ENFIELD 1861 MUSKETOON
Caliber: 58.
Barrel: 24".
Weight: 7 lbs. **Length:** 40½" overall.
Stock: Walnut.
Sights: Fixed front, adjustable rear.
Features: Percussion muzzleloader, made to original 1861 English patterns. Made by Gibbs Rifle Co., distributed by Navy Arms.
Price: $450.00

Parker-Hale Whitworth

PARKER-HALE WHITWORTH MILITARY TARGET RIFLE
Caliber: 45.
Barrel: 36".
Weight: 9¼ lbs. **Length:** 52½" overall.
Stock: Walnut. Checkered at wrist and forend.
Sights: Hooded post front, open step-adjustable rear.
Features: Faithful reproduction of the Whitworth rifle, only bored for 45-cal. Trigger has a detented lock, capable of being adjusted very finely without risk of the sear nose catching on the half-cock bent and damaging both parts. Introduced 1978. Made by Gibbs Rifle Co., distributed by Navy Arms.
Price: $815.00

Parker-Hale Limited Edition Whitworth Sniping Rifle
Same as the Parker-Hale Whitworth Military Target Rifle except has replica of the Model 1860 brass telescope sight in fully adjustable mount. Made by Gibbs Rifle Co., distributed by Navy Arms.
Price: $995.00

PARKER-HALE VOLUNTEER RIFLE

Caliber: .451".
Barrel: 32".
Weight: 9½ lbs. **Length:** 49" overall.
Stock: Walnut, checkered wrist and forend.
Sights: Globe front, adjustable ladder-type rear.
Features: Recreation of the type of gun issued to volunteer regiments during the 1860s. Rigby-pattern rifling, patent breech, detented lock. Stock is glass bedded for accuracy. Made by Gibbs Rifle Co., distributed by Navy Arms.
Price: $750.00
Price: Three-band Volunteer $815.00

PENNSYLVANIA FULL-STOCK RIFLE

Caliber: 45 or 50.
Barrel: 32" rifled, ¹⁵⁄₁₆" dia.
Weight: 8½ lbs.
Stock: Walnut.
Sights: Fixed.
Features: Available in flint or percussion. Blued lock and barrel, brass furniture. Offered complete or in kit form. From The Armoury.
Price: Flint $250.00
Price: Percussion $225.00

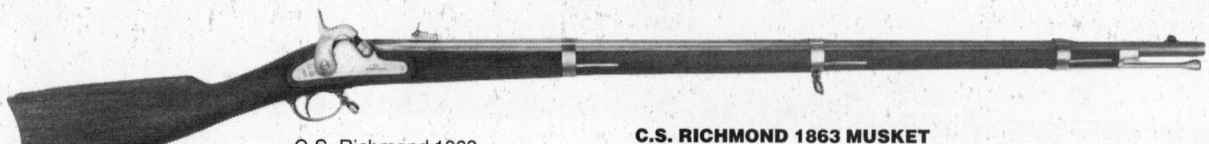

C.S. Richmond 1863

C.S. RICHMOND 1863 MUSKET

Caliber: 58.
Barrel: 40".
Weight: 11 lbs. **Length:** 56¼" overall.
Stock: European walnut with oil finish.
Sights: Blade front, adjustable folding leaf rear.
Features: Reproduction of the three-band Civil War musket. Sling swivels attached to trigger guard and middle barrel band. Lock plate marked "1863" and "C.S. Richmond." All metal left in the white. Brass buttplate and forend cap. Imported by Euroarms of America.
Price: $650.00

ROBERTS 98 MAUSER MUZZLE LOADER

Caliber: 45, 50, 54.
Barrel: 26".
Weight: 8 lbs. **Length:** 46" overall.
Stock: Walnut-finished hardwood.
Sights: None furnished; comes with Weaver-style one-piece scope mount.
Features: Uses 98 Mauser bolt action. Wilson #3 tapered barrel; Mark II low profile safety. Announced 1993. Made in U.S. Available from Sile Distributors.
Price: About $336.00

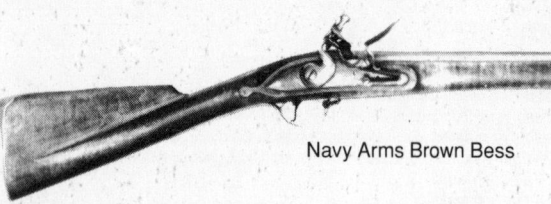

Navy Arms Brown Bess

SECOND MODEL BROWN BESS MUSKET

Caliber: 75, uses .735" round ball.
Barrel: 42", smoothbore.
Weight: 9½ lbs. **Length:** 59" overall.
Stock: Walnut (Navy); walnut-stained hardwood (Dixie).
Sights: Fixed.
Features: Polished barrel and lock with brass trigger guard and buttplate. Bayonet and scabbard available. From Navy Arms, Dixie Gun Works.
Price: Finished .... $475.00 to $850.00
Price: Kit (Dixie Gun Works, Navy Arms) ... $495.00 to $510.00
Price: Carbine (Navy Arms) $635.00

SHARPS PERCUSSION RIFLES

Caliber: 54.
Barrel: 28".
Weight: 9 lbs. **Length:** 46" overall.
Stock: Checkered walnut.
Sights: Blade front, ladder-type adjustable rear.
Features: Blued barrel, color case-hardened receiver and buttplate. Imported from Italy by E.M.F.
Price: Rifle or carbine $860.00

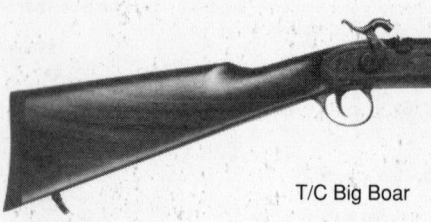

T/C Big Boar

THOMPSON/CENTER BIG BOAR RIFLE

Caliber: 58.
Barrel: 26" octagon; 1:48 twist.
Weight: 7¾ lbs. **Length:** 42½" overall.
Stock: American black walnut; rubber buttpad; swivels.
Sights: Bead front, fullt adjustable open rear.
Features: Percussion lock; single trigger with wide bow trigger guard. Comes with soft leather sling. Introduced 1991. From Thompson/Center.
Price: $340.00

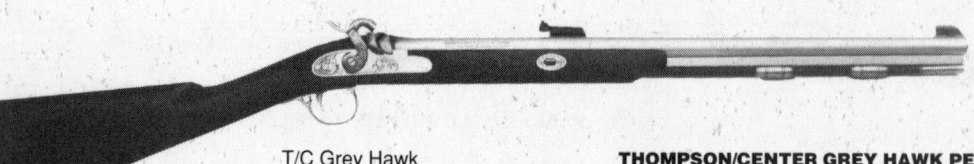

T/C Grey Hawk

THOMPSON/CENTER GREY HAWK PERCUSSION RIFLE

Caliber: 50.
Barrel: 24"; 1:48 twist.
Weight: 7 lbs. **Length:** 41" overall.
Stock: Black Rynite with rubber recoil pad.
Sights: Bead front, fully adjustable open hunting rear.
Features: Stainless steel barrel, lock, hammer, trigger guard, thimbles; blued sights. Percussion only. Introduced 1993. From Thompson/Center Arms.
Price: $275.00

T/C Hawken

THOMPSON/CENTER HAWKEN RIFLE
Caliber: 45, 50 or 54.
Barrel: 28" octagon, hooked breech.
Stocks: American walnut.
Sights: Blade front, rear adjustable for windage and elevation.
Features: Solid brass furniture, double-set triggers, button rifled barrel, coil-type mainspring. From Thompson/Center.
Price: Percussion model (45-, 50- or 54-cal.) $375.00
Price: Flintlock model (50-cal.) $385.00
Price: Percussion kit $275.00
Price: Flintlock kit $295.00

THOMPSON/CENTER HIGH PLAINS SPORTER
Caliber: 50.
Barrel: 24".
Weight: 7 lbs. **Length:** 41" overall.
Stock: Black walnut with pistol grip, rubber recoil pad, sling swivel studs.
Sights: Blade front with open hunting-style rear, or T/C hunting-style tang peep sight.
Features: Percussion lock only. Single hunting-style trigger with wide bow trigger guard. Color case-hardened lock plate. Introduced 1992. From Thompson/Center.
Price: With open sights $340.00
Price: With tang sight $345.00

THOMPSON/CENTER NEW ENGLANDER RIFLE
Caliber: 50, 54.
Barrel: 28", round.
Weight: 7 lbs., 15 oz.
Stock: American walnut or Rynite.
Sights: Open, adjustable.
Features: Color case-hardened percussion lock with engraving, rest blued. Also accepts 12-ga. shotgun barrel. Introduced 1987. From Thompson/Center.
Price: Right-hand model $270.00
Price: As above, Rynite stock $255.00
Price: Left-hand model $290.00
Price: Accessory 12-ga. barrel, right-hand $130.00

T/C Pennsylvania Hunter

Thompson/Center Pennsylvania Hunter Carbine
Similar to the Pennsylvania Hunter except has 21" barrel, weighs 6.5 lbs., and has an overall length of 38". Designed for shooting patched round balls. Available in percussion or flintlock styles. Introduced 1992. From Thompson/Center.
Price: Percussion $310.00
Price: Flintlock $325.00
Price: Accessory barrels $155.00

THOMPSON/CENTER PENNSYLVANIA HUNTER RIFLE
Caliber: 50.
Barrel: 31", half-octagon, half-round.
Weight: About 7½ lbs. **Length:** 48" overall.
Stock: Black walnut.
Sights: Open, adjustable.
Features: Rifled 1:66 for round ball shooting. Available in flintlock or percussion. From Thompson/Center.
Price: Percussion $320.00
Price: Flintlock $335.00

Thompson/Center Renegade Hunter
Similar to standard Renegade except has single trigger in a large-bow shotgun-style trigger guard, no brass trim. Available in 50- or 54-caliber. Color case-hardened lock, rest blued. Introduced 1987. From Thompson/Center.
Price: $310.00

THOMPSON/CENTER RENEGADE RIFLE
Caliber: 50 and 54.
Barrel: 26", 1" across the flats.
Weight: 8 lbs.
Stock: American walnut.
Sights: Open hunting (Patridge) style, fully adjustable for windage and elevation.
Features: Coil spring lock, double-set triggers, blued steel trim. From Thompson/Center.
Price: Percussion model $335.00
Price: Flintlock model, 50-cal. only $345.00
Price: Percussion kit $245.00
Price: Flintlock kit $260.00
Price: Left-hand percussion, 50- or 54-cal. $345.00

THOMPSON/CENTER SCOUT RIFLE
Caliber: 50 and 54.
Barrel: 21", interchangeable, 1:20 twist.
Weight: 7 lbs., 4 oz. **Length:** 38⅝" overall.
Stocks: American black walnut stock and forend.
Sights: Bead front, adjustable semi-buckhorn rear.
Features: Patented in-line ignition system with special vented breech plug. Patented trigger mechanism consists of only two moving parts. Interchange-

able barrels. Wide grooved hammer. Brass trigger guard assembly, brass barrel band and buttplate. Ramrod has blued hardware. Comes with q.d. swivels and suede leather carrying sling. Drilled and tapped for standard scope mounts. Introduced 1990. From Thompson/Center.
Price: 50- or 54-cal. $395.00
Price: With black Rynite stock $295.00
Price: Extra barrel, 50- or 54-cal. $160.00

T/C Thunder Hawk

THOMPSON/CENTER THUNDER HAWK RIFLE
Caliber: 50.
Barrel: 21"; 1:38" twist.

Weight: 6.75 lbs. **Length:** 38.75" overall.
Stock: American walnut with rubber recoil pad.
Sights: Bead on ramp front, adjustable leaf rear.
Features: Uses modern in-line ignition system, adjustable trigger. Knurled striker handle indicators for Safe and Fire. Black wood ramrod. Drilled and tapped for T/C scope mounts. Introduced 1993. From Thompson/Center Arms.
Price: $275.00

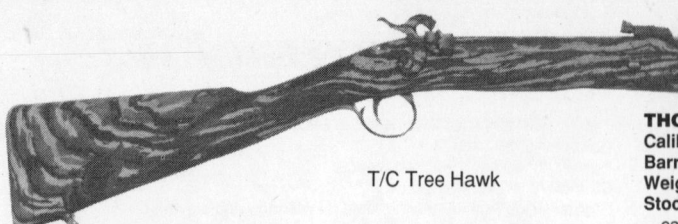

T/C Tree Hawk

THOMPSON/CENTER WHITE MOUNTAIN CARBINE
Caliber: 45, 50 and 54.
Barrel: 21", half-octagon, half-round.
Weight: 6½ lbs. **Length:** 38" overall.
Stock: American black walnut.
Sights: Open hunting (Patridge) style, fully adjustable rear.
Features: Percussion or flintlock. Single trigger, large trigger guard; rubber buttpad; rear q.d. swivel, front swivel mounted on thimble; comes with sling. Introduced 1989. From Thompson/Center.
Price: Percussion **$335.00**
Price: Flintlock **$355.00**

THOMPSON/CENTER TREE HAWK CARBINE
Caliber: 50.
Barrel: 21".
Weight: 6.75 lbs. **Length:** 38" overall.
Stock: Rynite composition with choice of Realtree or Mossy Oak Bottomland camouflage.
Sights: Bead front, fully adjustable open hunting-style rear.
Features: All hardware (except sling swivels and barrel wedge) finished in camouflage, including the polymer-coated fiberglass ramrod. Single trigger, wide bow trigger guard, rubber recoil pad, camo sling. Introduced 1992. From Thompson/Center.
Price: 50-cal. percussion only **$340.00**
Price: Accessory 12-gauge barrel **$165.00**

Traditions Buckskinner

TRADITIONS DEERHUNTER RIFLE
Caliber: 50.
Barrel: 26", octagonal, ¹⁵/₁₆" flats; 1:48" or 1:66" twist.
Weight: 5 lbs., 14 oz. **Length:** 39¼" overall.
Stock: Stained beech with rubber buttpad, sling swivels.
Sights: Blade front, rear adjustable for windage.
Features: Flint or percussion with color case-hardened lock. Hooked breech, oversized trigger guard, blackened furniture, wood ramrod. Imported by Traditions, Inc.
Price: Percussion, 1:48" twist **$165.00**
Price: Flintlock, 1:66" twist **$182.00**
Price: Percussion kit **$149.00**

Traditions Frontier Carbine
Similar to the Frontier Rifle except has 24" barrel, is 40½" overall, weighs 6½ lbs. Available in 50-caliber percussion only. From Traditions, Inc.
Price: **$254.00**

TRADITIONS BUCKSKINNER CARBINE
Caliber: 50.
Barrel: 21", ¹⁵/₁₆" flats, half octagon, half round.
Weight: 6 lbs. **Length:** 36¼" overall.
Stock: Beech or black laminated.
Sights: Beaded blade front, hunting-style open rear click adjustable for windage and elevation.
Features: Uses V-type mainspring, single trigger. Non-glare hardware. Comes with leather sling. From Traditions, Inc.
Price: Flintlock **$290.00**
Price: Flintlock, laminated stock **$337.00**
Price: Percussion **$274.00**
Price: Percussion, laminated stock **$320.00**
Price: Percussion, left-hand **$290.00**

TRADITIONS FRONTIER SCOUT RIFLE
Caliber: 36, 45, 50.
Barrel: 24" (36-cal.), 26" (45, 50); ⅞" flats.
Weight: 6 lbs. **Length:** 39⅛" overall (24" barrel).
Stock: Beech.
Sights: Blade Front, primitive-style adjustable rear.
Features: Scaled-down version of the Frontier rifle for smaller shooters. Percussion only. Color case-hardened lock plate. From Traditions, Inc.
Price: **$232.00**

Traditions Frontier

TRADITIONS HAWKEN RIFLE
Caliber: 50, 54.
Barrel: 32¼"; 1" flats.
Weight: 9 lbs. **Length:** 50" overall.
Stock: Walnut with cheekpiece.
Sights: Hunting style, click adjustable for windage and elevation.
Features: Fiberglass ramrod, double-set triggers, polished brass furniture. From Traditions, Inc.
Price: Percussion **$412.00**

TRADITIONS HAWKEN WOODSMAN RIFLE
Caliber: 50 and 54.
Barrel: 28"; ¹⁵/₁₆" flats.
Weight: 7 lbs. **Length:** 45.75" overall.
Stock: Walnut-stained hardwood.

TRADITIONS FRONTIER RIFLE
Caliber: 45, 50.
Barrel: 28", ¹⁵/₁₆" flats.
Weight: 8 lbs. **Length:** 44¾" overall.
Stock: Beech.
Sights: Beaded blade front, hunting-style rear click adjustable for windage and elevation.
Features: Adjustable sear engagement with fly and bridle, V-type mainspring; double-set triggers. Brass furniture. From Traditions, Inc.
Price: Percussion **$254.00**
Price: Flintlock **$274.00**
Price: Kit, 50-caliber percussion **$165.00**

Sights: Beaded blade front, hunting-style open rear adjustable for windage and elevation.
Features: Percussion only. Brass patchbox and furniture. Double triggers. From Traditions, Inc.
Price: 50 or 54 . . . . **$292.00**
Price: 50-cal., left-hand **$309.00**
Price: Kit **$210.00**

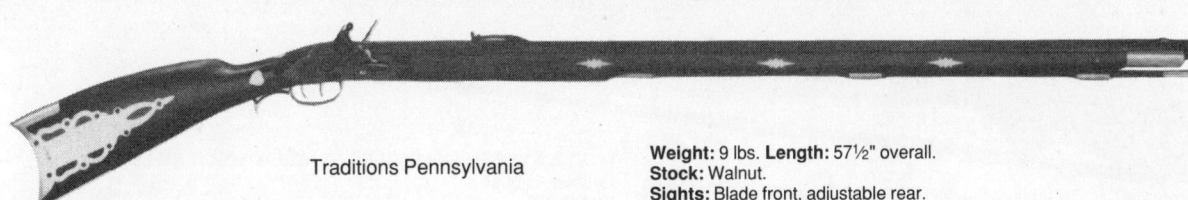

Traditions Pennsylvania

TRADITIONS PENNSYLVANIA RIFLE
Caliber: 45, 50.
Barrel: 40¼", ⅞" flats.

TRADITIONS PIONEER RIFLE/CARBINE
Caliber: 50, 54.
Barrel: 27¼"; ¹⁵/₁₆" flats.
Weight: 7 lbs. **Length:** 44" overall.
Stock: Beech with pistol grip, recoil pad.

TRADITIONS WHITETAIL SERIES RIFLES
Caliber: 50, 54 (percussion only).
Barrel: 21", 26", ¹⁵/₁₆" flats.
Weight: 5 lbs., 14 oz. (rifle). **Length:** 39¼" overall (rifle).
Stock: Walnut-stained hardwood, rubber recoil pad; or synthetic.
Sights: Beaded blade front with flourescent dot, fully adjustable hunting-style rear.
Features: Flint or percussion. Color case-hardened, engraved lock with V-type mainspring, offset hammer. Barrel drilled and tapped for scope mounting (percussion only). Oversized trigger guard, sling swivels, blackened furniture, inletted wedge plates. Imported by Traditions, Inc.
Price: Flintlock, wood stock, rifle or carbine $274.00
Price: Flintlock, synthetic stock, stainless barrel $337.00
Price: Percussion, wood stock, 50 or 54 . . . . $257.00
Price: As above, synthetic stock $290.00
Price: Carbine, percussion, wood stock $257.00
Price: As above, synthetic stock $290.00
Price: Carbine, percussion, synthetic stock, stainless barrel $320.00

Weight: 9 lbs. **Length:** 57½" overall.
Stock: Walnut.
Sights: Blade front, adjustable rear.
Features: Brass patchbox and ornamentation. Double-set triggers. From Traditions, Inc.
Price: Flintlock $495.00
Price: Percussion $467.00

Sights: German silver blade front, buckhorn rear with elevation ramp.
Features: V-type mainspring, adjustable single trigger; blackened furniture; color case-hardened lock; large trigger guard. From Traditions, Inc.
Price: Percussion only, rifle $227.00
Price: Carbine. 24" barrel, 50-cal. only $227.00

TRADITIONS T93 CUSTOM IN-LINE RIFLE, CARBINE
Caliber: 50.
Barrel: 21", 28", round.
Weight: 7 lbs., 14 oz. (rifle). **Length:** 44¼" overall (rifle).
Stock: Stained beech.
Sights: Beaded blade front, click adjustable rear.
Features: Closed breech in-line percussion action, ambidextrous and half-cock safety. Comes with blackened furniture, swivel studs, unbreakable ramrod, oversized trigger guard. Polished blue finish. From Traditions, Inc.
Price: Rifle or carbine $432.00

TRYON RIFLE
Caliber: 50, 54.
Barrel: 34", octagon; 1:63 twist.
Weight: 9 lbs. **Length:** 49" overall.
Stock: European walnut with steel furniture.
Sights: Blade front, fixed rear.
Features: Reproduction of an American plains rifle with double-set triggers and back-action lock. Imported from Italy by Dixie Gun Works.
Price: $595.00

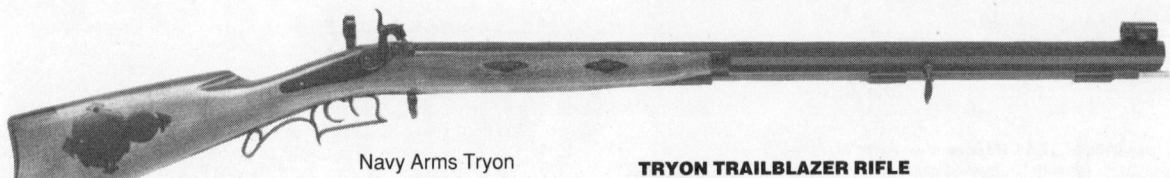

Navy Arms Tryon

Navy Arms Tryon Creedmoor Target Model
Similar to the standard Tryon rifle except 45-caliber only, 33" octagon barrel, globe front sight with inserts, fully adjustable match rear. Has double-set triggers, sling swivels. Imported by Navy Arms.
Price: $680.00

TRYON TRAILBLAZER RIFLE
Caliber: 50.
Barrel: 32", 1" flats.
Weight: 9 lbs. **Length:** 48" overall.
Stock: European walnut with cheekpiece.
Sights: Blade front, semi-buckhorn rear.
Features: Reproduction of a rifle made by George Tryon about 1820. Double-set triggers, back action lock, hooked breech with long tang. From Armsport, Navy Arms.
Price: About $455.00
Price: 50-, 54-cal., 28", 30" bbl. (Armsport) $825.00
Price: Deluxe model with silver finish (Armsport) $895.00

Ultra Light Model 90

UBERTI SANTA FE HAWKEN RIFLE
Caliber: 50 or 54.
Barrel: 32", octagonal.
Weight: 9.8 lbs. **Length:** 50" overall.
Stock: Walnut, with beavertail cheekpiece.
Sights: German silver blade front, buckhorn rear.
Features: Browned finish, color case-hardened lock, double triggers, German silver ferrule, wedge plates. Imported by Uberti USA.
Price: $495.00

ULTRA LIGHT ARMS MODEL 90 MUZZLELOADER
Caliber: 45, 50.
Barrel: 28", button rifled; 1:48 twist.
Weight: 6 lbs.
Stock: Kevlar/graphite, colors optional.
Sights: Hooded blade front on ramp, Williams aperture rear adjustable for windage and elevation.
Features: In-line ignition system with top loading port. Timney trigger; integral side safety. Comes with recoil pad, sling swivels and hard case. Introduced 1990. Made in U.S. by Ultra Light Arms.
Price: $950.00

White Systems Super 91

White Systems Original 68 Blackpowder Rifle

Similar to the Super 91 model except made of blued ordnance steel. Uses Insta-Fire Straight-Pull Hammer percussion ignition. Has 24" barrel, Posi-safe thumb safety, adjustable trigger. Fully adjustable hunting rear sight, black composite stock with recoil pad, swivel studs; Delron ramrod. Drilled and tapped for scope mounting. Weighs 7½ lbs. Available in 45-caliber (1:20" twist) or 50-caliber (1:24" twist). Reintroduced 1993. From White Systems, Inc.
Price: **$599.00**

WHITE SYSTEMS SUPER 91 BLACKPOWDER RIFLE

Caliber: 45 or 50.
Barrel: 26".
Weight: 7½ lbs. **Length:** 43.5" overall.
Stock: Black laminate or black composite; recoil pad, swivel studs.
Sights: Bead front on ramp, fully adjustable open rear.
Features: Insta-Fire straight-line ignition system; all stainless steel construction; side-swing safety; fully adjustable trigger; full barrel under-rib with two ramrod thimbles. Introduced 1991. Made in U.S. by White Systems, Inc.
Price: Laminated or composite stock **$699.00**

White Systems Whitetail

WHITE SYSTEMS WHITETAIL RIFLE

Caliber: 45 or 50.
Barrel: 22".
Weight: 6.5 lbs. **Length:** 39.5" overall.
Stock: Black composite; classic style; recoil pad, swivel studs.
Sights: Bead front on ramp, fully adjustable open rear.
Features: Insta-Fire straight-line ignition; action and trigger safeties; adjustable trigger; stainless steel. Introduced 1992. Made in U.S. by White Systems, Inc.
Price: Blue, composite stock **$499.00**
Price: Stainless, composite stock **$549.00**

White Systems Bison Blackpowder Rifle

Similar to the blued Whitetail model except in 50-caliber (1:24" twist) or 54-caliber (1:28" twist) with 22" ball barrel. Uses Insta-Fire in-line percussion system, double safety. Adjustable sight, walnut-finished hardwood stock, matte blue metal finish, Delron ramrod, swivel studs. Drilled and tapped for scope mounting. Weighs 7¼ lbs. Introduced 1993. From White Systems, Inc.
Price: **$399.00**

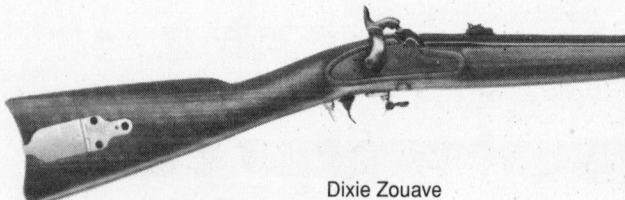

Dixie Zouave

Mississippi Model 1841 Percussion Rifle

Similar to Zouave rifle but patterned after U.S. Model 1841. Imported by Dixie Gun Works, Euroarms of America, Navy Arms.
Price: . . . . **$430.00** to **$463.00**

ZOUAVE PERCUSSION RIFLE

Caliber: 58, 59.
Barrel: 32½".
Weight: 9½ lbs. **Length:** 48½" overall.
Stock: Walnut finish, brass patchbox and buttplate.
Sights: Fixed front, rear adjustable for elevation.
Features: Color case-hardened lockplate, blued barrel. From Navy Arms, Dixie Gun Works, Euroarms of America (M1863), E.M.F.
Price: About . . . . **$325.00** to **$540.00**
Price: Kit (Euroarms 58-cal. only) **$263.00**

BLACKPOWDER SHOTGUNS

Cabela's 12-Gauge

CVA TRAPPER PERCUSSION

Gauge: 12.
Barrel: 28". Choke tubes (Imp. Cyl., Mod., Full).
Weight: NA.
Length: 46" overall.
Stock: English-style straight grip of walnut-finished hardwood.
Sights: Brass bead front.
Features: Single blued barrel; color case-hardened lockplate and hammer; screw adjustable sear engagements, V-type mainspring; brass wedge plates; color case-hardened and engraved trigger guard and tang. From CVA.
Price: Finished **$339.95**

CABELA'S BLACKPOWDER SHOTGUNS

Gauge: 10, 12, 20.
Barrel: 28½" (10-, 12-ga.), Imp. Cyl., Mod., Full choke tubes; 27½" (20-ga.), Imp. Cyl., Mod. choke tubes.
Weight: 6½ to 7 lbs. **Length:** 45" overall (28½" barrel).
Stock: American walnut with checkered grip; 12- and 20-gauge have straight stock, 10-gauge has pistol grip.
Features: Blued barrels, engraved, color case-hardened locks and hammers, brass ramrod tip. From Cabela's.
Price: 10-gauge **$379.95**
Price: 12-gauge **$359.95**
Price: 20-gauge **$329.95**

BLACKPOWDER SHOTGUNS

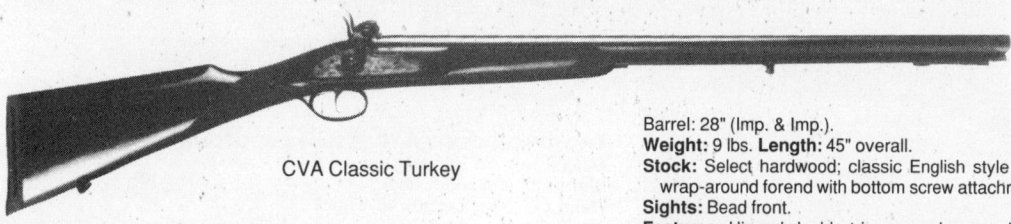

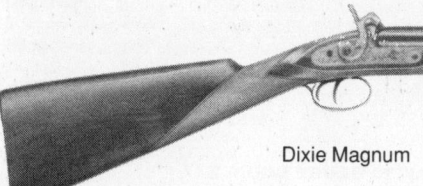

CVA Classic Turkey

CVA CLASSIC TURKEY DOUBLE SHOTGUN
Gauge: 12.

Barrel: 28" (Imp. & Imp.).
Weight: 9 lbs. **Length:** 45" overall.
Stock: Select hardwood; classic English style with checkered straight grip, wrap-around forend with bottom screw attachment.
Sights: Bead front.
Features: Hinged double triggers; color case-hardened and engraved lockplates, trigger guard and tang. Rubber recoil pad. Not suitable for steel shot. Introduced 1990. Imported by CVA.
Price: **$404.95**

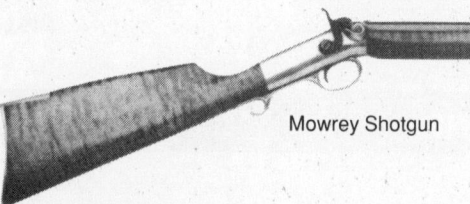

Dixie Magnum

DIXIE MAGNUM PERCUSSION SHOTGUN
Gauge: 10, 12.

Barrel: 30" (Imp. Cyl. & Mod.) in 10-ga.; 28" in 12-ga.
Weight: 6¼ lbs. **Length:** 45" overall.
Stock: Hand-checkered walnut, 14" pull.
Features: Double triggers, light hand engraving. Case-hardened locks in 12-ga.; polished steel in 10-ga. with sling swivels. From Dixie Gun Works.
Price: Upland **$399.00**
Price: 12-ga. kit **$350.00**
Price: 10-ga. **$495.00**
Price: 10-ga. kit **$375.00**

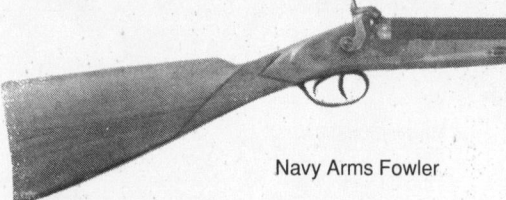

Mowrey Shotgun

MOWREY SHOTGUN
Gauge: 12, 28.

Barrel: 28" (28-gauge, Cyl.); 32" (12-gauge, Cyl.); octagonal.
Weight: About 8 lbs. **Length:** 48" overall (32" barrel).
Stock: Curly maple.
Sights: Bead front.
Features: Brass or steel frame; shotgun butt. Made in U.S. by Mowrey Gun Works.
Price: Finished **$350.00**
Price: Kit **$300.00**

Navy Arms Fowler

NAVY ARMS FOWLER SHOTGUN
Gauge: 12.
Barrel: 28".
Weight: 7 lbs., 12 oz. **Length:** 45" overall.
Stock: Walnut-stained hardwood.
Features: Color case-hardened lockplates and hammers; checkered stock. Imported by Navy Arms.
Price: Fowler model, 12-ga. only **$325.00**

NAVY ARMS STEEL SHOT MAGNUM SHOTGUN
Gauge: 10.
Barrel: 28" (Cyl. & Cyl.).
Weight: 7 lbs., 9 oz. **Length:** 45½" overall.
Stock: Walnut, with cheekpiece.
Features: Designed specifically for steel shot. Engraved, polished locks; sling swivels; blued barrels. Introduced 1991. Imported by Navy Arms.
Price: **$510.00**

> Consult our Directory pages for the location of firms mentioned.

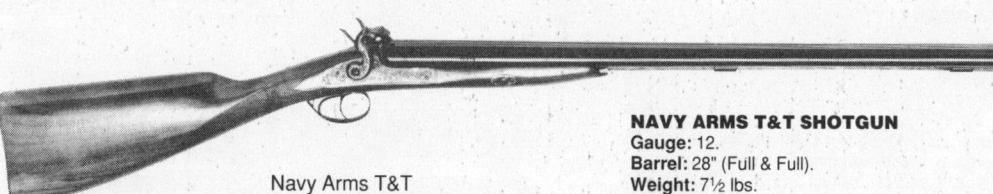

Navy Arms T&T

NAVY ARMS T&T SHOTGUN
Gauge: 12.
Barrel: 28" (Full & Full).
Weight: 7½ lbs.
Stock: Walnut.
Sights: Bead front.
Features: Color case-hardened locks, double triggers, blued steel furniture. From Navy Arms.
Price: **$480.00**

NAVY ARMS MORTIMER FLINTLOCK SHOTGUN
Gauge: 12.
Barrel: 36".
Weight: 7 lbs. **Length:** 53" overall.
Stock: Walnut, with cheekpiece.
Features: Waterproof pan, roller frizzen, external safety. Color case-hardened lock, rest blued. Introduced 1991. Imported by Navy Arms.
Price: **$670.00**

BLACKPOWDER SHOTGUNS

T/C Tree Hawk

THOMPSON/CENTER NEW ENGLANDER SHOTGUN
Gauge: 12.
Barrel: 28" (Imp. Cyl.), round.
Weight: 5 lbs., 2 oz.
Stock: Select American black walnut with straight grip.
Features: Percussion lock is color case-hardened, rest blued. Also accepts 26" round 50- and 54-cal. rifle barrel. Introduced 1986. From Thompson/Center.
Price: Right-hand $270.00
Price: Right-hand, Rynite stock $255.00
Price: Left-hand $310.00
Price: Accessory rifle barrel, right-hand, 50 or 54 . . . . $130.00
Price: As above, left-hand $140.00

THOMPSON/CENTER TREE HAWK SHOTGUN
Gauge: 12.
Barrel: 28" (Full choke tube).
Weight: 6.75 lbs. **Length:** 45" overall.
Stock: Rynite composition with choice of Realtree or Mossy Oak Bottomland camouflage.
Sights: Bead front.
Features: All hardware (except sling swivels and barrel wedge) finished in camouflage, including the polymer-coated fiberglass ramrod. Single trigger, wide bow trigger guard, rubber recoil pad, camo sling. Accessory Imp. Cyl. and Mod. choke tubes available. Introduced 1992. From Thompson/Center.
Price: 12-gauge, percussion only $345.00
Price: Accessory 50-caliber barrel $160.00

TRAIL GUNS KODIAK 10-GAUGE DOUBLE
Gauge: 10.
Barrel: 20", 30¾" (Cyl. bore).
Weight: About 9 lbs. **Length:** 47⅛" overall.
Stock: Walnut, with cheek rest. Checkered wrist and forend.
Features: Chrome-plated bores; engraved lockplates, brass bead front and middle sights; sling swivels. Introduced 1980. Imported from Italy by Trail Guns Armory, Inc.
Price: $425.00

AIRGUNS—HANDGUNS

AIRROW MODEL 6A AIR PISTOL
Caliber: #2512 10.75" arrow.
Barrel: 10.75".
Weight: 1.75 lbs. **Length:** 16.5" overall.
Power: CO₂ or compressed air.
Stocks: Checkered composition.
Sights: Bead front, fully adjustable Williams rear.
Features: Velocity to 375 fps. Pneumatic air trigger. Floating barrel. All aircraft aluminum and stainless steel construction; Mil-spec materials and finishes. Announced 1993. From Swivel Machine Works, Inc.
Price: About $499.00

Airrow Model 6A

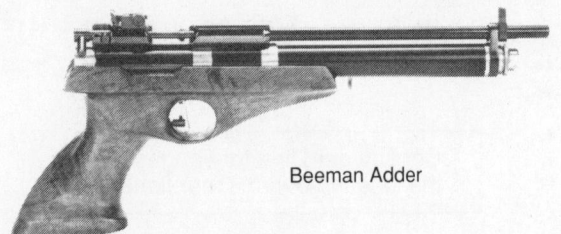

Beeman Adder

BEEMAN P1 MAGNUM AIR PISTOL
Caliber: 177, 5mm, 22, single shot.
Barrel: 8.4".
Weight: 2.5 lbs. **Length:** 11" overall.
Power: Top lever cocking; spring piston.
Stocks: Checkered walnut.
Sights: Blade front, square notch rear with click micrometer adjustments for windage and elevation. Grooved for scope mounting.
Features: Dual power for 177 and 20-cal.: low setting gives 350-400 fps; high setting 500-600 fps. Rearward expanding mainspring simulates firearm recoil. All Colt 45 auto grips fit gun. Dry-firing feature for practice. Optional wooden shoulder stock. Introduced 1985. Imported by Beeman.
Price: 177, 5mm, 22-cal. $384.50
Price: 177, 5mm, stainless/blue finish $434.50

Beeman P2 Match Air Pistol
Similar to the Beeman P1 Magnum except shoots only 177 or 5mm pellets; completely recoilless single-stroke pneumatic action. Weighs 2.2 lbs. Choice of thumbrest match grips or standard style. Introduced 1990.
Price: 177, 5mm, standard grip $425.00
Price: 177, match grip $455.00

BEEMAN ADDER AIR PISTOL
Caliber: 20, 25, single shot.
Barrel: 10.5"; 12-groove rifling.
Weight: 3 lbs. **Length:** 16.5" overall.
Power: Pre-charged pneumatic, internal air chamber.
Stocks: Smooth, select hardwood.
Sights: Micrometer click adjustable. Built-in scope dovetail.
Features: Two-stage trigger. Steel body, highly polished, blued and accented with solid brass. Introduced 1992. Imported by Beeman.
Price: 20-, 25-cal. $529.00

Beeman P-1

BEEMAN/FEINWERKBAU C5 CO₂ RAPID FIRE PISTOL
Caliber: 177.
Barrel: 7.25".
Weight: 2.42 lbs.
Power: NA.
Stocks: Anatomical match.
Sights: Match.
Features: Velocity 510 fps. Has special trigger shape with swivel action, longitudinal positioning. Introduced 1990. Imported by Beeman.
Price: Right-hand **$1,485.00**
Price: Left-hand **$1,570.00**

BEEMAN/FEINWERKBAU C20 CO₂ PISTOL
Caliber: 177, single shot.
Barrel: 10.1", 12-groove rifling.
Weight: 2.5 lbs. **Length:** 16" overall.
Power: Special CO₂ cylinder.
Stock: Stippled walnut with adjustable palm shelf.
Sights: Blade front, open rear adjustable for windage and elevation. Notch size adjustable for width. Interchangeable front blades.
Features: Fully adjustable trigger; can be set for dry firing. Separate gas chamber for uniform power. Cylinders interchangeable even when full. Short-barrel model also available. Introduced 1988. Imported by Beeman.
Price: Right-hand, regular or Mini **$1,130.00**
Price: Left-hand **$1,195.00**

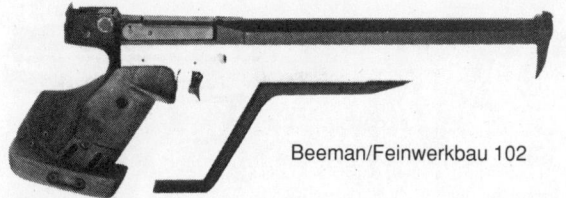

Beeman/Feinwerkbau 102

BEEMAN/FEINWERKBAU 65 MKII AIR PISTOL
Caliber: 177, single shot.
Barrel: 6.1" or 7.5", removable bbl. wgt. available.
Weight: 42 oz. **Length:** 13.3" or 14.1" overall.
Power: Spring, sidelever cocking.
Stocks: Walnut, stippled thumbrest; adjustable or fixed.
Sights: Front, interchangeable post element system, open rear, click adjustable for windage and elevation and for sighting notch width. Scope mount available.
Features: New shorter barrel for better balance and control. Cocking effort 9 lbs. Two-stage trigger, four adjustments. Quiet firing, 525 fps. Programs instantly for recoil or recoilless operation. Permanently lubricated. Steel piston ring. Special switch converts trigger from 17.6-oz. pull to 42-oz. let-off. Imported by Beeman.
Price: Right-hand **$1,065.00**
Price: Left-hand, 6.1" barrel **$1,149.00**
Price: Model 65 Mk. I (7.5" bbl.) **$1,065.00**

Beeman HW70

Benjamin Sheridan Pneumatic

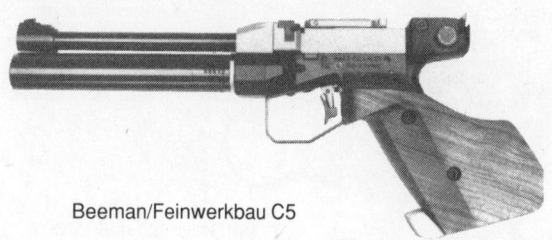

Beeman/Feinwerkbau C5

BEEMAN/FEINWERKBAU C25 CO₂ PISTOL
Caliber: 177, single shot.
Barrel: 10.1"; 12-groove rifling.
Weight: 2.5 lbs. **Length:** 16.5" overall.
Power: Vertical, interchangeable CO₂ bottles.
Stocks: Stippled walnut with adjustable palm shelf.
Sights: Blade front, rear micrometer adjustable. Notch size adjustable for width; interchangeable front blades.
Features: Fully adjustable trigger; can be set for dry firing. Has special vertical CO₂ cylinder and weight rail for balance. Short-barrel model (C25 Mini) also available. Introduced 1992. Imported by Beeman.
Price: Right-hand **$1,295.00**
Price: Left-hand **$1,295.00**
Price: C25 Mini **$1,285.00**

BEEMAN/FEINWERKBAU 102 PISTOL
Caliber: 177, single shot.
Barrel: 10.1", 12-groove rifling.
Weight: 2.5 lbs. **Length:** 16.5" overall.
Power: Single-stroke pneumatic, underlever cocking.
Stocks: Stippled walnut with adjustable palm shelf.
Sights: Blade front, open rear adjustable for windage and elevation. Notch size adjustable for width. Interchangeable front blades.
Features: Velocity 460 fps. Fully adjustable trigger. Cocking effort 12 lbs. Introduced 1988. Imported by Beeman.
Price: Right-hand **$1,325.00**
Price: Left-hand **$1,395.00**

BEEMAN WOLVERINE PISTOL
Caliber: 177, 20, 25, single shot.
Barrel: 10.5"; 12-groove rifling.
Weight: 3 lbs. **Length:** 16.5" overall.
Power: Pre-charged pneumatic, internal air chamber.
Stocks: Stippled walnut.
Sights: Blade front, micrometer click adjustable rear. Built-in scope dovetail.
Features: Match trigger. Solid brass rear receiver cap. Introduced 1992. Imported by Beeman.
Price: 177, 20, 25 . . . . **$698.00**

BEEMAN HW70 AIR PISTOL
Caliber: 177, single shot.
Barrel: 6¼", rifled.
Weight: 38 oz. **Length:** 12¾" overall.
Power: Spring, barrel cocking.
Stocks: Plastic, with thumbrest.
Sights: Hooded post front, square notch rear adjustable for windage and elevation. HW70A has scope base.
Features: Adjustable trigger, 24-lb. cocking effort, 410 fps MV; automatic barrel safety. Imported by Beeman.
Price: HW70 (open sights) **$189.98**
Price: HW70A (open sights, scope base) **$194.50**

BENJAMIN SHERIDAN PNEUMATIC PELLET PISTOLS
Caliber: 177, 20, 22, single shot.
Barrel: 9⅜", rifled brass.
Weight: 38 oz. **Length:** 13⅛" overall.
Power: Under-lever pneumatic, hand pumped.
Stocks: Walnut stocks and pump handle.
Sights: High ramp front, fully adjustable notch rear.
Features: Velocity to 525 fps (variable). Bolt action with cross-bolt safety. Choice of black or nickel finish. Made in U.S. by Benjamin Sheridan Co.
Price: Black finish, HB17 (177), HB20 (20), HB22 (22) **$104.95**
Price: Nickel finish, H17 (177), H20 (20), H22 (22) **$111.50**

Benjamin Sheridan CO₂

BRNO Aeron-Tau

BSA SCORPION AIR PISTOL

Caliber: 177 or 22, single shot.
Barrel: 7¾".
Weight: 3½ lbs. **Length:** 15¾" overall.
Power: Spring piston, barrel cocking.
Stocks: Moulded synthetic with thumbrest.
Sights: Globe front, adjustable open rear.
Features: Velocity to 600 fps (177); 400 fps (22). Two-stage trigger. Barrel extension to ease cocking effort. Polished blue finish. Imported from England by Air Rifle Specialists.
Price: **$190.00**

Crosman Auto Air II

Crosman Model 1008

BENJAMIN SHERIDAN CO₂ PELLET PISTOLS

Caliber: 177, 20, 22, single shot.
Barrel: 6⅜", rifled brass.
Weight: 29 oz. **Length:** 9.8" overall.
Power: 12-gram CO₂ cylinder.
Stocks: Walnut on nickeled model, checkered plastic on black guns.
Sights: High ramp front, fully adjustable notch rear.
Features: Velocity to 500 fps. Turn-bolt action with cross-bolt safety. Gives about 40 shots per CO₂ cylinder. Black or nickel finish. Made in U.S. by Benjamin Sheridan Co.
Price: Black finish, EB17 (177), EB20 (20), EB22 (22) **$96.50**
Price: Nickel finish, E17 (177), E20 (20), E22 (22) **$109.50**

BRNO AERON-TAU CO₂ PISTOL

Caliber: 177.
Barrel: 10".
Weight: 37 oz. **Length:** 12.5" overall.
Power: 12.5-gram CO₂ cartridges.
Stocks: Stippled hardwood with palm rest.
Sights: Blade front, open fully adjustable rear.
Features: Comes with extra seals and counterweight. Blue finish. Imported by Century International Arms.
Price: About **$299.00**

BSA Scorpion

CROSMAN AUTO AIR II PISTOL

Caliber: BB, 17-shot magazine, 177 pellet, single shot.
Barrel: 8⅝" steel, smoothbore.
Weight: 13 oz. **Length:** 10¾" overall.
Power: CO₂ Powerlet.
Stocks: Grooved plastic.
Sights: Blade front, adjustable rear; highlighted system.
Features: Velocity to 480 fps (BBs), 430 fps (pellets). Semi-automatic action with BBs, single shot with pellets. Silvered finish. Introduced 1991. From Crosman.
Price: About **$28.00**

CROSMAN MODEL 357 AIR PISTOL

Caliber: 177, 6- and 10-shot pellet clips.
Barrel: 4" (Model 357-4), 6" (Model 357-6), rifled steel; 8" (Model 357-8), rifled brass.
Weight: 32 oz. (6"). **Length:** 11⅜" overall (357-6).
Power: CO₂ Powerlet.
Stocks: Checkered wood-grain plastic.
Sights: Ramp front, fully adjustable rear.
Features: Average 430 fps (Model 357-6). Break-open barrel for easy loading. Single or double action. Vent. rib barrel. Wide, smooth trigger. Two cylinders come with each gun. Model 357-8 has matte gray finish, black grips. From Crosman.
Price: 4" or 6", about **$45.00**
Price: 8", about **$50.00**
Price: Model 1357 (same gun as above, except shoots BBs, has 6-shot clip), about **$45.00**

CROSMAN MODEL 1008 REPEAT AIR

Caliber: 177, 8-shot pellet clip
Barrel: 4.25", rifled steel.
Weight: 17 oz. **Length:** 8.625" overall.
Power: CO₂ Powerlet.
Stocks: Checkered plastic.
Sights: Post front, adjustable rear.
Features: Velocity about 430 fps. Break-open barrel for easy loading; single or double semi-automatic action; two 8-shot clips included. Optional carrying case available. Introduced 1992. From Crosman.
Price: About **$43.00**
Price: With case, about **$50.00**

CAUTION: PRICES CHANGE, CHECK AT GUNSHOP.

Crosman 1322

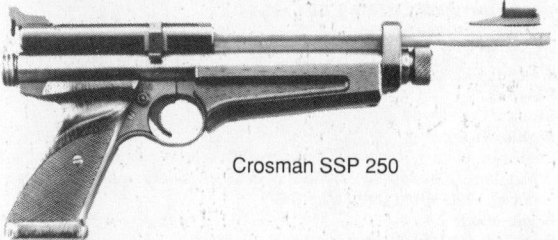

Crosman SSP 250

CZ Model 3

CROSMAN MODEL 1322, 1377 AIR PISTOLS
Caliber: 177 (M1377), 22 (M1322), single shot.
Barrel: 8", rifled steel.
Weight: 39 oz. **Length:** 13⅝".
Power: Hand pumped.
Sights: Blade front, rear adjustable for windage and elevation.
Features: Moulded plastic grip, hand size pump forearm. Cross-bolt safety. Model 1377 also shoots BBs. From Crosman.
Price: About $50.00

CROSMAN MODEL SSP 250 PISTOL
Caliber: 177, 20, 22, single shot.
Barrel: 9⅞", rifled steel.
Weight: 3 lbs., 1 oz. **Length:** 14" overall.
Power: CO_2 Powerlet.
Stocks: Composition; black, with checkering.
Sights: Hooded front, fully adjustable rear.
Features: Velocity about 560 fps. Interchangeable accessory barrels. Two-stage trigger. High/low power settings. From Crosman.
Price: About $48.00

CZ MODEL 3 AIR PISTOL
Caliber: 177, single shot.
Barrel: 7.25".
Weight: 44 oz. **Length:** 13.75" overall.
Power: Spring piston, barrel cocking.
Stocks: High-impact plastic; ambidextrous, with thumbrest.
Sights: Hooded front, fully adjustable rear.
Features: Velocity about 420 fps. Externally adjustable trigger; removable screwdriver threaded into receiver. Imported from the Czech Republic by Action Arms.
Price: $79.00

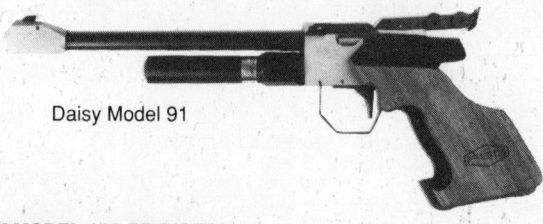

Daisy Model 91

DAISY MODEL 91 MATCH PISTOL
Caliber: 177, single shot.
Barrel: 10.25", rifled steel.
Weight: 2.5 lbs. **Length:** 16.5" overall.
Power: CO_2, 12-gram cylinder.
Stocks: Stippled hardwood; anatomically shaped and adjustable.
Sights: Blade and ramp front, changeable-width rear notch with full micrometer adjustments.
Features: Velocity to 476 fps. Gives 55 shots per cylinder. Fully adjustable trigger. Introduced 1991. Imported by Daisy Mfg. Co.
Price: About $600.00

Daisy Model 288

DAISY MODEL 188 BB PISTOL
Caliber: BB.
Barrel: 9.9", steel smoothbore.
Weight: 1.67 lbs. **Length:** 11.7" overall.
Stocks: Copolymer; checkered with thumbrest.
Sights: Blade and ramp front, open fixed rear.
Features: 24-shot repeater. Spring action with under-barrel cocking lever. Grip and receiver of Nylafil-copolymer material. Introduced 1979. From Daisy Mfg. Co.
Price: About $25.00

DAISY MODEL 288 AIR PISTOL
Caliber: 177 pellets, 24-shot.
Barrel: Smoothbore steel.
Weight: .8 lb. **Length:** 12.1" overall.
Power: Single stroke spring air.
Stocks: Moulded resin with checkering and thumbrest.
Sights: Blade and ramp front, open fixed rear.
Features: Velocity to 215 fps. Cross-bolt trigger block safety. Black finish. Introduced 1993. From Daisy Mfg. Co.
Price: About $26.00

Daisy Model 500

> Consult our Directory pages for the location of firms mentioned.

DAISY MODEL 500 RAVEN AIR PISTOL
Caliber: 177 pellets, single shot.
Barrel: Rifled steel.
Weight: 36 oz. **Length:** 8.5" overall.
Power: CO_2.
Stocks: Moulded plastic with checkering.
Sights: Blade front, fixed rear.
Features: Velocity up to 500 fps. Hammer-block safety. Resembles semi-auto centerfire pistol. Barrel tips up for loading. Introduced 1993. From Daisy Mfg. Co.
Price: About $65.00

Daisy/Power Line 45

Daisy/Power Line 93

DAISY/POWER LINE 717 PELLET PISTOL
Caliber: 177, single shot.
Barrel: 9.61".
Weight: 2.8 lbs. **Length:** 13½" overall.
Stocks: Moulded wood-grain plastic, with thumbrest.
Sights: Blade and ramp front, micro-adjustable notch rear.
Features: Single pump pneumatic pistol. Rifled steel barrel. Cross-bolt trigger block. Muzzle velocity 385 fps. From Daisy Mfg. Co. Introduced 1979.
Price: About **$80.00**

Daisy/Power Line 747 Pistol
Similar to the 717 pistol except has a 12-groove rifled steel barrel by Lothar Walther. Velocity of 360 fps. Manual cross-bolt safety.
Price: About **$160.00**

DAISY/POWER LINE MATCH 777 PELLET PISTOL
Caliber: 177, single shot.
Barrel: 9.61" rifled steel by Lothar Walther.
Weight: 32 oz. **Length:** 13½" overall.
Power: Sidelever, single pump pneumatic.
Stocks: Smooth hardwood, fully contoured with palm and thumbrest.
Sights: Blade and ramp front, match-grade open rear with adjustable width notch, micro. click adjustments.
Features: Adjustable trigger; manual cross-bolt safety. MV of 385 fps. Comes with cleaning kit, adjustment tool and pellets. From Daisy Mfg. Co.
Price: About **$330.00**

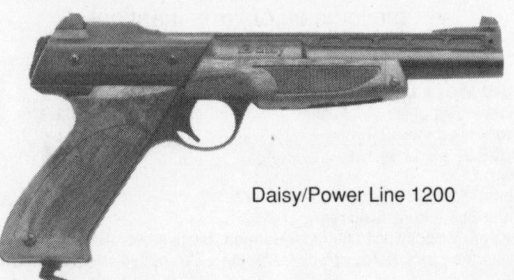

Daisy/Power Line 1200

DAISY/POWER LINE 44 REVOLVER
Caliber: 177 pellets, 6-shot.
Barrel: 6", rifled steel; interchangeable 4" and 8".
Weight: 2.7 lbs.
Power: CO_2.
Stocks: Moulded plastic with checkering.
Sights: Blade on ramp front, fully adjustable notch rear.
Features: Velocity up to 400 fps. Replica of 44 Magnum revolver. Has swingout cylinder and interchangeable barrels. Introduced 1987. From Daisy Mfg. Co.
Price: **$65.00**

DAISY/POWER LINE 45 AIR PISTOL
Caliber: 177, 13-shot clip.
Barrel: 5", rifled steel.
Weight: 1.25 lbs. **Length:** 8.5" overall.
Power: CO_2.
Stocks: Checkered plastic.
Sights: Fixed.
Features: Velocity 400 fps. Semi-automatic repeater with double-action trigger. Manually operated lever-type trigger block safety; magazine safety. Introduced 1990. From Daisy Mfg. Co.
Price: About **$75.00**
Price: Model 645 (nickel-chrome plated), about **$83.00**

DAISY/POWER LINE 93 PISTOL
Caliber: 177, BB, 15-shot clip.
Barrel: 5", steel.
Weight: 17 oz. **Length:** NA.
Power: CO_2.
Stocks: Checkered plastic.
Sights: Fixed.
Features: Velocity to 400 fps. Semi-automatic repeater. Manual lever-type trigger-block safety. Introduced 1991. From Daisy Mfg. Co.
Price: About **$75.00**
Price: Model 693 (nickel-chrome plated), about **$83.00**

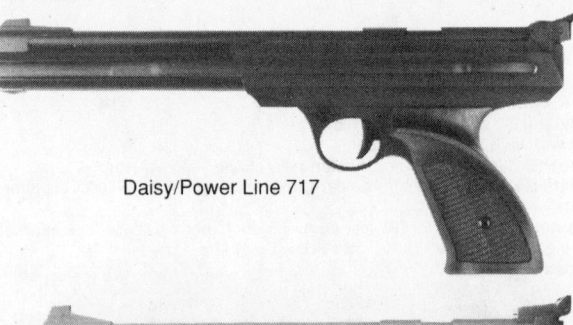

Daisy/Power Line 717

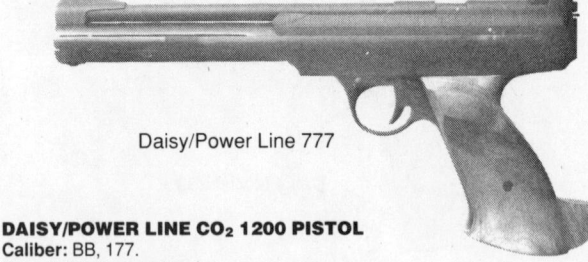

Daisy/Power Line 777

DAISY/POWER LINE CO₂ 1200 PISTOL
Caliber: BB, 177.
Barrel: 10½", smooth.
Weight: 1.6 lbs. **Length:** 11.1" overall.
Power: Daisy CO_2 cylinder.
Stocks: Contoured, checkered moulded wood-grain plastic.
Sights: Blade ramp front, fully adjustable square notch rear.
Features: 60-shot BB reservoir, gravity feed. Cross-bolt safety. Velocity of 420-450 fps for more than 100 shots. From Daisy Mfg. Co.
Price: About **$39.00**

"GAT" AIR PISTOL
Caliber: 177, single shot.
Barrel: 7½" cocked, 9½" extended.
Weight: 22 oz.
Power: Spring piston.
Stocks: Cast checkered metal.
Sights: Fixed.
Features: Shoots pellets, corks or darts. Matte black finish. Imported from England by Stone Enterprises, Inc.
Price: **$21.95**

MARKSMAN 1010 REPEATER PISTOL
Caliber: 177, 18-shot repeater.
Barrel: 2½", smoothbore.
Weight: 24 oz. **Length:** 8¼" overall.
Power: Spring.
Features: Velocity to 200 fps. Thumb safety. Black finish. Uses BBs, darts or pellets. Repeats with BBs only. From Marksman Products.
Price: Matte black finish **$24.95**
Price: Model 1010X (as above except nickel-plated) **$32.95**

MARKSMAN 1015 SPECIAL EDITION AIR PISTOL
Caliber: 177, 24-shot repeater.
Barrel: 3.8", rifled.
Weight: 22 oz. **Length:** 10.3" overall.
Power: Spring-air.
Stocks: Checkered brown composition.
Sights: Fixed.
Features: Velocity about 230 fps. Skeletonized trigger, extended barrel with "ported compensator." Shoots BBs, pellets, darts or bolts. From Marksman Products.
Price: **$29.95**

Marksman 1015

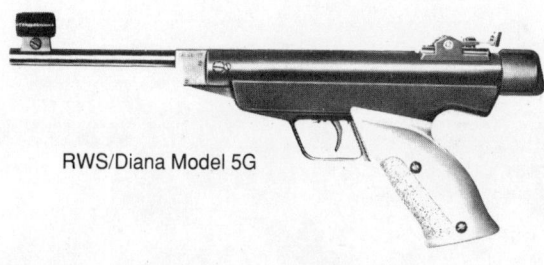
Record Jumbo

RECORD JUMBO DELUXE AIR PISTOL
Caliber: 177, single shot.
Barrel: 6", rifled.
Weight: 1.9 lbs. **Length:** 7.25" overall.
Power: Spring-air, lateral cocking lever.
Stocks: Smooth walnut.
Sights: Blade front, fully adjustable open rear.
Features: Velocity to 322 fps. Thumb safety. Grip magazine compartment for extra pellet storage. Introduced 1983. Imported from Germany by Great Lakes Airguns.
Price: **$107.50**

RWS/DIANA MODEL 5G AIR PISTOL
Caliber: 177, single shot.
Barrel: 7".
Weight: 2¾ lbs. **Length:** 16" overall.
Power: Spring-air, barrel cocking.
Stocks: Plastic, thumbrest design.
Sights: Tunnel front, micro-click open rear.
Features: Velocity of 410 fps. Two-stage trigger with automatic safety. Imported from Germany by Dynamit Nobel-RWS, Inc.
Price: **$200.00**

RWS/Diana Model 5G

RWS/DIANA MODEL 6M MATCH AIR PISTOL
Caliber: 177, single shot.
Barrel: 7".
Weight: 3 lbs. **Length:** 16" overall.
Power: Spring-air, barrel cocking.
Stocks: Walnut-finished hardwood with thumbrest.
Sights: Adjustable front, micro. click open rear.
Features: Velocity of 410 fps. Recoilless double piston system, movable barrel shroud to protect from sight during cocking. Imported from Germany by Dynamit Nobel-RWS, Inc.
Price: Right-hand **$475.00**
Price: Left-hand **$530.00**

RWS GAMO PR-45 AIR PISTOL
Caliber: 177, single shot.
Barrel: 8.3".
Weight: 25 oz. **Length:** 11" overall.
Power: Pre-compressed air.
Stocks: Composition.
Sights: Blade front, adjustable rear.
Features: Velocity to 430 fps. Recoilless and vibration free. Manual safety. Imported from Spain by Dynamit Nobel-RWS, Inc.
Price: **$130.00**
Price: Compact model (adjustable walnut grips, adjustable trigger, swiveling trigger shoe) **$200.00**

RWS/Diana Model 6G Air Pistols
Similar to the Model 6M except does not have the movable barrel shroud. Has click micrometer rear sight, two-stage adjustable trigger, interchangeable tunnel front sight. Available in right- or left-hand models.
Price: Right-hand **$350.00**
Price: Left-hand **$390.00**

Sharp Model U-FP

SHARP MODEL U-FP CO2 PISTOL
Caliber: 177, single shot.
Barrel: 8", rifled steel.
Weight: 2.4 lbs. **Length:** 11.6" overall.
Power: 12-gram CO_2 cylinder.
Stocks: Smooth hardwood. Walnut target stocks available.
Sights: Post front, fully adjustable target rear.
Features: Variable power adjustment up to 545 fps. Adjustable trigger. Also available with adjustable field sight. Imported from Japan by Great Lakes Airguns.
Price: **$228.50**
Price: With walnut target grips **$257.00**

STEYR CO2 MATCH 91 PISTOL
Caliber: 177, single shot.
Barrel: 9".
Weight: 38.7 oz. **Length:** 15.3" overall.
Power: Pre-compressed CO_2 cylinders.
Stocks: Fully adjustable Morini match with palm shelf; stippled walnut.
Sights: Interchangeable blade in 4mm, 4.5mm or 5mm widths, fully adjustable open rear with interchangeable 3.5mm or 4mm leaves.
Features: Velocity about 500 fps. Adjustable trigger, adjustable sight radius from 12.4" to 13.2". Imported from Austria by Nygord Precision Products.
Price: About **$1,050.00**

STEYR LP5 MATCH PISTOL

Caliber: 177, 5-shot magazine.
Barrel: NA.
Weight: 40.2 oz. **Length:** 13.39" overall.
Power: Pre-compressed CO_2 cylinders.
Stocks: Adjustable Morini match with palm shelf; stippled walnut.
Sights: Movable 2.5mm blade front; 2-3mm interchangeable in .2mm increments; fully adjustable open match rear.
Features: Velocity about 500 fps. Fully adjustable trigger; has dry-fire feature. Barrel and grip weights available. Introduced 1993. Imported from Austria by Nygord Precision Products.
Price: About $1,250.00

WALTHER CP 3 AIR PISTOL

Caliber: 177, single shot.
Barrel: 9".
Weight: 40 oz. **Length:** 14¾" overall.
Power: CO_2.
Stocks: Full target-type stippled wood with adjustable hand shelf.
Sights: Target post front, fully adjustable target rear.
Features: Velocity of 520 fps, CO_2 powered; target-quality trigger; comes with adaptor for charging with standard CO_2 air tanks, case, and accessories. Introduced 1983. Imported from Germany by Interarms.
Price: $1,360.00
Price: Model LPM-1 Match $1,667.00
Price: Model CPM-1 . . . . $1,405.00

AIRGUNS—LONG GUNS

AIR ARMS SM 100 AIR RIFLE

Caliber: 177, 22, single shot.
Barrel: 22", 12-groove Lothar Walther.
Weight: 8½ lbs. **Length:** 39½" overall.
Power: Pre-charged compressed air from diving tank.
Stock: Walnut-finished beech.
Sights: None furnished.
Features: Velocity to 1000 fps (177), 800 fps (22). PFTE-coated lightweight striker for consistent shots. Blued barrel and air chamber. Imported from England by Air Rifle Specialists.
Price: $750.00
Price: For left-hand stock add $60.00
Price: Model XM 100 (same as SM100 except walnut stock) $940.00
Price: For left-hand stock add $60.00

Air Arms TM 100 Air Rifle

Similar to the SM 100 except is target model with hand-picked barrel for best accuracy. Target-type walnut stock with adjustable cheekpiece and adjustable buttplate. Stippled grip and forend. Available in 177 or 22 (special order), right- or left-hand models. Variable power settings. Two-stage adjustable trigger; 22" barrel. Imported from England by Air Rifle Specialists.
Price: $1,170.00
Price: Left-hand $1,230.00

Air Arms NJR 100 Air Rifle

Similar to the SM 100 except designed for Field Target competition. Hand-picked Walther barrel for best accuracy. Walnut Field Target thumbhole stock has adjustable forend, cheekpiece and buttpad. Has lever-type bolt, straight blade trigger. Imported from England by Air Rifle Specialists, Beeman.
Price: $1,670.00
Price: Left-hand $1,730.00
Price: Right-hand (Beeman) $1,795.00
Price: Left-hand (Beeman) $1,895.00

Airrow Model 8S1P .

AIRROW MODEL 8S1P STEALTH AIR GUN

Caliber: #2512 16" arrow.
Barrel: 16".
Weight: 4.4 lbs. **Length:** 30.1" overall.
Power: CO_2 or compressed air; variable power.
Stock: Telescoping CAR-15-type.
Sights: 1.5-5x variable power scope.
Features: Velocity to 650 fps with 260-grain arrow. Pneumatic air trigger. All aircraft aluminum and stainless steel construction. Mil-spec materials and finishes. Waterproof case. Introduced 1991. From Swivel Machine Works, Inc.
Price: About $1,699.00

AIRROW MODEL 8SRB STEALTH AIR GUN

Caliber: 177, 22, 25, 38.
Barrel: 19.7".
Weight: 6 lbs. **Length:** 34" overall.
Power: CO_2 or compressed air; variable power.
Stock: Telescoping CAR-15-type.
Sights: 3.5-10x A.O. variable power scope.
Features: Velocity 1100 fps in all calibers. Pneumatic air trigger. All aircraft aluminum and stainless steel construction. Mil-spec materials and finishes. Introduced 1992. From Swivel Machine Works, Inc.
Price: About $2,599.00

ARS AR6 REPEATING AIR RIFLE

Caliber: 22, 6-shot repeater.
Barrel: 23¼".
Weight: 6¾ lbs. **Length:** 38¼" overall.
Power: Pre-compressed air from diving tank or CO_2.
Stock: Walnut with checkered grip; rubber buttpad.
Sights: Blade front, adjustable peep rear.
Features: Velocity to 1100 fps with 25-grain pellet. Receiver grooved for scope mounting. Imported from Korea by Air Rifle Specialists.
Price: $550.00

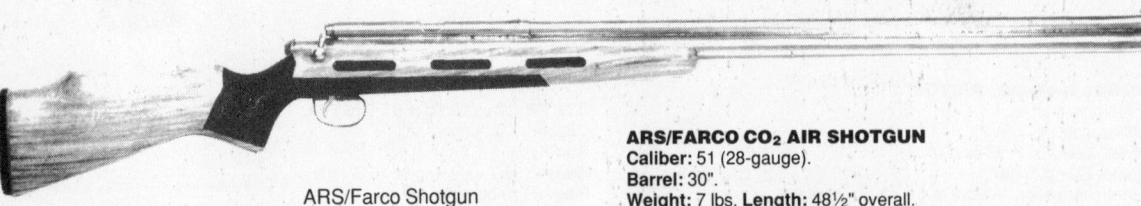

ARS/Farco Shotgun

ARS/FARCO CO_2 AIR SHOTGUN

Caliber: 51 (28-gauge).
Barrel: 30".
Weight: 7 lbs. **Length:** 48½" overall.
Power: 10-oz. refillable CO_2 tank.
Stock: Hardwood.
Sights: Bead front, fixed dovetail rear.
Features: Gives over 100 ft. lbs. energy for taking small game. Imported from Korea by Air Rifle Specialists.
Price: $395.00

CAUTION: PRICES CHANGE, CHECK AT GUNSHOP.

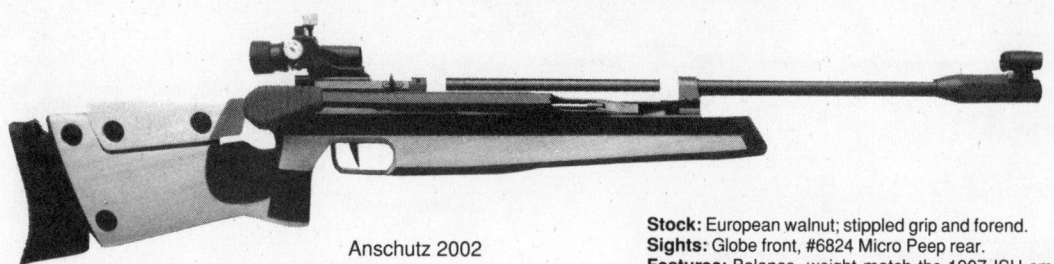

Anschutz 2002

ANSCHUTZ 2002 MATCH AIR RIFLE
Caliber: 177, single shot.
Barrel: 26".
Weight: 10½ lbs. **Length:** 44½" overall.

Stock: European walnut; stippled grip and forend.
Sights: Globe front, #6824 Micro Peep rear.
Features: Balance, weight match the 1907 ISU smallbore rifle. Uses #5019 match trigger. Recoil and vibration free. Fully adjustable cheekpiece and buttplate. Introduced 1988. Imported from Germany by Precision Sales International.
Price: Right-hand **$1,999.00**
Price: Left-hand, hardwood stock **$2,039.00**
Price: Model 2002D RT (Running Target) **$2,094.00**

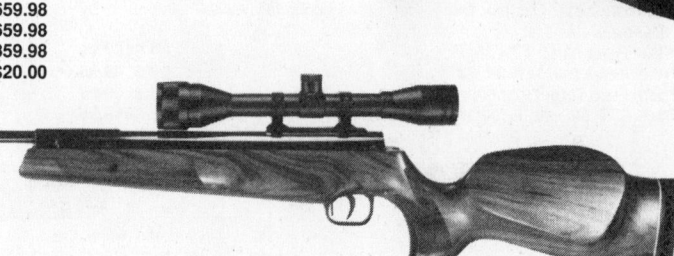

Beeman Wolf Pup Deluxe

BEEMAN AIR WOLF AIR RIFLE
Caliber: 177, 20, 22, 25, single shot.
Barrel: 21"; 12-groove rifling.
Weight: 5.7 lbs. **Length:** 37" overall.
Power: Pre-charged pneumatic, internal air chamber.
Stock: Select walnut, adult-scaled stock; hand checkered.
Sights: None furnished; grooved for scope mounting
Features: Up to 150 shots per air charge. Imported by Beeman.
Price: **$659.98**
Price: Wolf Pup (15.5" bbl., 5 lbs.) **$659.98**
Price: Wolf Pup Deluxe (thumbhole stock) **$859.98**
Price: For 20-cal., add **$20.00**

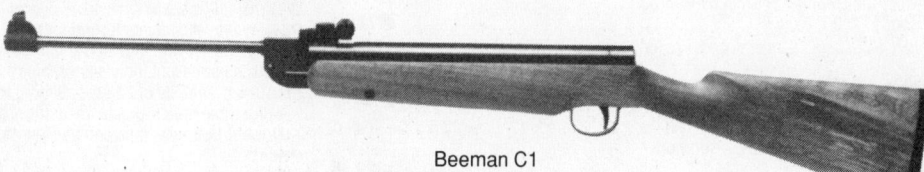

Beeman Classic

BEEMAN CLASSIC MAGNUM AIR RIFLE
Caliber: 20, 25, single shot.
Barrel: 15"; 12-groove rifling.
Weight: 8.6 lbs. **Length:** 44.5" overall.
Power: Gas-spring; barrel cocking action. Adjustable power.
Stock: Walnut.
Sights: None furnished. Built-in base and 1" rings included.
Features: Two-stage adjustable trigger. Automatic safety. Also available in 22-caliber on special order. Imported by Beeman.
Price: Special order only **$965.00**

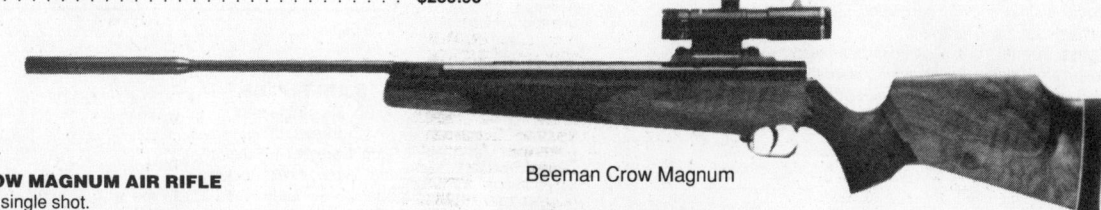

Beeman C1

BEEMAN CARBINE MODEL C1
Caliber: 177 or 22, single shot.
Barrel: 14"; 12-groove rifling.
Weight: 6¼ lbs. **Length:** 38" overall.
Power: Spring-piston, barrel cocking.
Stock: Walnut-stained beechwood with rubber buttpad.
Sights: Blade front, rear click-adjustable for windage and elevation.
Features: Velocity 830 fps. Adjustable trigger. Receiver grooved for scope mounting. Imported by Beeman.
Price: **$289.98**

Beeman Crow Magnum

BEEMAN CROW MAGNUM AIR RIFLE
Caliber: 20, 25, single shot.
Barrel: 16"; 10-groove rifling.
Weight: 8.5 lbs. **Length:** 46" overall.
Power: Gas-spring; adjustable power to 32 foot pounds muzzle energy. Barrel-cocking.
Stock: Classic-style walnut; hand checkered.
Sights: For scope use only; built-in base and 1" rings included.
Features: Adjustable two-stage trigger. Automatic safety. Also available in 22-caliber on special order. Introduced 1992. Imported by Beeman.
Price: **$1,195.00**

BEEMAN FX-1 AIR RIFLE
Caliber: 177, single shot.
Barrel: 18", rifled.
Weight: 6.6 lbs. **Length:** 43" overall.
Power: Spring-piston, barrel cocking.
Stock: Walnut-stained hardwood.
Sights: Tunnel front with interchangeable inserts; rear with rotating disc to give four sighting notches.
Features: Velocity 680 fps. Match-type adjustable trigger. Receiver grooved for scope mounting. Imported by Beeman.
Price: **$189.95**

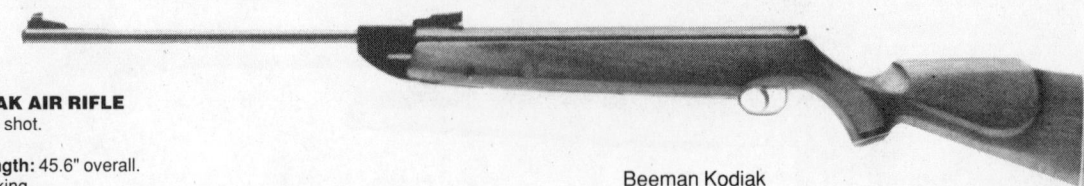

Beeman Kodiak

BEEMAN KODIAK AIR RIFLE
Caliber: 25, single shot.
Barrel: 17.6".
Weight: 9 lbs. **Length:** 45.6" overall.
Power: Barrel cocking.
Stock: Stained hardwood.
Sights: Blade front, open fully adjustable rear.
Features: Velocity to 820 fps. Up to 30 foot pounds muzzle energy. Introduced 1993. Imported by Beeman.
Price: **$549.95**

BEEMAN R1 AIR RIFLE
Caliber: 177, 20 or 22, single shot.
Barrel: 19.6", 12-groove rifling.
Weight: 8.5 lbs. **Length:** 45.2" overall.
Power: Spring-piston, barrel cocking.
Stock: Walnut-stained beech; cut-checkered pistol grip; Monte Carlo comb and cheekpiece; rubber buttpad.
Sights: Tunnel front with interchangeable inserts, open rear click-adjustable for windage and elevation. Grooved for scope mounting.
Features: Velocity of 940-1050 fps (177), 860 fps (20), 800 fps (22). Non-drying nylon piston and breech seals. Adjustable metal trigger. Milled steel safety. Right- or left-hand stock. Available with adjustable cheekpiece and buttplate at extra cost. Custom and Super Laser versions available. Imported by Beeman.
Price: Right-hand, 177, 20, 22 . . . . **$489.95**
Price: Left-hand, 177, 20, 22 . . . . **$549.95**
Price: Field Target, right-hand, 177, 20 . . . . **$669.95**
Price: 177, 20, with Tyrolean walnut stock **$649.95**

BEEMAN R1 LASER AIR RIFLE
Caliber: 177, 20, 22, 25, single shot.
Barrel: 16.1" or 19.6".
Weight: 8.4 lbs. **Length:** 41.7" overall (16.1" barrel).
Power: Spring-piston, barrel cocking.
Stock: Laminated wood with Monte Carlo comb and cheekpiece; checkered p.g. and forend; rubber buttpad.
Sights: Tunnel front with interchangeable inserts, open adjustable rear.
Features: Velocity up to 1150 fps (177). Special powerplant components. Built from the Beeman R1 rifle by Beeman.
Price: 177, 20, 22, 25 . . . . **$979.50**

Beeman R7 Air Rifle
Similar to the R8 model except has lighter ambidextrous stock, match-grade trigger block; velocity of 680-700 fps; barrel length 17"; weight 5.8 lbs. Milled steel safety. Imported by Beeman.
Price: 177, 20 . . . . **$299.98**

BEEMAN RX-1 GAS-SPRING MAGNUM AIR RIFLE
Caliber: 177, 20, 22, 25, single shot.
Barrel: 19.6"; 12-groove rifling.
Weight: 8.8 lbs.
Power: Gas-spring piston air; single stroke barrel cocking.
Stock: Walnut-finished hardwood, hand checkered, with cheekpiece. Adjustable cheekpiece and buttplate.
Sights: Tunnel front, click-adjustable rear.
Features: Velocity adjustable to about 1200 fps. Uses special sealed chamber of air as a mainspring. Gas-spring cannot take a set. Introduced 1990. Imported by Beeman.
Price: 177 or 22, regular, right-hand **$539.95**
Price: 20 or 25, regular, right hand **$539.95**

BEEMAN SUPER 7 AIR RIFLE
Caliber: 22, 7-shot repeater.
Barrel: 19", 12-groove rifling.
Weight: 7.2 lbs. **Length:** 41" overall.
Power: Pre-charged pneumatic, external air reservoir.
Stock: Walnut; high cheekpiece; rubber buttpad.
Sights: None furnished; drilled and tapped; 1" ring scope mounts included.
Features: Two-stage adjustable trigger; 7-shot rotary magazine. Receiver of anodized aircraft aluminum. All working parts either hardened or stainless steel. Imported by Beeman.
Price: **$1,560.00**

BEEMAN R1 CARBINE
Caliber: 177, 20, 22, 25, single shot.
Barrel: 16.1".
Weight: 8.6 lbs. **Length:** 41.7" overall.
Power: Spring-piston, barrel cocking.
Stock: Stained beech; Monte Carlo comb and checkpiece; cut checkered p.g.; rubber buttpad.
Sights: Tunnel front with interchangeable inserts, open adjustable rear; receiver grooved for scope mounting.
Features: Velocity up to 1050 fps (177). Non-drying nylon piston and breech seals. Adjustable metal trigger. Machined steel receiver end cap and safety. Right- or left-hand stock. Imported by Beeman.
Price: 177, 20, 22, 25, right-hand **$489.95**
Price: As above, left-hand **$549.95**

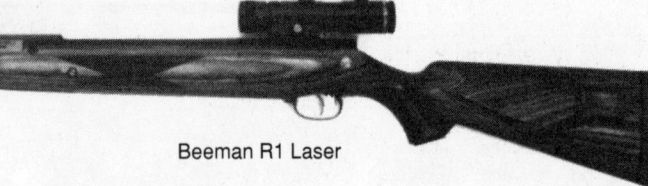

Beeman R1 Laser

BEEMAN R8 AIR RIFLE
Caliber: 177, single shot.
Barrel: 18.3".
Weight: 7.2 lbs. **Length:** 43.1" overall.
Power: Barrel cocking, spring-piston.
Stock: Walnut with Monte Carlo cheekpiece; checkered pistol grip.
Sights: Globe front, fully adjustable rear.
Features: Velocity of 735 fps. Similar to the R1. Nylon piston and breech seals. Adjustable match-grade, two-stage, grooved metal trigger. Milled steel safety. Rubber buttpad. Imported by Beeman.
Price: **$379.98**

> Consult our Directory pages for the location of firms mentioned.

BEEMAN R10 AIR RIFLES
Caliber: 177, 20, 22, single shot.
Barrel: 16.1"; 12-groove rifling.
Weight: 7.9 lbs. **Length:** 46" overall.
Power: Spring-piston, barrel cocking.
Stock: Standard—walnut-finished hardwood with Monte Carlo comb, rubber buttplate; Deluxe has white spacers at grip cap, buttplate, checkered grip, cheekpiece, rubber buttplate.
Sights: Tunnel front with interchangeable inserts, open rear click adjustable for windage and elevation. Receiver grooved for scope mounting.
Features: Over 1000 fps in 177-cal. only; 26-lb. cocking effort; milled steel safety and body tube. Right- and left-hand models. Similar in appearance to the Beeman R8. Introduced 1986. Imported by Beeman.
Price: 177, 20 or 22 Standard **$389.98**
Price: 20, Standard **$389.98**
Price: 177, 20, 22, Deluxe, right-hand **$439.88**
Price: 177, 20, 22, Deluxe, left-hand **$498.50**

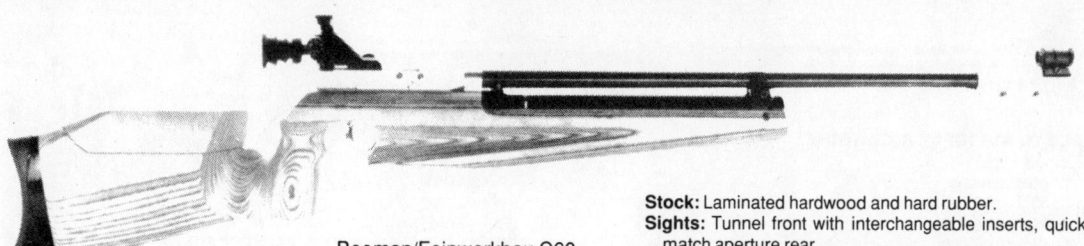

Beeman/Feinwerkbau C60

BEEMAN/FEINWERKBAU C60 CO₂ RIFLE
Caliber: 177.
Barrel: 16.9". With barrel sleeve, 25.4".
Weight: 10 lbs. **Length:** 42.6" overall.

Stock: Laminated hardwood and hard rubber.
Sights: Tunnel front with interchangeable inserts, quick release micro. click match aperture rear.
Features: Similar features, performance as Beeman/FWB 601. Virtually no cocking effort. Right- or left-hand. Running target version available. Introduced 1987. Imported from Germany by Beeman.
Price: Right-hand $1,495.00
Price: Left-hand $1,655.00
Price: Running Target, right-hand $1,475.00
Price: Running Target, left-hand $1,599.00
Price: Mini C60, right-hand $1,495.00

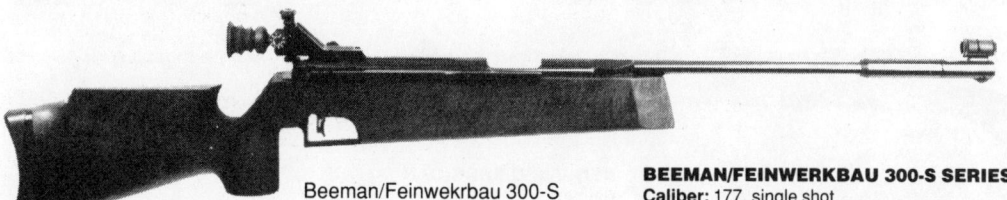

Beeman/Feinwekrbau 300-S

BEEMAN/FEINWERKBAU 300-S MINI-MATCH
Caliber: 177, single shot.
Barrel: 17⅛".
Weight: 8.8 lbs. **Length:** 40" overall.
Power: Spring piston, single stroke sidelever cocking.
Stock: Walnut. Stippled grip, adjustable buttplate. Scaled-down for youthful or slightly built shooters.
Sights: Globe front with interchangeable inserts, micro. adjustable rear. Front and rear sights move as a single unit.
Features: Recoilless, vibration free. Grooved for scope mounts. Steel piston ring. Cocking effort about 9½ lbs. Barrel sleeve optional. Left-hand model available. Introduced 1978. Imported by Beeman.
Price: Right-hand $1,195.00
Price: Left-hand $1,298.00

BEEMAN/HW30 AIR RIFLE
Caliber: 177, 22, single shot.
Barrel: 17" (177), 16.9" (20); 12-groove rifling.
Weight: 5.5 lbs.
Power: Spring piston; single-stroke barrel cocking.
Stock: Walnut-finished hardwood.
Sights: Blade front, adjustable rear.
Features: Velocity about 660 fps (177). Double-jointed cocking lever. Cast trigger guard. Synthetic non-drying breech and piston seals. Introduced 1990. Imported by Beeman.
Price: 177 . . . . $196.50
Price: 20 . . . . $209.95

BEEMAN/FEINWERKBAU 300-S SERIES MATCH RIFLE
Caliber: 177, single shot.
Barrel: 19.9", fixed solid with receiver.
Weight: Approx. 10 lbs. with optional bbl. sleeve. **Length:** 42.8" overall.
Power: Single stroke sidelever, spring piston.
Stock: Match model—walnut, deep forend, adjustable buttplate.
Sights: Globe front with interchangeable inserts. Click micro. adjustable match aperture rear. Front and rear sights move as a single unit.
Features: Recoilless, vibration free. Five-way adjustable match trigger. Grooved for scope mounts. Permanent lubrication, steel piston ring. Cocking effort 9 lbs. Optional 10-oz. barrel sleeve. Available from Beeman.
Price: Right-hand $1,195.00
Price: Left-hand $1,298.00

BEEMAN/FEINWERKBAU MODEL 601 AIR RIFLE
Caliber: 177, single shot.
Barrel: 16.6".
Weight: 10.8 lbs. **Length:** 43" overall.
Power: Single stroke pneumatic.
Stock: Special laminated hardwoods and hard rubber for stability.
Sights: Tunnel front with interchangeable inserts, click micrometer match apperture rear.
Features: Recoilless action; double supported barrel; special, short rifled area frees pellet from barrel faster so shooter's motion has minimum effect on accuracy. Fully adjustable match trigger. Trigger and sights blocked when loading latch is open. Imported by Beeman. Introduced 1984.
Price: Right-hand $1,598.00
Price: Left-hand $1,765.00
Price: Right-hand, walnut stock $1,598.00

Beeman/Feinwerkbau 601 Running Target
Similar to the standard Model 601. Has 16.9" barrel (33.7" with barrel sleeve); special match trigger, short loading gate which allows scope mounting. No sights—built for scope use only. Introduced 1987.
Price: Right-hand $1,595.00
Price: Left-hand $1,725.00
Price: Running target scope mounts $159.95

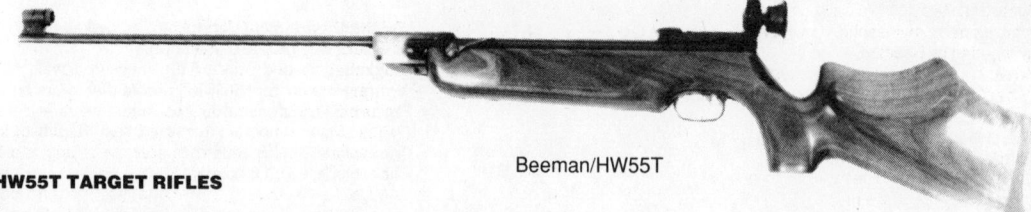

Beeman/HW55T

BEEMAN/HW55MM, HW55T TARGET RIFLES
Caliber: 177, single shot.
Barrel: 18½".
Weight: 7.8 lbs. **Length:** 43½" overall.
Power: Spring piston, barrel cocking.
Stock: Walnut. Pistol grip, high comb, beavertail forend on 55MM; 55T has Tyrolean style.
Sights: Globe front with four interchangeable inserts, fully adjustable match aperture rear.

Features: Trigger fully adjustable and removable. Nylon piston seals. Imported by Beeman.
Price: HW55MM $609.95
Price: HW55T $679.95

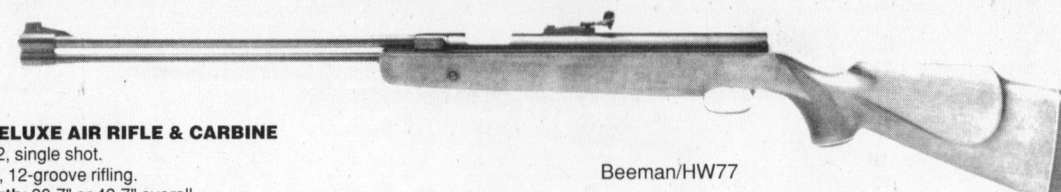

BEEMAN/HW77 DELUXE AIR RIFLE & CARBINE

Caliber: 177, 20 or 22, single shot.
Barrel: 14.5" or 18.5", 12-groove rifling.
Weight: 8.9 lbs. **Length:** 39.7" or 43.7" overall.
Power: Spring-piston; under-lever cocking.
Stocks: Walnut-stained beech; rubber buttplate, cut checkering on grip; cheek-piece.
Sights: Blade front, open adjustable rear.
Features: Velocity 830 fps. Fixed-barrel with fully opening, direct loading breech. Extended under-lever gives good cocking leverage. Adjustable trigger. Grooved for scope mounting. Carbine has 14.5" barrel, weighs 8.7 lbs., and is 39.7" overall. Imported by Beeman.
Price: Right-hand, 177, 20, 22 . . . . $529.00
Price: Left-hand, 177, 20, 22 . . . . $579.00
Price: With Tyrolean walnut stock, right-hand $645.00

Beeman/HW77

BEEMAN/HW50 LIGHT/SPORTER TARGET RIFLE

Caliber: 177, single shot.
Barrel: 18.4"; 12-groove rifling.
Weight: 6.9 lbs. **Length:** 43.1" overall.
Power: Spring piston; single-stroke barrel cocking.
Stock: Walnut-finished hardwood.
Sights: Blade front, adjustable rear.
Features: Velocity about 705 fps. Synthetic non-drying breech and piston seals. Double-jointed cocking lever. Introduced 1990. Imported by Beeman.
Price: $214.98

Benjamin Sheridan CO₂

BENJAMIN SHERIDAN PNEUMATIC (PUMP-UP) AIR RIFLES

Caliber: 177 or 22, single shot.
Barrel: 19⅜", rifled brass.
Weight: 5½ lbs. **Length:** 36¼" overall.
Power: Under-lever pneumatic, hand pumped.
Stock: American walnut stock and forend.
Sights: High ramp front, fully adjustable notch rear.
Features: Variable velocity to 800 fps. Bolt action with ambidextrous push-pull safety. Black or nickel finish. Introduced 1991. Made in the U.S. by Benjamin Sheridan Co.
Price: Black finish, Model 397 (177), Model 392 (22) $125.50
Price: Nickel finish, Model S397 (177), Model S392 (22) $134.00

BENJAMIN SHERIDAN CO₂ AIR RIFLES

Caliber: 177, 20 or 22, single shot.
Barrel: 19⅜", rifled brass.
Weight: 5 lbs. **Length:** 36½" overall.
Power: 12-gram CO₂ cylinder.
Stock: American walnut with buttplate.
Sights: High ramp front, fully adjustable notch rear.
Features: Velocity to 680 fps (177). Bolt action with ambidextrous push-pull safety. Gives about 40 shots per cylinder. Black or nickel finish. Introduced 1991. Made in the U.S. by Benjamin Sheridan Co.
Price: Black finish, Model G397 (177), Model G392 (22) $114.50
Price: Nickel finish, Model GS397 (177), Model GS392 (22) $122.00
Price: Black finish, Model FB9 (20) $124.00
Price: Nickel finish, Model F9 (20) $131.95

BRNO Aeron-Tau

BRNO AERON-TAU-2000 AIR RIFLE

Caliber: 177, single shot
Barrel: 23".

Weight: 6 lbs., 8 oz. **Length:** 40" overall.
Power: 12.5-gram CO₂ cartridges.
Stock: Synthetic match style with adjustable comb and buttplate.
Sights: Globe front with interchangeable inserts, fully adjustable open rear.
Features: Adjustable trigger. Rear sight converts to aperture on receiver. Comes with sling, extra seals, CO₂ cartridges, large CO₂ bottle, counterweight. Introduced 1993. Imported by Century International Arms.
Price: About $312.00

BRNO Model 631

BRNO 630 SERIES AIR RIFLES

Caliber: 177 single shot.
Barrel: 20.75".

Weight: 6 lbs., 15 oz. **Length:** 45.75" overall.
Power: Spring piston, barrel cocking.
Stock: Beechwood (Model 630); checkered, walnut stained (Model 631).
Sights: Hooded front, fully adjustable rear; grooved for scope mount.
Features: Velocity about 600 fps. Automatic safety; externally adjustable trigger; sling swivels. Imported from the Czech Republic by Action Arms, Ltd.
Price: Model 630 (Standard) $95.00
Price: Model 631 (Deluxe) $119.00

BSA SUPERSTAR AIR RIFLE

Caliber: 177 or 22, single shot.
Barrel: 18½".
Weight: 7¾ lbs. **Length:** 42½" overall.
Power: Under-lever cocking spring piston or optional sealed gas Ram.
Stock: Walnut-stained European beech; checkered grip, rubber buttpad.

Sights: Globe front, open adjustable rear.
Features: Velocity up to 1000 fps (177); 800 fps (22). Adjustable two-stage trigger. Polished blue finish. Introduced 1991. Imported from England by Air Rifle Specialists.
Price: Spring piston model $385.00
Price: With sealed gas Ram $510.00

CAUTION: PRICES CHANGE, CHECK AT GUNSHOP.

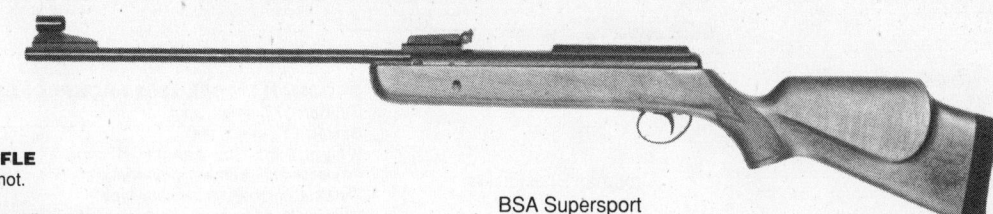

BSA SUPERSPORT AIR RIFLE
Caliber: 177, 22 or 25, single shot.
Barrel: 18½".
Weight: 7 lbs. **Length:** 41¾" overall.
Power: Spring piston or optional sealed gas Ram.
Stock: Walnut-stained European beech.
Sights: Globe front, adjustable open rear.
Features: Velocity up to 1010 fps (177); 830 fps (22); 700 fps (25). Adjustable two-stage trigger. Polished blue finish. Checkered pistol grip, rubber buttpad.

BSA Supersport

Introduced 1991. Imported from England by Air Rifle Specialists.
Price: Spring piston model **$250.00**
Price: With sealed gas Ram **$375.00**

Crosman Model 664X

CROSMAN MODEL 66 POWERMASTER
Caliber: 177 (single shot pellet) or BB, 200-shot reservoir.
Barrel: 20", rifled steel.

Weight: 3 lbs. **Length:** 38½" overall.
Power: Pneumatic; hand pumped.
Stock: Wood-grained ABS plastic; checkered p.g. and forend.
Sights: Ramp front, fully adjustable open rear.
Features: Velocity about 645 fps. Bolt action, cross-bolt safety. Introduced 1983. From Crosman.
Price: About **$42.00**
Price: Model 66RT (as above with Realtree camo finish), about **$50.00**
Price: Model 664X (as above, with 4x scope) **$50.00**

Crosman Model 262

CROSMAN MODEL 262 SPORTER AIR RIFLE
Caliber: 177 pellet, single shot.
Barrel: 21.75", rifled steel.

Weight: 4 lbs. 14 oz.
Power: CO_2 Powerlet.
Stock: Hardwood.
Sights: Fixed front, adjustable rear.
Features: Easy-loading pellet port, two-stage trigger. Also available as Youth model with overall length of 33.75". Introduced 1990. From Crosman.
Price: About **$80.00**

Crosman Model 760

CROSMAN MODEL 760 PUMPMASTER
Caliber: 177 pellets (single shot) or BB (200-shot reservoir).
Barrel: 19½", rifled steel.
Weight: 2 lbs., 12 oz. **Length:** 33.5" overall.
Power: Pneumatic, hand pumped.
Stock: Walnut-finished ABS plastic stock and forend.
Features: Velocity to 590 fps (BBs, 10 pumps). Short stroke, power determined by number of strokes. Post front sight and adjustable rear sight. Cross-bolt safety. Introduced 1966. From Crosman.
Price: About **$32.00**

CROSMAN MODEL 781 SINGLE PUMP
Caliber: 177 pellets (5-shot pellet clip) or BB (195-shot BB reservoir).
Barrel: 19½"; steel.
Weight: 2 lbs., 14 oz. **Length:** 35.8" overall.
Power: Pneumatic, single pump.
Stock: Wood-grained ABS plastic; checkered pistol grip and forend.
Sights: Blade front, open adjustable rear.
Features: Velocity of 405 fps (pellets). Uses only one pump. Hidden BB reservoir holds 195 shots; pellets loaded via 5-shot clip. Introduced 1984. From Crosman.
Price: About **$35.00**

CROSMAN MODEL 782 BLACK DIAMOND AIR RIFLE
Caliber: 177 pellets (5-shot clip) or BB (195-shot reservoir).
Barrel: 18", rifled steel.
Weight: 3 lbs.
Power: CO_2 Powerlet.
Stock: Wood-grained ABS plastic; checkered grip and forend.
Sights: Blade front, open adjustable rear.
Features: Velocity up to 595 fps (pellets), 650 fps (BB). Black finish with white diamonds. Introduced 1990. From Crosman.
Price: About **$40.00**

CROSMAN MODEL 788 BB SCOUT RIFLE
Caliber: BB only, 20-shot magazine.
Barrel: 14", steel.
Weight: 2 lbs. 7 oz. **Length:** 31½" overall.
Power: Pneumatic; hand pumped.
Stock: Wood-grained ABS plastic, checkered p.g. and forend.
Sights: Blade front, open adjustable rear.
Features: Variable pump power—three pumps give MV of 330 fps, six pumps 437 fps, 10 pumps 465 fps (BBs, average). Steel barrel, cross-bolt safety. Introduced 1978. From Crosman.
Price: About **$25.00**

CROSMAN MODEL 1077 REPEATAIR RIFLE
Caliber: 177 pellets, 12-shot clip
Barrel: 20.3", rifled steel.
Weight: 3 lbs., 11 oz. **Length:** 38.8" overall.
Power: CO_2 Powerlet.
Stock: Textured synthetic.
Sights: Blade front, fully adjustable rear.
Features: Velocity 590 fps. Removable 12-shot clip. True semi-automatic action. Introduced 1993. From Crosman.
Price: About **$60.00**

Crosman Backpacker

CROSMAN MODEL 2100 CLASSIC AIR RIFLE
Caliber: 177 pellets (single shot), or BB (200-shot BB reservoir).
Barrel: 21", rifled.
Weight: 4 lbs., 13 oz. **Length:** 39¾" overall.
Power: Pump-up, pneumatic.
Stock: Wood-grained checkered ABS plastic.
Features: Three pumps give about 450 fps, 10 pumps about 755 fps (BBs). Cross-bolt safety; concealed reservoir holds over 200 BBs. From Crosman.
Price: About **$55.00**

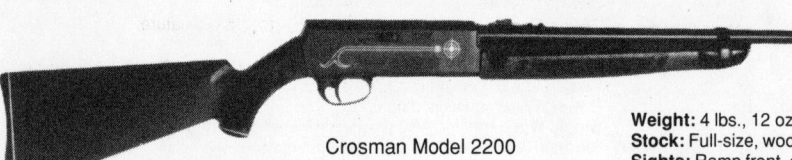

Crosman Model 2200

CROSMAN MODEL 2200 MAGNUM AIR RIFLE
Caliber: 22, single shot.
Barrel: 19", rifled steel.

DAISY/POWER LINE 130 AIR RIFLE
Caliber: 177, single shot.
Barrel: 18", rifled steel.
Weight: 5.9 lbs. **Length:** 41" overall.
Power: Spring-air, barrel cocking.
Stock: European-style hardwood.
Sights: Hooded front with blade on ramp, micrometer adjustable open rear.
Features: Velocity up to 800 fps. Introduced 1990. Imported from Spain by Daisy Mfg. Co.
Price: About **$175.00**

Daisy Model 840

DAISY MODEL 840
Caliber: 177 pellet single shot; or BB 350-shot.
Barrel: 19", smoothbore, steel.

Daisy/Power Line 856

DAISY/POWER LINE 880 PUMP-UP AIRGUN
Caliber: 177 pellets, BB.
Barrel: Rifled steel with shroud.
Weight: 4.5 lbs. **Length:** 37¾" overall.
Power: Pneumatic pump-up.
Stock: Wood-grain moulded plastic with Monte Carlo cheekpiece.
Sights: Ramp front, open rear adjustable for elevation.
Features: Crafted by Daisy. Variable power (velocity and range) increase with pump strokes. 10 strokes for maximum power. 100-shot BB magazine. Cross-bolt trigger safety. Positive cocking valve. From Daisy Mfg. Co.
Price: About **$60.00**

CROSMAN MODEL 1389 BACKPACKER RIFLE
Caliber: 177, single shot.
Barrel: 14", rifled steel.
Weight: 3 lbs. 3 oz. **Length:** 31" overall.
Power: Hand pumped, pneumatic.
Stock: Composition, skeletal type.
Sights: Blade front, rear adjustable for windage and elevation.
Features: Velocity to 560 fps. Detachable stock. Receiver grooved for scope mounting. Metal parts blued. From Crosman.
Price: About **$54.00**

Weight: 4 lbs., 12 oz. **Length:** 39" overall.
Stock: Full-size, wood-grained ABS plastic with checkered grip and forend.
Sights: Ramp front, open step-adjustable rear.
Features: Variable pump power—three pumps give 395 fps, six pumps 530 fps, 10 pumps 595 fps (average). Full-size adult air rifle. Has white line spacers at pistol grip and buttplate. Introduced 1978. From Crosman.
Price: About **$55.00**

DAISY/POWER LINE 753 TARGET RIFLE
Caliber: 177, single shot.
Barrel: 20.9", Lothar Walther.
Weight: 6.4 lbs. **Length:** 39.75" overall.
Power: Recoilless pneumatic, single pump.
Stock: Walnut with adjustable cheekpiece and buttplate.
Sights: Globe front with interchangeable inserts, diopter rear with micro. click adjustments.
Features: Includes front sight reticle assortment, web shooting sling. From Daisy Mfg. Co.
Price: About **$350.00**

Weight: 2.7 lbs. **Length:** 36.8" overall.
Stock: Moulded wood-grain stock and forend.
Sights: Ramp front, open, adjustable rear.
Features: Single pump pneumatic rifle. Muzzle velocity 335 fps (BB), 300 fps (pellet). Steel buttplate; straight pull bolt action; cross-bolt safety. Forend forms pump lever. Introduced 1978. From Daisy Mfg. Co.
Price: About **$40.00**

DAISY/POWER LINE 856 PUMP-UP AIRGUN
Caliber: 177 pellets (single shot) or BB (100-shot reservoir).
Barrel: Rifled steel with shroud.
Weight: 2.7 lbs. **Length:** 37.4" overall.
Power: Pneumatic pump-up.
Stock: Moulded wood-grain with Monte Carlo cheekpiece.
Sights: Ramp and blade front, open rear adjustable for elevation.
Features: Velocity from 315 fps (two pumps) to 650 fps (10 pumps). Shoots BBs or pellets. Heavy die-cast metal receiver. Cross-bolt trigger-block safety. Introduced 1984. From Daisy Mfg. Co.
Price: About **$45.00**

DAISY MODEL 990 DUAL-POWER AIR RIFLE
Caliber: 177 pellets (single shot) or BB (100-shot magazine).
Barrel: Rifled steel.
Weight: 4.1 lbs. **Length:** 37.4" overall.
Power: Pneumatic pump-up and 12-gram CO_2.
Stock: Moulded woodgrain.
Sights: Ramp and blade front, adjustable open rear.
Features: Velocity to 650 fps (BB), 630 fps (pellet). Choice of pump or CO_2 power. Shoots BBs or pellets. Heavy die-cast receiver dovetailed for scope mount. Cross-bolt trigger block safety. Introduced 1993. From Daisy Mfg. Co.
Price: About **$65.00**

Daisy Model 1894

DAISY MODEL 1894
Caliber: BB, 40-shot magazine.
Barrel: 17.5".

Weight: 2.2 lbs. **Length:** 39.5" overall.
Power: Spring air.
Stock: Moulded woodgrain plastic.
Sights: Blade on ramp front, adjustable open rear.
Features: Velocity 300 fps. Side loading port; slide safety; die-cast receiver. Made in U.S. From Daisy Mfg. Co.
Price: **$50.00**

Daisy Red Ryder

DAISY 1938 RED RYDER CLASSIC
Caliber: BB, 650-shot repeating action.
Barrel: Smoothbore steel with shroud.

Weight: 2.2 lbs. **Length:** 35.4" overall.
Stock: Walnut stock burned with Red Ryder lariat signature.
Sights: Post front, adjustable V-slot rear.
Features: Walnut forend. Saddle ring with leather thong. Lever cocking. Gravity feed. Controlled velocity. One of Daisy's most popular guns. From Daisy Mfg. Co.
Price: About **$44.00**

DAISY/POWER LINE 853
Caliber: 177 pellets.
Barrel: 20.9"; 12-groove rifling, high-grade solid steel by Lothar Walther™, precision crowned; bore size for precision match pellets.
Weight: 5.08 lbs. **Length:** 38.9" overall.
Power: Single-pump pneumatic.
Stock: Full-length, select American hardwood, stained and finished; black buttplate with white spacers.
Sights: Globe front with four aperture inserts; precision micrometer adjustable rear peep sight mounted on a standard ⅜" dovetail receiver mount.
Features: Single shot. From Daisy Mfg. Co.
Price: About **$200.00**

DAISY/POWER LINE 922
Caliber: 22, 5-shot clip.
Barrel: Rifled steel with shroud.
Weight: 4.5 lbs. **Length:** 37¾" overall.
Stock: Moulded wood-grained plastic with checkered p.g. and forend, Monte Carlo cheekpiece.
Sights: Ramp front, fully adjustable open rear.
Features: Muzzle velocity from 270 fps (two pumps) to 530 fps (10 pumps). Straight-pull bolt action. Separate buttplate and grip cap with white spacers. Introduced 1978. From Daisy Mfg. Co.
Price: About **$75.00**
Price: Models 970/920 (same as Model 922 except with hardwood stock and forend), about **$120.00**

DAISY/POWER LINE EAGLE 7856 PUMP-UP AIRGUN
Caliber: 177 (pellets), BB, 100-shot BB magazine.
Barrel: Rifled steel with shroud.
Weight: 2¾ lbs. **Length:** 37.4" overall.
Power: Pneumatic pump-up.
Stock: Moulded wood-grain plastic.
Sights: Ramp and blade front, open rear adjustable for elevation.
Features: Velocity from 315 fps (two pumps) to 650 fps (10 pumps). Finger grooved forend. Cross-bolt trigger-block safety. Introduced 1985. From Daisy Mfg. Co.
Price: With 4x scope, about **$60.00**

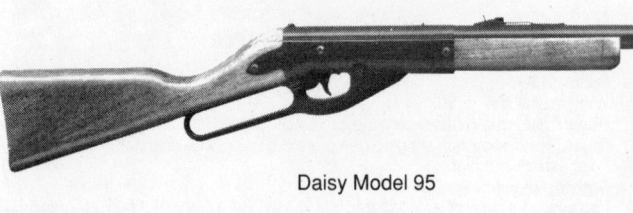

Daisy Model 95

DAISY/YOUTH LINE RIFLES

Model:	95	111	105
Caliber:	BB	BB	BB
Barrel:	18"	18"	13½"
Length:	35.2"	34.3"	29.8"
Power:	Spring	Spring	Spring
Capacity:	700	650	400
Price: About	**$40.00**	**$35.00**	**$30.00**

Features: Model 95 stock and forend are wood; 105 and 111 have plastic stocks. From Daisy Mfg. Co.

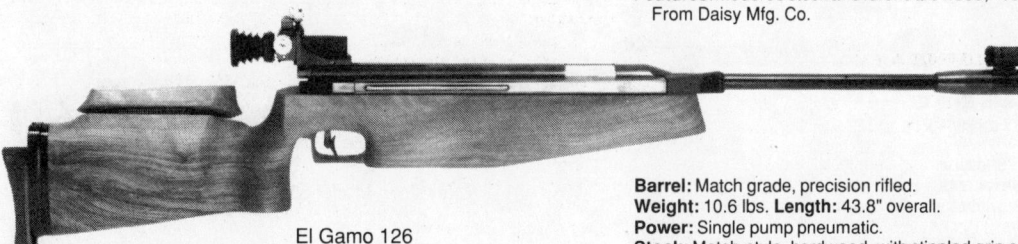

El Gamo 126

EL GAMO 126 SUPER MATCH TARGET RIFLE
Caliber: 177, single shot.

Barrel: Match grade, precision rifled.
Weight: 10.6 lbs. **Length:** 43.8" overall.
Power: Single pump pneumatic.
Stock: Match-style, hardwood, with stippled grip and forend.
Sights: Hooded front with interchangeable elements, fully adjustable match rear.
Features: Velocity of 590 fps. Adjustable trigger; easy loading pellet port; adjustable buttpad. Introduced 1984. Imported from Spain by Daisy Mfg. Co.
Price: About **$750.00**

FAMAS SEMI-AUTO AIR RIFLE
Caliber: 177, 10-shot magazine.
Barrel: 19.2".
Weight: About 8 lbs. **Length:** 29.8" overall.
Power: 12 gram CO_2.
Stock: Synthetic bullpup design.
Sights: Adjustable front, aperture rear.
Features: Velocity of 425 fps. Duplicates size, weight and feel of the centerfire MAS French military rifle in caliber 223. Introduced 1988. Imported from France by Century International Arms.
Price: About **$275.00**

"GAT" AIR RIFLE
Caliber: 177, single shot.
Barrel: 17¼" cocked, 23¼" extended.
Weight: 3 lbs.
Power: Spring piston.
Stock: Composition.
Sights: Fixed.
Features: Velocity about 450 fps. Shoots pellets, darts, corks. Imported from England by Stone Enterprises, Inc.
Price: **$34.95**

Marksman/Anschutz 380

MARKSMAN 28 INTERNATIONAL AIR RIFLE
Caliber: 177, single shot.
Barrel: 17".
Weight: 5¾ lbs.
Power: Spring-air, barrel cocking.
Stock: Hardwood.
Sights: Hooded front, adjustable rear.
Features: Velocity of 580-620 fps. Introduced 1989. Imported from Germany by Marksman Products.
Price: **$199.00**

MARKSMAN 40 INTERNATIONAL AIR RIFLE
Caliber: 177, single shot.
Barrel: 18⅜".
Weight: 7⅓ lbs.
Power: Spring-air, barrel cocking.
Stock: Hardwood.
Sights: Hooded front, adjustable rear.
Features: Velocity of 700-720 fps. Introduced 1989. Imported from Germany by Marksman Products.
Price: **$225.00**

MARKSMAN/ANSCHUTZ MODEL 380 MATCH AIR RIFLE
Caliber: 177, single shot.
Barrel: 20.75".
Weight: 10.75 lbs.
Power: Spring piston, sidelever cocking.
Stock: Match-style, walnut, with adjustable cheekpiece, adjustable buttplate.
Sights: Tunnel front with interchangeable inserts, match diopter rear.
Features: Velocity of 600-640 fps. Fully adjustable trigger. Recoilless and vibration free. Introduced 1990. Imported from Germany by Marksman Products.
Price: Right-hand only **$1,250.00**

MARKSMAN MODEL 45 AIR RIFLE
Caliber: 177, single shot.
Barrel: 19.1".
Weight: 7.3 lbs. **Length:** 46.75" overall.
Power: Spring-air, barrel cocking.
Stock: Stained hardwood with Monte Carlo cheekpiece, butt pad.
Sights: Hooded front, fully adjustable micrometer rear.
Features: Velocity 900-930 fps. Adjustable trigger; automatic safety. Introduced 1993. Imported from Spain by Marksman Products.
Price: **$189.00**

MARKSMAN 58-S SILHOUETTE RIFLE
Caliber: 177, single shot.
Barrel: 16".
Weight: 8.5 lbs.
Power: Spring-air, barrel cocking.
Stock: Hardwood with stippled grip; ambidextrous.
Sights: None furnished.
Features: Velocity 910-940 fps. Adjustable Rekord trigger. Removable full-length barrel sleeve. Introduced 1989. Imported from Germany by Marksman Products.
Price: **$390.00**

Consult our Directory pages for the location of firms mentioned.

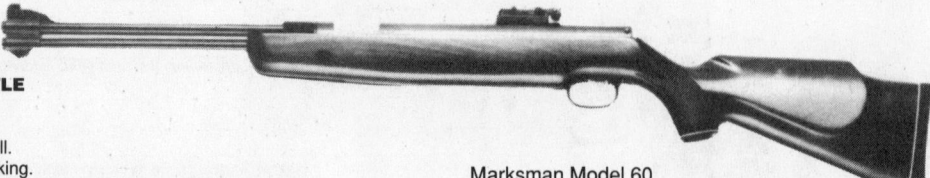

Marksman 58-S

MARKSMAN 56-FTS FIELD TARGET RIFLE
Caliber: 177, single shot.
Barrel: 19⅝".
Weight: 8.8 lbs.
Power: Spring-air, barrel cocking.
Stock: Hardwood with stippled grip; ambidextrous, with adjustable cheekpiece, adjustable buttplate.
Sights: None furnished.
Features: Velocity of 910-940 fps. Introduced 1989. Imported from Germany by Marksman Products.
Price: **$450.00**

MARKSMAN MODEL 60 AIR RIFLE
Caliber: 177, single shot.
Barrel: 18.5", rifled.
Weight: 8.9 lbs. **Length:** 44.75" overall.
Power: Spring piston, under-lever cocking.
Stock: Walnut-stained beech with Monte Carlo comb, hand-checkered pistol grip, rubber butt pad.
Sights: Blade front, open, micro. adjustable rear.
Features: Velocity of 810-840 fps. Automatic button safety on rear of receiver. Receiver grooved for scope mounting. Fully adjustable Rekord trigger. Introduced 1990. Imported from Germany by Marksman Products.
Price: **$439.00**
Price: Model 61 Carbine (14.5" barrel) **$439.00**

Marksman Model 60

CAUTION: PRICES CHANGE, CHECK AT GUNSHOP.

MARKSMAN 70 AIR RIFLE

Caliber: 177, 20 or 22, single shot.
Barrel: 19.75".
Weight: 8 lbs. **Length:** 45.5" overall.
Power: Spring air, barrel cocking.
Stock: Stained hardwood with Monte Carlo cheekpiece, rubber buttpad, cut checkered p.g.
Sights: Hooded front, open fully adjustable rear.
Features: Velocity of 910-940 fps (177), 810-840 fps (20), 740-780 fps (22); adjustable Rekord trigger. Introduced 1988. Imported from Germany by Marksman Products.
Price: 177 (Model 70T) **$329.00**
Price: 20 (Model 72) **$345.00**
Price: (Model 71) **$329.00**

Marksman 1750 BB

MARKSMAN 1790 BIATHLON TRAINER

Caliber: 177, single shot.
Barrel: 15", rifled.
Weight: 4.7 lbs.
Power: Spring-air, barrel cocking.
Stock: Synthetic.
Sights: Hooded front, match-style diopter rear.
Features: Velocity of 450 fps. Endorsed by the U.S. Shooting Team. Introduced 1989. From Marksman Products.
Price: **$66.95**

RWS/DIANA MODEL 24 AIR RIFLE

Caliber: 177, 22, single shot.
Barrel: 17", rifled.
Weight: 6 lbs. **Length:** 42" overall.
Power: Spring air, barrel cocking.
Stock: Beech.
Sights: Hooded front, adjustable rear.
Features: Velocity of 700 fps (177). Easy cocking effort; blue finish. Imported from Germany by Dynamit Nobel-RWS, Inc.
Price: **$185.00**
Price: Model 24C **$185.00**

RWS/DIANA MODEL 36 AIR RIFLE

Caliber: 177, 22, single shot.
Barrel: 19", rifled.
Weight: 8 lbs. **Length:** 45" overall.
Power: Spring air, barrel cocking.
Stock: Beech.
Sights: Hooded front (interchangeable inserts avail.), adjustable rear.
Features: Velocity of 1000 fps (177-cal.). Comes with scope mount; two-stage adjustable trigger. Imported from Germnay by Dynamit Nobel-RWS, Inc.
Price: **$345.00**
Price: Model 36 Carbine (same as Model 36 except has 15" barrel) **$345.00**

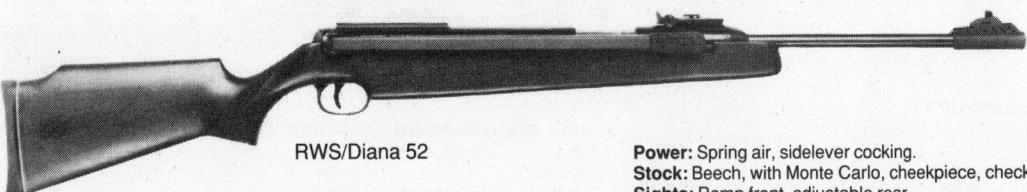

RWS/Diana 52

RWS/DIANA MODEL 52 AIR RIFLE

Caliber: 177, 22, single shot.
Barrel: 17", rifled.
Weight: 8½ lbs. **Length:** 43" overall.

Marksman 55 Air Rifle

Similar to the Model 70T except has uncheckered hardwood stock, no cheekpiece, plastic buttplate. Adjustable Rekord trigger. Overall length is 45.25", weight is 7½ lbs. Available in 177-caliber only.
Price: **$279.00**
Price: Model 59T (as above, carbine) **$279.00**

MARKSMAN 1740 AIR RIFLE

Caliber: 177 or 18-shot BB repeater.
Barrel: 15½", smoothbore.
Weight: 5 lbs., 1 oz. **Length:** 36½" overall.
Power: Spring, barrel cocking.
Stock: Moulded high-impact ABS plastic.
Sights: Ramp front, open rear adjustable for elevation.
Features: Velocity about 450 fps. Automatic safety; fixed front, adjustable rear sight; positive feed BB magazine; shoots 177-cal. BBs, pellets and darts. From Marksman Products.
Price: **$47.95**
Price: Model 1780 (deluxe sights, rifled barrel, shoots only pellets) . . **$62.95**

MARKSMAN 1750 BB BIATHLON REPEATER RIFLE

Caliber: BB, 18-shot magazine.
Barrel: 15", smoothbore.
Weight: 4.7 lbs.
Power: Spring piston, barrel cocking.
Stock: Moulded composition.
Sights: Tunnel front, open adjustable rear.
Features: Velocity of 450 fps. Automatic safety. Positive Feed System loads a BB each time gun is cocked. Introduced 1990. From Marksman Products.
Price: **$54.95**

RWS/Diana Model 34 Air Rifle

Similar to the Model 24 except has 19" barrel, weighs 7.5 lbs. Gives velocity of 1000 fps (177), 800 fps (22). Adjustable trigger, synthetic seals. Comes with scope rail.
Price: 177 or 22 . . . . **$245.00**

RWS/Diana Model 26 Air Rifle

Similar to the Model 24 except weighs 6.25 lbs., gives velocity of 750 fps (177), 500 fps (22). Automatic safety, scope rail, synthetic seals.
Price: 177 or 22 . . . . **$195.00**

RWS/Diana Model 28 Air Rifle

Similar to the Model 26 except has Monte Carlo stock with cheekpiece, rubber recoil pad and two-stage trigger. Velocity of 750 fps (177), 500 fps (22).
Price: 177 or 22 . . . . **$205.00**

RWS/DIANA MODEL 45 AIR RIFLE

Caliber: 177, single shot.
Weight: 7¾ lbs. **Length:** 46" overall.
Power: Spring air, barrel cocking.
Stock: Walnut-finished hardwood with rubber recoil pad.
Sights: Globe front with interchangeable inserts, micro. click open rear with four-way blade.
Features: Velocity of 820 fps. Dovetail base for either micrometer peep sight or scope mounting. Automatic safety. Imported from Germany by Dynamit Nobel-RWS, Inc.
Price: **$280.00**

Power: Spring air, sidelever cocking.
Stock: Beech, with Monte Carlo, cheekpiece, checkered grip and forend.
Sights: Ramp front, adjustable rear.
Features: Velocity of 1100 fps (177). Blue finish. Solid rubber buttpad. Imported from Dynamit Nobel-RWS, Inc.
Price: **$450.00**
Price: Model 48 (same as Model 52 except no Monte Carlo, cheekpiece or checkering) **$400.00**
Price: Model 54, recoilless action **$635.00**

RWS/DIANA MODEL 70 MATCH AIR RIFLE
Caliber: 177, single shot.
Barrel: 13.5".
Weight: 4.5 lbs. **Length:** 33" overall.
Power: Spring air, barrel cocking.
Stock: Beech, match-type.
Sights: Tunnel front with interchangeable inserts, fully adjustable peep rear.
Features: Velocity of 450 fps. Adjustable trigger. Designed and scaled for junior shooters. Introduced 1990. Imported from Germany by Dynamit Nobel-RWS, Inc.
Price: **$190.00**

RWS/Diana Model 72 Air Rifle
Similar to the Model 70 except has recoilless action. Introduced 1990.
Price: **$340.00**

RWS/Diana 75 T01

RWS/DIANA MODEL 75 T01 MATCH AIR RIFLE
Caliber: 177, single shot.
Barrel: 19".
Weight: 11 lbs. **Length:** 43.7" overall.
Power: Spring air, sidelever cocking.
Stock: Oil-finished beech with stippled grip, adjustable buttplate, accessory rail. Conforms to ISU rules.
Sights: Globe front with five inserts, fully adjustable match peep rear.
Features: Velocity of 574 fps. Fully adjustable trigger. Model 75 HV has stippled forend, adjustable cheekpiece. Uses double opposing piston system for recoilless operation. Imported from Germany by Dynamit Nobel-RWS, Inc.
Price: Model 75 T01 . . . . **$950.00**

RWS/Diana Model 75S T01 Air Rifle
Similar to the Model 75 T01 except has beech stock specially shaped for standing and three-position shooting. Buttplate is vertically adjustable with curved and straight spacers for individual fit, adjustable cheekpiece. Introduced 1990.
Price: Right-hand **$1,150.00**
Price: Left-hand **$1,245.00**

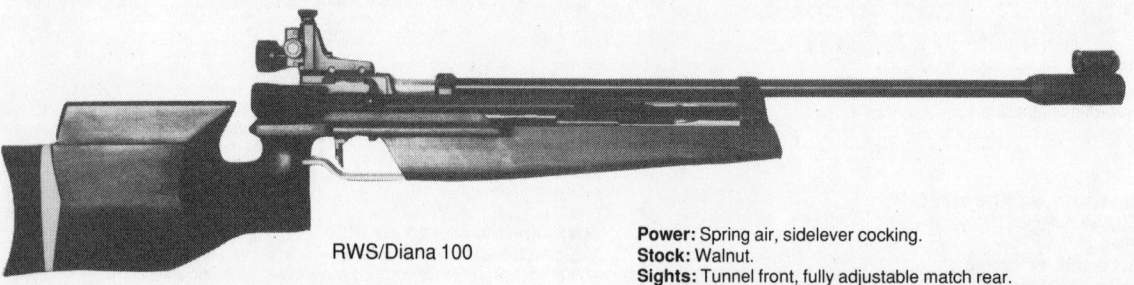

RWS/Diana 100

RWS/DIANA MODEL 100 MATCH AIR RIFLE
Caliber: 177, single shot.
Barrel: 19".
Weight: 11 lbs. **Length:** 43" overall.
Power: Spring air, sidelever cocking.
Stock: Walnut.
Sights: Tunnel front, fully adjustable match rear.
Features: Velocity of 580 fps. Single-stroke cocking; cheekpiece adjustable for height and length; recoilless operation. Cocking lever secured against rebound. Introduced 1990. Imported from Germany by Dynamit Nobel-RWS, Inc.
Price: Right-hand only **$1,400.00**

RWS GAMO CF-20 AIR RIFLE
Caliber: 177, single shot.
Barrel: 17.7".
Weight: 6.6 lbs. **Length:** 43.3" overall.
Power: Barrel cocking, spring piston.
Stock: Hardwood.
Sights: Blade on ramp front, fully adjustable open rear.
Features: Velocity to 800 fps. Cocking effort of 33 lbs. Grooved receiver, synthetic seals, dual safeties; sdjustable two-stage trigger. Imported from Spain by Dynamit Nobel-RWS, Inc.
Price: **$190.00**

RWS GAMO EXPOMATIC 2000 AIR RIFLE
Caliber: 177, 25-shot magazine.
Barrel: 17.7".
Weight: 5.5 lbs. **Length:** 40.9" overall.
Power: Barrel cocking, spring piston.
Stock: Hardwood.
Sights: Blade front, fully adjustable open rear.
Features: Velocity to 600 fps. Cocking effort of 20 lbs. Dual safeties, grooved receiver, synthetic seals. Magazine tube holds 25 pellets, loads automatically. Imported from Spain by Dynamit Nobel-RWS, Inc.
Price: **$150.00**

RWS Gamo Delta

RWS GAMO DELTA AIR RIFLE
Caliber: 177.
Barrel: 15.73".
Weight: 5.3 lbs. **Length:** 37" overall.
Power: Barrel cocking, spring piston.
Stock: Carbon fiber.
Sights: Blade front, fully adjustable open rear.
Features: Velocity to 565 fps. Has 20-lb. cocking effort. Synthetic seal; dual safeties; grooved for scope mounting. Imported from Spain by Dynamit Nobel-RWS, Inc.
Price: **$105.00**

RWA GAMO HUNTER 440 AIR RIFLE
Caliber: 177, single shot.
Barrel: 18".
Weight: 6.75 lbs. **Length:** 43" overall.
Power: Spring piston, barrel cocking.
Stock: Hardwood.
Sights: Hooded blade on ramp front, fully adjustable rear.
Features: Velocity 1000 fps. Monte Carlo stock with cheekpiece; scope rail; dual safeties. Imported from Spain by Dynamit Nobel-RWS.
Price: **$205.00**

SHERIDAN PNEUMATIC (PUMP-UP) AIR RIFLES
Caliber: 20 (5mm), single shot.
Barrel: 19⅜", rifled brass.
Weight: 6 lbs. **Length:** 36½" overall.
Power: Under-lever pneumatic, hand pumped.
Stock: Walnut with buttplate and sculpted forend.

Sights: High ramp front, fully adjustable notch rear.
Features: Variable velocity to 675 fps. Bolt action with ambidextrous push-pull safety. Blue finish (Blue Streak) or nickel finish (Silver Streak). Introduced 1991. Made in the U.S. by Benjamin Sheridan Co.
Price: Blue Streak, Model CB9 . . . . **$139.95**
Price: Silver streak, Model C9 . . . . **$148.50**

Sterling HR81

STERLING SPRING PISTON AIR RIFLES
Caliber: 177, 20, 22, single shot.
Barrel: 18½", Lothar Walther, steel.
Weight: 9 lbs. **Length:** 42" overall.
Power: Spring piston with under-barrel lever.

Stock: American walnut (HR81); HR83 has walnut with checkpiece and hand-checkered grip. Rubber buttpad.
Sights: Standard—tunnel-type front, fully adjustable open rear; Deluxe has tunnel-type front, Williams fully adjustable peep rear with ¼-minute click-stop knobs.
Features: Velocity to 740 fps (177). Spring-loaded bolt action with adjustable single stage match trigger. Introduced 1983. Made in the U.S. by Benjamin Sheridan Co.
Price: Standard models, HR81-17 (177), HR81-20 (20), HR81-22 (22) **$341.95**
Price: Deluxe models, HR83-17W (177), HR83-20W (20),
HR83-22W (22) **$481.95**

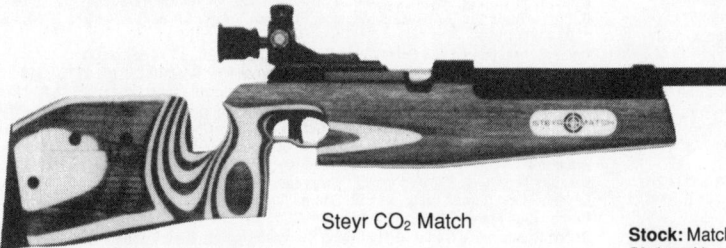

Steyr CO₂ Match

STEYR CO₂ MATCH AIR RIFLE MODEL 91
Caliber: 177, single shot.
Barrel: 23.75", (13.75" rifled).
Weight: 10.5 lbs. **Length:** 51.7" overall.
Power: CO₂.

Stock: Match. Laminated wood. Adjustable buttplate and cheekpiece.
Sights: None furnished; comes with scope mount.
Features: Velocity 577 fps. CO₂ cylinders are refillable; about 320 shots per cylinder. Designed for 10-meter shooting. Introduced 1990. Imported from Austria by Nygord Precision Products.
Price: About **$1,300.00**
Price: Left-hand, about **$1,400.00**
Price: Running Target Rifle, right-hand, about **$1,325.00**
Price: As above, left-hand, about **$1,425.00**

THEOBEN CLASSIC AIR RIFLE
Caliber: 177 or 22, single shot.
Barrel: 19½".
Weight: 7¾ lbs. **Length:** 44" overall.
Power: Gas ram piston. Variable power.
Stock: Walnut with checkered grip and forend.
Sights: None furnished. Comes with scope mount.
Features: Velocity to 1100 fps (177) and 900 fps (22). Barrel-cocking action. Polished blue finish on metal, oil-finished stock. Adjustable trigger. Imported from England by Air Rifle Specialists.
Price: **$830.00**
Price: For left-hand stock add **$60.00**
Price: Grand Prix model (same as Classic except has thumbhole stock with adjustable buttplate) **$940.00**
Price: For left-hand stock add **$60.00**

Theoben Eliminator Air Rifle
Similar to the Theoben Classic except has a longer, more sturdily built action with longer piston stroke for more power. Has walnut thumbhole stock with adjustable buttplate and comes with sling. Imported from England by Air Rifle Specialists.
Price: **$1,500.00**
Price: Left-hand stock, add **$60.00**

Theoben Imperator SLR 88 Air Rifle
Sporter version of the Theoben Imperator FT in 22-caliber only. Has conventional sporter stock of oil-finished walnut with checkered grip and forend. Has 7-shot clip. Velocity up to 725 fps. Imported from England by Air Rifle Specialists.
Price: **$1,680.00**

THEOBEN IMPERATOR FT AIR RIFLE
Caliber: 177, single shot.
Barrel: 16".
Weight: 8½ lbs. **Length:** 42" overall.
Power: Under-lever cocking gas Ram piston. Variable power.
Stock: Hand-checkered European walnut, thumbhole design with adjustable forend block, roll-over cheekpiece, adjustable rubber buttpad.
Sights: None furnished. Comes with scope mount.
Features: Velocity up to 900 fps. Stippled grip and forend panels. Adjustable match-grade trigger. Imported from England by Air Rifle Specialists.
Price: **$1,500.00**

CONSULT
SHOOTER'S MARKETPLACE
Page 231, This Issue

WALTHER CG90 AIR RIFLE
Caliber: 177, single shot.
Barrel: 18.9".
Weight: 10.2 lbs. **Length:** 44" overall.
Power: CO₂ cartridge.
Stock: Match type of European walnut; stippled grip.
Sights: Globe front, fully adjustable match rear.
Features: Uses tilting-block action. Introduced 1989. Imported from Germany by Interarms.
Price: **$1,748.00**

WALTHER LG-90 MATCH AIR RIFLE
Caliber: 177, single shot.
Barrel: 25.5".
Weight: 13 lbs. **Length:** 44¾" overall.
Power: Spring air, barrel cocking.
Stock: Walnut match design with stippled grip and forend, adjustable cheekpiece, rubber buttpad.
Features: Has the same weight and contours as the Walther U.I.T. rimfire target rifle. Comes complete with sights, accessories and muzzle weight. Imported from Germany by Interarms.
Price: **$1,317.00**

A

A.A. Arms, Inc. 4811 Persimmon Court, Monroe, NC 28110/704-289-5356/FAX: 704-289-5859
Accu-Tek, 4525 Carter Ct., Chino, CA 91710/714-627-2404
Accuracy Gun Shop, 1240 Hunt Ave., Columbus, GA 31907/404-561-6386
Accuracy Gun Shop, Inc., 5903 Boulder Highway, Las Vegas, NV 89122/702-458-3330
Action Arms Ltd., P.O. Box 9573, Philadelphia, PA 19124/215-744-0100
Adventure A.G.R., 3040 Sashabaw Rd., Waterford, MI 48329/313-673-3090
Ahlman's Custom Gun Shop, Inc., Rt. 1, Box 20, Morristown, MN 55052/507-685-4244
Aimpoint U.S.A., 580 Herndon Parkway, Suite 500, Herndon, VA 22070/703-471-6828
Aimtech Mount Systems, 101 Inwood Acres, Thomasville, GA 31792/912-226-4313
Air Arms (See Air Rifle Specialists)
Air Gun Rifle Repair, 6420 1st Ave. W., Sebring, FL 33870/813-655-0516
Air Gun Shop, The, 2312 Elizabeth St., Billings, MT 59102/406-656-2983
Air Guns Unlimited, 15866 Main St., La Puente, CA 91744/818-333-4991
Air Rifle Specialists, 311 East Water St., Elmira, NY 14901/607-734-7340
Air Venture Air Guns, 9752 Flower St., Bellflower, CA 90706/213-867-6355
Airgun Centre, Ltd., 3230 Garden Meadow Dr., Lawrenceburg, IN 47025/812-637-1463
Airgun Repair Centre, Ltd., P.O. Box 6249, Cincinnati, OH 45206-0249/812-637-1463
Airport Sports Shop, Inc., 585 Kelly Blvd., North Attleboro, MA 02760/617-695-7071
Alexander, Gunsmith, W.R., 3795 Forsythe Way, Tallahassee, FL 32308/904-893-1847
All Game Sport Center, 6076 Guinea Pike, Milford, OH 45150/513-575-0134
Allen County Gun Works, 900 E. Pettit Ave., Ft. Wayne, IN 46806/219-744-5690
Allison & Carey Gun Works, 10218 S.E. Powell Blvd., Portland, OR 97266/503-760-3388
Alpine Arms Corp., 6716 Fort Hamilton Pkwy., Brooklyn, NY 11219/718-833-2228
Alpine Range, 5482 Shelby Rd., Fort Worth, TX 76140/817-478-6613
Al's Gun & Reel Shop, Inc., 318 E. Front St., North Platte, NE 69101/308-534-2660
A&M Sales, 23 W. North Ave., North Lake, IL 60164/708-562-8190
AMAC (American Military Arms Corp.), 2202 Redmond Rd., Jacksonville, AR 72076/501-982-1633
American Arms, Inc., 715 E. Armour Rd., N. Kansas City, MO 64116/816-474-3161/FAX: 816-474-3161
American Derringer Corp., 127 N. Lacy Dr., Waco, TX 76705/817-799-9111
Ammo Load, Inc., 1560 E. Edinger, Suite G, Santa Ana, CA 92705/714-558-8858
AMT (Arcadia Machine & Tool, Inc.), 6226 Santos Diaz St., Irwindale, CA 91702/818-334-6629
Andersen Gunsmithing, 2485 Petaluma Blvd. N.,Petaluma, CA 94952/707-764-5744
Anderson, Inc., Andy, 2125 Northwest Expressway, Oklahoma City, OK 73112/405-842-3305
Anderson Manufacturing Co., Inc., 2741 N. Crosby Rd., Oak Harbor, WA 98277/206-675-7300
Anschutz (See Precision Sales Intl., Inc.)
Antonowicz, Frank, 8349 Kentucky Ave. North, Minneapolis, MN 55445
Apple Town Gun Shop, Rt. 104, Williamson, NY 14589/315-589-3311
Argonaut Gun Shop, 607 McHenry Ave., Modesto, CA 95350/209-522-5876
Arizaga (See Mandall Shooting Supplies)
Armadillo Air Gun Repair, 5892 Hampshire Rd., Corpus Christi, TX 78408/512-289-5458
Armes de Chasse, Phone: 215-388-1146 or FAX: 215-388-1147
Armoury, Inc., The, Route 202, New Preston, CT 06777/203-868-0001
Armscorp. USA, Inc., 4424 John Ave., Baltimore, MD 21227/301-247-6200
Armscor (See Ruko Products)
Armsport, Inc. 3950 NW 49th St., Miami, FL 33142/305-635-7850
Armurie De L'Outaouqis, 28 Rue Bourque, Hull, Quebec, CANADA J84 181
Arrieta (See Quality Arms, Inc./Wingshooting Adventures)
ASI, 6226 Santos Diaz St., Irwindale, CA 91702/818-334-6629
A-Square Co., Inc., One Industrial Pk., Bedford, KY 40006/502-255-7456
Astra-Unceta Y Cia, S.A. (See E.A.A. Corp.)
Atlantic & Pacific Guns, 4859 Virginia Beach Blvd., Virginia Beach, VA 23454/804-340-6269
Atlantic Guns, Inc., 944 Bonifant St., Silver Springs, MD 20910/301-585-4448/301-279-7963
Atlas Gun Repair, 4908 E. Judge Perez Dr., Violet, LA 70092/504-277-4229
Auto Electric & Parts, Inc., 24 W. Baltimore Ave., Media, PA 19063/215-565-2432
Auto-Ordnance Corp., Williams Ln., West Hurley, NY 12491/914-679-7225
Autumn Sales, Inc., 1320 Lake St., Fort Worth, TX 76102/817-335-1634
AYA (See Armes de Chasse)

B

Bachelder Master Gunmakers, 1229 Michigan N.E., Grand Rapids, MI 49503/616-459-3636
Badgers Shooters Supply, Inc., 106 S. Harding St., Owen, WI 54460/715-229-2101
Bain & Davis, 307 East Valley Blvd., San Gabriel, CA 91776/213-283-7449
Bait & Tackle Shop, The, Rt. 1, Box 5B, Fairmont, WV 26554/304-363-0183
Baity's Custom Gunworks, 414 Second St., North Wilksboro, NC 28659/919-667-8785
Baltimore Gunsmiths, 218 South Broadway, Baltimore, MD 21231/301-276-6908
Barrett Firearms Mfg., Inc., 8211 Manchester Hwy., Murfreesboro, TN 37133
Barrows Point Trading Post, Rt. 4 West, Quechee, VT 05059/802-295-1050
Bausch & Lomb, Inc., 300 N. Lone Hill Ave., San Dimas, CA 91773
B&B Supply Co., 4501 Minnehaha Ave., Minneapolis, MN 56406/612-724-5230
Beards Sport Shop, 811 Broadway, Cape Girardeau, MO 63701/314-334-2266
Beauchamp & Son, Inc., 160 Rossiter Rd., Richmond, MA 01254
Bedlan's Sporting Goods, Inc., 1318 E. Street, P.O. Box 244, Fairbury, NE 68352/402-729-6112
Beeman Precision Airguns, Inc., 3440-GD Airway Dr., Santa Rosa, CA 95403/707-578-7900
Belleplain Supply, Inc., Box 222, Handsmill Rd., Belleplain, NJ 08270/609-861-2345
Bellrose & Son, L.E., 21 Forge Pond Rd., Granby, MA 01033-0184/413-467-9695
Bell's Legendary County Ware, 22 Circle Dr., Bellmore, NY 11701/516-679-1158
Ben's Gun Shop, 1151 S. Cedar Ridge Rd., Duncanville, TX 75137/214-780-1807
Benelli Armi S.p.A. (See E.A.A. Corp./Heckler & Koch, Inc./Sile Distributors)
Benjamin/Sheridan Co., 2600 Chicory Rd., Racine, WI 53403/414-554-7900
Benson Gun Shop, 35 Middle Country Rd., Coram L.I., NY 11727/516-736-0065
Beretta U.S.A., 17601 Beretta Dr.. Accokeek, MD 20607/301-283-2191

Beretta U.S.A., c/o Bolsa Gunsmithing, 7404 Bolsa Ave., Westminster, CA 92683/714-894-9100 (California only)
Bernardelli SpA (See Magnum Research, Inc.)
Bersa S.A. (See Eagle Imports)
Bertuzzi (See Moore & Co., William Larkin)
Brown, E. Arthur, 3404 Pawnee Drive, Alexandria, MN 56308/612-762-8847
Bickford Arms, 127 N. Main St., Joplin, MO 64801/417-781-6440
Big Bear Arms, 2714 Fairmount St., Dallas, TX/214-871-7061/FAX: 214-754-0449
Billings Gunsmiths, 1940 Grand Ave., Billings, MT 59102/406-652-3104
Billy Freds, P.O. Box 7646, Amarillo, TX 79109/806-352-2519
Blaser Jagdwaffen GmbH (See Autumn Sales, Inc.)
Blue Ridge Outdoor Sports, Inc., 2314 Spartanburg Hwy., E. Flatrock, NC 28726/704-697-3006
Blount, Inc., Sporting Equipment Division, Outers/Weaver Operation, N5549 CTH "Z", Onalaska, WI 54650/608-781-3358/800-635-7656
Blythe's Sport Shop, Inc., 2810 N. Calmut Ave., Valparaiso, IN 46383/219-462-4412
Bob's Crosman Repair, 2510 E. Henry Ave., Cudahy, WI 53110/414-769-8256
Bob's Gun & Tackle Shop, (Blaustein & Reich, Inc.), 746 Granby St., Norfolk, VA 23510/804-627-8311/804-622-9786
Bob's Repair, 750 Contor, Idaho Falls, ID 83401/208-522-4959
Boggus Gun Shop, 1402 W. Hopkins St., San Marcos, TX 78666/512-392-3513
Bohemia Arms Co., 17101 Los Modelos, Fountain Valley, CA 92708/714-963-0809; FAX: 714-963-0809
Bolsa Gunsmithing, 7404 Bolsa Ave., Westminster, CA 92683/714-894-9100
Boracci, E. John, Village Sport Center, 38-10 Merrick Rd., Seaford L.I., NY 11783/516-221-8229
Borgheresi, Enrique, 106 E. Tallalah, P.O. Box 8063, Greenville, SC 29604/803-271-2664
Boudreaux, Gunsmith, Preston, 412 W. School St., Lake Charles, LA 70605/318-478-8908
Bradys Sportsmans Surplus, P.O. Box 4166, Missoula, MT 59806/460-721-5500
Braverman Arms Co., 912 Penn Ave., Wilkinsburg, PA 15221/412-241-1344
Brazdas Top Guns, 307 Bertrand Dr., Lafayette, LA 70506/318-233-4137
Brenner Sport Shop, Charlie, 344 St. George Ave., Rahway, NJ 07065/201-382-4066
Bretton (See Mandall Shooting Supplies)
Bridge Sportsmen's Center, 1319 Spring St., Paso Robles, CA 93446/805-238-4407
British Sporting Arms, RR 1 Box 130, Millbrook, NY 12545/914-677-8303
BRNO (See Action Arms, Ltd./Bohemia Arms Co./Century International Arms, Inc.)
Broadway Arms, 4116 E. Broadway, N. Little Rock, AR 72203
Brock's Gunsmithing, Inc., North 2104 Division St., Spokane, WA 99207/509-328-9788
Browning (See page 466)
Bryco Arms, 17692 Cowan, Irvine, CA 92714/714-252-7621
Brunswick Gun Shop, 31 Bath Rd., Brunswick, ME 04011/207-729-8322
Brunton U.S.A., 620 E. Monroe Ave., Riverton, WY 82501/307-856-6559
Bryan & Associates, 201 S. Gossett St., Anderson, SC 29624/803-225-4475
Bryco Arms (See Jennings Firearms, Inc.)
BSA Guns Ltd. (See Air Rifle Specialists)
B-Square Co., 2708 St. Louis Ave., Fort Worth, TX 76110/817-923-0964
B&T, Inc., 1777 Central Ave., Albany, NY 12205/518-869-7934
Buffalo Gun Center, Inc., 3385 Harlem Rd., Buffalo, NY 14225/716-833-2581
Bullseye Gun Works, 7949 E. Frontage Rd.. Overland Park, KS 66204/913-648-4867
Burby, Inc. Guns & Gunsmithing, Rt. 7 South RR #3, Box 345, Middlebury, VT 05753/802-388-7365
Burgins Gun Shop, RD #1 Box 66, Sidney Center, NY 13839/607-829-8668
Burris (Canada Repairs), Harvey Trace Scope Repair, 11915-132nd Ave., Edmonton, Alberta TSE 1AB/403-454-1397
Burris Co., Inc., 331 E. 8th St., Greeley, CO 80631/303-356-1670
Burton Hardware, 200 N. Huntington, Sulphur, LA 70663/318-527-0794
Bushnell, 300 N. Lone Hill Ave., San Dimas, CA 91773/714-592-8000
B&W Gunsmithing, 505 Main Ave. N.W., Cullman, AL 35055/205-737-9595

C

Cabanas (See Mandall Shooting Supplies, Inc.)
Caddo Arms & Cycle, 1400 Fairfield Ave., Shreveport, LA 71101/318-424-9011
Calico Light Weapon Systems, 405 E. 19th St., Bakersfield, CA 93305/805-323-1327
Cal's Customs, 110 E. Hawthorne, Fallbrook, CA 92028/619-728-5230
Camdex, Inc., 2330 Alger, Troy, MI 48083/313-528-2300
Cape Oufitters, Rte. #2, Beuton Hill Rd., Cape Girardeau, MO 63701/314-335-1403
Capitol Sports & Western Wear, 1092 Helena Ave., Helena, MT 59601/406-443-2978
Carl's Gun Shop, Route 1, Box 131, El Dorado Springs, MO 64744/417-876-4168
Carpenters Gun Works, RD 1 Box 43D, Newton Rd., Proctorsville, VT 05153/802-226-7690
Carroll's Gun Shop, Inc., 1610 N. Alabama Rd., Wharton, TX 77488/409-532-3175
Carter's Country, 8925 Katy Freeway, Houston, TX 77024/713-461-1844
Casey's Gun Shop, 59 Des E Rables, P.O. Box 100, Rogersville, New Brunswick E0A 2T0 CANADA/506-775-6822
Catfish Guns, 900 Jeffco-Executive Park, Imperial, MO 63052/314-464-1217
CBC (See Magtech Recreational Products, Inc.)
Central Ohio Police Supply, c/o Wammes Guns, 225 South Main St., Bellefontaine, OH 43311
Century Gun Dist., Inc., 1467 Jason Rd., Greenfield, IN 46140/317-462-4524
Century Intl. Arms, Inc., 48 Lower Newton St., St. Albans, VT 05478/802-527-1252
Cervera, Albert J., Rt. 1 Box 808, Hanover, VA 23069/804-994-5783
C-H Tool & Die Corp. (See 4-D Die Co.)
Chalmette Jewelry & Guns, 507 W. St. Bernard Hwy., Chalmette, LA 70043/504-279-5585
Chaney Rifle Works, Tinker Street, Waldron, IN 46182/Phone and FAX: 317-525-6181
Chapuis Armes (See Armes de Chasse)
Charlie's Sporting Goods, Inc., 7401-H Menaul Blvd. N.E., Albuquerque, NM 87110/505-884-4545
Charlton Co., Ltd., M.D., Box 153, Brentwood Bay, B.C., CANADA V0S 1A0/604-652-5266
Charter Arms Corp. (CHARCO), 26 Beaver St., Ansonia, CT 06401/203-735-4686/FAX: 203-735-6569

Cheney Firearms Co., 915 E. 1050 N., Bountiful, UT 84010/801-295-4396
Cherry Corners, Inc., 11136 Congress Rd., P.O. Box 38, Lodi, OH 44254/216-948-1238
Cherry's Gun Shop, 302 S. Farmerville St., Ruston, LA 71270/318-255-5678
Chet Paulson Outfitters, 6409 South Sprague, Tacoma, WA 98409/206-475-4868
ChinaSports, Inc., 2010 S. Lynx Pl., Ontario, CA 91761/714-923-1411
Chipmunk (See Oregon Arms, Inc.)
Christopher Firearms Co., Inc., E., Rt. 128 & Ferry St., Miamitown, OH 45041/513-353-1321
Chuck's Gun Shop, Box 9112 Espinosa Rd., Ranchos De Taos, NM 87557/505-758-8594
Chung, Gunsmith, Mel, 8 Ing Rd., Kaunakakai, HI 96748/808-553-5888
Churchill (See Ellett Brothers)
Cimarron Arms (See Uberti USA, Inc.)
Clapps Gun Shop, P.O. Box 578, Orchard Heights, VT 05301/802-254-4663
Claridge Hi-Tec, Inc., 19350 Business Ctr. Dr. Suite 200, Northridge, CA 91324/818-700-9093
Clark Custom Guns, Inc., 11462 Keatchie Rd., Keithville, LA 71047/318-925-0836
Cogdell's, Inc., 615 N. Valley Mills Dr., Waco, TX 76710/817-772-8224
Colabaugh Gunsmith, Inc., Craig, R.D. 4, Box 4168 Gumm St., Stroudsburg, PA 18360/717-992-4499
Coleman, Inc., Ron, 1600 North I-35 #106, Carrollton, TX 75006/214-245-3030
Coliseum Gun Traders, Ltd., 1180 Hempstead Turnpike, Uniondale, NY 11553/718-833-2228
Colt Mfg., Inc., 150 Huyshope Ave., Hartford, CT 06010/203-236-6311
Coonan Arms, Inc., 830 Hampden Ave., St. Paul, MN 55114/612-646-6672
Cooper Arms, 4072 East Side Hwy., Stevensville, MT 59870/800-732-GUNS
Corbin, Inc., 600 Industrial Circle, White City, OR 97503/503-826-5211
Colabaugh, Craig, R.D. #4, Box 4168, Gumm St., Stroudsburg, PA/717-992-4499
Cosmi (See New England Arms Co.)
Covey's Precision Gunsmith, 700 N. Main St., Roswell, NM 88201/505-623-6565
CR Specialty, 1701 Baltimore Ave., Kansas City, MO 64108/816-221-3550
Creekside Gun Shop, East Main Street, Holcomb, NY 14469/716-657-6131
Crosman Airguns (See page 466)
Crosman Corp., Rt. 5 and 20, E. Bloomfield, NY 14443/716-657-6161; FAX: 716-657-5405
Cruceleguia Hermanos (See Mandall Shooting Supplies, Inc.)
Cumberland Arms, Rt. 1, Box 1150, Manchester, TN 37355
Cumberland Knife & Gun Works, 5661 Bragg Blvd., Fayetteville, NC 28303/919-867-0009
Custom Chronograph, Inc., 5305 Reese Hill Rd., Sumas, WA 98295/206-988-7801
Custom Firearms Shop, The, 1133 Indiana Ave., Sheboygan, WI 53081/414-457-3320
Custom Gun Service, 1104 Upas Ave., McAllen, TX 78501/512-686-4670
Custom Gun Shop, 10558 115 St., Edmonton, Alberta, CANADA T5H 3K6/403-426-4417
Custom Gun Works, 4952 Johnston St., Lafayette, LA 70503/318-984-0721
CVA (Connecticut Valley Arms Co.), Customer Service, 5988 Peachtree Corners East, Norcross, GA 30071/404-449-4687
Cylinder & Slide, Inc., 245 E. 4th St. Box 937, Fremont, NE 68025/402-721-4277
CZ (See Action Arms, Ltd.)

D

Daenzer, Charles E., 142 Jefferson Ave., Otisville, MI 48463/313-631-2415
Daewoo Precision Industries, Ltd. (See Firstshot, Inc.)
Daisy Mfg. Co., 2111 South 8th St., Rogers, AR 72756/501-636-1200
Dakota (See EMF Co., Inc.)
Dakota Arms, Inc., HC 55, Box 326, Sturgis, SD 57785/605-347-4686
Dale's Guns & Archery Center, 3915 Eighteenth Ave., S.W., Rochester, MN 55902/507-289-8308
Daly, Charles (See Outdoor Sports Headquarters, Inc.)
Damiano's Field & Stream, 172 N. Highland Ave., Ossining, NY 10562/914-941-6005
Danny's Gun Repair, Inc., 811 East Market St., Louisville, KY 40206/502-583-7100
Darnall's Gun Works, RR #3, Bloomington, IL 61704/309-379-4331
Daryl's Gun Shop, Inc., R.R. #2 Highway 30 West, State Center, IA 50247/515-483-2656
Davco Stores, 305 Broadway, Box 152, Monticello, NY 12701/914-794-5225
Davidson's Canada, 71 Princess Street, Peterborough, Ontario, CANADA K9J 6Z6/705-742-5408
Davis Industries, 15150 Sierra Bonita Ln., Chino, CA 91710/714-591-4726
D&D Sporting Goods, 108 E. Main, Tishomingo, OK 73460/405-371-3571
Dean's Place, Route 41, Box 61, Hockessin, DE 19707/302-239-5959
Deer Creek Rifle Co., Tinker Street, Waldron, IN 46182/317-525-6181
Delhi Small Arms, 22B Argyle Ave., Delhi, Ontario, CANADA N4B 1J3/519-582-0522
Delisle Thompsoon Sport Goods, Ltd., 1814A Loren Ave., Saskatoon, Saskatchewan, CANADA/306-653-2171
Denver Arms, Ltd., P.O. Box 4640, Pagosa Springs, CO 81157/303-731-2295
Denver Instrument Company, 6542 Fig St., Arvada, CO 80004/800-321-1135
Desert Industries, Inc., 3245 E. Patrick Ln., Suite H, Las Vegas, NV 89120/702-597-1066
Destination North Software, 804 Surry Rd., Wenatchee, WA 98801/501-662-6602
D&H Precision Tooling, 7522 Barnard Mill Rd., Ringwood, IL 60072/815-653-4011
Diana (See Dynamit Nobel-RWS, Inc.)
Dillon Precision Prods., Inc., 7442 E. Butherus Dr., Scottsdale, AZ 85260/602-948-8009
Dixie Gun Works, Inc., Hiway 51 S., Union City, TN 38261
D&J Coleman Service, 4811 Guadalupe Ave., Hobbs, NM 88240/505-392-5318
D&L Gunsmithing/Guns & Ammo, 3615 Summer Ave., Memphis, TN 38122/901-327-4384
D&L Shooting Supplies, 2663 W. Shore Rd., Warwick, RI 02886/401-738-1889
D Max Industries, 1701 W. Valley Hwy. N., Auburn, WA 98071/206-939-5137
Dollar Drugs, Inc., 15A West 3rd, Lee's Summit, MO 64063/816-524-7600
Don & Tim's Gun Shop, 3724 Northwest Loop 410 and Fredricksburg, San Antonio, TX 78229/512-736-0263
Don's Gun Shop, 1085 Tunnel Rd., Ashville, NC 28805/704-298-4867
Don's Sport Shop, Inc., 7803 E. McDowell Rd., Scottsdale, AZ 85257/602-946-5313
Don's Sporting Goods, 120 Second Ave. South, Lewiston, MT 59457/406-538-9408
Dorn's Outdoor Center, 4388 Mercer University Drive, Macon, GA 31206/912-474-1991
Down Under Gunsmiths, 318 Driveway, Fairbanks, AK 99701/907-456-8500
Dress Ranch & Home, Inc., 1147 W. Broadway, Moses Lake, WA 98837/509-765-9231
Dubbs, Gunsmith, Dale R., Box 54, Route 1, Hwy. 90, Seminole, AL 36574/205-946-3245
Dundee Custom Gunsmithing, 1501 Oregon Ave., Medford, OR 97504/503-773-1800
Dynamit Nobel-RWS, Inc., 105 Stonehurst Ct., Northvale, NJ 07647/201-767-1995

E

E.A.A. (European American Armory Corp.), 4480 E. 11th Ave., Hialeah, FL 33013
Eagle Arms, Inc., 131 E. 22nd Ave., Coal Valley, IL 61240/309-799-5619
Eagle Imports, Inc., c/o Bolsa Gunsmithing, 7404 Bolsa Ave., Westminster, CA 92683/714-894-9100
Eagle Imports, Inc., c/o Walker Arms Co., 499 Dallas Road 820, Selma, AL 36701/205-872-6231
Ed's Gun & Tackle Shop, Inc., 2727 Canton Rd. (Hwy. 5), Marietta, GA 30066/404-425-8461
Efinger Sporting Goods, 513 W. Union Ave. Rt. 28, Bound Brook, NJ 08805/908-356-0604
Elbe Arms Co., Inc., 610 East 27th St., Cheyenne, WY 82001/307-634-5731
Ellett Bros., Churchill Repairs, 201 Clark St., Chapin, SC 29036/803-345-2199
Emerging Technologies, Inc., 716 Main St., Little Rock, AR 72201
EMF Co., Inc., 1900 East Warner Ave. 1-D, Santa Ana, CA 92705/714-261-6611/FAX: 714-756-0133
Enstad & Douglas, 211 Hedges, Oregon City, OR 97045/503-655-3751
Epps, Ellwood, Highway 11 N. R.R. 3, Orilla, Ontario, CANADA L0K 1G0/705-689-5333
Erma Werke GmbH (See Mandall Shooting Supplies, Inc./PSI, Inc.)
Ernie's Gun Shop, Ltd., 1031 Marion St., Winnipeg, Manitoba, CANADA R2J 0L1/204-233-1928
Euroarms of America, Inc., 208 East Piccadilly, Winchester, VA, 22601/703-662-1863
Europtik, Ltd., 5437 Laurel Canyon Blvd., North Hollywood, CA 91617/818-761-1593
Eversull Gunsmith, Inc., K., 4800 Hwy. 121, Boyce, LA 71409/318-793-8728
Ewell Cross Gun Shop, Inc., 8240 Interstate 30W, Ft. Worth, TX 76108/817-246-4622
Eyster Heritage Gunsmiths, Inc., Ken, 6441 Bishop Rd., Centerburg, OH 43011/614-625-6131

F

Fabarm SpA (See St. Lawrence Sales, Inc.)
Fabrica D'Armi Sabatti S.R.L. (See E.A.A. Corp.)
Famas (See Century International Arms, Inc.)
FAS (See Nygord Precision Products)
Fausti & Figlie s.n.c., Stefano (See American Arms, Inc.)
F&D Guns, 5140 Westwood Drive, Harvester, MO 63303/314-441-5897
Feather Industries, Inc., 2300 Central Ave. #K, Boulder, CO 80301/303-442-7021
Federal Eng. Corp., 2335 S. Michigan Ave., Chicago, IL 60616/312-842-1063
Federal Firearms Co., Inc., Box 145, Thom's Run Rd., Oakdale, PA 15071/412-221-0300
Federal Ordnance, 1443 Potrero Ave., So. El Monte, CA 91733/818-350-4161
FEG (See Century International Arms, Inc./K.B.I., Inc.)
Felton, James, Custom Gunsmith, 1033 Elizabeth St., Eugene, OR 97402/503-689-1687
FERLIB (See New England Arms Co./Quality Arms, Inc.)
Fiocchi of America, Nygord Precision Products, 15735 Starthern Unit 5, Van Nuys, CA 91406/818-352-3027
Firearms Co. Ltd./Alpine (See Mandall Shooting Supplies, Inc.)
Firearms Repair & Refinish Shoppe, 639 Hoods Mill Rd., Woodbine, MD 21797/301-795-5859
Firearms Service Center, 2140 Old Shepherdsville Rd., Louisville, KY 40218/502-458-1148
Firearms Unlimited, Inc., 4360 Corporate Square, Naples, FL 33942/813-643-2922
Firstshot, Inc., 4101 Far Green Rd., Harrisburg, PA 17110/717-238-2575
Fix Gunshop, Inc., Michael D., R.D. 11, Box 192, Reading, PA 19607/215-775-2067
Flaig's Inc., 2200 Evergreen Rd., Pittsburgh, PA 15209/412-821-1717
Flintrop Arms Corp., 4034 W. National Ave. West, Milwaukee, WI 53215/414-383-2626
Foothills Shooting Center, 7860 W. Jewell Ave., Lakewood, CO 80226/303-985-4417
Forster Products, Inc., 82 E. Lanark Ave., Lanark, IL 61046/815-493-6360/FAX: 815-493-2371
4-D Die Co./C-H Tool & Die, 711 N. Sandusky St., Mount Vernon, OH 43050/614-397-7214/FAX: 614-397-6600
Four Seasons, 76 R Winn St., Woburn, MA 01801/617-932-3133/3255
Fox & Company, 2211 Dutch Valley Rd., Knoxville, TN 37918/615-687-7411
Franchi S.p.A., Luigi (See American Arms, Inc.)
Francotte & CIE S.A., Auguste (See Armes de Chasse)
Franklin Sports, Inc., 575 Hawthorne Ave., Athens, GA 30606/404-543-7803
Fred's Gun Shop, 1364 Ridgewood Dr., Mobile, AL 36608/205-344-1079
Freedom Arms Reworks Dept., #1 Freedom Ln., Freedom, WY 83120
Freer's Gun Shop, Building B-1, 8928 Spring Branch Drve, Houston, TX 77080/713-467-3016
Fremont Tool Works, 1214 Praire, Ford, KS 67842/316-369-2338 (after 5 p.m.)
Fricano, Gunsmith, J., 15258 Moreland, Grand Haven, MI 49417/616-846-4458
Friedman's Army Surplus, 2617 Nolenville Rd., Nashville, TN 37211/615-244-1653
Frontier Gun & Sport, 9 Canbero Road West, Font Hill, Ontario, CANADA L0S 1E0/416-892-6962
Frontiersman's Sports, 6925 Wayzeta Blvd., Minneapolis, MN 55426/612-544-3775
FWB (Feinwerkbau) (See Beeman Precision Airguns, Inc.)

G

Galaxy Imports Ltd., Inc., 303 Sherwood, Victoria, TX 77901
Gamba U.S.A., 925 Wilshire Blvd., Santa Monica, CA 90401/310-917-2255/FAX: 310-917-2253
Gamo (See Daisy Mfg. Co./Dynamit Nobel-RWS, Inc.)
Gander Mountain, Inc., P.O. Box 128, Highway W, Wilmot, WI 53192/414-862-2331
Garbi, Armas Urki (See Moore & Co., William Larkin)
Garfield Gunsmithing, 237 Wessington Ave., Garfield, NJ 07026/201-478-0171
Garrett Gunsmiths, Inc., Peter, 838 Monmouth St., Newport, KY 41071-1821/606-261-1855
Gart Brothers Sporting Goods, 1000 Broadway, Denver, CO 80203/303-861-1122
Gary's Gun Shop, 700 S. Minnesota Ave., Sioux Falls, SD 57104/605-332-6119
Gat Guns, 14N 915 Route 25, East Dundee, IL 60118/708-428-4867
Gaucher Armes S.A. (See Mandall Shooting Supplies, Inc.)
Geake & Son, Inc., 23510 Woodward Ave., Ferndale MI 48220/313-542-0498
Gemini Arms Ltd., 324 Jackson Ave., Syosset, NY 11791/516-921-0134
Gene's Gunsmithing, Box 34 GRP 326 R.R. 3, Selkirk, Manitoba, CANADA R1A 2A8/204-757-2003
Gene Taylor's Sportsman Supply, Inc., 445 W. Gunnison Ave., Grand Junction, CO 81505/303-242-8165
GFR Corp., Rt. 11, Andover, NH 03216/603-735-5300
G.H. Gun Shop, 323 W. "B" St., McCook, NE 69001/308-345-1250
Gibbs Rifle Company, Inc., R.R. #2, Box 214, Hoffman Rd., Cannon Hill Industrial Park, Martinsburg, WV 25401/304-274-0458
G.I. Loan Shop, 1004 W. Second St., Grand Island, NE 68801/308-382-9573
Gilman-Mayfield, 1552 N. 1st, Fresno, CA 93703/209-237-2500
Girard, Florent, Gunsmith, 598 Verreault, Chicoutimi, Quebec, CANADA G7H 2B8/418-696-3329
Glenn's Reel & Rod Repair, 2210 E. 9th St., Des Moines, IA 50316/515-262-2990
Glock, Gesell Schaft m.b.h., P.O. Box 50, A-2232 Deutsch-Wagram, Austria (International)
Glock, Inc., 6000 Highlands Pkwy, Smyrna, GA 30082/404-447-4466
Gonic Arms, Inc., 134 Flagg Rd., Gonic, NH 03867/603-332-8456
Gordon's Wigwam, 501 S. St. Francis, Wichita, KS 67202/316-264-5311

Gorenflo Gunsmithing, 1821 State St., Erie, PA 16501/814-452-4855
Great Lakes Airguns, 6175 S. Park Ave., Hamburg, NY 14075/716-648-6666
Green Acres Sporting Goods, Inc., 8774 Normandy Blvd., Jacksonville, FL 32221/904-786-5166
Greene's Gun Shop, 4778 Monkey Hill Rd., Oak Harbor, WA 98277/206-675-3421
Grenada Gun Works, Hwy. 8 East, Grenada, MS 38901/601-226-9272
Grendel, Inc., 550 St. Johns St., Cocoa, FL 32922
Grice Gun Shop, Inc., 216 Reed St., P.O. 2028, Clearfield, PA 16830/814-765-9273
Griffiths & Sons, E.J., 1014 N. McCullough St., Lima OH 45801/419-228-2141
Grulla Armes (See American Arms, Inc./Hanus Birdguns, Bill)
Grundman's, Inc., 75 Wildwood Ave., Rio Dell, CA 95562/707-764-5744
G&S Gunsmithing, 220 N. Second St., Eldridge, IA 52748/319-285-4153
GSI, Inc., 108 Morrow Ave., Trussville, AL 35173/205-655-8299
G.U. Inc., 4325 S. 120th, Omaha, NE 68137/402-330-4492/FAX: 402-330-8029
Gun Ace Gunsmithing, 3395 So. 5175 West, P.O. Box 1606, Cedar City, UT 84721/801-586-7421
Gun Center, The, 5733 Buckeystown Pike, Frederick, MD 21701/301-694-6887
Gun City, Inc., 212 West Main, Bismarck, ND 58501/701-223-2304
Gun City USA, Inc., 573 Murfreesboro Rd., Nashville, TN 37210/615-256-6127
Gun Corral, The, 2827 East College Ave., Decatur, GA 30030/404-299-0288
Gun Doc, Inc., 5405 N.W. 82nd Ave., Miami, FL 33166/305477-2777
Gun Exchange, Inc., 5317 W. 65th St., Little Rock, AR 72209/501-562-4668
Gun Hospital, The, 45 Vineyard Ave., E. Providence, RI 02914/401-438-3495
Gun Parts Corp., P.O. Box 2, West Hurley, NY 12491/914-679-2417
Gun Rack, Inc., The, 213 Richland Ave., Aiken, SC 29801/803-648-7100
Gun Room, The, 201 Clark St., Chapin, SC 29036/803-345-2199
Gun Shop, Inc., The, 8945 Biscayne Blvd., Miami Shores, FL 33138/305-757-1422
Gun Shop, The, 5550 South 900 East, Salt Lake City, UT 84117/801-263-3633
Gun South, Inc. (See GSI, Inc.)
Gun & Stuff, Inc., 3055 N. Broadway, Wichita, KS 67219/316-838-2448
Gun & Tackle Store, The, 6041 Forrest Ln., Dallas, TX 75230/214-239-8181
Gun Works, The, 4325 S. 120th St., Omaha, NE 68127/402-339-2249
Gunshop, Inc., The, 44633 N. Sierra Hwy., Lancaster CA 93534/805-942-8377
Gunsmith, The, 2205 Nord Ave., Chico, CA 95926/916-343-4550
Gunsmith Co., The, 3435 S. State St., Salt Lake City, UT 84115/801-467-8244
Gunsmith, Inc., The, 1410 Sunset Blvd., West Columbia, SC 29169/803-791-0250
Gunsmithing Limited, 57 Unquowa Rd., Fairfield, CT 06430/203-254-0436
Gunsmithing Specialties, Co., 110 North Washington St., Papillion, NE 68046/402-339-1222
Gun World, 392 Fifth Street, Elko, NV 89801/702-458-3330
Gustaf, Carl (See PSI, Inc.)

H

Hagstrom, E.G., 2008 Janis Dr., Memphis, TN 38116/910-398-5333
Hallowell & Co., 340 West Putnum Ave., Greenwich, CT 006830/203-869-2190/FAX: 203-869-0692
Hal's Gun Supply, 505 Main Ave., Cullman, AL 35055/205-734-7546
Hammerli (See Hammerli-U.S.A./Marent, Rudolph)
Hammerli-U.S.A., 19296 Oak Grove Circle, Groveland, CA 95321/209-962-5311
Hampel's, Inc., 710 Randolph, Traverse City, MI 49684/616-946-5485
Hanus, Bill, P.O. Box 533, Newport, OR 97365
Harrington & Richardson (See Gun Parts Corp./parts only)
Harry's Army & Navy Store, 691 NJSH Rt. 130, Robbinsville, NJ 08691/609-585-5450
Hart & Son, Robert W., 401 Montgomery Street, Nescopeck, PA 18635/717-752-3655
Hart's Gun Supply, Ed, U.S. Route 15 N., Bath, NY 14810/607-776-4228
Haskell Mfg., Inc, 399 Lester Ave., Lima, OH 45801/419-225-8297
Hatfield Gun Co., Inc., 224 N. 4th St., St. Joseph, MO 64501/816-279-8688
Hawken Shop, The, P.O. Box 593, Oak Harbor, WA 98277/206-679-4657/FAX: 206-675-1114
Heckler & Koch, Inc., 21480 Pacific Blvd., Sterling, VA 22170/703-450-1900
Heckman Arms Company, Chagrin Valley Firearms, 32 N. Main St, Chagrin, OH 44022/216-289-9182
Helwan (See Interarms)
Hemlock Gun Shop, Box 149, Rt. 590 W., Lakeville, PA 18438/717-226-9410
Hemlock Gun Shop, Star Rt. 1, Box 128, Hawley, PA 18428/717-226-9410
Henry's Airguns, 1204 W. Locust, Belvidere, IL 61008/815-547-5091
Herold's Gun Shoppe, 1498 E. Main Street, Box 350, Waynesboro, PA 17268/717-762-4010
Heym GmbH & Co. (See JägerSport Ltd./Swarovski Optik North America Ltd.)
Hill's Hardware & Sporting Goods, 1234 S. Second St., Union City, TN 38261/901-885-1510
Hill's, Inc., 1720 North Blvd., Raleigh, NC 27604/919-833-4884
Hobb's Bicycle & Gun Sales, 406 E. Broadway, Hobbs, NM 88240/505-393-9815
Hodson & Son Pell Gun Repair, 4500 S. 100 E., Anderson, IN 46013/317-643-2055
Hoffman's Gun Center, Inc., 2600 Berlin Turnpike, Newington, CT 06111/203-666-8827
Hollywood Engineering (M&M Engineering), 10642 Arminta St., Sun Valley, CA 91352/818-842-8376
Holmes Firearms Corp., Bill Holmes, 1100 E. Township, Fayetteville, AR 72703
Horchler's Gun Shop, Ratlum Mt. Rd. RFD PO, Collinsville, CT 06022/203-379-1977
Hornady Manufacturing Co., 3625 Old Potash Hwy., Grand Island, NE 68802/308-382-1390/800-338-3220
Houma Gun Works, 1520 Grand Caillou Rd., Houma, LA 70363/504-872-2782
Howa Machinery, Ltd. (See Interarms/Weatherby Inc.)
H&R 1871, Inc., Service Dept., Industrial Rowe, Gardner, MA 01440
H-S Precision, Inc., 1301 Turbine Dr., Rapid City, SD 57701/605-341-3006
Huntington Die Specialties, 601 Oro Dam Blvd., Oroville, CA 95965/916-534-1210/FAX: 916-534-1212
Huntington Sportsman's Store, 601 Oro Dam Blvd., P.O. Box 991, Oroville, CA 95965/916-534-8000
Hutchinson's Gun Repair, 507 Clifton St., Pineville, LA 71360/318-640-4315
Hutch's, 50 E. Main St., Lehi, UT 84043/801-768-3461

I

IAI (See AMT)
Iberia Firearms, Inc., 3929 S.R. 309, Galion, OH 44833/419-468-3746
IGA (See Stoeger Industries)
IMI/Desert Eagle (See Magnum Research, Inc.)
Imatronic, Inc., 1275 Paramount Pkwy., Batavia, IL 60510/708-406-1920

Imbert & Smithers, Inc., 1148 El Camino Real, San Carlos, CA 94070/415-593-4207
Incor, Inc., P.O. Box 132, Addison, TX 75001/214-931-3500
INDESAL (See American Arms, Inc.)
Interarms, 10 Prince St., Alexandria, VA 22314/703-548-1400
Intermountain Arms & Tackle, Inc., 105 East Idaho St., Meridian, ID 83642/208-888-4911
Intratec, 12405 SW 130th St., Miami, FL 33186/FAX: 305-253-7207
Ithaca Aquisition Corp./Ithaca Gun Co., 891 Route 34B, King Ferry, NY 13081/315-364-7171
Iver Johnson, 2202 Redmond Rd., Jacksonville, AR 72076/501-982-1633

J

Jackalope Gun Shop, 1048 South 5th St., Douglas, WY 82633/307-358-3441
Jack First Distributors, 44633 Sierra Highway, P.O. Box 542, Lancaster, CA 93534/805-945-6981
Jack's Lock & Gun Shop, 32 4th St., Fond Du Lac, WI 54935/414-922-4420
Jackson, Inc., Bill, 9501 U.S. 19 N., Pinellas Park, FL 34666/813-576-4169
Jacobson's Gun Center, 607 Broad Street, Story City, IA 50248/515-733-2995
Jaeger, Inc., Paul/Dunn's, 1 Madison Ave., Grand Junction, TN 38039/901-764-6909
JägerSports Ltd., One Wholesale Way, Cranston, RI 02920/401-944-9682; FAX: 401-946-2587
Jason Empire, Inc., 9200 Cody, Overland Park, KS 66214/913-888-0220
Jay's Sports, Inc., North 88 West 15263 Main St., Menomonee Falls, WI 53051/414-251-0550
Jennings Firearms, Inc., 17692 Cowen, Irvine, CA 92714/714-252-7621; FAX: 714-252-7626
Jensen's Custom Ammunition/Lathrops Shooting Supplies, 5146 E. Pima, Tuscon, AZ 85712/602-325-3346
J&G Gunsmithing, 625 Vernon St., Roseville, CA 95678/916-782-7075
Jim's Gun & Service Center, 514 Tenth Ave. S.E., Aberdeen, SD 57401/605-225-9111
Jim's Sporting Goods, 1307 Malcolm Ave., Newport, AR 72112/501-523-5165
Jim's Trading Post, #10 Southwest Plaza, Pine Bluff, AR 71603/501-534-8591
J.O. Arms & Ammunition Co., 5709 Hartsdale, Huston, TX 77036/713-789-0745/FAX: 713-789-7513
Joe's Gun Shop, 4430 14th St., Dorr, MI 49323/616-877-4615
Joe's Gun Shop, 5215 W. Edgemont Ave., Phoenix, AZ 85035/602-233-0694
John Q's Quality Gunsmithing, 5165 Auburn Blvd., Sacramento, CA 95841/916-344-7669
Johnson Gunsmithing, Don, N15515 Country Rd. 566, Powers, MI 49874/906-497-5757
Johnson, Iver (See AMAC)
Johnson Service, Inc., W., 3654 N. Adrian Rd., Adrian, MI 49221/517-265-2545
Jordan Gun & Pawn Shop, Rt. 3, Box 19, Tifton, GA 31794/912-382-4251
Jordan Gun Shop, 28 Magnolia Dr., Tifton, GA 31794/912-382-4251
Jovino Co., Inc., John, 5 Center Market Pl., New York, NY 10013/212-925-4881
JSL, Ltd. (See Specialty Shooters Supply, Inc.)
J.T. Gunshop, Inc., d/b/a Carolina Gun & Sports, 145 Dexter Ave., Beckley, WV 25801/304-256-1217
Junior's Gun & Lock Shop, 100 E. Grand St., Ponca City, OK 74601/405-762-4553

K

Kahles Scopes, c/o Swarovski Optik, One Wholesale Way, Cranston, RI 02920/401-942-3380
Karrer's Gunatorium, 5323 N. Argonne Rd., Spokane, WA 99212/509-924-3030
Kassnar (See K.B.I., Inc.)
K.B.I., Inc., 5398 Linglestown Rd., Harrisburg, PA 17112/717-540-4645/FAX: 717-540-5801
KDF, Inc., 2485 Hwy. 46 N., Seguin, TX 78155/512-379-8141
Keeley, John L., 679 Ridge Rd., Spring City, PA 19475/215-495-6874
Keidel's Gunsmithing Service, 927 Jefferson Ave., Washington, PA 15301/412-222-6379
Keller Gunsmithing, 147 N. Miami Ave., Bradford, OH 45308/513-448-2424
Keller's Co., Inc., Rt. 4, Box 1257, Burlington, CT 06013/203-583-2220
Keng's Firearms Specialty, Inc., 875 Wharton Drive SW, Atlanta, GA 30336/404-691-7611/FAX: 404-505-8445
Kesselring Gun Shop, 400 Pacific Hwy., 99 North, Burlington, WA 98233/206-724-3113
Kick's Sport Center, 300 Goodge St., Claxton, GA 30417/912-739-1734
Kimel Industries, P.O. Box 335, Matthews, NC 28106/704-821-7663
King's Gun Shop, Inc., Rt. 1 Box 78, Franklin, VA 23851/804-562-4725
King's Gun Works, Inc., 1837 W. Glenoaks Blvd., Glendale, CA 91201/818-956-6010
Kintrek, Owensboro, KY/502-686-8137
Kirkpatrick, Gunsmith, Larry, 707 79th St., Lubbock, TX 79404/806-745-5308
Klelon, Gunsmith, Dave, 57 Kittleberger Park, Webster, NY 14580/716-872-2256
K&M Services, 2525 Primrose Lane, York, PA 17404/717-764-1461
Kopp, Professional Gunsmith, Terry K., Hwy. 13, Lexington, MO 64067/816-259-2636
Korth (See Mandall Shooting Supplies, Inc.)
Kotila Gun Shop, Rt. #2, Box 212, Cokato, MN 55321/612-286-5636
Kowa Optimed, Inc., 20001 S. Vermont Ave., Torrance, CA 90502/310-327-1913/800-966-5692
Krebs Gunsmithing, 7417 N. Milwaukee Ave., Niles, IL 60714/708-647-6994
Krico/Kriegeskorte GmbH, A. (See Mandall Shooting Supplies, Inc.)
Krieghoff International, Inc., Customer Service Manager, 7528 Easton Road, Ottsville, PA 18942/215-847-5173

L

La Armeria Metropolitana In, Ave Dediego 799 Capparra, San Juan, Puerto Rico 00921/809-782-6378
Labs Air Gun Shop, 2307 N. 62nd St., Omaha, NE 68104/402-553-0990
Lafayette Shooters, 3530 Amb Caffrey Parkway, Lafayette, LA 70503/318-988-1191
Laibs Gunsmithing, North Hwy. 23, R.R. 1, Spicer, MN 56288/612-796-2686
Lakefield Arms Ltd., Taylors Service Center, RR #1, Box 112, Mokane, MO 65059/314-676-5675
Lakefield Arms Ltd., c/o The Gun Room, 201 Clark St., Chapin, SC 29036/803-345-2199
L.A.R. Manufacturing, Inc., 4133 W. Farm Rd., West Jordan, UT 84088/801-255-7106
L'Armurier Alain Bouchard, Inc., 293 Rue Notre Dame, St. Chryostome Quebec J0S 1R0 CANADA
Laser Devices, Inc., 2 Harris Ct., A4, Monterey, CA 93940
Lawsons Custom Firearms, Inc., Art, 313 S. Magnolia Ave., Ocala, FL 32671/904-629-7793
Lee Precision, Inc., 4275 Hwy. U, Hartford, WI 53027/414-673-3075

LeFever & Sons, Inc., Frank, RD 1, Lee Center, NY 13363/315-337-6722

Leo's Custom Stocks, 1767 Washington Ave., Library, PA 15129/412-835-4126

Les Gun & Tackle Shop, 1423 New Boston Rd., Texarkana, TX 75501/214-793-2201

Leupold, 600 NW Meadow Dr., Beaverton, OR 97006/503-646-9171

Levan's Sport Goods, 433 N. Ninth St., Lebanon, PA 17042/717-273-3148

Lewis Arms at Riley's, 1575 Hooksett Rd., Hooksett, NH 03106/603-485-7334

Lew's Mountaineer Gunsmithing, Route 2, Box 330A, Charleston, WV 25314/304-344-3745

Ljutic Industries, Inc., 732 N. 16th Ave., Suite #22, Yakima, WA 98902/509-248-0476

Ljutic Industries, Inc., Paul's Gun Shop, 307 S. Riverview Dr., E. Peoria, IL 61611

Llama (See SGS Importers International, Inc.)

L&M Firing Line, Inc., 20 S. Potomac St., Aurora, CO 80012/303-363-0041

Lock Stock & Barrel, 775 S.E. 6th St. (rear), Grants Pass, OR 97526/503-474-0775

Loftin & Taylor, 2619 N. Main St., Jacksonville, FL 32206/904-353-9634

Log Cabin Sport Shop, 8010 Lafayette Rd., Rt. 1, Lodi, OH 44254/216-948-1082

Lolo Sporting Goods, 1026 Main St., Lewiston, ID 83501/208-743-1031

Lone Star Guns, Inc., 2452 Avenue "K", Plano, TX 75074/214-424-4501

Longacres, Inc., 358 Chestnut St., Abilene, TN 79602/915-672-9521

Long Beach Uniform Co., Inc., 2789 Long Beach Blvd., Long Beach, CA 90806/213-424-0220

Long Gunsmithing Ltd., W.R., 2007 Brook Rd. North, Coburg, Ontario CANADA K9A 4W4/416-372-5955

Longs Gunsmiths, Ltd., W.R., P.O. Box 876, Cobourg, CANADA K9A 4S3/416-372-5955

Lorcin Engineering Co., Inc., 10427 San Sevaine Way Unit A, Mira Loma, CA 91752/714-360-1406/FAX:714-360-0623

Lounsbury Sporting Goods, Bob, 104 North St., Middletown, NY 10940/914-343-1808

L&S Technologies, Inc., P.O. Box 223, 101 Inwood Acres, Thomasville, GA 31792/Phone and FAX: 912-226-4313

Lusignant Armurier, A. Richard, 15820 St. Michel, St. Hyacinthe, Quebec, CANADA, J2T 3R7/514-773-7997

Lutter, Robert E., 3547 Auer Dr., Ft. Wayne, IN 46835/219-485-8319

Lyman (Blackpowder Products Only), Dixon Muzzle Loading, RD 1, Box 175, Kempton, PA 19529

Lyman Products Corp., 147 West St., Middlefield, CT 06455/203-349-3421

M

Mac-1, 13972 VanNess, Gardena, CA 90249/213-327-3581

Magasin Latulippe, Inc., 637 St. Vallier O, P.O. Box 395, Quebec, CANADA G1K 6W8/418-529-0024

Magma Engneering, ¼ Mile East of Ellsworth on Ocotillo Rd., Queen Creek, AZ 85242/602-987-9008

Magnum Gun Service, 357 Welsh Track Rd., Newark, DE 19702/302-454-0141

Magnum Research, Inc., 7110 University Ave. NE, Minneapolis, MN 55432/612-574-1868

Magtech Recreational Products, Las Vegas, NV 89119/702-795-7191

Mandall Shooting Supplies, 3616 N. Scottsdale Rd., Scottsdale, AZ 85252/602-945-2553

Mannlicher (See GSI, Inc.)

Marble Arms Corp., 420 Industrial Park, Gladstone, MI 49837/906-428-3710

Marent, Rudolph, 9711 Tiltree St., Houston, TX 77075/713-946-7028

Marine Gun & Lock Shop, 1525 Piney Green Rd., Jacksonville, NC 28546/919-353-9114

Marksman Products, 5482 Argosy Dr., Huntington Beach, CA 92649/714-898-7535

Marlin Firearms Co., 100 Kenna Dr., North Haven, CT 06473

Marlin Service Dept., Howards Gun Shop, 100 E. International Airport Rd., Anchorage, AK 99501/907-562-3030

Marlin Service Dept., Mel Chung, Gunsmith, #8 Ing Rd., Kaunakaki, HI 96748/808-553-5888

Marocchi F.lli S.p.A. (See PSI, Inc./Sile Distributors)

Marshall Gun Shop, 1345 Chambers Rd., Dellwood, MO 63135/314-522-8359

Martin Gun Shop, Henry, 206 Kay Lane, Shreveport, LA 71115/318-797-1119

Martins Gun Shop, 3600 Laurel Ave., Natchez, MS 39120/601-442-0784

Mashburn Arms Co., Inc., 1218-20 North Pennsylvania Ave., Oklahoma City, OK 73107/405-236-5151

Master Gunsmiths, Inc., 21621 Ticonderoga, Houston, TX 77044/713-459-1631

Matt's 10K Gunsmithing, Inc., 5906 Castle Rd., Duluth, MN 55803/218-721-4210

Mauser (See Precision Imports, Inc.)

Maverick Arms, Inc., Industrial Blvd., Eagle Pass, TX 78853/512-773-9007

May & Company, Inc., P.O. Box 1111, 838 W. Capitol St., Jackson, MS 39209/601-354-5781

McBride's Guns, Inc., 2915 San Gabriel, Austin, TX 78705/512-472-3532

McClelland Gun Shop, 1533 Centerville Rd., Dallas, TX 75228-2597/214-321-0231

McDaniel Co., Inc., B., 8880 Pontiac Tr., P.O. Box 119, South Lyon, MI 48178/313-437-8989

McGuns, W.H., Central Ave. & 2215 Osborn St., Humboldt, TN 38343/901-784-5742

McMillan Gunworks, Inc., 302 W. Melinda Dr., Phoenix, AZ 85027/602-582-9627/FAX: 602-582-5178

MCS, Inc., 34 Delmar Dr., Brookfield, CT 06804/203-775-1013; FAX: 203-775-9462

MEC (Mayville Engineering Co.), 715 South St., Mayville, WI 53050/414-387-4500

Merkel Freres (See GSI, Inc./Hanus Birdguns, Bill)

Merrill Pistol (See RPM)

Metro Rod & Reel, 236 S.E. Grand Ave., Portland, OR 97214/503-232-3193

Meydag, Peter, 12114 East 16th, Tulsa, OK 74128/918-437-1928

Miclean, Bill, 499 Theta Ct., San Jose, CA 95123/408-224-1445

Midwest Sport Distributors, Box 129, Fayette, MO 65248

Midwest Sporting Goods Co., Inc., 8565 Plainfield Rd., Lyons, IL 60534/708-447-4848

Midwestern Shooters Supply, Inc., 150 Main St., Lomira, WI 53048/414-269-4995

Mike's Crosman Service, 5995 Renwood Dr., Winston-Salem, NC 27106/919-922-1031

Millers Gun Shop, 915 23rd St., Gulfport, MS 39501/601-864-1765

Miller's Gun Shop, 1009 N. 9th St., Stroudsburg, PA 18360/717-424-5540

Miller's Sport Shop, 2 Summit View Dr., Mountaintop, PA 18707/717-474-6931

Millie "D" Enterprises, 1241 W. Calle Concordia, Tucson, AZ 85737/602-297-4887

Milliken's Gun Shop, Rt. 4, Box 167, Elm Grove, WV 26003/304-242-0827

Mines Gun Shack, Rt. 4 Box 4623, Tullahoma, TN 37388/615-455-1414

Mirador Optical Corp., 4051 Glencoe Ave., Marina Del Rey, CA 90292/310-821-5587

Miroku, B.C./Daly, Charles (See Bell's Legendary Country Wear/British Sporting Arms/Outdoor Sports Headquarters)

Mitchell Arms, Inc., 3400-I W. MacArthur Blvd., Suite I, Santa Ana, CA 92704/714-957-5711 (Rifles only)

MK Arms, Inc., P.O. Box 16411, Irvine, CA 92713/714-261-2767

MKS Supply (See Stallard, Haskell, Iberia)

M&M Engineering (See Hollywood Engineering)

M.O.A. Corp., 175 Carr Dr., Brookville, OH 45309/513-833-5559

Moates Sport Shop, Bob, 10418 Hull St. Rd., Midlothian, VA 23113/804-276-2293

Modern Guncraft, 148 N. Branford Rd., Collinsville, CT 06492/203-265-1015

Modern Muzzleloading, Inc., 234 Airport Rd., Centerville, IA 52544/515-856-2623

Moneymaker Gun Craft, Inc., 1420 Minitary Ave., Omaha, NE 68131/402-556-0226

Montana Armory, Inc., 100 Centennial Dr., Big Timber, MT 59011/406-932-4353

Montana Gun Works, 3017 10th Ave. S., Great Falls, MT 59405/406-761-4346

Moore & Co., William Larkin, c/o Freddie Bruner, 1610 Friendship Lane, Escondido, CA 92026/619-738-8413

Moore & Co., William Larkin, c/o Ken Eversull, Tracemont Farms, 4800 Hwy 121, Boyce, LA 71409/318-793-8728

Moore & Co., William Larkin, c/o John F. Rowe, 2501 Rockwood Rd., Box 86, Enid, OK 73702/405-233-5942

Moreau, Gunsmith, Pete, 1296 Orchard Rd., Essexville, MI 48732

Morini (See Nygord Precision Products)

Morrison, Carl Bill, Middle Rd., Bradford, ME 04410/207-327-1116

Mossberg & Sons, O.F. (See page 466)

Mowrey Gun Works, Tinker Street, Waldron, IN 46182/Phone and FAX: 317-525-6181

Mueschke Manufacturing Co., 1003 Columbia St., Houston, TX 77008/713-869-7073

Mulvey's Marine & Sport Shop, 994 E. Broadway, Monticello, NY 12701/914-794-2000

N

N.A. Guns, Inc., 10220 Florida Blvd., Baton Rouge, LA 70815/504-272-3620

Nagel Gun Shop, Inc., 6201 San Pedro Ave., San Antonio, TX 78216/512-342-5420/512-342-9893

Navy Arms Co., 689 Bergen Blvd., Ridgefield, NJ 07657/201-945-2500

Nelson's Engine Shop, 620 State St., Cedar Falls, IA 50613/319-266-4497

Nevada Air Guns, 3297 "J" Las Vegas Blvd. N., N. Las Vegas, NV 89115/702-643-8532

New Advantage Arms Corp., Inc., 7545 University Ave., La Mesa, CA 91941/619-589-8565

Newby, Stewart, Gunsmith, Main & Cross Streets, New Burgh, Ontario CANADA K0K 2S0/613-378-6613

New England Arms, Co., 60 Industrial Rowe, Gardner, MA 01440/508-632-9393 FAX: 508-632-2300

New England Firearms Co., Inc. (See H&R 1871)

New England Firearms, c/o Walker Arms, Highway 80 West-Route #2, Selma, AL 36701/205-872-6231

Nichols Sports Optics (See G.U. Inc.)

Nicholson's Gunsmithing, 35 Center St., Shelton, CT 06484/203-924-5635

Nikon, Inc., Repair Dept., 19601 Hamilton Ave., Torrance, CA 90502

Norckauer Assoc., 10220 Florida Blvd., Baton Rouge, LA 70815/504-272-3620

Norica (See American Arms, Inc./K.B.I., Inc.)

Norinco (See Century International Arms, Inc./China Sports, Inc./Interarms/Midwest Sport Distributors/Sportarms of Florida)

North American Arms, 1800 North 300 West, Spanish Fork, UT 84660/801-798-7401

Northern Precision Airguns, 1161 Grove St., Tawas City, MI 48763/517-362-6944

Northern Virginia Gun Works, Inc., 7518-K Fullerton Road, Springfield, VA 22153/703-644-6504

Northland Sport Center, 1 Mile W. on U.S. 2, Bagley, MN 56621/218-694-2464

Northwest Arms Service, 720 S. Second St., Atwood, KS 67730/913-626-3700

Nu-Line Guns, Inc., 1053 Caulks Hill Rd., Harvester, MO 63303/314-441-4500/314-447-4501

Nusbaum Enterprises, Inc., 1364 Ridgewood Dr., Mobile, AL 38808/205-344-1079

Nygord Precision Products, 6278 Hamilton Lane, La Crescenta, CA 91214/Phone and FAX: 818-352-3027

O

Oakland Custom Arms, 4690 W. Walton Blvd., Waterford, MI 48329/313-674-8261

Oehler Research, Inc., 1308 Barclay, Austin, TX 78746/512-327-6900

Old Dominion Engraver, Inc., 100 Progress Dr., Lynchburg, VA 24502/804-237-4450 Ext. 17

Old West Arms, 7024 West ColFAX: Ave., Lakewood, CO 80215/303-232-1423

Old Western Scrounger, Inc., 12924 Hwy. A-12, Montague, CA 96064/916-459-5445

Olympic Arms, Inc. (See Safari Arms/SGW)

On Target Gunshop, Inc., 6984 West Main St., Kalamazoo, MI 49009/616-375-4570

Oregon Arms, Inc., 165 Schulz Rd., Central Point, OR 97502/503-664-5586

Oshman's Sporting Goods, Inc., 7729 Westheimer, Houston, TX 77029/713-780-3235

Ott's Gun Service, Rt. 2, Box 169A, Atmore, AL 36502/205-862-2588

Ott's Gunsmith Service, RR 1, Box 259, Decatur, IL 62526/217-875-3468

Outdoor America Store, 1925 N. MacArthur Blvd., Oklahoma City, OK 73127/405-789-0051

Outdoor Sports Headquarters, Inc., 967 Watertower Ln., Dayton, OH 45449/513-865-5855

Outdoorsman Sporting Goods Co., The, 105 W. State St., Geneva, IL 60134/312-232-4680

Outdoorsman, Inc., Village West Shopping Center, Fargo, ND 58103/701-282-0131

Outers Operation, N5549 CTH Z, P.O. Box 39, OnAlaska, WI 54650

Outpost, The, 2451 E. Maple Rapids Rd., Eureka, MI 58833/517-224-9562

P

Pachmayr, Ltd., 1875 South Mountain Ave., Monrovia, CA 91016/818-357-7771

Pacific International Service Co., Mountain Way, P.O. Box 3, Janesville, CA 96114/916-253-2218

P.A.C.T., Inc., P.O. Box 531525, Grand Prairie, TX 75050/214-641-0049

Paducah Shooters Supply, Inc., 3919 Cairo St., Paducah, KY 42001/502-443-3758

Para-Ordnance Mfg., Inc., C.S.G.S., Inc., Rd 1, Main Street, Holcomb, NY 14469/716-657-6131

Para-Ordnance Mfg., Inc., P.I.S.C.O., Inc., Mountain Way, Janesville, CA 96114/916-253-2218

Pardini Armi Commerciale S.r.l. (See MCS, Inc.)

Parker-Hale (See Navy Arms Co.)

Parker Reproductions, 124 River Rd., Middlesex, NJ 08846

Pasadena Gun Center, 206 East Shaw, Pasadena, TX 77506/713-472-0417

Paschall's, 709 Walston, Kingston, NC 28501/919-527-4135

Pearson's Gun Shop, 408 Owasco Rd., Auburn, NY 13021/315-252-4840

Pedersoli Davide & C. (See Beauchamp & Son, Inc./Dixie Gun Works/EMF Co., Inc./Navy Arms Co./Trail Guns Armory Inc.)

Pederson & Son, C.R., 2717 S. U.S. 31, Ludington, MI 49431/616-843-2061

Pekin Gun & Sporting Goods, 1304 Derby St., Pekin, IL 61554/309-347-6060

Pentax Corp., 35 Inverness Dr. E., Englewood, CO 80112/303-799-8000

Perazzi U.S.A., Inc., 1207 S. Shamrock Ave., Monrovia, CA 91016/818-303-0068

Peregrine Industries, Inc., 7601 Woodwind Dr., Huntington Beach, CA 92647-1310/714-847-4700
Perry's of Wendell, Inc., P.O. Box 826, Wendell, NC 27591/919-365-6391
Perugini-Visini & Co. s.r.l. (See Moore & Co., William Larkin)
Peters Stahl GmbH (See McMillian Gunworks, Inc./Safari-SGW)
Pete's Gun Shop, 31 Columbia St., Adams, MA 01220/413-743-0780
Phelps Mfg. Co., Box 2266, Evansville, IN 47741
Phillips, D.J., Gunsmith, Rt. 1, N31-W22087 Shady Ln., Pewaukee, WI 53072/414-691-2165
Phoenix Armoury, Inc., 248 Miami Ave., Norristown, PA 19403/215-539-0733
Phoenix Arms, 1420 S. Archibald Ave., Ontario, CA 91761/714-947-4843
PHOXX Shooters Supply, 5813 Watt Ave., N. Highlands, CA 95660/916-348-9827
Pintos Gun Shop, 835 N. Central Bldg. B, Kent, WA 98032/206-859-6333
Pioneer Marketing & Research, 216 Haddon Ave., Westmont, NJ 08108/609-854-2424
Piotti (See Moore & Co., William Larkin)
Plaza Gunworks, Inc., 983 Gasden Highway, Birmingham, AL 35235/205-836-6206
Poly Technologies, Inc. (See Keng's Firearms Specialty, Inc.)
Ponsness-Warren, South 763, Hwy. 41, Rathdrum, ID 83858
Poor Borch's, Inc., 1204 E. College Dr., Marshall, MN 56258/507-532-4880
Potter Gunsmithing, 13960 Boxhorn Dr., Muskego, WI 53150/414-425-4830
Precision Airgun Sales, 31812 Bainbridge Rd., Solon, OH 44139/216-248-7550
Precision Arms & Gunsmithing Ltd., Hwy. 27 & King Road Box 809, Nobleton, Ontario, CANADA L0G-1N0
Precision Gunsmithing, 2723 W. 6th St., Amarillo, TX 79106/806-376-7223
Precision Gun Works, 4717 State Rd. 44, Oshkosh, WI 54904/414-233-2274
Precision Imports, Inc./Mauser, 5040 Space Center Drive, San Antonio, TX 78155/512-666-3033
Precision Pellet, 1018 Erwin Dr., Joppa, MD 21085/410-679-8179
Precision Reloading, Inc., 165 Crooked S Road, Stafford Springs, CT 06076/800-223-0900
Precision Sales Intl., Inc., c/o Pacific International Service Co., Box 3-Mountain Way, Janesville, CA 96114/916-253-2218
Precision Sales, c/o Uncle Fred's Gun Shop, 1 East St., Southampton, MA 01073/413-527-1660
Precision Sport Optics, 15571 Producer Ln., Unit G, Huntington Beach, CA 92649/714-891-1309/FAX: 714-892-6920
Precision Sports, Div. of Cortland Line Co., 3736 Kellogg Rd., Cortland, NY 13045/607-756-2851
Preuss Gun Shop, 4545 E. Shepherd, Clovis, CA 93612/209-299-6248
Princess Anne Marine & Sport Center, 2371 Virginia Beach Blvd., Virginia Beach, VA 23454/804-340-6269
Professional Armaments, Inc., 4555 S. 300 West, Murray, UT 84107/801-268-2598
PSI, Inc., P.O. Box 1776, Westfield, MA 01086/413-562-5055/FAX: 413-562-5056

Q

Quality Arms, Inc., 2000 Dari Ashford Suite 490, Houston, TX 77077
Quality Firearms, Inc., 4530 NW 135 Street, Opa Locka, FL 33054

R

Rajo Corporation, 2025 W. Franklin St., Evansville, IN 47712/812-422-6945
Ralph's Gun Shop, Box 662 Canora, Saskatoon, Saskatchewan, CANADA S0A 0L0/306-244-2023
Ram-Line, Inc., 10601 West 48 Ave., Wheatridge, CO 80033/303-467-0300
Randy's Gun Repair, P.O. Box 106, Tabusintac, N.B. CANADA E0C 2A0
Ranging, Inc., Routes 5 & 20, East Bloomfield, NY 14443/716-657-6161
Ransom Intl. Corp., 1040-A Sandretto Dr., Prescott, AZ 86302/602-778-7899/FAX: 602-778-7993
Rapids Gun Shop, 7811 Buffalo Ave., Niagra Falls, NY 14304/716-283-7873
Ray's Gunsmith Shop, 3199 Elm Ave., Grand Junction, CO 81504/303-434-6162
Ray's Liquor and Sporting Goods, 1956 Solano St., Box 677, Corning, CA 96021/916-824-5625
Ray's Rod & Reel Service, 414 Pattie St., Wichita, KS 67211/316-267-9462
Ray's Sport Shop, Inc., 559 Route 22 North, Plainfield, NJ 07060/908-561-4400
Ray's Sporting Goods, 730 Singleton Blvd., Dallas, TX 75212/214-747-7916
RCBS, 605 Oro Dam Blvd., Oroville, CA 95965/800-533-5000
R.D.P. Tool Co., Inc., 49162 McCoy Ave., East Liverpool, OH 43920/216-385-5129
Redding Reloading, Inc., 1089 Starr Rd., Cortland, NY 13045/607-753-3331
Redfield, Inc., 5800 E. Jewell Ave., Denver, CO 80224/303-757-6411/FAX: 303-756-2338
Red's Gunsmithing, P.O. Box 1251, Chickaloon, AK 99674/907-745-4500
Red Willow Tool & Armory, Inc., 4004 Highway 93 North, Stevensville, MT 59870/406-777-5401/FAX: 406-777-5402
Reliable Gun & Tackle, Ltd., 3227 Fraser St., Vancouver, British Columbia CANADA V5V 4B8/604-874-4710
Reloaders Specialty Mfg., 7602 Carlton Rd., Coopersburg, PA 18036/215-838-9507
Reloading Center, 515 W. Main St., Burley, ID 83318/208-678-5053
Remington Arms Co. (See page 466)
Repair Station, The, 2254 North Atlantic St., Franklin Park, IL 60131/708-455-2003
Reynolds Gun Shop, 314 N. Western Ave., Peoria, IL 61606/309-674-5790
Reynolds Gun Shop, Inc., 3502A S. Broadway, Tyler, TX 75702/214-592-1531
Rice Hardware, 15 S.W. First Ave., Gainesville, FL 32601/904-377-0892
Richland Gun Shop, 207 Park St., Richland, PA 17087/717-866-4246
Richmond Gun Shop, 517 E. Main St., Richmond, VA 23219/804-644-7207
Rigby & Co., John (See Griffin & Howe, Inc.)
River Bend Sport Shop, 230 Farmsite Dr., Waupaca, WI 54981/715-258-3583
Rizzini, F.LLI (See Moore & Co., William Larkin)
Robinson's Sporting Goods, Ltd., 1307 Broad St., Victoria, British Columbia CANADA V8W 2A8/604-385-3429
Rogers Ltd. International, 891 Dixwell Ave., Hamden, CT 06514/203-865-8484/FAX: 800-847-7492
Ron's Gun Repair, 1517 E. 10th St., Sioux Falls, SD 57103/605-338-7398
Ross Sporting Goods, 204 W. Main St, Farmington, NM 87401/505-325-1062
Rossi S.A. Metalurgica E Municoes, Amadeo (See Interarms)
Roy's Antiques & Things, Route 1 Box 303, Mountain Rest, SC 29664/803-638-5340
Roy's Sport Shop, 10 Second St. NE, Watertown, SD 57201/605-886-7508
RPM (R&R Sporting Arms, Inc.), 15481 N. Twin Lakes Dr., Tucson, AZ 85337/602-725-1233
R&R Shooters Supply, W6553 North Rd., Mauston, WI 53948/608-847-4562

Rue's Gunsmithing, 427 Broadway, El Cajon, CA 92021/619-447-2169
Ruger (See Sturm Ruger & Co.)
Ruko Products, Suite 102, Walnutport, PA 18088/215-767-1339
Rusk Gun Shop, Inc., 6904 Watts Rd., Madison, WI 53719/608-274-8740
Russel's Sporting Goods, 6624 Centre St. S., Calgary, Alberta, CANADA T2H 0C6/403-269-5566
RWS (See Dynamit Nobel-RWS, Inc.)

S

Safari Arms/SGW, 624 Old Pacific Hwy SE, Olympia WA 98503/206-456-3471; FAX: 206-491-3447
Saffle Repair Service, 312 Briar Wood Dr., Jackson, MS 39206/601-956-4968
Sako, Ltd. (See Stoeger Industries)
San Marko (See Cape Outfitters)
Sanders Custom Gun Shop, P.O. Box 5967-2031, Bloomingdale Ave., Augusta, GA 30906/404-798-5220
Sanders Gun Shop, 3001 Fifth St., P.O. Box 4181, Meridian, MS 39301/601-485-5301
Saskatoon Gunsmith Shoppe, Ltd., 2310 Avenue "C" N., Saskatoon, Saskatchewan, CANADA S7L 5X5/306-242-6747
Sauer (See G.U. Inc./Simmons Enterprises, Ernie/Simmons Gun Repair)
Savage Arms, Inc., Davidson's Canada, 584 Neal Drive, Peterborough, Ontario, CANADA K9J 6Z6/705-742-5408
Savage Arms, Inc., Randy's Gun Repair, P.O. Box 106, Tabusintac, NB, CANADA E0C 2A0/506-779-4768
Savage Arms, Inc., Red's Gunsmithing, 1230 East 68th Ave. #102, Anchorage, AK 99518/907-344-4867
Savage Arms, Inc., Repair Station, W.R. Longs Gunsmiths Ltd., Brook Road North, Coburg, Ontario, CANADA K9A 453/416-372-5955
Savage Arms, Inc., Shop 2, #8 Ing Road, Kaunakakai, HI 96748/808-553-5888
Savage Arms, Inc., Springdale Rd., Westfield, MA 01085/413-568-7001
Scalzo's Sporting Goods, 207 Odell Ave., Endicott, NY 13760/607-746-7586
Scattergun Technologies, 518 3rd Avenue South, Nashville, TN 37210/615-254-1441
Scharch Mfg., Inc., 10325 Co. Rd. 120 Unit "C", Salida, CO 81201/719-539-7242/FAX: 719-539-3021
Schmidt, Herbert (See Sportarms of Florida)
Schmidt & Bender (See Jaeger, Inc., Paul)
Schultheis Sporting Goods, 6 Main St., Arkport, NY 14807/607-295-7485
Sea Gull Marina, 1400 Lake, Two Rivers, WI 54241/414-794-7533
Seecamp Co., Inc., L.W., 301 Brewster Rd., Milford, CT 06460
Selin Gunsmith, Ltd., Del, 2803 28th Street, Vernon, British Columbia, CANADA V1T 4Z5/604-545-6413
S.E.M. Gun Works, 3204 White Horse Rd., Greenville, SC 29611/803-295-2948
SGS Importers International, Inc., 1907 Hwy. 35, Ocean, NJ 07712/908-531-9424; FAX: 908-531-1520
Shaler Eagle, R.R. 8 Box 407, Jonesbrough, TN 37659/615-753-7620
Shamburg's Wholesale Spt. Gds., 403 Frisco Ave., Clinton, OK 73601/405-323-0209
Shapel & Son, 1708 N. Liberty, Boise, ID 83704/208-375-6159
Sharps Arms Co., Inc., C., 100 Centennial Dr., Big Timber, MT 59011/406-932-4353
Shepherd Scope Ltd., RR 2 Box 23, Waterloo, NE 68069/402-779-2424
Sheridan Products, Inc. (See Benjamin/Sheridan Co.)
Shiloh Rifle Mfg. Co., Inc., 201 Centennial Dr., Big Timber, MT 59011
Shockey, H., 204 E. Farmington Rd., Hanna City, IL 61536/309-565-4524
Shooters Supply, 1120 Tieton Dr., Yakima, WA 98902
Shooting Gallery, The, 1619 Penna, Weirton, WV 26062/304-723-3298
Siegle's Gunshop, Inc., 508 W. MacArthur Blvd., Oakland, CA 94609/415-655-8789
Sievert's Guns 4107 W. Northern, Pueblo, CO 81005/719-564-0035
SIG (See Mandall Shooting Supplies Inc.)
SIG-Sauer (See Sigarms, Inc.)
Sigarms, Inc., Industrial Dr., Corporate Park, Exeter, NH 03833/603-722-2302
Sile Distributors, 8 Centre Market Place, New York, NY 10013
Sillman, Hal, Associated Services, 1514 NE 205 Terrace, Miami, FL 33170/305-651-4450
Simmons Enterprises, c/o The Gun Works, 8540 I St., Omaha, NE 68127/402-339-2249
Simmons Enterprises, Ernie, 709 East Elizabethtown Rd., Manheim, PA 17545/717-664-4040
Simmons Gun Repair/Sauer, 700 S. Rodgers Rd., Olathe, KS 66083/913-782-3131
Simmons Outdoor Corp., 14530 SW 119 Ave., Miami, FL 33186/305-252-0477
Sipes Gun Shop, 919 High St, Little Rock, AR 72202/501-376-8940
SKB Arms Co. (See G.U. Inc./Hanus Birdguns, Bill/Simmons Enterprises, Ernie)
Skeet's Gun Shop, Rt. 3, Box 235, Tahlequah, OK 74464/918-456-4749
Skeet Hill Gun Shop, R.L., 209 Raymond St., Verona, MS 38879/601-566-8353
S.K. Guns, Inc., 3041A Main Ave., Fargo, ND 58103/701-293-4867
Smith & Smith Gun Shop, Inc., 2589 Oscar Johnson Drive, Charleston Heights, SC 29405/803-744-2024
Smith & Wesson (See page 466)
Smith's Lawn & Marine Svc., 9100 Main St., Clarence, NY 14031/716-633-7868
Sodak Sport & Bait, 319 8th Ave. N.W., Aberdeen, SD 57401/605-225-2737
Solothurn (See Sile Distributors)
Solvay Home & Outdoor Center, 102 First St., Solvay, NY 13209/315-468-6285
Southland Gun Works, Inc., 1134 Hartsville Rd., Darlington, SC 29532/803-393-6291
Southwest Airguns, Box 132 Route 8, Lake Charles, LA 70605-9304/318-474-6038
Southwest Shooters Supply, Inc., 1940 Linwood Blvd., Oklahoma City, OK 73106/405-235-4476/405-235-7022
Specialty Shooters Supply, Inc., 3325 Griffin Rd., Suite 9mm, Ft. Lauderdale, FL 33317
Sportarms of Florida, 5555 N.W. 36 Ave., Miami, FL 33142/305-635-2411
Sport Shop, The, 100 Will Roger Dr., Kingfisher, OK 73750/405-375-5130
Sportarms of Florida, 5555 NW 36 Ave., Miami, FL 33142/305-635-2411
Sporting Arms Mfg., Inc., 801 Hall Ave., Littlefield, TX 79339/806-385-5665
Sporting Goods, Inc., 232 North Lincoln St., Hastings, NE 68901/402-462-6132
Sports Mart, The, 828 Ford St., Ogdensburg, NY 13669/315-393-2865
Sports Shop, The, 8055 Airline Hwy., Baton Rouge, LA 70815/504-927-2600
Sports World, Inc., 5800 S. Lewis Ave., Suite 154, Tulsa, OK 74105/918-742-4027
Sportsman's Center, U.S. Hwy. 130, Box 731, Bordentown, NJ 08505/609-298-5300
Sportsman's Depot, 644 Miami St., Urban, OH 43078/513-653-4429
Sportsman's Exchange, Inc., 560 South "C" St., Oxnard, CA 93030/805-483-1917
Sportsman's Haven, Rt. 4, Box 541, 14695 E. Pike Rd., Cambridge, OH 43725/614-432-7243

WARRANTY SERVICE CENTER DIRECTORY

Sportsman's Paradise Gunsmith, 640 Main St., Pineville, LA 71360/318-443-6041

Sportsman's Shop, 101 W. Main St., New Holland, PA 17557/717-354-4311

Sportsman's Surplus, Trumpers Shopping Center, P.O. Box 4166, Missoula, MT 59806/406-721-5500

Sportsmen's Repair Ctr., Inc., 106 S. High St., Box 134, Columbus Groves, OH 45830/419-659-5818

Springfield, Inc., 420 W. Main St., Geneseo, IL 61254/309-944-5631

Spradlin's, 113 Arthur, Pueblo, CO 81004/719-543-9462/fs

Stallard Arms, Inc., 728 FairFAX: Ave., Mansfield, OH 44906/419-747-6095

Stalwart Corp., 756 N. Garfield, Pocatello, ID 83204/208-232-7899

Star Bonifacio Echeverria S.A. (See Interarms)

Star Machine Works, 418 10th Ave., San Diego, CA 92101/619-232-3216

Starnes, Gunmaker, Ken, 32900 SW Laurelview Rd., Hillsboro, OR 97123/503-628-0705

Steel City Arms, Inc. (See Desert Industries, Inc.)

Steyr Airguns (See Nygord Precision Products)

Steyr-Daimler-Puch (See GSI, Inc.)

Steyr-Mannlicher (See GSI, Inc.)

St. Lawrence Sales, Inc., 12 West Fint St., Lake Orion, MI 48035/313-693-7760

Stan's Gun Repair, RR #2 Box 48, Westbrook, MN 56183-9521/507-274-5649

Stocker's Shop, 5199 Mahoning Ave., Warren, OH 44483/216-847-9579

Stoeger Industries (See page 466)

Stratemeyer, H.P., Winch Hill Rd., P.O. Box 489, Langdon, NH 03602/603-835-6130

Sturm, Ruger & Co., Guild Rd., Newport, NH 03773/603-863-3300

Sundance Industries, Inc., 25163 W. Ave. Stanford, Valencia, CA 91355/805-257-4807

Surplus Center, 621 S.E. Cass, Roseburg, OR 97470/503-672-4312

Survival Arms, 4500 Pine Cone Place, Cocao, FL 32922/407-633-4880

Swarovski Optik, One Wholesale Way, Cranston, RI 02920/401-942-3380

Swift Instruments, Inc., 952 Dorchester Ave., Boston, MA 02125

Swift Instruments, Inc., (West Coast Only), 1190 North 4th Street, San Jose, CA 95112

Swivel Machine Works, Inc., 167 Cherry St., Suite 286, Milford, CT 06460/203-926-1840

T

Tanfoglio S.r.l., Fratelli/Witness (See E.A.A. Corp.)

Tanner (See Mandall Shooting Supplies, Inc.)

Tapco, Inc., P.O. Box 818, Smyrna, GA 30081/404-435-9782

Tasco Sales, Inc., 7600 NW 26th St., Miami, FL 33122/305-591-3670

Taurus Firearms, Inc., 16175 NW 49th Ave., Miami, FL 33014/305-624-1115

Taylor's Sporting Goods, Gene, 445 W. Gunnison Ave., Grand Junction, CO 81505/303-242-8165

Taylor's Technical Gunsmithing Co., 14 Stalwart Industrial Drive, Gormely, Ontario CANADA L0H 1G0/416-888-9391

Taylor & Vadney, Inc., 303 Central Ave., Albany, NY 12206/518-472-9183

Ted's Gun & Reel Repair, 311 Natchitoches St. Box 1635, W. Monroe, LA 71291/318-323-0661

Ten Ring Service, 2227 West Lou Dr., Jacksonville, FL 32216/904-724-7419

Texas Gun Shop, Inc., 4518 S. Padre Island Dr., Corpus Christi, TX 78411/512-854-4424

Texas Longhorn Arms, Inc., 3830 FM 2218, Richmond, TX 77469/713-341-0775

The Way It Was Sporting, 620 Chestnut Street, Moorestown, NJ 08057/609-234-0212

Theoben Engineering (See Air Rifle Specialists)

Thompson/Center Arms (See page 466)

Thompson's Gunshop, Inc., 10254-84th St., Alto, MI 49302/616-868-6156

Thunder Mountain Arms, P.O. Box 593, Oak Harbor, WA 98277/206-679-4657/FAX: 206-675-1114

Tikka (See Stoeger Industries)

300 Gunsmith Service, 6850 South Yosemite Ct., Englewood, CO 80112/303-773-0300

Tokarev (See Sportarms of Florida)

Traders, The, 685 E. 14th St., San Leandro, CA 94577/415-569-0555

Tradewinds, 2339 Tacoma Ave. S., Tacoma, WA 98402/206-272-4887

Trading Post, The, 412 Erie St. S., Massillon, OH 44646/216-833-7761

Traditions, Inc., 500 Main St., Deep River, CT 06417/203-526-9555

Trail Guns Armory, 1422 E. Main St., League City, TX 77573/713-332-5833/FAX: 713-332-5833

Treaster, Inc., Verne, 3604 West 16th St., Indianapolis, IN 46222/317-638-6921

Treptow, Inc., Herman, 209 S. Main St., Milltown, NJ 08850/908-828-0184

Trident Ltd., 564 Kantz Rd., Springdale, AZ 72764/501-361-2803

Trijicon, Inc., 37716 Hills Tech Drive, Farmington Hills, MI 48331

U

Uberti USA (West Coast Only), Tabor Engineering, 527 San Mateo Ave., San Bruno, CA 94066

Uberti USA, Inc., 362 Limerock Rd., Lakeville, CT 06039/203-435-8068

Ultra Light Arms, Inc., 214 Price St., Granville, WV 26534/304-599-5687

Unertl Optical Co., John, 1224 Freedom Rd., Mars, PA 16046/412-776-9700

Ugartechea S.A., Ignacio (See Hanus Birdguns, Bill/Mandall Shooting Supplies, Inc./Precision Sports)

Unique/M.A.P.F. (See Nygord Precision Products)

Unique Sporting Goods, First United Federal Bldg., Edensburg, PA 15931/814-472-4123

Upper Missoui Trading Co., Inc., 304 Harold St., Crofton, NE 68730/402-388-4844

Upton's Gun Shop, 810 Croghan St., Fremont, OH 43420/419-332-1326

U.S. Repeating Arms Co. (See Winchester)

V

Valley Gun Shop, 7719 Hartford Rd., Baltimore, MD 21234/410-668-2171

Valley Gunsmithing, John A. Foster, 619 Second St., Webster City, IA 50595/515-832-5102

Van Burens Gun Shop, 2706 Sylvania Ave., Toledo, OH 43613/419-475-9526

Van's Gunsmith Service, Rt. 69A, Parish, NY 13131/315-625-7251

Voere (See JägerSports, Ltd./Swarovski Optik North America, Ltd.)

Vostok (See Nygord Precision Products)

W

Walker Arms Co., Inc., Hwy. 80 West, Rt. 2, Box 73, Selma, AL 36701/205-872-6231

Wallace Gatlin Gun Repair, Rt. 2, Box 73, Oxford, AL 36203/205-831-6993

Walther GmbH, Carl (See Interarms)

Warren's Sports Hdqts., 240 W. Main St., Washington, NC 27889/919-946-0960

Weapon Works, The, 7017 N. 19th Ave., Phoenix, AZ 85021/602-995-3010

Weatherby, Inc. (See page 466)

Weaver Scope Repair Service, 1121 Larry Mahan Dr., Suite B, El Paso, TX 79925/915-593-1005

Weihrauch KG, Hermann (See Beeman Precision Airguns, Inc./E.A.A. Corp.)

Weinberger Gunsmithing, Herbert, 30 W. Prospect St., Waldwick, NJ 07436/201-447-0025

Wessel Gun Service, 4000 E. 9-Mile Rd., Warren, MI 48091/313-756-2660

Wesson Firearms Co., Inc., Attn: OSR, Maple Tree Industrial Center, Rt. 20, Wilbraham Rd., Palmer, MA 01069/413-267-4081

Western Ordnance Intl. Corp., 325 S. Westwood, Suite #1, Mesa, AZ 85210/602-964-1799

Westgate Gunsports, Inc., 10116-175th Street, Edmonton, Alberta, CANADA T5S 1A1

West Luther Gun Repair, R.R. #1, Conn, Ontario, CANADA/519-848-6260

Wheeler Gun Shop, C., 1908 George Washington Way Bldg. F, Richland, WA 99352/509-946-4634

White Dog Gunsmithing, 62 Central Ave., Ilion, NY 13357/315-894-6211

White Systems, Inc., 810 W. 100 North, Roosevelt, UT 84066/Phone and FAX: 801-722-3085

Wholesale Shooters Supplies, 751 W. Brubaker Valley Rd., Lititz, PA 17543/717-626-8574

Wholesale Sports, 12505-97 St., Edmonton, Alberta, CANADA T5G 4A4417

Wichita Arms, Inc., 444 Ellis St., Wichita, KS 67211/316-265-0661/FAX: 316-265-0760

Wichita Guncraft, Inc., 4607 Barnett Rd., Wichita Falls, TX 76310/817-692-5622

Wilderness Sport & Electronics, 14430 S. Pulaski Rd., Midlothian, IL 60445/708-389-1776

Wildey, Inc., 458 Danbury Rd., New Milford, CT 06776/203-355-9000/FAX: 203-354-7759

Wilkinson Arms, 26884 Pearl Rd., Parma, ID 83660/208-722-6771

Willborn Outdoors & Feed, 505 Main Avenue N.W., Cullman, AL 35055/205-737-9595

Williams Gun Shop, 7389 Lapeer Rd., Davison, MI 48423/313-742-2120

Williams Gun Sight Co., 7389 Lapeer Rd., Davison, MI 48423/313-653-2131

Williams Gunsmithing, 1480 Houlihan Rd., Saginaw, MI 48601/517-777-1240

Williamson Gunsmith Service, 117 West Pipeline Rd., Hurst, TX 76053/817-285-0064

Will's Gun Shop, 5603 N. Hubbard Lake Rd., Spruce, MI 48762/517-727-2500

Winchester (See page 466)

Windsor Gun Shop, 8410 Southeastern Ave., Indianapolis, IN 46239/317-862-2512

Wingshooting Adventures, 4320 Kalamazoo Ave. SE, Grand Rapids, MI 49508/616-455-7810/FAX: 616-455-5212

Wisner's Gun Shop, Inc., 287 NW Chehalis Ave., Chehalis, WA 98532/206-748-8942

Wolf Custom Gunsmithing, Gregory, c/o Albright's Gun Shop, 36 E. Dover St., Easton, MD 21601/301-820-8811

Wolfer Brothers, Inc., 1701 Durham, Houston, TX 77007/713-869-7640

Woodman's Sporting Goods, 223 Main Street, Norway, ME 04268/207-743-6602

Wortner Gun Works, Ltd., 433 Queen St., Chatham, Ont., M7M 5K5/519-352-0924

Wyoming Arms Mfg. Corp., 210 Hwy. 20 South, Thermopolis, WY 82443/307-864-5503

Y

Ye Olde Blk Powder Shop, 994 W. Midland Rd., Auburd, MI 48611/517-662-2271

Ye Olde Gun Shop, 12 Woodlawn Ave., Bradford, PA 16701/814-368-3034

Ye Olde Gun Shoppe, P.O. Box 358, Sitka, AK 99835/907-747-5720

Z

Zabala Hermanos S.A. (See American Arms, Inc.)

Zanes Gun Rack, 4167 N. High St., Columbus, OH 43214/614-263-0369

Zanoletti, Pietro (See Mandall Shooting Supplies, Inc.)

Zastava Arms (See Interarms)

Zeiss Optical, Inc., Carl, Sports Optics Repair Shop, 1015 Commerce St., Petersburg, VA 23803/804-861-0033/800-446-1807

Zoli USA, Inc., Antonio, 1426 E. Tillman Rd., Ft. Wayne, IN 46816

BR=Browning ■**CR**=Crosman ■**MO**=Mossberg ■**RE**=Remington ■**ST**=Stoeger ■**SW**=Smith & Wesson ■**TC**=Thompson/Center ■**WN**=Winchester ■**WE**=Weatherby

SERVICE CENTER	CITY	BR	CR	MO	RE	ST	SW	TC	WN	WE
ALABAMA										
B&W Gunsmithing	Cullman				●					
Dubbs, Gunsmith, Dale R.	Seminole				●					
Fred's Gun Shop	Mobile	●			●					
Hal's Gun Supply	Cullman	●		●						
Nusbaum Enterprises, Inc.	Mobile	●								
Ott's Gun Service	Atmore				●	●				
Plaza Gunworks, Inc.	Birmingham				●	●	●			
Walker Arms Co., Inc.	Selma	●		●	●	●	●	●	●	
Wallace Gatlin Gun	Oxford				●				●	
Willborn Outdoors & Feed	Cullman								●	●
ALASKA										
Down Under Gunsmiths	Fairbanks	●			●					
Red's Gunsmithing	Chickaloon	●	●		●		●	●	●	
Ye Olde Gun Shoppe	Sitka				●					●
ARIZONA										
Don's Sport Shop, Inc.	Scottsdale	●			●			●	●	
Jensen's Custom Ammunition/Lathrops	Tucson	●			●		●	●	●	
Joe's Gun Shop	Phoenix		●							
Millie "D" Enterprises	Tucson		●		●					
Weapon Works, The	Phoenix									●
ARKANSAS										
Broadway Arms	North Little Rock		●		●				●	
Gun Exchange, Inc.	Little Rock		●		●					
Jim's Sporting Goods	Newport				●		●			
Jim's Trading Post	Pine Bluff	●			●					
Sipes Gun Shop	Little Rock	●			●					
CALIFORNIA										
Air Guns Unlimited	La Puente		●							
Air Venture Air Guns	Bellflower		●							
Andersen Gunsmithing	Petaluma				●					
Argonaut Gun Shop	Modesto				●					
Bain & Davis	San Gabriel		●	●	●					
Beeman Precision Arms, Inc.	Santa Rosa		●		●					
Bolsa Gunsmithing	Westminster	●			●					
Bridge Sportsman's Ctr.	Paso Robles					●				
Cal's Customs	Fallbrook		●		●					
Gilman-Mayfield	Fresno				●					
Grundman's	Rio Dell				●					
Gunshop, Inc., The	Lancaster				●				●	
Gunsmith, The	Chico				●					

SERVICE CENTER	CITY	BR	CR	MO	RE	ST	SW	TC	WN	WE
CALIFORNIA										
Huntington Sportsman's Store	Oroville	●			●				●	
Imbert & Smithers, Inc.	San Carlos	●			●				●	
Jack First Distributors	Lancaster			●				●	●	
J&G Gunsmithing	Roseville	●			●					
John Q's Quality Gunsmithing	Sacramento	●			●					
King's Gun Works, Inc.	Glendale									
Long Beach Uniform Co., Inc.	Long Beach									
Mac-1	Gardena						●			
Miclean, Bill	San Jose									
Pacific International Service Co.	Janesville	●	●	●	●	●	●	●	●	
Pachmayr Gun Works	Monrovia				●					
PHOXX Shooters Supply	N. Highlands									
Preuss Gun Shop	Clovis	●	●							
Ray's Liquor and Sporting Goods	Corning	●	●				●			
Rue's Gunsmithing	El Cajon		●							
Siegle's Gunshop, Inc.	Oakland	●	●	●	●	●	●		●	
Sportsman's Exchange, Inc.	Oxnard	●	●		●					
Traders, The	San Leandro									
COLORADO										
Foothills Shooting Ctr.	Lakewood	●			●				●	
Gart Brothers Sporting Goods	Denver	●		●	●				●	
L&M Firing Line, Inc.	Aurora						●			
Old West Arms	Lakewood				●			●		
Ray's Gunsmith Shop	Grand Junction	●	●					●		
Sievert's Guns	Pueblo				●					
Spradlin's	Pueblo				●					
Taylor's Sporting Goods, Gene	Grand Junction				●					●
300 Gunsmith Service	Englewood				●				●	
CONNECTICUT										
Gunsmithing Limited	Fairfield	●			●					
Hoffman's Gun Center, Inc.	Newington				●				●	
Horchler's Gun Shop	Collinsville		●		●					
Keller's Co., Inc.	Burlington				●					
Modern Guncraft	Collinsville		●							
Nicholson's Gunsmithing	Shelton				●					
DELAWARE										
Dean's Place	Hockessin				●					
Magnum Gun Service	Newark				●				●	
FLORIDA										
Air Gun Rifle Repair	Sebring		●							
Alexander, Gunsmith, W.R.	Tallahassee						●			
Firearms Unlimited, Inc.	Naples									●

See page 460 for Service Center addresses.

Legend: ■BR=Browning ■CR=Crosman ■MO=Mossberg ■RE=Remington ■ST=Stoeger ■SW=Smith & Wesson ■TC=Thompson/Center ■WN=Winchester ■WE=Weatherby

SERVICE CENTER	CITY	BR	CR	MO	RE	ST	SW	TC	WN	WE
Green Acres Sporting Goods, Inc.	Jacksonville	●	●	●	●		●			
Gun Doc. Inc.	Miami			●	●					
Gun Shop, Inc., The	Miami Shores		●	●	●					
Jackson, Inc., Bill	Pinellas Park									
Lawsons Custom Firearms, Inc., Art	Ocala	●		●	●					
Loftin & Taylor	Jacksonville			●	●					
Rice Hardware	Gainesville		●	●	●					
Sillman, Hal, Associated Services	Miami								●	
Ten Ring Service	Jacksonville							●		
GEORGIA										
Accuracy Gun Shop	Columbus	●		●	●				●	
Dorn's Outdoor Center	Macon	●		●	●				●	
Ed's Gun & Tackle Shop, Inc.	Marietta	●	●	●	●					
Franklin Sports, Inc.	Athens	●			●					
Gun Corral, Inc.	Decatur			●	●		●		●	
Jordan Gun & Pawn Shop	Tifton	●			●					
Kick's Sport Center	Claxton				●				●	
Sanders Custom Gun Shop	Augusta									
HAWAII										
Chung, Gunsmith, Mel	Kaunakakai	●	●	●	●				●	
IDAHO										
Bob's Repair	Idaho Falls									●
Intermountain Arms & Tackle, Inc.	Meridian	●	●	●	●				●	
Lolo Sporting Goods	Lewiston	●		●					●	
Quality Firearms	Nampa	●	●		●				●	
Reloading Center	Burley			●	●					
Shapel & Son	Boise				●				●	
ILLINOIS										
A&M Sales	North Lake		●	●	●					
Darnall's Gun Works	Bloomington			●	●				●	
Gat Guns	East Dundee			●	●					
Henry's Airguns	Belvidere		●	●						
Krebs Gunsmithing	Niles				●					
Midwest Sporting Goods Co., Inc.	Lyons			●			●			
Ott's Gunsmith Service	Decatur		●	●	●					
Outdoorsman Sporting Goods Co.	Geneva		●		●					
Pekin Gun & Sporting Goods	Pekin			●	●					
Repair Station, The	Franklin Park		●							
Reynolds Gun Shop	Peoria	●								
Shockey, H.	Hanna City	●	●							
Wilderness Sport & Electronics	Midlothian		●							
INDIANA										
Airgun Centre, Ltd.	Lawrenceburg		●		●					
Allen County Gun Works	Ft. Wayne	●	●	●	●				●	
Blythe's Sport Shop, Inc.	Valparaiso		●	●	●					
Hodson & Son Pell Gun Repair	Anderson		●							
Lutter, Robert E.	Ft. Wayne									

SERVICE CENTER	CITY	BR	CR	MO	RE	ST	SW	TC	WN	WE
Rajo Corporation	Evansville		●				●			
Treaster, Inc.	Indianapolis			●	●					
Windsor Gun Shop	Indianapolis		●	●	●					
IOWA										
Daryl's Gun Shop, Inc.	State Center				●					
Glenn's Reel & Rod Repair	Des Moines		●		●					
G&S Gunsmithing	Eldridge				●					
Jacobson's Gun Center	Story City									●
Nelson's Engine Shop	Cedar Falls			●	●					
Valley Gunsmithing, John A. Foster	Webster City								●	
KANSAS										
Bullseye Gun Works	Overland Park				●					
Gordon's Wigwam	Wichita	●	●		●		●			
Gun & Stuff, Inc.	Wichita				●					
Northwest Arms Service	Atwood			●	●					
Ray's Rod & Reel Service	Wichita		●		●					
Simmons Gun Repair	Olathe				●				●	
KENTUCKY										
Danny's Gun Repair, Inc.	Louisville	●	●	●	●				●	
Firearms Service Center	Louisville		●		●					
Garrett Gunsmiths, Inc.	Newport	●			●					
Paducah Shooters Supply, Inc.	Paducah				●					
LOUISIANA										
Atlas Gun Repair	Violet	●			●					
Boudreaux, Gunsmith	Lake Charles				●					
Brazdas Top Guns	Lafayette				●					
Burton Hardware	Sulphur				●					
Caddo Arms & Cycle	Shreveport				●				●	
Chalmette Jewelry & Guns	Chalmette	●			●					
Cherry's Gun Shop	Ruston				●					
Clark Custom Guns, Inc.	Keithville						●			
Custom Gun Works	Lafayette			●	●					
Eversull Gunsmith, Inc., K.	Boyce	●		●	●					
Houma Gun Works	Houma	●	●	●	●					
Hutchinson's Gun Repair	Pineville			●						
Lafayette Shooters	Lafayette				●					
Martin Gun Shop	Shreveport				●					
N.A. Guns, Inc.	Baton Rouge	●			●					
Southwest Airguns	Lake Charles		●							
Sports Shop, The	Baton Rouge	●			●					
Sportsman's Paradise Gunsmith	Pineville				●					
Ted's Gun & Reel Repair	W. Monroe								●	
MAINE										
Brunswick Gun Shop	Brunswick				●		●		●	
Morrison, Carl Bill	Bradford				●		●		●	
Woodman's Sporting Goods	Norway								●	

See page 460 for Service Center addresses.

Legend: BR=Browning CR=Crosman MO=Mossberg RE=Remington ST=Stoeger SW=Smith & Wesson TC=Thompson/Center WN=Winchester WE=Weatherby

SERVICE CENTER	CITY	BR	CR	MO	RE	ST	SW	TC	WN	WE
MARYLAND										
Atlantic Guns, Inc.	Silver Springs	●		●	●		●			
Baltimore Gunsmiths	Baltimore			●	●					
Firearms Repair & Refinish Shoppe	Woodbine									●
Gun Center, The	Frederick		●							
Precision Pellet	Joppa		●							
Valley Gun Shop	Baltimore	●		●	●	●	●		●	
Wolf Custom Gunsmithing, Gregory. c/o Albright's Gun Shop	Easton	●			●					
MASSACHUSETTS										
Airport Sports Shop. Inc.	North Attleboro									●
Bellrose & Son. L.E.	Granby		●		●					
Four Seasons	Woburn			●	●	●	●		●	
Pete's Gun Shop	Adams			●	●					
MICHIGAN										
Adventure A.G.R.	Waterford			●	●					●
Bachelder Master Gunmakers	Grand Rapids	●	●	●	●	●	●		●	
Daenzer. Charles E.	Otisville		●							
Fricano. Gunsmith. J.	Grand Haven		●							
Geake & Son. Inc.	Ferndale				●	●				
Hampel's. Inc.	Traverse City				●	●	●			
Joe's Gun Shop	Dorr	●		●	●					
Johnson Gunsmithing. Don	Powers			●	●					
Johnson Service. Inc.. W.	Adrian			●	●					
McDaniel Co... Inc.. B.	South Lyon			●	●					
Moreau. Gunsmith. Pete	Essexvile		●	●	●					
Northern Precision Airguns	Tawas City		●							
Oakland Custom Arms	Waterford				●	●	●			
On Target Gunshop. Inc.	Kalamazoo	●	●		●					
Outpost. The	Eureka				●					
Pederson & Son. C.R.	Ludington		●	●	●	●	●			
Thompson's Gunshop. Inc.	Alto	●		●	●	●	●			
Wessel Gun Service	Warren	●	●		●					
Williams Gun Sight Co.	Davison		●		●				●	
Will's Gun Shop	Saginaw				●					
Ye Olde Blk Powder Shop	Spruce							●		●
	Auburd									
MINNESOTA										
Ahlman's Custom Gun Shop. Inc.	Morristown	●		●	●	●	●		●	
Antonowicz. Frank	Minneapolis	●								
B&B Supply Co.	Minneapolis				●					
Dale's Guns & Archery Center	Rochester				●					
Gun Shop. The	Excelsior				●					
Frontiersman's Sports	Minneapolis	●								
Kotila Gun Shop	Cokato				●					
Laibs Gunsmithing	Spicer				●					
Matt's 10K Gunsmithing. Inc.	Duluth				●					
Northland Sport Center	Bagley									

SERVICE CENTER	CITY	BR	CR	MO	RE	ST	SW	TC	WN	WE
Poor Borch's, Inc.	Marshall				●					
Stan's Gun Repair	Westbrook				●					
MISSISSIPPI										
Grenada Gun Works	Grenada				●					
Martins Gun Shop	Natchez			●	●					
May & Company. Inc.	Jackson		●							
Millers Gun Shop	Gulfport		●							
Saffle Repair Service	Jackson							●		
Sanders Gun Shop	Meridian			●	●					
Skeet Hill Gun Shop. R.L.	Verona	●							●	
MISSOURI										
Beards Sport Shop	Cape Girardeau			●	●					
Bickford Arms	Joplin			●	●		●			●
Carl's Gun Shop	El Dorado Springs			●	●		●			●
Catfish Guns	Imperial						●			
CR Specialty	Kansas City	●								
Dollar Drugs. Inc.	Lee's Summit		●							
F&D Guns	Harvester			●	●		●			●
Kopp. Prof. Gunsmith. Terry K.	Lexington	●			●					
Marshall Gun Shop	Dellwood				●		●			●
Nu-Line Guns. Inc.	Harvester	●			●			●		●
MONTANA										
Air Gun Shop. The	Billings									
Billings Gunsmiths	Billings		●							●
Bradys Sportsmans Surplus	Missoula			●	●					●
Capitol Sports & Western Wear	Helena			●	●		●			
Don's Sporting Goods	Lewiston									
Montana Gun Works	Great Falls							●		
Sportsman's Surplus	Missoula									
NEBRASKA										
Al's Gun & Reel Shop. Inc.	North Platte			●	●				●	●
Bedlan's Sporting Goods. Inc.	Fairbury		●	●						
Cylinder & Slide. Inc.	Fremont	●			●					
G.H. Gun Shop	McCook									
G.I. Loan Shop	Grand Island								●	●
Gun Works. The	Omaha	●			●					
Gunsmithing Specialties. Co.	Papillion									
Labs Air Gun Shop	Omaha									
Moneymaker Gun Craft. Inc.	Omaha		●	●	●		●	●	●	●
Sporting Goods. Inc.	Hastings			●	●					●
Upper Missouri Trading Co.. Inc.	Crofton								●	
NEVADA										
Accuracy Gun Shop. Inc.	Las Vegas		●	●	●					●
Gun World	Elko									
Nevada Air Guns	N. Las Vegas		●							

See page 460 for Service Center addresses.

■BR=Browning ■CR=Crosman ■MO=Mossberg ■RE=Remington ■ST=Stoeger ■SW=Smith & Wesson ■TC=Thompson/Center ■WN=Winchester ■WE=Weatherby

SERVICE CENTER	CITY	BR	CR	MO	RE	ST	SW	TC	WN	WE
NEW HAMPSHIRE										
Lewis Arms at Riley's	Hooksett	●		●	●				●	●
Stratemeyer, H.P.	Langdon			●	●				●	
NEW JERSEY										
Belleplain Supply, Inc.	Belleplain	●								
Brenner Sport Shop, Charlie	Rahway		●							
Efinger Sporting Goods	Bound Brook			●	●					
Garfield Gunsmithing	Garfield	●		●	●					
Harry's Army & Navy Store	Robbinsville	●	●	●	●				●	
Ray's Sport Shop, Inc.	Plainfield	●		●	●				●	
Sportsman's Center	Bordentown				●					
The Way It Was Sporting	Moorestown	●			●					
Treptow, Inc., Herman	Milltown				●					
Weinberger Gunsmithing, Herbert	Waldwick				●					
NEW MEXICO										
Charlie's Sporting Goods, Inc.	Albuquerque	●		●	●				●	
Chuck's Gun Shop	Ranchos De Taos			●	●					
Covey's Precision Gunsmith	Roswell									
D&J Coleman Service	Hobbs		●	●	●		●			
Hobb's Bicycle & Gun Sales	Hobbs			●	●		●			
Ross Sporting Goods	Farmington								●	
NEW YORK										
Alpine Arms Corp.	Brooklyn									
Apple Town Gun Shop	Williamson			●	●					
B&T, Inc.	Albany		●							
Benson Gun Shop	Coram L.I.			●	●					
Boracci, E. John, Village Sport Ctr.	Seaford L.I.		●		●					
Buffalo Gun Center, Inc.	Buffalo			●	●					
Burgins Gun Shop	Sidney Center			●	●					
Centre Firearms Co., Inc.	New York City						●			
Coliseum Gun Traders, Ltd.	Uniondale			●	●					
Creekside Gun Shop	Holcomb	●	●		●					●
Damiano's Field & Stream	Ossining				●		●			
Davco Stores, 305 Broadway	Monticello		●	●						
Gemini Arms Ltd.	Syosset									
Hart's Gun Supply, Ed	Bath				●			●		
Jovino Co., Inc., John	New York				●					
Kielon, Gunsmith, Dave	Webster			●					●	
LeFever & Sons, Inc., Frank	Lee Center									
Lounsbury Sporting Goods, Bob	Middletown		●	●						
Mulvey's Marine & Sport Shop	Monticello		●							
Pearson's Gun Shop	Auburn			●						
Rapids Gun Shop	Niagra Falls		●		●					
Scalzo's Sporting Goods	Endicott				●					
Schultheis Sporting Goods	Arkport			●						
Smith's Lawn & Marine Svc.	Clarence		●							
Solvay Home & Outdoor Center	Solvay									
Sports Mart, The	Ogdensburg									●

SERVICE CENTER	CITY	BR	CR	MO	RE	ST	SW	TC	WN	WE
Taylor & Vadney, Inc.	Albany		●							
Van's Gunsmith Service	Parish				●					
White Dog Gunsmithing	Ilion				●					
NORTH CAROLINA										
Baity's Custom Gunworks	North Wilksboro			●	●		●		●	
Blue Ridge Outdoor Sports, Inc.	E. Flatrock	●		●	●		●		●	●
Cumberland Knife & Gun Works	Fayetteville				●				●	
Don's Gun Shop	Ashville			●						
Hill's, Inc.	Raleigh	●			●					
Marine Gun & Lock Shop	Jacksonville									
Mike's Crosman Service	Winston-Salem		●							
Paschall's	Kingston				●					
Perry's of Wendell, Inc.	Wendell				●					
Warren's Sports Hdqts.	Washington				●					
NORTH DAKOTA										
Gun City, Inc.	Bismarck	●	●	●	●				●	
Outdoorsman, Inc.	Fargo	●	●	●	●					●
S.K. Guns, Inc.	Fargo									
OHIO										
Airgun Centre, Ltd.	Cincinnati		●							
All Game Sport Center	Milford		●					●		
Central Ohio Police Supply, c/o Wammes Guns	Bellefontaine									
Cherry Corners, Inc.	Lodi				●					
Eyster Heritage Gunsmiths, Ken	Centerburg	●							●	
Griffiths & Sons, E.J.	Lima			●						
Heckman Arms Company, Chagrin Valley Firearms	Chagrin								●	
Keller Gunsmithing	Bradford				●					
Log Cabin Sport Shop	Lodi							●		
Precision Airgun Sales	Solon		●							
Sportsman's Depot	Urban		●		●					
Sportsman's Haven	Cambridge		●		●		●		●	●
Sportsmen's Repair Ctr., Inc.	Columbus Groves						●			
Stocker's Shop	Warren		●		●					
Trading Post, The	Massillon				●		●	●	●	
Upton's Gun Shop	Fremont									
VanBurnes Gun Shop	Toledo		●		●		●			
Zanes Gun Rack	Columbus									
OKLAHOMA										
Anderson, Inc., Andy	Oklahoma City				●				●	
D&D Sporting Goods	Tishomingo									
Junior's Gun & Lock Shop	Ponca City									
Mashburn Arms Co. Inc.	Oklahoma City		●					●		
Meydag, Peter	Tulsa									
Outdoor America Store	Oklahoma City		●		●				●	
Shamburg's Wholesale Spt. Gds.	Clinton									
Skeet's Gun Shop	Tahlequah									

See page 460 for Service Center addresses.

Warranty Service Centers (cont.)

■BR=Browning ■CR=Crosman ■MO=Mossberg ■RE=Remington ■ST=Stoeger ■SW=Smith & Wesson ■TC=Thompson/Center ■WN=Winchester ■WE=Weatherby

SERVICE CENTER	CITY	BR	CR	MO	RE	ST	SW	TC	WN	WE
Southwest Shooters Supply, Inc.	Oklahoma City	●								
Sport Shop, The	Kingfisher		●							
Sports World, Inc.	Tulsa	●			●		●		●	
OREGON										
Allison & Carey Gun Works	Portland	●		●	●				●	
Dundee Custom Gunsmithing	Medford		●	●						
Enstad & Douglas	Oregon City			●	●			●		
Felton, James	Eugene				●					
Lock, Stock & Barrel	Grants Pass								●	
Metro Rod & Reel	Portland									
Starnes, Gunmaker, Ken	Hillsboro		●		●					
Surplus Center	Roseburg	●		●	●					
PENNSYLVANIA										
Auto Electric & Parts, Inc.	Media		●							
Braverman Arms Co.	Wilkinsburg				●					
Colabaugh Gunsmith, Inc., Craig	Stroudsburg				●					
Federal Firearms Co., Inc.	Oakdale									
Fix Gunshop, Inc., Michael D.	Reading									
Flaig's Inc.	Pittsburgh									
Gorenflo Gunsmithing	Erie									
Grice Gun Shop, Inc.	Clearfield		●	●						
Hart & Son, Robert W.	Nescopeck									
Hemlock Gun Shop	Lakeville		●							
Hemlock Gun Shop	Hawley		●							
Herold's Gun Shoppe	Waynesboro	●			●					
Keeley, John L.	Spring City			●						
Keidel's Gunsmithing Service	Washington				●				●	
Leo's Custom Stocks	Library			●						
Levan's Sport Goods	Lebanon		●							
Miller's Sport Shop	Mountaintop			●						
Phoenix Armoury, Inc.	Norristown		●							
Richland Gun Shop	Richland			●						
Somerset Sports Shop	Somerset				●					
Sportsman's Shop	New Holland		●		●					
Unique Sporting Goods	Edensburg				●					
Wholesale Shooters Supplies	Lititz									
Ye Olde Gun Shop	Bradford		●	●						
RHODE ISLAND										
D&L Shooting Supplies	Warwick	●	●		●				●	
Gun Hospital, The	E. Providence		●							
SOUTH CAROLINA										
Borgheresi, Enrique	Greenville		●							
Bryan & Associates	Anderson									
Gun Rack, Inc., The	Aiken				●		●			
Gun Room, The	Chapin									
Gunsmith, Inc., The	West Columbia			●	●					
Roy's Antiques & Things	Mountain Rest		●	●						
S.E.M. Gun Works	Greenville		●							

SERVICE CENTER	CITY	BR	CR	MO	RE	ST	SW	TC	WN	WE
Smith & Smith Gun Shop, Inc.	Charleston Hghts.	●								
Southland Gun Works, Inc.	Darlington				●					
SOUTH DAKOTA										
Gary's Gun Shop	Sioux Falls				●					
Jim's Gun & Service Center	Aberdeen				●				●	
Ron's Gun Repair	Sioux Falls			●	●				●	
Roy's Sport Shop	Watertown			●	●					●
Sodak Sport & Bait	Aberdeen	●			●				●	
TENNESSEE										
D&L Gunsmithing/Guns & Ammo	Memphis	●		●	●		●		●	
Fox & Company	Knoxville				●					
Friedman's Army Surplus	Nashville		●		●				●	
Gun City USA, Inc.	Nashville	●	●	●	●		●	●		●
Hagstrom, E.G.	Memphis				●					
Hill's Hardware & Sporting Goods	Union City									●
McGuns, W.H.	Humboldt	●			●					
Mines Gun Shack	Tullahoma				●					
Shaler Eagle	Jonesbrough									
TEXAS										
Alpine Range	Fort Worth	●			●				●	
Armadillo Air Gun Repair	Corpus Christi		●							
Ben's Gun Shop	Duncanville		●		●				●	
Billy Freds	Amarillo	●			●					
Boggus Gun Shop	San Marcos				●		●			
Carroll's Gun Shop, Inc.	Wharton				●				●	
Carter's Country	Houston			●	●					●
Cogdell's, Inc.	Waco									
Coleman, Inc., Ron	Carrollton	●			●				●	
Custom Gun Service	McAllen				●		●		●	
Don & Tim's Gun Shop	San Antonio				●				●	
Ewell Cross Gun Shop, Inc.	Ft. Worth	●			●		●		●	
Freer's Gun Shop	Houston	●			●					
Gun & Tackle Store, The	Dallas				●		●			
Kirkpatrick, Gunsmith, Larry	Lubbock									
Les Gun & Tackle Shop	Texarkana				●			●		
Lone Star Guns, Inc.	Plano				●					
Longacres, Inc.	Abilene									
Master Gunsmiths, Inc.	Houston	●			●		●		●	
McBride's Guns, Inc.	Austin	●			●				●	
McClelland Gun Shop	Dallas				●		●		●	
Mueschke Manufacturing Co.	Houston									●
Nagel Gun Shop, Inc.	San Antonio				●			●	●	
Oshman's Sporting Goods, Inc.	Houston									
Pasadena Gun Center	Pasadena				●		●		●	
Precision Gunsmithing	Amarillo									
Ray's Sporting Goods	Dallas				●					●
Reynolds Gun Shop, Inc.	Tyler				●					
Texas Gun Shop, Inc.	Corpus Christi									

See page 460 for Service Center addresses.

Warranty Service Centers (cont.)

■BR=Browning ■CR=Crosman ■MO=Mossberg ■RE=Remington ■ST=Stoeger ■SW=Smith & Wesson ■TC=Thompson/Center ■WN=Winchester ■WE=Weatherby

SERVICE CENTER	CITY	BR	CR	MO	RE	ST	SW	TC	WN	WE
Custom Firearms Shop, The	Sheboygan	●		●	●					
Flintrop Arms Corp.	Milwaukee	●		●	●					
Gander Mountain, Inc.	Wilmot						●			●
Jack's Lock & Gun Shop	Fond Du Lac		●							
Jay's Sports, Inc.	Menomonee Falls	●			●				●	
Midwestern Shooters Supply, Inc.	Lomira	●		●	●					
Phillips, D.J., Gunsmith	Pewaukee			●	●					
Potter Gunsmithing	Muskego			●	●					
Precision Gun Works	Oshkosh			●	●					
River Bend Sport Shop	Waupaca						●			
R&R Shooters Supply	Mauston		●							●
Rusk Gun Shop, Inc.	Madison	●		●	●					●
Sea Gull Marina	Two Rivers		●							
WYOMING										
Elbe Arms Co. Inc.	Cheyenne			●	●					
Jackalope Gun Shop	Douglas			●	●					
CANADA										
Armurie De L'Outaouqis	Hull, PQ			●	●		●		●	
Casey's Gun Shop	Rogersville, NB	●		●	●		●		●	
Charlton Co., Ltd.	Brentwood Bay, BC						●		●	
Custom Gun Shop	Edmonton, AB	●		●	●				●	
Davidson's Canada	Peterborough, ON			●	●				●	
Delhi Small Arms	Delhi, ON								●	
Delisle Thompson Sport Goods	Saskatoon, SK				●				●	
Epps, Ellwood	Orilla, ON							●		
Ernie's Gun Shop, Ltd.	Winnipeg, MB			●	●				●	
Frontier Gun & Sport	Font Hill, ON								●	
Gene's Gunsmithing	Selkirk, MB	●		●	●					
Girard, Florent, Gunsmith	Chicoutimi, PQ							●		
L'Armurier Alain Bouchard, Inc.	St. Chryostome, PQ	●		●	●					
Long Gunsmithing Ltd., W.R.	Coburg, ON	●			●					
Lusignant Armurier, A. Richard	St. Hyacinthe, PQ			●	●					●
Magasin Latulippe, Inc.	Quebec, PQ	●			●					
Newby, Stewart, Gunsmith	New Burgh, ON				●					
Precision Arms & Gunsmithing Ltd.	Nobleton, ON			●	●				●	
Ralph's Gun Shop	Saskatoon, SK				●				●	
Randy's Gun Repair	Tabustinac, NB				●				●	
Reliable Gun & Tackle, Ltd.	Vancouver, BC	●			●					
Robinson's Sporting Goods, Ltd.	Victoria, BC								●	
Russel's Sporting Goods	Calgary, AB			●	●					
Saskatoon Gunsmith Shoppe, Ltd.	Saskatoon, SK			●	●				●	
Selin Gunsmith, Ltd., Del	Vernon, BC						●		●	
Taylor's Technical Gunsmithing Co.	Gormley, ON				●				●	
Westgate Gunsports, Inc.	Edmonton, AB			●	●				●	
West Luther Gun Repair	Conn, ON									
Wholesale Sports	Edmonton, AB				●				●	
Wortner Gun Works, Ltd.	Chatham, ON		●						●	

SERVICE CENTER	CITY	BR	CR	MO	RE	ST	SW	TC	WN	WE
Wichita Guncraft, Inc.	Wichita Falls			●	●				●	
Williamson Gunsmith Service	Hurst			●	●					
Wolfer Brothers, Inc.	Houston		●							
UTAH										
Gun Ace Gunsmithing	Cedar City	●			●					
Gun Shop, The	Salt Lake City			●	●					
Gunsmith Co., The	Salt Lake City			●	●					
Hutch's	Lehi		●	●				●		
Professional Armaments, Inc.	Murray		●	●	●		●			
VERMONT										
Barrows Point Trading Post	Quechee				●					
Burby, Inc. Guns & Gunsmithing	Middlebury				●				●	
Carpenters Gun Works	Proctorsville		●	●						
Clapps Gun Shop	Orchard Heights							●		
VIRGINIA										
Atlantic & Pacific Guns	Virginia Beach	●		●	●					
Bob's Gun & Tackle Shop, (Blaustein & Reich, Inc.)	Norfolk	●		●	●		●		●	
Cervera, Albert J.	Hanover	●	●							
King's Gun Shop, Inc.	Franklin	●		●	●					
Moates Sport Shop, Bob	Midlothian	●								
Northern Virginia Gun Works, Inc.	Springfield				●					
Old Dominion Engraver, Inc.	Lynchburg									
Princess Anne Marine & Sport Center	Virginia Beach			●	●					
Richmond Gun Shop	Richmond				●					
WASHINGTON										
Brock's Gunsmithing, Inc.	Spokane			●	●					
Chet Paulson Outfitters	Tacoma	●		●	●					
Dress Ranch & Home, Inc.	Moses Lake			●	●					
Greene's Gun Shop	Oak Harbor				●					
Karrer's Gunatorium	Spokane			●	●		●			
Kesselring Gun Shop	Burlington	●		●	●					
Pintos Gun Shop	Kent				●					
Shooters Supply	Yakima									
Wisner's Gun Shop, Inc.	Chehalis		●	●	●		●	●		
Wheeler Gun Shop, C.	Richland		●	●	●					●
WEST VIRGINIA										
Bait & Tackle Shop, The	Fairmont		●		●					
J.T. Gunshop, Inc., d/b/a Carolina Gun & Sports	Beckley								●	
Lew's Mountaineer Gunsmithing	Charleston				●		●		●	
Milliken's Gun Shop	Elm Grove			●					●	
Shooting Gallery, The	Weirton		●							
WISCONSIN										
Badgers Shooters Supply, Inc.	Owen				●					
Bob's Crosman Repair	Cudahy		●							

See page 460 for Service Center addresses.

METALLIC SIGHTS

Sporting Leaf and Open Sights

BURRIS SPORTING REAR SIGHT Made of spring steel, supplied with multi-step elevator for coarse adjustments and notch plate with lock screw for finer adjustments.
Price: **$15.95**
LYMAN No. 16 Middle sight for barrel dovetail slot mounting. Folds flat when scope or peep sight is used. Sight notch plate adjustable for elevation. White triangle for quick aiming. 3 heights: A—.400" to .500", B—.345" to .445", C—.500" to .600".
Price: **$13.50**
MARBLE FALSE BASE #72, #73, #74 New screw-on base for most rifles replaces factory base. ³⁄₈" dovetail slot permits installation of any folding rear sight. Can be had in sweat-on models also.
Price: **$7.25**
MARBLE CONTOUR RAMP #14R For late model Rem. 725, 740, 760, 742 rear sight mounting. ⁹⁄₁₆" between mounting screws. Accepts all sporting rear sights.
Price: **$14.40**
MARBLE FOLDING LEAF Flat-top or semi-buckhorn style. Folds down when scope or peep sights are used. Reversible plate gives choice of "U" or "V" notch. Adjustable for elevation.
Price: **$13.35**
Price: Also available with both windage and elevation adjustment . . . **$15.30**
MARBLE SPORTING REAR With white enamel diamond, gives choice of two "U" and two "V" notches or different sizes. Adjustment in height by means of double step elevator and sliding notch piece. For all rifles; screw or dovetail installation.
Price: . . . . **$13.35-$15.20**
MARBLE #20 UNIVERSAL New screw or sweat-on base. Both have .100" elevation adjustment. In five base sizes. Three styles of U-notch, square notch, peep. Adjustable for windage and elevation.
Price: Screw-on **$20.55**
Price: Sweat-on **$18.90**
MILLETT RIFLE SIGHT Open, fully adjustable rear sight fits standard ³⁄₈" dovetail cut in barrel. Choice of white outline or target rear blades, .360". Front with white or orange bar, .343", .400", .430", .460", .500", .540".
Price: Rear sight **$52.95**
Price: Front sight **$11.75**
MILLETT SCOPE-SITE Open, adjustable or fixed rear sights dovetail into a base integral with the top scope-mounting ring. Blaze orange front ramp sight is integral with the front ring half. Rear sights have white outline aperture. Provides fast, short-radius, Patridge-type open sights on the top of the scope. Can be used with all Millett rings, Weaver-style bases, Ruger 77 (also fits Redhawk), Ruger Ranch Rifle, No. 1, No. 3, Rem. 870, 1100; Burris, Leupold and Redfield bases.
Price: Scope-Site top only, windage only **$29.65**
Price: As above, fully adjustable **$62.95**
Price: Scope-Site Hi-Turret, fully adjustable, low, medium, high **$62.95**
WICHITA MULTI RANGE SIGHT SYSTEM Designed for silhouette shooting. System allows you to adjust the rear sight to four repeatable range settings, once it is pre-set. Sight clicks to any of the settings by turning a serrated wheel. Front sight is adjustable for weather and light conditions with one adjustment. Specify gun when ordering.
Price: Rear sight **$93.50**
Price: Front sight **$69.95**
WILLIAMS DOVETAIL OPEN SIGHT (WDOS) Open rear sight with windage and elevation adjustment. Furnished with "U" notch or choice of blades. Slips into dovetail and locks with gib lock. Heights from .281" to .531".
Price: With blade **$14.95**
Price: Less Blade **$9.35**
WILLIAMS GUIDE OPEN SIGHT (WGOS) Open rear sight with windage and elevation adjustment. Bases to fit most military and commercial barrels. Choice of square "U" or "V" notch blade, ³⁄₁₆", ¼", ⁵⁄₁₆", or ³⁄₈" high.
Price: With blade **$19.95**
Price: Extra blades, each **$5.60**
Price: Less blade **$14.35**
WILLIAMS WGOS OCTAGON Open rear sight for 1" octagon barrels. Installs with two 6-48 screws and uses same hole spacing as most T/C muzzleloading rifles. Four heights, choice of square, U, V, B blade.
Price: **$19.95**

Micrometer Receiver Sights

BEEMAN/WEIHRAUCH MATCH APERTURE SIGHT Micrometer ¼-minute click adjustment knobs with settings indicated on scales.
Price: **$119.95**

BEEMAN/FEINWERKBAU MATCH APERTURE SIGHTS Locks into one of four eye-relief positions. Micrometer ¼-minute click adjustments; may be set to zero at any range. Extra windage scale visible beside eyeshade. Primarily for use at 5 to 20 meters.
Price: **$199.98**
BEEMAN SPORT APERTURE SIGHT Positive click micrometer adjustments. Standard units with flush surface screwdriver adjustments. Deluxe version has target knobs. For air rifles with grooved receivers.
Price: Standard **$34.98**
Price: Deluxe **$44.98**
LYMAN No. 57 ¼-minute clicks. Stayset knobs. Quick release slide, adjustable zero scales. Made for almost all modern rifles.
Price: **$65.00**
LYMAN No. 66 Fits close to the rear of flat-sided receivers, furnished with Stayset knobs. Quick release slide, ¼-min. adjustments. For most lever or slide action or flat-sided automatic rifles.
Price: **$65.00**
LYMAN No. 66U Light weight, designed for most modern shotguns with a flat-sided, round-top receiver. ¼-minute clicks. Requires drilling, tapping. Not for Browning A-5, Rem. M11.
Price: **$65.00**
LYMAN 90MJT RECEIVER SIGHT Mounts on standard Lyman and Williams FP bases. Has ¼-minute audible micrometer click adjustments, target knobs with direction indicators. Adjustable zero scales, quick release slide. Large ⁷⁄₈" diameter aperture disk.
Price: **$79.95**
MILLETT ASSAULT RIFLE SIGHTS Fully adjustable, heat-treated nickel steel peep aperture receiver sight for Mini-14. Has fine windage and elevation adjustments; replaces original.
Price: Rear sight **$51.45**
Price: Front sight **$17.85**
WILLIAMS FP Internal click adjustments. Positive locks. For virtually all rifles, T/C Contender, Heckler & Koch HK-91, Ruger Mini-14, plus Win., Rem. and Ithaca shotguns.
Price: From **$53.25**
Price: With Target Knobs **$63.25**
Price: With Square Notched Blade **$56.00**
Price: With Target Knobs & Square Notched Blade **$66.15**
Price: FP-GR (for dovetail-grooved receivers, 22s and air guns) **$53.25**
WILLIAMS TARGET FP Similar to the FP series but developed for most bolt-action rimfire rifles. Target FP High adjustable from 1.250" to 1.750" above centerline of bore; Target FP Low adjustable from .750" to 1.250". Attaching bases for Rem. 540X, 541-S, 580, 581, 582 (#540); Rem. 510, 511, 512, 513-T, 521-T (#510); Win. 75 (#75); Savage/Anschutz 64 and Mark 12 (#64). Some rifles require drilling, tapping.
Price: High or Low, with Base **$84.10**
Price: As above, less Base **$72.00**
Price: Base only **$12.10**
Price: FP-T/C Scout rifle, from **$53.25**
WILLIAMS 5-D SIGHT Low cost sight for shotguns, 22s and the more popular big game rifles. Adjustment for windage and elevation. Fits most guns without drilling or tapping. Also for British SMLE, Winchester M94 Side Eject.
Price: From **$29.95**
Price: With Shotgun Aperture **$29.95**
WILLIAMS GUIDE (WGRS) Receiver sight for 30 M1 Carbine, M1903A3 Springfield, Savage 24s, Savage-Anschutz rifles and Weatherby XXII. Utilizes military dovetail; no drilling. Double-dovetail windage adjustment, sliding dovetail adjustment for elevation.
Price: **$29.95**

Front Sights

LYMAN HUNTING SIGHTS Made with gold or white beads ¹⁄₁₆" to ³⁄₃₂" wide and in varying heights for most military and commercial rifles. Dovetail bases.
Price: **$9.80**
MARBLE STANDARD Ivory, red, or gold bead. For all American-made rifles, ¹⁄₁₆" wide bead with semi-flat face which does not reflect light. Specify type of rifle when ordering.
Price: **$8.00**
MARBLE-SHEARD "GOLD" Shows up well even in darkest timber. Shows same color on different colored objects; sturdily built. Medium bead. Various models for different makes of rifles so specify type of rifle when ordering.
Price: **$10.18**
MARBLE CONTOURED Same contour and shape as Marble-Sheard but uses standard ¹⁄₁₆" or ³⁄₃₂" bead, ivory, red or gold. Specify rifle type.
Price: **$9.25**
MARBLE PATRIDGE Gold-faced Patridge front sight is available in .250" or .34" widths and heights from .260" to .538".
Price: **$10.18**

CAUTION: PRICES CHANGE, CHECK AT GUNSHOP.

POLY-CHOKE Rifle front sights available in six heights and two widths. Model A designed to be inserted into the barrel dovetail; Model B is for use with standard .350" ramp; both have standard ⅜" dovetails. Gold or ivory color ⅟₁₆" bead. From Marble Arms.
Price: **$6.45**

WILLIAMS RISER BLOCKS For adding .250" height to front sights when using a receiver sight. Two widths available: .250" for Williams Streamlined Ramp or .340" on all standard ramps having this base width. Uses standard ⅜" dovetail.
Price: **$4.95**

Globe Target Front Sights

LYMAN 20 MJT TARGET FRONT Has ⅞" diameter, one-piece steel globe with ⅜" dovetail base. Height is .700" from bottom of dovetail to center of aperture; height on 20 LJT is .750". Comes with seven Anschutz-size steel inserts—two posts and five apertures .126" through .177".
Price: 20 MJT or 20 LJT **$36.00**

LYMAN No. 17A TARGET Includes seven interchangeable inserts: four apertures, one transparent amber and two posts .50" and .100" in width.
Price: **$28.00**
Price: Insert set **$9.95**

LYMAN NO. 93 MATCH Has ⅞" diameter, fits any rifle with a standard dovetail mounting block. Comes with seven target inserts and accepts most Anschutz accessories. Hooked locking bolt and nut allows quick removal, installation. Base available in .860" (European) and .562" (American) hole spacing.
Price: **$45.00**

Ramp Sights

LYMAN SCREW-ON RAMP Used with 8-40 screws but may also be brazed on. Heights from .10" to .350". Ramp without sight.
Price: **$15.95**

MARBLE FRONT RAMPS Available in either screw-on or sweat-on style, five heights: ³⁄₁₆", ⁵⁄₁₆", ⅜", ⁷⁄₁₆", ⁹⁄₁₆". Standard ⅜" dovetail slot.
Price: **$15.40**
Price: Hoods for above ramps **$3.35**

WILLIAMS SHORTY RAMP Companion to "Streamlined" ramp, about ½" shorter. Screw-on or sweat-on. It is furnished in ⅛", ³⁄₁₆", ⁹⁄₃₂", and ⅜" heights without hood only.
Price: **$12.50**
Price: With dovetail lock **$14.85**

WILLIAMS STREAMLINED RAMP Available in screw-on or sweat-on models. Furnished in ⁹⁄₁₆", ⁷⁄₁₆", ⅜", ⁵⁄₁₆", ³⁄₁₆" heights.
Price: **$14.95**
Price: Sight hood **$3.50**

WILLIAMS STREAMLINED FRONT SIGHTS Narrow (.250" width) for Williams Streamlined ramps and others with ¼" top width; medium (.340" width) for all standard factory ramps. Available with white, gold or flourescent beads, ⅟₁₆" or ³⁄₃₂".
Price: . . . . **$7.90 to $8.20**

Handgun Sights

BO-MAR DELUXE BMCS Gives ⅜" windage and elevation adjustment at 50 yards on Colt Gov't 45; sight radius under 7". For GM and Commander models only. Uses existing dovetail slot. Has shield-type rear blade.
Price: **$65.95**

BO-MAR LOW PROFILE RIB & ACCURACY TUNER Streamlined rib with front and rear sights; 7⅛" sight radius. Brings sight line closer to the bore than standard or extended sight and ramp. Weight 5 oz. Made for Colt Gov't 45, Super 38, and Gold Cup 45 and 38.
Price: **$123.00**

BO-MAR COMBAT RIB For S&W Model 19 revolver with 4" barrel. Sight radius 5¾", weight 5½ oz.
Price: **$110.00**

BO-MAR FAST DRAW RIB Streamlined full-length rib with integral Bo-Mar micrometer sight and serrated fast draw sight. For Browning 9mm, S&W 39, Colt Commander 45, Super Auto and 9mm.
Price: **$110.00**

BO-MAR HUNTER REAR SIGHT Replacement rear sight in two models— S&W K and L frames use 2¾" Bo-Mar base with ⁷⁄₁₆" overhang, has two screw holes; S&W N frame has 3" base, three screw holes. A .200" taller front blade is required.
Price: **$86.00**

BO-MAR WINGED RIB For S&W 4" and 6" length barrels—K-38, M10, HB 14 and 19. Weight for the 6" model is about 7¼ oz.
Price: **$123.00**

BO-MAR COVER-UP RIB Adjustable rear sight, winged front guards. Fits right over revolver's original front sight. For S&W 4" M-10HB, M-13, M-58, M-64 & 65, Ruger 4" models SDA-34, SDA-84, SS-34, SS-84, GF-84, GF-84.
Price: **$117.00**

C-MORE SIGHTS Replacement front sight blades offered in two types and five styles. Made of Du Pont Acetal, they come in a set of five high-contrast

colors: blue, green, pink, red and yellow. Easy to install. Patridge style for Colt Python (all barrels), Ruger Super Blackhawk (7½"), Ruger Blackhawk (4⅝"); ramp style for Python (all barrels), Blackhawk (4⅝"), Super Blackhawk (7½" and 10½"). From Mag-na-port Int'l.
Price: Per set **$19.95**

MMC COMBAT FIXED REAR SIGHT (Colt 1911-Type Pistols) This veteran MMC sight is well known to those who prefer a true combat sight for "carry" guns. Steel construction for long service. Choose from a wide variety of front sights.
Price: Combat Fixed Rear, plain **$18.45**
Price: As above, white outline **$23.65**
Price: Combat Front Sight for above, six styles, from **$5.15**

MMC M/85 ADJUSTABLE REAR SIGHT Designed to be compatible with the Ruger P-85 front sight. Fully adjustable for windage and elevation.
Price: M/85 Adjustable Rear Sight, plain **$52.45**
Price: As above, white outline **$57.70**

MMC STANDARD ADJUSTABLE REAR SIGHT Available for Colt 1911 type, Ruger Standard Auto, and now for S&W 469, and 659 pistols. No front sight change is necessary, as this sight will work with the original factory front sight.
Price: Standard Adjustable Rear Sight, plain leaf **$46.05**
Price: Standard Adjustable Rear Sight, white outline **$51.15**

MMC MINI-SIGHT Miniature size for carrying, fully adjustable, for maximum accuracy with your pocket auto. MMC's Mini-Sight will work with the factory front sight. No machining is necessary; easy installation. Available for Walther PP, PPK, and PPK/S pistols. Will also fit fixed sight Browning Hi-Power (P-35).
Price: Mini-Sight, plain **$58.45**
Price: Mini-Sight, white bar **$63.45**

MEPROLIGHT SIGHTS Replacement tritium open sights for popular handguns and AR-15/M-16 rifles. Both front and rear sights have tritium inserts for illumination in low-light conditions. Inserts give constant non-glare green light for 5 years, even in cold weather. For most popular auto pistols, revolvers, some rifles and shotguns. Contact Hesco, Inc. for complete details.
Price: Shotgun bead front sight **$22.95**
Price: M-16 front sight only **$32.95**
Price: H&K SR9, MP5 front sight only **$49.95**
Price: Colt Python, King Cobra, Ruger GP-100 adj. sights **$124.95**
Price: Most other front and rear fixed sights **$89.95**
Price: Adj. sights for Beretta, Browning, Colt Gov't., Glock, Ruger P-Series, SIG, Taurus PT-92 . . . . **$139.95**

MILLETT BAR-DOT-BAR TRITIUM SIGHTS Combo set uses the Series 100 fully adjustable sight system with horizontal tritium inserts on the rear, a single insert on the front. Available for: Ruger P-85, SIG Sauer P220, P225/226, Browning Hi-Power, Colt GM, CZ/TZ, TA-90, Glock 17, 19, 20, 21, 22, 23, S&W (2nd, 3rd generations), Beretta 84, 85, 92SB, Taurus PT-92.
Price: **$135.00**
Price: Beretta, Taurus **$143.50**

MILLETT 3-DOT SYSTEM SIGHTS The 3-Dot System sights use a single white dot on the front blade and two dots flanking the rear notch. Fronts available in Dual-Crimp and Wide Stake-On styles, as well as special applications. Adjustable rear sight available for most popular auto pistols and revolvers.
Price: Front, from **$15.25**
Price: Adjustable rear, from . . . . **$46.96 to $52.95**

MILLETT REVOLVER FRONT SIGHTS All-steel replacement front sights with either white or orange bar. Easy to install. For Ruger GP-100, Redhawk, Security-Six, Police-Six, Speed-Six, Colt Trooper, Diamondback, King Cobra, Peacemaker, Python, Dan Wesson 22 and 15-2.
Price: . . . . **$12.95 to $15.25**

MILLETT DUAL-CRIMP FRONT SIGHT Replacement front sight for automatic pistols. Dual-Crimp uses an all-steel two-point hollow rivet system. Available in eight heights and four styles. Has a skirted base that covers the front sight pad. Easily installed with the Millett Installation Tool Set. Available in Blaze Orange Bar, White Bar, Serrated Ramp, Plain Post.
Price: **$15.25**

MILLETT STAKE-ON FRONT SIGHT Replacement front sight for automatic pistols. Stake-On sights have skirted base that covers the front sight pad. Easily installed with the Millet Installation Tool Set. Available in seven heights and four styles—Blaze Orange Bar, White Bar, Serrated Ramp, Plain Post.
Price: **$15.25**

OMEGA OUTLINE SIGHT BLADES Replacement rear sight blades for Colt and Ruger single action guns and the Interarms Virginian Dragoon. Standard Outline available in gold or white notch outline on blue metal. From Omega Sales, Inc.
Price: **$8.95**

OMEGA MAVERICK SIGHT BLADES Replacement "peep-sight" blades for Colt, Ruger SAs, Virginian Dragoon. Three models available—No. 1, Plain; No. 2, Single Bar; No. 3, Double Bar Rangefinder. From Omega Sales, Inc.
Price: Each **$6.95**

TRIJICON NIGHT SIGHTS Three-dot night sight system uses tritium inserts in the front and rear sights. Tritium "lamps" are mounted in silicone rubber inside a metal cylinder. A polished crystal sapphire provides protection and clarity. Inlaid white outlines provide 3-dot aiming in daylight also. Available for most popular handguns with fixed or adjustable sights. From Trijicon, Inc.
Price: . . . . **$19.95 to $175.00**

CAUTION: PRICES CHANGE, CHECK AT GUNSHOP.

THOMPSON/CENTER SILHOUETTE SIGHTS Replacement front and rear sights for the T/C Contender. Front sight has three interchangeable blades. Rear sight has three notch widths. Rear sight can be used with existing soldered front sights.
Price: Front sight **$30.40**
Price: Rear sight **$77.25**
WICHITA SERIES 70/80 SIGHT Provides click windage and elevation adjustments with precise repeatability of settings. Sight blade is grooved and angled back at the top to reduce glare. Available in Low Mount Combat or Low Mount Target styles for Colt 45s and their copies, S&W 645, Hi-Power, CZ 75 and others.
Price: Rear sight, target or combat **$66.75**
Price: Front sight, Patridge or ramp **$10.45**
WICHITA GRAND MASTER DELUXE RIBS Ventilated rib has wings machined into it for better sight acquisition. Made of stainless steel, sights blued. Uses Wichita Multi-Range rear sight, adjustable front sight. Made for revolvers with 6" barrel.
Price: Model 301 (adj. sight K-frames with custom bbl. of 1.000"-1.032" dia., L- and N-frames with 1.062"-1.100" bbl.) **$160.00**
Price: Model 302 (fixed sight K-frames; M10, 65, 13 with 1.000" bbl., N-frame with 1.062" bbl.) **$160.00**
Price: Model 303 (Model 29, 629 with factory bbl., adj. sight K-, L-, N-frames) **$160.00**
WICHITA DOUBLE MASTER RIB Ventilated rib has wings machined on either side of fixed front post sight for better acquisition and is relieved for Mag-na-ports. Milled to accept Weaver See-Thru-style rings. Made of blued steel. Has Wichita Multi-Range rear sight system. Made for Model 29/629 with factory barrel, and all adjustable-sight K-, L- and N-frames.
Price: Model 403 . . . . **$140.00**

Shotgun Sights

ACCURA-SITE For shooting shotgun slugs. Three models to fit most shotguns—"A" for vent. rib barrels, "B" for solid ribs, "C" for plain barrels. Rear sight has windage and elevation provisions. Easily removed and replaced. Includes front and rear sights. From All's, The Jim Tembeils Co.
Price: . . . . **$27.95 to $34.95**
FIRE FLY EM-109 SL SHOTGUN SIGHT Made of aircraft-grade aluminum, this ¼-oz. "channel" sight has a thick, sturdy hollowed post between the side rails to give a Patridge sight picture. All shooting is done with both eyes open, allowing the shooter to concentrate on the target, not the sights. The hole in the sight post gives reduced-light shooting capability and allows for fast, precise aiming. For sport or combat shooting. Model EM-109 fits all vent. rib and double barrel shotguns and muzzleloaders with octagon barrel. Model MOC-110 fits all plain barrel shotguns without screw-in chokes. From JAS, Inc. Add $3 postage.
Price: **$29.95**
LYMAN Three sights of over-sized ivory beads. No. 10 Front (press fit) for double barrel or ribbed single barrel guns...**$5.00**; No. 10D Front (screw fit) for non-ribbed single barrel guns (comes with wrench)...**$6.50**; No. 11 Middle (press fit) for double and ribbed single barrel guns...**$5.00**.
MMC M&P COMBAT SHOTGUN SIGHT SET A durable, protected ghost ring aperture, combat sight made of steel. Fully adjustable for windage and elevation.
Price: M&P Sight Set (front and rear) **$73.45**
Price: As above, installed **$83.95**
MARBLE SHOTGUN BEAD SIGHTS No. 214—Ivory front bead, ¹¹⁄₆₄", tapered shank...**$3.70**; No. 223—Ivory rear bead, .080", tapered shank...**$3.75**; No. 217—Ivory front bead, ¹¹⁄₆₄", threaded shank...**$4.00**; No.

223-T—Ivory rear bead, .080", threaded shank...**$5.30**. Reamers, taps and wrenches available from Marble Arms.
MILLETT SHURSHOT SHOTGUN SIGHT A sight system for shotguns with ventilated rib. Rear sight attaches to the rib, front sight replaces the front bead. Front has an orange face, rear has two orange bars. For 870, 1100 or other models.
Price: Front and rear **$20.95**
Price: Adjustable front and rear **$27.40**
POLY-CHOKE Replacement front shotgun sights in four styles—Xpert, Poly Bead, Xpert Mid Rib sights, and Bev-L-Block. Xpert Front available in 3x56, 6x48 thread, ³⁄₃₂" or ⁵⁄₃₂" shank length, gold, ivory...**$4.55**; or Sun Spot orange bead...**$4.85**; Poly Bead is standard replacement ⅛" bead, 6x48...**$2.75**; Xpert Mid Rib in tapered carrier (ivory only) **$4.00**, or 3x56 threaded shank (gold only)...**$2.75**; Hi and Lo Blok sights with 6x48 thread, gold or ivory...**$4.55** or Sun Spot Orange...**$4.85**. From Marble Arms.
SLUG SIGHTS Made of non-marring black nylon, front and rear sights stretch over and lock onto the barrel. Sights are low profile with blaze orange front blade. Adjustable for windage and elevation. For plain-barrel (non-ribbed) guns in 12-, 16- and 20-gauge, and for shotguns with ⁵⁄₁₆" and ⅜" ventilated ribs. From Innovision Ent.
Price: **$11.95**
WILLIAMS GUIDE BEAD SIGHT Fits all shotguns, ⅛" ivory, red or gold bead. Screws into existing sight hole. Various thread sizes and shank lengths.
Price: **$4.50**
WILLIAMS SLUGGER SIGHTS Removable aluminum sights attach to the shotgun rib. High profile front, fully adjustable rear. Fits ¼", ⁵⁄₁₆" or ⅜" (special) ribs.
Price: **$34.95**

Sight Attachments

MERIT IRIS SHUTTER DISC Eleven clicks give 12 different apertures. No. 3 Disc and Master, primarily target types, 0.22" to .125"; No. 4, ½" dia. hunting type, .025" to .155". Available for all popular sights. The Master Deluxe, with flexible rubber light shield, is particularly adapted to extension, scope height, and tang sights. All Merit Deluxe models have internal click springs; are hand fitted to minimum tolerance.
Price: Master Deluxe **$63.00**
Price: No. 3 Disc **$52.00**
Price: No. 4 Hunting Disc **$45.00**
MERIT LENS DISC Similar to Merit Iris Shutter (Model 3 or Master) but incorporates provision for mounting prescription lens integrally. Lens may be obtained locally from your optician. Sight disc is ⁷⁄₁₆" wide (Model 3), or ¾" wide (Master). Model 3 Target.
Price: **$65.00**
Price: Master Deluxe **$75.00**
MERIT OPTICAL ATTACHMENT For revolver and pistol shooters, instantly attached by rubber suction cup to regular or shooting glasses. Any aperture .020" to .156".
Price: Deluxe (swings aside) **$63.00**
WILLIAMS APERTURES Standard thread, fits most sights. Regular series ⅜" to ½" O.D., .050" to .125" hole. "Twilight" series has white reflector ring. .093" to .125" inner hole.
Price: Regular series **$4.50**
Price: Twilight series **$6.15**
Price: Wide open ⁵⁄₁₆" aperture for shotguns fits 5-D or Foolproof sights (specify model) **$7.95**

CHOKES & BRAKES

Briley Screw-In Chokes
Installation of these choke tubes requires that all traces of the original choking be removed, the barrel threaded internally with square threads and then the tubes are custom fitted to the specific barrel diameter. The tubes are thin and, therefore, made of stainless steel. Cost of installation for single-barrel guns (pumps, autos), lead shot, 12-gauge, **$129.00**, 20-gauge **$139.00**; steel shot **$159.00** and **$169.00**, all with three chokes; un-single target guns run **$190.00**; over/unders and side-by-sides, lead shot, 12-gauge, **$349.00**, 20-gauge **$369.00**; steel shot **$449.00** and **$469.00**, all with five chokes. For 10-gauge auto or pump with two steel shot chokes, **$149.00**; over/unders, side-by-sides with three steel shot chokes, **$329.00**. For 16-gauge auto or pump, three lead shot chokes, **$239.00**; over/unders, side-by-sides with five lead shot chokes, **$429.00**. The 28 and 410-bore run **$159.00** for autos and pumps with three lead shot chokes, **$429.00** for over/unders and side-by-sides with five lead shot chokes.

Cellini Stabilizer System
Designed for handgun, rifle and shotgun applications, the Cellini Stabilizer System is available as a removable factory-installed accessory. Overall length is 1¾", weight is 2 oz., and is said to reduce muzzle jump to nearly zero, even for automatic weapons. If installed by the maker, cost starts at **$185.00** for rifles; double shotguns, **$180.00**; handguns **$165.00**; single barrel shotguns start at **$75.00**. From Vito Cellini.

Cutts Compensator
The Cutts Compensator is one of the oldest variable choke devices available. Manufactured by Lyman Gunsight Corporation, it is available with a steel body. A series of vents allows gas to escape upward and downward. For the 12-ga. Comp body, six fixed-choke tubes are available: the Spreader—popular with Skeet shooters; Improved Cylinder; Modified; Full; Superfull, and Magnum Full. Full, Modified and Spreader tubes are available for 12 or 20, and an Adjustable Tube, giving Full through Improved Cylinder chokes, is offered in 12 and 20 gauges. Cutts Compensator, complete with wrench, adaptor and any single tube **$69.80**; with adjustable tube **$91.00**. All single choke tubes **$23.00** each. No factory installation available.

Fabian Bros. Muzzle Stabilizer
A muzzlebrake/flash hider system that installs without gunsmithing on most military-type rifles, except Ruger Mini-14 and the Uzi Carbine. Adjustable for right- or left-handed shooters to eliminate muzzle rise and sideswing. No increase in sound level. Fabian Bros. offers a low-cost barrel threading service for the Mini-14 and Uzi Carbine. Available for most popular military-type rifles and carbines. Standard model, **$39.95**; Semi-Custom model (Cobray M11, MAC-10, Valmet), **$79.95**; Deluxe (M1A/M-14, M-60), **$79.95**; stainless steel, **$44.95**. All prices do not include shipping.

Gentry Quiet Muzzle Brake
Developed by gunmaker David Gentry, the "Quiet Muzzle Brake" is said to reduce recoil by up to 85 percent with no loss of accuracy or velocity. There is no increase in noise level because the noise and gasses are directed away from the shooter. The barrel is threaded for installation and the unit is blued to match the barrel finish. Price, installed, is **$150.00**. Add **$15.00** for stainless steel, **$25.00** for knurled cap to protect threads.

Intermountain Arms Recoil Brake
The Custom Compact Recoil Brake is said to reduce felt recoil by 50 percent in most calibers. Machined with an expansion chamber to maximize efficiency. There are 42 ports to direct gases away from the shooter. Individually machined, polished and blued to match each barrel. Adds 1¾ inches to the barrel. Blued or stainless steel, **$169.00**. From Intermountain Arms.

KDF Slim Line Muzzle Brake
Works on the same principle as the KDF Recoil Arrestor except has 30 pressure ports, is closer to the carrel contour, and is made of a stronger steel. Price, installed, is **$179.00**. From KDF, Inc.

Lyman CHOKE
The Lyman CHOKE is similar to the Cutts Comp in that it comes with fixed-choke tubes or an adjustable tube, with or without recoil chamber. The adjustable tube version sells for **$49.95** with recoil chamber, in 12- or 20-gauge. Lyman also offers Single-Choke tubes at **$23.00**. This device may be used with or without a recoil-reduction chamber; cost of the latter is **$12.00** extra. Available in 12- or 20-gauge only. No factory installation offered.

Mag-na-port
Electrical Discharge Machining works on any firearm except those having non-conductive shrouded barrels. EDM is a metal erosion technique using carbon electrodes that control the area to be processed. The Mag-na-port venting process utilizes small trapezoidal openings to direct powder gases upward and outward to reduce recoil.
No effect is had on bluing or nickeling outside the Mag-na-port area so no refinishing is needed. Cost for the Mag-na-port treatment is **$65.00** for revolvers, **$90.00** for auto pistols, **$115.00** for rifles, not including shipping, handling and insurance.

Poly-Choke
Marble Arms Corp., manufacturer of the Poly-Choke adjustable shotgun choke, now offers two models in 12-, 16-, 20-, and 28-gauge—the Ventilated and Standard style chokes. Each provides nine choke settings including Xtra-Full and Slug. The Ventilated model reduces 20 percent of a shotgun's recoil, the company claims, and is priced at **$85.50**. The Standard Model is **$77.25**. Postage not included. Contact Marble Arms for more data.

Reed-Choke
Reed-Choke is a system of interchangeable choke tubes that can be installed in any single or double-barreled shotgun, including over/unders. The existing chokes are bored out, the muzzles over-bored and threaded for the tubes. A choice of three Reed-Choke tubes are supplied—Skeet, Imp. Cyl., Mod., Imp. Mod., or Full. Flush fitting, no notches exposed. Designed for thin-walled barrels. Made from 174 stainless steel. Cost of the installation is **$179.95** for single-barrel guns, **$229.95** for doubles. Extra tubes cost **$40.00** each. Postage and handling charges are **$8.50**.

Pro-port
A compound ellipsoid muzzle venting process similar to Mag-na-porting, only exclusively applied to shotguns. Like Mag-na-porting, this system reduces felt recoil, muzzle jump, and shooter fatigue. Very helpful for trap doubles shooters. Pro-Port is a patented process and installation is available in both the U.S. and Canada. Cost for the Pro-Port process is **$110.00** for over/unders (both barrels); **$80.00** for only the top or bottom barrel; and **$69.00** for single-barrel shotguns. Prices do not include shipping and handling. From Pro-port Ltd.

SSK Arrestor Brake
This is a true muzzlebrake with an expansion chamber. It takes up about 1 inch of barrel and reduces velocity accordingly. Some Arrestors are added to a barrel, increasing its length. Said to reduce the felt recoil of a 458 to that approaching a 30-06. Can be set up to give zero muzzle rise in any caliber, and can be added to most guns. For handgun or rifle. Prices start at **$95.00**. Contact SSK Industries for full data.

Techni-Port
The Techni-Port recoil compensation system is intended for revolvers, single shot pistols and rifles. This is a machined process which involves back-boring the muzzle (with a 30-degree internal crown) and cutting an oval port on each side of the barrel. The process is said to reduce muzzle jump up to 60 percent and felt recoil up to 50 percent, with no reduction in velocity or accuracy. Cost of the Techni-Port process is **$99.95**, plus **$16.00** for return freight and insurance. Available from Delta Vectors, Inc.

Walker Choke Tubes
This interchangeable choke tube system uses an adaptor fitted to the barrel without swaging. Therefore, it can be fitted to any single-barreled gun. The choke tubes use the conical-parallel system as used on all factory-choked barrels. These tubes can be used in Winchester, Mossberg, Smith & Wesson, Weatherby, or similar barrels made for the standard screw-in choke system. Available for 10-, 12-, 16- and 20-gauge. Factory installation (single barrel) with standard Walker choke tube is **$95.00**, **$190.00** for double barrels with two choke tubes. A full range of constriction is available. Contact Walker Arms for more data.

Walker Full Thread Choke Tubes
An interchangeable choke tube system using fully threaded inserts. No swaging, adaptor or change in barrel exterior dimensions. Available in 12- or 20-gauge. Factory installation cost: **$95.00** with one tube; extra tubes **$20.00** each. Contact Walker Arms Co. for more data.

Maker and Model	Magn.	Field at 100 Yds. (feet)	Relative Bright-ness	Eye Relief (in.)	Length (in.)	Tube Dia. (in.)	W&E Adjust-ments	Weight (ozs.)	Price	Other Data
ACTION ARMS										[1]56mm objective. Variable intensity LED red aiming dot. Average battery life 20 to 4500 hours. Waterproof, nitrogen-filled aluminum tube. Fits most standard 1" rings. Both Ultra Dot models avail. in black and satin chrome. Imported by Action Arms Ltd.
Micro-Dot										
1.5-4.5x LER Pistol	1.5-4.5	80-26	—	12-24	8.8	1	Int.	9.5	$255.00	
1.5-4.5x Rifle	1.5-4.5	80-26	—	3	9.8	1	Int.	10.5	259.00	
2-7x32	2-7	54-18	—	3	11	1	Int.	12.1	275.00	
3-9x40	3-9	40-14	—	3	12.2	1	Int.	13.3	289.00	
4x-12x[1]	4-12	—	—	3	14.3	1	Int.	18.3	395.00	
Ultra-Dot 25 1x	—	—	—	—	5.1	1	Int.	4.0	139.00	
Ultra-Dot 30 1x	—	—	—	—	5.1	30mm	Int.	3.9	179.00	
ADCO										[1]Multi-Color Dot system changes from red to green. [2]For airguns, paintball, rimfires. Uses common lithium wafer battery. All come with extension tube for mounting. Black or matte nickel finish. Optional 2x booster available. Five year warranty. From ADCO Sales.
MiRAGE Ranger 1"	0	—	—	—	5.2	1	Int.	4.5	139.00	
MiRAGE Ranger 30mm	0	—	—	—	5.5	30mm	Int.	5.5	165.00	
MiRAGE Sportsman[1]	0	—	—	—	5.2	1	Int.	4.5	219.00	
MiRAGE Competitor[1]	0	—	—	—	5.5	30mm	Int.	5.5	249.00	
IMP Sight[2]	0	—	—	—	4.5	—	Int.	2	35.00	
AIMPOINT										Illuminates red dot in field of view. Noparallax (dot does not need to be centered). Unlimited field of view and eye relief. On/off, adj. intensity. Dot covers 3" @ 100 yds. Mounts avail. for all sights and scopes. [1]Comes with 30mm rings, battery, lens cloth. [2]Requires 1" rings. Black or stainless finish. 3x scope attachment (for rifles only), **$129.95.** [3]Projects red dot of visible laser light onto target. Black finish (LSR-2B) or stainless (LSR-2S); or comes with rings and accessories. Optional toggle switch, **$34.95.** Lithium battery life up to 15 hours. [4]Black finish (AP 5000-B) or stainless (AP 5000-S); avail. with regular 3-min. or 10-min. Mag Dot as B2 or S2. [5]Black finish; 2x magnification scope with floating dot. [6]For Beretta, Browning, Colt Gov't., Desert Eagle, Glock, Ruger, SIG-Sauer, S&W. [7]For Colt, S&W. From Aimpoint.
Series 3000 Short[2]	0	—	—	—	5.5	1	Int.	5.5	269.00	
Series 3000 Long[2]	0	—	—	—	6⅞	1	Int.	5.8	269.95	
Laserdot[3]	—	—	—	—	3.5	1	Int.	4.0	319.95	
Series 5000[4]	0	—	—	—	5.75	30mm	Int.	5.8	319.95	
Series 5000/2x[1]	2	—	—	—	7	30mm	Int.	9	399.95	
AP 2P[5]	2	—	—	—	8.5	1	Int.	8.3	324.95	
Autolaser[6]	—	—	—	—	3.75	1	Int.	4.3	351.00	
Revolver Laser[7]	—	—	—	—	3.5	1	Int.	3.6	339.00	
APPLIED LASER SYSTEMS										Visible laser diode with 100,000 hour life. Class IIIa; deep red color; 80% of beam image in 1" square at 50ft.; 100-yd. effective range; all metal construction; over 2½-hour battery life at continuous duty. From Applied Laser Systems.
T2	—	—	—	—	2.8	—	Int.	2.2	210.00	
AR15	—	—	—	—	2	—	Int.	3	315.00	
Colt 1911	—	—	—	—	2	—	Int.	4	315.00	
Beretta 92F	—	—	—	—	2	—	Int.	4	315.00	
RM 870	—	—	—	—	3	—	Int.	3	315.00	
Glock	—	—	—	—	.75	—	Int.	.8	385.00	
Mini Aimer	—	—	—	—	1.5	—	Int.	.8	370.00	
ARMSON O.E.G.										Shows red dot aiming point. No batteries needed. Standard model fits 1" ring mounts (not incl.). Other models available for many popular shotguns, para-military rifles and carbines. [1]Daylight Only Sight with ⅜" dovetail mount for 22s. Does not contain tritium. From Trijicon, Inc.
Standard	0	—	—	—	5⅛	1	Int.	4.3	211.00	
22 DOS[1]	0	—	—	—	3¾	—	Int.	3.0	121.00	
22 Day/Night	0	—	—	—	3¾	—	Int.	3.0	167.00	
M16/AR-15	0	—	—	—	5⅛	—	Int.	5.5	250.00	
Colt Pistol	0	—	—	—	3¾	—	Int.	3.0	250.00	
BAUSCH & LOMB										[1]Adj. objective, sunshade. [2]Also in matte finish, **$533.95.** [3]Also in matte finish, **$499.95.** [4]Also in matte finish, silver finish, **$319.95.** [5]Also in matte finish, **$297.95.** [6]50mm objective; matte finish **$369.95. Contact Bushnell for details.**
Elite 4000										
40-6244A[1]	6-24	18-4.5	—	3	16.9	1	Int.	20.2	587.95	
40-2104G[2]	2.5-10	41.5-10.8	—	3	13.5	1	Int.	16	513.95	
40-1636G[3]	1.5-6	61.8-16.1	—	3	12.8	1	Int.	15.4	479.95	
40-1040	10	10.5	—	3.6	13.8	1	Int.	22.1	1,389.95	
Elite 3000										
30-4124A	4-12	26.9-9	—	3	13.2	1	Int.	15.2	349.95	
30-3940G[4]	3-9	33.8-11.5	—	3	12.6	1	Int.	13.1	301.95	
30-2732G[5]	2-7	44.6-12.7	—	3	11.6	1	Int.	11.7	281.95	
30-3950G[6]	3-9	31.5-10.5	—	3	15.7	1	Int.	19	359.95	
BEEMAN										All scopes have 5-pt. reticle, all glass, fully coated lenses. [1]Pistol scope; cast mounts included. [2]Pistol scope; silhouette knobs. [3]Rubber armor coating; built-in double adj. mount, parallax-free setting. [4]Objective focus, built-in double-adj. mount; matte finish. [5]Objective focus. [6]Also available with color reticle. [7]Includes cast mounts. [8]Objective focus; silhouette knobs; matte finish. [9]Also in "L" models with reticle lighted by ambient light or tiny add-on illuminator. Lighted models slightly higher priced. Imported by Beeman.
Blue Ring 20[1]	1.5	14	150	11-16	8.3	¾	Int.	3.6	59.95	
Blue Ribbon 25[2]	2	19	150	10-24	9¹⁄₁₆	1	Int.	7.4	154.95	
SS-1[3]	2.5	30	61	3.25	5½	1	Int.	7	198.50	
SS-2[4,6,7,8,9]	3	34.5	74	3.5	6.8	1.38	Int.	13.6	285.95	
Blue Ribbon 50R[5]	2.5	33	245	3.5	12	1	Int.	11.8	198.95	
Blue Ring 10	4	27	69	3.0	10.6	1	Int.	9.5	109.95	
Blue Ribbon 66R[6,8,9]	2-7	62-16	384-31	3	11.4	1	Int.	14.9	298.50	
Blue Ring 3	3-9	39-13	172-20	3.0	12.8	1	Int.	12.7	129.95	
SS-3[3,4]	1.5-4	44.6-24.6	172-24	3	5.75	⅞	Int.	8.5	299.95	
Blue Ribbon 68R	4-12	30.5-11	150-13.5	3	14.4	1	Int.	15.2	429.95	
Blue Ribbon 54R[5]	4	29	96	3.5	12	1	Int.	12.3	229.95	
SS-2[4,6,8]	4	24.6	41	5	7	1.38	Int.	13.7	299.95	
B-SQUARE										Blue or stainless finish. From B-Square.
BSL-1	—	—	—	—	2.75	.75	Int.	2.25	259.95	

Maker and Model	Magn.	Field at 100 Yds. (feet)	Relative Bright-ness	Eye Relief (in.)	Length (in.)	Tube Dia. (in.)	W&E Adjust-ments	Weight (ozs.)	Price	Other Data
BURRIS										
Fullfield										
1½x[9]	1.6	62	—	3¼	10¼	1	Int.	9.0	229.95	All scopes avail. in Plex reticle. Steel-on-steel click adjustments. [1]Dot reticle $13 extra. [2]Post crosshair reticle $13 extra. [3]Matte satin finish $20 extra. [4]Available with parallax adjustment $28 extra (standard on 10x, 12x, 4-12x, 6-12x, 6-18x, 6x HBR and 3-12x Signature). [5]Silver Safari finish $30 extra. [6]Target knobs $20 extra, standard on silhouette models, LER and XER with P.A., 6x HBR. [7]Sunshade avail. [8]Avail. with Fine Plex reticle. [9]Available with Heavy Plex reticle. [10]Available with Posi-Lock. [11]Available with Peep Plex reticle.
2½x[9]	2.5	55	—	3¼	10¼	1	Int.	9.0	237.95	
4x[1,2,3]	3.75	36	—	3¼	11¼	1	Int.	11.5	255.95	
6x[1,3]	5.8	23	—	3¼	13	1	Int.	12.0	274.95	
12x[1,4,6,7,8]	11.8	10.5	—	3¼	15	1	Int.	15	346.95	
1¾-5x[1,2,9]	1.7-4.6	66-25	—	3¼	10⅞	1	Int.	13	295.95	
2-7x[1,2,3]	2.5-6.8	47-18	—	3¼	12	1	Int.	14	322.95	
3-9x[1]	3.3-8.7	38-15	—	3¼	12⅝	1	Int.	15	331.95	
3.7-10x50mm[3,5]	3.7-9.7	29.5-11	—	3-3.25	14	1	Int.	19	408.95	
4-12x[1,4,8,11]	4.4-11.8	27-10	—	3¼	15	1	Int.	18	406.95	
6-18x[1,3,4,6,7,8]	6.5-17.6	16-7	—	3¼	15.8	1	Int.	18.5	422.95	
Mini Scopes										
4x[4,5]	3.6	24	—	3¾-5	8¼	1	Int.	7.8	205.95	
6x[1,4]	5.5	17	—	3¾-5	9	1	Int.	8.2	219.95	
6x HBR P.A.[1,5,8]	6.0	13	—	4.5	11¼	1	Int.	13.0	283.95	
2-7x	2.5-6.9	32-14	—	3¾-5	12	1	Int.	10.5	281.95	
3-9x[5]	3.6-8.8	25-11	—	3¾-5	12⅝	1	Int.	11.5	289.95	
4-12x[1,4,6]	4.5-11.6	19-8	—	3¾-4	15	1	Int.	15	383.95	
Signature Series										LER=Long Eye Relief; IER=Intermediate Eye Relief; XER=Extra Eye Relief. From Burris.
1.5-6x[2,3,5,9,10]	1.7-5.8	70-20	—	3½-4	10.8	1	Int.	13.0	381.95	
4x[3]	4.0	30	—	3	12⅛	1	Int.	14	325.95	
6x[3]	6.0	20	—	3	12⅛	1	Int.	14	353.95	
2-8x[3,5,11]	2.1-7.7	53-17	—	3-3.25	11.75	1	Int.	14	443.95	
3-9x[3,5,10]	3.3-8.8	36-14	—	3	12⅞	1	Int.	15.5	455.95	
2½-10x[3,5,10]	2.7-9.5	37-10.5	—	3-3¾	14	1	Int.	19.0	511.95	
3-12x[3,10]	3.3-11.7	34-9	—	3	14¼	1	Int.	21	369.95	
6-24x[1,3,5,6,8,10]	6.6-23.8	17-6	—	3-2½	16.0	1	Int.	22.7	600.95	
Handgun										
1½-4x LER[1,5]	1.6-3.	16-11	—	11-25	10¼	1	Int.	11	315.95	
2½-7x LER[3,4,5]	2-6.5	21-7	—	7-27	9.5	1	Int.	12.6	308.95	
3-9x LER[4,5]	3.4-8.4	12-5	—	22-14	11	1	Int.	14	347.95	
1x LER[1]	1.1	27	—	10-24	8¾	1	Int.	6.8	194.95	
2x LER[4,5,6]	1.7	21	—	10-24	8¾	1	Int.	6.8	201.95	
3x LER[4,6]	2.7	17	—	10-20	8⅞	1	Int.	6.8	217.95	
4x LER[1,4,5,6]	3.7	11	—	10-22	9⅝	1	Int.	9.0	224.95	
7x IER[1,4,5,6]	6.5	6.5	—	10-16	11¼	1	Int.	10	248.95	
10x IER[1,4,6]	9.5	4	—	8-12	13½	1	Int.	14	308.95	
Scout Scope										
1½x XER[3,9]	1.5	22	—	7-18	9	1	Int.	7.3	199.95	
2¾x XER[3,9]	2.7	15	—	7-14	9⅜	1	Int.	7.5	205.95	
BUSHNELL										
Trophy										[1]45mm objective. [2]Wide angle. [3]Also silver finish, **$175.95**. [4]Also silver finish, **$209.95**. [5]56mm objective. [6]Selective red L.E.D. dot for low light hunting. **Only selected models shown. Contact Bushnell for details.**
73-2545[1]	2.5-10	39-10	—	3	13.75	1	Int.	14	259.95	
73-1500[2]	1.75-5	68-23	—	3.5	10.8	1	Int.	12.3	209.95	
73-2733[2]	2-7	63-18	—	3	10	1	Int.	11.3	177.95	
73-4124[2]	4-12	32-11	—	3	12.5	1	Int.	16.1	245.95	
73-3940[2]	3-9	42-14	—	3	11.7	1	Int.	13.2	169.95	
73-6184	6-18	17.3-6	—	3	14.8	1	Int.	17.9	277.95	
Trophy Handgun										
73-0232[3]	2	20	—	9-26	8.7	1	Int.	7.7	163.95	
73-2632[4]	2-6	21-7	—	9-26	9.1	1	Int.	9.6	199.95	
Banner Armor-Sight										
65-3940	3-9	39-13	—	3	12	1	Int.	12.5	349.95	
Banner Standard										
71-2520	2.5	44	—	3.6	10	1	Int.	7.5	78.95	
71-3956[5]	3-9	37-12	—	3.5	13.7	1	Int.	17.3	241.95	
71-1040	10	12	—	3	14.7	1	Int.	14.3	197.95	
Lite-Site										
71-3940[6]	3-9	36-13	—	3.1	12.8	1	Int.	15.5	289.95	
Sportview										
74-1545	1.5-4.5	69-24	—	3	10.7	1	Int.	8.6	78.95	
74-2532	2.5	44	—	3.5	10.75	1	Int.	9	78.95	
74-3145	3.5-10	36-13	—	3	12.75	1	Int.	13.9	125.90	
74-1403	4	29	—	4	11.75	1	Int.	11.5	47.95	
74-3938	3-9	42-14	—	3	12.7	1	Int.	12.5	98.95	
74-3720	3-7	23-11	—	2.6	11.3	.75	Int.	5.7	37.95	
CHARLES DALY										[1]Pistol scope. [2]Adj. obj. From Outdoor Sports Headquarters.
4x32	4	28	—	3.25	11.75	1	Int.	9.5	70.00	
4x32[2]	4	28	—	3	9	1	Int.	8.5	129.00	
4x40 WA	4	36	—	3.25	13	1	Int.	11.5	98.00	
2.5x20[1]	2.5	17	—	3	7.3	1	Int.	7.25	80.00	
2.5x32	2.5	47	—	3	12.25	1	Int.	10	80.00	
2-7x32 WA	2-7	56-17	—	3	11.5	1	Int.	12	125.00	
3-9x40	3-9	35-14	—	3	12.5	1	Int.	11.25	77.00	
3-9x40 WA	3-9	36-13	—	3	12.75	1	Int.	12.5	125.00	
4-12x40 WA	4-12	30-11	—	3	13.75	1	Int.	14.5	133.00	
2x20[1]	2	16	—	16-25	8.75	1	Int.	6.5	107.00	

Maker and Model	Magn.	Field at 100 Yds. (feet)	Relative Brightness	Eye Relief (in.)	Length (in.)	Tube Dia. (in.)	W&E Adjustments	Weight (ozs.)	Price	Other Data
FROM JENA										[1]Military scope with adjustable parallax. Fixed powers have 26mm tubes, variables have 30mm tubes. Some models avail. with steel tubes. All lenses multi-coated. Dust and water tight
4x36	4	39	—	3.5	11.6	26mm	Int.	14	695.00	
6x36	6	21	—	3.5	12	26mm	Int.	14	795.00	
6x42	6	21	—	3.5	13	26mm	Int.	15	860.00	
8x56	8	18	—	3.5	14.4	26mm	Int.	20	890.00	
1.5-6x42	1.5-6	61.7-23	—	3.5	12.6	30mm	Int.	17	975.00	
2-8x42	2-8	52-17	—	3.5	13.3	30mm	Int.	17	1,050.00	
2.5-10x56	2.5-10	40-13.6	—	3.5	15	30mm	Int.	21	1,195.00	
3-12x56	3-12	NA	—	NA	NA	30mm	Int.	NA	1,195.00	
4-16x56	4-16	NA	—	NA	NA	30mm	Int.	NA	1,225.00	
3-9x40	3-9	NA	—	NA	NA	1	Int.	NA	1,120.00	
2.5-10x46	2.5-10	NA	—	NA	NA	30mm	Int.	NA	1,150.00	
4-16x56[1]	4-16	NA	—	NA	NA	30mm	Int.	NA	1,490.00	
GLOBAL INDUSTRIES										[1]With adj. obj.; [2]Also 4x40, 4x40 with adj. obj.; [3]Also with adj. obj.; [4]Also 2-7x40, 2-7x40 with adj. obj.; [5]Also 3-9x40, 3-9x40 with adj. obj.; [6]Also 4x30, 4x40; [7]Also 10x40.
30mm Superb Series WA										
1.5x20	1.5	78.73	69.64	3.9	9.4	1.18	Int.	12.3	318.56	
4x42	4	31.16	43.40	4.5	12.2	1.18	Int.	14.6	392.27	
6x42	6	19	19.29	3.7	12.2	1.18	Int.	14.6	408.51	
8x56	8	13.12	19.29	3.7	13.5	1.18	Int.	19.0	449.74	
15x56[1]	15	8.5	5.38	3.3	15.9	1.18	Int.	25.7	673.13	
30mm Variables										**30mm Superb Series:** All models can be ordered with target or external knobs, magnifying reticle (European style), objective adjustment (O.A.), and choice of six reticles. Variables—IPC, extra-heavy construction of 6061 T-6 alloy. Fogproof, recoil-proof coated optics. **American Series:** Special reticles (12), target knobs, BDC objective lens adjustment feature can be added to any scope at extra cost. Sunshades also avail. 12x thru 24x can be made on special order. German-type speed focus avail. as option on all American Series scopes. Waterproof, fogproof, recoil-proof, fully coated. **European 1":** All wide angle with choice of 12 reticles, obj. adj. avail. on some models. BDC and target knobs avail. on all as options. Sunshades, locking lens covers, speed focus also optional. **Partial listing of models shown.** Contact Global Industries for full details.
1-4x20	1-4	101-30.1	157-9.8	4.3-3.3	9.4	1.18	Int.	11.1	460.98	
2-8x42	2-8	46.9-16	173-11	4.5-3.5	13.3	1.18	Int.	17.4	522.82	
2.5-10	2.5-10	42.6-13	111.1-69	4.3-3.3	13.3	1.18	Int.	17.4	541.56	
3-12x56	3-12	37.7-10.8	137-16	3.9-3.3	14.3	1.18	Int.	25.7	673.13	
4-20x42	4-20	26-6	40-4	3.3-3.0	17.7	1.18	Int.	23.8	704.50	
American 1" Series WA										
Adirondack 1x20	1	—	—	—	—	1	Int	—	168.65	
Raton 2.5x32	2.5	33.0	161	3.5	11.7	1	Int.	9.2	169.60	
Las Vegas 4x32[2]	4	29.0	64	3.3	11.7	1	Int.	9.2	172.40	
Kalispell 6x40[3]	6	18.5	45	3.2	13.0	1	Int.	10.2	198.29	
Pecos 8x40 O.A.	8	13.5	25	3.0	13.0	1	Int.	10.2	253.83	
San Antonio 10x40 O.A.	10	12.5	16	3.0	13.0	1	Int.	10.4	257.23	
Variables										
Abeline 1-3x20	1-3	—	—	—	—	1	Int.	—	237.98	
Shiloh 1.5-4.5x20	1.5-4.5	—	—	—	—	1	Int.	—	241.73	
Denver 2-7x32[4]	2-7	—	—	—	—	1	Int.	—	226.24	
Santa Fe 3-9x32[5]	3-9	43.5-15	114-13	3.3-3.0	12.2	1	Int.	12.0	221.91	
Sutter's Creek 4-12x40 O.A.	4-12	30.5-11	100-12.3	3.0	15.8	1	Int.	15.0	301.71	
European 1" Series										
Jutland 4x20[6]	4	33	25	3.2	11.0	1	Int.	10.5	208.82	
Grenoble 6x40	6	26	43.56	3	13.2	1	Int.	13.7	244.29	
Rhineland 8x56	8	20	49	3.2	13.5	1	Int.	17.2	310.05	
Hamburg 10x56 O.A.[7]	10	—	—	3.2	13.5	1	Int.	17.2	375.46	
Brunswick 15x56 O.A.	15	—	—	3.1	13.5	1	Int.	17.6	414.30	
INTERAIMS										Intended for handguns. Comes with rings. Dot size less than 1½" @ 100 yds. Waterproof. Battery life 50-10,000 hours. Black or nickel finish Imported by Stoeger.
One V	0	—	—	—	4.5	1	Int.	4	139.95	
One V	0	—	—	—	4.5	1	Int.	4	139.95	
KAHLES										[1]Steel tube. [2]Ballistic cam system with military rangefinder. Waterproof, nitrogen filled. Choice of reticles. Imported from Austria by Kahles USA.
K4x32-L	4	33	—	—	11.3	1	Int.	11.2	555.00	
K6x42-L	6	23	—	—	12.5	1	Int.	13	615.00	
K7x56-L	7	19.7	—	—	14.4	26mm	Int.	16.1	695.00	
K8x56-L	8	17.1	—	—	14.4	1	Int.	16.1	715.00	
K1.1-4.5x20-L	1.1-4.5	78.7-30	—	—	10.5	30mm	Int.	12.6	685.00	
K1.5-6x42-L	1.5-6	61-21	—	—	12.5	30mm	Int.	15.8	785.00	
K2.2-9x42-L	2.2-9	39.5-15	—	—	13.3	30mm	Int.	15.5	945.00	
K3-12x56-L	3-12	30-11	—	—	15.2	30mm	Int.	18	1,045.00	
K2.5x20-S[1]	2.5	54	—	—	9.6	1	Int.	12.6	525.00	
KZF84-6[1,2]	6	23	—	—	12.5	1	Int.	17.6	995.00	
KZF84-10[1,2]	10	13	—	—	13.25	1	Int.	18	1,045.00	
KASSNAR VISTASCOPES										Waterproof, fogproof, shockproof. Four-post reticle. From K.B.I.
HI0405	4	26	—	4	12	1	Int.	9.1	NA	
HI0413	3-9	28-12	—	3.4-2.9	12	1	Int.	9.8	NA	
HI0480 Compact	4	21	—	4.1	9.9	1	Int.	9.1	NA	
HI0499 Pistol	4	9	—	14.5	9.5	1	Int.	9.5	NA	
HI0502 Pistol	2.5	12.6	—	13	8.9	1	Int.	9.1	NA	
KILHAM										Unlimited eye relief; internal click adjustments; crosshair reticle. Fits Thompson/Center rail mounts, for S&W K, N, Ruger Blackhawk, Super, Super Single-Six, Contender.
Hutson Handgunner II	1.7	8	—	5½	7/8	Int.	5.1	119.95		
Hutson Handgunner	3	8	—	10-12	6	7/8	Int.	5.3	119.95	
LASER AIM										[1]Laser sight. Battery life 45 min. Dot size 2" @ 300 ft. [2]Dot size 1" @ 300 ft. [3]Red dot sight. Dot size 3" @ 300 ft. (LA99), 6" (LA9750), 10" (LA9750-10). From Emerging Technologies, Inc.
LA5[1]	—	—	—	—	2	.75	Int.	1.2	239.00	
LA5 Magnum[1,2]	—	—	—	—	2.75	.75	Int.	1.3	265.00	
LA7[1]	—	—	—	—	1.5	1.5	Int.	1.7	265.00	
LA99[3]	—	—	—	—	5.25	1	Int.	NA	135.00	
LA9750[3]	—	—	—	—	5.25	50mm	Int.	NA	230.00	
LA-9750-10[3]	—	—	—	—	5.25	50mm	Int.	NA	230.00	
LASER DEVICES										Projects high intensity beam of laser light onto target as an aiming point. Adj. for w. & e. [1]Diode laser system. From Laser Devices, Inc.
He Ne FA-6	—	—	—	—	6.2	—	Int.	11	229.50	
He Ne FA-9	—	—	—	—	12	—	Int.	16	299.00	
He Ne FA-9P	—	—	—	—	9	—	Int.	14	299.00	

CAUTION: PRICES CHANGE, CHECK AT GUNSHOP.

Maker and Model	Magn.	Field at 100 Yds. (feet)	Relative Brightness	Eye Relief (in.)	Length (in.)	Tube Dia. (in.)	W&E Adjustments	Weight (ozs.)	Price	Other Data
Laser Devices (cont.)										
FA-4[1]	—	—	—	—	4.5	—	Int.	3.5	299.00	
LASERSIGHT										Projects a highly visible beam of concentrated laser light onto the target. Adjustable for w.& e. Visible up to 500 yds. at night. For handguns, rifles, shotguns. Uses two standard 9V batteries. From Imatronic Lasersight.
LS45	0	—	—	—	7.5	—	Int.	8.5	245.00	
LS25	0	—	—	—	6	¾	Int.	3.5	270.00	
LS55	0	—	—	—	7	1	Int.	7	299.00	
LEATHERWOOD										Compensates for bullet drop via external circular cam. Matte gray finish. Designed specifically for the M1A/M-14 rifle. Quick Detachable model for rifles with Weaver-type bases. From North American Specialties.
ART II	3.0-8.8	31-12	—	3.5	13.9	1	Int.	42	750.00	
LEATHERWOOD-MEOPTA, INC.										ART CZ-4 and CZ-6 have range-finding reticles with hold-over marks, multi-coated optics. Black or gray finish. From Leatherwood-Meopta, Inc.
ART II	3.0-8.8	31-12	—	3.5	13.9	1	Int.	42	750.00	
ART CZ-4	4	32	—	—	11	1	Int.	13.4	257.90	
ART CZ-6	6	21	—	—	13.7	1	Int.	18.3	287.90	
LEUPOLD										Constantly centered reticles, choice of Duplex, tapered CPC, Leupold Dot, Crosshair and Dot. CPC and Dot reticles extra. [1]2x and 4x scopes have from 12"-24" of eye relief and are suitable for handguns, top ejection arms and muzzleloaders. [2]3x9 Compact, 6x Compact, 12x, 3x9, 3.5x6x20 come with adjustable objective. [3]Target scopes have 1-min. divisions with ¼-min. clicks, and adjustable objectives. 50-ft. Focus Adaptor available for indoor target ranges, **$51.80**. Sunshade for all adjustable objective scopes, **$19.60-37.50**. [4]Also available in matte finish for about **$22.00** extra. [5]Silver finish about **$22.00** extra. [6]Matte finish. Partial listing shown. **Contact Leupold for complete details.**
Vari-X III 3.5x10 STD Police	3.5-10	29.5-10.7	—	3.6-4.6	12.5	1	Int.	13.5	610.70	
M8-2X EER[1]	1.7	21.2	—	12-24	7.9	1	Int.	6.0	246.40	
M8-2X EER Silver[1]	1.7	21.2	—	12-24	7.9	1	Int.	6.0	267.90	
M8-4X EER[1]	3.7	9	—	12-24	8.4	1	Int.	7.0	333.90	
M8-4X EER Silver[1]	3.7	9	—	12-24	8.4	1	Int.	7.0	333.90	
Vari-X 2.5-8 EER	2.5-8.0	13-4.3	—	11.7-12	9.7	1	Int.	10.9	501.10	
M8-2.5X Compact	2.3	39.5	—	4.9	8.0	1	Int.	6.5	273.20	
M8-4X Compact	3.6	25.5	—	4.5	9.2	1	Int.	7.5	292.90	
2-7x Compact	2.5-6.6	41.7-16.5	—	5-3.7	9.9	1	Int.	8.5	373.20	
3-9x Compact	3.2-8.6	34-13.5	—	4.0-3.0	11-11.3	1	Int.	11.0	387.50	
M8-4X[4]	4.0	24	—	4.0	10.7	1	Int.	9.3	292.90	
M8-6X[6]	5.9	17.7	—	4.3	11.4	1	Int.	10.0	310.90	
M8-6x 42mm	6.0	17	—	4.5	12	1	Int.	11.3	408.90	
M8-12x A.O. Varmint	11.6	9.1	—	4.2	13.0	1	Int.	13.5	508.90	
BR-24X[3]	24.0	4.7	—	3.2	13.8	1	Int.	15.3	803.60	
BR-36X[3]	36.0	3.2	—	3.4	14.1	1	Int.	15.6	841.10	
Vari-X 3-9x Compact EFR A.O.	3.8-8.6	34.0-13.5	—	4.0-3.0	11.0	1	Int.	11	442.90	
Vari-X-II 1x4	1.6-4.2	70.5-28.5	—	4.3-3.8	9.2	1	Int.	9.0	330.40	
Vari-X-II 2x7[4,5]	2.5-6.6	42.5-17.8	—	4.9-3.8	11.0	1	Int.	10.5	373.20	
Vari-X-II 3x9[1,4,5]	3.3-8.6	32.3-14.0	—	4.1-3.7	12.3	1	Int.	13.5	376.80	
Vari-X-II 3-9x50mm[4]	3.3-8.6	32.3-14	—	4.7-3.7	12	1	Int.	13.6	437.50	
Vari-X-II 4-12 A.O. Matte	4.4-11.6	22.8-11.0	—	5.0-3.3	12.3	1	Int.	13.5	489.30	
Vari-X-III 1.5x5	1.5-4.5	66.0-23.0	—	5.3-3.7	9.4	1	Int.	9.5	487.50	
Vari-X-III 1.75-6x 32	1.9-5.6	47-18	—	4.8-3.7	9.8	1	Int.	11	507.10	
Vari-X-III 2.5x8[4]	2.6-7.8	37.0-13.5	—	4.7-3.7	11.3	1	Int.	11.5	525.00	
Vari-X-III 3.5-10x50 A.O.	3.3-9.7	29.5-10.7	—	4.6-3.6	12.4	1	Int.	13.0	696.40	
Vari-X-III 3.5-10x50[2,4]	3.3-9.7	29.5-10.7	—	4.6-3.6	12.4	1	Int.	14.4	641.10	
Vari-X-III 4.5-14	4.7-13.7	20.8-7.4	—	5.0-3.7	12.4	1	Int.	14.5	632.10	
Vari-X-III 6.5-20 A.O. Varmint	6.5-19.2	14.2-5.5	—	5.3-3.6	14.2	1	Int.	17.5	717.90	
Vari-X-III 6.5-20x Target EFR A.O.	6.5-19.2	—	—	5.3-3.6	14.2	1	Int.	16.5	708.90	
Mark 4 M3-6x	6	17.7	—	4.5	13.1	30mm	Int.	21	1,419.60	
Mark 4 M1-10x[6]	10	11.1	—	3.6	13⅛	1	Int.	21	1,419.60	
Mark 4 M1-16x[6]	16	6.6	—	4.1	12⅞	1	Int.	22	1,419.60	
Mark 4 M3-10x[6]	10	11.1	—	3.6	13⅛	1	Int.	21	1,419.60	
Vari-X-III 6.5x20[2]	6.5-19.2	14.2-5.5	—	5.3-3.6	14.2	1	Int.	16.0	637.50	
Rimfire										
Vari-X-II 2-7x RF Special	3.6	25.5	—	4.5	9.2	1	Int.	7.5	373.20	
Shotgun										
M8 2x EER	1.7	21.2	—	12-24	7.9	1	Int.	6.0	269.60	
M8 4x	3.7	9.0	—	12-24	8.4	1	Int.	6.0	314.30	
Vari-X-II 1x4	1.6-4.2	70.5-28.5	—	4.3-3.8	9.2	1	Int.	9.0	353.60	
Vari-X-II 2x7	2.5-6.6	42.5-17.8	—	4.9-3.8	11.0	1	Int.	9.0	398.20	
McMILLAN										42mm obj. lens; ¼-MOA clicks; nitrogen filled, fogproof, waterproof; etched duplex-type reticle. [1]Tactical Scope with external adj. knobs, military reticle; 60+ min. adj.
Vision Master 2.5-10x	2.5-10	14.2-4.4	—	4.3-3.3	13.3	30mm	Int.	17.0	$1,500	
Vision Master Model I[1]	2.5-10	14.2-4.4	—	4.3-3.3	13.3	30mm	Int.	17.0	$1,200	
MIRADOR										[1]Wide Angle scope. Multi-coated objective lens. Nitrogen filled; waterproof; shockproof. From Mirador Optical Corp.
RXW 4x40[1]	4	37	—	3.8	12.4	1	Int.	12	179.95	
RXW 1.5-5x20[1]	1.5-5	46-17.4	—	4.3	11.1	1	Int.	10	188.95	
RXW 3-9x40	3-9	43-14.5	—	3.1	12.9	1	Int.	13.4	251.95	
NICHOLS										[1]Matte finish; also avail. with high gloss. [2]Adj. obj. [3]Stainless; also 3-9x40, blue, **$144.00**. [4]50-yd. parallax, with 22 rings; also with adj. obj., **$130.00**. [5]Also in stainless. [6]50-yd. parallax, **$90.00**. [7]Also 3-9x40, **$124.00**. Imported by G.U., Inc.
"Light" Series										
1.5-5x20 WA	1.5-5	80.8-24.2	—	3.2-4.5	9.5	1	Int.	10.1	264.00	
2-7x32 WA	2-7	60.4-17.5	—	3.3-4.2	10.0	1	Int.	11.3	280.00	
3-9x40 WA	3-9	40.2-13.3	—	3.2-3.9	11.7	1	Int.	12.9	290.00	
3-10x44 WA	3-10	40.2-12.1	—	3.1-4.0	11.9	1	Int.	14.1	310.00	
4-12x44 WA A.O.	4-12	30.1-10	—	3.1-3.6	12.3	1	Int.	16.7	320.00	
"Magnum Target"										
12x44[2]	12	8.7	—	3.1	14.3	1	Int.	19.1	525.00	
24x44[2]	24	4.3	—	2.9	14.3	1	Int.	18.4	525.00	
6-20x44[2]	6-20	17.4-5.4	—	3.1-3.0	14.4	1	Int.	19.8	577.00	
"Classic"										
4x40 WA	4	37.0	—	3.8	13.0	1	Int.	11.6	140.00	

Maker and Model	Magn.	Field at 100 Yds. (feet)	Relative Brightness	Eye Relief (in.)	Length (in.)	Tube Dia. (in.)	W&E Adjustments	Weight (ozs.)	Price	Other Data
Nichols (cont.)										
6x40 WA	6	24.5	—	3.3	13.0	1	Int.	11.6	142.00	
1.5-4.5x WA	1.5-4.5	54.0-22.0	—	3.4-3.3	11.5	1	Int.	10.9	163.00	
2-7x32 WA	2-7	36.7-15.8	—	2.8-2.6	11.7	1	Int.	10.9	163.00	
3-9x32 WA[3]	3-9	39.3-13.1	—	3.4-2.9	11.4	1	Int.	10.5	163.00	
4-12x40	4-12	30.0-11.0	—	3.9-3.2	12.3	1	Int.	12.3	170.00	
"Air Gun/Rimfire"										
4x32[4]	4	28.5	—	3.1	12.2	1	Int.	10.7	105.00	
2-7x32 WA A.O.	2-7	36.7-15.7	—	2.8-2.6	11.8	1	Int.	10.5	187.00	
"Classic Handgun"										
2x20[5]	2	17.0	—	8.6-19.5	7.4	1	Int.	7.5	135.00	
2-7x28[5]	2-7	40.0-9.7	—	8.9-19.5	9.0	1	Int.	9.0	260.00	
"Bullet"										
4x32[6]	4	28.5	—	3.1	12.2	1	Int.	10.7	82.00	
3-9x32[7]	3-9	34.5-23.6	—	3.1-3.0	12.6	1	Int.	11.2	118.00	
NIKON										
4x40	4	26.7	—	3.5	11.7	1	Int.	11.7	295.00	Super multi-coated lenses and blackening of all internal metal parts for maximum light gathering capability; positive 1/4-MOA; fogproof; waterproof; shockproof; luster and matte finish. [1]Also available in matte silver finish, **$448.00**. From Nikon, Inc.
1.5-4.5x20	1.5-4.5	67.8-22.5	—	3.7-3.2	10.1	1	Int.	9.5	387.00	
1.5-4.5x24 EER	1.5-4.4	13.7-5.8	—	24-18	8.9	1	Int.	9.3	387.00	
2-7x32	2-7	46.7-13.7	—	3.9-3.3	11.3	1	Int.	11.3	426.00	
3-9x40[1]	3-9	33.8-11.3	—	3.6-3.2	12.5	1	Int.	12.5	433.00	
3.5-10x50	3.5-10	25.5-8.9	—	3.9-3.8	13.7	1	Int.	15.5	653.00	
4-12x40 A.O.	4-12	25.7-8.6	—	3.6-3.2	14	1	Int.	16.6	563.00	
4-12x50 A.O.	4-12	25.4-8.5	—	3.6-3.5	14.0	1	Int.	18.3	712.00	
6.5-20x44	6.5-19.4	16.2-5.4	—	3.5-3.1	14.8	1	Int.	19.6	653.00	
2x20 EER	2	22	—	26.4	8.1	1	Int.	6.3	234.00	
OAKSHORE ELECTRONICS										
UltraDOT[1]	0	—	—	—	5	1	Int.	3.9	139.00	[1]Also 30mm tube, **$199**. [2]Variable intensity red dot appears in center of the duplex crosshair. Waterproof; nitrogen filled; coated lenses; 1/2-MOA dot at 100 yds. From Oakshore Electronic Sights, Inc.
MicroDOT 1.5-4.5x LER[2]	1.5-4.5	14.9-6.9	—	12-24	9	1	Int.	10	259.00	
MicroDOT 1.5-4.5x[2]	1.5-4.5	73.8-24.6	—	3	9.8	1	Int.	10.5	259.00	
MicroDOT 2-7x[2]	2-7	48.2-13.8	—	3	11	1	Int.	12	279.00	
MicroDOT 3-9x[2]	3-9	37-12.5	—	3	12.3	1	Int.	13.4	299.00	
MicroDOT 4-12x[2]	1.5-4.5	28.1-9.2	—	3	14.4	1	Int.	21	399.00	
PENTAX										
1.5-5x	1.5-5	66-25	—	3-3 1/4	11	1	Int.	13	310.00	Multi-coated lenses, fogproof, waterproof, nitrogen-filled. Penta-Plex reticle. Click 1/3-1/2-MOA adjustments. Matte finish **$20.00** extra. [1]Also in matte chrome **$260.00**. [2]Also in matte chrome **$390.00**. [3]ProFinish (matte) **$500**. [4]ProFinish (matte) **$530.00**; satin chrome **$550.00**. [5]Chrome-Matte finish **$400.00**. [6]ProFinish (matte) **$460.00**; satin chrome **$480.00**. [7]Gloss finish; matte, **$290.00**. [8]Gloss finish; mattte, **$560.00**. Imported by Pentax Corp.
4x	4	35	—	3 1/4	11.6	1	Int.	12.2	280.00	
6x	6	20	—	3 1/4	13.4	1	Int.	13.5	310.00	
2-7x	2-7	42.5-17	—	3-3 1/4	12	1	Int.	14	360.00	
3-9x	3-9	33-13.5	—	3-3 1/4	13	1	Int.	15	380.00	
2.5x Lightseeker[7]	2.5	55	—	3-3.5	10	1	Int.	9	280.00	
2-8x Lightseeker[6]	2-8	53-17	—	3.5	11 7/8	1	Int.	14	450.00	
3-9x Lightseeker[4]	3-9	36-14	—	3	12.7	1	Int.	15	540.00	
3-10x Lightseeker[8]	3.5-10	29.5-11	—	3-3.25	14	1	Int.	19.5	540.00	
3-9x Mini	3-9	26.5-10.5	—	3 3/4	10.4	1	Int.	13	320.00	
4-12x Mini[3]	4-12	19-8	—	3.75-4	11.3	1	Int.	11.3	410.00	
6-18x[3]	6-18	16-7	—	3-3.25	15.8	1	Int.	15.8	460.00	
Pistol										
2x LER[1]	2	21	—	10-24	8 3/4	1	Int.	6.8	240.00	
1.5-4x LER[2]	1.5-4	16-11	—	11-25	10	1	Int.	11	360.00	
2 1/2-7x[5]	2.5-7	12.0-7.5	—	11-28	12	1	Int.	12.5	400.00	
RWS										
300	4	—	—	8	12 3/4	1	Int.	11	160.00	Air gun scopes. All have Dyna-Plex reticle. Model 800 is for air pistols. Imported from Japan by Dynamit Nobel-RWS.
350	4	—	—	8	10	1	Int.	10	125.00	
400	2-7	—	—	8	12 3/4	1	Int.	12	170.00	
CS-10	2.5	—	—	8	5 3/4	1	Int.	7	125.00	
REDFIELD										
Ultimate Illuminator 3-9x	3.4-9.1	27-9	—	3-3.5	15.1	30mm	Int.	20.5	652.95	*Accutrac feature avail. on these scopes at extra cost. Traditionals have round lenses. 4-Plex reticle is standard. [1]"Magnum Proof." Specially designed for magnum and auto pistols. Uses "Double Dovetail" mounts. Also in nickel-plated finish, 2 1/2x, **$204.95**, 4x, **$253.95**. [2]With matte finish **$545.95**. [3]Also available with matte finish at extra cost. [4]All Golden Five Star scopes come with Butler Creek flip-up lens covers. [5]Black anodized finish, also in nickel finish, **$303.95**. [6]56mm adj. objective; European #4 or 4-Plex reticle; comes with 30mm steel rings with Rotary Dovetail System. 1/4-min. click adj. Also in matte finish, **$754.95**. [7]Also available nickel-plated **$342.95**. [8]Also with RealTree camo finish **$581.95**. [9]With RealTree camo finish **$426.95**. [10]Also available with RealTree camo finish **$196.95**. [11]With RealTree camo finish **$264.95**. [12]Also with RealTree camo finish **$412.95**; with matte finish **$403.95**. [13]With RealTree camo finish **$314.95**. Selected models shown. **Contact Redfield for full data.**
Ultimate Illuminator 3-12x[6]	2.9-11.7	27-10.5	—	3-3 1/2	15.4	30mm	Int.	23	745.95	
Illuminator Trad. 3-9x	2.9-8.7	33-11	—	3 1/2	12 3/4	1	Int.	17	505.95	
Illuminator Widefield 4x	4.2	28	—	3-3.5	11.7	1	Int.	13.5	376.95	
Illuminator Widefield 2-7x	2.0-6.8	56-17	—	3-3.5	11.7	1	Int.	13.5	498.95	
Illuminator Widefield 3-9x*[2,8]	2.9-8.7	38-13	—	3 1/2	12 3/4	1	Int.	17	560.95	
Tracker 4x[3,10]	3.9	28.9	—	3 1/2	11.02	1	Int.	9.8	169.95	
Tracker 6x[3]	6.2	18	—	3.5	12.4	1	Int.	11.1	190.95	
Tracker 2-7x[3]	2.3-6.9	36.6-12.2	—	3 1/2	12.20	1	Int.	11.6	216.95	
Tracker 3-9x[3,11]	3.0-9.0	34.4-11.3	—	3 1/2	14.96	1	Int.	13.4	244.95	
Traditional 4x 3/4"	4	24 1/2	27	3 1/2	9 3/8	3/4	Int.	—	161.95	
Traditional 2 1/2x	2 1/2	43	64	3 1/2	10 1/4	1	Int.	8 1/2	161.95	
Golden Five Star 4x[4]	4	28.5	58	3.75	11.3	1	Int.	9.75	236.95	
Golden Five Star 6x[4]	6	18	40	3.75	12.2	1	Int.	11.5	254.95	
Golden Five Star 2-7x[4]	2.4-7.4	42-14	207-23	3-3.75	11.25	1	Int.	12	303.95	
Golden Five Star 3-9x[4,7]	3.0-9.1	34-11	163-18	3-3.75	12.50	1	Int.	13	372.95	
Golden Five Star 3-9x 50mm[4,12]	3.0-9.1	36.0-11.5	—	3-3.5	12.8	1	Int.	16	359.95	
Golden Five Star 4-12x A.O.*[4]	3.9-11.4	27-9	112-14	3-3.75	13.8	1	Int.	16	416.95	
Golden Five Star 6-18x A.O.*[4]	6.1-18.1	18.6	50-6	3-3.75	14.3	1	Int.	18	439.95	

Maker and Model	Magn.	Field at 100 Yds. (feet)	Relative Bright-ness	Eye Relief (in.)	Length (in.)	Tube Dia. (in.)	W&E Adjust-ments	Weight (ozs.)	Price	Other Data
Redfield (cont.)										
I.E.R. 1-4x Shotgun[13]	1.3-3.8	48-16	—	6	10.2	1	Int.	12	297.95	
Compact Scopes										
Golden Five Star Compact 4x	3.8	28	—	3.5	9.75	1	Int.	8.8	225.95	
Golden Five Star Compact 6x	6.3	17.6	—	3.5	10.70	1	Int.	9.5	252.95	
Golden Five Star Compact 2-7x	2.4-7.1	40-16	—	3-3.5	9.75	1	Int.	9.8	300.95	
Golden Five Star Compact 3-9x	3.3-9.1	32-11.25	—	3-3.5	10.7	1	Int.	10.5	317.95	
Golden Five Star Compact 4-12x	4.1-12.4	22.4-8.3	—	3-3.5	12	1	Int.	13	402.95	
Pistol Scopes										
2½xMP[1]	2.5	9	64	14-19	9.8	1	Int.	10.5	224.95	
4xMP[1]	3.6	9	—	12-22	9¹¹⁄₁₆	1	Int.	11.1	239.95	
2-6x[5]	2-5.5	25-7	—	10-18	10.4	1	Int.	11	283.95	
Widefield Low Profile Compact										
Widefield 4xLP Compact	3.7	33	—	3.5	9.35	1	Int.	10	279.95	
Widefield 3-9x LP Compact	3.3-9	37.0-13.7	—	3-3.5	10.20	1	Int.	13	355.95	
Low Profile Scopes										
Widefield 2¾xLP	2¾	55½	69	3½	10½	1	Int.	8	260.95	
Widefield 4xLP	3.6	37½	84	3½	11½	1	Int.	10	290.95	
Widefield 6xLP	5.5	23	—	3½	12¾	1	Int.	11	315.95	
Widefield 1¾x-5xLP	1¾-5	70-27	136-21	3½	10¾	1	Int.	11½	357.95	
Widefield 2x-7xLP*	2-7	49-19	144-21	3½	11¾	1	Int.	13	366.95	
Widefield 3x-9xLP*[9]	3-9	39-15	112-18	3½	12½	1	Int.	14	407.95	
SCHMIDT & BENDER										
Vari-M 1¼-4x20[1]	1¼-4	96-16	—	3¼	10.4	30mm	Int.	12.3	619.99	[1]All steel. 30-year warranty. All have ⅓-min. click adjustment, centered reticles, nitrogen filling. Most models avail. in aluminum with mounting rail. Available from Paul Jaeger, Inc./Dunn's.
Vari-M 1½-6x42	1½-6	60-19.5	—	3¼	12.2	30mm	Int.	17.5	684.99	
Vari-M 2½-10x56	2½-10	37.5-12	—	3¼	14.6	30mm	Int.	21.9	804.99	
All Steel 4-12x42	4-12	34.7-12	—	3¼	13.25	30mm	Int.	23	736.99	
SHEPHERD										
3940-E	3-9	43.5-15	178-20	3.3	13	1	Int.	17	597.00	[1]Also avail. as 310-1, 310-E, **$453.28**. [2]Also avail. as 310-P1, 310-P2, 310-P3, 310-Pla, 310-PE1, 310-P22, 310-P22 Mag., 310-PE, **453.28** [3]27-4 has 9" stadia circles, traj. for 22 rifles. [4]Click adj. for shotgun, carbine, blackpowder. All have patented Dual Reticle system with rangefinder bullet drop compensation; multi-coated lenses, waterproof, shockproof, nitrogen filled, matte finish. From Shepherd Scope, Ltd.
310-2[1,2]	3-10	35.3-11.6	178-16	3-3.75	12.8	1	Int.	18	453.28	
27-4[3]	2.5-7.5	42-14	164-18	2.5-3	11.6	1	Int.	16.3	389.00	
CBS[4]	1.5-5	82.5-27.5	45.5-40.9	2.5-3.25	11	1	Int.	14.9	500.00	
SIMMONS										
44 Mag										
M-1043	2-7	56-16	—	3.3	11.8	1	Int.	13	256.95	[1]Matte; also polished finish. [2]Silver; also black matte or polished. [3]Black polish finish. [4]Granite finish; black polish **$216.95**; silver **$218.95**; also with 50mm obj., black granite **$336.95**. [5]Camouflage. [6]Black polish. [7]With ring mounts. **Only selected models shown. Contact Simmons Outdoor Corp. for complete details.**
M-1044	3-10	36.2-10.5	—	3.4-3.3	13.1	1	Int.	16.3	268.95	
M-1045	4-12	27-9	—	3	12.6	1	Int.	19.5	280.95	
Prohunter										
7700[1]	2-7	58-17	—	3.25	11.6	1	Int.	12.4	159.95	
7710[2]	3-9	40-15	—	3	12.6	1	Int.	13.4	169.95	
7715[3]	4-12	—	—	—	—	1	Int.	—	179.95	
7720	6-18	38-13	—	2.5	12.5	1	Int.	13.5	209.95	
7725	4.5	26	—	3	9.9	1	Int.	9.9	109.95	
Whitetail Classic										
WTC10[4]	4	36.8	—	4	12.3	1	Int.	9.8	139.95	
WTC11[4]	1.5-5	80-23.5	—	3.4-3.2	12.6	1	Int.	11.8	174.95	
WTC12[4]	2.5-8	46.5-14.5	—	3.2-3	12.6	1	Int.	12.8	189.95	
WTC13[4]	3.5-10	35-12	—	3.2-3	12.4	1	Int.	12.8	209.95	
WTC14[4]	2-10	50-11	—	3	12.8	1	Int.	16.9	256.95	
Deerfield										
21006	4	28	—	4	12.0	1	Int.	9.1	74.95	
21010	3-9	38-12	—	3.4	12.6	1	Int.	12.3	91.95	
21029	3-9	32-11	—	3.4	12.6	1	Int.	12.3	104.95	
21031	4-12	28-11	—	3-2.8	13.9	1	Int.	14.6	139.95	
Gold Medal Silhouette										
23000	12	8.7	—	3.1-3	14.5	1	Int.	18.3	449.95	
23001	24	4.3	—	3	14.5	1	Int.	18.3	455.95	
23002	6-20	17.4-5.4	—	3	14.5	1	Int.	18.3	499.95	
Gold Medal Handgun										
22002[6]	2.5-7	9.7-4.0	—	8.9-19.4	9.25	1	Int.	9.0	319.95	
22004[6]	2	3.9	—	8.6-19.5	7.3	1	Int.	7.4	219.95	
22006[6]	4	8.9	—	9.8-18.7	9	1	Int.	8.8	249.95	
Shotgun										
21005	2.5	29	—	4.6	7.1	1	Int.	7.2	85.95	
7790	4	16	—	5.5	8.8	1	Int.	9.2	139.95	
Rimfire										
1022[7]	4	36	—	3.5	11.5	¾	Int.	10	74.95	
21007[7]	4	29	—	3.5	12.0	¾	Int.	11.5	108.95	
STEINER										
Penetrator										Waterproof, fogproof, nitrogen filled, accordion-type eye cup. From Pioneer Marketing & Research, Inc.
6x42	6	20.4	—	3.1	14.8	26mm	Int.	14	889.00	
1.5x6x42	1.5-6	64-21	—	3.1	12.8	30mm	Int.	17	1,099.00	

CAUTION: PRICES CHANGE, CHECK AT GUNSHOP.

Maker and Model	Magn.	Field at 100 Yds. (feet)	Relative Brightness	Eye Relief (in.)	Length (in.)	Tube Dia. (in.)	W&E Adjustments	Weight (ozs.)	Price	Other Data
Steiner (cont.)										
3-12x56	3-12	29-10	—	3.1	14.8	30mm	Int.	21	1,299.00	
SWAROVSKI HABICHT										All models offered in either steel or lightweight alloy tubes. Weights shown are for lightweight versions. Choice of nine constantly centered reticles. Eyepiece recoil mechanism and rubber ring shield to protect face. American-style plex reticle available in 2.2-9x42 and 3-12x56 traditional European scopes. Imported by Swarovski Optik North America Ltd.
4x32	4	33	—	3¼	11.3	1	Int.	15	625.00	
6x42	6	23	—	3¼	12.6	1	Int.	17.9	690.00	
8x56	8	17	—	3¼	14.4	1	Int.	23	819.00	
1.5-6x42	1.5-6	61-21	—	3¼	12.6	30mm	Int.	16	900.00	
2.2-9x42	2.2-9	39.5-15	—	3¼	13.3	30mm	Int.	15.5	1,050.00	
3-12x56	3-12	30-11	—	3¼	15.25	1	Int.	18	1,165.00	
AL Scopes										
4x32A	4	30	—	3.2	11.5	1	Int.	10.8	495.00	
6x36A	6	21	—	3.2	11.9	1	Int.	11.5	530.00	
1.5-4.5x20A	1.5-4.5	75-25.8	—	3.5	9.53	1	Int.	10.6	595.00	
3-9x36	3-9	39-13.5	—	3.3	11.9	1	Int.	13	640.00	
SWIFT										All Swift scopes, with the exception of the 4x15, have Quadraplex reticles and are fogproof and waterproof. The 4x15 has crosshair reticle and is non-waterproof. [1]Available in black or silver finish—same price. From Swift Instruments.
600 4x15	4	16.2	—	2.4	11	¾	Int.	4.7	22.00	
601 3-7x20	3-7	25-12	—	3-2.9	11	1	Int.	5.6	52.00	
650 4x32	4	29	—	3.5	12	1	Int.	9	78.00	
653 4x40WA[1]	4	35.5	—	3.75	12.25	1	Int.	12	95.00	
654 3-9x32	3-9	35.75-12.75	—	3	12.75	1	Int.	13.75	94.00	
656 3-9x40WA[1]	3-9	42.5-13.5	—	2.75	12.75	1	Int.	14	102.00	
657 6x40	6	18	—	3.75	13	1	Int.	10	99.50	
660 4x20	4	25	—	4	11.8	1	Int.	9	79.00	
664 4-12x40[1]	4-12	27-9	—	3-2.8	13.3	1	Int.	14.8	142.00	
665 1.5-4.5x21	1.5-4.5	69-24.5	—	3.5-3	10.9	1	Int.	9.6	97.50	
666 Shotgun 1x20	1	113	—	3.2	7.5	1	Int.	9.6	99.50	
Pistol Scopes										
661 4x32	4	90	—	10-22	9.2	1	Int.	9.5	110.50	
662 2.5x32	2.5	14.3	—	9-22	8.9	1	Int.	9.3	99.95	
663 2x20[1]	2	18.3	—	9-21	7.2	1	Int.	8.4	105.00	
TASCO										[1]Water, fog & shockproof; fully coated optics; ¼-min. click stops; haze filter caps; lifetime warranty. [2]30/30 range finding reticle. [3]World Class Wide Angle; Supercon multi-coated optics; Opti-Centered® 30/30 range finding reticle; lifetime warranty. [4]⅓ greater zoom range. [5]Trajectory compensating scopes, Opti-Centered® stadia reticle. [6]Anodized finish. [7]True one-power scope. [8]Coated optics; crosshair reticle; ring mounts included to fit most 22, 10mm receivers. [9]Fits Remington 870, 1100, 11-87. [10]Electronic dot reticle with rheostat; coated optics; adj. for windage and elevation; waterproof, shockproof, fogproof; Lithium battery; 3x power booster avail.; matte black or matte aluminum finish; dot or T-3 reticle. [11]TV view. [12]Also matte aluminum finish. [13]Also with crosshair reticle. [14]Also 30/30 reticle. [15]Dot size 1.5" at 100 yds.; waterproof. [16]Stainless finish. [17]Black matte or stainless finish. **Contact Tasco for details on complete line.**
World Class										
WA4x40	4	36	100.0	3	13	1	Int.	11.5	160.00	
WA4x32ST[16]	4	34	—	3	—	1	Int.	10.5	160.00	
WA13.5x20[1,3,10]	1-3.5	115-31	400.0-32.4	3.5	9.75	1	Int.	10.2	229.00	
WA1.75-5x20[1,3]	1.75-5	72-24	129.9-16.0	3	10⅝	1	Int.	9.8	257.00	
WA2.5x40	2.5-8	44-14	—	3	—	1	Int.	14.25	199.00	
WA27x32[1,3,9]	2-7	56-17	256.0-20.2	3.25	11.5	1	Int.	12	191.00	
WA39x40[1,3,6,11]	3-9	43.5-15	176.8-19.3	3⅛	12.75	1	Int.	12.5	199.00	
World Class Compact										
CW4x32LE	4	25	64	5	10.0	1	Int.	9.5	183.00	
CW28x32	2-8	55-16	—	3	10.5	1	Int.	11.5	214.00	
World Class Airgun										
AG4x40A	4	36	—	3	13	1	Int.	14	267.00	
AG39x50WA	3-9	41-14	—	3	15	1	Int.	17.5	428.00	
World Class Electronic										
ER39x40WA	3-9	41-14	176.8-19.3	3	12.75	1	Int.	16	458.00	
World Class Mag IV-44										
WC2510x44[6]	2.5-10	41-11	—	3.5	12.5	1	Int.	14.4	272.00	
World Class TS										
TS24x44	24	4.5	—	3	14	1	Int.	17.9	430.00	
TS624x44	6-24	15-4.5	—	3	14	1	Int.	18.5	510.00	
World Class TR										
TR39x40WA	3-9	41-14	—	3	12.75	1	Int.	12.5	275.00	
World Class Pistol										
PWC2x22[12]	2	25	—	11-20	8.75	1	Int.	7.3	206.00	
PWC4x28[12]	4	8	—	12-19	9.45	1	Int.	7.9	252.00	
Mag IV										
W312x40[1,2,4]	3-12	33-11	176.8-10.8	3	12⅛	1	Int.	12	183.00	
W416x40[1,2,4]	4-16	25.5-7	100.0-6.2	3	14.25	1	Int.	16.75	229.00	
W624x40	6-24	17-4	—	3	15.25	1	Int.	16.8	290.00	
Titan										
TT1.56x42	1.5-6	59-20	748-49	3.5-4	12	30mm	Int.	16.4	612.00	
TT39x42	3-9	37-13	196-22	3.5-4	12.5	30mm	Int.	16.8	733.00	
Golden Antler										
GA4x32TV	4	32	—	3	13	1	Int.	12.7	79.00	
GA2.510x44TV	2.5-10	35-9	—	3.5	12.5	1	Int.	14.4	214.00	
GA39x32TV[11]	3-9	39-13	—	3	—	1	Int.	12.2	102.00	
Silver Antler										
SA2.5x32	2.5	42	—	3¼	11	1	Int.	10	86.00	
SA4x40	4	32	—	3	12	1	Int.	12.5	99.00	
SA39x40	3-9	39-13	—	3	12.5	1	Int.	13	135.00	
SA2.150x44	2.5-10	35-9	—	3.5	—	1	Int.	14.4	214.00	
Rubber Armored										
RC39x40A	3-9	35-12	—	3.25	12.5	1	Int.	14.3	206.00	
TR Scopes										
TR39x40WA	3-9	41-14	—	3	13	1	Int.	12.5	275.00	
TR416x40	4-16	26-7	—	3	14.25	1	Int.	16.8	298.00	
TR624x40	6-24	17-4	—	3	15.5	1	Int.	17.5	336.00	
Shotgun Scopes										
WA1.75-5x20[9]	1.75-5	74-24	—	3	10.5	1	Int.	10	257.00	

CAUTION: PRICES CHANGE, CHECK AT GUNSHOP.

Maker and Model	Magn.	Field at 100 Yds. (feet)	Relative Brightness	Eye Relief (in.)	Length (in.)	Tube Dia. (in.)	W&E Adjustments	Weight (ozs.)	Price	Other Data
Tasco (cont.)										
WA13.5x20[9]	1-3.5	103-31	—	3	9	1	Int.	12	229.00	
Airgun										
AG4x20	4	20	—	2.5	10.75	.75	Int.	5	48.00	
AG4x32	4	28	—	3	12	1	Int.	13	220.00	
AG4x32N	4	30	—	3	—	1	Int.	13.5	128.00	
AG39x50WA	3-9	27-9	—	3	15	1	Int.	17.5	428.00	
Rimfire										
RF4x15[8]	4	22.5	13.6	2.5	11	.75	Int.	4	17.00	
RF4x32	4	31	—	3	12.5	1	Int.	12.6	91.00	
RF37x20	3-7	24-11	—	2.5	11.5	.75	Int.	5.7	49.00	
P1.5x15	1.5	22.5	—	9.5-20.75	8.75	.75	Int.	3.25	37.00	
Propoint										
PDP2[10,12]	1	25-12	—	—	5	30mm	Int.	5.5	267.00	
PDP3[10,12]	1	40	—	—	5	30mm	Int.	5.5	367.00	
PDP4[17]	1	82	—	—	—	45mm	Int.	6.14	458.00	
PB1[13]	3	35	—	3	5.5	30mm	Int.	6.3	183.00	
PB3	2	30	—	—	1.25	30mm	Int.	2.6	214.00	
Proclass										
P2x22S[14]	2	23-18	—	10-24	6.5	30mm	Int.	7.7	291.00	
P3x22[14,17]	3	13-6	—	12-24	8.25	30mm	Int.	8.5	283.00	
World Class Plus										
WCP4x44	4	32	—	3¼	12.75	1	Int.	13.5	310.00	
WCP3.510x50	3.5-10	30-10.5	—	3¾	13	1	Int.	17.1	489.00	
WCP6x44	6	21	—	3.25	12.75	1	Int.	13.6	310.00	
WCP39x44	3-9	39-14	—	3.5	12.75	1	Int.	15.8	370.00	
LaserPoint[15]	—	—	—	—	2	⅝	Int.	.75	458.00	
THOMPSON/CENTER RECOIL PROOF PISTOL SCOPES										
8312 Compact Rail[2]	2.5	15	64	9-21	7.25	1	Int.	6.6	160.00	[1]Also silver finish, **$265.00** (#8316); with rail mount, black, **$257.00** (#8317); with lighted reticle, black, **$295.00** (#8326); with rail, lighted reticle, black, **$300.00** (#8327). [2]With lighted reticle, **$225.00** (#8322); silver, **$235.00** (#8323); with lighted reticle, rail mount, black, **$235.00** (#8320). [3]With lighted reticle, **$295.00** (#8626). [4]With rail mount, lighted reticle, **$170** (#8640). From Thompson/Center.
8315 Compact[1]	2.5-7	15-5	125-16	8-21	9.25	1	Int.	9.2	250.00	
Rifle Scopes										
8621 Compact	1.5-5	61-20	177-16	3	10	1	Int.	8.5	220.00	
8623 Compact WA[3]	3-9	33-11	113-13	3	10.75	1	Int.	9.9	241.00	
8624 Compact[4]	4	26	64	3	10	1	Int.	8.2	183.00	
TRIJICON SPECTRUM										
6x56[1]	6	24	—	3.0	14.1	1	Int.	20.3	579.00	[1]Self-luminous low-light reticle glows in poor light; allows choice of red, amber or green via a selector ring on objective end. [2]Advanced Combat Optical Gunsight for AR-15, M-16, with integral mount. [3]Reticle glows red in low light. From Trijicon, Inc.
1-3x20[1]	1-3	94-33	—	3.7-4.9	9.6	1	Int.	13.2	594.00	
3-9x40[1]	3-9	35-14	—	3.3-3.0	13.1	1	Int.	16.0	569.00	
3-9x56[1]	3-9	35-14	—	3.3-3.0	14.2	1	Int.	21.5	649.00	
ACOG 3.5x35	3.5	29	—	2.4	8.0	—	Int.	14.0	995.00	
ACOG 4x32[2]	4	37	—	1.5	5.8	—	Int.	9.7	695.00	
4x32 Red[3]	4	29	—	3.3	11.6	1	Int.	10.2	298.00	
UNERTL										
1" Target	6,8,10	16-10	17.6-6.25	2	21½	¾	Ext.	21	233.00	[1]Dural ¼-MOA click mounts. Hard coated lenses. Non-rotating objective lens focusing. [2]¼-MOA click mounts. [3]With target mounts. [4]With calibrated head. [5]Same as 1" Target but without objective lens focusing. [6]Price with ¼-MOA click mounts. [7]With new Posa mounts. [8]Range focus unit near rear of tube. Price is with Posa or standard mounts. Magnum clamp. From Unertl.
1¼" Target[1]	8,10,12,14	12-16	15.2-5	2	25	¾	Ext.	21	302.00	
1½" Target	8,10,12,14, 16,18,20	11.5-3.2	—	2¼	25½	¾	Ext.	31	326.00	
2" Target[2]	8,10,12,14, 16,18,24, 30,36	8	22.6-2.5	2¼	26¼	1	Ext.	44	431.00	
Varmint, 1¼"[3]	6,8,10,12	1-7	28-7.1	2½	19½	⅞	Ext.	26	296.00	
Ultra Varmint, 2"[4]	8,10,12,15	12.6-7	39.7-11	2½	24	1	Ext.	34	420.00	
Small Game[5]	4,6	25-17	19.4-8.4	2¼	18	¾	Ext.	16	175.00	
Vulture[6]	8	11.2	29	3-4	15⅝	1	Ext.	15½	333.00	
	10	10.9	18½	—	16⅛	1				
Programmer 200[7]	8,10,12,14, 16,18,20, 24,30,36	11.3-4	39-1.9	—	26½	1	Ext.	45	532.00	
BV-20[8]	20	8	4.4	4.4	17⅞	1	Ext.	21¼	390.00	
U.S. OPTICS										
SN/TR-1 System										
10x	10	11.3	—	3.8	14.5	30mm	Int.	24	695.00	Extra-heavy thickness tubes; extra-long turrets; recoil shoulder on turret; individual adj. w&e rebound spring; up to 300 m.o.a. elevation travel; ranging reticles; front or rear focal plane reticle location; up to 40mm dia. tube; up to 77mm obj. lens; multi-coated lenses. Made in U.S. by United States Optical Technologies, Inc.
15x	15	8.6	—	4.3	16.5	30mm	Int.	27	749.00	
20x	20	5.8	—	3.8	18.0	30mm	Int.	29	795.00	
24x	24	5.0	—	3.4	18.0	30mm	Int.	31	849.00	
30x	30	4.6	—	3.5	18.0	30mm	Int.	32	895.00	
36x	36	4.0	—	3.6	18.0	30mm	Int.	32	949.00	
40x	40	3.6	—	3.7	18.0	30mm	Int.	32	1,020.00	
50x	50	3.0	—	3.8	18.0	30mm	Int.	32	1,099.00	
Variables										
4-20x	4-20	26.8-5.8	—	5.4-3.8	18.0	30mm	Int.	24	884.71	
12-48x	12-48	—	—	4.4-4.8	18.4	30mm	Int.	36	1,250.00	
8-36x	8-36	—	—	4.6-4.9	18.0	30mm	Int.	35	1,105.00	
Tactical Format										
2.5-10x	2.5-10	—	—	43-11	12.8	30mm	Int.	18	924.48	
1-4x	1-4	118-25	—	4.8-4.4	9.4	30mm	Int.	18	535.00	
SN-6	6,8,10	—	—	4.2-4.8	9.2	30mm	Int.	18	748.00	
SN-7	4	27.5	—	5.2	7	30mm	Int.	18	426.00	
SN-8	4	28.8	—	5.2	7	30mm	Int.	18	642.00	
WEATHERBY										
Supreme 1¾-5x20	1.7-5	66.6-21.4	—	3.4	10.7	1	Int.	11	254.00	Lumiplex reticle in all models. Blue-black, nonglare finish. From Weatherby.

Maker and Model	Magn.	Field at 100 Yds. (feet)	Relative Bright-ness	Eye Relief (in.)	Length (in.)	Tube Dia. (in.)	W&E Adjust-ments	Weight (ozs.)	Price	Other Data
Weatherby (cont.)										
Supreme 2-7x34	2.1-6.8	59-16	—	3.4	11¼	1	Int.	10.4	263.00	
Supreme 4x44	3.9	32	—	3	12½	1	Int.	11.6	263.00	
Supreme 3-9x44	3.1-8.9	36-13	—	3.5	12.7	1	Int.	11.6	310.00	
WEAVER										
K2.5	2.5	35	—	3.7	9.5	1	Int.	7.3	117.61	Micro-Trac adjustment system with ¼-minute clicks on all models. All have Dual-X reticle. One-piece aluminum tube, satin finish, nitrogen filled, multi-coated lenses, waterproof. [1]Also avilable in matte finish: K4, **$133.95**; V9, **$174.41**; V10, **$185.57**. From Weaver.
K4[1]	3.7	26.5	—	3.3	11.3	1	Int.	10	127.52	
K6	5.7	18.5	—	3.3	11.4	1	Int.	10	138.95	
V3	1.1-2.8	88-32	—	3.9-3.7	9.2	1	Int.	8.5	154.13	
V9[1]	2.8-8.7	33-11	—	3.5-3.4	12.1	1	Int.	11.1	166.10	
V10[1]	2.2-9.6	38.5-9.5	—	3.4-3.3	12.2	1	Int.	11.2	176.64	
KT15	14.6	7.5	—	3.2	12.9	1	Int.	14.7	276.84	
WILLIAMS										
Twilight Crosshair TNT	1½-5	57¾-21	177-16	3½	10¾	1	Int.	10	206.65	[1]Matte or glossy black finish. TNT models. From Williams Gunsight Co.
Twilight Crosshair TNT	2½	32	64	3¾	11¼	1	Int.	8½	146.25	
Twilight Crosshair TNT	4	29	64	3½	11¾	1	Int.	9½	152.90	
Twilight Crosshair TNT	2-6	45-17	256-28	3	11½	1	Int.	11½	206.65	
Twilight Crosshair TNT	3-9	36-13	161-18	3	12¾	1	Int.	13½	217.15	
Guideline II										
4x[1]	4	29	64	3.6	11¾	1	Int.	9½	222.00	
1.5-5x[1]	1.5-5	57¾-21	177-16	3.5	10¾	1	Int.	10	267.00	
2-6x[1]	2-6	45½-10¾	256-28	3	11½	1	Int.	11½	267.00	
3-9x[1]	3-9	36½-12¾	161.2-17.6	3.1-2.9	12¾	1	Int.	13½	296.00	
Pistol Scopes										
Twilight 1.5x TNT	1.5	19	177	18-25	8.2	1	Int.	6.4	151.25	
Twilight 2x TNT	2	17.5	100	18-25	8.5	1	Int.	6.4	153.50	
ZEISS										
Diatal C 4x32	4	30	—	3.5	10.6	1	Int.	11.3	680.00	All scopes have ¼-minute click-stop adjustments. Choice of Z-Plex or fine crosshair reticles. Rubber armored objective bell, rubber eyepiece ring. Lenses have T-Star coating for highest light transmission. Z-Series scopes offered in non-rail tubes with duplex reticles only; 1" and 30mm. Imported from Germany by Carl Zeiss Optical, Inc.
Diatal C 6x32	6	20	—	3.5	10.6	1	Int.	11.3	715.00	
Diatal C 10x36	10	12	—	3.5	12.7	1	Int.	14.1	835.00	
Diatal Z 6x42	6	22.9	—	3.5	12.7	1.02 (26mm)	Int.	13.4	910.00	
Diatal Z 8x56	8	18	—	3.5	13.8	1.02 (26mm)	Int.	17.6	1,015.00	
Diavari C 1.5-4.5	1.5-4.5	72-27	—	3.5	11.8	1	Int.	13.4	930.00	
Divari Z 2.5x10x48	2.5-10	33-11.7	—	3.2	14.5	30mm	Int.	24	1,405.00	
Diavari C 3-9x36	3-9	36-13	—	3.5	11.2	1	Int.	15.2	975.00	
Diavari ZA 1.5-6x42	1.5-6	65.5-22.9	—	3.5	12.4	1.18 (30mm)	Int.	18.5	1,230.00	
Diavari Z 3-12x56	3-12	27.6-9.9	—	3.2	15.3	1.18 (30mm)	Int.	25.8	1,405.00	

Hunting scopes in general are furnished with a choice of reticle—crosshairs, post with crosshairs, tapered or blunt post, or dot crosshairs, etc. The great majority of target and varmint scopes have medium or fine crosshairs but post or dot reticles may be ordered. W—Windage E—Elevation MOA—Minute of angle or 1" (approx.) at 100 yards, etc.

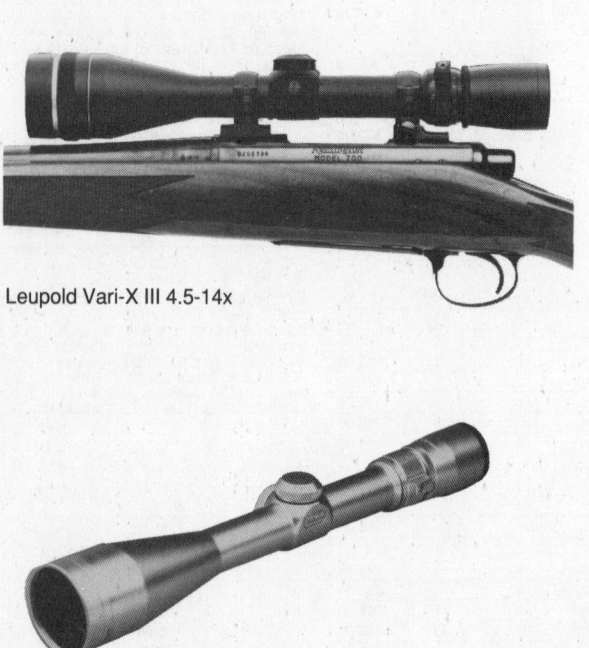

Leupold Vari-X III 4.5-14x

Nikon 3-9x40 Silver Matte

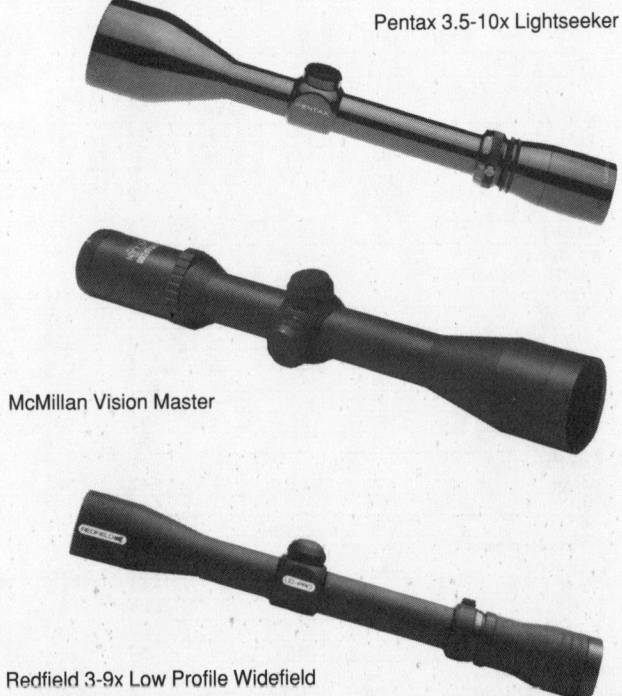

Pentax 3.5-10x Lightseeker

McMillan Vision Master

Redfield 3-9x Low Profile Widefield

CAUTION: PRICES CHANGE, CHECK AT GUNSHOP.

SCOPE MOUNTS

Maker, Model, Type	Adjust.	Scopes	Price
ACTION ARMS	No	1" split rings	**From $12.00**
For UZI, Galil, Ruger Mk. II, Mini-14, Win. 94, AR-15, Rem. 870, Ithaca 37, and many other popular rifles, handguns. Accept Weaver rings. All allow use of iron sights; some include rings; many in satin stainless finish. **Partial list shown.** From Action Arms.			
AIMPOINT	No	1"	49.95-89.95
Laser Mounts[1]		1", 30mm	51.95
Mounts/rings for all Aimpoint sights and 1" scopes. For many popular revolvers, auto pistols, shotguns, military-style rifles/carbines, sporting rifles. Most require no gunsmithing. [1]Mounts Aimpoint Laser-dot below barrel; many popular handguns, military-style rifles. Contact Aimpoint.			
AIMTECH			
Handguns			
AMT Auto Mag II, III	No	1"	56.99-64.95
Auto Mag IV	No	1"	64.95
Astra revolvers	No	1"	63.25
Beretta/Taurus auto	No	1"	63.25
Browning Buck Mark/Challenger II	No	1"	56.99
Browning Hi-Power	No	1"	63.25
Glock 17, 17L, 19, 22, 23	No	1"	63.25
Govt. 45 Auto	No	1"	63.25
Rossi revolvers	No	1"	63.25
Ruger Blackhawk/Super	No	1"	63.25
Ruger Mk I, Mk II	No	1"	49.95
S&W K,L,N frame	No	1"	63.25
S&W Model 41 Target	No	1"	63.25
S&W Model 52 Target	No	1"	63.25
S&W 45, 9mm autos	No	1"	56.99
S&W 422/622/2206	No	1"	56.99
Taurus revolvers	No	1"	63.25
TZ/CZ/P9 9mm	No	1"	63.25
Rifles			
AR-15	No	1"	21.95
Browning A-Bolt	No	1"	19.95
Knight MK85	No	1"	21.95
Remington 700	No	1"	19.95
Ruger 10/22	No	1"	19.95
Savage 110G	No	1"	19.95
Winchester 70	No	1"	19.95
Winchester 94	No	1"	19.95
Shotguns			
Benelli Super 90	No	1"	37.95
Ithaca 37	No	1"	37.95
Mossberg 500	No	1"	37.95
Mossberg 835 Ultimag	No	1"	37.95
Mossberg 5500	No	1"	37.95
Remington 870/1100	No	1"	37.95
Winchester 1300/1400	No	1"	37.95
Mount scopes, lasers, electronic sights using Weaver-style base. All mounts allow use of iron sights; no gunsmithing. Available in satin black or satin stainless finish. **Partial listing shown.** Contact maker for full details. From L&S Technologies, Inc.			
A.R.M.S.			
FN FAL LAR	No	Weaver-type rail	98.00
FN FAL LAR Para.	No	—	120.00
M21/14	No	—	135.00
M16A1/A2/AR-15	No	Weaver-type rail	59.95
Multibase Weaver Rail[1]	No	—	59.95
Ring Inserts	No	30mm to 1"	29.00
STANAG Rings	No	30mm	65.00
Throw Lever Weaver Rings	No	1"	78.75
#19 Weaver/STANAG Throw Lever Rail	No	—	140.00
[1]For rifles with detachable carry handle, other Weaver rails. From A.R.M.S., Inc.			
ARMSON			
AR-15[1]	No	1"	39.00
Mini-14[2]	No	1"	56.00
H&K[3]	No	1"	74.00
UZI[4]	No	1"	74.00
[1]Fastens with one nut. [2]Models 181, 182, 183, 184, etc. [3]Claw mount. [4]Claw mount, bolt cover still easily removable. From Trijicon, Inc.			
ARMSPORT			
100 Series[1]	No	1" rings. Low, med., high	10.75
104 22-cal.	No	1"	10.75
201 See-Thru	No	1"	13.00
1-Piece Base[2]	No	—	5.50
2-Piece Base[2]	No	—	2.75
[1]Weaver-type rings. [2]Weaver-type base; most popular rifles. Made in U.S. From Armsport.			

Maker, Model, Type	Adjust.	Scopes	Price
B-SQUARE			
Pistols			
Beretta/Taurus 92/99[6]	—	1"	69.95
Browning Buck Mark[6]	No	1"	49.95
Colt 45 Auto	E only	1"	69.95
Colt Python/MkIV, 4",6",8"[1,6]	E	1"	59.95
Dan Wesson Clamp-On[2,6]	E	1"	59.95
Ruger 22 Auto Mono-Mount[3]	No	1"	49.95
Ruger Single-Six[4]	No	1"	49.95
Ruger Blackhawk, Super B'hwk[8]	W&E	1"	59.95
Ruger GP-100[9]	No	1"	59.95
Ruger Redhawk[8]	W&E	1"	59.95
S&W 422/2206[9]	No	1"	59.95
Taurus 66[9]	No	1"	59.95
S&W K, L, N frame[2,6]	No	1"	59.95
T/C Contender (Dovetail Base)	W&E	1"	49.95
Rifles			
Charter AR-7	No	1"	49.95
Mini-14 (dovetail/NATO Stanag)[5,6]	W&E	1"	59.95
M-94 Side Mount	W&E	1"	49.95
RWS, Beeman/FWB Air Rifles	E only	—	69.95
SMLE Side Mount with rings	W&E	1"	69.95
Rem. Model Seven, 600, 660, etc.[6]	No	1" One-piece base	9.95
Military			
AK-47/AKM/AKS/SKS-56[10]	No	1"	59.95
AK-47, SKS-56[11]	No	1"	69.95
M1-A[7]	W&E	1"	99.50
AR-15/16[6,7]	W&E	1"	59.95
FN-LAR/FAL[6,7]	E only	1"	149.50
HK-91/93/94[6,7]	E only	1"	99.50
Shotguns[6]			
Ithaca 37[6]	No	1"	49.95
Mossberg 500, 712, 5500[6]	No	1"	49.95
Rem. 870/1100 (12 & 20 ga.)[6]	No	1"	49.95
Rem. 870, 1100 (and L.H.)[6]	No	1"	49.95
BSL Laser Mounts			
Scope Tube Clamp[12,13,16]	No	—	39.95
45 Auto[12,13,16]	No	—	69.95
SIG P226[12,13,16]	No	—	69.95
Beretta 92F/Taurus PT99[12,13,16]	No	—	69.95
Colt King Cobra, Python, MkV[12,13,16]	No	—	39.95
S&W L Frame[13,16]	No	—	39.95
Taurus 66/69[12,14,16]	No	—	69.95
S&W K,L,N Frames[12,14,16]	No	—	69.95
Beretta 92F/Taurus PT99[12,15,16]	No	—	79.95
Ruger P85[12,15,16]	No	—	79.95

[1]Clamp-on, blue finish; stainless finish **$59.95**. [2]Blue finish; stainless finish **$59.95**. [3]Clamp-on; blue; stainless finish **$59.95**. [4]Dovetail; stainless finish **$59.95**. [5]No gunsmithing, no sight removal; blue; stainless finish **$79.95**. [6]Weaver-style rings. Rings not included with Weaver-type bases; stainless finish add $10. [7]NATO Stanag dovetail model, **$99.50**. [8]Blue; stainless **$69.95**. [9]Blue; stainless **$69.95**. [10]Handguard mounts. [11]Receiver mounts. [12]Stainless finish add $10. [13]Under-barrel mount, no gunsmithing. [14]Ejector rod mount. [15]Guide rod mount. [16]Used with B-Square BSL-1 Laser Sight only. Mounts for many shotguns, airguns, military and law enforcement guns also available. **Partial listing of mounts shown here. Contact B-Square for more data.**

B-Square makes mounts for the following military rifles: AK47/AKS, Egyptian Hakim, French MAS 1936, M91 Argentine Mauser, Model 98 Brazilian and German Mausers, Model 93, Spanish Mauser (long and short), Model 1916 Mauser, Model 38 and 96 Swedish Mausers, Model 91 Russian (round and octagon receivers), Chinese SKS 56, SMLE No. 1, Mk. III, 1903 Springfield, U.S. 30-cal. Carbine, and others. Those following replace gun's rear sight: AK47/AKS, P14/1917 Enfield, FN49, M1 Garand, M1-A/M14 (no sight removal), SMLE No. 1, Mk III/No. 4 & 5, Mk. 1, 1903/1903-A3 Springfield, Beretta AR 70 (no sight removal).

Maker, Model, Type	Adjust.	Scopes	Price
BEEMAN			
Double Adjustable	W&E	1"	29.98
Deluxe Ring Mounts	No	1"	29.98
Professional Mounts	W&E	1"	149.95
Dampamount	No	1"	89.95
All grooved receivers and scope bases on all known air rifles and 22-cal. rimfire rifles (1/2" to 5/8"—6mm to 15mm).			
BOCK			
Swing ALK[1]	W&E	1", 26mm, 30mm	224.00
Safari KEMEL[2]	W&E	1", 26mm, 30mm	149.00
Claw KEMKA[3]	W&E	1", 26mm, 30mm	224.00
ProHunter Fixed[4]	No	1", 26mm, 30mm	95.00

Maker, Model, Type	Adjust.	Scopes	Price
BOCK (cont.)			
Dovetail 22[5]	No	1", 26mm	59.00

[1]Q.D.; pivots right for removal. For Steyr-Mannlicher, Win. 70, Rem. 700, Mauser 98, Dakota, Sako, Sauer 80, 90. Magnum has extra-wide rings, same price. [2]Heavy-duty claw-type; reversible for front or rear removal. For Steyr-Mannlicher rifles. [3]True claw mount for bolt-action rifles. Also in extended model. For Steyr-Mannlicher, Win. 70, Rem. 700. Also avail. as Gunsmith Bases—bases not drilled or contoured—same price. [4]Extra-wide rings. [5]Fit most 22 rimfires with dovetail receivers. Imported from Germany by GSI, Inc.

Maker, Model, Type	Adjust.	Scopes	Price
BUEHLER			
One Piece (T)[1]	W only	1" split rings, 3 heights	Complete—89.50
		1" split rings, engraved	Rings only—140.00
		26mm split rings, 2 heights	Rings only—59.00
		30mm split rings, 1 height	Rings only—77.00
One Piece Micro Dial (T)[1]	W&E	1" split rings	Complete—115.50
Two Piece (T)[1]	W only	1" split rings	Complete—89.50
Two Piece Dovetail (T)[2]	W only	1" split rings	Complete—110.50
One Piece Pistol (T)[3]	W only	1" split rings	Complete—$89.50
One Piece Pistol Stainless (T)[1]	W only	1" stainless rings	Complete—115.50
One Piece Ruger Mini-14 (T)[4]	W only	1" split rings	Complete—110.50
One Piece Pistol M83 Blue[4,5]	W only	1" split rings	Complete—102.50
One Piece Pistol M83 Silver[4,5]	W only	1" stainless rings	Complete—118.50

[1]Most popular models. [2]Sako dovetail receivers. [3]15 models. [4]No drilling & tapping. [5]Aircraft alloy, dyed blue or to match stainless; for Colt Diamondback, Python, Trooper, Ruger Blackhawk, Single-Six, Security-Six, S&W K-frame, Dan Wesson.

Maker, Model, Type	Adjust.	Scopes	Price
BURRIS			
Supreme One Piece (T)[1]	W only	1" split rings, 3 heights	1 piece base—25.95
Trumount Two Piece (T)	W only	1" split rings, 3 heights	2 piece base—23.95
Trumount Two Piece Ext.	W only	1" split rings	29.95
Browning Auto Mount[2]	No	1" split rings	19.95
Rings Mounts[3]	No	1" rings—20.95	
L.E.R. Mount Bases[4]	W only	1" split rings	23.95
L.E.R. No Drill-No Tap Bases[4,7,8]	W only	1" split rings	37.95-48.95
Extension Rings[5]	No	1" scopes	41.95-48.95
Ruger Ring Mount[6]	W only	1" split rings	36.95-41.95
Std. 1" Rings	—	Low, medium, high heights	33.95-41.95
Zee Rings	—	Fit Weaver bases; medium and high heights	27.95-35.95

[1]Most popular rifles. Universal rings, mounts fit Burris, Universal, Redfield, Leupold and Browning bases. Comparable prices. [2]Browning Standard 22 Auto rifle. [3]Grooved receivers. [4]Universal dovetail; accept Burris, Universal, Redfield, Leupold rings. For Dan Wesson, S&W, Virginian, Ruger Blackhawk, Win. 94. [5]Medium standard front, extension rear, per pair. Low standard front, extension rear, per pair. [6]Mini scopes, scopes with 2" bell, for M77R. [7]Selected rings and bases available with matte Safari or silver finish. [8]For S&W K,L,N frames, Colt Python, Dan Wesson with 6" or longer barrels.

Maker, Model, Type	Adjust.	Scopes	Price
BUSHNELL			
Detachable (T) mounts only[1]	W only	1" split rings, uses Weaver base	Rings—15.95
22 mount	No	1" only	Rings—6.95

[1]Most popular rifles. Includes windage adjustment.

Maker, Model, Type	Adjust.	Scopes	Price
CAPE OUTFITTERS			
Quick Detachable	No	1" split rings, lever quick detachable	99.95

Double rifles; Rem. 700-721, Colt Sauer, Sauer 200, Kimber, Win. 61-63-07-100-70, Browning High Power, 22, BLR, BAR, BBR, A-Bolt; Wea. Mark V, Vanguard; Modern Muzzle Loading, Knight, Thompson/Center, CVA rifles, Dixie rifles. All steel; returns to zero. From Cape Outfitters.

Maker, Model, Type	Adjust.	Scopes	Price
CLEAR VIEW			
Universal Rings, Mod. 101[1]	No	1" split rings	21.95
Standard Model[2]	No	1" split rings	21.95
Broad View[3]	No	1"	21.95
22 Model[4]	No	3/4", 7/8", 1"	13.95
SM-94 Winchester[5]	No	1" split rings	23.95
94 EJ[6]	No	1" split rings	21.95

[1]Most rifles by using Weaver-type base; allows use of iron sights. [2]Most popular rifles; allows use of iron sights. [3]Most popular rifles; low profile, wide field of view. [4]22 rifles with grooved receiver. [5]Side mount. [6]For Winchester Angle Eject. From Clear View Mfg.

Maker, Model, Type	Adjust.	Scopes	Price
CONETROL			
Huntur[1]	W only	1", 26mm, 26.5mm solid or split rings, 3 heights	59.91
Gunnur[2]	W only	1", 26mm, 26.5mm solid or split rings, 3 heights	74.91
Custum[3]	W only	1", 26mm, 26.5mm solid or split rings, 3 heights	89.91
One Piece Side Mount Base[4]	W only	1", 26mm, 26.5mm solid or split rings, 3 heights	—
DapTar Bases[5]	W only	1", 26mm, 26.5mm solid or split rings, 3 heights	—
Pistol Bases, 2 or 3-ring[6]	W only	1" scopes	—
Fluted Bases[7]	W only	Standard Conetrol rings	99.99
30mm Rings[8]	W only	30mm	49.98-69.96

[1]All popular rifles, including metric-drilled foreign guns. Price shown for base, two rings. Matte finish. [2]Gunnur grade has mirror-finished rings, satin-finish base. Price shown for base, two rings. [3]Custum grade has mirror-finished rings and mirror-finished, streamlined base. Price shown for base, two rings. [4]Win. 94, Krag, older split-bridge Mannlicher-Schoenauer, Mini-14, etc. Prices same as above. [5]For all popular guns with integral mounting provision, including Sako, BSA, Ithacagun, Ruger, Tikka, H&K, BRNO—$29.97-$44.97—and many others. Also for grooved-receiver rimfires and air rifles. Prices same as above. [6]For XP-100, T/C Contender, Colt SAA, Ruger Blackhawk, S&W. [7]Sculptured two-piece bases as found on fine custom rifles. Price shown is for base alone. Also available unfinished—$74.91, or finished but unblued—$87.95. [8]30mm rings made in projectionless style, medium height only. Three-ring mount available for T/C Contender and other pistols in Conetrol's three grades.

Maker, Model, Type	Adjust.	Scopes	Price
EAW			
Quick Detachable Top Mount	W&E	1", 26mm	259.99
	W&E	1"/26mm with front extension ring	259.99
	W&E	30mm	279.99
	W&E	30mm with front extension ring.	279.99

Also 30mm rings to fit Burris, Redfield or Leupold-type bases, low and high, $112.00; 1" or 26mm rings only, $95.00 Most popular rifles. Elevation adjusted with variable-height sub-bases for rear ring. Imported by Paul Jaeger, Inc.

Maker, Model, Type	Adjust.	Scopes	Price
GENTRY			
Feather-Light Rings	No	1", 30mm	75.00

Maker, Model, Type	Adjust.	Scopes	Price
GRACE			
Swan G-3	No	Weaver-type	259.95

For HK G-3 guns. All-steel; provides iron sight see-through. From Grace Tool, Inc.

Maker, Model, Type	Adjust.	Scopes	Price
GRIFFIN & HOWE			
Standard Double Lever (S)	No	1" or 26mm split rings.	305.00

All popular models (Garand $215). All rings $75. Top ejection rings available. Price installed for side mount.

Maker, Model, Type	Adjust.	Scopes	Price
HOLDEN			
Wide Ironsighter™	No	1" split rings	27.95
Ironsighter Center Fire[1]	No	1" split rings	27.95
Ironsighter S-94	No	1" split rings	32.95
Ironsighter 22-Cal. Rimfire			
Model #500[2]	No	1" split rings	19.95
Model #600[3]	No	7/8" split rings also fits 3/4"	15.95
Series #700[5]	No	1" split rings	27.95
Model 732, 777[6]	No	1" split rings	56.95
Ironsighter Handguns[4]	No	1" split rings	32.95-56.95
Blackpowder Mount[7]	No	1" split rings	27.95-56.95

[1]Most popular rifles, including Ruger Mini-14, H&R M700, and muzzleloaders. Rings have oval holes to permit use of iron sights. [2]For 1" dia. scopes. [3]For 3/4" or 7/8" dia. scopes. [4]For 1" dia. extended eye relief scopes. [5]702—Browning A-Bolt; 709—Marlin 39A. [6]732—Ruger 77/22 R&RS, No. 1, Ranch Rifle; 777 fits Ruger 77R, RS. Both 732, 777 fit Ruger integral bases. [7]Fits most popular blackpowder rifles; one model for Holden Ironsighter mounts, one for Weaver rings. Adj. rear sight is integral. Some models in stainless finish. From J.B. Holden Co.

Maker, Model, Type	Adjust.	Scopes	Price
KENPATABLE MOUNT			
Shotgun Mount	No	1", laser or red dot device	49.95

Wrap-around design; no gunsmithing required. Models for Browning BPS, A-5 12-ga., Sweet 16, 20, Rem. 870/1100 (LTW and L.H.), S&W 916, Mossberg 500, Ithaca 37 & 51 12-ga., S&W 1000/3000, Win. 1400. From KenPatable Ent.

Maker, Model, Type	Adjust.	Scopes	Price
KRIS MOUNTS			
Side-Saddle[1]	No	1", 26mm split rings	12.98
Two Piece (T)[2]	No	1", 26mm split rings	8.98

Maker, Model, Type	Adjust.	Scopes	Price
Kris (cont.)			
One Piece (T)[3]	No	1", 26mm split rings	12.98

[1]One-piece mount for Win. 94. [2]Most popular rifles and Ruger. [3]Blackhawk revolver. Mounts have oval hole to permit use of iron sights.

KWIK-SITE			
KS-See-Thru[1]	No	1"	25.95
KS-22 See-Thru[2]	No	1"	22.95
KS-W94[3]	No	1"	30.95
Imperial Bench Rest	No	1"	30.95
KS-WEV	No	1"	21.95
KS-WEV-HIGH	No	1"	21.95
KS-T22 1"[4]	No	1"	22.95
KS-FL Flashlite[5]	No	Mini or C cell flashlight	49.95
KS-T88[6]	No	1"	10.95
KS-T89	No	30mm	14.95
KSN 22 See-Thru	No	1", 7/8"	19.95
KSN-T22	No	1", 7/8"	19.95
KSN-M16 See-Thru	No	1"	99.95
KSB Base Set	—	—	5.65
Combo Bases & Rings	No	1"	26.75

[1]Most rifles. Allows use of iron sights. [2]22-cal. rifles with grooved receivers. Allows use of iron sights. [3]Model 94, 94 Big Bore. No drilling or tapping. Also in adjustable model $49.95. [4]Non-see-through model for grooved receivers. [5]Allows Mag Lite or C or D, Mini Mag Lites to be mounted atop See-Thru mounts. [6]Fits any Redfield, Tasco, Weaver or universal-style Kwik-Site dovetail base. Bright blue, black matte or satin finish. Standard, high heights.

LASER AIM	No	Laser Aim	29.00-69.00

Mounts Laser Aim above or below barrel. Avail. for most popular handguns, rifles, shotguns, including militaries. From Emerging Technologies, Inc.

LASERSIGHT	No	LS45 only	29.95-149.00

For the LS45 Lasersight. Allows LS45 to be mounted alongside any 1" scope. Universal adapter attaches to any full-length Weaver-type base. For most popular military-type rifles, Mossberg, Rem. shotguns, Python, Desert Eagle, S&W N frame, Colt 45ACP. From Imatronic Lasersight.

LEUPOLD			
STD Bases[1]	W only	One- or two-piece bases	22.90
STD Rings[2]	—	1" super low, low, medium, high	32.00
STD Handgun mounts[3]	No	—	57.90
Dual Dovetail Bases[1,4]	No	—	22.90
Dual Dovetail Rings[10]	—	1", super low, low	32.00
Ring Mounts[5,6,7]	No	7/8", 1"	81.10
22 Rimfire[10]	No	7/8", 1"	60.00
Gunmaker Base[8]	W only	1"	16.00
Gunmaker Ring Blanks[9]	—	1"	22.00
Quick Release Rings	—	1", low, med., high	32.00
Quick Release Bases[11]	No	1", one- or two-piece	66.00
Airgun Ringmount[12]	No	1"	92.00

[1]Rev. front and rear combinations; matte finish $22.90. [2]Avail. polished, matte or silver (low, med. only) finish. [3]Base and rear two rings; Casull, Ruger, S&W, T/C; add $5.00 for silver finish. [4]Rem. 700, Win. 70-type actions. [5]For Ruger No. 1, 77, 77/22; interchangeable with Ruger units. [6]Sako. [7]For dovetailed rimfire rifles. [8]Must be drilled, tapped for each action. [9]Unfinished bottom, top completed; sold singly. [10]Most dovetail-receiver 22s. [11]BSA Monarch, Rem. 40X, 700, 721, 725, Ruger M77, S&W 1500, Weatherby Mark V, Vanguard, Win M70. [12]Receiver grooves 9.5mm to 11.0mm; matte finish.

LEATHERWOOD			
Bridge Bases[1]	No	ART II or all dovetail rings	15.00
M1A/M-14 Q.D.	No	ART II or all dovetail rings	105.00
AR-15/M-16 Base	No	ART II or all dovetail rings	25.00
FN-FAL Base	No	ART II or all dovetail rings	100.00
FN Para. Base	No	ART II or all dovetail rings	110.00
Steyr SSG Base	No	ART II or all dovetail rings	55.00

[1]Many popular bolt actions. Mounts accept Weaver or dovetail-type rings. From North American Specialties.

MARLIN			
One Piece QD (T)	No	1" split rings	14.95
Most Marlin lever actions.			

MILLETT			
Black Onyx Smooth	—	1", low, medium, high	29.65
Chaparral Engraved	—	1", low, medium, high engraved	43.95
One-Piece Bases[6]	Yes	1"	23.95
Universal Two-Piece Bases			
700 Series	W only	Two-piece bases	23.95

Maker, Model, Type	Adjust.	Scopes	Price
Millett (cont.)			
FN Series	W only	Two-piece bases	23.95
70 Series[1]	W only	1", two-piece bases	23.95
Angle-Loc Rings[2]	W only	1", low, medium, high	30.65-44.95
Ruger 77 Rings[3]	—	1"	44.95
Shotgun Rings[4]	—	1"	26.95
Handgun Bases, Rings[5]	—	1"	32.95-61.35
30mm Rings[7]	—	30mm	35.95
Extension Rings[8]	—	1"	33.95

Rem. 40X, 700, 722, 725, Ruger 77 (round top), Weatherby, FN Mauser, FN Brownings, Colt 57, Interarms Mark X, Parker-Hale, Sako (round receiver), many others. [1]Fits Win. M70, 70XTR, 670, Browning BBR, BAR, BLR, A-Bolt, Rem. 7400/7600, Four, Six, Marlin 336, Win. 94 A.E., Sav. 110. [2]To fit Weaver-type bases. [3]Engraved. Smooth $30.65. [4]For Rem. 870, 1100; smooth. [5]Two and three-ring sets for Colt Python, Trooper, Diamondback, Peacekeeper, Dan Wesson, Ruger Redhawk, Super Redhawk. [6]Turn-in bases and Weaver-style for most popular rifles and T/C Contender, XP-100 pistols. [7]Both Weaver and turn-in styles; three heights. [8]Med. or high; ext. front—std. rear, ext. rear—std. front, ext. front—ext. rear; $38.95 for double extension. Some models available in nickel at extra cost. From Millett Sights.

OAKSHORE			
Handguns			
Browning Buck Mark	No	1"	29.00
Colt Cobra, Diamondback, Python, 1911	No	1"	38.00-52.00
Ruger 22 Auto, GP100	No	1"	33.00-49.00
S&W N Frame	No	1"	45.00-60.00
S&W 422	No	1"	35.00-38.00
Rifles			
Colt AR-15	No	1"	26.00-34.00
H&K 91, 93, 94, MP-5, G-3	No	1"	56.00
Galil	No	1"	75.00
Marlin 336 & 1800 Series	No	1"	21.00
Win. 94	No	1"	39.00
Shotguns			
Mossberg 500	No	1"	40.00
Rem. 870, 1100	No	1"	33.00-52.00
Rings	No	1", med., high	5.20-9.80

See Through offered in some models. Black or silver finish; 1" rings also avail. for 3/8" grooved receivers (See Through). From Oakshore Electronic Sights, Inc.

PEM'S			
22T Mount[1]	No	1"	17.95
The Mount[2]	Yes	1"	27.50

[1]Fit all 3/8" dovetail on rimfire rifles. [2]Base and ring set; for over 100 popular rifles; low, medium rings. From Pem's.

RAM-LINE			
Mini-14 Mount	Yes	1"	24.97

No drilling or tapping. Use std. dovetail rings. Has built-in shell deflector. Made of solid black polymer. From Ram-Line, Inc.

REDFIELD			
American Rings[8]	No	1", low, med., high	16.95
American Bases[8]	No	—	2.65-5.09
American Widefield See-Thru[9]	No	1"	16.95
JR-SR (T)[1]	W only	3/4", 1", 26mm, 30mm	JR—20.95-52.95 SR—20.95-39.95
Ring (T)[2]	No	3/4" and 1"	27.95
Three-Ring Pistol System SMP[3]	No	1" split rings (three)	56.95-62.95
Widefield See-Thru Mounts	No	1"	16.95
Ruger Rings[4]	No	1", med., high	35.95
Ruger 30mm[5]	No	1"	46.95
Midline Ext. Rings	No	1"	20.95
Steel "WS" Rings[6]	W	1", 30mm	26.95-39.95
Steel 22 Ring Mount, Base[7]	No	3/4", 1"	13.95-29.95

[1]Low, med. & high, split rings. Reversible extension front rings for 1". 2-piece bases for Sako. Colt Sauer bases $39.95. Med. Top Access JR rings nickel-plated, $29.95. SR two-piece ABN mount nickel-plated, $22.95; RealTree Camo rings, med. high $31.95; RealTree Camo JR bases $25.95; RealTree bases $25.95. [2]Split rings for grooved 22s. See-Thru mounts $16.95. [3]Used with MP scopes for: S&W K, L or N frame, XP-100, T/C Contender, Ruger receivers. [4]For Ruger Model 77 rifles, medium and high; medium only for M77/22. [5]For Model 77. Also in matte finish, $44.95. [6]Nickel-plated, $37.95. [7]For 22 rifles with grooved receivers. Fits all radius dovetails. [8]Aluminum 22 groove mount $14.95; base and medium rings $17.95. [9]Fits American or Weaver-style base.

S&K			
Insta-Mount (T) bases and rings[1]	W only	Use S&K rings only	25.00-99.00
Conventional rings and bases[2]	W only	1" split rings	From 50.00
Skulptured Bases, Rings[2]	W only	1", 26mm, 30mm	From 50.00

[1]1903, A3, M1 Carbine, Lee Enfield #1, Mk. III, #4, #5, M1917, M98 Mauser, FN Auto, AR-15, AR-180, M-14, M-1, Ger. K-43, Mini-14, M1-A, Krag, AKM, AK-47, Win. 94, SKS Type 56, Daewoo, H&K. [2]Most popular rifles already drilled and tapped. Horizontally and vertically split rings, matte or high gloss.

Maker, Model, Type	Adjust.	Scopes	Price
SSK INDUSTRIES			
T'SOB	No	1"	65.00-145.00
Quick Detachable	No	1"	From 160.00

Custom installation using from two to four rings (included). For T/C Contender, most 22 auto pistols, Ruger and other S.A. revolvers, Ruger, Dan Wesson, S&W, Colt DA revolvers. Black or white finish. Uses Kimber rings in two- or three-ring sets. In blue or SSK Khrome. For T/C Contender or most popular revolvers. Standard, non-detachable model also available, from $65.00.

Maker, Model, Type	Adjust.	Scopes	Price
SAKO			
QD Dovetail	W only	1" only	67.00-140.00

Sako, or any rifle using Sako action, 3 heights available. Stoeger, importer.

Maker, Model, Type	Adjust.	Scopes	Price
TASCO			
World Class			
Universal "W" Ringmount[1]	No	1", 30mm	27.00-59.00
Ruger[2]	No	1", 30mm	35.00-59.00
22, Air Rifle[3]	No	1", 30mm	28.00-66.00
Center-Fire Ringmount[4]	No	1", 26mm, 30mm	46.00-66.00
Desert Eagle Ringmount[5]	No	1", 30mm	51.00-72.00
Ringsets[6]	No	1", 26mm, 30mm	26.00-56.00
Bases[7]	Yes	—	26.00-46.00
Pro-Mount Handgun Base[8]	No	—	9.00-37.00

[1]Steel; low, high only; also high-profile see-through; fit Tasco, Weaver, other universal bases; black gloss or satin chrome. [2]Low, high only; for Redhawk and Super, No.1, Mini-14 & Thirty, 77, 77/22; blue or stainless. [3]Low, med., high; [3]⁄[8]" grooved receivers; black or satin chrome. [4]Low, med., high; for Tasco W.C. bases, some dovetail; black gloss only. [5]For Desert Eagle pistols, 22s, air rifles with deep dovetails. [6]Low, med., high; black gloss, matte satin chrome; also Traditional Ringsets **$31.00** (1"), **$42.00** (26mm), **$53.00** (30mm). [7]For popular rifles and shotguns; one-piece, two-piece, Q.D., long and short action, extension. Handgun bases have w&e adj. [8]For many popular handguns, blue or stainless. From Tasco.

Maker, Model, Type	Adjust.	Scopes	Price
THOMPSON/CENTER			
Contender 9741[1]	No	2[1]⁄[2], 4 RP	17.00
S&W 9747[2]	No	Lobo or RP	17.00
Ruger 9748[3]	No	Lobo or RP	17.00
Hawken 9749[4]	No	Lobo or RP	17.00
Hawken/Renegade 9754[5]	No	Lobo or RP	17.00
New Englander 9757	No	Lobo or RP	17.00
Quick Release System[6]	No	1"	Rings 48.00
			Base 24.50

[1]T/C rail mount scopes; all Contenders except vent. rib. [2]All S&W K and Combat Masterpiece, Hi-Way Patrolman, Outdoorsman, 22 Jet, 45 Target 1955. Requires drilling, tapping. [3]Blackhawk, Super Blackhawk, Super Single-Six. Requires drilling, tapping. [4]45 or 50 cal.; replaces rear sight. [5]Rail mount scopes; 54-cal. Hawken, 50, 54, 56-cal. Renegade. Replaces rear sight. [6]For Contender pistol, Carbine, Scout, all M/L long guns. From Thompson/Center.

Maker, Model, Type	Adjust.	Scopes	Price
UNERTL			
[1]⁄[4] Click[1]	Yes	[3]⁄[4]", 1" target scopes	Per set 115.00

[1]Unertl target or varmint scopes. Posa or standard mounts, less bases. From Unertl.

Maker, Model, Type	Adjust.	Scopes	Price
WARNE			
Quick Detachable Thumb Knob	No	1", 3 heights	67.80
		26mm 2 heights	82.80
		30mm 2 heights	82.80
Traditional Double Lever	No	1", 3 heights	89.50
		26mm 2 heights	103.00
		30mm 2 heights	103.00
Adjustable Double Lever	No	1", 3 heights	99.50
		26mm 2 heights	111.50
		30mm 2 heights	111.50
Grooved Receiver[1]	No	1", 3 heights	67.80-99.50
Machine Screw[2]	—	—	67.80-99.50
BRNO[3]	No	ZKK[4] 1", 3 heights	99.50
		ZKK[4] 30mm 2 heights	111.50
		MDL 1[5] 1" 2 heights	99.50
		MDL 1[5] 30mm 2 heights	111.50
		MDL 2	67.80-99.50
Ruger[3,6]	No	M77 1", 2 heights	99.50
		M77 30mm, 2 heights	111.50
		Other 1", 4 heights	99.50
		Other 30mm, 3 heights	111.50
Sako[3,6,7]	No	1", 4 heights	99.50
		30mm, 3 heights	111.50

Maker, Model, Type	Adjust.	Scopes	Price
Warne (cont.)			
Steyr[3,6]	No	SSG 1", 2 heights	99.50
		SSG 30mm, 2 heights	111.50
Two-Piece Bases (pr.)	—	—	25.00
One-Piece Base	—	—	32.00
Ruger Pistol Kit[8,9]	—	—	47.00

Vertically split rings with dovetail clamp, precise repeat to zero. Fit most popular rifles, handguns. Regular blue, matte blue, silver finish. [1]In 3 styles for 22-cal. [3]⁄[8]" dovetailed receivers. [2]Non q.d. [3]Adjustable double lever only. [4]19mm dovetail. [5]16mm dovetail. [6]Use standard rings if bases required. [7]For dovetail receiver. [8]For Bull barrel only. [9]Not including rings. From Warne Mfg. Co.

Maker, Model, Type	Adjust.	Scopes	Price
WEAVER			
Detachable Mounts			
Top Mount[1]	No	[7]⁄[8]", 1"	25.49-26.51
Side Mount[2]	No	1", 1" Long	31.18-36.87
Pivot Mount[3]	No	1"	39.96
Tip-Off Mount[4]	No	[7]⁄[8]", 1"	22.69-28.93
See-Thru Mount			
Traditional[6]	No	1"	26.51
Symmetrical[6]	No	1"	17.61-21.44
Detachable[5]	No	1"	26.51
Tip-Off[4]	No	1", [7]⁄[8]"	17.67-21.51
Pro View[6]	No	1"	17.67-18.44
Mount Base System[7]			
Blue Finish	No	1"	76.71
Stainless Finish	No	1"	107.31
Shotgun Converta-Mount System[8]	No	1"	76.71
Rifle Mount System[9]	No	1"	34.02
Paramount Mount Systems[10]			
Bases, pair	Yes	1"	26.36
Rings, pair	No	1"	34.22

[1]Nearly all modern rifles. Low, med., high. 1" extension **$30.96**. 1" low, med., high stainless steel **$40.53**. [2]Nearly all modern rifles, shotguns. [3]Most modern big bore rifles; std., high. [4]22s with [3]⁄[8]" grooved receivers. [5]Nearly all modern rifles. 1" See-Thru extension **$30.96**. [6]Most modern big bore rifles. Some in stainless finish **$20.22-21.44**. [7]No drilling, tapping. For Colt Python, Trooper, 357, Officer's Model, Ruger Blackhawk & Super, Mini-14, Security-Six, 22 auto pistols, Single-Six 22, Redhawk, Blackhawk SRM 357, S&W current K, L with adj. sights. [8]For Rem. 870, 1100, 11-87, Browning A-5, BPS, Ithaca 37, 87, Beretta A303, Beretta A-390, Winchester 1200-1500, Mossberg 500. [9]For some popular sporting rifles. [10]Dovetail design mount for Rem. 700, Win. 70, FN Mauser, low, med., high rings; std., extension bases. From Weaver.

Maker, Model, Type	Adjust.	Scopes	Price
WIDEVIEW			
Premium 94 Angle Eject	No	1"	24.00
Premium See-Thru	No	1"	22.00
22 Premium See-Thru	No	[3]⁄[4]", 1"	16.00
Universal Ring Angle Cut	No	1"	24.00
Universal Ring Straight Cut	No	1"	22.00
Solid Mounts			
Lo Ring Solid[1]	No	1"	16.00
Hi Ring Solid[1]	No	1"	16.00
SR Rings	—	1", 30mm	16.00
22 Grooved Receiver	No	1"	16.00
94 Side Mount	No	1"	26.00
Blackpowder Mounts[2]	No	1"	30.00

[1]For Weaver-type bases. Models for many popular rifles. Low ring, high ring and grooved receiver types. [2]No drilling, tapping; for T/C Renegade, Hawken, CVA guns; for guns drilled and tapped, **$16.00**. From Wideview Scope Mount Corp.

Maker, Model, Type	Adjust.	Scopes	Price
WILLIAMS			
Sidemount with HCO Rings[1]	No	1", split or extension rings	69.25
Sidemount, offset rings[2]	No	Same	57.00
Sight-Thru Mounts[3]	No	1", [7]⁄[8]" sleeves	23.95
Streamline Mounts	No	1" (bases form rings).	23.95
Guideline Handgun[4]	No	1" split rings.	79.95

[1]Most rifles, Br. S.M.L.E. (round rec.) **$13.45** extra. [2]Most rifles including Win. 94 Big Bore. [3]Many modern rifles, including CVA Apollo, others with 1" octagon barrels. [4]No drilling, tapping required; heat treated alloy. For Ruger Blackhawk, Super Blackhawk, Redhawk; S&W N frame, M29 with 10[5]⁄[8]" barrel (**$79.95**); S&W K, L frames; Colt Python, King Cobra; Ruger MkII Bull Barrel; Streamline Top Mount for T/C Contender, Scout Rifle, CVA Apollo (**$39.95**), High Top Mount with sub-base (**$49.95**). From Williams Gunsight Co.

Maker, Model, Type	Adjust.	Scopes	Price
YORK			
M-1 Garand	Yes	1"	39.95

Centers scope over the action. No drilling, tapping or gunsmithing. Uses standard dovetail rings. From York M-1 Conversions.

NOTES

(S)—Side Mount (T)—Top Mount; 22mm=.866"; 25.4mm=1.024"; 26.5mm=1.045"; 30mm=1.81"

CAUTION: PRICES CHANGE, CHECK AT GUNSHOP.

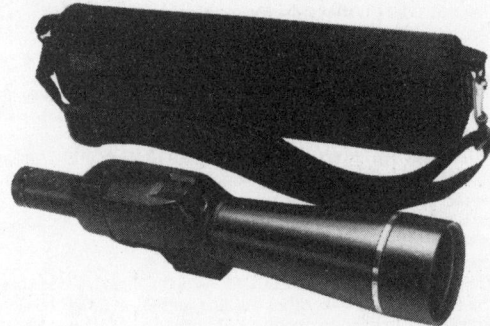

Bausch & Lomb 77mm Elite

Leupold 12-40x60mm Variable

BAUSCH & LOMB DISCOVERER—15x to 60x zoom, 60mm objective. Constant focus throughout range. Field at 1000 yds. 38 ft (60x), 150 ft. (15x). Comes with lens caps. Length 17½"; weight 48.5 oz.
Price: **$329.95**
BAUSCH & LOMB ELITE—15x to 45x zoom, 60mm objective. Field at 1000 yds., 119-62 ft. Length is 12.2"; weight, 26.5 oz. Waterproof, armored. Tripod mount. Comes with black case.
Price: **$589.95**
BAUSCH & LOMB 77MM ELITE—20x, 30x or 20-60x zoom, 77mm objective. Field of view at 1000 yds. 175 ft. (20x), 78 ft. (30x), 108-62 ft. (zoom). Weight 51 oz. (20x, 30x), 54 oz. (zoom); length 16.8". Interchangeable bayonet-style eyepieces. Built-in peep sight.
Price: **$640.00**
Price: With EDPrime Glass **$1,400.00**
Price: 20-60x zoom eyepiece **$350.00**
Price: 20x wide angle eyepiece **$250.00**
Price: 30x eyepiece **$230.00**
BURRIS 20x SPOTTER—20x, 50mm objective. Straight type. Field at 100 yds. 15 ft. Length 10"; weight 21 oz. Rubber armor coating, multi-coated lenses, 22mm eye relief. Recessed focus adjustment. Nitrogen filled. Retractable sunshade.
Price: 20x 50mm **$478.95**
Price: 24x 60mm **$507.95**
Price: 30x 60mm **$536.95**
BUSHNELL BANNER SENTRY—18-36x zoom, 50mm objective. Field at 1000 yds. 115-78 ft. Length 14.5", weight 27 oz. Black rubber armored. Built-in peep sight. Comes with tripod.
Price: **$177.95**
BUSHNELL COMPACT COMPETITOR—20x, 40mm objective. Field at 1000 yds. 141 ft. Focuses down to 40 ft. for indoor use. Tripod mount. Length 10.5"; weight 14.5 oz. Comes with tripod.
Price: **$117.95**
BUSHNELL SPACEMASTER—15x-45x zoom. Rubber armored, prismatic. 60mm objective. Field at 1000 yds. 125-65 ft. Minimum focus 20 ft. Length with caps 11.6"; weight 38.4 oz.
Price: With tripod and carrying case **$572.95**
Price: Interchangeable eyepieces—15x, 20x, 25x, 60x, each **$61.95**
Price: 22x Wide Angle **$71.95**
Price: 15-45x zoom eyepiece **$129.95**
BUSHNELL STALKER—10x to 30x zoom, 50mm objective. Field at 1000 yds. 142 ft. (10x) to 86 ft. (30x). Length 10.5". Weight 16 oz. Camo armored. Comes with tripod.
Price: **$337.95**
KOWA TSN-1-45˚—Offset-type. 77mm objective, 25x, fixed and zoom eyepieces; field at 1000 yds. 94 ft.; relative brightness 9.6; length 15.4"; weight 48.8 oz. Lens shade and caps. Straight-type (TSN-2) also available with similar specs and prices.
Price: Without eyepiece **$535.00**
Price: 20x-60x zoom eyepiece **$222.00**
Price: 20x eyepiece (wide angle) **$182.00**
Price: 25x, 40x eyepiece **$114.00, $128.00**
Price: 25x LER eyepiece **$170.00**
Price: 30x eyepiece (wide angle) **$195.00**
Price: 60x eyepiece **$187.00**
Price: 77x eyepiece **$190.00**
Price: TSN-2 (straight), no eyepiece **$510.00**

KOWA TS-601—45˚ off-set type. 60mm multi-coated objective, 25x fixed and zoom eyepieces; field at 1000 yds. 93 ft.; relative brightness 5.8; length 14.8"; weight 37 oz. Comes with lens shade and caps. Straight-type also available (TS-602).
Price: Without eyepiece **$425.00**
Price: 25x eyepiece **$89.00**
Price: 20x eyepiece (wide angle) **$104.00**
Price: 40x eyepiece **$92.00**
Price: 25x-60x zoom eyepiece **$194.00**
Price: 25x LER eyepiece **$170.00**
KOWA TS-9C—Straight-type. 50mm objective, 20x compact model; fixed power eyepieces; objective focusing down to 17 ft.; field at 1000 yds. 157 ft.; relative brightness 6.3; length 9.65"; weight 22.9 oz. Lens caps.
Price: With 20x eyepiece **$193.00**
Price: 15x, 20x eyepieces, each **$35.00, $33.00**
Price: 11x-33x zoom eyepiece **$111.00**
Price: As above, rubber armored, 20x (TS-9R) **$212.00**
Price: TS-9B (45˚ offset), 20x **$236.00**
LEATHERWOO-MEOPTA C-Z SPOTTING SCOPE—25x, 70mm objective. Field at 1000 yards 101 ft. Length 13.7", weight 2.4 lbs. Comes with soft case.
Price: **$199.50**
LEUPOLD 12-40x60 VARIABLE—60mm objective, 12-40x. Field at 100 yds. 17.5-5.3 ft.; eye relief 1.2" (20x). Overall length 11.5", weight 32 oz. Rubber armored.
Price: **$883.90**
LEUPOLD 20x50 COMPACT—50mm objective, 20x. Field at 100 yards 11.5 ft.; eye relief 1"; length 9.4"; weight 20.5 oz.
Price: Armored model **$576.80**
Price: Packer Tripod **$87.50**
LEUPOLD 25x50 COMPACT—50mm objective, 25x. Field at 100 yds. 8.3 ft.; eye relief 1"; length overall 9.4"; weight 20.5 oz.
Price: Armored model **$616.10**
Price: Armored, with reticle **$633.90**
Price: Packer Tripod **$87.50**
LEUPOLD 30x60 COMPACT—60mm objective, 30x. Field at 100 yds. 6.4 ft.; eye relief 1"; length overall 12.9"; weight 26 oz.
Price: Armored model **$633.90**
Price: Packer Tripod **$87.50**
MIRADOR TTB SERIES—Draw tube armored spotting scopes. Available with 75mm or 80mm objective. Zoom model (28x-62x, 80mm) is 11⅞" (closed), weighs 50 oz. Field at 1000 yds. 70-42 ft. Comes with lens covers.
Price: 28-62x80mm **$953.95**
Price: 32x80mm **$809.95**
Price: 26-58x75mm **$863.95**
Price: 30x75mm **$719.95**
MIRADOR SSD SPOTTING SCOPES—60mm objective, 15x, 20x, 22x, 25x, 40x, 60x, 20-60x; field at 1000 yds. 37 ft.; length 10¼"; weight 33 oz.
Price: 25x **$548.95**

Price: 22x Wide Angle **$557.95**
Price: 20-60x Zoom **$701.95**
Price: As above, with tripod, case **$854.95**
MIRADOR SIA SPOTTING SCOPES—Similar to the SSD scopes except with 45° eyepiece. Length 12¼"; weight 39 oz.
Price: 25x **$701.95**
Price: 22x Wide Angle **$710.95**
Price: 20-60x Zoom **$854.95**
MIRADOR SSA SPOTTING SCOPES—Lightweight, slender version of the SSD series with 50mm objective. Length 11⅛"; weight 28 oz.
Price: 20x **$413.95**
Price: 18x Wide Angle **$422.95**
Price: 16-48x Zoom **$566.95**
MIRADOR SSR SPOTTING SCOPES—50mm or 60mm objective. Similar to SSD except rubber armored in black or camouflage. Length 11⅛"; weight 31 oz.
Price: Black, 20x **$449.95**
Price: Black, 18x Wide Angle **$458.95**
Price: Black, 16-48x Zoom **$602.95**
Price: Black, 20x, 60mm, EER **$611.95**
Price: Black, 22x Wide Angle, 60mm **$602.95**
Price: Black, 20-60x Zoom **$746.95**
MIRADOR SSF FIELD SCOPES—Fixed or variable power, choice of 50mm, 60mm, 75mm objective lens. Length 9¾"; weight 20 oz. (15-32x50).
Price: 20x50mm **$287.95**
Price: 25x60mm **$341.95**
Price: 30x75mm **$413.95**
Price: 15-32x50mm Zoom **$449.95**
Price: 18-40x60mm Zoom **$503.95**
Price: 22-50x75mm Zoom **$575.95**
MIRADOR SRA MULTI ANGLE SCOPES—Similar to SSF Series except eyepiece head rotates for viewing from any angle.
Price: 20x50mm **$449.95**
Price: 25x60mm **$512.95**
Price: 30x75mm **$566.95**
Price: 15-32x50mm Zoom **$611.95**
Price: 18-40x60mm Zoom **$674.95**
Price: 22-50x75mm Zoom **$728.95**
MIRADOR SIB FIELD SCOPES—Short-tube, 45° scopes with porro prism design. 50mm and 60mm objective. Length 10¼"; weight 18.5 oz. (15-32x50mm); field at 1000 yds. 129-81 ft.
Price: 20x50mm **$359.95**
Price: 25x60mm **$422.95**
Price: 15-32x50mm Zoom **$521.95**
Price: 18-40x60mm Zoom **$584.95**
NICHOLS "BACKPACKER" COMPACT—25x, 50mm objective. Field at 1000 yds. 101.2 ft. Overall length 8.76"; weight 20.6 oz. Gray finish. Comes with tripod.
Price: **$157.00**
NICHOLS "GRANDSLAM"—25x, 50mm objective. Field at 1000 yds. 91.6 ft. Overall length 12.2"; weight 24.7 oz. Gray finish. Comes with tripod.
Price: **$255.00**
Price: 17x-52x Zoom, with 25x lens, tripod **$443.00**
NIKON SPOTTING SCOPE—60mm objective, 20x fixed power or 15-45x zoom. Field at 1000 yds. 145 ft. (20x). Black rubber armored. Straight eyepiece. Weighs 44.2 oz., length 12.1" (20x).
Price: 20x60 fixed **$384.00**
Price: 15-45x zoom **$570.00**
PENTAX 30x60 HG—60mm objective lens, 30x. Field of view 86 ft. at 1000 yds. Length 12.1"; weight 35 oz. Waterproof, rubber armor, multi-coated lenses. Comes with lens cap, case, neck strap.
Price: **$600.00**
REDFIELD 25x WATERPROOF SPOTTER—60mm objective, 25x fixed power. Black rubber armor coat. Field at 1000 yds. 100 ft. Length 12.5"; weight 24 oz. Comes with lens covers, vinyl carrying case.
Price: **$416.95**
Price: As above, with adjustable tripod, aluminum carrying case with shoulder strap **$576.95**
REDFIELD WATERPROOF 20-45x SPOTTER—60mm objective, 20-45x. Field at 1000 yds. 45-63 ft. Length 12.5"; weight 23 oz. Black rubber armor coat. With vinyl carrying case.
Price: **$462.95**
Price: As above, with adjustable tripod, aluminum carrying case with shoulder strap **$613.95**
REDFIELD REGAL II—Regal II has 60mm objective, interchangeable 25x and 18x-40x zoom eyepieces. Field at 1000 yds.•125 ft. (25x). Dual rotation of eyepiece and scope body. With aluminum carrying case, tripod.
Price: **$718.95**
REDFIELD REGAL IV—Conventional straight through viewing. Regal IV has 60mm objective and interchangeable 25x and 20x-60x zoom eyepieces. Field at 1000 yds. 94 ft. (25x). With tripod and aluminum carrying case.
Price: Regal IV with black rubber Armorcoat **$755.95**

REDFIELD REGAL VI—60mm objective, 25x fixed and 20x-60x interchangeable eyepieces. Has 45° angled eyepiece, front-mounted focus ring, 180° tube rotation. Field at 1000 yds. 94 ft. (25x); length 12¼"; weight 40 oz. Comes with tripod, aluminum carrying case.
Price: Regal VI **$793.95**
SIMMONS 1204 COMPACT—50mm objective, 12-36x zoom. Camouflage rubber armored finish. Ocular focus and variable power magnification.
Price: With tripod **$243.95**
Price: Model 1205 (black non-armored finish) **$206.95**
SIMMONS 1207 COMPACT—50mm objective, 25x fixed power. Ocular focus. Green rubber-armored finish.
Price: With tripod **$199.95**
Price: Model 1206 (black rubber-armored finish) **$199.95**
SIMMONS 1208 COMPACT—50mm objective, 25x fixed power. Ocular focus. Non-reflective finish.
Price: With tripod **$169.95**
SWAROVSKI HABICHT HAWK 30x75S TELESCOPE—75mm objective, 30x. Field at 1000 yds. 90 ft. Minimum focusing distance 65 ft. Length: closed 13", extended 20.9"; weight 47 oz. Precise recognition of smallest details even at dusk. Leather or rubber covered, with caps and carrying case.
Price: **$865.00**
SWAROVSKI 25-40x75 TELESCOPE—75mm objective, variable power from 25x to 40x with a field of 90 ft. (25x) and 66 ft. (40x). Minimum focusing distance 66 ft. Length: closed 14.2", extended 21.7"; weight 50 oz. Rubber covered.
Price: Standard **$1,075.00**
SWIFT LEOPARD M837—50mm objective, 25x. Length 9¹¹⁄₁₆" to 10½". Weight with tripod 28 oz. Rubber armored. Comes with tripod.
Price: **$145.00**
SWIFT TELEMASTER M841—60mm objective. 15x to 60x variable power. Field at 1000 yds. 160 feet (15x) to 40 feet (60x). Weight 3.4 lbs.; length 18" overall.
Price: **$399.50**
SWIFT M700R—10x-40x, 40mm objective. Field of 210 feet at 10x, 70 feet at 40x. Length 16.3", weight 21.4 oz. Has 45° eyepiece.
Price: **$180.00**
SWIFT SEARCHER M839—60mm objective, 20x, 40x. Field at 1000 yds. 118 ft. (30x), 59 ft. (40x). Length 12.6"; weight 3 lbs. Rotating eyepiece head for straight or 45° viewing.
Price: **$435.00**
Price: 30x, 50x eyepieces, each **$50.00**
Price: Tripod, from **$64.00**
TASCO CW50TZB, CW50TZBC ZOOM SPOTTING SCOPES—50mm objective lens, 12-36x zoom. Field at 100 yds. 16-9 ft. Available in black or brown camo rubber armor. With panhead lever tripod.
Price: CW50TZB (brown) **$283.00**
Price: CW50TZBC (camo) **$283.00**
TASCO CW50TR COMPACT SPOTTING SCOPE—50mm objective lens, 25x fixed power. Field at 100 yds. 11 ft. Comes with panhead lever tripod.
Price: **$214.00**
TASCO 17EB SPOTTING SCOPE—60mm objective lens, 20-60x zoom with black metal tripod, micro-adjustable elevation control. Built-in sights.
Price: **$214.00**
TASCO 20EB SPOTTING SCOPE—50mm objective lens, 15-45x zoom. Field at 1000 yds. 95-42 ft.; includes tripod with pan-head lever. Built-in sights.
Price: **$115.00**
TASCO 9002T WORLD CLASS SPOTTING SCOPE—60mm objective lens, 15-60x zoom. Field at 1000 yds. 160 ft. (15x). Fully multi-coated optics, includes camera adaptor, camera case, tripod with pan-head lever.
Price: **$612.00**
UNERTL "FORTY-FIVE"—54mm objective. 20x (single fixed power). Field at 100 yds. 10',10"; eye relief 1"; focusing range infinity to 33 ft. Weight about 32 oz.; overall length 15¾". With lens covers.
Price: With multi-layer lens coating **$390.00**
Price: With mono-layer magnesium coating **$325.00**
UNERTL RIGHT ANGLE—63.5mm objective, 24x. Field at 100 yds., 7 ft. Relative brightness, 6.96. Eye relief ½". Weight 41 oz.; length closed 19". Push-pull and screw-focus eyepiece. 16x and 32x eyepieces **$70.00** each.
Price: **$350.00**
UNERTL STRAIGHT PRISMATIC—Same as Unertl Right Angle except straight eyepiece and weight of 40 oz.
Price: **$290.00**
UNERTL 20x STRAIGHT PRISMATIC—54mm objective, 20x. Field at 100 yds. 8.5 ft. Relative brightness 6.1. Eye relief ½". Weight 36 oz.; length closed 13½". Complete with lens covers.
Price: **$270.00**
UNERTL TEAM SCOPE—100mm objective. 15x, 24x, 32x eyepieces. Field at 100 yds. 13 to 7.5 ft. Relative brightness, 39.06 to 9.79. Eye relief 2" to 1½". Weight 13 lbs.; length 29⅞" overall. Metal tripod, yoke and wood carrying case furnished (total weight 80 lbs.).
Price: **$1,500.00**

CAUTION: PRICES CHANGE, CHECK AT GUNSHOP.

PERIODICAL PUBLICATIONS

Action Pursuit Games Magazine (M)
CFW Enterprises, Inc., 4201 W. Vanowen Pl., Burbank, CA 91505. $2.95 single copy U.S., $3.50 Canada. Editor: Randy Kamiya, 818-845-2656. World's leading magazine of paintball sports.

Airgun World
10 Sheet St., Windsor, Berks., SL4 1BG, England. £19.20 (£26.00 overseas) for 12 issues. Monthly magazine catering exclusively to the airgun enthusiast.

Alaska Magazine
Alaska Publishing Properties Inc., 808 E St., Suite 200, Anchorage, AK 99501. $26.00 yr. Hunting, Fishing and Life on the Last Frontier articles of Alaska and western Canada. Outdoors Editor, Ken Marsh.

American Airgunner (Q)
P.O. Box 1459, Abilene, TX 79604-1459. $15 yr. Anything and everything about airguns.

American Firearms Industry
Nat'l. Assn. of Federally Licensed Firearms Dealers, 2455 E. Sunrise Blvd., Ft. Lauderdale, FL 33304. $25.00 yr. For firearms retailers, distributors and manufacturers.

American Handgunner*
591 Camino de la Reina, Suite 200, San Diego, CA 92108. $16.75 yr. Articles for handgun enthusiasts, competitors, police and hunters.

American Hunter (M)
National Rifle Assn., 1600 Rhode Island Ave., NW, Washington, DC 20036. Publications Div., 470 Spring Park Pl., Suite 1000, Herndon, VA 22070. $25.00 yr. Wide scope of hunting articles.

American Rifleman (M)
National Rifle Assn., 1600 Rhode Island Ave., NW, Washington, DC 20036. Publications Div., 470 Spring Park Pl., Suite 1000, Herndon, VA 22070. $25.00 yr. Firearms articles of all kinds.

American Survival Guide
McMullen and Yee Publishing, Inc., 774 S. Placentia Ave., Placentia, CA 92670-6846. 12 issues $26.95/714-572-2255; FAX: 714-572-1864.

American West*
American West Management Corp., 7000 E. Tanque Verde Rd., Suite #30, Tucson, AZ 85715. $15.00 yr.

Arms Collecting (Q)
Museum Restoration Service, P.O. Drawer 390, Bloomfield, Ont., Canada K0K 1G0 and P.O. Box 70, Alexandria Bay, NY 13607. $15.00 yr.; $41.50 3 yrs.; $75.00 5 yrs.

Australian Shooters' Journal
Sporting Shooter's Assn. of Australia, P.O. Box 2066, Kent Town SA 5071, Australia. $40.00 yr. locally; $50.00 yr. overseas surface mail only. Hunting and shooting articles.

The Backwoodsman Magazine
P.O. Box 627, Westcliffe, CO 81252. $14.00 for 6 issues per yr.; $26.00 for 2 yrs.; sample copy $2.50. Subjects include muzzle-loading, woodslore, primitive survival, trapping, homesteading, blackpowder cartridge guns, 19th century how-to.

Black Powder Times
P.O. Box 842, Mount Vernon, WA 98273. $15.00 yr.; add $2 per year for Canada, $5 per year other foreign. Tabloid newspaper for blackpowder activities; test reports.

The Blade Magazine*
P.O. Box 22007, Chattanooga, TN 37422. $17.99 for 8 issues. Foreign price $35.00. A magazine for all enthusiasts of the edged blade.

The Caller (Q) (M)
National Wild Turkey Federation, P.O. Box 530, Edgefield, SC 29824. Tabloid newspaper for members; 4 issues per yr.

The Cast Bullet*(M)
Official journal of The Cast Bullet Assn. Director of Membership, 4103 Foxcraft Dr., Traverse City, MI 49684. Annual membership dues $14, includes 6 issues.

Combat Handguns*
Harris Publications, Inc., 1115 Broadway, New York, NY 10010. Single copy $2.95 U.S.A.; $3.25 Canada.

The Derringer Peanut (M)
The National Association of Derringer Collectors, P.O. Box 160671, San Antonio, TX 78280-2871. A newsletter dedicated to developing the best derringer information. Write for details.

Deutsches Waffen Journal
Journal-Verlag Schwend GmbH, Postfach 100340, D7170 Schwäbisch Hall, Germany/0791-404-500; FAX:0791-404-505. DM97.10 yr. (interior); DM114.60 (abroad), postage included. Antique and modern arms and equipment. German text.

The Engraver (M) (Q)
P.O. Box 4365, Estes Park, CO 80517. Mike Dubber, editor. The journal of firearms engraving.

Ducks Unlimited, Inc. (M)
1 Waterfowl Way, Memphis, TN 38120

The Field
6 Sheet Street, Windsor, Berkshire, SL4 1BG, England. £35.00 sterling U.S. (approx. $70.00) yr. Hunting and shooting articles, and all country sports.

Field & Stream
Times Mirror Magazines, Two Park Ave., New York, NY 10016. $11.94 yr. Articles on hunting and fishing.

FIRE
Euro-Editions, Boulevard Du Triomphe 132, B1160 Brussels, Belgium. Belg. Franc 1500 for 6 issues. Arms, shooting, ammunition. French text.

Fur-Fish-Game
A.R. Harding Pub. Co., 2878 E. Main St., Columbus, OH 43209. $15.95 yr. "Gun Rack" column by Don Zutz.

Gray's Sporting Journal
Gray's Sporting Journal, Inc., P.O. Box 1207, Augusta, GA 30903. $34.95 per yr. for 6 consecutive issues. Hunting and fishing journals.

Gun List
700 E. State St., Iola, WI 54990. $24.95 yr. (26 issues); $46.50 2 yrs. (52 issues). Indexed market publication for firearms collectors and active shooters; guns, supplies and services.

The Gun Report
World Wide Gun Report, Inc., Box 38, Aledo, IL 61231-0038. $29.95 yr. For the antique and collectable gun dealer and collector.

Gunmaker (M)†
ACGG, P.O. Box 812, Burlington, IA 52601-0812. The journal of custom gunmaking.

The Gunrunner
Div. of Kexco Publ. Co. Ltd., Box 565G, Lethbridge, Alb., Canada T1J 3Z4. $23.00 yr. Monthly newspaper, listing everything from antiques to artillery.

Gun Show Calendar (Q)
700 E. State St., Iola, WI 54990. $12.95 yr. (4 issues). Gun shows listed chronologically by date, and alphabetically by state.

Gun Tests
11 Commerce Blvd., Palm Coast, FL 32142. The consumer resource for the serious shooter. Write for information.

Gun Week†
Second Amendment Foundation, P.O. Box 488, Station C, Buffalo, NY 14209. $32.00 yr. U.S. and possessions; $40.00 yr. other countries. Tabloid paper on guns, hunting, shooting and collecting.

Gun World
Gallant/Charger Publications, Inc., 34249 Camino Capistrano, Capistrano Beach, CA 92624. $20.00 yr. For the hunting, reloading and shooting enthusiast.

Guns & Ammo
Petersen Publishing Co., 6420 Wilshire Blvd., Los Angeles, CA 90048. $21.94 yr. Guns, shooting, and technical articles.

Guns
Guns Magazine, P.O. Box 85201, San Diego, CA 92138. $19.95 yr. In-depth articles on a wide range of guns, shooting equipment and related accessories for gun collectors, hunters and shooters.

Guns Review
Ravenhill Publishing Co. Ltd., Box 35, Standard House, Bonhill St., London EC 2A 4DA, England. £20.00 sterling (approx. U.S. $38 USA & Canada) yr. For collectors and shooters.

Handgunning (Q)
PJS Publications, News Plaza, P.O. Box 1790, Peoria, IL 61656. Cover price $3.95; subscriptions $19.95 for 6 issues. Various recreational uses of handguns; hunting, silhouette, practical pistol and target shooting.

Handloader*
Wolfe Publishing Co., 6471 Airpark Dr., Prescott, AZ 86301. $19.00 yr. The journal of ammunition reloading.

HUNT Magazine*
TimberLine-B, Inc., P.O. Box 58069, Renton, WA 98058. $19.97 yr.; Canadian and foreign countries add U.S. $12 for postage. Geared to the serious hunter, with action hunting articles.

Hunting Horizons
Wolfe Publishing Co., 6471 Airpark Dr., Prescott, AZ 86301. $34.00 yr. Dedicated to the finest pursuit of the hunt.

The Insider Gun News
The Gunpress Publishing Co., 1347 Webster St. NE, Washington, DC 20017. Editor, John D. Aquilino. $50.00 yr. (12 issues). Newsletter by former NRA communications director.

INSIGHTS*
NRA, 1600 Rhode Island Ave., NW, Washington, DC 20036. Editor, John E. Robbins. $10.00 yr., which includes NRA junior membership; $10.00 for adult subscriptions (12 issues). Plenty of details for the young hunter and target shooter; emphasizes gun safety, marksmanship training, hunting skills.

International Shooting Sport*/UIT Journal
International Shooting Union (UIT), Bavariaring 21, D-8000 Munich 2, Fed. Rep. of Germany. Europe: (Deutsche Mark) DM44.00 yr.; outside Europe: DM50.00 yr. (air mail postage included.) For international sport shooting.

Internationales Waffen-Magazin
Habegger-Verlag Zürich, Postfach 9230 CH-8036 Zürich, Switzerland. SF 91.00 (approx. U.S. $61.00) surface mail for 10 issues. Modern and antique arms. German text; English summary of contents.

The Journal of the Arms & Armour Society (M)
E.J.B. Greenwood (Hon. Sec.), Field House, Upper Dicker, Hailsham, East Sussex, BN27 3PY, England. $20.00 yr. Articles for the historian and collector.

Journal of the Historical Breechloading Smallarms Assn.
Published annually. Imperial War Museum, Lambeth Road, London SE1 6HZ, England. $13.00 yr. Articles for the collector plus mailings of lecture transcripts, short articles on specific arms, reprints, newsletters, etc.; a surcharge is made for airmail.

Knife World
Knife World Publications, P.O. Box 3395, Knoxville, TN 37927. $15.00 yr.; $25.00 2 yrs. Published monthly for knife enthusiasts and collectors. Articles on custom and factory knives; other knife-related interests.

Law and Order
Law and Order Magazine, 1000 Skokie Blvd., Wilmette, IL 60091. $20.00 yr. Articles for law enforcement professionals.

Machine Gun News
Lane Publishing, P.O. Box 759, Dept. GD, Hot Springs, AR 71902/501-623-4951. $29.95 yr.; $3.50 sample copy. The magazine for full-auto enthusiasts, full-auto news, how to solve functioning problems, machinegun shoots from around the country and free classifieds for subscribers.

Man At Arms*
P.O. Box 460, Lincoln, RI 02865. $24.00 yr.; $46.00 2 yrs. plus $8.00 for foreign subscribers. The N.R.A. magazine of arms collecting-investing, with excellent articles for the collector of antique arms and militaria.

MAN/MAGNUM
S.A. Man (Pty) Ltd., P.O. Box 35204, Northway, Durban 4065, Republic of South Africa. SA Rand 78.00 for 12 issues. Africa's only publication on hunting, shooting, firearms, bushcraft, knives, etc.

The Marlin Collector (M)
R.W. Paterson, 407 Lincoln Bldg., 44 Main St., Champaign, IL 61820.

Muzzle Blasts (M)
National Muzzle Loading Rifle Assn., P.O. Box 67, Friendship, IN 47021. $30.00 yr. annual membership. For the blackpowder shooter.

Muzzleloader Magazine*
  Rebel Publishing Co., Inc., Dept. Gun, Route 5, Box 347-M, Texarkana, TX 75501. $14.00 U.S.; $17.00 U.S. for foreign subscribers a yr. The publication for blackpowder shooters.

National Defense (M)*
  American Defense Preparedness Assn., Two Colonial Place, Suite 400, 2101 Wilson Blvd., Arlington, VA 22201-3061/703-522-1820; FAX: 703-522-1885. $35.00 yr. Articles on both military and civil defense field, including weapons, materials technology, management.

National Knife Magazine (M)
  Natl. Knife Coll. Assn., 7201 Shallowford Rd., P.O. Box 21070, Chattanooga, TN 37421. Membership $35 yr.; $64.00 International yr.

National Rifle Assn. Journal (British) (Q)
  Natl. Rifle Assn. (BR.), Bisley Camp, Brookwood, Woking, Surrey, England. GU24, OPB. £15.50 Sterling including air postage.

National Wildlife*
  Natl. Wildlife Fed., 1400 16th St. NW, Washington, DC 20036, $16.00 yr. (6 issues); *International Wildlife*, 6 issues, $16.00 yr. Both, $22.00 yr., includes all membership benefits. Write attn.: Membership Services Dept., for more information.

New Zealand GUNS*
  Waitekauri Publishing, P.O. 45, Waikino 3060, New Zealand. $NZ90.00 (6 issues) yr. Covers the hunting and firearms scene in New Zealand.

New Zealand Wildlife (Q)
  New Zealand Deerstalkers Assoc., Inc., P.O. Box 6514, Wellington, N.Z. $30.00 (N.Z.). Hunting, shooting and firearms/game research articles.

North American Hunter* (M)
  P.O. Box 3401, Minnetonka, MN 55343. $18.00 yr. (7 issues). Articles on all types of North American hunting.

Outdoor Life
  Times Mirror Magazines, Two Park Ave., New York, NY 10016. Special 1-yr. subscription, $11.97. Extensive coverage of hunting and shooting. Shooting column by Jim Carmichel.

La Passion des Courteaux (Q)
  Phenix Editions, 25 rue Mademoiselle, 75015 Paris, France. French text.

Petersen's HUNTING Magazine
  Petersen Publishing Co., 8490 Sunset Blvd., Los Angeles, CA 90069. $19.94 yr.; Canada $29.34 yr.; foreign countries $29.94 yr. Hunting articles for all game; test reports.

P.I. Magazine
  America's Private Investigation Journal, 755 Bronx Dr., Toledo, OH 43609. Chuck Klein, firearms editor with column about handguns.

Point Blank
  Citizens Committee for the Right to Keep and Bear Arms (sent to contributors), Liberty Park, 12500 NE 10th Pl., Bellevue, WA 98005

POINTBLANK (M)
  Natl. Firearms Assn., Box 4384 Stn. C, Calgary, AB T2T 5N2, Canada. Official publication of the NFA.

The Police Marksman*
  6000 E. Shirley Lane, Montgomery, AL 36117. $17.95 yr. For law enforcement personnel.

Police Times (M)
  Membership Records, 3801 Biscayne Blvd., Miami, FL 33137.

Popular Mechanics
  Hearst Corp., 224 W. 57th St., New York, NY 10019. $15.94 yr. Firearms, camping, outdoor oriented articles.

Precision Shooting
  Precision Shooting, Inc., 37 Burnham St., East Hartford, CT 06108. $25.00 yr. Journal of the International Benchrest Shooters, and target shooting in general. Also considerable coverage of varmint shooting, as well as big bore, small bore, schuetzen, lead bullet and wildcats.

Rifle*
  Wolfe Publishing Co., 6471 Airpark Dr., Prescott, AZ 86301. $19.00 yr. The sporting firearms journal.

Rod & Rifle Magazine
  Lithographic Serv. Ltd., P.O. Box 38-138, Wellington, New Zealand. $50.00 yr. (6 issues). Hunting, shooting and fishing articles.

Safari* (M)
  Safari Magazine, 4800 W. Gates Pass Rd., Tucson, AZ 85745/602-620-1220. $30.00 (6 times). The journal of big game hunting, published by Safari Club International. Also publish *Safari Times*, a monthly newspaper, included in price of $30.00 field membership.

Second Amendment Reporter
  Second Amendment Foundation, James Madison Bldg., 12500 NE 10th Pl., Bellevue, WA 98005. $15.00 yr. (non-contributors).

Shooting Industry
  Publisher's Dev. Corp., 591 Camino de la Reina, Suite 200, San Diego, CA 92108. $50.00 yr. To the trade $25.00.

Shooting Sports Retailer*
  SSR Publishing, Inc., P.O. Box 25, Cuba, NY 14727-0025/716-968-3858. 6 issues yr. Free to

qualifying retailers, wholesalers, manufacturers, distributors; $30 annually for all other subscribers; $35 for foreign subscriptions; single copy $5.

Shooting Sports USA
  National Rifle Assn. of America, 1600 Rhode Island Ave., NW, Washington, DC 20036. Annual subscriptions for NRA members are $5 for classified shooters and $10 for non-classified shooters. Non-NRA member subscriptions are $15. Covering events, techniques and personalities in competitive shooting.

The Shooting Times & Country Magazine (England)†
  10 Sheet St., Windsor, Berkshire SL4 1BG, England. £65 (approx. $98.00) yr.; £79 yr. overseas (52 issues). Game shooting, wild fowling, hunting, game fishing and firearms articles. Britain's best selling field sports magazine.

Shooting Times
  PJS Publications, News Plaza, P.O. Box 1790, Peoria, IL 61656. $19.98 yr. Guns, shooting, reloading; articles on every gun activity.

The Shotgun News‡
  Snell Publishing Co., Box 669, Hastings, NE 68902. $20.00 yr.; all other countries $100.00 yr. Sample copy $3.00. Gun ads of all kinds.

SHOT Business
  Flintlock Ridge Office Center, 11 Mile Hill Rd., Newtown, CT 06470-2359/203-426-1320; FAX: 203-426-1087. For the shooting, hunting and outdoor trade retailer.

Shotgun Sports
  P.O. Box 6810, Auburn, CA 95603/916-889-2220; FAX:916-889-9106. $26.00 yr. Trapshooting how-to's, shotshell reloading, shotgun patterning, shotgun tests and evaluations, Sporting Clays action, waterfowl/upland hunting.

The Sixgunner (M)
  Handgun Hunters International, P.O. Box 357, MAG, Bloomingdale, OH 43910

The Skeet Shooting Review
  National Skeet Shooting Assn., P.O. Box 680007, San Antonio, TX 78268. $15.00 yr. (Assn. membership of $20.00 includes mag.) Competition results, personality profiles of top Skeet shooters, how-to articles, technical, reloading information.

Soldier of Fortune
  Subscription Dept., P.O. Box 348, Mt. Morris, IL 61054. $24.95 yr.; $34.95 Canada; $45.95 foreign.

Sporting Clays Magazine*
  5211 South Washington Ave., Titusville, FL 32780. $26.00 yr. (6 issues).

Sporting Goods Business
  Miller Freeman, Inc., 1515 Broadway, New York, NY 10036. Trade journal.

Sporting Goods Dealer
  Two Park Ave., New York, NY 10016. $100.00 yr. Sporting goods trade journal.

Sporting Gun
  Bretton Court, Bretton, Peterborough PE3 8DZ, England. £24.00 (approx. U.S. $36.00), airmail £33.00 yr. For the game and clay enthusiasts.

Sports Afield
  The Hearst Corp., 250 W. 55th St., New York, NY 10019. $13.97 yr. Tom Gresham on firearms, ammunition; Grits Gresham on shooting and Thomas McIntyre on hunting.

The Squirrel Hunter
  P.O. Box 368, Chireno, TX 75937. $14.00 yr. Articles about squirrel hunting.

TACARMI
  Via E. De Amicis, 25; 20123 Milano, Italy. $120.00 yr. approx. Antique and modern guns. (Italian text.)

Trap & Field
  1200 Waterway Blvd., Indianapolis, IN 46202. $22.00 yr. Official publ. Amateur Trapshooting Assn. Scores, averages, trapshooting articles.

Turkey Call* (M)
  Natl. Wild Turkey Federation, Inc., P.O. Box 530, Edgefield, SC 29824. $20.00 with membership (6 issues per yr.)

The U.S. Handgunner* (M)
  U.S. Revolver Assn., 96 West Union St., Ashland, MA 01721. $8.00 yr. General handgun and competition articles. Bi-monthly sent to members.

U.S. Airgun Magazine
  2603 Rollingbrook, Benton, AR 72015. Cover the sport from hunting, 10-meter, field target and collecting. Write for details.

The Varmint Hunter Magazine (Q)
  The Varmint Hunters Assn., Box 730, Lone Grove, OK 73443/405-657-3098. $24.00 yr.

VDB-Aktuell (Q)
  GFI-Verlag, Theodor-Heuss-Ring 62, 5000 Koln 1, Germany. For hunters, target shooters and outdoor people. (German text.)

Wild Sheep (M) (Q)
  Foundation for North American Wild Sheep, 720 Allen Ave., Cody, WY 82414. Official journal of the foundation.

Women & Guns
  P.O. Box 488, Sta. C, Buffalo, NY 14209. $24.00 yr. U.S.; (12 issues). Only magazine edited by and for women gun owners.

---

*Published bi-monthly †Published weekly ‡Published three times per month. All others are published monthly.
M=Membership requirements; write for details. Q=Published Quarterly.

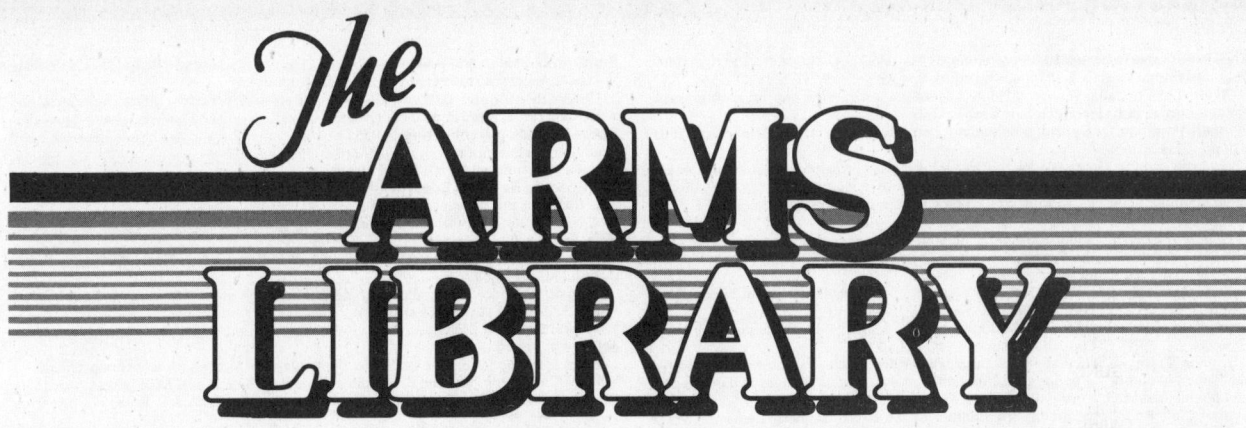

The ARMS LIBRARY

FOR COLLECTOR • HUNTER • SHOOTER • OUTDOORSMAN

BALLISTICS and HANDLOADING

*ABC's of Reloading, 5th Edition, by Dean A. Grennell, DBI Books, Inc., Northbrook, IL, 1993. 288 pp., illus. Paper covers. $18.95.

The definitive guide to every facet of cartridge and shotshell reloading.

Ammunition Making, by George E. Frost, National Rifle Association of America, Washington, D.C., 1990. 160 pp., illus. Paper covers. $17.95.

Reflects the perspective of "an insider" with half a century's experience in successful management of ammunition manufacturing operations.

Ballistic Science for the Law Enforcement Officer, by Charles G. Wilber, Ph.D., Charles C. Thomas, Springfield, IL, 1977. 309 pp., illus. $80.00.

A scientific study of the ballistics of civilian firearms.

Basic Handloading, by George C. Nonte, Jr., Outdoor Life Books, New York, NY, 1982. 192 pp., illus. Paper covers. $6.95.

How to produce high-quality ammunition using the safest, most efficient methods known.

Black Powder Guide, 2nd Edition, by George C. Nonte, Jr., Stoeger Publishing Co., So. Hackensack, NJ, 1991. 288 pp., illus. Paper covers. $12.95.

How-to instructions for selection, repair and maintenance of muzzleloaders, making your own bullets, restoring and refinishing, shooting techniques.

Big Bore Rifles And Cartridges, Wolfe Publishing Co., Prescott, AZ, 1991. Paper cover. $26.00.

This book covers cartridges from 8mm to .600 Nitro with over 60 chapters containing loading tables and commentary.

The Bullet Swage Manual. MDSU/I, by Ted Smith, Corbin Manufacturing and Supply Co., White City, OR, 1988. 45 pp., illus. Paper covers. $10.00.

A book that fills the need for information on bullet swaging.

Cartridge Case Measurements, by Dr. Arthur J. Mack, Amrex Enterprises, Vienna, VA, 1990. 300 pp., illus. Paper covers. $49.95.

Lists over 5000 cartridges of all kinds. Gives basic measurements (rim, head, shoulder, neck, length, plus bullet diameter) in both English and Metric. Hundreds of experimental and wildcats.

*Cartridges of the World, 7th Edition, by Frank Barnes, edited by Mike Bussard, DBI Books, Inc., Northbrook, IL, 1993. 464 pp., illus. Paper covers. $21.95

Completely revised edition of the general purpose reference work for which collectors, police, scientists and laymen reach first for answers to cartridge identification questions. (September '93)

Cast Bullets, by Col. E. H. Harrison, A publication of the National Rifle Association of America, Washington, DC, 1979. 144 pp., illus. Paper covers. $12.95.

An authoritative guide to bullet casting techniques and ballistics.

The Complete Handloader, by John Wootters, Stackpole Books, Harrisburg, PA, 1989. 224 pp., illus. $29.95.

One of the deans of gun writers shares a lifetime of experience and recommended procedures on handloading for rifles, handguns, and shotguns.

The Complete Handloader for Rifles, Handguns and Shotguns, by John Wootters, Stackpole Books, Harrisburg, PA, 1988. 214 pp., illus. $29.95.

Loading-bench know-how.

Discover Swaging, by David R. Corbin, Stackpole Books, Harrisburg, PA, 1979. 283 pp., illus. $18.95.

A guide to custom bullet design and performance.

Extended Ballistics for the Advanced Rifleman, by Art Blatt, Pachmayr, Inc., Los Angeles, CA, 1986. 379 pp. Spiral bound. $15.95.

Enhanced data on all factory centerfire rifle loads from Federal, Hornady, Norma, Remington, Weatherby, and Winchester.

Firearms Pressure Factors, by Dr. Lloyd Brownell, Wolfe Publishing Co., Prescott, AZ, 1990. 200 pp., illus. $14.00.

The only book available devoted entirely to firearms and pressure. Contains chapters on secondary explosion effect, modern pressure measuring techniques in revolvers and rifles, and Dr. Brownell's series on pressure factors.

*Game Loads and Practical Ballistics for the American Hunter, by Bob Hagel, Wolfe Publishing Co., Prescott, AZ, 1992. 310 pp., illus. $27.90.

Hagel's knowledge gained as a hunter, guide and gun enthusiast is gathered in this informative text.

Gibbs' Cartridges and Front Ignition Loading Technique, by Roger Stowers, Wolfe Publishing Co., Prescott, AZ, 1991. 64 pp., illus. Paper covers. $14.95.

The story of this innovative gunsmith who designed his own wildcat cartridges known for their flat trajectories, high velocity and accuracy.

The Gun Digest Black Powder Loading Manual, Revised Edition, by Sam Fadala, DBI Books, Inc., Northbrook, IL, 1991. 320 pp., illus. Paper covers. $16.95.

Revised and expanded edition of this landmark loading book first published in 1982. Covers 600 loads for 120 of the most popular blackpowder rifles, handguns and shotguns.

Handbook of Bullet Swaging No. 7, by David R. Corbin, Corbin Manufacturing and Supply Co., White City, OR, 1986. 199 pp., illus. Paper covers. $10.00.

This handbook explains the most precise method of making quality bullets.

Handbook for Shooters and Reloaders, by P.O. Ackley, Salt Lake City, UT, 1970, (Vol. I), 567 pp., illus. (Vol. II), a new printing with specific new material. 495 pp., illus. $15.95 each.

Handbook of Metallic Cartridge Reloading, by Edward Matunas, Winchester Press, Piscataway, NJ, 1981. 272 pp., illus. $19.95.

Up-to-date, comprehensive loading tables prepared by four major powder manufacturers.

Handgun Reloading, The Gun Digest Book of by Dean A. Grennell and Wiley M. Clapp, DBI Books, Inc., Northbrook, IL, 1987. 256 pp., illus. Paper covers. $15.95.

Detailed discussions of all aspects of reloading for handguns, from basic to complex. New loading data.

*Handloader's Digest 1994, 13th Edition, edited by Bob Bell, DBI Books, Inc., Northbrook, IL, 1993. 448 pp., illus. Paper covers. $20.95

Top writers in the field contribute helpful information on techniques and components. Greatly expanded and fully indexed catalog of all currently available loading tools, accessories and components.

Handloader's Guide, by Stanley W. Trzoniec, Stoeger Publishing Co., So. Hackensack, NJ, 1985. 256 pp., illus. Paper covers. $14.95.

The complete step-by-step fully illustrated guide to handloading ammunition.

Handloader's Manual of Cartridge Conversions, by John J. Donnelly, Stoeger Publishing Co., So. Hackensack, NJ, 1986. Unpaginated. $34.95.

From 14 Jones to 70-150 Winchester in English and American cartridges, and from 4.85 U.K. to 15.2x28R Gevelot in metric cartridges. Over 900 cartridges described in detail.

Handloading, by Bill Davis, Jr., NRA Books, Wash., D.C., 1980. 400 pp., illus. Paper covers. $15.95.

A complete update and expansion of the NRA Handloader's Guide.

Handloading for Hunters, by Don Zutz, Winchester Press, Piscataway, NJ, 1977. 288 pp., illus. $30.00.

Precise mixes and loads for different types of game and for various hunting situations with rifle and shotgun.

Hatcher's Notebook, by S. Julian Hatcher, Stackpole Books, Harrisburg, PA, 1992. 488 pp., illus. $29.95.

A reference work for shooters, gunsmiths, ballisticians, historians, hunters and collectors.

The Home Guide to Cartridge Conversions, by Maj. George C. Nonte Jr., The Gun Room Press, Highland Park, NJ, 1976. 404 pp., illus. $24.95.
Revised and updated version of Nonte's definitive work on the alteration of cartridge cases for use in guns for which they were not intended.

Hornady Handbook of Cartridge Reloading, Hornady Mfg. Co., Grand Island, NE, 1981. 650 pp., illus. $15.95.
New edition of this famous reloading handbook. Latest loads, ballistic information, etc.

The Ideal Handbook of Useful Information for Shooters, No. 15, originally published by Ideal Manufacturing Co., reprinted by Wolfe Publishing Co., Prescott, AZ, 1991. 142 pp., illus. Paper covers. $10.95.
A facsimile reprint of one of the early Ideal Handbooks.

***The Ideal Handbook, No. 5,** Facsimile reprint by Armory Publications, Oceanside, CA, 1993. 80 pp., illus. Paper covers. $12.95.
A limited reprinting of the rare 1893 edition of the handbook issued by the Ideal manufacturing Co., of New Haven, CT.

***Loading the Black Powder Rifle Cartridge,** by Paul A Matthews, Wolfe Publishing Co., Prescott, AZ, 1993. 121 pp., illus. Paper covers. $22.50.
Author Matthews brings the black powder cartridge shooter valuable information on the basics, including cartridge care, lubes and moulds, powder charges and developing and testing loads in his usual authoritative style.

Lyman Cast Bullet Handbook, 3rd Edition, edited by C. Kenneth Ramage, Lyman Publications, Middlefield, CT, 1980. 416 pp., illus. Paper covers. $18.95.
Information on more than 5000 tested cast bullet loads and 19 pages of trajectory and wind drift tables for cast bullets.

Lyman Black Powder Handbook, ed. by C. Kenneth Ramage, Lyman Products for Shooters, Middlefield, CT, 1975. 239 pp., illus. Paper covers. $14.95.
Comprehensive load information for the modern blackpowder shooter.

Lyman Pistol & Revolver Handbook, edited by C. Kenneth Ramage, Lyman Publications, Middlefield, CT, 1978. 280 pp., illus. Paper covers. $14.95.
An extensive reference of load and trajectory data for the handgun.

***Lyman Reloading Handbook No. 47,** edited by Edward A. Matunas, Lyman Publications, Middlefield, CT, 1992. 480 pp., illus. Paper covers. $19.95.
"The world's most comprehensive reloading manual." Complete "How to Reload" information. Expanded data section with all the newest rifle and pistol calibers.

Lyman Shotshell Handbook, 3rd Edition, edited by C. Kenneth Ramage, Lyman Publications, Middlefield, CT, 1984. 312 pp., illus. Paper covers. $18.95.
Has 2000 loads, including slugs and buckshot, plus feature articles and a full color I.D. section.

Manual of Pistol and Revolver Cartridges, Volume 2, Centerfire U.S. and British Calibers, by Hans A. Erlmeier and Jakob H. Brandt, Journal-Verlag, Wiesbaden, Germany, 1981. 270 pp., illus. $34.95.
Catalog system allows cartridges to be traced by caliber or alphabetically.

Metallic Cartridge Reloading, 2nd Edition, by Edward A. Matunas, DBI Books, Inc., Northbrook, IL., 1988. 320 pp., illus. Paper covers. $17.95.
A true reloading manual with a wealth of invaluable technical data provided by a recognized expert.

Modern Handloading, by Maj. Geo. C. Nonte, Winchester Press, Piscataway, NJ, 1972. 416 pp., illus. $15.00.
Covers all aspects of metallic and shotshell ammunition loading, plus more loads than any book in print.

Modern Practical Ballistics, by Art Pejsa, Pejsa Ballistics, Minneapolis, MN, 1990. 150 pp., illus. $24.95.
Covers all aspects of ballistics and new, simplified methods. Clear examples illustrate new, easy but very accurate formulas.

Nosler Reloading Manual No. 3, edited by Gail Root, Nosler Bullets, Inc., Bend, OR, 1989. 516 pp., illus. $21.95.
All-new book. New format including featured articles and cartridge introductions by well-known shooters, gun writers and editors.

The Paper Jacket, by Paul Matthews, Wolfe Publishing Co., Prescott, AZ, 1991. Paper covers. $13.50.
Up-to-date and accurate information about paper-patched bullets.

Pet Loads, by Ken Waters, Wolfe Publishing Co., Prescott, AZ, 3rd edition, 1986. 2 volumes of 636 pp. Limp fabricoid covers. $34.95.
Ken Water's favorite loads that have appeared in "Handloader" magazine.

Practical Handgun Ballistics, by Mason Williams, Charles C. Thomas, Publisher, Springfield, IL, 1980. 215 pp., illus. $55.00.
Factual information on the practical aspects of ammunition performance in revolvers and pistols.

Precision Handloading, by John Withers, Stoeger Publishing Co., So. Hackensack, NJ, 1985. 224 pp., illus. Paper covers. $12.95.
An entirely new approach to handloading ammunition.

Propellant Profiles New and Expanded, 3rd Edition, Wolfe Publishing Co., Prescott, AZ, 1991. Paper covers. $16.95.

Rediscover Swaging, by David R. Corbin, Corbin Manufacturing and Supply, Inc., Phoenix, OR, 1983. 240 pp., illus. $18.50.
A new textbook on the subject of bullet swaging.

Reloader's Guide, 3rd Edition, by R.A. Steindler, Stoeger Publishing Co., So. Hackensack, NJ, 1984. 224 pp., illus. Paper covers. $11.95.
Complete, fully illustrated step-by-step guide to handloading ammunition.
The very latest in reloading information for the shotgunner.

***Reloading for Shotgunners, 3rd Edition,** by Edward A. Matunas, DBI Books, Inc., Northbrook, IL, 1993. 288 pp., illus. Paper covers. $16.95. (October '93)
Expanded reloading tables with over 2,000 loads. Bushing charts for every major press and component maker. All new presentation on all aspects of shotshell reloading by one of the top experts in the field.

Sierra Handgun Manual, 3rd Edition, edited by Kenneth Ramage, Sierra Bullets, Santa Fe Springs, CA, 1990. 704 pp., illus. 3-ring binder. $19.95.
New listings for XP-100 and Contender pistols and TCU cartridges...part of a new single shot section. Covers the latest loads for 10mm Auto, 455 Super Mag, and Accurate powders.

Sierra Rifle Manual, 3rd Edition, edited by Kenneth Ramage, Sierra Bullets, Santa Fe Springs, CA, 1990. 856 pp., illus. 3-ring binder. $24.95.
Updated load information with new powder listings and a wealth of inside tips.

Sixgun Cartridges and Loads, by Elmer Keith, The Gun Room Press, Highland Park, NJ, 1986. 151 pp., illus. $24.95.
A manual covering the selection, uses and loading of the most suitable and popular revolver cartridges. Originally published in 1936. Reprint.

Small Arms Design and Ballistics, Volume 1, by Col. Townsend Whelen, Wolfe Publishing Co., Prescott, AZ, 1991. 352 pp., illus. $45.00.
Reprinting of this sought-after book dealing with small arms in general; barrels in general; breech actions; stocks and sights; ammunition, etc.

Small Arms Design and Ballistics, Volume 2, by Col. Townsend Whelen, Wolfe Publishing Co., Prescott, AZ, 1991. 314 pp., illus. $45.00.
Covers interior and exterior ballistics; trajectories; wounding effects; pressures and velocities; recoil, jump and vibration; shotgun ballistics; handloading ammunition, etc.

Speer Reloading Manual Number 11, edited by members of the Speer research staff, Omark Industries, Lewiston, ID, 1987. 621 pp., illus. $13.95.
Reloading manual for rifles and pistols.

The Sporting Ballistics Book, by Charles W. Matthews, Bill Matthews, Inc., Lakewood, CO, 1992. 182 pp. Wirebound. $19.95.
A useful book for those interested in doing their own exterior-ballistic calculations without the aid of a computer.

Why Not Load Your Own? by Col. T. Whelen, A. S. Barnes, New York, 1957, 4th ed., rev. 237 pp., illus. $10.95.
A basic reference on handloading, describing each step, materials and equipment. Loads for popular cartridges are given.

***Wildcat Cartridges, Volume I,** Wolfe Publishing Company, Prescott, AZ, 1992. 125 pp. Soft cover. $16.95.
From *Handloader* magazine, the more popular and famous wildcats are profiled.

***Wildcat Cartridges, Volume II,** compiled from *Handloader* and *Rifle* magazine articles written by featured authors, Wolfe Publishing Co., Prescott, AZ, 1992. 971 pp., illus. Paper covers. $34.95.
This volume details rifle and handtgun cartridges from the 14-221 to the 460 Van Horn. A comprehensive work containing loading tables and commentary.

Yours Truly, Harvey Donaldson, by Harvey Donaldson, Wolfe Publ. Co., Inc., Prescott, AZ, 1980. 288 pp., illus. $19.50.
Reprint of the famous columns by Harvey Donaldson which appeared in "Handloader" from May 1966 through December 1972.

COLLECTORS

The American Cartridge, by Charles R. Suydam, Borden Publishing Co., Alhambra, CA, 1986. 184 pp., illus. $12.50.
An illustrated study of the rimfire cartridge in the United States.

Antique Guns: The Collector's Guide, by John E. Traister, Stoeger Publishing Co., So. Hackensack, NJ, 1988. 320 pp., illus. Paper covers. $16.95.
Covers all categories, history, craftsmanship, firearms components, gunmakers and values on the gun-trading market.

Arms & Accoutrements of the Mounted Police 1873-1973, by Roger F. Phillips and Donald J. Klancher, Museum Restoration Service, Ont., Canada, 1982. 224 pp., illus. $49.95.
A definitive history of the revolvers, rifles, machine guns, cannons, ammunition, swords, etc. used by the NWMP, the RNWMP and the RCMP during the first 100 years of the Force.

Arms Makers of Eastern Pennsylvania: The Colonial Years to 1790, by James B. Whisker and Roy F. Chandler, Acorn Press, Bedford, PA, 1984. Unpaginated. $10.00.
Definitive work on Eastern Pennsylvania gunmakers.

Arms Makers of Maryland, by Daniel D. Hartzler, George Shumway, York, PA, 1975. 200 pp., illus. $45.00.
A thorough study of the gunsmiths of Maryland who worked during the late 18th and early 19th centuries.

Astra Automatic Pistols, by Leonardo M. Antaris, FIRAC Publishing Co., Sterling, CO, 1989. 248 pp., illus. $45.00.
Charts, tables, serial ranges, etc. The definitive work on Astra pistols.

Basic Documents on U.S. Marital Arms, commentary by Col. B. R. Lewis, reissue by Ray Riling, Phila., PA, 1956 and 1960. *Rifle Musket Model 1855.* The first issue rifle of musket caliber, a muzzle loader equipped with the Maynard Primer, 32 pp. $2.50. *Rifle Musket Model 1863.* The typical Union muzzle-loader of the Civil War, 26 pp. $1.75. *Breech-Loading Rifle Musket Model 1866.* The first of our 50-caliber breechloading rifles, 12 pp. $1.75. *Remington Navy Rifle Model 1870.* A commercial type breech-loader made at Springfield, 16 pp. $1.75. *Lee Straight Pull Navy Rifle Model 1895.* A magazine cartridge arm of 6mm caliber. 23 pp. $3.00. *Breech-Loading Arms* (five models) 27 pp. $2.75. *Ward-Burton Rifle Musket 1871*-16 pp. $2.50. *U.S. Magazine Rifle and Carbine (cal. 30) Model 1892* (the Krag rifle) 36 pp. $3.00.

Beretta Automatic Pistols, by J.B. Wood, Stackpole Books, Harrisburg, PA, 1985. 192 pp., illus. $24.95.
Only English-language book devoted entirely to the Beretta line. Includes all important models.

Blacksmith Guide to Ruger Flat-top & Super Blackhawks, by H.W. Ross, Jr., Blacksmith Corp., Chino Valley, AZ, 1990. 96 pp., illus. Paper covers. $9.95.
A key source on the extensively collected Ruger Blackhawk revolvers.

***Blue Book of Gun Values, 14th edition,** compiled by S.P. Fjestad, Investment Rarities, Inc., Minneapolis, MN, 1993. 621 pp., illus. Soft covers. $24.95.
Uses percentage grading system to determine each gun's value based on its unique condition.

The Book of the Springfield, by Edward C. Crossman and Roy F. Dunlap, Wolfe Publishing Co., Prescott, AZ, 1990. 567 pp., illus. $49.00.
A textbook covering the military, sporting and target rifles chambered for the caliber 30 Model 1906 cartridge; their metallic and telescopic sights and ammunition used in them.

Boy's Single-Shot Rifles, by James J. Grant, Wolfe Publishing Co., Prescott, AZ, 1991. 597 pp., illus. $36.00.
The bible for those single shots that became the prized possessions of boys growing up in the early part of the century.

Breech-Loading Carbines of the United States Civil War Period, by Brig. Gen. John Pitman, Armory Publications, Tacoma, WA, 1987. 94 pp., illus. $29.95.
The first in a series of previously unpublished manuscripts originated by the late Brigadier General John Putnam. Exploded drawings showing parts actual size follow each sectioned illustration.

The Bren Gun Saga, by Thomas B. Dugelby, Collector Grade Publications, Toronto, Canada, 1986. 300 pp., illus. $50.00.
Contains information on all models of Bren guns used by all nations.

Browning Dates of Manufacture, compiled by George Madis, Art and Reference House, Brownsboro, TX, 1989. 48 pp. $5.00.
Gives the date codes and product codes for all models from 1824 to the present.

Bullard Arms, by G. Scott Jamieson, The Boston Mills Press, Ontario, Canada, 1989. 244 pp., illus. $35.00.
The story of a mechanical genius whose rifles and cartridges were the equal to any made in America in the 1880s.

Burning Powder, compiled by Major D.B. Wesson, Wolfe Publishing Company, Prescott, AZ, 1992. 110 pp. Soft cover. $10.95.

A rare booklet from 1932 for Smith & Wesson collectors.

The Burnside Breech Loading Carbines, by Edward A. Hull, Andrew Mowbray, Inc., Lincoln, RI, 1986. 95 pp., illus. $16.00.

No. 1 in the "Man at Arms Monograph Series." A model-by-model historical/technical examination of one of the most widely used cavalry weapons of the American Civil War based upon important and previously unpublished research.

California Gunsmiths 1846-1900, by Lawrence P. Sheldon, Far Far West Publ., Fair Oaks, CA, 1977. 289 pp., illus. $29.65.

A study of early California gunsmiths and the firearms they made.

Carbines of the Civil War, by John D. McAulay, Pioneer Press, Union City, TN, 1981. 123 pp., illus. Paper covers. $7.95.

A guide for the student and collector of the colorful arms used by the Federal cavalry.

Cartridges for Breechloading Rifles, by A. Mattenheimer, Armory Publications, Oceanside, CA, 1989. 90 pp. with two 15"x19" color lithos containing 163 drawings of cartridges and firearms mechanisms. $29.95.

Reprinting of this German work on cartridges. Text in German and English.

***Cartridges of the World, 7th Edition,** by Frank C. Barnes, edited by Mike Bussard, DBI Books, Inc., Northbrook, IL, 1993. 464 pp., illus. Paper covers. $21.95 (September '93)

Completely revised edition of the general purpose reference work for which collectors, police, scientists and laymen reach first for answers to cartridge identification questions.

Cast Iron Toy Guns and Capshooters, by Samuel H. Logan, and Charles W. Best, Samuel Logan, Davis, CA, 1991. 251 pp., illus. $55.00.

Covers 1860s to 1950 with some 1,250 toys shown with brief descriptions, estimated dates of production and indication of rarity.

A Catalog Collection of 20th Century Winchester Repeating Arms Co., compiled by Roger Rule, Alliance Books, Inc., Northridge, CA, 1985. 396 pp., illus. $29.95.

Reflects the full line of Winchester products from 1901-1931 with emphasis on Winchester firearms.

Civil War Breech Loading Rifles, by John D. McAulay, Andrew Mowbray, Inc., Lincoln, RI, 1991. 144 pp., illus. Paper covers. $15.00.

All the major breech-loading rifles of the Civil War and most, if not all, of the obscure types are detailed, illustrated and set in their historical context.

Civil War Carbines, by A.F. Lustyik, World Wide Gun Report, Inc., Aledo, IL, 1962. 63 pp., illus. Paper covers. $3.50.

Accurate, interesting summary of most carbines of the Civil War period, in booklet form, with numerous good illus.

Civil War Carbines Volume 2: The Early Years, by John D. McAulay, Andrew Mowbray, Inc., Lincoln, RI, 1991. 144 pp., illus. Paper covers. $15.00.

Covers the carbines made during the exciting years leading up to the outbreak of war and used by the North and South in the conflict.

***Civil War Pistols,** by John D. McAulay, Andrew Mowbray Inc., Lincoln, RI, 1992. 166 pp., illus. $38.50.

A survey of the handguns used during the American Civil War.

***A Collector's Guide to United States Combat Shotguns,** by Bruce N. Canfield, Andrew Mowbray Inc., Lincoln, RI, 1992. 184 pp., illus. Paper covers. $24.00

This book provides full coverage of combat shotguns, from the earliest examples right up to the Gulf War and beyond.

A Collector's Guide to Winchester in the Service, by Bruce N. Canfield, Andrew Mowbray, Inc., Lincoln, RI, 1991. 192 pp., illus. $38.00.

The firearms produced by Winchester for the national defense. From Hotchkiss to the M14, each firearm is examined and illustrated.

A Collector's Guide to the M1 Garand and the M1 Carbine, by Bruce N. Canfield, Andrew Mowbray, Inc., Publisher, Lincoln, RI, 1988. 144 pp., illus., paper covers. $22.98.

A comprehensive guide to the most important and ubiquitous American arms of WWII and Korea.

A Collector's Guide to the '03 Springfield, by Bruce N. Canfield, Andrew Mowbray Inc, Lincoln, RI, 1989. 160 pp., illus. $35.00.

A comprehensive guide follows the '03 through its unparalleled tenure of service. Covers all of the interesting variations, modifications and accessories of this highly collectible military rifle.

Collector's Illustrated Encyclopedia of the American Revolution, by George C. Neumann and Frank J. Kravic, Rebel Publishing Co., Inc., Texarkana, TX, 1989. 286 pp., illus. $29.95.

A showcase of more than 2,300 artifacts made, worn, and used by those who fought in the War for Independence.

Colonial Frontier Guns, by T.M. Hamilton, Pioneer Press, Union City, TN, 1988. 176 pp., illus. Paper covers. $13.95.

A complete study of early flint muskets of this country.

The Colt-Burgess Magazine Rifle, by Samuel L. Maxwell Sr., Samuel L. Maxwell, Bellvue, WA, 1985. 176 pp., illus. $35.00.

Serial numbers, engraved arms, newly discovered experimental models, etc.

Colt Firearms, by James E. Serven, Wolfe Publishing, Prescott, AZ, 1991. 400 pp., illus. $45.00.

An illustrated history of the Colt company and its firearms including the story of the Gatling gun and an outline of Colt automatic weapons.

***Colt 45 Service Pistol Models of 1911 and 1911A1,** by Charles W. Clawson, Charles W. Clawson, Fort Wayne, IN, 1991. 429 pp., illus. $65.00.

Complete military history, development and production 1900 through 1945 plus foreign pistols, gallery pistols, revolvers, cartridge development, and much more.

Colt Heritage, by R.L. Wilson, Simon & Schuster, 1979. 358 pp., illus. $75.00.

The official history of Colt firearms 1836 to the present.

Colt Peacemaker British Model, by Keith Cochran, Cochran Publishing Co., Rapid City, SD, 1989. 160 pp., illus. $35.00.

Covers those revolvers Colt squeezed in while completing a large order of revolvers for the U.S. Cavalry in early 1874, to those magnificent cased target revolvers used in the pistol competitions at Bisley Commons in the 1890s.

Colt Peacemaker Encyclopedia, by Keith Cochran, Keith Cochran, Rapid City, SD, 1986. 434 pp., illus. $59.95.

A must book for the Peacemaker collector.

***Colt Peacemaker Encyclopedia, Volume 2,** by Keith Cochran, Cochran Publishing Co., SD, 1992. 416 pp., illus. $60.00.

Included in this volume are extensive notes on engraved, inscribed, historical and noted revolvers, as well as those revolvers used by outlaws, lawmen, movie and television stars.

Colt Peacemaker Yearly Variations, by Keith Cochran, Keith Cochran, Rapid City, SD, 1987. 96 pp., illus. $17.95.

A definitive, precise listing for each year the Peacemaker was manufactured from 1873-1940.

Colt Pistols 1836-1976, by R.L. Wilson in association with R.E. Hable, Jackson Arms, Dallas, TX, 1976. 380 pp., illus. $125.00.

A magnificently illustrated book in full color featuring Colt firearms from the famous Hable collection.

Colt Revolvers and the Tower of London, by Joseph G. Rosa, Royal Armouries of the Tower of London, London, England, 1988. 72 pp., illus. Soft covers. $15.00.

Details the story of Colt in London through the early cartridge period.

Colt Revolvers and the U.S. Navy 1865-1889, by C. Kenneth Moore, Dorrance and Co., Bryn Mawr, PA, 1987. 140 pp., illus. $29.95.

The Navy's use of all Colt handguns and other revolvers during this era of change.

Colt Single Action Army Revolvers and the London Agency, by C. Kenneth Moore, Andrew Mowbray Publishers, Lincoln, RI, 1990. 144 pp., illus. $35.00.

Drawing on vast documentary sources, this work chronicles the relationship between the London Agency and the Hartford home office.

The Colt U.S. General Officers' Pistols, by Horace Greeley IV, Andrew Mowbray Inc., Lincoln, RI, 1990. 199 pp., illus. $38.00.

These unique weapons, issued as a badge of rank to General Officers in the U.S. Army from WWII onward, remain highly personal artifacts of the military leaders who carried them. Includes serial numbers and dates of issue.

Colt's Dates of Manufacture 1837-1978, by R.L. Wilson, published by Maurie Albert, Coburg, Australia; N.A. distributor I.D.S.A. Books, Hamilton, OH, 1983. 61 pp. $10.00.

An invaluable pocket guide to the dates of manufacture of Colt firearms up to 1978.

***Colt's 100th Anniversary Firearms Manual 1836-1936: A Century of Achievement,** Wolfe Publishing Co., Prescott, AZ, 1992. 100 pp., illus. Paper covers. $12.95.

Originally published by the Colt Patent Firearms Co., this booklet covers the history, manufacturing procedures and the guns of the first 100 years of the genius of Samuel Colt.

Colt's SAA Post War Models, George Garton, revised edition, Gun Room Press, Highland Park, NJ, 1987. 166 pp., illus. $29.95.

The complete facts on Colt's famous post war single action army revolver using factory records to cover types, calibers, production numbers and many variations of this popular firearm.

The Colt Whitneyville-Walker Pistol, by Lt. Col. Robert D. Whittington, Brownlee Books, Hooks, TX, 1984. 96 pp., illus. Limited edition. $20.00.

A study of the pistol and associated characters 1846-1851.

***Compliments of Col. Ruger: A Study of Factory Engraved Single Action Revolvers,** by John C. Dougan, Taylor Publishing Co., El Paso, TX, 1992. 238 pp., illus. $46.50.

Clearly detailed black and white photographs and a precise text present an accurate istory of the Sturm, Ruger & Co. single-action revolver engraving project.

Confederate Revolvers, by William A. Gary, Taylor Publishing Co., Dallas, TX, 1987. 174 pp., illus. $45.00.

Comprehensive work on the rarest of Confederate weapons.

***Coykendall's 2nd Sporting Collectible Price Guide,** by Ralf Coykendall, Jr., Lyons & Burford Publlishers, New York, NY, 1992. 223 pp., illus. Paper covers. $16.95.

The all-new second volume with new sections on knives and sporting magazines.

***Cowboy Collectibles and Western Memorabilia,** by Bob Bell and Edward Vebell, Schiffer Publishing, Atglen, PA, 1992. 160 pp., illus. Paper covers. $29.95.

The exciting era of the cowboy and the wild west collectibles including rifles, pistols, gun rigs, etc.

Dance & Brothers; Texas Gunmakers of the Confederacy, by Gary Wiggins, Moss Publications, Orange, VA, 1986. 151 pp., illus. $29.95.

Presents a thorough and detailed study of the legendary Texas gunmakers, Dance & Brothers.

The Deringer in America, Volume 1, The Percussion Period, by R.L. Wilson and L.D. Eberhart, Andrew Mowbray Inc., Lincoln, RI, 1985. 271 pp., illus. $48.00.

A long awaited book on the American percussion deringer.

Description & Rules for the Management of the Springfield Rifle, Carbine and Army Revolver Caliber .45, originally published by the U.S. Ordnance Department, reprinted by Wolfe Publishing, Co., Prescott, AZ, 1991. 69 pp., illus. Paper covers. $10.50.

Reprint of the 1898 government manual giving complete directions, dimensions, care and use for these guns.

Development of the Henry Cartridge and Self-Contained Cartridges for the Toggle-Link Winchesters, by R. Bruce McDowell, A.M.B., Metuchen, NJ, 1984. 69 pp., illus. Paper covers. $10.00.

From powder and ball to the self-contained metallic cartridge.

***The Devil's Paintbrush: Sir Hiram Maxim's Gun,** by Dolf Goldsmith, 2nd Edition, expanded and revised, Collector Grade Publications, Toronto, Canada, 1993. 384 pp., illus. $69.95

The classic work on the world's first true automatic machine gun.

Early Indian Trade Guns: 1625-1775, by T.M. Hamilton, Museum of the Great Plains, Lawton, OK, 1968. 34 pp., illus. Paper covers. $7.95.

Detailed descriptions of subject arms, compiled from early records and from the study of remnants found in Indian country.

Encyclopedia and Price Guide of American Paper Shotshells, compiled by Dick Iverson, prices by Bob Strauss, Circus Promotions Corp., Spring, TX, 1991. 436 pp., illus. Paper covers. $25.00.

Pages of headstamps, head types, dimensions, color listed, and 3,100 individual prices.

***Encyclopedia of Ruger Rimfire Semi-Automatic Pistols: 1949-1992,** by Chad Hiddleson, Krause Publications, Iola, WI, 1993. 250 pp., illus. $29.95.

Covers all physical aspects of Ruger 22-caliber pistols including important features such as boxes, grips, muzzlebrakes, instruction manuals, serial numbers, etc.

English Pistols: The Armories of H.M. Tower of London Collection, by Howard L. Blackmore, Arms and Armour Press, London, England, 1985. 64 pp., illus. Soft covers. $14.95.

All the pistols described and pictured are from this famed collection.

European Firearms in Swedish Castles, by Kaa Wennberg, Bohuslaningens Boktryckeri AB, Uddevalla, Sweden, 1986. 156 pp., illus. $45.00.

The famous collection of Count Keller, the Ettersburg Castle collection, and others. English text.

Evolution of the Winchester, by R. Bruce McDowell, Armory Publications, Tacoma, WA, 1986. 200 pp., illus. $37.50.

Historic lever-action, tubular-magazine firearms.

Fifteen Years in the Hawken Lode, by John D. Baird, The Gun Room Press, Highland Park, NJ, 1976. 120 pp., illus. $24.95.

A collection of thoughts and observations gained from many years of intensive study of the guns from the shop of the Hawken brothers.

***'51 Colt Navies,** by Nathan L. Swayze, The Gun Room Press, Highland Park, NJ, 1993. 243 pp., illus. $59.95.

The Model 1851 Colt Navy, its variations and markings.

Firearms and Tackle Memorabilia, by John Delph, Schiffer Publishing, Ltd., West Chester, PA, 1991. 124 pp., illus. $39.95.

A collector's guide to signs and posters, calendars, trade cards, boxes, envelopes, and other highly sought after memorabilia. With a value guide.

*__The Firearms of Tipu Sultan 1785-1799,__ by Robin Wigington, Robin Wigington, Warwickshire, England, 1993. 148 pp., illus. Limited edition. $95.00.

A general survey of the characteristics of the arms with references to the man they were made for, Tipu Sultan himself, and the craftsmen who made them.

Flayderman's Guide to Antique American Firearms...and Their Values, 5th Edition, by Norm Flayderman, DBI Books, Inc., Northbrook, IL, 1990. 624 pp., illus. Soft covers. $27.95.

Updated edition of this bible of the antique gun field.

The .45-70 Springfield, by Joe Poyer and Craig Riesch, North Cape Publications, Tustin, CA, 1991. 112 pp., illus. Soft covers. $14.95.

A definitive work on the 45-70 Springfield. Organized by serial number and date of production to aid the collector in identifying models and rifle parts.

The 45/70 Trapdoor Springfield Dixie Collection, compiled by Walter Crutcher and Paul Oglesby, Pioneer Press, Union City, TN, 1975. 600 pp., illus. Paper covers. $9.95.

An illustrated listing of the 45-70 Springfields in the Dixie Gun Works Collection. Little known details and technical information is given, plus current values.

Frank and George Freund and the Sharps Rifle, by Gerald O. Kelver, Gerald O. Kelver, Brighton, CO, 1986. 60 pp., illus. Paper covers. $12.00.

Pioneer gunmakers of Wyoming Territory and Colorado.

French Military Weapons, 1717-1938, Major James E. Hicks, N. Flayderman & Co., Publishers, New Milford, CT, 1973. 281 pp., illus. $24.95.

Firearms, swords, bayonets, ammunition, artillery, ordnance equipment of the French army.

George Schreyer, Sr. and Jr., Gunmakers of Hanover, Pennsylvania, by George Shumway, George Shumway Publishers, York, PA, 1990. 160pp., illus. $45.00.

This monograph is a detailed photographic study of almost all known surviving long rifles and smoothbore guns made by highly regarded gunsmiths George Schreyer, Sr. and Jr.

The German Assault Rifle 1935-1945, by Peter R. Senich, Paladin Press, Boulder, CO, 1987. 328 pp., illus. $49.95.

A complete review of machine carbines, machine pistols and assault rifles employed by Hitler's Wehrmacht during WWII.

*__German Machineguns,__ by Daniel D. Musgrave, Revised edition, Ironside International Publishers, Inc. Alexandria, VA, 1992. 586 pp., 650 illus. $49.95.

The most definitive book ever written on German machineguns. Covers the introduction and development of machineguns in Germany from 1899 to the rearmament period after World War II,

German Military Pistols 1904-1930, by Fred A. Datig, Michael Zomber Co., Culver City, CA, 1990. 88 pp., illus. Paper covers. $14.95.

Monograph #2 in the series "The Luger Pistol Its History & Development from 1893-1945."

German Military Rifles and Machine Pistols, 1871-1945, by Hans Dieter Gotz, Schiffer Publishing Co., West Chester, PA, 1990. 245 pp., illus. $35.00.

This book portrays in words and pictures the development of the modern German weapons and their ammunition including the scarcely known experimental types.

German Pistols and Holsters 1934-1945, Vol. 2, by Robert Whittington, Brownlee Books, Hooks, TX, 1990. 312 pp., illus. $55.00.

This volume addresses pistols only: military (Heer, Luftwaffe, Kriegsmarine & Waffen-SS), captured, commercial, police, NSDAP and government.

German 7.9mm Military Ammunition, by Daniel W. Kent, Daniel W. Kent, Ann Arbor, MI, 1991. 244 pp., illus. $35.00.

The long-awaited revised edition of a classic among books devoted to ammunition.

German Pistols and Holsters, 1934-1945, Volume 4, by Lt. Col. Robert D. Whittington, 3rd, U.S.A.R., Brownlee Books, Hooks, TX, 1991. 208 pp. $30.00.

Pistols and holsters issued in 412 selected armed forces, army and Waffen-SS units including information on personnel, other weapons and transportation.

The Government Models: The Development of the Colt Model of 1911, by William H.D. Goddard, Andrew Mowbray, Inc., Publishers, Lincoln, RI, 1988. 223 pp., illus. $58.50.

An authoritative source on the world's most popular military sidearm.

*__Great Irish Gunmakers: Messrs. Rigby 1760-1869,__ by D.H.L. Back, Historical Firearms, Norwich, England, 1993. 196 pp., illus. $150.00.

The history of this famous firm of Irish gunmakers illustrated with a wide selection of Rigby arms.

Guide to Ruger Single Action Revolvers Production Dates, 1953-73, by John C. Dougan, Blacksmith Corp., Chino Valley, AZ, 1991. 22 pp., illus. Paper covers. $9.95.

A unique pocket-sized handbook providing production information for the popular Ruger single-action revolvers manufactured during the first 20 years.

Gun Collecting, by Geoffrey Boothroyd, Sportsman's Press, London, 1989. 208 pp., illus. $29.95.

The most comprehensive list of 19th century British gunmakers and gunsmiths ever published.

Gun Collector's Digest, 5th Edition, edited by Joseph J. Schroeder, DBI Books, Inc., Northbrook, IL, 1989. 224 pp., illus. Paper covers. $15.95.

The latest edition of this sought-after series.

Gunmakers of London 1350-1850, by Howard L. Blackmore, George Shumway Publisher, York, PA, 1986. 222 pp., illus. $35.00.

A listing of all the known workmen of gun making in the first 500 years, plus a history of the guilds, cutlers, armourers, founders, blacksmiths, etc. 260 gunmarks are illustrated.

The Gunsmiths of Manhattan, 1625-1900: A Checklist of Tradesmen, by Michael H. Lewis, Museum Restoration Service, Bloomfield, Ont., Canada, 1991. 40 pp., illus. Paper covers. $4.95.

This listing of more than 700 men in the arms trade in New York City prior to about the end of the 19th century will provide a guide for identification and further research.

Gunsmiths of Ohio—18th & 19th Centuries: Vol. I, Biographical Data, by Donald A. Hutslar, George Shumway, York, PA, 1973. 444 pp., illus. $45.00.

An important source book, full of information about the old-time gunsmiths of Ohio.

*__Gun Tools, Their History and Identification,__ by James B. Shaffer, Lee A. Rutledge and R. Stephen Dorsey, Collector's Library, Eugene, OR, 1992. 375 pp., illus. $32.00.

Written history of foreign and domestic gun tools from the flintlock period to World War II.

The Handgun, by Geoffrey Boothroyd, David and Charles, North Pomfret, VT, 1989. 566 pp., illus. $60.00.

Every chapter deals with an important period in handgun history from the 14th century to the present.

The Hawken Rifle: Its Place in History, by Charles E. Hanson, Jr., The Fur Press, Chadron, NE, 1979. 104 pp., illus. Paper covers. $6.00.

A definitive work on this famous rifle.

Hawken Rifles, The Mountain Man's Choice, by John D. Baird, The Gun Room Press, Highland Park, NJ, 1976. 95 pp., illus. $24.95.

Covers the rifles developed for the Western fur trade. Numerous specimens are described and shown in photographs.

High Standard: A Collector's Guide to the Hamden & Hartford Target Pistols, by Tom Dance, Andrew Mowbray, Inc., Lincoln, RI, 1991. 192 pp., illus. Paper covers. $24.00.

From Citation to Supermatic, all of the production models and specials made from 1951 to 1984 are covered according to model number or series.

*__Hi-Standard Autoloading Pistols 1951-1984,__ by James V. Spacek, Jr., James V. Spacek, Jr., Berlin, CT, 1993. 60 pp., illus. Paper covers. $10.00.

Information on takedown styles, serial numbers, production numbers, model charts and magazine references. Includes a price guide.

Historic Pistols: The American Martial Flintlock 1760-1845, by Samuel E. Smith and Edwin W. Bitter, The Gun Room Press, Highland Park, NJ, 1986. 353 pp., illus. $45.00.

Covers over 70 makers and 163 models of American martial arms.

Historical Hartford Hardware, by William W. Dalrymple, Colt Collector Press, Rapid City, SD, 1976. 42 pp., illus. Paper covers. $5.50.

Historically associated Colt revolvers.

The History and Development of Small Arms Ammunition, Volume 1, by George A. Hoyem, Armory Publications, Oceanside, CA, 1991. 230 pp., illus. $75.00.

Military musket, rifle, carbine and primitive machine gun cartridges of the 18th and 19th centuries, together with the firearms that chambered them.

The History and Development of Small Arms Ammunition, Volume 2, by George A. Hoyem, Armory Publications, Oceanside, CA, 1991. 303 pp., illus. $65.00.

Covers the blackpowder military centerfire rifle, carbine, machine gun and volley gun ammunition used in 28 nations and dominions, together with the firearms that chambered them.

The History and Development of Small Arms Ammunition (British Sporting Rifle) Volume 3, by George A. Hoyem, Armory Publications, Oceanside, CA, 1991. 300 pp., illus. $60.00.

Concentrates on British sporting rifle cartridges that run from the 4-bore through the .600 Nitro to the .297/.230 Morris.

The History of Smith and Wesson, by Roy G. Jinks, Willowbrook Enterprises, Springfield, MA, 1988. 290 pp., illus. $23.95.

Revised 10th Anniversary edition of the definite book on S&W firearms.

*__The History of Winchester Firearms 1866-1992,__ sixth edition, updated, expanded, and revised by Thomas Henshaw, New Win Publishing, Clinton, NJ, 1993. 280 pp., illus. $24.95.

This classic is the standard reference for all collectors and others seeking the facts about any Winchester firearm, old or new.

How to Buy and Sell Used Guns, by John Traister, Stoeger Publishing Co., So. Hackensack, NJ, 1984. 192 pp., illus. Paper covers. $10.95.

A new guide to buying and selling guns.

Illustrations of United States Military Arms 1776-1903 and Their Inspector's Marks, compiled by Turner Kirkland, Pioneer Press, Union City, TN, 1988. 37 pp., illus. Paper covers. $4.95.

Reprinted from the 1949 Bannerman catalog. Valuable information for both the advanced and beginning collector.

An Introduction the Civil War Small Arms, by Earl J. Coates and Dean S. Thomas, Thomas Publishing Co., Gettysburg, PA, 1990. 96 pp., illus. Paper covers. $6.95.

The small arms carried by the individual soldier during the Civil War.

Iver Johnson's Arms & Cycle Works Handguns, 1871-1964, by W.E. "Bill" Goforth, Blacksmith Corp., Chino Valley, AZ, 1991. 160 pp., illus. Paper covers. $14.95.

Covers all of the famous Iver Johnson handguns from the early solid-frame pistols and revolvers to optional accessories, special orders and patents.

James Reid and His Catskill Knuckledusters, by Taylor Brown, Andrew Mowbray Publishers, Lincoln, RI, 1990. 288 pp., illus. $24.95.

A detailed history of James Reid, his factory in the picturesque Catskill Mountains, and the pistols which he manufactured there.

Japanese Handguns, by Frederick E. Leithe, Borden Publishing Co., Alhambra, CA, 1985. 160 pp., illus. $19.95.

This book is an identification guide to all models and variations of Japanese handguns.

The Kentucky Rifle: A True American Heritage in Picture, by The Kentucky Rifle Association, The Forte Group of Creative Companies, Inc., Alexandria, VA, second edition, 1985. 110 pp., illus. $27.50.

This classic essay reveals both the beauty and the decorative nature of the Kentucky by providing detailed photographs of some of the most significant examples of American rifles, pistols, and accoutrements.

Kentucky Rifles and Pistols 1756-1850, compiled by members of the Kentucky Rifle Association, Wash., DC, Golden Age Arms Co., Delaware, OH, 1976. 275 pp., illus. $45.00.

Profusely illustrated with more than 300 examples of rifles and pistols never before published.

Know Your Broomhandle Mausers, by R.J. Berger, Blacksmith Corp., Southport, CT, 1985. 96 pp., illus. Paper covers. $9.95.

An interesting story on the big Mauser pistol and its variations.

Krag Rifles, by William S. Brophy, The Gun Room Press, Highland Park, NJ, 1980. 200 pp., illus. $35.00.

The first comprehensive work detailing the evolution and various models, both military and civilian.

The Krieghoff Parabellum, by Randall Gibson, Midland, TX, 1988. 279 pp., illus. $40.00.

A comprehensive text pertaining to the Lugers manufactured by H. Krieghoff Waffenfabrik.

Levine's Guide to Knives And Their Values, 3rd Edition, by Bernard Levine, DBI Books, Inc., Northbrook, IL, 1993. 480 pp., illus. Paper covers. $24.95

All the basic tools for identifying, valuing and collecting folding and fixed blade knives.

Longrifles of North Carolina, by John Bivens, George Shumway Publisher, York, PA, 1988. 256 pp., illus. $45.00.

Covers art and evolution of the rifle, immigration and trade movements. Committee of Safety gunsmiths, characteristics of the North Carolina rifle.

Longrifles of Pennsylvania, Volume 1, Jefferson, Clarion & Elk Counties, by Russel H. Harringer, George Shumway Publisher, York, PA, 1984. 200 pp., illus. $45.00.

First in series that will treat in great detail the longrifles and gunsmiths of Pennsylvania.

*__Luger Holsters and Accessories of the 20th Century,__ by Eugene J. Bender, Eugene J. Bender, Margate, FL, 1993. 640 pp., illus. $65.00.

A major new book for collectors, dealers, and historians, with over 1,000 photographs.

Lugers at Random, by Charles Kenyon, Jr., Handgun Press, Glenview, IL, 1990. 420 pp., illus. $39.95.

A new printing of this classic and sought-after work on the Luger pistol. A boon to the Luger collector/shooter.

*__The Luger Pistol Its History & Development From 1893 to 1947; Monograph IV: The Swiss Variations 1897-1947,__ by Fred A. Datig, Fred A. Datig, Los Angeles, CA, 1992. 88 pp., illus. Paper covers. $14.95.

A definitive work on the Swiss variations of this most collectible pistol.

Luger: The Multi-National Pistol, by Charles Kenyon, Jr., Richard Ellis Publications, Moline, IL, 1991. 192 pp., illus. $69.95 (hardcover); $150.00 (leather bound).

A fresh approach to this historical handgun. A must for the serious collector.

The Luger Book, by John Walter, Sterling Publishing Co., New York, NY, 1991. 287 pp., illus. $19.95.

The encyclopedia of the Borchardt and Borchardt-Luger handgun 1885-1985.

Marlin Firearms: A History of the Guns and the Company That Made Them, by Lt. Col. William S. Brophy, USAR, Ret., Stackpole Books, Harrisburg, PA, 1989. 672 pp., illus. $59.95.

The definitive book on the Marlin Firearms Co. and their products.

Massachusetts Military Shoulder Arms 1784-1877, by George D. Moller, Andrew Mowbray Publisher, Lincoln, RI, 1989. 250 pp., illus. $24.00.

A scholarly and heavily researched study of the military shoulder arms used by Massachusetts during the 90-year period following the Revolutionary War.

Mauser Bolt Rifles, by Ludwig Olson, F. Brownell & Son, Inc., Montezuma, IA, 1976. 364 pp., illus. $47.50.

The most complete, detailed, authoritative and comprehensive work ever done on Mauser bolt rifles.

Mauser Rifles and Pistols, by Walter H.B. Smith, Wolfe Publishing Co., Prescott, AZ, 1990. 234 pp., illus. $30.00.

A handbook covering Mauser history and the amrs Mauser manufactured.

Military Pistols of Japan, by Fred L. Honeycutt, Jr., Julin Books, Palm Beach Gardens, FL, 1991. 168 pp., illus. $34.00.

Covers every aspect of military pistol production in Japan through WWII.

The Military Remington Rolling Block Rifle, by George Layman, Wolfe Publishing Company, Prescott, AZ, 1992. 250 pp., illus. Soft cover. $21.00.

A reference work for the collector, tracing the history of this military rifle and disclosing previously unpublished data.

Military Rifles of Japan, 4th Edition, by F.L. Honeycutt, Julin Books, Lake Park, FL, 1989. 208 pp., illus. $42.00.

A new revised and updated edition. Includes the early Murata-period markings, etc.

Military Small Arms of the 20th Century, 6th Edition, by Ian V. Hogg, DBI Books, Inc., Northbrook, IL, 1991. 352 pp., illus. Paper covers. $19.95.

Fully revised and updated edition of the standard reference in its field.

M1 Carbine, by Larry Ruth, Gunroom Press, Highland Park, NJ, 1987. 291 pp., illus. Cloth $24.95; Paper $19.95.

The origin, development, manufacture and use of this famous carbine of World War II.

The M1 Garand: Post World War, by Scott A. Duff, Scott A. Duff, Export, PA, 1990. 139 pp., illus. Soft covers. $17.95.

A detailed account of the activities at Springfield Armory through this period. International Harvester, H&R, Korean War production and quantities delivered. Serial numbers.

*Modern Guns Identification & Values, 9th Edition, by Russell & Steve Quertermous, Collector Books, Paducah, KY, 1992. 480 pp., illus. Paper covers. $12.95.

Over 2,250 models of rifles, handguns and shotguns from 1900 to the present are described and priced in excellent and very good condition with suggested retail prices for those models still in production.

*Modern Gun Values, The Gun Digest Book of 9th Edition, by Jack Lewis, DBI Books, Inc., Northbrook, IL. 560 pp., illus. Paper covers. $20.95.

Updated and expanded edition of the book that has become the standard for valuing modern firearms.

More Single Shot Rifles, by James C. Grant, The Gun Room Press, Highland Park, NJ, 1976. 324 pp., illus. $25.00.

Details the guns made by Frank Wesson, Milt Farrow, Holden, Borchardt, Stevens, Remington, Winchester, Ballard and Peabody-Martini.

*Mortimer, the Gunmakers, 1753-1923, by H. Lee Munson, Andrew Mowbray Inc., Lincoln, RI, 1992. 320 pp., illus. $65.00.

Seen through a single, dominant, English gunmaking dynasty this fascinating study provides a window into the classical era of firearms artistry.

The Muzzle-Loading Cap Lock Rifle, by Ned H. Roberts, reprinted by Wolfe Publishing Co., Prescott, AZ, 1991. 432 pp., illus. $30.00.

Originally published in 1940, this fascinating study of the muzzle-loading cap lock rifle covers rifles on the frontier to hunting rifles, including the famous Hawken.

The Navy Luger, by Joachim Gortz and John Walter, Handgun Press, Glenview, IL, 1988. 128 pp., illus. $24.95.

The 9mm Pistole 1904 and the Imperial German Navy. A concise illustrated history.

The Northwest Gun, by Charles E. Hanson, Jr., Nebraska State Historical Society, Lincoln, NE, 1976. 85 pp., illus., paper covers. $6.00.

Number 2 in the Society's "Publications in Anthropology." Historical survey of rifles which figured in the fur trade and settlement of the Northwest.

The P-08 Parabellum Luger Automatic Pistol, edited by J. David McFarland, Desert Publications, Cornville, AZ, 1982. 20 pp., illus. Paper covers. $8.00.

Covers every facet of the Luger, plus a listing of all known Luger models.

The P.38 Pistol, Volume 3, by Warren H. Buxton, Ucross Books, Los Alamos, NM, 1991. 270 pp., illus. $54.50.

The postwar distribution of the P.38 pistol.

Paterson Colt Pistol Variations, by R.L. Wilson and R. Phillips, Jackson Arms Co., Dallas, TX, 1979. 250 pp., illus. $35.00.

A book about the different models and barrel lengths in the Paterson Colt story.

Pennsylvania Longrifles of Note, by George Shumway, George Shumway, Publisher, York, PA, 1977. 63 pp., illus. Paper covers. $10.00.

Illustrates and describes samples of guns from a number of Pennsylvania rifle-making schools.

Pistols of the World, 3rd Edition, by Ian Hogg and John Weeks, DBI Books, Inc., Northbrook, IL, 1992. 320 pp., illus. Paper covers. $19.95.

A totally revised edition of one of the leading studies of small arms.

The Pitman Notes on U.S. Martial Small Arms and Ammunition, 1776-1933, Volume 2, Revolvers and Automatic Pistols, by Brig. Gen. John Pitman, Thomas Publications, Gettysburg, PA, 1990. 192 pp., illus. $29.95.

A most important primary source of information on United States military small arms and ammunition.

The Plains Rifle, by Charles Hanson, Gun Room Press, Highland Park, NJ, 1989. 169 pp., illus. $29.95.

All rifles that were made with the plainsman in mind, including pistols.

*The Powder Flask Book, by Ray Riling, R&R Books, Livonia, NY, 1993. 514 pp., illus. $70.00.

The complete book on flasks of the 19th century. Exactly scaled pictures of 1,600 flasks are illustrated.

*Prices Paid for British Sporting Rifle Cartridges, by Bill Fleming, Armory Publications, Oceanside, CA, 1992. 31 pp. Paper covers. $15.00.

A list reflecting the relative scarcity of case types, particular load variations, and unusual headstamps of cartridges for British sporting rifles.

Proving Ground History of the Carbine Caliber .30, M1, by G.P. Grant, Desert Publications, Cornville, AZ, 1990. 21 pp., illus. Paper covers. $5.49.

Reprint of the Addenda to Volume 2, Historical Data, Aberdeen Proving Ground, MD. Added to this is "Weapons Usage in Korea" by S.L.A. Marshall.

The Rare and Valuable Antique Arms, by James E. Serven, Pioneer Press, Union City, TN, 1976. 106 pp., illus. Paper covers. $4.95.

A guide to the collector in deciding which direction his collecting should go, investment value, historic interest, mechanical ingenuity, high art or personal preference.

Reloading Tools, Sights and Telescopes for Single Shot Rifles, by Gerald O. Kelver, Brighton, CO, 1982. 163 pp., illus. Paper covers. $15.00.

A listing of most of the famous makers of reloading tools, sights and telescopes with a brief description of the products they manufactured.

Revolvers of the British Services 1854-1954, by W.H.J. Chamberlain and A.W.F. Taylerson, Museum Restoration Service, Ottawa, Canada, 1989. 80 pp., illus. $27.50.

Covers the types issued among many of the United Kingdom's naval, land or air services.

Rhode Island Arms Makers & Gunsmiths, by William O. Archibald, Andrew Mowbray, Inc., Lincoln, RI, 1990. 108 pp., illus. $16.50.

A serious and informative study of an important area of American arms making.

*Rifles of the World, by John Walter, DBI Books, Inc., Northbrook, IL, 1993. 320 pp., illus. Paper covers. $19.95.

Compiled as a companion valume to *Pistols of the World*, this brand new reference work covers all centerfire military and commercial rifles produced from the perfection of the metal-case cartridge in the 1870's to the present time.

*The Rock Island '03, by C.S. Ferris, C.S. Ferris, Arvada, CO, 1993. 58 pp., illus. Paper covers. $12.50.

A monograph of interenst to the collector or historian concentrating on the U.S. M1903 rifle made by the less publicized of our two producing facilities.

Ruger, edited by Joseph Roberts, Jr., the National Rifle Association of America, Washington, D.C., 1991. 109 pp. illus. Paper covers. $14.95.

The story of Bill Ruger's indelible imprint in the history of sporting firearms.

Ruger Rimfire Handguns 1949-1982, by J.C. Munnell, G.D.G.S. Inc., McKeesport, PA, 1982. 189 pp., illus. Paper covers. $13.50.

Updated edition with additional material on the semi-automatic pistols and the New Model revolvers.

*Sam Colt's Own Record 1847, by John Parsons, Wolfe Publishing Co., Prescott, AZ, 1992. 167 pp., illus. $24.50.

Chronologically presented, the correspondence published here completes the account of the manufacture, in 1847, of the Walker Model Colt revolver.

Scottish Arms Makers, by Charles E. Whitelaw, Arms and Armour Press, London, England, 1982. 363 pp., illus. $29.95.

An important and basic addition to weapons reference literature.

Sharps Firearms, by Frank Seller, Frank M. Seller, Denver, CO, 1982. 358 pp., illus. $45.00.

Traces the development of Sharps firearms with full range of guns made including all martial variations.

Shot Shell Boxes: Prices Realized at Auction 1985-1990 compiled by Bob Strauss, Circus Promotions Corp., Spring, TX, 2nd edition, 1990. 148 pp., illus. Paper covers. $12.00.

Actual prices realized at all major cartridge and other auctions over the past five years.

The Shotshell in the United States, by Richard J. Iverson, Circus Promotions Corp., Jefferson, ME, 1988. 193 pp., illus. Paper covers. $35.00.

Lists manufacturers, distributors, trade brands, headstamps, gauges, shot sizes, colors and configurations.

Simeon North: First Official Pistol Maker of the United States, by S. North and R. North, The Gun Room Press, Highland Park, NJ, 1972. 207 pp., illus. $9.95.

Reprint of the rare first edition.

*The SKS Type 45 Carbines, by Duncan Long, Desert Publications, El Dorado, AZ, 1992. 110 pp., illus. Paper covers.

Covers the history and practical aspects of operating, maintaining and modifying this abundantly available rifle.

Small Arms of the World, 12th Edition, fully updated and revised, by Edward C. Ezell, Marboro Book Corp., New York, NY, 1990. 894 pp., illus. $16.95.

An encyclopedia of global weapons with over 3,500 entries.

Southern Derringers of the Mississippi Valley, by Turner Kirkland, Pioneer Press, Tenn., 1971. 80 pp., illus., paper covers. $5.00.

A guide for the collector, and a much-needed study.

Soviet Russian Postwar Military Pistols and Cartridges, by Fred A. Datig, Handgun Press, Glenview, IL, 1988. 152 pp., illus. $29.95.

Thoroughly researched, this definitive sourcebook covers the development and adoption of the Makarov, Stechkin and the new PSM pistols. Also included in this source book is coverage on Russian clandestine weapons and pistol cartridges.

Sporting Collectibles, by Jim and Vivian Karsnitz, Schiffer Publishing Ltd., West Chester, PA, 1992. 160 pp., illus. Paper covers. $29.95.

The fascinating world of hunting related collectibles presented in an informative text.

The Springfield 1903 Rifles, by Lt. Col. William S. Brophy, USAR, Ret., Stackpole Books Inc., Harrisburg, PA, 1985. 608 pp., illus. $49.95.

The illustrated, documented story of the design, development, and production of all the models, appendages, and accessories.

Springfield Shoulder Arms 1795-1865, by Claud E. Fuller, S. & S. Firearms, Glendale, NY, 1986. 76 pp., illus. Paper covers. $15.00.

Exact reprint of the scarce 1930 edition of one of the most definitive works on Springfield flintlock and percussion muskets ever published.

*Stevens Pistols & Pocket Rifles, by K.L. Cope, Museum Restoration Service, Alexandria Bay, NY, 1992. 114 pp., illus. $24.50.

This is the story of the guns and the man who designed them and the company which he founded to make them.

The Sumptuous Flaske, by Herbert G. Houze, Andrew Mowbray, Inc., Lincoln, RI, 1989. 158 pp., illus. Soft covers. $35.00.

Catalog of a recent show at the Buffalo Bill Historical Center bringing together some of the finest European and American powder flasks of the 16th to 19th centuries.

Textbook of Automatic Pistols, by R.K. Wilson, Wolfe Publishing Co., Prescott, AZ, 1990. 349 pp., illus. $54.00.

Reprint of the 1943 classic being a treatise on the history, development and functioning of modern military self-loading pistols.

Thoughts on the Kentucky Rifle in its Golden Age, by Joe Kindig, George Shumway, Publisher, York, PA, 1984. 561 pp., illus. $85.00.

A new printing of the classic work on Kentucky rifles.

The Trapdoor Springfield, by M.D. Waite and B.D. Ernst, The Gun Room Press, Highland Park, NJ, 1983. 250 pp., illus. $39.95.

The first comprehensive book on the famous standard military rifle of the 1873-92 period.

UK and Commonwealth FALS, by R. Blake Stevens, Collector Grade Publications, Toronto, Canada, 1987. 260 pp., illus. $36.00.

The complete story of the L1A1 in the UK, Australia and India.

Underhammer Guns, by H.C. Logan, Stackpole Books, Harrisburg, PA, 1965. 250 pp., illus. $20.00.

A full account of an unusual form of firearm dating back to flintlock days. Both American and foreign specimens are included.

United States Martial Flintlocks, by Robert M. Reilly, Andrew Mowbray, Inc., Lincoln, RI, 1986. 263 pp., illus. $39.50.

A comprehensive illustrated history of the flintlock in America from the Revolution to the demise of the system.

U.S. Breech-Loading Rifles and Carbines, Cal. 45, by Gen. John Pitman, Thomas Publications, Gettysburg, PA, 1992. 192 pp., illus. $29.95.

The third volume in the Pitman Notes on U.S. Martial Small Arms and Ammunition, 1776-1933. This book centers on the "Trapdoor Springfield" models.

U.S. Military Arms Dates of Manufacture from 1795, by George Madis, David Madis, Dallas, TX, 1989. 64 pp. Soft covers. $5.00.

Lists all U.S. military arms of collector interest alphabetically, covering about 250 models.

U.S. Military Small Arms 1816-1865, by Robert M. Reilly, The Gun Room Press, Highland Park, NJ, 1983. 270 pp., illus. $39.95.

Covers every known type of primary and secondary martial firearms used by Federal forces.

U.S. Naval Handguns, 1808-1911, by Fredrick R. Winter, Andrew Mowbray Publishers, Lincoln, RI, 1990. 128 pp., illus. $26.00.

The story of U.S. Naval Handguns spans an entire century—included are sections on each of the important naval handguns within the period.

Walther Models PP and PPK, 1929-1945, by James L. Rankin, assisted by Gary Green, James L. Rankin, Coral Gables, FL, 1974. 142 pp., illus. $35.00.

Complete coverage on the subject as to finish, proofmarks and Nazi Party inscriptions.

Walther P-38 Pistol, by Maj. George Nonte, Desert Publications, Cornville, AZ, 1982. 100 pp., illus. Paper covers. $9.95.

Complete volume on one of the most famous handguns to come out of WWII. All models covered.

Walther Volume II, Engraved, Presentation and Standard Models, by James L. Rankin, J.L. Rankin, Coral Gables, FL, 1977. 112 pp., illus. $35.00.

The new Walther book on embellished versions and standard models. Has 88 photographs, including many color plates.

Walther, Volume III, 1908-1980, by James L. Rankin, Coral Gables, FL, 1981. 226 pp., illus. $35.00.

Covers all models of Walther handguns from 1908 to date, includes holsters, grips and magazines.

Webley Revolvers, by Gordon Bruce and Christien Reinhart, Stocker-Schmid, Zurich, Switzerland, 1988. 256 pp., illus. $69.50.

A revised edition of Dowell's "Webley Story."

Westley Richards Guns and Rifles, a reprint of the Westley Richards firm's centennial catalog of 1912, by Armory Publications, Oceanside, CA, 1988. 211 pp., illus. Paper covers. $27.95.

A century of gun and rifle manufacture, 1812-1912.

The Whitney Firearms, by Claud Fuller, Standard Publications, Huntington, WV, 1946. 334 pp., many plates and drawings, $40.00.

An authoritative history of all Whitney arms and their maker. Highly recommended. An exclusive with Ray Riling Arms Books Co.

Winchester: An American Legend, by R.L. Wilson, Random House, New York, NY, 1991. 403 pp., illus. $65.00.

The official history of Winchester firearms from 1849 to the present.

The Winchester Book, by George Madis, David Madis Gun Book Distributor, Dallas, TX, 1986. 650 pp., illus. $45.50.

A new, revised 25th anniversary edition of this classic book on Winchester firearms. Complete serial ranges have been added.

Winchester Catalogue of 1899, reprinted by Wolfe Publishing Co., Prescott, AZ, 1990. 158 pp., illus. Paper covers. $10.50

More than just a price list! This text contains explanations of parts, assembly and disassembly, testing techniques, and evaluations of selected models.

Winchester Dates of Manufacture 1849-1984, by George Madis, Art & Reference House, Brownsboro, TX, 1984. 59 pp. $5.95.

A most useful work, compiled from records of the Winchester factory.

Winchester Engraving, by R.L. Wilson, Beinfeld Books, Springs, CA, 1989. 500 pp., illus. $115.00.

A classic reference work, of value to all arms collectors.

The Winchester Handbook, by George Madis, Art & Reference House, Lancaster, TX, 1982. 287 pp., illus. $19.95.

The complete line of Winchester guns, with dates of manufacture, serial numbers, etc.

*The Winchester Model 94: The First 100 Years, by Robert C. Renneberg, Krause Publications, Iola, WI, 1991. 208 pp., illus. $34.95.

Covers the design and evolution from the early years up to the many different editions that exist today.

*Winchester Slide-Action Rifles, Volume 1: Model 1890 & 1906, by Ned Schwing, Krause Publications, Iola, WI, 1992. 352 pp., illus. $39.95.

First book length treatment of models 1890 & 1906 with over 50 charts and tables showing significant new information about caliber style and rarity.

Winchester's 30-30, Model 94, by Sam Fadala, Stackpole Books, Inc., Harrisburg, PA, 1986. 223 pp., illus. $24.95.

The story of the rifle America loves.

World War 2 Small Arms, by John Weeks, Chartwell Books, Inc., Secaucus, NJ, 1989. 144 pp., illus. $10.95.

Assesses the weapons of each of the major combatant nations, their production, history, design and features.

EDGED WEAPONS

A.G. Russell's Knife Trader's Guide, by A.G. Russell, Paul Wahl Corp., Bogata, NJ, 1991. 160 pp., illus. Paper covers. $10.00.

Recent sales prices of many popular collectible knives.

The American Eagle Pommel Sword: The Early Years 1793-1830, by Andrew Mowbray, Publisher, Lincoln, RI, 1988. 224 pp., illus. $45.00.

Provides an historical outline, a collecting structure and a vast new source of information for this rapidly growing field.

American Knives; The First History and Collector's Guide, by Harold L. Peterson, The Gun Room Press, Highland Park, NJ, 1980. 178 pp., illus. $24.95.

A reprint of this 1958 classic. Covers all types of American knives.

American Primitive Knives 1770-1870, by G.B. Minnes, Museum Restoration Service, Ottawa, Canada, 1983. 112 pp., illus. $24.95.

Origins of the knives, outstanding specimens, structural details, etc.

American Socket Bayonets and Scabbards, by Robert M. Reilly, Andrew Mowbray, Inc., Lincoln, RI, 1990. 209 pp., illus. $40.00.

A comprehensive illustrated history of socket bayonets, scabbards and frogs in America from the Colonial period through the Civil War period.

The American Sword, 1775-1945, by Harold L. Peterson, Ray Riling Arms Books, Co., Phila., PA, 1980. 286 pp. plus 60 pp. of illus. $45.00.

1977 reprint of a survey of swords worn by U.S. uniformed forces, plus the rare "American Silver Mounted Swords, (1700-1815)."

Blades and Barrels, by H. Gordon Frost, Wallon Press, El Paso, TX, 1972. 298 pp., illus. $19.95.

The first full scale study about man's attempts to combine an edged weapon with a firearm.

The Book of the Sword, by Richard F. Burton, Dover Publications, New York, NY, 1987. 199 pp., illus. Paper covers.

Traces the swords origin from its birth as a charged and sharpened stick through diverse stages of development.

Borders Away, Volume 1: With Steel, by William Gilkerson, Andrew Mowbray, Inc., Lincoln, RI, 1991. 184 pp., illus. $48.00.

A comprehensive study of naval armament under fighting sail. This first voume covers axes, pikes and fighting blades in use between 1626-1826.

The Bowie Knife, by Raymond Thorp, Phillips Publications, Wiliamstown, NJ, 1992. 167 pp., illus. $9.95.

After forty-five years, the classic work on the Bowie knife is once again available.

Bowie Knives, by Robert Abels, Sherwood International Corp., Northridge, CA, 1988. 30 pp., illus. Paper covers. $14.95.

Reprint of the classic work on Bowie knives.

Collecting the Edged Weapons of Imperial Germany, by Thomas M. Johnson and Thomas T. Wittmann, Johnson Reference Books, Fredricksburg, VA, 1989. 363 pp., illus. $39.50.

An in-depth study of the many ornate military, civilian, and government daggers and swords of the Imperial era.

*Collector's Guide to Ames U.S. Contract Military Edged Weapons: 1832-1906, by Ron G. Hickox, Pioneer Press, Union City, IN, 1993. 70 pp., illus. Paper covers. $14.95.

While this book deals primarily with edged weapons made by the Ames Manufacturing Company, this guide refers to other manufactureres of United States swords.

Collector's Handbook of World War 2 German Daggers, by LtC. Thomas M. Johnson, Johnson Reference Books, Fredericksburg, VA, 2nd edition, 1991. 252 pp., illus. Paper covers. $20.00.

Concise pocket reference guide to Third Reich daggers and accoutrements in a convenient format. With value guide.

The Complete Bladesmith: Forging Your Way to Perfection, by Jim Hrisoulas, Paladin Press, Boulder, CO, 1987. 192 pp., illus. $25.00.

Novice as well as experienced bladesmith will benefit from this definitive guide to smithing world-class blades.

The Craft of the Japanese Sword, by Leon & Hiroko Kapp, Yoshindo Yoshihara, Kodanska Interantional, Tokyo, Japan, 1990. 167 pp., illus. $34.95.

The first book in English devoted entirely to contemporary sword manufacturing in Japan.

Custom Knifemaking, 55D by Tim McCreight, Stackpole Books, Inc., Harrisburg, PA, 1985. 224 pp., illus. $14.95.

Ten projects from a master craftsman.

How to Make Knives, by Richard W. Barney & Robert W. Loveless, Beinfeld Publ., Inc., No. Hollywood, CA, 1977. 178 pp., illus. $17.95.

A book filled with drawings, illustrations, diagrams, and 500 how-to-do-it photos.

The Japanese Sword, by Kanzan Sato, Kodansha International Ltd. and Shibundo, Tokyo, Japan, 1983. 210 pp., illus. $27.95.

The history and appreciation of the Japanese sword, with a detailed examination of over a dozen of Japan's most revered blades.

Kentucky Knife Traders Manual No. 6, by R.B. Ritchie, Hindman, KY, 1980. 217 pp., illus. Paper covers. $10.00.

Guide for dealers, collectors and traders listing pocket knives and razor values.

Knife and Tomakawk Throwing: The Art of the Experts, by Harry K. McEvoy, Charles E. Tuttle, Rutland, VT, 1989. 150 pp., illus. Soft covers. $8.95.

The first book to employ side-by-side the fascinating art and science of knives and tomahawks.

Knifemaking, The Gun Digest Book of by Jack Lewis and Roger Combs, DBI Books, Inc., Northbrook, IL, 1989. 256 pp., illus. Paper covers. $15.95.

All the ins and outs from the world of knifemaking in a brand new book.

Knife Throwing a Practical Guide, by Harry K. McEvoy, Charles E. Tuttle Co., Rutland, VT, 1973. 108 pp., illus. Paper covers. $8.95.

If you want to learn to throw a knife this is the "bible."

Knives, 4th Edition, The Gun Digest Book of by Jack Lewis and Roger Combs, DBI Books, Inc., Northbook, IL, 1992. 256 pp., illus. Paper covers. $15.95.

All new edition covers practically every aspect of the knife world.

*Knives '94, 14th Edition, by Ken Warner, DBI Books, Inc., Northbrook, IL, 1993. 288 pp., illus. Paper covers. $17.95.

Visual presentation of current factory and custom designs in straight and folding patterns, in swords, miniatures and commercial cutlery. (September '93)

*Levine's Guide to Knives And Their Values, 3rd Edition, by Bernard Levine, DBI Books, Inc., Northbook, IL, 1989. 512 pp., illus. Paper covers. $24.95.

All the basic tools for identifying, valuing and collecting folding and fixed blade knives.

The Master Bladesmith: Advanced Studies in Steel, by Jim Hrisoulas, Paladin Press, Boulder, CO, 1990. 296 pp., illus. $45.00.

The author reveals the forging secrets that for centuries have been protected by guilds.

Military Swords of Japan 1868-1945, by Richard Fuller and Ron Gregory, Arms and Armour Press, London, England, 1986. 127 pp., illus. Paper covers. $18.95.

A wide-ranging survey of the swords and dirks worn by the armed forces of Japan until the end of World War II.

On Damascus Steel, by Dr. Leo S. Figiel, Atlantis Arts Press, Atlantis, FL, 1991. 145 pp., illus. $65.00.

The historic, technical and artistic aspects of Oriental and mechanical Damascus. Persian and Indian sword blades, from 1600-1800, which have never been published, are illustrated.

*****Randall Made Knives: The History of the Man and the Blades,** by Robert L. Gaddis, Paladin Press, Boulder, CO, 1993. 304 pp., illus. $50.00.

The authorized history of Bo Randall and his blades, told in his own words and those of the people who knew him best.

Rice's Trowel Bayonet, reprinted by Ray Riling Arms Books, Co., Phila., PA, 1968. 8 pp., illus. Paper covers. $3.00.

A facsimile reprint of a rare circular originally published by the U.S. government in 1875 for the information of U.S. troops.

The Samurai Sword, by John M. Yumoto, Charles E. Tuttle Co., Rutland, VT, 1958. 191 pp., illus. $18.95.

A must for anyone interested in Japanese blades, and the first book on this subject written in English.

Scottish Swords from the Battlefield at Culloden, by Lord Archibald Campbell, The Mowbray Co., Providence, RI, 1973. 63 pp., illus. $15.00.

A modern reprint of an exceedingly rare 1894 privately printed edition.

Secrets of the Samurai, by Oscar Ratti and Adele Westbrook, Charles E. Tuttle Co., Rutland, VT, 1983. 483 pp., illus. $35.00.

A survey of the martial arts of feudal Japan.

Sword of the Samurai, by George R. Parulski, Jr., Paladin Press, Boulder, CO, 1985. 144 pp., illus. $34.95.

The classical art of Japanese swordsmanship.

Swords for the Highland Regiments 1757-1784, by Anthony D. Darling, Andrew Mowbray, Inc., Publisher, Lincoln, RI, 1988. 62 pp., illus. $18.00.

The basket-hilted swords used by private highland regiments in the 18th century British army.

Swords from Public Collections in the Commonwealth of Pennsylvania, edited by Bruce S. Bazelon, Andrew Mowbray Inc., Lincoln, RI, 1987. 127 pp., illus. Paper covers. $12.00.

Contains new information regarding swordmakers of the Philadelphia area.

Swords of Germany 1900/1945, by John R. Angolia, Johnson Reference Books, Fredericksburg, VA, 1990. 460 pp., illus. $37.95.

If you have an interest in edged weapons of Imperial and Nazi Germany, this is a highly recommended book.

The Scottish Dirk, by James D. Forman, Museum Restoration Service, Bloomfield, Ont., Canada, 1991. 60 pp., illus. Paper covers. $4.95.

More than 100 dirks are illustrated with a text that sets the dirk and Sgian Dubh in their socio-historic content following design changes through more than 300 years of evolution.

Swords and Blades of the American Revolution, by George C. Neumann, Rebel Publishing Co., Inc., Texarkana, TX, 1991. 288 pp., illus. $35.95.

The encyclopedia of bladed weapons—swords, bayonets, spontoons, halberds, pikes, knives, daggers, axes—used by both sides, on land and sea, in America's struggle for independence.

Tomahawks Illustrated, by Robert Kuck, Robert Kuck, New Knoxville, OH, 1977. 112 pp., illus. Paper covers. $15.00.

A pictorial record to provide a reference in selecting and evaluating tomahawks.

World Bayonets, 1800 to the Present, by Anthony Carter, Sterling Publishing Co., New York, NY, 1990. 72 pp., illus. $24.95.

An incredible bayonet-fancier's buying encyclopedia. Includes buying and selling prices, plus over 250 closeup photos.

GENERAL

Advanced Muzzleloader's Guide, by Toby Bridges, Stoeger Publishing Co., So. Hackensack, NJ, 1985. 256 pp., illus. Paper covers. $14.95.

The complete guide to muzzle-loading rifles, pistols and shotguns—flintlock and percussion.

Air Gun Digest, 2nd Edition, by J.I. Galan, DBI Books, Inc., Northbrook, IL, 1988. 256 pp., illus. Paper covers. $15.95.

Everything from A to Z on air gun history, trends and technology.

The AK47 Story, by Edward Ezell, Stackpole Books, Harrisburg, PA, 1988. 256 pp., illus. $16.95.

Evolution of the Kalashnikov weapons.

American Gunsmiths, by Frank M. Sellers, The Gun Room Press, Highland Park, NJ, 1983. 349 pp. $39.95.

A comprehensive listing of the American gun maker, patentee, gunsmith and entrepreneur.

American and Imported Arms, Ammunition and Shooting Accessories, Catalog No. 18 of the Shooter's Bible, Stoeger, Inc., reprinted by Fayette Arsenal, Fayetteville, NC, 1988. 142 pp., illus. Paper covers. $10.95.

A facsimile reprint of the 1932 Stoeger's Shooter's Bible.

America's Great Gunmakers, by Wayne van Zwoll, Stoeger Publishing Co., So. Hackensack, NJ, 1992. 288 pp., illus. Paper covers. $16.95.

This book traces in great detail the evolution of guns and ammunition in America and the men who formed the companies that produced them.

*****Another Country: Personal Adventures of the 20th Century,** by Jeff Cooper, Gunsite Press, Paulden, AZ, 1992. 318 pp., illus. $28.00.

The narratives are autobiographical and tell of this 20th century man's experiences that could not and may not be repeated by anyone, anywhere, in any age to come.

Archer's Digest, 5th Edition, edited by Roger Combs, DBI Books, Inc., Northbrook, IL, 1990. 256 pp., illus. Paper covers. $15.95.

Authoritative information on all facets of the archer's sport.

Armed and Female, by Paxton Quigley, E.P. Dutton, New York, NY, 1989. 237 pp., illus. $16.95.

The first complete book on one of the hottest subjects in the media today, the arming of the American woman.

Arms and Equipment of the British Army, 1886, edited by John Walter, Presidio Press, Novato, CA, 1991. $30.00.

Victorian military equipment from the Enfield to the Snider.

Arsenal of Freedom, The Springfield Armory, 1890-1948: A Year-by-Year Account Drawn from Official Records, compiled and edited by Lt. Col. William S. Brophy, USAR Ret., Andrew Mowbray, Inc., Lincoln, RI, 1991. 400 pp., illus. Soft covers. $29.95.

A "must buy" for all students of American military weapolns, equipment and accoutrements.

*****Assault Weapons, 3rd Edition, The Gun Digest Book of** edited by Jack Lewis, DBI Books, Inc., Northbrook, IL, 1993. 256 pp., illus. Paper covers. $17.95.

An in-depth look at the history and uses of these arms.

Be an Expert Shot with Rifle or Shotgun, by Clair Rees, Winchester Press, Piscataway, NJ, 1984. 192 pp., illus. $19.95.

The illustrated self-coaching method that turns shooters into fine marksmen.

Beginner's Guide to Guns and Shooting, Revised Edition, by Clair F. Rees, DBI Books, Inc., Northbrook, IL, 1988. 224 pp., illus. Paper covers. $14.95.

The "how to" book for beginning shooters. The perfect teaching tool for America's youth, the future of our sport, for novices of any age.

A Bibliography of American Sporting Books, compiled by John C. Phillips, James Cummins, Bookseller, New York, NY, 1991. 650 pp. Edition limited to 250 numbered copies. $75.00.

A reprinting of the very scarce 1930 edition originally published by the Boone & Crockett Club.

Black Powder Loading Manual, Revised Edition, by Sam Fadala, DBI Books, Inc., Northbrook, IL, 1991. 320 pp., illus. Paper covers. $16.95.

Revised and expanded edition of this landmark loading book first published in 1982. Covers 600 loads for 120 of the most popular blackpowder rifles, handguns and shotguns.

Bows and Arrows of the Native Americans, by Jim Hamm, Lyons & Burford Publishers, New York, NY, 1991. 156 pp., illus. $19.95.

A complete step-by-step guide to wooden bows, sinew-backed bows, composite bows, strings, arrows and quivers.

*****Cartridges of the World, 7th Edition,** by Frank Barnes, edited by Mike Bussard, DBI Books, Inc., Northbrook, IL, 1993. 464 pp., illus. Paper covers. $21.95

Completely revised edition of the general purpose reference work for which collectors, police, scientists and laymen readh first for answers to cartridge identification questions. (September '93)

Civil War Chief of Sharpshooters Hiram Berdan, Military Commander and Firearms Inventor, by Roy M. Marcot, Northwood Heritage Press, Irvine, CA, 1990. 400 pp., illus. $59.95.

Details the life and career of Col. Hiram Berdan and his U.S. Sharpshooters.

Colonial Riflemen in the American Revolution, by Joe D. Huddleston, George Shumway Publisher, York, PA, 1978. 70 pp., illus. $25.00.

This study traces the use of the longrifle in the Revolution for the purpose of evaluating what effects it had on the outcome.

Combat Handgunnery, 3rd Edition, The Gun Digest Book of by Chuck Karwan, DBI Books, Inc., Northbrook, IL, 1992. 256 pp., illus. Paper covers. $15.95.

This all-new edition looks at real world combat handgunnery from three different perspectives–military, police and civilian.

Competitive Shooting, by A.A. Yuryev, introduction by Gary L. Anderson, NRA Books, The National Rifle Assoc. of America, Wash., DC, 1985. 399 pp., illus. $29.95.

A unique encyclopedia of competitive rifle and pistol shooting.

The Complete Black Powder Handbook, Revised Edition, by Sam Fadala, DBI Books, Inc., Northbrook, IL, 1990. 320 pp., illus. Soft covers. $17.95.

Expanded and refreshed edition of the definitive book on the subject of blackpowder.

Complete Book of Shooting: Rifles, Shotguns, Handguns, by Jack O'Connor, Stackpole Books, Harrisburg, PA, 1983. 392 pp., illus. $24.95.

A thorough guide to each area of the sport, appealing to those with a new or ongoing interest in shooting.

The Complete Guide to Game Care and Cookery, Revised Edition, by Sam Fadala, DBI Books, Inc., Northbrook, IL, 1989. 320 pp., illus. Paper covers. $16.95.

Over 500 detailed photos and hundreds of tested recipes anyone can master.

Crossbows, Edited by Roger Combs, DBI Books, Inc., Northbrook, IL, 1986. 192 pp., illus. Paper covers. $14.95.

Complete, up-to-date coverage of the hottest bow going—and the most controversial.

Death from Above: The German FG42 Paratrooper Rifle, by Thomas B. Dugelby and R. Blake Stevens, Collector Grade Publications, Toronto, Canada, 1990. 147 pp., illus. $39.95.

The first comprehensive study of all seven models of the FG42.

The Emma Gees, by Herbert W. McBride, Lancer Publications, Mt. Ida, AR, 1988. 218 pp., illus. $18.95.

The author's service with the Machine Gun Section of the 21st Battalion Canadian Expeditionary Force in World War I.

Encyclopedia of Modern Firearms, Vol. 1, compiled and publ. by Bob Brownell, Montezuma, IA, 1959. 1057 pp. plus index, illus. $60.00. Dist. By Bob Brownell, Montezuma, IA 50171.

Massive accumulation of basic information of nearly all modern arms pertaining to "parts and assembly." Replete with arms photographs, exploded drawings, manufacturers' lists of parts, etc.

*****The Encyclopedia of Sporting Firearms,** by David E. Petzal, Facts on File, New York, NY, 1992. 237 pp., illus. $50.00.

The best and most authoritative single-volume reference to handguns, rifles and shotguns now available.

Firearms Engraving as Decorative Art, by Dr. Fredric A. Harris, Barbara R. Harris, Seattle, WA, 1989. 172 pp., illus. $95.00.

The origin of American firearms engraving motifs in the decorative art of the Middle East. Illustrated with magnificent color photographs.

Flayderman's Guide to Antique American Firearms...and Their Values, 5th Edition, by Norm Flayderman, DBI Books, Inc., Northbrook, IL, 1990. 624 pp., illus. Soft covers. $27.95.

Updated edition of this bible of the antique gun field.

The Frontier Rifleman, by H.B. LaCrosse Jr., Pioneer Press, Union City, TN, 1989. 183 pp., illus. Soft covers. $14.95.

The Frontier rifleman's clothing and equipment during the era of the American Revolution, 1760-1800.

The Gargantuan Gunsite Gossip, by Jeff Cooper, Gunsite Press, Paulden, AZ, 1990. 702 pp., illus. Paper covers. $25.00.

All the items that appeared in the *Gunsight Newsletter* and in a column in the *Guns & Ammo* magazine is in this book.

The Gatling Gun: 19th Century Machine Gun to 21st Century Vulcan, by Joseph Berk, Paladin Press, Boulder, CO, 1991. 136 pp., illus. $29.95.
Here is the fascinating on-going story of a truly timeless weapon, from its beginnings during the Civil War to its current role as a state-of-the-art modern combat system.

Good Friends, Good Guns, Good Whiskey: The Selected Works of Skeeter Skelton, by Skeeter Skelton, PJS Publications, Peoria, IL, 1989. 347 pp. $21.95.
A guidebook to the world of Skeeter Skelton.

Great Shooters of the World, by Sam Fadala, Stoeger Publishing Co., So. Hackensack, NJ, 1991. 288 pp., illus. Paper covers. $18.95.
This book offers gun enthusiasts an overview of the men and women who have forged the history of firearms over the past 150 years.

Guerrilla Warfare Weapons, by Terry Gander, Sterling Publishing Co., Inc., 1990. 128 pp., illus. Paper covers. $9.95.
The latest and sophisticated armaments of the modern underground fighter's armory.

Gun Digest, 1994, 48th Edition, edited by Ken Warner, DBI Books, Inc., Northbrook, IL, 1993. 544 pp., illus. Paper Covers. $21.95.
All-new edition of the world's best selling gun book; the only one to make the *USA Today* list of best-selling sports books.

Gunshot Injuries: How They Are Inflicted, Their Complications and Treatment, by Col. Louis A. La Garde, 2nd revised edition, Lancer Militaria, Mt. Ida, AR, 1991. 480 pp., illus. $34.95.
A classic work which was the standard textbook on the subject at the time of World War I.

Guns Illustrated, 1994, 26th Edition, edited by Harold A. Murtz, DBI Books, Inc., Northbrook, IL, 1993. 320 pp., illus. Paper covers. $18.95.
Truly the Journal of Gun Buffs, this all-new edition consists of articles of interest to every shooter as well as a complete catalog of all U.S. and imported firearms with latest specs and prices.

Guns of the Empire, by George Markham, Arms & Armour Press, London, England, 1991. 160 pp., illus. $29.95
The firearms that carved out the worldwide British Empire come together in a riveting display of handguns, rifles, and automatics.

Guns of the Wild West, by George Markham, Arms & Armour Press, London, England, 1991. 160 pp., illus. $19.95.
The handguns, longarms and shotguns of the Gold Rush, the American Civil War, and the Armed Forces.

Gun Talk, edited by Dave Moreton, Winchester Press, Piscataway, NJ, 1973. 256 pp., illus. $9.95.
A treasury of original writing by the top gun writers and editors in America. Practical advice about every aspect of the shooting sports.

The Gun That Made the Twenties Roar, by Wm. J. Helmer, rev. and enlarged by George C. Nonte, Jr., The Gun Room Press, Highland Park, NJ, 1977. Over 300 pp., illus. $24.95.
Historical account of John T. Thompson and his invention, the infamous "Tommy Gun."

The Gunfighter, Man or Myth? by Joseph G. Rosa, Oklahoma Press, Norman, OK, 1969. 229 pp., illus. (including weapons). Paper covers. $12.95.
A well-documented work on gunfights and gunfighters of the West and elsewhere. Great treat for all gunfighter buffs.

Gunproof Your Children/Handgun Primer, by Massad Ayoob, Police Bookshelf, Concord, NH, 1989. Paper covers. $4.95.
Two books in one. The first, keeping children safe from unauthorized guns in their hands; the second, a compact introduction to handgun safety.

Guns & Shooting: A Selected Bibliography, by Ray Riling, Ray Riling Arms Books Co., Phila., PA, 1982. 434 pp., illus. Limited, numbered edition. $75.
A limited edition of this superb bibliographical work, the only modern listing of books devoted to guns and shooting.

Guns, Loads, and Hunting Tips, by Bob Hagel, Wolfe Publishing Co., Prescott, AZ, 1986. 509 pp., illus. $19.95.
A large hardcover book packed with shooting, hunting and handloading wisdom.

Guns of the Elite, by George Markham, Arms and Armour Press, Poole, England, 1987. 184 pp., illus. $24.95.
Special Forces firearms, 1940 to the present.

Guns of the First World War, Rifle, Handguns and Ammunition from the Text Book of Small Arms, 1909, edited by John Walter, Presidio Press, Novato, CA, 1991. $30.00.
Details of the Austro-Hung. Mann., French Lebels, German Mausers, U.S. Springfields, etc.

Guns of the Reich, by George Markham, Arms & Armour Press, London, England, 1989. 175 pp., illus. $24.95.
The pistols, rifles, submachine guns, machineguns and support weapons of the German armed forces, 1939-1945.

Gunshot Wounds, by Vincent J.M. DiMaio, M.D., Elsevier Science Publishing Co., New York, NY, 1985. 331 pp., illus. $70.00.
Practical aspects of firearms, ballistics, and forensic techniques.

***Gun Trader's Guide, 16th Edition,** published by Stoeger Publishing Co., S. Hackensack, NJ, 1993. 528 pp., illus. Paper covers. $18.95.
Complete guide to identification of modern firearms with current values.

***Handloader's Digest, 1994, 13th Edition,** edited by Bob Bell, DBI Books, Inc., Northbrook, IL, 1993. 448 pp., illus. $20.95.
Top writers in the field contribute helpful information on techniques and components. Greatly expanded and fully indexed catalog of all currently available reloading tools, accessories and components.

"Hell, I Was There!," by Elmer Keith, Petersen Publishing Co., Los Angeles, CA, 1979. 308 pp., illus. $24.95.
Adventures of a Montana cowboy who gained world fame as a big game hunter.

***An Historical Guide to Arms and Armor,** by Stephen Bull, edited by Tony North, Facts On File, Inc., New York, NY, 1992. 224 pp., illus. $35.00
Traces the history of protective military apparel throughout the centuries, providing a chronicle as rich in texture as it is broad in scope.

***Lasers and Night Vision Devices,** by Duncan Long, Desert Publications, El Dorado, AZ, 1993. 150 pp., illus. Paper covers. $29.95.
A comprehensive look at the evolution of devices that allow firearms to be operated in low light conditions and at night.

The Last Book: Confessions of a Gun Editor, by Jack O'Connor, Amwell Press, Clinton, NJ, 1984. 247 pp., illus. $30.00.
Jack's last book. Semi-autobiographical.

The Law Enforcement Book of Weapons, Ammunition and Training Procedures, Handguns, Rifles and Shotguns, by Mason Williams, Charles C. Thomas, Publisher, Springfield, IL, 1977. 496 pp., illus. $135.00.
Data on firearms, firearm training, and ballistics.

The Lewis Gun, by J. David Truby, Paladin Press, Boulder, CO, 1988. 206 pp., illus. $39.95.
The development and employment of this much loved and trusted weapon throughout the early decades of this century.

The Manufacture of Gunflints, by Sydney B.J. Skertchly, facsimile reprint with new introduction by Seymour de Lotbiniere, Museum Restoration Service, Ontario, Canada, 1984. 90 pp., illus. $24.50.
Limited edition reprinting of the very scarce London edition of 1879.

Master Tips, by J. Winokur, Potshot Press, Pacific Palisades, CA, 1985. 96 pp., illus. Paper covers. $11.95.
Basics of practical shooting.

Meditations on Hunting, by Jose Ortega y Gasset, Charles Scribner's Sons, New York, NY, 1985. 132 pp. Paper covers. $9.95.
Anticipates with profound accuracy the direction and basic formations of discipline which does not yet exist, a true ecology of men. A new printing of this 1942 classic.

Metallic Silhouette Shooting, 2nd Edition, The Gun Digest Book of by Elgin Gates, DBI Books, Inc., Northbrook, IL, 1988. 256 pp., illus. Paper covers. $15.95.
Examines all aspects of this fast growing sport including history, rules and meets.

Military Rifle & Machine Gun Cartridges, by Jean Huon, Paladin Press, Boulder, CO, 1990. 392 pp., illus. $34.95.
Describes the primary types of military cartridges and their principal loadings, as well as their characteristics, origin and use.

Military Small Arms of the 20th Century, 6th Edition, by Ian V. Hogg, DBI Books, Inc., Northbrook, IL, 1991. 352 pp., illus. Paper covers. $19.95.
Fully revised and updated edition of the standard reference in its field.

***Modern Gun Values, 9th Edition, The Gun Digest Book of** by Jack Lewis, DBI Books, Inc., Northbrook, IL, 1993. 560 pp., illus. Paper covers. $20.95.
Updated and expanded edition of the book that's become the standard for valuing modern firearms.

Modern Law Enforcement Weapons & Tactics, 2nd Edition, by Tom Ferguson, DBI Books, Inc., Northbrook, IL, 1991. 256 pp., illus. Paper covers. $17.95.
An in-depth look at the weapons and equipment used by law enforcement agencies of today.

The More Complete Cannoneer, by M.C. Switlik, Museum & Collectors Specialties Co., Monroe, MI, 1990. 199 pp., illus. $19.95.
Compiled agreeably to the regulations for the U.S. War Department, 1861, and containing current observations on the use of antique cannon.

***L.D. Nimschke Firearms Engraver,** by R.L. Wilson, R&R Books, Livonia, NY, 1992. 108 pp., illus. $100.00.
The personal work record of one of the 19th century America's foremost engravers. Augmented by a comprehensive text, photographs of deluxe-engraved firearms, and detailed indexes.

No Second Place Winner, by Wm. H. Jordan, publ. by the author, Shreveport, LA (Box 4072), 1962. 114 pp., illus. $15.95.
Guns and gear of the peace officer, ably discussed by a U.S. Border Patrolman for over 30 years, and a first-class shooter with handgun, rifle, etc.

NRA Firearms Fact Book, by the editors of NRA, National Rifle Association, Wash., DC, 1991. 330 pp., illus. Paper covers. $10.95.
The second, revised edition of the classic *NRA Firearms and Ammunition Fact Book.* Covers gun collecting, firearms safety, ballistics and general references.

Outdoor Life Gun Data Book, by F. Philip Rice, Outdoor Life Books, New York, NY, 1987. 412 pp., illus. $27.95.
All the facts and figures that hunters, marksmen, handloaders and other gun enthusiasts need to know.

***Pin Shooting: A Complete Guide,** by Mitchell A. Ota, Wolfe Publishing Co., Prescott, AZ, 1992. 145 pp., illus. Paper covers. $14.95.
Traces the sport from its humble origins to today's thoroughly enjoyable social event, including the mammoth eight-day Second Chance Pin Shoot in Michigan.

E.C. Prudhomme, Master Gun Engraver, A Retrospective Exhibition: 1946-1973, intro. by John T. Amber, The R. W. Norton Art Gallery, Shreveport, LA, 1973. 32 pp., illus. Paper covers. $5.00.
Examples of master gun engravings by Jack Prudhomme.

A Rifleman Went to War, by H. W. McBride, Lancer Militaria, Mt. Ida, AR, 1987. 398 pp., illus. $24.95.
The classic account of practical marksmanship on the battlefields of World War I.

Second to None, edited by John Culler and Chuck Wechsler, Live Oak Press, Inc., Camden, SC, 1988. 227 pp., illus. $39.95.
The most popular articles from *Sporting Classics* magazine on great sporting firearms.

Shooter's Bible, 1940, Stoeger Arms Corp., Stoeger, Inc., So. Hackensack, NJ, 1990. 512 pp., illus. Soft covers. $16.95.
Reprint of the Stoeger Arms Corp. catalog No. 33 of 1940.

***Shooter's Bible 1994, No. 85,** edited by William S. Jarrett, Stoeger Publishing Co., So. Hackensack, NJ, 1993. 576 pp., illus. Paper covers. $19.95.
"The World's Standard Firearms Reference Book."

Shooting, by Edward A. Matunas, Stackpole Books, Harrisburg, PA, 1986. 416 pp., illus. $31.95.
How to become an expert marksman with rifle, shotgun, handgun, muzzle loader and bow.

Shots Fired in Anger, by Lt. Col. John George, The National Rifle Association of America, Washington, D.C., 2nd printing, 1991. 535 pp., illus. $19.95.
A rifleman's view of the war in the Pacific, 1942-45.

Small Arms Today, 2nd Edition, by Edward C. Ezell, Stackpole Books, Harrisburg, PA, 1988. 479 pp., illus. Paper covers. $19.95.
Latest reports on the world's weapons and ammunition.

***Sniping in France,** by Major H. Hesketh-Prichard, Lancer Militaria, Mt. Ida, AR, 1993. 224 pp., illus. $24.95.
The author was a well-known British adventurer and big game hunter. He was called upon in the early days of "The Great War" to develop a program to offset an initial German advantage in sniping. How the British forces came to overcome this advantage.

The SPIW: Deadliest Weapon that Never Was, by R. Blake Stevens, and Edward C. Ezell, Collector Grade Publications, Inc., Toronto, Canada, 1985. 138 pp., illus. $29.95.
The complete saga of the fantastic flechette-firing Special Purpose Individual Weapon.

***1992 Standard Catalog of Firearms,** edited by Ned Schwing, Howard Madaus and Herbert Houze, Krause Publications. Iola, WI, 1992. 725 pp., illus. Soft covers. $24.95.
A firearms price guide covering guns from 1836-date.

Steindler's New Firearms Dictionary, by R.A. Steindler, Stackpole Books, Inc., Harrisburg, PA, 1985. 320 pp., illus. $24.95.
Completely revised and updated edition of this standard work.

The Street Smart Gun Book, by John Farnam, Police Bookshelf, Concord, NH, 1986. 45 pp., illus. Paper covers. $11.95.
Weapon selection, defensive shooting techniques, and gunfight-winning tactics from one of the world's leading authorities.

Stress Fire, Vol. 1: Stress Fighting for Police, by Massad Ayoob, Police Bookshelf, Concord, NH, 1984. 149 pp., illus. Paper covers. $9.95.
Gunfighting for police, advanced tactics and techniques.

*__Survival Guns__, by Mel Tappan, Desert Publications, El Dorado, AZ, 1993. 456 pp., illus. Paper covers. $21.95.
Discusses in a frank and forthright manner which handguns, rifles and shotguns to buy for personal defense and securing food, and the ones to avoid.

Thompson Guns 1921-1945, Anubis Press, Houston, TX, 1980. 215 pp., illus. Paper covers. $11.95.
Facsimile reprinting of five complete manuals on the Thompson submachine gun.

Triggernometry, by Eugene Cunningham, Caxton Printers Ltd., Caldwell, ID, 1970. 441 pp., illus. $17.95.
A classic study of famous outlaws and lawmen of the West—their stature as human beings, their exploits and skills in handling firearms. A reprint.

U.S. Marine Corp Rifle and Pistol Marksmanship, 1935, reprinting of a government publication, Lancer Militaria, Mt. Ida, AR, 1991. 99 pp., illus. Paper covers. $11.95.
The old corps method of precision shooting.

U.S. Marine Corps Scout/Sniper Training Manual, Lancer Militaria, Mt. Ida, AR, 1989. Soft covers. $14.95.
Reprint of the original sniper training manual used by the Marksmanship Training Unit of the Marine Corps Development and Education Command in Quantico, Virginia.

U.S. Marine Corps Sniping, Lancer Militaria, Mt. Ida, AR, 1989. Irregular pagination. Soft covers. $14.95.
A reprint of the official Marine Corps FMFM1-3B.

Unrepentant Sinner, by Charles Askins, Tejano Publications, San Antonio, TX, 1985. 322 pp., illus. Soft covers. $17.95.
The autobiography of Colonel Charles Askins.

Vietnam Weapons Handbook, by David Rosser-Owen, Patrick Stephens, Wellingborough, England, 1986. 136 pp., illus. Paper covers. $9.95.
Covers every weapon used by both sides.

Warsaw Pact Weapons Handbook, by Jacques F. Baud, Paladin Press, Boulder, CO, 1989. 168 pp., illus. Soft covers. $20.00.
The most complete handbook on weapons found behind the Iron Curtain.

Weapons of the Waffen-SS, by Bruce Quarrie, Sterling Publishing Co., Inc., 1991. 168 pp., illus. $24.95.
An in-depth look at the weapons that made Hitler's Waffen-SS the fearsome fighting machine it was.

*__Weatherby: The Man, The Gun, The Legend__, by Grits and Tom Gresham, Cane River Publishing Co., Natchitoches, LA, 1992. 290 pp., illus. $24.95.
A fascinating look at the life of the man who changed the course of firearms development in America.

The Winchester Era, by David Madis, Art & Reference House, Brownsville, TX, 1984. 100 pp., illus. $14.95.
Story of the Winchester company, management, employees, etc.

With British Snipers to the Reich, by Capt. C. Shore, Lander Militaria, Mt. Ida, AR, 1988. 420 pp., illus. $24.95.
One of the greatest books ever written on the art of combat sniping.

You Can't Miss, by John Shaw and Michael Bane, John Shaw, Memphis, TN, 1983. 152 pp., illus. Paper covers. $12.95.
The secrets of a successful combat shooter; how to better defensive shooting skills.

GUNSMITHING

The Art of Engraving, by James B. Meek, F. Brownell & Son, Montezuma, IA, 1973. 196 pp., illus. $33.95.
A complete, authoritative, imaginative and detailed study in training for gun engraving. The first book of its kind—and a great one.

Artistry in Arms, The R. W. Norton Gallery, Shreveport, LA, 1970. 42 pp., illus. Paper covers. $5.00.
The art of gunsmithing and engraving.

Barrels & Actions, by Harold Hoffman, H&P Publishers, San Angelo, TX, 1990. 309 pp., illus. Sprial bound. $25.95.
A manual on barrel making.

*__Black Powder Hobby Gunsmithing__, by Sam Fadala and Dale Storey, DBI Books, Inc., Northbrook, IL. 256 pp., illus. Paper covers. $17.95.
A how-to guide for gunsmithing blackpowder pistols, rifles and shotguns from two men at the top of their respective fields. (Spring '94)

Checkering and Carving of Gun Stocks, by Monte Kennedy, Stackpole Books, Harrisburg, PA, 1962. 175 pp., illus. $34.95.
Revised, enlarged cloth-bound edition of a much sought-after, dependable work.

The Colt .45 Automatic Shop Manual, by Jerry Kuhnhausen, VSP Publishers, McCall, ID, 1987. 200 pp., illus. Paper covers. $19.95.
Covers repairing, accurizing, trigger/sear work, action tuning, springs, bushings, rebarreling, and custom .45 modification.

The Colt Double Action Revolvers: A Shop Manual, Volume 1, by Jerry Kuhnhausen, VSP Publishers, McCall, ID, 1988. 224 pp., illus. Paper covers. $22.95.
Covers D, E, and I frames.

The Colt Double Action Revolvers: A Shop Manual, Volume 2, by Jerry Kuhnhausen, VSP Publishers, McCall, ID, 1988. 156 pp., illus. Paper covers. $17.95.
Covers J, V, and AA models.

*__The Complete Metal Finishing Book__, by Harold Hoffman, H&P Publishers, San Angelo, TX, 1992. 364 pp., illus. Paper covers. $28.95.
Instructions for the different metal finishing operations that the normal craftsman or shop will use. Primarily firearm related.

The Complete Rehabilitation of the Flintlock Rifle and Other Works, by T.B. Tyron, Limbo Library, Taos, NM, 1972. 112 pp., illus. Paper covers. $6.95.
A series of articles which first appeared in various issues of the "American Rifleman" in the 1930s.

Do-It-Yourself Gunsmithing, by Jim Carmichel, Outdoor Life-Harper & Row, New York, NY, 1977. 371 pp., illus. $24.95.
The author proves that at-home gunsmithing is relatively easy and can be highly satisfying.

Exploded Handgun Drawings, The Gun Digest Book of edited by Harold A. Murtz, DBI Books, Inc., Northbrook, IL. 1992. 512 pp., illus. Paper covers. $19.95.
Exploded or isometric drawings for 494 of the most popular handguns.

*__Exploded Long Gun Drawings, The Gun Digest Book of__ edited by Harold A. Murtz, DBI Books, Inc., Northbrook, IL. 512 pp., illus. Paper covers. $19.95.
Containing almost 500 rifle and shotgun exploded drawings. An invaluable aid to both professionals and hobbyists.

Firearms Assembly/Disassembly, Part I: Automatic Pistols, Revised Edition, The Gun Digest Book of by J.B. Wood, DBI Books, Inc., Northbrook, IL, 1990. 480 pp., illus. Soft covers. $17.95.
Covers 58 popular autoloading pistols plus nearly 200 variants of those models integrated into the text and completely cross-referenced in the index.

Firearms Assembly/Disassembly Part II: Revolvers, Revised Edition, The Gun Digest Book of by J.B. Wood, DBI Books, Inc., Northbrook, IL, 1990. 480 pp., illus. Soft covers. $17.95.
Covers 49 popular revolvers plus 130 variants. The most comprehensive and professional presentation available to either hobbyist or gunsmith.

*__Firearms Assembly/Disassembly Part III: Rimfire Rifles, Revised Edition, The Gun Digest Book of__ by J. B. Wood, DBI Books, Inc., Northbrook, IL. 480 pp., illus. Paper covers. $18.95.
Greatly expanded edition covering 65 popular rimfire rifles plus over 100 variants all completely cross-referenced in the index. (Spring '94)

Firearms Assembly/Disassembly Part IV: Centerfire Rifles, Revised Edition, The Gun Digest Book of by J.B. Wood, DBI Books, Inc., Northbrook, IL, 1991. 480 pp., illus. Paper covers. $17.95.
Covers 54 popular centerfire rifles plus 300 variants. The most comprehensive and professional presentation available to either hobbyist or gunsmith.

Firearms Assembly/Disassembly, Part V: Shotguns, Revised Edition, The Gun Digest Book of by J.B. Wood, DBI Books, Inc., Northbrook, IL, 1992. 480 pp., illus. Paper covers. $17.95.
Covers 46 popular shotguns plus over 250 variants. The most comprehensive and professional presentation available to either hobbyist or gunsmith.

Firearms Assembly/Disassembly Part VI: Law Enforcement Weapons, The Gun Digest Book of by J.B. Wood, DBI Books, Inc., Northbrook, IL, 1981. 288 pp., illus. Paper covers, $15.95.
Step-by-step instructions on how to completely dismantle and reassemble the most commonly used firearms found in law enforcement arsenals.

Firearms Assembly 3: The NRA Guide to Rifle and Shotguns, NRA Books, Wash., DC, 1980. 264 pp., illus. Paper covers. $11.50.
Text and illustrations explaining the takedown of 125 rifles and shotguns, domestic and foreign.

Firearms Assembly 4: The NRA Guide to Pistols and Revolvers, NRA Books, Wash., DC, 1980. 253 pp., illus. Paper covers. $11.50.
Text and illustrations explaining the takedown of 124 pistol and revolver models, domestic and foreign.

Firearms Bluing and Browning, By R.H. Angier, Stackpole Books, Harrisburg, PA. 151 pp., illus. $16.95.
A world master gunsmith reveals his secrets of building, repairing and renewing a gun, quite literally, lock, stock and barrel. A useful, concise text on chemical coloring methods for the gunsmith and mechanic.

First Book of Gunsmithing, by John E. Traister, Stackpole Books, Harrisburg, PA, 1981. 192 pp., illus. $18.95.
Beginner's guide to gun care, repair and modification.

Gun Owner's Book of Care, Repair & Improvement, by Roy Dunlap, Outdoor Life-Harper & Row, NY, 1977. 336 pp., illus. $12.95.
A basic guide to repair and maintenance of guns, written for the average firearms owner.

Guns and Gunmaking Tools of Southern Appalachia, by John Rice Irwin, Schiffer Publishing Ltd., 1983. 118 pp., illus. Paper covers. $9.95.
The story of the Kentucky rifle.

*__Gunsmithing Tips and Projects__, a collection of the best articles from the *Handloader* and *Rifle* magazines, by various authors, Wolfe Publishing Co., Prescott, AZ, 1992. 443 pp., illus. Paper covers. $25.00.
Includes such subjects as shop, stocks, actions, tuning, triggers, barrels, customizing, etc.

Gunsmith Kinks, by F.R. (Bob) Brownell, F. Brownell & Son, Montezuma, IA, 1st ed., 1969. 496 pp., well illus. $18.95.
A widely useful accumulation of shop kinks, short cuts, techniques and pertinent comments by practicing gunsmiths from all over the world.

Gunsmith Kinks 2, by Bob Brownell, F. Brownell & Son, Publishers, Montezuma, IA, 1983. 496 pp., illus. $18.95.
A collection of gunsmithing knowledge, shop kinks, new and old techniques, shortcuts and general know-how straight from those who do them best—the gunsmiths.

Gunsmithing, by Roy F. Dunlap, Stackpole Books, Harrisburg, PA, 1990. 742 pp., illus. $29.95.
A manual of firearm design, construction, alteration and remodeling. For amateur and professional gunsmiths and users of modern firearms.

Gunsmithing at Home, by John E. Traister, Stoeger Publishing Co., So. Hackensack, NJ, 1985. 256 pp., illus. Paper covers. $14.95.
Over 25 chapters of explicit information on every aspect of gunsmithing.

Gunsmithing With Simple Hand Tools, by Andrew Dubino, Stackpole Books, Harrisburg, PA, 1987. 205 pp., illus. $19.95.
How to repair, improve, and add a touch of class to the guns you own.

The Gunsmith's Manual, by J.P. Stelle and Wm. B. Harrison, The Gun Room Press, Highland Park, NJ, 1982. 376 pp., illus. $19.95.
For the gunsmith in all branches of the trade.

The Mauser M91 Through M98 Bolt Actions: A Shop Manual, by Jerry Kuhnhausen, VSP Books, McCall, ID, 1991. 224 pp., illus. Paper covers. $22.95.
An essential book if you work on or plan to work on a Mauser action.

The NRA Gunsmithing Guide—Updated, by Ken Raynor and Brad Fenton, National Rifle Association, Wash., DC, 1984. 336 pp., illus. Paper covers. $15.95.
Material includes chapters and articles on all facets of the gunsmithing art.

Pistolsmithing, The Gun Digest Book of, by Jack Mitchell, DBI Books, Inc., Northbrook, IL, 1980. 256 pp., illus. Paper covers. $14.95.
An expert's guide to the operation of each of the handgun actions with all the major functions of pistolsmithing explained.

Pistolsmithing, by George C. Nonte, Jr., Stackpole Books, Harrisburg, PA, 1974. 560 pp., illus. $29.95.
A single source reference to handgun maintenance, repair, and modification at home, unequaled in value.

Practical Gunsmithing, by Edward A. Matunas, Stackpole Books, Harrisburg, PA, 1989. 352 pp., illus. $31.95.
A complete guide to maintaining, repairing, and improving firearms.

Recreating the American Longrifle, by William Buchele, et al., George Shumway, Publisher, York, PA, 1983. 175 pp., illus. Paper covers. $20.00.
Includes full-scale plans for building a Kentucky rifle.

*__The Remington M870 and M1100/M11-87 Shotguns: A Shop Manual__, by Jerry Kuhnhausen, VSP Publishers, McCall, ID, 1992. 226 pp., illus. Paper covers. $26.95.

Covers everything about gunsmithing the most popular Remington shotguns from fitting a recoil pad to installing choke tubes, and everything in between.

Riflesmithing, The Gun Digest Book of, by Jack Mitchell, DBI Books, Inc., Northbrook, IL, 1982. 256 pp., illus. Paper covers. $14.95.

The art and science of rifle gunsmithing. Covers tools, techniques, designs, finishing wood and metal, custom alterations.

Ruger Double Action Revolvers, Vol. 1, Shop Manual, by Jerry Kuhnhausen, VSP Publishers, McCall, ID, 1989. 176 pp., illus. Soft covers. $18.95.

Covers the Ruger Six series of revolvers: Security-Six, Service-Six, and Speed-Six. Includes step-by-step function checks, disassembly, inspection, repairs, rebuilding, reassembly, and custom work.

The S&W Revolver: A Shop Manual, by Jerry Kuhnhausen, VSP Publishers, McCall, ID, 1987. 152 pp., illus. Paper covers. $17.95.

Covers accurizing, trigger jobs, action tuning, rebarreling, barrel setback, forcing cone angles, polishing and rebluing.

Shotgun Gunsmithing, The Gun Digest Book of, by Ralph Walker, DBI Books, Inc., Northbrook, IL, 1983. 256 pp., illus. Paper covers. $14.95.

The principles and practices of repairing, individualizing and accurizing modern shotguns by one of the world's premier shotgun gunsmiths.

Survival Gunsmithing, by J.B. Wood, Desert Publications, Cornville, AZ, 1986. 92 pp., illus. Paper covers. $9.95.

A guide to repair and maintenance of many of the most popular rifles, shotguns and handguns.

The Trade Gun Sketchbook, by Charles E. Hanson, The Fur Press, Chadron, NE, 1979. 48 pp., illus. Paper covers. $4.00.

Complete full-size plans to build seven different trade guns from the Revolution to the Indian Wars and a two-thirds size for your son.

The Trade Rifle Sketchbook, by Charles E. Hanson, The Fur Press, Chadron, NE, 1979. 48 pp., illus. Paper covers. $4.00.

Includes full-scale plans for 10 rifles made for Indian and mountain men; from 1790 to 1860, plus plans for building three pistols.

HANDGUNS

American Police Handgun Training, by Charles R. Skillen and Mason Williams, Charles C. Thomas, Springfield, IL, 1980. 216 pp., illus. $50.00.

Deals comprehensively with all phases of current handgun training procedures in America.

Askins on Pistols and Revolvers, by Col. Charles Askins, NRA Books, Wash., DC, 1980. 144 pp., illus. Paper covers. $14.95.

A book full of practical advice, shooting tips, technical analysis and stories of guns in action.

Blue Steel and Gun Leather, by John Bianchi, Beinfeld Publishing, Inc., No. Hollywood, CA, 1978. 200 pp., illus. $14.95.

A complete and comprehensive review of holster uses plus an examination of available products on today's market.

Browning Hi-Power Pistols, Desert Publications, Cornville, AZ, 1982. 20 pp., illus. Paper covers. $9.00.

Covers all facets of the various military and civilian models of the Browning Hi-Power pistol.

Colt Automatic Pistols, by Donald B. Bady, Borden Publ. Co., Alhambra, CA, 1974, 368 pp., illus. $19.95.

The rev. and enlarged ed. of a key work on a fascinating subject. Complete information on every automatic marked with Colt's name.

The Colt .45 Auto Pistol, compiled from U.S. War Dept. Technical Manuals, and reprinted by Desert Publications, Cornville, AZ, 1978. 80 pp., illus. Paper covers. $9.95.

Covers every facet of this famous pistol from mechanical training, manual of arms, disassembly, repair and replacement of parts.

The Combat .45 Automatic, by Bill Wilson, Wilson's Gun Shop, Tampa, FL, 1988. 241 pp., illus. Soft covers. $14.95.

A guide to purchasing, modifying and using the .45 automatic.

Combat Handgunnery, 3nd Edition, The Gun Digest Book of by Chuck Karwan, DBI Books, Inc., Northbrook, IL, 1992. 256 pp., illus. Paper covers. $15.95.

This all-new edition looks at real world combat handgunnery from three different perspectives—military, police and civilian.

Combat Handgun Shooting, by James D. Mason, Charles C. Thomas Publisher, Springfield, IL, 1990. 280 pp., illus. $47.00.

The most detailed and exciting book on this sport to date.

Combat Pistols, by Terry Gander, Sterling Publishing Co., Inc., 1991. Paper covers. $9.95.

The world's finest and deadliest pistols are shown close-up, with detailed specifications, muzzle velocity, rate of fire, ammunition, etc.

The Complete Book of Combat Handgunning, by Chuck Taylor, Desert Publications, Cornville, AZ, 1982. 168 pp., illus. Paper covers. $16.95.

Covers virtually every aspect of combat handgunning.

Competitive Pistol Shooting, by Laslo Antal, A&C Black, Cambs, England, 1989. 176 pp., illus. Soft covers. $24.00.

Covers free pistol, air pistol, rapid fire, etc.

*The Custom Government Model Pistol, by Layne Simpson, Wolfe Publishing Co., Prescott, AZ, 1992. 639 pp., illus. $24.50.

This book is about one of the world's greatest firearms and the things pistolsmiths do to make it even better.

The CZ-75 Family: The Ultimate Combat Handgun, by J.M. Ramos, Paladin Press, Boulder, CO, 1990. 100 pp., illus. Soft covers. $16.00.

And in-depth discussion of the early-and-late model CZ-75s, as well as the many newest additions to the Czech pistol family.

Experiments of a Handgunner, by Walter Roper, Wolfe Publishing Co., Prescott, AZ, 1989. 202 pp., illus. $37.00.

A limited edition reprint. A listing of experiments with functioning parts of handguns, with targets, stocks, rests, handloading, etc.

Exploded Handgun Drawings, The Gun Digest Book of, edited by Harold A. Murtz, DBI Books, Inc., Northbrook, IL. 1992. 512 pp., illus. Paper covers. $19.95.

Exploded or isometric drawings for 494 of the most popular handguns.

Fast and Fancy Revolver Shooting, by Ed. McGivern, Anniversary Edition, Winchester Press, Piscataway, NJ, 1984. 484 pp., illus. $18.95.

A fascinating volume, packed with handgun lore and solid information by the acknowledged dean of revolver shooters.

Firearms Assembly/Disassembly, Part I: Automatic Pistols, Revised Edition, The Gun Digest Book of, by J.B. Wood, DBI Books, Inc., Northbrook, IL, 1990. 480 pp., illus. Soft covers. $17.95.

Covers 58 popular autoloading pistols plus nearly 200 variants of those models

integrated into the text and completely cross-referenced in the index.

Firearms Assembly/Disassembly Part II: Revolvers, Revised Edition, The Gun Digest Book of, by J.B. Wood, DBI Books, Inc., Northbrook, IL, 1990. 480 pp., illus. Soft covers. $17.95.

Covers 49 popular revolvers plus 130 variants. The most comprehensive and professional presentation available to either hobbyist or gunsmith.

.45 ACP Super Guns, by J.M. Ramos, Paladin Press, Boulder, CO, 1991. 144 pp., illus. Paper covers. $20.00.

Modified .45 automatic pistols for competition, hunting and personal defense.

The .45, The Gun Digest Book of by Dean A. Grennell, DBI Books, Inc., Northbrook, IL, 1989. 256 pp., illus. Paper covers. $15.95.

Definitive work on one of America's favorite calibers.

Hallock's .45 Auto Handbook, by Ken Hallock, The Mihan Co., Oklahoma City, OK, 1981. 178 pp., illus. Paper covers. $11.95.

For gunsmiths, dealers, collectors and serious hobbyists.

Handgun Digest, 2nd Edition, by Dean A. Grennell, DBI Books, Inc., Northbrook, IL, 1991. 256 pp., illus. Paper covers. $16.95.

Full coverage of all aspects of handguns and handgunning from a highly readable, knowledgeable author.

Handgun Reloading, The Gun Digest Book of, by Dean A. Grennell and Wiley M. Clapp, DBI Books, Inc., Northbrook, IL, 1987. 256 pp., illus. Paper covers. $15.95.

Detailed discussions of all aspects of reloading for handguns, from basic to complex. New loading data.

*Handguns '94, 6th Edition, edited by Jack Lewis, DBI Books, Inc., Northbrook, IL, 1993. 320 pp., illus. Paper covers. $18.95

What's new in handguns for 1994 plus informative and interesting articles on all aspects of handguns.

Handguns of the World, by Edward C. Ezell, Marboro Book, Corp., Rockleigh, NJ, 1991. 704 pp., illus. $16.95.

A comprehensive international guide to military revolvers and self-loaders.

High Standard Automatic Pistols 1932-1950, by Charles E. Petty, The Gunroom Press, Highland Park, NJ, 1989. 124 pp., illus. $19.95.

A definitive source of information for the collector of High Standard arms.

*How to Become a Master Handgunner: The Mechanics of X-Count Shooting, by Charles Stephens, Paladin Press, Boulder, CO, 1993. 64 pp., illus. Paper covers. $10.00.

Offers a simple formula for success to the handgunner who strives to master the technique of shooting accurately.

Hunting for Handgunners, by Larry Kelly and J.D. Jones, DBI Books, Inc., Northbrook, IL, 1990. 256 pp., illus. Paper covers. $15.95.

Covers the entire spectrum of hunting with handguns in an amusing, easy-flowing manner that combines entertainment with solid information.

Instinct Combat Shooting, by Chuck Klein, Chuck Klein, The Goose Creek, IN, 1989. 49 pp., illus. Paper covers. $10.95.

Defensive handgunning for police.

Know Your Czechoslovakian Pistols, by R.J. Berger, Blacksmith Corp., Chino Valley, AZ, 1989. 96 pp., illus. Soft covers. $9.95.

A comprehensive reference which presents the fascinating story of Czech pistols.

Know Your 45 Auto Pistols—Models 1911 & A1, by E.J. Hoffschmidt, Blacksmith Corp., Southport, CT, 1974. 58 pp., illus. Paper covers. $9.95.

A concise history of the gun with a wide variety of types and copies.

Know Your Walther P.38 Pistols, by E.J. Hoffschmidt, Blacksmith Corp., Southport, CT, 1974. 77 pp., illus. Paper covers. $9.95.

Covers the Walther models Armee, M.P., H.P., P.38—history and variations.

Know Your Walther PP & PPK Pistols, by E.J. Hoffschmidt, Blacksmith Corp., Southport, CT, 1975. 87 pp., illus. Paper covers. $9.95.

A concise history of the guns with a guide to the variety and types.

Luger: The Multi-National Pistol, by Charles Kenyon, Jr., Richard Ellis Publications, Moline, IL, 1991. 192 pp. $69.95 (hardcover); $150.00 (leather bound).

A fresh approach to this most historical handgun.

Luger Variations, by Harry E. Jones, Harry E. Jones, Torrance, CA, 1975. 328 pp., 160 full page illus., many in color. $45.00.

A rev. ed. of the book known as "The Luger Collector's Bible."

The Mauser Self-Loading Pistol, by Belford & Dunlap, Borden Publ. Co., Alhambra, CA. Over 200 pp., 300 illus., large format. $24.95.

The long-awaited book on the "Broom Handles," covering their inception in 1894 to the end of production. Complete and in detail: pocket pistols, Chinese and Spanish copies, etc.

Metallic Silhouette Shooting, 2nd Edition, The Gun Digest Book of, by Elgin Gates, DBI Books, Inc., Northbrook, IL, 1988. 256 pp., illus. Paper covers. $15.95.

All about the rapidly growing sport. With a history and rules of the International Handgun Metallic Silhouette Association.

Modern American Pistols and Revolvers, by A.C. Gould, Wolfe Publishing Co., Prescott, AZ, 1988. 222 pp., illus. $37.00.

A limited edition reprint. An account of the development of those arms as well as the manner of shooting them.

*The Modern Technique of the Pistol, by Gregory Boyce Morrison, Gunsite Press, Paulden, AZ, 1991. 153 pp., illus. $45.00.

The theory of effective defensive use of modern handguns.

The New Handbook of Handgunning, by Paul B. Weston, Charles C. Thomas, Publisher, Springfield, IL, 1980. 102 pp., illus. $35.00.

A step-by-step, how-to manual of handgun shooting.

*9mm Handguns, 2nd Edition, The Gun Digest Book of, edited by Steve Comus, DBI Books, Inc., Northbrook, IL, 1993. 256 pp., illus. Paper covers. $17.95.

Covers the 9mmP cartridge and the guns that have been made for it in greater depth than any other work available. (October '93)

*9mm Parabellus; The History & Developement of the World's 9mm Pistols & Ammunition, by Klaus-Peter Konig and Martin Hugo, Schiffer Publishing Ltd., Atglen, PA, 1993. 304 pp., illus. $39.95.

Detailed history of 9mm weapons from Belguim, Italy, Germany, Israel, France, USA, Czechoslovakia, Hungary, Poland, Brazil, Finland and Spain.

*P-38 Automatic Pistol, by Gene Gangarosa, Jr., Stoeger Publishing Co., S. Hackensack, NJ, 1993. 272 pp., illus. Paper covers. $16.95

This book traces the origins and development of the P-38, including the momentous political forces of the World War II era that caused its near demise and, later, its rebirth.

Pistol & Revolver Guide, 3rd Ed., by George C. Nonte, Stoeger Publ. Co., So. Hackensack, NJ, 1975. 224 pp., illus. Paper covers. $11.95.

The standard reference work on military and sporting handguns.

The Pistol Book, by John Walter, 2nd edition, 1991. Sterling Publishing Co., Inc., 1991. 176 pp., illus. $29.95.

Beretta, Colt, Mauser—plus a wealth of information and specs on other worldwide manufacturers of pistols and ammunition.

Pistol Guide, by George C. Nonte, Jr., Stoeger Publishing Co., So. Hackensack, NJ, 1991. 280 pp., illus. Paper covers. $13.95.
Covers handling and marksmanship, care and maintenance, pistol ammunition, how to buy a used gun, military pistols, air pistols and repairs.
Pistols of the World, 3rd Edition, by Ian Hogg and John Weeks, DBI Books, Inc., Northbrook, IL, 1992. 320 pp., illus. Paper covers. $19.95.
A totally revised edtion of one of the leading studies of small arms.
Pistolsmithing, The Gun Digest Book of, by Jack Mitchell, DBI Books, Inc., Northbrook, IL, 1980, 288 pp., illus. Paper covers. $14.95.
An expert's guide to the operation of each of the handgun actions with all the major functions of pistolsmithing explained.
Police Handgun Manual, by Bill Clede, Stackpole Books, Inc., Harrisburg, PA, 1985. 128 pp., illus. $18.95.
How to get street-smart survival habits.
Powerhouse Pistols—The Colt 1911 and Browning Hi-Power Source book, by Duncan Long, Paladin Press, Boulder, CO, 1989. 152 pp., illus. Soft covers. $19.95.
The author discusses internal mechanisms, outward design, test-firing results, maintenance and accessories.
Report of Board on Tests of Revolvers and Automatic Pistols. From the Annual Report of the Chief of Ordnance, 1907. Reprinted by J.C. Tillinghast, Marlow, NH, 1969. 34 pp., 7 plates, paper covers. $9.95.
A comparison of handguns, including Luger, Savage, Colt, Webley-Fosbery and other makes.
Revolver Guide, by George C. Nonte, Jr., Stoeger Publishing Co., So. Hackensack, NJ, 1991. 288 pp., illus. Paper covers. $10.95.
A detailed and practical encyclopedia of the revolver, the most common handgun to be found.
***The Ruger P-85 Family of Handguns,** by Duncan Long, Desert Publications, El Dorado, AZ, 1993. 128 pp., illus. Paper covers. $14.95.
A full-fledged documentary on a remarkable series of Sturm Ruger handguns. The P-85 emerged as the "Volksgun" of the '90s, offering great reliability with affordability.
The Ruger .22 Automatic Pistol, Standard/Mark I/Mark II Series, by Duncan Long, Paladin Press, Boulder, CO, 1989. 168 pp., illus. Paper covers. $12.00.
The definitive book about the pistol that has served more than 1 million owners so well.
The Semiautomatic Pistols in Police Service and Self Defense, by Massad Ayoob, Police Bookshelf, Concord, NH, 1990. 25 pp., illus. Soft covers. $9.95.
First quantitative, documented look at actual police experience with 9mm and 45 police service automatics.
***The Sharpshooter—How to Stand and Shoot Handgun Metallic Silhouettes,** by Charles Stephens, Yucca Tree Press, Las Cruces, NM, 1993. 86 pp., illus. Paper covers. $7.95.
A narration of some of the author's early experiences in silhouette shooting, plus how-to information.
Shoot a Handgun, by Dave Arnold, PVA Books, Canyon County, CA, 1983. 144 pp., illus. Paper covers. $11.95.
A complete manual of simplified handgun instruction.
Shoot to Win, by John Shaw, Blacksmith Corp., Southport, CT, 1985. 160 pp., illus. Paper covers. $11.95.
The lessons taught here are of interest and value to all handgun shooters.
***Shooting,** by J.H. FitzGerald, Wolfe Publishing Co., Prescott, AZ, 1993. 421 pp., illus. $29.00
Exhaustive coverage of handguns and their use for target shooting, defense, trick shooting, and in police work by an noted firearms expert.
Sixgun Cartridges and Loads, by Elmer Keith, reprint edition by The Gun Room Press, Highland Park, NJ, 1984. 151 pp., illus. $24.95.
A manual covering the selection, use and loading of the most suitable and popular revolver cartridges.
Sixguns, by Elmer Keith, Wolfe Publishing Company, Prescott, AZ, 1992. 336 pp. Hardcover. $34.95.
The history, selection, repair, care, loading, and use of this historic frontiersman's friend–the one-hand firearm.
Skeeter Skelton on Handguns, by Skeeter Skelton, PJS Publications, Peoria, IL, 1980. 122 pp., illus. Soft covers. $5.00.
A treasury of facts, fiction and fables.
Successful Pistol Shooting, by Frank and Paul Leatherdale, The Crowood Press, Ramsbury, England, 1988. 144 pp., illus. $34.95.
Easy-to-follow instructions to help you achieve better results and gain more enjoyment from both leisure and competitive shooting.
Textbook of Pistols & Revolvers, by Julian Hatcher, Wolfe Publishing Co., Prescott, AZ, 1988. 533 pp., illus. $65.00.
A limited edition reprint. Hatcher wrote this shooters' bible in 1935 and it remains a classic full of invaluable information.
***Webley & Scott Automatic Pistols,** by Gordon Bruch, Stocker-Schmid Publishing Co., Dietikon, Switzerland, 1992. 256 pp., illus. $69.50.
The fundamental representation of the history and development of all Webley & Scott automatic pistols.
World's Deadliest Rimfire Battleguns, by J.M. Ramos, Paladin Press, Boulder, CO, 1990. 184 pp., illus. Paper covers. $14.00.
This heavily illustrated book shows international rimfire assault weapon innovations from World War II to the present.

HUNTING

NORTH AMERICA

Advanced Deer Hunting, by John Weiss, Stackpole Books, Harrisburg, PA, 1988. 352 pp., illus. $28.95.
New strategies based on the latest studies of whitetail behavior.
Advanced Wild Turkey Hunting & World Records, by Dave Harbour, Winchester Press, Piscataway, NJ, 1983. 264 pp., illus. $19.95.
The definitive book, written by an authority who has studied turkeys and turkey calling for over 40 years.
Alaska Safari, by Harold Schetzle, Great Northwest Publishing and Distributing Co., Inc., Anchorage, AK, 1990. 366 pp., illus. $35.00.
The most comprehensive and up-to-date guide to Alaska big game hunting currently available.
Alaska Wilderness Hunter, by Harold Schetzle, Great Northwest Publishing and Distributing Co., Anchorage, AK, 1987. 224 pp., illus. $35.00.
A superb collection of Alaska hunting adventures by master guide Harold Schetzle.
Alaskan Yukon Trophies Won and Lost, by G.O. Young, Wolfe Publishing Co., Prescott, AZ, 1989. 273 pp., illus. $35.00.
A new printing of the classic book on Alaskan big game hunting.
All About Bears, by Duncan Gilchrist, Stoneydale Press Publishing Co., Stevensville, MT, 1989. 176 pp., illus. $19.95.
Covers all kinds of bears—black, grizzly, Alaskan brown, polar and leans on a lifetime of hunting and guiding experiences to explore proper hunting techniques.
All About Deer in America, edited by Robert Elman, Winchester Press, Piscataway, NJ, 1976. 256 pp., illus. $15.95.
Twenty of America's great hunters share the secrets of their hunting success.
All-American Deer Hunter's Guide, edited by Jim Zumbo and Robert Elman, Winchester Press, Piscataway, NJ, 1983. 320 pp., illus. $29.95.
The most comprehensive, thorough book yet published on American deer hunting.
All Season Hunting, by Bob Gilsvik, Winchester Press, Piscataway, NJ, 1976. 256 pp., illus. $14.95.
A guide to early-season, late-season and winter hunting in America.
American Duck Shooting, by George Bird Grinnell, Stackpole Books, Harrisburg, PA, 1991. 640 pp., illus. Paper covers. $17.95.
First published in 1901 at the height of the author's career. Describes 50 species of waterfowl, and discusses hunting methods common at the turn of the century.
***Awesome Antlers of North America,** by Odie Sudbeck, HTW Publications, Seneca, KS, 1993. 150 pp., illus. $35.00.
500 world-class bucks in color and black and white. This book starts up where the Boone & Crockett recordbook leaves off.
***Bare November Days,** by George Bird Evans et al, Countrysport Press, Traverse City, MI, 1992. 136 pp., illus. $39.50.
A new, original anthology, a tribute to ruffed grouse, king of upland birds.
The Bear Hunter's Century, by Paul Schullery, Stackpole Books, Harrisburg, PA, 1989. 240 pp., illus. $19.95.
Thrilling tales of the bygone days of wilderness hunting.
Bear Hunting, by Jerry Meyer, Stackpole Books, Harrisburg, PA, 1983. 224 pp., illus. $16.95.
First complete guide on the how-to's of bear hunting. Information on every type of bear found in the U.S. and Canada.
Bear in Their World, by Erwin Bauer, an Outdoor Life Book, New York, NY, 1985. 254 pp., illus. $32.95.
Covers all North American bears; including grizzlies, browns, blacks, and polars.
The Best of Babcock, by Havilah Babcock, selected and with an introduction by Hugh Grey, The Gunnerman Press, Auburn Hills, MI, 1985. 262 pp., illus. $19.95.
A treasury of memorable pieces, 21of which have never before appeared in book form.
The Best of Nash Buckingham, by Nash Buckingham, selected, edited and annotated by George Bird Evans, Winchester Press, Piscataway, NJ, 1973. 320 pp., illus. $17.95.
Thirty pieces that represent the very cream of Nash's output on his whole range of outdoor interests—upland shooting, duck hunting, even fishing.
***The Best of Sheep Hunting,** by John Batten, Amwell Press, Clinton, NJ, 1992. 616 pp., illus. $47.50.
This "Memorial Edition" is a collection of 40 articles and appendices covering sheep hunting in the North American area of Canada, Alaska, the West and Midwest as well as Africa and Europe.
Big Game, Big Country, by Dr. Chauncey Guy Suits, Great Northwest Publishing and Distributing Co., Anchorage, AK, 1987. 224 pp., illus. $29.50.
Chronicles more than a decade of high-quality wilderness hunting by one of this country's more distinguished big game hunters.
Big Game of North America, Ecology and Management, by Wildlife Management Institute, Stackpole Books, Harrisburg, PA, 1983. 512 pp., illus. $34.95.
An outstanding reference for professionals and students of wildlife management.
Big Game Trails in the Far North, by Col. Philip Neuweiler, Great Northwest Publishing and Distributing Co., Inc., Anchorage, AK, 1990. 320 pp., illus. $35.00.
This book is the result of 50 years hunting big game in the Far North.
Bird Hunting with Dalrymple, by Byron W. Dalrymple, Stackpole Books, Harrisburg, PA, 1987. 256 pp., illus. $24.95.
The rewards of shotgunning across North America.
***Birds on the Horizon,** by Stuart Williams, Countrysport Press, Traverse City, MI, 1993. 288 pp., illus. $49.50.
Wingshooting adventures around the world.
***Blacktail Trophy Tactics,** by Boyd Iverson, Stoneydale Press, Stevensville, MI, 1992. 166 pp., illus. Paper covers. $14.95.
A comprehensive analysis of blacktail deer habits, describing a deer's and man's use of scents, still hunting, tree techniques, etc.
The Bobwhite Quail Book, Compiled by Lamar Underwood, Amwell Press, Clinton, NJ, 1981. 442 pp., illus. $25.00.
An anthology of the finest stories on Bobwhite quail ever assembled under one cover.
***Boone & Crockett Club's 21st Big Game Awards,** edited by Gary Sitton & Jack Reneau, Missoula, MT, 1992. 537 pp., illus. $39.95.
A book of the Boone & Crockett Club containing tabulations of outstanding North American big game trophies accepted during the 21st awards entry period of 1989-1991.
Bowhunter's Digest, 3rd Edition, by Chuck Adams, DBI Books, Inc., Northbrook, IL, 1990. 288 pp., illus. Soft covers. $15.95.
All-new edition covers all the necessary equipment and how to use it, plus the fine points on how to improve your skill.
Brown Feathers, by Steven J. Julak, Stackpole Books, Harrisburg, PA, 1988. 224 pp., illus. $16.95.
Waterfowling tales and upland dreams.
Bugling for Elk, by Dwight Schuh, Stoneydale Press Publishing Co., Stevensville, MT, 1983. 162 pp., illus. $18.95.
A complete guide to early season elk hunting.
Call of the Quail: A Tribute to the Gentleman Game Bird, by Michael McIntosh, et al., Countrysport Press, Traverse City, MI, 1990. 175 pp., illus. $39.50.
A new anthology on quail hunting.
Calling All Elk, by Jim Zumbo, Jim Zumbo, Cody, WY, 1989. 169 pp., illus. Paper covers. $14.95.
The only book on the subject of elk hunting that covers every aspect of elk vocalization.
Campfires and Game Trails: Hunting North American Big Game, by Craig Boddington, Winchester Press, Piscataway, NJ, 1985. 295 pp., illus. $23.95.
How to hunt North America's big game species.
Come October, by Gene Hill et al, Countrysport Press, Inc., Traverse City, MI, 1991. 176 pp., illus. $39.50.
A new and all-original anthology on the woodcock and woodcock hunting.
The Complete Book of Hunting: A Guide to Game Hunting, Wildfowling and Competition Shooting, edited by David Petzal, W.H. Smith, Publishers, New York, NY, 1988. 192 pp., illus. $14.98.

Equipment, game and dogs, plus techniques and reading the land.

The Complete Book of the Wild Turkey, by Roger M. Latham, Stackpole Books, Harrisburg, PA, 1978. 228 pp., illus. $14.95.
A new revised edition of the classic on American wild turkey hunting.

The Complete Guide to Bowhunting Deer, by Chuck Adams, DBI Books, Inc., Northbrook, IL, 1984. 256 pp., illus. Paper covers. $15.95.
Plenty on equipment, bows, sights, quivers, arrows, clothes, lures and scents, stands and blinds, etc.

The Complete Guide to Game Care and Cookery, Revised Edition, by Sam Fadala, DBI Books, Inc., Northbrook, IL, 1989. 320 pp., illus. Paper covers. $16.95.
Over 500 detailed photos and hundreds of tested recipes anyone can master.

The Complete Smoothbore Hunter, by Brook Elliot, Winchester Press, Piscataway, NJ, 1986. 240 pp., illus. $16.95.
Advice and information on guns and gunning for all varieties of game.

The Complete Turkey Hunt, by William Morris Daskal, El-Bar Enterprises Publishers, New York, NY, 1982. 129 pp., illus. Paper covers. $7.95.
Covers every aspect of turkeys and turkey hunting, by an expert.

Complete Turkey Hunting, by John Phillips, Stackpole Books, Harrisburg, PA, 1988. 320 pp., illus. $24.95.
The definitive work on hunting America's largest game bird.

Confessions of an Outdoor Maladroit, by Joel M. Vance, Amwell Press, Clinton, NJ, 1983. $20.00.
Anthology of some of the wildest, irreverent, and zany hunting tales ever.

Covey Rises and Other Pleasures, by David H. Henderson, Amwell Press, Clinton, NJ, 1983. 155 pp., illus. $17.50.
A collection of essays and stories concerned with field sports.

Coveys and Singles: The Handbook of Quail Hunting, by Robert Gooch, A.S. Barnes, San Diego, CA, 1981. 196 pp., illus. $11.95.
The story of the quail in North America.

Deer and Deer Hunting: The Serious Hunter's Guide, by Dr. Robert Wegner, Stackpole Books, Harrisburg, PA, 1984. 384 pp., illus. $24.95.
In-depth information from the editor of "Deer & Deer Hunting" magazine. Major bibliography of English language books on deer and deer hunting from 1838-1984.

Deer and Deer Hunting Book 2, by Dr. Robert Wegner, Stackpole Books, Harrisburg, PA, 1987. 400 pp., illus. $29.95.
Strategies and tactics for the advanced hunter.

Deer and Deer Hunting, Book 3, by Dr. Robert Wegner, Stackpole Books, Harrisburg, PA, 1990. 368 pp., ilus. $29.95.
This comprehensive volume covers natural history, deer hunting lore, profiles of deer hunters, and discussion of important issues facing deer hunters today.

The Deer Book, edited by Lamar Underwood, Amwell Press, Clinton, NJ, 1982. 480 pp., illus. $25.00.
An anthology of the finest stories on North American deer ever assembled under one cover.

Deer Hunter's Guide to Guns, Ammunition, and Equipment, by Edward A. Matunas, an Outdoor Life Book, distributed by Stackpole Books, Harrisburg, PA, 1983. 352 pp., illus. $24.95.
Where to hunt for North American deer. An authoritative guide that will help every deer hunter get maximum enjoyment and satisfaction from his sport.

Deer Hunting, by R. Smith, Stackpole Books, Harrisburg, PA, 1978. 224 pp., illus. Paper covers. $14.95.
A professional guide leads the hunt for North America's most popular big game animal.

Deer Hunting Coast to Coast, by C. Boddington and R. Robb, Safari Press, Long Beach, CA, 1989. 248 pp., illus. $24.95.
Join the authors as they hunt whitetail deer in eastern woodlot, southern swamps, midwestern prairies, and western river bottom; mule deer in badland, deserts, and high alpine basins; blacktails in oak grasslands and coastal jungles.

Deer in Their World, by Erwin Bauer, Stackpole Books, Harrisburg, PA, 1984. 256 pp., illus. $29.95.
More than 250 natural habitat deer photos. Substantial natural history of North American deer.

The Deer of North America, edited by Leonard Lee Rue, Stackpole Books, Harrisburg, PA, 1989. 544 pp., illus. $32.95.
Updated and expanded edition of this definitive work on North American deer.

The Desert Bighorn, its Life History, Ecology, and Management, edited by Gale Monson and Lowel Sumner, U. of Arizona Press, Tucson, AZ, 1985. 370 pp., illus. Paper covers. $14.95.
There is nothing else around that can tell you anywhere near as much about desert sheep.

***Doves and Dove Shooting,** by Byron W. Dalrymple, New Win Publishing, Inc., Hampton, NJ, 1992. 256 pp., illus. $17.95.
The author reveals in this classic book his penchant for observing, hunting, and photographing this elegantly fashioned bird.

Dove Hunting, by Charley Dickey, Galahad Books, NY, 1976. 112 pp., illus. $10.00.
This indispensable guide for hunters deals with equipment, techniques, types of dove shooting, hunting dogs, etc.

Doves and Dove Shooting, by Byron Dalrymple, New Win Publishing, Inc., Hampton, NJ, 1991. 256 pp., illus. $17.95.
The classic book on the subject in a new printing.

Drummer in the Woods, by Burton L. Spiller, Stackpole Books, Harrisburg, PA, 1990. 240 pp., illus. Soft covers. $16.95.
Twenty-one wonderful stories on grouse shooting by "the Poet Laureate of Grouse."

Duck Decoys and How to Rig Them, by Ralf Coykendall, revised by Ralf Coykendall, Jr., Nick Lyons Books, New York, NY, 1990. 137 pp., illus. Paper covers. $12.95.
Sage and practical advice on the art of decoying ducks and geese.

The Duck Hunter's Handbook, by Bob Hinman, revised, expanded, updated edition, Winchester Press, Piscataway, NJ, 1985. 288 pp., illus. $15.95.
The duck hunting book that has it all.

The Duck-Huntingest Gentlemen, by Keith C. Russell et al., Winchester Press, Piscataway, NJ, 1980. 284 pp., illus. $17.95.
A collection of stories on waterfowl hunting.

Ducks of the Mississippi Flyway, ed. by John McKane, North Star Press, St. Cloud, MN, 1969. 54 pp., illus. Paper covers. $10.00.
A duck hunter's reference. Full color paintings of some 30 species, plus descriptive text.

Early American Waterfowling, 1700's-1930, by Stephen Miller, Winchester Press, Piscataway, NJ, 1986. 256 pp., illus. $27.95.
Two centuries of literature and art devoted to the nation's favorite hunting sport.

Eastern Upland Shooting, by Dr. Charles C. Norris, Countrysport Press, Traverse City, MI, 1990. 424 pp., illus. $29.50.
A new printing of this 1946 classic with a new, original Foreword by the author's friend and hunting companion, renowned author George Bird Evans.

The Education of Pretty Boy, by Havilah Babcock, The Gunnerman Press, Auburn Hills, MI, 1985. 160 pp., illus. $19.95.
Babcock's only novel, a heartwarming story of an orphan boy and a gun-shy setter.

Elk and Elk Hunting, by Hart Wixom, Stackpole Books, Harrisburg, PA, 1986. 288 pp., illus. $29.95.
Your practical guide to fundamentals and fine points of elk hunting.

Elk Hunting in the Northern Rockies, by Ed. Wolff, Stoneydale Press, Stevensville, MT, 1984. 162 pp., illus. $18.95.
Helpful information about hunting the premier elk country of the northern Rocky Mountain states—Wyoming, Montana and Idaho.

***Elk Hunting with the Experts,** by Bob Robb, Stoneydale Press, Stevensville, MT, 1992. 176 pp., illus. Paper covers. $15.95.
A complete guide to elk hunting in North America by America's top elk hunting expert.

***Elk Rifles, Cartridges and Hunting Tactics,** by Wayne van Zwoll, Larsen's Outdoor Publishing, Lakeland, FL, 1992. 414 pp., illus. $24.95.
The definitive work on which rifles and cartridges are proper for hunting elk plus the tactics for hunting them.

***Encyclopedia of Deer,** by G. Kenneth Whitehead, Safari Press, Huntington, CA, 1993. 704 pp., illus. $130.00.
This massive tome will be the reference work on deer for well into the next century.

Fair Chase, by Jim Rikhoff, Amwell Press, Clinton, NJ, 1984. 323 pp., illus. $25.00.
A collection of hunting experiences from the Arctic to Africa, Mongolia to Montana, taken from over 25 years of writing.

Field Dressing Big Game, by James Churchill, Stackpole Books, Harrisburg, PA, 1989. 88 pp., illus. Soft covers. $10.95.
Dressing, caping, skinning and butchering instructions.

Field Dressing Small Game and Fowl, by James Churchill, Stackpole Books, Harrisburg, PA, 1987. 112 pp., illus. Paper covers. $10.95.
The illustrated guide to dressing 20 birds and animals.

Field Judging Trophy Animals, by William Shuster, Stackpole Books, Harrisburg, PA, 1987. 132 pp., illus. Paper covers. $8.95.
Expert advice and practical suggestions.

Firelight, by Burton L. Spiller, Gunnerman Press, Auburn Hills, MI, 1990. 196 pp., illus. $19.95.
Enjoyable tales of the outdoors and stalwart companions.

Fireside Waterfowler, edited by David E. Wesley and William G. Leitch, A Ducks Unlimited Book, Stackpole Books, Harrisburg, PA, 1987. 357 pp., illus. $29.95.
Fundamentals of duck and goose hunting.

For Whom the Ducks Toll, by Keith C. Russell, et al., Winchester Press, Piscataway, NJ, 1984. 288 pp., illus. Slipcased, limited and signed edition. $30.00. Trade edition, $16.95.
A select gathering of memorable waterfowling tales by the author and 68 of his closest friends.

The Formidable Game, by John H. Batten, Amwell Press, Clinton, NJ. 1983. 264 pp., illus. $175.00.
Deluxe, limited, signed and numbered edition. Big game hunting in India, Africa and North America by a world famous hunter.

***Fresh Looks at Deer Hunting,** by Byron W. Dalrymple, New Win Publishing, Inc., Hampton, NJ, 1993. 288 pp., illus. $24.95.
Tips and techniques abound throughout the pages of this latest work by Mr. Dalrymple whose name is synonymous with hunting proficiency.

Fur Trapping In North America, by Steven Geary, Winchester Press, Piscataway, NJ, 1985. 160 pp., illus. Paper covers. $10.95.
A comprehensive guide to techniques and equipment, together with fascinating facts about fur bearers.

A Gallery of Waterfowl and Upland Birds, by Gene Hill, with illustrations by David Maass, Petersen Prints, Los Angeles, CA, 1978. 132 pp., illus. $44.95.
Gene Hill at his best. Liberally illustrated with 51 full-color reproductions of David Maass' finest paintings.

Game in the Desert Revisited, by Jack O'Connor, Amwell Press, Clinton, NJ, 1984. 306 pp., illus. $27.50.
Reprint of a Derrydale Press classic on hunting in the Southwest

Getting the Most Out of Modern Waterfowling, by John O. Cartier, St. Martin's Press, NY, 1974. 396 pp., illus. $22.50.
The most comprehensive, up-to-date book on waterfowling imaginable.

The Grand Passage: A Chronicle of North American Waterfowling, by Gene Hill, et al., Countrysport Press, Traverse City, MI, 1990. 175 pp., illus. $39.50.
A new original anthology by renowned sporting authors on our world of waterfowling.

The Grand Spring Hunt for America's Wild Turkey Gobbler, by Bart Jacob with Ben Conger, Winchester Press, Piscataway, NJ, 1985. 176 pp., illus. $15.95.
The turkey book for novice and expert alike.

Grizzlies Don't Come Easy, by Ralph Young, Winchester Press, Piscataway, NJ, 1981. 200 pp., illus. $15.95.
The life story of a great woodsman who guided famous hunters such as O'Connor, Keith, Fitz, Page and others.

Grizzly Country, by Andy Russell, A.A. Knopf, NYC, 1973, 302 pp., illus. $15.95.
Many-sided view of the grizzly bear by a noted guide, hunter and naturalist.

Grouse and Grouse Hunting, by Frank Woolner, Nick Lyons Books, N.Y., NY, 1987. 192 pp., illus. $18.95.
An authoritative and affectionate portrait of one of America's greatest game birds.

Grouse of North America, by Tom Huggler, NorthWord Press, Inc., Minocqua, WI, 1990. 160 pp., illus. $29.95.
A cross-continental hunting guide.

Grouse Hunter's Guide, by Dennis Walrod, Stackpole Books, Harrisburg, PA, 1985. 192 pp., illus. $16.95.
Solid facts, observations, and insights on how to hunt the ruffed grouse.

Gun Clubs & Decoys of Back Bay & Currituck Sound, by Archie Johnson and Bud Coppedge, CurBac Press, Virginia Beach, VA, 1991. 224 pp., illus. $40.00.
This book identifies and presents a photographic history of over 100 hunting clubs and lodges on Back Bay, VA and Currituck Sound, NC.

Gunning for Sea Ducks, by George Howard Gillelan, Tidewater Publishers, Centreville, MD, 1988. 144 pp., illus. $14.95.
A book that introduces you to a practically untouched arena of waterfowling.

***Heartland Trophy Whitetails,** by Odie Sudbeck, HTW Publications, Seneca, KS, 1992. 130 pp., illus. $35.00.
A completely revised and expanded edition which includes over 500 photos of Boone & Crockett class whitetail, major mulies and unusual racks.

Horned and Antlered Game, by Erwin Bauer, Stackpole Books, Harrisburg, PA, 1987. 256 pp., illus. $32.95.
This book features spectacular color photographs and text brimming with animal lore.

Horns in the High Country, by Andy Russell, Alfred A. Knopf, NY, 1973. 259 pp., illus. Paper covers. $12.95.
A many-sided view of wild sheep and their natural world.

How to Get Your Deer, by John O. Cartier, Stackpole Books, Harrisburg, PA, 1986. 320 pp., illus. $24.95.
An authoritative guide to deer hunting that shows you how to match wits with your quarry and win.
How to Hunt, by Dave Bowring, Winchester Press, Piscataway, NJ, 1982. 208 pp., illus. Paper covers. $10.95; cloth, $15.00.
A basic guide to hunting big game, small game, upland birds, and waterfowl.
Hunt High, by Duncan Gilchrist, Outdoor Expeditions & Books, Cowallis, MT, 1992. 192 pp., illus. Limited, signed edition. $34.95.
High country lore and how-to information on hunting Rocky Mountain Goats, Bighorn Sheep, Chamois, and Tahr.
The Hunters and the Hunted, by George Laycock, Outdoor Life Books, New York, NY, 1990. 280 pp., illus. $34.95.
The pursuit of game in America from Indian times to the present.
A Hunter's Fireside Book, by Gene Hill, Winchester Press, Piscataway, NJ, 1972. 192 pp., illus. $16.95.
An outdoor book that will appeal to every person who spends time in the field—or who wishes he could.
***A Hunter's Road,** by Jim Fergus, Henry Holt & Co., NY, 1992. 290 pp. $22.50
A journey with gun and dog across the American uplands.
***Hunt High for Rocky Mountain Goats, Bighorn Sheep, Chamois & Tahr,** by Duncan Gilchrist, Stoneydale Press, Stevensville, MT, 1992. 192 pp., illus. Paper covers. $19.95.
The source book for hunting mountain goats.
The Hunter's Shooting Guide, by Jack O'Connor, Outdoor Life Books, New York, NY, 1982. 176 pp., illus. Paper covers. $5.95.
A classic covering rifles, cartridges, shooting techniques for shotguns/rifles/handguns.
The Hunter's World, by Charles F. Waterman, Winchester Press, Piscataway, NJ, 1983. 250 pp., illus. $29.95.
A classic. One of the most beautiful hunting books that has ever been produced.
Hunting America's Game Animals and Birds, by Robert Elman and George Peper, Winchester Press, Piscataway, NJ, 1975. 368 pp., illus. $16.95.
A how-to, where-to, when-to guide—by 40 top experts—covering the continent's big, small, upland game and waterfowl.
Hunting and Stalking Deer Throughout the World, by Kenneth G. Whitehead, Batsford Books, London, 1982. 336 pp., illus. $35.00.
Comprehensive coverage of deer hunting areas on a country-by-country basis, dealing with every species in any given country.
***Hunting Boar, Hogs & Javelinas,** by Bob Gooch, Atlantic Publishing Co., Tabor City, NC, 1989. 204 pp., illus. Paper covers. $9.95.
Thorough in explaining where, when and how to hunt these elusive creatures, along with a state-by-state hunting guide and a list of recipes.
Hunting Ducks and Geese, by Steven Smith, Stackpole Books, Harrisburg, PA, 1984. 160 pp., illus. $15.95.
Hard facts, good bets, and serious advice from a duck hunter you can trust.
Hunting for Handgunners, by Larry Kelly and J.D. Jones, DBI Books, Inc., Northbrook, IL, 1990. 256 pp., illus. Soft covers. $15.95.
A definitive work on an increasingly popular sport.
Hunting Fringeland Deer, by David Richey, Stackpole Books, Harrisburg, PA, 1987. 208 pp., illus. $24.95.
Tactics for trail watching, stillhunting and driving whitetails in farmlands, edge country and populated areas.
Hunting in Many Lands, edited by Theodore Roosevelt and George Bird Grinnell, et al., Boone & Crockett Club, Dumphries, VA, 1990. 447 pp., illus. $40.00.
A limited edition reprinting of the original Boone & Crockett Club 1895 printing.
Hunting in the Southlands, edited by Lamar Underwood, Amwell Press, Clinton, NJ, 1987. 565 pp., illus. $35.00.
An anthology of the best stories of southern hunts including dove, turkey, waterfowl, deer, quail and more.
Hunting North America's Big Game, by Bob Hagel, Stackpole Books, Harrisburg, PA, 1987. 220 pp., illus. $27.95.
Complete coverage on how to approach, track, and shoot game in different terrains.
Hunting Open-Country Mule Deer, by Dwight Schuh, Sage Press, Nampa, ID, 1989. 180 pp., illus. $18.95.
A guide taking Western bucks with rifle and bow.
Hunting Predators for Hides and Profits, by Wilf E. Pyle, Stoeger Publishing Co., So. Hackensack, NJ, 1985. 224 pp., illus. Paper covers. $11.95.
The author takes the hunter through every step of the hunting/marketing process.
Hunting the Alaskan Brown Bear, by John Eddy, Wolfe Publishing Co., Prescott, AZ, 1988. 253 pp., illus. $47.00.
A limited edition reprint of the best book on the big brown bear of the North.
Hunting the American Wild Turkey, by Dave Harbour, Stackpole Books, Harrisburg, PA, 1975. 256 pp., illus. $14.95.
The techniques and tactics of hunting North America's largest, and most popular, woodland game bird.
Hunting the Southwest, by Jack Samson, The Amwell Press, Clinton, NJ, 1985. 172 pp., illus. In slipcase $27.50.
The most up-to-date look at one of the most difficult and diverse hunting areas in the world today.
Hunting Superbucks, by Kathy Etling, Grolier Book Clubs, Danbury, CT, 1989. 444 pp., illus. $32.95.
How to find and hunt today's trophy mule and whitetail deer.
Hunting Trips in North America, by F.C. Selous, Wolfe Publishing Co., Prescott, AZ, 1988. 395 pp., illus. $52.00.
A limited edition reprint. Coverage of caribou, moose and other big game hunting in virgin wilds.
Hunting Trophy Deer, by John Wootters, Winchester Press, Piscataway, NJ, 1983. 265 pp., illus. $15.95.
All the advice you need to succeed at bagging trophy deer.
Hunting Upland Gamebirds, by Steve Smith, Stackpole Books, Harrisburg, PA, 1987. 176 pp., illus. $16.95.
What the wingshooter needs to know about the birds, the game, and the new clay games.
Hunting Wild Turkeys in the Everglades, by Frank P. Harben, Harben Publishing Co., Safety Harbor, FL, 1983. 341 pp., illus. Paper covers. $8.95.
Describes techniques, ways and means of hunting this wary bird.
***Hunting Wild Turkeys in the West,** by John Higley, Stoneydale Press, Stevensville, MT, 1992. 154 pp., illus. Paper covers. $12.95.
Covers the basics of calling, locating and hunting turkeys in the western states.
Hunting Wild Turkeys with Ray Eye, by Michael Pearce and Ray Eye, Stackpole Books, Harrisburg, PA, 1990. 208 pp., illus. $22.95.
Whether you hunt in spring or fall, with a gun or bow and arrow, alone or with a partner, you will find in this book a wealth of practical information.
I Don't Want to Shoot an Elephant, by Havilah Babcock, The Gunnerman Press, Auburn Hills, MI, 1985. 184 pp., illus. $19.95.
Eighteen delightful stories that will enthrall the upland gunner for many pleasurable hours.
In Search of the Wild Turkey, by Bob Gooch, Greatlakes Living Press, Ltd., Waukegan, IL, 1978. 182 pp., illus. $9.95.
A state-by-state guide to wild turkey hot spots, with tips on gear and methods for bagging your bird.
Indian Hunts and Indian Hunters of the Old West, by Dr. Frank C. Hibben, Safari Press, Long Beach, CA, 1989. 228 pp., illus. $24.95.
Tales of some of the most famous American Indian hunters of the Old West as told to the author by an old Navajo hunter.
Instinctive Shooting, by G. Fred Asbell, Stackpole Books, Harrisburg, PA, 1988. 132 pp., illus. Paper covers. $13.95.
Expert advice on applying instinctive shooting to bowhunting. Written by the president of the Pope & Young Club.
Jack O'Connor's Gun Book, by Jack O'Connor, Wolfe Publishing Company, Prescott, AZ, 1992. 208 pp. Hardcover. $26.00.
Jack O'Connor imparts a cross-section of his knowledge on guns and hunting. Brings back some of his writings that have here-to-fore been lost.
Jaybirds Go to Hell on Friday, by Havilah Babcock, The Gunnerman Press, Auburn Hills, MI, 1985. 149 pp., illus. $19.95.
Sixteen jewels that reestablish the lost art of good old-fashioned yarn telling.
Jim Dougherty's Guide to Bowhunting Deer, by Jim Dougherty, DBI Books, Inc., Northbrook, IL, 1992. 256 pp., illus. Paper covers. $15.95.
Dougherty sets down some important guidelines for bowhunting and bowhunting equipment.
A Listening Walk...and Other Stories, by Gene Hill, Winchester Press, Piscataway, NJ, 1985. 208 pp., illus. $15.95.
Vintage Hill. Over 60 stories.
Making Game: An Essay on Woodcock, by Guy De La Valdene, Willow Creek Press, Oshkosh, WI, 1985. 202 pp., illus. $35.00.
The most delightful book on woodcock yet published.
Marsh Tales, by William N. Smith, Tidewater Publishers, Centreville, MD, 1985. 228 pp., illus. $15.95.
Market hunting, duck trapping, and gunning.
Matching the Gun to the Game, by Clair Rees, Winchester Press, Piscataway, NJ, 1982. 272 pp., illus. $17.95.
Covers selection and use of handguns, blackpowder firearms for hunting, matching rifle type to the hunter, calibers for multiple use, tailoring factory loads to the game.
Measuring and Scoring North American Big Game Trophies, by Wm. H. Nesbitt and Philip L. Wright, The Boone and Crockett Club, Alexandria, VA, 1986. 176 pp., illus. $15.00.
The Boone and Crockett Club official scoring system, with tips for field evaluation of trophies.
Meat on the Table: Modern Small-Game Hunting, by Galen Geer, Paladin Press, Boulder, CO, 1985. 216 pp., illus. $16.95.
All you need to know to put meat on your table from this comprehensive course in modern small-game hunting.
Mixed Bag, by Jim Rikhoff, National Rifle Association of America, Wash., DC, 1981. 284 pp., illus. Paper covers. $9.95.
Reminiscences of a master raconteur.
Modern Pheasant Hunting, by Steve Grooms, Stackpole Books, Harrisburg, PA, 1982. 224 pp., illus. Paper covers. $10.95.
New look at pheasants and hunters from an experienced hunter who respects this splendid gamebird.
Modern Waterfowl Guns and Gunning, by Don Zutz, Stoeger Publishing Co., So. Hackensack, NJ, 1985. 224 pp., illus. Paper covers. $11.95.
Up-to-date information on the fast-changing world of waterfowl guns and loads.
Montana—Land of Giant Rams, by Duncan Gilchrist, Stoneydale Press Publishing Co., Stevensville, MT, 1990. 208 pp., illus. $19.95.
Latest information on Montana bighorn sheep and why so many Montana bighorn rams are growing to trophy size.
***Montana—Land of Giant Rams, Volume 2,** by Duncan Gilchrist, Outdoor Expeditions and Books, Corvallis, MT, 1992. 208 pp., illus. $34.95.
The reader will find stories of how many of the top-scoring trophies were taken.
More Alaska Bear Tales, by Larry Kamut, Alaska Northwest Books, Bothell, WA, 1991. 295 pp., illus. Paper covers. $12.95.
Action-packed stories for everyone with an interest in the most powerful animal roaming the North American wilderness.
More and Better Pheasant Hunting, by Steve Smith, Winchester Press, Piscataway, NJ, 1986. 192 pp., illus. $15.95.
Complete, fully illustrated, expert coverage of the bird itself, the dogs, the hunt, the guns, and the best places to hunt.
More Grouse Feathers, by Burton L. Spiller, Crown Publ., NY, 1972. 238 pp., illus. $25.00.
Facsimile of the original Derrydale Press issue of 1938. Guns and dogs, the habits and shooting of grouse, woodcock, ducks, etc. Illus. by Lynn Bogue Hunt.
More Than a Trophy, by Dennis Walrod, Stackpole Books, Harrisburg, PA, 1983. 256 pp., illus. Paper covers. $12.95.
Field dressing, skinning, quartering, and butchering to make the most of your valuable whitetail, blacktail or mule deer.
***More Tracks: 78 Years of Mountains, People & Happinesss** by Howard Copenhaver, Stoney dale Press, Stevensville, MT, 1992. 150 pp., illus. $18.95.
A collection of stories by one of the back country's best storytellers about the people who shared with Howard his great adventure in the high places and wild Montana country.
Mostly Huntin', by Bill Jordan, Everett Publishing Co., Bossier City, LA, 1987. 254 pp., illus. $21.95.
Jordan's hunting adventures in North America, Africa, Australia, South America and Mexico.
Mostly Tailfeathers, by Gene Hill, Winchester Press, Piscataway, NJ, 1975. 192 pp., illus. $15.95.
An interesting, general book about bird hunting.
Movin' Along with Charley Dickey, by Charlie Dickey, Winchester Press, Piscataway, NJ, 1985. 224 pp., illus. $14.95.
More wisdom, wild tales, and wacky wit from the Sage of Tallahassee.
"Mr. Buck": The Autobiography of Nash Buckingham, by Nash Buckingham, Countrysport Press, Traverse City, MI, 1990. 288 pp., illus. $39.50.
A lifetime of shooting, hunting, dogs, guns, and Nash's reflections on the sporting life,

along with previously unknown pictures and stories written especially for this book.

Murry Burnham's Hunting Secrets, by Murry Burnham with Russell Tinsley, Winchester Press, Piscataway, NJ, 1984. 244 pp., illus. $17.95.

One of the great hunters of our time gives the reasons for his success in the field.

The Muzzleloading Hunter, by Rick Hacker, Stackpole Books, Harrisburg, PA, 1989. 295 pp., illus. $19.95.

The book for anyone interested in the rapidly growing sport of hunting with a muzzleloader.

My Health is Better in November, by Havilah Babcock, University of S. Carolina Press, Columbia, SC, 1985. 284 pp., illus. $19.95.

Adventures in the field set in the plantation country and backwater streams of SC.

My Lost Wilderness: Tales of an Alaskan Woodsman, by Ralph Young, Winchester Press, Piscataway, NJ, 1983. 193 pp., illus. $22.50.

True tales of an Alaskan hunter, guide, fisherman, prospector, and backwoodsman.

New England Grouse Shooting, by William Harnden Foster, Willow Creek Press, Oshkosh, WI, 1983. 213 pp., illus. $45.00.

A new release of a classic book on grouse shooting.

North American Big Game Animals, by Byron W. Dalrymple and Erwin Bauer, Outdoor Life Books/Stackpole Books, Harrisburg, PA, 1985. 258 pp., illus. $29.95.

Complete illustrated natural histories. Habitat, movements, breeding, birth and development, signs, and hunting.

North American Elk: Ecology and Management, edited by Jack Ward Thomas and Dale E. Toweill, Stackpole Books, Harrisburg, PA, 1982. 576 pp., illus. $39.95.

The definitive, exhaustive, classic work on the North American elk.

The North American Waterfowler, by Paul S. Bernsen, Superior Publ. Co., Seattle, WA, 1972. 206 pp. Paper covers. $4.95.

The complete inside and outside story of duck and goose shooting. Big and colorful, illus. by Les Kouba.

Northeast Upland Hunting Guide, by Jim Capossela, Stackpole Books, Harrisburg, PA, 1991. 120 pp., illus. Paper covers. $12.95.

Useful strategies and techniques for bagging all the region's most popular upland game.

Of Bears and Man, by Mike Cramond, University of Oklahoma Press, Norman, OK, 1986. 433 pp., illus. $29.95.

The author's lifetime association with bears of North America. Interviews with survivors of bear attacks.

The Old Man and the Boy and The Old Man Grows Older, by Robert Ruark, Stackpole Books, Harrisburg, PA, 1989. 620 pp., illus. Soft covers. $17.95.

Two novels in one volume. Classic tales of the coming of age of a boy and young man as he is nurtured and educated by his remarkable sportsman grandfather.

The Old Pro Turkey Hunter, by Gene Nunnery, Gene Nunnery, Meridian, MS, 1980. 144 pp., illus. $12.95.

True facts and old tales of turkey hunters.

1001 Hunting Tips, by Robert Elman, Winchester Press, Piscataway, NJ, 1983. 544 pp., illus. $22.95.

New edition, updated and expanded. A complete course in big and small game hunting, wildfowling and hunting upland birds.

The Only Good Bear is a Dead Bear, by Jeanette Hortick Prodgers, Falcon Press, Helena, MT, 1986. 204 pp. Paper covers. $7.95.

A collection of the West's best bear stories.

Opening Shots and Parting Lines: The Best of Dickey's Wit, Wisdom, and Wild Tales for Sportsmen, by Charley Dickey, Winchester Press, Piscataway, NJ, 1983. 208 pp., illus. $14.95.

Selected by the writer who has entertained millions of readers in America's top sporting publications—49 of his best pieces.

The Outdoor Life Bear Book, edited by Chet Fish, an Outdoor Life book, distributed by Stackpole Books, Harrisburg, PA, 1983. 352 pp., illus. $26.95.

All-time best personal accounts of terrifying attacks, exciting hunts, and intriguing natural history.

The Outdoor Life Deer Hunter's Encyclopedia, by John Madson, et al., Stackpole Books, Harrisburg, PA, 1985. 800 pp., illus. $49.95.

The largest, most comprehensive volume of its kind ever published.

Outdoor Yarns & Outright Lies, by Gene Hill and Steve Smith, Stackpole Books, Harrisburg, PA, 1984. 168 pp., illus. $16.95.

Fifty or so stories by two good sports.

The Outlaw Gunner, by Harry M. Walsh, Tidewater Publishers, Cambridge, MD, 1973. 178 pp., illus. $15.95.

A colorful story of market gunning in both its legal and illegal phases.

Pheasant Hunter's Harvest, by Steve Grooms, Lyons & Burford Publishers, New York, NY, 1990. 180 pp. $18.95.

A celebration of pheasant, pheasant dogs and pheasant hunting. Practical advice from a passionate hunter.

Picking Your Shots, by Steve Smith, Stackpole Books, Harrisburg, PA, 1986. 160 pp., illus. $16.95.

Stories of dogs and birds, and guns and days afield.

Pinnell and Talifson: Last of the Great Brown Bear Men, by Marvin H. Clark, Jr., Great Northwest Publishing and Distributing Co., Spokane, WA, 19880. 224 pp., Illus. $39.95.

The story of these famous Alaskan guides and some of the record bears taken by them.

Predator Caller's Companion, by Gerry Blair, Winchester Press, Piscataway, NJ, 1981. 280 pp., illus. $18.95.

Predator calling techniques and equipment for the hunter and trapper.

Predators of North America, by Erwin Bauer, Stackpole Books, Harrisburg, PA, 1988. 256 pp., illus. $34.95.

Pronghorn, North America's Unique Antelope, by Charles L. Cadieux, Stackpole Books, Harrisburg, PA, 1986. 256 pp., illus. $24.95.

The practical guide for hunters.

Quail Hunting in America, by Tom Huggler, Stackpole Books, Harrisburg, PA, 1987. 288 pp., illus. $19.95.

Tactics for finding and taking bobwhite, valleys, Gambel's Mountain, scaled-blue, and Mearn's quail by season and habitat.

Radical Elk Hunting Strategies, by Mike Lapinski, Stoneydale Press Publishing Co., Stevensville, MT, 1988. 161 pp., illus. $18.95.

Secrets of calling elk in close.

Ranch Life and the Hunting Trail, by Theodore Roosevelt, Readex Microprint Corp., Dearborn, MI, 1966. 186 pp. With drawings by Frederic Remington. $22.50.

A facsimile reprint of the original 1899 Century Co. edition. One of the most fascinating books of the West of that day.

Records of North American Big Game 1932, by Prentis N. Grey, Boone and Crockett Club, Dumfries, VA, 1988. 178 pp., illus. $79.95.

A reprint of the book that started the Club's record keeping for native North American big game.

Records of North American Big Game, 9th Edition, 1988, edited by William H. Nesbitt and Jack Reneau, Boone and Crockett Club, Dumfries, VA, 1989. 512 pp., illus. $49.95.

A special Centennial Year edition of useful statistics and good reading about our native big game animals. With a special full-color section.

Records of North American Whitetailed Deer, by the editors of the Boone and Crockett Club, Dumfries, VA, 1987. 256 pp., illus. Flexible covers. $15.00.

Contains data on 1293 whitetail trophies over the all-time record book minimum, listed and ranked by state or province and divided into typical and non-typical categories.

Ridge Runners & Swamp Rats, by Charles F. Waterman, Amwell Press, Clinton, NJ, 1983. 347 pp., illus. $25.00.

Tales of hunting and fishing.

The Rifles, the Cartridges, and the Game, by Clay Harvey, Stackpole Books, Harrisburg, PA, 1991. 254 pp., illus. $32.95.

Engaging reading combines with exciting photos to present the hunt with an intense level of awareness and respect.

Ringneck! Pheasants & Pheasant Hunting, by Ted Janes, Crown Publ., NY, 1975. 120 pp., illus. $15.95.

A thorough study of one of our more popular game birds.

Ruffed Grouse, edited by Sally Atwater and Judith Schnell, Stackpole Books, Harrisburg, PA, 1989. 370 pp., illus. $59.95.

Everything you ever wanted to know about the ruffed grouse. More than 25 wildlife professionals provided in-depth information on every aspect of this popular game bird's life. Lavishly illustrated with over 300 full-color photos.

Shadows of the Tundra, by Tom Walker, Stackpole Books, Harrisburg, PA, 1990. 192 pp., illus. $19.95.

Alaskan tales of predator, prey, and man.

***Sheep & Sheep Hunting,** by Jack O'Connor, Safari Press, Huntington Beach, CA, 1992. 308 pp., illus. $35.00.

A new printing of the definitive book on wild sheep.

Shorebirds: The Birds, The Hunters, The Decoys, by John M. Levinson & Somers G. Headley, Tidewater Publishers, Centreville, MD, 1991. 160 pp., illus. $49.95.

A thorough study of shorebirds and the decoys used to hunt them. Photographs of more than 200 of the decoys created by prominent carvers are shown.

Shots at Big Game, by Craig Boddington, Stackpole Books, Harrisburg, PA, 1989. 198 pp., illus. $24.95.

How to shoot a rifle accurately under hunting conditions.

Small Game & Varmint Hunting, by Wilf E. Pyle, Stoeger Publishing Co., So. Hackensack, NJ, 1989. 288 pp., illus. Soft covers. $16.95.

Provides information on modern techniques and methods needed for successful hunting of small game.

Sport and Travel; East and West, by Frederick Courteney Selous, Wolfe Publishing Co., Prescott, AZ, 1988. 311 pp., illus. $29.00.

A limited edition reprint. One of the few books Selous wrote covering North American hunting. His daring in Africa is equalled here as he treks after unknown trails and wild game.

Spring Turkey Hunting, by John M. McDaniel, Stackpole Books, Harrisburg, PA, 1986. 224 pp., illus. $21.95.

The serious hunter's guide.

***Sunlight and Shadows,** by Gene Hill, Petersen Publishing Co., Los Angeles, CA, 1990. 173 pp., illus. $24.50.

Essays and stories on the out-of-doors.

Squirrels and Squirrel Hunting, by Bob Gooch. Tidewater Publ., Cambridge, MD, 1973. 148 pp., illus. $9.95.

A complete book for the squirrel hunter, beginner or old hand. Details methods of hunting, squirrel habitat, management, proper clothing, care of the kill, cleaning and cooking.

Strayed Shots and Frayed Lines, edited by John E. Howard, Amwell Press, Clinton, NJ, 1982. 425 pp., illus. $25.00.

Anthology of some of the finest, funniest stories on hunting and fishing ever assembled.

Successful Goose Hunting, by Charles L. Cadieux, Stone Wall Press, Inc., Washington, DC, 1986. 223 pp., illus. $24.95.

Here is a complete book on modern goose hunting by a lifetime waterfowler and professional wildlifer.

Successful Handgun Hunting, by Phil W. Johnson. The Shooting Sports Press, Minneapolis, MN, 1988. 216 pp., illus. $19.95.

The definitive work on the most exciting sport in America.

Supreme Duck Shooting Stories, by William Hazelton, The Gunnerman Press, Auburn Hills, MI, 1989. 160 pp. $19.95.

Originally published in 1931, this is about duck hunting as it was.

Taking Big Bucks, by Ed Wolff, Stoneydale Press, Stevensville, MT, 1987. 169 pp., illus. $18.95.

Solving the whitetail riddle.

Tales of Alaska's Big Bears, by Jim Rearden, Wolfe Publishing Co., Prescott, AZ, 1989. 125 pp., illus. Soft covers. $12.95.

A collection of bear yarns covering nearly three-quarters of a century.

Tales of Quails 'n Such, by Havilah Babcock, University of S. Carolina Press, Columbia, SC, 1985. 237 pp. $19.95.

A group of hunting stories, told in informal style, on field experiences in the South in quest of small game.

They Left Their Tracks, by Howard Coperhaver, Stoneydale Press Publishing Co., Stevensville, MT, 1990. 190 pp., illus. $18.95.

Recollections of 60 years as an outfitter in the Bob Marshall Wilderness.

Timberdoodle, by Frank Woolner, Nick Lyons Books, N. Y., NY, 1987. 168 pp., illus. $18.95.

The classic guide to woodcock and woodcock hunting.

Track of the Kodiak, by Marvin H. Clark, Great Northwest Publishing and Distributing Co., Anchorage, AK, 1984. 224 pp., illus. $39.95.

A full perspective on Kodiak Island bear hunting.

Tracking Wounded Deer, by Richard P. Smith, Stackpole Books, Harrisburg, PA, 1988. 159 pp., illus. Paper covers. $15.95.

How to find and tag deer shot with bow or gun.

Trail and Campfire, edited by George Bird Grinnel and Theodore Roosevelt, The Boone and Crockett Club, Dumfries, VA, 1989. 357 pp., illus. $39.50.

Reprint of the Boone and Crockett Club's 3rd book published in 1897.

Trail of the Eagle, by Bud Conkle, as told to Jim Rearden, Great Northwest Publishing & Distributing Co., Anchorage, AK, 1991. 280 pp., illus. $29.50.

Hunting Alaska with master guide Bud Conkle.

Trophy Hunter in Asia, by Elgin T. Gates, Charger Productions Inc., Capistrano Beach, CA, 1982. 272 pp., illus. $19.95.

Fascinating high adventure with Elgin Gates, one of America's top trophy hunters.

Trophy Rams of the Brooks Range Plus Secrets of a Sheep and Mountain Goat Guide,

by Duncan Gilchrist, Pictorial Histories Publishing Co., Missoula, MT, 1984. 176 pp., illus. $19.95.

Covers hunting a remote corner of the Brooks Range for virgin herds of dall rams.

The Turkey Hunter's Book, by John M. McDaniel, Amwell Press, Clinton, NJ, 1980. 147 pp., illus. Paper covers. $9.95.

One of the most original turkey hunting books to be published in many years.

Turkey Hunter's Digest, by Dwain Bland, DBI Books, Inc., Northbrook, IL, 1986. 256 pp., illus. Paper covers. $15.95.

Describes and pictures all varieties of turkey. Offers complete coverage on calls, calling techniques, appropriate guns, bows, cameras and other equipment.

Turkey Hunter's Guide, by Byron W. Dalrymple, et al., a publication of The National Rifle Association, Washington, DC, 1979. 96 pp., illus. Paper covers. $9.95.

Expert advice on turkey hunting hotspots, guns, guides, and calls.

Turkey Hunting, Spring and Fall, by Doug Camp, Outdoor Skills Bookshelf, Nashville, TN, 1983. 165 pp., illus. Paper covers. $12.95.

Practical turkey hunting, calling, dressing and cooking, by a professional turkey hunting guide.

Turkey Hunting with Gerry Blair, by Gerry Blair, Krause Publications, Iola, WI, 1991. 280 pp., illus. $19.95.

Turkey types, guns, camouflage, calls, bowhunting, field care, spring tactics and fall tactics.

The Upland Gunner's Book, edited by George Bird Evans, The Amwell Press, Clinton, NJ, 1985. 263 pp., illus. In slipcase. $27.50.

An anthology of the finest stories ever written on the sport of upland game hunting.

The Waterfowl Gunner's Book, edited by F. Phillips Williamson, The Amwell Press, Clinton, NJ, 1986. 282 pp., illus. In slipcase. $35.00.

An anthology of the finest duck hunting stories ever gathered under one cover.

***Wegner's Bibliography on Dear and Deer Hunting,** by Robert Wegner, St. Hubert's Press, Deforest, WI, 1993. 333 pp., 16 full-page illustrations. $45.00.

A comprehensive annotated compilation of books in English pertaining to deer and their hunting 1413-1991.

Western Hunting Guide, by Mike Lapinski, Stoneydale Press Publishing Co., Stevensville, MT, 1989. 168 pp., illus. $18.95.

A complete where-to-go and how-to-do-it guide to Western hunting.

White-Tailed Deer: Ecology and Management, by Lowell K. Halls, Stackpole Books, Harrisburg, PA, 1984. 864 pp., illus. $59.95.

The definitive work on the world's most popular big game animal.

Whitetails, by Leonard Lee Rue III, Stackpole Books, Harrisburg, PA, 1991. 320 pp., illus. $32.95.

Answers to all your questions on life cycle, feeding patterns, antlers, scrapes and rubs, behavior during the rut, and habitat.

The Wild Bears, by George Laycock, Outdoor Life Books, N. Y., NY, 1987. 272 pp., illus. Soft covers. $19.95.

The story of the grizzly, brown and black bears, their conflicts with man, and their chances of survival in the future.

The Wild Turkey Book, edited and with special commentary by J. Wayne Fears, Amwell Press, Clinton, NJ, 1982. 303 pp., illus. $22.50.

An anthology of the finest stories on wild turkey ever assembled under one cover.

Wilderness Hunting and Wildcraft, by Townsend Whelen, Wolfe Publishing Co., Prescott, AZ, 1988. 338 pp., illus. $39.00.

A limited edition reprint. Plentiful information on sheep and mountain hunting with horses and on life histories of big game animals.

The Wildfowler's Quest, by George Reiger, Lyons & Burford, Publishers, New York, NY, 1989. 320 pp., illus. $24.95.

A richly evocative look into one man's passionate pursuit of ducks, geese, turkey, woodcock, and other wildfowl all over the world.

Wind on the Water, as told to Jim Rearden, Great Northwest Publishing & Distributing Co., Anchorage, AK, 1991. 280 pp., illus. $19.95.

The true-life account of a pioneering couple, Bud and Lenora Conkle, in the wilds. Hunting stories as well as takes of the trapline, winter hardship and wilderness life in the far North.

***Wings for the Heart,** by Jerry A. Lewis, West River Press, Corvallis, MT, 1991. 324 pp., illus. Paper covers. $14.95.

A delightful book on hunting Montan's upland birds and waterfowl.

The Wings of Dawn, by George Reiger, Lyons & Burford, Publishers, New York, NY, 1989. 320 pp., illus. Soft covers. $15.95.

This memorable and rich portrait of the waterfowler's world includes the history of the sport, natural history of all types of ducks and geese, useful hunting advice, and more.

Woodcock, by John Alden Knight, Gunnerman Press, Auburn Hills, MI, 1989. 160 pp., illus. $21.95.

A new printing of one of the finest books ever written on the subject.

Woodcock Shooting, by Steve Smith, Stackpole Books, Inc., Harrisburg, PA, 1988. 142 pp., illus. $16.95.

A definitive book on woodcock hunting and the characteristics of a good woodcock dog.

AFRICA/ASIA

***Aagaard's Africa: A Hunter Remembers,** by Finn Aagaard, National Rifle Association, Washington, DC, 1991. 196 pp., illus. $16.95.

Tales of life and livelihood in Kenya in the twilight of its glory days is told by native Kenyan Finn Aagaard.

***The African Adventures: A Return to the Silent Places,** by Peter Hathaway Capstick, St. Martin's Press, New York, NY, 1992. 220 pp., illus. $22.95.

This book brings to life four turn-of-the-century adventurers and the savage frontier they braved. Frederick Selous, Constatine "Iodine" Ionides, Johnny Boyes and Jim Sutherland.

African Game Trails, by Theodore Roosevelt, St. Martin's Press, New York, NY, 1988. 583 pp., illus. $19.95.

The 1908 safari of President Teddy Roosevelt and his son Kermit to East Africa.

African Hunter, by James Mellon, Safari Press, Long Beach, CA, 1988. 522 pp., illus. $100.00.

The most ardent and intricately detailed book on African game hunting to appear in 50 years.

African Hunter, by Baron Bror von Blixen-Finecke, St. Martin's Press, New York, NY, 1986. 284 pp., illus. $14.95.

Reprint of the scarce 1938 edition. An African hunting classic.

African Hunting and Adventure, by William Charles Baldwin, Books of Zimbabwe, Bulawayo, 1981. 451 pp., illus. $75.00.

Facsimile reprint of the scarce 1863 London edition. African hunting and adventure from Natal to the Zambezi.

African Rifles & Cartridges, by John Taylor, The Gun Room Press, Highland Park, NJ, 1977. 431 pp., illus. $35.00.

Experiences and opinions of a professional ivory hunter in Africa describing his knowledge of numerous arms and cartridges for big game. A reprint.

The African Safari, by P. Jay Fetner, St. Martin's Press, Inc., N. Y., NY, 1987. 700 pp., illus. $70.00.

A lavish, superbly illustrated, definitive work that brings together the practical elements of planning a safari with a proper appreciation for the animals and their environment.

After Big Game in Central Africa, by Edouard Foa, St. Martin's Press, New York, NY, 1989. 400 pp., illus. $16.95.

Reprint of the scarce 1899 edition. This sportsman covered 7200 miles, mostly on foot—from Zambezi delta on the east coast to the mouth of the Congo on the west.

Bell of Africa, compiled and edited by Townsend Whelen, Safari Press, Huntington Beach, CA, 1990. 236 pp., illus. $24.95.

The autobiography of W.D.M. Bell compiled and edited by his lifetime friend from Bell's own papers.

The Big Game Hunters, by Michael Brander, St. Martin's Press, New York, NY, 1989. 192 pp., illus. $24.95.

The adventures of 19 sportsmen of yore in Asia, Africa, and America.

Big Game Hunting and Collecting in East Africa 1903-1926, by Kalman Kittenberger, St. Martin's Press, New York, NY, 1989. 496 pp., illus. $16.95.

One of the most heart stopping, charming and funny accounts of adventure in the Kenya Colony ever penned.

Big Game Hunting Around the World, by Bert Klineburger and Vernon W. Hurst, Exposition Press, Jericho, NY, 1969. 376 pp., illus. $30.00.

The first book that takes you on a safari all over the world.

Big Game Hunting in North-Eastern Rhodesia, by Owen Letcher, St. Martin's Press, New York, NY, 1986. 272 pp., illus. $15.95.

A classic reprint and one of the very few books to concentrate on this fascinating area, a region that today is still very much safari country.

***Big Game Shooting in Cooch Behar, the Duars and Assam,** by The Maharajah of Cooch Behar, Wolfe Publishing Co., Prescott, AZ, 1993. 461 pp., illus. $118.00.

A reprinting of the book that has become legendary. This is the Maharajah's personal diary of killing 365 tigers.

The Book of the Lion, by Sir Alfred E. Pease, St. Martin's Press, New York, NY, 1986. 305 pp., illus. $15.95.

Reprint of the finest book ever published on the subject. The author describes all aspects of lion history and lion hunting, drawing heavily on his own experiences in British East Africa.

Claws of Africa, by Roger Courtney, Trophy Room Books, Agoura, CA, 1990. 272 pp., illus. $65.00.

A classic account of the experiences of a professional "White Hunter," one of a carefully selected band of men who acted as official guides to hunters and shooting parties throughout Equatorial Africa in the 1940s and 1950s.

Death in a Lonely Land, by Peter Capstick, St. Martin's Press, New York, NY, 1990. 284 pp., illus. $19.95.

Twenty-three stories of hunting as only the master can tell them.

Death in the Dark Continent, by Peter Capstick, St. Martin's Press, New York, NY, 1983. 238 pp., illus. $15.95.

A book that brings to life the suspense, fear and exhilaration of stalking ferocious killers under primitive, savage conditions, with the ever present threat of death.

Death in the Long Grass, by Peter Hathaway Capstick, St. Martin's Press, New York, NY, 1977. 297 pp., illus. $15.95.

A big game hunter's adventures in the African bush.

Death in the Silent Places, by Peter Capstick, St. Martin's Press, New York, NY, 1981. 243 pp., illus. $15.95.

The author recalls the extraordinary careers of legendary hunters such as Corbett, Karamojo Bell, Stigand and others.

East Africa and its Big Game, by Captain Sir John C. Willowghby, Wolfe Publishing Co., Prescott, AZ, 1990. 312 pp., illus. $52.00.

A deluxe limited edition reprint of the very scarce 1889 edition of a narrative of a sporting trip from Zanzibar to the borders of the Masai.

East of the Sun and West of the Moon, by Theodore and Kermit Roosevelt, Wolfe Publishing Co., Prescott, AZ, 1988. 284 pp., illus. $25.00.

A limited edition reprint. A classic on Marco Polo sheep hunting. A life experience unique to hunters of big game.

Elephant, by Commander David Enderby Blunt, The Holland Press, London, England, 1985. 260 pp., illus. $35.00.

A study of this phenomenal beast by a world-leading authority.

Elephant Hunting in East Equatorial Africa, by Arthur H. Neumann, Books of Zimbabwe, Bulawayo, 1982. 455 pp., illus. $85.00.

Facsimile reprint of the scarce 1898 London edition. An account of three years ivory hunting under Mount Kenya.

Elephant Hunting in Portuguese East Africa, by Jose Pardal, Safari Press, Huntington Beach, CA, 1990. 256 pp., illus. $60.00.

This book chronicles the hunting-life story of a nearly vanished breed of man—those who single-handedly hunted elephants for prolonged periods of time.

Elephants of Africa, by Dr. Anthony Hall-Martin, New Holland Publishers, London, England, 1987. 120 pp., illus. $75.00.

A superbly illustrated overview of the African elephant with reproductions of paintings by the internationally acclaimed wildlife artist Paul Bosman.

Ends of the Earth, by Roy Chapman Andrews, Wolfe Publishing Co., Prescott, AZ, 1988. 230 pp., illus. $27.00.

A limited edition reprint. Includes adventures in China and hunting in Mongolia. Andrews was a distinguished hunter and scout.

First Wheel, by Bunny Allen, Amwell Press, Clinton, NJ, 1984. Limited, signed and numbered edition in the NSFL "African Hunting Heritage Series." 292 pp., illus. $100.00.

A white hunter's diary, 1927-47.

Green Hills of Africa, by Ernest Hemingway. Charles Scribner's Sons, NY, 1963. 285 pp., illus. Paper covers. $11.95.

A famous narrative of African big game hunting, that was first published in 1935.

Gun and Camera in Southern Africa, by H. Anderson Bryden, Wolfe Publishing Co., Prescott, AZ, 1989. 201 pp., illus. $37.00.

A limited edition reprint. The year was 1893 and author Bryden wandered for a year in Bechuanaland and the Kalahari Desert hunting the white rhino, lechwe, eland, and more.

***Horned Death,** by John F. Burger, Safari Press, Huntington Beach, CA, 1992. 343 pp., illus. $35.00.

The classic work on hunting the African buffalo.

Horn of the Hunter, by Robert Ruark, Safari Press, Long Beach, CA, 1987. 315 pp., illus. $35.00.

Ruark's most sought-after title on African hunting, here in reprint.

Hunting Big Game, 2 volumes, by Townsend Whelen, Wolfe Publishing Co., Prescott, AZ, 1989. Volume I, Africa and Asia, 339 pp., illus.; Volume 2, The America's, 282 pp., illus. $90.00.
A limited edition reprint. Articles and stories by F.C. Selous, Sir Samuel Baker, Arthur H. Neumann, Theodore Roosevelt and others.

Hunting in Many Lands, by Theodore Roosevelt and George Bird Grinnel, The Boone and Crockett Club, Dumfries, VA, 1987. 447 pp., illus. $40.00.
Limited edition reprint of this 1895 classic work on hunting in Africa, India, Mongolia, etc.

***Hunting in the Sudan, An Anthology,** compiled by Tony Sanchez-Arino, Safari Press, Huntington Beach, CA, 1992. 350 pp., illus. Limited, signed and numbered edition in a slipcase. $125.00.
The finest selection of junting stories ever compiled on hunting in this great game country.

Hunting in Tanzania, An Anthology, by Tony Sanchez-Arino, Safari Press, Huntington Beach, CA, 1991. 416 pp., illus. Limited, signed and numbered edition, in a slipcase. $125.00.
The finest selection of hunting stories ever compiled on that great East African game country, Tanzania.

***Hunting in Zimbabwe, An Anthology,** by Tony Sanchez-Arino, Safari Press, Huntington Beach, CA, 1992. 350 pp., illus. Limited, signed and numbered edition, in a slipcase. $125.00.
The finest selection of hunting stories ever compiled on hunting in this gread game country.

Hunting the Elephant in Africa, by Captain C.H. Stigand, St. Martin's Press, New York, NY, 1986. 379 pp., illus. $14.95.
A reprint of the scarce 1913 edition; vintage Africana at its best.

Jaguar Hunting in the Mato Grosso and Bolivia, by T. Almedia, Safari Press, Long Beach, CA, 1989. 256 pp., illus. $35.00.
Not since Sacha Siemel has there been a book on jaguar hunting like this one.

The Jim Corbett Collection, by Jim Corbett. Safari Press, Huntington, CA, 1991. 1124 pp., illus., five volumes in slipcase. $105.00.
This slip-cased set of Jim Corbett's works includes: *Jungle Lore, The Man-Eating Leopard of Rudraprayag, My India, Man-Eaters of Kumaon, Tree Tops,* and *Temple Tiger.*

***Jim Corbett's India,** stories selected by R.E. Hawkins, Oxford University Press, New York, NY, 1993. 250 pp. $24.95.
Stories and extracts from Jim Corbett's writings on tiger hunting by his publisher and editor.

Karamojo Safari, by W.D.M. Ball, Safari Press, Huntington Beach, CA, 1990. 288 pp., illus. $24.95.
The story of Bell's caravan travels through Karamojo, his exciting elephant hunts, and his life among the uncivilized and uncorrupted natives.

Lake Ngami, by Charles Anderson, New Holland Press, London, England, 1987. 576 pp., illus. $35.00.
Originally published in 1856. Describes two expeditions into what is now Botswana, depicting every detail of landscape and wildlife.

Last Horizons: Hunting, Fishing and Shooting on Five Continents, by Peter Capstick, St. Martin's Press, New York, NY, 1989. 288 pp., illus. $19.95.
The first in a two volume collection of hunting, fishing and shooting tales from the selected pages of The American Hunter, Guns & Ammo and Outdoor Life.

The Last Ivory Hunter: The Saga of Wally Johnson, by Peter Capstick, St. Martin's Press, New York, NY, 1988. 220 pp., illus. $18.95.
A grand tale of African adventure by the foremost hunting author of our time. Wally Johnson spent half a century in Mozambique hunting white gold—ivory.

Last of the Ivory Hunters, by John Taylor, Safari Press, Long Beach, CA, 1990. 354 pp., illus. $29.95.
Reprint of the classic book "Pondoro" by one of the most famous elephant hunters of all time.

The Man-Eaters of Tsavo, by Lt. Col. J.H. Patterson, St. Martin's Press, New York, NY, 1986. 346 pp., illus. $14.95.
A reprint of the scarce original book on the man-eating lions of Tsavo.

Memories of an African Hunter, by Denis D. Lyell, St. Martin's Press, New York, NY, 1986. 288 pp., illus. $15.95.
A reprint of one of the truly great writers on African hunting. A gripping and highly readable account of Lyell's many years in the African bush.

Peter Capstick's Africa: A Return to the Long Grass, by Peter Hathaway Capstick, St. Martin's Press, N. Y., NY, 1987. 213 pp., illus. $29.95.
A first-person adventure in which the author returns to the long grass for his own dangerous and very personal excursion.

The Recollections of an Elephant Hunter 1864-1875, by William Finaughty, Books of Zimbabwe, Bulawayo, Zimbabwe, 1980. 244 pp., illus. $85.00.
Reprint of the scarce 1916 privately published edition. The early game hunting exploits of William Finaughty in Matabeleland and Nashonaland.

Robert Ruark's Africa, by Robert Ruark, Countrysport Press, Inc., Traverse City, MI, 1991. 256 pp., illus. $29.50.
A new release of previously uncollected stories of the wanderings through Africa of this giant in American sporting literature.

Safari: A Chronicle of Adventure, by Bartle Bull, Viking/Penguin, London, England, 1989. 383 pp., illus. $40.00.
The thrilling history of the African safari, highlighting some of Africa's best-known personalities.

Safari Rifles: Double, Magazine Rifles and Cartridges for African Hunting, by Craig Boddington, Safari Press, Huntington Beach, CA, 1990. 416 pp., illus. $37.50.
A wealth of knowledge on the safari rifle. Historical and present double-rifle makers, ballistics for the large bores, and much, much more.

Safari: The Last Adventure, by Peter Capstick, St. Martin's Press, New York, NY, 1984. 291 pp., illus. $15.95.
A modern comprehensive guide to the African Safari.

Sands of Silence, by Peter H. Capstick, Saint Martin's Press, New York, NY, 1991. 224 pp., illus. $35.00.
Join the author on safari in Nambia for his latest big-game hunting adventures.

The Shamba Raiders: Memories of a Game Warden, by Bruce Kinlock, Safari Press, Long Beach, CA, 1988. 405 pp., illus. $35.00.
Thrilling stories of encounters with rogue elephants, buffalo and other dangerous animals.

Sourdough and Swahili, by Bud Branham, The Amwell Press, Clinton, NJ, 1990. 265 pp., illus. $35.00.
A professional hunter's experiences on two continents.

South Pacific Trophy Hunter, by Murray Thomas, Safari Press, Long Beach, CA, 1988. 181 pp., illus. $37.50.
A record of a hunter's search for a trophy of each of the 15 major game species in the South Pacific region.

***Sport on the Pamirs and Turkestan Steppes,** by Major C.S. Cumberland, Moncrieff & Smith, Victoria, Autralia, 1992. 278 pp., illus. $45.00.
The first in a series of facsimile reprints of great trophy hunting books by Moncrieff & Smith.

Tales of the Big Game Hunters, selected and introduced by Kenneth Kemp, The Sportsman's Press, London, 1986. 209 pp., illus. $15.00.
Writings by some of the best known hunters and explorers, among them: Frederick Courteney Selous, R.G. Gordon Cumming, Sir Samuel Baker, and elephant hunters Neumann and Sutherland.

Tanzania Safari, by Brian Herne, Amwell Press, Clifton, NJ, 1982. 259 pp., illus. Limited, signed and numbered edition. $125.00.
The story of Tanzania and hunting safaris, professional hunters, and a little history, too.

***Those Were the Days,** by Rudolf Sand, Safari Press, Huntington Beach, CA, 1993. 300 pp., illus. $100.00.
Travel with Rudolf Sand to the pinnacles of the world in his pursuit of wild sheep and goats.

Uganda Safaris, by Brian Herne, Winchester Press, Piscataway, NJ, 1979. 236 pp., illus. $12.95.
The chronicle of a professional hunter's adventures in Africa.

***Use Enough Gun,** by Robert Ruark, Safari Press, Huntington Beach, CA, 1992. 333 pp., illus. $30.00.
A record of a lifetime's bag hunting big game.

The Wanderings of an Elephant Hunter, by W.D.M. Bell, Safari Press, Huntington Beach, CA, 1990. 187 pp., illus. $24.95.
The greatest of elephant books by the greatest-of-all elephant hunter.

A White Hunters Life, by Angus MacLagan, an African Heritage Book, published by Amwell Press, Clinton, NJ, 1983. 283 pp., illus. Limited, signed, and numbered deluxe edition, in slipcase. $100.00.
True to life, a sometimes harsh yet intriguing story.

Wild Ivory, by Horace S. Mazet, Nautulus Books, No. Plainfield, NJ, 1971. 280 pp., illus. $30.00.
The true story of the last of the old elephant hunters.

Wild Sports of Southern Africa, by William Cornwallis Harris, New Holland Press, London, England, 1987. 376 pp., illus. $35.00.
Originally published in 1863, describes the author's travels in Southern Africa.

With a Rifle in Mongolia, by Count Hoyos-Sprizenstein, Safari Press, Long Beach, CA, 1987. 144 pp., illus. In slipcase. $85.00.
First English edition of the author's 1911 expedition to Mongolia and China.

RIFLES

The Accurate Varmint Rifle, by Boyd Mace, Precision Shooting, Inc., Whitehall, NY, 1991. 184 pp., illus. $22.95.
A long overdue and long needed work on what factors go into the selection of components for and the susequent assembly of...the accurate varmint rifle.

The AK-47 Assault Rifle, Desert Publications, Cornville, AZ, 1981. 150 pp., illus. Paper covers. $10.00.
Complete and practical technical information on the only weapon in history to be produced in an estimated 30,000,000 units.

The AR-15/M16, A Practical Guide, by Duncan Long. Paladin Press, Boulder, CO, 1985. 168 pp., illus. Paper covers. $16.95.
The definitive book on the rifle that has been the inspiration for so many modern assault rifles.

***Assault Weapons, 3rd Edition, The Gun Digest Book of,** edited by Jack Lewis, DBI Books, Inc., Northbrook, IL, 1993. 256 pp., illus. Paper covers. $17.95
An in-depth look into the history and uses of these arms.

The Big-Bore Rifle, by Michael McIntosh, Countrysport Press, Traverse City, MI, 1990. 224 pp., illus. $39.50.
The book of fine magazine and double rifles 375 to 700 calibers.

Big Game Rifles and Cartridges, by Elmer Keith, reprint edition by The Gun Room Press, Highland Park, NJ, 1984. 161 pp., illus. $29.95.
Reprint of Elmer Keith's first book, a most original and accurate work on big game rifles and cartridges.

The Black Rifle, M16 Retrospective, R. Blake Stevens and Edward C. Ezell, Collector Grade Publications, Toronto, Canada, 1987. 400 pp., illus. $59.95
The complete story of the M16 rifle and its development.

***The Bolt Action, Volume I,** by Stuart Otteson, Wolfe Publishing Co., Prescott, AZ, 1992. 288 pp., illus. $22.50.
A design analysis of 16 bolt actions including Mauser, Springfield, Enfield, Remington, Winchester, etc.

The Bolt Action, Volume 2, by Stuart Otteson, Wolfe Publishing Co., Inc. Prescott, AZ, 1985. 289 pp., illus. $22.50.
Covers 17 bolt actions from Newton to Ruger.

Bolt Action Rifles, revised edition, by Frank de Haas, DBI Books, Inc., Northbrook, IL, 1984. 448 pp., illus. Paper covers. $18.95.
A revised edition of the most definitive work on all major bolt-action rifle designs. Detailed coverage of over 110 turnbolt actions, including how they function, takedown and assembly, strengths and weaknesses, dimensional specifications.

The Book of the Garand, by Maj.-Gen. J.S. Hatcher, The Gun Room Press, Highland Park, NJ, 1977. 292 pp., illus. $26.95.
A new printing of the standard reference work on the U.S. Army M1 rifle.

The Book of the Rifle, by T.F. Fremantle, Wolfe Publishing Co., Prescott, AZ, 1988. 558 pp., illus. $54.00.
A limited edition reprint. This book records the point of the rifle's evolution at the opening of the 19th century.

The Book of the Twenty-Two: The All American Caliber, by Sam Fadala, Stoeger Publishing Co., So. Hackensack, NJ, 1989. 288 pp., illus. Soft covers. $16.95.
The All American Caliber from BB caps up to the powerful 226 Barnes. It's about ammo history, plinking, target shooting, and the quest for the one-hole group.

The Breech-Loading Single-Shot Rifle, by Major Ned H. Roberts and Kenneth L. Waters, Wolfe Publishing Co., Prescott, AZ, 1987. 333 pp., illus. $32.50.
A comprehensive history of the evolution of Scheutzen and single shot rifles.

Combat Rifles of the 21st Century, by Duncan Long, Paladin Press, Boulder, CO, 1991. 115 pp., illus. Paper covers. $15.00.
An inside look at the U.S. Army's program to develop a super advanced combat rifle to replace the M16.

***Exploded Long Gun Drawings, The Gun Digest Book of** edited by Harold A. Murtz, DBI Books, Inc., Northbrook, IL. 512 pp., illus. Paper covers. $19.95.
Containing almost 500 rifle and shotgun exploded drawings. An invaluable aid to both professionals and hobbyists.

The Fighting Rifle, by Chuck Taylor, Paladin Press, Boulder, CO, 1983. 184 pp., illus. Paper covers. $16.95.
The difference between assault and battle rifles and auto and light machine guns.

***Firearms Assembly/Disassembly Part III: Rimfire Rifles, Revised Edition, The Gun Digest Book of** by J. B. Wood, DBI Books, Inc., Northbrook, IL. 480 pp., illus. Paper covers. $18.95.
Covers 65 popular rimfires plus over 100 variants, all cross-referenced in the index. (Spring '94)

Firearms Assembly/Disassembly Part IV: Centerfire Rifles, Revised Edition, The Gun Digest Book of, by J.B. Wood, DBI Books, Inc., Northbrook, IL, 1991. 480 pp., illus. Paper covers. $17.95.
Covers 54 popular centerfire rifles plus 300 variants. The most comprehensive and professional presentation available to either hobbyist or gunsmith.

F.N.-F.A.L. Auto Rifles, Desert Publications, Cornville, AZ, 1981. 130 pp., illus. Paper covers. $13.95.
A definitive study of one of the free world's finest combat rifles.

A Forgotten Heritage; The Story of a People and the Early American Rifle, by Harry P. Davis, The Gun Room Press, Highland Park, NJ, 1976. 199 pp., illus. $12.95.
Reprint of a very scarce history, originally published in 1941, the Kentucky rifle and the people who used it.

The Golden Age of Single-Shot Rifles, by Edsall James, Pioneer Press, Union City, TN, 1975. 33 pp., illus. Paper covers. $2.75.
A detailed look at all of the fine, high quality sporting single shot rifles that were once the favorite of target shooters.

The History and Development of the M16 Rifle and Its Cartridge, by David R. Hughes, Armory Publications, Oceanside, CA, 1990. 294 pp., illus. $49.95.
Study of small caliber rifle development culminating in the M16 with encyclopedic coverage of the .223/5.56mm cartridge.

***Illustrated Handbook of Rifle Shooting,** by A.L. Russell, Museum Restoration Service, Alexandria Bay, NY, 1992. 194 pp., illus. $24.50.
A new printing of the 1869 edition by one of the leading military marksman of the day.

Keith's Rifles for Large Game, by Elmer Keith, The Gun Room Press, Highland Park, NJ, 1986. 406 pp., illus. $39.95.
Covers all aspects of selecting, equipping, use and care of high power rifles for hunting big game, especially African.

Know Your M1 Garand, by E. J. Hoffschmidt, Blacksmith Corp., Southport, CT, 1975, 84 pp., illus. Paper covers. $9.95.
Facts about America's most famous infantry weapon. Covers test and experimental models, Japanese and Italian copies, National Match models.

Know Your Ruger 10/22 Carbine, by William E. Workman, Blacksmith Corp., Chino Valley, AZ, 1991. 96 pp., illus. Paper covers. $9.95.
The story and facts about the most popular 22 autoloader ever made.

***The Lee Enfield No. 1 Rifles,** by Alan M. Petrillo, Excaliber Publications, Latham, NY, 1992. 64 pp., illus. Paper covers. $10.95.
Highlights the SMLE rifles from the Mark 1-VI.

***The Lee Enfield Number 4 Rifles,** by Alan M. Petrillo, Excalibur Publications, Latham, NY, 1992. 64 pp., illus. Paper covers. $10.95.
A pocket-sized, bare-bones reference devoted entirely to the .303 World War II and Korean War vintage service rifle.

Legendary Sporting Rifles, by Sam Fadala, Stoeger Publishing Co., So. Hackensack, NJ, 1992. 288 pp., illus. Paper covers. $16.95.
Covers a vast span of time and technology beginning with the Kentucky Long-rifle.

The M-14 Rifle, facsimile reprint of FM 23-8, Desert Publications, Cornville, AZ, 50 pp., illus. Paper $7.95.
Well illustrated and informative reprint covering the M-14 and M-14E2.

***Military Bolt Action Rifles, 1841-1918,** by Donald B. Webster, Museum Restoration Service, Alexander Bay, NY, 1993. 150 pp., illus. $27.50.
A photographic survey of the principal rifles and carbines of the European and Asiatic powers of the last half of the 19th century and the first years of the 20th century.

Military and Sporting Rifle Shooting, by Captain E.C. Crossman, Wolfe Publishing Co., Prescott, AZ, 1988. 449 pp., illus. $45.00.
A limited edition reprint. A complete and practical treatise covering the use of rifles.

The Mini-14, by Duncan Long, Paladin Press, Boulder, CO, 1987. 120 pp., illus. Paper covers. $10.00.
History of the Mini-14, the factory-produced models, specifications, accessories, suppliers, and much more.

Modern Military Bullpup Rifles, by T.B. Dugelby, Collector Grade Publications, Toronto, Canada, 1984. 97 pp., illus. $25.00.
The EM-2 concept comes to age.

Modern Sportsman's Gun and Rifle, by J.H. Walsh ("Stonehenge"), Wolfe Publishing Co., Prescott, AZ, 1988. In two volumes, Vol. 1, 459 pp., Vol. 2, 546 pp., illus. $110.00.
A limited edition reprint. An extremely rare set of books first published in 1880s. Covers game, sporting and match rifles, and revolvers.

M1 Carbine Owner's Manual, M1, M2 & M3 .30 Caliber Carbines, Firepower Publications, Cornville, AZ, 1984. 102 pp., illus. Paper covers. $9.95.
The complete book for the owner of an M1 Carbine.

More Single Shot Rifles and Actions, by Frank de Haas, Frank de Haas, Orange City, IA, 1989. 146 pp., illus. Soft covers. $29.95.
A definitive book with in-depth studies, illustrations, drawings and descriptions of over 45 obsolete single shot rifles and actions.

The Pennsylvania Rifle, by Samuel E. Dyke, Sutter House, Lititz, PA, 1975. 61 pp., illus. Paper covers. $5.00.
History and development, from the hunting rifle of the Germans who settled the area. Contains a full listing of all known Lancaster, PA, gunsmiths from 1729 through 1815.

The Remington 700, by John F. Lacy, Taylor Publishing Co., Dallas, TX, 1990. 208 pp., illus. $44.95.
Covers the different models, limited editions, chamberings, proofmarks, serial numbers, military models, and much more.

The Revolving Rifles, by Edsall James, Pioneer Press, Union City, TN, 1975. 23 pp., illus. Paper covers. $2.50.
Valuable information on revolving cylinder rifles, from the earliest matchlock forms to the latest models of Colt and Remington.

Rifle and Marksmanship, by Judge H.A. Gildersleeve, reprinted by W.S. Curtis, Buckinghamshire, England, 1986. 131 pp., illus. $25.00.
Reprint of a book first published in 1878 in New York, catering to the shooter of early breechloaders and late muzzleloaders.

The Rifle Book, by John Walter, Arms & Armour Press, London, England, 1990. 158 pp. illus. $29.95.
The comprehensive one-volume guide to the world's shoulder guns.

***Rifle Guide,** by Sam Fadala, Stoeger Publishing Co., S. Hackensack, NJ, 1993. 288 pp., illus. Paper covers. $16.95.
This comprehensive, fact-filled book beckons to both the seasoned rifleman as well as the novice shooter.

The Rifle in America, by Philip B. Sharpe, Wolfe Publishing Co., Prescott, AZ, 1988. 641 pp., illus. $59.00.
A limited edition reprint. A marvelous volume packed with information for the man who is interested in rifles, from the man whose life was guns.

***The Rifle: Its Development for Big-Game Hunting,** by S.R. Truesdell, Safari Press, Huntington Beach, CA, 1992. 274 pp., illus. $35.00.
The full story of the development of the big-game rifle from 1834-1946.

Rifle Shooting as a Sport, by Bernd Klingner, A.S. Barnes and Co., Inc., San Diego, CA, 1980. 186 pp., illus. Paper covers. $15.00.
Basic principles, positions and techniques by an international expert.

Rifleman's Handbook: A Shooter's Guide to Rifles, Reloading & Results, by Rick Jamison, NRA Publications, Washington, DC, 1990. 303 pp., illus. $21.95.
Helpful tips on precision reloading, how to squeeze incredible accuracy out of an "everyday" rifle, etc.

Riflesmithing, The Gun Digest Book of, by Jack Mitchell, DBI Books, Inc., Northbrook, IL, 1982. 256 pp., illus. Paper covers. $14.95.
Covers tools, techniques, designs, finishing wood and metal, custom alterations.

***Rifles of the World,** by John Walter, DBI Books, Inc., Northbrook, IL, 1993. 320 pp., illus. Paper covers. $19.95.
Compiled as a companion volume to *Pistols of the World*, this brand new reference work covers all centerfire military and commercial rifles produced from the perfection of the metal-case cartridge in the 1870's to the present time.

Ned H. Roberts and the Schuetzen Rifle, edited by Gerald O. Kelver, Brighton, CO, 1982. 99 pp., illus. $15.00.
A compilation of the writings of Major Ned H. Roberts which appeared in various gun magazines.

Schuetzen Rifles, History and Loading, by Gerald O. Kelver, Gerald O. Kelver, Publisher, Brighton, CO, 1972. Illus. $15.00.
Reference work on these rifles, their bullets, loading, telescopic sights, accuracy, etc. A limited, numbered ed.

Semi-Auto Rifles: Data and Comment, edited by Robert W. Hunnicutt, The National Rifle Association, Washington, DC, 1988. 156 pp., illus. Paper covers. $15.95.
A book for those who find military-style self-loading rifles interesting for their history, intriguing for the engineering that goes into their design, and a pleasure to shoot.

Single-Shot Actions, Their Design and Construction, by Frank and Mark Delisse, Dehaas Books, Orange City, IA 1991. 247 pp., illus. $35.00.
Covers the best single shot rifles of the past plus a potpourri of modern single shot rifle actions.

Single-Shot Rifle Finale, by James Grant, Wolfe Publishing Co., Prescott, AZ, 1992. 556 pp., illus. $36.00.
The master's 5th book on the subject and his best.

Single Shot Rifles and Actions, by Frank de Haas, Orange City, IA, 1990. 352 pp., illus. Soft covers. $25.00.
The definitive book on over 60 single shot rifles and actions.

The Springfield Rifle M1903, M1903A1, M1903A3, M1903A4, Desert Publications, Cornville, AZ, 1982. 100 pp., illus. Paper covers. $10.00.
Covers every aspect of disassembly and assembly, inspection, repair and maintenance.

Sixty Years of Rifles, by Paul A. Matthews, Wolfe Publishing Co., Prescott, AZ, 1991. 224 pp., illus. $19.50.
About rifles and the author's experience and love affair with shooting and hunting.

The Sturm, Ruger 10/22 Rifle and .44 Magnum Carbine, by Duncan Long, Paladin Press, Boulder, CO, 1988. 108 pp., illus. Paper covers. $12.00.
An in-depth look at both weapons detailing the elegant simplicity of the Ruger design. Offers specifications, troubleshooting procedures and ammunition recommendations.

U.S. Rifle M14–From John Garand to the M21, by R. Blake Stevens, Collector Grade Publications, Inc., Toronto, Canada, revised second edition, 1991. 350 pp., illus. $47.50.
A classic, in-depth examination of the development, manufacture and fielding of the last wood-and-metal ("lock, stock, and barrel") battle rifle to be issued to U.S. troops.

***War Baby!: The U.S. Caliber 30 Carbine, Volume I,** by Larry Ruth, Collector Grade Publications, Toronto, Canada, 1992. 512 pp., illus. $69.95.
Volume 1 of the in-depth story of the phenomenally popular U.S. caliber 30 carbine. Concentrates on design and production of the military 30 carbine during World War II.

***War Baby Comes Home: The U.S. Caliber 30 Carbine, Volume 2,** by Larry Ruth, Collector Grade Pulications, Toronto, Canada, 1993. 386 pp., illus. $49.95.
The triumphant competion of Larry Ruth's two-volume in-depth series on the most popular U.S. military small arm in history.

The Winchester Model 94: The First 100 Years, by Robert C. Renneberg, Krause Publications, Iola, WI, 1991. 207 pp., illus. $34.95.
Covers the design and evolution from the early years up to today.

SHOTGUNS

The American Shotgun, by Charles Askins, Wolfe Publishing Co., Prescott, AZ, 1988. 321 pp., illus. $39.00.
A limited edition reprint. Askins covers shotguns and patterning extremely well.

The American Shotgun, by David F. Butler, edited by C. Kenneth Ramage, Lyman Publications, Middlefield, CT, 1973. 243 pp., illus. Paper covers. $14.95.
A comprehensive history of the American smoothbore's evolution from Colonial times to the present day.

American Shotgun Design and Performance, by L.R. Wallack, Winchester Press, Piscataway, NJ, 1977. 184 pp., illus. $16.95.
An expert lucidly recounts the history and development of American shotguns and explains how they work.

The American Single Barrel Trap Gun, by Frank F. Conley, Frank F. Conley, Carmel Valley, CA, 1989. 241 pp., illus. $39.95.
History, serial numbers, collecting and how they were made. Covers Baker, Fox, Ithaca, Levefer, Meriden, Parker, L.C. Smith, etc.

Best Guns, by Michael McIntosh, Countrysport, Inc., Traverse City, MI, 1989. 288 pp., illus. $39.50.
Devoted to the best shotguns ever made in the United States and the best presently being made in the world.

*__Black's Wing & Clay, 1992-93 Annual Edition__, JFB, Inc., Red Bank, NJ, 1992. 177 pp., illus. Paper covers. $10.00.
The sportsman's annual guide to wing & clay shooting locations. Over fifty pages of charts, graphs, maps indexes and valuable how-to information for the shotgunner.

The British Shotgun, Volume 1, 1850-1870, by I.M. Crudington and D.J. Baker, Barrie & Jenkins, London, England, 1979. 256 pp., illus. $59.95.
An attempt to trace, as accurately as is now possible, the evolution of the shotgun during its formative years in Great Britain.

The British Shotgun, Volume 2, 1871-1890, by I.M. Crudginton and D.J. Baker, Ashford Press, Southampton, England, 1989. 250 pp., illus. $59.95.
The second volume of a definitive work on the evolution and manufacture of the British shotgun.

Clay Pigeon Shooting for Beginners and Enthusiasts, by John King, The Sportsman's Press, London, England, 1991. 94 pp., illus. $24.95.
John King has devised this splendid guide to clay pigeon shooting in the same direct style in which he teaches at his popular Barbury Shooting School near Swindon.

Clay Shooting, by Peter Croft, Ward Lock, London, England, 1990. 160 pp., illus, $29.95.
A complete guide to Skeet, trap and sporting shooting.

*__Clay Target Handbook__ by Jerry Meyer, Lyons & Buford, Publisher, New York, NY, 1993. 182 pp., illus. $22.95.
Contains in-depth, how-to-do-it information on trap, Skeet, sporting clays, international trap, international Skeet and clay target games played around the country.

Clay Target Shooting, by Paul Bentley, A&C Black, London, England, 1987. 144 pp., illus. $25.00.
Practical book on clay target shooting written by a very successful international competitor, providing valuable professional advice and instruction for shooters of all disciplines.

Cradock on Shotguns, by Chris Cradock, Banford Press, London, England, 1989. 200 pp., illus. $45.00.
A definitive work on the shotgun by a British expert on shotguns.

The Defensive Shotgun, by Louis Awerbuck, S.W.A.T. Publications, Cornville, AZ, 1989. 77 pp., illus. Soft covers. $12.95.
Cuts through the myths concerning the shotgun and its attendant ballistic effects.

The Double Shotgun, by Don Zutz, Winchester Press, Piscataway, NJ, 1985. 304 pp., illus. $19.95.
Revised, updated, expanded edition of the history and development of the world's classic sporting firearms.

*__Ed Scherer on Sporting Clays__, by Ed Scherer, Ed Scherer, Elk Grove, WI, 1993. 200 pp., illus. Paper covers. $29.95.
Covers footwork, gun fit, master eye checks, recoil reduction, noise abatement, eye and ear protection, league shooting, shot sizes and chokes.

*__Exploded Long Gun Drawings, The Gun Digest Book of__ edited by Harold A. Murtz, DBI Books, Inc., Northbrook, IL. 512 pp., illus. Paper covers. $19.95.
Containing almost 500 rifle and shotgun exploded drawings. An invaluable aid to both professionals and hobbyists.

Field, Cover and Trap Shooting, by Adam H. Bogardus, Wolfe Publishing Co., Prescott, AZ, 1988. 446 pp., illus. $43.00.
A limited edition reprint. Hints for skilled marksmen as well as young sportsmen. Includes haunts and habits of game birds and waterfowl.

Finding the Extra Target, by Coach John R. Linn & Stephen A. Blumenthal, Shotgun Sports, Inc., Auburn, CA, 1989. 126 pp., illus. Paper covers. $14.95.
The ultimate training guide for all the clay target sports.

Firearms Assembly/Disassembly, Part V: Shotguns, Revised Edition, The Gun Digest Book of, by J.B. Wood, DBI Books, Inc., Northbrook, IL, 1992. 480 pp., illus. Paper covers. $17.95.
Covers 46 popular shotguns plus over 250 variants. The most comprehensive and professional presentation available to either hobbyist or gunsmith.

*__A.H. Fox "The Finest Gun in the World"__, by Michael McIntosh, Countrysport Press, Traverse City, MI, 1993. 392 pp., illus. $49.95.
The first full-length biography of famed American gunmaker Ansley H. Fox and the detailed history of one of America's finest shotguns.

*__Fucili D'Autore (The Best Guns)__, by Marco E. Nobili, London Guns, Ltd., Santa Barbara, CA, 1992. 845 pp., illus. $125.00.
An exhaustive study on Italian luxury-grade shotguns and their makers, with information on European makers as well. Text in English and Italian.

The Golden Age of Shotgunning, by Bob Hinman, Wolfe Publishing Co., Inc., Prescott, AZ, 1982. $17.95.
A valuable history of the late 1800s detailing that fabulous period of development in shotguns, shotshells and shotgunning.

Hartman on Skeet, By Barney Hartman, Stackpole Books, Harrisburg, PA, 1973. 143 pp., illus. $14.95.
A definitive book on Skeet shooting by a pro.

The Ithaca Gun Company From the Beginning, by Walter Claude Snyder, Cook & Uline Publishing Co., Spencerport, NY, 1991. 256 pp., illus. $59.95.
The entire "familyk of Ithaca Gun Company products is described together with a photo gallery section containing many previously unpublished photographs of the gun makers.

L.C. Smith Shotguns, by Lt. Col. William S. Brophy, The Gun Room Press, Highland Park, NJ, 1979. 244 pp., illus. $35.00.
The first work on this very important American gun and manufacturing company.

Lefever: Guns of Lasting Fame, by Robert W. (Bob) Elliot and Jim Cobb, Robert W. (Bob) Elliot, Lindale, TX, 1986. 174 pp., illus. $35.00.
Hundreds of photographs, patent drawings and production figures are given on this famous maker's shotguns.

A Manual of Clayshooting, by Chris Cradock, Hippocrene Books, Inc., New York, NY, 1983. 192 pp., illus. $39.95.
Covers everything from building a range to buying a shotgun, with lots of illus. & dia.

The Modern Shotgun, by Major Sir Charles Burrard, Ashford Press, Southampton, England, 1986 reprint of this 3-volume set. The set, $150.00.
Reprinting of the most classic and informative work on the shotgun.

The Mysteries of Shotgun Patterns, by George G. Oberfell and Charles E. Thompson, Oklahoma State University Press, Stillwater, OK, 1982. 164 pp., illus. Paper covers. $25.00.
Shotgun ballistics for the hunter in non-technical language.

The Orvis Wing-Shooting Handbook, by Bruce Bowlen, Nick Lyons Books, New York, NY, 1985. 83 pp., illus. Paper covers. $8.95.
Proven techniques for better shotgunning.

Police Shotgun Manual, by Bill Clede, Stackpole Books, Harrisburg, PA, 1986. 128 pp., illus. $18.95.
Latest shotgun techniques for tough situations.

Purdey's, the Guns and the Family, by Richard Beaumont, David and Charles, Pomfert, VT, 1984. 248 pp., illus. $39.95.
Records the history of the Purdey family from 1814 to today, how the guns were and are built and daily functioning of the factory.

Recreating the Double Barrel Muzzle-Loading Shotgun, by William R. Brockway, George Shumway Publisher, York, PA, 1985. 198 pp., illus. Paper covers. $20.00.
Treats the making of double guns of classic type.

*__Reloading for Shotgunners, 3rd Edition__, by Edward A. Matunas, DBI Books, Inc., Northbrook, IL, 1993. 288 pp., illus. Paper covers. $16.95.
Expanded reloading tables with over 2,000 loads. Bushing charts for every major press and component maker. All new presentation on all aspects of shotshell reloading by one of the top experts in the field.

Robert Churchill's Game Shooting, edited by MacDonald Hastings, Countrysport Press, Traverse City, MI, 1990. 252 pp., illus. $29.50.
A new revised edition of the definitive book on the Churchill method of instinctive wingshooting for game and Sporting Clays.

75 Years with the Shotgun, by C.T. (Buck) Buckman, Valley, Publ., Fresno, CA, 1974. 141 pp., illus. $10.00.
An expert hunter and trapshooter shares experiences of a lifetime.

*__Scherer on Skeet 2__, by Ed Scherer, Ed. Scherer, Waukesha, WI, 1993. 121 pp., illus. Paper covers. $19.95.
A "teaching" book, featuring the eight Skeet stations plus shootoff doubles.

Shooting at Clays, by Alan Jarrett, Stanley Paul, London, England, 1991. 176 pp., illus. $34.95.
This book unravels the complexities of clay pigeon shooting.

The Shooting Field with Holland & Holland, by Peter King, Quiller Press, London, England, new & enlarged edition, 1990. 184 pp., illus. $49.95.
The story of a company which has produced excellence in all aspects of gunmaking.

The Shotgun in Combat, by Tony Lesce, Desert Publications, Cornville, AZ, 1979. 148 pp., illus. Paper covers. $10.00.
A history of the shotgun and its use in combat.

*__Shotgun Digest, 4th Edition__, edited by Jack Lewis, DBI Books, Inc., Northbrook, IL, 1993. 256 pp., illus. Paper covers. $16.95.
The all-new edition looking at what's happening with shotguns and shotgunning today.

Shotgun Gunsmithing, The Gun Digest Book of, by Ralph Walker, DBI Books, Inc., Northbrook, IL, 1983. 256 pp., illus. Paper covers. $14.95.
The principles and practices of repairing, individualizing and accurizing modern shotguns by one of the world's premier shotgun gunsmiths.

Shotgun Stuff, by Don Zutz, Shotgun Sports, Inc., Auburn, CA, 1991. 172 pp., illus. Paper covers. $19.95.
This book gives shotgunners all the "stuff" they need to achieve better performance and get more enjoyment from their favorite smoothbore.

Shotgunner's Notebook: The Advice and Reflections of a Wingshooter, by Gene Hill, Countrysport Press, Traverse City, MI, 1990. 192 pp., illus. $24.50.
Covers the shooting, the guns and the miscellany of the sport.

Shotgunning: The Art and the Science, by Bob Brister, Winchester Press, Piscataway, NJ, 1976. 321 pp., illus. $17.95.
Hundreds of specific tips and truly novel techniques to improve the field and target shooting of every shotgunner.

Shotgunning Trends in Transition, by Don Zutz, Wolfe Publishing Co., Prescott, AZ, 1990. 314 pp., illus. $29.50.
This book updates American shotgunning from post WWII to present.

Shotguns and Cartridges for Game and Clays, by Gough Thomas, edited by Nigel Brown, A & C Black, Ltd., Cambs, England, 1989. 256 pp., illus. Soft covers. $24.95.
Gough Thomas' well-known and respected book for game and clay pigeon shooters in a thoroughly up-dated edition.

Shotguns by Keith, by Elmer Keith, Wolfe Publishing Co., Prescott, AZ, 1988. 305 pp., illus. $39.00.
A limited edition reprint. The master reveals his knowledge again.

Sidelocks & Boxlocks, by Geoffrey Boothroyd, Sand Lake Press, Amity, OR, 1991. 271 pp., illus. $29.95.
The story of the classic British shotgun.

The Sporting Clay Handbook, by Jerry Meyer, Lyons and Burford Publishers, New York, NY, 1990. 140 pp., illus. Soft covers. $14.95.
Introduction to the fastest growing, and most exciting, gun game in America.

Sporting Clays, The Gun Digest Book of, by Jack Lewis, DBI Books, Inc., Northbrook, IL, 1991. 224 pp., illus. Paper covers. $16.95.
A superb introduction to the fastest growing gun game in America.

Sporting Clays, by Michael Pearce, Stackpole Books, Harrisburg, PA, 1991. 192 pp., illus. $16.95.
Expert techniques for every kind of clays course.

The Story of the Sporting Gun, by Ranulf Rayner, Trafalgar Square, North Pomfret, VT, 1991. 96 pp., illustrated. $75.00.
This magnificent volume traces the story of game shooting from the early development of the shotgun to the present day.

Trap & Skeet Shooting, 2nd Edition, The Gun Digest Book of, by Art Blatt, DBI Books, Inc., Northbrook, IL, 1989. 288 pp., illus. Paper covers. $16.95.
This new edition contains valuable info. for the inter. and adv. competition shooter.

Turkey Hunter's Digest, by Dwain Bland, DBI Books, Inc., Northbrook, IL, 1986. 256 pp., illus. Paper covers. $15.95.
Describes and pictures all varieties of turkey. Offers complete coverage on calls, calling techniques, appropriate guns, bows, cameras and other equipment.

U.S. Shotguns, All Types, reprint of TM9-285, Desert Publications, Cornville, AZ, 1987. 257 pp., illus. Paper covers. $9.95.
Covers operation, assembly and disassembly of nine shotguns used by the U.S. armed forces.

*__U.S. Winchester Trench and Riot Guns and Other U.S. Military Combat Shotguns__, by Joe Poyer, North Cape Publications, Tustin, CA, 1992. 124 pp., illus. Paper covers. $15.95.
A detailed history of the use of military shotguns, and the acquisition procedures used by the U.S. Army's Ordnance Department in both World Wars.

The Winchester Model Twelve, by George Madis, David Madis, Dallas, TX, 1984. 176 pp., illus. $19.95.
A definitive work on this famous American shotgun.

The Winchester Model 42, by Ned Schwing, Krause Pub., Iola, WI, 1990. 159 pp., illus. $39.95.
Behind-the-scenes story of the model 42's invention and its early development. Production totals and manufacturing dates; reference work.

Winchester Shotguns and Shotshells, by Ronald W. Stadt, Armory Publications, Tacoma, WA, 1984. 184 pp., illus. $34.95.
From the hammer and double guns to the Model 59.

Winchester's Finest, the Model 21, by Ned Schwing, Krause Publicatons, Inc., Iola, WI, 1990. 360 pp., illus. $49.95.
The classic beauty and the interesting history of the Model 21 Winchester shotgun.

The World's Fighting Shotguns, by Thomas F. Swearengen, T. B. N. Enterprises, Alexandria, VA, 1979. 500 pp., illus. $34.95.
The complete military and police reference work from the shotgun's inception to date, with up-to-date developments.

ARMS ASSOCIATIONS

UNITED STATES

ALABAMA

Alabama Gun Collectors Assn.
Secretary, P.O. Box 6080, Tuscaloosa, AL 35405

ALASKA

Alaska Gun Collectors Assn., Inc.
Gereth Stillman, Pres., 1554 Myrtle, Eagle River, AK 99577

ARIZONA

Arizona Arms Assn.
Don DeBusk, President, 4837 Bryce Ave., Glendale, AZ 85301

CALIFORNIA

California Waterfowl Assn.
4630 Northgate Blvd., #150, Sacramento, CA 95834
Greater Calif. Arms & Collectors Assn.
Donald L. Bullock, 8291 Carburton St., Long Beach, CA 90808-3302
Los Angeles Gun Ctg. Collectors Assn.
F.H. Ruffra, 20810 Amie Ave., Apt. #9, Torrance, CA 90503

COLORADO

Colorado Gun Collectors Assn.
L.E.(Bud) Greenwald, 2553 S. Quitman St., Denver, CO 80219/303-935-3850

CONNECTICUT

Ye Connecticut Gun Guild, Inc.
Dick Fraser, P.O. Box 425, Windsor, CT 06095

FLORIDA

Tampa Bay Arms Collectors' Assn.
John Tuvell, 2461-67th Ave., S., St., Petersburg, FL 33712
Unified Sportsmen of Florida
P.O. Box 6565, Tallahassee, FL 32314

GEORGIA

Georgia Arms Collectors Assn., Inc.
Michael Kindberg, President, P.O. Box 277, Alpharetta, GA 30239-0277

ILLINOIS

Illinois State Rifle Assn.
P.O. Box 27, Kankakee, IL 60901
Illinois Gun Collectors Assn.
T.J. Curl, Jr., P.O. Box 971, Kankakee, IL 60901
Mississippi Valley Gun & Cartridge Coll. Assn.
Bob Filbert, P.O. Box 61, Port Byron, IL 61275/309-523-2593
Sauk Trail Gun Collectors
Gordell M. Matson, P.O. Box 1113, Milan, IL 61264
Wabash Valley Gun Collectors Assn., Inc.
Jerry D. Holycross, RR #6, Box 341, Danville, IL 61832

INDIANA

Indiana Sportsmen's Council-Legislative
Maurice Latimer, P.O. Box 93, Bloomington, IN 47402
Indiana State Rifle & Pistol Assn.
Thos. Glancy, P.O. Box 552, Chesterton, IN 46304
Southern Indiana Gun Collectors Assn., Inc.
Sheila McClary, 309 W. Monroe St., Boonville, IN 47601/812-897-3742

IOWA

Beaver Creek Plainsmen Inc.
Steve Murphy, Secy., P.O. Box 298, Bondurant, IA 50035

Central States Gun Collectors Assn.
Avery Giles, 1104 S. 1st Ave., Marshtown, IA 50158

KANSAS

Kansas Cartridge Collectors Assn.
Bob Linder, Box 84, Plainville, KS 67663

KENTUCKY

Kentuckiana Arms Collectors Assn.
Ralph Handy, President, Box 1776, Louisville, KY 40201
Kentucky Gun Collectors Assn., Inc.
Ruth Johnson, Box 64, Owensboro, KY 42302/502-729-4197

LOUISIANA

Washitaw River Renegades
Sandra Rushing, P.O. Box 256, Main St., Grayson, LA 71435

MARYLAND

Baltimore Antique Arms Assn.
Stanley I. Kellert, 8340 Dubbs Dr., Severn, MD 21144

MASSACHUSETTS

Bay Colony Weapons Collectors, Inc.
John Brandt, Box 111, Hingham, MA 02043
Massachusetts Arms Collectors
John J. Callan, Jr., 1887 Main St., Leicester, MA 01524-1943/508-892-3837

MISSISSIPPI

Mississippi Gun Collectors Assn.
Jack E. Swinney, P.O. Box 16323, Hattiesburg, MS 39402

MISSOURI

Mineral Belt Gun Collectors Assn.
D.F. Saunders, 1110 Cleveland Ave., Monett, MO 65708
Missouri Valley Arms Collectors Assn., Inc.
L.P Brammer II, Membership Secy., P.O. Box 33033, Kansas City, MO 64114

MONTANA

Montana Arms Collectors Assn.
Lewis E. Yearout, 308 Riverview Dr. East, Great Falls, MT 59404
The Winchester Arms Collectors Assn.
Richard Berg, P.O. Box 6754, Great Falls, MT 59406

NEW HAMPSHIRE

New Hampshire Arms Collectors, Inc.
Frank H. Galeucia, Rt. 28, Box 44, Windham, NH 03087

NEW JERSEY

Englishtown Benchrest Shooters Assn.
Michael Toth, 64 Cooke Ave., Carteret, NJ 07008
Jersey Shore Antique Arms Collectors
Joe Sisia, P.O. Box 100, Bayville, NJ 08721
New Jersey Arms Collectors Club, Inc.
Angus Laidlaw, President, 230 Valley Rd., Montclair, NJ 07042/201-746-0939

NEW YORK

Empire State Arms Collectors Assn.
P.O. Box 2328, Rochester, NY 14623
Iroquois Arms Collectors Assn.
Bonnie Robinson, Show Secy., P.O. Box 142, Ransomville, NY 14131/716-791-4096
Mid-State Arms Coll. & Shooters Club
Jack Ackerman, 24 S. Mountain Terr., Binghamton, NY 13903

NORTH CAROLINA

North Carolina Gun Collectors Assn.
Jerry Ledford, 3231-7th St. Dr. NE, Hickory, NC 28601

OHIO

Ohio Gun Collectors Assn.
P.O. Box 24170, Cincinnati, OH 45224-0170
The Stark Gun Collectors, Inc.
William I. Gann, 5666 Waynesburg Dr., Waynesburg, OH 44688

OKLAHOMA

Indian Territory Gun Collector's Assn.
P.O. Box 4491, Tulsa, OK 74159

OREGON

Oregon Arms Collectors Assn., Inc.
Phil Bailey, P.O. Box 13000-A, Portland, OR 97213
Oregon Cartridge Collectors Assn.
Gale Stockton, 52 N.W. 2nd, Gresham, OR 97030

PENNSYLVANIA

Presque Isle Gun Collectors Assn.
James Welch, 156 E. 37 St., Erie, PA 16504

SOUTH CAROLINA

Belton Gun Club, Inc.
J.K. Phillips, 195 Phillips Dr., Belton, SC 29627
South Carolina Shooting Assn.
P.O. Box 12658, Columbia, SC 29211-2658
Membership Div.: William Strozier, Secretary, P.O. Box 70, Johns Island, SC 29457-0070

SOUTH DAKOTA

Dakota Territory Gun Coll. Assn., Inc.
Curt Carter, Castlewood, SD 57223

TENNESSEE

Smoky Mountain Gun Coll. Assn., Inc.
Hugh W. Yabro, President, P.O. Box 23225, Knoxville, TN 37933
Tennessee Gun Collectors Assn., Inc.
M.H. Parks, 3556 Pleasant Valley Rd., Nashville, TN 37204

TEXAS

Houston Gun Collectors Assn., Inc.
P.O. Box 741429, Houston, TX 77274-1429
Texas Cartridge Collectors Assn., Inc.
James C. Sartor, Sec./Tres., 5606 Duxbury St., Houston, TX 77035
Texas Gun Collectors Assn.
13201 Wells Fargo Trail, Austin, TX 78737
Texas State Rifle Assn.
P.O. Drawer 710549, Dallas, TX 75371

WASHINGTON

Washington Arms Collectors, Inc.
J. Dennis Cook, P.O. Box 7335, Tacoma, WA 98407

WISCONSIN

Great Lakes Arms Collectors Assn., Inc.
Edward C. Warnke, 2913 Woodridge Lane, Waukesha, WI 53188
Wisconsin Gun Collectors Assn., Inc.
Lulita Zellmer, P.O. Box 181, Sussex, WI 53089

WYOMING

Wyoming Weapons Collectors
P.O. Box 284, Laramie, WY 82070/307-745-4652 or 745-9530

NATIONAL ORGANIZATIONS

Amateur Trapshooting Assn.
601 W. National Rd., Vandalia, OH 45377

American Coon Hunters Assn.
Opal Johnston, P.O. Cadet, Route 1, Box 492, Old Mines, MO 63630

American Custom Gunmakers Guild
Jan Billeb, Exec. Director, P.O. Box 812, Burlington, IA 52601-0812/319-752-6114

American Defense Preparedness Assn.
Two Colonial Place, 2101 Wilson Blvd., Suite 400, Arlington, VA 22201-3061

American Pistolsmiths Guild
Hamilton S. Bowen, President, P.O. Box 67, Louisville, TN 37777

American Police Pistol & Rifle Assn.
3801 Biscayne Blvd., Miami, FL 33137

American Single Shot Rifle Assn.
Gary Staup, Secy., 709 Carolyn Dr., Delphos, OH 45833/419-692-3866

American Society of Arms Collectors
George E. Weatherly, P.O. Box 2567, Waxahachie, TX 75165

Association of Firearm and Toolmark Examiners
Eugenia A. Bell, Secy., 7857 Esterel Dr., LaJolla, CA 92037; Membership Secy., Andrew B. Hart, 80 Mountain View Ave., Rensselaer, NY 12144

Boone & Crockett Club
241 South Fraley Blvd., P.O. Box 547, Dumfries, VA 22026

Browning Collectors Assn.
Bobbie Hamit, P.O. Box 526, Aurora, NE 68818/402-694-6602

The Cast Bullet Assn., Inc.
Ralland J. Fortier, Membership Director, 4103 Foxcraft Dr., Traverse City, MI 49684

Citizens Committee for the Right to Keep and Bear Arms
Natl. Hq., Liberty Park, 12500 NE Tenth Pl., Bellevue, WA 98005

Colt Collectors Assn.
3200 Westminster, Dallas, TX 75205

Ducks Unlimited, Inc.
One Waterfowl Way, Memphis, TN 38120

Fifty Caliber Shooters Assn.
11469 Olive St. Rd., Suite 50, St. Louis, MO 63141

Firearms Coalition
Box 6537, Silver Spring, MD 20906/301-871-3006

Firearms Engravers Guild of America
Robert Evans, Secy., 332 Vine St., Oregon City, OR 97045

Foundation for North American Wild Sheep
720 Allen Ave., Cody, WY 82414

Garand Collectors Assn.
P.O. Box 181, Richmond, KY 40475

Golden Eagle Collectors Assn.
Chris Showler, 11144 Slate Creek Rd., Grass Valley, CA 95945

Gun Owners of America
8001 Forbes Place, Suite 102, Springfield, VA 22151/703-321-8585

Handgun Hunters International
J.D. Jones, Director, P.O. Box 357 MAG, Bloomingdale, OH 43910

Harrington & Richardson Gun Coll. Assn.
George L. Cardet, 525 NW 27th Ave., Suite 201, Miami, FL 33125

Hopkins & Allen Arms & Memorabilia Society (HAAMS)
1309 Pamela Circle, Delphos, OH 45833

International Benchrest Shooters
Joan Borden, RD 1, Box 244A, Tunkhannock, PA 18657

International Cartridge Coll. Assn., Inc.
Charles Spano, P.O. Box 5297, Ormond Beach, FL 32174-5297

IHMSA (Intl. Handgun Metallic Silhouette Assn.)
Frank Scotto, 127 Winthrop Terr., Meriden, CT 06450

IPPA (International Paintball Players Assn.)
P.O. Box 90974, Los Angeles, CA 90009/310-322-3107

Jews for the Preservation of Firearms Ownership (JPFO)
2872 S. Wentworth Ave., Milwaukee, WI 53207/414-769-0760

The Mannlicher Collectors Assn.
Rev. Don L. Henry, Secy., P.O. Box 7144, Salem, OR 97303

Marlin Firearms Collectors Assn., Ltd.
Dick Paterson, Secy., 407 Lincoln Bldg., 44 Main St., Champaign, IL 61820

Miniature Arms Collectors/Makers Society, Ltd.
Donald A. Beck, Secretary, 3329 Palm St., Granite City, IL 62040/618-877-5284

M1 Carbine Collectors Assn. (M1-CCA)
P.O. Box 4895, Stateline, NV 89449

National Association of Buckskinners
Tim Pray, 1981 E. 94th Ave., Thornton, CO 80229

The National Association of Derringer Collectors
P.O. Box 160671, San Antonio, TX 78280

National Assn. of Federally Licensed Firearms Dealers
Andrew Molchan, 2455 E. Sunrise, Ft. Lauderdale, FL 33304

National Association to Keep and Bear Arms
P.O. Box 78336, Seattle, WA 98178

National Automatic Pistol Collectors Assn.
Tom Knox, P.O. Box 15738, Tower Grove Station, St. Louis, MO 63163

National Bench Rest Shooters Assn., Inc.
Pat Baggett, 2027 Buffalo, Levelland, TX 79336

National Firearms Assn.
P.O. Box 160038, Austin, TX 78716

National Muzzle Loading Rifle Assn.
Box 67, Friendship, IN 47021

National Reloading Manufacturers Assn.
One Centerpointe Dr., Suite 300, Lake Oswego, OR 97035

National Rifle Assn. of America
1600 Rhode Island Ave., NW, Washington, DC 20036

National Shooting Sports Foundation, Inc.
Robert T. Delfay, President, Flintlock Ridge Office Center, 11 Mile Hill Rd., Newtown, CT 06470-2359/203-426-1320; FAX: 203-426-1087

National Skeet Shooting Assn.
Mike Hampton, Exec. Director, P.O. Box 680007, San Antonio, TX 78268-0007

National Sporting Clays Association
P.O. Box 680007, San Antonio, TX 78268/800-877-5338

National Wild Turkey Federation, Inc.
P.O. Box 530, Edgefield, SC 29824

North American Hunting Club
P.O. Box 3401, Minnetonka, MN 55343

North-South Skirmish Assn., Inc.
Stevan F. Meserve, Exec. Secretary, 204 W. Holly Ave., Sterling, VA 22170-4006

Remington Society of America
Leon W. Wier Jr., President, 22526 Leyte Dr., Torrance, CA 90505

Rocky Mountain Elk Foundation
P.O. Box 8249, Missoula, MT 59807-8249

Ruger Collector's Assn., Inc.
P.O. Box 1441, Yazoo City, MS 39194

Safari Club International
Philip DeLone, Admin. Dir., 4800 W. Gates Pass Rd., Tucson, AZ 85745/602-620-1220

Sako Collectors Assn., Inc.
Karen Reed, 1725 Woodhill Ln., Bedford, TX 76021

Second Amendment Foundation
James Madison Building, 12500 NE 10th Pl., Bellevue, WA 98005

Smith & Wesson Collectors Assn.
George Linne, 2711 Miami St., St. Louis, MO 63118

The Society of American Bayonet Collectors
P.O. Box 234, East Islip, NY 11730-0234

Southern California Schuetzen Society
Dean Lillard, 34657 Ave. E., Yucaipa, CA 92399

Sporting Arms & Ammunition Manufacturers Institute (SAAMI)
Flintlock Ridge Office Center, 11 Mile Hill Rd., Newtown, CT 06470-2359/203-426-1320; FAX: 203-426-1087

Sporting Clays of America (SCA)
Linda Fairchild, Director of Membership Services, 9 Mott Ave., Suite 103, Norwalk, CT 06850/203-831-8483; FAX: 203-831-8497

The Thompson/Center Assn.
Joe Wright, President, Box 792, Northboro, MA 01532/508-393-3834

USPSA/IPSC
Dave Stanford, P.O. Box 811, Sedro Woolley, WA 98284/206-855-2245

U.S. Revolver Assn.
Chick Shuter, 96 West Union St., Ashland, MA 01721

The Varmint Hunters Assn., Inc.
Box 730, Lone Grove, OK 73443/405-657-3098

Weatherby Collectors Assn., Inc.
P.O. Box 128, Moira, NY 12957

The Wildcatters
P.O. Box 170, Greenville, WI 54942

Winchester Arms Collectors Assn.
Richard Berg, Executive Secy., P.O. Box 6754, Great Falls, MT 59406

The Women's Shooting Sports Foundation (WSSF)
Glynne Moseley, 1505 Highway 6 South, Suite 103, Houston, TX 77077

AUSTRALIA

Sporting Shooters Assn. of Australia, Inc.
P.O. Box 2066, Kent Town, SA 5071, Australia

CANADA

ALBERTA

Canadian Historical Arms Society
P.O. Box 901, Edmonton, Alb., Canada T5J 2L8

National Firearms Assn.
Natl. Hq: P.O. Box 1779, Edmonton, Alb., Canada T5J 2P1

ONTARIO

Tri-County Antique Arms Fair
P.O. Box 122, RR #1, North Lancaster Ont., Canada K0C 1Z0

EUROPE

ENGLAND

Arms and Armour Society
E.J.B. Greenwood, Field House, Upper Dicker, Hailsham, East Sussex, BN27 3PY, England

Historical Breechloading Smallarms Assn.
D.J. Penn M.A., Imperial War Museum, Lambeth Rd., London SE 1 6HZ, England.
Journal and newsletter are $12 a yr., plus surcharge for airmail.

National Rifle Assn.
(Great Britain) Bisley Camp, Brookwood, Woking Surrey GU24 OPB, England/0483.797777

FRANCE

Syndicat National de l'Arqueuserie du Commerce de l'Arme Historique
B.P. No. 3, 78110 Le Vesinet, France

GERMANY

Deutscher Schützenbund
Lahnstrasse 120, W-6200 Wiesbaden-Klarenthal, Germany

NEW ZEALAND

New Zealand Deerstalkers Assn.
Michael Watt, P.O. Box 6514, Wellington, New Zealand

SOUTH AFRICA

Historical Firearms Soc. of South Africa
P.O. Box 145, 7725 Newlands, Republic of South Africa

SAGA (S.A. Gunowners' Assn.)
P.O. Box 35204, Northway 4065, Republic of South Africa

DIRECTORY
OF THE
ARMS TRADE

The **Product Directory** contains a total of 53 product categories. A black bullet preceding the manufacturer's name indicates the availability of a Warranty Service Center address, which can be found on page 460.

The **Manufacturers' Directory** lists the manufacturers alphabetically with their addresses, phone numbers and FAX numbers, if available.

DIRECTORY OF THE ARMS TRADE INDEX

PRODUCT DIRECTORY

AMMUNITION, COMMERCIAL

Action Arms Ltd.
ACTIV Industries, Inc.
A-Square Co., Inc.
Black Hills Ammunition
Blammo Ammo
Blount, Inc. Sporting Equipment
   Division
Bottom Line Shooting Supplies
Buck Stix
Buck-X, Inc
The BulletMakers Workshop
California Magnum
CBC
Century International Arms, Inc.
ChinaSports, Inc.
Cor-Bon Bullet & Ammo Co.
Daisy Mfg. Co.
Diana
Denver Bullets, Inc.
Dynamit Nobel-RWS, Inc.
Eley Ltd.
Elite Ammunition
Enguix Import-Export
Estate Cartridge, Inc.
Federal Cartridge Co.
Fiocchi of America, Inc.
FN Herstal
Gamo
Garrett Cartridges, Inc.
GDL Enterprises
Glaser Safety Slug, Inc.
"Gramps"Antique Cartridges
Hansen Cartridge Co.
Hirtenberger Aktiengesellschaft
Hornady Mfg. Co.
ICI-America
IMI
Jones, J.D.
Kent Cartridge Mfg. Co. Ltd.
Lapua Ltd.

Lethal Force Institute
M&D Munitions Ltd.
Maionchi-L.M.I.
MAGTECH Recreational
   Products, Inc.
Markell, Inc.
Master Class Bullets
Men—Metallwerk
   Elisenhuette, GmbH
Midway Arms, Inc.
New England Ammunition Co.
Neutralizer Police Munitions
Old Western Scrounger, Inc.
Omark Industries
Paragon Sales & Services, Inc.
PMC/Eldorado Cartridge Corp.
Police Bookshelf
Pony Express Reloaders
Precision Delta Corp.
Precision Prods. of Wash., Inc.
Pro Load Ammunition, Inc.
Ravell Ltd.
Remington Arms Co., Inc.
Rocky Fork Enterprises
Royal Arm International Products
Rucker Ammunition Co.
RWS
Safari Gun Co.
Sherwood Intl. Export Corp.
SOS Products Co.
Speer Products
Star Reloading Co., Inc.
3-D Ammunition & Bullets
3-Ten Corp.
USAC
Valor Corp.
Weatherby, Inc.
Winchester Div., Olin Corp.
Wosenitz VHP, Inc.
Zero Ammunition Co., Inc.

AMMUNITION, CUSTOM

AFSCO Ammunition
All American Bullets
Ballistica Maximus North
Ballistica Maximus South
Beeman Precision Airguns, Inc.
Bertram Bullet Co.
Bottom Line Shooting Supplies
Brynin, Milton
Buck Stix
The BulletMakers Workshop
Cartridges Unlimited
Country Armourer, The
Cubic Shot Shell Co., Inc.
Custom Hunting Ammo & Arms
Custom Tackle & Ammo
Dakota Arms
Deadeye Sport Center
DKT, Inc.
E.A.A. Corp.
Eagle Flight Bullet Co.
Elite Ammunition
Elko Arms, L. Kortz
Ellis Sport Shop, E.W.
Epps "Orillia" Ltd., Ellwood
Estate Cartridge, Inc.
Fitz Pistol Grip Co.
Freedom Arms, Inc.
Gammog, Gregory B. Gally
GDL Enterprises
"Gramps" Antique Cartridges
Granite Custom Bullets
Hardin Specialty Dist.
Heidenstrom Bullets
Hindman, Ace
Hirtenberger Aktiengesellschaft
Horizons Unlimited
Jensen's Custom Ammunition

Jensen's Firearm Academy
Jett & Co., Inc.
Kaswer Custom, Inc.
Keeler, R.H.
Kent Cartridge Mfg. Co. Ltd.
KJM Brass Group
Lindsley Arms Cartridge Co.
Lomont Precision Bullets, Kent
MagSafe Ammo Co.
Marple & Associates, Dick
McMurdo, Lynn
M&D Munitions Ltd.
Monte Kristo Pistol Grip Co.
Mountain South
Newman Gunshop
Old Western Scrounger, Inc.
Personal Protection Systems Ltd.
Precision Delta Corp.
Precision Munitions, Inc.
Sanders Custom Gun Service
Sandia Die & Cartridge Co.
SOS Products Co.
Specialty Gunsmithing
Spence, George W.
SSK International
Star Custom Bullets
State Arms Gun Co.
Stewart's Gunsmithing
3-D Ammunition & Bullets
Three-Ten Corp.
Vitt/Boos
Weaver Arms Corp.
Westley Richards & Co.
Worthy Products, Inc.
Wosenitz VHP, Inc.
Wyoming Armory, Inc.

AMMUNITION, FOREIGN

Action Arms Ltd.
AFSCO Ammunition
Bertram Bullet Co.
Bottom Line Shooting Supplies

Brenneke KG, Wilhelm
The BulletMakers Workshop
Cartridges Unlimited
CBC

Champion's Choice, Inc.
Cubic Shot Shell Co., Inc.
Diana
Dynamit Nobel-RWS, Inc.
Enguix Import-Export
Estate Cartridge, Inc.
Fiocchi of America, Inc.
FN Herstal
Gamo
"Gramps" Antique Cartridges
Hansen Cartridge Co.
Hirtenberger Aktiengesellschaft
IMI
K.B.I., Inc.
Lapua Ltd.
Maionchi-L.M.I.

MAGTECH Recreational
   Products, Inc.
Merkuria Ltd.
New England Arms Co.
Old Western Scrounger, Inc.
Paragon Sales & Services, Inc.
PMC/Eldorado Cartridge Corp.
Precision Delta Corp.
R.E.T. Enterprises
Rocky Fork Enterprises
RWS
Safari Gun Co.
Sako, Ltd.
Samco Global Arms, Inc.
T.F.C. S.p.A.

AMMUNITION COMPONENTS—BULLETS, POWDER, PRIMERS

Acadian Ballistic Specialties
Accuracy Unlimited (Glendale, AZ)
Accurate Arms Co., Inc.
ACTIV Industries, Inc.
Alaska Bullet Works
Allred Bullet Co.
Alpha LaFranck
American Bullets
A-Square Co., Inc.
American Products Co.
Armfield Custom Bullets
Ballard Built Custom Bullets
Ballistic Products, Inc.
Banaczkowski Bullets
Barnes Bullets, Inc.
Bell Reloading, Inc.
Berger Bullets, Ltd.
Berry's Bullets
Bertram Bullet Co.
Bitterroot Bullet Co.
Black Hills Shooters Supply
Black Mountain Bullets
Blount, Inc. Sporting Equipment
   Division
Blue Mountain Bullets
Brenneke KG, Wilhelm
Brown Co., E. Arthur
Brownells, Inc.
BRP, Inc.
Bruno Shooters Supply
Buckeye Custom Bullets
Buck Stix
Buffalo Bullet Co., Inc.
Buffalo Rock Shooters Supply
Bullet, Inc.
Bull-X, Inc.
Bullseye Bullets
Burling Bullets
Buzztail Brass
Calhoon Varmint Bullets, James
Canadian Custom Bullets
Carnahan Bullets
Cartridge Co., C.W.
Cartridges Unlimited
Canyon Cartridge Corp.
CFVentures
Champion's Choice, Inc.
Cheddite France S.A.
CheVron Bullets
Circle M Custom Bullets
Classic Brass
Competitor Corp., Inc.
Cook Bullets
Cook Engineering Service
Cor-Bon Bullet & Ammo Co.
Crawford Co., Inc., R.M.
Creative Cartridge Co.
Cummings Bullets
Custom Bullets by Hoffman
Cutsinger Benchrest Bullets
D&J Bullet Co. & Custom
   Gun Shop, Inc.
Denver Bullets, Inc.
DKT, Inc.
Dohring Bullets
DuPont
E.A.A. Corp.
Ed's Custom Bullets
Eichelberger Bullets, Wm.
Eiland Custom Bullets
Enguix Import-Export

Eureka Bullets
Federal Cartridge Co.
Finch Custom Bullets
Fiocchi of America, Inc.
Fitz Pistol Grip Co.
Fowler Bullets
Foy Custom Bullets
Freedom Arms, Inc.
Fusilier Bullets
G&C Bullet Co., Inc.
Gise Bullets
GOEX, Inc.
Gotz Bullets
Grand Falls Bullets
Granite Custom Bullets
Green Bay Bullets
Greenwalt Rifles
Grizzly Bullets
Group Tight Bullets
Gun City
Hammets VLD Bullets
Hansen Cartridge Co.
Harris Enterprises
Harrison Bullet Works
Hawk Co.
Hawk Laboratories, Inc.
Heidenstrom Bullets
Hercules, Inc.
Higgs Bullets
High Country Custom Bullets
Hirtenberger Aktiengesellschaft
Hobson Precision
   Manufacturing Co.
Hodgdon Powder Co., Inc.
Hornady Mfg. Co.
HT Bullets
Idaho Bullets
Imperical Magnum Corp.
IMR Powder Co.
IMI
J-4, Inc.
Jensen Bullets
Jensen's Custom Ammunition
Jensen's Firearms Acadamy
Jester Bullets
JLK Bullets
Ka Pu Kapili
Kasmarsnik Bullets
Kaswer Custom, Inc.
Keith's Bullets
Ken's Kustom Kartridge
Kent Cartridge Mfg. Co. Ltd.
Keystone Bullets
KJM Brass Group
Kodiak Custom Bullets
Kustom Kast Bullets
Lachaussee, S.A.
Lage Uniwad, Inc.
Lane Bullets
Lapua Ltd.
Lathrop's, Inc.
Lindsley Arms Cartridge Co.
Lomont Precision Bullets, Kent
Magnus Bullets
Maine Custom Bullets
Maionchi-L.M.I.
Marchmon Bullets
Master Class Bullets
McKenzie Bullet Co.
McMurdo, Lynn
M&D Munitions Ltd.

MEC
Merkuria Ltd.
Michael's Antiques
Miller Enterprises, Inc.
Mitchell Bullets, R.F.
MoLoc Bullets
Montana Precision Swaging
Mulhern, Rick
Mullins Ammo
Murmur Corp.
Mushroom Express Bullet Co.
Nagel's Bullets
NAK Custom Bullets
National Bullet Co.
Naval Ordanance Works
Necromancer Industries, Inc.
Newman Gunshop
Norma
Northern Precision Custom
     Swaged Bullets
Nosler, Inc.
O'Connor Rifle Products Co., Ltd.
Old Wagon Bullets
Old Western Scrounger, Inc.
Omark Industries
Ordnance Works, The
Pace Marketing, Inc.
Page Custom Bullets
Patchbox & Museum of
     the Great Divide, The
Patrick Bullets
Patriot Manufacturing
Pattern Control
Phillippi Custom Bullets, Justin
Polywad, Inc.
Pomeroy, Robert
Pony Express Reloaders
Precision Components & Guns
Precision Delta Corp.
Precision Munitions, Inc.
Precision Reloading, Inc.
Prescott Projectile Co.
Price Bullets, Patrick W.
Rainier Ballistic Corp.
Ranch Products
Ravell Ltd.
Red Willow Tool & Armory, Inc.
Redwood Bullet Works
Reloading Specialties
Remington Arms Co., Inc.
Rencher Bullets
Renner Co., R.J./Radical Concepts
R.I.S. Co., Inc.
Rolston, Jr., Fred
Rossi, Amadeo

Rubright Bullets
Rucker Ammunition Co.
Sako, Ltd.
Scharch Mfg., Inc.
Scot Powder Co. of Ohio, Inc.
Schmidtman Custom Ammunition
Schneider Bullets
Shappy Bullets
Sheidan USA, Inc., Austin
Sioux Bullets
Small Group Bullets
SOS Products Co.
Southern Ammunition Co., Inc.
Specialty Gunsmithing
Stanley Bullets
Star Custom Bullets
Stark's Bullets Manufacturing
Stevi Machine, Inc.
Stewart's Gunsmithing
Swift Bullet Co.
Taracorp Industries
TCCI
T.F.C. S.p.A.
3-D Ammunition & Bullets
Thompson Precision
TMI Products
Tooley, David
Trico Plastics
Trophy Bonded Bullets, Inc.
True Flight Bullet Co.
USAC
Vann Custom Bullets
Vihtavuori Oy
Vincent's Shop
Vitt/Boos
Warren Muzzleloading Co., Inc.
Watson Trophy Match Bullets
Weisner Bullets
Whitestone Lumber Corp.
White Systems, Inc.
Widener's Reloading &
     Shooting Supply
Williams Bullet Co., J.R.
Winchester Div., Olin Corp.
Windjammer Tournament
     Wads, Inc.
Winkle Bullets
Woodland Bullets
Worthy Products, Inc.
Wosenitz VHP, Inc.
Wyant Bullets
Wyoming Casting Co.
Wyoming Custom Bullets
Zero Ammunition Co., Inc.

ANTIQUE ARMS DEALERS

Ad Hominem
Ammunition Consulting
     Services, Inc.
Antique American Firearms
Antique Arms Co.
Aplan Antiques & Art, James O.
Arms, Jackson
Beeman Precision Airguns, Inc.
Boggs, Wm.
British Arms Co. Ltd.
Buckskin Machine Works
Cape Outfitters
Carlson, Douglas R.
Chadick's Ltd.
Champlin Firearms, Inc.
Classic Guns, Inc.
Colonial Repair
Condon, Inc., David
Corry, John
Cullity Restoration, Daniel
D&D Gunsmiths, Ltd.
Dilliott Gunsmithing, Inc.
Dyson & Son Ltd., Peter
Ed's Gun House
Epps "Orillia" Ltd., Ellwood
Fagan & Co., William
Fish, Marshall F.
Flayderman & Co., N.
Flintlock Muzzle Loading
     Gun Shop, The
Frielich Police Equipment
Fulmer's Antique Firearms, Chet
Glass, Herb
Goergen Gun Shop, Inc.
Golden Age Arms Co.
Gun Works, The

Hallowell & Co.
Hansen & Co.
Hunkeler, A.
Jackson Arms
Kelley's
Ledbetter Airguns, Riley
LeFever Arms Co., Inc.
Lever Arms Service Ltd.
Lock's Philadelphia Gun Exchange
Log Cabin Sport Shop
Martin's Gun Shop
Mendez, John A.
Montana Outfitters
Museum of Historical Arms, Inc.
Muzzleloaders Etcetera, Inc.
New England Arms Co.
New Orleans Arms Co.
Paragon Sales & Services, Inc.
Patchbox & Museum
     of the Great Divide, The
Pioneer Guns
Pony Express Sport Shop, Inc.
P.S.M.G. Gun Co.
Ravell Ltd.
Retting, Inc., Martin B.
Rutgers Book Center
Semmer, Charles
Sherwood Intl. Export Corp.
S&S Firearms
Steves House of Guns
Stott's Creek Armory, Inc.
Ward & Van Valkenburg
Wiest, M.C.
Wood, Frank S.
Yearout, Lewis E.

APPRAISERS—GUNS, ETC.

Ahlman Guns
Ammunition Consulting
     Services, Inc.
Amodei, Jim
Antique Arms Co.
Aplan Antiques & Art, James O.
Beeman Precision Airguns, Inc.
Blue Book Publications, Inc.
Bustani Appraisers, Leo
Butterfield & Butterfield
Camilli, Lou
Cannon's Guns
Chadick's Ltd.
Christie's East
Christopher Firearms Co., Inc., E.
Clark Firearms Engraving
Classic Guns, Inc.
Clements' Custom
     Leathercraft, Chas
Condon, Inc., David
Cullity Restoration, Daniel
Custom Tackle & Ammo
D&D Gunsmiths, Ltd.
Dixon Muzzleloading Shop, Inc.
D.O.C. Specialists, Inc.
Ed's Gun House
Ellis Sport Shop, E.W.
Epps "Orillia" Ltd., Ellwood
Eversull Co., Inc., K.
Fagan & Co., William
Fish, Marshall F.-Mfg. Gunsmith
Flayderman & Co., Inc., N.
Forgett, Valmore J., Jr.
Fredrick Gun Shop
Frontier Arms Co., Inc.
Goergen's Gun Shop, Inc.
Golden Age Arms Co.
Gonzalez Guns, Ramon B.
Goodwin, Fred
Greenwald, Leon E. "Bud"
Griffin & Howe, Inc.
Guns
Hallowell & Co.
Hansen & Co.
Holster Shop, The
Hughes, Steven Dodd
Irwin, Campbell H.
Jaeger, Inc., Paul/Dunn's
Jonas Appraisals & Taxidermy, Jack

Kelley's
Ledbetter Airguns, Riley
LeFever Arms Co., Inc.
Lock's Philadelphia Gun Exchange
Mack's Sport Shop
Mac's .45 Shop
Marple & Associates, Dick
Martin's Gun Shop
McGowan Rifle Barrels
Montana Outfitters
Museum of Historical Arms, Inc.
Muzzleloaders Etcetera, Inc.
Navy Arms Co.
Novak's .45 Shop, Wayne
Orvis Co., The
Parke-Bernet
Parker-Hale
Pentheny de Pentheny
Perazzi U.S.A., Inc.
Pettinger Books, Gerald
Pony Express Sport Shop, Inc.
Precision Arms International, Inc.
P.S.M.G. Gun Co.
R.E.T. Enterprises
Richards, John
Safari Outfitters Ltd.
Shell Shack
Shooting Gallery, The
Silver Ridge Gun Shop
S.K. Guns, Inc.
Sotheby's
S&S Firearms
Stott's Creek Armory, Inc.
Stratco, Inc.
Strawbridge, Victor W.
Thurston Sports, Inc.
Tillinghast, James C.
Ulrich, Doc & Bud
Unick's Gunsmithing
Vic's Gun Refinishing
Vintage Industries, Inc.
Wayne Firearms for Collectors and
     Investors, James
Whildin & Sons Ltd., E.H.
Whitestone Lumber Corp.
Wiest, M.C.
Wood, Frank S.
Yearout, Lewis E.

AUCTIONEERS—GUNS, ETC.

Ammunition Consulting
     Services, Inc.
Bourne Co., Inc., Richard A.
Butterfield & Butterfield
Christie's East
Fagan & Co., William
Goodwin, Fred

Kelley's
"Little John's" Antique Arms
Parke-Bernet
Silver Ridge Gun Shop
Sotheby's
Tillinghast, James C.

BOOKS (Publishers and Dealers)

ADC, Inc.
American Handgunner Magazine
Aplan Antiques & Art, James O.
Armory Publications
Arms & Armour Press, Ltd.
Beeman Precision Airguns, Inc.
Blacksmith Corp.
Blacktail Mountain Books
Blue Book Publications, Inc.
Brownell's, Inc.
Calibre Press, Inc.
Colorado Sutlers Arsenal
Corbin, Inc.
DBI Books, Inc.
Executive Protection Institute
Flores Publications, Inc., J.
Fortress Publications, Inc.
Golden Age Arms Co.
"Gramps" Antique Cartridges
Gun City
Guncraft Sports, Inc.
Gun Hunter Books
Gun Room Press, The
GUNS Magazine
Gunnerman Books
Handgun Press
H&P Publishing
Hodgdon Powder Co., Inc.
Hungry Horse Books
Ironside International
     Publishers, Inc.
Jackson Arms
King & Co.

Krause Publications
Lane Publishing
LBT
Madis, David
Magma Engineering Co.
Martin, J.
McKee Publications
Mountain South
NECO
New Win Publishing, Inc.
NgraveR Co., The
North American Pine
     Training Center
Old Western Scrounger, Inc.
Outdoorsman's Bookstore, The
Paladin Press
Pease Accuracy, Bob
Pejsa Ballistics
Petersen Publishing Co.
Pettinger Books, Gerald
PFRB Co.
Pranger, Ed G.
Quack Decoy Corp.
Ravell Ltd.
R.G.-G., Inc.
Riling Arms Books Co., Ray
Rutgers Book Center
Rutgers Gun & Boat Center
Safari Press, Inc.
S.A.F.E.
Shootin' Accessories, Ltd.
Stackpole Books
Stoeger Publishing Co.

Survival Books/The Larder
Thomas, Charles C.
Threat Management Institute
Trafalgar Square
Trotman, Ken
Vintage Industries, Inc.

VSP Publishers
Wahl Corp., Paul
Weisz Antique Gun Parts
Wilderness Sound Productions Ltd.
Wolfe Publishing Co.

BULLET AND CASE LUBRICANTS

Armite Laboratories
Blackhawk East
Blackhawk Mountain
Blackhawk West
Blount, Inc. Sporting Equipment
  Division
Bullet Swaging Supply, Inc.
Camp-Cap Products
CFVentures
Cooper-Woodward
Corbin, Inc.
Dillon Precision Prods., Inc.
Fitz Pistol Grip Co.
GAR
Gozon Corp.
Guardsman Products
Hollywood Engineering
Hornady Mfg. Co.
Huntington Die Specialties
INTEC International, Inc.
Javelina Products
Lane Bullets, Inc.
LBT

Lee Precision, Inc.
Lighthouse Mfg. Co., Inc.
Lithi Bee Bullet Lube
Magma Engineering Co.
Micro-Lube
Monte Kristo Pistol Grip Co.
M&N Bullet Lube
Ox-Yoke Originals, Inc.
Ravell Ltd.
RCBS
Reardon Products
SAECO
Shay's Gunsmithing
Shooters Accessory Supply
Slipshot MTS Group
Small Custom Mould & Bullet Co.
Tamarack Products, Inc.
Thompson Bullet Lube Co.
Thompson/Center Arms
Watson Trophy Match Bullets
White Systems, Inc.
Young Country Arms

BULLET SWAGE DIES AND TOOLS

Advance Car Mover Co.
Blount, Inc. Sporting Equipment
  Division
Bruno Shooters Supply
Brynin, Milton
Bullet Swaging Supply, Inc.
C-H Tool & Die Corp./4-D Custom
  Die Co.
Corbin, Inc.
Fitz Pistol Grip Co.

Hollywood Engineering
Lachaussee, S.A.
MoLoc Bullets
Monte Kristo Pistol Grip Co.
NECO
Necromancer Industries, Inc.
Rorschach Precision Products
Speer Products
Sport Flite Manufacturing Co.

CARTRIDGES FOR COLLECTORS

Ad Hominem
Ammunition Consulting
  Services, Inc.
Baekgaard Ltd.
Cameron's
Campbell, Dick
Duffy, Chas. E.
Ed's Gun House
Eichelberger Bullets, Wm.
Epps "Orillia" Ltd., Ellwood
First Distributors, Inc., Jack
Forty Five Ranch Enterprises
Gun City
"Gramps" Antique Cartridges
Hansen & Co.

Idaho Ammunition Service
Kelley's
Lock's Philadelphia Gun Exchange
Montana Outfitters
Mountain Bear Rifle Works, Inc.
Muzzleloaders Etcetera, Inc.
Old Western Scrounger, Inc.
Paragon Sales & Services, Inc.
Ranch Products
Ravell Ltd.
San Francisco Gun Exchange
Tillinghast, James C.
Ward & Van Valkenburg
Yearout, Lewis E.

CASES, CABINETS, RACKS AND SAFES—GUN

A&B Industries, Inc.
Abel Safe & File, Inc.
Airmold, W.R. Grace & Co.-Conn.
Alco Carrying Cases
Allen Co., Bob
Allen Co., Inc.
Allen Sportswear, Bob
American Display Co.
American Security Products Co.
Americase
Ansen Enterprises
Arizona Custom Case
Arkfeld Mfg. & Dist. Co., Inc.
Art Jewel Enterprises Ltd.
Ashby Turkey Calls
Bandera Gun Locker
Barramundi Corp.
Bill's Custom Cases
Big Sky Racks, Inc.
Big Spring Enterprises "Bore Stores"
Black Sheep Brand
Boyt
Brauer Bros. Mfg. Co.
Browning Arms Co.
Brunsport, Inc.
Bucheimer, J.M.
Bushmaster Hunting & Fishing
Cannon Safe, Inc.
Cascade Fabrication
Chipmunk
CoBalt Mfg., Inc.

Crane & Crane Ltd.
Dara-Nes, Inc.
Dee Zee Alumna Sports
Doskocil Mfg. Co., Inc.
DTM International, Inc.
Elk River, Inc.
EMF Co., Inc.
English Inc., A.G.
Enhanced Presentations, Inc.
Epps "Orillia" Ltd., Ellwood
Eversull Co., Inc., K.
Fort Knox Security Products
Frontier Safe Co.
Galati Internationl
GAR
Granite Custom Bullets
Gun-Ho Sports Cases
Gun Vault, Inc.
Gusdorf Corp.
Hafner Creation, Inc.
Hall Plastics, Inc., John
Harrison-Hurtz Enterprises, Inc.
Homak Mfg. Co., Inc.
Huey Gun Cases, Marvin
Hugger Hooks Co.
Hunter Co., Inc.
Hunting Classics Ltd.
Impact Case Co.
Johnson Gunsmithing, Inc., Neal G.
Johnston Bros.
Jumbo Sports Products

Kalispel Case Line
Kane Products, Inc.
KK Air International
Knock on Wood Antiques
Kodiak Safe
Kolpin Mfg., Inc.
Lakewood Products, Inc.
Liberty Safe
Maloni, Russ
Marsh, Mike
Maximum Security Corp.
McGuire, Bill
McWelco Products
Morton Booth Co.
Mountain States Engraving
M/S Deepeeka Exports Pvt. Ltd.
National Security Safe Co., Inc.
Nesci Enterprises, Inc.
Nielsen Custom Cases
Oregon Arms, Inc.
Otto, Tim
Outa-Site Gun Carriers
Outdoor Connection, Inc., The
Palmer Metal Products
Penguin Industries, Inc.
Perazzi U.S.A., Inc.
Pflumm Gun Mfg. Co.
PistolPAL Products

Protecto Plastics
Prototech Industries, Inc.
Quality Arms, Inc.
Red Head, Inc.
Russwood Custom Pistol Grips
San Angelo Sports Products, Inc.
Savana Sports, Inc.
Schulz Industries
Sonderman, Robert B.
Sportsman's Communicators
Sun Welding Safe Co.
Sweet Home, Inc.
Tinks & Ben Lee Hunting Products
Tread Corp.
Unick's Gunsmithing
Verdemont Fieldsports
Waller & Son, Inc., W.
WAMCO, Inc.
Warren, Kenneth W.
Weatherby, Inc.
Weather Shield Sports
  Equipment, Inc.
Wellington Outdoors
Wilson Case, Inc.
Woodstream
Zanotti Armor
Ziegel Engineering

CHOKE DEVICES, RECOIL ABSORBERS AND RECOIL PADS

Action Products, Inc.
Answer Products Co.
Arms Ingenuity Co.
Baker, Stan
B-Square Co.
Briley Mfg., Inc.
Butler Creek Corp.
C&H Research
Cape Outfitters
Cation
Cellini, Inc., Vito Francesca
Clinton River Gun Serv., Inc.
Colonial Arms, Inc.
Danuser Machine Co.
Delta Vectors, Inc.
E.A.A. Corp.
Fabian Bros. Sporting Goods, Inc.
FAPA Corp.
Franchi S.p.A., Luigi
Frontier Arms Co., Inc.
Gentry Custom Gunmaker, David
Great 870 Co., The
Griggs Products
Harper, William E.
Hastings Barrels
Intermountain Arms
Jaeger, Inc., Paul/Dunn's

Jenkins Recoil Pads, Inc.
KDF, Inc.
Kick Eez
LaRocca Gun Works, Inc.
London Guns Ltd.
Mag-Na-Port Int'l, Inc.
Marble Arms Corp.
McGowen Rifle Barrels
MCRW Associates
Moneymaker Guncraft Corp.
Morrow, Bud
Nelson/Weather-rite
Nu-Line Guns, Inc.
Oakland Custom Arms, Inc.
One Of A Kind
Pachmayr Ltd.
Palsa Outdoor Products
Pro-Port Ltd.
Protektor Model Co.
Ravell Ltd.
Royal Arm International Products
Shotguns Unlimited
S.K. Guns, Inc.
Thompson/Center Arms
Trulock Tool
Upper Missouri Trading Co.

CHRONOGRAPHS AND PRESSURE TOOLS

Canons Delcour
Chronotech
Competition Electronics, Inc.
Custom Chronograph, Inc.
D&H Precision Tooling
Dedicated Systems

Lachaussee, S.A.
Oehler Research, Inc.
P.A.C.T., Inc.
Shooting Chrony, Inc.
Stratco, Inc.
Tepeco

CLEANING AND REFINISHING SUPPLIES

Acculube II, Inc.
Accupro Gun Care
Accuracy Products, S.A.
ADCO International
American Gas & Chemical Co., Ltd.
Armoloy Co. of Ft. Worth
Belltown, Ltd.
Beretta, Dr. Franco
Big 45 Frontier Gun Shop
Bill's Gun Repair
Birchwood Laboratories, Inc.
Blount, Inc. Sporting Equipment
  Division
Break-Free
Bridgers Best
Brobst, Jim
Browning Arms Co.
Bruno Shooters Supply
Chopie Mfg., Inc.
Clenzoil Corp.
Corbin, Inc.
Crane & Crane Ltd.
Creedmoor Sports, Inc.
Crouse's Country Cover
Custom Products
Decker Shooting Products
M/S Deepeeka Exports Pvt. Ltd.

Dewey Mfg. Co., Inc., J.
Dri-Slide, Inc.
Du-Lite Corp.
Dutchman's Firearms, Inc., The
Dykstra, Doug
Eezox, Inc.
Faith Associates, Inc.
Flitz International Ltd.
Flouramics, Inc.
Forster Products
Forty-Five Ranch
Frontier Products Co.
G96 Products Co., Inc.
Golden Age Arms Co.
Gozon Corp.
Graves Co.
Guardsman Products
Gun Works, The
Half Moon Rifle Shop
Heatbath Corp.
Hoppe's Div.
INTEC International, Inc.
Iosso Marine Products
Jantz Supply
J-B Bore Cleaner
Johnson Gunsmithing, Inc., Neal G.
Johnston Bros.

Jonad Corp.
Kleen-Bore, Inc.
Kopp, Terry K.
Lee Supplies, Mark
LEM Gun Specialties, Inc.
LPS Laboratories, Inc.
LT Industries, Inc.
Marble Arms Corp.
Micro Sight Co.
Mountain View Sports, Inc.
Munger, Robert D.
Muscle Products Corp./Firepower
   Lubricants
Nesci Enterprises, Inc.
Northern Precision Custom
   Swaged Bullets
Old World Oil Products
Omark Industries
Outers Laboratories, Div. of Blount
Ox-Yoke Originals, Inc.
Parker Gun Finishes
Pendleton Royal
Pflumm Gun Mfg. Co.
P&M Sales and Service
Precision Sports
Prolix®
Pro-Shot Products, Inc.
Radiator Specialty Co.
Ravell Ltd.
R&S Industries Corp.
Rice, Keith

Richards Classic Oil Finish, John
Rickard, Inc., Pete
RIG Products Co.
Robar Co.'s, Inc., The
Rusteprufe Laboratories
Rusty Duck Premium Gun Care
   Products
San Angelo Sports Products, Inc.
Scott, Inc., Tyler
Shooter's Choice
Shootin' Accessories, Ltd.
Slipshot MTS Group
Speer Products
Sports Support Systems, Inc.
Stoney Point Products, Inc.
Svon Corp.
TDP Industries, Inc.
TETRA Gun Lubricants
Texas Platers Supply Co.
T.F.C. S.p.A.
Treso, Inc.
United States Products Co.
Valor Corp.
Van Gorden & Son, Inc., C.S.
Verdemont Fieldsports
Watson Trophy Match Bullets
WD-40 Co.
White Rock Tool & Die
Williams Shootin' Iron Service
Young Country Arms
Z-Coat Industrial Coatings, Inc.

COMPUTER SOFTWARE—BALLISTICS

ADC, Inc.
AmBr Software Group Ltd.
Arms, Peripheral Data Systems
Ballistic Program Co., Inc., The
Best Load
Blount, Inc. Sporting Equipment
   Division
Canons Delcour
Corbin Applied Technology
Corbin, Inc.
Country Armourer, The
Data Tech Software Systems
Destination North Software
Exe, Inc.

Ford, Jack
J.I.T. Ltd.
Lachaussee, S.A.
Lee Precision, Inc.
Load From A Disk
Magma Engineering Co.
Maionchi-L.M.I.
Oehler Research, Inc.
P.A.C.T., Inc.
Pejsa Ballistics
Ravell Ltd.
Regional Associates
Sierra Bullets
Vancini, Carl A./Bestload

CUSTOM GUNSMITHS

Accuracy Gun Shop
Accuracy Unlimited (Glendale, AZ)
Accurate Plating & Weaponry, Inc.
Ackley Rifle Barrels, P.O.
Adair Custom Shop, Bill
Ahlman Guns
Ahrends, Kim
Aldis Gunsmithing & Shooting
   Supply
Alpine's Precision Gunsmithing &
   Indoor Shooting Range
American Custom Gunmakers Guild
Amrine's Gun Shop
Answer Products Co.
Apel, Dietrich
Armament Gunsmithing Co., Inc.
Arms Craft Gunsmithing
Arms Ingenuity Co.
Armscorp. USA, Inc.
Armurier Hiptmayer
Arrieta, S.L.
Art's Gun & Sport Shop, Inc.
A&W Repair
AWC Systems Technology
B&C
Bain & Davis, Inc.
Baity's Custom Gunworks
Barnes Bullets, Inc.
Barton Technology
Barta's Gunsmithing
Baumannize, Inc.
Beaver Lodge
Beeman Precision Airguns, Inc.
Behlert Precision
Beitzinger, George
Belding's Custom Gun Shop
Bell & Carlson, Inc.
Bellm Contenders
Benchmark Guns
Bengtson Arms Co., L.
Biesen, Al
Biesen, Roger
Billeb, Stephen L.
Billings Gunsmiths, Inc.
Bolden's
Boltin, John M.

Borovnik KG, Ludwig
Bowerly, Kent
Brace, Larry D.
Brgoch, Frank
Briganti & Co., A.
Briley Mfg., Inc.
Broken Gun Ranch
Brown Precision, Inc.
Bruno Shooters Supply
Buck Stix
Buckhorn Gun Works
Buckskin Machine Works
Budin, Dave
Burgess and Son Gunsmiths, R.W.
Burkhart Gunsmithing, Don
Burres, Jack
Bustani Appraisers, Leo
Cache La Poudre Rifleworks
CAM Enterprises
Camilli, Lou
Campbell, Dick
Cannon's Guns
Carter's Gun Shop
Caywood, Shane J.
Chicasaw Gun Works
Christopher Firearms Co., Inc., E.
Chuck's Gun Shop
Clark Custom Guns, Inc.
Clark Firearms Engraving
Classic Arms Corp.
Classic Guns, Inc.
Clinton River Gun Service, Inc.
Cloward's Gun Shop
Cochran, Oliver
Colonial Repair
Competitive Pistol Shop, The
Conrad, C.A.
Cook, John
Corkys Gun Clinic
Costa, David
Cox, C. Ed
Creekside Gun Shop, Inc.
Cumberland Knife & Gun Works
Curtis Custom Shop
Custom Barrel Electropolishing
Custom Checkering Service

Custom Firearms
Custom Gun Products
Custom Gunsmiths
Custom Gun Stocks
Custom Shop, The
Dangler, Homer L.
Darlington Gun Works, Inc.
Davis Service Center, Bill
D.D. Custom Rifles
D&D Gunsmiths, Ltd.
Dever Co., Jack
Devereaux, R.H. "Dick"
DGS, Inc.
Dilliott Gunsmithing, Inc.
Donnelly, C.P.
Dowtin Gunworks
Duffy, Charles E.
Duncan's Gun Works, Inc.
Dyson & Son Ltd., Peter
E.A.A. Corp.
Eagle Flight Bullet Co.
Echols & Co., D'Arcy
Eckelman Gunsmithing
Echols & Co., D'Arcy
Eggleston, Jere D.
EMF Co., Inc.
Emmons, Bob
Erhardt, Dennis
Eversull Co., Inc., K.
Eyster Heritage Gunsmiths, Inc.,
   Ken
Fanzoj GmbH
Farmer-Dressell, Sharon
Fautheree, Andy
Fellowes, Ted
Ferris Firearms
First Distributors, Inc., Jack
Fish, Marshall F.-Mfg. Gunsmith
Fisher, Jerry A.
Flaig's
Fleming Firearms
Flynn's Custom Guns
Fogle, James W.
Forster, Kathy
Forster, Larry L.
Forthofer's Gunsmithing &
   Knifemaking
Forty-Niner Trading Co.
Francesca Stabilizer's, Inc.
Francotte & Cie S.A., Auguste
Frank Custom Gun Service, Ron
Fredrick Gun Shop
Frontier Arms Co., Inc.
Furr Arms
Gander Mountain, Inc.
Garrett Accur-Lt. D.F.S. Co.
Gator Guns & Repair
Genecco Gun Works, K.
Gentry Custom Gunmaker, David
Gillmann, Edwin
Gilman-Mayfield, Inc.
Giron, Robert E.
Goens, Dale W.
Goodling's Gunsmithing
Goodwin, Fred
Gordie's Gun Shop
Grace, Charles E.
Graybill's Gun Shop
Green, Roger M.
Greenwalt Rifles
Greg Gunsmithing Repair
Griffin & Howe, Inc.
Gun Shop, The
Guns
Gunsite Gunsmithy
Gunsmithing Ltd.
Gun Works, The
Gutridge, Inc.
Hagn Rifles & Actions, Martin
Hallberg Gunsmith, Fritz
Hammans, Charles E.
Hammond Custom Guns Ltd., Guy
Hank's Gun Shop
Hanson's Gun Center, Dick
Hardison, Charles
Hart & Son, Inc., Robert W.
Hecht, Hubert J.
Heilmann, Stephen
Heinie Specialty Products
Hensler, Jerry
Hensley, Darwin
Heppler, Keith
Heppler's Machining
High Bridge Arms, Inc.
Hill, Loring F.
Hiptmayer, Klaus
H&L Gun Works

Hoag, James W.
Hobaugh, Wm.
Hobbie Gunsmithing, Duane A.
Hodgson, Richard
Hoehn's Shooting Supply
Hoenig & Rodman
Hofer Jagdwaffen, P.
Holland, Dick
Hollis Gun Shop
Horst, Alan K.
Huebner, Corey O.
Hughes, Steven Dodd
Hunkeler, Al
Huntington Die Specialties
Hyper-Single, Inc.
Intermountain Arms
Irwin, Campbell H.
Ivanoff, Thomas G.
Jackalope Gun Shop
Jaeger, Inc., Paul/Dunn's
Jarrett Rifles, Inc.
Jet Comp Systems
Jim's Gun Shop
Johnson Gunsmithing, Inc., Neal G.
Johnston, James
Jones, J.D.
Juenke, Vern
Jurras, L.E.
K-D, Inc.
KDF, Inc.
Kehr, Roger
Keith's Custom Gunstocks
Ken's Gun Specialties
King's Gun Works
Klein Custom Guns, Don
Kleinendorst, K.W.
Kneiper Custom Rifles, Jim
Knippel, Richard
Kopp, Terry K.
Korzinek Riflesmith, J.
LaFrance Specialties
Lair, Sam
Lampert, Ron
LaRocca Gun Works, Inc.
Lawson Co., Harry
Lee's Red Ramps
LeFever Arms Co., Inc.
Liberty Antique Gunworks
Lilja Precision Rifle Barrels
Lind Custom Guns, Al
Linebaugh Custom Sixguns
   & Rifle Works
Lock's Philadelphia Gun Exchange
Long, George F.
Mac's .45 Shop
Mag-Na-Port Int'l, Inc.
Mahoney, Philip Bruce
Mahony, Philip Bruce
Makinson, Nicholas
Mandarino, Monte
Manley Shooting Supplies, Lowell
Marent, Rudolf
Martin's Gun Shop
Masker, Seely
Mathews & Son, Inc., Geo. E.
Mazur Restoration, Pete
McCament, Jay
McGowen Rifle Barrels
McGuire, Bill
McMillan Gunworks, Inc.
MCS, Inc.
Mercer Custom Stocks, R.M.
Mid-America Recreation, Inc.
Miller Arms, Inc.
Miller Co., David
Miller Custom
Miller, Tom
Mills Jr., Hugh B.
Moeller, Steve
Monell Custom Guns
Moneymaker Guncraft Corp.
Moreton/Fordyce Enterprises
Morrison Custom Rifles, J.W.
Morrow, Bud
Mountain Bear Rifle Works, Inc.
Mowreys Guns & Gunsmithing
Mullis Guncraft
Mustra's Custom Guns, Inc., Carl
Nastoff's 45 Shop Inc., Steve
Nelson, Stephen E.
Nettestad Gun Works
New England Custom Gun Service
Newman Gunshop
Nickels, Paul R.
Nicklas, Ted
Nolan, Dave
Norman Custom Gunstocks, Jim

North American Shooting Systems
North Fork Custom Gunsmithing
Novak's .45 Shop, Wayne
Nowlin Custom Barrels Mfg.
Nu-Line Guns, Inc.
Oakland Custom Arms, Inc.
Old World Gunsmithing
Olson, Vic
Orvis Co., The
Ottmar, Maurice
Pace Marketing, Inc.
Pachmayr Ltd.
Pagel Gun Works, Inc.
Pasadena Gun Center
Paterson Gunsmithing
Pell, John T.
PEM's Mfg. Co.
Pence Precision Barrels
Penrod Precision
Pentheny de Pentheny
Peterson Gun Shop, Inc., A.W.
Powell & Son (Gunmakers) Ltd.,
  William
Power Custom, Inc.
Practical Tools, Inc.
Precision Arms International, Inc.
Professional Gunsmiths of America
Pro-Port Ltd.
P&S Gun Service
Quality Firearms of Idaho, Inc.
Rice, Keith
Ridgetop Sporting Goods
Ries, Chuck
Rifle Shop, The
Rigby & Co., John
Rizzini Battista
RMS Custom Gunsmithing
Robar Co.'s, Inc., The
Roberts Jr., Wm. A.
Robinson, Don
Rocky Mountain Rifle Works Ltd.
Rogers Gunsmithing, Bob
Royal Arm International Products
Rupert's Gun Shop
Russell's Rifle Shop
Ryan, Chad L.
Sanders Custom Gun Service
Sandy's Custom Gunshop
Schaefer, Roy V.
Schiffman, Curt
Schiffman, Mike
Schiffman, Norman
Schumakers Gun Shop, William
Schwartz Custom Guns, Wayne E.
Scott Fine Guns, Inc., Thad
Scott/McDougall Custom Gunsmiths
Shane's Gunsmithing
Shaw, Inc., E.R.
Shaw's Finest in Guns
Shay's Gunsmithing
Shell Shack
Shockley, Harold H.
Shootin' Shack, Inc.
Shooting Gallery, The
Shooting Specialties
Shotgun Shop, The
Shotguns Unlimited
Silver Ridge Gun Shop
Sipes Gun Shop
Siskiyou Gun Works
S.K. Guns, Inc.
Sklany, Steve
Skeoch, Brian R.
Slezak, Jerome F.

Small Arms Mfg. Co.
Smith, Art
Snapp's Gunshop
SOS Products Co.
Spender Reblue Service
Sportsmen's Exchange & Western
  Gun Traders, Inc.
Spradlin's
Springfield, Inc.
SSK Industries
Starnes, Ken
Steelman's Gun Shop
Steffens, Ron
Storey, Dale A.
Stott's Creek Armory, Inc.
Strawbridge, Victor W.
Stroup, Earl R.
Swann, D.J.
Swenson's 45 Shop, A.D.
S.W.I.F.T.
Swift River Gunworks, Inc.
Szweda, Robert
300 Gunsmith Service, Inc.
Talmage, William G.
Tank's Rifle Shop
Taylor & Robbins
Tennessee Valley Mfg.
Ten-Ring Precision, Inc.
Tertin, James A.
Texas Platers Supply
Thurston Sports, Inc.
Titus, Daniel
Tom's Gun Repair
Tom's Gunshop
Tooley, David
Trevallion Gunstocks
T.S.W. Conversion, Inc.
Unick's Gunsmithing
Upper Missouri Trading Co.
Van Epps, Milton
Van Horn, Gil
Vest, John
Vic's Gun Refinishing
Vintage Arms, Inc.
Volquartsen Custom Ltd.
Waffen-Weber Custom Gunsmithing
Walker Arms Co., Inc.
Wallace's
Wardell Precision Handguns Ltd.
Weaver Arms Corp.
Weaver's Gun Shop
Weems, Cecil
Wells Custom Gunsmith, R.A.
Wells Sport Store
Werth, T.W.
Wessinger Custom Guns &
  Engraving
West, Robert G.
Westchester Carbide
Western Ordnance Int'l Corp.
Westley Richards & Co.
White Owl Enterprises
White Rock Tool & Die
White Systems, Inc.
Wichita Arms, Inc.
Wiebe, Duane
Williams Gun Sight Co.
Williamson Precision Gunsmithing
Wilson's Gun Shop
Winter, Robert M.
Wisner's Gun Shop, Inc.
Wood, Frank S.
Yankee Gunsmith
Zeeryp, Russ

Francesca Stabilizer's, Inc.
Fullmer, Geo. M.
Gentry Custom Gunmaker, David
Goodwin, Fred
Gordie's Gun Shop
Graybill's Gun Shop
Green, Roger M.
Greenwalt Rifles
Griffin & Howe, Inc.
Guns
Gunsmithing Ltd.
Gutridge, Inc.
Hagn Rifles & Actions, Martin
Hecht, Hubert J.
Heilmann, Stephen
Heppler's Machining
Hiptmayer, Klaus
Hoag, James W.
Highline Machine Co.
Hobaugh, Wm. H.
Hyper-Single, Inc.
Intermountain Arms
Ivanoff, Thomas G.
Jaeger, Inc., Paul/Dunn's
Jamison's Forge Works
Jeffredo Gunsight
Johnson Gunsmithing, Inc., Neal G.
Johnston, James
Jones, Neil
K-D, Inc.
Kilham & Co.
Klein Custom Guns, Don
Kleinendorst, K.W.
Kopp, Terry K.
Lampert, Ron
Lawson Co., Harry
Lock's Philadelphia Gun Exchange
Mac's .45 Shop
Mains Enterprises, Inc.
McCament, Jay
McCormick's Custom Gun Bluing
McFarland, Stan
Mid-America Recreation, Inc.
Morrison Custom Rifles, J.W.
Morrow, Bud
Mullis Guncraft
Nettestad Gun Works
New England Custom Gun Service
Noreen, Peter H.
North Fork Custom Gunsmithing
Pace Marketing, Inc.

Pagel Gun Works, Inc.
Parker Gun Finishes
Pasadena Gun Center
Penrod Precision
Pentheny de Pentheny
Precise Metal Finishing
Precise Metalsmithing Enterprises
Precision Metal Finishing, John
  Westrom
Precision Specialties
P&S Gun Service
Rice, Keith
Rifle Shop, The
Robar Co.'s, Inc., The
Royal Arm International Products
Shell Shack
Shirley Co. Gun & Riflemakers Ltd., J.A.
Shockley, Harold H.
Silver Ridge Gun Shop
S.K. Guns, Inc.
Skeoch, Brian R.
Smith, Art
Snapp's Gunshop
Sportsmatch Ltd.
Strawbridge, Victor W.
Steffens, Ron
Talley, Dave
Ten-Ring Precision, Inc.
Tom's Gun Repair
Thompson, Randall
T.S.W. Conversions, Inc.
Unick's Gunsmithing
Van Horn, Gil
Van Patten, J.W.
Vic's Gun Refinishing
Waffen-Weber Custom Gunsmithing
Waldron, Herman
Wallace's
Westchester Carbide
Wells Sport Store
Werth, T.W.
Wessinger Custom Guns &
  Engraving
Western Design
White Owl Enterprises
White Rock Tool & Die
Wiebe, Duane
Wisner's Gun Shop, Inc.
Westrom, John
Wood, Frank S.

DECOYS

A&M Waterfowl, Inc.
Ammunition Consulting
  Services, Inc.
Baekgaard Ltd.
Belding's Custom Gun Shop
Burnham Bros.
Carry-Lite, Inc.
Deer Me Products Co.
Fair Game International
Farm Form, Inc.
Feather Flex Decoys
Flambeau Products Corp.
G&H Decoys, Inc.
Herter's Manufacturing, Inc.

Hiti-Schuch, Atelier Wilma
Iron Mountain Knife Co.
Klingler Woodcarving
Molin Industries, Tru-Nord Division
North Wind Decoys Co.
Penn's Woods Products, Inc.
Quack Decoy Corp.
Ravell Ltd.
Robinson Firearms Mfg. Ltd.
Royal Arms
Sports Innovations, Inc.
Tanglefree Industries
Waterfield Sports, Inc.
Woods Wise Products

ENGRAVERS, ENGRAVING TOOLS

Adair Custom Shop, Bill
Adams, John J.
Ahlman Guns
Alfano, Sam
Allard, Gary
Altamont Co.
Anthony and George Ltd.
Artistic Engraving
Baron Technology, Inc.
Bates Engraving, Billy
Bell Originals, Sid
Bledsoe, Weldon
Bleile, C. Roger
Boessler, Erich
Bone Engraving, Ralph
Bratcher, Dan
Brgoch, Frank
Brooker, Dennis
Brownell Checkering Tools, W.E.
Burgess, Byron
CAM Enterprises
Christopher Firearms Co., Inc., E.
Churchill, Winston
Clark Firearms Engraving
Clark, Frank
Creek Side Metal & Woodcrafters

Davidson, Jere
Delorge, Ed
Dolbare, Elizabeth
Drain, Mark
Dubber, Michael W.
Dyson & Son Ltd., Peter
Engraving Artistry
Evans Engraving, Robert
Eversull Co., Inc., K.
Eyster Heritage Gunsmiths, Inc.,
  Ken
Fanzoj GesmbH
Firearms Engraver's Guild of
  America
Flannery Engraving Co., Jeff W.
Floatstone Mfg. Co.
Fogle, James W.
Fountain Products
Francolini, Leonard
Frank Knives
French, J.R.
Gene's Custom Guns
George, Tim and Christy
Glimm, Jerome C.
Golden Age Arms Co.
Gournet, Geoffroy

CUSTOM METALSMITHS

Ackley Rifle Barrels, P.O.
Ahlman Guns
Aldis Gunsmithing & Shooting
  Supply
Apel, Dietrich
Armurier Hiptmayer
Baron Technology, Inc.
Barta's Gunsmithing
Beitzinger, George
Bellm Contenders
Benchmark Guns
Biesen, Al
Billingsley & Brownell
Brace, Larry D.
Briganti & Co., A.
Brown Precision, Inc.
Bustani Appraisers, Leo
Campbell, Dick
Carter's Gun Shop
Checkmate Refinishing

Chuck's Gun Shop
Classic Guns, Inc.
Clinton River Gun Serv., Inc.
Colonial Repair
Condor Mfg. Co.
Costa, David
Craftguard
Crandall Tool & Machine Co.
Cullity Restoration, Daniel
Custom Gun Products
Custom Gunsmiths
D&D Gunsmiths, Ltd.
D&H Precision Tooling
Duncan's Gunworks, Inc.
Dyson & Son Ltd., Peter
Eyster Heritage Gunsmiths, Inc.,
  Ken
First Distributors, Inc., Jack
Flaig's
Fisher, Jerry A.

Grant, Howard V.
Griffin & Howe, Inc.
GRS Corp.
Gun Room, The
Guns
Gurney, F.R.
Gwinnell, Bryson J.
Hale, Peter
Hand Engravers Supply Co.
Hands, Barry Lee
Harris Hand Engraving, Paul A.
Harwood, Jack O.
Hendricks, Frank E.
Hiptmayer, Heidemarie
Horst, Alan K.
Ingle, Ralph W.
Jaeger, Inc., Paul/Dunn's
Johns, Bill
Kamyk Engraving Co., Steve
Kehr, Roger
Kelly, Lance
Klingler Woodcarving
Koevenig's Engraving Service
Kudlas, John M.
Leibowitz, Leonard
Letschnig, Franz
Lindsay, Steve
Lutz Engraving, Ron
Mains Enterprises, Inc.
Maki School of Engraving, Robert E.
Marek, George
Master Engravers, Inc.
McDonald, Dennis
McKenzie, Lynton
Mele, Frank
Mid-America Recreation, Inc.
Mittermeier, Inc., Frank
Moschetti, Mitchell R.
Mountain States Engraving
Nelson, Gary K.
New Orleans Arms Co.
New Orleans Jewelers Supply Co.
NgraveR Co., The
Oker's Engraving
Old Dominion Engravers
Pachmayr Ltd.
Palmgren Steel Products

Pedersen & Son, C.R.
Pilgrim Pewter, Inc.
Pilkington, Scott
Piquette, Paul R.
Potts, Wayne E.
Pranger, Ed G.
P&S Gun Service
Rabeno, Martin
Ravell Ltd.
Reed, Dave
Reno, Wayne & Karen
Riggs, Jim
Roberts, J.J.
Rohner, Hans and John
Rosser, Bob
Rundell's Gun Shop
Runge, Robert P.
Sampson, Roger
Schiffman, Mike
Shaw's Finest in Guns
Sherwood, George
Sinclair, W.P.
Singletary, Kent
Skaggs, R.E.
Smith, Mark A.
Smith, Ron
Theis, Terry
Thiewes, George W.
Thirion Hand Engraving, Denise
Tuscano, Tony
Valade, Robert B.
Vest, John
Viramontez, Ray
Vohres, David
Waffen-Weber Custom Gunsmithing
Wagoner, Vernon G.
Wallace's
Wallace, Terry
Warenski, Julie
Warren, Kenneth W.
Welch, Sam
Wells, Rachel
Wessinger Custom Guns & Engraving
Willig Custom Engraving, Claus
Wood, Mel

GAME CALLS

Adventure Game Calls
Arkansas Mallard Duck Calls
Ashby Turkey Calls
Baekgaard Ltd.
Blakemore Game Calls, Jim
Bostick Wildlife Calls, Inc.
Buck Stix
Burnham Bros.
Carter's Wildlife Calls, Inc., Garth
Cedar Hill Game Call Co.
Crawford Co., Inc., R.M.
D-Boone Ent., Inc.
Dr. O's Products Ltd.
Duck Call Specialists
Faulk's Game Call Co., Inc.
Flow-Rite of Tennessee, Inc.
Green Head Game Call Co.
Hally Caller
Haydel's Game Calls, Inc.
Herter's Manufacturing, Inc.
Hunter's Specialties, Inc.
Keowee Game Calls
Kingyon, Paul L.
Knight & Hale Game Calls
Lohman Mfg. Co., Inc.
Mallardtone Game Calls
Marsh, Johnny
Moss Double Tone, Inc.
Mountain Hollow Game Calls

M/S Deepeeka Exports Pvt. Ltd.
Oakman Turkey Calls
Olt Co., Philip S.
Penn's Woods Products, Inc.
Primos Wild Game Calls, Inc.
Quaker Boy, Inc.
Rickard, Inc., Pete
Robbins Scent, Inc.
Safari Gun Co.
Salter Calls, Inc., Eddie
San Angelo Sports Products, Inc.
Savana Sports, Inc.
Sceery Co., E.J.
Scobey Duck & Goose Calls, Glynn
Scotch Hunting Products Co., Inc.
Scruggs' Game Calls, Stanley
Simmons Outdoor Corp.
SOS Products Co.
Sports Innovations, Inc.
Stewart Game Calls, Inc., Johnny
Sure-Shot Game Calls, Inc.
Tanglefree Industries
Tink's & Ben Lee Hunting Products
Tink's Safariland Hunting Corp.
Wellington Outdoors
Wilderness Sound Productions Ltd.
Wittasek, Dipl.-Ing. Norbert
Woods Wise Products
Wyant's Outdoor Products, Inc.

GUN PARTS, U.S. AND FOREIGN

Ad Hominem
Amherst Arms
Armscorp. USA, Inc.
Aztec International Ltd.
Badger Shooters Supply, Inc.
Baumannize, Inc.
Behlert Precision
Bob's Gun Shop
Bustani Appraisers, Leo
Can Am Enterprises
Caspian Arms
Century International Arms, Inc.
Clark Custom Guns, Inc.
Colonial Repair
Condor Mfg. Co.

Defense Moulding Enterprises
Delta Arms Ltd.
Dibble, Derek A.
Dressel Jr., Paul G.
Duffy, Charles E.
Eagle International, Inc.
Ed's Gun House
EMF Co., Inc.
Fabian Bros. Sporting Goods, Inc.
FAPA Corp.
Farmer-Dressel, Sharon
Federal Ordnance, Inc.
First Distributors, Inc., Jack
Fleming Firearms
Forrest, Inc., Tom

Frazier Brothers Enterprises
Gentry Custom Gunmaker, David
Global Industries
Greider Precision
Gun Parts Corp., The
Guns
Gun Shop, The
Hallberg Gunsmith, Fritz
Hastings Barrels
Hoehn's Shooting Supply
Irwin, Campbell H.
Jaeger, Inc., Paul/Dunn's
J.O. Arms & Ammunition Co.
GJohnson Gunsmithing, Inc., Neal G.
K&T Co.
Keng's Firaarms Specialty, Inc.
Kimber, Inc.
Kopp, Terry K.
Krico/Kriegeskorte GmbH, A.
Lock's Philadelphia Gun Exchange
Lodewick, Walter H.
London Guns Ltd.
Mac's .45 Shop
Mag-Pack Corp.
Markell, Inc.
McCormick Corp., Chip
McKee Publications
MEC-GAR S.R.L.
Merkuria Ltd.
Morrow, Bud
Nu-Line Guns, Inc.
Old Western Scrounger, Inc.
Olympic Arms, Inc.
Pace Marketing, Inc.
Parts & Surplus
Perazzi U.S.A., Inc.
Pre-Winchester 92-90-62 Parts Co.
Quality Firearms of Idaho, Inc.

Quality Parts Co.
Ram-Line, Inc.
Ranch Products
Randco UK
Ravell Ltd.
Retting, Inc., Martin B.
Rizzini Battista
Ruvel & Co., Inc.
Safari Arms, Inc./SGW
Sarco, Inc.
Shell Shack
Scherer
Sheridan USA, Inc., Austin
Sherwood Intl. Export Corp.
Smires, Clifford L.
Southern Ammunition Co., Inc.
Southern Armory, The
Springfield, Inc.
Springfield Sporters, Inc.
S&S Firearms
Starnes, Ken
Su-Press-On, Inc.
Tank's Rifle Shop
Taurus, S.A., Forjas
Tradewinds, Inc.
Triple-K Mfg. Co., Inc.
T.S.W. Conversions, Inc.
Twin Pine Armory
Vintage Industries, Inc.
Walker Arms Co., Inc.
Wardell Precision Handguns Ltd.
Weaver's Gun Shop
Weisz Antique Gun Parts
Westfield Engineering
Wisner's Gun Shop, Inc.
Wolff Co., W.C.
Zoli USA, Inc., Antonio

GUNS, AIR

•Action Arms Ltd.
•Airgun Repair Centre
•Air Rifle Specialists
•Air Venture
•Beeman Precision Airguns, Inc.
•Benjamin/Sheridan Co.
Brass Eagle, Inc.
•BSA Guns Ltd.
Champion's Choice, Inc.
Component Concepts, Inc.
Crawford Co., Inc., R.M.
•Crosman Corp.
Crosman Products of Canada Ltd.
•Daisy Mfg. Co.
•Diana
•Dynamit Nobel-RWS, Inc.
•FWB
•Gamo
•GFR Corp.
•Great Lakes Airguns
GZ Paintball Sports Products
Hartmann & Weiss GMBH
Hebard Guns, Gil
Hy-Score Arms Co. Ltd.
•Interarms
I.S.S.

•Mac-1 Distributors
•Marksman Products
Merkuria Ltd.
National Survival Game, Inc.
Nationwide Airgun Repairs
•Old Western Scrounger, Inc.
•Pardini Armi Commerciale Srl
Penguin Industries, Inc.
•PSI, Inc.
Ravell Ltd.
•RWS
Savana Sports, Inc.
S.G.S. Sporting Guns Srl
Sheridan USA, Inc., Austin
Specialized Weapons, Inc.
Sportsmatch Ltd.
•Steyr-Mannlicher
Stone Enterprises Ltd.
•Swivel Machine Works, Inc.
Tapco, Inc.
•Taurus, S.A., Forjas
Tippman Pneumatics, Inc.
Valor Corp.
•Walther GmbH, Carl
Webley and Scott Ltd.
•Weihrauch KG, Hermann

GUNS, FOREIGN—IMPORTERS (Manufacturers)

Action Arms Ltd. (BRNO; CZ)
Air Rifle Specialists (Air Arms; BSA Guns Ltd.; Theoben Engineering)
Air Venture (airguns)
American Arms, Inc. (Fausti & Figlie s.n.c., Stefano; Franchi S.P.A., Luigi; Grulla Armes; Hermanos S.A., Zabala; INDESAL; Norica, Avnda Otaloa; blackpowder arms)
Armes de Chasse (AYA; Chapuis Armes; Francotte & Cie S.A., Auguste)
Armoury, Inc., The (blackpowder)
Armscorp USA, Inc.
Armsport, Inc. (Armsport, Inc.; blackpowder arms)
Autumn Sales, Inc. (Blaser Jagdwaffen GmbH)
Beauchamp & Son, Inc. (Pedersoli Davide & C.)
Beeman Precision Airguns, Inc. (Air Arms; Beeman Precision Airguns, Inc.; FWB; Weihrauch KG, Hermann)
Bell's Legendary Country Wear

(Miroku, B.C./Daly, Charles; Powell & Son, Ltd., William)
Beretta U.S.A. Corp. (Beretta Firearms, Pietro)
Bohemia Arms Co. (BRNO)
British Arms Co. Ltd.
British Sporting Arms (Miroku, B.C./Daly, Charles)
Browning Arms Co. (Browning Arms Co.)
B-West Imports, Inc.
Cabela's (Pedersoli Davide & C.; blackpowder arms)
California Armory, Inc.
Cape Outfitters (San Marco; blackpowder arms)
Century International Arms, Inc. (BRNO; Famas; FEG; Norinco)
ChinaSports, Inc. (Norinco)
Cimarron Arms (Uberti, Aldo; blackpowder arms)
CVA (blackpowder arms)
Daisy Mfg. Co. (Daisy Mfg. Co.; Gamo)
Dixie Gun Works (Pedersoli Davide & C.; blackpowder arms)

Dynamit Nobel-RWS, Inc. (Diana, Gamo, RWS)
E.A.A. Corp. (Astra-Unceta Y Cia, S.A.; Benelli Armi S.p.A.; Fabrica D'Armi Sabatti S.R.L.; Tanfoglio S.r.l., Fratelli/Witness; Weihrauch KG, Hermann)
Eagle Imports, Inc. (Bersa S.A.)
Ellett Bros. (Churchill)
EMF Co., Inc. (Dakota, Pedersoli Davide & C.; blackpowder arms)
Euroarms of America, Inc. (blackpowder arms)
Firstshot, Inc. (Daewoo Precision Industries Ltd.)
Glock, Inc. (Glock GmbH)
Griffin & Howe, Inc. (Rigby & Co., John)
Great Lakes Airguns (Sharp airguns)
GSI, Inc. (Merkel Freres, Steyr-Daimler-Puch, Steyr-Mannlicher AG)
G.U., Inc. (Sauer, SKB Arms Co.)
Hammerli USA (Hammerli Ltd.)
Hanus Birdguns, Bill (Grulla Armes; Merkel Freres; SKB Arms Co.; Ugartechea S.A., Ignacio; Weatherby, Inc.)
Heckler & Koch, Inc. (Benelli Armi S.p.A.; Heckler & Koch, GmbH)
Interarms (Helwan; Howa Machinery Ltd.; Interarms; Norinco; Rossi, Amadeo; Star Bonifacio Echeverria S.A.; Walther GmbH, Carl; Zastava Arms)
JägerSport, Ltd. (Heym GmbH & Co., Friedrich Wilh.; Voere-KGH m.b.H.)
J.O. Arms & Ammunition Co. (J.O. Arms & Ammunition Co.)
K.B.I., Inc. (FEG; Kassnar; K.B.I., Inc.; Norica, Avnda Otaola)
Keng's Firearms Specialty, Inc. (Poly Technologies, Inc.)
Krieghoff International, Inc. (Krieghoff Gun Co., H.)
K-Sports Imports, Inc.
London Guns Ltd.
Magnum Research, Inc. (Bernardelli Vincenzo S.p.A.; IMI/Desert Eagle)
MAGTECH Recreational Products, Inc. (CBC)
Mandall Shooting Supplies, Inc. (Ariziga; Bretton; Cabanas; Crucelegoi, Hermanos; Erma Werke GmbH; Firearms Co. Ltd./Alpine; Gaucher Armes S.A.; Korth; Krico/Kriegeskorte GmbH, A.; SIG; Tanner; Ugartechea S.A., Ignacio; Zanoletti, Pietro; Zoli, Antonio; blackpowder arms)
Marent, Rudolf (Hammerli Ltd.)
Marksman Products (Marksman Products)
McMillan Gunworks, Inc. (Peters Stahl GmbH)
MCS, Inc. (Pardini Armi Commerciale Srl)
MEC-Gar U.S.A., Inc. (MEC-Gar s.r.l.)

Midwest Sport Distributors (Norinco)
Mitchell Arms, Inc. (Mitchell Arms, Inc.; blackpowder arms)
Moore & Co., Wm. Larkin (Bertuzzi; Garbi, Armas Urki; Perugini-Visini & Co. s.r.l.; Piotti; Rizzini, F.LLI)
Navy Arms Co. (Navy Arms Co; Pedersoli Davide & C.; Uberti, Aldo; blackpowder arms)
New England Arms Co. (Cosmi Americo & Figlio s.n.c.; FERLIB; premium high-grade shotguns)
Nygord Precision Products (FAS, Morini; Steyr airguns, Unique/M.A.P.F.; Vostok)
Outdoor Sports Headquarters, Inc. (Miroku, B.C./Daly, Charles)
Para-Ordnance Mfg., Inc. (Para-Ordnance Mfg., Inc.)
Parker Div. Reagent Chemicals (Parker Reproductions)
Perazzi U.S.A., Inc. (Perazzi m.a.p. S.p.A.)
Pragotrade (BRNO, CZ)
Precision Imports, Inc. (Mauser-Werke)
PSI, Inc. (Anschutz GmbH; Erma Werke GmbH; Gustaf, Carl; Marocchi F.lli S.p.A.)
Precision Sports (Ugartechea S.A., Ignacio)
Quality Arms, Inc. (Arrieta, S.L.; FERLIB)
Ruko Products (Armscor)
Safari Arms/SGW (Peters Stahl GmbH)
SGS Importers International, Inc. (Llama Gabilondo Y Cia)
Sigarms, Inc. (SIG-Sauer)
Sile Distributors (Benelli Armi S.p.A.; Marocchi F.lli S.p.A.; Solothurn)
Simmons Enterprises, Ernie (Sauer, SKB Arms Co.)
Specialty Shooters Supply, Inc. (JSL Ltd.)
Sportarms of Florida (Norinco; Schmidt, Herbert; Tokarav)
St. Lawrence Sales, Inc. (Fabarm S.p.A.)
Springfield, Inc. (Springfield, Inc.)
Stoeger Industries (IGA, Sako Ltd., Tikka)
Stone Enterprises Ltd. (air guns)
Swarovski Optik North America Ltd. (Heym GmbH & Co., Friedrich Wilh.; Voere-KGH m.b.H.)
Taurus Firearms Inc. (Taurus International Firearms)
Tradewinds, Inc. (blackpowder arms)
Trail Guns Armory, Inc. (Pedersoli Davide & C.; blackpowder arms)
Uberti USA, Inc. (Uberti, Aldo; blackpowder arms)
Vintage Arms, Inc.
Weatherby, Inc. (Howa Machinery Ltd.; Weatherby, Inc.)
Wingshooting Adventures (Arrieta, S.L.)
Zoli U.S.A., Inc., Antonio (Zoli, Antonio)

GUNS, FOREIGN—MANUFACTURERS (Importers)

•Air Arms (Air Rifle Specialists; Beeman Precision Airguns, Inc.)
•Anschutz GmbH (PSI, Inc.)
•Ariziga (Mandall Shooting Supplies, Inc.)
•Armscor (Ruko Products)
•Armsport, Inc. (Armsport, Inc.)
•Arrieta, S.L. (Quality Arms, Inc.; Wingshooting Adventures)
•Astra-Unceta Y Cia, S.A. (E.A.A. Corp.)
ATIS Armi S.A.S.
•AYA (Armes de Chasse)
•Beeman Precision Airguns, Inc. (Beeman Precision Airguns, Inc.)
•Benelli Armi S.p.A. (E.A.A. Corp.; Heckler & Koch, Inc.; Sile Distributors)
•Beretta Firearms, Pietro (Beretta U.S.A. Corp.)
Beretta, Dr. Franco

•Bernardelli Vincenzo S.p.a. (Magnum Research, Inc.)
•Bersa S.A. (Eagle Imports, Inc.)
•Bertuzzi (Moore & Co., Wm. Larkin)
•Blaser Jagdwaffen GmbH (Autumn Sales, Inc.)
Bondini Paolo (blackpowder arms)
•Bretton (Mandall Shooting Supplies, Inc.)
•BRNO (Action Arms Ltd.; Bohemia Arms Co.; Century International Arms, Inc.)
•Browning Arms Co. (Browning Arms Co.)
•BSA Guns Ltd. (Air Rifle Specialists)
•Cabanas (Mandall Shooting Supplies, Inc.)
•CBC (MAGTECH Recreational Products, Inc.)
•Chapuis Armes (Armes de Chasse)
•Churchill (Ellett Bros.)

•Cosmi Americo & Figlio s.n.c. (New England Arms Co.)
•Crucelegui Hermanos (Mandall Shooting Supplies, Inc.)
•CVA (blackpowder arms)
•CZ (Action Arms Ltd.)
•Daewoo Precision Industries Ltd. (Firstshot, Inc.)
•Dakota (EMF Co., Inc.)
•Daisy Mfg. Co. (Daisy Mfg. Co.)
•Diana (Dynamit Nobel-RWS, Inc.)
Dumoulin, Ernest
Elko Arms, L. Kortz
•Erma Werke GmbH (Mandall Shooting Supplies, Inc.; PSI, Inc.)
•Fabarm S.p.A. (St. Lawrence Sales, Inc.)
•Fabrica D'Armi Sabatti S.R.L. (E.A.A. Corp.)
•Famas (Century International Arms, Inc.)
•FAS (Nygord Precision Products)
•Fausti & Figlie s.n.c., Stefano (American Arms, Inc.)
•FEG (Century International Arms, Inc.; K.B.I., Inc.)
•FERLIB (New England Arms Co.; Quality Arms, Inc.)
•Firearms Co. Ltd./Alpine (Mandall Shooting Supplies, Inc.)
FN Herstal
Frankonia Jagd
•Franchi S.p.A, Luigi (American Arms, Inc.)
•Francotte & Cie S.A., Auguste (Armes de Chasse)
•FWB (Beeman Precision Airguns, Inc.)
•Gamba S.p.A., Renato
•Gamo (Daisy Mfg. Co.; Dynamit Nobel-RWS, Inc.)
•Garbi, Armas Urki (Moore & Co., Wm. Larkin)
•Gaucher Armes S.A. (Mandall Shooting Supplies, Inc.)
•Glock GmbH (Glock, Inc.)
•Grulla Armes (American Arms, Inc.; Hanus Birdguns, Bill)
•Gustaf, Carl (PSI, Inc.)
•Hammerli Ltd. (Hammerli USA; Marent, Rudolph)
Hartmann & Weiss GmbH
•Heckler & Koch, GmbH (Heckler & Koch, Inc.)
•Helwan (Interarms)
•Heym GmbH & Co., Friedrich Wilh. (JägerSport, Ltd.; Swarovski Optik North America Ltd.)
•Howa Machinery Ltd. (Interarms; Weatherby, Inc.)
•IGA (Stoeger Industries)
•IMI/Desert Eagle (Magnum Research, Inc.)
•INDESAL (American Arms, Inc.)
•Interarms (Interarms)
•J.O. Arms & Ammunition Co. (J.O. Arms & Ammunition Co.)
•JSL Ltd. (Specialty Shooters Supply, Inc.)
•Kassnar (K.B.I., Inc.)
•K.B.I., Inc. (K.B.I., Inc.)
•Korth (Mandall Shooting Supplies, Inc.)
•Krico/Kriegeskorte GmbH, A. (Mandall Shooting Supplies, Inc.)
•Krieghoff Gun Co., H. (Krieghoff International, Inc.)
•Lakefield Arms Ltd.
Lanber Armes S.A.
Laurona Armes S.A.
Lebeau-Courally
•Llama Gabilondo Y Cia (SGS Importers International, Inc.)
•Marksman Products (Marksman Products)
•Marocchi F.lli S.p.A. (PSI, Inc.; Sile Distributors)
•Mauser-Werke (Precision Imports, Inc.)
•MEC-Gar s.r.l. (MEC-Gar U.S.A., Inc.)
•Merkel Freres (GSI, Inc.; Hanus Birdguns, Bill)
•Miroku, B.C./Daly, Charles (Bell's Legendary Country Wear; British Sporting Arms; Outdoor Sports Headquarters)

•Mitchell Arms, Inc. (Mitchell Arms, Inc.)
•Morini (Nygord Precision Products)
•Navy Arms Co. (Navy Arms Co.)
•Norica, Avnda Otaola (American Arms, Inc.; K.B.I., Inc.)
•Norinco (Century International Arms, Inc.; ChinaSports, Inc.; Interarms; Midwest Sport Distributors; Sportarms of Florida)
•Para-Ordnance Mfg., Inc. (Para-Ordnance Mfg., Inc.)
•Pardini Armi Commerciale Srl (MCS, Inc.)
•Parker Reproductions (Parker Div. Reagent Chemical)
•Pedersoli Davide & C. (Beauchamp & Son, Inc.; Cabela's; Dixie Gun Works; EMF Co., Inc.; Navy Arms Co.; Trail Guns Armory, Inc.)
•Perazzi m.a.p. S.p.A. (Perazzi U.S.A., Inc.)
•Perugini-Visini & Co. s.r.l. (Moore & Co., Wm. Larkin)
•Peters Stahl GmbH (McMillan Gunworks, Inc.; Safari Arms/SGW)
•Piotti (Moore & Co., Wm. Larkin)
•Poly Technologies, Inc. (Keng's Firearms Specialty, Inc.)
Powell & Son (Gunmakers) Ltd., William (Bell's Legendary Country Wear)
•Rigby & Co., John (Griffin & Howe, Inc.)
•Rizzini, F.LLI (Moore & Co., Wm. Larkin)
•Rossi, Amadeo (Interarms)
•RWS (Dynamit Nobel-RWS, Inc.)
•Sako Ltd. (Stoeger Industries)
•San Marco (Cape Outfitters)
Sardius Industries Ltd.
•Sauer (G.U., Inc.; Simmons Enterprises, Ernie)
•Schmidt, Herbert (Sportarms of Florida)
•SIG (Mandall Shooting Supplies, Inc.)
•SIG-Sauer (Sigarms, Inc.)
•SKB Arms Co. (G.U., Inc.; Hanus Birdguns, Bill; Simmons Enterprises, Ernie)
•Solothurn (Sile Distributors)
•Springfield, Inc. (Springfield, Inc.)
•Star Bonifacio Echeverria S.A. (Interarms)
•Steyr airguns (Nygord Precision Products)
•Steyr-Daimler-Puch (GSI, Inc.)
•Steyr-Mannlicher AG (GSI, Inc.)
•Tanfoglio S.r.l., Fratelli/Witness (E.A.A. Corp.)
•Tanner (Mandall Shooting Supplies, Inc.)
•Taurus International Firearms (Taurus Firearms, Inc.)
Techni-Mec
T.F.C. S.p.A.
•Theoben Engineering (Air Rifle Specialists)
•Tikka (Stoeger Industries)
•Tokarav (Sportarms of Florida)
•Uberti, Aldo (Cimarron Arms; Navy Arms Co.; Uberti USA, Inc.)
•Ugartechea S.A., Ignacio (Hanus Birdguns, Bill; Mandall Shooting Supplies, Inc.; Precision Sports)
•Unique/M.A.P.F. (Nygord Precision Products)
Verney-Carron
•Voere-KGH m.b.H. (JägerSport, Ltd.; Swarovski Optik North America Ltd.)
•Vostok (Nygord Precision Products)
•Walther GmbH, Carl (Interarms)
•Weatherby, Inc. (Hanus Birdguns, Bill; Weatherby, Inc.)
•Weihrauch KG, Hermann (Beeman Precision Airguns, Inc.; E.A.A. Corp.)
Westley Richards & Co.
•Zanoletti, Pietro (Mandall Shooting Supplies, Inc.)
•Zabala Hermanos S.A. (American Arms, Inc.)
•Zastava Arms (Interarms)
•Zoli, Antonio (Mandall Shooting Supplies, Inc.; Zoli USA, Inc., Antonio)

•See page 460 for Warranty Service Center Addresses

GUNS, U.S.-MADE

- Accu-Tek
- AMAC
- American Arms, Inc.
- American Derringer Corp.
- AMT
- Armscorp USA, Inc.
- A-Square Co., Inc.
- Auto-Ordnance Corp.
- Barrett Firearms Mfg., Inc.
- Beretta U.S.A. Corp.
- Brown Co., E. Arthur
- Browning Arms Co. (Parts & Service)
- Bryco Arms
- Calico Light Weapon Systems
  California Armory, Inc.
- Century Gun Dist., Inc.
- Century International Arms, Inc.
- Charter Arms
- Claridge Hi-Tec, Inc.
  Clifton Arms
  Colt Blackpower Arms Co.
- Colt's Mfg. Co., Inc.
- Competitor Corp., Inc.
  Connecticut Valley Classics
- Coonan Arms, Inc.
- Cooper Arms
- CVA
- Dakota Arms, Inc.
- Davis Industries
- Desert Industries, Inc.
- Eagle Arms, Inc.
- EMF Co., Inc.
  Falcon Industries, Inc.
- Feather Industries, Inc.
- Federal Engineering Corp.
- Freedom Arms, Inc.
  Gentry Custom Gunmaker, David
- Gibbs Rifle Co., Inc.
  Gilbert Equipment Co., Inc.
- Gonic Arms, Inc.
- Grendel, Inc.
- H&R 1871, Inc.
- Hatfield Gun Co., Inc.
- Hawken Shop, The
  HJS Arms, Inc.
- H-S Precision, Inc.
- IAI
- Intratec
- Ithaca Aquisition Corp./Ithaca Gun Co.
- Jennings Firearms Inc.
- J.O. Arms & Ammunition Co.
- Johnson, Iver
  Jones, J.D.
- KDF, Inc.
  Kimber, Inc.
  Kimel Industries
  Knight's Mfg. Co.
- L.A.R. Manufacturing, Inc.

- Laseraim Arms
- Ljutic Industries, Inc.
- Lorcin Engineering Co., Inc.
- Magnum Research, Inc.
- Marlin Firearms Co.
- Maverick Arms, Inc.
- McMillan Gunworks, Inc.
- Mitchell Arms, Inc.
- MK Arms, Inc.
- M.O.A. Corp.
- Montana Armory, Inc.
- Mossberg & Sons, Inc., O.F.
- Mowrey Gun Works
- Navy Arms Co.
- New Advantage Arms Corp.
- New England Firearms
- North American Arms
- Olympic Arms, Inc.
- Oregon Arms, Inc.
- Parker-Hale
- Phelps Mfg. Co.
- Phoenix Arms
  Precision Arms International, Inc.
  Quality Parts Co.
- Ram-Line, Inc.
  Ravell Ltd.
- Red Willow Tool & Armory, Inc.
- Remington Arms Co., Inc.
  Rocky Mountain Arms, Inc.
- RPM
- Safari Arms/SGW
- Savage Arms, Inc.
- Scattergun Technologies, Inc.
- Seecamp Co., Inc., L.W.
- Sharps Arms Co., Inc., C.
  Shilen Rifles, Inc.
- Shiloh Rifle Mfg.
- Smith & Wesson
- Sporting Arms Mfg., Inc.
- Springfield, Inc.
  SSK Industries
- Sturm, Ruger & Co., Inc.
- Sundance Industries, Inc.
- Survival Arms, Inc.
- Taurus Firearms, Inc.
  Texas Arms
- Texas Longhorn Arms, Inc.
- Thompson/Center Arms
- Ultra Light Arms, Inc.
  U.S. Arms Corp.
  U.S. Repeating Arms Co.
  Valor Corp.
- Wesson Firearms Co., Inc.
- White Systems, Inc.
- Wichita Arms, Inc.
- Wildey, Inc.
  Wilkinson Arms
  Wyoming Armory, Inc.

GUNS AND GUN PARTS, REPLICA AND ANTIQUE

Antique Arms Co.
Armi San Paolo
Armsport, Inc.
Beauchamp & Son, Inc.
Bondini Paolo
Bill's Gun Repair
Billings Gunsmiths, Inc.
Buckskin Machine Works
Burgess & Son Gunsmiths, R.W.
Cache La Poudre Rifleworks
Champlin, R. MacDonald
Century International Arms, Inc.
Colonial Repair
Day & Sons, Inc., Leonard
Delhi Gun House
Delta Arms Ltd.
Dilliott Gunsmithing, Inc.
Dixie Gun Works
Dixon Muzzleloading Shop, Inc.
Dyson & Son Ltd., Peter
EMF Co., Inc.
Federal Ordnance, Inc.
First Distributors, Inc., Jack
Flintlocks, Inc.
Forster Products
Franchi S.p.A., Luigi
Furr Arms
Getz Barrel Co.
Global Industries
Golden Age Arms Co.
Goodwin, Fred
Gun Parts Corp., The
Guns

Gun Works, The
Hallberg Gunsmith, Fritz
House of Muskets, Inc., The
Hunkeler, A.
Ken's Gun Specialties
Kopp, Terry K.
Liberty Antique Gunworks
Lock's Philadelphia Gun Exchange
Lodewick, Walter H.
Log Cabin Sport Shop
Lucas, Edw. E.
Mowrey Gun Works
Munsch Gunsmithing, Tommy
Muzzleloaders Etcetera, Inc.
Navy Arms Co.
OMR Feinmechanik, Jagd-und Sportwaffen, GmbH
Parker-Hale
PEM's Mfg. Co.
Pony Express Sport Shop, Inc.
Precise Metalsmithing Enterprises
Pre-Winchester Parts Co.
Quality Firearms of Idaho, Inc.
Ram-Line, Inc.
Randco UK
Ravell Ltd.
Sarco, Inc.
Shiloh Rifle Mfg.
Silver Ridge Gun Shop
Sklany, Steve
S&S Firearms
Stott's Creek Armory, Inc.
Taylor's & Co., Inc.

Track of the Wolf, Inc.
Unick's Gunsmithing
Upper Missouri Trading Co.
Vintage Industries, Inc.

Wayne Firearms for Collectors & Investors, James
Wescombe
Winchester Sutler, Inc., The

GUNS, SURPLUS—PARTS AND AMMUNITION

Ammunition Consulting Services, Inc.
Armscorp. USA, Inc.
Aztec International Ltd.
Ballistica Maximus North
Ballistica Maximus South
Bondini Paolo
Braun, M.
British Arms Co. Ltd.
Century International Arms, Inc.
ChinaSports, Inc.
Delta Arms Ltd.
Ed's Gun House
Federal Ordnance, Inc.
First Distributors, Inc., Jack
Fleming Firearms
Forrest, Inc., Tom
Garcia National Gun Traders, Inc.
Gibbs Rifle Co., Inc.
Gun Parts Corp., The
Hallberg Gunsmith, Fritz
Interarms
Lever Arms Service Ltd.

Lock's Philadelphia Gun Exchange
Moreton/Fordyce Enterprises
Navy Arms Co.
Oil Rod and Gun Shop
Old Western Scrounger, Inc.
Paragon Sales & Services, Inc.
Parker-Hale
Parts & Surplus
Pre-Winchester Parts Co.
Quality Firearms of Idaho, Inc.
Randall Firearms Research
Ravell Ltd.
Sarco, Inc.
Shell Shack
Sherwood Intl. Export Corp.
Southern Ammunition Co., Inc.
Springfield Sporters, Inc.
T.F.C. S.p.A.
Thurston Sports, Inc.
U.S. Arms Corp.
Westfield Engineering
Whitestone Lumber Corp.

GUNSMITHS, CUSTOM (see Custom Gunsmiths)

GUNSMITHS, HANDGUN (see Pistolsmiths)

GUNSMITH SCHOOLS

Brooker, Dennis
Colorado School of Trades
Cylinder & Slide, Inc.
Lassen Community College, Gunsmithing Dept.
Modern Gun Repair School
Montgomery Community College
Murray State College
North American Correspondence Schools
Nowlin Custom Barrels Mfg.

Pennsylvania Gunsmith School
Piedmont Community College
Pine Technical College
Professional Gunsmiths of America, Inc.
Ravell Ltd.
Southeastern Community College
Trinidad State Junior College Gunsmithing Dept.
Yavapai College

GUNSMITH SUPPLIES, TOOLS, SERVICES

Ackley Rifle Barrels
Aldis Gunsmithing & Shooting Supply
Alley Supply Co.
American Pistolsmiths Guild
Atlantic Mills, Inc.
Bald Eagle Precision Machine Co.
Bellm Contenders
Bengtson Arms Co., L.
Biesen, Al
Biesen, Roger
Blue Ridge Machinery & Tools, Inc.
Brownell's, Inc.
Brown Products, Inc., Ed
B-Square Co.
Buckhorn Gun Works
Buehler Scope Mounts
Can Am Enterprises
C-H Tool & Die Corp./4-D Custom Die
Chapman Manufacturing Co., The
Choate Machine & Tool Co., Inc.
Clymer Manufacturing Co., Inc.
Colonial Arms, Inc.
Conetrol Scope Mounts
Crouse's Country Cover
Cumberland Arms
Custom Checkering Service
Custom Gun Products
D&D Gunsmiths, Ltd.
Dan's Whetstone Co., Inc.
Davidson Products, Inc.
Dayton Traister
Decker Shooting Products
Dem-Bart Hand Checkering Tools, Inc.
de Treville & Co., Stan
Dremel Mfg. Co.
Duffy, Charles E.
Du-Lite Corp.
The Dutchman's Firearms, Inc.
E.A.A. Corp.
Echols & Co., D'Arcy
Edmund Scientific Co.
Ed's Gun House

Eilan S.A.L.
Faith Associates, Inc.
FERLIB di Ferraglio Libero & Co.
First Distributors, Inc., Jack
Fisher, Jerry A.
Flashette Co.
Flitz International Ltd.
Forgreens Tool Mfg., Inc.
Forster, Kathy
Forster Products
Frazier Brothers Enterprises
Garrett Accur-Lt. D.F.S. Co.
Global Industries
Grace Metal Products, Inc.
Graybill's Gun Shop
Greenwalt Rifles
GRS Corp.
Gunline Tools
Guns
Gun-Tec
Gutridge, Inc.
Half Moon Rifle Shop
Henriksen Tool Co., Inc.
Huey Gun Cases, Marvin
Iosso Marine Products
Ivanoff, Thomas G.
Jantz Supply
JGS Precision Tool Mfg.
K-D, Inc.
Kasenit Co., Inc.
Kleinendorst, K.W.
Kopp, Terry K.
Korzinek Riflesmith, J.
LaRocca Gun Works, Inc.
Lea Mfg. Co.
Lee Supplies, Mark
Lortone, Inc.
Marsh, Mike
MCRW Associates
MCS, Inc.
MDS, Inc.
Menck, Thomas W.
Metalife Industries
Millett Sights
Milliron Custom Mittermeier, Inc.

MMC
Morrow, Bud
Newman Gunshop
NGraveR Co., The
Nitex, Inc.
N&J Sales
Nowlin Custom Barrels Mfg.
Ole Frontier Gunsmith Shop
Pace Marketing, Inc.
Palmgren Steel Products
PanaVise Products, Inc.
Pease Accuracy, Bob
PEM's Mfg. Co.
Power Custom, Inc.
Precise Metal Finishing
Precision Arms International, Inc.
Precision Specialties
Prolix®
Ravell Ltd.
Reardon Products
Robar Co.'s, Inc., The
Roto/Carve
Russell Knives, Inc., A.G.
Scott/McDougall Custom Gunsmiths
Shaw's Finest in Guns
Sheridan USA, Inc., Austin

Shirley Co. Gun & Riflemakers Ltd.
S.K. Guns, Inc.
Smith Whetstone Co., Inc.
Spyderco, Inc.
Starrett Co., L.S.
Stoney Point Products, Inc.
Stuart Products, Inc.
Sure Shot of LA, Inc.
TDP Industries, Inc.
Texas Platers Supply
Tom's Gun Repair
Trulock Tool
Turnbull Restoration, Doug
Unick's Gunsmithing
Walker Arms Co., Inc.
Washita Mountain Whetstone Co.
Weaver's Gun Shop
Wessinger Custom Guns &
  Engraving
Westfield Engineering
Westrom, John
Wilcox All-Pro Tools & Supply
Will-Burt Co.
Williams Gun Sight Co.
Williams Shootin' Iron Service
Yavapai College

HANDGUN ACCESSORIES

Action Arms Ltd.
ADCO International
Adventurer's Outpost
Ajax Custom Grips, Inc.
American Bullets
American Pistolsmiths Guild
Ansen Enterprises
Auto-Ordnance Corp.
Bar-Sto Precision Machine
Baumannize, Inc.
Behlert Precision
Bob's Tactical Indoor Shooting
  Range & Gun Shop
Boonie Packer Products
Brauer Bros. Mfg. Co.
Brownells, Inc.
Brown Products, Inc., Ed
B-Square Co.
Bucheimer, J.M.
Centaur Systems, Inc.
Central Specialties Ltd.
Champion's Choice, Inc.
Clark Custom Guns, Inc.
Clymer Manufacturing Co., Inc.
Cobra Gunskin
C3 Systems
Dade Screw Machine Products
Doskocil Mfg. Co., Inc
E.A.A. Corp.
Eagle Imports, Inc.
Eagle International, Inc.
E&L Mfg., Inc.
EMF Co., Inc.
Faith Associates, Inc.
Feminine Protection, Inc.
Ferris Firearms
Fleming Firearms
Frielich Police Equipment
Glock, Inc.
Greider Precision
Gremmel Enterprises
Gun-Alert/Master Products, Inc.
Guncraft Sports, Inc.
Gunfitters, The
Gun-Ho Sports Cases
Hebard Guns, Gil
Heinie Specialty Products
Hill Speed Leather, Ernie
H.K.S. Products
Holster Shop, The
Jeffredo Gunsight
Jet Comp Systems
Jett & Co., Inc.
J.O. Arms & Ammunition Co.
Johnson Gunsmithing, Inc., Neal G.
Jones, J.D.
Jumbo Sports Products
Keller Co., The
King's Gun Works
K&K Ammo Wrist Band
KLP, Inc.
Kopp, Terry K.
Lakewood Products, Inc.
La Prade

LaRocca Gun Works, Inc.
Laseraim
Lee's Red Ramps
Lighthouse Mfg. Co., Inc.
Loch Leven Industries
Lohman Mfg. Co., Inc.
Mac's .45 Shop
Mag-Na-Port Int'l, Inc.
Magnolia Sports, Inc.
Magnum Research, Inc.
Mag-Pack Corp.
Maloni, Russ
Masen Co., John
Master Products, Inc.
McCormick Corp., Chip
MEC-Gar S.R.L.
Menck, Thomas W.
Merit Corp.
Merkuria Ltd.
Michaels of Oregon Co.
MTM Molded Products Co., Inc.
Mustra's Custom Guns, Inc., Carl
N.C. Ordnance Co.
Nielsen Custom Cases
No-Sho Mfg. Co.
Novak's .45 Shop, Wayne
Owen, Harry
Pace Marketing, Inc.
Pachmayr Ltd.
Pardini Armi Commerciale Srl
Peregrine Industries, Inc.
PistolPAL Products
Power Custom, Inc.
Practical Tools, Inc.
Precision Arms International, Inc.
Ranch Products
Ravell Ltd.
Royal Arm International Products
Russwood Custom Pistol Grips
Sheridan USA, Inc., Austin
Sile Distributors
Sling 'N Things, Inc.
Sonderman, Robert
Southwind Sanctions
Specialized Weapons, Inc.
Sport Specialties
SSK Industries
TacTell, Inc.
Tapco, Inc.
Taurus, S.A., Forjas
T.F.C. S.p.A.
Thompson/Center Arms
Triple-K Mfg. Co.
Tyler Mfg.-Dist., Melvin
Valor Corp.
Volquartsen Custom Ltd.
Wessinger Custom Guns &
  Engraving
Western Design
Whitestone Lumber Corp.
Wilson's Gun Shop
Wichita Arms, Inc.

HANDGUN GRIPS

African Import Co.
Ahrends, Kim
Ajax Custom Grips, Inc.
Altamont Co.
American Gripcraft
Art Jewel Enterprises Ltd.
Barami Corp.
Bear Hug Grips, Inc.
Bell Originals, Inc., Sid
Bob's Gun Shop
Boone's Custom Ivory Grips, Inc.
CAM Enterprises
Champion's Choice, Inc.
Cobra Gunskin
Cole-Grip
Colonial Repair
Custom Firearms
Desert Industries, Inc.
E.A.A. Corp.
Eagle Imports, Inc.
EMF Co., Inc.
Eyears
Fitz Pistol Grip Co.
Forrest, Inc., Tom
Greene, M.L.
Guns
Harrison-Hurtz Enterprises, Inc.
Herrett's Stocks, Inc.
Hogue Grips
Holster Shop, The
Johnson Gunsmithing, Inc., Neal G.
Linebaugh Custom Sixguns & Rifle
  Works
Logan Security Products Co.

Mac's .45 Shop
Maloni, Russ
Masen Co., John
Monte Kristo Pistol Grip Co.
N.C. Ordnance Co.
Newell, Robert H.
Old Western Scrounger, Inc.
Pace Marketing, Inc.
Pachmayr Ltd.
Pardini Armi Commerciale Srl
Pilgrim Pewter, Inc.
Ravell Ltd.
Renner Co., R.J./Radical Concepts
Rosenberg & Sons, Jack A.
Royal Arm International Products
Royal Arms
Roy's Custom Grips
Russwood Custom Pistol Grips
Safari Gun Co.
Safariland Ltd., Inc.
Savana Sports, Inc.
Sheridan USA, Inc., Austin
Sile Distributors
Sonderman, Robert B.
Spegel, Craig
Taurus, S.A., Forjas
Taurus Firearms, Inc.
Tyler Mfg.-Dist., Melvin
Valor Corp.
Vintage Industries, Inc.
Volquartsen Custom Ltd.
Wallace's
Wayland Precision Wood Products

HEARING PROTECTORS

Bausch & Lomb, Inc.
Bilsom Intl., Inc.
Blount, Inc. Sporting Equipment
  Division
Champion's Choice, Inc.
Clark Co., Inc., David
Cobra Gunskin
E-A-R, Inc.
Fitz Pistol Grip Co.
Flents Products Co., Inc.
Johnson Gunsmithing, Inc., Neal G.
MCRW Associates

North Specialty Products
Paterson Gunsmithing
Peltor, Inc.
R.E.T. Enterprises
Rockwood Corp., Speedwell Div.
Safari Gun Co.
Safariland Ltd., Inc.
Safety Direct
Smith & Wesson
Valor Corp.
Willson Safety Prods. Div.

HOLSTERS AND LEATHER GOODS

A&B Industries, Inc.
Action Products, Inc.
Aker Leather Products
Alessi Holsters, Inc.
American Sales & Mfg. Co.
Arratoonian, Andy
Artistry in Leather
Baker's Leather Goods, Roy
Bandcor Industries
Barami Corp.
Beeman Precision Airguns, Inc.
Bianchi International, Inc.
Blocker's Custom Holsters, Ted
Bob's Tactical Indoor Shooting
  Range & Gun Shop
Brauer Bros. Mfg. Co.
Brown, H.R.
Brownells, Inc.
Browning Arms Co.
Bucheimer, J.M.
Carvajal Belts & Holsters
Cathey Enterprises, Inc.
Chace Leather Products
Clements' Custom Leathercraft,
  Chas
Cobra Gunskin
Cobra Line SRL
Cobra Sport
Colonial Repair
Crawford Co., Inc., R.M.
Creedmoor Sports, Inc.
Dakota Corp.
Davis Leather Co., G. Wm.
Delhi Gun House
DeSantis Holster & Leather Goods
Easy Pull/Outlaw Products
Ekol Leather Care
El Paso Saddlery Co.
EMF Co., Inc.
Epps "Orillia" Ltd., Ellwood
Eutaw Co., Inc., The
Faust, Inc., T.G.
Fobus International Ltd.

Fury Cutlery
Galati International
GALCO International Ltd.
Glock, Inc.
GML Products, Inc.
Gould & Goodrich
Gunfitters, The
Gun Leather Limited
Gusty Winds Corp.
Gun Works, The
Hafner Creations, Inc.
Hebard Guns, Gil
Henigson & Associates, Steve
High North Products, Inc.
Hill Speed Leather, Ernie
Holster Outpost
Holster Shop, The
Horseshoe Leather Products
Hoyt Holster Co., Inc.
Hume, Don
Hunter Co., Inc.
J.O. Arms & Ammunition Co.
John's Custom Leather
Jumbo Sports Products
Kane Products, Inc.
Kirkpatrick Leather Co.
KLP, Inc.
Kolpin Mfg., Inc.
L.A.R. Manufacturing, Inc.
Law Concealment Systems, Inc.
Lawrence Leather Co.
Leather Arsenal
Lethal Force Institute
Lone Star Gunleather
Magnolia Sports, Inc.
Markell, Inc.
MCRW Associates
Michaels of Oregon Co.
Mixson Leathercraft, Inc.
Nelson Combat Leather, Bruce
Nielsen Custom Cases
Noble Co., Jim
No-Sho Mfg. Co.

Null Holsters Ltd., K.L.
October Country
Ojala Holsters, Arvo
Oklahoma Leather Products, Inc.
Old West Reproductions, Inc.
Pace Marketing, Inc.
Pathfinder Sports Leather
Police Bookshelf
Proline Handgun Leather
PW Gunleather
Red Head, Inc.
Red River Frontier Outfitters
Renegade
Ringler Custom Leather Co.
Rybka Custom Leather Equipment, Thad
Safari Gun Co.
Safariland Ltd., Inc.
Safety Speed Holster, Inc.
Savana Sports, Inc.
Schulz Industries
Shadow Concealment Systems
Sheridan USA, Inc., Austin
Shoemaker & Sons, Inc., Tex

Shurkatch Corp.
Sile Distributors
Silhouette Leathers
Smith Saddlery, Jesse W.
Southwind Sanctions
Sparks, Milt
Stalker, Inc.
Strong Holster Co.
Stuart, V. Pat
Tabler Marketing
Texas Longhorn Arms, Inc.
Torel, Inc.
Triple-K Mfg. Co., Inc.
Tyler Mfg.-Dist., Melvin
Uberti USA, Inc.
Valor Corp.
Venus Industries
Viking Leathercraft, Inc.
Walt's Custom Leather
Whinnery, Walt
Wild Bill's Originals
Whitestone Lumber Corp.
Winchester Sutler, Inc., The

HUNTING AND CAMP GEAR, CLOTHING, ETC.

Ace Sportswear, Inc.
Action Products, Inc.
Adventure 16, Inc.
All Weather Outerwear
Allen Co., Bob
Allen Sportswear, Bob
American Import Co., The
Armor
Atsko/Sno-Seal, Inc.
Bagmaster Mfg. Inc.
Barbour, Inc.
Barteaux Machetes, Inc.
Bauer, Eddie
Bausch & Lomb, Inc.
Bean, L.L.
Bear Archery
Beaver Park Products, Inc
Better Concepts Co.
Bilsom Intl., Inc.
Boss Manufacturing Co.
Brell Mar Products
Browning Arms Co.
Brown Manufacturing
Brunton U.S.A.
Buck Stop Lure Co., Inc.
Cabela's
Camofare Co.
Camp-Cap Products
Carhartt, Inc.
Catoctin Cutlery
Chameleon Camouflage Systems
Coulston Int. Corp.
Chimere, Inc.
Chippewa Shoe Co.
Churchill Glove Co., James
Clarkfield Enterprises, Inc.
Cobra Gunskin
Coghlan's Ltd.
Crawford Co., Inc., R.M.
Creedmoor Sports, Inc.
Coleman Co., Inc.
Counter Assault
Dakota Corp.
Danner Shoe Mfg. Co.
DeckSlider of Florida
Deer Me Products
Dr. O's Products Ltd.
Dunham Co.
Duofold, Inc.
Duxbak, Inc.
Dynalite Products, Inc.
E-A-R, Inc.
Erickson's Mfg., Inc., C.W.
Finerty, Raymond F.
Fish-N-Hunt, Inc.
Forrest Tool Co.
Fox River Mills, Inc.
Frankonia Jagd
Fury Cutlery
Game Winner, Inc.
Gander Mountain, Inc.
G&H Decoys, Inc.
Gerber Legendary Blades
Glacier Glove
Gozon Corp.
Hawken Shop, The
Herrett's Stocks, Inc.
Hinman Outfitters, Bob
Hodgman, Inc.
Houtz & Barwick

Hunter's Specialties, Inc.
Hunting Classics Ltd.
Innovision Enterprises
Johanssons Vapentillbehor, Bert
Just Brass, Inc.
Kamik Outdoor Footwear
K&M Industries, Inc.
Keowee Game Calls
LaCrosse Footwear, Inc.
Langenberg Hat Co.
Mack's Sport Shop
MAG Instrument, Inc.
Marathon Rubber Prods. Co., Inc.
Melton Shirt Co., Inc.
Millenium Safety Products
Molin Industries
Nelson/Weather-Rite
Noble Co., Jim
Northlake Boot Co.
Original Mink Oil, Inc.
Orvis Co., The
Palsa Outdoor Products
Partridge Sales Ltd., John
PAST Sporting Goods, Inc
Pendleton Woolen Mills
Porta Blind, Inc.
Primos Wild Game Calls, Inc.
Pro-Mark
Pyramid, Inc.
Randolph Engineering, Inc.
Ranger Footwear
Ranger Mfg. Co., Inc.
Rattlers Brand
Red Ball
Red Head, Inc.
Red River Frontier Outfitters
Refrigiwear, Inc.
Re-Heater, Inc.
Remington Footwear Co.
Rocky
Safari Gun Co.
Safesport Manufacturing Co.
Safety Direct
San Angelo Sports Products, Inc.
Savana Sports, Inc.
Scansport, Inc.
Scotch Hunting Products Co., Inc.
Servus Footwear Co.
Slings 'N Things, Inc.
Smith Whetstone Co., Inc.
Streamlight, Inc.
Survival Books/The Larder
Swanndri New Zealand
Torel, Inc.
Trail Timer Co.
Teledyne Co.
10-X Products Group
Thompson, Norm
Tink's Safariland Hunting Corp.
Torel, Inc.
Venus Industries
Wakina by Pic
Walker Shoe Co.
Walls Industries
Willson Safety Prods. Div.
Wolverine Boots & Shoes Div.
Woolrich Woolen Mills
Wyoming Knife Corp.
Yellowstone Wilderness Supply

KNIVES AND KNIFEMAKER'S SUPPLIES FACTORY AND MAIL ORDER

Adventure 16, Inc.
African Import Co.
Aitor-Cuchilleria Del Norte, S.A.
American Target Knives
Aristocrat Knives
Art Jewel Enterprises Ltd.
Atlanta Cutlery Corp.
B&D Trading Co., Inc.
Barteaux Machetes, Inc.
Bean, L.L.
Benchmark Knives
Beretta U.S.A. Corp.
Blackjack Knives
Blue Ridge Knives
Blue Ridge Machinery & Tools, Inc.
Boker USA, Inc.
Bowen Knife Co.
Browning Arms Co.
Brunton U.S.A.
Buck Knives, Inc.
Buster's Custom Knives
CAM Enterprises
Camillus Cutlery Co.
Campbell, Dick
Case & Sons Cutlery Co., W.R.
Catoctin Cutlery
Chicago Cutlery Co.
Christopher Firearms Co., Inc., E.
Clements' Custom Leathercraft, Chas
Coast Cutlery Co.
Cold Steel, Inc.
Coleman Co., Inc.
Collins Brothers Div.
Colonial Knife Co.
Compass Industries, Inc.
Crawford Co., Inc., R.M.
Creative Craftsman, Inc., The
Crosman Blades
Cutco Cutlery
Cutlery Shoppe
Damascus-U.S.A.
Dan's Whetstone Co., Inc.
Degen Knives
Delhi Gun House
Diamontd Machining Technology, Inc.
EdgeCraft Corp.
EK Knife Co.
Empire Cutlery Corp.
Eze-Lap Diamond Prods.
Fitz Pistol Grip Co.
Forrest Tool Co.
Forthofer's Gunsmithing & Knifemaking
Fortune Products, Inc.
Frank Knives
Frost Cutlery Co.
Fury Cutlery
Gerber Legendary Blades
Golden Age Arms Co.
Gutmann Cutlery Co., Inc.
Hawken Shop, The
H&B Forge Co.
Harrington Cutlery, Inc., Russell
Henckels Zwillingswerk, Inc., J.A.

Hubertus Schneidwarenfabrik
Hunting Classics Ltd.
Hy-Score Arms Co. Ltd.
Ibberson (Sheffield) Ltd., George
Iron Mountain Knife Co.
J.A. Blades, Inc.
Jantz Supply
Jenco Sales, Inc.
KA-BAR Knives
Kasenit Co., Inc.
Kellogg's Professional Products
Ken's Finn Knives
Kershaw Knives
Knife Importers, Inc.
Koval Knives, Inc.
Lamson & Goodnow Mfg. Co.
Lansky Sharpeners & Crock Stick
Leatherman Tool Group, Inc.
Linder Solingen Knives
Mar Knives, Inc., Al
Matthews Cutlery
Molin Industries
Monte Kristo Pistol Grip Co.
Murphy Co., Inc., R.
Normark Corp.
North American Specialties
Outdoor Edge Cutlery Corp.
Plaza Cutlery, Inc.
Precise International
Queen Cutlery Co.
Randall-Made Knives
R&C Knives & Such
Ravell Ltd.
Reno, Wayne and Karen
Russell Knives, Inc., A.G.
Safesport Manufacturing Co.
Scansport, Inc.
Schiffman, Mike
Schrade Cutlery Corp.
Schrimsher's Custom Knifemaker's Supply, Bob
Sheffield Knifemakers Supply
Sheridan USA, Inc., Austin
Smith & Wesson
Smith Saddlery, Jesse W.
Smith Whetstone Co., Inc.
Soque River Knives
Spyderco, Inc.
Survival Books/The Larder
Swiss Army Knives, Inc.
T.F.C. S.p.A.
Track of the Wolf, Inc.
Tru-Balance Knife Co.
United Cutlery Corp.
Utica Cutlery Co.
Valor Corp.
Venus Industries
Walt's Custom Leather
Washita Mountain Whetstone Co.
Weber Jr., Rudolf
Wenoka/Seastyle
Western Cutlery Co.
Whinnery, Walt
White Owl Enterprises
Wostenholm
Wyoming Knife Corp.

LABELS, BOXES, CARTRIDGE HOLDERS

Accuracy Products, S.A.
Anderson Manufacturing Co., Inc.
Arkfeld Mfg. & Dist. Co., Inc.
Cabinet Mtn. Outfitter
Del Rey Products
Fitz Pistol Grip Co.
Flambeau Products Corp.
Huey Gun Cases, Marvin
J&J Products Co.

KLP, Inc.
Kolpin Mfg., Inc.
Lakewood Products, Inc.
Monte Kristo Pistol Grip Co.
Peterson Instant Targets Co.
Ravell Ltd.
Scharch Mfg., Inc.
Stalwart Corp.

LOAD TESTING AND PRODUCT TESTING, (Chronographing, Ballistic Studies)

ADC, Inc.
Ballistic Research
Bustani Appraisers, Leo
Clerke Co., J.A.
Corbin Applied Technology
D&H Precision Tooling
Farr Studio, Inc.
Jensen Bullets
Jones, J.D.
Jurras, L.E.
Lachaussee, S.A.
Lomont Precision Bullets

Maionchi-L.M.I.
McMurdo, Lynn
Neutralizer Police Munitions
Pejsa Ballistics
Rupert's Gun Shop
Russell's Rifle Shop
Schumakers Gun Shop, William
SSK Industries
Star Custom Bullets
White Laboratory, Inc., H.P.
Wildcatters, The

MISCELLANEOUS

Actions, Rifle
Hall Manufacturing
Accurizing, Rifle
Stoney Baroque Shooters Supply
Adapters, Cartridge
Alex, Inc.
Owen, Harry
Adapters, Shotshell
PC Co. (Plummer 410 conversion)
Airgun Accessories
Beeman Precision Airguns, Inc.
(Beeman Pell Seat, Pell Size)
BSA Guns Ltd.
Assault Rifle Accessories
Feather Industries, Inc.
Ram-Line, Inc.
Body Armor
A&B Industries, Inc.
Faust, Inc., T.G.
Second Chance Body Armor
Bore Collimator
Alley Supply Co. (Sweany
Site-A-Line)
Bore Illuminator
Flashette Co. (gun cleaning aid)
Bore Lights
MDS, Inc.
Brass Catcher
M.A.M. Products, Inc. (free
standing for all auto pistols
and/or semi-auto rifles)
Bullets, Rubber
CIDCO
Calendar, Gun Show
Stott's Creek Armory, Inc.
Cannons, Miniature Replicas
Furr Arms
R.G.-G., Inc.
Convert-A-Pell
Jett & Co., Inc.
Dehumidifiers
Buenger Enterprises
Hydrosorbent Products
Deer Drag
D&H Prods. Co., Inc.
Dryers
Buenger Enterprises
(thermo-electric)
Peet Shoe Dryer, Inc. (electric
boot, shoe, hip, chest wader)
E-Z Loader
Del Rey Products (for 22-cal.
rifles)
Firearm Historian
Kennerknecht, Rick "KK"
Firearm Restoration
Adair Custom Shop, Bill
Border Guns & Leather
Johns, Bill
Liberty Antique Gunworks
Mazur Restoration, Pete
Moeller, Steve
FFL Record Keeping
Basics Information Systems, Inc.
R.E.T. Enterprises
Flares
Aztec International Ltd.
Gatling Guns
Furr Arms
Hunting Trips
J/B Adventures & Safaris, Inc.
Professional Hunter Specialties
(African safaris)
Mongaso Wild Life Safaris
Hypodermic Rifles/Pistols
Multipropulseurs
Insert Barrels
Owen, Harry/Sport Specialties
IR Detection Systems
GTS Enterprises, Inc.
Locks, Gun
Brown Manufacturing
Master Lock Co.
Military Equipment/Accessories
Alpha 1 Drop Zone
Monte Carlo Pad
Hoppe's Div.
Photographers, Gun
Bilal, Mustafa
Hanusin, John
Macbean, Stan
Payne Photography, Robert
Semmer, Charles
Smith, Michael
Weyer International

Power Tools, Rotary Flexible Shaft
Foredom Electric Co.
Racks, Gun and Bow
All Rite Products, Inc.
Saddle Rings, Studs
Silver Ridge Gun Shop
Safety Devices
Gun-Alert/Master Products, Inc.
(gun safety cover)
P&M Sales and Service
Safeties
Harper, William E./The Great 870
Co. (for Rem. 870P)
Taylor & Robbins (sidelever f. rifle)
Scents and Lures
Buck Stop Lure Co., Inc.
Cabinet Mtn. Outfitter
Dr. O's Products Ltd.
Mountain Hollow Game Calls
Rickard, Inc., Pete
Robbins Scent, Inc.
Tink's Safariland Hunting Corp.
Wildlife Research Center, Inc.
Scoring Plug
RIG Products
Scrimshaw
Boone's Custom Ivory Grips, Inc.
Dolbare, Elizabeth
Gun Room, The
Marek, George
Reno, Wayne and Karen
Sherwood, George
Self-Defense Sprays
Counter Assault
Shell Catcher
Condor Mfg. Co.
Shell Dispenser
Loadmaster
Shooting Range Equipment
Caswell International Corp.
Silencers
AWC Systems Technology
Ciener, Jonathan Arthur
Developmental Concepts
DLO Mfg.
Fleming Firearms
Norrell Arms, John
Precision Arms International, Inc.
S&H Arms Mfg. Co.
S.C.R.C.
Sound Technology
Ward Machine
Slings and Swivels
Boonie Packer Products
Butler Creek Corp.
DTM International, Inc.
Leather Arsenal
Michaels of Oregon Co.
Outdoor Connection, Inc., The
Palsa Outoor Products
Pathfinder Sports Leather
Schulz Industries
Sile Distributors
Torel, Inc.
Speedloader, Shotgun
Armstec, Inc.
Treestands and Steps
A&J Products
Amacker International, Inc.
Apache Products, Inc.
Dr. O's Products Ltd.
Silent Hunter
Summit Specialties, Inc.
Trax America, Inc.
Treemaster
Warren & Sweat Mfg. Co.
Trophies
Blackinton & Co., Inc., V.H.
Ventilation
ScanCo Environmental Systems
(indoor range filtration)
Video Tapes
Calibre Press, Inc. (police survival)
Dangler, Homer L. (Kentucky
rifles)
Eastman Products, R.T. (outdoor
adventure)
Foothills Video Productions, Inc.
MagSafe Ammo Co.
New Historians Productions, The
(muzzle-loading)
Trail Visions (woodcock hunting)
Wilderness Sound Productions
Xythos-Miniature Revolver
Andres & Dworsky

MUZZLE-LOADING GUNS, BARRELS AND EQUIPMENT

Accuracy Unlimited (Littleton, CO)
Adkins, Luther
All American Bullets
•Anderson Manufacturing Co., Inc.
Armi San Paolo
•Armoury, Inc., The
•Armsport, Inc.
Barton, Michael D.
•Beauchamp & Son, Inc.
Beaver Lodge
Bentley, John
Blackhawk East
Blackhawk Mountain
Blackhawk West
•Blount, Inc. Sporting Equipment
Division
Bridgers Best
Buckskin Machine Works
Buffalo Bullet Co., Inc.
Burgess and Son Gunsmiths, R.W.
Butler Creek Corp.
Cache La Poudre Rifleworks
•Cape Outfitters
Camas Hot Springs Mfg.
Chopie Mfg., Inc.
CONKKO
Cousin Bob's Mountain Products
•Cumberland Arms
•Cumberland Knife & Gun Works
•CVA
Dangler, Homer L.
Dan's Whetstone Co., Inc.
Day & Sons, Inc., Leonard
Dayton Traister
deHaas Barrels
•Denver Arms, Ltd.
DGS, Inc.
Dixon Muzzleloading Shop, Inc.
Ed's Gun House
•EMF Co., Inc.
•Euroarms of America, Inc.
Eutaw Co., Inc., The
Fautheree, Andy
Fellowes, Ted
Fish, Marshall F.-Mfg. Gunsmith
Flintlock Muzzle Loading Gun
Shop, The
Flintlocks, Etc.
•Forster Products
Frontier
Getz Barrel Co.
•Gibbs Rifle Co., Inc.
Golden Age Arms Co.
•Gonic Arms, Inc.
Green Bay Bullets
•Gun Works, The
•Hatfield Gun Co., Inc.
•Hawken Shop, The
Hege Jagd-u. Sporthandels, GmbH
Hodgdon Powder Co., Inc.
•Hornady Mfg. Co.
House of Muskets, Inc., The
Hunkeler, A.
Jamison's Forge Works
K&M Industries, Inc.
Kolpin Mfg., Inc.

Kwik-Site Co.
Lite Tek International
•Log Cabin Sport Shop
•Lyman Products Corp.
McCann's Muzzle-Gun Works
•Mitchell Arms, Inc.
•Modern MuzzleLoading, Inc.
•Montana Armory, Inc.
•Mossberg & Sons, Inc., O.F.
Mountain State Muzzleloading
Supplies
•Mowrey Gun Works
MMP
Mt. Alto Outdoor Products
Mushroom Express Bullet Co.
Muzzleloaders Etcetera, Inc.
Neumann GmbH
Newman Gunshop
October Country
Oklahoma Leather Products, Inc.
Olde Pennsylvania
Ox-Yoke Originals, Inc.
Parker Gun Finishes
Patchbox & Museum of the Great
Divide, The
•Pedersoli Davide & C.
Peterson Gun Shop, Inc., A.W.
Peterson Instant Targets, Inc.
Phyl-Mac
Robinson Firearms Mfg. Ltd.
R.V.I.
Scott, Inc., Tyler
Selsi Co., Inc.
Safari Gun Co.
S&B Industries
•Sharps Arms Co., Inc., C.
Shooter's Choice
•Sile Distributors
Siler Locks
Single Shot, Inc.
Slings 'N Things, Inc.
South Bend Replicas, Inc.
Southern Bloomer Mfg. Co.
SPG Bullet Lubricant
Storey, Dale A.
•Sturm, Ruger & Co., Inc.
Taylor's & Co., Inc.
TDP Industries, Inc.
Tennessee Valley Mfg.
TETRA Gun Lubricants
•Thompson/Center Arms
•Thunder Mountain Arms
Tiger-Hunt
Track of the Wolf, Inc.
•Traditions, Inc.
•Trail Guns Armory, Inc.
•Uberti USA, Inc.
•Ultra Light Arms, Inc.
•Upper Missouri Trading Co.
Warren Muzzleloading Co., Inc.
Wescombe
•White Systems, Inc.
Winchester Sutler, Inc., The
Young Country Arms
Ziegel Engineering

PISTOLSMITHS

Accuracy Gun Shop
Accuracy Unlimited (Glendale, AZ)
Accurate Plating & Weaponry, Inc.
Ahlman Guns
Aldis Gunsmithing & Shooting
Supply
Alpha Precision, Inc.
American Pistolsmiths Guild
Amodei, Jim
Armament Gunsmithing Co., Inc.
Bain & Davis, Inc.
Baity's Custom Gunworks
Banks, Ed
Bar-Sto Precision Machine
Barta's Gunsmithing
Bengtson Arms Co., L.
Border Guns & Leather
Bowen Classic Arms Corp.
Brian, C.T.
Briley Mfg., Inc.
Broken Gun Ranch
Brown Products, Inc., Ed
Campbell, Dick
Cannon's Guns
Caraville Manufacturing
Carter's Gun Shop

Cellini, Inc., Vito Francesca
Chesire & Perez Dist.
Chuck's Gun Shop
Clark Custom Guns, Inc.
Colonial Repair
Corkys Gun Clinic
Curtis Custom Shop
Custom Gunsmiths
Cylinder & Slide, Inc.
Davis Service Center, Bill
D&D Gunsmiths, Ltd.
D&L Sports
D.O.C. Specialists, Inc.
Duncan's Gunworks, Inc.
E.A.A. Corp.
EMF Co., Inc.
Ferris Firearms
First Distributors, Inc., Jack
Fisher Custom Firearms
Francesca Stabilizer's, Inc.
Frielich Police Equipment
Frontier Arms Co., Inc.
Garthwaite, Jim
Greider Precision
Guncraft Sports, Inc.
Gunsite Gunsmithy

•See page 460 for Warranty Service Center Addresses

Gunsmithing Ltd.
Gutridge, Inc.
Hamilton, Keith
Hank's Gun Shop
Hanson's Gun Center, Dick
Hardison, Charles
Hebard Guns, Gil
Heinie Specialty Products
High Bridge Arms, Inc.
Highline Machine Co.
Hindman, Ace
Hoag, James W.
Irwin, Campbell H.
Ivanoff, Thomas G.
Ken's Gun Specialties
Jarvis Gunsmithing, Inc.
Johnston, James
Jones, J.D.
Jungkind, Reeves C.
Kilham & Co.
Kimball, Gary
Kopec Enterprises, John
Kopp, Terry K.
La Clinique du .45
LaFrance Specialties
LaRocca Gun Works, Inc.
Laughridge, William R.
Lawson, John G.
Lee's Red Ramps
Linebaugh Custom Sixguns & Rifle
 Works
Lock's Philadelphia Gun Exchange
Long, George F.
Mac's .45 Shop
Mahony, Philip Bruce
Martz, John V.
Marvel, Alan
McMillan Gunworks, Inc.
MCS, Inc.
Mid-America Recreation, Inc.
Miller Custom
Mitchell's Accuracy Shop
MJK Gunsmithing, Inc.
Moran, Jerry
Mountain Bear Rifle Works, Inc.
Mullis Guncraft
Mustra's Custom Guns, Inc., Carl
Nastoff's 45 Shop Inc., Stev
North Fork Custom Gunsmithing
Novak's .45 Shop, Wayne
Nowlin Custom Barrels Mfg.
Nu-Line Guns, Inc.
Nygord Precision Products
Oglesby & Oglesby
 Gunmakers, Inc.

Old West Reproductions
Pace Marketing, Inc.
Pachmayr Ltd.
Pardini Armi Commerciale Srl
Paris, Frank J.
Peacemaker Specialists
PEM's Mfg. Co.
Performance Specialists
Phillips & Bailey, Inc.
Pierce Pistols
Plaxco, J. Michael
Practical Tools, Inc.
Precision Arms International, Inc.
Precision Specialties
Randco UK
Ravell Ltd.
Ries, Chuck
Riggs, Jim
Robar Co.'s, Inc., The
Rogers Gunsmithing, Bob
Scott/McDougall Custom Gunsmiths
Seecamp Co., Inc., L.W.
Shell Shack
Shooter Shop, The
Singletary, Kent
Sipes Gun Shop
Sight Shop, The
S.K. Guns, Inc.
Slings & Arrows
Spokhandguns, Inc.
Springfield, Inc.
SSK Industries
Starnes, Ken
Steger, James R.
Strawbridge, Victor W.
Stroup, Earl R.
Swenson's 45 Shop, A.D.
300 Gunsmith Service, Inc.
Ten-Ring Precision, Inc.
Thompson, Randall
Thurston Sports, Inc.
Tom's Gun Repair
T.S.W. Conversions, Inc.
Ulrich, Doc & Bud
Unick's Gunsmithing
Vic's Gun Refinishing
Volquartsen Custom Ltd.
Wallace's
Walters Industries
Wardell Precision Handguns Ltd.
Wessinger Custom Guns &
 Engraving
Williamson Precision Gunsmithing
Woods Pistolsmithing
Yavapai College

G&C Bullet Co., Inc.
"Gramps" Antique Cartridges
Graphics Direct
Green, Arthur S.
Hanned Line, The
HEBB Resources
Heidenstrom Bullets
Hensley & Gibbs
Hindman, Ace
Hoehn's Shooting Supply
•Hollywood Engineering
Hondo Industries
•Hornady Mfg. Co.
•Huntington Die Specialties
INTEC International, Inc.
Iosso Marine Products
JGS Precision Tool Mfg.
Jones, Neil
KAPRO MFG. Co., Inc.
King & Co.
•K&M Services
Lachaussee, S.A.
LeClear Industries
•Lee Precision, Inc.
Liberty Metals
Lighthouse Mfg. Co., Inc.
Lortone, Inc.
Loweth Firearms, Richard
•Lyman Products Corp.
•Magma Engineering Co.
McKillen & Heyer, Inc.
MCRW Associates
•MCS, Inc.
•MEC
Midway Arms, Inc.
MMP
Monte Kristo Pistol Grip Co.
Mountain South
MTM Molded Products Co., Inc.
Multi-Scale Charge Ltd.
NECO
Necromancer Industries, Inc.
Newman Gunshop
Niemi Enterprises, W.B.
Old West Bullet Moulds
•Old Western Scrounger, Inc.
Omark Industries
Pattern Control
Pend Oreille Sport Shop
Peterson Instant Targets, Inc.
Plum City Ballistic Range
•Ponsness/Warren
Precision Castings & Equipment,
 Inc.
•Precision Reloading, Inc.

Quinetics Corp.
Rapine Bullet Mould Mfg. Co.
Ravell Ltd.
Raytech
•RCBS
•R.D.P. Tool Co., Inc.
•Redding Reloading, Inc.
Riebe Co., W.J.
Roberts Products
Rochester Lead Works, Inc.
Rooster Laboratories
Rorschach Precision Products
Rucker Ammunition Co.
SAECO
Safari Gun Co.
Sandia Die & Cartridge Co.
S.C.A.P. Industries
•Scharch Mfg., Inc.
Scot Powder Co. of Ohio, Inc.
Shooters Accessory Supply
Sierra Bullets
Sierra Specialty Prod. Co.
Silver Eagle Machining
Simmons, Jerry
Sinclair International, Inc.
Skip's Machine
Slipshot MTS Group
Small Custom Mould & Bullet Co.
SOS Products Co.
Speer Products
Sportsman Supply Co.
•Stalwart Corp.
•Star Machine Works
Stoney Point Products, Inc.
Taracorp Industries
TETRA Gun Lubricants
Thompson Bullet Lube Co.
Timber Heirloom Products
Trammco, Inc.
Tru-Square Metal Products
T&S Industries, Inc.
Varner's Service
Vega Tool Co.
VibraShine, Inc.
Vibra-Tek Co.
Webster Scale Mfg. Co.
Welsh, Bud
Westfield Engineering
Whitestone Lumber Corp.
Whitetail Design & Engineering Ltd.
Widener's Reloading & Shooting
 Supply
•William's Gun Shop, Ben
Wilson, Co, L.E.
Young Country Arms

REBORING AND RERIFLING

Ackley Rifle Barrels, P.O.
Bellm Contenders
Chuck's Gun Shop
DKT, Inc.
H&S Liner Service
Ivanoff, Thomas G.
Jackalope Gun Shop
Jaeger, Inc., Paul/Dunn's
K-D, Inc.
Kopp, Terry K.
LaBounty Precision Reboring
Matco, Inc.
Mid-America Recreation, Inc.

Morrow, Bud
Ozark Gun Works
Pac-Nor Barreling
Pence Precision Barrels
Redman's Rifling & Reboring
Ridgetop Sporting Goods
Sharon Rifle Barrel Co.
Shaw, Inc., E.R.
Swift River Gunworks, Inc.
300 Gunsmith Service, Inc.
Tom's Gun Repair
Van Patten, J.W.
West, Robert G.

RELOADING TOOLS AND ACCESSORIES

Accuracy Components Co.
Advance Car Mover Co., Inc.
•Ammo Load, Inc.
•AMT
Andela Tool & Machinery, Inc.
•ASI
Ballisti-Cast, Inc.
Ballistic Products, Inc.
Barlett, J.
Ben's Machines
•Blount, Inc. Sporting Equipment
 Division
•Brown Co., E. Arthur
Brynin, Milton
Buck Stix
C&D Special Products
•Camdex, Inc.
Carbide Die & Mfg. Co., Inc.
•C-H Tool & Die Corp./4-D Custom
 Die Co.
CheVron Case Master
Claybuster
Coats, Mrs. Lester

Colorado Shooter's Supply
Competitor Corp., Inc.
Conetrol Scope Mounts
CONKKO
•Corbin, Inc.
Custom Products
•Dakota Arms
D.C.C. Enterprises
•Denver Instrument Co.
•Destination North Software
Dever Co., Jack
Dewey Mfg. Co., Inc., J.
•Dillon Precision Prods., Inc.
Eagan, Donald V.
Efemes Enterprises
Engineered Accessories
Enguix Import-Export
Fisher Enterprises
Fitz Pistol Grip Co.
Flambeau Products Corp.
Forgreens Tool Mfg., Inc.
•Forster Products
•Fremont Tool Works

RESTS—BENCH, PORTABLE—AND ACCESSORIES

Adventure 16, Inc.
Armor Metal Products
Bald Eagle Precision Machine Co.
Blount, Inc. Sporting Equipment
 Division
B-Square Co.
Champion's Choice, Inc.
Clift Mfg., L.R.
Clifton Arms, Inc.
Cravener's Gun Shop
Davidson Products, Inc.
Desert Mountain Mfg.
Forster Products
Greenwalt Rifles
Harris Engineering, Inc.
Hart & Son, Inc., Robert W.
Hidalgo, Tony

Holden Co., J.B.
Hoppe's Div.
Johnson Gunsmithing, Inc., Neal G.
MCRW Associates
Millett Sights
Newman Gunshop
Protektor Model Co.
Ransom International Corp
Sinclair International, Inc.
Sportsman Supply Co.
Sports Support Systems, Inc.
Sure Shot of LA, Inc.
Thompson Target Technology
Ultra Light Arms, Inc.
Verdemont Fieldsports
World of Targets

RIFLE BARREL MAKERS (See also Muzzle-Loading Guns, Barrels and Equipment)

Ackley Rifle Barrels, P.O.
American Bullets
Bellm Contenders
Borovnik KG, Ludwig
Bullberry Barrel Works, Ltd.
Bustani Appraisers, Leo
Carter's Gun Shop
Camas Hot Springs Mfg.
Cincinnati Swaging
Clark Custom Guns, Inc.
Clerke Co., J.A.
Competition Limited
DKT, Inc.
Donnelly, C.P.
Douglas Barrels, Inc.
Federal Ordnance, Inc.
Frank Custom Gun Service, Ron
Getz Barrel Co.

Graybill's Gun Shop
Green Mountain Rifle Barrel Co.,
 Inc.
H-S Precision, Inc.
Half Moon Rifle Shop
Hart Rifle Barrels, Inc.
Hastings Barrels
K-D, Inc.
KOGOT
Kopp, Terry K.
Krieger Barrels, Inc.
LaBounty Precision Reboring
Lilja Precision Rifle Barrels
Lock's Philadelphia Gun Exchange
Marquart Precision Co., Inc.
Matco, Inc.
McGowen Rifle Barrels
McMillan Rifle Barrels

Mid-America Recreation, Inc.
Oakland Custom Arms, Inc.
Obermeyer Rifled Barrels
Olympic Arms, Inc.
Pell, John T.
Pence Precision Barrels
Ravell Ltd.
Robar Co.'s, Inc., The
Rocky Mountain Rifle Works Ltd.
Safari Arms, Inc./SGW
Schneider Rifle Barrels, Inc., Gary
Sharon Rifle Barrel Co.

Shaw, Inc., E.R.
Shilen Rifles, Inc.
Small Arms Mfg. Co.
Siskiyou Gun Works
Societa Armi Bresciane Srl
Springfield, Inc.
Strutz Rifle Barrels, Inc., W.C.
Unique/M.A.P.F.
Verney-Carron
White Systems, Inc.
Wilson Arms Co., The

SCOPES, MOUNTS, ACCESSORIES, OPTICAL EQUIPMENT

Ackley Rifle Barrels
•Action Arms Ltd.
•ADCO International
Adventurer's Outpost
•Aimpoint, Inc.
•Aimtech Mount Systems
•Air Venture
Ajax Custom Grips, Inc.
Alley Supply Co.
Anderson Manufacturing Co., Inc.
Apel GmbH, Ernst
Applied Laser Systems, Inc.
A.R.M.S., Inc.
•Armscorp. USA, Inc.
Armurier Hiptmayer
Baumannize, Inc.
•Bausch & Lomb, Inc.
Beaver Park Products, Inc.
•Beeman Precision Airguns, Inc.
Bellm Contenders
•Blount, Inc. Sporting Equipment
   Division
B.M.F. Activator, Inc.
Brownells, Inc.
Brunton U.S.A.
•B-Square Co.
Buehler Scope Mounts
•Burris Co., Inc.
•Bushnell
Butler Creek Corp.
California Armory, Inc.
California Grip
Camp-Cap Products
•Cape Outfitters
Celestron International
•Clark Custom Guns, Inc.
Clearview Mfg. Co., Inc.
Combat Military Ordnance Ltd.
Compass Industries, Inc.
Conetrol Scope Mounts
Creedmoor Sports, Inc.
Del-Sports, Inc.
D&H Prods. Co., Inc.
•E.A.A. Corp.
E&L Mfg., Inc.
Ednar, Inc.
Eggleston, Jere D.
•Europtik Ltd.
Farr Studio, Inc.
•Flaig's
•Forster Products
Fujinon, Inc.
Galati International
Global Industries
Grace Tool, Inc.
Greenwalt Rifles
Griffin & Howe, Inc.
•GSI, Inc.
•G.U., Inc.
Hakko Co. Ltd.
Hermann Leather Co., H.J.
Hertel & Reuss
Hiptmayer, Klaus
Holden Co., J.B.
•Imatronic, Inc.
•Jaeger, Inc., Paul/Dunn's
•Jason Empire, Inc.
Jeffredo Gunsight
Johnson Gunsmithing, Inc., Neal G.
•Kahles USA
K-D, Inc.
•Keng's Firearms Specialty, Inc.
KenPatable Ent., Inc.
•Kesselring Gun Shop
Kilham & Co.
Kimber, Inc.
Kmount
•Kowa Optimed, Inc.
Kris Mounts
KVH Industries, Inc.
Kwik Mount Corp.
Kwik-Site Co.

•L&S Technologies, Inc.
Laseraim
•Laser Devices, Inc.
Leatherwood-Meopta, Inc.
Lectro Science, Inc.
Lee Supplies, Mark
Lee Co., T.K.
Leica USA, Inc.
•Leupold
Lite Tek International
Lohman Mfg. Co., Inc.
London Guns Ltd.
•Mac-1 Distributors
Mac's .45 Shop
McKee, Arthur
McMillan Optical Gunsight Co.
Meier Works
Midway Arms, Inc.
Military Armament Corp.
Millett Sights
•Mirador Optical Corp.
Muzzle-Nuzzle Co.
New Democracy, Inc.
Newman Gunshop
•Nichols Sports Optics
Night Vision Equipment Co., Inc.
•Nikon, Inc.
North American Specialties
•Nygord Precision Products
Oakshore Electronic Sights, Inc.
•Old Western Scrounger, Inc.
Olympic Optical Co.
OMR Feinmechanik, Jagd-und
   Sportwaffen, GmbH
Optolyth-USA, Inc.
Orchard Park Enterprise
Outdoor Connection, Inc., The
Pace Marketing, Inc.
•Pachmayr Ltd.
PECAR Herbert Schwarz, GmbH
PEM's Mfg. Co.
•Pentax Corp.
Pilkington Gun Co.
Precise Metalsmithing Enterprises
•Precision Sport Optics
Premier Reticles
•Ram-Line, Inc.
Ranch Products
Randolph Engineering, Inc.
•Ranging, Inc.
Ravell Ltd.
•Redfield, Inc.
Robar Co.'s, Inc., The
Rocky Mountain High Sports
   Glasses
Royal Arm International Products
Sanders Custom Gun Service
•Schmidt & Bender
Seattle Binocular & Scope Repair
   Co.
Selsi Co,, Inc.
•Shepherd Scope Ltd.
Sheridan USA, Inc., Austin
•Shooters Supply
•Simmons Enterprises, Ernie
Simmons Outdoor Corp.
S&K Mfg. Co.
Societa Armi Bresciane Srl.
•Specialized Weapons, Inc.
Speer Products
Sportsmatch Ltd.
•Springfield, Inc.
Sure Shot of LA, Inc.
•Swift Instruments, Inc.
•Tapco, Inc.
•Tasco Sales, Inc.
Tele-Optics
Tele-Optics, Inc.
•Thompson/Center Arms
•Trijicon, Inc.
•Unertl Optical Co., Inc., John
United Binocular Co.

United States Optics Technologies,
   Inc.
Valor Corp.
Warne Manufacturing Co.
WASP Shooting Systems
•Weatherby, Inc.
Weaver Products
•Weaver Scope Repair Service

Wells Custom Gunsmith, R.A.
Western Design
Westfield Engineering
•White Systems, Inc.
Wideview Scope Mount Corp.
•Williams Gun Sight Co.
•Zeiss Optical, Inc., Carl

SHOOTING/TRAINING SCHOOLS

Alpine Precision Gunsmithing &
   Indoor Shooting Range
American Pistol Institute
American Small Arms Academy
Auto Arms
Bob's Tactical Indoor Shooting
   Range & Gun Shop
Chapman Academy of Practical
   Shooting
Chelsea Gun Club of New York
   City, Inc.
CQB Training
Daisy Mfg. Co.
Defense Training International, Inc.
Dowtin Gunworks
Executive Protection Institute
Firearm Training Center, The
Firearms Academy of Seattle
Francesca Stabilizer's, Inc.
G.H. Enterprises Ltd.
Guardian Group International
Guncraft Sports, Inc.
Gunfitters, The
InSights Training Center, Inc.
International Shootists, Inc.
Jensen's Firearms Acadamy
Lethal Force Institute

McMurdo, Lynn
Mendez, John A.
North American Shooting Systems
Northeast Training Institute, Inc.
North Mountain Pine Training
   Center
Pacific Pistolcraft
Police Bookshelf
Quack Decoy Corp.
Quigley's Personal Protection
   Strategies, Paxton
River Road Sporting Clays
Robar Co.'s, Inc., The
Rossi S.A. Metalurgica E
   Municoes, Amadeo
S.A.F.E.
Shooter's World
Shotgun Shop, The
Sipes Gun Shop
Slings & Arrows
Specialty Gunsmithing
Starlight Training Center, Inc.
S.W.I.F.T.
Tactical Training Center
Threat Management Institute
Western Missouri Shooters Alliance
Yavapai Firearms Academy Ltd.

SIGHTS, METALLIC

Alley Supply Co.
All's, The Jim J. Tembelis Co., Inc.
Alpec Team, Inc.
Andela Tool & Machine, Inc.
Armurier Hiptmayer
Bo-Mar Tool & Mfg. Co.
Bradley Gunsight Co.
Burris Co., Inc.
Cape Outfitters
Carter's Gun Shop
Champion's Choice, Inc.
Colonial Repair
E.A.A. Corp.
Engineered Accessories
Fausti & Figlie s.n.c., Stefano
Fautheree, Andy
Francesca Stabilizer's, Inc.
Guardian Group International
Gun Doctor, The
Heinie Specialty Products
Hesco-Meprolight
Hiptmayer, Klaus
Imatronic, Inc.
Innovision Enterprises
Jaeger, Inc., Paul/Dunn's
J.O. Arms & Ammunition Co.
Johnson Gunsmithing, Inc., Neal G.
Kopp, Terry K.
Lofland, James W.
London Guns Ltd.

L.P.A. Snc
Lyman Products Corp.
Marble Arms Corp.
McKee, Arthur
MCS, Inc.
Meier Works
Meprolight
Merit Corp.
Mid-America Recreation, Inc.
Millett Sights
MMC
Newman Gunshop
Novak's .45 Shop, Wayne
OMR Feinmechanik, Jagd-und
   Sportwaffen, GmbH
Pachmayr Ltd.
PEM's Mfg. Co.
Peterson Instant Targets, Inc.
Ravell Ltd.
Robar Co.'s, Inc., The
RPM
Sheridan USA, Inc., Austin
Slug Site Co.
Tanfoglio S.r.l., Fratelli
T.F.C. S.p.A.
Trijicon, Inc.
Vintage Arms, Inc.
WASP Shooting Systems
Wichita Arms, Inc.
Williams Gun Sight Co.

STOCKS (Commercial and Custom)

Angelo & Little Custom Gun Stock
   Blanks
Apel, Dietrich
Arms Ingenuity Co.
Armurier Hiptmayer
Balickie, Joe
Barta's Gunsmithing
Bartlett, Don
Barton, Michael D.
Beeman Precision Airguns, Inc.
Belding's Custom Gun Shop
Benchmark Guns
Biesen, Al
Biesen, Roger
Billeb, Stephen L.
Bishop, E.C.
B.M.F. Activator, Inc.
Bob's Gun Shop
Boltin, John M.
Borovnik KG, Ludwig
Bowerly, Kent
Boyds' Gunstock Industries, Inc.
Brace, Larry D.

Brgoch, Frank
Brown Precision, Inc.
Buckhorn Gun Works
Bullberry Barrel Works, Ltd.
Burkhart Gunsmithing, Don
Burres, Jack
Butler Creek Corp.
Cali'co Hardwoods, Inc.
Camilli, Lou
Campbell, Dick
Cape Outfitters
Caywood, Shane J.
Chicasaw Gun Works
Churchill, Winston
Clifton Arms, Inc.
Clinton River Gun Serv., Inc.
Cloward's Gun Shop
Cochran, Oliver
Coffin, Charles H.
Coffin, Jim
Conrad, C.A.
Costa, David
Crane Sales Co., George S.

•See page 460 for Warranty Service Center Addresses

Creedmoor Sports, Inc.
Custom Checkering Service
Custom Gun Products
Custom Gun Stocks
Dahl's Custom Stocks
Dangler, Homer L.
D&D Custom Rifles
D&D Gunsmiths, Ltd.
Desert Industries, Inc.
Dever Co., Jack
Devereaux, R.H. "Dick"
Dillon, Ed
Dowtin Gunworks
Dressel Jr., Paul G.
Duane Custom Stocks, Randy
Dutchman's Firearms, Inc., The
Duncan's Gunworks, Inc.
E.A.A. Corp.
Echols & Co., D'Arcy
Eggleston, Jere D.
Emmons, Bob
Erhardt, Dennis
Eversull Co., Inc., K.
Fajen, Inc., Reinhart
Farmer-Dressel, Sharon
Fiberpro Rifle Stocks
Fibron Products
Fisher, Jerry A.
Flaig's
Folks, Donald E.
Forster, Kathy
Forster, Larry L.
Frank Custom Gun Service, Ron
Game Haven Gunstocks
Garrett Accur-Lt. D.F.S. Co.
Gene's Custom Guns
Gentry Custom Gunmaker, David
Glaser Safety Slug, Inc.
Goens, Dale W.
Golden Age Arms Co.
Gordie's Gun Shop
Goudy Classic Stocks, Gary
Grace, Charles E.
Green, Roger M.
Greene, M.L.
Greenwalt Rifles
Griffin & Howe, Inc.
Gun Shop, The
Gunsmithing Ltd.
Halstead, Rick
Hank's Gun Shop
Hanson's Gun Center, Dick
Harper's Custom Stocks
Hecht, Hubert J.
Heilmann, Stephen
Hensley, Darwin
Heppler, Keith M.
Heydenberk, Warren R.
Hillmer Custom Gunstocks, Paul D.
Hiptmayer, Klaus
Hoenig & Rodman
H-S Precision, Inc.
Huebner, Corey O.
Hughes, Steven Dodd
Intermountain Arms
Ivanoff, Thomas G.
Jackalope Gun Shop
Jaeger, Inc., Paul/Dunn's
Jamison's Forge Works
Jarrett Rifles, Inc.
Johnson Gunsmithing, Inc., Neal G.
Johnson Wood Products
Keith's Custom Gunstocks
Ken's Rifle Blanks
Klein Custom Guns, Don
Klingler Woodcarving
Knippel, Richard
Kopp, Terry K.
Lawson Co., Harry
Lind Custom Guns, Al
Lynn's Custom Gunstocks
Makinson, Nicholas
Mandarino, Monte
Masen Co., John
McCullough, Ken
McCament, Jay

McDonald, Dennis
McFarland, Stan
McGuire, Bill
McMillan Fiberglass Stocks, Inc.
McMillan Rifle Barrels
Mercer Custom Stocks, R.M.
Mid-America Recreation, Inc.
Miller Gun Woods
Monell Custom Guns
Morrison Custom Rifles, J.W.
Morrow, Bud
MPI Stocks
Muzzelite Corp.
Nettestad Gun Works
New England Custom Gun Service
Newman Gunshop
Nickels, Paul R.
Nicklas, Ted
Norman Custom Gunstocks, Jim
Oakland Custom Arms, Inc.
Old World Gunsmithing
One Of A Kind
Or-Un
Orvis Co., The
Ottmar, Maurice
Pachmayr Ltd.
Pasadena Gun Center
Paulsen Gunstocks
PEM's Mfg. Co.
Pentheny de Pentheny
Perazzi U.S.A., Inc.
P&S Gun Service
Reiswig, Wallace E.
Richards Micro-Fit Stocks
R&J Gun Shop
RMS Custom Gunsmithing
Robar Co.'s, Inc., The
Robinson, Don
Robinson Firearms Mfg. Ltd.
Roto Carve
Royal Arm International Products
Royal Arms
Ryan, Chad L.
Schaefer, Roy V.
Schiffman, Curt
Schiffman, Mike
Schwartz Custom Guns, David W.
Shaw's Finest in Guns
Sherk, Dan A.
Shooting Gallery, The
Sile Distributors
Six Enterprises
Skeoch, Brian R.
Snider Stocks, Walter S.
Speedfeed, Inc.
Speiser, Fred D.
Strawbridge, Victor W.
Swan, D.J.
Szweda, Robert
Talmage, William G.
Tecnolegno S.p.A.
T.F.C. S.p.A.
Tiger-Hunt
Tirelli
Tom's Gun Repair
Tom's Gun Shop
Trevallion Gunstocks
Tucker, James C.
Vest, John
Vic's Gun Refinishing
Vintage Industries, Inc.
Waffen-Weber Custom Gunsmithing
Wallace's
Weatherby, Inc.
Weems, Cecil
Wenig Custom Gunstocks, Inc.
Werth, T.W.
West, Robert G.
Western Gunstock Mfg. Co.
Westminster Arms Ltd.
Windish, Jim
Winter, Robert M.
Wright's Hardwood Sawmill
Yee, Mike
York M-1 Conversions
Zeeryp, Russ

TARGETS, BULLET AND CLAYBIRD TRAPS

Abbott Industries
Action Target, Inc.
Aldis Gunsmithing & Shooting Supply
American Whitetail Target Systems
Applied Laser Systems
Armor Metal Products
Aztec International Ltd.
Barsotti, Bruce
Birchwood Laboratories, Inc.
Blount, Inc. Sporting Equipment Division
Caswell International Corp.
Champion's Choice, Inc.
Champion Target Co.
Clay Target Enterprises
Cunningham Co., Eaton
Dapkus Co., J.G.
Datumtech Corp.
Detroit-Armor Corp.
Diamond Mfg. Co.
Dutchman's Firearms, Inc., The
Epps "Orillia" Ltd., Ellwood
Federal Champion Target Co.
Freeman Animal Targets
G.H. Enterprises Ltd.
Hiti-Schuch, Atelier Wilma
Hunterjohn
Innovision Enterprises
Johnson Gunsmithing, Inc., Neal G.

Kennebec Journal
Kleen-Bore, Inc.
Littler Sales Co.
Maki Industries
MTM Molded Products Co., Inc.
National Target Co.
North American Shooting Systems
Nu-Teck
Outers Laboratories
Ox-Yoke Originals, Inc.
Primos Wild Game Calls, Inc.
Quack Decoy Corp.
Red Star Target Co.
Remington Arms Co., Inc.
Richards, John
River Road Sporting Clays
Rockwood Corp., Speedwell Div.
Rocky Mountain Target Co.
R-Tech Corp.
Schaefer Shooting Sports
Seligman Shooting Products
Shooting Arts Ltd
Shotgun Shop, The
Stoney Baroque Shooters Supply
Thompson Target Technology
Verdemont Fieldsports
White Flyer
White Flyer Targets
World of Targets

TAXIDERMY

Jonas Appraisals & Taxidermy, Jack
Kulis Freeze Dry Taxidermy
Shell Shack

Parker, Mark D.
Piedmont Community College
World Trek, Inc.

TRAP AND SKEET SHOOTER'S EQUIPMENT

Allen Sportswear, Bob
Baker, Stan
Blount, Inc. Sporting Equipment Division
C&H Research
Clymer Manufacturing Co., Inc.
D&H Prods. Co., Inc.
Danuser Machine Co.
F.A.I.R. Tecni-Mec SNC di Isidoro Rizzini
Ganton Manufacturing Ltd.
G.H. Enterprises Ltd.
Great 870 Co., The
Griggs Products
Hafner Creations, Inc.
Hall Plastics, Inc., John
Harper, William E.
Hoppe's Div.
Jenkins Recoil Pads, Inc.
K&T Co.
Loadmaster
Lynn's Custom Gunstocks
Magnum Research, Inc.
Maionchi-L.M.I.

Meadow Industries
Moneymaker Guncraft Corp.
MTM Molded Products Co., Inc.
Noble Co., Jim
Outers Laboratories
PAST Sporting Goods, Inc.
Perazzi U.S.A., Inc.
Pro-Port Ltd.
Protektor Model Co.
Quack Decoy Corp.
Ravell Ltd.
Remington Arms Co., Inc.
Rhodeside, Inc.
Shootin' Accessories, Ltd.
Shooting Specialties
Shotgun Shop, The
Speer Products
10-X Products Group
Titus, Daniel
Trius Traps
Universal Clay Pigeon Traps
Winchester Div., Olin Corp.
Ziegel Engineering

TRIGGERS, RELATED EQUIPMENT

Boyds' Gunstock Industries, Inc.
Canjar Co., M.H.
Central Specialties Ltd.
Clark Custom Guns, Inc.
Custom Products
Cycle Dynamics, Inc.
Dayton Traister
E.A.A. Corp.
Electronic Trigger Systems, Inc.
Flaig's
Forster Products
Gentry Custom Gunmaker, David
Greenwalt Rifles
Hart & Son, Inc., Robert W.
Johnson Gunsmithing, Inc., Neal G.
Jones, Neil
Krieger Barrels, Inc.
Lee's Red Ramps

London Guns, Ltd.
Mac's .45 Shop
Mahony, Philip Bruce
Mid-America Recreation, Inc.
Miller Single Trigger Mfg. Co.
Newman Gunshop
Pace Marketing, Inc.
Pachmayr Ltd.
Pease Accuracy, Bob
PEM's Mfg. Co.
Penrod Precision
Perazzi U.S.A., Inc.
Royal Arms
S&B Industries
Shilen Rifles, Inc.
Taurus, S.A., Forjas
Timney Mfg., Inc.
Tyler Mfg.-Dist., Melvin

MANUFACTURERS' DIRECTORY

A

A&B Industries, Inc., 7920-28 Hamilton Ave., Cincinnati, OH 45231/513-522-2992, 800-346-6699; FAX: 513-522-0916
A&J Products, Inc., 5791 Hall Rd., Muskegon, MI 49442-1964
A&M Waterfowl, Inc., 301 Burke Dr., Ripley, TN 38063/901-635-4003; FAX: 901-635-2320
A&W Repair, 2930 Schneider Dr., Arnold, MO 63010/314-287-3725
Abbott Industries, 3368 Miller St., Philadelphia, PA 19134/215-426-3435; FAX: 215-426-1718
Abel Safe & File, Inc., 124 West Locust St., Fairbury, IL 61739/815-692-2131; FAX: 815-692-3350
A.B.S. III, 9238 St. Morritz Dr., Fern Creek, KY 40291
Acadian Ballistic Specialties, Rt. 1, Box 1-D, Galliano, LA 70354
Accu-Tek, 4525 Carter Ct., Chino, CA 91710/714-627-2404; FAX: 714-627-7817
Acculube II, Inc., 22261 68th Ave. S., Kent, WA 98032-1914/206-395-7171
Accupro Gun Care, 15512-109 Ave., Surrey, BC U3R 7E8, CANADA/604-583-7807
Accuracy Components Co., P.O. Box 60034, Renton, WA 98058/206-255-4577
Accuracy Den, The, 25 Bitterbrush Rd., Reno, NV 89523/702-345-0225
Accuracy Gun Shop, 3651 University Ave., San Diego, CA 92104/619-282-8500
Accuracy Products, S.A., 14 rue de Lawsanne, Brussels, 1060 BELGIUM/32-2-539-34-42; FAX: 32-2-539-39-60
Accuracy Unlimited, 7479 S. DePew St., Littleton, CO 80123
Accuracy Unlimited, 16036 N. 49 Ave., Glendale, AZ 85306/602-978-9089
Accura-Site (See All's, The Jim Tembellis Co., Inc.)
Accurate Arms Co., Inc., Rt. 1, Box 167, McEwen, TN 37101/615-729-4207; FAX 615-729-4217
Accurate Plating & Weaponry, Inc., 1937 Calumet St., Clearwater, FL 34625/813-449-9112
Ace Sportswear, Inc., 700 Quality Rd., Fayetteville, NC 28306/919-323-1223
Ackley Rifle Barrels, P.O. (See Bellm Contenders)
Action Ammo Ltd. (See Action Arms Ltd.)
Action Arms Ltd., P.O. Box 9573, Philadelphia, PA 19124/215-744-0100; FAX: 215-533-2188
Action Products, Inc., 22 N. Mulberry St., Hagerstown, MD 21740/301-797-1414
Action Target, Inc., P.O. Box 636, Provo, UT 84603/801-377-8033; FAX: 801-377-8096
Actions by "T", Teddy Jacobson, 16315 Redwood Forest Ct., Sugarland, TX 77478/713-277-4008
ACTIV Industries, Inc., 1000 Zigor Rd., P.O. Box 339, Kearneysville, WV 25430/304-725-0451; FAX: 304-725-2080
Ad Hominem, RR 3, Orillia, Ont. L3V 6H3, CANADA/705-689-5303
Adair Custom Shop, Bill,, 2886 Westridge, Carrollton, TX 75006
Adams, John J., P.O. Box 467, Corinth, VT 05039/802-439-5904
ADC, Inc., 32654 Coal Creek Rd., Scappoose, OR 97056-2601/503-543-5088
ADCO International, 1 Wyman St., Woburn, MA 01801-2341/617-935-1799; FAX: 617-932-4807
Adkins, Luther, 1292 E. McKay Rd., Shelbyville, IN 46176-9353/317-392-3795
Advance Car Mover Co., Rowell Div., P.O. Box 1, 240 N. Depot St., Juneau, WI 53039/414-386-4464
Adventure 16, Inc., 4620 Alvarado Canyon Rd., San Diego, CA 92120/619-283-6314
Adventure Game Calls, R.D. 1, Leonard Rd., Spencer, NY 14883/607-589-4611
Adventurer's Outpost, P.O. Box 70, Cottonwood, AZ 86326/800-762-7471; FAX: 602-634-8781
African Import Co., 20 Braunecker Rd., Plymouth, MA 02360/508-746-8552
AFSCO Ammunition, 731 W. Third St., P.O. Box L, Owen, WI 54460/715-229-2516
Ahlman Guns, Rt. 1, Box 20, Morristown, MN 55052/507-685-4243; FAX: 507-685-4247
Ahrends, Kim, Custom Firearms, Box 203, Clarion, IA 50525/515-532-3449
Aimpoint, Inc., 580 Herndon Parkway, Suite 500, Herndon, VA 22070/703-471-6828; FAX: 703-689-0575
Aimtech Mount Systems, 101 Inwood Acres, Thomasville, GA 31792/912-226-4313; FAX: 912-227-0222
Air Arms (See U.S. importers—Air Rifle Specialists; Beeman Precision Airguns, Inc.)
Air Rifle Specialists, 31 East Water St., Elmira, NY 14901/607-734-7340; FAX: 607-733-3261
Air Venture, 9752 E. Flower St., Bellflower, CA 90706/213-867-6344
Airgun Repair Centre, 3227 Garden Meadows, Lawrenceburg, IN 47025/812-637-1463
Airmold, W.R. Grace & Co.-Conn., Becker Farms Ind. Park, P.O. Box 610, Roanoke Rapids, NC 27870/919-536-2171; FAX: 919-536-2201
Airrow (See Swivel Machine Works, Inc.)
Aitor-Cuchilleria Del Norte, S.A., Izelaieta, 17, 48260 Ermua (Vizcaya), SPAIN/43-17-08-50; FAX: 43-17-00-01
Ajax Custom Grips, Inc., Div. of A. Jack Rosenberg & Sons, 9130 Viscount Row, Dallas, TX 75247/214-630-8893
Aker Leather Products, 2248 Main St., Suite 6, Chula Vista, CA 91911/619-423-5182
Alaska Bullet Works, P.O. Box 54, Douglas, AK 99824/907-789-3834
Alcas Cutlery Corp. (See Cutco Cutlery)
Alco Carrying Cases, 601 W. 26th St., New York, NY 10001/212-675-5820
Aldis Gunsmithing & Shooting Supply, 502 S. Montezuma St., Prescott, AZ 86303/602-445-6723; FAX: 602-445-6763
Alessi Holsters, Inc., 2465 Niagara Falls Blvd., Amherst, NY 14228-3527/716-691-5615
Alex, Inc., Box 3034, Bozeman, MT 59772/406-282-7396; FAX: 406-282-7396
Alfano, Sam, 36180 Henry Gaines Rd., Pearl River, LA 70452/504-863-3364; FAX: 504-863-7715
All American Bullets, 889 Beatty St., Medford, OR 97501/503-770-5649
All American Lead Shot Corp., P.O. Box 224566, Dallas, TX 75062
All Rite Products, Inc., 5752 N. Silver Stone Circle, Mountain Green, UT 84040/801-586-7100
All Weather Outerwear, 1270 Broadway, Rm 1005, New York, NY 10001/212-244-2690
All's, The Jim J. Tembelis Co., Inc., 280 E. Fernau Ave., Oshkosh, WI 54901/414-426-1080; FAX: 414-426-1080
Allard, Gary, Creek Side Metal & Woodcrafters, Fishers Hill, VA 22626/703-465-3903
Allen Co., Bob, 214 SW Jackson, Des Moines, IA 50315/515-283-2191; 800-685-7020
Allen Sportswear, Bob, P.O. Box 477, Des Moines, IA 50302
Allen Co., Inc., 525 Burbank St., Broomfield, CO 80020/303-469-1857
Alley Supply Co., P.O. Box 848, Gardnerville, NV 89410/702-782-3800
Allred Bullet Co., 932 Evergreen Drive, Logan, UT 84321/801-752-6983
American Display Co., 55 Cromwell St., Providence, RI 02907/401-331-2464; FAX: 401-421-1264
Alpec Team, Inc., 55 Oak Ct., Danville, CA 94526/510-820-1763; FAX: 510-820-8738
Alpha LaFranck Enterprises, P.O. Box 81072, Lincoln, NE 68501/402-466-3193
Alpha 1 Drop Zone, 2121 N. Tyler, Wichita, KS 67212/316-729-0800

Alpha Precision, Inc., 2765-B Preston Rd. NE, Good Hope, GA 30641/404-267-6163
Alpine's Precision Gunsmithing & Indoor Shooting Range, 2401 Government Way, Coeur d'Alene, ID 83814/208-765-3559
Altamont Co., 901 N. Church St., P.O. Box 309, Thomasboro, IL 61878/217-643-3125; FAX: 217-643-7973
AMAC, Iver Johnson, 2202 Redmond Rd., Jacksonville, AR 72076/501-982-1633; FAX: 501-982-8075
Amacker International, Inc., 1212 Main St., Amacker Park, Delhi, LA 71232/318-878-9061; FAX: 318-878-5532
AmBr Software Group Ltd., The, 2205 Maryland Ave., Baltimore, MD 21218/301-243-7717; FAX: 301-366-8742
American Arms, Inc., 715 E. Armour Rd., N. Kansas City, MO 64116/816-474-3161; FAX: 816-474-1225
American Bullets, 2190 C. Coffee Rd., Lithonia, GA 30058/404-482-4253
American Custom Gunmakers Guild, P.O. Box 812, Burlington, IA 52601/319-752-6114
American Derringer Corp., P.O. Box 8983, Waco, TX 76714/800-642-7817, 817-799-9111; FAX: 817-799-7935
American Gas & Chemical Co., Ltd., 220 Pegasus Ave., Northvale, NJ 07647/201-767-7300
American Gripcraft, 3230 S. Dodge 2, Tucson, AZ 85713/602-790-1222
American Handgunner Magazine, 591 Camino de la Reina, Suite 200, San Diego, CA 92108/619-297-5350; FAX: 619-297-5353
American Import Co., The, 1453 Mission St., San Francisco, CA 94103/415-863-1506
American Military Arms Corp. (See AMAC)
American Pistol Institute, P.O. Box 401, Paulden, AZ 86334/602-636-4565; FAX: 602-636-1236
American Pistolsmiths Guild, P.O. Box 67, Louisville, TN 37777/615-984-3583
American Products Co., 14729 Spring Valley Road, Morrison, IL 61270/815-772-3336; FAX: 815-772-7921
American Sales & Mfg. Co., P.O. Box 677, Laredo, TX 78042/210-723-6893; FAX: 210-725-0672
American Security Products Co., 11925 Pacific Ave., Fontana, CA 92335/714-685-9680, 800-421-6142
American Small Arms Academy, P.O. Box 12111, Prescott, AZ 86304/602-778-5623
American Target Knives, 1030 Brownwood NW, Grand Rapids, MI 49504/616-453-1998
American Whitetail Target Systems, P.O. Box 41, 106 S. Church St., Tennyson, IN 47637/812-567-4527
Americase, P.O. Box 271, Waxahachie, TX 75165/800-972-2737
Amherst Arms, P.O. Box 1457, Englewood, FL 34295/813-475-2020
Ammo Load, Inc., 1560 East Edinger, Suite G., Santa Ana, CA 92705/714-558-8858; FAX: 714-569-0319
Amm-O-Mart, Ltd., P.O. Box 125, Hawkesbury, Ont., K6A 2R8 CANADA/613-632-9300
Ammunition Consulting Services, Inc., P.O. Box 1303, St. Charles, IL 60174/708-377-3431; FAX: 708-377-4680
Amodei, Jim (See D.O.C. Specialists, Inc.)
Amrine's Gun Shop, 937 La Luna, Ojai, CA 93023/805-646-2376
AMT, 6226 Santos Diaz St., Irwindale, CA 91702/818-334-6629; FAX: 818-969-5247
Analog Devices, Box 9106, Norwood, MA 02062
Andela Tool & Machine, Inc., RD3, Box 246, Richfield Springs, NY 13439
Anderson Manufacturing Co., Inc., P.O. Box 2640, 2741 N. Crosby Rd., Oak Harbor, WA 98277/206-675-7300; FAX: 206-675-3939
Andres & Dworsky, Bergstrasse 18, A-3822 Karlstein, Thaya, Austria, EUROPE, 0 28 44-285
Angelo & Little Custom Gun Stock Blanks, Chaffin Creek Rd., Darby, MT 59829/406-821-4530
Anschutz GmbH, Postfach 1128, D-7900 Ulm, Donau, GERMANY (U.S. importer—PSI, Inc.)
Ansen Enterprises, Inc., 1506 W. 228th St., Torrance, CA 90501-5105/213-534-1837
Answer Products Co., 1519 Westbury Drive, Davison, MI 48423/313-653-2911
Anthony and George Ltd., Rt. 1, P.O. Box 45, Evington, VA 24550/804-821-8117
Antique American Firearms (See Carlson, Douglas R.)
Antique Arms Co., 1110 Cleveland Ave., Monett, MO 65708/417-235-6501
AO Safety Products, Div. of American Optical Corp. (See E-A-R, Inc.)
Apache Products, Inc., 2208 Mallory Place, Monroe, LA 71201/318-325-1761; FAX: 318-325-4813
Apel GmbH, Ernst, Am Kirschberg 3, D-8708 Gerbrunn, GERMANY/0(9 31)-70 71 91; FAX: 0(9 31)70 71 92
Apel, Dietrich, New England Custom Gun Service, RR 2, Box 122W, Brook Rd., W. Lebanon, NH 03784/603-469-3565; FAX: 603-469-3471
Aplan Antiques & Art, James O., HC 80, Box 793-25, Piedmont, SD 57769/605-347-5016
Applied Case Systems, Inc., 2160 NW Vine St., Bldg. A, Grants Pass, OR 97526/503-479-0484; FAX: 503-476-5105
Applied Laser Systems, 2160 NW Vine St., Grants Pass, OR 97526/503-479-0484; FAX: 503-476-5105
Arcadia Machine & Tool, Inc. (See AMT)
Aristocrat Knives, 9608 Van Nuys Blvd.,104, Panorama City, CA 91402/818-892-6534; FAX: 818-830-7333
Arizaga (See U.S. importer—Mandall Shooting Supplies, Inc.)
Arizona Ammo & Arms, 2631 Sierra Lane, Kingman, AZ 86401
Arizona Custom Case, 1015 S. 23rd St., Phoenix, AZ 85034/602-273-0220
Arkansas Mallard Duck Calls, Rt. Box 182, England, AR 72046/501-842-3597
Arkfeld Mfg. & Dist. Co., Inc., P.O. Box 54, Norfolk, NE 68702-0054/402-371-9430; 800-533-0676
Armament Gunsmithing Co., Inc., 525 Rt. 22, Hillside, NJ 07205/908-686-0960
Armes de Chasse, P.O. Box 827, Chadds Ford, PA 19317/215-388-1146; FAX: 215-388-1147
Armfield Custom Bullets, 4775 Caroline Drive, San Diego, CA 92115/619-582-7188
Armi San Paolo, via Europa 172-A, I-25062 Concesio, (BS) ITALY/030-2751725
Armite Laboratories, 1845 Randolph St., Los Angeles, CA 90001/213-587-7768; FAX: 213-587-5075
Armoloy Co. of Ft. Worth, 204 E. Daggett St., Fort Worth, TX 76104/817-332-5604; FAX: 817-335-6517
Armor (See Buck Stop Lure Co., Inc.)
Armor Metal Products, P.O. Box 4609, Helena, MT 59604/406-442-5560
Armory Publications, P.O. Box 4206, Oceanside, CA 92052-4206/619-757-3930; FAX: 619-722-4108
Armoury, Inc., The, Rt. 202, Box 2340, New Preston, CT 06777/203-868-0001
A.R.M.S., Inc., 375 West St., West Bridgewater, MA 02379/508-584-7816; FAX: 508-588-8045
Arms, Peripheral Data Systems, 15110 SW Boones Ferry Rd., Suite 225, Lake Oswego, OR 97035/800-366-5559, 503-697-0533; FAX: 503-697-3337
Arms & Armour Press, Ltd. Villiers House, 41-47 Strand, London WC2N 5JE/ENGLAND
Arms Corp. of the Phillipines, 550E Delos Santos Ave., Cubau, Quezon City, PHILLIPINES

Arms Craft Gunsmithing, 1106 Linda Dr., Arroyo Grande, CA 93420/805-481-2830
Arms Ingenuity Co., P.O. Box 1, 51 Canal St., Weatogue, CT 06089/203-658-5624
Armscor (See U.S. importer—Ruko Products)
Armscor Precision, 225 Lindbergh St., San Mateo, CA 94401/415-347-9556; FAX: 415-347-7634
Armscorp USA, Inc., 4424 John Ave., Baltimore, MD 21227/301-247-6200
Armsport, Inc., 3950 NW 49th St., Miami, FL 33142/305-635-7850; FAX: 305-633-2877
Armstec, Inc., 339 East Ave., Rochester, NY 14604/800-262-2832
Armurier Hiptmayer, RR 112 750, P.O. Box 136, Eastman, Quebec JOE 1P0 CANADA/514-297-2492
Arratoonian, Andy (See Horseshoe Leather Products)
Arrieta, S.L., Morkaiko, 5, Elgoibar, E-20870, SPAIN/(43) 74 31 50; FAX: (43) 74 31 54 (U.S. importers—Quality Arms, Inc.; Wingshooting Adventures)
Artistry in Leather (See Stuart, V. Pat)
Art Jewel Enterprises Ltd., Eagle Business Ctr., 460 Randy Rd., Carol Stream, IL 60188/708-260-0400
Art's Gun & Sport Shop, Inc., 6008 Hwy. Y, Hillsboro, MO 63050
ASI, 6226 Santos Dias St., Irwindale, CA 91706/818-334-6629
A-Square Co., Inc., RR2, Box 357D, Bedford, KY 40006-9667/502-255-7456; FAX: 502-255-7657
Ashby Turkey Calls, HCR 5, Box 345, Houston, MO 65483/417-967-3787
Astra-Unceta Y Cia, S.A., Apartado 3, 48300 Guernica, Espagne, SPAIN (U.S. importer—E.A.A. Corp.)
ATIS Armi S.A.S., via Gussalli 24, Zona Industriale-Loc. Fornaci, 25020, Brescia, ITALY
Atlanta Cutlery Corp., 2143 Gees Mill Rd., Box 839XE, Conyers, GA 30207/800-241-3595
Atlanta Discount Ammo (See Bottom Line Shooting Supplies)
Atlantic Mills, Inc., 1325 Washington Ave., Asbury Park, NJ 07712/201-774-4882
Atlantic Research Marketing Systems (See A.R.M.S., Inc.)
Atsko/Sno-Seal, Inc., 2530 Russell SE, Orangeburg, SC 29115/803-531-1820; FAX: 803-531-2139
Audette, Creighton, 19 Highland Circle, Springfield, VT 05156/802-885-2331
Auto Arms, 738 Clearview, San Antonio, TX 78228/512-434-5450
Automatic Equipment Sales, 627 E. Railroad Ave., Salesburg, MD 21801
Auto-Ordnance Corp., Williams Lane, West Hurley, NY 12491/914-679-7225; FAX: 914-679-2698
Automatic Weaponry (See Scattergun Technologies, Inc.)
Autumn Sales, Inc. (Blaser), 1320 Lake St., Fort Worth, TX 76102/817-335-1634; FAX: 817-338-0119
AWC Systems Technology, P.O. Box 41938, Phoenix, AZ 85080-1938/602-780-1050
AYA (See U.S. importer—Armes de Chasse)
Aztec International Ltd., P.O. Box 1384, Clarkesville, GA 30523/404-754-8282

B

B&C (See Bell & Carlson, Inc.)
B&D Trading Co., Inc., 3935 Fair Hill Rd., Fair Oaks, CA 95628/916-967-9366
Badger Shooters Supply, Inc., 202 N. Harding, Owen, WI 54460/715-229-2101; FAX: 715-229-2332
Baer Custom, Inc., Les, 3737 14th Ave., Rock Island, IL 61201/309-794-1166; FAX: 309-794-9882
Baekgaard Ltd., 1855 Janke Dr., Northbrook, IL 60062/708-498-3040; FAX: 708-493-3106
Bagmaster Mfg., Inc., 2731 Sutton Ave., St. Louis, MO 63143/314-781-8002
Bain & Davis, Inc., 307 E. Valley Blvd., San Gabriel, CA 91776-3522/818-573-4241, 213-283-7449
Baity's Custom Gunworks, 414 2nd St., N. Wilkesboro, NC 28659/919-667-8785
Baker's Leather Goods, Roy, P.O. Box 893, Magnolia, AR 71753/501-234-0344
Baker, Stan, 10,000 Lake City Way, Seattle, WA 98125/206-522-4575
Balaance Co., 340-39 Ave. S.E. Box 505, Calgary, AB, T2G 1X6 CANADA
Bald Eagle Precision Machine Co., 101 Allison St., Lock Haven, PA 17745/717-748-6772; FAX: 717-748-4443
Balickie, Joe, 408 Trelawney Lane, Apex, NC 27502/919-362-5185
Ballard Built, P.O. Box 1443, Kingsville, TX 78364/512-592-0853
Ballisti-Cast, Inc., Box 383, Parshall, ND 58770/701-862-3324
Ballistic Products, Inc., 20015 75th Ave. North, Corcoran, MN 55340/612-494-9237; FAX: 612-494-9236
Ballistic Program Co., Inc., The, 2417 N. Patterson St., Thomasville, GA 31792/912-228-5739, 800-368-0835
Ballistic Research, 1108 W. May Ave., McHenry, IL 60050/815-385-0037
Ballistica Maximus North, 107 College Park Plaza, Johnstown, PA 15904/814-266-8380
Ballistica Maximus South, 3242 Mary St., Suite S-318, Miami, FL 33133/305-446-5549
Banaczkowski Bullets, 56 Victoria Dr., Mount Barker, S.A. 5251 AUSTRALIA
Bandcor Industries, Div. of Man-Sew Corp., 6108 Sherwin Dr., Port Richey, FL 34668/813-848-0432
Bandera Gun Locker, 2146 NE 4th St., Bend, OR 97701/800-441-6773
Bang-Bang Boutique (See Holster Shop, The)
Banks, Ed, 2762 Hwy. 41 N., Ft. Valley, GA 31030/912-987-4665
Barnes Bullets, Inc., P.O. Box 215, American Fork, UT 84003/801-756-4222
Bar-Sto Precision Machine, 73377 Sullivan Rd., P.O. Box 1838, Twentynine Palms, CA 92277/619-367-2747; FAX: 619-367-2407
Barami Corp., 6250 E. 7 Mile Rd., Detroit, MI 48234/313-891-2536
Barbour, Inc., 55 Meadowbrook Dr., Milford, NH 03055/603-673-1313; FAX: 603-673-6510
Barlett, J., 6641 Kaiser Ave., Fontana, CA 92336-3265
Barnett International, P.O. Box 934, 1967 Gunn Highway, Odessa, FL 33556/813-920-2241
Baron Technology, 62 Spring Hill Rd., Trumbull, CT 06611/203-452-0515; FAX: 203-452-0663
Barramundi Corp., P.O. Drawer 4259, Homosassa Springs, FL 32687/904-628-0200
Barrett Firearms Mfg., Inc., P.O. Box 1077, Murfreesboro, TN 37133/615-896-2938; FAX: 615-896-7313
Barsotti, Bruce (See River Road Sporting Clays)
Barta's Gunsmithing, 10231 US Hwy. 10, Cato, WI 54206/414-732-4472
Barteaux Machete, 1916 SE 50th Ave., Portland, OR 97215-3238/503-233-5880
Bartlett, Don, 3704 E. Pine Needle Ave., Colbert, WA 99005/509-467-5009
Barton, Michael D. (See Tiger-Hunt)
Basics Information Systems, Inc., 1141 Georgia Ave., Suite 515, Wheaton, MD 20902/301-949-1070
Bates Engraving, Billy, 2302 Winthrop Dr., Decatur, AL 35603/205-355-3690
Bauer, Eddie, 15010 NE 36th St., Redmond, WA 98052
Baumannize Custom, 4784 Sunrise Hwy., Bohemia, NY 11716/800-472-4387; FAX: 516-567-0001
Baumgartner Bullets, 3011 S. Alane St., W. Valley City, UT 84120
Bausch & Lomb Sports Optics Div. (See Bushnell)
Bausch & Lomb, Inc., 42 East Ave., Rochester, NY 14603/800-828-5423
Bean, L.L., 386 Main St., Freeport, ME 04032/207-865-3111
Bear Archery, RR 4, 4600 Southwest 41st Blvd., Gainesville, FL 32601/904-376-2327
Bear Hug Grips, Inc., 17230 County Rd. 338, Buena Vista, CO 81211/800-232-7710
Bear Machine Co., 1108 Society Building, 159 S. Main, Akron, OH 44308/216-376-3747
Beauchamp & Son, Inc., 160 Rossiter Rd., Richmond, MA 01254
Beaver Lodge (See Fellowes, Ted)
Beaver Park Products, Inc., 840 J St., Penrose, CO 81240/719-372-6744
Beeman Precision Airguns, Inc., 3440 Airway Dr., Santa Rosa, CA 95403/707-578-7900; FAX: 707-578-4751
Behlert Precision, P.O. Box 288, 7067 Easton Rd., Pipersville, PA 18947/215-766-8681; FAX: 215-766-8681
Beitzinger, George, 116-20 Atlantic Ave., Richmond Hill, NY 11419/718-847-7661
Belding's Custom Gun Shop, 10691 Sayers Rd., Munith, MI 49259/517-596-2388
Bell & Carlson, Inc., 509 N. 5th St., Atwood, KS 67730/913-626-3204; FAX: 913-626-9602
Bell Originals, Inc., Sid, 7776 Sharkham Rd., Tully, NY 13159-9333/607-842-6431
Bell Reloading, Inc., 1725 Harlin Lane Rd., Villa Rica, GA 30180
Bell's Legendary Country Wear, 22 Circle Dr., Bellmore, NY 11710/516-679-1158
Bell's Gun & Sport Shop, 3309-19 Mannheim Rd, Franklin Park, IL 60131
Bellm Contenders, P.O. Ackley Rifle Barrels, P.O. Box 459, Cleveland, UT 84518/801-653-2530
Belltown, Ltd., 11 Camps Rd., Kent, CT 06757/203-354-5750
Ben's Machines, 1151 S. Cedar Ridge, Duncanville, TX 75137/214-780-1807
Benchmark Guns, 12593 S. Ave. 5 East, Yuma, AZ 85365
Benchmark Knives (See Gerber Legendary Blades)
Benchrest & Bucks, 6601 Kirby Drive 527, Houston, TX 77005/713-669-0925
Benelli Armi, S.p.A., Via della Stazione, 61029 Urbino, ITALY (U.S. importers—E.A.A. Corp.; Heckler & Koch, Inc.; Sile Distributors)
Bengtson Arms Co., L., 6345-B E. Akron St., Mesa, AZ 85205/602-981-6375
Benjamin Air Rifle Co. (See Benjamin/Sheridan Co.)
Benjamin/Sheridan Co., 2600 Chicory Rd., Racine, WI 53403/414-554-7900
Bentley, John, 128-D Watson Dr., Turtle Creek, PA 15145
Beretta Firearms, Pietro, 25063 Gardone V.T., ITALY (U.S. importer—Beretta U.S.A. Corp.)
Beretta U.S.A. Corp., 17601 Beretta Drive, Accokeek, MD 20607/301-283-2191
Beretta, Dr. Franco, via Rossa, 4, Concesio (BC), Italy I-25062/030-2751955; FAX: 030-218-0414
Berger Bullets, Ltd., 4234 N. 63rd Ave., Phoenix, AZ 85033/602-846-5791; FAX: 602-848-0780
Bergman & Williams, 2450 Losee Rd., Suite F, Las Vegas, NV 89030/702-642-1901
Bernardelli Vincenzo S.p.A., Via Matteotti 125, Gardone V.T., ITALY I-25063/30-8912851-2-3 (U.S. importer—Magnum Research, Inc.)
Berry's Bullets, Div. of Berry's Mfg., Inc., Box 100, Bloomington, CA 92316/714-823-5222; FAX: 714-823-4715
Bersa S.A., Gonzales Castillo 312, 1704 Ramos Mejia, ARGENTINA (U.S. importer—Eagle Imports, Inc.)
Bertram Bullet Co., P.O. Box 313, Seymour, Victoria 3660, AUSTRALIA/61-57-922912; FAX: 61-47-991650
Best Load, P.O. Box 4354, Stamford, CT 06907
Better Concepts Co., 663 New Castle Rd., Butler, PA 16001/412-285-9000
Bertuzzi (See U.S. importer—Moore & Co., Wm. Larkin)
Bianchi International, Inc., 100 Calle Cortez, Temecula, CA 92590/714-676-5621
Biesen, Al, 5021 Rosewood, Spokane, WA 99208/509-328-9340
Biesen, Roger, 5021 W. Rosewood, Spokane, WA 99208/509-328-9340
Big 45 Frontier Gun Shop, 515 Cliff Ave., Valley Springs, SD 57068/605-757-6248; FAX: 605-757-6248
Big Sky Racks, Inc., P.O. Box 729, Bozeman, MT 59771-0729/406-586-9393
Big Spring Enterprises "Bore Stores", P.O. Box 1115, Big Spring Rd., Yellville, AR 72687/501-449-5297; FAX: 501-449-4446
Bilal, Mustafa, 5429 Russell Ave. NW, Suite 202, Seattle, WA 98107/206-782-4164
Bill's Custom Cases, P.O. Box 2, Dunsmuir, CA 96025/916-235-0177
Bill's Gun Repair, 1007 Burlington St., Mendota, IL 61342/815-539-5786
Billeb, Stephen L., 1100 N. 7th St., Burlington, IA 52601/319-753-2110
Billings Gunsmiths, Inc., 1940 Grand Ave., Billings, MT 59102/406-652-3104
Billingsley & Brownell, P.O. Box 25, Dayton, WY 82836/307-655-9344
Bilsom Intl., Inc., 109 Carpenter Dr., Sterling, VA 20164/703-834-1070
Birchwood Laboratories, Inc., 7900 Fuller Rd., Eden Prairie, MN 55344/612-937-7933; FAX: 612-937-7979
Bishop, E.C., P.O. Box 7, Warsaw, MO 65355/816-438-5121; FAX: 816-4387-2201
Bismuth Cartridge Co., 3500 Maple Ave., Suite 1650, Dallas, TX 75129/800-759-3333; 214-521-5882
Bitterroot Bullet Co., Box 412, Lewiston, ID 83501-0412/208-743-5635
Black Hills Ammunition, P.O. Box 3090, Rapid City, SD 57709/605-348-5150; FAX: 605-348-9827
Black Hills Shooters Supply, P.O. Box 4220, Rapid City, SD 57709/605-348-4477; FAX: 605-348-5037
Black Sheep Brand, 3220 W. Gentry Parkway, Tyler, TX 75702/214-592-3853
Blackhawk East, P.O. Box 2274, Loves Park, IL 61131
Blackhawk Mountain, P.O. Box 210, Conifer, CO 80433
Blackhawk West, P.O. Box 285, Hiawatha, KS 66434
Blackinton & Co., Inc., V.H., 221 John L. Dietsch, Attleboro Falls, MA 02763-3000/508-699-4436; FAX: 508-695-5349
Blackjack Knives, 1307 W. Wabash, Effingham, IL 62401/217-347-7700; FAX: 217-347-7737
Blacksmith Corp., 830 N. Road 1 E., Box 1752, Chino Valley, AZ 86323/602-636-4456; FAX: 602-636-4457
Blacktail Mountain Books, 42 First Ave. West, Kalispell, MT 59901/406-257-5573
Blakemore Game Calls, Jim, Rt. 2, Box 544, Cape Girardeau, MO 63701
Blammo Ammo, P.O. Box 1677, Seneca, SC 29679/803-882-1768
Blaser Jagdwaffen GmbH, D-7972 Isny Im Allgau, GERMANY (U.S. importer—Autumn Sales, Inc.)
Bledsoe, Weldon, 6812 Park Place Dr., Fort Worth, TX 76118/817-589-1704
Bleile, C. Roger, 5040 Ralph Ave., Cincinnati, OH 45238/513-251-0249
Blocker's Holsters, Inc., Ted, 5360 NE 112, Portland, OR 97220/503-254-9950
Blount, Inc., Sporting Equipment Div., 2299 Snake River Ave., P.O. Box 856, Lewiston, ID 83501/800-627-3640, 208-746-2351
Blue and Gray Products, Inc. (See Ox-Yoke Originals, Inc.)
Blue Book Publications, Inc., One Appletree Square, Minneapolis, MN 55425/800-877-4867; FAX: 612-853-1486
Blue Mountain Bullets, HCR 77, P.O. Box 231, John Day, OR 97845/503-820-4594
Blue Point Mfg., Co., P.O. Box 722, Massena, NY 13662
Blue Ridge Knives, Rt. 6, Box 185, Marion, VA 24354/703-783-6143; FAX: 703-783-9298
Blue Ridge Machinery & Tools, Inc., P.O. Box 536-GD, Hurricane, WV 25526/304-562-3538; FAX: 304-562-5311
Bluebonnet Specialty, P.O. Box 737, Palestine, TX 75802/214-723-2075
BMC Supply, Inc., 26051-179th Ave. S.E., Kent, WA 98042
B.M.F. Activator, Inc., 803 Mill Creek Run, Plantersville, TX 77363/409-894-2005, 800-527-2881
Bo-Mar Tool & Mfg. Co., Rt. 12, Box 405, Longview, TX 75605/903-759-4784; FAX: 903-759-9141
Bob's Gun Shop, P.O. Box 200, Royal, AR 71968/501-767-1970
Bob's Tactical Indoor Shooting Range & Gun Shop, 122 Lafayette Rd., Salisbury, MA 01952/508-465-5561
Boessler, Erich, Am Vogeltal 3, 8732 Munnerstadt, GERMANY/9733-9443
Boggs, Wm., 1816 Riverside Dr. C, Columbus, OH 43212/614-486-6965
Bohemia Arms Co., 17101 Los Modelos, Fountain Valley, CA 92708/714-963-0809; FAX: 714-963-0809
Boker USA, Inc., 14818 West 6th Ave., Suite 10A, Golden, CO 80401-5045/303-279-5997; FAX: 303-279-5919
Bolden's, 1295 Lassen Dr., Hanford, CA 93230/209-582-6937
Boltin, John M., P.O. Box 644, Estill, SC 29918/803-625-2185
Bondini Paolo, Via Sorrento, 345, San Carlo di Cesena, ITALY I-47020/0547 663 240; FAX: 0547 663 780
Bone Engraving, Ralph, 718 N. Atlanta, Owasso, OK 74055/918-272-9745
Boone's Custom Ivory Grips, Inc., 562 Coyote Rd., Brinnon, WA 98320/206-796-4330

Boonie Packer Products, P.O. Box 12204, Salem, OR 97309/800-477-3244; FAX: 503-581-3191
Border Guns & Leather, P.O. Box 1423, 110 E. Spruce St., Deming, NM 88031
Borovnik KG, Ludwig, 9170 Ferlach, Bahnhofstrasse 7, AUSTRIA
Boss Manufacturing Co., 221 W. First St., Kewanee, IL 61443/309-852-2131
Bostick Wildlife Calls, Inc., P.O. Box 728, Estill, SC 29918/803-625-2210, 803-625-4512
Bottom Line Shooting Supplies, P.O. Box 258, Clarkesville, GA 30523/706-754-9000; FAX: 706-754-7263
Bourne Co., Inc., Richard A., P.O. Box 141, Hyannis Port, MA 02647/508-775-0797
Bowen Classic Arms Corp., P.O. Box 67, Louisville, TN 37777/615-984-3583
Bowen Knife Co., P.O. Box 590, Blackshear, GA 31516/912-449-4794
Bowerly, Kent, HCR Box 1903, Camp Sherman, OR 97730/503-595-6028
Bowlin, Gene, Rt. 1, Box 890, Snyder, TX 79549
Boyds' Gunstock Industries, Inc., 3rd & Main, Box 305, Geddes, SD 57342/605-337-2123; FAX: 605-337-3363
Boyt, 509 Hamilton, Iowa Falls, IA 50126/515-648-4626
Brace, Larry D., 771 Blackfoot Ave., Eugene, OR 97404/503-688-1278
Bradley Gunsight Co., P.O. Box 140, Plymouth, VT 05056/203-589-0531; FAX: 203-582-6294
Brass Eagle, Inc., 7050A Bramalea Rd., Unit 19, Mississauga, Ont. L4Z 1C7, CANADA/416-848-4844
Bratcher, Dan, 311 Belle Air Pl., Carthage, MO 64836/417-358-1518
Brauer Bros. Mfg. Co., 2020 Delmar Blvd., St. Louis, MO 63103/314-231-2864; FAX: 314-249-4952
Braun, M., 32, rue Notre-Dame, 2440 LUXEMBURG
Break-Free, P.O. Box 25020, Santa Ana, CA 92799/714-953-1900
Brell Mar Products, Inc., 5701 Hwy. 80 West, Jackson, MS 39209
Brenneke KG, Wilhelm, Ilmenauweg 2, P.O. Box 16 46, D-3012 Langenhagen, GERMANY/1-772288
Bretton, 19 rue Victor Grignard, Z.I. Montreynaud, 42-St. Et., FRANCE (U.S. importer—Mandall Shooting Supplies, Inc.)
Brgoch, Frank, 1580 S. 1500 East, Bountiful, UT 84010/801-295-1885
Brian, C.T., 1101 Indiana Ct., Decatur, IL 62521/217-429-2290
Bricker Bullets, Box 509M RD3, Manheim, PA 17545/717-665-4332
Bridgers Best, P.O. Box 1410, Berthoud, CO 80513
Briganti & Co., A., 475 Rt. 32, Highland Mills, NY 10930/914-928-9573
Briley Mfg., Inc., 1230 Lumpkin, Houston, TX 77043/B713-932-6995; FAX: 713-932-1043
British Arms Co. Ltd., P.O. Box 7, Latham, NY 12110/518-783-0773
British Sporting Arms, RR1, Box 130, Millbrook, NY 12545/914-677-8303
BRNO (See U.S. importers—Action Arms Ltd.; Bohemia Arms Co.; Century International Arms, Inc.)
Brobst, Jim, 299 Poplar St., Hamburg, PA 19526/215-562-2103
Broken Gun Ranch, RR2, Box 92, Spearville, KS 67876/316-385-2587
Brooker, Dennis, Rt. 1, Box 12A, Derby, IA 50068/515-533-2103
Brown Manufacturing, P.O. Box 9219, Akron, OH 44305/800-837-GUNS
Brown Co., E. Arthur, 3404 Pawnee Dr., Alexandria, MN 56308/612-762-8847
Brown Precision, Inc., 7786 Molinos Ave., Los Molinos, CA 96055/916-384-2506; FAX: 916-384-1638
Brown Products, Ed, Inc., Rt. 2, Box 2922, Perry, MO 63462/314-565-3261; FAX: 565-2791
Brown, H.R. (See Silhouette Leathers)
Brownell Checkering Tools, W.E., 9390 Twin Moutain Circle, San Diego, CA 92126/619-695-2479; FAX: 619-695-2479
Brownells, Inc., 200 S. Front St., Montezuma, IA 50171/515-623-5401; FAX: 515-623-3896
Browning Arms Co. (Gen. Offices), 1 Browning Place, Morgan, UT 84050/801-876-2711; FAX: 801-876-3331
Browning Arms Co. (Parts & Service), 3005 Arnold Tenbrook Rd., Arnold, MO 63010-9406/314-287-6800; FAX: 314-287-9751
BRP, Inc. High Performance Cast Bullets, 1210 Alexander Rd., Colorado Springs, CO 80909/719-633-0658
Bruno Shooters Supply, 106 N. Wyoming St., Hazleton, PA 18201/717-455-2211; FAX: 717-455-2211
Brunsport, Inc., 1131 Bayview Dr., Quincy, IL 62301/217-223-8844
Brunton U.S.A., 620 E. Monroe Ave., Riverton, WY 82501/307-856-6559; FAX: 307-856-1840
Bryco Arms (See U.S. distributor—Jennings Firearms, Inc.)
Bryant, A.V., 72 Whiting Road, E. Hartford, CT 06118
Brynin, Milton, P.O. Box 383, Yonkers, NY 10710/914-779-4333
BSA Guns Ltd., Armoury Rd. Small Heath, Birmingham, ENGLAND B11 2PX/(011)21 772 8543; FAX: (011)21 773-0845 (U.S. importer—Air Rifle Specialists)
B-Square Co., P.O. Box 11281, 2708 St. Louis Ave., Ft. Worth, TX 76110/817-923-0964, 800-433-2909; FAX: 817-926-7012
Bucheimer, J.M., Jumbo Sports Products, 721 N. 20th St., St. Louis, MO 63103/314-241-1020
Buck Knives, Inc., 1900 Weld Blvd., El Cajon, CA 92020/619-449-1100; FAX: 619-562-5774
Buck Stix—SOS Products Co., Box 3, Neenah, WI 54956
Buck Stop Lure Co., Inc., 3600 Grow Rd. NW, P.O. Box 636, Stanton, MI 48888/517-762-5091; FAX: 517-762-5124
Buckeye Custom Bullets, 6490 Stewart Rd., Elida, OH 45807/419-641-4463
Buckhorn Gun Works, Rt. 6, Box 2230, Rapid City, SD 57702/605-787-6289
Buckskin Machine Works, A. Hunkeler, 3235 S. 358th St., Auburn, WA 98001/206-927-5412
Budin, Dave, Main St., Margaretville, NY 12455/914-568-4103; FAX: 914-586-4105
Buehler Scope Mounts, 17 Orinda Way, Orinda, CA 94563/510-254-3201; FAX: 510-254-9720
Buenger Enterprises, Box 5286, Oxnard, CA 93031/805-985-0541
Buffalo Bullet Co., Inc., 12637 Los Nietos Rd. Unit A, Santa Fe Springs, CA 90670/310-944-0322; FAX: 310-944-5054
Buffalo Rock Shooters Supply, R.R. 1, Ottawa, IL 61350/815-433-2471
Bullberry Barrel Works, Ltd., 2430 W. Bullberry Ln. 67-5, Hurricane, UT 84737/801-635-9866
Bull-X, Inc., 520 N. Main St., Farmer City, IL 61842/309-928-2574, 800-248-3845 orders only
Bullet, Inc., 3745 Hiram Alworth Rd., Dallas, GA 30132
Bullet Swaging Supply, Inc., P.O. Box 1056, 303 McMillan Rd, West Monroe, LA 71291/318-387-7257; FAX: 318-387-7779
The BulletMakers Workshop, RFD 1 Box 1755, Brooks, ME 04921
Bullseye Bullets, 1610 State Road 60, Suite 12, Valrico, FL 33594/813-654-6563
Burgess, Byron, 1816 Gathe Dr., San Luis Obispo, CA 93405/805-543-7274
Burgess & Son Gunsmiths, R.W., P.O. Box 3364, Warner Robins, GA 31099/912-328-7487
Burkhart Gunsmithing, Don, P.O. Box 852, Rawlins, WY 82301/307-324-6007
Burling Bullets, 306 Range St., Elizabethton, TN 37643/615-542-8162
Burnham Bros., P.O. Box 669, 912 Hi-way 1431 West, Marble Falls, TX 78654/512-693-3112
Burres, Jack, 10333 San Fernando Rd., Pacoima, CA 91331/818-899-8000
Burris Co., Inc., P.O. Box 1747, Greeley, CO 80631/303-356-1670; FAX: 303-356-8702
Bushmann Hunters/Safaris, P.O. Box 110639, Aurora, CO 80011
Bushmaster Hunting & Fishing, 451 Alliance Ave., Toronto, Ont. M6N 2J1 CANADA/416-763-4040; FAX: 416-763-0623
Bushnell, Bausch & Lomb Sports Optics Div., 9200 Cody, Overland Park, KS 66214/913-888-0220
Bushwacker Backpack & Supply Co. (See Counter Assault)
Bustani Appraisers, Leo, P.O. Box 8125, W. Palm Beach, FL 33407/305-622-2710
Buster's Custom Knives, P.O. Box 214, Richfield, UT 84701/801-896-5319
Butler Creek Corp., 290 Arden Dr., Belgrade, MT 59714/406-388-1356; FAX: 406-388-7204
Butterfield & Butterfield, 220 San Bruno Ave., San Francisco, CA 94103/415-861-7500
Buzztail Brass, 5306 Bryant Ave., Klamath Falls, OR 97603/503-884-1072
B-West Imports, Inc., 5132 E. Pima St., Tucson, AZ 85712/602-881-3525; FAX: 602-322-5704

C

C3 Systems, 678 Killingly St., Johnston, RI 02919
C&D Special Products (Claybuster), 309 Sequoya Dr., Hopkinsville, KY 42240/800-922-6287, 800-284-1746
C&H Research, 115 Sunnyside Dr., Box 351, Lewis, KS 67552/316-324-5445
Cabanas (See U.S. importer—Mandall Shooting Supplies, Inc.)
Cabela's, 812-13th Ave., Sidney, NE 69160/308-254-5505; FAX: 308-254-7809
Cabinet Mtn. Outfitter, P.O. Box 766, Plains, MT 59859/406-826-3970
Cache La Poudre Rifleworks, 140 N. College, Ft. Collins, CO 80524/303-482-6913
Cadre Supply (See Parts & Surplus)
Calhoon Varmint Bullets, James, 6035 Penworth Rd., S.E., Calgary, Alberta, T2A 4E9 CANADA/403-235-2959
Calibre Press, Inc., 666 Dundee Rd., Suite 1607, Northbrook, IL 60062-2760/800-323-0037; FAX: 708-498-6869
Cali'co Hardwoods, Inc., 1648 Airport Blvd., Windsor, CA 95492/707-546-4045; FAX: 707-546-4027
Calico Light Weapon Systems, 405 E. 19th St., Bakersfield, CA 93305/805-323-1327; FAX: 805-323-7844
California Armory, Inc., 881 W. San Bruno Ave., San Bruno, CA 94066/415-871-4886; FAX: 415-871-0713
California Grip, 1323 Miami Ave., Clovis, CA 93612/209-299-1316
California Magnum, 20746 Dearborn St., Chatsworth, CA 91313/818-341-7302; FAX: 818-341-7304
California Sight, P.O. Box 4607, Pagosa Springs, CO 81157/303-731-5003
CAM Enterprises, 5090 Iron Springs Rd., Box 2, Prescott, AZ 86301/602-776-9640
Camas Hot Springs Mfg., P.O. Box 639, Hot Springs, MT 59845/406-741-3756
Camdex, Inc., 2330 Alger, Troy, MI 48083/313-528-2300
Cameron's, 16690 W. 11th Ave., Golden, CO 80401/303-279-7365; FAX: 303-628-5413
Camilli, Lou, 4700 Oahu Dr. NE, Albuquerque, NM 87111/505-293-5259
Camillus Cutlery Co./Western Cutlery Co., 54 Main St., Camillus, NY 13031/315-672-8111; FAX: 315-672-8832
Camofare Co., 712 Main St. 2800, Houston, TX 77002/713-229-9253
Camp-Cap Products, P.O. Box 173, Chesterfield, MO 63006/314-532-4340
Campbell, Dick, 20,000 Silver Ranch Rd., Conifer, CO 80433/303-697-0150
Canadian Custom Bullets, Box 52, Anola Man. R0E 0A0 CANADA
Can Am Enterprises, Box 27, Fruitland, Ont. LOR ILO, CANADA/416-643-4357
Canjar Co., M.H., 500 E. 45th Ave., Denver, CO 80216/303-295-2638
Cannon Safe, Inc., 9358 Stephens St., Pico Rivera, CA 90660/213-692-0636, 800-242-1055, 800-222-1055 (CA)
Cannon's Guns, Box 1036, Polson, MT 59860/406-883-3583
Canons Delcour, Rue J.B. Cools, B-4040 Herstal, BELGIUM/32.(0)41.40.13.40; FAX: 32(0)412.40.22.88
Canyon Cartridge Corp., P.O. Box 152, Albertson, NY 11507/FAX: 516-294-8946
Cape Outfitters, Rt. 2, Box 437C, Cape Girardeau, MO 63701/314-335-4103; FAX: 314-335-1555
Caraville Manufacturing, P.O. Box 4545, Thousand Oaks, CA 91359/805-499-1234
Carbide Die & Mfg. Co., Inc., 15615 E. Arrow Hwy., Irwindale, CA 91706/818-337-2518
Carhartt, Inc., P.O. Box 600, Dearborn, MI 48121/800-358-3825; FAX: 313-271-3455
Carlson, Douglas R., Antique American Firearms, P.O. Box 71035, Dept. GD, DesMoines, IA 50325/515-224-6552
Carnahan Bullets, 17645 110th Ave. SE, Renton, WA 98055
Carry-Lite, Inc., 5203 W. Clinton Ave., Milwaukee, WI 53223/414-355-3520
Carter's Gun Shop, 225 G St., Penrose, CO 81240/719-372-6240
Carter's Wildlife Calls, Inc., Garth, P.O. Box 821, Cedar City, UT 84720/801-586-7639
Cartridges Unlimited, 190 Bull's Bridge Rd., South Kent, CT 06785/203-927-3053
Carvajal Belts & Holsters, 422 Chestnut, San Antonio, TX 78202/210-222-1634
Cascade Bullet Co., Inc., 413 Main St., Klamath Falls, OR 97601/503-884-9316
Cascade Fabrication, 1090 Bailey Hill Rd. Unit A, Eugene, OR 97402/503-485-3433; FAX: 503-485-3543
Cascade Shooters, 2155 N.W. 12th St., Redwood, OR 97756
Case & Sons Cutlery Co., W.R., Owens Way, Bradford, PA 16701/814-368-4123; FAX: 814-362-4877
Caspian Arms, 14 North Main St., Hardwick, VT 05843/802-472-6454
Cast Bullet Assoc., Inc., The, 4103 Foxcraft Dr., Traverse City, MI 49684
Caswell International Corp., 1221 Marshall St. NE, Minneapolis, MN 55413/612-379-2000
Catco-Ambush, Inc., P.O.Box 300, Corte Madera, CA 94926
Cathey Enterprises, Inc., P.O. Box 2202, Brownwood, TX 76804/915-643-2553; FAX: 915-643-3653
Cation, 32360 Edward, Madison Heights, MI 48071/313-588-0160
Catoctin Cutlery, P.O. Box 188, Smithsburg, MD 21783/301-824-7416; FAX: 301-824-6138
Caywood, Shane J., P.O. Box 321, Minocqua, WI 54548
CBC, Avenida Industrial, 3330, Santo Andre-SP-BRAZIL 09080/11-449-5600 (U.S. importer—MAGTECH Recreational Products, Inc.)
CCI, Div. of Blount, Inc., 2299 Snake River Ave., P.O. Box 856, Lewiston, ID 83501/800-627-3640, 208-746-2351
Cedar Hill Game Call Co., Rt. 2, Box 236, Downsville, LA 71234/318-982-5632
Celestron International, P.O. Box 3578, Torrance, CA 90503
Centaur Systems, Inc., 1602 Foothill Rd., Kalispell, MT 59901/406-755-8609; FAX: 406-755-8609
Central Specialties Ltd., 1122 Silver Lake Road, Cary, IL 60013/708-537-3300; FAX: 708-537-3615
Century Gun Dist., Inc., 1467 Jason Rd., Greenfield, IN 46140/317-462-4524
Century International Arms, Inc., 48 Lower Newton St., St. Albans, VT 05478/802-527-1252; FAX: 802-527-0470
CF Ventures, 509 Harvey Dr., Bloomington, IN 47403-1715
C-H Tool & Die Corp. (See 4-D Custom Die Co.)
Chace Leather Products, 507 Alden St., Fall River, MA 02722/508-678-7556; FAX: 508-675-9666
Chadick's Ltd., P.O. Box 100, Terrell, TX 75160/214-563-7577
Chameleon Camouflage Systems, 15199 S. Maplelane Rd., Oregon City, OR 97045/503-657-2266
Champion Target Co., 232 Industrial Parkway, Richmond, IN 47374/800-441-4971
Champion's Choice, Inc., 223 Space Park South, Nashville, TN 37211/615-834-6666; FAX: 615-831-2753
Champlin Firearms, Inc., P.O. Box 3191, Woodring Airport, Enid, OK 73701/405-237-7388; FAX: 405-242-6922
Champlin, R. MacDonald, P.O. Box 132, Candia, NH 03034
Chapman Academy of Practical Shooting, 4350 Academy Rd., Hallsville, MO 65255/314-696-5544; FAX: 314-696-2266
Chapman Manufacturing Co., The, 471 New Haven Rd., P.O. Box 250, Durham, CT 06422/203-349-9228; FAX: 203-349-0084
Chapuis Armes, 21 La Gravoux, BP15, 42380 St. Bonnet-le-Chateau, FRANCE/(33)77.50.06.96 (U.S. importer—Armes de Chasse)
CHARCO, 26 Beaver St., Ansonia, CT 06401/203-377-8080

Charter Arms (See CHARCO)
Checkmate Refinishing, 8232 Shaw Rd., Brooksville, FL 34602/904-799-5774
Cheddite France, S.A., 99 Route de Lyon, F-26500 Bourg Les Valence, FRANCE/75 56 45 45; FAX: 75 56 98 89
Chelsea Gun Club of New York City, Inc., 237 Ovington Ave., Apt. D53, Brooklyn, NY 11209/718-836-9422, 718-833-2704
Chem-Pak, Inc., 11 Oates Ave., P.O. Box 1685, Winchester, VA 22601/800-336-9828; FAX: 703-722-3993
Cherokee Gun Accessories (See Glaser Safety Slug, Inc.)
Chesapeake Importing & Distributing Co. (See CIDCO)
Chesire & Perez Dist., 425 W. Allen Ave., San Dimas, CA 91773-1485
CheVron Bullets, RR1, Ottawa, IL 61350/815-433-2471
CheVron Case Master (See CheVron Bullets)
Chicago Cutlery Co., 1536 Beech St., Terre Haute, IN 47804/800-457-2665
Chicasaw Gun Works (See Cochran, Oliver)
Chimere, Inc., 4406 Exchange Ave., Naples, FL 33942/813-643-4222
ChinaSports, Inc., 2010 S. Lynx Place, Ontario, CA 91761/714-923-1411; FAX: 714-923-0775
Chipmunk (See Oregon Arms, Inc.)
Chippewa Shoe Co., P.O. Box 2521, Ft. Worth, TX 76113/817-332-4385
Choate Machine & Tool Co., Inc., P.O. Box 218, Bald Knob, AR 72010/501-724-6193, 800-972-6390; FAX: 501-724-5873
Chopie Mfg., Inc., 700 Copeland Ave., LaCrosse, WI 54603/608-784-0926
Christie's East, 219 E. 67th St., New York, NY 10021/212-606-0400
Christopher Firearms Co., Inc., E., Route 128 & Ferry St., Miamitown, OH 45041/513-353-1321
Chronotech, 1655 Siamet Rd. Unit 6, Mississauga, Ont. L4W 1Z4 CANADA/416-625-5200; FAX: 416-625-5190
Chuck's Gun Shop, P.O. Box 597, Waldo, FL 32694/904-468-2264
Churchill (See U.S. importer—Ellett Bros.)
Churchill Glove Co., James, P.O. Box 298, Centralia, WA 98531
Churchill, Winston, Twenty Mile Stream Rd., RFD P.O. Box 29B, Proctorsville, VT 05153/802-226-7772
Chu Tani Ind., Inc., Box 3782, Chula Vista, CA 92011
CIDCO, 21480 Pacific Blvd., Sterling, VA 22170/703-444-5353
Ciener, Inc., Jonathan Arthur, 8700 Commerce St., Cape Canaveral, FL 32920/407-868-2200; FAX: 407-868-2201
Cimarron Arms, 1106 Wisterwood G, Houston, TX 77043/713-468-2007; FAX: 713-461-8320
Cincinnati Swaging, 2605 Marlington Ave., Cincinnati, OH 45208
Circle M Custom Bullets, 2718 Button Willow Parkway, Abilene, TX 97606/915-698-3106
Claridge Hi-Tec, Inc., 19350 Business Center Dr., Northridge, CA 91324/818-700-9093; FAX: 818-700-0026
Clark Co., Inc., David, P.O. Box 15054, Worcester, MA 01615-0054/508-756-6216; FAX: 508-753-5827
Clark Custom Guns, Inc., P.O. Box 530, 11462 Keatchie Rd., Keithville, LA 71047/318-925-0836; FAX: 318-925-9425
Clark Firearms Engraving, P.O. Box 80746, San Marino, CA 91118/818-287-1652
Clark, Frank, 3714-27th St., Lubbock, TX 79410/806-799-1187
Clarkfield Enterprises, Inc., 1032 10th Ave., Clarkfield, MN 56223/612-669-7140
Classic Arms Corp., P.O. Box 106, Dunsmuir, CA 96025-0106/916-235-2000
Classic Brass, 14 Grove St., Plympton, MA 02367/FAX: 617-585-5673
Classic Guns, Inc., Frank S. Wood, 3230 Medlock Bridge Rd., Suite 110, Norcross, GA 30092/404-242-7944
Clay Target Enterprises, 300 Railway Ave., Campbell, CA 95008/408-379-4829
Clearview Mfg. Co., Inc., 413 S. Oakley St., Fordyce, AR 71742/501-352-8557; FAX: 501-352-8557
Clements' Custom Leathercraft, Chas, 1741 Dallas St., Aurora, CO 80010-2018/303-364-0403
Clenzoil Corp., P.O. Box 80226, Canton, OH 44708/216-833-9758
Clerke Co., J.A., P.O. Box 627, Pearblossom, CA 93553-0627/805-945-0713
Clift Welding Supply & Cases, 1332-A Colusa Hwy., Yuba City, CA 95993/916-755-3390; FAX: 916-755-3393
Clifton Arms, Inc., P.O. Box 1471, Medina, TX 78055/210-589-2666; FAX: 210-589-2661
Clinton River Gun Serv., Inc., 30016 S. River Rd., Mt. Clemens, MI 48045/313-468-1090
Cloward's Gun Shop, 4023 Aurora Ave. N, Seattle, WA 98103/206-632-2072
Clymer Manufacturing Co., Inc., 1645 W. Hamlin Rd., Rochester Hills, MI 48309/313-853-5555; FAX: 313-853-1530
Coast Cutlery Co., 609 SE Ankeny, Portland, OR 97214/503-234-4545
Coats, Mrs. Lester, 300 Luman Rd., Space 125, Phoenix, OR 97535/503-535-1611
CoBalt Mfg., Inc., 15121 35 W., Unit 106-07, Denton, TX 76205/817-382-8986
Cobra Gunskin, 133-30 32nd Ave., Flushing, NY 11354/718-762-8181; FAX: 718-762-0890
Cobra Sport s.r.l., Via Caduti Nei Lager No. 1, 56020 San Romano, Montopoli v/Arno (Pi), ITALY/0039-571-450490; FAX: 0039-571-450492
Cochran, Oliver, Box 868, Shady Spring, WV 25918
Coffin, Charles H., 3719 Scarlet Ave.,Odessa, TX 79762/915-366-4729
Coffin, Jim, 250 Country Club Lane, Albany, OR 97321/503-928-4391
Coghlan's Ltd., 121 Irene St., Winnipeg, Man., CANADA R3T 4C7/204-284-9550
Cold Steel, Inc., 2128 Knoll Dr., Unit D, Ventura, CA 93003/800-255-4716, 800-624-2363
Cole-Grip, 16135 Cohasset St., Van Nuys, CA 91406/818-782-4424
Coleman Co., Inc., 250 N. St. Francis, Wichita, KS 67201
Collins Brothers Div. (See Bowen Knife Co.)
Colonial Arms, Inc., P.O. Box 636, Selma, AL 36702-0636/205-872-9455; FAX: 205-872-9540
Colonial Knife Co., P.O. Box 3327, Providence, RI 02909/401-421-1600; FAX: 401-421-2047
Colonial Repair, P.O. Box 372, Hyde Park, MA 02136-9998/617-469-4951
Colorado School of Trades, 1575 Hoyt St., Lakewood, CO 80215/800-234-4594; FAX: 303-233-4723
Colorado Shooter's Supply, 138 S. Plum, P.O. Box 132, Fruita, CO 81521/303-858-9191
Colorado Sutlers Arsenal, Box 991, Granby, CO 80446/303-887-3813
Colt Blackpowder Arms Co., 5 Centre Market Place, New York, NY 10013/212-925-4881; FAX: 212-966-4986
Colt's Mfg. Co., Inc., P.O. Box 1868, Hartford, CT 06144-1868/203-236-6311; FAX: 203-244-1449
Combat Military Ordnance Ltd., 3900 Hopkins St., Savannah, GA 31405/912-238-1900; FAX: 912-236-7570
Combat Shop, The (See Jet Comp Systems)
Companhia Brasileira de Cartuchos (See CBC)
Compass Industries, Inc., 104 East 25th St., New York, NY 10010/212-473-2614
Competition Electronics, Inc., 3469 Precision Dr., Rockford, IL 61109/815-874-8001; FAX: 815-874-8181
Competition Limited, 1664 S. Research Loop Rd., Tucson, AZ 85710/602-722-6455
Competitive Pistol Shop, The, 5233 Palmer Dr., Ft. Worth, TX 76117-2433/817-834-8479
Competitor Corp., Inc., P.O. Box 244, 293 Townsend Rd., West Groton, MA 01472/508-448-3521; FAX: 603-673-4540
Component Concepts, Inc., 10240 SW Nimbus Ave., Suite L-8, Portland, OR 97223/503-684-9262; FAX: 503-620-4285
Condon, Inc., David, P.O. Box 312, 14502-G Lee Rd., Chatilly, VA 22021/703-631-7748 or 109 E. Washington St., Middleburg, VA 22117/703-687-5642
Condor Mfg. Co., 418 W. Magnolia Ave., Glendale, CA 91204/818-240-3173
Conetrol Scope Mounts, 10225 Hwy. 123 S., Seguin, TX 78155/210-379-3030, 800-CONETROL
CONKKO, P.O. Box 40, Broomall, PA 19008/215-356-0711
Connecticut Valley Arms Co. (See CVA)
Connecticut Valley Classics, P.O. Box 2068, 12 Taylor Lane, Westport, CT 06880/203-435-4600
Conrad, C.A., 3964 Ebert St., Winston-Salem, NC 27127/919-788-5469
Continental Kite & Key (See CONKKO)
Cook Bullets, 1846 Rosemeade Parkway 188, Carrollton, TX 75007/214-394-8725
Cook Engineering Service, 891 Highbury Rd., Vermont VICT 3133 AUSTRALIA
Coonan Arms, Inc., 830 Hampden Ave., St. Paul, MN 55114/612-646-0902; FAX: 612-646-0902
Cooper Arms, P.O. Box 114, Stevensville, MT 59870/406-777-5534
Cooper-Woodward, P.O. Box 1788, East Helena, MT 59635/406-475-3321
Cor-Bon, Inc., 4828 Michigan Ave.,P.O. Box 10126, Detroit, MI 48210/313-894-2373
Corbin Applied Technology, P.O. Box 2171, White City, OR 97503/503-826-5211
Corbin, Inc., 600 Industrial Circle, P.O. Box 2659, White City, OR 97503/503-826-5211; FAX: 503-826-8669
Corkys Gun Clinic, 111 North 11th Ave., Greeley, CO 80631/303-330-0516
Corry, John, 861 Princeton Ct., Neshanic Station, NJ 08853/308-369-8019
Cosmi Americo & Figlio s.n.c., Via Flaminia 307, Ancona, ITALY I-60020/071-888208; FAX: 071-887008 (U.S. importer—New England Arms Co.)
Costa, David, P.O. Box 428, Island Pond, VT 05846
Coulston Products, Inc., P.O. Box 30, Easton, PA 18044-0030/215-253-0167; FAX: 215-252-1511
Counter Assault, Box 4721, Missoula, MT 59806/406-728-6241; FAX: 406-728-8800
Country Armourer, The, P.O. Box 308, Ashby, MA 01431/508-386-7789
Cousin Bob's Mountain Products, 7119 Ohio River Blvd., Ben Avon, PA 15202/412-766-5114; FAX: 412-766-5114
Cox, C. Ed, RD 2, Box 192, Prosperity, PA 15329/412-228-4984
CP Specialties, 1814 Mearns Rd., Warminster, PA 18974
CQB Training, P.O. Box 1739, Manchester, MO 63011
Craftguard, 3624 Logan Ave., Waterloo, IA 50703/319-232-2959
Crandall Tool & Machine Co., 1545 N. Mitchell St., P.O. Box 569, Cadillac, MI 49601/616-775-5562
Crane & Crane Ltd., 105 N. Edison Way 6, Reno, NV 89502-2355/702-856-1516; FAX: 702-856-1616
Crane Sales Co., George S., P.O. Box 385, Van Nuys, CA 91409/818-505-8337
Cravener's Gun Shop, 1627-5th Ave., Ford City, PA 16226/412-763-8312
Crawford Co., Inc., R.M., P.O. Box 277, Everett, PA 15537/814-652-6536; FAX: 814-652-9526
Creative Cartridge Co., 56 Morgan Rd., Canton, CT 06019/203-693-2529
Creative Craftsman, Inc., The, 95 Highway 29 North, P.O. Box 331, Lawrenceville, GA 30246/404-963-2112
Creedmoor Sports, Inc., P.O. Box 1040, Oceanside, CA 92051/619-757-5529
Creek Side Metal & Woodcrafters (See Allard, Gary)
Creekside Gun Shop, Inc., Main St., Holcomb, NY 14469/716-657-6338; FAX: 716-657-7900
Crosman Blades (See Coleman Co., Inc.)
Crosman Corp., Rt. 5 and 20, E. Bloomfield, NY 14443/716-657-6161; FAX: 716-657-5405
Crosman Products of Canada Ltd., 1173 N. Service Rd. West, Oakville, Ontario, LCM 2V9 CANADA/416-827-1822
Crouse's Country Cover, P.O. Box 160, Storrs, CT 06268/203-423-0702
Crucelegui Hermanos (See U.S. importer—Mandall Shooting Supplies, Inc.)
CRW Products, Inc., Box 2123, Des Moines, IA 50310
Cubic Shot Shell Co., Inc., 98 Fatima Dr., Campbell, OH 44405/216-755-0349; FAX: 216-755-0349
Cullity Restoration, Daniel, 209 Old County Rd., East Sandwich, MA 02537/508-888-1147
Cumberland Arms, Rt. I, Box 1150 Shafer Rd., Blantons Chapel, Manchester, TN 37355
Cumberland Knife & Gun Works, 5661 Bragg Blvd., Fayetteville, NC 28303/919-867-0009
Cummings Bullets, 1417 Esperanza Way, Escondido, CA 92027
Cummingham Co., Eaton, Admiral Blvd. at Oak, Kansas City, MO 64106/816-842-2600
Curtis Custom Shop, RR1, Box 193A, Wallingford, KY 41093/703-659-4265
Custom Barrel Electropolishing, 11609 Galayda St., Houston, TX 77086/713-448-5300; FAX: 713-448-7298
Custom Bullets by Hoffman, 2604 Peconic Ave., Seaford, NY 11783
Custom Checkering Service, Kathy Forster, 2124 SE Yamhill St., Portland, OR 97214/503-236-5874
Custom Chronograph, Inc., 5305 Reese Hill Rd., Sumas, WA 98295/206-988-7801
Custom Firearms (See Ahrends, Kim)
Custom Gun Products, 5021 W. Rosewood, Spokane, WA 99208/509-328-9340
Custom Gun Stocks, Rt. 6, P.O. Box 177, McMinnville, TN 37110/615-668-3912
Custom Gunsmiths, 4303 Friar Lane, Colorado Springs, CO 80907/719-599-3366
Custom Hunting Ammo & Arms, 2900 Fisk Rd., Howell, MI 48843/517-546-9498
Custom Shop, The, 890 Cochrane Crescent, Peterborough, Ont. K9H 5N3 CANADA/705-742-6693
Custom Tackle and Ammo, P.O. Box 1886, Farmington, NM 87499/505-632-3539
Cutco Cutlery, P.O. Box 810, Olean, NY 14760/716-372-3111
Cutlery Shoppe, 5461 Kendall St., Boise, ID 83706-1248/800-231-1272
Cutsinger Bench Rest Bullets, RR 8, Box 161-A, Shelbyville, IN 46176/317-729-5360
CVA, 5988 Peachtree Corners East, Norcross, GA 30071/404-449-4687; FAX: 404-242-8546
C.W. Cartridge Co., 242 Highland Ave., Kearney, NJ 07032/201-998-1030 or 71 Hackensack St., Wood-Ridge, NJ 07075
Cycle Dynamics, Inc., 74 Garden St., Feeding Hills, MA 01030/413-786-0141
Cylinder & Slide, Inc., William R. Laughridge, 245 E. 4th St., Fremont, NE 68025/402-721-4277; FAX: 402-721-0263
CZ (See U.S. importer—Action Arms Ltd.)

D

D&D Gunsmiths, Ltd., 363 E. Elmwood, Troy, MI 48083/313-583-1512
D&H Precision Tooling, 7522 Barnard Mill Rd., Ringwood, IL 60072/815-653-4011
D&H Prods. Co., Inc., 465 Denny Rd., Valencia, PA 16059/412-898-2840
D&J Bullet Co. & Custom Gun Shop, Inc., Rt. 1, Box 223 A-1, Flatwoods, KY 41139/606-836-2663; FAX: 606-836-2663
D&L Sports, P.O. Box 651, Gillette, WY 82717/307-686-4008
D&R Distributing, 308 S.E. Valley St., Myrtle Creek, OR 97457/503-863-6850
Dade Screw Machine Products, 2319 NW 7th Ave., Miami, FL 33127/305-573-5050
Daewoo Precision Industries Ltd., 34-3 Yeoeuido-Dong, Yeongdeungoo-GU, 15th Fl., Seoul, KOREA (U.S. importer—Firstshot, Inc.)
Dahl's Custom Stocks, Rt. 4, P.O. Box 558, Lake Geneva, WI 53147/414-248-2464
Daisy Mfg. Co., P.O. Box 220, Rogers, AR 72756
Dakota (See U.S. importer—EMF Co., Inc.)
Dakota Arms, HC55, Box 326, Sturgis, SD 57785/605-347-4686; FAX: 605-347-4459
Dakota Corp., P.O. Box 543, Rutland, VT 05702/800-451-4167; FAX: 802-773-3919
Daly, Charles (See Miroku, B.C./Daly, Charles)
Damascus-U.S.A., RR 3, Box 39-A, Edenton, NC 27932/919-482-4992; FAX: 919-482-4723
Dan's Whetstone Co., Inc., 109 Remington Terrace, Hot Springs, AR 71913/501-767-1616; FAX: 501-767-9598
Dangler, Homer L., Box 254, Addison, MI 49220/517-547-6745
Danner Shoe Mfg. Co., 12722 NE Airport Way, Portland, OR 97230/503-251-1100; FAX: 503-251-1119
Danuser Machine Co., 550 E. Third St., P.O. Box 368, Fulton, MO 65251/314-642-2246; FAX: 314-642-2240
Dapkus Co., J.G., P.O. Box 293, Durham, CT 06422

Dara-Nes, Inc. (See Nesci Enterprises, Inc.)
Darlington Gun Works, Inc., P.O. Box 698, 516 S. 52 Bypass, Darlington, SC 29532/803-393-3931
Data Tech Software Systems, 19312 East Eldorado Drive, Aurora, CO 80013
Datumtech Corp., 2275 Wehrle Dr., Buffalo, NY 14221
Davidson Products, 2020 Huntington Dr., Las Cruces, NM 88801/505-522-5612
Davidson's, 2703 High Point Rd., Greensboro, NC 27403/800-367-4867, 919-292-5161; FAX: 919-252-2552
Davidson, Jere, Rt. 1, Box 132, Rustburg, VA 24588/804-821-3637
Davis Industries, 11186 Venture Dr., Mira Loma, CA 91752/909-360-5598
Davis Leather Co., G. Wm., 3990 Valley Blvd., Unit D, Walnut, CA 91789/714-598-5620
Davis Products, Mike, 643 Loop Dr., Moses Lake, WA 98837/509-765-6178, 800-765-6178 orders only
Davis Service Center, Bill, 10173 Croydon Way 9, Sacramento, CA 95827/916-369-6789
Day & Sons, Inc., Leonard, P.O. Box 122, Flagg Hill Rd., Heath, MA 01346/413-337-8369
Dayton Traister, P.O. Box 593, Oak Harbor, WA 98277
DBASE Consultants (See Peripheral Data Systems)
DBI Books, Inc., 4092 Commercial Ave., Northbrook, IL 60062/708-272-6310; FAX: 708-272-2051
D-Boone Ent., Inc., 5900 Colwyn Dr., Harrisburg, PA 17109
D.C.C. Enterprises, 259 Wynburn Ave., Athens, GA 30601
D.D. Custom Rifles, R.H. "Dick" Devereaux, 5240 Mule Deer Dr., Colorado Springs, CO 80919/719-548-8468
Dead Eyes Sport Center, RD 1, Box 147B, Shickshin, PA 18655/717-256-7432
de Treville & Co., Stan, 4129 Normal St., San Diego, CA 92103/619-298-3393
Decker Shooting Products, 1729 Laguna Ave., Schofield, WI 54476/715-359-5873
DeckSlider of Florida, 27641-2 Reahard Ct., Bonita Springs, FL 33923/800-782-1474
Dedicated Systems, 105-B Cochrane Circle, Morgan Hill, CA 95037/408-779-2808; FAX: 408-779-2673
Deepeeka Exports Pvt. Ltd., D-78, Saket, Meerut-250-006, INDIA/0121-74483; FAX: 0121-74483
Deer Me Products Co., Box 34, 1208 Park St., Anoka, MN 55303/612-421-8971; FAX: 612-422-0536
Dee Zee Alumna Sports, 1572 NE 58th Ave., P.O. Box 3090, Des Moines, IA 50316/515-265-7331
Defense Moulding Enterprises, 16781 Daisey Ave., Fountain Valley, CA 92708/714-842-5062
Defense Training International, Inc., 749 S. Lemay, Ste. A3-337, Ft. Collins, CO 80524/303-482-2520
Degen Knives, 9608 Van Nuys Blvd., 104, Panorama City, CA 91402/818-892-6534; FAX: 818-830-7333
deHaas Barrels, RR 3, Box 77, Ridgeway, MO 64481/816-872-6308
Del Rey Products, P.O. Box 91561, Los Angeles, CA 90009/213-823-0494
Del-Sports, Inc., Box 685, Main St., Margaretville, NY 12455/914-586-4103; FAX: 914-586-4105
Delhi Gun House, 1374 Kashmere Gate, Delhi, INDIA 110 006/(011)237375 239116; FAX: 91-11-2917344
Delorge, Ed, 2231 Hwy. 308, Thibodaux, LA 70301/504-447-1633
Delta Co. Ammo Bunker, 1209 16th Place, Yuma, AZ 85364/602-783-4563
Delta Arms Ltd., P.O. Box 68, Sellers, SC 29592-0068/803-752-7426, 800-677-0641; 800-274-1611
Delta Enterprises, 284 Hagemann Drive, Livermore, CA 94550
Delta Vectors, Inc., 7119 W. 79th St., Overland Park, KS 66204/913-642-0307
Dem-Bart Checkering Tools, Inc., 6807 Hwy. 2, Bickford Ave., Snohomish, WA 98290/206-568-7356; FAX: 206-568-3134
Denver Arms, Ltd., P.O. Box 4640, Pagosa Springs, CO 81157/303-731-2295
Denver Bullets, Inc., 1811 W. 13th Ave., Denver, CO 80204/303-893-3146
Denver Instrument Co., 6542 Fig St., Arvada, CO 80004/800-321-1135, 303-431-7255
DeSantis Holster & Leather Goods, P.O. Box 2039, New Hyde Park, NY 11040-0701/516-354-8000; FAX: 516-354-7501
Desert Industries, Inc., 3245 E. Patrick Ln., Suite H, Las Vegas, NV 89120/702-597-1066; FAX: 702-434-9495
Desert Mountain Mfg., P.O. Box 184, Coram, MT 59913/406-387-5381
Destination North Software, 804 Surry Road, Wenatchee, WA 98801/509-662-6602
Detroit-Armor Corp., 720 Industrial Dr. 112, Cary, IL 60013/708-639-7666
Developmental Concepts, Rt. 4, New Henderson Rd., Clinton, TN 37716/615-945-1428
Dever Co., Jack, 8590 NW 90, Oklahoma City, OK 73132/405-721-6393
Devereaux, R.H. "Dick" (See D.D. Custom Rifles)
Dewey Mfg. Co., Inc., J., P.O. Box 2014, Southbury, CT 06488/203-598-7912; FAX: 203-598-3119
DGS, Inc., Dale A. Storey, 1117 E. 12th, Casper, WY 82601/307-237-2414
Diamond Machining Technology, Inc., 85 Hayes Memorial Dr., Marlborough, MA 01752/508-481-5944; FAX: 508-485-3924
Diamond Mfg. Co., P.O. Box 174, Wyoming, PA 18644/800-233-9601
Diana (See U.S. importer—Dynamit Nobel-RWS, Inc.)
Dibble, Derek A., 555 John Downey Dr., New Britain, CT 06051/203-224-2630
Dilliott Gunsmithing, Inc., 657 Scarlett Rd., Dandridge, TN 37725/615-397-9204
Dillon Precision Products, Inc., 7442 E. Butherus Dr., Scottsdale, AZ 85260/602-948-8009
Dillon, Ed, 1035 War Eagle Dr. N., Colorado Springs, CO 80919/719-598-4929; FAX: 719-598-4929
Division Lead Co., 7742 W. 61st Pl., Summit, IL 60502
Dixie Gun Works, Hwy. 51 South, Union City, TN 38261/901-885-0700, order 800-238-6785; FAX: 901-885-0440
Dixon Muzzleloading Shop, Inc., RD 1, Box 175, Kempton, PA 19529/215-756-6271
DKT, Inc., 14623 Vera Drive, Union, MI 49130-9744/616-641-7120; FAX: 616-641-2015
DLO Mfg., 415 Howe Ave., Shelton, CT 06484/203-924-2952
Dohring Bullets, 100 W. 8 Mile Rd., Ferndale, MI 48220
Dolbare, Elizabeth, 39 Dahlia, Casper, WY 82604/307-266-5924
Donnelly, C.P., 405 Kubli Rd., Grants Pass, OR 97527/503-846-6604
Doskocil Mfg. Co., Inc., P.O. Box 1246, Arlington, TX 76004/817-467-5116
Douglas Barrels, Inc., 5504 Big Tyler Rd., Charleston, WV 25313-1398/304-776-1341; FAX: 304-776-8560
Dowtin Gunworks, Rt. 4, Box 930A, Flagstaff, AZ 86001/602-779-1898
Dr. O's Products Ltd., P.O. Box 111, Niverville, NY 12130/518-784-3333; FAX: 518-784-2800
Drain, Mark, SE 3211 Kamilche Point Rd., Shelton, WA 98584/206-426-5452
Dremel Mfg. Co., 4915-21st St., Racine, WI 53406
Dressel Jr., Paul G., 209 N. 92nd Ave., Yakima, WA 98908/509-966-9233
Dri-Slide, Inc., 411 N. Darling, Fremont, MI 49412/616-924-3950
DTM International, Inc., 40 Joslyn Rd., P.O. Box 5, Lake Orion, MI 48035/313-693-6670
D.O.C. Specialists, Inc., Doc & Bud Ulrich, Jim Amodei, 2209 S. Central Ave., Cicero, IL 60650/708-652-3606; FAX: 708-652-2516
Du-Lite Corp., 171 River Rd., Middletown, CT 06457/203-347-2505
Duane Custom Stocks, Randy, 110 W. North Ave., Winchester, VA 22601/703-667-9461; FAX: 703-722-3993
Dubber, Michael W., P.O. Box 312, Evansville, IN 47702/812-424-9000; FAX: 812-424-6551
Duck Call Specialists, P.O. Box 124, Jerseyville, IL 62052/618-498-4692
Duffy, Charles E., Williams Lane, West Hurley, NY 12491/914-679-2997
Dumoulin, Ernest, Rue Florent Boclinville 8-10, 13-4041 Votten, BELGIUM/41 27 78 92
Duncan's Gun Works, Inc., 1619 Grand Ave., San Marcos, CA 92069/619-727-0515
Dunham Co., P.O. Box 813, Brattleboro, VT 05301/802-254-2316
Duofold, Inc., 120 W. 45th St., 15th Floor, New York, NY 10036
DuPont (See IMR Powder Co.)
Durward, John, 448 Belgreen Way, Waterloo, Ontario N2L 5X5 CANADA
Dutchman's Firearms, Inc., The, 4143 Taylor Blvd., Louisville, KY 40215/502-366-0555
Duxbak, Inc., 903 Woods Rd., Cambridge, MD 21613/301-228-2990, 800-334-1845
Dybala Gun Shop, P.O. Box 1024, FM 3156, Bay City, TX 77414/409-245-0866
Dykstra, Doug, 411 N. Darling, Fremont, MI 49412/616-924-3950
Dynalite Products, Inc., 215 S. Washington St., Greenfield, OH 45123/513-981-2124
Dynamit Nobel-RWS, Inc., 81 Ruckman Rd., Closter, NJ 07624/201-767-1995; FAX: 201-767-1589
Dyson & Son Ltd., Peter, 29-31 Church St., Honley, Huddersfield, W. Yorkshire HD7 2AH, ENGLAND/0484-661062; FAX: 0484 663709

E

E&L Mfg., Inc., 39042 N. School House Rd., Cave Creek, AZ 85331/602-488-2598; FAX: 602-488-0813
E.A.A. Corp., 4480 E. 11th Ave., Hialeah, FL 33013/305-688-4442; FAX: 305-688-5656
Eagan, Donald V., P.O. Box 196, Benton, PA 17814/717-925-6134
Eagle Arms, Inc., 131 E. 22nd Ave., P.O. Box 457, Coal Valley, IL 61240/309-799-5619; FAX: 309-799-5150
Eagle Flight Bullet Co., 925 Lakeville St., Suite 123, Petaluma, CA 94954/707-762-6955
Eagle Imports, Inc., 1907 Highway 35, Ocean, NJ 07712/908-531-8375; FAX: 908-531-1520
Eagle International, Inc., 5195 W. 58th Ave., Suite 300, Arvada, CO 80002/303-426-8100
Eagle Products Co., 1520 Adelia Ave., S. El Monte, CA 91733
E-A-R, Inc., Div. of Cabot Safety Corp., 5457 W. 79th St., Indianapolis, IN 46268/800-327-3431; FAX: 800-488-8007
Eastman Products, R.T., P.O. Box 1531, Jackson, WY 83001
Easy Pull Outlaw Products, 316 1st St. East, Polson, MT 59860/406-883-6822
Echols & Co., D'Arcy, 164 W. 580 S., Providence, UT 84332/801-753-2367
Eckelman Gunsmithing, 3125 133rd St. SW, Fort Ripley, MN 56449/218-829-3176
Edenpine, Inc. c/o Six Enterprises, Inc., 320 D Turtle Creek Ct., San Jose, CA 95125/408-999-0201; FAX: 408-999-0216
Ed's Gun House, Rt. 1, Box 62, Minnesota City, MN 55959/507-689-2925
EdgeCraft Corp., P.O. Box 3000, Avondale, PA 19311/215-268-0500, 800-342-3255; FAX: 215-268-3545
Edmisten Co., P.O. Box 1293, Boone, NC 28607
Edmund Scientific Co., 101 E. Gloucester Pike, Barrington, NJ 08033/609-543-6250
Ednar, Inc., 2-4-8 Kayabacho, Nihonbashi, Chuo-ku, Tokyo, JAPAN/81(Japan)-3-3667-1651
Eds Custom Bullets, 431 North 75 East, North Salt Lake, UT 84054/801-295-3960
Eezox, Inc., P.O. Box 772, Waterford, CT 06385-0772/203-447-8282; FAX: 203-447-3484
Efemes Enterprises, P.O. Box 691, Colchester, VT 05446
Eggleston, Jere D., 400 Saluda Ave., Columbia, SC 29205/803-799-3402
Eichelberger Bullets, Wm., 158 Crossfield Rd., King of Prussia, PA 19406
Eilan S.A.L., Paseo San Andres N8, Eibar, SPAIN 20600/(34)43118916; FAX: (34)43 114038
Eiland Custom Bullets, P.O. Box 688, Buena Vista, CO 81211/303-429-8850
EK Knife Co., 601 N. Lombardy St., Richmond, VA 23220/804-257-7272
Ekol Leather Care, P.O. Box 2652, West Lafayette, IN 47906/317-463-2250; FAX: 317-463-7004
El Paso Saddlery Co., P.O. Box 27194, El Paso, TX 79926/915-544-2233; FAX: 915-544-2535
Eldorado Cartridge Corp. (See PMC/Eldorado Cartridge Corp.)
Electronic Trigger Systems, Inc., 4124 Thrushwood Lane, Minnetonka, MN 55345/612-935-7829
Electro Prismatic Collimators, Inc., 1441 Manatt St., Lincoln, NE 68521
Eley Ltd., P.O. Box 705, Witton, Birmingham, B6 7UT, ENGLAND/21-356-8899; FAX: 21-331-4173
Elite Ammunition, P.O. Box 3251, Oakbrook, IL 60522/708-366-9006
Elk River, Inc., 1225 Paonia St., Colorado Springs, CO 80915/719-574-4407
Elko Arms, Dr. L. Kortz, 28 rue Ecole Moderne, B-7060 Soignies, BELGIUM/(32)67-33-29-34
Ellett Bros., P.O. Box 128, Columbia, SC 29036/803-345-1820; FAX: 803-345-1820
Ellis Sport Shop, E.W., RD 1, Route 9N, P.O. Box 315, Corinth, NY 12822/518-654-6444
EMF Co., Inc., 1900 E. Warner Ave. Suite 1-D, Santa Ana, CA 92705/714-261-6611; FAX: 714-956-0133
Empire Cutlery Corp., 12 Kruger Ct., Clifton, NJ 07013/201-472-5155; FAX: 201-779-0759
Engineered Accessories, 1307 W. Wabash Ave., Effingham, IL 62401/217-347-7700; FAX: 217-347-7737
English, Inc., A.G., 708 S. 12th St., Broken Arrow, OK 74012/918-251-3399
Englishtown Sporting Goods Co., Inc., David J. Maxham, 38 Main St., Englishtown, NJ 07726/201-446-7717
Engraving Artistry, 36 Alto Rd., RFD 2, Burlington, CT 06013/203-673-6837
Enguix Import-Export, Alpujarras 58, Alzira, Valencia, SPAIN 46600/(96) 241 43 95; FAX: (96) 241 43 95
Enhanced Presentations, Inc., 5929 Market St., Wilmington, NC 28405/919-799-1622; FAX: 919-799-5004
The Ensign-Bickford Co., 660 Hopmeadow St., Simsbury, CT 06070
Epps "Orillia" Ltd., Ellwood, RR 3, Hwy. 11 North, Orillia, Ont. L3V 6H3, CANADA/705-689-5333
Erhardt, Dennis, 3280 Green Meadow Dr., Helena, MT 59601/406-442-4533
Erickson's Mfg., Inc., C.W., 530 Garrison Ave. N.E., Buffalo, MN 55313/612-682-3665; FAX: 612-682-4328
Erma Werke GmbH, Johan Ziegler St., 13/15/FeldiglSt., D-8060 Dachau, GERMANY (U.S. importers—Mandall Shooting Supplies, Inc.; PSI, Inc.)
Essex Arms, P.O. Box 345, Island Pond, VT 05846/802-723-4313
Estate Cartridge, Inc., 2778 FM 830, Willis, TX 77378/409-856-7277; FAX: 409-856-5486
Eureka Bullets, Hill House, Taylors Arm, NSW 2447 AUSTRALIA
Euroarms of America, Inc., 208 E. Piccadilly St., Winchester, VA 22601/703-662-1863; FAX: 703-662-4464
European American Armory Corp. (See E.A.A. Corp.)
Europtik Ltd., P.O. Box 319, Dunmore, PA 18512/717-347-6049, 800-873-5362; FAX: 717-969-4330
Eutaw Co., Inc., The, P.O. Box 608, U.S. Hwy. 176 West, Holly Hill, SC 29059/803-496-3341
Evans Engraving, Robert, 332 Vine St., Oregon City, OR 97045/503-656-5693
Eversull Co., Inc., K., 1 Tracemont, Boyce, LA 71409/318-793-8728; FAX: 318-793-5483
Exe, Inc., 18830 Partridge Circle, Eden Prairie, MN 55346/612-944-7662
Executive Protection Institute, Rt. 2, Box 3645, Berryville, VA 22611/703-955-1128
Eyears Insurance, 4926 Annhurst Rd., Columbus, OH 43228-1341
Eyster Heritage Gunsmiths, Inc., Ken, 6441 Bishop Rd., Centerburg, OH 43011/614-625-6131
Eze-Lap Diamond Prods., P.O. Box 2229, 15164 Weststate St., Westminster, CA 92683//714-847-1555

F

4-D Custom Die Co., 711 N. Sandusky St., P.O. Box 889, Mt. Vernon, OH 43050-0889/614-397-7214; FAX: 614-397-6600
Fabarm S.p.A., Via G. Zola N.33, Brescia, ITALY 25136/(030)2004805; FAX: (030)2004816 (U.S. importer—St. Lawrence Sales, Inc.)
Fabian Bros. Sporting Goods, Inc., 1510 Morena Blvd., Suite G, San Diego, CA 92110/619-275-0816; FAX: 619-276-8733

Fabrica D'Armi Sabatti S.R.L., via Dante 179, 25068 Sarezzo, Brescia, ITALY (U.S. importer—E.A.A. Corp.)
Fagan & Co., William, 22952 15 Mile Rd., Mt. Clemens, MI 48043/313-465-4637; FAX: 313-792-6996
Fair Game International, P.O. Box 77234-34053, Houston, TX 77234/713-941-6269
F.A.I.R. Techni-Mec s.n.c. Di Isidoro Rizzini & C., Via Gitti 41, 25060 Marcheno (BS), ITALY
Faith Associates, Inc., 1139 S. Greenville Hwy., Hendersonville, NC 28792/704-692-1916; FAX: 704-697-6827
Fajen, Inc., Reinhart, 1000 Red Bud Dr., P.O. Box 338, Warsaw, MO 65355/816-438-5111; FAX: 816-438-5175
Falcon Industries, Inc., P.O. Box 1310, Huntington Beach, CA 92647-1310/714-847-4700; 714-847-4141
Famas (See U.S. importer—Century International Arms, Inc.)
Fanzoj GmbH, Griesgasse 1, 9170 Ferlach, AUSTRIA 9170/(43) 04227-2283; FAX: (43) 04227-2867
FAPA Corp., P.O. Box 1439, New London, NH 03257/603-735-5652; FAX: 603-735-5154
Farm Form Decoys, Inc., 1602 Biovu, Galveston, TX 77551/409-744-0762, 409-765-6361; FAX: 409-765-8513
Farmer-Dressel, Sharon, 209 N. 92nd Ave., Yakima, WA 98908/509-966-9233
Far North Outfitters, Box 1252, Bethel, AK 99559
Farr Studio, Inc., 1231 Robinhood Rd., Greeneville, TN 37743/615-638-8825
FAS, Via E. Fermi, 8, 20019 Settimo Milanese, Milano, ITALY (U.S. importer—Nygord Precision Products)
Faulk's Game Call Co., Inc., 616 18th St., Lake Charles, LA 70601/318-436-9726
Faust, Inc., T.G., 544 Minor St., Reading, PA 19602/215-375-8549; FAX: 215-375-4488
Fausti & Figlie s.n.c., Stefano, Via Martini Zudipeudente, 70, Marcheno, 25060 ITALY (U.S. importer—American Arms, Inc.)
Fautheree, Andy, P.O. Box 4607, Pagosa Springs, CO 81157/303-731-5003
Feather Flex Decoys, 1655 Swan Lake Rd., Bossier City, LA 71111/318-746-8596; FAX: 318-742-4815
Feather Industries, Inc., 2300 Central Ave. K, Boulder, CO 80301/303-442-7021; FAX: 303-447-0944
Federal Cartridge Co., 900 Ehlen Dr., Anoka, MN 55303/612-422-2840
Federal Champion Target Co., 232 Industrial Parkway, Richmond, IN 47374/800-441-4971; FAX: 317-966-7747
Federal Engineering Corp., 1090 Bryn Mawr, Bensenville, IL 60106/708-860-1938
Federal Ordnance, Inc., 1443 Potrero Ave., S. El Monte, CA 91733/818-350-4161; FAX: 818-444-3875
FEG, Budapest, Soroksariut 158, H-1095 HUNGARY (U.S. importers—Century International Arms, Inc.; K.B.I., Inc.)
Feinwerkbau Westinger & Altenburger GmbH & Co. KG (See FWB)
Fellowes, Ted, Beaver Lodge, 9245 16th Ave. SW, Seattle, WA 98106/206-763-1698
Feminine Protection, Inc., 10514 Shady Trail, Dallas, TX 75220/214-351-4500
Ferdinand, Inc., P.O. Box 5, 201 Main St., Harrison, ID 83833/208-689-3012; FAX: 208-689-3142
Ferguson, Bill, P.O. Box 1238, Sierra Vista, AZ 85636/602-452-0533; FAX: 602-458-9125
FERLIB di Ferraglio Libero & C., Via Costa 46, 25063 Gardone V.T. (Brescia), ITALY/30 89 12 586; FAX: 30 89 12 586 (U.S. importers—New England Arms Co., Quality Arms, Inc.)
Ferris Firearms, 1827 W. Hildebrand, San Antonio, TX 78201/210-734-0304
Fiberpro Rifle Stocks, Div. of Fibers West, 10977 San Diego Mission Rd., San Diego, CA 92108/619-282-4211; FAX: 619-282-0598
Fibron Products, Inc., 170 Florida St., Buffalo, NY 14208/716-886-2378; FAX: 716-886-2394
Finch Custom Bullets, 40204 La Rochelle, Prairieville, LA 70769
Finerty, Raymond F., 803 N. Downing St., P.O. Box 914, Piqua, OH 45356/800-543-8952
Fiocchi of America, Inc., Rt. 2, P.O. Box 90-8, Ozark, MO 65721/417-725-4118; FAX: 417-725-1039
Firearm Training Center, The, 9555 Blandville Rd., West Paducah, KY 42086/502-554-5886
Firearms Academy of Seattle, P.O. Box 6691, Lynnwood, WA 98036/206-827-0533
Firearms Co. Ltd./Alpine (See U.S. importer—Mandall Shooting Supplies, Inc.)
Firearms Engraver's Guild of America, 332 Vine St., Oregon City, OR 97045/503-656-5693
Firearms Safety Products, Inc. (See FSPI)
First Distributors, Jack, Inc., 44633 Sierra Hwy., Lancaster, CA 93534/805-945-6981; FAX: 805-942-0844
Firstshot, Inc., 4101 Far Green Rd., Harrisburg, PA 17110/717-238-2575
Fish, Marshall F., Rt. 22 N., P.O. Box 2439, Westport, NY 12993/518-962-4897
Fish-N-Hunt, Inc., 5651 Beechnut St., Houston, TX 77096/713-777-3285; FAX: 713-777-9884
Fisher Custom Firearms, 2199 S. Kittredge Way, Aurora, CO 80013/303-755-3710
Fisher Enterprises, 655 Main St. 305, Edmonds, WA 98020/206-776-4365
Fisher, Jerry A., 535 Crane Mt. Rd., Big Fork, MT 59911/406-837-1024
Fitz Pistol Grip Co., P.O. Box 610, Douglas City, CA 96024/916-623-4019
Flaig's, 2200 Evergreen Rd., Millvale, PA 15209/412-821-1717
Flambeau Products Corp., P.O. Box 97, Middlefield, OH 44062/216-632-1631; FAX: 216-632-1581
Flannery Engraving Co., Jeff W., 11034 Riddles Run Rd., Union, KY 41091/606-384-3127
Flashette Co., 4725 S. Kolin Ave., Chicago, IL 60632/312-927-1302
Flayderman & Co., Inc., N., P.O. Box 2446, Ft. Lauderdale, FL 33303/305-761-8855
Fleming Firearms, 7720 E. 126 St. N., Collinsville, OK 74021/918-665-3624
Flents Products Co., Inc., P.O. Box 2109, Norwalk, CT 06852/203-866-2581; FAX: 203-854-9322
Flintlock Muzzle Loading Gun Shop, The, 1238 "G" S. Beach Blvd., Anaheim, CA 92804/714-821-6655
Flintlocks, Etc. (See Beauchamp & Son, Inc.)
Flitz International Ltd., 821 Mohr Ave., Waterford, WI 53185/414-534-5898; FAX: 414-534-2991
Floatstone Mfg. Co., 106 Powder Mill Rd., P.O. Box 765, Canton, CT 06019/203-693-1977
Flores Publications, J., P.O. Box 830131, Miami, FL 33283/305-559-4652
Flouramics, Inc., 103 Pleasant Ave., Upper Saddle River, NJ 07458/201-825-8110
Flow-Rite of Tennessee, Inc., 107 Allen St., Bruceton, TN 38317/901-586-2271; FAX: 901-586-2300
Flynn's Custom Guns, P.O. Box 7461, Alexandria, LA 71306/318-455-7130
FN Herstal, Voie de Liege 33, Herstal 4040, BELGIUM/(32)41.40.82.83; FAX: (32)40.86.79
Fobus International Ltd., Kfar Hess, ISRAEL 40692/FAX: 972-52-911716
Fogle, James W., RR 2, P.O. Box 258, Herrin, IL 62948/618-988-1795
Folks, Donald E., 205 W. Lincoln St., Pontiac, IL 61764/815-844-7901
Foothills Video Productions, Inc., P.O. Box 651, Spartanburg, SC 29304/803-573-7023, 800-782-5358
Ford, Jack, 1430 Elkwood, Missouri City, TX 77489/713-499-9984
Foredom Electric Co., Rt. 6, 16 Stony Hill Rd., Bethel, CT 06801/203-792-8622
Forgett Jr., Valmore J., 689 Bergen Blvd., Ridgefield, NJ 07657/201-945-2500
Forgreens Tool Mfg., Inc., P.O. Box 990, Robert Lee, TX 76945/915-453-2800
Forrest Tool Co., P.O. Box 768, 44380 Gordon Lane, Mendocino, CA 95460/707-937-2141; FAX: 717-937-1817
Forrest, Inc., Tom, P.O. Box 326, Lakeside, CA 92040/619-561-5800; FAX: 619-561-0227
Forster, Kathy (See Custom Checkering Service)
Forster Products, 82 E. Lanark Ave., Lanark, IL 61046/815-493-6360; FAX: 815-493-2371
Forster, Larry L., P.O. Box 212, 220 First St. NE, Gwinner, ND 58040-0212/701-678-2475
Fort Knox Security Products, 1051 N. Industrial Park Rd., Orem, UT 84057/801-224-7233
Forthofer's Gunsmithing & Knifemaking, 711 Spokane Ave., Whitefish, MT 59937/406-862-2674
Fortress Publications, Inc., P.O. Box 9241, Stoney Creek, Ont. L8G 3X9, CANADA/416-662-3505
Fortune Products, Inc., Box 1308, Friendswood, TX 77546/713-996-0729; FAX: 713-996-1034
Forty Five Ranch Enterprises, Box 1080, Miami, OK 74355-1080/918-542-5875
Forty-Niner Trading Co., P.O. Box 792, Manteca, CA 95336/209-823-7263
Fouling Shot, The, 6465 Parfet St., Arvada, CO 80004
Fountain Products, 492 Prospect Ave., West Springfield, MA 01089/413-781-4651; FAX: 413-733-8217
Fowler Bullets, 4003 Linwood Rd., Gastonia, NC 28052/704-867-3259
Fox River Mills, Inc., P.O. Box 298, 227 Poplar St., Osage, IA 50461/515-732-3798; FAX: 515-732-5128
Foy Custom Bullets, 104 Wells Ave., Daleville, AL 36322
Francesca, Inc., 3115 Old Ranch Rd., San Antonio, TX 78217/512-826-2584; FAX: 512-826-8211
Francesca Stabilizer's, Inc., 3115 Old Ranch Rd., San Antonio, TX 78217/512-826-2584
Franchi S.p.A., Luigi, Via del Serpente, 12, 25020 Fornaci, ITALY (U.S. importer—American Arms, Inc.)
Francolini, Leonard, 106 Powder Mill Rd., P.O. Box 765, Canton, CT 06019/203-693-1977
Francotte & Cie S.A., Auguste, rue du Trois Juin 109, 4400 Herstal-Liege, BELGIUM/41-48.13.18 (U.S. importer—Armes de Chasse)
Frank Custom Gun Service, Ron, 7131 Richland Rd., Ft. Worth, TX 76118/817-284-4426
Frank Knives, Box 984, Whitefish, MT 59937/406-862-2681; FAX: 406-862-2681
Frankonia Jagd, Hofmann & Co., P.O. Box 6780, D-8700 Wurzburg 1, GERMANY/09302-200; FAX: 09302-20200
Frazier Brothers Enterprises, 1118 N. Main St., Franklin, IN 46131/317-736-4000; FAX: 317-736-4000
Fredrick Gun Shop, 10 Elson Dr., Riverside, RI 02915/401-433-2805
Freedom Arms, Inc., P.O. Box 1776, Freedom, WY 83120/307-883-2468; FAX: 307-883-2005
Freeman Animal Targets, 2559 W. Morris St., Plainsfield, IN 46168/317-271-5314; FAX: 317-271-9106
Fremont Tool Works, 1214 Prairie, Ford, KS 67842/316-369-2338
French, J.R., 1712 Creek Ridge Ct., Irving, TX 75060/214-254-2654
Frielich Police Equipment, 211 East 21st St., New York, NY 10010/212-254-3045
Frontier, 2910 San Bernardo, Laredo, TX 78040/512-723-5409
Frontier Arms Co., Inc., 401 W. Rio Santa Cruz, Green Valley, AZ 85614-3932
Frontier Products Co., 164 E. Longview Ave., Columbus, OH 43202/614-262-9357
Frontier Safe Co., Envirotemp Corp., 1317 Chute St., Fort Wayne, IN 46803/219-422-4801
Frost Cutlery Co., P.O. Box 21353, Chattanooga, TN 37421/615-894-6079; FAX: 615-894-9576
FSPI, 5885 Glenridge Dr. Suite 220A, Atlanta, GA 30328/404-843-2881; FAX: 404-843-0271
Fujinon, Inc., 10 High Point Dr., Wayne, NJ 07470/201-633-5600
Fullmer, Geo M., 2499 Mavis St., Oakland, CA 94601/510-533-4193
Fulmer's Antique Firearms, Chet, P.O. Box 792, Rt. 2 Buffalo Lake, Detroit Lakes, MN 56501/218-847-7712
Furr Arms, 91 N. 970 W., Orem, UT 84057/801-226-3877; FAX: 801-226-0085
Fury Cutlery, 801 Broad Ave., Ridgefield, NJ 07657/201-943-5920; FAX: 201-943-1579
Fusilier Bullets, 10010 N. 6000 W., Highland, UT 84003/801-756-6813
FWB, Neckarstrasse 43, 7238 Oberndorf a. N., GERMANY/07423-814-0; FAX: 07423-814-89 (U.S. importer—Beeman Precision Airguns, Inc.)

G

G96 Products Co., Inc., 237 River St., Paterson, NJ 07524/201-684-4050; FAX: 201-684-3848
G&C Bullet Co., Inc., 8835 Thornton Rd., Stockton, CA 95209
G&H Decoys, Inc., P.O. Box 1208, Hwy. 75 North, Henryetta, OK 74437/918-652-3314
Galati International, P.O. Box 326, Catawissa, MO 63015/314-257-4837; FAX: 314-257-2268
Galaxy Imports Ltd., Inc., P.O. Box 3361, Victoria, TX 77903/512-573-4867; FAX: 512-576-9622
GALCO International Ltd., 2019 W. Quail Ave., Phoenix, AZ 85027/602-258-8295; FAX: 602-582-6854
Gamba S.p.A., Renato, Via Artigiani, 93, 25063 Gardone V.T. (Brescia), ITALY
Game Haven Gunstocks, 13750 Shire Rd., Wolverine, MI 49799/616-525-8257
Game Winner, Inc., 2625 Cumberland Parkway, Suite 220, Atlanta, GA 30339/404-434-9210; FAX: 404-434-9215
Gammog, Gregory B. Gally, 16009 Kenny Rd., Laurel, MD 20707/301-725-3838
Gamo (See U.S. importers—Daisy Mfg. Co.; Dynamit Nobel-RWS, Inc.)
Gander Mountain, Inc., P.O. Box 128, Hwy."W," Wilmot, WI 53192/414-862-2331,Ext. 6425
Ganton Manufacturing Ltd., Depot Lane, Seamer Rd., Scarborough, North Yorkshire, Y012 4EB ENGLAND/0723-371910; FAX: 0723-501671
GAR, 139 Park Lane, Wayne, NJ 07470/201-256-7641
Garbi, Armas Urki, 12-14, 20.600 Eibar (Guipuzcoa) SPAIN/43-11 38 73 (U.S. importer—Moore & Co. Wm. Larkin)
Garcia National Gun Traders, Inc., 225 SW 22nd Ave., Miami, FL 33135/305-642-2355
Garrett Accur-Lt. D.F.S. Co., P.O. Box 8675, 1413B East Olive Ct., Ft. Collins, CO 80524/303-224-3067
Garrett Cartridges, Inc., P.O. Box 178, Chehalis, WA 98532/206-736-0702
Garthwaite, Jim, Rt. 2, Box 310, Watsontown, PA 17777/717-538-1566
Gator Guns & Repair, 6255 Spur Hwy., Kenai, AK 99611/907-283-7947
Gaucher Armes, S.A., 46, rue Desjoyaux, 42000 Saint-Etienne, FRANCE/77 33 38 92 (U.S. importer—Mandall Shooting Supplies, Inc.)
GDL Enterprises, 409 Le Gardeur, Slidell, LA 70460/504-649-0693
Genco, P.O. Box 5704, Asheville, NC 28803
Gene's Custom Guns, P.O. Box 10534, White Bear Lake, MN 55110/612-429-5105
Gene's Gun Shop, Rt. 1 Box 890, Snyder, TX 79549/915-573-2323
Genecco Gun Works, K., 10512 Lower Sacramento Rd., Stockton, CA 95210/209-951-0706
General Lead, Inc., 1022 Grand Ave., Phoenix, AZ 85007
Gentry Custom Gunmaker, David, 314 N. Hoffman, Belgrade, MT 59714/406-388-4867
George & Ray's Primer Sealant, 2950 NW 29th, Portland, OR 97210/800-553-3022
George, Tim, Rt. 1, P.O. Box 45, Evington, VA 24550/804-821-8117
Gerber Legendary Blades, 14200 SW 72nd Ave., Portland, OR 97223/503-639-6161; FAX: 503-684-7008
Getz Barrel Co., P.O. Box 88, Beavertown, PA 17813/717-658-7263
GFR Corp., P.O. Box 430, Andover, NH 03216/603-735-5300
G.H. Enterprises Ltd., Bag 10, Okotoks, Alberta T0L 1T0 CANADA/403-938-6070
Gibbs Rifle Co., Inc., Cannon Hill Industrial Park, Rt. 2, Box 214 Hoffman Rd., Martinsburg, WV 25401/304-274-0458; FAX: 304-274-0078
Gilbert Equipment Co., Inc., 960 Downtowner Rd., Mobile, AL 36609/205-344-3322
Gillmann, Edwin, 33 Valley View Dr., Hanover, PA 17331/717-632-1662
Gilman-Mayfield, Inc., 3279 E. Shields, Fresno, CA 93703/209-237-2500
Giron, Robert E., 1328 Pocono St., Pittsburgh, PA 15218/412-731-6041
Gise Bullets, P.O. Box 772, Santa Clara, CA 95052
Glacier Glove, 4890 Aircenter Circle 206, Reno, NV 89502/702-825-8225; FAX: 702-825-6544
Glaser Safety Slug, Inc., P.O. Box 8223, Foster City, CA 94404/415-345-7677; FAX: 415-345-8217
Glass, Herb, P.O. Box 25, Bullville, NY 10915/914-361-3021

Glimm, Jerome C., 19 S. Maryland, Conrad, MT 59425/406-278-3574
Global Industries, 1501 E. Chapman Ave., 306, Fullerton, CA 92631/714-879-8922
Glock GmbH, P.O. Box 50, A-2232 Deutsch Wagram, AUSTRIA (U.S. importer—Glock, Inc.)
Glock, Inc., 6000 Highlands Parkway, Smyrna, GA 30082/404-432-1202
GML Products, Inc., 394 Laredo Dr., Birmingham, AL 35226/205-979-4867
Goens, Dale W., P.O. Box 224, Cedar Crest, NM 87008/505-281-5419
Goergen's Gun Shop, Inc., Rt. 2, Box 182BB, Austin, MN 55912/507-433-9280
GOEX, Inc., 1002 Springbrook Ave., Moosic, PA 18507/717-457-6724; FAX: 717-457-1130
Golden Age Arms Co., 115 E. High St., Ashley, OH 43003/614-747-2488
Gonic Arms, Inc., 134 Flagg Rd., Gonic, NH 03839/603-332-8456, 603-332-8457
Gonzalez Guns, Ramon B., P.O. Box 370, Monticello, NY 12701/914-794-4515
Goodling's Gunsmithing, R.D. 1, Box 1097, Spring Grove, PA 17362/717-225-3350
Goodwin, Fred, Silver Ridge Gun Shop, Sherman Mills, ME 04776/207-365-4451
Gordie's Gun Shop, 1401 Fulton St., Streator, IL 61364/815-672-7202
Gotz Bullets, 7313 Rogers St., Rockford, IL 61111
Goudy Classic Stocks, Gary, 263 Hedge Rd., Menlo Park, CA 94025-1711/415-322-1338
Gould & Goodrich, P.O. Box 1479, Lillington, NC 27546/919-893-2071; FAX: 919-893-4742
Gozon Corp., P.O. Box 6278, Fulsom, CA 95763/916-983-1807; FAX: 916-983-9500
Gournet, Geoffroy, 820 Paxinosa Ave., Easton, PA 18042/215-559-0710
Gozon Corp., P.O. Box 6278, Folsom, CA 95630/FAX: 916-983-9500
Grace & Co.-Conn., W.R. (See Airmold, W.R. Grace & Co.-Conn.)
Grace, Charles E., 10144 Elk Lake Rd., Williamsburg, MI 49690/616-264-9483
Grace Metal Products, Inc., P.O. Box 67, Elk Rapids, MI 49629/616-264-8133
Grace Tool, Inc., 3661 E. 44th St., Tucson, AZ 85713/602-747-0213
"Gramps" Antique Cartridges, Box 341, Washago, Ont. L0K 2B0 CANADA/705-689-5348
Grand Falls Bullets, Inc., 1120 Forest Dr., Blue Springs, MO 64015/816-229-0112
Granger, Georges, 66 cours Fauriel, 42100 Saint Etienne, FRANCE/(77)25 14 73
Granite Custom Bullets, Box 190, Philipsburg, MT 59858/406-859-3245
Grant, Howard V., Hiawatha 15, Woodruff, WI 54568/715-356-7146
Graphics Direct, 18336 Gault St., Reseda, CA 91335/818-344-9002
Graves Co., 1800 Andrews Av., Pompano Beach, FL 33069/800-327-9103; FAX: 305-960-0301
Graybill's Gun Shop, 1035 Ironville Pike, Columbia, PA 17512/717-684-6220
The Great 870 Co., P.O. Box 6309, El Monte, CA 91734
Great Lakes Airguns, 6175 S. Park Ave., Hamburg, NY 14075/716-648-6666; FAX: 716-648-0393
Green, Arthur S., 485 S. Rovertson Blvd., Beverly Hills, CA 90211/310-274-1283
Green Bay Bullets, 1860 Burns Ave., Green Bay, WI 54313/414-494-5166
Green Genie, Box 114, Cusseta, GA 31805
Green Head Game Call Co., RR 1, Box 33, Lacon, IL 61540/309-246-2155
Green Mountain Rifle Barrel Co., Inc., RFD 2, Box 8 Center, Conway, NH 03813/603-356-2047; FAX: 603-356-2048
Green, Roger M., P.O. Box 984, 435 E. Birch, Glenrock, WY 82637/307-436-9804
Greene, M.L., 17200 W. 57th Ave., Golden, CO 80403/303-279-2383
Greenwald, Leon E. "Bud", 2553 S. Quitman St., Denver, CO 80219/303-935-3850
Greg Gunsmithing Repair, 3732 26th Ave. North, Robbinsdale, MN 55422/612-529-8103
Greg's Superior Products, P.O. Box 46219, Seattle, WA 98146
Greider Precision, 431 Santa Marina Ct., Escondido, CA 92029/619-480-8892
Gremmel Enterprises, 271 Sterling Dr., Eugene, OR 97404/503-688-3319
Grendel, Inc., P.O. Box 560909, Rockledge, FL 32953/800-274-7427, 407-636-1211; FAX: 407-633-6710
Griffin & Howe, Inc., 33 Claremont Rd., Bernardsville, NJ 07924/908-766-2287; FAX: 908-766-1068
Griffin & Howe, Inc., 36 W. 44th St., Suite 1011, New York, NY 10036/212-921-0980
Grifon, Inc., 58 Guinam St., Waltham, MS 02154
Griggs Products, P.O. Box 789, 270 S. Main St., Suite 103, Bountiful, UT 84010/801-295-9696
Grip-Master, P.O. Box 32, Westbury, NY 11490/800-752-0164; FAX: 516-997-5142
Grizzly Bullets, 2137 Hwy. 200, Trout Creek, MT 59874/406-847-2627
Group Tight Bullets, 482 Comerwood Court, San Francisco, CA 94080/415-583-1550
GRS Corp., Glendo, P.O. Box 1153, 900 Overlander St., Emporia, KS 66801/316-343-1084
Grulla Armes, Apartado 453, Avda Otaloa, 12, Eiber, SPAIN (U.S. importers—American Arms, Inc.; Hanus Birdguns, Bill)
GSI, Inc., 108 Morrow Ave., P.O. Box 129, Trussville, AL 35173/205-655-8299; FAX: 205-655-7078
GTS Enterprises, Inc., Dynaray Marketing Div., 50 W. Hillcrest Dr., Suite 215, Thousand Oaks, CA 91360/805-373-0921
G.U., Inc., 4325 S. 120th St., Omaha, NE 68137/402-330-4492
Guardian Group International, 21 Warren St., Suite 3E, New York, NY 10007/212-619-3838
Guardsman Products, 411 N. Darling, Fremont, MI 49412/616-924-3950
Gun City, 212 W. Main Ave., Bismarck, ND 58501/701-223-2304
Gun Doctor, The, 435 East Maple, Roselle, IL 60172/708-894-0668
Gun Doctor, The, P.O. Box 39242, Downey, CA 90242
Gun Hunter Books, Div. of Gun Hunter Trading Co., 5075 Heisig St., Beaumont, TX 77705/409-835-3006
Gun Leather Limited, 116 Lipscomb, Ft. Worth, TX 76104/817-334-0225; 800-247-0609
Gun List (See Krause Publications)
Gun Parts Corp., The, Williams Lane, West Hurley, NY 12491/914-679-2417; FAX: 914-679-5849
Gun Room, The, 1121 Burlington, Muncie, IN 47302/317-282-9073; FAX: 317-282-9073
Gun Room Press, The, 127 Raritan Ave., Highland Park, NJ 08904/908-545-4344; FAX: 908-545-6686
Gun Shop, The, 5550 S. 900 East, Salt Lake City, UT 84117/801-263-3633
Gun Shop, The, 62778 Spring Creek Rd., Montrose, CO 81401
Gun Shop, The, Shop 31 320 West St., Durban 4001 SOUTH AFRICA
Gun South, Inc. (See GSI, Inc.)
Gun Vault, Inc., 200 Larkin Dr., Unit E, Wheeling, IL 60090/708-215-6606; FAX: 708-215-7550
Gun Works, The, 236 Main St., Springfield, OR 97477/503-741-4118
Gun-Alert/Master Products, Inc., 1010 N. Maclay Ave., San Fernando, CA 91340/818-365-0864; FAX: 818-365-1308
Gun-Ho Sports Cases, 110 E. 10th St., St. Paul, MN 55101/612-224-9491
Gun-Tec, P.O. Box 8125, W. Palm Beach, FL 33407
Guncraft Books (See Guncraft Sports, Inc.)
Guncraft Sports, Inc., 10737 Dutchtown Rd., Knoxville, TN 37932/615-966-4545
Gunfitters, The, P.O. 426, Cambridge, WI 53523-0426/608-764-8128
Gunline Tools, P.O. Box 478, Placentia, CA 92670/714-528-5252; FAX: 714-572-4128
Gunnerman Books, P.O. Box 214292, Auburn Hills, MI 48321/313-879-2779
Guns, 81 E. Streetsboro St., Hudson, OH 44236/216-650-4563
GUNS Magazine, 591 Camino de la Reina, Suite 200, San Diego, CA 92108/619-297-5350; FAX: 619-297-5353
Guns Unlimited, Inc. (See G.U., Inc.)
Gunsight, The, 1712 North Placentia Ave., Fullerton, CA 92631
Gunsite Gunsmithy, P.O. Box 451, Paulden, AZ 86334/602-636-4565; FAX: 602-636-1236
The Gunsmith in Elk River, 14021 Victoria Lane, Elk River, MN 55330/612-441-7761
Gunsmithing Ltd., 57 Unquowa Rd., Fairfield, CT 06430/203-254-0436
Gurney, F.R., Box 13, Sooke, BC V0S 1N0 CANADA/604-642-5282
Gusdorf Corp., 11440 Lackland Rd., St. Louis, MO 63146/314-567-5249
Gustaf, Carl (See U.S. importer—PSI, Inc.)
Gusty Winds Corp., 2950 Bear St., Suite 120, Costa Mesa, CA 92626/714-536-3587
Gutmann Cutlery Co., Inc., 120 S. Columbus Ave., Mt. Vernon, NY 10553/914-699-4044
Gutridge, Inc., 2143 Gettler St., Dyer, IN 46311/219-865-8617
Gwinnell, Bryson J., P.O. Box 248C, Maple Hill Rd., Rochester, VT 05767/802-767-3664
GZ Paintball Sports Products, P.O. Box 430, Andover, NH 03216/603-735-5300; FAX: 603-735-5154

H

H&B Forge Co., Rt. 2 Geisinger Rd., Shiloh, OH 44878/419-895-1856
H&H Engineering, Box 642, Narberty, PA 19072
H&L Gun Works, 817 N. Highway 90 1109, Sierra Vista, AZ 85635/602-452-0702
H&P Publishing, 7174 Hoffman Rd., San Angelo, TX 76905/915-655-5953
H&R 1871, Inc., 60 Industrial Rowe, Gardner, MA 01440/508-632-9393; FAX: 508-632-2300
H&S Liner Service, 515 E. 8th, Odessa, TX 79761/915-332-1021
Hafner Creations, Inc., Rt. 1, P.O. Box 248A, Lake City, FL 32055/904-755-6481
Hagn Rifles & Actions, Martin, P.O. Box 444, Cranbrook, B.C. VIC 4H9, CANADA/604-489-4861
Hakko Co. Ltd., 5F Daini-Tsunemi Bldg., 1-13-12, Narimasu, Itabashiku Tokyo 175, JAPAN/(03)5997-7870-2
Hale, Peter, 800 E. Canyon Rd., Spanish Fork, UT 84660/801-798-8215
Half Moon Rifle Shop, 490 Halfmoon Rd., Columbia Falls, MT 59912/406-892-4409
Hall Manufacturing, 1801 Yellow Leaf Rd., Clanton, AL 35045/205-755-4094
Hall Plastics, Inc., John, P.O. Box 1526, Alvin, TX 77512/713-489-9709
Hallberg Gunsmith, Fritz, 33 S. Main, Payette, ID 83661
Hallowell & Co., 340 W. Putnam Ave., Greenwich, CT 06830/203-869-2190; FAX: 203-869-0692
Hally Caller, 443 Wells Rd., Doylestown, PA 18901/215-345-6354
Halstead, Rick, P.O. Box 63, Grinnell, IA 50112/515-236-5904
Hamilton, Keith, P.O. Box 871, Gridley, CA 95948/916-846-2316
Hammans, Charles E., P.O. Box 788, 2022 McCracken, Stuttgart, AR 72106/501-673-1388
Hammerli USA, 19296 Oak Grove Circle, Groveland, CA 95321/209-962-5311; FAX: 209-962-5931
Hämmerli Ltd., Seonerstrasse 37, CH-5600 Lenzburg, SWITZERLAND/064-50 11 44; FAX: 064-51 38 27 (U.S. importer—Hammerli USA; Marent, Rudolph)
Hammets VLD Bullets, P.O. Box 479, Rayville, LA 71269/318-728-2019
Hammond Custom Guns Ltd., Guy, 619 S. Pandora, Gilbert, AZ 85234/602-892-3437
Hand Engravers Supply Co., 601 Springfield Dr., Albany, GA 31707/912-432-9683
Handgun Press, P.O. Box 406, Glenview, IL 60025/708-657-6500
HandiCrafts Unltd. (See Clements' Custom Leathercraft, Chas)
Handloader's Journal, 60 Cottage St. 11, Hughesville, PA 17737
Hands, Barry Lee, 26184 E. Shore Route, Bigfork, MT 59911/406-837-0035
Hank's Gun Shop, Box 370, 50 West 100 South, Monroe, UT 84754/801-527-4456
Hanned Line, The, P.O. Box 161565, Cupertino, CA 95016-1565/916-324-9089
Hanned Precision (See Hanned Line, The)
Hansen & Co. (See Hansen Cartridge Co.)
Hansen Cartridge Co., 244 Old Post Rd., Southport, CT 06490/203-789-7337
Hanson's Gun Center, Dick, 233 Everett Dr., Colorado Springs, CO 80911
Hanus Birdguns, Bill, P.O. Box 533, Newport, OR 97365
Hanusin, John, 3306 Commercial, Northbrook, IL 60062/708-564-2706
Hardin Specialty Dist., P.O. Box 338, Radcliff, KY 40159-0338/502-351-6649
Hardison, Charles, P.O. Box 356, 200 W. Baseline Rd., Lafayette, CO 80026 0356/303-666-5171
Harper, William E. (See Great 870 Co., The)
Harper's Custom Stocks, 928 Lombrano St., San Antonio, TX 78207/512-732-5780
Harrington & Richardson (See H&R 1871, Inc.)
Harrington Cutlery, Inc., Russell, Subs. of Hyde Mfg. Co., 44 River St., Southbridge, MA 01550/617-765-0201
Harris Engineering, Inc., Rt. 1, Barlow, KY 42024/502-334-3633; FAX: 502-334-3000
Harris Enterprises, P.O. Box 105, Bly, OR 97622/503-353-2625
Harris Hand Engraving, Paul A., 10630 Janet Lee, San Antonio, TX 78230/512-391-5121
Harrison Bullet Works, 6437 E. Hobart Street, Mesa, AZ 85205/602-985-7844
Harrison-Hurtz Enterprises, Inc., P.O. Box 268, Wymore, NE 68466/402-645-3378; FAX: 402-645-3606
Hart & Son, Inc., Robert W., 401 Montgomery St., Nescopeck, PA 18635/717-752-3655; FAX: 717-752-1088
Hart Rifle Barrels, Inc., RD 2, Apulia Rd., P.O. Box 182, Lafayette, NY 13084/315-677-9841
Hartmann & Weiss GmbH, Rahlstedter Bahnhofstr. 47, 2000 Hamburg 73, GERMANY/(40) 677 55 85; FAX: (40) 677 55 92
Harwood, Jack O., 1191 S. Pendlebury Lane, Blackfoot, ID 83221/208-785-5368
Haselbauer Products, Jerry, P.O. Box 27629, Tucson, AZ 85726/602-883-3391
Hastings Barrels, 320 Court St., Clay Center, KS 67432/913-632-3169; FAX: 913-632-6554
Hatfield Gun Co., Inc., 224 N. 4th St., St. Joseph, MO 64501/816-279-8688; FAX: 816-279-2716
Hawk Co., P.O. Box 1843, Glenrock, WY 82637/307-436-5561
Hawk Laboratories, Inc., P.O. Box 1843, Glenrock, WY 82637/307-436-5561
Hawken Shop, The (See Dayton Traister)
Haydel's Game Calls, Inc., 5018 Hazel Jones Rd., Bossier City, LA 71111/318-746-3586; FAX: 318-746-3711
Heatbath Corp., P.O. Box 2978, Springfield, MA 01101/413-543-3381
Hebard Guns, Gil, 125-129 Public Square, Knoxville, IL 61448
HEBB Resources, P.O. Box 999, Mead, WA 99021-09996/509-466-1292
Hecht, Hubert J., Waffen-Hecht, P.O. Box 2635, Fair Oaks, CA 95628/916-966-1020
Heckler & Koch GmbH, Postfach 1329, D-7238 Oberndorf, Neckar, GERMANY (U.S. importer—Heckler & Koch, Inc.)
Heckler & Koch, Inc., 21480 Pacific Blvd., Sterling, VA 20166/703-450-1900; FAX: 703-450-8160
Hege Jagd-u. Sporthandels, GmbH, P.O. Box 101461, W-7770 Ueberlingen a.Bodensee, GERMANY
Heidenstrom Bullets, Urds GT 1 Heroya, 3900 Porsgrunn, NORWAY
Heilmann, Stephen, P.O. Box 657, Grass Valley, CA 95945/916-272-8758
Heinie Specialty Products, 323 W. Franklin St., Havana, IL 62644/309-543-4535; FAX: 309-543-2521
Helwan (See U.S. importer—Interarms)
Henckels Zwillingswerk, Inc., J.A., 9 Skyline Dr., Hawthorne, NY 10532/914-592-7370
Hendricks, Frank E., Master Engravers, Inc., HC03, Box 434, Dripping Springs, TX 78620/512-858-7828
Henigson & Associates, Steve, 2049 Kerwood Ave., Los Angeles, CA 90025/213-305-8288
Henriksen Tool Co., Inc., 8515 Wagner Creek Rd., Talent, OR 97540/503-535-2309
Henry Customs, J., P.O. Box 3281, Texas City, TX 77592
Hensler, Jerry, 6614 Country Field, San Antonio, TX 78240
Hensley & Gibbs, Box 10, Murphy, OR 97533/503-862-2341
Hensley, Darwin, P.O. Box 179, Brightwood, OR 97011/503-622-5411
Heppler, Keith's Custom Gunstocks, Keith M., 540 Banyan Circle, Walnut Creek, CA 94598/510-934-3509
Heppler's Machining, 2240 Calle Del Mundo, Santa Clara, CA 95054/408-748-9166; FAX: 408-988-7711
Hercules, Inc., Hercules Plaza, 1313 N Market St., Wilmington, DE 19894/302-594-5000
Heritage Firearms, 4600 NW 135th St., Opa Locka, FL 33054/305-687-6721
Hermann Leather Co., H.J., Rt. 1, P.O. Box 525, Skiatook, OK 74070/918-396-1226
Herrett's Stocks, Inc., P.O. Box 741, Twin Falls, ID 83303/208-733-1498
Hertel & Reuss, Werk für Optik und Feinmechanik GmbH, Quellhofstrabe 67, 3500 Kassel, GERMANY/0561-83006; FAX: 0561-893308

Herter's Manufacturing, Inc., 111 E. Burnett St., P.O. Box 518, Beaver Dam, WI 53916/414-887-1765; FAX: 414-887-8444
Hesco-Meprolight, 2821 Greenville Rd., LaGrange, GA 30240/706-884-7967; FAX: 706-882-4683
Heydenberk, Warren R., 1059 W. Sawmill Rd., Quakertown, PA 18951/215-538-2682
Heym GmbH & Co., Friedrich Wilh, Coburger Str.8, D-8732 Munnerstadt, GERMANY (U.S. importers—JägerSport, Ltd.; Swarovski Optik North America Ltd.)
Hickman, Jaclyn, Box 1900, Glenrock, WY 82637
Hidalgo, Tony, 12701 SW 9th Pl., Davie, FL 33325/305-476-7645
Higgs Bullets, 403 E. Broadway, Denver City, TX 79323/806-592-8794
High Bridge Arms, Inc., 3185 Mission St., San Francisco, CA 94110/415-282-8358
High Country Custom Bullet, 19822 NW Sauvie Island Rd., Portland, OR 97231/503-621-3721
High North Products, Inc., P.O. Box 2, Antigo, WI 54409
Highline Machine Co., 654 Lela Place, Grand Junction, CO 81504/303-434-4971
Hill, Loring F., 304 Cedar Rd., Elkins Park, PA 19117
Hill Speed Leather, Ernie, 4507 N. 195th Ave., Litchfield Park, AZ 85340/602-853-9222; FAX: 602-853-9235
Hillmer Custom Gunstocks, Paul D., 7251 Hudson Heights, Hudson, IA 50643/319-988-3941
Hindman, Ace, 1880 1/2 Upper Turtle Creek Rd., Kerrville, TX 78028/512-257-4290
Hinman Outfitters, Bob, 1217 W. Glen, Peoria, IL 61614/309-691-8132
Hiptmayer, Heidemarie, RR 112 750, P.O. Box 136, Eastman, Quebec J0E 1PO, CANADA/514-297-2492
Hiptmayer, Klaus, RR 112 750, P.O. Box 136, Eastman, Quebec J0E 1P0, CANADA/514-297-2492
Hirtenberger Aktiengesellschaft, Leobersdorferstrasse 31, A-2552 Hirtenberg, AUSTRIA
HiTek International, 490 El Camino Real, Redwood City, CA 94063/800-54-NIGHT; FAX: 415-363-1408
Hiti-Schuch, Atelier Wilma, A-8863 Predlitz, Pirming Y1 AUSTRIA/0353418278
HJS Arms, Inc., P.O. Box 3711, Brownsville, TX 78523-3711/800-453-2767, 210-542-2767
H.K.S. Products, 7841 Founion Dr., Florence, KY 41042/606-342-7841
Hoag, James W., 8523 Canoga Ave., Suite C, Canoga Park, CA 91304/818-998-1510
Hobaugh, Wm. H. (See Rifle Shop, The)
Hobbie Gunsmithing, Duane A., 2412 Pattie Ave., Wichita, KS 67216/316-264-8266
Hobson Precision Mfg. Co., Rt. 1, Box 220-C, Brent, AL 35034/205-926-4662
Hodgdon Powder Co., Inc., P.O. Box 2932, Shawnee Mission, KS 66201/913-362-9455; FAX: 913-362-1307
Hodgman, Inc., 1750 Orchard Rd., Montgomery, IL 60538/708-897-7555; FAX: 708-897-7558
Hodgson, Richard, 9081 Tahoe Lane, Boulder, CO 80301
Hoehn's Shooting Supply, 75 Greensburg Ct., St. Charles, MO 63304/314-441-4231
Hoenig & Rodman, 6521 Morton Dr., Boise, ID 83704/208-375-1116
Hofer Jagdwaffen, Buchsenmachermeister,P., F.-Lange Strasse 13, A-9170, Ferlach, AUSTRIA/04227-3683
Hoffman New Ideas, 821 Northmoor Rd., Lake Forest, IL 60045/312-234-4075
Hogue Grips, P.O. Box 2038, Atascadero, CA 93423/FAX: 805-466-7329
Holden Co., J.B., P.O. Box 700320, 975 Arthur, Plymouth, MI 48170/313-455-4850; FAX: 313-455-4212
Holland, Dick, 422 NE 6th St., Newport, OR 97365/503-265-7556
Hollis Gun Shop, 917 Rex St., Carlsbad, NM 88220/505-835-3782
Hollywood Engineering, 10642 Arminta St., Sun Valley, CA 91352/818-842-8376
Holster Outpost, 950 Harry St., El Cajon, CA 92020/619-588-1222
Holster Shop, The, 720 N. Flagler Dr., Ft. Lauderdale, FL 33304/305-463-7910; FAX: 305-761-1483
Homak Mfg. Co., Inc., 3800 W. 45th, Chicago, IL 60632/312-523-3100
Hondo Ind., 510 S. 52nd St.,I04, Tempe, AZ 85281
Hoppe's Div., Penguin Industries, Inc., Airport Industrial Mall, Coatesville, PA 19320/251-384-6000
Horizons Unlimited, 8351 Roswell Rd., Suite 168, Atlanta, GA 30350/404-683-1269; FAX: 404-993-9770
Hornady Mfg. Co., P.O. Box 1848, Grand Island, NE 68801/800-338-3220, 308-382-1390
Horseshoe Leather Products, Andy Arratoonian, The Cottage Sharow, Ripon HG4 5BP ENGLAND/0765-605858
Horst, Alan K., 3221 2nd Ave. N., Great Falls, MT 59401/406-454-1831
Horton Dist. Co., Inc., Lew, 15 Walkup Dr., Westboro, MA 01581/508-366-7400
House of Muskets, Inc., The, P.O. Box 4640, Pagosa Springs, CO 81157/303-731-2295
Houtz & Barwick, P.O. Box 435, W. Church St., Elizabeth City, NC 27909/800-775-0337, 919-335-4191; FAX: 919-335-1152
Howa Machinery, Ltd., Sukaguchi, Shinkawa-cho, Nishikasugai-gun, Aichi 452, JAPAN (U.S. importers—Interarms; Weatherby, Inc.)
Howell Machine, 815 1/2 D St., Lewiston, ID 83501/208-743-7418
Hoyt Holster Co., Inc., P.O. Box 69, Coupeville, WA 98239-0069/206-678-6640; FAX: 206-678-6549
H-S Precision, Inc., 1301 Turbine Dr., Rapid City, SD 57701/605-341-3006; FAX: 605-342-8964
HT Bullets, 244 Belleville Rd., New Bedford, MA 02745/508-999-3338
Hubertus Schneidwarenfabrik, P.O. Box 180 106, Solingen, D-W-5650 GERMANY/01149-212-59-19-94: FAX: 01149-212-59-19-92
Huebner, Corey O., P.O. Box 2074, Missoula, MT 59804/406-721-9647
Huey Gun Cases, Marvin, P.O. Box 22456, Kansas City, MO 64113/816-444-1637
Hugger Hooks Co., 3900 Easley Way, Golden, CO 80403/303-279-0600
Hughes, Steven Dodd, P.O. Box 11455, Eugene, OR 97440/503-485-8869
Hume, Don, P.O. Box 351, Miami, OK 74355/918-542-6604
Hungry Horse Books, 4605 Hwy. 93 South, Whitefish, MT 59937/406-862-7997
Hunkeler, A. (See Buckskin Machine Works)
Hunter Co., Inc., 3300 W. 71st Ave., Westminster, CO 80030/303-427-4626
Hunter's Specialties, Inc., 6000 Huntington Ct. NE, Cedar Rapids, IA 52402-1268/319-395-0321
Hunterjohn, P.O. Box 477, St. Louis, MO 63166/314-531-7250
Hunting Classics Ltd., P.O. Box 2089, Gastonia, NC 28053/704-867-1307; FAX: 704-867-0491
Huntington Die Specialties, 601 Oro Dam Blvd., Oroville, CA 95965/916-534-1210; FAX: 916-534-1212
Hy-Score Arms Co. Ltd., 40 Stonar Industrial Estate, Sandwich, Kent CT13 9LN, ENGLAND/0304-61.12.21
Hydrosorbent Products, P.O. Box 437, Ashley Falls, MA 01222/413-229-2967; FAX: 413-229-8743
Hyper-Single, Inc., 520 E. Beaver, Jenks, OK 74037/918-299-2391

I

IAI, 6226 Santos Diaz St., Irwindale, CA 91702/818-334-1200
Ibberson (Sheffield) Ltd., George, 25-31 Allen St., Sheffield, S3 7AW ENGLAND/0742-766123; FAX: 0742-738465
ICI-America, P.O. Box 751, Wilmington, DE 19897/302-575-3000
Idaho Ammunition Service, 2816 Mayfair Dr., Lewiston, ID 83501/208-743-0270
Idaho Bullets, Box 2532, Orofino, ID 83544/208-476-5046
IGA (See U.S. importer—Stoeger Industries)
Illinois Lead Shop, 7742 W. 61st Place, Summit, IL 60501
Imatronic, Inc., 1275 Paramount Pkwy., P.O. Box 520, Batavia, IL 60510/708-406-1920; FAX: 708-879-6749
IMI, P.O. Box 1044, Ramat Hasharon 47100, ISRAEL/972-3-5485222 (U.S. importer—Magnum Research, Inc.)
Impact Case Co., P.O. Box 9912, Spokane, WA 99209-0912/509-467-3303; FAX: 509-326-5436
Imperial Magnum Corp., 1417 Main St., Oroville, WA 98844/604-495-3131; FAX: 604-495-2816
IMR Powder Co., Box 247E, Xplo Complex, RTS, Plattsburgh, NY 12901/518-561-9530; FAX: 518-563-0044
I.N.C., Inc. (See Kick Eez)
Incor, Inc., P.O. Box 132, Addison, TX 75001/214-931-3500; FAX: 214-458-1626
Independent Machine & Gun Shop, 1416 N. Hayes, Pocatello, ID 83201
INDESAL, P.O. Box 233, Eibar, SPAIN 20600/43-751800; FAX: 43-751962 (U.S. importer—American Arms, Inc.)
Industria de la Escopeta S.A.L. (See INDESAL)
Info-Arm, P.O. Box 1262, Champlain, NY 12919
Ingle, Ralph W., 4 Missing Link, Rossville, GA 30741/404-866-5589
Innovision Enterprises, 728 Skinner Dr., Kalamazoo, MI 49001/616-382-1681; FAX: 616-382-1830
InSights Training Center, Inc., 240 NW Gilman Blvd., Issaquah, WA 98027/206-391-4834
INTEC International, Inc., P.O. Box 5828, Sparks, NV 89432-5828
Interarms, 10 Prince St., Alexandria, VA 22314/703-548-1400
Intermountain Arms & Tackle, Inc., 105 E. Idaho St., Meridian, ID 83642/208-888-4911; FAX: 208-888-4381
International Shooters Service (See I.S.S.)
International Shootists, Inc., P.O. Box 5354, Mission Hills, CA 91345/818-891-1723
Intratec, 12405 SW 130th St., Miami, FL 33186/305-232-1821; FAX: 305-253-7207
Iosso Products, 1485 Lively Blvd., Elk Grove Villiage, IL 60007/708-437-8400
Iron Mountain Knife Co., P.O. Box 2146, Sparks, NV 89432-2146/800-22-KNIFE, 702-356-3632
Ironside International Publishers, Inc., P.O. Box 55, 800 Slaters Lane, Alexandria, VA 22313/703-684-6111; FAX: 703-683-5486
Irwin, Campbell H., 140 Hartland Blvd., East Hartland, CT 06027/203-653-3901
Irwindale Arms, Inc. (See IAI)
Israel Military Industries Ltd. (See IMI)
I.S.S., P.O. Box 185234, Ft. Worth, TX 76181/817-595-2090
I.S.W., 106 E. Cairo Dr., Tempe, AZ 85282
Ithaca Aquisition Corp., Ithaca Gun Co., 891 Route 34B, King Ferry, NY 13081/315-364-7171; FAX: 315-364-5134
Ivanoff, Thomas G. (See Tom's Gun Repair)

J

J-4, Inc., 1700 Via Burton, Anaheim, CA 92806
J&J Products Co., 9240 Whitmore, El Monte, CA 91731/818-571-5228; FAX: 818-571-8704
J&R Enterprises, 4550 Scotts Valley Rd., Lakeport, CA 95453
J.A. Blades, Inc. (See Christopher Firearms Co., Inc., E.)
Jackalope Gun Shop, 1048 S. 5th St., Douglas, WY 82633/307-358-3441
Jackson Arms, 6209 Hillcrest Ave., Dallas, TX 75205
JACO Precision Co., 11803 Indian Head Dr., Austin, TX 78753/512-836-4418
Jaeger, Inc., Paul/Dunn's, P.O. Box 449, 1 Madison Ave., Grand Junction, TN 38039/800-223-8667; FAX: 901-764-6503
JägerSport, Ltd., One Wholesale Way, Cranston, RI 02920/401-944-9682; FAX: 401-946-2587
Jamison's Forge Works, 4527 Rd. 6.5 NE, Moses Lake, WA 98837/509-762-2659
Jantz Supply, P.O. Box 584-GD, Davis, OK 73030/405-369-2316; FAX: 405-369-3082
Jarrett Rifles, Inc., 383 Brown Rd., Jackson, SC 29831/803-471-3616
Jarvis Gunsmithing, Inc., 1123 Cherry Orchard Lane, Hamilton, MT 59840/406-961-4392
JAS, Inc., P.O. Box 0, Rosemount, MN 55068/612-890-7631
Jason Empire, Inc., 9200 Cody, Overland Park, KS 66214-3259/913-888-0220; FAX: 913-888-0222
Javelina Products, P.O. Box 337, San Bernardino, CA 92402/714-882-5847; FAX: 714-434-6937
J/B Adventures & Safaris, Inc., P.O. Box 3397, Englewood, CO 80155/303-771-0977
J-B Bore Cleaner, 299 Poplar St., Hamburg, PA 19526/215-562-2103
Jeffredo Gunsight, P.O. Box 669, San Marcos, CA 92079/619-728-2695
Jenco Sales, Inc., P.O. Box 1000, Manchaca, TX 78652/512-282-2800; FAX: 512-282-7504
Jenkins Recoil Pads, Inc., RR 2, P.O. Box 471, Olney, IL 62450/618-395-3416
Jennings Firearms, Inc., 17692 Cowan, Irvine, CA 92714/714-252-7621; FAX: 714-252-7626
Jensen Bullets, 86 North, 400 West, Blackfoot, ID 83221/208-785-5590
Jensen's Custom Ammunition, 5146 E. Pima, Tucson, AZ 85712/602-325-3346; FAX: 602-322-5704
Jensen's Firearms Academy, 1280 W. Prince, Tucson, AZ 85705/602-293-8516
Jerry's Sport Center, P.O. Box 121 Main St., Forest City, PA 18421
Jester Bullets, Rt. 1 Box 27, Orienta, OK 73737
Jet Comp Systems, Rt. 1, Box 112-C, Surry, VA 23883/804-357-0881
Jett & Co., Inc., RR 3, Box 167-B, Litchfield, IL 62056/217-324-3779
JGS Precision Tool Mfg., 1141 S. Summer Rd., Coos Bay, OR 97420/503-267-4331; FAX:503-267-5996
Jim's Gun Shop (See Spradlin's)
Jim's Precision, Jim Ketchum, 1725 Moclips Dr., Petaluma, CA 94952/707-762-3014
J.I.T., Ltd., P.O. Box 749, Glenview, IL 60025/708-998-0937
JLK Bullets, RR1, Box 310C, Dover, AR 72837/501-331-4194
J.O. Arms & Ammunition Co., 5709 Hartsdale, Houston, TX 77036/713-789-0745; FAX: 713-789-7513
Johanssons Vapentillbehor, Bert, S-430 20 Veddige, SWEDEN
John's Custom Leather, 523 S. Liberty St., Blairsville, PA 15717/412-459-6802
Johns, Bill, 1412 Lisa Rae, Round Rock, TX 78664/512-255-8246
Johnson Gunsmithing, Inc., Neal G., 111 Marvin Dr., Hampton, VA 23666/804-838-8091; FAX: 804-838-8157
Johnson Wood Products, RR 1, Strawberry Point, IA 52076/319-933-4930
Johnson, Iver (See AMAC)
Johnston Bros., 1889 Rt. 9, Unit 22, Toms River, NJ 08755/800-257-2595; FAX: 800-257-2534
Johnston, James (See North Fork Custom Gunsmithing)
Jonad Corp., 2091 Lakeland Ave., Lakewood, OH 44107/216-226-3161
Jonas Appraisals & Taxidermy, Jack, 10050 E. Harvard Ave. B711, Denver, CO 80231/303-368-1939
Jones Custom Products, Neil, RD 1, Box 483A, Saegertown, PA 16443/814-763-2769; FAX: 814-763-4228
J.D. Jones, 721 Woodvue Lane, Wintersville, OH 43952/614-264-0176
Joy Enterprises (See Fury Cutlery)
J.P. Enterprises, Inc., P.O. Box 26324, Shoreview, MN 55126
JP Sales, Box 307, Anderson, TX 77830
JRW, 2425 Taffy Ct., Nampa, ID 83687
JSL Ltd., 35 Church St., Hereford HR1 2LR ENGLAND/0432-355416; FAX: 0432-355242 (U.S. importer—Specialty Shooters Supply, Inc.)
Juenke, Vern, 25 Bitterbush Rd., Reno, NV 89523/702-345-0225
Jumbo Sports Products (See Bucheimer, J.M.)

Jungkind, Reeves C., 5001 Buckskin Pass, Austin, TX 78745/512-442-1094
Jurras, L.E.,P.O. Box 680, Washington, IN 47501/812-254-7698
Just Brass, Inc., 121 Henry St., P.O. Box 112, Freeport, NY 11520/516-378-8588
J.V.B., Inc., 109 6th St. NE, Little Falls, MN 56345/612-632-5120

K

K&K Ammo Wrist Band, R.D. 1, P.O. Box 448-CA18, Lewistown, PA 17044/717-242-2329
K&M Industries, Inc., Box 66, 510 S. Main, Troy, ID 83871/208-835-2281; FAX: 208-835-5211
K&M Services, P.O. Box 363, 2525 Primrose Lane, York, PA 17404/717-764-1461
K&T Co., Div. of T&S Industries, Inc., 1027 Skyview Dr., W. Carrollton, OH 45449/513-859-8414
KA-BAR Knives, 31100 Solon Rd., Solon, OH 44139/216-248-7000; 800-321-9336; FAX: 216-248-8651
Kahles USA, P.O. Box 81071, Warwick, RI 02888/800-752-4537: FAX: 717-540-8567
Kalispel Case Line, P.O. Box 267, Cusick, WA 99119/509-445-1121
Kamik Outdoor Footwear, 554 Montee de Liesse, Montreal, Quebec, H4T 1P1 CANADA/514-341-3950
Kamyk Engraving Co., Steve, 9 Grandview Dr., Westfield, MA 01085/413-568-0457
Kane Products, Inc., 5572 Brecksville Rd., Cleveland, OH 44131/216-524-9962
Ka Pu Kapili, P.O. Box 745, Honokaa, HI 96727/808-776-1644; FAX: 808-776-1731
Kapro Mfg. Co., Inc., P.O. Box 88, Tallevast, FL 34270/813-755-0085
Kasenit Co., Inc., 13 Park Ave., Highland Mills, NY 10930/914-928-9595; FAX: 914-928-7292
Kasmarsik Bullets, 152 Crstler Rd., Chehalis, WA 98532
Kassnar (See U.S. importer—K.B.I., Inc.)
Kaswer Custom, Inc., 13 Surrey Drive, Brookfield, CT 06804/203-775-0564; FAX: 203-775-6872
K.B.I., Inc., P.O. Box 6346, Harrisburg, PA 17112/717-540-8518; FAX: 717-540-8567
K-D, Inc., 665 W. 300 South, Price, UT 84501/801-653-2530
KDF, Inc., 2485 Hwy. 46 N., Seguin, TX 78155/512-379-8141; FAX: 512-379-5420
Keeler, R.H., 817 "N" St., Port Angeles, WA 98362/206-457-4702
Kehr, Roger, 2131 Agate Ct. SE, Lacy, WA 98503/206-456-0831
Keith's Bullets, 942 Twisted Oak, Algonquin, IL 60102/708-658-3520
Keith's Custom Gunstocks (See Heppler, Keith M.)
Keller Co., The, 4215 McEwen Rd., Dallas, TX 75244/214-788-4254
Kelley's, P.O. Box 125, Woburn, MA 01801/617-935-3389
Kellogg's Professional Products, 325 Pearl St., Sandusky, OH 44870/419-625-6551; FAX: 419-625-6167
Kelly, Lance, 1723 Willow Oak Dr., Edgewater, FL 32132/904-423-4933
Ken's Kustom Kartridges, 331 Jacobs Rd., Hubbard, OH 44425/216-534-4595
Ken's Finn Knives, Rt. 1, Box 338, Republic, MI 49879/906-376-2132
Ken's Gun Specialties, Rt. 1, Box 147, Lakeview, AR 72642/501-431-5606
Ken's Rifle Blanks, Ken McCullough, Rt. 2, P.O. Box 85B, Weston, OR 97886/503-566-3879
Keng's Firearms Specialty, Inc., 875 Wharton Dr. SW, Atlanta, GA 30336/404-691-7611; FAX: 404-505-8445
Kennebec Journal, 274 Western Ave., Augusta, ME 04330/207-622-6288
Kennerknecht, Rick, "KK", Randall Firearms Historian, P.O. Box 1586, Lomita, CA 90717-5586/310-781-9199; FAX: 310-781-9266
KenPatable Ent., Inc., P.O. Box 19422, Louisville, KY 40219/502-239-5447
Kent Cartridge Mfg. Co. Ltd., Unit 16, Branbridges Industrial Estate, East Peckham, Tonbridge, Kent, TN12 5HF ENGLAND/622-872255; FAX: 622-873645
Keowee Game Calls, 608 Hwy. 25 North, Travelers Rest, SC 29690/803-834-7204
Kershaw Knives, 25300 SW Parkway Ave., Wilsonville, OR 97070/503-682-1966; FAX: 503-682-7168
Kesselring Gun Shop, 400 Hwy. 99 North, Burlington, WA 98233/206-724-3113; FAX: 206-724-7003
Keystone Bullets, RD 1, Box 312, New Bloomfield, PA 17068/717-582-8347
Kick Eez, P.O. Box 12767, Wichita, KS 67277/316-721-9570; FAX: 316-721-5260
Kilham & Co., Main St., P.O. Box 37, Lyme, NH 03768/603-795-4112
Kimball, Gary, 1526 N. Circle Dr., Colorado Springs, CO 80909/719-634-1274
Kimber, Inc., 16709 NE Union Rd., Ridgefield, WA 98642/206-573-4783
Kimel Industries, 3800 Old Monroe Rd., P.O. Box 335, Matthews, NC 28105/800-438-9288
King & Co., P.O. Box 1242, Bloomington, IL 61701/309-473-3964
King's Gun Works, 1837 W. Glenoaks Blvd., Glendale, CA 91201/818-956-6010
Kingyon, Paul L., 607 N. 5th St., Burlington, IA 52601/319-752-4465
Kirkpatrick Leather Co., 1910 San Bernardo, Laredo, TX 78040/512-723-6631; FAX: 512-725-0672
KJM Brass Group, P.O. Box 162, Marietta, GA 30061
KK Air International (See Impact Case Co.)
K.K. Arms Co., Star Route Box 671, Kerrville, TX 78028/512-257-4718
Kleen-Bore, Inc., 20 Ladd Ave., Northampton, MA 01060/413-586-7240; FAX: 413-586-0236
Klein Custom Guns, Don, 433 Murray Park Dr., Ripon, WI 54971/414-748-2931
Kleinendorst, K.W., RR 1, Box 1500, Hop Bottom, PA 18824/717-289-4687; FAX: 717-289-4687
Klingler Woodcarving, P.O. Box 141, Thistle Hill, Cabot, VT 05647/802-426-3811
KLP, Inc., 215 Charles Dr., Holland, MI 49424/616-396-2575; FAX: 616-396-1287
Kmount, P.O. Box 19422, Louisville, KY 40259/502-239-5447
Kneiper Custom Gums, Jim, 334 Summit Vista, Carbondale, CO 81623/303-963-9880
Knife Importers, Inc., P.O. Box 1000, Manchaca, TX 78652/512-282-6860
Knight & Hale Game Calls, Box 468 Industrial Park, Cadiz, KY 42211/502-522-3651; FAX: 502-522-0211
Knight's Mfg. Co., 7750 9th St. SW, Vero Beach, FL 32968/407-562-5697; FAX: 407-569-2955
Knippel, Richard, 5924 Carnwood, Riverbank, CA 95367/209-869-1469
Knock on Wood Antiques, 355 Post Rd., Darien, CT 06820/203-655-9031
Kodiak Custom Bullets, 8261 Henry Circle, Anchorage, AK 99507/907-349-2282
Kodiak Safe, 468 N. 1200 W., Lindon, UT 84042/801-785-9113
Koevenig's Engraving Service, Box 55 Rabbit Gulch, Hill City, SD 57745/605-574-2239
KOGOT, 410 College, Trinidad, CO 81082/719-846-9406
Kolbe Precision, Riccarton Farm, Newcastleton SCOTLAND U.K.
Kolpin Mfg., Inc., P.O. Box 107, 205 Depot St., Fox Lake, WI 53933/414-928-3118; FAX: 414-928-3687
Kopec Enterprises, John (See Peacemaker Specialists)
Kopp Publishing Co., Div. of Koppco Industries, 1301 Franklin, Lexington, MO 64067/816-259-2636
Kopp, Terry, 1301 Franklin, Lexington, MO 64067/816-259-2636
Korth, Robert-Bosch-Str. 4, P.O. Box 1320, 2418 Ratzeburg, GERMANY/0451-4991497; FAX: 0451-4993230 (U.S. importer—Mandall Shooting Supplies, Inc.)
Korzinek Riflesmith, J., RD 2, Box 73, Canton, PA 17724/717-673-8512
Koval Knives, 460 D Schrock Rd., Columbus, OH 43229/614-888-6486; FAX: 614-888-8218
Kowa Optimed, Inc., 20001 S. Vermont Ave., Torrance, CA 90502/310-327-1913; FAX: 310-327-4177
Krause Publications, 700 E. State St., Iola, WI 54990/715-445-2214; FAX: 715-445-4087
Krico/Kriegeskorte GmbH, A., Kronacherstr. 63, 85 W. Fürth-Stadeln, D-8510 GERMANY/0911-796092; FAX: 0911-796074 (U.S. importer—Mandall Shooting Supplies, Inc.)
Krieger Barrels, Inc., N114 W18697 Clinton Dr., Germantown, WI 53022/414-255-9593; FAX: 414-255-9586
Kriegeskorte GmbH., A. (See Krico/Kriegeskorte GmbH., A.)
H. Krieghoff Gun Co., Bosch Str. 22, 7900 Ulm, GERMANY (U.S. importer—Krieghoff International, Inc.)
Krieghoff International, Inc., 7528 Easton Rd., Ottsville, PA 18942/215-847-5173; FAX: 215-847-8691
Kris Mounts, 108 Lehigh St., Johnstown, PA 15905
K-Sports Imports, Inc., 290 Pioneer Place, Pomona, CA 91768/909-468-5871; FAX: 909-468-5870
Kudlas, John M., 622 14th St. SE, Rochester, MN 55904/507-288-5579
Kulis Freeze Dry Taxidermy, 725 Broadway Ave., Bedford, OH 44146/216-232-8352; FAX: 216-232-7305
Kustom Kast Bullets, 18533 Roscoe Blvd. S. 137, Northridge, CA 91324
KVH Industries, Inc., 110 Enterprise Center, Middletown, RI 02840/401-847-3327; FAX: 401-849-0045
Kwik Mount Corp., P.O. Box 19422, Louisville, KY 40259/502-239-5447
Kwik-Site Co., 5555 Treadwell, Wayne, MI 48184/313-326-1500; FAX: 313-326-4120

L

L&S Technologies, Inc. (See Aimtech Mount Systems)
La Clinique du .45, 1432 Rougemont, Chambly, Quebec, J3L 2L8 CANADA/514-658-1144
La Prade, Rt. 5, P.O. Box 240AD, Tazewell, TN 37879
LaBounty Precision Reboring, P.O. Box 186, 7968 Silver Lk. Rd., Maple Falls, WA 98266/206-599-2047
Lachaussee, S.A., 29 Rue Kerstenne, Ans, B-4430 BELGIUM/041-63 88 77
LaCrosse Footwear, Inc., P.O. Box 1328, La Crosse, WI 54602/608-782-3020
LaFrance Specialties, P.O. Box 178211, San Diego, CA 92117/619-293-3373
Lage Uniwad, Inc., P.O. Box 446, Victor, IA 52327/319-647-3232
Lair, Sam, 520 E. Beaver, Jenks, OK 74037/918-299-2391
Lake Center, P.O. Box 38, St. Charles, MO 63302/314-946-7500
Lakefield Arms Ltd., 248 Water St., Lakefield, Ont. K0L 2H0, CANADA/705-652-6735, 705-652-8000; FAX: 705-652-8431
Lakewood Products, Inc., P.O. Box 1527, 1445 Eagle St., Rhinelander, WI 54501/715-369-3445
Ron Lampert, Rt. 1, Box 177, Guthrie, MN 56461/218-854-7345
Lamson & Goodnow Mfg. Co., 45 Conway St., Shelburne Falls, MA 03170/413-625-6331
Lanber Armes S.A., Calle Zubiaurre 5, Zaldibar, SPAIN/34-4-6827702; FAX: 34-4-6827999
Lane Bullets, Inc., 1011 S. 10th St., Kansas City, KS 66105/913-621-6113, 800-444-7468
Lane Publishing, P.O. Box 759, Hot Springs, AR 71902/501-623-4951; FAX: 501-623-9832
Langenberg Hat Co., P.O. Box 1860, Washington, MO 63090/800-428-1860; FAX: 314-239-3151
Lan Orchards, 3601 10th St. SE, Ewenatchee, WA 98801
Lansky Sharpeners & Crock Stick, P.O. Box 800, Buffalo, NY 14231/716-877-7511; FAX: 716-877-6955
Lapua Ltd., P.O. Box 5, Lapua, FINLAND SF-62101/64-310111
L.A.R. Manufacturing, Inc., 4133 W. Farm Rd., West Jordan, UT 84088/801-255-7106; FAX: 801-569-1972
LaRocca Gun Works, Inc., 51 Union Place, Worcester, MA 01608/508-754-2887; FAX: 508-754-2887
Laseraim (Emerging Technologies, Inc.), P.O. Box 3548, Little Rock, AR 72203/501-375-2227; FAX: 501-372-1445
Laseraim Arms, Sub. of Emerging Technologies, Inc., P.O. Box 3548, Little Rock, AR 72203/501-375-2227; FAX: 501-372-1445
Laser Devices, Inc., 2 Harris Ct. A-4, Monterey, CA 93940/408-373-0701; FAX: 408-373-0903
Lassen Community College, Gunsmithing Dept., P.O. Box 3000, Hwy. 139, Susanville, CA 96130/916-257-6181 ext. 109; FAX: 916-257-8964
Lathrop's, Inc., 5146 E. Pima, Tucson, AZ 85712/602-881-0226, 800-875-4867
Laughridge, William R. (See Cylinder & Slide, Inc.)
Laurona Armas S.A., Apartado 260, Avda Otaloa 25, Eibar, SPAIN/34-43-700600; FAX: 34-43-700616
Law Concealment Systems, Inc., P.O. Box 3952, Wilmington, NC 28406/919-791-6656, 800-373-0116 orders
Lawrence Leather Co., P.O. Box 1479, Lillington, NC 27546/919-893-2071; FAX: 919-893-4742
Lawson Co., Harry, 3328 N. Richey Blvd., Tucson, AZ 85716/602-326-1117
Lawson, John G. (See Sight Shop, The)
LBT, HCR 62, Box 145, Moyie Springs, ID 83845/208-267-3588
Lea Mfg. Co., 237 E. Aurora St., Waterbury, CT 06720/203-753-5116
Lead Bullets Technology (See LBT)
Leather Arsenal, 27549 Middleton Rd., Middleton, ID 83644/208-585-6212
Leatherman Tool Group, Inc., P.O. Box 20595, Portland, OR 97220/503-253-7826; FAX: 503-253-7830
Leatherwood-Meopta, Inc., 719 Ryan Plaza, Suite 103, Arlington, TX 76011/817-965-3253
Lebeau-Courally, Rue St. Gilles, 386, 4000 Liege, BELGIUM/041 52 48 43; FAX: 041 52 20 08
LeClear Industries, 1126 Donald Ave., P.O. Box 484, Royal Oak, MI 48068/313-588-1025
Lectro Science, Inc., 6410 W. Ridge Rd., Erie, PA 16506/814-833-6487; FAX: 814-833-0447
Ledbetter Airguns, Riley, 1804 E. Sprague St., Winston Salem, NC 27107-3521/919-784-0676
Leding Loader, RR 1, Box 645, Ozark, AR 72949
Lee Precision, Inc., 4275 Hwy. U, Hartford, WI 53027/414-673-3075
Lee Supplies, Mark, 9901 France Ct., Lakeville, MN 55044/612-461-2114
Lee's Red Ramps, Box 291240, Phelan, CA 92329-1240/619-868-5731
Lee Co., T.K., One Independence Plaza, Suite 520, Birmingham, AL 35209
LeFever Arms Co., Inc., RD 2, Box 31, Lee Center, NY 13363/315-337-6722; FAX: 315-337-1543
Leibowitz, Leonard, 1205 Murrayhill Ave., Pittsburgh, PA 15217/412-361-5455
Leica USA, Inc., 156 Ludlow Ave., Northvale, NJ 07647/201-767-7500; FAX: 201-767-8666
LEM Gun Specialties, P.O. Box 87031, College Park, GA 30337
Lenahan Family Enterprise, P.O. Box 46, Manitou Springs, CO 80829
Lethal Force Institute (See Police Bookshelf)
Letschnig, Franz, RR 1, Martintown, Ont. K0C 1S0, CANADA/613-528-4843
Leupold, P.O. Box 688, Beaverton, OR 97075/503-526-1491
Lever Arms Service Ltd., 2131 Burrard St., Vancouver, B.C. V6J 3H7 CANADA/604-736-0004; FAX: 604-738-3503
Liberty Antique Gunworks, 19 Key St., P.O. Box 183, Eastport, ME 04631/207-853-4116
Liberty Metal, 2233 East 16th St., Los Angeles, CA 90021/213-581-9171
Liberty Safe, 316 W. 700 S., Provo, UT 84601/801-373-0727
Lighthouse Mfg. Co., Inc., 443 Ashwood Place, Boca Raton, FL 33431/407-394-6011
Lilja Precision Rifle Barrels, P.O. Box 372, Plains, MT 59859/406-826-3084; FAX: 406-826-3083
Lincoln, Dean, Box 1886, Farmington, NM 87401
Lind Custom Guns, Al, 7821 76th Ave. SW, Tacoma, WA 98498/206-584-6361
Linder Solingen Knives, 4401 Sentry Dr., Tucker, GA 30084/404-939-6915
Lindner Custom Bullets, 325 Bennetts Pond La., Mattituck, NY 11952
Lindsay, Steve, RR 2 Cedar Hills, Kearney, NE 68847/308-236-7885
Lindsley Arms Ctg. Co., P.O. Box 757, 20 College Hill Rd., Henniker, NH 03242/603-428-3127
Linebaugh Custom Sixguns & Rifle Works, P.O. Box 1263, Cody, WY 82414/307-587-8010
Lite Tek International, 133-30 32nd Ave., Flushing, NY 11354/718-463-0650; FAX: 718-762-0890
Lithi Bee Bullet Lube, 2161 Henry St., Muskegon, MI 49441/616-755-4707
"Little John's" Antique Arms, 1740 W. Laveta, Orange, CA 92668

Littler Sales Co., 20815 W. Chicago, Detroit, MI 48228/313-273-6888; FAX: 313-273-1099
Ljutic Industries, Inc., 732 N. 16th Ave., Yakima, WA 98902/509-248-0476; FAX: 509-457-5141
Llama Gabilondo Y Cia, Apartado 290, E-01080, Victoria, SPAIN (U.S. importer—SGS Importers International, Inc.)
Load From A Disk, 9826 Sagedale, Houston, TX 77089/713-484-0935
Loadmaster, P.O. Box 1209, Warminster, Wilts. BA12 9XJ ENGLAND/(0985)218544; FAX: (0985)214111
Loch Leven Industries, P.O. Box 2751, Santa Rosa, CA 95405/707-573-8735
Lock's Philadelphia Gun Exchange, 6700 Rowland Ave., Philadelphia, PA 19149/215-332-6225; FAX: 215-332-4800
Lodewick, Walter H., 2816 NE Halsey St., Portland, OR 97232/503-284-2554
Lofland, James W., 2275 Larkin Rd., Boothwyn, PA 19061/215-485-0391
Log Cabin Sport Shop, 8010 Lafayette Rd., Lodi, OH 44254/216-948-1082
Logan, Harry M., Box 745, Honokaa, HI 96727/808-776-1644
Logan Security Products Co., 4926 Annhurst Rd., Columbus, OH 43228-1341
Lohman Mfg. Co., Inc., 4500 Doniphan Dr., P.O. Box 220, Neosho, MO 64850/417-451-4438; FAX: 417-451-2576
Lomont Precision Bullets, 4236 W. 700 South, Poneto, IN 46781/219-694-6792; FAX: 219-694-6797
London Guns Ltd., Box 3750, Santa Barbara, CA 93130/805-683-4141; FAX: 805-683-1712
Lone Star Gunleather, 1301 Brushy Bend Dr., Round Rock, TX 78681/512-255-1805
Long, George F., 1500 Rogue River Hwy., Ste. F, Grants Pass, OR 97527/503-476-7552
Lorcin Engineering Co., Inc., 10427 San Sevaine Way, Ste. A, Mira Loma, CA 91752/714-360-1406; FAX: 714-360-0623
Lortone, Inc., 2856 NW Market St., Seattle, WA 98107/206-789-3100
Loweth, Richard, 29 Hedgegrow Lane, Kirby Muxloe, Leics. LE9 9BN ENGLAND
L.P.A. Snc, Via V. Alfieri 26, Gardone V.T. BS, ITALY 25063/(30)8911481; FAX: (30)8910951
LPS Laboratories, Inc., 4647 Hugh Howell Rd., P.O. Box 3050, Tucker, GA 30084/404-934-7800
LT Industries, Inc., 20504 Hillgrove Ave., Maple Heights, OH 44137/216-587-5005
Lucas, Edward E., 32 Garfield Ave., East Brunswick, NJ 08816/201-251-5526
Lutz Engraving, Ron, E. 1998 Smokey Valley Rd., Scandinavia, WI 54977/715-467-2674
Lyman Products Corp., Rt. 147 West St., Middlefield, CT 06455
Lynn's Custom Gunstocks, RR 1, Brandon, IA 52210/319-474-2453

M

M&D Munitions Ltd., 127 Verdi St., Farmingdale, NY 11735/516-752-1038; FAX: 516-752-1905
M&M Engineering (See Hollywood Engineering)
M&N Bullet Lube, P.O. Box 495, 151 NE Jefferson St., Madras, OR 97741/503-255-3750
MA Systems, P.O. Box 489, Chouteau, OK 74337/918-479-6378
Mac-1 Distributors, 13972 Van Ness Ave., Gardena, CA 90249/310-327-3582
Mac's .45 Shop, P.O. Box 2028, Seal Beach, CA 90740/310-438-5046
Macbean, Stan, 754 North 1200 West, Orem, UT 84057/801-224-6446
Macks Sport Shop, P.O. Box 1155, Kodiak, AK 99615/907-486-4276
Madis, David, 2453 West Five Mile Pkwy., Dallas, TX 75233/214-330-7169
MAG Instrument, Inc., 1635 S. Sacramento Ave., Ontario, CA 91761/714-947-1006; FAX: 714-947-3116
Mag-Na-Port International, Inc., 41302 Executive Dr., Harrison Twp., MI 48045-3448/313-469-6727; FAX: 313-469-0723
Mag-Pack Corp., P.O. Box 846, Chesterland, OH 44026
Magma Engineering Co., P.O. Box 161, Queen Creek, AZ 85242/602-987-9008; FAX: 602-987-0148
Magnolia Sports, Inc., 211 W. Main, Magnolia, AR 71753/800-530-7816; FAX: 501-234-8117
Magnum Power Products, Inc., P.O. Box 17768, Fountain Hills, AZ 85268
Magnum Research, Inc., 7110 University Ave., Minneapolis, MN 55432/612-574-1868; FAX: 612-574-0109
Magnus Bullets, P.O.Box 239, Toney, AL 35773/205-828-5089
MagSafe Ammo Co., Box 5692, 2725 Friendly Grove Rd NE, Olympia, WA 98506/206-357-6383
MAGTECH Recreational Products, Inc., 5030 Paradise Rd., Suite C211, Las Vegas, NV 89119/702-795-7191, 800-460-7191; FAX: 702-795-2769
Mahony, Philip Bruce, 67 White Hollow Rd., Lime Rock, CT 06039-2418/203-435-9341
Maine Custom Bullets, RFD 1, Box 1755, Brooks, ME 04921
Mains Enterprises, Inc., 3111 S. Valley View Blvd., Suite B120, Las Vegas, NV 89102-7790/702-876-6278; FAX: 702-876-1269
Maionchi-L.M.I., Via Di Coselli-Zona Industriale Di Guamo, Lucca, ITALY 55060/011 39-583 94291
Maki Industries, 26-10th St. SE, Medicine Hat, AB T1A 1P7 CANADA/403-526-7997
Maki School of Engraving, Robert E., P.O. Box 947, Northbrook, IL 60065/708-724-8238
Makinson, Nichola, RR 3, Komoka, Ont. N0L 1R0 CANADA/519-471-5462
Malcolm Enterprises, 1023 E. Prien Lake Rd., Lake Charles, LA 70601
Mallardtone Game Calls, 2901 16th St., Moline, IL 61265/309-762-8089
M.A.M. Products, Inc., 153 B Cross Slope Court, Englishtown, NJ 07726/908-536-3604
Mandall Shooting Supplies, Inc., 3616 N. Scottsdale Rd., Scottsdale, AZ 85252/602-945-2553; FAX: 602-949-0734
Maxi-Mount, 2405 Somrack Dr., Willoughby Hills, OH 44094/216-946-3105
Mandarino, Monte, 205 Fifth Ave. East, Kalispell, MT 59901/406-257-6208
Manley Shooting Supplies, Lowell, 3684 Pine St., Deckerville, MI 48427/313-376-3665
Manufacture D'Armes Des Pyrenees Francaises (See Unique/M.A.P.F.)
Mar Knives, Inc., Al, 5755 SW Jean Rd., Suite 101, Lake Oswego, OR 97035/503-635-9229
Marathon Rubber Prods. Co., Inc., 510 Sherman St., Wausau, WI 54401/715-845-6255
Marble Arms Corp., 420 Industrial Park, P.O. Box 111, Gladstone, MI 49837/906-428-3710; FAX: 906-428-3711
Marchmon Bullets, 8191 Woodland Shore Dr., Brighton, MI 48116
Marek, George, 55 Arnold St., Westfield, MA 01085/413-562-5673
Marent, Rudolf, 9711 Tiltree St., Houston, TX 77075/713-946-7028
Markell, Inc., 422 Larkfield Center 235, Santa Rosa, CA 95403/707-573-0792; FAX: 707-573-9867
Marksman Products, 5482 Argosy Dr., Huntington Beach, CA 92649/714-898-7535, 800-822-8005; FAX: 714-891-0782
Marlin Firearms Co., 100 Kenna Dr., New Haven, CT 06473/203-239-5621; FAX: 203-234-7991
Marocchi F.lli S.p.A., Via Galileo Galilei, I-25068 Zanano di Sarezzo, ITALY (U.S. importers—PSI, Inc.; Sile Distributors)
Marple & Associates, Dick, 21 Dartmouth St., Hooksett, NH 03106/603-627-1837; FAX: 603-641-4837
Marquart Precision Co., Inc., Rear 136 Grove Ave., Box 1740, Prescott, AZ 86302/602-445-5646
Marsh, Johnny, 1007 Drummond Dr., Nashville, TN 37211/615-833-3259
Marsh, Mike, Croft Cottage, Main St., Elton, Derbyshire DE4 2BY, ENGLAND/0629 650 669
Marshall Enterprises, 792 Canyon Rd., Redwood City, CA 94062
Martin Bookseller, J., P.O. Drawer AP, Beckley, WV 25802/304-255-4073; FAX: 304-255-4077
Martin's Gun Shop, 937 S. Sheridan Blvd., Lakewood, CO 80226/303-922-2184
Martz, John V., 8060 Lakeview Lane, Lincoln, CA 95648/916-645-2250
Marvel, Alan, 3922 Madonna Rd., Jarretsville, MD 21084/301-557-6545
Masen Co., John, P.O. Box 5050, Suite 165, Lewisville, TX 75057/817-430-8732
Masker, Seely, 54 Woodshire S., Getzville, NY 14068/716-689-8894
Master Class Bullets, 4110 Alder St., Eugene, OR 97405/503-687-1263
Master Engravers, Inc. (See Hendricks, Frank E.)
Master Lock Co., 2600 N. 32nd St., Milwaukee, WI 53245/414-444-2800
Master Products, Inc. (See Gun-Alert/Master Products, Inc.)
Matco, Inc., 1003-2nd St., N. Manchester, IN 46962/219-982-8282
Mathews & Son, Inc., George E., 10224 S. Paramount Blvd., Downey, CA 90241/310-862-6719
Matthews Cutlery, 4401 Sentry Dr., Tucker, GA 30084
Mauser-Werke Oberndorf, P.O. Box 1349, 7238 Oberndorf, Neckar, GERMANY (U.S. importer—Precision Imports, Inc.)
Maverick Arms, Inc., 7 Grasso Ave., P.O. Box 497, North Haven, CT 06473/203-288-6491; FAX: 203-288-2404
Maximum Security Corp., 32841 Calle Perfecto, San Juan Capistrano, CA 92675/714-493-3684; FAX: 714-496-7733
Mayville Engineering Co. (See MEC)
Mazur Restoration, Pete, 13083 Drummer Way, Grass Valley, CA 95949/916-268-2412
MCA Sports, P.O. Box 8868, Palm Springs, CA 92263/619-770-2005
McCament, Jay, 1730-134th St. Ct. S., Tacoma, WA 98444/206-531-8832
McCann's Muzzle-Gun Works, 14 Walton Dr., New Hope, PA 18938/215-862-9180
McCormick Corp., Chip, 1825 Fortview Rd., Ste. 115, Austin, TX 78704/512-462-0004; FAX: 512-462-0009
McCormick's Custom Gun Bluing, 609 NE 104th Ave., Vancouver, WA 98664/206-896-4232
McCullough, Ken (See Ken's Rifle Blanks)
McDonald, Dennis, 8359 Brady St., Peosta, IA 52068/319-556-7940
McFarland, Stan, 2221 Idella Ct., Grand Junction, CO 81505/303-243-4704
McGowen Rifle Barrels, 5961 Spruce Lane, St. Anne, IL 60964/815-937-9816; FAX: 815-937-4024
McGuire, Bill, 1600 N. Eastmont Ave., East Wenatchee, WA 98802/509-884-6021
McKee Publications, 121 Eatons Neck Rd., Northport, NY 11768/516-575-8850
McKee, Arthur, 121 Eatons Neck Rd., Northport, NY 11768/516-757-8850
McKenzie, Lynton, 6940 N. Alvernon Way, Tucson, AZ 85718/602-299-5090
McKillen & Heyer, Inc., 35535 Euclid Ave. Suite 11, Willoughby, OH 44094/216-942-2044
McMillan Fiberglass Stocks, Inc., 21421 N. 14th Ave., Phoenix, AZ 85027/602-582-9635; FAX: 602-581-3825
McMillan Gunworks, Inc., 302 W. Melinda Lane, Phoenix, AZ 85027/602-582-9627; FAX: 602-582-5178
McMillan Optical Gunsight Co., 28638 N. 42nd St., Cave Creek, AZ 85331/602-585-7868; FAX: 602-585-7872
McMillan Rifle Barrels, Bill Wiseman & Co., Inc., P.O. Box 3427, Bryan, TX 77805/409-690-3456; FAX: 409-690-0156
McMurdo, Lynn (See Specialty Gunsmithing)
MCRW Associates, R.R. 1 Box 1425, Sweet Valley, PA 18656
MCS, Inc., 34 Delmar Dr., Brookfield, CT 06804/203-775-1013; FAX: 203-775-9462
McWelco Products, 6730 Santa Fe Ave., Hesperia, CA 92345/619-244-8876; FAX: 619-244-9398
MDS, Inc., 1640 Central Ave., St. Petersburg, FL 33712/813-894-3512
Meadow Industries, P.O. Box 754, Locust Grove, VA 22508/703-972-2175
Measurement Group, Inc., Box 27777, Raleigh, NC 27611
MEC, Inc., 715 South St., Mayville, WI 53050/414-387-4500
MEC-Gar S.R.L., Via Madonnina 64, Gardone V.T. (BS), ITALY 25063/39-30-8911719; FAX: 39-30-8910065 (U.S. importer—MEC-Gar U.S.A., Inc.)
MEC-Gar U.S.A., Inc., Box 112, 500B Monroe Turnpike, Monroe, CT 06468/203-635-8662; FAX: 203-635-8662
Meier Works, P.O. Box 423, Tijeras, NM 87059/505-281-3783
Mele, Frank, Rt. 1 P.O. Box 349, Springfork Rd., Granville, TN 38564/615-653-4414
Melton Shirt Co., Inc., 56 Harvester Ave., Batavia, NY 14020/716-343-8750
Men-Metallwerk Elisenhuette, GmbH, P.O. Box 1263, W-5408 Nassau, GERMANY/2604-7819
Menck, Thomas W., 5703 S. 77th St., Ralston, NE 68127-4201
Mendez, John A., P.O. Box 1534, Radio City Station, New York, NY 10019/212-315-2580
Meprolight (See Hesco-Meprolight)
Mercer Custom Stocks, R.M., 216 S. Whitewater Ave., Jefferson, WI 53549/414-674-3839
Merit Corp., Box 9044, Schenectady, NY 12309/518-346-1420
Merkel Freres, Strasse 7 October, 10, Suhl, GERMANY (U.S. importers—GSI, Inc.; Hanus Birdguns, Bill)
Merkuria Ltd., Argentinska 38, 17005 Praha 7, CZECH REPUBLIC/422-875117; FAX: 422-809152
Metalife Industries, Box 53 Mong Ave., Reno, PA 16343/814-436-7747; FAX: 814-676-5662
Michael's Antiques, Box 591, Waldoboro, ME 04572
Michaels of Oregon Co., P.O. Box 13010, Portland, OR 97213/503-255-6890; FAX: 503-255-0746
Micro Sight Co., 242 Harbor Blvd., Belmont, CA 94002/415-591-0769; FAX: 415-591-7531
Micro-Lube, Rt. 2, P.O. Box 201, Deming, NM 88030/505-546-9116
Mid-America Recreation, Inc., 1328 5th Ave., Moline, IA 52807/309-764-5089; FAX: 309-764-2722
Midway Arms, Inc., P.O. Box 1483, Columbia, MO 65205/314-445-6363; FAX: 314-446-1018
Midwest Gun Sport, 1108 Herbert Dr., Zebulon, NC 27597/919-269-5570
Midwest Sport Distributors, Box 129, Fayette, MO 65248
Military Armament Corp., P.O. Box 120, Mt. Zion Rd., Lingleville, TX 76461/817-965-3253
Millenium Safety Products, P.O. Box 9802-916, Austin, TX 78766/512-346-3876
Miller Arms, Inc., P.O. Box 260 Purl St., St. Onge, SD 57779/605-642-5160
Miller Custom, 210 E. Julia, Clinton, IL 61727/217-935-9362
Miller Co., David, 3131 E. Greenlee Rd., Tucson, AZ 85716/602-326-3117
Miller Engineering, R&D Engineering & Manufacturing, P.O. Box 6342, Virginia Beach, VA 23456/804-468-1402
Miller Enterprises, Inc., 1557 E. Main St., Brownsburg, IN 46112/317-852-8187
Miller Gun Woods, 1440 Peltier Dr., Point Roberts, WA 98281/206-945-7014
Miller Single Trigger Mfg. Co., R.D.1, P.O. Box 99, Millersburg, PA 17061/717-692-3704
Miller, Tom (See Huntington Die Specialties)
Millett Sights, 16131 Gothard St., Huntington Beach, CA 92647/714-842-5575, 714-847-5245; FAX: 714-843-5707
Milliron Custom Machine Carving, Earl, 1249 NE 166th Ave., Portland, OR 97230/503-252-3725
Mills Jr., Hugh B., 3615 Canterbury Rd., New Bern, NC 28560/919-637-4631
Miniature Machine Co. (See MMC)
Mirador Optical Corp., 4501 Glencoe Ave., Marina Del Rey, CA 90292/310-821-5587; FAX: 310-305-0386
Miroku, B.C./Daly, Charles (See U.S. importers—Bell's Legendary Country Wear; British Sporting Arms; Outdoor Sports Headquarters)
Mitchell Arms, Inc., 3400 W. MacArthur Blvd., Ste. 1, Santa Ana, CA 92704/714-957-5711; FAX: 714-957-5732
Mitchell Bullets, R.F., 430 Walnut St., Westernport, MD 21562
Mitchell's Accuracy Shop, 68 Greenridge Dr., Stafford, VA 22554/703-659-0165
Mittermeier, Inc., Frank, P.O. Box 2G, 3577 E. Tremont Ave., Bronx, NY 10465/718-828-3843
Mixson Leathercraft, Inc., 7435 W. 19th Ct., Hialeah, FL 33014/305-821-5190; FAX: 305-558-9318
MJK Gunsmithing, Inc., 417 N. Huber Ct., E. Wenatchee, WA 98802/509-884-7683
MK Arms, Inc., 9112 Hyde Park Dr., Huntington Beach, CA 92646-2327/714-261-2767

MKS Supply, Inc., 1015 Springmill Rd., Mansfield, OH 44906/419-747-1088
MMC, 606 Grace Ave., Ft. Worth, TX 76111/817-831-0837
MMP, Rt. 6, Box 384, Harrison, AR 72601/501-741-5019; FAX: 501-741-3104
M.O.A. Corp., 2451 Old Camden Pike, Eaton, OH 45320/513-456-3669
M.O.A. Maximum, P.O. Box 185, Dayton, OH 45404/513-456-3669
Modern Gun Repair School, 2538 N. 8th St., P.O. Box 5338, Dept. GJY94, Phoenix, AZ 85010/602-990-8346
Modern MuzzleLoading, Inc., 234 Airport Rd., P.O. Box 130, Centerville, IA 52544/515-856-2626; FAX: 515-856-2628
Moeller, Steve, 1213 4th St., Fulton, IL 61252/815-589-2300
Molin Industries, Tru-Nord Division, P.O. Box 365, 204 North 9th St., Brainerd, MN 56401/218-829-2870
MoLoc Bullets, P.O. Box 2810, Turlock, CA 95381/209-632-1644
Monell Custom Guns, Red Mill Road, Pine Bush, NY 12566/914-744-3021
Moneymaker Guncraft Corp., 1420 Military Ave., Omaha, NE 68131/402-556-0226
Mongaso Wild Life Safaris, P.O. Box 67641 Station O, Vancouver B.C., V5W 3V1 CANADA
Montana Armory, Inc., 100 Centennial Dr., Big Timber, MT 59011/406-932-4353
Montana Outfitters, Lewis E. Yearout, 308 Riverview Dr. E., Great Falls, MT 59404/406-761-0859
Montana Precision Swaging, P.O. Box 4746, Butte, MT 59702/406-782-7502
Monte Kristo Pistol Grip Co., P.O. Box 85, Whiskeytown, CA 96095/916-623-4019
Montgomery Community College, P.O. Box 787, Troy, NC 27371/919-572-3691
Moore & Co., Wm. Larkin, 31360 Via Colinas, Suite 109, Westlake Village, CA 91361/818-889-4160; FAX: 818-889-1986
Moran, Jerry, P.O. Box 357, Mt. Morris, MI 45458-0357
Moreton/Fordyce Enterprises, P.O. Box 940, Saylorsburg, PA 18353/717-992-5742
Morini (See U.S. importer—Nygord Precision Products)
Morrison Custom Rifles, J.W., 4015 W. Sharon, Phoenix, AZ 85029/602-978-3754
Morrow, Bud, 11 Hillside Lane, Sheridan, WY 82801-9729/307-674-8360
Morton Booth Co., P.O. Box 123, Joplin, MO 64802/417-673-1962
Mo's Competitor Supplies (See MCS, Inc.)
MPC, 188 Freeport Rd., Butler, PA 16001/800-227-7049, 412-283-0567; FAX: 412-283-8310
Moschetti, Mitchell R. , P.O. Box 27065, Denver, CO 80227/303-733-9593
Moss Double Tone, Inc., P.O. Box 1112, 2101 S. Kentucky, Sedalia, MO 65301/816-827-0827
Mossberg & Sons, Inc., O.F, 7 Grasso Ave., North Haven, CT 06473/203-288-6491; FAX: 203-288-2404
Mountain Bear Rifle Works, Inc., 100 B Ruritan Rd., Sterling, VA 20164/703-430-0420
Mountain Hollow Game Calls, Box 121, Cascade, MD 21719/301-241-3282
Mountain South, P.O. Box 381, Barnwell, SC 29812/FAX: 803-259-3227
Mountain State Muzzleloading Supplies, Box 154-1, Rt. 2, Williamstown, WV 26187/304-375-7842; FAX: 304-375-3737
Mountain States Engraving, Kenneth W. Warren, P.O. Box 2842, Wenatchee, WA 98802/509-663-6123
Mountain View Sports, Inc., Box 188, Troy, NH 03465/603-357-9690; FAX: 603-357-9691
Mowreys Guns and Gunsmithing, P.O. Box 246, Waldron, IN 46182/317-525-6181; FAX: 317-525-6181
Mowreys Guns & Supplies, RD 1, Box 82, Canajoharie, NY 13317/518-673-3483
MPI Stocks, P.O. Box 83266, Portland, OR 97283-0266/503-226-1215
Mt. Alto Outdoor Products, Rt. 735, Howardsville, VA 24562
MTM Molded Products Co., Inc., 3370 Obco Ct., Dayton, OH 45414/513-890-7461; FAX: 513-890-1747
Mulhern, Rick, Rt. 5, Box 152, Rayville, LA 71269/318-728-2688
Mullins Ammo, Rt. 2, Box 304K, Clintwood, VA 24228/703-926-6772
Mullis Guncraft, 3523 Lawyers Road E., Monroe, NC 28110/704-283-6683
Multipax, 8086 S. Yale, Suite 286, Tulsa, OK 74136/918-496-1999; FAX: 918-492-7465
Multiplex International, 26 S. Main St., Concord, NH 03301/FAX: 603-796-2223
Multipropulseurs, La Bertrandiere, 42580 L'Etrat, FRANCE/77 74 01 30; FAX: 77 93 19 34
Multi-Scale Charge Ltd., P.O. Box 101 LP, Niagara Falls, NY14303/416-566-1255; FAX: 416-276-6295
Mundy, Thomas A., 69 Robbins Road, Somerville, NJ 08876/201-722-2199
Munger, Robert D. (See Rusteprufe Laboratories)
Munsch Gunsmithing, Tommy, Rt. 2, P.O. Box 248, Little Falls, MN 56345/612-632-6695
Murmur Corp., 2823 N. Westmoreland Ave., Dallas, TX 75222/214-630-5400
Murphy Co., Inc., R., 13 Groton-Harvard Rd., P.O. Box 376, Ayer, MA 01432/617-772-3481
Murray State College, 100 Faculty Dr., Tishomingo, OK 73460/405-371-2371
Muscle Products Corp. (See MPC)
Museum of Historical Arms, Inc., 1038 Alton Rd., Miami Beach, FL 33139/305-672-7480
Mushroom Express Bullet Co., 601 W. 6th St., Greenfield, IN 46140/317-462-6332
Mustra's Custom Guns, Inc., Carl, 1002 Pennsylvania Ave., Palm Harbor, FL 34683/813-785-1403
Muzzle-Nuzzle Co., 609 N. Virginia Ave., Roswell, NM 88201/505-624-1260
Muzzlelite Corp., P.O. Box 987, DeLeon Springs, FL 32130
Muzzleload Magnum Products (See MMP)
Muzzleloaders Etcetera, Inc., 9901 Lyndale Ave. S., Bloomington, MN 55420/612-884-1161

N

N&J Sales, Lime Kiln Rd., Northford, CT 06472/203-484-0247
Nagel's Bullets, 9 Wilburn, Baytown, TX 77520
Nastoff's 45 Shop, Inc., Steve, 12288 Mahoning Ave., P.O. Box 446, North Jackson, OH 44451
National Bullet Co., 1585 E. 361 St., Eastlake, OH 44095/216-951-1854; FAX: 216-951-7761
National Security Safe Co., Inc., P.O. Box 39, 620 S. 380 E., American Fork, UT 84003/801-756-7706
National Survival Game, Inc., P.O. Box 1439, New London, NH 03257/603-735-6165; FAX: 603-735-5154
National Target Co., 4690 Wyaconda Rd., Rockville, MD 20852/800-827-7060, 301-770-7060; FAX: 301-770-7892
Nationwide Airgun Repairs (See Airgun Repair Centre)
Naval Ordnance Works, Rt. 2, Box 919, Sheperdstown, WV 25443/304-876-0998
Navy Arms Co., 689 Bergen Blvd., Ridgefield, NJ 07657/201-945-2500; FAX: 201-945-6859
N.C. Ordnance Co., P.O. Box 3254, Wilson, NC 27895/919-237-2440
Necessary Concepts, Inc., P.O. Box 571, Deer Park, NY 11729/516-321-8509
NECO, 1316-67th St., Emeryville, CA 94608/510-450-0420
Necromancer Industries, Inc., 14 Communications Way, West Newton, PA 15089/412-872-8722
Nelson Combat Leather, Bruce, P.O. Box 8691 CRB, Tucson, AZ 85738/602-825-9047
Nelson, Gary K., 975 Terrace Dr., Oakdale, CA 95361/209-847-4590
Nelson, Stephen, 7365 NW Spring Creek Dr., Corvallis, OR 97330/503-745-5232
Nelson/Weather-Rite, 14760 Santa Fe Trail Dr., Lenexa, KS 66215/913-492-3200
Nesci Enterprises, Inc., P.O. Box 119, Summit St., East Hampton, CT 06424/203-267-2588
Nettestad Gun Works, RR 1, Box 160, Pelican Rapids, MN 56572/218-863-4301
Neumann GmbH, Untere Ringstr. 17, 8506 Langenzenn, GERMANY/09101-8258
Neutralizer Police Munitions, 5029 Middle Rd., Horseheads, NY 14845-9568/607-739-8362; FAX: 607-594-3900
New Advantage Arms Corp., 2843 N. Alvernon Way, Tucson, AZ 85712/602-881-7444; FAX: 602-323-0949
New Democracy, Inc., 719 Ryan Plaza, Suite 103, Arlington, TX 76011
New England Ammunition Co., 1771 Post Rd. East, Suite 223, Westport, CT 06880/203-254-8048
New England Arms Co., Box 278, Lawrence Lane, Kittery Point, ME 03905/207-439-0593; FAX: 207-439-6726
New England Custom Gun Service (See Apel, Dietrich)
New England Firearms, 60 Industrial Rowe, Gardner, MA 01440/508-632-9393; FAX: 508-632-2300
New Historians Productions, The, 131 Oak St., Royal Oak, MI 48067/313-544-7544
New Orleans Arms Co., 5001 Treasure St., New Orleans, LA 70186/504-944-3371
New Orleans Jewelers Supply Co., 206 Charters St., New Orleans, LA 70130/504-523-3839
New Win Publishing, Inc., Box 5159, Clinton, NJ 08809/201-735-9701; FAX: 201-735-9703
Newark Electronics, 4801 N. Ravenswood Ave., Chicago, IL 60640
Newell, Robert H., 55 Coyote, Los Alamos, NM 87544/505-662-7135
Newman Gunshop, Rt. 1, Box 90F, Agency, IA 52530/515-937-5775
NgraveR Co., The, 67 Wawecus Hill Rd., Bozrah, CT 06334/203-823-1533
Nichols Sports Optics, P.O. Box 37669, Omaha, NE 68137/402-339-3530; FAX: 402-330-8029
Nickels, Paul R., 4789 Summerhill Rd., Las Vegas, NV 89121/702-435-5318
Nicklas, Ted, 5504 Hegel Rd., Goodrich, MI 48438/313-797-4493
Nielsen Custom Cases, P.O. Box 26297, Las Vegas, NV 89126/800-377-1341, 702-878-5611; FAX: 702-877-4433
Niemi Engineering, W.B., Box 126 Center Road, Greensboro, VT 05841/802-533-7180 days, 802-533-7141 evenings
Night Vision Equipment Co., Inc., P.O. Box 266, Emmaus, PA 18049/215-391-9101
Nikon, Inc., 1300 Walt Whitman Rd., Melville, NY 11747/516-547-4200
Nitex, Inc., P.O. Box 1706, Uvalde, TX 78801/512-278-8843
No-Sho Mfg. Co., 10727 Glenfield Ct., Houston, TX 77096/713-723-5332
Noble Co., Jim, 1305 Columbia St., Vancouver, WA 98660/206-695-1309
Nolan, Dave, Fox Valley Range, P.O. Box 155, Dundee, IL 60118/708-426-5921
Noreen, Peter H., 5075 Buena Vista Dr., Belgrade, MT 59714/406-586-7383
Norica, Avnda Otaola, 16, Apartado 68, 20600 Eibar, SPAIN (U.S. importers—American Arms, Inc.; K.B.I., Inc.)
Norinco, 7A, Yun Tan N Beijing, CHINA (U.S. importers—Century International Arms, Inc.; ChinaSports, Inc.; Interarms; Midwest Sport Distributors; Sportarms of Florida)
Norma (See U.S. importer—Paul Co., The)
Norman Custom Gunstocks, Jim, 14281 Cane Rd., Valley Center, CA 92082/619-749-6252
Normark Corp., 1710 E. 78th St., Minneapolis, MN 55423/612-869-3291
Normington Co., Box 6, Rathdrum, ID 83858
Norrell Arms, John, 2608 Grist Mill Rd., Little Rock, AR 72207/501-225-7864
North American Arms, 1800 North 300 West, Spanish Fork, UT 84660/800-821-5783, 801-897-7401; FAX: 801-798-9418
North American Correspondence Schools, The Gun Pro School, Oak & Pawney St., Scranton, PA 18515/717-342-7701
North American Shooting Systems, P.O. Box 306, Osoyoos, B.C. V0H 1V0 CANADA
North American Specialties, 25442 Trabuco Rd., 105-328, El Torro, CA 92630/714-979-4867; FAX: 714-979-1520
North Fork Custom Gunsmithing, James Johnston, 428 Del Rio Rd., Roseburg, OR 97470/503-673-4467
North Mountain Pine Training Center (See Executive Protection Institute)
North Specialty Products, 2664-B Saturn St., Brea, CA 92621/714-524-1665
North Wind Decoys Co., 1005 N. Tower Rd., Fergus Falls, MN 56537/218-736-4378; FAX: 218-736-4378
Northeast Training Institute, Inc., 1142 Rockland St., Suite 380, Reading, PA 19604/215-373-1940
Northern Precision Custom Swaged Bullets, 337 S. James St., Carthage, NY 13619/315-493-3456
Northlake Boot Co., 1810 Columbia Ave., Franklin, TN 37064/615-794-1556
Nosler, Inc., P.O. Box 671, Bend, OR 97709/800-285-3701, 503-382-3921; FAX: 503-388-4667
Novak's .45 Shop, Wayne, 1206 1/2 30th St., P.O. Box 4045, Parkersburg, WV 25101/304-485-9295
Nowlin Custom Barrels Mfg., Rt. 1, Box 308, Claremore, OK 74017/918-342-0689; FAX: 918-342-0624
Nu-Line Guns, Inc., 1053 Caulks Hill Rd., Harvester, MO 63303/314-441-4500; FAX: 314-447-5018
Null Holsters Ltd., K.L., Hill City Station, Resaca, GA 30735/404-625-5643; FAX: 404-625-9392
Numrich Arms Corp., 203 Broadway, W. Hurley, NY 12491
Nu-Teçk, 30 Industrial Park Rd., Box 37, Centerbrook, CT 06409/203-767-3573; FAX: 203-767-9137
NW Sinker and Tackle, P.O. Box 1931, Myrtle Creek, OR 97457
Nygord Precision Products, P.O. Box 8394, La Crescenta, CA 91224/818-352-3027; FAX: 818-352-3027

O

Oakland Custom Arms, Inc., 4690 W. Walton Blvd., Waterford, MI 48329/313-674-8261
Oakman Turkey Calls, RD 1, Box 825, Harrisonville, PA 17228/717-485-4620
Oakshore Electronic Sights, Inc., P.O. Box 4470, Ocala, FL 32678-4470/904-629-7112; FAX: 904-629-1433
Obermeyer Rifled Barrels, 23122 60th St., Bristol, WI 53104/414-843-3537; FAX: 414-843-2129
O'Connor Rifle Products Co., Ltd., 2008 Maybank Hwy., Charleston, SC 29412/803-795-8590
October Country, P.O. Box 969, Dept. GD, Hayden Lake, ID 83835/208-772-2068
Oehler Research, Inc., P.O. Box 9135, Austin, TX 78766/512-327-6900
Oglesby & Oglesby Gunmakers, Inc., RR 5, Springfield, IL 62707/217-487-7100
Oil Rod and Gun Shop, 69 Oak St., East Douglas, MA 01516/508-865-2005
Ojala Holsters, Arvo, P.O. Box 98, N. Hollywood, CA 91603/503-669-1404
Oker's Engraving, 365 Bell Rd., P.O. Box 126, Shawnee, CO 80475/303-838-6042
Oklahoma Leather Products, Inc., 500 26th NW, Miami, OK 74354/918-542-6651
Old Dominion Engravers, 100 Progress Drive, Lynchburg, VA 24502/804-237-4450
Old Wagon Bullets, 32 Old Wagon Rd., Wilton, CT 06897
Old West Bullet Moulds, P.O. Box 519, Flora Vista, NM 87415
Old West Reproductions, Inc., 446 Florence S. Loop, Florence, MT 59833/406-273-2615
Old Western Scrounger, Inc., 12924 Hwy. A-l2, Montague, CA 96064/916-459-5445
Old World Gunsmithing, 2901 SE 122nd St., Portland, OR 97236/503-760-7681
Old World Oil Products, 3827 Queen Ave. N., Minneapolis, MN 55412/612-522-5037
Olde Pennsylvania, P.O. Box 912, New Kensington, PA 15068/412-337-1552
Ole Frontier Gunsmith Shop, 2617 Hwy. 29 S., Cantonment, FL 32533/904-477-8074
Olsen Development Lab, 111 Lakeview Ave., Blackwood, NJ 08012
Olson, Vic, 5002 Countryside Dr., Imperial, MO 63052/314-296-8086
Olt Co., Philip S., P.O. Box 550, Pekin, IL 61554/309-348-3633; FAX: 309-348-3300
Olympic Arms, Inc., 624 Old Pacific Hwy. SE, Olympia, WA 98503/206-456-3471; FAX: 206-491-3447
Olympic Optical Co., P.O. Box 752377, Memphis, TN 38175-2377/901-794-3890
Omark, Div. of Blount, Inc., 2299 Snake River Ave., P.O. Box 856, Lewiston, ID 83501/800-627-3640, 208-746-2351
Omnishock, 2219 Verde Oak Drive, Hollywood, CA 90068
OMR Feinmechanik, Jagd-und Sportwaffen, GmbH, Postfach 1231, Schutzenstr. 20, D-5400 Koblenz, GERMANY/0261-31865-15351
One Of A Kind, 15610 Purple Sage, San Antonio, TX 78255/512-695-3364

Optolyth-USA, Inc., 18805 Melvista Lane, Hillsboro, OR 97123/503-628-0246; FAX: 503-628-0797
Orchard Park Enterprise, P.O. Box 563, Orchard Park, NY 14227/616-656-0356
Ordnance Works, The, 2969 Pidgeon Point Road, Eureka, CA 95501/707-443-3252
Oregon Arms, Inc., 114 E. Jackson, P.O. Box 1104, Medford, OR 97501/503-560-4040
Original Mink Oil, Inc., P.O. Box 20191, 11021 NE Beach St., Portland, OR 97220/503-255-2814
Or-Un, Tahtakale Menekse Han 18, Istanbul, TURKEY 34460/901-522-5912; FAX: 901-522-7973
Orvis Co., The, Rt. 7, Manchester, VT 05254/802-362-3622 ext. 283; FAX: 802-362-3525
Ottmar, Maurice, Box 657, 113 E. Fir, Coulee City, WA 99115/509-632-5717
Otto, Tim, 320 Fairhaven Rd., Alameda, CA 94501-5963
Outa-Site Gun Carriers, 219 Market, Laredo, TX 78040/210-722-4678; FAX: 210-726-4858
Outdoor Connection, Inc., The, 201 Douglas, P.O. Box 7751, Waco, TX 76712/800-533-6076; 817-772-5575; FAX: 817-776-6076
Outdoor Edge Cutlery Corp., 2888 Bluff St., Suite 130, Boulder, CO 80301/303-530-3855; FAX: 303-530-3855
Outdoor Sports Headquarters, Inc., 967 Watertower Lane, Dayton, OH 45449/513-865-5855; FAX: 513-865-5962
Outdoorsman's Bookstore, The, Llangorse, Brecon, County Powys LD3 7UE, U.K./44-87484-660; FAX: 44-87484-650
Outers Laboratories, Div. of Blount, Inc., Route 2, Onalaska, WI 54650/608-781-5800
Owen, Harry, Sport Specialties, 100 N. Citrus Ave. 412, W. Covina, CA 91791-1614/818-968-5806
Ox-Yoke Originals, Inc., 34 Main St., Milo, ME 04463/800-231-8313; FAX: 207-943-2416
Ozark Gun Works, 335 Cemetary Rd., Rogers, AR 72756/FAX: 501-631-6944

P

P&M Sales and Service, 5724 Gainsborough Pl., Oak Forest, IL 60452/708-687-7149
P&P Tool Co., 125 W. Market St., Morrison, IL 61270/815-772-7618
P&S Gun Service, 2138 Old Shepardsville Rd., Louisville, KY 40218/502-456-9346
Pac-Nor Barreling, 99299 Overlook Rd., P.O. Box 6188, Brookings, OR 97415/503-469-7330; FAX: 503-469-7331
Pace Marketing, Inc., 9474 NW 48th St., Sunrise, FL 33351-5137/305-741-4361; FAX: 305-741-2901
Pachmayr Ltd., 1875 S. Mountain Ave., Monrovia, CA 91016/818-357-7771, 800-423-9704; FAX: 818-358-7251
Pacific Pistolcraft, 1810 E. Columbia Ave., Tacoma, WA 98404/206-474-5465
Pacific Tool Co., P.O. Box 2048, Ordnance Plant Rd., Grand Island, NE 68801
Paco's (See Small Custom Mould & Bullet Co.)
P.A.C.T., Inc., P.O. Box 531525, Grand Prairie, TX 75053/214-641-0049
Page Custom Bullets, P.O. Box 25, Port Moresby Papua, NEW GUINEA
Pagel Gun Works, Inc., 1407 4th St. NW, Grand Rapids, MN 55744/218-326-3003
Palmer Manufacturing Co., C., Inc., P.O. Box 220, West Newton, PA 15089/412-872-8200; FAX: 412-872-8302
Palmer Metal Products, 2930 N. Campbell Ave., Chicago, IL 60618/800-788-7725; FAX: 312-267-8080
Palmgren Steel Products, 8383 S. Chicago Ave., Chicago, IL 60617/312-721-9675; FAX: 312-721-9739
Palsa Outdoor Products, P.O. Box 81336, Lincoln, NE 68501/402-456-9281, 800-456-9281; FAX: 402-488-2321
PanaVise Products, Inc., 1485 Southern Way, Sparks, NV 89431/702-353-2900; FAX: 702-353-2929
Para-Ordnance Mfg., Inc., 3411 McNicoll Ave., Unit 14, Scarborough, Ont. M1V 2V6, CANADA/416-297-7855; FAX: 416-297-1289
Paragon Sales & Services, Inc., P.O. Box 2022, Joliet, IL 60434/815-725-9212; FAX: 815-725-8974
Pardini Armi Commerciale Srl, Via Italica 154, 55043 Lido Di Camaiore Lu, ITALY/584-90121; FAX: 584-90122 (U.S. importer—MCS, Inc.)
Paris, Frank J., 13945 Minock Dr., Redford, MI 48239/313-255-0888
Parke-Bernet (See Sotheby's)
Parker Div. Reagent Chemical (See Parker Reproductions)
Parker Gun Finishes, 9337 Smokey Row Rd., Strawberry Plains, TN 37871/615-933-3286
Parker Reproductions, 124 River Rd., Middlesex, NJ 08846/908-469-0100; FAX: 908-469-9692
Parker, Mark D., 1240 Florida Ave. 7, Longmont, CO 80501/303-772-0214
Parker-Hale (See U.S. distributor-Navy Arms Co.)
Parts & Surplus, P.O. Box 22074, Memphis, TN 38122/901-683-4007
Partridge Sales Ltd., John, Trent Meadows, Rugeley, Staffordshire, WS15 2HS ENGLAND/0889-584438
Pasadena Gun Center, 206 E. Shaw, Pasadena, TX 77506/713-472-0417; FAX: 713-472-1322
PAST Sporting Goods, Inc., P.O. Box 1035, Columbia, MO 65205/314-445-9200
Patchbox & Museum of the Great Divide, The, 600 Farm Rd., Kalispell, MT 59901/406-756-8851
Paterson Gunsmithing, 438 Main St., Paterson, NJ 07502/201-345-4100
Pathfinder Sports Leather, 2920 E. Chambers St., Phoenix, AZ 85040/602-276-0016
Patrick Bullets, P.O. Box 172, Warwick QSLD 4370 AUSTRALIA
Patriot Manufacturing, P.O. Box 50065, Lighthouse Point, FL 33074/305-783-4849
Pattern Control, 114 N. Third St., Garland, TX 75040/214-494-3551
Paul Co., The, Rt. 1, Box 177A, Wellsville, KS 66092/913-883-4444
Paulsen Gunstocks, Rt. 71, Box 11, Chinook, MT 59523/406-357-3403
Payne Photography, Robert, P.O. Box 141471, Austin, TX 78714/512-272-4554; FAX: 512-929-0714
PC Co., 5942 Secor Rd., Toledo, OH 43623/419-472-6222
Peacemaker Specialists, John Kopec Enterprises, P.O. Box 157, Whitmore, CA 96096/916-472-3438
Pease Accuracy, Bob, P.O. Box 310787, New Braunfels, TX 78131/210-625-1342
Peasley, David, P.O. Box 604, 2067 S. Hiway 17, Alamosa, CO 81101
PECAR Herbert Schwarz, GmbH, Kreuzbergstrasse 6, Berlin 61, 1000 GERMANY/004930-785-7383; FAX: 004930-785-1934
Pedersen & Son, C.R., 2717 S. Pere Marquette Hwy., Ludington, MI 49431/616-843-2061
Pedersoli Davide & C., Via Artigiani 53, Gardone V.T. (BS) ITALY 25063/030-8912402; FAX: 030-8911019 (U.S. importers—Beauchamp & Son, Inc.; Cabela's; Dixie Gun Works, EMF Co., Inc.; Navy Arms Co.; Trail Guns Armory, Inc.)
Peet Shoe Dryer, Inc., 130 S. 5th St., St. Maries, ID 83861/800-222-PEET; FAX: 208-245-5441
Pejsa Ballistics, 2120 Kenwood Pkwy., Minneapolis, MN 55405/612-374-3337; FAX: 612-374-3337
Pell, John T., 410 College, Trinidad, CO 81082/719-846-9406
Peltor, Inc., 63 Commercial Way, E. Providence, RI 02914/401-438-4800; FAX: 800-EAR-FAX1
PEM's Mfg. Co., 5063 Waterloo Rd., Atwater, OH 44201/216-947-3721
Pence Precision Barrels, 7567 E. 900 S., S. Whitley, IN 46787/219-839-4745
Pend Oreille Sport Shop, 3100 Hwy. 200 East, Sandpoint, ID 83864/208-263-2412
Pendleton Royal, 4/7 Highgate St., Birmingham, ENGLAND B12 0X5/44 21 440 3060; FAX: 44 21 446 4165
Pendleton Woolen Mills, P.O. Box 3030, 220 N.W. Broadway, Portland, OR 97208/503-226-4801
Penguin Industries, Inc., Airport Industrial Mall, Coatesville, PA 19320/215-384-6000
Penn's Woods Products, Inc., 19 W. Pittsburgh St., Delmont, PA 15626/412-468-8311
Pennsylvania Gunsmith School, 812 Ohio River Blvd., Avalon, Pittsburgh, PA 15202/412-766-1812
Penrod Precision, 312 College Ave., P.O. Box 307, N. Manchester, IN 46962/219-982-8385
Pentax Corp., 35 Inverness Dr. E., Englewood, CO 80112/303-799-8000
Pentheny de Pentheny, 2352 Baggett Ct., Santa Rosa, CA 95401/707-573-1390
Pepperbox Gun Shop, P.O. Box 922, E. Moline, IL 61244
Perazzi m.a.p. S.P.A., Via Fontanelle 1/3, 1-25080 Botticino Mattina, ITALY (U.S. importer—Perazzi USA, Inc.)
Perazzi USA, Inc., 1207 S. Shamrock Ave., Monrovia, CA 91016/818-303-0068
Peregrine Industries (See Falcon Industries, Inc.)
Performance Specialists, 308 Eanes School Rd., Austin, TX 78746/512-327-0119
Peripheral Data Systems (See Arms)
Personal Protection Systems, RD 5, Box 5027-A, Moscow, PA 18444/717-842-1766
Perugini Visini & Co. s.r.l., Via Camprelle, 126, 25080 Nuvolera (Bs.), ITALY (U.S. importer—Moore & Co., Wm. Larkin)
Peters Stahl GmbH, Stettiner Str. 42, D-4790 Paderborn, GERMANY/05251-750025-27; FAX: 05251-75611 (U.S. importers—McMillan Gunworks, Inc.; Safari Arms/SGW)
Petersen Publishing Co., 6420 Wilshire Blvd., Los Angeles, CA 90048
Peterson Gun Shop, Inc., A.W., 4255 W. Old U.S. 441, Mt. Dora, FL 32757-3299/904-383-4258
Peterson Instant Targets, Inc. (See Lyman Products Corp.)
Pettinger Books, Gerald, Rt. 2, Box 125, Russell, IA 50238/515-535-2239
Pflumm Gun Mfg. Co., 6139 Melrose Ln., Shawnee, KS 66203/800-888-4867
PFRB Co., P.O. Box 1242, Bloomington, IL 61701/309-473-3964
Phelps Mfg. Co., Box 2266, Evansville, IN 47714/812-476-8791
Phillippi Custom Bullets, Justin, P.O. Box 773, Ligonier, PA 15658/412-238-9671
Phillips & Bailey, Inc., 815A Yorkshire St., Houston, TX 77022/713-699-4288
Phoenix Arms Co. Ltd. (See Hy-Score Arms Co. Ltd.)
Phoenix Arms, 1420 S. Archibald Ave., Ontario, CA 91761/714-947-4843
Phyl-Mac, 609 NE 104th Ave., Vancouver, WA 98664/206-256-0579
Piedmont Community College, P.O. Box 1197, Roxboro, NC 27573/919-599-1181
Pierce Pistols, 2326 E. Hwy. 34, Newnan, GA 30263/404-253-8192
Pilgrim Pewter, Inc. (See Bell Originals, Sid)
Pilkington Gun Co., P.O. Box 1296, Muskogee, OK 74402/918-683-9418
Pilkington, Scott, Little Trees Ramble, P.O. Box 97, Monteagle, TN 37356/615-924-3475; FAX: 615-924-3442
Pine Technical College, 1100 4th St., Pine City, MN 55063/800-521-7463; FAX: 612-629-6766
Pioneer Guns, 5228 Montgomery Rd., Norwood, OH 45212/513-631-4871
Piotti (See U.S. importer—Moore & Co., Wm. Larkin)
Piquette, Paul R., 80 Bradford Dr., Feeding Hills, MA 01030/413-781-8300, Ext. 682
PistolPAL Products, 2930 N. Campbell Ave., Chicago, IL 60618/800-788-7725; FAX: 312-267-8080
Plaxco, J. Michael, Rt. 1, P.O. Box 203, Roland, AR 72135/501-868-9787
Plaza Cutlery, Inc., 3333 Bristol, 161, South Coast Plaza, Costa Mesa, CA 92626/714-549-3932
Plum City Ballistic Range, N2162 80th St., Plum City, WI 54761-8622/715-647-2539
PMC/Eldorado Cartridge Corp., P.O. Box 62508, 12801 U.S. Hwy. 95 S., Boulder City, NV 89006-2508/702-294-0025; FAX: 702-294-0121
Police Bookshelf, P.O. Box 122, Concord, NH 03301/603-224-6814; FAX: 603-226-3554
Poly Technologies, Inc. (See U.S. importer—Keng's Firearms Specialty, Inc.)
Polywad, Inc., P.O. Box 7916, Macon, GA 31209/912-477-0669
Pomeroy, Robert, RR1, Box 50, E. Corinth, ME 04427/207-285-7721
Ponsness/Warren, P.O. Box 8, Rathdrum, ID 83858/208-687-2231; FAX: 208-687-2233
Pony Express Reloaders, 608 E. Co. Rd. D, Suite 3, St. Paul, MN 55117/612-483-9406
Pony Express Sport Shop, Inc., 16606 Schoenborn St., North Hills, CA 91343/818-895-1231
Porta Blind, Inc., 2700 Speedway, Wichita Falls, TX 76308/800-842-5545
Potts, Wayne E., 912 Poplar St., Denver, CO 80220/303-355-5462
Powder Horn, Inc., The, P.O. Box 114 Patty Drive, Cusseta, GA 31805/404-989-3257
Powell & Son (Gunmakers) Ltd., William, 35-37 Carrs Lane, Birmingham B4 7SX ENGLAND/21-643-0689; FAX: 21-631-3504 (U.S. importer—Bell's Legendary Country Wear)
Power Custom, Inc., RR 2, P.O. Box 756AB, Gravois Mills, MO 65037/314-372-5684
Power Plus Enterprises, P.O. Box 6070, Columbus, GA 31907-0058/404-561-1717
PPC Corp., 627 E. 24th St., Paterson, NJ 07514/201-278-5428
Practical Tools, Inc., Austin Behlerts, P.O. Box 133, Pipersville, PA 18947/215-766-7301
Pragotrade, 307 Humberline Dr., Rexdale, Ontario, CANADA M9W 5V1/416-675-1322
Pranger, Ed G., 1414 7th St., Anacortes, WA 98221/206-293-3488
Pre-Winchester 92-90-62 Parts Co., P.O. Box 8125, W. Palm Beach, FL 33407
Precise International, 15 Corporate Dr., Orangeburg, NY 10962/914-365-3500
Precise Metalsmithing Enterprises, 146 Curtis Hill Rd., Chehalis, WA 98532/206-748-3743; FAX: 206-748-8102
Precision Airgun Sales, Inc., 5139 Center Rd., Maple Hts., OH 44137-1906
Precision Arms International, Inc., Rt. 17, Box 456, Bldg. 810, Saluda, VA 23149/804-758-5233; FAX: 804-758-2690
Precision Cartridge, 176 Eastside Rd., Deer Lodge, MT 59722/800-397-3901, 406-846-3900
Precision Cast Bullets, 101 Mud Creek Lane, Ronan, MT 59864/406-676-5135
Precision Castings & Equipment, Inc., P.O. Box 326, Jasper, IN 47547-0135/812-634-9167
Precision Components and Guns, Rt. 55, P.O. Box 337, Pawling, NY 12564/914-855-3040
Precision Delta Corp., P.O. Box 128, Ruleville, MS 38771/601-756-2810; FAX: 601-756-2590
Precision Imports, Inc., 5040 Space Center Dr., San Antonio, TX 78218/512-666-3033; FAX: 512-666-2723
Precision Metal Finishing, John Westrom, P.O. Box 3186, Des Moines, IA 50316/515-288-8680; FAX: 515-288-8680
Precision Munitions, Inc., P.O. Box 326, Jasper, IN 47547
Precision Ordnance, 1316 E. North St., Jackson, MI 49202
Precision Reloading, Inc., P.O. Box 122, Stafford Springs, CT 06076/203-684-7979; FAX: 203-684-6788
Precision Sales International, Inc. (See PSI, Inc.)
Precision Shooting, 102 Brandon Rd., Yonkers, NY 10704/914-776-1581
Precision Shooting, Inc., 5735 Sherwood Forest Dr., Akron, OH 44319
Precision Small Parts, Inc., 155 Carlton Rd., Charlottesville, VA 22902/804-293-6124
Precision Specialties, 131 Hendom Dr., Feeding Hills, MA 01030/413-786-3365; FAX: 413-786-3365
Precision Sport Optics, 15571 Producer Lane, Unit G, Huntington Beach, CA 92649/714-891-1309; FAX: 714-892-6920
Precision Sports, 3736 Kellogg Rd., P.O. Box 5588, Cortland, NY 13045-5588/607-756-2851, 800-847-6787; FAX: 607-753-8835
Premier Reticles, 920 Breckenridge Lane, Winchester, VA 22601-6707
Prescott Projectile Co., 1808 Meadowbrook Road, Prescott, AZ 86303
Price Bullets, Patrick W., 16520 Worthley Drive, San Lorenzo, CA 94580/415-278-1547
Primos Wild Game Calls, Inc., P.O. Box 12785, Jackson, MS 39236-2785/601-366-1288; FAX: 601-362-3274
Pro Load Ammunition, Inc., 5180 E. Seltice Way, Post Falls, ID 83854/208-773-9444; FAX: 208-773-9441
Pro-Mark, Div. of Wells Lamont, 6640 W. Touhy, Chicago, IL 60648/312-647-8200
Pro-Port Ltd., 41302 Executive Dr., Harrison Twp., MI 48045-3448/313-469-7323; FAX: 313-469-0425
Pro-Shot Products, Inc., P.O. Box 763, Taylorville, IL 62568/217-824-9133; FAX: 217-824-8861
Professional Firearms Record Book Co. (See PFRB Co.)

Professional Gunsmiths of America, Inc., 1301 Franklin, P.O. Box 224E, Lexington, MO 64067/816-259-2636
Professional Hunter Supplies (See Star Custom Bullets)
Proline Handgun Leather, P.O. Box 112154, Tacoma, WA 98411/206-564-6652
Prolix®, 15578 Mojave Dr. Unit D, Victorville, CA 92392/800-248-LUBE, 619-243-3129; FAX: 619-241-0148
Protecto Plastics, Div. of Penguin Ind., Airport Industrial Mall, Coatesville, PA 19320/215-384-6000
Protektor Model Co., 7 Ash St., Galeton, PA 16922/814-435-2442
Prototech Industries, Inc., Rt. 1, Box 81, Delia, KS 66418/913-771-3571
ProWare,Inc., 15847 NE Hancock St., Portland, OR 97230/503-239-0159
PSI, Inc., P.O. Box 1776, Westfield, MA 01086/413-562-5055; FAX: 413-562-5056
P.S.M.G. Gun Co., 10 Park Ave., Arlington, MA 02174/617-646-8845; FAX: 617-646-2133
PW Gunleather, P.O. Box 450432, Atlanta, GA 30345/404-822-1640; FAX: 404-822-1704
Pyromid, Inc., 3292 S. Highway 97, Redmond, OR 97786

Q

Quack Decoy Corp., 4 Mill St., Cumberland, RI 02864/401-723-8202
Quaker Boy, Inc., 5455 Webster Rd., Orchard Parks, NY 14127/716-662-3979
Qualigraphics, Inc., 25 Ruta Ct., P.O. Box 2306, S. Hackensack, NJ 07606/201-440-9200
Quality Arms, Inc., Box 19477, Dept. GD, Houston, TX 77224/713-870-8377; FAX: 713-870-8524
Quality Firearms of Idaho, Inc., 114 13th Ave. S., Nampa, ID 83651/208-466-1631
Quality Parts Co., 999 Roosevelt Trail, Bldg. 3, Windham, ME 04062/800-556-7928, 207-892-2005; FAX: 207-892-8068
Quartz-Lok, 13137 N. 21st Lane, Phoenix, AZ 85029
Queen Cutlery Co., 507 Chestnut St., Titusville, PA 16354/800-222-5233
Quigley's Personal Protection Strategies, Paxton, 9903 Santa Monica Blvd., 300 Beverly Hills, CA 90212/310-281-1762
Quinetics Corp., P.O. Box 13237, San Antonio, TX 78213/512-684-8561; FAX: 512-684-2912

R

R&C Knives & Such, P.O. Box 1047, Manteca, CA 95336/209-239-3722
R&J Gun Shop, 133 W. Main St., John Day, OR 97845/503-575-2130
R&S Industries Corp., 8255 Brentwood Industrial Dr., St. Louis, MO 63144/314-781-5400
Rabeno, Martin, 92 Spook Hole Rd., Ellenville, NY 12428/914-647-4567
Radiator Specialty Co., 1900 Wilkinson Blvd., P.O. Box 34689, Charlotte, NC 28234/800-438-6947; FAX: 800-421-9525
Radical Concepts, 19205 Parthenia St., Suite D, Northridge, CA 91324
Radix Research & Mktg., Box 247, Woodland Park, CO 80863
Rainier Ballists Corp., 4500 15th St. East, Tacoma, WA 98424/800-638-8722; FAX: 206-922-7854
Ram-Line, Inc., 10601 W. 48th Ave., Wheat Ridge, CO 80033/303-467-0300; FAX: 303-467-9833
Ranch Products, P.O. Box 145, Malinta, OH 43535/313-277-3118; FAX: 313-565-8536
Randall Firearms Research, P.O. Box 1586, Lomita, CA 90717-5586/310-325-0102; FAX: 310-325-0298
Randall-Made Knives, P.O. Box 1988, Orlando, FL 32802/407-855-8075
Randco UK, 286 Gipsy Rd., Welling, Kent DA16 1JJ, ENGLAND/44 81 303 4118
Randolph Engineering, Inc., 275 Centre St., Unit 17, Holbrook MA 02343/617-961-6070, 800-541-1405; FAX: 617-767-5239
Ranger Footwear, 1100 E. Main St., Endicott, NY 13760/800-688-6148
Ranger Mfg. Co., Inc., 1536 Crescent Dr., Augusta, GA 30919/404-738-3469
Ranger Shooting Glasses, 275 Centre St., Unit 17, Holbrook, MA 02343/800-541-1405, 617-961-6070; FAX: 617-767-5239
Ranging, Inc., Routes 5 & 20, East Bloomfield, NY 14443/716-657-6161
Ransom International Corp., P.O. Box 3845, 1040-A Sandretto Dr., Prescott, AZ 86302/602-778-7899; FAX: 602-778-7993
Rapine Bullet Mould Mfg. Co., P.O. Box 1119, East Greenville, PA 18041/215-679-5413
Rattlers Brand, P.O. Box 311, Thomaston, GA 30286/800-652-1341; FAX: 404-647-2742
Ravell Ltd., 289 Diputacion St., 08009, Barcelona SPAIN
Raytech, Div. of Lyman Products Corp., Rt. 32 Stafford Ind. Park, Box 6, Stafford Springs, CT 06076/203-684-4273; FAX: 203-684-7938
RCBS, Div. of Blount, Inc., 605 Oro Dam Blvd., Oroville, CA 95965/800-533-5000, 916-533-5191
R.D.P. Tool Co., Inc., 49162 McCoy Ave., East Liverpool, OH 43920/216-385-5129
Reagent Chemical & Research, Inc. (See Calico Hardwoods, Inc.)
Reardon Products, P.O. Box 126, Morrison, IL 61270/815-772-3155
Rebec's Reloading, P.O. Box 30550, Santa Barbara, CA 93130
Re-Heater, Inc., 15828 S. Broadway, C, Gardena, CA 90248
Red Ball, 100 Factory St., Nashua, NH 03060/603-881-4420
Red Diamond Dist. Co., 1304 Snowdon Dr., Knoxville, TN 37912
Red Head, Inc., P.O. Box 7100, Springfield, MO 65801/417-864-5430
Red River Frontier Outfitters, P.O. Box 241, Dept. GD, Tujunga, CA 91043/818-821-3167
Red Star Target Co., 4519 Brisebois Dr. NW, Calgary AB T2L 2G3 CANADA/403-289-7939; FAX: 403-289-3275
Red Willow Tool & Armory, Inc., 4004 Hwy. 93 North, Stevensville, MT 59870/406-777-5401; FAX: 406-777-5402
Redding Reloading, Inc., 1089 Starr Rd., Cortland, NY 13045/607-753-3331; FAX: 607-756-8445
Redfield, Inc., 5800 E. Jewell Ave., Denver, CO 80224/303-757-6411; FAX: 303-756-2338
Redman's Rifling & Reboring, Rt. 3, Box 330A, Omak, WA 98841/509-826-5512
Redwood Bullet Works, 3559 Bay Rd., Redwood City, CA 94063/415-367-6741
Reed, Dave, Rt. 1, Box 374, Minnesota City, MN 55959/507-689-2944
Refrigiwear, Inc., 71 Inip Dr., Inwood, Long Island, NY 11696
Regional Associates, P.O. Box 9849, Alexandria, VA 22304/703-780-6189
Reiswig, Wallace E., Claro Walnut Gunstock Co., 1235 Stanley Ave., Chico, CA 95928/916-342-5188
Reloaders Equipment Co., 4680 High St., Ecorse, MI 48229
Reloading Specialties, Inc., 209 S.W. 2nd Ave. Box 1130, Pine Island, MN 55963/507-356-8500
Remington Arms Co., Inc., 1007 Market St., Wilmington, DE 19898/302-773-5291
Remington Footwear Co., 1810 Columbia Ave., Franklin, TN 37604/800-332-2688
Rencher Bullets, 5161 NE 5th St., Redmond, OR 97756
Renegade, P.O. Box 31546, Phoenix, AZ 85046/602-482-6777
Renner Co./Radical Concepts, R.J., P.O. Box 10731, Canoga Park, CA 91309/818-700-8131
Reno, Wayne, 2808 Stagestop Rd., Jefferson, CO 80456/719-836-3452
R.E.T. Enterprises, 2608 S. Chestnut, Broken Arrow, OK 74012/918-251-GUNS; FAX: 918-251-0587
Retting, Inc., Martin B., 11029 Washington, Culver City, CA 90232/213-837-2412
R.G.-G., Inc., P.O. Box 1261, Conifer, CO 80433-1261
Rhodeside, Inc., 1704 Commerce Dr., Piqua, OH 45356/513-773-5781
Rice, Keith (See White Rock Tool & Die)
Richards Classic Oil Finish, John, Rt. 2, Box 325, Bedford, KY 40006/502-255-7222
Richards Micro-Fit Stocks, 8331 N. San Fernando Rd., P.O. Box 1066, Sun Valley, CA 91352/818-767-6097
Rickard, Inc., Pete, RD 1, Box 292, Cobleskill, NY 12043/800-282-5663; FAX: 518-234-2454
Ridgetop Sporting Goods, P.O. Box 306, 42907 Hilligoss Ln. East, Eatonville, WA 98328/206-832-6422
Riebe Co., W.J., 3434 Tucker Rd., Boise, ID 83703
Ries, Chuck, 415 Ridgecrest Dr., Grants Pass, OR 97527/503-476-5623
Rifle Shop, The, Wm. H. Hobaugh, P.O. Box M, Philipsburg, MT 59858/406-859-3515
RIG Products, 87 Coney Island Dr., Sparks, NV 89431-1990/702-331-5666; FAX: 702-331-5669
Rigby & Co., John, 66 Great Suffolk St., London SE1 OBU, ENGLAND (U.S. importer—Griffin & Howe, Inc.)
Riggs, Jim, 206 Azalea, Boerne, TX 78006/210-249-8567
Riling Arms Books Co., Ray, 6844 Gorsten St., P.O. Box 18925, Philadelphia, PA 19119/215-438-2456
Ringler Custom Leather Co., P.O. Box 206, Cody, WY 82414/307-645-3255
R.I.S. Co., Inc., 718 Timberlake Circle, Richardson, TX 75080/214-235-0933
River Road Sporting Clays, Bruce Barsotti, P.O. Box 3016, Gonzales, CA 93926/408-675-2473
Rizzini Battista, Via 2 Giugno 7/7Bis-25060 Marcheno (Brescia), ITALY
Rizzini, F.LLI (See U.S. importer—Moore & Co. Wm. Larkin)
RLCM Enterprises, 110 Hill Crest Drive, Burleson, TX 76028
RMS Custom Gunsmithing, 4120 N. Bitterwell, Prescott Valley, AZ 86314/602-772-7626
Robar Co.'s, Inc., The, 21438 N. 7th Ave., Suite B, Phoenix, AZ 85027/602-581-2648; FAX: 602-582-0059
Robbins Scent, Inc., P.O. Box 779, Connellsville, PA 15425/412-628-2529; FAX: 412-628-9598
Roberts Jr., William A., Rt. 14, P.O. Box 75, Athens, AL 35611/205-232-7027
Roberts Products, 25238 SE 32nd, Issaquah, WA 98027/206-392-8172
Roberts, J.J., 7808 Lake Dr., Manassas, VA 22111/703-330-0448
Robinson Firearms Mfg. Ltd., RR2, Suite 51, Comp. 24, Winfield, B.C. CANADA V0H 2C0/604-766-5353
Robinson, Don, Pennsylvania Hse., 36 Fairfax Crescent, Southowram, Halifax, W. Yorkshire HX3 9SQ, ENGLAND/0422-364458
Rochester Lead Works, 76 Anderson Ave., Rochester, NY 14607/716-442-8500
Rockwood Corp., Speedwell Division, 136 Lincoln Blvd., Middlesex, NJ 08846/908-560-7171
Rocky Fork Enterprises, P.O. Box 427, 878 Battle Rd., Nolensville, TN 37135/615-941-1307
Rocky Mountain Arms, Inc., 600 S. Sunset, Unit C, Longmont, CO 80501/303-768-8522; FAX: 303-678-8766
Rocky Mountain High Sports Glasses, 8121 N. Central Park Ave., Skokie, IL 60076/708-679-1012; FAX: 708-679-0184
Rocky Mountain Rifle Works Ltd., 1707 14th St., Boulder, CO 80302/303-443-9189
Rocky Mountain Target Co., 3 Aloe Way, Leesburg, FL 34788/904-365-9598
Rocky, Div. of Wm. Brooks Shoe Co., 294 Harper St., Nelsonville, OH 45764/614-753-1951; FAX: 614-753-4042
Rogers Gunsmithing, Bob, P.O. Box 305, 344 S. Walnut St., Franklin Grove, IL 61031/815-456-2685; FAX: 815-288-7142
Rohner, Hans and John, 710 Sunshine Canyon, Boulder, CO 80302/303-444-3841
Rolston Jr., Fred, 210 E. Cummins, Tecumseh, MI 49286/517-423-6002
Rooster Laboratories, P.O. Box 412514, Kansas City, MO 64141/816-474-1622; FAX: 816-474-1307
Rorschach Precision Products, P.O. Box 151613, Irving, TX 75015/214-790-3487
Rosenberg & Sons, Jack A., 12229 Cox Lane, Dallas, TX 75234/214-241-6302
Rosser, Bob, 142 Ramsey Dr., Albertville, AL 35950/205-878-5388
Rossi S.A. Metalurgica E Municoes, Amadeo, Rua Amadeo Rossi, 143, Sao Leopoldo, RS, BRAZIL 93 030/0512-92-5566 (U.S. importer—Interarms)
Roto Carve, 2754 Garden Ave., Janesville, IA 50647
Royal Arms, 5126 3rd Ave. N., Great Falls, MT 59401/406-453-1149
Royal Labs, Ltd., P.O. Box 2043, 710 Elm St., Truth or Consequences, NM 87901
Roy's Custom Grips, Rt. 3, Box 174-E, Lynchburg, VA 24504/804-385-6667
RPM, 15481 N. Twin Lakes Dr., Tucson, AZ 85737/602-825-1233; FAX: 602-825-3333
RSR Corp., 1111 West Mocking Bird Lane, Dallas, TX 75247
R-Tech Corp., P.O. Box 1281, Cottage Grove, OR 97424/503-942-5126; FAX: 503-942-8624
Rubright Bullets, 1008 S. Quince Rd., Walnutport, PA 18088/215-767-1339
Rucker Ammunition Co., P.O. Box 479, Terrell, TX 75160
Ruger (See Sturm, Ruger & Co.)
Ruko Products, Inc., 2245 Kenmore Ave., Suite 102, Buffalo, NY 14207/716-874-2707; FAX: 416-826-1353
Rundell's Gun Shop, 6198 Frances Rd., Clio, MI 48420/313-687-0559
Robert P. Runge, 94 Grove St., Ilion, NY 13357/315-894-3036
Rupert's Gun Shop, 2202 Dick Rd., Suite B, Fenwick, MI 48834/517-248-3252
Russell Knives, Inc., A.G., 1705 Hwy. 71 North, Springdale, AR 72764/501-751-7341
Russell's Rifle Shop, Rt. 5, P.O. Box 92, Georgetown, TX 78626/512-778-5338
Rusteprufe Laboratories, Robert D. Munger, 1319 Jefferson Ave., Sparta, WI 54656/608-269-4144
Rusty Duck Premium Gun Care Products, 7785 Founion Dr., Florence, KY 41042/606-342-5553
Rutgers Book Center, 127 Raritan Ave., Highland Park, NJ 08904/908-545-4344; FAX: 908-545-6686
Rutgers Gun & Boat Center, 127 Raritan Ave., Highland Park, NJ 08904/908-545-4344; FAX: 908-545-6686
Ruvel & Co., Inc., 4128-30 W. Belmont Ave., Chicago, IL 60641/312-286-9494
R.V.I., P.O. Box Q-1, 1300 Boblett St., Blaine, WA 98230/206-595-2933
RWS (See U.S. importer—Dynamit Nobel-RWS, Inc.)
Ryan, Chad L., RR 3, Box 72, Cresco, IA 52136/319-547-4384
Rybka Custom Leather Equipment, Thad, 32 Havilah Hill, Odenville, AL 35120

S

S&B Industries, 11238 McKinley Rd., Montrose, MI 48457/313-639-5491
S&H Arms Mfg. Co., Rt. 3, Box 689, Berryville, AR 72616/501-545-3511
S&K Mfg. Co., P.O. Box 247, Pittsfield, PA 16340/814-563-7808; FAX: 814-563-7808
S&S Firearms, 74-11 Myrtle Ave., Glendale, NY 11385/718-497-1100
SAECO (See Redding Reloading, Inc.)
Safari Arms/SGW (See Olympic Arms, Inc.)
Safari Gun Co., 6410 Brandon Ave., Springfield, VA 22150/703-569-1097
Safari Outfitters Ltd., 71 Ethan Allan Hwy., Ridgefield, CT 06877/203-544-9505
Safari Press, Inc., 15621 Chemical Lane B, Huntington Beach, CA 92649/714-894-9080; FAX: 714-894-4949
Safariland Ltd., Inc., 3120 E. Mission Blvd., P.O. Box 51478, Ontario, CA 91761/714-923-7300; FAX: 714-923-7400
S.A.F.E., P.O. Box 864, Post Falls, ID 83854/208-773-3624
Safesport Manufacturing Co., 1100 W. 45th Ave., Denver, CO 80211/303-433-6506; FAX: 303-433-4112
Safety Direct, 56 Coney Island Dr., Sparks, NV 89431/702-354-4451
Safety Speed Holster, Inc., 910 S. Vail Ave., Montebello, CA 90640/213-723-4140; FAX: 213-726-6973
Sako Ltd., P.O. Box 149, SF-11101, Riihimaki, FINLAND (U.S. importer—Stoeger Industries)
Salter Calls, Inc., Eddie, Hwy. 31 South-Brewton Industrial Park, Brewton, AL 36426/205-867-2584; FAX: 206-867-9005

Samco Global Arms, Inc., 6995 NW 43rd St., Miami, FL 33166/305-593-9782
Sampson, Roger, 430 N. Grove, Mora, MN 55051/612-679-4868
San Angelo Sports Products, Inc., 909 W. 14th St., San Angelo, TX 76903/915-655-7126; FAX: 915-653-6720
San Francisco Gun Exchange, 124 Second St., San Francisco, CA 94105/415-982-6097
San Marco (See U.S. importer—Cape Outfitters)
Sanders Custom Gun Service, 2358 Tyler Ln., Louisville, KY 40205/502-454-3338
Sanders Gun and Machine Shop, 145 Delhi Road, Manchester, IA 52057
Sandia Die & Ctg. Co., 37 Atancacio Rd. NE, Albuquerque, NM 87123/505-298-5729
Sandy's Custom Gunshop, Rt. 1, P.O. Box 4, Rockport, IL 62370/217-437-4241
Sarco, Inc., 323 Union St., Stirling, NJ 07980/908-647-3800
Sardius Industries Ltd., 72 Rokach St., Ramat Gan, ISRAEL 52542/972-3-7521353
Sauer (See U.S. importers—G.U., Inc.; Simmons Enterprises, Ernie)
Sauer Sporting Rifles, P.O. Box 37669, Omaha, NE 68137
Saunders Gun & Machine Shop, R.R. 2, Delhi Road, Manchester, IA 52057
Savage Arms, Inc., Springdale Rd., Westfield, MA 01085/413-568-7001; FAX: 413-562-7764
Savana Sports, Inc., 5763 Ferrier St., Montreal, Quebec, CANADA/514-739-1753; FAX: 514-739-1755
Scanco Environmental Systems, 5000 Highlands Parkway, Suite 180, Atlanta, GA 30082/404-431-0025; FAX: 404-431-0028
Scansport, Inc., P.O. Box 700, Enfield, NH 03748/603-632-7654
Scattergun Technologies, Inc., 518 3rd Ave. S., Nashville, TN 37210/615-254-1441
Sceery Co., E.J., 2308 Cedros Circle, Sante Fe, NM 87505/505-983-2125
Schaefer Shooting Sports, 2280 Grand Ave., Baldwin, NY 11510/516-379-4900; FAX: 516-379-6701
Schaefer, Roy V., 101 Irving Rd., Eugene, OR 97404/503-688-4333
Scharch Mfg., Inc., 10325 Co. Rd. 120, Unit C, Salida, CO 81201/719-539-7242
Scherer, Box 250, Ewing, VA 24248/615-733-2615; FAX: 615-733-2073
Schiffman, Curt, 3017 Kevin Cr., Idaho Falls, ID 83402/208-524-4684
Schiffman, Mike, 8233 S. Crystal Springs, McCammon, ID 83250/208-254-9114
Schiffman, Norman, 3017 Kevin Cr., Idaho Falls, ID 83402/208-524-4684
Schmidpke, Karl, P.O. Box 51692, New Berlin, WI 53151
Schmidt & Bender (See Jaeger, Inc., Paul/Dunn's)
Schmidt, Herbert (See U.S. importer—Sportarms of Florida)
Schmidtman Custom Ammunition, 6 Gilbert Court, Cotati, CA 94931
Schneider Bullets, 3655 West 214th St., Fairview Park, OH 44126
Schneider Rifle Barrels, Inc., Gary, 12202 N. 62nd Pl., Scottsdale, AZ 85254/602-948-2525
Schrade Cutlery Corp., Rt. 209 North, Ellenville, NY 12428/914-647-7600
Schrimsher's Custom Knifemaker's Supply, Bob, P.O. Box 308, Emory, TX 75440/903-473-3330; FAX: 903-473-2235
Schulz Industries, 16247 Minnesota Ave., Paramount, CA 90723/213-439-5903
Schumakers Gun Shop, William, 512 Prouty Corner Lp. A, Colville, WA 99114/509-684-4848
Schwartz Custom Guns, David W., 2505 Waller St., Eau Claire, WI 54703/715-832-1735
Schwartz Custom Guns, Wayne E., 970 E. Britton Rd., Morrice, MI 48857/517-625-4079
Scobey Duck & Goose Calls, Glynn, Rt. 3, Box 37, Newbern, TN 38059/901-643-6241
Scot Powder Co., 1200 Talley Road, Wilmington, DE 19809/302-764-9779
Scot Powder Co. of Ohio, Inc., 430 Powder Plant Rd., McArthur, OH 45651/614-596-2706; FAX: 614-596-4050
Scotch Hunting Products Co., Inc., 6619 Oak Orchard Rd., Elba, NY 14058/716-757-9958; FAX: 716-757-9066
Scott Fine Guns, Inc., Thad, P.O. Box 412, Indianola, MS 38751/601-887-5929
Scott, Inc., Tyler, 313 Rugby Ave., Terrace Park, OH 45174/513-831-7603
Scott/McDougall Custom Gunsmiths, 880 Piner Rd., Suite 50, Santa Rosa, CA 95403/707-546-2264
S.C.R.C., P.O. Box 660, Kary, TX 77492-0660/713-492-6332; FAX: 713-578-3134
Scruggs' Game Calls, Stanley, Rt. 1, Hwy. 661, Cullen, VA 23934/804-542-4241, 800-323-4828
Seattle Binocular & Scope Repair Co., P.O. Box 46094, Seattle, WA 98146/206-932-3733
Second Chance Body Armor, P.O. Box 578, Central Lake, MI 49622/616-544-5721; FAX: 616-544-9824
Security Awareness & Firearms Education (See S.A.F.E.)
Seebeck Assoc., R.E., P.O. Box 59752, Dallas, TX 75229
Seecamp Co., Inc., L.W., P.O. Box 255, New Haven, CT 06502/203-877-3429
Seligman Shooting Products, Box 133, Seligman, AZ 86337/602-422-3607
Selsi Co., Inc., 40 Veterans Blvd., Carlstadt, NJ 07072-0497/201-935-5851
Semmer, Charles, 7885 Cyd Dr., Denver, CO 80221/303-429-6947
Service Armament, 689 Bergen Blvd., Ridgefield, NJ 07657
Servus Footwear Co., 1136 2nd St., Rock Island, IL 61204-3610/309-786-7741; FAX: 309-786-9808
SGS Importers International, Inc., 1907 Hwy. 35, Ocean, NJ 07712/908-531-9424; FAX: 908-531-1520
S.G.S. Sporting Guns Srl., F1 Milanofiori, Assago, 20090 ITALY/2-8241144-5; FAX: 2-8254644
Shane's Gunsmithing, P.O. Box 321, Hwy. 51 S., Minocqua, WI 54548/715-356-5414
Shappy Bullets, 76 Milldale Ave., Plantsville, CT 06479/203-621-3704
Sharon Rifle Barrel Co., 14396 D. Tuolumne Rd., Sonora, CA 95370/209-532-4139
Sharps Arms Co., Inc., C. (See Montana Armory, Inc.)
Shaw's Finest in Guns, 1255 N. Broadway 351, Escondido, CA 92026-2858
Shaw, Inc., E.R. (See Small Arms Mfg. Co.)
Shay's Gunsmithing, 931 Marvin Ave., Lebanon, PA 17042
Sheffield Knifemakers Supply, P.O. Box 141, Deland, FL 32721/904-775-6453; FAX: 904-774-5754
Shell Shack, 113 E. Main, Laurel, MT 59044/406-628-8986
Shepherd Scope Ltd., Box 189, Waterloo, NE 68069/402-779-2424; FAX: 402-779-4010
Sheridan Products, Inc. (See Benjamin/Sheridan Co.)
Sheridan USA, Inc., Austin, P.O. Box 577, Durham, CT 06422
Sherk, Dan A., 1311-105 Ave., Dawson Creek, B.C. V1G 2L9, CANADA/604-782-3720
Sherwood Intl. Export Corp., 18714 Parthenia St., Northridge, CA 91324/818-349-7600
Sherwood, George, 46 N. River Dr., Roseburg, OR 97470/503-672-3159
Shilen Rifles, Inc., P.O. Box 1300, 205 Metro Park Blvd., Ennis, TX 75119/214-875-5318; FAX: 214-875-1442
Shiloh Rifle Mfg., 201 Centennial Dr., Big Timber, MT 59011/406-932-4454; FAX: 406-932-5627
Shirley Co. Gun & Riflemakers Ltd., J.A., P.O. Box 368, High Wycombe, Bucks. HP13 6YN, ENGLAND/0494-446883; FAX: 0494-463685
Shockley, Harold H., 204 E. Farmington Rd., Hanna City, IL 61536/309-565-4524
Shoemaker & Sons, Inc., Tex, 714 W. Cienega Ave., San Dimas, CA 91750/714-592-2071; FAX: 714-592-2378
Shooter Shop, The, 221 N. Main, Butte, MT 59701/406-723-3842
Shooter's Choice, 16770 Hilltop Park Place, Chagrin Falls, OH 44022/216-543-8808; FAX: 216-543-8811
Shooter's Edge, Inc., P.O.Box 769, Trinidad, CO 81082
Shooter's World, 3828 N. 28th Ave., Phoenix, AZ 85017/602-266-0170
Shooters Accessory Supply (See Corbin, Inc.)
Shooters Supply, 1120 Tieton Dr., Yakima, WA 98902/509-452-1181
Shootin Accessories, Ltd., P.O. Box 6810, Auburn, CA 95604/916-889-2220
Shootin' Shack, Inc., 1065 Silver Beach Rd., Riviera Beach, FL 33403/407-842-0990
Shooting Arts Ltd., Box 621399, Littleton, CO 80162/303-933-2539
Shooting Chrony, Inc., P.O. Box 101 LP, Niagara Falls, NY 14304/416-276-6292; FAX: 416-276-6295
Shooting Gallery, The, 8070 Southern Blvd., Boardman, OH 44512/216-726-7788
Shooting Specialties (See Titus, Daniel)
Shotgun Shop, The, 14145 Proctor Ave., Suite 3, Industry, CA 91746/818-855-2737; FAX: 818-855-2735
Shotguns Unlimited, 2307 Fon Du Lac Rd., Richmond, VA 23229/804-752-7115
Shurkatch Corp., P.O. Box 850, Richfield Springs, NY 13439/315-858-1470; FAX: 315-858-2969
Siegrist Gun Shop, 8754 Turtle Road, Whittemore, MI 48770
Sierra Bullets, 1400 W. Henry St., Sedalia, MO 65301/816-827-6300; FAX: 816-827-4999
Sierra Specialty Prod. Co., 1344 Oakhurst Ave., Los Altos, CA 94024
SIG, CH-8212 Neuhausen, SWITZERLAND (U.S. importer—Mandall Shooting Supplies, Inc.)
SIG-Sauer (See U.S. importer—Sigarms, Inc.)
Sigarms, Inc., Industrial Drive, Exeter, NH 03833/603-772-2302; FAX: 603-772-9082
Sight Shop, The, John G. Lawson, 1802 E. Columbia Ave., Tacoma, WA 98404/206-474-5465
Sile Distributors, Inc., 7 Centre Market Pl., New York, NY 10013/212-925-4389; FAX: 212-925-3149
Silencio (See Safety Direct)
Silent Hunter, 1100 Newton Ave., W. Collingswood, NJ 08107/609-854-3276
Siler Locks, 7 Acton Woods Rd., Candler, NC 28715/704-667-9991
Silhouette Leathers, P.O. Box 1161, Gunnison, CO 81230/303-641-6639
Silver Eagle Machining, 18007 N. 69th Ave., Glendale, AZ 85308
Silver Ridge Gun Shop (See Goodwin, Fred)
Silver-Tip Corp., Rt. 1, Box 211-C, Liberty, MS 39645/601-384-5830
Simmons Enterprises, Ernie, 709 East Elizabethtown Rd., Manheim, PA 17545/717-664-4040
Simmons, Jerry, 715 Middlebury St., Goshen, IN 46526/219-533-8546
Simmons Outdoor Corp., 2571 Executive Ctr. Circle E, Tallahassee, FL 32301/904-878-5100; FAX: 904-878-0300
Sinclair, Fred, 2330 Wayne Haven St., Fort Wayne, IN 46803/219-493-1858
Sinclair International, Inc., 2330 Wayne Haven St., Fort Wayne, IN 46803/219-493-1858; FAX: 219-493-2530
Sinclair, W.P., Box 1209, Warminster, Wiltshire BA12 9XJ, ENGLAND/01044-985-218544; FAX: 01044-985-214111
Single Shot, Inc. (See Montana Armory, Inc.)
Singletary, Kent, 7516 W. Sells, Phoenix, AZ 85033/602-789-6004
Sioux Bullets, P.O. Box 3696, Midland, TX 79702
Sipes Gun Shop, 7415 Asher Ave., Little Rock, AR 72204/501-565-8480
Siskiyou Gun Works (See Donnelly, C.P.)
Six Enterprises, 320-D Turtle Creek Ct., San Jose, CA 95125/408-999-0201; FAX: 408-999-0216
Skaggs, R.E., P.O. Box 34, 1217 S. Church, Princeton, IL 61356/815-875-8207
SKB Arms Co., C.P.O. Box 1401, Tokyo, JAPAN (U.S. importers—G.U., Inc.; Hanus Birdguns, Bill; Simmons Enterprises, Ernie)
S.K. Guns, Inc., 3041A Main Ave., Fargo, ND 58103/701-293-4867; FAX: 701-232-0001
Skeoch, Brian R., P.O. Box 279, Glenrock, WY 82637/307-436-9804
Skip's Machine, 364 29 Road, Grand Junction, CO 81501/303-245-5417
Sklany, Steve, 566 Birch Grove Dr., Kalispell, MT 59901/406-755-4257
SKR Industries, POB 1382, San Angelo, TX 76902/915-658-3133
S.L.A.P. Industries, P.O. Box 1121, Parklands 2121, SOUTH AFRICA
Slezak, Jerome F., 1290 Marlowe, Lakewood (Cleveland), OH 44107/216-221-1668
Slings & Arrows, RD 1, Box 91A, Barnet, VT 05821/802-633-3314; FAX: 802-684-1108
Slings 'N Things, Inc., 8909 Bedford Circle, Suite 11, Omaha, NE 68134/402-571-6954; FAX: 402-571-7082
Slipshot MTS Group, P.O. Box 5, Postal Station D, Etobicoke, Ont., CANADA M9A 4X1/FAX: 416-762-0962
Slug Site Co., Ozark Wilds, Rt. 2, Box 158, Versailles, MO 65084/314-378-6430
Small Arms Mfg. Co., 611 Thoms Run Rd., Bridgeville, PA 15017/412-221-4343; FAX: 412-221-8443
Small Custom Mould & Bullet Co., Box 17211, Tucson, AZ 85731
Small Group Bullets, P.O. Box 20, Mertzon, TX 76941/915-835-4751
Smires, Clifford L., 28269 Old Schoolhouse Rd., Columbus, NJ 08022/609-298-3158
Smith & Wesson, 2100 Roosevelt Ave., Springfield, MA 01102/413-781-8300
Smith Saddlery, Jesse W., N. 1325 Division, Spokane, WA 99202/509-325-0622
Smith Whetstone Co., Inc., 1700 Sleepy Valley Rd., P.O. Box 5095, Hot Springs, AR 71902-5095/501-321-2244; FAX: 501-321-9232
Smith, Art, 4124 Thrushwood Lane, Minnetonka, MN 55345/612-935-7829
Smith, Mark A., 200 N. 9th, Sinclair, WY 82334/307-324-7929
Smith, Michael, 620 Nye Circle, Chattanooga, TN 37405/615-267-8341
Smith, Ron, 5869 Straley, Ft. Worth, TX 76114/817-732-6768
Smokey Valley Rifles (See Lutz Engraving, Ron)
Snapp's Gunshop, 6911 E. Washington Rd., Clare, MI 48617/517-386-9226
Snider Stocks, Walter S., Rt. 2 P.O. Box 147, Denton, NC 27239
Sno-Seal (See Atsko, Sno-Seal)
Societa Armi Bresciane Srl., Via Artigiani 93, Gardone Val Trompia, ITALY 25063/30-8911640, 30-8911648
Solothurn (See U.S. importer—Sile Distributors)
Sonderman, Robert, 735 Kenton Dr., Charleston, IL 61920/217-345-5429
Soque River Knives, P.O. Box 880, Clarkesville, GA 30523/706-754-8500
SOS Products Co. (See Buck Stix—SOS Products Co.)
Sotheby's, 1334 York Ave. at 72nd St., New York, NY 10021
Sound Technology, P.O. Box 1132, Kodiak, AK 99615/907-486-8448
South Bend Replicas, Inc., 61650 Oak Rd., South Bend, IN 46614/219-289-4500
South Central Research Corp. (See S.C.R.C.)
Southeastern Community College, 1015 S. Gear Ave., West Burlington, IA 52655/319-752-2731
Southern Ammunition Co., Inc., Rt. 1, Box 6B, Latta, SC 29565/803-752-7751; FAX: 803-752-2022
Southern Armory, The, Rt. 2, Box 134, Woodlawn, VA 24381/703-236-7835; FAX: 703-236-3714
Southern Bloomer Mfg. Co., P.O. Box 1621, Bristol, TN 37620/615-878-6660
Southwest Institute of Firearms Training (See S.W.I.F.T.)
Southwind Sanctions, P.O. Box 445, Aledo, TX 76008/817-441-8917
Sparks, Milt, 605 E. 44th St. No. 2, Boise, ID 83714-4800
Specialized Weapons, Inc. (See Tapco, Inc.)
Specialty Gunsmithing, Lynn McMurdo, P.O. Box 404, Afton, WY 83110/307-886-5535
Specialty Shooters Supply, Inc., 3325 Griffin Rd., Suite 9mm, Fort Lauderdale, FL 33317
Speedfeed, Inc., P.O. Box 258, Lafayette, CA 94549/510-284-2929; FAX: 510-284-2879
Speer Products, Div. of Blount, Inc., P.O. Box 856, Lewiston, ID 83501/208-746-2351
Spegel, Craig, P.O. Box 108, Bay City, OR 97107/503-377-2697
Speiser, Fred D., 2229 Dearborn, Missoula, MT 59801/406-549-8133
Spence, George W., 115 Locust St., Steele, MO 63877/314-695-4916
Spencer Reblue Service, 1820 Tupelo Trail, Holt, MI 48842/517-694-7474
SPG Lubricants, Box 761-H, Livingston, MT 59047
Sphinx Engineering SA, Ch. des Grandes-Vies 2, CH-2900 Porrentruy, SWITZERLAND/41 66 66 73 81; FAX: 41 66 66 30 90
SPI, 215 Poppleton St., Birmingham, MI 48009-5725
Spokhandguns, Inc., 1206 Fig St., Benton City, WA 99320/509-588-5255
Sport Flite Manufacturing Co., P.O. Box 1082, Bloomfield Hills, MI 48303/313-647-3747
Sport Specialties (See Owen, Harry)
Sportarms of Florida, 5555 NW 36 Ave., Miami, FL 33142/305-635-2411; FAX: 305-634-4536
Sporting Arms Mfg., Inc., 801 Hall Ave., Littlefield, TX 79339/806-385-5665; FAX: 806-385-3394

Sports Innovations, Inc., P.O. Box 5181, 8505 Jacksboro Hwy., Wichita Falls, TX 76307/817-723-6015
Sports Support Systems, Inc., 28416 Pacheco, Mission Viejo, CA 92692/714-367-0343
Sportsman Supply Co., 714 East Eastwood, P.O. Box 650, Marshall, MO 65340/816-886-9393
Sportsman's Communicators, 588 Radcliffe Ave., Pacific Palisades, CA 90272/800-538-3752
Sportsmatch Ltd., 16 Summer St., Leighton Buzzard, Bedfordshire, LU7 8HT ENGLAND/0525-381638; FAX: 0525-851236
Sportsmen's Exchange & Western Gun Traders, Inc., 560 S. "C" St., Oxnard, CA 93030/805-483-1917
Spradlin's, 113 Arthur St., Pueblo, CO 81004/719-543-9462
Springfield, Inc., 25144 Ridge Rd., Colona, IL 61241/309-441-6002; FAX: 309-441-6003
Springfield Sporters, Inc., RD 1, Penn Run, PA 15765/412-254-2626; FAX: 412-254-9173
Spyderco, Inc., P.O. Box 800, Golden, CO 80402/800-525-7770
SSK Co., 220 N. Belvidere Ave., York, PA 17404/717-854-2897
SSK Industries, 721 Woodvue Lane, Wintersville, OH 43952/614-264-0176; FAX: 614-264-2257
St. Lawrence Sales, Inc., 12 W. Fint St., Lake Orion, MI 48035/313-693-7760; 313-693-7718
Stackpole Books, P.O. Box 1831, Harrisburg, PA 17105/717-234-5041; FAX: 717-234-1359
Stafford Bullets, 1920 Tustin Ave., Philadelphia, PA 19152
Stalker, Inc., P.O. Box 21, Fishermans Wharf Rd., Malakoff, TX 75148/903-489-1010
Stalwart Corp., P.O. Box 357, Pocatello, ID 83204/208-232-7899
Stanley Bullets, 2085 Heatheridge Ln., Reno, NV 89509
Star Bonifacio Echeverria S.A., Torrekva 3, Eibar, SPAIN 20600/43-117340; FAX: 43-111524 (U.S. importer—Interarms)
Star Custom Bullets, P.O. Box 608, 468 Main St., Ferndale, CA 95536/707-786-4040; FAX: 707-786-9117
Star Machine Works, 418 10th Ave., San Diego, CA 92101/619-232-3216
Star Reloading Co., Inc., 5520 Rock Hampton Ct., Indianapolis, IN 46268/317-872-5840
Stark's Bullet Mfg., 2580 Monroe St., Eugene, OR 97405
Starlight Training Center, Inc., Rt. 1, P.O. Box 88, Bronaugh, MO 64728/417-843-3555
Starnes, Ken, 32900 SW Laurelview Rd., Hillsboro, OR 97123/503-628-0705
Starrett Co., L.S., 121 Crescent St., Athol, MA 01331/617-249-3551
Starshot Holduxa, Bolognise 125, Miraflores, Lima PERU
State Arms Gun Co., 815 S. Division St., Waunakee, WI 53597/608-849-5800
Steel Reloading Components Inc., P.O. Box 812, Washington, IN 47501/812-254-3775; FAX: 812-254-7269
Steelman's Gun Shop, 10465 Beers Rd., Swartz Creek, MI 48473/313-735-4884
Steffens, Ron, 18396 Mariposa Creek Rd., Willits, CA 95490/707-485-0873
Stegall, James B., 26 Forest Rd., Wallkill, NY 12589
Steger, James R., 1131 Dorsey Pl., Plainfield, NJ 07062
Steves House of Guns, Rt. 1, Minnesota City, MN 55959/507-689-2573
Stevi Machine, Inc., 4004 Hwy. 93 North, Stevensville, MT 59870/406-777-5401
Stewart Game Calls, Inc., Johnny, P.O. Box 7954, 5100 Fort Ave., Waco, TX 76714/817-772-3261
Stewart's Gunsmithing, P.O. Box 5854, Pietersburg North 0750, Transvaal, SOUTH AFRICA/01521-89401
Steyr Mannlicher AG, Mannlicherstrasse 1, P.O.B. 1000, A-4400 Steyr, AUSTRIA/0043-7252-67331; FAX: 0043-7252-68621 (U.S. importer—GSI, Inc.)
Steyr-Daimler-Puch, Schonauerstrasse 5, A-4400 Steyr AUSTRIA (U.S. importer—GSI, Inc.)
Stoeger Industries, 55 Ruta Ct., S. Hackensack, NJ 07606/201-440-2700, 800-631-0722; FAX: 201-440-2707
Stoeger Publishing Co. (See Stoeger Industries)
Stone Enterprises Ltd., Rt. 609, P.O. Box 335, Wicomico Church, VA 22579/804-580-5114; FAX: 804-580-8421
Stoney Baroque Shooters Supply, John Richards, Rt. 2, Box 325, Bedford, KY 40006/502-255-7222
Stoney Point Products, Inc., 124 Stoney Point Rd., Courtland, MN 56021/507-354-3360; FAX: 507-354-7236
Storey, Dale A. (See DGS, Inc.)
Stott's Creek Armory, Inc., RR1, Box 70, Morgantown, IN 46160/317-878-5489
Stratco, Inc., 200 E. Center St., Kalispell, MT 59901/406-755-4034; FAX: 406-257-4753
Strawbridge, Victor W., 6 Pineview Dr., Dover, NH 03820/603-742-0013
Streamlight, Inc., 1030 W. Germantown Pike, Norristown, PA 19403/215-631-0600
Strong Holster Co., 105 Maplewood Ave., Gloucester, MA 01930/508-281-3300; FAX: 508-281-6321
Stroup, Earl R., 30506 Flossmoor Way, Hayward, CA 94544/415-471-1549
Strutz Rifle Barrels, Inc., W.C., P.O. Box 611, Eagle River, WI 54521/715-479-4766
Stuart Products, Inc., P.O. Box 1587, Easley, SC 29641/803-859-9360
Stuart, V. Pat, Rt. 1, Box 242-B, P.O. Box 232, Weyers Cave, VA 24486/703-234-0816
Sturm, Ruger & Co., Inc., Lacey Place, Southport, CT 06490/203-259-7843
Su-Press-On, Inc., P.O. Box 09161, Detroit, MI 48209/313-842-4222 7:30-11p.m. Mon-Thurs.
Summit Specialties, Inc., P.O. Box 786, Decatur, AL 35602/205-353-0634
Sundance Industries, Inc., 25163 W. Avenue Stanford, Valencia, CA 91355/805-257-4807
Sun Jammer Products, Inc., 9600 N. IH-35, Austin, TX 78753/512-837-8696
Sun Welding Safe Co., 290 Easy St. No.3, Simi Valley, CA 93065/805-584-6678
Super Vel, Hamilton Rd., Rt. 2, P.O. Box 1398, Fond du Lac, WI 54935
Sure Shot of LA, Inc., 103 Coachman Dr., Houma, LA 70360/504-876-6709
Sure-Shot Game Calls, Inc., P.O. Box 816, 6835 Capitol, Groves, TX 77619/409-962-1636; FAX: 409-962-5465
Survival Arms, Inc., 4500 Pine Cone Place, Cocoa, FL 32922/407-633-4880; FAX: 407-633-4975
Survival Books, The Larder, 11106 Magnolia Blvd., North Hollywood, CA 91601/818-763-0804
Svon Corp., 280 Eliot St., Ashland, MA 01721/508-881-8852
Swampfire Shop, The (See Peterson Gun Shop, Inc., A.W.)
Swann, D.J., 5 Orsova Close, Eltham North, Vic. 3095, AUSTRALIA/03-431-0323
Swanndri New Zealand, 152 Elm Ave., Burlingame, CA 94010/415-347-6158
SwaroSports, Inc. (See JägerSports, Ltd.)
Swarovski Optik North America Ltd., One Wholesale Way, Cranston, RI 02920/401-946-2220; FAX: 800-426-3089
Sweet Home, Inc., P.O. Box 900, Orrville, OH 44667-0900
Swenson's 45 Shop, A.D., P.O. Box 606, Fallbrook, CA 92028
S.W.I.F.T., 4610 Blue Diamond Rd., Las Vegas, NV 89118/702-897-1100
Swift Bullet Co., P.O. Box 27, 201 Main St., Quinter, KS 67752/913-754-3959; FAX: 913-754-2359
Swift Instruments, Inc., 952 Dorchester Ave., Boston, MA 02125/617-436-2960; FAX: 617-436-3232
Swift River Gunworks, Inc., 450 State St., Belchertown, MA 01007/413-323-4052
Swiss Army Knives, Inc., 151 Long Hill Crossroads, 37 Canal St., Shelton, CT 06484/800-243-4032
Swivel Machine Works, Inc., 167 Cherry St., Suite 286, Milford, CT 06460/203-926-1840; FAX: 203-726-9431
Szweda, Robert (See RMS Custom Gunsmithing)

T

3-D Ammunition & Bullets, 112 W. Plum St., P.O. Box J, Doniphan, NE 68832/402-845-2285; FAX: 402-845-6546
3-Ten Corp., P.O. Box 269, Feeding Hills, MA 01030/413-789-2086
10-X Products Group, 2915 Lyndon B. Johnson Freeway, Suite 133, Dallas, TX 75234/214-243-4016
300 Gunsmith Service, Inc., 6850 S. Yosemite Ct., Englewood, CO 80112/303-773-0300
Tabler Marketing, 2554 Lincoln Blvd. 555, Marina Del Rey, CA 90291-5082/818-366-7485; FAX: 818-831-3441
TacTell, Inc., P.O. Box 5654, Maryville, TN 37802/615-982-7855
Tactical Training Center, 574 Miami Bluff Ct., Loveland, OH 45140/513-677-8229
Talley, Dave, P.O. Box 821, Glenrock, WY 82637/307-436-8724
Talmage, William G., RR16, Box 102A, Brazil, IN 47834/812-442-0804
Tamarack Prods.,Inc., P.O. Box 625, Wauconda, IL 60084/708-526-9333
Tanfoglio S.r.l., Fratelli, via Valtrompia 39, 41, 25068 Gardone V.T., Brescia, ITALY/30-8910361; FAX: 30-8910183 (U.S. importer—E.A.A. Corp.)
Tanglefree Industries, 16102 Duggans Rd., Grass Valley, CA 95949
Tank's Rifle Shop, 1324 Ohio St., P.O. Box 474, Fremont, NE 68025/402-727-1317
Tanner (See U.S. importer—Mandall Shooting Supplies, Inc.)
Tapco, Inc., P.O. Box 546, Smyrna, GA 30081/404-435-9782, 800-359-6195; FAX: 404-333-9798
Taracorp Industries, Inc., 16th & Cleveland Blvd., Granite City, IL 62040/618-451-4400
Targot Man, Inc., 49 Gerald Dr., Manchester, CT 06040/203-646-8335; FAX: 203-646-8335
Tasco Sales, Inc., 7600 NW 84th Ave., Miami, FL 33122/305-591-3670; FAX: 305-592-5895
Taurus Firearms, Inc., 16175 NW 49th Ave., Miami, FL 33014/305-624-1115; FAX: 305-623-7506
Taurus International Firearms (See U.S. importer—Taurus Firearms, Inc.)
Taurus, S.A., Forjas, Avenida Do Forte 511, Porto Alegre, BRAZIL 91360/55 512-40 22 44
Taylor & Robbins, P.O. Box 164, Rixford, PA 16745/814-966-3233
Taylor's & Co., Inc., 299 Broad Ave., Winchester, VA 22602/703-722-2017; FAX: 703-722-2018
TCCI. P.O. Box 302, Phoenix, AZ 85001/602-237-3823; FAX: 602-237-3858
TDP Industries, Inc., 603 Airport Blvd., Doylestown, PA 18901/215-345-8687
Techni-Mec, Via Gitti s.n., 25060 Marcheno, ITALY
Tecnolegno S.p.A., Via A. Locatelli, 6, 10, 24019 Zogno, ITALY/0345-91114; FAX: 0345-93254
Tele-Optics, 5514 W. Lawrence Ave., Chicago, IL 60630/312-283-7757
Tele-Optics, Inc., P.O. Box 176, 219 E. Higgins Rd., Gilberts, IL 60136/708-426-7444
Teledyne Co., 290 E. Prairie St., Crystal Lake, IL 60014
Ten-Ring Precision, Inc., 1449 Blue Crest Lane, San Antonio, TX 78232/512-494-3063; FAX: 512-494-3066
Tennessee Valley Mfg., P.O. Box 1175, Corinth, MS 38834/601-286-5014
Tepeco, P.O. Box 342, Friendswood, TX 77546/713-482-2702
Testing Systems, Inc., 220 Pegasus Ave., Northvale, NJ 07647
TETRA Gun Lubricants, 1812 Margaret Ave., Annapolis, MD 21401/410-268-6451; FAX: 410-268-8377
Texas Arms, P.O. Box 154906, Waco, TX 76715/817-776-5294
Texas Longhorn Arms, Inc., 5959 W. Loop South, Suite 424, Bellaire, TX 77401/713-660-6323; FAX: 713-660-0493
Texas Platers Supply, 2453 W. Five Mile Parkway, Dallas, TX 75233/214-330-7168
T.F.C. S.p.A., Via G. Marconi 118, B, Villa Carcina, Brescia 25069, ITALY/030-881271; FAX: 030-881826
Theis, Terry, P.O. Box 535, Fredericksburg, TX 78624/512-997-6778
Theoben Engineering (See U.S. importer—Air Rifle Specialists)
Thiewes, George W., 1846 Allen Lane, St. Charles, IL 60174/708-584-1383
Things Unlimited, 235 N. Kimbau, Casper, WY 82601/307-234-5277
Thirion Hand Engraving, Denise, P.O. Box 408, Graton, CA 95444/707-829-1876
Thomas, Charles C., 2600 S. First St., Springfield, IL 62794/217-789-8980; FAX: 217-789-9130
Thompson Bullet Lube Co., P.O. Box 472343, Garland, TX 75047/214-271-8063; FAX: 214-840-6743
Thompson Precision, 110 Mary St., P.O. Box 251, Warren, IL 61087/815-745-3625
Thompson Target Technology, 618 Roslyn Ave., SW, Canton, OH 44710/216-453-7707; FAX: 216-478-4723
Thompson, Norm, 18905 NW Thurman St., Portland, OR 97209
Thompson, Randall (See Highline Machine Co.)
Thompson/Center Arms, Farmington Rd., P.O. Box 5002, Rochester, NH 03867/603-332-2394
Threat Management Institute, 1 St. Francis Place 2801, San Francisco, CA 94107/415-777-0303
Thunder Mountain Arms, P.O. Box 593, Oak Harbor, WA 98277/206-679-4657; FAX: 206-675-1114
Thunderbird Cartridge Co., Inc., (See TCCI)
Thurston Sports, Inc., RD 3 Donovan Rd., Auburn, NY 13021/315-253-0966
Tiger-Hunt, Michael D. Barton, Box 379, Beaverdale, PA 15921/814-472-5161
Tikka (See U.S. importer—Stoeger Industries)
Tillinghast, James C., P.O. Box 405DG, Hancock, NH 03449/603-525-4049
Timber Heirloom Products, 618 Roslyn Ave. SW, Canton, OH 44710/216-453-7707; FAX: 216-478-4723
Timney Mfg., Inc., 3065 W. Fairmont Ave., Phoenix, AZ 85017/602-274-2999; FAX: 602-241-0361
Tink's Safariland Hunting Corp., P.O. Box 244, Madison, GA 30650/404-342-4915
Tinks & Ben Lee Hunting Products (See Wellington Outdoors)
Tioga Engineering Co., Inc., P.O. Box 913, 13 Cone St., Wellsboro, PA 16901/717-662-2730
Tippman Pneumatics, Inc., 3518 Adams Center Rd., Fort Wayne, IN 46806/219-749-6022; FAX: 219-749-6619
Tirelli, Snc Di Tirelli Primo E.C., Via Matteotti No. 359, Gardone V.T., Brescia, ITALY 25063/030-8912819; FAX: 030-832240
Titus, Daniel, Shooting Specialties, 872 Penn St., Bryn Mawr, PA 19010/215-525-8829
TMI Products, 930 S. Plumer Ave., Tucson, AZ 85719/602-792-1075; FAX: 602-792-0093
Tokarav (See U.S. importer—Sportarms of Florida)
Tom's Gun Repair, Thomas G. Ivanoff, 76-6 Rt. Southfork Rd., Cody, WY 82414/307-587-6949
Tom's Gunshop, 3601 Central Ave., Hot Springs, AR 71913/501-624-3856
Tomboy, Inc., P.O. Box 846, Dallas, OR 97338/503-623-8405
Tooley, David, 516 Creek Meadow Dr., Gastonia, NC 28054
Torel, Inc., 1053 N. South St., P.O. Box 592, Yoakum, TX 77995/512-293-2341; FAX: 512-293-3413
Totally Dependable Products (See TDP Industries, Inc.)
Track of the Wolf, Inc., P.O. Box 6, Osseo, MN 55369-0006/612-424-2500; FAX: 612-424-9860
Tradewinds, Inc., P.O. Box 1191, 2339-41 Tacoma Ave. S., Tacoma, WA 98401/206-272-4887
Traditions, P.O. Box 235, Deep River, CT 06417/203-526-9555; FAX: 203-526-4564
Trafalgar Square, P.O. Box 257, N. Pomfret, VT 05053/802-457-1911
Traft Gunshop, P.O. Box 1078, Buena Vista, CO 81211
Trail Guns Armory, Inc., 1422 E. Main St., League City, TX 77573/713-332-5833; FAX: 713-332-5833
Trail Timer Co., 1992-A Suburban Ave., P.O. Box 19722, St. Paul, MN 55119/612-738-0925

Trail Visions, 5800 N. Ames Terrace, Glendale, WI 53209/414-228-1328
Trammco, 839 Gold Run Rd., Boulder, CO 80302
Trappers Trading, P.O. Box 26946, Austin, TX 78755/800-788-9334
Trax America, Inc., P.O. Box 898, 1150 Eldridge, Forrest City, AR 72335/800-232-2327
Tread Corp., 1764 Granby St. NE, Roanoke, VA 24012/703-982-6881
Treemaster, P.O. Box 247, Guntersville, AL 35976/205-878-3597
Treso, Inc., P.O. Box 4640, Pagosa Springs, CO 81157/303-731-2295
Trevallion Gunstocks, 9 Old Mountain Rd., Cape Neddick, ME 03902/207-361-1130
Trico Plastics, 590 S. Vincent Ave., Azusa, CA 91702
Trijicon, Inc., P.O. Box 2130, Farmington Hills, MI 48333/313-553-4960; FAX: 313-553-6129
Trinidad State Junior College, Gunsmithing Dept., 600 Prospect St., Trinidad, CO 81082/719-846-5631; FAX: 719-846-5667
Triple-K Mfg. Co., Inc., 2222 Commercial St., San Diego, CA 92113/619-232-2066; FAX: 619-232-7675
Trius Traps, P.O. Box 25, 221 S. Miami Ave., Cleves, OH 45002/513-941-5682; FAX: 513-941-7970
Trophy Bonded Bullets, Inc., 900 S. Loop W., Suite 190, Houston, TX 77054/713-645-4499; FAX: 713-741-6393
Trotman, Ken, 135 Ditton Walk, Unit 11, Cambridge CB5 8QD, ENGLAND/0223-211030; FAX: 0223-212317
Tru-Balance Knife Co., 2155 Tremont Blvd. NW, Grand Rapids, MI 49504/616-453-3679
Tru-Square Metal Prods., Inc., 640 First St. SW, P.O. Box 585, Auburn, WA 98001/206-833-2310
True Flight Bullet Co., 5581 Roosevelt St., Whitehall, PA 18052/800-875-3625; FAX: 215-262-7806
Trulock Tool, Broad St., Whigham, GA 31797/912-762-4678
T.S.W. Conversions, Inc., E. 115 Crain Rd., Paramus, NJ 07650-4017/201-265-1618
Tucker, James C., P.O. Box 38790, Sacramento, CA 95838/916-923-0571
Turnbull Restoration, Doug, 6426 County Rd. 30, Holcomb, NY 14469/716-657-6338
Tuscano, Tony, P.O. Box 461, Wickliffe, OH 44092/216-943-1175
Twin Pine Armory, P.O. Box 58, Hwy. 6, Adna, WA 98522/206-748-4590; FAX: 205-748-7011
Tyler Mfg.-Dist., Melvin, 1326 W. Britton Rd., Oklahoma City, OK 73114/405-842-8044

U

Uberti USA, Inc., 362 Limerock Rd., P.O. Box 469, Lakeville, CT 06039/203-435-8068; FAX: 203-435-8146
Uberti, Aldo, Casella Postale 43, I-25063 Gardone V.T., ITALY (U.S. importers—Cimarron Arms; Navy Arms Co; Uberti USA, Inc.)
Ugartechea S.A., Ignacio, Chonta 26, Eibar, SPAIN 20600/43-121257; FAX: 43-121669 (U.S. importers—Hanus Birdguns, Bill; Mandall Shooting Supplies, Inc.; Precision Sports)
Ulrich, Doc & Bud (See D.O.C. Specialists, Inc.)
Ultra Light Arms, Inc., P.O. Box 1270, 214 Price St., Granville, WV 26534/304-599-5687
Uncle Mike's (See Michaels of Oregon Co.)
Unertl Optical Co., Inc., John, 308 Clay Ave., P.O. Box 818, Mars, PA 16046-0818/412-625-3810
Unick's Gunsmithing, 5005 Center Rd., Lowellville, OH 44436/216-536-8015
Unique/M.A.P.F., 10, Les Allees, 64700 Hendaye, FRANCE 64700/33-59 20 71 93 (U.S. importer—Nygord Precision Products)
United Binocular Co., 9043 S. Western Ave., Chicago, IL 60620
United Cutlery Corp., 1425 United Blvd., Sevierville, TN 37862/615-428-2532
United States Ammunition Co. (See USAC)
United States Products Co., 518 Melwood Ave., Pittsburgh, PA 15213/412-621-2130
Universal Clay Pigeon Traps, Unit 5, Dalacre Industrial Estate, Wilbarston,ENGLAND LE16 8QL/011-44536771625; FAX: 011-44536771625
Upper Missouri Trading Co., 304 Harold St., Crofton, NE 68730/402-388-4844
USAC, 4500-15th St. East, Tacoma, WA 98424/206-922-7589
U.S. Arms Corp., 444 Brickell Ave., Suite P-26, Miami, FL 33131/305-371-7211
U.S. Optics Technologies, Inc., Div. of Zeitz Optics, U.S.A., 1501 E. Chapman Ave., Suite 306, Fullerton, CA 92631/714-879-8922; FAX: 714-449-0941
U.S. Repeating Arms Co., Inc., 275 Winchester Ave., New Haven, CT 06511/203-789-5000; FAX: 203-789-5071
Utica Cutlery Co., 820 Noyes St., Utica, NY 13503/315-733-4663
Uvalde Machine & Tool, P.O. Box 1604, Uvalde, TX 78802

V

Valade, Robert B., 931 3rd Ave., Seaside, OR 97138/503-738-7672
Valmet (See Tikka/U.S. importer—Stoeger Industries)
Valor Corp., 5555 NW 36th Ave., Miami, FL 33142/305-633-0127
Van Epps, Milton, Rt. 69-A, Parish, NY 13131/315-625-7251
Van Gorden & Son, Inc., C.S., 1815 Main St., Bloomer, WI 54724/715-568-2612
Van Horn, Gil, P.O. Box 207, Llano, CA 93544
Van Patten, J.W., P.O. Box 145, Foster Hill, Milford, PA 18337/717-296-7069
Vancini/Bestload, Carl A., P.O. Box 4354, Stamford, CT 06907/FAX: 203-978-0796
Vann Custom Bullets, 330 Grandview Ave., Novato, CA 94947
Varner's Service, 102 Shaffer Rd., Antwerp, OH 45813/419-258-8631
Vega Tool Co., 1840 Commerce St. Unit H, Boulder, CO 80301/303-443-4750
Venco Industries, Inc. (See Shooter's Choice)
Venus Industries, P.O. Box 246, Sialkot-1, PAKISTAN/FAX: 92 432 85579
Verdemont Fieldsports, P.O. Box 9337, San Bernardino, CA 92427/714-880-8255; FAX: 714-880-8255
Verney-Carron, B.P. 72, 54 Boulevard Thiers, 42002 St. Etienne Cedex 1, FRANCE/33-77791500; FAX: 33-77790702
Vest, John, P.O. Box 1552, Susanville, CA 96130/916-257-7228
VibraShine, Inc., Rt. 1, P.O. Box 64, Mt. Olive, MS 39119/601-733-5614; FAX: 601-733-2226
Vibra-Tek Co., 1844 Arroya Rd., Colorado Springs, CO 80906/719-634-8611; FAX: 719-634-6886
Vic's Gun Refinishing, 6 Pineview Dr., Dover, NH 03820/603-742-0013
Vihtavuori Oy, SF-41330 Vihtavuori, FINLAND/358-41-779-211; FAX: 358-41-771643
Vihtavuori Oy/Kaltron-Pettibone, 1241 Ellis St., Bensenville, IL 60106/708-350-1116; FAX: 708-350-1606
Viking Leathercraft, Inc., 1579A Jayken Way, Chula Vista, CA 91911/800-262-6666; FAX: 619-429-8268
Viking Video Productions, P.O. Box 251, Roseburg, OR 97470
Vincent's Shop, 210 Antoinette, Fairbanks, AK 99701
Vintage Arms, Inc., 6003 Saddle Horse, Fairfax, VA 22030/703-968-0779
Vintage Industries, Inc., P.O. Box 872, Casselberry, FL 32718-0872/FAX: 407-699-4919; FAX: 407-699-8419
Viramontez, Ray, 601 Springfield Dr., Albany, GA 31707/912-432-9683
Vitt/Boos, 2178 Nichols Ave., Stratford, CT 06497/203-375-6859
Voere-KGH m.b.H., P.O. Box 416, A-6333 Kufstein, Tirol, AUSTRIA/05372-62547; FAX: 5372-65752 (U.S. importers—JagerSport, Ltd.; Swarovski Optik North America Ltd.)
Volquartsen Custom Ltd., RR 1, Box 33A, P.O. Box 271, Carroll, IA 51401/712-792-4238; FAX: 712-792-2542
Vorhes, David, 3042 Beecham St., Napa, CA 94558/707-226-9116
Vostok (See U.S. importer—Nygord Precision Products)
VSP Publishers, P.O. Box 887, McCall, ID 83638/208-634-4104

W

Waffen-Frankonia (See Frankonia Jagd)
Waffen-Weber Custom Gunsmithing, 4-1691 Powick Rd., Kelowna, B.C. CANADA V1X 4L1/604-762-7575; FAX: 604-861-3655
Wagoner, Vernon G., 2325 E. Encanto, Mesa, AZ 85213/602-835-1307
Wahl Corp., Paul, P.O. Box 6, Bogota, NJ 07603-0006/201-342-9245; FAX: 201-487-9329
Wakina by Pic, 24813 Alderbrook Dr., Santa Clarita, CA 91321/805-295-8194
Waldron, Herman, Box 475, 80 N. 17th St., Pomeroy, WA 99347/509-843-1404
Walker Arms Co., Inc., 499 County Rd. 820, Selma, AL 36701/205-872-6231
Walker Mfg., Inc., 8296 S. Channel, Harsen's Island, MI 48028
Walker Shoe Co., P.O. Box 1167, Asheboro, NC 27203-1167/919-625-1380
Wallace's, Star Rt.1, Box 76, Grandin, MO 63943/314-593-4773
Wallace, Terry, 385 San Marino, Vallejo, CA 94589/707 642 7041
Waller & Son, Inc., W., 142 New Canaan Ave., Norwalk, CT 06850/203-838-4083
Walls Industries, P.O. Box 98, Cleburne, TX 76031/817-645-4366
Walt's Custom Leather, Walt Whinnery, 1947 Meadow Creek Dr., Louisville, KY 40218/502-458-4361
Walters Industries, 6226 Park Lane, Dallas, TX 75225/214-691-6973
Walther GmbH, Carl, B.P. 4325, D-89033 Ulm, GERMANY (U.S. importer—Interarms)
WAMCO, Inc., Mingo Loop, P.O. Box 337, Oquossoc, ME 04964-0337/207-864-3344
Ward & Van Valkenburg, 114 32nd Ave. N., Fargo, ND 58102/701-232-2351
Ward Machine, 5620 Lexington Rd., Corpus Christi, TX 78412/512-992-1221
Wardell Precision Handguns Ltd., 48851 N. Fig Springs Rd., New River, AZ 85027/602-465-7995
Warenski, Julie, 590 E. 500 N., Richfield, UT 84701/801-896-5319; FAX: 801-896-5319
Warne Manufacturing Co., 9039 SE Jannsen Rd., Clackamas, OR 97015/503-657-5590; FAX: 503-657-5695
Warren & Sweat Mfg. Co., P.O. Box 350440, Grand Island, FL 32735/904-669-3166; FAX: 904-669-7272
Warren Muzzleloading Co., Inc., Hwy. 21 North, Ozone, AR 72854/501-292-3268
Warren, Kenneth W. (See Mountain States Engraving)
Washita Mountain Whetstone Co., P.O. Box 378, Lake Hamilton, AR 71951/501-525-3914
WASP Shooting Systems, Rt. 1, Box 147, Lakeview, AR 72642/501-431-5606
Waterfield Sports, Inc., 13611 Country Lane, Burnsville, MN 55337/612-435-8339
Watson Trophy Match Bullets, 2404 Wade Hampton Blvd., Greenville, SC 29615/803-244-7948
Wayland Precision Wood Products, P.O. Box 1142, Mill Valley, CA 94942/415-381-3543
Wayne Firearms for Collectors and Investors, James, 2608 N. Laurent, Victoria, TX 77901/512-578-1258; FAX: 512-578-3559
Wayne Specialty Services, 260 Waterford Drive, Florissant, MO 63033/413-831-7083
WD-40 Co., P.O. Box 80607, San Diego, CA 92138/619-275-1400; FAX: 619-275-5823
Weather Shield Sports Equipment, Inc., Rt. 3, Petoskey Rd., Charlevoix, MI 49720
Weatherby, Inc., 2781 Firestone Blvd., South Gate, CA 90280/213-569-7186, 800-227-2023; FAX: 213-569-5025
Weaver Arms Corp., P.O. Box 8, Dexter, MO 63841/314-568-3101
Weaver Products, Div. of Blount, Inc., P.O. Box 39, Onalaska, WI 54650/800-635-7656; FAX: 608-781-0368
Weaver Scope Repair Service, 1121 Larry Mahan Dr., Suite B, El Paso, TX 79925/915-593-1005
Weaver's Gun Shop, P.O. Box 8, Dexter, MO 63841/314-568-3101
Weber Jr., Rudolf, P.O. Box 160106, D-5650 Solingen, GERMANY/0212-592136
Webley and Scott Ltd., Frankley Industrial Park, Tay Rd., Rubery Rednal, Birmingham B45 OPA, U.K./021-453-1864; FAX: 021-457-7846
Webster Scale Mfg. Co., P.O. Box 188, Sebring, FL 33870/813-385-6362
Weems, Cecil, P.O. Box 657, Mineral Wells, TX 76067/817-325-1462
Weihrauch KG, Hermann, Industriestrasse 11, 8744 Mellrichstadt, GERMANY/09776-497-498 (U.S. importers—Beeman Precision Airguns, Inc.; E.A.A. Corp.)
Weisz Antique Gun Parts, P.O. Box 311, Arlington, VA 22210/703-243-9161
Welch, Sam, CVSR 2110, Moab, UT 84532/801-259-8131
Wellington Outdoors, P.O. Box 244, Madison, GA 30650/404-342-4915; FAX: 404-342-4656
Wells Sport Store, 110 N. Summit St., Prescott, AZ 86301/602-445-3655
Wells Custom Gunsmith, R.A., 3452 1st Ave., Racine, WI 53402/414-639-5223
Wells, Rachel, 110 N. Summit St., Prescott, AZ 86301/602-445-3655
Wells Creek Knife & Gun Works, 32956 State Hwy. 38, Scottsburg, OR 97473/503-587-4202
Welsh, Bud, 80 New Road, E. Amherst, NY 14051/716-688-6344
Wenig Custom Gunstocks, Inc., 103 N. Market St., Lincoln, MO 65338/816-547-3334; FAX: 816-547-2881
Wenoka/Seastyle, P.O. Box 10969, Riviera Beach, FL 33419/407-845-6155; FAX: 407-842-4247
Werth, T.W., 1203 Woodlawn Rd., Lincoln, IL 62656/217-732-1300
Wescombe, P.O. Box 488, Glencoe, CA 95232/209-293-7010
Wessinger Custom Guns & Engraving, 268 Limestone Rd., Chapin, SC 29036/803-345-5677
Wesson Firearms Co., Inc., Maple Tree Industrial Center, Rt. 20, Wilbraham Rd., Palmer, MA 01069/413-267-4081; FAX: 413-267-3601
West, Robert G., 3973 Pam St., Eugene, OR 97402/503-344-3700
Westchester Carbide, 148 Wheeler Ave., Pleasantville, NY 10570/914-769-1445
Western Design, 1629 Via Monserate, Fallbrook, CA 92028/619-723-9279
Western Gunstock Mfg. Co., 550 Valencia School Rd., Aptos, CA 95003/408-688-5884
Western Missouri Shooters Alliance, P.O. Box 11144, Kansas City, MO 64119/816-597-3950; FAX: 816-229-7350
Western Ordnance Int'l Corp., 325 S. Westwood St. 1, Mesa, AZ 85210/602-964-1799
Westfield Engineering, 6823 Watcher St., Commerce, CA 90040/FAX: 213-928-8270
Westley Richards & Co., 40 Grange Rd., Birmingham, ENGLAND B29 6AR/010-214722953
Westminster Arms Ltd., 9375 Freemont Way, Reno, NV 89506/916-827-2179
Westrom, John (See Precise Metal Finishing)
Weyer International, 2740 Nebraska Ave., Toledo, OH 43607/419-534-2020; FAX: 419-534-2697
Whildin & Sons Ltd., E.H., 76 Autumn Dr., Tolland, CT 06084/203-870-8713
Whinnery, Walt (See Walt's Custom Leather)
White Flyer Targets, 124 River Rd., Middlesex, NJ 08846/908-469-0100; FAX: 908-469-9692
White Flyer, Div. of Reagent Chemical & Research, Inc., 9139 W. Redfield Rd., Peoria, AZ 85381/800-647-2898
White Laboratory, Inc., H.P., 3114 Scarboro Rd., Street, MD 21154/410-838-6550; FAX: 410-838-2802
White Owl Enterprises, Rt. 4, Box 266 GD, Abilene, KS 67410/913-263-2613, 2616; FAX: 913-263-1426
White Rock Tool & Die, 6400 N. Brighton Ave., Kansas City, MO 64119/816-454-0478
White Systems, Inc., P.O. Box 190, Roosevelt, UT 84066/801-722-3085; FAX: 801-722-3085
Whitehead, James D., 204 Cappucino Way, Sacramento, CA 95838
Whitestone Lumber Corp., 148-02 14th Ave., Whitestone, NY 11357/718-746-4400; FAX: 718-767-1748
Whitetail Design & Engineering Ltd., 9421 E. Mannsiding Rd., Clare, MI 48617/517-386-3932

Whits Shooting Stuff, Box 1340, Cody, WY 82414
Wichita Arms, Inc., 923 E. Gilbert, P.O. Box 11371, Wichita, KS 67211/316-265-0661; FAX: 316-265-0760
Widener's Reloading & Shooting Supply, Inc., P.O. Box 3009 CRS, Johnson City, TN 37602/615-282-6786; FAX: 615-282-6651
Wideview Scope Mount Corp., 26110 Michigan Ave., Inkster, MI 48141/313-274-1238; FAX: 313-274-2814
Wiebe, Duane, Casper Mt. Rt., Box 40, Casper, WY 82601/307-237-0615; FAX: 307-266-4143
Wiest, M.C., 10737 Dutchtown Rd., Knoxville, TN 37932/615-966-4545
Wilcox All-Pro Tools & Supply, RR 1, Montezuma, IA 50171/515-623-3138
Wild Bill's Originals, P.O. Box 13037, Burton, WA 98013/206-463-5738
Wildcatters, The, P.O. Box 170, Greenville, WI 54942
Wilderness Sound Products Ltd., 4015 Main St. A, Springfield, OR 97478/503-741-0263; FAX: 503-741-7648
Wildey, Inc., P.O. Box 475, Brookfield, CT 06804/203-355-9000; FAX: 203-354-7759
Wildlife Research Center, Inc., 4345 157th Ave. NW, Anoka, MN 55304/612-427-3350
Wilkinson Arms, 26884 Pearl Rd., Parma, ID 83660/208-722-6771
Will-Burt Co., 169 S. Main, Orrville, OH 44667
William's Gun Shop, Ben, 1151 S. Cedar Ridge, Duncanville, TX 75137/214-780-1807
Williams Bullet Co., J.R., 2008 Tucker Rd., Perry, GA 31069/912-987-0274
Williams Gun Sight Co., 7389 Lapeer Rd., Box 329, Davison, MI 48423/313-653-2131, 800-530-9028; FAX: 313-658-2140
Williams Shootin' Iron Service, The Lynx-Line, 8857 Bennett Hill Rd., Central Lake, MI 49622/616-544-6615
Williamson Precision Gunsmithing, 117 W. Pipeline, Hurst, TX 76053/817-285-0064
Willig Custom Engraving, Claus, D-97422 Schweinfurt, Siedlerweg 17, GERMANY/01149-9721-41446
Willson Safety Prods. Div., P.O. Box 622, Reading, PA 19603
Wilson Arms Co., The, 63 Leetes Island Rd., Branford, CT 06405/203-488-7297; FAX: 203-488-0135
Wilson Case, Inc., P.O. Box 1106, Hastings, NE 68902-1106/800-322-5493; FAX: 402-463-5276
Wilson, Inc., L.E., Box 324, 404 Pioneer Ave., Cashmere, WA 98815/509-782-1328
Wilson's Gun Shop, Box 578, Rt. 3, Berryville, AR 72616/501-545-3635; FAX: 501-545-3310
Winchester (See U.S. Repeating Arms Co., Inc.)
Winchester Div., Olin Corp., 427 N. Shamrock, E. Alton, IL 62024/618-258-3566; FAX: 618-258-3180
Winchester Press (See New Win Publishing, Inc.)
Winchester Sutler, Inc., The, 270 Shadow Brook Lane, Winchester, VA 22603/703-888-3595
Windish, Jim, 2510 Dawn Dr., Alexandria, VA 22306/703-765-1994
Windjammer Tournament Wads, Inc., 750 W. Hampden Ave. Suite 170, Englewood, CO 80110/303-781-6329
Wingshooting Adventures, 4320 Kalamazoo Ave. SE, Grand Rapids, MI 49508/616-455-7810; FAX: 616-455-5212
Winkle Bullets, R.R. 1 Box 316, Heyworth, IL 61745
Winter & Associates (See Olde Pennsylvania)
Winter, Robert M., RR 2, P.O. Box 484, Menno, SD 57045/605-387-5322
Wisner's Gun Shop, Inc., 287 NW Chehalis Ave., Chehalis, WA 98532/206-748-8942; FAX: 206-748-7011
Wittasek, Dipl.-Ing. Norbert, Seilergasse 2, Wien, 1010 AUSTRIA/0222-513-7001
Wolfe Publishing Co., 6471 Airpark Dr., Prescott, AZ 86301/602-445-7810, 800-899-7810; FAX: 602-778-5124
W.C. Wolff Co., P.O. Box I, Newtown Square, PA 19073/215-359-9600
Wolverine Boots & Shoes Div., Wolverine World Wide, 9341 Courtland Dr., Rockford, MI 49351/616-866-1561
Wood, Frank (See Classic Guns)
Wood, Mel, P.O. Box 1255, Sierra Vista, AZ 85636/602-455-5541

Woodland Bullets, 638 Woodland Dr., Manheim, PA 17545/717-665-4332
Woods Pistolsmithing, 3840 Dahlgren Ct., Ellicott City, MD 21042/410-465-7979
Woods Wise Products, P.O. Box 681552, 2200 Bowman Rd., Franklin, TN 37068/800-735-8182; FAX: 615-790-3581
Woodstream, P.O. Box 327, Lititz, PA 17543/717-626-2125; FAX: 717-626-1912
Woolrich Woolen Mills, Mill St., Woolrich, PA 17779/717-769-6464
World of Targets, Div. of Steidle Corp., 9200 Floral Ave., Cincinnati, OH 45242/513-791-0917; FAX: 513-792-0004
World of Targets (See Birchwood Laboratories, Inc.)
World Trek, Inc., 2648 McCormick Ave., Pueblo, CO 81001/719-546-2121; FAX: 719-543-6886
Worthy Products, Inc., RR 1, P.O. Box 213, Martville, NY 13111/315-324-5298
Wosenitz VHP, Inc., Box 741, Dania, FL 33004/305-923-3748; FAX: 305-925-2217
Wostenholm (See Ibberson [Sheffield] Ltd., George)
Wright's Hardwood Sawmill, 8540 SE Kane Rd., Gresham, OR 97080/503-666-1705
Wyant Bullets, Gen. Del., Swan Lake, MT 59911
Wyant's Outdoor Products, Inc., P.O. Box 1325, Harrisonburg, VA 22801-1325/FAX: 702-833-4021
Wyoming Armory, Inc., Box 28, Farson, WY 82932/307-273-5556
Wyoming Casting Co., 305 Commerce Dr. 10D, P.O. Box 1492, Gillette, WY 82717/307-687-7779, 800-821-2167
Wyoming Custom Bullets, 1626 21st St., Cody, WY 82414
Wyoming Knife Corp., 101 Commerce Dr., Ft. Collins, CO 80524/303-224-3454

Y

Yankee Gunsmith, 2901 Deer Flat Dr., Copperas Cove, TX 76522/817-547-8433
Yavapai College, 1100 E. Sheldon St., Prescott, AZ 86301/602-776-2359; FAX: 602-776-2193
Yavapai Firearms Academy Ltd., P.O. Box 27290, Prescott Valley, AZ 86312/602-772-8262
Yearout, Lewis E. (See Montana Outfitters)
Yee, Mike, 29927 56 Pl. S., Auburn, WA 98001/206-839-3991
Yellowstone Wilderness Supply, P.O. Box 129, W. Yellowstone, MT 59758/406-646-7613
York M-1 Conversions, 803 Mill Creek Run, Plantersville, TX 77363/800-527-2881, 713-477-8442
Young Country Arms, P.O. Box 3615, Simi Valley, CA 93093

Z

Zabala Hermanos S.A., P.O. Box 97, Eibar, SPAIN 20600 (U.S. importer—American Arms, Inc.)
Zanoletti, Pietro, Via Monte Gugielpo, 4, I-25063 Gardone V.T., ITALY (U.S. importer—Mandall Shooting Supplies, Inc.)
Zanotti Armor, 123 W. Lone Tree Rd., Cedar Falls, IA 50613/319-232-9650
Zastava Arms (See U.S. importer—Interarms)
Z-Coat Industrial Coatings, Inc., 3375 U.S. Hwy. 98 S. No. A, Lakeland, FL 33803-8365/813-665-1734
Zeeryp, Russ, 1601 Foard Dr., Lynn Ross Manor, Morristown, TN 37814/615-586-2357
Zeiss Optical, Inc., Carl, 1015 Commerce St., Petersburg, VA 23803/804-861-0033; FAX: 804-862-3734
Zero Ammunition Co., Inc., 1601 22nd St. SE, P.O. Box 1188, Cullman, AL 35055-1188/800-545-9376; FAX: 205-739-4683
Ziegel Engineering, 2108 Lomina Ave., Long Beach, CA 90815/310-596-9481; FAX: 310-598-4734
Zim's Inc., 4370 S. 3rd West, Salt Lake City, UT 84107
Zoli USA, Inc., Antonio, P.O. Box 6190, Fort Wayne, IN 46896/219-447-4603
Zoli, Antonio, Via Zanardelli 39, Casier Postal 21, 23, I-25063 Gardone V.T., ITALY (U.S. importers—Mandall Shooting Supplies, Inc.; Zoli USA, Inc., Antonio)